Seventeenth-Century Prose and Poetry

SECOND EDITION, ENLARGED

SELECTED AND EDITED BY

Alexander M. Witherspoon
LATE OF YALE UNIVERSITY

Frank J. Warnke
UNIVERSITY OF GEORGIA

HARCOURT BRACE JOVANOVICH, INC.

New York   San Diego   Chicago   San Francisco   Atlanta

London   Sydney   Toronto

MORRIS W. CROLL. "The Baroque Style in Prose," by Morris W. Croll, from *Studies in English Philology: A Miscellany in Honor of Frederick Klaeber*, edited by Kemp Malone and Martin B. Ruud, University of Minnesota Press, Minneapolis. Copyright 1929 by the University of Minnesota. Reprinted by permission of the publisher.

T. S. ELIOT. "The Metaphysical Poets," from *Selected Essays: New Edition* by T. S. Eliot, copyright, 1932, 1936, 1950, by Harcourt, Brace & World, Inc.; © 1960, by T. S. Eliot. Reprinted by permission of Harcourt, Brace & World, Inc., and Faber and Faber Ltd.

BEN JONSON. Selections from *Conversations with Drummond of Hawthornden* by Ben Jonson, edited by R. F. Patterson. Copyright 1923 by Blackie & Son Limited. Reprinted by permission of the publisher.

LOUIS L. MARTZ. Introduction from *The Anchor Anthology of Seventeenth-Century Verse*, Vol. 1, by Louis L. Martz. Copyright © 1963, 1969 by Louis L. Martz. Reprinted by permission of Doubleday & Company, Inc.

JOSEPH A. MAZZEO. "Metaphysical Poetry and the Poetic of Correspondence," from *Renaissance and Seventeenth-Century Studies* by Joseph A. Mazzeo. Columbia University Press, 1964. Reprinted by permission of Columbia University Press and Routledge & Kegan Paul Ltd.

EDWARD TAYLOR. "Preparatory Meditations," Second Series, Nos. 12, 143, and 146, are reprinted from *The Poems of Edward Taylor*, edited by Donald E. Stanford, Yale University Press, 1960, by permission of Yale University Press. Preface to "God's Determinations Touching His Elect," "The Joy of Church Fellowship," "Huswifery," "The Ebb and Flow," Prologue to "Preparatory Meditations," and "Preparatory Meditations," First Series, Nos. 1, 6, 29, 38, and Second Series, Nos. 3 and 7, are reprinted from *The Poetical Works of Edward Taylor*, edited by Thomas H. Johnson, Rockland Editions, 1939, copyright 1943 by Princeton University Press, by permission of Princeton University Press. "Preparatory Meditations," First Series, Nos. 29 and 32, are reprinted from "Poems by Edward Taylor," by Barbara D. Simison, *Yale University Library Gazette*, 28–29 (Jan.–Apr., July–Oct., 1954), by permission of the *Yale University Library Gazette* and Barbara D. Simison.

THOMAS TRAHERNE. Selections from "Centuries of Meditations" from *Centuries, Poems, and Thanksgivings* by Thomas Traherne, edited by H. M. Margoliouth, Oxford University Press, 1958. Reprinted by permission of the publisher.

FRANK J. WARNKE. "Art as Play," from *Versions of Baroque* by Frank J. Warnke. Yale University Press, 1972. Reprinted by permission of Yale University Press and the author.

AUSTIN WARREN. "Interlude: Baroque Art and the Emblem," from *Richard Crashaw: A Study in Baroque Sensibility* by Austin Warren. Louisiana State University Press, 1939; reissued by the University of Michigan Press, and by Faber and Faber, 1957. Reprinted by permission of Faber and Faber Ltd. and the author.

A NOTE ON THE COVER: The coat of arms reproduced on the cover of this book is that of the Worshipful Company of Stationers and Papermakers of London. This ancient City Company was originally a guild of stationers and craftsmen who made and dealt in parchment, paper, quill pens, and materials for binding books. In 1557, eighty-one years after printing was first introduced into England, the Stationers were granted a charter which gave them the monopoly of the "Art or Mystery of Printing." At the same time they received their coat of arms from the College of Heralds. For many years it was the custom to enter the titles of books to be printed by members of the Company in the Stationers' Register, which is thus a record of the first printing of most of the famous works known to students of the literature of the sixteenth and seventeenth centuries. Edward Arber's *A Transcript of the Register of the Company of Stationers* (1550–1640, 5 vols., 1875–94; 1650–1708, 3 vols., 1913–14) is a primary resource of scholarship in English studies. The Court records of the Company have been edited by W. W. Greg and E. Boswell (Vol. I) and William A. Jackson (Vol. II), 1930–57.

ISBN: 0–15–580237–2

Library of Congress Catalog Card Number: 82–083867

PRINTED IN THE UNITED STATES OF AMERICA

PREFACE

ORE than half a century has gone by since the appearance of the first edition of *A Book of Seventeenth-Century Prose* (1929) by Robert P. Tristram Coffin and Alexander M. Witherspoon, and more than three decades have passed since the revision and expansion of that anthology by the original editors into *Seventeenth-Century Prose and Poetry* (1946). Almost twenty years ago, in 1963, changing critical standards and the increased sophistication of both instructors and students prompted Witherspoon and Frank J. Warnke to produce the second edition of the anthology, greatly expanding the selections from several of the most important prose authors (Sir Thomas Browne, Izaak Walton, Thomas Traherne) and poets (Donne, Jonson, Herrick, Herbert, Milton, Marvell, and Dryden), and adding selections from a number of significant minor poets, including Lord Herbert of Cherbury, Phineas and Giles Fletcher, and the New England metaphysical poet Edward Taylor.

The past two decades have seen a rich production of scholarly and critical works dealing with English literature of the seventeenth century, particularly with regard to such figures as Donne, Herbert, Milton, Crashaw, and Marvell, and this revision of the second edition of *Seventeenth-Century Prose and Poetry* reflects recent scholarship both in the expanded bibliographies and in the several additions to the Critical Miscellany that serves as an appendix to the volume.

The bibliographies, which have been kept brief enough to be practicable and helpful, draw upon the whole new library of research and criticism that has come into existence during recent years. Wherever possible, the text followed is that of the best seventeenth-century edition of an author. Spelling, capitalization, and punctuation have, in general, been brought into conformity with modern usage except where an author's eccentricities or inconsistencies seem to justify the retention of the original forms. The number of notes has been reduced in order to provide more space for the literature itself, and to avoid trespassing upon the right of the instructor or the student to do his own work.

In 1963 the editors expressed their gratitude to Douglas Bush for his kindness in examining the plan and manuscript of that edition. The editor reiterates that gratitude.

In general, this revised and expanded edition of *Seventeenth-Century Prose and Poetry* provides, it is believed, as large and rich a body of material as can be conveniently compassed in a year's course, with a minimum of interference on the part of the twentieth-century editors.

F.J.W.

CONTENTS

PROSE

JAMES HOWELL

JOHN EARLE

OWEN FELLTHAM

POETRY

JOHN DONNE

BEN JONSON

JOHN FLETCHER

JOHN WEBSTER

RICHARD CORBET

PHINEAS FLETCHER

ROBERT HERRICK

FRANCIS QUARLES

HENRY KING

GEORGE HERBERT

JOHN MILTON

SIR JOHN SUCKLING

JAMES GRAHAM
First Marquis of Montrose

APPENDIX
A Critical Miscellany

PROSE

Seventeenth-Century Prose

I

THE most striking feature of seventeenth-century prose is its variety. We moderns, conditioned to think of a good prose style as distinguished chiefly by either the clarity and precision with which it conveys information or the force and originality with which it expresses an individual personality, are easily confused by the writings of an age which was obsessed by the search for absolute truth, but which found that that truth assumed an almost infinite variety of masks. At first glance there seem to be few connections between the terse pithiness of Francis Bacon's essays and the torrential flow of Robert Burton's eccentric masterpiece on the madness of humanity. Izaak Walton's idyllic picture of country life and Sir Thomas Browne's great meditation on mortality are expressed in manners as different from each other as are the visions of their authors. Nowhere in English literature do we find a wider range of mood, attitude, and emphasis; style is the man, and the men of the seventeenth century were remarkable for nothing if not for their individuality—an individuality largely uncramped by any prescriptive conception of what a prose style might or might not be allowed to do.

Nevertheless, at the distance of three hundred years we are able to discern, if not certain shared features, at least certain shared motives—a certain identity of purpose which distinguishes these writers from their Elizabethan forebears and their Augustan descendants alike. The ideals and rules of the Elizabethan age remain operative to varying degrees throughout the seventeenth century, and, even more noticeably, the norms of the eighteenth century may be perceived in the process of formulation, but nevertheless, from the late 1590's until slightly after 1660, English prose is remarkable for the richness, the multiplicity, one might almost say the peculiarity, of its accomplishment. The true defining feature of seventeenth-century prose is the individual accent which it almost always displays, and this accent, as we shall see, is intimately related to the opportunities, revelations, and frustrations of the age which produced it—an age which, perhaps more than any other since antiquity, deserves that term so loved by (and so often abused by) historians of every sort: an age of transition.

There is a very special sense in which, to us, the seventeenth century appears as the "age of transition" *par excellence*, for ours is the world which that era made the transition to. Western Europe was, as Douglas Bush has justly remarked,[1] more than half medieval in its attitudes in 1600, more than half modern in 1700. The seventeenth is the century which saw the establishment of the foundations of modern science, the definitive

---

1 D. Bush, *English Literature in the Earlier Seventeenth Century* (New York, rev. ed., 1962), p. 1. An extremely valuable work for the student of the period.

destruction of a view of the world which had persisted from the time of the ancients, the justification of experience as the true basis of knowledge, and the dissipation of religious concepts as guiding factors in politics and philosophy.

In science and philosophy, in religion and politics, a new spirit was stirring in the opening years of the seventeenth century, a spirit which questioned the inherited authorities—Aristotle, Ptolemy, Galen, and the rest—who had for so long held absolute dominion over the mind of European man. Through the observations and calculations of Galileo and Kepler, the heliocentric theory of Copernicus became, instead of an eccentric and amusing idea, a proposition which all thoughtful men were obliged, if not to accept, at least to consider seriously. Gilbert's studies of magnetism (1600) and Harvey's discovery of the circulation of the blood (1616) opened new realms to the human imagination as well as to the human understanding. A feature shared by all the great men of science in the earlier seventeenth century was a reliance on experience, a utilization of the methods of observation and experimentation, which contrasted strongly with the intellectual methods of earlier centuries. It was precisely this kind of approach to the problems of experience which was so effectively popularized by Sir Francis Bacon —himself not a great scientist, but certainly the greatest propagandist that science has ever had.

It is not difficult to see a relationship between the new emphases of the scientists and the direction in which speculative thought in the period began to move: the rationalism of Descartes, the materialism of Hobbes, the emphasis on the "inner light" of personal experience cultivated by the more radical Protestant sects, the successful attack on the principle of absolute monarchy—all these phenomena surely arose from the same grand mutation in the human spirit, a mutation which we may regard as the origin of the modern world. The seventeenth century closed with the fruition of these new modes of vision. Building on the foundation of Descartes, the great philosophers of the latter part of the century—Spinoza, Locke, Leibniz—established modern philosophy and anticipated both the idealistic and the empirical tendencies of the eighteenth century. And Sir Isaac Newton utilized the discoveries of Kepler to create the classical physics which was to remain unchallenged until our own time.

II

SCHEMATICALLY, the seventeenth century may seem, from our vantage point, to be distinguished chiefly by the consistent triumphs which modernism achieved in its course, and we might well expect to find in its prose literature—in both matter and style—a thoroughgoing rejection of past ways of thought and past forms of expression. In fact we find no such thing. The destruction of an old world view and the forging of a new are processes which generate a good deal of heat and smoke, and in the literature of the age, as in its thought, we find that the old and the new exist side by side. The physiological discoveries of Harvey stirred considerable interest, but so did the medicine of Paracelsus, based on an original and highly imaginative application of mystical and magical doctrines of extreme antiquity, opposed in every way to the spirit of the new science. Kepler discovered the laws of celestial motion, but at the same time speculated as to how these laws might lead him to an understanding of the mysterious "harmony of the world." Sir Thomas Browne, in his *Pseudodoxia Epidemica*, heroically took up arms against the legions of "vulgar errors"—but managed to perpetuate at least as many quaint legends as he destroyed. Conditioned by a heritage of centuries of belief in the necessity of the citation of authorities, the men of the seventeenth century propounded the boldest innovations in politics and religion—but always in the name of some distinguished precedent in Classical antiquity or primitive Christianity. Any brief scrutiny of the technique of disputation employed by that most independent of men, John Milton, will demonstrate how thoroughly intertwined, in the seventeenth century, were originality of idea and the appeal to authority and tradition.

We find that the prose style of the seventeenth-century authors is strikingly original, and yet that it is at the same time a style which keeps up the semblance of continuity with the past. Most significantly, the prose style of the first two-thirds of the century seldom violates three basic principles established by tradition: *copia*, citation of authorities, and the doctrine of imitation. *Copia*, or fullness of rhetorical expression, is more than a stylistic habit inculcated by the precedent of ancient oratory; it is intimately related to one of the major compulsions of seventeenth-century man—the need to strive for total statement, for an expression of both idea and self which is as complete and as exhaustive as the manifold resources of language can make it. Implicit in the rhetorical *copia* of the Baroque artist is an attitude toward language which is universes removed from the modern "scientific" conception of language, which is, for most of us, so thoroughly accepted as to constitute an unexamined assumption. The *word* itself, for Donne, for Browne, for Taylor, is a modification of precise meaning and hence a modification of emotion. The endless catalogues of approximate synonyms which make up such a striking proportion of Burton's *Anatomy of Melancholy* are there not because a bookish and unhappy scholar had the academic habit of verbosity, but because Burton the thinker, physician, and artist assumed that a line of thought was not complete until all the possible changes of connotation had been rung on his particularly extensive set of verbal chimes. In the same manner, the following passage from Browne's *Hydriotaphia* exhibits a richness of linguistic orchestration which only the tone-deaf could stigmatize as prolix:

> If we begin to die when we live, and long life be but a prolongation of death, our life is a sad composition; we live with death and die not in a moment. How many pulses made up the life of Methuselah were work for Archimedes: common counters sum up the life of Moses his man. Our days become considerable like petty sums by minute accumulations; where numerous fractions make up but small round numbers, and our days of a span long make not one little finger.

Mere statement of the theme is not enough; it must be tried on our pulses, presented to our reasoning capacities, tested against the length of our little finger. Or again:

> Pious spirits who passed their days in raptures of futurity made little more of this world than the world that was before it, while they lay obscure in the chaos of pre-ordination and night of their fore-beings. And if any have been so happy as truly to understand Christian annihilation, extasis, exolution, liquefaction, transformation, the kiss of the Spouse, gustation of God, and ingression into the divine shadow, they have already had an handsome anticipation of heaven; the glory of the world is surely over, and the earth in ashes unto them.

To Browne's strongly verbal imagination, the very conception of the pre-existence of the soul was not completely uttered until it had assumed both Latin and Saxon garb, and the evocation of the mystical experience required, beyond any doubt, at least eight synonyms. Communication is the aim of the seventeenth-century prose artist, but it is communication at an exalted spiritual level which would strike terror into the heart of the modern social scientist.

The urge toward what one might call "absolute expression" is thus at the root of the expansive luxuriance of much of the prose of the period. Nevertheless we must recognize that one of the major aspects of *copia*, the citation of authorities, is the manifestation of a conviction which reaches back into medieval antiquity—the conviction that the appeal to authority is one of the firmest bases of argument. The Bible, the Church Fathers, the Classics, medieval physicians, contemporary theologians—all are ransacked by the seventeenth-century writer. Burton is surely the great exemplar for this habit of mind: "I have only this of Macrobius to say of myself," he writes of his method:

> *Omne meum, nihil meum*, 'tis all mine and none mine. As a good housewife out of divers fleeces weaves one piece of cloth, a bee gathers wax and honey out of many flowers and makes a new bundle of all . . . I have laboriously collected this *cento* out of divers writers and that *sine iniuria*, I have wronged no authors but given every man his own. . . .

And so he proceeds, loading every rift of his giant *Anatomy of Melancholy* with Latin ore—the reinforcement itself usually reinforced with his own racy translations.

But if Burton exemplifies the habit of citation at its most extreme, every other major writer of his age displays the same trait to one degree or another. Donne's sermons are stiff with the great names of the Church, both those familiar and those forgotten. Milton's argument for freedom of thought and utterance in the *Areopagitica* (1644) is as pertinent now as it was three hundred years ago, but the fabric of that argument is interwoven with the early history of the Church and illustrative cases from the great days of Greece and Rome. Even Bacon himself, conqueror of the Goliath of authority, lards the pages of his essays with copious exempla from the Classical world. And when Izaak Walton gives advice on the art of angling, he has his authorities for it.

The habit of citation and the doctrine of imitation are intimately related in the history of English prose. What the former was to matter, the latter was to manner, for, to follow for a moment the reasoning of the age before the scientific revolution, if the ancients were the great and exclusive source of our knowledge, then those same ancients were the sole reliable models for literary style. In the sixteenth century, the ancient model set before the prose writer had been Cicero. He had been deemed to be effectively without rival in stylistic excellence, and his influence had reigned supreme over writers in the vernacular as well as those who used Latin. Early in the seventeenth century his hegemony came to an end.

The anti-Ciceronian movement in English prose has many sources: the balanced magniloquence of the Ciceronian manner, with its smooth regularity of rhythm and sentence structure, had become less than adequate to the expression of the varied needs and moods of the new century; a style which was in essence oratorical was now felt to be unsuited to writing which, like much seventeenth-century work, had a specifically utilitarian motive; and the beginnings of a new emphasis on individual experience more or less necessitated the formulation of prose styles which, in their individuality and immediacy, could give voice to that experience. We have noted that, despite the emergence of the new science, despite Bacon's attack on the ancient authorities, the centuries-old habit of citation continued unabated in the seventeenth-century writers, even in Bacon himself. By the same token, the recognition of the inadequacy of Ciceronian prose style for the purposes of their own age did not lead the writers of the early 1600's to abandon the doctrine of imitation, either in theory or practice. With a characteristic vigor and ingenuity they simply found new models to imitate. The anti-Ciceronian movement, which affected to at least some degree almost every important English prose writer of the first two-thirds of the seventeenth century, went by many names in its own time: often it was called "Attic" in the mistaken belief that it was modeled on the oratorical style of Demosthenes, a figure whose prestige equaled that of the rejected Cicero; sometimes it was called "Senecan," and with far more justice, for Seneca was in fact, with Tacitus, the great Classical model to whom the anti-Ciceronians turned. Seventeenth-century writers had yet other influential models, though often unavowed ones, nearer to them in time and space in Justus Lipsius and in the great figure of Montaigne, whose essays had been available since 1603 in the brilliant English translation of John Florio. Although modern literary historians often follow the lead of the seventeenth century and refer to the anti-Ciceronian style as "Attic" or "Senecan," the term "Baroque" has also established itself quite firmly in their usage,[2] and it has many advantages as a designation for a phenomenon which was as varied as it was far-reaching. Many of the connotations of this term are, furthermore, appropriate to a complex of prose styles which are striking in their individuality, their irregularity, and their eccentricity.

Bacon gives expression to one of the consistent critical attitudes of the Baroque prose artist when, in *The Advancement of Learning* (1605), he stigmatizes as one of the "vanities in studies" that type of "delicate learning" in which men begin "to hunt more after words than matter, and more after the choiceness of the phrase, and the round and clean composition of the sentence, and the sweet falling of the clauses, and the varying and illustration of their works with tropes and figures than after the weight of matter, worth of subject, soundness of argument, life of invention, or depth of judgment." *Things, not words:* the phrase becomes a battle cry for the anti-Ciceronian writers, and the seriousness of temperament implicit in this exaltation of subject matter over style is surely related both to the new scientific attitude and to the newly revived spirit of religious gravity which rather paradoxically coincided with it.

The foregoing observations make it clear that dedication to truthful content did not compel the anti-Ciceronian writers to become lesser artists than their predecessors. Some authors of the early seventeenth century tended, it is true, toward formlessness and awkwardness as a result of their revolt against Ciceronian formalism; a greater number, as the century progressed, tended to make of "Attic" terseness and irregularity a convention as artificial, as affectedly self-conscious, as the worst extremes of Ciceronianism against which Erasmus had spoken a century before. But the great artists of Baroque prose created an instrument in which manner and matter are almost perfectly blended, in which prose style is not the oratorical refashioning of conclusions already reached but rather the white-hot expression of ideas in the process of formation. Sentence structure, rhythm, and imagery all trace the very movements of the inquiring mind; like their contemporaries the Metaphysical poets, the Baroque prose writers give a voice to what Donne, in one of the *Songs and Sonnets,* calls "a naked, thinking heart." Again like their poetic coevals, these writers abandon predetermined forms to create

2 See M. W. Croll, "The Baroque Style in Prose," in Appendix, pp. 1065–1077.

new forms uniquely suited to the expression of their vision. That vision itself is very much like that of the Metaphysical poets: concerned with the contradictions of experience, analytical, desperately involved, it finds its natural form in paradox, in colloquialism, in extended conceit, in dramatic contrast.

Although the style of the anti-Ciceronians inevitably displays a greater variety than that of the Ciceronians, it is possible to perceive certain general categories into which their works fall. There is, to begin with, the pithy, dense, dignified manner of Bacon, equally well-suited to the utterance of his generalized worldly advice in the *Essays* and to the exposition of his program in *The Advancement of Learning*. We might look at a brief example of this manner:

> Men in great place are thrice servants: servants of the sovereign or state, servants of fame, and servants of business. So as they have no freedom, neither in their persons, nor in their actions, nor in their times. It is a strange desire, to seek power and lose liberty, or to seek power over others and to lose power over a man's self. The rising unto place is laborious, and by pains men come to greater pains; and it is sometimes base, and by indignities men come to dignities. The standing is slippery, and the regress is either a downfall or at least an eclipse, which is a melancholy thing. . . .

This passage, the opening of the essay "Of Great Place," impresses us first with its abrupt and attention-catching first phrase, reminiscent almost of those memorable first lines which distinguish so many of Donne's lyrics. The pervasive use of paradox recalls not only Donne but the entire Metaphysical succession. The variant repetition of the central idea, the tentative, searching metaphors, and the irregular syntax are all related to that quest for immediacy which is one of the great distinguishing marks of all Baroque style.

Another category of seventeenth-century prose is the loose, associational, almost irresponsible manner of which the major exponent is Burton:

> Never so much cause of laughter as now, never so many fools and madmen. 'Tis not one Democritus will serve turn to laugh in these days; we have now need of a "Democritus to laugh at Democritus"; one jester to flout at another, one fool to fleer at another: a great stentorian Democritus, as big as that Rhodian Colossus. For now, as Salisburiensis said in his time, *totus mundus histrionem agit*, the whole world plays the fool; we have a new theater, a new scene, a new comedy of errors, a new company of personate actors, *volupiae sacra*, as Calcagninus willingly feigns in his Apologues, are celebrated all the world over, where all the actors were madmen and fools, and every hour changed habits or took that which came next.

Later in the century we find a rather similar manner in the idiosyncratic and voluminous writings of Thomas Fuller. This highly personal, natural style (which may owe something to the example of Montaigne) lends itself to few generalizations with regard to technique, for it inevitably bears the stamp of individual temperament even more strongly than do the other anti-Ciceronian styles.

A final stylistic category which requires attention is the extreme Senecan style, more clipped and terse than Burton's, more self-consciously mannered than Bacon's. It enjoyed an enormous vogue in the early part of the century, and is typified by John Earle's *Microcosmography* (1628) and Owen Felltham's *Resolves* (1628). The opening sentences of Felltham's essay "Of Dreams" exemplify the qualities of wit and metaphor, the asymmetrical juxtaposition of long and short utterances, and the irregular rhythm which are characteristic of extreme Senecanism:

> Dreams are notable means of discovering our own inclinations. The wise man learns to know himself as well by the night's black mantle as the searching beams of day. In sleep we have the naked and natural thoughts of our souls; outward objects interpose not, either to shuffle in occasional cogitations, or hale out the included fancy. The mind is then shut up in the borough of the body; none of the *Cinque Ports* of the *Isle of Man* are then open, to in-let any strange disturbers.

But not all prose of the Baroque era can be designated as "anti-Ciceronian." Two of the giants of seventeenth-century prose, John Milton and Jeremy Taylor, remain true to the essential tenets of Ciceronian imitation, and their sonorous periods, regular rhythms, and sensuous imagery lend an indispensable voice to the harmonies of Baroque prose. The great rhetorical set piece is not really typical of the seventeenth century, but that century would be very much poorer if it lacked such men as Taylor, and such prose as this from his *Holy Dying*:

> Since we stay not here, being people but of a day's abode, and our age is like that of a fly and contemporary with a gourd, we must look somewhere else for an abiding city, a place in another country to fix our house in, whose walls and foundation is God, where we must ever rest, or else be restless forever. For whatsoever ease we can have or fancy here is shortly to be changed into sadness or tediousness: it goes away too soon, like the periods of our life: or stays too long, like the sorrows of a sinner: its own weariness, or a contrary disturbance, is its load; or it is eased by its revolution into vanity and forgetfulness; and where either there is sorrow or an end of joy, there can be no true felicity: which because it must be had by some instrument and in some period of our duration, we must carry up our affections to the mansions prepared for us above, where eternity is the measure, felicity is the state, angels are the company, the Lamb is the light, and God is the portion and inheritance.

As might be expected, Ciceronian and anti-Ciceronian streams come together in the work of some of the greatest figures of the century, and the result, as in the writings of John Donne and Sir Thomas Browne, is an art of unique and haunting beauty in which the whole spirit of the age finds perhaps its fullest expression. In the *Devotions upon Emergent Occasions*, as in the *Religio Medici*, constructions of the most elevated formality exist beside expressions of the most intimate familiarity; oratorical periods are succeeded by statements of piercing immediacy; and the total effect is of contrast, drama, intensity —a potent embodiment of the passionate and often self-contradictory preoccupations of the era. The following passage from Donne's *Sermon XIV* betrays, in its sophisticated devices and its tendency toward regular rhythm, its indebtedness to the oratorical tradition, but its striking metaphors and asymmetrical structure are fully typical of the Baroque temperament:

> Ask where that iron is that is ground off a knife or axe; ask that marble that is worn off of the threshold in the church porch by continual treading; and with that iron and with that marble thou mayst find thy father's skin and body; *contrita sunt*, the knife, the marble, the skin, the body are ground away, trod away; they are destroyed. Who knows the revolutions of dust? Dust upon the king's highway and dust upon the king's grave are both, or neither, dust royal and may change places. Who knows the revolutions of dust?

III

WE HAVE already noted that Baroque prose owes many of its qualities to the concerns of the age—the scientific revolution, the decline of traditional authorities, and a heightened religious awareness. It would be unwise to yield to the temptation of establishing a simple cause-and-effect relationship between the Baroque prose styles and the stimuli of intellectual history. Although these styles owe much to the fears, hopes, and beliefs of the men who employed them, they owe something also to the rhythms of literary history itself, to an internal development quite independent of external influences. In particular, the radical stylistic innovations of the earlier seventeenth century seem connected to the quasi-regular alternation, characteristic of western European literature and art from the time of antiquity onward, between two opposed conceptions of art and the role of the artist. To one of these conceptions tradition has given the name *Classicism*—that kind of art which is distinguished by relative impersonality and objectivity, restraint, decorum, more or less severe limitation of means, and a strong tendency to employ set and invariable forms and genres. Scholars and historians show less unanimity in the designation of the opposed conception of art: the terms *Romanticism* and *Baroque* have often been suggested, but their utility as terms referring to historically delimited artistic periods makes it undesirable that their significance be blurred by being used as universals. One might perhaps use the term *Expressionism*—as long as it remains clear that the term is used in a sweeping and broadly defined sense that has little to do with the minor European literary movement of the early twentieth century which went by that name. *Expressionism*, used as a constant, refers to that kind of literature which is opposed to Classicism and is distinguished by relative subjectivity and individualism, lack of restraint and decorum, an expansive and sometimes idiosyncratic attitude toward means, and a tendency to evolve unique forms and new genres.

When either conception of art and the artist has been dominant for a certain length of time, it tends toward an exaggeration and excess of its own qualities and thus prepares the way for a reaction against it—a movement toward the vitally opposed counter-principle. Just as, in the later eighteenth century, a Neoclassicism which had grown outworn and brittle yielded to the new expressive forms of Romanticism, so did Renaissance literature in the 1590's, having pushed to the extreme limit its features of luxuriance and formalism, give way to the analytic, intense, and angular forms of Baroque literature.

One apparent contradiction manifests itself in opposition to the view of Baroque prose style as one of the recurrent manifestations of the literary tendency opposed to Classicism: Expressionism (or *Mannerism*, to use another term recently introduced to designate this phenomenon) is often defined in terms of a preoccupation with style as an end, and we have already seen that the anti-Ciceronian element in Baroque prose is vociferously concerned with the exaltation of content over form, of truth over manner of expression. But there is a difference between an author's role and his conception of that role; the practitioners of the extreme Senecan style, for example, were usually at least as self-conscious as stylists as were the Ciceronians whom they decried. Any reading of the major Baroque prose artists—Donne, Bacon, Browne, even the ostensibly haphazard Burton—reveals a man who is determined to express himself completely, in his full individualism, and knows that an absolute and profound mastery of his medium is necessary to that full expression.

IV

WHATEVER the importance of the process of artistic reaction in eliciting a new prose style, whatever its importance in determining the general nature of that style, the specific details of style are related to the historical moment of its formation—to questions and beliefs and values which are extra-artistic. The new science, the new philosophy, and the new quickening of the religious spirit determined among them the particular directions of seventeenth-century prose. We should look more closely at a few aspects of these phenomena as they affected literature.

In the year 1600, in Rome, the philosopher Giordano Bruno was burned at the stake. The heretical cosmological doctrines which brought this fate upon him went beyond the heliocentric theory advanced by Copernicus a half-century before, a theory disturbing enough in itself; Bruno revived and promulgated the heterodox idea that an infinity of universes surrounds us, and that the earth, for so long viewed as the central and dominant feature of a divinely planned cosmos, is not only not central in location but is actually no more than an insignificant speck of dust lost in physical infinity. Representing as he does the radical destruction of the traditional view of the world, Bruno may be regarded as the doomed prophet of the scientific revolution which was, in the course of the fifty years after his death, to achieve almost complete fulfillment. The scientific revolution meant more than the destruction of the ancient authorities, more even than the establishment of new methods and new horizons in human thought; it meant no less than the annihilation of an entire system of symbol and correspondence which had, for centuries, given man not only his philosophy but also his poetry.

Renaissance man, like his medieval forebears, lived in a universe of never failing significance: man himself, viewed as a "microcosm," or "little world," mirrored in every detail of his bodily construction the physical organization of the "macrocosm," or "great world," whether that macrocosm was conceived of as the earth or as the entire universe. Thus the sciences of medicine and psychology were traditionally based on the real correspondences which it was felt existed between bodily features and the elements of the creation: earth, air, fire, and water, for example, corresponded to the four "humors," or liquids, which determined man's mental as well as physical health. Thus also the political system of monarchy found its divine and natural justification in the conception of the universe as an ordered whole of interrelated analogies: the king was to the state as the head was to the body or as God was to His creation; treason was accordingly a crime not only against the state but against the universe and against God Himself. It was a supremely comforting and aesthetically satisfying world view: God, the "circle whose circumference is everywhere and whose center is nowhere," gave His form of perfection to all His creation—to the flawless circles described by the planets in their orbits around the earth, to the round earth itself, to the round head of man— that head which was the seat of his Godlike reason. In a fallen world of change, decay, and death, man could at least look up to the heavens and see, beyond the sphere of the moon, a universe in which he was assured neither corruption nor change could take place. It was this beautiful and orderly world which seventeenth-century science destroyed. Kepler demonstrated in his laws of celestial motion that the planets describe orbits which are in fact not perfect circles but ellipses; Galileo, in his *Sidereus Nuntius* of 1610, reported his discovery of new celestial bodies and thus called into question the whole belief in superlunar perfection and permanence. Between them these founders of modern astronomy gave a terrifying kind of credibility to the Copernican theory.

It would be an historical error of major dimensions, however, to conceive of the intellectual history of the early seventeenth century as a simple conflict between the enlightened modernists and the benighted traditionalists, as an uncomplicated opposition between Bruno and Galileo on the one hand and their ecclesiastical persecutors on the other. The old view interpenetrates the new vision in the thought of almost every one of these fathers of science: Kepler established the laws of movement of the heavenly bodies, but continued to conceive of these bodies as occupied each by its private angel. In his *De Magnete* (1600), Gilbert established the study of magnetism and electricity and made the crucial distinction between "argument" and "experiment"—but also made it clear that he continued to view the world as an animate being, in full accord with the inherited conception. And Harvey's great discovery of the circulation of the blood was inspired in part by his awareness of the universal significance of the circle as a symbol of perfection.

If such men as these found it impossible completely to slough off the conventional vision of the world, we can imagine the difficulties encountered by less original and less brilliant thinkers. So it is that the literature influenced most strongly by the new science is not, except in the anomalous case of Bacon, a literature of assurance, confidence, and promise; rather it is a literature of conflict, contradiction, worry, and pessimism. Scientific innovation was a strong element in the formation of that early-century mood to which historians have given the name "Jacobean melancholy," for the typical writer or intellectual of the time could not believe that the theories of the new science, if true, meant anything other than the impending, and promised, end of the world. Thus Sir Thomas Browne, in the great concluding chapter of the *Hydriotaphia* (1658), writes: " 'Tis too late to be ambitious. The great mutations of the world are acted, or time may be too short for our designs." Donne's most ambitious poems, *The Anniversaries* (1611–12), take their form initially as meditations on the new science as a portent of the decay of the world. The degree to which these theories permeated the imagination of the time is suggested by compulsive references throughout the *Devotions upon Emergent Occasions* (1624). At the same time, these troubled men responded to the positive aspects of the new philosophy as well: Browne's *Pseudodoxia* (1646) is a specifically Baconian undertaking, and it is possible to regard Donne's whole achievement in prose and poetry as to some extent the application to his own mind and soul of the principles of observation and experimentation.

V

THE heightened religious sensibility of the Baroque age is due in part to the disturbing implications of the new science and the new philosophy. In fear men sought refuge in the eternal verities proclaimed by traditional religious teachings. To an even greater degree, however, this religious reawakening is to be regarded as a natural consequence of the Reformation. There is, inevitably, a considerable historical lag between the introduction of any important spiritual movement and the full impact of that movement on the life and thought of people in general; thus the moral and theological earnestness of the great reformers did not make itself significantly felt until close to the end of the sixteenth century. The seventeenth century is the great age of religious intensity as it is the great age of religious controversy. Protestantism, especially in such extreme manifestations as Puritanism, rejected the whole idea of extraneous ornamentation in literary style as violently as it did the popish symbols of images and incense in divine worship. And moderate Anglicanism felt obliged, to a certain extent, to assert its authentic Protestantism through a comparable sobriety and plainness of manner: George Herbert's *A Priest to the Temple* (1652) will serve as a fair example of this tendency in the standard prose of the period. At the same time, within the Anglican persuasion itself, an opposed tendency was making itself felt: the flamboyant idiosyncrasy of Donne's pulpit style was an expression of a general quality in the current of European religious feeling of the seventeenth century. The pulpit style which spread in that century from Catholic Italy to Protestant England and Sweden, highly individual, strongly dependent on the *concetto predicabile*, or "preachable conceit," is a peculiarly colorful variety of Baroque prose. Essentially anti-Ciceronian, it is nevertheless anything but plain. Still, it is interesting to note that its very vividness attracted a certain degree of censure from the earliest years of the century onward, and that well before the crucial year 1660 the ornate style of pulpit oratory had yielded to the ever increasing taste for the sober and the reserved.

Individuality of expression, as well as plainness of expression, was implied in the Puritan system of values. But the average Puritan Parliamentarian of 1642 would have felt a thrill of horror at the prospect of what yet more extreme individualists were to preach concerning man's soul, the Bible, and the organization of society. Before the Commonwealth period had reached its disappointing end, the so-called "Levellers" and "Diggers" had promulgated egalitarian and protosocialist ideas across the land, and such sects as the Quaker had made the doctrine of "inner light" the basis for a whole view of behavior and salvation. Extreme Protestant individualism attains its last literary expression, and one of its greatest, in Bunyan, in whose masterpiece, *Pilgrim's Progress*, however, innate taste and the great example of the English Bible combine to curb any potential eccentricities of manner and thus contribute to a style notable for its purity, directness, and extraordinary felicity.

If Protestantism contributed to English prose a taste for plainness and a sanction for individualism, the Catholic tradition, in its larger sense, contributed other elements. The Counter-Reformation's recommendation of appeals to the senses as aids to religious devotion found its echoes in England, even among men to whom the idea of "popery" was an abomination, and the practice of formal meditation, initiated in Spain and Italy in the sixteenth century, left its mark on much English religious prose of the period. The movement of Donne's *Devotions*—from the concrete and vivid evocation of a scene or object through the metaphorical or analytic examination of its significance to a radically reoriented emotional state—relates not only to the Metaphysical style in poetry but also to the entire Catholic tradition of meditation.

The characteristic forms and genres of prose literature in the Baroque age reveal at the same time the diverse interests and points of view of its authors and the common seriousness of purpose which unites them. English prose of the seventeenth century is essentially, as we have seen, a prose of utility; the varied purposes of the writers almost never include a specifically aesthetic motive or a specific dedication to entertainment. Treatises, tracts, and pamphlets; sermons, devotions, and prayers; biographical, historical, and scientific studies—such are the shapes assumed by prose art in one of its greatest periods. Prose fiction, as such, shows almost nothing of the vigor it was to assume early in the next century; in fact, it has conspicuously less importance than it had in the age of Elizabeth. The greatest piece of fictional prose produced by the century—*Pilgrim's Progress*—is dominated by religious motives which are anything but artistic; it is an artistic masterpiece almost in spite of itself. Even the prose genres which seem most clearly aimed at diverting their readers and nothing more—the essay and the character-book—partake of the general moral or practical preoccupations of the age. Bacon's *Essays* are subtitled "Counsels," and Fuller's characters take their being in a rigidly moral view of human society.

But the single-minded pursuit of truth, whether sacred or secular, which is the all-dominating concern of the writers of the first two-thirds of the seventeenth century, in no way interferes with the aesthetic effect of their creations. For Browne, for Burton, for Bacon, for Donne, the complete utterance of the vision of truth inevitably requires the utilization of all the conceivable implements available to the artist. Totality of statement is their common aim, and this totality can never be divided by such dichotomies as that of reason versus emotion or science versus art. T. S. Eliot, in an influential essay,[3] has suggested that the "unified sensibility" is the basis of the effects of much seventeenth-century poetry; the same sensibility is at the root of the prose written between 1600 and 1660. The separation of intellectually perceived truth from its embodiment in emotionally committed or persuasive prose was, to the Baroque artist, inconceivable. To their incapacity for compartmentalizing the manifold personality we owe our rich heritage of earlier seventeenth-century prose—a body of writing which, though always more than art, is never less than art.

VI

FOR PROSE, as for almost every other aspect of thought and art in seventeenth-century England, 1660, the year of the restoration of Charles II, constitutes an absolute watershed. If totality of statement serves as the common defining feature of Baroque prose, specialization and the rigid exclusion of the seemingly irrelevant define Augustan prose. Abraham Cowley's *Proposition for the Advancement of Experimental Philosophy* (1661) shows the marks of the new sensibility as clearly in its reserved and conversational manner of expression as in its advocacy of the experimental method in learning. And the personality which emerges from the same writer's *Essays* (1668) is, if more tolerant, urbane, and generally sane than that of the giants of the early century, notably less complex and passionate. Almost all the important writers of the last third of the century—with the major exceptions of John Bunyan and Thomas Traherne—are united by a common practicality of outlook, evenness of temper, and studied plainness of style: Cowley and Temple, Pepys and Evelyn, Dryden and Halifax are very different personalities with very different interests, but they all display an aversion to mystery, mysticism, paradox, and enthusiasm which is the measure of their difference from their Baroque predecessors.

It is a commonplace of intellectual history to attribute the change in the English temper around 1660 to the definitive triumph of the scientific spirit, as symbolized in

3 "The Metaphysical Poets." See Appendix, pp. 1061–1065.

the establishment of the Royal Society (1662). Few commonplaces have a more absolute validity. Unquestionably the great shift in intellectual orientation implicit in the spread of the methods of the new science had an effect on every phase of European thought and, inevitably, on every aspect of European art. A less circuitous, less luxuriant, and more precisely ordered approach to the organization of a literary work is one important result of the triumph of the scientific habit of mind; a rigid separation of the emotive qualities of language from the informative and descriptive qualities is another. These qualities of orderliness and restraint, rather than plainness as such, mark the transition from Baroque to Augustan prose; "plain" writing, as we have seen, is to be found in abundance in the period before 1660, but even its plainness aims at emotional immediacy and intellectual abundance.

Even more important than these effects of science upon prose style was the impact of the scientific outlook upon the inherited religious sensibility of the century. The new astronomy and the new philosophy (that of Descartes and Hobbes, for example) had alike set God at an infinitely great remove from human experience. From being an ever present vital principle, that "warm gale and gentle ventilation" felt by Sir Thomas Browne, the Deity had become a kind of glorified watchmaker in the distant heavens, a being whose handiwork operated on the basis of built-in rational laws and who was best understood and worshiped through the observation and understanding of His creation. A glance at the dominant prose genres of the period 1660–1700—essays, diaries, brief biographies, history, and literary criticism—will reveal to how great an extent the study of man in his social and political milieu had become the proper study of mankind.

Despite the central position of the scientific spirit in the formation of the new sensibility, we should not overlook other phenomena which contributed to its formation. In a sense, the religious passions of the early century, which had burst into flame with the great Civil War, had through their very intensity burned themselves out. From sheer exhaustion as much as anything else, the people of England turned away from austerity, ecstasy, and prophecy alike; the tolerant and low-keyed mood of Halifax's *Trimmer* (1688) expressed the spirit of the Restoration more faithfully than did the vatic stance of *Paradise Lost* (1667). Milton's masterpiece stands with *Pilgrim's Progress* (1678) and *Centuries of Meditations* (c. 1670) as a last great monument of the older sensibility.

Chance as well as historical process played a role in the creation of the Restoration temper. For some eleven years, from the execution of Charles I in 1649 until the restoration of Charles II in 1660, an appreciable number of English aristocrats and intellectuals had been in self-imposed exile in Paris. Inevitably they were subject there to the influence of seventeenth-century French civilization with its strong emphasis on order and restraint, its rigid interpretation of Classical decorum, and its feeling for the supremacy of rules—all features which had contributed to the characteristic literary expressions of the age of Louis XIV. To a certain extent, the Neoclassical ideals which were, at least officially, to dominate English literature for the century after 1660 may be regarded as imported ideals. Their firm establishment in English culture of the Augustan age was facilitated by still another historical circumstance—the successive domination of the English literary scene by three great literary dictators with Classical tastes: Dryden, Pope, and Johnson. Another development in English prose which may be traced at least partially to the influence of French culture is the enormous importance assumed by literary theory and criticism, activities which had been almost completely slighted by the Baroque writers. In Augustan England, as in the France of Louis XIV, Racine, and Boileau, a self-conscious concern with the nature of the literary work and with its relations to other forms of knowledge and expression made itself consistently felt. The growth of English literary criticism, related at once to the spirit of French Classicism and to the analytic temper of a scientific age, no doubt owed something as well to the character of the greatest writer of the Restoration period—John Dryden.

Dryden did more than any single writer to make certain the triumph of Neoclassical attitudes and values in his age and in that which followed, but he was in no sense rigid or narrow in either his conception of literature or his capacity to judge individual works. His feeling for decorum, order, and the rules is consistently modified by a wide-ranging taste and generous quantities of common sense. The combination of breadth of vision, depth of analytic insight, and flexibility of attitude makes Dryden the first of the great English literary critics. The prose in which he expresses his views on literature is a consummately efficient instrument, fashioned for its purpose more neatly than anything known before it in England. It is difficult to find, in the closely woven texture and seemingly inevitable organization of his essays, a single brief passage which will epitomize its qualities, but perhaps the following few sentences from the *Essay of Dramatic Poesy* (1668) will suggest the clarity, ease, vigor, and precision which he regularly achieved.

> The old rule of logic might have convinced him, that contraries, when placed near, set off each other. A continued gravity keeps the spirit too much bent; we must refresh it sometimes, as we bait in a journey that we may go on with greater ease. A scene of mirth, mixed with tragedy, has the same effect upon us which our music has betwixt the acts; which we find a relief to us from the best plots and language of the stage, if the discourses have been long. I must therefore have stronger arguments, ere I am convinced that compassion and mirth in the same subject destroy each other; and in the meantime cannot but conclude, to the honor of our nation, that we have invented, increased, and perfected a more pleasant way of writing for the stage, than was ever known to the ancients or moderns of any nation. . . .

This is, in the good sense of the phrase, modern prose—closer in many ways to the writing of our own century than to that of the generation before Dryden. Its strengths are those of good modern prose, as are, by the same token, its weaknesses. For every gain there is a corresponding loss, and we shall listen in vain in Dryden's harmonious achievement for the mighty cadences of the Baroque artists. The pomp and the desperate passion alike had vanished from English prose to be replaced by the fluent, civilized medium of communication which Dryden was the first to perfect. Seventeenth-century men had created the modern world, and Dryden gave that world its language. What was lost in the process is not irretrievably lost for the reader who will turn to Browne or Burton, Donne or Bacon, Walton or Bunyan. The "century of genius" left its monument behind in words of genius available to us all.

BIBLIOGRAPHY
[A selective list]

D. BUSH. *English Literature in the Earlier Seventeenth Century, 1600–1660* (New York, rev. ed., 1962).
W. G. CRANE. *Wit and Rhetoric in the Renaissance* (New York, 1937).

R. COLIE. *Paradoxia Epidemica* (Princeton, 1966).

M. W. CROLL. *Style, Rhetoric, and Rhythm,* ed. J. Max Patrick, R. O. Evans, *et al.* (Princeton, 1966).

S. FISH. *Self-Consuming Artifacts* (Berkeley, Calif., 1972).

R. F. JONES. *Ancients and Moderns* (St. Louis, 1936). Excellent on the impact of science in the seventeenth century.

E. N. S. THOMPSON. *Literary Bypaths of the Renaissance* (New Haven, 1924). A study of character-books and similar phenomena.

J. WEBBER. *The Eloquent "I"* (Madison, Wisc., 1968).

B. WILLEY. *The Seventeenth-Century Background* (London, 1934). A very useful study of seventeenth-century thought.

G. WILLIAMSON. *The Senecan Amble* (Chicago, 1951). Examines the rise of the Senecan style in prose.

F. P. WILSON. *Elizabethan and Jacobean* (Oxford, 1945).

Nicholas Breton

[*c.* 1555–*c.* 1626]

THE facts of Breton's[1] early life are obscure, but we know that he was eight or nine years old at the time of the death of his father, a prosperous London merchant, and that his mother's subsequent marriage to the poet George Gascoigne led to a considerable diminution of Breton's patrimony. He himself refers to his having studied at Oxford, although this fact cannot be definitely substantiated, and it is also believed that he traveled widely on the Continent at one time.

Breton seems to have been a friend of Shakespeare and Ben Jonson, and he was one of the poets to whom Mary, Countess of Pembroke, extended her patronage. He was one of Lady Pembroke's "outer circle," and may at one time have been a member of her "little court." He was, in any case, acquainted with the members of this group, and gives some account of them in his *Wit's Trenchmour*.[2] Like others of Lady Pembroke's group, he dedicated several of his works to her. The relationship between the two ceased in about 1601, and scholars have conjectured—on the basis of references in *Wit's Trenchmour* to the rejection of his suit by a high-born lady—that Breton's attentions may have offended the Countess by going beyond the limit of distant adoration permitted a poet by his patroness.

Breton occupies a curiously transitional position in English literature. Starting his career as a typical Elizabethan, he practiced the characteristic literary forms of that age —pastorals, satires, letter-books, political pamphlets, and a vast quantity of miscellaneous poetry. At some point in the opening years of the seventeenth century, he turned his attention primarily to prose, typifying in this respect a general tendency displayed by popular literature at the turn of the century. He produced, in his *Fantastics*, a work which informs with the Elizabethan qualities of delicacy, grace, and feeling for nature the burgeoning seventeenth-century genre of the character-book. The character-book, as developed later in the century by Overbury, Earle, and Fuller, presents the reader with a witty compendium of human types. In *Fantastics* the characters described are rather such unreal yet definite entities as love, money, the four seasons, the twelve hours of the day, and the months of the year. Breton's treatment, furthermore, aims at descriptive elaboration rather than witty condensation; he displays neither the analytic capacity nor the occasional malice of the later character writers, and the result is a work which has continuing value for its imaginative particularity and its vivid portrayal of the manners and customs of the English countryside three centuries ago. In both these respects it anticipates a greater work, one which was certainly influenced by it to some

1 The name is pronounced "Briton."　　　　　　　　　　2 A lively popular dance.

degree—Izaak Walton's *Complete Angler* (1653). Like Walton's, Breton's pages breathe for all their pastoral idealization an air of concrete reality which is relatively rare in the period.

Among Breton's numerous other prose works may be mentioned *A Post with a Mad Packet of Letters* and *A Mad World, my Masters*. Essentially a popular writer, never within reach of greatness, Breton has importance both as a writer of singular sweetness and ease and as a highly significant figure bridging the very different eras of Elizabeth and James.

N. BRETON. *Works in Verse and Prose*, ed. A. Grosart, 2 vols. (London, 1879). Though not absolutely complete, this must still rank as the definitive edition of Breton's works.

————. *Poems*, ed. J. Robertson (Liverpool, 1952). Contains the best bibliography and study of the canon.

E. BLUNDEN. In *Votive Tablets* (London, 1931).

N. E. MONTROSE. *Nicholas Breton As a Pamphleteer* (Philadelphia, 1929). Probably the most considerable study of Breton as a prose writer.

F R O M

FANTASTICS: SERVING FOR A PERPETUAL PROGNOSTICATION

[TEXT: *first edition, 1626*]

JANUARY

IT IS now January, and Time begins to turn the wheel of his revolution. The woods begin to lose the beauty of their spreading boughs, and the proud oak must stoop to the axe. The squirrel now surveyeth the nut and the maple, and the hedgehog rolls up himself like a football. An apple and a nutmeg make a gossip's cup, and the ale and the faggot are the victualler's merchandise. The northern black dust[3] is the during fuel, and the fruit of the grape heats the stomach of the aged. Down beds and quilted caps[4] are now in the pride of their service, and the cook and the pantler[5] are men of no mean office. The ox and the fat wether now furnish the market, and the coney is so ferreted that she cannot keep in her burrow. The currier[6] and the lime-rod[7] are the death of the fowl, and the falcon's bells ring the death of the mallard. The trotting gelding makes a way through the mire, and the hare and the hound put the huntsman to his horn. The barren doe subscribes to the dish, and the smallest seed[8] makes sauce to the greatest flesh. The dried grass is the horse's ordinary, and the meal of the beans makes him go through with his travel. Fishermen now have a cold trade and travellers a foul journey. The cook room now is not the worst place in the ship, and the shepherd hath a bleak seat on the mountain. The blackbird leaveth not a berry on the thorn, and the garden earth is turned up for her roots. The water floods run over the proud banks, and the gaping oyster leaves his shell in the streets, while the proud peacock leaps into the pie. Muscovia commodities are now much in request, and the water spaniel is a necessary servant. The load-horse to the mill hath his full back-burden, and the thresher in the barn tries the strength of his flail. The woodcock and the pheasant pay their lives for their feed, and the hare after a course makes his hearse in a pie. The shoulder of a hog is a shoeing-horn to good drink,[9] and a cold alms makes a beggar shrug. To conclude, I hold it a time of little comfort, the rich man's charge and the poor man's misery. Farewell.

---

3 Coal, brought by sea from Newcastle.
4 Coverlets.   5 Pantryman.
6 A harquebus, or a man armed with one.
7 A lime twig; a branch smeared with an adhesive substance to catch birds for food.

8 Mustard, for the roast beef.
9 Salt bacon helps down drink.

FEBRUARY

IT IS now February, and the sun is gotten up a cock-stride of his climbing. The valleys now are painted white, and the brooks are full of water. The frog goes to seek out the paddock, and the crow and the rook begin to mislike their old makes.[10] Forward coneys begin now to kindle, and the fat grounds are not without lambs. The gardener falls to sorting of his seeds, and the husbandman falls afresh to scouring of his plowshare. The term-travellers[11] make the shoemaker's harvest, and the chandler's cheese makes the chalk walk apace.[12] The fishmonger sorts his ware against Lent, and a lamb-skin is good for a lame arm. The waters now alter the nature of their softness, and the soft earth is made stony hard. The air is sharp and piercing, and the winds blow cold. The taverns and the inns seldom lack guests, and the ostler knows how to gain by his hay. The hunting horse is at the heels of the hound, while the ambling nag carrieth the physician and his footcloth. The blood of youth begins to spring, and the honor of art is gotten by exercise. The trees a little begin to bud, and the sap begins to rise up out of the root. Physic now hath work among weak bodies, and the apothecary's drugs are very gainful. There is hope of a better time not far off, for this in itself is little comfortable. And for the small pleasure that I find in it, I will thus briefly conclude of it: it is the poor man's pick-purse and the miser's cut-throat, the enemy to pleasure and the time of patience. Farewell.

MARCH

IT IS now March, and the northern wind drieth up the southern dirt. The tender lips are now masked for fear of chapping, and the fair hands must not be ungloved. Now riseth the sun a pretty step to his fair height, and Saint Valentine calls the birds together where nature is pleased in the variety of love. The fishes and the frogs fall to their manner of generation, and the adder dies to bring forth her young. The air is sharp, but the sun is comfortable and the day begins to lengthen. The forward gardens give the fine sallets, and a nosegay of violets is a present for a lady. Now beginneth nature, as it were, to wake out of her sleep and send the traveller to survey the walks of the world. The sucking rabbit is good for weak stomachs, and the diet for the

rheum doth many a great cure. The farrier now is the horse's physician, and the fat dog feeds the falcon in the mew.[13] The tree begins to bud and the grass to peep abroad, while the thrush with the blackbird make a charm in the young springs. The milkmaid with her best-beloved talk away weariness to the market, and in an honest meaning kind words do not hurt. The football now trieth the legs of strength, and merry matches continue good-fellowship. It is a time of much work and tedious to discourse of, but in all I find of it, I thus conclude in it: I hold it the servant of nature and the schoolmaster of art, the hope of labor and the subject of reason. Farewell.

APRIL

IT IS now April, and the nightingale begins to tune her throat against May. The sunny showers perfume the air and the bees begin to go abroad for honey. The dew, as in pearls, hangs upon the tops of the grass, while the turtles sit billing upon the little green boughs. The trout begins to play in the brooks, and the salmon leaves the sea to play in the fresh waters. The garden-banks are full of gay flowers, and the thorn and the plum send forth their fair blossoms. The March colt begins to play, and the cosset lamb[14] is learned to butt. The poets now make their studies in the woods, and the youth of the country make ready for the morris-dance. The little fishes lie nibbling at a bait, and the porpoise plays in the pride of the tide. The shepherd's pipe entertains the Princess of Arcadia, and the healthful soldier has a pleasant march. The lark and the lamb look up at the sun, and the laborer is abroad by the dawning of the day. Sheep's eyes in lambs' heads[15] tell kind hearts strange tales, while faith and troth make the true lover's knot. The aged hairs find a fresh life, and the youthful cheeks are as red as a cherry. It were a world to set down the worth of this month, but in sum, I thus conclude: I hold it the heaven's blessing and the earth's comfort. Farewell.

MAY

IT IS now May, and the sweetness of the air refresheth every spirit. The sunny beams bring forth fair blossoms, and the dripping clouds water Flora's great garden. The male deer puts out the velvet head, and the pagged[16] doe is near her fawning. The sparhawk now is drawn out of the mew, and the fowler makes

---

10 Mates.   11 Scholars.
12 Salted cheese runs up the scores chalked up against customers in the alehouses.

13 Cage.   14 A lamb reared by hand.
15 The wanton glances of lovelorn maidens.
16 Pregnant.

ready his whistle for the quail. The lark sets the morning watch, and the evening the nightingale. The barges, like bowers, keep the streams of the sweet rivers, and the mackerel with the shad are taken prisoners in the sea. The tall young oak is cut down for the maypole. The scythe and the sickle are the mower's furniture, and fair weather makes the laborer merry. The physician now prescribes the cold whey, and the apothecary gathers the dew for a medicine. Butter and sage make the wholesome breakfast, but fresh cheese and cream are meat for a dainty mouth, and the strawberry and the peasecod want no price in the market. The chicken and the duck are fattened for the market, and many a gosling never lives to be a goose. It is the month wherein nature hath her full of mirth and the senses are filled with delights. I conclude, it is from the heavens a grace and to the earth a gladness. Farewell.

JUNE

IT IS now June, and the haymakers are mustered to make an army for the field where, not always in order, they march under the bag [17] and the bottle, when betwixt the fork and the rake there is seen great force of arms. Now doth the broad oak comfort the weary laborer while under his shady boughs he sits singing to his bread and cheese. The hay-cock is the poor man's lodging, and the fresh river is his gracious neighbor. Now the falcon and the tassel try their wings at the partridge, and the fat buck fills the great pasty. The trees are all in their rich array, but the seely [18] sheep is turned out of his coat. The roses and sweet herbs put the distiller to his cunning, while the green apples on the tree are ready for the great-bellied wives. Now begins the hare to gather up her heels, and the fox looks about him for fear of the hound. The hook and the sickle are making ready for the harvest. The meadow grounds gape for rain, and the corn in the ear begins to harden. The little lads make pipes of the straw, and they that cannot dance will yet be hopping. The air now groweth somewhat warm, and the cool winds are very comfortable. The sailor now makes merry passage, and the nimble footman runs with pleasure. In brief, I thus conclude: I hold it a sweet season, the senses' perfume and the spirit's comfort. Farewell.

JULY

IT IS now July, and the sun is gotten up to his height, whose heat parcheth the earth and burns up the grass on the mountains. Now begins the cannon of heaven to rattle, and when the fire is put to the charge, it breaketh out among the clouds. The stones of congealed water cut off the ears of the corn, and the black storms affright the faint-hearted. The stag and the buck are now in the pride of their time, and the hardness of their heads makes them fit for the horner. [19] Now hath the sparhawk the partridge in the foot, and the ferret doth tickle the coney in the burrow. Now doth the farmer make ready his team, and the carter with his whip hath no small pride in his whistle. Now do the reapers try their backs and their arms, and the lusty youths pitch the sheaves into the cart. The old partridge calls her covey in the morning, and in the evening the shepherd falls to folding of his flock. The sparrows make a charm upon the green bushes till the fowler come and take them by the dozens. The smelt now begins to be in season, and the lamprey out of the river leaps into a pie. The soldier now hath a hot march, and the lawyer sweats in his lined gown. The pedlar now makes a long walk, and the aqua-vitæ bottle sets his face on a fiery heat. In sum, I thus conclude of it: I hold it a profitable season, the laborer's gain and the rich man's wealth. Farewell.

AUGUST

IT IS now August, and the sun is somewhat towards his declination, yet such is his heat as hardeneth the soft clay, dries up the standing ponds, withereth the sappy leaves, and scorcheth the skin of the naked. Now begin the gleaners to follow the corn cart, and a little bread to a great deal of drink maketh the traveller's dinner. The melon and the cucumber is now in request, and oil and vinegar give attendance on the sallet herbs. The alehouse is more frequented than the tavern, and a fresh river is more comfortable than a fiery furnace. The bath is now much visited by diseased bodies, and in the fair rivers swimming is a sweet exercise. The bow and the bowl pick many a purse, and the cocks with their heels spurn away many a man's wealth. The pipe and the tabor is now lustily set on work, and the lad and the lass will have no lead on their heels. The new wheat makes the gossip's cake, and the bride cup is carried above the heads of the whole parish. The furmenty [20] pot welcomes home the harvest cart, and the garland of flowers crowns the captain of the reapers. Oh, 'tis the merry time,

17 Wineskin. 18 Innocent.

19 Horn merchant.
20 Frumenty—hulled wheat boiled in milk and seasoned.

wherein honest neighbors make good cheer and God is glorified in his blessings on the earth. In sum, for that I find, I thus conclude: I hold it the world's welfare and the earth's warming-pan. Farewell.

SEPTEMBER

IT IS now September, and the sun begins to fall much from his height. The meadows are left bare by the mouths of hungry cattle, and the hogs are turned into the cornfields. The winds begin to knock the apples' heads together on the trees, and the fallings are gathered to fill the pies for the household. The sailors fall to work to get afore the wind, and if they spy a storm it puts them to prayer. The soldier now begins to shrug at the weather, and the camp dissolved, the companies are put to garrison. The lawyer now begins his harvest, and the client pays for words by weight. The inns now begin to provide for guests, and the night-eaters in the stable pinch the traveller in his bed. Paper, pen, and ink are much in request, and the quarter-sessions take order with the way-layers. Coals and wood make toward the chimney, and ale and sack are in account with good fellows. The butcher now knocks down the great beeves, and the poulter's feathers make toward the upholster. Walflet oysters are the fishwives' wealth, and pippins fine are the costermonger's rich merchandise. The flail and the fan fall to work in the barn, and the corn market is full of the bakers. The porkets now are driven to the woods, and the home-fed pigs make pork for the market. In brief, I thus conclude of it: I hold it the winter's forewarning and the summer's farewell.

OCTOBER

IT IS now October, and the lofty winds make bare the trees of their leaves, while the hogs in the woods grow fat with the fallen acorns. The forward deer begin to go to rut, and the barren doe groweth good meat. The basket-makers now gather their rods, and the fishers lay their leaps [21] in the deep. The load-horses go apace to the mill, and the meal-market is seldom without people. The hare on the hill makes the greyhound a fair course, and the fox in the woods calls the hounds to a full cry. The multitude of people raiseth the price of wares, and the smooth tongue will sell much. The sailor now bestirreth his stumps, while the merchant liveth in fear of the weather. The great feasts are now at hand for the city, but the poor must not beg for fear of the stocks. A fire and a pair [22] of cards keep the

21 Baskets or nets to catch fish in.   22 Set.

guests in the ordinary, and tobacco is held very precious for the rheum. The coaches now begin to rattle in the streets, but the cry of the poor is unpleasing to the rich. Muffs and cuffs are now in request, and the shuttlecock with the battledore is a pretty house exercise. Tennis and balloon [23] are sports of some charge, and a quick bandy [24] is the court-keeper's commodity. Dancing and fencing are now in some use, and kind hearts and true lovers lie close to keep off cold. The titmouse now keeps in the hollow tree, and the blackbird sits close in the bottom of a hedge. In brief, for the little pleasure I find in it, I thus conclude of it: I hold it a messenger of ill news and a second service to a cold dinner. Farewell.

NOVEMBER

IT IS now November, and according to the old proverb,

Let the thresher take his flail,
And the ship no more sail,

for the high winds and the rough seas will try the ribs of the ship and the hearts of the sailors. Now come the country people all wet to the market, and the toiling carriers are pitifully moiled. [25] The young hern [26] and the shoulerd [27] are now fat for the great feast, and the woodcock begins to make toward the cockshoot. [28] The warreners [29] now begin to pile their harvest, and the butcher after a good bargain drinks a health to the grazier. The cook and the comfitmaker make ready for Christmas, and the minstrels in the country beat their boys for false fingering. Scholars before breakfast have a cold stomach to their books, and a master without art is fit for an A B C. A red herring and a cup of sack make war in a weak stomach, and the poor man's fast is better than the glutton's surfeit. Trenchers and dishes are now necessary servants, and a lock to the cupboard keeps a bit for a need. Now begins the goshawk to weed the wood of the pheasant, and the mallard loves not to hear the bells of the falcon. The winds now are cold and the air chill, and the poor die through want of charity. Butter and cheese begin to raise their prices, and kitchen stuff is a commodity that every man is not acquainted with. In sum, with a conceit of the chilling cold of it, I thus conclude in it:

23 A balloon game.   24 An old form of hockey.
25 Daubed with dirt.   26 Heron.
27 The shoveler, a kind of duck.
28 An open space with nets stretched across to catch woodcock or other game.
29 Rabbit catchers.

I hold it the discomfort of nature and reason's patience. Farewell.

DECEMBER

IT IS now December, and he that walks the streets shall find dirt on his shoes, except he go all in boots. Now doth the lawyer make an end of his harvest and the client of his purse. Now capons and hens, beside turkeys, geese and ducks, besides beef and mutton, must all die for the great feast, for in twelve days a multitude of people will not be fed with a little. Now plums and spice, sugar and honey, square it among pies and broth, and Gossip I drink to you, and you are welcome, and I thank you, and how do you, and I pray you be merry. Now are the tailors and tire-makers[30] full of work against the holidays, and music now must be in tune or else never. The youth must dance and sing and the aged sit by the fire. It is the law of nature and no contradiction in reason. The ass that hath borne all the year must now take a little rest, and the lean ox must feed till he be fat. The footman now shall have many a foul step, and the ostler shall have work enough about the heels of the horses, while the tapster, if he take not heed, will lie drunk in the cellar. The prices of meat will rise apace, and the apparel of the proud will make the tailor rich. Dice and cards will benefit the butler, and if the cook do not lack wit he will sweetly lick his fingers. Starchers and launderers will have their hands full of work, and periwigs and paintings will not be a little set by.

> Strange stuffs will be well sold,
> Strange tales well told,
> Strange sights much sought,
> Strange things much bought,
> And what else as falls out.

To conclude, I hold it the costly purveyor of excess and the after-breeder of necessity, the practice of folly and the purgatory of reason. Farewell.

---

30 Headdress makers.

Sir Walter Ralegh

[*c.* 1554–1618]

ORN in Devonshire, Ralegh (though he spelled his name in a variety of ways, he never used the modern spelling "Raleigh") studied briefly at Oxford, fought in the Continental wars of religion, and resided in the Middle Temple as a law student. In 1578 he was engaged in a privateering expedition against the Spaniards, undertaken by his half-brother, Sir Humphrey Gilbert. On his return to London he attached himself to the Earls of Leicester and Oxford. He attracted the attention of Queen Elizabeth, soon became her favorite, and was knighted by her in 1584. The romantic anecdotes associated with Ralegh's life—his laying down his cloak for the Queen to walk on, his introduction of tobacco into England, and the rest—often tend to obscure the positive achievements of his genius. He was instrumental in sending out voyages of exploration and colonization to Virginia; he gave his patronage to Edmund Spenser; and he was active in the intellectual and literary life of late sixteenth-century London.

In 1592, as a result of marrying one of Elizabeth's maids of honor, Elizabeth Throckmorton, he fell from favor, but his boundless energy continued to assert itself in politics, exploration (he led an expedition to South America in search of gold in 1595 and wrote an account of it in his *Discovery of Guiana*), and philosophical speculation. It is unlikely that a formally organized "School of Night," composed of Ralegh, the poet Chapman, the mathematician Harriot, and others of a free-thinking, "atheistical" cast of mind, ever existed as such, but it is certain that Ralegh, like his friends, was of a questioning and skeptical temper.

Little of this skepticism is perceptible in his most important prose work, the *History of the World*, for the greatness of this noble fragment consists precisely in the stately grandeur with which it enunciates the commonplaces of the Elizabethan world view. Perhaps nothing in Ralegh's life is more typical of his Elizabethan ambition and expansiveness than is this extraordinary work, conceived when he was imprisoned in the Tower of London under sentence of death. His intransigent advocacy of a policy of hostility toward Spain had aroused the enmity of James I, who had him committed to the Tower on trumped-up charges of treason shortly after his accession to the throne in 1603. In 1616, motivated by the desire to alleviate his own fiscal problems, James released Ralegh from the Tower so that he might undertake one more voyage of exploration. Ralegh sailed again to Guiana, but a skirmish with Spanish settlers there sealed his doom. On his return to England he was once more condemned to death by James, who yielded to the demands of the Spanish ambassador Gondomar. He was executed on October 29, 1618.

Ralegh has many claims to immortality—as gallant, as statesman, as explorer, as historian, as poet. But it is as a combination of all these that he is best remembered. More than any of his great, and greater, contemporaries, he stands as a symbol of the vigorous and versatile Elizabethan genius.

E. THOMPSON. *Sir Walter Ralegh* (New Haven, 1936). An excellent biography.

M. C. BRADBROOK. *The School of Night* (Cambridge, 1936). A study of Ralegh's literary and philosophical relations.

E. A. STRATHMAN. *Sir Walter Ralegh, a Study in Elizabethan Skepticism* (New York, 1951). A useful study of Ralegh's thought.

A. L. ROWSE. *Sir Walter Ralegh: His Family and Private Life* (New York, 1962). The latest and fullest account.

F R O M

THE HISTORY OF THE WORLD

[TEXT: *first complete edition, 1621*]

How unfit and how unworthy a choice I have made of myself to undertake a work of this mixture mine own reason, though exceeding weak, hath sufficiently resolved me. For had it been begotten then with my first dawn of day, when the light of common knowledge began to open itself to my younger years and before any wound received either from fortune or time, I might yet well have doubted that the darkness of age and death would have covered over both it and me long before the performance. For beginning with the creation, I have proceeded with the History of the World; and lastly, purposed, some few sallies excepted, to confine my discourse within this our renowned Island of Great Britain. I confess that it had better sorted with my disability the better part of whose times are run out in other travels to have set together as I could the unjointed and scattered frame of our English affairs than of the universal, in whom, had there been no other defect (who am all defect) than the time of day, it were enough; the day of a tempestuous life drawn on to the very evening ere I began. But those inmost and soul-piercing wounds which are ever aching while un-cured, with the desire to satisfy those few friends which I have tried by the fire of adversity, the former enforcing, the latter persuading, have caused me to make my thoughts legible and myself the subject of every opinion, wise or weak.

· · · · · · · · · · · ·

Now for King Henry the Eighth, if all the pictures and patterns of a merciless prince were lost in the world, they might all again be painted to the life out of the story of this king. For how many servants did he advance in haste, but for what virtue no man could suspect and with the change of his fancy ruined again, no man knowing for what offence! To how many others of more desert gave he abundant flowers from whence to gather honey, and in the end of harvest burnt them in the hive! How many wives did he cut off and cast off as his fancy and affection changed! How many princes of the blood, whereof some of them for age could hardly crawl towards the block, with a world of others of all degrees of whom our common chronicles have kept the accompt, did he execute! Yea, in his very death-bed, and when he was at the point to have given his accompt to God for the abundance of blood already spilt, he imprisoned the Duke of Norfolk, the father, and executed the Earl of Surrey, the son; the one, whose deservings he knew not how to value, having never omitted anything that concerned his own honor and the king's service; the other, never having committed anything worthy of his least displeasure; the one exceeding valiant and advised; the other no less valiant than learned, and of excellent hope. But besides the sorrows which he heaped upon the fatherless and widows at home and besides the vain enterprises abroad, wherein it is thought that he consumed more treasure than all our victorious kings did in their several conquests, what causeless and cruel wars did he make upon his own nephew King James the Fifth! What laws and wills did he devise to establish this kingdom in his own issues! using his sharpest weapons to cut off and cut down those branches which sprang from the same root that himself did. And in the end, not withstanding these his so many irreligious provisions, it pleased God to take away all his own without increase, though, for themselves in their several kinds, all princes of eminent virtue.

.   .   .   .

But for myself I shall never be persuaded that God hath shut up all the light of learning within the lanthorn of Aristotle's brains or that it was ever said unto him as unto Esdras, *Accendam in corde tuo lucernam intellectus*, that God hath given invention but to the heathen and that they only invaded nature and found the strength and bottom thereof, the same nature having consumed all her store and left nothing of price to after ages. That these and these be the causes of these and these effects time hath taught us and not reason, and so hath experience without art. The cheesewife knoweth it as well as the philosopher that sour rennet doth coagulate the milk into a curd. But if we ask a reason of this cause why the sourness doth it, whereby it doth it, and the manner how, I think that there is nothing to be found in vulgar philosophy to satisfy this and many other like vulgar questions. But man to cover his ignorance in the least things, who cannot give a true reason for the grass under his feet, why it should be green rather than red or of any other color, that could never yet discover the way and reason of nature's working in those which are far less noble creatures than himself, who is far more noble than the heavens themselves, "man," saith Solomon, "that can hardly discern the things that are upon the earth and with great labor find out the things that are before us," that hath so short a time in the world as he no sooner begins to learn than to die, that hath in his memory but borrowed knowledge, in his understanding, nothing truly, that is ignorant of the essence of his own soul and which the wisest of the naturalists, if Aristotle be he, could never so much as define but by the action and effect, telling us what it works (which all men know as well as he) but not what it is, which neither he nor any else doth know, but God that created it—"For though I were perfect, yet I know not my soul," saith Job—man, I say, that is but an idiot in the next cause of his own life and in the cause of all actions of his life, will, notwithstanding, examine the art of God in creating the world, of God, who, saith Job, "is so excellent as we know him not," and examine

the beginning of the work which had end before mankind had a beginning of being.[1]

BUT as men once fallen away from undoubted truth do then after wander for evermore in vices unknown and daily travel towards their eternal perdition; so did these gross and blind idolaters every age after other descend lower and lower and shrink and slide downwards from the knowledge of one true and very God and did not thereby err in worshipping mortal men only but they gave divine reverence and had the same respect to beasts, birds, fishes, fowls, winds, earth, water, air, fire, to the morning, to the evening, to plants, trees, and roots, to passions and affections of the mind, to paleness, sickness, sorrows, yea, to the most unworthy and basest of all these. Which barbarous blasphemy Rhodius Anaxandrides derideth in this manner:

> *Bovem colis, ego deis macto bovem.*
> *Tu maximum anguillam deum putas; ego*
> *Obsoniorum credidi suavissimum.*
> *Carnes suillas tu caves, at gaudeo*
> *His maxime; canem colis quem verbero*
> *Edentem ubi deprehendo forte obsonium.*

I sacrifice to god the beef which you adore.
I broil th' Egyptian eels which you, as god, implore;
You fear to eat the flesh of swine, I find it sweet.
You worship dogs, to beat them I think meet
When they my store devour.

And in this manner Juvenal:

> *Porrum aut cæpe nefas violare aut frangere morsu.*
> *O sanctas gentes quibus hæc nascuntur in hortis numina!*

The Egyptians think it sin to root up or to bite
Their leeks or onions, which they serve with holy rite.
O happy nations which of their own sowing
Have store of gods in every garden growing![2]

But in so great a confusion of vanities, where among the heathens themselves there is no agreement or certainty, it were hard to find out from what example the beginnings of these inventions were borrowed, or after what ancient pattern they erected their building, were it not certain that the Egyptians had knowledge of the first age and of whatsoever was done therein, partly from some inscriptions upon stone or metal remaining after the Flood, and partly from Mizraim,

1 From the Preface.
2 Section iii of Chapter VI, Of Idolatrous Corruptions.

the son of Cham, who had learnt the same of Cham, and Cham of his father, Noah. For all that the Egyptians write of their ancient kings and date of times cannot be feigned. And though other nations after them had by imitation their Jupiters also, their Saturns, Vulcans, and Mercuries, with the rest, which St. Augustine out of Varro, Eusebius out of many profane histories, Cicero, Diodorus Siculus, Arnobius, and many more have observed, to wit, the Phœnicians, Phrygians, Cretans, Greeks, and other nations; yet was Cain, the son of Adam, as some very learned men conceive, called and reputed for the first and ancient Jupiter, and Adam for the first Saturn; for Jupiter was said to have invented the founding of cities; and the first city of the world was built by Cain, which he called Enoch, of whom were the *Henochii* before remembered. And so much may be gathered out of Plato in Protagoras, which also Hyginus in his 275 chapter confirmeth. For, besides that many cities were founded by divers men, *tamen primam latissimam a primo et antiquissimo Iove ædificatam*, "yet the first and largest was built by the first and most ancient Iupiter," seated in the east parts, or in India, according to that of Moses: "And Cain dwelt towards the east side of Eden," etc., where also the *Henochii* were found after the Flood. And therefore was Jupiter by the Athenians called *Polieus*, a founder of cities, and *Herceios*, an encloser or strengthener of cities, say Phornutus and Pausanias, and that to Jupiter *Herceios* there were in very many places altars and temples erected. And that there were cities built before the Flood Plato also witnesseth, as may be gathered in this his affirming that soon after mankind began to increase they built many cities, which as his meaning he delivereth in plain terms in his third book of laws; for he saith that cities were built an exceeding space of time before the destruction by the great Flood.

This first Jupiter of the ethnics was then the same Cain, the son of Adam, who marrying his own sister, as also Jupiter is said to have done, inhabited the East, where Stephanus, *De Urbibus*, placeth the city Henochia. And besides this City of Henoch, Philo Judæus conceiveth that Cain built six others, as Maich, Jared, Tehe, Jesca, Selet, and Gebat. But where Philo had this I know not. Now as Cain was the first Jupiter and from whom also the ethnics had the invention of sacrifice, so were Jubal, Tubal, and Tubal Cain, inventors of pastorage, smiths'-craft, and music, the same which were called by the ancient profane writers, Mercurius, Vulcan, and Apollo. And as there is a likelihood of name

between Tubal Cain and Vulcan, so doth Augustine expound the name of Noema or Naamath, the sister of Tubal Cain, to signify Venusta or beautiful, Voluptas or pleasure; as the wife of Vulcan is said to be Venus, the lady of pleasure and beauty. And as Adam was the ancient and first Saturn, Cain, the eldest Jupiter, Eva, Rhea, and Noema or Naamath, the first Venus; so did the fable of the dividing of the world between the three brethren, the sons of Saturn, arise from the true story of the dividing of the earth between the three sons of Noah; so also was the fiction of those golden apples kept by a dragon, taken from the serpent which tempted Evah; so was paradise itself transported out of Asia into Africa and made the garden of the Hesperides; the prophecies that Christ should break the serpent's head and conquer the power of hell occasioned the fables of Hercules killing the serpent of Hesperides and descending into hell and captivating Cerberus; so out of the taking up of Enoch by God was borrowed the conversion of their heroes, the inventors of religion and such arts as the life of man had profit by, into stars and heavenly signs and withal, that leaving of the world and ascension of Astræa, of which Ovid:

Ultima cœlestum terras Astræa reliquit.

Astræa last of heavenly wights the earth did leave.[3]

For the rest, if we seek a reason of the succession and continuance of this boundless ambition in mortal men, we may add to that which hath been already said that the kings and princes of the world have always laid before them the actions but not the ends of those great ones which preceded them. They are always transported with the glory of the one, but they never mind the misery of the other till they find the experience in themselves. They neglect the advice of God while they enjoy life or hope of it; but they follow the counsel of Death upon his first approach. It is he that puts into man all the wisdom of the world without speaking a word, which God, with all the words of his law, promises, or threats doth infuse. Death, which hateth and destroyeth man, is believed; God, which hath made him and loves him, is always deferred. "I have considered," saith Solomon, "all the works that are under the sun, and behold, all is vanity and vexation of spirit." But who believes it, till Death tells it us! It was Death, which opening the conscience of Charles the Fifth, made him enjoin his son Philip to restore Navarre, and King Francis the First of France to command

3 Section iv of Chapter VI.

that justice should be done upon the murderers of the Protestants in Merindol and Cabrieres, which till then he neglected. It is therefore Death alone that can suddenly make man to know himself. He tells the proud and insolent that they are but abjects and humbles them at the instant, makes them cry, complain, and repent, yea, even to hate their fore-passed happiness. He takes the account of the rich and proves him a beggar, a naked beggar, which hath interest in nothing but in the gravel that fills his mouth. He holds a glass before the eyes of the most beautiful and makes them see therein their deformity and rottenness, and they acknowledge it.

O eloquent, just, and mighty Death! whom none could advise thou hast persuaded; what none have dared thou hast done; and whom all the world hath flattered thou only hast cast out of the world and despised. Thou hast drawn together all the far-stretched greatness, all the pride, cruelty, and ambition of man and covered it all over with these two narrow words, *Hic jacet.*

Lastly, whereas this book by the title it hath calls itself The First Part of the General History of the World, implying a second and third volume, which I also intended and have hewn out; besides many other discouragements persuading my silence, it hath pleased God to take that glorious prince[4] out of the world to whom they were directed; whose unspeakable and never enough lamented loss hath taught me to say with Job, *Versa est in luctum cithara mea et organum meum in vocem flentium.*[5]

4 Prince Henry, the king's eldest son, had been Ralegh's patron. He died in 1612, at the age of 18.

5 My harp is turned to mourning, and my organ into the voice of them that weep. (This is the close of Chapter VI of the Fifth Book and the end of the History.)

Lancelot Andrewes
[1555-1626]

BISHOP ANDREWES, one of the most notable figures produced by the Anglican Church in its greatest period, was born in London and educated at the Merchant Tailors' School and at Pembroke Hall, Cambridge. Ordained in 1580, he became chaplain to Queen Elizabeth a few years later. He was made Dean of Westminster in 1601, and, during the reign of James I, rose to positions of great ecclesiastical eminence, becoming successively Bishop of Chichester (1605), of Ely (1609), and of Winchester (1618). Both his enormous learning and his mastery of English prose made themselves felt in the great authorized version of the Bible, in the preparation of which he was one of the more distinguished collaborators.

Despite his possession of rank and power and his prominence as an intellectual ornament of the court of James, Andrewes maintained throughout his life an unchallenged reputation for personal sanctity and devotional seriousness. He counted among his friends such men as Hooker, Bacon, Selden, Grotius, and George Herbert, and the posthumous edition of his *XCVI Sermons* was undertaken at the command of the king himself.

If the *Preces Privatæ*, or *Private Devotions* (translated and published in 1647 and 1648), display Andrewes' saintly character more immediately and fully, the sermons remain his chief literary monument. In the sermons emotional intensity and intellectual power are enhanced rather than undercut by a style remarkable for its wit, its tense angularity, and its pithy condensation. Although these are the qualities of "Metaphysical" poetry and prose, a comparison of Andrewes' sermons and Donne's discloses more differences than similarities. Whereas Donne is personal, dramatic, extravagant, and emotional, Andrewes is impersonal, quiet, and rational, purposefully devoted to an analysis designed to wring from the chosen text every last drop of theological significance. The effect of absolute sincerity which throbs in the Bishop's Senecan periods is not the result of any overt emotional indulgence on his part; it comes rather from that sense of the embodiment of the universal in the concrete and particular, which is such a distinctive possession of the finest seventeenth-century artists. And Andrewes, for all the very different commitments of his devoted life, was consummately an artist.

L. ANDREWES. *96 Sermons*, 5 vols. (Oxford and London, 1870–74). Still the only complete edition of the sermons.
————. *Two Sermons of the Resurrection* (Cambridge, 1932).
P. A. WELSBY. *Lancelot Andrewes, 1555–1626* (London, 1958). A recent biography.
T. S. ELIOT. *For Lancelot Andrewes* (New York, 1928). A valuable essay on Andrewes

gives its title to this collection. The essay is reprinted in Eliot's *Selected Essays* (New York, 1950).

K. N. COLVILLE. *Fame's Twilight* (London, 1923). The essay on Andrewes contains an able analysis of his style.

H. ROSS WILLIAMSON. *Four Stuart Portraits* (London, 1949).

W. F. MITCHELL. *English Pulpit Oratory from Andrewes to Tillotson* (London, 1932).

FROM

XCVI SERMONS

[TEXT: *first edition, 1629*]

A SERMON PREACHED BEFORE THE KING'S MAJESTY, AT WHITE-HALL, ON WEDNESDAY, THE TWENTY-FIFTH OF DECEMBER, A.D. MDCXXII., BEING CHRISTMAS-DAY.

Behold there came wise men from the East to Jerusalem,
Saying, Where is the King of the Jews that is born? For we have
seen His star in the East, and are come to worship Him.
MATTHEW ii. 1, 2.

Ecce magi ab Oriente venerunt Jerosolymam,
Dicentes, Ubi est Qui natus est Rex Judæorum? vidimus enim
stellam Ejus in Oriente, et venimus adorare Eum. Latin Vulg.

THERE be in these two verses two principal points, as was observed when time was; 1. The persons that arrived at Jerusalem, 2. and their errand. The persons in the former verse, whereof hath been treated heretofore. Their errand in the latter, whereof we are now to deal.

Their errand we may best learn from themselves out of their *dicentes,*[1] etc. Which, in a word, is to worship Him. Their errand our errand, and the errand of this day.

This text may seem to come a little too soon, before the time; and should have stayed till the day it was spoken on, rather than on this day. But if you mark them well, there are in the verse four words that be *verba diei hujus,* "proper and peculiar to this very day." 1. For first, *natus est*[2] is most proper to this day of all days, the day of His Nativity. 2. Secondly, *vidimus stellam;*[3] for on this day it was first seen, appeared first.

3. Thirdly, *venimus;*[4] for this day they set forth, began their journey. 4. And last, *adorare Eum;*[5] for "when He brought His only-begotten Son into the world, He gave in charge, Let all the Angels of God worship Him." (Heb. i. 6.) And when the Angels to do it, no time more proper for us to do it as then. So these four appropriate it to this day, and none but this.

The main heads of their errand are 1. *Vidimus stellam,* the occasion; 2. and *Venimus adorare,* the end of their coming. But for the better conceiving it I will take another course, to set forth these points to be handled.

I. Their faith first: faith—in that they never ask "Whether He be," but "Where He is born"; for that born He is, that they steadfastly believe.

II. Then "the work or service"(Phil. ii. 17) of this faith, as St. Paul calleth it; "the touch or trial," "δοχίμιον," (1 Peter i. 7), as St. Peter; the *ostende mihi,*[6] (James ii. 18), as St. James; of this their faith in these five. 1. Their confessing of it in *venerunt dicentes. Venerunt,* they were no sooner come, but *dicentes,* they tell it out; confess Him and His birth to be the cause of their coming. 2. Secondly, as confess their faith, so the ground of their faith; *vidimus enim,* for they had "seen" His star; and His star being risen, by it they knew He must be risen too. 3. Thirdly, as St. Paul calls them in Abraham's, *vestigia fidei,* "the steps of their faith," (Rom. iv. 12), in *venimus,* "their coming"—coming such a journey, at such a time, with such speed. 4. Fourthly, when they were come, their diligent enquiring Him out by *ubi est?*[7] for here is the place of it, asking after Him to find where He was. 5. And last, when they had found Him, the end of their seeing, coming, seeking; and all for no other end but to

---

1 Sayings.   2 He is born.
3 We have seen the star.

4 We have come.   5 To adore Him.
6 Show me.   7 Where is He?

worship Him. Here they say it, at the 11th verse they do it in these two acts; 1. *procidentes*, their "falling down," 2. and *obtulerunt*, their "offering" to Him. Worship Him with their bodies, worship Him with their goods; their worship and ours the true worship of Christ.

The text is of a star, and we may make all run on a star, that so the text and day may be suitable, and Heaven and earth hold a correspondence. St. Peter calls faith "the day-star rising in our hearts," (2. Peter i. 19), which sorts well with the star in the text rising in the sky. That in the sky manifesting itself from above to them; this in their hearts manifesting itself from below to Him, to Christ. Manifesting itself by these five: 1. by *ore fit confessio*, "the confessing of it," (Rom. x. 10); 2. by *fides est substantia*, "the ground of it," (Heb. xi. 1); 3. by *vestigia fidei*, "the steps of it" (Rom. iv. 12) in their painful coming; 4. by their *ubi est?* "careful enquiring"; 5. and last, by *adorare Eum*, "their devout worshiping." These five, as so many beams of faith, the day-star risen in their hearts. To take notice of them. For every one of them is of the nature of a condition, so as if we fail in them, *non lucet nobis stella hæc*, "we have no part in the light, or conduct of this star." Neither in *stellam*, "the star itself," nor in *Ejus*, "in Him Whose the star is"; that is, not in Christ neither.

We have now got us a star on earth for that in Heaven, and these both lead us to a third. So as upon the matter three stars we have, and each his proper manifestation. 1. The first in the firmament; that appeared unto them, and in them to us—a figure of St. Pauls' Επεφάνη χάρις, "the grace of God appearing, and bringing salvation to all men," (Tit. ii. 11), Jews and Gentiles and all. 2. The second here on earth is St. Peter's *Lucifer in cordibus;* and this appeared in them, and so must in us. Appeared 1. in their eyes—*vidimus;* 2. in their feet—*venimus;* 3. in their lips—*dicentes ubi est;* 4. in their knees—*procidentes*, "falling down"; 5. in their hands—*obtulerunt*, "by offering." These five every one a beam of this star. 3. The third in Christ Himself. St. John's star. "The generation and root of David, the bright morning Star, Christ." And He, His double appearing. 1. One at this time now, when He appeared in great humility; and we see and come to Him by faith. 2. The other, which we wait for, even "the blessed hope, and appearing of the great God and our Saviour" (Tit. ii. 13) in the majesty of His glory.

These three: 1. The first that manifested Christ to them; 2. The second that manifested them to Christ;

3. The third Christ Himself, in Whom both these were as it were in conjunction. Christ "the bright morning Star" of that day which shall have no night; the *beatifica visio*, 'the blessed sight' of which day is the *consummatum est*[8] of our hope and happiness for ever.

Of these three stars the first is gone, the third yet to come, the second only is present. We to look to that, and to the five beams of it. That is it must do us all the good, and bring us to the third.

I. St. Luke calleth faith the "door of faith." (Acts xiv. 27). At this door let us enter. Here is a coming, and "he that cometh to God," and so he that to Christ, "must believe, that Christ is": so do these. They never ask *an sit*, but *ubi sit?* Not "whether," but "where He is born." They that ask *ubi Qui natus?* take *natus* for granted, presuppose that born He is. Herein is faith— faith of Christ's being born, the third article of the Christian Creed.

And what believe they of Him? Out of their own words here; 1. first that *natus*, that "born" He is, and so Man He is—His human nature. 1. And as His nature, so His office in *natus est Rex*, "born a King." They believe that too. 3. But *Judæorum* may seem to be a bar; for then, what have they to do with "the King of the Jews"? They be Gentiles, none of His lieges, no relation to Him at all: what do they seeking or worshiping Him? But weigh it well, and it is no bar. For this they seem to believe: He is so *Rex Judæorum*, "King of the Jews," as He is *adorandus a Gentibus*, "the Gentiles to adore Him." And though born in Jewry, yet Whose birth concerned them though Gentiles, though born far off in the "mountains of the East." They to have some benefit by Him and His birth, and for that to do Him worship, seeing *officium fundatur in beneficio*[9] ever. 4. As thus born in earth, so a star He hath in Heaven of His own—*stellam Ejus*, "His star"; He the owner of it. Now we know the stars are the stars of Heaven, and He that Lord of them Lord of Heaven too; and so to be adored of them, of us, and of all. St. John puts them together; "the root and generation of David," His earthly; and "the bright morning star," (Rev. xxii. 16), His Heavenly or Divine generation. *Hæc est fides Magorum*,[10] this is the mystery of their faith. In *natus est*, man; in *stellam Ejus*, God. In *Rex*, "a King," though of the Jews, yet the good of Whose Kingdom should extend and stretch itself far and wide to Gentiles and all; and He of all to be adored. This, for *corde*

---

8 It is consummated.
9 Favor is founded on service.
10 This is the faith of the Magi.

creditur,[11] the day-star itself in their hearts. Now to the beams of this star.

II. Next to *corde creditur* is *ore fit confessio*, "the confession" of this faith. It is in *venerunt dicentes*, they came with it in their mouths. *Venerunt*, they were no sooner come, but they spake of it so freely, to so many, as it came to Herod's ear and troubled him not a little that any King of the Jews should be worshiped beside himself. So then their faith is no bosom-faith, kept to themselves without ever a *dicentes*, without saying any thing of it to anybody. No; *credidi, propter quod locutus sum*, "they believed, and therefore they spake." (Psa. cxvi. 10). The star in their hearts cast one beam out at their mouths. And though Herod, who was but *Rex factus*,[12] could evil brook to hear of *Rex natus*,[13]—must needs be offended at it, yet they were not afraid to say it. And though they came from the East, those parts to whom and their King the Jews had long time been captives and their underlings, they were not ashamed neither to tell, that One of the Jews' race they came to seek; and to seek Him to the end "to worship Him." So neither afraid of Herod, nor ashamed of Christ; but professed their errand, and cared not who knew it. This for their confessing Him boldly.

But faith is said by the Apostle to be ὑπόστασις,[14] and so there is a good "ground"; and ἔλεγχος,[15] and so hath a good "reason" for it. (Heb. xi. 1.). This puts the difference between *fidelis* and *credulus*, or as Solomon terms him, *fatuus qui credit omni verbo*,[16] (Pro. xiv. 15); between faith and lightness of belief. Faith hath ever a ground; *vidimus enim*,—an *enim*, a reason for it, and is ready to render it. How came you to believe? *Audivimus enim*, "for we have heard an Angel," (Luke ii. 20), say the shepherds. *Vidimus enim*, "for we have seen a star," say the Magi, and this is a well-grounded faith. We came not of our own heads, we came not before we saw some reason for it—saw that which set us on coming; *Vidimus enim stellam Ejus*.

Vidimus stellam—we can well conceive that; any that will but look up, may see a star. But how could they see the *Ejus* of it, that it was His? Either that it belonged to any, or that He it was it belonged to. This passeth all perspective;[17] no astronomy could shew them this. What by course of nature the stars can produce, that they by course of art or observation may discover.

But this birth was above nature. No trigon, triplicity, exaltation could bring it forth. They are but idle that set figures for it. The star should not have been His, but He the star's, if it had gone that way. Some other light then, they saw this *Ejus* by.

Now with us in Divinity there be but two in all; 1. *Vespertina*, and 2. *Matutina lux. Vespertina*, "the owl-light" of our reason or skill is too dim to see it by. No remedy then but it must be as Esay calls it, *matutina lux*, "the morning-light," the light of God's law must certify them of the *Ejus* of it. There, or not at all to be had whom this star did portend.

And in the Law, there we find it in the twenty-fourth of Numbers. (Num. xxiv. 17.) One of their own Prophets that came from whence they came, "from the mountains of the East," was ravished in spirit, "fell in a trance, had his eyes opened," and saw the *Ejus* of it many an hundred years before it rose. Saw *orietur in Jacob*, that there it should "rise," which is as much as *natus est* here. Saw *stella*, that he should be "the bright morning-Star," and so might well have a star to represent Him. Saw *sceptrum in Israel*, which is just as much as *Rex Judæorum*, that it should portend a King there—such a King as should not only "smite the corners of Moab," that is Balak their enemy for the present; but "should reduce and bring under Him all the sons of Seth," that is all the world; for all are now Seth's sons, Cain's were all drowned in the flood. Here now is the *Ejus* of it clear. A Prophet's eye might discern this; never a Chaldean of them all could take it with his astrolabe. Balaam's eyes were open to see it, and he helped to open their eyes by leaving behind him this prophecy to direct them how to apply it, when it should arise to the right *Ejus* of it.

But these had not the law. It is hard to say that the Chaldee paraphrase was extant long before this. They might have had it. Say, they had it not: if Moses was so careful to record this prophecy in his book, it may well be thought that some memory of this so memorable a prediction was left remaining among them of the East, his own country where he was born and brought up. And some help they might have from Daniel too, who lived all his time in Chaldea and Persia, and prophesied among them of such a King, and set the just time of it.

And this, as it is conceived, put the difference between the East and the West. For I ask, was it *vidimus in Oriente*[18] with them? Was it not *vidimus in*

---

11 It is believed with the heart.
12 A king made.   13 A king born.
14 Ground.   15 Proof.
16 The simple believeth every word.
17 The science of optics.

18 We have seen in the east.

Occidente?[19] In the West such a star—it or the fellow of it was seen nigh about that time, or the Roman stories deceive us. Toward the end of Augustus' reign such a star was seen, and much scanning there was about it. Pliny saith it was generally holden, that star to be *faustum sydus,* a "lucky comet," and portended good to the world, which few or no comets do. And Virgil, who then lived, would needs take upon him to set down the *ejus* of it, ... *Ecce Dionæi, etc.*—entitled Cæsar to it. And verily there is no man that can without admiration read his sixth Eclogue, of a birth that time expected, that should be the offspring of the gods, and that should take away their sins. Whereupon it hath gone for current—the East and West, *Vidimus* both.

But by the light of their prophecy, the East, they went straight to the right *Ejus.* And for want of this light the West wandered, and gave it a wrong *ejus;* as Virgil, applying it to little Salonine: and as evil hap was, while he was making his verses, the poor child died; and so his star shot, vanished, and came to nothing. Their *vidimus* never came to a *venimus;* they neither went, nor worshiped Him as these here did.

But by this we see, when all is done, hither we must come for our morning-light; to this book, to the word of prophecy. All our *vidimus stellam* is as good as nothing without it. That star is past and gone, long since; "Heaven and earth shall pass, but this word shall not pass." Here on this, we to fix our eye and to ground our faith. Having this, though we neither hear Angel nor see star, we may by the grace of God do full well. For even they that have had both those, have been fain to resolve into this as their last, best, and chiefest point of all. Witness St. Peter: he saith he, and they with him, "saw Christ's glory, and heard the voice from Heaven in the Holy Mount," (2 Peter i. 17–19). What then? After both these, *audivimus* and *vidimus,* both senses, he comes to this, *Habemus autem firmiorem, etc.* "We have a more sure word of prophecy" than both these; *firmiorem,* a "more sure," a more clear, than them both. And *si híc legimus*[20]— for *legimus* is *vidimus,* "if here we read it written," it is enough to ground our faith, and let the star go.

And yet, to end this point; both these, the star and the prophecy, they are but *circumfusa lux*[21]—without both. Besides these there must be a light within in the eye; else, we know, for all them nothing will be seen. And that must come from Him, and the enlightening of His Spirit. Take this for a rule; no knowing of *Ejus*

absque Eo, "of His without Him," Whose it is. Neither of the star, without Him That created it; nor of the prophecy, without Him That inspired it. But this third coming too; He sending the light of His Spirit within into their minds, they then saw clearly this the star, now the time, He the Child That this day was born.

He That sent these two without, sent also this third within, and then it was *vidimus* indeed. The light of the star in their eyes, the "word of prophecy" in their ears, the beam of His Spirit in their hearts; these three made up a full *vidimus.* And so much for *vidimus stellam Ejus,* the occasion of their coming.

Now to *venimus,* their coming itself. And it follows well. For it is not a star only, but a load-star; and whither should *stella Ejus ducere,* but *ad Eum?* "Whither lead us, but to Him Whose the star is?" The star to the star's Master.

All this while we have been at *dicentes,* "saying" and seeing; now we shall come to *facientes,*[22] see them do somewhat upon it. It is not saying nor seeing will serve St. James; he will call, and be still calling for *ostende mihi,* "shew me thy faith by some work." (James ii. 18.) And well may he be allowed to call for it this day; it is the day of *vidimus,* appearing, being seen. You have seen His star, let Him now see your star another while. And so they do. Make your faith to be seen; so it is— their faith in the steps of their faith. And so was Abraham's first by coming forth of his country; as these here do, and so "walk in the steps of the faith of Abraham" (Rom. iv. 12), do his first work.

It is not commended to stand "gazing up into Heaven" (Acts i. 11) too long; not on Christ Himself ascending, much less on His star. For they sat not still gazing on the star. Their *vidimus* begat *venimus;* their seeing made them come, come a great journey. *Venimus* is soon said, but a short word; but many a wide and weary step they made before they could come to say *Venimus,* Lo, here "we are come"; come, and at our journey's end. To look a little on it. In this their coming we consider, 1. First, the distance of the place they came from. It was not hard by as the shepherds—but a step to Bethlehem over the fields; this was riding many a hundred miles, and cost them many a day's journey. 2. Secondly, we consider the way that they came, if it be pleasant, or plain and easy; for if it be, it is so much the better. 1. This was nothing pleasant, for through deserts, all the way waste and desolate. 2. Nor secondly, easy either; for over the rocks and crags of both Arabias, specially Petræa, their journey lay. 3. Yet

19 We have seen in the west.
20 If here we read.   21 Surrounding light.   22 Doing.

if safe—but it was not, but exceeding dangerous, as lying through the midst of the "black tents of Kedar," (Cant. i. 5), a nation of thieves and cut-throats; to pass over the hills of robbers, infamous then, and infamous to this day. No passing without great troop or convoy. 4. Last we consider the time of their coming, the season of the year. It was no summer progress. A cold coming they had of it at this time of the year, just the worst time of the year to take a journey, and specially a long journey in. The ways deep, the weather sharp, the days short, the sun farthest off, *in solstitio brumali*, "the very dead of winter." [23] *Venimus*, "we are come," if that be one, *venimus*, "we are now come," come at this time, that sure is another.

And these difficulties they overcame, of a wearisome, irksome, troublesome, dangerous, unseasonable journey; and for all this they came. And came it cheerfully and quickly, as appeareth by the speed they made. It was but *vidimus, venimus*, with them; "they saw," and "they came"; no sooner saw, but they set out presently. So as upon the first appearing of the star, as it might be last night, they knew it was Balaam's star; it called them away, they made ready straight to begin their journey this morning. A sign they were highly conceited of [24] His birth, believed some great matter of it, that they took all these pains, made all this haste that they might be there to worship Him with all the possible speed they could. Sorry for nothing so much as that they could not be there soon enough, with the very first, to do it even this day, the day of His birth. All considered, there is more in *venimus* than shews at the first sight. It was not for nothing it was said in the first verse, *ecce venerunt;* their coming hath an *ecce* [25] on it, it well deserves it.

And we, what should we have done? Sure these men of the East shall rise in judgment against the men of the West, (Matt. viii. 11), that is us, and their faith against ours in this point. With them it was but *vidimus, venimus;* with us it would have been but *veniemus* [26] at most. Our fashion is to see and see again before we stir a foot, specially if it be to the worship of Christ. Come such a journey at such a time? No; but fairly have put it off to the spring of the year, till the days longer, and the ways fairer, and the weather warmer, till better traveling to Christ. Our Epiphany would sure have fallen in Easter-week at the soonest.

But then for the distance, desolateness, tediousness, and the rest, any of them were enough to mar our *venimus* quite. It must be no great way, first, we must come; we love not that. Well fare the shepherds, yet they came but hard by; rather like them than the Magi. Nay, not like them neither. For with us the nearer, lightly the farther off; our proverb is you know, "The nearer the Church, the farther from God."

Nor it must not be through no desert, over no Petræa. If rugged or uneven the way, if the weather ill-disposed, if any never so little danger, it is enough to stay us. To Christ we cannot travel, but weather and way and all must be fair. If not, no journey, but sit still and see farther. As indeed, all our religion is rather *vidimus*, a contemplation, than *venimus*, a motion, or stirring to do aught.

But when we do it, we must be allowed leisure. Ever *veniemus*, never *venimus;* ever coming, never come. We love to make no very great haste. To other things perhaps; not to *adorare*, the place of the worship of God. Why should we? Christ is no wild-cat. What talk ye of twelve days? And if it be forty days hence, ye shall be sure to find His Mother and Him; she cannot be churched [27] till then. What needs such haste? The truth is, we conceit Him and His birth but slenderly, and our haste is even thereafter. But if we be at that point, we must be out of this *venimus;* they like enough to leave us behind. Best get us a new Christmas in September; we are not like to come to Christ at this feast. Enough for *venimus*.

But what is *venimus* without *invenimus?* [28] And when they come, they hit not on Him at first. No more must we think, as soon as ever we be come, to find him straight. They are fain to come to their *ubi est?* We must now look back to that. For though it stand before in the verse, here is the right place of it. They saw before they came, and came before they asked; asked before they found, and found before they worshiped. Between *venimus*, "their coming," and *adorare*, "their worshiping," there is the true place of *dicentes, ubi est?*

Where, first, we note a double use of their *dicentes*, these wise men had. 1. As to manifest what they knew, *natus est*, "that He is born," so to confess and ask what they knew not, the place where. We to have the like.

2. Secondly, set down this; that to find where He is, we must learn of these to ask where He is, which we

---

23 This passage is the source of the images which begin T. S. Eliot's poem The Journey of the Magi.
24 That they were very concerned with.
25 Behold.   26 We shall come.

27 Undergo ritual purification after childbirth.
28 We find.

full little set ourselves to do. If we stumble on Him, so it is; but for any asking we trouble not ourselves, but sit still as we say, and let nature work; and so let grace too, and so for us it shall. I wot well, it is said in a place of Esay, "He was found," *a non quærentibus,* "of some that sought Him not," (Isa. lxv. 1), never asked *ubi est?* But it is no good holding by that place. It was their good hap that so did. But trust not to it, it is not everybody's case, that. It is better advice you shall read in the Psalm, *hæc est generatio quærentium,* "there is a generation of them that seek Him." (Ps. xxiv. 6.) Of which these were, and of that generation let us be. Regularly there is no promise of *invenietis* but to *quærite,* of finding but to such as "seek." It is not safe to presume to find Him otherwise.

I thought there had been small use of *ubi est?* Yet there is except we hold the ubiquity, that Christ is *ubi non,* "any where." But He is not so. Christ hath His *ubi,* His proper place where He is to be found; and if you miss of that, you miss of Him. And well may we miss, saith Christ Himself, there are so many will take upon them to tell us where, and tell us of so many *ubis.* *Ecce híc,* "Look you, here He is"; *Ecce illíc,* nay then, "there." *In deserto,* "in the desert." Nay, *in penetralibus,* "in such a privy conventicle," (Matt. xxiv. 23), you shall be sure of Him. And yet He, saith He Himself, in none of them all. There is then yet place for *ubi est?* I speak not of His natural body but of His mystical—that is Christ too.

How shall we then do? Where shall we get this "where" resolved? Where these did. They said it to many, and oft, but gat no answer, till they had got together a convocation of Scribes, and they resolved them of Christ's *ubi.* For they in the East were nothing so wise, or well seen, as we in the West are now grown. We need call no Scribes together, and get them tell us, "where." Every artisan hath a whole Synod of Scribes in his brain, and can tell where Christ is better than any learned man of them all. Yet these were wise men; best learn where they did.

And how did the Scribes resolve it then? Out of Micah. As before to the star they join Balaam's prophecy, so now again to His *orietur,* that such a one should be born, they had put Micah's *et tu Bethlehem,* the place of His birth.[29] Still helping, and giving light as it were to the light of Heaven, by a more clear light, the light of the Sanctuary.

Thus then to do. And to do it ourselves, and not seek Christ *per alium;*[30] set others about it as Herod did

these, and sit still ourselves. For so, we may hap never find Him no more than he did.

And now we have found "where," what then? It is neither in seeking nor finding, *venimus* nor *iuvenimus;* the end of all, the cause of all is in the last words, *adorare Eum,* "to worship Him." That is all in all, and without it all our seeing, coming, seeking, and finding is to no purpose. The Scribes they could tell, and did tell where He was, but were never the nearer for it, for they worshiped Him not. For this end to seek Him.

This is acknowledged: Herod, in effect, said as much. He would know where He were fain, and if they will bring him word where, he will come too and worship Him, that he will. None of that worship. If he find Him, his worshiping will prove worrying; as did appear by a sort of silly poor lambs that he worried, when he could not have his will on Christ. (Matt. ii. 16.) Thus he at His birth.

And at His death, the other Herod, he sought Him too; but it was that he and his soldiers might make themselves sport with Him. (Luke xxiii. 11.) Such seeking there is otherwhile. And such worshiping; as they in the judgment-hall worshiped Him with *Ave Rex,*[31] and then gave Him a bob blindfold. (John xix. 3.) The world's worship of Him for the most part.

But we may be bold to say, Herod was "a fox." (Luke xiii. 32.) These mean as they say; to worship Him they come, and worship Him they will. Will they so? Be they well advised what they promise, before they know whether they shall find Him in a worshipful taking or no? For full little know they, where and in what case they shall find Him. What, if in a stable, laid there in a manger, and the rest suitable to it; in as poor and pitiful a plight as ever was any, more like to be abhorred than adored of such persons? Will they be as good as their word, trow?[32] Will they not step back at the sight, repent themselves of their journey, and wish themselves at home again? But so find Him, and so finding Him, worship Him for all that? If they will, verily then great is their faith. This, the clearest beam of all.

"The Queen of the South," (Matt. xii. 42), who was a figure of these Kings of the East, she came as great a journey as these. But when she came, she found a King indeed, King Solomon in all his royalty. Saw a glorious King, and a glorious court about him. Saw him, and heard him; tried him with many hard questions, received satisfaction of them all. This was worth her coming. Weigh what she found, and what these here—

29 See Micah 5:2.   30 Through another.   31 Hail, King!   32 Do you believe?

as poor and unlikely a birth as could be, ever to prove a King, or any great matter. No sight to comfort them, nor a word for which they any whit the wiser; nothing worth their travel. Weigh these together, and great odds will be found between her faith and theirs. Theirs the greater far.

Well, they will take Him as they find Him, and all this notwithstanding, worship Him for all that. The Star shall make amends for the manger, and for *stella Ejus* they will dispense with *Eum*.[33]

And what is it to worship? Some great matter sure it is, that Heaven and earth, the stars and Prophets, thus do but serve to lead them and conduct us to. For all we see ends in *adorare*. *Scriptura et mundus ad hoc sunt, ut colatur Qui creavit, et adoretur Qui inspiravit;* "the Scripture and world are but to this end, that He That created the one and inspired the other might be but worshiped." Such reckoning did these seem to make of it here. And such the great treasurer of the Queen Candace. These came from the mountains in the East; he from the uttermost part of Æthiopia came, (Acts viii. 27), and came for no other end but only this—to worship; and when they had done that, home again. *Tanti est adorare*.[34] Worth the while, worth our coming if coming we do but that, but worship and nothing else. And so I would have men account of it.

To tell you what it is in particular, I must put you over to the eleventh verse,[35] where it is set down what they did when they worshiped. It is set down in two acts προσχυνεῖν, and προσφέρειν, "falling down," and "offering." Thus did they, thus we to do; we to do the like when we will worship. These two are all, and more than these we find not.

We can worship God but three ways, we have but three things to worship Him withal. 1. The soul He hath inspired; 2. the body He hath ordained us; 3. and the wordly goods He hath vouchsafed to bless us withal. We to worship Him with all, seeing there is but one reason for all.

If He breathed into us our soul, but framed not our body, but some other did that, neither bow your knee nor uncover your head, but keep on your hats, and sit even as you do hardly. But if He hath framed that body of yours and every member of it, let Him have the honor both of head and knee, and every member else.

Again, if it be not He That gave us our wordly goods but somebody else, what He gave not, that withhold from Him and spare not. But if all come from Him, all to return to Him. If He send all, to be worshiped with all. And this in good sooth is but *rationabile obsequium*,[36] as the Apostle calleth it (Rom. xii. 1.) No more than reason would, we should worship Him with all.

Else if all our worship be inward only, with our hearts and not our hats as some fondly imagine, we give Him but one of three; we put Him to His thirds, bid Him be content with that, He gets no more but inward worship. That is out of the text quite. For though I doubt not but these here performed that also, yet here it is not. St. Matthew mentions it not, it is not to be seen, no *vidimus* on it. And the text is a *vidimus*, and of a star; that is, of an outward visible worship to be seen of all. There is a *vidimus* upon the worship of the body, it may be seen—*procidentes*. Let us see you fall down. So is there upon the worship with our wordly goods, that may be seen and felt—*offerentes*. Let us see whether, and what you offer. With both which, no less than with the soul, God is to be worshiped. "Glorify God with your bodies, for they are God's," (1. Cor. vi. 20), saith the Apostle. "Honor God with your substance, for He hath blessed your store," (Prov. iii. 9), saith Solomon. It is the precept of a wise King, of one there; it is the practice of more than one, of these three here. Specially now; for Christ hath now a body, for which to do Him worship with our bodies. And now He was made poor to make us rich, and so *offerentes* will do well, comes very fit.

To enter farther into these two would be too long, and indeed they be not in our verse here, and so for some other treatise at some other time.

There now remains nothing but to include ourselves, and bear our part with them, and with the Angels, and all who this day adored Him.

This was the load-star of the Magi, and what were they? Gentiles. So are we. But if it must be ours, then we are to go with them; *vade, et fac similiter*, "go, and do likewise." (Luke x. 37.) It is *Stella gentium*, but *idem agentium*[37] "the Gentiles" star,' but "such Gentiles as overtake these and keep company with them." In their *dicentes*, "confessing their faith freely"; in their *vidimus*, "grounding it throughly"; in their *venimus*, "hasting to come to Him speedily"; in their *ubi est?* "enquiring Him out diligently"; and in their *adorare Eum*, "worshiping Him devoutly." *Per omnia* doing as these did; worshiping and thus worshiping, celebrating and thus celebrating the feast of His birth.

We cannot say *vidimus stellam;* the star is gone long

33 Him. 34 It is worth so much to worship.
35 Matthew 2:11.

36 Reasonable service. 37 Such as do likewise.

since, not now to be seen. Yet I hope for all that, that *venimus adorare*, "we be come thither to worship." It will be the more acceptable, if not seeing it we worship though. It is enough we read of it in the text; we see it there. And indeed as I said, it skills not[38] for the star in the firmament, if the same Day-Star be risen in our hearts that was in theirs, and the same beams of it to be seen, all five. For then we have our part in it no less, nay full out as much as they. And it will bring us whither it brought them, to Christ. Who at His second appearing in glory shall call forth these wise

38 Matters not.

men and all that have ensued[39] the steps of their faith, and that upon the reason specified in the text; for I have seen their star shining and shewing forth itself by the like beams; and as they came to worship Me, so am I come to do them worship. A *venite* then, for a *venimus* now. Their star I have seen, and give them a place above among the stars. They fell down: I will lift them up, and exalt them. And as they offered to Me, so am I come to bestow on them, and to reward them with the endless joy and bliss on My Heavenly Kingdom.

To which, etc.

39 Followed.

Francis Bacon

[1561–1626]

I F RALEGH is the symbol of Elizabethan vitality and romance, Bacon is the more
important symbol of Elizabethan intellectual greatness. One of the finest legal
minds of his day, he is also of abiding importance as a statesman, as a master of
prose style, and, most of all, as the philosopher of science who did more than
any other man to lay the foundation for the triumph of the scientific attitude in seventeenth-century England. Bacon was the younger son of Sir Nicholas Bacon, Lord
Keeper of the Great Seal. He entered Trinity College, Cambridge, at the age of twelve
and there he first developed his lifelong antipathy to the philosophy of Aristotle, or,
more accurately, to the persistent medieval habit of mind which made of Aristotelianism
an all-embracing orthodoxy which might not be questioned by speculation or experimentation. He left Cambridge in 1575, without taking a degree, and began the study of
law at Gray's Inn in London. After three years in Paris with the English ambassador,
Sir Amias Paulet, Bacon completed his law studies and was admitted as barrister in 1582.

Bacon seems, at this stage in his career, to have been divided by conflicting aspirations
—toward the life of philosophy and toward the life of public service. Both ambitions
were doomed to frustration for some time. Despite the brilliance of his legal activities,
despite his friendship with the Earl of Essex—then at the height of his influence as
favorite of the queen—and despite his family connection with the powerful Lord
Burghley, he was unable to obtain either an important government post which would
enable him to put his ideas into practice or the type of sinecure which would enable
him to devote himself to thought. Queen Elizabeth, who seems to have distrusted him,
finally made him a member of her Learned Counsel, and it was in this capacity that he
was obliged to take an active part in the prosecution for treason of his former friend
Essex—a part which he pursued with a devoted energy which has caused many members
of later generations to criticize him for lack of human warmth.

It was not until the accession of James I that Bacon's political fortunes began their
dramatic rise. He was knighted in 1603, and between that time and 1621 he was made
successively Solicitor-General, Attorney-General, Privy Councillor, Lord Keeper, Lord
High Chancellor, Baron Verulam of Verulam, and Viscount St. Albans. At the height
of his power he was, next to the king, the most powerful man in England. Bacon's
decline as a public figure was even more dramatic than his ascent. In 1621 he was
arraigned before Parliament for accepting bribes and was deprived of office, fined, and
condemned to imprisonment at the king's pleasure. Bacon pleaded guilty to the charges,
but defended himself on the ground that bribery had never influenced his judgments.
Unquestionably he was guilty of moral laxity, but in this respect he was not more

reprehensible than most other magistrates of his time. The true reason for his fall lay in Parliament's hostility to the untouchable king and his favorite, the equally untouchable Buckingham; its hostility reached out to strike an important figure who did lie within its reach. Bacon himself later remarked: "I was the justest judge that was in England these fifty years, but it was the justest censure in Parliament that was these 200 years." Released from prison almost immediately and his fine remitted, Bacon retired to private life. He died a few years later of pneumonia contracted while performing experiments in refrigeration with snow.

Throughout the years of his public service, Bacon's activity in literature and philosophy had been prodigious. In 1597 he published his first *Essays*, which were expanded and extensively revised in later editions. In 1605 appeared his *Advancement of Learning*, a preliminary survey of the ground which he proposed to conquer in his projected *Instauratio Magna*, which was to be the complete exposition of his philosophy. Although this work was never completed, we know its general plan: the first part was to be a general survey of the state of knowledge; the second an exposition and defense of a new method of inquiry—the inductive; the remainder of the work was to consist mainly of an application of the new method to the materials of human knowledge. "I have taken all knowledge to be my province," the young Bacon had written to Lord Burghley. Having expounded his new method in the *Novum Organum*, the aging philosopher, realizing that he would not live to make good this last great boast of Renaissance universality, translated his *Advancement of Learning* into Latin as *De Augmentis Scientiarum* (1623); the rest of his great scheme remained unfulfilled, but he had achieved enough to announce the modern world.

Glorified by the later seventeenth century, Bacon has inspired universal respect but little affection among later generations. The Essex affair and the disgrace at the hands of Parliament have injured his reputation, and our own century, living in the scientific paradise of which he was the prophet, has tended unjustly to blame him for the bad dreams which haunt that paradise. But no one can question his intellectual eminence, and it is impossible to contemplate his vision of progress and fulfillment—whether in the *Advancement* or in his unfinished Utopian fiction *The New Atlantis*—without recognizing much that is poetic and much more that is heroic.

F. BACON. *Works*, ed. J. Spedding, R. L. Ellis, and D. D. Heath, 7 vols. (London, 1857–59). *Life and Letters*, 7 vols. (London, 1861–74). The definitive edition.

————. *Essays, the Advancement of Learning, the New Atlantis and Other Pieces*, ed. R. F. Jones (New York, 1937).

M. STURT. *Francis Bacon* (New York, 1932). Biography.

F. H. ANDERSON. *Francis Bacon: His Career and Thought* (New York, 1962).

————. *The Philosophy of Francis Bacon* (Chicago, 1948).

R. F. JONES. *Ancients and Moderns* (St. Louis, 2nd ed., 1961). An examination of Bacon's influence in seventeenth-century thought.

B. WILLEY. *The Seventeenth-Century Background* (London, 1934). Contains good chapters on Bacon.

G. WILLIAMSON. *The Senecan Amble* (Chicago, 1951). A study of prose style which gives considerable attention to Bacon.

FROM

ESSAYS OR COUNSELS, CIVIL AND MORAL

[TEXT: *third edition, 1625*]

OF TRUTH

WHAT is truth? said jesting Pilate;[1] and would not stay for an answer. Certainly there be that delight in giddiness,[2] and count it a bondage to fix a belief; affecting free-will in thinking, as well as in acting. And though the sects of philosophers of that kind[3] be gone, yet there remain certain discoursing wits,[4] which are of the same veins, though there be not so much blood in them as was in those of the ancients. But it is not only the difficulty and labor which men take in finding out of truth; nor again, that when it is found, it imposeth upon[5] men's thoughts, that doth bring lies in favor; but a natural though corrupt love of the lie itself. One of the later school of the Grecians examineth the matter, and is at a stand to think what should be in it, that men should love lies; where neither they make for pleasure, as with poets; nor for advantage, as with the merchant, but for the lie's sake. But I cannot tell: this same truth is a naked and open daylight, that doth not show the masks and mummeries and triumphs of the world half so stately and daintily[6] as candle-lights. Truth may perhaps come to the price of a pearl, that showeth best by day, but it will not rise to the price of a diamond or carbuncle, that showeth best in varied lights. A mixture of a lie doth ever add pleasure. Doth any man doubt that if there were taken out of men's minds vain opinions, flattering hopes, false valuations, imaginations as one would, and the like, but it would leave the minds of a number of men poor shrunken things, full of melancholy and indisposition, and unpleasing to themselves? One of the fathers,[7] in great severity, called poesy *vinum dæmonum*,[8] because it filleth the imagination, and yet it is but with the shadow of a lie. But it is not the lie that passeth through the mind, but the lie that sinketh in, and

settleth in it, that doth the hurt, such as we spake of before. But howsoever these things are thus in men's depraved judgments and affections, yet truth, which only doth judge itself, teacheth that the inquiry of truth, which is the love-making, or wooing of it, the knowledge of truth, which is the presence of it, and the belief of truth, which is the enjoying of it, is the sovereign good of human nature. The first creature of God, in the works of the days, was the light of the sense: the last was the light of reason: and His sabbath work ever since is the illumination of His Spirit. First, He breathed light upon the face of the matter, or chaos; then He breathed light into the face of man; and still He breatheth and inspireth light into the face of His chosen. The poet[9] that beautified the sect[10] that was otherwise inferior to the rest saith yet excellently well: "It is a pleasure to stand upon the shore, and to see ships tossed upon the sea: a pleasure to stand in the window of a castle, and to see a battle, and the adventures thereof below: but no pleasure is comparable to the standing upon the vantage ground of truth" (a hill not to be commanded,[11] and where the air is always clear and serene), "and to see the errors, and wanderings, and mists, and tempests, in the vale below": so always that this prospect be with pity, and not with swelling or pride. Certainly, it is heaven upon earth to have a man's mind move in charity, rest in providence, and turn upon the poles of truth.

To pass from theological and philosophical truth to the truth of civil business; it will be acknowledged even by those that practise it not, that clear and round dealing[12] is the honor of man's nature, and that mixture of falsehood is like alloy in coin of gold and silver, which may make the metal work the better, but it embaseth it. For these windings and crooked courses are the goings of the serpent; which goeth basely upon the belly, and not upon the feet. There is no vice that doth so cover a man with shame as to be found false and

---

1 St. John 18:38.   2 *I.e.*, a whirl of thoughts.
3 The Greek Skeptics, who taught that absolute certainty in knowledge is impossible.
4 Rambling and talkative persons.
5 Puts a restraint upon.   6 Elegantly.
7 Perhaps St. Augustine, in his Confessions.
8 Wine of devils.

9 Lucretius, of the first century B.C., in Book II of his *De Rerum Natura*.
10 The Epicureans.
11 *I.e.*, impregnable.
12 Square dealing.

perfidious; and therefore Montaigne[13] saith prettily, when he inquired the reason why the word of the lie should be such a disgrace, and such an odious charge, saith he, "If it be well weighed, to say that a man lieth, is as much as to say that he is brave towards God and a coward towards men." For a lie faces God, and shrinks from man. Surely the wickedness of falsehood and breach of faith cannot possibly be so highly expressed, as in that it shall be the last peal to call the judgments of God upon the generations of men, it being foretold that when Christ cometh, he shall not "find faith upon the earth."[14]

OF DEATH[15]

MEN fear death as children fear to go in the dark; and as that natural fear in children is increased with tales, so is the other. Certainly, the contemplation of death as the wages of sin, and passage to another world, is holy and religious; but the fear of it, as a tribute due unto nature, is weak. Yet in religious meditations there is sometimes mixture of vanity and of superstition. You shall read in some of the friars' books of mortification that a man should think with himself what the pain is if he have but his finger's end pressed or tortured, and thereby imagine what the pains of death are, when the whole body is corrupted and dissolved; when many times death passeth with less pain than the torture of a limb; for the most vital parts are not the quickest of sense. And by him[16] that spake only as a philosopher, and natural man, it was well said, *Pompa mortis magis terret, quam mors ipsa.*[17] Groans and convulsions, and a discolored face, and friends weeping, and blacks[18] and obsequies, and the like, show death terrible. It is worthy the observing that there is no passion in the mind of man so weak, but it mates and masters the fear of death; and therefore death is no such terrible enemy when a man hath so many attendants about him that can win the combat of him. Revenge triumphs over death; love slights it; honor aspireth to it; grief flieth to it; fear preoccupateth it; nay, we read,

after Otho the emperor had slain himself, pity, which is the tenderest of affections, provoked many to die out of mere compassion to their sovereign, and as the truest sort of followers. Nay, Seneca adds niceness[19] and satiety: *Cogita quamdiu eadem feceris; mori velle, non tantum fortis, aut miser, sed etiam fastidiosus potest.*[20] A man would die, though he were neither valiant nor miserable, only upon a weariness to do the same thing so oft over and over. It is no less worthy to observe, how little alteration in good spirits the approaches of death make: for they appear to be the same men till the last instant. Augustus Cæsar died in a compliment, *Livia, conjugii nostri memor, vive et vale;*[21] Tiberius in dissimulation, as Tacitus saith of him, *Jam Tiberium vires et corpus, non dissimulatio, deserebant;*[22] Vespasian in a jest, sitting upon the stool, *Ut puto Deus fio:*[23] Galba with a sentence, *Feri, si ex re sit populi Romani,*[24] holding forth his neck; Septimius Severus in dispatch, *Adeste, si quid mihi restat agendum.*[25] And the like. Certainly the Stoics bestowed too much cost upon death, and by their great preparations made it appear more fearful. Better, saith he, *qui finem vitæ extremum inter munera ponat naturæ.*[26] It is as natural to die as to be born; and to a little infant, perhaps, the one is as painful as the other. He that dies in an earnest pursuit, is like one that is wounded in hot blood; who for the time scarce feels the hurt; and therefore a mind fixed and bent upon somewhat that is good, doth avert the dolors of death. But, above all, believe it, the sweetest canticle is *Nunc dimittis,*[27] when a man hath obtained worthy ends and expectations. Death hath this also, that it openeth the gate to good fame, and extinguisheth envy: *Extinctus amabitur idem.*[28]

13 In his Essays, II, 18. Montaigne was the greatest of Bacon's predecessors in the field of the essay.

14 St. Luke 18:8.

15 First published in the second edition, 1612.

16 The reference is thought to be to Seneca's Epistles, III, 3, 14.

17 The circumstances connected with death terrify us more than death itself.

18 Black draperies.

19 Fastidiousness.

20 Consider how long you have done the same things; a man may wish to die not only because he is brave, or unhappy, but also because he is simply tired of living.

21 Livia, mindful of our marriage, live on, and fare thee well.

22 His physical powers and vitality were deserting Tiberius, but not his duplicity.

23 I think I am becoming a god.

24 Strike, if it be for the good of the Roman people.

25 Make haste, if anything remains for me to do.

26 Who considers the end of life one of nature's blessings. —Juvenal, Satires, X, 358.

27 Now lettest thou thy servant depart in peace.—St. Luke 2:29.

28 The same man (who was envied while alive) shall be loved when dead.—Horace, Epistles, II, 1, 14.

OF PARENTS AND CHILDREN[29]

THE joys of parents are secret, and so are their griefs and fears; they cannot utter the one, nor will they not utter the other. Children sweeten labors, but they make misfortunes more bitter; they increase the cares of life, but they mitigate the remembrance of death. The perpetuity by generation is common to beasts; but memory, merit, and noble works, are proper to men: and surely a man shall see the noblest works and foundations have proceeded from childless men, which have sought to express the images of their minds where those of their bodies have failed; so the care of posterity is most in them that have no posterity. They that are the first raisers of their houses are most indulgent towards their children, beholding them as the continuance, not only of their kind, but of their work; and so both children and creatures.

The difference in affection of parents towards their several children is many times unequal, and sometimes unworthy, especially in the mother; as Solomon saith, "A wise son rejoiceth the father, but an ungracious son shames the mother."[30] A man shall see, where there is a house full of children, one or two of the eldest respected, and the youngest made wantons;[31] but in the midst some that are as it were forgotten, who, many times, nevertheless, prove the best. The illiberality of parents, in allowance towards their children, is an harmful error, makes them base, acquaints them with shifts, makes them sort[32] with mean company, and makes them surfeit more when they come to plenty: and, therefore, the proof is best when men keep their authority towards their children, but not their purse. Men have a foolish manner (both parents, and schoolmasters, and servants) in creating and breeding an emulation between brothers during childhood, which many times sorteth to[33] discord when they are men, and disturbeth families. The Italians make little difference between children and nephews, or near kinsfolks; but so they be of the lump, they care not, though they pass not through their own body; and, to say truth, in nature it is much a like matter; insomuch that we see a nephew sometimes resembleth an uncle or a kinsman more than his own parent, as the blood happens. Let parents choose betimes the vocations and courses they mean their children should take, for then they are most flexible, and let them not too much apply themselves to the disposition of their children, as thinking they will take best to that which they have most mind to. It is true that if the affection[34] or aptness of the children be extraordinary, then it is good not to cross it; but generally the precept is good, *Optimum elige, suave et facile illud faciet consuetudo.*[35] Younger brothers are commonly fortunate, but seldom or never where the elder are disinherited.

OF MARRIAGE AND SINGLE LIFE[36]

HE THAT hath wife and children hath given hostages to fortune; for they are impediments to great enterprises, either of virtue or mischief. Certainly the best works, and of greatest merit for the public, have proceeded from the unmarried or childless men, which both in affection and means have married and endowed the public. Yet it were great reason that those that have children should have greatest care of future times, unto which they know they must transmit their dearest pledges. Some there are who, though they lead a single life, yet their thoughts do end with themselves, and account future times impertinences. Nay, there are some other that account wife and children but as bills of charges. Nay more, there are some foolish rich covetous men that take a pride in having no children, because they may be thought so much the richer. For perhaps they have heard some talk, "Such an one is a great rich man," and another except to it, "Yea, but he hath a great charge of children"; as if it were an abatement to his riches. But the most ordinary cause of a single life is liberty, especially in certain self-pleasing and humorous[37] minds, which are so sensible of every restraint, as they will near to think their girdles and garters to be bonds and shackles. Unmarried men are best friends, best masters, best servants, but not always best subjects, for they are light to run away, and almost all fugitives are of that condition. A single life doth well with churchmen, for charity will hardly water the ground where it must first fill a pool. It is indifferent for judges and magistrates, for if they be facile and corrupt, you shall have a servant five times worse than a wife. For soldiers, I find the generals commonly in their hortatives put men in mind of their

---

29 First published in 1612.
30 Proverbs 10:1.
31 Spoiled children.
32 Associate.
33 Grows into.

34 Tendency, inclination.
35 Choose the best; custom will make it pleasant and easy.
36 First published in 1612.
37 Eccentric.

wives and children; and I think the despising of marriage amongst the Turks maketh the vulgar soldier more base. Certainly wife and children are a kind of discipline of humanity; and single men, though they be many times more charitable, because their means are less exhaust, yet, on the other side, they are more cruel and hard-hearted (good to make severe inquisitors), because their tenderness is not so oft called upon. Grave natures, led by custom, and therefore constant, are commonly loving husbands, as was said of Ulysses, *Vetulam suam prœtulit immortalitati.*[38] Chaste women are often proud and froward, as presuming upon the merit of their chastity. It is one of the best bonds, both of chastity and obedience, in the wife if she think her husband wise, which she will never do if she find him jealous. Wives are young men's mistresses, companions for middle age, and old men's nurses, so as a man may have a quarrel[39] to marry when he will. But yet he was reputed one of the wise men that made answer to the question when a man should marry: "A young man not yet, an elder man not at all." It is often seen that bad husbands have very good wives; whether it be that it raiseth the price of their husbands' kindness when it comes, or that the wives take a pride in their patience. But this never fails, if the bad husbands were of their own choosing, against their friends' consent; for then they will be sure to make good their own folly.

OF LOVE[40]

THE stage is more beholding[41] to love than the life of man. For as to the stage, love is ever matter of comedies, and now and then of tragedies; but in life it doth much mischief, sometimes like a siren, sometimes like a fury. You may observe, that amongst all the great and worthy persons whereof the memory remaineth, either ancient or recent, there is not one that hath been transported to the mad degree of love; which shows that great spirits and great business do keep out this weak passion. You must except, nevertheless, Marcus Antonius,[42] the half partner of the empire of Rome, and Appius Claudius,[43] the decemvir and law-

giver; whereof the former was indeed a voluptuous man, and inordinate; but the latter was an austere and wise man. And therefore it seems (though rarely) that love can find entrance, not only into an open heart, but also into a heart well fortified, if watch be not well kept. It is a poor saying of Epicurus, *Satis magnum alter alteri theatrum sumus:*[44] as if man, made for the contemplation of heaven and all noble objects, should do nothing but kneel before a little idol, and make himself a subject, though not of the mouth, as beasts are, yet of the eye, which was given him for higher purposes. It is a strange thing to note the excess of this passion, and how it braves[45] the nature and value of things by this, that the speaking in a perpetual hyperbole is comely in nothing but in love. Neither is it merely in the phrase. For whereas it hath been well said that the arch-flatterer, with whom all the petty flatterers have intelligence, is a man's self, certainly the lover is more. For there was never proud man thought so absurdly well of himself as the lover doth of the person loved; and therefore it was well said, "That it is impossible to love and to be wise." Neither doth this weakness appear to others only, and not to the party loved, but to the loved most of all, except the love be reciproque. For it is a true rule, that love is ever rewarded, either with the reciproque, or with an inward and secret contempt; by how much the more men ought to beware of this passion, which loseth not only other things, but itself. As for the other losses, the poet's relation doth well figure them, "That he[46] that preferred Helena, quitted the gifts of Juno and Pallas." For whosoever esteemeth too much of amorous affection, quitteth both riches and wisdom. This passion hath his floods in the very times of weakness, which are great prosperity and great adversity, though this latter hath been less observed. Both which times kindle love, and make it more fervent, and therefore show it to be the child of folly. They do best who, if they cannot but admit love, yet make it keep quarter, and sever it wholly from their serious affairs and actions of life. For if it check[47] once with business, it troubleth men's fortunes, and maketh men that they can nowise be true to their own ends. I know not how, but martial men are given to love. I think it is but as they are given to wine, for perils commonly ask to be paid in

38 He preferred his aged wife [Penelope] to immortality.
39 Pretext, reason.   40 First published in 1612.
41 Beholden, attached.
42 In love with Cleopatra, queen of Egypt.
43 Appius Claudius sought to get possession of Virginia, daughter of a plebeian, Virginius. The father slew his daughter to prevent her falling into the hands of Appius.

44 Each of us is to the other a sufficiently large theater.
45 Insults.
46 Paris, son of Priam, king of Troy. His infatuation with and abduction of Helen led to the Trojan War.
47 Interfere.

pleasures. There is in man's nature a secret inclination and motion towards love of others, which if it be not spent upon some one or a few, doth naturally spread itself towards many, and maketh men become humane and charitable, as it is seen sometimes in friars. Nuptial love maketh mankind, friendly love perfecteth it, but wanton love corrupteth and embaseth it.

OF GREAT PLACE [48]

MEN in great place are thrice servants—servants of the sovereign or state, servants of fame, and servants of business. So as they have no freedom, neither in their persons, nor in their actions, nor in their times. It is a strange desire to seek power and to lose liberty; or to seek power over others, and to lose power over a man's self. The rising unto place is laborious, and by pains men come to greater pains; and it is sometimes base, and by indignities men come to dignities. The standing is slippery, and the regress is either a downfall, or at least an eclipse, which is a melancholy thing. *Cum non sis qui fueris, non esse cur velis vivere.* [49] Nay, retire men cannot when they would, neither will they when it were reason; but are impatient of privateness even in age and sickness, which require the shadow; like old townsmen, that will be still sitting at their street-door, though thereby they offer age to scorn. Certainly great persons had need to borrow other men's opinions to think themselves happy; for if they judge by their own feeling, they cannot find it; but if they think with themselves what other men think of them, and that other men would fain be as they are, then they are happy as it were by report, when, perhaps, they find the contrary within. For they are the first that find their own griefs, though they be the last that find their own faults. Certainly men in great fortunes are strangers to themselves, and while they are in the puzzle of business they have no time to tend their health either of body or mind. *Illi mors gravis incubat, qui notus nimis omnibus, ignotus moritur sibi.* [50] In place there is licence to do good and evil; whereof the latter is a curse: for in evil the best condition is not to will, the second not to can. [51] But power to do good is the true

and lawful end of aspiring; for good thoughts, though God accept them, yet towards men are little better than good dreams, except they be put in act; and that cannot be without power and place, as the vantage and commanding ground. Merit and good works is the end of man's motion, and conscience [52] of the same is the accomplishment of man's rest: for if a man can be partaker of God's theater, [53] he shall likewise be partaker of God's rest. *Et conversus Deus, ut aspiceret opera, quæ fecerunt manus suæ, vidit quod omnia essent bona nimis;* [54] and then the Sabbath.

In the discharge of thy place set before thee the best examples; for imitation is a globe of precepts. And after a time set before thee thine own example; and examine thyself strictly whether thou didst not best at first. Neglect not also the examples of those that have carried themselves ill in the same place; not to set off thyself by taxing [55] their memory, but to direct thyself what to avoid. Reform, therefore, without bravery [56] or scandal of former times and persons; but yet set it down to thyself, as well to create good precedents as to follow them. Reduce things to the first institution, and observe wherein and how they have degenerate; but yet ask counsel of both times—of the ancient time what is best, and of the latter time what is fittest. Seek to make thy course regular, that men may know beforehand what they may expect; but be not too positive and peremptory; and express thyself well when thou digressest from thy rule. Preserve the right of thy place, but stir not questions of jurisdiction; and rather assume thy right in silence, and *de facto*, [57] than voice it with claims and challenges. Preserve likewise the rights of inferior places; and think it more honor to direct in chief than to be busy in all. Embrace and invite helps and advices touching the execution of thy place; and do not drive away such as bring thee information as meddlers, but accept of them in good part. The vices of authority are chiefly four: delays, corruption, roughness, and facility. [58] For delays, give easy access, keep times appointed, go through with that which is in hand, and interlace not business but of necessity. For corruption, do not only bind thine own hands or thy servants' hands from taking, but bind the hands of suitors also from offering. For integrity used doth the

---

48 First published in 1612.

49 Since you are not what you were, there is no reason why you should wish to live longer.

50 Death lies heavily upon him who, well known to all others, dies unknown to himself.

51 Know.

52 Consciousness.

53 Spectacle; *i.e.*, can see what God saw.

54 Genesis 1:31, quoted from the Vulgate: "And God, having looked upon the works which his hands had made, saw that all were very good."

55 Censuring.   56 Ostentation.

57 As a matter of course.   58 Easiness to be led.

one, but integrity professed, and with a manifest detestation of bribery, doth the other. And avoid not only the fault, but the suspicion. Whosoever is found variable, and changeth manifestly without manifest cause, giveth suspicion of corruption. Therefore, always when thou changest thine opinion or course, profess it plainly, and declare it, together with the reasons that move thee to change, and do not think to steal it.[59] A servant or a favorite, if he be inward,[60] and no other apparent cause of esteem, is commonly thought but a by-way to close corruption. For roughness, it is a needless cause of discontent: severity breedeth fear, but roughness breedeth hate. Even reproofs from authority ought to be grave, and not taunting. As for facility, it is worse than bribery; for bribes come but now and then; but if importunity or idle respects lead a man, he shall never be without. As Solomon saith, "To respect persons is not good; for such a man will transgress for a piece of bread."[61]

It is most true that was anciently spoken: "A place showeth the man." And it showeth some to the better and some to the worse. *Omnium consensu capax imperii, nisi imperasset,*[62] saith Tacitus of Galba; but of Vespasian he saith, *Solus imperantium Vespasianus mutatus in melius:*[63] though the one was meant of sufficiency,[64] the other of manners and affection.[65] It is an assured sign of a worthy and generous spirit, whom honor amends; for honor is, or should be, the place of virtue; and as in nature things move violently to their place, and calmly in their place, so virtue in ambition is violent, in authority settled and calm. All rising to great place is by a winding stair; and if there be factions, it is good to side[66] a man's self whilst he is in the rising, and to balance himself when he is placed. Use the memory of thy predecessor fairly and tenderly; for if thou dost not, it is a debt will sure be paid when thou art gone. If thou have colleagues, respect them; and rather call them when they look not for it, than exclude them when they have reason to look to be called. Be not too sensible or too remembering of thy place in conversation and private answers to suitors; but let it rather be said, "When he sits in place he is another man."

OF TRAVEL[67]

TRAVEL, in the younger sort, is a part of education; in the elder, a part of experience. He that travelleth into a country before he hath some entrance into the language, goeth to school, and not to travel. That young men travel under some tutor or grave servant, I allow[68] well; so that he be such a one that hath the language, and hath been in the country before; whereby he may be able to tell them what things are worthy to be seen in the country where they go, what acquaintances they are to seek, what exercises or discipline[69] the place yieldeth; for else young men shall go hooded, and look abroad little. It is a strange thing that in sea voyages, where there is nothing to be seen but sky and sea, men should make diaries; but in land travel, wherein so much is to be observed, for the most part they omit it; as if chance were fitter to be registered than observation. Let diaries, therefore, be brought in use. The things to be seen and observed are: the courts of princes, specially when they give audience to ambassadors; the courts of justice, while they sit and hear causes; and so of consistories ecclesiastic; the churches and monasteries, with the monuments which are therein extant; the walls and fortifications of cities and towns; and so the havens and harbors, antiquities and ruins, libraries, colleges, disputations,[70] and lectures, where any are; shipping and navies; houses and gardens of state and pleasure, near great cities; armories, arsenals, magazines, exchange, burses, warehouses, exercises of horsemanship, fencing, training of soldiers, and the like; comedies, such whereunto the better sort of persons do resort; treasuries of jewels and robes; cabinets and rarities; and, to conclude, whatsoever is memorable in the places where they go; after all which the tutors or servants ought to make diligent inquiry. As for triumphs, masks, feasts, weddings, funerals, capital executions, and such shows, men need not to be put in mind of them; yet are they not to be neglected. If you will have a young man to put his travel into a little room, and in short time to gather much, this you must do: first, as was said, he must have some entrance into the language before he goeth; then he must have such a servant, or tutor, as knoweth the country, as was

59 Do it by stealth.   60 Confidential.
61 Proverbs 28:21.
62 Everyone would have thought him capable of ruling—if he had not ruled.
63 Of the emperors, Vespasian alone changed for the better (when in power).
64 Ability.   65 Disposition.
66 Be on the side of.

67 First published in 1625.
68 Approve.
69 Learning.
70 Formal philosophical debates, which were a regular part of the academic discipline in Renaissance Europe.

likewise said; let him carry with him also some card,[71] or book, describing the country where he travelleth, which will be a good key to his inquiry. Let him keep also a diary; let him not stay long in one city or town, more or less as the place deserveth, but not long; nay, when he stayeth in one city or town, let him change his lodging from one end and part of the town to another, which is a great adamant[72] of acquaintance; let him sequester himself from the company of his countrymen, and diet in such places where there is good company of the nation where he travelleth. Let him, upon his removes from one place to another, procure recommendation to some person of quality residing in the place whither he removeth, that he may use his favor in those things he desireth to see or know. Thus he may abridge his travel with much profit. As for the acquaintance which is to be sought in travel, that which is most of all profitable is acquaintance with the secretaries and employed men of ambassadors; for so in travelling in one country he shall suck the experience of many. Let him also see and visit eminent persons in all kinds, which are of great name abroad, that he may be able to tell how the life agreeth with the fame. For quarrels, they are with care and discretion to be avoided. They are commonly for mistresses, healths, place, and words. And let a man beware how he keepeth company with choleric and quarrelsome persons, for they will engage him into their own quarrels. When a traveller returneth home, let him not leave the countries where he hath travelled altogether behind him, but maintain a correspondence by letters with those of his acquaintance which are of most worth. And let his travel appear rather in his discourse than in his apparel or gesture; and in his discourse let him be rather advised in his answers, than forward to tell stories. And let it appear that he doth not change his country manners[73] for those of foreign parts, but only prick in some flowers of that he hath learned abroad into the customs of his own country.

OF FRIENDSHIP[74]

IT HAD been hard for him that spake it to have put more truth and untruth together in few words than in that speech, "Whosoever is delighted in solitude, is either a wild beast or a god."[75] For it is most true, that a natural and secret hatred and aversion towards society in any man hath somewhat of the savage beast; but it is most untrue that it should have any character at all of the divine nature, except it proceed, not out of a pleasure in solitude, but out of a love and desire to sequester a man's self for a higher conversation: such as is found to have been falsely and feignedly in some of the heathen; as Epimenides, the Candian;[76] Numa, the Roman;[77] Empedocles, the Sicilian;[78] and Apollonius of Tyana;[79] and truly and really in divers of the ancient hermits and holy fathers of the church. But little do men perceive what solitude is, and how far it extendeth; for a crowd is not company, and faces are but a gallery of pictures, and talk but a tinkling cymbal, where there is no love. The Latin adage meeteth with it a little, *Magna civitas, magna solitudo;*[80] because in a great town friends are scattered, so that there is not that fellowship, for the most part, which is in less neighborhoods: but we may go further, and affirm most truly, that it is a mere and miserable solitude to want true friends, without which the world is but a wilderness; and even in this sense also of solitude, whosoever in the frame of his nature and affections is unfit for friendship, he taketh it of the beast, and not from humanity.

A principal fruit of friendship is the ease and discharge of the fullness and swellings of the heart, which passions of all kinds do cause and induce. We know diseases of stoppings and suffocations are the most dangerous in the body; and it is not much otherwise in the mind; you may take sarza[81] to open the liver, steel to open the spleen, flower of sulphur for the lungs, castoreum[82] for the brain; but no receipt openeth the heart but a true friend, to whom you may impart griefs, joys, fears, hopes, suspicions, counsels, and whatsoever lieth upon the heart to oppress it, in a kind of civil shrift or confession.

71 Chart, map.   72 Loadstone.
73 The manners of his own country.
74 First published in 1612, and entirely rewritten for the edition of 1625.

75 Aristotle's Politics, I.
76 A Cretan poet and sage of the sixth century B.C., who is reputed to have slept in a cave without waking for fifty-seven years.
77 A legendary king of Rome, said to have been taught in a cave by the muse Egeria.
78 A Sicilian philosopher of the sixth century B.C., who is said to have thrown himself into the crater of Mt. Etna so that his sudden disappearance might cause people to consider him a god.
79 A Pythagorean philosopher of the first century A.D., famous as a magician.
80 A great city, a great solitude.   81 Sarsaparilla.
82 A glandular secretion of the beaver.

It is a strange thing to observe how high a rate great kings and monarchs do set upon this fruit of friendship whereof we speak: so great, as they purchase it many times at the hazard of their own safety and greatness: for princes, in regard of the distance of their fortune from that of their subjects and servants, cannot gather this fruit, except (to make themselves capable thereof) they raise some persons to be as it were companions, and almost equals to themselves, which many times sorteth to inconvenience. The modern languages give unto such persons the name of favorites, or privadoes, as if it were matter of grace, or conversation; but the Roman name attaineth the true use and cause thereof, naming them *participes curarum;* [83] for it is that which tieth the knot; and we see plainly that this hath been done, not by weak and passionate princes only, but by the wisest and most politic that ever reigned, who have oftentimes joined to themselves some of their servants, whom both themselves have called friends, and allowed others likewise to call them in the same manner, using the word which is received between private men.

L. Sylla, when he commanded Rome, raised Pompey (after surnamed the Great) to that height that Pompey vaunted himself for Sylla's over-match, for when he had carried the consulship for a friend of his, against the pursuit of Sylla, and that Sylla did a little resent thereat, and began to speak great, Pompey turned upon him again, and in effect bade him be quiet; for that more men adored the sun rising than the sun setting. With Julius Cæsar, Decimus Brutus had obtained that interest, as he set him down in his testament for heir in remainder after his nephew; and this was the man that had power with him to draw him forth to his death. For when Cæsar would have discharged the senate, in regard of some ill presages, and specially a dream of Calpurnia, this man lifted him gently by the arm out of his chair, telling him he hoped he would not dismiss the senate till his wife had dreamt a better dream; and it seemeth his favor was so great, as Antonius, in a letter which is recited verbatim in one of Cicero's Philippics, calleth him *venefica, witch:* as if he had enchanted Cæsar. Augustus raised Agrippa (though of mean birth) to that height, as, when he consulted with Mæcenas about the marriage of his daughter Julia, Mæcenas took the liberty to tell him, that he must either marry his daughter to Agrippa, or take away his life: there was no third way, he had made him so great. With Tiberius Cæsar, Sejanus had ascended to that height, as they two were termed and

83 Partners in cares.

reckoned as a pair of friends. Tiberius, in a letter to him, saith, *Hæc pro amicitiâ nostrâ non occultavi;* [84] and the whole senate dedicated an altar to Friendship, as to a goddess, in respect of the great dearness of friendship between them two. The like, or more, was between Septimius Severus and Plautianus; for he forced his eldest son to marry the daughter of Plautianus, and would often maintain Plautianus in doing affronts to his son; and did write also, in a letter to the senate, by these words: "I love the man so well, as I wish he may over-live me." Now, if these princes had been as a Trajan, or a Marcus Aurelius, a man might have thought that this had proceeded of an abundant goodness of nature; but being men so wise, of such strength and severity of mind, and so extreme lovers of themselves, as all these were, it proveth most plainly that they found their own felicity (though as great as ever happened to mortal men) but as an half-piece, except they might have a friend to make it entire; and yet, which is more, they were princes that had wives, sons, nephews; and yet all these could not supply the comfort of friendship.

It is not to be forgotten what Comineus [85] observeth of his first master, Duke Charles the Hardy, namely, that he would communicate his secrets with none; and least of all, those secrets which troubled him most. Whereupon he goeth on, and saith, that towards his latter time that closeness did impair and a little perish his understanding. Surely Comineus might have made the same judgment also, if it had pleased him, of his second master, Louis the Eleventh, whose closeness was indeed his tormentor. The parable of Pythagoras is dark, but true, *Cor ne edito*—"eat not the heart." Certainly, if a man would give it a hard phrase, those that want friends to open themselves unto are cannibals of their own hearts: but one thing is most admirable (wherewith I will conclude this first fruit of friendship), which is, that this communicating of a man's self to his friend works two contrary effects; for it redoubleth joys, and cutteth griefs in halves: for there is no man that imparteth his joys to his friend, but he joyeth the more; and no man that imparteth his griefs to his friend, but he grieveth the less. So that it is, in truth, of operation upon a man's mind of like virtue as the alchemists used to attribute to their stone [86] for man's

84 Because of our friendship, I have not concealed these things from you.

85 Philippe de Comines, French historian and diplomat of the fifteenth century.

86 The philosopher's stone.

body, that it worketh all contrary effects, but still to the good and benefit of nature: but yet, without praying in aid of[87] alchemists, there is a manifest image of this in the ordinary course of nature; for, in bodies, union strengthened and cherisheth any natural action, and, on the other side, weakeneth and dulleth any violent impression; and even so is it of minds.

The second fruit of friendship is healthful and sovereign for the understanding, as the first is for the affections; for friendship maketh indeed a fair day in the affections from storm and tempests, but it maketh daylight in the understanding, out of darkness and confusion of thoughts. Neither is this to be understood only of faithful counsel, which a man receiveth from his friend; but before you come to that, certain it is, that whosoever hath his mind fraught with many thoughts, his wits and understanding do clarify and break up in the communicating and discoursing with another; he tosseth his thoughts more easily; he marshalleth them more orderly; he seeth how they look when they are turned into words: finally, he waxeth wiser than himself; and that more by an hour's discourse than by a day's meditation. It was well said by Themistocles to the king of Persia, "That speech was like cloth of Arras, opened and put abroad; whereby the imagery doth appear in figure; whereas in thoughts they lie, but as in packs." Neither is this second fruit of friendship, in opening the understanding, restrained only to such friends as are able to give a man counsel (they indeed are best), but even without that a man learneth of himself, and bringeth his own thoughts to light, and whetteth his wits as against a stone, which itself cuts not. In a word, a man were better relate himself to a statue or picture, than to suffer his thoughts to pass in smother.

Add now, to make this second fruit of friendship complete, that other point which lieth more open, and falleth within vulgar observation: which is faithful counsel from a friend. Heraclitus saith well in one of his enigmas, "Dry light is ever the best": and certain it is, that the light that a man receiveth by counsel from another, is drier and purer than that which cometh from his own understanding and judgment; which is ever infused and drenched in his affections and customs. So as there is as much difference between the counsel that a friend giveth, and that a man giveth himself, as there is between the counsel of a friend and of a flatterer; for there is no such flatterer as is a man's self,

and there is no such remedy against flattery of a man's self as the liberty of a friend. Counsel is of two sorts; the one concerning manners, the other concerning business: for the first, the best preservative to keep the mind in health, is the faithful admonition of a friend. The calling of a man's self to a strict account is a medicine sometimes too piercing and corrosive; reading good books of morality is a little flat and dead; observing our faults in others is sometimes improper for our case; but the best receipt (best I say to work and best to take) is the admonition of a friend. It is a strange thing to behold what gross errors and extreme absurdities many (especially of the greater sort) do commit for want of a friend to tell them of them, to the great damage both of their fame and fortune: for, as St. James saith, they are as men "that look sometimes into a glass, and presently forget their own shape and favor."[88] As for business, a man may think, if he will, that two eyes see no more than one; or, that a gamester seeth always more than a looker-on; or, that a man in anger is as wise as he that hath said over the four and twenty letters;[89] or, that a musket may be shot off as well upon the arm as upon a rest; and such other fond and high imaginations, to think himself all in all. But when all is done, the help of good counsel is that which setteth business straight: and if any man think that he will take counsel, but it shall be by pieces, asking counsel in one business of one man, and in another business of another man, it is well (that is to say, better, perhaps, than if he asked none at all); but he runneth two dangers; one, that he shall not be faithfully counselled; for it is a rare thing, except it be from a perfect and entire friend, to have counsel given, but such as shall be bowed and crooked to some ends which he hath that giveth it: the other, that he shall have counsel given, hurtful and unsafe (though with good meaning), and mixed partly of mischief, and partly of remedy; even as if you would call a physician, that is thought good for the cure of the disease you complain of, but is unacquainted with your body; and, therefore, may put you in a way for a present cure, but overthroweth your health in some other kind, and so cure the disease, and kill the patient. But a friend, that is wholly acquainted with a man's estate, will beware, by furthering any present business, how he dasheth upon other inconvenience; and therefore, rest not upon

---

87 *Praying in aid of* is a legal term meaning *being an advocate of.*

88 St. James 1:23, 24.
89 In the alphabet of Bacon's day there were only twenty-four letters, *i* and *j* being the same, as were *u* and *v*.

scattered counsels; they will rather distract and mis-lead, than settle and direct.

After these two noble fruits of friendship (peace in the affections, and support of the judgment), followeth the last fruit, which is like the pomegranate, full of many kernels; I mean aid, and bearing a part in all actions and occasions. Here the best way to represent to life the manifold use of friendship, is to cast and see how many things there are which a man cannot do himself: and then it will appear that it was a sparing speech of the ancients to say, "that a friend is another himself": for that a friend is far more than himself. Men have their time, and die many times in desire of some things which they principally take to heart; the bestowing of a child, the finishing of a work, or the like. If a man have a true friend, he may rest almost secure that the care of those things will continue after him; so that a man hath, as it were, two lives in his desires. A man hath a body, and that body is confined to a place: but where friendship is, all offices of life are, as it were, granted to him and his deputy; for he may exercise them by his friend. How many things are there, which a man cannot, with any face or comeli-ness, say or do himself? A man can scarce allege his own merits with modesty, much less extol them: a man cannot sometimes brook to supplicate, or beg, and a number of the like: but all these things are graceful in a friend's mouth, which are blushing in a man's own. So again, a man's person hath many proper relations which he cannot put off. A man cannot speak to his son but as a father; to his wife but as a husband; to his enemy but upon terms: whereas a friend may speak as the case requires, and not as it sorteth with the person. But to enumerate these things were endless; I have given the rule, where a man cannot fitly play his own part; if he have not a friend, he may quit the stage.

OF YOUTH AND AGE[90]

A MAN that is young in years may be old in hours, if he have lost no time; but that happeneth rarely. Generally, youth is like the first cogitations, not so wise as the second: for there is a youth in thoughts, as well as in ages; and yet the invention of young men is more lively than that of old, and imaginations stream into their minds better, and, as it were, more divinely. Natures that have much heat, and great and violent desires and perturbations, are not ripe for action till

they have passed the meridian of their years: as it was with Julius Cæsar and Septimius Severus; of the latter of whom it is said, *Juventutem egit erroribus, imo furor-ibus plenam;*[91] and yet he was the ablest emperor, almost, of all the list; but reposed natures may do well in youth, as it is seen in Augustus Cæsar, Cosmus duke of Florence, Gaston de Foix,[92] and others. On the other side, heat and vivacity in age is an excellent composi-tion[93] for business. Young men are fitter to invent than to judge, fitter for execution than for counsel, and fitter for new projects than for settled business; for the experience of age, in things that fall within the compass of it, directeth them; but in new things abuseth[94] them. The errors of young men are the ruin of business; but the errors of aged men amount but to this, that more might have been done, or sooner.

Young men, in the conduct and manage of actions, embrace more than they can hold, stir more than they can quiet; fly to the end, without consideration of the means and degrees; pursue some few principles which they have chanced upon absurdly; care[95] not to in-novate, which draws unknown inconveniences; use extreme remedies at first; and that, which doubleth all errors, will not acknowledge or retract them, like an unready horse, that will neither stop nor turn. Men of age object too much, consult too long, adventure too little, repent too soon, and seldom drive business home to the full period, but content themselves with a medio-crity of success. Certainly it is good to compound employments of both; for that will be good for the present, because the virtues of either age may correct the defects of both; and good for succession, that young men may be learners, while men in age are actors; and, lastly, good for externe[96] accidents, be-cause authority followeth old men, and favor and popularity youth: but, for the moral part, perhaps, youth will have the pre-eminence, as age hath for the politic. A certain rabbin, upon the text, "Your young men shall see visions, and your old men shall dream dreams,"[97] inferreth that young men are admitted nearer to God than old, because vision is a clearer revelation than a dream; and certainly, the more a man drinketh of the world, the more it intoxicateth: and age doth profit rather in the powers of understanding,

90 First published in 1612.

91 He spent his youth in folly, nay, in madness.

92 Probably the Duc de Nemours, who commanded the French armies in Italy, and was killed fighting the Spaniards in 1512.

93 Temperament.   94 Deceives.
95 Hesitate.   96 External.
97 Joel 2:28.

than in the virtues of the will and affections. There be some have an over-early ripeness in their years, which fadeth betimes: these are, first, such as have brittle wits, the edge whereof is soon turned: such as was Hermogenes the rhetorician, whose books are exceeding subtle, who afterwards waxed stupid: a second sort is of those that have some natural dispositions, which have better grace in youth than in age; such as is a fluent and luxuriant speech, which becomes youth well, but not age: so Tully saith of Hortensius, *Idem manebat, neque idem decebat:*[98] the third is of such as take too high a strain at the first, and are magnanimous more than tract of years can uphold; as was Scipio Africanus, of whom Livy saith, in effect, *Ultima primis cedebant.*[99]

OF STUDIES[100]

STUDIES serve for delight, for ornament, and for ability. Their chief use for delight is in privateness and retiring; for ornament, is in discourse; and for ability, is in the judgment and disposition of business. For expert men can execute, and perhaps judge of particulars, one by one; but the general counsels, and the plots and marshalling of affairs come best from those that are learned. To spend too much time in studies is sloth; to use them too much for ornament is affectation; to make judgment wholly by their rules is the humor of a scholar. They perfect nature, and are perfected by experience: for natural abilities are like natural plants, that need pruning by study; and studies themselves do give forth directions too much at large, except they be bounded in by experience. Crafty[101] men contemn studies, simple men admire them, and wise men use them; for they teach not their own use; but that is a wisdom without them and above them, won by

observation. Read not to contradict and confute, nor to believe and take for granted, nor to find talk and discourse, but to weigh and consider. Some books are to be tasted, others to be swallowed, and some few to be chewed and digested; that is, some books are to be read only in parts; others to be read, but not curiously;[102] and some few to be read wholly, and with diligence and attention. Some books also may be read by deputy, and extracts made of them by others; but that would[103] be only in the less important arguments and the meaner sort of books; else distilled books are, like common distilled waters, flashy[104] things. Reading maketh a full man; conference a ready man; and writing an exact man. And, therefore, if a man write little, he had need have a great memory; if he confer little, he had need have a present wit; and if he read little, he had need have much cunning, to seem to know that he doth not. Histories make men wise; poets, witty; the mathematics, subtile; natural philosophy, deep; moral, grave; logic and rhetoric, able to contend. *Abeunt studia in mores.*[105] Nay, there is no stond or impediment in the wit but may be wrought out by fit studies, like as diseases of the body may have appropriate exercises. Bowling is good for the stone[106] and reins, shooting for the lungs and breast, gentle walking for the stomach, riding for the head, and the like. So if a man's wit be wandering, let him study the mathematics; for in demonstrations, if his wit be called away never so little, he must begin again. If his wit be not apt to distinguish or find differences, let him study the schoolmen; for they are *Cymini sectores.*[107] If he be not apt to beat over matters, and to call up one thing to prove and illustrate another, let him study the lawyer's cases. So every defect of the mind may have a special receipt.

98 He remained the same when it was no longer becoming.
99 His latter days were not equal to his first.
100 First published in 1597.
101 By *crafty* Bacon presumably means *sly.*

102 Carefully.   103 Should.
104 Flat, or showy.
105 Studies pass into (that is, form) manners.
106 Of the bladder or reins (kidneys).
107 Dividers of cuminseed; that is, hairsplitters. See St. Matthew 23:23.

THE ADVANCEMENT OF LEARNING

[TEXT: *first edition, 1605*]

BOOK I
[The Errors and Vanities of Learning]

Now I proceed to those errors and vanities which have intervened amongst the studies themselves of the learned; which is that which is principal and proper to the present argument; wherein my purpose is not to make a justification of the errors, but, by a censure and separation of the errors, to make a justification of that which is good and sound, and to deliver that from the aspersion of the other. For we see that it is the manner of men to scandalize and deprave that which retaineth the state and virtue, by taking advantage upon that which is corrupt and degenerate: as the Heathens in the primitive church used to blemish and taint the Christians with the faults and corruptions of heretics. But nevertheless I have no meaning at this time to make any exact animadversion of the errors and impediments in matters of learning which are more secret and remote from vulgar opinion; but only to speak unto such as do fall under, or near unto, a popular observation.

There be therefore chiefly three vanities in studies, whereby learning hath been most traduced. For those things we do esteem vain, which are either false or frivolous, those which either have no truth or no use: and those persons we esteem vain, which are either credulous or curious; and curiosity is either in matter or words: so that in reason as well as in experience, there fall out to be these three distempers (as I may term them) of learning; the first, fantastical learning; the second, contentious learning; and the last, delicate learning; vain imaginations, vain altercations, and vain affectations; and with the last I will begin. Martin Luther, conducted (no doubt) by an higher Providence, but in discourse of reason finding what a province he had undertaken against the Bishop of Rome and the degenerate traditions of the church, and finding his own solitude, being no ways aided by the opinions of his own time, was enforced to awake all antiquity, and to call former times to his succors to make a party against the present time; so that the ancient authors, both in divinity and in humanity, which had long time slept in libraries, began generally to be read and revolved. This by consequence did draw on a necessity of a more exquisite travail in the languages original wherein those authors did write, for the better understanding of those authors and the better advantage of pressing and applying their words. And thereof grew again a delight in their manner of style and phrase, and an admiration of that kind of writing; which was much furthered and precipitated by the enmity and opposition that the propounders of those (primitive but seeming new) opinions had against the schoolmen; who were generally of the contrary part, and whose writings were altogether in a differing style and form; taking liberty to coin and frame new terms of art to express their own sense and to avoid circuit of speech, without regard to the pureness, pleasantness, and (as I may call it) lawfulness of the phrase or word. And again, because the great labor then was with the people, (of whom the Pharisees were wont to say, *Execrabilis ista turba, quæ non novit legem*),[1] for the winning and persuading of them, there grew of necessity in chief price and request eloquence and variety of discourse, as the fittest and forciblest access into the capacity of the vulgar sort. So that these four causes concurring, the admiration of ancient authors, the hate of the schoolmen, the exact study of languages, and the efficacy of preaching, did bring in an affectionate study of eloquence and copie[2] of speech, which then began to flourish. This grew speedily to an excess; for men began to hunt more after words than matter; and more after the choiceness of the phrase, and the round and clean composition of the sentence, and the sweet falling of the clauses, and the varying and illustration of their works with tropes and figures, than after the weight of matter, worth of subject, soundness of argument, life of invention, or depth of judgment. Then grew the flowing and watery vein of Osorius, the Portugal bishop, to be in price. Then did Sturmius spend such infinite and curious pains upon Cicero the orator and Hermogenes the

---

1 This wretched crowd which has not known the law.
2 Copia, fullness of rhetorical expression.

rhetorician, besides his own books of periods and imitation and the like. Then did Car of Cambridge, and Ascham, with their lectures and writings almost deify Cicero and Demosthenes, and allure all young men that were studious unto that delicate and polished kind of learning. Then did Erasmus take occasion to make the scoffing echo; *Decem annos consumpsi in legendo Cicerone*,[3] and the echo answered in Greek, *one*, *Asine*.[4] Then grew the learning of the schoolmen to be utterly despised as barbarous. In sum, the whole inclination and bent of those times was rather towards copie than weight.

Here therefore [is] the first distemper of learning, when men study words and not matter: whereof though I have represented an example of late times, yet it hath been and will be *secundum majus et minus* in all time. And how is it possible but this should have an operation to discredit learning, even with vulgar capacities, when they see learned men's works like the first letter of a patent or limned book; which though it hath large flourishes, yet it is but a letter? It seems to me that Pygmalion's frenzy is a good emblem or portraiture of this vanity: for words are but the images of matter; and except they have life of reason and invention, to fall in love with them is all one as to fall in love with a picture.

But yet notwithstanding it is a thing not hastily to be condemned, to clothe and adorn the obscurity even of philosophy itself with sensible and plausible elocution. For hereof we have great examples in Xenophon, Cicero, Seneca, Plutarch, and of Plato also in some degree; and hereof likewise there is great use; for surely to the severe inquisition of truth, and the deep progress into philosophy, it is some hinderance, because it is too early satisfactory to the mind of man, and quencheth the desire of further search, before we come to a just period; but then if a man be to have any use of such knowledge in civil occasions, of conference, counsel, persuasion, discourse, or the like; then shall he find it prepared to his hands in those authors which write in that manner. But the excess of this is so justly contemptible, that as Hercules, when he saw the image of Adonis, Venus' minion, in a temple, said in disdain, *Nil sacri es*,[5] so there is none of Hercules' followers in learning, that is, the more severe and laborious sort of inquirers into truth, but will despise those delicacies and affectations, as indeed capable of no divineness.

3 I have spent ten years reading Cicero.
4 "Ass" (Greek *one*, Latin *asine*).
5 You are no divinity.

And thus much of the first disease or distemper of learning.

The second, which followeth, is in nature worse than the former; for as substance of matter is better than beauty of words, so contrariwise vain matter is worse than vain words: wherein it seemeth the reprehension of St. Paul was not only proper for those times, but prophetical for the times following; and not only respective to divinity, but extensive to all knowledge: *Devita profanas vocum novitates, et oppositiones falsi nominis scientiæ*.[6] For he assigneth two marks and badges of suspected and falsified science; the one, the novelty and strangeness of terms; the other, the strictness of positions, which of necessity doth induce oppositions, and so questions and altercations. Surely, like as many substances in nature which are solid do putrefy and corrupt into worms, so it is the property of good and sound knowledge to putrefy and dissolve into a number of subtile, idle, unwholesome, and (as I may term them) vermiculate questions, which have indeed a kind of quickness and life of spirit, but no soundness of matter or goodness of quality. This kind of degenerate learning did chiefly reign amongst the schoolmen; who having sharp and strong wits, and abundance of leisure, and small variety of reading; but their wits being shut up in the cells of a few authors (chiefly Aristotle their dictator) as their persons were shut up in the cells of monasteries and colleges; and knowing little history, either of nature or time; did out of no great quantity of matter, and infinite agitation of wit, spin out unto us those laborious webs of learning which are extant in their books. For the wit and mind of man, if it work upon matter, which is the contemplation of the creatures of God, worketh according to the stuff, and is limited thereby; but if it work upon itself, as the spider worketh his web, then it is endless, and brings forth indeed cobwebs of learning, admirable for the fineness of thread and work, but of no substance or profit.

This same unprofitable subtility or curiosity is of two sorts; either in the subject itself that they handle, when it is a fruitless speculation or controversy (whereof there are no small number both in divinity and philosophy), or in the manner or method of handling of a knowledge; which amongst them was this; upon every particular position or assertion to frame objections, and to those objections, solutions; which solutions were for the most part not confutations, but

6 Shun profane novelties of terms and falsely named oppositions of science.

distinctions: whereas indeed the strength of all sciences is, as the strength of the old man's faggot, in the bond. For the harmony of a science, supporting each part the other, is and ought to be the true and brief confutation and suppression of all the smaller sort of objections; but on the other side, if you take out every axiom, as the sticks of the faggot, one by one, you may quarrel with them and bend them and break them at your pleasure: so that as was said of Seneca, *Verborum minutiis rerum frangit pondera,*[7] so a man may truly say of the schoolmen, *Quæstionum minutiis scientiarum frangunt soliditatem.*[8] For were it not better for a man in a fair room to set up one great light, or branching candlestick of lights, than to go about with a small watch candle into every corner? And such is their method, that rests not so much upon evidence of truth proved by arguments, authorities, similitudes, examples, as upon particular confutations and solutions of every scruple, cavillation, and objection; breeding for the most part one question as fast it solveth another; even as in the former resemblance, when you carry the light into one corner, you darken the rest: so that the fable and fiction of Scylla seemeth to be a lively image of this kind of philosophy or knowledge; which was transformed into a comely virgin for the upper parts; but then *Candida succinctam latrantibus inguina monstris,*[9] so the generalities of the schoolmen are for a while good and proportionable; but then when you descend into their distinctions and decisions, instead of a fruitful womb for the use and benefit of man's life, they end in monstrous altercations and barking questions. So as it is not possible but this quality of knowledge must fall under popular contempt, the people being apt to contemn truth upon occasion of controversies and altercations, and to think they are all out of their way which never meet: and when they see such digladiation about subtilities and matter of no use nor moment, they easily fall upon that judgment of Dionysius of Syracusa, *Verba ista sunt senum otiosorum.*[10]

Notwithstanding certain it is, that if those schoolmen to their great thirst of truth and unwearied travail of wit had joined variety and universality of reading and contemplation, they had proved excellent lights, to the great advancement of all learning and knowledge.

But as they are, they are great undertakers indeed, and fierce with dark keeping; but as in the inquiry of the divine truth their pride inclined to leave the oracle of God's word and to vanish in the mixture of their own inventions, so in the inquisition of nature they ever left the oracle of God's works and adored the deceiving and deformed images which the unequal mirror of their own minds or a few received authors or principles did represent unto them. And thus much for the second disease of learning.

For the third vice or disease of learning, which concerneth deceit or untruth, it is of all the rest the foulest; as that which doth destroy the essential form of knowledge, which is nothing but a representation of truth: for the truth of being and the truth of knowing are one, differing no more than the direct beam and the beam reflected. This vice therefore brancheth itself into two sorts; delight in deceiving, and aptness to be deceived; imposture and credulity; which, although they appear to be of a diverse nature, the one seeming to proceed of cunning, and the other of simplicity, yet certainly they do for the most part concur: for as the verse noteth,

Percontatorem fugito, nam garrulus idem est,

an inquisitive man is a prattler, so upon the like reason a credulous man is a deceiver: as we see it in fame, that he that will easily believe rumors will as easily augment rumors and add somewhat to them of his own; which Tacitus wisely noteth, when he saith, *Fingunt simul creduntque,*[11] so great an affinity hath fiction and belief.

This facility of credit, and accepting or admitting things weakly authorized or warranted, is of two kinds, according to the subject: for it is either a belief of history (as the lawyers speak, matter of fact), or else of matter of art and opinion. As to the former, we see the experience and inconvenience of this error in ecclesiastical history; which hath too easily received and registered reports and narrations of miracles wrought by martyrs, hermits, or monks of the desert, and other holy men, and their relics, shrines, chapels, and images: which though they had a passage for a time, by the ignorance of the people, the superstitious simplicity of some, and the politic toleration of others, holding them but as divine poesies; yet after a period of time, when the mist began to clear up, they grew to be esteemed but as old wives' fables, impostures of the clergy,

7 He broke up the weight of matters by minute verbal points.
8 They broke up the solidity of the sciences by the minuteness of their questions.
9 Her loins were surrounded by barking monsters.
10 These are the words of idle old men.
11 They make up a story as fast as they believe one.

illusions of spirits, and badges of antichrist, to the great scandal and detriment of religion.

So in natural history, we see there hath not been that choice and judgment used as ought to have been; as may appear in the writings of Plinius, Cardanus, Albertus, and divers of the Arabians; being fraught with much fabulous matter, a great part not only untried but notoriously untrue, to the great derogation of the credit of natural philosophy with the grave and sober kind of wits. Wherein the wisdom and integrity of Aristotle is worthy to be observed; that having made so diligent and exquisite a history of living creatures, hath mingled it sparingly with any vain or feigned matter; and yet on the other side hath cast all prodigious narrations which he thought worthy the recording into one book; excellently discerning that matter of manifest truth, such whereupon observation and rule was to be built, was not to be mingled or weakened with matter of doubtful credit; and yet again that rarities and reports that seem uncredible are not to be suppressed or denied to the memory of men.

And as for the facility of credit which is yielded to arts and opinions, it is likewise of two kinds; either when too much belief is attributed to the arts themselves, or to certain authors in any art. The sciences themselves which have had better intelligence and confederacy with the imagination of man than with his reason, are three in number; Astrology, Natural Magic, and Alchemy; of which sciences nevertheless the ends or pretences are noble. For astrology pretendeth to discover that correspondence or concatenation which is between the superior globe and the inferior: natural magic pretendeth to call and reduce natural philosophy from variety of speculations to the magnitude of works: and alchemy pretendeth to make separation of all the unlike parts of bodies which in mixtures of nature are incorporate. But the derivations and prosecutions to these ends, both in the theories and in the practices, are full of error and vanity; which the great professors themselves have sought to veil over and conceal by enigmatical writings, and referring themselves to auricular traditions, and such other devices to save the credit of impostures. And yet surely to alchemy this right is due, that it may be compared to the husbandman whereof Æsop makes the fable, that when he died told his sons that he had left unto

them gold buried under ground in his vineyard; and they digged over all the ground, and gold they found none, but by reason of their stirring and digging the mould about the roots of their vines, they had a great vintage the year following: so assuredly the search and stir to make gold hath brought to light a great number of good and fruitful inventions and experiments, as well for the disclosing of nature as for the use of man's life.

And as for the overmuch credit that hath been given unto authors in sciences, in making them dictators, that their words should stand, and not counsels to give advice; the damage is infinite that sciences have received thereby, as the principal cause that hath kept them low, at a stay without growth or advancement. For hence it hath comen that in arts mechanical the first deviser comes shortest, and time addeth and perfecteth; but in sciences the first author goeth furthest, and time leeseth and corrupteth. So we see, artillery, sailing, printing, and the like, were grossly managed at the first, and by time accommodated and refined; but contrariwise the philosophies and sciences of Aristotle, Plato, Democritus, Hippocrates, Euclides, Archimedes, of most vigor at the first, and by time degenerate and imbased; whereof the reason is no other, but that in the former many wits and industries have contributed in one; and in the later many wits and industries have been spent about the wit of some one, whom many times they have rather depraved than illustrated. For as water will not ascend higher than the level of the first spring-head from whence it descendeth, so knowledge derived from Aristotle, and exempted from liberty of examination, will not rise again higher than the knowledge of Aristotle. And therefore, although the position be good, *Oportet discentem credere*,[12] yet it must be coupled with this, *Oportet edoctum judicare*,[13] for disciples do owe unto masters only a temporary belief and a suspension of their own judgment until they be fully instructed, and not an absolute resignation or perpetual captivity: and therefore to conclude this point, I will say no more but, so let great authors have their due, as time which is the author of authors be not deprived of his due, which is further and further to discover truth.

12 It is fitting for a learner to believe.
13 It is fitting for an educated man to judge.

FROM

NOVUM ORGANUM,[1] [1620]

[IDOLS AND FALSE NOTIONS]

19. THERE are and can be only two ways of searching into and discovering truth. The one flies from the senses and particulars to the most general axioms, and from these principles, the truth of which it takes for settled and immovable, proceeds to judgment and to the discovery of middle axioms. And this way is now in fashion. The other derives axioms from the senses and particulars, rising by a gradual and unbroken ascent, so that it arrives at the most general axioms last of all. This is the true way, but as yet untried.

38. The Idols[2] and false notions which are now in possession of the human understanding, and have taken deep root therein, not only so beset men's minds that truth can hardly find entrance, but even after entrance obtained, they will again in the very instauration of the sciences meet and trouble us, unless men being forewarned of the danger fortify themselves as far as may be against their assaults.

39. There are four classes of Idols which beset men's minds. To these for distinction's sake I have assigned names—calling the first class *Idols of the Tribe;* the second, *Idols of the Cave;* the third, *Idols of the Market-place;* the fourth, *Idols of the Theater.*

40. The formation of ideas and axioms by true induction is no doubt the proper remedy to be applied for the keeping off and clearing away of Idols. To point them out, however, is of great use; for the doctrine of Idols is to the interpretation of Nature what the doctrine of the refutation of Sophisms is to common Logic.

41. The *Idols of the Tribe* have their foundation in human nature itself, and in the tribe or race of men. For it is a false assertion that the sense of man is the measure of things. On the contrary, all perceptions as well of the sense as of the mind are according to the measure of the individual and not according to the measure of the universe. And the human understanding is like a false mirror, which, receiving rays irregularly, distorts and discolors the nature of things by mingling its own nature with it.

42. The *Idols of the Cave* are the idols of the individual man. For every one (besides the errors common to human nature in general) has a cave or den of his own, which refracts and discolors the light of nature; owing either to his own proper and peculiar nature; or to his education and conversation with others; or to the reading of books, and the authority of those whom he esteems and admires; or to the differences of impressions, accordingly as they take place in a mind preoccupied and predisposed or in a mind indifferent and settled; or the like. So that the spirit of man (according as it is meted out to different individuals) is in fact a thing variable and full of perturbation, and governed as it were by chance. Whence it was well observed by Heraclitus that men look for sciences in their own lesser worlds, and not in the greater or common world.

43. There are also Idols formed by the intercourse and association of men with each other, which I call *Idols of the Market-place,* on account of the commerce and consort of men there. For it is by discourse that men associate; and words are imposed according to the apprehension of the vulgar. And therefore the ill and unfit choice of words wonderfully obstructs the understanding. Nor do the definitions or explanations wherewith in some things learned men are wont to guard and defend themselves, by any means set the matter right. But words plainly force and overrule the understanding, and throw all into confusion, and lead men away into numberless empty controversies and idle fancies.

44. Lastly, there are Idols which have immigrated into men's minds from the various dogmas of philosophies, and also from wrong laws of demonstration. These I call *Idols of the Theater;* because in my judgment all the received systems are but so many stage-plays, representing worlds of their own creation after an unreal and scenic fashion. Nor is it only of the

---

1 The *Novum Organum,* though in Latin and hence not a specimen of seventeenth-century English prose, is so important a part of Bacon's thought and writing that a few extracts from it are included here. The translation is that of R. L. Ellis and James Spedding.

2 *Idol* is from the Greek *eidōlon,* and means *phantom, apparition, specter.* The word as Bacon uses it here has no reference to false gods or images.

systems now in vogue, or only of the ancient sects and philosophies, that I speak; for many more plays of the same kind may yet be composed and in like artificial manner set forth; seeing that errors the most widely different have nevertheless causes for the most part alike. Neither again do I mean this only of entire systems, but also of many principles and axioms in science, which by tradition, credulity, and negligence have come to be received.

But of these several kinds of Idols I must speak more largely and exactly, that the understanding may be duly cautioned.

53. The *Idols of the Cave* take their rise in the peculiar constitution, mental or bodily, of each individual; and also in education, habit, and accident. Of this kind there is a great number and variety. But I will instance those the pointing out of which contains the most important caution, and which have most effect in disturbing the clearness of the understanding.

54. Men become attached to certain particular sciences and speculations, either because they fancy themselves the authors and inventors thereof, or because they have bestowed the greatest pains upon them and become most habituated to them. But men of this kind, if they betake themselves to philosophy and contemplations of a general character, distort and color them in obedience to their former fancies; a thing especially to be noticed in Aristotle, who made his natural philosophy a mere bond-servant to his logic, thereby rendering it contentious and well-nigh useless. . . .

56. There are found some minds given to an extreme admiration of antiquity, others to an extreme love and appetite for novelty; but few so duly tempered that they can hold the mean, neither carping at what has been well laid down by the ancients, nor despising what is well introduced by the moderns. This, however, turns to the great injury of the sciences and philosophy; since these affectations of antiquity and novelty are the humors of partisans rather than judgments; and truth is to be sought for not in the felicity of any age, which is an unstable thing, but in the light of nature and experience, which is eternal. . . .

58. Let such then be our provision and contemplative prudence for keeping off and dislodging the *Idols of the Cave*, which grow for the most part either out of the predominance of a favorite subject, or out of an excessive tendency to compare or to distinguish, or out of partiality for particular ages, or out of the large-ness or minuteness of the objects contemplated. And generally let every student of nature take this as a rule —that whatever his mind seizes and dwells upon with peculiar satisfaction is to be held in suspicion, and that so much the more care is to be taken in dealing with such questions to keep the understanding even and clear.

59. But the *Idols of the Market-place* are the most troublesome of all: idols which have crept into the understanding through the alliance of words and names. For men believe that their reason governs words; but it is also true that words react on the understanding; and this it is that has rendered philosophy and the sciences sophistical and inactive. Now words, being commonly framed and applied according to the capacity of the vulgar, follow those lines of division which are most obvious to the vulgar understanding. And whenever an understanding of greater acuteness or a more diligent observation would alter those lines to suit the true divisions of nature, words stand in the way and resist the change. Whence it comes to pass that the high and formal discussions of learned men end oftentimes in disputes about words and names; with which (according to the use and wisdom of the mathematicians) it would be more prudent to begin, and so by means of definitions reduce them to order. Yet even definitions cannot cure this evil in dealing with natural and material things; since the definitions themselves consist of words, and those words beget others: so that it is necessary to recur to individual instances, and those in due series and order; as I shall say presently when I come to the method and scheme for the formation of notions and axioms.

60. The Idols imposed by words on the understanding are of two kinds. They are either names of things which do not exist (for as there are things left unnamed through lack of observation, so likewise are there names which result from fantastic suppositions and to which nothing in reality corresponds), or they are names of things which exist, but yet confused and ill-defined, and hastily and irregularly derived from realities. Of the former kind are Fortune, the Prime Mover,[3] Planetary Orbits, Element of Fire, and like fictions which owe their origin to false and idle theories. And this class of idols is more easily expelled, because to get rid of them it is only necessary that all theories should be steadily rejected and dismissed as obsolete.

3 The *primum mobile*, or outermost sphere, which set in motion the other celestial spheres.

But the other class, which springs out of a faulty and unskillful abstraction, is intricate and deeply rooted. Let us take for example such a word as *humid;* and see how far the several things which the word is used to signify agree with each other; and we shall find the word *humid* to be nothing else than a mark loosely and confusedly applied to denote a variety of actions which will not bear to be reduced to any constant meaning. For it both signifies that which easily spreads itself round any other body; and that which in itself is indeterminate and cannot solidize; and that which readily yields in every direction; and that which easily divides and scatters itself; and that which easily unites and collects itself; and that which readily flows and is put in motion; and that which readily clings to another body and wets it; and that which is easily reduced to a liquid, or being solid easily melts. Accordingly when you come to apply the word—if you take it in one sense, flame is humid; if in another, air is not humid; if in another, fine dust is humid; if in another, glass is humid. So that it is easy to see that the notion is taken by abstraction only from water and common and ordinary liquids, without any due verification.

There are, however, in words certain degrees of distortion and error. One of the least faulty kinds is that of names of substances, especially of lowest species and well-deduced (for the notion of *chalk* and of *mud* is good, of *earth* bad); a more faulty kind is that of actions, as *to generate, to corrupt, to alter;* the most faulty is of qualities (except such as are the immediate objects of the sense), as *heavy, light, rare, dense,* and the like. Yet in all these cases some notions are of necessity a little better than others, in proportion to the greater variety of subjects that fall within the range of the human sense.

61. But the *Idols of the Theater* are not innate, nor do they steal into the understanding secretly, but are plainly impressed and received into the mind from the play-books of philosophical systems and the perverted rules of demonstration. To attempt refutations in this case would be merely inconsistent with what I have already said: for since we agree neither upon principles nor upon demonstrations there is no place for argument. And this is so far well, inasmuch as it leaves the honor of the ancients untouched. For they are no wise disparaged—the question between them and me being only as to the way. For as the saying is, the lame man who keeps the right road outstrips the runner who takes a wrong one. Nay, it is obvious that when a man runs the wrong way, the more active and swift he is the further he will go astray.

But the course I propose for the discovery of sciences is such as leaves but little to the acuteness and strength of wits, but places all wits and understandings nearly on a level. For as in the drawing of a straight line or perfect circle, much depends on the steadiness and practice of the hand, if it be done by aim of hand only, but if with the aid of rule or compass, little or nothing; so is it exactly with my plan. But though particular confutations would be of no avail, yet touching the sects and general divisions of such systems I must say something; something also touching the external signs which show that they are unsound; and finally something touching the causes of such great infelicity and of such lasting and general agreement in error; that so the access to truth may be made less difficult, and the human understanding may the more willingly submit to its purgation and dismiss its idols.

62. *Idols of the Theater,* or of Systems, are many, and there can be and perhaps will be yet many more. For were it not that now for many ages men's minds have been busied with religion and theology; and were it not that civil governments, especially monarchies, have been averse to such novelties, even in matters speculative; so that men labor therein to the peril and harming of their fortunes—not only unrewarded, but exposed also to contempt and envy; doubtless there would have arisen many other philosophical sects like to those which in great variety flourished once among the Greeks. For as on the phenomena of the heavens many hypotheses may be constructed, so likewise (and more also) many various dogmas may be set up and established on the phenomena of philosophy. And in the plays of this philosophical theater you may observe the same thing which is found in the theater of the poets, that stories invented for the stage are more compact and elegant, and more as one would wish them to be, than true stories out of history.

In general, however, there is taken for the material of philosophy either a great deal out of a few things, or a very little out of many things; so that on both sides philosophy is based on too narrow a foundation of experiment and natural history, and decides on the authority of too few cases. For the rational school of philosophers snatches from experience a variety of common instances, neither duly ascertained nor diligently examined and weighed, and leaves all the rest to meditation and agitation of wit. . . .

John Donne

[1572–1631]

BORN of a staunchly Roman Catholic family, Donne studied at Oxford and possibly also at Cambridge but left without taking a degree because his religion prevented him from taking the oath of allegiance to the Protestant Crown required by law. During the early 1590's he was in London, where his activities included the study of law at the Inns of Court, an intensive study of theology in order to determine to his own satisfaction the validity of Protestant and Catholic claims to religious truth, and at least a certain amount of sensual indulgence. The evidence of some of the *Songs and Sonnets* and love elegies written during this period has led some critics to exaggerate to a kind of mythic importance the conception of "Jack Donne the Rake." The poems make it clear that the love of women was important for Donne at that time, but at the same time they give ample documentation of that "hydroptic immoderate thirst of human languages and learning" which he attributed to himself.

At some point in the early 1590's Donne spent a year or so in foreign travel, and he accompanied Essex on his Spanish expeditions in 1596 and 1597. By 1598 he had been made secretary to Sir Thomas Egerton, Lord Keeper of the Great Seal, had probably at least nominally accepted the Anglican faith, and seemed assured of a brilliant career in the public service. His prospects were rudely dashed in 1601, when he fell passionately in love with Anne More, niece of Sir Thomas Egerton and daughter of Sir George More, Chancellor of the Garter. Sir George was adamantly opposed to the match, and when Donne and Anne were secretly married he obtained not only the poet's dismissal but also, briefly, his imprisonment. The period from his release until 1615 was the most desperate in Donne's life: deprived of his post and having spent his patrimony, he was dependent on the help of friends and patrons for the support of himself, his wife, and their numerous children. In 1609 Anne's father relented to the extent of assisting them a little, but the degree of Donne's despair at points before that time is suggested by his *Biathanatos* (not published until 1646), "a declaration of that paradox . . . that self-homicide is not so naturally a sin that it may never be otherwise."

By 1607 Donne's religious doubts seem to have been as settled as they ever were to be; in that year he assisted Thomas Morton, Dean of Gloucester, in attacks on the Roman Church. In 1610 he published, possibly at the request of the king, *Pseudo-Martyr*, a tract urging English Catholics to take the oath of allegiance, and in 1611 *Ignatius His Conclave*, a satirical attack on the Jesuits. As early as 1607 Donne had been urged by Morton to take holy orders, and in the years that followed, King James became so convinced of Donne's usefulness to him as a divine that he saw to it that all doors of secular preferment were closed to him. In 1615 he was ordained a minister of the

Anglican Church and promptly was named chaplain to the king. In 1617 Anne Donne died.

The works which have gained for Donne immortality as a prose writer belong to the period of his divine service. In 1621 he was named Dean of St. Paul's and soon became recognized as the greatest preacher in the great age of English preaching. His sermons, like the great *Devotions Upon Emergent Occasions*, religious meditations inspired by his serious illness of 1623, display the characteristic qualities of his poetry— dramatic immediacy, compelling rhythm, imaginative richness, and intellectual subtlety. His amorous poetry had explored the spiritual implications of physical love with an ingenuity and intensity which are unparalleled; his mature religious prose investigates man's relation to God in language which never loses the accents of human passion. There is an ultimate consistency in Donne's temperament: the Dean of St. Paul's, like the young libertine of thirty years before, is in search of some surpassing unity which will give final satisfaction to a passionate nature thirsting for infinity.

It is the expression of this passion and the evocation of its object which make the sermons and *Devotions* live for the modern reader, despite all the trappings of citation and theological definition in which they appear. The recurrent obsessions of Donne's prose—the vision of death, for example, more than Baudelairean in its terrifying intensity, or the theme of brotherhood—take their meaning from the ever present context—finite man's paradoxical desire for a union with the infinity of God. The fine psychology, the probing self-examination, the wide-ranging intellect—all are in the service of an aspiration which is, however different its terms may be in different historical periods, as universal as it is gloriously impossible.

J. DONNE. *The Sermons*, ed. G. R. Potter and E. M. Simpson, 9 vols. (Berkeley, Calif., 1953–59). Recent and definitive.

———. *Devotions Upon Emergent Occasions*, ed. J. Sparrow (Cambridge, 1923).

———. *Poetry and Prose*, ed. F. J. Warnke (New York, 1967).

E. GOSSE. *Life and Letters of John Donne*, 2 vols. (London, 1899).

I. HUSAIN. *The Dogmatic and Mystical Theology of John Donne* (New York, 1938).

E. M. SIMPSON. *A Study of the Prose Works of John Donne* (rev. ed., Oxford, 1948). The most thorough study of the prose.

C. M. COFFIN. *John Donne and the New Philosophy* (New York, 1937). Examines Donne's philosophical milieu.

R. C. BALD. *John Donne: a Life* (Oxford, 1970).

E. LeCOMTE. *Grace for a Witty Sinner* (New York, 1965).

J. WEBBER. *Contrary Music: the Prose Style of John Donne* (Madison, Wisc., 1963).

J. CAREY. *John Donne: Life, Mind and Art* (New York, 1981).

(SEE ALSO Donne bibliography in poetry section.)

DEVOTIONS UPON EMERGENT OCCASIONS

[TEXT: *first edition, 1624*]

MEDITATIONS

Insultus morbi primus;
The first alteration, the first
grudging of the sickness.

I. MEDITATION

VARIABLE and therefore miserable condition of man! this minute I was well, and am ill this minute. I am surprised with a sudden change and alteration to worse, and can impute it to no cause, nor call it by any name. We study health, and we deliberate upon our meats and drink and air and exercises, and we hew and we polish every stone that goes to that building; and so our health is a long and regular work. But in a minute a cannon batters all, overthrows all, demolishes all; a sickness unprevented for all our diligence, unsuspected for all our curiosity, nay, undeserved, if we consider only disorder, summons us, seizes us, possesses us, destroys us in an instant. O miserable condition of man! which was not imprinted by God, who, as he is immortal himself, had put a coal, a beam of immortality into us, which we might have blown into a flame but blew it out by our first sin; we beggared ourselves by hearkening after false riches, and infatuated ourselves by hearkening after false knowledge. So that now we do not only die but die upon the rack, die by the torment of sickness; nor that only but are pre-afflicted, super-afflicted with these jealousies and suspicions and apprehensions of sickness, before we can call it a sickness. We are not sure we are ill; one hand asks the other by the pulse, and our eye asks our own urine how we do. O multiplied misery! we die and cannot enjoy death because we die in this torment of sickness; we are tormented with sickness, and cannot stay till the torment come, but pre-apprehensions and presages prophesy those torments which induce that death before either come; and our dissolution is conceived in these first changes, quickened in the sickness itself, and born in death, which bears date from these first changes. Is this the honor which man hath by being a little world[1] that he hath these earthquakes in himself, sudden shakings; these lightnings, sudden flashes; these thunders, sudden noises; these eclipses, sudden offuscations and darkening of his senses; these blazing stars, sudden fiery exhalations; these rivers of blood, sudden red waters? Is he a world to himself only therefore that he hath enough in himself not only to destroy and execute himself but to presage that execution upon himself, to assist the sickness, to antedate the sickness, to make the sickness the more irremediable by sad apprehensions, and, as if he would make a fire the more vehement by sprinkling water upon the coals, so to wrap a hot fever in cold melancholy lest the fever alone should not destroy fast enough without this contribution nor perfect the work —which is destruction—except we joined an artificial sickness of our own melancholy to our natural, our unnatural fever? O perplexed discomposition, O riddling distemper! O miserable condition of man!

Decubitus sequitur tandem;
The patient takes his bed.

III. MEDITATION

WE ATTRIBUTE but one privilege and advantage to man's body above other moving creatures, that he is not as others grovelling but of an erect, of an upright form naturally built and disposed to the contemplation of heaven. Indeed it is a thankful form, and recompenses that soul which gives it with carrying that soul so many feet higher towards heaven. Other creatures look to the earth; and even that is no unfit object, no unfit contemplation for man, for thither he must come; but because man is not to stay there as other creatures are, man in his natural form is carried to the contemplation of that place which is his home, heaven. This is man's prerogative; but what state hath he in this dignity? A fever can fillip him down, a fever can

1 The medieval conception of man as a microcosm, a "little world."

depose him; a fever can bring that head which yesterday carried a crown of gold five feet towards a crown of glory as low as his own foot today. When God came to breathe into man the breath of life, he found him flat upon the ground; when he comes to withdraw that breath from him again, he prepares him to it by laying him flat upon his bed. Scarce any prison so close that affords not the prisoner two or three steps. The anchorites that barked themselves up in hollow trees and immured themselves in hollow walls, that perverse man that barrelled himself in a tub, all could stand or sit and enjoy some change of posture. A sick-bed is a grave, and all that the patient says there is but a varying of his own epitaph. Every night's bed is a type of the grave; at night we tell our servants at what hour we will rise, here we cannot tell ourselves at what day, what week, what month. Here the head lies as low as the foot; the head of the people as low as they whom those feet trod upon; and that hand that signed pardons is too weak to beg his own, if he might have it for lifting up that hand. Strange fetters to the feet, strange manacles to the hands, when the feet and hands are bound so much the faster by how much the cords are slacker; so much the less able to do their offices by how much more the sinews and ligaments are the looser. In the grave I may speak through the stones, in the voice of my friends and in the accents of those words which their love may afford my memory; here I am mine own ghost and rather affright my beholders than instruct them; they conceive the worst of me now and yet fear worse; they give me up for dead now and yet wonder how I do when they wake at midnight and ask how I do tomorrow. Miserable and (though common to all) inhuman posture where I must practice my lying in the grave by lying still and not practice my resurrection by rising any more!

Medicusque vocatur;
The physician is sent for.

IV. MEDITATION

IT IS too little to call a man a little world; except God, man is a diminutive to nothing. Man consists of more pieces, more parts than the world, than the world doth, nay, than the world is. And if those pieces were extended and stretched out in man as they are in the world, man would be the giant and the world the dwarf; the world but the map and the man the world.

If all the veins in our bodies were extended to rivers and all the sinews to veins of mines and all the muscles that lie upon one another to hills and all the bones to quarries of stones and all the other pieces to the proportion of those which correspond to them in the world, the air would be too little for this orb of man to move in, the firmament would be but enough for this star; for as the whole world hath nothing to which something in man doth not answer, so hath man many pieces of which the whole world hath no representation. Enlarge this meditation upon this great world, man, so far as to consider the immensity of the creatures this world produces; our creatures are our thoughts, creatures that are born giants, that reach from east to west, from earth to heaven, that do not only bestride all the sea and land but span the sun and firmament at once; my thoughts reach all, comprehend all. Inexplicable mystery! I their creator am in a close prison, in a sick-bed, anywhere, and any one of my creatures, my thoughts, is with the sun and beyond the sun, overtakes the sun and overgoes the sun in one pace, one step, everywhere. And then as the other world produces serpents and vipers, malignant and venomous creatures and worms and caterpillars that endeavor to devour that world which produces them and monsters compiled and complicated of divers parents and kinds; so this world, ourselves, produces all these in us in producing diseases and sicknesses of all those sorts, venomous and infectious diseases, feeding and consuming diseases, and manifold and entangled diseases made up of many several ones. And can the other world name so many venomous, so many consuming, so many monstrous creatures as we can diseases of all these kinds? O miserable abundance! O beggarly riches! how much do we lack of having remedies for every disease when as yet we have not names for them! But we have a Hercules against these giants, these monsters; that is, the physician; he musters up all the forces of the other world to succor this, all nature to relieve man. We have the physician, but we are not the physician. Here we shrink in our proportion, sink in our dignity in respect of very mean creatures who are physicians to themselves. The hart that is pursued and wounded, they say, knows an herb which being eaten throws off the arrow. A strange kind of vomit! The dog that pursues it, though he be subject to sickness, even proverbially knows his grass that recovers him. And it may be true that the drugger is as near to man as to other creatures; it may be that obvious and present simples easy to be had would cure him; but the apothecary is not so near him nor the physician so near him as they two are to other creatures; man hath not that innate instinct to apply those natural medicines to his present danger as those inferior creatures have; he is not his own apothecary, his own physician, as they are. Call back therefore thy meditation again and bring it down. What's become of man's great extent and proportion when himself shrinks himself and consumes himself to a handful of dust? what's become of his soaring thoughts, his compassing thoughts when himself brings himself to the ignorance, to the thoughtlessness, of the grave? His diseases are his own, but the physician is not; he hath them at home, but he must send for the physician.

Solus adest;
The physician comes.

V. MEDITATION

AS SICKNESS is the greatest misery, so the greatest misery of sickness is solitude, when the infectiousness of the disease deters them who should assist from coming; even the physician dares scarce come. Solitude is a torment which is not threatened in hell itself. Mere vacuity, the first agent, God, the first instrument of God, nature, will not admit; nothing can be utterly empty but so near a degree towards vacuity as solitude, to be but one they love not. When I am dead and my body might infect, they have a remedy, they may bury me; but when I am but sick and might infect, they have no remedy but their absence and my solitude. It is an excuse to them that are great and pretend and yet are loth to come; it is an inhibition to those who would truly come, because they may be made instruments and pestiducts to the infection of others by their coming. And it is an outlawry, an excommunication upon the patient and separates him from all offices, not only of civility but of working charity. A long sickness will weary friends at last, but a pestilential sickness averts them from the beginning. God himself would admit a figure of society, as there is a plurality of persons in God though there be but one God; and all his external actions testify a love of society and communion. In heaven there are orders of angels and armies of martyrs and in that house many mansions; in earth, families, cities, churches, colleges, all plural things; and lest either of these should not be company enough alone, there is an association of both, a communion of

saints which makes the militant and triumphant church one parish; so that Christ was not out of his diocese when he was upon the earth nor out of his temple when he was in our flesh. God, who saw that all that he made was good, came not so near seeing a defect in any of his works as when he saw that it was not good for man to be alone; therefore he made him a helper, and one that should help him so as to increase the number and give him her own and more society. Angels, who do not propagate nor multiply, were made at first in an abundant number, and so were stars; but for things of this world, their blessing was increase; for I think, I need not ask leave to think that there is no phœnix; nothing singular, nothing alone. Men that inhere upon nature only are so far from thinking that there is anything singular in this world as that they will scarce think that this world itself is singular but that every planet and every star is another world like this; they find reason to conceive not only a plurality in every species in the world but a plurality of worlds; so that the abhorrers of solitude are not solitary, for God and nature and reason concur against it. Now a man may counterfeit the plague in a vow and mistake a disease for religion by such a retiring and recluding of himself from all men as to do good to no man, converse with no man. God hath two testaments, two wills; but this is a schedule, and not of his, a codicil, and not of his, not in the body of his testaments but interlined and postscribed by others, that the way to the communion of saints should be by such a solitude as excludes all doing of good here. That is a disease of the mind, as the height of an infectious disease of the body is solitude, to be left alone. For this makes an infectious bed equal, nay, worse than a grave, that though in both I be equally alone, in my bed I know it and feel it, and shall not in my grave; and this too, that in my bed my soul is still in an infectious body, and shall not in my grave be so.

Metuit;
The physician is afraid.

VI. MEDITATION

I OBSERVE the physician with the same diligence as he the disease; I see he fears, and I fear with him; I overtake him, I overrun him in his fear, and I go the faster because he makes his pace slow; I fear the more because he disguises his fear, and I see it with the more sharpness because he would not have me see it. He knows that his fear shall not disorder the practice and exercise of his art, but he knows that my fear may disorder the effect and working of his practice. As the ill affections of the spleen complicate and mingle themselves with every infirmity of the body, so doth fear insinuate itself in every action or passion of the mind; and as wind in the body will counterfeit any disease and seem the stone and seem the gout, so fear will counterfeit any disease of the mind. It shall seem love, a love of having; and it is but a fear, a jealous and suspicious fear of losing. It shall seem valor in despising and under-valuing danger; and it is but fear in an overvaluing of opinion and estimation and a fear of losing that. A man that is not afraid of a lion is afraid of a cat; not afraid of starving and yet is afraid of some joint of meat at the table presented to feed him; not afraid of the sound of drums and trumpets and shot and those which they seek to drown, the last cries of men, and is afraid of some particular harmonious instrument; so much afraid as that with any of these the enemy might drive this man, otherwise valiant enough, out of the field. I know not what fear is, nor I know not what it is that I fear now; I fear not the hastening of my death, and yet I do fear the increase of the disease; I should belie nature if I should deny that I feared this; and if I should say that I feared death, I should belie God. My weakness is from nature, who hath but her measure; my strength is from God, who possesses and distributes infinitely. As then every cold air is not a damp, every shivering is not a stupefaction; so every fear is not a fearfulness, every declination is not a running away, every debating is not a resolving, every wish that it were not thus is not a murmuring nor a dejection, though it be thus; but as my physician's fear puts not him from his practice, neither doth mine put me from receiving from God and man and myself spiritual and civil and moral assistances and consolations.

Socios sibi jungier instat;

The physician desires to have others joined with him.

VII. MEDITATION

THERE is more fear, therefore more cause. If the physician desire help, the burden grows great. There is a growth of the disease, then; but there must be an autumn too; but whether an autumn of the disease or me, it is not my part to choose; but if it be of me, it is of both; my disease cannot survive me. I may overlive it. Howsoever, his desiring of others argues his candor and his ingenuity; if the danger be great, he justifies his proceedings, and he disguises nothing that calls in witnesses; and if the danger be not great, he is not ambitious that is so ready to divide the thanks and the honor of that work which he began alone with others. It diminishes not the dignity of a monarch that he derive a part of his care upon others; God hath not made many suns, but he hath made many bodies that receive and give light. The Romans began with one king; they came to two consuls; they returned in extremities to one dictator. Whether in one or many, the sovereignty is the same in all states; and the danger is not the more, and the providence is the more, where there are more physicians; as the state is happier where businesses are carried by more counsels than can be in one breast how large soever. Diseases themselves hold consultations and conspire how they can multiply and join with one another and exalt one another's force so; and shall we not call physicians to consultations? Death is in an old man's door, he appears and tells him so, and death is at a young man's back and says nothing; age is a sickness, and youth is an ambush; and we need so many physicians as may make up a watch and spy every inconvenience. There is scarce anything that hath not killed somebody; a hair, a feather hath done it; nay, that which is our best antidote against it hath done it, the best cordial hath been deadly poison. Men have died of joy and almost forbidden their friends to weep for them, when they have seen them die laugh-ing. Even that tyrant, Dionysius—I think the same that suffered so much after—who could not die of that sorrow of that high fall from a king to a wretched private man, died of so poor a joy as to be declared by the people at a theater that he was a good poet. We say often that a man may live of a little; but, alas, of how much less may a man die! And therefore the more assistants the better. Who comes to a day of hearing in a cause of any importance with one advo-cate? In our funerals we ourselves have no interest; there we cannot advise, we cannot direct; and though some nations, the Egyptians in particular, built them-selves better tombs than houses because they were to dwell longer in them; yet amongst ourselves the greatest man of style whom we have had, the Con-queror, was left, as soon as his soul left him, not only without persons to assist at his grave but without a grave. Who will keep us then we know not; as long as we can, let us admit as much help as we can; another and another physician is not another and another indication and symptom of death but another and another assistant and proctor of life. Nor do they so much feed the imagination with apprehension of danger as the understanding with comfort. Let not one bring learning, another diligence, another religion, but every one bring all; and as many ingredients enter into a receipt, so may many men make the receipt. But why do I exercise my meditation so long upon this of having plentiful help in time of need? Is not my meditation rather to be inclined another way, to condole and commiserate their distress who have none? How many are sicker perchance than I and laid in their woeful straw at home—if that corner be a home —and have no more hope of help, though they die, than of preferment, though they live! Nor do more expect to see a physician then than to be an officer after! of whom the first that takes knowledge is the sexton that buries them, who buries them in oblivion too! For they do but fill up the number of the dead in the bill, but we shall never hear their names till we read them in the book of life with our own. How many are sicker perchance than I, and thrown into hospitals, where, as fish left upon the sand must stay the tide, they must wait the physician's hour of visiting, and then can be but visited! How many are sicker perchance than all we and have not this hospital to cover them, not this straw to lie in, to die in, but have their gravestone under them and breathe out their souls in the ears and in the eyes of passengers, harder than their bed, the flint of the street! that taste of no part of our physic but a sparing diet, to whom ordinary porridge would be julep enough, the refuse of our servants bezoar² enough, and the offscouring of our kitchen tables cordial enough! O my soul, when thou art not enough awake to bless thy God enough for his plentiful mercy in affording thee many helpers, remember how many lack them and help them to them or to those other things which they lack as much as them.

2 A precious substance which, in ancient Hebrew lore, cut rocks apart and opened the sightless eyes of nestlings. Here some rare and expensive drug is meant which may have been a sort of laxative.

Et rex ipse suum mittit;
The king sends his own physician.

VIII. MEDITATION

STILL when we return to that meditation that man is a world, we find new discoveries. Let him be a world, and himself will be the land, and misery the sea. His misery (for misery is his, his own; of the happiness even of this world he is but tenant, but of misery the freeholder; of happiness he is but the farmer, but the usufructuary, but of misery the lord, the proprietary), his misery, as the sea, swells above all the hills and reaches to the remotest parts of this earth, man; who of himself is but dust and coagulated and kneaded into earth by tears; his matter is earth, his form misery. In this world that is mankind the highest ground, the eminentest hills, are kings; and have they line and lead enough to fathom this sea and say my misery is but this deep? Scarce any misery equal to sickness, and they are subject to that equally with their lowest subject. A glass is not the less brittle because a king's face is represented in it, nor a king the less brittle because God is represented in him. They have physicians continually about them and therefore sickness, or the worst of sickness, continual fear of it. Are they gods? He that called them so cannot flatter. They are gods, but sick gods; and God is presented to us under many human affections as far as infirmities. God is called angry and sorry and weary and heavy, but never a sick God; for then he might die like men as our gods do. The worst that they could say in reproach and scorn of the gods of the heathen was that perchance they were asleep; but gods that are so sick as that they cannot sleep are in an infirmer condition. A god, and need a physician? A Jupiter, and need an Esculapius? that must have rhubarb to purge his choler lest he be too angry and agaric to purge his phlegm lest he be too drowsy? that as Tertullian says of the Egyptian gods, plants and herbs, that "God was beholden to man for growing in his garden," so we must say of these gods their eternity, an eternity of threescore and ten years, is in the apothecary's shop and not in the metaphorical deity? But their deity is better expressed in their humility than in their height; when abounding and overflowing as God in means of doing good they descend as God to a communication of their abundances with men according to their necessities, then they are gods. No man is well that understands not, that values not his being well, that hath not a cheerfulness and a joy in it; and whosoever hath this joy hath a desire to communicate, to propagate that which occasions his happiness and his joy to others; for every man loves witnesses of his happiness, and the best witnesses are experimental witnesses, they who have tasted of that in themselves which makes us happy. It consummates therefore, it perfects the happiness of kings to confer, to transfer, honor and riches, and, as they can, health upon those that need them.

*Spirante columba supposita pedibus
revocantur ad ima vapores;*

They apply pigeons to draw the
vapors from the head.

XII. MEDITATION

WHAT will not kill a man if a vapor will! How great an elephant how small a mouse destroys! To die by a bullet is the soldier's daily bread; but few men die by hail-shot. A man is more worth than to be sold for single money, a life to be valued above a trifle. If this were a violent shaking of the air by thunder or by cannon, in that case the air is condensed above the thickness of water, of water baked into ice, almost petrified, almost made stone, and no wonder that kills; but that which is but a vapor, and a vapor not forced but breathed, should kill, that our nurse should overlay us, and air that nourishes us should destroy us! But that it is a half atheism to murmur against nature, who is God's immediate commissioner, who would not think himself miserable to be put into the hands of nature, who does not only set him up for a mark for others to shoot at but delights herself to blow him up like a glass till she see him break, even with her own breath? Nay, if this infectious vapor were sought for or travelled to, as Pliny hunted after the vapor of Etna and dared and challenged death in the form of a vapor to do his worst, and felt the worst—he died; or if this vapor were met withal in an ambush and we surprised with it out of a long shut well or out of a new opened mine, who would lament, who would accuse when we had nothing to accuse, none to lament against but fortune, who is less than a vapor? But when ourselves are the well that breathes out this exhalation, the oven that spits out this fiery smoke, the mine that spews out this suffocating and strangling damp, who can ever after this aggravate his sorrow by this circumstance, that it was his neighbor, his familiar friend, his brother that destroyed him and destroyed him with a whispering and a calumniating breath when we ourselves do it ourselves by the same means, kill ourselves with our own vapors? Or if these occasions of this self-destruction had any contribution from our own wills, any assistance from our own intentions, nay, from our own errors, we might divide the rebuke and chide ourselves as much as them. Fevers upon willful distempers of drink and surfeits, consumptions upon intemperances and licentiousness, madness upon misplacing or overbending our natural faculties proceed from ourselves and so as that ourselves are in the plot; and we are not only passive, but active too, to our own destruction. But what have I done either to breed or to breathe these vapors? They tell me it is my melancholy; did I infuse, did I drink in melancholy into myself? It is my thoughtfulness; was I not made to think? It is my study; doth not my calling call for that? I have done nothing willfully, perversely toward it, yet must suffer in it, die by it. There are too many examples of men that have been their own executioners and that have made hard shift to be so. Some have always had poison about them in a hollow ring upon their finger and some in their pen that they used to write with; some have beat out their brains at the wall of their prison, and some have eaten the fire out of their chimneys; and one is said to have come nearer our case than so, to have strangled himself, though his hands were bound, by crushing his throat between his knees. But I do nothing upon myself, and yet am mine own executioner. And we have heard of death upon small occasions and by scornful instruments. A pin, a comb, a hair pulled hath gangrened and killed; but when I have said a vapor, if I were asked again what is a vapor, I could not tell, it is so insensible a thing; so near nothing is that that reduces us to nothing. But extend this vapor, rarefy it from so narrow a room as our natural bodies to any politic body, to a state. That which is fume in us is in a state rumor; and these vapors in us, which we consider here pestilent and infectious fumes, are in a state infectious rumors, detracting and dishonorable calumnies, libels. The heart in that body is the king, and the brain his council; and the whole magistracy that ties all together is the sinews which proceed from thence; and the life of all is honor and just respect and due reverence; and therefore, when these vapors, these venomous rumors, are directed against these noble parts, the whole body suffers. But yet for all their privileges, they are not privileged from our misery; that as the vapors most pernicious do arise in our own bodies, so do the most dishonorable rumors and those that wound a state most arise at home. What ill air that I could have met in the street, what charnel, what shambles, what dung-hill, what vault, could have hurt me so much as these homebred vapors? What fugitive, what almsman of any foreign state, can do so much harm as a detractor, a libeller, a scornful jester at home? For as they that write of poisons and of creatures naturally disposed to the ruin of man do as well mention the flea as the viper, because the flea, though he kill none, he does all the harm he can; so even these libellous and licentious jesters utter the venom they have, though sometimes virtue, and always power, be a good pigeon to draw this vapor from the head and from doing any deadly harm there.

Ingeniumque malum numeroso stigmate fassus
pellitur ad pectus morbique suburbia morbus;

The sickness declares the infection
and malignity thereof by spots.

XIII. MEDITATION

WE SAY that the world is made of sea and land, as though they were equal; but we know that there is more sea in the western than in the eastern hemisphere. We say that the firmament is full of stars, as though it were equally full; but we know that there are more stars under the northern than under the southern pole. We say the elements of man are misery and happiness, as though he had an equal proportion of both, and the days of man vicissitudinary, as though he had as many good days as ill, and that he lived under a perpetual equinoctial, night and day equal, good and ill fortune in the same measure. But it is far from that; he drinks misery, and he tastes happiness; he mows misery, and he gleans happiness; he journeys in misery, he does but walk in happiness; and, which is worst, his misery is positive and dogmatical, his happiness is but disputable and problematical. All men call misery misery, but happiness changes the name by the taste of man. In this accident that befalls me, now that this sickness declares itself by spots to be a malignant and pestilential disease, if there be a comfort in the declaration that thereby the physicians see more clearly what to do, there may be as much discomfort in this, that the malignity may be so great as that all that they can do

shall do nothing; that an enemy declares himself then when he is able to subsist and to pursue and to achieve his ends is no great comfort. In intestine conspiracies, voluntary confessions do more good than confessions upon the rack; in these infections, when nature herself confesses and cries out by these outward declarations which she is able to put forth of herself, they minister comfort; but when all is by the strength of cordials, it is but a confession upon the rack, by which, though we come to know the malice of that man, yet we do not know whether there be not as much malice in his heart then as before his confession; we are sure of his treason, but not of his repentance; sure of him, but not of his accomplices. It is a faint comfort to know the worst when the worst is remediless, and a weaker than that to know much ill and not to know that that is the worst. A woman is comforted with the birth of her son, her body is eased of a burden; but if she could prophetically read his history, how ill a man, perchance how ill a son he would prove, she should receive a greater burden into her mind. Scarce any purchase that is not clogged with secret encumbrances; scarce any happiness that hath not in it so much of the nature of false and base money as that the allay [3] is more than the metal. Nay, is it not so (at least much towards it) even in the exercise of virtues? I must be poor and want before I can exercise the virtue of gratitude; miserable and in torment before I can exercise the virtue of patience. How deep do we dig and for how coarse gold! And what other touchstone have we of our gold but comparison, whether we be as happy as others, or as ourselves at other times? O poor step toward being well, when these spots do only tell us that we are worse than we were sure of before!

Idque notant criticis medici evenisse diebus;

The physicians observe these accidents to have
fallen upon the critical days.

XIV. MEDITATION

I WOULD not make man worse than he is nor his condition more miserable than it is. But could I though I would? As a man cannot flatter God nor overpraise him, so a man cannot injure man nor undervalue him. Thus much must necessarily be presented to his remembrance, that those false happinesses which he hath in this world have their times and their seasons

3 Alloy.

and their critical days; and they are judged and denominated according to the times when they befall us. What poor elements are our happinesses made of if time, time which we can scarce consider to be anything, be an essential part of our happiness! All things are done in some place; but if we consider place to be no more but the next hollow superficies of the air, alas! how thin and fluid a thing is air, and how thin a film is a superficies, and a superficies of air! All things are done in time too, but if we consider time to be but the measure of motion, and howsoever it may seem to have three stations, past, present, and future, yet the first and last of these are not—one is not now, and the other is not yet—and that which you call present is not now the same that it was when you began to call it so in this line—before you sound that word present or that monosyllable now, the present and the now is past. If this imaginary half-nothing, time, be of the essence of our happiness, how can they be thought durable! Time is not so; how can they be thought to be! Time is not so; not so considered in any of the parts thereof. If we consider eternity, into that time never entered; eternity is not an everlasting flux of time, but time is a short parenthesis in a long period; and eternity had been the same as it is, though time had never been. If we consider, not eternity, but perpetuity; not that which had no time to begin in but which shall outlive time and be when time shall be no more, what a minute is the life of the durablest creature compared to that! and what a minute is man's life in respect of the sun's or of a tree! and yet how little of our life is occasion, opportunity to receive good in! and how little of that occasion do we apprehend and lay hold of! How busy and perplexed a cobweb is the happiness of man here that must be made up with a watchfulness to lay hold upon occasion, which is but a little piece of that which is nothing, time! And yet the best things are nothing without that. Honors, pleasures, possessions presented to us out of time, in our decrepit and distasted and unapprehensive age, lose their office and lose their name; they are not honors to us that shall never appear nor come abroad into the eyes of the people to receive honor from them who give it, nor pleasures to us who have lost our sense to taste them, nor possessions to us who are departing from the possession of them. Youth is their critical day that judges them, that denominates them, that inanimates and informs them, and makes them honors and pleasures and possessions; and when they come in an unapprehensive age, they come as a cordial

when the bell rings out, as a pardon when the head is off. We rejoice in the comfort of fire, but does any man cleave to it at midsummer? We are glad of the freshness and coolness of a vault, but does any man keep his Christmas there? or are the pleasures of the spring acceptable in autumn? If happiness be in the season or in the climate, how much happier then are birds than men, who can change the climate and accompany and enjoy the same season ever!

Et properare meum clamant e turre propinqua obstreperæ campanæ aliorum in funere funus;

From the bells of the church adjoining, I am daily remembered of my burial in the funerals of others.

XVI. MEDITATION

WE HAVE a convenient author[4] who writ a discourse of bells when he was prisoner in Turkey. How would he have enlarged himself if he had been my fellow prisoner in this sick-bed so near to that steeple which never ceases no more than the harmony of the spheres, but is more heard! When the Turks took Constantinople, they melted the bells into ordnance; I have heard both bells and ordnance but never been so much affected with those as with these bells. I have lain near a steeple in which there are said to be more than thirty bells and near another where there is one so big as that the clapper is said to weigh more than six hundred pounds, yet never so affected as here. Here the bells can scarce solemnize the funeral of any person but that I knew him or knew that he was my neighbor. We dwelt in houses near to one another before, but now he is gone into that house into which I must follow him. There is a way of correcting the children of great persons, that other children are corrected in their behalf and in their names, and this works upon them who indeed had more deserved it. And when these bells tell me that now one and now another is buried, must not I acknowledge that they have the correction due to me and paid the debt I owe? There is a story of a bell in a monastery which, when any of the house was sick to death, rung always voluntarily, and they knew the inevitableness of the danger by that. It rung once when no man was sick, but the next day one of the house fell from the steeple and died, and the bell held the reputation of a prophet still. If these bells that

4 Magius.

warn to a funeral now were appropriated to none, may not I by the hour of the funeral supply? How many men that stand at an execution, if they would ask, for what dies that man? should hear their own faults condemned and see themselves executed by attorney! We scarce hear of any man preferred but we think of ourselves that we might very well have been that man; why might not I have been that man that is carried to his grave now? Could I fit myself to stand or sit in any man's place, and not to lie in any man's grave? I may lack much of the good parts of the meanest, but I lack nothing of the mortality of the weakest; they may have acquired better abilities than I, but I was born to as many infirmities as they. To be an incumbent by lying down in a grave, to be a doctor by teaching mortification by example, by dying, though I may have seniors, others may be older than I, yet I have proceeded apace in a good university and gone a great way in a little time by the furtherance of a vehement fever; and whomsoever these bells bring to the ground today, if he and I had been compared yesterday, perchance I should have been thought likelier to come to this preferment then than he. God hath kept the power of death in his own hands lest any man should bribe death. If man knew the gain of death, the ease of death, he would solicit, he would provoke death to assist him by any hand which he might use. But as when men see many of their own professions preferred, it ministers a hope that that may light upon them; so when these hourly bells tell me of so many funerals of men like me, it presents, if not a desire that it may, yet a comfort whensoever mine shall come.

Nunc lento sonitu dicunt, morieris;
Now this bell tolling softly for another
says to me, Thou must die.

XVII. MEDITATION

PERCHANCE he for whom this bell tolls may be so ill as that he knows not it tolls for him; and perchance I may think myself so much better than I am as that they who are about me and see my state may have caused it to toll for me, and I know not that. The church is catholic, universal, so are all her actions; all that she does belongs to all. When she baptizes a child, that action concerns me; for that child is thereby connected to that body which is my head too and ingrafted into that body whereof I am a member. And when she buries a man, that action concerns me. All mankind is of one author, and is one volume; when one man dies, one chapter is not torn out of the book, but translated into a better language; and every chapter must be so translated. God employs several translators; some pieces are translated by age, some by sickness, some by war, some by justice; but God's hand is in every translation, and his hand shall bind up all our scattered leaves again for that library where every book shall lie open to one another. As therefore the bell that rings to a sermon calls not upon the preacher only but upon the congregation to come, so this bell calls us all; but how much more me who am brought so near the door by this sickness! There was a contention as far as a suit—in which piety and dignity, religion and estimation, were mingled—which of the religious orders should ring to prayers first in the morning; and it was determined that they should ring first that rose earliest. If we understand aright the dignity of this bell that tolls for our evening prayer, we would be glad to make it ours by rising early, in that application, that it might be ours as well as his, whose indeed it is. The bell doth toll for him that thinks it doth; and though it intermit again, yet from that minute that that occasion wrought upon him he is united to God. Who casts not up his eye to the sun when it rises? but who takes off his eye from a comet when that breaks out? Who bends not his ear to any bell which upon any occasion rings? but who can remove it from that bell which is passing a piece of himself out of this world? No man is an island entire of itself; every man is a piece of the continent, a part of the main. If a clod be washed away by the sea, Europe is the less, as well as if a promontory were, as well as if a manor of thy friend's or of thine own were. Any man's death diminishes me, because I am involved in mankind, and therefore never send to know for whom the bell tolls; it tolls for thee. Neither can we call this a begging of misery or a borrowing of misery, as though we were not miserable enough of ourselves but must fetch in more from the next house, in taking upon us the misery of our neighbors. Truly it were an excusable covetousness if we did, for affliction is a treasure, and scarce any man hath enough of it. No man hath affliction enough that is not matured and ripened by it and made fit for God by that affliction. If a man carry treasure in bullion or in a wedge of gold and have none coined into current money, his treasure will not defray him as he travels. Tribulation is treasure in the nature of it, but it is not current money in the use of it, except we get nearer and nearer our home, heaven, by it. Another man may be sick too, and sick to death, and this affliction may lie in his bowels as gold in a mine and be of no use to him; but this bell that tells me of his affliction digs out and applies that gold to me, if by this consideration of another's danger I take mine own into contemplation and so secure myself by making my recourse to my God, who is our only security.

---

*Atque annuit ille qui per eos clamat, linquas
iam, Lazare, lectum;*

God prospers their practice, and he by them calls
Lazarus out of his tomb, me out of my bed.

XXI. MEDITATION

IF MAN had been left alone in this world at first, shall I think that he would not have fallen? If there had been no woman, would not man have served to have been his own tempter? When I see him now subject to infinite weaknesses, fall into infinite sin without any foreign temptations, shall I think he would have had none if he had been alone? God saw that man needed a helper if he should be well; but to make woman ill the Devil saw that there needed no third. When God and we were alone in Adam, that was not enough; when the Devil and we were alone in Eve, it was enough. O what a giant is man when he fights against himself, and what a dwarf when he needs or exercises his own assistance for himself! I cannot rise out of my bed till the physician enable me, nay, I cannot tell that I am able to rise till he tell me so. I do nothing, I know nothing of myself; how little and how impotent a piece of the world is any man alone! And how much less a piece of himself is that man! So little as that when it falls out, as it falls out in some cases, that more misery and more oppression would be an ease to a man, he cannot give himself that miserable addition of more misery. A man that is pressed to death and might be eased by more weights, cannot lay those more weights upon himself. We can sin alone and suffer alone, but not repent, not be absolved, without another. Another tells me I may rise; and I do so. But is every rising a preferment? or is every present preferment a station? I am readier to fall to the earth, now

I am up, than I was when I lay in the bed. O perverse way, irregular motion of man! even rising itself is the way to ruin! How many men are raised, and then do not fill the place they are raised to! No corner of any place can be empty; there can be no vacuity. If that man do not fill the place, other men will; complaints of his insufficiency will fill it; nay, such an abhorring is there in nature of vacuity that, if there be but an imagination of not filling in any man, that which is but imagination neither will fill it, that is, rumor and voice, and it will be given out—upon no ground but imagination, and no man knows whose imagination— that he is corrupt in his place or insufficient in his place, and another prepared to succeed him in his place. A man rises sometimes and stands not because he doth not or is not believed to fill his place; and sometimes he stands not because he overfills his place. He may bring so much virtue, so much justice, so much integrity to the place as shall spoil the place, burthen the place; his integrity may be a libel upon his predecessor and cast an infamy upon him and a burthen upon his successor to proceed by example and to bring the place itself to an undervalue and the market to an uncertainty. I am up, and I seem to stand, and I go round; and I am a new argument of the new philosophy[5] that the earth moves round. Why may I not believe that the whole earth moves in a round motion, though that seem to me to stand, when as I seem to stand to my company, and yet am carried in a giddy and circular motion as I stand? Man hath no center but misery; there, and only there, he is fixed and sure to find himself. How little soever he be raised, he moves, and moves in a circle giddily; and as in the heavens there are but a few circles that go about the whole world, but many epicycles and other lesser circles but yet circles; so of those men which are raised and put into circles few of them move from place to place and pass through many and beneficial places, but fall into little circles, and within a step or two are at their end and not so well as they were in the center from which they were raised. Everything serves to exemplify, to illustrate man's misery. But I need go no farther than myself. For a long time I was not able to rise; at last I must be raised by others; and now I am up, I am ready to sink lower than before.

5 Galileo's.

SERMON XV, FOLIO OF 1640[1]

"The last enemy that shall be destroyed is death."

THIS is a text of the resurrection, and it is not Easter yet; but it is Easter Eve; all Lent is but the vigil, the eve of Easter. To so long a festival as never shall end, the resurrection, we may well begin the eve betimes. Forty years long was God grieved for that generation which he loved; let us be content to humble ourselves forty days to be fitter for that glory which we expect. In the book of God there are many songs; there is but one lamentation. And that one Song of Solomon, nay, some one of David's hundred and fifty psalms is longer than the whole Book of Lamentations. Make way to an everlasting Easter by a short Lent, to an undeterminable glory by a temporary humiliation. You must weep these tears, tears of contrition, tears of mortification, before God will wipe all tears from your eyes; you must die this death, this death of the righteous, the death to sin, before this last enemy, death, shall be destroyed in you and you made partakers of everlasting life in soul and body too.

Our division shall be but a short and our whole exercise but a larger paraphrase upon the words. The words imply, first, that the kingdom of Christ, which must be perfected, must be accomplished—because all things must be subdued unto him—is not yet perfected, not accomplished yet. Why? what lacks it? It lacks the bodies of men which yet lie under the dominion of another. When we shall also see by that metaphor which the Holy Ghost chooseth to express that in, which is that there is *hostis* and so *militia*, an enemy and a war, and therefore that kingdom is not perfected, that he places perfect happiness and perfect glory in perfect peace. But then how far is any state consisting of many men, how far the state and condition of any one man in particular from this perfect peace! How truly a warfare is this life if the kingdom of heaven itself have not this peace in perfection! And it hath it not, *quia hostis*, because there is an enemy: though that enemy shall not overthrow it, yet because it plots and works and machinates and would overthrow it, this is a defect in that peace.

Who then is this enemy? An enemy that may thus far think himself equal to God, that as no man ever

saw God and lived so no man ever saw this enemy and lived, for it is death, and in this may think himself in number superior to God, that many men live who shall never see God. But *quis homo* is David's question, which was never answered, "Is there any man that lives and shall not see death?" An enemy that is so well victualled against man as that he cannot want as long as there are men, for he feeds upon man himself. And so well armed against man as that he cannot want munition while there are men, for he fights with our weapons; our own faculties, nay, our calamities, yea, our own pleasures are our death. And therefore he is *novissimus hostis*, saith the text, the last enemy.

We have other enemies; Satan about us, sin within us; but the power of both those this enemy shall destroy; but when they are destroyed, he shall retain a hostile and triumphant dominion over us. But *usque quo, Domine?* How long, O Lord? for ever? No, *abolebitur*. We see this enemy all the way, and all the way we feel him; but we shall see him destroyed; *abolebitur*. But how? or when? At and by the resurrection of our bodies. For as upon my expiration, my transmigration from hence, as soon as my soul enters into heaven I shall be able to say to the angels, I am of the same stuff as you, spirit and spirit, and therefore let me stand with you and look upon the face of your God and my God; so at the resurrection of this body, I shall be able to say to the angel of the great council, the Son of God, Christ Jesus himself, I am of the same stuff as you, body and body, flesh and flesh, and therefore let me sit down with you at the right hand of the Father in an everlasting security from this last enemy, who is now destroyed, death. And in these seven steps we shall pass apace and yet clearly through this paraphrase.

We begin with this, that the kingdom of heaven hath not all that it must have to a consummate perfection till it have bodies too. In those infinite millions of millions of generations in which the holy, blessed, and glorious Trinity enjoyed themselves one another and no more, they thought not their glory so perfect but that it might receive an addition from creatures; and therefore they made a world, a material world, a corporeal world; they would have bodies. In that noble part of the world which Moses calls the firmament, that great expansion from God's chair to his footstool, from heaven to earth, there was a defect which God did not supply that day nor the next, but the fourth day he did; for that day he made those bodies, those great and lightsome bodies, the sun and moon and stars and placed them in the firmament. So also the heaven of heavens, the presence chamber of God himself, expects the presence of our bodies.

No state upon earth can subsist without those bodies, men of their own. For men that are supplied from others may either in necessity or in indignation be withdrawn, and so that state which stood upon foreign legs sinks. Let the head be gold and the arms silver and the belly brass, if the feet be clay, men that may slip and molder away, all is but an image, all is but a dream of an image. For foreign helps are rather crutches than legs. There must be bodies, men, and able bodies, able men; men that eat the good things of the land, their own figs and olives; men not macerated with extortions. They are glorified bodies that make up the kingdom of heaven, bodies that partake of the good of the state that make up the state, bodies, able bodies; and lastly, bodies inanimated with one soul. one vegetative soul—all must be compassionate of one another's misery—and especially the immortal soul, one supreme soul, one religion. For God hath made us under good princes a great example of all that, abundance of men, men that live like men, men united in one religion; so we need not go far for an example of a slippery and uncertain being, where they must stand upon other men's men and must overload all men with exactions and distortions and convulsions and earthquakes in the multiplicity of religions.

The kingdom of heaven must have bodies; kingdoms of the earth must have them; and if upon the earth thou beest in the way to heaven, thou must have a body too, a body of thine own, a body of thy possession; for thy body hath thee, and not thou it, if thy body tyrannize over thee. If thou canst not withdraw thine eye from an object of temptation or withhold thy hand from subscribing against thy conscience nor turn thine ear from a popular and seditious libel, what hast thou towards a man? Thou hast no soul, nay, thou hast no body. There is a body, but thou hast it not; it is not thine, it is not in thy power. Thy body will rebel against thee even in a sin; it will not perform a sin when and where thou wouldst have it. Much more will it rebel against any good work, till thou have imprinted *stigmata Jesu*, the marks of the Lord Jesus, which were but exemplar in him but are essential and neces-

sary to thee, abstinences and such discreet disciplines and mortifications as may subdue that body to thee and make it thine; for till then it is but thine enemy and maintains a war against thee; and war and enemy is the metaphor which the Holy Ghost hath taken here to express a want, a kind of imperfectness even in heaven itself. *Bellum simbolum mali.* As peace is of all goodness, so war is an emblem, a hieroglyphic, of all misery; and that is our second step in this paraphrase.

If the feet of them that preach peace be beautiful (and "O how beautiful are the feet of them that preach peace?" The Prophet Isaiah asks the question, 52:7, and the Prophet Nahum asks it, 1:15, and the Apostle St. Paul asks it, Rom. 10:15; they all ask it, but none answers it), who shall answer us if we ask, how beautiful is his face who is the author of this peace when we shall see that in the glory of heaven, the center of all true peace? It was the inheritance of Christ Jesus upon the earth, he had it at his birth, he brought it with him, "Glory be to God on high, peace upon earth." It was his purchase upon earth, "He made peace"—indeed he bought peace—"through the blood of his cross." It was his testament when he went from earth: "Peace I leave with you, my peace I give unto you." Divide with him in that blessed inheritance, partake with him in that blessed purchase, enrich thyself with that blessed legacy, his peace.

Let the whole world be in thy consideration as one house; and then consider in that, in the peaceful harmony of creatures, in the peaceful succession and connection of causes and effects, the peace of nature. Let this kingdom where God hath blessed thee with a being be the gallery, the best room of that house, and consider in the two walls of that gallery, the church and the state, the peace of a royal and a religious wisdom; let thine own family be a cabinet in this gallery, and find in all the boxes thereof, in the several duties of wife and children and servants the peace of virtue, and of the father and mother of all virtues, active discretion, passive obedience, and then lastly, let thine own bosom be the secret box and reserve in this cabinet; and then the best jewel in the best cabinet and that in the best gallery of the best house that can be had, peace with the creature,[2] peace in the church, peace in the state, peace in thy house, peace in thy heart is a fair model and a lovely design even of the heavenly Jerusalem which is *visio pacis* where there is no object but peace.

And therefore the Holy Ghost to intimate to us that

2 Creation; nature.

happy perfectness which we shall have at last, and not till then, chooses the metaphor of an enemy and enmity to avert us from looking for true peace from anything that presents itself in the way. Neither truly could the Holy Ghost imprint more horror by any word than that which intimates war as the word enemy does. It is but a little way that the poet hath got in description of war, *iam seges est*, that now that place is plowed where the great city stood; for it is not so great a depopulation to translate a city from merchants to husbandmen, from shops to plows, as it is from many husbandmen to one shepherd; and yet that hath been often done. And all that, at most, is but a depopulation; it is not a devastation that Troy was plowed. But when the Prophet Isaiah comes to the devastation, to the extermination of a war, he expresses it first thus: "Where there were a thousand vineyards at a cheap rate all the land shall become briars and thorns." That is much; but there is more: "The earth shall be removed out of her place; that land, that nation, shall no more be called that nation nor that land." But yet more than that too; not only not that people but no other shall ever inhabit it: "It shall never be inhabited from generation to generation, neither shall shepherds be there; not only no merchant nor husbandman but no depopulators; none but owls and ostriches and satyrs,"—indeed God knows what, *ochim* and *ziim*, words which truly we cannot translate.

In a word, the horror of war is best discerned in the company he keeps, in his associates. And when the Prophet Gad brought war into the presence of David, there came with him famine and pestilence. And when famine entered, we see the effects; it brought mothers to eat their children of a span long; that is, as some expositors take it, to take medicines to procure abortions to cast their children, that they might have children to eat. And when war's other companion, the pestilence, entered, we see the effects of that too; in less than half the time that it was threatened for, it devoured three-score and ten thousand of David's men; and yet for all the vehemence, the violence, the impetuousness of this pestilence, David chose this pestilence rather than a war. *Militia* and *malitia* are words of so near a sound as that the Vulgate edition takes them as one. For where the prophet, speaking of the miseries that Jerusalem had suffered, says, *finita militia eius*, let her warfare be at an end, they read, *finita malitia eius*, let her misery be at an end; war and misery is all one thing. But is there any of this in heaven? Even the saints in heaven lack something of the consummation of their happiness, *quia hostis*, because they have an enemy. And that is our third and next step.

Michael and his angels fought against the Devil and his angels; though that war ended in victory, yet— taking that war, as divers expositors do, for the fall of angels—that kingdom lost so many inhabitants as that all the souls of all that shall be saved shall but fill up the places of them that fell, and so make that kingdom but as well as it was before that war. So ill effects accompany even the most victorious war. There is no war in heaven, yet all is not well, because there is an enemy; for that enemy would kindle a war again but that he remembers how ill he sped last time he did so. It is not an enemy that invades neither but only detains. He detains the bodies of the saints which are in heaven and therefore is an enemy to the kingdom of Christ; he that detains the souls of men in superstition, he that detains the hearts and allegiance of subjects in an hesitation, a vacillation, an irresolution where they shall fix them, whether upon their sovereign or a foreign power, he is in the notion and acceptation of enemy in this text, an enemy, though no hostile act be done. It is not a war, it is but an enemy, not an invading but a detaining enemy; and then this enemy is but one enemy, and yet he troubles and retards the consummation of that kingdom.

Antichrist [3] alone is enemy enough; but never carry this consideration beyond thyself. As long as there remains in thee one sin or the sinful gain of that one sin, so long there is one enemy; and where there is one enemy, there is no peace. Gardeners that husband their ground to the best advantage sow all their seeds in such order one under another that their garden is always full of that which is then in season. If thou sin with that providence, with that seasonableness that all thy spring, thy youth, be spent in wantonness, all thy summer, thy middle-age, in ambition and the ways of preferment, and thy autumn, thy winter, in indevotion and covetousness, though thou have no farther taste of licentiousness in thy middle-age (thou hast thy satiety in that sin) nor of ambition in thy last years (thou hast accumulated titles and honor), yet all the way thou hast had one enemy, and therefore never any perfect peace. But who is this one enemy in this text? As long as we put it off and as loth as we are to look this enemy in the face, yet we must, though it be death. And this is *vestigium quartum*, the fourth and the next step in this paraphrase.

3 In popular medieval belief the supreme opponent of Christ, to appear before the end of the world.

Surge et descende in domum figuli, says the Prophet Jeremiah, that is, say the expositors, to the consideration of thy mortality. It is *surge*, *descende*, arise and go down, a descent with an ascension. Our grave is upward, and our heart is upon Jacob's ladder; in the way and nearer to heaven. Our daily funerals are some emblems of that; for though we be laid down in the earth after, yet we are lifted up upon men's shoulders before. We rise in the descent to death, and so we do in the descent to the contemplation of it. In all the potter's house is there one vessel made of better stuff than clay? There is his matter. And of all forms a circle is the perfectest. And art thou loth to make up that circle with returning to the earth again?

Thou must, though thou be loth. *Fortasse*, says St. Augustine, that word of contingency, of casualty, perchance, *in omnibus ferme rebus præterquam in morte locum habet*. It hath room in all human actions excepting death. He makes his example thus: such a man is married, where he would or at least where he must, where his parents or his guardian will have him. Shall he have children? *Fortasse*, says he, they are a young couple, perchance they shall. And shall those children be sons? *Fortasse*, they are of a strong constitution, perchance they shall. And shall those sons live to be men? *Fortasse*, they are from healthy parents, perchance they shall. And when they have lived to be men, shall they be good men? Such as good men may be glad they may live? *Fortasse*, still; they are of virtuous parents, it may be they shall. But when they are come to that *morientur*, shall those good men die? here, says that father, the *fortasse* vanishes; here it is *omnino, certe, sine dubitatione;* infallibly, inevitably, irrecoverably they must die. Doth not a man die even in his birth? The breaking of prison is death, and what is our birth but a breaking of prison? As soon as we were clothed by God our very apparel was an emblem of death. In the skins of dead beasts he covered the skins of dying men. As soon as God set us on work our very occupation was an emblem of death; it was to dig the earth; not to dig pitfalls for other men but graves for ourselves. Hath any man here forgot today that yesterday is dead? And the bell tolls for today and will ring out anon; and for as much of every one of us as appertains to this day. *Quotidie morimur, et tamen nos esse æternos putamus*, says St. Jerome; we die every day, and we die all the day long; and because we are not absolutely dead, we call that an eternity, an eternity of dying. And is there comfort in that state? Why that is the state of hell itself, eternal dying, and not dead!

But for this there is enough said by the moral man [4] that we may respite divine proofs for divine points anon for our several resurrections; for this death is merely natural, and it is enough that the moral man says, *mors lex, tributum, officium mortalium*. First it is *lex;* you were born under that law, upon that condition to die; so it is a rebellious thing not to be content to die, it opposes the law. Then it is *tributum*, an imposition which nature the queen of this world lays upon us and which she will take when and where she list; here a young man, there an old man, here a happy, there a miserable man, and so it is a seditious thing not to be content to die, it opposes the prerogative. And lastly, it is *officium;* men are to have their turns, to take their time, and then to give way by death to successors; and so it is *incivile, inofficiosum*, not to be content to die, it opposes the frame and form of government. It comes equally to us all and makes us all equal when it comes. The ashes of an oak in the chimney are no epitaph of that oak to tell me how high or how large it was; it tells me not what flocks it sheltered while it stood, nor what men it hurt when it fell. The dust of great persons' graves is speechless too, it says nothing, it distinguishes nothing; as soon the dust of a wretch whom thou wouldst not as of a prince whom thou couldst not look upon will trouble thine eyes if the wind blow it thither; and when a whirlwind hath blown the dust of the churchyard into the church, and the man sweeps out the dust of the church into the churchyard, who will undertake to sift those dusts again and to pronounce, this is the patrician, this is the noble flour, and this the yeomanly, this the plebeian bran. So is the death of Jezebel (Jezebel was a queen) expressed; they shall not say, this is Jezebel; not only not wonder that it is nor pity that it should be, but they shall not say, they shall not know, this is Jezebel. It comes to all, to all alike; but not alike welcome to all. To die too willingly out of impatience to wish or out of violence to hasten death, or to die too unwillingly, to murmur at God's purpose revealed by age or by sickness, are equal distempers; and to harbor a disobedient lothness all the way, or to entertain it at last, argues but an irreligious ignorance; an ignorance that death is in nature but *expiratio*, a breathing out, and we do that every minute; an ignorance that God himself took a day to rest in, and a good man's grave is his Sabbath; an ignorance that Abel, the best of those whom we can compare with him, was the first that died. Howsoever, whensoever, all times are God's times; *vocantur boni ne*

4 Seneca.

diutius vexentur a noxiis, mali ne diutius bonos persequantur, God calls the good to take them from their dangers, and God takes the bad to take them from their triumph. And therefore neither grudge that thou goest, nor that worse stay, for God can make his profit of both; *aut ideo vivit ut corrigatur, aut ideo ut per illum bonus exerceatur;* God reprieves him to mend him or to make another better by his exercise; and not to exult in the misery of another but to glorify God in the ways of his justice let him know, *quantumcunque sero, subito ex hac vita tollitur qui finem prævidere nescit,* how long soever he live, how long soever he lie sick, that man dies a sudden death who never thought of it. If we consider death in St. Paul's *statutum est,* "It is decreed that all men must die," there death is indifferent; if we consider it in his *mori lucrum,* "that it is an advantage to die," there death is good; and so much the Vulgate edition seems to intimate when (Deut. 30:19), whereas we read I have set before you life and death, that reads it *vitam et bonum,* life and that which is good. If then death be at the worst indifferent and to the good, good, how is it *hostis,* an enemy to the kingdom of Christ? For that also is *vestigium quintum,* the fifth and next step in this paraphrase.

First God did not make death, says the wise man; and therefore St. Augustine makes a reasonable prayer to God, *Ne permittas, Domine, quod non fecisti dominari creaturæ quam fecisti,* suffer not, O Lord, death whom thou didst not make to have dominion over me whom thou didst. Whence then came death? The same wise man hath showed us the father, through envy of the Devil came death into the world; and a wiser than he, the Holy Ghost himself, hath showed us the mother, "By sin came death into the world." But yet if God have naturalized death, taken death into the number of his servants, how is death an enemy? First, he was an enemy in invading Christ, who was not in his commission because he had no sin; and still he is an enemy because still he adheres to the enemy. Death hangs upon the edge of every persecutor's sword, and upon the sting of every calumniator's and accuser's tongue. In the bull of Phalaris, in the bulls of Bashan, in the bulls of Babylon, the shrewdest bull of all, in temporal, in spiritual persecutions ever since God put an enmity between man and the serpent, from the time of Cain who began in a murther to the time of Antichrist who proceeds in massacres, death hath adhered to the enemy, and so is an enemy.

Death hath a commission, *stipendium peccati mors est,* "The reward of sin is death," but where God gives a *supersedeas* upon that commission, *Vivo ego, nolo mortem,* "As I live saith the Lord, I would have no sinner die," not die the second death, yet death proceeds to that execution; and whereas the enemy whom he adheres to, the serpent himself, hath power but *in calcaneo,* upon the heel, the lower, the mortal part, the body of man, "Death is come up into our windows," saith the prophet, into our best lights, our understandings, and benights us there either with ignorance before sin or with senselessness after; and a sheriff that should burn him who were condemned to be hanged were a murderer, though that man must have died. To come in by the door, by the way of sickness upon the body, is, but to come in at the window by the way of sin is not death's commission; God opens not that window.

So then he is an enemy, for they that adhere to the enemy are enemies; and adhering is not only a present subministration of supply to the enemy—for that death doth not—but it is also a disposition to assist the enemy then when he shall be strong enough to make benefit of that assistance. And so death adheres; when sin and Satan have weakened body and mind, death enters upon both. And in that respect he is *ultimus hostis,* the last enemy, and that is *sextum vestigium,* our sixth and next step in this paraphrase.

Death is the last and in that respect the worst enemy. In an enemy that appears at first, when we are or may be provided against him, there is some of that which we call honor; but in the enemy that reserves himself unto the last and attends our weak estate, there is more danger. Keep it where I intend it, in that which is my sphere, the conscience. If mine enemy meet me betimes in my youth in an object of temptation (so Joseph's enemy met him in Potiphar's wife), yet I do not adhere to this enemy, dwell upon a delightful meditation of that sin, if I do not fuel and foment that sin, assist and encourage that sin, by high diet, wanton discourse, other provocation, I shall have reason on my side, and I shall have grace on my side, and I shall have the history of a thousand that have perished by that sin on my side; even spittles[5] will give me soldiers to fight for me by their miserable example against that sin; nay, perchance sometimes the virtue of that woman whom I solicit will assist me. But when I lie under the hands of that enemy that hath reserved himself to the last, to my last bed, then when I shall be able to stir no limb in any other measure than a fever or a palsy shall shake them, when everlasting darkness shall have an

5 Hospitals.

inchoation in the present dimness of mine eyes, and the everlasting gnashing in the present chattering of my teeth, and the everlasting worm in the present gnawing of the agonies of my body and anguishes of my mind, when the last enemy shall watch my remediless body and my disconsolate soul there, there, where not the physician in his way, perchance not the priest in his shall be able to give any assistance, and when he hath sported himself with my misery upon that stage, my death-bed, shall shift the scene and throw me from that bed into the grave and there triumph over me God knows how many generations, till the Redeemer, my Redeemer, the Redeemer of all me, body as well as soul, come again, as death is *novissimus hostis,* the enemy which watches me at my last weakness and shall hold me when I shall be no more till the angel come who shall say and swear that time shall be no more, in that consideration, in that apprehension, he is the powerfullest, the fearfullest enemy; and yet even there this enemy *abolebitur,* he shall be destroyed, which is *septimum vestigium,* our seventh and last step in this paraphrase.

This destruction, this abolition of this last enemy, is by the resurrection; for the text is part of an argument for the resurrection. And truly, it is a fair intimation and testimony of an everlasting end in that state of the resurrection (that no time shall end it) that we have it presented to us in all the parts of time; in the past, in the present, and in the future. We had a resurrection in prophecy; we have a resurrection in the present working of God's spirit; we shall have a resurrection in the final consummation. The prophet speaks in the future, "He will swallow up death in victory," there it is *abolebit;* all the evangelists speak historically of matter of fact, in them it is *abolevit;* and here in this apostle, it is in the present, *aboletur,* now he is destroyed. And this exhibits unto us a threefold occasion of advancing our devotion in considering a threefold resurrection: first, a resurrection from dejections and calamities in this world, a temporal resurrection; secondly, a resurrection from sin, a spiritual resurrection; and then a resurrection from the grave, a final resurrection.

A calamitate; when the prophets speak of a resurrection in the Old Testament, for the most part their principal intention is upon a temporal restitution from calamities that oppress them then. Neither doth Calvin carry those emphatical words which are so often cited for a proof of the last resurrection, "That he knows his Redeemer lives, that he knows he shall stand the last man upon earth, that though his body be destroyed, yet in his flesh and with his eyes he shall see God," to any higher sense than so, that how low soever he be brought, to what desperate state soever he be reduced in the eyes of the world, yet he assures himself of a resurrection, a reparation, a restitution to his former bodily health and worldly fortune which he had before. And such a resurrection we all know Job had.

In that famous and most considerable prophetical vision which God exhibited to Ezekiel, where God set the prophet in a valley of very many and very dry bones and invites the several joints to knit again, ties them with their old sinews and ligaments, clothes them in their old flesh, wraps them in their old skin, and calls life into them again, God's principal intention in that vision was thereby to give them an assurance of a resurrection from their present calamity, not but that there is also good evidence of the last resurrection in that vision too; thus far God argues with them *a re nota;* from that which they knew before, the final resurrection; he assures them that which they knew not till then, a present resurrection from those pressures; remember by this vision that which you all know already, that at the last I shall reunite the dead and dry bones of all men in a general resurrection; and then if you remember, if you consider, if you look upon that, can you doubt but that I who can do that can also recollect you from your present desperation and give you a resurrection to your former temporal happiness? And this truly arises pregnantly, necessarily out of the prophet's answer; God asks him there, "Son of man, can these bones live?" and he answers, *Domine, tu nosti,* "O Lord God, thou knowest." The prophet answers according to God's intention in the question. If that had been for their living in the last resurrection, Ezekiel would have answered God as Martha answered Christ when he said, "Thy brother Lazarus shall rise again," "I know that he shall rise again at the resurrection at the last day." But when the question was whether men so macerated, so scattered in this world, could have a resurrection to their former temporal happiness here, that puts the prophet to his *Domine, tu nosti,* it is in thy breast to propose it, it is in thy hand to execute it, whether thou do it or do it not, thy name be glorified; it falls not within our conjecture which way it shall please thee to take for this resurrection, *Domine, tu nosti,* thou Lord and thou only knowest; which is also the sense of those words, "Others were tortured and accepted not a deliverance, that they might obtain a better resurrection." A present deliverance had been a resurrection, but to be more sure of a better hereafter, they less respected that; according to that of our Savior, "He that finds his life, shall lose it"; he that fixeth himself too earnestly upon this resurrection shall lose a better.

This is then the prophetical resurrection for the future, but a future in this world: that if the rulers take counsel against the Lord, the Lord shall have their counsel in derision; if they take arms against the Lord, the Lord shall break their bows and cut their spears in sunder; if they hiss and gnash their teeth and say, we have swallowed him up, if we be made their by-word, their parable, their proverb, their libel, the theme and burden of their songs, as Job complains; yet whatsoever fall upon me, damage, distress, scorn, or *hostis ultimus*, death itself, that death which we consider here, death of possessions, death of estimation, death of health, death of contentment, yet *abolebitur*, it shall be destroyed in a resurrection, in the return of the light of God's countenance upon me even in this world. And this is the first resurrection.

But this first resurrection, which is but from temporal calamities, doth so little concern a true and established Christian whether it come or no (for still Job's basis is his basis and his center, *etiamsi occiderit*, though he kill me, kill me, kill me, in all these several deaths and give me no resurrection in this world, yet I will trust in him) as that, as though this first resurrection were no resurrection, not to be numbered among the resurrections, St. John calls that which we call the second, which is from sin, the first resurrection: "Blessed and holy is he who hath part in the first resurrection," and this resurrection Christ implies when he says, "Verily, verily, I say unto you, the hour is coming, and now is, when the dead shall hear the voice of the Son of God; and they that hear it shall live." That is, by the voice of the word of life, the Gospel of repentance, they shall have a spiritual resurrection to a new life.

St. Augustine and Lactantius both were so hard in believing the roundness of the earth that they thought that those *homines pensiles*, as they call them, those men that hang upon the other cheek of the face of the earth, those Antipodes whose feet are directly against ours, must necessarily fall from the earth, if the earth be round. But whither should they fall? If they fall, they must fall upwards, for heaven is above them too, as it is to us. So if the spiritual Antipodes of this world, the sons of God that walk with feet opposed in ways contrary to the sons of men, shall be said to fall, when they fall to repentance, to mortification, to a religious negligence and contempt of the pleasures of this life; truly their fall is upwards, they fall towards heaven. "God gives breath unto the people upon the earth," says the prophet, *et spiritum his qui calcant illam*. Our translation carries that no farther but that "God gives breath to people upon the earth and spirit to them that walk thereon"; but Iranæus makes a useful difference between *afflatus* and *spiritus*, that God gives breath to all upon earth, but his spirit only to them who tread in a religious scorn upon earthly things.

Is it not a strange phrase of the apostle, "Mortify your members: fornication, uncleanness, inordinate affections"? He does not say, mortify your members against those sins, but he calls those very sins the members of our bodies, as though we were elemented and compacted of nothing but sin till we come to this resurrection, this mortification, which is indeed our vivification; "till we bear in our body the dying of our Lord Jesus, that the life also of Jesus may be made manifest in our body." God may give the other resurrection from worldly misery, and not give this. A widow may be rescued from the sorrow and solitariness of that state by having a plentiful fortune; there she hath one resurrection; but "the widow that liveth in pleasure is dead while she lives"; she hath no second resurrection; and so in that sense even this chapel may be a churchyard, men may stand and sit and kneel, and yet be dead; and any chamber alone may be a Golgotha, a place of dead men's bones, of men not come to this resurrection, which is the renunciation of their beloved sin.

It was inhumanly said by Vitellius upon the death of Otho, when he walked in the field of carcasses where the battle was fought, O how sweet a perfume is a dead enemy! But it is a divine saying to thy soul, O what a savor of life unto life is the death of a beloved sin! What an angelic comfort was that to Joseph and Mary in Egypt after the death of Herod, "Arise, for they are dead that sought the child's life!" And even that comfort is multiplied upon my soul when the spirit of God says to thee, arise, come to this resurrection; for that Herod, that sin, that sought the life, the everlasting life of this child, the child of God, thy soul, is dead, dead by repentance, dead by mortification. The highest cruelty that story relates, or poets imagine, is when a persecutor will not afford a miserable man death, not to be so merciful to him as to take his life. Thou hast made thy sin thy soul, thy life;

inanimated all thy actions, all thy purposes with that sin. *Miserere animæ tuæ*, be so merciful to thyself as to take away that life by mortification, by repentance, and thou art come to this resurrection. And though a man may have the former resurrection and not this, peace in his fortune and yet not peace in his conscience, yet whosoever hath this second hath an infallible seal of the third resurrection too, a fullness of glory in body as well as in soul. For *spiritus maturam efficit carnem et capacem incorruptalæ;* this resurrection by the spirit mellows the body of man and makes that capable of everlasting glory, which is the last weapon by which the last enemy, death, shall be destroyed; *a morte.*

Upon that pious ground that all Scriptures were written for us as we are Christians, that all Scriptures conduce to the proof of Christ and of the Christian state, it is the ordinary manner of the fathers to make all that David speaks historically of himself and all that the prophet speaks futurely of the Jews, if those places may be referred to Christ, to refer them to Christ primarily and but by reflection and in a second consideration upon David, or upon the Jews. Thereupon do the fathers, truly I think more generally more unanimely than in any other place of Scripture, take that place of Ezekiel which we spake of before to be primarily intended of the last resurrection and but secondarily of the Jews' restitution. But Gasper Sanctius, a learned Jesuit—that is not so rare, but an ingenuous Jesuit too—though he be bound by the Council of Trent to interpret the Scriptures according to the fathers, yet he here acknowledges the whole truth, that God's purpose was to prove by that which they did know, which was the general resurrection, that which they knew not, their temporal restitution. Tertullian is vehement at first, but after, more supple. *Allegoricæ Scripturæ*, says he, *resurrectionem subradiant aliæ, aliæ determinant;* some figurative places of Scripture do intimate a resurrection, and some manifest it; and of those manifest places he takes this vision of Ezekiel to be one. But he comes after to this, *Sit et corporum et rerum, et mea nihil interest;* let it signify a temporal resurrection, so it may signify the general resurrection of our bodies too, says he, and I am well satisfied; and then the truth satisfies him, for it doth signify both. It is true that Tertullian says, *De vacuo similitudo non competit;* if the vision be but a comparison, if there were no such thing as a resurrection, the comparison did not hold. *De nullo parabola non convenit,* says he, and truly; if there were no resurrection to which that parable might have relation, it were no parable. All that is true; but there was a resurrection always known to them, always believed by them, and that made their present resurrection from that calamity the more easy, the more intelligible, the more credible, the more discernible to them.

Let therefore God's method be thy method; fix thyself firmly upon that belief of the general resurrection, and thou wilt never doubt of either of the particular resurrections, either from sin, by God's grace, or from worldly calamities, by God's power. For the last resurrection is the ground of all. By that *vere victa mors*, says Irenæus, this last enemy, death, is truly destroyed, because his last spoil, the body, is taken out of his hands. The same body, *eadem ovis*, as the same father notes, Christ did not fetch another sheep to the flock in the place of that which was lost, but the same sheep. God shall not give me another, a better body at the resurrection, but the same body made better; for *si non haberet caro salvari, neutiquam verbum Dei caro factum fuisset*, if the flesh of man were not to be saved, the anchor of salvation would never have taken the flesh of man upon him.

The punishment that God laid upon Adam, *in dolore et in sudore*, "In sweat and in sorrow shalt thou eat thy bread," is but *donec reverteris*, "till man return to dust." But when man is returned to dust, God returns to the remembrance of that promise, "Awake and sing, ye that dwell in the dust." A mercy already exhibited to us in the person of our Savior Christ Jesus, in whom *per primitias benedixit campo*, says St. Chrysostom, as God by taking a handful for the first fruits gave a blessing to the whole field; so he hath sealed the bodies of all mankind to his glory by pre-assuming the body of Christ to that glory. For by that there is now *commercium inter cœlum et terram*; there is a trade driven, a staple established between heaven and earth; *ibi caro nostra, hic spiritus eius;* thither have we sent our flesh, and hither hath he sent his spirit.

This is the last abolition of this enemy death; for after, the bodies of the saints he cannot touch, the bodies of the damned he cannot kill, and if he could, he were not therein their enemy but their friend. This is that blessed and glorious state of which, when all the apostles met to make the creed, they could say no more but *credo resurrectionem*, "I believe the resurrection of the body"; and when those two reverend fathers to whom it belongs shall come to speak of it upon the day proper for it in this place, and if all the bishops that ever met in councils should meet them here, they could but second the apostles' *credo* with their *anathema*, we believe, and woe be unto them that do not believe the resurrection of the body; but in going about to express it the lips of an angel would be uncircumcised lips, and the tongue of an archangel would stammer. I offer not therefore at it. But in respect of and with relation to that blessed state according to the doctrine and the practice of our church, we do pray for the dead; for the militant church upon earth and the triumphant church in heaven and the whole catholic church in heaven and earth; we do pray that God will be pleased to hasten that kingdom, that we with all others departed in the true faith of his holy name may have this perfect consummation, both of body and soul, in his everlasting glory. Amen.

SERMON XXIII, FOLIO OF 1640[1]

"For now we see through a glass darkly, but then face to face; now I know in part, but then I shall know even as also I am known."

THESE two terms in our text, *nunc* and *tunc*, now and then, now in a glass, then face to face, now in part, then in perfection, these two secular terms, of which one designs the whole age of this world from the creation to the dissolution thereof, for all that is comprehended in this word *now*, and the other designs the everlastingness of the next world, for that incomprehensibleness is comprehended in the other word *then*—these two words that design two such ages are now met in one day, in this day in which we celebrate all resurrections in the root in the resurrection of our Lord and Savior Christ Jesus blest forever. For the first term, *now*, "Now in a glass, now in part," is intended most especially of that very act which we do now at this present, that is, of the ministry of the Gospel, of declaring God in his ordinance, of preaching his word, "Now," in this ministry of his Gospel, "we see in a glass, we know in part"; and then the *then*, the time of seeing face to face and knowing as we are known is intended of that time which we celebrate this day, the day of resurrection, the day of judgment, the day of the actual possession of the next life. So that this day this whole Scripture is fulfilled in your ears; for now, now in this preaching, you have some sight, and then, then when that day comes which in the first root thereof we celebrate this day, you shall have a perfect sight of all; "Now we see through a glass," etc.

That therefore you may the better know him when you come to see him face to face than by having seen him in a glass now, and that your seeing him now in his ordinance may prepare you to see him then in his essence, proceed we thus in the handling of these words. First, that there is nothing brought into comparison, into consideration, nothing put into the balance, but the sight of God, the knowledge of God; it is not called a better sight, nor a better knowledge, but there is no other sight, no other knowledge proposed or mentioned or intimated or imagined but this; all other sight is blindness, all other knowledge is ignorance; and then we shall see how there is a twofold sight of God and a twofold knowledge of God proposed to us here; a sight and a knowledge here in this life, and another manner of sight and another manner of knowledge in the life to come; for here we see God *in speculo*, in a glass, that is, by reflection, and here we know God *in ænigmate*, says our text, darkly, so we translate it, that is, by obscure presentations, and therefore it is called a knowledge but in part; but in heaven our sight is face to face, and our knowledge is to know as we are known.

For our sight of God here, our theater, the place where we sit and see him, is the whole world, the whole house and frame of nature, and our medium, our glass, is the book of creatures, and our light, by which we see him, is the light of natural reason. And then for our knowledge of God here, our place, our academy, our university is the church, our medium is the ordinance of God in his church, preaching and sacraments; and our light is the light of faith. Thus we shall find it to be for our sight and for our knowledge of God here. But for our sight of God in heaven, our place, our sphere is heaven itself, our medium is the patefaction, the manifestation, the revelation of God himself, and our light is the light of glory. And then for our knowledge of God there, God himself is all; God himself is the place, we see him in him; God is our medium, we see him by him; God is our light; not a light which is his, but a light which is he; not a light which flows from him, no, nor a light which is in him, but that light which is he himself. "Lighten our darkness, we beseech thee, O Lord, O Father of lights, that

1 Preached at St. Paul's on Easter Day, 1628.

in thy light we may see light," that now we see this through this thy glass, thy ordinance, and by the good of this hereafter face to face.

The sight is so much the noblest of all the senses as that it is all the senses. As the reasonable soul of man, when it enters, becomes all the soul of man, and he hath no longer a vegetative and a sensitive soul[2] but all is that one reasonable soul; so, says St. Augustine, and he exemplifies it by several pregnant places of Scripture, *Visus per omnes sensus recurrit,* all the senses are called seeing; as there is *videre et audire,* "St. John turned to see the sound"; and there is *gustate et videte,* "Taste and see how sweet the Lord is"; and so of the rest of the senses, all is sight. Employ then this noblest sense upon the noblest object, see God; see God in everything, and then thou needst not take off thine eye from beauty, from riches, from honor, from anything. St. Paul speaks here of a diverse seeing of God. Of seeing God in a glass, and seeing God face to face; but of not seeing God at all, the apostle speaks not at all.

When Christ took the blind man by the hand, though he had then begun his cure upon him, yet he asked him if he saw aught. Something he was sure he saw; but it was a question whether it were to be called a sight, for he saw men but as trees. The natural man[3] sees beauty and riches and honor, but yet it is a question whether he sees them or no, because he sees them but as a snare. But he that sees God in them sees them to be beams and evidences of that beauty, that wealth, that honor, that is in God, that is in God himself. The other blind man that importuned Christ, "Jesus, thou son of David, have mercy upon me," when Christ asked him, "What wilt thou that I shall do unto thee?" had presently that answer, "Lord, that I may receive my sight"; and we may easily think that if Christ had asked him a second question, "What wouldst thou see when thou hast received thy sight?" he would have answered, "Lord, I will see thee"; for when he had his sight and Christ said to him, "Go thy way," he had no way to go from Christ, but, as the text says there, "He followed him." All that he cared for was seeing, all that he cared to see was Christ. Whether he would see a peace or a war may be a statesman's problem; whether he would see plenty or scarcity of some com-modity may be a merchant's problem; whether he would see Rome or Spain grow in greatness may be a Jesuit's problem; but whether I had not rather see God than anything is no problematical matter. All sight is blindness, that was our first; all knowledge is ignorance till we come to God, is our next consideration.

The first act of will is love, says the School;[4] for till the will love, till it would have something, it is not a will. But then, *amare nisi nota non possumus;* it is impossible to love anything till we know it. First our understanding must present it as *verum,* as a known truth, and then our will embraces it as *bonum,* as good, and worthy to be loved. Therefore the philosopher[5] concludes easily, as a thing that admits no contradiction, that naturally all men desire to know, that they may love. But then, as the addition of an honest man varies the signification with the profession and calling of the man—for he is an honest man at court that oppresses no man with his power, and at the exchange he is the honest man that keeps his word, and in an army the valiant man is the honest man—so the addition of learning and understanding varies with the man; the divine, the physician, the lawyer are not qualified, not denominated by the same kind of learning. But yet, as it is for honesty, there is no honest man at court or exchange or army if he believe not in God; so there is no knowledge in the physician nor lawyer if he know not God. Neither does any man know God except he know him so as God hath made himself known, that is, in Christ. Therefore, as St. Paul desires to know nothing else, so let no man pretend to know anything but Christ crucified; that is, crucified for him, made his. In the eighth verse of this chapter he says, "Prophecy shall fail, and tongues shall fail, and knowledge shall vanish"; but this knowledge of God in Christ made mine, by being crucified for me, shall dwell with me forever. And so from this general consideration all sight is blindness, all knowledge is ignorance, but of God, we pass to the particular consideration of that twofold sight and knowledge of God expressed in this text, "Now we see through a glass," etc.

First then we consider—before we come to our knowledge of God—our sight of God in this world, and that is, says our apostle, *in speculo,* "We see as in a glass." But how do we see in a glass? Truly, that is not easily determined. The old writers in the optics said that when we see a thing in a glass, we see not the

---

2 A reference to the Neoplatonic conception of the three souls in man, the three ascending stages of being, represented in the verbs, *esse, sentire, intelligere.* The vegetative and sensitive souls are fused and made a part of the third, the immortal soul.

3 The man without religion.

4 The medieval Schoolmen.

5 Augustine.

thing itself but a representation only; all the later men say we do see the thing itself but not by direct but by reflected beams. It is a useless labor for the present to reconcile them. This may well consist with both, that as that which we see in a glass assures us that such a thing there is, for we cannot see a dream in a glass, nor a fancy, nor a chimera, so this sight of God, which our apostle says we have in a glass, is enough to assure us that a God there is.

This glass is better than the water; the water gives a crookedness and false dimensions to things that it shows; as we see by an oar when we row a boat, and as the poet describes a wry and distorted face, *qui faciem sub aqua, Phœbe, natantis habes*, that he looked like a man that swam under water. But in the glass which the apostle intends we may see God directly, that is, see directly that there is a God. And therefore St. Cyril's addition in this text is a diminution; *videmus quasi in fumo*, says he, we see God as in a smoke; we see him better then so; for it is a true sight of God, though it be not a perfect sight, which we have this way. This way our theater, where we sit to see God, is the whole frame of nature; our medium, our glass in which we see him is the creature; and our light by which we see him is natural reason.

Aquinas calls this theater, where we sit and see God, the whole world; and David compasses the world and finds God everywhere and says at last, "Whither shall I fly from thy presence? If I ascend up into heaven, thou art there"; at Babel they thought to build to heaven; but did any man ever pretend to get above heaven? Above the power of the winds, or the impression of other malignant meteors, some high hills are got. But can any man get above the power of God? "If I take the wings of the morning, and dwell in the uttermost parts of the sea, there thy right hand shall hold me and lead me." If we sail to the waters above the firmament, it is so too. Nay, take a place which God never made, a place which grew out of our sins, that is, hell; yet, "If we make our bed in hell, God is there too." It is a woeful inn to make our bed in, hell; and so much the more woeful as it is more than an inn, an everlasting dwelling. But even there God is; and so much more strangely than in any other place because he is there without any emanation of any beam of comfort from him who is the God of all consolation or any beam of light from him who is the Father of all lights. In a word, whether we be in the eastern parts of the world, from whom the truth of religion is passed, or in the western, to which it is not yet come;

whether we be in the darkness of ignorance, or darkness of the works of darkness, or darkness of oppression of spirit in sadness; the world is the theater that represents God, and everywhere every man may, nay, must see him.

The whole frame of the world is the theater, and every creature the stage, the medium, the glass in which we may see God. "Moses made the laver in the tabernacle of the looking glasses of women." Scarce can you imagine a vainer thing—except you will except the vain lookers-on in that action—than the looking glasses of women; and yet Moses brought the looking glasses of women to a religious use, to show them that came in the spots of dirt which they had taken by the way, that they might wash themselves clean before they passed any farther.

There is not so poor a creature but may be the glass to see God in. The greatest flat glass that can be made cannot represent anything greater than it is. If every gnat that flies were an archangel, all that could but tell me that there is a God; and the poorest worm that creeps tells me that. If I should ask the basilisk,[6] how camest thou by those killing eyes? he would tell me, thy God made me so; and if I should ask the slow-worm, how camest thou to be without eyes? he would tell me, thy God made me so. The cedar is no better a glass to see God in than the hyssop upon the wall; all things that are, are equally removed from being nothing; and whatsoever hath any being is by that very being a glass in which to see God, who is the root and the fountain of all being. The whole frame of nature is the theater, the whole volume of creatures is the glass, and the light of nature, reason, is our light; which is another circumstance.

Of these words, John 1:9, "That was the true light that lighteth every man that cometh into the world," the slackest sense that they can admit gives light enough to see God by. If we spare St. Chrysostom's sense, that that light is the light of the Gospel and of grace, and that that light considered in itself and without opposition in us does enlighten, that is, would enlighten every man if that man did not wink at that light; if we forbear St. Augustine's sense, that light enlightens every man, that is, every man that is enlightened is enlightened by that light; if we take but St. Cyril's sense, that this light is the light of natural reason, which, without all question, "enlighteneth every man that comes into the world"; yet have we

6 The reptile of fable whose eyes were deadly enough to slay.

light enough to see God by that light in the theater of nature and in the glass of creatures. God affords no man the comfort, the false comfort of atheism. He will not allow a pretending atheist the power to flatter himself so far as seriously to think there is no God. He must pull out his own eyes and see no creature before he can say, he sees no God; he must be no man and quench his reasonable soul before he can say to himself, there is no God. The difference between the reason of man and the instinct of the beast is this, that the beast does but know, but the man knows that he knows. The bestial atheist will pretend that he knows there is no God; but he cannot say that he knows that he knows it; for his knowledge will not stand the battery of an argument from another nor a ratiocination from himself. He dares not ask himself, who is it that I pray to in a sudden danger if there be no God? Nay, he dares not ask, who is it that I swear by in a sudden passion if there be no God? Whom do I tremble at and sweat under at midnight and whom do I curse by next morning if there be no God? It is safely said in the School, *media perfecta ad quæ ordinantur*, how weak soever those means which are ordained by God seem to be, and be indeed in themselves, yet they are strong enough to those ends and purposes for which God ordained them.

And so for such a sight of God as we take the apostle to intend here, which is to see that there is a God, the frame of nature, the whole world is our theater, the book of creatures is our medium, our glass, and natural reason is light enough. But then for the other degree, the other notification of God, which is the knowing of God, though that also be first to be considered in this world, the means is of a higher nature than served for the sight of God; and yet whilst we are in this world it is but *in ænigmate*, in an obscure riddle, a representation, darkly, and in part, as we translate it.

As the glass which we spoke of before was proposed to the sense, and so we might see God, that is, see that there is a God, this *ænigma* that is spoken of now, this dark similitude and comparison, is proposed to our faith; and so far we know God, that is, believe in God in this life but by enigmas, by dark representations and allusions. Therefore says St. Augustine that Moses saw God, in that conversation which he had with him in the mount, *sevocatus ab omni corporis sensu*, removed from all benefit and assistance of bodily senses—he needed not that glass, the help of the creature; and more than so, *ab omni significativo ænigmate spiritus,*

removed from all allusions or similitudes or representations of God which might bring God to the understanding and so to the belief; Moses knew God by a more immediate working than either sense or understanding or faith. Therefore says that father, *per speculum et ænigma*, by this which the apostle calls a glass and this which he calls *ænigma*, a dark representation, *intelliguntur omnia accommodata ad notificandum deum*, he understands all things by which God hath notified himself to man, by the glass to his reason, by the *ænigma* to his faith. And so for this knowing of God by way of believing in him—as for seeing him our theater was the world, the creature was our glass, and reason was our light—our academy to learn this knowledge is the church, our medium is the ordinance and institution of Christ in his church, and our light is the light of faith in the application of those ordinances in that church.

This place then where we take our degrees in this knowledge of God, our academy, our university for that, is the church; for, though as there may be some few examples given of men that have grown learned who never studied at university; so there may be some examples of men enlightened by God and yet not within that covenant which constitutes the church; yet the ordinary place for degrees is the university, and the ordinary place for illumination in the knowledge of God is the church. Therefore did God, who ever intended to have his kingdom of heaven well peopled, so powerfully, so miraculously enlarge his way to it, the church, that it prospered as a wood which no felling, no stubbing could destroy. We find in the acts of the church five thousand martyrs executed in a day; and we find in the Acts of the Apostles five thousand brought to the church by one sermon; still our christenings were equal to our burials at least.

Therefore when Christ says to the church, "Fear not, little flock," it was not *quia de magno minuitur, sed quia de pusillo crescit*, says Chrysologus, not because it should fall from great to little, but rise from little to great. Such care had Christ of the growth thereof; and then such care of the establishment and power thereof as that the first time that ever he names the church he invests it with an assurance of perpetuity. "Upon this rock will I build my church, and the gates of hell shall not prevail against it"; therein is denoted the strength and stability of the church in itself and then the power and authority of the church upon others in those often directions, *dic ecclesiæ*, complain to the church, and consult with the church, and then, *audi ecclesiam,* harken to the church, be judged by the church, hear not them that hear not the church, and then *ejice de ecclesia*, let them that disobey the church be cast out of the church. In all which we are forbidden private conventicles, private spirits, private opinions. For, as St. Augustine says well—and he cites it from another whom he names not, *quidam dixit*—if a wall stand single, not joined to any other wall, he that makes a door through the wall and passes through that door, *adhuc foris est*, for all this is without still, *nam domus non est*, one wall makes not a house; one opinion makes not catholic doctrine, one man makes not a church; for this knowledge of God the church is our academy; there we must be bred; and there we may be bred all our lives and yet learn nothing. Therefore, as we must be there, so there we must use the means; and the means in the church are the ordinances and institutions of the church.

The most powerful means is the Scripture; but the Scripture in the church. Not that we are discouraged from reading the Scripture at home; God forbid we should think any Christian family to be out of the church. At home the Holy Ghost is with thee in the reading of the Scriptures; but there he is with thee as a remembrancer; "The Holy Ghost shall bring to your remembrance whatsoever I have said unto you," says our Savior; here in the church he is with thee as a doctor to teach thee; first learn at church and then meditate at home; receive the seed by hearing the Scriptures interpreted here, and water it by returning to those places at home. When Christ bids you "Search the Scriptures," he means you should go to them who have a warrant to search, a warrant in their calling. To know which are Scriptures, to know what the Holy Ghost says in the Scriptures, apply thyself to the church. Not that the church is a judge above the Scriptures, for the power and the commission which the church hath, it hath from the Scriptures, but the church is a judge above thee, which are the Scriptures and what is the sense of the Holy Ghost in them.

So then thy means are the Scriptures; that is thy evidence. But then this evidence must be sealed to thee in the sacraments and delivered to thee in preaching, and so sealed and delivered to thee in the presence of competent witnesses, the congregation. When St. Paul was carried up *in raptu*, in an ecstasy, into paradise, that which he gained by this powerful way of teaching is not expressed in a *vidit* but an *audivit*; it is not said that he saw but that he heard unspeakable things. The eye is the Devil's door before the ear; for though he

do enter at the ear, by wanton discourse, yet he was at the eye before; we see, before we talk, dangerously. But the ear is the Holy Ghost's first door, he assists us with ritual and ceremonial things which we see in the church; but ceremonies have their right use when their right use hath first been taught by preaching. Therefore to hearing does the apostle apply faith; and as the church is our academy, and our medium the ordinances of the church, so the light by which we see this, that is, know God so as to make him our God, is faith; and that is our other consideration in this part.

Those heretics against whom St. Chrysostom and others of the fathers writ, the *Anomœi*, were inexcusable in this that they said they were able to know God in this life as well as God knew himself; but in this more especially lay their impiety, that they said that they were able to do all this by the light of nature without faith. By the light of nature in the theater of the world, by the medium of creatures, we see God; but to know God by believing, not only him, but in him, is only in the academy of the church, only through the medium of the ordinances there, and only by the light of faith.

The School does ordinarily design four ways of knowing God; and they make the first of these four ways to be by faith; but then by faith they mean no more but an assent that there is a God; which is but that which in our former considerations we called the seeing of God; and which indeed needs not faith; for the light of nature will serve for that, to see God so. They make their second way contemplation, that is, an union of God in this life; [7] which is truly the same thing that we mean by faith; for we do not call an assent to the Gospel, faith, but faith is the application of the Gospel to ourselves; not an assenting that Christ died but an assurance that Christ died for all. Their third way of knowing God is by apparition; as when God appeared to the patriarchs and others in fire, in angels, or otherwise. And their fourth way is *per apertam visionem*, by his clear manifestation of himself in heaven.

Their first way, by assenting only, and their third way of apparition, are weak and uncertain ways. The other two, present faith and future vision, are safe ways, but admit this difference, that that of future vision is *gratiæ consummantis*, such a knowledge of God as when it is once had can never be lost nor diminished;

7 The Neoplatonic conception of ecstasy, the mystic experience in which the soul of the contemplator of God was fused with the divine essence.

but knowledge by faith in this world is *gratiæ communis*, it is an effect and fruit of that grace which God shed upon the whole communion of saints, that is, upon all those who in this academy, the church, do embrace the medium, that is, the ordinances of the church; and this knowledge of God, by this faith, may be diminished or increased; for it is but *in ænigmate*, says our text, darkly, obscurely; clearly in respect of the natural man, but yet but obscurely in respect of that knowledge of God which we shall have in heaven; for, says the apostle, "As long as we walk by faith, and not by sight, we are absent from the Lord." Faith is a blessed presence, but compared with heavenly vision it is but an absence; though it create and constitute in us a possibility, a probability, a kind of certainty of salvation, yet that faith which the best Christian hath is not so far beyond that sight of God which the natural man hath as that sight of God which I shall have in heaven is above that faith which we have now in the highest exaltation. Therefore there belongs a consideration to that which is added by our apostle here, that the knowledge which I have of God here, even by faith through the ordinances of the church, is but a knowledge in part. "Now I know in part."

That which we call in part the Syriac translates *modicum ex multis;* though we know by faith, yet, for all that faith, it is but a little of a great deal that we know yet, because though faith be good evidence, yet faith is but "the evidence of things not seen"; and there is better evidence of them when they are seen. For if we consider the object, we cannot believe so much in God nor of our happiness in him as we shall see then. For when it is said that the heart comprehends it not, certainly faith comprehends it not neither. And if we consider the manner, faith itself is but darkness in respect of the vision of God in heaven. For those words of the prophet, "I will search Jerusalem with candles," are spoken of the times of the Christian church and of the best men in the Christian church; yet they shall be searched with candles, some darkness shall be found in them. To the Galatians well instructed and well established the apostle says, "Now, after ye have known God, or rather are known of God"; the best knowledge that we have of God here, even by faith, is rather that he knows us than that we know him. And in this text it is in his own person that the apostle puts the instance, "Now I"—I, an apostle taught by Christ himself—"know but in part." And therefore, as St. Augustine saith, *Sunt quasi cunabula caritatis dei, quibus diligimus proximum*, the love which we bear to our neighbor is but as the infancy, but as the cradle of that love which we bear to God; so the sight of God which we have *in speculo*, in the glass, that is, in nature, is but *cunabula fidei*, but the infancy, but the cradle of that knowledge which we have in faith; and yet that knowledge which we have in faith is but *cunabula visionis*, the infancy and cradle of that knowledge which we shall have when we come to see God face to face. Faith is infinitely above nature, infinitely above works, even above those works which faith itself produces, as parents are to children and the tree to the fruit. But yet faith is as much below vision and seeing God face to face. And therefore, though we ascribe willingly to faith more than we can express, yet let no man think himself so infallibly safe because he finds that he believes in God as he shall be when he sees God; the faithfullest man in the church must say, *Domine, adauge*, "Lord, increase my faith"; he that is least in the kingdom of heaven shall never be put to that. All the world is but *speculum*, a glass, in which we see God; the church itself and that which the ordinance of the church begets in us, faith itself, is but *ænigma*, a dark representation of God to us till we come to that state, to see God face to face and to know as also we are known.

Now as for the sight of God here our theater was the world, our medium and glass was the creature, and our light was reason, and then for our knowledge of God here our academy was the church, our medium the ordinances of the church, and our light the light of faith; so we consider the same terms, first, for the sight of God, and then for the knowledge of God in the next life. First, the sphere, the place where we shall see him, is heaven; he that asks me what heaven is means not to hear me, but to silence me; he knows I cannot tell him; when I meet him there, I shall be able to tell him, and then he will be as able to tell me; yet then we shall be but able to tell one another this, this that we enjoy is heaven, but the tongues of angels, the tongues of glorified saints, shall not be able to express what that heaven is; for even in heaven our faculties shall be finite. Heaven is not a place that was created; for all place that was created shall be dissolved. God did not plant a paradise for himself and remove to that as he planted a paradise for Adam and removed him to that; but God is still where he was before the world was made. And in that place where there are more suns than there are stars in the firmament, for all the saints are suns, and more light in another sun, the sun of righteousness, the sun of glory, the Son of God, than in all them in that illustration, that emanation, that effusion of beams of glory, which began not to shine 6,000 years ago, but 6,000 millions of millions ago, had been 6,000 millions of millions before that, in those eternal, in those uncreated heavens, shall we see God.

This is our sphere and that which we are fain to call our place; and then our medium, our way to see him is *patefactio sui*, God's laying himself open, his manifestation, his revelation, his evisceration, and embowelling of himself to us there. Doth God never afford this patefaction, this manifestation of himself in his essence, to any in this life? We cannot answer yea, nor no, without offending a great part in the School,[8] so many affirm, so many deny that God hath been seen in his essence in this life. There are those that say that it is *fere de fide*, little less than an article of faith that it hath been done; and Aquinas denies it so absolutely as that his followers interpret him *de absoluta potentia*, that God by his absolute power cannot make a man a mortal man and under the definition of a mortal man capable of seeing his essence; as we may truly say that God cannot make a beast remaining in that nature capable of grace or glory. St. Augustine speaking of discourses that passed between his mother and him not long before her death, says, *Perambulavimus cuncta mortalia et ipsum cœlum*, we talked ourselves above this earth and above all the heavens; *venimus in mentes nostras et transcendimus eas*, we came to the consideration of our own minds and our own souls, and we got above our own souls; that is, to the consideration of that place where our souls should be forever; and we could consider God then; but then we could not see God in his essence. As it may be fairly argued that Christ suffered not the very torments of very hell, because it is essential to the torments of hell to be eternal, they were not torments of hell if they received an end; so it is fairly argued too that neither Adam in his ecstasy in paradise nor Moses in his conversation in the mount nor the other apostles in the transfiguration of Christ nor St. Paul in his rapture to the third heavens saw the essence of God, because he that is admitted to that sight of God can never look off nor lose that sight again. Only in heaven shall God proceed to this patefaction, this manifestation, this revelation of himself; and that by the light of glory.

The light of glory is such a light as that our Schoolmen dare not say confidently that every beam of it is

not all of it. When some of them say that some souls see some things in God and others, others, because all have not the same measure of the light of glory, the rest cry down that opinion and say that as the essence of God is indivisible and he that sees any of it sees all of it, so is the light of glory communicated entirely to every blessed soul. God made light first, and three days after that light became a sun, a more glorious light. God gave me the light of nature when I quickened in my mother's womb by receiving a reasonable soul; and God gave me the light of faith when I quickened in my second mother's womb, the church, by receiving my baptism; but in my third day, when my mortality shall put on immortality, he shall give me the light of glory by which I shall see himself. To this light of glory the light of honor is but a glow-worm; and majesty itself but a twilight; the cherubims and seraphims are but candles; and the Gospel itself, which the apostle calls the glorious Gospel, but a star of the least magnitude. And if I cannot tell what to call this light by which I shall see it, what shall I call that which I shall see by it, the essence of God himself! And yet there is something else than this sight of God intended in that which remains; I shall not only see God face to face, but I shall know him—which, as you have seen all the way, is above sight—and know him even as also I am known.

In this consideration God alone is all; in all the former there was a place and a means and a light; here, for this perfect knowledge of God, God is all those. "Then," says the apostle, "God shall be all in all." *Hic agit omnia in omnibus*, says St. Jerome; here God does all in all; but here he does all by instruments; even in the infusing of faith he works by the ministry of the Gospel. But there he shall be all in all, do all in all immediately by himself; for Christ shall deliver up the kingdom to God even the Father. His kingdom is the administration of his church by his ordinances in the church. At the resurrection there shall be an end of that kingdom; no more church; no more working upon men by preaching, but God himself shall be all in all. *Ministri quasi larvæ dei*, says Luther. It may be somewhat too familiarly, too vulgarly said, but usefully; the ministry of the Gospel is but as God's vizard; for by such a liberty the apostle here calls it *ænigma*, a riddle, or, as Luther says too, God's picture; but in the resurrection God shall put off that vizard and turn away that picture and show his own face. Therefore is it said that "in heaven there is no temple, but God himself is the temple"; God is service and music and psalm

8 The Scholiasts made the experience of ecstasy an article of faith; see preceding note.

and sermon and sacrament and all. *Erit vita de verbo sine verbo;* we shall live upon the word, and hear never a word; live upon him who, being the word, was made flesh, the eternal Son of God. *Hic non est omnia in omnibus, sed pars in singulis;* here God is not all in all; where he is at all in any man that man is well; *in Solomone sapientia,* says that father;[9] it was well with Solomon because God was wisdom with him and patience in Job and faith in Peter and zeal in Paul; but there was something in all these which God was not. But in heaven he shall be so all in all *ut singuli sanctorum omnes virtutes habeant,* that every soul shall have every perfection in itself; and the perfection of these perfections shall be that their sight shall be face to face and their knowledge as they are known.

Since St. Augustine calls it a debt, a double debt, a debt because she asked it, a debt because he promised it, to give, even a woman, Paulina, satisfaction in that high point and mystery, how we should see God face to face in heaven, it cannot be unfit in this congregation to ask and answer some short questions concerning that. Is it always a declaration of favor when God shows his face? No. "I will set my face against that soul that eateth blood and cut him off." But when there is light joined with it, it is a declaration of favor; this was the blessing that God taught Moses for Aaron to bless the people with, "The Lord make his face to shine upon thee and be gracious to thee." And there we shall see him face to face by the light of his countenance, which is the light of glory. What shall we see by seeing him so, face to face? Not to enlarge ourselves into Gregory's wild speculation, *Qui videt videntem omnia omnia videt,* because we shall see him that sees all things we shall see all things in him (for then we should see the thoughts of men), rest we in the testimony of a safer witness, a council, *In speculo divinitatis quicquid eorum intersit illucescet;* in that glass we shall see whatsoever we can be the better for seeing. First, all things that they believed here they shall see there; and therefore, *discamus in terris quorum scientia nobiscum perseveret in cœlis,* let us meditate upon no other things on earth than we would be glad to think on in heaven; and this consideration would put many frivolous and many fond thoughts out of our mind, if men and women would love another but so as that love might last in heaven.

This then we shall get concerning ourselves by seeing God face to face; but what concerning God? Nothing but the sight of the humanity of Christ, which

9 St. Jerome.

only is visible to the eye. So Theodoret, so some others have thought; but that answers not the *sicut est;* and we know we shall see God—not only the body of Christ—as he is in his essence. Why? Did all that are said to have seen God face to face see his essence? No. In earth God assumed some material things to appear in and is said to have been face to face when he was seen in those assumed forms. But in heaven there is no material thing to be assumed, and if God be seen face to face there, he is seen in his essence. St. Augustine sums it up fully upon those words, *in lumine tuo,* "in thy light we shall see light," *te scilicet in te,* we shall see thee in thee; that is, says he, face to face.

And then what is it to know him as we are known? First, is that it which is intended here that we shall know God so as we are known? It is not expressed in the text so. It is only that we shall know so; not that we shall know God so. But the frame, and context of the place, hath drawn that unanimous exposition from all, that it is meant of our knowledge of God then. A comprehensive knowledge of God it cannot be; to comprehend is to know a thing as well as that thing can be known; and we can never know God so but that he will know himself better. Our knowledge cannot be so dilated, nor God condensed and contracted so as that we can know him that way, comprehensively. It cannot be such a knowledge of God as God hath of himself, nor as God hath of us; for God comprehends us and all this world and all the worlds that he could have made and himself. But it is *nota similitudinis, non æqualitatis;* as God knows me, so I shall know God; but I shall not know God so as God knows me. It is not *quantum* but *sicut;* not as much but as truly; as the fire does as truly shine as the sun shines, though it shine not out so far nor to so many purposes. So then I shall know God so as that there shall be nothing in me to hinder me from knowing God; which cannot be said of the nature of man, though regenerate, upon earth, no, nor of the nature of an angel in heaven left to itself, till both have received a super-illustration from the light of glory.

And so it shall be a knowledge so like his knowledge as it shall produce a love like his love, and we shall love him as he loves us. For as St. Chrysostom and the rest of the fathers whom Œcumenius hath compacted interpret it, *Cognoscam practice, id est, accurrendo,* I shall know him, that is, embrace him, adhere to him. *Qualis sine fine festivitas!* what a holiday this shall be which no working day shall ever follow! By knowing and loving the unchangeable, the immutable God, *mutabimur in immutabilitatem*, we shall be changed into an unchangeableness, says that father [10] that never said anything but extraordinarily. He says more, *dei præsentia si in inferno appareret*, if God could be seen and known in hell, hell in an instant would be heaven.

How many heavens are there in heaven? how is heaven multiplied to every soul in heaven where infinite other happinesses are crowned with this, this sight and this knowledge of God there? And how shall all those heavens be renewed to us every day, *qui non mirabimur hodie*, that shall be as glad to see and to know God millions of ages after every day's seeing and knowing as the first hour of looking upon his face. And as this seeing, and this knowing of God crowns all other joys and glories even in heaven, so this very crown is crowned; there grows from this a higher glory, which is, *participes erimus divinæ naturæ*, words of which Luther says that both testaments afford none equal to

10 St. Augustine; Donne holds him highest in esteem among all the church fathers, and he quotes him the most frequently of all.

them, that we shall be made partakers of the divine nature; immortal as the Father, righteous as the Son, and full of all comfort as the Holy Ghost.

Let me dismiss you with an easy request of St. Augustine, *Fieri non potest ut seipsum non diligat qui deum diligit;* that man does not love God that loves not himself; do but love yourselves; *immo solus se diligere novit qui deum diligit*, only that man that loves God hath the art to love himself; do but love yourselves; for if he love God, he would live eternally with him, and if he desire that and endeavor it earnestly, he does truly love himself and not otherwise. And he loves himself who, by seeing God in the theater of the world and in the glass of the creature by the light of reason and knowing God in the academy of the church by the ordinances thereof through the light of faith, endeavors to see God in heaven by the manifestation of himself through the light of glory and to know God himself, in himself, and by himself as he is all in all, contemplatively, by knowing as he is known and practically, by loving as he is loved.

SERMON LXXII, FOLIO OF 1640[1]

"And Jesus walking by the Sea of Galilee saw two brethren, Simon called Peter and Andrew his brother, casting a net into the sea, for they were fishers. And he saith unto them, 'Follow me, and I will make you fishers of men'; and they straightway left their nets and followed him."

WE ARE now in our order proposed at first come to our second part from the consideration of these persons, Peter and Andrew, in their former state and condition before and at their calling to their future estate in promise, but an infallible promise, Christ's promise, if they followed him; "Follow me, and I will make you fishers of men." In which part we shall best come to our end, which is your edification, by these steps. First, that there is an humility enjoined them in the *sequere*, follow, come after; that though they be brought to a high calling, that do not make them proud nor tyrannous over men's consciences; and then even this humility is limited, *sequere me*, follow me; for there may be a pride even in humility, and a man may follow a dangerous guide; our guide here is Christ, *sequere me*, follow me. And then we shall see

1 This and the preceding Sermon lxxi Donne expanded in 1630 from a sermon preached at the Hague in 1619.

the promise itself, the employment, the function, the preferment; in which there is no new state promised them, no innovation—they were fishers, and they shall be fishers still—but there is an improvement, a bettering, a reformation—they were fishermen before, and now they shall be fishers of men; to which purpose we shall find the world to be the sea and the Gospel their net. And lastly, all this is presented to them, not as it was expressed in the former part with a *for;* it is not follow me, for I will prefer you; he will not have that the reason of their following; but yet it is follow me, and I will prefer you; it is a subsequent addition of his own goodness, but so infallible a one as we may rely upon; whosoever doth follow Christ, speeds well. And into these considerations will fall all that belongs to this last part, "Follow me, and I will make you fishers of men."

First then, here is an impression of humility in following, in coming after, *sequere*, follow, press not to come before; and it had need be first, if we consider how early, how primary a sin pride is, and how soon it possesses us. Scarce any man, but if he look back seriously into himself and into his former life and revolve his own history, but that the first act which he can remember in himself, or can be remembered of by others, will be some act of pride. Before ambition or covetousness or licentiousness is awake in us, pride is working; though but a childish pride, yet pride; and this parents rejoice at in their children, and call it spirit, and so it is, but not the best. We enlarge not therefore the consideration of this word *sequere*, follow, come after, so far as to put our meditations upon the whole body and the several members of this sin of pride; nor upon the extent and diffusiveness of this sin, as it spreads itself over every other sin (for every sin is complicated with pride so as every sin is a rebellious opposing of the law and will of God); nor to consider the weighty heinousness of pride, how it aggravates every other sin, how it makes a musket a cannon bullet and a pebble a millstone; but after we have stopped a little upon that useful consideration that there is not so direct and diametrical a contrariety between the nature of any sin and God as between him and pride, we shall pass to that which is our principal observation in this branch, how early and primary a sin pride is, occasioned by this, that the commandment of humility is first given, first enjoined in our first word, *sequere*, follow.

But first, we exalt that consideration, that nothing is so contrary to God as pride, with this observation, that God in the Scriptures is often by the Holy Ghost invested and represented in the qualities and affections of man; and to constitute a commerce and familiarity between God and man, God is not only said to have bodily lineaments, eyes and ears and hands and feet, and to have some of the natural affections of man, as joy in particular—"The Lord will rejoice over thee for good, as he rejoiced over thy fathers," and so pity too—"The Lord was with Joseph and extended kindness unto him," but some of those inordinate and irregular passions and perturbations, excesses and defects of man are imputed to God by the Holy Ghost in the Scriptures. For so laziness, drowsiness is imputed to God—"Awake Lord, why sleepest thou?" so corruptibleness and deterioration and growing worse by ill company is imputed to God—*cum perverso perverteris*. God is said to grow froward with the froward, and that he learns to go crookedly with them that go crookedly; and prodigality and wastefulness is imputed to God—"Thou sellest thy people for naught, and dost not increase thy wealth by their price"; so sudden and hasty choler—"Kiss the Son lest he be angry and ye perish *in ira brevi*, though his wrath be kindled but a little"; and then illimited and boundless anger, a vindictive irreconcilableness is imputed to God—"I was but a

little displeased"—(but it is otherwise now), "I am very sore displeased"; so there is *ira devorans*—"wrath that consumes like stubble"; so there is *ira multiplicata*—"plagues renewed and indignation increased," so God himself expresses it—"I will fight against you in anger and in fury"; and so for his inexorableness, his irreconcilableness—"O Lord God of Hosts, *quousque*, how long wilt thou be angry against the prayer of thy people?"—God's own people, God's own people praying to their own God, and yet their God irreconcilable to them. Scorn and contempt is imputed to God; which is one of the most enormous and disproportioned weaknesses in man; that a worm that crawls in the dust, that a grain of dust that is hurried with every blast of wind should find anything so much inferior to itself as to scorn it, to deride it, to contemn it; yet scorn and derision and contempt is imputed to God—"He that sitteth in the heavens shall laugh, the Lord shall have them in derision," and again—"I will laugh at your calamity, I will mock you when your fear cometh." Nay, beloved, even inebriation, excess in that kind, drunkenness, is a metaphor which the Holy Ghost hath mingled in the expressing of God's proceedings with man; for God does not only threaten to make his enemies drunk—and to make others drunk is a circumstance of drunkenness, so Jerusalem being in his displeasure complains, *inebriavit absinthio*—"He hath made me drunk with wormwood," and again—"They shall be drunk with their own blood, as with new wine," nor only to express his plentiful mercies to his friends and servants, does God take that metaphor—*inebriabo animam sacerdotis*, "I will make the soul of the priest drunk," fill it, satiate it, and again—"I will make the weary soul, and the sorrowful soul drunk"; but not only all this—though in all this God have a hand—not only towards others, but God in his own behalf complains of the scant and penurious sacrificer, *non inebriasti me*, "Thou hast not made me drunk with thy sacrifices." And yet, though for the better applying of God to the understanding of man the Holy Ghost impute to God these excesses and defects of man, laziness and drowsiness, deterioration, corruptibleness by ill conversation, prodigality and wastefulness, sudden choler, long irreconcilableness, scorn, inebriation, and many others in the Scriptures; yet in no place of the Scripture is God for any respect said to be proud; God in the Scriptures is never made so like man as to be made capable of pride; for this had not been to have God like man, but like the Devil.

God is said in the Scriptures to apparel himself

gloriously—"God covers him with light as with a garment"; and so of his spouse the church it is said—"Her clothing is of wrought gold, and her raiment of needle work," and, as though nothing in this world were good enough for her wearing, she is said "to be clothed with the sun." But glorious apparel is not pride in them whose conditions require it and whose revenues will bear it. God is said in the Scriptures to appear with greatness and majesty—"A stream of fire came forth before him; thousand thousands ministered unto him, and ten thousand times ten thousand stood before him." And so Christ shall come at judgment with his hosts of angels in majesty and in glory. But these outward appearances and acts of greatness are not pride in those persons to whom there is a reverence due, which reverence is preserved by this outward splendor, and not otherwise. God is said in the Scriptures to triumph over his enemies and to be jealous of his glory—"The Lord, whose name is Jealous, is a jealous God"; but for princes to be jealous of their glory, studious of their honor, for any private man to be jealous of his good name, careful to preserve an honest reputation, is not pride. For pride is *appetitus celsitudinis perversus*, it is an inordinate desire of being better than we are.

Now there is a lawful, nay, a necessary desire of being better and better; and that not only in spiritual things—for so every man is bound to be better and better, better today than yesterday, and tomorrow than today, and he that grows not in religion withers, there is no standing at a stay, he that goes not forward in godliness goes backward, and he that is not better is worse; but even in temporal things too there is a liberty given us, nay, there is a law, an obligation laid upon us, to endeavor by industry in a lawful calling to mend and improve, to enlarge ourselves and spread even in worldly things. The first commandment that God gave man was not prohibitive; God in that forbade man nothing, but enlarged him with that *crescite et multiplicamini*, increase and multiply, which is not only in the multiplication of children, but in the enlargement of possessions too; for so it follows in the same place, not only *replete* but *dominamini*, not only to replenish the world but subdue and take dominion over it, that is, make it your own. For *terram dedit filiis hominum*, as God has given sons to men, so God gives the possession of this world to the sons of men. For so when God delivers that commandment the second time to Noah for the reparation of the world, *crescite et multiplicamini*, increase and multiply, he accom-

panies it with that reason, "The fear of you and the dread of you shall be upon all, and all are delivered into your hands"; which reason can have no relation to the multiplying of children, but to the enlarging of possessions. God planted trees in paradise in a good state at first; at first with ripe fruits upon them; but God's purpose was that even those trees, though well then, should grow greater. God gives many men good estates from their parents at first; yet God's purpose is that they should increase those estates. He that leaves no more than his father left him, if the fault be in himself, shall hardly make a good account of his stewardship to God; for he hath but kept his talent in a handkerchief. And "the slothful man is even brother to the waster." The Holy Ghost in Solomon scarce prefers him that does not get more before him that wastes all. He makes them brethren; almost all one. "Cursed be he that does the work of God negligently," that does any commandment of God by halves; and this negligent and lazy man, this in-industrious and illaborious man that takes no pains, he does one part of God's commandment, he does multiply, but he does not the other, he does not increase; he leaves children enow, but he leaves them nothing; not in possessions and maintenance, nor in vocation and calling.

And truly, howsoever "the love of money be the root of all evil"—he cannot mistake who told us so, howsoever "they that will be rich," that resolve to be rich by any means, "shall fall into many temptations," howsoever a hasty desire of being suddenly and prematurely rich be a dangerous and an obnoxious thing, a pestilent and contagious disease (for what a perverse and inordinate anticipation and prevention[2] of God and nature is it to look for our harvest in May, or to look for all grains at once? and such a perverseness is the hasty desire of being suddenly and prematurely rich), yet to go on industriously in an honest calling and giving God his leisure and giving God his portion all the way in tithes and in alms and then still to lay up something for posterity is that which God does not only permit and accept from us, but command to us and reward in us. And certainly, that man shall not stand so right in God's eye at the last day that leaves his children to the parish as he that leaves the parish to his children, if he have made his purchases out of honest gain in a lawful calling and not out of oppression.

In all which I would be rightly understood; that is, that I speak of such poverty as is contracted by our

2 Forestalling.

own laziness or wastefulness. For otherwise poverty that comes from the hand of God is as rich a blessing as comes from his hand. He that is poor with a good conscience, that hath labored and yet not prospered, knows to whom to go and what to say, "Lord, thou hast put gladness into my heart more than in the time when corn and wine increased" (more now than when I had more); "I will lay me down and sleep, for thou Lord only makest me to dwell in safety." Does every rich man dwell in safety? Can every rich man lie down in peace and sleep? No, nor every poor man neither; but he that is poor with a good conscience can. And though he that is rich with a good conscience may in a good measure do so too (sleep in peace), yet not so out of the sphere and latitude of envy and free from the machinations and supplantations and underminings of malicious men that feed upon the confiscations and build upon the ruins of others as the poor man is.

Though then St. Chrysostom call riches *absurditatis parentes*, the parents of absurdities, that they make us do not only ungodly but inhuman things, not only irreligious but unreasonable things, uncomely and absurd things, things which we ourselves did not suspect that we could be drawn to; yet there is a growing rich which is not covetousness, and there is a desire of honor and preferment which is not pride. For pride is, as we said before, *appetitus perversus*, a perverse and inordinate desire; but there is a desire of honor and preferment regulated by rectified reason; and rectified reason is religion. And therefore, as we said, however other affections of man may be and are by the Holy Ghost in Scriptures in some respects ascribed to God, yet never pride. Nay, the Holy Ghost himself seems to be straitened and in a difficulty when he comes to express God's proceedings with a proud man and his detestation of him and aversion from him. There is a considerable, a remarkable, indeed a singular manner of expressing it (perchance you find not the like in all the Bible), where God says, "Him that hath a high look and a proud heart I will not" (in our last), "I cannot" (in our former translation). Not what? Not as it is in those translations, "I cannot suffer him, I will not suffer him"; for that word of suffering is but a voluntary word supplied by the translators; in the original it is as it were an abrupt breaking off on God's part from the proud man and, if we may so speak, a kind of froward departing from him. God does not say of the proud man, I cannot work upon him, I cannot mend him, I cannot pardon him, I cannot suffer him, I cannot stay with him, but merely "I cannot," and no more; I

cannot tell what to say of him, what to do for him— "Him that hath a proud heart I cannot"; pride is so contrary to God as that the proud man and he can meet in nothing. And this consideration hath kept us thus long from that which we made our first and principal collection, that this commandment of humility was imprinted in our very first word, *sequere*, follow, be content to come after, to denote how early and primary a sin pride is and how soon it entered into the world and how soon into us; and that consideration we shall pursue now.

We know that light is God's eldest child, his firstborn of all creatures; and it is ordinarily received that the angels are twins with the light, made then when light was made. And then the first act that these angels that fell did was an act of pride. They did not thank nor praise God for their creation, which should have been their first act; they did not solicit nor pray to God for their sustentation, their melioration, their confirmation (so they should have proceeded); but the first act those first creatures did was an act of pride, a proud reflecting upon themselves, a proud overvaluing of their own condition and an acquiescence in that, in an imaginary possibility of standing by themselves without any farther relation or beholdingness to God. So early, so primary a sin is pride as that it was the first act of the first of creatures.

So early, so primary a sin as that whereas all pride is but a comparative pride, this first pride in the angels was a positive, a radical pride. The pharisee is but proud "that he is not as other men are"; that is but a comparative pride. No king thinks himself great enough, yet he is proud that he is independent, sovereign, subject to none. No subject thinks himself rich enough, yet he is proud that he is able to oppress others that are poorer, *et gloriatur in malo quia potens est*, he boasteth himself in mischief because he is a mighty man. But all these are but comparative prides; and there must be some subjects to compare with before a king can be proud, and some inferiors before the magistrate, and some poor before the rich man can be proud. But this pride in those angels in heaven was a positive pride; there were no other creatures yet made with whom these angels could compare themselves and before whom these angels could prefer themselves; and yet before there was any other creature but themselves, any other creature to undervalue or insult [3] over, these angels were proud of themselves. So early, so primary a sin is pride.

3 Note the closeness of the meaning to the Latin; exult.

So early, so primary as that in that ground which was for goodness next to heaven, that is, paradise, pride grew very early too. Adam's first act was not an act of pride, but an act of lawful power and jurisdiction, in naming the creatures; Adam was above them all, and he might have called them what he would; there had lien[4] no action, no appeal, if Adam had called a lion a dog or an eagle an owl. And yet we dispute with God why he should not make all us vessels of honor, and we complain of God that he hath not given us all, all the abundances of this world. Comparatively Adam was better than all the world beside, and yet we find no act of pride in Adam when he was alone. Solitude is not the scene of pride; the danger of pride is in company, when we meet to look upon another. But in Adam's wife, Eve, her first act that is noted was an act of pride, a harkening to that voice of the serpent, "Ye shall be as gods." As soon as there were two, there was pride. How many may we have known, if we have had any conversation in the world, that have been content all the week at home alone with their workaday faces as well as with their workaday clothes, and yet on Sundays, when they come to church and appear in company, will mend both, their faces as well as their clothes. Not solitude but company is the scene of pride; and therefore I know not what to call that practice of the nuns in Spain who though they never see man yet will paint. So early, so primary a sin is pride as that it grew instantly from her whom God intended for a helper, because he saw "that it was not good for man to be alone." God sees that it is not good for man to be without health, without wealth, without power and jurisdiction and magistracy; and we grow proud of our helpers, proud of our health and strength, proud of our wealth and riches, proud of our office and authority over others.

So early, so primary a sin is pride as that out of every mercy and blessing which God affords us (and "His mercies are new every morning"), we gather pride; we are not the more thankful for them, and yet we are the prouder of them. Nay, we gather pride not only out of those things which mend and improve us, God's blessings and mercies, but out of those actions of our own that destroy and ruin us we gather pride; sins overthrow us, demolish us, destroy and ruin us; and yet we are proud of our sins. How many men have we heard boast of their sins, and, as St. Augustine confesses of himself, belie themselves and boast of more sins than ever they committed? Out of everything, out

4 Past particle of *lie;* Biblical.

of nothing sin grows. Therefore was this commandment in our text, *sequere,* follow, come after, well placed first; for we are come to see even children strive for place and precedency, and mothers are ready to go to the Heralds[5] to know how cradles shall be ranked, which cradle shall have the highest place; nay, even in the womb there was contention for precedency; Jacob took hold of his brother Esau's heel and would have been born before him.

And as our pride begins in our cradle it continues in our graves and monuments. It was a good while in the primitive church before any were buried in the church; the best contented themselves with the churchyards. After, a holy ambition (may we call it so), a holy pride brought them *ad limina,* to the church threshold, to the church door, because some great martyrs were buried in the porches and devout men desired to lie near them, as one prophet did to lie near another, "Lay my bones beside his bones." But now persons whom the Devil kept from church all their lives, Separatists, libertines, that never came to any church, and persons whom the Devil brought to church all their lives (for such as come merely out of the obligation of the law and to redeem that vexation, or out of custom or company or curiosity or a perverse and sinister affection to the particular preacher, though they come to God's house, come upon the Devil's invitation), such as one devil, that is, worldly respect, brought to church in their lives, another devil, that is, pride and vainglory, brings to church after their deaths in an affectation of high places and sumptuous monuments in the church. And such as have given nothing at all to any pious uses or have determined their alms and their dole which they have given in that one day of their funeral and no farther have given large annuities, perpetuities, for newpainting their tombs and for new flags and 'scutcheons every certain number of years.

O the earliness! O the lateness! how early a spring and no autumn! how fast a growth and no declination of this branch of this sin, pride, against which this first word of ours, *sequere,* follow, come after, is opposed! This love of place and precedency, it rocks us in our cradles, it lies down with us in our graves. There are diseases proper to certain things, rots to sheep, murrain to cattle. There are diseases proper to certain places, as the sweat was to us. There are diseases proper to certain times, as the plague is in divers parts of the eastern countries, where they know assuredly when it will

5 The College of Heralds.

begin and end. But for this infectious disease of precedency and love of place, it is over all places, as well
cloisters as courts, and over all men, as well spiritual as
temporal, and over all times, as well the apostles' as
ours. The apostles disputed often, who should be
greatest; and it was not enough to them that Christ
assured them, "that they should sit upon the twelve
thrones and judge the twelve Tribes"; it was not
enough for the sons of Zebedee to be put into that
commission, but their friends must solicit the office to
place them high in that commission; their mother
must move that one may sit at Christ's right hand and
the other at his left in the execution of that commission. Because this sin of pride is so early and primary a
sin, is this commandment of humility first enjoined,
and because this sin appears most generally in this love
of place and precedency, the commandment is expressed in that word, *sequere*, follow, come after. But
then, even this humility is limited, for it is *sequere me*,
follow me, which was proposed for our second consideration, *sequere me*.

There may be a pride in humility, and an overweening of ourselves in attributing too much to our
own judgment in following some leaders; for so we
may be so humble as to go after some man, and yet so
proud as to go before the church, because that man
may be a schismatic. Therefore Christ proposes a safe
guide, himself, *sequere me*, follow me. It is a dangerous
thing when Christ says, *vade post me*, "get thee behind
me"; for that is accompanied with a shrewd name of
increpation, "Satan, get thee behind me, Satan!"
Christ speaks it but twice in the Gospel; once to Peter,
whom because he then did the part of an adversary
Christ called Satan, and once to Satan himself because
he pursued his temptations upon him; for there is a
going behind Christ, which is a casting out of his
presence without any future following, and that is a
fearful station, a fearful retrogradation; but when
Christ says, not *vade retro*, "get thee behind me," see
my face no more, but *sequere me*, follow me, he means
to look back upon us; so "the Lord turned and looked
upon Peter, and Peter wept bitterly," and all was well;
when he bids us follow him, he directs us in a good
way and by a good guide.

The Carthusian Friars thought they descended into
as low pastures as they could go when they renounced
all flesh and bound themselves to feed on fish only;
and yet another order follows them in their superstitious singularity and goes beyond them, *Foliantes*,
the *Feuillans*, they eat neither flesh nor fish, nothing

but leaves and roots; and as the Carthusians in a proud
humility despise all other orders that eat flesh so do the
Feuillans the Carthusians that eat fish. There is a pride
in such humility. That order of friars that called themselves *Ignorantes*, ignorant men, that pretended to know
nothing, sunk as low as they thought it possible into
an humble name and appellation; and yet the Minorites
(Minorites that are less than any) think they are gone
lower, and then the Minims (Minims that are less than
all) lower than they. And when one would have
thought that there had not been a lower step than that,
another sect went beyond all, beyond the Ignorants
and the Minorites and the Minims and all and called
themselves *Nullanos*, Nothings. But yet even these
diminutives, the Minorites and Minims and *Nullans*, as
little, as less, as least, as very nothing as they profess
themselves, lie under this disease which is opposed in
the *sequere me*, follow, come after, in our text; for no
sort nor condition of men in the world are more contentious, more quarrelsome, more vehement for place
and precedency than these orders of friars are there
where it may appear, that is, in their public processions,
as we find by those often troubles which the superiors
of the several orders and bishops in their several dioceses and some of those councils which they call general
have been put to for the ranking and marshalling of
these contentious and wrangling men. Which makes
me remember the words in which the eighteenth of
Elizabeth's injunctions is conceived, that to take away
fond courtesy, that is, needless compliment, and to take
away challenging of places (which it seems were frequent and troublesome then), to take away fond
courtesy and challenging of places, processions themselves were taken away, because in those processions
these orders of friars that pretended to follow and come
after all the world did thus passionately and with so
much scandalous animosity pursue the love of place
and precedency. Therefore is our humility limited,
sequere me, follow me, follow Christ. How is that
done?

Consider it in doctrinal things first, and then in
moral; first, how we are to follow Christ in believing,
and then how in doing, in practicing. First, in doctrinal
things there must have gone somebody before, else it
is no following; take heed therefore of going on with
thine own inventions, thine own imaginations, for
this is no following; take heed of accompanying the
beginners of heresies and schisms; for these are no
followings where none have gone before. Nay, there
have not gone enow before to make it a path to follow

in except it have had a long continuance and been much trodden in. And therefore to follow Christ doctrinally is to embrace those doctrines in which his church hath walked from the beginning and not to vex thyself with new points not necessary to salvation. That is the right way, and then thou art well entered; but that is not all; thou must walk in the right way to the end, that is, to the end of thy life. So that to profess the whole Gospel and nothing but Gospel for Gospel and profess this to thy death, for no respect, no dependence upon any great person, to slacken in any fundamental point of thy religion, nor to be shaken with hopes or fears in thy age when thou wouldst fain live at ease and therefore thinkest it necessary to do as thy supporters do; to persevere to the end in the whole Gospel, this is to follow Christ in doctrinal things.

In practical things, things that belong to action, we must also follow Christ in the right way and to the end. They are both (way and end) laid together, *sufferentiam Job audivistis, et finem Domini vidistis;* "You have heard of the patience of Job, and you have seen the end of the Lord"; and you must go Job's way to Christ's end. Job hath beaten a path for us to show us all the way; a path that affliction walked in, and seemed to delight in it, in bringing the Sabæan upon his oxen, the Chaldean upon his camels, the fire upon his sheep, destruction upon his servants, and at last, ruin upon his children. One affliction makes not a path; iterated, continued calamities do; and such a path Job hath showed us, not only patience but cheerfulness; more, thankfulness for our afflictions, because they were multiplied. And then we must set before our eyes as the way of Job so the end of the Lord; now the end of the Lord was the cross; so that to follow him to the end is not only to bear afflictions, though to death, but it is to bring our crosses to the cross of Christ. How is that progress made? For it is royal progress, not a pilgrimage, to follow Christ to his cross. Our Savior saith, "He that will follow me, let him take up his cross and follow me." You see four stages, four resting, baiting places in this progress. It must be a cross, and is must be my cross, and then it must be taken up by me, and with this cross of mine thus taken up by me I must follow Christ, that is, carry my cross to his.

First it must be a cross, *tollat crucem;* for every man hath afflictions, but every man hath not crosses. Only those afflictions are crosses, "whereby the world is crucified to us, and we to the world." The afflictions of the wicked exasperate them, enrage them, stone and pave them, obdurate and petrify them; but they do not crucify them. The afflictions of the godly crucify them. And when I come to that conformity with my Savior as to fulfill his sufferings in my flesh (as I am when I glorify him in a Christian constancy and cheerfulness in my afflictions), then I am crucified with him, carried up to his cross. And as Elisha in raising the Shunamite's dead child put his mouth upon the child's mouth, his eyes and his hands upon the hands and the eyes of the child; so when my crosses have carried me up to my Savior's cross, I put my hands into his hands and hang upon his nails, I put mine eyes upon his and wash off all my former unchaste looks and receive a sovereign tincture and a lively verdure and a new life into my dead tears from his tears. I put my mouth upon his mouth, and it is I that say, "My God, my God, why hast thou forsaken me?" and it is I that recover again and say, "Into thy hands, O Lord, I commend my spirit." Thus my afflictions are truly a cross when those afflictions do truly crucify me, supple me and mellow me and knead me and roll me out to a conformity with Christ. It must be this cross, and then it must be my cross that I must take up, *tollat suam.*

Other men's crosses are not my crosses; no man hath suffered more than himself needed. That is a poor treasure which they boast of in the Roman Church, that they have their exchequer, all the works of supererogation, of the martyrs in the primitive church that suffered so much more than was necessary for their own salvation, and those superabundant crosses and merits they can apply to me. If the treasure of the blood of Christ Jesus be not sufficient, Lord, what addition can I find to match them, to piece out them! And if it be sufficient of itself, what addition need I seek? Other men's crosses are not mine, other men's merits cannot save me. Nor is any cross mine own which is not mine by a good title; if I be not possessor *bona fide,* if I came not well by that cross. And *quid habeo quod non accepi?* is a question that reaches even to my crosses; what have I that I have not received! Not a cross; and from whose hands can I receive any good thing but from the hands of God? So that that only is my cross which the hand of God hath laid upon me. Alas! that cross of present bodily weakness which the former wantonnesses of my youth have brought upon me is not my cross; that cross of poverty which the wastefulness of youth hath brought upon me is not my cross; for these, weakness upon wantonness, want upon wastefulness, are nature's crosses, not God's, and they would fall naturally, though there were (which is an impossible supposition) no God. Except God therefore take these crosses in the way as they fall into his hands and sanctify them so and then lay them upon me, they are not my crosses; but if God do this, they are. And then this cross thus prepared I must take up; *tollat*.

Foreign crosses, other men's merits are not mine; spontaneous and voluntary crosses contracted by my own sins are not mine; neither are devious and remote and unnecessary crosses my crosses. Since I am bound to take up my cross, there must be a cross that is mine to take up; that is, a cross prepared for me by God and laid in my way, which is temptations or tribulations in my calling; and I must not go out of my way to seek a cross; for so it is not mine nor laid for my taking up. I am not bound to hunt after a persecution, nor to stand it and not fly, nor to affront a plague and not remove, nor to open myself to an injury and not defend. I am not bound to starve myself by inordinate fasting, nor to tear my flesh by inhuman whippings and flagellations. I am bound to take up my cross; and that is only mine which the hand of God hath laid for me, that is, in the way of my calling, temptations, and tribulations incident to that.

If it be mine, that is, laid for me by the hand of God and taken up by me, that is, voluntarily embraced, then *sequatur*, says Christ, I am bound to follow him with that cross, that is, to carry my cross to his cross. And if at any time I faint under this cross in the way, let this comfort me, that even Christ himself was eased by Simon of Cyrene in the carrying of his cross; and in all such cases I must fly to the assistance of the church and of good men that God, since it is his burden, will make it lighter, since it is his yoke, easier, and since it is his cross, more supportable, and give me the issue with the temptation. When all is done, with this cross thus laid for me and taken up by me, I must follow Christ; Christ to his end; his end is his cross; that is, I must bring my cross to his; lay down my cross at the foot of his; confess that there is no dignity, no merit in mine but as it receives an impression, a sanctification from his. For if I could die a thousand times for Christ, this were nothing if Christ had not died for me before. And this is truly to follow Christ both in the way and to the end as well in doctrinal things as in practical. And this is all that lay upon these two, Peter and Andrew, "Follow me." Remains yet to be considered, what they shall get by this; which is our last consideration.

They shall be fishers. And what shall they catch? Men. They shall be fishers of men. And then for that the world must be their sea, and their net must be the Gospel. And here in so vast a sea and with so small a net there was no great appearance of much gain. And in this function, whosoever they should catch, they should catch little for themselves. The apostleship as it was the fruitfullest, so it was the barrenest vocation; they were to catch all the world; there is their fecundity; but the apostles were to have no successors, as apostles; there is their barrenness. The apostleship was not intended for a function to raise house and families; the function ended in their persons; after the first, there were no more apostles.

And therefore it is an usurpation, an imposture, an illusion, it is a forgery, when the Bishop of Rome will proceed by apostolical authority and with apostolical dignity and apostolical jurisdiction; if he be St. Peter's successor in the bishopric of Rome, he may proceed with episcopal authority in his diocese. If he be; for, though we do not deny that St. Peter was at Rome and Bishop of Rome, though we receive it with an historical faith induced by the consent of ancient writers; yet when they will constitute matter of faith out of matter of fact and because St. Peter was *de facto* Bishop of Rome, therefore we must believe as an article of faith such an infallibility in that church as that no successor of St. Peter's can ever err; when they stretch it to matter of faith, then for matter of faith we require Scriptures; and then we are confident, and justly confident, that though historically we do believe it, yet out of Scriptures, which is a necessary proof in articles of faith, they can never prove that St. Peter was Bishop of Rome or ever at Rome. So then, if the present Bishop of Rome be St. Peter's successor as Bishop of Rome, he hath episcopal jurisdiction there; but he is not St. Peter's successor in his apostleship; and only that apostleship was a jurisdiction over all the world. But the apostleship was an extraordinary office instituted by Christ for a certain time and to certain purposes and to continue in ordinary use. As also the office of the prophet was in the Old Testament an extraordinary office and was not transferred then nor does not remain now in the ordinary office of the minister.

And therefore they argue impertinently and collect and infer sometimes seditiously that say the prophet proceeded thus and thus, therefore the minister may and must proceed so too; the prophets would chide the kings openly and threaten the kings publicly and proclaim the fault of the kings in the ears of the people confidently, authoritatively, therefore the minister may and must do so. God sent that particular Prophet Jeremiah with that extraordinary commission, "Behold I have this day set thee over the nations and over the kingdoms to root out and to pull down, to destroy and throw down, and then to build and to plant again"; but God hath given none of us his ministers in our ordinary function any such commission over nations and over kingdoms. Even in Jeremiah's commission there seems to be a limitation of time; "Behold this day I have set thee over them," where that addition, this day, is not only the date of the commission, that it passed God's hand that day, but this day is the term, the duration of the commission, that it was to last but that day, that is, as the phrase of that language is, that time for which it was limited. And therefore as they argue perversely, frowardly, dangerously that say the minister does not his duty that speaks not as boldly and as publicly too and of kings and great persons as the prophets did, because theirs was an extraordinary, ours an ordinary office—and no man will think that the justices in their sessions or the judges in their circuits may proceed to executions without due trial by a court of law because marshals in time of rebellion and other necessities may do so, because the one hath but an ordinary, the other an extraordinary commission— so do they deceive themselves and others that pretend in the Bishop of Rome an apostolical jurisdiction, a jurisdiction over all the world, whereas howsoever he may be St. Peter's successor as Bishop of Rome, yet he is no successor to St. Peter as an apostle; upon which only the universal power can be grounded and without which that universal power falls to the ground. The apostolical faith remains spread over all the world, but apostolical jurisdiction is expired with their persons.

These twelve Christ calls fishers. Why fishers? Because it is a name of labor, of service, and of humiliation; and names that taste of humiliation and labor and service are most properly ours (fishers we may be); names of dignity and authority and command are not so properly ours (apostles we are not in any such sense as they were); nothing inflames nor swells nor puffs us up more than that leaven of the soul, that empty, airy, frothy love of names and titles. We have known men part with ancient lands for new titles and with old manors for new honors; and as a man that should bestow all his money upon a fair purse and then have nothing to put into it; so whole estates have melted away for titles and honors and nothing left to support them. And how long last they? How many winds blast them? That name of God in which Moses was sent to Pharaoh is by our translators and expositors ordinarily said to be, "I am that I am, go and say, 'I am hath sent me!'" says God there; but in truth in the original the name is conceived in the future, it is, "I shall be." Every man is that he is; but only God is sure that he shall be so still. Therefore Christ calls them by a name of labor and humiliation. But why by that name of labor and humiliation, fishers?

Because it was *nomen primitivum*, their own, their former name. The Holy Ghost pursues his own way and does here in Christ as he does often in other places, he speaks in such forms and such phrases as may most work upon them to whom he speaks. Of David, that was a shepherd before, God says, he took him to feed his people. To those Magi of the East, who were given to the study of the stars, God gave a star to be their guide to Christ at Bethlehem. To those who followed him to Capernaum for meat, Christ took occasion by that to preach to them of the spiritual food of their souls. To the Samaritan woman, whom he found at the well, he preached of the water of life. To the men in our text accustomed to a joy and gladness, when they took great or great store of fish, he presents his comforts agreeably to their taste; they should be fishers still. Christ puts no man out of his way—for sinful courses are no way but continual deviations—to go to heaven. Christ makes heaven all things to all men that he might gain all. To the mirthful man he presents heaven as all joy; and to the ambitious man, as all glory; to the merchant it is a pearl; and to the husbandman it is a rich field. Christ hath made heaven all things to all men that he might gain all, and he puts no man out of his way to come thither. These men he calls fishers.

He does not call them from their calling, but he mends them in it. It is not an innovation; God loves not innovations; old doctors, old disciples, old words and forms of speech in his service God loves best. But it is a renovation though not an innovation, and renovations are always acceptable to God; that is, the renewing of a man's self in a consideration of his first estate, what he was made for and wherein he might be most serviceable to God. Such a renewing it is as could not be done without God; no man can renew himself, regenerate himself; no man can prepare that work, no man can begin it, no man can proceed in it of himself. The desire and the actual beginning is from the preventing[6] grace of God, and the constant proceeding is from the concomitant and subsequent and continual

6 Foreseeing.

succeeding grace of God; for there is no conclusive, no consummative grace in this life; no such measure of grace given to any man as that that man needs no more or can lose or frustrate none of that. The renewing of these men in our text Christ takes to himself; *faciam vos*, "I will make ye fishers of men"; no worldly respects must make us such fishers; it must be a calling from God; and yet, as the other evangelist in the same history expresses it, it is *faciam fieri vos*, "I will cause ye to be made fishers of men," that is, I will provide an outward calling for you too. Our calling to this man-fishing is not good, *nisi Dominus faciat et fieri faciat*, except God make us fishers by an eternal, and make his church to make us so too, by an external calling. Then we are fishers of men, and then we are successors to the apostles, though not in their apostleship yet in this fishing. And then for this fishing the world is the sea, and our net is the Gospel.

The world is a sea in many respects and assimilations. It is a sea as it is subject to storms and tempests; every man—and every man is a world[7]—feels that. And then it is never the shallower for the calmness, the sea is as deep, there is as much water in the sea, in a calm as in a storm; we may be drowned in a calm and flattering fortune, in prosperity, as irrecoverably as in a wrought sea, in adversity; so the world is a sea. It is a sea as it is bottomless to any line which we can sound it with and endless to any discovery that we can make of it. The purposes of the world, the ways of the world, exceed our consideration; but yet we are sure the sea hath a bottom, and sure that it hath limits that it cannot overpass; the power of the greatest in the world, the life of the happiest in the world, cannot exceed those bounds which God hath placed for them; so the world is a sea. It is a sea as it hath ebbs and floods and no man knows the true reason of those floods and those ebbs. All men have changes and vicissitudes in their bodies (they fall sick) and in their estates (they grow poor) and in their minds (they become sad) at which changes (sickness, poverty, sadness) themselves wonder, and the cause is wrapped up in the purpose and judgment of God only and hid even from them that have them; and so the world is a sea. It is a sea as the sea affords water enough for all the world to drink but such water as will not quench the thirst. The world affords conveniences enow to satisfy nature, but these increase our thirst with drinking, and our desire grows

and enlarges itself with our abundance, and though we sail in a full sea, yet we lack water; so the world is a sea. It is a sea if we consider the inhabitants. In the sea the greater fish devour the less; and so do the men of this world too. And as fish, when they mud themselves, have no hands to make themselves clean, but the current of the waters must do that; so have the men of this world no means to clean themselves from those sins which they have contracted in the world, of themselves, till a new flood, waters of repentance drawn up and sanctified by the Holy Ghost, work that blessed effect in them.

All these ways the world is a sea, but especially is it a sea in this respect, that the sea is no place of habitation, but a passage to our habitations. So the apostle expresses the world, "Here we have no continuing city, but we seek one to come"; we seek it not here, but we seek it whilst we are here, else we never find it. Those are the two great works which we are to do in this world: first to know that this world is not our home, and then to provide us another home whilst we are in this world. Therefore the prophet says, "Arise and depart, for this is not your rest." Worldly men that have no farther prospect promise themselves some rest in this world ("Soul, thou hast much goods laid up for many years, take thine ease, eat, drink, and be merry," says the rich man), but this is not your rest; indeed no rest; at least not yours. You must depart, depart by death, before ye come to that rest; but then you must arise before you depart; for except ye have a resurrection to grace here before you depart, you shall have no resurrection to glory in the life to come when you are departed.

Now, in this sea every ship that sails must necessarily have some part of the ship under water; every man that lives in this world must necessarily have some of his life, some of his thoughts, some of his labors spent upon this world; but that part of the ship by which he sails is above water; those meditations and those endeavors which bring us to heaven are removed from this world and fixed entirely upon God. And in this sea we are made fishers of men, of men in general; not rich men, to profit by them, nor of poor men, to pierce them the more sharply because affliction hath opened a way into them; not of learned men, to be over-glad of their approbation of our labors, nor of ignorant men, to affect them with an astonishment or admiration of our gifts. But we are fishers of men, of all men, of that which makes them men, their souls. And for this fishing in this sea this Gospel is our net.

7 This is Donne's favorite figure of the microcosm. In this old medieval concept the body of man was supposed to repeat in detail all the physical characteristics of the universe.

Eloquence is not our net; traditions of men are not our net; only the Gospel is. The Devil angles with hooks and baits; he deceives and he wounds in the catching; for every sin hath his sting. The Gospel of Christ Jesus is a net; it hath leads and corks; it hath leads, that is, the denouncing of God's judgments and a power to sink down and lay flat any stubborn and rebellious heart; and it hath corks, that is, the power of absolution and application of the mercies of God that swim above all his works, means to erect a humble and contrite spirit above all the waters of tribulation and affliction. A net is *res nodosa*, a knotty thing; and so is the Scripture, full of knots, of scruple, and perplexity and anxiety and vexation if thou wilt go about to entangle thyself in those things which appertain not to thy salvation; but knots of a fast union and inseparable alliance of thy soul to God and to the fellowship of his saints if thou take the Scriptures as they were intended for thee, that is, if thou beest content to rest in those places which are clear and evident in things necessary. A net is a large thing, past thy fathoming if thou cast it from thee, but if thou draw it to thee, it will lie upon thy arm. The Scriptures will be out of thy reach and out of thy use, if thou cast and scatter them upon reason, upon philosophy, upon morality, to try how the Scriptures will fit all them, and believe them but so far as they agree with thy reason. But draw the Scripture to thine own heart and to thine own actions, and thou shalt find it made for that; all the promises of the Old Testament made and all accomplished in the New Testament for the salvation of thy soul hereafter and for thy consolation in the present application of them.

Now this that Christ promises here is not here promised in the nature of wages due to our labor and to our fishing. There is no merit in all that we can do. "The wages of sin is death"; death is due to sin, the proper reward of sin; but the apostle does not say there that eternal life is the wages of any good work of ours. "The wages of sin is death, but eternal life is the gift of God through Jesus Christ our Lord." Through Jesus Christ, that is, as we are considered in him; and in him who is a savior, a redeemer, we are not considered but as sinners. So that God's purpose works no otherwise upon us but as we are sinners; neither did God mean ill to any man till that man was in his sight a sinner. God shuts no man out of heaven by a lock on the inside except that man have clapped the door after him and never knocked to have it opened again, that is, except that he has sinned and

never repented. Christ does not say in our text, follow me, for I will prefer you; he will not have that the reason, the cause. If I would not serve God except I might be saved for serving him, I shall not be saved though I serve him; my first end in serving God must not be myself but he and his glory. It is but an addition from his own good self, *et faciam*, follow me, and I will do this; but yet it is as certain and infallible as a debt or as an effect upon a natural cause; those propositions in nature are not so certain; the earth is at such a time just between the sun and the moon, therefore the moon must be eclipsed; the moon is at such a time just between the earth and the sun, therefore the sun must be eclipsed; for upon the sun and those other bodies God can and hath sometimes wrought miraculously and changed the natural courses of them; the sun stood still in Joshua, and there was an unnatural eclipse at the death of Christ; but God cannot by any miracle so work upon himself as to make himself not himself, unmerciful or unjust; and out of his mercy he makes this promise, do this, and thus it shall be with you, and then of his justice he performs that promise which was made merely and only out of mercy; if we do it, though not because we do it, we shall have eternal life.

Therefore did Andrew and Peter faithfully believe such a net should be put into their hands. Christ had vouchsafed to fish for them and caught them with that net, and they believed that he that made them fishers of men would also enable them to catch others with that net. And that is truly the comfort that refreshes us in all our lucubrations and night-studies through the course of our lives, that that God that sets us to sea will prosper our voyage, that he, whether he fix us upon our own or send us to other congregations, will open the hearts of those congregations to us and bless our labors to them. And as St. Paul's *væ si non* lies upon us wheresoever we are—woe be unto us if we do not preach—so, as St. Paul says too, we were of all men the most miserable if we preached without hope of doing good. With this net St. Paul caught three thousand souls in one day at one sermon and five thousand in another. With this net St. Paul fished all the Mediterranean Sea and caused the Gospel of Christ Jesus to abound from Jerusalem round about to Illyricum. This is the net with which if ye be willing to be caught, that is, to lay down all your hopes and affiances in the gracious promises of his Gospel, then you are fishers reserved for that great marriage feast which is the kingdom of heaven; where whosoever is a dish is a guest too; whosoever is served in at the table sits at the table; whosoever is caught by this net is called to this feast; and there your soul shall be satisfied with marrow and with fatness in an infallible assurance of an everlasting and undeterminable term in inexpressible joy and glory. Amen.

SELECTIONS FROM OTHER SERMONS

DECAY OF THE WORLD

As THE world is the whole frame of the world, God hath put into it a reproof, a rebuke, lest it should seem eternal, which is a sensible decay and age in the whole frame of the world and every piece thereof. The seasons of the year irregular and distempered; the sun fainter and languishing; men less in stature and shorter-lived. No addition but only every year new sorts, new species of worms and flies and sicknesses which argue more and more putrefaction of which they are engendered. And the angels of heaven which did so familiarly converse with men in the beginning of the world, though they may not be doubted to perform to us still their ministerial assistances, yet they seem so far to have deserted this world as that they do not appear unto us as they did to those of our fathers. St. Cyprian observed this in his time, when writing to Demetrianus, who imputed all those calamities which afflicted the world then to the impiety of the Christians who would not join with them in the worship of their gods, Cyprian went no farther for the cause of these calamities but *ad senescentem mundum,* to the age and impotency of the whole world; and therefore, says he, *Imputent senes Christianis quod minus valeant in senectutem;* old men were best accuse Christians that they are more sickly in their age than they were in their youth; is the fault in our religion, or in their decay? *Canos in pueris videmus, nec ætas in senectute desinit sed incipit a senectute;* we see gray hairs in children, and we do not die old, and yet we are born old. Lest the world, as the world signifies the whole frame of the world, should glorify itself or flatter and abuse us with an opinion of eternity, we may admit usefully, though we do not conclude peremptorily, this observation to be true, that there is a reproof, a rebuke born in it, a sensible decay and mortality of the whole world.[1]

WRETCHED MAN

FIRE and air, water and earth are not the elements of man; inward decay and outward violence, bodily pain and sorrow of heart may be rather styled his elements; and though he be destroyed by these, yet he consists of nothing but these. As the good qualities of all creatures are not for their own use, for the sun sees not his own glory, nor the rose smells not her own breath, but all their good is for man; so the ill conditions of the creature are not directed upon themselves, the toad poisons not itself, nor does the viper bite itself; but all their ill pours down upon men. As though man could be a microcosm, a world in himself, no other way except all the misery of the world fell upon him. . . . If a man do but prick a finger and bind it above that part so that the spirits or that which they call the *balsamum* of the body[2] cannot descend by reason of that ligature to that part, it will gangrene; and (which is an argument and an evidence that mischiefs are more operative, more insinuating, more penetrative, more diligent than remedies against mischiefs are) when the spirits and *balsamum* of the body cannot pass by that ligature to that wound, yet the gangrene will pass from that wound by that ligature to the body, to the heart, and destroy. In every part of the body death can find a door or make a breach; mortal diseases breed in every part. . . . Behold God hath walled us with mud walls, and wet mud walls, that waste away faster than God meant at first they should. And by sins this flesh that is but the loam and plaster of thy tabernacle, thy body, that, all that, that in the entire substance is corrupted. Those gums and spices which should embalm thy flesh when thou art dead are spent upon that diseased body whilst thou art alive. Thou seemest in the eye of the world to walk in silks, and thou dost but walk in cerecloth; thou hast a desire to please some eyes, when thou hast much to do, not to displease every nose; and thou wilt solicit an adulterous entrance into their beds,

---

1 Sermon xxxvi, folio of 1640.

2 Donne was well read in the medical science of Paracelsus.

who, if they should but see thee go into thine own bed, would need no other mortification nor answer to thy solicitation. Thou pursuest the works of the flesh, and hast none, for thy flesh is but dust held together by plasters; dissolution and putrefaction is gone over thee alive; thou hast over-lived thine own death and art become thine own ghost and thine own hell.[3]

We understand the frame of man's body better when we see him naked than apparelled, howsoever; and better by seeing him cut up than by seeing him do any exercise alive; one dissection, one anatomy teaches more of that than the marching or drilling of a whole army of living men. Let every one of us therefore dissect and cut up himself, and consider what he was before God raised him friends to bring those abilities and good parts which he had into knowledge and into use and into employment; what he was before he had by education and study and industry imprinted those abilities in his soul; what he was before that soul was infused into him, capable of such education; what he was when he was but in the list and catalogue of creatures and might have been left in the state of a worm or a plant or a stone; what he was when he was not so far but only in the vast and inexpressible and unimaginable depth of nothing at all.[4]

When I consider what I was in my parents' loins, a substance unworthy of a word, unworthy of a thought; when I consider what I am now, a volume of diseases bound up together, a dry cinder, if I look for natural, for radical moisture, and yet a sponge, a bottle of overflowing rheums, if I consider accidentals, an aged child, a gray-headed infant, and but a ghost of mine own youth; when I consider what I shall be at last by the hand of death in my grave, first but putrefaction and then not so much as putrefaction, I shall not be able to send forth so much as an ill air, not any air at all, but shall be all insipid, tasteless, savorless dust, for a while all worms and after a while not so much as worms, sordid, senseless, nameless dust; when I consider the past and present and future state of this body in this world; I am able to conceive, able to express the worst that can befall it in nature and the worst that can be inflicted upon it by man or fortune; but the least degree of glory that God hath prepared for that body in heaven I am not able to express, not able to conceive.[5]

3 Sermon xx, folio of 1649.
4 Sermon xii, folio of 1660.
5 Sermon xxii, folio of 1640.

Shall we that are but worms, but silk-worms, but glow-worms at best, chide God that he hath made slow-worms and other venomous creeping things? Shall we that are nothing but boxes of poison in ourselves reprove God for making toads and spiders in the world? Shall we that are all discord quarrel the harmony of his creation or his providence? Can an apothecary make a sovereign treacle of vipers and other poisons, and cannot God admit offenses and scandals into his physic? Scandals and offenses, temptations and tribulations are our leaven that ferment us and our lees that preserve us. Use them to God's glory and to thine own establishing.[6]

Begin therefore to pay these debts to thyself betimes; for, as we told you at beginning, some of you are to tender at noon, some at evening. Even at your noon and warmest sunshine of prosperity you owe yourselves a true information how you came by that prosperity, who gave it you, and why he gave it. Let not the olive boast of her own fatness nor the fig-tree of her own sweetness nor the vine of her own fruitfulness, for we are all but brambles. Let no man say, I could not miss a fortune, for I have studied all my youth; how many men have studied more nights than he hath done hours and studied themselves blind and mad in the mathematics and yet wither in beggary in a corner! Let him never add, but I studied in a useful and gainful profession; how many have done so too and yet never compassed the favor of a judge! And how many that have had all that have struck upon a rock even at full sea and perished there! In their grandfathers and great-grandfathers, in a few generations, whosoever is greatest now must say, with this staff came I over Jordan; nay, without any staff came I over Jordan, for he had in them at first a beginning of nothing. As for spiritual happiness, *non volentis nec currentis sed miserantis Dei*, it is not in him that would run nor in him that doth but only in God that prospers his course; so for the things of this world it is in vain to rise early and to lie down late and to eat the bread of sorrow, for *nisi Dominus ædificaverit, nisi Dominus custodierit*, except the Lord build the house, they labor in vain; except the Lord keep the city, the watchman waketh but in vain. Come not therefore to say, I studied more than my fellows and therefore am richer than my fellows but say, God that gave me my contemplations at first gave me my practice after and hath given me his blessing now. How many men have

6 Sermon xvii, folio of 1649.

worn their brains upon their studies and spent their time and themselves therein! How many men have studied more in thine own profession and yet for diffidence in themselves or some disfavor from others have not had thy practice! How many men have been equal to thee in study, in practice, and in getting too, and yet upon a wanton confidence that that world would always last or upon the burden of many children and an expensive breeding of them or for other reasons which God hath found in his ways are left upon the sand at last in a low fortune! Whilst the sun shines upon thee in all these, pay thyself the debt of knowing whence and why all this came, for else thou canst not know how much or how little is thine, nor thou canst not come to restore that which is none of thine but unjustly wrung from others. Pay therefore this debt of surveying thine estate, and then pay thyself thine own too by a cheerful enjoying and using that which is truly thine, and do not deny nor defraud thyself of those things which are thine and so become a wretched debtor to thy back or to thy belly, as though the world had not enough or God knew not what were enough for thee.

Pay this debt to thyself of looking into thy debts, of surveying, of severing, of serving thyself with that which is truly thine at thy noon, in the best of thy fortune and in the strength of thine understanding; that when thou comest to pay thy other, thy last debt to thyself, which is to open a door out of this world by the dissolution of body and soul, thou have not all thy money to tell over when the sun is ready to set, all the account to make of every bag of money and of every quillet of land, whose it is and whether it be his that looks for it from thee or his from whom it was taken by thee, whether it belong to thine heir that weeps joyful tears behind the curtain or belong to him that weeps true and bloody tears in the hole in a prison. There will come a time when that land that thou leavest shall not be his land, when it shall be nobody's land, when it shall be no land, for the earth must perish; there will be a time when there shall be no manors, no acres in the world, and yet there shall lie manors and acres upon thy soul, when land shall be no more, when time shall be no more, and thou pass away, not into the land of the living, but of eternal death. Then the accuser will be ready to interline the schedules of thy debts, thy sins, and insert false debts by abusing an over-tenderness which may be in thy conscience then, in thy last sickness, in thy death-bed. Then he will be ready to add a cipher more to thy debts and

make hundreds thousands and abuse the faintness which may be in thy conscience then, in thy last sickness, in thy death-bed. Then he will be ready to abuse even thy confidence in God and bring thee to think that, as a pirate ventures boldly home, though all that he hath be stolen, if he be rich enough to bribe for a pardon, so, howsoever those families perish whom thou hast ruined and those whole parishes whom thou hast depopulated, thy soul may go confidently home too, if thou bribe God then with an hospital or a fellowship in a college or a legacy to any pious use in appearance and in the eye of the world.[7]

SIN

THE wanton and licentious man sighs out his soul, weeps out his soul, swears out his soul in every place where his lust or his custom or the glory of victory in overcoming and deluding puts him upon such solicitations. In the corrupt taker his soul goes out that it may leave him insensible of his sin and not trouble him in his corrupt bargain; and in a corrupt giver ambitious of preferment his soul goes out with his money, which he loves well, but not so well as his preferment; this year his soul and his money goes out upon one office, and next year more soul and more money upon another; he knows how his money will come in again; for they will bring it that have need of his corruptness in his offices. But where will this man find his soul, thus scattered upon every woman corruptly won, upon every office corruptly usurped, upon every quillet[8] corruptly bought, upon every fee corruptly taken?

Thus it is when a soul is scattered upon the daily practice of any one predominant and habitual sin. But when it is indifferently scattered upon all, how much more is it so! In him that swallows sins in the world as he would do meats at a feast, passes through every dish and never asks physician the nature, the quality, the danger, the offense of any dish; that baits at every sin that rises, and pours himself into every sinful mold he meets; that knows not when he began to spend his soul nor where nor upon what sin he laid it out; no, nor whether he have, whether he ever had any soul or no; but hath lost his soul so long ago in rusty and in incoherent sins (not sins that produced one another as in David's case—and yet that is a fearful state, that concatenation of sins, that pedigree of sins—but in sins

7 Sermon ix, folio of 1640.
8 A narrow strip of land.

which he embraces merely out of an uneasiness to sin and not out of a love, no, nor out of a temptation to that sin in particular), that in these incoherent sins hath so scattered his soul as that he hath not soul enough left to seek out the rest.[9]

For every one of us well-nigh hath married himself to some particular sin, some beloved sin that he can hardly divorce himself from; nay, no man keeps his faith to that one sin that he hath married himself to, but mingles himself with other sins also. Though covetousness whom he loves as the wife of his bosom have made him rich, yet he will commit adultery with another sin, with ambition; and he will part even with those riches for honor. Though ambition be his wife, his married sin, yet he will commit adultery with another sin, with licentiousness, and he will endanger his honor to fulfill his lust; ambition may be his wife, but lust is his concubine.[10]

Have we not secular sins, sins of our own age, our own time, and yet sin by precedent of former as well as create precedents for future? And not only silver and gold but vessels of iron and brass were brought into the treasury of the Lord; not only the glorious sins of high places and national sins and secular sins; but the wretchedest beggar in the street contributes to this treasure, the treasure of sin, and to this mischievous use, to increase this treasure, the treasure of sin, is a subsidy man. He begs in Jesus' name and for God's sake; and in the same name curses him that does not give. He counterfeits a lameness, or he loves his lameness and would not be cured; for his lameness is his stock, it is his demesne.[11]

There are some sins so rooted, so riveted in men, so incorporated, so consubstantiated in the soul by habitual custom as that those sins have contracted the nature of ancient possessions. As men call manors by their names, so sins have taken names from men and from places; Simon Magus gave the name to a sin, and so did Gehazi, and Sodom did so. There are sins that run in names, in families, in blood; hereditary sins, entailed sins; and men do almost prove their gentry by those sins, and are scarce believed to be rightly born if they have not those sins; these are great possessions, and men do much more easily part with Christ than

9   Sermon xxi, folio of 1640.
10   Sermon iii, folio of 1640.
11   Sermon v, folio of 1660.

with these sins. But then there are less sins, light sins, vanities; and yet even these come to possess us and separate us from Christ. How many men neglect this ordinary means of their salvation, the coming to these exercises, not because their undoing lies on it, or their discountenancing, but merely out of levity, of vanity, of nothing! They know not what to do else, and yet do not this. You hear of one man that was drowned in a vessel of wine; but how many thousands in ordinary water! And he was no more drowned in that precious liquor than they in that common water. A gad of steel does no more choke a man than a feather, than a hair; men perish with whispering sins, nay, with silent sins, sins that never tell the conscience they are sins, as often as with crying sins. And in hell there shall meet as many men that never thought what was sin as that spent all their thoughts in the compassing of sin; as many who in a slack inconsideration never cast a thought upon that place as that by searing their conscience overcame the sense and fear of the place. Great sins are great possessions; but levities and vanities possess us too; and men had rather part with Christ than with any possessions.[12]

As a spider builds always where he knows there is most access and haunt of flies, so the Devil that hath cast these light cobwebs into thy heart knows that that heart is made of vanities and levities; and he that gathers into his treasure whatsoever thou wastest out of thine, how negligent soever thou be, he keeps thy reckoning exactly and will produce against thee at last as many lascivious glances as shall make up an adultery, as many covetous wishes as shall make up a robbery, as many angry words as shall make up a murder; and thou shalt have dropt and crumbled away thy soul with as much irrecoverableness as if thou hadst poured it out all at once; and thy merry sins, thy laughing sins shall grow to be crying sins even in the ears of God; and though thou drown thy soul here drop after drop, it shall not burn spark after spark but have all the fire, and all at once and all eternally, in one entire and intense torment.[13]

We say sometimes, and not altogether improperly, that a man walks clean, if in a foul way he contract but a few spots of dirt; but yet this is not absolute cleanness. A house is not clean except cobwebs be swept down; a man is not clean except he remove the lightest

12   Sermon xvii, folio of 1640.
13   Sermon xxiv, folio of 1660.

and slightest occasions of provocation. It is the speech of the greatest to the greatest, of Christ to the church, *Capite vulpeculas*, "Take us the little foxes, for they devour the vine." It is not a cropping, a pilling, a retarding of the growth of the vine that is threatened, but a devouring, though but from little foxes. It is not so desperate a state to have thy soul attempted by that lion that seeks whom he may devour (for then, in great and apparent sins, thou wilt be occasioned to call upon the lion of the tribe of Judah to thine assistance) as it is to have thy soul eaten up by vermin, by the custom and habit of small sins. God punished the Egyptians with little things, with hailstones and frogs and grasshoppers; and Pharaoh's conjurers, that counterfeited all Moses' greater works, failed in the least, in the making of lice. A man may stand a great temptation and satisfy himself in that and think he hath done enough in the way of spiritual valor, and then fall as irrecoverably under the custom of small. I were as good lie under a millstone as under a hill of sand; for howsoever I might have blown away every grain of sand, if I had watched it as it fell, yet when it is a hill I cannot blow it nor shove it away. And when I shall think to say to God, I have done no great sins, God shall not proceed with me by weight but by measure, nor ask how much but how long I have sinned.[14]

A house is not clean, though all the dust be swept together, if it lie still in a corner within doors; a conscience is not clean by having recollected all her sins in the memory, for they may fester there and gangrene even to desperation till she have emptied them in the bottomless seas of the blood of Christ Jesus and the mercy of his Father by this way of confession. But a house is not clean neither, though the dust be thrown out, if there hang cobwebs about the walls in how dark corners soever. A conscience is not clean, though the sins brought to our memory by this examination be cast upon God's mercy and the merits of his Son by confession, if there remain in me but a cobweb, a little but a sinful delight in the memory of those sins which I had formerly committed. How many men sin over the sins of their youth again in their age by a sinful delight in remembering those sins and a sinful desire that their bodies were not past them! How many men sin over some sins but imaginarily, and yet damnably, a hundred times, which they never sinned actually at all, by filling their imaginations with such thoughts as these, how would I be revenged of such an enemy, if I

14 Sermon xii, folio of 1640.

were in such a place of authority! How easily could I overthrow such a wasteful young man and compass his land, if I had but money to feed his humors! Those sins which we have never been able to do actually to the harm of others we do as hurtfully to our own souls by a sinful desire of them and a sinful delight in them.[15]

And for sin itself I would not, I do not extenuate my sin, but let me have fallen not seven times a day but seventy times a minute, yet what are my sins to all those sins that were upon Christ! The sins of all men and all women and all children, the sins of all nations, all the East and West and all the North and South, the sins of all times and ages, of nature, of law, of grace, the sins of all natures, sins of the body and sins of the mind, the sins of all growth and all extensions, thoughts and words and acts and habits and delight and glory and contempt and the very sin of boasting, nay, of belying ourselves in sin; all these sins, past, present, and future, were once upon Christ, and in that depth of sin mine are but a drop to his ocean; in that treasure of sin mine are but single money to his talent.[16]

DEATH

Now if all this earth were made in that minute, may not all come to the general dissolution in this minute? Or may not thy acres, thy miles, thy shires shrink into feet, and so few feet as shall but make up thy grave? When he who was a great lord must be a cottager; and not so well; for a cottager must have so many acres to his cottage; but in this case a little piece of an acre, five feet, is become the house itself; the house and the land; the grave is all. Lower than that; the grave is the land and the tenement and the tenant too. He that lies in it becomes the same earth that he lies in. They all make but one earth, and but a little of it.[17]

Truly, to see the hand of a great and mighty monarch, that hand that hath governed the civil sword, the sword of justice at home, and drawn and sheathed the foreign sword, the sword of war abroad, to see that hand lie dead and not be able to nip or fillip away one of his own worms (and then *quis homo*, what man, though he be one of those men of whom God hath said, "Ye are gods," yet *quis homo*, "What man is there

15 Sermon xlix, folio of 1649.
16 Sermon xx, folio of 1640.
17 Sermon xxviii, folio of 1649.

that lives and shall not see death"?), to see the brain of a great and religious counsellor (and God bless all from making, all from calling any great that is not religious), to see that brain that produced means to becalm gusts at council tables, storms in Parliament, tempests in popular commotions, to see that brain produce nothing but swarms of worms and no proclamation to disperse them, to see a reverend prelate that hath resisted heretics and schismatics all his life fall like one of them by death and perchance be called one of them when he is dead—to recollect all—to see great men made no men, to be sure that they shall never come to us, not to be sure that we shall know them when we come to them, to see the lieutenants and images of God, kings, the sinews of the state, religious counsellors, the spirit of the church, zealous prelates, and then to see vulgar, ignorant, wicked, and facinorous men thrown all by one hand of death into one cart, into one common tideboat, one hospital, one almshouse, one prison, the grave, in whose dust no man can say, this is the king, this is the slave, this is the bishop, this is the heretic, this is the counsellor, this is the fool, even this miserable equality of so unequal persons by so foul a hand is the subject of this lamentation, even *quia mortuus*, because Lazarus was dead, "Jesus wept." [18]

Even those bodies that were the temples of the Holy Ghost come to this dilapidation, to ruin, to rubbish, to dust; even the Israel of the Lord and Jacob himself hath no other specification, no other denomination but that, *vermis Jacob*, thou worm of Jacob. Truly the consideration of this posthume death, this death after burial, that after God, with whom are the issues of death, hath delivered me from the death of the womb by bringing me into the world and from the manifold deaths of the world by laying me in the grave, I must die again in an incineration of this flesh and in a dispersion of that dust; that that monarch who spread over many nations alive must in his dust lie in a corner of that sheet of lead, and there but so long as the lead will last; and that private and retired man that thought himself his own forever and never came forth must in his dust of the grave be published and—such are the revolutions of the grave—be mingled with the dust of every highway and of every dunghill and swallowed in every puddle and pond; this is the most inglorious and contemptible vilification, the most deadly and peremptory nullification of man, that we can consider. [19]

18 Sermon xvi, folio of 1640.
19 From Death's Duel, the last sermon of Donne, published

Except an epitaph tell me who lies there, I cannot tell by the dust, nor by the epitaph know which is the dust it speaks of, if another have been laid before or after in the same grave. Nor can any epitaph be confident in saying here lies, but here was laid. For so various, so vicissitudinary is all this world as that even the dust of the grave hath revolutions. As the motions of an upper sphere [20] imprint a motion in the lower sphere other than naturally it would have; so the changes of this life work after death. And as envy supplants and removes us alive, a shovel removes us and throws us out of our grave after death. No limbec, [21] no weights can tell you, this is dust royal, this plebeian dust. No commission, no inquisition can say, this is catholic, this is heretical dust. All lie alike. [22]

Every puff of wind within these walls may blow the father into the son's eyes or the wife into her husband's or his into hers or both into their children's or their children's into both. Every grain of dust that flies here is a piece of a Christian; you need not distinguish your pews by figures; you need not say, I sit within so many of such a neighbor, but I sit within so many inches of my husband's or wife's or child's or son's grave. Ambitious men never made more shift for places in court than dead men for graves in churches; and as in our later times we have seen two and two almost in every place and office, so almost every grave is oppressed with twins. [23]

And thy skin shall come to that absolute corruption as that, though a hundred years after thou art buried one may find thy bones and say, this was a tall man, this was a strong man, yet we shall soon be past saying upon any relic of thy skin, this was a fair man; corruption seizes the skin, all outward beauty quickly. . . .

When of the whole body there is neither eye nor ear nor any member left, where is the body? And what should an eye do there where there is nothing to be seen but loathsomeness? or a nose there where there is

in 1632 and reprinted in the folio of 1660 as Sermon xxvi; Donne, sick unto death, preached it before Charles I at Whitehall at the beginning of Lent, 1631, a few days before he died; it was this sermon, "called by his Majesty's household the Doctor's own funeral sermon," that Walton mentions in his Life.

20 The *primum mobile*, the outside globe which, in Ptolemaic astronomy, gave motion to the rest.
21 Alembic; the alchemist's apparatus for distilling.
22 Sermon xxviii, folio of 1649.
23 Sermon xxi, folio of 1660.

nothing to be smelt but putrefaction? or an ear where in the grave they do not praise God? Doth not that body that boasted but yesterday of that privilege above all creatures that it only could go upright, lie today so flat upon the earth as the body of a horse or of a dog? And doth it not tomorrow lose his other privilege, of looking up to heaven? Is it not farther removed from the eye of heaven, the sun, than any dog or horse by being covered with the earth, which they are not? Painters have presented to us with some horror the skeleton, the frame of the bones of a man's body; but the state of a body in the dissolution of the grave no pencil can present to us. Between that excremental jelly that thy body is made of at first and that jelly which thy body dissolves to at last there is not so noisome, so putrid a thing in nature. . . .

Ask where that iron is that is ground off a knife or axe; ask that marble that is worn off of the threshold in the church porch by continual treading; and with that iron and with that marble thou mayst find thy father's skin and body; *contrita sunt*, the knife, the marble, the skin, the body are ground away, trod away; they are destroyed. Who knows the revolutions of dust? Dust upon the king's highway and dust upon the king's grave are both, or neither, dust royal and may change places. Who knows the revolutions of dust?

Destroyed by worms. It makes the destruction the more contemptible; thou that wouldst not admit the beams of the sun upon thy skin, and yet hast admitted the pollutions of sin; thou that wouldst not admit the breath of air upon thy skin, and yet hast admitted the spirit of lust and unchaste solicitations to breathe upon thee in execrable oaths and blasphemies to vicious purposes; thou whose body hath—as far as it can—putrefied and corrupted even the body of thy Savior in an unworthy receiving thereof in this skin, in this body, must be the food of worms, the prey of destroying worms. After a low birth thou mayst pass an honorable life, after a sentence of an ignominious death thou mayst have an honorable end; but in the grave canst thou make these worms silk-worms? They were bold and early worms that ate up Herod before he died: they are bold and everlasting worms which after thy skin and body is destroyed shall remain as long as God remains in an eternal gnawing of thy conscience, long, long after the destroying of skin and body by bodily worms.[24]

If in death there be no remembrance of God, if this remembrance perish in death, certainly it decays in the nearness to death; if there be a possession in death, there is an approach in age; and therefore "Remember now thy Creator in the days of thy youth." There are spiritual lethargies that make a man forget his name, forget that he was a Christian and what belongs to that duty. God knows what forgetfulness may possess thee upon thy death-bed and freeze thee there; God knows what rage, what distemper, what madness may scatter thee then; and though in such cases God reckon with his servants according to that disposition which they used to have towards him before and not according to those declinations from him which they show in such distempered sicknesses, yet God's mercy towards them can work but so that he returns to those times when those men did remember him before. But if God can find no such time that they never remembered him, then he seals their former negligence with a present lethargy; they neglected God all their lives, and now in death there is no remembrance of him, nor there is no remembrance in him; God shall forget him eternally; and when he thinks he is come to his *consummatum est*, the bell tolls and will ring out and there is an end of all in death, by death he comes to his *sæcula sæculorum*, to the beginning of that misery which shall never end.[25]

I take no farther occasion from this circumstance but to arm you with consolation; how low soever God be pleased to cast you, though it be to the earth, yet he does not so much cast you down in doing that as bring you home. Death is not a banishing of you out of this world; but it is a visitation of your kindred that lie in the earth; neither are any nearer of kin to you than the earth itself and the worms of the earth. You heap earth upon your souls and encumber them with more and more flesh by a superfluous and luxuriant diet; you add earth to earth in new purchases and measure not by acres but by manors, nor by manors but by shires; and there is a little quillet, a little close, worth all these, a quiet grave. And therefore when thou readest that God makes thy bed in thy sickness, rejoice in this, not only that he makes that bed where thou dost lie but that bed where thou shalt lie; that that God that made the whole earth is now making thy bed in the earth, a quiet grave, where thou shalt sleep in peace till the angel's trumpet wake thee at the resurrection to that judgment where thy peace shall

---

24 Sermon xiv, folio of 1649.

25 Sermon liii, folio of 1640.

be made before thou comest and writ and sealed in the blood of the Lamb.[26]

Quis homo? What is that man that hungers and thirsts not, that labors not, that sickens not? I can tell you of many that never felt any of these; but contract the question to that one of death, *quis homo?* What man is he that shall not taste death? And I know of none. Whether we consider the summer solstice when the day is sixteen hours and the night but eight or the winter solstice when the night is sixteen hours and the day but eight, still all is but twenty-four hours, and still the evening and morning make but a day. The patriarchs in the Old Testament had their summer day, long lives; we are in the winter, short-lived; but *quis homo?* Which of them or us come not to our night in death? If we consider violent deaths, casual deaths, it is almost a scornful thing to see with what wantonness and sportfulness death plays with us; we have seen a man cannon-proof in the time of war and slain with his own pistol in the time of peace. We have seen a man recovered after his drowning and live to hang himself. But for that one kind of death which is general— though nothing be in truth more against nature than dissolution and corruption which is death—we are come to call that death natural death than which, indeed, nothing is more unnatural; the generality makes it natural. Moses says that man's age is seventy, and eighty is labor and pain; and yet himself was more than eighty and in good state and habitude when he said so. No length, no strength enables us to answer this *quis homo?* What man? etc.

Take a flat map, a globe *in plano*, and here is east and there is west as far asunder as two points can be put. But reduce this flat map to roundness, which is the true form, and then east and west touch one another, and all are one. So consider man's life aright to be a circle, *Pulvis es* and *in pulverem reverteris*, "Dust thou art and to dust thou must return"; *nudus egressus, nudus revertar*, "Naked, I came, and naked I must go"; in this circle, the two points meet, the womb and the grave are but one point, they make but one station, there is but a step from that to this. This brought in that custom amongst the Greek emperors that ever at the day of their coronation they were presented with several sorts of marble that they might then bespeak their tomb. And this brought in that custom into the primitive church that they called the martyrs' days

wherein they suffered *natalitia martyrum*, their birthdays; birth and death is all one.

Their death was a birth to them into another life, into the glory of God; it ended one circle and created another; for immortality and eternity is a circle too; not a circle where two points meet but a circle made at once; this life is a circle made with a compass that passes from point to point; that life is a circle stamped with a print, an endless and perfect circle as soon as it begins. Of this circle the mathematician is our great and good God; the other circle we make up ourselves; we bring the cradle and grave together by a course of nature. . . .

As every man must die, so every man may see that he must die; as it cannot be avoided, so it may be understood. A beast dies, but he does not see death; St. Basil says he saw an ox weep for the death of his yokefellow; but St. Basil might mistake the occasion of that ox's tears. Many men die too and yet do not see death; the approaches of death amaze and stupefy them; they feel no collucation with powers and principalities upon their death-bed; that is true; they feel no terrors in their consciences, no apprehensions of judgment, upon their death-bed; that is true; and this we call going away like a lamb. But the Lamb of God had a sorrowful sense of death; his soul was heavy unto death, and he had an apprehension that his Father had forsaken him. . . .

If I can say that the blood of the Savior runs in my veins, that the breath of his Spirit quickens all my purposes, that all my deaths have their resurrection, all my sins their remorses, all my rebellions their reconciliations, I will hearken no more after this question; as it is intended *de morte naturali*, of a natural death, I know I must die that death; what care I? nor *de morte spirituali*, the death of sin, I know I do and shall die so; why despair I? But I will find out another death, *mortem raptus*, a death of rapture and of ecstasy, that death which St. Paul died more than once, the death which St. Gregory speaks of, *divina contemplatio quoddam sepulchrum animæ*. The contemplation of God and heaven is a kind of burial and sepulchre and rest of the soul; and in this death of rapture and ecstasy, in this death of the contemplation of my interest in my Savior I shall find myself and all my sins interred and entombed in his wounds, and like a lily in paradise out of red earth I shall see my soul rise out of his blade in a candor and in an innocence contracted there acceptable in the sight of his Father.[27]

26 Sermon xlvi, folio of 1640.

27 Sermon xxvii, folio of 1640.

DAMNATION

WHEN God who is all blessing hath learned to curse us and being of himself spread as an universal honeycomb over all takes an impression, a tincture, an infusion, of gall from us, what extraction of wormwood can be so bitter, what exaltation of fire can be so raging, what multiplying of talents can be so heavy, what stiffness of destiny can be so inevitable, what confection of gnawing worms, of gnashing teeth, of howling cries, of scalding brimstone, of palpable darkness can be so, so insupportable, so inexpressible, so unimaginable as the curse and malediction of God?[28]

"It is a fearful thing to fall into the hands of the living God"; but to fall out of the hands of the living God is a horror beyond our expression, beyond our imagination.

That God should let my soul fall out of his hand into a bottomless pit and roll an unremovable stone upon it and leave it to that which it finds there (and it shall find that there which it never imagined till it came thither) and never think more of that soul, never have more to do with it; that of that providence of God that studies the life of every weed and worm and ant and spider and toad and viper there should never, never any beam flow out upon me; that that God who looked upon me when I was nothing and called me when I was not, as though I had been, out of the womb and depth of darkness, will not look upon me now when though a miserable and banished and damned creature, yet I am his creature still and contribute something to his glory even in my damnation; that that God who hath often looked upon me in my foulest uncleanness and when I had shut out the eye of day, the sun, and the eye of the night, the taper, and the eyes of all the world with curtains and windows and doors did yet see me and see me in mercy by making me see that he saw me and sometimes brought me to a present remorse and for that time to a forbearing of that sin, should so turn himself from me to his glorious saints and angels as that no saint nor angel nor Christ Jesus himself should ever pray him to look towards me, never remember him that such a soul there is; that that God who hath so often said to my soul, *Quare morieris?* why wilt thou die? and so often sworn to my soul, *Vivit Dominus*, as the Lord liveth, I would not have thee die but live, will neither let me die nor let

me live, but die an everlasting life and live an everlasting death; that that God who, when he could not get into me by standing and knocking, by his ordinary means of entering, by his word, his mercies, hath applied his judgments and hath shaked the house, this body, with agues and palsies, and set this house on fire with fevers and calentures and frighted the master of the house, my soul, with horrors and heavy apprehensions and so made an entrance into me; that that God should frustrate all his own purposes and practices upon me and leave me and cast me away as though I had cost him nothing; that this God at last should let this soul go away as a smoke, as a vapor, as a bubble; and that then this soul cannot be a smoke, a vapor, nor a bubble but must lie in darkness as long as the Lord of light is light itself, and never spark of that light reach to my soul; what Tophet is not paradise, what brimstone is not amber, what gnashing is not a comfort, what gnawing of the worm is not a tickling, what torment is not a marriage-bed to this damnation, to be secluded eternally, eternally, eternally from the sight of God?[29]

THE RESURRECTION OF THE BODY

NO MAN is superannuated in the grave that he is too old to enter into heaven where the master of the house is the ancient of days. No man is bed-rid with age in the grave that he cannot rise. It is not with God as it is with man; we do, but God does not forget the dead; and as long as God is with them they are with him. "As he puts all thy tears into his bottles," so he puts all the grains of thy dust into his cabinet, and the winds that scatter, the waters that wash them away carry them not out of his sight. "He remembers that we are but dust," but dust then when we lie in the grave; and yet he remembers us. But his memory goes farther than so; he remembers that we were but dust alive at our best; "They die," says David, "and they return to their own dust." It is not an entering into a new state when they die, but a returning to their old; they return to dust; and it is not to that dust which is cast upon them in the grave, for that may be another man's dust, but to that dust which they carried about them in their bodies; they return, and to dust, and to their own dust.[30]

28 Sermon xxvi, folio of 1649.

29 Sermon lxxvii, folio of 1640.
30 Sermon xxvi, folio of 1640.

In the general resurrection upon natural death God shall work upon this dispersion of our scattered dust as in the first fall, which is the divorce by way of reunion, and in the second, which is putrefaction, by way of reformation; so in this third, which is dispersion, by way of recollection; where man's buried flesh hath brought forth grass and that grass fed beasts and those beasts fed men and those men fed other men, God that knows in which box of his cabinet all this seed-pearl lies, in what corner of the world every atom, every grain of every man's dust sleeps, shall recollect that dust and then recompact that body and then reinanimate that man.[31]

Where be all the atoms of that flesh which a corrosive hath eaten away or a consumption hath breathed and exhaled away from our arms and other limbs? In what wrinkle, in what furrow, in what bowel of the earth lie all the grains of the ashes of a body burnt a thousand years since? In what corner, in what ventricle of the sea lies all the jelly of a body drowned in the general Flood? What coherence, what sympathy, what dependence maintains any relation, any correspondence, between that arm that was lost in Europe and that leg that was lost in Africa or Asia scores of years between? One humor of our dead body produces worms, and those worms suck and exhaust all other humor, and then all dies, and all dries and molders into dust, and that dust is blown into the river, and that puddled water tumbled into the sea, and that ebbs and flows in infinite revolutions, and still, still God knows in what cabinet every seed-pearl lies, in what part of the world every grain of every man's dust lies; and *sibilat populum suum*, as his prophet speaks in another case, he whispers, he hisses, and he beckons for the bodies of his saints, and in the twinkling of an eye that body that was scattered over all the elements is set down at the right hand of God in a glorious resurrection. A dropsy hath extended me to an enormous corpulency and unwieldiness; a consumption hath attenuated me to a feeble macilency[32] and leanness, and God raises me a body such as it should have been if these infirmities had not intervened and deformed it.[33]

Here a bullet will ask a man, where's your arm? and a wolf will ask a woman, where's your breast? A sentence in the Star-Chamber will ask him, where's your

ear,[34] and a month's close prison will ask him, where's your flesh? A fever will ask him, where's your red? and a morphew[35] will ask him, where's your white? But when after all this, . . . "I shall see God," I shall see him in my flesh, which shall be mine as inseparably —in the effect, though not in the manner—as the hypostatical union of God and man in Christ makes our nature and Godhead one person in him. My flesh shall no more be none of mine than Christ shall not be man as well as God.[36]

AT THE BIER OF A KING

WHEN you shall find that hand that had signed to one of you a patent for title, to another for pension, to another for pardon, to another for dispensation, dead; that hand that settled possessions by his seal in the Keeper and rectified honors by the sword in his Marshall and distributed relief to the poor in his Almoner and health to the diseased by his immediate touch,[37] dead; that hand that balanced his own three kingdoms so equally as that none of them complained of one another nor of him, and carried the keys of all the Christian world[38] and locked up and let out armies in their due season, dead; how poor, how faint, how pale, how momentary, how transistory, how empty, how frivolous, how dead things, must you necessarily think titles and possessions and favors and all when you see that hand which was the hand of destiny, of Christian destiny, of the Almighty God, lie dead? It was not so hard a hand when we touched it last nor so cold a hand when we kissed it last. That hand which was wont to wipe away all tears from our eyes doth now but press and squeeze us as so many sponges filled one with one, another with another cause of tears. . . .

When you have performed this *ingredimini*, that you have gone in and mourned upon him, and performed the *egredimini*, you have gone forth and laid his sacred body in consecrated dust and come to another *egredimini*, to a going forth in many several ways; some to the service of their new master and some to the enjoying of their fortunes conferred by their old; some to the raising of new hopes; some to the burying of old

31 Sermon xxi, folio of 1640.   32 Emaciation.
33 Sermon i, folio of 1649.

34 The inhuman custom of cutting off a man's ears for seditious utterance was quite common in the century.
35 A scurfy eruption.   36 Sermon xiv, folio of 1649.
37 English monarchs as late as Anne touched those afflicted with scrofula, the "King's evil."
38 James was "Defender of the Faith."

and all; some to new and busy endeavors in court; some to contented retirings in the country; let none of us go so far from him or from one another in any of our ways but that all we that have served him may meet once a day, the first time we see the sun, in the ears of Almighty God, with humble and hearty prayer that he will be pleased to hasten that day in which it shall be an addition, even to the joy of that place as perfect as it is, and as infinite as it is, to see that face again, and to see those eyes open there which we have seen closed here. Amen.[39]

TO THE HONORABLE COMPANY OF THE VIRGINIAN PLANTATION, 1622

BELOVED in him whose kingdom and Gospel you seek to advance in this plantation, our Lord and Savior Christ Jesus, if you seek to establish a temporal kingdom there, you are not rectified if you seek to be kings in either acceptation of the word; to be a king signifies liberty and independency and supremacy, to be under no man, and to be a king signifies abundance and omnisufficiency, to need no man. If those that govern there would establish such a government as should not depend upon this, or if those that go thither propose to themselves an exemption from laws, to live at their liberty; this is to be kings, to divest allegiance, to be under no man. And if those that adventure thither propose to themselves present benefit and profit, a sudden way to be rich and an abundance of all desirable commodities from thence, this is to be sufficient of themselves and to need no man; and to be under no man and to need no man are the two acceptations of being kings. Whom liberty draws to go, or present profit draws to adventure, are not yet in the right way. O if you could once bring a catechism to be as good ware amongst them as a bugle, as a knife, as a hatchet! O if you would be as ready to hearken at the return of a ship, how many Indians were converted to Christ Jesus, as what trees or drugs or dyes that ship

had brought, then you were in your right way, and not till then; liberty and abundance are characters of kingdoms, and a kingdom is excluded in the text; the apostles were not to look for it in their employment nor you in this your plantation. . . .

God says to you, no kingdom, not ease, not abundance; nay, nothing at all yet; the plantation shall not discharge the charges, not defray itself yet; but yet already now at first it shall conduce to great uses; it shall redeem many a wretch from the jaws of death,[40] from the hands of the executioner, upon whom perchance a small fault or perchance a first fault or perchance a fault heartily and sincerely repented, perchance no fault but malice had otherwise cast a present and ignominious death. It shall sweep your streets and wash your doors from idle persons and the children of idle persons, and employ them. And truly, if the whole country were but such a Bridewell[41] to force idle persons to work, it has a good use. But it is already not only a spleen to drain the ill humors of the body, but a liver to breed good blood; already the employment breeds mariners; already the place gives assays,[42] nay, freights of merchantable commodities; already it is a mark for the envy and for the ambition of our enemies. I speak but of our doctrinal, not national enemies. As they are Papists they are sorry we have this country; and surely twenty lectures in matter of controversy do not so much vex them as one ship that goes and strengthens that plantation. Neither can I recommend it to you by any better rhetoric than their malice. They would gladly have it, and therefore let us be glad to hold it. . . .

Those amongst you that are old now shall pass out of this world with this great comfort that you contributed to the beginning of that commonwealth and of that church, though they live not to see the growth thereof to perfection. Apollos[43] watered but Paul planted; he that began the work was the greater man. And you that are young now may live to see the enemy as much impeached by that place and your friends, yea, children as well accommodated in that place as any other. You shall have made this island which is but as the suburbs of the Old World a bridge, a gallery to the New, to join all to that world that shall never grow old, the kingdom of heaven; you shall add

---

39 From Sermon xxxiii, folio of 1649, "preached at Denmark House, some few days before the body of King James was removed thence, to his burial, Apr. 26, 1625." The death of James I was to Donne, as it was to George Herbert and many another man of letters and religion, a personal tragedy. It is one of Donne's best sermons that he preaches here by the body of his friend.

40 An allusion to the practice, soon to grow to greater proportions, of populating the New World plantations out of English prisons.

41 A famous London prison.   42 Returns of profit.

43 Successor of Paul at Corinth; see I Corinthians 3:4–6.

persons to this kingdom and to the kingdom of heaven and add names to the books of our chronicles and to the book of life. . . .

When I by way of exhortation all this while have seemed to tell you what should be done by you, I have, indeed, but told the congregation what hath been done already. Neither do I speak to move a wheel that stood still, but to keep the wheel in due motion; nor persuade you to begin, but to continue a good work; nor propose foreign, but your own examples to do still as you have done hitherto. For for that, that which is especially in my contemplation, the conversion of the people, as I have received so I can give this testimony that of those persons who have sent in moneys and concealed their names the greatest part, almost all have limited their devotion and contribution upon that point, the propagation of religion and the conversion of the people, for the building and beautifying of the house of God and for the instruction and education of their young children. Christ Jesus himself "is yesterday and today and the same forever." In the advancing of his glory be you so too, yesterday and today and the same forever here; and hereafter, when time shall be no more, no more yesterday, no more today, yet forever and ever you shall enjoy that joy and that glory which no ill accident can attain to diminish or eclipse it.44

GUY FAWKES DAY

WHY did these men rage and imagine a vain thing? What they did historically we know; they made that house which is the hive of the kingdom from whence all her honey comes, that house where justice herself is conceived in their preparing of laws and inanimated and quickened and born by the royal assent there given, they made that whole house one murdering piece and charged that piece with peers, with people, with princes, with the king and meant to discharge it upward at the face of heaven, to shoot God at the face of God, him of whom God hath saith, *Dii estis*, you are gods, at the face of God that had said so, as though

they would have reproached the God of heaven and not have been beholden to him for such a king, but shoot him up to him and bid him take his king again with a *nolumus hunc regnare*, we will not have this king to reign over us.45

THE DIVIDED MIND

I NEGLECT God and his angels for the noise of a fly, for the rattling of a coach, for the whining of a door; I talk on in the same posture of praying, eyes lifted up, knees bowed down, as though I prayed to God; and if God or his angels should ask me when I thought last of God in that prayer, I cannot tell. Sometimes I find that I had forgot what I was about, but when I began to forget it I cannot tell. A memory of yesterday's pleasures, a fear of tomorrow's dangers, a straw under my knee, a noise in mine ear, a light in mine eye, an anything, a nothing, a fancy, a chimera in my brain troubles me in my prayer. So certainly is there nothing, nothing in spiritual things perfect in this world.46

THE WORLD A MUSICAL INSTRUMENT

GOD made this whole world in such an uniformity, such a correspondency, such a concinnity of parts as that it was an instrument perfectly in tune. We may say the trebles, the highest strings were disordered first; the best understandings, angels and men, put this instrument out of tune. God rectified all again by putting in a new string, *semen mulieris*, the seed of the woman, the Messias. And only by sounding that string in your ears become we *musicum carmen*, true music, true harmony, true peace to you.47

Heaven and earth are as a musical instrument; if you touch a string below, the motion goes to the top. Any good done to Christ's poor members upon earth affects him in heaven.48

44 This sermon, preached November 13, 1622, was printed three times in Donne's lifetime; it is not found in the folios. It has been called by Jessop "the first missionary sermon ever preached in England since Britain became a Christian land." The deputy treasurer of this Virginian Company was the saintly Nicholas Ferrar, friend and publisher of George Herbert.

45 Sermon xliii, folio of 1649. This sermon, preached on the fifth of November, "Gunpowder Day," 1622, took the fancy of King James, and he ordered Donne to write him out a copy of it from his notes. Donne intended it for Paul's Cross, the outdoor preaching place which suited the Dean well because of the crowds that pressed to hear him; but inclement weather forced him to give it in the Cathedral.

46 Sermon lxxx, folio of 1640.

47 Sermon ii, folio of 1660.

48 Sermon x, folio of 1660.

THE LAMP OF CHRIST EXTINGUISHED BY REASON

THEY had a precious composition for lamps amongst the ancients, reserved especially for tombs, which kept light for many hundreds of years; we have had in our age experience in some casual openings of ancient vaults of finding such lights as were kindled, as appeared by their inscriptions, fifteen or sixteen hundred years before; but as soon as that light comes to our light it vanishes. So this eternal and this supernatural light, Christ and faith, enlightens, warms, purges, and does all the profitable offices of fire and light if we keep it in the right sphere, in the proper place, that is, if we consist in points necessary to salvation and revealed in the Scripture; but when we bring this light to the common light of reason, to our inferences and consequences, it may be in danger to vanish itself and perchance extinguish our reason too; we may search so far and reason so long of faith and grace as that we may lose not only them but even our reason too and sooner become mad than good.[49]

THE NEED OF FAITH

IF I twist a cable of infinite fathoms in length, if there be no ship to ride by it nor anchor to hold it by, what use is there of it? If manor thrust manor and title flow into title and bags pour out into chests, if I have no anchor—faith in Christ, if I have not a ship to carry to haven—a soul to save, what's my long cable to me? If I add number to number, a span, a mile long, if at the end of all that long line of numbers, there be nothing that notes pounds or crowns or shillings, what's that long number but so many millions of millions of nothing? If my span of life become a mile of life, my penny a pound, my pint a gallon, my acre a shire, yet if there be nothing of the next world at the end, so much peace of conscience, so much joy, so much glory, still all is but nothing multiplied, and that is still nothing at all.[50]

THE FOLLY OF THE ATHEIST

POOR intricated soul! Riddling, perplexed, labyrinthical soul! Thou couldst not say that thou believest

49 Sermon xxxvi, folio of 1649.
50 Sermon xxxi, folio of 1649.

not in God if there were no God! Thou couldst not believe in God if there were no God! If there were no God, thou couldst not speak, thou couldst not think, not a word, not a thought, no, not against God! Thou couldst not blaspheme the name of God, thou couldst not swear if there were no God! For all thy faculties however depraved and perverted by thee are from him; and except thou canst seriously believe that thou art nothing, thou canst not believe that there is no God. If I should ask thee at a tragedy where thou shouldst see him that hath drawn blood lie weltering and surrounded in his own blood, is there a God now? if thou couldst answer me, no, these are but inventions and representations of men, and I believe a God never the more for this; if I should ask thee at a sermon where thou shouldst hear the judgments of God formerly denounced and executed, re-denounced and applied to present occasions, is there a God now? if thou couldst answer me, no, these are but inventions of state to supple and regulate congregations and keep people in order, and I believe a God never the more for this; be as confident as thou canst in company, for company is the atheist's sanctuary; I respite thee not till the day of judgment when I may see thee upon thy knees, upon thy face begging of the hills that they would fall down and cover thee from the fierce wrath of God to ask thee then, is there a God now? I respite thee not till the day of thine own death, when thou shalt have evidence enough that there is a God, though no other evidence but to find a Devil, and evidence enough that there is a heaven, though no other evidence but to feel hell, to ask thee then, is there a God now? I respite thee but a few hours, but six hours, but till midnight. Wake then; and then dark and alone hear God ask thee then, remember that I asked thee now, is there a God? And if thou darest, say no.[51]

SANCTIFIED PASSIONS

AS THE prophets and the other secretaries of the Holy Ghost in penning the books of the Scriptures do for the most part retain and express in their writings some impressions and some air of their former professions, those that had been bred in courts and cities, those that had been shepherds and herdsmen, those that had been fishers, and so of the rest, ever inserting into their writings some phrases, some metaphors, some allusions taken from that profession which they had

51 Sermon xlviii, folio of 1640.

exercised before; so that soul that hath been transported upon any particular worldly pleasure, when it is entirely turned upon God and in the contemplation of his all-sufficiency and abundance, doth find in God fit subject and just occasion to exercise the same affection piously and religiously which had before so sinfully transported and possessed it.

A covetous person who is now truly converted to God, he will exercise a spiritual covetousness still, he will desire to have him all, he will have a good security, the seal and assurance of the Holy Ghost; and he will have his security often renewed by new testimonies and increases of those graces in him; he will have witnesses enough, he will have the testimony of all the world by his good life and conversation; he will gain every way at God's hand; he will have wages of God, for he will be his servant; he will have a portion from God, for he will be his son; he will have a reversion, he will be sure that his name is in the book of life; he will have pawns, the seals of the sacraments, nay, he will have a present possession; all that God hath promised, all that Christ hath purchased, all that the Holy Ghost hath the stewardship and dispensation of, he will have all in present by the appropriation and investiture of an actual and applying faith; a covetous person converted will be spiritually covetous still.

So will a voluptuous man who is turned to God find plenty and deliciousness enough in him to feed his soul as with marrow and fatness, as David expresses it; and so an angry and passionate man will find zeal enough in the house of God to eat him up.[52]

THE UPRIGHT MAN

If I had a secular glass, a glass that would run an age,[53] if the two hemispheres of the world were composed in the form of such a glass and all the world calcined and burnt to ashes and all the ashes and sands and atoms of the world put into that glass, it would not be enough to tell the godly man what his treasure and the object of his heart is. A parrot or a stare,[54] docile birds and of pregnant imitation, will sooner be brought to relate us the wisdom of a council table than any Ambrose or

any Chrysostom, men that have gold and honey in their names, shall tell us what the sweetness, what the treasure of heaven is, and what that man's peace that hath set his heart upon that treasure.[55]

That soul that is accustomed to direct herself to God upon every occasion, that as a flower at sun-rising conceives a sense of God in every beam of his and spreads and dilates itself towards him in a thankfulness in every small blessing that he sheds upon her, that soul that as a flower at the sun's declining contracts and gathers in and shuts up herself as though she had received a blow whensoever she hears her Savior wounded by an oath or blasphemy or execration, that soul who, whatsoever string be strucken in her, bass or treble, her high or her low estate, is ever turned toward God, that soul prays sometimes when it does not know it prays.[56]

When thou kneelest down at thy bedside to shut up the day at night or to begin it in the morning, thy servants, thy children, thy little flock about thee, there thou buildest a church too. And therefore sanctify that place, wash it with thy tears and with a repentant consideration that in that bed thy children were conceived in sin, that in that bed thou hast turned marriage which God afforded thee for remedy and physic to voluptuousness and licentiousness, that thou hast made that bed which God gave thee for rest and for reparation of thy weary body to be as thy dwelling and delight and the bed of idleness and stupidity.[57]

Upon this earth a man cannot possibly make one step in a straight and a direct line. The earth itself being round, every step we make upon it must necessarily be a segment, an arc of a circle. But yet though no piece of a circle be a straight line, yet if we take any piece, nay, if we take the whole circle, there is no corner, no angle in any piece in any entire circle. A perfect rectitude we cannot have in any ways in this world; in every calling there are some inevitable temptations. But though we cannot make up our circle of a straight line—that is impossible to human frailty; yet we may pass on without angles and corners, that is, without disguises in our religion and without the love of craft and falsehood and circumvention in our civil actions. A compass is a necessary thing in a ship, and the help of that compass brings the ship home

52 Sermon xviii, folio of 1660.
53 An hourglass. Donne had one by him as he preached; he often alludes to it; in many of his sermons he reversed it.
54 A starling. Like the parrot, it could be taught to mimic very simple words.

55 Sermon v, folio of 1660.
56 Sermon ix, folio of 1640.
57 Sermon xi, folio of 1649.

safe, and yet that compass hath some variation, it doth not look directly north; neither is that star which we call the North Pole or by which we know the North Pole the very pole itself; but we call it so, and we make our uses of it and our conclusions by it as if it were so because it is the nearest star to that pole. He that comes as near uprightness as infirmities admit is an upright man, though he have some obliquities. To God himself we may always go in a direct line, a straight, a perpendicular line; for God is vertical to me over my head now and vertical now to them that are in the East and West Indies; to our Antipodes, to them that are under our feet, God is vertical over their heads then when he is over us.[58]

Find God pleased with thee, and thou hast a hook in the nostrils of every Leviathan, power cannot shake thee; thou hast a wood to cast into the waters of Marah, the bitterness of the times cannot hurt thee; thou hast a rock to dwell upon, and the dream of a fortune's wheel cannot overturn thee. But if the Lord be angry, he needs no trumpets to call armies; if he do but *sibilare muscam*, hiss and whisper for the fly and the bee, there is nothing so little in his hand as cannot discomfort thee, discomfit thee, dissolve and pour out, attenuate and annihilate the very marrow of thy soul. Everything is his, and therefore everything is he.[59]

THE UNFADING FLOWER

THEN was there truly a rose amongst thorns when through his crown of thorns you might see his title *Iesus Nazarenus*. For in that very name *Nazarenus* is involved the signification of a flower; the very word signifies a flower. Isaiah's flower in the crown of pride fades and is removed; this flower in the crown of thorns fades not nor could be removed; for, for all the importunity of the Jews, Pilate would not suffer that title to be removed or to be changed.[60]

THE PARADOX OF CHRIST

THAT that Jesus whose father and mother and brothers and sisters they knew must be believed to be of another family and to have a father in another place

and yet he to be as old as his father, and to have another proceeding from him and yet he to be no older than that person who proceeded from him; that that Jesus whom they knew to be that carpenter's son and knew his work must be believed to have set up a frame that reached to heaven out of which no man could and in which any man might be saved; was it not as easy to believe that those tears which they saw upon his cheeks were pearls, that those drops of blood which they saw upon his back were rubies, that that spittle which they saw upon his face was enamel, that those hands which they saw buffet him were reached out to place him in a throne, and that that voice which they heard cry, *crucifige*, "Crucify him," was a *vivat rex*, "Long live Jesus of Nazareth, King of the Jews," as to believe that from that man, that worm and no man, ingloriously traduced as a conjurer, ingloriously apprehended as a thief, ingloriously executed as a traitor, they should look for glory and all glory and everlasting glory?[61]

THE IMAGE OF GOD

NO IMAGE but the image of God can fit our soul. Every other seal is too narrow, too shallow for it. The magistrate is sealed with the lion; the wolf will not fit that seal. The magistrate hath a power in his hands, but not oppression. Princes are sealed with the crown; the mitre will not fit that seal. Powerfully and graciously they protect the church and are supreme heads of the church; but they minister not the sacraments of the church. They give preferments but they give not the capacity of preferment. They give order who shall have; but they give not orders by which they are enabled to have that have. Men of inferior and laborious callings in the world are sealed with the cross; a rose or a bunch of grapes will not answer that seal. Ease and plenty in age must not be looked for without crosses and labor and industry in youth. All men, prince and people, clergy and magistrate are sealed with the image of God, with the profession of a conformity to him. And worldly seals will not answer that nor fill up that seal. We should wonder to see a mother in the midst of many sweet children passing her time in making babies and puppets for her own delight. We should wonder to see a man whose chambers and galleries were full of curious masterpieces thrust in a village fair to look upon six-penny pictures and

58 Sermon lxvii, folio of 1640.
59 Sermon xx, folio of 1649.
60 Sermon xxxiii, folio of 1649.

61 Sermon iv, folio of 1660.

three-farthing prints. We have all the image of God at home, and we all make babies, fancies of honor, in our ambitions. The masterpiece is our own, in our own bosom; and we thrust in country fairs, that is, we endure the distempers of any unseasonable weather in night-journeys and watchings. We endure the oppositions and scorns and triumphs of a rival and competitor that seeks with us and shares with us. We endure the guiltiness and reproach of having deceived the trust which a confident friend reposes in us and solicit his wife or daughter. We endure the decay of fortune, of body, of soul, of honor, to possess lower pictures, pictures that are not originals, not made by the hand of God, nature, but artificial beauties. And for that body we give a soul, and for that drug which might have been bought where they bought it for a shilling we give an estate. The image of God is more worth than all substances; and we give it for colors, for dreams, for shadows.[62]

GOD IN ALL THINGS

HERE God shows this inconsiderate man his book of creatures, which he may run and read; that is, he may go forward in his vocation and yet see that every creature calls him to a consideration of God. Every ant that he sees asks him, where had I this providence and industry? Every flower that he sees asks him, where had I this beauty, this fragrancy, this medicinal virtue in me? Every creature calls him to consider what great things God hath done in little subjects. But God opens to him also here in his church his book of Scriptures; and in that book every word cries out to him, every merciful promise cries to him, why am I here to meet thee, to wait upon thee, to perform God's purpose towards thee if thou never consider me, never apply me to thyself? Every judgment of his anger cries out, why am I here if thou respect me not, if thou make not thy profit of performing those conditions which are annexed to those judgments and which thou mightst perform if thou wouldst consider it? Yea, here God opens another book to him, his manual, his bosom, his pocket book, his *vade mecum*, the abridgment of all nature and all law, his own heart and conscience. And this book, though he shut it up and clasp it never so hard, yet it will sometimes burst open of itself; though he interline it with other studies and knowledges, yet

the text itself in the book itself, the testimonies of the conscience, will shine through and appear.[63]

THE BOOKS OF GOD

ALL other authors we distinguish by tomes, by parts, by volumes; but who knows the volumes of this author, how many volumes of spheres involve one another, how many tomes of God's creatures there are? Hast thou not room, hast thou not money, hast thou not understanding, hast thou not leisure for great volumes, for the books of heaven, for the mathematics? nor for the books of courts, the politics? Take but the georgics, the consideration of the earth, a farm, a garden, nay, seven foot of earth, a grave; and that will be book enough. Go lower; every worm in the grave; lower; every weed upon the grave is an abridgment of all. Nay, lock up all doors and windows, see nothing but thyself; nay let thyself be locked up in a close prison that thou canst not see thyself, and do but feel thy pulse; let thy pulse be intermitted and stupefied that thou feel not that. And do but think; and a worm, a weed, thyself, thy pulse, thy thought, are all testimonies that all, this all and all the parts thereof are *opus*, a work made, and *opus eius*, his work, made by God.[64]

THE SIGHT OF GOD

AMOROUS soul, ambitious soul, covetous soul, voluptuous soul, what wouldst thou have in heaven? What doth thy holy amorousness, thy holy covetousness, thy holy ambition, and voluptuousness most carry thy desire upon? Call it what thou wilt; think it what thou canst; think it something that thou canst not think; and all this thou shalt have if thou have any resurrection unto life.[65]

As it is said of old cosmographers that when they had said all that they knew of a country and yet much more was to be said, they said that the rest of those countries were possessed with giants or witches or spirits or wild beasts so that they could pierce no farther into that country; so when we have traveled as far as we can with safety, that is, as far as ancient or

---

62 Sermon xxix, folio of 1649.

63 Sermon xxx, folio of 1640.
64 Sermon xxxi, folio of 1649.
65 Sermon xxii, folio of 1640.

modern expositors lead us in the discovery of these new heavens and new earth, yet we must say at last that it is a country inhabited with angels and archangels, with cherubims and seraphims, and that we can look no farther into it with these eyes. Where it is locally, we inquire not; we rest in this, that it is the habitation prepared for the blessed saints of God; heavens where the moon is more glorious than our sun and the sun as glorious as he that made it; for it is he himself, the Son of God, the sun of glory. A new earth where all their waters are milk and all their milk, honey; where all their grass is corn and all their corn, manna; where all their glebe, all there clods of earth are gold and all their gold of innumerable carats; where all their minutes are ages and all their ages, eternity; where everything is every minute in the highest exaltation, as good as it can be and yet superexalted and infinitely multiplied by every minute's addition; every minute infinitely better than ever it was before. Of these new heavens and this new earth we must say at last that we can say nothing; for, "The eye of man hath not seen nor ear heard nor heart conceived the state of this place." We limit and determine our consideration with that horizon with which the Holy Ghost hath limited us, that it is that new heavens and new earth "wherein dwelleth righteousness."

Here then the Holy Ghost intends the same new heavens and new earth which he does in the Apocalypse and describes there by another name, the new Jerusalem. But here the Holy Ghost does not proceed as there to enamor us of the place by a promise of improvement of those things which we have and love here, but by a promise of that which here we have not at all. There and elsewhere the Holy Ghost applies himself to the natural affections of men. To those that are affected with riches he says that that new city shall be all gold and in the foundations all manner of precious stones; to those that are affected with beauty he promises an everlasting association with that beautiful couple, that fair pair, which spend their time in that contemplation and that protestation, *Ecce, tu pulchra, dilecta mea; ecce, tu pulcher;* "Behold, thou art fair, my beloved," says he; and then she replies, "Behold, thou art fair too"; noting the mutual complacency between Christ and his church there. To those which delight in music he promises continual singing and every minute a new song. To those whose thoughts are exercised upon honor and titles, civil or ecclesiastical, he promises priesthood, and if that be not honor enough, a royal priesthood. And to those who look after military honor, triumph after their victory in the militant church. And to those that are carried with sumptuous and magnific feasts, a marriage supper of the Lamb where not only all the rarities of the whole world but the whole world itself shall be served in; the whole world shall be brought to that fire and served at that table. But here the Holy Ghost proceeds not that way, by improvement of things, which we have and love here, riches or beauty or music or honor or feasts; but by an everlasting possession of that which we hunger and thirst and pant after here and cannot compass, that is, justice or righteousness; for both these our present word denotes, and both these we want here and shall have both forever in these new heavens and new earth.[66]

"No man ever saw God and lived"; and yet I shall not live till I see God; and when I have seen him I shall never die. What have I ever seen in this world that hath been truly the same thing that it seemed to me? I have seen marble buildings, and a chip, a crust, a plaster, a face of marble hath pilled[67] off, and I see brick bowels within. I have seen beauty, and a strong breath from another tells me that that complexion is from without, not from a sound constitution within. I have seen the state of princes, and all that is but ceremony; and I would be loth to put a master of ceremonies to define ceremony and tell me what it is and to include so various a thing as ceremony in so constant a thing as a definition. I see a great officer, and I see a man of mine own profession, of great revenues; and I see not the interest of the money that was paid for it, I see not the pensions nor the annuities that are charged upon that office or that church. As he that fears God fears nothing else so he that sees God sees everything else. When we shall see God *sicut est*, as he is, we shall see all things *sicut sunt*, as they are; for that's their essence as they conduce to his glory. We shall be no more deluded with outward appearances. For when this sight which we intend here comes, there will be no delusory thing to be seen. All that we have made as though we saw in this world will be vanished, and I shall see nothing but God and what is in him; and him

---

66 From the sermon which Donne preached, and Walton heard Donne "weep and preach," at the funeral of Magdalen Herbert, Lady Danvers, mother of George Herbert and lifelong friend and benefactress of Donne. Some of Donne's finest verses were addressed to her; it was at her house in Chelsea that Donne took refuge from the plague in 1625.

67 Shed.

I shall see *in carne*, in the flesh, which is another degree of exaltation in mine exaltation.

I shall see him *in carne sua*, in his flesh. And this was one branch in St. Augustine's great wish that he might have seen Rome in her state, that he might have heard St. Paul preach, that he might have seen Christ in the flesh. St. Augustine hath seen Christ in the flesh one thousand two hundred years, in Christ's glorified flesh; but it is with the eyes of his understanding and in his soul. Our flesh, even in the resurrection, cannot be a spectacle, a perspective glass to our soul. We shall see the humanity of Christ with our bodily eyes then glorified; but that flesh, though glorified, cannot make us see God better nor clearer than the soul alone hath done all the time from our death to our resurrection. But as an indulgent father or as a tender mother when they go to see the king in any solemnity or any other thing of observation and curiosity delights to carry their child which is flesh of their flesh and bone of their bone with them, and though the child cannot comprehend it as well as they, they are as glad that the child sees it as that they see it themselves; such a gladness shall my soul have that this flesh, which she will no longer call her prison nor her tempter but her friend, her companion, her wife, that this flesh, that is, I, in the reunion and redintegration of both parts shall see God; for then one principal clause in her rejoicing and acclamation shall be that this flesh is her flesh; *in carne mea*, "in my flesh I shall see God." [68]

Erimus sicut angeli, says Christ, "There we shall be as angels." The knowledge which I have by nature shall have no clouds; here it hath. That which I have by grace shall have no reluctance, no resistance; here it hath. That which I have by revelation shall have no suspicion, no jealousy; here it hath. Sometimes it is hard to distinguish between a respiration from God and a suggestion from the Devil. There our curiosity shall have this noble satisfaction, we shall know how the angels know by knowing as they know. We shall not pass from author to author as in a grammar school nor from art to art as in an university; but as that general which knighted his whole army God shall create us all doctors in a minute. That great liberty, those infinite volumes of the books of creatures, shall be taken away, quite away; no more nature; those reverend manuscripts written with God's own hand, the Scriptures themselves, shall be taken away, quite away; no more preaching, no more reading of Scriptures. And that great school-mistress, experience and observation, shall be removed; no new thing to be done, and in an instant I shall know more than they all could reveal unto me. I shall know not only as I know already that a bee-hive, that an ant-hill, is the same book in *decimo sexto* as a kingdom is in folio, that a flower that lives but a day is an abridgment of that king that lives out his threescore and ten years; but I shall know too that all these ants and bees and flowers and kings and kingdoms, howsoever they may be examples and comparisons to one another, yet they are all as nothing, altogether nothing, less than nothing, infinitely less than nothing to that which shall then be the subject of my knowledge, for it is the knowledge of the glory of God. [69]

What a dim vespers of a glorious festival, what a poor half-holiday is Methusalem's nine hundred years to eternity! what a poor account hath that man made that says, this land hath been in my name and in my ancestor's from the Conquest! what a yesterday is that! not six hundred years. If I could believe the transmigration of souls and think that my soul had been successively in some creature or other since the creation, what a yesterday is that! not six thousand years. What a yesterday for the past, what a tomorrow for the future is any term that can be comprehended in cipher or counters! But as how abundant a life soever any man hath in this world for temporal abundances, I have life more abundantly than he if I have the spiritual life of grace; so what measure soever I have of this spiritual life of grace in this world, I shall have that more abundantly in heaven; for there my term shall be a term for three lives, for those three, that as long as the Father and the Son and the Holy Ghost live I shall not die. [70]

How barren a thing is arithmetic! And yet arithmetic will tell you how many single grains of sand will fill this hollow vault to the firmament. How empty a thing is rhetoric! And yet rhetoric will make absent and remote things present to your understanding. How weak a thing is poetry! And yet poetry is a counterfeit creation and makes things that are not as though they were. How infirm, how impotent are all assistances if they be put to express this eternity! [71]

68 Sermon xiv, folio of 1649.

69 Sermon xxv, folio of 1660.
70 Sermon vii, folio of 1640.
71 Sermon xxvi, folio of 1640.

A state but of one day, because no night shall over-take or determine it, but such a day as is not of a thousand years, which is the longest measure in the Scriptures, but of a thousand millions of millions of generations. *Qui nec præceditur hesterno nec excluditur crastino,* a day that hath no *pridie* nor *postridie;* yesterday doth not usher it in, nor tomorrow shall not drive it out. Methusalem with all his hundreds of years was but a mushroom of a night's growth to this day, and all the four monarchies with all their thousands of years and all the powerful kings and all the beautiful queens of this world were but as a bed of flowers, some gathered at six, some at seven, some at eight, all in one morning in respect of this day. In all the two thousand years of nature before the law given by Moses and the two thousand years of law before the Gospel given by Christ and the two thousand of grace which are run-ning now—of which last hour we have heard three quarters strike, more than fifteen hundred of this last two thousand spent—in all this six thousand and in all those which God may be pleased to add, *in domo patris,* in this house of his Father's, there was never heard quarter clock to strike, never seen minute glass to turn.[72]

Heirs of heaven! which is not a gavel-kind[73]—every son, every man alike—but it is an universal primogeniture, every man full, so full as that every man hath all in such measure as that there is nothing in heaven which any man in heaven wants. Heirs of the joys of heaven! joy in a continual dilation of thy heart to receive augmentation of that which is infinite in the accumulation of essential and accidental joy. Joy in a continual melting of indissoluble bowels, in joyful and yet compassionate beholding thy Savior, rejoicing at thy being there and almost lamenting, in a kind of affection which we can call by no name, that thou couldst not come thither but by those wounds which are still wounds though wounds glorified. Heirs of the joy and heirs of the glory of heaven! where if thou look down and see kings fighting for crowns, thou canst look off as easily as from boys at stool-ball for points here, and from kings triumphing after victories as easily as a philosopher from a pageant of children here. Where thou shalt not be subject to any other title of dominion in others but Jesus of Nazareth King of the Jews, nor ambitious of any other title in thyself but that which thou possessest, to be the child of God. Heirs of joy, heirs of glory, and heirs of the eternity of heaven! where in the possession of this joy and this glory the angels which were there almost six thousand years before thee, and so prescribe, and those souls which shall come at Christ's last coming and so enter but then, shall not survive thee, but they and thou and all shall live as long as he that gives you all that life, as God himself.[74]

---

72 Sermon lxxiii, folio of 1640.

73 A system of land-tenure involving equal division of the intestate's property among all his sons, as opposed to the system of primogeniture by which the whole real estate of the intestate passes to the eldest son.

74 Sermon xxxiv, folio of 1640.

Ben Jonson

[1572?–1637]

Our chief authority for the facts of Jonson's early life is Jonson himself, in his colorful conversations with William Drummond of Hawthornden, as recorded by the latter. Jonson, the posthumous son of a minister, studied for a short time at Westminster School under William Camden, whom he was always to revere. He was obliged to work for a while at his stepfather's craft of brick-laying, and fought in the wars in the Low Countries, where, according to his own account, he killed an enemy in single combat. By 1598 he was active in the theatrical life of London as actor and playwright; his first important play, *Every Man in His Humour*, was presented in that year with Shakespeare as one of the players. It was in 1598 also that he killed a fellow actor in a duel and narrowly escaped hanging by claiming "benefit of clergy." This danger past, he was kept quite consistently in trouble by his robust and quarrelsome nature: in the early 1600's he was a prominent figure in the "War of the Theatres" with Marston and Dekker, and his part in *Eastward Ho*, with its satire against the Scots, aroused the ire of Scottish King James. In general, however, he enjoyed James's favor, and throughout most of that monarch's reign Jonson was the chief purveyor of the masques which were the staple of court entertainment—carrying on at the same time a running warfare with the architect and stage designer Inigo Jones, his chief rival in that department.

According to the *Conversations with William Drummond*, Jonson "was a Papist" for some twelve years after his imprisonment in 1598, but in 1610 he returned to the Anglican fold with little sign of spiritual conflict, draining the communion cup to symbolize the completeness of his reconciliation. Despite the sincere and simple piety of some of his religious verse, religious feeling is not one of the major wellsprings of Jonson's imposing and varied art. Greatest as a comic dramatist, he achieved in *Volpone* (1606), *Epicoene* (1609), and *The Alchemist* (1610) masterpieces quite sufficient to preserve his name as long as there is an English literature. But he inspires at least respect as a tragic dramatist, and he counts as one of the supreme masters of the lyric in the early seventeenth century. Jonson's prose, as typified by *Timber*, has the fluency, clarity, and chiseled excellence which characterize his achievement in other types of literature. The critical ideas which he expresses are, of course, not new, but they have a great deal of historical importance as being among the first manifestations of a new emphasis in the tradition of classicism —more rigorous and form-conscious than that of the Renaissance—which was to gain a slow dominance throughout the seventeenth century and achieve a complete triumph by its end.

Perhaps it was Jonson's position as the prophet of classicism which gave him such an unquestioned influence over the young poets of the earlier seventeenth century. Perhaps it was his vast erudition (although he never attended the university, he was finally awarded degrees by both Oxford and Cambridge), or his easy mastery of so many literary forms. Almost certainly it was his supremely confident, all-overpowering personality. At any rate, from his various chambers of authority in the Sun, the Dog, the Triple Tun, and the other taverns memorialized by Herrick, he exerted the powers of a literary dictator, and to be "sealed of the Tribe of Ben" was an honor coveted by almost every young poet. His declining years were saddened by illness, by neglect at court after the death of James, and by public indifference to his later plays. But he had comfort in the respect given him by the younger poets, his "sons," and in the memory of the friendship of the great contemporaries who had preceded him into death—Bacon and Chapman and Donne and Shakespeare.

C. H. HERFORD and P. SIMPSON, eds. *Ben Jonson*, 11 vols. (Oxford, 1925–52). The definitive edition.

B. JONSON. *Timber, or Discoveries* and *Conversations with William Drummond*, ed. G. B. Harrison (New York, 1923).

J. PALMER. *Ben Jonson* (New York, 1934). Biography.

M. CHUTE. *Ben Jonson of Westminster* (New York, 1953). A shorter biography.

FROM

CYNTHIA'S REVELS

[TEXT: *second edition, 1616*]

CRITES

A CREATURE of a most perfect and divine temper: one in whom the humors and elements are peaceably met, without emulation of precedency. He is neither too fantastically melancholy, too slowly phlegmatic, too lightly sanguine, nor too rashly choleric; but in all so composed and ordered as it is clear nature went about some full work, she did more than make a man when she made him. His discourse is like his behavior, uncommon, but not unpleasing; he is prodigal of neither. He strives rather to be that which men call judicious than to be thought so; and is so truly learned that he affects not to show it. He will think and speak his thought both freely; but as distant from depraving another man's merit as proclaiming his own. For his valor, 'tis such that he dares as little to offer any injury as receive one. In sum, he hath a most ingenious and sweet spirit, a sharp and seasoned wit, a straight judgment, and a strong mind. Fortune could never break him, nor make him less. He counts it his pleasure to despise pleasures, and is more delighted with good deeds than goods. It is a competency to him that he can be virtuous. He doth neither covet nor fear, he hath too much reason to do either; and that commends all things to him.

FROM

TIMBER:

Or Discoveries Made Upon Men and Matter

[TEXT: *first edition, 1641*]

CENSURA DE POETIS [1]

NOTHING in our age, I have observed, is more preposterous than the running judgments upon poetry and poets; when we shall hear those things commended and cried up for the best writings which a man would scarce vouchsafe to wrap any wholesome drug in; he would never light his tobacco with them. And those men almost named for miracles, who yet are so vile that if a man should go about to examine and correct them, he must make all they have done but one blot. Their good is so entangled with their bad as forcibly one must draw on the other's death with it. A sponge dipped in ink will do all:—

> "—— *Comitetur Punica librum*
> *Spongia.* ——" [2]

Et paulò post,

> "*Non possunt . . . multæ . . . lituræ*
> *. . . una litura potest.*" [3]

Yet their vices have not hurt them; nay, a great many they have profited, for they have been loved for nothing else. And this false opinion grows strong against the best men, if once it take root with the ignorant. Cestius, in his time, was preferred to Cicero, so far as the ignorant durst. They learned him without book, and had him often in their mouths; but a man cannot imagine that thing so foolish or rude but will find and enjoy an admirer; at least a reader or spectator. The puppets are seen now in despite of the players; Heath's [4] epigrams and the Sculler's [5] poems have their applause. There are never wanting that dare

prefer the worst preachers, the worst pleaders, the worst poets; not that the better have left to write or speak better, but that they that hear them judge worse; *Non illi pejus dicunt, sed hi corruptius judicant.* Nay, if it were put to the question of the Water-rhymer's works, against Spenser's, I doubt not but they would find more suffrages; because the most favor common vices, out of a prerogative the vulgar have to lose their judgments and like that which is naught.

Poetry, in this latter age, hath proved but a mean mistress to such as have wholly addicted themselves to her, or given their names up to her family. They who have but saluted her on the by, and now and then tendered their visits, she hath done much for, and advanced in the way of their own professions (both the law and the gospel) beyond all they could have hoped or done for themselves without her favor. Wherein she does emulate the judicious but preposterous bounty of the time's grandees, who accumulate all they can upon the parasite or freshman in their friendship; but think an old client or honest servant bound by his place to write and starve.

Indeed, the multitude commend writers as they do fencers or wrastlers, who if they come in robustiously and put for it with a deal of violence, are received for the braver fellows; when many times their own rudeness is a cause of their disgrace, and a slight touch of their adversary gives all that boisterous force the foil. But in these things the unskillful are naturally deceived, and judging wholly by the bulk, think rude things greater than polished, and scattered more numerous than composed. Nor think this only to be true in the sordid multitude, but the neater sort of our gallants; for all are the multitude, only they differ in clothes, not in judgment or understanding.

DE SHAKESPEARE NOSTRATI

I REMEMBER the players have often mentioned it as an honor to Shakespeare, that in his writing (whatsoever he penned) he never blotted out a line. My answer hath been, "Would he had blotted a thousand!"

---

1 The headings of the different sections are taken from the *marginalia* in the *editio princeps.*
2 Let a Punic sponge accompany the book.—Martial, Epigrams, iv. 10. 5.
3 No number of erasures will emend it; one general wiping-out is necessary.
4 John Heath, flourished 1615.
5 John Taylor, the Water-Poet, 1580–1653.

which they thought a malevolent speech. I had not told posterity this but for their ignorance who chose that circumstance to commend their friend by wherein he most faulted; and to justify mine own candor, for I loved the man, and do honor his memory on this side idolatry as much as any. He was, indeed, honest, and of an open and free nature; had an excellent phantasy, brave notions, and gentle expressions, wherein he flowed with that facility that sometimes it was necessary he should be stopped. "*Sufflaminandus erat,*"[6] as Augustus said of Haterius. His wit was in his own power; would the rule of it had been so, too! Many times he fell into those things could not escape laughter, as when he said in the person of Cæsar, one speaking to him, "Cæsar, thou dost me wrong." He replied, "Cæsar did never wrong but with just cause"; and such like, which were ridiculous.[7] But he redeemed his vices, with his virtues. There was ever more in him to be praised than to be pardoned.

INGENIORUM DISCRIMINA

Nota 1.—In the difference of wits I have observed there are many notes; and it is a little maistry to know them to discern what every nature, every disposition will bear; for before we sow our land we should plow it. There are no fewer forms of minds than of bodies amongst us. The variety is incredible, and therefore we must search. Some are fit to make divines, some poets, some lawyers, some physicians; some to be sent to the plow, and trades.

There is no doctrine will do good where nature is wanting. Some wits are swelling and high; others low and still; some hot and fiery; others cold and dull; one must have a bridle, the other a spur.

Nota 2.—There be some that are forward and bold; and these will do every little thing easily. I mean that is hard by and next them, which they will utter unretarded without any shamefastness. These never perform much, but quickly. They are what they are on the sudden; they show presently, like grain that, scattered on the top of the ground, shoots up, but takes no root; has a yellow blade, but the ear empty. They are wits of good promise at first, but there is an *ingenistitium;*[8] they stand still at sixteen, they get no higher.

Nota 3.—You have others that labor only to ostentation: and are ever more busy about the colors and

surface of a work than in the matter and foundation, for that is hid, the other is seen.

Nota 4.—Others that in composition are nothing but what is rough and broken; *Quæ per salebras, altaque saxa cadunt.*[9] And if it would come gently, they trouble it of purpose. They would not have it run without rubs, as if that style were more strong and manly that struck the ear with a kind of unevenness. These men err not by chance, but knowingly and willingly; they are like men that affect a fashion by themselves; have some singularity in a ruff, cloak, or hat-band; or their beards specially cut to provoke beholders, and set a mark upon themselves. They would be reprehended while they are looked on. And this vice, one that is authority with the rest, loving, delivers over to them to be imitated; so that oft-times the faults which he fell into the others seek for. This is the danger, when vice becomes a precedent.

Nota 5.—Others there are that have no composition at all; but a kind of tuning and rhyming fall in what they write. It runs and slides, and only makes a sound. Women's poets they are called, as you have women's tailors.

> "They write a verse as smooth, as soft as cream,
>   In which there is no torrent, nor scarce stream."

You may sound these wits and find the depth of them with your middle finger. They are cream-bowl or but puddle-deep.

Nota 6.—Some that turn over all books, and are equally searching in all papers; that write out of what they presently find or meet, without choice. By which means it happens that what they have discredited and impugned in one week, they have before or after extolled the same in another. Such are all the essayists, even their master Montaigne. These, in all they write, confess still what books they have read last, and therein their own folly so much, that they bring it to the stake raw and undigested; not that the place did need it neither, but that they thought themselves furnished and would vent it.

Nota 7.—Some again, who, after they have got authority, or, which is less, opinion, by their writings, to have read much, dare presently to feign whole books and authors, and lie safely. For what never was will not easily be found, not by the most curious.

Nota 8.—And some, by a cunning protestation against all reading, and false vendition of their own

6 He ought to have been clogged.
7 Cf. Julius Cæsar, III. i. 47.
8 "A wit-stand"; marginal note in Folio.

9 Which fall over rough crags and high rocks.

naturals,[10] think to divert the sagacity of their readers from themselves, and cool the scent of their own fox-like thefts; when yet they are so rank as a man may find whole pages together usurped from one author; their necessities compelling them to read for present use, which could not be in many books; and so come forth more ridiculously and palpably guilty than those who, because they cannot trace, they yet would slander their industry.

Nota 9.—But the wretcheder are the obstinate contemners of all helps and arts; such as presuming on their own naturals (which, perhaps, are excellent), dare deride all diligence, and seem to mock at the terms when they understand not the things; thinking that way to get off wittily with their ignorance. These are imitated often by such as are their peers in negligence, though they cannot be in nature; and they utter all they can think with a kind of violence and indisposition, unexamined, without relation either to person, place, or any fitness else; and the more willful and stubborn they are in it the more learned they are esteemed of the multitude, through their excellent vice of judgment, who think those things the stronger that have no art; as if to break were better than to open, or to rend asunder gentler than to loose.

Nota 10.—It cannot but come to pass that these men who commonly seek to do more than enough may sometimes happen on something that is good and great; but very seldom: and when it comes it doth not recompense the rest of their ill. For their jests, and their sentences (which they only and ambitiously seek for) stick out, and are more eminent, because all is sordid and vile about them; as lights are more discerned in a thick darkness than a faint shadow. Now, because they speak all they can (however unfitly), they are thought to have the greater copy; where the learned use ever election and a mean, they look back to what they intended at first, and make all an even and proportioned body. The true artificer will not run away from nature as he were afraid of her, or depart from life and the likeness of truth, but speak to the capacity of his hearers. And though his language differ from the vulgar somewhat, it shall not fly from all humanity, with the Tamerlanes and Tamerchams of the late age, which had nothing in them but the scenical strutting and furious vociferation to warrant them to the ignorant gapers. He knows it is his only art so to carry it, as none but artificers perceive it. In

the meantime, perhaps, he is called barren, dull, lean, a poor writer, or by what contumelious word can come in their cheeks, by these men who, without labor, judgment, knowledge, or almost sense, are received or preferred before him. He gratulates them and their fortune. Another age, or juster men, will acknowledge the virtues of his studies, his wisdom in dividing, his subtlety in arguing, with what strength he doth inspire his readers, with what sweetness he strokes them; in inveighing, what sharpness; in jest, what urbanity he uses; how he doth reign in men's affections; how invade and break in upon them, and make[11] their minds like the thing he writes. Then in his elocution to behold what word is proper, which hath ornament, which height, what is beautifully translated, where figures are fit, which gentle, which strong, to show the composition manly; and how he hath avoided faint, obscure, obscene, sordid, humble, improper or effeminate phrase; which is not only praised of the most, but commended (which is worse), especially for that it is naught.

STILI EMINENTIA

IT IS no wonder men's eminence appears but in their own way. Virgil's felicity left him in prose, as Tully's forsook him in verse. Sallust's orations are read in the honor of story, yet the most eloquent Plato's speech, which he made for Socrates, is neither worthy of the patron nor the person defended. Nay, in the same kind of oratory, and where the matter is one, you shall have him that reasons strongly, open negligently; another that prepares well, not fit so well. And this happens not only to brains, but to bodies. One can wrastle well, another run well, a third leap or throw the bar, a fourth lift or stop a cart going; each hath his way of strength. So in other creatures—some dogs are for the deer, some for the wild boar, some are fox-hounds, some otter-hounds. Nor are all horses for the coach or saddle, some are for the cart and panniers.

SCRIPTORUM CATALOGUS

CICERO is said to be the only wit that the people of Rome had equaled to their empire: *Ingenium par imperio.* We have had many, and in their several ages (to take in but the former *seculum*) Sir Thomas More, the elder Wyatt, Henry Earl of Surrey, Chaloner,[12]

---

10 Boastful display of their own natural abilities.

11 Folio: "makes."

12 Sir Thomas Chaloner, diplomatist and author, 1521–1565.

Smith,[13] Eliot,[14] Bishop Gardiner, were for their times admirable; and the more, because they began eloquence with us. Sir Nicolas Bacon was singular, and almost alone, in the beginning of Queen Elizabeth's times. Sir Philip Sidney and Mr. Hooker (in different matter) grew great masters of wit and language, and in whom all vigor of invention and strength of judgment met. The Earl of Essex, noble and high; and Sir Walter Ralegh, not to be contemned, either for judgment or style; Sir Henry Savile,[15] grave, and truly lettered; Sir Edwin Sandys,[16] excellent in both; Lord Egerton, the Chancellor, a grave and great orator, and best when he was provoked; but his learned and able, though unfortunate, successor[17] is he who hath filled up all numbers, and performed that in our tongue which may be compared or preferred either to insolent Greece or haughty Rome. In short, within his view, and about his times, were all the wits born that could honor a language or help study. Now things daily fall, wits grow downward, and eloquence grows backward; so that he may be named and stand as the mark and ἀκμή of our language.

DE MALIGNITATE STUDENTIUM

THERE be some men are born only to suck out the poison of books: *Habent venenum pro victu; imo, pro deliciis.*[18] And such are they that only relish the obscene and foul things in poets, which makes the profession taxed. But by whom? Men that watch for it; and, had they not had this hint, are so unjust valuers of letters as they think no learning good but what brings in gain. It shows they themselves would never have been of the professions they are, but for the profits and fees. But if another learning, well used, can instruct to good life, inform manners, no less persuade and lead men than they threaten and compel, and have no reward, is it therefore the worst study? I could never think the study of wisdom confined only to the philosopher, or of piety[19] to the divine, or of state to the politic; but

13 Sir Thomas Smith, Secretary of State, scholar, author, 1513–1577.
14 Sir Thomas Eliot, or Elyot, author of The Book Named the Governor, 1531.
15 Historian and scholar, 1549–1622. His translation of Tacitus drew warm praise from Jonson.
16 Statesman and author of *Europæ Speculum* (on the religious condition of Europe); 1561–1629.
17 Sir Francis Bacon.
18 "They have poison for their food, even for their dainties."
19 Folio: "poetry."

that he which can feign a commonwealth (which is the poet) can gown it with counsels, strengthen it with laws, correct it with judgments, inform it with religion and morals, is all these. We do not require in him mere elocution, or an excellent faculty in verse, but the exact knowledge of all virtues and their contraries, with ability to render the one loved, the other hated, by his proper embattling them. The philosophers did insolently to challenge only to themselves that which the greatest generals and gravest counsellors never durst. For such had rather do than promise the best things.

POESIS ET PICTURA

POETRY and pictures are arts of a like nature, and both are busy about imitation. It was excellently said of Plutarch, poetry was a speaking picture, and picture a mute poesy. For they both invent, feign, and devise many things, and accommodate all they invent to the use and service of nature. Yet of the two the pen is more noble than the pencil; for that can speak to the understanding, the other but to the sense. They both behold pleasure and profit as their common object; but should abstain from all base pleasures, lest they should err from their end, and, while they seek to better men's minds, destroy their manners. They both are born artificers, not made. Nature is more powerful in them than study.

DE PICTURA

WHOSOEVER loves not picture is injurious to truth and all the wisdom of poetry. Picture is the invention of heaven, the most ancient and most akin to nature. It is itself a silent work, and always of one and the same habit; yet it doth so enter and penetrate the inmost affection (being done by an excellent artificer) as sometimes it o'ercomes the power of speech and oratory. There are divers graces in it, so are there in the artificers. One excels in care, another in reason, a third in easiness, a fourth in nature and grace. Some have diligence and comeliness, but they want majesty. They can express a human form in all the graces, sweetness, and elegancy, but they miss the authority. They can hit nothing but smooth cheeks; they cannot express roughness or gravity. Others aspire to truth so much as they are rather lovers of likeness than beauty. Zeuxis and Parrhasius are said to be contemporaries; the first found out the reason of lights and shadows in picture, the other more subtly examined the lines.

DE STILO

IN picture light is required no less than shadow; so in style, height as well as humbleness. But beware they be not too humble, as Pliny pronounced of Regulus's writings. You would think them written, not on a child, but by a child.[20] Many, out of their own obscene apprehensions, refuse proper and fit words—as *occupy*, *nature*, and the like; so the curious industry in some, of having all alike good, hath come nearer a vice than a virtue.

DE PROGRESSIONE PICTURÆ

PICTURE took her feigning from poetry; from geometry her rule, compass, lines, proportion, and the whole symmetry. Parrhasius was the first won reputation by adding symmetry to picture; he added subtlety to the countenance, elegancy to the hair, love-lines to the face, and by the public voice of all artificers, deserved honor in the outer lines. Eupompus[21] gave it splendor by numbers and other elegancies. From the optics[22] it drew reasons, by which it considered how things placed at distance and afar off should appear less; how above or beneath the head should deceive the eye, etc. So from thence it took shadows, recession,[23] light, and heightenings. From moral philosophy it took the soul, the expression of senses, perturbations, manners, when they would paint an angry person, a proud, an inconstant, an ambitious, a brave, magnanimous, a just, a merciful, a compassionate, an humble, a dejected, a base, and the like. They made all heightenings bright, all shadows dark, all swellings from a plane, all solids from breaking. See where he [Vitruvius] complains of their painting Chimæras,[24] by the vulgar unaptly called grotesque, saying that men who were born truly to study and emulate nature did nothing but make monsters against nature, which Horace so laughed at.[25] The art plastic was molding in clay or potter's earth anciently. This is the parent of statuary, sculpture, graving, and picture; cutting in brass and marble, all serve under her. Socrates taught Parrhasius and Clito, two noble statuaries, first to express manners by their looks in imagery. Polygnotus and Aglaophon[26] were ancienter. After them Zeuxis, who was the lawgiver to all painters after Parrhasius. They were contemporaries, and lived both about Philip's time, the father of Alexander the Great. There lived in this latter age six famous painters in Italy, who were excellent and emulous of the ancients—Raphael de Urbino, Michael Angelo Buonarotti, Titian, Antony of Correggio, Sebastian of Venice, Julio Romano, and Andrea del Sarto.

DE STILO ET OPTIMO SCRIBENDI GENERE

FOR a man to write well, there are required three necessaries—to read the best authors, observe the best speakers, and much exercise of his own style. In style, to consider what ought to be written, and after what manner, he must first think and excogitate his matter, then choose his words, and examine the weight of either. Then take care, in placing and ranking both matter and words, that the composition be comely; and to do this with diligence and often. No matter how slow the style be at first, so it be labored and accurate; seek the best, and be not glad of the forward conceits,[27] or first words, that offer themselves to us; but judge of what we invent, and order what we approve. Repeat often what we have formerly written; which beside that it helps the consequence, and makes the juncture better, it quickens the heat of the imagination, that often cools in the time of setting down, and gives it new strength, as if it grew lustier by the going back. As we see in the contention of leaping, they jump farthest that fetch their race largest; or, as in throwing a dart or javelin, we force back our arms to make our loose the stronger. Yet, if we have a fair gale of wind, I forbid not the steering out of our sail, so the favor of the gale deceive us not. For all that we invent doth please us in the conception or birth, else we would never set it down. But the safest is to return to our judgment, and handle over again those things the easiness of which might make them justly suspected. So did the best writers in their beginnings; they imposed upon themselves care and industry; they did nothing rashly: they obtained first to write well, and then custom made it easy and a habit. By little and little their matter showed itself to them more plentifully; their words answered, their composition followed; and all, as in a well-ordered family, presented itself in the place. So that the sum of all is, ready writing makes not good

---

20 Regulus, a lawyer, wrote a eulogy on his dead son, which, according to Pliny (Epistles, iv. 7) moved the hearer to mirth rather than sadness.

21 A Greek painter contemporary with Parrhasius and Zeuxis.

22 Perspective.

23 Folio: "recessor." Schelling's correction.

24 *De Architectura*, vii. 5.   25 *De Arte Poetica*, 1–5.

26 Aglaophon was father and teacher of Polygnotus, an artist of Thasos. They were contemporaries of Socrates.

27 First notions.

writing, but good writing brings on ready writing. Yet, when we think we have got the faculty, it is even then good to resist it, as to give a horse a check sometimes with a bit, which doth not so much stop his course as stir his mettle. Again, whither a man's genius is best able to reach, thither it should more and more contend, lift and dilate itself; as men of low stature raise themselves on their toes, and so oft-times get even, if not eminent. Besides, as it is fit for grown and able writers to stand of themselves, and work with their own strength, to trust and endeavour by their own faculties, so it is fit for the beginner and learner to study others and the best. For the mind and memory are more sharply exercised in comprehending another man's things than our own; and such as accustom themselves and are familiar with the best authors shall ever and anon find somewhat of them in themselves, and in the expression of their minds, even when they feel it not, be able to utter something like theirs, which hath an authority above their own. Nay, sometimes it is the reward of a man's study, the praise of quoting another man fitly; and though a man be more prone and able for one kind of writing than another, yet he must exercise all. For as in an instrument, so in style, there must be a harmony and consent of parts.

PRÆCIPIENDI MODI

I TAKE this labor in teaching others, that they should not be always to be taught, and I would bring my precepts into practice, for rules are ever of less force and value than experiments; yet with this purpose, rather to show the right way to those that come after than to detect any that have slipped before by error. And I hope it will be more profitable; for men do more willingly listen, and with more favor, to precept than reprehension. Among divers opinions of an art, and most of them contrary in themselves, it is hard to make election; and, therefore, though a man cannot invent new things after so many, he may do a welcome work yet to help posterity to judge rightly of the old. But arts and precepts avail nothing, except nature be beneficial and aiding. And therefore these things are no more written to a dull disposition, than rules of husbandry to a barren soil. No precepts will profit a fool, no more than beauty will the blind, or music the deaf. As we should take care that our style in writing be neither dry nor empty, we should look again it be not winding, or wanton with far-fetched descriptions: either is a vice. But that is worse which proceeds out of want than that which riots out of plenty. The remedy of fruitfulness is easy, but no labor will help the contrary. I will like and praise some things in a young writer which yet, if he continue in, I cannot but justly hate him for the same. There is a time to be given all things for maturity, and that even your country husbandman can teach, who to a young plant will not put the pruning-knife, because it seems to fear the iron, as not able to admit the scar. No more would I tell a green writer all his faults, lest I should make him grieve and faint, and at last despair. For nothing doth more hurt than to make him afraid of all things as he can endeavor nothing. Therefore youth ought to be instructed betimes, and in the best things; for we hold those longest we take soonest, as the first scent of a vessel lasts, and the tinct the wool first receives. Therefore a master should temper his own powers, and descend to the other's infirmity. If you pour a glut of water upon a bottle, it receives little of it; but with a funnel, and by degrees, you shall fill many of them, and spill little of your own; to their capacity they will all receive and be full. And as it is fit to read the best authors to youth first, so let them be of the openest and clearest, as Livy before Sallust, Sidney before Donne. And beware of letting them taste Gower or Chaucer at first, lest, falling too much in love with antiquity, and not apprehending the weight, they grow rough and barren in language only. When their judgments are firm, and out of danger, let them read both the old and the new; but no less take heed that their new flowers and sweetness do not as much corrupt as the others' dryness and squalor, if they choose not carefully Spenser, in affecting the ancients, writ no language; yet I would have him read for his matter, but as Virgil read Ennius. The reading of Homer and Virgil is counselled by Quintilian[28] as the best way of informing youth and confirming man. For, besides that the mind is raised with the height and sublimity of such a verse, it takes spirit from the greatness of the matter, and is tincted with the best things. Tragic and lyric poetry is good too, and comic with the best, if the manners of the reader be once in safety. In the Greek poets, as also in Plautus, we shall see the economy and disposition of poems better observed than in Terence and the later [Greek poets],[29] who thought the sole grace and virtue of their fable the sticking in of sentences, as ours do the forcing in of jests.

28 Cf. *Institutes,* i. 8. 5–9.
29 Schelling's correction of the Folio reading: "and the latter who thought," etc.

PRÆCEPTA ELEMENTARIA

IT is not the passing through these learnings that hurts us, but the dwelling and sticking about them. To descend to those extreme anxieties and foolish cavils of grammarians, is able to break a wit in pieces, being a work of manifold misery and vainness, to be *elementarii senes.*[30] Yet even letters are, as it were, the bank of words, and restore themselves to an author as the pawns of language. But talking and eloquence are not the same: to speak, and to speak well, are two things. A fool may talk, but a wise man speaks; and out of the observation, knowledge, and the use of things, many writers perplex their readers and hearers with mere nonsense. Their writings need sunshine. Pure and neat language I love, yet plain and customary. A barbarous phrase hath often made me out of love with a good sense, and doubtful[31] writing hath wracked me beyond my patience. The reason why a poet is said that he ought to have all knowledges is that he should not be ignorant of the most, especially of those he will handle. And indeed, when the attaining of them is possible, it were a sluggish and base thing to despair; for frequent imitation of anything becomes a habit quickly. If a man should prosecute as much as could be said of everything, his work would find no end.

DE ORATIONIS DIGNITATE

SPEECH is the only benefit man hath to express his excellency of mind above other creatures. It is the instrument of society; therefore Mercury, who is the president of language, is called *deorum hominumque interpres.* In all speech, words and sense are as the body and the soul. The sense is as the life and soul of language, without which all words are dead. Sense is wrought out of experience, the knowledge of human life and actions, or of the liberal arts, which the Greeks called Ἐγκυκλοπαιδείαν. Words are the people's, yet there is a choice of them to be made; for *verborum delectus origo est eloquentiæ.* They are to be chose according to the persons we make speak, or the things we speak of. Some are of the camp, some of the council-board, some of the shop, some of the sheepcot, some of the pulpit, some of the bar, etc. And herein is seen their elegance and propriety, when we use them fitly and draw them forth to their just strength and nature by way of translation or metaphor. But in this translation we must only serve necessity (*nam temere nihil*

30 Gray-beards still at their A B C's.   31 Ambiguous.

transfertur a prudenti[32]) or commodity, which is a kind of necessity: that is, when we either absolutely want a word to express by, and that is necessity; or when we have not so fit a word, and that is commodity;[33] as when we avoid loss by it, and escape obsceneness, and gain in the grace and property which helps significance. Metaphors far-fet hinder to be understood; and affected, lose their grace. Or when the person fetcheth his translations from a wrong place: as if a privy councillor should at the table take his metaphor from a dicing-house, or ordinary, or a vintner's vault; or a justice of peace draw his similitudes from the mathematics; or a divine from a bawdy-house, or taverns; or a gentleman of Northamptonshire, Warwickshire, or the Midland, should fetch all the illustrations to his country neighbors from shipping, and tell them of the main-sheet and the bowline. Metaphors are thus many times deformed, as in him that said, *Castratam morte Africani rempublicam;* and another, *Stercus curiæ Glauciam,* and *Cana nive conspuit Alpes.*[34] All attempts that are new in this kind are dangerous, and somewhat hard, before they be softened with use. A man coins not a new word without some peril and less fruit; for if it happens to be received, the praise is but moderate; if refused, the scorn is assured. Yet we must adventure; for things at first hard and rough are by use made tender and gentle. It is an honest error that is committed, following great chiefs.

Custom is the most certain mistress of language, as the public stamp makes the current money. But we must not be too frequent with the mint, every day coining, nor fetch words from the extreme and utmost ages; since the chief virtue of a style is perspicuity, and nothing so vicious in it as to need an interpreter. Words borrowed of antiquity do lend a kind of majesty to style, and are not without their delight sometimes; for they have the authority of years, and out of their intermission do win themselves a kind of grace-like newness. But the eldest of the present, and newest of the past language, is the best. For what was the ancient language, which some men so dote upon, but the ancient custom? Yet when I name custom, I understand not the vulgar custom; for that were a precept no less dangerous to language then life, if we should speak or live after the manners of the vulgar: but that I call custom of speech, which is the consent of the

32 A wise man does not use a metaphor rashly.—Quintilian, Institutes, viii. 6. 4.
33 Convenience.
34 Cf. Institutes, viii, 6. 15–17; and Horace, Satires, ii. 5. 41.

learned; as custom of life, which is the consent of the good. Virgil was most loving of antiquity; yet how rarely doth he insert *aquai* and *pictai!* Lucretius is scabrous[35] and rough in these; he seeks them as some do Chaucerisms with us, which were better expunged and banished. Some words are to be culled out for ornament and color, as we gather flowers to straw houses or make garlands; but they are better when they grow to our style; as in a meadow, where, though the mere grass and greenness delights, yet the variety of flowers doth heighten and beautify. Marry, we must not play or riot too much with them, as in paronomasies;[36] nor use too swelling or ill-sounding words, *quæ per salebras altaque saxa cadunt*.[37] It is true, there is no sound but shall find some lovers, as the bitterest confections are grateful to some palates. Our composition must be more accurate in the beginning and end than in the midst, and in the end more than in the beginning; for through the midst the stream bears us. And this is attained by custom more than care or diligence. We must express readily and fully, not profusely. There is difference between a liberal and a prodigal hand. As it is a great point of art, when our matter requires it, to enlarge and veer out all sail, so to take it in and contract it is of no less praise, when the argument doth ask it. Either of them hath their fitness in the place. A good man always profits by his endeavor, by his help, yea, when he is absent; nay, when he is dead, by his example and memory: so good authors in their style. A strict and succinct style is that where you can take away nothing without loss, and that loss to be manifest.

The *brief* style is that which expresseth much in little; the *concise* style, which expresseth not enough, but leaves somewhat to be understood; the *abrupt* style, which hath many breaches, and doth not seem to end but fall. The *congruent* and *harmonious* fitting of parts in a sentence hath almost the fastening and force of knitting and connection; as in stones well squared, which will rise strong a great way without mortar.

Periods, *periodi*, are beautiful when they are not too long; for so they have their strength too, as in a pike or javelin. As we must take the care that our words and sense be clear, so if the obscurity happen through the hearer's or reader's want of understanding, I am not to answer for them, no more than for their not listening or marking; I must neither find them ears nor mind. But a man cannot put a word so in sense but something

about it will illustrate it, if the writer understand himself; for order helps much to perspicuity, as confusion hurts. *Rectitudo lucem adfert; obliquitas et circumductio offuscat*.[38] We should therefore speak what we can the nearest way, so as we keep our gait, not leap; for too short may as well be not let into the memory, as too long not kept in. *Obscuritas offundit tenebras*.[39] Whatsoever loseth the grace and clearness, converts into a riddle; the obscurity is marked, but not the value. That perisheth, and is passed by, like the pearl in the fable. Our style should be like a skein of silk, to be carried and found by the right thread, not ravelled and perplexed: then all is a knot, a heap. There are words that do as much raise a style as others can depress it. Superlation[40] and overmuchness amplifies; it may be above faith, but never above a mean. It was ridiculous in Cestius, when he said of Alexander—

"Fremit oceanus, quasi indignetur, quod terras relinquas."[41]

But propitiously from Virgil—

"Credas innare revulsas
Cycladas."[42]

He doth not say it was so, but seemed to be so. Although it be somewhat incredible, that is excused before it be spoken. But there are hyperboles which will become one language, that will by no means admit another. As *Eos esse Populi Romani exercitus, qui cœlum possint perrumpere*,[43] who would say with us but a madman? Therefore we must consider in every tongue what is used, what received. Quintilian warns us that in no kind of translation, or metaphor, or allegory, we make a turn from what we began; as if we fetch the original of our metaphor from sea and billows, we end not in flames and ashes: it is a most foul inconsequence. Neither must we draw out our allegory too long, lest either we make ourselves obscure, or fall into affectation, which is childish. But why do men depart at all from the right and natural ways of speaking? Sometimes for necessity, when we are driven, or think it

35 Harsh.   36 Puns.
37 Which fall over rough crags and high rocks.

38 Directness enlightens; obliquity and circumlocution darken.
39 Obscurity spreads darkness.   40 Exaggeration.
41 The ocean roars, as if indignant that you quit the land.—Seneca, *Suasoria*, i. 11.
42 You would believe that the uprooted Cyclades were swimming in the sea.—Æneid, viii. 691.
43 To be those armies of the people of Rome that might break through the heavens.

fitter, to speak that in obscure words, or by circumstance, which uttered plainly would offend the hearers; or to avoid obsceneness, or sometimes for pleasure, and variety, as travellers turn out of the highway, drawn either by the commodity[44] of a footpath, or the delicacy or freshness of the fields. And all this is called ἐσχηματισμένη, or figured language.

ORATIO IMAGO ANIMI

LANGUAGE most shows a man: Speak, that I may see thee. It springs out of the most retired and inmost parts of us, and is the image of the parent of it, the mind. No glass renders a man's form or likeness so true as his speech. Nay, it is likened to a man; and as we consider feature and composition in a man, so words in language; in the greatness, aptness, sound structure, and harmony of it.

DE POETICA

WE HAVE spoken sufficiently of oratory, let us now make a diversion to poetry. Poetry, in the primogeniture, had many peccant humors, and is made to have more now, through the levity and inconstancy of men's judgments. Whereas, indeed, it is the most prevailing eloquence, and of the most exalted charact.[45] Now the discredits and disgraces are many it hath received through men's study of depravation or calumny; their practice being to give it diminution of credit by lessening the professors' estimation,[46] and making the age afraid of their liberty; and the age is grown so tender of her fame, as she calls all writings "aspersions." That is the state word, the phrase of court, Placentia College, which some call Parasites Place, the Inn of Ignorance.

Whilst I name no persons, but deride follies, why should any man confess or betray himself? why doth not that of Saint Jerome come into their mind, *Ubi generalis est de vitiis disputatio, ibi nullius esse personæ injuriam?*[47] It is such an inexpiable crime in poets to tax vices generally, and no offence in them, who by their exception confess they have committed them particularly. Are we fallen into those times that we must not

Auriculas teneras mordaci rodere vero?[48]

44 Convenience.   45 Distinguishing mark.
46 The estimation in which the professors of poetry are commonly held.
47 When the discussion of faults is general, no one receives any injury.
48 Gnaw tender little ears with biting truth.—Cf. Persius, Satires, i. 107.

Remedii votum semper verius erat, quam spes.[49] If men may by no means write freely, or speak truth, but when it offends not, why do physicians cure with sharp medicines, or corrosives? Is not the same equally lawful in the cure of the mind that is in the cure of the body? Some vices, you will say, are so foul that it is better they should be done than spoken. But they that take offence where no name, character, or signature doth blazon them seem to me like affected as women, who if they hear anything ill spoken of the ill of their sex, are presently moved, as if the contumely respected their particular; and on the contrary, when they hear good of good women, conclude that it belongs to them all. If I see anything that toucheth me, shall I come forth a betrayer of myself presently? No, if I be wise, I'll dissemble it; if honest, I'll avoid it, lest I publish that on my own forehead which I saw there noted without a title. A man that is on the mending hand will either ingenuously confess or wisely dissemble his disease. And the wise and virtuous will never think anything belongs to themselves that is written, but rejoice that the good are warned not to be such; and the ill to leave to be such. The person offended hath no reason to be offended with the writer, but with himself; and so to declare that properly to belong to him which was so spoken of all men, as it could be no man's several, but his that would wilfully and desperately claim it. It sufficeth I know what kind of persons I displease, men bred in the declining and decay of virtue, betrothed to their own vices; that have abandoned or prostituted their good names; hungry and ambitious of infamy, invested in all deformity, enthralled to ignorance and malice, of a hidden and concealed malignity, and that hold a concomitancy with all evil.

WHAT IS A POET?

A POET is that which by the Greeks is called κατ' ἐξοχήν, ὁ ποιητής, a maker, or a feigner: his art, an art of imitation or feigning; expressing the life of man in fit measure, numbers, and harmony; according to Aristotle from the word ποιεῖν, which signifies to make or feign. Hence he is called a poet, not he which writeth in measure only, but that feigneth and formeth a fable, and writes things like the truth. For the fable and fiction is, as it were, the form and soul of any poetical work or poem.

49 The desire for remedy was always truer than the hope.

FROM

BEN JONSON'S CONVERSATIONS WITH DRUMMOND OF HAWTHORNDEN

[TEXT: *based on the edition of R. F. Patterson, London, 1923*]

1. That he had an intention to perfect an epic poem entitled Heroologia, of the worthies of his country roused by Fame, and was to dedicate it to his country; it is all in couplets, for he detesteth all other rimes. Said he had written a discourse of poesie both against Campion and Daniel, especially this last, where he proves couplets to be the bravest sort of verses, especially when they are broken, like hexameters; and that cross rimes and stanzas (because the purpose would lead him beyond eight lines to conclude) were all forced.

2. He recommended to my reading Quintilian (who, he said, would tell me the faults of my verses as if he had lived with me) and Horace, Plinius 2dus Epistles, Tacitus, Juvenal, Martial, whose epigram *"Vitam quæ faciunt beatiorem,* etc." he hath translated.

3. His censure of the English poets was this, that Sidney did not keep a decorum in making every one speak as well as himself.

Spenser's stanzas pleased him not, nor his matter, the meaning of which allegory he had delivered in papers to Sir Walter Ralegh.

Samuel Daniel was a good honest man, had no children, but no poet.

That Michael Drayton's *Poly-Olbion* (if he had performed what he promised, to write the deeds of all the worthies) had been excellent. His long verses pleased him not.

That Sylvester's translation of Du Bartas was not well done, and that he wrote his verses before it ere he understood to confer. Nor that of Fairfax his.[1]

That the translations of Homer and Virgil in long alexandrines were but prose.

That John Harington's Ariosto, under all translations, was the worst. That when Sir John Harington desired him to tell the truth of his Epigrams, he answered him that he loved not the truth, for they were Narrations and not Epigrams.

That Warner, since the king's coming to England, had marred all his *Albion's England.*

That Donne's *Anniversary* was profane and full of blasphemies; that he told Mr. Donne, if it had been written of the Virgin Mary, it had been something; to which he answered that he described the Idea of a Woman, and not as she was.

That Donne, for not keeping of accent, deserved hanging.

That next himself only Fletcher and Chapman could make a masque.

That Shakespeare wanted art. . . .

4. His judgment of stranger poets was that he thought not Bartas a poet but a verser, because he wrote not fiction.

He cursed Petrarch for redacting verses to sonnets, which he said were like that tyrant's bed, where some who were too short were racked, others too long cut short.

That Guarini, in his *Pastor Fido,* kept not decorum, in making shepherds speak as well as himself could.

That Lucan, taken in parts, was good divided, read altogether merited not the name of a poet. . . .

That the best pieces of Ronsard were his odes.

All this was to no purpose, for he neither doth understand French nor Italian. . . .

6. His censure of my verses was that they were all good, especially my Epitaph of the Prince,[2] save that they smelled too much of the schools and were not after the fancy of the time, for a child says he may write after the fashion of the Greek and Latin verses in running; yet that he wished, to please the king, that piece of *Forth Feasting* had been his own.

1 Joshua Sylvester's translation of Guillaume Du Bartas' religious epic *La Semaine* appeared in 1605–06; Edward Fairfax's translation of Tasso's *Gerusalemme Liberata* appeared in 1600.

2 Drummond's elegy on the death of Prince Henry, eldest son of King James I (1612); *Forth Feasting* was a panegyric written on the occasion of the king's visit to Scotland (1617).

7. He esteemeth John Donne the first poet in the world in some things; his verses of the Lost Chain he hath by heart, and that passage of *The Calm*, That dust and feathers do not stir, all was so quiet. Affirmeth Donne to have written all his best pieces ere he was 25 years old.

Sir Henry Wotton's verses of a happy life he hath by heart, and a piece of Chapman's translation of the 13 of the Iliad, which he thinketh well done.

That Donne said to him he wrote that Epitaph on Prince Henry, "Look to me, Faith," to match Sir Edward Herbert in obscureness.

He hath by heart some verses of Spenser's *Calendar*, about wine, between Colin and Percy.

8. The conceit of Donne's *Transformation* or *Metempsychosis* was that he sought the soul of that apple which Eva pulled, and thereafter made it the soul of a bitch, then of a she-wolf, and so of a woman; his general purpose was to have brought in all the bodies of the heretics from the soul of Cain, and at last left it in the body of Calvin. Of this he never wrote but one sheet and now, since he was made Doctor, repenteth highly and seeketh to destroy all his poems.[3] . . .

10. For a heroic poem, he said, there was no such ground as King Arthur's fiction and that S. P. Sidney had an intention to have transformed all his *Arcadia* to the stories of King Arthur.

11. His acquaintance and behavior with poets living with him.

Daniel was at jealousies with him.

Drayton feared him, and he esteemed not of him.

That Francis Beaumont loved too much himself and his own verses. . . .

He beat Marston, and took his pistol from him.

Sir W. Alexander was not half kind unto him, and neglected him because a friend to Drayton.

That Sir R. Aytoun loved him dearly. . . .

That Chapman and Fletcher were loved of him.

Overbury was first his friend, then turned his mortal enemy.

12. Particulars of the actions of other poets, and apothegms.

That the Irish having robbed Spenser's goods and burned his house and a little child new born, he and his wife escaped, and after, he died for lack of bread in King Street and refused 20 pieces sent to him by my lord of Essex and said, He was sorry, he had no time to spend them.

That in that paper S. W. Ralegh had of the allegories of his *Faerie Queen*, by the Blating Beast the Puritans were understood, by the false Duessa the Q. of Scots.

That Southwell was hanged, yet so he had written that piece of his, *The Burning Babe*, he would have been content to destroy many of his.

Franc. Beaumont died ere he was 30 years of age.

Sir John Roe was an infinite spender, and used to say, when he had no more to spend he could die. He died in his arms of the pest, and he furnished his charges, 20 lbs., which was given him back.

That Drayton was challenged[4] for entitling one book *Mortimuriados*.

That S. J. Davies played in an epigram on Drayton, who in a sonnet concluded his mistress might been the Tenth Worthy, and said, he used a phrase like Dametas in *Arcadia*, who said, for wit his mistress might be a giant.

Donne's grandfather on the mother side was Heywood the epigrammatist.

That Donne himself, for not being understood, would perish.

That Sir W. Ralegh esteemed more of fame than conscience.

The best wits of England were employed for making of his *History*. Ben himself had written a piece to him of the Punic war, which he altered and set in his book. S. W. hath written the life of Queen Elizabeth, of which there is copies extant.

Sir P. Sidney had translated some of the Psalms, which went abroad under the name of the Countess of Pembroke.

Marston wrote his father-in-law's preachings, and his father-in-law his comedies.

Shakespeare, in a play, brought in a number of men saying they had suffered shipwreck in Bohemia, where there is no sea near by some 100 miles.

Daniel wrote *Civil Wars*, and yet hath not one battle in all his book.

The Countess of Rutland was nothing inferior to her father, S. P. Sidney, in poesy. Sir Th. Overbury was in love with her, and caused Ben to read his *Wife* to her, which he, with an excellent grace, did, and

---

3 In this passage Jonson describes Donne's early satiric poem Metempsychosis or The Progress of the Soul.

4 Taken to task. Jonson questions the propriety of applying such a title to a poem in a single book.

praised the author. That the morn thereafter he discorded with Overbury, who would have him intend a suit that was unlawful. The lines my lady kept in remembrance, "He comes too near who comes to be denied." Beaumont wrote that elegy on the death of the Countess of Rutland. . . .

Owen is a poor pedantic schoolmaster, sweeping his living from the posteriors of little children, and hath no thing good in him, his epigrams being bare narrations.

Chapman hath translated Musaeus in his verses, like his Homer.

Fletcher and Beaumont, ten years since, hath written *The Faithful Shepherdess*, a tragicomedy, well done.

Dyer died unmarried.

S. P. Sidney was no pleasant man in countenance, his face being spoiled with pimples, and of high blood, and long; that my Lord Lisle, now Earl of Leicester his eldest son, resembleth him.[5]

13. Of his own life, education, birth, actions.

His grandfather came from Carlisle, and he thought from Anandale to it; he served King Henry VIII and was a gentleman. His father lost all his estate under Queen Mary, having been cast in prison and forfeited, at last turned minister; so he was a minister's son. He himself was posthumous born, a month after his father's decease, brought up poorly, put to school by a friend (his master Camden), after taken from it, and put to another craft (I think was to be a wright or bricklayer), which he could not endure, then went he to the Low Countries, but returning soon he betook himself to his wonted studies. In his service in the Low Countries he had, in the face of both the camps, killed an enemy and taken *opima spolia* from him, and since his coming to England, being appealed to the fields, he had killed his adversary, which had hurt him in the arm, and whose sword was ten inches longer than his; for the which he was imprisoned and almost at the gallows. Then took he his religion by trust, of a priest who visited him in prison. Thereafter he was twelve years a Papist.

He was Master of Arts in both the universities, by their favor, not his study.

He married a wife who was a shrew, yet honest; five years he had not bedded with her, but remained with my Lord D'Aubigny.

5 The now-extinct Elizabethan genitive is a source of confusion in this passage, which actually refers to "My Lord Lisle's (now Earl of Leicester's) eldest son." Lisle was the brother of Sidney.

In the time of his close imprisonment, under Queen Elizabeth, his judges could get nothing of him to all their demands but aye and no. They placed two damned villains to catch advantage of him with him, but he was advertised by his keeper; of the spies he hath an epigram.

When the king came in England, at that time the pest was in London, he being in the country at Sir Robert Cotton's house with old Camden, he saw in a vision his eldest son (then a child and at London) appear unto him with the mark of a bloody cross on his forehead, as if it had been cutted with a sword, at which amazed he prayed unto God, and in the morning he came to Mr. Camden's chamber to tell him, who persuaded him it was but an apprehension of his fantasy at which he should not be disjected; in the meantime comes there letters from his wife of the death of that boy in the plague. He appeared to him (he said) of a manly shape, and of that growth that he thinks he shall be at the resurrection.

He was delated by Sir James Murray to the king for writing something against the Scots in a play, *Eastward Hoe*, and voluntarily imprisoned himself with Chapman and Marston, who had written it amongst them. The report was that they should then [have] had their ears cut and noses. After their delivery he banqueted all his friends; there was Camden, Selden, and others; at the midst of the feast his old mother drank to him, and shew him a paper which she had (if the sentence had taken execution) to have mixed in the prison among his drink, which was full of lusty strong poison, and that she was no churl, she told, she minded first to have drunk of it herself.

He had many quarrels with Marston, beat him, and took his pistol from him, wrote his *Poetaster* on him; the beginning of them were that Marston represented him in the stage.

In his youth given to venery. He thought the use of a maid nothing in comparison to the wantonness of a wife, and would never have an other mistress. He said two accidents strange befell him: one, that a man made his own wife to court him, whom he enjoyed two years ere he knew of it, and one day finding them by chance was passingly delighted with it; another, lay diverse times with a woman who shew him all that he wished, except the last act, which she would never agree unto.

Sir W. Ralegh sent him governor with his son, anno 1613, to France. This youth, being knavishly inclined, among other pastimes (as the setting of the favor of damosels on a cod-piece), caused him to be drunken, and dead drunk, so that he knew not where he was, thereafter laid him on a car, which he made to be drawn by pioneers through the streets, at every corner showing his governor stretched out, and telling them that he was a more lively image of the Crucifix than any they had; at which sport young Ralegh's mother delighted much (saying, his father, young, was so inclined), though the father abhorred it. . . .

After he was reconciled with the Church and left off to be a recusant,[6] at his first communion, in token of true reconciliation, he drank out all the full cup of wine. . . .

He hath consumed a whole night in lying looking to his great toe, about which he hath seen Tartars and Turks, Romans and Carthaginians, fight in his imagination. . . .

6 A person, especially a Roman Catholic, who refused to accept the authority of the Church of England.

15. His opinion of verses.

That he wrote all his first in prose, for so his master, Camden, had learned him.

That verses stood by sense without either colors[7] or accent, which yet other times he denied. . . .

19. He is a great lover and praiser of himself, a contemner and scorner of others, given rather to lose a friend than a jest, jealous of every word and action of those about him (especially after drink, which is one of the elements in which he liveth), a dissembler of ill parts which reign in him, a bragger of some good that he wanteth, thinketh nothing well but what either he himself or some of his friends and countrymen hath said and done, he is passionately kind and angry, careless either to gain or keep, vindicative, but, if he be well answered, at himself. . . .

7 Figures of rhetoric.

Robert Burton

[1577–1640]

I N STRIKING contrast to Bacon, Jonson, and Donne, Robert Burton led a life which was uneventful to the point of monotony. Born in Leicestershire, he entered Brasenose College, Oxford, in 1593, became a student of Christ Church in 1599, and took his degree there in 1602. Subsequently, after taking orders, he enjoyed the benefits of a couple of ecclesiastical livings, but he scarcely stirred from Oxford for the rest of his life—a life spent in the Bodleian Library absorbing those countless authors ancient and modern who were to supply him with the texture of that "*cento* out of divers writers" by which he lives in English literature.

"I write of melancholy, by being busy to avoid melancholy," he tells us in the preface to his work, and indeed it is likely that only an urgent personal need could have disturbed the quiet tenor of his scholar's life sufficiently to goad him into composing the massive *Anatomy of Melancholy*. The book was his life, and the copious revisions of the five editions which appeared in Burton's lifetime reveal the extent to which the book grew with his own personality. It appeared under the name of "Democritus Junior," and Democritus, the laughing philosopher, serves to supply Burton not only with a pseudonym and a meaningful *persona* but also with a governing figure for the entire work. The degree to which the mask of Democritus was necessary to Burton, in a personal as well as a literary sense, is suggested by the oft-cited story of his going to the bridge at Oxford to amuse himself by listening to the bargemen swear. Overtly an imitation of his Greek forebear laughing at human folly at the port of Abdera, the story also hints at something isolated and desperate in Burton's own nature: that inherited tendency to melancholy to which he himself confesses, which required extreme remedies—universal laughter, and an incredibly vast labor.

Readers have often observed the inherent paradox of the *Anatomy*—that this most derivative of books, larded at every point with quotation, citation, and example, is at the same time one of the most completely original and individual works to be found in any language. It is paradoxical in another sense too: this richly humorous work, prized by every generation for its eccentricity and its "quaintness," is a serious and profound work of scholarship and science. Sir William Osler has called it "the greatest medical treatise ever written by a layman," and more recently Bergen Evans has drawn attention to its qualities as a study in abnormal psychology which anticipates many of the findings of modern psychiatry. In its combination of scientific seriousness and human warmth, the work is typical of both its author and its age—an age which could not conceive of the separation of science and art any more than it could conceive of the separation of reason and emotion. In style the *Anatomy* is one of the most important examples of the early seventeenth-century revolt against Ciceronian formalism and regularity in prose style; the torrential, seemingly haphazard sentences actually serve to suggest something of the tentative, searching quality of the author's thought and also to convey his insights with an extraordinary degree of immediacy and fidelity.

With the exception of the academic Latin play *Philosophaster* (1606) and a handful of mediocre occasional verses, Burton wrote nothing except the *Anatomy*. As a selective list of the book's admirers—Dr. Johnson, Coleridge, Lamb, Byron, Keats (who found in it the story of his *Lamia*)—would indicate, it was enough.

R. BURTON. *The Anatomy of Melancholy*, ed. H. Jackson, 3 vols. (London, 1932). Probably the best modern edition.

————. *The Anatomy of Melancholy*, ed. F. Dell and P. Jordan-Smith (New York, 1929). A version which gives the Latin citations in English translation.

F. MADAN, ed. *Robert Burton and the Anatomy of Melancholy: Papers by Sir William Osler, Professor Edward Bensly, and Others* (Oxford, 1926). Valuable especially for Osler's appreciative essay.

W. R. MUELLER. *The Anatomy of Robert Burton's England* (Berkeley, Calif., 1952).

B. EVANS. *The Psychiatry of Robert Burton* (New York, 1944). A provocative consideration of Burton's ideas.

L. BABB. *Sanity in Bedlam* (East Lansing, Mich., 1959). A recent and excellent study.

FROM

THE ANATOMY OF MELANCHOLY

[TEXT: *sixth edition, 1651*]

THE AUTHOR'S ABSTRACT OF MELANCHOLY [1]

When I go musing all alone,
Thinking of divers things foreknown,
When I build castles in the air,
Void of sorrow and void of fear,
Pleasing myself with phantasms sweet,
Methinks the time runs very fleet.
    All my joys to this are folly,
    Naught so sweet as melancholy.

[1] This curious manifesto, which the seventeenth-century Spectator prefixes to his great work, may be doggerel; Burton was no poet; but it nevertheless furnishes another seventeenth-century prose artist and poet as well with the inspiration for two of his best poems. In verse form, in phrasing sometimes, and in the pattern of the contemplative attitude in general, *L'Allegro* and *Il Penseroso* have their wellspring here; but even more noteworthy is Milton's rehandling of the one half of Burton's antiphonal. In a mosaic of flat colors the finely perspective eye of the young Puritan, as much a lover of the studious life as Burton, saw the makings of a painting full of the nuances and chiaroscuro of oil.

When I lie waking all alone
Recounting what I have ill done,
My thoughts on me then tyrannize,
Fear and sorrow me surprise,
Whether I tarry still or go,
Methinks the time moves very slow.
    All my griefs to this are jolly,
    Naught so sad as melancholy.
When to myself I act and smile,
With pleasing thoughts the time beguile,
By a brook side or wood so green,
Unheard, unsought for, or unseen,
A thousand pleasures do me bless
And crown my soul with happiness.
    All my joys besides are folly,
    None so sweet as melancholy.
When I lie, sit, or walk alone,
I sigh, I grieve, making great moan
In a dark grove or irksome den,
With discontents and Furies then
A thousand miseries at once
Mine heavy heart and soul ensconce.

All my griefs to this are jolly,
None so sour as melancholy.
Methinks I hear, methinks I see
Sweet music, wondrous melody,
Towns, palaces, and cities fine;
Here now, then there; the world is mine;
Rare beauties, gallant ladies shine,
Whate'er is lovely or divine,
    All other joys to this are folly,
    None so sweet as melancholy.
Methinks I hear, methinks I see
Ghosts, goblins, fiends; my fantasy
Presents a thousand ugly shapes,
Headless bears, black men, and apes,
Doleful outcries and fearful sights
My sad and dismal soul affrights.
    All my griefs to this are jolly,
    None so damned as melancholy.
Methinks I court, methinks I kiss,
Methinks I now embrace my mistress.
O blessed days! O sweet content!
In paradise my time is spent.
Such thoughts may still my fancy move,
So may I ever be in love.
    All my joys to this are folly,
    Naught so sweet as melancholy.
When I recount love's many frights,
My sighs and tears, my waking nights,
My jealous fits, O mine hard fate
I now repent, but 'tis too late!
No torment is so bad as love,
So bitter to my soul can prove.
    All my griefs to this are jolly,
    Naught so harsh as melancholy.
Friends and companions get you gone,
'Tis my desire to be alone;
Ne'er well but when my thoughts and I
Do domineer my privacy.
No gem, no treasure like to this,
'Tis my delight, my crown, my bliss.
    All my joys to this are folly,
    Naught so sweet as melancholy.
'Tis my sole plague to be alone,
I am a beast, a monster grown,
I will no light nor company;
I find it now my misery.
The scene is turned, my joys are gone;
Fear, discontent, and sorrows come.
    All my griefs to this are jolly,
    Naught so fierce as melancholy.

I'll not change life with any king,
I ravished am. Can the world bring
More joy than still to laugh and smile,
In pleasant toys time to beguile?
Do not, O do not trouble me!
So sweet content I feel and see.
    All my joys to this are folly,
    None so divine as melancholy.
I'll change my state with any wretch
Thou canst from gaol or dunghill fetch.
My pain's past cure, another hell;
I may not in this torment dwell.
Now desperate I hate my life,
Lend me a halter or a knife!
    All my griefs to this are jolly,
    Naught so damned as melancholy.

DEMOCRITUS JUNIOR TO THE READER

GENTLE READER, I presume thou wilt be very inquisitive to know what antic or personate actor this is that so insolently intrudes upon this common theatre to the world's view, arrogating another man's name, whence he is, why he doth it, and what he hath to say. Although as he said, *Primum si noluero, non respondebo, quis coacturus est?*—I am a free man born and may choose whether I will tell, who can compel me? —if I be urged, I will as readily reply as that Egyptian in Plutarch when a curious fellow would needs know what he had in his basket, *Quam vides velatim, quid inquiris in rem absconditam?* It was therefore covered because he should not know what was in it. Seek not after that which is hid. If the contents please thee and be for thy use, suppose the man in the moon or whom thou wilt to be the author. I would not willingly be known. Yet in some sort to give thee satisfaction, which is more than I need, I will show a reason both of this usurped name, title, and subject. And first of the name of Democritus, lest any man by reason of it should be deceived, expecting a pasquil, a satire, some ridiculous treatise—as I myself should have done— some prodigious tenet or paradox of the earth's motion, of infinite worlds, *in infinito vacuo, ex fortuita atomorum collisione*, in an infinite waste, so caused by an accidental collision of motes in the sun, all which Democritus held, Epicurus and their master Lucippus of old maintained, and are lately revived by Copernicus, Brunus, and some others. Besides it hath been always an ordinary custom, as Gellius observes, "for later writers and impostors to broach many absurd and insolent fictions under the name of so noble a philosopher as Democritus to get themselves credit and by that means the more to be respected," as artificers usually do, *Novo qui marmori ascribunt Praxitelem suo.* 'Tis not so with me.

> *Non hic Centauros, non Gorgonas, Harpyasque*
> *Invenias, hominem pagina nostra sapit.*
>   No centaurs here or gorgons look to find,
>   My subject is of man and humankind.

Thou thyself art the subject of my discourse.

> *Quicquid agunt homines, votum, timor, ira, voluptas,*
> *Gaudia, discursus, nostri farrago libelli.*
>   Whate'er men do, vows, fears, in ire, in sport,
>   Joys, wanderings are the sum of my report.

My intent is no otherwise to use his name than Mercurius Gallobelgicus, Mercurius Britannicus use the name of Mercury, Democritus Christianus, etc. Although there be some other circumstances for which I have masked myself under this vizard and some peculiar respects which I cannot well express until I have set down a brief character of this our Democritus, what he was, with an epitome of his life.

Democritus, as he is described by Hippocrates and Laertius, was a little wearish old man, very melancholy by nature, averse from company in his latter days, and much given to solitariness, a famous philosopher in his age, *coævus* with Socrates, wholly addicted to his studies at the last and to a private life, wrote many excellent works, a great divine according to the divinity of those times, an expert physician, a politician, an excellent mathematician, as *Diacosmus* and the rest of his works do witness. He was much delighted with the studies of husbandry, saith Columella, and often I find him cited by Constantinus and others treating of that subject. He knew the natures, differences of all beasts, plants, fishes, birds, and as some say, could understand the tunes and voices of them. In a word, he was *omnifariam doctus,* a general scholar, a great student; and to the intent he might better contemplate, I find it related by some that he put out his eyes and was in his old age voluntarily blind, yet saw more than all Greece besides, and writ of every subject, *Nihil in toto opificio naturæ de quo non scripsit.* A man of an excellent wit, profound conceit; and to attain knowledge the better in his younger years, he travelled to Egypt and Athens

to confer with learned men, "admired of some, despised of others." After a wandering life, he settled at Abdera, a town in Thrace, and was sent for thither to be their law-maker, recorder, or town-clerk, as some will, or as others, he was there bred and born. Howsoever it was, there he lived at last in a garden in the suburbs wholly betaking himself to his studies and a private life, "saving that sometimes he would walk down to the haven and laugh heartily at such variety of ridiculous objects which there he saw." Such a one was Democritus.

But in the meantime, how doth this concern me or upon what reference do I usurp his habit? I confess indeed that to compare myself unto him for aught I have yet said were both impudency and arrogancy. I do not presume to make any parallel, *Antistat mihi millibus trecentis, parvus sum, nullus sum, altum nec spiro, nec spero.* Yet thus much I will say of myself, and that I hope without all suspicion of pride or self-conceit, I have lived a silent, sedentary, solitary, private life, *mihi et Musis,* in the university as long almost as Xenocrates in Athens, *ad senectam fere,* to learn wisdom as he did, penned up most part in my study. For I have been brought up a student in the most flourishing college of Europe, *augustissimo collegio*[2] and can brag with Jovius, almost, *in ea luce domicilii Vaticani, totius orbis celeberrimi, per 37 annos multa opportunaque didici;* for thirty years I have continued, having the use of as good libraries as ever he had, a scholar, and would be therefore loth, either by living as a drone to be an unprofitable or unworthy a member of so learned and noble a society or to write that which should be any way dishonorable to such a royal and ample foundation. Something I have done, though by my profession a divine; yet *turbine raptus ingenii,* as he said, out of a running wit, an unconstant, unsettled mind I had a great desire (not able to attain to a superficial skill in any) to have some smattering in all, to be *aliquis in omnibus, nullus in singulis;* which Plato commends, out of him Lipsius approves and furthers "as fit to be imprinted in all curious wits, not to be a slave of one science or dwell altogether in one subject as most do, but to rove abroad, *centum puer artium,* to have an oar in every man's boat, to taste of every dish, and sip of every cup," which, saith Montaigne, was well performed by Aristotle and his learned countryman Adrian Turnebus. This roving humor—though not with like success

2 Christ Church, Oxford. Cardinal Wolsey had designed this expressly to be "the most magnificent college in Christendom."

—I have ever had, and like a ranging spaniel that barks at every bird he sees, leaving his game, I have followed all saving that which I should, and may justly complain and truly *qui ubique est, nusquam est*, which Gesner did in modesty, that I have read many books, but to little purpose for want of good method; I have confusedly tumbled over divers authors in our libraries with small profit for want of art, order, memory, judgment. I never travelled but in map or card,[3] in which my unconfined thoughts have freely expatiated as having ever been especially delighted with the study of cosmography. Saturn was lord of my geniture, culminating, etc., and Mars, principal *significator* of manners in partile conjunction with mine ascendant, both fortunate in their houses, etc. I am not poor, I am not rich; *nihil est, nihil deest*, I have little, I want nothing. All my treasure is in Minerva's tower. Greater preferment as I could never get, so am I not in debt for it. I have a competency, *laus Deo*, from my noble and munificent patrons, though I live still a collegiate student as Democritus in his garden and lead a monastic life, *ipse mihi theatrum*, sequestered from those tumults and troubles of the world, *et tanquam in specula positus*, as he said, in some high place above you all like *Stoicus sapiens, omnia sæcula, præterita, præsentiaque videns, uno velut intuitu*, I hear and see what is done abroad, how others run, ride, turmoil, and macerate themselves in court and country, far from those wrangling lawsuits, *aulæ vanitatem, fori ambitionem, ridere mecum soleo*. I laugh at all, "only secure lest my suit go amiss, my ships perish," corn and cattle miscarry, trade decay; "I have no wife nor children good or bad to provide for." A mere spectator of other men's fortunes and adventures and how they act their parts, which methinks are diversely presented unto me as from a common theatre or scene. I hear new news every day and those ordinary rumors of war, plagues, fires, inundations, thefts, murders, massacres, meteors, comets, spectrums, prodigies, apparitions, of towns taken, cities besieged in France, Germany, Turkey, Persia, Poland, etc., daily musters and preparations and such like which these tempestuous times afford, battles fought, so many men slain, monomachies,[4] shipwrecks, piracies and sea-fights, peace, leagues, stratagems, and fresh alarums. A vast confusion of vows, wishes, actions, edicts, petitions, lawsuits, pleas, laws, proclamations, complaints, grievances are daily brought to our ears. New books every day, pamphlets, currantoes,[5] stories, whole catalogues of volumes of all sorts, new paradoxes, opinions, schisms, heresies, controversies in philosophy, religion, etc. Now come tidings of weddings, maskings, mummeries, entertainments, jubilees, embassies, tilts and tournaments, trophies, triumphs, revels, sports, plays. Then again, as in a new-shifted scene, treasons, cheating tricks, robberies, enormous villainies in all kinds, funerals, burials, deaths of princes, new discoveries, expeditions; now comical, then tragical matters. Today we hear of new lords and officers created, tomorrow of some great men deposed, and then again of fresh honors conferred; one is let loose, another imprisoned; one purchaseth, another breaketh; he thrives, his neighbor turns bankrupt; now plenty, then again dearth and famine; one runs, another rides, wrangles, laughs, weeps, etc. Thus I daily hear, and such like, both private and public news amidst the gallantry and misery of the world; jollity, pride, perplexities and cares, simplicity and villainy, subtlety, knavery, candor and integrity mutually mixed and offering themselves. I rub on *privus privatus;* as I have still lived so I now continue *statu quo prius*, left to a solitary life and mine own domestic discontents; saving that sometimes, *ne quid mentiar*, as Diogenes went into the city and Democritus to the haven to see fashions, I did for my recreation now and then walk abroad, look into the world, and could not choose but make some little observation, *non tam sagax observator ac simplex recitator*, not as they did to scoff or laugh at all but with a mixed passion.

Bilem sæpe, jocum vestri movere tumultus.

I did sometime laugh and scoff with Lucian and satirically tax with Menippus, lament with Heraclitus, sometimes again I was *petulanti splene cachinno*, and then again, *urere bilis jecur*, I was much moved to see that abuse which I could not amend. In which passion howsoever I may sympathize with him or them, 'tis for no such respect I shroud myself under his name, but either in an unknown habit to assume a little more liberty and freedom of speech, or if you will needs know, for that reason and only respect which Hippocrates relates at large in his Epistle to Damagetus wherein he doth express how coming to visit him one day, he found Democritus in his garden at Abdera in the suburbs under a shady bower with a book on his knees, busy at his study, sometimes writing, sometime walking.

3 Chart. 4 Single combats.

5 Newspapers. They originated in the early seventeenth century.

The subject of his book was melancholy and madness. About him lay the carcasses of many several beasts newly by him cut up and anatomized, not that he did contemn God's creatures, as he told Hippocrates, but to find out the seat of this *atra bilis* or melancholy, whence it proceeds and how it was engendered in men's bodies, to the intent he might better cure it in himself, by his writings and observations teach others how to prevent and avoid it. Which good intent of his Hippocrates highly commended. Democritus Junior is therefore bold to imitate, and because he left it imperfect and it is now lost, *quasi succenturiator Democriti*, to revive again, prosecute, and finish in this treatise.

You have had a reason of the name. If the title and inscription offend your gravity, were it a sufficient justification to accuse others, I could produce many sober treatises, even sermons themselves, which in their fronts carry more fantastical names. Howsoever it is a kind of policy in these days to prefix a fantastical title to a book which is to be sold. For as larks come down to a day-net, many vain readers will tarry and stand gazing like silly passengers at an antic picture in a painter's shop that will not look at a judicious piece. And indeed, as Scaliger observes, "nothing more invites a reader than an argument unlooked for, unthought of, and sells better than a scurril pamphlet, *tum maxime cum novitas excitat palatum.*" Many men, saith Gellius, "are very conceited in their inscriptions," and able, as Pliny quotes out of Seneca, to make him loiter by the way "that went in haste to fetch a midwife for his daughter now ready to lie down." For my part, I have honorable precedents for this which I have done. I will cite one for all, Anthony Zara, *Pap. Episc.*, his Anatomy of Wit, in four sections, members, subsections, etc., to be read in our libraries.

If any man except against the matter or manner of treating of this my subject and will demand a reason of it, I can allege more than one. I write of melancholy, by being busy to avoid melancholy. There is no greater cause of melancholy than idleness, "no better cure than business," as Rhasis holds. And howbeit *stultus labor est ineptiarum*, to be busied in toys is to small purpose, yet hear that divine Seneca, better *aliud agere quam nihil*, better do to no end than nothing. I writ therefore and busied myself in this playing labor, *otiosaque diligentia ut vitarem torporem feriandi*, with Vectius in Macrobius, *atque otium in utile verterem negotium.*

—*Simul et iucunda et idonea dicere vitæ,*
Lectorem delectando simul atque momendo.

To this end I write like them, saith Lucian, that "recite to trees and declaim to pillars for want of auditors." As Paulus Ægineta ingeniously confesseth, "not that anything was unknown or omitted, but to exercise myself"; which course if some took, I think it would be good for their bodies and much better for their souls; or peradventure, as others do, for fame, to show myself, *Scire tuum nihil est, nisi te scire hoc sciat alter*. I might be of Thucydides' opinion, "to know a thing and not to express it is all one as if he knew it not." When I first took this task in hand, *et quod ait ille, impellente genio negotium suscepi*, this I aimed at; *vel ut lenirem animum scribendo*, to ease my mind by writing, for I had *gravidum cor, fœtum caput*, a kind of impostume in my head which I was very desirous to be unladen of and could imagine no fitter evacuation than this. Besides I might not well refrain, for *ubi dolor, ibi digitus*, one must needs scratch where it itches. I was not a little offended with this malady, shall I say my Mistress Melancholy, my Egeria, or my *malus genius*, and for that cause, as he that is stung with a scorpion, I would expel *clavum clavo*, comfort one sorrow with another, idleness with idleness, *ut ex vipera theriacum*, make an antidote out of that which was the prime cause of my disease. Or as he did of whom Felix Plater speaks that thought he had some of Aristophanes' frogs in his belly, still crying *Brececcecex, coax, coax, oop, oop*, and for that cause studied physic seven years and travelled over most part of Europe to ease himself. To do myself good I turned over such physicians as our libraries would afford, or my private friends impart, and have taken this pains. And why not? Cardan confesseth he writ his book *De consolatione* after his son's death to comfort himself; so did Tully write of the same subject with like intent after his daughter's departure, if it be his at least, or some imposter's put out in his name, which Lipsius probably suspects. Concerning myself I can peradventure affirm with Marius in Sallust, "that which others hear or read of I felt and practised myself. They get their knowledge by books, I mine by melancholizing," *experto crede Roberto*.[6] Something I can speak out of experience, *ærumnabilis experientia me docuit*, and with her in the poet, *Haud ignara mali miseris succurrere disco*. I would help others out of a fellowfeeling, and as that virtuous lady did of old, "being a leper herself, bestow all her portion to build an hospital for lepers," I will spend my time and knowledge, which are my greatest fortunes, for the common good of all.

6 Burton refers to himself here by his first name.

Yea, but you will infer that this is *actum agere*, an unnecessary work, *crambem bis coctam apponere*, the same again and again in other words. To what purpose? "Nothing is omitted that may well be said," so thought Lucian in the like theme. How many excellent physicians have written just volumes and elaborate tracts of this subject! no news here, that which I have is stolen from others, *Dicitque mihi mea pagina, fur es*. If that severe doom of Synesius be true, "It is a greater offence to steal dead men's labors than their clothes," what shall become of most writers! I hold up my hand at the bar amongst others and am guilty of felony in this kind, *habes confitentem rerum*, I am content to be pressed with the rest. 'Tis most true, *tenet insanabile multos scribendi cacoethes*, and "there is no end of writing of books," as the wiseman found of old, in this scribbling age especially wherein "the number of books is without number," as a worthy man saith, "presses be oppressed," and out of an itching humor that every man hath to show himself, desirous of fame and honor —*scribimus indocti doctique*—he will write no matter what and scrape together it boots not whence. "Bewitched with this desire of fame," *etiam mediis in morbis*, to the disparagement of their health and scarce able to hold a pen, they must say something "and get themselves a name," saith Scaliger, "though it be to the downfall and ruin of many others." To be counted writers, *scriptores ut salutentur*, to be thought and held Polymathes and Polyhistors, *apud imperitum vulgus ob ventosæ nomen artis*, to get a paper kingdom. *Nulla spe quæstus sed ampla famæ*, in this precipitate, ambitious age, *nunc ut est sæculum, inter immaturam eruditionem, ambitiosum et præceps*—'tis Scaliger's censure—and they that are scarce auditors, *vix auditores*, must be masters and teachers before they be capable and fit hearers. They will rush into all learning, *togatam, armatam*, divine, human authors, rake over all indexes and pamphlets for notes, as our merchants do strange havens for traffic, write great tomes, *cum non sint re vera doctiores, sed loquaciores*, when as they are not thereby better scholars but greater praters. They commonly pretend public good, but as Gesner observes, 'tis pride and vanity that eggs them on, no news, or aught worthy of note, but the same in other terms. *Ne feriarentur fortasse typographi, vel ideo scribendum est aliquid ut se vixisse testentur*. As apothecaries we make new mixtures every day, pour out of one vessel into another; and as those old Romans robbed all the cities of the world to set out their bad sited Rome, we skim off the cream of other men's wits, pick the choice flowers of their tilled gardens to set out our own sterile plots. *Castrant alios ut libros suos per se graciles alieno adipe suffarciant*, so Jovius inveighs. They lard their lean books with the fat of others' works. *Ineruditi fures*, etc. A fault that every writer finds, as I do now, and yet faulty themselves, *trium literarum homines*, all thieves; they pilfer out of old writers to stuff up their new comments, scrape Ennius' dung-hills, and out of Democritus' pit, as I have done. By which means it comes to pass "that not only libraries and shops are full of our putrid papers but every close-stool and jakes," *Scribunt carmina quæ legunt cacantes;* they serve to put under pies, to lap spice in, and keep roast meat from burning. With us in France, saith Scaliger, "every man hath liberty to write but few ability. Heretofore learning was graced by judicious scholars, but now noble sciences are vilified by base and illiterate scribblers" that either write for vainglory, need, to get money, or as parasites to flatter and collogue with some great men; they put out *burras, quisquiliasque ineptiasque*. "Amongst so many thousand authors you shall scarce find one by reading of whom you shall be any whit better but rather much worse," *quibus inficitur potius quam perficitur*, by which he is rather infected than any way perfected.

> *—Qui talia legit,*
> *Quid didicit tandem, quid scit nisi somnia, nugas?*

So that oftentimes it falls out, which Callimachus taxed of old, a great book is a great mischief. Cardan finds fault with Frenchmen and Germans for their scribbling to no purpose, *non inquit ab edendo deterreo, modo novum aliquid inveniant*, he doth not bar them to write, so that it be some new invention of their own; but we weave the same web still, twist the same rope again and again. Or if it be a new invention, 'tis but some bauble or toy which idle fellows write for as idle fellows to read, and who so cannot invent? "He must have a barren wit that in this scribbling age can forge nothing. Princes show their armies, rich men vaunt their buildings, soldiers their manhood, and scholars vaunt their toys"; they must read, they must hear, whether they will or no.

> *Et quodcunque semel chartis illeverit, omnes*
> *Gestiet a furno reduntes scire lacuque,*
> *Et pueros et anus——*
> What once is said and writ all men must know,
> Old wives and children as they come and go.

"What a company of poets hath this year brought

out," as Pliny complains to Sossius Sinesius; "this April every day some or other have recited." What a catalogue of new books all this year, all this age, I say, have our Frankfort marts, our domestic marts brought out? Twice a year *Proferunt se nova ingenia et ostentant,* we stretch our wits out and set them on sale, *magno conatu nihil agimus.* So that, which Gesner most desires, if a speedy reformation be not had by some princes' edicts and grave supervisors to restrain this liberty, it will run on *in infinitum. Quis tam avidus librorum helluo,* who can read them! As already, we shall have a vast chaos and confusion of books; we are oppressed with them, our eyes ache with reading, our fingers with turning. For my part, I am one of the number, *nos numerus sumus,* I do not deny it. I have only this of Macrobius to say of myself, *Omne meum, nihil meum,* 'tis all mine and none mine. As a good housewife out of divers fleeces weaves one piece of cloth, a bee gathers wax and honey out of many flowers and makes a new bundle of all,

Floriferis ut apes in saltibus omnia libant,

I have laboriously collected this *cento* out of divers writers and that *sine iniuria,* I have wronged no authors but given every man his own; which Jerome so much commends in Nepotian, he stole not whole verses, pages, tracts, as some do nowadays, concealing their authors' names, but still said this was Cyprian's, that Lactantius', that Hilarius', so said Minutius Felix, so Victorinus, thus far Arnobius. I cite and quote mine authors—which, howsoever some illiterate scribblers account pedantical, as a cloak of ignorance, and opposite to their affected fine style, I must and will use— *sumsi, non surripui;* and what Varro, *lib. 6, De re rust.,* speaks of bees, *minime maleficæ, nullius opus vellicantes faciunt deterius,* I can say of myself, whom have I injured? The matter is theirs most part and yet mine, *apparet unde sumptum sit,* which Seneca approves, *aliud tamen quam unde sit sumptum apparet,* which nature doth with the aliment of our bodies, incorporate, digest, assimilate, I do *concoquere quod hausi,* dispose of what I take. I make them pay tribute to set out this my *Macaronicon.* The method only is mine own. I must usurp that of Wecker *e Ter., nihil dictum quod non dictum prius, methodus sola artificem ostendit.* We can say nothing but what hath been said, the composition and method is ours only and shows a scholar. Oribasius, Aetius, Avicenna, have all out of Galen, but to their own method, *diverso stilo, non diversa fide;* our poets steal from Homer, he spews, saith Ælian, they lick it

up. Divines use Austin's words verbatim still, and our story-dressers do as much. He that comes last is commonly best,

—donec quid grandius ætas
Postera sorsque ferat melior.—

Though there were many giants of old in physic and philosophy, yet I say with Didacus Stella, "A dwarf standing on the shoulders of a giant may see farther than a giant himself"; I may likely add, alter, and see farther than my predecessors; and it is no great prejudice for me to endite after others than for Ælianus Montaltus, that famous physician, to write *de morbis capitis* after Jason Pratensis, Heurnius, Hildesheim, etc. Many horses to run a race; one logician, one rhetorician, after another. Oppose then what thou wilt,

Allatres licet usque nos et usque,
Et gannitibus improbis lacessas.

I solve it thus. And for those other faults of barbarism, Doric dialect, extemporanean style, tautologies, apish imitation, a rhapsody of rags gathered together from several dung-hills, excrements of authors, toys and fopperies confusedly tumbled out without art, invention, judgment, wit, learning, harsh, raw, rude, fantastical, absurd, insolent, indiscreet, ill-composed, undigested, vain, scurril, idle, dull and dry; I confess all ('tis partly affected). Thou canst not think worse of me than I do of myself. 'Tis not worth the reading, I yield it, I desire thee not to lose time in perusing so vain a subject; I should be peradventure loth myself to read him or thee so writing, 'tis not *operæ pretium.* All I say is this, that I have precedents for it, which Isocrates calls *perfugium iis qui peccant,* others as absurd, vain, idle, illiterate, etc. *Nonnulli alii idem fecerunt,* others have done as much, it may be more, and perhaps thou thyself, *Novimus et qui te,* etc., we have all our faults; *scimus, et hanc veniam,* etc., thou censurest me, so have I done others and may do thee, *Cedimus inque vicem,* etc., 'tis *lex talionis, quid pro quo.* Go now censure, criticize, scoff and rail!

Nasutus sis usque licet, sis denique nasus,
Non potes in nugas dicere plura meas,
Ipse ego quam dixi, etc.
Wer'st thou all scoffs and flouts, a very Momus,
Than we ourselves, thou canst not say worse of us.

Thus, as when women scold, have I cried whore first, and in some men's censures I am afraid I have overshot myself. *Laudare se vani, vituperare stulti,* as I do not arrogate, I will not derogate. *Primus vestrum non sum, nec imus,* I am none of the best, I am none of the meanest of you. As I am an inch or so many feet, so many parasangs after him or him, I may be peradventure an ace before thee. Be it therefore as it is, well or ill, I have assayed, put myself upon the stage, I must abide the censure, I may not escape it. It is most true, *stilus virum arguit,* our style bewrays us, and as hunters find their game by the trace, so is a man's genius descried by his works, *Multo melius ex sermone quam lineamentis, de moribus hominum iudicamus;* 'twas old Cato's rule. I have laid myself open (I know it) in this treatise, turned my inside outward, I shall be censured, I doubt not, for to say truth with Erasmus, *nihil morosius hominum iudiciis,* there's naught so peevish as men's judgments, yet this is some comfort, *ut palata, sic iudicia,* our censures are as various as our palates.

Tres mihi convivæ prope dissentire videntur
Poscentes vario multum diversa palato, etc.

Our writings are as so many dishes, our readers guests, our books like beauty; that which one admires, another rejects; so are we approved as men's fancies are inclined.

Pro captu lectoris habent sua fata libelli.

That which is most pleasing to one is *amaracum sui,* most harsh to another. *Quot homines, tot sententiæ,* so many men, so many minds; that which thou condemnest he commends.

Quod petis, id sane est invisum acidumque duobus.

He respects matter, thou art wholly for words; he loves a loose and free style, thou art all for neat composition, strong lines, hyperboles, allegories; he desires a fine frontispiece, enticing pictures, such as Jeron. Natali the Jesuit hath cut to the dominicals to draw on the reader's attention, which thou rejectest; that which one admires, another explodes[7] as most absurd and ridiculous. If it be not point blank to his humor, his method, his conceit, *Si quid forsan omissum, quod is animo conceperit, si quæ dictio,* etc., if aught be omitted, or added which he likes or dislikes, thou art *mancipium paucæ lectionis,* an idiot, an ass, *nullus es,* or *plagiarius,* a trifler, a trivant, thou art an idle fellow; or else 'tis a thing of mere industry, a collection without wit or invention, a very toy. *Facilia sic putant omnes quæ iam facta, nec de salebris cogitant, ubi via strata;* so men are

7 The Latin meaning, to hiss off the stage.

valued, their labors vilified by fellows of no worth themselves, as things of nought; who could not have done as much? *unusquisque abundat sensu suo,* every man abounds in his own sense; and whilst each particular party is so affected, how should one please all?

Quid dem, quid non dem? Renuis tu quod iubet ille.

How shall I hope to express myself to each man's humor and conceit or to give satisfaction to all? Some understand too little, some too much, *Qui similiter in legendos libros, atque in salutandos homines irruunt, non cogitantes quales, sed quibus vestibus induti sint,* as Austin observes, not regarding what but who write, *orexin habet auctoris cælebritas,* not valuing the mettle but the stamp that is upon it, *cantharum aspiciunt, non quid in eo.* If he be not rich, in great place, polite and brave, a great doctor, or full fraught with grand titles, though never so well qualified, he is a dunce; but as Baronius hath it of Cardinal Caraffa's works, he is a mere hog that rejects any man for his poverty. Some are too partial as friends to overween, others come with a prejudice to carp, vilify, detract, and scoff; *qui de me forsan, quidquid est, omni contemptu contemptius iudicant;* some as bees for honey, some as spiders to gather poison. What shall I do in this case? As a Dutch host, if you come to an inn in Germany and dislike your fare, diet, lodging, etc., replies in a surly tone, *aliud tibi quæras diversorium,* if you like not this, get you to another inn; I resolve, if you like not my writing, go read something else. I do not much esteem thy censure, take thy course, 'tis not as thou wilt, nor as I will. But when we have both done, that of Plinius Secundus to Trajan will prove true, "Every man's witty labor takes not, except the matter, subject, occasion, and some commending favorite happen to it." If I be taxed, exploded by thee and some such, I shall haply be approved and commended by others, and so have been, *expertus loquor,* and may truly say with Jovius in like case—*absit verbo jactantia*—*heroum quorundam, pontificum, et virorum nobilium familiaritatem et amicitiam, gratasque gratias, et multorum bene laudatorum laudes sum inde promeritus,* as I have been honored by some worthy men, so have I been vilified by others, and shall be. At the first publishing of this book, which Probus of Persius' satires, *editum librum continuo mirari homines, atque avide deripere cæperunt,* I may in some sort apply to this my work. The first, second, and third edition were suddenly gone, eagerly read and, as I have said, not so much approved by some as scornfully rejected by others. But it was Democritus his fortune, *Idem admirationi et irrisioni habitus.* 'Twas Seneca's fate, that superintendent of wit, learning, judgment, *ad stuporem doctus,* the best of Greek and Latin writers, in Plutarch's opinion, that "renowned corrector of vice," as Fabius terms him, "and painful omniscious philosopher, that writ so excellently and admirably well," could not please all parties or escape censure. How is he vilified by Caligula, Agellius, Fabius, and Lipsius himself, his chief propugner! *In eo pleraque pernitiosa,* saith the same Fabius, many childish tracts and sentences he hath, *sermo illaboratus,* too negligent often and remiss, as Agellius observes, *oratio vulgaris et protrita, dicaces et ineptæ sententiæ, eruditio plebeia,* an homely shallow writer as he is. *In partibus spinas et fastidia habet,* saith Lipsius, and as in all his other works so especially in his epistles, *aliæ in argutiis et ineptiis occupantur, intricatus alicubi, et parum compositus, sine copia rerum hoc fecit,* he jumbles up many things together unmethodically after the Stoics' fashion, *parum ordinavit, multa accumulavit,* etc. If Seneca be thus lashed, and many famous men that I could name, what shall I expect? How shall I that am *vix umbra tanti philosophi* hope to please! "No man so absolute," Erasmus holds, "to satisfy all, except antiquity, prescription, etc., set a bar." But as I have proved in Seneca, this will not always take place, how shall I evade! 'Tis the common doom of all writers, I must, I say, abide it; I seek applause; *Non ego ventosæ venor suffragia plebis;* again, *non sum adeo informis,* I would not be vilified.

> —*laudatus abunde,*
> *Non fastiditus si tibi, lector, ero.*

I fear good men's censures and to their favorable acceptance I submit my labors,

> —*et linguas mancipiorum*
> *Contemno.*—

As the barking of a dog, I securely contemn those malicious and scurril obloquies, flouts, calumnies of railers and detractors; I scorn the rest. What therefore have I said *pro tenuitate mea* I have said.

One or two things yet I was desirous to have amended if I could concerning the manner of handling this my subject, for which I must apologize, *deprecari,* and upon better advice give the friendly reader notice. It was not mine intent to prostitute my Muse in English or to divulge *secreta Minervæ,* but to have exposed this more contract in Latin, if I could have got

it printed. Any scurril pamphlet is welcome to our mercenary stationers in English, they print all,

> —*cuduntque libellos*
> *In quorum foliis vix simia nuda cacaret;*

but in Latin they will not deal; which is one of the reasons Nicholas Carr in his oration of the paucity of English writers gives that so many flourishing wits are smothered in oblivion, lie dead and buried in this our nation. Another main fault is that I have not revised the copy and amended the style, which now flows remissly as it was first conceived; but my leisure would not permit, *Feci nec quod potui, nec quod volui,* I confess it is neither as I would or as it should be.

> *Cum relego scripsisse pudet, quia plurima cerno*
> *Me quoque quæ fuerunt iudice digna lini.*
> When I peruse this tract which I have writ,
> I am abashed and much I hold unfit.

Et quod gravissimum, in the matter itself many things I disallow at this present which when I writ, *Non eadem est ætas, non mens;* I would willingly retract much, etc., but 'tis too late, I can only crave pardon now for what is amiss.

I might indeed—had I wisely done—observed that precept of the poet,

> —*nonumque prematur in annum,*

and have taken more care. Or as Alexander the physician would have done by lapis lazuli, fifty times washed before it be used, I should have revised, corrected and amended this tract; but I had not, as I said, that happy leisure, no *amanuenses* or assistants. Pancrates in Lucian, wanting a servant as he went from Memphis to Coptus in Egypt, took a door bar and after some superstitious words pronounced—Eucrates the relator was then present—made it stand up like a serving-man, fetch him water, turn the spit, serve in supper, and what work he would besides; and when he had done that service he desired, turned his man to a stick again. I have no such skill to make new men at my pleasure or means to hire them, no whistle to call like the master of a ship and bid them run, etc. I have no such authority, no such benefactors as that noble Ambrosius was to Origen, allowing him six or seven *amanuenses* to write out his dictates. I must for that cause do my business myself, and was therefore enforced, as a bear doth her whelps, to bring forth this confused lump; I had not time to lick it into form, as she doth her young ones, but even so to publish it as it was first written, *quidquid in buccam venit*, in an extemporean style, as I do commonly all other exercises, *effudi quidquid dictavit genius meus*, out of a confused company of notes and writ with as small deliberation as I do ordinarily speak, without all affectation of big words, fustian phrases, jingling terms, tropes, strong lines, that like Acestes' arrows caught fire as they flew, strains of wit, brave heats, eulogies, hyperbolical exornations, elegancies, etc., which many so much affect. I am *aquæ potor*, drink no wine at all, which so much improves our modern wits, a loose, plain, rude writer, *ficum voco ficum, et ligonem ligonem*, and as free, as loose, *idem calamo quod in mente*, I call a spade a spade, *animis hæc scribo, non auribus*, I respect matter, not words, remembering that of Cardan, *verba propter res, non res propter verba*, and seeking with Seneca, *quid scribam, non quemadmodum*, rather what than how to write. For as Philo thinks, "He that is conversant about matter neglects words, and those that excel in this art of speaking have no profound learning,"

> *Verba nitent phaleris, at nullus verba medullas*
> *Intus habent—.*

Besides, it was the observation of that wise Seneca, "when you see a fellow careful about his words and neat in his speech, know this for a certainty, that man's mind is busied about toys, there's no solidity in him." *Non est ornamentum virile concinnitas:* as he said of a nightingale,

> *—vox es, præterea nihil*, etc.

I am therefore in this point a professed disciple of Apollonius, a scholar of Socrates, I neglect phrases and labor wholly to inform my reader's understanding, not to please his ears; 'tis not my study or intent to compose neatly, which an orator requires, but to express myself readily and plainly as it happens. So that, as a river runs sometimes precipitate and swift, then dull and slow, now direct, then *per ambages*, now deep, then shallow, now muddy, then clear, now broad, then narrow, doth my style flow; now serious, then light, now comical, then satirical, now more elaborate, then remiss, as the present subject required or as at that time I was affected. And if thou vouchsafe to read this treatise, it shall seem no otherwise to thee than the way to an ordinary traveler, sometimes fair, sometimes foul, here champaign, there enclosed, barren in one place, better soil in another. By woods, groves, hills, dales, plains, etc., I shall lead thee *per ardua montium et lubrica vallium et roscida cespitum et glebosa camporum*, through variety of objects, that which thou shalt like and surely dislike.

For the matter itself or method, if it be faulty, consider I pray you that of Columella, *Nihil perfectum, aut a singulari consummatum industria*, no man can observe all, much is defective no doubt, may be justly taxed, altered, and avoided in Galen, Aristotle, those great masters. *Boni venatoris*, one holds, *plures feras capere, non omnes;* he is a good huntsman can catch some, not all. I have done my endeavor. Besides, I dwell not in this study, *Non hic sulcos ducimus, non hoc pulvere desudamus;* I am but a smatterer, I confess, a stranger; here and there I pull a flower; I do easily grant, if a rigid censurer should criticize on this which I have writ, he should not find three sole faults, as Scaliger in Terence, but 300, so many as he hath done in Cardan's Subtleties, as many notable errors as Gul. Laurembergius, a late professor of Rostock, discovers in that Anatomy of Laurentius, or Barocius the Venetian in Sacroboscus. And although this be a sixth edition, in which I should have been more accurate, corrected all those former escapes, yet it was *magni laboris opus*, so difficult and tedious that as carpenters do find out of experience 'tis much better build a new sometimes than repair an old house, I could as soon write as much more as alter that which is written. If aught therefore be amiss—as I grant there is—I require a friendly admonition, no bitter invective,

> *Sint Musis sociæ charites, furia omnis abesto.*

Otherwise as in ordinary controversies, *funem contentionis nectamus; sed cui bono?* We may content and likely misuse each other; but to what purpose? We are both scholars, say,

> *—Arcades ambo,*
> *Et cantare pares, et respondere parati.*

If we do wrangle, what shall we get by it? Trouble and wrong ourselves, make sport to others. If I be convict of an error, I will yield, I will amend. *Si quid bonis moribus, si quid veritati dissentaneum, in sacris vel humanis literis a me dictum sit, id nec dictum esto.* In the meantime I require a favorable censure of all faults omitted, harsh compositions, pleonasms of words, tautological repetitions—though Seneca bear me out, *nunquam nimis dicitur quod nunquam satis dicitur*—perturbations of tenses, numbers, printer's faults, etc. My translations are sometimes rather paraphrases than interpretations, *non ad verbum*, but as an author I use more liberty; and that's only taken which was to my purpose. Quotations are often inserted in the text, which makes the style more harsh, or in the margin as it happened. Greek authors, Plato, Plutarch, Athenæus, etc., I have cited out of their interpreters, because the original was not so ready. I have mingled *sacra profanis* but I hope not profaned, and in repetition of authors' names ranked them *per accidens*, not according to chronology; sometimes neoterics before ancients, as my memory suggested. Some things are here altered, expunged in this sixth edition, others amended, much added, because many good authors in all kinds are come to my hands since, and 'tis no prejudice, no such indecorum, or oversight.

Nunquam ita quidquam bene subducta ratione ad vitam fuit,
Quin res, ætas, usus, semper aliquid apportent novi,
Aliquid moneant, ut illa quæ scire te credas, nescias,
Et quæ tibi putaris prima, in experiundo ut repudies.
　　Ne'er was aught yet at first contrived so fit
　　But use, age, or something would alter it,
　　Advise thee better, and upon peruse
　　Make thee not say, and what thou tak'st, refuse.

But I am now resolved never to put this treatise out again; *ne quid nimis*, I will not hereafter add, alter, or retract, I have done.

The last and greatest exception is that I being a divine have meddled with physic,

　　—Tantumne est ab re tua otii tibi,
　　Aliena ut cures, eaque nihil quæ ad te attinent?

which Menedemus objected to Chremes; I have so much leisure or little business of mine own as to look after other men's matters which concern me not. What have I to do with physic! *Quod medicorum est promittant medici.* The Lacedemonians were once in council about state matters; a debauched fellow spake excellent well and to the purpose; his speech was generally approved. A grave senator steps up and by all means would have it repealed, though good, because *dehonestabatur pessimo auctore*, it had no better an author; let some good man relate the same, and then it should pass. This counsel was embraced, *factum est*, and it was registered forthwith, *et sic bona sententia mansit, malus auctor mutatus est.* Thou sayest as much of me, *stomachosus* as thou art, and grantest peradventure this which I have written in physic not to be amiss, had another done it, a professed physician, or so; but

why should I meddle with this tract! Hear me speak. There be many other subjects, I do easily grant, both in humanity and divinity, fit to be treated of, of which, had I written *ad ostentationem* only, to show myself, I should have rather chosen and in which I have been more conversant; I could have more willingly luxuriated and better satisfied myself and others; but that at this time I was fatally driven upon this rock of melancholy and carried away by this bystream which as a rillet is deducted from the main channel of my studies; in which I have pleased and busied myself at idle hours as a subject most necessary and commodious. Not that I prefer it before divinity, which I do acknowledge to be the queen of professions and to which all the rest are as handmaids, but that in divinity I saw no such great need. For had I written positively, there be so many books in that kind, so many commentators, treatises, pamphlets, expositions, sermons that whole teams of oxen cannot draw them; and had I been as forward and ambitious as some others I might have haply printed a sermon at Paul's Cross, a sermon in St. Mary's *Oxon.*, a sermon in Christ Church, or a sermon before the right honorable, right reverend, a sermon before the right worshipful, a sermon in Latin, in English, a sermon with a name, a sermon without, a sermon, a sermon, etc. But I have been ever as desirous to suppress my labors in this kind as others have been to press and publish theirs. To have written in controversy had been to cut off an hydra's head; *lis litem, generat*, one begets another, so many duplications, triplications, and swarms of questions *in sacro bello hoc quod stili mucrone agitur* that having once begun I should never make an end. One had much better, as Alexander the sixth pope long since observed, provoke a great prince than a begging friar, a Jesuit or a seminary priest I will add, for *inexpugnabile genus hoc hominum*, they are an irrefragable society, they must and will have the last word; and that with such eagerness, impudence, abominable lying, falsifying, and bitterness in their questions they proceed that as he said, *furore cæcus, an rapit vis acrior, an culpa? responsum date.* Blind fury or error or rashness or what it is that eggs them I know not, I am sure many times, which Austin perceived long since, *tempestate contentionis serenitas caritatis obnubilatur*, with this tempest of contention the serenity of charity is over-clouded, and there be too many spirits conjured up already in this kind in all science and more than we can tell how to lay which do so furiously rage and keep such a racket that as Fabius said, "It had been much better for some of them to have been born dumb and altogether illiterate than so far to dote to their own destruction."

At melius fuerat non scribere, namque tacere
Tutum semper erit,—

'tis a general fault, so Severinus the Dane complains in physic, "unhappy men as we are we spend our days in unprofitable questions and disputations," intricate subtleties, *de lana caprina*, about moonshine in the water, "leaving in the meantime those chiefest treasures of nature untouched wherein the best medicines for all manner of diseases are to be found and do not only neglect them ourselves but hinder, condemn, forbid, and scoff at others that are willing to inquire after them." These motives at this present have induced me to make a choice of this medicinal subject.

If any physician in the meantime shall infer *ne sutor ultra crepidam* and find himself grieved that I have intruded into his profession, I will tell him in brief, I do not otherwise by them than they do by us. If it be for their advantage, I know many of their sect which have taken orders in hope of a benefice, 'tis a common transition; and why may not a melancholy divine, that can get nothing but by simony, profess physic? Drusianus an Italian—Crusianus, but corruptly, Trithemius calls him—"because he was not fortunate in his practice, forsook his profession and writ afterwards in divinity." Marcilius Ficinus was *semel et simul*, a priest and a physician at once, and T. Linacre in his old age took orders. The Jesuits profess both at this time, divers of them *permissu superiorum*, surgeons, panders, bawds, and midwives, etc. Many poor country vicars, for want of other means, are driven to their shifts, to turn mountebanks, quacksalvers, empirics; and if our greedy patrons hold us to such hard conditions as commonly they do, they will make most of us work at some trade as Paul did, at last turn taskers, maltsters, costermongers, graziers, sell ale as some have done, or worse. Howsoever in undertaking this task I hope I shall commit no great error or indecorum; if all be considered aright, I can vindicate myself with Georgius Braunus and Hieronymus Hemingius, those two learned divines; who—to borrow a line or two of mine elder brother—drawn by a "natural love, the one of pictures and maps, prospectives and chorographical delights writ that ample theatre of cities; the other to the study of genealogies, penned *Theatrum Genealogicum*." Or else I can excuse my studies with Lessius the Jesuit in like case; it is a disease of the soul on which I am to treat, and as much appertaining to a divine as

to a physician; and who knows not what an agreement there is betwixt these two professions? A good divine either is or ought to be a good physician, a spiritual physician at least, as our Savior calls himself and was indeed, Mat. 4:23, Luke 5:18, Luke 7:21. They differ but in object, the one of the body, the other of the soul, and use divers medicines to cure. One amends *animam per corpus*, the other *corpus per animam*, as our Regius Professor of Physic well informed us in a learned lecture of his not long since. One helps the vices and passions of the soul, anger, lust, desperation, pride, presumption, etc., by applying that spiritual physic; as the other uses proper remedies in bodily diseases. Now this being a common infirmity of body and soul and such a one that hath as much need of spiritual as corporal cure, I could not find a fitter task to busy myself about, a more apposite theme, so necessary, so commodious, and generally concerning all sorts of men that should so equally participate of both and require a whole physician. A divine in this compound mixed malady can do little alone, a physician in some kinds of melancholy much less; both make an absolute cure.

Alterius sic altera poscit opem.

And 'tis proper to them both and I hope not unbeseeming me who am by my profession a divine and by mine inclination a physician. I had Jupiter in my fixed house; I say with Beroaldus, *Non sum medicus nec medicinæ prorsus expers*, in the theoric of physic I have taken some pains, not with an intent to practise but to satisfy myself, which was a cause likewise of the first undertaking of this subject.

If these reasons do not satisfy thee, good reader, as Alexander Munificus, that bountiful prelate, sometime Bishop of Lincoln, when he had built six castles, *ad invidiam operis eluendam*, saith Mr. Camden, to take away the envy of his work—which very words Nubrigensis hath of Roger, the rich Bishop of Salisbury, who in King Stephen's time built Shirburn Castle and that of Devises—to divert the scandal of imputation which might thence be inferred built so many religious houses. If this my discourse be overmedicinal or savor too much of humanity, I promise thee that I will hereafter make thee amends in some treatise of divinity. But this I hope shall suffice when you have more fully considered of the matter of this my subject, *rem substratam*, melancholy, madness, and of the reasons following, which were my chief motives, the generality of the disease, the necessity of the cure,

and the commodity or common good that will arise
to all men by the knowledge of it, as shall at large
appear in the ensuing preface. And I doubt not but
that in the end you will say with me that to anatomize
this humor aright through all the members of this our
microcosmos is as great a task as to reconcile those
chronological errors in the Assyrian monarchy, find
out the quadrature of a circle, the creeks and sounds of
the northeast or northwest passages, and all out as good
a discovery as that hungry Spaniard's of *Terra Australis
Incognita*, as great trouble as to perfect the motion of
Mars and Mercury, which so crucifies our astronomers,
or to rectify the Gregorian calendar. I am so affected
for my part and hope as Theophrastus did by his
characters "That our posterity, O friend Policles, shall
be the better for this which we have written by correcting and rectifying what is amiss in themselves by
our examples and applying our precepts and cautions
to their own use." And as that great captain Zisca
would have a drum made of his skin when he was dead
because he thought the very noise of it would put his
enemies to flight, I doubt not but that these following
lines when they shall be recited or hereafter read will
drive away melancholy, though I be gone, as much as
Zisca's drum could terrify his foes. Yet one caution let
me give by the way to my present or future reader
who is actually melancholy, that he read not the
symptoms of prognostics in this following tract lest by
applying that which he reads to himself, aggravating,
appropriating things generally spoken to his own
person, as melancholy men for the most part do, he
trouble or hurt himself and get in conclusion more
harm than good. I advise them therefore warily to
peruse that tract. *Lapides loquitur*, so said Agrippa, *de
occ. Phil., et caveant lectores ne cerebrum iis excutiat*. The
rest I doubt not they may securely read and to their
benefit. But I am over-tedious, I proceed.

Of the necessity and generality of this which I have
said, if any man doubt, I shall desire him to make a
brief survey of the world as Cyprian advised Donate,
"Supposing himself to be transported to the top of
some high mountain and thence to behold the tumults
and chances of this wavering world, he can't choose
but either laugh at, or pity it." St. Jerome out of a
strong imagination, being in the wilderness, conceived
with himself that he then saw them dancing in Rome;
and if thou shalt either conceive or climb to see, thou
shalt soon perceive that all the world is mad, that it is
melancholy, dotes; that it is—which Epichthonius
Cosmopolites expressed not so many years since in a

map—made like a fool's head—with that motto, *Caput
heleboro dignum*—a crazed head, *cavea stultorum*, a fools'
paradise, or as Apollonius, a common prison of gulls,
cheaters, flatterers, etc., and needs to be reformed.
Strabo in the ninth book of his Geography compares
Greece to the picture of a man, which comparison of
his Nic. Gerbelius in his exposition of Sophianus' map
approves; the breast lies open from those Acrocerau-
nian Hills in Epirus to the Sunian Promontory in
Attica; Pagæ and Megara are the two shoulders; that
Isthmus of Corinth the neck; and Peloponnesus the
head. If this allusion hold, 'tis sure a mad head; Morea
may be Moria; and to speak what I think the inhabitants of modern Greece swerve as much from reason
and true religion at this day as that Morea doth from
the picture of a man. Examine the rest in like sort, and
you shall find that kingdoms and provinces are melancholy, cities and families, all creatures, vegetal, sensible,
and rational, that all sorts, sects, ages, conditions, are
out of tune, as in Cebes' table, *omnes errorem bibunt*,
before they come into the world, they are intoxicated
by error's cup, from the highest to the lowest have
need of physic; and those particular actions in Seneca
where father and son prove one another mad may be
general; Porcius Latro shall plead against us all. For
indeed who is not a fool, melancholy, mad!—*Qui nil
molitur inepte*, who is not brainsick! Folly, melancholy,
madness are but one disease, delirium is a common
name to all. Alexander Gordonius, Jason Pratensis,
Savonarola, Guianerius, Montaltus, confound them as
differing *secundum magis et minus*, so doth David, Psal.
75:4, "I said unto the fools, deal not so madly," and
'twas an old Stoical paradox, *omnes stultos insanire*, all
fools are mad, though some madder than others. And
who is not a fool, who is free from melancholy? Who
is not touched more or less in habit or disposition? If
in disposition, "ill dispositions beget habits if they persevere," saith Plutarch, habits either are or turn to
diseases. 'Tis the same which Tully maintains in the
second of his *Tusculanes, omnium insipientum animi in
morbo sunt, et perturbatorum*, fools are sick and all that
are troubled in mind. For what is sickness but as
Gregory Tholosanus defines it, "A dissolution or perturbation of the bodily league which health combines."
And who is not sick or ill disposed! in whom doth not
passion, anger, envy, discontent, fear, and sorrow
reign! Who labors not of this disease! Give me but a
little leave, and you shall see by what testimonies, confessions, arguments I will evince it, that most men are
mad, that they had as much need to go a pilgrimage

to the Anticyræ—as in Strabo's time they did—as in our days they run to Compostella, our Lady of Sichem, or Loretto, to seek for help; that it is like to be as prosperous a voyage as that of Guiana, and that there is much more need of hellebore than of tobacco.

That men are so misaffected, melancholy, mad, giddy-headed, hear the testimony of Solomon, Eccl. 2:12, "And I turned to behold wisdom, madness, and folly," etc., and ver. 23, "All his days are sorrow, his travail grief, and his heart taketh no rest in the night." So that take melancholy in what sense you will, properly or improperly, in disposition or habit, for pleasure or for pain, dotage, discontent, fear, sorrow, madness, for part or all, truly or metaphorically, 'tis all one. Laughter itself is madness according to Solomon, and as St. Paul hath it, "worldly sorrow brings death. The hearts of the sons of men are evil, and madness is in their hearts while they live," Eccl. 9:3. "Wise men themselves are no better," Eccl. 1:18. "In the multitude of wisdom is much grief, and he that increaseth wisdom increaseth sorrow," cap. 2:17. He hated life itself, nothing pleased him; he hated his labor, all, as he concludes, is "sorrow, grief, vanity, vexation of spirit." And though he were the wisest man in the world, *sanctuarium sapientiæ*, and had wisdom in abundance, he will not vindicate himself or justify his own actions. "Surely I am more foolish than any man and have not the understanding of a man in me," Pro. 30:2. Be they Solomon's words or the words of Agur the son of Jakeh, they are canonical. David a man after God's own heart, confesseth as much of himself, Ps. 73:21, 22, "So foolish was I and ignorant I was even as a beast before thee." And condemns all fools, Ps. 53 and 32:9 and 49:20. He compares them to "beasts, horses, and mules, in which there is no understanding." The Apostle Paul accuseth himself in like sort, II Cor. 11:21, "I would you would suffer a little my foolishness, I speak foolishly." "The whole head is sick," saith Isaiah, "and the heart is heavy," cap. 1:5, and makes lighter of them "than of oxen and asses; the ox knows his owner," etc. Read Deut. 32:6, Jer. 4, Amos 3:1, Ephes. 5:6. "Be not mad, be not deceived, foolish Galatians, who hath bewitched you?" How often are they branded with this epithet of madness and folly! No word so frequent amongst the fathers of the church and divines; you may see what an opinion they had of the world and how they valued men's actions.

I know that we think far otherwise and hold them most part wise men that are in authority, princes, magistrates, rich men; they are wise men born, all

politicians and statesmen must needs be so, for who dare speak against them? And on the other, so corrupt is our judgment we esteem wise and honest men fools. Which Democritus well signified in an epistle of his to Hippocrates. The "Abderites account virtue madness," and so do most men living. Shall I tell you the reason of it? Fortune and Virtue, Wisdom and Folly, their seconds, upon a time contended in the Olympics; every man thought that Fortune and Folly would have the worst and pitied their cases. But it fell out otherwise. Fortune was blind and cared not where she struck nor whom, without laws, *audabatarum instar*, etc. Folly rash and inconsiderate esteemed as little what she said or did. Virtue and Wisdom gave place, were hissed out and exploded by the common people; Folly and Fortune admired, and so are all their followers ever since. Knaves and fools commonly fare and deserve best in worldlings' eyes and opinions. Many good men have no better fare in their ages. Achish, I Sam. 21:14, held David for a madman. Elisha and the rest were no otherwise esteemed, David was derided of the common people, Ps. 71:7, "I am become a monster to many." And generally we are accounted fools for Christ, I Cor. 4:10. "We fools thought his life madness and his end without honor," Wisd. 5:4. Christ and his apostles were censured in like sort, Joh. 10, Mar. 3, Act. 26. And so were all Christians in Pliny's time, *fuerunt et alii similis dementiæ*, etc. And called not long after *vesaniæ sectatores, eversores hominum, polluti novatores, fanatici, canes, malefici, venefici, Gallilæi homunciones*, etc. 'Tis an ordinary thing with us to account honest, devout, orthodox, divine, religious, plaindealing men, idiots, asses, that cannot or will not lie and dissemble, shift, flatter, *accommodare se ad eum locum ubi nati sunt*, make good bargains, supplant, thrive, *patronis inservire, sollennes ascendendi modos apprehendere, leges, mores, consuetudines recte, observare, candide laudare, fortiter defendere, sententias amplecti, dubitare de nullis, credere omnia, accipere omnia, nihil reprehendere, cæteraque quæ promotionem ferunt et securitatem, quæ sine ambage felicem reddunt hominem, et vere sapientem apud nos*, that cannot temporize as other men do, hand and take bribes, etc., but fear God and make a conscience of their doings. But the Holy Ghost that knows better how to judge, he calls them fools. "The fool hath said in his heart," Ps. 53:1. "And their ways utter their folly," Ps. 49:13. "For what can be more mad than for a little worldly pleasure to procure unto themselves eternal punishment!" as Gregory and others inculcate unto us.

Yea, even all those great philosophers the world hath ever had in admiration, whose works we do so much esteem, that gave precepts of wisdom to others, inventors of arts and sciences, Socrates, the wisest man of his time by the Oracle of Apollo, whom his two scholars Plato and Xenephon so much extol and magnify with those honorable titles, "best and wisest of all mortal men, the happiest, and most just, and as Alcibiades incomparably commends him; Achilles was a worthy man, but Bracides and others were as worthy as himself, Antenor and Nestor were as good as Pericles, and so of the rest, but none present, before, or after Socrates, *nemo veterum neque eorum qui nunc sunt*, were ever such, will match, or come near him. Those seven wise men of Greece, those Britain Druids, Indian *Brachmanni*, Ethiopian Gymnosophists, *Magi* of the Persians, Apollonius, of whom Philostratus, *non doctus, sed natus sapiens*, wise from his cradle, Epicurus so much admired by his scholar Lucretius,

> *Qui genus humanum ingenio superavit, et omnes*
> *Perstrinxit stellas exortus ut ætherius sol.*
> Whose wits excelled the wits of men as far
> As the sun-rising doth obscure a star.

Or that so much renowned Empedocles,

> *Ut vix humana videtur stirpe creatus.*

All those of whom we read such hyperbolical eulogies, as of Aristotle, that he was wisdom itself in the abstract, a miracle of nature, breathing libraries, as Eunapius of Longinus, lights of nature, giants for wit, quintessence of wit, divine spirits, eagles in the clouds, fallen from heaven, gods, lamps of the world, dictators,

> *Nulla ferant talem sæcula futura virum,*

monarchs, miracles, superintendents of wit and learning, "*Oceanus, Phœnix, Atlas, monstrum, portentum hominis, orbis universi musæum, ultimus humanæ naturæ conatus, naturæ maritus.*

> *—merito cui doctior orbis*
> *Submissis defert fascibus imperium,*

as Ælian writ of Protagoras and Gorgias,—we may say of them all, *tantum a sapientibus abfuerunt quantum a viris pueri*, they were children in respect, infants, not eagles but kites, novices, illiterate *eunuchi sapientiæ*. And although they were the wisest and most admired in their age, as he censured Alexander I do them, there were 10,000 in his army as worthy captains—had they

been in place of command—as valiant as himself; there were myriads of men wiser in those days, and yet all short of what they ought to be. Lactantius in his Book of Wisdom proves them to be dizzards, fools, asses, madmen, so full of absurd and ridiculous tenets and brain-sick positions that to his thinking never any old woman or sick person doted worse. Democritus took all from Leucippus and left, saith he, "the inheritance of his folly to Epicurus," *insanienti dum sapientiæ*, etc. The like he holds of Plato, Aristippus, and the rest, making no difference "betwixt them and beasts, saving that they could speak." Theodoret in his tract *De cur Græc. affect.* manifestly evinces as much of Socrates, whom though that Oracle of Apollo confirmed to be the wisest man then living and saved him from the plague, whom 2,000 years have admired, of whom some will as soon speak evil as of Christ, yet, *re vera*, he was an illiterate idiot, as Aristophanes calls him, *irrisor et ambitiosus*, as his master Aristotle terms him, *scurra Atticus*, as Zeno, an enemy to all arts and sciences, as Athenæus, to philosophers and travellers, an opinionative ass, a caviller, a kind of pedant; for his manners, as Theod. Cyrensis describes him, a sodomite, an atheist, so convicted by Anytus, *iracundus et ebrius, dicax*, etc., a pot-companion by Plato's own confession, a sturdy drinker; and that of all others he was most sottish, a very madman in his actions and opinions. Pythagoras was part philosopher, part magician, or part witch. If you desire to hear more of Apollonius, a great wise man sometime paralleled by Julian the Apostate to Christ, I refer you to that learned tract of Eusebius against Hierocles, and for them all to Lucian's Piscator, Icaromenippus, Necyomantia. Their actions, opinions in general were so prodigious, absurd, ridiculous, which they broached and maintained, their books and elaborate treatises were full of dotage, which Tully, *ad Atticum*, long since observed, *delirant plerumque scriptores in libris suis*, their lives being opposite to their words, they commended poverty to others and were most covetous themselves, extolled love and peace and yet persecuted one another with virulent hate and malice. They could give precepts for verse and prose but not a man of them, as Seneca tells them home, could moderate his affections. Their music did show us *flebiles modos*, etc., how to rise and fall; but they could not so contain themselves as in adversity not to make a lamentable tone. They will measure ground by geometry, set down limits, divide and subdivide but cannot yet prescribe *quantum homini satis* or keep within compass of reason and discretion. They can square circles but understand not the state of their own souls, describe right lines and crooked, etc., but know not what is right in this life, *quid in vita rectum sit,* ignorant; so that as he said,

Nescio an Anticyram ratio illis destinet omnem,

I think all the Anticyræ will not restore them to their wits. If these men now that held Zenodotus' heart, Crates' liver, Epictetus' lanthorn were so sottish and had no more brains than so many beetles, what shall we think of the commonalty! what of the rest!

Yea, but will you infer, that is true of heathens if they be conferred with Christians, 1 Cor. 3:19. "The wisdom of this world is foolishness with God, earthly and devilish," as James calls it, 3:15. "They were vain in their imaginations, and their foolish heart was full of darkness," Rom. 1:21, 22. "When they professed themselves wise, became fools." Their witty works are admired here on earth whilst their souls are tormented in hell-fire. In some sense, *Christiani Crassiani,* Christians are Crassians, and if compared to that wisdom, no better than fools. *Quis est sapiens? Solus deus,* Pythagoras replies; "God is only wise," Rom. 16. Paul determines, "only good," as Austin well contends, "and no man living can be justified in his sight." "God looked down from heaven upon the children of men to see if any did understand," Psalm 53:2, 3, but all are corrupt, err. Rom. 3:12, "None doth good, no not one." Job aggravates this, 4:18, "Behold he found no steadfastness in his servants and laid folly upon his angels, 19. How much more on them that dwell in houses of clay!" In this sense we are all as fools, and the Scripture alone is *arx Minervæ;* we and our writings are shallow and imperfect. But I do not so mean; even in our ordinary dealings we are no better than fools. All our actions, as Pliny told Trajan, "upbraid us of folly," our whole course of life is but matter of laughter; we are not soberly wise; and the world itself, which ought at least to be wise by reason of his antiquity, as Hugo de Prato Florido will have it, *semper stultizat,* "is every day more foolish than other; the more it is whipped, the worse it is, and, as a child, will still be crowned with roses and flowers." We are apish in it, *asini bipedes,* and every place is full *inversorum Apuleiorum,* of metamorphosed and two-legged asses, *inversorum Silenorum,* childish, *pueri instar bimuli, tremula patris dormientis in ulna.* Jovianus Pontus, *Antonio Dial.,* brings in some laughing at an old man that by reason of his age was a little fond, but as he admonisheth there, *Ne mireris, mi hospes, de hoc sene,*

marvel not at him only, for *tota hæc civitas delirium,* all our town dotes in like sort, we are a company of fools. Ask not with him in the poet, *Larvæ hunc intemperiæ insaniæque agitant senem?* What madness ghosts this old man but what madness ghosts us all? For we are *ad unum omnes,* all mad, *semel insanivimus omnes,* not once but always so, *et semel et simul et semper,* ever and altogether as bad as he; and not *senex bis puer, delira anus,* but say it of us all, *semper pueri,* young and old, all dote, as Lactantius proves out of Seneca; and no difference betwixt us and children, saving that *maiora ludimus et grandioribus pupis,* they play with babies of clouts and such toys, we sport with greater babies. We cannot accuse or condemn one another, being faulty ourselves, *deliramenta loqueris,* you talk idly, or as Mitio upbraided Demea, *insanis, aufer te,* for we are as mad our own selves, and it is hard to say which is the worst. Nay, 'tis universally so,

Vitam regit fortuna, non sapientia.

When Socrates had taken great pains to find out a wise man and to that purpose had consulted with philosophers, poets, artificers, he concludes all men were fools; and though it procured him both anger and much envy, yet in all companies he would openly profess it. When Supputius in Pontanus had travelled all over Europe to confer with a wise man, he returned at last without his errand and could find none. Cardan concurs with him, "few there are, for aught I can perceive, well in their wits." So doth Tully, "I see everything to be done foolishly and unadvisedly."

Ille sinistrorsum, hic dextrorsum, unus utrique
Error, sed variis illudit partibus omnes.
One reels to this, another to that wall.
'Tis the same error that deludes them all.

They dote all, but not alike, Μανία γὰρ οὐ πᾶσιν ὁμοία, not in the same kind. "One is covetous, a second lascivious, a third ambitious, a fourth envious," etc., as Damasippus the Stoic hath well illustrated in the poet,

Desipiunt omnes æque ac tu.

'Tis an inbred malady in every one of us, there is *seminarium stultitiæ,* a seminary of folly, "which if it be stirred up or get a head will run *in infinitum* and infinitely varies as we ourselves are severally addicted," saith Balthazar Castilio; and cannot so easily be rooted out, it takes such fast hold, as Tully holds, *altæ radices stultitiæ;* so we are bred, and so we continue. Some say there be two main defects of wit, error and ignorance, to which all others are reduced; by ignorance we know not things necessary, by error we know them falsely. Ignorance is a privation, error a positive act. From ignorance comes vice, from error heresy, etc. But make how many kinds you will, divide and subdivide, few men are free or that do not impinge on some kind or other. *Sic plerumque agitat stultos inscitia,* as he that examines his own and other men's actions shall find.

Charon in Lucian, as he wittily feigns, was conducted by Mercury to such a place where he might see all the world at once; after he had sufficiently viewed and looked about, Mercury would needs know of him what he had observed. He told him that he saw a vast multitude and a promiscuous, their habitations like mole-hills, the men as emmets, "he could discern cities like so many hives of bees wherein every bee had a sting, and they did nought but sting one another, some domineering like hornets, bigger than the rest, some like filching wasps, others as drones." Over their heads were hovering a confused company of perturbations, hope, fear, anger, avarice, ignorance, etc., and a multitude of diseases hanging which they still pulled on their pates. Some were brawling, some fighting, riding, running, *sollicite ambientes, callide litigantes,* for toys and trifles and such momentary things. Their towns and provinces mere factions, rich against poor, poor against rich, nobles against artificers, they against nobles, and so the rest. In conclusion he condemned them all for madmen, fools, idiots, asses, *O stulti, quænam hæc est amentia!* O fools! O madmen! he exclaims, *insana studia, insani labores,* etc.! Mad endeavors, mad actions, mad, mad, mad! *O sæculum insipiens et infacetum!* a giddy-headed age. Heraclitus the philosopher, out of a serious meditation of men's lives, fell a-weeping and with continual tears bewailed their misery, madness, and folly. Democritus on the other side burst out a-laughing, their whole life seemed to him so ridiculous, and he was so far carried with this ironical passion that the citizens of Abdera took him to be mad and sent therefore ambassadors to Hippocrates the physician, that he would exercise his skill upon him. But the story is set down at large by Hippocrates in his Epistle to Damagetus, which, because it is not impertinent to this discourse, I will insert verbatim almost as it is delivered by Hippocrates himself, with all the circumstances belonging unto it.

When Hippocrates was now come to Abdera, the people of the city came flocking about him, some weeping, some entreating of him that he would do his best. After some little repast, he went to see Democritus, the people following him, whom he found, as before, in his garden in the suburbs all alone, "sitting upon a stone under a plane tree, without hose or shoes, with a book on his knees, cutting up several beasts, and busy at his study." The multitude stood gazing round about to see the congress. Hippocrates, after a little pause, saluted him by his name, whom he resaluted, ashamed almost that he could not call him likewise by his or that he had forgot it. Hippocrates demanded of him what he was doing. He told him that he was "busy in cutting up several beasts to find out the cause of madness and melancholy." Hippocrates commended his work, admiring his happiness and leisure. And why, quoth Democritus, have not you that leisure? Because, replied Hippocrates, domestical affairs hinder, necessary to be done, for ourselves, neighbors, friends; expenses, diseases, frailties and mortalities which happen; wife, children, servants, and such businesses that deprive us of our time. At this speech Democritus profusely laughed, his friends and the people standing by, weeping in the meantime and lamenting his madness. Hippocrates asked the reason why he laughed. He told him at the vanity and fopperies of the time, to see men so empty of all virtuous actions to hunt so far after gold, having no end of ambition; to take such infinite pains for a little glory and to be favored of men; to make such deep mines into the earth for gold, and many times to find nothing, with loss of their lives and fortunes. Some to love dogs, others horses, some to desire to be obeyed in many provinces, and yet themselves will know no obedience. Some to love their wives dearly at first, and after a while to forsake and hate them, begetting children with much care and cost for their education, yet when they grow to man's estate to despise, neglect, and leave them naked to the world's mercy. Do not these behaviors express their intolerable folly? When men live in peace, they covet war, detesting quietness, deposing kings and advancing others in their stead, murdering some men to beget children of their wives. How many strange humors are in men! When they are poor and needy, they seek riches; and when they have them, they do not enjoy them but hide them under ground or else wastefully spend them. O wise Hippocrates! I laugh at such things being done, but much more when no good comes of them and when they are done to so ill purpose. There is no truth or justice found amongst them, for they daily plead one against another, the son against the father and the mother, brother against brother, kindred and friends of the same quality; and all this for riches whereof after death they cannot be possessors. And yet notwithstanding they will defame and kill one another, commit all unlawful actions, contemning God and men, friends and country. They make great account of many senseless things, esteeming them as a great part of their treasure, statues, pictures, and such like movables, dear bought and so cunningly wrought as nothing but speech wanteth in them; and yet they hate living persons speaking to them. Others affect difficult things; if they dwell on firm land, they will remove to an island and thence to land again, being no way constant to their desires. They commend courage and strength in wars, and let themselves be conquered by lust and avarice; they are, in brief, as disordered in their minds as Thersites was in his body. And now methinks, O most worthy Hippocrates, you should not reprehend my laughing, perceiving so many fooleries in men; for no man will mock his own folly, but that which he seeth in a second, and so they justly mock one another. The drunkard calls him a glutton whom he knows to be sober. Many men love the sea, others husbandry; briefly, they cannot agree in their own trades and professions, much less in their lives and actions.

When Hippocrates heard these words so readily uttered without premeditation to declare the world's vanity, full of ridiculous contrariety, he made answer that necessity compelled men to many such actions and divers wills ensuing from divine permission, that we might not be idle, being nothing so odious to them as sloth and negligence. Besides, men cannot foresee future events in this uncertainty of human affairs; they would not marry, if they could foretell the causes of their dislike and separation; or parents, if they knew the hour of their children's death, so tenderly provide for them; or an husbandman sow if he thought there would be no increase; or a merchant adventure to sea if he foresaw shipwreck; or be a magistrate if presently to be deposed. Alas! worthy Democritus, every man hopes the best, and to that end he doth it, and therefore no such cause or ridiculous occasion of laughter.

Democritus hearing this poor excuse laughed again aloud, perceiving he wholly mistook him and did not well understand what he had said concerning perturbations and tranquillity of the mind. Insomuch that if men would govern their actions by discretion and providence, they would not declare themselves fools as now they do and he should have no cause of laughter; but, quoth he, they swell in this life as if they were immortal and demi-gods, for want of understanding. It were enough to make them wise if they would but consider the mutability of this world and how it wheels about, nothing being firm and sure. He that is now above, tomorrow is beneath; he that sat on this side today, tomorrow is hurled on the other. And not considering these matters they fall into many inconveniences and troubles, coveting things of no profit and thirsting after them, tumbling headlong into many calamities. So that if men would attempt no more than what they can bear they should lead contented lives and learning to know themselves would limit their ambition; they would perceive then that nature hath enough without seeking such superfluities and unprofitable things which bring nothing with them but grief and molestation. As a fat body is more subject to diseases so are rich men to absurdities and fooleries, to many casualties and cross inconveniences. There are many that take no heed what happeneth to others by bad conversation and therefore overthrow themselves in the same manner through their own fault, not foreseeing dangers manifest. These are things—O more than mad! quoth he—that give me matter of laughter, by suffering the pains of your impieties, as your avarice, envy, malice, enormous villainies, mutinies, insatiable desires, conspiracies, and other incurable vices; besides, your dissimulation and hypocrisy, bearing deadly hatred one to the other, and yet shadowing it with a good face, flying out into all filthy lusts and transgressions of all laws both of nature and civility. Many things which they have left off, after a while they fall to again, husbandry, navigation; and leave again, fickle and inconstant as they are. When they are young, they would be old, and old, young. Princes commend a private life, private men itch after honor. A magistrate commends a quiet life, a quiet man would be in his office and obeyed as he is. And what is the cause of all this but that they know not themselves. Some delight to destroy, one to build, another to spoil one country to enrich another and himself. In all these things they are like children, in whom is no judgment or counsel, and resemble beasts, saving that beasts are better than they, as being contented with nature. When shall you see a lion hide gold in the ground or a bull contend for a better pasture! when a boar is thirsty, he drinks what will serve him and no more; and when his belly is full, he ceaseth to eat. But men are immoderate in both; as in lust they covet carnal copulation at set times; men always, ruinating thereby the health of their bodies. And doth it not deserve laughter to see an amorous fool torment himself for a wench, weep, howl for a misshapen slut, a dowdy sometimes, that might have his choice of the finest beauties? Is there any remedy for this in physic? I do anatomize and cut up these poor beasts to see these distempers, vanities, and follies; yet such proof were better made on man's body, if my kind nature would endure it. Who from the hour of his birth is most miserable, weak, and sickly; when he sucks he is guided by others, when he is grown great practiceth unhappiness and is sturdy, and when old, a child again and repenteth him of his life past. And here being interrupted by one that brought books, he fell to it again that all were mad, careless, stupid. To prove my former speeches look into courts or private houses. Judges give judgment according to their own advantage, doing manifest wrong to poor innocents to please others. Notaries alter sentences and for money lose their deeds. Some make false moneys, others counterfeit false weights. Some abuse their parents, yea, corrupt their own sisters, others make long libels and pasquils, defaming men of good life and extol such as are lewd and vicious. Some rob one, some another; magistrates make laws against thieves and are the veriest thieves themselves. Some kill themselves, others despair, not obtaining their desires. Some dance, sing, laugh, feast and banquet, whilst others sigh, languish, mourn and lament, having neither meat, drink, nor clothes. Some prank up their bodies and have their minds full of execrable vices. Some trot about to bear false witness and say anything for money; and though judges know of it, yet for a bribe they wink at it and suffer false contracts to prevail against equity. Women are all day a-dressing to pleasure other men abroad and go like sluts at home, not caring to please their own husbands whom they should. Seeing men are so fickle, so sottish, so intemperate, why should not I laugh at those to whom folly seems wisdom, will not be cured, and perceive it not!

It grew late, Hippocrates left him; and no sooner was he come away but all the citizens came about flocking to know how he liked him. He told them in brief that notwithstanding those small neglects of his attire, body, diet, the world had not a wiser, a more learned, a more honest man and they were very much deceived to say that he was mad.

Thus Democritus esteemed of the world in his time,

and this was the cause of his laughter. And good cause he had.

Olim iure quidem, nunc plus, Democrite, ride;
Quin rides? vita hæc nunc magis ridicula est.
Democritus did well to laugh of old,
  Good cause he had, but now much more,
This life of ours is more ridiculous
  Than that of his or long before.

Never so much cause of laughter as now, never so many fools and madmen. 'Tis not one Democritus will serve turn to laugh in these days, we have now need of a "Democritus to laugh at Democritus," one jester to flout another, one fool to fleer at another. A great stentorian Democritus as big as that Rhodian Colossus. For now, as Salisburiensis said in his time, *totus mundus histrionem agit*, the whole world plays the fool; we have a new theater, a new scene, a new comedy of errors, a new company of personate actors, *volupiæ sacra*, as Calcagninus wittily feigns in his Apologues, are celebrated all the world over, where all the actors were madmen and fools and every hour changed habits or took that which came next. He that was a mariner today, is an apothecary tomorrow; a smith one while, a philosopher another, in his *volupiæ ludis;* a king now with his crown, robes, sceptre, attendants, by and by drove a loaded ass before him like a carter, etc. If Democritus were alive now, he should see strange alterations, a new company of counterfeit vizards, whistlers, Cuman asses, maskers, mummers, painted puppets, outsides, fantastic shadows, gulls, monsters, giddy-heads, butterflies. And so many of them are indeed, if all be true that I have read. For when Jupiter and Juno's wedding was solemnized of old, the gods were all invited to the feast and many noblemen besides. Amongst the rest came Chrysalus, a Persian prince, bravely attended, rich in golden attires, in gay robes, with a majestical presence, but otherwise an ass. The gods seeing him come in such pomp and state rose up to give him place *ex habitu hominem metientes;* but Jupiter perceiving what he was, a light, fantastic, idle fellow, turned him and his proud followers into butterflies. And so they continue still, for aught I know to the contrary, roving about in pied coats and are called *chrysalides* by the wiser sort of men; that is, golden outsides, drones, flies, and things of no worth. Multitudes of such, etc.,

—ubique invenies
Stultos avaros, sycophantas prodigos.

Many additions, much increase of madness, folly, vanity, should Democritus observe, were he now to travel or could get leave of Pluto to come see fashions, as Charon did in Lucian, to visit our cities of Moronia Pia, and Moronia Felix; sure I think he would break the rim of his belly with laughing.

Si foret in terris rideret Democritus, seu, etc.

A satirical Roman in his time thought all vice, folly, and madness were at full sea,[8]

Omne in præcipiti vitium stetit.—

Josephus the historian taxeth his countrymen Jews for bragging of their vices, publishing their follies, and that they did contend amongst themselves who should be most notorious in villainies; but we flow higher in madness, far beyond them,

Mox daturi progeniem vitiosiorem,

and the latter end—you know whose oracle it is—is like to be worst. 'Tis not to be denied, the world alters every day, *Ruunt urbes, regna transferuntur*, etc., *variantur habitus, leges innovantur*, as Petrarch observes, we change language, habits, laws, customs, manners, but not vices, not diseases, not the symptoms of folly and madness; they are still the same. And as a river we see keeps the like name and place but not water and yet ever runs,

Labitur et labetur in omne volubilis ævum;

our times and persons alter, vices are the same, and ever will be; look how nightingales sang of old, cocks crowed, kine lowed, sheep bleated, sparrows chirped, dogs barked, so they do still; we keep our madness still, play the fools still, *nec dum finitus Orestes*, we are of the same humors and inclinations as our predecessors were, you shall find us all alike, much at one, we and our sons,

Et nati natorum, et qui nascuntur ab illis,

and so shall our posterity continue to the last. But to speak of times present.

If Democritus were alive now and should but see the superstition of our age, our religious madness, as Meteran calls it, *religiosam insaniam*, so many professed Christians yet so few imitators of Christ, so much talk of religion, so much science, so little conscience, so much knowledge, so many preachers, so little

practice, such variety of sects, such have and hold of all sides,

—obvia signis signa, etc.,

such absurd and ridiculous traditions and ceremonies; if he should meet a Capuchin, a Franciscan, a pharisaical Jesuit, a man-serpent, a shave-crowned monk in his robes, a begging friar, or see their three-crowned sovereign lord the pope, poor Peter's successor, *servus servorum Dei*, to depose kings with his foot, to tread on emperors' necks, make them stand barefoot and bare-legged at his gates, hold his bridle and stirrup, etc.,— O that Peter and Paul were alive to see this!—if he should observe a prince creep so devoutly to kiss his toe, and those red-cap cardinals, poor parish priests of old, now princes' companions; what would he say? *Cælum ipsum petitur stultitia*. Had he met some of our devout pilgrims going barefoot to Jerusalem, our lady of Loretto, Rome, St. Iago, St. Thomas' shrine, to creep to those counterfeit and maggot-eaten relics. Had he been present at a mass and seen such kissing of paxes, crucifixes, cringes, duckings, their several attires and ceremonies, pictures of saints, indulgences, pardons, vigils, fasting, feasts, crossing, knocking, kneeling at *Ave Marias*, bells, with many such,

—jucunda rudi spectacula plebi,

praying in gibberish, and mumbling of beads. Had he heard an old woman say her prayers in Latin, their sprinkling of holy water, and going a procession,

—incedunt monachorum agmina mille,
Quid memorem vexilla, cruces, idolaque culta, etc.

their breviaries, bulls, hallowed beads, exorcisms, pictures, curious crosses, fables, and baubles. Had he read the Golden Legend, the Turks' Alcoran, or Jews' Talmud, the Rabbins' Comments, what would he have thought? How dost thou think he might have been affected? Had he more particularly examined a Jesuit's life amongst the rest, he should have seen an hypocrite profess poverty and yet possess more goods and lands than many princes, to have infinite treasures and revenues, teach others to fast, and play the gluttons themselves, like watermen that row one way and look another. Vow virginity, talk of holiness, and yet indeed a notorious bawd and famous fornicator, *lascivum pecus*, a very goat. Monks by profession, such as give over the world and the vanities of it, and yet a Machiavellian rout interested in all manner of state. Holy men, peace-makers, and yet composed of envy, lust, ambition, hatred and malice, fire-brands, *adulta patriæ pestis*, traitors, assassins, *hac itur ad astra*, and this is to supererogate and merit heaven for themselves and others! Had he seen on the adverse side some of our nice and curious schismatics in another extreme abhor all ceremonies and rather lose their lives and livings than do or admit anything Papists have formerly used though in things indifferent—they alone are the true church, *sal terræ, cum sint omnium insulsissimi*. Formalists, out of fear and base flattery like so many weathercocks turn round, a rout of temporizers, ready to embrace and maintain all that is or shall be proposed in hope of preferment. Another Epicurean company, lying at lurch as so many vultures, watching for a prey of church goods, and ready to rise by the downfall of any. As Lucian said in like case, what dost thou think Democritus would have done, had he been spectator of these things?

Or had he but observed the common people follow like so many sheep one of their fellows drawn by the horns over a gap, some for zeal, some for fear, *quo se cunque rapit tempestas*, to credit all, examine nothing, and yet ready to die before they will abjure any of those ceremonies to which they have been accustomed; others out of hypocrisy frequent sermons, knock their breasts, turn up their eyes, pretend zeal, desire reformation, and yet professed usurers, gripers, monsters of men, harpies, devils in their lives, to express nothing less?

What would he have said to see, hear, and read so many bloody battles, so many thousands slain at once, such streams of blood able to turn mills, *unius ob noxam furiasque*, or to make sport for princes, without any just cause, "for vain titles," saith Austin, "precedency, some wench, or such like toy, or out of desire of domineering, vainglory, malice, revenge, folly, madness," goodly causes all, *ob quas universus orbis bellis et cædibus misceatur*, whilst statesmen themselves in the meantime are secure at home, pampered with all delights and pleasures, take their ease, and follow their lusts, not considering what intolerable misery poor soldiers endure, their often wounds, hunger, thirst, etc.; the lamentable cares, torments, calamities, and oppressions that accompany such proceedings, they feel not, take no notice of it. "So wars are begun by the persuasion of a few debauched, hare-brain, poor, dissolute, hungry captains, parasitical fawners, unquiet hotspurs, restless innovators, green-heads, to satisfy one man's private spleen, lust, ambition, avarice," etc., *tales rapiunt scelerata in prælia causæ. Flos hominum*, proper men, well proportioned, carefully brought up, able

both in body and mind, sound, led like so many beasts to the slaughter in the flower of their years, pride, and full strength, without all remorse and pity sacrificed to Pluto, killed up as so many sheep for devils' food, 40,000 at once. At once, said I?—that were tolerable, but these wars last always and for many ages; nothing so familiar as this hacking and hewing, massacres, murders, desolations,

—ignoto cælum clangore remugit.

They care not what mischief they procure so that they may enrich themselves for the present; they will so long blow the coals of contention till all the world be consumed with fire. The siege of Troy lasted ten years, eight months, there died 870,000 Grecians, 670,000 Trojans at the taking of the city, and after were slain 276,000 men, women, and children, of all sorts. Cæsar killed a million, Mahomet the second Turk 300,000 persons. Sicinius Dentatus fought in an hundred battles, eight times in single combat he overcame, had forty wounds before, was rewarded with 140 crowns, triumphed nine times for his good service. M. Sergius had 32 wounds; Scæva the centurion I know not how many; every nation hath their Hectors, Scipios, Cæsars and Alexanders. Our Edward the Fourth was in 26 battles afoot. And as they do all, he glories in it, 'tis related to his honor. At the siege of Jerusalem 1,100,000 died with sword and famine. At the battle of Cannæ 70,000 men were slain, as Polybius records, and as many at Battle Abbey[9] with us. And 'tis no news to fight from sun to sun as they did, as Constantine and Licinius, etc. At the siege of Ostend, the Devil's Academy, a poor town in respect, a small fort, but a great grave, 120,000 men lost their lives, besides towns, dorpes,[10] and hospitals full of maimed soldiers; there were engines, fireworks, and whatsoever the Devil could invent to do mischief with 2,500,000 iron bullets shot of 40 pound weight, three or four millions of gold consumed. "Who," saith mine author, "can be sufficiently amazed at their flinty hearts, obstinacy, fury, blindness, who without any likelihood of good success hazard poor soldiers and lead them without pity to the slaughter, which may justly be called the rage of furious beasts that run without reason upon their own deaths." *Quis malus genius, quæ furia, quæ pestis*, etc., what plague, what fury brought so devilish, so brutish a thing as war into men's minds? Who made so soft and peaceable a creature born to love, mercy, meekness, so to rave,

9 Hastings. 10 Villages.

rage like beasts, and run on to their own destruction? how may nature expostulate with mankind, *Ego te divinum animal finxi,* etc., I made thee a harmless, quiet, a divine creature! How may God expostulate, and all good men! Yet *horum facta,* as one condoles, *tantum admirantur et heroum numero habent;* these are brave spirits, the gallants of the world, these admired alone, triumph alone, have statues, crowns, pyramids, obelisks to their eternal fame, that immortal genius attends on them, *hac itur ad astra.* When Rhodes was besieged *fossæ urbis cadaveribus repletæ sunt,* the ditches were full of dead carcasses; and as when the said Solyman Great Turk beleaguered Vienna, they lay level with the top of the walls. This they make a sport of and will do it to their friends and confederates, against oaths, vows, promises, by treachery or otherwise—

dolus an virtus? quis in hoste requirat?—

leagues and laws of arms (*silent leges inter arma*) for their advantage, *omnia jura, divina, humana, proculcata plerumque sunt;* God's and men's laws are trampled under foot, the sword alone determines all; to satisfy their lust and spleen they care not what they attempt say, or do,

Rara fides probitasque viris qui castra sequuntur,

nothing so common as to have "father fight against son, brother against brother, kinsman against kinsman, kingdom against kingdom, province against province, Christians against Christians," *a quibus nec unquam cogitatione fuerunt læsi,* of whom they never had offense in thought, word, or deed. Infinite treasures consumed, towns burned, flourishing cities sacked and ruinated, *quodque animus meminisse horret,* goodly countries depopulated and left desolate, old inhabitants expelled, trade and traffic decayed, maids deflowered,

Virgines nondum thalamis iugatæ,
Et comis nondum positis ephebi;

chaste matrons cry out with Andromache, *Concubitum mox cogar pati eius qui interemit Hectorem,* they shall be compelled peradventure to lie with them that erst killed their husband; to see rich, poor, sick, sound, lords, servants, *eodem omnes incommodo macti,* consumed all or maimed, etc., *et quidquid gaudens scelere animus audet et perversa mens,* saith Cyprian, and whatsoever torment, misery, mischief, hell itself, the Devil, fury, and rage can invent to their own ruin and destruction; so abominable thing is war, as Gerbelius concludes, *adeo fœda et abominanda res est bellum, ex quo*

hominum cædes, vastationes, etc., the scourge of God, cause, effect, fruit and punishment of sin, and not *tonsura humani generis,* as Tertullian calls it, but *ruina.* Had Democritus been present at the late civil wars in France, those abominable wars,

—bellaque matribus detestata,

"where in less than ten years ten hundred thousand men were consumed," saith Collignius, twenty thousand churches overthrown; nay, the whole kingdom subverted, as Richard Dinoth adds. So many myriads of the commons were butchered up with sword, famine, war, *tanto odio utrinque ut barbari ad horrendam lanienam obstupescerent,* with such feral hatred, the world was amazed at it. Or at our late Pharsalian fields in the time of Henry the Sixth betwixt the houses of Lancaster and York an hundred thousand men slain, one writes, another, ten thousand families were rooted out, "that no man can but marvel," saith Comineus, "at that barbarous inhumanity, feral madness, committed betwixt men of the same nation, language, and religion." *Quis furor, O cives?* "Why do the Gentiles so furiously rage?" saith the Prophet David, Psal. 2:1. But we may ask, why do the Christians so furiously rage?

Arma volunt, quare poscunt, rapiuntque iuventus?

Unfit for Gentiles, much less for us so to tyrannize, as the Spaniards in the West Indies that killed up in 42 years, if we may believe Bartholomæus a Casa their own bishop, 12 millions of men, with stupendous and exquisite torments; neither should I lie, said he, if I said 50 millions. I omit those French massacres, Sicilian evensongs, the Duke of Alva's tyrannies, our Gunpowder machinations, and that fourth fury, as one calls it, the Spanish Inquisition, which quite obscures those ten persecutions,

—sævit toto Mars impius orbe,

is not this *mundus furiosus,* a mad world, as he terms it, *insanum bellum?* are not these madmen, as Scaliger concludes, *qui in prælio acerba morte, insaniæ suæ memoriam pro perpetuo teste relinquunt posteritati,* which leave so frequent battles, as perpetual memorials of their madness to all succeeding ages? Would this, think you, have enforced our Democritus to laughter, or rather made him turn his tune, alter his tone, and weep with Heraclitus, or rather howl, roar, and tear his hair in commiseration, stand amazed; or as the poets feign that Niobe was for grief quite stupefied and turned to a stone? I have not yet said the worst, that which is more absurd and mad, in their tumults, seditions, civil and unjust wars, *quod stulte suscipitur, impie geritur, misere finitur,* such wars I mean; for all are not to be condemned, as those fantastical Anabaptists vainly conceive. Our Christian tactics are all out as necessary as the Roman *acies* or Grecian *phalanx;* to be a soldier is a most noble and honorable profession (as the world is) not to be spared, they are our best walls and bulwarks, and I do therefore acknowledge that of Tully to be most true, "All our civil affairs, all our studies, all our pleading, industry, and their commendation lies under the protection of warlike virtues, and whensoever there is any suspicion of tumult, all our arts cease"; wars are most behoveful, *et bellatores agricolis civitati sunt utiliores,* as Tyrius defends; and valor is much to be commended in a wise man. But they mistake most part, *auferre, trucidare, rapere, falsis nominibus virtutem vocant,* etc.,—'twas Galgacus' observation in Tacitus—they term theft, murder, and rapine, virtue, by a wrong name; rapes, slaughters, massacres, etc., *jocus et ludus,* are pretty pastimes, as Ludovicus Vives notes. "They commonly call the most hare-brain bloodsuckers, strongest thieves, the most desperate villains, treacherous rogues, inhuman murderers, rash, cruel, and dissolute caitiffs, courageous and generous spirits, heroical and worthy captains, brave men-at-arms, valiant and renowned soldiers, possessed with a brute persuasion of false honor," as Pontus Huter in his Burgundian history complains. By means of which it comes to pass that daily so many voluntaries offer themselves, leaving their sweet wives, children, friends, for sixpence (if they can get it) a day, prostitute their lives and limbs, desire to enter upon breaches, lie sentinel, *perdue,* give the first onset, stand in the forefront of the battle, marching bravely on with a cheerful noise of drums and trumpets, such vigor and alacrity, so many banners streaming in the air, glittering armors, motions of plumes, woods of pikes and swords, variety of colors, cost and magnificence as if they went in triumph, now victors to the Capitol and with such pomp as when Darius' army marched to meet Alexander at Issus. Void of all fear they run into eminent dangers, cannon's mouth, etc., *ut vulneribus suis ferrum hostium hebetent,* saith Barletius, to get a name of valor, honor, and applause, which lasts not neither, for it is but a mere flash, this fame, and like a rose *intra diem unum extinguitur,* 'tis gone in an instant. Of 50,000 proletaries slain in a battle scarce fifteen are recorded in history, or one alone, the general perhaps; and after a while his and their names are likewise blotted out, the whole battle itself is forgotten. Those Grecian orators, *summa vi ingenii et eloquentiæ,* set out the renowned overthrows at Thermopylæ, Salamis, Marathon, Mycale, Mantinea, Chæronea, Platea. The Romans record their battle at Cannæ and Pharsalian fields, but they do but record, and we scarce hear of them. And yet this supposed honor, popular applause, desire of immortality by this means, pride and vainglory spurs them on many times rashly and unadvisedly to make away themselves and multitudes of others. Alexander was sorry because there were no more worlds for him to conquer; he is admired by some for it, *animosa vox videtur, et regia,* 'twas spoken like a prince. But as wise Seneca censures him, 'twas *vox iniquissima et stultissima,* 'twas spoken like a Bedlam fool. And that sentence which the same Seneca appropriates to his father Philip and him I apply to them all, *Non minores fuere pestes mortalium quam inundatio, quam conflagratio, quibus,* etc., they did as much mischief to mortal men as fire and water, those merciless elements when they rage. Which is yet more to be lamented, they persuade them this hellish course of life is holy, they promise heaven to such as venture their lives *bello sacro* and that by these bloody wars, as Persians, Greeks, and Romans of old, as modern Turks do now their commons to encourage them to fight, *ut cadant infeliciter,* "if they die in the field, they go directly to heaven and shall be canonized for saints,"—O diabolical invention!—put in the chronicles, *in perpetuam rei memoriam,* to their eternal memory. When as in truth, as some hold it, it were much better, since wars are the scourge of God for sin by which he punisheth mortal men's peevishness and folly, such brutish stories were suppressed, because *ad morum institutionem nihil habent,* they conduce not at all to manners or good life. But they will have it thus nevertheless, and so they put a note of "divinity upon the most cruel and pernicious plague of human kind," adore such men with grand titles, degrees, statues, images, honor, applaud, and highly reward them for their good service, no greater glory than to die in the field. So Africanus is extolled by Ennius; Mars and Hercules, and I know not how many besides of old were deified, went this way to heaven, that were indeed bloody butchers, wicked destroyers, and troublers of the world, prodigious monsters, hell-hounds, feral plagues, devourers, common executioners of human kind, as Lactantius truly proves, and Cyprian to Donat, such as were desperate in wars and precipitately made away themselves—like those Celts in Damascen, with ridiculous valor, *ut dedecorosum putarent muro ruenti se subducere*, a disgrace to run away for a rotten wall now ready to fall on their heads—such as will not rush on a sword's point or seek to shun a cannon's shot are base cowards and no valiant men. By which means, *Madet orbis mutuo sanguine*, the earth wallows in her own blood, *Sævit amor ferri et scelerati insania belli*, and for that which, if it be done in private, a man shall be rigorously executed "and which is no less than murder itself, if the same fact be done in public in wars, it is called manhood, and the party is honored for it."—*Prosperum et felix scelus virtus vocatur.*—We measure all as Turks do, by the event, and most part, as Cyprian notes, in all ages, countries, places, *sævitiæ magnitudo impunitatem sceleris acquirit*, the foulness of the fact vindicates the offender. One is crowned for that for which another is tormented,

Ille crucem sceleris pretium tulit, hic diadema,

made a knight, a lord, an earl, a great duke, as Agrippa notes, for which another should have hung in gibbets as a terror to the rest,

et tamen alter,
Si fecisset idem, caderet sub iudice morum.

A poor sheep-stealer is hanged for stealing of victuals, compelled peradventure by necessity of that intolerable cold, hunger and thirst, to save himself from starving. But a great man in office may securely rob whole provinces, undo thousands, pill and pole, oppress *ad libitum*, flay, grind, tyrannize, enrich himself by the spoils of the commons, be uncontrollable in his actions, and after all be recompensed with turgent titles, honored for his good service, and no man dare to find fault or mutter at it.

How would our Democritus have been affected to see a wicked caitiff or "fool, a very idiot, a fungus, a golden ass, a monster of men, to have many good men, wise men, learned men to attend upon him with all submission as an appendix to his riches for that respect alone because he hath more wealth and money and to honor him with divine titles and bombast epithets," to smother him with fumes and eulogies whom they know to be a dizzard, a fool, a covetous wretch, a beast, etc., "because he is rich!" To see *sub exuviis leonis onagrum*, a filthy loathsome carcass, a Gorgon's head puffed up by parasites assume this unto himself, glorious titles, in worth an infant, a Cuman ass, a painted sepulchre, an Egyptian temple! To see a withered face, a diseased, deformed, cankered, complexion, a rotten carcass, a viperous mind, and Epicurean soul set out with orient pearls, jewels, diadems, perfumes, curious elaborate works, as proud of his clothes as a child of his new coats; and a goodly person, of an angel-like divine countenance, a saint, an humble mind, a meek spirit clothed in rags, beg, and now ready to be starved! To see a silly contemptible sloven in apparel, ragged in his coat, polite in speech, of a divine spirit, wise! another neat in clothes, spruce, full of courtesy, empty of grace, wit, talk nonsense!

To see many lawyers, advocates, so many tribunals, so little justice; so many magistrates, so little care of the common good; so many laws, yet never more disorders; *tribunal litium segetem*, the tribunal a labyrinth, so many thousand suits in one court sometimes, so violently followed! To see *iniustissimum sæpe iuri præsidentem, impium religioni, imperitissimum eruditioni, otiosissimum labori, monstrosum humanitati!* To see a lamb executed, a wolf pronounce sentence, *latro* arraigned, and *fur* sit on the bench, the judge severely punish others and do worse himself, *eundem furtum facere et punire, rapinam plectere, quum sit ipse raptor!* Laws altered, misconstrued, interpreted *pro* and *con*, as the judge is made by friends, bribed, or otherwise affected as a nose of wax, good today, none tomorrow; or firm in his opinions, cast in his! Sentence prolonged, changed *ad arbitrium iudicis*, still the same case, "one thrust out of his inheritance, another falsely put in by favor, false forged deeds or wills." *Incisæ leges negliguntur*, laws are made and not kept; or if put in execution, they be some silly ones that are punished. As put case it be fornication, the father will disinherit or abdicate his child, quite cashier him (out! villain, begone! come no more in my sight), a poor man is miserably tormented with loss of his estate perhaps, goods, fortunes, good name, forever disgraced, forsaken, and must do penance to the utmost; a mortal sin, and yet make the worst of it, *Nunquid aliud fecit*, saith Tranio in the poet, *nisi quod faciunt summis nati generibus?* he hath done no more than what gentlemen usually do.

Neque novum, neque mirum, neque secus quam alii solent.

For in a great person, right worshipful sir, a right honorable grandee, 'tis not a venial sin, no, not a *peccadillo*, 'tis no offense at all, a common and ordinary thing, no man takes notice of it; he justifies it in public and peradventure brags of it.

Nam quod turpe bonis, Titio, Seioque, decebat
Crispinum—

many poor men, younger brothers, etc., by reason of bad policy and idle education—for they are likely brought up in no calling—are compelled to beg or steal, and then hanged for theft; than which what can be more ignominious! *Non minus enim turpe principi multa supplicia quam medico multa funera*, 'tis the governor's fault. *Libentius verberant quam docent*, as schoolmasters do rather correct their pupils than teach them when they do amiss. "They had more need provide there should be no more thieves and beggars, as they ought with good policy, and take away the occasions than let them run on as they do to their own destruction," root out likewise those causes of wrangling, a multitude of lawyers, and compose controversies, *lites lustrales et seculares*, by some more compendious means. Whereas now for every toy and trifle they go to law, *Mugit litibus insanum forum, et sævit invicem discordantium rabies*, they are ready to pull out one another's throats; and for commodity "to squeeze blood," saith Jerome, "out of their brother's heart," defame, lie, disgrace, backbite, rail, bear false witness, swear, forswear, fight and wrangle, spend their goods, lives, fortunes, friends, undo one another, to enrich an harpy advocate that preys upon them both and cries, *Eia, Socrates! Eia, Xantippe!* or some corrupt judge that like the kite in Æsop, while the mouse and frog fought, carried both away. Generally they prey one upon another as so many ravenous birds, brute beasts, devouring fishes, no medium, *omnes hic aut captantur aut captant; aut cadavera quæ lacerantur, aut corvi qui lacerant*, either deceive or be deceived; tear others, or be torn in pieces themselves; like so many buckets in a well, as one riseth another falleth, one's empty, another's full; his ruin is a ladder to the third; such are our ordinary proceedings. What's the market? A place according to Anacharsis wherein they cozen one another, a trap. Nay, what's the world itself? A vast chaos, a confusion of manners, as fickle as the air, *domicilium insanorum*, a turbulent troop full of impurities, a mart of walking spirits, goblins, the theater of hypocrisy, a shop of knavery, flattery, a nursery of villainy, the scene of babbling, the school of giddiness, the academy of vice; a warfare, *ubi velis nolis pugnandum, aut vincas aut succumbas*, in which kill or be killed; wherein every man is for himself, his private ends, and stands upon his own guard. No charity, love, friendship, fear of God, alliance, affinity, consanguinity, Christianity can contain them, but if they be any ways offended or that string of commodity be touched, they fall foul. Old friends become bitter enemies on a sudden

for toys and small offenses, and they that erst were willing to do all mutual offices of love and kindness now revile and persecute one another to death with more than Vatinian hatred and will not be reconciled. So long as they are behoveful, they love, or may bestead each other; but when there is no more good to be expected, as they do by an old dog, hang him up or cashier him. Which Cato counts a great indecorum, to use men like old shoes or broken glasses which are flung to the dunghill; he could not find in his heart to sell an old ox, much less turn away an old servant. But they instead of recompense, revile him, and when they have made him an instrument of their villainy, as Bajazet the second emperor of the Turks did by Acomethes Bassa, make him away, or instead of reward hate him to death, as Silius was served by Tiberius. In a word, every man for his own ends. Our *summum bonum* is commodity, and the goddess we adore *Dea Moneta*, Queen Money, to whom we daily offer sacrifice, which steers our hearts, hands, affections, all, that most powerful goddess, by whom we are reared, depressed, elevated, esteemed the sole commandress of our actions, for which we pray, run, ride, go, come, labor, and contend as fishes do for a crumb that falleth into the water. It's not worth, virtue (that's *bonum theatrale*), wisdom, valor, learning, honesty, religion, or any sufficiency for which we are respected, but money, greatness, office, honor, authority; honesty is accounted folly; knavery, policy; men admired out of opinion, not as they are but as they seem to be. Such shifting, lying, cogging, plotting, counterplotting, temporizing, flattering, cozening, dissembling "that of necessity one must highly offend God if he be conformable to the world, *Cretizare cum Crete* or else live in contempt, disgrace and misery." One takes upon him temperance, holiness, another austerity, a third an affected kind of simplicity, when as indeed he and he and he and the rest are hypocrites, ambodexters, outsides, so many turning pictures, a lion on the one side, a lamb on the other. How would Democritus have been affected to see these things!

To see a man turn himself into all shapes like a chameleon or as Proteus, *omnia transformans sese in miracula rerum*, to act twenty parts and persons at once for his advantage, to temporize and vary like Mercury the planet, good with good, bad with bad; having a several face, garb, and character for everyone he meets; of all religions, humors, inclinations; to fawn like a spaniel, *mentitis et mimicis obsequiis*, rage like a lion, bark like a cur, fight like a dragon, sting like a serpent, as meek as a lamb, and yet again grin like a tiger, weep like a crocodile, insult over some, and yet others domineer over him, here command, there crouch, tyrannize in one place, be baffled in another, a wise man at home, a fool abroad to make others merry.

To see so much difference betwixt words and deeds, so many parasangs betwixt tongue and heart, men like stage-players act variety of parts, give good precepts to others, soar aloft, whilst they themselves grovel on the ground.

To see a man protest friendship, kiss his hand, *quem mallet truncatum videre*, smile with an intent to do mischief, or cozen him whom he salutes, magnify his friend unworthy with hyperbolical eulogies; his enemy, albeit a good man, to vilify and disgrace him, yea, all his actions, with the utmost livor and malice can invent.

To see a servant able to buy out his master, him that carries the mace more worth than the magistrate, which Plato, *lib*. 11, *de leg*., absolutely forbids, Epictetus abhors. An horse that tills the land fed with chaff, an idle jade have provender in abundance; him that makes shoes go barefoot himself, him that sells meat almost pined; a toiling drudge starve, a drone flourish.

To see men buy smoke for wares, castles built with fools' heads, men like apes follow the fashions in tires, gestures, actions. If the king laugh, all laugh;

> —*Rides? majore cachinno*
> *Concutitur, flet si lachrymas conspexit amici.*

Alexander stooped, so did his courtiers; Alphonsus turned his head, and so did his parasites. Sabina Poppea, Nero's wife, wore amber-colored hair, so did all the Roman ladies in an instant, her fashion was theirs.

To see men wholly led by affection, admired and censured out of opinion without judgment; an inconsiderate multitude, like so many dogs in a village, if one bark, all bark without a cause; as fortune's fan turns, if a man be in favor or commended by some great one, all the world applauds him; if in disgrace, in an instant all hate him, and as at the sun when he is eclipsed, that erst took no notice now gaze and stare upon him.

To see a man wear his brains in his belly, his guts in his head, an hundred oaks on his back, to devour 100 oxen at a meal, nay, more, to devour houses and towns, or as those *anthropophagi*, to eat one another.

To see a man roll himself up like a snowball, from base beggary to right worshipful and right honorable titles, unjustly to screw himself into honors and offices;

another to starve his genius, damn his soul to gather wealth, which he shall not enjoy, which his prodigal son melts and consumes in an instant.

To see the κακοζηλίαν of our times, a man bend all his forces, means, time, fortunes, to be a favorite's favorite's favorite, etc., a parasite's parasite's parasite that may scorn the servile world as having enough already.

To see an hirsute beggar's brat that lately fed on scraps, crept, and whined, crying to all and for an old jerkin ran on errands, now ruffle in silk and satin, bravely mounted, jovial and polite, now scorn his old friends and familiars, neglect his kindred, insult over his betters, domineer over all.

To see a scholar crouch and creep to an illiterate peasant for a meal's meat; a scrivener better paid for an obligation; a falconer receive greater wages than a student; a lawyer get more in a day than a philosopher in a year, better reward for an hour than a scholar for a twelvemonth's study; him that can paint Thais, play on a fiddle, curl hair, etc., sooner get preferment than a philologer or a poet.

To see a fond mother like Æsop's ape, hug her child to death, a wittol wink at his wife's honesty and too perspicacious in all other affairs; one stumble at a straw, and leap over a block; rob Peter, and pay Paul; scrape unjust sums with one hand, purchase great manors by corruption, fraud, and cozenage, and liberally to distribute to the poor with the other, give a remnant to pious uses, etc. Penny wise, pound foolish; blind men judge of colors; wise men silent, fools talk; find fault with others, and do worse themselves; denounce that in public which he doth in secret; and which Aurelius Victor gives out of Augustus, severely censure that in a third, of which he is most guilty himself.

To see a poor fellow, or an hired servant venture his life for his new master that will scarce give him his wages at a year's end; a country colone toil and moil, till and drudge for a prodigal idle drone that devours all the gain or lasciviously consumes with fantastical expenses; a noble man in a bravado to encounter death and for a small flash of honor to cast away himself; a worldling tremble at an executioner, and yet not fear hell-fire; to wish and hope for immortality, desire to be happy, and yet by all means avoid death, a necessary passage to bring him to it.

To see a foolhardy fellow like those old Danes, *qui decollari malunt quam verberari*, die rather than be punished, in a sottish humor embrace death with alacrity yet scorn to lament his own sins and miseries or his dearest friend's departures.

To see wise men degraded, fools preferred, one govern towns and cities, and yet a silly woman over-rules him at home; command a province, and yet his own servants or children prescribe laws to him, as Themistocles' son did in Greece; "What I will," said he, "my mother will, and what my mother will my father doth." To see horses ride in a coach, men draw it; dogs devour their masters; towers build masons; children rule; old men go to school; women wear the breeches; sheep demolish towns, devour men, etc. And in a word, the world turned upside downward. *O viveret Democritus!* . . .

[THE UTOPIA OF DEMOCRITUS JUNIOR]

I WILL yet, to satisfy and please myself, make an Utopia of mine own, a New Atlantis, a poetical commonwealth of mine own, in which I will freely domineer, build cities, make laws, statutes, as I list myself. And why may I not? *Pictoribus atque poetis,* etc.—you know what liberty poets ever had, and besides, my predecessor Democritus was a politician, a recorder of Abdera, a law-maker, as some say; and why may not I presume so much as he did? Howsoever I will adventure. For the site, if you will needs urge me to it, I am not fully resolved, it may be in *Terra Australis Incognita,*[11] there is room enough (for of my knowledge neither that hungry Spaniard,[12] nor Mercurius Britannicus, have yet discovered half of it), or else one of those floating islands in Mare del Zur,[13] which, like the Cyanean Isles in the Euxine Sea, alter their place, and are accessible only at set times, and to some few persons; or one of the Fortunate Isles, for who knows yet where, or which they are? There is room enough in the inner parts of America and northern coasts of Asia. But I will choose a site, whose latitude shall be forty-five degrees (I respect not minutes) in the midst of the temperate zone, or perhaps under the Equator, that paradise of the world, *ubi semper virens laurus,*[14] etc., where is a perpetual spring: the longitude for some reasons I will conceal. Yet "be it known to all men by these presents," that if any honest gentleman will send

in so much money as Cardan allows an astrologer for casting a nativity, he shall be a sharer, I will acquaint him with my project; or if any worthy man will stand for any temporal or spiritual office or dignity (for, as he said of his archbishopric of Utopia, 'tis *sanctus ambitus,*[15] and not amiss to be sought after), it shall be freely given without all intercessions, bribes, letters, etc., his own worth shall be the best spokesman; and because we shall admit of no deputies or advowsons, if he be sufficiently qualified, and as able as willing to execute the place himself, he shall have present possession. It shall be divided into twelve or thirteen provinces, and those by hills, rivers, roadways, or some more eminent limits exactly bounded. Each province shall have a metropolis, which shall be so placed as a center almost in a circumference, and the rest at equal distances, some twelve Italian miles asunder, or thereabout, and in them shall be sold all things necessary for the use of man, *statis horis et diebus;*[16] no market towns, markets or fairs, for they do but beggar cities (no village shall stand above six, seven, or eight miles from a city); except those emporiums which are by the seaside, general staples, marts, as Antwerp, Venice, Bergen of old, London, etc. Cities most part shall be situate upon navigable rivers or lakes, creeks, havens; and for their form, regular, round, square, or long square, with fair, broad, and straight streets, houses uniform, built of brick and stone, like Bruges, Brussels, Rhegium Lepidi, Berne in Switzerland, Milan, Mantua, Crema, Cambalu in Tartary, described by M. Polus, or that Venetian Palma. I will admit very few or no suburbs, and those of baser building, walls only to keep out man and horse, except it be in some frontier towns, or by the seaside, and those to be fortified after the latest manner of fortification, and situated upon convenient havens, or opportune places. In every so built city, I will have convenient churches, and separate places to bury the dead in, not in churchyards; a *citadella* (in some, not all) to command it, prisons for offenders, opportune market-places of all sorts, for corn, meat, cattle, fuel, fish; commodious courts of justice, public halls for all societies, bourses, meeting-places, armories, in which shall be kept engines for quenching of fire, artillery gardens, public walks, theaters, and spacious fields allotted for all gymnics, sports, and honest recreations, hospitals of all kinds, for children, orphans, old folks, sick men, madmen, soldiers,

---

11 The Unknown Southern Land (Australia).
12 Ferdinando de Quiros, 1612. [Burton.]
13 The South Sea (Pacific Ocean).
14 Where the laurel is ever green.

15 A holy ambition; quoted from the prefatory letter in Sir Thomas More's *Utopia.*
16 At stated hours and on stated days.

pesthouses, etc., not built *precario*, or by gouty bene-factors, who, when by fraud and rapine they have ex-torted all their lives, oppressed whole provinces, societies, give something to pious uses, build a satis-factory almshouse, school, or bridge, etc., at their last end, or before perhaps, which is no otherwise than to steal a goose and stick down a feather, rob a thousand to relieve ten; and those hospitals so built and main-tained, not by collections, benevolences, donaries, for a set number (as in ours), just so many and no more at such a rate, but for all those who stand in need, be they more or less, and that *ex publico ærario*,[17] and so still maintained; *non nobis solum nati sumus*,[18] etc. I will have conduits of sweet and good water aptly disposed in each town, common granaries, as at Dresden in Misnia, Stettin in Pomerland, Nuremberg, etc.; col-leges of mathematicians, musicians, and actors, as of old at Lebedus in Ionia, alchemists,[19] physicians, artists, and philosophers, that all arts and sciences may sooner be perfected and better learned; and public historio-graphers, as amongst those ancient Persians, *qui in commentarios referebant quæ memoratu digna gerebantur*, in-formed and appointed by the state to register all famous acts, and not by each insufficient scribbler, partial or parasitical pedant, as in our times. I will pro-vide public schools of all kinds, singing, dancing, fencing, etc., especially of grammar and languages, not to be taught by those tedious precepts ordinarily used, but by use, example, conversation, as travelers learn abroad, and nurses teach their children: as I will have all such places, so will I ordain public governors, fit officers to each place, treasurers, ædiles, quæstors, over-seers of pupils, widows' goods, and all public houses, etc., and those once a year to make strict accounts of all receipts, expenses, to avoid confusion, *et sic fiet ut non absumant* (as Pliny to Trajan), *quod pudeat dicere*.[20] They shall be subordinate to those higher officers and governors of each city, which shall not be poor trades-men and mean artificers, but noblemen and gentlemen, which shall be tied to residence in those towns they dwell next, at such set times and seasons: for I see no reason (which Hippolytus complains of) "that it should be more dishonorable for noblemen to govern the city than the country, or unseemly to dwell there now than of old." I will have no bogs, fens, marshes, vast woods,

deserts, heaths, commons, but all enclosed (yet not depopulated, and therefore take heed you mistake me not); for that which is common, and every man's, is no man's; the richest countries are still enclosed, as Essex, Kent, with us, etc., Spain, Italy; and where enclosures are least in quantity, they are best husbanded, as about Florence in Italy, Damascus in Syria, etc., which are liker gardens than fields. I will not have a barren acre in all my territories, not so much as the tops of moun-tains: where nature fails, it shall be supplied by art: lakes and rivers shall not be left desolate. All common highways, bridges, banks, corrivations[21] of waters, aqueducts, channels, public works, building, etc., out of a common stock, curiously[22] maintained and kept in repair; no depopulations, engrossings, alterations of wood, arable, but by the consent of some supervisors that shall be appointed for that purpose, to see what reformation ought to be had in all places, what is amiss, how to help it, *Et quid quæque ferat regio, et quid quæque recuset*,[23] what ground is aptest for wood, what for corn, what for cattle, gardens, orchards, fishponds, etc., with a charitable division in every village (not one domineering house greedily to swallow up all, which is too common with us), what for lords, what for tenants; and because they shall be better encouraged to improve such lands they hold, manure, plant trees, drain, fence, etc., they shall have long leases, a known rent, and known fine, to free them from those intoler-able exactions of tyrannizing landlords. These super-visors shall likewise appoint what quantity of land in each manor is fit for the lord's demesnes, what for holding of tenants, how it ought to be husbanded— *Ut Magnetes equis, Minyæ gens cognita remis*[24]—how to be manured, tilled, rectified,

> *Hic segetes veniunt, illic felicius uvæ,*
> *Arborei fœtus alibi, atque injussa virescunt*
> *Gramina,*[25]

and what proportion is fit for all callings, because pri-vate possessors are many times idiots, ill husbands,

---

17 From the public treasury.

18 We are not born for ourselves alone.

19 Not to make gold, but for matters of physic. [Burton.]

20 And so they shall not squander the funds, which one is ashamed even to speak of.

21 Junctions.   22 Studiously, neatly.

23 And what each locality will bear, and what it refuses to bear.

24 As the Magnesians, famous for horses, the Argonauts, for oarsmanship.

25 From Virgil's Georgics, I, translated by Dryden as follows:

> This ground with Bacchus, that with Ceres suits,
> The other loads the trees with happy fruits,
> A fourth, with grass unbidden, decks the ground.

oppressors, covetous, and know not how to improve their own, or else wholly respect their own, and not public good.

Utopian parity is a kind of government to be wished for rather than effected. *Respub. Christianopolitana,*[26] Campanella's City of the Sun, and that New Atlantis,[27] witty fictions, but mere chimeras, and Plato's community in many things is impious, absurd, and ridiculous, it takes away all splendor and magnificence. I will have several orders, degrees of nobility, and those hereditary, not rejecting younger brothers in the meantime, for they shall be sufficiently provided for by pensions, or so qualified, brought up in some honest calling, they shall be able to live of themselves. I will have such a proportion of ground belonging to every barony; he that buys the land shall buy the barony, he that by riot consumes his patrimony and ancient demesnes shall forfeit his honors. As some dignities shall be hereditary, so some again by election, or by gift (besides free offices, pensions, annuities), like our bishoprics, prebends, the bassas' palaces in Turkey, the procurators' houses and offices in Venice, which, like the golden apple, shall be given to the worthiest and best deserving both in war and peace, as a reward of their worth and good service, as so many goals for all to aim at (*honos alit artes*),[28] and encouragements to others. For I hate those severe, unnatural, harsh, German, French, and Venetian decrees, which exclude plebeians from honors; be they never so wise, rich, virtuous, valiant, and well qualified, they must not be patricians, but keep their own rank; this is *naturæ bellum inferre,*[29] odious to God and men, I abhor it. My form of government shall be monarchical;

> *nunquam libertas gratior exstat*
> *Quam sub rege pio,* etc.[30]

Few laws, but those severely kept, plainly put down, and in the mother tongue, that every man may understand. Every city shall have a peculiar trade or privilege, by which it shall be chiefly maintained: and parents shall teach their children, one of three at least, bring up and instruct them in the mysteries of their own trade. In each town these several tradesmen shall be so aptly disposed, as they shall free the rest from

danger or offense: fire-trades, as smiths, forge-men, brewers, bakers, metal-men, etc. shall dwell apart by themselves: dyers, tanners, fellmongers,[31] and such as use water, in convenient places by themselves: noisome or fulsome for bad smells, as butchers' slaughterhouses, chandlers, curriers, in remote places and some back lanes. Fraternities and companies I approve of, as merchants' bourses, colleges of druggers, physicians, musicians, etc., but all trades to be rated in the sale of wares, as our clerks of the market do bakers and brewers; corn itself, what scarcity soever shall come, not to exceed such a price. Of such wares as are transported or brought in, if they be necessary, commodious, and such as nearly concern man's life, as corn, wood, coals, etc., and such provision we cannot want,[32] I will have little or no custom paid, no taxes; but for such things as are for pleasure, delight, or ornament, as wine, spice, tobacco, silk, velvet, cloth of gold, lace, jewels, etc., a greater impost. I will have certain ships sent out for new discoveries every year, and some discreet men appointed to travel into all neighbor kingdoms by land, which shall observe what artificial inventions and good laws are in other countries, customs, alterations, or aught else, concerning war or peace, which may tend to the common good. Ecclesiastical discipline, *penes episcopos,*[33] subordinate as the other. No impropriations, no lay patrons of church livings, or one private man, but common societies, corporations, etc., and those rectors of benefices to be chosen out of the universities, examined and approved, as the *literati* in China.[34] No parish to contain above a thousand auditors. If it were possible, I would have such priests as should imitate Christ, charitable lawyers should love their neighbors as themselves, temperate and modest physicians, politicians contemn the world, philosophers should know themselves, noblemen live honestly, tradesmen leave lying and cozening, magistrates corruption, etc.; but this is impossible, I must get such as I may. I will therefore have of lawyers, judges, advocates, physicians, chirurgeons,[35] etc., a set number, and every man, if it be possible, to plead his own cause, to tell that tale to the judge which he doth to his advocate, as at Fez in Africa, Bantam, Aleppo, Ragusa, *suam quisque causam dicere tenetur.*[36] Those advocates, chirurgeons, and physicians which are allowed, to be maintained out of the common treasure, no fees to be

26 The "Christianopolitan Republic," described in the *Christianopolis* of Johann Valentin Andrea, a seventeenth-century Protestant theologian and Rosicrucian philosopher.
27 Of Sir Francis Bacon.   28 Honor fosters the arts.
29 To make war on nature.
30 Liberty is never more gratifying than under a virtuous king.

31 Dealers in hides.   32 Do without.
33 In the hands of the bishops.
34 *I.e.,* by competitive examinations.   35 Surgeons.
36 Everyone is expected to plead his own cause.

given or taken upon pain of losing their places; or if they do, very small fees, and when the cause is fully ended. He that sues any man shall put in a pledge, which, if it be proved he hath wrongfully sued his adversary, rashly or maliciously, he shall forfeit and lose. Or else, before any suit begin, the plaintiff shall have his complaint approved by a set delegacy to that purpose; if it be of moment, he shall be suffered as before to proceed, if otherwise, they shall determine it. All causes shall be pleaded *suppresso nomine*, the parties' names concealed, if some circumstances do not otherwise require. Judges and other officers shall be aptly disposed in each province, villages, cities, as common arbitrators to hear causes and end all controversies, and those not single, but three at least on the bench at once, to determine or give sentence, and those again to sit by turns or lots, and not to continue still in the same office. No controversy to depend above a year, but without all delays and further appeals to be speedily dispatched, and finally concluded in that time allotted. These and all other inferior magistrates to be chosen as the *literati* in China, or by those exact suffrages of the Venetians, and such again not to be eligible, or capable of magistracies, honors, offices, except they be sufficiently qualified for learning, manners, and that by the strict approbation of deputed examinators: first scholars to take place, then soldiers; for I am of Vegetius his opinion, a scholar deserves better than a soldier, because *unius ætatis sunt quæ fortiter fiunt, quæ vero pro utilitate reipub. scribuntur, æterna:* a soldier's work lasts for an age, a scholar's forever. If they misbehave themselves, they shall be deposed, and accordingly punished, and whether their offices be annual or otherwise, once a year they shall be called in question, and give an account; for men are partial and passionate, merciless, covetous, corrupt, subject to love, hate, fear, favor, etc., *omne sub regno graviore regnum:* [37] like Solon's Areopagites, or those Roman censors, some shall visit others, and be visited *invicem* [38] themselves, they shall oversee that no prowling officer, under color of authority, shall insult over his inferiors, as so many wild beasts, oppress, domineer, flay, grind, or trample on, be partial or corrupt, but that there be *æquabile jus*, justice equally done, live as friends and brethren together; and which Sesellius would have and so much desires in his kingdom of France, "a diapason and sweet harmony of kings, princes, nobles, and plebeians so mutually tied and involved in love, as well as laws

and authority, as that they never disagree, insult or encroach one upon another." If any man deserve well in his office, he shall be rewarded,

> *quis enim virtutem amplectitur ipsam,*
> *Præmia si tollas?* [39]

He that invents anything for public good in any art or science, writes a treatise, or performs any noble exploit at home or abroad, shall be accordingly enriched, honored, and preferred. I say with Hannibal in Ennius, *Hostem qui feriet erit mihi Carthaginensis*, let him be of what condition he will, in all offices, actions, he that deserves best shall have best.

Tilianus in Philonius, out of a charitable mind no doubt, wished all his books were gold and silver, jewels and precious stones, to redeem captives, set free prisoners, and relieve all poor distressed souls that wanted means; religiously done, I deny not, but to what purpose? Suppose this were so well done, within a little after, though a man had Crœsus' wealth to bestow, there would be as many more. Wherefore I will suffer no beggars, rogues, vagabonds, or idle persons at all, that cannot give an account of their lives how they maintain themselves. If they be impotent, lame, blind, and single, they shall be sufficiently maintained in several hospitals, built for that purpose; if married and infirm, past work, or by inevitable loss or some such-like misfortune cast behind, by distribution of corn, house-rent free, annual pensions or money, they shall be relieved, and highly rewarded for their good service they have formerly done; if able, they shall be enforced to work. "For I see no reason" (as he said) [40] "why an epicure or idle drone, a rich glutton, a usurer, should live at ease, and do nothing, live in honor, in all manner of pleasures, and oppress others, whenas in the meantime a poor laborer, a smith, a carpenter, an husbandman that hath spent his time in continual labor, as an ass to carry burdens, to do the commonwealth good, and without whom we cannot live, shall be left in his old age to beg or starve, and lead a miserable life worse than a jument." [41] As all conditions shall be tied to their task, so none shall be over-tired, but have their set times of recreations and holidays, *indulgere genio,* [42] feasts and merry meetings, even to the meanest artificer, or basest servant, once a week to sing or dance (though not all at once), or do

---

37 Every throne is subject to a greater throne.
38 In turn.

39 For who would choose virtue for its own sake if you were to take away the reward?
40 The passage is from Book II of More's Utopia.
41 Mare.   42 Follow their own bent.

whatsoever he shall please; like that *Saccarum festum* amongst the Persians, those Saturnals in Rome, as well as his master. If any be drunk, he shall drink no more wine or strong drink in a twelvemonth after. A bankrupt shall be *catomidiatus in amphitheatro*,[43] publicly shamed, and he that cannot pay his debts, if by riot or negligence he have been impoverished, shall be for a twelvemonth imprisoned; if in that space his creditors be not satisfied, he shall be hanged. He that commits sacrilege shall lose his hands; he that bears false witness, or is of perjury convict, shall have his tongue cut out, except he redeem it with his head. Murder, adultery, shall be punished by death, but not theft, except it be some more grievous offense, or notorious offenders: otherwise they shall be condemned to the galleys, mines, be his slaves whom they have offended, during their lives. I hate all hereditary slaves, and that *duram Persarum legem*,[44] as Brisonius calls it; or as Ammianus, *impendio formidatas et abominandas leges, per quas ob noxam unis omnis propinquitas perit*, hard law that wife and children, friends and allies, should suffer for the father's offense.

No man shall marry until he be 25, no woman till she be 20, *nisi aliter dispensatum fuerit*.[45] If one die, the other party shall not marry till six months after; and because many families are compelled to live niggardly, exhaust and undone by great dowers, none shall be given at all, or very little, and that by supervisors rated; they that are foul shall have a greater portion; if fair, none at all, or very little: howsoever, not to exceed such a rate as those supervisors shall think fit. And when once they come to those years, poverty shall hinder no man from marriage, or any other respect, but all shall be rather enforced than hindered, except they be dismembered, or grievously deformed, infirm, or visited with some enormous hereditary disease in body or mind; in such cases upon a great pain or mulct, man or woman shall not marry, other order shall be taken for them to their content. If people over-abound, they shall be eased by colonies.

No man shall wear weapons in any city. The same attire shall be kept, and that proper to several callings, by which they shall be distinguished. *Luxus funerum*[46] shall be taken away, that intempestive expense moderated, and many others. Brokers, takers of pawns, biting usurers, I will not admit; yet because *hic cum*

hominibus non cum diis agitur, we converse here with men, not with gods, and for the hardness of men's hearts, I will tolerate some kind of usury. If we were honest, I confess, *si probi essemus*, we should have no use of it, but being as it is, we must necessarily admit it. Howsoever most divines contradict it, *Dicimus inficias, sed vox ea sola reperta est*,[47] it must be winked at by politicians. And yet some great doctors approve of it, Calvin, Bucer, Zanchius, P. Martyr, because by so many grand lawyers, decrees of emperors, princes' statutes, customs of commonwealths, churches' approbations, it is permitted, etc., I will therefore allow it. But to no private persons, nor to every man that will, to orphans only, maids, widows, or such as by reason of their age, sex, education, ignorance of trading, know not otherwise how to employ it; and those so approved, not to let it out apart, but to bring their money to a common bank which shall be allowed in every city, as in Genoa, Geneva, Nuremberg, Venice, at 5, 6, 7, not above 8 per centum, as the supervisors, or *ærarii præfecti*,[48] shall think fit. And as it shall not be lawful for each man to be an usurer that will, so shall it not be lawful for all to take up money at use, not to prodigals and spendthrifts, but to merchants, young tradesmen, such as stand in need, or know honestly how to employ it, whose necessity, cause, and condition the said supervisors shall approve of.

I will have no private monopolies, to enrich one man and beggar a multitude, multiplicity of offices, of supplying by deputies; weights and measures the same throughout, and those rectified by the *primum mobile* and sun's motion, threescore miles to a degree according to observation, 1000 geometrical paces to a mile, five foot to a pace, twelve inches to a foot, etc., and from measures known it is an easy matter to rectify weights, etc., to cast up all, and resolve bodies by algebra, stereometry.[49] I hate wars if they be not *ad populi salutem*,[50] upon urgent occasion. *Odimus accipitrem, quia semper vivit in armis*.[51] Offensive wars, except the cause be very just, I will not allow of. For I do highly magnify that saying of Hannibal to Scipio, in Livy: "It had been a blessed thing for you and us, if God had given that mind to our predecessors, that you had been content with Italy, we with Africa. For neither Sicily nor Sardinia are worth such cost and

---

43 Horsed and flogged in the amphitheater.
44 Hard law of the Persians.
45 Unless it shall have been otherwise arranged.
46 Display at funerals.
47 We say No, but it proves to be only a word.
48 Managers of the treasury.
49 The art of measuring solid bodies.
50 For the safety of the people.
51 We hate the hawk because it lives always in battle.

pains, so many fleets and armies, or so many famous captains' lives." *Omnia prius tentanda,* fair means shall first be tried. *Peragit tranquilla potestas, Quod violenta nequit.*[52] I will have them proceed with all moderation: but hear you, Fabius my general, not Minucius, *nam qui consilio nititur plus hostibus nocet, quam qui sine animi ratione, viribus.*[53] And in such wars to abstain as much as is possible from depopulations, burning of towns, massacring of infants, etc. For defensive wars, I will have forces still ready at a small warning, by land and sea, a prepared navy, soldiers *in procinctu, et quam Bonfinius apud Hungaros suos vult, virgam ferream,*[54] and money, which is *nervus belli,*[55] still in a readiness, and a sufficient revenue, a third part as in old Rome and Egypt, reserved for the commonwealth; to avoid those heavy taxes and impositions, as well to defray this charge of wars, as also all other public defalcations, expenses, fees, pensions, reparations, chaste sports, feasts, donaries, rewards, and entertainments. All things in this nature especially I will have maturely done, and with great deliberation: *ne quid temere, ne quid remisse ac timide fiat.*[56] *Sed quo feror hospes?*[57] To prosecute the rest would require a volume. *Manum de tabella,*[58] I have been over-tedious in this subject; I could have here willingly ranged, but these straits wherein I am included will not permit. . . .

LOVE OF LEARNING, OR, OVERMUCH STUDY.
With a Digression of the Misery of Scholars, and Why the Muses Are Melancholy[59]

LEONARTUS FUCHSIUS, *Instit., lib.* 3, *sect.* 1, *cap.* 1, Felix Plater, *lib.* 3, *de mentis alienat.,* Herc. de Saxonia, *Tract. post. de melanch., cap.* 3, speak of a peculiar fury which comes by overmuch study. Fernelius, *lib.* 1, *cap.*

18, puts study, contemplation and continual meditation, as an especial cause of madness, and in his 86 *consul.* cites the same words. . . . And 'tis the common tenet of the world that learning dulls and diminisheth the spirits and so *per consequens* produceth melancholy.

Two main reasons may be given of it why students should be more subject to this malady than others. The one is, they live a sedentary, solitary life, *sibi et Musis,* free from bodily exercise and those ordinary disports which other men use; and many times if discontent and idleness concur with it, which is too frequent, they are precipitated into this gulf on a sudden. But the common cause is overmuch study; too much learning, as Festus told Paul, hath made thee mad; 'tis that other extreme which effects it. So did Trincavellius, *lib.* 1, *consil.* 12 and 13, find by his experience in two of his patients, a young baron, and another that contracted this malady by too vehement study. So Forestus, *observat., l.* 10, *observ.* 13, in a young divine in Louvain, that was mad and said "he had a Bible in his head." Marsilius Ficinus, *de sanit. tuend., lib.* 1, *cap.* 1, 3, 4, and *l.* 2, *cap.* 16, gives many reasons "why students dote more often than others." The first is their negligence. "Other men look to their tools, a painter will wash his pencils, a smith will look to his hammer, anvil, forge; an husbandman will mend his plow-irons, and grind his hatchet if it be dull; a falconer or huntsman will have an especial care of his hawks, hounds, horses, dogs, etc.; a musician will string and unstring his lute, etc.; only scholars neglect that instrument, their brain and spirits I mean, which they daily use and by which they range over all the world, which by much study is consumed." *Vide,* saith Lucian, *ne funiculum nimis intendendo, aliquando abrumpas;* see thou twist not the rope so hard till at length it break. Ficinus in his fourth chap. gives some other reasons; Saturn and Mercury, the patrons of learning, are both dry planets. And Origanus assigns the same cause why mercurialists are so poor and most part beggars; for that their president Mercury had no better fortune himself. The destinies of old put poverty upon him as a punishment; since when poetry and beggary are *gemelli,* twin-born brats, inseparable companions:

> "And to this day is every scholar poor,
> Gross gold from them runs headlong to the boor."

Mercury can help them to knowledge, but not to money. The second is contemplation, "which dries the brain and extinguisheth natural heat; for whilst the spirits are intent to meditation above in the head,

---

52 Calm strength accomplishes what violence cannot.
53 For he who relies on strategy injures his enemy more than one who depends on unintelligent force.
54 Ready for action, and, what Bonfinius wants for his Hungarians, an iron rod.
55 The sinews of war.
56 That nothing be done rashly, nothing remissly, or timidly.
57 But whither am I, a mere novice, drifting?
58 Enough! Hands off the paper!
59 This is Subsection 15 of the Third Member of Section 2, Partition I, The Causes of Melancholy.

the stomach and liver are left destitute, and thence come black blood and crudities by defect of concoction, and for want of exercise the superfluous vapors cannot exhale," etc. The same reasons are repeated by Gomesius, *lib.* 4, *cap.* 1, *de sale*, Nymannus, *orat. de Imag.*, Jo. Voschius, *lib.* 2, *cap.* 5, *de peste*. And something more they add, that hard students are commonly troubled with gouts, catarrhs, rheums, cachexia, bradiopepsia, bad eyes, stone, and colic, crudities, oppilations, vertigo, winds, consumptions, and all such diseases as come by overmuch sitting; they are most part lean, dry, ill-colored, spend their fortunes, lose their wits and many times their lives, and all through immoderate pains and extraordinary studies. If you will not believe the truth of this, look upon great Tostatus' and Thomas Aquinas' works, and tell me whether those men took pains? peruse Austin, Jerome, etc., and many thousands besides.

> *Qui cupit optatam cursu contingere metam,*
> *Multa tulit, fecitque, puer, sudavit et alsit.*
> He that desires this wished goal to gain
> Must sweat and freeze before he can attain,

and labor hard for it. So did Seneca by his own confession, *ep.* 8, "Not a day that I spend idle, part of the night I keep mine eyes open, tired with waking, and now slumbering, to their continual task." Hear Tully, *pro Archia poeta*, "Whilst others loitered and took their pleasures, he was continually at his book." So they do that will be scholars, and that to the hazard, I say, of their healths, fortunes, wits, and lives. How much did Aristotle and Ptolemy spend? *unius regni pretium* they say, more than a king's ransom; how many crowns *per annum*, to perfect arts, the one about his History of Creatures, the other on his Almagest? How much time did Thebet Benchorat employ to find out the motion of the eighth sphere? Forty years and more, some write. How many poor scholars have lost their wits or become dizzards, neglecting all worldly affairs and their own health, wealth, *esse* and *bene esse*, to gain knowledge? For which, after all their pains, in the world's esteem they are accounted ridiculous and silly fools, idiots, asses, and (as oft they are) rejected, contemned, derided, doting and mad. . . . Go to Bedlam and ask. Or if they keep their wits, yet they are esteemed scrubs and fools by reason of their carriage; "after seven years' study."

> —*statua taciturnius exit,*
> *Plerumque et risum populi quatit.*—

Because they cannot ride an horse, which every clown can do, salute and court a gentlewoman, carve at table, cringe, and make congés, which every common swasher can do, *hos populus ridet*, etc., they are laughed to scorn and accounted silly fools by our gallants. Yea, many times, such is their misery, they deserve it. A mere scholar, a mere ass. . . . Thus they go commonly meditating unto themselves, thus they sit, such is their action and gesture. Fulgosus, *l.* 8, *c.* 7, makes mention how Th. Aquinas supping with King Lewis of France, upon a sudden knocked his fist upon the table and cried, *Conclusum est contra Manichæos!* his wits were a-woolgathering, as they say, and his head busied about other matters; when he perceived his error, he was much abashed. Such a story there is of Archimedes in Vitruvius, that having found out the means to know how much gold was mingled with the silver in King Hiero's crown, ran naked forth of the bath and cried εὑρηκα! I have found; "and was commonly so intent to his studies that he never perceived what was done about him. When the city was taken and the soldiers now ready to rifle his house, he took no notice of it." St. Bernard rode all day long by the Lemnian Lake, and asked at last where he was, Marullus, *lib.* 2, *cap.* 4. It was Democritus' carriage alone that made the Abderites suppose him to have been mad and send for Hippocrates to cure him; if he had been in any solemn company, he would upon all occasions fall a-laughing. Theophrastus saith as much of Heraclitus, for that he continually wept, and Laertius of Menedemus Lampsacus, because he ran like a madman, "saying he came from hell as a spy to tell the devils what mortal men did." Your greatest students are commonly no better; silly, soft fellows in their outward behavior, absurd, ridiculous to others, and no whit experienced in worldly business; they can measure the heavens, range over the world, teach others wisdom, and yet in bargains and contracts they are circumvented by every base tradesman. Are not these men fools? and how should they be otherwise "but as so many sots in schools when, as he well observed, they neither hear nor see such things as are commonly practiced abroad?" How should they get experience, by what means? "I knew in my time many scholars," saith Æneas Sylvius, in an epistle of his to Kaspar Schlick, chancellor to the emperor, "excellent well learned, but so rude, so silly that they had no common civility nor knew how to manage their domestic or public affairs." "Paglarensis was amazed and said his farmer had surely cozened him when he heard him tell that his sow had eleven pigs and his ass had but one foal." To say the best of this profession, I can give no other testimony of them in general than that of Pliny of Isæus; "He is yet a scholar, than which kind of men there is nothing so simple," so sincere, none better; they are most part harmless, honest, upright, innocent, plain-dealing men.

Now because they are commonly subject to such hazards and inconveniences as dotage, madness, simplicity, etc., Jo. Voschius would have good scholars to be highly rewarded and had in some extraordinary respect above other men, "to have greater privileges than the rest, that adventure themselves and abbreviate their lives for the public good." But our patrons of learning are so far nowadays from respecting the Muses and giving that honor to scholars or reward which they deserve and are allowed by those indulgent privileges of many noble princes that after all their pains taken in the universities, cost and charge, expenses, irksome hours, laborious tasks, wearisome days, dangers, hazards (barred *interim* from all pleasures which other men have, mewed up like hawks all their lives), if they chance to wade through them, they shall in the end be rejected, contemned, and, which is their greatest misery, driven to their shifts, exposed to want, poverty, and beggary. . . .

If there were nothing else to trouble them, the conceit of this alone were enough to make them all melancholy. Most other trades and professions, after some seven years' 'prenticeship, are enabled by their craft to live of themselves. A merchant adventures his goods at sea, and though his hazard be great, yet if one ship return of four, he likely makes a saving voyage. An husbandman's gains are almost certain; *quibus ipse Jupiter nocere non potest* ('tis Cato's hyperbole, a great husband himself); only scholars methinks are most uncertain, unrespected, subject to all casualties, and hazard. For first, not one of a many proves to be a scholar, all are not capable and docile, *ex omni ligno non fit Mercurius.* We can make majors and officers every year, but not scholars; kings can invest knights and barons, as Sigismund the Emperor confessed; universities can give degrees; and *Tu quod es, e populo quilibet esse potest;* but he nor they nor all the world can give learning, make philosophers, artists, orators, poets; we can soon say, as Seneca well notes, *O virum bonum, O divitem,* point at a rich man, a good, an happy man, a proper man, *sumptuose vestitum, calamistratum, bene olentem, magno temporis impendio constat hæc laudatio, O virum literatum!* but 'tis not so easily performed to find out a learned man. Learning is not so quickly got;

though they may be willing to take pains, to that end sufficiently informed, and liberally maintained by their patrons and parents, yet few can compass it. Or if they be docile, yet all men's wills are not answerable to their wits, they can apprehend, but will not take pains; they are either seduced by bad companions, *vel in puellam impingunt vel in poculum,* and so spend their time to their friends' grief and their own undoings. Or put case they be studious, industrious, of ripe wits, and perhaps good capacities, then how many diseases of body and mind must they encounter? No labor in the world like unto study. It may be, their temperature will not endure it, but striving to be excellent to know all, they lose health, wealth, wit, life, and all. Let him yet happily escape all these hazards, *æreis intestinis,* with a body of brass, and is now consummate and ripe, he hath profited in his studies, and proceeded with all applause, after many expenses, he is fit for preferment; where shall he have it? he is as far to seek it as he was (after twenty years' standing) at the first day of his coming to the university. For what course shall he take, being now capable and ready? The most parable and easy, and about which many are employed, is to teach a school, turn lecturer or curate, and for that he shall have falconer's wages, ten pounds *per annum,* and his diet, or some small stipend, so long as he can please his patron or the parish; if they approve him not—for usually they do but a year or two—as inconstant as they that cried "Hosanna!" one day and "Crucify him!" the other, serving-man-like, he must go look a new master. If they do, what is his reward? . . . Like an ass, he wears out his time for provender and can show a stum rod, *togam tritam et laceram,* saith Hædus, an old torn gown, an ensign of his infelicity; he hath his labor for his pain, a modicum to keep him till he be decrepit, and that is all. *Grammaticus non est felix,* etc. If he be a trencher chaplain in a gentleman's house, as it befell Euphormio, after some seven years' service he may perchance have a living to the halves, or some small rectory with the mother of the maids at length, a poor kinswoman, or a cracked chambermaid, to have and to hold during the time of his life. But if he offend his good patron or displease his lady mistress in the meantime,

> *Ducetur planta velut ictus ab Hercule Cacus,*
> *Poneturque foras, si quid tentaverit unquam*
> *Hiscere—*

as Hercules did by Cacus, he shall be dragged forth of doors by the heels, away with him! If he bend his forces to some other studies with an intent to be *a secretis* to some nobleman or in such a place with an ambassador, he shall find that these persons rise like 'prentices one under another, and in so many tradesmen's shops, when the master is dead, the foreman of the shop commonly steps in his place. Now for poets, rhetoricians, historians, philosophers, mathematicians, sophisters, etc., they are like grasshoppers, sing they must in summer, and pine in the winter, for there is no preferment for them. Even so they were at first, if you will believe that pleasant tale of Socrates, which he told fair Phædrus under a plane tree at the banks of the River Ilissus; about noon when it was hot and the grasshoppers made a noise he took that sweet occasion to tell him a tale how grasshoppers were once scholars, musicians, poets, etc., before the Muses were born, and lived without meat and drink, and for that cause were turned by Jupiter into grasshoppers. And may be turned again *in Tithoni cicadas aut Lyciorum ranas* for any reward I see they are like to have! Or else in the meantime I would they could live as they did, without any viaticum, like so many *manucodiatæ*, those Indian birds of paradise, as we commonly call them, those I mean that live with the air and dew of heaven and need no other food. For being as they are, their "rhetoric only serves them to curse their bad fortunes," and many of them for want of means are driven to hard shifts; from grasshoppers they turn humblebees and wasps, plain parasites, and make the Muses mules to satisfy their hunger-starved paunches and get a meal's meat. To say truth, 'tis the common fortune of most scholars to be servile and poor, to complain pitifully, and lay open their wants to their respectless patrons, as Cardan doth, as Xilander, and many others, and, which is too common in those dedicatory epistles, for hope of gain, to lie, flatter, and with hyperbolical eulogiums and commendations to magnify and extol an illiterate unworthy idiot for his excellent virtues, whom they should rather, as Machiavel observes, vilify and rail at downright for his most notorious villainies and vices. So they prostitute themselves as fiddlers or mercenary tradesmen to serve great men's turns for a small reward. They are like Indians, they have store of gold, but know not the worth of it. For I am of Synesius' opinion, "King Hiero got more by Simonides' acquaintance than Simonides did by his." They have their best education, good institution, sole qualification from us, and when they have done well, their honor and immortality from us; we are the living tombs, registers, and as so many trumpeters of their

fames. What was Achilles without Homer? Alexander without Arrian and Curtius? who had known the Cæsars, but for Suetonius and Dion? . . . They are more beholden to scholars than scholars to them; but they under-value themselves, and so by those great men are kept down. Let them have that encyclopedian, all the learning in the world, they must keep it to themselves, "live in base esteem, and starve, except they will submit," as Budæus well hath it, "so many good parts, so many ensigns of arts, virtues, be slavishly obnoxious to some illiterate potentate, and live under his insolent worship or honor like parasites," *qui tanquam mures alienum panem comedunt.* For to say truth, *artes hæ non sunt lucrativæ,* as Guido Bonat, that great astrologer, could foresee, they be not gainful arts these, *sed esurientes et famelicæ,* but poor and hungry.

> *Dat Galenus opes, dat Justinianus honores,*
> *Sed genus et species cogitur ire pedes:*
> The rich physician, honored lawyers ride,
> Whilst the poor scholar foots it by their side.

Poverty is the Muses' patrimony, and as that poetical divinity teacheth us, when Jupiter's daughters were each of them married to the gods, the Muses alone were left solitary, Helicon forsaken of all suitors, and I believe it was because they had no portion.

> *Calliope longum cælebs cur vixit in ævum?*
> *Nempe nihil dotis, quod numeraret, erat.*
> Why did Calliope live so long a maid?
> Because she had no dowry to be paid.

Ever since, all their followers are poor, forsaken, and left unto themselves. In so much that, as Petronius argues, you shall likely know them by their clothes. "There came," saith he, "by chance into my company a fellow not very spruce to look on, that I could perceive by that note alone he was a scholar, whom commonly rich men hate. I asked him what he was; he answered, a poet; I demanded again why he was so ragged; he told me this kind of learning never made any man rich." . . . All which our ordinary students right well perceiving in the universities, how unprofitable these poetical, mathematical, and philosophical studies are, how little respected, how few patrons, apply themselves in all haste to those three commodious professions of law, physic, and divinity, sharing themselves between them, rejecting these arts in the meantime, history, philosophy, philology, or lightly passing them over as pleasant toys fitting only table talk and to furnish them with discourse. They are not so behoveful; he that can tell his money hath arithmetic enough; he is a true geometrician can measure out a good fortune to himself; a perfect astrologer that can cast the rise and fall of others and mark their errant motions to his own use; the best optics are to reflect the beams of some great men's favor and grace to shine upon him; he is a good engineer that alone can make an instrument to get preferment. This was the common tenet and practice of Poland, as Cromerus observed not long since, in the first book of his History; their universities were generally base, not a philosopher, a mathematician, an antiquary, etc., to be found of any note amongst them, because they had no set reward or stipend, but every man betook himself to divinity, *hoc solum in votis habens, opimum sacerdotium*, a good parsonage was their aim. . . .

Although many times, for aught I can see, these men fail as often as the rest in their projects and are as usually frustrate of their hopes. For let him be a doctor of the law, an excellent civilian of good worth, where shall he practice and expatiate? Their fields are so scant, the civil law with us so contracted, with prohibitions so few causes by reason of those all-devouring municipal laws, *quibus nihil illiteratius*, saith Erasmus, an illiterate and a barbarous study—for though they be never so well learned in it, I can hardly vouchsafe them the name of scholars, except they be otherwise qualified—and so few courts are left to that profession, such slender offices, and those commonly to be compassed at such dear rates, that I know not how an ingenious man should thrive amongst them. Now for physicians, there are in every village so many mountebanks, empirics, quacksalvers, Paracelsians, as they call themselves, *causifici et sanicidæ*, so Clenard terms them, wizards, alchemists, poor vicars, cast apothecaries, physicians' men, barbers, and good-wives professing great skill, that I make great doubt how they shall be maintained or who shall be their patients. Besides, there are so many of both sorts and some of them such harpies, so covetous, so clamorous, so impudent and, as he said, litigious idiots, . . . that they cannot well tell how to live one by another, but as he jested in the Comedy of Clocks, they were so many, *major pars populi arida reptant fame*, they are almost starved a great part of them and ready to devour their fellows, *et noxia calliditate se corripere*, such a multitude of pettifoggers and empirics, such impostors, that an honest man knows not in what sort to compose and behave

himself in their society, to carry himself with credit in so vile a rout, *scientiæ nomen, tot sumptibus partum et vigiliis, profiteri dispudeat, postquam*, etc.

Last of all, to come to our divines, the most noble profession and worthy of double honor but of all others the most distressed and miserable. If you will not believe me, hear a brief of it, as it was not many years since publicly preached at Paul's Cross by a grave minister then and now a reverend bishop of this land:[60] "We that are bred up in learning and destined by our parents to this end, we suffer our childhood in the grammar school, which Austin calls *magnam tyrannidem et grave malum* and compares it to the torments of martyrdom; when we come to the university, if we live of the college allowance, as Phalaris objected to the Leontines, πάντων ἐνδεεῖς, πλὴν λιμοῦ χαὶ φόβον, needy of all things but hunger and fear, or if we be maintained but partly by our parents' cost, do expend in unnecessary maintenance, books and degrees, before we come to any perfection, five hundred pounds or a thousand marks. If by this price of the expense of time, our bodies and spirits, our substance and patrimonies, we cannot purchase those small rewards which are ours by law and the right of inheritance, a poor parsonage or a vicarage of £50 *per annum*, but we must pay to the patron for the lease of a life—a spent and outworn life—either in annual pension or above the rate of a copy-hold and that with the hazard and loss of our souls by simony and perjury and the forfeiture of all our spiritual preferments in *esse* and *posse* both present and to come, what father after a while will be so improvident to bring up his son to his great charge to this necessary beggary? What Christian will be so irreligious to bring up his son in that course of life which by all probability and necessity *coget ad turpia*, enforcing to sin, will entangle him in simony and perjury, when as the poet saith, *Invitatus ad hæc aliquis de ponte negabit*, a beggar's brat taken from the bridge where he sits a-begging, if he knew the inconvenience, had cause to refuse it?" This being thus, have not we fished fair all this while that are initiate divines to find no better fruits of our labors? *Hoc est cur palles, cur quis non prandeat hoc est?* Do we macerate ourselves for this? Is it for this we rise so early all the year long? "Leaping," as he saith, "out of our beds when we hear the bell ring as if we had heard a thunderclap." If this be all the respect, reward, and honor we shall have, *frange leves calamos et scinde, Thalia, libellos!* let us give over our books and betake ourselves to some other

60 John Howson.

course of life! To what end should we study? *Quid me litterulas stulti docuere parentes?* what did our parents mean to make us scholars, to be as far to seek of preferment after twenty years' study as we were at first? Why do we take such pains? *Quid tantum insanis juvat impallescere chartis?* If there be no more hope of reward, no better encouragement, I say again, *Frange leves calamos et scinde, Thalia, libellos!* let's turn soldiers, sell our books and buy swords, guns, and pikes, or stop bottles with them, turn our philosophers' gowns, as Cleanthes once did, unto millers' coats, leave all and rather betake ourselves to any other course of life than to continue longer in this misery. . . .

Yea, but methinks I hear some man except at these words, that though this be true which I have said of the estate of scholars, and especially of divines, that it is miserable and distressed at this time, that the church suffers shipwreck of her goods, and that they have just cause to complain; there is a fault, but whence proceeds it? If the cause were justly examined, it would be retorted upon ourselves; if we were cited at that tribunal of truth, we should be found guilty and not able to excuse it. That there is a fault among us I confess, and were there not a buyer, there would not be a seller. But to him that will consider better of it, it will more than manifestly appear that the fountain of these miseries proceeds from these griping patrons. In accusing them I do not altogether excuse us; both are faulty, they and we; yet in my judgment, theirs is the greater fault, more apparent causes and much to be condemned. For my part, if it be not with me as I would or as it should, I do ascribe the cause, as Cardan did in the like case, *meo infortunio potius quam illorum sceleri*, to mine own infelicity rather than their naughtiness, although I have been baffled in my time by some of them and have as just cause to complain as another. Or rather indeed to mine own negligence; for I was ever like that Alexander in Plutarch, Crassus his tutor in philosophy, who though he lived many years familiarly with rich Crassus, was even as poor when from—which many wondered at—as when he came first to him; he never asked, the other never gave him anything; when he traveled with Crassus, he borrowed a hat of him, at his return restored it again. I have had some such noble friends' acquaintance and scholars', but most part,—common courtesies and ordinary respects excepted—they and I parted as we met; they gave me as much as I requested, and that was—. And as Alexander *ab Alexandro, Genial. dier., l. 6, c. 16,* made answer to Hieronimus Massainus that wondered

quum plures ignavos et ignobiles ad dignitates et sacerdotia promotos quotidie videret, when other men rose, still he was in the same state, *eodem tenore et fortuna cui mercedem laborum studiorumque deberi putaret,* whom he thought to deserve as well as the rest. He made answer that he was content with his present estate, was not ambitious, and although *objurgabundus suam segnitiem accusaret, cum obscuræ sortis homines ad sacerdotia et pontificatus evectos,* etc., he chid him for his backwardness, yet he was still the same. And for my part, though I be not worthy perhaps to carry Alexander's books, yet by some overweening and well-wishing friends the like speeches have been used to me; but I replied still with Alexander that I had had enough and more peradventure than I deserved; and with Libanius Sophista, that rather chose, when honors and offices by the emperor were offered unto him, to be *talis Sophista quam talis magistratus,* I had as lief be still Democritus Junior, *privus privatus, si mihi iam daretur optio, quam talis fortasse doctor, talis dominus.—Sed quorsum hæc?* For the rest 'tis on both sides *facinus detestandum* to buy and sell livings, to detain from the church that which God's and men's laws have bestowed on it; but in them most, and that from the covetousness and ignorance of such as are interested in this business. I name covetousness in the first place as the root of all these mischiefs, which Achan-like compels them to commit sacrilege and to make simoniacal compacts and what not to their own ends, that kindles God's wrath, brings a plague, vengeance, and an heavy visitation upon themselves and others. Some out of that insatiable desire of filthy lucre, to be enriched, care not how they come by it *per fas et nefas,* hook or crook, so they have it. And others when they have with riot and prodigality embezzled their estates, to recover themselves make a prey of the church, robbing it, as Julian the Apostate did, spoil parsons of their revenues in "keeping half back," as a great man amongst us observes, "and that maintenance on which they should live." By means whereof barbarism is increased and a great decay of Christian professors. For who will apply himself to these divine studies, his son, or friend, when after great pains taken, they shall have nothing whereupon to live! But with what event do they these things? . . . They toil and moil, but what reap they? They are commonly unfortunate families that use it, accursed in their progeny, and, as common experience evinceth, accursed themselves in all their proceedings. "With what face," as he quotes out of Aust., "can they expect a blessing or inheritance from Christ in heaven that defraud Christ of his inheritance here on earth!" I would our simoniacal patrons and such as detain tithes would read those judicious tracts of Sir Henry Spelman and Sir James Sempill, knights, those late elaborate and learned treatises of Dr. Tillesley and Mr. Montague, which they have written of that subject. But though they should read, it would be to small purpose, *clames licet et mare cælo confundas;* thunder, lighten, preach hell and damnation, tell them 'tis a sin, they will not believe it; denounce and terrify, they have "cauterized consciences," they do not attend; as the enchanted adder, they stop their ears. Call them base, irreligious, profane, barbarous, pagans, atheists, epicures—as some of them surely are—with the bawd in Plautus, *Euge! optime!* they cry and applaud themselves with that miser, *simul ac nummos contemplor in arca.* Say what you will, *quocunque modo rem,* as a dog barks at the moon, to no purpose are your sayings. Take your heaven, let them have money. A base, profane, hypocritical rout! For my part, let them pretend what zeal they will, counterfeit religion, blear the world's eyes, bombast themselves, and stuff out their greatness with church spoils, shine like so many peacocks; so cold is my charity, so defective in this behalf that I shall never think better of them than that they are rotten at core, their bones are full of epicurean hypocrisy and atheistical marrow, they are worse than heathens. . . . The eagle in Æsop, seeing a piece of flesh now ready to be sacrificed, swept it away with her claws and carried it to her nest; but there was a burning coal stuck to it by chance, which unawares consumed her, young ones, nest and all together. Let our simoniacal church-chopping patrons and sacrilegious harpies look for no better success.

A second cause is ignorance and from thence contempt, *successit odium in literas ab ignorantia vulgi,* which Junius well perceived; this hatred and contempt of learning proceeds out of ignorance, as they are themselves barbarous, idiots, dull, illiterate, and proud, so they deem others.

> *Sint Mæcenates, non deerunt, Flacce, Marones.*

Let there be bountiful patrons, and there will be painful scholars in all sciences. But when they contemn learning and think themselves sufficiently qualified if they can write and read, scamble at a piece of evidence, or have so much Latin as that emperor had *qui nescit dissimulare, nescit vivere,* they are unfit to do their country service, to perform or undertake any action or employment which may tend to the good of a commonwealth, except it be to fight or to do country justice with common sense, which every yeoman can likewise do. And so they bring up their children rude as they are themselves, unqualified, untaught, uncivil most part. *Quis e nostra juventute legitime instituitur literis? Quis oratores aut philosophos tangit? Quis historiam legit, illam rerum agendarum quasi animam? Præcipitant parentes vota sua,* etc., 'twas Lipsius' complaint to his illiterate countrymen, it may be ours. Now shall these men judge of a scholar's worth that have no worth, that know not what belongs to a student's labors, that cannot distinguish between a true scholar and a drone? or him that by reason of a voluble tongue, a strong voice, a pleasing tone, and some trivantly Polyanthean helps, steals and gleans a few notes from other men's harvests and so makes a fairer show than he that is truly learned indeed, that thinks it no more to preach than to speak "or to run away with an empty cart," as a grave man said.[61] And thereupon vilify us and our pains, scorn us, and all learning. Because they are rich and have other means to live, they think it concerns them not to know or to trouble themselves with it; a fitter task for younger brothers or poor men's sons to be pen and ink-horn men, pedantical slaves, and no whit beseeming the calling of a gentleman, as Frenchmen and Germans commonly do, neglect therefore all human learning; what have they to do with it! Let mariners learn astronomy, merchants' factors study arithmetic, surveyors get them geometry, spectacle-makers optics, landleapers geography, town-clerks rhetoric; what should he do with a spade that hath no ground to dig! or they with learning that have no use of it! Thus they reason and are not ashamed to let mariners, 'prentices, and the basest servants be better qualified than themselves. In former times kings, princes, and emperors were the only scholars, excellent in all faculties.

Julius Cæsar mended the year[62] and writ his own Commentaries, . . . Antonius, Hadrian, Nero, Severus, Jul., etc., Michael the Emperor, and Isacius were so much given to their studies that no base fellow would take so much pains. Orion, Perseus, Alphonsus, Ptolemæus, famous astronomers; Sabor, Mithridates, Lysimachus, admired physicians; Plato's kings all; Evax, that Arabian prince, a most expert jeweler, and an exquisite philosopher. The kings of Egypt were priests of old and chosen from thence,—*Idem rex*

61 Dr. King, Bishop of London.
62 Revised the calendar.

hominum, Phœbique sacerdos. But those heroical times are past; the Muses are now banished in this bastard age *ad sordida tuguriola,* to meaner persons, and confined alone almost to universities. In those days scholars were highly beloved, honored, esteemed; as old Ennius by Scipio Africanus, Virgil by Augustus, Horace by Mæcenas; princes' companions, dear to them, as Anacreon to Polycrates, Philoxenus to Dionysius, and highly rewarded. Alexander sent Xenocrates the Philosopher 50 talents because he was poor, *visu rerum, aut eruditione præstantes viri, mensis olim regum adhibiti,* as Philostratus relates of Hadrian and Lampridius of Alexander Severus. Famous clerks came to these princes' courts *velut in Lycæum,* as to an university, and were admitted to their tables *quasi divum epulis accumbentes;* Archilaus that Macedonian king would not willingly sup without Euripides—amongst the rest he drank to him at supper one night and gave him a cup of gold for his pains—*delectatus poeta suavi sermone;* and it was fit it should be so, because, as Plato in his Protagoras well saith, a good philosopher as much excels other men as a great king doth the commons of his country; and again, *quoniam illis nihil deest, et minime egere solent, et disciplinas quas profitentur, soli a contemptu vindicare possunt,* they needed not to beg so basely, as they compel scholars in our times to complain of poverty or crouch to a rich chuff for a meal's meat, but could vindicate themselves and those arts which they professed. Now they would and cannot. For it is held by some of them as an axiom that to keep them poor will make them study; they must be dieted, as horses to a race, not pampered, *Alendos volunt, non saginandos, ne melioris mentis flammula extinguatur;* a fat bird will not sing, a fat dog cannot hunt, and so by this depression of theirs some want means, others will, all want encouragement as being forsaken almost and generally contemned. 'Tis an old saying, *Sint Mæcenates, non deerunt, Flacce, Marones,* and 'tis a true saying still. Yet oftentimes, I may not deny it, the main fault is in ourselves. Our academics too frequently offend in neglecting patrons, as Erasmus well taxeth, or making ill choice of them; *negligimus oblatos aut amplectimur parum aptos;* or if we get a good one, *non studemus mutuis officiis favorem eius alere,* we do not ply and follow him as we should. *Idem mihi accidit adolescenti,* saith Erasmus acknowledging his fault, *et gravissime peccavi,* and so may I say myself, I have offended in this and so peradventure have many others. We did not *spondere magnatum favoribus qui cœperunt nos amplecti,* apply ourselves with that readiness we should; idleness, love of

liberty, *immodicus amor libertatis effecit ut diu cum perfidis amicis,* as he confesseth, *et pertinaci paupertate colluctarer,* bashfulness, melancholy, timorousness cause many of us to be too backward and remiss. So some offend in one extreme but too many on the other, we are most part too forward, too solicitous, too ambitious, too impudent; we commonly complain *deesse Mæcenates,* want of encouragement, want of means, when as the true defect is in our own want of worth, our insufficiency. Did Mæcenas take notice of Horace or Virgil till they had showed themselves first? or had Bavius and Mevius any patrons? *Egregium specimen dent,* saith Erasmus, let them approve themselves worthy first, sufficiently qualified for learning and manners, before they presume or impudently intrude and put themselves on great men as too many do; with such base flattery, parasitical colloguing, such hyperbolical eulogies they do usually insinuate that it is a shame to hear and see. . . . So we offend, but the main fault is in their harshness, defect of patrons. How beloved of old and how much respected was Plato by Dionysius! How dear to Alexander was Aristotle, Demaratus to Philip, Solon to Crœsus, Anaxarchus and Trebatius to Augustus, Cassius to Vespasian, Plutarch to Trajan, Seneca to Nero, Simonides to Hiero! how honored!

> *Sed hæc prius fuere, nunc recondita*
> *Senent quiete,*

those days are gone,

> *Et spes, et ratio studiorum in Cæsare tantum;*

as he said of old, we may truly say now, he is our amulet, our sun, our sole comfort and refuge, our Ptolemy, our common Mæcenas, *Jacobus munificus, Jacobus pacificus, mysta Musarum, rex Platonicus, grande decus, columenque nostrum,*[63] a famous scholar himself, and the sole patron, pillar, and sustainer of learning. But his worth in this kind is so well known that, as Paterculus of Cato, *Iam ipsum laudare nefas sit,* and which Pliny to Trajan, *Seria te carmina honorque æternus annalium, non hæc brevis et pudenda prædicatio colet.* But he is now gone, the sun of ours set, and yet no night follows,

> *—Sol occubuit, nox nulla secuta est.*

63 This is, of course, James I.

We have such another in his room [64]

> *—aureus alter*
> *Avulsus, simili frondescit virga metallo,*

and long may he reign and flourish amongst us!

Let me not be malicious and lie against my genius, I may not deny but that we have a sprinkling of our gentry, here and there one excellently well learned, like those Fuggeri in Germany, Dubartas, Du Plessis, Sadael in France, Picus Mirandola, Schottus, Barotius in Italy,

> *Apparent rari nantes in gurgite vasto.*

But they are but few in respect of the multitude, the major part—and some again excepted that are indifferent—are wholly bent for hawks and hounds and carried away many times with intemperate lust, gaming, and drinking. If they read a book at any time, *si quod est interim otii a venatu, poculis, alea, scortis,* 'tis an English chronicle, Sir Huon of Bordeaux, Amadis de Gaul, etc., a play-book, or some pamphlet of news, and that at such seasons only when they cannot stir abroad to drive away time. Their sole discourse is dogs, hawks, horses, and what news? If someone have been a traveler in Italy or as far as the emperor's court, wintered in Orleans, and can court his mistress in broken French, wear his clothes neatly in the newest fashion, sing some choice outlandish tunes, discourse of lords, ladies, towns, palaces, and cities, he is complete and to be admired. Otherwise he and they are much at one; no difference betwixt the master and the man but worshipful titles; wink and choose betwixt him that sits down—clothes excepted—and him that holds the trencher behind him. Yet these men must be our patrons, our governors too sometimes, statesmen, magistrates, noble, great, and wise, by inheritance.

Mistake me not, I say again, *vos, O patricius sanguis,* you that are worthy senators, gentlemen, I honor your names and persons, and with all submissiveness, prostrate myself to your censure and service. There are amongst you, I do ingenuously confess, many well-deserving patrons and true patriots of my knowledge, besides many hundreds which I never saw, no doubt, or heard of, pillars of our commonwealth, whose worth, bounty, learning, forwardness, true zeal in religion, and good esteem of all scholars ought to be consecrated to all posterity. But of your rank there are a debauched, corrupt, covetous, illiterate crew again no better than stocks, *merum pecus—testor Deum, non mihi*

64 Charles I.

videri dignos ingenui hominis appellatione—barbarous Thracians, *et quis ille Thrax qui hoc neget?* a sordid, profane, pernicious company, irreligious, impudent, and stupid, I know not what epithets to give them, enemies to learning, confounders of the church, and the ruin of a commonwealth. Patrons they are by right of inheritance and put in trust freely to dispose of such livings to the church's good; but (hard task-masters they prove) they take away their straw and compel them to make their number of brick. They commonly respect their own ends, commodity is the steer of all their actions, and him they present in conclusion as a man of greatest gifts that will give most; no penny, no pater-noster, as the saying is. *Nisi preces auro fulcias, amplius irritas, ut Cerberus offa,* their attendants and officers must be bribed, feed, and made, as Cerberus is with a sop by him that goes to hell. It was an old saying, *omnia Romæ venalia,* 'tis a rag of popery which will never be rooted out; there is no hope, no good to be done without money. A clerk may offer himself, approve his worth, learning, honesty, religion, zeal, they will commend him for it; but—*probitas laudatur, et alget.* If he be a man of extraordinary parts, they will flock afar off to hear him, as they did in Apuleius, to see Psyche: . . . many mortal men came to see fair Psyche, the glory of her age, they did admire her, commend, desire her for her divine beauty, and gaze upon her; but as on a picture; none would marry her *quod indotata;* fair Psyche had no money. So they do by learning;

> *—didicit iam dives avarus*
> *Tantum admirari, tantum laudare disertos,*
> *Ut pueri Junonis avem—.*
> Your rich men have now learned of latter days
> T'admire, commend, and come together
> To hear and see a worthy scholar speak,
> As children do a peacock's feather.

He shall have all the good words that may be given, a proper man, and 'tis pity he hath no preferment, all good wishes, but inexorable, indurate as he is, he will not prefer him, though it be in his power, because he is *indotatus,* he hath no money. Or if he do give him entertainment, let him be never so well qualified, plead affinity, consanguinity, sufficiency, he shall serve seven years, as Jacob did for Rachel, before he shall have it. If he will enter at first, he must get in at that simoniacal gate, come off soundly, and put in good security to perform all covenants, else he will not deal with or admit him. But if some poor scholar, some parson chaff will offer himself, some trencher chaplain that will take it to the halves, thirds, or accept of what he will give, he is welcome; be conformable, preach as he will have him, he likes him before a million of others; for the best is always best cheap. And then as Jerome said to Cromatius, *patella dignum operculum*, such a patron, such a clerk; the cure is well supplied, and all parties pleased. So that is still verified in our age which Chrysostom complained of in his time, *Qui opulentiores sunt, in ordinem parasitorum cogunt eos, et ipsos tanquam canes ad mensas suas enutriunt, eorumque impudentes ventres iniquarum cænarum reliquiis differtiunt, iisdem pro arbitrio abutentes;* rich men keep these lecturers and fawning parasites like so many dogs at their tables, and filling their hungry guts with offals of their meat, they abuse them at their pleasure and make them say what they propose. "As children do by a bird or a butterfly in a string, pull in and let him out as they list, do they by their trencher chaplains, prescribe, command their wits, let in and out as to them it seems best." If the patron be precise, so must his chaplain be, if he be papistical, his clerk must be so too or else be turned out. These are those clerks which serve the turn whom they commonly entertain and present to church livings, whilst in the meantime we that are university men, like so many hide-bound calves in a pasture, tarry out our time, wither away as a flower ungathered in a garden, and are never used, or as so many candles, illuminate ourselves alone, obscuring one another's light, and are not discerned here at all, the least of which, translated to a dark room, or to some country benefice, where it might shine apart, would give a fair light and be seen over all. Whilst we lie waiting here as those sick men did at the Pool of Bethesda till the angel stirred the water, expecting a good hour, they step between and beguile us of our preferment. I have not yet said, if after long expectation, much expense, travel, earnest suit of ourselves and friends, we obtain a small benefice at last, our misery begins afresh; we are suddenly encountered with the flesh, world, and Devil, with a new onset; we change a quiet life for an ocean of troubles, we come to a ruinous house, which before it be habitable must be necessarily to our great damage repaired; we are compelled to sue for dilapidations or else sued ourselves, and, scarce yet settled, we are called upon for our predecessor's arrearages; first-fruits, tenths, subsidies are instantly to be paid, benevolence, procurations, etc., and which is most to be feared, we light upon a cracked title, as it befell Clenard of Brabant; for his rectory and charge of his Beginæ; he was no sooner inducted but instantly sued, *cœpimusque,* saith he, *strenue litigare et implacabili bello confligere;* at length after ten years' suit, as long as Troy's siege, when he had tired himself and spent his money, he was fain to leave all for quietness' sake and give it up to his adversary. Or else we are insulted over and trampled on by domineering officers, fleeced by those greedy harpies to get more fees; we stand in fear of some precedent lapse; we fall amongst refractory, seditious sectaries, peevish Puritans, perverse Papists, a lascivious rout of atheistical epicures that will not be reformed, or some litigious people ("those wild beasts of Ephesus" must be fought with) that will not pay their dues without much repining or compelled by long suit; *Laici clericis oppido infesti,* an old axiom, all they think well gotten that is had from the church, and by such uncivil, harsh dealings they make their poor minister weary of his place, if not of his life. And put case they be quiet honest men, make the best of it, as often it falls out, from a polite and terse academic he must turn rustic, rude, melancholize alone, learn to forget, or else, as many do, become maltsters, graziers, chapmen, etc., now banished from the academy, all commerce of the Muses, and confined to a country village, as Ovid was from Rome to Pontus, and daily converse with a company of idiots and clowns. . . .

AIR RECTIFIED. WITH A DIGRESSION OF THE AIR [65]

As a long-winged hawk when he is first whistled off the fist mounts aloft, and for his pleasure fetcheth many a circuit in the air, still soaring higher and higher till he be come to his full pitch, and in the end, when the game is sprung, comes down amain and stoops upon a sudden, so will I, having come at last into these ample fields of air wherein I may freely expatiate and exercise myself for my recreation, a while rove, wander round about the world, mount aloft to those etherial orbs and celestial spheres, and so descend to my former elements again. In which progress I will first see whether that relation of the friar of Oxford [66] be true concerning those northern parts under the Pole—if I meet *obiter* with the Wandering Jew, Elias Artifex, or Lucian's Icaromenippus, they shall be my guides—

65 This is Member 3 of Section 2 of Partition 2, The Cure of Melancholy.
66 Nicholas de Lynna, cited by Mercator in his map.

whether there be such 4 Euripes and a great rock of loadstones which may cause the needle in the compass still to bend that way, and what should be the true cause of the variation of the compass. Is it a magnetical rock, or the Pole Star, as Cardan will, or some other star in the Bear, as Marsilius Ficinus, or a magnetical meridian, as Maurolicus, *vel situs in vena terræ*, as Agricola, or the nearness of the next continent, as Cabeus will, or some other cause, as Scaliger, Cortesius, Conimbricenses, Peregrinus, contend; why at the Azores it looks directly north, otherwise not? In the Mediterranean or Levant, as some observe, it varies 7 grad. by and by 12 and then 22. In the Baltic Seas, near Rasceburg in Finland, the needle runs round if any ships come that way, though Martin Ridley write otherwise, that the needle near the Pole will hardly be forced from his direction. 'Tis fit to be inquired whether certain rules may be made of it, as 11 *grad. Lond. variat. alibi* 36, etc., and that which is more prodigious, the variation varies in the same place, now taken accurately 'tis so much after a few years quite altered from that it was. Till we have better intelligence, let our D. Gilbert and Nicholas Cabeus the Jesuit, that have both written great volumes of this subject, satisfy these inquisitors. Whether the sea be open and navigable by the Pole Arctic, and which is the likeliest way, that of Bartison the Hollander, under the Pole itself, which for some reasons I hold best, or by *Fretum* Davis, or Nova Zembla. Whether Hudson's discovery be true of a new-found ocean, any likelihood of Button's Bay in 50 degrees, Hubberd's Hope in 60, that of *ut ultra* near Sir Thomas Roe's welcome in Northwest Fox, being that the sea ebbs and flows constantly there 15 foot in 12 hours, as our new cards inform us that California is not a cape but an island, and the west winds make the neap tides equal to the spring, or that there be any probability to pass by the Straits of Anian to China by the Promontory of Tabin. If there be, I shall soon perceive whether Marcus Polus the Venetian's narration be true or false of that great City of Quinsay and Cambalu; whether there be any such places, or that, as Matth. Riccius the Jesuit hath written, China and Cataia be all one, the great Cham of Tartary and the King of China be the same, Xuntain and Quinsay and the City of Cambalu be that new Peking, or such a wall 400 leagues long to part China from Tartary; whether Presbyter John be in Asia or Africa; M. Polus Venetus puts him in Asia; the most received opinion is that he is emperor of the *Abissines*, which of old was Ethiopia, now Nubia,

under the Equator in Africa. Whether Guinea be an island or part of the continent, or that hungry Spaniard's discovery of *Terra Australis Incognita*, or *Magellanica*, be as true as that of Mercurius Britannicus, or his of Utopia, or his of Lucinia. And yet in likelihood it may be so, for without all question it, being extended from the Tropic of Capricorn to the Circle Antarctic and lying as it doth in the Temperate Zone, cannot choose but yield in time some flourishing kingdoms to succeeding ages, as America did unto the Spaniards. Shouten and Le Meir have done well in the discovery of the Straits of Magellan, in finding a more convenient passage to *Mare Pacificum*. Methinks some of our modern Argonauts should prosecute the rest. As I go by Madagascar, I would see that great bird rucke, that can carry a man and horse or an elephant, with that Arabian phœnix described by Adricomius, see the pelicans of Egypt, those Scythian gryphes in Asia, and afterwards in Africa examine the fountains of Nilus, whether Herodotus, Seneca, Plin., *lib.* 5, *cap.* 9, Strabo, *lib.* 5, give a true cause of his annual flowing, Pagaphetta discourse rightly of it or of Niger and Senegal; examine Cardan, Scaliger's reasons, and the rest. Is it from those Etesian winds or melting of snow in the mountains under the Equator—for Jordan yearly overflows when the snow melts in Mount Libanus—or from those great dropping perpetual showers which are so frequent to the inhabitants within the tropics when the sun is vertical and cause such vast inundations in Senegal, Maragnan, Orinoco, and the rest of those great rivers in *Zona Torrida*, which have all commonly the same passions at set times; and by good husbandry and policy hereafter no doubt may come to be as populous, as well tilled, as fruitful as Egypt itself or Cauchinthina. I would observe all those motions of the sea and from what cause they proceed, from the moon, as the vulgar hold, or earth's motion, which Galileus in the fourth dialogue of his system of the world so eagerly proves and firmly demonstrates, or winds, as some will. Why in that quiet Ocean of Zur, *in Mari Pacifico*, it is scarce perceived, in our British seas most violent, in the Mediterranean and Red Sea so vehement, irregular, and diverse. Why the current in that Atlantic Ocean should still be in some places from, in some again towards the north, and why they come sooner than go. And so from Moabar to Madagascar in that Indian Ocean the merchants come in three weeks, as Scaliger discusseth; they return scarce in three months with the same or like winds; the continual current is from east to west. Whether Mount

Athos, Pelion, Olympus, Ossa, Caucasus, Atlas be so high as Pliny, Solinus, Mela relate, above clouds, meteors, *ubi nec auræ nec venti spirant* (insomuch that they that ascend die suddenly very often, the air is so subtile) 1,250 paces high according to that measure of Dicearchus, or 78 miles perpendicularly high, as Jacobus Mazonius, sec. 3 and 4, expounding that place of Aristotle about Mount Caucasus, and as Blancanus the Jesuit contends out of Clavius' and Nonius' demonstrations *de Crepusculis*, or rather 32 stadiums, as the most received opinion is, or 4 miles, which the height of no mountain doth perpendicularly exceed and is equal to the greatest depths of the sea, which is, as Scaliger holds, 1,280 paces, exer. 38, others 100 paces. I would see those inner parts of America, whether there be any such great city of Manoa or Eldorado in that golden empire, where the highways are as much beaten, one reports, as between Madrid and Valladolid in Spain; or any such Amazons as he relates or gigantical Patagones in Chica; with that miraculous mountain Ybouyapab in the northern Brazil, *cuius jugum sternitur in amœnissimam planitiem,* etc., or that Pariacacca so high elevated in Peru. The pike of Teneriffe how high it is, 70 miles or 50, as Patricius holds, or 9, as Snellius demonstrates in his Eratosthenes. See that strange Cirknickzerksey Lake in Carniola, whose waters gush so fast out of the ground that they will overtake a swift horseman and by and by with as incredible celerity are supped up; which Lazius and Warnerus make an argument of the Argonauts sailing underground. And that vast den or hole called Esmellen in Muscovia *quæ visitur horrendo hiatu,* etc., which if anything casually fall in, makes such a roaring noise that no thunder or ordnance or warlike engine can make the like; such another is Gilber's Cave in Lapland, with many the like. I would examine the Caspian Sea and see where and how it exonerates[67] itself after it hath taken in Volga, Jaxares, Oxus, and those great rivers; at the mouth of Oby, or where? What vent the Mexican lake hath, the Titicacan in Peru, or that circular pool in the vale of Terapeia, of which Acosta, *l.* 3, *c.* 16, hot in a cold country, the spring of which boils up in the middle twenty foot square and hath no vent but exhalation; and that of *Mare Mortuum* in Palestina, of Thrasymene at Peruzium in Italy; the Mediterranean itself. For from the ocean at the Straits of Gibraltar there is a perpetual current into the Levant and so likewise by the Thracian Bosphorus out of the Euxine or Black Sea, besides all those great rivers of Nilus, Padus, Rhodanus, etc., how is this water consumed, by the sun, or otherwise? I would find out with Trajan the fountains of Danubius, of Ganges, Oxus, see those Egyptian pyramids, Trajan's bridge, Grotto de Sibylla, Lucullus' fish-ponds, the temple of Nidrose, etc. And, if I could, observe what becomes of swallows, storks, cranes, cuckoos, nightingales, redstarts, and many other kind of singing birds, water-fowls, hawks, etc.; some of them are only seen in summer, some in winter; some are observed in the snow and at no other times; each have their seasons. In winter not a bird is in Muscovy to be found, but at the spring in an instant the woods and hedges are full of them, saith Herbastein; how comes it to pass? Do they sleep in winter, like Gesner's Alpine mice; or do they lie hid, as Olaus affirms, "in the bottom of lakes and rivers, *spiritum continentes?* often so found by fishermen in Poland and Scandia, two together, mouth to mouth, wing to wing; and when the spring comes they revive again, or if they be brought into a stove or to the fireside." Or do they follow the sun, as Peter Martyr, *legat. Babylonica, l.* 2, manifestly convicts out of his own knowledge? For when he was ambassador in Egypt, he saw swallows, Spanish kites, and many such European birds in December and January very familiarly flying and in great abundance about Alexandria, *ubi floridæ tunc arbores ac viridariæ.* Or lie they hid in the caves, rocks, and hollow trees, as most think, in deep tin-mines or sea-cliffs, as Mr. Carew gives out? I conclude of them all, for my part, as Munster doth of cranes and storks; whence they come, whither they go, *incompertum adhuc,* as yet we know not. We see them here, some in summer, some in winter. "Their coming and going is sure in the night. In the plains of Asia," saith he, "the storks meet on such a set day, he that comes last is torn in pieces, and so they get them gone." Many strange places, Isthmi, Euripi, Chersonesi, creeks, havens, promontories, straits, lakes, baths, rocks, mountains, places, and fields where cities have been ruined or swallowed, battles fought, creatures, sea-monsters, *remora,* etc., minerals, vegetals, zoöphytes[68] were fit to be considered in such an expedition and amongst the rest that of Herbastein his Tartar lamb, Hector Boethius' goose-bearing tree in the Orcades, to which Cardan, *lib.* 7, *cap.* 36, *de rerum varietat.,* subscribes; Vertomannus' wonderful

---

67 Unburdens; frequently the seventeenth-century word is exactly the Latin in its meaning.

68 Plantlike animals, such as sponges, jellyfish, or starfish.

palm,[69] that fly in Hispaniola that shines like a torch in the night that one may well see to write; those spherical stones in Cuba which nature hath so made and those like birds, beasts, fishes, crowns, swords, saws, pots,[70] etc., usually found in the metal-mines in Saxony about Mansfield and in Poland near Nokow and Pallukie, as Munster and others relate. Many rare creatures and novelties each part of the world affords. Amongst the rest, I would know for a certain whether there be any such men as Leo Suavius in his comment on Paracelsus' *de sanit. tuend.* and Gaguinus records in his description of Muscovy, "that in Lucomoria, a province in Russia, lie fast asleep as dead all winter, from the 27 of November, like frogs and swallows, benumbed with cold, but about the 24 of April in the spring they revive again and go about their business." I would examine that demonstration of Alexander Piccolomineus, whether the earth's superficies be bigger than the sea's; or that of Archimedes be true, the superficies of all water is even. Search the depth and see that variety of sea-monsters and fishes, mermaids, sea-men, horses, etc., which it affords. Or whether that be true which Jordanus Brunus scoffs at, that if God did not detain it, the sea would overflow the earth by reason of his higher site, and which Josephus Blancanus the Jesuit in his interpretation on those mathematical places of Aristotle foolishly fears and in a just tract proves by many circumstances that in time the sea will waste away the land and all the globe of the earth shall be covered with waters; *risum teneatis, amici?* what the sea takes away in one place it adds in another. Methinks he might rather suspect the sea should in time be filled by land, trees grow up, carcasses, etc., that all-devouring fire, *omnia devorans et consumens,* will sooner cover and dry up the vast ocean with sand and ashes. I would examine the true seat of that terrestrial paradise and where Ophir was whence Solomon did fetch his gold; from Peruana which some suppose, or that *aurea* Chersonesus, as Dominicus Niger, Arius Montanus, Goropius, and others will. . . .

I would have a convenient place to go down with Orpheus, Ulysses, Hercules, Lucian's Menippus, at St. Patrick's purgatory, at Trophonius' den, Hecla in Iceland, Etna in Sicily, to descend and see what is done in the bowels of the earth; do stones and metals grow there still? how come fir trees to be digged out from tops of hills as in our mosses and marshes all over Europe? How come they to dig up fish-bones, shells, beams, iron-works many fathoms under ground and anchors in mountains far remote from all seas? *Anno* 1460 at Berne in Switzerland, 50 fathoms deep, a ship was digged out of a mountain where they got metal ore, in which were 48 carcasses of men, with other merchandise. That such things are ordinarily found in tops of hills, Aristotle insinuates in his meteors, Pomponius Mela in his first book, *c. de Numidia,* and familiarly in the Alps, saith Blancanus the Jesuit, the like is to be seen. Came this from earthquakes or from Noah's Flood, as Christians suppose, or is there a vicissitude of sea and land? as Anaximenes held of old the mountains of Thessaly would become seas, and seas again mountains? The whole world belike should be new molded, when it seemed good to those all-commanding powers, and turned inside out, as we do haycocks in harvest, top to bottom, or bottom to top, or as we turn apples to the fire, move the world upon his center, that which is under the poles now should be translated to the equinoctial, and that which is under the Torrid Zone to the Circle Arctic and Antarctic another while, and so be reciprocally warmed by the sun; or if the worlds be infinite and every fixed star a sun with his compassing planets, as Brunus and Campanella conclude, cast three or four worlds into one; or else of one old world make three or four new, as it shall seem to them best. To proceed, if the earth be 21,500 miles in compass, its diameter is 7,000 from us to our Antipodes, and what shall be comprehended in all that space? What is the center of the earth? is it pure element only, as Aristotle decrees, inhabited, as Paracelsus thinks, with creatures whose chaos is the earth; or with fairies, as the woods and waters, according to him, are with nymphs or as the air with spirits? Dionisiodorus, a mathematician in Pliny, that sent a letter *ad superos* after he was dead from the center of the earth to signify what distance the same center was from the superficies of the same, viz. 42,000 stadiums, might have done well to have satisfied all these doubts. Or is it the place of hell, as Virgil in his *Æneides,* Plato, Lucian, Dante, and others poetically describe it, and as many of our divines think? In good earnest, Anthony Rusca, one of the society of that Ambrosian College in Milan, in his great volume *de Inferno, lib.* 1, *cap.* 47, is stiff in this tenet, 'tis a corporeal fire-tow, *cap.* 5, *l.* 2,

---

69 The coconut, "that bears fruits to eat, wood to burn, bark to make ropes, wine and water to drink, oil and sugar, and leaves and tiles to cover houses, flowers for clothes."

70 Many of these may well have been fossils, miraculous enough to a century that still took the Book of Genesis as history. See also below.

as he there disputes. "Whatsoever philosophers write," saith Surius, "there be certain mouths of hell and places appointed for the punishment of men's souls, as at Hecla in Iceland, where the ghosts of dead men are familiarly seen and sometimes talk with the living. God would have such visible places that mortal men might be certainly informed that there be such punishments after death and learn hence to fear God." Kranzius, *Dan. hist.*, lib. 2, cap. 24, subscribes to this opinion of Surius, so doth Colerus, cap. 12, lib. de immortal. animæ—out of the authority belike of St. Gregory, Durand, and the rest of the Schoolmen, who derive as much from Etna in Sicily, Lypara, Hyera, and those sulphureous vulcanian islands—making Terra del Fuego and those frequent volcanoes in America, of which Acosta, lib. 3, cap. 24, that fearful Mount Hecklebirg in Norway, an especial argument to prove it, "where lamentable screeches and howlings are continually heard which strike a terror to the auditors; fiery chariots are commonly seen to bring in the souls of men in the likeness of crows, and devils ordinarily go in and out." Such another proof is that place near the pyramids in Egypt by Cairo, as well to confirm this as the resurrection, mentioned by Kornmanus, *mirac. mort.*, lib. 1, cap. 38, Camerarius, oper. suc., cap. 37, Bredenbachius, pereg. ter. sanct., and some others, "where once a year dead bodies arise about March and walk, and after a while hide themselves again; thousands of people come yearly to see them." But these and such like testimonies others reject as fables, illusions of spirits, and they will have no such local known place more than Styx or Phlegethon, Pluto's court, or that poetical Infernus, where Homer's soul was seen hanging on a tree, etc., to which they ferried over in Charon's boat or went down at Hermione in Greece, *compendiaria ad inferos via*, which is the shortest cut *quia nullum a mortuis naulum eo loci exposcunt*, saith Gerbelius, and besides there were no fees to be paid. Well then, is it hell, or purgatory, as Bellarmine; or *limbus patrum*, as Gallucius will, and as Rusca will—for they have made maps of it—or Ignatius' parlor? Virgil, sometime Bishop of Salzburg, as Aventinus, anno 745, relates, by Bonifacius, Bishop of Mentz, was therefore called in question, because he held Antipodes—which they made a doubt whether Christ died for—and so by that means took away the seat of hell or so contracted it that it could bear no proportion to heaven and contradicted that opinion of Austin, Basil, Lactantius, that held the earth round as a trencher (whom Acosta and common experience

more largely confute) but not as a ball; and Jerusalem where Christ died the middle of it; or Delos, as the fabulous Greeks feigned; because when Jupiter let two eagles loose to fly from the world's ends east and west, they met at Delos. But that scruple of Bonifacius is now quite taken away by our latter divines; Franciscus Ribera in *cap*. 14, *Apocalyps*. will have hell a material and local fire in the center of the earth, 200 Italian miles in diameter, as he defines it out of those words, *exivit sanguis de terra*—*per stadia mille sexcenta*, etc. But Lessius, lib. 13, de moribus divinis, cap. 24, will have this local hell far less, one Dutch mile in diameter, all filled with fire and brimstone; because, as he there demonstrates, that space cubically multiplied will make a sphere able to hold eight hundred thousand millions of damned bodies, allowing each body six foot square, which will abundantly suffice; *cum certum sit, inquit, facta subductione, non futuros centies mille milliones damnandorum*. But if it be no material fire, as Scotus, Thomas, Bonaventure, Soncinas, Voscius, and others argue, it may be there or elsewhere, as Keckerman disputes, *System. Theol.*, for sure somewhere it is, *certum est alicubi, etsi definitus circulus non assignetur*. I will end the controversy in Austin's words, "Better doubt of things concealed than to contend about uncertainties, where Abraham's bosom is and hell fire. . . ."

In the meantime let us consider of that which is *sub dio* and find out a true cause, if it be possible, of such accidents, meteors, alterations as happen above ground. Whence proceed that variety of manners and a distinct character, as it were, to several nations? Some are wise, subtle, witty; others dull, sad and heavy; some big, some little, as Tully, *de Fato*, Plato in *Timæo*, Vegetius and Bodin proves at large, *method.*, cap. 5; some soft and some hardy, barbarous, civil, black, dun, white,— is it from the air, from the soil, influence of stars, or some other secret cause? Why doth Africa breed so many venomous beasts, Ireland none? Athens owls, Crete none? Why hath Daulis and Thebes no swallows —so Pausanias informeth us—as well as the rest of Greece, Ithaca no hares, Pontus asses, Scythia swine? whence come this variety of complexions, colors, plants, birds, beasts, metals, peculiar almost to every place? Why so many thousand strange birds and beasts proper to America alone, as Acosta demands, lib. 4, cap. 36; were they created in the six days, or ever in Noah's Ark? If there, why are they not dispersed and found in other countries? It is a thing, saith he, hath long held me in suspense; no Greek, Latin, Hebrew ever heard of them before and yet as differing from our

European animals as an egg and a chestnut; and which is more, kine, horses, sheep, etc., till the Spaniards brought them, were never heard of in those parts. How comes it to pass that in the same site, in one latitude, to such as are *periœci*, there should be such difference of soil, complexion, color, metal, air, etc.? The Spaniards are white, and so are Italians, when as the inhabitants about *Caput Bonæ Spei* are blackamoors, and yet both alike distant from the Equator; nay, they that dwell in the same parallel line with these Negroes, as about the Straits of Magellan, are white-colored, and yet some in Presbyter John's country in Ethiopia are dun; they in Zeilan and Malabar, parallel with them again, black. Manamotapa in Africa and St. Thomas' Isle are extreme hot, both under the Line, coal-black their inhabitants; whereas in Peru they are quite opposite in color, very temperate, or rather cold, and yet both alike elevated. Moscow in 53 degrees of latitude extreme cold, as those northern countries usually are, having one perpetual hard frost all winter long; and in 52 deg. lat. sometimes hard frost and snow all summer, as in Button's Bay, etc., or by fits; and yet England near the same latitude and Ireland, very moist, warm, and more temperate in winter than Spain, Italy, or France. Is it the sea that causeth this difference and the air that comes from it? Why then is Ister so cold near the Euxine, Pontus, Bithynia, and all Thrace? *Frigidas regiones* Maginus calls them, and yet their latitude is but 42, which should be hot. Quevira, or Nova Albion, in America, bordering on the sea, was so cold in July that our Englishmen could hardly endure it. At Noremberga in 45 lat. all the sea is frozen ice, and yet in a more southern latitude than ours. New England and the Island of Cambrial Colchos, which that noble gentleman, Mr. Vaughan, or Orpheus Junior, describes in his Golden Fleece, is in the same latitude with Little Britain in France, and yet their winter begins not till January, their spring till May; which search he accounts worthy of an astrologer; is this from the easterly winds, or melting of ice and snow dissolved within the Circle Arctic? or that the air being thick, is longer before it be warm by the sunbeams, and once heated like an oven will keep itself from cold? Our climes breed lice. Hungary and Ireland *male audiunt* in this kind; come to the Azores, by a secret virtue of that air they are instantly consumed, and all our European vermin almost, saith Ortelius. Egypt is watered with Nilus not far from the sea, and yet there it seldom or never rains. Rhodes, an island of the same nature, yields not a cloud, and yet our

islands ever dropping and inclining to rain. The Atlantic Ocean is still subject to storms, but in Del Zur, or *Mari Pacifico*, seldom or never any. Is it from tropic stars, *apertio portarum*, in the dodecatemories or constellations, the moon's mansions, such aspects of planets, such winds, or dissolving air, or thick air, which causeth this and the like differences of heat and cold? . . . Arica in Chile is by report one of the sweetest places that ever the sun shined upon, *Olympus terræ*, an heaven on earth. How incomparably do some extol Mexico in Nova Hispania, Peru, Brazil, etc.? In some again hard, dry, sandy, barren, a very desert, and still in the same latitude. Many times we find great diversity of air in the same country by reason of the site to seas, hills, or dales, want of water, nature of soil, and the like; as in Spain Arragon is *aspera et sicca*, harsh and evil inhabited, Estremadura is dry, sandy, barren most part, extreme hot by reason of his plains, Andalusia another paradise, Valencia a most pleasant air and continually green; so is it about Granada, on the one side fertile plains, on the other continual snow to be seen all summer long on the hill tops. That their houses in the Alps are three quarters of the year covered with snow, who knows not? That Teneriffe is so cold at the top, extreme hot at the bottom. . . . But this diversity of air in places equally site,[71] elevated, and distant from the Pole can hardly be satisfied with that diversity of plants, birds, beasts which is so familiar with us; with Indians, everywhere, the sun is equally distant, the same vertical stars, the same irradiations of planets, aspects alike, the same nearness of seas, the same superficies, the same soil, or not much different. . . . How comes or wherefore is this *temeraria siderum dispositio*, this rash placing of stars, or as Epicurus will, *fortuita*, or accidental? Why are some big, some little, why are they so confusedly, unequally situated in the heavens and set so much out of order? In all other things nature is equal, proportionable, and constant; there be *iustæ dimensiones et prudens partium dispositio*, as in the fabric of man, his eyes, ears, nose, face, members are correspondent, *cur non idem cælo opere omnium pulcherrimo?* Why are the heavens so irregular, *neque paribus molibus, neque paribus intervallis*, whence is this difference? *Diversos*, he concludes, *efficere locorum genios*, to make diversity of countries, soils, manners, customs, characters, and constitutions among us, *ut quantum vicinia ad caritatem addat, sidera distrahant ad perniciem*, and so by this means *fluvio vel monte distincti sunt dissimiles*, the same places almost shall be distinguished in manners.

71 Situated.

But this reason is weak and most insufficient. The fixed stars are removed since Ptolemy's time 26 gr. from the first of Aries, and if the earth be immovable, as their site varies, so should countries vary, and divers alterations would follow. But this we perceive not; as in Tully's time with us in Britain, *cœlum visu fœdum, et in quo facile generatur nubes*, etc., 'tis so still. Wherefore Bodin, *Theat. Nat.*, lib. 2, and some others will have all these alterations and effects immediately proceed from those *genii*, spirits, angels, which rule and domineer in several places; they cause storms, thunder, lightning, earthquakes, ruins, tempests, great winds, floods, etc. The philosophers of Conimbra will refer this diversity to the influence of that empyrean heaven; for some say the eccentricity of the sun is come nearer to the earth than in Ptolemy's time, the virtue therefore of all the vegetals is decayed, men grow less, etc. There are [those] that observe new motions of the heavens, new stars, *palantia sidera*, comets, clouds, call them what you will, like those Medicean, Bourbonian, Austrian planets lately detected, which do not decay but come and go, rise higher and lower, hide and show themselves amongst the fixed stars, amongst the planets, above and beneath the moon at set times, now nearer, now farther off, together, asunder; as he that plays upon a sackbut by pulling it up and down alters his tones and tunes, do they their stations and places, though to us undiscerned; and from those motions proceed, as they conceive, divers alterations. Clavius conjectures otherwise, but they be but conjectures. About Damascus in Cœli-Syria is a paradise by reason of the plenty of waters, *in promptu causa est*, and the deserts of Arabia barren because of rocks, rolling seas of sands, and dry mountains, *quod inaquosa*, saith Adricomius, *montes habens asperos, saxosos, præcipites, horroris et mortis speciem præ se ferentes*, uninhabitable therefore of men, birds, beasts, void of all green trees, plants, and fruits, a vast, rocky, horrid wilderness, which by no art can be manured, 'tis evident. Bohemia is cold for that it lies all along to the north. But why should it be so hot in Egypt, or there never rain? Why should those Etesian and north-eastern winds blow continually and constantly so long together in some places at set times, one way still, in the dog-days only; here perpetual drought, there dropping showers; here foggy mists, there a pleasant air; here terrible thunder and lightning at such set seasons, here frozen seas all the year; there open in the same latitude, to the rest no such thing, nay, quite opposite is to be found? Sometimes, as in Peru, on the one side of the mountains it is hot, on the other

cold, here snow, there wind, with infinite such. Fromundus in his Meteors will excuse or solve all this by the sun's motion, but when there is such diversity to such as [are] *periœci*, or very near site, how can that position hold?

Who can give a reason of this diversity of meteors? that it should rain stones, frogs, mice, etc., rats, which they call *lemmer* in Norway and are manifestly observed, as Munster writes, by the inhabitants to descend and fall with some feculent showers and like so many locusts consume all that is green. Leo Afer speaks as much of locusts, about Fez in Barbary there be infinite swarms in their fields upon a sudden. So at Arles in France, 1553, the like happened by the same mischief, all their grass and fruits were devoured, *magna incolarum admiratione et consternatione*, as Valleriola, *obser. med.*, lib. 1, obser. 1, relates, *cœlum subito obumbrabant*, etc.; he concludes, it could not be from natural causes, they cannot imagine whence they come but from heaven. Are these and such creatures, corn, wood, stones, worms, wool, blood, etc., lifted up into the middle region by the sunbeams, as Baracellus the physician disputes, and thence let fall with showers, or there engendered? Cornelius Gemma is of that opinion that they are conceived by celestial influences. Others suppose they are immediately from God or prodigies raised by art, and illusions of spirits which are princes of the air; to whom Bodin, *lib. 2, Theat. Nat.*, subscribes. In fine, of meteors in general Aristotle's reasons are exploded by Bernardinus Telesius, by Paracelsus his Principles confuted and other causes assigned, sal, sulphur, mercury, in which his disciples are so expert that they can alter elements and separate at their pleasure, make perpetual motions, not as Cardan, Tasneir, Peregrinus by some magnetical virtue but by mixture of elements; imitate thunder, like Salmoneus, snow, hail, the sea's ebbing and flowing, give life to creatures, as they say, without generation, and what not. P. Nonius Saluciensis and Kepler take upon them to demonstrate that no meteors, clouds, fogs, vapors, arise higher than 50 or 80 miles and all the rest to be purer air or element of fire. Which Cardan, Tycho, and John Pena manifestly confute by refractions and many other arguments, there is no such element of fire at all. If, as Tycho proves, the moon be distant from us 50 and 60 semidiameters of the earth, and, as Peter Nonius will have it, the air be so angust,[72] what proportion is there betwixt the other three elements and it? to what use serves it? is it full of spirits which inhabit it, as the

72 Narrow.

Paracelsians and Platonists hold, the higher the more noble, full of birds, or a mere vacuum to no purpose? It is much controverted betwixt Tycho Brahe and Christopher Rotman, the Landgrave of Hesse's mathematician, in their astronomical epistles, whether it be the same *diaphanum*, clearness, matter of air and heavens, or two distinct essences. Christopher Rotman, John Pena, Jordanus Brunus, with many other late mathematicians, contend it is the same and one matter throughout, saving that the higher still the purer it is and more subtile; as they find by experience in the top of some hills in America; if a man ascend, he faints instantly for want of thicker air to refrigerate the heart. Acosta, *l.* 3, *c.* 9, calls this mountain Periacacca in Peru, it makes men cast and vomit, he saith, that climb it, as some other of those Andes do in the deserts of Chile for 500 miles together and for extremity of cold to lose their fingers and toes. Tycho will have two distinct matters of heaven and air; but to say truth, with some small qualification, they have one and the selfsame opinion about the essence and matter of heavens; that it is not hard and impenetrable, as Peripatetics hold, transparent, of a *quinta essentia*,[73] "but that it is penetrable and soft as the air itself is, and that the planets move in it, as birds in the air, fishes in the sea." This they prove by motion of comets and otherwise, though Claremontius in his Anti-Tycho stiffly oppose, which are not generated, as Aristotle teacheth, in the aerial region, of a hot and dry exhalation, and so consumed; but as Anaxagoras and Democritus held of old, of a celestial matter, and as Tycho, Eliseus Rœslin, Thaddeus Haggesius, Pena, Rotman, Fracastorius demonstrate by their progress, parallaxes, refractions, motions of the planets, which interfere and cut one another's orbs, now higher, and then lower, as ♂[74] amongst the rest, which sometimes, as Kepler confirms by his own and Tycho's accurate observations, comes nearer the earth than the ◯,[75] and is again eftsoons aloft in Jupiter's orb; and other sufficient reasons, far above the moon; exploding in the meantime that element of fire, those fictitious first watery movers, those heavens, I mean, above the firmament, which Delrio, Ludovicus Imola, Patricius, and many of the fathers affirm; those monstrous orbs of eccentrics and *eccentre epicycles deserentes*,—which howsoever Ptolemy, Alhasen, Vitellio, Purbachius, Maginus, Clavius, and many of their associates stiffly maintain to be real orbs, eccentric, concentric, circles equant, etc.,—are absurd and ridiculous. For who is so mad to think that there should be so many circles like subordinate wheels in a clock all impenetrable and hard, as they feign, add, and subtract at their pleasure? Maginus makes eleven heavens, subdivided into their orbs and circles, and all too little to serve those particular appearances; Fracastorius 72 homocentrics; Tycho Brahe, Nicholas Ramerus, Heliseus Rœslin, have peculiar hypotheses of their own inventions; and they be but inventions, as most of them acknowledge, as we admit of equators, tropics, colures, circles, Arctic and Antarctic, for doctrine's sake, though Ramus thinks them all unnecessary; they will have them supposed only for method and order. Tycho hath feigned I know not how many sub-divisions of epicycles in epicycles, etc., to calculate and express the moon's motion. But when all is done, as a supposition and no otherwise; not, as he holds, hard, impenetrable subtile, transparent, etc., or making music, as Pythagoras maintained of old and Robert Constantine of late, but still quiet, liquid, open, etc.

If the heavens then be penetrable, as these men deliver, and no lets,[76] it were not amiss in this aerial progress to make wings and fly up, which that Turk in Busbequius made his fellow-citizens in Constantinople believe he would perform; and some new-fangled wits, methinks, should some time or other find out; or if that may not be, yet with a Galileo's glass or Icaromenippus' wings in Lucian command the spheres and heavens and see what is done amongst them. . . . Examine likewise *an cœlum sit coloratum?* Whether the stars be of that bigness, distance, as astronomers relate, so many in number, 1,026 or 1,725, as I. Bayerus; or as some rabbins, 29,000 myriads; or as Galileo discovers by his glasses, infinite, and that *via lactea* a confused light of small stars like so many nails in a door; or all in a row like those 12,000 isles of the Maldives in the Indian Ocean? Whether the least visible star in the eighth sphere be 18 times bigger than the earth, and as Tycho calculates, 14,000 semidiameters distant from it? Whether they be thicker parts of the orbs, as Aristotle delivers, or so many habitable worlds, as Democritus? Whether they have light of their own, or from the sun, or give light round, as Patricius discourseth? *An æque distent a centro mundi?* Whether light be of their essence; and that light be a substance or an accident? Whether they be hot by themselves, or by accident cause heat? Whether there be such a precession

---

73 The "fifth essence," by means of which the alchemists hoped to change the nature of material substances composed of the four elements.

74 Mars.   75 The sun.   76 Barriers, hindrances.

of the equinoxes as Copernicus holds, or that the eighth sphere move? *An bene philosophentur* R. Bacon *et* J. Dee, *Aphorism. de multiplicatione specierum?* Whether there be any such images ascending with each degree of the Zodiac in the east, as Aliacensis feigns? *An aqua super cœlum?* as Patricius and Schoolmen will, a crystalline watery heaven, which is certainly to be understood of that in the middle region? For otherwise, if at Noah's Flood the water came from thence, it must be above an hundred years falling down to us, as some calculate. Besides, *an terra sit animata?* which some so confidently believe with Orpheus, Hermes, Averroes, from which all other souls of men, beasts, devils, plants, fishes, etc., are derived and into which again, after some revolutions, as Plato in his *Timæus*, Plotinus in his *Enneades* more largely discuss, they return (see Chalcidius and Bennius, Plato's commentators) as all philosophical matter *in materiam primam.* Keplerus, Patricius, and some other neoterics have in part revived this opinion, and that every star in heaven hath a soul, angel, or intelligence to animate or move it, etc. Or to omit all smaller controversies as matters of less moment and examine that main paradox of the earth's motion now so much in question. Aristarchus Samius, Pythagoras maintained it of old, Democritus and many of their scholars. Didacus Astunica, Anthony Fascarinus, a Carmelite, and some other commentators will have Job to insinuate as much, *cap. 9, ver. 6, qui commovet terram de loco suo*, etc., and that this one place of Scripture makes more for the earth's motion than all the other prove against it; whom Pineda confutes, most contradict. Howsoever, it is revived since by Copernicus, not as a truth but a supposition, as he confesseth himself in the preface to Pope Nicholas, but now maintained in good earnest by Calcagninus, Telesius, Kepler, Rotman, Gilbert, Digges, Galileus, Campanella, and especially by Lansbergius, *naturæ, rationi, et veritati consentaneum*, by Origanus, and some others of his followers. For if the earth be the center of the world, stand still, and the heavens move, as the most received opinion is, which they call *inordinatam cœli dispositionem*, though stiffly maintained by Tycho, Ptolemeus, and their adherents, *quis ille furor?* etc., what fury is that, saith Dr. Gilbert, *satis animose*, as Cabeus notes, that shall drive the heavens about with such incomprehensible celerity in 24 hours, when as every point of the firmament and in the Equator must needs move, so Clavius calculates, 176,660 in one 246th part of an hour; and an arrow out of a bow must go seven times about the earth whilst a man can say an *Ave Maria* if it keep the same space or compass the earth 1,884 times in an hour, which is *supra humanam cogitationem*, beyond human conceit, *ocyor et jaculo, et ventos, æquante sagitta.* A man could not ride so much ground, going 40 miles a day, in 2,904 years as the firmament goes in 24 hours; or so much in 203 years as the said firmament in one minute; *quod incredible videtur.* And the Pole Star, which to our thinking scarce moveth out of his place, goeth a bigger circuit than the sun, whose diameter is much larger than the diameter of the heaven of the sun and 20,000 semidiameters of the earth from us with the rest of the fixed stars, as Tycho proves. To avoid therefore these impossibilities, they ascribe a triple motion of the earth, the sun immovable in the center of the whole world, the earth center of the moon alone, above ♀ and ☿, beneath, ♄, ♃, ♂,[77] or as Origanus and others will, one single motion to the earth still placed in the center of the world, which is more probable, a single motion to the firmament, which moves in 30 or 26 thousand years; and so the planets, Saturn in 30 years absolves his sole and proper motion, Jupiter in 12, Mars in 3, etc., and so solve all appearances better than any way whatsoever, calculate all motions, be they in *longum* or *latum*, direct, stationary, retrograde, ascent or descent, without epicycles, intricate eccentrics; etc., *rectius commodiusque per unicum motum terræ*, saith Lansbergius, much more certain than by those Alphonsine or any such tables which are grounded from those other suppositions. And 'tis true, they say, according to optic principles, the visible appearances of the planets do so indeed answer to their magnitudes and orbs and come nearest to mathematical observations and precedent calculations; there is no repugnancy to physical axioms because no penetration of orbs. But then between the sphere of Saturn and the firmament[78] there is such an incredible and vast space of distance—7,000,000 semidiameters of the earth, as Tycho calculates—void of stars. And besides, they do so enhance the bigness of the stars, enlarge their circuit to solve those ordinary objections of parallaxes and retrogradations of the fixed stars, that alteration of the poles, elevation in several places or latitude of cities here on earth; for, say they, if a man's eye were in the firmament, he should not at all discern that great annual motion of the earth, but it would still appear *punctum indivisibile* and seem to be fixed in one place, of the same bigness; that it is quite

77 Venus, Mercury, Saturn, Jupiter, Mars.
78 The planets Uranus, Neptune, and Pluto had not yet been discovered.

opposite to reason, to natural philosophy, and all out as absurd as disproportional, so some will, as prodigious as that of the sun's swift motion of heavens. But *hoc posito*, to grant this their tenet of the earth's motion, if the earth move, it is a planet and shines to them in the moon and to the other planetary inhabitants as the moon and they do to us upon the earth. But shine she doth, as Galileo, Kepler, and others prove, and then *per consequens* the rest of the planets are inhabited as well as the moon, which he grants in his dissertation with Galileo's *Nuncius Sidereus*, "that there be Jovial and Saturn inhabitants," etc., and those several planets have their several moons about them as the earth hath hers, as Galileus hath already evinced by his glasses, four about Jupiter, two about Saturn (Sitius the Florentine, Fortunius Licetus, and Jul. Cæsar la Galla cavil at it) yet Kepler, the emperor's mathematician, confirms out of his experience that he saw as much by the same help and more about Mars, Venus; and the rest they hope to find out peradventure even amongst the fixed stars, which Brunus and Brutius have already averred. Then, I say, the earth and they be planets alike, inhabited alike, moved about the sun, the common center of the world alike, and it may be those two green children which Nubrigensis speaks of in his time, that fell from heaven, came from thence; and that famous stone that fell from heaven in Aristotle's time, Olymp. 84, *anno tertio, ad Capuæ Fluenta*, recorded by Laertius and others, or ancile or buckler in Numa's time, recorded by Festus. We may likewise insert with Campanella and Brunus that which Pythagoras, Aristarchus Samius, Heraclitus, Epicurus, Melissus, Democritus, Leucippus maintained in their ages, there be infinite worlds and infinite earths or systems *in infinito æthere*, which Eusebius collects out of their tenets, because infinite stars and planets like unto this of ours, which some stick not still to maintain and publicly defend, *sperabundus expecto innumerabilium mundorum in æternitate perambulationem*, etc. (Nic. Hill, *Londinensis, philos. Epicur.*) For if the firmament be of such an incomparable bigness as these Copernical giants will have it, *infinitum, aut infinito proximum*, so vast and full of innumerable stars, as being infinite in extent, one above another, some higher, some lower, some nearer, some farther off, and so far asunder, and those so huge and great, insomuch, that if the whole sphere of Saturn and all that is included in it, *totum aggregatum*, as Fromundus of Louvain in his tract *de immobilitate terræ* argues, *evehatur inter stellas, videri a nobis non poterat, tam immanis est distantia inter tellurem*

et fixas, sed instar puncti, etc. If our world be small in respect, why may we not suppose a plurality of worlds, those infinite stars visible in the firmament to be so many suns with particular fixed centers, to have likewise their subordinate planets, as the sun hath his dancing still round him? Which Cardinal Cusanus, Walkarinus, Brunus, and some others have held, and some still maintain, *animæ Aristotelismo innutritæ, et minutis speculationibus assuetæ, secus forsan*, etc. Though they seem close to us, they are infinitely distant, and so *per consequens* there are infinite habitable worlds; what hinders? Why should not an infinite cause, as God is, produce infinite effects? as Nic. Hill, *Democrit. philos.*, disputes. Kepler, I confess, will by no means admit of Brunus' infinite worlds or that the fixed stars should be so many suns with their compassing planets, yet the said Kepler betwixt jest and earnest in his perspectives, lunar geography, *et somnio suo, dissertat. cum nunc sider.*, seems in part to agree with this and partly to contradict; for the planets, he yields them to be inhabited, he doubts of the stars; and so doth Tycho in his astronomical epistles out of a consideration of their vastity and greatness break out into some such like speeches, that he will never believe those great and huge bodies were made to no other use than this that we perceive, to illuminate the earth, a point insensible in respect of the whole. But who shall dwell in these vast bodies, earths, worlds "if they be inhabited? rational creatures?" as Kepler demands, "or have they souls to be saved? or do they inhabit a better part of the world than we do? Are we or they lords of the world? And how are all things made for man?" *Difficile est nodum hunc expedire, eo quod nondum omnia quæ huc pertinent explorata habemus;* 'tis hard to determine; this only he proves, that we are in *præcipuo mundi sinu*, in the best place, best world, nearest the heart of the sun. Thomas Campanella, a Calabrian monk, in his second book *de sensu rerum, cap. 4*, subscribes to this of Keplerus; that they are inhabited he certainly supposeth, but with what kind of creatures he cannot say, he labors to prove it by all means, and that there are infinite worlds, having made apology for Galileus, and dedicates this tenet of his to Cardinal Cajetanus. Others freely speak, mutter, and would persuade the world, as Marinus Marcenus complains, that our modern divines are too severe and rigid against mathematicians, ignorant and peevish in not admitting their true demonstrations and certain observations, that they tyrannize over art, science, and all philosophy in suppressing their labors, saith Pomponatius, forbidding them to write, to speak a truth, all to maintain their superstition and for their profit's sake. As for those places of Scripture which oppugn it, they will have spoken *ad captum vulgi*, and if rightly understood and favorably interpreted, not at all against it, and as Otho Casman, *Astrol., cap. 1, part. 1*, notes, many great divines, besides Porphyrius, Proclus, Simplicius, and those heathen philosophers, *doctrina et ætate venerandi, Mosis Genesin mundanam popularis nescio cuius ruditatis, quæ longa absit a vera philosophorum eruditione, insimulant;* for Moses makes mention but of two planets, ☉ and ☾,[79] no 4 elements, etc. Read more in him, in Grossius, and Junius. But to proceed, these and such like insolent and bold attempts, prodigious paradoxes, inferences must needs follow, if it once be granted which Rotman, Kepler, Gilbert, Diggeus, Origanus, Galileus, and others maintain of the earth's motion, that 'tis a planet and shines as the moon doth, which contains in it "both land and sea as the moon doth"; for so they find by their glasses that *maculæ in facie lunæ,* "the brighter parts are earth, the dusky sea," which Thales, Plutarch, and Pythagoras formerly taught, and manifestly discern hills and dales and such like concavities, if we may subscribe to and believe Galileo's observations. But to avoid these paradoxes of the earth's motion, which the Church of Rome hath lately condemned as heretical, as appears by Blancanus' and Fromundus' writings, our latter mathematicians have rolled all the stones that may be stirred; and to solve all appearances and objections have invented new hypotheses and fabricated new systems of the world out of their own Dædalean heads. Fracastorius will have the earth stand still as before; and to avoid that supposition of eccentrics and epicycles, he hath coined 72 homocentrics to solve all appearances. Nicholas Ramerus will have the earth the center of the world, but movable, and the eighth sphere immovable, the five upper planets to move about the sun, the sun and moon about the earth. Of which orbs, Tycho Brahe puts the earth the center immovable, the stars immovable, the rest with Ramerus, the planets without orbs to wander in the air, keep time and distance, true motion, according to that virtue which God hath given them. Heliseus Rœslin censureth both, with Copernicus (whose hypothesis *de terræ motu* Philippus Lansbergius hath lately vindicated and demonstrated with solid arguments in a just volume, Jansonius Cæsius hath illustrated in a sphere). The said Johannes Lansbergius, 1633, hath since defended his assertion

79 The sun and the moon.

against all the cavils and calumnies of Fromundus his Anti-Aristarchus, Baptista Morinus, and Petrus Bartholinus; Fromundus, 1634, hath written against him again, J. Rosseus of Aberdeen, etc. (sound drums and trumpets), whilst Rœslin, I say, censures all and Ptolemæus himself as insufficient; one offends against natural philosophy, another against optic principles, a third against mathematical, as not answering to astronomical observations; one puts a great space betwixt Saturnus' orb and the eighth sphere, another too narrow. In his own hypothesis he makes the earth as before, the universal center, the sun to the five upper planets, to the eighth sphere he ascribes diurnal motion, eccentrics and epicycles to the seven planets, which had been formerly exploded; and so

Dum vitant stulti vitia in contraria currunt,

as a tinker stops one hole and makes two, he corrects them and doth worse himself; reforms some, and mars all. In the meantime the world is tossed in a blanket amongst them, they hoist the earth up and down like a ball, make it stand and go at their pleasures; one saith the sun stands, another he moves; a third comes in, taking them all at rebound, and lest there should be any paradox wanting, he finds certain spots and clouds in the sun by the help of glasses which multiply, saith Keplerus, a thing seen a thousand times bigger *in plano* and makes it come 32 times nearer to the eye of the beholder; but see the demonstration of this glass in Tarde, by means of which the sun must turn round upon his own center, or they about the sun. Fabricius puts only three and those in the sun; Apelles 15 and those without the sun, floating like the Cyanean Isles in the Euxine Sea. Tarde the Frenchman hath observed 33 and those neither spots nor clouds, as Galileus' *Epist. ad Velserum* supposeth, but planets concentric with the sun and not far from him with regular motions. Christopher Scheiner, a German-Swiss Jesuit, Ursica Rosa, divides them *in maculas et faculas,* and will have them to be fixed *in solis superficie* and to absolve their periodical and regular motion in 27 or 28 days, holding withal the rotation of the sun upon his center; and are all so confident that they have made schemes and tables of their motions. The Hollander in his *dissertatiuncula cum Apelle* censures all; and thus they disagree amongst themselves, old and new, irreconcilable in their opinions; thus Aristarchus, thus Hipparchus, thus Ptolemæus, thus Albateginus, thus Alfraganus, thus Tycho, thus Ramerus, thus Rœslinus, thus Fracastorius, thus Copernicus and his adherents, thus Clavius and Maginus, etc., with their followers vary and determine of these celestial orbs and bodies; and so whilst these men contend about the sun and moon, like the philosophers in Lucian, it is to be feared the sun and moon will hide themselves and be as much offended as she was with those and send another message to Jupiter by some newfangled Icaromenippus to make an end of all those curious controversies and scatter them abroad.

But why should the sun and moon be angry or take exceptions at mathematicians and philosophers? when as the like measure is offered unto God himself by a company of theologasters. They are not contented to see the sun and moon, measure their site and biggest distance in a glass, calculate their motions, or visit the moon in a poetical fiction or a dream, as he saith, *Audax facinus et memorabile nunc incipiam, neque hoc sæculo usurpatum prius, quid in lunæ regno hac nocte gestum sit exponam, et quo nemo unquam nisi somniando pervenit,* but he and Menippus, or as Peter Cuneus, *Bona fide agam, nihil eorum quæ scripturus sum, verum esse scitote,* etc., *quæ nec facta, nec futura sunt, dicam, stili tantum et ingenii causa,* not in jest but in good earnest these gigantical Cyclopes will transcend spheres, heaven, stars into that empyrean heaven, soar higher yet, and see what God himself doth. The Jewish Talmudists take upon them to determine how God spends his whole time, sometimes playing with Leviathan, sometimes overseeing the world, etc., like Lucian's Jupiter, that spent much of the year in painting butterflies' wings and seeing who offered sacrifice, telling the hours when it should rain, how much snow should fall in such a place, which way the wind should stand in Greece, which way in Africa. In the Turks' Alcoran Mahomet is taken up to heaven upon a Pegasus sent a purpose for him as he lay in bed with his wife, and after some conference with God is set on ground again. The pagans paint him and mangle him after a thousand fashions; our heretics, schismatics, and some Schoolmen come not far behind; some paint him in the habit of an old man and make maps of heaven, number the angels, tell their several names, offices; some deny God and his providence, some take his office out of his hand, will bind and loose in heaven, release, pardon, forgive, and be quartermaster with him; some call his Godhead in question, his power, and attributes, his mercy, justice, providence; they will know with Cecilius why good and bad are punished together, war, fires, plagues infest all alike, why wicked men flourish, good are poor, in prison, sick, and ill at ease. Why doth he suffer so much mischief and evil to be done if he be able to help? why doth he not assist good or resist bad, reform our wills, if he be not the author of sin, and let such enormities be committed unworthy of his knowledge, wisdom, government, mercy, and providence, why lets he all things be done by fortune and chance? Others as prodigiously inquire after his omnipotency, *an possit plures similes creare deos? an ex scarabæo deum?* etc., *et quo demum ruetis sacrificuli?* Some by visions and revelations take upon them to be familiar with God and to be of privy council with him; they will tell how many and who shall be saved, when the world shall come to an end, what year, what month, and whatsoever else God hath reserved unto himself and to his angels. Some again, curious fantastics, will know more than this, and inquire with Epicurus, what God did before the world was made? was he idle? Where did he bide? What did he make the world of? Why did he then make it and not before? If he made it new, or to have an end, how is he unchangeable, infinite, etc.? Some will dispute, cavil, and object, as Julian did of old, whom Cyril confutes, as Simon Magus is feigned to do in that dialogue betwixt him and Peter; and Ammonius the philosopher in that dialogical disputation with Zacharias the Christian. If God be infinitely and only good, why should he alter or destroy the world? If he confound that which is good, how shall himself continue good? If he pull it down because evil, how shall he be free from the evil that made it evil? etc. With many such absurd and brainsick questions, intricacies, froth of human wit, and excrements of curiosity, etc., which, as our Saviour told his inquisitive disciples, are not fit for them to know. But hoo! I am now gone quite out of sight, I am almost giddy with roving about. I could have ranged farther yet; but I am an infant and not able to dive into these profundities or sound these depths; not able to understand, much less to discuss. I leave the contemplation of these things to stronger wits, that have better ability and happier leisure to wade into such philosophical mysteries. For put case I were as able as willing, yet what can one man do? . . . When God sees his time, he will reveal these mysteries to mortal men and show that to some few at last which he hath concealed so long. For I am of his mind that Columbus did not find out America by chance but God directed him at that time to discover it; it was contingent to him, but necessary to God; he reveals and conceals to whom and when he will. And which one said of histories and records of former times, "God in his providence to check our presumptuous inquisition wraps up all things in uncertainty, bars us from long antiquity, and bounds our search within the compass of some few ages." Many good things are lost which our predecessors made use of, as Pancirola will better inform you; many new things are daily invented to the public good; so kingdoms, men and knowledge ebb and flow, are hid and revealed, and when you have all done, as the preacher concluded, *Nihil est sub sole novum*. But my melancholy spaniel's quest, my game is sprung, and I must suddenly come down and follow.

Jason Pratensis, in his book *de morbis capitis* and chapter of melancholy, hath these words out of Galen, "Let them come to me to know what meat and drink they shall use, and besides that, I will teach them what temper of ambient air they shall make choice of, what wind, what countries they shall choose, and what avoid." Out of which lines of his thus much we may gather, that to this cure of melancholy, amongst other things, the rectification of air is necessarily required. This is performed either in reforming natural or artificial air. Natural is that which is in our election to choose or avoid, and 'tis either general, to countries, provinces; particular, to cities, towns, villages, or private houses. What harm those extremes of heat or cold do in this malady I have formerly showed. The medium must needs be good where the air is temperate, serene, quiet, free from bogs, fens, mists, all manner of putrefaction, contagious and filthy noisome smells. The Egyptians by all geographers are commended to be *hilares*, a conceited and merry nation; which I can ascribe to no other cause than the serenity of their air. They that live in the Orcades are registered by Hector Boethius and Cardan to be fair of complexion, long-lived, most healthful, free from all manner of infirmities of body and mind by reason of a sharp purifying air which comes from the sea. The Bœotians in Greece were dull and heavy, *crassi Bœoti*, by reason of a foggy air in which they lived,

Bœotum in crasso iurares aere natum,

Attica most acute, pleasant, and refined. The clime changeth not so much customs, manners, wits, as Aristotle, *Polit.*, *lib. 6, cap. 4*, Vegetius, Plato, Bodin, *method. hist.*, *cap. 5*, hath proved at large, as constitutions of their bodies and temperature itself. In all particular provinces we see it confirmed by experience, as the air is so are the inhabitants, dull, heavy, witty, subtile, neat, cleanly, clownish, sick, and sound. In Périgord in France the air is subtile, healthful, seldom

any plague, or contagious disease, but hilly and barren; the men sound, nimble, and lusty; but in some parts of Guienne, full of moors and marshes, the people dull, heavy, subject to many infirmities. Who sees not a great difference betwixt Surrey, Sussex, and Romney Marsh, the wolds in Lincolnshire and the fens? He therefore that loves his health, if his ability will give him leave, must often shift places and make choice of such as are wholesome, pleasant, and convenient. There is nothing better than change of air in this malady and generally for health to wander up and down, as those *Tartari Zamolhenses* that live in hordes and take opportunity of times, places, seasons. The kings of Persia had their summer and winter houses; in winter ar Sardis, in summer at Susa; now at Persepolis, then at Pasargada. Cyrus lived seven cold months at Babylon, three at Susa, two at Ecbatana, saith Xenophon, and had by that means a perpetual spring. The Great Turk sojourns sometimes at Constantinople, sometimes at Adrianople, etc. The kings of Spain have their Escurial in heat of summer, Madrid for an wholesome seat, Valladolid, a pleasant site, etc., a variety of *secess*, as all princes and great men have, and their several progresses to this purpose. Lucullus the Roman had his house at Rome, at Baiæ, etc. When Cn. Pompeius, Marcus Cicero, saith Plutarch, and many noblemen in the summer came to see him, at supper Pompeius jested with him that it was an elegant and pleasant village, full of windows, galleries, and all offices fit for a summer house, but in his judgment very unfit for winter; Lucullus made answer that the lord of the house had wit like a crane that changeth her country with the season; he had other houses furnished and built for that purpose all out as commodious as this. So Tully had his Tusculan, Plinius his Lauretan village, and every gentleman of any fashion in our times hath the like. The Bishop of Exeter had 14 several houses all furnished in times past. In Italy, though they bide in cities in winter, which is more gentlemanlike, all the summer they come abroad to their countryhouses to recreate themselves. Our gentry in England live most part in the country, except it be some few castles, building still in bottoms, saith Jovius, or near woods—*corona arborum virentium*, you shall know a village by a tuft of trees at or about it —to avoid those strong winds wherewith the island is infested and cold winter blasts. Some discommend moated houses as unwholesome; so Camden saith of Ewelme, that it was therefore unfrequented *ob stagni vicini halitus;* and all such places as be near lakes or rivers. But I am of opinion that these inconveniences will be mitigated or easily corrected by good fires, as one reports of Venice, that *graveolentia* and fog of the moors is sufficiently qualified by those innumerable smokes. Nay more, Thomas Philol. Ravennas, a great physician, contends that the Venetians are generally longer-lived than any city in Europe and live many of them 120 years. But it is not water simply that so much offends as the slime and noisome smells that accompany such overflowed places, which is but at some few seasons after a flood and is sufficiently recompensed with sweet smells and aspects in summer, *Ver pinget vario gemmantia prata colore*, and many other commodities of pleasure and profit; or else may be corrected by the site if it be somewhat remote from the water, as Lindley, Orton-super-Montem, Drayton, or a little more elevated, though nearer, as Caucut, as Amington, Polesworth, Weddington, to insist in such places best to me known, upon the River of Anker in Warwickshire, Swarston, and Drakesly-upon-Trent. Or howsoever they be unseasonable in winter or at some times, they have their good use in summer. If so be that their means be so slender as they may not admit of any such variety but must determine once for all and make one house serve each season, I know no men that have given better rules in this behalf than our husbandry writers. Cato and Columella prescribe a good house to stand by a navigable river, good highways, near some city, and in a good soil; but that is more for commodity than health.

The best soil commonly yields the worst air, a dry sandy plat is fittest to build upon and such as is rather hilly than plain, full of downs, a Cotswold country, as being most commodious for hawking, hunting, wood, waters, and all manner of pleasures. Périgord in France is barren, yet by reason of the excellency of the air and such pleasures that it affords much inhabited by the nobility; as Nuremberg in Germany, Toledo in Spain. Our countryman Tusser will tell us so much, that the fieldone is for profit, the woodland for pleasure and health, the one commonly a deep clay, therefore noisome in winter, and subject to bad highways, the other a dry sand. Provision may be had elsewhere, and our towns are generally bigger in the woodland than the fieldone, more frequent and populous, and gentlemen more delight to dwell in such places. Sutton Coldfield in Warwickshire, where I was once a grammar scholar, may be a sufficient witness, which stands, as Camden notes, *loco ingrato et sterili*, but in an excellent air and full of all manner of pleasures. Wadley in

Berkshire is situate in a vale, though not so fertile a soil as some vales afford, yet a most commodious site, wholesome, in a delicious air, a rich and pleasant seat. So Segrave in Leicestershire, which town I am now bound to remember,[80] is sited in a champaign at the edge of the wolds and more barren than the villages about it, yet no place likely yields a better air. And he that built that fair house Wollerton in Nottinghamshire is much to be commended, though the tract be sandy and barren about it, for making choice of such a place. Constantine, *lib. 2, cap. de agricult.*, praiseth mountains, hilly, steep places above the rest by the seaside and such as look toward the north upon some great river, as Farmack in Derbyshire on the Trent, environed with hills, open only to the north, like Mount Edgecombe in Cornwall, which Mr. Carew so much admires for an excellent seat; such as is the general site of Bohemia; *serenat Boreas*, the north wind clarifies, "but near lakes or marshes, in holes, obscure places, or to the south and west he utterly disapproves," those winds are unwholesome, putrefying, and make men subject to diseases. The best building for health, according to him, is in "high places and in an excellent prospect," like that of Cuddeston in Oxfordshire, which place I must *honoris ergo* mention, is lately and fairly built in a good air, good prospect, good soil, both for profit and pleasure, not so easily to be matched. P. Crescentius, in his *lib.* 1 *de agric., cap.* 5, is very copious in this subject how a house should be wholesomely sited, in a good coast, good air, wind, etc. Varro, *de re rust., lib.* 1, *cap.* 12, forbids lakes and rivers, marshy and manured grounds; they cause a bad air, gross diseases, hard to be cured; "if it be so that he cannot help it, better," as he adviseth, "sell thy house and land than lose thine health." He that respects not this in choosing of his seat or building his house is *mente captus*, mad, Cato saith, "and his dwelling next to hell itself," according to Columella; he commends in conclusion the middle of an hill, upon a descent. . . . If it be so the natural site may not be altered of our city, town, village, yet by artificial means it may be helped. In hot countries therefore they make the streets of their cities very narrow, all over Spain, Africa, Italy, Greece, and many cities of France, in Languedoc especially, and Provence, those southern parts; Montpelier, the habitation and university of physicians, is so built with high houses, narrow streets to divert the sun's scalding rays, which

80 John Bancroft of Christ Church and Bishop of Oxford, Burton's former tutor, had a house there which Burton probably visited.

Tacitus commends, *l.* 15, *Annal.*, as most agreeing to their health "because the height of buildings and narrowness of streets keep away the sunbeams." Some cities use galleries or arched cloisters towards the street, as Damascus, Bologna, Padua, Berne in Switzerland, Westchester with us, as well to avoid tempests as the sun's scorching heat. They build on high hills in hot countries for more air, or to the seaside, as Baiæ, Naples, etc. In our northern coasts we are opposite, we commend straight, broad, open, fair streets as most befitting and agreeing to our clime. We build in bottoms for warmth; and that site of Mitylene in the island of Lesbos in the Ægean Sea, which Vitruvius so much discommends, magnificently built with fair houses, *sed imprudenter positam*, unadvisedly sited because it lay along to the south and when the south wind blew the people were all sick, would make an excellent site in our northern climes.

Of that artificial site of houses I have sufficiently discoursed. If the air of the dwelling may not be altered, yet there is much in choice of such a chamber or room, in opportune opening and shutting of windows, excluding foreign air and winds, and walking abroad at convenient times. Crato, a German, commends east and south site—disallowing cold air and northern winds in this case, rainy weather and misty days—free from putrefaction, fens, bogs, and muck-hills. If the air be such, open no windows, come not abroad. Montanus will have his patient not to stir at all if the wind be big or tempestuous, as most part in March it is with us; or in cloudy, lowering, dark days, as in November, which we commonly call the black month; or stormy, let the wind stand how it will, *consil.* 27 and 30, he must not open a casement in bad weather or in a boisterous season, *consil.* 299, he especially forbids us to open windows to a south wind. The best sites for chamber windows in my judgment are north, east, south; and which is the worst, west. Levinus Lemnius, *lib.* 3, *cap.* 3, *de occult. nat. mir.*, attributes so much to air and rectifying of wind and windows that he holds it alone sufficient to make a man sick or well, to alter body and mind. "A clear air cheers up the spirits, exhilarates the mind; a thick, black, misty, tempestuous, contracts, overthrows." Great heed is therefore to be taken at what times we walk, how we place our windows, lights, and houses, how we let in or exclude this ambient air. The Egyptians, to avoid immoderate heat, make their windows on the top of the house like chimneys with two tunnels to draw a through air. In Spain they commonly make great opposite windows

without glass, still shutting those which are next to the sun. So likewise in Turkey and Italy—Venice excepted, which brags of her stately glazed palaces—they use paper windows to like purpose, and lie *sub dio* in the top of their flat-roofed houses, so sleeping under the canopy of heaven. In some parts of Italy they have windmills to draw a cooling air out of hollow caves and disperse the same through all the chambers of their palaces to refresh them, as at Costoza, the house of Cæsareo Trento, a gentleman of Vicenza, and elsewhere. Many excellent means are invented to correct nature by art. If none of these courses help, the best way is to make artificial air, which howsoever is profitable and good, still to be made hot and moist and to be seasoned with sweet perfumes, pleasant and lightsome as may be; to have roses, violets, and sweet-smelling flowers ever in their windows, posies in their hand. Laurentius commends water-lilies, a vessel of warm water to evaporate in the room, which will make a more delightsome perfume if there be added orange-flowers, pills of citron, rosemary, cloves, bays, rose-water, rose-vinegar, benzoin, labdanum, styrax, and such like gums which make a pleasant and acceptable perfume. Bessardus Bisantinus prefers the smoke of juniper to melancholy persons, which is in great request with us at Oxford to sweeten our chambers. Guianerius prescribes the air to be moistened with water and sweet herbs boiled in it, vine and sallow-leaves, etc., to besprinkle the ground and posts with rose-water, rose-vinegar, which Avicenna much approves. Of colors it is good to behold green, red, yellow, and white, and by all means to have light enough, with windows in the day, wax candles in the night, neat chambers, good fires in winter, merry companions; for though melancholy persons love to be dark and alone, yet darkness is a great increaser of the humor.

Although our ordinary air be good by nature or art, yet it is not amiss, as I have said, still to alter it; no better physic for a melancholy man than change of air and variety of places, to travel abroad and see fashions. Leo Afer speaks of many of his countrymen so cured without all other physic. Amongst the Negroes "there is such an excellent air that if any of them be sick elsewhere and brought thither, he is instantly recovered, of which he was often an eye-witness." Lipsius, Zuinger, and some other add as much of ordinary travel. No man, saith Lipsius in an epistle to Phil. Lanoius, a noble friend of his now ready to make a voyage, "can be such a stock or stone whom that pleasant speculation of countries, cities, towns, rivers, will not affect." Seneca the philosopher was infinitely taken with the sight of Scipio Africanus' house near Linternum to view those old buildings, cisterns, baths, tombs, etc. And how was Tully pleased with the sight of Athens to behold those ancient and fair buildings with a remembrance of their worthy inhabitants! Paulus Æmilius, that renowned Roman captain, after he had conquered Perseus, the last king of Macedonia, and now made an end of his tedious wars, though he had been long absent from Rome and much there desired, about the beginning of autumn, as Livy describes it, made a pleasant peregrination all over Greece accompanied with his son Scipio and Athenæus, the brother of King Eumenes, leaving the charge of his army with Sulpicius Gallus. By Thessaly he went to Delphos, thence to Megaris, Aulis, Athens, Argos, Lacedæmon, Megalopolis, etc. He took great content, exceeding delight in that his voyage, as who doth not that shall attempt the like though his travel be *ad jactationem magis quam ad usum reipub.*, as one well observes, to crack, gaze, see fine sights and fashions, spend time, rather than for his own or public good, as it is to many gallants that travel out their best days together with their means, manners, honesty, religion, yet it availeth howsoever. For peregrination charms our senses with such unspeakable and sweet variety that some count him unhappy that never traveled, a kind of prisoner, and pity his case that from his cradle to his old age beholds the same still, still, still the same, the same. Insomuch that Rhasis, *cont.*, *lib.* 1, *tract.* 2, doth not only commend but enjoin travel and such variety of objects to a melancholy man "and to lie in divers inns, to be drawn into several companies." Montaltus, *cap.* 36, and many neoterics are of the same mind. Celsus adviseth him therefore that will continue his health to have *varium vitæ genus*, diversity of callings, occupations to be busied about, "sometimes to live in the city, sometimes in the country, now to study or work, to be intent, then again to hawk or hunt, swim, run, ride, or exercise himself." A good prospect alone will ease melancholy, as Gomesius contends, *l.* 2, *c.* 7, *de Sale.* The citizens of Barcelona, saith he, otherwise penned in, melancholy, and stirring little abroad are much delighted with that pleasant prospect their city hath into the sea, which like that of old Athens besides Ægina, Salamina, and many pleasant islands had all the variety of delicious objects. So are those *Neapolitanes* and inhabitants of Genoa to see the ships, boats, and passengers go by, out of their windows, their whole cities being sited on the side of an hill, like Pera by Constantinople, so that each house almost hath a free prospect to the sea, as some part of London to the Thames. Or to have a free prospect all over the city at once, as at Granada in Spain and Fez in Africa, the river running betwixt two declining hills, the steepness causeth each house almost as well to oversee as to be overseen of the rest. Every country is full of such delightsome prospects as well within land as by sea, as Hermon and Rama in Palestina, Colalto in Italy, the top of Tagetus or Acrocorinthus, that old decayed castle in Corinth, from which Peloponnesus, Greece, the Ionian and Ægean Seas were *semel et simul*, at one view, to be taken. In Egypt the square top of the Great Pyramid, 300 yards in height, and so the Sultan's Palace in Grand Cairo, the country being plain, hath a marvellous fair prospect as well over Nilus as that great city five Italian miles long and two broad by the river side. From Mount Sion in Jerusalem the Holy Land is of all sides to be seen. Such high places are infinite. With us those of the best note are Glastonbury Tower, Bever Castle, Rodway Grange, Walsby in Lincolnshire, where I lately received a real kindness by the munificence of the Right Honorable my noble lady and patroness, the Lady Frances, Countess Dowager of Exeter.[81] And two amongst the rest, which I may not omit for vicinity's sake, Oldbury in the confines of Warwickshire, where I have often looked about me with great delight, at the foot of which hill I was born; and Hanbury in Staffordshire, contiguous to which is Falde, a pleasant village and an ancient patrimony belonging to our family, now in the possession of mine elder brother, William Burton, Esquire. Barclay the Scot commends that of Greenwich Tower for one of the best prospects in Europe, to see London on the one side, the Thames, ships, and pleasant meadows on the other. There be those that say as much and more of St. Mark's steeple in Venice. Yet these are at too great a distance; some are especially affected with such objects as be near, to see passengers go by in some great roadway or boats in a river, *in subjectum forum despicere*, to oversee a fair, a market-place, or out of a pleasant window into some thoroughfare street to behold a continual concourse, a promiscuous rout coming and going, or a multitude of spectators at a theater, a mask, or some such like show. But I rove. The sum is this, that variety of actions, objects, air, places, are excellent good in this infirmity and all others, good for man, good for beast. Constantine the

81 She gave Burton a church living.

Emperor, *lib.* 18, *c.* 13, *ex Leontio,* "holds it an only cure for rotten sheep and any manner of sick cattle." Lælius a Fonte Ægubinus, that great doctor, at the latter end of many of his consultations—as commonly he doth set down what success his physic had—in melancholy most especially approves of this above all other remedies whatsoever, as appears, *consult.* 69, *consult.* 229, etc., "Many other things helped, but change of air was that which wrought the cure and did most good."

CHARITY COMPOSED OF ALL THREE KINDS, PLEASANT, PROFITABLE, HONEST[82]

BESIDES this love that comes from profit, pleasant, honest (for one good turn asks another in equity), that which proceeds from the law of nature, or from discipline and philosophy, there is yet another love compounded of all these three, which is charity, and includes piety, dilection, benevolence, friendship, even all those virtuous habits; for love is the circle equant of all other affections, of which Aristotle dilates at large in his Ethics, and is commanded by God, which no man can well perform, but he that is a Christian, and a true regenerate man; this is, "To love God above all, and our neighbor as ourself;" for this love is *lychnus accendens et accensus,* a communicating light, apt to illuminate itself as well as others. All other objects are fair, and very beautiful, I confess; kindred, alliance, friendship, the love that we owe to our country, nature, wealth, pleasure, honor, and such moral respects, &c., of which read copious Aristotle in his morals; a man is beloved of a man, in that he is a man; but all these are far more eminent and great, when they shall proceed from a sanctified spirit, that hath a true touch of religion, and a reference to God. Nature binds all creatures to love their young ones; a hen to preserve her brood will run upon a lion, a hind will fight with a bull, a sow with a bear, a silly sheep with a fox. So the same nature urgeth a man to love his parents (*dii me pater omnes oderint, ni te magis quam oculos amem meos!*), and this love cannot be dissolved, as Tully holds, "without detestable offense:" but much more God's commandment, which enjoins a filial love, and an obedience in this kind. "The love of brethren is great, and like an arch of stones, where if one be dis-

placed, all comes down," no love so forcible and strong, honest, to the combination of which, nature, fortune, virtue, happily concur; yet this love comes short of it. *Dulce et decorum pro patriâ mori,* it cannot be expressed, what a deal of charity that one name of country contains. *Amor laudis et patria pro stipendio est;* the Decii did *se devovere,* Horatii, Curii, Scævola, Regulus Codrus, sacrifice themselves for their country's peace and good.

> *Una dies Fabios ad bellum miserat omnes,*
> *Ad bellum missos perdidit una dies.*
> One day the Fabii stoutly warred,
> One day the Fabii were destroyed.

Fifty thousand Englishmen lost their lives willingly near Battle Abbey, in defense of their country. P. Æmilius, 1.6. speaks of six senators of Calais that came with halters in their hands to the king of England, to die for the rest. This love makes so many writers take such pains, so many historiographers, physicians, &c., or at least, as they pretend, for common safety, and their country's benefit. *Sanctum nomen amicitiæ, sociorum communio sacra;* friendship is a holy name, and a sacred communion of friends. "As the sun is in the firmament, so is friendship in the world," a most divine and heavenly band. As nuptial love makes, this perfects mankind, and is to be preferred (if you will stand to the judgment of Cornelius Nepos) before affinity or consanguinity, *plus in amicitiâ valet similitudo morum quam affinitas,* &c. the cords of love bind faster than any other wreath whatsoever. Take this away, and take all pleasure, joy, comfort, happiness, and true content out of the world; 'tis the greatest tie, the surest indenture, strongest band, and, as our modern Maro decides it, is much to be preferred before the rest.

> Hard is the doubt, and difficult to deem,
> When all three kinds of love together meet;
> And do dispart the heart with power extreme,
> Whether shall weigh the balance down; to wit,
> The dear affection unto kindred sweet,
> Or raging fire of love to women kind,
> Or zeal of friends, combin'd by virtues meet;
> But of them all the band of virtuous mind,
> Methinks the gentle heart should most assured bind.

> For natural affection soon doth cease,
> And quenched is with Cupid's greater flame;
> But faithful friendship doth them both suppress,
> And them with mastering discipline doth tame,
> Through thoughts aspiring to eternal fame.

82 This is the Third Member of Section 1, Partition III, Love-Melancholy.

For as the soul doth rule the earthly mass,
And all the service of the body frame,
So love of soul doth love of body pass,
No less than perfect gold surmounts the meanest brass.[83]

A faithful friend is better than gold, a medicine of misery, an only possession; yet this love of friends, nuptial, heroical, profitable, pleasant, honest, all three loves put together, are little worth, if they proceed not from a true Christian illuminated soul, if it be not done *in ordine ad Deum*, for God's sake. "Though I had the gift of prophecy, spake with tongues of men and angels, though I feed the poor with all my goods, give my body to be burned, and have not this love, it profiteth me nothing," 1 Cor. xiii. 1, 3. 'tis *splendidum peccatum*, without charity. This is an all-apprehending love, a deifying love, a refined, pure, divine love, the quintessence of all love, the true philosopher's stone, *Non potest enim*, as Austin infers, *veraciter amicus esse hominis, nisi fuerit ipsius primitus veritatis.* He is no true friend that loves not God's truth. And therefore this is true love indeed, the cause of all good to mortal men that reconciles all creatures, and glues them together in perpetual amity and firm league; and can no more abide bitterness, hate, malice, than fair and foul weather, light and darkness, sterility and plenty may be together; as the sun in the firmament (I say), so is love in the world; and for this cause, 'tis love without an addition, love, love of God, and love of men. "The love of God begets the love of man; and by this love of our neighbor, the love of God is nourished and increased." By this happy union of love, "all well governed families and cities are combined, the heavens annexed, and divine souls complicated, the world itself composed, and all that is in it conjoined in God, and reduced to one. This love causeth true and absolute virtues, the life, spirit, and root of every virtuous action, it finisheth prosperity, easeth adversity, corrects all natural incumbrances, inconveniences, sustained by faith and hope, which with this our love make an indissoluble twist, a Gordian knot, an equilateral triangle, and yet the greatest of them is love," 1 Cor. xiii. 13, "which inflames our souls with a divine heat, and being so inflamed, purged, and so purgeth, elevates to God, makes an atonement, and reconciles us unto him." That other love infects the soul of man, this cleanseth; that depresses, this rears; that causeth cares and troubles, this quietness of mind; this informs, that

83 Spenser, The Faerie Queene, Book IV, canto 9, stanzas 1–2.

deforms our life; that leads to repentance, this to heaven. For if once we be truly linked and touched with this charity, we shall love God above all, our neighbor as ourself, as we are enjoined, Mark xii. 31. Matt. xix. 19. perform those duties and exercises, even all the operations of a good Christian.

"This love suffereth long, it is bountiful, envieth not, boasteth not itself, is not puffed up, it deceiveth not, it seeketh not his own things, is not provoked to anger, it thinketh not evil, it rejoiceth not in iniquity, but in truth. It suffereth all things, believeth all things, hopeth all things," 1 Cor. xiii. 4, 5, 6, 7; "it covereth all trespasses," Prov. x. 12; "a multitude of sins," 1 Pet. iv. 8, as our Saviour told the woman in the Gospel, that washed his feet, "many sins were forgiven her, for she loved much," Luke vii. 47; "it will defend the fatherless and the widow," Isa. i. 17; "will seek no revenge, or be mindful of wrong," Levit. xix. 18; "will bring home his brother's ox if he go astray, as it is commanded," Deut. xxii. 1; "will resist evil, give to him that asketh, and not turn from him that borroweth, bless them that curse him, love his enemy," Matt. v; "bear his brother's burthen," Gal. vi. 7. He that so loves will be hospitable, and distribute to the necessities of the saints; he will, if it be possible, have peace with all men, "feed his enemy if he be hungry, if he be athirst give him drink;" he will perform those seven works of mercy, "he will make himself equal to them of the lower sort, rejoice with them that rejoice, weep with them that weep," Rom. xii; he will speak truth to his neighbor, be courteous and tender-hearted, "forgiving others for Christ's sake, as God forgave him," Eph. iv. 32; "he will be like minded," Phil. ii. 2. "Of one judgment; be humble, meek, long-suffering," Colos. iii. "Forbear, forget and forgive," 12, 13. 23. and what he doth shall be heartily done to God, and not to men. "Be pitiful and courteous," 1 Pet. iii. "Seek peace and follow it." He will love his brother, not in word and tongue, but in deed and truth, 1 John iii. 18. "and he that loves God, Christ will love him that is begotten of him," 1 John v. 1, &c. Thus should we willingly do, if we had a true touch of this charity, of this divine love, if we could perform this which we are enjoined, forget and forgive, and compose ourselves to those Christian laws of love.

io felix hominum genus,
Si vestros animos amor
Quo cœlum regitur regat

"Angelical souls, how blessed, how happy should we

be, so loving, how might we triumph over the devil, and have another heaven upon earth!"

But this we cannot do; and which is the cause of all our woes, miseries, discontent, melancholy, want of this charity. We do *invicem angariare*, contemn, consult, vex, torture, molest, and hold one another's noses to the grindstone hard, provoke, rail, scoff, calumniate, challenge, hate, abuse (hard-hearted, implacable, malicious, peevish, inexorable as we are), to satisfy our lust or private spleen, for toys, trifles, and impertinent occasions, spend ourselves, goods, friends, fortunes, to be revenged on our adversary, to ruin him and his. 'Tis all our study, practice, and business how to plot mischief, mine, countermine, defend and offend, ward ourselves, injure others, hurt all; as if we were born to do mischief, and that with such eagerness and bitterness, with such rancor, malice, rage, and fury, we prosecute our intended designs, that neither affinity or consanguinity, love or fear of God or men can contain us: no satisfaction, no composition will be accepted, no offices will serve, no submission; though he shall upon his knees, as Sarpedon did to Glaucus in Homer, acknowledging his error, yield himself with tears in his eyes, beg his pardon, we will not relent, forgive, or forget, till we have confounded him and his, "made dice of his bones," as they say, see him rot in prison, banish his friends, followers, *et omne invisum genus*, rooted him out and all his posterity. Monsters of men as we are, dogs, wolves, tigers, fiends, incarnate devils, we do not only contend, oppress, and tyrannize ourselves, but as so many firebrands, we set on, and animate others: our whole life is a perpetual combat, a conflict, a set battle, a snarling fit. *Eris dea* is settled in our tents, *Omnia de lite*, opposing wit to wit, wealth to wealth, strength to strength, fortunes to fortunes, friends to friends, as at a sea-fight, we turn our broadsides, or two millstones with continual attrition, we fire ourselves, or break another's back and both are ruined and consumed in the end. Miserable wretches, to fat and enrich ourselves, we care not how we get it, *Quocunque modo rem;* how many thousands we undo, whom we oppress, by whose ruin and downfall we arise, whom we injure, fatherless children, widows, common societies, to satisfy our own private lust. Though we have myriads, abundance of wealth and treasure (pitiless, merciless, remorseless, and uncharitable in the highest degree), and our poor brother in need, sickness, in great extremity, and now ready to be starved for want of food, we had rather, as the fox told the ape, his tail should sweep the ground still, than

cover his buttocks; rather spend it idly, consume it with dogs, hawks, hounds, unnecessary buildings, in riotous apparel, ingurgitate, or let it be lost, than he should have part of it; rather take from him that little which he hath, than relieve him.

Like the dog in the manger, we neither use it ourselves, let others make use of or enjoy it; part with nothing while we live; for want of disposing our household, and setting things in order, set all the world together by the ears after our death. Poor Lazarus lies howling at his gates for a few crumbs, he only seeks chippings, offals; let him roar and howl, famish, and eat his own flesh, he respects him not. A poor decayed kinsman of his sets upon him by the way in all his jollity, and runs begging bareheaded by him, conjuring by those former bonds of friendship, alliance, consanguity, &c., uncle, cousin, brother, father,

—*Per ego has lachrymas, dextramque tuam te,*
Si quidquam de te merui, fuit aut tibi quidquam
Dulce meum, misere mei.

"Show some pity for Christ's sake, pity a sick man, an old man," &c., he cares not, ride on: pretend sickness, inevitable loss of limbs, goods, plead suretyship, or shipwreck, fires, common calamities, show thy wants and imperfections.

Et si per sanctum juratus dicat Osyrim,
Credite, non ludo, crudeles tollite claudum.

"Swear, protest, take God and all his angels to witness, *quære peregrinum*, thou art a counterfeit crank, a cheater, he is not touched with it, *pauper ubique jacet*, ride on, he takes no notice of it." Put up a supplication to him in the name of a thousand orphans, a hospital, a spittel, a prison, as he goes by, they cry out to him for aid, ride on, *surdo narras*, he cares not, let them eat stones, devour themselves with vermin, rot in their own dung, he cares not. Show him a decayed haven, a bridge, a school, a fortification, &c., or some public work, ride on; good your worship, your honor, for God's sake, your country's sake, ride on. But show him a roll wherein his name shall be registered in golden letters, and commended to all posterity, his arms set up, with his devices to be seen, then peradventure he will stay and contribute; or if thou canst thunder upon him, as Papists do, with satisfactory and meritorious works, or persuade him by this means he shall save his soul out of hell, and free it from purgatory (if he be of any religion), then in all likelihood he will listen and stay; or that he have no children, no near kinsman, heir, he cares for, at least, or cannot well tell otherwise how or where to bestow his possessions (for carry them with him he cannot), it may be then he will build some school or hospital in his life, or be induced to give liberally to pious uses after his death. For I dare boldly say, vainglory, that opinion of merit, and this enforced necessity, when they know not otherwise how to leave, or what better to do with them, is the main cause of most of our good works. I will not urge this to derogate from any man's charitable devotion, or bounty in this kind to censure any good work; no doubt there be many sanctified, heroical and worthy-minded men, that in true zeal, and for virtue's sake (divine spirits), that out of commiseration and pity extend their liberality, and as much as in them lies do good to all men, clothe the naked, feed the hungry, comfort the sick and needy, relieve all, forget and forgive injuries, as true charity requires; yet most part there is *simulatum quid*, a deal of hypocrisy in this kind, much default and defect. Cosmo de' Medici, that rich citizen of Florence, ingenuously confessed to a near friend of his, that would know of him why he built so many public and magnificent palaces, and bestowed so liberally on scholars, not that he loved learning more than others, "but to eternize his own name, to be immortal by the benefit of scholars; for when his friends were dead, walls decayed, and all inscriptions gone, books would remain to the world's end." The lanthorn in Athens was built by Zenocles, the theater by Pericles, the famous port Pyræum by Musicles, Pallas Palladium by Phidias, the Pantheon by Callicratidas; but these brave monuments are decayed all, and ruined long since, their builders' names alone flourish by meditation of writers. And as he said of that Marian oak, now cut down and dead, *nullius Agricolæ manu culta stirps tam diuturna quam quæ poetæ versu seminari potest*, no plant can grow so long as that which is *ingenio sata*, set and manured by those ever-living wits. Allong Backuth, that weeping oak, under which Deborah, Rebecca's nurse, died, and was buried, may not survive the memory of such everlasting monuments. Vainglory and emulation (as to most men) was the cause efficient, and to be a trumpeter of his own fame, Cosmo's sole intent so to do good, that all the world might take notice of it. Such for the most part is the charity of our times, such our benefactors, Mecænases and patrons. Show me amongst so many myriads, a truly devout, a right, honest, upright, meek, humble, a patient, innocuous, innocent, a merciful, a loving, a charitable man! *Probus quis nobiscum vivit?*

Show me a Caleb or a Joshua! *Dic mihi Musa virum*—show a virtuous woman, a constant wife, a good neighbor, a trusty servant, an obedient child, a true friend, &c. Crows in Africa are not so scant. He that shall examine this iron age wherein we live, where love is cold, *et jam terras Astrea reliquit*, justice fled with her assistants, virtue expelled,

> ——*Justitiæ soror,*
> *Incorrupta fides, nudaque veritas,*—

all goodness gone, where vice abounds, the devil is loose, and see one man vilify and insult over his brother, as if he were an innocent, or a block, oppress, tyrannize, prey upon, torture him, vex, gall, torment and crucify him, starve him, where is charity? He that shall see men swear and forswear, lie and bear false witness, to advantage themselves, prejudice others, hazard goods, lives, fortunes, credit, all, to be revenged on their enemies, men so unspeakable in their lusts, unnatural in malice, such bloody designments, Italian blaspheming, Spanish renouncing, &c., may well ask where is charity? He that shall observe so many lawsuits, such endless contention, such plotting, undermining, so much money spent with such eagerness and fury, every man for himself, his own ends, the devil for all: so many distressed souls, such lamentable complaints, so many factions, conspiracies, seditions, oppressions, abuses, injuries, such grudging, repining, discontent, so much emulation, envy, so many brawls, quarrels, monomachies, &c., may well require what is become of charity? when we see and read of such cruel wars, tumults, uproars, bloody battles, so many men slain, so many cities ruinated, &c. (for what else is the subject of all our stories almost, but bills, bows, and guns!) so many murders and massacres, &c., where is charity? Or see men wholly devote to God, churchmen, professed divines, holy men, "to make the trumpet of the gospel the trumpet of war," a company of hell-born Jesuits, and fiery-spirited friars, *facem præferre* to all seditions: as so many firebrands set all the world by the ears (I say nothing of their contentions and railing books, whole ages spent in writing one against another, and that with such virulency and bitterness, *Bionæis sermonibus et sale nigro*), and by their bloody inquisitions, that in thirty years, Bale saith, consumed 39 princes, 148 earls, 235 barons, 14,755 commons; worse than those ten persecutions, may justly doubt where is charity? *Obsecro vos quales hi demum Christiani!* Are these Christians? I beseech you tell me: he that shall observe and see these things, may say to them as

Cato to Cæsar, *credo quæ de inferis dicuntur falsa existimas*, "sure I think thou art of opinion there is neither heaven nor hell." Let them pretend religion, zeal, make what shows they will, give alms, peace-makers, frequent sermons, if we may guess at the tree by the fruit they are no better than hypocrites, epicures, atheists, with the "fool in their hearts they say there is no God." 'Tis no marvel then if being so uncharitable, hard-hearted as we are, we have so frequent and so many discontents, such melancholy fits, so many bitter pangs, mutual discords, all in a combustion, often complaints, so common grievances, general mischiefs, *si tantæ in terris tragædiæ, quibus labefactatur et miserè laceratur humanum genus*, so many pestilences, wars, uproars, losses, deluges, fires, inundations, God's vengeance and all the plagues of Egypt, come upon us, since we are so currish one towards another, so respectless of God, and our neighbors, and by our crying sins pull these miseries upon our own heads. Nay more, 'tis justly to be feared, which Josephus once said of his countrymen Jews, "if the Romans had not come when they did to sack their city, surely it had been swallowed up with some earthquake, deluge, or fired from heaven as Sodom and Gomorrah: their desperate malice, wickedness and peevishness was such." 'Tis to be suspected, if we continue these wretched ways, we may look for the like heavy visitations to come upon us. If we had any sense or feeling of these things, surely we should not go on as we do, in such irregular courses, practice all manner of impieties; our whole carriage would not be so averse from God. If a man would but consider, when he is in the midst and full career of such prodigious and uncharitable actions, how displeasing they are in God's sight, how noxious to himself, as Solomon told Joab, 1 Kings ii. "The Lord shall bring this blood upon their heads." Prov. i. 27, "sudden desolation and destruction shall come like a whirlwind upon them: affliction, anguish, the reward of his hand shall be given him," Isa. iii. 11, &c., "they shall fall into the pit they have digged for others," and when they are scraping, tyrannizing, getting, wallowing in their wealth, "this night, O fool, I will take away thy soul," what a severe account they must make; and how "gracious on the other side a charitable man is in God's eyes," *haurit sibi gratiam.* Matt. v. 7, "Blessed are the merciful, for they shall obtain mercy: he that lendeth to the poor, gives to God," and how it shall be restored to them again; "how by their patience and long-suffering they shall heap coals on their enemies' heads," Rom. xii. "and he that followeth after

righteousness and mercy, shall find righteousness and glory"; surely they would check their desires, curb in their unnatural, inordinate affections, agree amongst themselves, abstain from doing evil, amend their lives, and learn to do well. "Behold how comely and good a thing it is for brethren to live together in union: it is like the precious ointment, &c. How odious to contend one with the other!" *Miseri quid luctatiunculis hisce volumus? ecce mors supra caput est, et supremum illud tribunal, ubi et dicta et facta nostra examinanda sunt: Sapiamus!* "Why do we contend and vex one another? behold death is over our heads, and we must shortly give an account of all our uncharitable words and actions: think upon it: and be wise."

HOW LOVE TYRANNIZETH OVER MEN. LOVE, OR HEROICAL MELANCHOLY, HIS DEFINITION, PART AFFECTED[84]

YOU have heard how this tyrant Love rageth with brute beasts and spirits; now let us consider what passions it causeth amongst men.

Improbe amor, quid non mortalia pectora cogis? How it tickles the hearts of mortal men, *horresco referens*, I am almost afraid to relate, amazed and ashamed, it hath wrought such stupend and prodigious effects, such foul offenses. Love indeed (I may not deny) first united provinces, built cities, and by a perpetual generation makes and preserves mankind, propagates the Church; but if it rage, it is no more love, but burning lust, a disease, frenzy, madness, hell. *Est orcus ille, vis est immedicabilis, est rabies insana;* 'tis no virtuous habit this, but a vehement perturbation of the mind, a monster of nature, wit, and art, as Alexis in Athenæus sets it out, *viriliter audax, muliebriter timidum, furore præceps, labore infractum, mel felleum, blanda percussio,* etc. It subverts kingdoms, overthrows cities, towns, families, mars, corrupts, and makes a massacre of men; thunder and lightning, wars, fires, plagues, have not done that mischief to mankind, as this burning lust, this brutish passion. Let Sodom and Gomorrah, Troy (which Dares Phrygius and Dictys Cretensis will make good), and I know not how many cities bear record, *et fuit ante Helenam,* etc.; all succeeding ages will subscribe: Joanna of Naples in Italy, Fredegunde and

---

84 This is a portion of Subsection 2 of the First Member of Section 2, Partition III, Love-Melancholy.

Brunhalt in France, all histories are full of these basilisks. Besides those daily monomachies, murders, effusion of blood, rapes, riot, and immoderate expense, to satisfy their lusts, beggary, shame, loss, torture, punishment, disgrace, loathsome diseases that proceed from thence, worse than calentures and pestilent fevers, those often gouts, pox, arthritis, palsies, cramps, sciatica, convulsions, aches, combustions, etc., which torment the body, that feral melancholy which crucifies the soul in this life, and everlastingly torments in the world to come.

Notwithstanding they know these and many such miseries, threats, tortures, will surely come upon them, rewards, exhortations, *e contra;* yet either out of their own weakness, a depraved nature, or love's tyranny, which so furiously rageth, they suffer themselves to be led like an ox to the slaughter; (*Facilis descensus Averni*) they go down headlong to their own perdition, they will commit folly with beasts, men "leaving the natural use of women," as Paul saith, "burned in lust one towards another, and man with man wrought filthiness. . . ."

I come at last to that heroical love, which is proper to men and women, is a frequent cause of melancholy, and deserves much rather to be called burning lust, than by such an honorable title. There is an honest love, I confess, which is natural, *laqueus occultus captivans corda hominum, ut a mulieribus non possint separari,* a secret snare to captivate the hearts of men, as Christopher Fonseca proves, a strong allurement, of a most attractive, occult, adamantine property and powerful virtue, and no man living can avoid it. *Et qui vim non sensit amoris, aut lapis est, aut bellua.* He is not a man but a block, a very stone, *aut numen, aut Nebuchadnezzar,* he hath a gourd for his head, a *pepon*[85] for his heart, that hath not felt the power of it, and a rare creature to be found, one in an age, *Qui nunquam visæ flagravit amore puellæ;* for *semel insanivimus omnes,* dote we either young or old, as he said, and none are excepted but Minerva and the Muses: so Cupid in Lucian complains to his mother Venus, that amongst all the rest his arrows could not pierce them. But this nuptial love is a common passion, an honest, for men to love in the way of marriage; *ut materia appetit formam, sic mulier virum.* You know marriage is honorable, a blessed calling, appointed by God Himself in Paradise; it breeds true peace, tranquillity, content, and happiness, *qua nulla est aut fuit unquam sanctior conjunctio,* as Daphnæus in Plutarch could well prove, *et*

85 Pumpkin.

quæ generi humano immortalitatem parat, when they live without jarring, scolding, lovingly as they should do.

> *Felices ter et amplius*
> *Quos irrupta tenent copula, nec ullis*
> *Divulsus querimoniis*
> *Suprema citius solvit amor die.*

> Thrice happy they, and more than that,
> Whom bond of love so firmly ties,
> That without brawls till death them part,
> 'Tis undissolv'd and never dies.

As Seneca lived with his Paulina, Abraham and Sarah, Orpheus and Eurydice, Arria and Pætus, Artemisia and Mausolus, Rubenius Celer, that would needs have it engraven on his tomb, he had led his life with Ennea, his dear wife, forty-three years eight months, and never fell out. There is no pleasure in this world comparable to it, 'tis *summum mortalitatis bonum, hominum divumque voluptas, Alma Venus; latet enim in muliere aliquid majus potentiusque omnibus aliis humanis voluptatibus,* as one holds, there's something in a woman beyond all human delight; a magnetic virtue, a charming quality, an occult and powerful motive. The husband rules her as head, but she again commands his heart, he is her servant, she his only joy and content: no happiness is like unto it, no love so great as this of man and wife, no such comfort as *placens uxor,* a sweet wife:

> *Omnis amor magnus, sed aperto in conjuge major;*

when they love at last as fresh as they did at first, *caraque caro consenescit conjugi,* as Homer brings Paris kissing Helen, after they had been married ten years, protesting withal that he loved her as dear as he did the first hour that he was betrothed. And in their old age, when they make much of one another, saying, as he did to his wife in the poet,

> *Uxor, vivamus quod viximus, et moriamur,*
> *Servantes nomen sumpsimus in thalamo;*
> *Nec ferat ulla dies ut commutemur in ævo,*
> *Quin tibi sim juvenis, tuque puella mihi.*

> Dear wife, let's live in love, and die together,
> As hitherto we have in all good will:
> Let no day change or alter our affections,
> But let's be young to one another still.

Such should conjugal love be, still the same, and as they are one flesh, so should they be of one mind, as in an aristocratical government, one consent, Geryon-like,[86] *coalescere in unum*, have one heart in two bodies, will and nill the same. A good wife, according to Plutarch, should be as a looking-glass to represent her husband's face and passion: if he be pleasant, she should be merry; if he laugh, she should smile; if he look sad, she should participate of his sorrow, and bear a part with him, and so they should continue in mutual love one towards another.

> *Et me ab amore tuo deducet nulla senectus,*
>   *Sive ego Tithonus, sive ego Nestor ero.*
>   No age shall part my love from thee, sweet wife,
>   Though I live Nestor or Tithonus' life.

And she again to him, as the bride saluted the bridegroom of old in Rome, *Ubi tu Caius, ego semper Caia*, Be thou still Caius, I'll be Caia.

'Tis a happy state this indeed, when the fountain is blessed (saith Solomon, Prov. v. 18), "and he rejoiceth with the wife of his youth, and she is to him as the loving hind and pleasant roe, and he delights in her continually." But this love of ours is immoderate, inordinate, and not to be comprehended in any bounds. It will not contain itself within the union of marriage, or apply to one object, but is a wandering, extravagant, a domineering, a boundless, an irrefragable, a destructive passion: sometimes this burning lust rageth after marriage, and then it is properly called jealousy; sometimes before, and then it is called heroical melancholy; it extends sometimes to corrivals, etc., begets rapes, incests, murders: *Marcus Antonius compressit Faustinam sororem, Caracalla Juliam novercam, Nero matrem, Caligula sorores, Cinyras Myrrham filiam, etc.* But it is confined within no terms of blood, years, sex, or whatsoever else. Some furiously rage before they come to discretion or age. Quartilla in Petronius never remembered she was a maid; and the Wife of Bath, in Chaucer, cracks,

> Since I was twelve years old, believe,
>   Husbands at kirk-door had I five.

Aretine's Lucretia sold her maidenhead a thousand times before she was twenty-four years old, *plus millies vendiderant virginitatem, etc., neque te celabo, non deerant qui ut integram ambirent.* Rahab, that harlot, began to be a professed quean[87] at ten years of age, and was but fifteen when she hid the spies, as Hugh Broughton

86 Geryon, in Greek myth, was a king who had three heads.
87 Whore.

proves, to whom Serrarius the Jesuit, *quæst. 6 in cap. 2 Josue*, subscribes. Generally women begin *pubescere*, as they call it, or *catulire*, as Julius Pollux cites, *lib. 2, cap. 3, Onomast.* out of Aristophanes, at fourteen years old, then they do offer themselves, and some plainly rage. Leo Afer saith, that in Africa a man shall scarce find a maid at fourteen years of age, they are so forward, and many amongst us after they come into the teens do not live without husbands, but linger. What pranks in this kind the middle age have played is not to be recorded, *Si mihi sint centum linguæ, sint oraque centum*, no tongue can sufficiently declare, every story is full of men and women's insatiable lust, Neros, Heliogabali, Bonosi, etc. *Cælius Aufilenum, et Quintius Aufilenam depereunt*, etc. They neigh after other men's wives (as Jeremy, *cap.* v, 8, complaineth) like 'fed horses, or range like town bulls, *raptores virginum et viduarum*, as many of our great ones do. Solomon's wisdom was extinguished in this fire of lust, Samson's strength enervated, piety in Lot's daughters quite forgot, gravity of priesthood in Eli's sons, reverend old age in the Elders that would violate Susanna, filial duty in Absalom to his stepmother, brotherly love in Amnon towards his sister. Human, divine laws, precepts, exhortations, fear of God and men, fair, foul means, fame, fortunes, shame, disgrace, honor cannot oppose, stave off, or withstand the fury of it, *omnia vincit amor*, etc. No cord or cable can so forcibly draw, or hold so fast, as love can do with a twined thread. The scorching beams under the equinoctial, or extremity of cold within the circle Arctic, where the very seas are frozen, cold or torrid zone cannot avoid or expel this heat, fury, and rage of mortal men.

> *Quo fugis? ah, demens! nulla est fuga, tu licet usque*
>   *Ad Tanaim fugias, usque sequetur amor.*

Of women's unnatural, unsatiable lust, what country, what village doth not complain? Mother and daughter sometimes dote on the same man; father and son, master and servant on one woman.

> *Sed amor, sed ineffrenata libido,*
>   *Quid castum in terris intentatumque reliquit?*

What breach of vows and oaths, fury, dotage, madness, might I reckon up! Yet this is more tolerable in youth, and such as are still in their hot blood; but for an old fool to dote, to see an old lecher, what more odious, what can be more absurd? and yet what so common? Who so furious? *Amare ea ætate si occeperint, multo insaniunt acrius.* Some dote then more than ever they did in their youth. How many decrepit, hoary, harsh, writhen, bursten-bellied, crooked, toothless, bald, blear-eyed, impotent, rotten old men shall you see flickering still in every place? One gets him a young wife, another a courtesan, and when he can scarce lift his leg over a sill, and hath one foot already in Charon's boat, when he hath the trembling in his joints, the gout in his feet, a perpetual rheum in his head, a continuate cough, "his sight fails him, thick of hearing, his breath stinks," all his moisture is dried up and gone, may not spit from him, a very child again, that cannot dress himself, or cut his own meat, yet he will be dreaming of, and honing after wenches; what can be more unseemly? Worse it is in women than in men; when she is *ætate declivis, diu vidua, mater olim, parum decore matrimonium sequi videtur,* an old widow, a mother so long since (in Pliny's opinion), she doth very unseemly seek to marry; yet whilst she is so old a crone, a beldam, she can neither see nor hear, go nor stand, a mere carcass, a witch, and scarce feel, she caterwauls, and must have a stallion, a champion, she must and will marry again, and betroth herself to some young man, that hates to look on her but for her goods, abhors the sight of her; to the prejudice of her good name, her own undoing, grief of friends, and ruin of her children.

But to enlarge or illustrate this power and effects of love is to set a candle in the sun. . . .

Sir Thomas Overbury

[1581–1613]

Sᴏ Thomas Overbury's name lives through a combination of scandal and chance. Educated at Queen's College, Oxford, and at the Middle Temple, he became a close friend of the King's favorite, Robert Carr, later Earl of Somerset, and was knighted in 1608. Shortly afterward he traveled in France and the Low Countries, where he wrote his *Observations upon the State of the Seventeen Provinces.* He returned to London, where he seemed assured of a brilliant future. Somerset, however, became interested in Frances Howard, Countess of Essex, and Overbury got himself fatally involved in the intrigue. He aroused Somerset's hostility through his poem "A Wife," designed to dissuade him from marrying the Countess (after the favorite had procured the annulment of her marriage to Essex), and finally managed to alienate the King himself, through an alleged insult to the Queen. Caught in a web of intrigue, Overbury was finally imprisoned in the Tower, where, seemingly through the instigation of the Countess, he was slowly poisoned to death. He died in 1613 and was buried in the Tower, but news of the scandal soon leaked out and implicated the Earl and the Countess, who were, however, cleared in 1616. The details of the affair remain murky to this day.

Shortly after Overbury's death, "A Wife" was published, together with a group of character sketches allegedly penned by the unfortunate knight. Their immediate and enormous popularity had a strong influence on the growth of the character genre in the early seventeenth century. Although the writing of "characters" was an activity fully consonant with Overbury's temperament as a courtier and wit, and although there is little doubt that some of the sketches are his own work, modern scholarship has established that a good many of the characters are from the hands of a variety of seventeenth-century literary figures. Some of the most striking of the "Overburian" characters were written by the dramatist John Webster, and others were by Thomas Dekker and John Donne.

The "character" is a genre of great antiquity which, however, achieved its final definition in the seventeenth century. The first formal character sketches were composed by the Athenian Theophrastus in the time of Aristotle; they were revived in the late Renaissance by various writers, including Joseph Hall in England (*Characters of Virtues and Vices,* 1608). In large part the "character" is to be regarded as a natural prose development of the Elizabethan verse satire, but the influence of the notoriety of the Overbury case is scarcely to be underestimated in any history of the popularity of the form. The character is, as Overbury describes it in one of the sketches which may well be his own, "a quick and soft touch of many strings, all shutting up in one musical close . . . wit's descant on any plain song." It has its connections with the character of humors as developed in the comedies of Ben Jonson; it has its connections more generally with the analytic temper of the early seventeenth century and with an ever increasing tendency to put into the form of prose any perceptions and insights which did not inevitably require the complexities of poetic expression.

T. OVERBURY. *The Overburian Characters*, ed. W. J. Paylor (Oxford, 1936).

R. ALDINGTON, ed. *A Book of Characters* (London, 1924). Contains most of the Overburian group.

E. N. S. THOMPSON. *Literary Bypaths of the Renaissance* (New Haven, 1924). Includes a good essay on the character.

B. BOYCE. *Theophrastan Character in England to 1642* (Cambridge, Mass., 1947).

FROM

SIR THOMAS OVERBURY HIS WIFE . . .
New News and Divers More Characters

[TEXT: *ninth edition, 1616*]

A GOOD WOMAN

A GOOD woman is a comfort, like a man. She lacks of him nothing but heat. Thence is her sweetness of disposition, which meets his stoutness more pleasingly; so wool meets iron easier than iron, and turns resisting into embracing. Her greatest learning is religion, and her thoughts are on her own sex, or on men, without casting the difference. Dishonesty[1] never comes nearer than her ears, and then wonder stops it out, and saves virtue the labor. She leaves the neat youth, telling his luscious tales, and puts back the serving-man's putting forward, with a frown. yet her kindness is free enough to be seen, for it hath no guilt about it: and her mirth is clear, that you may look through it, into virtue, but not beyond. She hath not behavior at a certain[2] but makes it to her occasion. She hath so much knowledge as to love it, and if she have it not at home, she will fetch it; for this sometimes in a pleasant discontent she dares chide her sex, though she use it never the worse. She is much within, and frames outward things to her mind, not her mind to them. She wears good clothes, but never better; for she finds no degree beyond decency. She hath a content of her own, and so seeks not a husband, but finds him. She is indeed most, but not much of description, for she is direct and one, and hath not the variety of ill.

1 Unchastity.
2 A word is apparently omitted here.

Now she is given fresh and alive to a husband, and she does nothing more than love him, for she takes him to that purpose. So his good becomes the business of her actions, and she doth herself kindness upon him. After his, her chiefest virtue is a good husband. For she is he.

A COURTIER

TO ALL men's thinking is a man, and to most men the finest: all things else are defined by the understanding, but this by the senses; but his surest mark is that he is to be found only about princes. He smells; and putteth away much of his judgment about the situation of his clothes. He knows no man that is not generally known. His wit, like the marigold, openeth with the sun, and therefore he riseth not before ten of the clock. He puts more confidence in his words than meaning, and more in his pronunciation than his words. Occasion is his Cupid, and he hath but one receipt of making love. He follows nothing but inconstancy, admires nothing but beauty, honors nothing but fortune, loves nothing. The sustenance of his discourse is news, and his censure like a shot depends upon the charging. He is not, if he be out of court, but fish-like breathes destruction, if out of his own element. Neither his motion or aspect are regular, but he moves by the upper spheres, and is the reflection of higher substances.

If you find him not here, you shall in Paul's, with a pick-tooth in his hat, a cape-cloak, and a long stocking.

AN AMORIST

Is A MAN blasted or planet-strooken, and is the dog that leads blind Cupid; when he is at the best his fashion exceeds the worth of his weight. He is never without verses and musk confects, and sighs to the hazard of his buttons. His eyes are all white, either to wear the livery of his mistress' complexion or to keep Cupid from hitting the black. He fights with passion, and loseth much of his blood by his weapon; dreams, thence his paleness. His arms are carelessly used, as if their best use was nothing but embracements. He is untrussed, unbuttoned, and ungartered, not out of carelessness, but care; his farthest end being but going to bed. Sometimes he wraps his petition in neatness, but he goeth not alone; for then he makes some other quality moralize his affection, and his trimness is the grace of that grace. Her favor lifts him up as the sun moisture; when he disfavors, unable to hold that happiness, it falls down in tears. His fingers are his orators, and he expresseth much of himself upon some instrument. He answers not, or not to the purpose, and no marvel, for he is not at home. He scotcheth time with dancing with his mistress, taking up of her glove, and wearing her feather, he is confined to her color, and dares not pass out of the circuit of her memory. His imagination is a fool, and it goeth in a pied coat of red and white. Shortly he is translated out of a man into folly; his imagination is the glass of lust, and himself the traitor to his own discretion.

AN AFFECTATE TRAVELER

Is A speaking fashion; he hath taken pains to be ridiculous, and hath seen more than he hath perceived. His attire speaks French or Italian, and his gait cries, Behold me. He censures all things by countenances and shrugs, and speaks his own language with shame and lisping; he will choke rather than confess beer good drink, and his pick-tooth is a main part of his behavior. He chooseth rather to be counted a spy than not a politician, and maintains his reputation by naming great men familiarly. He chooseth rather to tell lies than not wonders, and talks with men singly; his discourse sounds big, but means nothing; and his boy is bound to admire him howsoever. He comes still from great personages, but goes with mean. He takes occasion to show jewels given him in regard of his virtue, that were bought in St. Martin's;[3] and not long after

3 St. Martin's-le-Grand, fashionable for laces and jewelry.

having with a mountebank's method pronounced them worth thousands, impawneth them for a few shillings. Upon festival days he goes to court, and salutes without resaluting; at night in an ordinary he canvasseth the business in hand, and seems as conversant with all intents and plots as if he begot them. His extraordinary account of men is first to tell them the ends of all matters of consequence and then to borrow money of them; he offers courtesies to show them, rather than himself, humble. He disdains all things above his reach, and preferreth all countries before his own. He imputeth his want and poverty to the ignorance of the time, not his own unworthiness; and concludes his discourse with half a period, or a word, and leaves the rest to imagination. In a word, his religion is fashion, and both body and soul are governed by fame; he loves most voices above truth.

AN OLD MAN

Is A thing that hath been a man in his days. Old men are to be known blindfolded: for their talk is as terrible as their resemblance. They praise their own times as vehemently as if they would sell them. They become wrinkled with frowning and facing youth; they admire their old customs, even to the eating of red herring, and going wetshod. They call the thumb under the girdle, gravity; and because they can hardly smell at all, their posies are under their girdles. They count it an ornament of speech to close the period with a cough: and it is venerable (they say) to spend time in wiping their driveled beards. Their discourse is unanswerable, by reason of their obstinacy; their speech is much, though little to the purpose. Truths and lies pass with an equal affirmation: for their memories several is won into one receptacle, and so they come out with one sense. They teach their servants their duties with as much scorn and tyranny as some people teach their dogs to fetch. Their envy is one of their diseases. They put off and on their clothes with that certainty, as if they know their heads would not direct them, and therefore custom should. They take a pride in halting and going stiffly, and therefore their staves are carved and tipped: they trust their attire with much of their gravity; and they dare not go without a gown in summer. Their hats are brushed, to draw men's eyes off from their faces; but above all, their pomanders are worn to most purpose, for their putrefied breath ought not to want either a smell to defend, or a dog to excuse.

A FINE GENTLEMAN

Is THE cinnamon tree, whose bark is more worth than his body. He hath read the book of good manners, and by this time each of his limbs may read it. He alloweth of no judge but the eye; painting, bolstering, and bombasting are his orators; by these also he proves his industry: for he hath purchased legs, hair, beauty, and straightness, more than nature left him. He unlocks maidenheads with his language, and speaks Euphues,[4] not so gracefully as heartily. His discourse makes not his behavior, but he buys it at court, as countrymen their clothes in Birchin Lane.[5] He is somewhat like a salamander, and lives in the flame of love, which pains he expresses comically; and nothing grieves him so much as the want of a poet to make an issue in his love; yet he sighs sweetly and speaks lamentably; for his breath is perfumed and his words are wind. He is best in season at Christmas; for the boar's head and reveler come together; his hopes are laden in his quality; and lest fiddlers should take him unprovided, he wears pumps in his pocket: and lest he should take fiddlers unprovided, he whistles his own galliard. He is a calendar of ten years, and marriage rusts him. Afterwards he maintains himself an implement of household by carving and ushering. For all this, he is judicial only in tailors and barbers, but his opinion is ever ready, and ever idle. If you will know more of his acts, the broker's shop is the witness of his valor, where lies wounded, dead, rent, and out of fashion, many a spruce suit, overthrown by his fantasticness.

A BRAGGADOCHIO WELSHMAN

Is THE oyster that the pearl is in, for a man may be picked out of him. He hath the abilities of the mind *in potentia*, and *actu* nothing but boldness. His clothes are in fashion before his body; and he accounts boldness the chiefest virtue; above all men he loves an herald, and speaks pedigrees naturally. He accounts none well descended that call him not cousin; and prefers Owen Glendower before any of the nine worthies. The first note of his familiarity is the confession of his valor; and so he prevents quarrels. He voucheth Welsh a pure and unconquered language, and courts ladies with the story of their chronicle. To conclude, he is precious in his own conceit, and upon St. Davie's day without comparison.

4 After the fashion of John Lyly's Euphues, 1580.
5 Where the old clothes shops were situated.

A PEDANT

HE TREADS in a rule, and one hand scans verses, and the other holds his sceptre. He dares not think a thought, that the nominative case governs not the verb; and he never had meaning in his life, for he traveled only for words. His ambition is criticism, and his example Tully. He values phrases, and elects them by the sound, and the eight parts of speech are his servants. To be brief, he is a heteroclite[6] for he wants the plural number, having only the single quality of words.

A GOOD WIFE

Is A man's best movable, a scion incorporate with the stock, bringing sweet fruit; one that to her husband is more than a friend, less than a trouble; an equal with him in the yoke. Calamities and troubles she shares alike, nothing pleases her that doth not him. She is relative in all; and he without her, but half himself. She is his absent hands, eyes, ears and mouth; his present and absent all. She frames her nature unto his howsoever: the hyacinth follows not the sun more willingly. Stubbornness and obstinacy are herbs that grow not in her garden. She leaves tattling to the gossips of the town, and is more seen than heard. Her household is her charge; her care to that makes her seldom non-resident. Her pride is but to be cleanly, and her thrift not to be prodigal. By her discretion she hath children, not wantons; a husband without her is a misery in man's apparel; none but she hath an aged husband, to whom she is both a staff and a chair. To conclude, she is both wise and religious, which makes her all this.

A PURITAN

Is A diseased piece of Apocrypha; bind him to the Bible, and he corrupts the whole text; ignorance and fat feed are his founders; his nurses, railing, rabies, and round breeches; his life is but a borrowed blast of wind; for between two religions, as between two doors, he is ever whistling. Truly whose child he is is yet unknown; for willingly his faith allows no father; only thus far his pedigree is found, Bragger and he flourished about a time first; his fiery zeal keeps him continually costive, which withers him into his own translation, and till he eat a Schoolman, he is hidebound; he ever prays against non-residents, but is himself the greatest discontinuer, for he never keeps near

6 An irregularly inflected noun.

his text; anything that the law allows, but marriage and March beer, he murmurs at; what it disallows and holds dangerous, makes him a discipline; where the gate stands open, he is ever seeking a stile; and where his learning ought to climb, he creeps through; give him advice, you run into traditions, and urge a modest course, he cries out councils. His greatest care is to condemn obedience, his last care to serve God handsomely and cleanly. He is now become so cross a kind of teaching that should the church enjoin clean shirts, he were lousy; more sense than single prayers is not his; nor more in those than still the same petitions; from which he either fears a learned faith, or doubts God understands not at first hearing. Show him a ring, he runs back like a bear; and hates square dealing as allied to caps; a pair of organs blow him out o' th' parish, and are the only clyster-pipes to cool him. Where the meat is best there he confutes most, for his arguing is but the efficacy of his eating; good bits he holds breed good positions, and the Pope he best concludes against in plum-broth. He is often drunk, but not as we are, temporally, nor can his sleep then cure him, for the fumes of his ambition make his very soul reel, and that small beer that should allay him (silence) keeps him more surfeited, and makes his heat break out in private houses; women and lawyers are his best disciples; the one, next fruit, longs for forbidden doctrine; the other, to maintain forbidden titles; both which he sows amongst them. Honest he dare not be, for that loves order; yet if he can be brought to ceremony, and made but master of it, he is converted.

A TINKER[7]

Is A movable: for he hath no abiding place; by his motion he gathers heat, thence his choleric nature. He seems to be very devout, for his life is a continual pilgrimage, and sometimes in humility goes barefoot, thereon making necessity a virtue. His house is as ancient as Tubal-cain's,[8] and so is a runagate[9] by antiquity; yet he proves himself a gallant, for he carries all his wealth upon his back; or a philosopher, for he bears all his substance about him. From his art was music first invented, and therefore he is always furnished with a song; to which his hammer keeping tune, proves that he was the first founder of the kettle-drum. Note, that where the best ale is, there stands his music most upon crotchets. The companion of his travel is some foul sun-burnt quean, that since the terrible

statute recanted gipsyism, and is turned pedlaress. So marches he all over England with his bag and baggage. His conversation is unreprovable; for he is ever mending. He observes truly the statutes, and therefore he can rather steal than beg, in which he is unremovably constant in spite of whips or imprisonment; and so a strong enemy to idleness, that in mending one hole, he had rather make three than want work, and when he hath done, he throws the wallet of his faults behind him. He embraceth naturally ancient custom, conversing in open fields, and lowly cottages. If he visit cities or towns, 'tis but to deal upon the imperfections of our weaker vessels. His tongue is very voluble, which with canting proves him a linguist. He is entertained in every place, but enters no further than the door, to avoid suspicion. Some would take him to be a coward; but believe it, he is a lad of mettle; his valor is commonly three or four years long, fastened to a pike in the end for flying off. He is very provident, for he will fight with but one at once, and then also he had rather submit than be counted obstinate. To conclude, if he 'scape Tyburn and Banbury, he dies a beggar.

A CHAMBERMAID

SHE is her mistress's she-secretary, and keeps the box of her teeth, her hair, and her painting very private. Her industry is upstairs and downstairs like a drawer: and by her dry hand you may know she is a sore starcher. If she lie at her master's bed's feet, she is quit of the green sickness forever; for she hath terrible dreams when she's awake, as if she were troubled with the nightmare. She hath a good liking to dwell in the country, but she holds London the goodliest forest in England to shelter a great belly. She reads Greene's[10] works over and over, but is so carried away with the Mirror of Knighthood[11] she is many times resolved to run out of herself, and become a lady-errant. If she catch a clap, she divides it so equally between the master and the serving-man as if she had cut out the getting of it by a thread; only the knave sumner makes her bowl booty, and overreach the master. The pedant of the house, though he promise her marriage, cannot grow further inward with her; she hath paid for her credulity often, and now grows wary. She likes the form of our marriage very well, in that a woman is

---

7 By J. Cocke.   8 See Genesis 4:22.
9 Vagabond.

10 Robert Greene (1560–1592), novelist, dramatist, and pamphleteer.
11 One of the romances of chivalry in Don Quixote's library; cf. Don Quixote, I. i. 6.

not tied to answer any articles concerning questions of virginity; her mind, her body, and clothes are parcels loosely packed together, and for want of good utterance, she perpetually laughs out her meaning. Her mistress and she help to make away time, to the idlest purpose that can be, either for love or money. In brief, these chambermaids are like lotteries: you may draw twenty ere one worth anything.

A WORTHY COMMANDER IN THE WARS[12]

IS ONE that accounts learning the nourishment of military virtue, and lays that as his first foundation. He never bloodies his sword but in heat of battle, and had rather save one of his own soldiers than kill ten of his enemies. He accounts it an idle, vainglorious, and suspected bounty to be full of good words; his rewarding, therefore, of the deserver arrives so timely that his liberality can never be said to be gouty-handed. He holds it next his creed that no coward can be an honest man, and dare die in 't. He doth not think his body yields a more spreading shadow after a victory than before; and when he looks upon his enemy's dead body 'tis with a kind of noble heaviness, not insultation. He is so honorably merciful to women in surprisal that only that makes him an excellent courtier. He knows the hazard of battles, not the pomp of ceremonies, are soldiers' best theaters, and strives to gain reputation, not by the multitude but by the greatness of his actions. He is the first in giving the charge and the last in retiring his foot. Equal toil he endures with the common soldier; from his example they all take fire, as one torch lights many. He understands in war there is no mean to err twice, the first and least fault being sufficient to ruin an army: faults, therefore, he pardons none; they that are presidents of disorder or mutiny repair it by being examples of his justice. Besiege him never so strictly, so long as the air is not cut from him, his heart faints not. He hath learned as well to make use of a victory as to get it, and pursuing his enemies like a whirlwind, carries all afore him; being assured if ever a man will benefit himself upon his foe, then is the time, when they have lost force, wisdom, courage, and reputation. The goodness of his cause is the special motive to his valor; never is he known to slight the weakest enemy that comes armed against him in the band of justice. Hasty and overmuch heat he accounts the stepdame to all great actions that will not suffer them to thrive; if he cannot overcome his enemy by force, he does it by time. If ever he shake

hands with war, he can die more calmly than most courtiers, for his continual dangers have been, as it were, so many meditations of death. He thinks not out of his own calling when he accounts life a continual warfare, and his prayers then best become him when armed *cap-a-pie*. He utters them like the great Hebrew general,[13] on horseback. He casts a smiling contempt upon calumny; it meets him as if glass should encounter adamant. He thinks war is never to be given o'er, but on one of these three conditions: an assured peace, absolute victory, or an honest death. Lastly, when peace folds him up, his silver head should lean near the golden sceptre and die in his prince's bosom.

A FAIR AND HAPPY MILKMAID[14]

IS A country wench, that is so far from making herself beautiful by art that one look of hers is able to put all face-physic out of countenance. She knows a fair look is but a dumb orator to commend virtue, therefore minds it not. All her excellencies stand in her so silently as if they had stolen upon her without her knowledge. The lining of her apparel (which is herself) is far better than the outsides of tissue:[15] for though she be not arrayed in the spoil of the silkworm, she is decked in innocency, a far better wearing. She doth not, with lying long abed, spoil both her complexion and conditions; nature hath taught her too immoderate sleep is rust to the soul: she rises therefore with chanticleer, her dame's cock, and at night makes the lamb her curfew. In milking a cow, and straining the teats through her fingers, it seems that so sweet a milk-press makes the milk the whiter or sweeter; for never came almond glove or aromatic ointment on her palm to taint it. The golden ears of corn fall and kiss her feet when she reaps them, as if they wished to be bound and led prisoners by the same hand that felled them. Her breath is her own, which scents all the year long of June, like a new made hay-cock. She makes her hand hard with labor, and her heart soft with pity; and when winter evenings fall early (sitting at her merry wheel), she sings a defiance to the giddy wheel of fortune. She doth all things with so sweet a grace it seems ignorance will not suffer her to do ill, being her mind is to do well. She bestows her year's wages at next fair; and in choosing her garments, counts no bravery in the world like decency. The garden and bee-hive are all her physic and chirurgery, and she

---

13 Probably Judas Maccabæus, "the foremost champion of his fellow-citizens;" cf. II Maccabees 15:20–39.

14 By John Webster.   15 Rich cloth.

12 By John Webster.

lives the longer for it. She dares go alone, and unfold sheep in the night, and fears no manner of ill, because she means none; yet to say truth, she is never alone, for she is still accompanied with old songs, honest thoughts, and prayers, but short ones; yet they have their efficacy, in that they are not palled[16] with ensuing idle cogitations. Lastly, her dreams are so chaste that she dare tell them; only a Friday's dream is all her superstition; that she conceals for fear of anger. Thus lives she, and all her care is that she may die in the springtime, to have store of flowers stuck upon her winding-sheet.

A JESUIT[17]

Is A larger spoon for a traitor to feed with the devil than any other order: unclasp him, and he's a gray wolf,[18] with a golden star in his forehead; so superstitiously he follows the Pope that he forsakes Christ in not giving Cæsar his due. His vows seem heavenly; but in meddling with state business, he seems to mix heaven and earth together. His best elements are confession and penance; by the first, he finds out men's inclinations; and by the latter, heaps wealth to his seminary. He sprang from Ignatius Loyola, a Spanish soldier; and though he were found out long since the invention of the cannon, 'tis thought he has not done less mischief. He is a false key to open princes' cabinets, and pry into their counsels; and where the Pope's excommunication thunders, he holds it not more sin the decrowning of kings than our Puritans do the suppression of bishops. His order is full of irregularity and disobedience; ambitious above all measure; for of late days, in Portugal and the Indies, he rejected the name of Jesuit, and would be called disciple. In Rome and other countries that give him freedom, he wears a mask upon his heart; in England he shifts it, and puts it upon his face. No place in our climate hides him so securely as a lady's chamber; the modesty of the pursuivant hath only forborne the bed, and so missed him. There is no disease in Christendom that may so properly be called the King's Evil.[19] To conclude, would you know him beyond the sea? In his seminary, he's a fox; but in the inquisition, a lion rampant.

16 Weakened.   17 By John Webster.
18 F. L. Lucas, in his edition of Webster's works, quotes Mr. C. G. Pritchard's description of the family-arms of St. Ignatius: "argent, a pot and chain sable between two gray wolves, rampant."
19 Scrofula: supposed to be cured by the king's touch.

AN EXCELLENT ACTOR[20]

WHATSOEVER is commendable to the grave orator is most exquisitely perfect in him, for by a full and significant action of body he charms our attention. Sit in a full theatre and you will think you see so many lines drawn from the circumference of so many ears, while the actor is the center. He doth not strive to make nature monstrous; she is often seen in the same scene with him, but neither on stilts nor crutches; and for his voice, 'tis not lower than the prompter, nor louder than the foil or target. By his action he fortifies moral precepts with examples, for what we see him personate we think truly done before us: a man of a deep thought might apprehend the ghost of our ancient heroes walked again, and take him at several times for many of them. He is much affected to painting, and 'tis a question whether that make him an excellent player, or his playing an exquisite painter. He adds grace to the poet's labors, for what in the poet is but ditty, in him is both ditty and music. He entertains us in the best leisure of our life—that is, between meals, the most unfit time either for study or bodily exercise. The flight of hawks and chase of wild beasts, either of them are delights noble; but some think this sport of men the worthier, despite all calumny. All men have been of his occupation; and indeed, what he doth feignedly, that do others essentially. This day one plays a monarch, the next a private person; here one acts a tyrant, on the morrow an exile; a parasite this man tonight, tomorrow a precisian; and so of divers others. I observe, of all men living, a worthy actor in one kind is the strongest motive of affection that can be; for, when he dies, we cannot be persuaded any man can do his parts like him. But, to conclude, I value a worthy actor by the corruption of some few of the quality as I would do gold in the ore—I should not mind the dross, but the purity of the metal.

A FRANKLIN[21]

HIS OUTSIDE is an ancient yeoman of England, though his inside may give arms (with the best gentlemen) and ne'er see the herald. There is no truer servant in the house than himself. Though he be master, he says not to his servants, Go to field, but, Let us go; and with his own eye doth both fatten his flock and set forward all manner of husbandry. He is taught by nature to be contented with a little; his own fold yields him both food and raiment; he is pleased with any

20 By John Webster.   21 By John Webster.

nourishment God sends, whilst curious gluttony ransacks, as it were, Noah's ark for food, only to feed the riot of one meal. He is ne'er known to go to law; understanding to be law-bound among men is like to be hide-bound among his beasts; they thrive not under it; in that such men sleep as unquietly as if their pillows were stuffed with lawyers' pen knives. When he builds, no poor tenant's cottage hinders his prospect;[22] they are indeed his alms-houses, though there be painted on them no such superscription; he never sits up late but when he hunts the badger, the vowed foe of his lambs; nor uses he any cruelty but when he hunts the hare, nor subtlety, but when he setteth snares for the snite, or pitfalls for the blackbird; nor oppression, but when in the month of July, he goes to the next river, and shears his sheep. He allows of honest pastime, and thinks not the bones of the dead anything bruised, or the worse for it, though the lasses dance in the churchyard after evensong. Rock Monday,[23] and the wake in summer, shrovings,[24] the wakeful catches on Christmas Eve, hoky,[25] or seed cake,[26] these he yearly keeps, yet holds them no relics

22 He does not pull down any cottage on this ground.
23 The Monday following Twelfth Night. Rock Day, or St. Distaff's Day, was the day after Twelfth Night. (Rock = distaff.) Spinning was resumed on this day, after the Christmas holidays.
24 The festivities attendant on Shrove Tuesday.
25 Hoky, *i.e.* hockey; the festival of harvest-home.
26 A feast in late October, following wheat-sowing.

of popery. He is not so inquisitive after news derived from the privy closet, when the finding an eyrie of hawks in his own ground, or the foaling of a colt come of a good strain, are tidings more pleasant, more profitable. He is lord paramount within himself, though he hold by never so mean a tenure; and dies the more contentedly (though he leave his heir young) in regard he leaves him not liable to a covetous guardian. Lastly, to end him; he cares not when his end comes, he needs not fear his audit, for his *quietus*[27] is in heaven.

WHAT A CHARACTER IS

IF I must speak the schoolmaster's language, I will confess that character comes from this infinite mood χαράξω, that signifieth to engrave, or make a deep impression. And for that cause, a letter (as A.B.) is called a character.

Those elements which we learn first, leaving a strong seal in our memories.

Character is also taken from an Egyptian hieroglyphic, for an impress, or short emblem; in little comprehending much.

To square out a character by our English level, it is a picture (real or personal) quaintly drawn, in various colors, all of them heightened by one shadowing.

It is a quick and soft touch of many strings, all shutting up in one musical close; it is wit's descant on any plain song.

27 The settling of his accounts.

Thomas Hobbes

[1588–1679]

ALTHOUGH Hobbes belongs, properly speaking, to the history of philosophy rather than to the history of English literature, he has, as a literary figure, at least three claims on our attention: he moved in literary circles as the friend of such men as Jonson, Bacon, Lord Herbert, Waller, Cowley, and Davenant; he proved himself, in his *Answer* to Davenant on the latter's *Gondibert,* to be an incisive literary theorist who in many ways anticipates the temper of the Restoration; and, most of all, he wrote his philosophical works in an admirable style in which coolness, terseness, and clarity are enlivened by a consistent play of irony and wit.

Born in the year of the Armada, Hobbes lived well into the world of the Restoration. He was born in Wiltshire, of yeoman stock, and early showed signs of great precocity. Educated at Magdalen Hall, Oxford, he manifested the same distaste for the outmoded curriculum of the university as did Bacon and Milton. After taking his degree in 1608, he supported himself by acting as tutor in the family of William Cavendish, Earl of Devonshire. From this time on he moved in circles socially considerably above his own, and his intellectual life was quickened by contact with gifted and prominent persons. From his early years he spent much time abroad in the service of the Cavendish family; he met Galileo in Florence in 1636, and was well acquainted with Mersenne and Gassendi in France. His discovery of Euclid in 1629 helped convert him to the philosophical life, but his interests turned more and more to the social and political aspects of philosophy. The greatest English philosopher between Bacon and Locke, he differs from Bacon in his extreme materialism and in his radically different method of inquiry, despite having served as Bacon's secretary for a period in the 1620's. For all the boldness of his thought, Hobbes was a timid man, and he fled to Paris at the beginning of the Civil War. Here, between the years 1648 and 1651, he evolved his masterpiece, the *Leviathan,* a complete exposition of his views concerning the nature of the state and man's relationship with it.

The *Leviathan* holds that man, in the state of nature, is a selfish and greedy animal, engaged in a ceaseless warfare with his fellows, a warfare which results in making the life of man "solitary, poor, nasty, brutish, and short." In order to ameliorate this situation man has established the social covenant through which he and his fellows jointly agree to give their sovereignty and power to "one man or assembly of men." This action enjoins upon all men the duty of unquestioning obedience to the supreme political power, and it makes absolute monarchy the only sensible kind of government. The *Leviathan* made Hobbes one of the most notorious men of his day; understandably enraging to parliamentarians and republicans, it found little more favor at the hands of royalists, for its hard-bitten view of human motivation left no room for such dignified doctrines as divine right.

Passionately anticlerical, with a reputation of being an atheist, Hobbes found it wise, in 1651, to leave Paris and return to England, where he made his submission to the Commonwealth. Forgiven for this apostasy by Charles II, he lived on into an old age embittered by controversy and the banning of his writings. Near the end of his life, he translated the *Iliad* and the *Odyssey;* the prophet of modern materialism retained to the end the quality of Renaissance universality.

T. HOBBES. *Leviathan,* ed. A. R. Waller (Cambridge, 1904).

————. "Answer to Davenant," in *Critical Essays of the Seventeenth Century,* ed. J. E. Spingarn, 3 vols. (Oxford, 1908–09).

SIR L. STEPHEN. *Hobbes* (London, 1904). Biography.

C. D. THORPE. *The Aesthetic Theory of Thomas Hobbes* (Ann Arbor, 1940).

B. WILLEY. (Cited under Bacon.)

S. I. MINTZ. *The Hunting of Leviathan* (New York, 1962). Examines seventeenth-century reactions to Hobbes' philosophy.

FROM

LEVIATHAN,

Or, The Matter, Form, and Power of a Commonwealth, Ecclesiastical and Civil

[TEXT: *first edition, 1651*]

THE INTRODUCTION

NATURE, the art whereby God hath made and governs the world, is by the art of man, as in many other things, so in this also imitated, that it can make an artificial animal. For seeing life is but a motion of limbs, the beginning whereof is in some principal part within, why may we not say that all *automata* (engines that move themselves by springs and wheels as doth a watch) have an artificial life? For what is the *heart* but a *spring;* and the *nerves* but so many *strings;* and the *joints* but so many *wheels,* giving motion to the whole body, such as was intended by the artificer? Art goes yet further, imitating that rational and most excellent work of nature, man. For by art is created that great *Leviathan* called a *commonwealth,* or State, in Latin *Civitas,* which is but an artificial man; though of greater stature and strength than the natural, for whose protection and defense it was intended; and in which the sovereignty is an artificial soul, as giving life and motion to the whole body; the magistrates and other officers of judicature and execution, artificial joints; reward and punishment, by which fastened to the seat of the sovereignty every joint and member is moved to perform his duty, are the nerves, that do the same in the body natural; the wealth and riches of all the particular members are the strength; *salus populi,* the people's safety, its business; counselors, by whom all things needful for it to know are suggested unto it, are the memory; equity and laws, an artificial reason and will; concord, health; sedition, sickness; and civil war, death. Lastly, the pacts and covenants, by which the parts of this body politic were at first made, set together, and united, resemble that *fiat,* or the first "Let us make man," pronounced by God in the Creation.

To describe the nature of this artificial man, I will consider—

First, the matter thereof, and the artificer; both which is man.

Secondly, how and by what covenants it is made;

what are the rights and just power or authority of a sovereign; and what it is that preserveth and dissolveth it.

Thirdly, what is a Christian commonwealth.

Lastly, what is the kingdom of darkness.

Concerning the first, there is a saying much usurped of late that wisdom is acquired, not by reading of books, but of men. Consequently whereunto, those persons that for the most part can give no other proof of being wise, take great delight to show what they think they have read in men by uncharitable censures of one another behind their backs. But there is another saying not of late understood, by which they might learn truly to read one another if they would take the pains; that is, *Nosce teipsum*, Read thyself: which was not meant, as it is now used, to countenance either the barbarous state of men in power towards their inferiors, or to encourage men of low degree to a saucy behavior towards their betters; but to teach us, that for the similitude of the thoughts and passions of one man to the thoughts and passions of another, whosoever looketh into himself, and considereth what he doth when he does think, opine, reason, hope, fear, etc., and upon what grounds, he shall thereby read and know what are the thoughts and passions of all other men upon like occasions. I say the similitude of passions, which are the same in all men, desire, fear, hope, etc., not the similitude of the objects of the passions, which are the things desired, feared, hoped, etc.; for these the constitution individual and particular education do so vary, and they are so easy to be kept from our knowledge, that the characters of man's heart, blotted and confounded as they are with dissembling, lying, counterfeiting, and erroneous doctrines, are legible only to him that searcheth hearts. And though by men's actions we do discover their design sometimes, yet to do it without comparing them with our own and distinguishing all circumstances by which the case may come to be altered, is to decipher without a key, and be for the most part deceived by too much trust or too much diffidence, as he that reads is himself a good or evil man.

But let one man read another by his actions never so perfectly, it serves him only with his acquaintance, which are but few. He that is to govern a whole nation must read in himself, not this or that particular man, but mankind; which, though it be hard to do, harder than to learn any language or science, yet when I shall have set down my own reading orderly and perspicuously, the pains left another will be only to consider

if he also find not the same in himself. For this kind of doctrine admitteth no other demonstration.

PART I. OF MAN

CHAPTER IV
Of Speech

. . . .

[THE IMPORTANCE OF DEFINITIONS]

SEEING that truth consisteth in the right ordering of names in our affirmations, a man that seeketh precise truth had need to remember what every name he useth stands for, and to place it accordingly, or else he will find himself entangled in words as a bird in lime twigs—the more he struggles the more belimed. And therefore in geometry, which is the only science that it hath pleased God hitherto to bestow on mankind, men begin at settling the significations of their words; which settling of significations they call definitions, and place them in the beginning of their reckoning.

By this, it appears how necessary it is for any man that aspires to true knowledge to examine the definitions of former authors; and either to correct them where they are negligently set down, or to make them himself. For the errors of definitions multiply themselves according as the reckoning proceeds, and lead men into absurdities, which at last they see, but cannot avoid without reckoning anew from the beginning, in which lies the foundation of their errors. From whence it happens that they which trust to books do as they that cast up many little sums into a greater, without considering whether those little sums were rightly cast up or not; and at last, finding the error visible and not mistrusting their first grounds, know not which way to clear themselves, but spend time in fluttering over their books, as birds that, entering by the chimney and finding themselves inclosed in a chamber, flutter at the false light of a glass window, for want of wit to consider which way they came in. So that in the right definition of names lies the first use of speech, which is the acquisition of science; and in wrong or no definitions lies the first abuse; from which proceed all false and senseless tenets, which make those men that take their instruction from the authority of books, and not from their own meditation, to be as much below the condition of ignorant men as men endued with true science are above it. For between true science and erroneous doctrines, ignorance is in the middle. Natural sense and imagination are not subject to absurdity. Nature itself cannot err, and as men abound in copiousness of language, so they become more wise or more mad than ordinary. Nor is it possible without letters for any man to become either excellently wise, or, unless his memory be hurt by disease or ill constitution of organs, excellently foolish. For words are wise men's counters,—they do but reckon by them; but they are the money of fools, that value them by the authority of an Aristotle, a Cicero, or a Thomas,[1] or any other doctor whatsoever, if but a man. . . .

CHAPTER XIII
Of the Natural Condition of Mankind, as Concerning Their Felicity and Misery

NATURE hath made men so equal in the faculties of body and mind as that though there be found one man sometimes manifestly stronger in body, or of quicker mind than another, yet when all is reckoned together, the difference between man and man is not so considerable as that one man can thereupon claim to himself any benefit to which another may not pretend as well as he. For as to the strength of body, the weakest has strength enough to kill the strongest, either by secret machination, or by confederacy with others that are in the same danger with himself.

And as to the faculties of the mind, setting aside the arts grounded upon words, and especially that skill of proceeding upon general and infallible rules, called science, which very few have, and but in few things as being not a native faculty, born with us, nor attained, as prudence, while we look after somewhat else, I find yet a greater equality amongst men than that of strength. For prudence is but experience; which equal time equally bestows on all men, in those things they equally apply themselves unto. That which may perhaps make such equality incredible is but a vain conceit of one's own wisdom, which almost all men think they have in a greater degree than the vulgar; that is, than all men but themselves and a few others, whom by fame or for concurring with themselves they approve. For such is the nature of men, that howsoever they may acknowledge many others to be more witty or more eloquent or more learned, yet they will hardly believe there be many so wise as

1 St. Thomas Aquinas, Italian scholastic (1225?–1274?).

themselves. For they see their own wit at hand, and other men's at a distance. But this proveth rather that men are in that point equal, than unequal. For there is not ordinarily a greater sign of the equal distribution of anything than that every man is contented with his share.

From this equality of ability ariseth equality of hope in the attaining of our ends. And therefore if any two men desire the same thing, which nevertheless they cannot both enjoy, they become enemies; and in the way to their end (which is principally their own conservation, and sometimes their delectation only), endeavor to destroy or subdue one another. And from hence it comes to pass, that where an invader hath no more to fear than another man's single power, if one plant, sow, build or possess a convenient seat, others may probably be expected to come prepared with forces united to dispossess and deprive him, not only of the fruit of his labor, but also of his life or liberty. And the invader again is in the like danger of another.

And from this diffidence of one another, there is no way for any man to secure himself so reasonable as anticipation; that is, by force or wiles to master the persons of all men he can, so long till he see no other power great enough to endanger him; and this is no more than his own conservation requireth, and is generally allowed. Also because there be some, that taking pleasure in contemplating their own power in the acts of conquest, which they pursue farther than their security requires; if others, that otherwise would be glad to be at ease within modest bounds, should not by invasion increase their power, they would not be able, long time, by standing only on their defense, to subsist. And by consequence, such augmentation of dominion over men, being necessary to a man's conservation, it ought to be allowed him.

Again, men have no pleasure, but on the contrary a great deal of grief, in keeping company, where there is no power able to overawe them all. For every man looketh that his companion should value him at the same rate he sets upon himself; and upon all signs of contempt or undervaluing, naturally endeavors, as far as he dares (which amongst them that have no common power to keep them in quiet, is far enough to make them destroy each other), to extort a greater value from his contemners, by damage; and from others, by the example.

So that in the nature of man, we find three principal causes of quarrel. First, competition; secondly, diffidence; thirdly, glory.

The first maketh men invade for gain; the second, for safety; and the third, for reputation. The first use violence, to make themselves masters of other men's persons, wives, children, and cattle; the second, to defend them; the third, for trifles, as a word, a smile, a different opinion, and any other sign of undervalue, either direct in their persons, or by reflection in their kindred, their friends, their nation, their profession, or their name.

Hereby it is manifest, that during the time men live without a common power to keep them all in awe, they are in that condition which is called war; and such a war as is of every man, against every man. For war consisteth not in battle only or the act of fighting; but in a tract of time, wherein the will to contend by battle is sufficiently known; and therefore the notion of time is to be considered in the nature of war, as it is in the nature of weather. For as the nature of foul weather lieth not in a shower or two of rain, but in an inclination thereto of many days together; so the nature of war consisteth not in actual fighting, but in the known disposition thereto during all the time there is no assurance to the contrary. All other time is peace.

Whatsoever therefore is consequent to a time of war, where every man is enemy to every man, the same is consequent to the time wherein men live without other security than what their own strength and their own invention shall furnish them withal. In such condition there is no place for industry, because the fruit thereof is uncertain; and consequently no culture of the earth; no navigation, nor use of the commodities that may be imported by sea; no commodious building; no instruments of moving and removing such things as require much force; no knowledge of the face of the earth; no account of time; no arts; no letters; no society; and, which is worst of all, continual fear, and danger of violent death; and the life of man, solitary, poor, nasty, brutish, and short.

It may seem strange to some man that has not well weighed these things, that nature should thus dissociate and render men apt to invade and destroy one another; and he may therefore, not trusting to this inference made from the passions, desire perhaps to have the same confirmed by experience. Let him therefore consider with himself; when taking a journey, he arms himself, and seeks to go well accompanied; when going to sleep, he locks his doors; when even in his house he locks his chests; and then when he knows there be laws and public officers, armed, to revenge all injuries shall be done him; what opinion he has of his fellow-subjects, when he rides armed; of his fellow-citizens, when he locks his doors; and of his children and servants, when he locks his chests. Does he not there as much accuse mankind by his actions as I do by my words? But neither of us accuse man's nature in it. The desires and other passions of man are in themselves no sin. No more are the actions that proceed from those passions, till they know a law that forbids them; which till laws be made they cannot know; nor can any law be made till they have agreed upon the person that shall make it.

It may peradventure be thought there was never such a time nor condition of war as this; and I believe it was never generally so over all the world; but there are many places where they live so now. For the savage people in many places of America, except the government of small families, the concord whereof dependeth on natural lust, have no government at all, and live at this day in that brutish manner, as I said before. Howsoever, it may be perceived what manner of life there would be, where there were no common power to fear, by the manner of life which men that have formerly lived under a peaceful government use to degenerate into in a civil war.

But though there had never been any time wherein particular men were in a condition of war one against another, yet in all times, kings and persons of sovereign authority, because of their independency, are in continual jealousies, and in the state and posture of gladiators; having their weapons pointing, and their eyes fixed on one another; that is, their forts, garrisons, and guns, upon the frontiers of their kingdoms; and continual spies upon their neighbors; which is a posture of war. But because they uphold thereby the industry of their subjects, there does not follow from it that misery which accompanies the liberty of particular men.

To this war of every man against every man, this also is consequent, that nothing can be unjust. The notions of right and wrong, justice and injustice, have there no place. Where there is no common power, there is no law; where no law, no injustice. Force and fraud are in war the two cardinal virtues. Justice and injustice are none of the faculties neither of the body nor mind. If they were, they might be in a man that were alone in the world, as well as his senses and passions. They are qualities that relate to men in society, not in solitude. It is consequent also to the same condition that there be no propriety, no dominion, no "mine" and "thine" distinct; but only that to be every man's that he can get; and for so long as he can keep it. And thus much for the ill condition which every man by mere nature is actually placed in; though with a possibility to come out of it, consisting partly in the passions, partly in his reason.

The passions that incline men to peace are fear of death, desire of such things as are necessary to commodious living, and a hope by their industry to obtain them. And reason suggesteth convenient articles of peace, upon which men may be drawn to agreement. These articles are they which otherwise are called the laws of nature. . . .

PART II.
OF COMMONWEALTH

CHAPTER XVII
Of the Causes, Generation, and Definition of a Commonwealth

THE final cause, end, or design of men, who naturally love liberty, and dominion over others in the introduction of that restraint upon themselves, in which we see them live in commonwealths, is the foresight of their own preservation, and of a more contented life thereby; that is to say, of getting themselves out from that miserable condition of war, which is necessarily consequent, as hath been shown in Chapter XIII, to the natural passions of men, when there is no visible power to keep them in awe, and tie them by fear of punishment to the performance of their covenants, and observation of those laws of nature set down in the fourteenth and fifteenth chapters.

For the laws of nature as justice, equity, modesty, mercy, and, in sum, doing to others as we would be done to, of themselves, without the terror of some power, to cause them to be observed, are contrary to our natural passions, that carry us to partiality, pride, revenge, and the like. And covenants, without the sword, are but words, and of no strength to secure a man at all. Therefore notwithstanding the laws of nature, which everyone hath then kept, when he has the will to keep them, when he can do it safely, if there be no power erected, or not great enough for our security; every man will and may lawfully rely on his own strength and art, for caution against all other men. And in all places, where men have lived by small families, to rob and spoil one another has been a trade,

and so far from being reputed against the law of nature that the greater spoils they gained, the greater was their honor; and men observed no other laws therein but the laws of honor; that is, to abstain from cruelty, leaving to men their lives, and instruments of husbandry. And as small families did then, so now do cities and kingdoms, which are but greater families for their own security, enlarge their dominions, upon all pretences of danger, and fear of invasion, or assistance that may be given to invaders, endeavor as much as they can to subdue or weaken their neighbors, by open force and secret arts, for want of other caution, justly; and are remembered for it in after ages with honor.

Nor is it the joining together of a small number of men that gives them this security; because in small numbers small additions on the one side or the other make the advantage of strength so great as is sufficient to carry the victory; and therefore gives encouragement to an invasion. The multitude sufficient to confide in for our security is not determined by any certain number, but by comparison with the enemy we fear; and is then sufficient when the odds of the enemy is not of so visible and conspicuous moment to determine the event of war, as to move him to attempt.

And be there never so great a multitude, yet if their actions be directed according to their particular judgments, and particular appetites, they can expect thereby no defense nor protection, neither against a common enemy, nor against the injuries of one another. For being distracted in opinions concerning the best use and application of their strength, they do not help, but hinder one another; and reduce their strength by mutual opposition to nothing; whereby they are easily not only subdued by a very few that agree together, but also when there is no common enemy they make war upon each other for their particular interests. For if we could suppose a great multitude of men to consent in the observation of justice, and other laws of nature, without a common power to keep them all in awe, we might as well suppose all mankind to do the same; and then there neither would be, nor need to be, any civil government or commonwealth at all; because there would be peace without subjection.

Nor is it enough for the security, which men desire should last all the time of their life, that they be governed and directed by one judgment, for a limited time, as in one battle or one war. For though they obtain a victory by their unanimous endeavor against a foreign enemy, yet afterwards, when either they have no common enemy, or he that by one part is held for an enemy, is by another part held for a friend, they must needs by the difference of their interests dissolve, and fall again into a war amongst themselves.

It is true that certain living creatures, as bees and ants, live sociably one with another, which are therefore by Aristotle numbered amongst political creatures and yet have no other direction than their particular judgments and appetites; nor speech, whereby one of them can signify to another what he thinks expedient for the common benefit; and therefore some man may perhaps desire to know why mankind cannot do the same. To which I answer,

First, that men are continually in competition for honor and dignity, which these creatures are not; and consequently amongst men there ariseth on that ground envy and hatred, and finally war; but amongst these not so.

Secondly, that amongst these creatures the common good differeth not from the private; and being by nature inclined to their private, they procure thereby the common benefit. But man, whose joy consisteth in comparing himself with other men, can relish nothing but what is eminent.

Thirdly, that these creatures, having not as man the use of reason, do not see, nor think they see any fault, in the administration of their common business; whereas amongst men there are very many that think themselves wiser, and abler to govern the public, better than the rest; and these strive to reform and innovate, one this way, another that way; and thereby bring it into distraction and civil war.

Fourthly, that these creatures, though they have some use of voice in making known to one another their desires and other affections, yet they want that art of words by which some men canre present to others that which is good in the likeness of evil; and evil in the likeness of good; and augment or diminish the apparent greatness of good and evil, discontenting men, and troubling their peace at their pleasure.

Fifthly, irrational creatures cannot distinguish between *injury* and *damage;* and therefore as long as they be at ease they are not offended with their fellows; whereas man is then most troublesome when he is most at ease; for then it is that he loves to show his wisdom, and control the actions of them that govern the commonwealth.

Lastly, the agreement of these creatures is natural; that of men is by covenant only, which is artificial; and therefore it is no wonder if there be somewhat else required besides covenant to make their agreement constant and lasting; which is a common power, to keep them in awe, and to direct their actions to the common benefit.

The only way to erect such a common power as may be able to defend them from the invasion of foreigners, and the injuries of one another, and thereby to secure them in such sort as that by their own industry and by the fruits of the earth they may nourish themselves and live contentedly, is to confer all their power and strength upon one man, or upon one assembly of men, that may reduce all their wills by plurality of voices unto one will; which is as much as to say, to appoint one man or assembly of men to bear their person; and everyone to own and acknowledge himself to be author of whatsoever he that so beareth their person shall act, or cause to be acted, in those things which concern the common peace and safety; and therein to submit their wills, everyone to his will, and their judgments, to his judgment. This is more than consent or concord; it is a real unity of them all, in one and the same person, made by covenant of every man with every man, in such manner as if every man should say to every man, "I authorize and give up my right of governing myself to this man, or to this assembly of men, on this condition, that thou give up thy right to him, and authorize all his actions in like manner." This done, the multitude so united in one person, is called a Commonwealth, in Latin, *Civitas.* This is the generation of that great Leviathan, or rather, to speak more reverently, of that mortal god, to which we owe, under the immortal God, our peace and defense. For by this authority, given him by every particular man in the commonwealth, he hath the use of so much power and strength conferred on him, that by terror thereof he is enabled to form the wills of them all to peace at home, and mutual aid against their enemies abroad. And in him consisteth the essence of the commonwealth; which, to define it, is "One person, of whose acts a great multitude, by mutual covenants one with another, have made themselves everyone the author, to the end he may use the strength and means of them all, as he shall think expedient, for their peace and common defense."

And he that carrieth this person is called sovereign, and said to have sovereign power; and everyone besides, his subject.

The attaining to this sovereign power is by two ways. One, by natural force; as when a man maketh his children to submit themselves and their children to his government, as being able to destroy them if they refuse; or by war subdueth his enemies to his will, giving them their lives on that condition. The other is when men agree amongst themselves to submit to some man or assembly of men, voluntarily, on confidence to be protected by him against all others. This latter may be called a political commonwealth, or commonwealth by institution; and the former, a commonwealth by acquisition. . . .

THE ANSWER TO DAVENANT'S PREFACE
BEFORE *GONDIBERT*

[TEXT: *first edition, Paris, 1650*]

SIR,

IF TO commend your poem, I should only say (in general terms) that in the choice of your argument, the disposition of the parts, the maintenance of the characters of your persons, the dignity and vigor of your expression you have performed all the parts of various experience, ready memory, clear judgment, swift and well governed fancy, though it were enough for the truth, it were too little for the weight and credit of my testimony. For I lie open to two exceptions, one of an incompetent, the other of a corrupted witness. Incompetent, because I am not a poet; and corrupted with the honor done me by your preface. The former obliges me to say something (by the way) of the nature and differences of poesy.

As philosophers have divided the universe (their subject) into three regions, celestial, aerial, and terrestrial; so the poets (whose work it is by imitating human life, in delightful and measured lines, to avert men from vice, and incline them to virtuous and honorable actions) have lodged themselves in the three regions of mankind, court, city, and country correspondent in some proportion, to those three regions of the world. For there is in princes and men of conspicuous power (anciently called heroes) a luster and influence upon the rest of men, resembling that of the heavens; and an insincereness, inconstancy, and troublesome humor of those that dwell in populous cities, like the mobility, blustering, and impurity of the air; and a plainness, and (though dull) yet a nutritive faculty in rural people, that endures a comparison with the earth they labor.

From hence have proceeded three sorts of poesy, heroic, scommatic,[1] and pastoral. Every one of these is distinguished again in the manner of representation, which sometimes is narrative, wherein the poet himself relateth, and sometimes dramatic, as when the persons are every one adorned and brought upon the

1 Satiric (literally, *scommatic* means derisive, scoffing).

theater, to speak and act their own parts. There is therefore neither more nor less than six sorts of poesy. For the heroic poem narrative (such as is yours) is called an epic poem; the heroic poem dramatic, is tragedy. The scommatic narrative, is satire; dramatic is comedy. The pastoral narrative, is called simply pastoral (anciently bucolic) the same dramatic, pastoral comedy. The figure therefore of an epic poem, and of a tragedy, ought to be the same, for they differ no more but in that they are pronounced by one, or many persons. Which I insert to justify the figure of yours, consisting of five books divided into songs or cantos, as five acts divided into scenes has ever been the approved figure of a tragedy.

They that take for poesy whatsoever is writ in verse, will think this division imperfect, and call in sonnets, epigrams, eclogues, and the like pieces (which are but essays, and parts of an entire poem) and reckon Empedocles and Lucretius (natural philosophers) for poets, and the moral precepts of Phocylides, Theognis, and the quatrains of Pybrach, and the history of Lucan, and others of that kind amongst poems; bestowing on such writers for honor the name of poets, rather then of historians or philosophers. But the subject of a poem is the manners of men, not natural causes; manners presented, not dictated; and manners feigned (as the name of poesy imports), not found in men. They that give entrance to fictions writ in prose, err not so much, but they err. For poesy requireth delightfulness, not only of fiction, but of style; in which if prose contend with verse, it is with disadvantage (as it were) on foot, against the strength and wings of Pegasus.

For verse amongst the Greeks was appropriated anciently to the service of their gods, and was the holy style; the style of the oracles; the style of the laws; and the style of men that publicly recommended to their gods, the vows and thanks of the people; which was done in their holy songs called hymns, and the composers of them were called prophets and priests before the name of poet was known. When afterwards the majesty of that style was observed, the poets chose it as best becoming their high invention. And for the antiquity of verse it is greater than the antiquity of letters. For it is certain Cadmus was the first that (from Phœnicia, a country that neighboreth Judea) brought the use of letters into Greece. But the service of the Gods, and the laws (which by measured sounds were easily committed to the memory) had been long time in use, before the arrival of Cadmus there.

There is besides the grace of style, another cause why the ancient poets chose to write in measured language, which is this. Their poems were made at first with intention to have them sung, as well epic as dramatic (which custom hath been long time laid aside, but began to be revived in part, of late years in Italy) and could not be made commensurable to the voice or instruments, in prose; the ways and motions whereof are so uncertain and undistinguished (like the way and motion of a ship in the sea) as not only to discompose the best composers, but also to disappoint sometimes the most attentive reader, and put him to hunt counter for the sense. It was therefore necessary for poets in those times, to write in verse.

The verse which the Greeks, and Latins (considering the nature of their own languages) found by experience most grave, and for an epic poem most decent, was their hexameter; a verse limited, not only in the length of the line, but also in the quantity of the syllables. Instead of which we use the line of ten syllables, recompensing the neglect of their quantity, with the diligence of rhyme. And this measure is so proper for an heroic poem, as without some loss of gravity and dignity, it was never changed. A longer is not far from ill prose, and a shorter, is a kind of whisking (you know) like the unlacing, rather then the singing of a muse. In an epigram or a sonnet, a man may vary his measures, and seek glory from a needless difficulty, as he that contrived verses into the forms of an organ, a hatchet, an egg, an altar, and a pair of wings; but in so great and noble a work as is an epic poem, for a man to obstruct his own way with unprofitable difficulties, is great imprudence. So likewise to choose a needless and difficult correspondence of rhyme, is but a difficult toy, and forces a man sometimes for the stopping of a chink to say somewhat he did never think; I cannot therefore but very much approve your stanza, wherein the syllables in every verse are ten, and the rhyme, alternate.

For the choice of your subject you have sufficiently justified yourself in your preface. But because I have observed in Virgil, that the honor done to Æneas and his companions, has so bright a reflection upon Augustus Cæsar, and other great Romans of that time, as a man may suspect him not constantly possessed with the noble spirit of those his heros, and believe you are not acquainted with any great man of the race of Gondibert, I add to your justification the purity of your purpose, in having no other motive of your labor, but to adorn virtue, and procure her lovers; then which there cannot be a worthier design and more becoming noble poesy.

In that you make so small account of the example of almost all the approved poets, ancient and modern, who thought fit in the beginning, and sometimes also in the progress of their poems, to invoke a muse, or some other deity, that should dictate to them, or assist them in their writings, they that take not the laws of art, from any reason of their own, but from the fashion of precedent times, will perhaps accuse your singularity. For my part, I neither subscribe to their accusation, nor yet condemn that heathen custom, otherwise than as necessary to their false religion. For their poets were their divines; had the name of prophets; exercised amongst the people a kind of spiritual authority; would be thought to speak by a divine spirit; have their works which they writ in verse (the divine style) pass for the word of God, and not of man; and to be harkened to with reverence. Do not our divines (excepting the style) do the same, and by us that are of the same religion cannot justly be reprehended for it? Besides, in the use of the spiritual calling of divines, there is danger sometimes to be feared, from want of skill, such as is reported of unskillful conjurers, that mistaking the rites and ceremonious points of their art, call up such spirits, as they cannot at their pleasure allay again; by whom storms are raised, that overthrow buildings, and are the cause of miserable wrecks at sea. Unskillful divines do oftentimes the like, for when they call unseasonably for zeal, there appears a spirit of cruelty; and by the like error instead of truth they raise discord; instead of wisdom, fraud; instead of reformation, tumult; and controversy instead of religion. Whereas in the heathen poets, at least in those whose works have lasted to the time we are in, there are none of those indiscretions to be found, that tended to subversion or disturbance of the commonwealths wherein they lived. But why a Christian should think it an ornament to his poem, either to profane the true God, or invoke a false one, I can imagine no cause, but a reasonless imitation of custom, of a foolish custom; by which a man, enabled to speak wisely from the principles of nature, and his own meditation, loves rather to be thought to speak by inspiration, like a bag-pipe.

Time and education begets experience; experience begets memory; memory begets judgment and fancy: judgment begets the strength and structure, and fancy begets the ornaments of a poem. The ancients therefore fabled not absurdly, in making memory the mother of the muses. For memory is the world (though not really, yet so as in a looking glass) in which the judgment (the severer sister) busieth herself in a grave and rigid examination of all the parts of nature, and in registering by letters, their order, causes, uses, differences and resemblances; whereby the fancy, when any work of art is to be performed, findeth her materials at hand and prepared for use, and needs no more than a swift motion over them, that what she wants, and is there to be had, may not lie too long unespied. So that when she seemeth to fly from one Indies to the other, and from heaven to earth, and to penetrate into the hardest matter, and obscurest places, into the future, and into herself, and all this in a point of time; the voyage is not very great, herself being all she seeks; and her wonderful celerity, consisteth not so much in motion, as in copious imagery discreetly ordered, and perfectly registered in the memory; which most men under the name of philosophy have a glimpse of, and is pretended to by many that grossly mistaking her embrace contention in her place. But so far forth as the fancy of man has traced the ways of true philosophy, so far it hath produced very marvelous effects to the benefit of mankind. All that is beautiful or defensible in building; or marvelous in engines and instruments of motion; whatsoever commodity men receive from the observation of the heavens, from the description of the earth, from the account of time, from walking on the seas; and whatsoever distinguisheth the civility of Europe, from the barbarity of the American savages, is the workmanship of fancy, but guided by the precepts of true philosophy. But where these precepts fail, as they have hitherto failed in the doctrine of moral virtue, there the architect (fancy) must take the philosophers part, upon herself. He therefore that undertakes an heroic poem (which is to exhibit a venerable and amiable image of heroic virtue) must not only be the poet, to place and con, but also the philosopher, to furnish and square his matter, that is, to make both body and soul, color and shadow of his poem out of his own store: which how well you have performed I am now considering.

Observing how few the persons be you introduce in the beginning, and how in the course of the actions of these (the number increasing) after several confluences they run all at last into the two principal streams of your poem, Gondibert and Oswald, methinks the fable is not much unlike the theater. For so, from several and far distant sources, do the lesser brooks of Lombardy, flowing into one another, fall all at last into the two main rivers, the Po and the Adice. It hath the same resemblance also with a man's veins, which proceeding from different parts, after the like concourse, insert themselves at last into the two principal veins of the body. But when I considered that also the actions of men, which singly are inconsiderable, after many conjunctures grow at last either into one great protecting power, or into two destroying factions; I could not but approve the structure of your poem, which ought to be no other then such as an imitation of human life requireth.

In the streams themselves I find nothing but settled valor, clean honor, calm counsel, learned diversion, and pure love; save only a torrent or two of ambition, which (though a fault) hath somewhat heroic in it, and therefore must have place in an heroic poem. To show the reader in what place he shall find every excellent picture of virtue you have drawn, is too long. And to show him one, is to prejudice the rest; yet I cannot forbear to point him to the description of love in the person of Birtha, in the seventh Canto of the second book. There hath nothing been said of that subject neither by the ancient nor modern poets comparable to it. Poets are painters: I would fain see another painter draw so true, perfect, and natural a love to the life, and make use of nothing but pure lines, without the help of any the least uncomely shadow, as you have done. But let it be read as a piece by itself, for in the almost equal height of the whole, the eminence of parts is lost.

There are some that are not pleased with fiction, unless it be bold not only to exceed the work, but also the possibility of nature; they would have impenetrable armors, enchanted castles, invulnerable bodies, iron men, flying horses, and a thousand other such things which are easily feigned by them that dare. Against such I defend you (without assenting to those that condemn either Homer or Virgil by dissenting only from those that think the beauty of a poem consisteth in the exorbitancy of the fiction. For as truth is the bound of historical, so the resemblance of truth is the utmost limit of poetical liberty. In old time amongst the heathens, such strange fictions and meta-morphoses were not so remote from the articles of their faith, as they are now from ours, and therefore we are not so unpleasant. Beyond the actual works of nature a poet may now go; but beyond the conceived possi-bility of nature, never. I can allow a geographer to make in the sea, a fish or a ship, which by the scale of his map would be two or three hundred miles long, and think it done for ornament, because it is done without the precincts of his undertaking; but when he paints an elephant so, I presently apprehend it as ignorance, and a plain confession of terra incognita.

As the description of great men and great actions is the constant design of a poet; so the descriptions of worthy circumstances are necessary accessions to a poem, and being well performed, are the jewels and most precious ornaments of poesy. Such in Virgil, are the funeral games of Anchises. The duel of Æneas and Turnus, etc.; And such in yours, are The Hunting. The Battle. The City Mourning. The Funeral. The House of Astragon. The Library. And the Temples. Equal to his, or those of Homer whom he imitated.

There remains now no more to be considered but the expression, in which consisteth the countenance and color of a beautiful muse; and is given her by the poet out of his own provision, or is borrowed from others. That which he hath of his own, is nothing but experience and knowledge of nature, and specially human nature; and is the true and natural color. But that which is taken out of the books (the ordinary boxes of counterfeit complexion) shows well or ill, as it hath more or less resemblance with the natural, and are not to be used (without examination) un-advisedly. For in him that professes the imitation of nature (as all poets do) what greater fault can there be, then to bewray an ignorance of nature in his poem; especially having a liberty allowed him, if he meet with any thing he cannot master, to leave it out?

That which giveth a poem the true and natural color, consisteth in two things, which are, to know well; that is, to have images of nature in the memory distinct and clear; and to know much. A sign of the first is perspicuity, property, and decency, which delight all sorts of men, either by instructing the ignorant or soothing the learned in their knowledge: A sign of the latter is novelty of expression, and pleaseth by excitation of the mind; for novelty causeth

admiration; and admiration, curiosity; which is a delightful appetite of knowledge.

There be so many words in use at this day in the English tongue, that, though of magnific sound, yet (like the windy blisters of a troubled water) have no sense at all; and so many others that lose their meaning by being ill coupled, that it is a hard matter to avoid them; for having been obtruded upon youth in the Schools (by such as make it, I think, their business there, as 'tis expressed by the best poet)

With terms to charm the weak and
pose the wise,[2]

they grow up with them, and gaining reputation with the ignorant, are not easily shaken off.

To this palpable darkness, I may also add the am-bitious obscurity of expressing more than is perfectly conceived; or perfect conception in fewer words than it requires. Which expressions, though they have had the honor to be called strong lines, are indeed no better than riddles, and not only to the reader, but also (after a little time) to the writer himself, dark and troublesome.

To the property of expression, I refer that clearness of memory, by which a poet when he hath once intro-duced any person whatsoever, speaking in his poem, maintaineth in him, to the end, the same character he gave to him in the beginning. The variation whereof, is a change of pace that argues the poet tired.

Of the indecencies of an heroic poem, the most re-markable are those that show disproportion either be-tween the persons and their actions, or between the manners of the poet and the poem. Of the first kind, is the uncomeliness of representing in great persons the inhuman vice of cruelty, or the sordid vices of lust and drunkenness. To such parts as those, the ancient ap-proved poets thought it fit to suborn, not the persons of men, but of monsters and beastly giants, such as Polyphemus, Cacus, and the centaurs. For it is sup-posed, a muse, when she is invoked to sing a song of that nature, should maidenly advise the poet to set such persons to sing their own vices upon the stage; for it is not so unseemly in a tragedy. Of the same kind it is to represent scurrility, or any action or language that moveth much laughter. The delight of an epic poem consisteth not in mirth but in admiration. Mirth and laughter is proper to comedy and satire. Great persons that have their minds employed on great designs have not leisure enough to laugh, and are pleased with the

---

[2] Gondibert, Lib. I. Cant. 5. [Hobbes]

contemplation of their own power and virtues, so as they need not the infirmities and vices of other men to recommend themselves to their own favor by comparison, as all men do when they laugh. Of the second kind, where the disproportion is between the poet, and the persons of his poem, one is in the dialect of the inferior sort of people which is always different from the language of the court. Another is to derive the illustration of any thing, from such metaphors or comparisons as cannot come into men's thoughts, but by mean conversation, and experience of humble or evil arts, which the persons of an epic poem cannot be thought acquainted with.

From knowing much, proceedeth the admirable variety and novelty of metaphors and similitudes, which are not possibly to be lighted on in the compass of a narrow knowledge. And the want whereof compelleth a writer to expressions that are either defaced by time or sullied with vulgar or long use. For the phrases of poesy, as the airs of music, with often hearing become insipid; the reader having no more sense of their force, than our flesh is sensible of the bones that sustain it. As the sense we have of bodies, consisteth in change and variety of impression, so also does the sense of language in the variety and changeable use of words. I mean not in the affectation of words newly brought home from travel, but in new (and withal, significant) translation to our purposes, of those that be already received, and in far fetched (but withal, apt, instructive, and comely) similitudes.

Having thus (I hope) avoided the first exception, against the incompetency of my judgment: I am but little moved with the second; which is, of being bribed by the honor you have done me, by attributing in your preface somewhat to my judgment. For I have used your judgment no less in many things of mine, which coming to light will thereby appear the better. And so you have your bribe again.

Having thus made way for the admission of my testimony, I give it briefly thus; I never yet saw poem that had so much shape of art, health of morality, and vigor and beauty of expression, as this of yours. And but for the clamor of the multitude that hide their envy of the present, under a reverence of antiquity, I should say further, that it would last as long as either the Æneid or Iliad, but for one disadvantage. And the disadvantage is this: The languages of the Greeks and Romans (by their colonies and conquest) have put off flesh and blood, and are become immutable, which none of the modern tongues are like to be. I honor

antiquity; but, that which is commonly called old time, is young time. The glory of antiquity is due, not to the dead, but to the aged.

And now, whilst I think on't, give me leave with a short discord to sweeten the harmony of the approaching close. I have nothing to object against your poem; but, dissent only from something in your preface, sounding to the prejudice of age. 'Tis commonly said, that old age is a return to childhood. Which methinks you insist on so long, as if you desired it should be believed. That's the note I mean to shake a little. That saying, meant only of the weakness of body, was wrested to the weakness of mind, by froward children, weary of the controlment of their parents, masters, and other admonitors. Secondly, the dotage and childishness they ascribe to age, is never the effect of time, but sometimes of the excesses of youth, and not a returning to, but a continual stay with childhood. For they that wanting the curiosity of furnishing their memories with the rarities of nature in their youth, and pass their time in making provision only for their ease and sensual delight, are children still, at what years soever; as they that coming into a populous city, never go out of their own inn, are strangers still, how long soever they have been there. Thirdly, there is no reason for any man to think himself wiser today than yesterday, which doth not equally convince he shall be wiser tomorrow than today.

Fourthly, you will be forced to change your opinion hereafter when you are old; and in the meantime you discredit all I have said before in your commendation, because I am old already. But no more of this.

I believe (Sir) you have seen a curious kind of perspective, where, he that looks through a short hollow pipe, upon a picture containing diverse figures, sees none of those that are there painted, but some one person made up of their parts, conveyed to the eye by the artificial cutting of a glass. I find in my imagination an effect not unlike it from your poem. The virtues you distribute there amongst so many noble persons represent (in the reading) the image but of one man's virtue to my fancy, which is your own; and that so deeply imprinted, as to stay forever there, and govern all the rest of my thoughts and affections in the way of honoring and serving you, to the utmost of my power, that am

SIR,

Your most humble,
and obedient Servant,
THOMAS HOBBES.

Paris, Jan. 10, 1650.

George Herbert

[1593–1633]

THE facts of George Herbert's life are told most winningly by Izaak Walton in the biography excerpted later in this volume. Walton, in his usual manner, tends to turn reality into an *exemplum*, a saint's life, but in the case of Herbert he may be readily forgiven, for there was much that was indeed saintly in the aristocratic parson of Bemerton. Herbert was born in Montgomeryshire in northern Wales, the fifth son of one of the greatest of the border families. His mother was Magdalen Herbert, the friend of Donne, and his eldest brother was Edward, later Lord Herbert of Cherbury, noted philosopher, diplomat, and gallant. The young Herbert was educated at Westminster School and at Trinity College, Cambridge. He received his B.A. in 1613 and his M.A. in 1616, after which he was appointed a fellow of his college.

Although Herbert seems always to have been of a serious and religious cast of mind, and although his strong-willed mother felt that he was ideally suited to the ministry, his ultimate acceptance of his vocation was preceded by a good deal of spiritual conflict. Strongly attracted to the life of the court with its fine clothes, elegant manners, and sophisticated atmosphere, Herbert recognized that his post as University Orator, to which he was called in 1620, might well lead to a distinguished career in the service of the king; more than once in the past, the position of Public Orator to the University of Cambridge had led to the post of Secretary of State. Herbert had particular reason to nourish high ambitions, for his exercise of his official duties, particularly his effective demolishment of the arguments of the Scottish Calvinist Andrew Melville, had attracted to him the favorable attention of both King James I and Bishop (later Archbishop) Laud. But the death of James in 1625, as well as the death of another patron, the Marquess of Hamilton, crushed Herbert's hopes, and his old attraction to the ministry asserted itself once more. At some time around 1626 he was ordained deacon; in 1629 he married Jane Danvers, the kinswoman of his mother's second husband; and in 1630 he was ordained a priest of the Church of England and appointed to the rectory of the country town of Bemerton near Salisbury.

The remaining three years of Herbert's life were notable for their devoted service and exemplary piety. Walton tells the story of Herbert's shutting himself into his church on the occasion of his induction as rector and lying prostrate before the altar while he made "rules to himself for the future manage of his life." To judge from the anecdotes which Walton further tells of Herbert's life as a country parson, he conducted himself fully in accordance with the kind of rules contained in *A Priest to the Temple*, his straightforward but curiously moving manual for the guidance of ministers in his position. It was outwardly a life of placid serenity which "holy Mr. Herbert" led in Bemerton in the company of his scarcely less saintly wife; it was a life of quiet service to God and man, relieved by the pleasures of music—playing the lute for his own enjoyment, or listening to the choir at Salisbury Cathedral—and the pleasures of friendship—one of his closest friends was Nicholas Ferrar, who had already established his meditative community at Little Gidding. But Herbert's inner life in those years must have been one of passionate excitement, for it was during that period that he composed almost all of *The Temple*, that magnificent sequence of devotional lyrics which records in detail finite man's approach to the infinite love of God and which must rank among the greatest of all expressions of the religious impulse. For the truest account of Herbert's real life, the reader must turn to that volume.

G. HERBERT. *Works*, ed. F. E. Hutchinson (Oxford, rev. ed., 1945). The definitive edition of the complete works in verse and prose.

H. C. BEECHING. *George Herbert's Country Parson* (Oxford, 1898). An edition of *A Priest to the Temple* under its alternative title.

M. BOTTRALL. *George Herbert* (London, 1954). Critical biography, with a good chapter on *A Priest to the Temple*.

M. M. ROSS. "George Herbert and the Humanist Tradition." *Univ. of Toronto Quarterly*, XVI (1947).

FROM

A PRIEST TO THE TEMPLE

[TEXT: *first edition, 1652*]

THE PARSON'S LIFE[1]

THE country parson is exceeding exact in his life, being holy, just, prudent, temperate, bold, grave in all his ways. And because the two highest points of life, wherein a Christian is most seen, are patience and mortification, patience in regard of afflictions, mortification in regard of lusts and affections and the stupefying and dreading of all the clamorous powers of the soul, therefore he hath thoroughly studied these that he may be an absolute master and commander of himself for all the purposes which God hath ordained him. Yet in these points he labors most in those things which are most apt to scandalize his parish. And first, because country people live hardly and therefore as feeling their own sweat and consequently knowing the price of money are offended much with any who by hard usage increase their travail, the country parson is very circumspect in avoiding all covetousness, neither being greedy to get nor niggardly to keep nor troubled to

1 Chapter III of A Priest to the Temple.

lose any worldly wealth, but in all his words and actions slighting and disesteeming it even to a wondering that the world should so much value wealth, which in the day of wrath hath not one dram of comfort for us. Secondly, because luxury is a very visible sin, the parson is very careful to avoid all the kinds thereof, but especially that of drinking, because it is the most popular vice; into which if he come, "he prostitutes himself" both to shame and sin and by having "fellowship with the unfruitful works of darkness" he disableth himself of authority "to reprove them." For sins make all equal whom they find together; and then they are worst who ought to be best. Neither is it for the servant of Christ to haunt inns or taverns or alehouses "to the dishonor of his person and office." The parson doth not so, but orders his life in such a fashion that when death takes him, as the Jews and Judas did Christ, he may say as he did, "I sat daily with you teaching in the Temple." Thirdly, because country people, as indeed all honest men, do much esteem their word, it being the life of buying and selling and dealing in the world, therefore the parson is very strict in keeping his word, though it be to his own hindrance, as knowing that if he be not so, he will quickly be discovered and disregarded; neither will they believe him in the pulpit whom they cannot trust in his conversation. As for oaths and apparel, the disorders thereof are also very manifest. The parson's yea is yea, and nay nay; and his apparel plain, but reverend and clean, without spots or dust or smell; the purity of his mind breaking out and dilating itself even to his body, clothes, and habitation.

THE PARSON IN HIS HOUSE[2]

THE parson is very exact in the governing of his house, making it a copy and model for his parish. He knows the temper and pulse of every person in his house, and accordingly either meets with their vices or advanceth their virtues. His wife is either religious, or night and day he is winning her to it. Instead of the qualities of the world, he requires only three of her: first, a training up of her children and maids in the fear of God with prayers and catechizing and all religious duties. Secondly, a curing and healing of all wounds and sores with her own hands; which skill either she brought with her or he takes care she learn it of some religious neighbor. Thirdly, a providing for her family in such sort as that neither they want a competent sustentation nor her husband be brought in debt. His children he first makes Christians and then commonwealth's men; the one he owes to his heavenly country, the other to his earthly, having no title to either except he do good to both. Therefore having seasoned them with all piety, not only of words in praying and reading but in actions, in visiting other sick children and tending their wounds and sending his charity by them to the poor and sometimes giving them a little money to do it themselves that they get a delight in it and enter favor with God, who weighs even children's actions, I Kings, 14:12, 13. He afterwards turns his care to fit all their dispositions with some calling, not sparing the eldest but giving him the prerogative of his father's profession, which happily[3] for his other children he is not able to do. Yet in binding them 'prentices, in case he think fit to do so, he takes care not to put them into vain trades and unbefitting the reverence of their father's calling, such as are taverns for men and lacemaking for women; because those trades, for the most

part, serve but the vices and vanities of the world which he is to deny and not augment. However, he resolves with himself never to omit any present good deed of charity in consideration of providing a stock for his children; but assures himself that money thus lent to God is placed surer for his children's advantage than if it were given to the Chamber of London.[4] Good deeds and good breeding are his two great stocks for his children; if God give anything above those and not spent in them, he blesseth God and lays it out as he sees cause. His servants are all religious, and were it not his duty to have them so, it were his profit, for none are so well served as by religious servants, both because they do best and because what they do is blessed and prospers. After religion, he teacheth them that three things make a complete servant: truth, and diligence, and neatness or cleanliness. Those that can read are allowed times for it, and those that cannot are taught; for all in his house are either teachers or learners or both, so that his family is a school of religion, and they all account that to teach the ignorant is the greatest alms. Even the walls are not idle, but something is written or painted there which may excite the reader to a thought of piety; especially the 101 Psalm, which is expressed in a fair table, as being the rule of a family. And when they go abroad, his wife among her neighbors is the beginner of good discourses, his children among children, his servants among other servants; so that as in the house of those that are skilled in music all are musicians, so in the house of a preacher all are preachers. He suffers not a lie or equivocation by any means in his house, but counts it the art and secret of governing to preserve a directness and open plainness in all things; so that all his house knows that there is no help for a fault done but confession. He himself or his wife takes account of sermons,[5] and how everyone profits, comparing this year with the last; and besides the common prayers of the family, he straitly requires of all to pray by themselves before they sleep at night and stir out in the morning, and knows what prayers they say, and till they have learned them makes them kneel by him, esteeming that this private praying is a more voluntary act in them than when they are called to others' prayers, and that which when they leave the family

---

4 A reference to the institution of orphanage; the Mayor and aldermen of London acted as trustees for the children of freemen.

5 Summarizes briefly.

they carry with them. He keeps his servants between love and fear, according as he finds them; but generally he distributes it thus: to his children he shows more love than terror, to his servants more terror than love; but an old good servant boards[6] a child. The furniture of his house is very plain, but clean, whole, and sweet, as sweet as his garden can make; for he hath no money for such things, charity being his only perfume, which deserves cost when he can spare it. His fare is plain and common, but wholesome; what he hath is little but very good; it consisteth most of mutton, beef, and veal; if he adds anything for a great day or a stranger, his garden or orchard supplies it or his barn and backside;[7] he goes no further for any entertainment, lest he go into the world, esteeming it absurd that he should exceed who teacheth others temperance. But those which his home produceth he refuseth not, as coming cheap and easy and arising from the improvement of things which otherwise would be lost. Wherein he admires and imitates the wonderful providence and thrift of the great householder of the world. For there being two things which, as they are, are unuseful to man, the one for smallness, as crumbs and scattered corn and the like, the other for the foulness, as wash and dirt and things thereinto fallen; God hath provided creatures for both; for the first, poultry; for the second, swine. These save man the labor and doing that which either he could not do or was not fit for him to do, by taking both sorts of food into them do as it were dress and prepare both for man in themselves by growing themselves fit for his table. The parson in his house observes fasting days; and particularly, as Sunday is his day of joy so Friday his day of humiliation, which he celebrates not only with abstinence of diet but also of company, recreation, and all outward contentments, and besides, with confession of sins and all acts of mortification. Now fasting days contain a treble obligation: first, of eating less that day than on other days; secondly, of eating no pleasing or over-nourishing things, as the Israelites did eat sour herbs; thirdly, of eating no flesh, which is but the determination of the second rule by authority to this particular. The two former obligations are much more essential to a true fast than the third and last; and fasting days were fully performed by keeping of the two former, had not authority interposed; so that to eat a little, and that unpleasant, is the natural rule of fasting, although it be flesh. For since fasting in Scripture language is an afflicting of our souls, if a piece of dry flesh at my table be more unpleasant to me than some fish there, certainly to eat the flesh, and not the fish, is to keep the fasting day naturally. And it is observable that the prohibiting of flesh came from hot countries where both flesh alone, and much more with wine, is apt to nourish more than in cold regions and where flesh may be much better spared, and with more safety than elsewhere, where both the people and the drink being cold and phlegmatic the eating of flesh is an antidote to both. For it is certain that a weak stomach, being prepossessed with flesh, shall much better brook and bear a draught of beer than if it had taken before either fish or roots or such things; which will discover itself by spitting and rheum or phlegm. To conclude, the parson, if he be in full health, keeps the three obligations, eating fish or roots, and that for quantity little, for quality unpleasant. If his body be weak and obstructed, as most students' are, he cannot keep the last obligation nor suffer others in his house that are so to keep it; but only the two former, which also in diseases of exinanition, as consumption, must be broken; for meat was made for man, not man for meat. To all this may be added, not for emboldening the unruly but for the comfort of the weak, that not only sickness breaks these obligations of fasting but sickliness also. For it is as unnatural to do anything that leads me to a sickness to which I am inclined as not to get out of that sickness, when I am in it, by any diet. One thing is evident, that an English body and a student's body are two great obstructed vessels; and there is nothing that is food, and not physic, which doth less obstruct than flesh moderately taken; as being immoderately taken, it is exceeding obstructive. And obstructions are the cause of most diseases.

THE PARSON'S COMPLETENESS[8]

THE country parson desires to be all to his parish, and not only a pastor but a lawyer also and a physician. Therefore he endures not that any of his flock should go to law, but in any controversy that they should resort to him as their judge. To this end he hath gotten himself some insight in things ordinarily incident and controverted by experience and by reading some initiatory treatises in the law, with Dalton's Justice of Peace and the Abridgments of the Statutes, as also by

6 Approaches, counts as a child.　　7 Backyard.　　8 Chapter XXIII.

discourse with men of that profession, whom he hath ever some cases to ask when he meets with them; holding that rule that to put men to discourse of that wherein they are most eminent is the most gainful way of conversation. Yet whenever any controversy is brought to him, he never decides it alone, but sends for three or four of the ablest of the parish to hear the cause with him, whom he makes to deliver their opinion first; out of which he gathers, in case he be ignorant himself, what to hold; and so the thing passeth with more authority and less envy. In judging he follows that which is altogether right; so that if the poorest man of the parish detain but a pin unjustly from the richest, he absolutely restores it as a judge; but when he hath so done, then he assumes the parson and exhorts to charity. Nevertheless, there may happen sometimes some cases wherein he chooseth to permit his parishioners rather to make use of the law than himself; as in cases of an obscure and dark nature, not easily determinable by lawyers themselves; or in cases of high consequence, as establishing of inheritances; or lastly, when the persons in difference are of a contentious disposition and cannot be gained but that they still fall from all compromises that have been made. But then he shows them how to go to law, even as brethren and not as enemies, neither avoiding therefore one another's company, much less defaming one another. Now as the parson is in law, so is he in sickness also; if there be any of his flock sick, he is their physician, or at least his wife, of whom instead of the qualities of the world he asks no other but to have the skill of healing a wound or helping the sick. But if neither himself nor his wife have the skill, and his means serve, he keeps some young practitioner in his house for the benefit of his parish, whom yet he ever exhorts not to exceed his bounds but in ticklish cases to call in help. If all fail, then he keeps in good correspondence with some neighbor physician and entertains him for the cure of his parish. Yet it is easy for any scholar to attain to such a measure of physic as may be of much use to him both for himself and others. This is done by seeing one anatomy, reading one book of physic, having one herbal by him. And let Fernelius be the physic author, for he writes briefly, neatly, and judiciously; especially let his Method of Physic be diligently perused, as being the practical part and of most use. Now both the reading of him and the knowing of herbs may be done at such times as they may be an help and a recreation to more divine studies, nature serving grace both in comfort of diversion and

the benefit of application when need requires; as also by way of illustration even as our Savior made plants and seeds to teach the people. For he was the true householder, who bringeth out of his treasure things new and old; the old things of philosophy, and the new of grace; and maketh the one serve the other. And I conceive our Savior did this for three reasons: first, that by familiar things he might make his doctrine slip the more easily into the hearts even of the meanest. Secondly, that laboring people, whom he chiefly considered, might have everywhere monuments of his doctrine, remembering in gardens his mustard-seed and lilies; in the field, his seed-corn and tares; and so not be drowned altogether in the works of their vocation but sometimes lift up their minds to better things, even in the midst of their pains. Thirdly, that he might set a copy for parsons. In the knowledge of simples, wherein the manifold wisdom of God is wonderfully to be seen, one thing would be carefully observed; which is to know what herbs may be used instead of drugs of the same nature and to make the garden the shop. For homebred medicines are both more easy for the parson's purse and more familiar for all men's bodies. So, where the apothecary useth either for loosening, rhubarb, or for binding, bolearmena, the parson useth damask or white roses for the one and plantain, shepherd's purse, knot-grass for the other, and that with better success. As for spices he doth not only prefer homebred things before them but condemns them for vanities and so shuts them out of his family, esteeming that there is no spice comparable, for herbs, to rosemary, thyme, savory, mints; and for seeds, to fennel and caraway seeds. Accordingly, for salves his wife seeks not the city but prefers her garden and fields before all outlandish gums. And surely hyssop, valerian, mercury, adder's tongue, yarrow, melilot, and Saint John's wort made into a salve, and elder, camomile, mallows, camphor, and smallage made into a poultice have done great and rare cures. In curing of any the parson and his family use to premise prayers, for this is to cure like a parson, and this raiseth the action from the shop to the church. But though the parson sets forward all charitable deeds, yet he looks not in this point of curing beyond his own parish, except the person be so poor that he is not able to reward the physician; for as he is charitable so he is just also. Now it is a justice and debt to the commonwealth he lives in not to encroach on others' professions but to live on his own. And justice is the ground of charity.

THE PARSON IN MIRTH[9]

THE country parson is generally sad, because he knows nothing but the cross of Christ, his mind being defixed on and with those nails wherewith his master was. Or if he have any leisure to look off from thence, he meets continually with two most sad spectacles, sin and misery; God dishonored every day and man afflicted.

9 Chapter XXVII.

Nevertheless, he sometimes refresheth himself, as knowing that nature will not bear everlasting droopings and that pleasantness of disposition is a great key to do good, not only because all men shun the company of perpetual severity but also for that when they are in company instructions seasoned with pleasantness both enter sooner and root deeper. Wherefore he condescends to human frailties both in himself and others, and intermingles some mirth in his discourses occasionally according to the pulse of the hearer.

Izaak Walton

[1593–1683]

ORN in Staffordshire, the son of a tavern-keeper, Walton was apprenticed at an early age to a relative who was a sempster, or tailor, in London. We know the general outline of Walton's life, but many details have remained obscure: although he was admitted to the Ironmongers' Company in 1618, he seems really to have made his living as a draper in London. We may be certain that he had little formal education, but he became a man of learning and cultivation through his own reading and his friendship with such men as Donne, of whom he was a parishioner, and Sir Henry Wotton. He was married in 1626; his wife bore him seven children, but they died in infancy and she followed them in 1640. Married again in 1647, he outlived his second wife by some twenty years. At some time near 1660 he retired to his native Staffordshire, where he owned property. During much of the time from 1662 until the end of his life he lived with his friend Bishop Morley, whose steward he may have been, first at Worcester and then at Winchester.

Walton may have dabbled in verse as a young man, but his true literary career began only when he was close to his fiftieth year, and it began partly through chance. At the request of Wotton, Walton had been gathering material on Donne's life, to be written by Wotton and prefixed to the edition of Donne's *LXXX Sermons* (1640). After the death of Wotton, however, Walton was asked to write the biography himself. He followed this biography with a life of Wotton (1651) and then with lives of Hooker (1665), Herbert (1670), and Sanderson (1678).

Walton subjected all the Lives to extensive revision, and this fact suggests the degree to which he conceived of the biographer's task as a specifically artistic one. In their easy, rhythmic fluency, their rich, concrete detail, and their masterly subjection of this detail to an overriding unity of theme, the *Lives* attain a high position in seventeenth-century prose art. They have been criticized from extra-artistic points of view, however: some readers have found too much sameness in the personalities attributed by Walton to his five worthies, and some have felt that the biographer imposed too much of his own serene and gentle temperament upon his various subjects. Modern scholarship has, of course, corrected some inaccuracies in Walton's work, and it cannot be denied that he presents us with an oversimplified picture of the complex Donne, but in general we must recognize that Walton deliberately chose subjects whom he found, in their holiness and their love of peace, congenial. Considering the limited facilities of the seventeenth-century biographer, as well as the lack of precedent for sound biographical method, we must admire Walton's research almost as much as his artistry.

Izaak Walton's masterpiece, *The Complete Angler* (1653), has much in common with the *Lives.* Like them it is a work of consummate and conscious artistry; like them it shows, in its final form, the effects of repeated stylistic revisions; like them it stands as the near-definitive embodiment of a traditional ideal. Essentially, the *Angler* is one of the supreme manifestations of the pastoral tradition in English literature: its landscapes, like its characters, retain a recognizable connection with observed and felt reality, and many of its episodes have the unmistakable taste of real experience rendered permanent through art, although both landscape and character are stylized to an impossible but infinitely desirable perfection. In the midst of an England torn by fanaticism, strife, and violence, Walton gave to the Arcadian dream of the quiet life a local habitation and a name. Such justly famous scenes as the anglers' meeting with the milkmaids revive the myth of the Golden Age with a sensitivity as delicate as it is poignant.

The Complete Angler went through numerous editions in the author's own lifetime, and the fifth edition (1676) contained an imitative addition written by the poet Charles Cotton, a friend of Walton in his later years. Its popularity has never since abated, and it remains at the present time one of the most widely read of seventeenth-century books. It is likely that its immortality derives neither from the charm of its quaint dialogue style nor from its unquestionable fascination as a guide to the angler's craft, but rather from the almost impeccable skill with which it recreates one of the most enduring and attractive of human ideals.

    I. WALTON. *The Complete Angler*, ed. J. Buchan (Oxford, 1935).
    ————. *Lives*, ed. S. B. Carter (London, 1951).
    G. KEYNES, ed. *The Compleat Walton* (London, 1929). A collection which includes all
        the major works.
    D. A. STAUFFER. *English Biography Before 1700* (Cambridge, Mass., 1930).
    D. NOVARR. *The Making of Walton's Lives* (Ithaca, N.Y., 1958). The most valuable
        study of Walton as a biographer.

THE COMPLETE ANGLER

[TEXT: *fourth edition, 1668*]

THE EPISTLE TO THE READER

To all readers of this discourse, but especially to the honest angler

I THINK fit to tell thee these following truths, that I did neither undertake, nor write, nor publish, and much less own, this discourse to please myself; and having been too easily drawn to do all to please others, as I proposed not the gaining of credit by this undertaking, so I would not willingly lose any part of that to which I had a just title before I begun it, and therefore desire and hope, if I deserve not commendation, yet I may obtain pardon.

And though this discourse may be liable to some exceptions, yet I cannot doubt but that most readers may receive so much pleasure or profit by it as may make it worthy the time of their perusal, if they be not very busy men. And this is all the confidence that I can put on concerning the merit of what is here offered to their consideration and censure; and if the last prove too severe, I have a liberty, and am resolved to neglect it.

And I wish the reader also to take notice that in writing of it I have made myself a recreation of a recreation; and that it might prove so to him, and not read dull and tediously, I have in several places mixed, not any scurrility, but some innocent, harmless mirth; of which, if thou be a severe, sour-complexioned man, then I here disallow thee to be a competent judge; for divines say there are offenses given and offenses not given but taken.

And I am the willinger to justify the pleasant part of it because though it is known I can be serious at seasonable times, yet the whole discourse is, or rather was, a picture of my own disposition, especially in such days and times as I have laid aside business and gone a-fishing with honest Nat. and R. Roe; but they are gone, and with them most of my pleasant hours, even as a shadow that passeth away and returns not.

And next let me add this, that he that likes not the book should like the excellent picture of the trout and some of the other fish; which I may take a liberty to commend, because they concern not myself.[1]

Next, let me tell the reader that in that which is the more useful part of this discourse, that is to say, the observations of the nature and breeding and seasons and catching of fish, I am not so simple as not to know that a captious reader may find exceptions against something said of some of these; and therefore I must entreat him to consider that experience teaches us to know that several countries alter the time, and I think almost the manner, of fishes' breeding, but doubtless of their being in season; as may appear by three rivers in Monmouthshire, namely, Severn, Wye, and Usk, where Camden (Brit. f. 633) observes that in the river Wye salmon are in season from September to April, and we are certain that in Thames and Trent, and in most other rivers they be in season the six hotter months.

Now for the art of catching fish, that is to say, how to make a man that was none to be an angler by a book, he that undertakes it shall undertake a harder task than Mr. Hales, a most valiant and excellent fencer, who in a printed book called A Private School of Defence undertook by it to teach that art or science, and was laughed at for his labor. Not but that many useful things might be learnt by that book, but he was laughed at because that art was not to be taught by words, but practice: and so must angling. And in this discourse I do not undertake to say all that is known or may be said of it, but I undertake to acquaint the reader with many things that are not usually known to every angler; and I shall leave gleanings and obser-vations enough to be made out of the experience of all that love and practice this recreation, to which I shall encourage them. For angling may be said to be so like the mathematics that it can never be fully learnt; at least not so fully but that there will still be more new experiments left for the trial of other men that succeed us.

But I think all that love this game may here learn something that may be worth their money, if they be not poor and needy men: and in case they be, I then wish them to forbear to buy it; for I write not to get money, but for pleasure, and this discourse boasts of no more; for I hate to promise much, and deceive the reader.

And however it proves to him, yet I am sure I have found a high content in the search and conference of what is here offered to the reader's view and censure. I wish him as much in the perusal of it. And so I might here take my leave, but will stay a little and tell him that whereas it is said by many that in fly-fishing for a trout, the angler must observe his twelve several flies for the twelve months of the year; I say he that follows that rule shall be as sure to catch fish and be as wise as he that makes hay by the fair days in an almanac, and no surer; for those very flies that use to appear about and on the water in one month of the year may the following year come almost a month sooner or later, as the same year proves colder or hotter; and yet in the following discourse I have set down the twelve flies that are in reputation with many anglers, and they may serve to give him some light concerning them. And he may note that there are in Wales and other countries peculiar flies, proper to the particular place or country; and doubtless, unless a man makes a fly to counterfeit that very fly in that place, he is like to lose his labor, or much of it; but for the generality, three or four flies neat and rightly made, and not too big, serve for a trout in most rivers all the summer. And for winter fly-fishing it is as useful as an almanac out of date. And of these (because as no man is born an artist, so no man is born an angler) I thought fit to give thee this notice.

When I have told the reader that in this third im-pression there are many enlargements, gathered both by my own observation and the communication of friends, I shall stay him no longer than to wish him a rainy evening to read this following discourse; and that, if he be an honest angler, the east wind may never blow when he goes a-fishing.

                                                    I. W.

---

1 The book was illustrated with cuts.

CHAPTER I
A Conference Betwixt an Angler, a Falconer,
and a Hunter, Each Commending
His Recreation

PISCATOR, VENATOR, AUCEPS

PISCATOR. You are well overtaken, gentlemen! A good morning to you both! I have stretched my legs up Tottenham Hill to overtake you, hoping your business may occasion you towards Ware this fine fresh May morning.

VENATOR. Sir, I for my part shall almost answer your hopes, for my purpose is to drink my morning's draught at the Thatched House in Hoddesden, and I think not to rest till I come thither, where I have appointed a friend or two to meet me. But for this gentleman that you see with me, I know not how far he intends his journey; he came so lately into my company that I have scarce had time to ask him the question.

AUCEPS. Sir, I shall by your favor bear you company as far as Theobald's, and there leave you, for then I turn up to a friend's house, who mews a hawk for me, which I now long to see.

VENATOR. Sir, we are all so happy as to have a fine, fresh, cool morning, and I hope we shall each be the happier in the others' company. And, gentlemen, that I may not lose yours, I shall either abate or amend my pace to enjoy it, knowing that, as the Italians say, "Good company in a journey makes the way to seem the shorter."

AUCEPS. It may do so, Sir, with the help of good discourse, which methinks we may promise from you that both look and speak so cheerfully. And for my part I promise you, as an invitation to it, that I will be as free and open hearted as discretion will allow me to be with strangers.

VENATOR. And, Sir, I promise the like.

PISCATOR. I am right glad to hear your answers, and in confidence you speak the truth, I shall put on a boldness to ask you, Sir, whether business or pleasure caused you to be so early up, and walk so fast, for this other gentleman hath declared he is going to see a hawk, that a friend mews for him.

VENATOR. Sir, mine is a mixture of both, a little business and more pleasure, for I intend this day to do all my business, and then bestow another day or two in hunting the otter, which a friend, that I go to meet, tells me is much pleasanter than any other chase whatsoever;

howsoever, I mean to try it; for tomorrow morning we shall meet a pack of otter-dogs of noble Mr. Sadler's upon Amwell Hill, who will be there so early that they intend to prevent[2] the sunrising.

PISCATOR. Sir, my fortune has answered my desires, and my purpose is to bestow a day or two in helping to destroy some of those villainous vermin. For I hate them perfectly, because they love fish so well, or rather, because they destroy so much; indeed so much that in my judgment all men that keep otter-dogs ought to have pensions from the king, to encourage them to destroy the very breed of those base otters, they do so much mischief.

VENATOR. But what say you to the foxes of the nation, would not you as willingly have them destroyed? for doubtless they do as much mischief as otters do.

PISCATOR. O, Sir, if they do, it is not so much to me and my fraternity as those base vermin the otters do.

AUCEPS. Why, Sir, I pray, of what fraternity are you, that you are so angry with the poor otters?

PISCATOR. I am, Sir, a brother of the angle, and therefore an enemy to the otter. For you are to note that we anglers all love one another, and therefore do I hate the otter both for my own and their sakes who are of my brotherhood.

VENATOR. And I am a lover of hounds. I have followed many a pack of dogs many a mile, and heard many merry huntsmen make sport and scoff at anglers.

AUCEPS. And I profess myself a falconer, and have heard many grave, serious men pity them, 'tis such a heavy, contemptible, dull recreation.

PISCATOR. You know, gentlemen, 'tis an easy thing to scoff at any art or recreation; a little wit, mixed with ill nature, confidence and malice, will do it; but though they often venture boldly, yet they are often caught even in their own trap, according to that of Lucian, the father of the family of scoffers:

Lucian, well skilled in scoffing, this hath writ,
Friend, that's your folly, which you think your wit:
This you vent oft, void both of wit and fear,
Meaning another, when yourself you jeer.

If to this you add what Solomon says of scoffers, that they are an abomination to mankind, let him that thinks fit scoff on, and be a scoffer still, I account them enemies to me, and to all that love virtue and angling.

And for you that have heard many grave, serious men

2 Anticipate.

pity anglers; let me tell you, Sir, there be many men that are by others taken to be serious and grave men which we contemn and pity. Men that are taken to be grave, because nature hath made them of a sour, complexion, money-getting men, men that spend all their time first in getting, and next in anxious care to keep it, men that are condemned to be rich, and then always busy or discontented. For these poor-rich-men, we anglers pity them perfectly, and stand in no need to borrow their thoughts to think ourselves happy. No, no, Sir, we enjoy a contentedness above the reach of such dispositions, and as the learned and ingenuous Montaigne says, like himself freely, "When my cat and I entertain each other with mutual apish tricks, as playing with a garter, who knows but that I make my cat more sport than she makes me? Shall I conclude her to be simple, that has her time to begin or refuse sportiveness as freely as I myself have? Nay, who knows but that it is a defect of my not understanding her language (for doubtless cats talk and reason with one another) that we agree no better and who knows but that she pities me for being no wiser, and laughs and censures my folly for making sport for her when we two play together?"

Thus freely speaks Montaigne concerning cats, and I hope I may take as great a liberty to blame any man, and laugh at him too, let him be never so serious, that hath not heard what anglers can say in the justification of their art and recreation. Which I may again tell you is so full of pleasure that we need not borrow their thoughts to think ourselves happy.

VENATOR. Sir, you have almost amazed me, for though I am no scoffer, yet I have—I pray let me speak it without offense—always looked upon anglers as more patient and more simple men than I fear I shall find you to be.

PISCATOR. Sir, I hope you will not judge my earnestness to be impatience. And for my simplicity, if by that you mean a harmlessness, or that simplicity which was usually found in the primitive Christians, who were, as most anglers are, quiet men, and followers of peace, men that were so simply wise as not to sell their consciences to buy riches and with them vexation and a fear to die; if you mean such simple men as lived in those times when there were fewer lawyers; when men might have had a lordship safely conveyed to them in a piece of parchment no bigger than your hand, though several sheets will not do it safely in this wiser age—I say, Sir, if you take us anglers to be such simple men as I have spoke of, then

myself and those of my profession will be glad to be so understood. But if by simplicity you meant to express a general defect in those that profess and practice the excellent art of angling, I hope in time to disabuse you, and make the contrary appear so evidently that, if you will but have patience to hear me, I shall remove all the anticipations that discourse, or time, or prejudice have possessed you with against that laudable and ancient art; for I know it is worthy the knowledge and practice of a wise man.

But, gentlemen, though I be able to do this, I am not so unmannerly as to engross all the discourse to myself; and therefore you two having declared yourselves, the one to be a lover of hawks, the other of hounds, I shall be most glad to hear what you can say in the commendation of that recreation which each of you love and practice; and having heard what you can say, I shall be glad to exercise your attention with what I can say concerning my own recreation, and by this means we shall make the way to seem the shorter. And if you like my motion, I would have Mr. Falconer to begin.

AUCEPS. Your motion is consented to with all my heart, and to testify it I will begin as you have desired me.

And first, for the element that I use to trade in, which is the air, an element of more worth than weight, an element that doubtless exceeds both the earth and water; for though I sometimes deal in both, yet the air is most properly mine, I and my hawks use that most, and it yields us most recreation; it stops not the high soaring of my noble, generous falcon, in it she ascends to such a height as the dull eyes of beasts and fish are not able to reach to; their bodies are too gross for such high elevations; in the air my troops of hawks soar up on high, and when they are lost in the sight of men, then they attend upon and converse with the gods; therefore I think my eagle is so justly styled Jove's faithful servant in ordinary. And that very falcon that I am now going to see deserves no meaner a title, for she usually in her flight endangers herself, like the son of Dædalus, to have her wings scorched by the sun's heat; but her mettle makes her careless of danger, for she then heeds nothing, but makes her nimble pinions cut the fluid air, and so makes her highway over the steepest mountains and deepest rivers, and in her glorious career looks with contempt upon those high steeples and magnificent palaces which we adore and wonder at; from which height I can make her to descend by a word from my mouth, which she both knows and obeys, to accept of meat from my hand, to own me for her master, to go home with me, and be willing the next day to afford me the like recreation.

And more, this element of air which I profess to trade in, the worth of it is such and it is of such necessity that no creature whatsoever, not only those numerous creatures that feed on the face of the earth, but those various creatures that have their dwelling within the waters, every creature that hath life in its nostrils stands in need of my element. The waters cannot preserve the fish without air, witness the not breaking of ice in an extreme frost; the reason is, for that if the inspiring and expiring organ of any animal be stopped, it suddenly yields to nature, and dies. Thus necessary is air to the existence both of fish and beasts, nay, even to man himself, that air or breath of life with which God at first inspired mankind, he, if he wants it, dies presently, becomes a sad object to all that loved and beheld him, and in an instant turns to putrefaction.

Nay more, the very birds of the air, those that be not hawks, are both so many and so useful and pleasant to mankind that I must not let them pass without some observations. They both feed and refresh him; feed him with their choice bodies, and refresh him with their heavenly voices. I will not undertake to mention the several kind of fowl by which this is done, and his curious palate pleased by day, and which with their very excrements afford him a soft lodging at night. These I will pass by, but not those little nimble musicians of the air that warble forth their curious ditties with which nature hath furnished them to the shame of art.

As first the lark, when she means to rejoice, to cheer herself and those that hear her, she then quits the earth, and sings as she ascends higher into the air, and having ended her heavenly employment, grows then mute and sad to think she must descend to the dull earth, which she would not touch but for necessity.

How doth the blackbird and throstle with their melodious voices bid welcome to the cheerful spring, and in their fixed months warble forth such ditties as no art or instrument can reach to!

Nay, the smaller birds also do the like in their particular seasons, as namely the laverock, the tit-lark, the little linnet, and the honest robin, that loves mankind both alive and dead.[3]

But the nightingale, another of my airy creatures,

3 A reference to the old tale of the Babes in the Wood.

breathes such sweet, loud music out of her little instrumental throat that it might make mankind to think miracles are not ceased. He that at midnight, when the very laborer sleeps securely, should hear, as I have very often, the clear airs, the sweet descants, the natural rising and falling, the doubling and redoubling of her voice, might well be lifted above earth, and say, "Lord, what music hast thou provided for the saints in heaven, when thou affordest men such music on earth!"

And this makes me the less to wonder at the many aviaries in Italy, or at the great charge of Varro his aviary, the ruins of which are yet to be seen in Rome, and is still so famous there that it is reckoned for one of those notables which men of foreign nations either record or lay up in their memories when they return from travel.

This for the birds of pleasure, of which very much more might be said. My next shall be of birds of political use. I think 'tis not to be doubted that swallows have been taught to carry letters betwixt two armies. But 'tis certain that when the Turks besieged Malta or Rhodes—I now remember not which it was—pigeons are then related to carry and recarry letters. And Mr. G. Sandys in his Travels (fol. 269) relates it to be done betwixt Aleppo and Babylon. But if that be disbelieved, 'tis not to be doubted that the dove was sent by Noah, to give him notice of land when to him all appeared to be sea, and the dove proved a faithful and comfortable messenger. And for the sacrifices of the law, a pair of turtle-doves or young pigeons were as well accepted as costly bulls and rams. And when God would feed the Prophet Elijah (1 Kings 17) after a kind of miraculous manner, he did it by ravens, who brought him meat morning and evening. Lastly, the Holy Ghost when he descended visibly upon our Savior, did it by assuming the shape of a dove. And to conclude this part of my discourse, pray remember these wonders were done by birds of the air, the element in which they and I take so much pleasure.

There is also a little contemptible, winged creature, an inhabitant of my aerial element, namely the laborious bee, of whose prudence, policy and regular government of their own commonwealth I might say much, as also of their several kinds, and how useful their honey and wax is both for meat and medicines to mankind; but I will leave them to their sweet labor, without the least disturbance, believing them to be all very busy amongst the herbs and flowers that we see nature puts forth this May morning.

And now to return to my hawks, from whom I have made too long a digression; you are to note that they are usually distinguished into two kinds; namely, the long-winged and the short-winged hawk; of the first kind, there be chiefly in use amongst us in this nation,

The gerfalcon and jerkin,
The falcon and tassel-gentle,
The laner and laneret,
The bockerel and bockeret,
The saker and saceret,
The merlin and jack merlin,
The hobby and jack.

There is the stelletto of Spain,
The blood-red rook from Turkey,
The waskite from Virginia.

And there is of short-winged hawks,
The eagle and iron,
The goshawk and tercel,
The sparhawk and musket,
The French pye of two sorts.

These are reckoned hawks of note and worth, but we have also of an inferior rank,

The stanyel, the rigtail,
The raven, the buzzard,
The forked kite, the bald buzzard,
The hen-driver, and others that I forbear to name.

Gentlemen, if I should enlarge my discourse to the observation of the eires, the brancher, the ramish hawk, the haggard, and the two sorts of lentners, and then treat of their several eyries, their mewings, rare order of casting, and the renovation of their feathers, their reclaiming, dieting, and then come to their rare stories of practice—I say, if I should enter into these, and many other observations that I could make, it would be much, very much pleasure to me. But lest I should break the rules of civility with you by taking up more than the proportion of time allotted to me, I will here break off and entreat you, Mr. Venator, to say what you are able in the commendation of hunting, to which you are so much affected. And if time will serve, I will beg your favor for a further enlargement of some of those several heads of which I have spoken. But no more at present.

VENATOR. Well, Sir, and I will now take my turn and will first begin with a commendation of the earth, as you have done most excellently of the air, the earth being that element upon which I drive my pleasant, wholesome, hungry trade. The earth is a solid, settled element, an element most universally beneficial both to man and beast, to men who have their several recreations upon it, as horse-races, hunting, sweet smells, pleasant walks. The earth feeds man and all those several beasts that both feed him and afford him recreation. What pleasure doth man take in hunting the stately stag, the generous buck, the wild boar, the cunning otter, the crafty fox, and the fearful hare! And if I may descend to a lower game, what pleasure is it sometimes with gins to betray the very vermin of the earth? as namely the fichat, the fulimart, the ferret, the pole-cat, the moldwarp, and the like creatures that live upon the face and within the bowels of the earth. How doth the earth bring forth herbs, flowers and fruits, both for physic and the pleasure of mankind! and above all, to me at least, the fruitful vine, of which when I drink moderately, it clears my brain, cheers my heart, and sharpens my wit. How could Cleopatra have feasted Mark Antony with eight wild boars roasted whole at one supper and other meat suitable, if the earth had not been a bountiful mother? But to pass by the mighty elephant, which the earth breeds and nourisheth and descend to the least of creatures, how doth the earth afford us a doctrinal example in the little pismire, who in the summer provides and lays up her winter provision, and teaches man to do the like! The earth feeds and carries those horses that carry us. If I would be prodigal of my time and your patience, what might not I say in commendations of the earth? That puts limits to the proud and raging sea, and by that means preserves both man and beast that it destroys them not; as we see it daily doth those that venture upon the sea and are there shipwrecked, drowned, and left to feed haddocks; when we that are so wise as to keep ourselves on earth, walk, and talk, and live, and eat, and drink, and go a-hunting. Of which recreation I will say a little, and then leave Mr. Piscator to the commmendation of angling.

Hunting is a game for princes and noble persons; it hath been highly prized in all ages; it was one of the qualifications that Xenophon bestowed on his Cyrus, that he was a hunter of wild beasts. Hunting trains up the younger nobility to the use of manly exercises in their riper age. What more manly exercise than hunting the wild boar, the stag, the buck, the fox or the hare? How doth it preserve health and increase strength and activity!

And for the dogs that we use, who can commend their excellency to that height which they deserve? How perfect is the hound at smelling, who never leaves or forsakes his scent, but follows it through so many changes and varieties of other scents, even over and in the water and into the earth! What music doth a pack of dogs then make to any man whose heart and ears are so happy as to be set to the tune of such instruments! How will a right greyhound fix his eye on the best buck in a herd, single him out and follow him, and him only through a whole herd of rascal game, and still know and then kill him! For my hounds, I know the language of them, and they know the language and meaning of one another as perfectly as we know the voices of those with whom we discourse daily.

I might enlarge myself in the commendation of hunting, and of the noble hound especially, as also of the docibleness of dogs in general; and I might make many observations of land-creatures, that for composition, order, figure and constitution approach nearest to the completeness and understanding of man; especially of those creatures which Moses in the Law permitted to the Jews, which have cloven hoofs and chew the cud, which I shall forbear to name because I will not be so uncivil with Mr. Piscator as not to allow him a time for the commendation of angling, which he calls an art. But doubtless 'tis an easy one. And, Mr. Auceps, I doubt we shall hear a watery discourse of it; but I hope it will not be a long one.

AUCEPS. And I hope so too, though I fear it will.

PISCATOR. Gentlemen, let not prejudice prepossess you. I confess my discourse is like to prove suitable to my recreation, calm and quiet; we seldom take the name of God into our mouths, but it is either to praise him or pray to him; if others use it vainly in the midst of their recreations, so vainly as if they meant to conjure, I must tell you it is neither our fault nor our custom; we protest against it. But pray remember I accuse nobody; for as I would not make a watery discourse, so I would not put too much vinegar into it, nor would I raise the reputation of my own art by the diminution or ruin of another's. And so much for the prologue to what I mean to say.

And now for the water, the element that I trade in. The water is the eldest daughter of the creation, the element upon which the Spirit of God did first move, the element which God commanded to bring forth living creatures abundantly, and without which those that inhabit the land, even all creatures that have breath in their nostrils, must suddenly return to putrefaction. Moses, the great lawgiver and chief philosopher, skilled in all the learning of the Egyptians, who was called the friend of God, and knew the mind of the Almighty, names this element the first in the creation; this is the element upon which the Spirit of God did first

move, and is the chief ingredient in the creation. Many philosophers have made it to comprehend all the other elements, but most allow it the chiefest in the mixtion of all living creatures.

There be [those] that profess to believe that all bodies are made of water and may be reduced back again to water only. They endeavor to demonstrate it thus:

Take a willow, or any like speedy-growing plant, newly rooted in a box or barrel full of earth, weigh them all together exactly when the tree begins to grow and then weigh all together after the tree is increased from its first rooting to weigh a hundred pound weight more than when it was first rooted and weighed; and you shall find this augment of the tree to be without the diminution of one dram of the earth. Hence they infer this increase of wood to be from water or rain or from dew, and not to be from any other element. And they affirm they can reduce this wood back again to water; and they affirm also, the same may be done in any animal or vegetable. And this I take to be a fair testimony of the excellency of my element of water.

The water is more productive than the earth. Nay, the earth hath no fruitfulness without showers or dews; for all the herbs and flowers and fruit are produced and thrive by the water; and the very minerals are fed by streams that run underground, whose natural course carries them to the tops of many high mountains, as we see by several springs breaking forth on the tops of the highest hills, and this is also witnessed by the daily trial and testimony of several miners.

Nay, the increase of those creatures that are bred and fed in the water are not only more and more miraculous, but more advantageous to man, not only for the lengthening of his life but for the preventing of sickness; for 'tis observed by the most learned physicians that the casting off of Lent and other fish days, which hath not only given the lie to so many learned, pious, wise founders of colleges, for which we should be ashamed, hath doubtless been the chief cause of those many putrid, shaking, intermitting agues unto which this nation of ours is now more subject than those wiser countries that feed on herbs, salads, and plenty of fish; of which it is observed in story that the greatest part of the world now do. And it may be fit to remember that Moses (Lev. 11:9; Deut. 14:9) appointed fish to be the chief diet for the best commonwealth that ever yet was.

And it is observable not only that there are fish, as namely the whale, three times as big as the mighty elephant, that is so fierce in battle, but that the mightiest feasts have been of fish. The Romans in the height of their glory have made fish the mistress of all their entertainments; they have had music to usher in their sturgeons, lampreys, and mullet, which they would purchase at rates rather to be wondered at than believed. He that shall view the writings of Macrobius or Varro may be confirmed and informed of this and of the incredible value of their fish and fish-ponds.

But, gentlemen, I have almost lost myself, which I confess I may easily do in this philosophical discourse. I met with most of it very lately, and I hope happily, in a conference with a most learned physician, a dear friend,[4] that loves both me and my art of angling. But, however, I will wade no deeper into these mysterious arguments but to pass to such observations as I can manage with more pleasure and less fear of running into error. But I must not yet forsake the waters, by whose help we have so many known advantages.

And first, to pass by the miraculous cures of our known baths, how advantageous is the sea for our daily traffic without which we could not now subsist! How does it not only furnish us with food and physic for the bodies but with such observations for the mind as ingenious persons would not want!

How ignorant had we been of the beauty of Florence, of the monuments, urns, and rarities that yet remain in and near unto old and new Rome, so many as it is said will take up a year's time to view, and afford to each of them but a convenient consideration! And therefore it is not to be wondered at that so learned and devout a father as St. Jerome, after his wish to have seen Christ in the flesh and to have heard St. Paul preach, makes his third wish to have seen Rome in her glory; and that glory is not yet all lost, for what pleasure is it to see the monuments of Livy, the choicest of the historians! of Tully, the best of orators! and to see the bay trees that now grow out of the very tomb of Virgil! These to any that love learning must be pleasing. But what pleasure is it to a devout Christian to see there the humble house in which Saint Paul was content to dwell! and to view the many rich statues that are there made in honor of his memory! nay, to see the very place in which St. Peter and he lie buried together! These are in and near to Rome. And how much more doth it please the pious curiosity of a Christian to see that place on which the blessed Savior of the world was pleased to humble himself and to take our nature upon him and to converse with men! to see Mount Sion, Jerusalem, and the very sepulchre of our

4 Dr. Wharton.

Lord Jesus! How may it beget and heighten the zeal of a Christian to see the devotions that are daily paid to him at that place! Gentlemen, lest I forget myself, I will stop here, and remember you that but for my element of water the inhabitants of this poor island must remain ignorant that such things have yet a being.

Gentlemen, I might both enlarge and lose myself in such like arguments; I might tell you that Almighty God is said to have spoken to a fish, but never to a beast; that he hath made a whale a ship, to carry and set his Prophet Jonah safe on the appointed shore. Of these I might speak, but I must in manners break off, for I see Theobald's House. I cry you mercy for being so long, and thank you for your patience.

AUCEPS. Sir, my pardon is easily granted you: I except against nothing that you have said: nevertheless I must part with you at this park-wall, for which I am very sorry; but I assure you, Mr. Piscator, I now part with you full of good thoughts, not only of yourself but your recreation. And so, gentlemen, God keep you both.

PISCATOR. Well, now, Mr. Venator, you shall neither want time nor my attention to hear you enlarge your discourse concerning hunting.

VENATOR. Not I, Sir. I remember you said that angling itself was of great antiquity and a perfect art and an art not easily attained to; and you have so won upon me in your former discourse that I am very desirous to hear what you can say further concerning those particulars.

PISCATOR. Sir, I did say so, and I doubt not but if you and I did converse together but a few hours to leave you possessed with the same high and happy thoughts that now possess me of it; not only of the antiquity of angling, but that it deserves commendations and that it is an art and an art worthy the knowledge and practice of a wise man.

VENATOR. Pray, Sir, speak of them what you think fit, for we have yet five miles to the Thatched House, during which walk I dare promise you my patience and diligent attention shall not be wanting. And if you shall make that to appear which you have undertaken first, that it is an art and an art worth the learning, I shall beg that I may attend you a day or two a-fishing and that I may become your scholar and be instructed in the art itself which you so much magnify.

PISCATOR. O, Sir, doubt not but that angling is an art! Is it not an art to deceive a trout with an artificial fly? a trout! that is more sharp-sighted than any hawk you have named and more watchful and timorous than your high-mettled merlin is bold! And yet I doubt not to catch a brace or two tomorrow for a friend's breakfast. Doubt not therefore, Sir, but that angling is an art 5 and an art worth your learning. The question is rather whether you be capable of learning it! for angling is somewhat like poetry, men are to be born so. I mean, with inclinations to it, though both may be heightened by practice and experience; but he that hopes to be a good angler must not only bring an inquiring, searching, observing wit, but he must bring a large measure of hope and patience and a love and propensity to the art itself; but having once got and practiced it, then doubt not but angling will prove to be so pleasant that it will prove, like virtue, a reward to itself.

VENATOR. Sir, I am now become so full of expectation that I long much to have you proceed and in the order that you propose.

PISCATOR. Then first, for the antiquity of angling, of which I shall not say much but only this: some say it is as ancient as Deucalion's Flood; others, that Belus, who was the first inventor of the godly and virtuous recreations, was the first inventor of angling; and some others say, for former times have had their disquisitions about the antiquity of it, that Seth, one of the sons of Adam, taught it to his sons, and that by them it was derived to posterity; others say that he left it engraven on those pillars which he erected and trusted to preserve the knowledge of the mathematics, music, and the rest of that precious knowledge and those useful arts, which by God's appointment or allowance and his noble industry were thereby preserved from perishing in Noah's Flood.

These, Sir, have been the opinions of several men, that have possibly endeavored to make angling more ancient than is needful or may well be warranted; but for my part, I shall content myself in telling you that angling is much more ancient than the incarnation of our Savior; for in the Prophet Amos mention is made of fish-hooks; and in the Book of Job—which was long before the days of Amos, for that book is said to be writ by Moses—mention is made also of fish-hooks, which must imply anglers in those times.

But, my worthy friend, as I would rather prove myself a gentleman by being learned and humble, valiant and inoffensive, virtuous and communicable, than by any fond ostentation of riches, or wanting those virtues myself, boast that these were in my ancestors—

5 This passage on the sharp-sighted trout is from the fifth edition.

and yet I grant that where a noble and ancient descent and such merit meet in any man it is a double dignification of that person—so if this antiquity of angling—which for my part I have not forced—shall, like an ancient family, be either an honor or an ornament to this virtuous art which I profess to love and practice, I shall be the gladder that I made an accidental mention of the antiquity of it; of which I shall say no more but proceed to that just commendation which I think it deserves.

And for that I shall tell you that in ancient times a debate hath risen—and it remains yet unresolved—whether the happiness of man in this world doth consist more in contemplation or action.

Concerning which some have endeavored to maintain their opinion of the first by saying, "that the nearer we mortals come to God by way of imitation the more happy we are." And they say, "that God enjoys himself only by a contemplation of his own infiniteness, eternity, power, and goodness," and the like. And upon this ground many cloisteral men of great learning and devotion prefer contemplation before action. And many of the fathers seem to approve this opinion, as may appear in their commentaries upon the words of our Savior to Martha, Luke 10:41, 42.

And on the contrary there want not men of equal authority and credit that prefer action to be the more excellent, as namely "experiments in physic and the application of it, both for the ease and prolongation of man's life"; by which each man is enabled to act and do good to others, either to serve his country or do good to particular persons; and they say also, "that action is doctrinal and teaches both art and virtue and is a maintainer of human society"; and for these and other like reasons to be preferred before contemplation.

Concerning which two opinions I shall forbear to add a third by declaring my own, and rest myself contented in telling you, my very worthy friend, that both these meet together and do most properly belong to the most honest, ingenuous, quiet, and harmless art of angling.

And first, I shall tell you what some have observed, and I have found to be a real truth, that the very sitting by the river's side is not only the quietest and fittest place for contemplation but will invite an angler to it. And this seems to be maintained by the learned Pet. du Moulin, who, in his discourse of the Fulfilling of Prophecies, observes that when God intended to reveal any future event or high notions to his prophets, he then carried them either to the deserts or the seashore, that having so separated them from amidst the press of people and business and the cares of the world he might settle their mind in a quiet repose and make them fit for revelation.

And this seems also to be intimated by the children of Israel (Psal. 137), who having in a sad condition banished all mirth and music from their pensive hearts and having hung up their then mute harps upon the willow-trees growing by the rivers of Babylon, sat down upon those banks bemoaning the ruins of Sion and contemplating their own sad condition.

And an ingenious Spaniard says, "That rivers and the inhabitants of the watery element were made for wise men to contemplate and fools to pass by without consideration." And though I will not rank myself in the number of the first, yet give me leave to free myself from the last by offering to you a short contemplation, first of rivers and then of fish; concerning which I doubt not but to give you many observations that will appear very considerable. I am sure they have appeared so to me and made many an hour pass away more pleasantly, as I have sat quietly on a flowery bank by a calm river and contemplated what I shall now relate to you.

And first concerning rivers, there be divers wonders reported of them by authors of such credit that we need not to deny them an historical faith.

As namely of a river in Epirus that puts out any lighted torch and kindles any torch that was not lighted. Some waters being drunk cause madness, some drunkenness, and some laughter to death. The River Selarus in a few hours turns a rod or wand to be stone. And our Camden mentions the like in England, and the like in Lochmere in Ireland. There is also a river in Arabia of which all the sheep that drink thereof have their wool turned into a vermilion color. And one of no less credit than Aristotle tells us of a merry river, the River Elusina, that dances at the noise of music, for with music it bubbles, dances, and grows sandy, and so continues till the music ceases, but then it presently returns to its wonted calmness and clearness. And Camden tells us of a well near to Kirby in Westmoreland that ebbs and flows several times every day; and he tells us of a river in Surrey—it is called Mole—that after it has run several miles, being opposed by hills, finds or makes itself a way under ground and breaks out again so far off that the inhabitants thereabout boast, as the Spaniards do of their River Anus, that they feed divers flocks of sheep upon a bridge. And lastly,—for I would not tire your patience

—one of no less authority than Josephus, that learned Jew, tells us of a river in Judea that runs swiftly all the six days of the week and stands still and rests all their Sabbath.

But I will lay aside my discourse of rivers and tell you some things of the monsters, or fish, call them what you will, that they breed and feed in them. Pliny the philosopher says, in the third chapter of his ninth book, that in the Indian Sea the fish called *balæna*, or whirlpool, is so long and broad as to take up more in length and breadth than two acres of ground; and of other fish, of two hundred cubits long; and that in the River Ganges there be eels of thirty feet long. He says there that these monsters appear in that sea only when the tempestuous winds oppose the torrents of water falling from the rocks into it and so turning what lay at the bottom to be seen on the water's top. And he says that the people of Cadara, an island near this place, make the timber for their houses of those fish bones. He there tells us that there are sometimes a thousand of these great eels found wrapt or interwoven together. He tells us there that it appears that dolphins love music and will come when called for by some men or boys that know and use to feed them; and that they can swim as swift as an arrow can be shot out of a bow; and much of this is spoken concerning the dolphin and other fish as may be found also in the learned Dr. Casaubon's Discourse of Credulity and Incredulity, printed by him about the year 1670.

I know, we islanders are averse to the belief of these wonders; but there be so many strange creatures to be now seen, many collected by John Tradescant and others added by my friend Elias Ashmole, Esq.,[6] who now keeps them carefully and methodically at his house near to Lambeth, near London, as may get some belief of some of the other wonders I mentioned. I will tell you some of the wonders that you may now see, and not till then believe, unless you think fit.

You may there see the hog-fish, the dog-fish, the dolphin, the coney-fish, the parrot-fish, the shark, the poison-fish, sword-fish, and not only other incredible fish, but you may there see the salamander, several sorts of barnacles, of solan-geese, the bird of paradise, such sorts of snakes, and such birds'-nests, and of so various forms and so wonderfully made as may beget wonder and amusement in any beholder; and so many hundred of other rarities in that collection as will make the other wonders I spake of the less incredible; for

6 He has his monument at Oxford, in the Ashmolean Museum.

you may note that the waters are nature's storehouse in which she locks up her wonders.[7]

But Sir, lest this discourse may seem tedious, I shall give it a sweet conclusion out of that holy poet, Mr. George Herbert, his divine Contemplation on God's Providence:

Lord, who hath praise enough, nay, who hath any!
None can express thy works, but he that knows them;
And none can know thy works, they are so many
And so complete, but only he that owes them.

We all acknowledge both thy power and love
To be exact, transcendant, and divine;
Who dost so strangely and so sweetly move,
Whilst all things have their end, yet none but thine.

Wherefore, most sacred Spirit, I here present
For me and all my fellows praise to thee;
And just it is that I should pay the rent,
Because the benefit accrues to me.

And as concerning fish in that psalm (Psal. 104) wherein for height of poetry and wonders the Prophet David seems even to exceed himself, how doth he there express himself in choice metaphors, even to the amazement of a contemplative reader, concerning the sea, the rivers, and the fish therein contained! And the great naturalist Pliny says, "That nature's great and wonderful power is more demonstrated in the sea than on the land." And this may appear by the numerous and various creatures inhabiting both in and about that element; as to the readers of Gesner, Rondeletius, Pliny, Ausonius, Aristotle, and others, may be demonstrated. But I will sweeten this discourse also out of a contemplation in divine Du Bartas, who says:

God quickened in the sea, and in the rivers
So many fishes of so many features
That in the waters we may see all creatures,
Even all that on the earth are to be found,
As if the world were in deep waters drowned.
For seas—as well as skies—have sun, moon, stars;
As well as air—swallows, rooks, and stares;
As well as earth—wines, roses, nettles, melons,
Mushrooms, pinks, gilliflowers, and many millions
Of other plants more rare, more strange than these,
As very fishes living in the seas;
As also rams, calves, horses, hares, and hogs,
Wolves, urchins, lions, elephants, and dogs;

Yea, men and maids, and which I most admire,
The mitred bishop and the cowled friar.
Of which, examples, but a few years since,
Were shown the Norway and Polonian prince.

These seem to be wonders, but have had so many confirmations from men of learning and credit that you need not doubt them. Nor are the number nor the various shapes of fishes more strange or more fit for contemplation than their different natures, inclinations, and actions; concerning which I shall beg your patient ear a little longer.

The cuttle-fish will cast a long gut out of her throat, which, like as an angler doth his line, she sendeth forth and pulleth in again at her pleasure according as she sees some little fish come near to her; and the cuttle-fish, being then hid in the gravel, lets the smaller fish nibble and bite the end of it, at which time she by little and little draws the smaller fish so near to her that she may leap upon her, and then catches and devours her. And for this reason some have called this fish the sea-angler.

And there is a fish called a hermit,[8] that at a certain age gets into a dead fish's shell and like a hermit dwells there alone, studying the wind and weather, and so turns her shell that she makes it defend her from the injuries that they would bring upon her.

There is also a fish called by Elian (in his 9th book of living creatures, chap. 16) the Adonis, or darling of the sea, so called because it is a loving and innocent fish, a fish that hurts nothing that hath life and is at peace with all the numerous inhabitants of that vast watery element. And truly I think most anglers are so disposed to most of mankind.

And there are also lustful and chaste fishes; of which I shall give you examples.

And first, what Du Bartas says of a fish called the sargus; which—because none can express it better than he does—I shall give you in his own words, supposing it shall not have the less credit for being verse, for he hath gathered this and other observations out of authors that have been great and industrious searchers into the secrets of nature:

The adult'rous sargus doth not only change
Wives every day in the deep streams, but, strange,
As if the honey of sea-love delight
Could not suffice his ranging appetite,
Goes courting she-goats on the grassy shore,
Horning their husbands that had horns before.

7 These three paragraphs above are inserted from the fifth edition.

8 The hermit-crab.

And the same author writes concerning the cantharus that which you shall also hear in his own words:

> But, contrary, the constant cantharus
> Is ever constant to his faithful spouse,
> In nuptial duties spending his chaste life,
> Never loves any but his own dear wife.

Sir, but a little longer, and I have done.

VENATOR. Sir, take what liberty you think fit, for your discourse seems to be music and charms me to an attention.

PISCATOR. Why then, Sir, I will take a little liberty to tell or rather to remember you what is said of turtle-doves; first, that they silently plight their troth and marry; and that then the survivor scorns, as the Thracian women are said to do, to outlive his or her mate; and this is taken for such a truth, and if the survivor shall ever couple with another, then not only the living, but the dead, be it either the he or the she, is denied the name and honor of a true turtle-dove.

And to parallel this land-rarity and teach mankind moral faithfulness and to condemn those that talk of religion and yet come short of the moral faith of fish and fowl, men that violate the law affirmed by St. Paul (Rom. 2:14, 15) to be writ in their hearts, and which, he says shall at the Last Day condemn and leave them without excuse—I pray hearken to what Du Bartas sings, for the hearing of such conjugal faithfulness will be music to all chaste ears, and therefore I pray hearken to what Du Bartas sings of the mullet:

> But for chaste love the mullet hath no peer;
> For if the fisher hath surprised her pheer,[9]
> As mad with woe, to shore she followeth,
> Pressed to consort him both in life and death.

On the contrary, what shall I say of the house-cock, which treads any hen, and then, contrary to the swan, the partridge and pigeon, takes no care to hatch, to feed, or cherish his own brood but is senseless, though they perish. And 'tis considerable[10] that the hen, which, because she also takes any cock, expects it not, who is sure the chickens be her own, hath by a moral impression her care and affection to her own brood more than doubled, even to such a height that our Savior in expressing his love to Jerusalem (Mat. 23:37) quotes her for an example of tender affection, as his Father had done Job for a pattern of patience.

9 Companion.
10 Worthy of consideration.

And to parallel this cock, there be divers fishes that cast their spawn on flags or stones and then leave it uncovered and exposed to become a prey and be devoured by vermin or other fishes. But other fishes, as namely the barbel, take such care for the preservation of their seed that, unlike to the cock, or the cuckoo, they mutually labor, both the spawner and the melter, to cover their spawn with sand or watch it or hide it in some secret place unfrequented by vermin or by any fish but themselves.

Sir, these examples may, to you and others, seem strange; but they are testified some by Aristotle, some by Pliny, some by Gesner, and by many others of credit, and are believed and known by divers, both of wisdom and experience, to be a truth; and indeed are, as I said at the beginning, fit for the contemplation of a most serious and a most pious man. And doubtless this made the Prophet David say, "They that occupy themselves in deep waters, see the wonderful works of God"; indeed such wonders and pleasures too as the land affords not.

And that they be fit for the contemplation of the most prudent and pious and peaceable men seems to be testified by the practice of so many devout and contemplative men, as the patriarchs and prophets of old, and of the apostles of our Savior in these later times; of which twelve he chose four that were fishermen, whom he inspired and sent to publish his blessed will to the Gentiles; "freedom from the encumbrances of the law and a new way to everlasting life"; this was the employment of these fishermen. Concerning which choice, some have made these observations:

First, that he never reproved these for their employment or calling as he did the scribes and the money-changers. And secondly, he found that the hearts of such men by nature were fitted for contemplation and quietness; men of mild and sweet and peaceable spirits, as indeed most anglers are. These men our blessed Savior, who is observed to love to plant grace in good natures, though indeed nothing be too hard for him, yet these men he chose to call from their irreprovable employment of fishing, and gave them grace to be his disciples and to follow him and do wonders. I say four of twelve.

And it is observable that it was our Savior's will that these our four fishermen should have a priority of nomination in the catalogue of his twelve apostles (Mat. 10), as namely, first, St. Peter, St. Andrew, St. James, and St. John, and then the rest in their order.

And it is yet more observable that when our blessed

Savior went up into the Mount, when he left the rest of his disciples and chose only three to bear him company at his transfiguration, that those three were all fishermen. And it is to be believed that all the other apostles, after they betook themselves to follow Christ, betook themselves to be fishermen too; for it is certain that the greater number of them were found together a-fishing by Jesus after his resurrection, as is recorded in the 21st chapter of St. John's Gospel.

And since I have your promise to hear me with patience, I will take a liberty to look back upon an observation that hath been made by an ingenious and learned man, who observes that God hath been pleased to allow those whom he himself hath appointed to write his holy will in Holy Writ yet to express his will in such metaphors as their former affections or practice had inclined them to; and he brings Solomon for an example, who before his conversion was remarkably carnally amorous; and after by God's appointment writ that spiritual, holy, amorous love-song, the Canticles, betwixt God and his church in which he says she "had eyes like the fish-pools of Heshbon."

And if this hold in reason, as I see none to the contrary, then it may be probably concluded that Moses, who I told you before writ the book of Job, and the Prophet Amos, who was a shepherd, were both anglers, for you shall in all the Old Testament find fish-hooks I think but twice mentioned, namely, by meek Moses, the friend of God, and by the humble Prophet Amos.

Concerning which last, namely the Prophet Amos, I shall make but this observation, that he that shall read the humble, lowly, plain style of that prophet and compare it with the high, glorious, eloquent style of the Prophet Isaiah, though they be both equally true, may easily believe him to be not only a shepherd, but a good-natured, plain fisherman.

Which I do the rather believe by comparing the affectionate, loving, lowly humble Epistles of St. Peter, St. James, and St. John, whom we know were all fishers, with the glorious language and high metaphors of St. Paul, who we may believe was not.

And for the lawfulness of fishing, it may very well be maintained by our Savior's bidding St. Peter cast his hook into the water and catch a fish for money to pay tribute to Cæsar. And let me tell you that angling is of high esteem and of much use in other nations. He that reads the voyages of Ferdinand Mendez Pinto shall find that there he declares to have found a king and several priests a-fishing.

And he that reads Plutarch shall find that angling was not contemptible in the days of Mark Antony and Cleopatra and that they in the midst of their wonderful glory used angling as a principal recreation. And let me tell you that in the Scripture angling is always taken in the best sense and that though hunting may be sometimes so taken, yet it is but seldom to be so understood. And let me add this more. He that views the ancient ecclesiastical canons shall find hunting to be forbidden to churchmen, as being a toilsome, perplexing recreation; and shall find angling allowed to clergymen, as being a harmless recreation, a recreation that invites them to contemplation and quietness.

I might here enlarge myself by telling you what commendations our learned Perkins bestows on angling; and how dear a lover and great a practicer of it our learned Dr. Whitaker was, as indeed many others of great learning have been. But I will content myself with two memorable men that lived near to our own time, whom I also take to have been ornaments to the art of angling.

The first is Dr. Nowel, sometime Dean of the Cathedral Church of St. Paul in London, where his monument stands yet undefaced; a man that in the reformation of Queen Elizabeth—not that of Henry VIII—was so noted for his meek spirit, deep learning, prudence, and piety that the then Parliament and convocation both chose, enjoined, and trusted him to be the man to make a catechism for public use, such a one as should stand as a rule for faith and manners to their posterity. And the good old man, though he was very learned, yet knowing that God leads us not to heaven by many nor by hard questions, like an honest angler, made that good, plain, unperplexed catechism which is printed with our good old service-book. I say, this good man was a dear lover and constant practicer of angling as any age can produce; and his custom was to spend besides his fixed hours of prayer, those hours which by command of the church were enjoined the clergy and voluntarily dedicated to devotion by many primitive Christians, besides those hours, this good man was observed to spend a tenth part of his time in angling; and also—for I have conversed with those which have conversed with him—to bestow a tenth part of his revenue, and usually all his fish, amongst the poor that inhabited near to those rivers in which it was caught, saying often, "that charity gave life to religion"; and at his return to his house would praise God he had spent that day free from worldly trouble, both harmlessly and in a recreation that became a churchman. And this good man was well content, if not desirous, that posterity should know he was an angler, as may appear by his picture, now to be seen and carefully kept in Brasenose College, to which he was a liberal benefactor; in which picture he is drawn leaning on a desk with his Bible before him, and on one hand of him his lines, hooks, and other tackling lying in a round; and on his other hand are his angle-rods of several sorts; and by them this is written, "that he died 13, Feb., 1601, being aged 95 years, 44 of which he had been Dean of St. Paul's Church; and that his age had neither impaired his hearing nor dimmed his eyes nor weakened his memory nor made any of the faculties of his mind weak or useless." 'Tis said that angling and temperance were great causes of these blessings; and I wish the like to all that imitate him and love the memory of so good a man.

My next and last example shall be that undervaluer of money, the late Provost of Eton College, Sir Henry Wotton, a man with whom I have often fished and conversed, a man whose foreign employments in the service of this nation and whose experience, learn-ing, wit, and cheerfulness made his company to be esteemed one of the delights of mankind. This man, whose very approbation of angling were sufficient to convince any modest censurer of it, this man was also a most dear lover and a frequent practicer of the art of angling; of which he would say, " 'Twas an employ-ment for his idle time, which was then not idly spent"; for angling was, after tedious study, "a rest to his mind, a cheerer of his spirits, a diverter of sadness, a calmer of unquiet thoughts, a moderator of passions, a procurer of contentedness; and that it begot habits of peace and patience in those that professed and prac-ticed it." Indeed, my friend, you will find angling to be like the virtue of humility, which has a calmness of spirit and a world of other blessings attending upon it.

Sir, this was the saying of that learned man, and I do easily believe, that peace and patience and a calm content did cohabit in the cheerful heart of Sir Henry Wotton, because I know that when he was beyond seventy years of age, he made this description of a part of the present pleasure that possessed him, as he sat quietly in a summer's evening on a bank a-fishing; it is a description of the spring, which, because it glides as soft and sweetly from his pen as that river does at this time, by which it was then made, I shall repeat it unto you:

This day Dame Nature seemed in love;
The lusty sap began to move;
Fresh juice did stir th' embracing vines;
And birds had drawn their valentines.

The jealous trout, that low did lie,
Rose at a well-dissembled fly;
There stood my friend with patient skill
Attending of his trembling quill.

Already were the eaves possessed
With the swift pilgrim's daubed nest;
The groves already did rejoice,
In Philomel's triumphing voice;

The showers were short, the weather mild,
The morning fresh, the evening smiled.
Joan takes her neat-rubbed pail, and now
She trips to milk the sand-red cow;

Where for some sturdy foot-ball swain
Joan strokes a syllabub or twain;
The fields and gardens were beset
With tulips, crocus, violet;

And now, though late, the modest rose
Did more than half a blush disclose.
Thus all looks gay and full of cheer
To welcome the new-liveried year.

These were the thoughts that then possessed the undisturbed mind of Sir Henry Wotton. Will you hear the wish of another angler and the commendation of his happy life, which he also sings in verse, *viz.* Jo. Davors, Esq.?

Let me live harmlessly and near the brink
    Of Trent or Avon have a dwelling-place,
Where I may see my quill or cork down sink
    With eager bite of perch, or bleak, or dace;
And on the world and my Creator think;
    Whilst some men strive ill-gotten goods t'embrace,
And others spend their time in base excess
Of wine or worse, in war and wantonness.

Let them that list these pastimes still pursue,
    And on such pleasing fancies feed their fill,
So I the fields and meadows green may view
    And daily by fresh rivers walk at will
Among the daisies and the violets blue,
    Red hyacinth, and yellow daffodil,
Purple Narcissus like the morning rays,
Pale gander-grass, and azure culver-keys.

I count it higher pleasure to behold
  The stately compass of the lofty sky,
And in the midst thereof, like burning gold,
  The flaming chariot of the world's great eye,
The watery clouds that in the air up-rolled
  With sundry kinds of painted colors fly;
And fair Aurora, lifting up her head,
Still blushing rise from old Tithonus' bed.

The hills and mountains raisèd from the plains,
  The plains extended level with the ground,
The grounds divided into sundry veins,
  The veins enclosed with rivers running round;
These rivers making way through nature's chains
  With headlong course into the sea profound;
The raging sea, beneath the valleys low,
Where lakes and rills and rivulets do flow.

The lofty woods, the forests wide and long,
  Adorned with leaves and branches fresh and green,
In whose cool bowers the birds with many a song
  Do welcome with their quire the summer's queen;
The meadows fair where Flora's gifts among
  Are intermixed with verdant grass between;
The silver-scalèd fish that softly swim
Within the sweet brook's crystal watery stream.

All these, and many more of his creation
  That made the heavens, the angler oft doth see,
Taking therein no little delectation,
  To think how strange, how wonderful they be,
Framing thereof an inward contemplation
  To set his heart from other fancies free;
And whilst he looks on these with joyful eye,
His mind is rapt above the starry sky.

Sir, I am glad my memory has not lost these last
verses, because they are somewhat more pleasant and
more suitable to May-Day than my harsh discourse.
And I am glad your patience hath held out so long as
to hear them and me; for both together have brought
us within the sight of the Thatched House. And I must
be your debtor, if you think it worth your attention,
for the rest of my promised discourse till some other
opportunity and a like time of leisure.

VENATOR. Sir, you have angled me on with much
pleasure to the Thatched House; and I now find your
words true, "that good company makes the way seem
short"; for trust me, Sir, I thought we had wanted
three miles of this house, till you showed it to me. But
now we are at it, we'll turn into it, and refresh ourselves with a cup of drink and a little rest.

PISCATOR. Most gladly, Sir, and we'll drink a
civil cup to all the otter-hunters that are to meet you
tomorrow.

VENATOR. That we will, Sir, and to all the lovers
of angling, too, of which number I am now willing to
be one myself; for, by the help of your good discourse
and company I have put on new thoughts both of the
art of angling and of all that profess it; and if you will
but meet me tomorrow at the time and place appointed
and bestow one day with me and my friends in hunting the otter, I will dedicate the next two days to wait
upon you, and we two will for that time do nothing
but angle and talk of fish and fishing.

PISCATOR. 'Tis a match, Sir, I'll not fail you, God
willing, to be at Amwell Hill tomorrow morning before sunrising.

CHAPTER II
Observations of the Otter and the Chub

VENATOR. My friend Piscator, you have kept time
with my thoughts, for the sun is just rising, and I myself just now come to this place, and the dogs have just
now put down an otter. Look! down at the bottom
of the hill there in that meadow chequered with water-
lilies and lady-smocks, there you may see what work
they make. Look! look! you may see all busy, men
and dogs, dogs and men, all busy.

PISCATOR. Sir, I am right glad to meet you, and
glad to have so fair an entrance into this day's sport,
and glad to see so many dogs, and more men, all in
pursuit of the otter. Let's compliment no longer but
join unto them. Come, honest Venator, let's be gone,
let's make haste; I long to be doing; no reasonable
hedge or ditch shall hold me.

VENATOR. Gentleman huntsman, where found you
this otter?

HUNTSMAN. Marry, Sir, we found her a mile from
this place, a-fishing. She has this morning eaten the
greatest part of this trout; she has only left thus much
of it as you see, and was fishing for more; when we
came we found her just at it. But we were here very
early, we were here an hour before sunrise, and have
given her no rest since we came. Sure she'll hardly
escape all these dogs and men. I am to have the skin if
we kill her.

VENATOR. Why, Sir, what's the skin worth?

HUNTSMAN. 'Tis worth ten shillings to make

gloves; the gloves of an otter are the best fortification for your hands that can be thought on against wet weather.

PISCATOR. I pray, honest huntsman, let me ask you a pleasant question. Do you hunt a beast or a fish?

HUNTSMAN. Sir, it is not in my power to resolve you; I leave it to be resolved by the College of Carthusians, who have made vows never to eat flesh. But I have heard the question hath been debated among many great clerks, and they seem to differ about it; yet most agree that his tail is fish; and if his body be fish too, then I may say that a fish will walk upon land, for an otter does so, sometimes five or six or ten miles in a night. But, Sir, I can tell you certainly that he devours much fish and kills and spoils much more than he eats. And I can tell you that this dog-fisher, for so the Latins call him, can smell a fish in the water a hundred yards from him—Gesner says much farther; and that his stones are good against the falling sickness; and that there is an herb, benione, which, being hung in a linen cloth near a fish-pond or any haunt that he uses, makes him to avoid the place; which proves he smells both by water and land. And I can tell you there is brave hunting this water-dog in Cornwall, where there have been so many that our learned Camden says there is a river called Ottersey[11] which was so named by reason of the abundance of otters that bred and fed in it.

And thus much for my knowledge of the otter, which you may now see above water at vent, and the dogs close with him; I now see he will not last long. Follow, therefore, my masters, follow! for Sweetlips was like to have him at this vent.

VENATOR. Oh me! all the horse are got over the river, what shall we do now? Shall we follow them over the water?

HUNTSMAN. No, Sir, no! be not so eager, stay a little and follow me, for both they and the dogs will be suddenly on this side again, I warrant you, and the otter too, it may be. Now have at him with Kilbuck, for he vents again.

VENATOR. Marry, so he is! for look! he vents in that corner. Now, now, Ringwood has him. Now he's gone again, and has bit the poor dog. Now Sweetlips has her; hold her, Sweetlips! now all the dogs have her, some above and some under water. But now, now she's tired and past losing. Come bring her to me, Sweetlips. Look! 'tis a bitch-otter, and she has lately whelped. Let's go to the place where she was put

11 Otterey.

down, and not far from it you will find all her young ones, I dare warrant you, and kill them all too.

HUNTSMAN. Come, gentlemen, come, all! let's go to the place where we put down the otter. Look you! hereabout it was that she kenneled; look you! here it was indeed; for here's her young ones, no less than five. Come, let's kill them all.

PISCATOR. No, I pray, Sir, save me one, and I'll try if I can make her tame, as I know an ingenious gentleman in Leicestershire, Mr. Nich. Seagrave, has done; who hath not only made her tame, but to catch fish and do many other things of much pleasure.

HUNTSMAN. Take one with all my heart. But let us kill the rest. And now let's go to an honest alehouse, where we may have a cup of good barley wine, and sing Old Rose, and all of us rejoice together.

VENATOR. Come, my friend Piscator, let me invite you along with us. I'll bear your charges this night, and you shall bear mine tomorrow; for my intention is to accompany you a day or two in fishing.

PISCATOR. Sir, your request is granted; and I shall be right glad both to exchange such a courtesy and also to enjoy your company.

VENATOR. Well, now let's go to your sport of angling.

PISCATOR. Let's be going with all my heart. God keep you all, gentlemen, and send you meet this day with another bitch-otter, and kill her merrily, and all her young ones too.

VENATOR. Now, Piscator, where will you begin to fish?

PISCATOR. We are not yet come to a likely place, I must walk a mile further yet before I begin.

VENATOR. Well then, I pray, as we walk tell me freely, how do you like mine host and the company? Is not mine host a witty man?

PISCATOR. Sir, I will tell you presently what I think of your host; but first I will tell you I am glad these otters were killed, and I am sorry there are no more otter-killers; for I know that the want of otter-killers and the not keeping the fence-months for the preservation of fish will in time prove the destruction of all rivers; and those very few that are left that make conscience of the laws of the nation and of keeping days of abstinence will be forced to eat flesh, or suffer more inconveniences than are yet foreseen.

VENATOR. Why, Sir, what be those that you call the fence-months?

PISCATOR. Sir, they be principally three, namely, March, April, and May, these being the usual months that salmon come out of the sea to spawn in most fresh rivers, and their fry would about a certain time return back to the salt water, if they were not hindered by weirs and unlawful gins which the greedy fishermen set and so destroy them by thousands, as they would, being so taught by nature, change the fresh for salt water. He that shall view the wise statutes made in the 13th of Edw. the I and the like in Rich. the II may see several provisions made against the destruction of fish. And though I profess no knowledge of the law, yet I am sure the regulation of these defects might be easily mended. But I remember that a wise friend of mine did usually say, "That which is everybody's business is nobody's business." If it were otherwise, there could not be so many nets and fish that are under the statute size sold daily amongst us, and of which the conservators of the waters should be ashamed.

But, above all, the taking fish in spawning-time may be said to be against nature; it is like the taking the dam on the nest when she hatches her young, a sin so against nature that Almighty God hath in the Holy Writ made a law against it.

But the poor fish have enemies enough besides such unnatural fishermen, as namely, the otters that I spake of, the cormorant, the bittern, the osprey, the sea-gull, the hern, the king-fisher, the gorara, the puet, the swan, goose, ducks, and the craber, which some call the water-rat; against all which any honest man may make a just quarrel, but I will not; I will leave them to be quarreled with and killed by others, for I am not of a cruel nature, I love to kill nothing but fish.

And, now to your question concerning your host, to speak truly, he is not to me a good companion; for most of his conceits were either Scripture jests or lascivious jests; for which I count no man witty; for the Devil will help a man that way inclined to the first; and his own corrupt nature, which he always carries with him, to the latter. But a companion that feasts the company with wit and mirth, and leaves out the sin which is usually mixed with them, he is the man; and indeed such a companion should have his charges borne; and to such company I hope to bring you this night; for at Trout Hall, not far from this place, where I purpose to lodge tonight, there is usually an angler that proves good company. And let me tell you, good company and good discourse are the very sinews of virtue. But for such discourse as we heard last night it infects others; the very boys will learn to talk and swear as they heard mine host and another of the company that shall be nameless; I am sorry he is a gentle-

man, for less religion will not save their souls than a beggar's; I think more will be required at the last great day. Well, you know what example is able to do, and I know what the poet says in the like case, which is worthy to be noted by all parents and people of civility:

> —Many a one
> Owes to his country his religion,
> And in another would as strongly grow,
> Had but his nurse or mother taught him so.

This is reason put into verse and worthy the consideration of a wise man. But of this no more; for though I love civility, yet I hate severe censures. I'll to my own art, and I doubt not but at yonder tree I shall catch a chub; and then we'll turn to an honest cleanly hostess that I know right well; rest ourselves there; and dress it for our dinner.

VENATOR. Oh, Sir! a chub is the worst fish that swims. I hoped for a trout to my dinner.

PISCATOR. Trust me, Sir, there is not a likely place for a trout hereabout, and we stayed so long to take our leave of your huntsmen this morning that the sun is got so high and shines so clear that I will not undertake the catching of a trout till evening. And though a chub be by you and many others reckoned the worst of fish, yet you shall see I'll make it a good fish by dressing it.

VENATOR. Why, how will you dress him?

PISCATOR. I'll tell you when I have caught him. Look you here, Sir, do you see—but you must stand very close—there lie upon the top of the water in this very hole twenty chubs. I'll catch only one, and that shall be the biggest of them all; and that I will do so I'll hold you twenty to one, and you shall see it done.

VENATOR. Ay, marry! Sir, now you talk like an artist, and I'll say you are one when I shall see you perform what you say you can do. But I yet doubt it.

PISCATOR. You shall not doubt me long, for you shall see me do it presently. Look! the biggest of these chubs has had some bruise upon his tail by a pike or some other accident; and that looks like a white spot; that very chub I mean to put into your hands presently; sit you but down in the shade, and stay but a little while, and I'll warrant you I'll bring him to you.

VENATOR. I'll sit down and hope well, because you seem to be so confident.

PISCATOR. Look you, Sir, there is a trial of my skill. There he is! that very chub that I showed you with the white spot on his tail. And I'll be as certain to make him a good dish of meat as I was to catch him.

I'll now lead you to an honest alehouse where we shall find a cleanly room, lavender in the windows, and twenty ballads stuck about the wall. There my hostess, which I may tell you is both cleanly and handsome and civil, hath dressed many a one for me, and shall now dress it after my fashion, and I warrant it good meat.

VENATOR. Come, Sir, with all my heart, for I begin to be hungry and long to be at it, and indeed to rest myself too; for though I have walked but four miles this morning, yet I begin to be weary; yesterday's hunting hangs still upon me.

PISCATOR. Well, Sir, and you shall quickly be at rest, for yonder is the house I mean to bring you to.

Come, hostess, how do you? Will you first give us a cup of your best drink, and then dress this chub as you dressed my last when I and my friend were here about eight or ten days ago? But you must do me one courtesy, it must be done instantly.

HOSTESS. I will do it, Mr. Piscator, and with all the speed I can.

PISCATOR. Now, Sir, has not my hostess made haste? and does not the fish look lovely?

VENATOR. Both, upon my word, Sir, and therefore let's say grace and fall to eating of it.

PISCATOR. Well, Sir, how do you like it?

VENATOR. Trust me, 'tis as good meat as I ever tasted. Now let me thank you for it, drink to you, and beg a courtesy of you; but it must not be denied me.

PISCATOR. What is it, I pray, Sir? You are so modest that methinks I may promise to grant it before it is asked.

VENATOR. Why, Sir, it is that from henceforth you would allow me to call you master and that really I may be your scholar; for you are such a companion and have so quickly caught and so excellently cooked this fish as makes me ambitious to be your scholar.

PISCATOR. Give me your hand; from this time forward I will be your master and teach you as much of this art as I am able; and will, as you desire me, tell you somewhat of the nature of most of the fish that we are to angle for, and I am sure I both can and will tell you more than any common angler yet knows.

CHAPTER III
How To Fish for and To Dress the Chavender or Chub

PISCATOR. The chub, though he eat well thus dressed, yet as he is usually dressed he does not. He is objected against, not only for being full of small forked bones dispersed through all his body, but that he eats waterish and that the flesh of him is not firm but short and tasteless. The French esteem him so mean as to call him *un villain;* nevertheless he may be so dressed as to make him very good meat; as, namely, if he be a large chub then dress him thus:

First, scale him, and then wash him clean, and then take out his guts; and to that end make the hole as little and near to his gills as you may conveniently, and especially make clean his throat from the grass and weeds that are usually in it, for if that be not very clean, it will make him to taste very sour; having so done, put some sweet herbs into his belly, and then tie him with two or three splinters to a spit and roast him, basted often with vinegar, or rather verjuice[12] and butter, with good store of salt, mixed with it.

Being thus dressed, you will find him a much better dish of meat than you or most folk, even than anglers themselves, do imagine. For this dries up the fluid watery humor with which all chubs do abound.

But take this rule with you, that a chub newly taken and newly dressed is so much better than a chub of a day's keeping after he is dead that I can compare him to nothing so fitly as to cherries newly gathered from a tree and others that have been bruised and lain a day or two in water. Being thus used and dressed presently, and not washed after he is gutted, for note that lying long in water and washing the blood out of any fish after they be gutted abates much of their sweetness, you will find the chub to be such meat as will recompense your labor.

Or you may dress the chavender or chub thus:

When you have scaled him and cut off his tail and fins and washed him very clean, then chine or slit him through the middle, as a salt-fish is usually cut; then give him three or four cuts or scotches on the back with your knife, and broil him on charcoal, or wood coal, that are free from smoke; and all the time he is a-broiling baste him with the best sweet butter, and good store of salt mixed with it; and to this add a little thyme cut exceedingly small or bruised into the butter. The cheven thus dressed hath the watery taste taken away for which so many except against him. Thus was the cheven dressed that you liked so well and commended so much. But note again that if this chub that you eat of had been kept till tomorrow, he had not been worth a rush. And remember that his throat be very clean,

12 Sour juice, as of crab apples or unripe grapes, at one time much used in cooking.

I say very clean, and his body not washed after he is gutted.

Well, scholar, you see what pains I have taken to recover the lost credit of the poor despised chub. And now I will give you some rules how to catch him; and I am glad to enter you into the art of fishing by catching a chub, for there is no fish better to enter a young angler, he is so easily caught; but then it must be this particular way:

Go to the same hole in which I caught my chub, where in most hot days you will find a dozen or twenty chevens floating near the top of the water. Get two or three grasshoppers as you go over the meadow, and get secretly behind the tree, and stand as free from motion as is possible, Then put a grasshopper on your hook, and let your hook hang a quarter of a yard short of the water, to which end you must rest your rod on some bough of the tree; and it is likely the chubs will sink down towards the bottom of the water at the shadow of your rod, for chub is the fearfullest of fishes, and will do so if but a bird flies over him and makes the least shadow on the water. But they will presently rise up to the top again and there lie soaring till some shadow affrights them again. When they lie upon the top of the water, look out the best chub, which you, setting yourself in a fit place, may very easily see, and move your rod as softly as a snail moves to that chub you intend to catch; let your bait fall gently upon the water three or four inches before him, and he will infallibly take the bait, and you will be as sure to catch him; for he is one of the leather-mouthed fishes, of which a hook does scarce ever lose his hold. And therefore give him play enough before you offer to take him out of the water. Go your way presently, take my rod, and do as I bid you, and I will sit down and mend my tackling till you return back.

VENATOR. Truly, my loving master, you have offered me as fair as I could wish. I'll go and observe your directions.

Look you, master, what I have done, that which joys my heart, caught just such another chub as yours was.

PISCATOR. Marry, and I am glad of it. I am like to have a towardly scholar of you. I now see that with advice and practice you will make an angler in a short time. Have but a love to it, and I'll warrant you.

VENATOR. But, master, what if I could not have found a grasshopper?

PISCATOR. Then I may tell you that a black snail, with his belly slit to show his white, or a piece of soft cheese, will usually do as well. Nay, sometimes a worm, or any kind of fly, as the ant-fly, the flesh-fly, or wall-fly, or the dor or beetle, which you may find under cow-turd, or a bob, which you will find in the same place, and in time will be a beetle; it is a short white worm, like to and bigger than a gentle, or a cod-worm, or a case-worm; any of these will do very well to fish in such a manner. And after this manner you may catch a trout in a hot evening. When as you walk by a brook and shall see or hear him leap at flies, then if you get a grasshopper, put it on your hook, with your line about two yards long, standing behind a bush or tree where his hole is, and make your bait stir up and down on the top of the water; you may, if you stand close, be sure of a bite, but not sure to catch him, for he is not a leather-mouthed fish. And after this manner you may fish for him with almost any kind of live fly, but especially with a grasshopper.

VENATOR. But before you go further, I pray, good master, what mean you by a leather-mouthed fish?

PISCATOR. By a leather-mouthed fish, I mean such as have their teeth in their throat, as the chub or cheven, and so the barbel, the gudgeon, and carp, and divers others have; and the hook being stuck into the leather or skin of the mouth of such fish does very seldom or never lose its hold. But on the contrary, a pike, a perch, or trout, and so some other fish which have not their teeth in their throats but in their mouths—which you shall observe to be very full of bones, and the skin very thin and little of it—I say, of these fish the hook never takes so sure hold but you often lose your fish, unless he have gorged it.

VENATOR. I thank you, good master, for this observation. But now what shall be done with my chub or cheven that I have caught?

PISCATOR. Marry, Sir, it shall be given away to some poor body; for I'll warrant you I'll give you a trout for your supper; and it is a good beginning of your art to offer your first-fruits to the poor, who will both thank you and God for it, which I see by your silence you seem to consent to. And for your willingness to part with it so charitably, I will also teach you more concerning chub-fishing. You are to note that in March and April he is usually taken with worms; in May, June, and July he will bite at any fly or at cherries or at beetles with their legs and wings cut off or at any kind of snail or at the black bee that breeds in clay walls; and he never refuses a grasshopper, on the top of a swift stream, nor, at the bottom, the young humble-bee that breeds in long grass and is ordinarily found by the mower of it. In August and in the cooler months a yellow paste made of the strongest cheese and pounded in a mortar with a little buttter and saffron, so much of it as being beaten small, will turn it to a lemon color. And some make a paste for the winter months, at which time the chub is accounted best, for then it is observed that the forked bones are lost or turned into a kind of gristle, especially if he be baked with a paste made of cheese and turpentine. He will bite also at a minnow or penk as a trout will; of which I shall tell you more hereafter, and of divers other baits. But take this for a rule, that in hot weather he is to be fished for towards the mid-water, or nearer the top; and in colder weather, nearer the bottom. And if you fish for him on the top, with a beetle or any fly, then be sure to let your line be very long and to keep out of sight. And having told you that his spawn is excellent and that the head of a large cheven, the throat being well washed, is the best part of him, I will say no more of this fish at the present, but wish you may catch the next you fish for.

And now my next observation and direction shall be concerning the trout, which I love to angle for above any fish. But lest you may judge me too nice in urging to have the chub dressed so presently after he is taken, I will commend to your consideration how curious former times have been in the like kind.

You shall read in Seneca his Natural Questions (*lib.* 3, *cap.* 17) that the ancients were so curious in the new-ness of their fish that that seemed not new enough that was not put alive into the guest's hand; and he says that to that end they did usually keep them living in glass bottles in their dining-rooms; and they did glory much in their entertaining of friends to have that fish taken from under their table alive that was instantly to be fed upon; and he says they took great pleasure to see their mullets change to several colors when they were dying. But enough of this, for I doubt I have stayed too long from giving you some observations of the trout and how to fish for him, which shall take up the next of my spare time.

CHAPTER IV
On the Nature and Breeding of the Trout, and How To Fish for Him, and the Milkmaid's Song

PISCATOR. The trout is a fish highly valued, both in this and foreign nations. He may be justly said, as the old poet said of wine and we English say of venison, to be a generous fish; a fish that is so like the buck that he also has his seasons, for it is observed that he comes in and goes out of season with the stag and buck. Ges-ner says his name is of a German offspring, and says he is a fish that feeds clean and purely, in the swiftest streams and on the hardest gravel, and that he may justly contend with all fresh water fish, as the mullet may with all sea fish, for precedency and daintiness of taste; and that being in right season, the most dainty palates have allowed precedency to him.

And before I go farther in my discourse, let me tell you that you are to observe that as there be some barren does that are good in summer so there be some barren trouts that are good in winter; but there are not many that are so, for usually they be in their perfec-tion in the month of May and decline with the buck. Now you are to take notice that in several countries, as in Germany and in other parts, compared to ours, fish do differ much in their bigness and shape and other ways; and so do trouts. It is well known that in the Lake Leman, the Lake of Geneva, there are trouts taken of three cubits long, as is affirmed by Gesner, a writer of good credit, and Mercator says the trouts that are taken in the Lake of Geneva are a great part of the merchandise of that famous city. And you are further to know that there be certain waters that breed trouts remarkable both for their number and smallness. I know a little brook in Kent that breeds them to a number incredible, and you may take them twenty or forty in an hour, but none greater than about the size of a gudgeon. There are also in divers rivers, especially that relate to or be near to the sea, as Win-chester or the Thames about Windsor, a little trout called a samlet or skegger trout, in both which places I have caught twenty or forty at a standing, that will bite as fast and as freely as minnows; these be by some taken to be young salmons, but in those waters they never grow to be bigger than a herring.

There is also in Kent near to Canterbury a trout called there a Fordidge trout, a trout that bears the name of the town where it is usually caught, that is accounted the rarest of fish, many of them near the bigness of a salmon, but known by their different color, and in their best season cut very white; and none of these have been known to be caught with an angle, unless it were one that was caught by Sir George Hastings, an excellent angler, and now with God; and he hath told me, he thought that trout bit not for hunger but wantonness; and it is the rather to be believed, because both he then and many others before him have been curious to search into their bellies, what the food was by which they lived; and have found out nothing by which they might satisfy their curiosity.

Concerning which you are to take notice that it is reported by good authors that grasshoppers and some fish have no mouths, but are nourished and take breath by the porousness of their gills, man knows not how; and this may be believed, if we consider that when the raven hath hatched her eggs, she takes no further care, but leaves her young ones to the care of the God of nature, who is said, in the Psalms, "to feed the young ravens that call upon him." And they be kept alive and fed by a dew, or worms that breed in their nests, or some other ways that we mortals know not.[13] And this may be believed of the Fordidge trout which, as it is said of the stork that he knows his season, so he knows his times, I think almost his day, of coming into that river out of the sea, where he lives and, it is like, feeds nine months of the year, and about three in the River of Fordidge. And you are to note that the townsmen are very punctual in observing the very time of beginning to fish for them; and boast much that their river affords a trout that exceeds all others. And just so doth Sussex boast of several fish, as namely a Shelsey cockle, a Chichester lobster, an Arundel mullet, and an Amerly trout.

And now for some confirmation of the Fordidge trout, you are to know that this trout is thought to eat nothing in the fresh water; and it may be the better believed because it is well known that swallows, which are not seen to fly in England for six months in the year but about Michaelmas leave us for a hotter climate, yet some of them that have been left behind their fellows have been found many thousands at a time in hollow trees, where they have been observed to live and sleep out the whole winter without meat; and so Albertus observes that there is one kind of frog that hath her mouth naturally shut up about the end of August and that she lives so all the winter; and though it be strange to some, yet it is known to too many among us to be doubted.

And so much for these Fordidge trouts, which never afford an angler sport, but either live their time of being in the fresh water by their meat formerly gotten in the sea, not unlike the swallow or frog, or by the virtue of the fresh water only; or as the birds of paradise and the chameleon are said to live, by the sun and the air.

[13] The first two sentences of this paragraph are taken largely from the fifth edition.

There is also in Northumberland a trout called a bull-trout, of a much greater length and bigness than any in these southern parts; and there is in many rivers that relate to the sea salmon-trouts, as much different from others both in shape and in their spots, as we see sheep differ one from another in their shape and bigness, and in the fineness of the wool; and certainly, as some pastures breed larger sheep, so do some rivers by reason of the ground over which they run breed larger trouts.

Now the next thing that I will commend to your consideration is that the trout is of a more sudden growth than other fish. Concerning which you are also to take notice that he lives not so long as the perch and divers other fishes do, as Sir Francis Bacon hath observed in his History of Life and Death.

And next you are to take notice that he is not like the crocodile, which if he lives never so long, yet always thrives till his death; but 'tis not so with the trout, for after he is come to his full growth, he declines in his body, but keeps his bigness or thrives only in his head till his death. And you are to know that he will about (especially before) the time of his spawning get almost miraculously through weirs and floodgates against the stream, even through such high and swift places as is almost incredible. Next, that the trout usually spawns about October or November, but in some rivers a little sooner or later. Which is the more observable because most other fish spawn in the spring or summer when the sun hath warmed both the earth and water and made it fit for generation. And you are to note that he continues many months out of season; for it may be observed of the trout that he is like the buck or the ox that will not be fat in many months, though he go in the very same pastures that horses do which will be fat in one month; and so you may observe that most other fishes recover strength and grow sooner fat and in season than the trout doth.

And next you are to note that till the sun gets to such a height as to warm the earth and the water the trout is sick and lean and lousy and unwholesome; for you shall in winter find him to have a big head and then to be lank and thin and lean; at which time many of them have sticking on them sugs, or trout-lice, which is a kind of a worm in shape like a clove or pin with a big head, and sticks close to him and sucks his moisture; those, I think, the trout breeds himself, and never thrives till he free himself from them, which is till warm weather comes; and then, as he grows stronger, he gets from the dead, still water into the sharp streams and the gravel and there rubs off these worms or lice, and then as he grows stronger, so he gets him into swifter and swifter streams, and there lies at the watch for any fly or minnow that comes near to him; and he especially loves the May-fly, which is bred of the cod-worm or caddis; and these make the trout bold and lusty, and he is usually fatter and better meat at the end of that month than at any time of the year.

Now you are to know that it is observed that usually the best trouts are either red or yellow, though some, as the Fordidge trout, be white and yet good; but that is not usual. And it is a note observable that the female trout hath usually a less head and a deeper body than the male trout, and is usually the better meat. And note that a hog-back and a little head to any fish, either trout, salmon, or other fish, is a sign that that fish is in season.

But yet you are to note that as you see some willows or palm-trees bud and blossom sooner than others do, so some trouts be in some rivers sooner in season; and as some hollies or oaks are longer before they cast their leaves, so are some trouts in some rivers longer before they go out of season.

And you are to note that there are several kinds of trouts. But these several kinds are not considered but by very few men; for they go under the general name of trouts; just as pigeons do in most places, though it is certain there are tame and wild pigeons; and of the tame there be helmits and runts and carriers and cropers, and indeed too many to name. Nay, the Royal Society have found and published lately that there be thirty and three kinds of spiders; and yet all, for aught I know, go under that one general name of spider. And it is so with many kinds of fish, and of trouts especially, which differ in their bigness and shape and spots and color. The great Kentish hens may be an instance, compared to other hens; and doubtless there is a kind of small trout which will never thrive to be big that breeds very many more than others do that be of a larger size. Which you may rather believe, if you consider that the little wren and titmouse will have twenty young ones at a time, when usually the noble hawk or the musical throstle or blackbird exceed not four or five.[14]

And now you shall see me try my skill to catch a trout; and at my next walking, either this evening or tomorrow morning, I will give you direction how you yourself shall fish for him.

VENATOR. Trust me, master, I see now it is a harder matter to catch a trout than a chub; for I have

14 This paragraph is partly from the fifth edition.

put on patience and followed you these two hours and not seen a fish stir, neither at your minnow nor your worm.

PISCATOR. Well, scholar, you must endure worse luck sometime, or you will never make a good angler. But what say you now? There is a trout now, and a good one too, if I can but hold him; and two or three turns more will tire him. Now you see he lies still, and the sleight is to land him. Reach me that landing-net. So, Sir, now he is mine own. What say you now? is not this worth all my labor and your patience?

VENATOR. On my word, master, this is a gallant trout; what shall we do with him?

PISCATOR. Marry, e'en eat him to supper. We'll go to my hostess from whence we came; she told me, as I was going out of door, that my brother Peter, a good angler and a cheerful companion, had sent word he would lodge there tonight and bring a friend with him. My hostess has two beds, and I know you and I may have the best. We'll rejoice with my brother Peter and his friend, tell tales, or sing ballads, or make a catch, or find some harmless sport to content us, and pass away a little time without offense to God or man.

VENATOR. A match, good master, let's go to that house, for the linen looks white and smells of lavender, and I long to lie in a pair of sheets that smell so. Let's be going, good master, for I am hungry again with fishing.

PISCATOR. Nay, stay a little, good scholar. I caught my last trout with a worm, now I will put on a minnow and try a quarter of an hour about yonder trees for another, and so walk towards our lodging. Look you, scholar, thereabout we shall have a bite presently, or not at all. Have with you, Sir! On my word, I have hold of him. Oh, it is a great logger-headed chub! Come, hang him upon that willow twig, and let's be going. But turn out of the way a little, good scholar, towards yonder high hedge. We'll sit whilst this shower falls so gently upon the teeming earth and gives yet a sweeter smell to the lovely flowers that adorn these verdant meadows.

Look! under that broad beech-tree I sate down when I was last this way a-fishing; and the birds in the adjoining grove seemed to have a friendly contention with an echo whose dead voice seemed to live in a hollow tree near to the brow of that primrose-hill. There I sat viewing the silver streams glide silently towards their center, the tempestuous sea, yet sometimes opposed by rugged roots and pebble-stones, which broke their waves and turned them into foam. And sometimes I beguiled time by viewing the harmless lambs, some leaping securely in the cool shade, whilst others sported themselves in the cheerful sun; and saw others craving comfort from the swollen udders of their bleating dams. As I thus sate these and other sights had so fully possessed my soul with content that I thought as the poet has happily expressed it,

> I was for that time lifted above earth,
> And possessed joys not promised in my birth.

As I left this place and entered into the next field, a second pleasure entertained me. 'Twas a handsome milkmaid that had cast away all care, and sung like a nightingale. Her voice was good, and the ditty fitted for it. 'Twas that smooth song which was made by Kit Marlowe, now at least fifty years ago. And the milkmaid's mother sung an answer to it which was made by Sir Walter Ralegh in his younger days.

They were old-fashioned poetry, but choicely good, I think much better than the strong lines that are now in fashion in this critical age. Look yonder! on my word, yonder they both be a-milking again. I will give her the chub and persuade them to sing those two songs to us.

God speed you, good woman. I have been a-fishing, and am going to Bleak Hall to my bed, and having caught more fish than will sup myself and my friend, I will bestow this upon you and your daughter, for I use to sell none.

MILK-WOMAN. Marry! God requite you, Sir, and we'll eat it cheerfully. And if you come this way a-fishing two months hence, a grace of God! I'll give you a syllabub of new verjuice, in a new-made hay-cock, for it. And my Maudlin shall sing you one of her best ballads, for she and I both love all anglers, they be such honest, civil, quiet men. In the meantime will you drink a draught of red cow's milk? You shall have it freely.

PISCATOR. No, I thank you, but I pray do us a courtesy that shall stand you and your daughter in nothing, and we will think ourselves still something in your debt. It is but to sing us a song that was sung by you and your daughter when I last passed over this meadow, about eight or nine days since.

MILK-WOMAN. What song was it, I pray? Was it Come, Shepherds, deck your herds? or As at noon Dulcina rested? or Phillida flouts me? or Chevy Chase?

PISCATOR. No, it is none of those. It is a song that your daughter sung the first part, and you sung the answer to it.

MILK-WOMAN. O, I know it now. I learned the first part in my golden age, when I was about the age of my poor daughter; and the latter part, which indeed fits me best now, but two or three years ago, when the cares of the world began to take hold of me. But you shall, God willing, hear them both; and sung as well as we can, for we both love anglers. Come, Maudlin, sing the first part to the gentlemen with a merry heart; and I'll sing the second, when you have done.

THE MILKMAID'S SONG

> Come live with me and be my love,
> And we will all the pleasures prove
> That valleys, groves, or hills, or fields,
> Or woods, and steepy mountains yields;
>
> Where we will sit upon the rocks
> And see the shepherds feed our flocks
> By shallow rivers to whose falls
> Melodious birds sing madrigals.
>
> And I will make thee beds of roses,
> And then a thousand fragrant posies,
> A cap of flowers, and a kirtle
> Embroidered all with leaves of myrtle;
>
> A gown made of the finest wool
> Which from our pretty lambs we pull,
> Slippers lined choicely for the cold
> With buckles of the purest gold,
>
> A belt of straw and ivy-buds,
> With coral clasps, and amber studs.
> And if these pleasures may thee move,
> Come live with me and be my love.
>
> Thy silver dishes for thy meat
> As precious as the gods do eat
> Shall on an ivory table be
> Prepared each day for thee and me.
>
> The shepherd swains shall dance and sing
> For thy delight each May morning.
> If these delights thy mind may move,
> Then live with me and be my love.

VENATOR. Trust me, master, it is a choice song, and sweetly sung by honest Maudlin. I now see it was not without cause that our good Queen Elizabeth did so often wish herself a milkmaid all the month of May, because they are not troubled with fears and cares, but sing sweetly all the day and sleep securely all the night. And without doubt honest, innocent, pretty Maudlin does so. I'll bestow Sir Thomas Overbury's milkmaid's wish upon her, "that she may die in the spring; and have good store of flowers stuck round about her winding-sheet."

THE MILKMAID'S MOTHER'S ANSWER

If all the world and love were young
And truth in every shepherd's tongue,
These pretty pleasures might me move
To live with thee and be thy love.

But time drives flocks from field to fold,
When rivers rage and rocks grow cold,
Then Philomel becometh dumb,
And age complains of cares to come.

The flowers do fade, and wanton fields
To wayward winter reckoning yields.
A honey tongue, a heart of gall
Is fancy's spring but sorrow's fall.

Thy gowns, thy shoes, thy beds of roses,
Thy cap, thy kirtle, and thy posies,
Soon break, soon wither, soon forgotten,
In folly ripe, in reason rotten.

Thy belt of straw and ivy-buds,
Thy coral clasps and amber studs,
All these in me no means can move
To come to thee and be thy love.

What should we talk of dainties then,
Of better meat than's fit for men?
These are but vain. That's only good
Which God hath blessed, and sent for food.

But could youth last and love still breed,
Had joys no date, nor age no need;
Then those delights my mind might move
To live with thee and be thy love.

PISCATOR. Well sung, good woman! I thank you. I'll give you another dish of fish one of these days, and then beg another song of you. Come, scholar! let Maudlin alone. Do not you offer to spoil her voice. Look! yonder comes mine hostess to call us to supper. How now? is my brother Peter come?

HOSTESS. Yes, and a friend with him. They are both glad to hear that you are in these parts, and long to see you, and are hungry and long to be at supper.

CHAPTER V
More Directions How To Fish for and How To Make for the Trout an Artificial Minnow and Fly, and Some Merriment

PISCATOR. Well met, brother Peter! I heard you and a friend would lodge here tonight, and that hath made me and my friend cast to lodge here too. My friend is one that would fain be a brother of the angle. He hath been an angler but this day, and I have taught him how to catch a chub by dapping with a grasshopper, and he hath caught a lusty one of nineteen inches long. But I pray, brother Peter, who is it that is your companion?

PETER. Brother Piscator, my friend is an honest countryman, and his name is Coridon, a most downright, witty, and merry companion that met me here purposely to eat a trout and to be pleasant, and I have not yet wet my line since I came from home. But I hope to fit him with a trout for his breakfast; for I'll be early up.

PISCATOR. Nay, brother, you shall not delay him so long, for look you, here is a trout will fix six reasonable bellies. Come, hostess, dress it presently; and get us what other meat the house will afford, and give us some of your best barley-wine, the good liquor that our honest forefathers did use to drink of, which preserved their health, and made them live so long and to do so many good deeds.

PETER. On my word, this trout is perfect in season. Come, I thank you, and here is a hearty draught to you, and to all the brothers of the angle wheresoever they be, and to my young brother's good fortune tomorrow. I will furnish him with a rod, if you will furnish him with the rest of the tackling. We will set him up, and make him a fisher.

And I will tell him one thing for his encouragement, that his fortune hath made him happy to be scholar to such a master, a master that knows as much both of the nature and breeding of fish as any man, and can also tell him as well how to catch and cook them from the minnow to the salmon as any that I ever met withal.

PISCATOR. Trust me, brother Peter, I find my scholar to be so suitable to my own humor, which is to be free and pleasant and civilly merry, that my resolution is to hide nothing that I know from him. Believe me, scholar, this is my resolution; and so here's to you a hearty draught, and to all that love us and the honest art of angling.

VENATOR. Trust me, good master, you shall not sow your seed in barren ground, for I hope to return you an increase answerable to your hopes; but however you shall find me obedient and thankful and serviceable to my best ability.

PISCATOR. 'Tis enough, honest scholar, come, let's to supper. Come, my friend Coridon, this trout looks lovely. It was twenty-two inches when it was taken, and the belly of it looked some part of it as yellow as a marigold and part of it as white as a lily. And yet methinks it looks better in this good sauce!

CORIDON. Indeed, honest friend, it looks well, and tastes well. I thank you for it, and so doth my friend Peter, or else he is to blame.

PETER. Yes, and so I do, we all thank you, and when we have supped, I will get my friend Coridon to sing you a song for requital.

CORIDON. I will sing a song, if anybody will sing another, else, to be plain with you, I will sing none. I am none of those that sing for meat, but for company. I say, " 'Tis merry in hall when men sing all."

PISCATOR. I'll promise you I'll sing a song that was lately made at my request by Mr. William Basse, one that hath made the choice songs of the Hunter in his Career and of Tom of Bedlam, and many others of note; and this that I will sing is in praise of angling.

CORIDON. And then mine shall be the praise of a countryman's life. What will the rest sing of?

PETER. I will promise you I will sing another song in praise of angling tomorrow night, for we will not part till then, but fish tomorrow, and sup together, and the next day every man leave fishing, and fall to his business.

VENATOR. 'Tis a match; and I will provide you a song or a catch against then too, which shall give some addition of mirth to the company; for we will be civil and merry too.

PISCATOR. 'Tis a match, my masters. Let's e'en say grace and turn to the fire, drink the other cup to whet our whistles, and so sing away all sad thoughts. Come on, my masters, who begins? I think it is best to draw cuts, and avoid contention.

PETER. It is a match. Look, the shortest cut falls to Coridon.

CORIDON. Well then, I will begin, for I hate contention:

CORIDON'S SONG

Oh the sweet contentment
The countryman doth find!
    Heigh trolollie lollie loe,
    Heigh trolollie lee.

That quiet contemplation
Possesseth all my mind.
    Then care away,
    And wend along with me.

For courts are full of flattery,
As hath too oft been tried;
    Heigh trolollie lollie loe, etc.
The city full of wantonness,
And both are full of pride.
    Then care away, etc.

But oh, the honest countryman
Speaks truly from his heart,
    Heigh trolollie lollie loe, etc.
His pride is in his tillage,
His horses, and his cart.
    Then care away, etc.

Our clothing is good sheep-skins,
Gray russet for our wives,
    Heigh trolollie lollie loe, etc.
'Tis warmth and not gay clothing
That doth prolong our lives.
    Then care away, etc.

The plowman, though he labor hard,
Yet on the holiday,
    Heigh trolollie lollie loe, etc.
No emperor so merrily
Does pass his time away.
    Then care away, etc.

To recompense our tillage
The heavens afford us showers,
    Heigh trolollie lollie loe, etc.
And for our sweet refreshments
The earth affords us bowers.
    Then care away, etc.

The cuckoo and the nightingale
Full merrily do sing,
    Heigh trolollie lollie loe, etc.
And with their pleasant roundelays
Bid welcome to the spring.
    Then care away, etc.

This is not half the happiness
The countryman enjoys,
    Heigh trolollie lollie loe, etc.
Though others think they have as much,
Yet he that says so lies:
    Then come away,
    Turn countrymen with me.

                                    JO. CHALKHILL

PISCATOR. Well sung, Coridon, this song was sung with mettle, and it was choicely fitted to the occasion; I shall love you for it as long as I know you; I would you were a brother of the angle, for a companion that is cheerful and free from swearing and scurrilous discourse is worth gold. I love such mirth as does not make friends ashamed to look upon one another next morning; nor men, that cannot well bear it, to repent the money they spend when they be warmed with drink. And take this for a rule: you may pick out such times and such companies that you make yourselves merrier for a little than a great deal of money; for " 'Tis the company and not the charge that makes the feast"; and such a companion you prove, I thank you for it.

But I will not compliment you out of the debt that I owe you, and therefore I will begin my song, and wish it may be so well liked:

THE ANGLER'S SONG

As inward love breeds outward talk,
The hound some praise, and some the hawk,
Some better pleased with private sport
Use tennis, some a mistress court:
    But these delights I neither wish
    Nor envy, while I freely fish.

Who hunts doth oft in danger ride;
Who hawks lures oft both far and wide;
Who uses games shall often prove
A loser; but who falls in love
    Is fettered in fond Cupid's snare.
    My angle breeds me no such care.

Of recreation there is none
So free as fishing is alone;
All other pastimes do no less
Than mind and body both possess;
    My hand alone my work can do,
    So I can fish and study too.

I care not, I, to fish in seas,
Fresh rivers best my mind do please,
Whose sweet calm course I contemplate
And seek in life to imitate.
    In civil bounds I fain would keep
    And for my past offenses weep.

And when the timorous trout I wait
To take, and he devours my bait,
How poor a thing sometimes I find
Will captivate a greedy mind;

And when none bite, I praise the wise
Whom vain allurements ne'er surprise.

But yet, though while I fish I fast,
I make good fortune my repast;
And thereunto my friend invite,
In whom I more than that delight,
    Who is more welcome to my dish
    Than to my angle was my fish.

As well content no prize to take
As use of taken prize to make;
For so our Lord was pleasèd when
He fishers made fishers of men;
    Where, which is in no other game,
    A man may fish and praise his name.

The first men that our Savior dear
Did choose to wait upon him here
Blest fishers were, and fish the last
Food was that he on earth did taste.
I therefore strive to follow those
Whom he to follow him hath chose.

CORIDON. Well sung, brother, you have paid your debt in good coin. We anglers are all beholden to the good man that made this song. Come, hostess, give us more ale, and let's drink to him.

And now let's everyone go to bed, that we may rise early. But first let's pay our reckoning, for I will have nothing to hinder me in the morning, for my purpose is to prevent the sunrising.

PETER. A match. Come, Coridon, you are to be my bed-fellow. I know, brother, you and your scholar will lie together. But where shall we meet tomorrow night? for my friend Coridon and I will go up the water towards Ware.

PISCATOR. And my scholar and I will go down towards Waltham.

CORIDON. Then let's meet here, for here are fresh sheets that smell of lavender, and I am sure we cannot expect better meat or better usage in any place.

PETER. 'Tis a match. Good-night to everybody.

PISCATOR. And so say I.

VENATOR. And so say I. . . .

And now, scholar, my direction for fly-fishing is ended with this shower, for it has done raining. And now look about you, and see how pleasantly that meadow looks; nay, and the earth smells so sweetly too. Come let me tell you what holy Mr. Herbert says of such days and flowers as these, and then we will thank God that we enjoy them, and walk to the river and sit down quietly, and try to catch the other brace of trouts.

> Sweet day, so cool, so calm, so bright,
> The bridal of the earth and sky,
> Sweet dews shall weep thy fall tonight,
>> For thou must die.
>
> Sweet rose whose hue, angry and brave,
> Bids the rash gazer wipe his eye,
> Thy root is ever in its grave,
>> And thou must die.
>
> Sweet spring, full of sweet days and roses,
> A box where sweets compacted lie,
> My music shows you have your closes,
>> And all must die.
>
> Only a sweet and virtuous soul
> Like seasoned timber never gives,
> But when the whole world turns to coal,
>> Then chiefly lives.

VENATOR. I thank you, good master, for your good direction for fly-fishing and for the sweet enjoyment of the pleasant day, which is so far spent without offense to God or man; and I thank you for the sweet close of your discourse with Mr. Herbert's verses, which, I have heard, loved angling; and I do the rather believe it, because he had a spirit suitable to anglers and to those primitive Christians that you love and have so much commended.

PISCATOR. Well, my loving scholar, and I am pleased to know that you are so well pleased with my direction and discourse.

And since you like these verses of Mr. Herbert's so well, let me tell you what a reverend and learned divine that professes to imitate him—and has indeed done so most excellently—that writ of our Book of Common Prayer; which I know you will like the better because he is a friend of mine and I am sure no enemy to angling.

> What! prayer by th' book? and common?
>> Yes, why not?
>>> The spirit of grace
>>> And supplication
>>> Is not left free alone
>>> For time and place,
>> But manner too; to read or speak by rote
>>> Is all alike to him that prays
>>> In's heart what with his mouth he says.

> They that in private by themselves alone
>> Do pray may take
>>> What liberty they please
>>> In choosing of the ways
>>> Wherein to make
> Their soul's most intimate affections known
>> To him that sees in secret, when
>> Th' are most concealed from other men.
>
> But he that unto others leads the way
>> In public prayer
>>> Should do it so
>>> As all that hear may know
>>> They need not fear
> To tune their hearts unto his tongue and say
>> Amen; nor doubt they were betrayed
>> To blaspheme when they should have prayed.
>
> Devotion will add life unto the letter;
>> And why should not
>>> That which authority
>>> Prescribed esteemèd be
>>> Advantage got?
> If th' prayer be good, the commoner the better,
>> Prayer in the church's words as well
>> As sense of all prayers bears the bell.
>
>> CH. HARVEY

And now, scholar, I think it will be time to repair to our angle-rods, which we left in the water to fish for themselves; and you shall choose which shall be yours; and it is an even lay one of them catches.

And let me tell you, this kind of fishing with a dead rod and laying night-hooks are like putting money to use; for they both work for the owners when they do nothing but sleep or eat or rejoice, as you know we have done this last hour and sate as quietly and as free from cares under this sycamore as Virgil's Tityrus and his Melibœus did under their broad beech-tree. No life, my honest scholar, no life so happy and so pleasant as the life of a well-governed angler; for when the lawyer is swallowed up with business and the statesman is preventing or contriving plots, then we sit on cowslip-banks, hear the birds sing, and possess ourselves in as much quietness as these silent silver streams which we now see glide so quietly by us. Indeed, my good scholar, we may say of angling, as Dr. Boteler said of strawberries, "Doubtless God could have made a better berry, but doubtless God never did"; and so if I might be judge, God never did make a more calm, quiet, innocent recreation than angling.

I'll tell you, scholar; when I sate last on this prim-rose-bank and looked down these meadows, I thought of them as Charles the Emperor did of the City of Florence: "That they were too pleasant to be looked on but only on holidays." As I then sate on this very grass, I turned my present thoughts into verse. 'Twas a wish, which I'll repeat to you:—

THE ANGLER'S WISH

I in these flowery meads would be;
These crystal streams should solace me,
To whose harmonious bubbling noise
I with my angle would rejoice,
Sit here, and see the turtle-dove
Court his chaste mate to acts of love;

Or on that bank feel the west wind
Breathe health and plenty; please my mind,

To see sweet dewdrops kiss these flowers,
And then washed off by April showers;
Here hear my Clora sing a song,
There see a blackbird feed her young,
Or a leverock build her nest;
Here give my weary spirits rest
And raise my low-pitched thoughts above
Earth or what poor mortals love;
　　Thus free from law-suits and the noise
　　Of princes' courts I would rejoice;

Or, with my Bryan and a book,
Loiter long days near Shawford-brook;
There sit by him, and eat my meat,
There see the sun both rise and set,
There bid good morning to next day;
There meditate my time away,
　　And angle on; and beg to have
　　A quiet passage to a welcome grave.

LIFE OF DR. JOHN DONNE

[TEXT: *fourth edition, 1675*]

MASTER John Donne was born in London in the year 1573,[1] of good and virtuous parents; and though his own learning and other multiplied merits may justly appear sufficiently to dignify both himself and his posterity, yet the reader may be pleased to know that his father was masculinely and lineally descended from a very ancient family in Wales, where many of his name now live that deserve and have great reputation in that country.

By his mother he was descended of the family of the famous and learned Sir Thomas More, sometime Lord Chancellor of England, as also from that worthy and laborious Judge Rastall, who left posterity the vast statutes of the law of this nation most exactly abridged.

He had his first breeding in his father's house, where a private tutor had the care of him until the tenth year of his age; and in his eleventh year was sent to the University of Oxford, having at that time a good command both of the French and Latin tongue. This and some other of his remarkable abilities made one then give this censure of him: "That this age had brought forth another Picus Mirandola," of whom story says, "That he was rather born, than made wise by study."

There he remained for some years in Hart Hall,

1 Recent research has put the birth date back to 1571, or possibly early 1572.

having for the advancement of his studies tutors of several sciences to attend and instruct him, till time made him capable and his learning expressed in public exercises declared him worthy to receive his first degree in the schools; which he forbore by advice from his friends, who being for their religion of the Romish persuasion were conscionably averse to some parts of the oath that is always tendered at those times and not to be refused by those that expect the titulary honor of their studies.

About the fourteenth year of his age he was transplanted from Oxford to Cambridge; where, that he might receive nourishment from both soils, he stayed till his seventeenth year; all which time he was a most laborious student, often changing his studies but endeavoring to take no degree for the reasons formerly mentioned.

About the seventeenth year of his age he was removed to London and then admitted into Lincoln's Inn with an intent to study the law; where he gave great testimonies of his wit, his learning, and of his improvement in that profession which never served him for other use than an ornament and self-satisfaction.

His father died before his admission into this society and being a merchant left him his portion in money (it was £3000). His mother and those to whose care he was committed were watchful to improve his knowledge and to that end appointed him tutors both in the mathematics and in all the other liberal sciences to attend him. But with these arts they were advised to instill into him particular principles of the Romish Church; of which those tutors professed (though secretly) themselves to be members.

They had almost obliged him to their faith, having for their advantage, besides many opportunities, the example of his dear and pious parents, which was a most powerful persuasion and did work much upon him, as he professeth in his preface to his Pseudo-Martyr, a book of which the reader shall have some account in what follows.

He was now entered into the eighteenth year of his age; and at that time had betrothed himself to no religion that might give him any other denomination than a Christian. And reason and piety had both persuaded him that there could be no such sin as schism if an adherence to some visible church were not necessary.

About the nineteenth year of his age he, being then unresolved what religion to adhere to and considering how much it concerned his soul to choose the most orthodox, did therefore, though his youth and health promised him a long life, to rectify all scruples that might concern that, presently lay aside all study of the law and of all other sciences that might give him a denomination; and begun seriously to survey, and consider the body of divinity as it was then controverted betwixt the Reformed and the Roman Church. And as "God's blessed Spirit did then awaken him to the search and in that industry did never forsake him"— they be his own words[2]—"so he calls the same Holy Spirit to witness this protestation; that in that disquisition and search he proceeded with humility and diffidence in himself, and by that which he took to be the safest way, namely, frequent prayers and an indifferent affection to both parties"; and indeed, truth had too much light about her to be hid from so sharp an inquirer; and he had too much ingenuity not to acknowledge he had found her.

Being to undertake this search, he believed the Cardinal Bellarmine to be the best defender of the Roman cause and therefore betook himself to the examination of his reasons. The cause was weighty, and willful delays had been inexcusable both towards God and his own conscience; he therefore proceeded in

2 Pseudo-Martyr, preface, 1610.

this search with all moderate haste, and about the twentieth year of his age did show the then Dean of Gloucester, whose name my memory hath now lost, all the cardinal's works marked with many weighty observations under his own hand; which works were bequeathed by him at his death as a legacy to a most dear friend.

About a year following he resolved to travel; and the Earl of Essex going first the Cadiz and after the Island voyages, the first anno 1596, the second 1597, he took the advantage of those opportunities, waited upon his lordship, and was an eye-witness of those happy and unhappy employments.

But he returned not back into England till he had stayed some years first in Italy and then in Spain, where he made many useful observations of those countries, their laws and manner of government, and returned perfect in their languages.

The time that he spent in Spain was at his first going into Italy designed for traveling to the Holy Land and for viewing Jerusalem and the sepulchre of our Savior. But at his being in the furthest parts of Italy, the disappointment of company or of a safe convoy or the uncertainty of returns of money into those remote parts denied him that happiness; which he did often occasionally mention with a deploration.

Not long after his return into England, that exemplary pattern of gravity and wisdom, the Lord Ellesmere, then Keeper of the Great Seal and Lord Chancellor of England, taking notice of his learning, languages, and other abilities and much affecting his person and behavior, took him to be his chief secretary, supposing and intending it to be an introduction to some more weighty employment in the state; for which, his lordship did often protest, he thought him very fit.

Nor did his lordship in this time of Master Donne's attendance upon him account him to be so much his servant as to forget he was his friend; and to testify it did always use him with much courtesy, appointing him a place at his own table, to which he esteemed his company and discourse to be a great ornament.

He continued that employment for the space of five years, being daily useful and not mercenary to his friends. During which time he—I dare not say unhappily—fell into such a liking as, with her approbation, increased into a love with a young gentlewoman that lived in that family who was niece to the Lady Ellesmere, and daughter to Sir George More, then Chancellor of the Garter and Lieutenant of the Tower.

Sir George had some intimation of it and, knowing prevention to be a great part of wisdom, did therefore remove her with much haste from that to his own house at Lothesley, in the County of Surrey; but too late, by reason of some faithful promises which were so interchangeably passed as never to be violated by either party.

These promises were only known to themselves, and the friends of both parties used much diligence and many arguments to kill or cool their affections to each other. But in vain; for love is a flattering mischief that hath denied aged and wise men a foresight of those evils that too often prove to be the children of that blind father, a passion, that carries us to commit errors with as much ease as whirlwinds remove feathers and begets in us an unwearied industry to the attainment of what we desire. And such an industry did, notwithstanding much watchfulness against it, bring them secretly together—I forbear to tell the manner how —and at last to a marriage too without the allowance of those friends whose approbation always was and ever will be necessary to make even a virtuous love become lawful.

And that the knowledge of their marriage might not fall like an unexpected tempest on those that were unwilling to have it so and that preapprehensions might make it the less enormous when it was known, it was purposely whispered into the ears of many that it was so, yet by none that could affirm it. But to put a period to the jealousies of Sir George—doubt often begetting more restless thoughts than the certain knowledge of what we fear—the news was in favor to Mr. Donne and with his allowance made known to Sir George by his honorable friend and neighbor Henry, Earl of Northumberland. But it was to Sir George so immeasurably unwelcome and so transported him that as though his passion of anger and inconsideration might exceed theirs of love and error he presently engaged his sister, the Lady Ellesmere, to join with him to procure her lord to discharge Mr. Donne of the place he held under his lordship. This request was followed with violence; and though Sir George were remembered that errors might be overpunished and desired therefore to forbear till second considerations might clear some scruples, yet he became restless until his suit was granted and the punishment executed. And though the Lord Chancellor did not at Mr. Donne's dismission give him such a commendation as the great Emperor Charles the Fifth did of his secretary Eraso, when he presented him to his son and successor, Philip the

Second, saying, "That in his Eraso he gave to him a greater gift than all his estate and all the kingdoms which he then resigned to him"; yet the Lord Chancellor said, "He parted with a friend and such a secretary as was fitter to serve a king than a subject."

Immediately after his dismission from his service, he sent a sad letter to his wife to acquaint her with it; and after the subscription of his name writ

"John Donne, Anne Donne, Undone,"

and God knows it proved too true.

For this bitter physic of Mr. Donne's dismission was not strong enough to purge out all Sir George's choler; for he was not satisfied till Mr. Donne and his sometime compupil in Cambridge that married him, namely, Samuel Brooke, who was after Doctor of Divinity, and Master of Trinity College, and his brother Mr. Christopher Brooke, sometime Mr. Donne's chamber-fellow in Lincoln's Inn, who gave Mr. Donne his wife and witnessed the marriage, were all committed to three several prisons.

Mr. Donne was first enlarged, who neither gave rest to his body or brain nor to any friend in whom he might hope to have an interest until he had procured an enlargement for his two imprisoned friends.

He was now at liberty; but his days were still cloudy; and being past these troubles, others did still multiply upon him; for his wife was, to her extreme sorrow, detained from him; and though with Jacob he endured not an hard service for her, yet he lost a good one and was forced to make good his title and to get possession of her by a long and restless suit in law; which proved troublesome and sadly chargeable to him whose youth and travel and needless bounty had brought his estate into a narrow compass.

It is observed, and most truly, that silence and submission are charming qualities and work most upon passionate men; and it proved so with Sir George; for these and a general report of Mr. Donne's merits, together with his winning behavior, which when it would entice had a strange kind of elegant irresistible art, these and time had so disappointed Sir George that as the world had approved his daughter's choice so he also could not but see a more than ordinary merit in his new son. And this at last melted him into so much remorse—for love and anger are so like agues as to have hot and cold fits, and love in parents, though it may be quenched, yet is easily rekindled and expires not till death denies mankind a natural heat—that he labored his son's restoration to his place, using to that end both his own and his sister's power to her lord; but with no success; for his answer was, "That though he was unfeignedly sorry for what he had done, yet it was inconsistent with his place and credit to discharge and readmit servants at the request of passionate petitioners."

Sir George's endeavor for Mr. Donne's readmission was by all means to be kept secret, for men do more naturally reluct for errors than submit to put on those blemishes that attend their visible acknowledgment. But however it was not long before Sir George appeared to be so far reconciled as to wish their happiness and not to deny them his parental blessing, but yet refused to contribute any means that might conduce to their livelihood.

Mr. Donne's estate was the greatest part spent in many and chargeable travels, books, and dear-bought experience; he out of all employment that might yield a support for himself and wife, who had been curiously and plentifully educated; both their natures generous and accustomed to confer and not to receive courtesies; these and other considerations, but chiefly that his wife was to bear a part in his sufferings, surrounded him with many sad thoughts and some apparent apprehensions of want.

But his sorrows were lessened and his wants prevented by the seasonable courtesy of their noble kinsman, Sir Francis Wolley, of Pirford in Surrey, who entreated them to a cohabitation with him; where they remained with much freedom to themselves and equal content to him for some years; and as their charge increased—she had yearly a child—so did his love and bounty.

It hath been observed by wise and considering men that wealth hath seldom been the portion and never the mark to discover good people, but that Almighty God, who disposeth all things wisely, hath of his abundant goodness denied it—he only knows why—to many whose minds he hath enriched with the greater blessings of knowledge and virtue as the fairer testimonies of his love to mankind; and this was the present condition of this man of so excellent erudition and endowments whose necessary and daily expenses were hardly reconcilable with his uncertain and narrow estate. Which I mention, for that at this time there was a most generous offer made him for the moderating of his worldly cares, the declaration of which shall be the next employment of my pen.

God hath been so good to his church as to afford it in every age some such men to serve at his altar as have been piously ambitious of doing good to mankind, a disposition that is so like to God himself that it owes itself only to him who takes a pleasure to behold it in his creatures. These times he did bless with many such; some of which still live to be patterns of apostolical charity and of more than human patience. I have said this because I have occasion to mention one of them in my following discourse, namely, Dr. Morton, the most laborious and learned Bishop of Durham, one that God hath blessed with perfect intellectuals and a cheerful heart at the age of 94 years—and is yet living —one that in his days of plenty had so large a heart as to use his large revenue to the encouragement of learning and virtue and is now—be it spoken with sorrow—reduced to a narrow estate, which he embraces without repining; and still shows the beauty of his mind by so liberal a hand as if this were an age in which tomorrow were to care for itself. I have taken a pleasure in giving the reader a short but true character of this good man, my friend, from whom I received this following relation.—He sent to Mr. Donne and entreated to borrow an hour of his time for a conference the next day. After their meeting, there was not many minutes passed before he spake to Mr. Donne to this purpose: "Mr. Donne, the occasion of sending for you is to propose to you what I have often revolved in my own thought since I last saw you. Which nevertheless I will not declare but upon this condition, that you shall not return me a present answer but forbear three days and bestow some part of that time in fasting and prayer; and after a serious consideration of what I shall propose, then return to me with your answer. Deny me not, Mr. Donne; for it is the effect of a true love, which I would gladly pay as a debt due for yours to me."

This request being granted, the doctor expressed himself thus:

"Mr. Donne, I know your education and abilities; I know your expectation of a state-employment; and I know your fitness for it; and I know too the many delays and contingencies that attend court-promises; and let me tell you that my love begot by our long friendship and your merits hath prompted me to such an inquisition after your present temporal estate as makes me no stranger to your necessities; which I know to be such as your generous spirit could not bear, if it were not supported with a pious patience. You know I have formerly persuaded you to waive your court-hopes and enter into holy orders; which I now again persuade you to embrace with this reason added to my former request. The king hath yesterday made me Dean of Gloucester, and I am also possessed of a benefice the profits of which are equal to those of my deanery; I will think my deanery enough for my maintenance—who am and resolve to die a single man —and will quit my benefice and estate you in it— which the patron is willing I shall do—if God shall incline your heart to embrace this motion. Remember, Mr. Donne, no man's education or parts make him too good for this employment, which is to be an ambassador for the God of glory, that God who by a vile death opened the gates of life to mankind. Make me no present answer, but remember your promise, and return to me the third day with your resolution."

At the hearing of this, Mr. Donne's faint breath and perplexed countenance gave a visible testimony of an inward conflict; but he performed his promise and departed without returning an answer till the third day, and then his answer was to this effect:

"My most worthy and most dear friend, since I saw you I have been faithful to my promise and have also meditated much of your great kindness, which hath been such as would exceed even my gratitude; but that it cannot do; and more I cannot return you; and I do that with an heart full of humility and thanks, though I may not accept of your offer. But, Sir, my refusal is not for that I think myself too good for that calling for which kings, if they think so, are not good enough; nor for that my education and learning, though not eminent, may not, being assisted with God's grace and humility, render me in some measure fit for it. But I dare make so dear a friend as you are my confessor; some irregularities of my life have been so visible to some men that though I have, I thank God, made my peace with him by penitential resolutions against them and by the assistance of his grace banished them my affections, yet this, which God knows to be so, is not so visible to man as to free me from their censures and it may be that sacred calling from a dishonor. And besides, whereas it is determined by the best of casuists that God's glory should be the first end and a maintenance the second motive to embrace that calling, and though each man may propose to himself both together; yet the first may not be put last without a violation of conscience, which he that searches the heart will judge. And truly my present condition is such that if I ask my own conscience whether it be reconcilable to that rule, it is at this time so perplexed about it that I can neither give myself nor you an

answer. You know, Sir, who says, 'Happy is that man whose conscience doth not accuse him for that thing which he does.' To these I might add other reasons that dissuade me; but I crave your favor that I may forbear to express them and thankfully decline your offer."

This was his present resolution; but the heart of man is not in his own keeping; and he was destined to this sacred service by an higher hand, a hand so powerful as at last forced him to a compliance. Of which I shall give the reader an account before I shall give a rest to my pen.

Mr. Donne and his wife continued with Sir Francis Wolley till his death. A little before which time Sir Francis was so happy as to make a perfect reconciliation betwixt Sir George and his forsaken son and daughter, Sir George conditioning by bond to pay to Mr. Donne £800 at a certain day as a portion with his wife or £20 quarterly for their maintenance as the interest for it till the said portion was paid.

Most of those years that he lived with Sir Francis he studied the civil and canon laws; in which he acquired such a perfection as was judged to hold proportion with many who had made that study the employment of their whole life.

Sir Francis being dead and that happy family dissolved, Mr. Donne took for himself a house in Micham, near to Croydon in Surrey, a place noted for good air and choice company. There his wife and children remained. And for himself he took lodgings in London near to Whitehall, whither his friends and occasions drew him very often and where he was as often visited by many of the nobility and others of this nation who used him in their counsels of greatest consideration and with some rewards for his better subsistence.

Nor did our own nobility only value and favor him, but his acquaintance and friendship was sought for by most ambassadors of foreign nations and by many other strangers whose learning or business occasioned their stay in this nation.

He was much importuned by many friends to make his constant residence in London, but he still denied it, having settled his dear wife and children at Micham and near some friends that were bountiful to them and him. For they, God knows, needed it. And that you may the better now judge of the then present condition of his mind and fortune, I shall present you with an extract collected out of some few of his many letters:

——"And the reason why I did not send an answer to

your last week's letter was because it then found me under too great a sadness; and at present 'tis thus with me; there is not one person but myself well of my family. I have already lost half a child, and with that mischance of hers my wife is fallen into such a discomposure as would afflict her too extremely but that the sickness of all her other children stupefies her. Of one of which, in good faith, I have not much hope. And these meet with a fortune so ill provided for physics and such relief that if God should ease us with burials, I know not how to perform even that. But I flatter myself with this hope, that I am dying too. For I cannot waste faster than by such griefs. As for,——

From my hospital
Aug. 10   at Micham,
JOHN DONNE"

Thus he did bemoan himself. And thus in other letters:

——"For we hardly discover a sin when it is but an omission of some good and no accusing act; with this or the former I have often suspected myself to be overtaken; which is with an over-earnest desire of the next life. And though I know it is not merely a weariness of this, because I had the same desire when I went with the tide and enjoyed fairer hopes than I now do. Yet I doubt worldly troubles have increased it. 'Tis now spring, and all the pleasures of it displease me; every other tree blossoms, and I wither. I grow older and not better; my strength diminisheth and my load grows heavier; and yet I would fain be or do something; but that I cannot tell what, is no wonder in this time of my sadness; for to choose is to do; but to be no part of any body is as to be nothing; and so I am and shall so judge myself, unless I could be so incorporated into a part of the world as by business to contribute some sustentation to the whole. This I made account, I began early when I understood the study of our laws; but was diverted by leaving that and embracing the worst voluptuousness, an hydroptic, immoderate desire of human learning and languages. Beautiful ornaments indeed to men of great fortunes; but mine was grown so low as to need an occupation. Which I thought I entered well into when I subjected myself to such a service as I thought might exercise my poor abilities. And there I stumbled and fell too. And now I am become so little or such a nothing that I am not a subject good enough for one of my own letters.—Sir, I fear my present discontent does not proceed from a

good root, that I am so well content to be nothing, that is, dead. But, Sir, though my fortune hath made me such as that I am rather a sickness or a disease of the world than any part of it and therefore neither love it nor life, yet I would gladly live to become some such thing as you should not repent loving me. Sir, your own soul cannot be more zealous for your good than I am, and God who loves that zeal in me will not suffer you to doubt it. You would pity me now if you saw me write, for my pain hath drawn my head so much awry and holds it so that my eye cannot follow my pen. I therefore receive you into my prayers with mine own weary soul and commend myself to yours. I doubt not but next week will bring you good news, for I have either mending or dying on my side. But if I do continue longer thus, I shall have comfort in this, that my blessed Savior in exercising his justice upon my two worldly parts, my fortune and my body, reserves all his mercy for that which most needs it, my soul! Which is, I doubt, too like a porter that is very often near the gate and yet goes not out. Sir, I profess to you truly that my loathness to give over writing now seems to myself a sign that I shall write no more——

Your poor friend, and
God's poor patient
Sept. 7   JOHN DONNE"

By this you have seen a part of the picture of his narrow fortune and the perplexities of his generous mind; and thus it continued with him for about two years; all of which time his family remained constantly at Micham; and to which place he often retired himself and destined some days to a constant study of some points of controversy betwixt the English and Roman Church, and especially those of supremacy and allegiance. And to that place and such studies he could willingly have wedded himself during his life but the earnest persuasion of friends became at last to be so powerful as to cause the removal of himself and family to London, where Sir Robert Drury, a gentleman of a very noble estate and a more liberal mind assigned him and his wife an useful apartment in his own large house in Drury Lane, and not only rent-free but was also a cherisher of his studies and such a friend as sympathized with him and his in all their joy and sorrows.

At this time of Mr. Donne's and his wife's living in Sir Robert's house the Lord Hay was by King James sent upon a glorious embassy to the then French King Henry the Fourth, and Sir Robert put on a sudden resolution to accompany him to the French court and to be present at his audience there. And Sir Robert put on as sudden a resolution to solicit Mr. Donne to be his companion in that journey. And this desire was suddenly made known to his wife, who was then with child and otherways under so dangerous a habit of body as to her health that she professed an unwillingness to allow him any absence from her, saying, "her divining soul boded her some ill in his absence," and therefore desired him not to leave her. This made Mr. Donne lay aside all thoughts of the journey and really to resolve against it. But Sir Robert became restless in his persuasions for it; and Mr. Donne was so generous as to think he had sold his liberty when he received so many charitable kindnesses from him, and told his wife so; who did therefore with an unwilling-willingness give a faint consent to the journey, which was proposed to be but for two months, for about that time they determined their return. Within a few days after this resolve the ambassador, Sir Robert, and Mr. Donne left London; and were the twelfth day got all safe to Paris. Two days after their arrival there, Mr. Donne was left alone in that room in which Sir Robert and he and some other friends had dined together. To this place Sir Robert returned within half an hour; and as he left, so he found Mr. Donne alone; but in such an ecstasy and so altered as to his looks as amazed Sir Robert to behold him. Insomuch that he earnestly desired Mr. Donne to declare what had befallen him in the short time of his absence. To which Mr. Donne was not able to make a present answer. But after a long and perplexed pause, did at last say, "I have seen a dreadful vision since I saw you. I have seen my dear wife pass twice by me through this room with her hair hanging about her shoulders and a dead child in her arms. This I have seen since I saw you." To which Sir Robert replied, "Sure, Sir, you have slept since I saw you; and this is the result of some melancholy dream, which I desire you to forget, for you are now awake." To which Mr. Donne's reply was, "I cannot be surer that I now live than that I have not slept since I saw you, and am as sure that at her second appearing she stopped and looked me in the face and vanished." Rest and sleep had not altered Mr. Donne's opinion the next day. For he then affirmed this vision with a more deliberate and so confirmed a confidence that he inclined Sir Robert to a faint belief that the vision was true. It is truly said that desire and doubt have no rest. And it proved so with Sir Robert, for he immediately sent a servant to Drury House with a charge to hasten back and bring him word whether Mrs. Donne were alive, and if alive, in what condition she was as to her health. The twelfth day the messenger returned with this account: that he found and left Mrs. Donne very sad and sick in her bed, and that after a long and dangerous labor she had been delivered of a dead child. And upon examination the abortion proved to be the same day and about the very hour that Mr. Donne affirmed he saw her pass by him in his chamber.

This is a relation that will beget some wonder. And it well may; for most of our world are at present possessed with an opinion that visions and miracles are ceased. And though 'tis most certain that two lutes, being both strung and tuned to an equal pitch and then one played upon, the other that is not touched being laid upon a table at a fit distance will, like an echo to a trumpet, warble a faint audible harmony in answer to the same tune. Yet many will not believe there is any such thing as a sympathy of souls; and I am well pleased that every reader do enjoy his own opinion. But if the unbelieving will not allow the believing reader of this story a liberty to believe that it may be true; then I wish him to consider, many wise men have believed that the ghost of Julius Cæsar did appear to Brutus and that both St. Austin and Monica, his mother, had visions in order to his conversion. And though these and many others too many to name have but the authority of human story, yet the incredible reader may find in the sacred story that Samuel did appear to Saul even after his death, whether really or not I undertake not to determine. And Bildad in the Book of Job says these words: "A spirit passed before my face, the hair of my head stood up, fear and trembling came upon me and made all my bones to shake." Upon which words I will make no comment but leave them to be considered by the incredulous reader; to whom I will also commend this following consideration, that there be many pious and learned men that believe our merciful God hath assigned to every man a particular guardian angel to be his constant monitor and to attend him in all his dangers, both of body and soul. And the opinion that every man hath his particular angel may gain some authority by the relation of St. Peter's miraculous deliverance out of prison, not by many but by one angel. And this belief may yet gain more credit by the reader's considering that when Peter after his enlargement knocked at the door of Mary the mother of John; and Rode the maidservant being surprised with joy that Peter was there did not let him in but ran in haste and told the disciples who were then and there met together that Peter was at the door. And they not believing it, said she was mad. Yet when she again affirmed it, though they then believed it not, yet they concluded and said, "It is his angel."

More observations of this nature and inferences from them might be made to gain the relation a firmer belief. But I forbear lest I that intended to be but a relater may be thought to be an engaged person for the proving what was related to me; and yet I think myself bound to declare that, though it was not told me by Mr. Donne himself, it was told me now long since by a person of honor and of such intimacy with him that he knew more of the secrets of his soul than any person then living. And I think they told me the truth; for it was told with such circumstances and such asseveration that, to say nothing of my own thoughts, I verily believe he that told it me did himself believe it to be true.

I forbear the reader's farther trouble as to the relation and what concerns it and will conclude mine with commending to his view a copy of verses given by Mr. Donne to his wife at the time that he then parted from her. And I beg leave to tell that I have heard some critics learned both in languages and poetry say that none of the Greek or Latin poets did ever equal them.

A VALEDICTION FORBIDDING TO MOURN

As virtuous men pass mildly away.
And whisper to their souls to go
Whilst some of their sad friends do say
The breath goes now, and some say no,

So let us melt and make no noise;
No wind-sighs or tear-floods us move,
'Twere profanation of our joys
To tell the laity our love.

Movings of th' earth cause harms and fears;
Men reckon what they did or meant,
But trepidation of the spheres,
Though greater far, is innocent.

Dull, sublunary lovers' love,
Whose soul is sense, cannot admit
Absence, because that doth remove
Those things that elemented it.

But we by a soul so much refined
That our souls know not what it is,
Inter-assurèd of the mind,
Care not hands, eyes, or lips to miss.

Our two souls, therefore, which are one,
Though I must go, endure not yet
A breach, but an expansion
Like gold to airy thinness beat.

If we be two, we are two so
As stiff twin-compasses are two.
Thy soul, the fixed foot, makes no show
To move, but does, if th' other do.

And though thine in the center sit,
Yet when my other far does roam,
Thine leans and hearkens after it
And grows erect as mine comes home.

Such thou must be to me, who must
Like th' other foot obliquely run.
Thy firmness makes my circle just,
And me to end where I begun.

I return from my account of the vision to tell the reader that both before Mr. Donne's going into France, at his being there, and after his return many of the nobility and others that were powerful at court were watchful and solicitous to the king for some secular employment for him. The king had formerly both known and put a value upon his company and had also given him some hopes of a state-employment, being always much pleased when Mr. Donne attended him, especially at his meals, where there were usually many deep discourses of general learning and very often friendly disputes or debates of religion betwixt his Majesty and those divines whose places required their attendance on him at those times, particularly the Dean of the Chapel, who then was Bishop Montague, the publisher of the learned and eloquent works of his Majesty, and the most reverend Doctor Andrews, the late learned Bishop of Winchester, who then was the king's almoner.

About this time there grew many disputes that concerned the oath of supremacy and allegiance in which the king had appeared and engaged himself by his public writings now extant. And his Majesty discoursing with Mr. Donne concerning many of the reasons which are usually urged against the taking of those oaths, apprehended such a validity and clearness in his stating the questions and his answers to them that his Majesty commanded him to bestow some time in drawing the arguments into a method and then to write his answers to them and having done that not to send but be his own messenger and bring them to him. To this he presently and diligently applied himself and within six weeks brought them to him under his own handwriting as they be now printed, the book bearing the name of Pseudo-Martyr, printed *anno* 1610.

When the king had read and considered that book he persuaded Mr. Donne to enter into the ministry; to which at that time he was, and appeared, very unwilling, apprehending it, such was his mistaking modesty, to be too weighty for his abilities; and though his Majesty had promised him a favor and many persons of worth mediated with his Majesty for some secular employment for him, to which his education had apted him, and particularly the Earl of Somerset when in his greatest height of favor; who being then at Theobald's with the king, where one of the clerks of the council died that night, the earl posted a messenger for Mr. Donne to come to him immediately and at Mr. Donne's coming said, "Mr. Donne, to testify the reality of my affection and my purpose to prefer you, stay in this garden till I go up to the king and bring you word that you are clerk of the council. Doubt not my doing this, for I know the king loves you, and know the king will not deny me." But the king gave a positive denial to all requests and, having a discerning spirit, replied, "I know Mr. Donne is a learned man, has the abilities of a learned divine, and will prove a powerful preacher. And my desire is to prefer him that way, and that way I will deny you nothing for him." After that time, as he professeth, "The king descended to a persuasion, almost to a solicitation of him to enter into sacred orders."[3] Which though he then denied not yet he deferred it for almost three years. All which time he applied himself to an incessant study of textual divinity and to the attainment of a greater perfection in the learned languages, Greek and Hebrew.

In the first and most blessed times of Christianity, when the clergy were looked upon with reverence and deserved it, when they overcame their opposers by high examples of virtue, by a blessed patience and long suffering, those only were then judged worthy the ministry whose quiet and meek spirits did make them look upon that sacred calling with an humble adoration and fear to undertake it; which indeed requires such great degrees of humility and labor and care that none but such were then thought worthy of that celestial dignity. And such only were then sought out and solicited to undertake it. This I have mentioned because forwardness and inconsideration could not in Mr. Donne, as in many others, be an argument of insufficiency or unfitness; for he had considered long and

3 From Donne's Book of Devotions.

had many strifes within himself concerning the strictness of life and competency of learning required in such as enter into sacred orders; and doubtless, considering his own demerits, did humbly ask God with St. Paul, "Lord, who is sufficient for these things?" and with meek Moses, "Lord, who am I?" And sure if he had consulted with flesh and blood, he had not for these reasons put his hand to that holy plow. But God who is able to prevail wrestled with him, as the angel did with Jacob, and marked him, marked him for his own, marked him with a blessing, a blessing of obedience to the motions of his blessed Spirit. And then—as he had formerly asked God with Moses, "Who am I?" —so now being inspired with an apprehension of God's particular mercy to him in the king's and other solicitations of him, he came to ask King David's thankful question, "Lord, who am I that thou art so mindful of me?" so mindful of me as to lead me for more than forty years through this wilderness of the many temptations and various turnings of a dangerous life, so merciful to me as to move the learnedest of kings to descend to move me to serve at the altar, so merciful to me as at last to move my heart to embrace this holy motion. Thy motions I will and do embrace. And I now say with the blessed Virgin, "Be it with thy servant as seemeth best in thy sight." And so, blessed Jesus, I do take the cup of salvation and will call upon thy name and will preach thy Gospel.

Such strifes as these St. Austin had when St. Ambrose endeavored his conversion to Christianity; with which he confesseth he acquainted his friend Alipius. Our learned author, a man fit to write after no mean copy, did the like. And declaring his intentions to his dear friend Dr. King, then Bishop of London, a man famous in his generation and no stranger to Mr. Donne's abilities, for he had been chaplain to the Lord Chancellor at the time of Mr. Donne's being his lordship's secretary, that reverend man did receive the news with much gladness; and after some expressions of joy and a persuasion to be constant in his pious purpose, he proceeded with all convenient speed to ordain him first deacon and then priest not long after.

Now the English Church had gained a second St. Austin, for I think none was so like him before his conversion, none so like St. Ambrose after it. And if his youth had the infirmities of the one, his age had the excellencies of the other, the learning and holiness of both.

And now all his studies which had been occasionally diffused were all concentered in divinity. Now he had a new calling, new thoughts, and a new employment for his wit and eloquence. Now all his earthly affections were changed into divine love, and all the faculties of his own soul were engaged in the conversion of others, in preaching the glad tidings of remission to repenting sinners and peace to each troubled soul. To these he applied himself with all care and diligence. And now such a change was wrought in him that he could say with David, "Oh how amiable are thy tabernacles, O Lord God of Hosts!" Now he declared openly "that when he required a temporal, God gave him a spiritual blessing." And that "he was now gladder to be a door-keeper in the house of God than he could be to enjoy the noblest of all temporal employments."

Presently after he entered into his holy profession, the king sent for him and made him his Chaplain in Ordinary and promised to take a particular care for his preferment.

And though his long familiarity with scholars and persons of greatest quality was such as might have given some men boldness enough to have preached to any eminent auditory, yet his modesty in this employment was such that he could not be persuaded to it but went, usually accompanied with some one friend, to preach privately in some village not far from London, his first sermon being preached at Paddington. This he did till his Majesty sent and appointed him a day to preach to him at Whitehall, and, though much were expected from him both by his Majesty and others, yet he was so happy (which few are) as to satisfy and exceed their expectations, preaching the word so as showed his own heart was possessed with those very thoughts and joys that he labored to distill into others. A preacher in earnest, weeping sometimes for his auditory, sometimes with them, always preaching to himself like an angel from a cloud, but in none, carrying some, as St. Paul was, to heaven in holy raptures and enticing others by a sacred art and courtship to amend their lives, here picturing a vice so as to make it ugly to those that practiced it and a virtue so as to make it be beloved even by those that loved it not; and all this with a most particular grace and an unexpressible addition of comeliness.

There may be some that may incline to think—such indeed as have not heard him—that my affection to my friend hath transported me to an immoderate commendation of his preaching. If this meets with any such, let me entreat, though I will omit many, yet that they will receive a double witness for what I say,

it being attested by a gentleman of worth, Mr. Chidley, a frequent hearer of his sermons, in part of a funeral elegy writ by him on Dr. Donne, and is a known truth, though it be in verse:

Each altar had his fire—
He kept his love but not his object; wit
He did not banish, but transplanted it,
Taught it both time and place, and brought it home
To piety, which it doth best become.
For say, had ever pleasure such a dress?
Have you seen crimes so shaped? or loveliness
Such as his lips did clothe religion in?
Had not reproof a beauty passing sin?
Corrupted nature sorrowed that she stood
So near the danger of becoming good.
And when he preached she wished her ears exempt
From piety that had such power to tempt.
How did his sacred flattery beguile
Men to amend!——

More of this and more witnesses might be brought, but I forbear and return.

That summer, in the very same month in which he entered into sacred orders and was made the king's chaplain, his Majesty then going his progress, was entreated to receive an entertainment in the University of Cambridge. And Mr. Donne attending his Majesty at that time, his Majesty was pleased to recommend him to the universitity, to be made Doctor in Divinity; Doctor Harsnet, after Archbishop of York, was then Vice-Chancellor, who knowing him to be the author of that learned book the Pseudo-Martyr, required no other proof of his abilities but proposed it to the university, who presently assented and expressed gladness that they had such an occasion to entitle him to be theirs.

His abilities and industry in his profession were so eminent and he so known and so beloved by persons of quality that within the first year of his entering into sacred orders he had fourteen advowsons[4] of several benefices presented to him. But they were in the country, and he could not leave his beloved London, to which place he had a natural inclination, having received both his birth and education in it and there contracted a friendship with many whose conversation multiplied the joys of his life. But an employment that might affix him to that place would be welcome; for he needed it.

Immediately after his return from Cambridge, his wife died, leaving him a man of a narrow unsettled

4 Rights to benefices.

estate and, having buried five, the careful father of seven children then living, to whom he gave a voluntary assurance never to bring them under the subjection of a step-mother; which promise he kept most faithfully, burying with his tears all his earthly joys in his most dear and deserving wife's grave, and betook himself to a most retired and solitary life.

In this retiredness, which was often from the sight of his dearest friends, he became crucified to the world and all those vanities, those imaginary pleasures that are daily acted on that restless stage; and they were as perfectly crucified to him. Nor is it hard to think, being passions may be both changed, and heightened by accidents, but that that abundant affection which once was betwixt him and her who had long been the delight of his eyes and the companion of his youth, her with whom he had divided so many pleasant sorrows and contented fears as common people are not capable of—not hard to think but that she being now removed by death, a commeasurable grief took as full a possession of him as joy had done; and so indeed it did. For now his very soul was elemented of nothing but sadness; now grief took so full a possession of his heart as to leave no place for joy. If it did, it was a joy to be alone where like a pelican in the wilderness he might bemoan himself without witness or restraint and pour forth his passions like Job in the days of his affliction, "Oh, that I might have the desire of my heart! Oh that God would grant the thing that I long for!" For then, "as the grave is become her house, so I would hasten to make it mine also, that we two might there make our beds together in the dark!" Thus as the Israelites sate mourning by the rivers of Babylon when they remembered Sion, so he gave some ease to his oppressed heart by thus venting his sorrows. Thus he began the day and ended the night, ended the restless night and began the weary day in lamentations. And thus he continued till a consideration of his new engagements to God and St. Paul's "Woe is me, if I preach not the Gospel," dispersed those sad clouds that had then benighted his hopes and now forced him to behold the light.

His first motion from his house was to preach where his beloved wife lay buried in St. Clement's Church, near Temple-Bar, London, and his text was a part of the Prophet Jeremy's lamentation, "Lo, I am the man that have seen affliction."

And indeed, his very words and looks testified him to be truly such a man; and they with the addition of his sighs and tears expressed in his sermon did so work upon the affections of his hearers as melted and molded them into a companionable sadness; and so they left the congregation; but then their houses presented them with objects of diversion; and his presented him with nothing but fresh objects of sorrow in beholding many helpless children, a narrow fortune, and a consideration of the many cares and casualties that attend their education.

In this time of sadness he was importuned by the grave benchers of Lincoln's Inn, who were once the companions and friends of his youth, to accept of their lecture, which by reason of Dr. Gataker's removal from thence was then void. Of which he accepted, being most glad to renew his intermitted friendship with those whom he so much loved and where he had been a Saul, though not to persecute Christianity or to deride it yet in his irregular youth to neglect the visible practice of it, there to become a Paul and preach salvation to his beloved brethren.

And now his life was as a shining light among his old friends. Now he gave an ocular testimony of the strictness and regularity of it; now he might say as St. Paul adviseth his Corinthians, "Be ye followers of me, as I follow Christ, and walk as ye have me for an example"; not the example of a busybody, but of a contemplative, a harmless, an humble, and an holy life and conversation.

The love of that noble society was expressed to him many ways. For besides fair lodgings that were set apart and newly furnished for him with all necessaries, other courtesies were also daily added; indeed, so many and so freely as if they meant their gratitude should exceed his merits; and in this love-strife of desert and liberality they continued for the space of two years, he preaching faithfully and constantly to them and they liberally requiting him. About which time the Emperor of Germany died and the Palsgrave,[5] who had lately married the Lady Elizabeth, the king's only daughter, was elected and crowned King of Bohemia, the unhappy beginning of many miseries in that nation.

King James, whose motto *beati pacifici* did truly speak the very thoughts of his heart, endeavored first to prevent and after to compose the discords of that discomposed state; and amongst other his endeavors did then send the Lord Hay, Earl of Doncaster, his ambassador to those unsettled princes; and by a special

5 The Elector Palatine (German *Pfalzgraf*), one of the Protestant princes of Germany. His acceptance of the crown of Bohemia occasioned the outbreak of the Thirty Years War.

command from his Majesty Dr. Donne was appointed to assist and attend that employment to the princes of the union, for which the earl was most glad, who had always put a great value on him and taken a great pleasure in his conversation and discourse. And his friends of Lincoln's Inn were as glad; for they feared that his immoderate study and sadness for his wife's death would, as Jacob said, make his days few and, respecting his bodily health, evil too; and of this there were many visible signs.

At his going, he left his friends of Lincoln's Inn and they him with many reluctations. For though he could not say as St. Paul to his Ephesians, "Behold you to whom I have preached the kingdom of God shall from henceforth see my face no more," yet he, believing himself to be in a consumption, questioned, and they feared it, all concluding that his troubled mind with the help of his unintermitted studies hastened the decays of his weak body. But God who is the God of all wisdom and goodness turned it to the best; for this employment, to say nothing of the event of it, did not only divert him from those too serious studies and sad thoughts but seemed to give him a new life by a true occasion of joy, to be an eye-witness of the health of his most dear and most honored mistress, the Queen of Bohemia, in a foreign nation and to be a witness of that gladness which she expressed to see him, who, having formerly known him a courtier, was much joyed to see him in a canonical habit and more glad to be an ear-witness of his excellent and powerful preaching.

About fourteen months after his departure out of England he returned to his friends of Lincoln's Inn with his sorrows moderated, and his health improved; and there betook himself to his constant course of preaching.

About a year after his return out of Germany, Dr. Cary was made Bishop of Exeter, and by his removal the deanery of St. Paul's being vacant, the king sent to Dr. Donne and appointed him to attend him at dinner the next day. When his Majesty was sate down, before he had eat any meat, he said after his pleasant manner, "Dr. Donne, I have invited you to dinner; and, though you sit not down with me, yet I will carve to you of a dish that I know you love well; for knowing you love London, I do therefore make you Dean of Paul's; and when I have dined, then do you take your beloved dish home to your study, say grace there to yourself, and much good may it do you."

Immediately after he came to his deanery, he employed workmen to repair and beautify the chapel, suffering, as holy David once vowed, "his eyes and temples to take no rest till he had first beautified the house of God."

The next quarter following, when his father-in-law Sir George More (whom time had made a lover and admirer of him) came to pay to him a conditioned sum of twenty pounds, he refused to receive it, and said, as good Jacob did, when he heard his beloved son Joseph was alive," It is enough. You have been kind to me and mine: I know your present condition is such as not to abound: and I hope mine is or will be such as not to need it: I will therefore receive no more from you upon that contract"; and in testimony of it freely gave him up his bond.

Immediately after his admission into his deanery, the vicarage of St. Dunstan in the West, London, fell to him by the death of Dr. White, the advowson of it having been given to him long before by his honorable friend, Richard Earl of Dorset, then the patron, and confirmed by his brother the late deceased Edward, both of them men of much honor.

By these and another ecclesiastical endowment which fell to him about the same time, given to him formerly by the Earl of Kent, he was enabled to become charitable to the poor, and kind to his friends, and to make such provision for his children that they were not left scandalous, as relating to their or his profession and quality.

The next Parliament, which was within that present year, he was chosen prolocutor to the convocation; and about that time was appointed by his Majesty, his most gracious master, to preach very many occasional sermons, as at St. Paul's Cross and other places. All which employments he performed to the admiration of the representative body of the whole clergy of this nation.

He was once, and but once, clouded with the king's displeasure; and it was about this time; which was occasioned by some malicious whisperer, who had told his Majesty that Dr. Donne had put on the general humor of the pulpits, and was become busy in insinuating a fear of the king's inclining to popery and a dislike of his government, and particularly for the king's then turning the evening lectures into catechizing and expounding the prayer of our Lord and of the belief and commandments. His Majesty was the more inclinable to believe this for that a person of nobility and great note, betwixt whom and Dr. Donne there had been a great friendship, was at this very time discarded the court (I shall forbear his name unless I had a fairer occasion) and justly committed to prison; which begot many rumors in the common people, who in this nation think they are not wise unless they be busy about what they understand not and especially about religion.

The king received this news with so much discontent and restlessness that he would not suffer the sun to set and leave him under this doubt but sent for Dr. Donne and required his answer to the accusation; which was so clear and satisfactory that the king said "he was right glad he rested no longer under the suspicion." When the king had said this, Doctor Donne kneeled down and thanked his Majesty and protested his answer was faithful and free from all collusion and therefore "desired that he might not rise till, as in like cases he always had from God, so he might have from his Majesty some assurance that he stood clear and fair in his opinion." At which the king raised him from his knees with his own hands and protested he believed him and that he knew he was an honest man and doubted not but that he loved him truly. And having thus dismissed him, he called some lords of his council into his chamber and said with much earnestness, "My doctor is an honest man. And, my Lords, I was never better satisfied with an answer than he hath now made me. And I always rejoice when I think that by my means he became a divine."

He was made dean the fiftieth year of his age; and in his fifty-fourth year a dangerous sickness seized him, which inclined him to a consumption. But God, as Job thankfully acknowledged, preserved his spirit and kept his intellectuals as clear and perfect as when that sickness first seized his body; but it continued long and threatened him with death; which he dreaded not.

In this distemper of body, his dear friend Doctor Henry King, then chief residenciary of that church and late Bishop of Chichester, a man generally known by the clergy of this nation and as generally noted for his obliging nature, visited him daily; and observing that his sickness rendered his recovery doubtful, he chose a seasonable time to speak to him to this purpose.

"Mr. Dean, I am by your favor no stranger to your temporal estate, and you are no stranger to the offer lately made us for the renewing a lease of the best prebends' corps belonging to our church, and you know 'twas denied for that our tenant being very rich offered to fine at so low a rate as held not proportion with his advantages. But I will either raise him to an higher sum or procure that the other residenciaries shall join to accept of what was offered. One of these

I can and will by your favor do without delay and without any trouble either to your body or mind; I beseech you to accept of my offer, for I know it will be a considerable addition to your present estate, which I know needs it."

To this, after a short pause, and raising himself upon his bed, he made this reply.

"My most dear friend, I most humbly thank you for your many favors and this in particular. But in my present condition I shall not accept of your proposal; for doubtless there is such a sin as sacrilege; if there were not, it could not have a name in Scripture. And the primitive clergy were watchful against all appearances of that evil; and indeed then all Christians looked upon it with horror and detestation, judging it to be even an open defiance of the power and providence of Almighty God and a sad presage of a declining religion. But instead of such Christians, who had selected times set apart to fast and pray to God for a pious clergy which they then did obey, our times abound with men that are busy and litigious about trifles and church ceremonies, and yet so far from a scrupling sacrilege that they make not so much as a *quære* what it is. But I thank God I have and dare not now upon my sick-bed, when Almighty God hath made me useless to the service of the church, make any advantages out of it. But if he shall again restore me to such a degree of health as again to serve at his altar, I shall then gladly take the reward which the bountiful benefactors of this church have designed me; for God knows my children and relations will need it. In which number my mother, whose credulity and charity has contracted a very plentiful to a very narrow estate, must not be forgotten. But, Doctor King, if I recover not, that little worldly estate that I shall leave behind me (that very little when divided into eight parts) must, if you deny me not so charitable a favor, fall into your hands as my most faithful friend and executor; of whose care and justice I make no more doubt than of God's blessing on that which I have conscientiously collected for them; but it shall not be augmented on my sick-bed; and this I declare to be my unalterable resolution."

The reply to this was only a promise to observe his request.

Within a few days his distempers abated; and as his strength increased so did his thankfulness to Almighty God, testified in his most excellent Book of Devotions, which he published at his recovery. In which the reader may see the most secret thoughts that then possessed his soul paraphrased and made public, a book that may not unfitly be called a sacred picture of spiritual ecstasies occasioned and appliable to the emergencies of that sickness; which book, being a composition of Meditations, Disquisitions, and Prayers, he writ on his sick-bed, herein imitating the holy patriarchs, who were wont to build their altars in that place where they had received their blessings.

This sickness brought him so near to the gates of death and he saw the grave so ready to devour him that he would often say his recovery was supernatural. But that God that then restored his health continued it to him till the fifty-ninth year of his life. And then in August, 1630, being with his eldest daughter, Mrs. Harvey at Abury Hatch in Essex, he there fell into a fever, which with the help of his constant infirmity (vapors from the spleen) hastened him into so visible a consumption that his beholders might say, as St. Paul of himself, "He dies daily"; and he might say with Job, "My welfare passeth away as a cloud, the days of my affliction have taken hold of me, and weary nights are appointed for me."

Reader, this sickness continued long, not only weakening but wearying him so much that my desire is he may now take some rest and that before I speak of his death thou wilt not think it an impertinent digression to look back with me upon some observations of his life, which, whilst a gentle slumber gives rest to his spirits, may, I hope, not unfitly exercise thy consideration.

His marriage was the remarkable error of his life; an error which, though he had a wit able and very apt to maintain paradoxes, yet he was very far from justifying it. And though his wife's competent years and other reasons might be justly urged to moderate severe censures, yet he would occasionally condemn himself for it. And doubtless it had been attended with an heavy repentance, if God had not blest them with so mutual and cordial affections as in the midst of their sufferings made their bread of sorrow taste more pleasantly than the banquets of dull and low-spirited people.

The recreations of his youth were poetry, in which he was so happy as if nature and all her varieties had been made only to exercise his sharp wit and high fancy; and in those pieces which were facetiously composed and carelessly scattered, most of them being written before the twentieth year of his age, it may appear by his choice metaphors that both nature and all the arts joined to assist him with their utmost skill.

It is a truth that in his penitential years, viewing some of those pieces that had been loosely (God knows too loosely) scattered in his youth, he wished they had been abortive or so short-lived that his own eyes had witnessed their funerals. But though he was no friend to them, he was not so fallen out with heavenly poetry as to forsake that. No, not in his declining age; witnessed then by many divine sonnets and other high, holy, and harmonious composures. Yea, even on his former sick-bed he wrote this heavenly hymn expressing the great joy that then possessed his soul in the assurance of God's favor to him when he composed it:

AN HYMN TO GOD THE FATHER

Wilt thou forgive that sin where I begun,
   Which was my sin, though it were done before?
Wilt thou forgive that sin through which I run
   And do run still, though still I do deplore?
   When thou hast done, thou hast not done,
          For I have more.

Wilt thou forgive that sin which I have won
   Others to sin and made my sin their door?
Wilt thou forgive that sin which I did shun
   A year or two but wallowed in a score?
   When thou hast done, thou hast not done,
          For I have more.

I have a sin of fear that when I've spun
   My last thread I shall perish on the shore.
But swear by thyself that at my death thy Son
   Shall shine as he shines now and heretofore.
   And having done that, thou hast done,
          I fear no more.

I have the rather mentioned this hymn for that he caused it to be set to a most grave and solemn tune and to be often sung to the organ by the choristers of St. Paul's Church in his own hearing, especially at the evening service, and at his return from his customary devotions in that place did occasionally say to a friend, "The words of this hymn have restored to me the same thoughts of joy that possessed my soul in my sickness when I composed it. And, Oh the power of church-music! that harmony added to this hymn has raised the affections of my heart and quickened my graces of zeal and gratitude; and I observe, that I always return from paying this public duty of prayer and praise to God with an inexpressible tranquillity of mind and a willingness to leave the world."

After this manner did the disciples of our Savior, and the best of Christians in those ages of the church nearest to his time offer their praises to Almighty God. And the reader of St. Augustine's life may there find that towards his dissolution he wept abundantly that the enemies of Christianity had broken in upon them and profaned and ruined their sanctuaries, and because their public hymns and lauds were lost out of their churches. And after this manner have many devout souls lifted up their hands and offered acceptable sacrifices unto Almighty God where Dr. Donne offered his and now lies buried.

But now, oh Lord, how is that place become desolate! } 1656

Before I proceed further, I think fit to inform the reader that not long before his death he caused to be drawn a figure of the body of Christ extended upon an anchor, like those which painters draw when they would present us with the picture of Christ crucified on the cross, his varying no otherwise than to affix him not to a cross but to an anchor, the emblem of hope. This he caused to be drawn in little and then many of those figures thus drawn to be engraven very small in helitropian stones and set in gold, and of these he sent to many of his dearest friends to be used as seals or rings and kept as memorials of him and of his affection to them.

His dear friends and benefactors, Sir Henry Goodyere and Sir Robert Drury, could not be of that number; nor could the Lady Magdalen Herbert, the mother of George Herbert, for they had put off mortality and taken possession of the grave before him. But Sir Henry Wotton and Dr. Hall, the then late deceased Bishop of Norwich, were; and so were Dr. Duppa, Bishop of Salisbury, and Dr. Henry King, Bishop of Chichester, lately deceased, men in whom there was such a commixture of general learning, of natural eloquence, and Christian humility that they deserve a commemoration by a pen equal to their own, which none have exceeded.

And in this enumeration of his friends, though many must be omitted, yet that man of primitive piety, Mr. George Herbert may not; I mean that George Herbert who was the author of the Temple, or Sacred Poems and Ejaculations, a book in which by declaring his own spiritual conflicts he hath comforted and raised many a dejected and discomposed soul and charmed them into sweet and quiet thoughts, a book by the frequent reading whereof and the assistance of that Spirit that seemed to inspire the author the reader may attain habits of peace and piety and all the gifts of the Holy Ghost and heaven, and may by still reading still keep those sacred fires burning upon the altar of so pure a heart as shall free it from the anxieties of this world and keep it fixed upon things that are above. Betwixt this George Herbert and Dr. Donne there was a long and dear friendship made up by such a sympathy of inclinations that they coveted and joyed to be in each other's company; and this happy friendship was still maintained by many sacred endearments; of which that which followeth may be some testimony:

To Mr. George Herbert, sent him with one of my seals of the anchor and Christ. (A sheaf of snakes used heretofore to be my seal, which is the crest of our poor family.)

> *Qui prius assuetus serpentum falce tabellas*
> *Signare, hæc nostræ symbola parva domus*
> *Adscitus domui Domini.——*

Adopted in God's family and so
  My old coat lost into new arms I go.
The cross my seal in baptism spread below
  Does by that form into an anchor grow.
Crosses grow anchors; bear as thou should'st do
  Thy cross, and that cross grows an anchor too.
But he that makes our crosses anchors thus
  Is Christ, who there is crucified for us.
Yet with this I may my first serpents hold.
  (God gives new blessings, and yet leaves the old)
The serpent may as wise my pattern be,
  My poison, as he feeds on dust that's me.

And as he rounds the earth to murder, sure
  He is my death; but on the cross my cure.
Crucify nature then; and then implore
  All grace from him, crucified there before.
When all is cross and that cross anchor grown,
  This seal's a catechism, not a seal alone.
Under that little seal great gifts I send,
  Both works and prayers, pawns and fruits of a friend.
Oh may that Saint that rides on our great seal,
  To you that bear his name large bounty deal!

JOHN DONNE

IN SACRAM ANCHORAM PISCATORIS
GEORGE HERBERT

> *Quod crux nequibat fixa clavique additi,*
> *Tenere Christum scilicet ne ascenderet*
> *Tuive Christum——*

Although the cross could not Christ here detain,
When nailed unto't, but he ascends again,

Nor yet thy eloquence here keep him still
But only whilst thou speak'st, this anchor will.
Nor canst thou be content unless thou to
This certain anchor add a seal; and so
The water and the earth both unto thee
Do owe the symbol of their certainty.
Let the world reel, we and all ours stand sure,
This holy cable's from all storms secure.

GEORGE HERBERT

I return to tell the reader that besides these verses to his dear Mr. Herbert and that hymn that I mentioned to be sung in the quire of St. Paul's Church, he did also shorten and beguile many sad hours by composing other sacred ditties; and he writ an hymn on his death-bed, which bears this title:

AN HYMN TO GOD, MY GOD, IN MY SICKNESS,
MARCH 23, 1630

Since I am coming to that holy room
Where with thy quire of saints for evermore
I shall be made thy music, as I come
I tune my instrument here at the door,
And what I must do then think here before.

Since my physicians by their loves are grown
Cosmographers and I their map who lie
Flat on this bed——

So in his purple wrapped receive me, Lord!
By these, his thorns, give me his other crown!
And as to other souls I preached thy word,
Be this my text, my sermon to mine own,
That he may raise therefore the Lord throws down.

If these fall under the censure of a soul whose too much mixture with earth makes it unfit to judge of these high raptures and illuminations, let him know that many holy and devout men have thought the soul of Prudentius to be most refined when not many days before his death he charged it to present his God each morning and evening with a new and spiritual song; justified by the example of King David and the good King Hezekiah, who upon the renovation of his years paid his thankful vows to Almighty God in a royal hymn which he concludes in these words, "The Lord was ready to save, therefore I will sing my songs to the stringed instruments all the days of my life in the temple of my God."

The latter part of his life may be said to be a continued study; for as he usually preached once a week, if not oftener, so after his sermon he never gave his eyes rest till he had chosen out a new text, and that night cast his sermon into form and his text into divisions; and the next day betook himself to consult the fathers, and so commit his meditations to his memory, which was excellent. But upon Saturday he usually gave himself and his mind a rest from the weary burthen of his week's meditations and usually spent that day in visitation of friends or some other diversions of his thoughts and would say, "that he gave both his body and mind that refreshment that he might be enabled to do the work of the day following, not faintly, but with courage and cheerfulness."

Nor was his age only so industrious, but in the most unsettled days of his youth his bed was not able to detain him beyond the hour of four in a morning; and it was no common business that drew him out of his chamber till past ten. All which time was employed in study; though he took great liberty after it; and if this seem strange, it may gain a belief by the visible fruits of his labors, some of which remain as testimonies of what is here written, for he left the resultance of 1400 authors most of them abridged and analyzed with his own hand; he left also six-score of his sermons, all written with his own hand, also an exact and laborious treatise concerning self-murther, called *Biathanatos*, wherein all the laws violated by that act are diligently surveyed and judiciously censured, a treatise written in his younger days which alone might declare him then not only perfect in the civil and canon law but in many other such studies and arguments as enter not into the consideration of many that labor to be thought great clerks and pretend to know all things.

Nor were these only found in his study, but all businesses that passed of any public consequence, either in this or any of our neighbor nations, he abbreviated either in Latin or in the language of that nation and kept them by him for useful memorials. So did he the copies of divers letters and cases of conscience that had concerned his friends, with his observations and solutions of them, and divers other businesses of importance, all particularly and methodically digested by himself.

He did prepare to leave the world before life left him, making his will when no faculty of his soul was damped or made defective by pain or sickness or he surprised by a sudden apprehension of death; but it was made with mature deliberation, expressing himself an impartial father by making his children's portions equal, and a lover of his friends, whom he remembered with legacies fitly and discreetly chosen and bequeathed. I cannot forbear a nomination of some of them; for methinks they be persons that seem to challenge a recordation in this place; as namely, to his brother-in-law, Sir Thomas Grimes, he gave that striking clock which he had long worn in his pocket. To his dear friend and executor, Dr. King, late Bishop of Chichester, that model of gold of the synod of Dort with which the States presented him at his last being at The Hague, and the two pictures of Padre Paulo and Fulgentio, men of his acquaintance when he traveled Italy and of great note in that nation for their remarkable learning. To his ancient friend, Dr. Brooke, that married him, Master of Trinity College in Cambridge, he gave the picture of the blessed Virgin and Joseph. To Dr. Winniff, who succeeded him in the deanery he gave a picture called the Skeleton. To the succeeding dean, who was not then known, he gave many necessaries of worth and useful for his house, and also several pictures and ornaments for the chapel, with a desire that they might be registered, and remain as a legacy to his successors. To the Earls of Dorset and Carlisle, he gave several pictures. And so he did to many other friends.—Legacies given rather to express his affection than to make any addition to their estates. But unto the poor he was full of charity, and unto many others who by his constant and long continued bounty might entitle themselves to be his almspeople, for all these he made provision; and so largely as having then six children living might to some appear more than proportionable to his estate. I forbear to mention any more lest the reader may think I trespass upon his patience. But I will beg his favor to present him with the beginning and end of his will:

"In the name of the blessed and glorious Trinity, Amen. I, John Donne, by the mercy of Jesus Christ and by the calling of the Church of England priest, being at this time in good health and perfect understanding (praised be God therefore) do hereby make my last will and testament in manner and form following:

"First, I give my gracious God an entire sacrifice of body and soul, with my most humble thanks for that assurance which his blessed Spirit imprints in me now of the salvation of the one and the resurrection of the other; and for that constant and cheerful resolution which the same Spirit hath established in me to live and die in the religion now professed in the Church of England. In expectation of that resurrection, I desire my body may be buried, in the most private manner that may be, in that place of St. Paul's Church, London, that the now residenciaries have at my request designed for that purpose, &c.——. And this my last will and testament, made in the fear of God, whose mercy I humbly beg and constantly rely upon in Jesus Christ, and in perfect love and charity with all the world, whose pardon I ask from the lowest of my servants to the highest of my superiors. Written all with my own hand and my name subscribed to every page, of which there are five in number."

Sealed Decemb. 13, 1630

Nor was this blessed sacrifice of charity expressed only at his death but in his life also by a cheerful and frequent visitation of any friend whose mind was dejected or his fortune necessitous. He was inquisitive after the wants of prisoners and redeemed many from thence that lay for their fees or small debts; he was a continual giver to poor scholars, both of this and foreign nations. Besides what he gave with his own hand, he usually sent a servant or a discreet and trusty friend to distribute his charity to all the prisons in London at all the festival times of the year, especially at the birth and resurrection of our Savior. He gave an hundred pounds at one time to an old friend whom he had known live plentifully and by a too liberal heart and carelessness become decayed in his estate. And when the receiving of it was denied by the gentleman saying, "He wanted not"; for the reader may note that as there be some spirits so generous as to labor to conceal and endure a sad poverty rather than expose themselves to those blushes that attend the confession of it so there be others to whom nature and grace have afforded such sweet and compassionate souls as to pity and prevent the distresses of mankind; which I have mentioned because of Mr. Donne's reply, whose answer was, "I know you want not what will sustain nature, for a little will do that; but my desire is that you who in the days of your plenty have cheered and raised the hearts of so many of your dejected friends would now receive this from me and use it as a cordial for the cheering of your own." And upon these terms it was received. He was an happy reconciler of many differences in the families of his friends and kindred—which he never undertook faintly, for such undertakings have usually faint effects—and they had such a faith in his judgment and impartiality that he never advised them to anything in vain. He was even to her death a most dutiful son to his mother, careful to provide for her supportation, of which she had been destitute but that God raised him up to prevent her necessities; who having sucked in the religion of the Roman Church with her mother's milk spent her estate in foreign countries to enjoy a liberty in it and died in his house but three months before him.

And to the end it may appear how just a steward he was of his Lord and Master's revenue I have thought fit to let the reader know that after his entrance into his deanery, as he numbered his years, he—at the foot of a private account to which God and his angels were only witnesses with him—computed first his revenue, then what was given to the poor and other pious uses, and lastly what rested for him and his; and having done that, he then blest each year's poor remainder with a thankful prayer, which for that they discover a more than common devotion the reader shall partake some of them in his own words:

So all is that remains this year

Deo opt. max. benigno
Largitori à me et ab iis
Quibus hæc à me reservantur,
Gloria et gratia in æternum.
Amen.

So that this year God hath blessed me and mine with

Multiplicatæ sunt super
Nos misericordiæ tuæ,
Domine.————

Da Domine, ut quæ ex immensa
Bonitate tua nobis elargiri
Dignatus sis, in quorumcunque
Manus devenerint, in tuam
Semper cedant gloriam.
Amen.

In fine horum sex annorum manet——

Quid habeo quod non accepi à Domino?
Largitur etiam ut quæ largitus est
Sua iterum fiant, bono eorum usu, ut
Quemadmodum nec officiis hujus mundi,
Nec loci in quo me posuit, dignitati, nec
Servis nec egenis in toto hujus anni
Curriculo mihi conscius sum me defuisse;
Ita et liberi, quibus quæ supersunt,
Supersunt, grato animo ea accipiant,
Et beneficum authorem recognoscant.
Amen.

But I return from my long digression. We left the author sick in Essex, where he was forced to spend much of that winter by reason of his disability to remove from that place. And having never for almost twenty years omitted his personal attendance on his Majesty in that month in which he was to attend and preach to him nor having ever been left out of the roll and number of Lent preachers, and there being then (in January, 1630) a report brought to London or raised there that Dr. Donne was dead, that report gave him occasion to write this following letter to a dear friend:

Sir,—

This advantage you and my other friends have by my frequent fevers, that I am so much the oftener at the gates of heaven, and this advantage by the solitude and close imprisonment that they reduce me to after, that I am so much the oftener at my prayers, in which I shall never leave out your happiness; and I doubt not among his other blessings, God will add some one to you for my prayers. A man would almost be content to die (if there were no other benefit in death) to hear of so much sorrow and so much good testimony from good men as I (God be blessed for it) did upon the report of my death; yet I perceive it went not through all; for one writ to me that some (and he said of my friends) conceived I was not so ill as I pretended but withdrew myself to live at ease, discharged of preaching. It is an unfriendly and, God knows, an ill-grounded interpretation; for I have always been sorrier when I could not preach than any could be they could not hear me. It hath been my desire, and God may be pleased to grant it, that I might die in the pulpit; if not that, yet that I might take my death in the pulpit, that is, die the sooner by occasion of those labors. Sir, I hope to see you presently after Candlemass, about which time will fall my Lent sermon at court, except my Lord Chamberlain believe me to be dead and so leave me out of the roll; but as long as I live and am not speechless, I would not willingly decline that service, I have better leisure to write than you to read; yet I would not willingly oppress you with too much letter. God so bless you and your son as I wish to

Your poor friend and servant
in Christ Jesus,
J. DONNE

Before that month ended, he was appointed to preach upon his old constant day, the first Friday in

Lent; he had notice of it and had in his sickness so prepared for that employment that as he had long thirsted for it so he resolved his weakness should not hinder his journey; he came therefore to London some few days before his appointed day of preaching. At his coming thither many of his friends—who with sorrow saw his sickness had left him but so much flesh as did only cover his bones—doubted his strength to perform that task and did therefore dissuade him from undertaking it, assuring him, however, it was like to shorten his life; but he passionately denied their requests, saying, "he would not doubt that that God who in so many weaknesses had assisted him with an unexpected strength would now withdraw it in his last employment," professing an holy ambition to perform that sacred work. And when to the amazement of some beholders he appeared in the pulpit, many of them thought he presented himself not to preach mortification by a living voice but mortality by a decayed body and a dying face. And doubtless many did secretly ask that question in Ezekiel; "Do these bones live? or can that soul organize that tongue to speak so long time as the sand in that glass will move towards its center and measure out an hour of this dying man's unspent life? Doubtless it cannot"; and yet, after some faint pauses in his zealous prayer, his strong desires enabled his weak body to discharge his memory of his preconceived meditations, which were of dying, the text being, "To God the Lord belong the issues from death." Many that then saw his tears and heard his faint and hollow voice professing they thought the text prophetically chosen and that Dr. Donne "had preached his own funeral sermon."

Being full of joy that God had enabled him to perform this desired duty, he hastened to his house; out of which he never moved till, like St. Stephen, he was carried by devout men to his grave.

The next day after his sermon, his strength being much wasted and his spirits so spent as indisposed him to business or to talk, a friend that had often been a witness of his free and facetious discourse asked him, "Why are you sad?" To whom he replied with a countenance so full of cheerful gravity as gave testimony of an inward tranquillity of mind and of a soul willing to take a farewell of this world and said:

"I am not sad, but most of the night past I have entertained myself with many thoughts of several friends that have left me here and are gone to that place from which they shall not return, and that within a few days I also shall go hence and be no more seen.

And my preparation for this change is become my nightly meditation upon my bed, which my infirmities have now made restless to me. But, at this present time, I was in a serious contemplation of the providence and goodness of God to me, to me who am less than the least of his mercies; and looking back upon my life past, I now plainly see it was his hand that prevented me from all temporal employment and that it was his will I should never settle nor thrive till I entered into the ministry; in which I have now lived almost twenty years (I hope to his glory) and by which, I most humbly thank him, I have been enabled to requite most of those friends which showed me kindness when my fortune was very low, as God knows it was; and as it hath occasioned the expression of my gratitude, I thank God most of them stood in need of my requital. I have lived to be useful and comfortable to my good father-in-law, Sir George More, whose patience God hath been pleased to exercise with many temporal crosses; I have maintained my own mother, whom it hath pleased God after a plentiful fortune in her younger days to bring to a great decay in her very old age. I have quieted the consciences of many that have groaned under the burthen of a wounded spirit, whose prayers I hope are available for me. I cannot plead innocency of life, especially of my youth. But I am to be judged by a merciful God who is not willing to see what I have done amiss. And, though of myself I have nothing to present to him but sins and misery, yet I know he looks not upon me now as I am of myself but as I am in my Savior and hath given me even at this present time some testimonies by his holy Spirit that I am of the number of his elect. I am therefore full of inexpressible joy and shall die in peace."

I must here look so far back as to tell the reader that at his first return out of Essex to preach his last sermon, his old friend and physician, Dr. Fox, a man of great worth, came to him to consult his health and that after a sight of him and some queries concerning his distempers he told him, "That by cordials and drinking milk every twenty days together there was a probability of his restoration to health"; but he passionately denied to drink it. Nevertheless, Dr. Fox, who loved him most entirely, wearied him with solicitations till he yielded to take it for ten days; at the end of which time he told Dr. Fox, "He had drunk it more to satisfy him than to recover his health and that he would not drink it ten days longer upon the best moral assurance of having twenty years added to his life, for he loved it not, and was so far from fearing death, which to others is the king of terrors, that he longed for the day of his dissolution."

It is observed that a desire of glory or commendation is rooted in the very nature of man and that those of the severest and most mortified lives, though they may become so humble as to banish self-flattery and such weeds as naturally grow there, yet they have not been able to kill this desire of glory, but that, like our radical heat, it will both live and die with us; and many think it should be so; and we want not sacred examples to justify the desire of having our memory to outlive our lives. Which I mention, because Dr. Donne, by the persuasion of Dr. Fox, easily yielded at this very time to have a monument made for him; but Dr. Fox undertook not to persuade him how or what monument it should be; that was left to Dr. Donne himself.

A monument being resolved upon, Dr. Donne sent for a carver to make for him in wood the figure of an urn, giving him directions for the compass and height of it, and to bring with it a board of the just height of his body. These being got, then without delay a choice painter was got to be in a readiness to draw his picture, which was taken as followeth: Several charcoal fires being first made in his large study, he brought with him into that place his winding-sheet in his hand and, having put off all his clothes, had this sheet put on him and so tied with knots at his head and feet and his hands so placed as dead bodies are usually fitted to be shrouded and put into their coffin or grave. Upon this urn he thus stood with his eyes shut and with so much of the sheet turned aside as might show his lean, pale, and death-like face, which was purposely turned toward the East, from whence he expected the second coming of his and our Savior, Jesus. In this posture he was drawn at his just height; and when the picture was fully finished, he caused it to be set by his bed-side, where it continued and became his hourly object till his death and was then given to his dearest friend and executor, Doctor Henry King, then chief residenciary of St. Paul's, who caused him to be thus carved in one entire piece of white marble, as it now stands in that church; and by Doctor Donne's own appointment these words were to be affixed to it as his epitaph:

JOHANNES DONNE

Sac. Theol. Profess.

*Post varia studia quibus ab annis tenerrimis
fideliter, nec infeliciter incubuit,
instinctu et impulsu Sp. Sancti, monitu
et hortatu*

*REGIS JACOBI, ordines sacros
amplexus, anno sui Jesu, 1614, et suæ ætatis 42,
decanatu hujus ecclesiæ indutus 27,
Novembris, 1621,*

*exutus morte ultimo die Martii, 1631,
hic licet in occiduo cinere aspicit eum
cujus nomen est Oriens.*

And now, having brought him through the many labyrinths and perplexities of a various life, even to the gates of death and the grave, my desire is he may rest till I have told my reader that I have seen many pictures of him in several habits and at several ages and in several postures. And I now mention this because I have seen one picture of him, drawn by a curious hand at his age of eighteen, with his sword and what other adornments might then suit with the present fashions of youth and the giddy gaieties of that age; and his motto then was,

> How much shall I be changed
> Before I am changed!

And if that young and his now dying picture were at this time set together, every beholder might say, "Lord! how much is Dr. Donne already changed, before he is changed!" And the view of them might give my reader occasion to ask himself with some amazement, "Lord! how much may I also that am now in health be changed, before I am changed! before this vile, this changeable body shall put off mortality!" and therefore to prepare for it.——But this is not writ so much for my reader's *memento* as to tell him that Dr. Donne would often in his private discourses and often publicly in his sermons mention the many changes both of his body and mind, especially of his mind from a vertiginous giddiness, and would as often say his great and most blessed change was from a temporal to a spiritual employment. In which he was so happy that he accounted the former part of his life to be lost and the beginning of it to be from his first entering into sacred orders and serving his most merciful God at his altar.

Upon Monday after the drawing of this picture he took his last leave of his beloved study, and being sensible of his hourly decay, retired himself to his bed-chamber; and that week sent at several times for many of his most considerable friends, with whom he took a solemn and deliberate farewell, commending to their considerations some sentences useful for the regulation of their lives, and then dismissed them, as good Jacob did his sons, with a spiritual benediction. The Sunday following he appointed his servants, that if there were any business yet undone that concerned him or themselves, it should be prepared against Saturday next; for after that day he would not mix his thoughts with anything that concerned this world; nor ever did, but, as Job, so he waited for the appointed day of his dissolution.

And now he was so happy as to have nothing to do but to die; to do which he stood in need of no longer time, for he had studied it long and to so happy a perfection that in a former sickness [6] he called God to witness, "He was that minute ready to deliver his soul into his hands if that minute God would determine his dissolution." In that sickness he begged of God the constancy to be preserved in that estate forever; and his patient expectation to have his immortal soul disrobed from her garment of mortality makes me confident he now had a modest assurance that his prayers were then heard and his petition granted. He lay fifteen days earnestly expecting his hourly change; and in the last hour of his last day, as his body melted away and vapored into spirit, his soul having, I verily believe, some revelation of the beatifical vision, he said, "I were miserable if I might not die"; and after those words, closed many periods of his faint breath by saying often, "Thy kingdom come, thy will be done." His speech, which had long been his ready and faithful servant, left him not till the last minute of his life, and then forsook him not to serve another master (for who speaks like him!) but died before him for that it was then become useless to him that now conversed with God on earth as angels are said to do in heaven, only by thoughts and looks. Being speechless and seeing heaven by that illumination by which he saw it, he did, as St. Stephen, look steadfastly into it, till he saw the Son of Man, standing at the right hand of God, his Father; and being satisfied with this blessed sight, as his soul ascended and his last breath departed from him, he closed his own eyes; and then disposed his hands and body into such a posture as required not the least alteration by those that came to shroud him.

Thus variable, thus virtuous was the life; thus excellent, thus exemplary was the death of this memorable man.

He was buried in that place of St. Paul's Church which he had appointed for that use some years before his death and by which he passed daily to pay his pub-

6 When he wrote his Devotions on Emergent Occasions.

lic devotions to Almighty God (who was then served twice a day by a public form of prayer and praises in that place). But he was not buried privately, though he desired it; for, beside an unnumbered number of others, many persons of nobility and of eminency for learning, who did love and honor him in his life, did show it at his death by a voluntary and sad attendance of his body to the grave, where nothing was so remarkable as a public sorrow.

To which place of his burial some mournful friend repaired, and as Alexander the Great did to the grave of the famous Achilles, so they strewed his with an abundance of curious and costly flowers, which course they (who were never yet known) continued morning and evening for many days, not ceasing till the stones that were taken up in that church to give his body admission into the cold earth (now his bed of rest) were again by the mason's art so leveled and firmed as they had been formerly and his place of burial undistinguishable to common view.

The next day after his burial some unknown friend, some one of the many lovers and admirers of his virtue and learning, writ this epitaph with a coal on the wall, over his grave.

> Reader! I am to let thee know,
> Donne's body only lies below;
> For, could the grave his soul comprise,
> Earth would be richer than the skies.

Nor was this all the honor done to his reverend ashes; for as there be some persons that will not receive a reward for that for which God accounts himself a debtor, persons that dare trust God with their charity, and without a witness, so there was by some grateful unknown friend, that thought Dr. Donne's memory ought to be perpetuated, an hundred marks sent to his two faithful friends and executors [7] towards the making of his monument. It was not for many years known by whom; but after the death of Dr. Fox, it was known that 'twas he that sent it; and he lived to see as lively a representation of his dead friend as marble can express, a statue indeed so like Dr. Donne that, as his friend, Sir Henry Wotton, hath expressed himself, it seems to breathe faintly; and posterity shall look upon it as a kind of artificial miracle.

He was of stature moderately tall, of a straight and equally-proportioned body, to which all his words and actions gave an inexpressible addition of comeliness.

7 Dr. King and Dr. Mountfort.

The melancholy and pleasant humor were in him so contempered that each gave advantage to the other and made his company one of the delights of mankind.

His fancy was inimitably high, equalled only by his great wit; both being made useful by a commanding judgment.

His aspect was cheerful and such as gave a silent testimony of a clear-knowing soul and of a conscience at peace with itself.

His melting eye showed that he had a soft heart, full of noble compassion, of too brave a soul to offer injuries and too much a Christian not to pardon them in others.

He did much contemplate—especially after he entered into his sacred calling—the mercies of Almighty God, the immortality of the soul, and the joys of heaven, and would often say, in a kind of sacred ecstasy, "Blessed be God that he is God only and divinely like himself."

He was by nature highly passionate but more apt to reluct at the excesses of it. A great lover of the offices of humanity and of so merciful a spirit that he never beheld the miseries of mankind without pity and relief.

He was earnest and unwearied in the search of knowledge; with which his vigorous soul is now satisfied and employed in a continual praise of that God that first breathed it into his active body, that body which once was a temple of the Holy Ghost and is now become a small quantity of Christian dust.

But I shall see it reanimated.

I. W.

FROM

THE LIFE OF MR. GEORGE HERBERT

[TEXT: *fourth edition of the Lives, 1675*]

GEORGE HERBERT was born the third day of April, in the year of our Redemption 1593. The place of his birth was near to the town of Montgomery, and in that castle that did then bear the name of that town and county; that castle was then a place of state and strength, and had been successively happy in the family of the Herberts, who had long possessed it, and, with it, a plentiful estate, and hearts as liberal to their poor neighbors. A family that had been blessed with men of remarkable wisdom, and a willingness to serve their country, and indeed to do good to all mankind, for which they were eminent. But, alas! this family did in the late rebellion suffer extremely in their estates, and the heirs of that castle saw it laid level with that earth that was too good to bury those wretches that were the cause of it.

The father of our George was Richard Herbert, the son of Edward Herbert, Knight, the son of Richard Herbert, Knight, the son of the famous Sir Richard Herbert of Colebrook, in the county of Monmouth, Banneret, who was the youngest brother of the memorable William Herbert, Earl of Pembroke, that lived in the reign of our King Edward the Fourth.

His mother was Magdalen Newport, the youngest daughter of Sir Richard, and sister to Sir Francis Newport, of High Arkall, in the county of Salop, Knight, and grandfather of Francis Lord Newport, now Comptroller of his Majesty's Household. A family that for their loyalty have suffered much in their estates, and seen the ruin of that excellent structure where their ancestors have long lived and been memorable for their hospitality.

This mother of George Herbert (of whose person, wisdom, and virtue I intend to give a true account in a seasonable place) was the happy mother of seven sons and three daughters, which she would often say was Job's number, and Job's distribution, and as often bless God that they were neither defective in their shapes or in their reason, and very often reprove them that did not praise God for so great a blessing. I shall give the reader a short account of their names, and not say much of their fortunes.

Edward, the eldest, was first made Knight of the Bath, at that glorious time of our late Prince Henry's being installed Knight of the Garter, and after many years' useful travel, and the attainment of many languages, he was by King James sent ambassador resident to the then French king, Lewis XIII. There he continued about two years, but he could not subject himself to a compliance with the humors of the Duke de

Luines, who was then the great and powerful favorite at Court, so that, upon a complaint to our king, he was called back into England in some displeasure; but at his return he gave such an honorable account of his employment, and so justified his comportment to the duke and all the Court, that he was suddenly sent back upon the same embassy, from which he returned in the beginning of the reign of our good King Charles I, who made him first Baron of Castle Island, and not long after of Cherbury, in the county of Salop. He was a man of great learning and reason, as appears by his printed book "De Veritate," and by his "History of the Reign of King Henry VIII," and by several other tracts.

The second and third brothers were Richard and William, who ventured their lives to purchase honor in the wars of the Low Countries, and died officers in that employment. Charles was the fourth, and died Fellow of New College in Oxford. Henry was the sixth, who became a menial servant to the Crown, in the days of King James, and hath continued to be so for fifty years, during all of which time he hath been Master of the Revels; a place that requires a diligent wisdom, with which God has blessed him. The seventh son was Thomas, who being made captain of a ship in that fleet with which Sir Robert Mansell was sent against Algiers, did there show a fortunate and true English valor. Of the three sisters I need not say more than that they were all married to persons of worth and plentiful fortunes, and lived to be examples of virtue, and to do good in their generations.

I now come to give my intended account of George, who was the fifth of those seven brothers.

George Herbert spent much of his childhood in a sweet content under the eye and care of his prudent mother, and the tuition of a chaplain or tutor to him and two of his brothers, in her own family (for she was then a widow), where he continued till about the age of twelve years; and being at that time well instructed in the rules of grammar, he was not long after commended to the care of Dr. Neale, who was then Dean of Westminster, and by him to the care of Mr. Ireland, who was then chief master of that school, where the beauties of his pretty behavior and wit shined and became so eminent and lovely in this his innocent age that he seemed to be marked out for piety, and to become the care of Heaven, and of a particular good angel to guard and guide him. And thus he continued in that school till he came to be perfect in the learned languages, and especially in the Greek tongue, in which he after proved an excellent critic.

About the age of fifteen (he being then a King's scholar) he was elected out of that school for Trinity College in Cambridge, to which place he was transplanted about the year 1608; and his prudent mother, well knowing that he might easily lose or lessen that virtue and innocence which her advice and example had planted in his mind, did therefore procure the generous and liberal Dr. Nevil, who was then Dean of Canterbury, and master of that college, to take him into his particular care, and provide him a tutor, which he did most gladly undertake; for he knew the excellences of his mother, and how to value such a friendship.

This was the method of his education till he was settled in Cambridge, where we will leave him in his study till I have paid my promised account of his excellent mother, and I will endeavor to make it short.

I have told her birth, her marriage, and the number of her children, and have given some short account of them. I shall next tell the reader that her husband died when our George was about the age of four years. I am next to tell that she continued twelve years a widow; that she then married happily to a noble gentleman, the brother and heir of the Lord Danvers, Earl of Danby, who did highly value both her person and the most excellent endowments of her mind.

In this time of her widowhood, she being desirous to give Edward, her eldest son, such advantages of learning and other education as might suit his birth and fortune, and thereby make him the more fit for the service of his country, did at his being of a fit age remove from Montgomery Castle with him, and some of her younger sons, to Oxford; and having entered Edward into Queen's College, and provided him a fit tutor, she commended him to his care; yet she continued there with him, and still kept him in a moderate awe of herself, and so much under her own eye, as to see and converse with him daily; but she managed this power over him without any such rigid sourness as might make her company a torment to her child, but with such a sweetness and compliance with the recreations and pleasures of youth, as did incline him willingly to spend much of his time in the company of his dear and careful mother; which was to her great content, for she would often say, "That as our bodies take a nourishment suitable to the meat on which we feed, so our souls do as insensibly take in vice by the example or conversation with wicked company"; and would therefore as often say, "That ignorance of vice was the best preservation of virtue; and that the very knowledge of wickedness was as tinder to inflame and kindle sin, and to keep it burning." For these reasons she endeared him to her own company, and continued with him in Oxford four years; in which time her great and harmless wit, her cheerful gravity, and her obliging behavior, gained her an acquaintance and friendship with most of any eminent worth or learning that were at that time in or near that university, and particularly with Mr. John Donne, who then came accidentally to that place in this time of her being there. It was that John Donne, who was after Dr. Donne, and Dean of St. Paul's, London, and he, at his leaving Oxford, writ and left there, in verse, a character of the beauties of her body and mind; of the first he says,

No Spring nor Summer beauty has such grace
As I have seen in an Autumnal face.

Of the latter he says,

In all her words to every hearer fit,
You may at revels or at councils sit.

The rest of her character may be read in his printed poems, in that elegy which bears the name of the "Autumnal Beauty." For both he and she were then past the meridian of man's life.

This amity, begun at this time and place, was not an amity that polluted their souls; but an amity made up of a chain of suitable inclinations and virtues, an amity like that of St. Chrysostom's to his dear and virtuous Olympias; whom, in his letters, he calls his saint; or an amity indeed more like that of St. Hierom to his Paula, whose affection to her was such that he turned poet in his old age, and then made her epitaph, "wishing all his body were turned into tongues, that he might declare her just praises to posterity." And this amity betwixt her and Mr. Donne was begun in a happy time for him, he being then near to the fortieth year of his age (which was some years before he entered into sacred Orders): a time when his necessities needed a daily supply for the support of his wife, seven children, and a family, and in this time she proved one of his most bountiful benefactors, and he as grateful an acknowledger of it. You may take one testimony for what I have said of these two worthy persons from this following letter and sonnet:—

MADAM,

Your favors to me are everywhere; I use them, and have them. I enjoy them at London, and leave them there, and yet find them at Micham. Such riddles as these become things unexpressible; and such is your goodness. I was almost sorry to find your servant here this day, because I was loth to have any witness of my not coming home last night, and indeed of my coming this morning: but my not coming was excusable, because earnest business detained me, and my coming this day is by the example of your St. Mary Magdalen, who rose early upon Sunday to seek that which she loved most, and so did I. And, from her and myself, I return such thanks as are due to one to whom we owe all the good opinion that they whom we need most have of us. By this messenger, and on this good day, I commit the enclosed holy hymns and sonnets (which for the matter, not the workmanship, have yet escaped the fire) to your judgment, and to your protection too, if you think them worthy of it, and I have appointed this enclosed sonnet to usher them to your happy hand.

Your unworthiest servant,
Unless your accepting him to be so
Have mended him,
Jo. Donne.

Micham, July 11, 1607.

TO THE LADY MAGDALEN HERBERT,
OF ST. MARY MAGDALEN.

Her of your name, whose fair inheritance
    Bethina was, and jointure Magdalo;
An active faith so highly did advance,
    That she once knew more than the Church did know,
The Resurrection; so much good there is
    Delivered of her, that some fathers be
Loth to believe one woman could do this;
    But think these Magdalens were two or three.
Increase their number, lady, and their fame;
    To their devotion add your innocence;
Take so much of th' example as of the name;
    The latter half; and in some recompense
That they did harbor Christ Himself a guest,
    Harbor these hymns, to His dear Name addrest.
                                    J. D.

These hymns are now lost to us, but doubtless they were such as they two now sing in heaven.

There might be more demonstrations of the friendship, and the many sacred endearments betwixt these two excellent persons (for I have many of their letters in my hand), and much more might be said of her great prudence and piety; but my design was not to write hers, but the Life of her son; and therefore I shall only tell my reader that about that very day twenty years that this letter was dated and sent her, I saw and heard this Mr. John Donne (who was then Dean of St. Paul's) weep and preach her funeral sermon in the parish church of Chelsea, near London, where she now rests in her quiet grave, and where we must now leave her, and return to her son George, whom we left in his study in Cambridge.

And in Cambridge we may find our George Herbert's behavior to be such, that we may conclude he consecrated the first-fruits of his early age to virtue and a serious study of learning. And that he did so, this following letter and sonnet, which were in the first year of his going to Cambridge sent his dear mother for a New Year's gift, may appear to be some testimony:—

. . . But I fear the heat of my late ague hath dried up those springs, by which scholars say the Muses used to take up their habitations. However, I need not their help to reprove the vanity of those many love-poems that are daily writ and consecrated to Venus, nor to bewail that so few are writ that look towards God and Heaven. For my own part, my meaning, dear mother, is in these sonnets to declare my resolution to be, that my poor abilities in poetry shall be all and ever consecrated to God's glory, and I beg you to receive this as one testimony.

My God, where is that ancient heat towards Thee,
　Wherewith whole shoals of martyrs once did burn,
Besides their other flames? Doth poetry
　Wear Venus' livery? only serve her turn?
Why are not sonnets made of Thee? and lays
　Upon Thine altar burnt? Cannot Thy love
Heighten a spirit to sound out Thy praise
　As well as any she? Cannot Thy Dove
Outstrip their Cupid easily in flight?
　Or, since Thy ways are deep, and still the same,
　Will not a verse run smooth that bears Thy Name!
Why doth that fire, which by Thy power and might
　Each breast does feel, no braver fuel choose
　Than that which one day worms may chance refuse?

Sure, Lord, there is enough in Thee to dry
　Oceans of ink; for, as the deluge did
Cover the earth, so doth Thy majesty:
　Each cloud distills Thy praise, and doth forbid

Poets to turn it to another use.
　Roses and lilies speak Thee; and to make
A pair of cheeks of them is Thy abuse.
　Why should I women's eyes for crystal take?
Such poor invention burns in their low mind
　Whose fire is wild, and doth not upward go
　To praise, and on Thee, Lord, some ink bestow.
Open the bones, and you shall nothing find
　In the best face but filth; when, Lord, in Thee
　The beauty lies in the discovery.

G. H.

This was his resolution at the sending this letter to his dear mother; about which time he was in the seventeenth year of his age; and as he grew older, so he grew in learning, and more and more in favor both with God and man; insomuch, that in this morning of that short day of his life, he seemed to be marked out for virtue, and to become the care of Heaven; for God still kept his soul in so holy a frame, that he may and ought to be a pattern of virtue to all posterity, and especially to his brethren of the clergy, of which the reader may expect a more exact account in what will follow.

I need not declare that he was a strict student, because that he was so there will be many testimonies in the future part of his life. I shall therefore only tell that he was made Bachelor of Arts in the year 1611; Major Fellow of the College, March 15, 1615; and that in that year he was also made Master of Arts, he being then in the twenty-second year of his age; during all which time, all, or the greatest diversion from his study, was the practice of music, in which he became a great master, and of which he would say, "That it did relieve his drooping spirits, compose his distracted thoughts, and raised his weary soul so far above the earth, that it gave him an earnest of the joys of heaven before he possessed them." And it may be noted, that from his first entrance into the college, the generous Dr. Nevil was a cherisher of his studies, and such a lover of his person, his behavior, and the excellent endowments of his mind, that he took him often into his own company, by which he confirmed his native gentleness; and if during this time he expressed any error, it was that he kept himself too much retired, and at too great a distance with all his inferiors; and his clothes seemed to prove that he put too great a value on his parts and parentage.

This may be some account of his disposition, and of the employment of his time till he was Master of Arts, which was anno 1615; and in the year 1619 he was chosen orator for the university. His two precedent orators were Sir Robert Naunton and Sir Francis Nethersole; the first was not long after made Secretary of State; and Sir Francis, not very long after his being orator, was made Secretary to the Lady Elizabeth, Queen of Bohemia. In this place of orator, our George Herbert continued eight years, and managed it with as becoming and grave a gaiety as any had ever before or since his time. For he had acquired great learning, and was blest with a high fancy, a civil and sharp wit, and with a natural elegance, both in his behavior, his tongue, and his pen. Of all which there might be very many particular evidences, but I will limit myself to the mention of but three.

And the first notable occasion of showing his fitness for this employment of orator was manifested in a letter to King James upon the occasion of his sending that university his book, called "Basilicon Doron"; and their orator was to acknowledge this great honor, and return their gratitude to his Majesty for such a condescension, at the close of which letter he writ—

Quid Vaticanam Bodleianamque objicis hospes!
Unicus est nobis Bibliotheca Liber.

This letter was writ in such excellent Latin, was so full of conceits, and all the expressions so suited to the genius of the king, that he inquired the orator's name, and then asked William, Earl of Pembroke, if he knew him; whose answer was, "That he knew him very well and that he was his kinsman; but he loved him more for his learning and virtue than for that he was of his name and family." At which answer the king smiled, and asked the earl leave "That he might love him too; for he took him to be the jewel of that university."

The next occasion he had and took to show his great abilities was with them, to show also his great affection to that Church in which he received his baptism, and of which he professed himself a member; and the occasion was this: there was one Andrew Melvin, a minister of the Scotch Church, and rector of St. Andrews, who, by a long and constant converse with a discontented part of that clergy which opposed episcopacy, became at last to be a chief leader of that faction; and had proudly appeared to be so to King James, when he was but king of that nation; who the second year after his coronation in England, convened a part of the bishops and other learned divines of his Church, to attend him at Hampton Court, in order to a friendly conference with some dissenting brethren, both of this and the Church of Scotland, of which

Scotch party Andrew Melvin was one; and he being a man of learning, and inclined to satirical poetry, had scattered many malicious bitter verses against our Liturgy, our ceremonies, and our Church government; which were by some of that party so magnified for the wit, that they were therefore brought into Westminster School, where Mr. George Herbert then, and often after, made such answers to them, and such reflections on him and his kirk, as might unbeguile any man that was not too deeply pre-engaged in such a quarrel.

But to return to Mr. Melvin at Hampton Court conference; he there appeared to be a man of an unruly wit, of a strange confidence, of so furious a zeal and of so ungoverned passions, that his insolence to the king and others at this conference lost him both his rectorship of St. Andrews and his liberty too; for his former verses and his present reproaches there used against the Church and State caused him to be committed prisoner to the Tower of London, where he remained very angry for three years. . . .

And, in order to my third and last observation of his great abilities, it will be needful to declare that about this time King James came very often to hunt at Newmarket and Royston, and was almost as often invited to Cambridge, where his entertainment was comedies suited to his pleasant humor, and where Mr. George Herbert was to welcome him with gratulations and the applauses of an orator, which he always performed so well that he still grew more into the king's favor, insomuch that he had a particular appointment to attend his Majesty at Royston; where, after a discourse with him, his Majesty declared to his kinsman, the Earl of Pembroke, "That he found the orator's learning and wisdom much above his age or wit." The year following, the king appointed to end his progress at Cambridge, and to stay there certain days; at which time he was attended by the great secretary of nature and all learning, Sir Francis Bacon (Lord Verulam), and by the ever memorable and learned Doctor Andrews, Bishop of Winchester, both which did at that time begin a desired friendship with our orator. Upon whom the first put such a value on his judgment, that he usually desired his approbation before he would expose any of his books to be printed, and thought him so worthy of his friendship, that having translated many of the prophet David's psalms into English verse, he made George Herbert his patron, by a public dedication of them to him, as the best judge of divine poetry. And for the learned bishop, it is observable, that at that time there fell to be a modest debate betwixt them two about predestination and sanctity of life; of both which the orator did, not long after, send the bishop some safe and useful aphorisms in a long letter written in Greek, which letter was so remarkable for the language and reason of it, that after the reading it the bishop put it into his bosom, and did often show it to many scholars both of this and foreign nations, but did always return it back to the place where he first lodged it, and continued it so near his heart till the last day of his life.

To these I might add the long and entire friendship betwixt him and Sir Henry Wotton and Dr. Donne, but I have promised to contract myself, and shall therefore only add one testimony to what is also mentioned in the Life of Dr. Donne—namely, that a little before his death he caused many seals to be made, and in them to be engraven the figure of Christ crucified on an anchor—the emblem of hope—and of which Dr. Donne would often say, *"Crux mihi anchora."* These seals he gave or sent to most of those friends on which he put a value; and at Mr. Herbert's death these verses were found wrapt up with that seal which was by the Doctor given to him:

> When my dear friend could write no more,
> He gave this seal, and so gave o'er.
>
> When winds and waves rise highest, I am sure;
> This anchor keeps my faith, that me secure.

At this time of being orator he had learnt to understand the Italian, Spanish, and French tongues very perfectly, hoping that as his predecessors so he might in time attain the place of a Secretary of State, he being at that time very high in the king's favor, and not meanly valued and loved by the most eminent and most powerful of the Court nobility. This, and the love of a Court conversation, mixed with a laudable ambition to be something more than he then was, drew him often from Cambridge to attend the king wheresoever the Court was, who then gave him a sinecure which fell into his Majesty's disposal, I think, by the death of the Bishop of St. Asaph. It was the same that Queen Elizabeth had formerly given to her favorite, Sir Philip Sidney, and valued to be worth £120 per annum. With this, and his annuity, and the advantage of his college, and of his oratorship, he enjoyed his genteel humor for clothes and Court-like company,

and seldom looked towards Cambridge unless the king were there, but then he never failed, and at other times left the manage of his orator's place to his learned friend Mr. Herbert Thorndike, who is now prebendary of Westminster.

I may not omit to tell that he had often designed to leave the university and decline all study, which he thought did impair his health; for he had a body apt to a consumption, and to fevers, and other infirmities, which he judged were increased by his studies, for he would often say, "He had too thoughtful a wit; a wit like a penknife in too narrow a sheath, too sharp for his body." But his mother would by no means allow him to leave the university or to travel, and though he inclined very much to both, yet he would by no means satisfy his own desires at so dear a rate as to prove an undutiful son to so affectionate a mother, but did always submit to her wisdom. And what I have now said may partly appear in a copy of verses in his printed poems; it is one of those that bear the title of "Affliction"; and it appears to be a pious reflection on God's providence, and some passages of his life, in which he says—

> Whereas my birth and spirit rather took
> The way that takes the town;
> Thou didst betray me to a lingering book,
> And wrap me in a gown.
> I was entangled in a world of strife,
> Before I had the power to change my life.
>
> Yet, for I threatened oft the siege to raise,
> Not simpering all mine age;
> Thou often didst with academic praise
> Melt and dissolve my rage.
> I took Thy sweetened pill, till I came near,
> I could not go away, nor persevere.
>
> Yet lest perchance, I should too happy be
> In my unhappiness,
> Turning my purge to food, Thou throwest me
> Into more sicknesses.
> Thus doth Thy power cross-bias me, not making
> Thine own gift good, yet me from my ways taking.
>
> Now I am here, what Thou wilt do with me
> None of my books will show:
> I read, and sigh, and wish I were a tree;
> For then sure I should grow
> To fruit or shade: at least some bird would trust
> Her household to me, and I should be just.

Yet, though Thou troublest me, I must be meek,
                In weakness must be stout;
Well, I will change my service, and go seek
                Some other master out.
Ah! my dear God! though I am clean forgot,
Let me not love Thee, if I love Thee not.

                                    G. H.

In this time of Mr. Herbert's attendance and expectation of some good occasion to remove from Cambridge to Court, God, in whom there is an unseen chain of causes, did in a short time put an end to the lives of two of his most obliging and most powerful friends, Lodowick Duke of Richmond, and James Marquis of Hamilton; and not long after him King James died also, and with them all Mr. Herbert's Court hopes, so that he presently betook himself to a retreat from London, to a friend in Kent, where he lived very privately, and was such a lover of solitariness as was judged to impair his health more than his study had done. In this time of retirement he had many conflicts with himself whether he should return to the painted pleasures of a Court life or betake himself to a study of divinity, and enter into sacred Orders, to which his dear mother had often persuaded him. These were such conflicts as they only can know that have endured them, for ambitious desires and the outward glory of this world are not easily laid aside; but at last God inclined him to put on a resolution to serve at His altar.

He did at his return to London acquaint a Court friend with his resolution to enter into sacred Orders, who persuaded him to alter it, as too mean an employment, and too much below his birth, and the excellent abilities and endowments of his mind. To whom he replied, "It hath been formerly adjudged that the domestic servants of the King of Heaven should be of the noblest families on earth; and though the iniquity of the late times have made clergymen meanly valued, and the sacred name of priest contemptible, yet I will labor to make it honorable, by consecrating all my learning, and all my poor abilities, to advance the glory of that God that gave them; knowing that I can never do too much for Him that hath done so much for me as to make me a Christian. And I will labor to be like my Saviour, by making humility lovely in the eyes of all men, and by following the merciful and meek example of my dear Jesus."

This was then his resolution, and the God of constancy, Who intended him for a great example of virtue, continued him in it; for within that year he was made deacon, but the day when or by whom I cannot learn; but that he was about that time made deacon is most certain; for I find by the records of Lincoln that he was made prebendary of Layton Ecclesia, in the diocese of Lincoln, July 15, 1626; and that this prebend was given him by John, then Lord Bishop of that See. And now he had a fit occasion to show that piety and bounty that was derived from his generous mother, and his other memorable ancestors, and the occasion was this.

This Layton Ecclesia is a village near to Spalden, in the county of Huntingdon, and the greatest part of the parish church was fallen down, and that of it which stood was so decayed, so little, and so useless, that the parishioners could not meet to perform their duty to God in public prayer and praises; and thus it had been for almost twenty years, in which time there had been some faint endeavors for a public collection to enable the parishioners to rebuild it, but with no success till Mr. Herbert undertook it; and he by his own and the contribution of many of his kindred and other noble friends, undertook the re-edification of it, and made it so much his whole business, that he became restless till he saw it finished as it now stands: being for the workmanship a costly mosaic, for the form an exact cross, and for the decency and beauty, I am assured, it is the most remarkable parish church that this nation affords. He lived to see it so wainscoted as to be exceeded by none; and, by his order, the reading pew and pulpit were a little distant from each other, and both of an equal height; for he would often say, "They should neither have a precedency or priority of the other; but that prayer and preaching, being equally useful, might agree like brethren, and have an equal honor and estimation."

Before I proceed farther, I must look back to the time of Mr. Herbert's being made prebendary, and tell the reader, that not long after, his mother being informed of his intentions to rebuild that church, and apprehending the great trouble and charge that he was likely to draw upon himself, his relations and friends, before it could be finished, sent for him from London to Chelsea (where she then dwelt), and at his coming said, "George, I sent for you to persuade you to commit simony, by giving your patron as good a gift as he has given you; namely, that you give him back his prebend; for, George, it is not for your weak body and empty purse to undertake to build churches." Of which he desired he might have a day's time to consider, and then make her an answer; and at his return to her the next day, when he had first desired her blessing, and she given it him, his next request was, "That she would, at the age of thirty-three years, allow him to become an undutiful son; for he had made a vow to God, that if he were able, he would rebuild that church"; and then showed her such reasons for his resolution that she presently subscribed to be one of his benefactors, and undertook to solicit William Earl of Pembroke to become another, who subscribed for fifty pounds; and not long after, by a witty and persuasive letter from Mr. Herbert, made it fifty pounds more. And in this nomination of some of his benefactors, James Duke of Lennox, and his brother Sir Henry Herbert, ought to be remembered; as also the bounty of Mr. Nicholas Ferrar, and Mr. Arthur Woodnot; the one a gentleman in the neighborhood of Layton, and the other a goldsmith in Foster Lane, London, ought not to be forgotten, for the memory of such men ought to outlive their lives. Of Mr. Ferrar I shall hereafter give an account in a more seasonable place; but before I proceed farther, I will give this short account of Mr. Arthur Woodnot. . . .

About the year 1629, and the thirty-fourth of his age, Mr. Herbert was seized with a sharp quotidian ague, and thought to remove it by the change of air: to which end he went to Woodford in Essex, but thither more chiefly to enjoy the company of his beloved brother, Sir Henry Herbert, and other friends then of that family. In his house he remained about twelve months, and there became his own physician, and cured himself of his ague by forbearing drink and not eating any meat—no, not mutton, nor a hen or pigeon, unless they were salted; and by such a constant diet he removed his ague, but with inconveniences that were worse, for he brought upon himself a disposition to rheums and other weaknesses, and a supposed consumption. And it is to be noted that in the sharpest of his extreme fits he would often say, "Lord, abate my great affliction, or increase my patience, but, Lord, I repine not; I am dumb, Lord, before Thee, because Thou doest it." By which, and a sanctified submission to the will of God, he showed he was inclinable to bear the sweet yoke of Christian discipline, both then and in the latter part of his life, of which there will be many true testimonies.

And now his care was to recover from his consumption by a change from Woodford into such an air as was most proper to that end: and his remove was to Dauntsey in Wiltshire, a noble house which stands in a choice air; the owner of it then was the Lord Danvers, Earl of Danby, who loved Mr. Herbert so very much that he allowed him such an apartment in it as might best suit with his accommodation and liking. And in this place, by a spare diet, declining all perplexing studies, moderate exercise and a cheerful conversation, his health was apparently improved to a good degree of strength and cheerfulness. And then he declared his resolution both to marry and to enter into the sacred Orders of priesthood. These had long been the desire of his mother and his other relations; but she lived not to see either, for she died in the year 1627. And though he was disobedient to her about Layton Church, yet in conformity to her will he kept his orator's place till after her death, and then presently declined it: and the more willingly that he might be succeeded by his friend Robert Creighton, who now is Dr. Creighton, and the worthy Bishop of Wells.

I shall now proceed to his marriage, in order to which it will be convenient that I first give the reader a short view of his person, and then an account of his wife, and of some circumstances concerning both.

He was for his person of a stature inclining towards tallness, his body was very straight, and so far from being encumbered with too much flesh, that he was lean to an extremity. His aspect was cheerful, and his speech and motion did both declare him a gentleman; for they were all so meek and obliging that they purchased love and respect from all that knew him.

These, and his other visible virtues, begot him much love from a gentleman of a noble fortune, and a near kinsman to his friend the Earl of Danby—namely, from Mr. Charles Danvers of Bainton, in the county of Wilts, Esq.; this Mr. Danvers having known him long and familiarly, did so much affect him that he often and publicly declared a desire that Mr. Herbert would marry any of his nine daughters (for he had so many), but rather his daughter Jane than any other, because Jane was his beloved daughter. And he had often said the same to Mr. Herbert himself, and that if he could like her for a wife, and she him for a husband, Jane should have a double blessing; and Mr. Danvers had so often said the like to Jane, and so much commended Mr. Herbert to her, that Jane became so much a platonic as to fall in love with Mr. Herbert unseen.

This was a fair preparation for a marriage, but alas! her father died before Mr. Herbert's retirement to Dauntsey; yet some friends to both parties procured their meeting, at which time a mutual affection entered into both their hearts, as a conqueror enters into a surprised city; and love having got such possession, governed and made there such laws and resolutions as neither party was able to resist, insomuch that she changed her name into Herbert the third day after this first interview.

This haste might in others be thought a love-frenzy, or worse; but it was not, for they had wooed so like princes, as to have select proxies, such as were true friends to both parties, such as well understood Mr. Herbert's and her temper of mind, and also their estates, so well before this interview, that the suddenness was justifiable by the strictest rules of prudence; and the more because it proved so happy to both parties; for the eternal Lover of Mankind made them happy in each other's mutual and equal affections and compliance; indeed so happy, that there never was any opposition betwixt them, unless it were a contest which should most incline to a compliance with the other's desires. And though this begot, and continued in them, such a mutual love and joy and content as was no way defective; yet this mutual content and love and joy did receive a daily augmentation by such daily obligingness to each other, as still added such new affluences to the former fullness of these divine souls as was only improvable in Heaven, where they now enjoy it.

About three months after this marriage, Dr. Curle, who was then rector of Bemerton in Wiltshire, was made Bishop of Bath and Wells, and not long after translated to Winchester, and by that means the presentation of a clerk to Bemerton did not fall to the Earl of Pembroke (who was the undoubted patron of it), but to the king, by reason of Dr. Curle's advancement; but Philip, then Earl of Pembroke (for William was lately dead), requested the king to bestow it upon his kinsman George Herbert; and the king said, "Most willingly to Mr. Herbert, if it be worth his acceptance." And the earl as willingly and suddenly sent it to him without seeking; but though Mr. Herbert had formerly put on a resolution for the clergy, yet at receiving this presentation, the apprehension of the last great account that he was to make for the cure of so many souls made him fast and pray often, and consider for not less than a month: in which time he had some resolutions to decline both the priesthood and that living. And in this time of considering, "he endured," as he would often say, "such spiritual conflicts as none can think but only those that have endured them."

In the midst of these conflicts, his old and dear friend Mr. Arthur Woodnot took a journey to salute him at Bainton (where he then was with his wife's friends and relations), and was joyful to be an eye-witness of his health and happy marriage. And after they had rejoiced together some few days they took a journey to Wilton, the famous seat of the Earls of Pembroke, at which time the king, the earl, and the whole Court were there or at Salisbury, which is near to it. And at this time Mr. Herbert presented his thanks to the earl for his presentation to Bemerton, but had not yet resolved to accept it, and told him the reason why; but that night the earl acquainted Dr. Laud, then Bishop of London, and after Archbishop of Canterbury, with his kinsman's irresolution. And the bishop did the next day so convince Mr. Herbert that the refusal of it was a sin, that a tailor was sent for to come speedily from Salisbury to Wilton to take measure and make him canonical clothes against next day; which the tailor did: and Mr. Herbert being so habited, went with his presentation to the learned Dr. Davenant, who was then Bishop of Salisbury, and he gave him institution immediately (for Mr. Herbert had been made deacon some years before); and he was also the same day (which was April 26, 1630) inducted into the good, and more pleasant than healthful, parsonage of Bemerton, which is a mile from Salisbury.

I have now brought him to the parsonage of Bemerton, and to the thirty-sixth year of his age, and must stop here and bespeak the reader to prepare for an almost incredible story of the great sanctity of the short remainder of his holy life; a life so full of charity, humility, and all Christian virtues, that it deserves the eloquence of St. Chrysostom to commend and declare it; a life, that if it were related by a pen like his, there would then be no need for this age to look back into times past for the examples of primitive piety; for they might be all found in the life of George Herbert. But now, alas! who is fit to undertake it? I confess I am not; and am not pleased with myself that I must; and profess myself amazed when I consider how few of the clergy lived like him then, and how many live so unlike him now; but it becomes not me to censure: my design is rather to assure the reader that I have used very great diligence to inform myself, that I might inform him of the truth of what follows; and though I cannot adorn it with eloquence, yet I will do it with sincerity.

When at his induction he was shut into Bemerton Church, being left there alone to toll the bell (as the law requires him), he stayed so much longer than an ordinary time before he returned to those friends that stayed expecting him at the church door, that his friend Mr. Woodnot looked in at the church window, and saw him lie prostrate on the ground before the altar; at which time and place (as he after told Mr. Woodnot) he set some rules to himself for the future manage of his life, and then and there made a vow to labor to keep them.

And the same night that he had his induction, he said to Mr. Woodnot: "I now look back upon my aspiring thoughts, and think myself more happy than if I had attained what then I so ambitiously thirsted for; and I can now behold the Court with an impartial eye, and see plainly that it is made up of fraud and titles and flattery, and many other such empty, imaginary, painted pleasures; pleasures that are so empty as not to satisfy when they are enjoyed. But in God and His service is a fullness of all joy and pleasure, and no satiety. And I will now use all my endeavors to bring my relations and dependents to a love and reliance on Him, who never fails those that trust Him. But above all I will be sure to live well, because the virtuous life of a clergyman is the most powerful eloquence to persuade all that see it to reverence and love, and at least to desire to live like him. And this I will do, because I know we live in an age that hath more need of good examples than precepts. And I beseech that God, who hath honored me so much as to call me to serve Him at His altar, that as by His special grace He hath put into my heart these good desires and resolutions; so He will, by His assisting grace, give me ghostly strength to bring the same to good effect. And I beseech Him that my humble and charitable life may so win upon others, as to bring glory to my Jesus, whom I have this day taken to be my Master and Governor; and I am so proud of His service, that I will always observe, and obey, and do His will, and always call Him Jesus my Master, and I will always contemn my birth or any title or dignity that can be conferred upon me, when I shall compare them with my title of being a priest, and serving at the altar of Jesus my Master."

And that he did so may appear in many parts of his book of Sacred Poems; especially in that which he calls "The Odor." In which he seems to rejoice in the thoughts of that word Jesus, and say, that the adding these words, my Master, to it, and the often repetition of them seemed to perfume his mind, and leave an Oriental fragrancy in his very breath. And for his unforced choice to serve at God's altar, he seems in another place of his poems ("The Pearl," Matt. xiii.) to rejoice and say—He knew the ways of learning,

knew what Nature does willingly, and what, when it is forced by fire, knew the ways of honor, and when glory inclines the soul to noble expressions; knew the Court, knew the ways of pleasure, of love, of wit, of music, and upon what terms he declined all these for the service of his Master Jesus, and then concludes, saying:

> That through these labyrinths, not my groveling wit,
> But Thy silk-twist, let down from Heaven to me,
> Did both conduct, and teach me, how by it
>   To climb to Thee.

The third day after he was made rector of Bemerton, and had changed his sword and silk clothes into a canonical coat, he returned so habited with his friend Mr. Woodnot to Bainton; and immediately after he had seen and saluted his wife, he said to her: "You are now a minister's wife, and must now so far forget your father's house as not to claim a precedence of any of your parishioners, for you are to know that a priest's wife can challenge no precedence or place, but that which she purchases by her obliging humility; and I am sure places so purchased do best become them. And let me tell you, that I am so good a herald as to assure you that this is truth." And she was so meek a wife as to assure him it was no vexing news to her, and that he should see her observe it with a cheerful willingness. And, indeed, her unforced humility, that humility that was in her so original as to be born with her, made her so happy as to do so, and her doing so begot her an unfeigned love and a serviceable respect from all that conversed with her; and this love followed her in all places as inseparably as shadows follow substances in sunshine.

It was not many days before he returned back to Bemerton to view the church and repair the chancel, and indeed to rebuild almost three parts of his house, which was fallen down or decayed by reason of his predecessors living at a better parsonage-house— namely, at Minal, sixteen or twenty miles from this place. At which time of Mr. Herbert's coming alone to Bemerton, there came to him a poor old woman with an intent to acquaint him with her necessitous condition, as also with some troubles of her mind; but after she had spoken some few words to him she was surprised with a fear, and that begot a shortness of breath, so that her spirits and speech failed her; which he perceiving, did so compassionate her, and was so humble that he took her by the hand, and said, "Speak, good mother, be not afraid to speak to me, for I am a man that will hear you with patience, and will relieve your necessities too if I be able, and this I will do willingly; and therefore, mother, be not afraid to acquaint me with what you desire." After which comfortable speech he again took her by the hand, made her sit down by him, and understanding she was of his parish, he told her, "He would be acquainted with her, and take her into his care." And having with patience heard and understood her wants—and it is some relief for a poor body to be but heard with patience—he, like a Christian clergyman, comforted her by his meek behavior and counsel; but because that cost him nothing he relieved her with money too, and so sent her home with a cheerful heart, praising God and praying for him. Thus worthy, and (like David's blessed man) thus lowly was Mr. George Herbert in his own eyes, and thus lovely in the eyes of others.

At his return that night to his wife at Bainton, he gave her an account of the passages betwixt him and the poor woman, with which she was so affected that she went next day to Salisbury, and there bought a pair of blankets, and sent them as a token of her love to the poor woman, and with them a message, "That she would see and be acquainted with her when her house was built at Bemerton."

There be many such passages both of him and his wife, of which some few will be related; but I shall first tell that he hasted to get the parish church repaired; then to beautify the chapel (which stands near his house), and that at his own great charge. He then proceeded to rebuild the greatest part of the parsonage-house, which he did also very completely and at his own charge; and having done this good work, he caused these verses to be writ upon or engraven in the mantel of the chimney in his hall:

TO MY SUCCESSOR

If thou chance for to find
A new house to thy mind,
   And build without thy cost:
Be good to the poor,
As God gives thee store,
   And then my labor's not lost.

We will now, by the reader's favor, suppose him fixed at Bemerton, and grant him to have seen the church repaired, and the chapel belonging to it very decently adorned at his own great charge (which is a real truth); and having now fixed him there, I shall proceed to give an account of the rest of his behavior both to his parishioners, and those many others that knew and conversed with him.

Doubtless Mr. Herbert had considered and given rules to himself for his Christian carriage both to God and man before he entered into Holy Orders. And it is not unlike but that he renewed those resolutions at his prostration before the holy altar, at his induction into the church of Bemerton; but as yet he was but a deacon, and therefore longed for the next Ember-week, that he might be ordained priest, and made capable of administering both the Sacraments. At which time the Rev. Dr. Humphrey Henchman, now Lord Bishop of London (who does not mention him but with some veneration for his life and excellent learning), tells me, "He laid his hand on Mr. Herbert's head, and alas! within less than three years, lent his shoulder to carry his dear friend to his grave."

And that Mr. Herbert might the better preserve those holy rules which such a priest as he intended to be ought to observe, and that time might not insensibly blot them out of his memory, but that the next year might show him his variations from this year's resolutions; he, therefore, did set down his rules, then resolved upon, in that order as the world now sees them printed in a little book called "The Country Parson," in which some of his rules are:

The Parson's Knowledge.
The Parson on Sundays.
The Parson Praying.
The Parson Preaching.
The Parson's Charity.
The Parson Comforting the Sick.
The Parson Arguing.
The Parson Condescending.
The Parson in his Journey.
The Parson in his Mirth.
The Parson with his Churchwardens.
The Parson Blessing the People.

And his behavior towards God and man may be said to be a practical comment on these and the other holy rules set down in that useful book: a book so full of plain, prudent, and useful rules, that that country parson that can spare twelve pence, and yet wants it, is scarce excusable, because it will both direct him what he ought to do, and convince him for not having done it.

At the death of Mr. Herbert, this book fell into the hands of his friend Mr. Woodnot, and he commended it into the trusty hands of Mr. Barnabas Oley, who published it with a most conscientious and excellent preface, from which I have had some of those truths that are related in this Life of Mr. Herbert. The text for his first sermon was taken out of Solomon's Proverbs, and the words were, "Keep thy heart with all diligence." In which first sermon he gave his parishioners many necessary, holy, safe rules for the discharge of a good conscience both to God and man; and delivered his sermon after a most florid manner, both with great learning and eloquence. But at the close of this sermon told them "that should not be his constant way of preaching, for since Almighty God does not intend to lead men to heaven by hard questions, he would not therefore fill their heads with unnecessary notions; but that for their sakes, his language and his expressions should be more plain and practical in his future sermons." And he then made it his humble request, "that they would be constant to the afternoon's service and catechizing," and showed them convincing reasons why he desired it; and his obliging example and persuasions brought them to a willing conformity with his desires.

The texts for all his future sermons, which God knows were not many, were constantly taken out of the Gospel for the day; and he did as constantly declare why the Church did appoint that portion of Scripture to be that day read, and in what manner the Collect for every Sunday does refer to the Gospel or to the Epistle then read to them; and that they might pray with understanding, he did usually take occasion to explain, not only the Collect for every particular Sunday, but the reasons of all the other Collects and responses in our Church service, and made it appear to them that the whole service of the Church was a reasonable and therefore an acceptable sacrifice to God; as, namely, that we begin with confession of ourselves to be vile, miserable sinners, and that we begin so, because till we have confessed ourselves to be such, we are not capable of that mercy which we acknowledge we need and pray for; but having in the prayer of our Lord begged pardon for those sins which we have confessed, and hoping, that as the priest hath declared our absolution, so by our public confession and real repentance we have obtained that pardon; then we dare and do proceed to beg of the Lord to open our lips that our mouths may show forth His praise, for till then we are neither able nor worthy to praise Him. But this being supposed, we are then fit to say, Glory be to the Father, and to the Son, and to the Holy Ghost; and fit to proceed to a further service of

our God in the Collects, and psalms, and lauds, that follow in the service. . . .

And by this account of his diligence to make his parishioners understand what they prayed, and why they praised and adored their Creator, I hope I shall the more easily obtain the reader's belief to the following account of Mr. Herbert's own practice, which was to appear constantly with his wife and three nieces (the daughters of a deceased sister) and his whole family twice every day at the Church prayers, in the chapel which does almost join to his parsonage-house. And for the time of his appearing, it was strictly at the canonical hours of ten and four; and then and there he lifted up pure and charitable hands to God in the midst of the congregation. And he would joy to have spent that time in that place where the honor of his Master Jesus dwelleth; and there, by that inward devotion which he testified constantly by a humble behavior and visible adoration, he, like Joshua, brought not only his own household thus to serve the Lord, but brought most of his parishioners and many gentlemen in the neighborhood constantly to make a part of his congregation twice a day; and some of the meaner sort of his parish did so love and reverence Mr. Herbert, that they would let their plough rest when Mr. Herbert's saint's-bell rung to prayers, that they might also offer their devotions to God with him, and would then return back to their plough. And his most holy life was such, that it begot such reverence to God and to him, that they thought themselves the happier when they carried Mr. Herbert's blessing back with them to their labor. Thus powerful was his reason and example to persuade others to a practical piety and devotion.

And his constant public prayers did never make him to neglect his own private devotions, nor those prayers that he thought himself bound to perform with his family, which always were a set form and not long; and he did always conclude them with that Collect which the Church hath appointed for the day or week. Thus he made every day's sanctity a step towards that kingdom where impurity cannot enter.

His chiefest recreation was music, in which heavenly art he was a most excellent master, and did himself compose many divine hymns and anthems, which he set and sung to his lute or viol; and though he was a lover of retiredness, yet his love to music was such, that he went usually twice every week on certain appointed days to the cathedral church in Salisbury; and at his return would say, "That his time spent in prayer and cathedral music elevated his soul, and was his heaven upon earth." But before his return thence to Bemerton, he would usually sing and play his part at an appointed private music-meeting; and, to justify this practice, he would often say, "Religion does not banish mirth, but only moderates and sets rules to it."

And as his desire to enjoy his heaven upon earth drew him twice every week to Salisbury, so his walks thither were the occasion of many happy accidents to others, of which I will mention some few.

In one of his walks to Salisbury, he overtook a gentleman that is still living in that city, and in their walk together Mr. Herbert took a fair occasion to talk with him, and humbly begged to be excused if he asked him some account of his faith, and said, "I do this, the rather because though you are not of my parish, yet I receive tithe from you by the hand of your tenant; and, sir, I am the bolder to do it, because I know there be some sermon-hearers that be like those fishes that always live in salt water, and yet are always fresh." After which expression Mr. Herbert asked him some needful questions, and having received his answer, gave him such rules for the trial of his sincerity, and for a practical piety, and in so loving and meek a manner, that the gentleman did so fall in love with him and his discourse, that he would often contrive to meet him in his walk to Salisbury, or to attend him back to Bemerton, and still mentions the name of Mr. George Herbert with veneration, and still praiseth God for the occasion of knowing him.

In another of his Salisbury walks, he met with a neighbor minister, and after some friendly discourse betwixt them, and some condolement for the decay of piety, and too general contempt of the clergy, Mr. Herbert took occasion to say, "One cure for these distempers would be for the clergy themselves to keep the Ember-weeks strictly, and beg of their parishioners to join with them in fasting and prayers for a more religious clergy.

"And another cure would be for themselves to restore the great and neglected duty of catechizing, on which the salvation of so many of the poor and ignorant lay people does depend, but principally that the clergy themselves would be sure to live unblamably; and that the dignified clergy especially, which preach temperance, would avoid surfeiting and take all occasions to express a visible humility and charity in their lives, for this would force a love and an imitation, and an unfeigned reverence from all that knew them to be such." (And for proof of this, we need no other testimony than the life and death of Dr. Lake, late Bishop of

Bath and Wells.) "This," said Mr. Herbert, "would be a cure for the wickedness and growing atheism of our age. And, my dear brother, till this be done by us, and done in earnest, let no man expect a reformation of the manners of the laity; for it is not learning, but this, this only, that must do it, and till then the fault must lie at our own doors."

In another walk to Salisbury he saw a poor man with a poorer horse, that was fallen under his load; they were both in distress, and needed present help, which Mr. Herbert perceiving, put off his canonical coat, and helped the poor man to unload, and after, to load his horse. The poor man blessed him for it, and he blessed the poor man, and was so like the good Samaritan, that he gave him money to refresh both himself and his horse, and told him, "That if he loved himself, he should be merciful to his beast." Thus he left the poor man, and at his coming to his musical friends at Salisbury, they began to wonder that Mr. George Herbert, who used to be so trim and clean, came into that company so soiled and discomposed; but he told them the occasion; and when one of the company told him "he had disparaged himself by so dirty an employment," his answer was, "That the thought of what he had done would prove music to him at midnight, and that the omission of it would have upbraided and made discord in his conscience whensoever he should pass by that place; for if I be bound to pray for all that be in distress, I am sure that I am bound, so far as it is in my power, to practice what I pray for. And though I do not wish for the like occasion every day, yet let me tell you, I would not willingly pass one day of my life without comforting a sad soul, or showing mercy, and I praise God for this occasion. And now let us tune our instruments."

Thus as our blessed Saviour, after His resurrection, did take occasion to interpret the Scriptures to Cleopas and that other disciple which He met with, and accompanied, in their journey to Emmaus; so Mr. Herbert, in his path towards heaven, did daily take any fair occasion to instruct the ignorant, or comfort any that were in affliction; and did always confirm his precepts, by showing humility and mercy, and ministering grace to the hearers.

And he was most happy in his wife's unforced compliance with his acts of charity, whom he made his almoner, and paid constantly into her hand a tenth penny of what money he received for tithe, and gave her power to dispose that to the poor of his parish, and with it a power to dispose a tenth part of the corn that came yearly into his barn; which trust she did most faithfully perform, and would often offer to him an account of her stewardship, and as often beg an enlargement of his bounty; for she rejoiced in the employment; and this was usually laid out by her in blankets and shoes for some such poor people as she knew to stand in most need of them. This as to her charity. And for his own, he set no limits to it, nor did ever turn his face from any that he saw in want, but would relieve them, especially his poor neighbors; to the meanest of whose houses he would go and inform himself of their wants, and relieve them cheerfully if they were in distress, and would always praise God, as much for being willing, as for being able to do it. And when he was advised by a friend to be more frugal, because he might have children, his answer was, "He would not see the danger of want so far off; but being the Scripture does so commend charity as to tell us that charity is the top of Christian virtues, the covering of sins, the fulfilling of the law, the life of faith; and that charity hath a promise of the blessings of this life, and of a reward in that life which is to come; being these and more excellent things are in Scripture spoken of thee, O Charity! and that being all my tithes and Church-dues are a deodate from thee, O my God, make me, O my God, so far to trust Thy promise, as to return them back to Thee! and by Thy grace I will do so, in distributing them to any of Thy poor members that are in distress, or do but bear the image of Jesus my Master. Sir," said he to his friend, "my wife hath a competent maintenance secured her after my death, and therefore as this is my prayer, so this my resolution shall, by God's grace, be unalterable."

This may be some account of the excellences of the active part of his life; and thus he continued till a consumption so weakened him as to confine him to his house, or to the chapel, which does almost join to it; in which he continued to read prayers constantly twice every day, though he were very weak; in one of which times of his reading his wife observed him to read in pain, and told him so, and that it wasted his spirits, and weakened him; and he confessed it did, but said, "His life could not be better spent than in the service of his Master Jesus, who had done and suffered so much for him; but," said he, "I will not be willful; for though my spirit be willing, yet I find my flesh is weak; and therefore Mr. Bostock shall be appointed to read prayers for me to-morrow, and I will now be only a hearer of them, till this mortal shall put on immor-

tality." And Mr. Bostock did the next day undertake and continue this happy employment till Mr. Herbert's death. This Mr. Bostock was a learned and virtuous man, an old friend of Mr. Herbert's, and then his curate to the church of Fulston, which is a mile from Bemerton, to which church Bemerton is but a chapel of ease. And this Mr. Bostock did also constantly supply the Church service for Mr. Herbert in that chapel when the music-meeting at Salisbury caused his absence from it.

About one month before his death, his friend Mr. Ferrar (for an account of whom I am by promise indebted to the reader, and intend to make him sudden payment), hearing of Mr. Herbert's sickness, sent Mr. Edmund Duncon (who is now rector of Fryer Barnet, in the county of Middlesex) from his house of Gidden Hall, which is near to Huntingdon, to see Mr. Herbert, and to assure him he wanted not his daily prayers for his recovery, and Mr. Duncon was to return back to Gidden with an account of Mr. Herbert's condition. Mr. Duncon found him weak, and at that time lying on his bed, or on a pallet; but at his seeing Mr. Duncon he raised himself vigorously, saluted him, and with some earnestness inquired the health of his brother Ferrar; of which Mr. Duncon satisfied him; and after some discourse of Mr. Ferrar's holy life, and the manner of his constant serving God, he said to Mr. Duncon: "Sir, I see by your habit that you are a priest, and I desire you to pray with me"; which being granted, Mr. Duncon asked him, "What prayers?" to which Mr. Herbert's answer was, "O sir, the prayers of my mother the Church of England; no other prayers are equal to them; but at this time I beg of you to pray only the Litany, for I am weak and faint"; and Mr. Duncon did so. After which, and some other discourse of Mr. Ferrar, Mrs. Herbert provided Mr. Duncon a plain supper and a clean lodging, and he betook himself to rest. This Mr. Duncon tells me; and tells me that at his first view of Mr. Herbert he saw majesty and humility so reconciled in his looks and behavior, as begot in him an awful reverence for his person, and says, "his discourse was so pious, and his motion so genteel and meek, that after almost forty years yet they remain still fresh in his memory."

The next morning Mr. Duncon left him, and betook himself a journey to Bath, but with a promise to return back to him within five days, and he did so; but before I shall say anything of what discourse then fell betwixt them two, I will pay my promised account of Mr. Ferrar.

Mr. Nicholas Ferrar (who got the reputation of being called St. Nicholas at the age of six years) was born in London, and doubtless had good education in his youth, but certainly was at an early age made Fellow of Clare Hall in Cambridge, where he continued to be eminent for his piety, temperance and learning. About the twenty-sixth year of his age he betook himself to travel, in which he added to his Latin and Greek a perfect knowledge of all the languages spoken in the western parts of our Christian world, and understood well the principles of their religion and of their manner, and the reasons of their worship. In this his travel he met with many persuasions to come into a communion with that Church which calls itself Catholic; but he returned from his travels as he went, eminent for his obedience to his mother, the Church of England. In his absence from England Mr. Ferrar's father (who was a merchant) allowed him a liberal maintenance, and, not long after his return into England, Mr. Ferrar had, by the death of his father or an elder brother, or both, an estate left him, that enabled him to purchase land to the value of four or five hundred pounds a year, the greatest part of which land was at Little Gidden [1] four or six miles from Huntingdon, and about eighteen from Cambridge; which place he chose for the privacy of it, and for the Hall, which had the parish church or chapel belonging and adjoining near to it; for Mr. Ferrar having seen the manners and vanities of the world, and found them to be, as Mr. Herbert says, a nothing between two dishes, did so contemn it, that he resolved to spend the remainder of his life in mortifications, and in devotion and charity, and to be always prepared for death; and his life was spent thus:

He and his family, which were like a little college, and about thirty in number, did most of them keep Lent and all Ember-weeks strictly, both in fasting and using all those mortifications and prayers that the Church hath appointed to be then used; and he and they did the like constantly on Fridays, and on the Vigils or Eves appointed to be fasted before the Saints' days; and this frugality and abstinence turned to the relief of the poor; but this was but a part of his charity, none but God and he knew the rest.

This family, which I have said to be in number about thirty, were a part of them his kindred; and the rest chosen to be of a temper fit to be moulded into a devout life; and all of them were for their dispositions

1 This is the "Little Gidding" which supplies the fourth of T. S. Eliot's Four Quartets (1943) with its title.

serviceable and quiet and humble, and free from scandal. Having thus fitted himself for his family, he did, about the year 1630, betake himself to a constant and methodical service of God, and it was in this manner: —He, being accompanied with most of his family, did himself use to read the common prayers (for he was a deacon) every day at the appointed hours of ten and four, in the parish church, which was very near his house, and which he had both repaired and adorned; for it was fallen into a great ruin, by reason of a depopulation of the village, before Mr. Ferrar bought the manor; and he did also constantly read the matins every morning at the hour of six, either in the church, or in an oratory which was within his own house; and many of the family did there continue with him after the prayers were ended, and there they spent some hours in singing hymns or anthems, sometimes in the church, and often to an organ in the oratory. And there they sometimes betook themselves to meditate, or to pray privately, or to read a part of the New Testament to themselves, or to continue their praying or reading the Psalms; and, in case the Psalms were not always read in the day, then Mr. Ferrar and others of the congregation did at night, at the ring of a watch-bell, repair to the church or oratory, and there betake themselves to prayers and lauding God, and reading the Psalms that had not been read in the day; and when these or any part of the congregation grew weary or faint, the watch-bell was rung, sometimes before and sometimes after midnight, and then another part of the family rose, and maintained the watch, sometimes by praying or singing lauds to God or reading the Psalms; and when after some hours they also grew weary and faint, then they rung the watch-bell, and were also relieved by some of the former, or by a new part of the society which continued their devotions (as hath been mentioned) until morning. And it is to be noted, that in this continued serving of God, the Psalter, or whole Book of Psalms, was in every four-and-twenty hours sung or read over, from the first to the last verse; and this was done as constantly as the sun runs his circle every day about the world, and then begins again the same instant that it ended.

Thus did Mr. Ferrar and his happy family serve God day and night—thus did they always behave themselves as in His presence. And they did always eat and drink by the strictest rules of temperance; eat and drink so as to be ready to rise at midnight, or at the call of a watch-bell, and perform their devotions to God. And it is fit to tell the reader, that many of the clergy that were more inclined to practical piety and devotion than to doubtful and needless disputations, did often come to Gidden Hall, and make themselves a part of that happy society, and stay a week or more, and then join with Mr. Ferrar and the family in these devotions, and assist and ease him or them in the watch by night. And these various devotions had never less than two of the domestic family in the night; and the watch was always kept in the church or oratory, unless in extreme cold winter nights, and then it was maintained in a parlor which had a fire in it, and the parlor was fitted for that purpose. And this course of piety, and great liberality to his poor neighbors, Mr. Ferrar maintained till his death, which was in the year 1639.

Mr. Ferrar's and Mr. Herbert's devout lives were both so noted, that the general report of their sanctity gave them occasion to renew that slight acquaintance which was begun at their being contemporaries in Cambridge; and this new holy friendship was long maintained without any interview, but only by loving and endearing letters. And one testimony of their friendship and pious designs may appear by Mr. Ferrar's commending "The Considerations of John Valdesso" (a book which he had met with in his travels, and translated out of Spanish into English) to be examined and censured by Mr. Herbert before it was made public; which excellent book Mr. Herbert did read, and returned back with many marginal notes, as they be now printed with it; and with them, Mr. Herbert's affectionate letter to Mr. Ferrar. . . .

After this account of Mr. Ferrar and John Valdesso, I proceed to my account of Mr. Herbert and Mr. Duncon, who, according to his promise, returned from the Bath the fifth day, and then found Mr. Herbert much weaker than he left him, and therefore their discourse could not be long; but at Mr. Duncon's parting with him, Mr. Herbert spoke to this purpose: "Sir, I pray give my brother Ferrar an account of the decaying condition of my body, and tell him I beg him to continue his daily prayers for me; and let him know that I have considered, that God only is what He would be; and that I am, by His grace, become now so like Him, as to be pleased with what pleaseth Him; and tell him that I do not repine, but am pleased with my want of health; and tell him, my heart is fixed on that place where true joy is only to be found; and that I long to be there, and do wait for my appointed change with hope and patience." Having said this, he did, with so sweet a humility as seemed to exalt him, bow down to Mr. Duncon, and, with a thoughtful and contented

look, say to him, "Sir, I pray deliver this little book to my dear brother Ferrar, and tell him he shall find in it a picture of the many spiritual conflicts that have passed betwixt God and my soul, before I could subject mine to the will of Jesus my Master, in whose service I have now found perfect freedom; desire him to read it, and then, if he can think it may turn to the advantage of any dejected poor soul, let it be made public; if not, let him burn it; for I and it are less than the least of God's mercies." Thus meanly did this humble man think of this excellent book, which now bears the name of "The Temple; or, Sacred Poems and Private Ejaculations," of which Mr. Ferrar would say, "There was in it the picture of a divine soul in every page, and that the whole book was such a harmony of holy passions as would enrich the world with pleasure and piety." And it appears to have done so; for there have been more than twenty thousand of them sold since the first impression.

And this ought to be noted, that when Mr. Ferrar sent this book to Cambridge to be licensed for the press, the Vice-Chancellor would by no means allow the two so much noted verses—

> Religion stands a tip-toe in our land,
> Ready to pass to the American strand,

to be printed, and Mr. Ferrar would by no means allow the book to be printed and want them; but after some time, and some arguments for and against their being made public, the Vice-Chancellor said, "I knew Mr. Herbert well, and know that he had many heavenly speculations, and was a divine poet; but I hope the world will not take him to be an inspired prophet, and therefore I license the whole book." So that it came to be printed without diminution or addition of a syllable, since it was delivered into the hands of Mr. Duncon, save only that Mr. Ferrar hath added that excellent preface that is printed before it.

At the time of Mr. Duncon's leaving Mr. Herbert (which was about three weeks before his death), his old and dear friend Mr. Woodnot came from London to Bemerton, and never left him till he had seen him draw his last breath, and closed his eyes on his deathbed. In this time of his decay he was often visited and prayed for by all the clergy that lived near to him, especially by his friends the bishop and prebendaries of the cathedral church in Salisbury; but by none more devoutly than his wife, his three nieces (then a part of his family), and Mr. Woodnot, who were the sad witnesses of his daily decay; to whom he would often speak to this purpose: "I now look back upon the pleasures of my life past, and see the content I have taken in beauty, in wit, and music, and pleasant conversation, are now all past by me like a dream, or as a shadow that returns not, and are now all become dead to me, or I to them; and I see that as my father and generation hath done before me, so I also shall now suddenly (with Job) make my bed also in the dark, and I praise God I am prepared for it; and I praise Him that I am not to learn patience now I stand in such need of it; and that I have practiced mortification, and endeavored to die daily that I might not die eternally, and my hope is that I shall shortly leave this valley of tears, and be free from all fevers and pain; and which will be a more happy condition, I shall be free from sin, and all the temptations and anxieties that attend it, and this being past, I shall dwell in the new Jerusalem, dwell there with men made perfect, dwell where these eyes shall see my Master and Saviour Jesus; and with Him see my dear mother, and all my relations and friends. But I must die, or not come to that happy place; and this is my content, that I am going daily towards it, and that every day which I have lived hath taken a part of my appointed time from me, and that I shall live the less time for having lived this and the day past." These, and the like expressions, which he uttered often, may be said to be his enjoyment of heaven before he enjoyed it. The Sunday before his death, he rose suddenly from his bed or couch, called for one of his instruments, took it into his hand, and said:

> My God, my God,
> My music shall find Thee,
>   And ev'ry string
> Shall have his attribute to sing.

And having tuned it, he played and sung:

> The Sundays of man's life,
>   Threaded together on Time's string,
> Make bracelets to adorn the wife
>   Of the eternal glorious King:
> On Sundays, Heaven's door stands ope;
>   Blessings are plentiful and rife,
> More plentiful than hope.

Thus he sung on earth such hymns and anthems as the angels and he and Mr. Ferrar now sing in heaven.

Thus he continued meditating and praying and rejoicing, till the day of his death, and on that day said to Mr. Woodnot: "My dear friend, I am sorry I have nothing to present to my merciful God but sin and misery; but the first is pardoned, and a few hours will now put a period to the latter, for I shall suddenly go hence, and be no more seen." Upon which expression, Mr. Woodnot took occasion to remember him of the re-edifying Layton Church, and his many acts of mercy, to which he made answer, saying, "They be good works if they be sprinkled with the blood of Christ, and not otherwise." After this discourse he became more restless, and his soul seemed to be weary of her earthly tabernacle, and this uneasiness became so visible that his wife, his three nieces, and Mr. Woodnot stood constantly about his bed, beholding him with sorrow, and an unwillingness to lose the sight of him whom they could not hope to see much longer. As they stood thus beholding him, his wife observed him to breathe faintly and with much trouble, and observed him to fall into a sudden agony, which so surprised her that she fell into a sudden passion, and required of him to know how he did? To which his answer was, "That he had passed a conflict with his last enemy, and had overcome him by the merits of his Master Jesus." After which answer he looked up and saw his wife and nieces weeping to an extremity, and charged them, "If they loved him, to withdraw into the next room, and there pray every one alone for him, for nothing but their lamentations could make his death uncomfortable." To which request their sighs and tears would not suffer them to make any reply, but they yielded him a sad obedience, leaving only with him Mr. Woodnot and Mr. Bostock. Immediately after they had left him he said to Mr. Bostock, "Pray, sir, open that door, then look into that cabinet, in which you may easily find my last will, and give it into my hand"; which being done, Mr. Herbert delivered it into the hand of Mr. Woodnot, and said, "My old friend, I here deliver you my last will, in which you will find that I have made you my sole executor for the good of my wife and nieces, and I desire you to show kindness to them as they shall need it. I do not desire you to be just, for I know you will be so for your own sake; but I charge you by the religion of our friendship to be careful of them." And having obtained Mr. Woodnot's promise to be so, he said, "I am now ready to die." After which words he said, "Lord, forsake me not now my strength faileth me, but grant me mercy for the merits of my Jesus. And now, Lord—Lord, now receive my soul." And with these words he breathed forth his divine soul without any apparent disturbance, Mr. Woodnot and

Mr. Bostock attending his last breath and closing his eyes.

Thus he lived and thus he died like a saint, unspotted of the world, full of alms-deeds, full of humility, and all the examples of a virtuous life, which I cannot conclude better than with this borrowed observation:—

> All must to their cold graves;
> But the religious actions of the just
> Smell sweet in death, and blossom in the dust.

Mr. George Herbert's have done so to this, and will doubtless do so to succeeding generations. I have but this to say more of him, that if Andrew Melvin died before him, then George Herbert died without an enemy. I wish—if God shall be so pleased—that I may be so happy as to die like him.

Iz. Wa.

There is a debt justly due to the memory of Mr. Herbert's virtuous wife, a part of which I will endeavor to pay by a very short account of the remainder of her life, which shall follow.

She continued his disconsolate widow about six years, bemoaning herself and complaining that she had lost the delight of her eyes; but more, that she had lost the spiritual guide for her poor soul; and would often say, "O that I had, like holy Mary, the mother of Jesus, treasured up all his sayings in my heart; but since I have not been able to do that, I will labor to live like him, that where he now is, I may be also." And she would often say (as the Prophet David for his son Absalom) "O that I had died for him!" Thus she continued mourning, till time and conversation had so moderated her sorrows, that she became the happy wife of Sir Robert Cook, of Highnam, in the county of Gloucester, Knight; and though he put a high value on the excellent accomplishments of her mind and body, and was so like Mr. Herbert, as not to govern like a master, but as an affectionate husband; yet she would, even to him, often take occasion to mention the name of Mr. George Herbert, and say, "That name must live in her memory, till she put off mortality." By Sir Robert she had only one child, a daughter, whose parts and plentiful estate make her happy in this world, and her well using of them gives a fair testimony that she will be so in that which is to come.

Mrs. Herbert was the wife of Sir Robert eight years, and lived his widow about fifteen; all which time she took a pleasure in mentioning and commending the excellences of Mr. George Herbert. She died in the year 1663, and lies buried at Highnam; Mr. Herbert in his own church, under the altar, and covered with a gravestone without any inscription.

This Lady Cook had preserved many of Mr. Herbert's private writings, which she intended to make public, but they and Highnam House were burnt together by the late rebels, and so lost to posterity.

James Howell

[1594?–1666]

IKE most of his fellow Welshmen who attended Oxford, James Howell matriculated at Jesus College. After receiving his degree, he was employed at the London glassworks of Sir Robert Mansell, and spent some six years on the Continent as foreign agent for that company. During these years of travel in France, Holland, Italy, and Spain, he managed to become an accomplished linguist and, in his own phrase, "a true Cosmopolite." But his familiarity with foreign tongues and customs did not in any sense dilute his patriotic pride as a Welshman, a pride which was to remain one of the most constant emotions of a life notable more for its variety and vicissitude than for any conspicuous success.

On his return to England Howell began the first of his generally fruitless attempts to obtain a post in the public service, attempts which were to constitute a kind of leitmotiv in his career. He applied unsuccessfully for a position in the diplomatic service, but was finally, in 1622, sent on a special mission to Madrid to carry out negotiations concerning an English vessel which had been seized. While he was there the Prince of Wales, accompanied by the Duke of Buckingham, arrived on his ill-fated mission to secure the hand of the Infanta of Spain. To Howell we owe one of the most colorful accounts of the prince's romantic undertaking, and to his encounter with the royal party Howell owed a number of acquaintances which he later tried, again unsuccessfully, to exploit in the advancement of his career.

By 1626 Howell had become secretary to Lord Scrope, and in 1627 he was elected Member of Parliament for Richmond in Yorkshire. In 1632 he accompanied the Earl of Leicester on a special mission to Denmark but once again failed to obtain any lasting employment. Again in the capital, Howell made a good many literary friends, among them Ben Jonson, Lord Herbert of Cherbury, and Sir Kenelm Digby. His *Dodona's Grove*, a political allegory, was published in 1640, and his *Instructions for Foreign Travel*, a more interesting book to the modern reader, in 1642. He finally became clerk of the King's Privy Council, but was suddenly, in 1643, committed by Parliament to the Fleet Prison, where he remained for the next eight years. Anthony à Wood maintains that the cause of his imprisonment was debt, but it is more probable that he was imprisoned for his royalist sympathies. In any case, his years in the Fleet transformed Howell into a writer of some importance: his *Epistolæ Ho-Elianæ, or Familiar Letters* (the title is designed to indicate the pronunciation of his name) are important not only in the history of letter-writing but also in the development of the essay. In all likelihood Howell's letters were almost all written in prison, the author drawing on his memories and his reading for the events and scenes which he described. Frequently, as in his disquisitions on wines, or on the languages of the world, Howell transforms his "letters" into full-scale essays. The *Epistolæ* were issued in four series, in 1645, 1647, 1650, and 1655.

Released in the general amnesty of 1650, Howell gave his allegiance to the Cromwell government but was nevertheless, on the restoration of Charles II, rewarded by being appointed Historiographer Royal, a position of which he was so inordinately proud that he left instructions that it be engraved on his gravestone, together, of course, with the fact of his Welsh birth.

Howell's style is easy, agreeable, and chatty, and these qualities perhaps explain his continuing popularity with readers of the eighteenth century. His reputation, however, has not survived undimmed into our own time. He is likely, for the modern reader, to be dwarfed by the giant figures of Burton, Donne, and Browne. Nevertheless, there is much in his work which makes vivid for us the stirring times in which he lived.

J. HOWELL. *Epistolæ Ho-Elianæ, or Familiar Letters,* ed. J. Jacobs, 2 vols. (London, 1890–92). The definitive edition.

W. H. VANN. *Notes on the Writings of James Howell* (Waco, Texas, 1924). An annotated bibliography which is very useful to any student of Howell.

FROM

EPISTOLÆ HO-ELIANÆ:
Familiar Letters, Domestic and Foreign

[TEXT: *third edition, 1655*]

VOLUME ONE

SECTION I

To Sir J. S.,[1] *At Leeds Castle*

SIR,

It was a quaint difference the ancients did put 'twixt a letter and an oration, that the one should be attired like a woman, the other like a man. The latter of the two is allowed large side robes, as long periods, parentheses, similes, examples, and other parts of rhetorical flourishes: but a letter or epistle should be short-coated, and closely couched; a hungerlin[2] becomes a letter more handsomely than a gown. Indeed we should write as we speak, and that's a true familiar letter which expresseth one's mind as if he were discoursing with the party to whom he writes in succinct and short terms. The tongue and the pen are both of them interpreters of the mind, but I hold the pen to be the more faithful of the two. The tongue *in udo posita,* being seated in a moist slippery place, may fail and falter in her sudden extemporal expressions; but the pen, having a greater advantage of premeditation, is not so subject to error, and leaves things behind it upon firm and authentic record. Now, letters, though they be capable of any subject, yet commonly they are either narratory, objurgatory, consolatory, monitory, congratulatory. The first consists of relations, the second of reprehensions, the third of comfort, the last two of counsel and joy; there are some who in lieu of letters write homilies, they preach when they should epistolize; there are others that turn them to tedious tractates; this is to make letters degenerate from their true nature. Some modern authors there are who have exposed their letters to the world, but most of them, I mean among your Latin epistolizers, go freighted with mere Bartholomew

1 Sir John Smith; knighted 1603, died 1632.
2 A short coat, introduced from Hungary.

ware,[3] with trite and trivial phrases only, lifted with pedantic shreds of schoolboy verses. Others there are among our next transmarine neighbors eastward, who write in their own language, but their style is so soft and easy that their letters may be said to be like bodies of loose flesh without sinews, they have neither joints of art nor arteries in them; they have a kind of simpering and lank hectic expressions made up of a bombast of words and finical affected compliments only. I cannot well away with such sleazy[4] stuff, with such cobweb compositions, where there is no strength of matter, nothing for the reader to carry away with him that may enlarge the notions of his soul. One shall hardly find an apothegm, example, simile, or anything of philosophy, history, or solid knowledge, or as much as one new created phrase, in a hundred of them; and to draw any observations out of them were as if one went about to distill cream out of froth; insomuch that it may be said of them, what was said of the echo, "That she is a mere sound, and nothing else."

I return you your Balzac[5] by this bearer, and when I found those letters, wherein he is so familiar with his king, so flat, and those to Richelieu, so puffed with profane hyperboles, and larded up and down with such gross flatteries, with others besides which he sends as urinals up and down the world to look into his water for discovery of the crazy condition of his body, I forbore him further.—So I am your most affectionate servitor,

J. H.

Westminster, 25 July 1625.

To Captain Francis Bacon, From Paris

Sir,

I received two of yours in Rouen with the bills of exchange there inclosed, and according to your directions I sent you those things which you wrote for.

I am now newly come to Paris, this huge magazine of men, the epitome of this large populous kingdom, and rendezvous of all foreigners. The structures here are indifferently fair, though the streets generally foul, all the four seasons of the year, which I impute first, to the position of the city being built upon an isle (the

Isle of France, made so by the branching and serpentine course of the river of Seine), and having some of her suburbs seated high, the filth runs down the channel and settles in many places within the body of the city, which lieth upon a flat; as also for a world of coaches, carts, and horses of all sorts that go to and fro perpetually, so that sometimes one shall meet with a stop half a mile long of those coaches, carts, and horses that can move neither forward nor backward by reason of some sudden encounter of others coming a cross-way, so that often times it will be an hour or two before they can disentangle. In such a stop the great Henry was so fatally slain by Ravillac.[6] Hence comes it to pass that this town (for Paris is a town, a city, and a university) is always dirty, and 'tis such a dirt that by perpetual motion is beaten into such a thick black unctuous oil that where it sticks no art can wash it off of some colors, insomuch that it may be no improper comparison to say, that an ill name is like the crot (the dirt) of Paris, which is indelible; besides the stain this dirt leaves, it gives also so strong a scent that it may be smelt many miles off if the wind be in one's face as he comes from the fresh air of the country. This may be one cause why the plague is always in some corner or other of this vast city, which may be called, as once Scythia was, *vagina populorum*, or (as mankind was called by a great philosopher) a great molehill of ants. Yet I believe this city is not so populous as she seems to be, for her form being round (as the whole kingdom is) the passengers wheel about and meet oftener than they use to do in the long continued streets of London, which makes London appear less populous than she is indeed, so that London for length (though not for latitude), including Westminster, exceeds Paris, and hath in Michaelmas term more souls moving within her in all places. 'Tis under one hundred years that Paris is become so sumptuous and strong in buildings; for her houses were mean until a mine of white stone was discovered hard by, which runs in a continued vein of earth and is digged out with ease, being soft, and is between a white clay and chalk at first, but being pulled up, with the open air it receives a crusty kind of hardness and so becomes perfect freestone; and before it is sent up from the pit they can reduce it to any form. Of this stone the Louvre, the king's palace, is built, which is a vast fabric, for the gallery wants not much of an Italian mile in length, and will easily lodge 3000 men, which some told me was the end for

---

3 Cheap ware, such as was offered for sale at Bartholomew Fair. See Ben Jonson's play of that name.

4 Flimsy.

5 Jean Louis Guez de Balzac, 1594–1655. His Letters had been published shortly before, and were probably models for Howell's.

6 Henry IV was slain by Ravillac, a Lay-Jesuit, on May 14, 1610.

which the last king made it so big, that lying at the fag-end of this great mutinous city, if she perchance should rise, the king might pour out of the Louvre so many thousand men unawares into the heart of her.

I am lodged here hard by the Bastille, because it is furthest off from those places where the English resort, for I would go on to get a little language as soon as I could. In my next I shall impart unto you what state news France affords.—In the interim, and always, I am, your humble servant,

J. H.

Paris, the 30 March 1620.

To Dr. Francis Mansell,[7] From Valencia

SIR,

Though it be the same glorious sun that shines upon you in England, which illuminates also this part of the hemisphere, though it be the sun that ripeneth your pippins and our pomegranates, your hops and our vineyards here, yet he dispenseth his heat in different degrees of strength; those rays that do but warm you in England, do half roast us here; those beams that irradiate only and gild your honey-suckled fields, do scorch and parch this chinky gaping soil, and so put too many wrinkles upon the face of our common mother the earth. O blessed clime, O happy England, where there is such a rare temperature of heat and cold, and all the rest of elementary qualities, that one may pass (and suffer little) all the year long without either shade in summer or fire in winter.

I am now in Valencia, one of the noblest cities of all Spain, situate in a large vegue or valley, above three score miles compass. Here are the strongest silks, the sweetest wines, the excellentest almonds, the best oils, and beautifulest females of all Spain, for the prime courtesans in Madrid and elsewhere are had hence. The very brute animals make themselves beds of rosemary and other fragrant flowers hereabouts; and when one is at sea, if the wind blows from the shore, he may smell this soil before he come in sight of it many leagues off, by the strong odoriferous scent it casts. As it is the most pleasant, so it is also the temperatest clime of all Spain, and they commonly call it the second Italy, which made the Moors, whereof many thousands were disterred and banished hence to Barbary, to think that paradise was in that part of the heavens which hung over this city. Some twelve miles off is old Sagunto, called now Morviedre, through which I

7 Principal of Jesus College, Oxford.

passed, and saw many monuments of Roman antiquities there: amongst others there is the temple dedicated to Venus, when the snake came about her neck, a little before Hannibal came thither. No more now, but that I heartily wish you were here with me, and I believe you would not desire to be a good while in England.—So I am,

Your J. H.

Valencia, 1 of March 1620.

To the Honorable Sir Robert Mansell, Vice-Admiral of England, From Venice

SIR,

As soon as I came to Venice, I applied myself to dispatch your business according to instructions, and Mr. Seymour was ready to contribute his best furtherance. These two Italians who are the bearers hereof, by report here, are the best gentlemen-workmen that ever blew crystal, one is allied to Antonio Miotti, the other is cousin to Mazalao; for other things they shall be sent in the ship *Lion*, which rides here at Malamocca, as I shall send you account by conveyance of Mr. Symns. Herewith I have sent a letter to you from Sir Henry Wotton,[8] the Lord Ambassador here, of whom I have received some favors. He wishes me to write that you have now a double interest in him; for whereas before he was only your servant, he is now your kinsman by your late marriage.

I was lately to see the arsenal of Venice, one of the worthiest things of Christendom; they say there are as many galleys, and galeasses of all sorts, belonging to Saint Mark, either in course, at anchor, in dock, or upon the careen, as there be days in the year; here they can build a complete galley in half a day, and put her afloat in perfect equipage, having all the ingredients fitted before-hand, as they did in three hours, when Henry the Third passed this way to France from Poland, who wished, that besides Paris and his parliament towns, he had this arsenal in exchange for three of his chiefest cities. There are three hundred people perpetually here at work, and if one comes young and grows old in Saint Mark's service, he hath a pension from the state during life. Being brought to see one of the Clarissimos that governs this arsenal, this huge sea store-house, amongst other matters reflecting upon England, he was saying: "That if Cavalier Don

8 Sir Henry Wotton, 1568–1639, the favorite ambassador of James I, and employed by him on the most important and delicate missions.

Roberto Mansell were now here, he thought verily the republic would make a proffer to him to be admiral of that fleet of galleys and galleons, which are now going against the Duke of Ossuna and the forces of Naples, you are so well known here."

I was, since I came hither, in Murano, a little island about the distance of Lambeth from London, where crystal glass is made, and 'tis a rare sight to see a whole street, where on the one side there are twenty furnaces together at work. They say here that although one should transplant a glass-furnace from Murano to Venice herself, or to any of the little assembly of islands about her, or to any other part of the earth besides, and use the same materials, the same workmen, the same fuel, the self-same ingredients every way, yet they cannot make crystal glass in that perfection, for beauty and luster, as in Murano. Some impute it to the quality of the circumambient air that hangs over the place, which is purified and attenuated by the concurrence of so many fires that are in those furnaces night and day perpetually, for they are like the vestal fire which never goes out. And it is well known that some airs make more qualifying impressions than others, as a Greek told me in Sicily of the air of Egypt, where there be huge common furnaces to hatch eggs by the thousands in camel's dung; for, during the time of hatching if the air happen to come to be overcast and grow cloudy, it spoils all; if the sky continue still, serene, and clear, not one egg in a hundred will miscarry.

I met with Camillo, your consaorman, here lately, and could he be sure of entertainment, he would return to serve you again, and, I believe, for less salary.

I shall attend your commands herein by the next, and touching other particulars, whereof I have written to Captain Bacon. So I rest, your most humble and ready servant,

J. H.

Venice, May the 30, 1621.

To Mr. Richard Altham at Gray's Inn, From Venice

GENTLE SIR,

—O dulcior illo
Melle quod in ceris Attica ponit apis.[9]

O thou who dost in sweetness far excel
That juice the Attic bee stores in her cell.

9 "*O dulcior illo*"; cf. Ovid's Tristia, V. iv. 30.

MY DEAR DICK,

I have now a good while since taken footing in Venice, this admired maiden city, so called because she was never deflowered by any enemy since she had a being, nor since her Rialto was first erected, which is now above twelve ages ago.

I protest unto you at my first landing I was for some days ravished with the high beauty of this maid, with her lovely countenance. I admired her magnificent buildings, her marvellous situation, her dainty smooth neat streets, whereon you may walk most days in the year in a silk stocking and satin slippers, without soiling them, nor can the streets of Paris be so foul as these are fair. This beauteous maid hath been often attempted to be vitiated; some have courted her, some bribed her, some would have forced her, yet she has still preserved her chastity entire; and though she hath lived so many ages, and passed so many shrewd brunts, yet she continueth fresh to this very day, without the least wrinkle of old age or any symptoms of decay, whereunto political bodies, as well as natural, use to be liable. Besides she hath wrestled with the greatest potentates upon earth. The Emperor, the King of France, and most of the other princes of Christendom, in that famous league of Cambray,[10] would have sunk her; but she bore up still within her lakes, and broke that league to pieces by her wit. The Grand Turk hath been often at her, and though he could not have his will of her, yet he took away the richest jewel she wore in her coronet and put it in his turban—I mean the kingdom of Cyprus, the only royal gem she had; he hath set upon her skirts often since, and though she closed with him sometimes, yet she came off still with her maidenhead, though some that envy her happiness would brand her to be of late times a kind of concubine to him, and that she gives him ready money once a year to lie with her, which she minceth by the name of present, though it be indeed rather a tribute.

I would I had you here with a wish, and you would not desire in haste to be at Gray's Inn, though I hold your walks to be the pleasantest place about London; and that you have there the choicest society. I pray present my kind commendations to all there, and service at Bishopsgate Street, and let me hear from you by the next post.—So I am, entirely yours,

J. H.

Venice, 5 June 1621.

10 Formed in 1508 by the Emperor, the Pope, France, and Spain, against Venice.

To Sir J. H.,[11] From Lyons

SIR,

I am now got over the Alps and returned to France. I had crossed and clambered up the Pyrenees to Spain before; they are not so high and hideous as the Alps, but for our mountains in Wales, as Eppint and Penwinmaur, which are so much cried up amongst us, they are molehills in comparison of these, they are but pigmies compared to giants, but blisters compared to imposthumes, or pimples to warts. Besides our mountains in Wales bear always something useful to man or beast, some grass at least; but these uncouth huge monstrous excrescences of nature, bear nothing (most of them) but craggy stones. The tops of some of them are blanched over all the year long with snows, and the people who dwell in the valleys, drinking for want of other this snow water, are subject to a strange swelling in the throat, called goitre, which is common amongst them.

As I scaled the Alps, my thoughts reflected upon Hannibal, who with vinegar and strong waters did eat out a passage through those hills, but of late years they have found a speedier way to do it by gunpowder.

Being at Turin, I was by some disaster brought to an extreme low ebb in money, so that I was forced to foot it along with some pilgrims, and with gentle pace and easy journeys to climb up those hills till I came to this town of Lyons, where a countryman of ours, one Mr. Lewis, whom I knew in Alicant, lives factor, so that now I want not anything for my accommodation.

This is a stately rich town, and a renowned mart for the silks of Italy and other Levantine commodities, and a great bank for money, and indeed the greatest of France. Before this bank was founded, which was by Henry the First, France had but little gold and silver, insomuch that we read how King John, their captive king, could not in four years raise sixty thousand crowns to pay his ransom to our King Edward. And Saint Lewis was in the same case when he was prisoner in Egypt, where he had left the Sacrament for a gage. But after this bank was erected it filled France full of money. They of Lucca, Florence, and Genoa, with the Venetian got quickly over the hills, and brought their moneys hither to get twelve in the hundred profit, which was the interest at first, though it be now much lower.

In this great mercantile town there be two deep navigable rivers, the Rhone and the Saone. The one hath a swift rapid course; the other slow and smooth. And one day as I walked upon their banks and observed so much difference in their course, I fell into a contemplation of the humors of the French and Spaniard, how they might be not improperly compared to these rivers,—the French to the swift, the Spaniard to the slow, river.

I shall write you no more letters until I present myself unto you for a speaking letter, which I shall do as soon as I may tread London stones.—Your affectionate servitor,

J. H.

Lyons, 6 November 1621.

SECTION II

To My Father[12]

SIR,

It hath pleased God, after almost three years' peregrination by land and sea, to bring me back safely to London; but although I am come safely, I am come sickly; for when I landed in Venice, after so long a sea-voyage from Spain, I was afraid the same deflection of salt rheum which fell from my temples into my throat in Oxford, and distilling upon the uvula impeached my utterance a little to this day, had found the same channel again, which caused me to have an issue made in my left arm for the diversion of the humor. I was well ever after till I came to Rouen, and there I fell sick of a pain in the head, which, with this issue, I have carried with me to England. Doctor Harvey,[13] who is my physician, tells me that it may turn to a consumption, therefore he hath stopped the issue, telling me there is no danger at all in it, in regard I have not worn it a full twelvemonth. My brother, I thank him, hath been very careful of me in this my sickness, and hath come often to visit me. I thank God I have passed the brunt of it, and am recovering, and picking up my crumbs apace. There is a flaunting French Ambassador come over lately, and I believe his errand is naught else but compliment, for the King

---

11 Jacobs thinks this is a misprint for Sir T. H. (Sir Thomas Hawkins, author of Unhappy Prosperity, and translator of Horace).

12 The Rev. Thomas Howell, minister of Abernant, Caermarthenshire, Wales.

13 Dr. William Harvey, discoverer of the circulation of the blood, 1578–1657.

of France being lately at Calais, and so in sight of England, he sent his ambassador, Monsieur Cadenet, expressly to visit our king; he had audience two days since, where he with his train of ruffling long-haired monsieurs carried himself in such a light garb, that after the audience, the king asked my Lord Keeper Bacon what he thought of the French Ambassador. He answered that he was a tall, proper man. "Aye," his Majesty replied, "but what think you of his head-piece? Is he a proper man for the office of an ambassador?" "Sir," said Bacon, "tall men are like high houses of four or five stories, wherein commonly the uppermost room is worst furnished."

So, desiring my brothers and sisters, with the rest of my cousins and friends in the country, may be acquainted with my safe return to England, and that you would please to let me hear from you by the next conveniency, I rest, your dutiful son,

J. H.

London, 2 February 1621.

SECTION III

To the Honorable Sir Thomas Savage, Knight and Baronet

Honorable Sir,

The great business of the match[14] was tending to a period, the articles reflecting both upon church and state being capitulated and interchangeably accorded on both sides, and there wanted nothing to consummate all things, when to the wonderment of the world the prince and the Marquis of Buckingham arrived at this court on Friday last upon the close of the evening. They alighted at my Lord of Bristol's house, and the marquis (Mr. Thomas Smith) came in first with a portmanteau under his arm, then (Mr. John Smith) the prince was sent for, who stayed a while the other side of the street in the dark. My Lord of Bristol, in a kind of astonishment, brought him up to his bedchamber, where he presently called for pen and ink, and dispatched a post that night to England to acquaint his Majesty how in less than sixteen days he was come safely to the court of Spain. That post went lightly laden, for he carried but three letters. The next day came Sir Francis Cottington and Mr. Porter, and dark

rumors ran in every corner how some great man was come from England, and some would not stick to say amongst the vulgar, it was the king. But towards the evening on Saturday the marquis went in a close coach to court, where he had private audience of this king, who sent Olivares to accompany him back to the prince, where he kneeled and kissed his hands, and hugged his thighs, and delivered how unmeasurably glad his Catholic Majesty was of his coming, with other high compliments, which Mr. Porter did interpret. About ten o'clock that night the king himself came in a close coach with intent to visit the prince, who, hearing of it, met him half way, and after salutations and divers embraces which passed in the first interview they parted late. I forgot to tell you that Count Gondomar, being sworn Councilor of State that morning, having been before but one of the Council of War, he came in great haste to visit the prince, saying he has strange news to tell him, which was that an Englishman was sworn Privy Councilor of Spain, meaning himself, who he said was an Englishman in his heart. On Sunday following, the king in the afternoon came abroad to take the air with the queen, his two brothers, and the Infanta, who were all in one coach; but the Infanta sat in the boot with a blue ribbon about her arm, of purpose that the prince might distinguish her. There were above twenty coaches besides of grandees, noblemen, and ladies that attended them. And now it was publicly known amongst the vulgar that it was the Prince of Wales who had come, and the confluence of people before my Lord of Bristol's house was so great and greedy to see the prince that to clear the way Sir Lewis Dives went out and took coach, and all the crowd of people went after him. So the prince himself a little after took coach, wherein there were the Earl of Bristol, Sir Walter Aston, and Count Gondomar, and so went to the Prado, a place hard by, of purpose to take the air, where they stayed till the king passed by. As soon as the Infanta saw the prince her color rose very high, which we hold to be an impression of love and affection, for the face is oftentimes a true index of the heart. Upon Monday morning after, the king sent some of his prime nobles and other gentlemen to attend the prince in quality of officers, as one to be his major-domo (his steward), another to be master of the horse, and so too inferior officers, so that there is a complete court now at my Lord of Bristol's house. But upon Sunday next the prince is to remove to the king's palace, where there is one of the chief quarters of the

---

14 The "Spanish Match," between the Prince of Wales (later Charles I) and the Infanta of Spain.

house providing for him. By the next opportunity you shall hear more.—In the interim I take my leave and rest your most humble and ready servitor,

J. H.

March 27, 1623.

To Captain Thomas Porter

NOBLE CAPTAIN,

My last unto you was in Spanish, in answer to one of yours in the same language, and amongst that confluence of English gallants, which upon the occasion of his Highness being here, are come to this court, I fed myself with hopes a long while to have seen you, but I find now that these hopes were imped with false feathers. I know your heart is here and your best affections, therefore I wonder what keeps back your person; but I conceive the reason to be that you intend to come like yourself, to come commander-in-chief of one of the castles of the crown, one of the ships royal. If you come so to this shore side, I hope you will have time to come to the court. I have at any time a good lodging for you, and my landlady is none of the meanest, and her husband hath many good parts. I heard her setting him forth one day and giving this character of him: "*Mi marido es buen musico, buen esgrimidor, buen escrivano, excellente arithmetico, salvo que no multiplica*" (My husband is a good musician, a good fencer, a good horseman, a good penman, and an excellent arithmetician, only he cannot multiply). For outward usage there is all industry used to give the prince and his servants all possible contentment, and some of the king's own servants wait upon them at table in the palace, where I am sorry to hear some of them jeer at the Spanish fare, and use other slighting speeches and demeanor. There are many excellent poems made here since the prince's arrival, which are too long to couch in a letter, yet I will venture to send you this one stanza of Lope de Vega:—

> Carlos Estuardo Soy
> Que siendo Amor mi guia
> Al cielo d'España voy
> Por ver mi Estrella María.[15]

15 Lope de Vega Carpio, poet and dramatist, 1562–1635. This verse, which Howell attributes to him, may be translated,

> Charles Stuart am I,
>   Whom Love has guided afar;
> To this heaven of Spain I am come,
>   To see Maria, my Star.

There are comedians once a week come to the palace, where under a great canopy the queen and the Infanta sit in the middle, our prince and Don Carlos on the queen's right hand, the king and the little cardinal on the Infanta's left hand. I have seen the prince have his eyes immovably fixed upon the Infanta half-an-hour together in a thoughtful, speculative posture, which sure would needs be tedious, unless affection did sweeten it; it was no handsome comparison of Olivares, that he watched her as a cat doth a mouse. Not long since the prince, understanding that the Infanta was used to go some mornings to the Casa de Campo, a summer house the king hath the other side the river, to gather May dew, he did rise betimes and went thither, taking your brother with him. They were let into the house and into the garden, but the Infanta was in the orchard, and there being a high partition wall between and the door doubly bolted, the prince got on top of the wall and sprung down a great height, and so made towards her; but she, spying him first of all the rest, gave a shriek and ran back. The old marquis that was then her guardian came towards the prince and fell on his knees, conjuring his Highness to retire, in regard he hazarded his head if he admitted any to her company. So the door was opened, and he came out under that wall over which he had got in. I have seen him watch a long hour together in a close coach in the open street to see her as she went abroad. I cannot say that the prince did ever talk with her privately, yet publicly often, my Lord of Bristol being interpreter, but the king always sat hard by to overhear all. Our cousin Archy[16] hath more privilege than any, for he often goes with his fool's coat where the Infanta is with her meninas and ladies of honor, and keeps a-blowing and blustering amongst them, and flirts out what he list.

One day they were discoursing what a marvelous thing it was that the Duke of Bavaria with less than 15,000 men, after a long toilsome march, should dare to encounter the Palsgrave's army consisting of above 25,000, and to give them an utter discomfiture, and take Prague presently after. Whereunto Archy answered that he would tell them a stranger thing than that. Was it not a strange thing, quoth he, that in the year '88 there should come a fleet of 140 sails from Spain to invade England, and that ten of these could not go back to tell what became of the rest? By the

16 Archy Armstrong, the Court Fool of James I.

next opportunity I will send you the Cordovan pockets and gloves you wrote for of Francisco Moreno's perfuming. So may my dear captain live long and love his

J. H.

Madrid, July 10, 1623.

To My Noble Friend, Sir John North, Knight

SIR,

I received lately one of yours, but it was of a very old date. We have our eyes here now all fixed upon Rome, greedily expecting the ratification, and lately a strong rumor ran it was come. In so much, Mr. Clerk, who was sent hither from the prince, being a-shipboard (and now lies sick at my Lord of Bristol's house of a calenture),[17] hearing of it, he desired to speak with him, for he had something to deliver him from the prince. My Lord Ambassador being come to him, Mr. Clerk delivered a letter from the prince, the contents whereof were: That whereas he had left certain proxies in his hand to be delivered to the King of Spain after the ratification was come, he desired and required him not to do it till he should receive further order from England. My Lord of Bristol hereupon went to Sir Walter Aston, who was in joint commission with him for concluding the match, and showing him the letter, what my Lord Aston said I know not, but my Lord of Bristol told him that they had a commission royal under the broad seal of England to conclude the match. He knew as well as he how earnest the king their master hath been any time this ten years to have it done, how there could not be a better pawn for the surrender of the Palatinate than the Infanta in the prince's arms, who could never rest till she did the work to merit love of our nation. He told him also how their own particular fortunes depended upon it; besides, if he should delay one moment to deliver the proxy after the ratification was come, according to agreement, the Infanta would hold herself so blemished in her honor that it might overthrow all things. Lastly, he told him that they incurred the hazard of their heads if they should suspend the executing of his Majesty's commission upon any order, but from that power which gave it, who was the king himself. Hereupon both the ambassadors proceeded still in preparing matters for the solemnizing of the marriage. The Earl of Bristol had caused

above thirty rich liveries to be made of watchet velvet, with silver lace up to the very capes of the cloaks; the best sorts whereof were valued at £80 a livery. My Lord Aston had also provided new liveries, and a fortnight after the said politic report was blown up the ratification came indeed complete and full. So the marriage day was appointed, a terrace covered all over with tapestry was raised from the king's palace to the next church, which might be about the same extent as from Whitehall to Westminster Abbey, and the king intended to make his sister a wife and his daughter (whereof the queen was delivered a little before) a Christian upon the same day. The grandees and great ladies had been invited to the marriage, and order was sent to all the port towns to discharge their great ordnance, and sundry other things were prepared to honor the solemnity; but when we were thus at the height of our hopes, a day or two before, there came Mr. Killegree, Gresley, Wood, and Davies, one upon the neck of another with a new commission to my Lord of Bristol immediately from his Majesty, countermanding him to deliver the proxy aforesaid, until a full and absolute satisfaction were had for the surrendry of the Palatinate under this king's hand and seal, in regard he desired his son should be married to Spain, and his son-in-law remarried to the Palatinate at one time. Hereupon all was dashed in pieces, and that frame which was rearing so many years was ruined in a moment. This news struck a damp in the hearts of all people here, and they wished that the postilions that brought it had all broke their necks on the way.

My Lord of Bristol hereupon went to court to acquaint the king with his new commission, and so proposed the restitution of the Palatinate. The king answered it was none of his to give. It is true he had a few towns there, but he held them as commissioner only for the emperor, and he could not command an emperor. Yet if his Majesty of Great Britain would put a treaty a-foot, he would send his own ambassadors to join. In the interim the earl was commanded not to deliver the aforesaid proxy of the prince for the *desposorios* or espousal until Christmas (and herein it seems his Majesty with you was not well informed, for those powers of proxies expired before). The king here said further that if his uncle the emperor, or the Duke of Bavaria, would not be conformable to reason he would raise as great an army for the Prince Palsgrave as he did under Spinola when he first invaded the Palatinate; and to secure this he would engage his

17 A violent tropical fever.

Contratation House[18] of the West Indies, with his Plate fleet, and give the most binding instrument that he could under his hand and seal. But this gave no satisfaction; therefore my Lord of Bristol, I believe, hath not long to stay here, for he is commanded to deliver no more letters to the Infanta nor demand any more audience, and that she should be no more styled Princess of England or Wales. The aforesaid caution which this king offered to my Lord of Bristol made me think of what I read of his grandfather Philip the Second, who having been married to our Queen Mary, and it being thought she was with child of him, and was accordingly prayed for at Paul's Cross, though it proved afterwards but a tympany, King Philip proposed to our Parliament that they would pass an act that he might be regent during his or her minority that should be born, and he would give caution to surrender the crown when he or she should come to age. The motion was hotly canvassed in the House of Peers, and like to pass, when the Lord Paget rose up and said, "Aye, but who shall sue the king's bond?" so the business was dashed. I have no more news to send you now, and I am sorry I have so much, unless it were better; for we that have business to negotiate here are like to suffer much by this rupture. Welcome be the will of God, to whose benediction I commend you, and rest, your most humble servitor,

J. H.

Madrid, August 25, 1623.

SECTION IV

To My Father, From London

SIR,

I received yours of the third of February, by the hands of my cousin, Thomas Guin of Trecastle.

It was my fortune to be on Sunday was fortnight at Theobald's, where his late Majesty King James departed this life and went to his last rest upon the day of rest, presently after sermon was done. A little before the break of day he sent for the prince, who rose out of his bed and came in his nightgown; the king seemed to have some earnest thing to say unto him, and so endeavored to rouse himself upon his pillow, but his spirits were so spent that he had not strength to make

18 The exchange in Seville where contracts were made in connection with the West Indian trade.

his words audible. He died of a fever which began with an ague, and some Scotch doctors mutter at a plaster the Countess of Buckingham applied to the outside of his stomach. It is thought the last breach of the match with Spain, which for many years he had so vehemently desired, took too deep an impression in him, and that he was forced to rush into a war now in his declining age, having lived in a continual uninterrupted peace his whole life, except some collateral aids he has sent his son-in-law. As soon as he expired the Privy Council sat, and in less than a quarter of an hour, King Charles was proclaimed at Theobald's Court Gate by Sir Edward Zouch, Knight Marshal, Master Secretary Conway dictating unto him: "That whereas it hath pleased God to take to his mercy our most gracious sovereign King James of famous memory, we proclaim Prince Charles his rightful and indubitable heir to be King of England, Scotland, France, and Ireland, etc." The Knight Marshal mistook, saying, "His rightful and dubitable heir," but he was rectified by the secretary. This being done, I took my horse instantly and came to London first, except one who was come a little before me, insomuch that I found the gates shut. His now Majesty took coach and the Duke of Buckingham with him, and came to St. James. In the evening he was proclaimed at Whitehall Gate, in Cheapside, and other places in a sad shower of rain; and the weather was suitable to the condition wherein he finds the kingdom, which is cloudy; for he is left engaged in a war with a potent prince, the people by long desuetude unapt for arms, the fleet royal in quarter repair, himself without a queen, his sister without a country, the crown pitifully laden with debts, and the purse of the state lightly ballasted, though it never had better opportunity to be rich than it had these last twenty years. But God Almighty I hope will make him emerge and pull this island out of all these plunges, and preserve us from worser times.

The plague is begun in Whitechapel, and as they say, in the same house, at the same day of the month, with the same number that died twenty-two years since when Queen Elizabeth departed.

There are great preparations for the funeral, and there is a design to buy all the cloth for mourning white and then to put it to the dyers in gross, which is like to save the crown a good deal of money; the drapers murmur extremely at the Lord Cranfield for it.

I am not settled yet in any stable condition, but I lie

windbound at the Cape of Good Hope, expecting some gentle gale to launch out into an employment.

So with my love to all my brothers and sisters at the Bryn, and near Brecknock, I humbly crave a continuance of your prayers and blessing to your dutiful son,

J. H.

London, December 11, 1625.

To Dr. Pritchard[19]

Sir,

Since I was beholden to you for your many favors in Oxford, I have not heard from you (*ne gry quidem*).[20] I pray let the wonted correspondence be now revived and receive new vigor between us.

My Lord Chancellor Bacon is lately dead of a long languishing weakness; he died so poor, so that he scarce left money to bury him, which, though he had a great wit, did argue no great wisdom, it being one of the essential properties of a wise man to provide for the main chance. I have read that it hath been the fortunes of all poets commonly to die beggars; but for an orator, a lawyer, and a philosopher, as he was, to die so, 'tis rare. It seems the same fate befell him that attended Demosthenes, Seneca, and Cicero (all great men), of whom the two first fell by corruption. The fairest diamond may have a flaw in it, but I believe he died poor out of a contempt of the pelf of fortune, as also out of an excess of generosity; which appeared as in divers other passages, so once when the king had sent him a stag, he sent up for the under-keeper, and having drunk the king's health unto him in a great silver-gilt bowl, he gave it him for his fee.

He writ a pitiful letter to King James not long before his death, and concludes, "Help me, dear sovereign lord and master, and pity me so far that I who have been born to a bag be not now in my age forced in effect to bear a wallet; nor I that desire to live to study may be driven to study to live." Which words, in my opinion, argued a little abjectness of spirit, as his former letter to the prince did of profaneness, wherein he hoped that as the Father was his creator, the Son will be his redeemer. I write not this to derogate from the noble worth of the Lord Viscount Verulam, who was a rare man, a man *recondite, scientie, et ad salutem literatum natus*, and I think the

eloquentest that was born in this isle. They say he shall be the last Lord Chancellor, as Sir Edward Coke was the last Lord Chief-Justice of England; for ever since they have been termed Lord Chief-Justices of the King's Bench, so hereafter they shall be only Keepers of the Great Seal, which for title and Office are deposable, but they say the Lord Chancellor's title is indelible.

I was lately at Gray's Inn with Sir Eubule, and he desired me to remember him unto you, as I do also salute *Meum Prichardum ex imis præcordiis, Vale κεφαλή μοι προσφιλεσάτη.*—Yours most affectionately while

J. H.

London, January 6, 1625.

To My Brother, Master Hugh Penry

Sir,

I thank you for your late letter, and the several good tidings sent me from Wales. In requital I can send you gallant news, for we have now a most noble new Queen of England, who in true beauty is beyond the long-wooed Infanta, for she was of a fading flaxen hair, big-lipped, and somewhat heavy-eyed; but this daughter of France, this youngest branch of Bourbon (being but in her cradle when the great Henry her father was put out of the world) is of a more lovely and lasting complexion, a dark brown; she hath eyes that sparkle like stars, and for her physiognomy she may be said to be a mirror of perfection. She had a rough passage in her transfretation to Dover Castle, and in Canterbury the king bedded first with her. There were a goodly train of choice ladies attended her coming upon the bowling-green on Barham Downs, upon the way, who divided themselves into two rows, and they appeared like so many constellations; but methought that the country ladies outshined the courtiers. She brought over with her two hundred thousand crowns in gold and silver as half her portion, and the other moiety is to be paid at the year's end. Her first suite of servants (by article) are to be French, and as they die English are to succeed. She is also allowed twenty-eight ecclesiastics of any order except Jesuits, a bishop for her almoner, and to have private exercise of her religion for her and her servants.

I pray convey the enclosed to my father by the next conveniency, and pray present my dear love to my sister. I hope to see you at Dyvinnock about Michaelmas, for I intend to wait upon my father, and will

---

19 Dr. Thomas Prichard, Vice-Principal of Jesus College, Oxford.

20 From Plautus, meaning "not even a grain's worth."

take my mother in the way; I mean Oxford. In the interim I rest your most affectionate brother,

J. H.

London, 16 May 1626.

SECTION V

To Sir J. S.,[21] Knight

SIR,

You writ to me lately for a footman, and I think this bearer will suit you. I know he can run well, for he hath run away twice from me, but he knew the way back again; yet though he hath a running head as well as running heels (and who will expect a footman to be a staid man?) I would not part with him were I not to go post to the North. There be some things in him that answer for his waggeries. He will come when you call him, go when you bid him, and shut the door after him. He is faithful and stout, and a lover of his master. He is a great enemy to all dogs if they bark at him in his running, for I have seen him confront a huge mastiff and knock him down. When you go a country journey, or have him run with you a-hunting, you must spirit him with liquor; you must allow him also something extraordinary for socks, else you must not have him to wait at your table; when his grease melts in running hard it is subject to fall into his toes. I send him you but for trial. If he be not for your turn, turn him over to me again when I come back.

The best news I can send you at this time is that we are like to have peace both with France and Spain, so that Harwich men, your neighbors, shall not hereafter need to fear the name of Spinola,[22] who struck such an apprehension into them lately that I understand they begin to fortify.

I pray present my most humble service to my good lady, and at my return from the North I will be bold to kiss her hands and yours, so I am, your much obliged servitor,

J. H.

London, 25 of May 1628.

To My Father, Mr. Ben Johnson

FATHER BEN, *Nullum fit magnum ingenium sine mixtura dementiæ*, there is no great wit without some mixture of madness, so saith the philosopher; nor was he a fool who answered, *nec parvum, sine mixtura stultitiæ*, nor small wit without some allay of foolishness. Touching the first it is verified in you, for I find that you have been oftentimes mad. You were mad when you writ your "Fox," and madder when you writ your "Alchemist"; you were mad when you writ "Catilin," and stark mad when you writ "Sejanus"; but when you writ your "Epigrams" and the "Magnetic Lady" you were not so mad. Insomuch that I perceive there be degrees of madness in you. Excuse me that I am so free with you. The madness I mean is that divine fury, that heating and heightening spirit which Ovid speaks of.

Est Deus in nobis agitante calescimus illo: that true enthusiasm which transports and elevates the souls of poets above the middle region of vulgar conceptions, and makes them soar up to heaven to touch the stars with their laurelled heads, to walk in the Zodiac with Apollo himself, and command Mercury upon their errand.

I cannot yet light upon Doctor Davies' Welsh Grammar. Before Christmas I am promised one. So desiring you to look better hereafter to your charcoal fire and chimney, which I am glad to be one that preserved from burning, this being the second time that Vulcan hath threatened you, it may be because you have spoken ill of his wife, and been too busy with his horns, I rest your son and contiguous neighbor,

J. H.

Westminster, 27 June 1629.

To My Noble Lady, the Lady Cor[23]

MADAM,

You spoke to me for a cook who had seen the world abroad, and I think the bearer hereof will fit your ladyship's turn. He can marinate fish, make jellies, he is excellent for a piquant sauce, and the haugou. Besides, madam, he is passing good for an olla. He will tell your ladyship that the reverend matron the olla-podrida hath intellectuals and senses. Mutton, beef, and bacon are to her as the will, understanding,

---

21 It is not known to whom these initials refer.
22 The Marquis de Spinola, Commander of the Spanish Army in the Low Countries.

23 Jacobs infers that the lady is Elizabeth, the widow of Sir Frederick Cornwallis, to whom another letter is addressed.

and memory are to the soul. Cabbage, turnips, arti-
chokes, potatoes, and dates are her five senses, and
pepper the common sense. She must have marrow to
keep life in her, and some birds to make her light. By
all means she must go adorned with chains of sausages.
He is also good at larding of meat after the mode of
France. Madam, you may make proof of him, and
if your ladyship find him too saucy or wasteful, you
may return him whence you had him. So I rest,
madam, your ladyship's most humble servitor,

J. H.

Westminster, 2 June 1630.

SECTION VI

*To Dr. Duppa, L.B., of Chichester, His Highness'
Tutor at St. James*

My Lord,

It is a well-becoming and very worthy work you
are about not to suffer Mr. Ben Johnson to go so
silently to his grave or rot so suddenly. Being newly
come to town and understanding that your "Johnsonus
Virbius" was in the press, upon the solicitation of Sir
Thomas Hawkins, I suddenly fell upon the ensuing
decastich, which, if your lordship please, may have
room amongst the rest.

UPON MY HONORED FRIEND AND F.,
MR. BEN JOHNSON

And is thy glass run out, is that oil spent
Which light to such strong sinewy labors lent?
Well, Ben; I now perceive that all the nine,
Though they their utmost forces should combine,
Cannot prevail 'gainst Night's three daughters, but
One still must spin, one wind, the other cut.
Yet in despite of distaff, clue, and knife,
Thou in thy strenuous lines hast got a life,
Which like thy bays shall flourish ev'ry age,
While sock or buskin shall ascend the stage.
Sic vaticinatur Hoellus.

So I rest, with many devoted respects to your lordship, as being your very humble servitor,

J. H.

London, 1 May 1636.[24]

24 The date, as often in Howell's Letters, is obviously
wrong, as Jonson died August 6, 1637.

VOLUME TWO

To Sir Thomas Hawk,[25] *Knight*

Sir,

I was invited yesternight to a solemn supper by
B. J.,[26] where you were deeply remembered. There
was good company, excellent cheer, choice wines, and
jovial welcome. One thing intervened which almost
spoiled the relish of the rest, that B. began to engross
all the discourse, to vapor extremely of himself, and
by vilifying others to magnify his own muse. T.
Ca.[27] buzzed me in the ear that, though Ben had
barreled up a great deal of knowledge, yet it seems
he had not read the "Ethics,"[28] which, among other
precepts of morality forbid self-commendation, declaring it to be an ill-favored solecism in good manners. It
made me think upon the lady (not very young) who,
having a good while given her guests neat entertainment, a capon being brought upon the table, instead
of a spoon she took a mouthful of claret and spouted
it into the poop of the hollow bird. Such an accident
happened in this entertainment, you know. "——
Proprio laus sordet in ore" (Be a man's breath never so
sweet, yet it makes one's praises stink if he makes his
own mouth the conduit-pipe of it). But for my part I
am content to dispense with the Roman infirmity of
B., now that time hath snowed upon his *pericranium*.
You know Ovid and (your) Horace were subject to
his humor, the first bursting out into

Jamq; opus exegi quod nec Jovis ira, nec ignis, etc.[29]

The other into

Exegi monumentum ære perennius, etc.[30]

As also Cicero, while he forced himself into this
hexameter—

O fortunatam natam, me consule Romam![31]

There is another reason that excuseth B., which is,
that if one be allowed to love the natural issue of his

25 Sir Thomas Hawkins.
26 That the initials refer to Ben Jonson has never been
questioned.
27 Either Thomas Carew, the poet, or Thomas Cary, his
contemporary.
28 The Nicomachean Ethics of Aristotle.
29 Ovid, Metamorphoses, xv. 871.
30 Horace, Odes, B. III. xxx. 1.
31 Quoted from Juvenal x. 122.

body, why not that of the brain, which is of a spiritual and more noble extraction? I preserve your manuscripts safe for you till you return to London. What news the times afford this bearer will impart unto you. So I am sir, your very humble and most faithful servitor,

J. H.

Westminster, 5 April 1636.

To My Honorable Friend, Sir C. C.[32]

SIR,

I was upon point of going abroad to steal a solitary walk, when yours of the twelfth current came to hand; the high researches and choice abstracted notions I found therein seemed to heighten my spirits and make my fancy fitter for my intended retirement and meditations; add hereunto, that the countenance of the weather invited me, for it was a still evening, it was also a clear open sky, not a speck or the least wrinkle appeared in the whole face of heaven, it was such a pure deep azure all the hemisphere over that I wondered what was become of the three regions of the air with their meteors. So having got into a close field, I cast my face upward, and fell to consider what a rare prerogative the optic virtue of the eye hath, much more the intuitive virtue of the thought, that the one in a moment can reach heaven and the other go beyond it. Therefore sure that philosopher was but a kind of frantic fool that would have plucked out both his eyes because they were a hindrance to his speculations. Moreover, I began to contemplate as I was in this posture the vast magnitude of the universe and what proportion this poor globe of earth might bear with it, for if those numberless bodies which stick in the vast roof of heaven, though they appear to us but as spangles, be some of them thousands of times bigger than the earth—take the sea with it to boot, for they both make but one sphere, surely the astronomers had reason to term this sphere an indivisible point and a thing of no dimension at all being compared to the whole world. I fell then to think that at the second general destruction, it is no more for God Almighty to fire this earth than for us to blow up a small squib or rather one small grain of gunpowder. As I was musing thus, I spied a swarm of gnats waving up and down the air about me, which I knew to be part of the universe as well as I; and methought it was a strange

32 Rather, Jacobs thinks, Sir S. C., Sir Sackville Crow, ambassador to Constantinople.

opinion of our Aristotle to hold that the least of those small insected ephemerans should be more noble than the sun, because it had a sensitive soul in it. I fell to think that the same porportion which these animalillios bore with me in point of bigness, the same I held with those glorious spirits which are near the throne of the Almighty, what then should we think of the magnitude of the Creator himself? Doubtless it is beyond the reach of any human imagination to conceive it. In my private devotions I presume to compare him to a great mountain of light, and my soul seems to discern some glorious form therein, but suddenly as she would fix her eyes upon the object, her sight is presently dazzled and disgregated with the refulgency and coruscations thereof.

Walking a little further I espied a young boisterous bull breaking over a hedge and ditch to a herd of kine in the next pasture, which made me think that if that fierce strong animal with others of that kind knew their own strength, they would never suffer man to be their master. Then looking upon them quietly grazing up and down, I fell to consider that the flesh which is daily dished upon our tables is but concocted grass, which is recarnified in our stomachs and transmuted to another flesh. I fell also to think what advantage those innocent animals had of man, which, as soon as nature casts them into the world, find their meat dressed, the cloth laid, and the table covered; they find their drink brewed and the buttery open, their beds made and their clothes ready; and though man hath the faculty of reason to make him a compensation for the want of these advantages, yet this reason brings with it a thousand perturbations of mind and perplexities of spirit, griping cares and anguishes of thought, which those harmless silly creatures were exempted from. Going on, I came to repose myself upon the trunk of a tree, and I fell to consider further what advantage that dull vegetable had of those feeding animals, as not to be so troublesome and beholding to nature, nor to be so subject to starving, to diseases, to the inclemency of the weather, and to be far longer-lived. I then spied a great stone, and sitting a while upon it, I fell to weigh in my thoughts that that stone was in a happier condition in some respects than either those sensitive creatures or vegetables I saw before, in regard that that stone, which propagates by assimilation, as the philosophers say, needed neither grass nor hay, or any aliment for restoration of nature, nor water to refresh its roots, or the heat of the sun to attract the moisture upwards to increase growth as the other did. As I directed my pace homeward, I spied a kite soaring high in the air, and gently gliding up and down the clear region so far above my head, I fell to envy the bird extremely and repine at his happiness that he should have a privilege to make a nearer approach to heaven than I.

Excuse me that I trouble you thus with these rambling meditations; they are to correspond with you in some part for those accurate fancies of yours you lately sent me. So I rest your entire and true servitor,

J. H.

Holborn, 17 March 1639.

To Mr. T. V.,[33] At Brussels

MY DEAR TOM,

Who would have thought poor England had been brought to this pass? Could it ever have entered into the imagination of man that the scheme and whole frame of so ancient and well-molded a government should be so suddenly struck off its hinges, quite out of joint, and tumbled into such a horrid confusion? Who would have held it possible that to fly from Babylon we should fall into such a Babel? That to avoid superstition some people should be brought to belch out such horrid profaneness as to call the temples of God the tabernacles of Satan? the Lord's Supper a twopenny ordinary? to make the communion table a manger, and the font a trough to water their horses in? to term the white decent robe of the presbyter the whore's smock? the pipes, through which nothing came but anthems and holy hymns, the Devil's bagpipes? The liturgy of the church, though extracted most of it out of the sacred text, called by some another kind of Alcoran; by others raw porridge; by some a piece forged in hell? Who would have thought to have seen in England the churches shut and the shops open upon Christmas Day? Could any soul have imagined that this isle would have produced such monsters as to rejoice at the Turk's good successes against Christians, and wish he were in the midst of Rome? Who would have dreamt ten years since, when Archbishop Laud did ride in state through London streets accompanying my Lord of London to be sworn Lord High Treasurer of England, that the miter should have now come to such a scorn, to such a national kind of hatred, as to put the whole island in a combustion; which makes me call to memory a

saying of the Earl of Kildare in Ireland, in the reign of Henry VIII, which earl, having deadly feud with the Bishop of Cassiles, burnt a church belonging to that diocese, and being asked, upon his examination before the Lord Deputy at the Castle of Dublin, why he had committed such a horrid sacrilege as to burn God's church, he answered, "I had never burned the church unless I had thought the bishop had been in it." Lastly, who would have imagined that the excise would have taken footing here? A word I remember in the last Parliament, save one, so odious that when Sir D. Carleton, then Secretary of State, did but name it in the House of Commons, he was like to be sent to the Tower, although he named it to no ill sense but to show what advantage of happiness the people of England had over nations having neither the gabells of Italy, the tallies of France, or the excise of Holland laid upon them, yet upon this he was suddenly interrupted, and called to the bar. Such a strange metamorphosis poor England is now come unto, and I am afraid our miseries are not come to their height, but the longest shadows stay till the evening.

The freshest news that I can write unto you is that the Kentish knight of your acquaintance, whom I wrote in my last had an apostasy in his brain, died suddenly this week of an impostume in his breast, as he was reading a pamphlet of his own that came from the press, wherein he showed a great mind to be nibbling with my trees; but he only showed his teeth, for he could not bite them to any purpose.

William Ro.[34] is returned from the wars, but he is grown lame in one of his arms, so he hath no mind to bear arms any more. He confesseth himself to be an egregious fool to leave his mercership and go to be a musketeer. It made me think upon the tale of the Gallego in Spain, who in the civil wars against Aragon, being in the field he was shot in the forehead, and being carried away to a tent, the surgeon searched his wound and found it mortal, so he advised him to send for his confessor, for he was no man for this world, in regard the brain was touched. The soldier wished him to search it again, which he did, and told him that he found he was hurt in the brain and could not possibly escape; whereupon the Gallego fell into a chafe, and said he lied; for he had no brain at all *por que si tuviera seso, nunca hunier a venido a esta a guerra,* for if I had had any brain, I would never have come to this war. All your friends here are well, except the

---

33 Thomas Vaughan, cousin of Howell, is Jacob's conjecture.

34 William Roberts, later Bishop of Bangor, is perhaps referred to.

maimed soldier, and remember you often, especially Sir J. Brown, a good gallant gentleman, who never forgets any who deserved to have a place in his memory. Farewell, my dear Tom, and God send you better days than we have here, for I wish you as much happiness as possibly man can have. I wish your mornings may be good, your noons better, your evenings and nights best of all. I wish your sorrows may be short, your joys lasting, and all your desires end in success. Let me hear once more from you before you remove thence, and tell me how the squares go in Flanders. So I rest, your entirely affectionate servitor,

J. H.

Fleet, 3 August 1644.[35]

VOLUME THREE

To Henry Hopkins, Esq.

SIR,

To usher in again old Janus, I send you a parcel of Indian perfume, which the Spaniard calls the holy herb, in regard of the various virtues it hath, but we call it tobacco. I will not say it grew under the King of Spain's window, but I am told it was gathered near his gold mines of Potosi (where they report that in some places there is more of that ore than earth), therefore it must needs be precious stuff. If moderately and seasonably taken (as I find you always do), 'tis good for many things; it helps digestion taken a while after meat, it makes one void rheum, breaks wind, and it keeps the body open. A leaf or two being steeped o'er night in a little white wine is a vomit that never fails in its operation. It is a good companion to one that converseth with dead men, for if one hath been poring long upon a book, or is toiled with the pen and stupefied with study, it quickeneth him, and dispels those clouds that usually o'erset the brain. The smoke of it is one of the wholesomest scents that is against all contagious airs, for it o'ermasters all other smells, as King James, they say, found true when, being once a-hunting, a shower of rain drove him into a pigsty for shelter, where he caused a pipeful to be taken of purpose. It cannot endure a spider or a flea, with such-like vermin, and if your hawk be troubled with any

such, being blown into his feathers it frees him. It is good to fortify and preserve the sight, the smoke being let in round about the balls of the eyes once a week, and frees them from all rheums, driving them back by way of repercussion. Being taken backward, it is excellent good against the colic, and taken into the stomach, 'twill heat and cleanse it; for I could instance in a great lord (my Lord of Sunderland, President of York), who told me that he taking it downward into his stomach, it made him cast up an impostume, bag and all, which had been a long time engendering out of a bruise he had received at football, and so preserved his life for many years. Now to descend from the substance of the smoke to the ashes. 'Tis well known that the medicinal virtues thereof are very many but they are so common that I will spare the inserting of them here. But if one would try a pretty conclusion how much smoke there is in a pound of tobacco, the ashes will tell him, for let a pound be exactly weighed, and the ashes kept charily and weighed afterwards, what wants of a pound weight in the ashes cannot be denied to have been smoke, which evaporated into air. I have been told that Sir Walter Ralegh won a wager of Queen Elizabeth upon this nicety.

The Spaniards and Irish take it most in powder or smutchin,[36] and it mightily refreshes the brain, and I believe there is as much taken in this way in Ireland as there is in pipes in England. One shall commonly see the serving maid upon the washing block, and the swain upon the plowshare, when they are tired with labor, take out their boxes of smutchin and draw it into their nostrils with a quill, and it will beget new spirits in them, with a fresh vigor to fall to their work again. In Barbary and other parts of Africa it is wonderful what a small pill of tobacco will do for those who use to ride post through the sandy deserts, where they meet not with anything that is potable or edible sometimes three days together; they use to carry small balls or pills of tobacco, which being put under the tongue, it affords them a perpetual moisture, and takes off the edge of the appetite for some days.

If you desire to read with pleasure all the virtues of this modern herb, you must read Doctor Thorius' *Pætalogia*, an accurate piece couched in a strenuous heroic verse full of matter, and continuing its strength from first to last, insomuch that for the bigness it may be compared to any piece of antiquity, and in my

---

35 The letter purports to come from the Fleet prison, in which Howell was incarcerated in 1642 by the Parliamentary party, and where he remained until the general amnesty of 1650.

opinion is beyond βατρακομνομαχία [37] or γαλεομνομαχία. [38]

So I conclude these rambling notions, presuming you will accept this small argument of my great respects unto you. If you want paper to light your pipe, this letter may serve the turn, and if it be true what the poets frequently sing, that affection is fire, you shall need no other than the clear flames of the donor's love to make ignition, which is comprehended in this distich—

> *"Ignis amor si sit, tobaccum accendere nostrum,*
> *Nulla petenda tibi fax nisi dantis amor."*

> "If love be fire, to light this Indian weed,
> The donor's love of fire may stand in stead."

So I wish you, as to myself, a most happy New Year; may the beginning be good, the middle better, and the end best of all.—Your most faithful and truly affectionate servant,

J. H.

1 January 1646.

To Sir William Boswell, At The Hague

SIR,

That black tragedy [39] which was lately acted here, as it hath filled most hearts among us with consternation and horror, so I believe it hath been no less resented abroad. For my own particular the more I ruminate upon it, the more it astonisheth my imagination and shaketh all the cells of my brain, so that sometimes I struggle with my faith and have much ado to believe it yet. I shall give over wondering at anything hereafter, nothing shall seem strange unto me, only I will attend with patience how England will thrive now that she has let blood in the basilical vein and cured, as they say, of the king's evil.

I had one of yours by Mr. Jacob Boeue, and I much thank you for the account you please to give me of what I sent you by his conveyance. Holland may now be proud, for there is a younger commonwealth in Christendom than herself. No more now but that I always rest, sir, your most humble servitor,

J. H.

Fleet, 20 of March 1648.

37 The Battle of the Frogs and the Mice, one of the Homeric poems.
38 The Battle of the Cats and the Mice, by Theodorus Prodromus, a Byzantine poet of the twelfth century.
39 The execution of Charles I, January 30, 1649.

VOLUME FOUR

To Sir James Crofts, Knight, At His House Near Lemster [40]

SIR,

Epistles, or (according to the word in use) Familiar Letters, may be called the larum bells of love; I hope this will prove so to you, and have power to awaken you out of that silence wherein you have slept so long; yet I would not have this larum make any harsh obstreperous sound, but gently summon you to our former correspondence; your returns to me shall be more than larum bells, they shall be like silver trumpets to rouse up my spirits, and make me take pen in hand to meet you more than half way in the old field of friendship.

It is recorded of Galen, one of nature's cabinet clerks, that when he slept his siesta (as the Spaniard calls it), or afternoon sleep, to avoid excess that way, he used to sit in such a posture that having a gold ball in his hand, and a copper vessel underneath, as soon as his senses were shut, and the phantasy began to work, the ball would fall down, the noise whereof would awake him, and draw the spring-lock back again to set the outward sense at liberty. I have seen in Italy a finger-ring which in the boss thereof had a watch, and there was such a trick of art in it that it might be so wound up that it would make a small pin to prick him who wore it at such an hour he pleased in the night. Let the pen between us have the virtue of that pin: but the pen hath a thousand virtues more. You know that *anser, apis, vitulus,* the goose, the bee, and the calf, do rule the world, the one affording parchment, the other two sealing-wax and the quills to write withal. You know also how the gaggling of geese did once preserve the Capitol from being surprised by my countryman Brennus, which was the first foreign force that Rome felt. But the goose quill doth daily greater things; it conserves empires (and the feathers of it get kingdoms; witness what exploits the English performed by it in France), the quill being the chiefest instrument of intelligence, and the ambassador's prime tool. Nay, the quill is the usefulest thing which preserves that noble virtue, friendship, who else would perish among men for want of practice.

I shall make no more sallies out of London this

40 Now Leominster, Herefordshire.

summer, therefore your letters may be sure where to find me. Matters are still involved here in a strange confusion, but the stars may let down milder influences; therefore cheer up, and reprieve yourself against better times, for the world would be irksome unto me if you were out of it: hap what will, you shall be sure to find me your ready and real servant,

J. H.

John Earle

[1600?–1665]

ORN at York some time around 1600, Earle entered Oxford at eighteen and received his M.A. there in 1624. There is some uncertainty as to his undergraduate college, but he was elected a fellow of Merton College shortly after his receipt of the degree. During these Oxford years Earle wrote his character-book, *Microcosmography*, which was published anonymously in 1628 and soon achieved great popularity. The volume went through ten editions in Earle's lifetime, and the editions of 1629 and 1633 added new characters to the original number. Although the authorship of the book was soon a matter of general knowledge, Earle's name did not appear on the book until 1732.

Earle's academic and ecclesiastical career began auspiciously; appointed proctor of the University in 1631, he then became chaplain to the Earl of Pembroke, who was at that time Chancellor of Oxford. Shortly thereafter he was made chaplain and tutor to the Prince of Wales (later Charles II), and then Chancellor of Salisbury Cathedral. Like the majority of royalist divines, Earle was deprived of his livings by Parliament, and he spent the years of Commonwealth rule in exile in France, where he continued in his capacity as chaplain to Charles II and also translated into Latin the *Eikon Basilike*, that potent piece of propaganda which the royalists ascribed to the martyred Charles I.

After the Restoration Earle was rewarded by being made successively Dean of Westminster, Bishop of Worcester, and Bishop of Salisbury. The sweet and reasonable temper which had always been one of his most marked characteristics led him consistently to counsel policies of moderation toward the defeated nonconformists. His advice was not accepted by the king and his advisers, but it earned for him the respect and admiration of the Puritan Richard Baxter. Indeed, throughout his life Earle had a remarkable capacity for winning the friendship and regard of diverse types of men. Falkland was a friend of his youth, as Pepys and Evelyn were friends of his later years; Walton compared him to the revered Hooker; and Clarendon said of him: "He was amongst the few excellent men who never had, nor never could have, an enemy, but such a one who was enemy to all learning and virtue and therefore would never make himself known."

Microcosmography is perhaps the best of the seventeenth-century English character-books. Fully as witty and incisive as the Overburian characters, Earle's characters show a greater thoughtfulness, a finer analytic capacity, and a more profound understanding of human motivation. A kind of affectionate irony is the dominant attitude which Earle brings to bear on his human comedy, but his tone is flexible enough to modulate into philosophical tenderness, as in his picture of "A Child," or something rather like tragic insight, as in his picture of "A Pot Poet." The range and depth of impression which the reader receives from these character sketches must also be attributed to Earle's style, probably the most distinguished to be found among the English character-writers: it is terse, pithy, and epigrammatic, in the Senecan tradition, but one has the impression that these qualities appear in Earle's work not as the result of fashion but because they are inevitably the expression of his thoughtfully ironic temper and his analytic cast of mind.

Earle's characters are further distinguished by the important role assumed among them by campus types and by personified localities, such as "Paul's Walk" or "A Bowling Alley." In general, they retain their validity for the modern reader because Earle has been able not only to present the character in its full particularity but also to perceive within the particular the unchanging universal.

J. EARLE. *Microcosmographie*, ed. H. Osborne (London, 1933).
B. BOYCE. *Theophrastan Character in England to 1642* (Cambridge, Mass., 1947).
R. ALDINGTON. (Cited under Overbury.)
E. N. S. THOMPSON. (Cited under Overbury.)

FROM

MICROCOSMOGRAPHY,
Or, A Piece of the World Discovered in Essays and Characters

[TEXT: *first complete edition, 1633*]

A CHILD

IS A man in a small letter, yet the best copy of Adam before he tasted of Eve or the apple; and he is happy whose small practice in the world can only write his character. He is nature's fresh picture newly drawn in oil, which time, and much handling, dims and defaces. His soul is yet a white paper[1] unscribbled with observations of the world, wherewith, at length, it becomes a blurred note-book. He is purely happy, because he knows no evil, nor hath made means by sin to be acquainted with misery. He arrives not at the mischief of being wise, nor endures evils to come, by foreseeing them. He kisses and loves all, and, when the smart of the rod is past, smiles on his beater. Nature and his parents alike dandle him, and tice him on with a bait of sugar to a draught of wormwood. He plays yet, like a young 'prentice the first day, and is not come to his task of melancholy. All the language he speaks yet is tears, and they serve him well enough to express his necessity. His hardest labor is his tongue, as if he were loth to use so deceitful an organ; and he is best company with it when he can but prattle. We laugh at his foolish sports, but his game is our earnest; and his drums, rattles, and hobby-horses, but the emblems and mocking of man's business. His father hath writ him as his own little story, wherein he reads those days of his life that he cannot remember, and sighs to see what innocence he has out-lived. The older he grows, he is a stair lower from God; and, like his first father, much worse in his breeches.[2] He is the Christian's example, and the old man's relapse; the one imitates his pureness, and the other falls into his simplicity. Could he put off his body with his little coat, he had got eternity without a burden, and exchanged but one heaven for another.

A YOUNG RAW PREACHER

IS A bird not yet fledged, that hath hopped out of his nest to be chirping on a hedge, and will be straggling

1 An interesting anticipation of John Locke's description of the infant's mind as a *tabula rasa*, or blank paper, in his *Essay Concerning the Human Understanding*, I, i, 15.

2 A pun on Genesis 3:7, which, in the Geneva Bible, says that after their first disobedience Adam and Eve "made themselves breeches."

abroad at what peril soever. His backwardness in the university hath set him thus forward; for had he not truanted there, he had not been so hasty a divine. His small standing and time hath made him a proficient only in boldness, out of which, and his table-book, he is furnished for a preacher. His collections of study are the notes of sermons, which, taken up at St. Mary's, he utters in the country: and if he write brachygraphy,[3] his stock is so much the better. His writing is more than his reading, for he reads only what he gets without book. Thus accomplished he comes down to his friends, and his first salutation is grace and peace out of the pulpit. His prayer is conceited, and no man remembers his college more at large. The pace of his sermon is a full career, and he runs wildly over hill and dale, till the clock stops him. The labor of it is chiefly in his lungs; and the only thing he has made in it himself is the faces. He takes on against the Pope without mercy, and has a jest still in lavender for Bellarmine:[4] yet he preaches heresy, if it comes in his way, though with a mind, I must needs say, very orthodox. His action is all passion, and his speech interjections. He has an excellent faculty in bemoaning the people, and spits with a very good grace. His style is compounded of twenty several men's, only his body imitates someone extraordinary. He will not draw his handkercher out of his place, nor blow his nose without discretion. His commendation is, that he never looks upon book; and indeed he was never used to it. He preaches but once a year, though twice on Sunday; for the stuff is still the same, only the dressing a little altered: he has more tricks with a sermon than a tailor with an old cloak, to turn it, and piece it, and at last quite disguise it with a new preface. If he have waded further in his profession, and would show reading of his own, his authors are postils,[5] and his School-divinity a catechism. His fashion and demure habit gets him in with some town-precisian, and makes him a guest on Friday nights. You shall know him by his narrow velvet cape, and serge-facing; and his ruff, next his hair, the shortest thing about him. The companion of his walk is some zealous tradesman, whom he astonisheth with strange points, which they both understand alike. His friends and much painfulness may prefer him to thirty pounds a year, and this means to a chambermaid; with whom we leave him

3 Shorthand writing.
4 Cardinal Robert Bellarmine, 1542–1621, Jesuit, and one of the ablest controversialists of his day.
5 Annotations of Scriptural passages.

now in the bonds of wedlock: next Sunday you shall have him again.

A MERE ALDERMAN

HE IS venerable in his gown, more in his beard, wherewith he sets not forth so much his own, as the face of a city. You must look on him as one of the town gates, and consider him not as a body, but a corporation. His eminency above others hath made him a man of worship, for he had never been preferred, but that he was worth thousands. He oversees the commonwealth as his shop, and it is an argument of his policy, that he has thriven by his craft. He is a rigorous magistrate in his ward; yet his scale of justice is suspected, lest it be like the balances in his warehouse. A ponderous man he is, and substantial, for his weight is commonly extraordinary, and in his preferment nothing rises so much as his belly. His head is of no great depth, yet well furnished; and when it is in conjunction with his brethren, may bring forth a city apothegm, or some such sage matter. He is one that will not hastily run into error, for he treads with great deliberation, and his judgment consists much in his pace. His discourse is commonly the annals of his mayoralty, and what good government there was in the days of his gold chain; though the door-posts were the only things that suffered reformation. He seems most sincerely religious, especially on solemn days; for he comes often to church to make a show and is a part of the choir hangings. He is the highest stair of his profession, and an example to his trade, what in time they may come to. He makes very much of his authority, but more of his satin doublet, which, though of good years, bears its age very well, and looks fresh every Sunday: but his scarlet gown is a monument, and lasts from generation to generation.

AN ANTIQUARY

HE IS a man strangely thrifty of time past, and an enemy indeed to his maw, whence he fetches out many things when they are now all rotten and stinking. He is one that hath that unnatural disease to be enamored of old age and wrinkles, and loves all things (as Dutchmen do cheese), the better for being moldy and worm-eaten. He is of our religion, because we say it is most ancient; and yet a broken statue would almost make him an idolater. A great admirer he is of the rust of old monuments, and reads only those characters where time hath eaten out the letters. He will go you forty miles to see a saint's well or a ruined abbey; and if there be a cross or stone foot-stool in the way, he'll be considering it so long, till he forget his journey. His estate consists much in shekels, and Roman coins; and he hath more pictures of Cæsar than James or Elizabeth. Beggars cozen him with musty things which they have raked from dunghills, and he preserves their rags for precious relics. He loves no library but where there are more spiders' volumes than authors', and looks with great admiration on the antique work of cobwebs. Printed books he contemns, as a novelty of this latter age, but a manuscript he pores over everlastingly, especially if the cover be all moth-eaten, and the dust make a parenthesis between every syllable. He would give all the books in his study (which are rarities all) for one of the old Roman bindings, or six lines of Tully in his own hand. His chamber is hung commonly with strange beasts' skins, and is a kind of charnel-house of bones extraordinary; and his discourse upon them, if you will hear him, shall last longer. His very attire is that which is the eldest out of fashion and you may pick a criticism out of his breeches. He never looks upon himself till he is gray-haired, and then he is pleased with his own antiquity. His grave does not fright him, for he has been used to sepulchres, and he likes death the better, because it gathers him to his fathers.

A TAVERN

IS A degree, or (if you will) a pair of stairs above an alehouse, where men are drunk with more credit and apology. If the vintner's nose be at door, it is a sign sufficient, but the absence of this is supplied by the ivy-bush: the rooms are ill breathed like the drinkers that have been washed well overnight, and are smelt-to fasting next morning; not furnished with beds apt to be defiled, but more necessary implements, stools, table, and a chamberpot. It is a broacher of more news than hogsheads, and more jests than news, which are sucked up here by some spongy brain, and from thence squeezed into a comedy. Men come here to make merry, but indeed make a noise, and this music above is answered with the clinking below. The drawers are the civilest people in it, men of good bringing up, and howsoever we esteem of them, none can boast more justly of their high calling. 'Tis the best theater of natures, where they are truly acted, not played, and the business is in the rest of the world up and down, to wit, from the bottom of the cellar to the great chamber. A melancholy man would find here matter to work upon, to see heads as brittle as glasses, and often broken; men come hither to quarrel, and come hither to be made friends: and if Plutarch will lend me his simile, it is even Telephus [6] his sword that makes wounds and cures them. It is the common consumption of the afternoon, and the murderer or maker-away of a rainy day. It is the torrid zone that scorches the face, and tobacco the gunpowder that blows it up. Much harm would be done, if the charitable vintner had not water ready for these flames. A house of sin you may call it, but not a house of darkness, for the candles are never out; and it is like those countries far in the North, where it is as clear at midnight as at mid-day. After a long sitting, it becomes like a street in a dashing shower, where the spouts are flushing above, and the conduits running below, while the jordans [7] like swelling rivers overflow their banks. To give you the total reckoning of it; it is the busy man's recreation, the idle man's business, the melancholy man's sanctuary, the stranger's welcome, the inns-a-court man's entertainment, the scholar's kindness, and the citizen's courtesy. It is the study of sparkling wits, and a cup of sherry their book, where we leave them.

A YOUNG MAN

HE IS now out of nature's protection, though not yet able to guide himself; but left loose to the world and fortune, from which the weakness of his childhood preserved him; and now his strength exposes him. He is, indeed, just of age to be miserable, yet in his own conceit first begins to be happy; and he is happier in this imagination, and his misery not felt is less. He sees yet but the outside of the world and men, and conceives them, according to their appearing, glister, and out of this ignorance believes them. He pursues all vanities for happiness, and enjoys them best in this fancy. His reason serves not to curb but understand his appetite, and prosecute the motions thereof with a more eager earnestness. Himself is his own temptation, and needs not Satan, and the world will come hereafter. He leaves repentance for gray hairs, and performs it in being covetous. He is mingled with the vices of the age as the fashion and custom, with which he longs to be acquainted, and sins to better his understanding. He conceives his youth as the season of his lust, and the hour wherein he ought to be bad; and because he would not lose his time, spends it. He

6 The son of Hercules and Auge, who was wounded by Achilles, and was healed by the rust of Achille's spear.
7 Chamber pots.

distastes religion as a sad thing, and is six years elder for a thought of heaven. He scorns and fears, and yet hopes for old age, but dare not imagine it with wrinkles. He loves and hates with the same inflammation, and when the heat is over is cool alike to friends and enemies. His friendship is seldom so steadfast but that lust, drink, or anger may overturn it. He offers you his blood today in kindness, and is ready to take yours tomorrow. He does seldom anything which he wishes not to do again, and is only wise after a misfortune. He suffers much for his knowledge, and a great deal of folly it is makes him a wise man. He is free from many vices, by being not grown to the performance, and is only more virtuous out of weakness. Every action is his danger, and every man his ambush. He is a ship without pilot or tackling, and only good fortune may steer him. If he scape this age, he has scaped a tempest, and may live to be a man.

AN UPSTART KNIGHT

Is A holiday clown, and differs only in the stuff of his clothes, not the stuff of himself. [His honor was some-what preposterous,][8] for he bare the king's sword before he had arms to wield it; yet being once laid o'er the shoulder with a knighthood, he finds the herald his friend. His father was a man of good stock, though but a tanner or usurer; he purchased the land, and his son the title. He has doffed off the name of a country fellow, but the look not so easy, and his face bears still a relish of churn-milk. He is guarded with more gold lace than all the gentlemen of the country, yet his body makes his clothes still out of fashion. His house-keeping is seen much in the distinct families of dogs, and serving-men attendant on their kennels, and the deepness of their throats is the depth of his dis-course. A hawk he esteems the true burden of nobility, and is exceeding ambitious to seem delighted in the sport, and have his fist gloved with his jesses.[9] A justice of peace he is to domineer in his parish, and do his neighbor wrong with more right. He will be drunk with his hunters for company, and stain his gentility with droppings of ale. He is fearful of being sheriff of the shire by instinct, and dreads the size-week as much as the prisoner. In sum, he's but a clod of his own earth, or his land is the dunghill and he the cock that crows over it: and commonly his race is quickly run, and his children's children, though they

8 First edition, 1628.
9 The straps of leather fastened to the hawk's legs, by which she is held on the fist.

scape hanging, return to the place from whence they came.

A GALLANT

Is ONE that was born and shaped for his clothes; and, if Adam had not fallen, had lived to no purpose. He gratulates therefore the first sin and fig-leaves that were an occasion of bravery.[10] His first care is his dress, the next his body, and in the uniting of these two lies his soul and its faculties. He observes London trulier than the terms, and his business is the street, the stage, the court, and those places where a proper man is best shown. If he be qualified in gaming extraor-dinary, he is so much the more gentle and complete, and he learns the best oaths for the purpose. These are a great part of his discourse, and he is as curious in their newness as the fashion. His other talk is ladies and such pretty things, or some jest at a play. His pick-tooth bears a great part in his discourse, so does his body, the upper parts whereof are as starched as his linen, and perchance use the same laundress. He has learned to ruffle his face from his boot, and takes great delight in his walk to hear his spurs jingle. Though his life pass somewhat slidingly, yet he seems very careful of the time, for he is still drawing his watch out of his pocket, and spends part of his hours in numbering them. He is one never serious but with his tailor, when he is in conspiracy for the next device. He is furnished with his jests, as some wanderer with sermons, some three for all congregations, one espe-cially against the scholar, a man to him much ridicu-lous, whom he knows by no other definition but silly fellow in black. He is a kind of walking mercer's shop, and shows you one stuff today and another tomorrow; an ornament to the rooms he comes in as the fair bed and hangings be; and is merely ratable accordingly, fifty or an hundred pounds as his suit is. His main ambition is to get a knighthood, and then an old lady; which if he be happy in, he fills the stage and a coach so much longer. Otherwise, himself and his clothes grow stale together, and he is buried commonly ere he dies in the gaol, or the country.

A CONSTABLE

Is A viceroy in the street, and no man stands more upon't that he is the king's officer. His jurisdiction extends to the next stocks, where he has commission for the heels only, and sets the rest of the body at

10 Fine dress.

liberty. He is a scarecrow to that alehouse where he drinks not his morning's draught, and apprehends a drunkard for not standing in the king's name. Beggars fear him more than the justice, and as much as the whipstock, whom he delivers over to his subordinate magistrates, the Bridewell-man and the beadle. He is a great stickler in the tumults of double jugs, and ventures his head by his place, which is broke many times to keep whole the peace. He is never so much in his majesty as in his nightwatch, where he sits in his chair of state, a shop-stall, and environed with a guard of halberts, examines all passengers. He is a very careful man in his office, but if he stay up after midnight you shall take him napping.

A DOWNRIGHT SCHOLAR

Is ONE that has much learning in the ore, unwrought and untried, which time and experience fashions and refines. He is good metal in the inside, though rough and unscoured without, and therefore hated of the courtier, that is quite contrary. The time has got a vein of making him ridiculous, and men laugh at him by tradition, and no unlucky absurdity but is put upon his profession, and done like a scholar. But his fault is only this, that his mind is somewhat too much taken up with his mind, and his thoughts not loaden with any carriage besides. He has not put on the quaint garb of the age, which is now a man's *imprimis and all the item*.[11] He has not humbled his meditations to the industry of compliment, nor afflicted his brain in an elaborate leg. His body is not set upon nice pins, to be turning and flexible for every motion, but his scrape is homely and his nod worse. He cannot kiss his hand and cry, Madam, nor talk idle enough to bear her company. His smacking of a gentlewoman is somewhat too savory, and he mistakes her nose for her lips. A very woodcock would puzzle him in carving, and he wants the logic of a capon. He has not the glib faculty of sliding over a tale, but his words come squeamishly out of his mouth, and the laughter commonly before the jest. He names this word college too often, and his discourse beats too much on the university. The perplexity of mannerliness will not let him feed, and he is sharp set at an argument when he should cut his meat. He is discarded for a gamester at all games but one and thirty, and at tables he reaches not beyond doublets. His fingers are not long and drawn out to handle a fiddle, but his fist is clenched with the

habit of disputing. He ascends a horse somewhat sinisterly, though not on the left side, and they both go jogging in grief together. He is exceedingly censured by the inns-a-court men for that heinous vice, being out of fashion. He cannot speak to a dog in his own dialect, and understands Greek better than the language of a falconer. He has been used to a dark room, and dark clothes, and his eyes dazzle at a satin suit. The hermitage of his study has made him somewhat uncouth in the world, and men make him worse by staring on him. Thus is he silly and ridiculous, and it continues with him for some quarter of a year out of the university. But practice him a little in men, and brush him o'er with good company, and he shall outbalance those glisterers, as far as a solid substance does a feather, or gold, gold-lace.

A PLAIN COUNTRY FELLOW

Is ONE that manures his ground well, but lets himself lie fallow and untilled. He has reason enough to do his business, and not enough to be idle or melancholy. He seems to have the punishment of Nebuchadnezzar, for his conversation is among beasts, and his talons none of the shortest, only he eats not grass, because he loves not sallets. His hand guides the plow, and the plow his thoughts, and his ditch and land-mark is the very mound of his meditations. He expostulates with his oxen very understandingly, and speaks Gee and Ree better than English. His mind is not much distracted with objects, but if a good fat cow come in his way, he stands dumb and astonished, and though his haste be never so great, will fix here half an hour's contemplation. His habitation is some poor thatched roof, distinguished from his barn by the loop-holes that let out smoke, which the rain had long since washed through, but for the double ceiling of bacon on the inside, which has hung there from his grandsire's time, and is yet to make rashers for posterity. His dinner is his other work, for he sweats at it as much as at his labor; he is a terrible fastener on a piece of beef, and you may hope to stave the guard off sooner. His religion is a part of his copyhold, which he takes from his landlord, and refers it wholly to his discretion. Yet if he give him leave he is a good Christian to his power, that is, comes to church in his best clothes, and sits there with his neighbors, where he is capable only of two prayers, for rain, and fair weather. He apprehends God's blessings only in a good year, or a fat pasture, and never praises him but on good ground. Sunday he esteems a day to make merry in, and thinks

---

11 All in all.

a bag-pipe as essential to it as evening-prayer, where he walks very solemnly after service with his hands coupled behind him, and censures[12] the dancing of his parish. His compliment with his neighbor is a good thump on the back, and his salutation commonly some blunt curse. He thinks nothing to be vices but pride and ill-husbandry, from which he will gravely dissuade the youth, and has some thrifty hob-nail proverbs to clout his discourse. He is a niggard all the week, except only market-day, where, if his corn sell well, he thinks he may be drunk with a good conscience. His feet never stink so unbecomingly as when he trots after a lawyer in Westminster-hall, and even cleaves the ground with hard scraping in beseeching his worship to take his money. He is sensible of no calamity but the burning of a stack of corn or the overflowing of a meadow, and thinks Noah's Flood the greatest plague that ever was, not because it drowned the world, but spoiled the grass. For death he is never troubled, and if he get in but his harvest before, let it come when it will, he cares not.

A PLAYER

HE KNOWS the right use of the world, wherein he comes to play a part and so away. His life is not idle, for it is all action, and no man need be more wary in his doings, for the eyes of all men are upon him. His profession has in it a kind of contradiction, for none is more disliked, and yet none more applauded; and he has this misfortune of some scholar, too much wit makes him a fool. He is like our painting gentle-women, seldom in his own face, seldomer in his clothes; and he pleases the better he counterfeits, except only when he is disguised with straw for gold-lace. He does not only personate on the stage, but sometimes in the street, for he is masked still in the habit of a gentleman. His parts find him oaths and good words, which he keeps for use and discourse, and makes show with them of a fashionable companion. He is tragical on the stage, but rampant in the tiring-house,[13] and swears oaths there which he never conned. The waiting-women spectators are over ears in love with him, and ladies send for him to act in their chambers. Your inns-of-court men were undone but for him, he is their chief guest and employment, and the sole business that makes them afternoon's-men. The poet only is his tyrant, and he is bound to make his friend's friend drunk at his charge. Shrove-Tuesday

he fears as much as the bawds, and Lent[14] is more damage to him than the butcher. He was never so much discredited as in one act,[15] and that was of Parliament, which gives hostlers privilege before him, for which he abhors it more than a corrupt judge. But to give him his due, one well-furnished actor has enough in him for five common gentlemen, and, if he have a good body, for six; and for resolution he shall challenge any Cato, for it has been his practice to die bravely.

A YOUNG GENTLEMAN OF THE UNIVERSITY

IS ONE that comes there to wear a gown, and to say hereafter, he has been at the university. His father sent him thither because he heard there were the best fencing and dancing schools; from these he has his education, from his tutor the oversight. The first element of his knowledge is to be shown the colleges, and initiated in a tavern by the way, which hereafter he will learn of himself. The two marks of his seniority is the bare velvet of his gown, and his proficiency at tennis, where when he can once play a set, he is a freshman no more. His study has commonly handsome shelves, his books neat silk strings, which he shows to his father's man, and is loth to untie or take down for fear of misplacing. Upon foul days for recreation he retires thither, and looks over the pretty book his tutor reads to him, which is commonly some short history, or a piece of Euphormio;[16] for which his tutor gives him money to spend next day. His main loitering is at the library, where he studies arms and books of honor, and turns a gentleman critic in pedigrees. Of all things he endures not to be mistaken for a scholar, and hates a black suit though it be made of satin. His companion is ordinarily some stale fellow, that has been notorious for an ingle to gold hat-bands,[17] whom he admires at first, afterwards scorns. If he have spirit or wit he may light of better company, and may learn some flashes of wit, which may do him knight's service in the country hereafter. But he is now gone to the inns-of-court, where he studies to forget what he learned before, his acquaintance and the fashion.

14 The theaters were not permitted to be open during Lent in the reign of James I.

15 There was an act passed in Elizabeth's reign which treated as vagabonds all actors not attached to some nobleman.

16 Euphormio Lusinius, pen-name of John Barclay, 1582–1621, author of the Argenis.

17 An ingle to gold hatbands; *i.e.*, a crony of noblemen at the university, who wore gold tassels on their caps.

12 Criticizes.   13 The dressing room.

A POT-POET

IS THE dregs of wit, yet mingled with good drink may have some relish. His inspirations are more real than others, for they do but feign a God, but he has his by him. His verse runs like the tap, and his invention, as the barrel, ebbs and flows at the mercy of the spigot. In thin drink he aspires not above a ballad, but a cup of sack inflames him, and sets his muse and nose afire together. The press is his mint, and stamps him now and then a sixpence or two in reward of the baser coin of his pamphlet. His works would scarce sell for three half-pence, though they are given oft for three shillings, but for the pretty title that allures the country gentleman; for which the printer maintains him in ale a fortnight. His verses are, like his clothes, miserable *centos*[18] and patches, yet their pace is not altogether so hobbling as an almanack's. The death of a great man or the burning of a house furnish him with an argument, and the nine muses are out straight[19] in mourning gowns, and Melpomene cries Fire! fire! His other poems are but briefs in rhyme, and like the poor Greeks collections to redeem from captivity. He is a man now much employed in commendations of our navy, and a bitter inveigher against the Spaniard. His frequentest works go out in single sheets, and are chanted from market to market to a vile tune and a worse throat; whilst the poor country wench melts like her butter to hear them. And these are the stories of some men of Tyburn, or a strange monster out of Germany; or, sitting in a bawdy-house, he writes God's judgments. He drops away at last in some obscure painted cloth,[20] to which himself made the verses, and his life, like a can too full, spills upon the bench. He leaves twenty shillings on the score, which my hostess loses.

A CONTEMPLATIVE MAN

IS A scholar in this great university the world; and the same his book and study. He cloisters not his meditations in the narrow darkness of a room, but sends them abroad with his eyes, and his brain travels with his feet. He looks upon man from a high tower, and sees him trulier at this distance in his infirmities and poorness. He scorns to mix himself in men's actions, as he would to act upon a stage; but sits aloft on the scaffold a censuring spectator. He will not lose his time by being busy, nor make so poor a use of the world as to hug and embrace it. Nature admits him as a partaker of her sports, and asks his approbation as it were of her own works and variety. He comes not in company, because he would not be solitary, but finds discourse enough with himself, and his own thoughts are his excellent playfellows. He looks not upon a thing as a yawning stranger at novelties, but his search is more mysterious and inward, and he spells heaven out of earth. He knits his observations together, and makes a ladder of them all to climb to God. He is free from vice, because he has no occasion to employ it, and is above those ends that make men wicked. He has learnt all can here be taught him, and comes now to heaven to see more.

A VULGAR-SPIRITED MAN

IS ONE of the herd of the world. One that follows merely the common cry, and makes it louder by one. A man that loves none but who are publicly affected, and he will not be wiser than the rest of the town. That never owns a friend after an ill name, or some general imputation, though he knows it most unworthy. That opposes to reason, "thus men say," and "thus most do," and "thus the world goes," and thinks this enough to poise the other. That worships men in place, and those only; and thinks all a great man speaks, oracles. Much taken with my lord's jest, and repeats you it all to a syllable. One that justifies nothing out of fashion, nor any opinion out of the applauded way. That thinks certainly all Spaniards and Jesuits very villains, and is still cursing the Pope and Spinola.[21] One that thinks the gravest cassock the best scholar and the best clothes the finest man. That is taken only with broad and obscene wit, and hisses anything too deep for him. That cries Chaucer for his money above all our English poets, because the voice has gone so, and he has read none. That is much ravished with such a nobleman's courtesy, and would venture his life for him, because he put off his hat. One that is foremost still to kiss the king's hand, and cries "God bless his Majesty!" loudest. That rails on all men condemned and out of favor, and the first that says "Away with the traitors!"—yet struck with much ruth at executions, and for pity to see a man die, could kill the hangman. That comes to London to see it, and the

---

18 A *cento* is a work made up of quotations from other authors.

19 Straightway.

20 Tapestry; cf. I Henry IV, IV. ii. 27, "slaves as ragged as Lazarus in the painted cloth."

21 Ambrose Spinola, 1569–1630, a general under Philip III of Spain.

pretty things in it, and, the chief cause of his journey, the bears. That measures the happiness of the kingdom by the cheapness of corn, and conceives no harm of state but ill trading. Within this compass, too, come those that are too much wedged into the world, and have no lifting thoughts above those things; that call to thrive well, to do well; and preferment only the grace of God. That aim all studies at this mark, and show you poor scholars as an example to take heed by. That think the prison and want, a judgment for some sin; and never like well hereafter of a jail-bird. That know no other content but wealth, bravery, and the town-pleasures; that think all else but idle speculation, and the philosophers madmen. In short, men that are carried away with all outwardnesses, shows, appearances, the stream, the people; for there is no man of worth but has a piece of singularity, and scorns something.

A PLODDING STUDENT

IS A kind of alchymist or persecutor of nature, that would change the dull lead of his brain into finer metal, with success many times as unprosperous, or at least not quitting the cost, to wit, of his own oil and candles. He has a strange forced appetite to learning, and to achieve it brings nothing but patience and a body. His study is not great but continual, and consists much in the sitting up till after midnight in a rug-gown and night-cap, to the vanquishing perhaps of some six lines; yet what he has, he has perfect, for he reads it so long to understand it till he gets it without book. He may with much industry make a breach into logic, and arrive at some ability in an argument; but for politer studies he dare not skirmish with them, and for poetry accounts it impregnable. His invention is no more than the finding out of his papers, and his few gleanings there; and his disposition of them is as just as the bookbinder's, a setting or gluing of them together. He is a great discomforter of young students, by telling them what travail it has cost him, and how often his brain turned at philosophy, and makes others fear studying as a cause of duncery. He is a man much given to apothegms, which serve him for wit, and seldom breaks any jest but which belonged to some Lacedæmonian or Roman in Lycosthenes.[22] He is like a dull carrier's horse, that will go a whole week together, but never out of a foot-pace; and he that sets forth on the Saturday shall overtake him.

22 The nom-de-plume of Conrad Wolfhart, German scholar, 1518–1561.

PAUL'S WALK[23]

IS THE land's epitome, or you may call it the lesser Isle of Great Britain. It is more than this, the whole world's map, which you may here discern in its perfectest motion, justling and turning. It is a heap of stones and men, with a vast confusion of languages; and were the steeple not sanctified, nothing liker Babel. The noise in it is like that of bees, a strange humming or buzz mixed of walking tongues and feet: it is a kind of still roar or loud whisper. It is the great exchange of all discourse, and no business whatsoever but is here stirring and a-foot. It is the synod of all pates politic, jointed and laid together in most serious posture, and they are not half so busy at the Parliament. It is the antic[24] of tails to tails, and backs to backs, and for vizards you need go no further than faces. It is the market of young lecturers, whom you may cheapen[25] here at all rates and sizes. It is the general mint of all famous lies, which are here like the legends of popery, first coined and stamped in the church. All inventions are emptied here, and not few pockets. The best sign of a temple in it is, that it is the thieves' sanctuary, which rob more safely in the crowd than a wilderness, whilst every searcher is a bush to hide them. It is the other expense of the day, after plays, tavern, and a bawdy-house; and men have still some oaths left to swear here. The visitants are all men without exceptions, but the principal inhabitants and possessors are stale knights and captains out of service; men of long rapiers and breeches, which after all turn merchants here and traffic for news. Some make it a preface to their dinner, and travel for a stomach; but thriftier men make it their ordinary, and board here very cheap. Of all such places it is least haunted with hobgoblins, for if a ghost would walk more, he could not.

A PRETENDER TO LEARNING

IS ONE that would make all others more fools than himself, for though he know nothing, he would not have the world know so much. He conceits nothing in learning but the opinion, which he seeks to purchase without it, though he might with less labor cure his ignorance than hide it. He is indeed a kind of

23 St. Paul's Cathedral was, during the sixteenth and seventeenth centuries, a general gathering-place for merchants and business men, and a public parade, especially about noon.
24 Grotesque dance, mummery.
25 Purchase, bargain for.

scholar-mountebank, and his art our delusion. He is tricked out in all the accoutrements of learning, and at the first encounter none passes better. He is oftener in his study than at his book, and you cannot pleasure him better than to deprehend him: yet he hears you not till the third knock, and then comes out very angry, as interrupted. You find him in his slippers and a pen in his ear, in which formality he was asleep. His table is spread wide with some classic folio, which is as constant to it as the carpet, and hath laid open in the same page this half year. His candle is always a longer sitter-up than himself, and the boast of his window at midnight. He walks much alone in the posture of meditation, and has a book still before his face in the fields. His pocket is seldom without a Greek Testament or Hebrew Bible, which he opens only in the church, and that when some stander-by looks over. He has sentences for company, some scatterings of Seneca and Tacitus, which are good upon all occasions. If he read anything in the morning, it comes up all at dinner; and as long as that lasts, the discourse is his. He is a great plagiary of tavern wit, and comes to sermons only that he may talk of Austin.[26] His parcels are the mere scrapings from company, yet he complains at parting what time he has lost. He is wondrously capricious to seem a judgment, and listens with a sour attention to what he understands not. He talks much of Scaliger,[27] and Casaubon,[28] and the Jesuits, and prefers some unheard of Dutch names before them all. He has verses to bring in upon these and these hints, and it shall go hard but he will wind in his opportunity. He is critical in a language he cannot construe, and speaks seldom under Arminius[29] in divinity. His business and retirement and caller-away is his study, and he protests no delight to it comparable. He is a great nomenclator[30] of authors, which he has read in general in the catalogue, and in particular in the title, and goes seldom so far as the dedication. He never talks of anything but learning, and learns all from talking. Three encounters with the same men pump him, and then he only puts in or

26 St. Augustine.
27 Julius Cæsar Scaliger, 1484–1558, Italian Latin poet and philologist, or his son, Joseph Scaliger, 1540–1609, the famous scholar of Leyden.
28 Isaac Casaubon, 1559–1614, French scholar, and first editor and translator of the Characters of Theophrastus.
29 Jacobus Arminius, Dutch theologian, 1560–1609, the great opponent of Calvinism.
30 A Roman slave whose function was to announce the names of the guests to the host.

gravely says nothing. He has taken pains to be an ass, though not to be a scholar, and is at length discovered and laughed at.

A BLUNT MAN

IS ONE whose wit is better pointed than his behavior, and that coarse and unpolished, not out of ignorance so much as humor. He is a great enemy to the fine gentleman, and these things of compliment, and hates ceremony in conversation, as the Puritan in religion. He distinguishes not betwixt fair and double dealing, and suspects all smoothness for the dress of knavery. He starts at the encounter of a salutation as an assault, and beseeches you in choler to forbear your courtesy. He loves not anything in discourse that comes before the purpose, and is always suspicious of a preface. Himself falls rudely still on his matter without any circumstance, except he use an old proverb for an introduction. He swears old, out-of-date, innocent oaths, as, By the mass! By our lady! and such like, and though there be lords present, he cries, My masters! He is exceedingly in love with his humor, which makes him always profess and proclaim it, and you must take what he says patiently, "because he is a plain man." His nature is his excuse still, and other men's tyrant; for he must speak his mind, and that is his worst, and craves your pardon most injuriously for not pardoning you. His jests best become him, because they come from him rudely and unaffected; and he has the luck commonly to have them famous. He is one that will do more than he will speak, and yet speak more than he will hear; for though he love to touch others, he is touchy himself, and seldom to his own abuses replies but with his fists. He is as squeazy[31] of his commendations as his courtesy, and his good word is like an eulogy in a satire. He is generally better favored than he favors, as being commonly well expounded in his bitterness, and no man speaks treason more securely. He chides great men with most boldness, and is counted for it an honest fellow. He is grumbling much in the behalf of the commonwealth, and is in prison oft for it with credit. He is generally honest, but more generally thought so, and his downrightness credits him, as a man not well bended and crookened[32] to the times. In conclusion, he is not easily bad in whom this quality is nature, but the counterfeit is most dangerous, since he is disguised in a humor that professes not to disguise.

31 Niggardly.   32 Crook-kneed.

Owen Felltham

[1602?–1668]

ERY little is known of the life of Felltham, but his *Resolves* (1623?) occupy an important place in the development of the English essay. He was apparently born in Sussex, of a propertied family, and some time in his early twenties traveled in the Low Countries. After returning to London he was associated with theatrical and poetic circles and apparently was well acquainted with such figures as Ben Jonson and Thomas Randolph. In the early 1620's he published his *Resolves, Divine, Moral, and Political,* and in the second edition expanded the original hundred essays of the work by the addition of another "century." The work was very popular in Felltham's own lifetime and went through numerous editions; to one of the later editions the author appended *Lusoria,* a collection of reasonably good verses which includes a satiric answer to Ben Jonson's "Come, Leave the Loathed Stage," as well as "When, Dearest, I but Think on Thee," a lyric of sufficient distinction to have been attributed to Suckling. His *Brief Character of the Low Countries,* which had appeared in a pirated edition in 1648, made its authorized appearance in 1652.

From around 1632 until the end of his life, Felltham seems to have been in the service of the Earl of Thomond as steward of the Earl's household at Great Billing, Northamptonshire. He died at that family's house in London.

The most certain fact with regard to Felltham's life and interests is his fanatical devotion to the royalist cause, an adherence marked more by ardor than by discretion. In his "Epitaph to the Eternal Memory of Charles the First . . . Inhumanely Murthered by a Perfidious Party of His Prevalent Subjects," occurs the famous line "Here Charles the First and Christ the Second lies." But the work through which Felltham's name lives displays a balance and sanity of temper which are very unlike the tone of that line; the *Resolves* introduce us to a likable, tolerant, and witty gentleman whose poetic sensitivity frequently kindles into memorable passages of beauty and perceptiveness, as in his Platonic description of the soul as "a shoot of everlastingness," a phrase which Henry Vaughan was to borrow and make immortal in his "The Retreat."

Felltham's merit as an essayist rests at least as much in his style as in his thought; he is a master of the "Senecan" style, with its aphoristic brevity, witty conciseness, and conversational rhythms. In reading the *Resolves,* however, one seldom has the impression that Felltham employs the Attic style for fashion's sake; the style seems rather the natural and appropriate garb for the author's disposition of mind, and his best passages have, like Browne's, an air of inevitability despite their originality.

Like many of the other prose artists of the seventeenth century, Felltham experienced a revival in the early nineteenth century, a period which prized him for his "quaintness."

He has not been subject, in our own time, to the re-examination which has elevated the prose of Donne and Browne to such a position of prominence, but the reader with a taste for the eccentric elegance of seventeenth-century prose will always give Felltham an honored, if small, place in his library.

O. FELLTHAM. *Resolves, Divine, Morall, and Politicall*, ed. O. Smeaton (London, 1904).

E. N. S. THOMPSON. *The Seventeenth-Century English Essay* (Iowa City, 1926).

F. S. TUPPER. "New Facts Regarding Owen Felltham," *MLN*, LIV (1939). An important contribution to Felltham biography.

F R O M

RESOLVES; DIVINE, MORAL, AND POLITICAL

[TEXT: *second edition, 1628*]

THE FIRST CENTURY[1]

OF PURITANS

I FIND many that are called Puritans;[2] yet few or none that will own the name. Whereof the reason sure is this, that 'tis for the most part held a name of infamy, and is so new, that it hath scarcely yet obtained a definition; nor is it an appellation derived from one man's name, whose tenents we may find digested into a volume; whereby we do much err in the application. It imports a kind of excellency above another, which man (being conscious of his own frail bendings) is ashamed to assume to himself. So that I believe there are men which would be Puritans, but indeed not any that are. One will have him one that lives religiously, and will not revel it in a shoreless excess. Another, him that separates from our divine assemblies. Another, him that in some tenents only is peculiar. Another, him that will not swear. Absolutely to define him, is a work, I think, of difficulty; some I know that rejoice at the name; but sure they be such as least understand it. As he is more generally in these times taken, I suppose we may call him a Church-rebel, or one that would exclude order, that his brain might rule. To decline offenses, to be careful and conscionable in our several actions, is a purity that every man ought to labor for, which we may well do without a sullen segregation from all society. If there be any privileges, they are surely granted to the children of the king, which are those that are the children of heaven. If mirth and recreations be lawful, sure such a one may lawfully use it. If wine were given to cheer the heart, why should I fear to use it for that end? Surely, the merry soul is freer from intended mischief than the thoughtful man. A bounded mirth is a patent, adding time and happiness to the crazed life of man. Yet if Laertius reports him rightly, Plato deserves a censure for allowing drunkenness at festivals; because, says he, as then, the gods themselves reach wines to present men. God delights in nothing more than in a cheerful heart, careful to perform him service. What parent is it that rejoiceth not to see his child pleasant, in the limits of a filial duty? I know, we read of Christ's weeping, not of his laughter: yet we see, he graceth a feast with his first miracle, and that a feast of joy; and can we think that such a meeting could pass without the noise of laughter? What a lump of quickened care is the melancholic man! Change anger into mirth, and the precept will hold good still: Be merry but sin not. As there be many that in their life assume too great a liberty, so I believe there are some that abridge themselves of what they might lawfully use. Ignorance is an ill steward, to provide for either soul or body. A man that submits to reverent order, that sometimes unbends himself in

---

1 This "first century" of essays in all the later editions of the Resolves is entitled the "second century" in the second edition, the text of which is here followed. The original edition (1623?) contained only the one hundred essays which comprise the "second century" of all editions after the second.

2 The term "Puritan" began to be applied about 1566 to those members of the Church of England who, not satisfied with the reforms that had been effected, wished a still "purer" church, and withdrew from its authority.

a moderate relaxation, and in all, labors to approve himself in the sereneness of a healthful conscience, such a Puritan I will love immutably. But when a man, in things but ceremonial, shall spurn at the grave authority of the Church, and out of a needless nicety be a thief to himself of those benefits which God hath allowed him, or out of a blind and uncharitable pride, censure and scorn others as reprobates, or out of obstinacy fill the world with brawls about undeterminable tenents, I shall think him one of those whose opinion hath fevered his zeal to madness and distraction. I have more faith in one Solomon, than in a thousand Dutch parlors of such opinionists. "Behold then; what I have seen good!—That it is comely to eat, and to drink, and to take pleasure in all his labor wherein he travaileth under the sun, the whole number of the days of his life, which God giveth him. For this is his portion. Nay, there is no profit to man, but that he eat, and drink, and delight his soul with the profit of his labor." [3] For, he that saw other things but *vanity*, saw this also, that it was the hand of God. Methinks the reading of Ecclesiastes should make a Puritan undress his brain, and lay off all those fanatic toys that jingle about his understanding. For my own part, I think the world hath not better men than some that suffer under that name; nor withal, more *scelestique* [4] villains. For when they are once elated with that pride, they so contemn others, that they infringe the laws of all human society.

OF REPREHENSION

To REPREHEND well, is both the hardest, and most necessary part of friendship. Who is it that will either not merit a check or endure one? Yet wherein can a friend more unfold his love, than in preventing dangers before their birth, or in reducing a man to safety which is traveling in the way to ruin? I grant, the manner of the application may turn the benefit into an injury; and then it both strengtheneth error and wounds the giver. Correction is never in vain. Vice is a miry deepness; if thou strivest to help one out and dost not, thy stirring him sinks him in the further. Fury is the madder for his chain. When thou chidest thy wandering friend, do it secretly, in season, in love —not in the ear of a popular convention. For many times, the presence of a multitude makes a man take

up an unjust defense, rather than fall in a just shame. Diseased eyes endure not an unmasked sun, nor does the wound but rankle more which is fanned by the public air. Nor can I much blame a man, though he shuns to make the vulgar his confessor; for they are the most uncharitable tell-tales that the burthened earth doth suffer. They understand nothing but the dregs of actions, and with spattering those abroad, they besmear a deserving fame. A man had better be convinced in private, than be made guilty by a proclamation. Open rebukes are for magistrates and courts of justice, for stelled chambers, and for scarlets in the thronged hall. Private are for friends; where all the witnesses of the offender's blushes are blind, and deaf, and dumb. We should do by them as Joseph thought to have done by Mary, seek to cover blemishes with secrecy. Public reproof is like striking of a deer in the herd, it not only wounds him to the loss of enabling blood, but betrays him to the hound, his enemy, and makes him, by his fellows, be pushed out of company. Even concealment of a fault argues some charity to the delinquent, and when we tell him of it in secret, it shows we wish he should amend, before the world comes to know his amiss. Next, it ought to be in season, neither when the brain is misted with arising fumes, nor when the mind is madded with unreined passions. Certainly, he is drunk himself that profanes reason so as to urge it to a drunken man. Nature unloosed in a flying speed cannot come off with a sudden stop.

Quis matrem, nisi mentis inops, in funere nati
Flere vetat? non hoc ulla monenda loco est.

He's mad, that dries a mother's eyes full tide
At her son's grave. There, 'tis no time to chide,

was the opinion of the smoothest poet. To admonish a man in the height of his passion is to call a soldier to counsel in the midst, in the heat of a battle. Let the combat slack, and then thou mayst expect a hearing. All passions are like rapid torrents: they swell the more for meeting with a dam in their violence. He that will hear nothing in the rage and roar of his anger will, after a pause, inquire of you. Seem you to forget him and he will the sooner remember himself. For it often falls out that the end of passion is the beginning of repentance. Then will it be easy to draw back a retiring man, as a boat is rowed with less labor, when it hath both a wind and tide to drive it. A word seasonably given, like a rudder, sometimes steers a

---

3 Ecclesiastes 2:24; 8:5.   4 Wicked.

man quite into another course. When the Macedonian Philip was capering in the view of his captives, says Demades, "Since fortune has made you like Agamemnon, why will you show yourself like Thersites?"[5] And this changed him to another man. A blow bestowed in the striking time is better than ten delivered unseasonably. There are some nicks in time, which whosoever finds, may promise to himself success. As in all things, so in this; especially if he do it as he ought, in love. It is not good to be too tetrical and virulent. Kind words make rough actions plausible. The bitterness of reprehension is in-sweetened with the pleasingness of compellations. If ever flattery might be lawful here is a cause that would give it admission. To be plain, argues honesty; but to be pleasing, argues discretion. Sores are not to be anguished with a rustic pressure, but gently stroked with a ladied hand. Physicians fire not their eyes at patients, but calmly minister to their diseases. Let it be so done, as the offender may see affection without arrogancy. Who blows out candles with too strong a breath does but make them stink, and blows them light again. To avoid this, it was ordained among the Lacedemonians that every transgressor should be, as it were, his own beadle; for his punishment was to compass an altar, singing an invective made against himself. It is not consonant that a member so unboned as the tongue is, should smart it with an iron lash. Every man that adviseth assumes, as it were, a transcendency over the other; which if it be not allayed with protestations and some self-including terms, grows hateful: that even the reprehension is many times the greater fault of the two. It will be good therefore, not to make the complaint our own, but to lay it upon some others, that not knowing his grounded virtues, will, according to this, be apt to judge of all his actions. Nor can he be a competent judge of another's crime that is guilty of the like himself. 'Tis unworthily done, to condemn that in others which we would not have but pardoned in ourselves. When Diogenes fell in the school of the Stoics, he answers his deriders with this question: "Why do you laugh at me for falling backward, when you yourselves do retrograde your lives?" He is not fit to cure a dimmed sight that looks upon another with a beamed eye. Freed, we may free others. And if we please them with praising some of their virtues, they will with much more ease be brought to know their vices. Shame will not let them be angry with

them, that so equally deal both the rod and laurel. If he be much our superior, 'tis good to do it sometimes in parables, as Nathan did to David.[6] So let him by collection give himself the censure. If he be an equal, let it appear affection, and the truth of friendship urging it. If he be our inferior, let it seem our care and desire to benefit him. Towards all, I would be sure to show humility and love. Though I find a little bluster for the present, I am confident I shall meet with thanks afterward,—and in my absence, his reverent report following me. If not, the best way to lose a friend is by seeking, by my love, to save him. 'Tis best for others that they hate me for vice; but if I must be hated, 'tis best for myself, that they hate me for my goodness. For then am I mine own antidote against all the poison they can spit upon me.

OF THE WORSHIP OF ADMIRATION

WHATSOEVER is rare and passionate carries the soul to the thought of eternity; and, by contemplation, gives it some glimpses of more absolute perfection than here 'tis capable of. When I see the royalty of a state show at some unwonted solemnity, my thoughts present me something more royal than this. When I see the most enchanting beauties that earth can show me, I yet think, there is something far more glorious; methinks I see a kind of higher perfection, peeping through the frailty of a face. When I hear the ravishing strains of a sweet-tuned voice, married to the warbles of the artful instrument, I apprehend by this a higher diapason; and do almost believe I hear a little deity whispering, through the pory substance of the tongue. But this I can but grope after. I can neither find nor say what it is. When I read a rarely sententious man, I admire him to my own impatiency. I cannot read some parts of Seneca above two leaves together. He raises my soul to a contemplation, which sets me a-thinking on more than I can imagine. So I am forced to cast him by, and subside to an admiration. Such effects works poetry, when it looks to towering virtues. It gives up a man to raptures, and inradiates the soul with such high apprehensions that all the glories which this world hath hereby appear contemptible; of which the soft-souled Ovid gives a touch when he complains the want.

5 Diodorus Siculus, xvi, 87.

6 See II Samuel 12.

Impetus ille sacer, qui vatum pectora nutrit,
Qui prius in nobis esse solebat abest.

That sacred vigor which had wont, alone,
To flame the poet's noble breast, is gone.

But this is when these excellencies incline to gravity and seriousness. For otherwise, light airs turns us into spriteful actions, which breathe away in a loose laughter, not leaving half that impression behind them, which serious considerations do. As if mirth were the excellency for the body, and meditation for the soul. As if one were for the contentment of this life: and the other eyeing to that of the life to come. All endeavors aspire to eminency; all eminencies do beget an admiration. And this makes me believe that contemplative admiration is a large part of the worship of the Deity. 'Tis an adoration purely of the spirit; a more sublime bowing of the soul to the Godhead. And this is it, which that Homer of philosophers avowed, could bring a man to perfect happiness, if to his contemplation he joined a constant imitation of God, in justice, wisdom, holiness. Nothing can carry us so near to God and Heaven as this. The mind can walk beyond the sight of the eye; and (though in a cloud) can lift us into Heaven, while we live. Meditation is the soul's perspective glass, whereby in her long remove, she discerneth God, as if he were nearer hand. I persuade no man to make it his whole life's business. We have bodies, as well as souls. And even this world, while we are in it, ought somewhat to be cared for. As those states are likely to flourish where execution follows sound advisements, so is man, when contemplation is seconded by action. Contemplation generates, action propagates. Without the first, the latter is defective. Without the last, the first is but abortive and embrious. Saint Bernard compares contemplation to Rachel, which was the more fair; but action to Leah, which was the more fruitful. I will neither always be busy and doing, nor ever shut up in nothing but thoughts. Yet that which some would call idleness, I will call the sweetest part of my life; and that is my thinking. Surely, God made so many varieties in his creatures, as well for the inward soul as the outward senses; though he made them primarily for his own free-will and glory. He was a monk of an honester age, that being asked how he could endure that life without the pleasure of books, answered: The nature of the creatures was his library; wherein when he pleased, he could muse upon God's deep oracles.

OF PREACHING

THE excess which is in the defect of preaching has made the pulpit slighted; I mean the much bad oratory we find it guilty of. 'Tis a wonder to me how men can preach so little and so long; so long a time, and so little matter; as if they thought to please by the inculcation of their vain tautologies. I see no reason that so high a princess as divinity is should be presented to the people in the sordid rags of the tongue; nor that he which speaks from the Father of Languages should deliver his embassage in an ill one. A man can never speak too well, where he speaks not too obscure. Long and distended clauses are both tedious to the ear, and difficult for their retaining. A sentence well couched takes both the sense and the understanding. I love not those cart-rope speeches that are longer than the memory of man to fathom. I see not but that divinity, put into apt significants, might ravish as well as poetry. The weighty lines men find upon the stage, I am persuaded have been the lures to draw away the pulpit's followers. We complain of drowsiness at a sermon, when a play of doubled length leads us on still with alacrity. But the fault is not all in ourselves. If we saw divinity acted, the gesture and variety would as much invigilate. But it is too high to be personated by humanity. The stage feeds both the ear and the eye; and through this latter sense the soul drinks deeper draughts. Things acted possess us more, and are, too, more retainable than the passable tones of the tongue. Besides here we meet with more compassed language, the *dulcia sermonis* molded into curious phrase; though 'tis to be lamented such wits are not set to the right tune, and consorted to divinity, who without doubt well decked, will cast a far more radiant lustre than those obscene scurrilities that the stage presents us with, though oe'd and spangled in their gaudiest tire. At a sermon well dressed, what understander can have a motion to sleep? Divinity well ordered casts forth a bait, which angles the soul into the ear; and how can that close, when such a guest sits in it? They are sermons but of baser metal, which lead the eyes to slumber. And should we hear a continued oration upon such a subject as the stage treats on, in such words as we hear some sermons, I am confident it would not only be far more tedious, but nauseous and contemptful. The most advantage they have of other places is in their good lives and actions. For 'tis certain, Cicero and Roscius are most complete when they both make but one man. He answered well, that after often asking, said still that action was the chiefest part of an orator. Surely, the oration is most powerful where the tongue is diffusive and speaks in a native decency even in every limb. A good orator should pierce the ear, allure the eye, and invade the mind of his hearer. And this is Seneca's opinion. Fit words are better than fine ones. I like not those that are injudiciously made, but such as be expressively significant, that lead the mind to something, beside the naked term. And he that speaks thus must not look to speak thus every day. A combed oration will cost both sweat and the rubbing of the brain. And combed I wish it, not frizzled, nor curled. Divinity should not lasciviate. Unwormwooded jests I like well, but they are fitter for the tavern than the majesty of a temple. Christ taught the people with authority. Gravity becomes the pulpit. Demosthenes confessed he became an orator by spending more oil than wine. This is too fluid an element to beget substantials. Wit procured by wine is, for the most part, like the sparklings in the cup when 'tis filling; they brisk it for a moment, but die immediately. I admire the valor of some men, that, before their studies, dare ascend the pulpit, and do there take more pains than they have done in their library. But having done this I wonder not that they there spend sometimes three hours but to weary the people into sleep. And this makes some such fugitive divines that, like cowards, they run away from their texts. Words are not all, nor matter is not all, nor gesture; yet together they are. 'Tis much moving in an orator when the soul seems to speak as well as the tongue. Saint Augustine says, Tully was admired more for his tongue than his mind; Aristotle, more for his mind than his tongue; but Plato for both. And surely nothing decks an oration more than a judgment able well to conceive and utter. I know God hath chosen by weak things to confound the wise; yet I see not but in all times a washed language hath much prevailed. And even the Scriptures (though I know not the Hebrew) yet I believe they are penned in a tongue of deep expressions; wherein, almost every word hath a metaphorical sense, which does illustrate by some allusion. How political is Moses in his Pentateuch! How philosophical Job! How massy and sententious is Solomon in his Proverbs! How quaint and flamingly amorous in the Canticles! How grave and solemn in his Ecclesiastes! that in the world there is not such another dissection of the world as it. How were the Jews astonished at Christ's doctrine! How eloquent

a pleader is Paul at the bar; in disputation how subtle! And he that reads the Fathers shall find them as if written with a crisped pen. Nor is it such a fault as some would make it, now and then to let a philosopher or a poet come in and wait and give a trencher at this banquet. Saint Paul is precedent for it. I wish no man to be too dark and full of shadow. There is a way to be pleasingly plain, and some have found it. Nor wish I any man to a total neglect of his hearers. Some stomachs rise at sweet meats. He prodigals a mine of excellency, that lavishes a terse oration to an aproned auditory. Mercury himself may move his tongue in vain, if he has none to hear him but a non-intelligent. They that speak to children assume a pretty lisping. Birds are caught by the counterfeit of their own shrill notes. There is a magic in the tongue can charm the wild man's motions. Eloquence is a bridle wherewith a wise man rides the monster of the world, the people. He that hears has only those affections that thy tongue will give him.

Thou mayst give smiles or tears, which joys do blot;
Or wrath to judges, which themselves have not.

You may see it in Lucan's words:

Flet, si flere jubes, gaudet, gaudere coactus;
Et te dante, capit judex quam non habet iram.

I grieve that anything so excellent as divinity is should fall into a sluttish handling. Sure, though other interposures do eclipse here, yet this is a principal. I never yet knew a good tongue that wanted ears to hear it. I will honor her in her plain trim; but I will wish to meet her in her graceful jewels; not that they give addition to her goodness, but that she is more persuasive in working out the soul it meets with. When I meet with worth which I cannot over-love, I can well endure that art, which is a means to heighten liking. Confections that are cordial are not the worse but the better for being gilded.

THAT NO MAN CAN BE GOOD TO ALL

I NEVER yet knew any man so bad but some have thought him honest, and afforded him love. Nor ever any so good, but some have thought him vile, and hated him. Few are so stigmatical as that they are not honest to some. And few again are so just as that they seem not to some unequal; either the ignorance, the envy, or the partiality of those that judge do constitute a various man. Nor can a man in himself always appear alike to all. In some, nature hath invested a disparity. In some, report hath foreblinded judgment. And in some, accident is the cause of disposing us to love or hate. Or, if not these, the variation of the body's humors. Or, perhaps, not any of these. The soul is often led by secret motions, and loves, she knows not why. There are impulsive privacies which urge us to a liking, even against the parliamental acts of the two houses—reason and common sense. As if there were some hidden beauty of a more magnetic force than all that the eye can see. And this, too, more powerful at one time than another. Undiscovered influences please us now with what we would sometimes contemn. I have come to the same man, that hath now welcomed me with a free expression of love and courtesies, and another time hath left me unsaluted at all. Yet, knowing him well, I have been certain of his sound affection, and have found this not an intended neglect, but an indisposedness, or a mind seriously busied within. Occasion reins the motions of the stirring mind. Like men that walk in their sleep, we are led about, we neither know whither nor how. I know there is a generation that do thus out of pride; and in strangers, I confess, I know not how to distinguish. For there is no disposition but hath a vanished vizor, as well as an unpencilled face. Some people cozen the world, are bad, and are not thought so. In some the world is cozened, believing them ill when they are not. Unless it hath been some few of a family, I have known the whole molehill of pismires (the world) in an error. For, though report once vented, like a stone cast into a pond, begets circle upon circle till it meets with the bank that bounds it, yet fame often plays the cur, and opens when she springs no game. Censures will not hold out weight, that have life only from the spongy cells of the common brain. Why should I definitively censure any man whom I know but superficially? as if I were a God, to see the inward soul. Nature, art, report, may all fail; yea, oftentimes probabilities. There is no certainty to discover man by, but time and conversation. Every man may be said in some sort to have two souls: one, the internal mind, the other, even the outward air of the face and body's gesture. And how infinitely in some shall they differ! I have known a wise look hide a fool within, and a merry face inhold a discontented

soul. Cleanthes[7] might well have failed in his judgment, had not accident have helped him to the obscured truth. He would undertake to read the mind in the body. Some, to try his skill, brought him a luxurious fellow that in his youth had been exposed to toil; seeing his face tanned and his hands leathered with a hardened skin, he was at a stand. Whereupon departing, the man sneezed, and Cleanthes says, Now I know the man, he is effeminate.[8] For great laborers rarely sneeze. Judgment is apt to err, when it passeth upon things we know not. Every man keeps his mind, if he lists, in a labyrinth. The heart of man, to man, is a room inscrutable, into which nature has made no certain window, but as himself shall please to open. One man shows himself to me; to another he is shut up. No man can either like all or be liked of all. God doth not please all. Nay, I think it may stand with divinity, as men are, to say he cannot. Man is infinitely more impotent. I will speak of every man as I find. If I hear he hath been ill to others, I will beware him, but not condemn him till I hear his own apology.

Qui statuit aliquid, parte inaudita altera,
Æquum licèt statuerit haud æquus est.[9]

Who judgment gives, and will but one side hear,
Though he judge right, is no good justicer.

The nature of many men is abstruse and not to be espied at an instant. And without knowing this, I know nothing that may warrant my sentence. As I will not too far believe reports from others, so I will never censure any man whom I know not internally; nor ever those, but sparing, and with modesty.

OF WOMEN

SOME are so uncharitable as to think all women bad; and others are so credulous as they believe they all are good. Sure, though every man speaks as he finds, there is reason to direct our opinion, without experience of the whole sex; which, in a strict examination, makes more for their honor than most men have acknowledged. At first, she was created his equal; only the difference was in the sex; otherwise they both were man. If we argue from the text that male and female

7 A Stoic philosopher of Assos in Troas, and successor to Zeno, *c.* 300 B.C. Cicero called him "father of the Stoics."
8 Diogenes Laertius, vii, ch. 5.
9 Seneca, Medea, 199.

made man, so the man being put first was worthier, I answer, so the evening and morning was the first day; yet few will think the night the better. That man is made her governor, and so above her, I believe rather the punishment of her sin, than the prerogative of his worth. Had they both stood, it may be thought, she had never been in that subjection; for then had it been no curse, but a continuance of her former estate, which had nothing but blessedness in it. Peter Martyr, indeed, is of opinion that man before the Fall had priority; but Chrysostom, he says, does doubt it. All will grant her body more admirable, more beautiful than man's; fuller of curiosities and noble Nature's wonders; both for conception, and fostering the producted birth. And can we think God would put a worser soul into a better body? When man was created, 'tis said, God made man; but when woman, 'tis said, God builded her; as if he had then been about a frame of rarer rooms, and more exact composition. And, without doubt, in her body she is much more wonderful, and by this we may think so in her mind. Philosophy tells us though the soul be not caused by the body, yet in the general it follows the temperament of it; so the comeliest outsides are naturally (for the most part) more virtuous within. If place can be any privilege, we shall find her built in Paradise, when man was made without it. 'Tis certain they are by constitution colder than the boiling man; so by this more temperate; 'tis heat that transports man to immoderation and fury; 'tis that which hurries him to a savage and libidinous violence. Women are naturally the more modest; and modesty is the seat and dwelling place of virtue. Whence proceed the most abhorred villainies, but from a masculine unblushing impudence? What a deal of sweetness do we find in a mild disposition! When a woman grows bold and daring, we dislike her, and say, she is too like a man; yet in ourselves we magnify what we condemn in her. Is not this injustice? Every man is so much the better by how much he comes nearer to God. Man in nothing is more like him than in being merciful. Yet woman is far more merciful than man; it being a sex wherein pity and compassion have dispersed far brighter rays. God is said to be love; and I am sure everywhere woman is spoken of for transcending in that quality. It was never found but in two men only,[10] that their love exceeded that of the feminine sex; and if you observe them you shall find they were

both of melting dispositions. I know when they prove bad, they are a sort of the vilest creatures, yet still the same reason gives it; for, *optima corrupta pessima*, the best things corrupted become the worst. They are things whose souls are of a more ductible temper than the harder metal of man; so may be made both better and worse. The representations of Sophocles and Euripides may be both true; and for the tongue-vice, talkativeness, I see not but at meetings men may very well vie words with them. 'Tis true, they are not of so tumultuous a spirit, so not so fit for great actions. Natural heat does more actuate the stirring genius of man. Their easy natures make them somewhat more unresolute; whereby men have argued them of fear and inconstancy. But men have always held the parliament, and have enacted their own wills, without ever hearing them speak; and then, how easy is it to conclude them guilty! Besides, education makes more difference between men and them than Nature; and all their aspersions are less noble for that they are only from their enemies, men. Diogenes snarled bitterly when, walking with another, he spied two women talking, and said, "See, the viper and the asp are changing poison." The poet was conceited that said, after they were made ill, that God made them fearful, that man might rule them; otherwise they had been past dealing with. Catullus his conclusion was too general, to collect a deceit in all women, because he was not confident of his own.

> *Nulli se dicit mulier mea nubere malle*
> *Quam mihi; non si se Jupiter ipse petat.*
> *Dicit: sed mulier Cupido quod dicit amanti,*
> *In vento et rapida scribere oportet aqua.*

My mistress swears, she'd leave all men for me:
Yea, though that Jove himself should suitor be.
She says it: but what women swear to kind
Loves, may be writ in rapid streams and wind.

I am resolved to honor virtue, in what sex soever I find it. And I think, in the general, I shall find it more in women than men, though weaker and more infirmly guarded. I believe they are better, and may be wrought to be worse. Neither shall the faults of many make me uncharitable to all; nor the goodness of some make me credulous of the rest. Though hitherto, I confess, I have not found more sweet and constant goodness in man than I have found in woman; and yet of these, I have not found a number.

10 David and Jonathan; see II Samuel 1:26.

OF APPREHENSION IN WRONGS

WE MAKE ourselves more injuries than are offered us; they many times pass for wrongs in our own thoughts that were never meant so by the heart of him that speaketh. The apprehension of wrong hurts more than the sharpest part of the wrong done. So, by falsely making of ourselves patients of wrong, we become the true and first actors. It is not good, in matters of discourtesy, to dive into a man's mind beyond his own comment, nor to stir upon a doubtful indignity without it, unless we have proofs that carry weight and conviction with them. Words do sometimes fly from the tongue that the heart did neither hatch nor harbor. While we think to revenge an injury, we many times begin one, and after that, repent our misconceptions. In things that may have a double sense, 'tis good to think the better was intended; so shall we still both keep our friends and quietness. If it be a wrong that is apparent, yet it is sometimes better to dissemble it than play the wasp and strive to return a sting. A wise man's glory is in passing by an offense, and this was Solomon's philosophy. A fool struck Cato in the bath, and when he was sorry for it, Cato had forgot it; for, says Seneca, *Melius putavit non agnoscere, quam ignoscere.*[11] He would not come so near revenge, as to acknowledge that he had been wronged. Light injuries are made none by a not regarding; which with a pursuing revenge, grow both to height and burthen. It stands not with the discretion of a generous spirit to return a punishment for every abuse. Some are such, as they require nothing but contempt to kill them. The cudgel is not of use when the beast but only barks. Though much sufferance be a stupidity, yet a little is of good esteem. We hear of many that are disturbed with a light offense, and we condemn them for it, because that which we call remedy slides into disease, and makes that live to mischief us, which else would die with giving life to safety. Yet, I know not what self-partiality makes us think ourselves behindhand if we offer not repayment in the same coin we received it. Of which, if they may stand for reasons, I think I may give you two. One is the sudden apprehension of the mind, which will endure anything with more patience than a disgrace, as if by the secret spirits of the air it conveyed a stab to the ethereal soul. Another is, because living among many, we would justify ourselves, to avoid their contempt; and these being most such as are not able to judge, we rather satisfy them by external actions than rely upon a judicious verdict, which gives us in for nobler by contemning it. Howsoever we may prize the revengeful man for spirit, yet without doubt it is princely to disdain a wrong, who, when ambassadors have offered undecencies, use not to chide, but to deny them audience, as if silence were the way-royal to reject a wrong. He enjoys a brave composedness that seats himself above the flight of the injurious claw. Nor does he by this show his weakness, but his wisdom. For, *Qui leviter sæviunt, sapiunt magis:*[12] The wisest rage the least. I love the man that is modestly valiant, that stirs not till he must needs, and then to purpose. A continued patience I commend not; 'tis different from what is goodness. For though God bears much, yet he will not bear always.

OF THE WASTE AND CHANGE OF TIME

I LOOK upon the lavish expenses of former ages with pity and admiration,[13] that those things men built for the honor of their name (as they thought) are either eaten up by the steely teeth of Time, or else, rest as monuments but of their pride and luxury. Great works undertaken for ostentation miss of their end, and turn to the author's shame; if not, the transitions of Time wear out the engraved names, and they last not much longer than Caligula's bridge[14] over the Baiæ. What is become of the Mausoleum, or the ship-bestriding Colossus? Where is Marcus Scaurus' theater? the bituminated walls of Babylon? and how little rests of the Egyptian Pyramids? and of these how diverse does report give in their builders, some ascribing them to one, some to another? Who would not pity the toils of virtue, when he shall find greater honor inscribed to loose Phryne[15] than to victorious Alexander? who, when he had razed the walls of Thebes, she offered to re-edify them, with condition this sentence might but on them be enlettered: "Alexander pulled them down, but Phryne did rebuild them!" From whence some have jested it unto a quarrel for

---

11 *De Ira*, ii, 32.

12 Plautus, Bacchides, 374.   13 Wonder.

14 Caligula, third Roman Emperor, built a bridge of boats between Baiæ and Puteoli, a distance of three miles, in imitation of the feat of Xerxes, and erected houses upon them.

15 A famous courtesan of antiquity.

fame betwixt a whore and a thief. Doubtless no fortification can hold against the cruel devastations of Time.
I could never yet find any estate exempted from this
mutability. Nay, those which we would have thought
had been held up with the strongest pillars of continuance have yet suffered the extremest changes. The
houses of the dead, and the urned bones, have sometimes met with rude hands, that have scattered them.
Who would have thought when Scanderbeg[16] was
laid in his tomb, that the Turks should after rifle it, and
wear his bones for jewels? Change is the great Lord of
the World; Time is his agent, that brings in all things,
to suffer his unstayed dominion.

> —Ille tot regum parens,
> Caret sepulchro Priamus, et flamma indiget,
> Ardente Troia—

> He that had a prince each son,
> Now finds no grave, and Troy in flames,
> He wants his funeral one.

We are so far from leaving anything certain to posterity
that we cannot be sure to enjoy what we have, while
we live. We live sometimes to see more changes in
ourselves than we could expect could happen to our
lasting offspring. As if none were ignorant of the fate
the poet asks:

> Divitis audita est cui non opulentia Crœsi?
> Nempe tamen vitam, captus ab hoste tulit,
> Ille, Syracusa modo formidatus in urbe,
> Vix humili duram repulit arte famem.

> Who has not heard of Crœsus' heaps of gold,
> Yet knows his foe did him a prisoner hold?
> He that once aw'd Sicilia's proud extent,
> By a poor art could famine scarce prevent.

We all put into the world, as men put money into a
lottery. Some lose all, and get nothing. Some with
nothing, get infinite prize; which, perhaps, venturing
again with hope of increase, they lose with grief, that
they did not rest contented. There is nothing that we
can confidently call our own; or that we can surely
say we shall either do or avoid. We have no power

16 Iskander (Alexander) Beg or Bey, the Turkish name and
title of George Castriota (1404–1467), a patriot of Albania
who defeated the Turks in many battles, and checked their
advance on Europe.

over the present; much less over the future, when we
shall be absent or dissolved. And, indeed, if we consider the world aright, we shall find some reason for
these continual mutations. If everyone had power to
transmit the certain possession of all his acquisitions to
his own succeeders, there would be nothing left for
the noble deeds of new aspirers to purchase; which
would quickly betray the world to an incommunicable
dullness, and utterly discourage the generous designs
of the stirring and more elementary spirit. As things
now are, every man thinks something may fall to his
share; and since it must crown some endeavors, he
imagines, why not his? Thus by the various treads of
men, every action comes to be done, which is requisite for the world's maintaining. But since nothing
here below is certain, I will never purchase anything
with too great a hazard. 'Tis ambition, not wisdom,
that makes princes hazard their whole estates for an
honor merely titular. If I find that lost, which I thought
to have kept, I will comfort myself with this: that I
knew the world was changeable; and that as God can
take away a less good, so he can, if he please, confer
me a greater.

OF IDLENESS

THE idle man is the barrenest piece of earth in the orb.
There is no creature that hath life, but is busied in
some action for the benefit of the restless world. Even
the most venomous and most ravenous things that
are, have their commodities as well as their annoy-
ances; and they are ever engaged in some action
which profiteth the world, and continues them in their
nature's courses. Even the vegetables, wherein calm
nature dwells, have their turns and times in fructify-
ing; they leaf, they flower, they seed. Nay, creatures
quite inanimate are (some) the most laborious in their
motion. With what a cheerly face the golden sun
chariots through the rounding sky! How perpetual is
the maiden moon, in her just and horned mutations!
The fire, how restless is his quick and catching flames!
in the air, what transitions! and how fluctuous are the
salted waves! Nor is the teeming earth weary, after so
many thousand years' productions! All which may
tutor the couch-stretched man, and raise the modest
red to showing through his unwashed face. Idleness is
the most corrupting fly that can blow in any human
mind. That ignorance is the most miserable which
knows not what to do. The idle man is like the dumb

jack in a virginal; while all the other dance out a winning music, this, like a member out of joint, sullens the whole body with an ill disturbing laziness. I do not wonder to see some of our gentry grown well-near the lewdest men of our land, since they are, most of them, so muffled in a non-employment. 'Tis action that does keep the soul both sweet and sound; while lying still does rot it to an ordured noisomeness. Augustine imputes Esau's loss of the blessing partly to his slothfulness, that had rather receive meat than seek it. Surely, exercise is the fattening food of the soul, without which she grows lank and thinly parted. That the followers of great men are so much debauched, I believe to be want of employment; for the soul, impatient of an absolute recess, preys upon the lewder actions. 'Tis true, men learn to do ill by doing what is next to it, nothing. I believe Solomon meant the field of the sluggard, as well for the emblem of his mind, as the certain index of his outward state. As the one is overgrown with thorns and briars, so is the other with vices and enormities. If any wonder how Egistus[17] grew adulterate, the exit of the verse will tell him— *Desidiosus erat.*[18] When one would brag the blessings of the Roman state, that since Carthage was razed, and Greece subjected, they might now be happy, as having nothing to fear, says the best Scipio: "We now are most in danger; for while we want business, and have no foe to awe us, we are ready to drown in the mud of vice and slothfulness." How bright does the soul grow with use and negotiation! With what proportioned sweetness does that family flourish, where but one laborious guide steereth in an ordered course! When Cleanthes had labored and gotten some coin, he shows it his companions, and tells them that he now, if he will, can nourish another Cleanthes. Believe it, industry is never wholly unfruitful. If it bring not joy with the incoming profit, it will yet banish mischief from thy busied gates. There is a kind of good angel waiting upon diligence, that ever carries a laurel in his hand to crown her. Fortune, they said of old, should not be prayed unto but with hands in motion. The bosomed fist beckons the approach of poverty, and leaves besides the noble head unguarded; but the lifted arm does frighten want, and is ever a shield to that noble director. How unworthy was that man of the world, that never did aught but only lived and

died! Though Epaminondas[19] was severe, he was yet exemplary, when he found a soldier sleeping in his watch, and ran him through with his sword, as if he would bring the two brothers, Death and Sleep, to a meeting; and when he was blamed for that as cruelty, he says, he did but leave him as he found him, dead. It is none of the meanest happiness to have a mind that loves a virtuous exercise; 'tis daily rising to blessedness and contentation. They are idle divines that are not heavened in their lives above the unstudious man. Everyone shall smell of that he is busied in; as those that stir among perfumes and spices shall, when they are gone, have still a grateful odor with them; so, they that turn the leaves of the worthy writer cannot but retain a smack of their long-lived author. They converse with virtue's soul, which he that writ, did spread upon his lasting paper. Every good line adds sinew to the virtuous mind; and withal heals that vice which would be springing in it. That I have liberty to do anything, I account it from the favoring Heavens. That I have a mind sometimes inclining to use that liberty well, I think I may without ostentation be thankful for it, as a bounty of the Deity. Sure, I should be miserable, if I did not love this business in my vacancy. I am glad of that leisure which gives me leisure to employ myself. If I should not grow better for it, yet this benefit, I am sure, would accrue, I should both keep myself from worse, and not have time to entertain the Devil in.

AGAINST COMPULSION

AS NOTHING prevaileth more than courtesy, so compulsion often is the way to lose. Too much importunity does but teach men how to deny. The more *we* desire to gain, the more do others desire that *they* may not lose. Nature is ever jealous of her own supremacy, and when she sees that others would under-tread it, she calls in all her powers for resistance. Certainly, they work by a wrong engine that seek to gain their ends by constraint. Cross two lovers, and you knit but their affection stronger. You may stroke the lion into a bondage, but you shall sooner hew him to pieces than beat him into a chain. The fox may praise the crow's meat from her bill, but cannot with his swiftness overtake her wing. Easy nature and free liberty will

17 Ægisthus, the seducer of Clytemnestra and murderer of Agamemnon. See the Agamemnon of Æschylus, and the Electra of Sophocles.
18 He was lazy.

19 The great Theban general who delivered Thebes from the yoke of Sparta in his battle with the Lacedæmonians at Leuctra, 371 B.C.

steal a man into a winy excess, when urged healths do but show him the way to refuse. The noblest weapon wherewith man can conquer is love and gentlest courtesy. How many have lost their hopes while they have sought to ravish with too rude a hand? Nature is more apt to be led by the soft motions of the musical tongue than the rustic threshings of a striking arm. Love of life and jollities will draw a man to more than the fear of death and torments. No doubt, nature meant Cæsar for a conqueror, when she gave him both such courage and such courtesy; both which put Marius into a muse. They which durst speak to him (he said), were ignorant of his greatness; and they which durst not, were so of his goodness. They are men the best composed, that can be resolute and remiss. For, as fearful natures are wrought upon by the sternness of a rough comportment, so the valiant are not gained on but by gentle affability and a show of pleasing liberty. Little fishes are twitched up with the violence of a sudden pull, when the like action cracks the line whereon a great one hangs. I have known denials that had never been given but for the earnestness of the requester. They teach the petitioned to be suspicious, and suspicion teaches him to hold and fortify. He that comes with "you must have me," is like to prove but a fruitless wooer. Urge a grant to some men, and they are inexorable; seem careless, and they will force the thing upon you. Augustus got a friend of Cinna by giving him a second life, whereas his death could at best but have removed an enemy. Hear but his exiled poet.

> Flectitur obsequio curvatus ab arbore ramus:
>   Franges, si vires experiere tuas.
> Obsequio tranantur aquæ, nec vincere possis
>   Flumina, si contra quam rapit unda nates.
> Obsequium tigresque domat, tumidosque leones:
>   Rustica paulatim taurus aratra subit.[20]

The trees' crookt branches, gently bent, grow right,
When as the hand's full vigor breaks them quite.
He safely swims, that waves along the flood,
While crossing streams is neither safe nor good.
Tigers and lions, mildness keeps in awe:
And, gently us'd, bulls yok'd, in plows will draw.

Certainly, the fair way is the best, though it be something the further about. It is less ill for a journey to be long than dangerous. To vex other men, I will think is but to tutor them how they should again vex me. I will never wish to purchase aught unequally: what is got against reason, is for the most part won by the meeting of a fool and knave. If aught be sought with reason, that may come with kindness; for then reason in their own bosoms will become a pleader for me; but I will be content to lose a little rather than be drawn to obtain by violence; the trouble and the hazard we avoid, may very well sweeten or outweigh a slender loss. Constraint is for extremities, when all ways else shall fail. But in the general, fairness has preferment. If you grant, the other may supply the desire; yet this does the like and purchaseth love, when that only leaves a loathsome hate behind it.

OF DREAMS

DREAMS are notable means of discovering our own inclinations. The wise man learns to know himself as well by the night's black mantle as the searching beams of day. In sleep we have the naked and natural thoughts of our souls; outward objects interpose not, either to shuffle in occasional cogitations, or hale out the included fancy. The mind is then shut up in the borough of the body; none of the *Cinque Ports* of the *Isle of Man* are then open, to in-let any strange disturbers. Surely, how we fall to vice or rise to virtue we may by observation find in our dreams. It was the wise Zeno that said, he could collect a man by his dreams,[21] for then the soul, stated in a deep repose, bewrayed her true affections, which, in the busy day, she would either not show or not note. It was a custom among the Indians, when their kings went to their sleep, to pray, with piping acclamations, that they might have happy dreams; and withal consult well for their subjects' benefit, as if the night had been a time wherein they might grow good and wise. And certainly, the wise man is the wiser for his sleeping, if he can order well in the day what the eyeless night presenteth him. Every dream is not to be counted of; nor yet are all to be cast away with contempt. I would neither be a Stoic, superstitious in all, nor yet an Epicure, considerate of none. If the physician may by them judge of the disease of the body, I see not but

20 Ovid, *Ars Amatoria*, ii, 179.

21 Plutarch, How a man may be aware of his progress in virtue, ch. 12.

the divine may do so concerning the soul. I doubt not but the genius of the soul is waking and motive even in the fastest closures of the imprisoning eyelids. But to presage from these thoughts of sleep is a wisdom that I would not reach to. The best use we can make of dreams is observation, and by that, our own correction or encouragement. For 'tis not doubtable but that the mind is working in the dullest depth of sleep. I am confirmed by Claudian.

> *Omnia quæ sensu volvuntur vota diurno,*
> *Tempore nocturno reddit amica quies.*
> *Venator, defessa toro cum membra reponit,*
> *Mens tamen ad sylvas, et sua lustra redit.*
> *Judicibus lites, aurigæ somnia currus,*
> *Vanaque nocturnis meta cavetur equis.*
> *Furto gaudet amans; permutat navita merces:*
> *Et vigil elapsas quærit avarus opes.*
> *Blandaque largitur frustra sitientibus ægris,*
> *Irriguus gelido pocula fonte sopor.*
> *Me quoque Musarum studium, sub nocte silenti,*
> *Artibus assiduis, sollicitare solet.*[22]

Day thoughts, transwinged from th' industrious breast,
All seem re-acted in the night's dumb rest.
When the tired huntsman his repose begins,
Then flies his mind to woods and wild beast dens.
Judges dream cases: champions seem to run,
With their night coursers, the vain bounds to shun.
Love hugs his rapes.—The merchant traffic minds.
The miser thinks he some lost treasure finds.
And to the thirsty sick, some potion cold,
Stiff flattering sleep inanely seems to hold.
Yea, and in the age of silent rest, even I,
Troubled with art's deep musings, nightly lie.

Dreams do sometimes call us to a recognition of our inclinations, which print the deeper in so undisturbed times. I could wish men to give them their consideration but not to allow them their trust, though sometimes 'tis easy to pick out a profitable moral. Antiquity had them in much more reverence and did oft account them prophecies, as is easily found in the sacred volume; and among the heathen nothing was more frequent. Astyages had two, of his daughter Mandana, the vine and her urine.[23] Calphurnia of her Cæsar,[24] Hecuba of Paris, and almost every prince among them had his fate showed in interpreted dreams. Galen[25] tells of one that dreamed his thigh was turned to stone, when soon after it was struck with a dead palsy. The aptness of the humors to the like effects might suggest something to the mind, then apt to receive. So that I doubt not but either to preserve health or amend the life, dreams may, to a wise observer, be of special benefit. I would neither depend upon any to incur a prejudice, nor yet cast them all away in a prodigal neglect and scorn. I find it of one that having long been troubled with the paining spleen, that he dreamt if he opened a certain vein between two of his fingers, he should be cured; which he, awaked, did and mended. But indeed, I would rather believe this, than be drawn to practice after it. These plain predictions are more rare, foretellings used to be lapped in more obscure folds; and now that art is lost, Christianity hath settled us to less inquisition; 'tis for a Roman soothsayer to read those darker spirits of the night, and tell that still dictator, his dream of copulation with his mother signified his subjecting the world to himself. 'Tis now so out of use that I think it not to be recovered. And were it not for the power of the Gospel in crying down the vains of men, it would appear a wonder how a science so pleasing to humanity should fall so quite to ruin.

OF POETS AND POETRY

SURELY he was a little wanton with his leisure that first invented poetry. 'Tis but a play which makes words dance in the evenness of a cadency; yet without doubt, being a harmony, it is nearer the mind than prose, for that itself is a harmony in height. But the words being rather the drossy part, conceit I take to be the principal. And here, though it digresseth from truth, it flies above her, making her more rare by giving curious raiment to her nakedness. The name the Grecians gave the men that wrote thus, showed how much they honored it; they called them Makers. And had some of them had power to put their conceits in act, how near would they have come to deity! And for the virtues of men, they rest not on the bare demeanor, but slide into imagination; so proposing things above us, they kindle the reader to wonder and imitation. And certainly, poets that write thus Plato never meant to banish. His own practice shows he

---

22 *Panegyricus de sexto Consulatus Honorii Augusti*, 1 ff.
23 Herodotus, i, 107–08.
24 Plutarch, Life of Cæsar, ch. 63.
25 Galen (104–193 A.D.), the greatest of ancient writers on medicine.

excluded not all. He was content to hear Antimachus recite his poem, when all the herd had left him;[26] and he himself wrote both tragedies and other pieces. Perhaps he found them a little too busy with his gods; and he being the first that made philosophy divine and rational, was modest in his own beginnings. Another name they had of honor, too, and that was *Vates*. Nor know I how to distinguish between the prophets and poets of Israel. What is Jeremiah's Lamentation, but a kind of Sapphic elegy? David's Psalms are not only poems but songs, snatches and raptures of a flaming spirit. And this indeed I observe to the honor of poets; I never found them covetous or scrapingly base. The Jews had not two such kings in all their catalogue as Solomon and his father, poets both. There is a largeness in their souls beyond the narrowness of other men; and why may we not then think this may embrace more both of heaven and God? I cannot but conjecture this to be the reason that they, most of them, are poor; they find their minds so solaced with their own flights that they neglect the study of growing rich; and this, I confess again, I think, turns them to vice and unmanly courses. Besides, they are for the most part mighty lovers of their palates, and this is known an impoverisher. Antigonus, in the tented field, found Antagoras cooking of a conger himself.[27] And they all are friends to the grape and liquor, though I think many, more out of a ductile nature and their love to pleasant company, than their affection to the juice alone. They are all of free natures, and are the truest definition of that philosopher's man, which gives him *animal risibile*. Their grossest fault is that you may conclude them sensual, yet this does not touch them all. Ingenious for the most part they are. I know there be some rhyming fools; but what have they to do with poetry? When Sallust would tell us that Sempronia's wit was not ill, says he, *Potuit versus facere, et jocum movere:*[28] She could make a verse and break a jest. Something there is in it more than ordinary in that it is all in such measured language as may be marred by reading. I laugh heartily at Philoxenus his jest, who passing by, and hearing some masons missensing his lines (with their ignorant sawing of them) falls to breaking their bricks amain; they ask the cause, and he replies, they spoil his work, and he theirs.[29] Certainly, a worthy poet is so far from being a fool

26 Plutarch, Life of Lysander, ch. 18.
27 Erasmus, Apothegms (Ed. Leyden, 1547), p. 359.
28 *Bellum Catilinæ*, ch. 25.
29 Erasmus, Apothegms, p. 678.

that there is some wit required in him that shall be able to read him well, and without the true accent, numbered poetry does lose of the gloss. It was a speech becoming an able poet of our own, when a lord read his verses crookedly, and he beseeched his lordship not to murder him in his own lines. He that speaks false Latin, breaks Priscian's head: but he that repeats a verse ill, puts Homer out of joint. One thing commends it beyond oratory, it ever complieth to the sharpest judgments. He is the best orator that pleaseth all, even the crowd and clowns. But poetry would be poor that they should all approve of. If the learned and judicious like it, let the throng bray. These, when 'tis best, will like it the least. So they contemn what they understand not, and the neglected poet falls by want. Calpurnius makes one complain the misfortune,

Frange, puer, calamos, et inanes desere Musas:
Et potius glandes, rubicundaque collige corna.
Duc ad mulctra greges, et lac venale per urbem
Non tacitus porta: Quid enim tibi fistula reddet,
Quo tutere famem? certe, mea carmina nemo
Præter ab his scopulis ventosa remurmurat Echo.[30]

Boy, break thy pipes, leave, leave thy fruitless muse:
Rather the mast, and blood-red cornel choose.
Go lead thy flocks to milking; sell and cry
Milk through the city: what can learning buy,
To keep back hunger? None my verses mind,
But Echo, babbling from these rocks and wind.

Two things are commonly blamed in poetry; nay, you take away that, if them; and these are lies and flattery. But I have told them in the worst words; for 'tis only to the shallow insight that they appear thus. Truth may dwell more clearly in an allegory or a moraled fable than in a bare narration. And for flattery, no man will take poetry literal; since in commendations, it rather shows what men should be, than what they are. If this were not, it would appear uncomely. But we all know, hyperboles in poetry do bear a decency, nay, a grace along with them. The greatest danger that I find in it is, that it wantons the blood and imagination, as carrying a man in too high a delight. To prevent these, let the wise poet strive to be modest in his lines. First, that he dash not the gods; next, that he injure not chastity, nor corrupt the ear with lasciviousness. When these are declined, I think a grave poem the deepest kind of writing. It wings the soul

30 Calpurnius Siculus, Eclogue IV, 23.

up higher than the slacked pace of prose. Flashes that do follow the cup, I fear me, are too sprightly to be solid; they run smartly upon the loose for a distance or two, but then being foul, they give in and tire. I confess I love the sober Muse and fasting; from the other, matter cannot come so clear but that it will be misted with the fumes of wine. Long poetry some cannot be friends withal; and indeed, it palls upon the reading. The wittiest poets have been all short and changing soon their subject, as Horace, Martial, Juvenal, Seneca and the two comedians. Poetry should be rather like a coranto, short and nimbly-lofty, than a dull lesson of a day long. Nor can it be but deadish, if distended; for when 'tis right, it centers conceit, and takes but the spirit of things, and therefore foolish poesy is of all writing the most ridiculous. When a goose dances and a fool versifies, there is sport alike. He is twice an ass, that is a rhyming one. He is something the less unwise, that is unwise but in prose. If the subject be history or contexted fable, then I hold it better put in prose or blanks; for ordinary discourse never shows so well in meter as in the strain it may seem to be spoken in; the commendation is, to do it to the life, nor is this any other than poetry in prose. Surely, though the world think not so, he is happy to himself that can play the poet. He shall vent his passions by his pen, and ease his heart of their weight; and he shall often raise himself a joy in his raptures, which no man can perceive but he. Sure Ovid found a pleasure in it, even when he wrote his Tristia. It gently delivers the mind of distempers, and works the thoughts to a sweetness in their searching conceit. I would not love it for a profession, and I would not want it for a recreation. I can make myself harmless, nay, amending mirth with it, while I should, perhaps, be trying of a worser pastime. And this I believe in it further, unless conversation corrupts his easiness, it lifts a man to nobleness, and is never in any rightly, but it makes him of a royal and capacious soul.

THE SECOND CENTURY

A RULE IN READING AUTHORS

SOME men read authors as our gentlemen use flowers, only for delight and smell, to please their fancy and refine their tongue. Others, like the bee, extract only the honey, the wholesome precepts, and this alone they bear away, leaving the rest, as little worth, of small value. In reading I will care for both, though for the last most; the one serves to instruct the mind, the other fits her to tell what she hath learned. Pity it is they should be divided. He that hath worth in him, and cannot express it, is a chest, keeping a rich jewel, and the key lost. Concealing goodness is vice. Virtue is better by being communicated. A good style with wholesome matter is a fair woman with a virtuous soul, which attracts the eyes of all. The good man thinks chastely and loves her beauty for her virtue, which he still thinks more fair for dwelling in so fair an outside. The vicious man hath lustful thoughts, and he would for her beauty fain destroy her virtue; but coming to solicit his purpose, finds such divine lectures from her angel's tongue, and those delivered with so sweet a pleasing modesty, that he thinks virtue is dissecting her soul to him, to ravish man with a beauty which he dreamed not of. So he could now curse himself for desiring that lewdly, which he hath learned since only to admire and reverence. Thus he goes away better, that came with an intent to be worse. Quaint phrases on a good subject are baits to make an ill man virtuous; how many vile men seeking these have found themselves convertites! I may refine my speech without harm; but I will endeavor more to reform my life. 'Tis a good grace both of oratory or the pen to speak or write proper; but that is the best work where the Graces and the Muses meet.

Sir Thomas Browne

[1605–1682]

Browne is a towering figure in English literature of the seventeenth century. Like another titan of the age, John Milton, he was born in the Cheapside district of London, but from that point on his life and thought present a consistent contrast to Milton's, for Browne was, in addition to being a devoted royalist and a persistent follower of the old ways of thought, a man who led a life as quiet and withdrawn as that of the poet of *Paradise Lost* was stormy and public. Educated at Winchester School, Browne entered Pembroke College (then known as Broadgates Hall), Oxford, in 1623. After some travel in Ireland and France, he undertook the study of medicine, and was in residence successively at the three great centers of medical education in the seventeenth century—the universities of Montpellier, Padua, and Leiden. Having received his medical degree from Leiden, he returned to England to practice his profession, first, possibly, in Halifax, Yorkshire, later in the town of Norwich, where he was to live from 1637 until his death.

Probably some time around 1635, Browne composed the *Religio Medici,* apparently as a private and personal attempt to sort out his beliefs concerning God and life. The appearance of two unauthorized editions of the work in 1642 induced Browne to publish it himself in an authorized edition the following year. Its success was immediate, and the publication of a Latin translation in 1644 (in Paris and Leiden) gave the author a European reputation. Despite the dubious attitude toward marriage expressed at one point in the *Religio,* Browne was married in 1641; his wife bore him ten children, only three of whom survived to adulthood. Throughout the violent years of the Civil Wars and the Commonwealth, Browne pursued his even ways as a provincial doctor, an antiquarian, and an amateur of scientific investigation. He remained quietly devoted to his royalist principles, but his general detachment from questions of the immediate and the topical is suggested by the titles of the works which he published during that period: *Pseudodoxia Epidemica: or Enquiries into very many Received Tenents and commonly presumed Truths* [popularly known as *Vulgar Errors*] (1646); and *Hydriotaphia, Urn Burial, or a Discourse of the Sepulchral Urns lately found in Norfolk, together with the Garden of Cyrus* (1658).

In 1671, on the occasion of a royal visit to Norwich, Dr. Browne, the first citizen of the town, was knighted. Eleven years later, on his seventy-seventh birthday, he died; it is not difficult to imagine the pleasure which this collector of paradoxes and strange phenomena would have derived from the curious neatness of that fact. Two posthumous works, *A Letter to a Friend* and *Christian Morals,* were published in 1690 and 1716 respectively.

Browne's pre-eminence as a prose writer derives in almost equal parts from his irresistibly attractive personality, his evocative and wide-ranging thought, and his incomparable artistic style. The *Religio Medici* is an extraordinarily complete expression of a human personality: not only in the thoroughness with which it exposes its author's vision of the world, but also in the self-satisfied equanimity with which Browne regards his own quirks and limitations—as when he admits the three charitable heresies of his early years, or solemnly advises us that "Where we desire to be informed, 'tis good to contest with men above ourselves; but to confirm and establish our opinions, 'tis best to argue with judgments below our own, that the frequent spoils and victories over their reasons may settle in ourselves an esteem and confirmed opinion of our own." Unusually tolerant and kindly for his strife-filled age, Browne turned his private examination of his soul into what amounts to a treatise on charity—and incidentally an ideal portrait of a Christian gentleman.

The thought of the *Religio* displays occasional Baconian elements (though not as many as the *Pseudodoxia Epidemica*), but essentially it is one of the last great expressions of the traditional world view inherited from the Middle Ages and the Renaissance. Sir Thomas delights in a paradox, in a sudden glimpse of those truths beyond reason which leave him with only an "O altitudo!" Equally at home in the visible and invisible worlds, Browne is, in the words of his own description of Man, "that great and true *Amphibium*, whose nature is disposed to live . . . in divided and distinguished worlds."

The wholeness of Browne's vision is exhibited most tellingly in the *Urn-Burial*, a work in which scientific reporting and archeological erudition modulate gradually but surely into the great last chapter, a sublime and eloquent meditation on the inevitability of death, the vanity of human strivings, and the goal of spiritual immortality. In the mighty peroration of *Urn-Burial*, as everywhere else in his work, Browne has found a rhetoric adequate to his theme. The style of *Urn-Burial* displays his usual traits—strongly marked rhythm, asymmetrical sentence structure, fullness of expression—but they are carried to unprecedented heights of intensity and passion.

The style of Browne's works, like the world view which it embodied, was doomed to extinction, and it found no imitators (unless we except Herman Melville two centuries later). But it stands as its own monument, something unique and irreplaceable in English literature.

T. BROWNE. *Works*, ed. G. Keynes, 6 vols. (London, 1928–31). The definitive edition of the complete works.

————. *Religio Medici*, ed. J. J. Denonain (Cambridge, 1953). The best edition of the work.

————. *Urne Buriall and the Garden of Cyrus*, ed. J. Carter (Cambridge, 1958). A companion volume to Denonain's edition, of comparable value.

J. S. FINCH. *Sir Thomas Browne* (New York, 1950). A good biography.

W. P. DUNN. *Sir Thomas Browne, a Study in Religious Philosophy* (Minneapolis, rev. ed., 1950).

F. L. HUNTLEY. *Sir Thomas Browne* (Ann Arbor, 1962).

E. S. MERTON. *Science and Imagination in Sir Thomas Browne* (New York, 1949).

R. SENCOURT. *Outflying Philosophy* (Hildesheim, 1924).

A. WARREN. "The Style of Sir Thomas Browne," *Kenyon Review*, XIII (1951).

J. BENNETT. *Sir Thomas Browne* (Cambridge, 1962).

L. NATHANSON. *The Strategy of Truth: a study of Sir Thomas Browne* (Chicago, 1967).

C. A. PATRIDES, ed. *Approaches to Sir Thomas Browne* (Columbia, Mo., 1982).

FROM

RELIGIO MEDICI[1]

[TEXT: *eighth edition, 1682*]

from THE FIRST PART

FOR my religion, though there be several circumstances that might persuade the world I have none at all, as the general scandal of my profession, the natural course of my studies, the indifferency of my behavior and discourse in matters of religion, neither violently defending one, nor with that common ardor and contention opposing another; yet, in despite hereof, I dare without usurpation assume the honorable style of a Christian. Not that I merely owe this title to the font, my education, or the clime wherein I was born, as being bred up either to confirm those principles my parents instilled into my unwary understanding, or by a general consent proceed in the religion of my country; but having in my riper years and confirmed judgment seen and examined all, I find myself obliged by the principles of grace, and the law of mine own reason, to embrace no other name but this. Neither doth herein my zeal so far make me forget the general charity I owe unto humanity, as rather to hate than pity Turks, Infidels, and (what is worse) Jews; rather contenting myself to enjoy that happy style, than maligning those who refuse so glorious a title.

But, because the name of a Christian is become too general to express our faith, there being a geography of religions as well as lands, and every clime distinguished not only by their laws and limits, but circumscribed by their doctrines and rules of faith; to be particular, I am of that reformed new-cast religion, wherein I dislike nothing but the name; of the same belief our Saviour taught, the Apostles disseminated, the Fathers authorized, and the Martyrs confirmed; but by the sinister ends of princes, the ambition and avarice of prelates, and the fatal corruption of times, so decayed, impaired, and fallen from its native beauty,

[1] *Religio Medici*, written when Browne was about thirty years old, is the attempt on the part of a young man who combined a devout religious disposition with an acute and inquiring intellect to clarify his beliefs by putting them in writing. It has been called the best answer of the time to the negativism and despair which tortured so many of Browne's contemporaries.

that it required the careful and charitable hands of these times to restore it to its primitive integrity. Now the accidental occasion whereupon, the slender means whereby, the low and abject condition of the person by whom so good a work was set on foot, which in our adversaries beget contempt and scorn, fills me with wonder, and is the very same objection the insolent pagans first cast at Christ and his disciples. . . .

I am, I confess, naturally inclined to that which misguided zeal terms superstition. My common conversation I do acknowledge austere, my behavior full of rigor, sometimes not without morosity; yet at my devotion I love to use the civility of my knee, my hat, and hand, with all those outward and sensible motions which may express or promote my invisible devotion. I should violate my own arm rather than a church; nor willingly deface the name of saint or martyr. At the sight of a cross or crucifix I can dispense with my hat, but scarce with the thought or memory of my Saviour. I cannot laugh at, but rather pity, the fruitless journeys of pilgrims, or contemn the miserable condition of friars; for, though misplaced in circumstances, there is something in it of devotion. I could never hear the Ave-Mary Bell without an elevation; or think it a sufficient warrant, because they erred in one circumstance, for me to err in all, that is, in silence and dumb contempt. Whilst, therefore, they directed their devotions to her, I offered mine to God, and rectified the errors of their prayers by rightly ordering mine own. . . .

I could never divide myself from any man upon the difference of an opinion, or be angry with his judgment for not agreeing with me in that from which perhaps within a few days I should dissent myself. I have no genius to disputes in religion, and have often thought it wisdom to decline them, especially upon a disadvantage, or when the cause of truth might suffer in the weakness of my patronage. Where we desire to be informed, 'tis good to contest with men above ourselves; but to confirm and establish our opinions, 'tis best to argue with judgments below our own, that the frequent spoils and victories over their reasons may settle in ourselves an esteem and confirmed opinion of our own. Every man is not a proper champion for truth, nor fit to take up the gauntlet in the cause of verity: many, from the ignorance of these maxims, and an inconsiderate zeal unto truth, have too rashly charged the troops of error, and remain as trophies unto the enemies of truth. A man may be in as just possession of truth as of a city, and yet be forced to surrender; 'tis therefore far better to enjoy her with peace, than to hazard her on a battle. If, therefore, there rise any doubts in my way, I do forget them, or at least defer them till my better settled judgment and more manly reason be able to resolve them; for I perceive every man's own reason is his best Œdipus,[2] and will, upon a reasonable truce, find a way to loose those bonds wherewith the subtleties of error have enchained our more flexible and tender judgments. In philosophy, where truth seems double-faced, there is no man more paradoxical than myself: but in divinity I love to keep the road; and, though not in an implicit, yet an humble faith, follow the great wheel of the church, by which I move, not reserving any proper poles or motion from the epicycle of my own brain. By this means I leave no gap for heresies, schisms, or errors, of which at present I hope I shall not injure truth to say I have no taint or tincture. . . .

As for those wingy mysteries in divinity, and airy subtleties in religion, which have unhinged the brains of better heads, they never stretched the *pia mater*[3] of mine. Methinks there be not impossibilities enough in religion for an active faith; the deepest mysteries ours contains have not only been illustrated, but maintained, by syllogism and the rule of reason. I love to lose myself in a mystery, to pursue my reason to an *O altitudo!*[4] 'Tis my solitary recreation to pose my apprehension with those involved enigmas and riddles of the Trinity, with incarnation, and resurrection. I can answer all the objections of Satan and my rebellious reason with that odd resolution I learned of Tertullian,

Certum est, quia impossibile est.[5] I desire to exercise my faith in the difficultest point; for to credit ordinary and visible objects is not faith, but persuasion. Some believe the better for seeing Christ's sepulchre; and, when they have seen the Red Sea, doubt not of the miracle. Now, contrarily, I bless myself and am thankful that I lived not in the days of miracles, that I never saw Christ nor his disciples. I would not have been one of those Israelites that passed the Red Sea, nor one of Christ's patients on whom he wrought his wonders; then had my faith been thrust upon me, nor should I enjoy that greater blessing pronounced to all that believe and saw not. 'Tis an easy and necessary belief, to credit what our eye and sense hath examined. I believe he was dead, and buried, and rose again; and desire to see him in his glory, rather than to contemplate him in his cenotaph or sepulchre. Nor is this much to believe; as we have reason, we owe this faith unto history: they only had the advantage of a bold and noble faith who lived before his coming, who upon obscure prophecies and mystical types could raise a belief, and expect apparent impossibilities. . . .

Natura nihil agit frustra[6] is the only indisputed axiom in philosophy. There are no grotesques in nature; not anything framed to fill up empty cantons, and unnecessary spaces. In the most imperfect creatures, and such as were not preserved in the ark, but, having their seeds and principles in the womb of nature, are everywhere, where the power of the sun is, in these is the wisdom of his hand discovered. Out of this rank Solomon chose the object of his admiration.[7] Indeed, what reason may not go to school to the wisdom of bees, ants, and spiders? what wise hand teacheth them to do what reason cannot teach us? Ruder heads stand amazed at those prodigious pieces of nature, whales, elephants, dromedaries and camels; these, I confess, are the colossus and majestic pieces of her hand: but in these narrow engines there is more curious mathematics; and the civility of these little citizens more neatly sets forth the wisdom of their Maker. Who admires not Regio-Montanus[8] his fly beyond his eagle, or wonders not more at the operation of two

2 The best solver of difficult problems. Œdipus solved the riddle of the Sphinx.

3 The vascular membrane that covers the brain.

4 Cf. Bacon, Advancement of Learning, II, xxv, 13: "In divinity many things must be left abrupt, and concluded with this: '*O altitudo sapientiæ et scientiæ Dei! quam incomprehensibilia sunt judicia ejus, et non investigabiles viæ ejus!*'" (Oh the depth of the riches both of the wisdom and knowledge of God! how unsearchable are his judgments, and his ways past finding out! —Romans 11:33).

5 It is certain, because impossible.

6 Nature does nothing in vain.

7 Proverbs 6:6: Go to the ant, thou sluggard; consider her ways, and be wise.

8 The German Johann Muller (1436–1475), reputed to have constructed an iron fly and a wooden eagle, both capable of flying.

souls in those little bodies, than but one in the trunk of a cedar? I could never content my contemplation with those general pieces of wonder, the flux and reflux of the sea, the increase of Nile, the conversion of the needle to the north; and have studied to match and parallel those in the more obvious and neglected pieces of nature, which without further travel I can do in the cosmography of myself. We carry with us the wonders we seek without us: there is all Africa and her prodigies in us; we are that bold and adventurous piece of nature, which he that studies wisely learns in a compendium what others labor at in a divided piece and endless volume.

Thus there are two books from whence I collect my divinity; besides that written one of God, another of his servant nature, that universal and public manuscript that lies expansed unto the eyes of all: those that never saw him in the one, have discovered him in the other. This was the scripture and theology of the heathens: the natural motion of the sun made them more admire him than its supernatural station did the children of Israel; the ordinary effects of nature wrought more admiration in them than in the other all his miracles. Surely the heathens knew better how to join and read these mystical letters than we Christians, who cast a more careless eye on these common hieroglyphics, and disdain to suck divinity from the flowers of nature. Nor do I so forget God as to adore the name of nature; which I define not, with the schools, to be the principle of motion and rest, but that straight and regular line, that settled and constant course the wisdom of God hath ordained the actions of his creatures, according to their several kinds. To make a revolution every day is the nature of the sun, because of that necessary course which God hath ordained it, from which it cannot swerve but by a faculty from that voice which first did give it motion. Now this course of nature God seldom alters or perverts, but like an excellent artist, hath so contrived his work, that with the selfsame instrument, without a new creation, he may effect his obscurest designs. Thus he sweeteneth the water with a wood, preserveth the creatures in the ark, which the blast of his mouth might have as easily created; for God is like a skillful geometrician, who, when more easily and with one stroke of his compass he might describe or divide a right line, had yet rather do this in a circle or longer way, according to the constituted and fore-laid principles of his art. Yet this rule of his he doth sometimes pervert, to acquaint the world with his prerogative, lest the arrogancy of our

reason should question his power, and conclude he could not. And thus I call the effects of nature the works of God, whose hand and instrument she only is; and therefore to ascribe his actions unto her, is to devolve the honor of the principal agent upon the instrument; which if with reason we may do, then let our hammers rise up and boast they have built our houses, and our pens receive the honor of our writings. I hold there is a general beauty in the works of God, and therefore no deformity in any kind or species of creature whatsoever. I cannot tell by what logic we call a toad, a bear, or an elephant ugly; they being created in those outward shapes and figures which best express the actions of their inward forms, and having passed that general visitation of God, who saw that all that he had made was good, that is, conformable to his will, which abhors deformity, and is the rule of order and beauty. There is no deformity but in monstrosity; wherein, notwithstanding, there is a kind of beauty; nature so ingeniously contriving the irregular parts, as they become sometimes more remarkable than the principal fabric. To speak yet more narrowly, there was never anything ugly or misshapen, but the chaos; wherein, notwithstanding, to speak strictly, there was no deformity, because no form; nor was it yet impregnant by the voice of God. Now nature is not at variance with art, nor art with nature, they being both servants of his providence. Art is the perfection of nature. Were the world now as it was the sixth day, there were yet a chaos. Nature hath made one world, and art another. In brief, all things are artificial; for nature is the art of God.

. . . .

That miracles are ceased, I can neither prove, nor absolutely deny, much less define the time and period of their cessation. That they survived Christ, is manifest upon the record of Scripture; that they outlived the Apostles also, and were revived at the conversion of nations many years after, we cannot deny, if we shall not question those writers whose testimonies we do not controvert in points that make for our own opinions. Therefore that may have some truth in it that is reported by the Jesuits of their miracles in the Indies; I could wish it were true, or had any other testimony than their own pens. They may easily believe those miracles abroad, who daily conceive a greater at home, the transmutation of those visible elements into the body and blood of our Saviour. For the conversion of water into wine, which he wrought in Cana, or, what the Devil would have had him done in the wilderness, of stones into bread, compared to this, will scarce deserve the name of a miracle: though indeed, to speak properly, there is not one miracle greater than another, they being the extraordinary effects of the hand of God, to which all things are of an equal facility; and to create the world, as easy as one single creature. For this is also a miracle, not only to produce effects against or above nature, but before nature; and to create nature, as great a miracle as to contradict or transcend her. We do too narrowly define the power of God, restraining it to our capacities. I hold that God can do all things; how he should work contradictions, I do not understand, yet dare not therefore deny. I cannot see why the angel of God should question Esdras[9] to recall the time past, if it were beyond his own power; or that God should pose[10] mortality in that which he was not able to perform himself. I will not say God cannot, but he will not, perform many things, which we plainly affirm he cannot. This, I am sure, is the mannerliest proposition, wherein, notwithstanding, I hold no paradox; for, strictly, his power is the same with his will, and they both, with all the rest, do make but one God.

Therefore that miracles have been, I do believe; that they may yet be wrought by the living, I do not deny; but have no confidence in those which are fathered on the dead. And this hath ever made me suspect the efficacy of relics, to examine the bones, question the habits and appurtenances of saints, and even of Christ himself. I cannot conceive why the cross that Helena found, and whereon Christ himself died, should have power to restore others unto life. I excuse not Constantine from a fall off his horse, or a mischief from his enemies, upon the wearing those nails on his bridle which our Saviour bore upon the cross in his hands. I compute among your *piæ fraudes*, nor many degrees before consecrated swords and roses, that which Baldwin, King of Jerusalem, returned the Genovese for their cost and pains in his war, to wit, the ashes of John the Baptist. Those that hold the sanctity of their souls doth leave behind a tincture and sacred faculty on their bodies, speak naturally of miracles, and do not salve the doubt. Now one reason I tender so little devotion unto relics is, I think, the slender and doubtful respect I have always held unto

antiquities. For that indeed which I admire, is far before antiquity, that is, eternity; and that is, God himself; who, though he be styled *the Ancient of Days*, cannot receive the adjunct of antiquity; who was before the world, and shall be after it, yet is not older than it; for in his years there is no climacter;[11] his duration is eternity, and far more venerable than antiquity.

But above all things I wonder how the curiosity of wiser heads could pass that great and indisputable miracle, the cessation of oracles; and in what swoon their reasons lay, to content themselves and sit down with such a far-fetched and ridiculous reason as Plutarch allegeth for it. The Jews, that can believe the supernatural solstice of the sun in the days of Joshua, have yet the impudence to deny the eclipse, which every pagan confessed, at his death: but for this, it is evident beyond all contradiction, the Devil himself confessed it. Certainly it is not a warrantable curiosity to examine the verity of Scripture by the concordance of human history, or seek to confirm the chronicle of Hester or Daniel, by the authority of Megasthenes or Herodotus. I confess, I have had an unhappy curiosity this way, till I laughed myself out of it with a piece of Justin, where he delivers that the children of Israel for being scabbed were banished out of Egypt. And truly since I have understood the occurrences of the world, and know in what counterfeit shapes and deceitful vizards times present represent on the stage things past, I do believe them little more than things to come. Some have been of my opinion, and endeavored to write the history of their own lives; wherein Moses hath outgone them all, and left not only the story of his life, but as some will have it, of his death also.

It is a riddle to me, how this story of oracles hath not wormed out of the world that doubtful conceit of spirits and witches; how so many learned heads should so far forget their metaphysics, and destroy the ladder and scale of creatures, as to question the existence of spirits. For my part, I have ever believed and do now know that there are witches: they that doubt of these, do not only deny them, but spirits; and are obliquely and upon consequence a sort not of infidels, but atheists. Those that to confute their incredulity desire to see apparitions, shall questionless never behold any, nor have the power to be so much as witches; the Devil hath them already in a heresy as capital as witchcraft; and to appear to them were but to convert

---

9 II Esdras 4:5: Then said he unto me, Go to, weigh me a weight of fire, or measure me a measure of wind, or call me again the day that is past.

10 To puzzle with a problem.

11 Climacteric; a critical period in human life in which some great change in health or fortune takes place.

them. Of all the delusions wherewith he deceives mortality, there is not any that puzzleth me more than the legerdemain of changelings. I do not credit those transformations of reasonable creatures into beasts, or that the Devil hath a power to transpeciate a man into a horse, who tempted Christ (as a trial of his divinity) to convert but stones into bread. I could believe that spirits use with man the act of carnality, and that in both sexes; I conceive they may assume, steal, or contrive a body, wherein there may be action enough to content decrepit lust, or passion to satisfy more active veneries; yet, in both, without a possibility of generation: and therefore that opinion that Antichrist should be born of the tribe of Dan by conjunction with the Devil, is ridiculous, and a conceit fitter for a rabbin than a Christian. I hold that the Devil doth really possess some men, the spirit of melancholy others, the spirit of delusion others; that, as the Devil is concealed and denied by some, so God and good angels are pretended by others, whereof the late defection of the Maid of Germany hath left a pregnant example.

Again, I believe that all that use sorceries, incantations, and spells, are not witches, or, as we term them, magicians. I conceive there is a traditional magic, not learned immediately from the Devil, but at second hand from his scholars, who, having once the secret betrayed, are able, and do empirically practice without his advice, they both proceeding upon the principles of nature; where actives, aptly conjoined to disposed passives, will under any master produce their effects. Thus I think at first a great part of philosophy was witchcraft; which, being afterward derived to one another, proved but philosophy, and was indeed no more but the honest effects of nature: what, invented by us, is philosophy, learned from him, is magic. We do surely owe the discovery of many secrets to the discovery of good and bad angels. I could never pass that sentence of Paracelsus without an asterisk or annotation; *Ascendens constellatum multa revelat quærentibus magnalia naturæ (i.e. opera Dei).*[12] I do think that many mysteries ascribed to our own inventions have been the courteous revelations of spirits; for those noble essences in heaven bear a friendly regard unto their fellow natures on earth; and therefore believe that those many prodigies and ominous prognostics, which fore-run the ruins of states, princes, and private persons, are the charitable premonitions of good angels,

which more careless inquiries term but the effects of chance and nature.

Now, besides these particular and divided spirits, there may be (for aught I know) an universal and common spirit to the whole world. It was the opinion of Plato, and it is yet of the Hermetical philosophers. If there be a common nature that unites and ties the scattered and divided individuals into one species, why may there not be one that unites them all? However, I am sure there is a common spirit that plays within us, yet makes no part of us; and that is, the spirit of God, the fire and scintillation of that noble and mighty essence, which is the life and radical heat of spirits, and those essences that know not the virtue of the sun; a fire quite contrary to the fire of hell. This is that gentle heat that brooded on the waters, and in six days hatched the world; this is that irradiation that dispels the mists of hell, the clouds of horror, fear, sorrow, despair; and preserves the region of the mind in serenity. Whosoever feels not the warm gale and gentle ventilation of this spirit, though I feel his pulse, I dare not say he lives: for truly, without this, to me there is no heat under the tropic; nor any light, though I dwelt in the body of the sun. . . .

Therefore for spirits, I am so far from denying their existence, that I could easily believe, that not only whole countries, but particular persons, have their tutelary and guardian angels. It is not a new opinion of the Church of Rome, but an old one of Pythagoras and Plato; there is no heresy in it; and if not manifestly defined in Scripture, yet is it an opinion of a good and wholesome use in the course and actions of a man's life, and would serve as an hypothesis to salve many doubts, whereof common philosophy affordeth no solution. Now, if you demand my opinion and metaphysics of their natures, I confess them very shallow; most of them in a negative way, like that of God; or in a comparative, between ourselves and fellow-creatures; for there is in this universe a stair, or manifest scale of creatures, rising not disorderly, or in confusion, but with a comely method and proportion. Between creatures of mere existence, and things of life, there is a large disproportion of nature; between plants, and animals or creatures of sense, a wider difference; between them and man, a far greater: and if the proportion hold one, between man and angels there should be yet a greater. We do not comprehend their natures, who retain the first definition of Porphyry, and distinguish them from ourselves by immortality; for before his fall, 'tis thought, man also

12 A constellation rising into view reveals many great secrets of nature to those who seek (that is, the works of God).

was immortal; yet must we needs affirm that he had a different essence from the angels. Having therefore no certain knowledge of their natures, 'tis no bad method of the schools, whatsoever perfection we find obscurely in ourselves, in a more complete and absolute way to ascribe unto them. I believe they have an extemporary knowledge, and upon the first motion of their reason do what we cannot without study or deliberation; that they know things by their forms, and define by specifical difference what we describe by accidents and properties; and therefore probabilities to us may be demonstrations unto them: that they have knowledge not only of the specifical, but numerical forms of individuals, and understand by what reserved difference each single hypostasis (besides the relation to its species) becomes its numerical self: that, as the soul hath a power to move the body it informs, so there's a faculty to move any, though inform none: ours upon restraint of time, place, and distance; but that invisible hand that conveyed Habakkuk to the lions' den,[13] or Philip to Azotus,[14] infringeth this rule, and hath a secret conveyance, wherewith mortality is not acquainted. If they have that intuitive knowledge, whereby as in reflection they behold the thoughts of one another, I cannot peremptorily deny but they know a great part of ours. They that, to refute the invocation of saints, have denied that they have any knowledge of our affairs below, have proceeded too far, and must pardon my opinion, till I can thoroughly answer that piece of Scripture, *At the conversion of a sinner the angels in heaven rejoice.* I cannot, with those in that great Father, securely interpret the work of the first day, *Fiat lux,* to the creation of angels; though I confess, there is not any creature that hath so near a glimpse of their nature as light in the sun and elements. We style it a bare accident; but, where it subsists alone, 'tis a spiritual substance, and may be an angel: in brief, conceive light invisible, and that is a spirit.

These are certainly the magisterial and masterpieces of the Creator, the flower, or (as we may say) the best part of nothing; actually existing, what we are but in hopes and probability. We are only that amphibious piece between a corporal and spiritual essence, that middle form that links those two together, and makes good the method of God and nature, that jumps not from extremes, but unites the incompatible distances by some middle and participating natures. That we

are the breath and similitude of God, it is indisputable, and upon record of Holy Scripture; but to call ourselves a microcosm, or little world, I thought it only a pleasant trope of rhetoric, till my near judgment and second thoughts told me there was a real truth therein. For first we are a rude mass, and in the rank of creatures which only are, and have a dull kind of being, not yet privileged with life, or preferred to sense or reason; next we live the life of plants, the life of animals, the life of men, and at last the life of spirits, running on in one mysterious nature those five kinds of existences which comprehend the creatures, not only of the world, but of the universe. Thus is man that great and true *amphibium*, whose nature is disposed to live, not only like other creatures in divers elements, but in divided and distinguished worlds: for though there be but one to sense, there are two to reason, the one visible, the other invisible; whereof Moses seems to have left description, and of the other so obscurely, that some parts thereof are yet in controversy. And truly, for the first chapters of Genesis, I must confess a great deal of obscurity; though divines have to the power of human reason endeavored to make all go in a literal meaning, yet those allegorical interpretations are also probable, and perhaps the mystical method of Moses, bred up in the hieroglyphical schools of the Egyptians.

Now for that immaterial world, methinks we need not wander so far as beyond the first movable; for even in this material fabric the spirits walk as freely exempt from the affection of time, place, and motion, as beyond the extremest circumference. Do but extract from the corpulency of bodies, or resolve things beyond their first matter, and you discover the habitation of angels, which if I call the ubiquitary and omnipresent essence of God, I hope I shall not offend divinity: for before the creation of the world God was really all things. For the angels he created no new world, or determinate mansion, and therefore they are everywhere where is his essence, and do live at a distance even in himself. That God made all things for man, is in some sense true, yet not so far as to subordinate the creation of those purer creatures unto ours, though as ministering spirits they do, and are willing to fulfill the will of God in these lower and sublunary affairs of man. God made all things for himself, and it is impossible he should make them for any other end than his own glory; it is all he can receive, and all that is without himself. For, honor being an external adjunct, and in the honorer rather than in the person honored, it

13 In the apocryphal book of Bel and the Dragon, verse 36.
14 Acts 8:39, 40.

was necessary to make a creature from whom he might receive this homage; and that is, in the other world, angels, in this, man; which when we neglect, we forget the very end of our creation, and may justly provoke God, not only to repent that he hath made the world, but that he hath sworn he would not destroy it. That there is but one world, is a conclusion of faith: Aristotle with all his philosophy hath not been able to prove it, and as weakly that the world was eternal. That dispute much troubled the pen of the ancient philosophers, but Moses decided that question, and all is salved with the new term of a creation, that is, a production of something out of nothing. And what is that? whatsoever is opposite to something; or more exactly, that which is truly contrary unto God: for he only is, all others have an existence with dependency, and are something but by a distinction. And herein is divinity conformant unto philosophy, and generation not only founded on contrarieties, but also creation; God, being all things, is contrary unto nothing, out of which were made all things, and so nothing became something, and omneity informed nullity into an essence.

The whole creation is a mystery, and particularly that of man. At the blast of his mouth were the rest of the creatures made, and at his bare word they started out of nothing: but in the frame of man (as the text describes it) he played the sensible operator, and seemed not so much to create, as make him. When he had separated the materials of other creatures, there consequently resulted a form and soul; but, having raised the walls of man, he was driven to a second and harder creation of a substance like himself, an incorruptible and immortal soul. For these two affections we have the philosophy and opinion of the heathens, the flat affirmative of Plato, and not a negative from Aristotle. There is another scruple cast in by divinity concerning its production, much disputed in the German auditories, and with that indifferency and equality of arguments as leave the controversy undermined. I am not of Paracelsus' mind, that boldly delivers a receipt to make a man without conjunction; yet cannot but wonder at the multitude of heads that do deny traduction, having no other argument to confirm their belief than that rhetorical sentence and *antimetathesis* of Augustine, *Creando infunditur, infundendo creatur*.[15] Either opinion will consist well enough with religion: yet I should rather incline to this, did not one objection

15 The soul is infused in the process of creation, and in being infused is created.

haunt me, not wrung from speculations and subtleties, but from common sense and observation; not picked from the leaves of any author, but bred amongst the weeds and tares of mine own brain; and this is a conclusion from the equivocal and monstrous productions in the conjunction of man with beast: for if the soul of man be not transmitted and transfused in the seed of the parents, why are not those productions merely beasts, but have also an impression and tincture of reason in as high a measure as it can evidence itself in those improper organs? Nor, truly, can I peremptorily deny that the soul, in this her sublunary estate, is wholly and in all acceptions inorganical; but that for the performance of her ordinary actions there is required not only a symmetry and proper disposition of organs, but a crasis and temper correspondent to its operations: yet is not this mass of flesh and visible structure the instrument and proper corpse of the soul, but rather of sense, and that the hand of reason. In our study of anatomy there is a mass of mysterious philosophy, and such as reduced the very heathens to divinity: yet, amongst all those rare discoveries and curious pieces I find in the fabric of man, I do not so much content myself, as in that I find not, that is, no organ or instrument for the rational soul; for in the brain, which we term the seat of reason, there is not anything of moment more than I can discover in the crany of a beast: and this is a sensible and no inconsiderable argument of the inorganity of the soul, at least in that sense we usually so receive it. Thus we are men, and we know not how: there is something in us that can be without us, and will be after us; though it is strange that it hath no history what it was before us, nor cannot tell how it entered in us.

Now, for these walls of flesh, wherein the soul doth seem to be immured before the resurrection, it is nothing but an elemental composition, and a fabric that must fall to ashes. *All flesh is grass*, is not only metaphorically, but literally, true; for all those creatures we behold are but the herbs of the field, digested into flesh in them, or more remotely carnified in ourselves. Nay further, we are what we all abhor, *Anthropophagi* and cannibals, devourers not only of men, but of ourselves; and that not in an allegory, but a positive truth; for all this mass of flesh which we behold came in at our mouths; this frame we look upon hath been upon our trenchers; in brief, we have devoured ourselves. I cannot believe the wisdom of Pythagoras did ever positively, and in a literal sense, affirm his metempsychosis, or impossible transmigration of the souls of men into beasts. Of all metamorphoses or transmigrations, I believe only one, that is of Lot's wife;[16] for that of Nebuchodonosor[17] proceeded not so far: in all others I conceive there is no further verity than is contained in their implicit sense and morality. I believe that the whole frame of a beast doth perish, and is left in the same state after death as before it was materialed unto life: that the souls of men know neither contrary nor corruption; that they subsist beyond the body, and outlive death by the privilege of their proper natures, and without a miracle; that the souls of the faithful, as they leave earth, take possession of heaven: that those apparitions and ghosts of departed persons are not the wandering souls of men, but the unquiet walks of devils, prompting and suggesting us unto mischief, blood, and villainy; instilling and stealing into our hearts that the blessed spirits are not at rest in their graves, but wander solicitous of the affairs of the world. But that those phantasms appear often, and do frequent cemeteries, charnel-houses, and churches, it is because those are the dormitories of the dead, where the Devil, like an insolent champion, beholds with pride the spoils and trophies of his victory over Adam.

This is that dismal conquest we all deplore, that makes us so often cry, O *Adam, quid fecisti?*[18] I thank God I have not those strait ligaments, or narrow obligations to the world, as to dote on life, or be convulsed and tremble at the name of death. Not that I am insensible of the dread and horror thereof; or by raking into the bowels of the deceased, continual sight of anatomies, skeletons, or cadaverous relics, like vespilloes,[19] or grave-makers, I am become stupid, or have forgot the apprehension of mortality; but that, marshaling all the horrors, and contemplating the extremities thereof, I find not anything therein able to daunt the courage of a man, much less a well-resolved Christian; and therefore am not angry at the error of our first parents, or unwilling to bear a part of this common fate, and like the best of them to die, that is, to cease to breathe, to take a farewell of the elements, to be a kind of nothing for a moment, to be within one instant of a spirit. When I take a full view and circle of myself without this reasonable moderator, and equal piece of justice, death, I do conceive myself the miserablest person extant. Were there not another life that

I hope for, all the vanities of this world should not intreat a moment's breath from me: could the Devil work my belief to imagine I could never die, I would not outlive that very thought. I have so abject a conceit of this common way of existence, this retaining to the sun and elements, I cannot think this is to be a man, or to live according to the dignity of humanity. In expectation of a better, I can with patience embrace this life, yet in my best meditations do often defy death; I honor any man that contemns it, nor can I highly love any that is afraid of it: this makes me naturally love a soldier, and honor those tattered and contemptible regiments that will die at the command of a sergeant. For a pagan there may be some motives to be in love with life; but for a Christian to be amazed at death, I see not how he can escape this dilemma, that he is too sensible of this life, or hopeless of the life to come.

Some divines count Adam thirty years old at his creation, because they suppose him created in the perfect age and stature of man. And surely we are all out of the computation of our age, and every man is some months elder than he bethinks him; for we live, move, have a being, and are subject to the actions of the elements, and the malice of diseases, in that other world, the truest microcosm, the womb of our mother. For besides that general and common existence we are conceived to hold in our chaos, and whilst we sleep within the bosom of our causes, we enjoy a being and life in three distinct worlds, wherein we receive most manifest graduations. In that obscure world and womb of our mother, our time is short, computed by the moon, yet longer than the days of many creatures that behold the sun; ourselves being not yet without life, sense, and reason; though for the manifestation of its actions, it awaits the opportunity of objects, and seems to live there but in its root and soul of vegetation. Entering afterwards upon the scene of the world, we arise up and become another creature, performing the reasonable actions of man, and obscurely manifesting that part of divinity in us; but not in complement and perfection, till we have once more cast our secondine, that is, this slough of flesh, and are delivered into the last world, that is, that ineffable place of Paul, that proper *ubi* of spirits. The smattering I have of the philosopher's stone (which is something more than the perfect exaltation of gold) hath taught me a great deal of divinity, and instructed my belief, how that immortal spirit and incorruptible substance of my soul may lie obscure, and sleep a while within this

16 Genesis 19:26.
17 Better known as Nebuchadnezzar. Cf. Daniel 4:33.
18 O Adam, what hast thou done?
19 Corpse-bearers.

house of flesh. Those strange and mystical transmigrations that I have observed in silkworms, turned my
philosophy into divinity. There is in these works of
nature, which seem to puzzle reason, something divine,
and hath more in it than the eye of a common spectator doth discover.

I am naturally bashful; nor hath conversation, age,
or travel, been able to effront or enharden me; yet I
have one part of modesty which I have seldom discovered in another, that is (to speak truly), I am not
so much afraid of death, as ashamed thereof. 'Tis the
very disgrace and ignominy of our natures, that in a
moment can so disfigure us, that our nearest friends,
wife, and children, stand afraid and start at us: the
birds and beasts of the field, that before in a natural
fear obeyed us, forgetting all allegiance, begin to prey
upon us. This very conceit hath in a tempest disposed
and left me willing to be swallowed up in the abyss
of waters, wherein I had perished unseen, unpitied,
without wondering eyes, tears of pity, lectures of
mortality, and none had said,

Quantum mutatus ab illo![20]

Not that I am ashamed of the anatomy of my parts, or
can accuse nature for playing the bungler in any part
of me, or my own vicious life for contracting any
shameful disease upon me, whereby I might not call
myself as wholesome a morsel for the worms as
any. . . .

I thank God, and with joy I mention it, I was never
afraid of hell, nor never grew pale at the description
of that place. I have so fixed my contemplations on
heaven, that I have almost forgot the idea of hell, and
am afraid rather to lose the joys of the one, than
endure the misery of the other: to be deprived of them
is a perfect hell, and needs, methinks, no addition to
complete our afflictions. That terrible term hath never
detained me from sin, nor do I owe any good action
to the name thereof. I fear God, yet am not afraid of
him: his mercies make me ashamed of my sins, before
his judgments afraid thereof. These are the forced and
secondary method of his wisdom, which he useth but
as the last remedy, and upon provocation; a course
rather to deter the wicked, than incite the virtuous to
his worship. I can hardly think there was ever any
scared into heaven; they go the fairest way to heaven

that would serve God without a hell; other mer-
cenaries, that crouch into him in fear of hell, though
they term themselves the servants, are indeed but the
slaves, of the Almighty.

And to be true, and speak my soul, when I survey
the occurrences of my life, and call into account the
finger of God, I can perceive nothing but an abyss and
mass of mercies, either in general to mankind, or in
particular to myself. And (whether out of the prejudice of my affection, or an inverting and partial
conceit of his mercies, I know not; but) those which
others term crosses, afflictions, judgments, misfortunes,
to me, who inquire farther into them than their visible effects, they both appear, and in event have ever
proved, the secret and dissembled favors of his affection. It is a singular piece of wisdom to apprehend
truly, and without passion, the works of God, and so
well to distinguish his justice from his mercy, as not to
miscall those noble attributes: yet it is likewise an
honest piece of logic, so to dispute and argue the proceedings of God, as to distinguish even his judgments
into mercies. For God is merciful unto all, because
better to the worst than the best deserve; and to say he
punisheth none in this world, though it be a paradox,
is no absurdity. To one that hath committed murther,
if the judge should only ordain a fine, it were a madness to call this a punishment, and to repine at the
sentence, rather than admire the clemency of the
judge. Thus, our offenses being mortal, and deserving
not only death, but damnation, if the goodness of
God be content to traverse and pass them over with a
loss, misfortune, or disease, what frenzy were it to
term this a punishment rather than an extremity of
mercy, and to groan under the rod of his judgments,
rather than admire the scepter of his mercies! Therefore to adore, honor, and admire him, is a debt of
gratitude due from the obligation of our nature, states,
and conditions; and with these thoughts, he that knows
them best, will not deny that I adore him. That I
obtain heaven, and the bliss thereof, is accidental, and
not the intended work of my devotion; it being a
felicity I can neither think to deserve, nor scarce
in modesty to expect. For these two ends of us
all, either as rewards or punishments, are mercifully
ordained and disproportionably disposed unto our
actions; the one being so far beyond our deserts, the
other so infinitely below our demerits. . . .

I believe many are saved, who to man seem reprobated; and many are reprobated, who, in the opinion

20 How greatly changed from what he was! (Æneid II,
274.)

and sentence of man, stand elected. There will appear at the last day strange and unexpected examples both of his justice and his mercy; and therefore to define either, is folly in man, and insolency even in the devils. Those acute and subtile spirits, in all their sagacity, can hardly divine who shall be saved; which if they could prognostic, their labor were at an end, nor need they compass the earth seeking whom they may devour. Those who, upon a rigid application of the law, sentence Solomon unto damnation, condemn not only him, but themselves, and the whole world: for, by the letter and written word of God, we are without exception in the state of death; but there is a prerogative of God, and an arbitrary pleasure above the letter of his own law, by which alone we can pretend unto salvation, and through which Solomon might be as easily saved as those who condemn him.

The number of those who pretend unto salvation, and those infinite swarms who think to pass through the eye of this needle, have much amazed me. That name and compellation of *little flock*, doth not comfort, but deject, my devotion; especially when I reflect upon mine own unworthiness, wherein, according to my humble apprehensions, I am below them all. I believe there shall never be an anarchy in heaven; but, as there are hierarchies amongst the angels, so shall there be degrees of priority amongst the saints. Yet is it (I protest) beyond my ambition to aspire unto the first ranks; my desires only are (and I shall be happy therein) to be but the last man, and bring up the rear in heaven.

Again, I am confident and fully persuaded, yet dare not take my oath, of my salvation. I am as it were sure, and do believe without all doubt, that there is such a city as Constantinople; yet for me to take my oath thereon were a kind of perjury, because I hold no infallible warrant from my own sense to confirm me in the certainty thereof. And truly, though many pretend an absolute certainty of their salvation, yet, when an humble soul shall contemplate her own unworthiness, she shall meet with many doubts, and suddenly find how little we stand in need of the precept of St. Paul, *Work out your salvation with fear and trembling*. That which is the cause of my election, I hold to be the cause of my salvation, which was the mercy and *beneplacit* of God, before I was, or the foundation of the world. *Before Abraham was, I am*, is the saying of Christ; yet is it true in some sense, if I say it of myself; for I was not only before myself, but Adam, that is, in the idea of God, and the decree of

that synod held from all eternity. And in this sense, I say, the world was before the creation, and at an end before it had a beginning; and thus was I dead before I was alive: though my grave be England, my dying place was Paradise: and Eve miscarried of me before she conceived of Cain.

Insolent zeals that do decry good works and rely only upon faith, take not away merit: for, depending upon the efficacy of their faith, they enforce the condition of God, and in a more sophistical way do seem to challenge heaven. It was decreed by God that only those that lapped in the water like dogs, should have the honor to destroy the Midianites; yet could none of those justly challenge, or imagine he deserved, that honor thereupon. I do not deny but that true faith, and such as God requires, is not only a mark or token, but also a means, of our salvation; but where to find this, is as obscure to me as my last end. And if our Saviour could object unto his own disciples and favorites, a faith, that, to the quantity of a grain of mustard-seed, is able to remove mountains; surely, that which we boast of, is not anything, or at the most, but a remove from nothing. This is the tenor of my belief; wherein though there be many things singular, and to the humor of my irregular self, yet, if they square not with maturer judgments, I disclaim them, and do no further father them, than the learned and best judgments shall authorize them.

from THE SECOND PART

Now for that other virtue of charity, without which faith is a mere notion, and of no existence, I have ever endeavored to nourish the merciful disposition and humane inclination I borrowed from my parents, and regulate it to the written and prescribed laws of charity. And if I hold the true anatomy of myself, I am delineated and naturally framed to such a piece of virtue; for I am of a constitution so general that it consorts and sympathizeth with all things. I have no antipathy, or rather idiosyncrasy, in diet, humor, air, anything. I wonder not at the French for their dishes of frogs, snails and toadstools, nor at the Jews for locusts and grasshoppers; but being amongst them, make them my common viands, and I find they agree with my stomach as well as theirs. I could digest a salad gathered in a churchyard, as well as in a garden. I cannot start at the presence of a serpent, scorpion, lizard, or salamander: at the sight of a toad or viper, I find in me no desire to take up a stone to destroy them. I feel not in myself those common antipathies that I can discover in others: those national repugnances do not touch me, nor do I behold with prejudice the French, Italian, Spaniard, or Dutch: but where I find their actions in balance with my countrymen's, I honor, love, and embrace them in the same degree. I was born in the eighth climate,[21] but seem for to be framed and constellated unto all. I am no plant that will not prosper out of a garden. All places, all airs, make unto me one country; I am in England everywhere, and under any meridian. I have been shipwrecked, yet am not enemy with the sea or winds; I can study, play, or sleep in a tempest. In brief, I am averse from nothing: my conscience would give me the lie if I should say I absolutely detest or hate any essence but the Devil: or so at least abhor anything, but that we might come to composition. If there be any among those common objects of hatred I do contemn and laugh at, it is that great enemy of reason, virtue and religion, the multitude: that numerous piece of monstrosity, which, taken asunder, seem men, and the reasonable creatures of God; but, confused together, make but one great beast, and a monstrosity more prodigious than hydra. It is no breach of charity to call these *fools;* it is the style all holy writers have afforded them, set down by Solomon in canonical Scripture,[22] and a point of our faith to believe so. Neither in the name of *multitude* do I only include the base and minor sort of people; there is a rabble even amongst the gentry, a sort of plebeian heads, whose fancy moves with the same wheel as these; men in the same level with mechanics, though their fortunes do somewhat gild their infirmities, and their purses compound for their follies. But as, in casting account, three or four men together come short in account of one man placed by himself below them; so neither are a troop of these ignorant *doradoes*[23] of that true esteem and value, as many a forlorn person, whose condition doth place him below their feet. Let us speak like politicians: there is a nobility without heraldry, a natural dignity, whereby one man is ranked with another, another filed before him, according to the quality of his desert, and pre-eminence of his good parts. Though the corruption of these times and the bias of present practice wheel another way, thus it was in the first and primitive common-wealths, and is yet in the integrity and cradle of well-ordered polities, till corruption getteth ground; ruder desires laboring after that which wiser considerations contemn, every one having a liberty to amass and heap up riches, and they a license or faculty to do or purchase anything. . . .

But to return from philosophy to charity: I hold not so narrow a conceit of this virtue, as to conceive that to give alms is only to be charitable, or think a piece of liberality can comprehend the total of charity. Divinity hath wisely divided the act thereof into many branches, and hath taught us in this narrow way many paths unto goodness; as many ways as we may do good, so many ways we may be charitable. There are infirmities not only of body, but of soul, and fortunes, which do require the merciful hand of our abilities. I cannot contemn a man for ignorance, but behold him with as much pity as I do Lazarus.[24] It is no greater charity to clothe his body, than apparel the nakedness of his soul. It is an honorable object to see the reasons of other men wear our liveries, and their borrowed understandings do homage to the bounty of ours: it is the cheapest way of beneficence, and, like the natural charity of the sun, illuminates another without obscuring itself. To be reserved and caitiff in this part of goodness, is the sordidest piece of covetousness, and more contemptible than pecuniary avarice. To this (as calling myself a scholar) I am obliged by the duty of my condition: I make not therefore my head a grave, but a treasure, of knowledge; I intend no monopoly, but a community in learning; I study not for my own sake only, but for theirs that study not for themselves. I envy no man that knows more than myself, but pity them that know less. I instruct no man as an exercise of my knowledge, or with an intent rather to nourish and keep it alive in mine own head than beget and propagate it in his: and in the midst of all my endeavors there is but one thought that dejects me, that my acquired parts must perish with myself, nor can be legacied among my honored friends. I cannot fall out or contemn a man for an error, or conceive why a difference in opinion should divide an affection; for controversies, disputes, and argumentations, both in philosophy and in divinity, if they meet with discreet and peaceable natures, do not infringe the laws of charity. In all disputes, so much as there is of passion, so much there is of nothing to the purpose; for then

21 A zone measured on the earth's surface which included England.
22 Proverbs 1:7, 22, 32, etc.
23 Rich men (literally, goldfish).

24 See St. Luke 16:19–31.

reason, like a bad hound, spends upon a false scent, and forsakes the question first started. And this is one reason why controversies are never determined; for, though they be amply proposed, they are scarce at all handled, they do so swell with unnecessary digressions; and the parenthesis on the party is often as large as the main discourse upon the subject. The foundations of religion are already established, and the principles of salvation subscribed unto by all: there remains not many controversies worth a passion; and yet never any disputed without, not only in divinity, but in inferior arts. What a βατραχομυομαχία[25] and hot skirmish is betwixt S. and T. in Lucian! How do grammarians hack and slash for the genitive case in *Jupiter!* How do they break their own pates to salve that of Priscian![26]

Si foret in terris, rideret Democritus.[27]

Yea, even amongst wiser militants, how many wounds have been given, and credits slain, for the poor victory of an opinion, or beggarly conquest of a distinction! Scholars are men of peace, they bear no arms, but their tongues are sharper than Actius his razor; their pens carry farther, and give a louder report than thunder: I had rather stand the shock of a basilisco,[28] than the fury of a merciless pen. It is not mere zeal to learning, or devotion to the muses, that wiser princes patron the arts, and carry an indulgent aspect unto scholars; but a desire to have their names eternized by the memory of their writings, and a fear of the revengeful pen of succeeding ages; for these are the men, that, when they have played their parts, and had their *exits*, must step out and give the moral of their scenes, and deliver unto posterity an inventory of their virtues and vices. And surely there goes a great deal of conscience to the compiling of an history: there is no reproach to the scandal of a story; it is such an authentic kind of falsehood that with authority belies our good names to all nations and posterity.

There is another offense unto charity, which no author hath ever written of, and few take notice of; and that's the reproach, not of whole professions, mysteries, and conditions, but of whole nations, wherein by opprobrious epithets we miscall each other, and by an uncharitable logic, from a disposition in a few, conclude a habit in all.

Le mutin Anglois, et le bravache Escossois,
Et le fol François,
Le poultron Romain, le larron de Gascongne,
L'Espagnol superbe, et l'Aleman yvrongne.[29]

St. Paul, that calls the Cretians liars,[30] doth it but indirectly, and upon quotation of their own poet. It is as bloody a thought in one way as Nero's was in another; for by a word we wound a thousand, and at one blow assassin the honor of a nation. It is as complete a piece of madness to miscall and rave against the times, or think to recall men to reason by a fit of passion. Democritus, that thought to laugh the times into goodness, seems to me as deeply hypochondriac as Heraclitus, that bewailed them. It moves not my spleen to behold the multitude in their proper humors, that is, in their fits of folly and madness; as well understanding that wisdom is not profaned unto the world, and 'tis the privilege of a few to be virtuous. They that endeavor to abolish vice, destroy also virtue; for contraries, though they destroy one another, are yet the life of one another. Thus virtue (abolish vice) is an idea. Again, the community of sin doth not disparage goodness; for when vice gains upon the major part, virtue, in whom it remains, becomes more excellent; and being lost in some, multiplies its goodness in others which remain untouched and persist entire in the general inundation. I can therefore behold vice without a satire, content only with an admonition, or instructive reprehension; for noble natures, and such as are capable of goodness, are railed into vice, that might as easily be admonished into virtue; and we should all be so far the orators of goodness, as to protect her from the power of vice, and maintain the cause of injured truth. No man can justly censure or condemn another, because indeed no man truly knows another. This I perceive in myself; for I am in the dark to all the world, and my nearest friends behold me but in a cloud. Those that know me but superficially, think less of me than I do of myself; those of my near acquaintance think more; God, who truly knows me, knows that I am nothing; for he only

25 Battle of frogs and mice.
26 The celebrated Roman grammarian. "To break Priscian's head" is to make a bad blunder in grammar.
27 If he were on earth, how Democritus would laugh! (Horace, Epistles II, Ep. 1, 194.)
28 A large piece of ordnance, called after the fabled basilisk, whose breath, and even whose look, was fatal.

29 The roistering Englishman, the swaggering Scotsman, and the mad Frenchman, the Roman coward, the thief of Gascony, the arrogant Spaniard, and the drunken German. (Joachim du Bellay, 1525–1560.)
30 Titus 1:12.

beholds me and all the world, who looks not on us through a derived ray, or a trajection of a sensible species,[31] but beholds the substance without the helps of accidents, and the forms of things as we their operations. Further, no man can judge another, because no man knows himself: for we censure others but as they disagree from that humor which we fancy laudable in ourselves, and commend others but for that wherein they seem to quadrate and consent with us. So that, in conclusion, all is but that we all condemn, self-love. 'Tis the general complaint of these times, and perhaps of those past, that charity grows cold; which I perceive most verified in those which most do manifest the fires and flames of zeal; for it is a virtue that best agrees with coldest natures, and such as are complexioned for humility. But how shall we expect charity towards others, when we are uncharitable to ourselves? *Charity begins at home*, is the voice of the world; yet is every man his greatest enemy, and, as it were, his own executioner. *Non occides*,[32] is the commandment of God, yet scarce observed by any man; for I perceive every man is his own Atropos, and lends a hand to cut the thread of his own days. . . .

There are wonders in true affection: it is a body of enigmas, mysteries, and riddles; wherein two so become one, as they both become two. I love my friend before myself, and yet methinks I do not love him enough: some few months hence my multiplied affection will make me believe I have not loved him at all. When I am from him, I am dead till I be with him; when I am with him, I am not satisfied, but would still be nearer him. United souls are not satisfied with embraces, but desire to be truly each other; which being impossible, their desires are infinite, and must proceed without a possibility of satisfaction. Another misery there is in affection, that whom we truly love like our own selves, we forget their looks, nor can our memory retain the idea of their faces; and it is no wonder, for they are ourselves, and our affection makes their looks our own. This noble affection falls not on vulgar and common constitutions, but on such as are marked for virtue: he that can love his friend with this noble ardor, will in a competent degree affect all. Now, if we can bring our affections to look beyond the body, and cast an eye upon the soul, we have found out the true object, not only of friendship,

but charity; and the greatest happiness that we can bequeath the soul, is that wherein we all do place our last felicity, salvation; which though it be not in our power to bestow, it is in our charity and pious invocations to desire, if not procure and further. I cannot contentedly frame a prayer for myself in particular, without a catalogue for my friends; nor request a happiness, wherein my sociable disposition doth not desire the fellowship of my neighbor. I never hear the toll of a passing bell, though in my mirth, without my prayers and best wishes for the departing spirit; I cannot go to cure the body of my patient, but I forget my profession, and call unto God for his soul; I cannot see one say his prayers, but, instead of imitating him, I fall into a supplication for him, who perhaps is no more to me than a common nature: and if God hath vouchsafed an ear to my supplications, there are surely many happy that never saw me, and enjoy the blessing of mine unknown devotions. To pray for enemies, that is, for their salvation, is no harsh precept, but the practice of our daily and ordinary devotions. I cannot believe the story of the Italian:[33] our bad wishes and uncharitable desires proceed no further than this life; it is the Devil, and the uncharitable votes of hell, that desire our misery in the world to come. . . .

I thank God, amongst those millions of vices I do inherit and hold from Adam, I have escaped one, and that a mortal enemy to charity, the first and father-sin, not only of man, but of the Devil, pride: a vice whose name is comprehended in a monosyllable, but in its nature not circumscribed with a world. I have escaped it in a condition that can hardly avoid it. Those petty acquisitions and reputed perfections that advance and elevate the conceits of other men, add no feathers unto mine. I have seen a grammarian tower and plume himself over a single line in Horace, and show more pride in the construction of one ode, than the author in the composure of the whole book. For my own part, besides the jargon and patois of several provinces, I understand no less than six languages; yet I protest I have no higher conceit of myself, than had our fathers before the confusion of Babel, when there was but one language in the world, and none to boast himself either linguist or critic. I have not only seen several

---

31 The visible representation of a substance *trajected* or transmitted by that substance.

32 Thou shalt not kill.

33 In his Pseudodoxia, VII, 19, Sir Thomas refers more specifically to this Italian, "who, after he had inveigled his enemy to disdain his faith for the redemption of his life, did presently poniard him, to prevent repentance, and assure his eternal death."

countries, beheld the nature of their climes, the chorography of their provinces, topography of their cities, but understood their several laws, customs, and policies; yet cannot all this persuade the dullness of my spirit unto such an opinion of myself as I behold in nimbler and conceited heads, that never looked a degree beyond their nests. I know the names, and somewhat more, of all the constellations in my horizon; yet I have seen a prating mariner, that could only name the pointers and the north star, out-talk me, and conceit himself a whole sphere above me. I know most of the plants of my country, and of those about me; yet methinks I do not know so many as when I did but know a hundred, and had scarcely ever simpled[34] further than Cheapside. For, indeed, heads of capacity, and such as are not full with a handful or easy measure of knowledge, think they know nothing till they know all; which being impossible, they fall upon the opinion of Socrates, and only know they know not anything. I cannot think that Homer pined away upon the riddle of the fishermen; or that Aristotle, who understood the uncertainty of knowledge, and confessed so often the reason of man too weak for the works of nature, did ever drown himself upon the flux and reflux of Euripus. We do but learn today what our better advanced judgments will unteach tomorrow; and Aristotle doth but instruct us, as Plato did him; that is, to confute himself. . . .

I was never yet once,[35] and commend their resolutions who never marry twice: not that I disallow of second marriage; as neither, in all cases, of polygamy, which, considering some times, and the unequal number of both sexes, may be also necessary. The whole world was made for man, but the twelfth part of man for woman: man is the whole world, and the breadth of God; woman the rib and crooked piece of man. I could be content that we might procreate like trees, without conjunction, or that there were any way to perpetuate the world without this trivial and vulgar way of union: it is the foolishest act a wise man commits in all his life: nor is there anything that will more deject his cooled imagination, when he shall consider what an odd and unworthy piece of folly he hath committed. I speak not in prejudice, nor am averse from that sweet sex, but naturally amorous of all that is beautiful. I can look a whole day with delight upon a handsome picture, though it be but of an horse. It is my temper, and I like it the better, to affect all harmony; and sure there is music even in the beauty, and the silent note which Cupid strikes, far sweeter than the sound of an instrument. For there is a music wherever there is a harmony, order, or proportion: and thus far we may maintain the music of the spheres; for those well-ordered motions, and regular paces, though they give no sound unto the ear, yet to the understanding they strike a note most full of harmony. Whosoever is harmonically composed delights in harmony; which makes me much distrust the symmetry of those heads which declaim against all church-music. For myself, not only from my obedience, but my particular genius, I do embrace it: for even that vulgar and tavern-music, which makes one man merry, another mad, strikes in me a deep fit of devotion, and a profound contemplation of the First Composer. There is something in it of divinity more than the ear discovers: it is an hieroglyphical and shadowed lesson of the whole world, and creatures of God; such a melody to the ear, as the whole world, well understood, would afford the understanding. In brief, it is a sensible fit of that harmony which intellectually sounds in the ears of God. I will not say, with Plato, the soul is an harmony, but harmonical, and hath its nearest sympathy unto music: thus some, whose temper of body agrees, and humors the constitution of their souls, are born poets, though indeed all are naturally inclined unto rhythm. This made Tacitus, in the very first line of his story,[36] fall upon a verse; and Cicero, the worst of poets, but declaiming for a poet, fall in the very first sentence upon a perfect hexameter.[37] I feel not in me those sordid and unchristian desires of my profession; I do not secretly implore and wish for plagues, rejoice at famines, revolve ephemerides[38] and almanacs in expectation of malignant aspects, fatal conjunctions, and eclipses. I rejoice not at unwholesome springs, nor unseasonable winters: my prayer goes with the husbandman's; I desire everything in its proper season, that neither men nor the times be put out of temper. Let me be sick myself, if sometimes the malady of my patient be not a disease unto me. I desire rather to cure his infirmities than my own necessities. Where I do him no good, methinks it is scarce honest gain; though I confess 'tis but the worthy salary of our well-intended endeavors. I am not only ashamed, but heartily sorry,

34 Gathered simples (herbs).
35 Before this sentence was published, however, Browne married, in 1641. He later had ten children.

36 The Annals.   37 In his *Pro Archia*.
38 Astronomical charts.

that, besides death, there are diseases incurable: yet not for my own sake, or that they be beyond my art, but for the general cause and sake of humanity, whose common cause I apprehend as mine own. . . .

For my conversation,[39] it is like the sun's, with all men, and with a friendly aspect to good and bad. Methinks there is no man bad, and the worst, best; that is, while they are kept within the circle of those qualities wherein they are good: there is no man's mind of such discordant and jarring a temper, to which a tunable disposition may not strike a harmony. *Magnæ virtutes, nec minora vitia;*[40] it is the posy of the best natures, and may be inverted on the worst; there are in the most depraved and venomous dispositions, certain pieces that remain untouched, which by an *antiperistasis*[41] become more excellent, or by the excellency of their antipathies are able to preserve themselves from the contagion of their enemy vices, and persist entire beyond the general corruption. For it is also thus in nature: the greatest balsams[42] do lie enveloped in the bodies of most powerful corrosives. I say, moreover, and I ground upon experience, that poisons contain within themselves their own antidote, and that which preserves them from the venom of themselves, without which they were not deleterious to others only, but to themselves also. But it is the corruption that I fear within me, not the contagion of commerce without me. 'Tis that unruly regiment within me, that will destroy me; 'tis I that do infect myself; the man without a navel[43] yet lives in me; I feel that original canker corrode and devour me; and therefore *Defenda me Dios de me,* "Lord deliver me from myself," is a part of my litany, and the first voice of my retired imaginations. There is no man alone, because every man is a microcosm,[44] and carries the whole world about him. *Nunquam minus solus quam cum solus,*[45] though it be the apothegm of a wise man, is yet true in the mouth of a fool. Indeed, though in a wilderness, a man is never alone, not only because he is with himself and his own thoughts, but because he is

39 Behavior, conduct.
40 Great virtues, and no smaller vices.
41 An opposition of contrary qualities by which one or both are intensified; or the intensification so produced.
42 Healing agents.   43 Adam.
44 The microcosm, or little world of man, is contrasted here, as elsewhere, with the macrocosm, or great world of the universe.
45 Never less alone than when alone. (Cicero, *de Officiis,* III, sec. 1.)

with the Devil, who ever consorts with our solitude, and is that unruly rebel that musters up those disordered motions which accompany our sequestered imaginations. And to speak more narrowly, there is no such thing as solitude, nor anything that can be said to be alone and by itself, but God, who is his own circle, and can subsist by himself; all others, besides their dissimilar and heterogeneous parts, which in a manner multiply their natures, cannot subsist without the concourse of God, and the society of that hand which doth uphold their natures. In brief, there can be nothing truly alone and by itself, which is not truly one; and such is only God: all others do transcend an unity, and so by consequence are many.

Now for my life, it is a miracle of thirty years, which to relate were not a history, but a piece of poetry, and would sound to common ears like a fable. For the world, I count it not an inn, but an hospital; and a place not to live, but to die in. The world that I regard is myself; it is the microcosm of my own frame that I cast mine eye on; for the other, I use it but like my globe, and turn it round sometimes for my recreation. Men that look upon my outside, perusing only my condition and fortunes, do err in my altitude; for I am above Atlas his shoulders. The earth is a point not only in respect of the heavens above us, but of that heavenly and celestial part within us; that mass of flesh that circumscribes me, limits not my mind: that surface that tells the heavens it hath an end, cannot persuade me I have any: I take my circle to be above three hundred and sixty; though the number of the arc do measure my body, it comprehendeth not my mind: whilst I study to find how I am a microcosm, or little world, I find myself something more than the great. There is surely a piece of divinity in us, something that was before the elements, and owes no homage unto the sun. Nature tells me I am the image of God, as well as Scripture: he that understands not thus much, hath not his introduction or first lesson, and is yet to begin the alphabet of man. Let me not injure the felicity of others, if I say I am as happy as any: *Ruat cœlum, fiat voluntas tua,*[46] salveth all; so that whatsoever happens, it is but what our daily prayers desire. In brief, I am content; and what should Providence add more? Surely this is it we call happiness, and this do I enjoy; with this I am happy in a dream, and as content to enjoy a happiness in a fancy, as others in a more apparent truth and realty. There is surely a nearer apprehension of anything that delights

46 Though the heavens fall, Thy will be done.

us in our dreams, than in our waked senses: without this I were unhappy; for my awaked judgment discontents me, ever whispering unto me, that I am from my friend; but my friendly dreams in the night requite me, and make me think I am within his arms. I thank God for my happy dreams, as I do for my good rest; for there is a satisfaction in them unto reasonable desires, and such as can be content with a fit of happiness: and surely it is not a melancholy conceit[47] to think we are all asleep in this world, and that the conceits of this life are as mere dreams to those of the next; as the phantasms of the night to the conceits of the day. There is an equal delusion in both, and the one doth but seem to be the emblem or picture of the other: we are somewhat more than ourselves in our sleeps, and the slumber of the body seems to be but the waking of the soul. It is the ligation[48] of sense, but the liberty of reason; and our waking conceptions do not match the fancies of our sleeps. At my nativity my ascendant[49] was the watery sign of Scorpius; I was born in the planetary hour of Saturn, and I think I have a piece of that leaden planet in me. I am no way facetious, nor disposed for the mirth and galliardize[50] of company; yet in one dream I can compose a whole comedy, behold the action, apprehend the jests, and laugh myself awake at the conceits thereof. Were my memory as faithful as my reason is then fruitful, I would never study but in my dreams; and this time also would I choose for my devotions: but our grosser memories have then so little hold of our abstracted understandings, that they forget the story, and can only relate to our awaked souls a confused and broken tale of that that hath passed. Aristotle, who hath written a singular tract Of Sleep, hath not, methinks, thoroughly defined it; nor yet Galen, though he seem to have corrected it; for those *noctambuloes* and nightwalkers, though in their sleep, do yet enjoy the action of their senses. We must therefore say that there is something in us that is not in the jurisdiction of Morpheus; and that those abstracted and ecstatic souls do walk about in their own corpse as spirits with the bodies they assume, wherein they seem to hear, see, and feel, though indeed the organs are destitute of sense, and their natures of those faculties that should inform them. Thus it is observed, that men some-

times, upon the hour of their departure, do speak and reason above themselves; for then the soul, beginning to be freed from the ligaments of the body, begins to reason like herself, and to discourse in a strain above mortality.

We term sleep a death; and yet it is waking that kills us, and destroys those spirits that are the house of life. 'Tis indeed a part of life that best expresseth death; for every man truly lives, so long as he acts his nature, or some way makes good the faculties of himself. Themistocles, therefore, that slew his soldier in his sleep, was a merciful executioner: 'tis a kind of punishment the mildness of no laws hath invented: I wonder the fancy of Lucan and Seneca did not discover it. It is that death by which we may be literally said to die daily; a death which Adam died before his mortality; a death whereby we live a middle and moderating point between life and death: in fine, so like death, I dare not trust it without my prayers, and an half adieu unto the world, and take my farewell in a colloquy with God. . . .

I conclude therefore, and say, there is no happiness under (or, as Copernicus will have it, above) the sun, nor any *crambe*[51] in that repeated verity and burthen of all the wisdom of Solomon, *All is vanity and vexation of spirit.* There is no felicity in that the world adores. Aristotle, whilst he labors to refute the Ideas of Plato, falls upon one himself; for his *summum bonum* is a chimera, and there is no such thing as his felicity. That wherein God himself is happy, the holy angels are happy, in whose defect the devils are unhappy, that dare I call happiness: whatsoever conduceth unto this, may with an easy metaphor deserve that name; whatsoever else the world terms happiness, is to me a story out of Pliny, a tale of Boccace or Malizspini, an apparition, or neat delusion, wherein there is no more of happiness than the name. Bless me in this life with but peace of my conscience, command of my affections, the love of thyself and my dearest friends, and I shall be happy enough to pity Cæsar. These are, O Lord, the humble desires of my most reasonable ambition, and all I dare call happiness on earth; wherein I set no rule or limit to thy hand or providence. Dispose of me according to the wisdom of thy pleasure: thy will be done, though in my own undoing.

47 Fancy, opinion.   48 Binding.
49 The sign of the zodiac rising over the horizon.
50 Excessive gaiety.

51 Tiresome repetition.

HYDRIOTAPHIA, URN-BURIAL.

[TEXT: *first edition, 1658, as corrected in Browne's hand*]

CHAPTER I

IN THE deep discovery of the subterranean world, a shallow part would satisfy some inquirers; who, if two or three yards were open about the surface, would not care to rake the bowels of Potosi,[1] and regions towards the center. Nature hath furnished one part of the earth, and man another. The treasures of time lie high, in urns, coins, and monuments, scarce below the roots of some vegetables. Time hath endless rarities, and shows of all varieties; which reveals old things in heaven, makes new discoveries in earth, and even earth itself a discovery. That great antiquity America lay buried for thousands of years, and a large part of the earth is still in the urn unto us.

Though, if Adam were made out of an extract of the earth, all parts might challenge a restitution, yet few have returned their bones far lower than they might receive them; not affecting the graves of giants, under hilly and heavy coverings, but content with less than their own depth, have wished their bones might lie soft, and the earth be light upon them. Even such as hope to rise again, would not be content with central interment, or so desperately to place their relics as to lie beyond discovery, and in no way to be seen again; which happy contrivance hath made communication with our forefathers, and left unto our view some parts which they never beheld themselves.

Though earth hath engrossed the name, yet water hath proved the smartest grave; which in forty days swallowed almost mankind, and the living creation; fishes not wholly escaping, except the salt ocean were handsomely contempered by a mixture of the fresh element.

Many have taken voluminous pains to determine the state of the soul upon disunion; but men have been most phantastical in the singular contrivances of their corporal dissolution: whilst the soberest nations have rested in two ways, of simple inhumation and burning.

That carnal interment or burying was of the elder date, the old examples of Abraham and the patriarchs are sufficient to illustrate; and were without competi-

1 The rich mountain of Peru. (Browne.)

tion, if it could be made out that Adam was buried near Damascus, or Mount Calvary, according to some tradition. God himself, that buried but one, was pleased to make choice of this way, collectible from Scripture expression, and the hot contest between Satan and the archangel, about discovering the body of Moses. But the practice of burning was also of great antiquity, and of no slender extent. For (not to derive the same from Hercules) noble descriptions there are hereof in the Grecian funerals of Homer, in the formal obsequies of Patroclus and Achilles; and somewhat elder in the Theban war, and solemn combustion of Meneceus, and Archemorus, contemporary unto Jair the eighth judge of Israel. Confirmable also among the Trojans, from the funeral pyre of Hector, burnt before the gates of Troy: and the burning of Penthesilea the Amazonian queen: and long continuance of that practice, in the inward countries of Asia; while as low as the reign of Julian, we find that the king of Chionia burnt the body of his son, and interred the ashes in a silver urn.

The same practice extended also far west; and, besides Herulians, Getes, and Thracians, was in use with most of the Celtæ, Sarmatians, Germans, Gauls, Danes, Swedes, Norwegians; not to omit some use thereof among Carthaginians and Americans. Of greater antiquity among the Romans than most opinion, or Pliny seems to allow: for (beside the old Table Laws of burning or burying within the city, of making the funeral fire with planed wood, or quenching the fire with wine), Manlius the consul burnt the body of his son: Numa, by special clause of his will, was not burnt but buried; and Remus was solemnly burnt, according to the description of Ovid.

Cornelius Sylla was not the first whose body was burned in Rome, but of the Cornelian family; which, being indifferently, not frequently used before, from that time spread, and became the prevalent practice. Not totally pursued in the highest run of cremation; for when even crows were funerally burnt, Poppæa the wife of Nero found a peculiar grave interment. Now as all customs were founded upon some bottom of reason, so there wanted not grounds for this; according to several apprehensions of the most rational dissolution. Some being of the opinion of Thales, that water was the original of all things, thought it most equal to submit unto the principle of putrefaction, and conclude in a moist relentment. Others conceived it most natural to end in fire, as due unto the master principle in the composition, according to the doctrine of Heraclitus; and therefore heaped up large piles, more actively to waft them toward that element, whereby they also declined a visible degeneration into worms, and left a lasting parcel of their composition.

Some apprehended a purifying virtue in fire, refining the grosser commixture, and firing out the ethereal particles so deeply immersed in it. And such as by tradition or rational conjecture held any hint of the final pyre of all things, or that this element at last must be too hard for all the rest, might conceive most naturally of the fiery dissolution. Others pretending no natural grounds, politicly declined the malice of enemies upon their buried bodies. Which consideration led Sylla unto this practice; who having thus served the body of Marius, could not but fear a retaliation upon his own; entertained after in the civil wars, and revengeful contentions of Rome.

But, as many nations embraced, and many left it indifferent, so others too much affected, or strictly declined this practice. The Indian Brachmans seemed too great friends unto fire, who burnt themselves alive, and thought it the noblest way to end their days in fire; according to the expression of the Indian, burning himself at Athens, in his last words upon the pyre unto the amazed spectators, "Thus I make myself immortal."

But the Chaldeans, the great idolaters of fire, abhorred the burning of their carcases, as a pollution of that deity. The Persian magi declined it upon the like scruple, and being only solicitous about their bones, exposed their flesh to the prey of birds and dogs. And the Parsees now in India, which expose their bodies unto vultures, and endure not so much as *feretra* or biers of wood, the proper fuel of fire, are led on with such niceties. But whether the ancient Germans, who burned their dead, held any such fear to pollute their deity of Herthus, or the Earth, we have no authentic conjecture.

The Egyptians were afraid of fire, not as a deity, but a devouring element, mercilessly consuming their bodies, and leaving too little of them; and therefore by precious embalmments, depositure in dry earths, or handsome inclosure in glasses, contrived the notablest ways of integral conservation. And from such Egyptian

scruples, imbibed by Pythagoras, it may be conjectured that Numa and the Pythagorical sect first waved the fiery solution.

The Scythians, who swore by wind and sword, that is, by life and death, were so far from burning their bodies, that they declined all interment, and made their graves in the air: and the Ichthyophagi, or fish-eating nations about Egypt, affected the sea for their grave; thereby declining visible corruption, and restoring the debt of their bodies. Whereas the old heroes, in Homer, dreaded nothing more than water or drowning; probably upon the old opinion of the fiery substance of the soul, only extinguishable by that element; and therefore the poet emphatically implieth the total destruction in this kind of death, which happened to Ajax Oileus.

The old Balearians had a peculiar mode, for they used great urns and much wood, but no fire in their burials, while they bruised the flesh and bones of the dead, crowded them into urns, and laid heaps of wood upon them. And the Chinese without cremation or urnal interment of their bodies, make use of trees and much burning, while they plant a pine-tree by their grave, and burn great numbers of printed draughts of slaves and horses over it, civilly content with their companies *in effigy*, which barbarous nations exact unto reality.

Christians abhorred this way of obsequies, and though they sticked not to give their bodies to be burned in their lives, detested that mode after death; affecting rather a depositure than absumption, and properly submitting unto the sentence of God, to return not unto ashes but unto dust again, comformable unto the practice of the patriarchs, the interment of our Saviour, of Peter, Paul, and the ancient martyrs. And so far at last declining promiscuous interment with Pagans, that some have suffered ecclesiastical censures, for making no scruple thereof.

The Musselman believers will never admit this fiery resolution. For they hold a present trial from their black and white angels in the grave; which they must have made so hollow, that they may rise upon their knees.

The Jewish nation, though they entertained the old way of inhumation, yet sometimes admitted this practice. For the men of Jabesh burnt the body of Saul; and by no prohibited practice, to avoid contagion or pollution, in time of pestilence, burnt the bodies of their friends.[2] And when they burnt not their dead

2 Amos vi: 10.

bodies, yet sometimes used great burnings near and about them, deducible from the expressions concerning Jehoram, Zedechias, and the sumptuous pyre of Asa. And were so little averse from Pagan burning, that the Jews lamenting the death of Cæsar, their friend and revenger on Pompey, frequented the place where his body was burnt for many nights together. And as they raised noble monuments and mausoleums for their own nation, so they were not scrupulous in erecting some for others, according to the practice of Daniel, who left that lasting sepulchral pile in Ecbatana, for the Median and Persian kings.

But even in times of subjection and hottest use, they conformed not unto the Roman practice of burning; whereby the prophecy was secured concerning the body of Christ, that it should not see corruption or a bone should not be broken; which we believe was also providentially prevented, from the soldier's spear and nails that passed by the little bones both in his hands and feet; not of ordinary contrivance, that it should not corrupt on the cross, according to the laws of Roman crucifixion; or an hair of his head perish, though observable in Jewish customs, to cut the hairs of malefactors.

Nor in their long cohabitation with Egyptians, crept into a custom of their exact embalming, wherein deeply slashing the muscles, and taking out the brains and entrails, they had broken the subject of so entire a resurrection, nor fully answered the types of Enoch, Elijah, or Jonah, which yet to prevent or restore, was of equal facility unto that rising power, able to break the fasciations and bands of death, to get clear out of the cerecloth, and an hundred pounds of ointment, and out of the sepulchre before the stone was rolled from it.

But though they embraced not this practice of burning, yet entertained they many ceremonies agreeable unto Greek and Roman obsequies. And he that observeth their funeral feasts, their lamentations at the grave, their music, and weeping mourners; how they closed the eyes of their friends, how they washed, anointed, and kissed the dead; may easily conclude these were not mere Pagan civilities. But whether that mournful burthen, and treble calling out after Absalom,[3] had any reference unto the last conclamation, and triple valediction, used by other nations, we hold but a wavering conjecture.

Civilians make sepulture but of the law of nations, others do naturally found it and discover it also in animals. They that are so thick-skinned as still to credit the story of the *Phœnix*, may say something for animal burning. More serious conjectures find some examples of sepulture in elephants, cranes, the sepulchral cells of pismires, and practice of bees,—which civil society carrieth out their dead, and hath exequies, if not interments.

CHAPTER II

THE solemnities, ceremonies, rites of their cremation or interment, so solemnly delivered by authors, we shall not disparage our reader to repeat. Only the last and lasting part in their urns, collected bones and ashes, we cannot wholly omit, or decline that subject, which occasion lately presented, in some discovered among us.

In a field of Old Walsingham, not many months past, were digged up between forty and fifty urns, deposited in a dry and sandy soil, not a yard deep, nor far from one another. Not all strictly of one figure, but most answering these described: some containing two pounds of bones, distinguishable in skulls, ribs, jaws, thigh bones, and teeth, with fresh impressions of their combustion; besides the extraneous substances, like pieces of small boxes, or combs handsomely wrought, handles of small brass instruments, brazen nippers, and in one some kind of opal.[4]

Near the same plot of ground, for about six yards compass, were digged up coals and incinerated substances, which begat conjecture that this was the *ustrina* or place of burning their bodies, or some sacrificing place unto the *manes*, which was properly below the surface of the ground, as the *aræ* and altars unto the gods and heroes above it.

That these were the urns of Romans from the common custom and place where they were found, is no obscure conjecture, not far from a Roman garrison, and but five miles from Brancaster, set down by ancient record under the name of Brannodunum. And where the adjoining town, containing seven parishes, in no very different sound, but Saxon termination, still retains the name of Burnham, which being an early station, it is not improbable the neighbor parts were filled with habitations, either of Romans themselves, or Britons Romanized, which observed the Roman customs.

3 2 Sam. xviii: 33.

4 In one sent me by my worthy friend, Dr. Thomas Witherley of Walsingham. (Browne.)

Nor is it improbable, that the Romans early possessed this country. For though we meet not with such strict particulars of these parts before the new institution of Constantine and military charge of the count of the Saxon shore, and that about the Saxon invasions, the Dalmatian horsemen were in the garrison of Brancaster; yet in the time of Claudius, Vespasian, and Severus, we find no less than three legions dispersed through the province of Britain. And as high as the reign of Claudius a great overthrow was given unto the Iceni, by the Roman lieutenant Ostorius. Not long after, the country was so molested, that, in hope of a better state, Prasutagus bequeathed his kingdom unto Nero and his daughters; and Boadicea, his queen, fought the last decisive battle with Paulinus. After which time, and conquest of Agricola, the lieutenant of Vespasian, probable it is, they wholly possessed this country, ordering it into garrisons or habitations best suitable with their securities; and so some Roman habitations not improbable in these parts, as high as the time of Vespasian, where the Saxons after seated, in whose thin-filled maps we yet find the name of Walsingham. Now if the Iceni were but Gammadims, Anconians, or men that lived in an angle, wedge, or elbow of Britain, according to the original etymology, this country will challenge the emphatical appellation, as most properly making the elbow or *iken* of Icenia.

That Britain was notably populous is undeniable, from that expression of Cæsar.[5] That the Romans themselves were early in no small numbers, seventy thousand, with their associates, slain by Boadicea, affords a sure account. And though not many Roman habitations are now known, yet some, by old works, rampiers, coins, and urns, do testify their possessions. Some urns have been found at Castor, some also about Southcreak, and, not many years past, no less than ten in a field at Buxton, not near any recorded garrison. Nor is it strange to find Roman coins of copper and silver among us; of Vespasian, Trajan, Adrian, Commodus, Antoninus, Severus, etc.; but the greater number of Dioclesian, Constantine, Constans, Valens, with many of Victorinus, Posthumius, Tetricus, and the thirty tyrants in the reign of Gallienus; and some as high as Adrianus have been found about Thetford, or Sitomagus, mentioned in the *Itinerary* of Antoninus, as the way from Venta or Castor unto London. But

5 Hominum infinita multitudo est, creberrimaque ædificia fere Gallicis consimilia. There is an infinite multitude of men, together with an abundance of buildings just like those of the Gauls.—Cæs. *De Bello Gal.* l. v. [c. 12.]

the most frequent discovery is made at the two Castors by Norwich and Yarmouth, at Burghcastle, and Brancaster.

Besides the Norman, Saxon, and Danish pieces of Cuthred, Canutus, William, Matilda, and others, some British coins of gold have been dispersedly found, and no small number of silver pieces near Norwich, with a rude head upon the obverse, and an ill-formed horse on the reverse, with inscriptions *Ic. Duro. T.*; whether implying Iceni, Durotriges, Tascia, or Trinobantes, we leave to higher conjecture. Vulgar chronology will have Norwich Castle as old as Julius Cæsar; but his distance from these parts, and its Gothic form of structure, abridgeth such antiquity. The British coins afford conjecture of early habitation in these parts, though the city of Norwich arose from the ruins of Venta; and though, perhaps, not without some habitation before, was enlarged, builded, and nominated by the Saxons. In what bulk or populosity it stood in the old East-Angle monarchy tradition and history are silent. Considerable it was in the Danish eruptions, when Sueno burnt Thetford and Norwich, and Ulfketel, the governor thereof, was able to make some resistance, and after endeavored to burn the Danish navy.

How the Romans left so many coins in countries of their conquests seems of hard resolution; except we consider how they buried them under ground when, upon barbarous invasions, they were fain to desert their habitations in most part of their empire, and the strictness of their laws forbidding to transfer them to any other uses. wherein the Spartans were singular, who, to make their copper money useless, contempered it with vinegar. That the Britons left any, some wonder, since their money was iron and iron rings before Cæsar; and those of after-stamp by permission, and but small in bulk and bigness. That so few of the Saxons remain, because, overcome by succeeding conquerors upon the place, their coins, by degrees, passed into other stamps and the marks of after-ages.

Than the time of these urns deposited, or precise antiquity of these relicks, nothing of more uncertainty; for since the lieutenant of Claudius seems to have made the first progress into these parts, since Boadicea was overthrown by the forces of Nero, and Agricola put a full end to these conquests, it is not probable the country was fully garrisoned or planted before; and, therefore, however these urns might be of later date, not likely of higher antiquity.

And the succeeding emperors desisted not from

their conquests in these and other parts, as testified by history and medal-inscription yet extant: the province of Britain, in so divided a distance from Rome, beholding the faces of many imperial persons, and in large account, no fewer than Cæsar, Claudius, Britannicus, Vespasian, Titus, Adrian, Severus, Commodus, Geta, and Caracalla.

A great obscurity herein, because no medal or emperor's coin enclosed, which might denote the date of their interments; observable in many urns, and found in those of Spitalfields, by London, which contained the coins of Claudius, Vespasian, Commodus, Antoninus, attended with lacrymatories,[6] lamps, bottles of liquor, and other appurtenances of affectionate superstition, which in these rural interments were wanting.

Some uncertainty there is from the period or term of burning, or the cessation of that practice. Macrobius affirmeth it was disused in his days; but most agree, though without authentic record, that it ceased with the Antonini,—most safely to be understood after the reign of those emperors which assumed the name of Antoninus, extending unto Heliogabalus. Not strictly after Marcus; for about fifty years later, we find the magnificent burning and consecration of Severus; and, if we so fix this period or cessation, these urns will challenge above thirteen hundred years.

But whether this practice was only then left by emperors and great persons, or generally about Rome, and not in other provinces, we hold not authentic account; for after Tertullian, in the days of Minucius, it was obviously objected upon Christians, that they condemned the practice of burning. And we find a passage in Sidonius, which asserteth that practice in France unto a lower account. And, perhaps, not fully discussed till Christianity fully established, which gave the final extinction to these sepulchral bonfires.

Whether they were the bones of men, or women, or children, no authentic decision from ancient custom in distinct places of burial. Although not improbably conjectured, that the double sepulture or burying-place of Abraham, had in it such intention. But from exility of bones, thinness of skulls, smallness of teeth, ribs, and thigh bones, not improbable that many thereof were persons of minor age, or women. Confirmable also from things contained in them. In most were found substances resembling combs, plates like boxes, fastened with iron pins, and handsomely over-wrought like the necks or bridges of musical instruments; long brass plates overwrought like the handles

6 Tear bottles.

of neat implements; brazen nippers, to pull away hair; and in one a kind of opal, yet maintaining a bluish color.

Now that they accustomed to burn or bury with them, things wherein they excelled, delighted, or which were dear unto them, either as farewells unto all pleasure, or vain apprehension that they might use them in the other world, is testified by all antiquity, observable from the gem or beryl ring upon the finger of Cynthia, the mistress of Propertius, when after her funeral pyre her ghost appeared unto him; and notably illustrated from the contents of that Roman urn preserved by Cardinal Farnese, wherein besides great number of gems with heads of gods and goddesses, were found an ape of agath, a grasshopper, an elephant of amber, a crystal ball, three glasses, two spoons, and six nuts of crystal; and beyond the content of urns, in the monument of Childerick the First, and fourth king from Pharamond, casually discovered three years past at Tournay, restoring unto the world much gold richly adorning his sword, two hundred rubies, many hundred imperial coins, three hundred golden bees, the bones and horse-shoes of his horse interred with him, according to the barbarous magnificence of those days in their sepulchral obsequies. Although, if we steer by the conjecture of many and Septuagint expression, some trace thereof may be found even with the ancient Hebrews, not only from the sepulchral treasure of David, but the circumcision knives which Joshua also buried.

Some men, considering the contents of these urns, lasting pieces and toys included in them, and the custom of burning with many other nations, might somewhat doubt whether all urns found among us, were properly Roman relicks, or some not belonging unto our British, Saxon, or Danish forefathers.

In the form of burial among the ancient Britons, the large discourses of Cæsar, Tacitus, and Strabo are silent. For the discovery whereof, with other particulars, we much deplore the loss of that letter which Cicero expected or received from his brother Quintus, as a resolution of British customs; or the account which might have been made by Scribonius Largus, the physician, accompanying the Emperor Claudius, who might have also discovered that frugal bit of the old Britons, which in the bigness of a bean could satisfy their thirst and hunger.

But that the Druids and ruling priests used to burn and bury, is expressed by Pomponius; that Bellinus, the brother of Brennus, and king of Britons, was burnt, is acknowledged by Polydorus, as also by Amandus Zierexensis in *Historia*, and Pineda in his *Universa Historia* (Spanish). That they held that practice in Gallia, Cæsar expressly delivereth. Whether the Britons (probably descended from them, of like religion, language, and manners) did not sometimes make use of burning, or whether at least such as were after civilized unto the Roman life and manners, conformed not unto this practice, we have no historical assertion or denial. But since, from the account of Tacitus, the Romans early wrought so much civility upon the British stock, that they brought them to build temples, to wear the gown, and study the Roman laws and language, that they conformed also unto their religious rites and customs in burials, seems no improbable conjecture.

That burning the dead was used in Sarmatia is affirmed by Gaguinus; that the Sueons and Goth-landers used to burn their princes and great persons, is delivered by Saxo and Olaus; that this was the old German practice, is also asserted by Tacitus. And though we are bare in historical particulars of such obsequies in this island, or that the Saxons, Jutes, and Angles burnt their dead, yet came they from parts where 'twas of ancient pratice; the Germans using it, from whom they were descended. And even in Jutland and Sleswick in Anglia Cymbrica, urns with bones were found not many years before us.

But the Danish and northern nations have raised an era or point of compute from their custom of burning their dead: some deriving it from Unguinus, some from Frotho the Great, who ordained by law, that princes and chief commanders should be committed unto the fire, though the common sort had the common grave interment. So Starkatterus, that old hero, was burnt, and Ringo royally burnt the body of Harold the king slain by him.

What time this custom generally expired in that nation, we discern no assured period; whether it ceased before Christianity, or upon their conversion, by Ansgarius the Gaul, in the time of Ludovicus Pius the son of Charles the Great, according to good computes; or whether it might not be used by some persons, while for an hundred and eighty years Paganism and Christianity were promiscuously embraced among them, there is no assured conclusion. About which times the Danes were busy in England, and particularly infested this country; where many castles and strongholds were built by them, or against them, and great number of names and families still derived from

them. But since this custom was probably disused before their invasion or conquest, and the Romans confessedly practiced the same since their possession of this island, the most assured account will fall upon the Romans, or Britons Romanized.

However, certain it is, that urns conceived of no Roman original, are often digged up both in Norway and Denmark, handsomely described, and graphically represented by the learned physician Wormius. And in some parts of Denmark in no ordinary number, as stands delivered by authors exactly describing those countries. And they contained not only bones, but many other substances in them, as knives, pieces of iron, brass, and wood, and one of Norway a brass gilded jew's-harp.

Nor were they confused or careless in disposing the noblest sort, while they placed large stones in circle about the urns or bodies which they interred: somewhat answerable unto the monument of Rollrich stones in England, or sepulchral monument probably erected by Rollo, who after conquered Normandy; where 'tis not improbable somewhat might be discovered. Meanwhile to what nation or person belonged that large urn found at Ashbury, containing mighty bones, and a buckler; what those large urns found at Little Massingham; or why the Anglesea urns are placed with their mouths downward, remains yet undiscovered.

CHAPTER III

PLAISTERED and whited sepulchres were anciently affected in cadaverous and corrupted burials; and the rigid Jews were wont to garnish the sepulchres of the righteous. Ulysses, in Hecuba, cared not how meanly he lived, so he might find a noble tomb after death. Great persons affected great monuments; and the fair and larger urns contained no vulgar ashes, which makes that disparity in those which time discovereth among us. The present urns were not of one capacity, the largest containing above a gallon, some not much above half that measure; nor all of one figure, wherein there is no strict conformity in the same or different countries; observable from those represented by Casalius, Bosio, and others, though all found in Italy; while many have handles, ears, and long necks, but most imitate a circular figure, in a spherical and round composure; whether from any mystery, best duration or capacity, were but a conjecture. But the common form with necks was a proper figure, making our last bed like our first; nor much unlike the urns of our nativity while we lay in the nether part of the earth, and inward vault of our microcosm. Many urns are red, these but of a black color, somewhat smooth, and dully sounding, which begat some doubt, whether they were burnt, or only baked in oven or sun, according to the ancient way, in many bricks, tiles, pots, and testaceous works; and, as the word *testa* is properly to be taken, when occurring without addition and chiefly intended by Pliny, when he commendeth bricks and tiles of two years old, and to make them in the spring. Nor only these concealed pieces, but the open magnificence of antiquity, ran much in the artifice of clay. Hereof the house of Mausolus was built, thus old Jupiter stood in the Capitol, and the *statua* of Hercules, made in the reign of Tarquinius Priscus, was extant in Pliny's days. And such as declined burning or funeral urns, affected coffins of clay, according to the mode of Pythagoras, and way preferred by Varro. But the spirit of great ones was above these circumscriptions, affecting copper, silver, gold, and porphyry urns, wherein Severus lay, after a serious view and sentence on that which should contain him. Some of these urns were thought to have been silvered over, from sparklings in several pots, with small tinsel parcels; uncertain whether from the earth, or the first mixture in them.

Among these urns we could obtain no good account of their coverings; only one seemed arched over with some kind of brick-work. Of those found at Buxton, some were covered with flints, some, in other parts, with tiles; those at Yarmouth Caster were closed with Roman bricks, and some have proper earthen covers adapted and fitted to them. But in the Homerical urn of Patroclus, whatever was the solid tegument, we find the immediate covering to be a purple piece of silk: and such as had no covers might have the earth closely pressed into them, after which disposure were probably some of these, wherein we found the bones and ashes half mortared unto the sand and sides of the urn, and some long roots of quich, or dog's-grass, wreathed about the bones.

No lamps, included liquors, lacrymatories, or tear bottles, attended these rural urns, either as sacred unto the *manes*, or passionate expressions of their surviving friends. While with rich flames, and hired tears, they solemnized their obsequies, and in the most lamented monuments made one part of their inscriptions. Some find sepulchral vessels containing liquors, which time

hath incrassated into jellies. For, besides these lacrymatories, notable lamps, with vessels of oils, and aromatical liquors, attended noble ossuaries; and some yet retaining a vinosity and spirit in them, which, if any have tasted, they have far exceeded the palates of antiquity. Liquors not to be computed by years of annual magistrates, but by great conjunctions and the fatal periods of kingdoms.[7] The draughts of consulary date were but crude unto these, and Opimian wine but in the must unto them.

In sundry graves and sepulchers we meet with rings, coins, and chalices. Ancient frugality was so severe, that they allowed no gold to attend the corpse, but only that which served to fasten their teeth. Whether the Opaline stone in this were burnt upon the finger of the dead, or cast into the fire by some affectionate friend, it will consist with either custom. But other incinerable substances were found so fresh, that they could feel no singe from fire. These, upon view, were judged to be wood; but, sinking in water, and tried by the fire, we found them to be bone or ivory. In their hardness and yellow colour they most resembled box, which, in old expressions, found the epithet of eternal, and perhaps in such conservatories might have passed uncorrupted.

That bay leaves were found green in the tomb of S. Humbert, after an hundred and fifty years, was looked upon as miraculous. Remarkable it was unto old spectators, that the cypress of the temple of Diana lasted so many hundred years. The wood of the ark, and olive-rod of Aaron, were older at the captivity; but the cypress of the ark of Noah was the greatest vegetable of antiquity, if Josephus were not deceived by some fragments of it in his days: to omit the moor logs and fir trees found underground in many parts of England; the undated ruins of winds, floods, or earthquakes, and which in Flanders still show from what quarter they fell, as generally lying in a northeast position.

But though we found not these pieces to be wood, according to first apprehensions, yet we missed not altogether of some woody substance; for the bones were not so clearly picked but some coals were found amongst them; a way to make wood perpetual, and a fit associate for metal, whereon was laid the foundation of the great Ephesian temple, and which were made the lasting tests of old boundaries and landmarks. Whilst we look on these, we admire not observations of coals found fresh after four hundred years.

7 About five hundred years.—Plato. (Browne.)

In a long-deserted habitation even eggshells have been found fresh, not tending to corruption.

In the monument of King Childerick the iron relicks were found all rusty and crumbling into pieces; but our little iron pins, which fastened the ivory works, held well together, and lost not their magnetical quality, though wanting a tenacious moisture for the firmer union of parts; although it be hardly drawn into fusion, yet that metal soon submitteth unto rust and dissolution. In the brazen pieces we admired not the duration, but the freedom from rust, and ill savor, upon the hardest attrition; but now exposed unto the piercing atoms of air, in the space of a few months, they begin to spot and betray their green entrails. We conceive not these urns to have descended thus naked as they appear, or to have entered their graves without the old habit of flowers. The urn of Philopœmen was so laden with flowers and ribbons, that it afforded no sight of itself. The rigid Lycurgus allowed olive and myrtle. The Athenians might fairly except against the practice of Democritus, to be buried up in honey, as fearing to embezzle a great commodity of their country, and the best of that kind in Europe. But Plato seemed too frugally politic, who allowed no larger monument than would contain four heroic verses, and designed the most barren ground for sepulture: though we cannot commend the goodness of that sepulchral ground which was set at no higher rate than the mean salary of Judas. Though the earth had confounded the ashes of these ossuaries, yet the bones were so smartly burnt, that some thin plates of brass were found half melted among them. Whereby we apprehend they were not of the meanest carcasses, perfunctorily fired, as sometimes in military, and commonly in pestilence, burnings; or after the manner of abject corpses, huddled forth and carelessly burnt, without the Esquiline Port at Rome; which was an affront continued upon Tiberius, while they but half burnt his body, and in the amphitheater, according to the custom in notable malefactors; whereas Nero seemed not so much to fear his death as that his head should be cut off and his body not burnt entire.

Some, finding many fragments of skulls in these urns, suspected a mixture of bones; in none we searched was there cause of such conjecture, though sometimes they declined not that practice.—The ashes of Domitian were mingled with those of Julia; of Achilles with those of Patroclus. All urns contained not single ashes; without confused burnings they affectionately compounded their bones; passionately endeavoring to continue their living unions. And when distance of death denied such conjunctions, unsatisfied affections conceived some satisfaction to be neighbors in the grave, to lie urn by urn, and touch but in their names. And many were so curious to continue their living relations, that they contrived large and family urns, wherein the ashes of their nearest friends and kindred might successively be received, at least some parcels thereof, while their collateral memorials lay in minor vessels about them.

Antiquity held too light thoughts from objects of mortality, while some drew provocatives of mirth from anatomies, and jugglers showed tricks with skeletons; when fiddlers made not so pleasant mirth as fencers, and men could sit with quiet stomachs, while hanging was played before them.[8] Old considerations made few mementos by skulls and bones upon their monuments. In the Egyptian obelisks and hieroglyphical figures it is not easy to meet with bones. The sepulchral lamps speak nothing less than sepulture, and in their literal draughts prove often obscene and antic pieces. Where we find *D. M.*[9] it is obvious to meet with sacrificing *pateras* and vessels of libation upon old sepulchral monuments. In the Jewish hypogæum and subterranean cell at Rome, was little observable beside the variety of lamps and frequent draughts of the holy candlestick. In authentic draughts of Anthony and Jerome we meet with thigh bones and death's-heads; but the cemeterial cells of ancient Christians and martyrs were filled with draughts of Scripture stories; not declining the flourishes of cypress, palms, and olive, and the mystical figures of peacocks, doves, and cocks; but iterately affecting the portraits of Enoch, Lazarus, Jonas, and the vision of Ezekiel, as hopeful draughts, and hinting imagery of the resurrection, which is the life of the grave, and sweetens our habitations in the land of moles and pismires.

Gentile inscriptions precisely delivered the extent of men's lives, seldom the manner of their deaths, which history itself so often leaves obscure in the records of memorable persons. There is scarce any philosopher but dies twice or thrice in Laërtius; nor almost any life without two or three deaths in Plutarch; which makes the tragical ends of noble persons more favorably

8 Ἀγχόνην παίζειν. A barbarous pastime at feasts [among the Thracians] when men stood upon a rolling globe, with their necks in a rope, and a knife in their hands, ready to cut it when the stone was rolled away; wherein if they failed, they lost their lives, to the laughter of their spectators.— Athenæus [iv. 42, p. 155]. (Browne.)

9 *Diis manibus.* (Browne.)

resented by compassionate readers who find some relief in the election of such differences.

The certainty of death is attended with uncertainties, in time, manner, places. The variety of monuments hath often obscured true graves; and cenotaphs confounded sepulchers. For beside their real tombs, many have found honorary and empty sepulchers. The variety of Homer's monuments made him of various countries. Euripides had his tomb in Africa but his sepulture in Macedonia. And Severus found his real sepulcher in Rome, but his empty grave in Gallia.

He that lay in a golden urn eminently above the earth, was not like to find the quiet of his bones. Many of these urns were broke by a vulgar discoverer in hope of enclosed treasure. The ashes of Marcellus were lost above ground, upon the like account. Where profit hath prompted, no age hath wanted such miners; for which the most barbarous expilators found the most civil rhetoric:—"Gold once out of the earth is no more due unto it;—what was unreasonably committed to the ground, is reasonably resumed from it;—let monuments and rich fabrics, not riches, adorn men's ashes;—the commerce of the living is not to be transferred unto the dead;—it is not injustice to take that which none complains to lose, and no man is wronged where no man is possessor."

What virtue yet sleeps in this *terra damnata* and aged cinders, were petty magic to experiment. These crumbling relics and long fired particles superannuate such expectations; bones, hairs, nails, and teeth of the dead, were the treasures of old sorcerers. In vain we revive such practices; present superstition too visibly perpetuates the folly of our forefathers, wherein unto old observation this island was so complete, that it might have instructed Persia.

Plato's historian of the other world lies twelve days incorrupted, while his soul was viewing the large stations of the dead. How to keep the corpse seven days from corruption by anointing and washing, without exenteration, were an hazardable piece of art, in our choicest practice. How they made distinct separation of bones and ashes from fiery admixture, hath found no historical solution; though they seemed to make a distinct collection, and overlooked not Pyrrhus his toe. Some provision they might make by fictile vessels, coverings, tiles, or flat stones, upon and about the body (and in the same field, not far from these urns, many stones were found under ground), as also by careful separation of extraneous matter, composing and raking up the burnt bones with forks, observable in that notable lamp of Galvanus. Marlianus, who had the sight of the *vas ustrinum* or vessel wherein they burnt the dead, found in the Esquiline field at Rome, might have afforded clearer solution. But their insatisfaction herein begat that remarkable invention in the funeral pyres of some princes, by incombustible sheets made with a texture of asbestos, incremable flax, or salamander's wool, which preserved their bones and ashes incommixed.

How the bulk of a man should sink into so few pounds of bones and ashes, may seem strange unto any who considers not its constitution, and how slender a mass will remain upon an open and urging fire of the carnal composition. Even bones themselves, reduced into ashes, do abate a notable proportion. And consisting much of a volatile salt, when that is fired out, make a light kind of cinders. Although their bulk be disproportionable to their weight, when the heavy principle of salt is fired out, and the earth almost only remaineth; observable in sallow, which makes more ashes than oak, and discovers the common fraud of selling ashes by measure, and not by ponderation.

Some bones make best skeletons, some bodies quick and speediest ashes. Who would expect a quick flame from hydropical Heraclitus? The poisoned soldier when his belly brake, put out two pyres in Plutarch. But in the plague of Athens, one private pyre served two or three intruders; and the Saracens burnt in large heaps, by the king of Castile, showed how little fuel sufficeth. Though the funeral pyre of Patroclus took up an hundred foot, a piece of an old boat burnt Pompey; and if the burthen of Isaac were sufficient for an holocaust, a man may carry his own pyre.

From animals are drawn good burning lights, and good medicines against burning. Though the seminal humor seems of a contrary nature to fire, yet the body completed proves a combustible lump, wherein fire finds flame even from bones, and some fuel almost from all parts; though the metropolis of humidity[10] seems least disposed unto it, which might render the skulls of these urns less burned than other bones. But all flies or sinks before fire almost in all bodies: when the common ligament is dissolved, the attenuable parts ascend, the rest subside in coal, calx, or ashes.

To burn the bones of the king of Edom for lime,[11] seems no irrational ferity; but to drink of the ashes of dead relations,[12] a passionate prodigality. He that hath

10 The brain.—Hippocrates. (Browne.)   11 Amos ii: 1.
12 As Artemisia of her husband Mausolus. (Browne.)

the ashes of his friend, hath an everlasting treasure; where fire taketh leave, corruption slowly enters. In bones well burnt, fire makes a wall against itself; experimented in cupels, and tests of metals, which consist of such ingredients. What the sun compoundeth, fire analyseth, not transmuteth. That devouring agent leaves almost always a morsel for the earth, whereof all things are but a colony; and which, if time permits, the mother element will have in their primitive mass again.

He that looks for urns and old sepulchral relics, must not seek them in the ruins of temples, where no religion anciently placed them. These were found in a field, according to ancient custom, noble or private burial; the old practice of the Canaanites, the family of Abraham, and the burying-place of Joshua, in the borders of his possessions; and also agreeable unto Roman practice to bury by highways, whereby their monuments were under eye;—memorials of themselves, and mementos of mortality unto living passengers; whom the epitaphs of great ones were fain to beg to stay and look upon them,—a language though sometimes used, not so proper in church inscriptions. The sensible rhetoric of the dead, to exemplarity of good life, first admitted the bones of pious men and martyrs within church walls, which in succeeding ages crept into promiscuous practice: while Constantine was peculiarly favored to be admitted into the church porch, and the first thus buried in England, was in the days of Cuthred.

Christians dispute how their bodies should lie in the grave. In urnal interment they clearly escaped this controversy. Though we decline the religious consideration, yet in cemeterial and narrower burying-places, to avoid confusion and cross-position, a certain posture were to be admitted: which even Pagan civility observed. The Persians lay north and south; the Megarians and Phœnicians placed their heads to the east; the Athenians, some think, towards the west, which Christians still retain. And Beda will have it to be the posture of our Saviour. That he was crucified with his face toward the west, we will not contend with tradition and probable account; but we applaud not the hand of the painter, in exalting his cross so high above those on either side: since hereof we find no authentic account in history, and even the crosses found by Helena, pretend no such distinction from longitude or dimension.

To be gnawed out of our graves, to have our skulls made drinking-bowls, and our bones turned into pipes, to delight and sport our enemies, are tragical abominations escaped in burning burials.

Urnal interments and burnt relics lie not in fear of worms, or to be an heritage for serpents. In carnal sepulture, corruptions seem peculiar unto parts; and some speak of snakes out of the spinal marrow. But while we suppose common worms in graves, 'tis not easy to find any there; few in churchyards above a foot deep, fewer or none in churches though in fresh-decayed bodies. Teeth, bones, and hair, give the most lasting defiance to corruption. In an hydropical body, ten years buried in the churchyard, we met with a fat concretion, where the niter of the earth, and the salt and lixivious liquor of the body, had coagulated large lumps of fat into the consistence of the hardest Castile soap, whereof part remaineth with us. After a battle with the Persians, the Roman corpses decayed in few days, while the Persian bodies remained dry and uncorrupted. Bodies in the same ground do not uniformly dissolve, nor bones equally molder; whereof in the opprobrious disease, we expect no long duration. The body of the Marquis of Dorset seemed sound and handsomely cerecloClthed, that after seventy-eight years was found uncorrupted. Common tombs preserve not beyond powder: a firmer consistence and compage of parts might be expected from arefaction, deep burial, or charcoal. The greatest antiquities of mortal bodies may remain in putrified bones, whereof, though we take not in the pillar of Lot's wife, or metamorphosis of Ortelius, some may be older than pyramids, in the putrified relics of the general inundation. When Alexander opened the tomb of Cyrus, the remaining bones discovered his proportion, whereof urnal fragments afford but a bad conjecture, and have this disadvantage of grave interments, that they leave us ignorant of most personal discoveries. For since bones afford not only rectitude and stability but figure unto the body, it is no impossible physiognomy to conjecture at fleshy appendencies, and after what shape the muscles and carnous parts might hang in their full consistencies. A full-spread *cariola*[13] shows a well-shaped horse behind; handsome formed skulls give some analogy to fleshy resemblance. A critical view of bones makes a good distinction of sexes. Even color is not beyond conjecture, since it is hard to be deceived in the distinction of Negroes' skulls. Dante's characters are to be found in skulls as well as faces. Hercules is not only known by his foot. Other parts make out their

13 That part in the skeleton of an horse, which is made by the haunch-bones. (Browne, in later editions.)

comproportions and inferences upon whole or parts. And since the dimensions of the head measure the whole body, and the figure thereof gives conjecture of the principal faculties, physiognomy outlives ourselves, and ends not in our graves.

Severe contemplators, observing these lasting relics, may think them good monuments of persons past, little advantage to future beings; and, considering that power which subdueth all things unto itself, that can resume the scattered atoms, or identify out of any thing, conceive it superfluous to expect a resurrection out of relics: but the soul subsisting, other matter, clothed with due accidents, may salve the individuality. Yet the saints, we observe, arose from graves and monuments about the holy city. Some think the ancient patriarchs so earnestly desired to lay their bones in Canaan, as hoping to make a part of that resurrection; and, though thirty miles from Mount Calvary, at least to lie in that region which should produce the first fruits of the dead. And if, according to learned conjecture, the bodies of men shall rise where their greatest relics remain, many are not like to err in the topography of their resurrection, though their bones or bodies be after translated by angels into the field of Ezekiel's vision, or as some will order it, into the valley of judgment, or Jehosaphat.

CHAPTER IV

CHRISTIANS have handsomely glossed the deformity of death by careful consideration of the body, and civil rites which take off brutal terminations: and though they conceived all reparable by a resurrection, cast not off all care of interment. And since the ashes of sacrifices burnt upon the altar of God were carefully carried out by the priests, and deposed in a clean field; since they acknowledged their bodies to be the lodging of Christ, and temples of the Holy Ghost, they devolved not all upon the sufficiency of soul-existence; and therefore with long services and full solemnities, concluded their last exequies, wherein to all distinctions the Greek devotion seems most pathetically ceremonious.

Christian invention hath chiefly driven at rites, which speak hopes of another life, and hints of a resurrection. And if the ancient Gentiles held not the immortality of their better part, and some subsistence after death, in several rites, customs, actions, and expressions, they contradicted their own opinions: wherein Democritus went high, even to the thought of a resurrection, as scoffingly recorded by Pliny. What can be more express than the expression of Phocylides? Or who would expect from Lucretius a sentence of Ecclesiastes? Before Plato could speak, the soul had wings in Homer, which fell not, but flew out of the body into the mansions of the dead; who also observed that handsome distinction of Demas and Soma, for the body conjoined to the soul, and body separated from it. Lucian spoke much truth in jest, when he said that part of Hercules which proceeded from Alcmena perished, that from Jupiter remained immortal. Thus Socrates was content that his friends should bury his body, so they would not think they buried Socrates; and, regarding only his immortal part, was indifferent to be burnt or buried. From such considerations, Diogenes might contemn sepulture, and, being satisfied that the soul could not perish, grow careless of corporal interment. The Stoics, who thought the souls of wise men had their habitation about the moon, might make slight account of subterraneous deposition; whereas the Pythagoreans and transcorporating philosophers, who were to be often buried, held great care of their interment. And the Platonics rejected not a due care of the grave, though they put their ashes to unreasonable expectations, in their tedious term of return and long set revolution.

Men have lost their reason in nothing so much as their religion, wherein stones and clouts make martyrs; and, since the religion of one seems madness unto another, to afford an account or rational of old rites requires no rigid reader. That they kindled the pyre aversely, or turning their face from it, was an handsome symbol of unwilling ministration. That they washed their bones with wine and milk; that the mother wrapped them in linen, and dried them in her bosom, the first fostering part and place of their nourishment; that they opened their eyes towards heaven before they kindled the fire, as the place of their hopes or original, were no improper ceremonies. Their last valediction, thrice uttered by the attendants, was also very solemn, and somewhat answered by Christians, who thought it too little, if they threw not the earth thrice upon the interred body. That, in strewing their tombs, the Romans affected the rose; the Greeks amaranthus and myrtle: that the funeral pyre consisted of sweet fuel, cypress, fir, larix, yew, and trees perpetually verdant, lay silent expressions of their surviving hopes. Wherein Christians, who deck their coffins with bays, have found a more elegant emblem; for that tree, seeming dead, will restore itself from the root, and its dry and exsuccous leaves resume their verdure again; which, if we mistake not, we have also observed in furze. Whether the planting of yew in churchyards hold not its original from ancient funeral rites, or as an emblem of resurrection, from its perpetual verdure, may also admit conjecture.

They made use of music to excite or quiet the affections of their friends, according to different harmonies. But the secret and symbolical hint was the harmonical nature of the soul; which, delivered from the body, went again to enjoy the primitive harmony of heaven, from whence it first descended; which, according to its progress traced by antiquity, came down by Cancer, and ascended by Capricornus.

They burnt not children before their teeth appeared, as apprehending their bodies too tender a morsel for fire, and that their gristly bones would scarce leave separable relics after the pyral combustion. That they kindled not fire in their houses for some days after was a strict memorial of the late afflicting fire. And mourning without hope, they had an happy fraud against excessive lamentation, by a common opinion that deep sorrows disturb their ghosts.

That they buried their dead on their backs, or in a supine position, seems agreeable unto profound sleep, and common posture of dying; contrary to the most natural way of birth; nor unlike our pendulous posture, in the doubtful state of the womb. Diogenes was singular, who preferred a prone situation in the grave; and some Christians like neither, who decline the figure of rest, and make choice of an erect posture.

That they carried them out of the world with their feet forward, not inconsonant unto reason, as contrary unto the native posture of man, and his production first into it; and also agreeable unto their opinions, while they bid adieu unto the world, not to look again upon it; whereas Mahometans who think to return to a delightful life again, are carried forth with their heads forward, and looking toward their houses.

They closed their eyes, as parts which first die, or first discover the sad effects of death. But their iterated clamations to excite their dying or dead friends, or revoke them unto life again, was a vanity of affection; as not presumably ignorant of the critical tests of death, by apposition of feathers, glasses, and reflection of figures, which dead eyes represent not: which, however not strictly verifiable in fresh and warm cadavers, could hardly elude the test, in corpses of four or five days.

That they sucked in the last breath of their expiring friends, was surely a practice of no medical institution, but a loose opinion that the soul passed out that way, and a fondness of affection, from some Pythagorical foundation, that the spirit of one body passed into another, which they wished might be their own.

That they poured oil upon the pyre, was a tolerable practice, while the intention rested in facilitating the accension. But to place good omens in the quick and speedy burning, to sacrifice unto the winds for a dispatch in this office, was a low form of superstition.

The archimime, or jester, attending the funeral train, and imitating the speeches, gesture, and manners of the deceased, was too light for such solemnities, contradicting their funeral orations and doleful rites of the grave.

That they buried a piece of money with them as a fee of the Elysian ferryman, was a practice full of folly. But the ancient custom of placing coins in considerable urns, and the present practice of burying medals in the noble foundations of Europe, are laudable ways of historical discoveries, in actions, persons, chronologies: and posterity will applaud them.

We examine not the old laws of sepulture, exempting certain persons from burial or burning. But hereby we apprehend that these were not the bones of persons planet-struck or burnt with fire from heaven; no relicks of traitors to their country, self-killers or sacrilegious malefactors; persons in old apprehension unworthy of the earth; condemned unto the Tartarus of hell, and bottomless pit of Plato, from whence there was no redemption.

Nor were only many customs questionable in order to their obsequies, but also sundry practices, fictions, and conceptions, discordant or obscure, of their state and future beings. Whether unto eight or ten bodies of men to add one of a woman, as being more inflammable, and unctuously constituted for the better pyral combustion, were any rational practice; or whether the complaint of Periander's wife be tolerable, that wanting her funeral burning, she suffered intolerable cold in hell, according to the constitution of the infernal house of Plato, wherein cold makes a great part of their tortures, it cannot pass without some question.

Why the female ghosts appear unto Ulysses, before the heroes and masculine spirits,—why the Psyche or soul of Tiresias is of the masculine gender, who, being blind on earth, sees more than all the rest in hell; why the funeral suppers consisted of eggs, beans, smallage, and lettuce, since the dead are made to eat asphodels about the Elysian meadows,—why, since there is no sacrifice acceptable, nor any propitiation for the covenant of the grave, men set up the deity of Morta, and fruitlessly adored divinities without ears, it cannot escape some doubt.

The dead seem all alive in the human Hades of Homer, yet cannot well speak, prophesy, or know the living, except they drink blood, wherein is the life of man. And therefore the souls of Penelope's paramours, conducted by Mercury, chirped like bats, and those which followed Hercules, made a noise but like a flock of birds.

The departed spirits know things past and to come; yet are ignorant of things present. Agamemnon foretells what should happen unto Ulysses; yet ignorantly enquires what is become of his own son. The ghosts are afraid of swords in Homer; yet Sibylla tells Æneas in Virgil, the thin habit of spirits was beyond the force of weapons. The spirits put off their malice with their bodies, and Cæsar and Pompey accord in Latin hell; yet Ajax, in Homer, endures not a conference with Ulysses: and Deiphobus appears all mangled in Virgil's ghosts, yet we meet with perfect shadows among the wounded ghosts of Homer.

Since Charon in Lucian applauds his condition among the dead, whether it be handsomely said of Achilles, that living contemner of death, that he had rather be a ploughman's servant, than emperor of the dead? How Hercules his soul is in hell, and yet in heaven; and Julius his soul in a star, yet seen by Æneas in hell?—except the ghosts were but images and shadows of the soul, received in higher mansions, according to the ancient division of body, soul, and image, or *simulacrum* of them both. The particulars of future beings must needs be dark unto ancient theories, which Christian philosophy yet determines but in a cloud of opinions. A dialogue between two infants in the womb concerning the state of this world, might handsomely illustrate our ignorance of the next, whereof methinks we yet discourse in Plato's den, and are but embryon philosophers.

Pythagoras escapes in the fabulous Hell of Dante, among that swarm of philosophers, wherein whilst we meet with Plato and Socrates, Cato is to be found in no lower place than purgatory. Among all the set, Epicurus is most considerable, whom men make honest without an Elysium, who contemned life without encouragement of immortality, and making nothing

after death, yet made nothing of the king of terrors.

Were the happiness of the next world as closely apprehended as the felicities of this, it were a martyrdom to live; and unto such as consider none hereafter, it must be more than death to die, which makes us amazed at those audacities that durst be nothing and return into their chaos again. Certainly such spirits as could contemn death, when they expected no better being after, would have scorned to live, had they known any. And therefore we applaud not the judgment of Machiavel, that Christianity makes men cowards, or that with the confidence of but half-dying, the despised virtues of patience and humility have abased the spirits of men, which Pagan principles exalted; but rather regulated the wildness of audacities, in the attempts, grounds, and eternal sequels of death; wherein men of the boldest spirits are often prodigiously temerarious. Nor can we extenuate the valor of ancient martyrs, who contemned death in the uncomfortable scene of their lives, and in their decrepit martyrdoms did probably lose not many months of their days, or parted with life when it was scarce worth the living. For (beside that long time past holds no consideration unto a slender time to come) they had no small disadvantage from the constitution of old age, which naturally makes men fearful; complexionally superannuated from the bold and courageous thoughts of youth and fervent years. But the contempt of death from corporal animosity, promoteth not our felicity. They may sit in the orchestra, and noblest seats of heaven, who have held up shaking hands in the fire, and humanly contended for glory.

Meanwhile Epicurus lies deep in Dante's Hell, wherein we meet with tombs enclosing souls which denied their immortalities. But whether the virtuous heathen, who lived better than he spake, or erring in the principles of himself, yet lived above philosophers of more specious maxims, lie so deep as he is placed, at least so low as not to rise against Christians, who believing or knowing that truth, have lastingly denied it in their practice and conversation—were a query too sad to insist on.

But all or most apprehensions rested in opinions of some future being, which, ignorantly or coldly believed, begat those perverted conceptions, ceremonies, sayings, which Christians pity or laugh at. Happy are they which live not in that disadvantage of time, when men could say little for futurity, but from reason: whereby the noblest minds fell often upon doubtful deaths, and melancholy dissolutions. With these hopes,

Socrates warmed his doubtful spirits against that cold potion; and Cato, before he durst give the fatal stroke, spent part of the night in reading the Immortality of Plato, thereby confirming his wavering hand unto the animosity of that attempt.

It is the heaviest stone that melancholy can throw at a man, to tell him he is at the end of his nature; or that there is no further state to come, unto which this seems progressional, and otherwise made in vain. Without this accomplishment, the natural expectation and desire of such a state, were but a fallacy in nature; unsatisfied considerators would quarrel the justice of their constitutions, and rest content that Adam had fallen lower; whereby, by knowing no other original, and deeper ignorance of themselves, they might have enjoyed the happiness of inferior creatures, who in tranquillity possess their constitutions, as having not the apprehension to deplore their own natures, and, being framed below the circumference of these hopes, or cognition of better being, the wisdom of God hath necessitated their contentment: but the superior ingredient and obscured part of ourselves, whereto all present felicities afford no resting contentment, will be able at last to tell us, we are more than our present selves, and evacuate such hopes in the fruition of their own accomplishments.

CHAPTER V

Now since these dead bones have already outlasted the living ones of Methuselah, and in a yard under ground, and thin walls of clay, out-worn all the strong and spacious buildings above it, and quietly rested under the drums and tramplings of three conquests: what prince can promise such diuturnity unto his relics, or might not gladly say,

Sic ego componi versus in ossa velim? [14]

Time, which antiquates antiquities, and hath an art to make dust of all things, hath yet spared these minor monuments.

In vain we hope to be known by open and visible conservatories, when to be unknown was the means of their continuation, and obscurity their protection. If they died by violent hands, and were thrust into their urns, these bones become considerable, and some old philosophers would honor them, whose souls they

conceived most pure, which were thus snatched from their bodies, and to retain a stronger propension unto them; whereas they weariedly left a languishing corpse, and with faint desires of reunion. If they fell by long and aged decay, yet wrapt up in the bundle of time, they fall into indistinction, and make but one blot with infants. If we begin to die when we live, and long life be but a prolongation of death, our life is a sad composition; we live with death, and die not in a moment. How many pulses made up the life of Methuselah, were work for Archimedes: common counters sum up the life of Moses his man. Our days become considerable, like petty sums, by minute accumulations; where numerous fractions make up but small round numbers; and our days of a span long, make not one little finger. [15]

If the nearness of our last necessity brought a nearer conformity into it, there were a happiness in hoary hairs, and no calamity in half-senses. But the long habit of living indisposeth us for dying; when avarice makes us the sport of death, when even David grew politicly cruel, and Solomon could hardly be said to be the wisest of men. But many are too early old, and before the date of age. Adversity stretcheth our days, misery makes Alcmena's nights, [16] and time hath no wings unto it. But the most tedious being is that which can unwish itself, content to be nothing, or never to have been, which was beyond the malcontent of Job, who cursed not the day of his life, but his nativity; content to have so far been, as to have a title to future being, although he had lived here but in an hidden state of life, and as it were an abortion.

What song the Sirens sang, or what name Achilles assumed when he hid himself among women, though puzzling questions, are not beyond all conjecture. What time the persons of these ossuaries entered the famous nations of the dead, and slept with princes and counselors, might admit a wide solution. But who were the proprietaries of these bones, or what bodies these ashes made up, were a question above antiquarism; not to be resolved by man, nor easily perhaps by spirits, except we consult the provincial guardians, or tutelary observators. Had they made as good provision for their names, as they have done for their relics, they had not so grossly erred in the art of perpetuation. But to subsist in bones, and be but

---

14 Thus, when I am turned to bones, I should wish to be laid to rest.

15 According to the ancient arithmetic of the hand, wherein the little finger of the right hand contracted, signified an hundred.—Pierius in *Hieroglyph.* (Browne.)

16 One night as long as three. (Browne.)

pyramidally extant, is a fallacy in duration. Vain ashes which in the oblivion of names, persons, times, and sexes, have found unto themselves a fruitless continuation, and only arise unto late posterity, as emblems of mortal vanities, antidotes against pride, vainglory, and madding vices. Pagan vainglories which thought the world might last for ever, had encouragement for ambition; and, finding no Atropos unto the immortality of their names, were never damped with the necessity of oblivion. Even old ambitions had the advantage of ours, in the attempts of their vainglories, who acting early, and before the probable meridian of time, have by this time found great accomplishment of their designs, whereby the ancient heroes have already outlasted their monuments and mechanical preservations. But in this latter scene of time, we cannot expect such mummies unto our memories, when ambition may fear the prophecy of Elias,[17] and Charles the Fifth can never hope to live within two Methuselahs of Hector.[18]

And therefore, restless unquiet for the diuturnity of our memories unto present considerations seems a vanity almost out of date, and superannuated piece of folly. We cannot hope to live so long in our names, as some have done in their persons. One face of Janus holds no proportion unto the other. 'Tis too late to be ambitious. The great mutations of the world are acted, or time may be too short for our designs. To extend our memories by monuments, whose death we daily pray for, and whose duration we cannot hope, without injury to our expectations in the advent of the last day, were a contradiction to our beliefs. We whose generations are ordained in this setting part of time, are providentially taken off from such imaginations; and, being necessitated to eye the remaining particle of futurity, are naturally constituted unto thoughts of the next world, and cannot excusably decline the consideration of that duration, which maketh pyramids pillars of snow, and all that's past a moment.

Circles and right lines limit and close all bodies, and the mortal right-lined circle[19] must conclude and shut up all. There is no antidote against the opium of time, which temporally considereth all things: our fathers find their graves in our short memories, and sadly tell us how we may be buried in our survivors.

Gravestones tell truth scarce forty years.[20] Generations pass while some trees stand, and old families last not three oaks. To be read by bare inscriptions like many in Gruter, to hope for eternity by enigmatical epithets or first letters of our names, to be studied by antiquaries, who we were, and have new names given us like many of the mummies, are cold consolations unto the students of perpetuity, even by everlasting languages.

To be content that times to come should only know there was such a man, not caring whether they knew more of him, was a frigid ambition in Cardan; disparaging his horoscopical inclination and judgment of himself. Who cares to subsist like Hippocrates' patients, or Achilles' horses in Homer, under naked nominations, without deserts and noble acts, which are the balsam of our memories, the *entelechia*[21] and soul of our subsistences? To be nameless in worthy deeds, exceeds an infamous history. The Canaanitish woman lives more happily without a name, than Herodias with one. And who had not rather have been the good thief than Pilate?

But the iniquity of oblivion blindly scattereth her poppy, and deals with the memory of men without distinction to merit of perpetuity. Who can but pity the founder of the pyramids? Herostratus lives that burnt the temple of Diana, he is almost lost that built it. Time hath spared the epitaph of Adrian's horse, confounded that of himself. In vain we compute our felicities by the advantage of our good names, since bad have equal durations, and Thersites is like to live as long as Agamemnon. Who knows whether the best of men be known, or whether there be not more remarkable persons forgot, than any that stand remembered in the known account of time? Without the favor of the everlasting register, the first man had been as unknown as the last, and Methuselah's long life had been his only chronicle.

Oblivion is not to be hired. The greater part must be content to be as though they had not been, to be found in the register of God, not in the record of man. Twenty-seven names make up the first story, and the recorded names ever since contain not one living century. The number of the dead long exceedeth all that shall live. The night of time far surpasseth the day, and who knows when was the equinox? Every hour adds

17 That the world may last but six thousand years. (Browne.)
18 Hector's fame lasting above two lives of Methuselah, before that famous prince was extant. (Browne.)
19 Θ The character of death. (Browne.)

20 Old ones being taken up, and other bodies laid under them. (Browne.)
21 The realization or complete expression of some function; informing spirit, soul. (Oxford English Dictionary.)

unto that current arithmetic, which scarce stands one moment. And since death must be the *Lucina*[22] of life, and even Pagans could doubt, whether thus to live were to die; since our longest sun sets at right descensions, and makes but winter arches, and therefore it cannot be long before we lie down in darkness, and have our light in ashes;[23] since the brother of death daily haunts us with dying mementos, and time that grows old in itself, bids us hope no long duration;—diuturnity is a dream and folly of expectation.

Darkness and light divide the course of time, and oblivion shares with memory a great part even of our living beings; we slightly remember our felicities, and the smartest strokes of affliction leave but short smart upon us. Sense endureth no extremities, and sorrows destroy us or themselves. To weep into stones are fables. Afflictions induce callosities; miseries are slippery, or fall like snow upon us, which notwithstanding is no unhappy stupidity. To be ignorant of evils to come, and forgetful of evils past, is a merciful provision in nature, whereby we digest the mixture of our few and evil days, and, our delivered senses not relapsing into cutting remembrances, our sorrows are not kept raw by the edge of repetitions. A great part of antiquity contented their hopes of subsistency with a transmigration of their souls,—a good way to continue their memories, while having the advantage of plural successions, they could not but act something remarkable in such variety of beings, and enjoying the fame of their passed selves, make accumulation of glory unto their last durations. Others, rather than be lost in the uncomfortable night of nothing, were content to recede into the common being, and make one particle of the public soul of all things, which was no more than to return into their unknown and divine original again. Egyptian ingenuity was more unsatisfied, contriving their bodies in sweet consistencies, to attend the return of their souls. But all was vanity, feeding the wind, and folly. The Egyptian mummies, which Cambyses or time hath spared, avarice now consumeth. Mummy is become merchandise, Mizraim cures wounds, and Pharaoh is sold for balsams.

In vain do individuals hope for immortality, or any patent from oblivion, in preservations below the moon; men have been deceived even in their flatteries above the sun, and studied conceits to perpetuate their names

in heaven. The various cosmography of that part hath already varied the names of contrived constellations; Nimrod is lost in Orion, and Osiris in the Dog-star. While we look for incorruption in the heavens, we find they are but like the earth;—durable in their main bodies, alterable in their parts; whereof, beside comets and new stars, perspectives[24] begin to tell tales, and the spots that wander about the sun, with Phaeton's favour, would make clear conviction.

There is nothing strictly immortal, but immortality. Whatever hath no beginning, may be confident of no end (all others have a dependent being and within the reach of destruction); which is the peculiar of that necessary Essence that cannot destroy itself; and the highest strain of omnipotency, to be so powerfully constituted as not to suffer even from the power of itself. But the sufficiency of Christian immortality frustrates all earthly glory, and the quality of either state after death, makes a folly of posthumous memory. God who can only destroy our souls, and hath assured our resurrection, either of our bodies or names hath directly promised no duration. Wherein there is so much of chance, that the boldest expectants have found unhappy frustration; and to hold long subsistence, seems but a scape in oblivion. But man is a noble animal, splendid in ashes, and pompous in the grave, solemnizing nativities and deaths with equal luster, nor omitting ceremonies of bravery in the infamy of his nature.

Life is a pure flame, and we live by an invisible sun within us. A small fire sufficeth for life, great flames seemed too little after death, while men vainly affected precious pyres, and to burn like Sardanapalus; but the wisdom of funeral laws found the folly of prodigal blazes, and reduced undoing fires unto the rule of sober obsequies, wherein few could be so mean as not to provide wood, pitch, a mourner, and an urn.

Five languages secured not the epitaph of Gordianus. The man of God lives longer without a tomb, than any by one, invisibly interred by angels, and adjudged to obscurity, though not without some marks directing human discovery. Enoch and Elias, without either tomb or burial, in an anomalous state of being, are the great examples of perpetuity, in their long and living memory, in strict account being still on this side death, and having a late part yet to act upon this stage of earth. If in the decretory term of the world, we shall not all die but be changed, according to received translation, the last day will make but few graves;

22 The goddess who presides over the birth of children.

23 According to the custom of the Jews, who place a lighted wax candle in a pot of ashes by the corpse.—*Leo*. (Browne, added in later editions.)

24 Telescopes.

at least quick resurrections will anticipate lasting sepultures. Some graves will be opened before they be quite closed, and Lazarus be no wonder. When many that feared to die, shall groan that they can die but once, the dismal state is the second and living death, when life puts despair on the damned; when men shall wish the coverings of mountains, not of monuments, and annihilations shall be courted.

While some have studied monuments, others have studiously declined them, and some have been so vainly boisterous, that they durst not acknowledge their graves; wherein Alaricus seems most subtle, who had a river turned to hide his bones at the bottom. Even Sylla, that thought himself safe in his urn, could not prevent revenging tongues, and stones thrown at his monument. Happy are they whom privacy makes innocent, who deal so with men in this world, that they are not afraid to meet them in the next; who, when they die, make no commotion among the dead, and are not touched with that poetical taunt of Isaiah.[25]

Pyramids, arches, obelisks, were but the irregularities of vainglory, and wild enormities of ancient magnanimity. But the most magnanimous resolution rests in the Christian religion, which trampleth upon pride, and sits on the neck of ambition, humbly pursuing that infallible perpetuity, unto which all others must diminish their diameters, and be poorly seen in angles of contingency.[26]

25 Isa. xiv: 16, etc. (Browne.)
26 *Angulus contingentiæ*, the least of angles. (Browne.)

Pious spirits who passed their days in raptures of futurity, made little more of this world, than the world that was before it, while they lay obscure in the chaos of preordination, and night of their forebeings. And if any have been so happy as truly to understand Christian annihilation, ecstasies, exolution, liquefaction, transformation, the kiss of the spouse, gustation of God, and ingression into the divine shadow, they have already had an handsome anticipation of heaven; the glory of the world is surely over, and the earth in ashes unto them.

To subsist in lasting monuments, to live in their productions, to exist in their names and predicament of chimeras, was large satisfaction unto old expectations, and made one part of their Elysiums. But all this is nothing in the metaphysics of true belief. To live indeed, is to be again ourselves, which being not only an hope, but an evidence in noble believers, 'tis all one to lie in St. Innocents'[27] church-yard, as in the sands of Egypt. Ready to be any thing, in the ecstasy of being ever, and as content with six foot as the *moles* of Adrianus.[28]

> —*tabesne cadavera solvat,*
> *An rogus, haud refert.*—Lucan [*Phars.* vii. 809].[29]

27 In Paris, where bodies soon consume. (Browne.)
28 A stately mausoleum or sepulchral pile, built by Adrianus in Rome, where now standeth the castle of St. Angelo. (Browne.)
29 Whether earth or the funeral fire consumes the corpses, it matters little.

Thomas Fuller

[1608–1661]

FULLER was one of the most popular as well as one of the most voluminous authors of the middle years of the seventeenth century. He was born in Northamptonshire, the son of a rector and the nephew of two churchmen who were later to become bishops of the Church of England. Educated at Queen's College, Cambridge, he maintained for many years his association with the university, but initiated, around 1634, a life as a kind of wandering ecclesiastic which led him to many parts of England before he was made, in 1642, curate of the Savoy Chapel in London. Fuller's moderate position at the time of the great conflict between king and parliament earned him certain extremist enemies on both sides; his loyalty to the king, however, was clear and unequivocal and it won him, in 1644, a position as chaplain to the infant princess Henrietta Anne. During the troubled years of the 1640's he resided at Exeter; after the surrender of that royalist stronghold he was obliged to remove to London, where he spent the rest of his life. After the restoration of Charles II he was made chaplain-in-extraordinary to the king. He died shortly thereafter, in 1661.

Although a devoted servant of the Church of England, Fuller was one of those rare phenomena of the seventeenth century, a professional writer. His earliest work, a poem entitled, with characteristic quaintness, *David's Heinous Sin, Hearty Repentance, and Heavy Punishment,* was followed in 1639 by an account of the Crusades entitled *The Holy War,* and in 1642 by *The Holy State,* one of the works on which his reputation rests. *The Holy State* belongs essentially to the tradition of the character-books, but its extremely didactic nature underlines at the same time a relationship to the sermon and the conduct-book. Basically, *The Holy State* (which consists of three books dealing with virtuous characters, one book—subtitled "The Profane State"—dealing with vicious characters, and one book dealing with abstractions) is a work of instruction for the middle classes, but Fuller's indomitable taste for anecdote gives the work an obstreperous vitality which is still operative today. Whatever his intellectual limitations (and they are many), the old preacher's love of life can still communicate itself, and this fact has given him a degree of immortality.

The twentieth-century reader is liable to patronize Fuller, and the foregoing sentences have perhaps a ring of condescension. A sympathetic perusal of his two most ambitious works (*The Church History of Britain*—1655, and *The History of the Worthies of England* —1662), however, makes condescension difficult. Fuller is a fanatically devoted researcher and antiquarian, and what he lacks in method or organizational power he compensates for in energy and enthusiasm. The *Church History* is an account of Britain from prehistoric times to 1649; the *Worthies* is a tour of England, with copious observations on the products, landmarks, marvels, and distinguished sons of each of its counties. In both works the thumbnail biographies, the appended anecdotes, and the witty asides are what charm the modern reader, and in both works the reader is certain to find himself ultimately bogged down in tedious detail and undigested observation. Fuller is, in all his works, best enjoyed in snatches. A similar limited charm may be found in his lesser works: *Good Thoughts in Bad Times* (1645), *Good Thoughts in Worse Times* (1647), *Mixed Contemplations in Better Times* (1660)—all manuals of devotion—and *A Pisgah-Sight of Palestine* (1650), an illustrated guide to the Holy Land. Never intellectually comparable to his great contemporaries, afflicted always by an inveterate immaturity, Fuller survives as a kind of genial joker in the company of somber titans.

T. FULLER. *The Holy State*, ed. M. G. Walten, 2 vols. (New York, 1938). The standard modern edition.

————. *Selections*, ed. E. K. Broadus (Oxford, 1929).

D. B. LYMAN. *The Great Tom Fuller* (Berkeley, Calif., 1935). A short biography.

S. C. ROBERTS. *Thomas Fuller, A Seventeenth-Century Worthy* (Manchester, 1953).

W. E. HOUGHTON. *The Formation of Thomas Fuller's Holy and Profane States* (Oxford, 1938).

E. N. S. THOMPSON. (Cited under Overbury.)

D. A. STAUFFER. (Cited under Walton.)

F R O M

THE HOLY STATE AND THE PROFANE STATE

[TEXT: *first edition, 1642*]

THE ELDER BROTHER

Is ONE who made haste to come into the world, to bring his parents the first news of male posterity; and is well rewarded for his tidings. His composition is then accounted the most precious when made of the loss of a double virginity.

1. He is thankful for the advantage God gave him at the starting in the race into this world. When twins have been even matched, one hath gained the goal but by his length. St. Augustine saith, that "it is every man's bounden duty solemnly to celebrate his birthday." If so, elder brothers may best afford good cheer on the festival.

2. He counts not his inheritance a writ of ease to free him from industry, as if only the younger brothers came into the world to work, the elder to compliment. These are the tops of their houses indeed; like cotlofts, highest and emptiest. Rather, he laboreth to furnish himself with all gentle accomplishment, being best able to go to the cost of learning. He need not fear to be

served as Ulric Fugger was (chief of the noble family of the Fuggers in Augsburg), who was disinherited of a great patrimony, only for his studiousness, and expensiveness in buying costly manuscripts.

3. He doth not so remember he is an heir that he forgets he is a son. Wherefore, his carriage to his parents is always respectful. It may chance that his father may be kept in a charitable prison, whereof his son hath the keys; the old man being only tenant for life, and the lands entailed on our young gentleman. In such a case, when it is in his power, if necessity requires, he enlargeth his father to such a reasonable proportion of liberty as may not be injurious to himself.

4. He rather desires his father's life than his living. This was one of the principal reasons (but God knows how true) why Philip II, King of Spain, caused, in the year 1568, Charles, his eldest son, to be executed for plotting his father's death, as was pretended. And a wit[1] in such difficult toys accommodated the numeral

---

1 Opmerus was the author thereof: Famianus Strada, *De Bello Belgico, lib.* 7, page 432. (Fuller.)

letters in Ovid's verse to the year wherein the prince suffered.

1568

FILIUs ante DIeM patrIos InqVIrIt In annos.

1568

Before the tIMe, the oVer-hasty son
Seeks forth hoVV near the father's LIfe Is Done.

But if they had no better evidence against him but this poetical synchronism, we might well count him a martyr.

5. His father's deeds and grants he ratifies and confirms. If a stitch be fallen in a lease, he will not widen it into a hole by caviling, till the whole strength of the grant run out thereat; or take advantage of the default of the clerk in writing, where the deed appears really done, and on a valuable consideration: he counts himself bound in honor to perform what, by marks and signs, he plainly understands his father meant, though he spake it not.

6. He reflecteth his luster to grace and credit his younger brethren. Thus Scipio Africanus, after his great victories against the Carthaginians, and conquering of Hannibal, was content to serve as a lieutenant[2] in the wars of Asia, under Lucius Scipio, his younger brother.

7. He relieveth his distressed kindred, yet so as he continues them in their calling. Otherwise, they would all make his house their hospital, his kindred their calling. When one, being a husbandman, challenged kindred of Robert Grosthead, Bishop of Lincoln, and thereupon requested favor of him to bestow an office on him, "Cousin," quoth the bishop, "if your cart be broken, I'll mend it; if your plow be old, I'll give you a new one, and seed to sow your land. But a husbandman I found you, and a husbandman I'll leave you." It is better to ease poor kindred in their profession than to ease them from their profession.

8. He is careful to support the credit and dignity of his family, neither wasting his paternal estate by his unthriftiness, nor marring it by parceling his ancient manors and demesnes amongst his younger children, whom he provides for by annuities, pensions, moneys, leases, and purchased lands. He remembers how, when our King Alfred divided the river of Lea (which parts Hertfordshire and Essex) into three streams, it became so shallow that boats could not row where

2 Plutarch, in the Life of Scipio. (Fuller.)

formerly ships did ride. Thus the ancient family of the Woodfords (which had long continued in Leicestershire, and elsewhere in England, in great account, estate, and livelihood) is at this day quite extinct. For when Sir Thomas Woodford, in the reign of King Henry VI, made almost an even partition of his means betwixt his five grandchildren, the house in short space utterly decayed; not any part of his lands now in the tenure[3] or name of any of his male line, some whereof lived to be brought to a low ebb of fortune. Yet, on the other side, to leave all to the eldest, and make no provision for the rest of their children, is against all rules of religion, forgetting their Christian name to remember their surname.

THE GOOD SCHOOLMASTER

THERE is scarce any profession in the commonwealth more necessary which is so slightly performed. The reasons whereof I conceive to be these: First, young scholars make this calling their refuge, yea, perchance, before they have taken any degree in the university, commence schoolmasters in the country, as if nothing else were required to set up this profession but only a rod and a ferula. Secondly, others who are able to use it only as a passage to better preferment, to patch the rents in their present fortune till they can provide a new one, and betake themselves to some more gainful calling. Thirdly, they are disheartened from doing their best with the miserable reward which in some places they receive, being masters to the children and slaves to their parents. Fourthly, being grown rich, they grow negligent, and scorn to touch the school but by the proxy of an usher. But see how well our schoolmaster behaves himself.

1. His genius inclines him with delight to his profession. Some men had as lief be schoolboys as schoolmasters, to be tied to the school as Cooper's Dictionary and Scapula's Lexicon are chained to the desk therein; and though great scholars, and skillful in other arts, are bunglers in this: but God of his goodness hath fitted several men for several callings, that the necessity of church and state, in all conditions, may be provided for. So that he who beholds the fabric thereof may say, God hewed out this stone, and appointed it to lie in this very place, for it would fit none other so well, and here it doth most excellent. And thus God moldeth some for a schoolmaster's life, undertaking it with desire

3 Burton, in his description of Leicestershire (Fuller.)

and delight, and discharging it with dexterity and happy success.

2. He studies his scholars' natures as carefully as they their books; and ranks their dispositions into several forms. And though it may seem difficult for him in a great school to descend to all particulars, yet experienced schoolmasters may quickly make a grammar of boys' natures, and reduce them all, saving some few exceptions, to these general rules:

(a) Those that are ingenious and industrious. The conjunction of two such planets in a youth presage much good unto him. To such a lad a frown may be a whipping, and a whipping a death; yea, where their master whips them once, shame whips them all the week after. Such natures he useth with all gentleness.

(b) Those that are ingenious and idle. These think, with the hare in the fable, that, running with snails (so they count the rest of their schoolfellows), they shall come soon enough to the post, though sleeping a good while before their starting. Oh, a good rod would finely take them napping!

(c) Those that are dull and diligent. Wines, the stronger they be, the more lees they have when they are new. Many boys are muddy-headed till they be clarified with age, and such afterwards prove the best. Bristol diamonds are both bright and squared and pointed by nature, and yet are soft and worthless; whereas orient ones in India are rough and rugged naturally. Hard, rugged, and dull natures of youth acquit themselves afterwards the jewels of the country, and therefore their dullness at first is to be borne with, if they be diligent. That schoolmaster deserves to be beaten himself who beats nature in a boy for a fault. And I question whether all the whipping in the world can make their parts, which are naturally sluggish, rise one minute before the hour nature hath appointed.

(d) Those that are invincibly dull and negligent also. Correction may reform the latter, not amend the former. All the whetting in the world can never set a razor's edge on that which hath no steel in it. Such boys he consigneth over to other professions. Shipwrights and boatmakers will choose those crooked pieces of timber which other carpenters refuse. Those may make excellent merchants and mechanics who will not serve for scholars.

3. He is able, diligent, and methodical in his teaching; not leading them rather in a circle than forwards. He minces his precepts for children to swallow, hanging clogs on the nimbleness of his own soul, that his scholars may go along with him.

4. He is and will be known to be an absolute monarch in his school. If cockering mothers proffer him money to purchase their sons an exemption from his rod (to live as it were in a peculiar, out of their master's jurisdiction), with disdain he refuseth it, and scorns the late custom, in some places, of commuting whipping into money, and ransoming boys from the rod at a set price. If he hath a stubborn youth, correction-proof, he debaseth not his authority by contesting with him, but fairly, if he can, puts him away before his obstinacy hath affected others.

5. He is moderate in inflicting deserved correction. Many a schoolmaster better answereth the name παιδοτρίβης than παιδαγωγός rather tearing his scholar's flesh with whipping than giving them good education. No wonder if his scholars hate the muses, being presented unto them in the shapes of fiends and furies. Junius complains *de insolenti carnificina*[4] of his schoolmaster, by whom *conscindebatur flagris septies aut octies in dies singulos*.[5] Yea, hear the lamentable verses of poor Tusser, in his own Life:

> From Paul's I went, to Eton sent,
> To learn straightways the Latin phrase,
> Where fifty-three stripes given to me
>   At once I had.

> For fault but small, or none at all,
> It came to pass thus beat I was;
> See, Udal,[6] see the mercy of thee
>   To me, poor lad.

Such an Orbilius[7] mars more scholars than he makes: their tyranny hath caused many tongues to stammer, which spake plain by nature, and whose stuttering at first was nothing else but fears quavering on their speech at their master's presence; and whose mauling them about their heads hath dulled those who in quickness exceeded their master.

6. He makes his school free to him who sues to him *in forma pauperis*. And surely learning is the greatest alms that can be given. But he is a beast who because the poor scholar cannot pay him wages, pays the scholar in his whipping. Rather are diligent lads to be encouraged with all excitements to learning. This

4 Harsh brutality.

5 He was scourged seven or eight times a day.

6 Nicholas Udal [or Udall], schoolmaster of Eton in the reign of King Henry VIII. (Fuller.)

7 Horace's teacher, whom he stigmatizes for the severe floggings which he gave his pupils.

minds me of what I have heard concerning Mr. Bust, that worthy late schoolmaster of Eton, who would never suffer any wandering begging scholar, such as justly the statute hath ranked in the forefront of rogues, to come into his school, but would thrust him out with earnestness (however privately charitable unto him) lest his schoolboys should be disheartened from their books, by seeing some scholars, after their studying in the university, preferred to beggary.

7. He spoils not a good school to make thereof a bad college, therein to teach his scholars logic. For besides that logic may have an action of trespass against grammar for encroaching on her liberties, syllogisms are solecisms taught in the school, and oftentimes they are forced afterwards in the university to unlearn the fumbling skill they had before.

8. Out of his school he is no whit pedantical in carriage or discourse; contenting himself to be rich in Latin, though he doth not jingle with it in every company wherein he comes.

To conclude, let this amongst other motives make schoolmasters careful in their place, that the eminencies of their scholars have commended the memories of their schoolmasters to posterity, who otherwise in obscurity had altogether been forgotten. Who had ever heard of R. Bond in Lancashire, but for the breeding of learned Ascham his scholar; or of Hartgrave in Brundley school, in the same county, but because he was the first to teach worthy Dr. Whitaker? Nor do I honor the memory of Mulcaster for anything so much as for his scholar, that gulf of learning, Bishop Andrewes. This made the Athenians, the day before the great feast of Theseus their founder, to sacrifice a ram to the memory of Conidas his schoolmaster that first instructed him.[8]

THE GOOD MERCHANT

Is ONE who by his trading claspeth the island to the continent, and one country to another; an excellent gardener, who makes England bear wine, and oil, and spices; yea, herein goes beyond nature, in causing that *omnis fert omnia tellus*. He wrongs neither himself nor the commonwealth, nor private chapmen[9] which buy commodities of him. As for his behavior towards the commonwealth, it far surpasses my skill to give any rules thereof; only this I know, that to export things of necessity, and to bring in foreign needless toys,

makes a rich merchant, and a poor kingdom. For the state loseth her radical moisture, and gets little better than sweat in exchange, except the necessaries which are exported be exceeding plentiful; which then, though necessary in their own nature, become superfluous through their abundance. We will content ourselves to give some general advertisements concerning his behavior towards his chapmen, whom he uses well in the quantity, quality, and price of the commodities he sells them.

1. He wrongs not the buyer in number, weight, or measure. These are the landmarks of all trading, which must not be removed; for such cozenage were worse than open felony. First, because they rob a man of his purse, and never bid him stand. Secondly, because highway thieves defy, but these pretend justice. Thirdly, as much as lies in their power, they endeavor to make God accessory to their cozenage, deceiving by pretending his weights. For God is the principal clerk of the market. "All the weights of the bag are his work."[10]

2. He never warrants any ware for good but what is so indeed. Otherwise he is a thief, and may be a murderer, if selling such things as are applied inwardly. Besides, in such a case he counts himself guilty if he selleth such wares as are bad, though without his knowledge, if avouching them for good; because he may, professeth, and is bound to be master in his own mystery,[11] and therefore in conscience must recompense the buyer's loss, except he gives him an item to buy it at his own adventure.

3. He either tells the faults in his ware, or abates proportionably in the price he demands; for then the low value shows the viciousness of it. Yet commonly when merchants depart with their commodities, we hear (as in funeral orations) all the virtues but none of the faults thereof.

4. He never demands out of distance of the price he intends to take; if not always within the touch, yet within the reach of what he means to sell for. Now we must know there be four several prices of vendible things. First, the price of the market, which ebbs and flows according to the plenty or scarcity of coin, commodities, and chapmen. Secondly, the price of friendship, which perchance is more giving than selling, and, therefore not so proper at this time. Thirdly, the price of fancy, as twenty pounds or more for a dog or hawk, when no such inherent worth can naturally be in them, but by the buyer's and seller's fancy reflecting on them.

8 Plutarch, in *Vita Thesei*. (Fuller.)   9 Pedlars.   10 Proverbs 16:11. (Fuller.)   11 Trade.

Yet I believe the money may be lawfully taken. First, because the seller sometimes on those terms is as loth to forego it as the buyer is willing to have it. And I know no standard herein whereby men's affections may be measured. Secondly, it being a matter of pleasure, and men able and willing, let them pay for it, *volenti non fit injuria*. Lastly, there is the price of the cozenage, which our merchant from his heart detests and abhors.

5. He makes not advantage of his chapman's ignorance, chiefly if referring himself to his honesty, where the seller's conscience is all the buyer's skill, who makes him both seller and judge, so that he doth not so much ask as order, what he must pay. When one told old Bishop Latimer that the cutler had cozened him, in making him pay twopence for a knife not (in those days) worth a penny, "No," quoth Latimer, "he cozened not me but his own conscience." On the other side St. Augustine tells us[12] of a seller, who out of ignorance asked for a book far less than it was worth, and the buyer (conceive himself to be the man if you please) of his own accord gave him the full value thereof.

6. He makes not the buyer pay the shot for his prodigality; as when the merchant through his own ignorance or ill husbandry hath bought dear, he will not bring in his unnecessary expenses on the buyer's score; and in such a case he is bound to sell cheaper than he bought.

7. Selling by retail, he may justify the taking of greater gain; because of his care, pains, and cost of fetching those wares from the fountain, and in parceling and dividing them. Yet because retailers trade commonly with those who have least skill what they buy, and commonly sell to the poorer sort of people, they must be careful not to grate on their necessity.

But how long shall I be retailing out rules to this merchant? It would employ a casuist an apprenticeship of years; take our Saviour's wholesale rule, "Whatsoever ye would have men do unto you, do you unto them; for this is the law and the prophets."[13]

THE GOOD YEOMAN

Is A gentleman in ore, whom the next age may see refined; and is the wax capable of a gentle impression, when the prince shall stamp it. Wise Solon (who accounted Tellus the Athenian the most happy man, for living privately on his own lands) would surely have

pronounced the English yeomanry a fortunate condition, living in the temperate zone betwixt greatness and want; an estate of people almost peculiar to England. France and Italy are like a die which hath no points between cinque and ace—nobility and peasantry. Their walls, though high, must needs be hollow, wanting filling-stones. Indeed Germany hath her boors, like our yeomen; but, by a tyrannical appropriation of nobility to some few ancient families, their yeomen are excluded from ever rising higher to clarify their bloods. In England, the temple of honor is bolted against none who have passed through the temple of virtue; nor is a capacity to be genteel denied to our yeoman who thus behaves himself.

1. He wears russet clothes, but makes golden payment, having tin in his buttons, and silver in his pocket. If he chance to appear in clothes above his rank, it is to grace some great man with his service, and then he blusheth at his own bravery. Otherwise he is the surest landmark, whence foreigners may take aim of the ancient English customs; the gentry more floating after foreign fashions.

2. In his house he is bountiful both to strangers and poor people. Some hold when hospitality died in England she gave her last groan amongst the yeomen of Kent. And still at our yeoman's table you shall have as many joints as dishes; no meat disguised with strange sauces; no straggling joint of a sheep in the midst of a pasture of grass, beset with salads on every side, but solid substantial food; no servitors (more nimble with their hands than the guests with their teeth) take away meat, before stomachs[14] are taken away. Here you have that which in itself is good, made better by the store of it, and best by the welcome to it.

3. He hath a great stroke in making a knight of the shire. Good reason, for he makes a whole line in the subsidy book, where whatsoever he is rated he pays without any regret, not caring how much his purse is let blood, so it be done by the advice of the physicians of the state.

4. He seldom goes far abroad, and his credit stretcheth further than his travel. He goes not to London, but *se defendendo*, to save himself of a fine, being returned of a jury; where seeing the king once, he prays for him ever afterwards.

5. In his own country he is a main man in juries, where, if the judge please to open his eyes in matter of law, he needs not to be led by the nose in matters of fact. He is very observant of the judge's *item*, when

12 *Lib.* 13 *de Trinitate, c.* 3. (Fuller.)   13 Matthew 7:12.

14 Appetites.

it follows the truths *imprimis;* otherwise (though not mutinous in a jury) he cares not whom he displeaseth so he pleaseth his own conscience.

6. He improveth his land to a double value by his good husbandry. Some grounds that wept with water, or frowned with thorns, by draining the one, and clearing the other, he makes both to laugh and sing with corn. By marl and limestone burnt he bettereth his ground, and his industry worketh miracles, by turning stones into bread. Conquest and good husbandry both enlarge the king's dominions; the one by the sword, making the acres more in number; the other by the plow, making the same acres more in value. Solomon saith, "The king himself is maintained by husbandry." Pythis,[15] a king, having discovered rich mines in his kingdom, employed all his people in digging of them, whence tilling was wholly neglected, insomuch as a great famine ensued. His queen, sensible of the calamities of the country, invited the king her husband to dinner, as he came home hungry from overseeing his workmen in the mines. She so contrived it that the bread and meat were most artificially made of gold; and the king was much delighted with the conceit thereof, till at last he called for real meat to satisfy his hunger. "Nay," said the queen, "if you employ all your subjects in your mines, you must expect to feed upon gold, for nothing else can your kingdom afford."

7. In time of famine he is the Joseph of the country, and keeps the poor from starving. Then he tameth his stacks of corn, which not his covetousness but providence hath reserved for time of need, and to his poor neighbors abateth somewhat of the high price of the market. The neighbor gentry court him for his acquaintance, which he either modestly waiveth, or thankfully accepteth, but no way greedily desireth. He insults not on the ruins of a decayed gentleman, but pities and relieves him; and as he is called Goodman, he desires to answer to the name, and to be so indeed.

8. In war, though he serveth on foot, he is ever mounted on an high spirit; as being a slave to none, and a subject only to his own prince. Innocence and independence make a brave spirit; whereas otherwise one must ask his leave to be valiant on whom he depends. Therefore if a state run up all to noblemen and gentlemen, so that the husbandmen be only mere laborers or cottagers (which one[16] calls but housed beggars),

it may have good cavalry, but never good bands of foot; so that their armies will be like those birds called *Apodes*, without feet, always only flying on their wings of horse. Wherefore to make good infantry, it requireth men bred, not in a servile or indigent fashion, but in some free and plentiful manner. Wisely therefore did that knowing prince, King Henry the Seventh, provide laws for the increase of his yeomanry, that his kingdom should not be like to coppice-woods, where the staddles[17] being left too thick, all runs to bushes and briers, and there's little clean underwood. For enacting that houses used to husbandry should be kept up with a competent proportion of land, he did secretly sow Hydra's teeth, whereupon (according to the poet's fiction)[18] should rise up armed men for the service of this kingdom.

OF APPAREL

CLOTHES are for necessity; warm clothes for health, cleanly for decency, lasting for thrift, and rich for magnificence. Now there may be a fault in their number, if too various; making, if too vain; matter, if too costly; and mind of the wearer, if he takes pride therein. We come therefore to some general directions.

1. It's a chargeable vanity to be constantly clothed above one's purse or place. I say constantly; for perchance sometimes it may be dispensed with. A great man, who himself was very plain in apparel, checked a gentleman for being over fine, who modestly answered, "Your Lordship hath better clothes at home, and I have worse." But sure no plea can be made when this luxury is grown to be ordinary. It was an arrogant act of Hubert, Archbishop of Canterbury, who, when King John had given his courtiers rich liveries, to ape the lion, gave his servants the like, wherewith the king was not a little offended. But what shall we say to the riot of our age, wherein (as peacocks are more gay than the eagle himself) subjects are grown braver than their sovereign?

2. 'Tis beneath a wise man always to wear clothes beneath men of his rank. True, there is a state sometimes in decent plainness. When a wealthy lord at a great solemnity had the plainest apparel, "Oh," said one, "if you had marked it well his suit had the richest pockets." Yet it argues no wisdom, in clothes always to stoop beneath his condition. When Antisthenes saw

---

15 Plutarch, *de Virtute Mulierum, exemplo ultimo.* (Fuller.)

16 Bacon's Henry VII, page 74. (Fuller.) See Bacon's essay Of the True Greatness of Kingdoms.

17 Young trees which are left standing.

18 See Ovid's Metamorphoses vii, 121.

Socrates in a torn coat, he showed a hole thereof to the people; "and lo," quoth he, "through this I see Socrates his pride."

3. He shows a light gravity who loves to be an exception from a general fashion. For the received custom in the place where we live is the most competent judge of decency; from which we must not appeal to our own opinion. When the French courtiers mourning for their King Henry the Second had worn cloth a whole year, all silks became so vile in every man's eyes that, if any was seen to wear them, he was presently accounted a mechanic or country fellow.

4. It's a folly for one Proteus-like never to appear twice in one shape. Had some of our gallants been with the Israelites in the wilderness, when for forty years their clothes waxed not old, they would have been vexed, though their clothes were whole, to have been so long in one fashion. Yet here I must confess I understand not what is reported of Fulgentius, that he used the same garment winter and summer, and never altered his clothes, *etiam in sacris peragendis*.

5. He that is proud of the rustling of his silks, like a madman laughs at the rattling of his fetters. For indeed, clothes ought to be our remembrancers of our lost innocency. Besides, why should any brag of what's but borrowed? Should the estridge snatch off the gallant's feather, the beaver his hat, the goat his gloves, the sheep his suit, the silkworm his stockings, and neat his shoes (to strip him no further than modesty will give leave), he would be left in a cold condition. And yet 'tis more pardonable to be proud, even of cleanly rags, than (as many are) of affected slovenness. The one is proud of a molehill, the other of a dunghill.

To conclude, sumptuary laws in this land to reduce apparel to a set standard of price and fashion, according to the several states of men, have long been wished, but are little to be hoped for. Some think private men's superfluity is a necessary evil in a state, the floating of fashions affording a standing maintenance to many thousands which otherwise would be at a loss for a livelihood, men maintaining more by their pride than by their charity.

OF BUILDING

HE THAT alters an old house is tied as a translator to the original, and is confined to the fancy of the first builder. Such a man were unwise to pluck down good old building, to erect, perchance, worse new. But those that raise a new house from the ground are blameworthy if they make it not handsome, seeing to them method and confusion are both at a rate. In building we must respect situation, contrivance, receipt, strength, and beauty. Of situation:

1. Chiefly choose a wholesome air. For air is a dish one feeds on every minute, and therefore it need be good. Wherefore great men, who may build where they please, as poor men where they can, if herein they prefer their profit above their health, I refer them to their physicians to make them pay for it accordingly.

2. Wood and water are two staple commodities where they may be had. The former I confess hath made so much iron that it must now be bought with the more silver, and grows daily dearer.[19] But 'tis as well pleasant as profitable so see a house cased with trees, like that of Anchises in Troy.

——*Quanquam secreta parentis*
  Anchisæ domus arboribusque obtecta recessit.[20]

The worst is, where a place is bald of wood, no art can make it a periwig. As for water, begin with Pindar's beginning, ἄριστον μὲν ὕδωρ.[21] The fort of Gogmagog Hills nigh Cambridge is counted impregnable but for want of water, the mischief of many houses where servants must bring the well on their shoulders.

3. Next, a pleasant prospect is to be respected. A medley view, such as of water and land at Greenwich, best entertains the eyes, refreshing the wearied beholder with exchange of objects. Yet I know a more profitable prospect, where the owner can only see his own land round about.

4. A fair entrance with an easy ascent gives a great grace to a building: where the hall is a preferment out of the court, the parlor out of the hall; not, as in some old buildings, where the doors are so low pigmies must stoop, and the rooms so high that giants may stand upright. But now we are come to contrivance.

5. Let not thy common rooms be several, nor thy several rooms be common. The hall, which is a Pandocheum,[22] ought to lie open, and so ought passages and stairs, provided that the whole house be not spent

---

19 Referring to the deforestation of England through the great use of wood as fuel in smelting the ore.
20 "Though my father Anchises' palace was retired in the privacy of embosoming trees."—Virgil, *Æneid*, II, 299.
21 Water is the best.—Olympian Odes, I, 1.
22 Literally, an inn; a reception room.

in paths; chambers and closets are to be private and retired.

6. Light, God's eldest daughter, is a principal beauty in a building: yet it shines not alike from all parts of heaven. An east window welcomes the infant beams of the sun, before they are of strength to do any harm, and is offensive to none but a sluggard. A south window in summer is a chimney with a fire in it, and needs the screen of a curtain. In a west window in summer time towards night, the sun grows low, and over-familiar, with more light than delight. A north window is best for butteries and cellars, where the beer will be sour for the sun's smiling on it. Thorough-lights are best for rooms of entertainment, and windows on one side for dormitories. As for receipt,

7. A house had better be too little for a day than too great for a year. And 'tis easier borrowing of thy neighbor a brace of chambers for a night than a bag of money for a twelvemonth. It is vain, therefore, to proportion the receipt to an extraordinary occasion, as those who by overbuilding their houses have dilapidated their lands, and their states have been pressed to death under the weight of their house. As for strength,

8. Country houses must be substantives, able to stand of themselves: not like city buildings supported by their neighbors on either side. By strength we mean such as may resist weather and time, not invasion, castles being out of date in this peaceable age. As for the making of moats round about, it is questionable whether the fogs be not more unhealthful than the fish brings profits, or the water defense. Beauty remains behind as the last to be regarded, because houses are made to be lived in, not looked on.

9. Let not the front look asquint on a stranger, but accost him right at his entrance. Uniformity also much pleaseth the eye; and 'tis observed that freestone, like a fair complexion, soonest waxeth old, whilst brick keeps her beauty longest.

10. Let the office-houses observe the due distance from the mansion-house. Those are too familiar which presume to be of the same pile with it. The same may be said of stables and barns; without which a house is like a city without out-works, it can never hold out long.

11. Gardens also are to attend in their place. When God (Gen. 2:9) planted a garden eastward, he made to grow out of the ground every tree pleasant to the sight, and good for food. Sure he knew better what was proper to a garden than those who now-a-days therein only feed the eyes, and starve both taste and smell.

To conclude, in building rather believe any man than an artificer in his own art for matter of charges; not that they cannot, but will not be faithful. Should they tell thee all the cost at the first, it would blast a young builder in the budding, and therefore they soothe thee up till it hath cost thee something to confute them. The spirit of building first possessed people after the Flood, which then caused the confusion of languages, and since of the estate of many a man.

OF MEMORY

IT IS the treasure house of the mind, wherein the monuments thereof are kept and preserved. Plato makes it the mother of the muses. Aristotle sets it one degree further, making experience the mother of arts, memory the parent of experience. Philosophers place it in the rear of the head; and it seems the mine of memory lies there, because there naturally men dig for it, scratching it when they are at a loss. This again is twofold; one, the simple retention of things; the other, a regaining them when forgotten

1. Brute creatures equal if not excel men in a bare retentive memory. Through how many labyrinths of woods, without other clue of thread than natural instinct, doth the hunted hare return to her mace?[23] How doth the little bee, flying into several meadows and gardens, sipping of many cups, yet never intoxicated, through an ocean (as I may say) of air, steadily steer herself home, without help of card or compass. But these cannot play an aftergame, and recover what they have forgotten, which is done by the meditation of discourse.

2. Artificial memory is rather a trick than an art, and more for the gain of the teacher than profit of the learners. Like the tossing of a pike, which is no part of the postures and motions thereof, and is rather for ostentation than use, to show the strength and nimbleness of the arm, and is often used by wandering soldiers as an introduction to beg. Understand it of the artificial rules which at this day are delivered by memory-mountebanks; for sure an art thereof may be made (wherein as yet the world is defective) and that no more destructive to natural memory than spectacles are to eyes, which girls in Holland wear from 12 years of age. But till this be found out, let us observe these plain rules.

23 Hiding place.

3. First, soundly infix in thy mind what thou desirest to remember. What wonder is it if agitation of business jog that out of thy head which was there rather tacked than fastened? Whereas those notions which get in by *violenta possessio* will abide there till *ejectio firma*, sickness or extreme age, dispossess them. It is best knocking in the nail overnight, and clinching it the next morning.

4. Overburden not thy memory to make so faithful a servant a slave. Remember Atlas was weary. Have as much reason as a camel, to rise when thou hast thy full load. Memory, like a purse, if it be over full that it cannot shut, all will drop out of it. Take heed of a gluttonous curiosity to feed on many things, lest the greediness of the appetite of thy memory spoil the digestion thereof. Beza's[24] case was peculiar and memorable; being above fourscore years of age he perfectly could say by heart any Greek chapter in St. Paul's Epistles, or anything else which he had learnt long before, but forgot whatsoever was newly told him; his memory like an inn retaining old guests, but having no room to entertain new.

5. Spoil not thy memory with thine own jealousy, nor make it bad by suspecting it. How canst thou find that true which thou wilt not trust? St. Augustine tells us of his friend Simplicius, who being asked, could tell all Virgil's verses backward and forward, and yet the same party vowed to God, that he knew not that he could do it till they did try him. Sure there is concealed strength in men's memories, which they take no notice of.

6. Marshal thy notions into a handsome method. One will carry twice more weight trussed and packed up in bundles than when it lies untowardly flapping and hanging about his shoulders. Things orderly fardled[25] up under heads are most portable.

7. Adventure not all thy learning in one bottom, but divide it betwixt thy memory and thy notebooks. He that with bias carries all his learning about him in his head will utterly be beggared and bankrupt, if a violent disease, a merciless thief, should rob and strip him. I know some have a commonplace against commonplace books, and yet perchance will privately make use of what publicly they declaim against. A commonplace book contains many notions in garrison, whence the owner may draw out an army into the field on competent warning.

8. Moderate diet and good air preserve memory; but what air is best I dare not define, when such great ones differ. Some say a pure and subtle air is best, another commends a thick and foggy air. For the Pisans sited in the fens and marsh of Arnus have excellent memories, as if the foggy air were a cap for their heads.

9. Thankfulness to God, for it continues the memory; whereas some proud people have been visited with such oblivion that they have forgotten their own names. Staupitius, tutor to Luther, and a godly man, in a vain ostentation of his memory repeated Christ's genealogy (Matt. 1) by heart in his sermon; but being out about the captivity of Babylon, "I see," saith he, "God resisteth the proud," and so betook himself to his book. Abuse not thy memory to be sin's register, nor make advantage thereof for wickedness, Excellently Augustine, *Quidam vero pessimi memoria sunt mirabili, qui tanto pejores sunt, quanto minus possunt, quæ male cogitant, oblivisci.*[26]

OF FANCY

IT IS an inward sense of the soul, for a while retaining and examining things brought in thither by the common sense. It is the most boundless and restless faculty of the soul: for whilst the understanding and the will are kept as it were in *libera custodia* to their objects of *verum et bonum*, the fancy is free from all engagements: it digs without spade, sails without ship, flies without wings, builds without charges, fights without bloodshed, in a moment striding from the center to the circumference of the world, by a kind of omnipotency creating and annihilating things in an instant; and things divorced in nature are married in fancy as in a lawless place. It is also most restless: whilst the senses are bound, and reason in a manner asleep, fancy, like a sentinel, walks the round, ever working, never wearied. The chief diseases of the fancy are, either that they are too wild and high soaring, or else too low and groveling, or else too desultory and over-voluble. Of the first,

1. If thy fancy be but a little too rank, age itself will correct it. To lift too high is no fault in a young horse, because with traveling he will mend it for his own ease. Thus lofty fancies in young men will come down to themselves, and in process of time the overplus will

24 Théodore Beza (Fr. de Bèze), French reformer and Calvinistic theologian (1519–1605).
25 Bundled.

26 Certain wicked men, in sooth, are remarkable for their memory, and are all the worse for being unable to forget the wicked things that they think upon. (*de Civitate Dei*, vii. 3.)

shrink to be but even measure. But if this will not do it, then observe these rules.

2. Take part always with thy judgment against thy fancy in anything wherein they shall dissent. If thou suspectest thy conceits too luxuriant, herein account thy suspicion a legal conviction, and damn whatsoever thou doubtest of. Warily Tully: *Bene monent, qui vetant quicquam facere, de quo dubitas, æquum sit an iniquum.*[27]

3. Take the advice of a faithful friend, and submit thy inventions to his censure. When thou pennest an oration, let him have the power of *index expurgatorius*, to expunge what he pleaseth; and do not thou, like a fond mother, cry if the child of thy brain be corrected for playing the wanton. Mark the arguments and reasons of his alterations; why *that* phrase least proper, *this* passage more cautious and advised; and after a while thou shalt perform the place in thine own person, and not go out of thyself for a censurer. If thy fancy be too low and humble,

4. Let thy judgment be king, but not tyrant over it, to condemn harmless, yea, commendable, conceits. Some for fear their orations should giggle, will not let them smile. Give it also liberty to rove, for it will not be extravagant. There is no danger that weak folks, if they walk abroad, will straggle far, as wanting strength.

5. Acquaint thyself with reading poets, for there fancy is in her throne; and in time, the sparks of the author's wit will catch hold on the reader, and inflame him with love, liking, and desire of imitation. I confess there is more required to teach one to write than to see a copy: however, there is a secret force of fascination in reading poems to raise and provoke fancy. If thy fancy be over-voluble, then

6. Whip this vagrant home to the first object whereon it should be settled. Indeed, nimbleness is the perfection of this faculty, but levity the bane of it. Great is the difference between a swift horse and a skittish, that will stand on no ground. Such is the ubiquitary fancy, which will keep long residence on no one subject, but is so courteous to strangers that it ever welcomes that conceit most which comes last; and new species supplant the old ones, before seriously considered. If this be the fault of thy fancy, I say whip it home to the first object whereon it should be settled. This do as often as occasion requires, and by degrees

the fugitive servant will learn to abide by his work without running away.

7. Acquaint thyself by degrees with hard and knotty studies, as School-divinity, which will clog thy overnimble fancy. True, at the first it will be as welcome to thee as a prison, and their very solutions will seem knots unto thee. But take not too much at once, lest thy brain turn edge. Taste it first as a potion for physic, and by degrees thou shalt drink it as beer for thirst: practice will make it pleasant. Mathematics are also good for this purpose. If beginning to try a conclusion, thou must make an end, lest thou losest thy pains that are past, and must proceed seriously and exactly. I meddle not with those bedlam-fancies, all whose conceits are antiques, but leave them for the physician to purge with hellebore.

8. To clothe low-creeping matter with high-flown language is not fine fancy, but flat foolery. It rather loads than raises a wren, to fasten the feathers of an estridge to her wings. Some men's speeches are like the high mountains in Ireland, having a dirty bog in the top of them: the very ridge of them in high words having nothing of worth, but what rather stalls than delights the auditor.

9. Fine fancies in manufactures invent engines rather pretty than useful; and commonly one trade is too narrow for them. They are better to project new ways than to prosecute old, and are rather skillful in many mysteries than thriving in one. They affect not voluminous inventions, wherein many years must constantly be spent to perfect them, except there be in them variety of pleasant employment.

10. Imagination, the work of the fancy, hath produced real effects. Many serious and sad examples hereof may be produced: I will only insist on a merry one. A gentleman having led a company of children beyond their usual journey, they began to be weary, and jointly cried to him to carry them; which, because of their multitude, he could not do, but told them he would provide them horses to ride on. Then cutting little wands out of the hedge as nags for them, and a great stake as a gelding for himself, thus mounted, fancy put metal into their legs, and they came cheerfully home.

11. Fancy runs most furiously when a guilty conscience drives it. One that owed much money, and had many creditors, as he walked London streets in the evening, a tenter-hook catched his cloak. "At whose suit?" said he, conceiving some bailiff had arrested him. Thus guilty consciences are afraid where no fear is,

---

[27] They counsel well who tell you not to do anything of whose propriety you are in doubt. (*de Officiis*, I. 9.)

and count every creature they meet a sergeant sent from God to punish them.

OF BOOKS

SOLOMON saith truly, "Of making many books there is no end,"[28] so insatiable is the thirst of men therein: as also endless is the desire of many in buying and reading them. But we come to our rules.

1. It is a vanity to persuade the world one hath much learning, by getting a great library. As soon shall I believe everyone is valiant that hath a well furnished armory. I guess good housekeeping by the smoking, not the number of the tunnels, as knowing that many of them, built merely for uniformity, are without chimneys, and more without fires. Once a dunce void of learning but full of books flouted a libraryless scholar with these words: "*Salve, doctor sine libris.*" But the next day the scholar coming into this jeerer's study, crowded with books; "*Salvete libri*," saith he, "*sine doctore.*"

2. Few books, well selected, are best. Yet, as a certain fool bought all the pictures that came out, because he might have his choice, such is the vain humor of many men in gathering of books: yet when they have done all, they miss their end, it being in the editions of authors as in the fashions of clothes, when a man thinks he hath gotten the latest and newest, presently another newer comes out.

3. Some books are only cursorily to be tasted of. Namely first, voluminous books, the task of a man's life to read them over; secondly, auxiliary books, only to be repaired to on occasions; thirdly, such as are mere pieces of formality, so that if you look on them, you look through them; and he that peeps through the casement of the index, sees as much as if he were in the house. But the laziness of those cannot be excused who perfunctorily pass over authors of consequence, and only trade in their tables and contents. These, like city-cheaters, having gotten the names of all country gentlemen, make silly people believe they have long lived in those places where they never were, and flourish with skill in those authors they never seriously studied.

4. The genius of the author is commonly discovered in the dedicatory epistle. Many place the purest grain in the mouth of the sack for chapmen to handle or buy: and from the dedication one may probably guess at the work, saving some rare and peculiar exceptions. Thus, when once a gentleman admired how so pithy, learned and witty a dedication was matched to a flat, dull, foolish book: "In truth," said another, "they may be well matched together, for I profess they are nothing akin."

5. Proportion an hour's meditation to an hour's reading of a staple author. This makes a man master of his learning, and dispirits the book into the scholar. The King of Sweden never filed his men above six deep in one company, because he would not have them lie in useless clusters in his army, but so that every particular soldier might be drawn out into service. Books that stand thin on the shelves, yet so as the owner of them can bring forth every one of them into use, are better than far greater libraries.

6. Learning hath gained most by those books by which the printers have lost. Arius Montanus, in printing the Hebrew Bible, commonly called the Bible of the King of Spain, much wasted himself, and was accused in the court of Rome for his good deed, and being cited thither, *Pro tantorum laborum præmio vix veniam impetravit.*[29] Likewise Christopher Plantin, by printing of his curious interlineary Bible, in Antwerp, through the unseasonable exactions of the king's officers, sunk and almost ruined his estate.[30] And our worthy English knight, who set forth the golden-mouthed father in a silver print, was a loser by it.[31]

7. Whereas foolish pamphlets prove most beneficial to the printers. When a French printer complained that he was utterly undone by printing a solid serious book of Rabelais concerning physic, Rabelais, to make him recompense, made that his jesting scurrilous work, which repaid the printer's loss with advantage. Such books the world swarms too much with. When one had set out with a witless pamphlet, writing *finis* at the end thereof, another wittily wrote beneath it,

——Nay, there thou liest, my friend.
In writing foolish books there is no end.

And surely such scurrilous scandalous papers do more than conceivable mischief. First, their lusciousness puts many palates out of taste, that they can never

---

28 Ecclesiastes 12:12.

29 With difficulty obtained pardon as a reward of his great labor.—Thuanus, *Obitus Virorum doctorum, anno* 1598. (Fuller.)

30 *Idem, in eodem oper,* 1589. (Fuller.)

31 Sir Henry Savile's edition of Chrysostom in eight volumes, 1610–1613.—See Hallam's Literature of Europe, Part III, ch. 1.

after relish any solid and wholesome writers; secondly, they cast dirt on the faces of many innocent persons, which dried on by continuance of time can never after be washed off; thirdly, the pamphlets of this age may pass for records with the next, because publicity uncontrolled, and what we laugh at, our children may believe: fourthly, grant the things true they jeer at, yet this music is unlawful in any Christian church, to play upon the sins and miseries of others, the fitter object of the elegies than the satires of all truly religious.

But what do I speaking against multiplicity of books in this age, who trespass in this nature myself? What was a learned man's compliment, may serve for my confession and conclusion: "*Multi mei similes hoc morbo laborant, ut cum scribere nescient tamen a scribendo temperare non possint.*"[32]

32 Many of my fellows are afflicted with this disease, who, though they know not how to write, are yet unable to refrain from writing.—Erasmus, Preface to the Works of Jerome, Series 3, vol. IV, p. 408. (Fuller.)

F R O M

THE CHURCH HISTORY OF BRITAIN

[TEXT: *first edition, 1655*]

from BOOK IV, CENTURY 14

GEOFFREY CHAUCER

WE MAY couple with him[1] his contemporary, Geoffrey Chaucer, born (some say) in Berkshire, others in Oxfordshire, most and truest in London. If the Grecian Homer had seven, let our English have three places contest for his nativity. Our Homer (I say) only herein he differed:

Mæonides nullas ipse reliquit opes:

Homer himself did leave no pelf,

whereas our Chaucer left behind him a rich and worshipful estate.

His father was a vintner in London; and I have heard his arms quarreled at, being argent and gules strangely contrived, and hard to be blazoned. Some more wits have made it the dashing of white and red wine (the parents of our ordinary claret) as nicking his father's profession. But were Chaucer alive, he would justify his own arms in the face of all his opposers, being not so devoted to the muses but he was also a son of Mars. He was the prince of English poets; married the daughter[2] of Payne Roët, king of arms in France,

1 John de Trevysa.
2 Chaucer's wife, according to the generally accepted theory, was Philippa, the daughter of Sir Payne Roët, a knight of Hainaut, and king of arms in Guienne in the reign of Edward III.

and sister to the wife of John of Gaunt, king of Castile.

He was a great refiner and illuminer of our English tongue (and if he left it so bad, how much worse did he find it?), witness Leland thus praising him:

Prædicat Aligerum merito Florentia Dantem,
Italia et numeros tota Petrarche tuos.
Anglia Chaucerum veneratur nostra poetam,
Cui veneres debet patria lingua suas.

Of Alger Dante, Florence doth justly boast,
Of Petrarch brags all the Italian coast,
England doth poet Chaucer reverence,
To whom our language owes its eloquence.

Indeed Verstegan,[3] a learned antiquary, condemns him for spoiling the purity of the English tongue, by the mixture of so many French and Latin words. But he who mingles wine with water, though he destroys the nature of water, improves the quality thereof.

I find this Chaucer fined in the temple two shillings for striking a Franciscan friar in Fleet street, and it seems his hands ever after itched to be revenged, and have his pennyworths out of them, so tickling religious orders with his tales, and yet so pinching them with his truths, that friars in reading his books know not how to dispose their faces betwixt crying and laughing. He lies buried in the south aisle of St. Peter's, Westminster, and since hath got the company of Spenser and Drayton (a pair-royal of poets) enough almost to make passengers' feet to move metrically, who go over the place where so much poetical dust is interred.

3 In his Restitution of Decayed Intelligence, p. 203. (Fuller.)

from BOOK IV, CENTURY 15

JOHN WYCLIFFE

HITHERTO the corpse of John Wycliffe had quietly slept in his grave, about one-and-forty years after his death, till his body was reduced to bones, and his bones almost to dust; for though the earth in the chancel of Lutterworth in Leicestershire, where he was interred, hath not so quick a digestion with the earth of Acel-dama, to consume flesh in twenty-four hours, yet such the appetite thereof, and all other English graves, [as] to leave small reversions of a body after so many years.

But now, such the spleen of the council of Constance, as they not only cursed his memory, as dying an obstinate heretic, but ordered that his bones (with this charitable caution, if it may be discerned from the bodies of other faithful people) to be taken out of the ground and thrown far off from any Christian burial.

In obedience hereunto, Richard Flemyng, Bishop of Lincoln, diocesan of Lutterworth, sent his officers (vultures with a quick sight-scent at a dead carcase) to ungrave him accordingly. To Lutterworth they come (sumner, commissary, official, chancellor, proctors, doctors, and the servants, so that the remnant of the body would not hold out a bone amongst so many hands), take what was left out of the grave, and burnt them to ashes, and cast them into Swift, a neighboring brook running hard by. Thus this brook hath conveyed his ashes into Avon, Avon into Severn, Severn into the narrow seas, they into the main ocean; and thus the ashes of Wycliffe are the emblem of his doctrine, which now is dispersed all the world over.

I know not whether the vulgar tradition be worth remembrance, that the brook into which Wycliffe his ashes were poured never since overflowed the banks. Were this true (as some deny it), as silly is the inference of Papists attributing this to divine providence, expressing itself pleased with such severity on a heretic, as simple the collection of some Protestants making it an effect of Wycliffe his sanctity. Such topical accidents are good for friend and foe, as they may be bowed to both; but in effect good to neither, seeing no solid judgment will build where bare fancy hath laid foundation.

FROM

THE HISTORY OF THE WORTHIES OF ENGLAND, ENDEAVORED BY THOMAS FULLER, D.D.

[TEXT: *first edition, 1662*]

BERKSHIRE

WILLIAM LAUD

WILLIAM LAUD was born at Reading in this county, of honest parentage, bred in St. John's College in Oxford, whereof he became president: successively Bishop of St. David's, Bath and Wells, London, and at last Archbishop of Canterbury. One of low stature but high parts; piercing eyes, cheerful countenance, wherein gravity and pleasantness were well compounded; admirable in his naturals, unblamable in morals, being very strict in his conversation. Of him I have written in my "Ecclesiastical History"; though I confess it was somewhat too soon for one with safety and truth to treat of such a subject. Indeed I could instance in some kind of coarse venison, not fit for food when first killed; and therefore cunning cooks bury it for some hours in the earth, till the rankness thereof being mortified thereby, it makes most palatable meat. So the memory of some persons newly deceased are neither fit for a writer's or reader's repast, until some competent time after their interment. However, I am confident that impartial posterity, on a serious review of all passages, will allow his name to be reposed amongst the heroes of our nation, seeing such as behold his expense on St. Paul's as but a cipher, will assign his other benefactions a very valuable signification; *viz.*, his erecting and endowing an almshouse in Reading, his increasing of Oxford library with books, and St. John's College with beautiful buildings. He was beheaded January 10, 1644.

ALFRED THE GREAT

ALFRED, the fourth son to King Athelwolf, was born at Wantage, a market town in this county; an excellent scholar, though he was past twelve years of age before he knew one letter in the book. And did not he run fast, who starting so late came soon to the mark? He was a curious poet, excellent musician, a valiant and successful soldier, who fought seven battles against the Danes in one year, and at last made them his subjects by conquest, and God's servants by Christianity. He gave the first institution, or (as others will have it) the best instauration, to the University of Oxford. A prince who cannot be painted to the life without his loss, no words reaching his worth.

He divided, 1. Every natural day (as to himself) into three parts: eight hours for his devotion, eight hours for his employment, eight hours for his sleep and refection. 2. His revenues into three parts: one for his expenses in war, a second for the maintenance of his court, and a third to be spent on pious uses. 3. His land into thirty-two shires, which number since is altered and increased. 4. His subjects into hundreds and tithings, consisting of ten persons, mutually pledges for their good behavior; such being accounted suspicious for their life and loyalty that could not give such security.

He left learning, where he found ignorance; justice, where he found oppression; peace, where he found distraction. And, having reigned about four and thirty years, he died, and was buried at Winchester, *anno* 901. He loved religion more than superstition, favored learned men more than lazy monks; which, perchance, was the cause that his memory is not loaden with miracles, and he not solemnly sainted with other Saxon kings who far less deserved it.

BEDFORDSHIRE

HENRY DE ESSEX

HE IS too well known in our English chronicles, being Baron of Raleigh in Essex, and hereditary standard-bearer of England. It happened in the reign of this king[1] there was a fierce battle fought in Flintshire, at Coleshull, betwixt the English and Welsh, wherein this Henry de Essex, *animum et signum simul abjecit* ("betwixt traitor and coward cast away both his courage and banner together"), occasioning a great overflow of English.

But he that had the baseness to do, had the boldness to deny the doing of, so foul a fact; until he was challenged in combat by Robert de Momford, a knight, eye-witness thereof, and by him overcome in a duel; whereupon his large inheritance was confiscated to the king, and he himself, partly thrust, partly going, into a convent, hid his head in a cowl, under which, betwixt shame and sanctity, he blushed out the remainder of his life.

CHESHIRE

CAPTAIN JOHN SMITH

JOHN SMITH, Captain, was born in this county, as Master Arthur Smith, his kinsman and my schoolmaster, did inform me. But whether or no related unto the worshipful family of the Smiths at Hatherton, I know not.

He spent the most of his life in foreign parts. First in Hungary, under the emperor, fighting against the Turks; three of which he himself killed in single duels; and therefore was authorized by Sigismund, King of Hungary, to bear three Turk's heads, as an augmentation to his arms. Here he gave intelligence to a besieged city in the night, by significant fireworks formed in the air, in legible characters, with many strange performances, the scene whereof is laid at such a distance, they are cheaper credited than confuted.

From the Turks in Europe he passed to the pagans in America, where, towards the latter end of the reign of Queen Elizabeth, such his perils, preservations, dangers, deliverances, they seem to most men above belief, to some beyond truth. Yet have we two witnesses to attest them, the prose and the pictures, both in his own book; and it soundeth much to the diminution of his deeds that he alone is the herald to publish and proclaim them.

Two captains being at dinner, one of them fell into a large relation of his own achievements, concluding his discourse with this question to his fellow, "And

1 Henry II, 1154–1189.

pray, Sir," said he, "what service have you done?" To whom he answered, "Other men can tell that." And surely such reports from strangers carry with them the greater reputation. However, moderate men must allow Captain Smith to have been very instrumental in settling the plantation in Virginia, whereof he was governor, as also admiral of New England.

He led his old age in London, where his having a prince's mind imprisoned in a poor man's purse rendered him to the contempt of such who were not ingenuous. Yet he efforted his spirits with the remembrance and relation of what formerly he had been, and what he had done. He was buried in Sepulchre's Church choir, on the south side thereof, having a ranting epitaph inscribed in a table over him, too long to transcribe. Only we will insert the first and last verses, the rather because the one may fit Alexander's life for his valor, the other his death for his religion:

> Here lies one conquer'd that hath conquer'd kings!
> Oh, may his soul in sweet Elysium sleep.

The orthography, poetry, history and divinity in this epitaph are much alike. He died on the 21st of June, 1631.

JOHN DOD

JOHN DOD was born at Shottliege, in this county (where his parents had a competent estate); bred in Jesus College in Cambridge, by nature a witty, by industry a learned, by grace a godly divine; successively minister of Hanwell in Oxford, Fenny-Compton in Warwick, Canons-Ashby and Fawsley in Northamptonshire, though for a time silenced in each of them.

A father (who shall pass nameless) is censured by some for his over-curiosity in his conceit rather than comment, Matt. 5:2. "And he opened his mouth, and taught them."—"For Christ," saith he, "taught them often, when he opened not his mouth, by his example, miracles, etc." Here I am sure, accordingly, Master Dod, when "his mouth was shut" (prohibiting preaching), instructed almost as much as before, by his holy demeanor and pious discourse; a good chemist, who could extract gold out of other men's lead; and how loose soever the premises of other men's discourse, piety was always his natural and unforced conclusion inferred thereupon.

For the rest, I refer the reader to Master Samuel Clark, by whom his life is written, wherein are many remarkable passages: I say Master Samuel Clark, with whose pen mine never did or shall interfere. Indeed, as the flocks of Jacob were distanced "three days' journeys" from those of Laban,[2] so (to prevent voluntary or casual commixtures) our styles are set more than a month's journey asunder.

The Jewish Rabbins have a fond and a false conceit, that Methusalem, who indeed died in the very year (and his death a sad prognostic) of the deluge, had a cabin built him in the outside of Noah's ark, where he was preserved by himself. But most true it is, that good Father Dod, though he lived to see the flood of our late civil wars, made to himself a cabin in his own contented conscience; and though his clothes were wetted with the waves (when plundered), he was dry in the deluge, such his self-solace in his holy meditations. He died, being eighty-six years of age, *anno* 1645.

When thieves break in a house and steal, the owner thereof knows for the present that he is robbed, but not of what or how much, till some days after he finds out by the want of such things which were taken from him. The vicinage of Fawsley, where Mr. Dod died, knew then they were bereft of a worthy treasure, though ignorant in the particulars of their losses, till daily discovery hath by this time made them sensible thereof.

CORNWALL

KING ARTHUR

KING ARTHUR, son of Uther Pendragon, was born in Tintagel castle in this county; and proved afterwards monarch of Great Britain. He may fitly be termed the British Hercules in three respects:

1. For his illegitimate birth, both being bastards, begotten on other men's wives, and yet their mothers honest women; deluded, the one by a miracle, the other by art magic of Merlin, in others personating their husbands.

2. Painful life; one famous for his twelve labors, the other for his twelve victories against the Saxons; and both of them had been greater, had they been made less, and the reports of them reduced within the compass of probability.

3. Violent and woeful death; our Arthur's being as

---

2 Genesis 30:36.

lamentable, and more honorable; not caused by feminine jealousy, but masculine treachery, being murdered by Modred, near the place where he was born:

As though no other place on Britain's spacious earth
Were worthy of his end, but where he had his birth. [3]

As for his Round Table, with his knights about it, the tale whereof hath trundled so smoothly along for many ages, it never met with much belief amongst the judicious. He died about the year 542.

And now to speak of the Cornish in general. They ever have been beheld men of valor. It seemeth in the reign of the aforesaid King Arthur they ever made up his vanguard, if I can rightly understand the barbarous verses of a Cornish poet: [4]

Nobilis Arcturus nos primos Cornubienses
Bellum facturus vocat (ut puta Cæsaris enses).
Nobis (non aliis reliquis) dat primitus ictum.

Brave Arthur, when he meant a field to fight,
Us Cornish men did first of all invite.
Only to Cornish (count them Cæsar's swords)
He the first blow in battle still affords.

But afterwards, in the time of King Canutus, the Cornish were appointed to make up the rear of our armies. Say not they were much degraded by this transposition from head to foot, seeing the judicious, in marshaling of an army, count the strength (and therefore the credit) to consist in the rear thereof.

But it must be pitied that this people, misguided by their leaders, have so often abused their valor in rebellions, and particularly in the reign of King Henry the Seventh, at Blackheath, where they did the greatest execution with their arrows, reported to be the length of a tailor's yard, the last of that proportion which ever were seen in England. However, the Cornish have since plentifully repaired their credit, by their exemplary valor and loyalty in our late civil wars.

LONDON

EDMUND SPENSER

EDMUND SPENSER, born in this city, was brought up in Pembroke Hall in Cambridge, where he be-
came an excellent scholar; but especially most happy in English poetry, as his works do declare; in which the many Chaucerisms used (for I will not say affected by him) are thought by the ignorant to be blemishes, known by the learned to be beauties, to his book, which notwithstanding had been more salable, if more conformed to our modern language.

There passeth a story commonly told and believed, that Spenser presenting his poems to Queen Elizabeth, she, highly affected therewith, commanded the Lord Cecil, her treasurer, to give him a hundred pounds; and when the treasurer (a good steward of the Queen's money) alleged that the sum was too much, "Then give him," quoth the queen, "what is reason"; to which the lord consented. But was so busied, belike, about matters of high concernment that Spenser received no reward; whereupon he presented this petition in a small piece of paper to the queen in her progress:

I was promis'd on a time,
To have reason for my rhyme;
From that time unto this season,
I receiv'd nor rhyme nor reason.

Hereupon the queen gave strict order (not without some check to her treasurer) for the present payment of the hundred pounds she first intended unto him.

He afterwards went over into Ireland, secretary to the Lord Gray, Lord Deputy thereof; and though that his office under his lord was lucrative, yet got he no estate; but, saith my author,[5] "*peculiari poetis fato, semper cum paupertate conflictatus est.*" So that it fared little better with him than with William Xilander the German (a most excellent linguist, antiquary, philosopher, and mathematician), who was so poor that (as Thuanus saith) he was thought, "*fami non fame scribere.*" [6]

Returning into England, he was robbed by the rebels of that little he had; and dying for grief in great want, *anno* 1598, was honorably buried nigh Chaucer in Westminster, where this distich concluded his epitaph on his monument:

Anglica te vivo vixit plausitque poesis,
Nunc moritura timet te moriente mori.

Whilst thou didst live, liv'd English poetry,
Which fears, now thou art dead, that she shall die.

---

3 Drayton's Polyolbion, First Song, lines 189, 190.
4 Michael Cornubiensis. (Fuller.)
5 Camden's Elizabeth, in *anno* 1598. (Fuller.)
6 *Fami non fame* [= *famæ*] *scribere*: to write for hunger, not for fame.

Nor must we forget, that the expense of his funeral and monument was defrayed at the sole charge of Robert, first of that name, Earl of Essex.

WESTMINSTER

BENJAMIN JONSON

BENJAMIN JONSON was born in this city. Though I cannot, with all my industrious inquiry, find him in his cradle, I can fetch him from his long coats. When a little child, he lived in Harts-horn-lane near Charing-cross, where his mother married a bricklayer for her second husband.

He was first bred in a private school in Saint Martin's Church; then in Westminster School; witness his own epigram;[7]

> Camden, most reverend head, to whom I owe
> All that I am in arts, all that I know;
> How nothing's that to whom my country owes
> The great renown and name wherewith she goes, etc.

He was statutably admitted into Saint John's College in Cambridge (as many years after incorporated an honorary member of Christ Church in Oxford), where he continued but few weeks for want of further maintenance, being fain to return to the trade of his father-in-law. And let them blush not that have, but those who have not, a lawful calling. He helped in the new structure of Lincoln's Inn, when, having a trowel in his hand, he had a book in his pocket.

Some gentlemen, pitying that his parts should be buried under the rubbish of so mean a calling, did by their bounty manumise[8] him freely to follow his own ingenious inclinations. Indeed his parts were not so ready to run of themselves as able to answer the spur; so that it may be truly said of him, that he had an elaborate wit wrought out in his own industry. He would sit silent in a learned company, and suck in (besides wine) their several humors into his observation. What was ore in others, he was able to refine to himself.

He was paramount in the dramatic part of poetry, and taught the stage an exact conformity to the laws of comedians. His comedies were above the *volge*

(which are only tickled with downright obscenity), and took not so well at the first stroke as at the rebound, when beheld the second time; yea, they will endure reading, and that with due commendation, so long as either ingenuity or learning are fashionable in our nation. If his later be not so spriteful and vigorous as his first pieces, all that are old will, and all that desire to be old should, excuse him therein.

He was not very happy in his children, and most happy in those which died first, though none lived to survive him. This he bestowed as part of an epitaph on his eldest son, dying in infancy:

> Rest in soft peace; and, ask'd, say here doth lie,
> Ben Jonson his best piece of poetry.[9]

He died *anno Domini* 1638; and was buried about the belfry, in the abbey church at Westminster.

WARWICKSHIRE

WILLIAM SHAKESPEARE

WILLIAM SHAKESPEARE was born at Stratford-on-Avon in this county; in whom three eminent poets may seem in some sort to be compounded. 1. Martial, in the warlike sound of his surname (whence some may conjecture him of military extraction) *Hasti-vibrans*, or Shake-speare. 2. Ovid, the most natural and witty of all poets; and hence it was that Queen Elizabeth, coming into a grammar school, made this extemporary phrase,

> Persius a crab-staff, bawdy Martial,
> Ovid a fine wag.

3. Plautus, who was an exact comedian, yet never any scholar, as our Shakespeare (if alive) would confess himself. Add to all these, that though his genius generally was jocular, and inclining him to festivity, yet he could (when so disposed) be solemn and serious, as appears by his tragedies; so that Heraclitus himself (I mean if secret and unseen) might afford to smile at his comedies, they were so merry; and Democritus scarce forbear to sigh at his tragedies, they were so mournful.

He was an eminent instance of the truth of that rule,

---

7 Epigram 14.　　　　　8 Set free.　　　　　9 Epigram 45.

"*Poeta non fit sed nascitur*" (one is not made but born a poet). Indeed his learning was very little; so that, as Cornish diamonds are not polished by any lapidary, but are pointed and smooth even as they are taken out of the earth, so nature itself was all the art which was used upon him.

Many were the wit-combats betwixt him and Ben Jonson; which two I behold like a Spanish great galleon and an English man-of-war; Master Jonson (like the former) was built far higher in learning; solid, but slow, in his performances. Shakespeare, with the English man-of-war, lesser in bulk, but lighter in sailing, could turn with all tides, tack about, and take advantage of all winds, by the quickness of his wit and invention. He died *anno Domini* 1616, and was buried at Stratford-upon-Avon, the town of his nativity.

John Milton

[1608–1674]

LMOST all of Milton's important prose works were written between 1641 and 1660, during the period of the struggle between king and parliament and the period of the Commonwealth and the Protectorate. It is a body of work elicited by a great man's passionate involvement with the issues of his day; like so much seventeenth-century prose, it aims at achieving practical and immediate results, and, like much of the other great prose of the time, it owes its permanence largely to a stylistic vigor and eloquence which surpass the outdated questions which aroused them. The two prose works here presented, however, stand apart from and above the greater part of Milton's prose not only for their stylistic pre-eminence but also for their concern with matters which are still very much alive and are likely to remain so—the proper ends and methods of education, and freedom of speech.

Milton himself asserts (in *Pro Populo Anglicano Defensio Secunda*, 1654), that his prose works of the 1640's were written in accordance with an orderly scheme for treating religious, domestic, and civil liberty. His breadth of mind and his generous ambitions give credence to the assertion, but one may be pardoned for suspecting that the sequence of these works and the subjects with which they deal were determined to a large degree by the particular events—political and personal—which affected the poet during those years. In 1639, on hearing of the open breach between Charles and his parliamentary opponents, Milton interrupted his travels in Italy to begin his return to England. (An account of Milton's earlier years is given in the introductory note which precedes this volume's selection from his poetry.) In 1641 he entered the lists on the Puritan side with *Of Reformation Touching Church-Discipline in England*, the first of his five antiepiscopal tracts. The others—*Of Prelatical Episcopacy*, *Animadversions upon the Remonstrant's Defense against Smectymnuus*, *The Reason of Church-Government Urged against Prelaty*, and *An Apology for Smectymnuus*—followed soon thereafter.

In 1642 Milton married Mary Powell, the young daughter of a royalist family. Their incompatibility manifested itself with pathetic swiftness, and Mary returned to her family's home only a few months after the marriage. In the next year Milton published *The Doctrine and Discipline of Divorce*, the first of a series of four tracts in which he argued a position which was, for its time, astonishingly liberal, especially in its contention that mental incompatibility was a valid basis for divorce. The years of the divorce controversy (1643–45) also saw the composition of his two most enduring prose works: the short treatise *Of Education*, and *Areopagitica* (both published in 1644). In 1645 Mary returned to her husband, and in the years that followed she bore him four children. His son John died in infancy, but his three daughters survived, the youngest becoming, during the years of his blindness, one of his amanuenses. Mary Powell Milton died in 1652.

Milton's defense of the execution of Charles I (*The Tenure of Kings and Magistrates*, 1649) led to his appointment as Secretary for Foreign Tongues to the Council of State, and his duties in that office involved the writing of *Eikonoklastes*, a reply to the *Eikon Basilike* doubtfully attributed to Charles, and the two weighty Latin tracts in defense of the Commonwealth government, *Defensio pro Populo Anglicano* and *Defensio Secunda*. These works, designed for an international audience, gained for Milton a European reputation, but they cost him his eyes. By 1652 his blindness had become total.

Milton's second marriage, to Katherine Woodcock, in 1656, ended some fifteen months later with her death following childbirth. In 1663 he was married a third time, to Elizabeth Minshull, who outlived him. After the death of Cromwell in 1658, as the doomed government careened toward its inevitable downfall, Milton summoned up his strength once more and, in *The Ready and Easy Way to Establish a Free Commonwealth*, published on the very eve of the Restoration, made a last despairing attempt to persuade his countrymen to retain republican principles. Imprisoned briefly at the time of the Restoration, Milton retired to private life embittered and disillusioned of his bright hopes for the future of his country and his countrymen. To this last period of his life belong the great poetic works of his full maturity, and during this time he wrote no important prose, his posthumously published *History of Britain* and *De Doctrina Christiana* having been brought to their essentially final form before 1660.

Milton's readers have often regretted the stern sense of public responsibility which led the poet, for some twenty years, to turn away from the poetic creation which he was born to achieve and to devote his time, energy, and eyes to the composition of prose tracts which are not only of no abiding interest but are also often repellent in their indulgence in the personal abuse so common in the controversial writing of the period. But, as many of his commentators have pointed out, Milton would not have been true to himself if he had turned his back on what he felt to be his duty, and the moral penetration of the last great poems is rooted firmly in the personal integrity of the poet. Then, too, Milton's experience of public life made an impression on his sensibility which was to show itself in many of the most memorable passages of *Paradise Lost*. Finally, however obsolete he may find the antiepiscopacy and divorce tracts, however unendearing the Latin defenses, the modern reader is scarcely likely to regret a decision which gave *Areopagitica* to our civilization.

Written specifically as a protest against the parliamentary order of June 14, 1643, which required that no book, pamphlet, or paper should be printed without a license from the proper authorities, *Areopagitica* moves from the particular occasion to become a definitive defense of the idea of a free press and free speech. Conceived in the form of a classical oration, the work has a massive dignity of style which can nevertheless modulate into savage irony or soaring imaginativeness. Most significantly, in its awareness of the individual nature of the search for truth and in its conviction that the knowledge of evil is a necessary condition for the knowledge of good, it stands with *Paradise Lost* as a classic statement of one of the central attitudes of western culture.

Areopagitica is essentially a doctrine in the tradition of Christian humanism, and that same tradition informs the tract *On Education*, a work which is, if immeasurably less eloquent, almost comparable in its intrinsic interest. However terrifying his schemes for training youth may appear to contemporary permissiveness, Milton expresses, in this as in his more immediately striking works, a vision of the possibility of human excellence which will continue to serve as an ideal to a culture which has been in part formed by it.

J. MILTON. *Works*, Columbia University Edition, 18 vols., with five supplements and index, 2 vols. (New York, 1931–38, 1940). The standard modern edition.

————. *Complete Prose Works*, general ed. D. M. Wolfe (New Haven, 1953–). Of the eight projected volumes of this important edition, three have appeared to date.

————. *Complete Poems and Major Prose*, ed. M. Y. Hughes (New York, 1957). An excellent volume for the student, with useful observations on Milton scholarship.

D. MASSON. *The Life of John Milton*, 7 vols. (rev. ed., London, 1881–96). A monument of detailed biography.

J. H. HANFORD, *John Milton: Englishman* (New York, 1949). A good short biography.

————. *A Milton Handbook* (4th ed., New York, 1946). A useful survey of scholarship and criticism.

M. KELLEY. *This Great Argument* (Princeton, N.J., 1941). A study of *Paradise Lost* in relation to *De Doctrina Christiana*.

D. M. WOLFE. *Milton in the Puritan Revolution* (New York, 1941).

A. BARKER. *Milton and the Puritan Dilemma* (Toronto, 1942).

OF EDUCATION

[TEXT: *first edition, 1644*]

TO MASTER SAMUEL HARTLIB[1]

MASTER HARTLIB,

I AM long since persuaded that to say or do aught worth memory and imitation, no purpose or respect[2] should sooner move us than simply the love of God and of mankind. Nevertheless, to write now the reforming of education, though it be one of the greatest and noblest designs that can be thought on, and for the want whereof this nation perishes, I had not yet at this time been induced but by your earnest entreaties and serious conjurements; as having my mind diverted for the present in the pursuance of some other assertions,[3] the knowledge and the use of which cannot but be a great furtherance both to the enlargements of truth and honest living with much more peace. Nor should the laws of any private friendship have prevailed with me to divide thus or transpose my former thoughts; but that I see those aims, those actions which have won you with me the esteem of a person sent hither by

some good providence from a far country to be the occasion and incitement of great good to this island, and, as I hear, you have obtained the same repute with men of most approved wisdom and some of the highest authority among us, not to mention the learned correspondence which you hold in foreign parts, and the extraordinary pains and diligence which you have used in this matter both here and beyond the seas, either by the definite will of God so ruling, or the peculiar sway of nature, which also is God's working. Neither can I think, that so reputed and so valued as you are, you would, to the forfeit of your own discerning ability, impose upon me an unfit and overponderous argument; but that the satisfaction which you profess to have received from those incidental discourses which we have wandered into hath pressed and almost constrained you into a persuasion, that what you require from me in this point I neither ought nor can in conscience defer beyond this time both of so much need at once and so much opportunity to try what God hath determined. I will not resist, therefore, whatever it is, either of divine or human obligement, that you lay upon me; but will forthwith set down in writing, as you request me, that voluntary idea, which hath long in silence presented itself to me, of a better education, in extent and comprehension far more

---

1 Samuel Hartlib, London merchant and philanthropist, connected with various projects for educational and social reform.

2 Consideration.

3 The Doctrine and Discipline of Divorce was published in 1643, the Areopagitica, in 1644.

large, and yet of time far shorter and of attainment far more certain than hath been yet in practice. Brief I shall endeavor to be; for that which I have to say, assuredly this nation hath extreme need should be done sooner than spoken. To tell you, therefore, what I have benefited herein among old renowned authors I shall spare; and to search what many modern Januas and Didactics,[4] more than ever I shall read, have projected, my inclination leads me not. But if you can accept of these few observations which have flowered off, and are, as it were, the burnishing of many contemplative years altogether spent in the search of religious and civil knowledge, and such as pleased you so well in the relating, I here give you them to dispose of.

The end, then, of learning is, to repair the ruins of our first parents by regaining to know God aright, and out of that knowledge to love him, to imitate him, to be like him, as we may the nearest by possessing our souls of true virtue, which, being united to the heavenly grace of faith, makes up the highest perfection. But because our understanding cannot in this body found itself but on sensible things, nor arrive so clearly to the knowledge of God and things invisible as by orderly conning over the visible and inferior creature, the same method is necessarily to be followed in all discreet teaching. And seeing every nation affords not experience and tradition enough for all kind of learning, therefore we are chiefly taught the languages of those people who have at any time been most industrious after wisdom; so that language is but the instrument conveying to us things useful to be known. And though a linguist should pride himself to have all the tongues that Babel cleft the world into, yet if he have not studied the solid things in them as well as the words and lexicons, he were nothing so much to be esteemed a learned man as any yeoman or tradesman competently wise in his mother-dialect only. Hence appear the many mistakes which have made learning generally so unpleasing and so unsuccessful. First, we do amiss to spend seven or eight years merely in scraping together so much miserable Latin and Greek as might be learned otherwise easily and delightfully in one year. And that which casts our proficiency therein so much behind is our time lost in too oft idle vacancies given both to schools and universi-

ties; partly in a preposterous[5] exaction, forcing the empty wits of children to compose themes, verses, and orations, which are the acts of ripest judgment, and the final work of a head filled by long reading and observing with elegant maxims and copious invention. These are not matters to be wrung from poor striplings, like blood out of the nose, or the plucking of untimely fruit; besides the ill habit which they get of wretched barbarizing against the Latin and Greek idiom with their untutored Anglicisms, odious to be read, yet not to be avoided without a well-continued and judicious conversing among pure authors, digested, which they scarce taste. Whereas, if after some preparatory grounds of speech by their certain forms got into memory they were led to the praxis hereof in some chosen short book lessoned thoroughly to them, they might then forthwith proceed to learn the substance of good things and arts in due order, which would bring the whole language quickly into their power. This I take to be the most rational and most profitable way of learning languages, and whereby we may best hope to give account to God of our youth spent herein.

And for the usual method of teaching arts,[6] I deem it to be an old error of universities, not yet well recovered from the scholastic grossness of barbarous ages, that instead of beginning with arts most easy (and those be such as are most obvious to the sense), they present their young unmatriculated novices at first coming with the most intellective abstractions of logic and metaphysics; so that they having but newly left those grammatic flats and shallows where they stuck unreasonably to learn a few words with lamentable construction, and now on the sudden transported under another climate, to be tossed and turmoiled with their unballasted wits in fathomless and unquiet deeps of controversy, do, for the most part, grow into hatred and contempt of learning, mocked and deluded all this while with ragged notions and babblements, while they expected worthy and delightful knowledge; till poverty or youthful years[7] call them importunately their several ways, and hasten them, with the sway of friends, either to an ambitious and mercenary, or ignorantly zealous divinity: some allured to the trade of law, grounding their purposes not on the prudent

---

4 The *Janua Linguorum Reserata*, and the *Didactica Magna* of the great German educator Comenius, which outline schemes of education not greatly dissimilar to Milton's own plan, although he seems here to disclaim any influence of Comenius.

5 Putting first that which should naturally and logically come last.
6 The various branches of learning which formed the curriculum for the B.A. degree.
7 The immaturity and impatience of youthful years.

and heavenly contemplation of justice and equity, which was never taught them, but on the promising and pleasing thoughts of litigious terms, fat contentions, and flowing fees; others betake them to state affairs with souls so unprincipled in virtue and true generous breeding that flattery, and courtships, and tyrannous aphorisms appear to them the highest points of wisdom, instilling their barren hearts with a conscientious slavery, if, as I rather think, it be not feigned; others, lastly, of a more delicious and airy spirit, retire themselves, knowing no better, to the enjoyments of ease and luxury, living out their days in feast and jollity, which, indeed, is the wisest and safest course of all these, unless they were with more integrity undertaken. And these are the errors, and these are the fruits of mis-spending our prime youth at the schools and universities, as we do, either in learning mere words, or such things chiefly as were better unlearnt.

I shall detain you no longer in the demonstration of what we should not do, but straight conduct you to a hillside, where I will point you out the right path of a virtuous and noble education; laborious indeed at the first ascent, but also so smooth, so green, so full of goodly prospect and melodious sounds on every side that the harp of Orpheus was not more charming. I doubt not but ye shall have more ado to drive our dullest and laziest youth, our stocks and stubs, from the infinite desire of such a happy nurture than we have now to haul and drag our choicest and hopefullest wits to that asinine feast of sow-thistles and brambles which is commonly set before them as all the food and entertainment of their tenderest and most docible age. I call, therefore, a complete and generous education, that which fits a man to perform justly, skillfully and magnanimously all the offices, both private and public, of peace and war. And how all this may be done between twelve and one-and-twenty, less time than is now bestowed in pure trifling at grammar and sophistry, is to be thus ordered:—

First, to find out a spacious house and ground about it fit for an academy, and big enough to lodge a hundred and fifty persons, whereof twenty or thereabout may be attendants, all under the government of one who shall be thought of desert sufficient, and ability either to do all, or wisely to direct and oversee it done. This place should be at once both school and university, not needing a remove to any other house of scholarship, except it be some peculiar college of law or physic where they mean to be practitioners; but as for those general studies which take up all our time from

Lilly[8] to the commencing,[9] as they term it, master of art, it should be absolute. After this pattern as many edifices may be converted to the use as shall be needful in every city throughout this land, which would tend much to the increase of learning and civility everywhere. This number, less or more, thus collected, to the convenience of a foot-company or interchangeably two troops of cavalry, should divide their day's work into three parts as it lies orderly—their studies, their exercise, and their diet.

For their studies: first, they should begin with the chief and necessary rules of some good grammar,[10] either that now used, or any better; and while this is doing, their speech is to be fashioned to a distinct and clear pronunciation, as near as may be to the Italian, especially in the vowels. For we Englishmen, being far northerly, do not open our mouths in the cold air wide enough to grace a southern tongue, but are observed by all other nations to speak exceeding close and inward; so that to smatter Latin with an English mouth is as ill a hearing as law French. Next, to make them expert in the usefullest points of grammar, and withal to season them and win them early to the love of virtue and true labor, ere any flattering seducement or vain principle seize them wandering, some easy and delightful book of education should be read to them, whereof the Greeks have store, as Cebes,[11] Plutarch,[12] and other Socratic discourses; but in Latin we have none of classic authority extant, except the two or three first books of Quintilian[13] and some select pieces elsewhere. But here the main skill and groundwork will be to temper them such lectures and explanations upon every opportunity as may lead and draw them in willing obedience, inflamed with the study of learning and the admiration of virtue, stirred up with high hopes of living to be brave men and worthy patriots, dear to God and famous to all ages: that they may despise and scorn all their childish and ill-taught qualities, to delight in manly and liberal exercises; which he who hath the art and proper eloquence to catch them with,

8 Lilly's Latin Grammar, the first and most famous of all English Latin grammars. William Lilly (1468?–1522) was the first headmaster of St. Paul's School.

9 Taking the degree of.   10 Latin grammar, of course.

11 Cebes of Thebes, one of Socrates' disciples. His Table was one of the most popular of the moral and philosophical allegories of the day.

12 Plutarch's *Moralia*, rather than the famous Parallel Lives, is probably referred to here.

13 The *Institutio Oratoria* of Quintilian (A.D. 35?–95), the famous treatise on education in general and oratory in particular.

what with mild and effectual persuasions, and what with the intimation of some fear, if need be, but chiefly by his own example, might in a short space gain them to an incredible diligence and courage, infusing into their young breasts such an ingenuous and noble ardor as would not fail to make many of them renowned and matchless men. At the same time, some other hour of the day, might be taught them the rules of arithmetic, and, soon after, the elements of geometry, even playing, as the old manner was. After evening repast till bed-time their thoughts would be best taken up in the easy grounds of religion and the story of Scripture. The next step would be the authors of agriculture, Cato,[14] Varro,[15] and Columella,[16] for the matter is most easy; and if the language is difficult, so much the better; it is not a difficulty above their years. And here will be an occasion of inciting and enabling them hereafter to improve the tillage of their country, to recover the bad soil, and to remedy the waste that is made of good; for this was one of Hercules' praises. Ere half these authors be read (which will soon be with plying hard and daily) they cannot choose but be masters of an ordinary prose: so that it will be then seasonable for them to learn in any modern author the use of the globes and all the maps, first with the old names and then with the new; or they might then be capable to read any compendious method of natural philosophy; and, at the same time, might be entering into the Greek tongue, after the same manner as was before prescribed for the Latin; whereby the difficulties of grammar being soon overcome, all the historical physiology of Aristotle and Theophrastus[17] are open before them, and, as I may say, under contribution. The like access will be to Vitruvius,[18] to Seneca's "Natural Questions,"[19] to Mela,[20]

Celsus,[21] Pliny,[22] or Solinus.[23] And having thus passed the principles of arithmetic, geometry, astronomy, and geography, with a general compact of physics, they may descend in mathematics to the instrumental science of trigonometry, and from thence to fortification, architecture, enginery, or navigation, And in natural philosophy they may proceed leisurely from the history of meteors, minerals, plants, and living creatures, as far as anatomy. Then also in course might be read to them out of some not tedious writer the institution of physic;[24] that they may know the tempers, the humors, the seasons, and how to manage a crudity,[25] which he who can wisely and timely do is not only a great physician to himself and to his friends, but also may at some time or other save an army by this frugal and expenseless means only, and not let the healthy and stout bodies of young men rot away under him for want of this discipline, which is a great pity, and no less a shame to the commander. To set forward all these proceedings in nature and mathematics, what hinders but that they may procure, as oft as shall be needful, the helpful experiences of hunters, fowlers, fishermen, shepherds, gardeners, apothecaries; and in other sciences, architects, engineers, mariners, anatomists, who, doubtless, would be ready, some for reward and some to favor such a hopeful seminary. And this would give them such a real tincture of natural knowledge as they shall never forget, but daily augment with delight. Then also those poets which are now counted most hard will be both facile and pleasant, Orpheus,[26] Hesiod,[27] Theocritus,[28] Aratus,[29] Nicander,[30]

14 Cato the Censor, 234–149 B.C., author of the *De Re Rustica*, a general work on agriculture.

15 Varro, 116–27 B.C., whose *Rerum Rusticarum* comprises three of his 620 volumes.

16 Columella, who flourished in the first century A.D., was the author of *De Re Rustica*, an encyclopædia of farming, in twelve books.

17 Theophrastus, 372–287 B.C., a pupil of Aristotle, and the most thorough botanist of the ancient world, author of the History of Plants and the Principles of Vegetable Life.

18 Vitruvius Pollio, Roman architect and engineer of the first century A.D., and author of *De Architectura*, the most influential of all works on architecture.

19 Seneca's *Naturalium Questionum*, dealing with astronomy and meteorology, was a favorite mediæval textbook.

20 Pomponius Mela (first century A.D.), author of *De Chorographia*, the most famous of Latin geographical treatises.

21 A. Cornelius Celsus (first century A.D.), whose *De Medicina* is the most extensive of ancient medical studies.

22 Pliny the Elder (A.D. 23–79), whose *Historia Naturalis* in thirty-seven books supplied the Middle Ages with most of their information and misinformation on natural science and related subjects.

23 Solinus (third century A.D.), an editor and redactor of Pliny.

24 The principles of medicine.   25 Indigestion.

26 Orpheus is a mythical personage, regarded as the most celebrated of Homer's predecessors. He is the reputed author of the *Argonautica* and many other works.

27 Hesiod flourished in the eighth century B.C. He was the author of the Theogony and the Works and Days.

28 Theocritus, the pastoral poet of Syracuse and the author of the famous Idyls, lived in the third century B.C.

29 Aratus, who flourished in the third century B.C., is the author of the *Prognostica*, from which St. Paul quotes, Acts 17:28.

30 Nicander of the second century B.C., is the author of *Theriaca* and *Alexipharmaca*, poems on subjects dealing with natural science.

Oppian,[31] Dionysius;[32] and, in Latin, Lucretius,[33] Manilius,[34] and the rural part of Virgil.[35]

By this time years and good general precepts will have furnished them more distinctly with that act of reason which in ethics is called proairesis,[36] that they may with some judgment contemplate upon moral good and evil. Then will be required a special reinforcement of constant and sound indoctrinating to set them right and firm, instructing them more amply in the knowledge of virtue and the hatred of vice, while their young and pliant affections are led through all the moral works of Plato, Xenophon, Cicero, Plutarch, Laertius,[37] and those Locrian[38] remnants; but still to be reduced[39] in their nightward studies wherewith they close the day's work under the determinate sentence of David or Solomon, or the evangels and apostolic Scriptures. Being perfect in the knowledge of personal duty, they may then begin the study of economics. And either now or before this they may have easily learned at any odd hour the Italian tongue. And soon after, but with wariness and good antidote, it would be wholesome enough to let them taste some choice comedies, Greek, Latin, or Italian; those tragedies also that treat of household matters, as Trachiniæ, Alcestis, and the like.[40] The next remove must be to the study of politics; to know the beginning, end, and

reasons of political societies, that they may not, in a dangerous fit of the commonwealth, be such poor shaken uncertain reeds, of such a tottering conscience as many of our great councilors have lately shown themselves, but steadfast pillars of the State. After this they are to dive into the grounds of law and legal justice, delivered first and with best warrant by Moses, and, as far as human prudence can be trusted, in those extolled remains of Grecian law-givers, Lycurgus, Solon, Zaleucus, Charondas;[41] and thence to all the Roman edicts and tables, with their Justinian;[42] and so down to the Saxon and common laws of England and the statutes. Sundays also and every evening may now be understandingly spent in the highest matters of theology and church history, ancient and modern; and ere this time at a set hour the Hebrew tongue might have been gained, that the Scriptures may be now read in their own original; whereto it would be no impossibility to add the Chaldee and the Syrian dialect.[43] When all these employments are well conquered, then will the choice histories, heroic poems, and Attic tragedies of stateliest and most regal argument, with all the famous political orations, offer themselves; which, if they were not only read, but some of them got by memory, and solemnly pronounced with right accent and grace, as might be taught, would endue them even with the spirit and vigor of Demosthenes or Cicero, Euripides or Sophocles. And now, lastly, will be the time to read with them those organic[44] arts which enable men to discourse and write perspicuously, elegantly, and according to the fitted style of lofty, mean,[45] or lowly. Logic, therefore, so much as is useful, is to be referred to this due place, with all her well-couched heads and topics, until it be time to open her contracted palm into a graceful and ornate rhetoric taught out of the rule of Plato, Aristotle,

31 Oppian, who lived early in the third century A.D., was in Milton's day accredited with two Greek hexameter poems, *Halieutica*, on fishing, and *Cynegetica*, on hunting. Modern scholarship has assigned the poems to two different persons of this name.

32 Dionysius surnamed Periegetes, from his poem *Periegesis*, a description of the whole earth, in hexameters. He probably lived about A.D. 300.

33 Lucretius (96–55 B.C.), author of the famous poem *De Rerum Natura*, in which he attacks the superstitious belief in gods.

34 Manilius, who lived in the time of Augustus, was the author of an astrological poem, *Astronomica*, in five books. He was famous for his mastery of the technique of verse.

35 The Eclogues and the Georgics of Virgil are referred to.

36 The process of choosing between right and wrong.

37 Diogenes Laertius (second century A.D.), author of the Lives of the Philosophers in ten books; the work is still the basis of most histories of ancient philosophy.

38 Timæus of Locri, in Italy, a Pythagorean philosopher, and reputed author of a work On the Soul of the World, now generally assigned to a much later author of the first century A.D.

39 Led back.

40 The *Trachiniæ* of Sophocles and the *Alcestis* of Euripides both deal with the affection, suffering, and sacrifice of faithful wives for their husbands.

41 Lycurgus (ninth century B.C.?), the lawgiver of Sparta; Solon, the Athenian legislator, of the seventh century B.C.; Zaleucus, the lawgiver of the Locrians, about 660 B.C.; Charondas, a lawgiver of Catania and other Sicilian and Italian cities, who lived about 500 B.C..

42 Justinian the Great, emperor of Constantinople (A.D. 483–565), codifier of the Roman law. His two collections of laws are known as the Institutes and the Digest.

43 The Chaldee (or Aramaic) dialect was the vernacular language of Palestine in the time of Christ. The Syrian (or Syriac) dialect is commonly called Christian Aramaic. The earliest extant manuscripts of the New Testament are in Syriac.

44 The more practical, and serving as means to an end.

45 Medium.

Phalereus,[46] Cicero, Hermogenes,[47] Longinus.[48] To which poetry would be made subsequent, or, indeed, rather precedent, as being less subtle and fine, but more simple, sensuous, and passionate; I mean not here the prosody of a verse, which they could not but have hit on before among the rudiments of grammar, but that sublime art which in Aristotle's Poetics, in Horace, and the Italian commentaries of Castelvetro,[49] Tasso,[50] Mazzoni,[51] and others, teaches what the laws are of a true epic poem, what of a dramatic, what of a lyric, what decorum is, which is the grand masterpiece[52] to observe. This would make them soon perceive what despicable creatures our common rhymers and play-writers be; and show them what religious, what glorious and magnificent use might be made of poetry, both in divine and human things. From hence, and not till now, will be the right season of forming them to be able writers and composers in every excellent matter, when they shall be thus fraught with an universal insight into things: or whether they be to speak in parliament or council, honor and attention would be waiting on their lips. There would then appear in pulpits other visages, other gestures, and stuff otherwise wrought, than we now sit under, oft-times to as great a trial of our patience as any other that they preach to us. These are the studies wherein our noble and our gentle youth ought to bestow their time in a disciplinary way from twelve to one-and-twenty, unless they rely more upon their ancestors dead than upon themselves living. In which methodical course it is so supposed they must proceed by the steady pace of learning onward, as at convenient times for memory's sake to retire back into the middle ward, and sometimes into the rear of what they have been taught, until

46 Phalereus (345–283 B.C.), one of the last of the popular orators of Athens. His only extant work, Elocution, is assigned to a later writer.

47 Hermogenes, the celebrated Greek rhetorician, flourished in the time of Marcus Aurelius, A.D. 161–180. His works on rhetoric were used as manuals in schools.

48 Longinus (A.D. 213–273), Greek critic and philosopher, is the reputed author of the celebrated treatise On the Sublime, a great part of which is extant.

49 Ludovico Castelvetro (1505–1571), one of the earliest and most important of Italian critics. His translation and exposition of Aristotle's Poetics (in Italian) was published at Vienna in 1570.

50 Tasso's commentaries on poets and poetry are in a six-volume work called Discourses on Epic Poetry.

51 Jacobo Mazzoni (1548–1598), one of the most important critics of Dante. His chief work is his Defense of the Divine Comedy of Dante.

52 The most important point.

they have confirmed and solidly united the whole body of their perfected knowledge, like the last embattling of a Roman legion. Now will be worth the seeing what exercises and recreations may best agree and become those studies.

The course of study hitherto briefly described is, what I can guess by reading, likest to those ancient and famous schools of Pythagoras, Plato, Isocrates, Aristotle, and such others, out of which were bred such a number of renowned philosophers, orators, historians, poets, and princes all over Greece, Italy, and Asia, besides the flourishing studies of Cyrene and Alexandria. But herein it shall exceed them, and supply a defect as great as that which Plato noted in the commonwealth of Sparta. Whereas that city trained up their youth most for war, and these in their academies and Lycæum all for the gown, this institution of breeding which I here delineate shall be equally good both for peace and war. Therefore, about an hour and a half ere they eat at noon should be allowed them for exercise, and due rest afterwards; but the time for this may be enlarged at pleasure, according as their rising in the morning shall be early. The exercise which I commend first is the exact use of their weapon,[53] to guard, and to strike safely with edge or point. This will keep them healthy, nimble, strong, and well in breath; is also the likeliest means to make them grow large and tall, and to inspire them with a gallant and fearless courage, which being tempered with seasonable lectures and precepts to make them of true fortitude and patience, will turn into a native and heroic valor, and make them hate the cowardice of doing wrong. They must be also practised in all the locks and gripes of wrestling, wherein Englishmen are wont to excel, as need may often be in fight to tug, to grapple, and to close. And this, perhaps, will be enough wherein to prove and heat their single strength. The interim of unsweating[54] themselves regularly, and convenient rest before meat, may both with profit and delight be taken up in recreating and composing their travailed spirits with the solemn and divine harmonies of music heard or learned, either whilst the skillful organist plies his grave and fancied descant in lofty fugues, or the whole symphony with artful and unimaginable touches adorn and grace the well-studied chords of some choice composer; sometimes the lute or soft organ-stop, waiting on elegant voices either to religious, martial, or civil ditties, which, if wise men and prophets be not extremely out, have a great power

53 Fencing.   54 Cooling off after exercise.

over dispositions and manners to smooth and make them gentle from rustic harshness and distempered passions. The like also would not be unexpedient after meat, to assist and cherish nature in her first concoction,[55] and send their minds back to study in good tune and satisfaction. Where having followed it under vigilant eyes until about two hours before supper, they are, by a sudden alarum or watchword, to be called out to their military motions, under sky or covert, according to the season, as was the Roman wont; first on foot, then, as their age permits, on horseback to all the art of cavalry; that having in sport, but with much exactness and daily muster, served out the rudiments of their soldiership in all the skill of embattling, marching, encamping, fortifying, besieging, and battering, with all the helps of ancient and modern stratagems, tactics, and warlike maxims, they may, as it were out of a long war, come forth renowned and perfect commanders in the service of their country. They would not then, if they were trusted with fair and hopeful armies, suffer them for want of just and wise discipline to shed away from about them like sick feathers, though they be never so oft supplied; they would not suffer their empty and unrecruitable[56] colonels of twenty men in a company to quaff out or convey into secret hoards the wages of a delusive list[57] and miserable remnant; yet in the meanwhile to be overmastered with a score or two of drunkards, the only soldiery left about them, or else to comply with all rapines and violences. No, certainly, if they knew aught of that knowledge which belongs to good men or good governors they would not suffer these things. But to return to our own institute. Besides these constant exercises at home, there is another opportunity of gaining experience to be won from pleasure itself abroad: in those vernal seasons of the year, when the air is calm and pleasant, it were an injury and sullenness against nature not to go out and see her riches, and partake in her rejoicing with heaven and earth. I should not, therefore, be a persuader to them of studying much then, after two or three years that they have well laid their grounds, but to ride out in companies with prudent and staid guides to all the quarters of the land, learning and observing all places of strength, all commodities[58] of building and of soil, for towns and tillage,

harbors, and ports for trade. Sometimes taking sea as far as to our navy, to learn there also what they can in the practical knowledge of sailing and sea-fight. These ways would try all their peculiar gifts of nature, and if there were any secret excellence among them, would fetch it out and give it fair opportunities to advance itself by, which could not but mightily redound to the good of this nation, and bring into fashion again those old admired virtues and excellencies with far more advantage now in this purity of Christian knowledge. Nor shall we then need the monsieurs of Paris to take our hopeful youth into their slight and prodigal custodies, and send them over back again transformed into mimics, apes, and kickshaws.[59] But if they desire to see other countries at three or four and twenty years of age, not to learn principles, but to enlarge experience and make wise observation, they will by that time be such as shall deserve the regard and honor of all men where they pass, and the society and friendship of those in all places who are best and most eminent. And perhaps then other nations will be glad to visit us for their breeding, or else to imitate us in their own country.

Now, lastly, for their diet there cannot be much to say, save only that it would be best in the same house; for much time else would be lost abroad, and many ill habits got; and that it should be plain, healthful, and moderate, I suppose is out of controversy.

Thus, Mr. Hartlib, you have a general view in writing, as your desire was, of that which at several times I had discoursed with you concerning the best and noblest way of education; not beginning, as some have done, from the cradle, which yet might be worth many considerations, if brevity had not been my scope. Many other circumstances also I could have mentioned, but this, to such as have the worth in them to make trial, for light and direction may be enough. Only I believe that this is not a bow for every man to shoot in[60] that counts himself a teacher, but will require sinews almost equal to those which Homer gave Ulysses; yet I am withal persuaded that it may prove much more easy in the assay than it now seems at distance, and much more illustrious: howbeit not more difficult than I imagine, and that imagination presents me with nothing but very happy and very possible according to best wishes, if God have so decreed, and this age have spirit and capacity enough to apprehend.

55 Digestion.   56 Unable to obtain recruits.
57 The list of a company that existed on paper only.
58 Suitable qualities.

59 Fantastic persons.   60 With.

AREOPAGITICA;[1]

A Speech of Mr. John Milton for the Liberty of Unlicensed Printing, to the Parliament of England

[TEXT: *first edition, 1644*]

THEY who to states[2] and governors of the Commonwealth direct their speech, High Court of Parliament, or, wanting[3] such access in a private condition, write that which they foresee may advance the public good, I suppose them, as at the beginning of no mean endeavor, not a little altered[4] and moved inwardly in their minds: some with doubt of what will be the success,[5] others with fear of what will be the censure;[6] some with hope, others with confidence of what they have to speak. And me perhaps each of these dispositions, as the subject was whereon I entered,[7] may have at other times variously affected; and likely might in these foremost expressions now also disclose which of them swayed most, but that the very attempt of this address thus made, and the thought of whom it hath recourse to, hath got the power within me to a passion far more welcome than incidental to a preface. Which though I stay not to confess ere any ask I shall be blameless, if it be no other than the joy and gratulation which it brings to all who wish and promote their country's liberty; whereof this whole discourse proposed will be a certain testimony, if not a trophy.[8] For this is not the liberty which we can hope, that no grievance ever should arise in the Commonwealth—that let no man in this world expect; but when complaints are freely heard, deeply considered, and speedily reformed, then is the utmost bound of civil liberty attained that wise men look for. To which if I now manifest by the very sound of this which I shall utter, that we are already in good part arrived, and yet from such a steep disadvantage of tyranny and superstition grounded into our principles as was beyond the manhood of a Roman recovery,[9] it will be attributed first, as is most due, to the strong assistance of God our deliverer, next to your faithful guidance and undaunted wisdom, Lords and Commons of England. Neither is it in God's esteem, the diminution of his glory, when honorable things are spoken of good men and worthy magistrates; which if I now first should begin to do, after so fair a progress of your laudable deeds, and such a long obligement upon the whole realm of your indefatigable virtues, I might be justly reckoned among the tardiest, and the unwillingest of them that praise ye. Nevertheless there being three principal things, without which all praising is but courtship[10] and flattery, First, when that only is praised which is solidly worth praise: next when greatest likelihoods are brought that such things are truly and really in those persons to whom they are ascribed; the other, when he who praises, by showing that such his actual persuasion is of whom he writes, can demonstrate that he flatters not; the former two of these I have heretofore endeavored, rescuing the employment from him who went about to impair your merits with a trivial and malignant encomium;[11]

---

1 The title is taken from the Λόγος Ἀρειοπαγιτικός (Areopagitic Oration) addressed by Isocrates to the Areopagus, or Great Council, of Athens. Isocrates, a contemporary of Plato, was physically and temperamentally unfitted to speak in public, and therefore composed his orations to be read. He was, however, the most famous teacher of oratory of his day. Like Milton's, his Areopagitic oration appeals to the highest instincts of the Athenian Council, and urges its members to reconsider certain of their acts. For another famous address in connection with the Areopagus (Mars' Hill), see St. Paul's speech, Acts 17.

2 Heads of states, statesmen.   3 Lacking.
4 Disturbed.   5 Outcome.
6 Opinion, judgment.
7 Milton's five pamphlets on church reform, his treatise on education, and two of his pamphlets on divorce had preceded the Areopagitica.
8 He may perhaps not win the trophy of victory in his argument for the freedom of the press, but he will have put his own feelings on record.

9 England, after all her reverses, had recovered herself, as all Rome's manhood could not recover Rome.
10 The fawning art of the courtier.
11 Joseph Hall, Bishop of Norwich, best known as "the first English satirist," had "impaired the merits" of Parliament in his Humble Remonstrance to the High Court of Parliament, against the antiepiscopal petition. The Humble Remonstrance started the famous Smectymnuus controversy, the name Smectymnuus being formed from the initials of the five writers who answered Hall's Remonstrance. The controversy grew apace with charges and countercharges, until Milton's Apology for Smectymnuus finally crushed Hall.

the latter[12] as belonging chiefly to mine own acquittal, that whom I so extolled I did not flatter, hath been reserved opportunely to this occasion. For he who freely magnifies what hath been nobly done, and fears not to declare as freely what might be done better, gives ye the best covenant of his fidelity; and that his loyalest affection and his hope waits on your proceedings. His highest praising is not flattery, and his plainest advice is a kind of praising; for though I should affirm and hold by argument that it would fare better with truth, with learning, and the Commonwealth, if one of your published Orders, which I should name, were called in; yet at the same time it could not but much redound to the luster of your mild and equal government, whenas private persons are hereby animated to think ye better pleased with public advice, than other statists[13] have been delighted heretofore with public flattery. And men will then see what difference there is between the magnanimity of a triennial[14] Parliament and that jealous haughtiness of prelates and Cabin[15] Counselors that usurped of late, whenas they shall observe ye in the midst of your victories and successes more gently brooking written exceptions against a voted Order than other Courts, which had produced nothing worth memory but the weak ostentation of wealth, would have endured the least signified dislike at any sudden Proclamation. If I should thus far presume upon the meek demeanor of your civil and gentle greatness, Lords and Commons, as what your published Order hath directly said, that to gainsay, I might defend myself with ease, if any should accuse me of being new or insolent, did they but know how much better I find ye esteem it to imitate the old and elegant humanity of Greece than the barbaric pride of a Hunnish and Norwegian stateliness. And out of those ages, to whose polite wisdom and letters we owe that we are not yet Goths and Jutlanders, I could name him[16] who from his private house wrote that discourse to the Parliament of Athens, that persuades them to change the form of democraty which was then established. Such honor was done in those days to men who professed the study of wisdom and eloquence, not only in their own country, but in other lands, that cities and signiories heard them gladly, and with great respect, if they had aught in public to admonish the state. Thus

did Dion Prusæus, a stranger and a private orator, counsel the Rhodians against a former edict;[17] and I abound with other like examples, which to set here would be superfluous. But if from the industry of a life wholly dedicated to studious labors, and those natural endowments haply not the worse for two and fifty degrees of northern latitude, so much must be derogated[18] as to count me not equal to any of those who had this privilege, I would obtain to be thought not so inferior, as yourselves are superior to the most of them who received their counsel: and how far you excel them, be assured, Lords and Commons, there can no greater testimony appear than when your prudent spirit acknowledges and obeys the voice of reason from what quarter so-ever it be heard speaking; and renders ye as willing to repeal any Act of your own setting forth as any set forth by your predecessors.

If ye be thus resolved, as it were injury to think ye were not, I know not what should withhold me from presenting ye with a fit instance wherein to show both that love of truth which ye eminently profess, and that uprightness of your judgment which is not wont to be partial to yourselves; by judging over again that Order[19] which ye have ordained to regulate Printing. "That no book, pamphlet, or paper shall be henceforth printed, unless the same be first approved and licensed by such, or at least one of such as shall be thereto appointed." For that part which preserves justly every man's copy[20] to himself, or provides for the poor, I touch not, only wish they be not made pretenses to abuse and persecute honest and painful[21] men, who offend not in either of these particulars. But that other clause of licensing books, which we thought had died with his brother quadragesimal and matrimonial[22] when the prelates expired,[23] I shall now attend with such a homily as shall lay before ye, first the inventors of it, to be those whom ye will be loth to own; next

17 Dion Prusæus, surnamed Chrysostomos (golden-mouthed) because of his eloquence; he attempted to dissuade the Rhodians from altering the names on their public statues so as to inscribe the names of the men then in power. He flourished in the first century B.C.
  18 Subtracted.   19 Dated June 14, 1643.
  20 Copyright.   21 Painstaking, laborious.
  22 Lenten and marriage licenses. The former had to do with regulating the eating of fish in Lent. Milton upheld the theory that marriage was wholly a civil ceremony and contract in which the church had properly no part.
  23 The prelates were deprived of their power by the bill for the Exclusion of Bishops from Parliament in 1642. Presbyterianism was substituted for Episcopacy as the established religion in 1646.

  12 The third of these.   13 Statesmen.
  14 Parliament was required to meet at least once every three years by the Act of February 15, 1641.
  15 Cabinet Counselors.   16 Isocrates.

what is to be thought in general of reading, whatever sort the books be; and that this order avails nothing to the suppressing of scandalous, seditious, and libelous books, which were mainly intended to be suppressed. Last, that it will be primely to the discouragement of all learning, and the stop of Truth, not only by disexercising and blunting our abilities in what we know already, but by hindering and cropping the discovery that might be yet further made both in religious and civil Wisdom.

I deny not, but that it is of greatest concernment in the Church and Commonwealth, to have a vigilant eye how books demean themselves as well as men; and thereafter to confine, imprison, and do sharpest justice on them as malefactors. For books are not absolutely dead things, but do contain a potency of life in them to be as active as that soul was whose progeny they are; nay, they do preserve as in a vial the purest efficacy and extraction of that living intellect that bred them. I know they are as lively, and as vigorously productive, as those fabulous dragon's teeth,[24] and being sown up and down, may chance to spring up armed men. And yet, on the other hand, unless wariness be used, as good almost kill a man as kill a good book: who kills a man kills a reasonable creature, God's image; but he who destroys a good book, kills reason itself, kills the image of God, as it were in the eye.[25] Many a man lives a burden to the earth; but a good book is the precious life-blood of a master spirit, embalmed and treasured up on purpose to a life beyond life. 'Tis true, no age can restore a life, whereof perhaps there is no great loss; and revolutions of ages do not oft recover the loss of a rejected truth, for the want of which whole nations fare the worse. We should be wary therefore what persecution we raise against the living labors of public men, how we spill that seasoned life of man, preserved and stored up in books; since we see a kind of homicide may be thus committed, sometimes a martyrdom, and if it extend to the whole impression, a kind of massacre, whereof the execution ends not in the slaying of an elemental life, but strikes at that ethereal and fifth essence,[26] the breath of

reason itself, slays an immortality rather than a life. But lest I should be condemned of introducing license, while I oppose licensing, I refuse not the pains to be so much historical as will serve to show what hath been done by ancient and famous commonwealths, against this disorder, till the very time that this project of licensing crept out of the Inquisition, was catched up by our prelates, and hath caught some of our presbyters.

In Athens, where books and wits were ever busier than in any other part of Greece, I find but only two sorts of writings which the magistrate cared to take notice of; those either blasphemous and atheistical, or libelous. Thus the books of Protagoras[27] were by the judges of Areopagus commanded to be burnt, and himself banished the territory for a discourse begun with his confessing not to know "whether there were gods, or whether not." And against defaming, it was agreed that none should be traduced by name, as was the manner of Vetus Comœdia,[28] whereby we may guess how they censured libeling: And this course was quick enough, as Cicero writes,[29] to quell both the desperate wits of other atheists, and the open way of defaming, as the event showed. Of other sects and opinions, though tending to voluptuousness, and the denying of Divine Providence, they took no heed. Therefore we do not read that either Epicurus, or that libertine school of Cyrene,[30] or what the Cynic impudence[31] uttered, was ever questioned by the laws. Neither is it recorded that the writings of those old comedians were suppressed, though the acting of them were forbid; and that Plato commended the reading of Aristophanes, the loosest of them all, to his royal scholar Dionysius, is commonly known, and may be excused, if holy Chrysostom,[32] as is reported, nightly studied so much the same author and had the art to cleanse a scurrilous vehemence into the style of a rousing sermon. That other leading city of Greece, Lacedæmon,

24 Jason, by Medea's direction, sowed the teeth of the Colchian dragon, whence armed men sprang up. (Ovid's Metamorphoses vii. 121 ff.) Similar accounts are to be found in the stories of Cadmus and of Deucalion.

25 Reason seems to be referred to as the image of God within the pupil of the eye.

26 An "elemental life" is an earthly, material existence, depending on the four elements; the fifth essence (*quinta essentia*) is not material, but spiritual.

27 Protagoras of Abdera, 480–410 B.C., the first of the "Sophists." See Plato's dialogue, Protagoras. His famous discourse is entitled "About Gods."

28 The old Greek comedy. For its license see Horace, *Ars Poetica*, 281 ff.

29 In his *De Natura Deorum*, i. 23.

30 A Greek city in West Africa. The Cyrenaic school, founded by Aristippus, about 370 B.C., held that pleasure was the *summum bonum*.

31 The Cynic school was founded by Antisthenes, the pupil of Socrates. Their zeal for leading a virtuous life caused them to be neglectful of ordinary social amenities, and gave rise to the charge of "impudence."

32 St. Chrysostom, Bishop of Constantinople, A.D. 347–407.

considering that Lycurgus their lawgiver was so addicted to elegant learning as to have been the first that
brought out of Ionia the scattered works of Homer,
and sent the poet Thales from Crete to prepare and
mollify the Spartan surliness with his smooth songs and
odes, the better to plant among them law and civility,
it is to be wondered how museless and unbookish they
were, minding nought but the feats of war. There
needed no licensing of books among them, for they
disliked all but their own laconic apothegms, and took
a slight occasion to chase Archilochus[33] out of their
city, perhaps for composing in a higher strain than
their own soldierly ballads and roundels could reach to.
Or if it were for his broad verses, they were not therein
so cautious, but they were as dissolute in their promiscuous conversing; whence Euripides affirms in *Andromache*, that their women were all unchaste. Thus much
may give us light after what sort [of] books were prohibited among the Greeks. The Romans also for many
ages trained up only to a military roughness, resembling most the Lacedæmonian guise, knew of
learning little but what their twelve Tables, and the
Pontific College with their augurs and flamins taught
them in religion and law, so unacquainted with other
learning, that when Carneades and Critolaus, with the
Stoic Diogenes coming ambassadors to Rome,[34] took
thereby occasion to give the city a taste of their philosophy, they were suspected for seducers by no less a
man than Cato the Censor, who moved it in the Senate to dismiss them speedily, and to banish all such
Attic babblers out of Italy. But Scipio and others of the
noblest senators withstood him and his old Sabine
austerity; honored and admired the men; and the censor himself at last, in his old age fell to the study of that
whereof before he was so scrupulous. And yet at the
same time, Nævius and Plautus, the first Latin comedians, had filled the city with all the borrowed scenes
of Menander and Philemon. Then began to be considered there also what was to be done to libelous
books and authors; for Nævius was quickly cast into
prison for his unbridled pen, and released by the
tribunes upon his recantation; we read also that libels
were burnt, and the makers punished by Augustus.
The like severity no doubt was used if aught were

impiously written against their esteemed gods. Except
in these two points, how the world went in books,
the magistrate kept no reckoning. And therefore
Lucretius without impeachment versifies his Epicurism
to Memmius, and had the honor to be set forth the
second time by Cicero, so great a father of the commonwealth; although himself disputes against that
opinion in his own writings. Nor was the satirical
sharpness, or naked plainness of Lucilius, or Catullus,
or Flaccus,[35] by any order prohibited. And for matters
of state, the story of Titus Livius, though it extolled
that part which Pompey held, was not therefore suppressed by Octavius Cæsar of the other faction. But
that Naso[36] was by him banished in his old age for the
wanton poems of his youth, was but a mere covert of
state over some secret cause; and besides, the books
were neither banished nor called in. From hence[37] we
shall meet with little else but tyranny in the Roman empire, that we may not marvel if not so often bad as
good books were silenced. I shall therefore deem to
have been large enough in producing what among the
ancients was punishable to write, save only which all
other arguments were free to treat on.

By this time the emperors were become Christians,
whose discipline in this point I do not find to have been
more severe than what was formerly in practice. The
books of those whom they took to be grand heretics
were examined, refuted, and condemned in the general Councils; and not till then were prohibited, or
burnt by authority of the emperor. As for the writings
of heathen authors, unless they were plain invectives
against Christianity, as those of Porphyrius and Proclus,[38] they met with no interdict that can be cited, till
about the year 400, in a Carthaginian Council, wherein
bishops themselves were forbid to read the books of
Gentiles, but heresies they might read: while others
long before them on the contrary scrupled more the
books of heretics than of Gentiles. And that the primitive Councils and Bishops were wont only to declare
what books were not commendable, passing no further, but leaving it to each one's conscience to read or
to lay by, till after the year 800, is observed already by
Padre Paolo,[39] the great unmasker of the Trentine

33 An early lyric poet of Ionia, traditional inventor of the
iambic measure.

34 Carneades of Cyrene on a special embassy to Rome in
155 B.C. gave two lectures on Justice, in the second of which
he refuted the arguments of the first. Cato resented this playing
with truth and insisted that the Senate dismiss him.

35 Horace (Quintus Horatius Flaccus).

36 The poet Ovid (Publius Ovidius Naso).

37 From the reign of Augustus.

38 Porphyrius and Proclus were Neoplatonists of the fourth
and fifth centuries A.D., respectively. Both were bitter enemies
of Christianity.

39 Pietro Paolo Sarpi, generally known as Fra Paolo, or
Paul of Venice. He wrote a History of the Council of Trent,

Council. After which time[40] the Popes of Rome, engrossing what they pleased of political rule into their own hands, extended their dominion over men's eyes, as they had before over their judgments, burning and prohibiting to be read what they fancied not; yet sparing in their censures, and the books not many which they so dealt with; till Martin V by his bull not only prohibited, but was the first that excommunicated[41] the reading of heretical books; for about that time Wycliffe and Huss growing terrible were they who first drove the Papal Court to a stricter policy of prohibiting. Which course Leo X[42] and his successors followed, until the Council of Trent and the Spanish Inquisition engendering together brought forth or perfected those Catalogues and expurging indexes that rake through the entrails of many an old good author with a violation worse than any could be offered to his tomb. Nor did they stay in matters heretical, but any subject that was not to their palate they either condemned in a Prohibition or had it straight into the new Purgatory of an Index. To fill up the measure of encroachment, their last invention was to ordain that no book, pamphlet, or paper should be printed (as if St. Peter had bequeathed them the keys of the press also out of Paradise) unless it were approved and licensed under the hands of two or three glutton friars. For example:

> "Let the Chancellor Cini be pleased to see if in this present work be contained aught that may withstand the printing.
> Vincent Rabbatta, Vicar of Florence."

> "I have seen this present work, and find nothing athwart the Catholic faith and good manners: in witness whereof I have given, etc.
> Nicolo Cini, Chancellor of Florence."

> "Attending the precedent relation, it is allowed that this present work of Davanzati may be printed.
> Vincent Rabbatta, etc."

> "It may be printed, July 15.
> Friar Simon Mompei d'Amelia,
> Chancellor of the holy office in Florence."

Sure they have a conceit, if he of the bottomless pit had not long since broke prison, that this quadruple exorcism would bar him down. I fear their next design will be to get into their custody the licensing of that which they say Claudius intended,[43] but went not through with. Vouchsafe to see another of their forms, the Roman stamp:

> "Imprimatur,[44] If it seem good to the reverend master of the holy Palace,
> Belcastro, Vicegerent."

> "Imprimatur, Friar Nicolo Rodolphi, Master of the holy Palace."

Sometimes five Imprimaturs are seen together dialogue-wise in the piazza of one title-page, complimenting and ducking each to other with their shaven reverences, whether the author who stands by in perplexity at the foot of his epistle shall to the press or to the sponge. These are the pretty responsories, these are the dear antiphonies, that so bewitched of late our prelates and their chaplains with the goodly echo they made; and besotted us to the gay imitation of a lordly Imprimatur, one from Lambeth House,[45] another from the west end of Paul's;[46] so apishly romanizing that the word of command still was set down in Latin; as if the learned grammatical pen that wrote it would cast no ink without Latin; or perhaps, as they thought, because no vulgar tongue was worthy to express the pure conceit of an Imprimatur; but rather, as I hope, for that our English, the language of men ever famous and foremost in the achievements of liberty, will not easily find servile letters enow to spell such a dictatory presumption English. And thus ye have the inventors and the original of book-licensing ripped up and drawn as lineally as any pedigree. We have it not, that can be heard of, from any ancient state, or polity, or church, nor by any statute left us by our ancestors elder or later; nor from the modern custom of any reformed

which met at intervals from 1545 to 1563, and the decrees of which were intended to offset the Protestant Confession of Faith formulated at Augsburg. Fra Paolo defended the republic of Venice against papal interference, and was excommunicated for his trouble in 1606.

40 After A.D. 800.

41 Punished with excommunication. The bull referred to, dating from about 1425, did not, however, mention the readers of Wycliffe and Huss.

42 Leo the Tenth was Giovanni de' Medici, and reigned as Pope during the ascendency of Martin Luther, 1513-1521.

43 A license to grant the privilege of breaking wind at table.

44 "Let it be printed."

45 The London residence of the Archbishop of Canterbury.

46 Probably the Stationers' Hall is meant. Its hostility to Milton was constantly in evidence.

city or church abroad; but from the most anti-christian council and the most tyrannous inquisition that ever inquired. Till then books were ever as freely admitted into the world as any other birth; the issue of the brain was no more stifled than the issue of the womb: no envious Juno sat cross-legged[47] over the nativity of any man's intellectual offspring; but if it proved a monster, who denies but that it was justly burnt, or sunk into the sea. But that a book, in worse condition than a peccant soul, should be to stand before a jury ere it be born to the world, and undergo yet in darkness the judgment of Radamanth and his colleagues,[48] ere it can pass the ferry backward into light, was never heard before, till that mysterious iniquity, provoked and troubled at the first entrance of Reformation, sought out new limbos and new hells wherein they might include our books also within the number of their damned. And this was the rare morsel so officiously snatched up, and so ill-favoredly imitated by our inquisiturient[49] bishops, and the attendant minorities[50] their chaplains. That ye like not now these most certain authors of this licensing order, and that all sinister intention was far distant from your thoughts, when ye were importuned the passing it, all men who know the integrity of your actions, and how ye honor Truth, will clear ye readily.

But some will say, What though the inventors were bad, the thing for all that may be good? It may be so; yet if that thing be no such deep invention, but obvious, and easy for any man to light on, and yet best and wisest commonwealths through all ages and occasions have forborne to use it, and falsest seducers and oppressors of men were the first who took it up, and to no other purpose but to obstruct and hinder the first approach of Reformation, I am of those who believe it will be a harder alchemy than Lullius[51] ever knew to sublimate any good use out of such an invention. Yet this only is what I request to gain from this reason, that it may be held a dangerous and suspicious fruit, as

certainly it deserves, for the tree that bore it, until I can dissect one by one the properties it has. But I have first to finish, as was propounded, what is to be thought in general of reading books, whatever sort they be, and whether be more the benefit or the harm that hence proceeds.

Not to insist upon the examples of Moses, Daniel, and Paul, who were skillful in all the learning of the Egyptians, Chaldeans, and Greeks, which could not probably be without reading their books of all sorts, in Paul especially, who thought it no defilement to insert into Holy Scripture the sentences of three Greek poets, and one of them a tragedian,[52] the question was notwithstanding sometimes controverted among the primitive doctors, but with great odds on that side which affirmed it both lawful and profitable, as was then evidently perceived, when Julian the Apostate[53] and subtlest enemy to our faith made a decree forbidding Christians the study of heathen learning: for, said he, they wound us with our own weapons, and with our own arts and sciences they overcome us. And indeed the Christians were put so to their shifts by this crafty means, and so much in danger to decline into all ignorance, that the two Apollinarii[54] were fain, as a man may say, to coin all the seven liberal sciences[55] out of the Bible, reducing it into divers forms of orations, poems, dialogues, even to the calculating of a new Christian grammar. But, saith the historian Socrates,[56] the providence of God provided better than the industry of Apollinarius and his son, by taking away that illiterate law with the life of him who devised it. So great an injury they then held it to be deprived of Hellenic learning; and thought it a persecution more undermining, and secretly decaying the Church, than the open cruelty of Decius or Diocletian. And perhaps it was the same politic drift that the Devil whipped St. Jerome in a Lenten dream, for reading Cicero; or else it was a phantasm bred by the fever which had then

---

47 Juno, goddess of birth, sat on the threshold cross-legged, muttering evil spells, at the birth of Hercules. See Ovid, Metamorphoses ix.

48 Radamanth, Minos, and Æacus are the three judges in Hades.

49 Desirous of being inquisitors.

50 Minorites; Franciscan friars adopted the name as a token of humility. Milton uses the term contemptuously, of course.

51 Raymond Lully (1235–1313), born at Palma, in the island of Majorca; famous for his knowledge of alchemy, chemistry, medicine, and logic.

52 The three are: Epimenides (sixth century A.D.), quoted in Titus 1:12; Aratus, in Acts 17:28; and Menander or Euripides, in I Corinthians 15:33.

53 Julian the Apostate (A.D. 331–363), nephew of Constantine the Great, whose apostasy consisted in his return to paganism upon his accession.

54 Father and son, of Alexandria; the son being Bishop of Alexandria.

55 The *trivium* (grammar, logic, rhetoric), and the *quadrivium* (arithmetic, music, geometry, and astronomy).

56 Called Scholasticus, of the fifth century A.D., the author of the History of the Christian Church from A.D. 306 to A.D. 439

seized him.[57] For had an angel been his discipliner, unless it were for dwelling too much upon Ciceronianisms, and had chastised the reading, not the vanity, it had been plainly partial; first to correct him for grave Cicero, and not for scurril Plautus, whom he confesses to have been reading, not long before; next to correct him only, and let so many more ancient fathers wax old in those pleasant and florid studies without the lash of such a tutoring apparition; insomuch that Basil teaches how some good use may be made of Margites, a sportful poem, not now extant, writ by Homer; and why not then of *Morgante*,[58] an Italian romance much to the same purpose. But if it be agreed we shall be tried by visions, there is a vision recorded by Eusebius,[59] far ancienter than this tale of Jerome to the nun Eustochium, and, besides, has nothing of a fever in it. Dionysius Alexandrinus was, about the year 240, a person of great name in the Church for piety and learning, who had wont to avail himself much against heretics by being conversant in their books; until a certain presbyter laid it scrupulously to his conscience, how he durst venture himself among those defiling volumes. The worthy man, loth to give offence, fell into a new debate with himself what was to be thought; when suddenly a vision sent from God (it is his own epistle that so avers it) confirmed him in these words: Read any books whatsoever come to thy hands, for thou art sufficient both to judge aright, and to examine each matter. To this revelation he assented the sooner, as he confesses because it was answerable to that of the Apostle to the Thessalonians, Prove all things, hold fast that which is good. And he might have added another remarkable saying of the same author: To the pure, all things are pure; not only meats and drinks, but all kind of knowledge whether of good or evil; the knowledge cannot defile, not consequently the books, if the will and conscience be not defiled. For books are as meats and viands are; some of good, some of evil substance; and yet God, in that unapocryphal vision, said without exception, Rise, Peter, kill and eat, leaving the choice to each man's discretion. Wholesome meats to a vitiated stomach differ little or nothing from unwholesome; and best books to a naughty mind are not appliable to occasions of evil. Bad meats will scarce breed good nourishment in the healthiest concoction; but herein the difference is of bad books, that they to a discreet and judicious reader serve in many respects to discover, to confute, to forewarn, and to illustrate. Whereof what better witness can ye expect I should produce than one of your own now sitting in Parliament, the chief of learned men reputed in this land, Mr. Selden;[60] whose volume of natural and national laws proves, not only by great authorities brought together, but by exquisite reasons and theorems almost mathematically demonstrative, that all opinions, yea, errors, known, read, and collated, are of main service and assistance toward the speedy attainment of what is truest. I conceive, therefore, that when God did enlarge the universal diet of man's body, saving ever the rules of temperance, he then also, as before, left arbitrary the dieting and repasting of our minds; as wherein every mature man might have to exercise his own leading capacity. How great a virtue is temperance, how much of moment through the whole life of man! Yet God commits the managing so great a trust, without particular law or prescription, wholly to the demeanor of every grown man. And therefore when he himself tabled the Jews from heaven, that omer,[61] which was every man's daily portion of manna, is computed to have been more than might have well sufficed for the heartiest feeder thrice as many meals. For those actions which enter into a man, rather than issue out of him, and therefore defile not, God uses not to captivate under a perpetual childhood of prescription, but trusts him with the gift of reason to be his own chooser; there were but little work left for preaching if law and compulsion should grow so fast upon those things which heretofore were governed only by exhortation. Solomon informs us that much reading is a weariness to the flesh; but neither he nor other inspired author tells us that such or such reading is unlawful; yet certainly had God thought good to limit us herein, it had been much more expedient to have told us what was unlawful than what was wearisome. As for the burning of those Ephesian books by St. Paul's converts, 'tis replied the books were magic, the Syriac so renders them. It was a private act, a voluntary act, and leaves us to a voluntary imitation: the men in remorse burnt those books which were their

---

57 St. Jerome (c. A.D. 345–420) in a letter to the nun, Eustochium, speaks of his illusion as arising from a fever. He ascribes the dream to the Devil, although it had to do with his being condemned in heaven to be whipped by angels for being a Ciceronian rather than a Christian.

58 The *Morgante Maggiore*, a mock-romance by Luigi Pulci, 1431–1487, burlesquing the poetry of chivalry. It is full of broad, coarse humor.

59 Bishop of Cæsarea in the early fourth century.

60 John Selden (1584–1654), the great legal and philological scholar.

61 See Exodus 16:16–36.

own; the magistrate by this example is not appointed: these men practised the books, another might perhaps have read them in some sort usefully. Good and evil we know in the field of this world grow up together almost inseparably; and the knowledge of good is so involved and interwoven with the knowledge of evil, and in so many cunning resemblances hardly to be discerned, that those confused seeds which were imposed upon Psyche as an incessant labor to cull out, and sort asunder, were not more intermixed.[62] It was from out the rind of one apple tasted, that the knowledge of good and evil, as two twins cleaving together, leaped forth into the world. And perhaps this is that doom which Adam fell into of knowing good and evil, that is to say of knowing good by evil. As therefore the state of man is, what wisdom can there be to choose, what continence to forbear, without the knowledge of evil? He that can apprehend and consider vice with all her baits and seeming pleasures, and yet abstain, and yet distinguish, and yet prefer that which is truly better, he is the true wayfaring Christian.[63] I cannot praise a fugitive and cloistered virtue, unexercised and unbreathed, that never sallies out and sees her adversary, but slinks out of the race, where that immortal garland is to be run for, not without dust and heat. Assuredly we bring not innocence into the world, we bring impurity much rather; that which purifies us is trial, and trial is by what is contrary. That virtue therefore which is but a youngling in the contemplation of evil, and knows not the utmost that vice promises to her followers, and rejects it, is but a blank virtue, not a pure; her whiteness is but an excremental[64] whiteness; which was the reason why our sage and serious poet Spenser, whom I dare be known to think a better teacher than Scotus[65] or Aquinas, describing true temperance under the person of Guion, brings him in with his palmer through the cave of Mammon, and the bower of earthly bliss, that he might see and know, and yet abstain. Since therefore the knowledge and survey of vice is in this world so

necessary to the constituting of human virtue, and the scanning of error to the confirmation of truth, how can we more safely and with less danger scout into the regions of sin and falsity than by reading all manner of tractates and hearing all manner of reason? And this is the benefit which may be had of books promiscuously read.

But of the harm that may result hence three kinds are usually reckoned. First, is feared the infection that may spread; but then all human learning and controversy in religious points must remove out of the world, yea, the Bible itself; for that oft-times relates blasphemy not nicely, it describes the carnal sense of wicked men not unelegantly, it brings in holiest men passionately murmuring against Providence through all the argument of Epicurus: in other great disputes it answers dubiously and darkly to the common reader: and ask a Talmudist what ails the modesty of his marginal Keri, that Moses and all the prophets cannot persuade him to pronounce the textual Chetiv.[66] For these causes we all know the Bible itself put by the Papist into the first rank of prohibited books. The ancientest fathers must be next removed, as Clement of Alexandria, and the Eusebian book of evangelic preparation, transmitting our ears through a hoard of heathenish obscenities to receive the Gospel. Who finds not that Irenæus,[67] Epiphanius,[68] Jerome, and others discover more heresies than they well confute, and that oft for heresy which is the truer opinion? Nor boots it to say for these, and all the heathen writers of greatest infection, if it must be thought so, with whom is bound up the life of human learning, that they writ in an unknown tongue, so long as we are sure those languages are known as well to the worst of men, who are both most able, and most diligent to instill the poison they suck, first into the courts of princes, acquainting them with the choicest delights, and criticisms of sins. As perhaps did that Petronius whom Nero called his Arbiter, the master of his revels; and the notorious ribald of Arezzo,[69] dreaded and yet dear

---

62 The famous story of Cupid and Psyche is an incidental tale in The Golden Ass of Apuleius, Books IV–VI. Walter Pater's translation of the story is the best known.

63 Milton later (in a copy of the Areopagitica now in the British Museum) corrected the word "wayfaring" to "warfaring."

64 Superficial.

65 Duns Scotus (1265–1308), the great English Franciscan Schoolman, and chief opponent of Thomas Aquinas (1225?–1274), the Seraphic Doctor, and the greatest of mediæval metaphysicians.

66 The original text of the Talmud (the great compilation of Jewish laws and traditions) is called the Chetiv ("written") and the marginal annotations are the Keri ("read"). The Talmud provides that "words which in the law are written obscenely must be changed to more civil words," a rule that seemed ridiculous to Milton. See his Apology for Smectymnuus.

67 Bishop of Lyons, A.D. 177.

68 Bishop of Constantia, A.D. 400.

69 Pietro Aretino (1492–1557), the "Scourge of Princes" as he called himself. He was not less famous for his obscene

to the Italian courtiers. I name not him for posterity's sake, whom Harry the Eighth named in merriment his Vicar of Hell.[70] By which compendious way all the contagion that foreign books can infuse will find a passage to the people far easier and shorter than an Indian voyage, though it could be sailed either by the north of Cataio[71] eastward, or of Canada westward, while our Spanish licensing gags the English press never so severely. But on the other side that infection which is from books of controversy in religion is more doubtful and dangerous to the learned than to the ignorant; and yet those books must be permitted untouched by the licenser. It will be hard to instance where any ignorant man hath been ever seduced by papistical book in English, unless it were commended and expounded to him by some of that clergy: and indeed all such tractates, whether false or true, are as the prophecy of Isaiah was to the eunuch, not to be understood without a guide.[72] But of our priests and doctors how many have been corrupted by studying the comments of Jesuits and Sorbonists, and how fast they could transfuse that corruption into the people, our experience is both late and sad. It is not forgot since the acute and distinct Arminius was perverted merely by the perusing of a nameless discourse written at Delft, which at first he took in hand to confute.[73] Seeing, therefore, that those books, and those in great abundance which are likeliest to taint both life and doctrine, cannot be suppressed without the fall of learning, and of all ability in disputation, and that these books of either sort are most and soonest catching to the learned, from whom to the common people whatever is heretical or dissolute may quickly be conveyed, and that evil manners are as perfectly learnt without books a thousand other ways which cannot be stopped, and evil doctrine not with books can propagate, except a teacher guide, which he might also do without writing, and so beyond prohibiting, I am not unable

to unfold how this cautelous[74] enterprise of licensing can be exempted from the number of vain and impossible attempts. And he who were pleasantly disposed could not well avoid to liken it to the exploit of that gallant man who thought to pound up the crows by shutting his park gate. Besides another inconvenience, if learned men be the first receivers out of books and dispreaders both of vice and error, how shall the licensers themselves be confided in, unless we can confer upon them, or they assume to themselves above all others in the land, the grace of infallibility and uncorruptedness? And again if it be true, that a wise man, like a good refiner, can gather gold out of the drossiest volume, and that a fool will be a fool with the best book, yea, or without book; there is no reason that we should deprive a wise man of any advantage to his wisdom, while we seek to restrain from a fool that which being restrained will be no hindrance to his folly. For if there should be so much exactness always used to keep that from him which is unfit for his reading, we should in the judgment of Aristotle not only, but of Solomon[75] and of our Saviour,[76] not vouchsafe him good precepts, and by consequence not willingly admit him to good books; as being certain that a wise man will make better use of an idle pamphlet than a fool will do of sacred Scripture.

'Tis next alleged we must not expose ourselves to temptations without necessity, and next to that, not employ our time in vain things. To both these objections one answer will serve, out of the grounds already laid, that to all men such books are not temptations, nor vanities, but useful drugs and materials wherewith to temper and compose effective and strong medicines, which man's life cannot want.[77] The rest, as children and childish men, who have not the art to qualify and prepare these working minerals, well may be exhorted to forbear, but hindered forcibly they cannot be by all the licensing that Sainted Inquisition could ever yet contrive: which is what I promised to deliver next, That this order of licensing conduces nothing to the end for which it was framed and hath almost prevented me[78] by being clear already while thus much hath been explaining. See the ingenuity[79] of Truth, who, when she gets a free and willing hand, opens

and lascivious writings than for his method of obtaining money from princes and great men, who supplied him with funds through fear of having his satirical shafts directed at themselves.

70 It is not known to whom Milton refers here. Cardinal Wolsey, Thomas Cromwell, the poet Skelton, and others have been suggested. The term, "Vicar of Hell," is, of course, a travesty of the Pope's title "Vicar of Christ."

71 Cathay.   72 See Acts 8:28–35.

73 Arminius, the Dutch theologian, was asked to confute an anti-Calvinistic treatise, but the result of his study of it was his complete conversion to the principles of the anti-Calvinists.

74 Dangerous, deceitful.

75 "Answer a fool according to his folly." Proverbs 26:5.

76 "Cast not your pearls before swine." Matthew 7:6.

77 Be without, dispense with.

78 Anticipated my proofs.

79 Ingenuousness, frankness; from Latin *ingenuus*, frank.

herself faster than the pace of method and discourse[80] can overtake her. It was the task which I began with, to show that no nation, or well instituted state, if they valued books at all, did ever use this way of licensing; and it might be answered, that this is a piece of prudence lately discovered. To which I return, that as it was a thing slight and obvious to think on, for if it had been difficult to find out, there wanted not among them long since, who suggested such a course; which they not following, leave us a pattern of their judgment that it was not the not knowing, but the not approving, which was the cause of their not using it. Plato, a man of high authority, indeed, but least of all for his commonwealth,[81] in the book of his laws, which no city ever yet received, fed his fancy by making many edicts to his airy burgomasters, which they who otherwise admire him wish had been rather buried and excused in the genial cups of an academic night-sitting.[82] By which laws he seems to tolerate no kind of learning, but by unalterable decree, consisting most of practical traditions, to the attainment whereof a library of smaller bulk than his own dialogues would be abundant. And there also enacts that no poet should be so much as read to any private man, what he had written, until the judges and law-keepers had seen it and allowed it. But that Plato meant this law peculiarly to that commonwealth which he had imagined, and to no other, is evident. Why was he not else a lawgiver himself, but a transgressor, and to be expelled by his own magistrates, but for the wanton epigrams and dialogues which he made, and his perpetual reading of Sophron Mimus,[83] and Aristophanes, books of grossest infamy, and also for commending the latter of them, though he were the malicious libeler of his chief friends, to be read by the tyrant Dionysius, who had little need of such trash to spend his time on? But that he knew this licensing of poems had reference and dependence to many other provisos there set down in his fancied republic, which in this world could have no place: and so neither he himself, nor any magistrate, or city ever imitated that course, which taken apart from those other collateral injunctions must needs be vain

and fruitless. For if they fell upon one kind of strictness, unless their care were equal to regulate all other things of like aptness to corrupt the mind, that single endeavor they knew would be but a fond labor; to shut and fortify one gate against corruption, and be necessitated to leave others round about wide open. If we think to regulate printing, thereby to rectify manners, we must regulate all recreations and pastimes, all that is delightful to man. No music must be heard, no song be set or sung, but what is grave and Doric.[84] There must be licensing dancers, that no gesture, motion, or deportment be taught our youth but what by their allowance shall be thought honest; for such Plato was provided of; it will ask more than the work of twenty licensers to examine all the lutes, violins, and the guitars in every house; they must not be suffered to prattle as they do, but must be licensed what they may say. And who shall silence all the airs and madrigals that whisper softness in chambers? The windows also, and the balconies must be thought on; there are shrewd[85] books with dangerous frontispieces set to sale; who shall prohibit them, shall twenty licensers? The villages also must have their visitors to inquire what lectures the bagpipe and the rebeck[86] reads even to the ballatry, and the gamut of every municipal fiddler, for these are the countryman's Arcadias, and his Monte Mayors.[87] Next, what more national corruption, for which England hears ill[88] abroad, than household gluttony: who shall be the rectors of our daily rioting? And what shall be done to inhibit the multitudes that frequent those houses where drunkenness is sold and harbored? Our garments also should be referred to the licensing of some more sober workmasters to see them cut into a less wanton garb. Who shall regulate all the mixed conversation of our youth, male and female together, as is the fashion of this country; who shall still appoint what shall be discoursed, what presumed, and no further? Lastly, who shall forbid and separate all idle resort, all evil company? These things will be, and must be; but how they shall be least hurtful, how least enticing, herein consists the grave and governing wisdom of a state. To sequester out of the

---

80 Reasoning.

81 Plato, in his Republic, describes an ideal state, which he intimates is impossible of realization.

82 A *symposium*, or drinking party such as Plato describes in his dialogue of that name.

83 Sophron Mimus, of Syracuse, fifth century B.C., whose mimes, coarse, animated, and amusing, were Plato's favorite reading at odd moments.

84 Of a martial character, as distinguished from the voluptuous quality of the Lydian mode, and the wild, loud tones of the Phrygian.

85 Mischievous.   86 The predecessor of the violin.

87 Jorge de Montemayor (1520?–1561), Portuguese poet, author of the prose pastoral *Diana Enamorada*, written in imitation of the Italian Sannazaro's *Arcadia*.

88 Is ill spoken of.

world into Atlantic and Utopian[89] polities, which never can be drawn into use, will not mend our condition; but to ordain wisely as in this world of evil, in the midst whereof God hath placed us unavoidably. Nor is it Plato's licensing of books will do this, which necessarily pulls along with it so many other kinds of licensing, as will make us all both ridiculous and weary, and yet frustrate; but those unwritten, or at least unconstraining laws of virtuous education, religious and civil nurture, which Plato there mentions as the bonds and ligaments of the commonwealth, the pillars and the sustainers of every written statute; these they be which will bear chief sway in such matters as these, when all licensing will be easily eluded. Impunity and remissness, for certain, are the bane of a commonwealth, but here the great art lies, to discern in what the law is to bid restraint and punishment, and in what things persuasion only is to work. If every action which is good or evil in man at ripe years were to be under pittance, and prescription, and compulsion, what were virtue but a name, what praise could be then due to well-doing, what gramercy to be sober, just, or continent? Many there be that complain of divine providence for suffering Adam to transgress; foolish tongues! when God gave him reason, he gave him freedom to choose, for reason is but choosing; he had been else a mere artificial Adam, such an Adam as he is in the motions.[90] We ourselves esteem not of that obedience, or love, or gift, which is of force. God therefore left him free, set before him a provoking[91] object, ever almost in his eyes; herein consisted his merit, herein the right of his reward, the praise of his abstinence. Wherefore did he create passions within us, pleasures round about us, but that these rightly tempered are the very ingredients of virtue? They are not skillful considerers of human things who imagine to remove sin by removing the matter of sin; for besides that it is a huge heap increasing under the very act of diminishing, though some part of it may for a time be withdrawn from some persons, it cannot from all, in such a universal thing as books are; and when this is done, yet the sin remains entire. Though ye take from a covetous man all his treasure, he has yet one jewel left, ye cannot bereave him of his covetousness. Banish all objects of lust, shut up all youth into the severest discipline that can be exercised in any hermitage, ye cannot make them chaste that came not thither so: such great care

and wisdom is required to the right managing of this point. Suppose we could expel sin by this means; look how much we thus expel of sin, so much we expel of virtue: for the matter of them both is the same; remove that, and ye remove them both alike. This justifies the high providence of God, who, though he commands us temperance, justice, continence, yet pours out before us, even to a profuseness, all desirable things, and gives us minds that can wander beyond all limit and satiety. Why should we then affect a rigor contrary to the manner of God and of nature, by abridging or scanting those means, which books freely permitted are, both to the trial of virtue, and the exercise of truth? It would be better done, to learn that the law must needs be frivolous, which goes to restrain things, uncertainly and yet equally working to good, and to evil. And were I the chooser, a dram of well doing should be preferred before many times as much the forcible hindrance of evil doing. For God sure esteems the growth and completing of one virtuous person, more then the restraint of ten vicious. And albeit whatever thing we hear or see, sitting, walking, traveling, or conversing, may be fitly called our book, and is of the same effect that writings are, yet grant the thing to be prohibited were only books, it appears that this Order hitherto is far insufficient to the end which it intends. Do we not see, not once or oftener, but weekly that continued court-libel[92] against the Parliament and City, printed, as the wet sheets can witness, and dispersed among us, for all that licensing can do? Yet this is the prime service a man would think, wherein this Order should give proof of itself. If it were executed, you'll say. But certain, if execution be remiss or blindfold now, and in this particular, what will it be hereafter and in other books? If then the Order shall not be vain and frustrate, behold a new labor, Lords and Commons, ye must repeal and proscribe all scandalous and unlicensed books already printed and divulged;[93] after ye have drawn them up into a list, that all may know which are condemned, and which not; and ordain that no foreign books be delivered out of custody, till they have been read over. This office will require the whole time of not a few overseers, and those no vulgar men. There be also books which are partly useful and excellent, partly culpable and pernicious; this work will ask as many more officials, to make expurgations, and expunctions, that the Commonwealth of

---

89 Referring to Plato's fabulous island of Atlantis (in his *Timæus* and *Critias*) and Sir Thomas More's Utopia.

90 Puppet shows.   91 Enticing.

92 Probably the *Mercurius Aulicus* (Court Mercury), a weekly newspaper of pronounced Royalist views.

93 Made public.

Learning be not damnified.[94] In fine, when the multitude of books increase upon their hands, ye must be fain to catalogue all those printers who are found frequently offending, and forbid the importation of their whole suspected typography. In a word, that this your Order may be exact, and not deficient, ye must reform it perfectly according to the model of Trent and Seville,[95] which I know ye abhor to do. Yet though ye should condescend[96] to this, which God forbid, the Order still would be but fruitless and defective to that end whereto ye meant it. If to prevent sects and schisms, who is so unread or so uncatechized in story, that hath not heard of many sects refusing books as a hindrance, and preserving their doctrine unmixed for many ages, only by unwritten traditions? The Christian faith, for that was once a schism, is not unknown to have spread all over Asia, ere any Gospel or Epistle was seen in writing. If the amendment of manners be aimed at, look into Italy and Spain, whether those places be one scruple the better, the honester, the wiser, the chaster since all the inquisitional rigor that hath been executed upon books.

Another reason, whereby to make it plain that this Order will miss the end it seeks, consider by the quality which ought to be in every licenser. It cannot be denied but that he who is made judge to sit upon the birth or death of books whether they may be wafted[97] into this world or not had need to be a man above the common measure, both studious, learned, and judicious; there may be else no mean mistakes in the censure of what is passable or not; which is also no mean injury. If he be of such worth as behooves him, there cannot be a more tedious and unpleasing journey-work,[98] a greater loss of time levied upon his head, than to be made the perpetual reader of unchosen books and pamphlets, oft-time huge volumes. There is no book that is acceptable unless at certain seasons; but to be enjoined the reading of that at all times, and in a hand scarce legible, whereof three pages would not down at any time in the fairest print, is an imposition which I cannot believe how he that values time, and his own studies, or is but of a sensible[99] nostril, should be able to endure. In this one thing I crave leave of the present

94 Made to suffer injury.
95 The Spanish Inquisition was formally instituted in Seville under Torquemada in 1481.
96 Give consent to.
97 Be permitted to cross the river which separates prenatal existence from this life.
98 Day-laborer's work (French *journée*); hack-work.
99 Sensitive.

licensers to be pardoned for so thinking, who doubtless took this office up, looking on it through their obedience to the Parliament, whose command perhaps made all things seem easy and unlaborious to them; but that this short trial hath wearied them out already, their own expressions and excuses to them who make so many journeys to solicit their license, are testimony enough. Seeing therefore those who now possess the employment, by all evident signs wish themselves well rid of it, and that no man of worth, none that is not a plain unthrift of his own hours is ever likely to succeed them, except he mean to put himself to the salary of a press corrector, we may easily foresee what kind of licensers we are to expect hereafter, either ignorant, imperious, and remiss, or basely pecuniary. This is what I had to show, wherein this Order cannot conduce to that end, whereof it bears the intention.

I lastly proceed from the no good it can do to the manifest hurt it causes, in being first the greatest discouragement and affront that can be offered to learning, and to learned men.

It was the complaint and lamentation of prelates, upon every least breath of a motion to remove pluralities, and distribute more equally Church revenues, that then all learning would be forever dashed and discouraged. But as for that opinion, I never found cause to think that the tenth part of learning stood or fell with the clergy; nor could I ever but hold it for a sordid and unworthy speech of any churchman who had a competency left him. If therefore ye be loth to dishearten heartily and discontent, not the mercenary crew of false pretenders to learning, but the free and ingenuous sort of such as evidently were born to study, and love learning for itself, not for lucre, or any other end, but the service of God and of truth, and perhaps that lasting fame and perpetuity of praise which God and good men have consented shall be the reward of those whose published labors advance the good of mankind, then know, that so far to distrust the judgment and the honesty of one who hath but a common repute in learning, and never yet offended, as not to count him fit to print his mind, without a tutor, and examiner, lest he should drop a schism, or something of corruption, is the greatest displeasure and indignity to a free and knowing spirit that can be put upon him. What advantage is it to be a man over it is to be a boy at school, if we have only escaped the ferula to come under the fescue[100] of an Imprimatur? If serious and elaborate writings, as if they were no more than the

100 Wand, staff; the teacher's "pointer."

theme of a grammar-lad under his pedagogue must not be uttered without the cursory eyes of a temporizing and extemporizing licenser? He who is not trusted with his own actions, his drift not being known to be evil, and standing to[101] the hazard of law and penalty, has no great argument to think himself reputed in the Commonwealth wherein he was born, for other than a fool or a foreigner. When a man writes to the world, he summons up all his reason and deliberation to assist him; he searches, meditates, is industrious, and likely consults and confers with his judicious friends; after all which done he takes himself to be informed in what he writes, as well as any that writ before him; if in this the most consummate act of his fidelity and ripeness, no years, no industry, no former proof of his abilities can bring him to that state of maturity, as not to be still mistrusted and suspected, unless he carry all his considerate diligence, all his midnight watchings, and expense of Palladian[102] oil, to the hasty view of an unleisured licenser, perhaps much his younger, perhaps far his inferior in judgment, perhaps one who never knew the labor of book-writing, and if he be not repulsed, or slighted, must appear in print like a puny[103] with his guardian, and his censor's hand on the back of his title to be his bail and surety, that he is no idiot, or seducer, it cannot be but a dishonor and derogation to the author, to the book, to the privilege and dignity of learning. And what if the author shall be one so copious of fancy as to have many things well worth the adding come into his mind after licensing, while the book is yet under the press, which not seldom happens to the best and diligentest writers; and that perhaps a dozen times in one book? The printer dares not go beyond his licensed copy; so often then must the author trudge to his leave-giver, that those his new insertions may be viewed; and many a jaunt will be made, ere that licenser, for it must be the same man, can either be found, or found at leisure; meanwhile either the press must stand still, which is no small damage, or the author lose his accuratest thoughts, and send the book forth worse than he had made it, which to a diligent writer is the greatest melancholy and vexation that can befall. And how can a man teach with authority, which is the life of teaching, how can he be a doctor in his book as he ought to be, or else had better be silent, whenas all he teaches, all he delivers,

is but under the tuition, under the correction of his patriarchal[104] licenser to blot or alter what precisely accords not with the hide-bound humor which he calls his judgment? When every acute reader upon the first sight of a pedantic license will be ready with these like words to ding[105] the book a quoit's distance from him, "I hate a pupil teacher, I endure not an instructor that comes to me under the wardship of an overseeing fist. I know nothing of the licenser, but that I have his own hand here for his arrogance; who shall warrant me his judgment?" "The State, sir," replies the stationer; but has a quick return, "The State shall be my governors, but not my critics; they may be mistaken in the choice of a licenser, as easily as this licenser may be mistaken in an author; this is some common stuff"; and he might add from Sir Francis Bacon,[106] that "such authorized books are but the language of the times." For though a licenser should happen to be judicious more than ordinary, which will be a great jeopardy of the next succession, yet this very office, and his commission, enjoins him to let pass nothing but what is vulgarly received already. Nay, which is more lamentable, if the work of any deceased author, though never so famous in his lifetime, and even to this day, come to their hands for license to be printed, or reprinted, if there be found in his book one sentence of a venturous edge, uttered in the height of zeal, and who knows whether it might not be the dictate of a divine spirit, yet not suiting with every low decrepit humor of their own, though it were Knox himself, the Reformer of a Kingdom, that spake it, they will not pardon him their dash.[107] the sense of that great man shall to all posterity be lost for the fearfulness, or the presumptuous rashness, of a perfunctory licenser. And to what an author[108] this violence hath been lately done, and in what book of greatest consequence to be faithfully published, I could now instance, but shall forbear till a more convenient season. Yet if these things be not resented seriously and timely by them who have the remedy in their power, but that such iron molds[109] as these shall have authority to gnaw out the choicest periods of exquisite books, and

---

101 Facing the peril of.

102 Learned; pertaining to Pallas Athene, the goddess of wisdom.

103 A minor (French *puis-né*, after-born).

104 Referring doubtless to Archbishop Laud, who was accused of desiring to be Patriarch of the Western Church.

105 Hurl.

106 The quotation is from Bacon's tract, An Advertisement Touching the Controversies in the Church of England.

107 A stroke of the pen to denote erasure.

108 It is not known to whom Milton refers.

109 Rust.

to commit such a treacherous fraud against the orphan remainders of worthiest men after death, the more sorrow will belong to that hapless race of men, whose misfortune it is to have understanding. Henceforth let no man care to learn, or care to be more than worldly wise; for certainly in higher matters to be ignorant and slothful, to be a common steadfast dunce will be the only pleasant life, and only in request.

And as it is a particular disesteem of every knowing person alive, and most injurious to the written labors and monuments of the dead, so to me it seems an undervaluing and vilifying of the whole nation. I cannot set so light by all the invention, the art, the wit, the grave and solid judgment which is in England, as that it can be comprehended in any twenty capacities how good soever, much less that it should not pass except their superintendence be over it, except it be sifted and strained with their strainers, that it should be uncurrent without their manual stamp. Truth and understanding are not such wares as to be monopolized and traded in by tickets and statutes and standards. We must not think to make a staple commodity of all the knowledge in the land, to mark and license it like our broadcloth, and our wool-packs. What is it but a servitude like that imposed by the Philistines,[110] not to be allowed the sharpening of our own axes and coulters, but we must repair from all quarters to twenty licensing forges. Had any one written and divulged erroneous things and scandalous to honest life, misusing and forfeiting the esteem had of his reason among men, if after conviction this only censure were adjudged him, that he should never henceforth write but what were first examined by an appointed officer, whose hand should be annexed to pass his credit for him, that now he might be safely read, it could not be apprehended less than a disgraceful punishment. Whence to include the whole nation, and those that never yet thus offended, under such a diffident and suspectful prohibition, may plainly be understood what a disparagement it is. So much the more, whenas debtors and delinquents may walk abroad without a keeper, but unoffensive books must not stir forth without a visible jailer in their title. Nor is it to the common people less than a reproach; for if we be so jealous[111] over them, as that we dare not trust them with an English pamphlet, what do we but censure them for a giddy, vicious, and ungrounded people; in such a sick and weak state of faith and discretion as to be able to

take nothing down but through the pipe[112] of a licenser. That this is care or love of them we cannot pretend, whenas in those popish places where the laity are most hated and despised the same strictness is used over them. Wisdom we cannot call it, because it stops but one breach of license, nor that neither: whenas those corruptions which it seeks to prevent break in faster at other doors which cannot be shut.

And in conclusion it reflects to the disrepute of our ministers also, of whose labors we should hope better, and of the proficiency which their flock reaps by them, than that after all this light of the Gospel which is, and is to be, and all this continual preaching, they should still be frequented with such an unprincipled, unedified, and laic rabble as that the whiff of every new pamphlet should stagger them out of their catechism and Christian walking. This may have much reason to discourage the ministers when such a low conceit is had of all their exhortations, and the benefiting of their hearers, as that they are not thought fit to be turned loose to three sheets of paper without a licenser; that all the sermons, all the lectures preached, printed, vented in such numbers, and such volumes, as have now well-nigh made all other books unsalable, should not be armor enough against one single Enchiridion,[113] without the castle of St. Angelo of an Imprimatur.

And lest some should persuade ye, Lords and Commons, that these arguments of learned men's discouragement at this your Order are mere flourishes, and not real, I could recount what I have seen and heard in other countries, where this kind of inquisition tyrannizes; when I have sat among their learned men, for that honor I had, and been counted happy to be born in such a place of philosophic freedom as they supposed England was, while themselves did nothing but bemoan the servile condition into which learning amongst them was brought; that this was it which had damped the glory of Italian wits; that nothing had been there written now these many years but flattery and fustian. There it was that I found and visited the famous Galileo,[114] grown old, a prisoner to the Inquisition, for thinking in astronomy otherwise than the Franciscan and Dominican licensers thought. And though I knew that England then was groaning

---

110 See I Samuel 13.   111 Suspicious.

112 The tube used to feed patients who are too weak to swallow.

113 The original means both dagger and hand-book. Milton plays on the double meaning.

114 Milton visited Galileo, then seventy-four years old, in 1638, during his visit to Florence.

loudest under the prelatical yoke, nevertheless I took it as a pledge of future happiness, that other nations were so persuaded of her liberty. Yet was it beyond my hope that those worthies were then breathing in her air, who should be her leaders to such a deliverance as shall never be forgotten by any revolution of time that this world hath to finish. When that was once begun, it was as little in my fear, that what words of complaint I heard among learned men of other parts uttered against the Inquisition, the same I should hear by as learned men at home uttered in time of Parliament against an order of licensing; and that so generally, that when I had disclosed myself a companion of their discontent, I might say, if without envy, that he whom an honest quæstorship had endeared to the Sicilians, was not more by them importuned against Verres[115] than the favorable opinion which I had among many who honor ye, and are known and respected by ye, loaded me with entreaties and persuasions, that I would not despair to lay together that which just reason should bring into my mind, toward the removal of an undeserved thralldom upon learning. That this is not therefore the disburdening of a particular fancy, but the common grievance of all those who had prepared their minds and studies above the vulgar pitch to advance truth in others, and from others to entertain it, thus much may satisfy. And in their name I shall for neither friend nor foe conceal what the general murmur is; that if it come to inquisitioning again and licensing, and that we are so timorous of ourselves, and so suspicious of all men, as to fear each book, and the shaking of every leaf, before we know what the contents are, if some who but of late were little better than silenced from preaching shall come now to silence us from reading, except what they please, it cannot be guessed what is intended by some but a second tyranny over learning; and will soon put it out of controversy that Bishops and Presbyters are the same to us both name and thing. That those evils of Prelaty, which before from five or six and twenty sees were distributively charged upon the whole people, will now light wholly upon learning, is not obscure to us: whenas now the pastor of a small unlearned parish on the sudden shall be exalted Archbishop over a large diocese of books, and yet not remove, but keep his other cure too, a mystical pluralist. He who but of late cried down the sole ordination of every novice Bachelor of Art, and denied

sole jurisdiction over the simplest parishioner, shall now at home in his private chair assume both these over worthiest and excellentest books and ablest authors that write them. This is not, ye Covenants[116] and Protestations that we have made, this is not to put down Prelaty; this is but to chop[117] an Episcopacy; this is but to translate the Palace Metropolitan[118] from one kind of dominion into another; this is but an old canonical sleight of commuting our penance. To startle thus betimes at a mere unlicensed pamphlet will after a while be afraid of every conventicle, and a while after will make a conventicle of every Christian meeting. But I am certain that a State governed by the rules of justice and fortitude, or a Church built and founded upon the rock of faith and true knowledge, cannot be so pusillanimous. While things are yet not constituted in Religion that freedom of writing should be restrained by a discipline imitated from the Prelates, and learnt by them from the Inquisition to shut us up all again into the breast of a licenser, must needs give cause of doubt and discouragement to all learned and religious men. Who cannot but discern the fineness of this politic drift, and who are the contrivers; that while Bishops were to be baited down, then all Presses might be open; it was the people's birthright and privilege in time of Parliament, it was the breaking forth of light. But now the Bishops abrogated and voided out the Church, as if our Reformation sought no more but to make room for others into their seats under another name, the episcopal arts begin to bud again, the cruse of truth must run no more oil, liberty of Printing must be enthralled again under a prelatical commission of twenty, the privilege of the people nullified, and which is worse, the freedom of learning must groan again, and to her old fetters: all this the Parliament yet sitting. Although their own late arguments and defenses against the Prelates might remember them that this obstructing violence meets for the most part with an event utterly opposite to the end which it drives at: instead of suppressing sects and schisms, it raises them and invests them with a reputation. "The punishing of wits enhances their authority," saith the Viscount St. Albans;[119] "and a forbidden writing is thought to be a certain spark of truth that

115 C. Cornelius Verres, against whom Cicero directed his famous orations because of his bad government in Sicily.

116 The Solemn League and Covenant, between England and Scotland, had been signed in 1643.

117 Barter, exchange.

118 The Archbishop of Canterbury was Metropolitan and Primate of All England.

119 From Bacon's tract already mentioned on page 407.

flies up in the faces of them who seek to tread it out."
This Order therefore may prove a nursing mother to
sects, but I shall easily show how it will be a stepdame
to Truth: and first by disenabling us to the maintenance of what is known already.

Well knows he who uses to consider, that our faith
and knowledge thrives by exercise, as well as our limbs
and complexion.[120] Truth is compared in Scripture to
a streaming fountain; if her waters flow not in a perpetual progression, they sicken into a muddy pool of
conformity and tradition. A man may be a heretic in
the truth; and if he believe things only because his
pastor says so, or the Assembly so determines, without
knowing other reason, though his belief be true, yet
the very truth he holds becomes his heresy. There is not
any burden that some would gladlier post off to another
than the charge and care of their Religion. There be,
who knows not that there be, of Protestants and professors[121] who live and die in as arrant an implicit faith
as any lay Papist of Loreto.[122] A wealthy man addicted
to his pleasure and to his profits, finds religion to be a
traffic so entangled, and of so many piddling accounts,
that of all mysteries[123] he cannot skill to keep a stock
going upon that trade. What should he do? Fain he
would have the name to be religious, fain he would
bear up with his neighbors in that. What does he therefore, but resolves to give over toiling, and to find himself out some factor, to whose care and credit he may
commit the whole managing of his religious affairs;
some divine of note and estimation that must be. To
him he adheres, resigns the whole warehouse of his
religion, with all the locks and keys into his custody;
and indeed makes the very person of that man his
religion; esteems his associating with him a sufficient
evidence and commendatory of his own party. So
that a man may say his religion is now no more within
himself, but is become a dividual movable,[124] and
goes and comes near him, according as that good man
frequents the house. He entertains him, gives him gifts,
feasts him, lodges him; his religion comes home at
night, prays, is liberally supped, and sumptuously laid
to sleep, rises, is saluted, and after the malmsey, or
some well-spiced brewage, and better breakfasted than
he whose morning appetite would have gladly fed on

120 Temperament, bodily constitution.
121 Those who make open profession of religion.
122 Near Ancona; one of the most frequented of mediæval
shrines.
123 Trades, occupations.
124 Something which may be separated from him and
removed.

green figs between Bethany and Jerusalem, his Religion walks abroad at eight, and leaves his kind enter-
tainer in the shop trading all day without his Religion.

Another sort there be, who when they hear that all
things shall be ordered, all things regulated and settled, nothing written but what passes through the
custom-house of certain publicans[125] that have the
tonnaging and poundaging of all free-spoken truth, will
straight give themselves up into your hands, make 'em
and cut 'em out what religion ye please: there be delights, there be recreations and jolly pastimes that will
fetch the day about from sun to sun, and rock the
tedious year as in a delightful dream. What need they
torture their heads with that which others have taken
so strictly and so unalterably into their own purveying?
These are the fruits which a dull ease and cessation of
our knowledge will bring forth among the people.
How goodly, and how to be wished were such an
obedient unanimity as this, what a fine conformity
would it starch us all into! Doubtless a staunch and
solid piece of framework, as any January could freeze
together.

Nor much better will be the consequence even
among the clergy themselves: it is no new thing never
heard of before for a parochial minister, who has his
reward, and is at his Hercules' pillars[126] in a warm
benefice, to be easily inclinable, if he have nothing else
that may rouse up his studies, to finish his circuit in an
English concordance and a topic folio,[127] the gather-
ings and savings of a sober graduateship, a harmony[128]
and a catena,[129] treading the constant round of certain
common doctrinal heads, attended with the uses,
motives, marks and means, out of which, as out of an
alphabet or sol-fa,[130] by forming and transforming,
joining and disjoining variously a little bookcraft,
and two hours' meditation, might furnish him un-
speakably to the performance of more than a weekly
charge of sermoning: not to reckon up the infinite
helps of interlinearies, breviaries, synopses, and other
loitering gear.[131] But as for the multitude of sermons
ready printed and piled up, on every text that is not
difficult, our London trading St. Thomas in his vestry,
and add to boot St. Martin, and St. Hugh, have not

125 Collectors of taxes.   126 Ultimate limit.
127 Commonplace book.
128 A synopsis of the four Gospels, in which all the
accounts are harmonized.
129 A "chain of extracts" from the writings of the fathers
arranged in sequence as a commentary on the Scriptures.
130 The musical scale or gamut.
131 Idle, worthless stuff.

within their hallowed limits more vendible ware of all sorts ready made:[132] so that penury he never need fear of pulpit provision, having where so plenteously to refresh his magazine. But if his rear and flanks be not impaled,[133] if his back door[134] be not secured by the rigid licenser, but that a bold book may now and then issue forth, and give the assault to some of his old collections in their trenches, it will concern him then to keep waking, to stand in watch, to set good guards and sentinels about his received opinions, to walk the round and counter-round with his fellow inspectors, fearing lest any of his flock be seduced, who also then would be better instructed, better exercised and disciplined. And God send that the fear of this diligence which must then be used do not make us affect the laziness of a licensing Church.

For if we be sure we are in the right, and do not hold the truth guiltily, which becomes not, if we ourselves condemn not our own weak and frivolous teaching, and the people for an untaught and irreligious gadding rout, what can be more fair than when a man judicious, learned, and of a conscience, for aught we know as good as theirs that taught us what we know, shall not privily from house to house, which is more dangerous, but openly by writing publish to the world what his opinion is, what his reasons, and wherefore that which is now thought cannot be sound? Christ urged it as wherewith to justify himself that he preached in public;[135] yet writing is more public than preaching; and more easy to refutation, if need be, there being so many whose business and profession merely it is to be the champions of Truth; which if they neglect, what can be imputed but their sloth, or inability?

Thus much we are hindered and disinured[136] by this course of licensing toward the true knowledge of what we seem to know. For how much it hurts and hinders the licensers themselves in the calling of their ministry, more than any secular employment, if they will discharge that office as they ought, so that of necessity they must neglect either the one duty or the other, I insist not, because it is a particular, but leave it to their own conscience, how they will decide it there.

There is yet behind of what I purposed to lay open,

the incredible loss and detriment that this plot of licensing puts us to, more than if some enemy at sea should stop up all our havens and ports and creeks, it hinders and retards the importation of our richest merchandise, Truth: nay, it was first established and put in practice by anti-christian malice and mystery[137] on set purpose to extinguish, if it were possible, the light of Reformation, and to settle falsehood; little differing from that policy wherewith the Turk upholds his Alcoran, by the prohibition of Printing. 'Tis not denied, but gladly confessed, we are to send our thanks and vows to Heaven, louder than most of nations for that great measure of truth which we enjoy, especially in those main points between us and the Pope, with his appurtenances the Prelates: but he who thinks we are to pitch our tent here, and have attained the utmost prospect of reformation, that the mortal glass[138] wherein we contemplate can show us, till we come to beatific vision, that man by this very opinion declares that he is yet far short of Truth.

Truth indeed came once into the world with her divine Master, and was a perfect shape most glorious to look on: but when he ascended, and his Apostles after him were laid asleep, then straight arose a wicked race of deceivers, who, as that story goes of the Egyptian Typhon with his conspirators, how they dealt with the good Osiris,[139] took the virgin Truth, hewed her lovely form into a thousand pieces, and scattered them to the four winds. From that time ever since, the sad friends of Truth, such as durst appear, imitating the careful[140] search that Isis made for the mangled body of Osiris, went up and down gathering up limb by limb still as they could find them. We have not yet found them all, Lords and Commons, nor ever shall do, till her Master's second coming; he shall bring together every joint and member, and shall mold them into an immortal feature of loveliness and perfection. Suffer not these licensing prohibitions to stand at every place of opportunity forbidding and disturbing them that continue seeking, that continue to do our obsequies to the torn body of our martyred saint. We boast our light; but if we look not wisely on the sun itself, it smites us into darkness. Who can discern those planets

132 The substance of the passage is that sermons are as numerous and as readily procurable in the neighborhoods of London churches as any other sort of ware.

133 Defended by stockades.   134 Postern.

135 See St. John 18:19.   136 Disaccustomed.

137 Underhand practices.

138 Alluding to I Corinthians 13:12, "For now we see through a glass darkly."

139 Typhon, the god of evil, was the antagonist of the good Osiris and his wife Isis. Typhon cut the body of Osiris in pieces and threw them into the Nile, whence they were collected after a prolonged search by Isis and their son, Horus.

140 Sorrowful.

that are oft combust,[141] and those stars of brightest magnitude that rise and set with the sun, until the opposite motion of their orbs bring them to such a place in the firmament where they may be seen evening or morning. The light which we have gained was given us, not to be ever staring on, but by it to discover onward things more remote from our knowledge. It is not the unfrocking of a priest, the unmitring of a bishop, and the removing him from off the Presbyterian shoulders that will make us a happy nation, no, if other things as great in the Church, and in the rule of life both economical[142] and political be not looked into and reformed. We have looked so long upon the blaze that Zuinglius[143] and Calvin hath beaconed up to us that we are stark blind. There be who perpetually complain of schisms and sects, and make it such a calamity that any man dissents from their maxims. 'Tis their own pride and ignorance which causes the disturbing, who neither will hear with meekness, nor can convince, yet all must be suppressed which is not found in their syntagma.[144] They are the troublers, they are the dividers of unity, who neglect and permit not others to unite those dissevered pieces which are yet wanting to the body of Truth. To be still searching what we know not by what we know, still closing up truth to truth as we find it (for all her body is homogeneal, and proportional),[145] this is the golden rule in theology as well as in arithmetic, and makes up the best harmony in a Church; not the forced and outward union of cold and neutral and inwardly divided minds.

Lords and Commons of England, consider what nation it is whereof ye are, and whereof ye are the governors: a nation not slow and dull, but of a quick, ingenious, and piercing spirit, acute to invent, subtle and sinewy to discourse, not beneath the reach of any point the highest that human capacity can soar to. Therefore the studies of Learning in her deepest sciences have been so ancient, and so eminent among us that writers of good antiquity and ablest judgment have been persuaded that even the school of Pythagoras and the Persian wisdom took beginning from the old philosophy of this island. And that wise and civil[146] Roman, Julius Agricola, who governed once here for Cæsar, preferred the natural wits of Britain before the labored studies of the French. Nor is it for nothing that the grave and frugal Transylvanian sends out yearly from as far as the mountainous borders of Russia, and beyond the Hercynian wilderness,[147] not their youth, but their staid men, to learn our language, and our theologic arts. Yet that which is above all this, the favor and the love of Heaven, we have great argument to think in a peculiar manner propitious and propending towards us. Why else was this nation chosen before any other, that out of her as out of Sion should be proclaimed and sounded forth the first tidings and trumpet of Reformation to all Europe? And had it not been the obstinate perverseness of our prelates against the divine and admirable spirit of Wycliffe, to suppress him as a schismatic and innovator, perhaps neither the Bohemian Huss and Jerome, no, nor the name of Luther, or of Calvin had been ever known: the glory of reforming all our neighbors had been completely ours. But now, as our obdurate clergy have with violence demeaned[148] the matter, we are become hitherto the latest and backwardest scholars, of whom God offered to have made us the teachers. Now once again by all concurrence of signs, and by the general instinct of holy and devout men, as they daily and solemnly express their thoughts, God is decreeing to begin some new and great period in his Church, even to the reforming of Reformation itself: what does he then but reveal himself to his servants, and as his manner is, first to his Englishmen; I say as his manner is, first to us, though we mark not the method of his counsels, and are unworthy. Behold now this vast city: a city of refuge, the mansion house of liberty, encompassed and surrounded with his protection; the shop of war hath not there more anvils and hammers waking, to fashion out the plates and instruments of armed Justice in defense of beleaguered Truth, than there be pens and heads there, sitting by their studious lamps, musing, searching, revolving new notions and ideas wherewith to present, as with their homage and their fealty, the approaching Reformation: others as fast reading, trying all things, assenting to the force of reason and convincement. What could a man require more from a nation so pliant and so prone to seek after knowledge?

141 A planet is said to be combust when, as viewed from the earth, it is so near the sun as to be invisible.

142 Having to do with the management of private life.

143 Zwingli (1484–1531), the Zurich reformer; Calvin (1509–1564), the Genevan reformer.

144 One's own personal beliefs.

145 Of the same nature throughout, and each part having a distinct proportion to each other and to the whole.

146 Cultured.

147 The Roman term for the forests and hills of southern and central Germany.

148 Conducted.

What wants there to such a towardly[149] and pregnant soil, but wise and faithful laborers, to make a knowing people, a nation of prophets, of sages, and of worthies? We reckon more than five months yet to harvest; there need not be five weeks; had we but eyes to lift up, the fields are white already. Where there is much desire to learn, there of necessity will be much arguing, much writing, many opinions; for opinion in good men is but knowledge in the making. Under these fantastic terrors of sect and schism, we wrong the earnest and zealous thirst after knowledge and understanding which God hath stirred up in this city. What some lament of, we rather rejoice at, should rather praise this pious forwardness among men, to reassume the ill-reputed care of their Religion into their own hands again. A little generous prudence, a little forbearance of one another, and some grain of charity might win all these diligences[150] to join and unite in one general and brotherly search after Truth; could we but forego this prelatical tradition of crowding free consciences and Christian liberties into canons and precepts of men. I doubt not, if some great and worthy stranger should come among us, wise to discern the mold and temper of a people, and how to govern it, observing the high hopes and aims, the diligent alacrity of our extended thoughts and reasonings in the pursuance of truth and freedom, but that he would cry out as Pyrrhus[151] did, admiring the Roman docility and courage, "If such were my Epirots, I would not despair the greatest design that could be attempted to make a Church or Kingdom happy." Yet these are the men cried out against for schismatics and sectaries; as if, while the temple of the Lord was building, some cutting, some squaring the marble, others hewing the cedars, there should be a sort[152] of irrational men who could not consider there must be many schisms and many dissections made in the quarry and in the timber ere the house of God can be built. And when every stone is laid artfully together, it cannot be united into a continuity, it can but be contiguous in this world; neither can every piece of the building be of one form; nay, rather the perfection consists in this, that out of many moderate varieties and brotherly dissimilitudes that are not vastly disproportional, arises the goodly and the graceful symmetry that commends the whole pile and structure. Let us therefore be more considerate

builders, more wise in spiritual architecture, when great reformation is expected. For now the time seems come, wherein Moses the great prophet may sit in heaven rejoicing to see that memorable and glorious wish of his fulfilled, when not only our seventy elders, but all the Lord's people, are become prophets.[153] No marvel then though some men, and some good men too, perhaps, but young in goodness, as Joshua then was, envy them. They fret, and out of their own weakness are in agony, lest these divisions and subdivisions will undo us. The adversary again applauds, and waits the hour; when they have branched themselves out, saith he, small enough into parties and partitions, then will be our time. Fool! he sees not the firm root, out of which we all grow, though into branches: nor will beware until he see our small divided maniples[154] cutting through at every angle of his ill-united and unwieldy brigade. And that we are to hope better of all these supposed sects and schisms, and that we shall not need that solicitude honest perhaps, though overtimorous of them that vex in this behalf, but shall laugh in the end, at those malicious applauders of our differences, I have these reasons to persuade me.

First, when a city shall be as it were besieged and blocked about, her navigable river infested, inroads and incursions round, defiance and battle oft rumored to be marching up even to her walls, and suburb trenches, that then the people, or the greater part, more than at other times, wholly taken up with the study of highest and most important matters to be reformed, should be disputing, reasoning, reading, inventing, discoursing, even to a rarity, and admiration, things not before discoursed or written of, argues first a singular goodwill, contentedness and confidence in your prudent foresight, and safe government, Lords and Commons; and from thence derives itself to a gallant bravery and well grounded contempt of their enemies, as if there were no small number of as great spirits among us, as his was, who when Rome was nigh besieged by Hannibal, being in the city, bought that piece of ground at no cheap rate, whereon Hannibal himself encamped his own regiment. Next, it is a lively and cheerful presage of our happy success and victory. For as in a body, when the blood is fresh, the spirits pure and vigorous, not only to vital, but to rational faculties, and those in the acutest, and the pertest[155] operations of wit and subtlety, it argues in what good plight and

---

149 Easily cultivated.   150 Labors, exertions, anxieties.
151 Pyrrhus, King of Epirus, defeated the Romans at Heraclea in 280 B.C.
152 Set, company.

153 See Numbers 11:27-29.
154 The Roman *manipulus* was a small company.
155 Sprightliest, nimblest.

constitution the body is, so when the cheerfulness of the people is so sprightly up, as that it has not only wherewith to guard well its own freedom and safety, but to spare, and to bestow upon the solidest and sublimest points of controversy and new invention, it betokens us not degenerated, nor drooping to a fatal decay, but casting off the old and wrinkled skin of corruption to outlive these pangs and wax young again, entering the glorious ways of truth and prosperous virtue destined to become great and honorable in these latter ages. Methinks I see in my mind a noble and puissant nation rousing herself like a strong man after sleep, and shaking her invincible locks. Methinks I see her as an eagle mewing[156] her mighty youth, and kindling her undazzled eyes at the full midday beam; purging and unscaling her long-abused sight at the fountain itself of heavenly radiance; while the whole noise of timorous and flocking birds, with those also that love the twilight, flutter about, amazed at what she means, and in their envious gabble would prognosticate a year of sects and schisms.

What would ye do then, should ye suppress all this flowery crop of knowledge and new lights sprung up and yet springing daily in this city, should ye set an oligarchy of twenty engrossers[157] over it, to bring a famine upon our minds again, when we shall know nothing but what is measured to us by their bushel? Believe it, Lords and Commons, they who counsel ye to such a suppressing do as good as bid ye suppress yourselves; and I will soon show how. If it be desired to know the immediate cause of all this free writing and free speaking, there cannot be assigned a truer than your own mild and free and humane government; it is the liberty, Lords and Commons, which your own valorous and happy counsels have purchased us, liberty which is the nurse of all great wits; this is that which hath rarefied and enlightened our spirits like the influence of heaven; this is that which hath enfranchised, enlarged, and lifted up our apprehensions degrees above themselves. Ye cannot make us now less capable, less knowing, less eagerly pursuing of the truth, unless ye first make yourselves, that made us so, less the lovers, less the founders of our true liberty. We can grow ignorant again, brutish, formal, and slavish, as ye found us; but you then must first become that which ye cannot be, oppressive, arbitrary, and tyrannous, as they were from whom ye have tried to free us. That

our hearts are now more capacious, our thoughts more erected to the search and expectation of greatest and exactest things, is the issue of your own virtue propagated in us; ye cannot suppress that unless ye reinforce an abrogated and merciless law, that fathers may dispatch at will their own children. And who shall then stick closest to ye, and excite others? not he who takes up arms for coat and conduct, and his four nobles of Danegelt.[158] Although I dispraise not the defense of just immunities, yet love my peace better, if that were all.[159] Give me the liberty to know, to utter, and to argue freely according to conscience, above all liberties.

What would be best advised, then, if it be found so hurtful and so unequal to suppress opinions for the newness, or the unsuitableness to a customary acceptance, will not be my task to say; I only shall repeat what I have learned from one of your own honorable number, a right noble and pious lord, who, had he not sacrificed his life and fortunes to the Church and Commonwealth, we had not now missed and bewailed a worthy and undoubted patron of this argument. Ye know him I am sure; yet I for honor's sake, and may it be eternal to him, shall name him the Lord Brooke.[160] He writing of Episcopacy, and by the way treating of sects and schisms, left ye his vote, or rather now the last words of his dying charge, which I know will ever be of dear and honored regard with ye, so full of meekness and breathing charity, that next to his last testament, who bequeathed love and peace to his disciples, I cannot call to mind where I have read or heard words more mild and peaceful. He there exhorts us to hear with patience and humility those, however they be miscalled, that desire to live purely, in such a use of God's ordinances as the best guidance of their conscience gives them, and to tolerate them, though in some disconformity to ourselves. The book itself will tell us more at large, being published to the world, and dedicated to the Parliament by him who both for

156 Molting; renewing.
157 Those who get a monopoly by buying up large quantities and thus command the market.

158 Alluding doubtless to John Hampden's refusal to pay ship-money. Danegelt was the old land-tax levied in order to protect the country from the Danes. Charles I appealed to the precedent of Danegelt in his attempts to impose ship-money. A noble was 6s. 8d.
159 If it were merely a question of being immune from paying a tax.
160 Robert, son of Fulke Greville, Lord Brooke, a supporter of the Parliamentary cause, and general in the Civil War. He was killed during an attack on Lichfield Cathedral, which was held by Royalist combatants, March 1, 1643. His book was A Discourse on Episcopacy. See Laud's Diary, March 2, 1643.

his life and for his death deserves that what advice he left be not laid by without perusal.

And now the time in special is by privilege to write and speak what may help to the further discussing of matters in agitation. The temple of Janus with his two controversal faces might now not unsignificantly be set open. And though all the winds of doctrine were let loose to play upon the earth, so Truth be in the field, we do injuriously by licensing and prohibiting to misdoubt her strength. Let her and Falsehood grapple; who ever knew Truth put to the worse in a free and open encounter. Her confuting is the best and surest suppressing. He who hears what praying there is for light and clearer knowledge to be sent down among us, would think of other matters to be constituted beyond the discipline of Geneva, framed and fabricked already to our hands. Yet when the new light which we beg for shines in upon us, there be who envy, and oppose, if it come not first in at their casements. What a collusion is this, whenas we are exhorted by the wise man to use diligence, to seek for wisdom as for hidden treasures early and late, that another order shall enjoin us to know nothing but by statute! When a man hath been laboring the hardest labor in the deep mines of knowledge, hath furnished out his findings in all their equipage, drawn forth his reasons as it were a battle arranged, scattered and defeated all objections in his way, calls out his adversary into the plain, offers him the advantage of wind and sun, if he please only that he may try the matter by dint of argument, for his opponents then to skulk, to lay ambushments, to keep a narrow bridge of licensing,[161] where the challenger should pass, though it be valor enough in soldiership, is but weakness and cowardice in the wars of Truth. For who knows not that Truth is strong, next to the Almighty; she needs no policies, nor stratagems, nor licensings to make her victorious, those are the shifts and the defenses that error uses against her power. Give her but room, and do not bind her when she sleeps, for then she speaks not true, as the old Proteus[162] did, who spake oracles only when he was caught and bound, but then rather she turns herself into all shapes, except her own, and perhaps tunes her voice according to the time, as Micaiah did before Ahab,[163] until she be adjured into her own likeness. Yet is it not impossible that she may have more shapes than one. What else is all that rank of things indifferent, wherein Truth may be on this side, or on the other, without being unlike herself? What but a vain shadow else is the abolition of those ordinances, that handwriting nailed to the cross, what great purchase is this Christian liberty which Paul so often boasts of? His doctrine is that he who eats, or eats not, regards a day, or regards it not, may do either to the Lord. How many other things might be tolerated in peace, and left to conscience, had we but charity, and were it not the chief stronghold of our hypocrisy to be ever judging one another! I fear yet this iron yoke of outward conformity hath left a slavish print upon our necks; the ghost of a linen decency[164] yet haunts us. We stumble and are impatient at the least dividing of one visible congregation from another, though it be not in fundamentals; and through our forwardness to suppress, and our backwardness to recover any enthralled piece of truth out of the gripe of custom, we care not to keep truth separated from truth, which is the fiercest rent and disunion of all. We do not see that, while we still affect by all means a rigid external formality, we may as soon fall again into a gross conforming stupidity, a stark and dead congealment of wood, and hay, and stubble forced and frozen together, which is more to the sudden degenerating of a Church than many subdichotomies[165] of petty schisms. Not that I can think well of every light separation, or that all in a Church is to be expected gold and silver and precious stones: it is not possible for man to sever the wheat from the tares, the good fish from the other fry; that must be the angels' ministry at the end of mortal things. Yet if all cannot be of one mind (as who looks they should be?), this doubtless is more wholesome, more prudent, and more Christian that many be tolerated, rather than all compelled. I mean not tolerated popery, and open superstition, which, as it extirpates all religious and civil supremacies, so itself should be extirpate, provided first that all charitable and compassionate means be used to win and regain the weak and the misled: that also which is impious or evil absolutely either against faith or manners no law can possibly permit that intends not to unlaw itself: but those neighboring

---

161 The allusion is to the tales of chivalry where knights often held a bridge in such manner.

162 The old man of the sea, in Greek mythology, who, to avoid having to prophesy, assumed many different shapes, until he was finally caught and bound.

163 See I Kings 22.

164 Referring to the controversies over ecclesiastical vestments, ceremonies, etc. Milton uses the words "linen decency" sarcastically, having in mind the directions of the Prayer-book with regard to linen cloths, surplices, etc.

165 Petty divisions.

differences, or rather indifferences, are what I speak of, whether in some point of doctrine or of discipline, which though they may be many, yet need not interrupt the unity of Spirit, if we could but find among us the bond of peace. In the meanwhile if anyone would write, and bring this helpful hand to the slow-moving Reformation which we labor under, if Truth have spoken to him before others, or but seemed at least to speak, who hath so bejesuited us that we should trouble that man with asking license to do so worthy a deed? and not consider this, that if it come to prohibiting, there is not aught more likely to be prohibited than truth itself; whose first appearance to our eyes, bleared and dimmed with prejudice and custom, is more unsightly and unplausible than many errors, even as the person is of many a great man slight and contemptible to see to. And what do they tell us vainly of new opinions, when this very opinion of theirs, that none must be heard but whom they like, is the worst and newest opinion of all others; and is the chief cause why sects and schisms do so much abound, and true knowledge is kept at distance from us; besides yet a greater danger which is in it. For when God shakes a kingdom with strong and healthful commotions to a general reforming, 'tis not untrue that many sectaries and false teachers are then busiest in seducing; but yet more true it is, that God then raises to his own work men of rare abilities, and more than common industry, not only to look back and revise what hath been taught heretofore, but to gain further and go on, some new enlightened steps in the discovery of truth. For such is the order of God's enlightening his Church, to dispense and deal out by degrees his beam, so as our earthly eyes may best sustain it. Neither is God appointed and confined, where and out of what place these his chosen shall be first heard to speak; for he sees not as man sees, chooses not as man chooses, lest we should devote ourselves again to set places, and assemblies, and outward callings of men; planting our faith one while in the old Convocation house,[166] and another while in the Chapel at Westminster; when all the faith and religion that shall be there canonized[167] is not sufficient without plain convincement and the

charity of patient instruction to supple the least bruise of conscience, to edify the meanest Christian, who desires to walk in the spirit, and not in the letter of human trust, for all the number of voices that can be there made; no, though Harry VII himself there, with all his liege tombs about him, should lend them voices from the dead, to swell their number. And if the men be erroneous who appear to be the leading schismatics, what withholds us but our sloth, our self-will, and distrust in the right cause, that we do not give them gentle meetings and gentle dismissions, that we debate not and examine the matter thoroughly with liberal and frequent audience; if not for their sakes, yet for our own? seeing no man who hath tasted learning, but will confess the many ways of profiting by those who not contented with stale receipts are able to manage, and set forth new positions to the world. And were they but as the dust and cinders of our feet, so long as in that notion they may yet serve to polish and brighten the armory of Truth, even for that respect they were not utterly to be cast away. But if they be of those whom God hath fitted for the special use of these times with eminent and ample gifts, and those perhaps neither among the Priests, nor among the Pharisees, and we in the haste of a precipitant zeal shall make no distinction, but resolve to stop their mouths, because we fear they come with new and dangerous opinions, as we commonly forejudge them ere we understand them, no less than woe to us, while thinking thus to defend the Gospel, we are found the persecutors.

There have been not a few since the beginning of this Parliament, both of the Presbytery and others, who by their unlicensed books to the contempt of an Imprimatur first broke that triple ice clung about our hearts, and taught the people to see day. I hope that none of those were the persuaders to renew upon us this bondage which they themselves have wrought so much good by contemning. But if neither the check that Moses gave to young Joshua, nor the countermand which our Saviour gave to young John, who was so ready to prohibit those whom he thought unlicensed, be not enough to admonish our elders how unacceptable to God their testy mood of prohibiting is, if neither their own remembrance what evil hath abounded in the Church by this let[168] of licensing, and what good they themselves have begun by transgressing it, be not enough, but that they will persuade, and execute the most Dominican part of the Inquisition over us, and are already with one foot in the stirrup so

166 The assembly of the clergy of the Church of England had the Chapter House of Westminster Abbey for its meeting place. When Presbyterianism was made the state religion in 1643, Parliament gave to the Assembly of Divines of the Presbyterian Church the powers and privileges formerly held by Convocation, and set aside Henry VII's Chapel in Westminster Abbey for its meeting place.

167 Pronounced to be orthodox.

168 Hindrance.

active at suppressing, it would be no unequal distribution in the first place to suppress the suppressors themselves: whom the change of their condition hath puffed up, more than their late experience of harder times hath made wise.

And as for regulating the Press, let no man think to have the honor of advising ye better than yourselves have done in that Order published next before this,[169] "that no book be Printed, unless the Printer's and the Author's name, or at least the Printer's be registered." Those which otherwise come forth, if they be found mischievous and libelous, the fire and the executioner will be the timeliest and the most effectual remedy that man's prevention can use. For this authentic[170] Spanish policy of licensing books, if I have said aught, will prove the most unlicensed book itself within a short while; and was the immediate image of a Star Chamber decree to that purpose made in those very times when that Court did the rest of those her pious works, for which she is now fallen from the stars with Lucifer. Whereby ye may guess what kind of state prudence, what love of the people, what care of Religion or good manners there was at the contriving, although with singular hypocrisy it pretended to bind books to their good behavior. And how it got the upper hand of your precedent Order so well constituted before, if we

may believe those men whose profession gives them cause to inquire most, it may be doubted there was in it the fraud of some old patentees and monopolizers in the trade of bookselling; who under pretense of the poor in their Company not to be defrauded, and the just retaining of each man his several copy, which God forbid should be gainsaid, brought divers glozing colors to the House, which were indeed but colors, and serving to no end except it be to exercise a superiority over their neighbors, men who do not therefore labor in an honest profession to which learning is indebted, that they should be made other men's vassals. Another end is thought was aimed at by some of them in procuring by petition this Order, that having power in their hands, malignant books might the easier scape abroad, as the event shows. But of these sophisms and elenchs[171] of merchandise I skill not. This I know, that errors in a good government and in a bad are equally almost incident; for what Magistrate may not be misinformed, and much the sooner, if liberty of Printing be reduced into the power of a few? But to redress willingly and speedily what hath been erred, and in highest authority to esteem a plain advertisement[172] more than others have done a sumptuous bribe, is a virtue (honored Lords and Commons) answerable to your highest actions, and whereof none can participate but greatest and wisest men.

169 The order of January 29, 1642 is referred to.
170 Peculiarly Spanish.

171 Fallacious arguments.   172 Notification.

Edward Hyde

FIRST EARL OF CLARENDON

[1609–1674]

CLARENDON'S career belongs at least as much to political as to literary history. Born in Wiltshire of a land-owning family, Edward Hyde entered Magdalen Hall, Oxford, in 1622. After an indifferent scholarly career, he received his B.A. in 1626 and moved to London to take up the study of law at the Middle Temple. In these early London years he proved to be as interested in letters as in law or politics, and he numbered among his friends not only the ubiquitous Jonson but also Selden, Earle, Davenant, Carew, and Waller. In particular, he was the friend of Lucius Cary, Viscount Falkland, whom he was to resemble in his devotion to king and church as in the moderation and sanity with which he was to express that devotion. Made a Member of Parliament in 1640, Hyde supported the parliamentarians in what he felt to be their justified resistance against the tyranny of Charles I; he supported the impeachment of Strafford in 1640 but not the sentence of death passed against that ill-fated figure. Loyalty to the Church of England and to the principles of monarchy and precedent, however, soon led to a break with the popular party, and by 1642 he was a firm supporter of the king in what had clearly become a civil war.

His destiny was to be very different from that of his friend Falkland, who fell in an early battle of the war, fighting for his king and church, but tormented internally by his clear understanding of the rights and wrongs on both sides. Hyde remained with the king in Oxford, counseling him always in the direction of moderation and legality. Unfortunately for both Charles and Britain, the king ignored his advice, and Hyde aroused the hostility of the extremists in the royalist party. Nevertheless, he was made Chancellor of the Exchequer and, in 1645, one of the Governors of the West. With the latter appointment he was obliged to move to Bristol, and in 1646 he accompanied Prince Charles to a place of safety in the Scilly Isles, where he began the enormous labor of his *History of the Rebellion*. At the outbreak of the Second Civil War in 1648 he followed the queen and the prince to their French exile, and, after the execution of Charles I, served the new king as faithfully as he had his father.

In 1658 Hyde was made Lord Chancellor of the exile government, and his skillful diplomacy did much to pave the way for the restoration of Charles II in 1660. At the restoration he received his reward by being elevated to the peerage and designated Chancellor of Oxford University. In 1661 he was made first Earl of Clarendon, and for the next six years he was virtual ruler of England. The years had, however, done much to alter the spirit of moderation which had once distinguished the friend of Falkland.

In opposition to Charles II, he advocated a policy of ruthless suppression toward Roman Catholics and dissenters and won Parliament to his way of thinking. A turn of the wheel of fortune, however, and Clarendon's power was at an end. The fiasco of the Dutch War led Parliament to seek a scapegoat, and Charles was only too willing to let his old servant become it. In 1667 Clarendon was dismissed and impeached; he fled the country, was voted a traitor by Parliament, and ended his life as an exile in France.

History has its ironies, however, and this disowned servant of the British state became the ancestor of three British queens. His daughter Anne, mistress of James, Duke of York, the brother of the king, had been secretly married to the Duke in 1660—despite the anger of her father and the resolute opposition of the queen mother. James succeeded his brother to the throne in 1685, and Anne became queen. After the revolution of 1688, her daughter Mary, with her husband William, came to the throne, and the monarchy passed to her other daughter Anne after William's death.

In another sense, too, historical irony re-established Clarendon. During the years of exile he turned once again to the literary pursuits which he had so long ignored: he undertook the writing of his autobiography—almost by definition an account of English history after 1648—and added it to his earlier account of the Civil War to produce his monumental *History of the Rebellion*. In form not so much a history as a patchwork of memoir and biography, the *History* succeeds nevertheless in being historical literature in the grand manner. It shows little understanding of the underlying religious causes of the great conflict, but the short biographical sketches of the protagonists in that conflict (which owe something to the traditions of the character-book) have an extraordinary vividness, and, for all of its author's personal bias, it occasionally shows something akin to the massive sense of destiny which marks Ralegh's *History of the World*.

E. HYDE, First Earl of Clarendon. *The History of the Rebellion and Civil Wars in England*, ed. W. D. Macray, 6 vols. (Oxford, 1888).

SIR H. CRAIK. *The Life of Edward, Earl of Clarendon*, 2 vols. (London, 1911). The standard biography.

L. C. KNIGHTS. "Reflections on Clarendon's *History of the Rebellion*," Scrutiny, XV (1948).

B. WORMALD. *Clarendon: Politics, History and Religion* (Cambridge, 1951).

C. V. WEDGWOOD. *Some Contemporary Accounts of the Great Civil War*, in Royal Society of Literature: Essays by Divers Hands, New Series, XXVI (London, 1953). Compares Clarendon's with other contemporary accounts of the conflict.

F R O M

THE HISTORY OF THE REBELLION

[TEXT: *Macray's edition, 1888*]

UNIVERSITY PLATE FOR THE KING

IT CANNOT be imagined how great advantage the King received by the Parliament's rejecting the King's messages for peace and their manner in doing All men's mouths were opened against them, the messages and answers being read in all churches; they who could not serve him in their persons contrived ways to supply him with money. Some eminent governors in the universities gave him notice that all the colleges were very plentifully supplied with plate, which would amount to a good value and lay useless in their treasuries, there being enough besides for their use; and there was not the least doubt but that whensoever his Majesty should think fit to require that treasure, it would all be sent to him. Of this the King had long thought, and when he was at Nottingham in that melancholic season, two gentlemen were dispatched away to Oxford and to Cambridge (two to each) with letters to the several Vice-Chancellors that they should move the heads and principals of the several colleges and halls that they would send their plate to the King, private advertisements being first sent to some confident persons to prepare and dispose those without whose consent the service could not be performed.

This whole affair was transacted with so great secrecy and discretion that the messengers returned from the two universities in as short a time as such a journey could well be made and brought with them all or very near all[1] their plate and a considerable sum of money, which was sent as a present to his Majesty from the several heads of colleges out of their own particular stores, some scholars coming with it and helping to procure horses and carts for the service; all which came safe to Nottingham at the time when there appeared no more expectation of a treaty and contributed much to raising the dejected spirits of the place.

DEATH AND CHARACTER OF HAMPDEN

THAT which would have been looked upon as a considerable recompense for a defeat could not but be thought a glorious crown of a victory, which was the death of Mr. Hampden; who, being shot into the shoulder with a brace of bullets which brake the bone, within three weeks after died with extraordinary pain, to as great a consternation of all that party as if their whole army had been defeated or cut off.

Many men observed—as upon signal turns of great affairs as this was such observations are frequently made—that the field in which the late skirmish was and upon which Mr. Hampden received his death's wound, Chalgrove Field, was the same place in which he had first executed the ordinance of the militia and engaged that county, in which his reputation was very great, in this rebellion. And it was confessed by the prisoners that were taken that day and acknowledged by all that upon the alarm that morning after their quarters were beaten up he was exceedingly solicitous

[1] Two colleges at Oxford are rather looked down on to this day because their plate dates from times prior to the Civil War.

to draw forces together to pursue the enemy, and being a colonel of foot, put himself among those horse as a volunteer, who were first ready, and that when the Prince made a stand all the officers were of opinion to stay till their body came up and he alone, being second to none but the general himself in the observance and application of all men, persuaded and prevailed with them to advance; so violently did his fate carry him to pay the mulct in the place where he had committed the transgression about a year before.

He was a gentleman of a good family in Buckinghamshire and born to a fair fortune and of a most civil and affable deportment. In his entrance into the world he indulged to himself all the license in sports and exercises and company which were used by men of the most jolly conversation. Afterwards, he retired to a more reserved and melancholic society, yet preserving his own natural cheerfulness and vivacity and, above all, a flowing courtesy to all men; though they who conversed nearly with him found him growing into a dislike of the ecclesiastical government of the church, yet most believed it rather a dislike of some churchmen and of some introducements of theirs which he apprehended might disquiet the public peace. He was rather of reputation in his own country than of public discourse or fame in the kingdom before the business of ship-money. But then he grew the argument of all tongues, every man inquiring who and what he was that durst at his own charge support the liberty and property of the kingdom and rescue his country from being made a prey to the court. His carriage, throughout that agitation, was with that rare temper and modesty that they who watched him narrowly to find some advantage against his person, to make him less resolute in his cause, were compelled to give him a just testimony. And the judgment that was given against him infinitely more advanced him than the service for which it was given. When this Parliament began, being returned knight of the shire for the county where he lived, the eyes of all men were fixed on him as their *patriæ pater* and the pilot that must steer their vessel through the tempests and rocks which threatened it. And I am persuaded, his power and interest at that time was greater to do good or hurt than any man's in the kingdom or than any man of his rank hath had in any time. For his reputation of honesty was universal, and his affections seemed so publicly guided that no corrupt or private ends could bias them.

He was of that rare affability and temper in debate

and of that seeming humility and submission of judgment as if he brought no opinions with him, but a desire of information and instruction; yet he had so subtle a way of interrogating and, under the notion of doubts, insinuating his objections that he left his opinions with those from whom he pretended to learn and receive them. And even with them who were able to preserve themselves from his infusions and discerned those opinions to be fixed in him with which they could not comply he always left the character of an ingenious and conscientious person. He was indeed a very wise man and of great parts and possessed with the most absolute spirit of popularity, that is, the most absolute faculties to govern the people, of any man I ever knew. For the first year of the Parliament he seemed rather to moderate and soften the violent and distempered humors than to inflame them. But wise and dispassioned men plainly discerned that that moderation proceeded [rather] from prudence and observation that the season was not ripe than that he approved of the moderation; and that he begat many opinions and motions the education whereof he committed to other men, so far disguising his own designs that he seemed seldom to wish more than was concluded; and in many gross conclusions which would hereafter contribute to designs not yet set on foot, when he found them sufficiently backed by majority of voices, he would withdraw himself before the question, that he might seem not to consent to so much visible unreasonableness; which produced as great a doubt in some, as it did approbation in others, of his integrity. What combination soever had been originally with the Scots for the invasion of England and what farther was entered into afterwards in favor of them and to advance any alteration in Parliament, no man doubts was at least with the privity of this gentleman.

After he was amongst those members accused by the King of high treason, he was much altered; his nature and carriage seeming much fiercer than it did before. And without question, when he first drew his sword, he threw away the scabbard; for he passionately opposed the overture made by the King for a treaty from Nottingham and as eminently any expedients that might have produced any accommodations in this that was at Oxford and was principally relied on to prevent any infusions which might be made into the Earl of Essex towards peace, or to render them ineffectual if they were made, and was indeed much more relied on by that party than the general himself.

In the first entrance into the troubles he undertook the command of a regiment of foot and performed the duty of a colonel on all occasions most punctually. He was very temperate in diet and a supreme governor over all his passions and affections and had thereby a great power over other men's. He was of an industry and vigilance not to be tired out or wearied by the most laborious and of parts not to be imposed upon by the most subtle or sharp and of a personal courage equal to his best parts; so that he was an enemy not to be wished wherever he might have been made a friend and as much to be apprehended where he was so as any man could deserve to be. And therefore his death was no less congratulated on the one party than it was condoled on the other. In a word, what was said of Cinna might well be applied to him: *Erat illi consilium ad facinus aptum; consilio autem neque lingua neque manu [s] deerat;* "he had a head to contrive and a tongue to persuade and a hand to execute any mischief." His death therefore seemed to be a great deliverance to the nation.[2]

CHARACTER AND DEATH OF LORD FALKLAND

HE HAD a courage of the most clear and keen temper and so far from fear that he was not without appetite of danger; and therefore upon any occasion of action he always engaged his person in those troops which he thought, by the forwardness of the commanders, to be most like to be farthest engaged; and in all such encounters he had about him a strange cheerfulness and companionableness, without at all affecting the execution that was then principally to be attended, in which he took no delight, but took pains to prevent it where it was not by resistance necessary. Insomuch that at Edgehill, when the enemy was routed, he was like to have incurred great peril by interposing to save those who had thrown away their arms and against whom, it may be, others were more fierce for their having thrown them away; insomuch as a man might think he came into the field only out of curiosity to see the face of danger, and charity to prevent the shedding of blood. Yet in his natural inclination he acknowledged he was addicted to the profession of a soldier; and shortly after he came to his fortune, and before he came to age, he went into the Low Countries with a resolution of procuring command and to give himself up to it; from which he was converted by the complete inactivity of that summer; and so he returned into England and shortly after entered that vehement

2 The Battle of Chalgrove Field was fought in June, 1643.

course of study we mentioned before, till the first alarum from the north; and then again he made ready for the field, and though he received some repulse in the command of a troop of horse of which he had a promise, he went a volunteer with the Earl of Essex.

From the entrance into this unnatural war his natural cheerfulness and vivacity grew clouded, and a kind of sadness and dejection of spirit stole upon him, which he had never been used to; yet being one of those who believed that one battle would end all differences and that there would be so great a victory on one side that the other would be compelled to submit to any conditions from the victor, which supposition and conclusion, generally sunk into the minds of most men, prevented the looking after many advantages that might then have been laid hold of, he resisted those indispositions *et in luctu bellum inter remedia erat.* But after the King's return from Brainford and the furious resolution of the two houses not to admit any treaty for peace, those indispositions, which had before touched him, grew into a perfect habit of uncheerfulness: and he who had been so exactly unreserved and affable to all men that his face and countenance was always present and vacant to his company and held any cloudiness and less pleasantness of the visage a kind of rudeness or incivility became, on a sudden, less communicable; and thence, very sad, pale, and exceedingly affected with the spleen. In his clothes and habit, which he had intended before always with more neatness and industry and expense than is usual to so great a mind he was not now only incurious but too negligent; and in his reception of suitors and the necessary or casual addresses to his place so quick and sharp and severe that there wanted not some men, who were strangers to his nature and disposition, who believed him proud and imperious, from which no mortal man was ever more free.

The truth is, as he was of a most incomparable gentleness, application, and even a demissness and submission to good and worthy and entire men so he was naturally—which could not but be more evident in his place, which objected him to another conversation and intermixture than his own election had done —*adversus malos injucundus;* and was so ill a dissembler of his dislike and disinclination to ill men that it was not possible for such not to discern it. There was once in the House of Commons such a declared acceptation of the good service an eminent member had done to them and, as they said, to the whole kingdom, that it was moved, he being present, "that the speaker might

in the name of the whole House give him thanks and then that every member might, as a testimony of his particular acknowledgement, stir or move his hat towards him"; the which, though not ordered, when very many did, the Lord Falkland, who believed the service itself not to be of that moment and that an honorable and generous person could not have stooped to it for any recompense, instead of moving his hat stretched both his arms out and clasped his hands together upon the crown of his hat and held it close down to his head that all men might see how odious that flattery was to him and the very approbation of the person, though at that time most popular.

When there was any overture or hope of peace, he would be more erect and vigorous and exceedingly solicitous to press anything which he thought might promote it, and sitting among his friends, often, after a deep silence and frequent sighs, would with a shrill and sad accent ingeminate the word *peace! peace!* and would passionately profess, "that the very agony of the war and the view of the calamities and desolation the kingdom did and must endure took his sleep from him and would shortly break his heart." This made some think, or pretend to think, "that he was so much enamored on peace that he would have been glad the King should have bought it at any price"; which was a most unreasonable calumny. As if a man that was himself the most punctual and precise in every circumstance that might reflect upon conscience or honor could have wished the King to have committed a trespass against either. And yet this senseless scandal made some impression upon him, or at least he used it for an excuse of the daringness of his spirit; for at the leaguer before Gloucester, when his friends passionately reprehended him for exposing his person unnecessarily to danger—for he delighted to visit the trenches and nearest approaches and to discover what the enemy did—as being so much beside the duty of his place that it might be understood rather against it, he would say merrily, "that his office could not take away the privileges of his age and that a secretary in war might be present at the greatest secret of danger"; but withal alleged seriously, "that it concerned him to be more active in enterprises of hazard than other men, that all might see that his impatiency for peace proceeded not from pusillanimity or fear to adventure his own person."

In the morning before the battle,[3] as always upon

3 The first Battle of Newbury was fought September 20–21, 1643.

action, he was very cheerful and put himself into the first rank of the Lord Byron's regiment, who was then advancing upon the enemy, who had lined the hedges on both sides with musketeers; from whence he was shot with a musket on the lower part of the belly, and in the instant falling from his horse, his body was not found till the next morning; till when there was some hope he might have been a prisoner, though his nearest friends, who knew his temper, received small comfort from that imagination. Thus fell that incomparable young man in the four and thirtieth year of his age, having so much dispatched the true business of life that the oldest rarely attain to that immense knowledge and the youngest enter not into the world with more innocence, and whosoever leads such a life need not care upon how short warning it be taken from him.

THE FIRST BATTLE OF NEWBURY

IT WAS disputed on all parts with great fierceness and courage; the enemy preserving good order and standing rather to keep the ground they were upon than to get more; by which they did not expose themselves to those disadvantages which any motion would have offered to the assailants. The King's horse, with a kind of contempt of the enemy, charged with wonderful boldness upon all grounds of inequality; and were so far too hard for the troops of the other side that they routed them in most places, till they had left the greatest part of their foot without any guard at all of horse. But then the foot behaved themselves admirably on the enemy's part and gave their scattered horse time to rally and were ready to assist and secure them upon all occasions. The London train-bands and auxiliary regiments—of whose inexperience of danger or any kind of service beyond the easy practice of their postures in the Artillery Garden men had till then too cheap an estimation—behaved themselves to wonder; and were, in truth, the preservation of that army that day. For they stood as a bulwark and rampire[4] to defend the rest; and when their wings of horse were scattered and dispersed, kept their ground so steadily that, though Prince Rupert himself led up the choice horse to charge them and endured their storm of small shot, he could make no impression upon their stand of pikes but was forced to wheel about. Of so sovereign benefit and use is that readiness, order, and dexterity in the use of their arms, which hath been so much neglected.

4 Rampart.

THE BATTLE OF NASEBY[5]

IT WAS about ten of the clock when the battle began, and the first charge was given by Prince Rupert, who with his own and his brother Prince Maurice's troop performed it with his usual vigor; and was so well seconded that he bore down all before him and was master of six pieces of the rebels' best cannon. The Lord Astley, with his foot, though against the hill, advanced upon their foot; who discharged their cannon at them, but overshot them, and so did their musketeers too. For the foot on either side hardly saw each other till they were within carbine shot, and so only gave one volley; the King's foot, according to their usual custom, falling in with their swords and the butt ends of their muskets; with which they did very notable execution, and put the enemy into great disorder and confusion. The right wing of horse and foot being thus fortunately engaged and advanced, the left wing, under Sir Marmaduke Langdale, in five bodies, advanced with equal resolution; and was encountered by Cromwell, who commanded the right wing of the enemy's horse, with seven bodies greater and more numerous than either of the other; and had, besides the odds in number, the advantage of the ground; for the King's horse were obliged to march up the hill before they could charge them. Yet they did their duty as well as the place and great inequality of numbers would enable them to do. But being flanked on both sides by the enemy's horse and pressed hard, before they could get to the top of the hill they gave back and fled farther and faster than became them. Four of the enemy's bodies, close and in good order, followed them, that they might not rally again; which they never thought of doing; and the rest charged the King's foot, who had till then so much the advantage over theirs; whilst Prince Rupert, with the right wing, pursued those horse which he had broken and defeated.

The King's reserve of horse, which was his own guards with himself in the head of them, were even ready to charge those horse who followed those of the left wing when on a sudden such a panic fear seized upon them that they all ran near a quarter of a mile without stopping; which happened upon an extraordinary accident which hath seldom fallen out and might well disturb and disorder very resolute troops, as these were, the best horse in the army. The King, as was said before, was even upon the point of charging

5 June 14, 1645.

the enemy in the head of his guards when the Earl of Carnewarth, who rode next to him, a man never suspected for infidelity nor yet one from whom the King would have received counsel in such a case, on a sudden laid his hand on the bridle of the King's horse, and swearing two or three full-mouthed Scots' oaths—for of that nation he was—said, "Will you go upon your death in an instant!" and before his Majesty understood what he would have, turned his horse round; upon which a word ran through the troops, "that they should *march* to the right hand"; which was both from charging the enemy and assisting their own men. Upon this they all turned their horses and rode upon the spur as if they were every man to shift for himself.

It is very true that upon the more soldierly word *stand*, which was sent to run after them, many of them returned to the King, though the former unlucky word carried more from him. And by this time Prince Rupert was returned with a good body of those horse which had attended him in his prosperous charge on the right wing; but they having, as they thought, acted their parts, could never be brought to rally themselves again in order or to charge the enemy. And that difference was observed shortly from the beginning of the war in the discipline of the King's troops and of those which marched under the command of Cromwell—for it was only under him and had never been notorious under Essex or Waller—that, though the King's troops prevailed in the charge and routed those they charged, they never rallied themselves again in order nor could be brought to make a second charge again the same day. Which was the reason that they had not an entire victory at Edgehill. Whereas Cromwell's troops, if they prevailed, or though they were beaten and routed, presently rallied again and stood in good order, till they received new orders. All that the King and Prince could do could not rally their broken troops which stood in sufficient numbers upon the field, though they often endeavored it with the manifest hazard of their own persons. So that in the end the King was compelled to quit the field and to leave Fairfax master of all his foot, cannon, and baggage; amongst which was his own cabinet where his most secret papers were and letters between the Queen and him; of which they shortly after made that barbarous use as was agreeable to their natures and published them in print, that is, so much of them as they thought would asperse either of their Majesties and improve the prejudice they had raised against them, and concealed other parts which would have

vindicated them from many particulars with which they had aspersed them.

CHARACTER OF CHARLES I

HE WAS very fearless in his person but not enterprising, and had an excellent understanding but was not confident enough of it; which made him oftentimes change his own opinion for a worse and follow the advice of men that did not judge so well as himself. And this made him more irresolute than the conjuncture of his affairs would admit. If he had been of a rougher and more imperious nature, he would have found more respect and duty. And his not applying some severe cures to approaching evils proceeded from the lenity of his nature and the tenderness of his conscience; which in all cases of blood made him choose the softer way and not hearken to severe counsels, how reasonably soever urged. This only restrained him from pursuing his advantage in the first Scottish expedition when, humanly speaking, he might have reduced that nation to the most entire obedience that could have been wished. But no man can say he had then many who advised him to it, but the contrary, by a wonderful indisposition all his council had to fighting or any other fatigue. He was always an immoderate lover of the Scottish nation, having not only been born there, but educated by that people and besieged by them always, having few English about him until he was king, and the major number of his servants being still of those, who he thought could never fail him. And then no man had such an ascendant over him, by the lowest and humblest insinuations, as Duke Hamilton had.

As he excelled in all other virtues so in temperance he was so strict that he abhorred all debauchery to that degree that, at a great festival solemnity where he once was, when very many of the nobility of the English and Scots were entertained, being told by one who withdrew from thence what vast draughts of wine they drank and "that there was one earl who had drunk most of the rest down and was not himself moved or altered," the King said, "that he deserved to be hanged"; and that earl coming shortly into the room where his Majesty was, in some gaiety to show how unhurt he was from that battle, the King sent one to bid him withdraw from his Majesty's presence; nor did he in some days after appear before the King.

There were so many miraculous circumstances contributed to his ruin that men might well think that heaven and earth conspired it, and that the stars designed it. Though he was from the first declension of his power so much betrayed by his own servants that there were very few who remained faithful to him, yet that treachery proceeded not from any treasonable purpose to do him any harm but from particular and personal animosities against other men. And afterwards, the terror all men were under of the Parliament and the guilt they were conscious of themselves made them watch all opportunities to make themselves gracious to those who could do them good; and so they became spies upon their master, and from one piece of knavery were hardened and confirmed to undertake another, till at last they had no hope of preservation but by the destruction of their master. And after all this, when a man might reasonably believe that less than a universal defection of three nations could not have reduced a great king to so ugly a fate, it is most certain that in that very hour when he was this wickedly murdered in the sight of the sun he had as great a share in the hearts and affections of his subjects in general, was as much beloved, esteemed, and longed for by the people in general of the three nations as any of his predecessors had ever been. To conclude, he was the worthiest gentleman, the best master, the best friend, the best husband, the best father, and the best Christian that the age in which he lived produced. And if he was not the greatest king, if he was without some parts and qualities which have made some kings great and happy, no other prince was ever unhappy who was possessed of half his virtues and endowments and so much without any kind of vice.

THE SPANISH TOROS[6]

As soon as the king comes, some officers clear the whole ground from the common people so that there is no man seen upon the plain but two or three algua-zils, magistrates with their small white wands. Then one of the four gates which lead into the streets is opened, at which the toreadors enter, all persons of quality richly clad, and upon the best horses in Spain, every one attended by eight or ten more lackeys, all clinquant with gold and silver lace, who carry the spears which their masters are to use against the bulls; and with this entry many of the common people break in, for which sometimes they pay very dear. The persons on horseback have all cloaks folded up upon their shoulder, the least disorder of which, much more the letting it fall, is a very great disgrace; and in that grave order they march to the place where the

6 This passage is not in the folio of 1702–04.

king sits, and after they have made the reverences, they place themselves at a good distance from one another and expect the bull. The bulls are brought in the night before from the mountains by people used to that work, who drive them into the town, when nobody is in the streets, into a pen made for them, which hath a door which opens into that large space, the key whereof is sent to the king; which the king, when he sees everything ready, throws to an alguazil, who carries it to the officer that keeps the door, and he causes it to be opened, when a single bull is ready to come out. When the bull enters, the common people, who sit over the door or near it, strike him or throw darts with sharp points of steel to provoke him to rage. He commonly runs with all his fury against the first man he sees on horseback, who watches him so carefully and avoids him so dexterously that, when the spectators believe him to be even between the horns of the bull, he avoids by the quick turn of his horse and with his lance strikes the bull upon a vein that runs through his pole, with which in a moment he falls down dead. But this fatal stroke can never be struck but when the bull comes so near upon the turn of the horse that his horn even touches the rider's leg and so is at such a distance that he can shorten his lance and use the full strength of his arm in the blow. And they who are the most skillful in the exercise do frequently kill the beast with such an exact stroke insomuch as in a day two or three fall in that manner; but if they miss the vein, it only gives a wound that the more enrages him. Sometimes the bull runs with so much fierceness—for if he escapes the first man, he runs upon the rest as they are in his way—that he gores the horse with his horns that his guts come out, and he falls before the rider can get from his back. Some-times, by the strength of his neck he raises horse and man from the ground and throws both down, and then the greatest danger is another gore upon the ground. In any of these disgraces, or any other by which the rider comes to be dismounted, he is obliged in honor to take his revenge upon the bull by his sword and upon his head, towards which the standers-by assist him by running after the bull and hocking him, by which he falls upon his hinder legs; but before that execution can be done, a good bull hath his revenge upon many poor fellows. . . . It is a wonderful thing to see with what steadiness those fellows will stand a full career of the bull, and by a little quick motion upon one foot avoid him and lay a hand upon his horn, as if he guided him from him; but then the next standers-by, who have not the same activity, commonly pay for it, and there is no day without much mischief. It is a very barbarous exercise and triumph in which so many men's lives are lost, and always ventured, but so rooted in the affections of that nation that it is not in the king's power, they say, to suppress it, though, if he disliked it enough, he might forbear to be present at it.

THE END OF MONTROSE[7]

HE [Montrose] said, "he was now again entered into the kingdom by his Majesty's command and with his authority. And what success soever it might have pleased God to have given him, he would always have obeyed any command he should have received from him." He advised them, "to consider well of the consequence before they proceeded against him and that all his actions might be examined and judged by the laws of the land or those of nations."

As soon as he had ended his discourse, he was ordered to withdraw; and, after a short space, was again brought in and told by the chancellor, "that he was on the morrow, being the one and twentieth of May, 1650, to be carried to Edinborough Cross and there to be hanged upon a gallows thirty-foot high for the space of three hours and then to be taken down and his head to be cut off upon a scaffold and hanged on Edinborough Tollbooth, and his legs and arms to be hanged up in other public towns of the kingdom, and his body to be buried at the place where he was to be executed, except the kirk should take off his excommunication; and then his body might be buried in the common place of burial." He desired, "that he might say somewhat to them"; but was not suffered, and so was carried back to the prison.

That he might not enjoy any ease or quiet during the short remainder of his life, their ministers came presently to insult over him with all the reproaches imaginable; pronounced his damnation; and assured him, "that the judgment he was the next day to undergo was but an easy prologue to that which he was to undergo afterward." After many such barbarities, they offered to intercede for him to the kirk upon his repentance and to pray with him; but he too well understood the form of their common prayers in those cases to be only the most virulent and insolent imprecations against the persons of those they prayed

against—"Lord, vouchsafe yet to touch the obdurate heart of this proud incorrigible sinner, this wicked, perjured, traitorous, and profane person who refuses to hearken to the voice of thy kirk," and the like charitable expressions—and therefore he desired them "to spare their pains, and to leave him to his own devotions." He told them, "that they were a miserable, deluded, and deluding people and would shortly bring that poor nation under the most insupportable servitude ever people had submitted to." He told them, "he was prouder to have his head set upon the place it was appointed to be than he could have been to have had his picture hung in the King's bedchamber; that he was so far from being troubled that his four limbs were to be hanged in four cities of the kingdom that he heartily wished that he had flesh enough to be sent to every city in Christendom as a testimony of the cause for which he suffered."

The next day they executed every part and circumstance of that barbarous sentence with all the inhumanity imaginable; and he bore it with all the courage and magnanimity, and the greatest piety, that a good Christian could manifest. He magnified the virtue, courage, and religion of the last King, exceedingly commended the justice and goodness and understanding of the present King and prayed, "that they might not betray him as they had done his father." When he had ended all he meant to say and was expecting to expire, they had yet one scene more to act of their tyranny. The hangman brought the book that had been published of his truly heroic actions whilst he had commanded in that kingdom, which book was tied in a small cord that was put about his neck. The Marquis smiled at this new instance of their malice and thanked them for it and said, "he was pleased that it should be there and was prouder of wearing it than ever he had been of the Garter"; and so renewing some devout ejaculations, he patiently endured the last act of the executioner.

THE BATTLE OF DUNBAR[8]

THE Scots did not intend to part with them [Cromwell's forces] so easily; they doubted not but to have the spoil of the whole army. And therefore they no sooner discerned that the whole army was upon their march, but they discamped and followed with their whole body all the night following and found themselves in the morning within a small distance of the enemy; for Cromwell was quickly advertised that the

7 The Marquis of Montrose, a Scottish supporter of Charles II, had been taken in an ill-starred uprising in favor of the King, April, 1650.

8 September 3, 1650.

Scots army was dislodged and marched after him; and thereupon he made a stand and put his men in good order. The Scots found they were not upon so clear a chase as they imagined, and placed themselves again upon such a side of a hill as they believed the English would not have the courage to attack them there.

But Cromwell knew them too well to fear them upon any ground when there were no trenches or fortifications to keep him from them; and therefore he made haste to charge them on all sides upon what advantage-ground soever they stood upon. Their horse did not sustain one charge but fled and were pursued with a great execution. The foot depended so much upon their ministers, who preached and prayed and assured them of the victory till the English were upon them; and some of their preachers were knocked in the head whilst they were promising the victory. Though there was so little resistance made that Cromwell did not want twenty men by that day's service, yet the execution was very terrible upon the enemy, the whole body of the foot being upon the matter cut in pieces; no quarter was given till they were weary of killing; so that there were between five and six thousand dead upon the place; and very few but they who escaped by the heels of their horse were without terrible wounds; of which very many died shortly after; especially such of their ministers who were not killed upon the place, as very many were, had very notable marks about the head and the face that anybody might know that they were not hurt by chance or in the crowd but by very good will. All the cannon, ammunition, carriages, and baggage were entirely taken, and Cromwell with his victorious army marched directly to Edinborough; where he found plenty of all things which he wanted and good accommodation for the refreshing his army, which stood in need of it.

DEFEAT OF VAN TROMP[9]

VAN TROMP all that night stood into the Texel; where he joined five and twenty more of their best ships; and with this addition, which made him one hundred and twenty sail, he faced the English; who kept still to the sea; and having got a little more room and the weather being a little clearer, tacked about, and were received by the Dutch with great courage and gallantry.

The battle continued very hot and bloody on both sides from six of the clock in the morning till one in

9 August, 1653.

the afternoon; when the Admiral of Holland, the famous Van Tromp, whilst he very signally performed the office of a brave and bold commander, was shot with a musket bullet into the heart, of which he fell dead without speaking word. And this blow killed the courage of the rest; who seeing many of their companions burned and sunk, and after having endured very hot service, before the evening fled and made all the sail they could towards the Texel; the English not being in a condition to pursue them; but found themselves obliged to retire to their own coast, both to preserve and mend their maimed and torn ships and refresh their wounded men.

This battle was the most bloody that had been yet fought, both sides rather endeavoring the destruction of their enemy's fleet than the taking their ships. On the Hollanders' part between twenty and thirty of their ships of war were fired or sunk, and above one thousand prisoners taken. The victory cost the English dear too; for four hundred common men and eight captains were slain outright and above seven hundred common men and five captains wounded. But they lost only one ship, which was burned; and two or three more, though carried home, were disabled for future service. The most sensible part of the loss to the Dutch was the death of their Admiral Van Tromp, who, in respect of his maritime experience and the frequent actions he had been engaged in, might very well be reckoned amongst the most eminent commanders at sea of that age and to whose memory his country is farther indebted than they have yet acknowledged.

BLAKE'S[10] LAST VICTORY AND DEATH

WITH this resolution they stood for the Canaries, and about the middle of April[11] came thither and found that the galleons were got thither before them and had placed themselves, as they thought, in safety. The smaller ships, being ten in number, lay in a semicircle moored along the shore; and the six great galleons—the fleet consisted of sixteen good ships—which could not come so near the shore lay with their broadsides toward the offing. And besides this good posture in which all the ships lay, they were covered with a strong castle well furnished with guns; and there were six or seven small forts raised in the most advantageous places of the bay, every one of them furnished with six good pieces of cannon; so that they were without the least apprehension of their want of security or

10 Admiral Robert Blake.
11 1657.

imagination that any men would be so desperate as to assault them upon such apparent disadvantage.

When the English fleet came to the mouth of the Bay of Santa Cruz and the generals saw in what posture the Spaniards lay, and thought it impossible to bring off any of the galleons; however, they resolved to burn them, which was by many thought to be equally impossible, and sent Captain Stayner with a squadron of the best ships to fall upon the galleons; which he did very resolutely; whilst other frigates entertained the forts and lesser breastworks with continual broadsides to hinder their firing. And so the generals coming up with the whole fleet, after full four hours' fight, they drove the Spaniards from their ships and possessed them; yet found that their work was not done and that it was not only impossible to carry away the ships which they had taken but that the wind that had brought them into the bay and enabled them to conquer the enemy would not serve to carry them out again; but that they lay exposed to all the cannon from the shore; which thundered upon them. However, they resolved to do what was in their power; and so, discharging their broadsides upon the forts and land, where they did great execution, they set fire to every ship, galleons and others, and burned every one of them; which they had no sooner done but the wind turned and carried the whole fleet without loss of one ship out of the bay and put them safe to sea again.

The whole action was so miraculous that all men who knew the place concluded that no sober men with what courage soever endued would ever undertake it; and they could hardly persuade themselves to believe what they had done; whilst the Spaniards comforted themselves with the belief that they were devils and not men which had destroyed them in such a manner. So much a strong resolution of bold and courageous men can bring to pass that no resistance and advantage of ground can disappoint them. And it can hardly be imagined how small loss the English sustained in this unparalleled action, no one ship being left behind and the killed and wounded not exceeding two hundred men, when the slaughter on board the [Spanish] ships and on the shore was incredible.

The fleet after this, having been long abroad, found it necessary to return home. And this was the last service performed by Blake; who sickened in his return and in the very entrance of the fleet into the Sound of Plymouth he expired. But he wanted no pomp when he was dead, Cromwell causing him to be brought up by land to London in all the state that could be; and then according to the method of that time, to encourage his officers to be killed that they might be pompously buried, he was, with all the solemnity possible and at the charge of the public, interred in Harry the Seventh's Chapel in the monument of the kings. . . . [He] was the first man that declined the old track and made it manifest that the science might be attained in less time than was imagined, and despised those rules which had been long in practice, to keep his ship and his men out of danger; which had been held in former times a point of great ability and circumspection, as if the principal art requisite in the captain of a ship had been to be sure to come home safe again. He was the first man who brought the ships to contemn castles on shore, which had been thought ever very formidable and were discovered by him only to make a noise and to fright those who could rarely be hurt by them. He was the first that infused that proportion of courage into the seamen by making them see by experience what mighty things they could do if they were resolved and taught them to fight in fire as well as upon water. And though he hath been very well imitated and followed, he was the first that drew the copy of naval courage and bold and resolute achievement.

DEATH AND CHARACTER OF CROMWELL

IT HAD been observed in England that, though from the dissolution of the last Parliament all things seemed to succeed at home and abroad to his wish, and his power and greatness to be better established than ever it had been, yet Cromwell never had the same serenity of mind he had been used to, after he had refused the crown; but was out of countenance and chagrin, as if he were conscious of not having been true to himself, and much more apprehensive of danger to his person than he had used to be. Insomuch as he was not so easy of access nor so much seen abroad and seemed to be in some disorder when his eyes found any stranger in the room; upon whom they were still fixed. When he intended to go to Hampton Court, which was his principal delight and diversion, it was never known till he was in the coach which way he would go; and was still hemmed in by his guards before and behind; and the coach in which he went was always thronged as full as it could be with his servants, who were armed; and he never returned the same way he went; and rarely lodged two nights together in one chamber but had many furnished and prepared to which his own key conveyed him and those he would have with him when he had a mind to go to bed. Which made his fears the more taken notice of and public, because he had never been accustomed to those precautions.

It is very true, he knew of many combinations to assassinate him by those who, he knew, wished the King no good. And when he had discovered the design of Syndercome, who was a very stout man and one who had been much in his favor and who had twice or thrice by wonderful and unexpected accidents been disappointed in the minute he made sure to kill him, and [had] caused him to be apprehended, his behavior was so resolute in his examination and trial as if he thought he should still be able to do it; and it was manifest that he had many more associates, who were undiscovered and as resolute as himself; and though he got him condemned to die, the fellow's carriage and words were such as if he knew well how to avoid the judgment; which made Cromwell believe that a party in the army would attempt his rescue; whereupon he gave strict charge, "that he should be carefully looked to in the Tower and three or four of the guard always with him day and night."

And at the day for his execution those troops he was most confident of were upon the Tower Hill, where the gallows were erected. But when the guard called him to arise in the morning, they found him dead in his bed; which gave trouble exceedingly to Cromwell; for besides that he hoped at his death, that to avoid the utmost rigor of it, he would have confessed many of his confederates, he now found himself under the reproach of having caused him to be poisoned, as not daring to bring him to public justice. Nor could he suppress that scandal, though it did appear upon examination that the night before, when he was going to bed in the presence of his guard, his sister came to take her leave of him; and whilst they spoke together at the bedside, he rubbed his nose with his hand, of which they then took no notice; and she going away, he put off his clothes, and leaped into his bed, with some snuffling in his nose, and said, "this was the last bed he should ever go into"; and seemed to turn to sleep, and never in the whole night made the least noise or motion, save that he sneezed once. When the physicians and surgeons opened his head, they found he had snuffed up through his nostrils some very well prepared poison, that in an instant curdled all the blood in that region, which presently suffocated him. The man was drawn by a horse to the gallows where he should have hanged, and buried under it with a stake driven through him, as is usual in the case of self-murderers. Yet this accident perplexed Cromwell very much; and though he was without the particular discovery which he expected, he made a general discovery by it that he himself was more odious in his army than he believed he had been.

He seemed to be much afflicted at the death of his friend the Earl of Warwick, with whom he had a fast friendship, though neither their humors nor their natures were like. And the heir of that house, who had married his youngest daughter, died about the same time; so that all his relation to or confidence in that family was at an end, the other branches of it abhorring his alliance. His domestic delights were lessened every day, and he plainly discovered that his son Falconbridge's heart was set upon an interest destructive to his, and grew to hate him perfectly. But that which broke his peace was the death of his daughter Claypole, who had been always his greatest joy and who had in her sickness, which was of a nature the physicians knew not how to deal with, had several conferences with him which exceedingly perplexed him. And though nobody was near enough to hear the particulars, yet her often mentioning in the pains she endured the blood her father had spilt made people conclude that she had presented his worst actions to his consideration. And though he never made the least show of remorse for any of those actions, it is very certain that either what she said or her death affected him wonderfully.

Whatever it was, about the middle of August he was seized on by a common tertian ague, from which he believed a little ease and divertisement at Hampton Court would have freed him. But the fits grew stronger, and his spirits much abated. So that he returned again to Whitehall, when his physicians began to think him in danger, though the preachers, who prayed always about him and told God Almighty what great things he had done for him and how much more need he had still of his service, declared as from God that he should recover. And he himself did not think he should die, till even the time that his spirits failed him, and then declared to them, "that he did appoint his son to succeed him, his eldest son Richard"; and so expired upon the third day of September (a day he thought always very propitious to him and on which he had triumphed for several victories), 1658; a day very memorable for the greatest storm of wind that had ever been known, for some hours before and after his death, which overthrew trees, houses, and made great wrecks at sea, and was so universal that there [were] terrible effects of it both in France and Flanders, where all people trembled at it; besides the wrecks all along the coast, many boats having been cast away in the very rivers; and within few days after, that circumstance of his death, that accompanied that storm, was known.

He was one of those men, *quos vituperare ne inimici quidem possunt nisi ut simul laudent;*[12] for he could never have done half that mischief without great parts of courage and industry and judgment. And he must have had a wonderful understanding in the natures and humors of men and as great a dexterity in the applying them; who, from a private and obscure birth—though of a good family—without interest of estate, alliance or friendship, could raise himself to such a height and compound and knead such opposite and contradictory tempers, humors, and interests into a consistence that contributed to his designs, and to their own destruction; whilst himself grew insensibly powerful enough to cut off those by whom he had climbed in the instant that they projected to demolish their own building. What Velleius Paterculus said of Cinna may very justly be said of him, *ausum eum quæ nemo auderet bonus perfecisse, quæ a nullo, nisi fortissimo, perfici possent.*[13] Without doubt, no man with more wickedness ever attempted anything or brought to pass what he desired more wickedly, more in the face and contempt of religion and moral honesty; yet wickedness as great as his could never have accomplished those designs without the assistance of a great spirit, an admirable circumspection and sagacity, and a most magnanimous resolution.

When he appeared first in the Parliament, he seemed to have a person in no degree gracious, no ornament of discourse, none of those talents which use to reconcile the affections of the standers-by. Yet

12 Whom his very enemies could not condemn without commending him at the same time.

13 He attempted those things which no good man durst have ventured on and achieved those in which none but a valiant and great man could have succeeded.

as he grew into place and authority, his parts seemed to be renewed, as if he had concealed faculties till he had occasion to use them; and when he was to act the part of a great man, he did it without any indecency through the want of custom.

After he was confirmed and invested Protector by the humble Petition and Advice, he consulted with very few upon any action of importance, nor communicated any enterprise he resolved upon with more than those who were to have principal parts in the execution of it; nor to them sooner than was absolutely necessary. What he once resolved, in which he was not rash, he would not be dissuaded from nor endure any contradiction of his power and authority; but extorted obedience from them who were not willing to yield it. . . .

To reduce three nations which perfectly hated him to an entire obedience to all his dictates, to awe and govern those nations by an army that was indevoted to him and wished his ruin, was an instance of a very prodigious address. But his greatness at home was but a shadow of the glory he had abroad. It was hard to discover which feared him most, France, Spain, or the Low Countries, where his friendship was current at the value he put upon it. And as they did all sacrifice their honor and their interest to his pleasure, so there is nothing he could have demanded that either of them would have denied him. . . .

He was not a man of blood, and totally declined Machiavel's method, which prescribes, upon any alteration of a government, as a thing absolutely necessary, to cut off all the heads of those, and extirpate their families, who are friends to the old [one]. And it was confidently reported that in the council of officers it was more than once proposed, "that there might be a general massacre of all the royal party as the only expedient to secure the government," but Cromwell would never consent to it; it may be, out of too much contempt of his enemies. In a word, as he had all the wickednesses against which damnation is denounced and for which hellfire is prepared, so he had some virtues which have caused the memory of some men in all ages to be celebrated; and he will be looked upon by posterity as a brave bad man.

Sir John Suckling

[1609–1642]

IT IS, of course, as the author of some of the most charming light lyrics in our language that Suckling is remembered, and his prose will never challenge the poetic basis of his fame. Nevertheless, the witty and casual letters which were printed in the posthumous collections of his works, *Fragmenta Aurea* (1646) and *Last Remains* (1659), have a certain value both as the embodiment of the libertine "naturalism" which had a distinct vogue in courtly circles of the Stuart era and as the expression of a personality who stands as one archetype of the cavalier, as Lovelace stands as another. Of a rich and aristocratic Norfolk family, Suckling was educated at Cambridge and, for a few weeks, at Gray's Inn. He did not exercise his legal training, however; instead he embarked, in 1628, on an extended grand tour which took him to France, Germany, Italy, and Spain. His talents as a linguist enabled him to absorb a variety of influences during his two years of travel. In 1631 he accompanied the Marquis of Hamilton to Germany and served with him under Gustavus Adolphus in the Thirty Years' War. Military service under the Protestant champion does not, however, seem to have had a sobering effect on his character; back in London, he became notorious for his passionate gambling (he is said to have invented the game of cribbage), his casual amours, and his scintillating wit. Extravagant to the point of eccentricity, he spent a small fortune on the mounting of his play *Aglaura* and a considerably larger fortune on the mounting of his famous troop of 100 horsemen to serve the king in the First Bishops' War in 1639. When Sir John's gorgeously outfitted horsemen shared in the general inglorious defeat of the king's forces at the Scottish border, Puritan merriment knew no bounds. Suckling, however, more than held his own in the interchange of epigrams which followed.

Deeply involved in a royalist plot to free Strafford in 1641, Suckling fled to Paris, where, a year later, his fortune gone and his future bleak, he died. According to Aubrey's account, he died by his own hand, and the story has at least a poetic validity, for Suckling had consistently shown himself to be one who, in the words of the lyric by another cavalier, had never feared to put it "unto the touch/ To win or lose it all." The casual, shallow brilliance of his life and verse are conspicuous in his letters as well.

SIR J. SUCKLING. *Works*, ed. A. H. Thompson (London, 1910).

LETTERS OF SIR JOHN SUCKLING

[TEXTS: *Fragmenta Aurea, 1658; The Last Remains, 1659*]

To a cousin who still loved young girls, and when they came to be marriageable, quitted them and fell in love with fresh, at his father's request, who desired he might be persuaded out of the humor, and marry.

HONEST CHARLES,[1]—Were there not fools enow before in the commonwealth of lovers, but that thou must bring up a new sect? Why delighted with the first knots of roses, and when they come to blow (can satisfy the sense and do the end of their creation) dost not care for them? Is there nothing in this foolish transitory world that thou canst find out to set thy heart upon but that which has newly left off making dirt-pies and is but preparing itself for loam and a green sickness? Seriously, Charles, and without ceremony, 'tis very foolish, and to love widows is as tolerable an humor and as justifiable as thine, for beasts that have been rid off their legs are as much for a man's use as colts that are unwayed and will not go at all.—Why the Devil such young things! Before these understand what thou wouldst have, others would have granted. Thou dost not marry them neither, nor anything else. 'Sfoot, it is the story of the jackanapes and the partridges; thou starest after a beauty till it is lost to thee, and then lettest out another, and starest after that till it is gone too. Never considering that it is here as in the Thames, and that while it runs up in the middle, it runs down on the sides; while thou contemplatest the coming-in tide and flow of beauty, that it ebbs with thee and that thy youth goes out at the same time. After all this too, she thou now art cast upon will have much ado to avoid being ugly. Pox on't! men will say thou wert benighted and wert glad of any inn. Well! Charles, there is another way, if you could find it out. Women are like melons, too green or too ripe are worth nothing; you must try till you find a right one. Taste all, but hark you—Charles, you shall not need to eat of all, for one is sufficient for a surfeit.

Your most humble servant.

I should have persuaded you to marriage, but to deal ingenuously, I am a little out of arguments that

1 Charles Suckling.

way at this present. 'Tis honorable, there's no question on't; but what more, in good faith, I cannot readily tell.

[*To Aglaura.*[2]]

MY DEAR DEAR,—Think I have kissed your letter to nothing, and now know not what to answer. Or that now I am answering, I am kissing you to nothing, and know not how to go on! For you must pardon, I must hate all I send you here, because it expresses nothing in respect of what it leaves behind with me. And oh! why should I write then? Why should I not come myself? Those tyrants, business, honor, and necessity, what have they to do with you and I? Why should we not do love's commands before theirs whose sovereignty is but usurped upon us! Shall we not smell to roses 'cause others do look on! or gather them 'cause there are prickles and something that would hinder us! Dear—I fain would—and know no hindrance but what must come from you, and why should any come! since 'tis not I but you must be sensible how much time we lose, it being long since I was not myself but *yours.*

[*A dissuasion from love.*]

JACK,—Though your disease be in the number of those that are better cured with time than precept, yet since it is lawful for every man to practice upon them that are forsaken and given over, which I take to be your state, I will adventure to prescribe to you; and of the innocence of the physic you shall not need to doubt, since I can assure you I take it daily myself.

To begin methodically, I should enjoin you to travel; for absence doth in a kind remove the cause, removing the object, and answers the physician's first recipes, vomiting and purging; but this would be too harsh, and indeed not agreeing to my way. I therefore advise you to see her as often as you can, for, besides that the rarity of visits endears them, this may bring you to surprise her and to discover little defects which,

2 This lady must remain unknown among the Celias and Delias and Corinnas of the time. Suckling addresses several letters to her. She has given her poetic name to his best-known play.

though they cure not absolutely, yet they qualify the fury of the fever. As near as you can, let it be unseasonably, when she is in sickness and disorder; for that will let you know she is mortal, and a woman, and the last would be enough to a wise man. If you could draw her to discourse of things she understands not, it would not be amiss.

Contrive yourself often into the company of the cried-up beauties; for if you read but one book, it will be no wonder if you speak or write that style; variety will breed distraction, and that will be a kind of diverting the humor.

I would not have you deny yourself the little things, for these agues are easier cured with surfeits than abstinence; rather, if you can, taste all; for that, as an old author saith, will let you see

> That the thing for which we woo
> Is not worth so much ado.

But since that here would be impossible, you must be content to take it where you can get it. And this for your comfort I must tell you, Jack, that mistress and woman differ no otherwise than Frontiniac and ordinary grapes; which, though a man loves never so well, yet if he surfeit of the last, he will care but little for the first.

I would have you leave that foolish humor, Jack, of saying you are not in love with her and pretending you care not for her; for smothered fires are dangerous, and malicious humors are best and safest vented and breathed out. Continue your affection to your rival still; that will secure you from one way of loving, which is in spite; and preserve your friendship with her woman; for who knows but she may help you to the remedy?

A jolly glass and right company would much conduce to the cure; for though in the Scripture (by the way, it is but Apocrypha) woman is resolved stronger than wine, yet whether it will be so or not when wit is joined to it, may prove a fresh question.

Marrying, as our friend the late ambassador hath wittily observed, would certainly cure it; but that is a kind of live pigeons laid to the soles of the feet, a last remedy, and, to say truth, worse than the disease.

But, Jack, I remember I promised you a letter, not a treaty;[3] I now expect you should be just, and as I have showed you how to get out of love, so you, according to our bargain, should teach me how to get

into it. I know you have but one way, and will prescribe me now to look upon Mistress Howard; but for that I must tell you aforehand that it is in love as in antipathy; the capers which will make my Lord of Dorset go from the table, another man will eat up. And, Jack, if you would make a visit to Bedlam, you shall find that there are rarely two there mad for the same thing.

> *Your humble servant.*

[A letter from the border.]

Sir,—We are now arrived at that river, about the uneven running of which my friend Master William Shakespeare makes Henry Hotspur quarrel so highly with his fellow rebels; and for his sake I have been something curious to consider the scantlet of ground that angry monsieur would have had in, but cannot find it could deserve his choler, nor any of the other side ours, did not the King think it did. The account I shall now give you of the war will be but imperfect, since I conceive it to be in the state that part of the four and twenty hours is in which we can neither call night nor day. I should judge it dawning towards earnest, did not the Lords Covenanters' letters to our Lords here something divide me. So, Sir, you may now imagine us walking up and down the banks of the Tweed like the Tower lions in their cages,[4] leaving the people to think what we would do if we were let loose. The enemy is not yet much visible. It may be it is the fault of the climate, which brings men as slowly forward as plants; but it gives us fears that the men of peace will draw all this to a dumb-show and so destroy a handsome opportunity which was now offered of producing glorious matter for future chronicle.

These are but conjectures, Sir. The last part of my letter I reserve for a great and known truth, which is that I am, Sir, *your most humble servant,* etc.

[A cavalier looks at Holland.[5]]

Will,[6]—It is reported here a-shipboard that the wind is, as women are, for the most part bad; that it altogether takes part with the water, for it crosses him continually that crosses the seas; that it is not good for a state-reserved politician to come to sea, for he is

---

3 A treatise.

4 The lions in the Tower were one of the sights of London.
5 This letter is folio 101, Ashmolean MS. 826, Bodleian Library. First printed by W. C. Hazlitt in 1874.
6 This is William Davenant, friend, fellow blade, poet laureate-to-be.

subject to lay forth his mind in very plain terms; that it is an ill gaming place, for four days together here has been very bad casting of all sides, and I think if we had tarried longer it would have been worse; that so much rope is a needless thing in a ship, for they drown here altogether, not hang; that if a wench at land, or a ship at sea, spring a leak, 'tis fit and necessary they should be pumped; that Dunkirk is the Papist's purgatory, for men are fain to pay money to be freed of it; or to speak more like a true Protestant, it is the water-hell; for if a man 'scape this, 'tis ten to one he shall be saved; that lying four nights a-shipboard is almost as bad as sitting up to lose money at threepenny gleek, and so pray tell Mr. Brett; and thus much for sea-news.

Since my coming ashore, I find that the people of this country are a kind of infidels, not believing in the Scripture; for though it be there promised there shall never be another Deluge, yet they do fear it daily and fortify against it; that they are nature's youngest children, and so consequently have the least portion of wit and manners; or rather that they are her bastards, and so inherit none at all. And sure their ancestors, when they begot them, thought on nothing but monkeys and boars and asses and such like ill-favored creatures; for their physiognomies are so wide from the rules of proportion that I should spoil my prose to let in the description of them. In a word, they are almost as bad as those of Leicestershire; their habits are as monstrous as themselves to all strangers. But by my troth, to speak the naked truth of them, the difference betwixt the dressing of their women and ours is only this: these bombast their tails, and ours their arms. As for the country the water and the King of France beleaguer it round; sometimes the Hollander gets ground upon them; sometimes they upon him. It is so even a level that a man must have more than the quantity of a grain of mustard-seed in faith to remove a mountain here, for there is none in the country. Their own turf is their firing altogether, and it is to be feared that they will burn up their country before doomsday. The air, what with their breathing in it and its own natural corruption, is so unwholesome that a man must resolve to be at the charge of an ague once a month. The plague is here constantly—I mean excise—and in so great a manner that the whole country is sick on't. Our very farts stand us in I know not how much excise to the States before we let them. To be learned here is capital treason of them, believing that *fortuna favet fatuis*, and therefore, that they may

have the better success in their wars, they choose burgomasters and burghers as we do our mayors and aldermen, by their great bellies, little wits, and full purses. Religion they use as a stuff cloak in summer, more for show than anything else; their *summum bonum* being altogether wealth. They wholly busy themselves about it; not a man here but would do that which Judas did for half the money. To be short, the country is stark nought, and yet too good for the inhabitants; but being our allies, I will forbear their character and rest.—*Your humble servant,*

J. Suckling

Leyden, Nov. 18, 1629.

The wine-drinkers to the water-drinkers, greeting:

Whereas by your ambassador two days since sent unto us we understand that you have lately had a plot to surprise, or to speak more properly, to take the waters, and in it have not only a little miscarried but also met with such difficulties that, unless you be speedily relieved, you are like to suffer in the adventure; we, as well out of pity to you as out of care to our state and commonwealth, knowing that women have ever been held necessary, and that nothing relisheth so well after wine, have so far taken it into our consideration that we have neglected no means, since we heard of it first, that might be for your contents or the good of the cause; and therefore to that purpose we have had divers meetings at the Bear at the Bridgefoot, and now at length have resolved to dispatch to you one of our cabinet council, Colonel Young, with some slight forces of canary and some few of sherry, which no doubt will stand you in good stead, if they do not mutiny and grow too headstrong for their commander; him Captain Puff of Barton shall follow with all expedition, with two or three regiments of claret; Monsieur de Granville, commonly called Lieutenant Strutt, shall lead up the rear of Rhenish and white. These succors thus timely sent we are confident will be sufficient to hold the enemy in play; and till we hear from you again we shall not think of a fresh supply. For the waters—though perchance they have driven you into some extremities and divers times forced their passages through some of your best-guarded places—yet have they, if our intelligence fail us not, hitherto had the worst of it still and evermore at length plainly run away from you.

Given under our hands at the Bear, this fourth of July.

To T[homas] C[arew].[7]

Though writing be as tedious to me as no doubt reading will be to thee, yet considering that I shall drive that trade thou speakest of to the Indies and for my beads and rattles have a return of gold and pearl,[8] I am content for thy sake and in private thus to do penance in a sheet.

Know then, dear Carew, that at eleven last night, flowing as much with love as thou hast ebbed, thy letter found me out. I read, considered, and admired, and did conclude at last that Horsley air did excel the waters of the Bath, just so much as love is a more noble disease than the pox.

No wonder if the countesses think time lost till they be there. Who would not be where such cures flow! The care thou hast of me, that I should traffic right, draws me by way of gratitude to persuade thee to bottle us some of that and send it hither to town; thy returns will be quicker than those to the Indies, nor needst thou fear a vent, since the disease is epidemical.

One thing more, who knows (wouldst thou be curious in search) but thou mayst find an air of contrary virtue about thy house, which may, as this destroys, so that create affection; if thou couldst,

> The lady of Highgate then should embrace
> The disease of the stomach and the word of disgrace.[9]
> Gredeline[10] and grass-green
>
> Shall sometimes be seen
> Its arms to entwine
> About the woodbine.

In honest prose thus: we would carry ourselves first and then our friends, manage all the little loves at court, make more Tower work, and be the Duke of B.[11] of our age, which without it, we shall never be. Think on 't, therefore, and be assured that if thou joinest me in the patent with thee, in the height of all my greatness I will be thine, all but what belongs to Desdemona, which is just, as I mean to venture at thy horse-race Saturday come seven-night.

J. S.

A letter to a friend[12] *to dissuade him from marrying a widow which he formerly had been in love with, and quitted.*

At this time when no hot planet fires the blood and when the lunatics of Bedlam themselves are trusted abroad, that you should run mad, is, Sir, not so much a subject for your friends' pity as their wonder. 'Tis true, love is a natural distemper, a kind of small-pox. Everyone either hath had it or is to expect it, and the sooner the better.

Thus far you are excused. But having been well cured of a fever, to court a relapse, to make love a second time in the same place, is, not to flatter you, neither better nor worse than to fall into a quagmire by chance, and ride into it afterwards on purpose. 'Tis not love, Tom, that doth the mischief, but constancy, for love is of the nature of a burning-glass, which kept still in one place, fireth; changed often, it doth nothing, a kind of glowing coal which with shifting from hand to hand a man easily endures. But then to marry, Tom! Why, thou hadst better to live honest. Love, thou knowest, is blind. What will he do when he hath fetters on, thinkest thou!

Dost thou know what marriage is? 'Tis curing of love the dearest way, or waking a losing gamester out of a winning dream, and after a long expectation of a strange banquet, a presentation of a homely meal. Alas! Tom, love seeds when it runs up to matrimony and is good for nothing. Like some fruit-trees it must be transplanted if thou wouldst have it active and bring forth anything.

Thou now perchance hast vowed all that can be vowed to any one face and thinkest thou hast left nothing unsaid to it. Do but make love to another, and if thou art not suddenly furnished with new language and fresh oaths, I will conclude Cupid hath used thee worse than ever he did any of his train.

After all this, to marry a widow, a kind of chewed meat! What a fantastical stomach hast thou, that canst not eat of a dish till another man hath cut of it! Who would wash after another, when he might have fresh water enough for asking?

Life is sometimes a long journey. To be tied to ride

7 This is the Cavalier poet of the immortal lines, "Ask me no more. . . ."

8 A commentary on the trading methods of our ancestors in the New World.

9 This is a nest of anagrams; the name concealed in the second line is Carew Ralegh, Suckling's friend; see note on Aubrey's Life of Ralegh.

10 Gridelin (cf. Fr., *gris-de-lin*, flaxen-gray). The name of a color, "a pale purple or gray violet; sometimes a pale red." (Oxford English Dictionary.)

11 Buckingham.

12 Thomas Carew again.

upon one beast still, and that half tired to thy hand too! Think upon that, Tom!

Well, if thou must needs marry (as who can tell to what height thou hast sinned), let it be a maid and no widow. For as a modern author hath wittily resolved in this case, 'tis better, if a man must be in prison, to lie in a private room than in the hole.

An answer to the letter.

Cease to wonder, honest Jack, and give me leave to pity thee, who laborest to condemn that which thou confessest natural, and the sooner had, the better.

Thus far there needs no excuse, unless it be on thy behalf, who stylest second thoughts (which are allowed the best) a relapse and talkest of a quagmire where no man ever stuck fast and accusest constancy of mischief in what is natural and advisedly undertaken.

'Tis confessed that love changed often doth nothing; nay, 'tis nothing; for love and change are incompatible; but where it is kept fixed to its first object, though it burn not, yet it warms and cherisheth, so as it needs no transplantation or change of soil to make it fruitful; and certainly if love be natural, to marry is the best recipe for living honest.

Yes, I know what marriage is and know you know it not by terming it the dearest way of curing love. For certainly there goes more charge to the keeping of a stable full of horses than one only steed. And much of vanity is therein besides; when, be the errand what it will, this one steed shall serve your turn as well as twenty more. Oh! if you could serve your steed so!

Marriage turns pleasing dreams to ravishing realities which outdo what fancy or expectation can frame unto themselves.

That love doth seed when it runs into matrimony is undoubted truth; how else should it increase and multiply, which is its greatest blessing!

'Tis not the want of love, nor Cupid's fault, if every day afford not new language and new ways of expressing affection. It rather may be caused through an excess of joy, which oftentimes strikes dumb.

These things considered, I will marry; nay, and to prove the second paradox false, I'll marry a widow, who is rather the chewer than the chewed. How strangely fantastical is he who will be an hour in plucking on a strait boot when he may be forthwith furnished with enough that will come on easily and do him as much credit and better service? Wine when

first broached drinks not half so well as after a while drawing. Would you not think him a madman who, whilst he might fair and easily ride on the beaten roadway, should trouble himself with breaking up the gaps? A well-wayed horse will safely convey thee to thy journey's end, when an unbacked filly may by chance give thee a fall. 'Tis prince-like to marry a widow, for 'tis to have a taster.

'Tis true, life may prove a long journey; and so, believe me it must do. A very long one too, before the beast you talk of prove tired. Think upon that, Jack!

Thus, Jack, thou seest my well taken resolution of marrying, and that a widow, not a maid; to which I am much induced out of what Pythagoras saith, in his 2d sect., *cuniculorum*, that it is better lying in the hole than sitting in the stocks.

[*A letter from Germany.*]

My Noble Lord,[13]

Your humble servant had the honor to receive from your hand a letter, and had the grace upon the sight of it to blush. I but then found my own negligence, and but now could have the opportunity to ask pardon for it. We have ever since been upon a march, and the places we are come to have afforded rather blood than ink; and of all things, sheets have been the hardest to come by, specially those of paper. If these few lines shall have the happiness to kiss your hand, they can assure that he that sent them knows none to whom he owes more obligation than to your lordship, and to whom he would more willingly pay it; and that it must be no less than necessity itself that can hinder him from often presenting it. Germany hath no whit altered me: I am still the humble servant of my Lord——that I was, and when I cease to be so, I must cease to be

John Suckling.

[*A sermon on malt.*[14]]

Certain drunkards, returning from a merry meeting at a country alehouse, by the way overtook a preacher, who in a sermon he had lately made against drunkenness, amongst other reproofs, as the sweet-sugared fellows constructed it, had termed them malt-worms.

---

13 The person to whom this letter was addressed has not been identified. It was obviously written about 1631 when Suckling was in Germany during the Thirty Years' War.

14 Printed from the text of the letter on the back of fol. 102 of Ashmolean MS. 826, Bodleian Library.

Wherefore they agreed to take him and by violence compel him to preach them a sermon, appointing him his theme to be

MALT

Preacher:

"There is no teaching without a division. This theme cannot well be divided into many parts, because it is but one word, nor yet into syllables, as being a monosyllable. It must therefore be quartered into four letters, and those being M. A. L. T. do form the word *malt,* my theme.

These four letters represent four distinct interpretations which we divines do much use: first, M, moral; secondly, A, allegorical; thirdly, L, literal; fourthly, T, tropological.

The moral is fitly placed first, if not to teach rude boisterous fellows good manners yet at least to procure your peaceable attention to the sermon; wherefore, M, Masters, A, all, L, listen, T, to the theme.

An allegory is when one thing is spoken and another thing meant. The thing here spoken is of malt, the thing meant is the oil of malt, which to the drunkards is so precious as that they account M, their meat, A, their ale, L, their liberty, T, their treasure.

Their literal sense hath ever been found suitable to the theme, confirmed by beggarly experience: M. A. L. T., much ale, little thought.

The tropological is manifested by the effect in the humor predominantly stirring up in some M, murther; in others A, adultery; in most L, loose-living; and in others some T, treachery; and consequently, M, misery, A, anguish, L, lamentation, T, tribulation.

For conclusion, I do seriously exhort all with repentance and amendment of life, and so you may escape the penalty due to such swinish livers; but I much fear that I lose my labor, my theme showing that it is M to A, a thousand pounds to a pot of ale, if I K L one knave of fifty will ever L T, leave to love potting. Nevertheless in regard of the discharge of my dutiful love unto you, my dearly beloved brethren, I do again and again exhort you one thing: M, mend; A, and; L, leave; T, tippling."

By this time the ale and his persuasion so wrought as they fell alseep, and the preacher closely crept away.

Jeremy Taylor

[1613–1667]

ORN the son of a Cambridgeshire barber, Taylor was educated at Perse School and at Cambridge, where he was a sizar of Gonville and Caius College. He remained at Cambridge from 1626 to 1635, taking holy orders in 1633 and proceeding to his M.A. in 1634. Having attracted the favorable attention of Archbishop Laud through his eloquence as a substitute preacher at St. Paul's, he was in 1636 made a fellow of All Souls' College, Oxford. Some time around 1639 he was married; his first wife died in 1651, and a few years later he was married to Joanna Bridges, who was reputed to be the illegitimate daughter of Charles I. He remained at Oxford for several years and was during that time attached as chaplain to the king's household. In 1645, however, while he was at Cardigan in Wales, he was captured and imprisoned by the Puritans. After his release he lived for some time under the patronage of the Earl of Carbery at his estate of Golden Grove in Carmarthenshire, Wales.

During his years at Golden Grove, in the late 1640's and early 1650's, Taylor produced most of his important works: *A Discourse of the Liberty of Prophesying* (1647), which exhibits his characteristic attitude of moderation and tolerance, going so far as to advocate the union of all Christian churches on the basis of the Apostles' Creed alone; *The Great Exemplar* (1649), which applies his eloquence to the life of Christ; and *The Rule and Exercises of Holy Living* (1650) and *The Rule and Exercises of Holy Dying* (1651), which are unquestionably his masterpieces. *Holy Dying*, which stands in a line of descent from both the Renaissance books of conduct and the medieval contemplations *de contemptu mundi*, shows at the same time a quality of personal involvement which no doubt owes something to the recent death of both Taylor's first wife and his patroness, Lady Carbery. It is essentially the work on which Taylor's reputation rests. A number of sermons date from the Golden Grove period also, for Taylor was active as a preacher both in Carmarthenshire and, from time to time, in London, where he became a friend of John Evelyn.

In 1655, for reasons which are not known, Taylor was arrested again and was briefly imprisoned. A few years later Lord Conway, at the suggestion of Evelyn, presented him with a lectureship in Lisburn in Ireland, where he was to spend much of his subsequent life. He was in London in 1660, however, and was active in the requisition to Charles II to return to the throne. After the restoration he was rewarded by being made Bishop of Down and Connor in Ireland, and it was in Ireland, after last years made uncomfortable by friction with the Presbyterians in his diocese, that he died.

It is difficult for the modern reader to understand the extraordinary enthusiasm for Taylor's works displayed by such romantics as Coleridge, Hazlitt, and Lamb, an enthusiasm which led to his being compared to Shakespeare, but it is in many ways regrettable that Taylor has not fully shared in the revival of interest in seventeenth-century prose writers which has elevated his contemporaries Donne and Browne to such heights in our own century. Both romantic admiration and modern relative indifference can be explained by the characteristic qualities of Taylor's prose style, and it is in his style rather than in his subject matter that we are likely to find the explanation for the vicissitudes of his reputation. Showing none of the vital, nervous, immediate quality which marks the rhythm, sentence structure, and diction of so many of his great contemporaries and which is so prized by modern readers, Taylor remains true to the oratorical and decorative traditions of earlier prose, and his greatest work tends toward a stiffly rhetorical texture alien to many modern tastes.

Nevertheless, Taylor continues to reward the reader who returns to him. The great set pieces with which *Holy Dying* abounds have more than antiquated rhetoric and unfashionable theology to offer; they exhibit a remarkable freshness of natural observation, a rich elegance of phrasing, and, above all, that gift which, as L. P. Smith has remarked, almost justifies the bizarre comparison to Shakespeare—the gift of profound, searching, and sharply illuminating metaphor.

J. TAYLOR. *Works*, ed. R. Heber, 15 vols. (London, 1822); rev. ed., C. P. Eden, 10 vols. (London, 1847–54). The definitive edition.

————. *Holy Living* and *Holy Dying*, ed. A. R. Waller, 2 vols. (London, 1900).

————. *The Golden Grove*, ed. L. P. Smith (Oxford, 1930). A volume of selections.

W. J. BROWN. *Jeremy Taylor* (London, 1925). A thorough treatment of Taylor's theology.

W. F. MITCHELL. *English Pulpit Oratory from Andrewes to Tillotson* (London, 1932).

C. J. STRANKS. *The Life and Writings of Jeremy Taylor* (London, 1952).

H. TREVOR HUGHES. *The Piety of Jeremy Taylor* (London, 1960).

FROM

THE RULE AND EXERCISES OF HOLY DYING

[TEXT: *seventh edition as revised by Rev. C. P. Eden, 1847*]

CHAPTER I
A GENERAL PREPARATION TOWARDS
A HOLY AND BLESSED DEATH,
BY WAY OF CONSIDERATION

SECTION I
Consideration of the Vanity and Shortness
of Man's Life

A MAN is a bubble, said the Greek proverb;[1] which Lucian[2] represents with advantages and its proper circumstances, to this purpose; saying, that all the world is a storm, and men rise up in their several generations, like bubbles descending *a Jove pluvio*, from God and the dew of heaven, from a tear and drop of man, from nature and providence: and some of these instantly sink into the deluge of their first parent, and are hidden in a sheet of water, having had no other business in the world but to be born that they might be able to die: others float up and down two or three turns, and suddenly disappear, and give their place to others: and they that live longest upon the face of the waters, are in perpetual motion, restless and uneasy; and, being crushed with the great drop of a cloud, sink into flatness and a froth; the change not being great, it being hardly possible it should be more a nothing than it was before. So is every man: he is born in vanity and sin; he comes into the world like morning mushrooms, soon thrusting up their heads into the air, and conversing with their kindred of the same production, and as soon they turn into dust and forgetfulness: some of them without any other interest in the affairs of the world but that they made their parents a little glad, and very sorrowful: others ride longer in the storm; it may be until seven years of

vanity be expired, and then peradventure the sun shines hot upon their heads, and they fall into the shades below, into the cover of death and darkness of the grave to hide them. But if the bubble stands the shock of a bigger drop, and outlives the chances of a child, of a careless nurse, of drowning in a pail of water, of being overlaid by a sleepy servant, or such little accidents, then the young man dances like a bubble, empty and gay, and shines like a dove's neck, or the image of a rainbow, which hath no substance, and whose very imagery and colors are fantastical; and so he dances out the gaiety of his youth, and is all the while in a storm, and endures only because he is not knocked on the head by a drop of bigger rain, or crushed by the pressure of a load of indigested meat, or quenched by the disorder of an ill-placed humor: and to preserve a man alive in the midst of so many chances and hostilities, is as great a miracle as to create him; to preserve him from rushing into nothing, and at first to draw him up from nothing, were equally the issues of an almighty power. And therefore the wise men of the world have contended who shall best fit man's condition with words signifying his vanity and short abode. Homer[3] calls a man "a leaf," the smallest, the weakest piece of a short-lived, unsteady plant: Pindar[4] calls him "the dream of a shadow": another, "the dream of the shadow of smoke": but St. James spake by a more excellent spirit, saying, "our life is but a vapor" (James 4:14, ἀτμὶς), viz., drawn from the earth by a celestial influence; made of smoke, or the lighter parts of water, tossed with every wind, moved by the motion of a superior body, without virtue in itself, lifted up on high or left below, according as it pleases the sun its foster-father. But it is lighter yet; it is but "appearing" (φαινομένη); a fantastic vapor, an apparition, nothing real: it is not so much as a mist, not the matter of a shower, nor substantial enough to make a cloud; but it is like Cassiopeia's chair, or Pelops' shoulder, or the circles of heaven, φαινόμενα, than which you cannot have a word

---

NOTE: The numerous classical, patristic, and other references in the margin, with which Taylor illustrated his observations, have in most cases been omitted, as having no intimate connection with the text of his work.

1 Πομφόλυξ ὁ ἄνθρωπος.   2 Charon, iii. 19.   3 Iliad, vi. 146.   4 Pyth. viii. 135.

that can signify a verier nothing. And yet the expression is one degree more made diminutive: a "vapor," and "fantastical," or a "mere appearance," and this but for a little while neither (πρὸς ὀλίγον); the very dream, the phantasm disappears in a small time, "like the shadow that departeth"; or "like a tale that is told"; or "as a dream when one awaketh." A man is so vain, so unfixed, so perishing a creature, that he cannot long last in the scene of fancy: a man goes off, and is forgotten, like the dream of a distracted person. The sum of all is this: that thou art a man, than whom there is not in the world any greater instance of heights and declensions, of lights and shadows, of misery and folly, of laughter and tears, of groans and death.

And because this consideration is of great usefulness and great necessity to many purposes of wisdom and the spirit, all the succession of time, all the changes in nature, all the varieties of light and darkness, the thousand thousands of accidents in the world, and every contingency to evey man, and to every creature, doth preach our funeral sermon, and calls us to look and see how the old sexton Time throws up the earth, and digs a grave where we must lay our sins or our sorrows, and sow our bodies, till they rise again in a fair or in an intolerable eternity. Every revolution which the sun makes about the world, divides between life and death; and death possesses both those portions by the next morrow; and we are dead to all those months which we have already lived, and we shall never live them over again: and still God makes little of our age. First we change our world, when we come from the womb to feel the warmth of the sun. Then we sleep and enter into the image of death, in which state we are unconcerned in all the changes of the world: and if our mothers or our nurses die, or a wild boar destroy our vineyards, or our king be sick, we regard it not, but during that state are as disinterest as if our eyes were closed with the clay that weeps in the bowels of the earth. At the end of seven years our teeth fall and die before us, representing a formal prologue to the tragedy; and still every seven years it is odds but we shall finish the last scene: and when nature, or chance, or vice, takes our body in pieces, weakening some parts and loosing others, we taste the grave and the solemnities of our own funerals, first in those parts that ministered to vice, and next in them that served for ornament, and in a short time even they that served for necessity become useless, and entangled like the wheels of a broken clock. Baldness is but a

dressing to our funerals, the proper ornament of mourning, and of a person entered very far into the regions and possession of death: and we have many more of the same signification; gray hairs, rotten teeth, dim eyes, trembling joints, short breath, stiff limbs, wrinkled skin, short memory, decayed appetite. Every day's necessity calls for a reparation of that portion which death fed on all night, when we lay in his lap, and slept in his outer chambers. The very spirits of a man prey upon the daily portion of bread and flesh, and every meal is a rescue from one death, and lays up for another; and while we think a thought, we die; and the clock strikes, and reckons on our portion of eternity: we form our words with the breath of our nostrils, we have the less to live upon for every word we speak.

Thus nature calls us to meditate of death by those things which are the instruments of acting it: and God by all the variety of his providence makes us see death everywhere, in all variety of circumstances, and dressed up for all the fancies and the expectation of every single person. Nature hath given us one harvest every year, but death hath two, and the spring and the autumn send throngs of men and women to charnel-houses; and all the summer long men are recovering from their evils of the spring, till the dog-days come, and then the Sirian star makes the summer deadly; and the fruits of autumn are laid up for all the year's provision, and the man that gathers them eats and surfeits, and dies and needs them not, and himself is laid up for eternity; and he that escapes till winter only stays for another opportunity which the distempers of that quarter minister to him with great variety. Thus death reigns in all the portions of our time; the autumn with its fruits provides disorders for us, and the winter's cold turns them into sharp diseases, and the spring brings flowers to strew our hearse, and the summer gives green turf and brambles to bind upon our graves. Calentures and surfeit, cold and agues, are the four quarters of the year, and all minister to death; and you can go no whither but you tread upon a dead man's bones.

The wild fellow in Petronius[5] that escaped upon a broken table from the furies of a shipwreck, as he was sunning himself upon the rocky shore espied a man rolled upon his floating bed of waves, ballasted with sand in the folds of his garment, and carried by his civil enemy, the sea, towards the shore to find a grave: and it cast him into some sad thoughts; that peradven-

5 *Satyricon,* cxv.

ture this man's wife in some part of the continent, safe and warm, looks next month for the good man's return; or, it may be, his son knows nothing of the tempest; or his father thinks of that affectionate kiss, which still is warm upon the good old man's cheek, ever since he took a kind farewell; and he weeps with joy to think how blessed he shall be when his beloved boy returns into the circle of his father's arms. These are the thoughts of mortals, this is the end and sum of all their designs: a dark night and an ill guide, a boisterous sea and a broken cable, a hard rock and a rough wind, dashed in pieces the fortune of a whole family, and they that shall weep loudest for the accident are not yet entered into the storm, and yet have suffered shipwreck. Then looking upon the carcase, he knew it, and found it to be the master of the ship, who the day before cast up the accounts of his patrimony and his trade, and named the day when he thought to be at home: see how the man swims who was so angry two days since; his passions are becalmed with the storm, his accounts cast up, his cares at an end, his voyage done, and his gains are the strange events of death, which whether they be good or evil, the men that are alive seldom trouble themselves concerning the interest of the dead.

But seas alone do not break our vessel in pieces: everywhere we may be shipwrecked. A valiant general, when he is to reap the harvest of his crowns and triumphs, fights unprosperously; or falls into a fever with joy and wine, and changes his laurel into cypress, his triumphal chariot to a hearse, dying the night before he was appointed to perish in the drunkenness of his festival joys. It was a sad arrest of the loosenesses and wilder feasts of the French court, when their King Henry the Second was killed really by the sportive image of a fight. And many brides have died under the hands of paranymphs[6] and maidens, dressing them for uneasy joy, the new and undiscerned chains of marriage, according to the saying of Bensirah, the wise Jew, "the bride went into her chamber, and knew not what should befall her there." Some have been paying their vows, and giving thanks for a prosperous return to their own house, and the roof hath descended upon their heads, and turned their loud religion into the deeper silence of a grave. And how many teeming mothers have rejoiced over their swelling wombs, and pleased themselves in becoming the channels of blessing to a family, and the midwife hath quickly bound their heads and feet, and carried

6 Bridesmaids.

them forth to burial! Or else the birthday of an heir hath seen the coffin of the father brought into the house, and the divided mother hath been forced to travail twice, with a painful birth, and a sadder death.

There is no state, no accident, no circumstance of our life, but it hath been soured by some sad instance of a dying friend: a friendly meeting often ends in some sad mischance, and makes an eternal parting: and when the poet Æschylus was sitting under the walls of his house, an eagle hovering over his bald head mistook it for a stone, and let fall his oyster, hoping there to break the shell, but pierced the poor man's skull.

Death meets us everywhere, and is procured by every instrument and in all chances, and enters in at many doors; by violence and secret influence, by the aspect of a star and the stink of a mist, by the emissions of a cloud and the meeting of a vapor, by the fall of a chariot and the stumbling at a stone, by a full meal or an empty stomach, by watching at the wine or by watching at prayers, by the sun or the moon, by a heat or a cold, by sleepless nights or sleeping days, by water frozen into the hardness and sharpness of a dagger, or water thawed into the floods of a river, by a hair or a raisin, by violent motion or sitting still, by severity or dissolution, by God's mercy or God's anger; by everything in providence and everything in manners, by everything in nature and everything in chance;

——*eripitur persona, manet res;*[7]

we take pains to heap up things useful to our life, and get our death in the purchase; and the person is snatched away, and the goods remain. And all this is the law and constitution of nature; it is a punishment to our sins, the unalterable event of providence, and the decree of heaven: the chains that confine us to this condition are strong as destiny, and immutable as the eternal laws of God.

I have conversed with some men who rejoiced in the death or calamity of others, and accounted it as a judgment upon them for being on the other side, and against them in the contention: but within the revolution of a few months, the same man met with a more uneasy and unhandsome death: which when I saw, I wept, and was afraid; for I knew that it must be so with all men; for we also shall die, and end our quarrels and contentions by passing to a final sentence.

7 Lucretius, *De Rerum Natura*, iii. 58: "The person is snatched away; the object remains."

SECTION II
The Consideration Reduced to Practice

IT WILL be very material to our best and noblest purposes if we represent this scene of change and sorrow a little more dressed up in circumstances, for so we shall be more apt to practice those rules the doctrine of which is consequent to this consideration. It is a mighty change that is made by the death of every person, and it is visible to us who are alive. Reckon but from the sprightfulness of youth, and the fair cheeks and full eyes of childhood, from the vigorousness and strong flexure of the joints of five-and-twenty to the hollowness and dead paleness, to the loathsomeness and horror of a three days' burial, and we shall perceive the distance to be very great and very strange. But so have I seen a rose newly springing from the clefts of its hood, and at first it was fair as the morning, and full with the dew of heaven as a lamb's fleece; but when a ruder breath had forced open its virgin modesty, and dismantled its too youthful and unripe retirements, it began to put on darkness, and to decline to softness and the symptoms of a sickly age; it bowed the head, and broke its stalk, and at night having lost some of its leaves and all its beauty, it fell into the portion of seeds and outworn faces. The same is the portion of every man and every woman, the heritage of worms and serpents, rottenness and cold dishonor, and our beauty so changed, that our acquaintance quickly knew us not; and that change mingled with so much horror, or else meets so with our fears and weak discoursings, that they who six hours ago tended upon us either with charitable or ambitious services, cannot without some regret stay in the room alone where the body lies stripped of its life and honor. I have read of a fair young German gentleman who, living, often refused to be pictured, but put off the importunity of his friends' desire by giving way that after a few days' burial they might send a painter to his vault, and if they saw cause for it, draw the image of his death unto the life: they did so, and found his face half eaten, and his midriff and backbone full of serpents; and so he stands pictured among his armed ancestors. So does the fairest beauty change, and it will be as bad with you and me; and then what servants shall we have to wait upon us in the grave? what friends to visit us? what officious people to cleanse away the moist and unwholesome cloud reflected upon our faces from the sides of the weeping vaults, which are the longest weepers for our funeral?

This discourse will be useful if we consider and practice by the following rules and considerations respectively.

1. All the rich and all the covetous men in the world will perceive, and all the world will perceive for them, that it is but an ill recompense for all their cares, that by this time all that shall be left will be this, that the neighbors shall say, "He died a rich man"; and yet his wealth will not profit him in the grave, but hugely swell the sad accounts of doomsday. And he that kills the Lord's people with unjust or ambitious wars for an unrewarding interest shall have this character, that he threw away all the days of his life, that one year might be reckoned with his name, and computed by his reign, or consulship; and many men by great labors and affronts, many indignities and crimes, labor only for a pompous epitaph and a loud title upon their marble; whilst those into whose possessions their heirs or kindred are entered, are forgotten, and lie unregarded as their ashes, and without concernment or relation, as the turf upon the face of their grave. A man may read a sermon, the best and most passionate that ever man preached, if he shall but enter into the sepulchres of kings. In the same Escurial where the Spanish princes live in greatness and power, and decree war or peace, they have wisely placed a cemetery where their ashes and their glory shall sleep till time shall be no more; and where our kings have been crowned, their ancestors lay interred, and they must walk over their grandsire's head to take his crown. There is an acre sown with royal seed, the copy of the greatest change, from rich to naked, from ceiled roofs to arched coffins, from living like gods to die like men. There is enough to cool the flames of lust, to abate the heights of pride, to appease the itch of covetous desires, to sully and dash out the dissembling colors of a lustful, artificial, and imaginary beauty. There the warlike and the peaceful, the fortunate and the miserable, the beloved and the despised princes mingle their dust, and pay down their symbol of mortality, and tell all the world, that when we die our ashes shall be equal to kings', and our accounts easier, and our pains or our crowns shall be less. To my apprehension it is a sad record, which is left by Athenæus concerning Ninus, the great Assyrian monarch, whose life and death is summed up in these words: "Ninus, the Assyrian, had an ocean of gold, and other riches more than the sand in the Caspian sea; he never saw

the stars, and perhaps he never desired it; he never
stirred up the holy fire among the Magi, nor touched
his god with the sacred rod according to the laws; he
never offered sacrifice, nor worshipped the deity, nor
administered justice, nor spake to his people, nor
numbered them; but he was most valiant to eat and
drink, and having mingled his wines he threw the
rest upon the stones. This man is dead: behold his
sepulchre; and now hear where Ninus is. Sometimes
I was Ninus, and drew the breath of a living man;
but now am nothing but clay. I have nothing, but
what I did eat, and what I served to myself in lust, that
was and is all my portion. The wealth with which I
was esteemed blessed, my enemies meeting together
shall bear away, as the mad Thyades carry a raw goat.
I am gone to hell; and when I went thither, I neither
carried gold, nor horse, nor silver chariot. I that wore
a mitre, am now a little heap of dust." I know not
anything that can better represent the evil condition of
a wicked man, or a changing greatness. From the
greatest secular dignity to dust and ashes his nature
bears him, and from thence to hell his sins carry him,
and there he shall be forever under the dominion of
chains and devils, wrath and an intolerable calamity.
This is the reward of an unsanctified condition, and a
greatness ill gotten or ill administered.

2. Let no man extend his thoughts or let his hopes
wander towards future and far-distant events and
accidental contingencies. This day is mine and yours,
but ye know not what shall be on the morrow: and
every morning creeps out of a dark cloud, leaving
behind it an ignorance and silence deep as midnight,
and undiscerned as are the phantasms that make a
chrisom-child to smile: so that we cannot discern
what comes hereafter, unless we had a light from
heaven brighter than the vision of an angel, even the
spirit of prophecy. Without revelation we cannot tell
whether we shall eat tomorrow, or whether a squinzy [8]
shall choke us: and it is written in the unrevealed folds
of divine predestination that many who are this day
alive shall tomorrow be laid upon the cold earth, and
the women shall weep over their shroud, and dress
them for their funeral. St. James in his epistle notes the
folly of some men his contemporaries, who were so
impatient of the event of tomorrow, or the accidents
of next year, or the good or evils of old age, that they
would consult astrologers and witches, oracles and
devils, what should befall them the next calends:
what should be the event of such a voyage, what God

8 Quinsy, a severe inflammation of the throat.

had written in his book concerning the success of
battles, the election of emperors, the heirs of families,
the price of merchandise, the return of the Tyrian
fleet, the rate of Sidonian carpets; and as they were
taught by the crafty and lying demons, so they would
expect the issue; and oftentimes by disposing their
affairs in order towards such events, really did produce
some little accidents according to their expectation;
and that made them trust the oracles in greater things,
and in all. Against this he opposes his counsel, that we
should not search after forbidden records, much less
by uncertain significations; for whatsoever is disposed
to happen by the order of natural causes or civil
counsels, may be rescinded by a peculiar decree of
providence, or be prevented by the death of the
interested persons; who, while their hopes are full, and
their causes conjoined, and the work brought forward, and the sickle put into the harvest, and the first-
fruits offered and ready to be eaten, even then if they
put forth their hand to an event that stands but at the
door, at that door their body may be carried forth to
burial, before the expectation shall enter into fruition.
When Richilda, the widow of Albert Earl of Ebers-
berg, had feasted the emperor Henry the Third and
petitioned in behalf of her nephew Welpho for some
lands formerly possessed by the earl her husband, just
as the emperor held out his hand to signify his consent, the chamber floor suddenly fell under them, and
Richilda falling upon the edge of a bathing vessel was
bruised to death, and stayed not to see her nephew
sleep in those lands which the emperor was reaching
forth to her, and placed at the door of restitution.

3. As our hopes must be confined, so must our
designs: let us not project long designs, crafty plots,
and diggings so deep that the intrigues of a design
shall never be unfolded till our grandchildren have
forgotten our virtues or our vices. The work of our
soul is cut short, facile, sweet, and plain, and fitted to
the small portions of our shorter life; and as we must
not trouble our inquiry, so neither must we intricate
our labor and purposes with what we shall never
enjoy. This rule does not forbid us to plant orchards
which shall feed our nephews with their fruit; for
by such provisions they do something towards an
imaginary immortality, and do charity to their relatives: but such projects are reproved which discompose our present duty by long and future designs;
such which by casting our labors to events at distance make us less to remember our death standing at
the door. It is fit for a man to work for his day's wages,

or to contrive for the hire of a week, or to lay a train to make provisions for such a time as is within our eye, and in our duty, and within the usual periods of man's life; for whatsoever is made necessary is also made prudent: but while we plot and busy ourselves in the toils of an ambitious war, or the levies of a great estate, night enters in upon us, and tells all the world how like fools we lived, and how deceived and miserably we died. Seneca[9] tells of Senecio Cornelius, a man crafty in getting, and tenacious in holding a great estate, and one who was as diligent in the care of his body as of his money, curious of his health, as of his possessions, that he all day long attended upon his sick and dying friend; but when he went away, was quickly comforted, supped merrily, went to bed cheerfully, and on a sudden being surprised by a squinzy, scarce drew his breath until the morning, but by that time died, being snatched from the torrent of his fortune, and the swelling tide of wealth, and a likely hope bigger than the necessities of ten men. This accident was much noted then in Rome, because it happened in so great a fortune, and in the midst of wealthy designs; and presently it made wise men to consider, how imprudent a person he is who disposes of ten years to come, when he is not lord of tomorrow.

4. Though we must not look so far off and pry abroad, yet we must be busy near at hand; we must with all arts of the spirit seize upon the present, because it passes from us while we speak, and because in it all our certainty does consist. We must take our waters as out of a torrent and sudden shower, which will quickly cease dropping from above, and quickly cease running in our channels here below; this instant will never return again, and yet it may be this instant will declare or secure the fortune of a whole eternity. The old Greeks and Romans taught us the prudence of this rule, but Christianity teaches us the religion of it. They so seized upon the present that they would lose nothing of the day's pleasure. "Let us eat and drink, for tomorrow we shall die"; that was their philosophy; and at their solemn feasts they would talk of death to heighten the present drinking, and that they might warm their veins with a fuller chalice, as knowing the drink that was poured upon their graves would be cold and without relish. "Break the beds, drink your wine, crown your heads with roses, and besmear your curled locks with nard; for God bids you to remember death": so the epigrammatist speaks

the sense of their drunken principles.[10] Something towards this signification is that of Solomon, "there is nothing better for a man than that he should eat and drink, and that he should make his soul enjoy good in his labor; for that is his portion; for who shall bring him to see that which shall be after him?" (Eccles. 2:24; 3:22.) But although he concludes all this to be vanity, yet because it was the best thing that was then commonly known that they should seize upon the present with a temperate use of permitted pleasures,[11] I had reason to say, that Christianity taught us to turn this into religion. For he that by a present and a constant holiness secures the present, and makes it useful to his noblest purpose, he turns his condition into his best advantage, by making his unavoidable fate become his necessary religion.

To the purpose of this rule is that collect of Tuscan hieroglyphics which we have from Gabriel Simeon: "Our life is very short, beauty is a cozenage, money is false and fugitive; empire is odious, and hated by them that have it not, and uneasy to them that have; victory is always uncertain, and peace most commonly is but a fraudulent bargain; old age is miserable, death is the period, and is a happy one if it be not soured by the sins of our life: but nothing continues but the effects of that wisdom which employs the present time in the acts of a holy religion and a peaceable conscience." For they make us to live even beyond our funerals, embalmed in the spices and odors of a good name, and entombed in the grave of the holy Jesus, where we shall be dressed for a blessed resurrection to the state of angels and beatified spirits.

5. Since we stay not here, being people but of a day's abode, and our age is like that of a fly and contemporary with a gourd, we must look somewhere else for an abiding city, a place in another country to fix our house in, whose walls and foundation is God, where we must find rest, or else be restless forever. For whatsoever ease we can have or fancy here is shortly to be changed into sadness or tediousness: it goes away too soon, like the periods of our life: or stays too long, like the sorrows of a sinner: its own weariness, or a contrary disturbance, is its load; or it is eased by its revolution into vanity and forgetfulness; and where either there is sorrow or an end of joy, there can be no true felicity: which because it must be had by some instrument and in some period

---

9 Epistles, ci.

10 Martial, Epigrams II. 59.

11 *Amici, dum vivimus, vivamus.* (Gruter, *Inscriptiones,* DCIX. 3.)

of our duration, we must carry up our affections to the mansions prepared for us above, where eternity is the measure, felicity is the state, angels are the company, the Lamb is the light, and God is the portion and inheritance.

SECTION III
Rules and Spiritual Arts of Lengthening Our Days, and to Take Off the Objection of a Short Life

1. IN THE accounts of a man's life, we do not reckon that portion of days in which we are shut up in the prison of the womb; we tell our years from the day of our birth: and the same reason that makes our reckoning to stay so long, says also that then it begins too soon. For then we are beholden to others to make the account for us; for we know not of a long time whether we be alive or no, having but some little approaches and symptoms of a life. To feed, and sleep, and move a little, and imperfectly, is the state of an unborn child; and when he is born, he does no more for a good while; and what is it that shall make him to be esteemed to live the life of a man? and when shall that account begin? For we should be loth to have the accounts of our age taken by the measures of a beast: and fools and distracted persons are reckoned as civilly dead; they are no parts of the commonwealth, not subject to laws, but secured by them in charity, and kept from violence as a man keeps his ox: and a third part of our life is spent, before we enter into a higher order, into the state of a man.

2. Neither must we think that the life of a man begins when he can feed himself, or walk alone, when he can fight, or beget his like; for so he is contemporary with a camel or a cow; but he is first a man when he comes to a certain, steady use of reason, according to his proportion: and when that is, all the world of men cannot tell precisely. Some are called at age at fourteen; some at one-and-twenty; some, never; but all men, late enough; for the life of a man comes upon him slowly and insensibly. But as when the sun approaches towards the gates of the morning, he first opens a little eye of heaven, and sends away the spirits of darkness, and gives light to a cock, and calls up the lark to matins, and by and by gilds the fringes of a cloud, and peeps over the eastern hills, thrusting out his golden horns, like those which decked the brows of Moses when he was forced to wear a veil because himself had seen the face of God;[12] and still while a man tells the story, the sun gets up higher, till he shows a fair face and a full light, and then he shines one whole day, under a cloud often, and sometimes weeping great and little showers, and sets quickly: so is a man's reason and his life. He first begins to perceive himself to see or taste, making little reflections upon his actions of sense, and can discourse of flies and dogs, shells and play, horses and liberty: but when he is strong enough to enter into arts and little institutions, he is at first entertained with trifles and impertinent things, not because he needs them, but because his understanding is no bigger, and little images of things are laid before him, like a cock-boat to a whale, only to play withal: but before a man comes to be wise, he is half dead with gouts and consumptions, with catarrhs and aches, with sore eyes and a worn-out body. So that if we must not reckon the life of a man but by the accounts of his reason, he is long before his soul be dressed; and he is not to be called a man without a wise and an adorned soul, a soul at least furnished with what is necessary towards his well-being: but by that time his soul is thus furnished, his body is decayed; and then you can hardly reckon him to be alive, when his body is possessed by so many degrees of death.

3. But there is yet another arrest. At first he wants strength of body, and then he wants the use of reason: and when that is come, it is ten to one but he stops by the impediments of vice, and wants the strengths of the spirit; and we know that body and soul and spirit are the constituent parts of every Christian man. And now let us consider what that thing is which we call years of discretion. The young man is past his tutors, and arrived at the bondage of a caitive spirit; he is run from discipline, and is let loose to passion; the man by this time hath wit enough to choose his vice, to act his lust, to court his mistress, to talk confidently, and ignorantly, and perpetually, to despise his betters, to deny nothing to his appetite, to do things that when he is indeed a man he must forever be ashamed of: for this is all the discretion that most men show in the first stage of their manhood; they can discern good from evil; and they prove their skill by leaving all that is good, and wallowing in the evils of folly and an unbridled appetite. And by this time the young man hath contracted vicious habits, and is a beast in manners, and therefore it will not be fitting to reckon

12 Exodus 34:29–35.

the beginning of his life; he is a fool in his understanding, and that is a sad death; and he is dead in trespasses and sins, and that is a sadder: so that he hath no life but a natural, the life of a beast or a tree; in all other capacities he is dead; he neither hath the intellectual nor the spiritual life, neither the life of a man nor of a Christian; and this sad truth lasts too long. For old age seizes upon most men while they still retain the minds of boys and vicious youth, doing actions from principles of great folly, and a mighty ignorance, admiring things useless and hurtful, and filling up all the dimensions of their abode with businesses of empty affairs, being at leisure to attend no virtue: they cannot pray, because they are busy, and because they are passionate; they cannot communicate, because they have quarrels and intrigues of perplexed causes, complicated hostilities, and things of the world, and therefore they cannot attend to the things of God: little considering that they must find a time to die in; when death comes, they must be at leisure for that. Such men are like sailors loosing from a port, and tossed immediately with a perpetual tempest lasting till their cordage crack, and either they sink, or return back again to the same place; they did not make a voyage, though they were long at sea. The business and impertinent affairs of most men steal all their time, and they are restless in a foolish motion: but this is not the progress of a man; he is no farther advanced in the course of a life, though he reckon many years; for still his soul is childish, and trifling like an untaught boy.

If the parts of this sad complaint find their remedy, we have by the same instruments also cured the evils and the vanity of a short life. Therefore,

1. Be infinitely curious you do not set back your life in the accounts of God by the intermingling of criminal actions, or the contracting vicious habits. There are some vices which carry a sword in their hand, and cut a man off before his time. There is a sword of the Lord, and there is a sword of man, and there is a sword of the Devil. Every vice of our own managing in the matter of carnality, of lust or rage, ambition or revenge, is a sword of Satan put into the hands of a man: these are the destroying angels; sin is the Apollyon, the destroyer that is gone out, not from the Lord, but from the tempter; and we hug the poison, and twist willingly with the vipers, till they bring us into the regions of an irrecoverable sorrow. We use to reckon persons as good as dead if they have lost their limbs and their teeth, and are confined to a hospital, and converse with none but surgeons and physicians, mourners and divines, those *pollinctores*, the dressers of bodies and souls to funeral: but it is worse when the soul, the principle of life, is employed wholly in the offices of death; and that man was worse than dead of whom Seneca tells, that, being a rich fool, when he was lifted up from the baths and set into a soft couch, asked his slaves, *An ego jam sedeo*, "do I now sit?" The beast was so drowned in sensuality and the death of his soul, that whether he did sit or no, he was to believe another. Idleness and every vice is as much of death as a long disease is, or the expense of ten years; and "she that lives in pleasures is dead while she liveth," saith the apostle; [13] and it is the style of the Spirit concerning wicked persons, "they are dead in trespasses and sins." [14] For as every sensual pleasure and every day of idleness and useless living lops off a little branch from our short life, so every deadly sin and every habitual vice does quite destroy us; but innocence leaves us in our natural portions and perfect period; we lose nothing of our life if we lose nothing of our soul's health; and therefore he that would live a full age, must avoid a sin, as he would decline the regions of death and the dishonors of the grave.

2. If we would have our life lengthened, let us begin betimes to live in the accounts of reason and sober counsels, of religion and the spirit, and then we shall have no reason to complain that our abode on earth is so short: many men find it long enough, and indeed it is so to all senses. But when we spend in waste what God hath given us in plenty, when we sacrifice our youth to folly, our manhood to lust and rage, our old age to covetousness and irreligion, not beginning to live till we are to die, designing that time to virtue which indeed is infirm to everything and profitable to nothing; then we make our lives short, and lust runs away with all the vigorous and healthful part of it, and pride and animosity steal the manly portion, and craftiness and interest possess old age: *velut ex pleno et abundanti perdimus*, we spend as if we had too much time, and knew not what to do with it: we fear everything, like weak and silly mortals; and desire strangely and greedily, as if we were immortal: we complain our life is short, and yet we throw away much of it, and are weary of many of its parts; we complain the day is long, and the night is long, and we want company, and seek out arts to drive the time away, and then weep because it is gone too soon. But so the treasure of the capitol is but a small

13 I Timothy 5:6.   14 Ephesians 2:1.

estate, when Cæsar comes to finger it, and to pay with it all his legions: and the revenue of all Egypt and the eastern provinces was but a little sum, when they were to support the luxury of Mark Antony, and feed the riot of Cleopatra; but a thousand crowns is a vast proportion to be spent in the cottage of a frugal person, or to feed a hermit. Just so is our life: it is too short to serve the ambition of a haughty prince or an usurping rebel; too little time to purchase great wealth, to satisfy the pride of a vain-glorious fool, to trample upon all the enemies of our just or unjust interest; but for the obtaining virtue, for the purchase of sobriety and modesty, for the actions of religion, God gave us time sufficient, if we make the "outgoings of the morning and evening," that is, our infancy and old age, to be taken into the computations of a man. Which we may see in the following particulars.

1. If, our childhood being first consecrated by a forward baptism, it be seconded by a holy education and a complying obedience; if our youth be chaste and temperate, modest and industrious, proceeding through a prudent and sober manhood to a religious old age; then we have lived our whole duration, and shall never die, but be changed, in a just time, to the preparations of a better and an immortal life.

2. If, besides the ordinary returns of our prayers and periodical and festival solemnities, and our seldom communions, we would allow to religion and the studies of wisdom those great shares that are trifled away upon vain sorrow, foolish mirth, troublesome ambition, busy covetousness, watchful lust, and impertinent amours, and balls and revellings and banquets, all that which was spent viciously, and all that time that lay fallow and without employment, our life would quickly amount to a great sum. Tostatus Abulensis was a very painful person, and a great clerk, and in the days of his manhood he wrote so many books, and they not ill ones, that the world computed a sheet for every day of his life; I suppose they meant, after he came to the use of reason and the state of a man; and John Scotus[15] died about the two-and-thirtieth year of his age; and yet besides his public disputations, his daily lectures of divinity in public and private, the books that he wrote, being lately collected and printed at Lyons, do equal the number of volumes of any two the most voluminous fathers of the Latin

church. Every man is not enabled to such employments, but every man is called and enabled to the works of a sober and religious life; and there are many saints of God that can reckon as many volumes of religion and mountains of piety, as those others did of good books. St. Ambrose (and I think, from his example, St. Augustine) divided every day into three "tertias" of employment: eight hours he spent in the necessities of nature and recreation; eight hours in charity and doing assistance to others, dispatching their businesses, reconciling their enmities, reproving their vices, correcting their errors, instructing their ignorances, transacting the affairs of his dioceses; and the other eight hours he spent in study and prayer. If we were thus minute and curious in the spending our time, it is impossible but our life would seem very long. For so have I seen an amorous person tell the minutes of his absence from his fancied joy, and while he told the sands of his hour-glass, or the throbs and little beatings of his watch, by dividing an hour into so many members, he spun out its length by number, and so translated a day into the tediousness of a month. And if we tell our days by canonical hours of prayer, our weeks by a constant revolution of fasting days or days of special devotion, and over all these draw a black cypress, a veil of penitential sorrow and severe mortification, we shall soon answer the calumny and objection of a short life. He that governs the day and divides the hours, hastens from the eyes and observation of a merry sinner; but loves to stand still, and behold and tell the sighs, and number the groans and sadly delicious accents of a grieved penitent. It is a vast work that any man may do if he never be idle: and it is a huge way that a man may go in virtue, if he never goes out of his way by a vicious habit or a great crime: and he that perpetually reads good books, if his parts be answerable, will have a huge stock of knowledge. It is so in all things else. Strive not to forget your time, and suffer none of it to pass undiscerned; and then measure your life, and tell me how you find the measure of its abode. However, the time we live is worth the money we pay for it, and therefore it is not to be thrown away.

3. When vicious men are dying, and scared with the affrighting truths of an evil conscience, they would give all the world for a year, for a month: nay, we read of some that called out with amazement, *inducias usque ad mane*, "truce but till the morning": and if that year or some few months were given, those men think they could do miracles in it. And let us awhile

---

15 Joannes Duns Scotus (1265?–1308?), the famous Doctor Subtilis, born at Dunse, Scotland. He was the founder of the scholastic system known as Scotism, and chief opponent of the system known as Thomism, founded by Thomas Aquinas.

suppose what Dives would have done, if he had been loosed from the pains of hell, and permitted to live on earth one year. Would all the pleasures of the world have kept him one hour from the temple? would he not perpetually have been under the hands of priests, or at the feet of the doctors, or by Moses' chair, or attending as near the altar as he could get, or relieving poor Lazarus, or praying to God, and crucifying all his sin? I have read of a melancholy person who saw hell but in a dream or vision, and the amazement was such that he would have chosen ten times to die rather than feel again so much of that horror; and such a person cannot be fancied but that he would spend a year in such holiness, that the religion of a few months would equal the devotion of many years even of a good man. Let us but compute the proportions. If we should spend all our years of reason so as such a person would spend that one, can it be thought that life would be short and trifling in which he had performed such a religion, served God with so much holiness, mortified sin with so great a labor, purchased virtue at such a rate and so rare an industry? It must needs be that such a man must die when he ought to die, and be like ripe and pleasant fruit falling from a fair tree, and gathered into baskets for the planter's use. He that hath done all his business, and is begotten to a glorious hope by the seed of an immortal spirit, can never die too soon, nor live too long.

Xerxes wept sadly, when he saw his army of two million three hundred thousand men, because he considered that within a hundred years all the youth of that army should be dust and ashes: and yet as Seneca[16] well observes of him, he was the man that should bring them to their graves; and he consumed all that army in two years, for whom he feared and wept the death after a hundred. Just so we do all. We complain that within thirty or forty years, a little more, or a great deal less, we shall descend again into the bowels of our mother, and that our life is too short for any great employment; and yet we throw away five-and-thirty years of our forty, and the remaining five we divide between art and nature, civility and customs, necessity and convenience, prudent counsels and religion: but the portion of the last is little and contemptible, and yet that little is all that we can prudently account of our lives. We bring that fate and that death near us, of whose approach we are so sadly apprehensive.

4. In taking the accounts of your life, do not reckon by great distances, and by the periods of pleasure, or the satisfaction of your hopes, or the stating your desires; but let every intermedial day and hour pass with observation. He that reckons he hath lived but so many harvests, thinks they come not often enough, and that they go away too soon: some lose the day with longing for the night, and the night in waiting for the day. Hope and fantastic expectations spend much of our lives: and while with passion we look for a coronation, or the death of an enemy, or a day of joy, passing from fancy to possession without any intermedial notices, we throw away a precious year, and use it but as the burden of our time, fit to be pared off and thrown away, that we may come at those little pleasures which first steal our hearts, and then steal our life.

5. A strict course of piety is the way to prolong our lives in the natural sense, and to add good portions to the number of our years: and sin is sometimes by natural causality, very often by the anger of God and the divine judgment, a cause of sudden and untimely death. Concerning which I shall add nothing to what I have somewhere else[17] said of this article, but only the observation of Epiphanius; that for three thousand three hundred and thirty-two years, even to the twentieth age, there was not one example of a son that died before his father; but the course of nature was kept, that he who was first born in the descending line did first die (I speak of natural death, and therefore Abel cannot be opposed to this observation), till that Terah the father of Abraham taught the people a new religion, to make images of clay and worship them, and concerning him it was first remarked, that "Haran died before his father Terah in the land of his nativity"; God by an unheard-of judgment and a rare accident punishing his newly invented crime by the untimely death of his son.

6. But if I shall describe a living man, a man that hath life that distinguishes him from a fool or a bird, that which gives him a capacity next to angels, we shall find that even a good man lives not long, because it is long before he is born to this life, and longer yet before he hath a man's growth. "He that can look upon death, and see its face with the same countenance with which he hears its story; that can endure all the labors of his life with his soul supporting his body; that can equally despise riches when he hath them and when he hath them not; that is not sadder if they lie in his neighbor's trunks, nor more brag if they

16 *De Brevitate Vitæ*, i. 16.

17 Life of Christ, Part III, Disc. 14.

shine round about his own walls; he that is neither moved with good fortune coming to him nor going from him; that can look upon another man's lands evenly and pleasedly as if they were his own, and yet look upon his own, and use them too, just as if they were another man's; that neither spends his goods prodigally and like a fool, nor yet keeps them avariciously and like a wretch; that weighs not benefits by weight and number, but by the mind and circumstances of him that gives them; that never thinks his charity expensive if a worthy person be the receiver; he that does nothing for opinion sake, but everything for conscience, being as curious of his thoughts as of his actings in markets and theaters, and is as much in awe of himself as of a whole assembly; he that knows God looks on, and contrives his secret affairs as in the presence of God and his holy angels; that eats and drinks because he needs it, not that he may serve a lust or load his belly; he that is bountiful and cheerful to his friends, and charitable and apt to forgive his enemies; that loves his country, and obeys his prince, and desires and endeavors nothing more than that he may do honor to God"; this person may reckon his life to be the life of a man, and compute his months, not by the course of the sun, but the zodiac and circle of his virtues; because these are such things which fools and children and birds and beasts cannot have; these are therefore the actions of life, because they are the seeds of immortality. That day in which we have done some excellent thing we may as truly reckon to be added to our life as were the fifteen years to the days of Hezekiah.[18]

SECTION IV
Consideration of the Miseries of Man's Life

As our life is very short, so it is very miserable; and therefore it is well it is short. God, in pity to mankind, lest his burden should be insupportable and his nature an intolerable load, hath reduced our state of misery to an abbreviature; and the greater our misery is, the less while it is like to last; the sorrows of a man's spirit being like ponderous weights, which by the greatness of their burden make a swifter motion, and descend into the grave to rest and ease our wearied limbs; for then only we shall sleep quietly, when those fetters are knocked off, which not only bound our souls in prison, but also ate the flesh till the very bones

18 Isaiah 38:7, 8.

opened the secret garments of their cartilages, discovering their nakedness and sorrow.

1. Here is no place to sit down in, but you must rise as soon as you are set, for we have gnats in our chambers, and worms in our gardens, and spiders and flies in the palaces of the greatest kings. How few men in the world are prosperous! What an infinite number of slaves and beggars, of persecuted and oppressed people, fill all corners of the earth with groans, and heaven itself with weeping prayers and sad remembrances! How many provinces and kingdoms are afflicted by a violent war, or made desolate by popular diseases! Some whole countries are remarked with fatal evils, or periodical sicknesses. Grand Cairo in Egypt feels the plague every three years returning like a quartan ague, and destroying many thousands of persons. All the inhabitants of Arabia the desert are in continual fear of being buried in huge heaps of sand, and therefore dwell in tents and ambulatory houses, or retire to unfruitful mountains, to prolong an uneasy and wilder life. And all the countries round about the Adriatic Sea feel such violent convulsions by tempests and intolerable earthquakes, that sometimes whole cities find a tomb, and every man sinks with his own house made ready to become his monument, and his bed is crushed into the disorders of a grave. Was not all the world drowned at one deluge and breach of the divine anger; and shall not all the world again be destroyed by fire?[19] Are there not many thousands that die every night, and that groan and weep sadly every day? But what shall we think of that great evil which for the sins of men God hath suffered to possess the greatest part of mankind? Most of the men that are now alive, or that have been living for many ages, are Jews, Heathens, or Turks; and God was pleased to suffer a base epileptic person, a villain and a vicious, to set up a religion which hath filled all the nearer parts of Asia, and much of Africa, and some part of Europe; so that the greatest number of men and women born in so many kingdoms and provinces are infallibly made Mahometans, strangers and enemies to Christ by whom alone we can be saved: this consideration is extremely sad, when we remember how universal and how great an evil it is, that so many millions of sons and daughters are born to enter into the possession of devils to eternal ages. These evils are miseries of great parts of mankind, and we cannot

19 Taylor's reference is to the prophecy in the Sibylline Oracles, III.

easily consider more particularly the evils which happen to us, being the inseparable affections or incidents to the whole nature of man.

2. We find that all the women in the world are either born for barrenness, or the pains of childbirth, and yet this is one of our greatest blessings; but such indeed are the blessings of this world, we cannot be well with nor without many things. Perfumes make our heads ache, roses prick our fingers, and in our very blood, where our life dwells, is the scene under which nature acts many sharp fevers and heavy sicknesses. It were too sad if I should tell how many persons are afflicted with evil spirits, with specters and illusions of the night; and that huge multitudes of men and women live upon man's flesh; nay, worse yet, upon the sins of men, upon the sins of their sons and of their daughters, and they pay their souls down for the bread they eat, buying this day's meal with the price of the last night's sin.

3. Or if you please in charity to visit a hospital, which is indeed a map of the whole world, there you shall see the effects of Adam's sin, and the ruins of human nature; bodies laid up in heaps like the bones of a destroyed town, *homines precarii spiritus et male hærentis*, men whose souls seem to be borrowed, and are kept there by art and the force of medicine, whose miseries are so great that few people have charity or humanity enough to visit them, fewer have the heart to dress them, and we pity them in civility or with a transient prayer, but we do not feel their sorrows by the mercies of a religious pity; and therefore as we leave their sorrows in many degrees unrelieved and uneased, so we contract by our unmercifulness a guilt by which ourselves become liable to the same calamities. Those many that need pity, and those infinities of people that refuse to pity, are miserable upon a several charge, but yet they almost make up all mankind.

4. All wicked men are in love with that which entangles them in huge varieties of troubles; they are slaves to the worst of masters, to sin and to the devil, to a passion, and to an imperious woman. Good men are forever prosecuted, and God chastises every son whom he receives, and whatsoever is easy is trifling and worth nothing, and whatsoever is excellent is not to be obtained without labor and sorrow; and the conditions and states of men that are free from great cares are such as have in them nothing rich and orderly, and those that have are stuck full of thorns and trouble. Kings are full of care; and learned men in all ages have been observed to be very poor, *et honestas*

miserias accusant, "they complain of their honest miseries."

5. But these evils are notorious and confessed; even they also whose felicity men stare at and admire, besides their splendor and the sharpness of their light, will with their appendant sorrows wring a tear from the most resolved eye; for not only the winter quarter is full of storms and cold and darkness, but the beauteous spring hath blasts and sharp frosts, the fruitful teeming summer is melted with heat, and burnt with the kisses of the sun her friend, and choked with dust, and the rich autumn is full of sickness; and we are weary of that which we enjoy, because sorrow is its biggest portion and when we remember that upon the fairest face is placed one of the worst sinks of the body, the nose, we may use it not only as a mortification to the pride of beauty, but as an allay to the fairest outside of condition which any of the sons and daughters of Adam do possess. For look upon kings and conquerors: I will not tell that many of them fall into the condition of servants, and their subjects rule over them, and stand upon the ruins of their families, and that to such persons the sorrow is bigger than usually happens in smaller fortunes; but let us suppose them still conquerors, and see what a goodly purchase they get by all their pains, and amazing fears and continual dangers. They carry their arms beyond Ister, and pass the Euphrates, and bind the Germans with the bounds of the river Rhine: I speak in the style of the Roman greatness; for nowadays the biggest fortune swells not beyond the limits of a petty province or two, and a hill confines the progress of their prosperity, or a river checks it: but whatsoever tempts the pride and vanity of ambitious persons is not so big as the smallest star which we see scattered in disorder and unregarded upon the pavement and floor of heaven. And if we would suppose the pismires had but our understandings, they also would have the method of a man's greatness, and divide their little molehills into provinces and exarchates: and if they also grew as vicious and as miserable, one of their princes would lead an army out and kill his neighbor ants, that he might reign over the next handful of a turf. But then if we consider at what price and with what felicity all this is purchased, the sting of the painted snake will quickly appear, and the fairest of their fortunes will properly enter into this account of human infelicities.

We may guess at it by the constitution of Augustus's fortune, who struggled for his power first with the Roman citizens, then with Brutus and Cassius and all the fortune of the republic; then with his colleague Mark Antony; then with his kindred and nearest relatives; and after he was wearied with slaughter of the Romans, before he could sit down and rest in his imperial chair, he was forced to carry armies into Macedonia, Galatia, beyond Euphrates, Rhine, and Danubius; and when he dwelt at home in greatness and within the circles of a mighty power, he hardly escaped the sword of the Egnatii, of Lepidus, Cæpio, and Murena; and after he had entirely reduced the felicity and grandeur into his own family, his daughter, his only child, conspired with many of the young nobility, and being joined with adulterous complications, as with an impious sacrament, they affrighted and destroyed the fortune of the old man, and wrought him more sorrow than all the troubles that were hatched in the baths and beds of Egypt between Antony and Cleopatra. This was the greatest fortune that the world had then or ever since, and therefore we cannot expect it to be better in a less prosperity.

6. The prosperity of this world is so infinitely soured with the overflowing of evils, that he is counted the most happy who hath the fewest; all conditions being evil and miserable, they are only distinguished by the number of calamities. The collector[20] of the Roman and foreign examples, when he had reckoned two-and-twenty instances of great fortunes, every one of which had been allayed with great variety of evils; in all his reading or experience, he could tell but of two who had been famed for an entire prosperity, Quintus Metellus, and Gyges the king of Lydia: and yet concerning the one of them he tells that his felicity was so inconsiderable (and yet it was the bigger of the two) that the oracle said that Aglaus Sophidius the poor Arcadian shepherd was more happy than he, that is, he had fewer troubles; for so indeed we are to reckon the pleasures of this life, the limit of our joy is the absence of some degrees of sorrow, and he that hath the least of this, is the most prosperous person. But then we must look for prosperity not in palaces or courts of princes, not in the tents of conquerors, or in the gaieties of fortunate and prevailing sinners; but something rather in the cottages of honest, innocent, and contented persons, whose mind is no bigger than their fortune, nor their virtue less than their security. As for others, whose fortune looks bigger, and allures fools to follow it like the wandering fires of the night, till they run into rivers or are broken upon rocks with staring and running after them, they are all in

20 Valerius Maximus, vii. 1.

the condition of Marius, than whose condition nothing was more constant, and nothing more mutable; if we reckon them amongst the happy, they are the most happy men; if we reckon them amongst the miserable, they are the most miserable. For just as is a man's condition, great or little, so is the state of his misery; all have their share; but kings and princes, great generals and consuls, rich men and mighty, as they have the biggest business and the biggest charge, and are answerable to God for the greatest accounts, so they have the biggest trouble; that the uneasiness of their appendage may divide the good and evil of the world, making the poor man's fortune as eligible as the greatest; and also restraining the vanity of man's spirit, which a great fortune is apt to swell from a vapor to a bubble; but God in mercy hath mingled wormwood with their wine, and so restrained the drunkenness and follies of prosperity.

7. Man never hath one day to himself of entire peace from the things of the world, but either something troubles him, or nothing satisfies him, or his very fullness swells him and makes him breathe short upon his bed. Men's joys are troublesome, and besides that the fear of losing them takes away the present pleasure, and a man hath need of another felicity to preserve this, they are also wavering and full of trepidation, not only from their inconstant nature, but from their weak foundation: they arise from vanity, and they dwell upon ice, and they converse with the wind, and they have the wings of a bird, and are serious but as the resolutions of a child, commenced by chance, and managed by folly, and proceed by inadvertency, and end in vanity and forgetfulness. So that as Livius Drusus said[21] of himself, he never had any play-days or days of quiet when he was a boy, for he was troublesome and busy, a restless and unquiet man; the same may every man observe to be true of himself; he is always restless and uneasy, he dwells upon the waters, and leans upon thorns, and lays his head upon a sharp stone.

SECTION V
This Consideration Reduced to Practice

---

1. THE effect of this consideration is this, that the sadnesses of this life help to sweeten the bitter cup of death. For let our life be never so long, if our strength were great as that of oxen and camels, if our sinews

21 Seneca, *De Brevitate Vitæ*, i. 6.

were strong as the cordage at the foot of an oak, if we were as fighting and prosperous people as Siccius Dentatus,[22] who was on the prevailing side in a hundred and twenty battles, who had three hundred and twelve public rewards assigned him by his generals and princes for his valor and conduct in sieges and sharp encounters, and, besides all this, had his share in nine triumphs; yet still the period shall be that all this shall end in death, and the people shall talk of us awhile, good or bad, according as we deserve, or as they please, and once it shall come to pass that concerning every one of us it shall be told in the neighborhood, that we are dead. This we are apt to think a sad story; but therefore let us help it with a sadder: for we therefore need not be much troubled that we shall die, because we are not here in ease, nor do we dwell in a fair condition; but our days are full of sorrow and anguish, dishonored, and made unhappy with many sins, with a frail and a foolish spirit, entangled with difficult cases of conscience, ensnared with passions, amazed with fears, full of cares, divided with curiosities and contradictory interests, made airy and impertinent with vanities, abused with ignorance and prodigious errors, made ridiculous with a thousand weaknesses, worn away with labors, loaded with diseases, daily vexed with dangers and temptations, and in love with misery; we are weakened with delights, afflicted with want, with the evils of myself and of all my family, and with the sadnesses of all my friends, and of all good men, even of the whole church; and therefore methinks we need not be troubled that God is pleased to put an end to all these troubles, and to let them sit down in a natural period, which, if we please, may be to us the beginning of a better life. When the prince of Persia wept because his army should all die in the revolution of an age, Artabanus told him that they should all meet with evils so many and so great that every man of them should wish himself dead long before that. Indeed it were a sad thing to be cut of the stone, and we that are in health tremble to think of it; but the man that is wearied with the disease looks upon that sharpness as upon his cure and remedy; and as none need to have a tooth drawn, so none could well endure it, but he that felt the pain of it in his head: so is our life so full of evils, that therefore death is no evil to them that have felt the smart of this, or hope for the joys of a better.

2. But as it helps to ease a certain sorrow, as a fire

22 Valerius Maximus, iii. 2.

draws out fire, and a nail drives forth a nail, so it instructs us in a present duty, that is, that we should not be so fond of a perpetual storm, nor dote upon the transient gauds and gilded thorns of this world. They are not worth a passion, nor worth a sigh or a groan, not of the price of one night's watching; and therefore they are mistaken and miserable persons, who, since Adam planted thorns round about paradise, are more in love with that hedge than all the fruits of the garden, sottish admirers of things that hurt them, of sweet poisons, gilded daggers, and silken halters. Tell them they have lost a bounteous friend, a rich purchase, a fair farm, a wealthy donative,[23] and you dissolve their patience; it is an evil bigger than their spirit can bear; it brings sickness and death; they can neither eat nor sleep with such a sorrow. But if you represent to them the evils of a vicious habit, and the dangers of a state of sin; if you tell them they have displeased God, and interrupted their hopes of heaven, it may be they will be so civil as to hear it patiently, and to treat you kindly, and first to commend, and then forget your story, because they prefer this world with all its sorrows before the pure unmingled felicities of heaven. But it is strange that any man should be so passionately in love with the thorns which grow on his own ground, that he should wear them for armlets, and knit them in his shirt, and prefer them before a kingdom and immortality. No man loves this world the better for his being poor; but men that love it because they have great possessions, love it because it is troublesome and chargeable, full of noise and temptation, because it is unsafe and ungoverned, flattered and abused; and he that considers the troubles of an overlong garment and of a crammed stomach, a trailing gown and a loaden table, may justly understand that all that for which men are so passionate, is their hurt and their objection, that which a temperate man would avoid, and a wise man cannot love.

He that is no fool but can consider wisely, if he be in love with this world, we need not despair but that a witty man might reconcile him with tortures, and make him think charitably of the rack, and be brought to dwell with vipers and dragons, and entertain his guests with the shrieks of mandrakes, cats, and screech-owls, with the filing of iron, and the harshness of rending of silk, or to admire the harmony that is made by a herd of evening wolves when they miss their draught of blood in their midnight revels. The groans

23 Gift.

of a man in a fit of the stone are worse than all these; and the distractions of a troubled conscience are worse than those groans; and yet a careless merry sinner is worse than all that. But if we could from one of the battlements of heaven espy how many men and women at this time lie fainting and dying for want of bread, how many young men are hewn down by the sword of war, how many poor orphans are now weeping over the graves of their father by whose life they were enabled to eat: if we could but hear how many mariners and passengers are at this present in a storm, and shriek out because their keel dashes against a rock, or bulges under them, how many people there are that weep with want, and are mad with oppression, or are desperate by too quick a sense of a constant infelicity; in all reason we should be glad to be out of the noise and participation of so many evils. This is a place of sorrows and tears, of great evils and constant calamity: let us remove from hence, at least in affections and preparation of mind.

Abraham Cowley

[1618–1667]

OWLEY has been overtaken by as perverse a fate as ever attended on a poet. He who was the most popular and admired poet of his day had within two generations become a byword and symbol of neglect. "Who now reads Cowley?" asked Pope, and he was quite sure of the answer. But the neglected poet has enjoyed a steadily rising reputation as one of the most agreeable as well as one of the most accomplished familiar essayists of his age.

Born in London, the seventh child of a stationer, Cowley early evinced a remarkable precocity in literature. His *Poetical Blossoms*, published when he was a fifteen-year-old student at Westminster School, is a consistently reputable volume which contains poems written when he was ten and twelve. Entering Trinity College, Cambridge, in 1636, Cowley continued his literary pursuits; he wrote three plays, one of which was performed at the college, and struck up a fast friendship with Richard Crashaw, whom he was later to memorialize in a moving elegy. Cowley was elected a Fellow of Trinity in 1640, but the shadow of the Civil War was already falling over the university. Before the arrival of the Puritan Commissioners at Cambridge, Cowley fled to Oxford, where the king's government was located, and shortly thereafter joined the exodus of royalist émigrés to Paris. After some years of service there as a secretary to the exiled Queen Henrietta Maria, Cowley returned to England, possibly on an intelligence mission for the royalist party. In any case, the Puritan government suspected his motives and imprisoned him in 1655. After his release he studied medicine, and, although this activity may have been designed to serve as a mask for further spying attempts, he received his M.D. in 1657. Cowley did not, after the Restoration, receive the kind of reward he had hoped for, but he was given some land by the queen and in 1663 he retired to it. It was in this retirement that Cowley wrote his essays, and it was there also that, at the age of 49, he died.

Cowley's interests were varied. Poet, essayist, and, to some extent, political intriguer, he was also a man of keen scientific interests, a great admirer of Bacon, an amateur of botany, and one of the guiding spirits behind the foundation of the Royal Society. His *Proposition for the Advancement of Experimental Philosophy* (1661) is a significant document of the triumph of the new scientific spirit in England—not only for the attitudes and aspirations which it expresses, but also for the clean, practical prose in which it expresses them, the kind of prose which the Royal Society was shortly to advocate as the only proper language for scientific discourse.

The "Philosophical College" which Cowley outlines in the *Proposition* is clearly an attempt to make practical reality out of Bacon's dream of "Solomon's House" in *The*

New Atlantis (as Cowley admits). But for all his admiration for the great Lord High Chancellor, Cowley shows in his *Several Discourses by Way of Essays, in Verse and Prose* no affinity with Bacon's essays. He abandons the pregnant sententiousness of Bacon's style for a manner which is almost startling in its relaxed modernity. Like the earlier practitioners of "Attic" prose, Cowley knows how to make the very shape of a sentence reveal his personality, but unlike them he is master of a style which is almost completely free of idiosyncrasy or affectation. Cowley was not the first Englishman to follow Montaigne into the realm of the distinctly personal essay; Sir William Cornwallis (*Essays*, 1600), for one, had preceded him. But Cowley was the first true master of the form in England, and from him the line of descent to Hazlitt and Lamb may clearly be traced.

A. COWLEY. *English Writings*, ed. A. R. Waller, 2 vols. (Cambridge, 1905–06).
————. *Essays and Other Prose Writings*, ed. A. B. Gough (Oxford, 1915).
A. H. NETHERCOT. *Abraham Cowley, the Muse's Hannibal* (London, 1931). The standard biography.
————. "The Essays of Abraham Cowley," *Journal of English and Germanic Philology*, XXIX (1930).

A PROPOSITION FOR THE ADVANCEMENT OF EXPERIMENTAL PHILOSOPHY

[TEXT: *first edition, 1661*]

TO THE HONORABLE SOCIETY FOR THE ADVANCEMENT OF EXPERIMENTAL PHILOSOPHY

THE author of the following discourse, having since his going into France allowed me to make it public, I thought I should do it most right by presenting it to your considerations; to the end that when it hath been fully examined by you, and received such additions or alterations as you shall think fit, the design thereof may be promoted by your recommending the practice of it to the nation.

I am,
Your most humble Servant,
P. P.[1]

THE PREFACE

ALL KNOWLEDGE must either be of God, or of his creatures, that is, of nature; the first is called from the object, divinity; the latter, natural philosophy, and is divided into the contemplation of the immediate or mediate creatures of God, that is, the creatures of his creature man. Of this latter kind are all arts for the use of human life, which are thus again divided: some are purely human, or made by man alone, and as it were entirely spun out of himself, without relation to other creatures: such are grammar and logic, to improve his natural qualities of internal and external speech; as likewise rhetoric and politics (or law) to fulfill and exalt his natural inclination to society. Other are mixed, and are man's creatures no otherwise than by the result which he effects by conjunction and application of the creatures of God. Of these parts of philosophy, that which treats of God Almighty (properly called divinity), which is almost only to be sought out of his revealed will, and therefore requires only the diligent and pious study of that, and of the best interpreters upon it; and that part which I call purely human, depending solely upon memory and wit, that is, reading and invention, are both excellently well provided for by the constitution of our universities. But the other two parts, the inquisition into the nature of God's creatures, and the application of them to human uses (especially the latter) seem to be very slenderly provided for, or rather almost totally neglected, except only some

1 The identity of "P. P." has not been discovered.

small assistances to physic and the mathematics. And therefore the founders of our colleges have taken ample care to supply the students with multitude of books, and to appoint tutors and frequent exercises, the one to interpret, and the other to confirm their reading, as also to afford them sufficient plenty and leisure for the opportunities of their private study, that the beams which they receive by lecture may be doubled by reflections of their own wit; but towards the observation and application, as I said, of the creatures themselves, they have allowed no instruments, materials, or conveniences. Partly, because the necessary expense thereof is much greater than of the other; and partly from that idle and pernicious opinion, which had long possessed the world, that all things to be searched in nature had been already found and discovered by the ancients, and that it were a folly to travel about for that which others had before brought home to us. And the great importer of all truths they took to be Aristotle, as if (as Macrobius[2] speaks foolishly of Hippocrates) he could neither deceive nor be deceived, or as if there had been not only no lies in him, but all verities. O true philosophers in one sense! and contended with a very little! Not that I would disparage the admirable wit, and worthy labors of many of the ancients, much less of Aristotle, the most eminent among them; but it were madness to imagine that the cisterns of men should afford us as much, and as wholesome waters, as the fountains of nature. As we understand the manners of men by conversation among them, and not by reading romances, the same is our case in the true apprehension and judgment of things. And no man can hope to make himself as rich by stealing out of others' trunks, as he might by opening and digging of new mines. If he conceive that all are already exhausted, let him consider that many lazily thought so hundred years ago, and yet nevertheless since that time whole regions of art have been discovered, which the ancients as little dreamt of as they did of America. There is yet many a *terra incognita* behind to exercise our diligence, and let us exercise it never so much, we shall leave work enough too for our posterity.

This therefore being laid down as a certain foundation, that we must not content ourselves with that inheritance of knowledge which is left us by the labor and bounty of our ancestors, but seek to improve those very grounds, and add to them new and greater purchases; it remains to be considered by what means we are most likely to attain the ends of this virtuous covetousness.

And certainly the solitary and inactive contemplation of nature, by the most ingenious persons living, in their own private studies, can never effect it. Our reasoning faculty as well as fancy, does but dream, when it is not guided by sensible objects. We shall compound where nature has divided, and divide where nature has compounded, and create nothing but either deformed monsters, or at best pretty but impossible mermaids. 'Tis like painting by memory and imagination, which can never produce a picture to the life. Many persons of admirable abilities (if they had been wisely managed and profitably employed) have spent their whole time and diligence in commentating upon Aristotle's philosophy, who could never go beyond him, because their design was only to follow, not grasp or lay hold on, or so much as touch nature, because they caught only at the shadow of her in their own brains. And therefore we see that for above a thousand years together nothing almost of ornament or advantage was added to the uses of human society, except only guns and printing, whereas since the industry of men has ventured to go abroad, out of books and out of themselves, and to work among God's creatures, instead of playing among their own, every age has abounded with excellent inventions, and every year perhaps might do so, if a considerable number of select persons were set apart, and well directed, and plentifully provided for the search of them. But our universities, having been founded in those former times that I complain of, it is no wonder if they be defective in their constitution as to this way of learning, which was not then thought on.

For the supplying of which defect, it is humbly proposed to his sacred Majesty, his most honorable Parliament, and Privy Council, and to all such of ish subjects as are willing and able to contribute anything towards the advancement of real and useful learning, that by their authority, encouragement, patronage and bounty, a Philosophical College may be erected, after this ensuing, or some such like model.

THE COLLEGE

THAT the Philosophical College be situated within one, two, or (at farthest) three miles to London, and,

---

2 Macrobius, a Latin author of about A.D. 400, author of a commentary on Cicero's Dream of Scipio, in which he refers to Hippocrates, the great physician of Cos, who lived in the fifth century B.C.

if it be possible to find that convenience, upon the side of the river, or very near it.

That the revenue of this College amount to £4000 a year.

That the company received into it be as follows:

1. Twenty philosophers or professors. 2. Sixteen young scholars, servants to the professors. 3. A chaplain. 4. A baily for the revenue. 5. A manciple or purveyor for the provisions of the house. 6. Two gardeners. 7. A master-cook. 8. An under-cook. 9. A butler. 10. An under-butler. 11. A chirurgeon. 12. Two lungs, or chemical servants. 13. A library-keeper who is likewise to be apothecary, druggist, and keeper of instruments, engines, etc. 14. An officer to feed and take care of all beasts, fowl, etc., kept by the College. 15. A groom of the stable. 16. A messenger to send upon and down for all uses of the College. 17. Four old women, to tend the chambers, keep the house clean, and such like services.

That the annual allowance for this company be as follows. 1. To every professor, and to the chaplain, £120. 2. To the sixteen scholars, £20 apiece, £10 for their diet, and £10 for their entertainment.[3] 3. To the baily, £30, besides allowance for his journeys. 4. To the purveyor or manciple, £30. 5. To each of the gardeners, £20. 6. To the master-cook, £20. 7. To the under-cook, £4. 8. To the butler, £10. 9. To the under-butler, £4. 10. To the chirurgeon, £30. 11. To the library-keeper, £30. 12. To each of the lungs, £12. 13. To the keeper of the beasts, £6. 14. To the groom, £5. 15. To the messenger, £12. 16. To the four necessary women, £10. For the manciple's table, at which all the servants of the house are to eat, except the scholars, £160. For three horses for the service of the College, £30.

All which amounts to £3285. So that there remains for keeping of the house and gardens, and operatories, and instruments and animals, and experiments of all sorts, and all other expenses, £715.

Which were a very inconsiderable sum for the great uses to which it is designed, but that I conceive the industry of the College will in a short time so enrich itself as to get a far better stock for the advance and enlargement of the work when it is once begun; neither is the continuance of particular men's liberality to be despaired of, when it shall be encouraged by the sight of that public benefit which will accrue to all mankind, and chiefly to our nation, by this foundation. Something likewise will arise from leases and

other casualties;[4] that nothing of which may be diverted to the private gain of the professors, or any other use besides that of the search of nature, and by it the general good of the world, and that care may be taken for the certain performance of all things ordained by the institution, as likewise for the protection and encouragement of the company, it is proposed:

That some person of eminent quality, a lover of solid learning, and no stranger in it, be chosen Chancellor or President of the College, and that eight Governors more, men qualified in the like manner, be joined with him, two of which shall yearly be appointed Visitors of the College, and receive an exact account of all expenses even to the smallest, and of the true estate of their public treasure, under the hands and oaths of the professors resident.

That the choice of the professors in any vacancy belong to the Chancellor and the Governors, but that the professors (who are likeliest to know what men of the nation are most proper for the duties of their society) direct their choice by recommending two or three persons to them at every election. And that if any learned person within his Majesty's dominions discover or eminently improve any useful kind of knowledge, he may upon that ground for his reward and the encouragement of others, be preferred, if he pretend[5] to the place, before anybody else.

That the Governors have power to turn out any professor who shall be proved to be either scandalous or unprofitable to the society.

That the College be built after this, or some such manner: That it consist of three fair quadrangular courts, and three large grounds, enclosed with good walls behind them. That the first court be built with a fair cloister, and the professors' lodgings or rather little houses, four on each side at some distance from one another, and with little gardens behind them, just after the manner of the Chartreux[6] beyond the sea. That the inside of the cloister be lined with a gravel walk, and that walk with a row of trees, and that in the middle there be a parterre of flowers, and a fountain.

That the second quadrangle just behind the first, be so contrived as to contain these parts. 1. A chapel. 2. A hall with two long tables on each side for the scholars and officers of the house to eat at, and with a pulpit and

3 The rest of their entertainment.

4 Incidental or occasional sources of revenue.
5 Lay a claim.
6 The Carthusian monks, of the famous monastery near Grenoble.

forms at the end for the public lectures. 3. A large and pleasant dining-room within the hall for the professors to eat in, and to hold their assemblies and conferences. 4. A public school-house. 5. A library. 6. A gallery to walk in, adorned with the pictures or statues of all the inventors of anything useful to human life; as printing, guns, America, etc., and of late in anatomy, the circulation of the blood, the milky veins, and such like discoveries in any art, with short elogies[7] under the portraitures: as likewise the figures of all sorts of creatures, and the stuffed skins of as many strange animals as can be gotten. 7. An anatomy chamber adorned with skeletons and anatomical pictures, and prepared with all conveniences for dissection. 8. A chamber for all manner of drugs and apothecaries' materials. 9. A mathematical chamber furnished with all sorts of mathematical instruments, being an appendix to the library. 10. Lodgings for the chaplain, chirurgeon, library-keeper and purveyor, near the chapel, anatomy chamber, library and hall.

That the third court be on one side of these, very large, but meanly built, being designed only for use and not for beauty too, as the others. That it contain the kitchen, butteries, brew-house, bake-house, dairy, lardry,[8] stables, etc., and especially great laboratories for chemical operations, and lodgings for the underservants.

That behind the second court be placed the garden, containing all sorts of plants that our soil will bear, and at the end a little house of pleasure, a lodge for the gardener, and a grove of trees cut out into walks.

That the second enclosed ground be a garden, destined only to the trial of all manner of experiments concerning plants, as their melioration, acceleration, retardation, conservation, composition, transmutation, coloration, or whatsoever else can be produced by art either for use or curiosity, with a lodge in it for the gardener.

That the third ground be employed in convenient receptacles for all sorts of creatures which the professors shall judge necessary for their more exact search into the nature of animals, and the improvement of their uses to us.

That there be likewise built in some place of the College where it may serve most for ornament of the whole, a very high tower for observation of celestial bodies, adorned with all sorts of dials and such like curiosities; and that there be very deep vaults made under ground, for experiments most proper to such places, which will be undoubtedly very many.

Much might be added, but truly I am afraid this is too much already for the charity or generosity of this age to extend to; and we do not design this after the model of Solomon's House[9] in my Lord Bacon (which is a project for experiments that can never be experimented) but propose it within such bounds of expense as have often been exceeded by the buildings of private citizens.

OF THE PROFESSORS, SCHOLARS, CHAPLAIN, AND OTHER OFFICERS

THAT of the twenty professors four be always traveling beyond seas, and sixteen always resident, unless by permission upon extraordinary occasions, and every one so absent leaving a deputy behind him to supply his duties.

That the four Professors itinerate[10] be assigned to the four parts of the world, Europe, Asia, Africa, and America, there to reside three years at least, and to give a constant account of all things that belong to the learning, and especially natural experimental philosophy, of those parts.

That the expense of all dispatches, and all books, simples,[11] animals, stones, metals, minerals, etc., and all curiosities whatsoever, natural or artificial, sent by them to the College, shall be defrayed out of the treasury, and an additional allowance (above the £120) made to them as soon as the College's revenue shall be improved.

That at their going abroad they shall take a solemn oath never to write anything to the College, but what after very diligent examination, they shall fully believe to be true, and to confess and recant it as soon as they find themselves in an error.

That the sixteen professors resident shall be bound to study and teach all sorts of natural, experimental philosophy, to consist of the mathematics, mechanics, medicine, anatomy, chemistry, the history of animals, plants, minerals, elements, etc.; agriculture, architecture, art military, navigation, gardening; the mysteries of all trades, and improvement of them; the facture[12] of all merchandises, all natural magic or divination; and briefly all things contained in the Catalogue of

7 Titles or descriptions.   8 The storeroom for meat.

9 See Bacon's New Atlantis.   10 Itinerant.
11 Medicinal herbs.   12 Manufacture.

Natural Histories annexed to my Lord Bacon's *Organon*.

That once a day from Easter to Michaelmas, and twice a week from Michaelmas to Easter, at the hours in the afternoon most convenient for auditors from London according to the time of the year, there shall be a lecture read in the Hall, upon such parts of natural experimental philosophy as the professors shall agree on among themselves, and as each of them shall be able to perform usefully and honorably.

That two of the professors by daily, weekly, or monthly turns shall teach the public schools according to the rules hereafter prescribed.

That all the professors shall be equal in all respects (except precedency, choice of lodging, and such like privileges, which shall belong to seniority in the College), and that all shall be masters and treasurers by annual turns, which two officers for the time being shall take place [13] of all the rest, and shall be *arbitri duarum mensarum.* [14]

That the master shall command all the officers of the College, appoint assemblies or conferences upon occasion, and preside in them with a double voice, [15] and in his absence the treasurer, whose business is to receive and disburse all moneys by the master's order in writing (if it be an extraordinary) after consent of the other professors.

That all professors shall sup together in the parlor within the hall every night, and shall dine there twice a week (to wit, Sundays and Thursdays) at two round tables for the convenience of discourse, which shall be for the most part of such matters as may improve their studies and professions, and to keep them from falling into loose or unprofitable talk shall be the duty of the two *arbitri mensarum,* who may likewise command any of the servant-scholars to read to them what he shall think fit, whilst they are at table: that it shall belong likewise to the said *arbitri mensarum* only to invite strangers, which they shall rarely do, unless they be men of learning or great parts, and shall not invite above two at a time to one table, nothing being more vain and unfruitful than numerous meetings of acquaintance.

That the professors resident shall allow the College £20 a year for their diet, whether they continue there all the time or not.

That they shall have once a week an assembly or conference concerning the affairs of the College and the progress of their experimental philosophy.

That if any one find out anything which he conceives to be of consequence, he shall communicate it to the assembly to be examined, experimented, approved, or rejected.

That if any one be author of an invention that may bring in profit, the third part of it shall belong to the inventor, and the two other to the society; and besides, if the thing be very considerable, his statue or picture with an elogy under it shall be placed in the gallery, and made a denizen of that corporation of famous men.

That all the professors shall be always assigned to some particular inquisition (besides the ordinary course of their studies) of which they shall give an account to the assembly, so that by this means there may be every day some operation or other made in all the arts, as chemistry, anatomy, mechanics, and the like, and that the College shall furnish for the charge of the operation.

That there shall be kept a register under lock and key, and not to be seen but by the professors, of all the experiments that succeed, signed by the persons who made the trial.

That the popular and received errors in experimental philosophy (with which, like weeds in a neglected garden, it is now almost overgrown) shall be evinced [16] by trial, and taken notice of in the public lectures, that they may no longer abuse the credulous, and beget new ones by consequence or similitude.

That every third year (after the full settlement of the foundation) the College shall give an account in print, in proper and ancient Latin, of the fruits of their triennial industry.

That every professor resident shall have his scholar to wait upon him in his chamber and at table, whom he shall be obliged to breed up in natural philosophy, and render an account of his progress to the assembly, from whose election he received him, and therefore is responsible to it, both for the care of his education, and the just and civil usage of him.

That the scholar shall understand Latin very well, and be moderately initiated in the Greek before he be capable of being chosen into the service, and that he shall not remain in it above seven years.

That his lodging shall be with the professor whom he serves.

That no professor shall be a married man or a divine,

13 Take precedence.   14 Presidents of the two tables.
15 Two votes.

16 Demonstrated and proved to be such.

or lawyer in practice; only physic he may be allowed to prescribe, because the study of that art is a great part of the duty of his place, and the duty of that is so great that it will not suffer him to lose much time in mercenary practice.

That the professors shall in the College wear the habit of ordinary Masters of Art in the universities, or of Doctors, if any of them be so.

That they shall all keep an inviolable and exemplary friendship with one another, and that the assembly shall lay a considerable pecuniary mulct[17] upon any one who shall be proved to have entered so far into a quarrel as to give uncivil language to his brother-professor; and that the perseverance in any enmity shall be punished by the Governors with expulsion.

That the chaplain shall eat at the master's table (paying his £20 a year as the others do), and that he shall read prayers once a day at least, a little before supper-time; that he shall preach in the chapel every Sunday morning, and catechize in the afternoon the scholars and the school-boys: that he shall every month administer the Holy Sacrament; that he shall not trouble himself and his auditors with the controversies of divinity, but only teach God in his just commandments, and in his wonderful works.

THE SCHOOL

THAT the school may be built so as to contain about two hundred boys.

That it be divided into four classes, not as others are ordinarily into six or seven, because we suppose that the children sent hither to be initiated in things as well as words, ought to have passed the two or three first, and to have attained the age of thirteen years, being already well advanced in the Latin grammar, and some authors.

That none, though never so rich, shall pay anything for their teaching; and that if any professor shall be convicted to have taken any money in consideration of his pains in the school, he shall be expelled with ignominy by the Governors; but if any persons of great estate and quality, finding their sons much better proficients in learning here than boys of the same age commonly are at other schools, shall not think fit to receive an obligation of so near concernment[18] without returning some marks of acknowledgment, they may, if they please (for nothing is to be demanded), bestow

some little rarity or curiosity upon the society in recompense of their trouble.

And because it is deplorable to consider the loss which children make of their time at most schools, employing, or rather casting away, six or seven years in the learning of words only, and that too very imperfectly:

That a method be here established for the infusing knowledge and language at the same time into them; and that this may be their apprenticeship in natural philosophy. This, we conceive, may be done by breeding them up in authors, or pieces of authors, who treat of some part of nature, and who may be understood with as much ease and pleasure, as those which are commonly taught; such are in Latin, Varro,[19] Cato,[20] Columella,[21] Pliny,[22] part of Celsus,[23] and of Seneca,[24] Cicero *De Divinatione, De Natura Deorum,* and several scattered pieces, Virgil's Georgics, Grotius,[25] Nemetianus,[26] Manilius;[27] and because the truth is we want good poets (I mean we have but few) who have purposely treated of solid and learned, that is, natural matters (the most part indulging to the weakness of the world, and feeding it either with the follies of love, or with the fables of gods and heroes), we conceive that one book ought to be compiled of all the scattered little parcels among the ancient poets that might serve for the advancement of natural science, and which would make no small or unuseful or unpleasant volume. To this we would have added the morals and rhetorics of Cicero, and the Institutions of Quintilian; and for the comedians, from whom almost all that necessary part of common discourse, and all the most intimate proprieties of the language are drawn, we conceive the boys may be made masters of them, as a part of their recreation and not of their

17 Fine.

18 Of such great value.

19 Marcus Terentius Varro (116–28 B.C.), author of the *De Re Rustica.*

20 Marcus Porcius Cato, the Elder, commonly called the Censor (234–149 B.C.), author of a treatise, *De Re Rustica.*

21 Columella, the most voluminous of Roman writers on agriculture, flourished in the first century A.D.

22 Pliny the Elder, author of the famous *Historia Naturalis* (A.D. 22–79).

23 Aulus Cornelius Celsus (flourished A.D. 50), author of the *De Medicina* and numerous other works.

24 Seneca's *Naturales Questiones* are here referred to.

25 Hugo Grotius, Dutch statesman and jurist (1583–1645), author, among many other works, of *De Jure Belli et Pacis.*

26 M. Aurelius Nemetianus, a Roman poet of Carthage, about A.D. 250. Only fragments of his various works on rural subjects are now extant.

27 Manilius, a Roman poet of the first century A.D., was author of the now fragmentary *Astronomica.*

task, if once a month, or at least once in two, they act one of Terence's comedies, and afterwards (the most advanced) some of Plautus his; and this is for many reasons one of the best exercises they can be enjoined, and most innocent pleasures they can be allowed. As for the Greek authors, they may study Nicander,[28] Oppianus[29] (whom Scaliger does not doubt to prefer above Homer himself, and place next to his adored Virgil); Aristotle's History of Animals, and other parts; Theophrastus[30] and Dioscorides[31] of plants, and a collection made out of several both poets and other Grecian writers. For the morals and rhetoric, Aristotle may suffice, or Hermogenes[32] and Longinus[33] be added for the latter; with the history of animals they should be showed anatomy as a divertisement, and made to know the figures and natures of those creatures which are not common among us, disabusing them at the same time of those errors which are universally admitted concerning many. The same method should be used to make them acquainted with all plants; and to this must be added a little of the ancient and modern geography, the understanding of the globes, and the principles of geometry and astronomy. They should likewise use to declaim in Latin and English, as the Romans did in Greek and Latin; and in all this travail be rather led on by familiarity, encouragement, and emulation, than driven by severity, punishment, and terror. Upon festivals and playtimes they should exercise themselves in the fields by riding, leaping, fencing, mustering and training after the manner of soldiers, etc., and to prevent all dangers and all disorder, there should always be two of the scholars with them to be as witnesses and directors of their actions; in foul weather it would not be amiss for them to learn to dance, that is, to learn just so much

(for all beyond is superfluous, if not worse) as may give them a graceful comportment of their bodies.

Upon Sundays and all days of devotion they are to be a part of the chaplain's province.

That for all these ends the College so order it, as that there may be some convenient and pleasant houses thereabouts, kept by religious, discreet, and careful persons, for the lodging and boarding of young scholars, that they have a constant eye over them to see that they be bred up there piously, cleanly, and plentifully, according to the proportion of their parents' expenses.

And that the College, when it shall please God either by their own industry and success, or by the benevolence of patrons, to enrich them so far, as that it may come to their turn and duty to be charitable to others, shall at their own charges erect and maintain some house or houses for the entertainment of such poor men's sons whose good natural parts may promise either use or ornament to the commonwealth, during the time of their abode at school, and shall take care that it shall be done with the same conveniences as are enjoyed even by rich men's children (though they maintain the fewer for that cause), there being nothing of eminent and illustrious to be expected from a low, sordid, and hospital-like[34] education.

CONCLUSION

IF I BE not much abused[35] by a natural fondness to my own conceptions (that στοργή of the Greeks, which no other language has a proper word for), there was never any project thought upon which deserves to meet with so few adversaries as this; for who can without impudent folly oppose the establishment of twenty well selected persons in such a condition of life that their whole business and sole profession may be to study the improvement and advantage of all other professions, from that of the highest general even to the lowest artisan? Who shall be obliged to employ their whole time, wit, learning, and industry, to these four, the most useful that can be imagined, and to no other ends; first, to weigh, examine, and prove all things of nature delivered to us by former ages; to detect, explode, and strike a censure through all false moneys with which the world has been paid and cheated so long, and (as I may say) to set the mark of the College upon all true coins that they may

28 Nicander, a Greek poet and physician, author of a poem *Theriaca*, on venomous animals, lived in the second century before Christ.

29 Oppianus, author of a Greek poem on fishing, and other similar works, lived in the second century A.D.

30 Theophrastus, a pupil of Aristotle, author of works on botany and other natural sciences.

31 Dioscorides, a Greek physician of Cilicia, flourished in the first century A.D. He is the author of *Materia Medica*, a treatise on plants useful in medicine.

32 Hermogenes, a Greek rhetorician (A.D. 175), author of a famous work on the Art of Rhetoric, completed before he was twenty-five.

33 Longinus, a Platonic philosopher of the third century A.D. He was the reputed author of the famous treatise On the Sublime.

34 Poverty-stricken.   35 Deceived, misled.

pass hereafter without any farther trial. Secondly, to recover the lost inventions, and, as it were, drowned lands of the ancients. Thirdly, to improve all arts which we now have. And lastly, to discover others which we yet have not. And who shall besides all this (as a benefit by the by) give the best education in the world (purely gratis) to as many men's children as shall think fit to make use of the obligation. Neither does it at all check or interfere with any parties in state or religion, but is indifferently to be embraced by all differences in opinion, and can hardly be conceived capable (as many good institutions have done)

even of degeneration into anything harmful. So that, all things considered, I will suppose this proposition shall encounter with no enemies; the only question is, whether it will find friends enough to carry it on from discourse and design to reality and effect; the necessary expenses of the beginning (for it will maintain itself well enough afterwards) being so great (though I have set them as low as is possible in order to so vast a work) that it may seem hopeless to raise such a sum out of those few dead relics of human charity and public generosity which are yet remaining in the world.

F R O M

SEVERAL DISCOURSES BY WAY OF ESSAYS, IN VERSE AND PROSE

[TEXT: *first edition, 1668*]

OF LIBERTY

THE liberty of a people consists in being governed by laws which they have made themselves, under whatsoever form it be of government; the liberty of a private man, in being master of his own time and actions, as far as may consist with the laws of God and of his country. Of this latter only we are here to discourse, and to enquire what estate of life does best seat us in the possession of it. This liberty of our own actions is such a fundamental privilege of human nature, that God himself, notwithstanding all his infinite power and right over us, permits us to enjoy it, and that, too, after a forfeiture made by the rebellion of Adam. He takes so much care for the entire preservation of it to us, that he suffers neither his providence nor eternal decree to break or infringe it. Now for our time, the same God, to whom we are but tenants-at-will for the whole, requires but the seventh part to be paid to him as a small quit-rent in acknowledgment of his title. It is man only that has the impudence to demand our whole time, though he neither gave it nor can restore it, nor is able to pay any considerable value for the least part of it. This birth-right of mankind above all other creatures some are forced by hunger to sell, like Esau,[1] for bread and

broth; but the greatest part of men make such a bargain for the delivery up of themselves, as Thamar[2] did with Judah; instead of a kid, the necessary provisions for human life, they are contented to do it for rings and bracelets. The great dealers in this world may be divided into the ambitious, the covetous, and the voluptuous, and that all these men sell themselves to be slaves, though to the vulgar it may seem a Stoical paradox,[3] will appear to the wise so plain and obvious, that they will scarce think it deserves the labor of argumentation. Let us first consider the ambitious, and those both in their progress to greatness, and after the attaining of it. There is nothing truer than what Sallust says,[4] *Dominationis in alios servitium suum mercedem dant:* They are content to pay so great a price as their own servitude to purchase the domination over others. The first thing they must resolve to sacrifice is their whole time; they must never stop, nor ever turn aside whilst they are in the race of glory, no, not like Atalanta for golden apples. Neither, indeed, can a man stop himself if he would when he's in this career. *Fertur equis auriga neque audit currus habenas.*[5]

---

[1] See Genesis 25:29–34.

[2] See Genesis 38:18.

[3] The Stoics made use of arguments and maxims, called paradoxes, which on the surface seemed untrue.

[4] The quotation is from the fragments of Sallust (86–34 B.C.))

[5] The charioteer is carried on by his steed, nor does the team heed the reins. (Virgil's Georgics, i. 514.)

Pray let us but consider a little what mean servile things men do for this imaginary food. We cannot fetch a greater example of it, than from the chief men of that nation which boasted most of liberty. To what pitiful baseness did the noblest Romans submit themselves for the obtaining of a prætorship, or the consular dignity! They put on the habit[6] of suppliants, and ran about on foot, and in dirt, through all the tribes to beg voices; they flattered the poorest artisans, and carried a *nomenclator* with them, to whisper in their ear every man's name, lest they should mistake it in their salutations; they shook the hand and kissed the cheek of every popular tradesman; they stood all day at every market in the public places to show and ingratiate themselves to the rout; they employed all their friends to solicit for them; they kept open tables in every street; they distributed wine and bread and money, even to the vilest of the people. *En Romanos rerum dominos!*[7] Behold the masters of the world begging from door to door. This particular humble way to greatness is now out of fashion, but yet every ambitious person is still in some sort a Roman candidate. He must feast and bribe, and attend and flatter, and adore many beasts, though not the beast with many heads.[8] Catiline,[9] who was so proud that he could not content himself with a less power than Sylla's,[10] was yet so humble for the attaining of it as to make himself the most contemptible of all servants, to be a public bawd, to provide whores, and something worse, for all the young gentlemen of Rome, whose hot lusts and courages and heads he thought he might make use of. And since I happen here to propose Catiline for my instance (though there be thousand of examples for the same thing), give me leave to transcribe the character which Cicero gives of this noble slave, because it is a general description of all ambitious men, and which Machiavel, perhaps, would say ought to be the rule of their life and actions. "This man" (says he,[11] as most of you may well remember) "had many artificial touches and strokes that looked like the beauty of great virtues; his intimate conversation was with the worst of men, and yet he seemed to be an admirer and lover of the best; he was furnished with all the nets of lust and luxury, and yet

wanted not the arms of labor and industry; neither do I believe that there was ever any monster in nature composed out of so many different and disagreeing parts. Who more acceptable sometimes to the most honorable persons, who more a favorite to the most infamous? Who sometimes appeared a braver champion, who at other times a bolder enemy to his country? Who more dissolute in his pleasures, who more patient in his toils? Who more rapacious in robbing, who more profuse in giving? Above all things, this was remarkable and admirable in him: the arts he had to acquire the good opinion and kindness of all sorts of men, to retain it with great complaisance, to communicate all things to them, to watch and serve all the occasions of their fortune, both with his money and his interest, and his industry; and if need were, not by sticking at any wickedness whatsoever that might be useful to them, to bend and turn about his own nature and laveer[12] with every wind, to live severely with the melancholy, merrily with the pleasant, gravely with the aged, wantonly with the young, desperately with the bold, and debauchedly with the luxurious; with this variety and multiplicity of his nature, as he had made a collection of friendships with all the most wicked and reckless of all nations, so by the artificial simulation of some virtues, he made a shift to ensnare some honest and eminent persons into his familiarity. Neither could so vast a design as the destruction of this empire have been undertaken by him, if the immanity[13] of so many vices had not been covered and disguised by the appearances of some excellent qualities."

I see, methinks, the character of an Anti-Paul,[14] who became all things to all men, that he might destroy all; who only wanted the assistance of fortune to have been as great as his friend Cæsar was a little after him. And the ways of Cæsar to compass the same ends (I mean till the civil war, which was but another manner of setting his country on fire) were not unlike these, though he used afterward his unjust dominion with more moderation than I think the other would have done. Sallust therefore who was well acquainted with them both, and with many such like gentlemen of his time, says,[15] "That it is the nature of ambition (*ambitio*

---

6 The white toga, whence is derived the term *candidati*.
7 See Virgil's *Æneid*, i. 282.　　8 The populace.
9 Lucius Sergius Catilina, against whom some of Cicero's most bitter philippics were delivered.
10 Lucius Cornelius Sulla, the dictator.
11 From Cicero's oration *Pro Cælio*, v. 12–vi. 14.

12 A term borrowed from the Dutch, meaning to sail so as to catch the wind, to tack.
13 Enormity.
14 Cf. the Apostle Paul's statement, "I am made all things to all men, that I might by all means save some." (I Cor. 9:22).
15 From Sallust's *De Catilinæ Conjuratione*, x.

multos mortales falsos fieri coegit, etc.) to make men liars and cheaters, to hide the truth in their breasts, and show, like jugglers, another thing in their mouths, to cut all friendships and enmities to the measure of their own interest, and to make a good countenance without the help of good will." And can there be freedom with this perpetual constraint? What is it but a kind of rack that forces men to say what they have no mind to? I have wondered at the extravagant and barbarous stratagem of Zopyrus,[16] and more at the praises which I find of so deformed an action; who, though he was one of the seven grandees of Persia, and the son of Megabyzus, who had freed before his country from an ignoble servitude, slit his own nose and lips, cut off his own ears, scourged and wounded his whole body, that he might, under pretense of having been mangled so inhumanely by Darius, be received into Babylon (then besieged by the Persians) and get into the command of it by the recommendation of so cruel a sufferance,[17] and their hopes of his endeavoring to revenge it. It is great pity the Babylonians suspected not his falsehood, that they might have cut off his hands too, and whipped him back again. But the design succeeded, he betrayed the city, and was made governor of it. What brutish master ever punished his offending slave with so little mercy as ambition did this Zopyrus? And yet how many are there in all nations who imitate him in some degree for a less reward; who, though they endure not so much corporal pain for a small preferment, or some honor (as they call it), yet stick not to commit actions, by which they are more shamefully and more lastingly stigmatized! But you may say, though these be the most ordinary and open ways to greatness, yet there are narrow, thorny and little-trodden paths too, through which some men find a passage by virtuous industry. I grant, sometimes they may; but then that industry must be such as cannot consist with liberty, though it may with honesty. Thou'rt careful, frugal, painful;[18] we commend a servant so, but not a friend.

Well then, we must acknowledge the toil and drudgery which we are forced to endure in this ascent, but we are epicures and lords when once we are gotten up into the high places. This is but a short apprenticeship, after which we are made free of a royal company. If we fall in love with any beauteous women, we must be content that they should be our mistresses whilst we woo them; as soon as we are wedded and enjoy, 'tis we shall be the masters.

I am willing to stick to this similitude in the case of greatness; we enter into the bonds of it, like those of matrimony; we are bewitched with the outward and painted beauty, and take it for better or worse, before we know its true nature and interior inconveniences. A great fortune (says Seneca[19]) is a great servitude; but many are of the opinion which Brutus imputes (I hope untruly) even to that patron of liberty, his friend Cicero: "We fear" (says he to Atticus), "death, and banishment, and poverty, a great deal too much. Cicero, I am afraid, thinks these to be the worst of evils, and if he have but some persons from whom he can obtain what he has a mind to, and others who will flatter and worship him, seems to be well enough contented with an honorable servitude, if anything indeed ought to be called honorable in so base and contumelious a condition." This was spoken as became the bravest man who was ever born in the bravest commonwealth. But with us generally no condition passes for servitude, that is accompanied with great riches, with honors, and with the service of many inferiors. This is but a deception of the sight through a false medium; for if a groom serve a gentleman in his chamber, that gentleman a lord, and that lord a prince, the groom, the gentleman, and the lord, are as much servants one as the other; the circumstantial difference of the one's getting only his bread and wages, the second a plentiful, and the third a superfluous estate, is no more intrinsical to this matter than the difference between a plain, a rich, and a gaudy livery. I do not say that he who sells his whole time and his own will for one hundred thousand is not a wiser merchant than he who does it for one hundred pounds; but I will swear they are both merchants, and that he is happier than both, who can live contentedly without selling that estate to which he was born. But this dependence upon superiors is but one chain of the lovers of power: *Amatorem trecentæ Pirithoum cohibent catenæ.*[20] Let's begin with him by break of day: for by that time he's besieged by two or three hundred suitors; and the hall and antechambers (all the outworks) possessed by the enemy; as soon as his chamber opens, they are ready to break into that, or to corrupt the guards, for entrance. This is so essential a part of greatness, that whosoever is without looks like a

16 The story of Zopyrus is in Herodotus, iii. 153–59.
17 Suffering.   18 Painstaking.

19 Seneca the Younger, *Liber de Consolatione*, xxvi.
20 Three hundred chains bind the lover Pirithous. (Horace, Odes, III. iv. 79.)

fallen favorite, like a person disgraced, and condemned to do what he please all the morning. There are some who, rather than want this, are contented to have their rooms filled up every day with murmuring and cursing creditors, and to charge bravely through a body of them to get to their coach. Now I would fain know which is the worst duty, that of any one particular person who waits to speak with the great man, or the great man's, who waits every day to speak with all the company. *Aliena negotia centum per caput et circum saliunt latus;*[21] a hundred businesses of other men (many unjust and most impertinent) fly continually about his head and ears, and strike him in the face like dors.[22] Let's contemplate him a little at another special scene of glory; and that is his table. Here he seems to be the lord of all nature: the earth affords him her best metals for his dishes, her best vegetables and animals for his food; the air and sea supply him with their choicest birds and fishes; and a great many men, who look like masters, attend upon him; and yet when all this is done, even all this is but a *table d'hoste;* 'tis crowded with people for whom he cares not, with many parasites, and some spies, with the most burdensome sort of guests, the endeavorers to be witty.

But everybody pays him great respect, everybody commends his meat, that is, his money; everybody admires the exquisite dressing and ordering of it, that is, his clerk of the kitchen, or his cook; everybody loves his hospitality, that is, his vanity. But I desire to know why the honest inn-keeper, who provides a public table for his profit, should be but of a mean profession; and he who does it for his honor, a munificent prince. You'll say, because one sells, and the other gives. Nay, both sell, though for different things; the one for plain money, the other for I know not what jewels, whose value is in custom and in fancy. If then his table be made a snare (as the Scripture speaks) to his liberty, where can he hope for freedom? There is always and everywhere some restraint upon him. He's guarded with crowds, and shackled with formalities. The half hat, the whole hat, the half smile, the whole smile, the nod, the embrace, the positive parting with a little bow, the comparative at the middle of the room, the superlative at the door; and if the person be *Pan huper sebastos,*[23] there's a *hypersuperlative*

ceremony then of conducting him to the bottom of the stairs, or to the very gate; as if there were such rules set to these leviathans as are to the sea, "Hitherto shalt thou go, and no further."[24] *Perditur hæc inter misero lux,*[25] Thus wretchedly the precious day is lost.

How many impertinent letters and visits must he receive, and sometimes answer, both too as impertinently! He never sets his foot beyond his threshold, unless, like a funeral, he have a train to follow him; as if, like the dead corpse, he could not stir till the bearers were all ready. "My life" (says Horace,[26] speaking to one of these magnificos) "is a great deal more easy and commodious than thine, in that I can go into the market and cheapen[27] what I please without being wondered at; and take my horse and ride as far as Tarentum, without being missed." 'Tis an unpleasant constraint to be always under the sight and observation and censure of others; as there may be vanity in it, so, methinks, there should be vexation too of spirit. And I wonder how princes can endure to have two or three hundred men stand gazing upon them whilst they are at dinner, and taking notice of every bit they eat. Nothing seems greater and more lordly than the multitude of domestic servants; but, even this too, if weighed seriously, is a piece of servitude. Unless you will be a servant to them (as many men are), the trouble and care of yours in the government of them all is much more than that of every one of them in their observance of you. I take the profession of a schoolmaster to be one of the most useful, and which ought to be of the most honorable in a commonwealth; yet certainly all his fasces and tyrannical authority over so many boys takes away his own liberty more than theirs.

I do but slightly touch upon all these particulars of the slavery of greatness; I shake but a few of their outward chains. Their anger, hatred, jealousy, fear, envy, grief, and all the *et cætera* of their passions, which are the secret but constant tyrants and torturers of their life, I omit here, because, though they be symptoms most frequent and violent in this disease, yet they are common, too, in some degree, to the epidemical disease of life itself. But, the ambitious man, though he be so many ways a slave (*O toties servus!*), yet he bears it bravely and heroically! he struts and looks big upon the stage; he thinks himself a real prince in his masking-habit, and deceives, too, all the foolish part

21 From Horace's Satires, II. vi. 34.
22 Dor is a species of beetle.
23 "Altogether superlatively reverend and august."

24 Job 38:11.   25 Horace, Satires, II. vi. 59.
26 Satires, I. vi. 104–117.   27 Bargain for.

of his spectators. He's a slave *in Saturnalibus.*[28] The covetous man is a downright servant, a draught-horse without bells or feathers; *ad metalla damnatus,* a man condemned to work in mines, which is the lowest and hardest condition of servitude; and, to increase his misery, a worker there for he knows not whom: "He heapeth up riches and knows not who shall enjoy them"; 'tis only sure that he himself neither shall nor can enjoy them. He's an indigent needy slave; he will hardly allow himself clothes and board-wages; *Unciatim vix demenso de suo suum defraudans genium comparsit miser;*[29] he defrauds not only other men, but his own genius; he cheats himself for money. But the servile and miserable condition of this wretch is so apparent, that I leave it, as evident to every man's sight, as well as judgment.

It seems a more difficult work to prove that the voluptuous man too is but a servant. What can be more the life of a free man, or as we say ordinarily, of a gentleman, than to follow nothing but his own pleasures? Why, I'll tell you who is that true free man, and true gentleman. Not he who blindly follows all his pleasures (the very name of follower is servile), but he who rationally guides them, and is not hindered by outward impediments in the conduct and enjoyment of them. If I want skill or force to restrain the beast that I ride upon, though I bought it, and call it my own, yet in the truth of the matter I am at that time rather his man, than he my horse. The voluptuous men (whom we are fallen upon) may be divided, I think, into the lustful and luxurious, who are both servants of the belly; the other, whom we spoke of before, the ambitious and the covetous, were κακὰ θηρία, evil wild beasts; these are γαστέρες ἀργαί, slow bellies,[30] as our translation renders it; but the word ἀργαί (which is a fantastical word, with two directly opposite significations) will bear as well the translation of quick or diligent bellies; and both interpretations may be applied to these men. Metrodorus[31] said that he had learnt Ἀληθῶς γαστρὶ χαρίζεσθαι, to give his belly just thanks for all his pleasures. This, by the calumniators of Epicurus his philosophy, was objected as one of the most scandalous of all their sayings; which, according to my charitable understanding may admit a very virtuous sense, which is, that he thanked his own belly for that moderation in the customary appetites of it, which can only give a man liberty and happiness in this world. Let this suffice at present to be spoken of those great *triumviri* of the world; the covetous man, who is a mean villain, like Lepidus; the ambitious, who is a brave one, like Octavius; and the voluptuous, who is a loose and debauched one, like Mark Antony. *Quisnam igitur liber. Sapiens, sibique imperiosus.*[32] Not Œnomaus,[33] who commits himself wholly to a charioteer that may break his neck, but the man,

> Who governs his own course with steady hand,
> Who does himself with sovereign power command;
> Whom neither death, nor poverty does fright,
> Who stands not awkwardly in his own light
> Against the truth: who can, when pleasures knock
> Loud at his door, keep firm the bolt and lock.
> Who can, though honor at his gate should stay
> In all her masking clothes, send her away,
> And cry, Be gone, I have no mind to play.

This I confess is a freeman: but it may be said, that many persons are so shackled by their fortune, that they are hindered from enjoyment of that manumission which they have obtained from virtue. I do both understand, and in part feel, the weight of this objection. All I can answer to it is, that we must get as much liberty as we can; we must use our utmost endeavors, and when all that is done, be contented with the length of that line which is allowed us. If you ask me what condition of life I think the most allowed, I should pitch upon that sort of people whom King James was wont to call the happiest of our nation; the men placed in the country by their fortune above an high-constable, and yet beneath the trouble of a justice of peace, in a moderate plenty, without any just argument for the desire of increasing it by the care of many relations, and with so much knowledge and love of piety and philosophy (that is of the study of God's laws, and of his creatures) as may afford him matter enough never to be idle though without business, and never to be melancholy though without sin or vanity.

I shall conclude this tedious discourse with a prayer

---

28 Slaves were allowed great freedom and general license during the Roman feast of Saturnalia, held in December in honor of Saturn.

29 From Terence's *Phormio,* I. i. 33.

30 The words are quoted from Paul's Epistle to Titus, 1:12.

31 An Epicurean philosopher who flourished during the third century B.C.

32 Who then is free? The wise man, and the man who is able to govern himself.

33 King of Pisa in Elis, and father of Hippodamia. He announced that he would bestow his daughter on the suitor who conquered him in a chariot race. His charioteer was at last overcome by Pelops.

of mine in a copy of Latin verses, of which I remember no other part, and (*pour faire bonne bouche*) with some other verses upon the same subjects.

Magne Deus, quod ad has vitæ brevis attinet horas,
Da mihi, da panem libertatemque, nec ultra
Sollicitas effundo preces, si quid datur ultra
Accipiam gratus; si non, contentus abibo.

For the few hours of life allotted me,
Give me (Great God) but bread and liberty,
I'll beg no more; if more thou're pleased to give,
I'll thankfully that overplus receive;
If beyond this no more be freely sent,
I'll thank for this, and go away content.

OF SOLITUDE

Nunquam minus solus quam cum solus[34] is now become a very vulgar saying. Every man, and almost every boy, for these seventeen hundred years has had it in his mouth. But it was at first spoken by the excellent Scipio, who was without question a most eloquent and witty person, as well as the most wise, most worthy, most happy, and the greatest of all mankind. His meaning no doubt was this; that he found more satisfaction to his mind, and more improvement of it, by solitude than by company; and to show that he spoke not this loosely or out of vanity, after he had made Rome mistress of almost the whole world, he retired himself from it by a voluntary exile, and at a private house in the middle of a wood near Linternum passed the remainder of his glorious life no less gloriously. This house Seneca went to see so long after with great veneration, and among other things describes his baths to have been of so mean a structure, that now, says he, the basest of the people would despise them, and cry out, "Poor Scipio understood not how to live." What an authority is here for the credit of retreat! And happy had it been for Hannibal, if adversity could have taught him as much wisdom as was learnt by Scipio from the highest prosperities. This would be no wonder, if it were as truly as it is colorably and wittily said by Monsieur de Montaigne, that ambition itself might teach us to love solitude; there's nothing does so much hate to have companions. 'Tis true, it loves to have its elbows free, it detests to have company on either side, but it delights above all

things in a train behind; aye, and ushers too before it. But the greatest part of men are so far from the opinion of that noble Roman, that, if they chance at any time to be without company, they're like a becalmed ship; they never move but by the wind of other men's breath, and have no oars of their own to steer withal. It is very fantastical and contradictory in human nature, that men should love themselves above all the rest of the world, and yet never endure to be with themselves. When they are in love with a mistress, all other persons are importunate and burdensome to them. *Tecum vivere amem, tecum obeam lubens,*[35] they would live and die with her alone.

Sic ego secretis possum bene vivere silvis
Qua nulla humano sit via trita pede,
Tu mihi curarum requies, tu nocte vel atra
Lumen et in solis tu mihi turba locis.[36]

With thee for ever I in woods could rest,
Where never human foot the ground has prest,
Thou from all shades the darkness canst exclude,
And from a desert banish solitude.

And yet our dear self is so wearisome to us that we can scarcely support its conversation for an hour together. This is such an odd temper of mind, as Catullus expresses towards one of his mistresses, whom we may suppose to have been of a very unsociable humor,

Odi et amo, quanam id faciam ratione requiris?
Nescio, sed fieri sentio, et excrucior.[37]

I hate, and yet I love thee too;
How can that be? I know not how;
Only that so it is I know,
And feel with torment that 'tis so.

It is a deplorable condition, this, and drives a man sometimes to pitiful shifts in seeking how to avoid himself.

The truth of the matter is, that neither he who is a fop in the world is a fit man to be alone nor he who has set his heart much upon the world, though he have never so much understanding; so that solitude can be well fitted and set right but upon a very few persons. They must have enough knowledge of the world to see the vanity of it, and enough virtue to despise all vanity; if the mind be possessed with any

34 Never less alone than when alone; Cicero, *De Republica,* i. 17.

35 With thee I should love to live; with thee I would gladly die; Horace, Odes, III. ix. 24.

36 Tibullus, IV. xiii. 9.   37 *De Amore Suo*, 83.

lust or passions, a man had better be in a fair than in a wood alone. They may, like petty thieves, cheat us perhaps, and pick our pockets in the midst of company; but like robbers they use to strip and bind, or murder us when they catch us alone. This is but to retreat from men, and fall into the hands of devils. 'Tis like the punishment of parricides among the Romans, to be sewn into a bag with an ape, a dog, and a serpent.

The first work therefore that a man must do to make himself capable of the good of solitude, is the very eradication of all lusts; for how is it possible for a man to enjoy himself while his affections are tied to things without himself? In the second place, he must learn the art and get the habit of thinking; for this too, no less than well speaking, depends upon much practice, and cogitation is the thing which distinguishes the solitude of a God from a wild beast. Now because the soul of man is not by its own nature or observation furnished with sufficient materials to work upon, it is necessary for it to have continual recourse to learning and books for fresh supplies, so that the solitary life will grow indigent, and be ready to starve, without them; but if once we be thoroughly engaged in the love of letters, instead of being wearied with the length of any day, we shall only complain of the shortness of our whole life.

> *O vita, stulto longa, sapienti brevis!*

> O life, long to the fool, short to the wise!

The first minister of state has not so much business in public as a wise man has in private; if the one have little leisure to be alone, the other has less leisure to be in company; the one has but part of the affairs of one nation, the other all the works of God and nature under his consideration. There is no saying shocks me so much as that which I hear very often, that a man does not know how to pass his time. 'Twould have been but ill spoken by Methusalem in the nine hundred sixty-ninth year of his life; so far it is from us, who have not time enough to attain the utmost perfection of any part of any science, to have cause to complain that we are forced to be idle for want of work. But this you'll say is work only for the learned; others are not capable either of the employments or divertisements that arrive from letters. I know they are not; and therefore cannot much recommend solitude to a man totally illiterate. But if any man be so unlearned as to want entertainment of the little inter-

vals of accidental solitude, which frequently occur in almost all conditions (except the very meanest of the people, who have business enough in the necessary provisions for life), it is truly a great shame both to his parents and himself; for a very small portion of any ingenious art will stop up all those gaps of our time; either music, or painting, or designing, or chemistry, or history, or gardening, or twenty other things will do it usefully and pleasantly; and if he happen to set his affections upon poetry (which I do not advise him to immoderately), that will overdo it; no wood will be thick enough to hide him from the importunities of company or business, which would abstract him from his beloved.

> ——*O qui me gelidis in vallibus Hæmi*
> *Sistat, et ingenti ramorum protegat umbra?* [38]

. . . .

OF OBSCURITY

> *Nam neque divitibus contingunt gaudia solis,*
> *Nec vixit male, qui natus moriensque fefellit.* [39]

> God made not pleasures only for the rich,
> Nor have those men without their share too lived,
> Who both in life and death the world deceived.

THIS seems a strange sentence thus literally translated, and looks as if it were in vindication of the men of business (for who else can deceive the world?); whereas it is in commendation of those who live and die so obscurely that the world takes no notice of them. This Horace calls deceiving the world, and in another place uses the same phrase,

> *Secretum iter et fallentis semita vitæ.* [40]

> The secret tracks of the deceiving life.

It is very elegant in Latin, but our English word will hardly bear up to that sense, and therefore Mr. Broom [41] translates it very well,

> Or from a life, led as it were by stealth.

---

38 Oh that someone would set me down in the cool valleys of Hæmus, and shelter me with a mighty shade of boughs. (Adapted from Virgil's Georgics, II. 489.)

39 Horace, Epistles, I. xvii. 9.

40 Horace, Epistles, I. xviii. 3.

41 Alexander Broom (Brome), 1620–1666. He collaborated with Ben Jonson and others in the translation of Horace.

Yet we say, in our language, a thing deceives our sight, when it passes before us unperceived, and we may say well enough out of the same author,

Sometimes with sleep, sometimes with wine we strive,
The cares of life and troubles to deceive.[42]

But that is not to deceive the world, but to deceive ourselves, as Quintilian says, *vitam fallere; to draw on still, and amuse,[43] and deceive our life, till it be advanced insensibly to the fatal period, and fall into that pit which nature hath prepared for it. The meaning of all this is no more than that most vulgar saying, *Bene qui latuit, bene vixit,* He has lived well who has lain well hidden. Which, if it be a truth, the world (I'll swear) is sufficiently deceived; for my part, I think it is, and that the pleasantest condition of life is *in incognito. What a brave privilege is it to be free from all contentions, from all envying or being envied, from receiving and from paying all kind of ceremonies! It is, in my mind, a very delightful pastime, for two good and agreeable friends to travel up and down together, in places where they are by nobody known, nor know anybody. It was the case of Æneas and his Achates, when they walked invisibly about the fields and streets of Carthage; Venus herself

A veil of thicken'd air around them cast,
That none might know or see them as they past.

The common story of Demosthenes' confession that he had taken great pleasure in hearing of a tanker-woman[44] say as he passed, "This is that Demosthenes," is wonderful ridiculous from so solid an orator. I myself have often met with that temptation to vanity (if it were any), but am so far from finding it any pleasure, that it only makes me run faster from the place, till I get, as it were, out of sight-shot. Democritus relates, and in such a manner as if he gloried in the good fortune and commodity[45] of it, that when he came to Athens nobody there did so much as take notice of him; and Epicurus lived there very well, that is, lay hid many years in his gardens, so famous since that time, with his friend Metrodorus; after whose death, making in one of his letters a kind commemoration of the happiness which they two had enjoyed together, he adds at last, that he thought it no disparagement to those great felicities of their life, that in the midst of the most talked-of and talking

country in the world, they had lived so long, not only without fame, but almost without being heard of. And yet within a very few years afterward, there were no two names of men more known or more generally celebrated. If we engage into a large acquaintance and various familiarities, we set open our gates to the invaders of most of our time; we expose our life to a quotidian ague of frigid impertinencies, which would make a wise man tremble to think of. Now, as for being known much by sight, and pointed at, I cannot comprehend the honor that lies in that. Whatsoever it be, every mountebank has it more than the best doctor, and the hangman more than the lord chief justice of a city. Every creature has it both of nature and art, if it be any ways extraordinary. It was as often said, "This is that Bucephalus," or, "This is that Incitatus," when they were led prancing through the streets, as "This is that Alexander," or "This is that Domitian"; and truly, for the latter, I take Incitatus to have been a much more honorable beast than his master, and more deserving the consulship, than he the empire. I love and commend a true good fame, because it is the shadow of virtue, not that it doth any good to the body which it accompanies, but 'tis an efficacious shadow, and, like that of St. Peter,[46] cures the diseases of others. The best kind of glory, no doubt, is that which is reflected from honesty, such as was the glory of Cato and Aristides; but it was harmful to them both, and is seldom beneficial to any man whilst he lives; what it is to him after his death, I cannot say, because I love not philosophy merely notional and conjectural, and no man who has made the experiment has been so kind as to come back to inform us. Upon the whole matter, I account a person who has a moderate mind and fortune, and lives in the conversation of two or three agreeable friends, with little commerce[47] in the world besides, who is esteemed well enough by his few neighbors that know him, and is truly irreproachable by anybody, and so after a healthful, quiet life, before the great inconveniences of old age, goes more silently out of it than he came in (for I would not have him so much as cry in the exit); this innocent deceiver of the world, as Horace calls him, this *muta persona,* I take to have been more happy in his part, than the greatest actors that fill the stage with show and noise, nay, even than Augustus himself, who asked with his last breath, whether he had not played his farce very well.

42 Horace, Satires, II. vii. 114.
43 Make use of, occupy.   44 A water-carrier.
45 Advantage.

46 Cf. Acts 5:15.   47 Intercourse.

OF GREATNESS

SINCE we cannot attain to greatness (says the Sieur de Montaigne), let's have our revenge by railing at it; this he spoke but in jest. I believe he desired it no more than I do, and had less reason, for he enjoyed so plentiful and honorable a fortune in a most excellent country, as allowed him all the real conveniences of it, separated and purged from the incommodities. If I were but in this condition, I should think it hard measure, without being convinced[48] of any crime, to be sequestered from it and made one of the principal officers of the state. But the reader may think that what I now say is of small authority, because I never was, nor ever shall be put to the trial. I can therefore only make my protestation,

> If ever I more riches did desire
> Than cleanliness and quiet do require,
> If e'er ambition did my fancy cheat,
> With any wish, so mean as to be great,
> Continue, Heav'n, still from me to remove
> The humble blessings of that life I love.

I know very many men will despise, and some pity me, for this humor, as a poor-spirited fellow; but I'm content; and, like Horace, thank God for being so. *Dii bene fecerunt inopis me quodque pusilli finxerunt animi.*[49] I confess, I love littleness almost in all things. A little convenient estate, a little cheerful house, a little company, and a very little feast; and if I were ever to fall in love again (which is a great passion, and therefore, I hope, I have done with it), it would be, I think, with prettiness, rather than with majestical beauty. I would neither wish that my mistress, nor my fortune, should be a *bona roba*,[50] nor, as Homer uses to describe his beauties, like a daughter of great Jupiter for the stateliness and largeness of her person; but as Lucretius says,

Parvula, pumilio, Χαρίτων μία tota merum sal.[51]

Where there is one man of this, I believe there are a thousand of Senecio's mind, whose ridiculous affectation of grandeur Seneca the Elder describes[52] to this effect. Senecio was a man of a turbid and confused wit, who could not endure to speak any but mighty words and sentences, till this humor grew at last into so notorious a habit, or rather disease, as became the sport of the whole town; he would have no servants but huge, massy fellows; no plate or household stuff, but thrice as big as the fashion; you may believe me, for I speak without raillery, his extravagancy came at last into such a madness, that he would not put on a pair of shoes, each of which was not big enough for both of his feet; he would eat nothing but what was great, nor touch any fruit but horse-plums and pound-pears; he kept a concubine that was a very giantess, and made her walk, too, always in chiopins,[53] till at last, he got the surname of *Senecio Grandio*, which, Messala said, was not his *cognomen*, but his *cognomentum*. When he declaimed for the three hundred Lacedæmonians, who alone opposed Xerxes his army of above three hundred thousand, he stretched out his arms, and stood on tiptoes, that he might appear the taller, and cried out, in a very loud voice: "I rejoice, I rejoice—." We wondered, I remember, what new great fortune had befallen his eminence, "Xerxes" (says he) "is all mine own. He who took away the sight of the sea, with the canvas veils of so many ships—" and then he goes on so, as I know not what to make of the rest, whether it be the fault of the edition, or the orator's own burly way of nonsense.

This is the character that Seneca gives of this hyperbolical fop, whom we stand amazed at; and yet there are very few men who are not in some things and to some degrees *Grandios*. Is anything more common than to see our ladies of quality wear such high shoes as they cannot walk in without one to lead them; and a gown as long again as their body, so that they cannot stir to the next room without a page or two to hold it up? I may safely say that all the ostentation of our grandees is just like a train of no use in the world, but horribly cumbersome and incommodious. What is all this, but a spice of *Grandio?* How tedious would this be if we were always bound to it! I do believe there is no king, who would not rather be deposed than endure every day of his reign all the ceremonies of his coronation. The mightiest princes are glad to fly often from these majestic pleasures (which is, methinks, no small disparagement to them) as it were for refuge, to the most contemptible divertisements, and meanest recreations of the vulgar, nay, even of children. One of the most powerful and

48 Convicted.

49 The gods have done well in that they have made me of a poor and lowly mind. (Horace, Satires, I. iv. 17.)

50 A vulgar term for a robust and handsome woman.

51 A tiny thing, a dainty thing, one of the Graces—all pure wit. (Lucretius, IV. 1158.)

52 In his *Suasoriarum Liber*, II. 17.

53 A kind of high shoe worn by ladies. (It. *Cioppini*.)

fortunate princes[54] of the world, of late could find no delight so satisfactory as the keeping of little singing birds, and hearing them, and whistling to them. What did the emperors of the whole world? If ever any men had the free and full enjoyment of all human greatness (nay, that would not suffice, for they would be gods too), they certainly possessed it; and yet, one of them,[55] who styled himself lord and god of the earth, could not tell how to pass his whole day pleasantly, without spending constant two or three hours in catching of flies, and killing them with a bodkin, as if his godship had been Beelzebub.[56] One of his predecessors, Nero (who never put any bounds, nor met with any stop to his appetite), could divert himself with no pastime more agreeable than to run about the streets all night in disguise, and abuse the women, and affront the men whom he met, and sometimes to beat them, and sometimes to be beaten by them; this was one of his imperial nocturnal pleasures. His chiefest in the day was to sing and play upon a fiddle, in the habit of a minstrel, upon the public stage. He was prouder of the garlands that were given to his divine voice (as they called it then) in those kinds of prizes, than all his forefathers were of their triumphs over nations. He did not at his death complain that so mighty an emperor and the last of all the Cæsarian race of deities should be brought to so shameful and miserable an end, but only cried out, "Alas, what pity 'tis that so excellent a musician should perish in this manner!" His uncle Claudius spent half his time at playing at dice; that was the main fruit of his sovereignty. I omit the madnesses of Caligula's delights, and the execrable sordidness of those of Tiberius. Would one think that Augustus himself, the highest and most fortunate of mankind, a person endowed too with many excellent parts of nature, should be so hard put to it sometimes for want of recreations, as to be found playing at nuts and bounding-stones with little Syrian and Moorish boys, whose company he took delight in, for their prating and their wantonness?

Was it for this that Rome's best blood be spilt,
With so much falsehood, so much guilt?
Was it for this that his ambition strove,
To equal Cæsar first, and after Jove?

Greatness is barren, sure, of solid joys;
Her merchandise (I fear) is all in toys;
She could not else, sure, so uncivil be,
To treat his universal Majesty,
    His new-created Deity,
    With nuts and bounding-stones and boys.

But we must excuse her for this meager entertainment. She has not really wherewithal to make such feasts as we imagine; her guests must be contented sometimes with but slender cates,[57] and with the same cold meats served over and over again, even till they become nauseous. When you have pared away all the vanity, what solid and natural contentment does there remain, which may not be had with five hundred pounds a year? Not so many servants or horses; but a few good ones, which will do all the business as well. Not so many choice dishes at every meal; but at several meals, all of them; which makes them both the more healthy and the more pleasant. Not so rich garments, nor so frequent changes, but as warm and as comely, and so frequent change too, as is every jot as good for the master, though not for the tailor or *valet de chambre*. Not such a stately palace, not gilt rooms, or the costliest sorts of tapestry, but a convenient brick house, with decent wainscot and pretty forest-work hangings. Lastly (for I omit all other particulars, and will end with that which I love most in both conditions), not whole woods cut in walks, nor vast parks, nor fountain, or cascade-gardens; but herb, and flower, and fruit gardens, which are more useful, and the water every whit as clear and wholesome as if it darted from the breasts of a marble nymph, or the urn of a river-god.

If, for all this, you like better the substance of that former estate of life, do but consider the inseparable accidents of both; servitude, disquiet, danger, and most commonly guilt, inherent in the one; in the other liberty, tranquillity, security, and innocence. And when you have thought upon this, you will confess that to be a truth which appeared to you before but a ridiculous paradox, that a low fortune is better guarded and attended than a high one. If, indeed, we look only upon the flourishing head of the tree, it appears a most beautiful object;

Sed quantum vertice ad auras
Etherias tantum radice ad Tartara tendit.[58]

As far as up towards Heav'n the branches grow,
So far the root sinks down to Hell below.

---

54 Louis XIII of France.   55 The Emperor Domitian.
56 Beelzebub, whose name signifies "lord of flies," was a sun-god of the Philistines.

57 Dainty foods.   58 Virgil's Georgics, II. 291.

Another horrible disgrace to greatness is, that it is for the most part in pitiful want and distress. What a wonderful thing is this! Unless it degenerate into avarice, and so cease to be greatness, it falls perpetually into such necessities as drive it into all the meanest and most sordid ways of borrowing, cozenage, and robbery; *mancipiis locuples eget æris Cappadocum rex.*[59] This is the case of almost all great men, as well as of the poor king of Cappadocia. They abound with slaves, but are indigent of money. The ancient Roman emperors, who had the riches of the whole world for their revenue, had wherewithal to live (one would have thought) pretty well at ease, and to have been exempt from the pressures of extreme poverty. But yet with most of them it was much otherwise, and they fell perpetually into such miserable penury, that they were forced to devour or squeeze most of their friends and servants, to cheat with infamous projects, to ransack and pillage all their provinces. This fashion of imperial grandeur is imitated by all inferior and subordinate sorts of it, as if it were a point of honor. They must be cheated of a third part of their estates, two other thirds they must expend in vanity, so that they remain debtors for all the necessary provisions of life, and have no way to satisfy those debts, but out of the succors and supplies of rapine. As riches increases (says Solomon), so do the mouths that devour it. The master mouth has no more than before. The owner, methinks, is like Ocnus in the fable,[60] who is perpetually winding a rope of hay, and an ass at the end perpetually eating it. Out of these inconveniences arises naturally one more, which is, that no greatness can be satisfied or contented with itself: still, if it could mount up a little higher, it would be happy; if it could gain but that point, it would obtain all its desires; but yet at last, when it had got up to the very top of the Pic of Teneriffe, it is in very great danger of breaking its neck downwards, but in no possibility of ascending upwards into the seat of tranquillity above the moon. The first ambitious men in the world, the old giants, are said to have made an heroical attempt of scaling heaven, in despite of the gods; and they cast Ossa upon Olympus and Pelion upon Ossa; two or three mountains more they thought would have done their business, but the thunder spoilt all the work, when they were come up to the third story.

And what a noble plot was crost!
And what a brave design was lost!

A famous person of their offspring, the late giant[61] of our nation, when, from the condition of a very inconsiderable captain, he had made himself lieutenant-general of an army of little Titans, which was his first mountain, and afterwards general, which was his second, and after that, absolute tyrant of three kingdoms, which was the third, and almost touched the heaven which he affected, is believed to have died with grief and discontent, because he could not attain to the honest name of a king, and the old formality of a crown, though he had before exceeded the power of a wicked usurpation. If he could have compassed that, he would perhaps have wanted something else that is necessary to felicity, and pined away for want of the title of an emperor or a god. The reason for this is, that greatness has no reality in nature, but a creature of the fancy, a notion that consists only in relation and comparison. It is indeed an idol; but St. Paul teaches us "that an idol is nothing in the world."[62] There is, in truth, no rising or meridian of the sun, but only in respect to several places; there is no right or left, no upper-hand in nature: everything is little, and everything is great, according as it is diversely compared. There may be perhaps some village in Scotland or Ireland where I might be a great man; and in that case I should be like Cæsar (you would wonder how Cæsar and I should be like one another in anything), and choose rather to be the first man of the village, than second at Rome. Our country is called Great Brittany, in regard only of a lesser of the same name; it would be but a ridiculous epithet for it when we consider it together with the kingdom of China. That too is but a pitiful rood of ground in comparison of the whole earth besides; and this whole globe of earth, which we account so immense a body, is but one point or atom in relation to those numberless worlds that are scattered up and down in the infinite space of the sky which we behold.

. . . .

THE DANGERS OF AN HONEST MAN IN MUCH COMPANY

IF TWENTY THOUSAND naked Americans were not able to resist the assaults of but twenty well-armed

---

59 Horace, *Epistles*, I. vi. 39.
60 Narrated in Pliny's *Historia Naturalis*, xxxv. 31.
61 Oliver Cromwell.   62 I Corinthians 8:4.

Spaniards, I see little possibility for one honest man to defend himself against twenty thousand knaves who are all furnished *cap-a-pie* with the defensive arms of worldly prudence, and the offensive too of craft and malice. He will find no less odds than this against him, if he have much to do in human affairs. The only advice therefore which I can give him, is to be sure not to venture his person any longer in the open campaign,[63] to retreat and entrench himself, to stop up all avenues, and draw up all bridges against so numerous an enemy. The truth of it is, that a man in much business must either make himself a knave, or else the world will make him a fool; and if the injury went no farther than the being laughed at, a wise man would content himself with the revenge of retaliation; but the case is much worse; for these civil cannibals too, as well as the wild ones, not only dance about such a taken stranger, but at last devour him. A sober man cannot get too soon out of drunken company, though they be never so kind and merry among themselves, 'tis not unpleasant only, but dangerous to him.

Do ye wonder that a virtuous man should love to be alone? It is hard for him to be otherwise; he is so when he is among ten thousand; neither is the solitude so uncomfortable to be alone without any other creature, as it is to be alone in the midst of wild beasts. Man is to man all kind of beasts: a fawning dog, a roaring lion, a thieving fox, a robbing wolf, a dissembling crocodile, a treacherous decoy, and a rapacious vulture. The civilest, methinks, of all nations, are those whom we account the most barbarous; there is some moderation and good nature in the Toupinambaltians,[64] who eat no men but their enemies, whilst we learned and polite Christian Europeans, like so many pikes and sharks, prey upon everything that we can swallow. It is the great boast of eloquence and philosophy, that they first congregated men dispersed, united them into societies, and built up the houses and the walls of cities. I wish they could unravel all they had woven, that we might have our woods and our innocence again, instead of our castles and our policies. They have assembled many thousands of scattered people into one body. 'Tis true, they have done so. They have brought them together into cities to cozen, and into armies to murder one another; they found them hunters and fishers of wild creatures, they have made them hunters and fishers of their brethren; they

boast to have reduced them to a state of peace, when the truth is, they have only taught them an art of war; they have framed, I must confess, wholesome laws for the restraint of vice, but they raised first that devil which now they conjure and cannot bind; though there were before no punishments for wickedness, yet there was less committed because there were no rewards for it. But the men who praise philosophy from this topic are much deceived; let oratory answer for itself; the tinkling perhaps of that may unite a swarm. It never was the work of philosophy to assemble multitudes, but to regulate only, and govern them when they were assembled; to make the best of an evil, and bring them, as much as possible, to unity again. Avarice and ambition only were the first builders of towns, and founders of empire. They said, "Go to, let us build us a city and a tower whose top may reach unto heaven, and let us make us a name, lest we be scattered abroad upon the face of the earth." What was the beginning of Rome, the metropolis of the world? What was it, but a concourse of thieves, and a sanctuary of criminals? It was justly named by the augury of no less than twelve vultures, and the founder cemented his walls with the blood of his brother. Not unlike to this was the beginning even of the first town[65] too in the world, and such is the original sin of most cities; their actual increase daily with their age and growth; the more people, the more wicked all of them; every one brings in his part to inflame the contagion, which becomes at last so universal and so strong that no precepts can be sufficient preservatives, nor anything secure our safety, but flight from among the infected. We ought in the choice of a situation to regard above all things the healthfulness of the place, and the healthfulness of it for the mind rather than for the body. But suppose (which is hardly to be supposed) we had antidote enough against this poison; nay, suppose farther, we were always and at all pieces[66] armed and provided both against the assaults of hostility and the mines of treachery, 'twill yet be an uncomfortable life to be ever in alarms; though we were compassed round with fire to defend ourselves from wild beasts, the lodging would be unpleasant, because we must always be obliged to watch that fire, and to fear no less the defects of our guard, than the diligences of our enemy. The sum of this is, that a virtuous man is in danger to be trod upon and destroyed in the crowd of his contraries; nay, which is worse, to be changed and

63 The level plains.
64 An ancient tribe of savages in northern Brazil.

65 Cain's city; see Genesis 4:17.   66 At all points.

corrupted by them; and that 'tis impossible to escape both these inconveniences without so much caution as will take away the whole quiet, that is, the happiness, of his life.

Ye see then, what he may lose; but, I pray, what can he get there? *Quid Romæ faciam? Mentiri nescio.*[67] What should a man of truth and honesty do at Rome? He can neither understand nor speak the language of the place; a naked man may swim in the sea, but 'tis not the way to catch fish there; they are likelier to devour him, than he them, if he bring no nets and use no deceits. I think therefore it was wise and friendly advice which Martial gave to Fabian, when he met him newly arrived at Rome.

Honest and poor, faithful in word and thought;
What has thee, Fabian, to the city brought?
Thou neither the buffoon, nor bawd canst play,
Nor with false whispers th' innocent betray:
Nor corrupt wives, nor from rich beldams get
A living by thy industry and sweat;
Nor with vain promises and projects cheat,
Nor bribe or flatter any of the great.
But you're a man of learning, prudent, just;
A man of courage, firm, and fit for trust.
Why, you may stay, and live unenvied here;
But (faith) go back, and keep you where you were.[68]

Nay, if nothing of all this were in the case, yet the very sight of uncleanness is loathsome to the cleanly; the sight of folly and impiety vexatious to the wise and pious.

Lucretius, by his favor, though a good poet, was but an ill-natured man, when he said, "It was delightful to see other men in a great storm."[69] And no less ill-natured should I think Democritus, who laughed at all the world, but that he retired himself so much out of it, that we may perceive he took no great pleasure in that kind of mirth. I have been drawn twice or thrice by company to go to Bedlam,[70] and have seen others very much delighted with the fantastical extravagancy of so many various madnesses, which upon me wrought so contrary an effect, that I always returned, not only melancholy, but even sick with the sight. My comparison there was perhaps too tender, for I meet a thousand madmen abroad, without any perturbation; though, to weigh the matter justly, the total loss of reason is less deplorable than

the total depravation of it. An exact judge of human blessings, of riches, honors, beauty, even of wit itself, should pity the abuse of them more than the want.

Briefly, though a wise man could pass never so securely through the great roads of human life, yet he will meet perpetually with so many objects and occasions of compassion, grief, shame, anger, hatred, indignation, and all passions but envy (for he will find nothing to deserve that), that he had better strike into some private path; nay, go so far, if he could, out of the common way, *ut nec facta audiat Pelopidarum;*[71] that he might not so much as hear of the actions of the sons of Adam. But whither shall we fly then? Into the deserts, like the ancient hermits.

Qua terra patet fera regnat Erinnys,
In facinus jurasse putes.[72]

One would think that all mankind had bound themselves by an oath to do all the wickedness they can; that they had all (as the Scripture speaks) sold themselves to sin; the difference only is that some are a little more crafty (and but a little, God knows) in making of the bargain. I thought when I went first to dwell in the country, that without doubt I should have met there with the simplicity of the old poetical Golden Age; I thought to have found no inhabitants there, but such as the shepherds of Sir Philip Sidney in Arcadia, or of Monsieur d'Urfé[73] upon the banks of Lignon; and began to consider with myself which way I might recommend no less to posterity the happiness and innocence of the men of Chertsey; but to confess the truth, I perceived quickly by infallible demonstrations that I was still in Old England, and not in Arcadia, or La Forest; that if I could not content myself with anything less than exact fidelity in human conversation, I had almost as good go back and seek it in the Court, or the Exchange, or Westminster Hall. I ask again then, whither shall we fly, or what shall we do? The world may so come in a man's way that he cannot choose but salute it; he must heed, though, not to go a whoring after it. If by any lawful vocation or just necessity men happen to be married to it, I can only give them St. Paul's advice. "Brethren, the time

---

67 What shall I do at Rome? I don't know how to lie. (From Juvenal, Satires, III. 41.)

68 Martial, Epigrams, IV. 5.   69 Lucretius, II. 1.

70 Bethlehem, the famous hospital for the insane in London.

71 From Cicero's Letter to Atticus, XV. xi. 3.

72 Ovid's Metamorphoses, I. 241. (As far as the earth extends, the fierce Fury reigns. You would think they had sworn allegiance to crime.)

73 Honoré d'Urfé (1567–1625), author of the famous romance, *L'Astrée*, in the vein of Sir Philip Sidney's Arcadia. The scene is laid on the banks of the Lignon in La Forest.

is short, it remains that they that have wives be as though they had none. But I would that all men were even as I myself." [74]

In all cases they must be sure that they do *mundum ducere*, and not *mundo nubere*. They must retain the superiority and headship over it; happy are they who can get out of the sight of this deceitful beauty, that they may not be led so much as into temptation, who have not only quitted the metropolis, but can abstain from ever seeing the next market town of their country.

OF MYSELF

IT IS a hard and nice subject for a man to write of himself; it grates his own heart to say anything of disparagement, and the reader's ears to hear anything of praise from him. There is no danger from me of offending him in this kind; neither my mind, nor body, nor my fortune, allow me any materials for that vanity. It is sufficient, for my own contentment, that they have preserved me from being scandalous, or remarkable on the defective side. But besides that, I shall here speak of myself, only in relation to the subject of these precedent discourses, and shall be likelier thereby to fall into the contempt than rise up to the estimation of most people.

As far as my memory can return back into my past life, before I knew or was capable of guessing what the world, or glories, or business of it were, the natural affections of my soul gave me a secret bent of aversion from them, as some plants are said to turn away from others, by an antipathy imperceptible to themselves, and inscrutable to man's understanding. Even when I was a very young boy at school, instead of running about on holidays and playing with my fellows, I was wont to steal from them, and walk into the fields, either alone with a book, or with some one companion, if I could find any of the same temper. I was then, too, so much an enemy to all constraint, that my masters could never prevail on me by any persuasions or encouragements to learn without book the common rules of grammar, in which they dispensed with me alone, because they found I made a shift to do the usual exercise out of my own reading and observation. That I was then of the same mind as I am now (which I confess, I wonder at myself) may

appear by the latter end of an ode, [75] which I made when I was but thirteen years old, and which was then printed with many other verses. The beginning of it is boyish, but of this part which I here set down (if a very little were corrected) I should hardly now be much ashamed.

9

This only grant me, that my means may lie
Too low for envy, for contempt too high.
    Some honor I would have
Not from great deeds, but good alone.
The unknown are better than ill known.
    Rumor can ope the grave.
Acquaintance I would have, but when 't depends
Not on the number, but the choice of friends.

10

Books should, not business, entertain the light,
And sleep, as undisturb'd as death, the night.
    My house a cottage, more
Than palace; and should fitting be
For all my use, no luxury.
    My garden painted o'er
With nature's hand, not art's; and pleasures yield,
Horace might envy in his Sabine field.

11

Thus would I double my life's fading space,
For he that runs it well, twice runs his race.
    And in this true delight,
These unbought sports, this happy state,
I would not fear nor wish my fate,
    But boldly say each night,
Tomorrow let my sun his beams display,
Or in clouds hide them; I have liv'd, today.

You may see by it, I was even then acquainted with the poets (for the conclusion is taken out of Horace[76]), and perhaps it was the immature and immoderate love of them which stamped first, or rather engraved, these characters in me; they were like letters cut into the bark of a young tree, which with the tree still grow proportionably. But, how this love came to be produced in me so early is a hard question. I believe I can tell the particular little chance that filled my head first with such chimes of verse as have never since left ringing there: for I remember when I began to

74 I Corinthians 7:29.

75 The poem from which Cowley quotes is entitled A Vote (*i.e.*, a wish, or prayer), and was included in his Sylva, 1636.
76 Horace's Odes, III. 29. 41–45.

read, and to take some pleasure in it, there was wont to lie in my mother's parlor (I know not by what accident, for she herself never in her life read any book but of devotion), but there was wont to lie Spenser's works; this I happened to fall upon, and was infinitely delighted with the stories of the knights, and giants, and monsters, and brave houses, which I found everywhere there, though my understanding had little to do with all this; and by degrees with the tinkling of the rhyme and dance of the numbers, so that I think I had read him all over before I was twelve years old, and was thus made a poet as irremediably as a child is made a eunuch. With these affections of mind, and my heart wholly set upon letters, I went to the university, but was soon torn from thence by that violent public storm[77] which could suffer nothing to stand where it did, but rooted up every plant, even from the princely cedars to me, the hyssop. Yet I had as good fortune as could have befallen me in such a tempest; for I was cast by it into the family of one of the best persons,[78] and into the court of one of the best princesses[79] of the world. Now though I was here engaged in ways most contrary to the original design of my life, that is, into much company and no small business, and into a daily sight of greatness, both militant and triumphant (for that was the state then of the English and French courts), yet all this was so far from altering my opinion, that it only added the confirmation of reason to that which was before but natural inclination. I saw plainly all the paint of that kind of life, the nearer I came to it; and that beauty which I did not fall in love with, when, for aught I knew, it was real, was not like to bewitch or entice me when I saw that it was adulterate. I met with several great persons, whom I liked very well, but could not perceive that any part of their greatness was to be liked or desired, no more than I would be glad or content to be in a storm, though I saw many ships which rid safely and bravely in it; a storm would not agree with my stomach, if it did with my courage. Though I was in a crowd of as good company as could be found anywhere, though I was in business of great and honorable trust, though I ate at the best table, and enjoyed the best conveniences for present subsistence that ought to be desired by a man of my condition in banishment and public distresses; yet I

could not abstain from renewing my old school-boy's wish in a copy of verses to the same effect.

> Well then; I now do plainly see
> This busy world and I shall ne'er agree, etc.[80]

And I never then proposed to myself any other advantage from his Majesty's happy restoration, but the getting into some moderately convenient retreat in the country; which I thought in that case I might easily have compassed, as well as some others, with no greater probabilities or pretenses, have arrived to extraordinary fortunes. But I had before written a shrewd prophecy against myself, and I think Apollo inspired me in the truth, though not in the elegance of it.

> Thou, neither great at Court nor in the war,
> Nor at th' Exchange shalt be, nor at the wrangling bar:
> Content thyself with the small barren praise
> Which neglected verse does raise, etc.[81]

However, by the failing of the forces which I had expected, I did not quit the design which I had resolved on: I cast myself into it a *corps perdu*, without making capitulations, or taking counsel of fortune. But God laughs at a man, who says to his soul, Take thy ease.[82] I met presently not only with many little encumbrances and impediments, but with so much sickness (a new misfortune to me) as would have spoiled the happiness of an emperor as well as mine. Yet I do neither repent nor alter my course. *Non ego perfidum dixi sacramentum.*[83] Nothing shall separate me from a mistress, which I have loved so long, and have now at last married; though she neither has brought me a rich portion, nor lived yet so quietly with me as I hoped from her.

> *Nec vos, dulcissima mundi*
> *Nomina, vos Musæ, libertas, otia, libri,*
> *Hortique sylvæque anima remanente relinquam.*[84]

> Nor by me e'er shall you,
> You of all names the sweetest and the best,
> You Muses, books, and liberty and rest,
> You gardens, fields, and woods forsaken be,
> As long as life itself forsakes not me.

---

77 The Civil War, which began in 1642.
78 Lord Jermyn, later Earl of St. Albans.
79 Queen Henrietta Maria, wife of Charles I.
80 From the poem entitled The Wish, in Cowley's The Mistress.
81 From Cowley's poem, Destiny, in his Pindaric Odes.
82 St. Luke 12:16–21.
83 I have not sworn a faithless oath. (Horace, Odes, II. 17.)
84 Presumably Cowley's own lines.

John Evelyn

[1620–1706]

BORN of a wealthy commercial family, Evelyn inherited a fortune which enabled him to spend his long life in pursuing the various interests suggested to him by his curious and alert mind. He studied at Balliol College, Oxford, but left the university without taking a degree shortly before the outbreak of the Civil War. In 1641 he embarked on his first trip to the Continent and, on his return, served briefly in the royalist army. In 1642 he returned to the Continent, and spent the next ten years in observant travel in Holland, Belgium, France, and Italy. In the course of his travels he met and courted the daughter of the English ambassador in Paris; the marriage produced nine children, but only one of them was destined to outlive the father. Evelyn returned to England in 1652, and he spent the rest of his life there, most of it on his estate near London.

During the waning years of the Puritan Interregnum, Evelyn lived quietly, engaging in private Anglican worship and enjoying the friendship of such men as Jeremy Taylor, Sir Thomas Browne, Sir William Temple, and Sir Christopher Wren. After the restoration Evelyn, who was on friendly terms with Charles II, served on a wide variety of governmental commissions and attained a degree of prominence as a public servant. Passionately interested (if such a term may be applied to a man of Evelyn's cool temperament) in architecture, city planning, the plastic arts, and gardening, Evelyn exhibited a similar interest in scientific experimentation. He was one of the organizers of the Royal Society, of which he was a charter member and of which he twice refused the presidency. His diary abounds with references to oddities and rare phenomena which came to his attention and which he found worthy of note.

Evelyn's successful and honored life drew to a quiet close, disturbed only by his injudicious lending of his house to the visiting Peter the Great of Russia in 1698. The Czar's boisterous antics managed to destroy the diarist's prize hedge with remarkable thoroughness.

Evelyn's writings reveal only partially the wide interests of his life: *A Character of England* (1659) is a satiric portrait of life and customs in England at the time of the Protectorate; *Fumifugium* (1661) is a protest against the nuisance of smoke in London; *Tyrannus, or the Mode* (1661) argues against the English imitation of French fashions in dress; and *Sylva* (1664) deals with the question of reforestation. None of these works holds any particular interest for the student of literature; the *Diary* alone assures Evelyn's place in literary history.

Not known to the public until 1818 and not printed in full until 1955, the set of writings which gives Evelyn a place beside Pepys as the chief diarist of the seventeenth century is far from being a personal document. It is not so much an account of the writer's personal emotions, reactions, experiences, and aspirations as a record of his observations and professional activities. In style, too, Evelyn's *Diary* stands in polar opposition to Pepys's: singularly lacking in warmth or distinctiveness, it is reserved and formal throughout. Apart from the intrinsic interest afforded by such vivid, though impersonal, passages as the famous description of the Great Fire of London, however, the *Diary* is of great value as a detailed account of seventeenth-century life as it was observed and experienced by a cultivated and keen-sighted gentleman.

J. Evelyn. *Diary*, ed. E. S. de Beer, 6 vols. (Oxford, 1955). The definitive edition, a monumental work.

A. Ponsonby. *John Evelyn* (London, 1933). A good biography.

M. Denny. "The Early Program of the Royal Society and John Evelyn," *Modern Language Quarterly*, I (1940).

F R O M

THE DIARY OF JOHN EVELYN

[*Based on the Bray edition, 1850*]

August 28, 1641. *Leyden*. Amongst all the rarities of this place, I was much pleased with a sight of their anatomy school, theater, and repository adjoining, which is well furnished with natural curiosities; skeletons from the whale and elephant to the fly and spider, which last is a very delicate piece of art; to see how the bones—if I may so call them of so tender an insect —could be separated from the mucilaginous parts of that minute animal. Amongst a great variety of other things, I was shown the knife newly taken out of a drunken Dutchman's guts by an incision in his side after it had slipped from his fingers into his stomach. The pictures of the chirurgeon and his patient, both living, were there.

I was brought acquainted with a Burgundian Jew, who had married an apostate Kentish woman. I asked him divers questions; he told me, amongst other things, that the world should never end, that our souls transmigrated, and that even those of the most holy persons did penance in the bodies of brutes after death, —and so he interpreted the banishment and savage life of Nebuchadnezzar; that all the Jews should rise again and be led to Jerusalem; that the Romans only were the occasion of our Saviour's death, whom he affirmed, as the Turks do, to be a great prophet, but not the Messiah. He showed me several books of their devotion, which he had translated into English for the instruction of his wife; he told me that when the

Messiah came, all the ships, barks, and vessels of Holland should, by the power of certain strange whirlwinds, be loosed from their anchors and transported in a moment to all the desolate ports and havens throughout the world, wherever the dispersion was, to convey their brethren and tribes to the holy city; with other such like stuff. He was a merry drunken fellow, but would by no means handle any money— for something I purchased of him—it being Saturday; but desired me to leave it in the window, meaning to receive it on Sunday morning.

October 5, 1641. *Antwerp*. There was nothing about this city which more ravished me than those delicious shades and walks of stately trees which render the fortified works of the town one of the sweetest places in Europe; nor did I ever observe a more quiet, clean, elegantly built, and civil place than this magnificent and famous City of Antwerp. In the evening, I was invited to Signor Duerte's, a Portuguese by nation, an exceeding rich merchant, whose palace I found to be furnished like a prince's. His three daughters entertained us with rare music, vocal and instrumental, which was finished with a handsome collation. I took leave of the ladies and of sweet Antwerp, as late as it was, embarking for Brussels on the Scheldt in a vessel, which delivered us to a second boat in another river drawn or towed by horses. In this passage we frequently changed our barge by reason of the bridges thwarting our course. Here I observed numerous families inhabiting their vessels and floating dwellings so built and divided by cabins as few houses on land enjoyed better accommodation, stored with all sorts of utensils, neat chambers, a pretty parlor, and kept so sweet that nothing could be more refreshing. The rivers on which they are drawn are very clear and still waters and pass through a most pleasant country on both banks.

FEBRUARY 8, 1643/4. *Paris.* I finished this day with a walk in the great garden of the Tuileries, rarely contrived for privacy, shade, or company, by groves, plantations, and that labyrinth of cypresses, not omitting the noble hedges of pomegranates, fountains, fishponds, and an aviary, but, above all, the artificial echo, redoubling the words so distinctly; and, as it is never without some fair nymph singing to its grateful returns, standing at one of the focuses, which is under a tree of a little cabinet of hedges, the voice seems to descend from the clouds, at another, as if it were underground. This being at the bottom of the garden, we were let into another, which being kept with all imaginable accurateness as to the orangery, precious shrubs, and rare fruits, seemed a paradise. From a terrace in this place we saw so many coaches, as one would hardly think could be maintained in the whole city, going, late as it was in the year, towards the course, which is a place adjoining of near an English mile long planted with the four rows of trees making a large circle in the middle. This course is walled about, near breast high, with squared freestone and has a stately arch at the entrance, with sculpture and statues about it, built by Mary de Medicis. Here it is that the gallants and ladies of the court take the air and divert themselves, as with us in Hyde Park, the circle being capable of containing a hundred coaches to turn commodiously and the larger of the plantations for five or six coaches abreast.

OCTOBER 7, 1644. *Marseilles.* The spectacle was to me new and strange to see so many hundreds of miserably naked persons, their heads being shaven close and having only high red bonnets, a pair of coarse canvas drawers, their whole backs and legs naked, doubly chained about their middle and legs, in couples, and made fast to their seats, and all commanded in a trice by an imperious and cruel seaman. One Turk amongst the rest he much favored, who waited on him in his cabin, but with no other dress than the rest, and a chain locked about his leg but not coupled. This galley was richly carved and gilded, and most of the rest were very beautiful. After bestowing some-

thing on the slaves, the captain sent a band of them to give us music at dinner where we lodged. I was amazed to contemplate how these miserable caitiffs lie in their galley crowded together; yet there was hardly one but had some occupation, by which, as leisure and calms permitted, they got some little money, insomuch as some of them have, after many years of cruel servitude, been able to purchase their liberty. The rising-forward and falling-back at their oar is a miserable spectacle, and the noise of their chains, with the roaring of the beaten waters, has something of strange and fearful in it to one unaccustomed to it. They are ruled and chastised by strokes on their backs and soles of their feet on the least disorder and without the least humanity, yet are they cheerful and full of knavery.

JUNE, 1645. *Venice.* Hence I passed through the Mercera, one of the most delicious streets in the world for the sweetness of it, and is all the way on both sides tapestried as it were with cloth of gold, rich damasks and other silks which the shops expose and hang before their houses from the first floor, and with that variety that for near half the year spent chiefly in this city I hardly remember to have seen the same piece twice exposed; to this add the perfumes, apothecaries' shops, and the innumerable cages of nightingales which they keep, that entertain you with their melody from shop to shop, so that shutting your eyes you could imagine yourself in the country, when indeed you are in the middle of the sea. It is almost as silent as the middle of a field, there being neither rattling of coaches nor trampling of horses.

JANUARY 22, 1648/9. I went through a course of chemistry at Sayes Court. Now was the Thames frozen over and horrid tempests of wind.

The villainy of the rebels proceeding now so far as to try, condemn, and murder our excellent King on the 30th of this month struck me with such horror that I kept the day of his martyrdom a fast and would not be present at the execrable wickedness, receiving the sad account of it from my brother George and Mr. Owen, who came to visit me this afternoon and recounted all the circumstances.

DECEMBER 4, 1653. Going this day to our church, I was surprised to see a tradesman, a mechanic, step up; I was resolved yet to stay and see what he would make of it. His text was from II Sam. 23 : 20: "And Benaiah went down also and slew a lion in the midst of a pit in the time of snow"; the purport was, that no danger was to be thought difficult, when God called for shedding of blood, inferring that now the saints were called to destroy temporal governments, with such feculent stuff; so dangerous a crisis were things grown to!

JULY 12, 1654. *Oxford.* We went to St. John's, saw the library and the two skeletons, which are finely cleansed and put together; observable is here also the store of mathematical instruments, chiefly given by the late Archbishop Laud, who built here a handsome quadrangle.

JULY 13, 1654. *Oxford.* We all dined at that most obliging and universally-curious Dr. Wilkins', at Wadham College. He was the first who showed me the transparent apiaries which he had built like castles and palaces and so ordered them one upon another as to take the honey without destroying the bees. These were adorned with a variety of dials, little statues, vanes, etc.; and he was so abundantly civil, finding me pleased with them, to present me with one of the hives which he had empty, and which I afterwards had in my garden at Sayes Court, where it continued many years and which his Majesty came on purpose to see and contemplate with much satisfaction. He had also contrived a hollow statue which gave a voice and uttered words by a long concealed pipe that went to his mouth while one speaks through it at a good distance. He had, above in his lodgings and gallery, variety of shadows, dials, perspectives, and many other artificial, mathematical, and magical curiosities, a way-wiser,[1] a thermometer, a monstrous magnet, conic, and other sections, a balance on a demi-circle, most of them his own; and that prodigious young scholar, Mr. Christopher Wren, who presented me with a piece of white marble which he had stained a lively red, very deep, as beautiful as if it had been natural.

MARCH 18, 1655. Went to London on purpose to hear that excellent preacher, Dr. Jeremy Taylor, on Matt. 14:17, showing what were the conditions of obtaining eternal life, also concerning abatements for unavoidable infirmities, how cast on the accounts of the cross. On the 31st, I made a visit to Dr. Jeremy Taylor to confer with him about some spiritual matters, using him thenceforward as my ghostly father. I beseech God Almighty to make me ever mindful of and thankful for his heavenly assistances!

APRIL 9, 1655. I went to see the great ship newly built by the Usurper, Oliver, carrying ninety-six brass guns, and 1000 tons burden. In the prow was Oliver on horseback, trampling six nations underfoot, a Scot, Irishman, Dutchman, Frenchman, Spaniard,

and English, as was easily made out by their several habits. A Fame held a laurel over his insulting[2] head; the word, *God with us.*

JULY 10, 1656. *Ipswich.* I had the curiosity to visit some Quakers here in prison; a new fanatic sect of dangerous principles, who show no respect to any man, magistrate, or other, and seem a melancholy, proud sort of people, and exceedingly ignorant. One of these was said to have fasted twenty days; but another, endeavoring to do the like, perished on the 10th, when he would have eaten, but could not.

JULY 11, 1656. Came home by Greenwich ferry, where I saw Sir J. Winter's project of charring sea-coal to burn out the sulphur and render it sweet. He did it by burning the coals in such earthen pots as the glass-men melt their metal, so firing them without consuming them, using a bar of iron in each crucible, or pot, which bar has a hook at one end, that so the coals being melted in a furnace with other crude sea-coals under them, may be drawn out of the pots sticking to the iron, whence they are beaten off in great half-exhausted cinders, which being rekindled make a clear pleasant chamber-fire deprived of their sulphur and arsenic malignity. What success it may have, time will discover.[3]

OCTOBER 19, 1657. I went to see divers gardens about London. Returning, I saw at Dr. Joyliffe's two Virginian rattlesnakes alive, exceeding a yard in length, small heads, slender tails, but in the middle nearly the size of my leg; when vexed, swiftly vibrating and shaking their tails, as loud as a child's rattle. This by the collision of certain gristly skins curiously jointed yet loose and transparent as parchment, by which they give warning, a providential precaution for other creatures to avoid them. The doctor tried their biting on rats and mice, which they immediately killed. But their vigor must needs be much exhausted here in another climate, and kept only in a barrel of bran.

AUGUST 14, 1658. We went to Durdans to a challenged match at bowls for £10, which we won.

AUGUST 18. To Sir Ambrose Browne, at Betchworth Castle, in that tempestuous wind which threw down my greatest trees at Sayes Court and did so much mischief all over England. It continued the whole night, in the southwest, and destroyed all our winter fruit.

SEPTEMBER 3. Died that arch-rebel, Oliver Cromwell, called Protector.

1 Direction-indicator, compass.   2 Exulting.   3 This is our coke.

OCTOBER 22. Saw the superb funeral of the Protector. He was carried from Somerset House in a velvet bed of state drawn by six horses housed with the same; the pall held by his new lords; Oliver lying in effigy in royal robes and crowned with a crown, scepter, and globe, like a king. The pendants and guidons were carried by the officers of the army; the imperial banners, achievements, etc., by the heralds in their coats; a rich caparisoned horse embroidered all over with gold; a knight of honor armed *cap-à-pie;* and, after all, his guards, soldiers, and innumerable mourners. In this equipage they proceeded to Westminster. But it was the joyfullest funeral I ever saw; for there were none that cried but dogs, which the soldiers hooted away with a barbarous noise, drinking and taking tobacco in the streets as they went.

MAY 29, 1660. This day his Majesty Charles the Second came to London, after a sad and long exile and calamitous suffering both of the King and the church, being seventeen years. This was also his birthday, and with a triumph of above 20,000 horse and foot, brandishing their swords and shouting with inexpressible joy; the ways strewed with flowers, the bells ringing, the streets hung with tapestry, fountains running with wine; the Mayor, aldermen, and all the companies in their liveries, chains of gold, and banners; lords and nobles clad in cloth of silver, gold, and velvet; the windows and balconies all set with ladies; trumpets, music, and myriads of people flocking, even so far as from Rochester, so as they were seven hours in passing the city, even from two in the afternoon till nine at night.

I stood in the Strand and beheld it and blessed God. And all this was done without one drop of blood shed and by that very army which rebelled against him; but it was the Lord's doing, for such a restoration was never mentioned in any history, ancient or modern, since the return of the Jews from the Babylonish captivity; nor so joyful a day and so bright ever seen in this nation, this happening when to expect or effect it was past all human policy.

JANUARY 30, 1660/1. This day—O stupendous and inscrutable judgments of God!—were the carcasses of those arch-rebels, Cromwell, Bradshaw, the judge who condemned his Majesty, and Ireton, son-in-law to the Usurper, dragged out of their superb tombs in Westminster among the kings to Tyburn and hanged on the gallows there from nine in the morning till six at night and then buried under that fatal and ignominious monument in a deep pit; thousands of people

who had seen them in all their pride being spectators. Look back at October 22, 1658, and be astonished! and fear God and honor the King; but meddle not with them who are given to change!

APRIL 23, 1661. This magnificent train on horseback, as rich as embroidery, velvet, cloth of gold and silver, and jewels could make them and their prancing horses, proceeded through the streets strewed with flowers, houses hung with rich tapestries, windows and balconies full of ladies; the London militia lining the ways and the several companies, with their banners and loud music ranked in their orders; the fountains running wine, bells ringing, with speeches made at the several triumphal arches; at that of the Temple Bar, near which I stood, the Lord Mayor was received by the Bailiff of Westminster, who, in a scarlet robe, made a speech. Thence, with joyful acclamations, his Majesty passed to Whitehall. Bonfires at night.

The next day, being St. George's, he went by water to Westminster Abbey. When his Majesty was entered, the dean and prebendaries brought all the regalia and delivered them to several noblemen to bear before the King, who met them at the west door of the church, singing an anthem to the choir. Then came the peers in their robes, and coronets in their hands, till his Majesty was placed on a throne elevated before the altar. Afterwards, the Bishop of London, the Archbishop of Canterbury being sick, went to every side of the throne to present the King to the people, asking if they would have him for their King and do him homage; at this, they shouted four times "God Save King Charles the Second!" Then an anthem was sung. His Majesty, attended by three bishops, went up to the altar, and he offered a pall and a pound of gold. Afterwards, he sat down in another chair during the sermon, which was preached by Dr. Morley, Bishop of Worcester.

After the sermon, the King took his oath before the altar to maintain the religion, Magna Charta, and laws of the land. The hymn *Veni, S. Sp.* followed and then the litany by two bishops. Then the Archbishop of Canterbury, present but much indisposed and weak, said, "Lift up your hearts"; at which the King rose up and put off his robes and upper garments and was in a waistcoat so opened in divers places that the Archbishop might commodiously anoint him, first in the palms of the hands, when an anthem was sung and a prayer read; then his breast and betwixt the shoulders, bending of both arms; and, lastly, on the crown of the head, with apposite hymns and prayers at each anointing; this done, the dean closed and buttoned up the waistcoat. After which was a coif put on and the cobbium, sindon or dalmatic, and over this a super-tunic of cloth of gold, with buskins and sandals of the same, spurs, and the sword; a prayer being first said over it by the Archbishop on the altar before it was girt on by the Lord Chamberlain. Then the armill, mantle, etc. Then the Archbishop placed the crown-imperial on the altar, prayed over it, and set it on his Majesty's head, at which all the peers put on their coronets. Anthems and rare music with lutes, viols, trumpets, organs, and voices were then heard, and the Archbishop put a ring on his Majesty's finger. The King next offered his sword on the altar, which being redeemed, was drawn and borne before him. Then the Archbishop delivered him the scepter, with the dove in one hand and in the other the scepter with the globe. The King kneeling, the Archbishop pronounced the blessing. His Majesty then ascending again his royal throne, whilst *Te Deum* was singing, all the peers did their homage by every one touching his crown, the Archbishop and the rest of the bishops first kissing the King, who received the holy sacrament and so dis-robed, yet with the crown-imperial on his head, and accompanied with all the nobility in the former order, he went on foot upon blue cloth, which was spread and reached from the west door of the Abbey to West-minster stairs, when he took water in a triumphal barge to Whitehall, where was extraordinary feasting.

OCTOBER 1, 1661. I broke fast this morning with the King at return in his smaller vessel, he being pleased to take me and only four more, who were noblemen, with him; but dined in his yacht, where we all ate to-gether with his Majesty. In the passage he was pleased to discourse to me about my book inveighing against the nuisance of the smoke of London[4] and proposing expedients how, by removing those particulars I mentioned, it might be reformed, commanding me to prepare a bill against the next session of Parliament, being, as he said, resolved to have something done in it.

NOVEMBER 26, 1661. I saw Hamlet, Prince of Denmark, played; but now the old plays began to disgust this refined age, since his Majesty's being so long abroad.

MAY 30, 1662. The Queen arrived with a train of Portuguese ladies in their monstrous farthingales, or *guard-infantes*, their complexions olivader[5] and suffi-ciently unagreeable. Her Majesty in the same habit, her fore-top long and turned aside very strangely. She was yet of the handsomest countenance of all the rest and, though low of stature, prettily shaped, languishing and excellent eyes, her teeth wronging her mouth by sticking a little too far out; for the rest lovely enough.

JULY 31, 1662. I sat with the commissioners about reforming buildings and streets of London, and we ordered the paving of the way from St. James's north, which was a quagmire, and also of the Haymarket about Piccadilly and agreed upon instructions to be printed and published for the better keeping the streets clean.

AUGUST 29, 1662. The council and fellows of the Royal Society went in a body to Whitehall to acknow-ledge his Majesty's royal grace in granting our charter and vouchsafing to be himself our founder; when the president gave an eloquent speech, to which his Ma-jesty gave a gracious reply and we all kissed his hand. Next day, we went in like manner with our address to my Lord Chancellor, who had much prompted our patent. He received us with extraordinary favor. In the evening, I went to the Queen-Mother's court, and had much discourse with her.

DECEMBER 21, 1663. One of his Majesty's chap-lains preached; after which, instead of the ancient, grave, and solemn wind music accompanying the organ, was introduced a concert of twenty-four violins between every pause after the French fantastical light way, better suiting a tavern or playhouse than a church. This was the first time of change, and now we no more heard the cornet which gave life to the organ; that instrument quite left off in which the English were so skillful.

OCTOBER 24, 1664. *Oxford.* I went to visit Mr. Boyle, now here, whom I found with Dr. Wallis and Dr. Christopher Wren in the tower of the Schools with an inverted tube, or telescope, observing the discus of the sun for the passing of Mercury that day before it; but the latitude was so great that nothing appeared; so we went to see the rarities in the Library, where the keepers showed me my name among the benefactors. They have a cabinet of some metals and pictures of the muscular parts of man's body. Thence to the new Theater, now building at an exceeding and royal expense by the Lord Archbishop of Canterbury,[6] to keep the acts in for the future, till now being in St. Mary's Church. The foundation had been newly laid and the whole designed by that incomparable genius, my worthy friend, Dr. Christopher Wren, who

---

4 The *Fumifugium.*   5 Olive.

6 Sheldon; this is the Sheldonian Theater.

showed me the model, not disdaining my advice in some particulars. Thence to see the picture on the wall over the altar at All Souls,[7] being the largest piece of fresco painting—or rather in imitation of it, for it is in oil of turpentine—in England, not ill designed by the hand of one Fuller; yet I fear it will not hold long. It seems too full of nakeds for a chapel.

SEPTEMBER 7, 1665. Came home, there perishing near 10,000 poor creatures weekly;[8] however, I went all along the city and suburbs from Kent Street to St. James's, a dismal passage, and dangerous to see so many coffins exposed in the streets, now thin of people; the shops shut up, and all in mournful silence, not knowing whose turn might be next. I went to the Duke of Albemarle for a pest-ship, to wait on our infected men, who were not a few.

SEPTEMBER 2, 1666. This fatal night, about ten, began the deplorable fire near Fish Street in London.

SEPTEMBER 3. I had public prayers at home. The fire continuing, after dinner I took coach with my wife and son and went to the Bankside in Southwark, where we beheld that dismal spectacle, the whole city in dreadful flames near the water-side; all the houses from the Bridge, all Thomas Street, and upwards towards Cheapside, down to the Three Cranes, were now consumed; and so returned exceeding astonished what would become of the rest.

The fire having continued all this night—if I may call that night which was light as day for ten miles round about after a dreadful manner—when conspiring with a fierce eastern wind in a very dry season, I went on foot to the same place; and saw the whole south part of the city burning from Cheapside to the Thames and all along Cornhill—for it likewise kindled back against the wind as well as forward—Tower Street, Fenchurch Street, Gracious Street, and so along to Baynard's Castle, and was now taking hold of St. Paul's Church, to which the scaffolds contributed exceedingly. The conflagration was so universal and the people so astonished that from the beginning, I know not by what despondency or fate, they hardly stirred to quench it; so that there was nothing heard or seen but crying out and lamentation, running about like distracted creatures without at all attempting to save even their goods, such a strange consternation there was upon them; so as it burned both in breadth and length the churches, public halls, Exchange,

hospitals, monuments, and ornaments, leaping after a prodigious manner from house to house and street to street at great distances one from the other. For the heat, with a long set of fair and warm weather, had even ignited the air and prepared the materials to conceive the fire, which devoured after an incredible manner, houses, furniture and everything. Here we saw the Thames covered with goods floating, all the barges and boats laden with what some had time and courage to save, as on the other side the carts, etc., carrying out to the fields, which for many miles were strewed with movables of all sorts, and tents erecting to shelter both people and what goods they could get away. Oh, the miserable and calamitous spectacle! such as haply the world had not seen since the foundation of it! nor can be outdone till the universal conflagration thereof. All the sky was of a fiery aspect, like the top of a burning oven, and the light seen above forty miles round about for many nights. God grant mine eyes may never behold the like, who now saw above 10,000 houses all in one flame! The noise and cracking and thunder of the impetuous flames, the shrieking of women and children, the hurry of people, the fall of towers, houses, and churches was like a hideous storm; and the air all about so hot and inflamed that at the last one was not able to approach it, so that they were forced to stand still and let the flames burn on, which they did, for near two miles in length and one in breadth. The clouds also of smoke were dismal and reached, upon computation, near fifty miles in length. Thus I left it this afternoon burning, a resemblance of Sodom, or the last day. It forcibly called to my mind that passage—*non enim hic habemus stabilem civitatem*, the ruins resembling the picture of Troy. London was, but is no more! Thus I returned.

SEPTEMBER 4. The burning still rages, and it is now gotten as far as the Inner Temple. All Fleet Street, the Old Bailey, Ludgate Hill, Warwick Lane, Newgate, Paul's Chain, Watling Street now flaming and most of it reduced to ashes; the stones of Paul's flew like grenados, the melting lead running down the streets in a stream, and the very pavements glowing with fiery redness, so as no horse nor man was able to tread on them, and the demolition had stopped all the passages, so that no help could be applied. The eastern wind still more impetuously driving the flames forward. Nothing but the almighty power of God was able to stop them; for vain was the help of man.

SEPTEMBER 5. It crossed towards Whitehall; but oh! the confusion there was then at that court! It

---

7 This painting was later covered up, forgotten and only fairly recently restored.

8 This is the apex of the Great Plague.

pleased his Majesty to command me, among the rest, to look after the quenching of Fetter Lane end, to preserve, if possible, that part of Holborn, whilst the rest of the gentlemen took their several posts, some at one part, and some at another; for now they began to bestir themselves, and not till now, who hitherto had stood as men intoxicated with their hands across, and began to consider that nothing was likely to put a stop but the blowing up of so many houses as might make a wider gap than any had yet been made by the ordinary method of pulling them down with engines. This some stout seamen proposed early enough to have saved near the whole city, but this some tenacious and avaricious men, aldermen, etc., would not permit because their houses must have been of the first. It was, therefore, now commanded to be practised; and my concern being particularly for the Hospital of St. Bartholomew near Smithfield, where I had many wounded and sick men, made me the more diligent to promote it; nor was my care for the Savoy less. It now pleased God by abating the wind and by the industry of the people, when almost all was lost infusing a new spirit into them, that the fury of it began sensibly to abate about noon, so as it came no farther than the Temple westward nor than the entrance of Smithfield north. But continued all this day and night so impetuous toward Cripplegate and the Tower as made us all despair. It also broke out again in the Temple; but the courage of the multitude persisting and many houses being blown up, such gaps and desolations were soon made as, with the former three days' consumption, the back fire did not so vehemently urge upon the rest as formerly. There was yet no standing near the burning and glowing ruins by near a furlong's space.

SEPTEMBER 7. I was infinitely concerned to find that goodly church, St Paul's, now a sad ruin and that beautiful portico, for structure comparable to any in Europe, as not long before repaired by the late King, now rent in pieces, flakes of vast stones split asunder, and nothing remaining entire but the inscription in the architrave showing by whom it was built, which had not one letter defaced! It was astonishing to see what immense stones the heat had in a manner calcined, so that all the ornaments, columns, friezes, capitals, and projectures of massy Portland stone flew off even to the very roof, where a sheet of lead covering a great space, no less than six acres by measure, was totally melted. The ruins of the vaulted roof falling broke into St. Faith's, which being filled with the

magazine of books belonging to the stationers and carried thither for safety they were all consumed, burning for a week following. It is also observable that the lead over the altar at the east end was untouched, and among the divers monuments the body of one bishop remained entire. Thus lay in ashes that most venerable church, one of the most ancient pieces of early piety in the Christian world, besides near one hundred more. The lead, iron-work, bells, plate, etc., melted, the exquisitely wrought Mercers' Chapel, the sumptuous Exchange, the august fabric of Christ Church, all the rest of the companies' halls, splendid buildings, arches, entries, all in dust; the fountains dried up and ruined, whilst the very waters remained boiling; the voragos of subterranean cellars, wells, and dungeons, formerly warehouses, still burning in stench and dark clouds of smoke; so that in five or six miles traversing about I did not see one load of timber unconsumed, nor many stones but were calcined white as snow.

The people, who now walked about the ruins appeared like men in some dismal desert, or rather in some great city laid waste by a cruel enemy; to which was added the stench that came from some poor creatures' bodies, beds, and other combustible goods. Sir Thomas Gresham's statue, though fallen from its niche in the Royal Exchange, remained entire, when all those of the kings since the Conquest were broken to pieces. Also the standard in Cornhill and Queen Elizabeth's effigies, with some arms on Ludgate, continued with but little detriment, whilst the vast iron chains of the city streets, hinges, bars, and gates of prisons were many of them melted and reduced to cinders by the vehement heat. Nor was I yet able to pass through any of the narrow streets, but kept the widest; the ground and air, smoke and fiery vapor, continued so intense that my hair was almost singed and my feet insufferably surbated. The bye-lanes and narrow streets were quite filled up with rubbish; nor could one have possibly known where he was but by the ruins of some church or hall that had some remarkable tower or pinnacle remaining.

I then went towards Islington and Highgate, where one might have seen 200,000 people of all ranks and degrees dispersed and lying along by their heaps of what they could save from the fire, deploring their loss and, though ready to perish for hunger and destitution, yet not asking one penny for relief, which appeared to me a stranger sight than any I had yet beheld. His Majesty and council indeed took all imaginable care for their relief by proclamation for the country to come in and refresh them with provisions.

JUNE 28, 1667. I went to Chatham, and thence to view not only what mischief the Dutch had done but how triumphantly their whole fleet lay within the very mouth of the Thames all from the North Foreland, Margate, even to the buoy of the Nore—a dreadful spectacle as ever Englishman saw and a dishonor never to be wiped off! Those who advised his Majesty to prepare no fleet this spring deserved—I know not what—but—

APRIL 2, 1668. To the Royal Society, where I subscribed 50,000 bricks towards building a college. Amongst other libertine libels, there was one now printed and thrown about, a bold petition of the poor whores to Lady Castlemaine.[9]

JULY 10, 1669. *Oxford.* The next day began the more solemn lectures in all the faculties, which were performed in the several schools, where all the inceptor-doctors did their exercises, the professors having first ended their reading. The assembly now returned to the Theater, where the *terræ filius*, the university buffoon, entertained the auditory with a tedious, abusive, sarcastical rhapsody most unbecoming the gravity of the university and that so grossly that unless it be suppressed, it will be of ill consequence, as I afterwards plainly expressed my sense of it both to the Vice-Chancellor and several heads of houses, who were perfectly ashamed of it and resolved to take care of it in the future. The old facetious way of rallying upon the questions was left off, falling wholly upon persons, so that it was rather licentious lying and railing than genuine and noble wit. In my life I was never witness of so shameful entertainment.[10]

MAY 26, 1671. The first thing we did[11] was to settle the form of a circular letter to the governors of all his Majesty's plantations and territories in the West Indies and islands thereof to give them notice to whom they should apply themselves on all occasions and to render us an account of their present state and government; but what we most insisted on was to know the condition of New England, which appearing to be very independent as to their regard to Old England or his Majesty, rich and strong as they now were, there were great debates in what style to write them; for the condition of that colony was such that they were able to contest with all other plantations about them, and there was a fear of their breaking from all dependence on this nation; his Majesty, therefore, commended this affair more expressly. We therefore thought fit, in the first place, to acquaint ourselves as well as we could of the state of that place by some whom we heard of that were newly come from thence and to be informed of their present posture and condition; some of our council were for sending them a menacing letter, which those who better understood the peevish and touchy humor of that colony were utterly against.

OCTOBER 17, 1671. *Norwich.* I went to see Sir Thomas Browne, with whom I had sometime corresponded by letter, though I had never seen him before; his whole house and garden being a paradise and cabinet of rarities, and that of the best collection, especially medals, books, plants, and natural things. Amongst other curiosities, Sir Thomas had a collection of the eggs of all the fowl and birds he could procure, that country, especially the promontory of Norfolk, being frequented, as he said, by several kinds which seldom or never go farther into the land, as cranes, storks, eagles, and variety of water-fowl. He led me to see all the remarkable places of this ancient city, being one of the largest, and certainly after London, one of the noblest of England for its venerable cathedral, number of stately churches, cleanness of the streets, and buildings of flint so exquisitely headed and squared as I was much astonished at; but he told me, they had lost the art of squaring the flints, in which they so much excelled, and of which the churches, best houses, and walls are built.

MARCH 24, 1672. I saw the surgeon cut off the leg of a wounded sailor, the stout and gallant man enduring it with incredible patience without being bound to his chair as usual on such painful occasions. I had hardly courage enough to be present. Not being cut off high enough, the gangrene prevailed, and the second operation cost the poor creature his life.

Lord! what miseries are mortal men subject to! and what confusion and mischief do the avarice, anger, and ambition of princes cause in the world!

DECEMBER 20, 1673. I had some discourse with certain strangers, not unlearned, who had been born not far from old Nineveh; they assured me of the ruins being still extant, and vast and wonderful were the

---

9 It was the belief of some that this was written by Evelyn himself.

10 Though the *terræ filius* is now extinct, degree-days at Oxford still see unlicensed baiting of the lions by the undergraduates.

11 This was a meeting of the Commission of Trade and Plantations.

buildings, vaults, pillars, and magnificent fragments; but they could say little of the Tower of Babel that satisfied me. But the description of the amenity and fragrancy of the country for health and cheerfulness delighted me, so sensibly they spoke of the excellent air and climate in respect of our cloudy and splenetic country.

AUGUST 30, 1680. He[12] told us that Nineveh was a vast city now all buried in her ruins, the inhabitants building on the subterranean city; that there were frequently found huge vases of fine earth, columns and other antiquities; that the straw which the Egyptians required of the Israelites was not to burn or cover the rows of bricks as we use but being chopped small to mingle with the clay, which being dried in the sun—for they bake not in the furnaces—would else cleave asunder; that in Persia are yet a race of *ignicolæ* who worship the sun and the fire as gods; that the women of Georgia and Mingrelia were universally and without any compare the most beautiful creatures for shape, features, and figure in the world, and therefore the Grand Seignior and bashaws had had from thence most of their wives and concubines; that there had within these hundred years been Amazons amongst them, that is to say, a sort or race of valiant women given to war.

OCTOBER 4, 1683. Following his Majesty this morning through the gallery, I went with the few who attended him into the Duchess of Portsmouth's dressing-room within her bed-chamber, where she was in her morning loose garment, her maids combing her, newly out of her bed, his Majesty and the gallants standing about her; but that which engaged my curiosity was the rich and splendid furniture of this woman's apartment, now twice or thrice pulled down and rebuilt to satisfy her prodigal and expensive pleasure whilst her Majesty's does not exceed some gentlemen's ladies' in furniture and accommodation. Here I saw the new fabric of French tapestry for design, tenderness of work, and incomparable imitation of the best paintings beyond anything I had ever beheld. Some pieces had Versailles, St. Germains, and other palaces of the French King, with huntings, figures, and landscapes, exotic fowls, and all to the life rarely done. Then for Japan cabinets, screens, pendule clocks, great vases of wrought plate, tables, stands, chimney-furniture, sconces, branches, braziers,

etc., all of massy silver and out of number, besides some of her Majesty's best paintings.

Surfeiting of this, I dined at Sir Stephen Fox's, and went contented home to my poor but quiet villa. What contentment can there be in the riches and splendor of this world purchased with vice and dishonor!

FEBRUARY 6, 1684/5. I can never forget the inexpressible luxury and profaneness, gaming, and all dissoluteness, and as it were, total forgetfulness of God, it being Sunday evening, which this day sennight I was witness of, the King sitting and toying with his concubines, Portsmouth, Cleveland, and Mazarine, etc., a French boy singing love songs, in that glorious gallery, whilst about twenty of the great courtiers and other dissolute persons were at basset round a large table, a bank of at least £2,000 in gold before them; upon which two gentlemen who were with me made reflections with astonishment. Six days after was all in the dust![13]

It was enjoined that those who put on mourning should wear it as for a father in the most solemn manner.

MARCH 5. To my grief I saw the new pulpit set up in the popish oratory at Whitehall for the Lent preaching, mass being publicly said and the Romanists swarming at court with greater confidence than had ever been seen in England since the Reformation so that everybody grew jealous as to what this would tend.

JULY 15, 1685. Of his faults he[14] professed great sorrow, and so died without any apparent fear. He would not make use of a cap or other circumstance, but, lying down, bid the fellow to do his Office better than to the late Lord Russell, and gave him gold; but the wretch made five chops before he had his head off; which so incensed the people that, had he not been guarded and got away, they would have torn him to pieces.

The Duke made no speech on the scaffold, which was on Tower Hill, but gave a paper containing not above five lines for the King, in which he disclaims all title to the crown, acknowledges that the late King, his father, had indeed told him he was but his base son, and so desired his Majesty to be kind to his wife and children.

Thus ended this *quondam* Duke, darling of his father and the ladies, being extremely handsome and adroit,

12 Sir John Chardin, born a Frenchman, knighted by Charles II, a man who had traveled widely in the East; Evelyn is reporting an address of his at the Royal Society.

13 Evelyn here refers to the King's death.
14 Monmouth.

an excellent soldier and dancer, a favorite of the people, of an easy nature, debauched by lust, seduced by crafty knaves who would have set him up only to make a property and taken the opportunity of the King being of another religion to gather a party of discontented men. He failed, and perished.

JANUARY 19, 1685/6. Dryden, the famous play-writer, and his two sons and Mrs. Nelly,[15] miss to the late——, were said to go to mass; such proselytes were no great loss to the church.

MARCH 7, 1689/90. I dined with Mr. Pepys, late Secretary to the Admiralty, where was that excellent shipwright and seaman—for so he had been and also a commissioner of the navy—Sir Anthony Deane. Amongst other discourse, and deploring the condition of our navy as now governed by inexperienced men since this Revolution, he mentioned what exceeding advantage we of this nation had by being the first who built frigates, the first of which ever built was that vessel which was afterwards called The Constant Warwick and was the work of Pett of Chatham for a trial of making a vessel that would sail swiftly; it was built with low decks, the guns lying near the water, and was so light and swift of sailing that in a short time, he told us, she had, ere the Dutch war was ended, taken as much money from privateers as would have laden her; and that more such being built did in a year or two scour the Channel from those of Dunkirk and others which had exceedingly infested it. He added that it would be the best and only infallible expedient to be masters of the sea and able to destroy the greatest navy of any enemy if, instead of building huge great ships and second and third rates, they would leave off building such high decks, which were for nothing but to gratify gentlemen-commanders, who must have all their effeminate accommodations, and for pomp; that it would be the ruin of our fleets if such persons were continued in command, they neither having experience nor being

15 Nell Gwynne.

capable of learning because they would not submit to the fatigue and inconvenience which those who were bred seamen would undergo in those so otherwise useful swift frigates.

FEBRUARY 4, 1692/3. Unheard-of stories of the universal increase of witches in New England; men, women, and children devoting themselves to the Devil so as to threaten the subversion of the government.—At the same time there was a conspiracy amongst the negroes in Barbadoes to murder all their masters discovered by overhearing a discourse of two of the slaves and so preventing the execution of the design.—Hitherto an exceeding mild winter.—France in the utmost misery and poverty for want of corn and subsistence, whilst the ambitious King is intent to pursue his conquests on the rest of his neighbors both by sea and land.

JANUARY 11, 1693/4. Supped at Mr. Edward Sheldon's, where was Mr. Dryden, the poet, who now intended to write no more plays, being intent on his translation of Virgil. He read to us his prologue and epilogue to his valedictory play now shortly to be acted.

APRIL 23, 1696. I went to Eton and dined with Dr. Godolphin, the provost. The schoolmaster assured me there had not been for twenty years a more pregnant youth in that place than my grandson.

JANUARY 30, 1697/8. The Czar of Muscovy being come to England and having a mind to see the building of ships, hired my house at Sayes Court and made it his court and palace new furnished for him by the King.

MAY 30, 1698. I dined at Mr. Pepys's, where I heard the rare voice of Mr. Pule, who was lately come from Italy, reputed the most excellent singer we had ever had. He sang several compositions of the late Dr. Purcell.

OCTOBER 31, 1705. I am this day arrived to the 85th year of my age. Lord, teach me so to number my days to come that I may apply them to wisdom!

John Aubrey

[1627?–1697]

L IKE Fuller before him and Anthony à Wood after him, Aubrey occupies an important but eccentric place in the development of English biography. Sickly in childhood, he was first educated at home by a private tutor; later he entered Trinity College, Oxford, but the combination of a smallpox epidemic and the civil disturbances of the 1640's caused him to leave, never to return. He inherited a comfortable fortune on the death of his father in 1652, but the habits of a disorderly and pleasure-loving life soon dissipated his estate and for much of his life he was obliged to depend on patrons. He never married, and in a "brief life" of himself he blames his mother for breaking up his projected marriage with an heiress. In every evident sense, Aubrey was a failure, but he enjoyed the friendship of such men as Sir Christopher Wren and William Penn, he had a gift for pleasure, and he left behind him in his *Brief Lives* a monument which has assured him a measure of immortality.

The *Brief Lives* were undertaken at the suggestion of Anthony à Wood, whom Aubrey assisted in research for the latter's *Athenæ Oxonienses*. Still in manuscript at Aubrey's death, the work is memorable, imperfect, untidy, and fitfully brilliant, a just index of its author's personality. As a biographer, Aubrey is often unreliable, frequently fragmentary, and usually haphazard; the *Lives* abound in "quæres" which the author never got around to answering and data which he never got around to verifying. But they are consistently absorbing as human accounts—rich in anecdote, gossip, and detail, and abounding in crisp, brilliant phrases which are capable, across the centuries, of bringing to life the worthies whom they document.

In the selections that follow, two lives—that of George Herbert and that of Cecil Calvert—appear in their entirety, and one life—that of Sir John Popham—practically so. In the excerpts from the others, the order and arrangement have been changed in a few instances where the change seemed to bring greater clarity. Aubrey, judging from his own literary habits, would be the last to care.

J. AUBREY. *Brief Lives*, ed. A. Clark, 2 vols. (London, 1898). The definitive edition.
————. *Brief Lives*, ed. O. L. Dick (London, 1949). A modern edition in one volume.
A. POWELL. *John Aubrey and His Friends* (New York, 1948). Biography.

BRIEF LIVES

[Based on the text of Andrew Clark, 1898]

SIR JOHN POPHAM
(1531–1607)

HE WAS of the Society of . . . and for several [years] addicted himself but little to the study of the laws but profligate company and was wont to take a purse with them. His wife considered her and his condition and at last prevailed with him to lead another life and to stick to the study of law; which, upon her importunity he did, being then about thirty years old. Spake to his wife to provide a very good entertainment for his comrades to take his leave of them; and after that day fell extremely hard to his study and profited exceedingly. He was a strong, stout man and could endure to sit at it day and night (the picture of a common lawyer:—He must have "an iron head, a brazen face, and a leaden breech."); became eminent in his calling, had good practice; called to be a serjeant, a judge: *vide Origines Juridicales.*

Sir . . . (John, I think) Dayrell of Littlecote in *com.* Wilts, having got his lady's waiting woman with child, when her travail came, sent a servant with a horse for a midwife whom he was to bring hoodwinked. She was brought and laid the woman, but as soon as the child was born, she saw the knight take the child and murther it, and burnt it in the fire in the chamber. She having done her business was extraordinarily rewarded for her pains and sent blindfold away. This horrid action did much run in her mind, and she had a desire to discover it but knew not where 'twas. She considered with herself the time that she was riding and how many miles might be rode at that rate in that time and that it must be some great person's house, for the room was 12 foot high; and she could know the chamber if she saw it. She went to a justice of peace, and search was made. The very chamber found. The knight was brought to his trial; and to be short, this judge had this noble house, park, and manor, and I think more for a bribe to save his life. Sir John Popham gave sentence according to law; but being a great person and a favorite, he procured a *noli prosequi.*

I have seen his picture; he was a huge, heavy, ugly man. He left a vast estate to his son, Sir Francis, I think ten thousand pounds, *per annum;* he lived like a hog, but his son John was a great waster, and died in his father's time.

He was the greatest house-keeper in England; would have at Littlecote 4 or 5 or more lords at a time. His wife (Harvey) was worth to him, I think, £60,000, and she was as vain as he, and she said that she had brought such an estate, and she scorned but she would live as high as he did; and in her husband's absence would have all the women of the country thither and feast them and make them drunk as she would be herself. They both died by excess; and by luxury and cozenage by their servants, when he died, there was, I think, a hundred thousand pound debt.

Old Sir Francis, he lived like a hog, at Hownstret in Somerset, all this while with a moderate pittance.

Mr. John would say that his wife's estate was ill got and that was the reason they prospered no better; she would say that the old judge got the estate unjustly, and thus they would twit one another, and that with matter of truth.

I remember this epitaph was made on Mr. John Popham:—

> Here lies he who not long since
> Kept a table like a prince
> Till Death came and took away,
> Then ask't the old man, What's to pay?

Memorandum:—at the hall in Wellington in the County of Somerset, the ancient seat of the Pophams, and which was this Sir John's, Lord Chief Justice (but *quære* if he did not buy it?), did hang iron shackles, of which the tradition of the country is that long ago one of the Pophams, lord of this place, was taken and kept a slave by the Turks for a good while and that by his lady's piety and continual prayers he was brought to this place by an invisible power, with these shackles on his legs, which were hung up as a memorial and continued till the house, being a garrison, was burnt. All the country people steadfastly believe the truth hereof.

Lord Chief Justice Popham first brought in [*i.e.* revived] brick building in London (*scil.* after Lincoln's Inn and St. James's); and first set afoot the Plantations,—e.g. Virginia (from Fabian Philips)—which he stocked or planted out of all the gaols of England.

SIR WALTER RALEGH
(1552–1618)

SIR WALTER RALEGH was of Oriel College. Mr. Child's father of Worcestershire was his chamber-fellow and lent him a gown, which he could never get, nor satisfaction for it.—From Mr. Child.

He was the first that brought tobacco into England and into fashion.—In our part of North Wilts, e.g. Malmesbury hundred, it came first into fashion by Sir Walter Long.

I have heard my grandfather Lyte say that one pipe was handed from man to man round about the table. They had first silver pipes; the ordinary sort made use of a walnut shell and a straw.

It was sold then for its weight in silver. I have heard some of our old yeomen neighbors say that when they went to Malmesbury or Chippenham market, they culled out their biggest shillings to lay in the scales against the tobacco.

Sir W. R., standing in a stand at Sir Robert Poyntz's part at Acton, took a pipe of tobacco, which made the ladies quit till he had done.

Within these 35 years 'twas scandalous for a divine to take tobacco.

Now the customs of it are the greatest his Majesty hath—Rider's Almanac (1682, *scilicet*)—"Since tobacco brought into England by Sir Walter Ralegh, 99 years, the custom whereof is now the greatest of all others and amounts to yearly . . . Mr. Michael Weeks of the Royal Society assures me out of the custom-house books that the custom of tobacco over all England is £400,000 *per annum*.

He [Sir Walter] was a tall, handsome and bold man; but his name was that he was damnable proud. . . . His beard turned up naturally.—I have heard my grandmother say that when she was young, they were wont to talk of this rebus, viz.,

The enemy to the stomach and the word of disgrace
Is the name of the gentleman with a bold face.[1]

Old Sir Thomas Malett, one of the justices of the

1 Raw-lye (lie).

King's Bench *tempore Caroli I et II*, knew Sir Walter; and I have heard him say that, notwithstanding his so great mastership in style and his conversation with the learnedest and politest persons, yet he spake broad Devonshire to his dying day. His voice was small as likewise were my schoolfellows', his grand-nephews.

Sir Walter Ralegh was a great chemist; and amongst some MSS. receipts I have seen some secrets from him. He studied most in his sea voyages, where he carried always a trunk of books along with him, and had nothing to divert him.

A person so much immersed in action all along and in fabrication of his own fortunes, till his confinement in the Tower, could have but little time to study but what he could spare in the morning. He was no slug; without doubt had a wonderful waking spirit and great judgment to guide it.

An attorney's father (that did my business in Herefordshire before I sold it[2]) married Dr. Burhill's widow. She said that he [Burhill] was a great favorite of Sir Walter Ralegh's and, I think, had been his chaplain; but all the greatest part of the drudgery of his book[3] for criticisms, chronology, and reading of Greek and Hebrew authors was performed by him for Sir Walter Ralegh, whose picture my friend has as part of the Doctor's goods.

I have heard old Major Cosh say that Sir W. Ralegh did not care to go on the Thames in a wherry boat; he would rather go round about over London Bridge.

My old friend James Harrington, Esq., was well acquainted with Sir Benjamin Ruddyer, who was an acquaintance of Sir Walter Ralegh's. He told Mr. J. H. that Sir Walter Ralegh, being invited to dinner to some great person where his son was to go with him, he said to his son, "Thou art expected today at dinner to go along with me, but thou art such a quarrelsome, affronting . . . that I am ashamed to have such a bear in my company." Mr. Walter humbled himself to his father and promised he would behave himself mightily mannerly. So away they went (and Sir Benjamin, I think, with them). He sat next to his father and was very demure at least half dinner time. Then said he, "I, this morning, not having the fear of God before my eyes but by the instigations of the Devil, went. . . ."[4] Sir Walter, being strangely surprised and put out of countenance at so great a table, gives his son a damned blow over the face. His son, as rude as he was, would

2 Aubrey's estate.   3 The History of the World.
4 Lines suppressed.

not strike his father, but strikes over the face the gentleman that sat next to him and said, "Box about! 'twill come to my father anon." 'Tis now a common-used proverb.

He loved . . .[4] one of the maids of honor (*quære* J. Ball, who? 'Twas his first lady). . . . She proved with child, and I doubt not but this hero took care of them both as also that the product was more than an ordinary mortal.

He was prisoner in the Tower . . . (*quære*) years;[5] *quære* where his lodgings were. He there, besides his compiling his History of the World, studied chemistry. The Earl of Northumberland was a prisoner at the same time, who was the patron to Mr. . . . Harriot and Mr. Warner, two of the best mathematicians then in the world, as also Mr. Hues, [author of] *De Globis*. Serjeant Hoskins, the poet, was a prisoner there too. I heard my cousin Whitney say that he saw him [Sir Walter] in the Tower. He had a velvet cap laced and a rich gown and trunk hose.

He took a pipe of tobacco a little before he went to the scaffold, which some formal persons were scandalized at, but I think 'twas well and properly done, to settle his spirits.

> Even such is time, which takes in trust
> Our youth, our joys, and all we have
> And pays us but with age and dust.
> Within the dark and silent grave,
> When we have wandered all our ways,
> Shuts up the story of our days.
> But from which grave and earth and dust
> The Lord will raise me up I trust.

These lines Sir Walter Raleigh wrote in his Bible the night before he was beheaded and desired his relations with these words, viz. "Beg my dead body which living is denied you; and bury it either in Sherburne or Exeter Church."

FRANCIS BACON
(1561–1626)

CHANCELLOR BACON:—The learned and great Cardinal Richelieu was a great admirer of the Lord Bacon.

In his Lordship's prosperity Sir Fulke Greville, Lord Brooke, was his great friend and acquaintance; but when he was in disgrace and want, he was so unworthy as to forbid his butler to let him have any more small

5 Thirteen years.

beer, which he had often sent for, his stomach being nice and the small beer of Gray's Inn not liking his palate. This has done his memory more dishonor than Sir Philip Sydney's friendship engraven on his monument hath done him honor.

Richard, Earl of Dorset, was a great admirer and friend of the Lord Chancellor Bacon and was wont to have Sir Thomas Billingsley along with him to remember and put down in writing my Lord's sayings at table.

At every meal according to the season of the year, he had his table strewed with sweet herbs and flowers, which he said did refresh his spirits and memory. . . . None of his servants durst appear before him without Spanish leather boots; for he would smell the neatsleather, which offended him.

His Lordship being at York House garden looking on fishers as they were throwing their net, asked them what they would take for their draught; they answered *so much*; his Lordship would offer them no more but *so much*. They drew up their net, and it were only 2 or 3 little fishes. His Lordship then told them it had been better for them to have taken his offer. They replied, they hoped to have had a better draught. "But," said his Lordship, "hope is a good breakfast but an ill supper."

When his Lordship was in disfavor, his neighbors hearing how much he was indebted, came to him with a motion to buy Oakwood of him. His Lordship told them, "He would not sell his feathers." . . . The Bishop of London did cut down a noble cloud of trees at Fulham. The Lord Chancellor told him that he was a good expounder of dark places.

Mr. Hobbes[6] told me that the cause of his Lordship's death was trying an experiment: viz., as he was taking the air in a coach with Dr. Witherborne, a Scotchman, physician to the King, towards Highgate, snow lay on the ground, and it came into my Lord's thoughts, why flesh might not be preserved in snow as in salt. They were resolved they would try the experiment presently. They alighted out of the coach and went into a poor woman's house at the bottom of Highgate Hill and bought a hen and made the woman exenterate it, and then stuffed the body with snow, and my Lord did help to do it himself. The snow so chilled him that he immediately fell so extremely ill that he could not return to his lodgings (I suppose then at Gray's Inn) but

6 Aubrey's friend and subject of his most ambitious life, author of Leviathan. Thomas Hobbes served as secretary to Bacon.

went to the Earl of Arundel's house at Highgate, where they put him into a good bed warmed with a pan, but it was a damp bed that had not been lain in about a year before, which gave him such a cold that in 2 or 3 days, as I remember he [Hobbes] told me, he died of suffocation.

RALPH KETTEL
(1563–1643)

RALPH KETTEL, D.D., *præses Coll. Trin. Oxon.*, was born at [King's Langley] in Hertfordshire.

The Doctor's fashion was to go up and down the college and peep in at the keyholes to see whether the boys did follow their books or no.

He observed that the houses that had the smallest beer had most drunkards, for it forced them to go into the town to comfort their stomachs; wherefore Dr. Kettel always had in his college excellent beer, not better to be had in Oxon; so that we[7] could not go to any other place but for the worse, and we had the fewest drunkards of any house in Oxford.

He was constantly at lectures and exercises in the hall to observe them, and brought along with him his hour-glass; and one time, being offended at the boys, he threatened them that if they would not do their exercises better he "would bring an hour-glass two hours long."

He was irreconcilable to long hair; called them hairy scalps, and as for periwigs, which were then very rarely worn, he believed them to be the scalps of men cut off after they were hanged and so tanned and dressed for use. When he observed the scholars' hair longer than ordinary, especially if they were scholars of the house, he would bring a pair of scissors in his muff, which he commonly wore, and woe be to them that sat on the outside of the table. I remember he cut Mr. Radford's hair with the knife that chips the bread on the buttery-hatch, and then he sang—this is in the old play—Henry VIII[8]—of Gammer Gurton's Needle—

"And was not Grim the collier finely trimmed?
Tonedi, tonedi!"

He dragged with one foot a little, by which he gave warning, like the rattlesnake, of his coming. Will. Egerton, Major-General Egerton's younger brother, a good wit and mimic, would go so like him that some-

time he would make the whole chapel rise up imagining he had been entering in.

As they were reading of inscribing and circumscribing figures, said he, "I will show you how to inscribe a triangle in a quadrangle. Bring a pig into the quadrangle, and I will set the college dog at him, and he will take the pig by the ear; then come I and take the dog by the tail and the hog by the tail, and so there you have a triangle in a quadrangle; *quod erat faciendum.*"

He preached every Sunday at his parsonage at Garsington, about 5 miles off. He rode on his bay gelding with his boy Ralph before him, with a leg of mutton commonly and some college bread. He did not care for the country revels because they tended to debauchery. Said he at Garsington revel, "Here is hey for Garsington! and hey for Cuddlesdon! and hey Hockley! but here's nobody cries, hey for God Almighty!"

Upon Trinity Sunday, our festival day, he would commonly preach at the college, whither a number of the scholars of other houses would come to laugh at him. In his prayer—where he was of course to remember Sir Thomas Pope, our founder, and the Lady Elizabeth his wife, deceased[9]—he would many times make a willful mistake and say, "Sir Thomas Pope, our confounder,"[10] but then presently recall himself.

He was a person of great charity. In his college where he observed diligent boys that he guessed had but a slender exhibition[11] from their friends he would many times put money in at their windows, that his right hand did not know what his left did.

He sang a shrill high treble; but there was one (J. Hoskins) who had a higher and would play the wag with the Dr. to make him strain his voice up to his.

'Tis probable this venerable Dr. might have lived some years longer and finished his century, had not those civil wars come on; which much grieved him that was wont to be absolute in the college to be affronted and disrespected by rude soldiers. I remember, being at the rhetoric lecture in the hall, a foot-soldier came in and broke his hour-glass. The Dr. indeed was just stepped out, but Jack Dowch pointed at it. Our grove was the Daphne for the ladies and their gallants to walk in, and many times my Lady Isabella Thynne (lay at Balliol College) would make her entry with a theorbo or lute played before her. I have heard her play on it in the grove myself, which she did rarely; for which Mr. Edmund Waller hath in his poems forever made her famous. One may say of her

---

7 Aubrey was at Trinity.
8 Henry VIII's time, he means—which is not very accurate.

9 This prayer is still said at Trinity.
10 Cofounder.   11 Financial assistance.

as Tacitus said of Agrippina, *Cuncta alia illi adfuere præter animum honestum*. She was most beautiful, most humble, charitable, etc., but she could not subdue one thing. I remember one time this lady, and fine Mrs. Fenshawe—she was wont, and my Lady Thynne, to come to our chapel mornings, half-dressed, like angels —(her great and intimate friend, who lay at our college)—would have a frolic to make a visit to the President. The old Dr. quickly perceived that they came to abuse him; he addresses his discourse to Mrs. Fenshawe, saying, "Madam, your husband and father I bred up here, and I knew your grandfather; I know you to be a gentlewoman, I will not say you are a whore; but get you gone for a very woman!" The dissoluteness of the times, as I have said, grieving the good old Doctor, his days were shortened, and died *Anno Domini* 1643 and was buried at Garsington; *quære* his epitaph.

WILLIAM HARVEY
(1578–1657)

I FIRST saw him at Oxford, 1642, after Edgehill fight but was then too young to be acquainted with so great a doctor. I remember he came several times to Trin. Coll. to George Bathurst, B.D., who had a hen to hatch eggs in his chamber, which they daily opened to discern the progress and way of generation.

He was always very contemplative and the first that I hear of that was curious in anatomy in England. He made dissections of frogs, toads, and a number of other animals, and had curious observations on them, which papers, together with his goods, in his lodgings at Whitehall were plundered at the beginning of the Rebellion, he being for the King and with him at Oxon; but he often said that of all the losses he sustained no grief was so crucifying to him as the loss of these papers, which for love or money he could not retrieve or obtain. When Charles I by reason of the tumults left London, he attended him and was at Edgehill with him; and during the fight the Prince and the Duke of York were committed to his care. He told me that he withdrew with them under a hedge and took out of his pocket a book and read; but he had not read very long before a bullet of a great gun grazed on the ground near him, which made him remove his station.

He did delight to be in the dark, and told me he could then best contemplate. He had a house hereto-fore at Combe, in Surrey, a good air and prospect, where he had caves made in the earth in which in summer time he delighted to meditate.

He was wont to say that man was but a great mischievous baboon. He would say that we Europeans knew not how to order or govern our women and that the Turks were the only people used them wisely.

He had been physician to the Lord Chancellor Bacon, whom he esteemed much for his wit and style but would not allow him to be a great philosopher. "He writes philosophy like a Lord Chancellor," said he to me, speaking in derision; "I have cured him."

I remember he kept a pretty young wench to wait on him, which I guess made use of for warmth sake as King David did and took care of her in his will as also of his man-servant.

For 20 years before he died he took no manner of care about his worldly concerns, but his brother Eliab, who was a very wise and prudent manager, ordered all not only faithfully but better than he could have done himself.

He was much and often troubled with the gout, and his way of cure was thus: he would then sit with his legs bare, if it were frost, on the leads of Cockaine House, put them into a pail of water, till he was almost dead with cold, and betake himself to his stove; and so 'twas gone.

He was hot-headed, and his thoughts working would many times keep him from sleeping; he told me that then his way was to rise out of his bed and walk about his chamber in his shirt till he was pretty cool, *i.e.*, till he began to have a horror [12] and then return to bed and sleep very comfortably.

I have heard him say that after his book of the Circulation of the Blood came out that he fell mightily in his practice and that 'twas believed by the vulgar that he was crack-brained; and all the physicians were against his opinion and envied him; many wrote against him, as Dr. Primige, Paracisanus, etc. (*Vide* Sir George Ent's book.) With much ado at last in about 20 or 30 years' time it was received in all the universities in the world; and, as Mr. Hobbes says in his book *De Corpore*, "He is the only man, perhaps, that ever lived to see his own doctrine established in his lifetime."

All his profession would allow him to be an excellent anatomist, but I never heard of any that admired his therapeutic way. I knew several practisers in London that would not have given 3*d.* for one of his bills; [13]

12 A chill.   13 Prescriptions.

and that a man could hardly tell by one of his bills what he did aim at.

Dr. Harvey told me, and anyone if he examines himself will find it to be true, that a man could not fancy—truthfully—that he is imperfect in any part that he has, *verbi gratia*, teeth, eye, tongue, *spina dorsi*, etc. Nature tends to perfection, and in matters of generation we ought to consult more with our sense and instinct than our reason and prudence, fashion of the country and interest. We see what contemptible products are of the prudent politics,[14] weak, fools, and rickety children, scandals to nature and their country. The heralds are fools—*tota errant via*. A blessing goes with a marriage for love upon a strong impulse.

I was at his funeral and helped to carry him into the vault.

THOMAS HOBBES
(1588–1670)

THOMAS HOBBES, *Malmesburiensis, Philosophus*, was born at his father's house in Westport, being that extreme house that points into or faces the horse-fair; the farthest house on the left hand as you go to Tedbury, leaving the church on your right.

The day of his birth was April the fifth, *Anno Domini* 1588, on a Friday morning, which that year was Good Friday. His mother fell in labor with him upon the fright of the invasion of the Spaniards.

T. H. so well profited in his learning that at fourteen years of age he went away a good school-scholar to Magdalen Hall in Oxford. It is not to be forgotten that before he went to the university he had turned Euripides' *Medea* out of Greek into Latin iambics, which he presented to his master. . . . Twenty odd years ago I searched all Mr. Latimer's papers but could not find them; the good housewives had sacrificed them.

I have heard his brother Edmund and Mr. Wayte, his schoolfellow, say that when he was a boy he was playsome enough but withal he had even then a contemplative melancholiness; he would get him into a corner and learn his lesson by heart presently. His hair was black, and his schoolfellows were wont to call him "Crow."

He was (*vide* his life[15]) 40 years old before he looked

14 Policies. Harvey would have little use for modern eugenics.
15 Written in Latin by Hobbes himself and included by Aubrey in his biography.

on geometry; which happened accidentally. Being in a gentleman's library in . . . Euclid's Elements lay open, and 'twas the 47 El. *libri* I. He read the proposition. "By"—he would now and then swear by way of emphasis—"G—!" said he, "this is impossible!" So he reads the demonstration of it, which referred him back to such a proposition; which proposition he read. *Et sic deinceps* that at last he was demonstratively convinced of that truth. This made him in love with geometry.

I have heard Mr. Hobbes say that he was wont to draw lines on his thigh and on the sheets abed and also multiply and divide. He would often complain that algebra, though of great use, was too much admired and so followed after, that it made men not contemplate and consider so much the nature and power of lines, which was a great hinderance to the growth of geometry.

LEVIATHAN: the manner of writing of which book, he told me, was thus: he walked much and contemplated, and had in the head of his staff a pen and ink-horn, carried always a notebook in his pocket, and as soon as a thought darted he presently entered it into his book, or otherwise he might perhaps have lost it. He had drawn the design of the book into chapters, etc., so he knew whereabout it would come in. Thus that book was made.

"He wrote and published the Leviathan far from the intention either of disadvantage to his Majesty or to flatter Oliver—who was not made Protector till three or four years after—on purpose to facilitate his return; for there is scarce a page in it that he does not upbraid him."

There was a report—and surely true—that in Parliament, not long after the King was settled, some of the bishops made a motion to have the good old gentleman burnt for a heretic. Which he hearing, feared that his papers might be searched by their order, and he told me he had burnt part of them.

It happened about two or three days after his Majesty's happy return that, as he was passing in his coach through the Strand, Mr. Hobbes was standing at Little Salisbury-House gate, where his lord then lived. The King espied him, put off his hat very kindly to him, and asked him how he did. About a week after he had oral conference with his Majesty at Mr. S. Cowper's, where, as he sat for his picture, he was diverted by Mr. Hobbes's pleasant discourse. Here his Majesty's favors were redintegrated to him, and order was given that he should have free access to his Majesty, who was always much delighted in his wit and smart repartees.

The wits at court were wont to bait him. But he feared none of them and would make his part good. The King would call him *the bear:* "Here comes the bear to be baited!"

In his youth, unhealthy, of an ill yellowish complexion, wet in his feet, and trod both his shoes the same way. . . . From forty or better he grew healthier, and then he had a fresh, ruddy complexion. . . . In his old age he was very bald—which claimed a veneration; yet within door he used to study and sit bareheaded, and said he never took cold in his head but that the greatest trouble was to keep off the flies from pitching on the baldness. His head was . . . inches in compass (I have the measure) and of a mallet form (approved by the physiologers).

Temperance and diet: he was, even in his youth (generally), temperate both as to wine and women— *et tamen hæc omnia mediocriter—*

> *Homo sum, humani nihil a me alienum puto.*

I have heard him say that he did believe he had been in excess in his life a hundred times; which, considering his great age, did not amount to above once a year. . . . After dinner he took a pipe of tobacco and then threw himself immediately on his bed, with his band off, and slept—took a nap of about half an hour.

Exercises: besides his daily walking he did twice or thrice a year play at tennis (at about 75 he did it), then went to bed there and was well rubbed. This he did believe would make him live two or three years the longer.

Singing: he had always books of prick-song lying on his table, e.g., of H. Lawes's etc., songs—which at night, when he was abed and the doors made fast, and was sure nobody heard him, he sang aloud—not that he had a very good voice—but for his health's sake. He did believe it did his lungs good and conduced much to prolong his life.

GEORGE HERBERT
(1593–1633)

MR. GEORGE HERBERT was kinsman (remote) and chaplain to Philip, Earl of Pembroke and Montgomery and Lord Chamberlain. His Lordship gave him a benefice at Bemerton, between Wilton and Salisbury, a pitiful little chapel of ease to Foughelston. The old house was very ruinous. Here he built a very handsome house for the minister, of brick, and made a good garden and walks. He lies in the chancel under no large nor yet very good marble gravestone without any inscription.

Scripsit:—Sacred poems, called The Church,[16] printed, Cambridge, 1633; a book entitled The Country Parson, not printed till about 1650, 8vo. He also wrote a folio in Latin, which because the parson of Hineham could not read, his widow, then wife to Sir Robert Cook, condemned to the uses of good housewifery.[17]

He was buried, according to his own desire, with the singing service for the burial of the dead by the singing men of Sarum.[18] Fr[ancis] Sambroke, attorney, then assisted as a chorister boy; my uncle, Thomas Danvers, was at the funeral. *Vide* in the register book at the office when he died, for the parish register is lost.

Memorandum:—in the chancel are many apt sentences of the Scripture. At his wife's seat, "My life is hid with Christ in God," Coloss. 3:3—he hath verses on this text in his poems. Above, in a little window blinded, within a veil (ill painted), "Thou art my hiding place," Psalm 32:7.

He married Jane, the third daughter of Charles Danvers of Bainton in *com.* Wilts, Esq., but had no issue by her. He was a very fine complexion and consumptive. His marriage, I suppose, hastened his death. My kinswoman was a handsome *bona roba* and ingenious.

When he was first married he lived a year or better at Dauntsey House. H. Allen of Dauntsey was well acquainted with him, who has told me that he had a very good hand on the lute and that he set his own lyrics or sacred poems. 'Tis an honor to the place to have had the heavenly and ingenious contemplation of this good man, who was pious even to prophesy;— e.g.,

> "Religion now on tiptoe stands
> Ready to go to the American strands."[19]

George Herbert:—[ask] cousin Nan Garnet *pro* [his] picture; if not, her aunt . . . Cook.

---

16 The Temple.
17 She used the pages for wrappers.
18 Old name of Salisbury.
19 Aubrey is not very exact in his quotations; the lines are:

> "Religion stands on tiptoe in our land,
> Ready to pass to the American strand."

Incidentally, this comment upon the exodus of the Puritans to the New World held up the publication of The Temple; the Vice-Chancellor wished it struck out, but finally let it go into print as a pious speculation rather than an inspired prophecy.

CECIL CALVERT
(1606–1675)

CECIL CALVERT, Lord Baltimore,[20] absolute lord and proprietary of Maryland and Avalon in America, son to Calvert, Secretary of Estate to King James, was a gentleman commoner of Trinity College, Oxon, contemporary with Mr. Francis Potter, B.D.

Now if I would be rich, I could be a prince. I could go into Maryland, which is one of the finest countries of the world; same climate with France; between Virginia and New England. I can have all the favor of my Lord Baltimore I could wish.—His brother is his lieutenant there; and a *very good-natured gentleman.*—Plenty of all things; ground there is 2,000 miles westwards.

I could be able I believe to carry a colony of rogues, another of ingenious artificers; and I doubt not one might make a shift to have 5 or 6 ingenious companions, which is enough.

JOHN MILTON
(1608–1674)

MR. JOHN MILTON was of an Oxfordshire family. His grandfather[21] . . . a Roman Catholic, of Holton, in Oxfordshire, near Shotover. His father was brought up in the University of Oxon, at Christ Church, and his father disinherited him because he kept not the Catholic religion. So thereupon he came to London and became a scrivener (brought up by a friend of his; was not an apprentice) and got a plentiful estate by it, and left it off many years before he died.—He was an ingenious man; delighted in music; composed many songs now in print, especially that of Oriana.

His son John was born in Bread Street, in London, at the Spread Eagle.[22] . . . *Anno Domini* 1619, he was ten years old, as by his picture; and was then a poet. His schoolmaster then was a Puritan in Essex who cut his hair short. He went to school to old Mr. Gill at Paul's School. Went, at his own charge only, to Christ's College in Cambridge at fifteen, where he stayed eight years at least. Then he traveled into France and Italy (had Sir H. Wotton's commendatory letters). At Geneva he contracted a great friendship with the learned Dr. Deodati of Geneva:—*vide* his

poems. He was acquainted with Sir Henry Wotton, ambassador at Venice, who delighted in his company. He was several years beyond sea and returned to England just upon the breaking out of the civil wars. From his brother, Christopher Milton:—when he went to school, when he was very young, he studied very hard and sat up very late, commonly till 12 or 1 a clock at night, and his father ordered the maid to sit up for him, and in those years (10) composed many copies of verses which might well become a riper age. And was a very hard student in the university and performed all his exercises there with very good applause.

He went to travel about the year 1638 and was abroad about a year's space, chiefly in Italy. Immediately after his return he took a lodging at Mr. Russell's, a tailor, in St. Bride's churchyard, and took into his tuition his sister's two sons, Edward and John Philips, the first 10, the other 9 years of age; and in a year's time made them capable of interpreting a Latin author at sight, etc. And within three years they went through the best of Latin and Greek poets—Lucretius and Manilius, and with him the use of the globes, and some rudiments of arithmetic and geometry of the Latins, Hesiod, Aratus, Dionysius Afer, Oppian, Apollonii *Argonautica*, and Quintus Calaber. Cato, Varro, and Columella, *De Re Rustica*, were the very first authors they learnt.—As he was severe on one hand so he was most familiar and free in his conversation to those to whom most sour in his way of education. N. B. he made his nephews songsters and sing from the time they were with him.

His sight began to fail him at first upon his writing against Salamasius, and before 'twas fully completed one eye absolutely failed. Upon the writing of other books after that, his other eye decayed. His eyesight was decaying about 20 years before his death; *quære*, when stark blind? His father read without spectacles at 84. His mother had very weak eyes and used spectacles presently after she was thirty years old.

His harmonical and ingenious soul did lodge in a beautiful and well-proportioned body:—

In toto nusquam corpore menda fuit.[23] Ovid.

He was a spare man. He was scarce so tall as I am—*quære, qot* feet I am high: *resp.*, of middle stature. He had auburn hair. His complexion exceedingly fair—he was so fair that they called him *the lady of Christ's College*. Oval face. His eye a dark gray. He had a

---

20 Second Baron Baltimore. 21 Richard Milton.
22 The name of the house.

23 Nowhere in his whole body was there a flaw.

delicate tuneable voice and had good skill. His father instructed him. He had an organ in his house; he played
on that most. Of a very cheerful humor.—He would be
cheerful even in his gout fits, and sing. He was very
healthy and free from all diseases; seldom took any
physic (only sometimes he took manna); only towards
his latter end he was visited with the gout spring and
fall. He had a very good memory; but I believe that his
excellent method of thinking and disposing did much
to help his memory. He pronounced the letter R,
littera canina, very hard—a certain sign of a satirical wit
—from John Dryden.

His exercise was chiefly walking. He was an early
riser (*scil.* at 4 a clock *mané*); yea, after he lost his sight.
He had a man read to him. The first thing he read was
the Hebrew Bible, and that was at 4 h. *mané* ½ h. +.
Then he contemplated. At 7 his man came to him again
and then read to him again, and wrote till dinner;
the writing was as much as the reading. His (2)
daughter, Deborah, could read to him Latin, Italian
and French, and Greek. Married in Dublin to one Mr.
Clarke (sells silk, etc.); very like her father. The other
sister is (1) Mary, more like her mother. After dinner
he used to walk 3 or 4 hours at a time—he always
had a garden where he lived; went to bed about 9.
Temperate man, rarely drank between meals. Extreme pleasant in his conversation, and at dinner, supper, etc.; but satirical.

From Mr. E. Philips:—all the time of writing his
Paradise Lost his vein began at the autumnal equinoctial and ceased at the vernal—or thereabouts; I believe
about May; and this was 4 or 5 years of his doing it.
He began about 2 years before the King came in and
finished about three years after the King's restoration.

In the 4th book of Paradise Lost there are about six
verses of Satan's exclamation to the sun which Mr. E.
Philips remembers about 15 or 16 years before ever his
poem was thought of. Which verses were intended for
the beginning of a tragedy which he had designed but
was diverted from it by other business.

[24] Whatever he wrote against monarchy was out of
no animosity to the King's person or out of any faction of interest but out of a pure zeal to the liberty of
mankind, which he thought would be greater under a
free state than under a monarchal government. His
being so conversant in Livy and the Roman authors
and the greatness he saw done by the Roman commonwealth and the virtue of their great commanders
induced him to.

24 This paragraph is not in Aubrey's hand.

He was visited much by learned; more than he did
desire. He was mightily importuned to go into France
and Italy. Foreigners came much to see him and much
admired him and offered him great preferments to
come over to them; and the only inducement of several foreigners that came over into England was chiefly
to see Oliver Protector and Mr. John Milton; and
would see the house and chamber where he was born.
He was much more admired abroad than at home. His
familiar learned acquaintance were Mr. Andrew Marvell, Mr. Skinner, Dr. Pagett, M.D., Mr. Skinner[25]
who was his disciple. John Dryden, Esq., Poet Laureate,
who very much admires him and went to him to have
leave to put his Paradise Lost into a drama in rhyme.[26]
Mr. Milton received him civilly and told him he would
give him leave to tag his verses.

He died of the gout struck in the 9th or 10th of
November, 1674, as appears by his apothecary's book.

SIR JOHN SUCKLING
(1609–1642)

HE WAS the greatest gallant of his time and the greatest
gamester both for bowling—(he was one of the best
bowlers of his time in England. He played at cards
rarely well and did use to practise by himself abed and
there studied how the best way of managing the cards
could be. His sisters coming to the Piccadilly bowling
green crying for the fear he should lose all [their]
portions)—and cards, so that no shopkeeper would
trust him for 6*d.*, as today, for instance, he might by
winning be worth £200, the next day he might not
be worth half so much, or perhaps be sometimes *minus
nihilo*. Sir William,[27] who was his intimate friend and
loved him entirely, would say that Sir John, when he
was at his lowest ebb in gaming, I mean when unfortunate, then would make himself most glorious in
apparel, and said that it exalted his spirits and that he
had then the best luck when he was most gallant and
his spirits were highest.

Anno Domini 163[9], when the expedition was into
Scotland, Sir John Suckling, at his own charge, raised
a troop of 100 very handsome, young, proper men

25 Cyriack Skinner, to whom Milton addressed a sonnet.
26 Dryden's opera, The State of Innocence.
27 Sir William Davenant, Poet Laureate, of whom Aubrey
says, on the authority of Samuel Butler, "He wrote with the
very spirit that Shakespeare, and seemed contented to be
thought his son."

whom he clad in white doublets and scarlet breeches and scarlet coats, hats, and . . . feathers, well horsed and armed. They say 'twas one of the finest sights in those days. But Sir John Mennis made a lampoon of it —*vide* the old collection of lampoons:

> "The ladies opened the windows to see
> So fine and goodly a sight-a," etc.

I think the lampoon says he made an inglorious charge against the Scots.

Quære in what army he was in the civil wars.

Memorandum:—he made a magnificent entertainment in London, at . . . for a great number of ladies of quality, all beauties and young, which cost him . . . hundreds of pounds, where were all the rarities that this part of the world could afford, and the last service of all was silk stockings and garters, and I think also gloves.

Anno Domini 1637, Sir John Suckling, William Davenant, Poet Laureate (not then knighted), and Jack Young came to the Bath. Sir John came like a young prince for all manner of equipage and convenience, and Sir W. Davenant told me that he had a cartload of books carried down, and 'twas there at Bath, that he writ the little tract in his book about Socinianism. 'Twas as pleasant a journey as ever men had; in the height of a long peace and luxury and in the venison season. The second night they lay at Marlborough, and walking on the delicate fine downs at the backside of the town whilst supper was making ready, the maids were drying of clothes on the bushes. Jack Young had espied a very pretty young girl and had got her consent for an assignation, which was about midnight, which they happened to overhear on the other side of the hedge, and were resolved to frustrate his design. They were wont every night to play at cards after supper a good while; but Jack Young pretended weariness, etc., and must needs go to bed, not to be persuaded by any means to the contrary. They had their landlady at supper with them; said they to her, "Observe this poor gentleman how he yawns, now is his mad fit coming upon him. We beseech you that you make fast his doors, and get somebody to watch and look to him, for about midnight he will fall to be most outrageous. Get the hostler or some strong fellow, to stay up, and we will well content him, for he is our worthy friend and a very honest gentleman, only perhaps twice a year he falls into these fits." Jack Young slept not, but was ready to go out as the clock struck to the hour of appointment, and then going to open the door he was disappointed, knocks, bounces, stamps, calls, "Tapster! chamberlain! hostler!" swears and curses dreadfully; nobody would come to him. Sir John and W. Davenant were expectant all this time and ready to die with laughter. I know not how he happened to get open the door and was coming downstairs. The hostler, a huge lusty fellow, fell upon him and held him and cried, "Good Sir, take God in your mind, you shall not go out to destroy yourself!" J. Young struggled and strived, insomuch that at last he was quite spent and dispirited and fain to go to bed to rest himself. In the morning the landlady of the house came to see how he did and brought him a caudle. "O Sir," said she, "you had a heavy fit last night, pray, Sir, be pleased to take some of this to comfort your heart." Jack Young thought the woman had been mad, and being exceedingly vexed, flirted the porringer of caudle in her face. The next day his comrades told him all the plot, how they crossbit him.

Sir John Suckling—from Mr. William Beeston—invented the game of cribbage. He sent his cards to all gaming places in the country, which were marked with private marks of his. He got £20,000 by this way. Sir Francis Cornwallis made Aglaura[28] except the end.

Anno . . . he went into France, where after some time being come to the bottom of his fund that was left, reflecting on the miserable and despicable condition he should be reduced to, having nothing left to maintain him, he (having a convenience for that purpose, lying at an apothecary's house in Paris) took poison, which killed him miserably with vomiting. He was buried in the Protestants' churchyard. This was, to the best of my remembrance, 1646.[29]

WILLIAM PENN
(1644–1718)

WILLIAM PENN, the eldest son of Sir William Penn, Knight, (Admiral both of the English navy before the restoration of the King and commanded as Captain-General under the D. Y.[30] in 1665 against the Dutch fleet), was born in London at Tower Hill, the 14 day

28 Suckling's best play, a tragedy, containing the immortal song, "Why so pale and wan, fond lover?"

29 Aubrey's best remembrance is not very good; the year is 1641.

30 James, Duke of York.

of October 1644. 'Twas upon a Monday, he thinks; but 'twas about 7 a clock in the morning.

His father was a very good man, but no Quaker; was very much against his son. His father was a man of excellent natural abilities not equaled in his time for the knowledge of naval affairs and instrumental to the raising of many families. Bred his son religiously; and, as the times grew loose, would have had his son of the fashion, and was therefore extreme bitter at his son's retirement. But this lasted not always; for in the conclusion of his life he grew not only kind but fond; made him the judge and ruler of his family; was sorry he had no more to leave him (and yet, in England and Ireland, he left him £1,500 *per annum*). But, which is most remarkable, he that opposed his son's way because of the cross that was in it to the world's latitude did himself embrace this faith, recommending to his son the plainness and self-denial of it, saying, "Keep to the plainness of your way, and you will make an end of the priests to the ends of the earth." And so he deceased, desiring that none but his son William should close his eyes (which he did). *Obiit anno ætatis* 49, 4 months.

[His son] went to school in London, a private school on that hill, and his father kept a tutor in the house. But first he went to school at Chigwell in Essex.

Mighty lively, but with innocence; and extremely tender under rebuke; and very early delighted in retirement; much given to reading and meditating of the Scriptures, and at 14 had marked over the Bible. Oftentimes at 13 and 14 in his meditations ravished with joy and dissolved into tears.

The first sense he had of God was when he was 11 years old at Chigwell, being retired in a chamber alone. He was so suddenly surprised with an inward comfort and, as he thought, an external glory in the room that he has many times said that from thence he had the seal of divinity and immortality, that there was a God, and that the soul of man was capable of enjoying his divine communications.—His schoolmaster was not of his persuasion.

To Christ's Church in Oxon, *anno* 1660, *anno ætatis* 16; stayed there about two years.

Anno 1662, went into France; stayed there two years. Returned and was entered of Lincoln's Inn.

About the plague, growing entirely solitary, was again diverted. Was employed by his father in a journey into Ireland to the Duke of Ormond's court; the diversions of which not being able to keep down the stronger motions of his soul to a more religious and retired life, upon the hearing of one Th[omas] Lowe, a tradesman of Oxon, at Cork, 1667, was so thoroughly convinced of the simplicity and self-denial of the way of the people called Quakers that from thence he heartily espoused that judgment and belief.

Since which time he has passed a life of great variety of circumstances both with respect to good and evil report; divers controversies oral and written, several imprisonments, one in Ireland, one in the Tower, 3rd in Newgate.

Traveled into Germany, Upper and Lower, *annis* 1671 and 1677, where several were affected with his way. (Did he gain any to him in France? *Neg.*[31])

Notwithstanding those many odd adventures of his life, he hath several times found favor from his Majesty and also the D. Y., with divers of the nobility and men of quality and learning in this kingdom.

His Majesty owing to his father £10,000, 16—, (which with the interest of it came not to less than £20,000), did in consideration thereof grant to him and his heirs a province in America, which his Majesty was pleased to name Pennsylvania,[32] the 4th day of March 168-, to which he is now going this next September, 1681.

His patent for Transylvania[33] is from the beginning of the 40th degree to 43 degrees in latitude and 5 degrees in longitude from Chesapeake Bay.

He speaks well the Latin and the French tongues and his own with great mastership. He often declares in the assemblies of his Friends and that with much eloquence and fervency of spirit—by which, and his perpetual attendance on K[ing] and P[rince] for the relief of his Friends, he often exposes his health to hazard.

He was chosen (balloted) November 9th, *nemine contradicente*, admitted Fellow of the Royal Society of London, with much respect.

August 26, 1682, Saturday. This day about 4 a clock P. M., W. Penn, Esq., went towards Deal to launch for Pennsylvania. God send him a prosperous and safe voyage!

31 Negative; no.
32 Penn gave Aubrey 600 acres in Pennsylvania, according to Aubrey, without his seeking or dreaming of it, and advised him to plant it with French Protestants "for seven years *gratis* and afterwards to pay such a rent."
33 Pennsylvania.

John Bunyan

[1628–1688]

I T FELL to the lot of John Bunyan, an obscure Bedfordshire tinker, to become the most popular religious writer in the language, the author of what is almost certainly the most widely read book by any English author. Born of humble parents in the village of Elstow, near Bedford, he differs from the other authors represented in this volume in the lowliness of his social origins. It is erroneous, however, to think of Bunyan as an uncultivated man or an untutored artist, as popular tradition has often maintained. He received at least some education at the local grammar school, and his mature works clearly show the effects of a habit of reading which made up in profundity for what it lacked in variety. Apart from the English Bible, which is the greatest single influence on Bunyan in both style and vision, literary influences which can be traced in his work include romances of chivalry, emblem-books, and popular books of religious devotion.

Bunyan was inducted into the parliamentary army at the age of sixteen and returned to his native shire some three years later. After misspent youthful years which he describes in his spiritual autobiography, *Grace Abounding to the Chief of Sinners*, with its harrowing account of such sins as swearing, dancing, and playing tip-cat on Sunday, Bunyan was converted to godliness. Married at the age of twenty or twenty-one, he tells us, with a pathos which is the more moving for being unconscious, of his wife's dowry—two religious books. These books, Arthur Dent's *The Plain Man's Pathway to Heaven* (1601) and Lewis Bayly's *The Practice of Piety* (1612), crystallized the young man's religious longings, and his baptism into the Baptist Church was shortly followed by his own assumption of the duties of a preacher. About 1656 his first wife died, after bearing him four children. He married again in 1659. During the 1650's Bunyan was not only active as a preacher; he also undertook the writing of the controversial and devotional books which were to fill such a large part of his life—they were to amount to some forty-eight separate works before he died.

Shortly after the Restoration of 1660, with its attendant suppression of the non-conformists, Bunyan was arrested for preaching without a license and was confined in Bedford jail—his original sentence of three months extended to twelve years because of his refusal to agree to stop preaching. The product of these years was *Grace Abounding*, probably the greatest of English spiritual autobiographies and a fascinating document of the Protestant spirit in the seventeenth century. Freed in 1672 by the Declaration of Indulgence, Bunyan resumed his active ministry, sometimes preaching even in London. In 1675, however, Charles II yielded to Parliament and repealed the Declaration. Bunyan was imprisoned again, this time for six months, and during this time he conceived and began his greatest work, *The Pilgrim's Progress*. Published in 1678, the work was an extraordinary popular success, and Bunyan suffered no further from king or prelate. The second part of *The Pilgrim's Progress*—mellower but also less gripping than its precursor—appeared in 1684. In the interim, *The Life and Death of Mr. Badman* (1680) and *The Holy War* (1682) also both allegorical works, had added to the author's stature. Bunyan died in 1688 of a severe cold contracted on a journey which he undertook in order to reconcile an estranged father and son.

The Pilgrim's Progress has sometimes been called the first English novel, and its vigor, its narrative sweep, and its vivid particularity unquestionably prefigure the great novels of the next century. At the same time, however, we must recognize that Bunyan was motivated by considerations very different from those of Smollett or Fielding; the novelistic elements of his masterpiece are always in the service of a religious and didactic purpose, and he is as much at ease with allegory as any medieval poet. The precise implications of his allegory—its relentless dwelling on man's worthlessness, on the impossibility of salvation through any efforts of one's own, on the fearful danger of damnation—are liable to be unpalatable to most modern readers, but the sincerity and urgency with which Bunyan holds his vision cannot but move us still. Finally, in the form which Bunyan's genius dictated to him he stumbled upon one of the great recurrent mythic patterns—that of the quest journey, in which death lies at the end but with a glorious rebirth beyond. Such patterns are always capable, beyond the narrow limits of doctrine or dogma, of stirring the imagination and the emotions of our race.

J. BUNYAN. *Grace Abounding to the Chief of Sinners*, ed. R. Sharrock (Oxford, 1962).

————. *Grace Abounding to the Chief of Sinners* and *The Pilgrim's Progress*, ed. J. Brown (Cambridge, 1907).

————. *The Pilgrim's Progress*, ed. L. L. Martz (New York, 1949).

————. *The Life and Death of Mr. Badman* and *The Holy War*, ed. J. Brown (Cambridge, 1905).

J. BROWN. *John Bunyan: His Life, Times, and Work*, rev. ed., F. M. Harrison (London, 1928).

G. B. HARRISON. *John Bunyan: A Study in Personality* (London, 1928). Biography.

W. Y. TINDALL. *John Bunyan, Mechanick Preacher* (New York, 1934). A biographical study from a different point of view.

R. SHARROCK. "Bunyan and the English Emblem Writers," *Review of English Studies*, X (1945).

H. TALON. *John Bunyan: The Man and His Works* (Cambridge, Mass., 1951).

O. E. WINSLOW. *John Bunyan* (New York, 1961). The most recent biography.

F R O M

THE PILGRIM'S PROGRESS:
From This World to That Which is to Come,
Delivered Under the Similitude of a Dream

[TEXT: *First Part, eleventh edition, 1688; Second Part, second edition, 1687*]

from
THE FIRST PART

[CHRISTIAN ESCAPES FROM THE CITY OF DESTRUCTION]

As I walked through the wilderness of this world, I lighted on a certain place where was a den, and I laid me down in that place to sleep: and, as I slept, I dreamed a dream.[1] I dreamed, and behold I saw a man clothed with rags, standing in a certain place, with his face from his own house, a book in his hand, and a great burden upon his back. I looked, and saw him open the book and read therein; and, as he read, he wept, and trembled; and not being able longer to contain, he brake out with a lamentable cry, saying, "What shall I do?"

In this plight, therefore, he went home and refrained himself as long as he could, that his wife and children should not perceive his distress; but he could not be silent long, because that his trouble increased. Wherefore at length he brake his mind to his wife and children; and thus he began to talk to them. "O my dear wife," said he, "and you the children of my bowels, I, your dear friend, am in myself undone by reason of a burden that lieth hard upon me; moreover, I am for certain informed that this our city will be burned with fire from heaven, in which fearful overthrow both myself, with thee my wife, and you my sweet babes, shall miserably come to ruin, except (the which yet I see not) some way of escape can be found,

whereby we may be delivered." At this his relations were sore amazed; not for that they believed that what he had said to them was true, but because they thought that some frenzy[2] distemper had got into his head; therefore, it drawing towards night, and they hoping that sleep might settle his brains, with all haste they got him to bed. But the night was as troublesome to him as the day; wherefore, instead of sleeping, he spent it in sighs and tears. So, when the morning was come, they would know how he did. He told them, "Worse and worse." He also set to talking to them again: but they began to be hardened. They also thought to drive away his distemper by harsh and surly carriages[3] to him; sometimes they would deride, sometimes they would chide, and sometimes they would quite neglect him. Wherefore he began to retire himself to his chamber, to pray for and pity them, and also to condole his own misery; he would also walk solitarily in the fields, sometimes reading, and sometimes praying: and thus for some days he spent his time.

Now, I saw, upon a time, when he was walking in the fields, that he was, as he was wont, reading in this book, and greatly distressed in his mind; and as he read, he burst out, as he had done before, crying, "What shall I do to be saved?"

I saw also that he looked this way and that way, as if he would run; yet he stood still, because, as I perceived, he could not tell which way to go. I looked then, and saw a man named Evangelist coming to him, and asked, "Wherefore dost thou cry?"

He answered, "Sir, I perceive by the book in my hand that I am condemned to die, and after that to come to judgment, and I find that I am not willing to do the first, nor able to do the second."

Then said Evangelist, "Why not willing to die, since this life is attended with so many evils?" The

---

1 The first sentence of The Pilgrim's Progress, like almost every other in the book, shows the influence of the King James Bible. In the early editions, as in all complete modern editions of the book, the quotations from the Bible and allusions to it are indicated in marginal notes. These are omitted here, to simplify the reading.

2 A rare and colloquial use of the noun as adjective.
3 Behavior.

man answered, "Because I fear that this burden that is upon my back will sink me lower than the grave, and I shall fall into Tophet.[4] And, sir, if I be not fit to go to prison, I am not fit to go to judgment, and from thence to execution; and the thoughts of these things make me cry."

Then said Evangelist, "If this be thy condition, why standest thou still?" He answered, "Because I know not whither to go." Then he gave him a parchment roll, and there was written within, "Fly from the wrath to come."

The man therefore read it, and looking upon Evangelist very carefully, said, "Whither must I fly?" Then said Evangelist, pointing with his finger over a very wide field, "Do you see yonder wicket-gate?" The man said, "No." Then said the other, "Do you see yonder shining light?" He said, "I think I do." Then said Evangelist, "Keep that light in your eye, and go up directly thereto: so shalt thou see the gate; at which when thou knockest it shall be told thee what thou shalt do."

So I saw in my dream that the man began to run. Now, he had not run far from his own door, but his wife and children perceiving it, began to cry after him to return; but the man put his fingers in his ears, and ran on, crying, "Life! life! eternal life!" So he looked not behind him, but fled towards the middle of the plain.

The neighbors also came out to see him run; and as he ran, some mocked, others threatened, and some cried after him to return; and, among those that did so, there were two that resolved to fetch him back by force. The name of the one was Obstinate, and the name of the other Pliable. Now by this time, the man was got a good distance from them; but, however, they were resolved to pursue him, which they did, and in a little time they overtook him. Then said the man, "Neighbors, wherefore are ye come?" They said, "To persuade you to go back with us." But he said, "That can by no means be; you dwell," said he, "in the City of Destruction, the place also where I was born. I see it to be so; and dying there, sooner or later, you will sink lower than the grave, into a place that burns with fire and brimstone: be content, good neighbors, and go along with me."

"What!" said Obstinate, "and leave our friends and our comforts behind us?"

"Yes," said Christian (for that was his name), "because that all which you shall forsake is not worthy

4 Hell.

to be compared with a little of that which I am seeking to enjoy; and if you will go along with me, and hold it, you shall fare as I myself; for there, where I go, is enough and to spare. Come away, and prove my words."

OBST. What are the things you seek, since you leave all the world to find them?

CHR. I seek an inheritance incorruptible, undefiled, and that fadeth not away, and it is laid up in heaven, and safe there, to be bestowed, at the time appointed, on them that diligently seek it. Read it so, if you will, in my book.

OBST. "Tush!" said Obstinate, "away with your book. Will you go back with us or no?"

CHR. "No, not I," said the other, "because I have laid my hand to the plow."

OBST. Come then, Neighbor Pliable, let us turn again, and go home without him; there is a company of these crazed-headed coxcombs, that, when they take a fancy by the end, are wiser in their own eyes than seven men that can render a reason.

PLI. "Then," said Pliable, "don't revile; if what the good Christian says is true, the things he looks after are better than ours; my heart inclines to go with my neighbor."

OBST. What! more fools still! Be ruled by me, and go back; who knows whither such a brain-sick fellow will lead you? Go back, go back, and be wise.

CHR. Nay, but do thou come with thy neighbor, Pliable; there are such things to be had which I spoke of, and many more glories besides. If you believe not me, read here in this book; and for the truth of what is expressed therein, behold all is confirmed by the blood of Him that made it.

PLI. "Well, Neighbor Obstinate," saith Pliable, "I begin to come to a point; I intend to go along with this good man, and to cast in my lot with him; but, my good companion, do you know the way to this desired place?"

CHR. I am directed by a man, whose name is Evangelist, to speed me to a little gate that is before us, where we shall receive instructions about the way.

PLI. Come, then, good neighbor, let us be going. Then they went both together.

OBST. "And I will go back to my place," said Obstinate; "I will be no companion of such misled, fantastical fellows."

Now, I saw in my dream, that, when Obstinate was gone back, Christian and Pliable went talking over the plain; and thus they began their discourse.

CHR. Come, Neighbor Pliable, how do you do? I am glad you are persuaded to go along with me. Had even Obstinate himself but felt what I have felt of the powers and terrors of what is yet unseen, he would not thus lightly have given us the back.

PLI. Come, Neighbor Christian, since there is none but us two here, tell me now further what the things are, and how to be enjoyed, whither we are going.

CHR. I can better conceive of them with my mind, than speak of them with my tongue; but yet, since you are desirous to know, I will read of them in my book.

PLI. And do you think that the words of your book are certainly true?

CHR. Yes, verily; for it was made by Him that cannot lie.

PLI. Well said; what things are they?

CHR. There is an endless kingdom to be inhabited, and everlasting life to be given us, that we may inhabit that kingdom for ever.

PLI. Well said; and what else?

CHR. There are crowns of glory to be given us, and garments that will make us shine like the sun in the firmament of heaven.

PLI. This is very pleasant; and what else?

CHR. There shall be no more crying, nor sorrow; for He that is owner of the place will wipe all tears from our eyes.

PLI. And what company shall we have there?

CHR. There we shall be with seraphims and cherubims,[5] creatures that will dazzle your eyes to look on them. There also you shall meet with thousands and ten thousands that have gone before us to that place; none of them are hurtful, but loving and holy; every one walking in the sight of God, and standing in his presence with acceptance for ever. In a word, there we shall see the elders with their golden crowns; there we shall see the holy virgins with their golden harps; there we shall see men that by the world were cut in pieces, burnt in flames, eaten of beasts, drowned in the seas, for the love that they bare to the Lord of the place, all well, and clothed with immortality as with a garment.

PLI. The hearing of this is enough to ravish one's heart. But are these things to be enjoyed? How shall we get to be sharers thereof?

CHR. The Lord, the Governor of the country, hath

recorded that in this book; the substance of which is, If we be truly willing to have it, He will bestow it upon us freely.

PLI. Well, my good companion, glad am I to hear of these things; come on, let us mend our pace.

CHR. I cannot go so fast as I would, by reason of this burden that is on my back.

Now, I saw in my dream, that just as they had ended this talk they drew near to a very miry slough, that was in the midst of the plain; and they, being heedless, did both fall suddenly into the bog. The name of the slough was Despond. Here, therefore, they wallowed for a time, being grievously bedaubed with dirt; and Christian, because of the burden that was on his back, began to sink in the mire.

PLI. Then said Pliable, "Ah! Neighbor Christian, where are you now?"

CHR. "Truly," said Christian, "I do not know."

PLI. At that Pliable began to be offended, and angrily said to his fellow, "Is this the happiness you have told me all this while of? If we have such ill speed at our first setting out, what may we expect 'twixt this and our journey's end? May I get out again with my life, you shall possess the brave country alone for me."[6] And, with that, he gave a desperate struggle or two, and got out of the mire on that side of the slough which was next[7] to his own house: so away he went, and Christian saw him no more.

Wherefore Christian was left to tumble in the Slough of Despond alone: but still he endeavored to struggle to that side of the slough that was still further from his own house, and next to the wicket-gate; the which he did, but could not get out, because of the burden that was upon his back: but I beheld in my dream, that a man came to him, whose name was Help, and asked him what he did there.

CHR. "Sir," said Christian, "I was bid go this way by a man called Evangelist, who directed me also to yonder gate, that I might escape the wrath to come; and as I was going thither I fell in here."

HELP. But why did not you look for the steps?

CHR. Fear followed me so hard, that I fled the next way and fell in.

HELP. Then said he, "Give me thy hand." So he gave him his hand, and he drew him out, and set him upon sound ground, and bid him go on his way.

Then I stepped to him that plucked him out, and said, "Sir, wherefore, since over this place is the way

---

5 *Seraphim* and *cherubim* are the Hebrew plural forms for *seraph* and *cherub*. The *s* was mistakenly added to the words by many older writers.

6 Alone for all I care.

7 Nearest, as elsewhere in this context.

from the City of Destruction to yonder gate, is it that this plat[8] is not mended, that poor travelers might go thither with more security?" And he said unto me, "This miry slough is such a place as cannot be mended; it is the descent whither the scum and filth that attends conviction for sin doth continually run, and therefore it was called the Slough of Despond; for still, as the sinner is awakened about his lost condition, there ariseth in his soul many fears, and doubts, and discouraging apprehensions, which all of them get together, and settle in this place. And this is the reason of the badness of this ground.

"It is not the pleasure of the King that this place should remain so bad. His laborers also have, by the direction of His Majesty's surveyors, been for above these sixteen hundred years employed about this patch of ground, if perhaps it might have been mended: yea, and to my knowledge," said he, "here have been swallowed up at least twenty thousand cart-loads, yea, millions of wholesome instructions, that have at all seasons been brought from all places of the King's dominions, and they that can tell say they are the best materials to make good ground of the place; if so be, it might have been mended, but it is the Slough of Despond still, and so will be when they have done what they can.

"True, there are, by the direction of the Lawgiver, certain good and substantial steps, placed even through the very midst of the slough; but at such time as this place doth much spew out its filth, as it doth against change of weather, these steps are hardly seen; or, if they be, men, through the dizziness of their heads, step besides, and then they are bemired to purpose,[9] notwithstanding the steps be there; but the ground is good when they are once got in at the gate."

Now, I saw in my dream, that by this time Pliable was got home to his house, so that his neighbors came to visit him; and some of them called him wise man for coming back, and some called him fool for hazarding himself with Christian: others, again, did mock at his cowardliness; saying, "Surely, since you began to venture, I would not have been so base to have given out for a few difficulties." So Pliable sat sneaking among them. But at last he got more confidence, and then they all turned their tales,[10] and began to deride poor Christian behind his back. And thus much concerning Pliable.

Now as Christian was walking solitarily by himself,

8 Plot.   9 To good purpose; i.e., thoroughly.
10 Turned their talk from Pliable to Christian.

he espied one afar off come crossing over the field to meet him; and their hap was to meet just as they were crossing the way of each other. The gentleman's name that met him was Mr. Worldly Wiseman: he dwelt in the town of Carnal Policy, a very great town, and also hard by from whence Christian came. This man, then, meeting with Christian, and having some inkling of him, for Christian's setting forth from the City of Destruction was much noised abroad, not only in the town where he dwelt, but also it began to be the town-talk in some other places—Master Worldly Wiseman, therefore, having some guess of him, by beholding his laborious going, by observing his sighs and groans, and the like, began thus to enter into some talk with Christian.

WORLD. How now, good fellow, whither way after this burdened manner?

CHR. A burdened manner indeed, as ever, I think, poor creature had. And whereas you ask me, Whither away, I tell you, Sir, I am going to yonder wicket-gate before me; for there, as I am informed, I shall be put into a way to be rid of my heavy burden.

WORLD. Hast thou a wife and children?

CHR. Yes; but I am so laden with this burden that I cannot take that pleasure in them as formerly; methinks I am as if I had none.

WORLD. Wilt thou hearken unto me if I give thee counsel?

CHR. If it be good, I will; for I stand in need of good counsel.

WORLD. I would advise thee, then, that thou with all speed get thyself rid of thy burden; for thou wilt never be settled in thy mind till then; nor canst thou enjoy the benefits of the blessing which God hath bestowed upon thee till then.

CHR. That is that which I seek for, even to be rid of this heavy burden; but get it off myself, I cannot; nor is there any man in our country that can take it off my shoulders; therefore am I going this way, as I told you, that I may be rid of my burden.

WORLD. Who bid thee go this way to be rid of thy burden?

CHR. A man that appeared to me to be a very great and honorable person; his name, as I remember, is Evangelist.

WORLD. I beshrew him for his counsel; there is not a more dangerous and troublesome way in the world than is that unto which he hath directed thee; and that thou shalt find, if thou will be ruled by his counsel. Thou hast met with something (as I perceive) already;

for I see the dirt of the Slough of Despond is upon thee; but that slough is the beginning of the sorrows that do attend those that go on in that way. Hear me, I am older than thou; thou art like to meet with, in the way which thou goest, wearisomeness, painfulness, hunger, perils, nakedness, sword, lions, dragons, darkness, and, in a word, death, and what not? These things are certainly true, having been confirmed by many testimonies. And why should a man so carelessly cast away himself, by giving heed to a stranger?

CHR. Why, Sir, this burden upon my back is more terrible to me than are all these things which you have mentioned; nay, methinks I care not what I meet with in the way, if so be I can also meet with deliverance from my burden.

WORLD. How camest thou by the burden at first?

CHR. By reading this book in my hand.

WORLD. I thought so; and it is happened unto thee as to other weak men, who, meddling with things too high for them, do suddenly fall into thy distractions; which distractions do not only unman men, as thine, I perceive, has done thee, but they run them upon desperate ventures to obtain they know not what.

CHR. I know what I would obtain; it is ease for my heavy burden.

WORLD. But why wilt thou seek for ease this way, seeing so many dangers attend it? Especially since (hadst thou but patience to hear me) I could direct thee to the obtaining of what thou desirest, without the dangers that thou in this way wilt run thyself into; yea, and the remedy is at hand. Besides, I will add that instead of those dangers thou shalt meet with much safety, friendship, and content.

CHR. Pray, Sir, open this secret to me.

WORLD. Why, in yonder village (the village is named Morality) there dwells a gentleman whose name is Legality, a very judicious man, and a man of a very good name, that has skill to help men off with such burdens as thine are from their shoulders: yea, to my knowledge, he hath done a great deal of good this way; ay, and besides, he hath skill to cure those that are somewhat crazed in their wits with their burdens. To him, as I said, thou mayest go, and be helped presently.[11] His house is not quite a mile from this place, and if he should not be at home himself, he hath a pretty young man to his son, whose name is Civility,[12] that can do it (to speak on) as well as the old gentle-

man himself; there, I say, thou mayest be eased of thy burden; and if thou art not minded to go back to thy former habitation, as indeed I would not wish thee, thou mayest send for thy wife and children to thee to this village, where there are houses now standing empty, one of which thou mayest have at reasonable rates; provision is there also cheap and good; and that which will make thy life the more happy is, to be sure, there thou shalt live by honest neighbors, in credit and good fashion.

Now was Christian somewhat at a stand; but presently he concluded, If this be true which this gentleman hath said, my wisest course is to take his advice; and with that he thus further spoke.

CHR. Sir, which is my way to this honest man's house?

WORLD. Do you see yonder high hill?

CHR. Yes, very well.

WORLD. By that hill you must go, and the first house you come at is his.

So Christian turned out of his way to go to Mr. Legality's house for help; but behold, when he was got now hard by the hill, it seemed so high, and also that side of it that was next the wayside did hang so much over, that Christian was afraid to venture further, lest the hill should fall on his head; wherefore there he stood still, and wotted not what to do. Also his burden now seemed heavier to him than while he was in his way. There came also flashes of fire out of the hill, that made Christian afraid that he should be burned. Here, therefore, he sweat and did quake for fear. And now he began to be sorry that he had taken Mr. Worldly Wiseman's counsel. And with that he saw Evangelist coming to meet him; at the sight also of whom he began to blush for shame. So Evangelist drew nearer and nearer; and coming up to him, he looked upon him with a severe and dreadful countenance, and thus began to reason with Christian.

EVAN. What dost thou here, Christian? said he: at which words Christian knew not what to answer; wherefore at present he stood speechless before him. Then said Evangelist further, Art not thou the man that I found crying without the walls of the City of Destruction?

CHR. Yes, dear Sir, I am the man.

EVAN. Did not I direct thee the way to the little wicket-gate?

CHR. Yes, dear Sir, said Christian.

EVAN. How is it, then, that thou art so quickly turned aside? For thou art now out of the way.

11 Quickly.
12 Theologically, civic virtue unredeemed by Faith.

CHR. I met with a gentleman so soon as I had got over the Slough of Despond, who persuaded me that I might, in the village before me, find a man that could take off my burden.

EVAN. What was he?

CHR. He looked like a gentleman, and talked much to me, and got me at last to yield; so I came hither: but when I beheld this hill, and how it hangs over the way, I suddenly made a stand, lest it should fall on my head.

EVAN. What said that gentleman to you?

CHR. Why, he asked me whither I was going, and I told him.

EVAN. And what said he then?

CHR. He asked me if I had a family, and I told him. But, said I, I am so loaden with the burden that is on my back, that I cannot take pleasure in them as formerly.

EVAN. And what said he then?

CHR. He bid me with speed get rid of my burden; and I told him 'twas ease that I sought. And, said I, I am therefore going to yonder gate, to receive further direction how I may get to the place of deliverance. So he said that he would show me a better way, and short, not so attended with difficulties as the way, Sir, that you set me in; which way, said he, will direct you to a gentleman's house that hath skill to take off these burdens; so I believed him, and turned out of that way into this, if haply I might be soon eased of my burden. But when I came to this place, and beheld things as they are, I stopped for fear (as I said) of danger: but I now know not what to do.

EVAN. Then, said Evangelist, stand still a little, that I may show thee the words of God. So he stood trembling. Then said Evangelist, "See that ye refuse not him that speaketh. For if they escaped not who refused him that spake on earth, much more shall not we escape, if we turn away from him that speaketh from heaven." He said, moreover, "Now the just shall live by faith: but if any man draw back, my soul shall have no pleasure in him." He also did thus apply them: Thou art the man that art running into this misery; thou hast begun to reject the counsel of the Most High, and to draw back thy foot from the way of peace, even almost to the hazarding of thy perdition.

Then Christian fell down at his feet as dead, crying, "Woe is me, for I am undone!" At the sight of which, Evangelist caught him by the right hand, saying, "All manner of sin and blasphemies shall be forgiven unto men." "Be not faithless, but believing." Then did Christian again a little revive, and stood up trembling, as at first, before Evangelist.

Then Evangelist proceeded, saying, Give more earnest heed to the things that I shall tell thee of. I will now show thee who it was that deluded thee, and who it was also to whom he sent thee. The man that met thee is one Worldly Wiseman, and rightly is he so called; partly because he favoreth only the doctrine of this world (therefore he always goes to the town of Morality to church): and partly because he loveth that doctrine best, for it saveth him best from the cross. And because he is of this carnal temper, therefore he seeketh to prevent my ways, though right. Now there are three things in this man's counsel that thou must utterly abhor.

1. His turning thee out of the way. 2. His laboring to render the cross odious to thee. 3. His setting thy feet in that way that leadeth unto the administration of death.

First, thou must abhor his turning thee out of the way; yea, and thine own consenting thereto: because this is to reject the counsel of God for the sake of the counsel of a Worldly Wiseman. The Lord says, "Strive to enter in at the strait gate," the gate to which I send thee; for "strait is the gate that leadeth unto life, and few there be that find it." From this little wicket-gate, and from the way thereto, hath this wicked man turned thee, to the bringing of thee almost to destruction; hate, therefore, his turning thee out of the way, and abhor thyself for hearkening to him.

Secondly, thou must abhor his laboring to render the cross odious unto thee; for thou art to prefer it before "the treasures in Egypt." Besides, the King of Glory hath told thee that he that "will save his life shall lose it"; and he that comes after him, "and hates not his father, and mother, and wife, and children, and brethren, and sisters, yea, and his own life also, he cannot be my disciple." I say, therefore, for man to labor to persuade thee that that shall be thy death, without which, the truth hath said, thou canst not have eternal life; this doctrine thou must abhor.

Thirdly, thou must hate his setting of thy feet in the way that leadeth to the ministration of death. And for this thou must consider to whom he sent thee, and also how unable that person was to deliver thee from thy burden.

He to whom thou wast sent for ease, being by name Legality, is the son of the bondwoman which now is in bondage with her children, and is, in a mystery,[13]

13 Symbolically.

this Mount Sinai, which thou has feared will fall on thy head. Now if she, with her children, are in bondage, how canst thou expect by them to be made free? This Legality, therefore, is not able to set thee free from thy burden. No man was as yet ever rid of his burden by him; no, nor ever is like to be: ye cannot be justified by the works of the law; for by the deeds of the law no man living can be rid of his burden: therefore, Mr. Worldly Wiseman is an alien, and Mr. Legality is a cheat; and for his son Civility, notwithstanding his simpering looks, he is but a hypocrite and cannot help thee. Believe me, there is nothing in all this noise that thou hast heard of these sottish men, but a design to beguile thee of thy salvation, by turning thee from the way in which I had set thee. After this, Evangelist called aloud to the heavens for confirmation of what he had said: and with that there came words and fire out of the mountain under which poor Christian stood, that made the hair of his flesh stand up. The words were thus pronounced: "As many as are of the works of the law are under the curse; for it is written, Cursed is every one that continueth not in all things which are written in the book of the law to do them."

Now Christian looked for nothing but death, and began to cry out lamentably; even cursing the time in which he met with Mr. Worldly Wiseman; still calling himself a thousand fools for hearkening to his counsel; he also was greatly ashamed to think that this gentleman's arguments, flowing only from the flesh, should have the prevalency with him as to cause him to forsake the right way. This done, he applied himself again to Evangelist in words and sense as follows:

CHR. Sir, what think you? Is there hopes? May I now go back and go up to the wicket-gate? Shall I not be abandoned for this, and sent back from thence ashamed? I am sorry I have hearkened to this man's counsel. But may my sin be forgiven?

EVAN. Then said Evangelist to him, Thy sin is very great, for by it thou hast committed two evils: thou hast forsaken the way that is good, to tread in forbidden paths; yet will the man at the gate receive thee, for he has good-will for men; only, said he, take heed that thou turn not aside again, "lest thou perish from the way, when his wrath is kindled but a little." Then did Christian address himself to go back; and Evangelist, after he had kissed him, gave him one smile, and bid him God-speed. So he went on with haste, neither spake he to any man by the way; nor, if any asked him, would he vouchsafe them an answer. He went like one that was all the while treading on forbidden ground, and could by no means think himself safe, till again he was got into the way which he left to follow Mr. Worldly Wiseman's counsel. So in process of time Christian got up to the gate. . . .

[SIMPLE, SLOTH, AND PRESUMPTION; FORMALIST AND HYPOCRISY]

NOW I saw in my dream, that the highway up which Christian was to go, was fenced on either side with a wall, and that wall was called Salvation. Up this way, therefore, did burdened Christian run, but not without great difficulty, because of the load on his back.

He ran thus till he came at a place somewhat ascending, and upon that place stood a cross, and a little below, in the bottom, a sepulchre. So I saw in my dream, that just as Christian came up with the cross, his burden loosed from off his shoulders, and fell from off his back, and began to tumble, and so continued to do, till it came to the mouth of the sepulchre, where it fell in, and I saw it no more.

Then was Christian glad and lightsome, and said, with a merry heart, "He hath given me rest by His sorrow, and life by His death." Then he stood still awhile to look and wonder; for it was very surprising to him, that the sight of the cross should thus ease him of his burden. He looked, therefore, and looked again, even till the springs that were in his head sent the waters down his cheeks. Now, as he stood looking and weeping, behold, three Shining Ones came to him and saluted him with "Peace be to thee." So the first said to him, "Thy sins be forgiven thee." The second stripped him of his rags, and clothed him with change of raiment. The third also set a mark in his forehead, and gave him a roll with a seal upon it, which he bid him look on as he ran, and that he should give it in at the Celestial Gate. So they went their way.

Then Christian gave three leaps for joy, and went on singing,

Thus far I did come loaden with my sin;
Nor could aught ease the grief that I was in
Till I came hither: What a place is this!
Must here be the beginning of my bliss?
Must here the burden fall from off my back?
Must here the strings that bound it to me crack?
Blest cross! blest sepulchre! blest rather be
The man that there was put to shame for me!

I saw then in my dream, that he went on thus, even until he came at a bottom, where he saw, a little out of the way, three men fast asleep, with fetters upon their heels. The name of the one was Simple, another Sloth, and the third Presumption.

Christian then seeing them lie in this case, went to them, if peradventure he might awake them, and cried, "You are like them that sleep on the top of a mast, for the Dead Sea is under you—a gulf that hath no bottom. Awake, therefore, and come away; be willing also, and I will help you off with your irons." He also told them, "If he that 'goeth about like a roaring lion' comes by, you will certainly become a prey to his teeth." With that they looked upon him, and began to reply in this sort: Simple said, "I see no danger;" Sloth said, "Yet a little more sleep;" and Presumption said, "Every fat[14] must stand upon his own bottom." And so they lay down to sleep again, and Christian went on his way.

Yet was he troubled to think that men in that danger should so little esteem the kindness of him that so freely offered to help them, both by awakening of them, counseling of them, and proffering to help them off with their irons. And as he was troubled thereabout, he espied two men come tumbling over the wall, on the left hand of the narrow way; and they made up apace to him. The name of the one was Formalist, and the name of the other Hypocrisy. So, as I said, they drew up unto him, who thus entered with them into discourse.

CHR. Gentlemen, whence came you, and whither do you go?

FORM. and HYP. We were born in the land of Vainglory, and are going for praise to Mount Sion.

CHR. Why came you not in at the gate which standeth at the beginning of the way? Know you not that it is written, that "he that cometh not in by the door, but climbeth up some other way, the same is a thief and a robber"?

FORM. and HYP. They said, That to go to the gate for entrance was by all their countrymen counted too far about; and that therefore their usual way was to make a short cut of it, and to climb over the wall, as they had done.

CHR. But will it not be counted a trespass against the Lord of the city whither we are bound, thus to violate his revealed will?

FORM. and HYP. They told him, that, as for that, he needed not to trouble his head thereabout; for what they did they had custom for; and could produce (if

need were) testimony that would witness it for more than a thousand years.

CHR. But, said Christian, will your practice stand a trial at law?

FORM. and HYP. They told him, That custom, it being of so long a standing as above a thousand years, would doubtless now be admitted as a thing legal by any impartial judge; and beside, said they, if we get into the way, what's matter which way we get in? If we are in, we are in; thou art but in the way, who, as we perceive, came in at the gate; and we are also in the way that came tumbling over the wall; wherein now is thy condition better than ours?

CHR. I walk by the rule of my Master; you walk by the rude working of your fancies. You are counted thieves already by the Lord of the way; therefore I doubt[15] you will not be found true men at the end of the way. You come in by yourselves without his direction, and shall go out by yourselves without his mercy.

To this they made him but little answer; only they bid him look to himself. Then I saw that they went on every man in his way, without much conference one with another; save that these two men told Christian, that as to laws and ordinances, they doubted not but they should as conscientiously do them as he; therefore, said they, we see not wherein thou differest from us but by the coat that is on thy back, which was, as we trow, given thee by some of thy neighbors, to hide the shame of thy nakedness.

CHR. By laws and ordinances you will not be saved, since you came not in by the door. And as for this coat that is on my back, it was given me by the Lord of the place whither I go; and that, as you say, to cover my nakedness with. And I take it as a token of his kindness to me; for I had nothing but rags before. And besides, thus I comfort myself as I go: Surely, think I, when I come to the gate of the city, the Lord thereof will know me for good, since I have his coat on my back, a coat that he gave me freely in the day that he stripped me of my rags. I have, moreover, a mark in my forehead, of which perhaps you have taken no notice, which one of my Lord's most intimate associates fixed there in the day that my burden fell off my shoulders. I will tell you, moreover, that I had then given me a roll, sealed, to comfort me by reading as I go on the way; I was also bid to give it in at the Celestial Gate, in token of my certain going in after it; all which things I doubt you want,[16]

14 Vat, tub.

15 Fear.

16 Fear that you do not have.

and want them because you came not in at the gate.

To these things they gave him no answer; only they looked upon each other and laughed. Then I saw that they went on all, save that Christian kept before, who had no more talk but with himself, and that sometimes sighingly and sometimes comfortably; also he would be often reading in the roll that one of the Shining Ones gave him, by which he was refreshed.

[THE HILL DIFFICULTY AND THE PALACE BEAUTIFUL]

I BEHELD, then, that they all went on till they came to the foot of the Hill Difficulty; at the bottom of which was a spring. There was also in the same place two other ways besides that which came straight from the gate; one turned to the left hand, and the other to the right, at the bottom of the hill; but the narrow way lay right up the hill, and the name of the going up the side of the hill is called Difficult. Christian now went to the spring, and drank thereof, to refresh himself, and then began to go up the hill, saying,

> The hill, though high, I covet to ascend,
> The difficulty will not me offend;
> For I perceive the way to life lies here.
> Come, pluck up heart, let's neither faint nor fear;
> Better, though difficult, the right way to go,
> Than wrong, though easy, where the end is woe.

The other two also came to the foot of the hill; but when they saw that the hill was steep and high, and that there was two other ways to go; and supposing also that these two ways might meet again, with that up which Christian went, on the other side of the hill, therefore they were resolved to go in those ways. Now the name of one of those ways was Danger, and the name of the other Destruction. So the one took the way which is called Danger, which did lead him into a great wood, and the other took directly up the way to Destruction, which led him into a wide field, full of dark mountains, where he stumbled and fell, and rose no more.

I looked then, after Christian, to see him go up the hill, where I perceived he fell from running to going,[17] and from going to clambering upon his hands and his knees, because of the steepness of the place. Now, about the midway to the top of the hill was a pleasant arbor, made by the Lord of the hill for the refreshing of weary travelers; thither, therefore, Christian got, where also he sat down to rest him. Then he pulled

17 Walking.

his roll out of his bosom, and read therein to his comfort; he also now began afresh to take a review of the coat or garment that was given him as he stood by the cross. Thus pleasing himself awhile, he at last fell into a slumber, and thence into a fast sleep, which detained him in that place until it was almost night; and in his sleep his roll fell out of his hand. Now, as he was sleeping, there came one to him, and awaked him, saying, "Go to the ant, thou sluggard; consider her ways, and be wise." And with that Christian suddenly started up, and sped him on his way, and went apace, till he came to the top of the hill.

Now, when he was got up to the top of the hill, there came two men running to meet him amain; the name of the one was Timorous, and the other, Mistrust; to whom Christian said, "Sirs, what's the matter you run the wrong way?" Timorous answered, that they were going to the City of Zion, and had got up that difficult place; "but," said he, "the further we go, the more danger we meet with; wherefore we turned, and are going back again."

"Yes," said Mistrust, "for just before us lies a couple of lions in the way, whether sleeping or waking we know not, and we could not think, if we came within reach, but they would presently pull us in pieces."

CHR. Then said Christian, "You make me afraid, but whither shall I fly to be safe? If I go back to mine own country, that is prepared for fire and brimstone, and I shall certainly perish there. If I can go to the Celestial City, I am sure to be in safety there. I must venture. To go back is nothing but death; to go forward is fear of death, and life everlasting beyond it. I will yet go forward." So Mistrust and Timorous ran down the hill, and Christian went on his way. But, thinking again of what he heard from the men, he felt in his bosom for his roll, that he might read therein, and be comforted; but he felt, and found it not. Then was Christian in great distress, and knew not what to do; for he wanted[18] that which used to relieve him, and that which should have been his pass into the Celestial City. Here, therefore, he began to be much perplexed, and knew not what to do. At last he bethought himself that he had slept in the arbor that is on the side of the hill; and, falling down upon his knees, he asked God's forgiveness for that foolish act, and then went back to look for his roll. But all the way he went back, who can sufficiently set forth the sorrow of Christian's heart! Sometimes he sighed,

18 Lacked.

sometimes he wept, and oftentimes he chid himself for being so foolish to fall asleep in that place, which was erected only for a little refreshment for his weariness. Thus, therefore, he went back, carefully looking on this side and on that, all the way as he went, if happily he might find the roll, that had been his comfort so many times in his journey. He went thus, till he came again within sight of the arbor where he sat and slept; but that sight renewed his sorrow the more, by bringing again, even afresh, his evil of sleeping unto his mind. Thus, therefore, he now went on bewailing his sinful sleep, saying, "O wretched man that I am! that I should sleep in the day-time! that I should sleep in the midst of difficulty! that I should so indulge the flesh as to use that rest for ease to my flesh which the Lord of the hill hath erected only for the relief of the spirits of pilgrims!

How many steps have I took in vain! Thus it happened to Israel, for their sin; they were sent back again by the way of the Red Sea; and I am made to tread those steps with sorrow, which I might have trod with delight, had it not been for this sinful sleep. How far might I have been on my way by this time! I am made to tread those steps thrice over, which I needed not to have trod but once; yea, now also I am like to be benighted, for the day is almost spent. Oh, that I had not slept!"

Now by this time he was come to the arbor again, where for a while he sat down and wept; but at last, as Christian would have it, looking sorrowfully down under the settle, there he espied his roll; the which he, with trembling and haste, catched up, and put into his bosom. But who can tell how joyful this man was when he had gotten his roll again! for this roll was the assurance of his life and acceptance at the desired haven. Therefore he laid it up in his bosom, gave thanks to God for directing his eye to the place where it lay, and with joy and tears betook himself again to his journey. But oh, how nimbly did he go up the rest of the hill! Yet, before he got up, the sun went down upon Christian; and this made him again recall the vanity of his sleeping to his remembrance; and thus he again began to condole with himself. "O thou sinful sleep: how, for thy sake, am I like to be benighted in my journey! I must walk without the sun; darkness must cover the path of my feet; and I must hear the noise of the doleful creatures, because of my sinful sleep." Now also he remembered the story that Mistrust and Timorous told him of, how they were frighted with the sight of the lions. Then said Christian

to himself again, "These beasts range in the night for their prey; and if they should meet with me in the dark, how should I shift[19] them? How should I escape being by them torn in pieces?" Thus he went on. But while he was thus bewailing his unhappy miscarriage, he lift up his eyes, and behold there was a very stately palace before him, the name of which was Beautiful; and it stood by the highway side.

So I saw in my dream that he made haste and went forward, that if possible he might get lodging there. Now, before he had gone far, he entered into a very narrow passage, which was about a furlong off the porter's lodge; and looking very narrowly before him as he went, he espied two lions in the way. "Now," thought he, "I see the dangers that Mistrust and Timorous were driven back by." (The lions were chained, but he saw not the chains.) Then he was afraid, and thought also himself to go back after them, for he thought nothing but death was before him. But the porter at the lodge, whose name is Watchful, perceiving that Christian made a halt as if he would go back, cried unto him, saying, "Is thy strength so small? Fear not the lions, for they are chained, and are placed there for trial of faith where it is, and for discovery of those that have none. Keep in the midst of the path, and no hurt shall come unto thee."

Then I saw that he went on, trembling for fear of the lions, but taking good heed to the directions of the porter; he heard them roar, but they did him no harm. Then he clapped his hands, and went on till he came and stood before the gate where the porter was. Then said Christian to the porter, "Sir, what house is this? And may I lodge here to-night?" The porter answered, "This house was built by the Lord of the hill, and he built it for the relief and security of pilgrims." The porter also asked whence he was, and whither he was going.

CHR. I am come from the City of Destruction, and am going to Mount Zion; but because the sun is now set, I desire, if I may, to lodge here to-night.

POR. What is your name?

CHR. My name is now Christian, but my name at the first was Graceless; I came of the race of Japheth, whom God will persuade to dwell in the tents of Shem.

POR. But how doth it happen you come so late? The sun is set.

CHR. I had been here sooner, but that, wretched man that I am! I slept in the arbor that stands on the

19 Escape.

hillside; nay, I had, notwithstanding that, been here much sooner, but that, in my sleep, I lost my evidence, and came without it to the brow of the hill; and then feeling for it, and finding it not, I was forced, with sorrow of heart, to go back to the place where I slept my sleep, where I found it, and now I am come.

POR. Well, I will call out one of the virgins of this place, who will, if she likes your talk, bring you in to the rest of the family, according to the rules of the house. So Watchful, the porter, rang a bell, at the sound of which came out at the door of the house a grave and beautiful damsel, named Discretion, and asked why she was called.

The porter answered, "This man is in a journey from the City of Destruction to Mount Zion, but being weary and benighted, he asked me if he might lodge here to-night; so I told him I would call for thee, who, after discourse had with him, mayest do as seemeth thee good, even according to the law of the house."

Then she asked him whence he was, and whither he was going; and he told her. She asked also how he got in the way; and he told her. Then she asked him what he had seen and met with in the way; and he told her. And last she asked his name; so he said, "It is Christian, and I have so much the more a desire to lodge here to-night, because, by what I perceive, this place was built by the Lord of the hill, for the relief and security of pilgrims." So she smiled, but the water stood in her eyes; and after a little pause, she said, "I will call forth two or three more of the family." So she ran to the door, and called out Prudence, Piety, and Charity, who, after a little more discourse with him, had him into the family; and many of them, meeting him at the threshold of the house, said, "Come in, thou blessed of the Lord; this house was built by the Lord of the hill, on purpose to entertain such pilgrims in." Then he bowed his head, and followed them into the house. So when he was come in and sat down, they gave him something to drink, and consented together, that until supper was ready, some of them should have some particular discourse with Christian, for the best improvement of time; and they appointed Piety, and Prudence, and Charity to discourse with him. . . .

Then I saw in my dream, that on the morrow he got up to go forwards, but they desired him to stay till the next day also; "and then," said they, "we will, if the day be clear, show you the Delectable Mountains," which, they said, would yet further add to his comfort, because they were nearer the desired haven

than the place where at present he was; so he consented and stayed. When the morning was up, they had him to the top of the house, and bid him look south; so he did: and behold, at a great distance, he saw a most pleasant mountainous country, beautified with woods, vineyards, fruits of all sorts, flowers also, with springs and fountains, very delectable to behold. Then he asked the name of the country. They said it was Immanuel's Land; "and it is as common," said they, "as this hill is, to and for all the pilgrims. And when thou comest there, from thence," said they, "thou mayest see to the gate of the Celestial City, as the shepherds that live there will make appear."

Now he bethought himself of setting forward, and they were willing he should. "But first," said they, "let us go again into the armory." So they did; and when he came there, they harnessed him from head to foot with what was of proof,[20] lest, perhaps, he should meet with assaults in the way. He being, therefore, thus accoutered, walketh out with his friends to the gate, and there he asked the porter if he saw any pilgrims pass by. Then the porter answered, "Yes."

CHR. "Pray, did you know him?" said he.

POR. I asked him his name, and he told me it was Faithful.

CHR. "Oh," said Christian, "I know him; he is my townsman, my near neighbor; he comes from the place where I was born. How far do you think he may be before?"

POR. He is got by this time below the hill.

CHR. "Well," said Christian, "good Porter, the Lord be with thee, and add to all thy blessings much increase, for the kindness that thou hast showed to me."

Then he began to go forward; but Discretion, Piety, Charity, and Prudence would accompany him down to the foot of the hill. So they went on together, reiterating their former discourses, till they came to go down the hill. Then said Christian, "As it was difficult coming up, so, so far as I can see, it is dangerous going down." "Yes," said Prudence, "so it is, for it is a hard matter for a man to go down into the Valley of Humiliation, as thou art now, and to catch no slip by the way." "Therefore," said they, "are we come out to accompany thee down the hill." So he began to go down, but very warily; yet he caught a slip or two.

Then I saw in my dream that these good companions, when Christian was gone down to the bottom

20 Armor of tried strength.

of the hill, gave him a loaf of bread, a bottle of wine, and a cluster of raisins; and then he went on his way.

[CHRISTIAN AND APOLLYON]

BUT now in this Valley of Humiliation poor Christian was hard put to it; for he had gone but a little way before he espied a foul fiend coming over the field to meet him; his name is Apollyon.[21] Then did Christian begin to be afraid, and to cast in his mind whether to go back or to stand his ground. But he considered again that he had no armor for his back; and therefore thought that to turn the back to him might give him the greater advantage with ease to pierce him with his darts. Therefore he resolved to venture and stand his ground; "for," thought he, "had I no more in mine eye than the saving of my life, it would be the best way to stand."

So he went on, and Apollyon met him. Now the monster was hideous to behold; he was clothed with scales, like a fish (and they are his pride), he had wings like a dragon, feet like a bear, and out of his belly came fire and smoke, and his mouth was as the mouth of a lion. When he was come up to Christian, he beheld him with a disdainful countenance, and thus began to question with him.

APOL. Whence come you? and whither are you bound?

CHR. I am come from the City of Destruction, which is the place of all evil, and am going to the City of Zion.

APOL. By this I perceive thou art one of my subjects, for all that country is mine, and I am the prince and god of it. How is it, then, that thou hast run away from thy king? Were it not that I hope thou mayest do me more service, I would strike thee now, at one blow, to the ground.

CHR. I was born, indeed, in your dominions, but your service was hard, and your wages such as a man could not live on, "for the wages of sin is death"; therefore, when I was come to years, I did as other considerate persons do, look out, if, perhaps, I might mend myself.

APOL. There is no prince that will thus lightly lose his subjects, neither will I as yet lose thee; but since thou complainest of thy service and wages, be content to go back: what our country will afford, I do here promise to give thee.

CHR. But I have let myself to another, even to the King of princes; and how can I with fairness, go back with thee?

APOL. Thou hast done in this, according to the proverb, "Change a bad for a worse"; but it is ordinary for those that have professed themselves His servants, after a while to give Him the slip, and return again to me. Do thou so too, and all shall be well.

CHR. I have given Him my faith, and sworn my allegiance to Him; how, then, can I go back from this, and not be hanged as a traitor?

APOL. Thou didst the same by me, and yet I am willing to pass by all, if now thou wilt yet turn again and go back.

CHR. What I promised thee was in my nonage; and, besides, I count that the Prince under whose banner now I stand is able to absolve me; yea, and to pardon also what I did as to my compliance with thee; and besides, O thou destroying Apollyon! to speak truth, I like His service, His wages, His servants, His government, His company, and country better than thine; and therefore leave off to persuade me further; I am His servant, and I will follow Him.

APOL. Consider, again, when thou art in cool blood, what thou art like to meet with in the way that thou goest. Thou knowest that, for the most part, His servants come to an ill end, because they are transgressors against me and my way. How many of them have been put to shameful death; and, besides, thou countest His service better than mine, whereas He never came yet from the place where He is to deliver any that served Him out of their hands; but as for me, how many times, as all the world very well knows, have I delivered, either by power or fraud, those that have faithfully served me, from Him and His, though taken by them; and so I will deliver thee.

CHR. His forbearing at present to deliver them is on purpose to try their love, whether they will cleave to Him to the end; and as for the ill end thou sayest they come to, that is most glorious in their account; for, for present deliverance, they do not much expect it, for they stay for their glory, and then they shall have it, when their Prince comes in His, and the glory of the angels.

APOL. Thou hast already been unfaithful in thy service to Him; and how dost thou think to receive wages of Him?

CHR. Wherein, O Apollyon! have I been unfaithful to him?

APOL. Thou didst faint at first setting out, when thou wast almost choked in the Gulf of Despond;

21 Destroyer (Greek). See Revelation 9:11 and 13:2.

thou didst attempt wrong ways to be rid of thy burden, whereas thou shouldst have stayed till thy Prince had taken it off; thou didst sinfully sleep and lose thy choice thing; thou wast, also, almost persuaded to go back, at the sight of the lions; and when thou talkest of thy journey, and of what thou hast heard and seen, thou art inwardly desirous of vainglory in all that thou sayest or doest.

CHR. All this is true, and much more which thou hast left out; but the Prince whom I serve and honor is merciful, and ready to forgive; but, besides, these infirmities possessed me in thy country, for there I sucked them in; and I have groaned under them, been sorry for them, and have obtained pardon of my Prince.

APOL. Then Apollyon broke out into a grievous rage, saying, "I am an enemy to this Prince; I hate His person, His laws, and people; I am come out on purpose to withstand thee."

CHR. Apollyon, beware what you do; for I am in the King's highway, the way of holiness; therefore take heed to yourself.

APOL. Then Apollyon straddled quite over the whole breadth of the way, and said, "I am void of fear in this matter: prepare thyself to die; for I swear by my infernal den, that thou shalt go no further; here will I spill thy soul."

And with that he threw a flaming dart at his breast; but Christian had a shield in his hand, with which he caught it, and so prevented the danger of that.

Then did Christian draw, for he saw it was time to bestir him: and Apollyon as fast made at him, throwing darts as thick as hail; by the which, notwithstanding all that Christian could do to avoid it, Apollyon wounded him in his head, his hand, and foot. This made Christian give a little back; Apollyon, therefore, followed his work amain, and Christian again took courage, and resisted as manfully as he could. This sore combat lasted for above half a day, even till Christian was almost quite spent; for you must know that Christian, by reason of his wounds, must needs grow weaker and weaker.

Then Apollyon, espying his opportunity, began to gather up close to Christian, and wrestling with him, gave him a dreadful fall; and with that Christian's sword flew out of his hand. Then said Apollyon, "I am sure of thee now." And with that he had almost pressed him to death, so that Christian began to despair of life: but as God would have it, while Apollyon was fetching his last blow, thereby to make a full end of this good man, Christian nimbly stretched out his hand for his sword, and caught it saying, "Rejoice not against me, O mine enemy: when I fall I shall arise"; and with that gave him a deadly thrust, which made him give back, as one that had received his mortal wound. Christian, perceiving that, made at him again, saying, "Nay, in all these things we are more than conquerors through Him that loved us." And with that Apollyon spread forth his dragon's wings, and sped him away, that Christian saw him no more.

In this combat no man can imagine, unless he had seen and heard as I did, what yelling and hideous roaring Apollyon made all the time of the fight—he spake like a dragon; and, on the other side, what sighs and groans burst from Christian's heart. I never saw him all the while give so much as one pleasant look, till he perceived he had wounded Apollyon with his two-edged sword; then, indeed, he did smile, and look upward; but it was the dreadfulest sight that ever I saw. . . .

[THE VALLEY OF THE SHADOW OF DEATH]

Now, at the end of this valley was another, called the Valley of the Shadow of Death, and Christian must needs go through it, because the way to the Celestial City lay through the midst of it. Now, this valley is a very solitary place. The prophet Jeremiah thus describes it: "A wilderness, a land of deserts and of pits, a land of drought, and of the shadow of death, a land that no man" (but a Christian) "passeth through, and where no man dwelt."

Now here Christian was worse put to it than in his fight with Apollyon: as by the sequel you shall see.

I saw then in my dream, that when Christian was got to the borders of the Shadow of Death, there met him two men, children of them that brought up an evil report of the good land,[22] making haste to go back; to whom Christian spake as follows:

CHR. Whither are you going?

MEN. They said, "Back! back! and we would have you to do so too, if either life or peace is prized by you."

CHR. "Why, what's the matter?" said Christian.

MEN. "Matter!" said they; "we were going that way as you are going, and went as far as we durst; and indeed we were almost past coming back; for had we gone a little further, we had not been here to bring the news to thee."

22 See Numbers 13.

CHR. "But what have you met with?" said Christian.

MEN. Why, we were almost in the Valley of the Shadow of Death; but that, by good hap, we looked before us, and saw the danger before we came to it.

CHR. "But what have you seen?" said Christian.

MEN. Seen! Why, the Valley itself, which is as dark as pitch; we also saw there the hobgoblins, satyrs, and dragons of the pit; we heard also in that Valley a continual howling and yelling, as of a people under unutterable misery, who there sat bound in affliction and irons; and over that Valley hangs the discouraging clouds of confusion. Death also doth always spread his wings over it. In a word, it is every whit dreadful, being utterly without order.

CHR. "Then," said Christian, "I perceive not yet, by what you have said, but that this is my way to the desired haven."

MEN. Be it thy way; we will not choose it for ours. So they parted, and Christian went on his way, but still with his sword drawn in his hand, for fear lest he should be assaulted.

I saw then in my dream so far as this Valley reached, there was on the right hand a very deep ditch; that ditch is it into which the blind hath led the blind in all ages, and have both there miserably perished. Again, behold, on the left hand, there was a very dangerous quag, into which, if even a good man falls, he finds no bottom for his foot to stand on. Into this quag King David once did fall, and had no doubt there been smothered, had not He that is able plucked him out.

The pathway was here also exceeding narrow, and therefore good Christian was the more put to it; for when he sought, in the dark, to shun the ditch on the one hand, he was ready to tip over into the mire on the other; also when he sought to escape the mire, without great carefulness he would be ready to fall into the ditch. Thus he went on, and I heard him here sigh bitterly; for, besides the danger mentioned above, the pathway was here so dark, that oft-times, when he lift up his foot to go forward, he knew not where nor upon what he should set it next.

About the midst of this Valley, I perceived the mouth of hell to be, and it stood also hard by the wayside. "Now," thought Christian, "what shall I do?" And ever and anon the flame and smoke would come out in such abundance, with sparks and hideous noises (things that cared not for Christian's sword, as did Apollyon before), that he was forced to put up his sword, and betake himself to another weapon, called All-prayer. So he cried in my hearing, "O Lord, I beseech thee, deliver my soul!" Thus he went on a great while, yet still the flames would be reaching towards him. Also he heard doleful voices, and rushings to and fro, so that sometimes he thought he should be torn in pieces, or trodden down like mire in the streets. This frightful sight was seen, and these dreadful noises were heard by him for several miles together; and, coming to a place where he thought he heard a company of fiends coming forward to meet him, he stopped, and began to muse what he had best to do. Sometimes he had half a thought to go back; then again he thought he might be half way through the Valley; he remembered also how he had already vanquished many a danger, and that the danger of going back might be much more than for to go forward; so he resolved to go on. Yet the fiends seemed to come nearer and nearer; but when they were come even almost at him, he cried out with a most vehement voice, "I will walk in the strength of the Lord God!" so they gave back, and came no further.

One thing I would not let slip; I took notice that now poor Christian was so confounded, that he did not know his own voice; and thus I perceived it. Just when he was come over against the mouth of the burning pit, one of the wicked ones got behind him, and stepped up softly to him, and whisperingly suggested many grievous blasphemies to him, which he verily thought had proceeded from his own mind. This put Christian more to it than anything that he met with before, even to think that he should now blaspheme Him that he loved so much before; yet, if he could have helped it, he would not have done it; but he had not the discretion either to stop his ears, or to know from whence those blasphemies came.

When Christian had traveled in this disconsolate condition some considerable time, he thought he heard the voice of a man, going before him, saying, "Though I walk through the Valley of the Shadow of Death, I will fear none ill, for Thou art with me."

Then was he glad, and that for these reasons:

First, Because he gathered from thence, that some who feared God were in this Valley as well as himself.

Secondly, For that he perceived God was with them, though in that dark and dismal state; "and why not," thought he, "with me? though, by reason of the impediment that attends this place, I cannot perceive it."

Thirdly, For that he hoped, could he overtake them, to have company by and by. So he went on, and called to him that was before; but he knew not what to answer; for that he also thought himself to be alone. And by and by the day broke; then said Christian, "He hath turned the shadow of death into the morning."

Now morning being come, he looked back, not of desire to return, but to see, by the light of the day, what hazards he had gone through in the dark. So he saw more perfectly the ditch that was on the one hand, and the quag that was on the other; also how narrow the way was which led betwixt them both; also now he saw the hobgoblins, and satyrs, and dragons of the pit, but all afar off (for after break of day, they came not nigh); yet they were discovered to him, according to that which is written, "He discovereth deep things out of darkness, and bringeth out to light the shadow of death."

Now was Christian much affected with his deliverance from all the dangers of his solitary way; which dangers, though he feared them more before, yet he saw them more clearly now, because the light of the day made them conspicuous to him. And about this time the sun was rising, and this was another mercy to Christian; for you must note, that though the first part of the Valley of the Shadow of Death was dangerous, yet this second part which he was yet to go, was, if possible, far more dangerous: for from the place where he now stood, even to the end of the Valley, the way was all along set so full of snares, traps, gins, and nets here, and so full of pits, pitfalls, deep holes, and shelvings down there, that, had it now been dark, as it was when he came the first part of the way, had he had a thousand souls, they had in reason been cast away; but, as I said just now, the sun was rising. Then, said he, "His candle shineth on my head, and by His light I go through darkness." In this light, therefore, he came to the end of the Valley. . . .

[CHRISTIAN MEETS FAITHFUL]

Now, as Christian went on his way, he came to a little ascent, which was cast up on purpose that pilgrims might see before them. Up there, therefore, Christian went, and looking forward, he saw Faithful before him, upon his journey. Then said Christian aloud, "Ho! ho! Soho! stay, and I will be your companion!" At that, Faithful looked behind him; to whom Christian cried again, "Stay, stay, till I come up to you." But Faithful answered, "No, I am upon my life, and the avenger of blood is behind me."

At this, Christian was somewhat moved, and putting to all his strength, he quickly got up with Faithful, and did also overrun him; so the last was first. Then did Christian vaingloriously smile, because he had gotten the start of his brother; but not taking good heed to his feet, he suddenly stumbled and fell, and could not rise again until Faithful came up to help him.

Then I saw in my dream they went very lovingly on together, and had sweet discourse of all things that had happened to them in their pilgrimage; and thus Christian began:

CHR. My honored and well-beloved Brother Faithful, I am glad that I have overtaken you; and that God has so tempered our spirits, that we can walk as companions in this so pleasant a path.

FAITH. I had thought, dear friend, to have had your company quite from our town; but you did get the start of me, wherefore I was forced to come thus much of the way alone.

CHR. How long did you stay in the City of Destruction, before you set out after me on your pilgrimage?

FAITH. Till I could stay no longer; for there was great talk presently after you were gone out, that our city would, in short time, with fire from heaven, be burned down to the ground.

CHR. What! did your neighbors talk so?

FAITH. Yes, 'twas for a while in everybody's mouth.

CHR. What! and did no more of them but you come out to escape the danger?

FAITH. Though there was, as I said, a great talk thereabout, yet I do not think they did firmly believe it. For in the heat of the discourse, I heard some of them deridingly speak of you and of your desperate journey (for so they called this your pilgrimage), but I did believe, and do still, that the end of our city will be with fire and brimstone from above; and therefore I have made my escape.

CHR. Did you hear no talk of Neighbor Pliable?

FAITH. Yes, Christian, I heard that he followed you till he came at the Slough of Despond, where, as some said, he fell in; but he would not be known to have so done; but I am sure he was soundly bedabbled with that kind of dirt.

CHR. And what said the neighbors to him?

FAITH. He hath, since his going back, been had greatly in derision, and that among all sorts of people; some do mock and despise him; and scarce will any set him on work. He is now seven times worse than if he had never gone out of the city.

CHR. But why should they be so set against him, since they also despise the way that he forsook?

FAITH. Oh, they say, "Hang him, he is a turncoat! he was not true to his profession." I think God has stirred up even his enemies to hiss at him, and make him a proverb, because he hath forsaken the way.

CHR. Had you no talk with him before you came out?

FAITH. I met him once in the streets, but he leered away on the other side, as one ashamed of what he had done; so I spake not to him.

CHR. Well, at my first setting out I had hopes of that man; but now I fear he will perish in the overthrow of the city; for "it is happened to him according to the true proverb, The dog is turned to his vomit again, and the sow that was washed to her wallowing in the mire."

FAITH. These are my fears of him too; but who can hinder that which will be?

CHR. Well, neighbor Faithful, said Christian, let us leave him and talk of things that more immediately concern ourselves. Tell me now what you have met with in the way as you came; for I know you have met with some things, or else it may be writ for a wonder.

FAITH. I escaped the Slough that I perceived you fell into, and got up to the gate without that danger; only I met with one whose name was Wanton, who had like to have done me a mischief.

CHR. It was well you escaped her net; Joseph was hard put to it by her, and he escaped her as you did; but it had like to have cost him his life. But what did she do to you?

FAITH. You cannot think (but that you know something) what a flattering tongue she had; she lay at me hard to turn aside with her, promising me all manner of content.

CHR. Nay, she did not promise you the content of a good conscience.

FAITH. You know what I mean; all carnal and fleshly content.

CHR. Thank God you have escaped her: the "abhorred of the Lord" shall fall into her ditch.

FAITH. Nay, I know not whether I did wholly escape her or no.

CHR. Why, I trow you did not consent to her desires?

FAITH. No, not to defile myself; for I remembered an old writing that I had seen, which said, "Her steps take hold of hell." So I shut mine eyes, because I would not be bewitched with her looks. Then she railed on me, and I went my way.

CHR. Did you meet with no other assault as you came?

FAITH. When I came to the foot of the hill called Difficulty, I met with a very aged man, who asked me what I was and whither bound. I told him that I was a pilgrim going to the Celestial City. Then said the old man, Thou lookest like an honest fellow; wilt thou be content to dwell with me for the wages that I shall give thee? Then I asked him his name and where he dwelt. He said his name was Adam the First, and that he dwelt in the town of Deceit. I asked him then what was his work and what the wages that he would give. He told me that his work was many delights; and his wages that I should be his heir at last. I further asked him what house he kept and what other servants he had. So he told me that his house was maintained with all the dainties in the world; and that his servants were those of his own begetting. Then I asked how many children he had. He said that he had but three daughters: "the lust of the flesh, the lust of the eyes, and the pride of life," and that I should marry them all if I would. Then I asked how long time he would have me live with him. And he told me, As long as he lived himself.

CHR. Well, and what conclusion came the old man and you to at last?

FAITH. Why, at first I found myself somewhat inclinable to go with the man, for I thought he spake very fair; but looking in his forehead, as I talked with him, I saw there written, "Put off the old man with his deeds."

CHR. And how then?

FAITH. Then it came burning hot into my mind, whatever he said and however he flattered, when he got me home to his house, he would sell me for a slave. So I bid him forbear to talk, for I would not come near the door of his house. Then he reviled me and told me that he would send such a one after me that should make my way bitter to my soul. So I turned to go away from him; but just as I turned myself to go thence, I felt him take hold of my flesh and give me such a deadly twitch back that I thought he had pulled part of me after himself. This made me cry, "Oh, wretched man!" So I went on my way up the hill.

Now when I had got about half way up, I looked

behind and saw one coming after me swift as the wind; so he overtook me just about the place where the settle stands.

CHR. Just there, said Christian, did I sit down to rest me; but being overcome with sleep, I there lost this roll out of my bosom.

FAITH. But, good brother, hear me out. So soon as the man overtook me, he was but a word and a blow, for down he knocked me and laid me for dead. But when I was a little come to myself again, I asked him wherefore he served me so. He said, because of my secret inclining to Adam the First: and with that he strook me another deadly blow on the breast and beat me down backward; so I lay at his foot as dead as before. So when I came to myself again, I cried him mercy; but he said, I know not how to show mercy; and with that knocked me down again. He had doubtless made an end of me, but that one came by and bid him forbear.

CHR. Who was that that bid him forbear?

FAITH. I did not know him at first, but as he went by I perceived the holes in his hands and his side; then I concluded that he was our Lord. So I went up the hill.

CHR. That man that overtook you was Moses. He spareth none, neither knoweth he how to show mercy to those that transgress his law.

FAITH. I know it very well; it was not the first time that he has met with me. It was he that came to me when I dwelt securely at home, and that told me he would burn my house over my head if I stayed there.

CHR. But did you not see the house that stood there on the top of the hill on the side of which Moses met you?

FAITH. Yes, and the lions too, before I came at it: but for the lions, I think they were asleep, for it was about noon; and because I had so much of the day before me, I passed by the porter and came down the hill.

CHR. He told me, indeed, that he saw you go by, but I wish you had called at the house, for they would have showed you so many rarities that you would scarce have forgot them to the day of your death. But pray tell me, did you meet nobody in the Valley of Humility?

FAITH. Yes, I met with one Discontent, who would willingly have persuaded me to go back again with him; his reason was, for that the valley was altogether without honor. He told me, moreover, that there to go was the way to disobey all my friends, as Pride, Arrogancy, Self-conceit, Worldly Glory, with others, who he knew, as he said, would be very much offended if I made such a fool of myself as to wade through this valley.

CHR. Well, and how did you answer him?

FAITH. I told him that although all these that he named might claim kindred of me, and that rightly (for indeed they were my relations according to the flesh); yet since I became a pilgrim they have disowned me, as I also have rejected them; and therefore they were to me now no more than if they had never been of my lineage. I told him, moreover, that as to this valley, he had quite misrepresented the thing; for "before honor is humility, and a haughty spirit before a fall." Therefore, said I, I had rather go through this valley to the honor that was so accounted by the wisest, than choose that which he esteemed most worthy our affections.

CHR. Met you with nothing else in that valley?

FAITH. Yes, I met with Shame; but of all the men that I met with in my pilgrimage, he, I think, bears the wrong name. The other would be said nay after a little argumentation (and somewhat else), but this bold-faced Shame would never have done.

CHR. Why, what did he say to you?

FAITH. What! why, he objected against religion itself; he said it was a pitiful, low, sneaking business for a man to mind religion; he said that a tender conscience was an unmanly thing; and that for a man to watch over his words and ways, so as to tie up himself from that hectoring liberty that the brave spirits of the times accustom themselves unto, would make him the ridicule of the times. He objected also that but few of the mighty, rich, or wise, were ever of my opinion; nor any of them neither before they were persuaded to be fools and to be of a voluntary fondness,[23] to venture the loss of all for nobody knows what. He, moreover, objected the base and low estate and condition of those that were chiefly the pilgrims of the times in which they lived: also their ignorance and want of understanding in all natural science. Yea, he did hold me to it at that rate also about a great many more things than here I relate; as that it was a *shame* to sit whining and mourning under a sermon, and a *shame* to come sighing and groaning home; that it was a *shame* to ask my neighbor forgiveness for petty faults, or to make restitution where I have taken from any. He said also that religion made a man grow strange to the great because of a few vices (which he

23 Foolishness.

called by finer names), and made him own and respect the base because of the same religious fraternity. And is not this, said he, a *shame*?

CHR. And what did you say to him?

FAITH. Say! I could not tell what to say at the first. Yea, he put me so to it that my blood came up in my face; even this Shame fetched it up and had almost beat me quite off. But at last I began to consider that "that which is highly esteemed among men is had in abomination with God." And I thought again, this Shame tells me what men are; but it tells me nothing what God or the Word of God is. And I thought, moreover, that at the day of doom we shall not be doomed to death or life according to the hectoring spirits of the world, but according to the wisdom and law of the Highest. Therefore, thought I, what God says is best, is best, though all the men in the world are against it. Seeing then that God prefers his religion; seeing God prefers a tender conscience; seeing they that make themselves fools for the kingdom of heaven are wisest; and that the poor man that loveth Christ is richer than the greatest man in the world that hates him; Shame, depart, thou art an enemy to my salvation! Shall I entertain thee against my sovereign Lord? How then shall I look him in the face at his coming? Should I now be ashamed of his ways and servants, how can I expect the blessing? But indeed this Shame was a bold villain; I could scarce shake him out of my company; yea, he would be haunting of me and continually whispering me in the ear, with some one or other of the infirmities that attend religion; but at last I told him it was but in vain to attempt further in this business; for those things that he disdained, in those did I see most glory; and so at last I got past this importunate one. And when I had shaken him off, then I began to sing:

> The trials that those men do meet withal
> That are obedient to the heavenly call,
> Are manifold and suited to the flesh,
> And come, and come, and come again afresh;
> That now, or sometime else, we by them may
> Be taken, overcome, and cast away.
> O, let the pilgrims, let the pilgrims then
> Be vigilant, and quit themselves like men.

CHR. I am glad, my brother, that thou didst withstand this villain so bravely; for of all, as thou sayest, I think he has the wrong name; for he is so bold as to follow us in the streets and to attempt to put us to shame before all men: that is, to make us ashamed of

that which is good; but if he was not himself audacious, he would never attempt to do as he does. But let us still resist him; for notwithstanding all his bravadoes he promoteth the fool and none else. "The wise shall inherit glory," said Solomon, "but shame shall be the promotion of fools."

FAITH. I think we must cry to him, for help against Shame, that would have us be valiant for truth upon the earth.

CHR. You say true; but did you meet nobody else in that valley?

FAITH. No, not I; for I had sunshine all the rest of the way through that, and also through the Valley of the Shadow of Death.

CHR. 'Twas well for you. I am sure it fared far otherwise with me. I had for a long season, as soon almost as I entered into that valley, a dreadful combat with that foul fiend Apollyon; yea, I thought verily he would have killed me, especially when he got me down and crushed me under him, as if he would have crushed me to pieces. For as he threw me, my sword flew out of my hand; nay, he told me he was sure of me: but I cried to God, and he heard me, and delivered me out of all my troubles. Then I entered into the Valley of the Shadow of Death, and had no light for almost half the way through it. I thought I should have been killed there, over and over; but at last day broke and the sun rose, and I went through that which was behind with far more ease and quiet. . . .

[CHRISTIAN AND FAITHFUL AT
VANITY FAIR]

THEN I saw in my dream, that when they were got out of the wilderness, they presently saw a town before them, and the name of that town is Vanity; and at the town there is a fair kept, called Vanity Fair:[24] it is kept all the year long; it beareth the name of Vanity Fair, because the town where it is kept is lighter than vanity; and also because all that is there sold, or that cometh thither, is vanity. As is the saying of the wise, "All that cometh is vanity."

24 When he coined the name of the fair, Bunyan gave the English language one of its most picturesque terms. In describing the fair he gives us a realistic picture of the ancient fairs of England, with all their hubbub, riot, and merriment, and, from a moralist's point of view, their thousand and one opportunities to waste time and money on "vanities." Bunyan probably had in mind the largest of all the fairs of his day, that of Stourbridge, which was held near Cambridge. Ben Jonson immortalized its chief rival, Bartholomew Fair, in his play of that name.

This fair is no new-erected business, but a thing of ancient standing; I will show you the original of it.

Almost five thousand years agone, there were pilgrims walking to the Celestial City, as these two honest persons are: and Beëlzebub, Apollyon, and Legion,[25] with their companions, perceiving by the path that the pilgrims made, that their way to the City lay through this town of Vanity, they contrived here to set up a fair; a fair wherein should be sold all sorts of vanity, and that it should last all the year long. Therefore at this fair are all such merchandise sold, as houses, lands, trades, places, honors, preferments, titles, countries, kingdoms, lusts, pleasures, and delights of all sorts, as whores, bawds, wives, husbands, children, masters, servants, lives, blood, bodies, souls, silver, gold, pearls, precious stones, and what not.

And, moreover, at this fair there is at all times to be seen jugglings, cheats, games, plays, fools, apes, knaves, and rogues, and that of every kind.

Here are to be seen, too, and that for nothing, thefts, murders, adulteries, false swearers, and that of a blood-red color.

And as in other fairs of less moment, there are the several rows of streets, under their proper names, where such wares are vended; so here likewise you have the proper places, rows, streets (*viz.* countries and kingdoms), where the wares of this fair are soonest to be found. Here is the Britain Row, the French Row, the Italian Row, the Spanish Row, the German Row, where several sorts of vanities are to be sold. But, as in other fairs, some one commodity is as the chief of all the fair, so the ware of Rome and her merchandise is greatly promoted in this fair; only our English nation, with some others, have taken a dislike thereat.

Now, as I said, the way to the Celestial City lies just through this town where this lusty[26] fair is kept; and he that will go to the City, and yet not go through this town, must needs "go out of the world." The Prince of princes Himself, when here, went through this town to His own country, and that upon a fair-day too; yea, and as I think, it was Beëlzebub, the chief lord of this fair, that invited Him to buy of his vanities; yea, would have made Him lord of the fair, would He but have done him reverence as He went through the town. Yea, because he was such a person of honor, Beëlzebub had him from street to street, and showed him all the kingdoms of the world in a little time, that he might, if possible, allure that

25 See St. Mark 5:9. 26 Joyous.

Blessed One to cheapen[27] and buy some of his vanities; but he had no mind to the merchandise, and therefore left the town without laying out so much as one farthing upon these vanities. This fair, therefore, is an ancient thing, of long standing, and a very great fair. Now these pilgrims, as I said, must needs go through this fair. Well, so they did: but, behold, even as they entered into the fair, all the people in the fair were moved, and the town itself as it were in a hubbub about them; and that for several reasons: for—

First, The pilgrims were clothed with such kind of raiment as was diverse from the raiment of any that traded in that fair. The people, therefore, of the fair made a great gazing upon them: some said they were fools, some they were bedlams, and some they were outlandish men.[28]

Secondly, And as they wondered at their apparel, so they did likewise at their speech; for few could understand what they said. They naturally spoke the language of Canaan, but they that kept the fair were the men of this world; so, that, from one end of the fair to the other, they seemed barbarians[29] each to the other.

Thirdly, But that which did not a little amuse the merchandisers was, that these pilgrims set very light by all their wares; they cared not so much as to look upon them; and if they called upon them to buy, they would put their fingers in their ears, and cry, "Turn away mine eyes from beholding vanity," and look upwards, signifying that their trade and traffic was in heaven.

One chanced mockingly, beholding the carriage[30] of the men, to say unto them, "What will ye buy?" But they, looking gravely upon him, said, "We buy the truth." At that there was an occasion taken to despise the men the more; some mocking, some taunting, some speaking reproachfully, and some calling upon others to smite them. At last things came to an hubbub and great stir in the fair, insomuch that all order was confounded. Now was word presently brought to the great one of the fair, who quickly came down, and deputed some of his most trusty friends to take these men into examination, about whom the fair was almost overturned. So the men were brought to examination; and they that sat upon them asked them whence they came, whither they went, and what they

27 Bargain. 28 Foreigners.
29 Used in the Classical and Biblical sense of "those who speak foreign tongues."
30 Behavior.

did there, in such an unusual garb? The men told them that they were pilgrims and strangers in the world, and that they were going to their own country, which was the heavenly Jerusalem; and that they had given no occasion to the men of the town, nor yet to the merchandisers, thus to abuse them, and to let[31] them in their journey, except it was for that, when one asked them what they would buy, they said they would buy the truth. But they that were appointed to examine them did not believe them to be any other than bedlams and mad, or else such as came to put all things into a confusion in the fair. Therefore they took them and beat them, and besmeared them with dirt, and then put them into the cage, that they might be made a spectacle to all the men of the fair.

There, therefore, they lay for some time, and were made the objects of any man's sport, or malice, or revenge, the great one of the fair laughing still at all that befell them. But the men being patient, and not rendering railing for railing, but contrariwise, blessing, and giving good words for bad, and kindness for injuries done, some men in the fair that were more observing, and less prejudiced than the rest, began to check and blame the baser sort for their continual abuses done by them to the men; they, therefore, in angry manner, let fly at them again, counting them as bad as the men in the cage, and telling them that they seemed confederates, and should be made partakers of their misfortunes. The other replied, that for aught they could see, the men were quiet, and sober, and intended nobody any harm; and that there were many that traded in their fair that were more worthy to be put into the cage, yea, and pillory too, than were the men they had abused. Thus, after divers words had passed on both sides, the men behaving themselves all the while very wisely and soberly before them, they fell to some blows among themselves, and did harm one to another. Then were these two poor men brought before their examiners again, and there charged as being guilty of the late hubbub that had been in the fair. So they beat them pitifully, and hanged irons upon them, and led them in chains up and down the fair, for an example and terror to others, lest any should speak in their behalf, or join themselves unto them. But Christian and Faithful behaved themselves yet more wisely, and received the ignominy and shame that was cast upon them, with so much meekness and patience, that it won to their side, though but few in comparison of the rest, several of the men in the

31 Hinder.

fair. This put the other party yet into a greater rage, insomuch that they concluded[32] the death of these two men. Wherefore they threatened, that neither the cage nor irons should serve their turn, but that they should die, for the abuse they had done, and for deluding the men of the fair.

Then were they remanded to the cage again, until further order should be taken with them. So they put them in, and made their feet fast in the stocks.

Here, therefore, they called again to mind what they had heard from their faithful friend Evangelist, and were the more confirmed in their way and sufferings, by what he told them would happen to them. They also now comforted each other, that whose lot it was to suffer, even he should have the best on it; therefore each man secretly wished that he might have that preferment: but committing themselves to the all-wise dispose of Him that ruleth all things, with much content they abode in the condition in which they were, until they should be otherwise disposed of.

Then a convenient time being appointed, they brought them forth to their trial, in order to their condemnation. When the time was come, they were brought before their enemies and arraigned. The Judge's name was Lord Hate-good. Their indictment was one and the same in substance, though somewhat varying in form, the contents whereof was this:

"That they were enemies to and disturbers of their trade; that they had made commotions and diversions in the town, and had won a party to their own most dangerous opinions, in contempt of the law of their prince."

Then Faithful began to answer, that he had only set himself against that which had set itself against Him that is higher than the highest. "And," said he, "as for disturbance, I make none, being myself a man of peace; the parties that were won to us, were won by beholding our truth and innocence, and they are only turned from the worse to the better. And as to the king you talk of, since he is Beëlzebub, the enemy of our Lord, I defy him and all his angels."

Then proclamation was made, that they that had aught to say for their lord the king against the prisoner at the bar, should forthwith appear and give in their evidence. So there came in three witnesses, to wit, Envy, Superstition, and Pickthank. They were then asked if they knew the prisoner at the bar; and what they had to say for their lord the king against him.

Then stood forth Envy, and said to this effect: "My

32 Determined upon.

Lord, I have known this man a long time, and will attest upon my oath before this honorable bench that he is—"

JUDGE. "Hold! Give him his oath." So they sware him. Then he said:

ENVY. My lord, this man, notwithstanding his plausible name, is one of the vilest men in our country. He neither regardeth prince nor people, law nor custom; but doth all that he can to possess all men with certain of his disloyal notions, which he in the general calls principles of faith and holiness. And, in particular, I heard him once myself affirm that Christianity and the customs of our town of Vanity were diametrically opposite, and could not be reconciled. By which saying, my lord, he doth at once not only condemn all our laudable doings, but us in the doing of them.

JUDGE. Then did the judge say to him, "Hast thou any more to say?"

ENVY. My lord, I could say much more, only I would not be tedious to the court. Yet, if need be, when the other gentlemen have given in their evidence, rather than anything shall be wanting that will dispatch him, I will enlarge my testimony against him. So he was bid stand by.

Then they called Superstition, and bid him look upon the prisoner. They also asked what he could say for their lord the king against him. Then they sware him; so he began.

SUPER. My lord, I have no great acquaintance with this man, nor do I desire to have farther knowledge of him; however, this I know, that he is a very pestilent fellow, from some discourse that, the other day, I had with him in this town; for then, talking with him, I heard him say, that our religion was naught, and such by which a man could by no means please God. Which sayings of his, my Lord, your Lordship very well knows, what necessarily thence will follow, to wit, that we do still worship in vain, are yet in our sins, and finally shall be damned; and this is that which I have to say.

Then was Pickthank sworn, and did say what he knew, in behalf of their lord the king against the prisoner at the bar.

PICK. My Lord, and you gentlemen all, this fellow I have known of a long time, and have heard him speak things that ought not to be spoke; for he hath railed on our noble prince Beëlzebub, and hath spoken contemptibly of his honorable friends, whose names are the Lord Old Man, the Lord Carnal Delight, the Lord Luxurious, the Lord Desire-of-Vain-Glory, my old Lord Lechery, Sir Having Greedy, with all the rest of our nobility; and he hath said, moreover, that if all men were of his mind, if possible, there is not one of these noblemen should have any longer a being in this town. Besides, he hath not been afraid to rail on you, my Lord, who are now appointed to be his judge, calling you an ungodly villain, with many other such like vilifying terms, with which he hath bespattered most of the gentry of our town.

When this Pickthank had told his tale, the Judge directed his speech to the prisoner at the bar, saying, "Thou runagate,[33] heretic, and traitor, hast thou heard what these honest gentlemen have witnessed against thee?"

FAITH. May I speak a few words in my own defense?

JUDGE. Sirrah! Sirrah! thou deservest to live no longer, but to be slain immediately upon the place; yet, that all men may see our gentleness towards thee, let us hear what thou, vile runagate, hast to say.

FAITH. 1. I say, then, in answer to what Mr. Envy hath spoken, I never said aught but this, that what rule, or laws, or customs, or people, were flat against the Word of God, are diametrically opposite to Christianity. If I have said amiss in this, convince me of my error, and I am ready here before you to make my recantation.

2. As to the second, to wit, Mr. Superstition, and his charge against me, I said only this, that in the worship of God there is required a divine faith; but there can be no divine faith without a divine revelation of the will of God. Therefore, whatever is thrust into the worship of God that is not agreeable to divine revelation, cannot be done but by a human faith, which faith will not be profitable to eternal life.

3. As to what Mr. Pickthank hath said, I say (avoiding terms, as that I am said to rail, and the like), that the prince of this town, with all the rabblement, his attendants, by this gentleman named, are more fit for a being in hell, than in this town and country: and so, the Lord have mercy upon me!

Then the Judge called to the jury (who all this while stood by, to hear and observe): "Gentlemen of the jury, you see this man about whom so great an uproar hath been made in this town. You have also heard what these worthy gentlemen have witnessed against him. Also you have heard his reply and confession. It lieth now in your breasts to hang him or save his life; but yet I think meet to instruct you in our law.

33 Renegade.

"There was an act made in the days of Pharaoh the Great, servant to our prince, that lest those of a contrary religion should multiply and grow too strong for him, their males should be thrown into the river. There was also an act made in the days of Nebuchadnezzar the Great, another of his servants, that whosoever would not fall down and worship his golden image, should be thrown into a fiery furnace. There was also an act made in the days of Darius, that whoso, for some time, called upon any god but him, should be cast into the lions' den. Now the substance of these laws this rebel has broken, not only in thought (which is not to be borne), but also in word and deed; which must therefore needs be intolerable.

"For that of Pharoah, his law was made upon supposition, to prevent mischief, no crime being yet apparent; but here is a crime apparent. For the second and third, you see he disputeth against our religion; and for the treason he hath confessed, he deserveth to die the death."

Then went the jury out, whose names were, Mr. Blind-man, Mr. No-good, Mr. Malice, Mr. Love-lust, Mr. Live-loose, Mr. Heady, Mr. High-mind, Mr. Enmity, Mr. Liar, Mr. Cruelty, Mr. Hate-light, and Mr. Implacable; who every one gave in his private verdict against him among themselves, and afterwards unanimously concluded to bring him in guilty before the Judge. And first, among themselves, Mr. Blind-man, the foreman, said, "I see clearly that this man is a heretic." Then said Mr. No-good, "Away with such a fellow from the earth." "Ay," said Mr. Malice, "for I hate the very looks of him." Then said Mr. Love-lust, "I could never endure him." "Nor I," said Mr. Live-loose, "for he would always be condemning my way." "Hang him, hang him," said Mr. Heady. "A sorry scrub," said Mr. High-mind. "My heart riseth against him," said Mr. Enmity. "He is a rogue," said Mr. Liar. "Hanging is too good for him," said Mr. Cruelty. "Let us dispatch him out of the way," said Mr. Hate-light. Then said Mr. Implacable, "Might I have all the world given me, I could not be reconciled to him; therefore, let us forthwith bring him in guilty of death." And so they did; therefore he was presently condemned to be had from the place where he was, to the place from whence he came, and there to be put to the most cruel death that could be invented.

They, therefore, brought him out, to do with him according to their law; and, first, they scourged him, then they buffeted him, then they lanced his flesh with knives; after that, they stoned him with stones, then pricked him with their swords; and, last of all, they burned him to ashes at the stake. Thus came Faithful to his end.

Now I saw that there stood behind the multitude a chariot and a couple of horses, waiting for Faithful, who (so soon as his adversaries had dispatched him) was taken up into it, and straightway was carried up through the clouds, with sound of trumpet, the nearest way to the Celestial Gate.

But as for Christian, he had some respite, and was remanded back to prison. So he there remained for a space; but He that overrules all things, having the power of their rage in His own hand, so wrought it about, that Christian for that time escaped them, and went his way. . . .

[CHRISTIAN, HOPEFUL, AND BY-ENDS]

NOW I saw in my dream, that Christian went not forth alone, for there was one whose name was Hopeful (being made so by the beholding of Christian and Faithful in their words and behavior, in their sufferings at the fair), who joined himself unto him, and, entering into a brotherly covenant, told him that he would be his companion. Thus, one died to bear testimony to the truth, and another rises out of his ashes, to be a companion with Christian in his pilgrimage. This Hopeful also told Christian, that there were many more of the men in the fair, that would take their time and follow after.

So I saw that quickly after they were got out of the fair, they overtook one that was going before them, whose name was By-ends: so they said to him, "What countryman, Sir? and how far go you this way?" He told them that he came from the town of Fair-speech, and he was going to the Celestial City, but told them not his name.

"From Fair-speech!" said Christian. "Is there any good that lives there?"

BY-ENDS. "Yes," said By-ends, "I hope."

CHR. "Pray, Sir, what may I call you?" said Christian.

BY-ENDS. I am a stranger to you, and you to me: if you be going this way, I shall be glad of your company; if not, I must be content.

CHR. "This town of Fair-speech," said Christian, "I have heard of; and, as I remember, they say, it is a wealthy place."

BY-ENDS. Yes, I will assure you that it is; and I have very many rich kindred there.

CHR. Pray, who are your kindred there? if a man may be so bold.

BY-ENDS. Almost the whole town; and in particular, my Lord Turn-about, my Lord Time-server, my Lord Fair-speech (from whose ancestors that town first took its name), also Mr. Smooth-man, Mr. Facing-both-ways, Mr. Any-thing; and the parson of our parish, Mr. Two-tongues, was my mother's own brother by father's side; and to tell you the truth, I am become a gentleman of good quality, yet my great-grandfather was but a waterman, looking one way and rowing another, and I got most of my estate by the same occupation.

CHR. Are you a married man?

BY-ENDS. Yes, and my wife is a very virtuous woman, the daughter of a virtuous woman; she was my Lady Feigning's daughter, therefore she came of a very honorable family, and is arrived to such a pitch of breeding, that she knows how to carry it to all, even to prince and peasant. It is true we somewhat differ in religion from those of the stricter sort, yet but in two small points: first, we never strive against wind and tide; secondly, we are always most zealous when religion goes in his silver slippers; we love much to walk with him in the street, if the sun shines, and the people applaud him.

Then Christian stepped a little aside to his fellow, Hopeful, saying, "It runs in my mind that this is one By-ends of Fair-speech; and if it be he, we have as very a knave in our company as dwelleth in all these parts." Then said Hopeful, "Ask him; methinks he should not be ashamed of his name." So Christian came up with him again, and said, "Sir, you talk as if you knew something more than all the world doth; and if I take not my mark amiss, I deem I have half a guess of you: Is not your name Mr. By-ends, of Fair-speech?"

BY-ENDS. This is not my name, but indeed it is a nickname, that is given me by some that cannot abide me: and I must be content to bear it as a reproach, as other good men have borne theirs before me.

CHR. But did you never give an occasion to men to call you by this name?

BY-ENDS. Never, never! The worst that ever I did to give them an occasion to give me this name was, that I had always the luck to jump in my judgment with the present way of the times, whatever it was, and my chance was to get thereby; but if things are thus cast upon me, let me count them a blessing; but let not the malicious load me therefore with reproach.

CHR. I thought, indeed, that you were the man that I heard of; and to tell you what I think, I fear this name belongs to you more properly than you are willing we should think it doth.

BY-ENDS. Well, if you will thus imagine, I cannot help it; you shall find me a fair company-keeper, if you will still admit me your associate.

CHR. If you will go with us, you must go against the wind and tide; the which, I perceive, is against your opinion; you must also own religion in his rags, as well as when in his silver slippers; and stand by him, too, when bound in irons, as well as when he walketh the streets with applause.

BY-ENDS. You must not impose, nor lord it over my faith; leave me to my liberty, and let me go with you.

CHR. Not a step further, unless you will do in what I propound as we.

"Then," said By-ends, "I shall never desert my old principles, since they are harmless and profitable. If I may not go with you, I must do as I did before you overtook me, even go by myself, until some overtake me that will be glad of my company."

Now I saw in my dream, that Christian and Hopeful forsook him, and kept their distance before him; but one of them looking back saw three men following Mr. By-ends, and behold, as they came up with him, he made them a very low *congé;* and they also gave him a compliment. The men's names were Mr. Hold-the-world, Mr. Money-love, and Mr. Save-all; men that Mr. By-ends had formerly been acquainted with; for in their minority they were schoolfellows, and were taught by one Mr. Gripe-man, a schoolmaster in Love-gain, which is a market town in the county of Coveting, in the north. This schoolmaster taught them the art of getting, either by violence, cozenage, flattery, lying, or by putting on a guise of religion; and these four gentlemen had attained much of the art of their master, so that they could each of them have kept such a school themselves.

Well, when they had, as I said, thus saluted each other, Mr. Money-love said to Mr. By-ends, "Who are they upon the road before us? (for Christian and Hopeful were yet within view)."

BY-ENDS. They are a couple of far countrymen, that, after their mode, are going on pilgrimage.

MONEY-LOVE. Alas! Why did they not stay, that we might have had their good company? for they, and we, and you, Sir, I hope, are all going on a pilgrimage.

BY-ENDS. We are so, indeed; but the men before us are so rigid, and love so much their own notions, and do also so lightly esteem the opinions of others, that let a man be never so godly, yet if he jumps not with them in all things, they thrust him quite out of their company.

SAVE-ALL. That's bad, but we read of some that are righteous overmuch; and such men's rigidness prevails with them to judge and condemn all but themselves. But, I pray, what, and how many, were the things wherein you differed?

BY-ENDS. Why, they, after their headstrong manner, conclude that it is duty to rush on their journey all weathers; and I am for waiting for wind and tide. They are for hazarding all for God at a clap; and I am for taking all advantages to secure my life and estate. They are for holding their notions, though all other men are against them; but I am for religion in what, and so far as the times, and my safety, will bear it. They are for religion when in rags and contempt; but I am for him when he walks in his golden slippers, in the sunshine, and with applause.

MR. HOLD-THE-WORLD. Ay, and hold you there still, good Mr. By-ends; for, for my part, I can count him but a fool, that, having the liberty to keep what he has, shall be so unwise as to lose it. Let us be wise as serpents; it's best to make hay when the sun shines; you see how the bee lieth still all winter, and bestirs her only when she can have profit with pleasure. God sends sometimes rain, and sometimes sunshine; if they be such fools to go through the first, yet let us be content to take fair weather along with us. For my part, I like that religion best that will stand with the security of God's good blessings unto us; for who can imagine, that is ruled by his reason, since God has bestowed upon us the good things of this life, but that he would have us keep them for his sake? Abraham and Solomon grew rich in religion. And Job says that a good man shall lay up gold as dust. But he must not be such as the men before us, if they be as you have described them.

MR. SAVE-ALL. I think that we are all agreed in this matter, and therefore there needs no more words about it. . . .

[BY-PATH MEADOW, DOUBTING CASTLE, AND GIANT DESPAIR]

Now, I beheld in my dream, that they had not journeyed far, but the river and the way for a time parted; at which they were not a little sorry; yet they durst not go out of the way. Now the way from the river was rough, and their feet tender, by reason of their travels; so the souls of the pilgrims were much discouraged because of the way. Wherefore, still as they went on, they wished for better way. Now, a little before them, there was on the left hand of the road a meadow, and a stile to go over into it; and that meadow is called By-path Meadow. Then said Christian to his fellow, "If this meadow lieth along by our wayside, let's go over into it." Then he went to the stile to see, and behold, a path lay along by the way, on the other side of the fence. "'Tis according to my wish," said Christian. "Here is the easiest going; come, good Hopeful, and let us go over."

HOPE. But how if this path should lead us out of the way?

CHR. "That's not like," said the other. "Look, doth it not go along by the wayside?" So Hopeful, being persuaded by his fellow, went after him over the stile. When they were gone over, and were got into the path, they found it very easy for their feet; and withal, they, looking before them, espied a man walking as they did (and his name was Vain-confidence); so they called after him, and asked him whither that way led. He said, "To the Celestial Gate." "Look," said Christian, "did I not tell you so? By this you may see we are right." So they followed, and he went before them. But, behold, the night came on, and it grew very dark; so that they that went behind lost the sight of him that went before.

He, therefore, that went before (Vain-confidence by name), not seeing the way before him, fell into a deep pit, which was on purpose there made, by the prince of those grounds, to catch vainglorious fools withal, and was dashed in pieces with his fall.

Now Christian and his fellow heard him fall. So they called to know the matter, but there was none to answer, only they heard a groaning. Then said Hopeful, "Where are we now?" Then was his fellow silent, as mistrusting that he had led him out of the way; and now it began to rain, and thunder, and lighten in a very dreadful manner; and the water rose amain.

Then Hopeful groaned in himself, saying, "Oh, that I had kept on my way!"

CHR. Who could have thought that this path should have led us out of the way?

HOPE. I was afraid on it at the very first, and therefore gave you that gentle caution. I would have spoken plainer, but that you are older than I.

CHR. Good brother, be not offended; I am sorry I have brought thee out of the way, and that I have put thee into such imminent danger; pray, my brother, forgive me; I did not do it of an evil intent.

HOPE. Be comforted, my brother, for I forgive thee; and believe, too, that this shall be for our good.

CHR. I am glad I have with me a merciful brother; but we must not stand thus: let's try to go back again.

HOPE. But, good brother, let me go before.

CHR. No, if you please, let me go first, that if there be any danger, I may be first therein, because by my means we are both gone out of the way.

HOPE. "No," said Hopeful, "you shall not go first; for your mind being troubled may lead you out of the way again." Then, for their encouragement, they heard the voice of one saying, "Let thine heart be towards the highway, even the way which thou wentest; turn again." But by this time the waters were greatly risen, by reason of which the way of going back was very dangerous. (Then I thought that it is easier going out of the way, when we are in, than going in when we are out.) Yet they adventured to go back, but it was so dark, and the flood was so high, that in their going back they had like to have been drowned nine or ten times.

Neither could they, with all the skill they had, get again to the stile that night. Wherefore, at last, lighting under a little shelter, they sat down there until the day brake, but, being weary, they fell asleep.

Now there was, not far from the place where they lay, a castle called Doubting Castle, the owner whereof was Giant Despair; and it was in his grounds they were now sleeping. Wherefore he, getting up in the morning early, and walking up and down in his fields, caught Christian and Hopeful asleep in his grounds. Then, with a grim and surly voice, he bid them awake; and asked them whence they were, and what they did in his grounds. They told him they were pilgrims, and that they had lost their way. Then said the Giant, "You have this night trespassed on me, by trampling in and lying on my ground, and therefore you must go along with me." So they were forced to go, because he was stronger than they. They also had but little to say, for they knew themselves in a fault. The Giant, therefore, drove them before him, and put them into his castle, into a very dark dungeon,[34] nasty and stinking to the spirits of these two men. Here, then, they lay from Wednesday morning till Saturday night, without one bit of bread, or drop of drink, or light, or any to ask how they did; they were, therefore, here in evil case, and were far from friends and acquaintance. Now in this place Christian had double sorrow, because 'twas through his unadvised counsel that they were brought into this distress.

Now, Giant Despair had a wife, and her name was Diffidence.[35] So when he was gone to bed, he told his wife what he had done; to wit, that he had taken a couple of prisoners and cast them into his dungeon, for trespassing on his grounds. Then he asked her also what he had best to do further to them. So she asked him what they were, whence they came, and whither they were bound; and he told her. Then she counseled him that when he arose in the morning he should beat them without mercy. So, when he arose, he getteth him a grievous crab-tree cudgel, and goes down into the dungeon to them, and there first falls to rating of them as if they were dogs, although they gave him never a word of distaste. Then he falls upon them, and beats them fearfully, in such sort that they were not able to help themselves, or to turn them upon the floor. This done, he withdraws and leaves them, there to condole their misery, and to mourn under their distress. So all that day they spent the time in nothing but sighs and bitter lamentations. The next night, she, talking with her husband about them further, and understanding they were yet alive, did advise him to counsel them to make away themselves. So when morning was come, he goes to them in a surly manner as before, and perceiving them to be very sore with the stripes that he had given them the day before, he told them, that since they were never like to come out of that place, their only way would be forthwith to make an end of themselves, either with knife, halter, or poison, "For why," said he, "should you choose life, seeing it is attended with so much bitterness?" But they desired him to let them go. With that he looked ugly upon them, and, rushing to them, had doubtless made an end of them himself, but that he fell into one of his fits (for he sometimes, in sunshiny weather, fell into fits), and lost for a time the use of his hand; wherefore he withdrew, and left them as before, to consider what to do. Then did the prisoners consult between themselves, whether 'twas best to take his counsel or no; and thus they began to discourse:

34 Since Bunyan wrote The Pilgrim's Progress in Bedford jail, his description of the dungeon was undoubtedly suggested by his own experience. It is possible that he may also have had in mind Spenser's account of the Red Cross Knight in the Cave of Despair (Faerie Queene, I, ix).

35 The word *diffidence* in Bunyan's day meant *distrust, want of confidence in others*, rather than *timidity, bashfulness*, etc.

CHR. "Brother," said Christian, "what shall we do? The life that we now live is miserable. For my part I know not whether is best, to live thus, or die out of hand. My soul chooseth strangling rather than life, and the grave is more easy for me than this dungeon. Shall we be ruled by the Giant?"

HOPE. "Indeed, our present condition is dreadful, and death would be far more welcome to me than thus forever to abide; but yet, let us consider, the Lord of the country to which we are going hath said, 'Thou shalt do no murder:' no, not to another man's person; much more, then, are we forbidden to take his counsel to kill ourselves. Besides, he that kills another, can but commit murder upon his body; but for one to kill himself is to kill body and soul at once. And, moreover, my brother, thou talkest of ease in the grave; but hast thou forgotten the hell, whither for certain the murderers go? For 'no murderer hath eternal life,' &c. And let us consider, again, that all the law is not in the hand of Giant Despair. Others, so far as I can understand, have been taken by him, as well as we; and yet have escaped out of his hand. Who knows, but that God that made the world may cause that Giant Despair may die? or that, at some time or other, he may forget to lock us in? or that he may, in a short time, have another of his fits before us, and may lose the use of his limbs? and if ever that should come to pass again, for my part, I am resolved to pluck up the heart of a man, and to try my utmost to get from under his hand. I was a fool that I did not try to do it before; but, however, my brother, let us be patient, and endure a while. The time may come that may give us a happy release; but let us not be our own murderers." With these words, Hopeful at present did moderate the mind of his brother; so they continued together (in the dark) that day, in their sad and doleful condition.

Well, towards evening, the Giant goes down into the dungeon again, to see if his prisoners had taken his counsel; but when he came there he found them alive; and truly, alive was all; for now, what for want of bread and water, and by reason of the wounds they received when he beat them, they could do little but breathe. But, I say, he found them alive; at which he fell into a grievous rage, and told them that, seeing they had disobeyed his counsel, it should be worse with them than if they had never been born.

At this they trembled greatly, and I think that Christian fell into a swoon; but, coming a little to himself again, they renewed their discourse about the Giant's counsel; and whether yet they had best take it or no. Now Christian again seemed to be for doing it, but Hopeful made his second reply as followeth:

HOPE. "My brother," said he, "remember thou not how valiant thou hast been heretofore? Apollyon could not crush thee, nor could all that thou didst hear, or see, or feel, in the Valley of the Shadow of Death. What hardship, terror, and amazement hast thou already gone through, and art thou now nothing but fears! Thou seest that I am in the dungeon with thee, a far weaker man by nature than thou art; also, this Giant has wounded me as well as thee, and hath also cut off the bread and water from my mouth; and with thee I mourn without the light. But let's exercise a little more patience; remember how thou playedst the man at Vanity Fair, and wast neither afraid of the chain or cage, nor yet of bloody death. Wherefore let us (at least to avoid the shame, that becomes not a Christian to be found in) bear up with patience as well as we can."

Now, night being come again, and the Giant and his wife being in bed, she asked him concerning the prisoners, and if they had taken his counsel. To which he replied, "They are sturdy rogues, they choose rather to bear all hardship, than to make away themselves." Then said she, "Take them into the castle-yard to-morrow, and show them the bones and skulls of those that thou hast already dispatched, and make them believe, ere a week comes to an end, thou also wilt tear them in pieces, as thou hast done their fellows before them."

So when the morning was come, the Giant goes to them again, and takes them into the castle-yard, and shows them, as his wife had bidden him. "These," said he, "were pilgrims as you are, once, and they trespassed in my grounds, as you have done; and when I thought fit, I tore them in pieces, and so, within ten days, I will do you. Go, get you down to your den again"; and with that he beat them all the way thither. They lay, therefore, all day on Saturday in a lamentable case, as before. Now, when night was come, and when Mrs. Diffidence and her husband, the Giant, were got to bed, they began to renew their discourse of their prisoners; and withal the old Giant wondered, that he could neither by his blows nor his counsel bring them to an end. And with that his wife replied, "I fear," said she, "that they live in hopes that some will come to relieve them, or that they have pick-locks about them, by the means of which they hope to escape." "And sayst thou so, my dear?" said the Giant; "I will, therefore, search them in the morning."

Well, on Saturday, about midnight, they began to pray, and continued in prayer till almost break of day.

Now, a little before it was day, good Christian, as one half amazed, brake out in this passionate speech: "What a fool," quoth he, "am I, thus to lie in a stinking dungeon, when I may as well walk at liberty! I have a key in my bosom, called Promise, that will, I am persuaded, open any lock in Doubting Castle." Then said Hopeful, "That's good news; good brother, pluck it out of thy bosom, and try."

Then Christian pulled it out of his bosom, and began to try at the dungeon door, whose bolt (as he turned the key) gave back, and the door flew open with ease, and Christian and Hopeful both came out. Then he went to the outward door that leads into the castle-yard, and, with his key, opened that door also. After, he went to the iron gate, for that must be opened too; but that lock went damnable hard, yet the key did open it. Then they thrust open the gate to make their escape with speed, but that gate, as it opened, made such a creaking that it waked Giant Despair, who, hastily rising to pursue his prisoners, felt his limbs to fail, for his fits took him again, so that he could by no means go after them. Then they went on, and came to the King's highway, and so were safe, because they were out of his jurisdiction.

Now, when they were gone over the stile, they began to contrive with themselves what they should do at that stile, to prevent those that shall come after, from falling into the hands of Giant Despair. So they consented to erect there a pillar, and to engrave upon the side thereof this sentence—"Over this stile is the way to Doubting Castle, which is kept by Giant Despair, who despiseth the King of the Celestial Country, and seeks to destroy the holy pilgrims." Many, therefore, that followed after, read what was written, and escaped the danger. . . .

[THE DELECTABLE MOUNTAINS]

THEY went then till they came to the Delectable Mountains, which mountains belong to the Lord of that hill of which we have spoken before; so they went up to the mountains, to behold the gardens and orchards, the vineyards and fountains of water; where also they drank and washed themselves, and did freely eat of the vineyards. Now there was on the tops of these mountains shepherds feeding their flocks, and they stood by the highway side. The pilgrims there-fore went to them, and leaning upon their staves (as is common with weary pilgrims, when they stand to talk with any by the way), they asked, "Whose Delectable Mountains are these? And whose be the sheep that feed upon them?"

SHEP. These mountains are Immanuel's Land, and they are within sight of His city; and the sheep also are His, and He laid down His life for them.

CHR. Is this the way to the Celestial City?

SHEP. You are just in your way.

CHR. How far is it thither?

SHEP. Too far for any but those that shall get thither indeed.

CHR. Is the way safe or dangerous?

SHEP. Safe for those for whom it is to be safe; but the transgressors shall fall therein.

CHR. Is there, in this place, any relief for pilgrims that are weary and faint in the way?

SHEP. The Lord of these mountains hath given us a charge not to be forgetful to entertain strangers; therefore the good of the place is before you.

I also saw in my dream, that when the Shepherds perceived that they were wayfaring men, they also put questions to them, to which they made answer as in other places; as, "Whence came you?" and, "How got you into the way?" and, "By what means have you so persevered therein?" For but few of them that begin to come hither, do show their face on these mountains. But when the Shepherds heard their answers, being pleased therewith, they looked very lovingly upon them, and said, "Welcome to the Delectable Mountains."

The Shepherds, I say, whose names were Knowledge, Experience, Watchful, and Sincere, took them by the hand, and had them to their tents, and made them partake of that which was ready at present. They said, moreover, "We would that ye should stay here awhile, to be acquainted with us; and yet more to solace yourselves with the good of these Delectable Mountains." They then told them, that they were content to stay; so they went to their rest that night, because it was very late.

Then I saw in my dream, that in the morning the Shepherds called up Christian and Hopeful to walk with them upon the mountains; so they went forth with them, and walked a while, having a pleasant prospect on every side. Then said the Shepherds one to another, "Shall we show these pilgrims some wonders?" So when they had concluded to do it, they had them first to the top of a hill called Error, which was very steep on the farthest side, and bid them look down to the bottom. So Christian and Hopeful looked down, and saw at the bottom several men dashed all to pieces by a fall that they had from the top. Then said Christian, "What meaneth this?" The Shepherds answered, "Have you not heard of them that were made to err, by hearkening to Hymeneus and Philetus, as concerning the faith of the resurrection of the body?" They answered, "Yes." Then said the Shepherds, "Those that you see lie dashed to pieces at the bottom of this mountain are they; and they have continued to this day unburied, as you see, for an example to others to take heed how they clamber too high, or how they come too near the brink of this mountain."

Then I saw that they had them to the top of another mountain, and the name of that is Caution, and bid them look afar off; which, when they did, they perceived, as they thought, several men walking up and down among the tombs that were there; and they perceived that the men were blind, because they stumbled sometimes upon the tombs, and because they could not get out from among them. Then said Christian, "What means this?"

The Shepherds then answered, "Did you not see a little below these mountains a stile, that led into a meadow, on the left hand of this way?" They answered, "Yes." Then said the Shepherds, "From that stile there goes a path that leads directly to Doubting Castle, which is kept by Giant Despair, and these men (pointing to them among the tombs), came once on pilgrimage, as you do now, even till they came to that same stile; and because the right way was rough in that place, they chose to go out of it into that meadow, and there were taken by Giant Despair, and cast into Doubting Castle; where, after they had been a while kept in the dungeon, he at last did put out their eyes, and led them among those tombs, where he has left them to wander to this very day, that the saying of the wise man might be fulfilled, "He that wandereth out of the way of understanding shall remain in the congregation of the dead." Then Christian and Hopeful looked upon one another, with tears gushing out, but yet said nothing to the Shepherds.

Then I saw in my dream, that the Shepherds had them to another place, in a bottom, where was a door in the side of a hill, and they opened the door, and bid them look in. They looked in, therefore, and saw that within it was very dark and smoky; they also thought that they heard there a rumbling noise as of fire, and a cry of some tormented, and that they smelt the scent of brimstone. Then said Christian, "What means this?" The Shepherds told them, "This is a by-way to hell, a way that hypocrites go in at; namely, such as sell their birthright, with Esau; such as sell their master, with Judas; such as blaspheme the gospel, with Alexander; and that lie and dissemble, with Ananias and Sapphira his wife." Then said Hopeful to the Shepherds, "I perceive that these had on them, even every one, a show of pilgrimage, as we have now; had they not?"

SHEP. Yes, and held it a long time too.

HOPE. How far might they go on in pilgrimage in their day, since they notwithstanding were thus miserably cast away?

SHEP. Some further, and some not so far, as these mountains.

Then said the pilgrims one to another, "We had need to cry to the Strong for strength."

SHEP. Ay, and you will have need to use it, when you have it, too.

By this time the pilgrims had a desire to go forwards, and the Shepherds a desire they should; so they walked together towards the end of the mountains. Then said the Shepherds one to another, Let us here show to the pilgrims the gates of the Celestial City, if they have skill to look through our perspective glass. The pilgrims then lovingly accepted the motion; so they had them to the top of a high hill, called Clear, and gave them their glass to look.

Then they essayed to look, but the remembrance of that last thing that the Shepherds had showed them, made their hands shake; by means of which impediment they could not look steadily through the glass; yet they thought they saw something like the gate, and also some of the glory of the place. Then they went away, and sang this song,

> Thus, by the Shepherds, secrets are revealed,
> Which from all other men are kept concealed.
> Come to the Shepherds, then, if you would see
> Things deep, things hid, and that mysterious be.

When they were about to depart, one of the Shepherds gave them a note of the way. Another of them bid them beware of the Flatterer. The third bid them take heed that they sleep not upon the Enchanted Ground. And the fourth bade them God speed. So I awoke from my dream.

And I slept, and dreamed again, and saw the same two pilgrims going down the mountains along the highway towards the city. Now, a little below these mountains, on the left hand, lieth the country of Conceit; from which country there comes into the way in which the pilgrims walked, a little crooked lane. Here, therefore, they met with a very brisk lad, that came out of that country; and his name was Ignorance. So Christian asked him from what parts he came, and whither he was going.

IGNOR. Sir, I was born in the country that lieth off there a little on the left hand, and am going to the Celestial City.

CHR. But how do you think to get in at the gate? for you may find some difficulty there.

IGNOR. "As other good people doth," saith he.

CHR. But what have you to show at that gate, that may cause that the gate should be opened to you?

IGNOR. I know my Lord's will, and have been a good liver; I pay every man his own; I pray, fast, pay tithes, and give alms, and have left my country for whither I am going.

CHR. But thou camest not in at the wicket-gate that is at the head of this way; thou camest in hither through that same crooked lane, and therefore, I fear, however thou mayest think of thyself, when the reckoning day shall come, thou wilt have laid to thy charge that thou art a thief and a robber, instead of getting admittance into the city.

IGNOR. Gentlemen, ye be utter strangers to me, I know you not; be content to follow the religion of your country, and I will follow the religion of mine. I hope all will be well. And as for the gate that you talk of all the world knows that that is a great way off of our country. I cannot think that any man in all our parts doth so much as know the way to it, nor need they matter whether they do or no, since we have, as you see, a fine, pleasant green lane, that comes down from our country, the next way into the way.

When Christian saw that the man was "wise in his own conceit," he said to Hopeful whisperingly, "There is more hope of a fool than of him." . . .

IGNOR. You go so fast I cannot keep pace with you. Do you go on before, I must stay a while behind. . . .

So I saw in my dream that they went on a pace before, and Ignorance he came hobbling after. . . .

[BEULAH LAND AND THE ARRIVAL AT THE CELESTIAL CITY]

NOW I saw in my dream that by this time the pilgrims were got over the Enchanted Ground, and entering into the country of Beulah, whose air was very sweet and pleasant; the way lying directly through it, they solaced themselves there for a season. Yea, here they heard continually the singing of birds, and saw every day the flowers appear in the earth, and heard the voice of the turtle in the land. In this country the sun shineth night and day; wherefore this was beyond the Valley of the Shadow of Death, and also out of the reach of Giant Despair, neither could they from this place so much as see Doubting Castle. Here they were within sight of the city they were going to; also here met them some of the inhabitants thereof. For in this land the Shining Ones commonly walked, because it was upon the borders of heaven. In this land also the contract between the bride and the bridegroom was renewed; yea, here, "As the bridegroom rejoiceth over the bride, so did their God rejoice over them." Here they had no want of corn and wine; for in this place they met with abundance of what they had sought for in all their pilgrimage. Here they heard voices from out of the city, loud voices, saying, "Say ye to the daughter of Zion, Behold, thy salvation cometh; behold, his reward is with him." Here all the inhabitants of the country called them "the holy people, the redeemed of the Lord, sought out," &c.

Now, as they walked in this land, they had more rejoicing than in parts more remote from the kingdom to which they were bound; and drawing near to the city, they had yet a more perfect view thereof. It was builded of pearls and precious stones, also the street thereof was paved with gold; so that by reason of the natural glory of the city, and the reflection of the sunbeams upon it, Christian with desire fell sick; Hopeful also had a fit or two of the same disease. Wherefore here they lay by it a while, crying out because of their pangs, "If you see my beloved, tell him that I am sick of love."

But being a little strengthened, and better able to bear their sickness, they walked on their way, and came yet nearer and nearer, where were orchards, vineyards, and gardens, and their gates opened into the highway. Now, as they came up to these places, behold the gardener stood in the way, to whom the pilgrims said, Whose goodly vineyards and gardens are these? He answered, They are the King's, and are planted here for his own delight, and also for the solace of pilgrims. So the gardener had them into the vineyards, and bid them refresh themselves with the dainties. He also showed them there the King's walks, and the arbors where he delighted to be; and here they tarried and slept.

Now I beheld in my dream that they talked more

in their sleep at this time than ever they did in all their journey; and being in a muse thereabout, the gardener said even to me, Wherefore musest thou at the matter? It is the nature of the fruit of the grapes of these vineyards to go down so sweetly as to cause "the lips of them that are asleep to speak."

So I saw that when they awoke, they addressed themselves to go up to the city. But, as I said, the reflections of the sun upon the city (for "the city was pure gold") was so extremely glorious, that they could not as yet with open face behold it, but through an instrument made for that purpose. So I saw that as they went on, there met them two men in raiment that shone like gold; also their faces shone as the light.

These men asked the pilgrims whence they came; and they told them. They also asked them where they had lodged, what difficulties and dangers, what comforts and pleasures they had met in the way; and they told them. Then said the men that met them, You have but two difficulties more to meet with, and then you are in the city.

Christian then and his companion asked the men to go along with them; so they told them they would. But, said they, you must obtain it by your own faith. So I saw in my dream that they went on together till they came in sight of the gate.

Now I further saw that betwixt them and the gate was a river,[36] but there was no bridge to go over; the river was very deep. At the sight therefore of this river, the pilgrims were much stunned; but the men that went with them said, You must go through, or you cannot come at the gate.

The pilgrims then began to inquire if there was no other way to the gate, to which they answered, Yes; but there hath not any, save two, to wit, Enoch and Elijah, been permitted to tread that path, since the foundation of the world, nor shall, until the last trumpet shall sound. The pilgrims then, especially Christian, began to despond in their minds, and looked this way and that, but no way could be found by them, by which they might escape the river. Then they asked the men if the waters were all of a depth. They said, No; yet they could not help them in that case; for, said they, you shall find it deeper or shallower, as you believe in the King of the place.

They then addressed themselves to the water; and entering, Christian began to sink, and crying out to his good friend Hopeful, he said, I sink in deep waters;

36 Death. [Bunyan's note.]

the billows go over my head, all his waves go over me! Selah.

Then said the other, Be of good cheer, my brother, I feel the bottom, and it is good. Then said Christian, Ah! my friend, the sorrows of death have compassed me about; I shall not see the land that flows with milk and honey; and with that a great darkness and horror fell upon Christian, so that he could not see before him. Also here he in great measure lost his senses, so that he could neither remember, nor orderly talk of any of those sweet refreshments that he had met with in the way of his pilgrimage. But all the words that he spake still tended to discover that he had horror of mind and heart-fears that he should die in that river, and never obtain entrance in at the gate. Here also, as they that stood by perceived, he was much in the troublesome thoughts of the sins that he had committed, both since and before he began to be a pilgrim. It was also observed that he was troubled with apparitions of hobgoblins and evil spirits, for ever and anon he would intimate so much by words. Hopeful therefore here had much ado to keep his brother's head above water; yea, sometimes he would be quite gone down, and then ere a while he would rise up again half dead. Hopeful also would endeavor to comfort him, saying, Brother, I see the gate, and men standing by to receive us; but Christian would answer, 'Tis you, 'tis you they wait for; you have been hopeful ever since I knew you. And so have you, said he to Christian. Ah, brother, said he, surely if I was right he would now arise to help me; but for my sins he hath brought me into the snare and hath left me. Then said Hopeful, My brother, you have quite forgot the text where it is said of the wicked, "There is no band in their death, but their strength is firm. They are not troubled as other men, neither are they plagued like other men." These troubles and distresses that you go through in these waters are no sign that God hath forsaken you, but are sent to try you, whether you will call to mind that which heretofore you have received of his goodness, and live upon him in your distresses.

Then I saw in my dream that Christian was as in a muse a while. To whom also Hopeful added this word, Be of good cheer; Jesus Christ maketh thee whole. And with that Christian brake out with a loud voice, Oh! I see him again, and he tells me, "When thou passest through the waters, I will be with thee; and through the rivers, they shall not overflow thee." Then they both took courage, and the enemy was after that as still as a stone, until they were gone over. Christian therefore presently found ground to stand upon, and so it followed that the rest of the river was but shallow. Thus they got over. Now upon the bank of the river on the other side, they saw the two shining men again, who there waited for them; wherefore, being come out of the river, they saluted them saying, "We are ministering spirits, sent forth to minister for those that shall be heirs of salvation." Thus they went along towards the gate. Now you must note that the city stood upon a mighty hill, but the pilgrims went up that hill with ease, because they had these two men to lead them up by the arms; also they had left their mortal garments behind them in the river, for though they went in with them, they came out without them. They therefore went up here with much agility and speed, though the foundation upon which the city was framed was higher than the clouds. They therefore went up through the regions of the air, sweetly talking as they went, being comforted, because they safely got over the river, and had such glorious companions to attend them.

The talk they had with the Shining Ones was about the glory of the place; who told them that the beauty and glory of it was inexpressible. There, said they, is the Mount Zion, the heavenly Jerusalem, the innumerable company of angels, and the spirits of just men made perfect. You are going now, said they, to the paradise of God, wherein you shall see the tree of life, and eat of the never-fading fruits thereof; and when you come there, you shall have white robes given you, and your walk and talk shall be every day with the King, even all the days of eternity. There you shall not see again such things as you saw when you were in the lower regions upon the earth, to wit, sorrow, sickness, affliction, and death, "for the former things are passed away." You are now going to Abraham, to Isaac, and Jacob, and to the prophets; men that God hath taken away from the evil to come, and that are now resting upon their beds, each one walking in his righteousness. The men then asked, What must we do in the holy place? To whom it was answered, You must there receive the comforts of all your toil, and have joy for all your sorrow; you must reap what you have sown, even the fruit of all your prayers, and tears, and sufferings for the King by the way. In that place you must wear crowns of gold, and enjoy the perpetual sight and vision of the Holy One, "for there you shall see him as he is." There also you shall serve him continually with praise, with shouting, and thanks-

giving, whom you desired to serve in the world, though with much difficulty, because of the infirmity of your flesh. There your eyes shall be delighted with seeing, and your ears with hearing the pleasant voice of the Mighty One. There you shall enjoy your friends again that are gone thither before you; and there you shall with joy receive every one that follows into the holy place after you. There also shall you be clothed with glory and majesty, and put into an equipage fit to ride out with the King of glory. When he shall come with sound of trumpets in the clouds, as upon the wings of the wind, you shall come with him; and when he shall sit upon the throne of judgment, you shall sit by him; yea, and when he shall pass sentence upon all the workers of iniquity, let them be angels or men, you also shall have a voice in that judgment, because they were his and your enemies. Also when he shall again return to the city, you shall go too, with sound of trumpet, and be ever with him.

Now while they were thus drawing towards the gate, behold a company of the heavenly host came out to meet them; to whom it was said, by the other two Shining Ones, "These are the men that have loved our Lord when they were in the world, and that have left all for His holy name; and He hath sent us to fetch them, and we have brought them thus far on their desired journey, that they may go in and look their Redeemer in the face with joy." Then the heavenly host gave a great shout, saying, "Blessed are they that are called unto the marriage supper of the Lamb." There came out also at this time to meet them, several of the King's trumpeters, clothed in white and shining raiment, who, with melodious noises, and loud, made even the heavens to echo with their sound. These trumpeters saluted Christian and his fellow with ten thousand welcomes from the world; and this they did with shouting, and sound of trumpet.

This done, they compassed them round on every side; some went before, some behind, and some on the right hand, some on the left (as it were to guard them through the upper regions), continually sounding as they went, with melodious noise, in notes on high: so that the very sight was to them that could behold it, as if heaven itself was come down to meet them. Thus, therefore, they walked on together; and as they walked, ever and anon these trumpeters, even with joyful sound, would, by mixing their music with looks and gestures, still signify to Christian and his brother, how welcome they were into their company, and with what gladness they came to meet them; and now were these two men, as it were, in heaven, before they came at it, being swallowed up with the sight of angels, and with hearing of their melodious notes. Here also they had the city itself in view, and they thought they heard all the bells therein to ring, to welcome them thereto. But above all, the warm and joyful thoughts that they had about their own dwelling there, with such company, and that for ever and ever. Oh, by what tongue or pen can their glorious joy be expressed! Thus they came up to the gate.

Now, when they were come up to the gate, there were written over it in letters of gold, "Blessed are they that do His commandments, that they may have right to the tree of life, and may enter in through the gates into the city."

Then I saw in my dream, that the Shining Men bid them call at the gate; the which, when they did, some from above looked over the gate, to wit, Enoch, Moses, and Elijah, etc., to whom it was said, "These pilgrims are come from the City of Destruction, for the love that they bear to the King of this place." And then the pilgrims gave in unto them each man his certificate, which they had received in the beginning; those, therefore, were carried in to the King, who, when He had read them, said, "Where are the men?" To whom it was answered, "They are standing without the gate." The King then commanded to open the gate, "That the righteous nation," said He, "which keepeth the truth may enter in."

Now I saw in my dream that these two men went in at the gate: and lo, as they entered, they were transfigured, and they had raiment put on that shone like gold. There was also that met them with harps and crowns, and gave them to them—the harps to praise withal, and the crowns in token of honor. Then I heard in my dream that all the bells in the city rang again for joy, and that it was said unto them, "Enter ye into the joy of our Lord." I also heard the men themselves, that they sang with a loud voice, saying, "Blessing, honor, glory, and power, be to Him that sitteth upon the throne, and to the Lamb, for ever and ever."

Now, just as the gates were opened to let in the men, I looked in after them, and, behold, the City shone like the sun; the streets also were paved with gold, and in them walked many men, with crowns on their heads, palms in their hands, and golden harps to sing praises withal.

There were also of them that had wings, and answered one another without intermission, saying, "Holy, holy, holy is the Lord." And after that they shut up the gates; which, when I had seen, I wished myself among them.

Now while I was gazing upon all these things, I turned my head to look back, and saw Ignorance come up to the riverside; but he soon got over, and that without half that difficulty which the other two men met with. For it happened that there was then in that place, one Vain-hope, a ferryman, that with his boat helped him over; so he, as the other, I saw did ascend the hill, to come up to the gate, only he came alone; neither did any man meet him with the least encouragement. When he was come up to the gate, he looked up to the writing that was above, and then began to knock, supposing that entrance should have been quickly administered to him; but he was asked by the men that looked over the top of the gate, "Whence came you? and what would you have?" He answered, "I have eat and drank in the presence of the King, and He has taught in our streets." Then they asked him for his certificate, that they might go in and show it to the King; so he fumbled in his bosom for one, and found none. Then said they, "Have you none?" But the man answered never a word. So they told the King, but He would not come down to see him, but commanded the two Shining Ones that conducted Christian and Hopeful to the City, to go out and take Ignorance, and bind him hand and foot, and have him away. Then they took him up, and carried him through the air, to the door that I saw in the side of the hill, and put him in there. Then I saw that there was a way to hell, even from the gates of heaven, as well as from the City of Destruction! So I awoke, and behold it was a dream.

from

THE SECOND PART[37]

[GREAT-HEART AND HIS COMPANIONS]

THE Interpreter then called for a man-servant of his, one Great-heart, and bid him take sword and helmet and shield; and take these my daughters, said he, and conduct them to the house called Beautiful, at which place they will rest next. So he took his weapons and went before them; and the Interpreter said, "Godspeed!" Those, also, that belonged to the family, sent

---

37 In the Second Part of The Pilgrim's Progress, Bunyan tells the story of the pilgrimage of Christian's wife, Christiana, and her children.

them away with many a good wish. So they went on their way and sung. . . .

Now, as they were going along, and talking, they espied a boy feeding his father's sheep. The boy was in very mean clothes, but of a very fresh and well-favored countenance; and as he sat by himself, he sung. "Hark," said Mr. Great-heart, "to what the shepherd's boy saith." So they hearkened, and he said,

> He that is down needs fear no fall;
>   He that is low, no pride;
> He that is humble, ever shall
>   Have God to be his guide.

> I am content with what I have,
>   Little be it, or much:
> And, Lord, contentment still I crave,
>   Because Thou savest such.

> Fullness to such, a burden is,
>   That go on pilgrimage;
> Here little, and hereafter bliss,
>   Is best from age to age.

Then said their guide, "Do you hear him? I will dare to say, that this boy lives a merrier life, and wears more of that herb called heart's-ease in his bosom, than he that is clad in silk and velvet; but we will proceed in our discourse." . . .

Then they got up and went forward. Now a little before them stood an oak; and under it, when they came to it, they found an old pilgrim fast asleep; they knew that he was a pilgrim by his clothes, and his staff, and his girdle.

So the guide, Mr. Great-heart, awaked him, and the old gentleman, as he lift up his eyes, cried out, "What's the matter? Who are you? and what is your business here?"

GREAT-HEART. Come, man, be not so hot, here are none but friends: yet the old man gets up, and stands upon his guard, and will know of them what they were. Then said the guide, "My name is Great-heart; I am the guide of these pilgrims, which are going to the Celestial Country."

HONEST. Then said Mr. Honest, "I cry you mercy; I feared that you had been of the company of those that some time ago did rob Little-faith of his money; but now I look better about me, I perceive you are honester people."

GREAT-HEART. Why, what would, or could you a-done to a-helped yourself, if we indeed had been of that company?

HON. Done! why I would have fought as long as breath had been in me; and had I so done, I am sure you could never have given me the worst on't; for a Christian can never be overcome, unless he shall yield of himself.

GREAT-HEART. "Well said, Father Honest," quoth the guide; "for by this I know thou are a cock of the right kind, for thou hast said the truth."

HON. And by this, also, I know that thou knowest what true pilgrimage is; for all others do think that we are the soonest overcome of any.

GREAT-HEART. Well, now we are so happily met, pray let me crave your name, and the name of the place you came from.

HON. My name I cannot; but I came from the Town of Stupidity; it lieth about four degrees beyond the City of Destruction.

GREAT-HEART. "Oh! are you that countryman, then? I deem I have half a guess of you; your name is Old Honesty, is it not?" So the old gentleman blushed, and said, "Not Honesty, in the abstract, but Honest is my name; and I wish that my nature shall agree to what I am called." . . .

Then they went on; and just at the place where Little-faith formerly was robbed, there stood a man with his sword drawn, and his face all bloody. Then said Mr. Great-heart, "What art thou?" The man made answer, saying, "I am one whose name is Valiant-for-truth. I am a pilgrim, and am going to the Celestial City. Now, as I was in my way, there were three men did beset me, and propounded unto me these three things: 1. Whether I would become one of them. 2. Or go back from whence I came. 3. Or die upon the place. To the first, I answered, I had been a true man a long season, and therefore it could not be expected that I now should cast in my lot with thieves. Then they demanded what I would say to the second. So I told them that the place from whence I came, had I not found incommodity there, I had not forsaken it at all; but finding it altogether unsuitable to me, and very unprofitable for me, I forsook it for this way. Then they asked me what I said to the third. And I told them, 'My life cost more dear far than that I should lightly give it away. Besides, you have nothing to do thus to put things to my choice; wherefore, at your peril be it if you meddle.' Then these three, to wit, Wild-head, Inconsiderate, and Pragmatic, drew upon me, and I also drew upon them.

"So we fell to it, one against three, for the space of above three hours. They have left upon me, as you see, some of the marks of their valor, and have also carried away with them some of mine. They are but just now gone. I suppose they might, as the saying is, hear your horse dash, and so they betook them to flight."

GREAT-HEART. But here was great odds, three against one.

VALIANT. 'Tis true; but *little* and *more* are nothing to him that has the truth on his side. "Though an host should encamp against me," said one, "my heart shall not fear; though war should rise against me, in this will I be confident." Besides, said he, I have read in some records, that one man has fought an army. And how many did Samson slay with the jaw-bone of an ass!

GREAT-HEART. Then said the guide, "Why did you not cry out, that some might a-came in for your succor?"

VALIANT. So I did, to my King, who, I knew, could hear, and afford invisible help, and that was sufficient for me.

GREAT-HEART. Then said Great-heart to Mr. Valiant-for-truth, "Thou hast worthily behaved thyself. Let me see thy sword." So he showed it him.

When he had taken it in his hand, and looked thereon a while, he said, "Ha! it is a right Jerusalem blade."

VALIANT. It is so. Let a man have one of these blades, with a hand to wield it and skill to use it, and he may venture upon an angel with it. He need not fear its holding, if he can but tell how to lay on. Its edges will never blunt. It will cut flesh and bones, and soul and spirit, and all.

GREAT-HEART. But you fought a great while; I wonder you was not weary.

VALIANT. I fought till my sword did cleave to my hand; and when they were joined together, as if a sword grew out of my arm, and when the blood ran through my fingers, then I fought with most courage.

GREAT-HEART. Thou hast done well. Thou hast "resisted unto blood, striving against sin." Thou shalt abide by us, come in and go out with us, for we are thy companions.

Then they took him, and washed his wounds, and gave him of what they had to refresh him; and so they went on together. Now, as they went on, because Mr. Great-heart was delighted in him, for he loved one greatly that he found to be a man of his hands, and because there were with his company them that were feeble and weak, therefore he questioned with him about many things. . . .

GREAT-HEART. And did none of these things discourage you?

VALIANT. No; they seemed but as so many nothings to me.

GREAT-HEART. How came that about?

VALIANT. Why, I still believed what Mr. Tell-true had said, and that carried me beyond them all.

GREAT-HEART. Then this was your victory, even your faith?

VALIANT. It was so. I believed, and therefore came out, got into the way, fought all that set themselves against me, and, by believing, am come to this place.

> Who would true valor see,[38]
>   Let him come hither;
> One here will constant be,
>   Come wind, come weather.
> There's no discouragement
> Shall make him once relent
> His first avowed intent
>   To be a pilgrim.
>
> Who so beset him round
>   With dismal stories,
> Do but themselves confound,—
>   His strength the more is;
> No lion can him fright,
> He'll with a giant fight;
> But he will have a right
>   To be a pilgrim.
>
> Hobgoblin nor foul fiend
>   Can daunt his spirit;
> He knows he at the end
>   Shall life inherit.
> Then fancies fly away,
> He'll fear not what men say;
> He'll labor night and day
>   To be a pilgrim.

By this time they were got to the Enchanted Ground, where the air naturally tended to make one drowsy; and that place was all grown over with briers and thorns, excepting here and there, where was an Enchanted Arbor, upon which, if a man sits, or in which, if a man sleeps, it is a question, say some, whether ever they shall rise or wake again in this world. Over this forest, therefore, they went, both

38 In this poem Bunyan seems to be parodying the song, "Under the Greenwood Tree," in Shakespeare's As You Like It, II, 5. One likes to think that he had Shakespeare's song in mind, and if so this is one of the very few instances in which literary influence other than that of the Bible, the religious chapbooks of the day, and a few broadside ballads can be detected in his works.

one with another, and Mr. Great-heart went before, for that he was the guide; and Mr. Valiant-for-truth, he came behind, being there a guard, for fear lest peradventure some fiend, or dragon, or giant, or thief, should fall upon their rear, and so do mischief. . . .

Now, when they were almost at the end of this ground, they perceived that, a little before them, was a solemn noise as of one that was much concerned. So they went on and looked before them; and behold they saw, as they thought, a man upon his knees, with hands and eyes lift up, and speaking, as they thought, earnestly to one that was above. They drew nigh, but could not tell what he said. So they went softly till he had done. When he had done, he got up, and began to run towards the Celestial City. Then Mr. Great-heart called after him, saying, "Soho! friend, let us have your company, if you go, as I suppose you do, to the Celestial City." So the man stopped, and they came up to him. But so soon as Mr. Honest saw him, he said, "I know this man." Then said Mr. Valiant-for-truth, "Prithee, who is it?" " 'Tis one," said he, "that comes from whereabouts I dwelt. His name is Stand-fast; he is certainly a right good pilgrim."

So they came up one to another; and presently Stand-fast said to old Honest, "Ho! Father Honest, are you there?" "Ay," said he, "that I am, as sure as you are there." "Right glad am I," said Mr. Stand-fast, "that I have found you on this road." "And as glad am I," said the other, "that I espied you upon your knees." Then Mr. Stand-fast blushed, and said, "But why, did you see me?" "Yes, that I did," quoth the other, "and with my heart was glad at the sight." "Why, what did you think?" said Stand-fast. "Think!" said old Honest, "what should I think? I thought we had an honest man upon the road, and therefore should have his company by and by." "If you thought not amiss," said Stand-fast, "how happy am I! But if I be not as I should, I alone must bear it." "That is true," said the other; "but your fear doth further confirm me, that things are right betwixt the Prince of Pilgrims and your soul; for, saith he, 'Blessed is the man that feareth always.' "

VALIANT. Well, but brother, I pray thee tell us what was it that was the cause of thy being upon thy knees even now? Was it for that some special mercies laid obligations upon thee, or how?

STAND-FAST. Why, we are, as you see, upon the Enchanted Ground; and as I was coming along, I was musing with myself of what a dangerous road the road in this place was, and how many that had come even

thus far on pilgrimage had here been stopped and been destroyed. I thought also of the manner of the death with which this place destroyeth men. Those that die here die of no violent distemper. The death which such die is not grievous to them; for he that goeth away in a sleep, begins that journey with desire and pleasure; yea, such acquiesce in the will of that disease.

HON. Then Mr. Honest, interrupting of him, said, "Did you see the two men asleep in the arbor?"

STAND-FAST. Ay, ay, I saw Heedless and Too-bold there; and, for aught I know, there they will lie till they rot. But let me go on in my tale. As I was thus musing, as I said, there was one in very pleasant attire, but old, who presented herself unto me, and offered me three things; to wit, her body, her purse, and her bed. Now, the truth is, I was both a-weary and sleepy; I am also as poor as a howlet,[39] and that, perhaps, the witch knew. Well, I repulsed her once and twice, but she put by my repulses, and smiled. Then I began to be angry; but she mattered that nothing at all. Then she made offers again, and said, if I would be ruled by her, she would make me great and happy; for, said she, "I am the mistress of the world, and men are made happy by me." Then I asked her name, and she told me it was Madam Bubble. This set me further from her: but she still followed me with enticements. Then I betook me, as you saw, to my knees; and with hands lift up, and cries, I prayed to Him that had said He would help. So, just as you came up, the gentlewoman went her way. Then I continued to give thanks for this my great deliverance; for I verily believe she intended no good, but rather sought to make stop of me in my journey.

HON. Without doubt her designs were bad. But stay, now you talk of her, methinks I either have seen her, or have read some story of her.

STAND-FAST. Perhaps you have done both.

HON. Madam Bubble! is she not a tall, comely dame, something of a swarthy complexion?

STAND-FAST. Right, you hit it, she is just such an one.

HON. Doth she not speak very smoothly, and give you a smile at the end of a sentence?

STAND-FAST. You fall right upon it again, for these are her very actions.

HON. Doth she not wear a great purse by her side; and is not her hand often in it, fingering her money, as if that was her heart's delight?

STAND-FAST. 'Tis just so; had she stood by all this

39 Owlet.

while, you could not more amply have set her forth before me, nor have better described her features.

HON. Then he that drew her picture was a good limner, and he that wrote of her said true.

GREAT-HEART. This woman is a witch, and it is by virtue of her sorceries that this ground is enchanted. Whoever doth lay their head down in her lap, had as good lay it down upon that block over which the axe doth hang; and whoever lay their eyes upon her beauty, are counted the enemies of God. This is she that maintaineth in their splendor all those that are the enemies of pilgrims. Yea, this is she that has bought off many a man from a pilgrim's life. She is a great gossiper; she is always, both she and her daughters, at one pilgrim's heels or other, now commending and then preferring[40] the excellences of this life. She is a bold and impudent slut; she will talk with any man. She always laugheth poor pilgrims to scorn; but highly commends the rich. If there be one cunning to get money in a place, she will speak well of him from house to house; she loveth banqueting and feasting mainly well; she is always at one full table or another. She has given it out in some places that she is a goddess, and therefore some do worship her. She has her times and open places of cheating; and she will say and avow it that none can show a good comparable to hers. She promiseth to dwell with children's children, if they will but love and make much of her. She will cast out of her purse gold like dust in some places, and to some persons. She loves to be sought after, spoken well of, and to lie in the bosoms of men. She is never weary of commending of her commodities, and she loves them most that think best of her. She will promise to some crowns and kingdoms, if they will but take her advice; yet many hath she brought to the halter, and ten thousand times more to hell.

STAND-FAST. "Oh," said Stand-fast, "what a mercy is it that I did resist! for whither might she a-drawn me!" . . .

[THE LAND OF BEULAH]

AFTER this, I beheld until they were come into the Land of Beulah, where the sun shineth night and day. Here, because they was weary, they betook themselves awhile to rest; and, because this country was common for pilgrims, and because the orchards and vineyards that were here belonged to the King of the Celestial Country, therefore they were licensed to make bold with any of His things.

40 Exhibiting.

But a little while soon refreshed them here; for the bells did so ring, and the trumpets continually sound so melodiously, that they could not sleep; and yet they received as much refreshing as if they had slept their sleep never so soundly. Here also all the noise of them that walked in the streets, was, "More pilgrims are come to town." And another would answer, saying, "And so many went over the water, and were let in at the golden gates to-day." They would cry again, "There is now a legion of Shining Ones just come to town, by which we know that there are more pilgrims upon the road; for here they come to wait for them, and to comfort them after all their sorrow." Then the pilgrims got up, and walked to and fro; but how were their ears now filled with heavenly noises, and their eyes delighted with celestial visions! In this land they heard nothing, saw nothing, felt nothing, smelt nothing, tasted nothing, that was offensive to their stomach or mind; only when they tasted of the water of the river over which they were to go, they thought that tasted a little bitterish to the palate, but it proved sweeter when 'twas down. . . .

Now the day drew on that Christiana must be gone. So the road was full of people to see her take her journey. But, behold, all the banks beyond the river were full of horses and chariots, which were come down from above to accompany her to the City Gate. So she came forth, and entered the river, with a beckon of farewell to those that followed her to the riverside. The last words that she was heard to say here was, "I come, Lord, to be with Thee, and bless Thee."

So her children and friends returned to their place, for that those that waited for Christiana had carried her out of their sight. So she went and called, and entered in at the gate with all the ceremonies of joy that her husband Christian had done before her. . . .

Then it came to pass, a while after, that there was a post in the town that inquired for Mr. Honest. So he came to the house where he was, and delivered to his hand these lines: "Thou art commanded to be ready against this day seven-night, to present thyself before thy Lord, at His Father's house." And for a token that my message is true, "All thy daughters of music shall be brought low." Then Mr. Honest called for his friends, and said unto them, "I die, but shall make no will. As for my honesty, it shall go with me; let him that comes after be told of this." When the day that he was to be gone was come, he addressed himself to go over the river. Now the river at that time overflowed the banks in some places; but Mr. Honest in his life-time had spoken to one Good-conscience to meet him there, the which he also did, and lent him his hand, and so helped him over. The last words of Mr. Honest were, "Grace reigns." So he left the world.

After this it was noised abroad, that Mr. Valiant-for-truth was taken with a summons by the same post as the other; and had this for a token that the summons was true, "That his pitcher was broken at the fountain." When he understood it, he called for his friends, and told them of it. Then said he, "I am going to my Father's; and though with great difficulty I am got hither, yet now I do not repent me of all the trouble I have been at to arrive where I am. My sword I give to him that shall succeed me in my pilgrimage, and my courage and skill to him that can get it. My marks and scars I carry with me, to be a witness for me, that I have fought His battles who now will be my re-warder." When the day that he must go hence was come, many accompanied him to the riverside, into which as he went he said, "Death, where is thy sting?" And as he went down deeper, he said, "Grave, where is thy victory?" So he passed over, and the trumpets sounded for him on the other side. . . .

FROM

GRACE ABOUNDING TO THE CHIEF OF SINNERS;
Or, A Brief Relation of the Exceeding Mercy of God in Christ,
to His Poor Servant, John Bunyan

[TEXT: *sixth edition, 1688*]

[FIRST STEPS IN THE PILGRIMAGE OF GRACE]

IN THIS my relation of the merciful working of God upon my soul, it will not be amiss, if, in the first place, I do, in a few words, give you a hint of my pedigree, and manner of bringing up; that thereby the goodness and bounty of God towards me may be the more advanced and magnified before the sons of men.

For my descent then, it was, as is well known by many, of a low and inconsiderable generation; my father's house being of that rank that is meanest and most despised of all the families in the land. Wherefore I have not here, as others, to boast of noble blood, or of an high-born state, according to the flesh; though, all things considered, I magnify the heavenly Majesty, for that by this door He brought me into this world, to partake of the grace and life that is in Christ by the Gospel.

But yet, notwithstanding the meanness and incon-siderableness of my parents, it pleased God to put it into their hearts to put me to school, to learn both to read and write; the which I also attained, according to the rate of other poor men's children; though, to my shame I confess, I did soon lose that little I learnt, even almost utterly, and that long before the Lord did work His gracious work of conversion upon my soul.

As for my own natural life, for the time that I was without God in the world, it was indeed according to the course of this world, and "the spirit that now worketh in the children of disobedience" (Eph. 2:2, 3). It was my delight to be "taken captive by the devil at his will" (II Tim. 2:26), being filled with all unright-eousness: the which did also so strongly work and put forth itself, both in my heart and life, and that from a child, that I had but few equals, especially considering my years, which were tender, being few, both for cursing, swearing, lying, and blaspheming the holy name of God.

Yea, so settled and rooted was I in these things, that they became as a second nature to me; the which, as I also have with soberness considered since, did so offend the Lord, that even in my childhood He did scare and affright me with fearful dreams, and did terrify me with dreadful visions; for often, after I had spent this and the other day in sin, I have in my bed been greatly afflicted, while asleep, with the apprehensions of devils and wicked spirits, who still, as I then thought, labored to draw me away with them, of which I could never be rid.

Also I should, at these years, be greatly afflicted and troubled with the thoughts of the fearful torments of hell fire; still fearing that it would be my lot to be found at last among those devils and hellish fiends, who are there bound down with the chains and bonds of darkness, unto the judgment of the great Day.

These things, I say, when I was but a child about nine or ten years old, did so distress my soul, that when in the midst of my many sports and childish vanities, amidst my vain companions, I was often much cast down and afflicted in my mind therewith, yet could I not let go my sins. Yea, I was also then so overcome with despair of life and heaven, that I should often wish either that there had been no hell, or that I had been a devil—supposing they were only tormentors; that if it must needs be that I went thither, I might be rather a tormentor, than be tormented myself.

A while after, these terrible dreams did leave me, which I also soon forgot; for my pleasures did quickly cut off the remembrance of them, as if they had never been: wherefore, with more greediness, according to the strength of nature, I did still let loose the reins to my lust, and delighted in all transgression against the law of God: so that, until I came to the state of marriage, I was the very ringleader of all the youth that kept me company, into all manner of vice and ungodliness.

Yea, such prevalency had the lusts and fruits of the flesh in this poor soul of mine, that had not a miracle of precious grace prevented, I had not only perished by the stroke of eternal justice, but had also laid myself open even to the stroke of those laws which bring some to disgrace and open shame before the face of the world.

In these days the thoughts of religion were very grievous to me; I could neither endure it myself, nor that any other should; so that, when I have seen some read in those books that concerned Christian piety, it would be as it were a prison to me. Then I said unto God, "Depart from me, for I desire not the knowledge of thy ways" (Job 21:14). I was now void of all good consideration, heaven and hell were both out of sight and mind; and as for saving and damning, they were least in my thoughts. O Lord, Thou knowest my life, and my ways were not hid from Thee.

Yet this I will remember, that though I could myself sin with the greatest delight and ease, and also take pleasure in the vileness of my companions; yet, even then, if I have at any time seen wicked things by those who professed goodness, it would make my spirit tremble. As once, above all the rest, when I was in my height of vanity, yet hearing one to swear that was reckoned for a religious man, it had so great a stroke upon my spirit, that it made my heart ache.

But God did not utterly leave me, but followed me still, not now with convictions, but judgments; yet such as were mixed with mercy. For once I fell into a creek of the sea, and hardly escaped drowning. Another time I fell out of a boat into Bedford River, but mercy yet preserved me alive. Besides, another time, being in the field with one of my companions, it chanced that an adder passed over the highway; so I, having a stick in my hand, struck her over the back; and having stunned her, I forced open her mouth with my stick, and plucked her sting out with my fingers; by which act, had not God been merciful unto me, I might, by my desperateness, have brought myself to mine end.

This also I have taken notice of, with thanksgiving: when I was a soldier, I, with others, were drawn out to go to such a place to besiege it; but when I was just ready to go, one of the company desired to go in my room; to which, when I had consented, he took my place; and coming to the siege, as he stood sentinel, he was shot into the head with a musket bullet, and died.

Here, as I said, were judgments and mercy, but neither of them did awaken my soul to righteousness; wherefore I sinned still, and grew more and more rebellious against God, and careless of mine own salvation.

Presently after this, I changed my condition into a married state, and my mercy was to light upon a wife whose father was counted godly. This woman and I, though we came together as poor as poor might be, not having so much household stuff as a dish or spoon betwixt us both, yet this she had for her part, The Plain Man's Pathway to Heaven, and The Practice of Piety, which her father had left her when he died. In these two books I should sometimes read with her, wherein I also found some things that were somewhat pleasing to me; but all this while I met with no conviction. She also would be often telling of me what a godly man her father was, and how he would reprove and correct vice, both in his house, and amongst his neighbors; what a strict and holy life he lived in his day, both in word and deed.

Wherefore these books with this relation, though they did not reach my heart, to awaken it about my sad and sinful state, yet they did beget within me some desires to religion: so that, because I knew no better, I fell in very eagerly with the religion of the times; to wit, to go to church twice a day, and that too with the foremost; and there should very devoutly both say and sing as others did, yet retaining my wicked life; but withal, I was so overrun with a spirit of superstition, that I adored, and that with great devotion, even all things, both the high place, priest, clerk, vestments, service, and what else belonging to the church; counting all things holy that were therein contained, and especially the priest and clerk most happy, and without doubt, greatly blessed, because they were the servants, as I then thought, of God, and were principal in the holy temple, to do His work therein.

The conceit grew so strong in little time upon my spirit, that had I but seen a priest, though never so sordid and debauched in his life, I should find my spirit fall under him, reverence him, and knit unto him; yea, I thought for the love I did bear unto them, supposing they were the ministers of God, I could have lain down at their feet, and have been trampled upon by them; their name, their garb, and work, did so intoxicate and bewitch me.

After I had been thus for some considerable time, another thought came in my mind; and that was, whether we were of the Israelites, or no? For finding in the Scriptures that they were once the peculiar people of God, thought I, if I were one of this race, my soul must needs be happy. Now again, I found within me a great longing to be resolved about this question, but could not tell how I should. At last I asked my father of it; who told me, No, we were not. Wherefore then I fell in my spirit as to the hopes of that, and so remained.

But all this while, I was not sensible of the danger and evil of sin; I was kept from considering that sin would damn me, what religion soever I followed, unless I was found in Christ. Nay, I never thought of Him, nor whether there was such an one, or no. Thus man, while blind, doth wander, but wearieth himself with vanity, for he knoweth not the way to the city of God (Eccles. 10:15).

But one day, amongst all the sermons our parson made, his subject was to treat of the Sabbath day, and of the evil of breaking that, either with labor, sports, or otherwise. Now I was, notwithstanding my religion, one that took much delight in all manner of vice, and especially that was the day that I did solace myself therewith, wherefore I fell in my conscience under his sermon, thinking and believing that he made that sermon on purpose to show me my evil doing; and at that time I felt what guilt was, though never before that I can remember; but then I was, for the present, greatly loaden therewith, and so went home when the sermon was ended, with a great burden on my spirit.

This, for that instant, did benumb the sinews of my best delights, and did embitter my former pleasures to me; but behold, it lasted not, for before I had well dined, the trouble began to go off my mind, and my heart returned to its old course: but oh! how glad was I, that this trouble was gone from me, and that the fire was put out, that I might sin again without control! Wherefore, when I had satisfied nature with my food, I shook the sermon out of my mind, and to my old custom of sports and gaming I returned with great delight.

But the same day, as I was in the midst of a game at cat,[1] and having struck it one blow from the hole, just as I was about to strike it the second time, a voice did suddenly dart from heaven into my soul, which said, "Wilt thou leave thy sins and go to heaven, or have thy sins and go to hell?" At this I was put to an exceeding maze; wherefore, leaving my cat upon the ground, I looked up to heaven, and was, as if I had, with the eyes of my understanding, seen the Lord Jesus looking down upon me, as being very hotly displeased with me, and as if He did severely threaten me with some grievous punishment for these and other my ungodly practices.

I had no sooner thus conceived in my mind, but suddenly this conclusion was fastened on my spirit, for the former hint did set my sins again before my face, that I had been a great and grievous sinner, and that it was now too late for me to look after heaven; for Christ would not forgive me, nor pardon my transgressions. Then I fell to musing upon this also; and while I was thinking on it, and fearing lest it should be so, I felt my heart sink in despair, concluding it was too late; and therefore I resolved in my mind I would go on in sin: for, thought I, if the case be thus, my state is surely miserable; miserable if I leave my sins, and but miserable if I follow them; I can but be damned, and if I must be so, I had as good be damned for many sins as be damned for few.

Thus I stood in the midst of my play, before all that then were present; but yet I told them nothing: but I say, I having made this conclusion, I returned desperately to my sport again; and I well remember, that presently this kind of despair did so possess my soul, that I was persuaded I could never attain to other

1 Tip-cat, a game in which a small cigar-shaped piece of wood, called a cat, is raised from the ground by tipping or striking one end with a stick, and then hit by the same player while it is in the air.

comfort than what I should get in sin; for heaven was gone already, so that on that I must not think. Wherefore I found within me a great desire to take my fill of sin, still studying what sin was yet to be committed, that I might taste the sweetness of it; and I made as much haste as I could to fill my belly with its delicates, lest I should die before I had my desire; for that I feared greatly. In these things, I protest before God, I lie not, neither do I feign this form of speech; these were really, strongly, and with all my heart, my desires; the good Lord, whose mercy is unsearchable, forgive me my transgressions.

And I am very confident that this temptation of the Devil is more usual amongst poor creatures than many are aware of, even to overrun their spirits with a scurvy and seared frame of heart, and benumbing of conscience; which frame, he stilly and slily supplieth with such despair, that though not much guilt attendeth souls, yet they continually have a secret conclusion within them that there is no hopes for them; "for they have loved sins, therefore after them they will go" (Jer. 2:25; and 18:12).

Now therefore I went on in sin with great greediness of mind, still grudging that I could not be so satisfied with it as I would. This did continue with me about a month, or more; but one day, as I was standing at a neighbor's shop-window, and there cursing and swearing, and playing the madman, after my wonted manner, there sat within the woman of the house, and heard me, who, though she was a very loose and ungodly wench, yet protested that I swore and cursed at that most fearful rate that she was made to tremble to hear me; and told me further, that I was the ungodliest fellow for swearing that ever she heard in all her life; and that I, by thus doing, was able to spoil all the youth in the whole town, if they came but in my company.

At this reproof I was silenced, and put to secret shame, and that too, as I thought, before the God of heaven; wherefore, while I stood there, and hanging down my head, I wished with all my heart that I might be a little child again, that my father might learn me to speak without this wicked way of swearing; for, thought I, I am so accustomed to it, that it is in vain for me to think of a reformation, for I thought it could never be.

But how it came to pass, I know not; I did from this time forward so leave my swearing, that it was a great wonder to myself to observe it; and whereas before, I knew not how to speak unless I put an oath before, and another behind, to make my words have authority, now, I could, without it, speak better, and with more pleasantness, than ever I could before. All this while I knew not Jesus Christ, neither did I leave my sports and play.

But quickly after this, I fell in company with one poor man that made profession of religion; who, as I then thought, did talk pleasantly of the Scriptures, and of the matters of religion; wherefore, falling into some love and liking to what he said, I betook me to my Bible, and began to take great pleasure in reading, but especially with the historical part thereof; for, as for Paul's epistles, and such like Scriptures, I could not away with them, being as yet ignorant, either of the corruptions of my nature, or of the want and worth of Jesus Christ to save me.

Wherefore I fell to some outward reformation, both in my words and life, and did set the Commandments before me for my way to heaven; which Commandments I also did strive to keep, as I thought, did keep them pretty well sometimes, and then I should have comfort; yet now and then should break one, and so afflict my conscience; but then I should repent, and say I was sorry for it, and promise God to do better next time, and there get help again, for then I thought I pleased God as well as any man in England.

Thus I continued about a year; all which time our neighbors did take me to be a very godly man, a new and religious man, and did marvel much to see such a great and famous alteration in my life and manners; and, indeed, so it was, though yet I knew not Christ, nor grace, nor faith, nor hope; for, as I have well seen since, had I then died, my state had been most fearful.

But, I say, my neighbors were amazed at this my great conversion from prodigious profaneness to something like a moral life; and, truly, so they well might; for this my conversion was as great as for Tom of Bedlam to become a sober man. Now, therefore, they began to praise, to commend, and to speak well of me, both to my face, and behind my back. Now I was, as they said, become godly; now I was become a right honest man. But, oh! when I understood that these were their words and opinions of me, it pleased me mighty well. For though as yet I was nothing but a poor painted hypocrite, yet I loved to be talked of as one that was truly godly, I was proud of my godliness, and, indeed, I did all I did, either to be seen of, or to be well spoken of, by men. And thus I continued for about a twelvemonth or more.

Now, you must know, that before this I had taken

much delight in ringing, but my conscience beginning to be tender, I thought such practice was but vain, and therefore forced myself to leave it, yet my mind hankered; wherefore I should go to the steeple house, and look on, though I durst not ring. But I thought this did not become religion neither, yet I forced myself, and would look on still; but quickly after, I began to think, "How, if one of the bells should fall?" Then I chose to stand under a main beam, that lay overthwart the steeple from side to side thinking there I might stand sure, but then I should think again, should the bell fall with a swing, it might first hit the wall, and then rebounding upon me, might kill me for all this beam. This made me stand in the steeple door; and now, thought I, I am safe enough; for, if a bell should then fall, I can slip out behind these thick walls, and so be preserved notwithstanding.

So, after this, I would yet go to see them ring, but would not go further than the steeple door; but then it came into my head, "How, if the steeple itself should fall?" And this thought, it may fall for aught I know, when I stood and looked on, did continually so shake my mind, that I durst not stand at the steeple door any longer, but was forced to flee, for fear the steeple should fall upon my head.

Another thing was my dancing; I was a full year before I could quite leave that; but all this while, when I thought I kept this or that Commandment, or did, by word or deed, anything that I thought were good, I had great peace in my conscience; and should think with myself, "God cannot choose but be now pleased with me"; yea, to relate it in mine own way, I thought no man in England could please God better than I.

But, poor wretch as I was, I was all this while ignorant of Jesus Christ, and going about to establish my own righteousness; and had perished therein, had not God, in mercy, showed me more of my state by nature.

But upon a day, the good providence of God did cast me to Bedford, to work on my calling, and in one of the streets of that town, I came where there were three or four poor women sitting at a door in the sun, and talking about the things of God; and being now willing to hear them discourse, I drew near to hear what they said, for I was now a brisk talker also myself in the matters of religion. But I may say, I heard, but I understood not; for they were far above, out of my reach. Their talk was about a new birth, the work of God on their hearts, also how they were convinced of their miserable state by nature; they talked how God had visited their souls with His love in the Lord Jesus, and with what words and promises they had been refreshed, comforted, and supported against the temptations of the Devil. Moreover, they reasoned of the suggestions and temptations of Satan in particular; and told to each other by which they had been afflicted, and how they were borne up under his assaults. They also discoursed of their own wretchedness of heart, of their unbelief; and did contemn, slight, and abhor their own righteousness, as filthy and insufficient to do them any good.

And methought they spake as if joy did make them speak; they spake with such pleasantness of Scripture language, and with such appearance of grace in all they said, that they were to me as if they had found a new world, as if they were people that dwelt alone, and were not to be reckoned amongst their neighbors (Num. 23:9).

At this I felt my own heart began to shake, and mistrust my condition to be naught; for I saw that in all my thoughts about religion and salvation, the new birth did never enter into my mind, neither knew I the comfort of the Word and promise, nor the deceitfulness and treachery of my own wicked heart. As for secret thoughts, I took no notice of them; neither did I understand what Satan's temptations were, nor how they were to be withstood and resisted, etc.

Thus, therefore, when I had heard and considered what they said, I left them, and went about my employment again, but their talk and discourse went with me; also my heart would tarry with them, for I was greatly affected with their words, both because of them I was convinced that I wanted[2] the true tokens of a truly godly man, and also because by them I was convinced of the happy and blessed condition of him that was such an one. . . .

2 Lacked.

Sir William Temple

[1628–1699]

THERE are curious contradictions in Temple's personality and career. By nature quiet, withdrawn, and peace-loving, he led an active though not conspicuously successful life as a statesman and diplomat, and he devoted much energy in his later years to defending the claims of the ancient learning against the modern in that warlike controversy of scholars which is known to intellectual history as the "battle of the books." Temple's father, like his father before him, was a civil servant in Ireland, and young Temple was brought up in England by an uncle. He attended Emmanuel College, Cambridge, where his tutor was the Platonist Ralph Cudworth, but he left without taking a degree. In 1648 he set out for France, where he was to reside for several years; on the way he stopped at the Isle of Wight to visit a young friend named Francis Osborne and immediately fell in love with Osborne's sister Dorothy. The story of their love is one of the most gentle and charming in literary history: her family opposed the match, but Dorothy was as firm-minded as she was witty, and the lovers were married on Christmas Day, 1654. Shortly before the wedding Dorothy suffered an attack of smallpox which marred her beauty, but nothing marred the exemplary quality of their relationship. The troubled course of their courtship is described in the memorable and delightful letters which Dorothy sent William during their separation; more than any other private documents of the seventeenth century, they evoke a sense of contemporaneity.

Temple took time off from his political activities to write on a wide variety of subjects. His treatises *Upon the Present State of Ireland* and *Upon the Original and Nature of Government* have little interest for the modern reader, and his notorious *Essay upon the Ancient and Modern Learning* is of interest only for its bizarre extremeness of position and for the fact that it elicited a work of genius, *The Battle of the Books*, from Temple's young relative and secretary, Jonathan Swift. It is for his less ambitious, more casual works that Temple is remembered in literary history, for he was a born essayist: diffuse, gossipy, and discursive. His essays *Of Poetry* and *Of Health and Long Life* have intelligence and charm, and they are expressed in an easy and felicitous style which at times reminds one of Cowley.

Temple was happier as a stylist and philosopher than as a literary historian or etymologist, although in the history of literary criticism he must be remembered as one of the first to consider literature with respect to man's environment and to considerations of historical change. Dr. Johnson spoke highly of him; Lamb loved him; and Thackeray was impressed by his "practiced and easy good breeding." The gentle reader cannot fail to be drawn to a quiet-loving man who considered the things pursued by most men as baubles beside "old wood to burn, old wine to drink, old friends to converse with, and old books to read," and whose three chief wishes were for health and peace and fair weather.

SIR W. TEMPLE. *Essays on Ancient and Modern Learning and on Poetry*, ed. J. E. Spingarn (Oxford, 1909).

————. *Three Essays*, ed. F. J. Fielden (Oxford, 1939). Contains "Of Poetry," "Of Popular Discontents," and "Of Health and Long Life."

H. E. WOODBRIDGE. *Sir William Temple: The Man and His Work* (New York, 1940). Biography.

C. MARBURG. *Sir William Temple: A Seventeenth-Century "Libertin"* (New Haven, Conn., 1932). A study of Temple's ideas.

OF POETRY

[TEXT: *third edition of Miscellanea, Part II, 1692*]

THE two common shrines to which most men offer up the application of their thoughts and their lives are profit and pleasure; and by their devotions to either of these they are vulgarly distinguished into two sects, and called either busy or idle men. Whether these terms differ in meaning or only in sound, I know very well may be disputed, and with appearance enough; since the covetous man takes perhaps as much pleasure in his gains as the voluptuous does in his luxury, and would not pursue his business unless he were pleased with it, upon the last account[1] of what he most wishes and desires, nor would care for the increase of his fortunes unless he proposed thereby that of his pleasures too, in one kind or another, so that pleasure may be said to be his end, whether he will allow to find it in his pursuit or no. Much ado there has been, many words spent, or (to speak with more respect to the ancient philosophers) many disputes have been raised upon this argument, I think to little purpose, and that all has been rather an exercise of wit than an inquiry after truth; and all controversies that can never end had better perhaps never begin. The best is to take words as they are most commonly spoken and meant, like coin as it most currently passes, without raising scruples upon the weight or the allay, unless the cheat or the defect be gross and evident. Few things in the world, or none, will bear too much refining; a thread too fine spun will easily break, and the point of a needle too finely filed. The usual acceptation takes profit and pleasure for two different things, and not only calls the followers or votaries of them by several

names of busy and of idle men, but distinguishes the faculties of the mind that are conversant about them, calling the operations of the first, wisdom, and of the other, wit, which is a Saxon word that is used to express what the Spaniards and Italians call *ingenio*, and the French, *esprit*, both from the Latin; but I think wit more peculiarly signifies that of poetry, as may occur upon remarks of the Runic language.[2] To the first of these are attributed the inventions or productions of things generally esteemed the most necessary, useful, or profitable to human life, either in private possessions or public institutions; to the other, those writings or discourses which are the most pleasing or entertaining to all that read or hear them. Yet, according to the opinion of those that link them together, as the inventions of sages and law-givers themselves do please as well as profit those who approve and follow them, so those of poets instruct and profit as well as please such as are conversant in them; and the happy mixture of both these makes the excellency in both those compositions, and has given occasion for esteeming, or at least for calling, heroic virtue and poetry divine.

The names given to poets, both in Greek and Latin, express the same opinion of them in those nations: the Greek signifying *makers* or *creators*, such as raise admirable frames and fabrics out of nothing, which strike with wonder and with pleasure the eyes and imaginations of those who behold them; the Latin makes the same word common to *poets* and to *prophets*. Now, as creation is the first attribute and highest

1 In making a final estimate.

2 See below, pp. 554 ff.

operation of divine power, so is prophecy the greatest emanation of divine spirit in the world. As the names in those two learned languages, so the causes of poetry, are by the writers of them made to be divine, and to proceed from a celestial fire or divine inspiration; and by the vulgar opinions, recited or related to in many passages of those authors, the effects of poetry were likewise thought divine and supernatural, and power of charms and enchantments were ascribed to it.

> *Carmina vel cælo possunt deducere lunam,*
> *Carminibus Circe socios mutavit Ulyssis,*
> *Frigidus in pratis cantando rumpitur anguis.*[3]

But I can easily admire poetry, and yet without adoring it: I can allow it to arise from the greatest excellency of natural temper or the greatest race of native genius, without exceeding the reach of what is human, or giving it any approaches of divinity, which is, I doubt, debased or dishonored by ascribing to it anything that is in the compass of our action or even comprehension, unless it be raised by an immediate influence from itself. I cannot allow poetry to be more divine in its effects than in its causes, nor any operation produced by it to be more than purely natural, or to deserve any other sort of wonder than those of music or of natural magic, however any of them have appeared to minds little versed in the speculations of nature, of occult qualities, and the force of numbers or of sounds. Whoever talks of drawing down the moon from heaven by the force of verses or of charms, either believes not himself, or too easily believes what others told him, or perhaps follows an opinion begun by the practice of some poet upon the facility of some people, who, knowing the time when an eclipse would happen, told them he would by his charms call down the moon at such an hour, and was by them thought to have performed it.

When I read that charming description in Virgil's eighth eclogue of all sorts of charms and fascinations by verses, by images, by knots, by numbers, by fire, by herbs, employed upon occasion of a violent passion from a jealous or disappointed love, I have recourse to the strong impressions of fables and of poetry, to the easy mistakes of popular opinions, to the force of imagination, to the secret virtues of several herbs, and

to the powers of sounds. And I am sorry the natural history or account of fascination has not employed the pen of some person of such excellent wit and deep thought and learning as Casaubon,[4] who writ that curious and useful treatise of enthusiasm, and by it discovered the hidden or mistaken sources of that delusion, so frequent in all regions and religions of the world, and which had so fatally spread over our country in that age in which this treatise was so seasonably published. 'Tis much to be lamented that he lived not to complete that work in the second part he promised, or that his friends neglected the publishing it, if it were left in papers, though loose and unfinished. I think a clear account of enthusiasm and fascination from their natural causes would very much deserve from mankind in general as well as from the commonwealth of learning; might perhaps prevent many public disorders, and save the lives of many innocent, deluded or deluding people, who suffer so frequently upon account of witches[5] and wizards. I have seen many miserable examples of this kind in my youth at home; and though the humor or fashion be a good deal worn out of the world within thirty or forty years past, yet it still remains in several remote parts of Germany, Sweden, and some other countries.

But to return to the charms of poetry, if the forsaken lover in that eclogue of Virgil had expected only from the force of her verses or her charms what is the burthen of the song—to bring Daphnis home from the town where he was gone and engaged in a new amour; if she had pretended only to revive an old fainting flame, or to damp a new one that was kindling in his breast, she might, for aught I know, have compassed such ends by the power of such charms, and without other than very natural enchantments. For there is no question but true poetry may have the force to raise passions and to allay them, to change and to extinguish them, to temper joy and grief, to raise love and fear, nay, to turn fear into boldness, and love into indifference and into hatred itself; and I easily believe that the disheartened Spartans were new animated, and recovered their lost courage, by the songs of Tyrtæus;[6]

---

3 Song can indeed draw down the moon from heaven; Circe by song transformed the comrades of Ulysses; by the power of song the cold snake in the meadows bursts its skin. (Virgil, Eclogues, viii, 69–71.)

4 Florence Estienne Méric Casaubon, 1599–1671, an English classical scholar, was the son of the great French scholar and theologian, Isaac Casaubon. His Treatise Concerning Enthusiasm appeared in 1655.

5 See Sir Thomas Browne's discussion of witches in his Religio Medici, pp. 337–38.

6 The war songs of Tyrtæus were given credit for animating the courage of the Spartans in their conflict with the Messenians in the seventh century B.C.

that the cruelty and revenge of Phalaris[7] were changed by the odes of Stesichorus[8] into the greatest kindness and esteem; and that many men were as passionately enamored by the charms of Sappho's[9] wit and poetry as by those of beauty in Flora[10] or Thais;[11] for 'tis not only beauty gives love, but love gives beauty to the object that raises it; and if the possession be strong enough, let it come from what it will, there is always beauty enough in the person that gives it. Nor is it any great wonder that such force should be found in poetry, since in it are assembled all the powers of eloquence, of music, and of picture, which are all allowed to make so strong impressions upon human minds. How far men have been affected with all or any of these needs little proof or testimony. The examples have been known enough in Greece and in Italy, where some have fallen downright in love with the ravishing beauties of a lovely object drawn by the skill of an admirable painter; nay, painters themselves have fallen in love with some of their own productions, and doted on them as on a mistress or a fond child, which distinguishes among the Italians the several pieces that are done by the same hand into several degrees of those made *con studio*, *con diligenza*, or *con amore*, whereof the last are ever the most excelling. But there needs no more instances of this kind than the stories related and believed by the best authors as known and undisputed: of the two young Grecians, one whereof ventured his life to be locked up all night in the temple, and satisfy his passion with the embraces and enjoyment of a statue of Venus that was there set up and designed for another sort of adoration; the other pined away and died for being hindered his perpetually gazing, admiring, and embracing a statue at Athens.

The powers of music are either felt or known by all men, and are allowed to work strangely upon the mind and the body, the passions and the blood, to raise joy and grief, to give pleasure and pain, to cure diseases and the mortal sting of the tarantula, to give motions to the feet as well as the heart, to compose disturbed thoughts, to assist and heighten devotions itself. We need no recourse to the fables of Orpheus or Amphion, or the force of their music upon fishes and beasts; 'tis enough that we find the charming of serpents, and the cure or allay of an evil spirit or possession attributed to it in Sacred Writ.[12]

For the force of eloquence, that so often raised and appeased the violence of popular commotions and caused such convulsions in the Athenian state, no man needs more to make him acknowledge it than to consider Cæsar, one of the greatest and wisest of mortal men, come upon the tribunal full of hatred and revenge, and with a determined resolution to condemn Labienus,[13] yet upon the force of Cicero's eloquence, in an oration for his defense, begin to change countenance, turn pale, shake to that degree that the papers he held fell out of his hand, as if he had been frighted with words that never was so with blows, and at last change all his anger into clemency, and acquit the brave criminal instead of condemning him.

Now if the strength of these three mighty powers be united in poetry, we need not wonder that such virtues and such honors have been attributed to it that it has been thought to be inspired, or has been called divine; and yet I think it will not be disputed that the force of wit and reasoning, the height of conceptions and expressions, may be found in poetry as well as in oratory, the life and spirit of representation or picture as much as in painting, and the force of sounds as well as in music. And how far these three natural powers together may extend, and to what effects, even such as may be mistaken for supernatural or magical, I leave it to such men to consider whose thoughts turn to such speculations as these, or who by their native temper and genius are in some degree disposed to receive the impressions of them. For my part, I do not wonder that the famous Doctor Harvey,[14] when he was reading Virgil, should sometimes throw him down upon the table, and say he had a devil; nor that the learned Méric Casaubon should find such charming pleasures and emotions as he describes, upon the reading some

---

7 Phalaris, ruler of Agrigentum in Sicily, a proverbially cruel tyrant of the sixth century B.C. He is reputed to have burnt his victims alive in a brazen bull.

8 Stesichorus, celebrated as one of the nine chiefs of ancient lyric verse, was a Greek poet contemporary with Sappho.

9 Sappho, the greatest of Greek poetesses, flourished about 600 B.C.

10 The Roman goddess of flowers.

11 An Athenian courtesan contemporary with Alexander the Great.

12 The reference is to the effect on King Saul of David's playing as narrated in I Samuel 16:14–23.

13 Temple's memory plays him false here. It was Cicero's speech in defense of Quintus Ligarius that wrought the change in Cæsar.

14 Dr. William Harvey, 1578–1658, whose discovery of the circulation of the blood was announced to the world in his great work, *De Motu Cordis*, 1628.

parts of Lucretius;[15] that so many should cry, and with downright tears, at some tragedies of Shakespeare, and so many more should feel such turns or curdling of their blood upon the reading or hearing some excellent pieces of poetry; nor that Octavia[16] fell into a swound at the recital made by Virgil of those verses in the sixth of his Æneids.

This is enough to assert the powers of poetry, and discover the ground of those opinions of old which derived it from divine inspiration, and gave it so great a share in the supposed effects of sorcery or magic. But as the old romances seem to lessen the honor of true prowess and valor in their knights by giving such a part in all their chief adventures to enchantment, so the true excellency and just esteem of poetry seems rather debased than exalted by the stories or belief of the charms performed by it, which among the northern nations grew so strong and so general that about five or six hundred years ago all the Runic poetry[17] came to be decried, and those ancient characters in which they were written to be abolished by the zeal of bishops and even by orders and decrees of state, which has given a great maim, or rather an irrecoverable loss, to the story of those northern kingdoms, the seat of our ancestors in all the western parts of Europe.

The more true and natural source of poetry may be discovered by observing to what god this inspiration was ascribed by the ancients, which was Apollo, or the sun, esteemed among them the god of learning in general, but more particularly of music and of poetry. The mystery of this fable means, I suppose, that a certain noble and vital heat of temper, but especially of the brain, is the true spring of these two arts or sciences. This was that celestial fire which gave such a pleasing motion and agitations to the minds of those men that have been so much admired in the world, that raises such infinite images of things so agreeable and delightful to mankind. By the influence of this sun are produced those golden and inexhausted mines of invention, which has furnished the world with treasures so highly esteemed and so universally known and used in all the regions that have yet been discovered. From this arises that elevation of genius which can never be produced by any art or study, by pains or by industry,

which cannot be taught by precepts or examples, and therefore is agreed by all to be the pure and free gift of heaven or of nature, and to be a fire kindled out of some hidden spark of the very first conception.

But though invention be the mother of poetry, yet this child is, like all others, born naked, and must be nourished with care, clothed with exactness and elegance, educated with industry, instructed with art, improved by application, corrected with severity, and accomplished with labor and with time, before it arrives at any great perfection or growth. 'Tis certain that no composition requires so many several ingredients, or of more different sorts than this, nor that to excel in any qualities there are necessary so many gifts of nature and so many improvements of learning and of art. For there must be an universal genius, of great compass as well as great elevation. There must be a sprightly imagination or fancy, fertile in a thousand productions, ranging over infinite ground, piercing into every corner, and by the light of that true poetical fire discovering a thousand little bodies or images in the world, and similitudes among them, unseen to common eyes, and which could not be discovered without the rays of that sun.

Besides the heat of invention and liveliness of wit, there must be the coldness of good sense and soundness of judgment, to distinguish between things and conceptions which at first sight or upon short glances seem alike; to choose among infinite productions of wit and fancy which are worth preserving and cultivating, and which are better stifled in the birth, or thrown away when they are born, as not worth bringing up. Without the forces of wit, all poetry is flat and languishing without the succors of judgment, 'tis wild and extravagant. The true wonder of poesy is that such contraries must meet to compose it: a genius both penetrating and solid; in expression both delicacy and force; and the frame or fabric of a true poem must have something both sublime and just, amazing and agreeable. There must be a great agitation of mind to invent, a great calm to judge and correct; there must be upon the same tree, and at the same time, both flower and fruit. To work up this metal into exquisite figure there must be employed the fire, the hammer, the chisel, and the file. There must be a general knowledge both of nature and of arts; and to go the lowest that can be, there are required genius, judgment, and application; for without this last all the rest will not serve turn, and none ever was a great poet that applied himself much to anything else.

---

15 Roman poet, c. 96–55 B.C., author of one of the great philosophical poems of the world, *De Rerum Natura* (On the Nature of Things).

16 Sister of Augustus and wife of Mark Antony. Virgil's sixth book describes the descent of Æneas into Hades.

17 See p. 553 below, and note.

When I speak of poetry I mean not an ode or an elegy, a song or a satire, nor by a poet the composer of any of these, but of a just poem;[18] and after all I have said, 'tis no wonder there should be so few that appeared in any parts or any ages of the world, or that such as have should be so much admired, and have almost divinity ascribed to them and to their works.

Whatever has been among those who are mentioned with so much praise or admiration by the ancients but are lost to us, and unknown any further than their names, I think no man has been so bold among those that remain to question the title of Homer and Virgil, not only to the first rank, but to the supreme dominion in this state, and from whom, as the great lawgivers as well as princes, all the laws and orders of it are or may be derived. Homer was without dispute the most universal genius that has been known in the world, and Virgil the most accomplished.[19] To the first must be allowed the most fertile invention, the richest vein, the most general knowledge, and the most lively expression; to the last, the noblest ideas, the justest institution, the wisest conduct, and the choicest elocution. To speak in the painter's terms, we find in the works of Homer the most spirit, force, and life; in those of Virgil, the best design, the truest proportions, and the greatest grace. The coloring in both seems equal, and, indeed, in both is admirable. Homer had more fire and rapture, Virgil more light and swiftness;[20] or at least the poetical fire was more raging in one, but clearer in the other, which makes the first more amazing and the latter more agreeable. The ore was richer in one, but in t'other more refined, and better allayed to make up excellent work. Upon the whole, I think it must be confessed that Homer was of the two, and perhaps of all others, the vastest, the sublimest, and the most wonderful genius; and that he has been generally so esteemed there cannot be a greater testimony given than what has been by some observed, that not only the greatest masters have found in his works the best and truest principles of all their sciences or arts, but that the noblest nations have derived from them the original of their several races, though it be hardly yet agreed whether his story be true or fiction. In short, these two immortal poets must be allowed to have so much excelled in their kinds as to have exceeded all comparison, to have even extinguished emulation, and in a manner confined true poetry not only to their two languages, but to their very persons. And I am apt to believe so much of the true genius of poetry in general, and of its elevation in these two particulars, that I know not whether of all the numbers of mankind that live within the compass of a thousand years, for one man that is born capable of making such a poet as Homer or Virgil, there may not be a thousand born capable of making as great generals of armies or ministers of state as any the most renowned in story.

I do not intend here to make a further critique upon poetry, which were too great a labor, nor to give rules for it, which were as great a presumption. Besides, there has been so much paper blotted upon these subjects in this curious and censuring age that 'tis all grown tedious or repetition. The modern French wits[21] (or pretenders) have been very severe in their censures and exact in their rules, I think to very little purpose; for I know not why they might not have contented themselves with those given by Aristotle and Horace, and have translated them rather than commented upon them, for all they have done has been no more, so as they seem, by their writings of this kind, rather to have valued themselves than improved anybody else. The truth is, there is something in the genius of poetry too libertine to be confined to so many rules; and whoever goes about to subject it to such constraints loses both its spirit and grace, which are ever native, and never learnt even of the best masters. 'Tis as if, to make excellent honey, you should cut off the wings of your bees, confine them to their hive or their stands, and lay flowers before them, such as you think the sweetest and like to yield the finest extraction; you had as good pull out their stings, and make arrant drones of them. They must range through fields as well as gardens, choose such flowers as they please, and by proprieties and scents they only know and distinguish. They must work up their cells with admirable

18 By "a just poem" Temple means an epic or other lengthy and ambitious work. See his comments on contemporary lyric and occasional verse in contrast to "heroic poetry," p. 556 below.

19 Compare Dryden's similar comments on Homer and Virgil in his Preface to the "Fables," pp. 632 ff. below.

20 The 1690 edition reads "sweetness," which seems more appropriate here.

21 Temple is referring to such critics as Rapin, Le Bossu, and Boileau. The latter's *L'Art Poétique*, 1674, a didactic poem written in imitation of Horace, contains the best formulation of the "rules," which stemmed from the works of Aristotle and Horace. Temple is one of a long line of attackers of these rules and of their French proponents. In spite of the justice of Temple's criticisms, the literary influence of France upon England was not without its beneficial effects in this period and in the succeeding generation.

art, extract their honey with infinite labor, and sever it from the wax with such distinction and choice as belongs to none but themselves to perform or to judge.

It would be too much mortification to these great arbitrary rulers among the French writers or our own to observe the worthy productions that have been formed by their rules, the honor they have received in the world, or the pleasure they have given mankind. But to comfort them, I do not know there was any great poet in Greece after the rules of that art laid down by Aristotle, nor in Rome after those by Horace, which yet none of our moderns pretend to have outdone. Perhaps Theocritus and Lucan[22] may be alleged against this assertion; but the first offered no further than at idylls or eclogues, and the last, though he must be avowed for a true and a happy genius, and to have made some very high flights, yet he is so unequal to himself, and his muse is so young, that his faults are too noted to allow his pretenses. *Feliciter audet*[23] is the true character of Lucan, as of Ovid *lusit amabiliter*.[24] After all, the utmost that can be achieved or, I think, pretended by any rules in this art is but to hinder some men from being very ill poets, but not to make any man a very good one. To judge who is so, we need go no further for instruction than three lines of Horace:

> *Ille meum qui pectus inaniter angit,*
> *Irritat, mulcet, falsis terroribus implet,*
> *Ut magus, et modo me Thebis, modo ponit Athenis.*[25]

He is a poet,

> Who vainly anguishes my breast,
> Provokes, allays, and with false terror fills,
> Like a magician, and now sets me down
> In Thebes, and now in Athens.

Whoever does not affect and move the same present passions in you that he represents in others, and at other times raise images about you, as a conjuror is said to do spirits, transport you to the places and to the persons he describes, cannot be judged to be a poet, though his measures are never so just, his feet never so smooth, or his sounds never so sweet.

But instead of critique or rules concerning poetry, I shall rather turn my thoughts to the history of it, and observe the antiquity, the uses, the changes, the decays, that have attended this great empire of wit.[26]

It is, I think, generally agreed to have been the first sort of writing that has been used in the world, and in several nations to have preceded the very invention or usage of letters. This last is certain in America, where the first Spaniards met with many strains of poetry, and left several of them translated into their language, which seem to have flowed from a true poetic vein before any letters were known in those regions. The same is probable of the Scythians, the Grecians, and the Germans. Aristotle says the Agathyrsi had their laws all in verse; and Tacitus, that the Germans had no annals nor records but what were so; and for the Grecian oracles delivered in them, we have no certain account when they began, but rather reason to believe it was before the introduction of letters from Phœnicia among them. Pliny tells it, as a thing known, that Pherecides was the first who writ prose in the Greek tongue, and that he lived about the same time of Cyrus, whereas Homer and Hesiod lived some hundreds of years before that age, and Orpheus, Linus, Musæus, some hundreds before them; and of the Sibyls, several were before any of those, and in times as well as places whereof we have no clear records now remaining. What Solon and Pythagoras writ is said to have been in verse, who were something older than Cyrus; and before them were Archilochus, Simonides, Tyrtæus, Sappho, Stesichorus, and several other poets famous in their times. The same thing is reported of Chaldæa, Syria, and China; among the ancient Western Goths, our ancestors, the Runic poetry seems to have been as old as their letters; and their laws, their precepts of wisdom as well as their records, their religious rites as well as their charms and incantations, to have been all in verse.

Among the Hebrews, and even in Sacred Writ, the most ancient is by some learned men esteemed to be the Book of Job,[27] and that it was written before the time

---

22 Lucan, a Latin poet during the reign of Nero, was the author of *Pharsalia*, which deals with the civil war between Cæsar and Pompey that terminated in the battle at Pharsalia with the total defeat of Pompey.

23 He ventures happily.   24 He ridiculed pleasantly.

25 This quotation, as well as the two foregoing Latin phrases, is taken from the same Epistle of Horace (II, i).

26 It is to be noted that in his history of poetry Temple draws chiefly on the ancient Classics, of which he was an ardent defender in the periodical controversies about the merits of ancient and of modern literature. Old English literature was not known in his day. Had it been, he could have adduced proof from the literature of his own island that poetry is of greater antiquity than literary prose.

27 Temple's discussion of the Book of Job as consisting chiefly of poetry and as having great value as literature is interesting in the evolution of the study of the Bible as a

of Moses, and that it was a translation into Hebrew, out of the old Chaldæan or Arabian language.[28] It may probably be conjectured that he was not a Jew, from the place of his abode, which appears to have been seated between the Chaldæans of one side and the Sabæans (who were of Arabia) on the other; and by many passages of that admirable and truly inspired poem, the author seems to have lived in some parts near the mouth of Euphrates, or the Persian Gulf, where he contemplated the wonders of the deep as well as the other works of nature common to those regions. Nor is it easy to find any traces of the Mosaical rites or institutions, either in the divine worship or the morals related to in those writings. For not only sacrifices and praises were more ancient in religious service than the age of Moses, but the opinion of one Deity, and adored without any idol or representation, was professed and received among the ancient Persians and Etruscans and Chaldæans. So that if Job was an Hebrew, 'tis probable he may have been of the race of Heber, who lived in Chaldæa, or of Abraham, who is supposed to have left that country for the profession or worship of one God, rather than from the branch of Isaac and Israel, who lived in the land of Canaan. Now I think it is out of controversy that the Book of Job was written originally in verse, and was a poem upon the subject of the justice and power of God, and in vindication of His providence against the common arguments of atheistical men, who took occasion to dispute it from the usual events of human things, by which so many ill and impious men seem happy and

prosperous in the course of their lives, and so many pious and just men seem miserable or afflicted. The Spanish translation of the Jews in Ferrara,[29] which pretends to render the Hebrew as near as could be, word for word, and for which all translators of the Bible since have had great regard, gives us the two first chapters and the last from the seventh verse in prose, as an historical introduction and conclusion of the work, and all the rest in verse, except the transitions from one part or person of this sacred dialogue to another.

But if we take the Books of Moses[30] to be the most ancient in the Hebrew tongue, yet the Song of Moses may probably have been written before the rest, as that of Deborah before the Book of Judges, being praises sung to God upon the victories or successes of the Israelites, related in both. And I never read the last without observing in it as true and noble strains of poetry and picture as in any other language whatsoever, in spite of all disadvantages from translations into so different tongues and common prose. If an opinion of some learned men both modern and ancient could be allowed, that Esdras was the writer or compiler of the first historical parts of the Old Testament,[31] though from the same divine inspiration as that of Moses and the other prophets, then the Psalms of David would be the first writings we find in Hebrew; and next to them the Song of Solomon, which was written when he was young, and Ecclesiastes when he was old.[32] So that from all sides, both sacred and profane, it appears that poetry was the first sort of writing known and used in the several nations of the world.

It may seem strange, I confess, upon the first thought, that a sort of style so regular and so difficult should have grown in use before the other so easy and so loose. But if we consider what the first end of writing was, it will appear probable from reason as well as

---

literary masterpiece. Such a view of the Scriptures was rare in his day. Sidney, in his Apology for Poetry, 1595, included in his discussion some of the poetical portions of the Bible. Milton, in his Reason of Church Government, 1642, refers to the Book of Job as "a brief model" of the epic poem, to the Song of Solomon as "a divine pastoral poem," and to the Apocalypse of St. John as "a high and stately tragedy." In general, however, the Bible was the Word of God, and it would have seemed profane and blasphemous to most of Temple's contemporaries to regard any portions of it as the productions of human wit or genius. With Temple's discussion of the poetry of the Bible compare Felltham's remarks on the subject in Of Poets and Poetry, p. 329.

28 Temple's speculations about the origins of the Book of Job are not sustained by modern scholarship. He was right in conjecturing that the character Job is not a Jew, but there is no reason to presuppose a non-Hebrew origin of the book itself. The prose prologue (chs. 1, 2) and epilogue (ch. 42:7–17) of the book are now considered to be the surviving fragments of a popular story of a comparatively early date, probably before the seventh century B.C. The poetic portion is now commonly assigned to the latter part of the fifth century B.C.

29 A version of the Old Testament in Spanish begun in the fifteenth century and published at Ferrara in 1553.

30 The "Books of Moses" (the first five books of the Bible, commonly called the Pentateuch) are not now ascribed to Moses, nor are they the "most ancient in the Hebrew tongue." Temple shows discernment, however, in recognizing the "Song of Moses" (Exodus 15:1–18) and that of Deborah (Judges 5) as being of separate composition from the rest of the books in which they are imbedded, and of an earlier date than their respective contexts.

31 Such an opinion is not now held. The Pentateuch is now recognized as the result of a long historical process, only the last stage of which began with the work of Ezra (Esdras) in the fifth century B.C.

32 Neither of these books is now attributed to Solomon.

experience. For the true and general end was but the help of memory in preserving that of words and of actions, which would otherwise have been lost and soon vanish away with the transitory passage of human breath and life. Before the discourses and disputes of philosophers began to busy or amuse the Grecian wits, there was nothing written in prose but either laws, some short sayings of wise men, or some riddles, parables, or fables, wherein were couched by the ancients many strains of natural or moral wisdom and knowledge; and besides these, some short memorials of persons, actions, and of times. Now 'tis obvious enough to conceive how much easier all such writings should be learnt and remembered in verse than in prose, not only by the pleasure of measures and of sounds, which gives a great impression to memory, but by the order of feet, which makes a great facility of tracing one word after another, by knowing what sort of foot or quantity must necessarily have preceded or followed the words we retain and desire to make up.

This made poetry so necessary before letters were invented, and so convenient afterwards; and shows that the great honor and general request wherein it has always been has not proceeded only from the pleasure and delight, but likewise from the usefulness and profit of poetical writings.

This leads me naturally to the subjects of poetry, which have been generally praise, instruction, story, love, grief, and reproach. Praise was the subject of all the songs and psalms mentioned in Holy Writ; of the hymns of Orpheus, of Homer, and many others; of the *Carmina Sæcularia* in Rome, composed all and designed for the honor of their gods; of Pindar, Stesichorus, and Tyrtæus, in the praises of virtue or virtuous men. The subject of Job is instruction concerning the attributes of God and the works of nature. Those of Simonides, Phocillides, Theognis and several other of the smaller Greek poets, with what passes for Pythagoras, are instructions in morality; the first book of Hesiod and Virgil's Georgics in agriculture, and Lucretius in the deepest natural philosophy. Story is the proper subject of heroic poems, as Homer and Virgil in their inimitable Iliads and Æneids; and fable, which is a sort of story, in the Metamorphoses of Ovid. The lyric poetry has been chiefly conversant about love, though turned often upon praise too; and the vein of pastorals and eclogues has run the same course, as may be observed in Theocritus, Virgil, and Horace, who was, I think, the first and last of true lyric poets among

the Latins. Grief has been always the subject of elegy, and reproach that of satire. The dramatic poesy has been composed of all these, but the chief end seems to have been instruction, and under the disguise of fables or the pleasure of story to show the beauties and the rewards of virtue, the deformities and misfortunes or punishment of vice, by examples of both, to encourage one and deter men from the other; to reform ill customs, correct ill manners, and moderate all violent passions. These are the general subjects of both parts, though comedy give us but the images of common life, and tragedy those of the greater and more extraordinary passions and actions among men. To go further upon this subject would be to tread so beaten paths that to travel in them only raises dust, and is neither of pleasure nor of use.

For the changes that have happened in poetry, I shall observe one ancient, and the others that are modern will be too remarkable, in the declines or decays of this great empire of wit. The first change of poetry was made by translating it into prose, or clothing it in those loose robes or common veils that disguised or covered the true beauty of its features and exactness of its shape. This was done first by Æsop in Greek, but the vein was much more ancient in the eastern regions, and much in vogue, as we may observe in the many parables used in the Old Testament as well as in the New. And there is a book of fables,[33] of the sort of Æsop's, translated out of Persian, and pretended to have been so into that language out of the ancient Indian; but though it seems genuine of the eastern countries, yet I do not take it to be so old nor to have so much spirit as the Greek. The next succession of poetry in prose seems to have been in the Milesian tales, which were a sort of little pastoral romances; and though much in request in old Greece and Rome, yet we have no examples that I know of them unless it be the *Longi Pastoralia*,[34] which gives a taste of the great delicacy and pleasure that was found so generally in those sort of tales. The last kind of poetry in prose is that which in latter ages has overrun the world under

33 Temple refers to *Le Livre des Lumières, ou la Conduite des Roys*, 1644, a French translation of a Persian version of the Arabic *Kalilah wa Dimnah*, a collection of animal stories stemming from a Sanskrit original. They are at least as old as the third century A.D. La Fontaine drew on this source for some of his fables. (Kalilah and Dimnah are the names of two jackals.)

34 The famous Greek pastoral romance of Daphnis and Chloë, ascribed to Longus, *c.* A.D. 200.

the name of romances, which though it seems modern and a production of the Gothic genius, yet the writing is ancient. The remainders of Petronius Arbiter[35] seem to be of this kind, and that which Lucian[36] calls his True History. But the most ancient that passes by the name is Heliodorus,[37] famous for the author's choosing to lose his bishopric rather than disown that child of his wit. The true spirit or vein of ancient poetry in this kind seems to shine most in Sir Philip Sidney,[38] whom I esteem both the greatest poet and the noblest genius of any that have left writings behind them and published in ours or any other modern language,—a person born capable not only of forming the greatest ideas, but of leaving the noblest examples, if the length of his life had been equal to the excellence of his wit and his virtues.

With him I leave the discourse of ancient poetry, and to discover the decays of this empire must turn to that of the modern, which was introduced after the decays or rather extinction of the old, as if, true poetry being dead, an apparition of it walked about. This mighty change arrived by no smaller occasions nor more ignoble revolutions than those which destroyed the ancient empire and government of Rome, and erected so many new ones upon their ruins, by the invasions and conquests, or the general inundations, of the Goths, Vandals, and other barbarous or northern nations, upon those parts of Europe that had been subject to the Romans. After the conquests made by Cæsar upon Gaul and the nearer parts of Germany, which were continued and enlarged in the times of Augustus and Tiberius by their lieutenants or generals, great numbers of Germans and Gauls resorted to the Roman armies and to the city itself, and habituated themselves there, as many Spaniards, Syrians, Grecians, had done before upon the conquest of those countries. This mixture soon corrupted the purity of the Latin tongue, so that in Lucian, but more in Seneca,

we find a great and harsh allay entered into the style of the Augustan Age. After Trajan and Adrian had subdued many German and Scythian nations on both sides of the Danube, the commerce of those barbarous people grew very frequent with the Romans; and I am apt to think that the little verses ascribed to Adrian were in imitation of the Runic poetry. The *Scythicas pati pruinas*[39] of Florus shows their race or climate, and the first rhyme that ever I read in Latin, with little allusions of letters or syllables, is in that of Adrian at his death:

> *O animula, vagula, blandula,*
> *Quæ nunc abibis in loca?*
> *Pallidula, lurida, timidula,*
> *Nec, ut soles, dabis joca.*[40]

'Tis probable the old spirit of poetry being lost or frighted away by those long and bloody wars with such barbarous enemies, this new ghost began to appear in its room even about that age,[41] or else that Adrian, who affected that piece of learning as well as others, and was not able to reach the old vein, turned to a new one, which his expeditions into those countries made more allowable in an emperor, and his example recommended to others. In the time of Boethius, who lived under Theodoric in Rome, we find the Latin poetry smell rank of this Gothic imitation, and the old vein quite seared up.

After that age learning grew every day more and more obscured by that cloud of ignorance which, coming from the North and increasing with the numbers and successes of those barbarous people, at length overshadowed all Europe for so long together. The Roman tongue began itself to fail or be disused, and by

35 The *Satyricon* of Petronius Arbiter is the most famous of ancient satirical romances. Only a few fragments of the original survive. The author is thought to have been Nero's confidant, Gaius Petronius, "the arbiter of elegance."

36 A Greek prose writer of the second century A.D., chiefly famous for his Dialogues of the Dead. His True History is a satire parodying tales of adventure.

37 The author of the *Æthiopica*, which relates the popular story of Theogenes and Chariclea, was, according to modern scholars, not the fourth-century bishop of Tricca in Thessaly, but a third-century author, a native of Syria.

38 Temple has in mind, of course, Sidney's Arcadia, 1590, the most fashionable and influential of English pastoral romances.

39 "To endure the Scythian winter." The phrase occurs in some verses to Hadrian (Adrian) by the poet Florus. Temple suggests that Hadrian, a poet and traveler as well as an emperor, learned the art of rhyme in Scythia or from Scythians.

40 Temple quotes the lines inaccurately, and probably from memory. They have been often translated and imitated; the paraphrase of them by Alexander Pope, entitled The Dying Christian to His Soul, is the best known. The lines Temple gives may be rendered: "O little wandering, playful soul, into what regions will you now depart—pale, wan, fearful—not jesting as you were wont to do?"

41 Temple's theory that rhyme came into European poetry only after the dissolution of the Roman Empire is upheld by modern scholarship. To so ardent a Classicist as he it could seem only a barbarous and degenerate feature of Latin poetry. His contemporary Milton, in his note on the verse of Paradise Lost, terms rhyme "no necessary adjunct or true ornament of poem or good verse, . . . but the invention of a barbarous age, to set off wretched matter and lame meter."

its corruption made way for the generation of three new languages, in Spain, Italy, and France. The courts of the princes and nobles, who were of the conquering nations, for several ages used their Gothic, or Frank, or Saxon tongues, which were mingled with those of Germany, where some of the Goths had sojourned long, before they proceeded to their conquests of the more southern or western parts. Wherever the Roman colonies had long remained and their language had been generally spoken, the common people used that still, but vitiated with the base allay of their provincial speech. This in Charlemagne's time was called in France *rustica Romana*, and in Spain, during the Gothic reigns there, *Romance;* but in England, from whence all the Roman soldiers, and great numbers of the Britons most accustomed to their commerce and language, had been drained for the defense of Gaul against the barbarous nations that invaded it about the time of Valentinian,[42] that tongue (being wholly extinguished as well as their own) made way for the entire use of the Saxon language. With these changes the ancient poetry was wholly lost in all these countries, and a new sort grew up by degrees, which was called by a new name of rhymes, with an easy change of the Gothic word *runes,*[43] and not from the Greek *rhythmos,* as is vulgarly supposed.

Runes was properly the name of the ancient Gothic letters or characters, which were invented first or introduced by Odin in the colony or kingdom of the Geats or Goths, which he planted in the northwest parts and round the Baltic Sea, as has been before related.[44] But because all the writings they had among them for many ages were in verse, it came to be the common name of all sorts of poetry among the Goths, and the writers or composers of them were called

runers or rhymers. They had likewise another name for them, or for some sorts of them, which was *Vüses* or *Wises;*[45] and because the sages of that nation expressed the best of their thoughts, and what learning and prudence they had, in these kind of writings, they that succeeded best and with most applause were termed *Wisemen.* The good sense or learning or useful knowledge contained in them was called wisdom, and the pleasant or facetious vein among them was called wit, which was applied to all spirit or race of poetry, where it was found in any men, and was generally pleasing to those that heard or read them.

Of these runes there were in use among the Goths above a hundred several sorts, some composed in longer, some in shorter lines, some equal and others unequal, with many different cadences, quantities, or feet, which in the pronouncing make many sorts of original or natural tunes. Some were framed with allusions of words or consonance of syllables or of letters, either in the same line or in the distich, or by alternate succession and resemblance, which made a sort of jingle that pleased the ruder ears of that people. And because their language was composed most of monosyllables, and of so great numbers, many must end in the same sound. Another sort of runes were made with the care and study of ending two lines, or each other of four lines, with words of the same sound, which being the easiest, requiring less art and needing less spirit, because a certain chime in the sounds supplied that want and pleased common ears, this in time grew the most general among all the Gothic colonies in Europe, and made rhymes or runes pass for the modern poetry in these parts of the world.

This was not used only in their modern languages, but, during those ignorant ages, even in that barbarous Latin which remained, and was preserved among the monks and priests, to distinguish them by some show of learning from the laity, who might well admire it, in what degree soever, and reverence the professors, when they themselves could neither write nor read even in their own language. I mean not only the vulgar laymen, but even the generality of nobles, barons, and princes among them; and this lasted till the ancient learning and languages began to be restored in Europe about two hundred years ago.

The common vein of the Gothic runes was what is

---

42 Emperor of Rome from A.D. 364 to 375.

43 Temple's knowledge of runes, although derived from the best authorities of his day, is faulty, and his etymology throughout this discussion has long since been discredited. There is no connection between *rhyme* (*rime*) and *rune.* *Rune* is the name given to any of the characters of the earliest Teutonic alphabet, which from the third century A.D. on was used especially by the Scandinavians and the Anglo-Saxons. For the etymology of *rune* see any dictionary or encyclopedia. The chief fact with regard to Temple's discussion of runes is that he was the first English critic to become interested in the languages and literatures of northern Europe, and to consider them in relation to the characteristics and development of English poetry.

44 In Temple's essay Upon Heroic Virtue, Section IV, where he also discusses Runic poetry.

45 Temple's etymology is again faulty. He has confused two words which are spelled alike but are of different origins and connotations. See the dictionary *s. v. wise*

termed dithyrambic,[46] and was of a raving or rambling sort of wit or invention, loose and flowing, with little art or confinement to any certain measures or rules; yet some of it wanted not the true spirit of poetry in some degree, or that natural inspiration which has been said to arise from some spark of poetical fire wherewith particular men are born. And such as it was it served the turn, not only to please, but even to charm the ignorant and barbarous vulgar where it was in use. This made the runers among the Goths as much in request and admired as any of the ancient and most celebrated poets were among the learned nations; for among the blind he that has one eye is a prince. They were, as well as the others, thought inspired, and the charms of their runic conceptions were generally esteemed divine, or magical at least.

The subjects of them were various, but commonly the same with those already observed in the true ancient poetry. Yet this vein was chiefly employed upon the records of bold and martial actions, and the praises of valiant men that had fought successfully or died bravely; and these songs or ballads were usually sung at feasts or in circles of young or idle persons, and served to inflame the humor of war, of slaughter, and of spoils among them. More refined honor or love had little part in the writings, because it had little in the lives or actions of those fierce people and bloody times. Honor among them consisted in victory; and love in rapes and in lust.

But as the true flame of poetry was rare among them, and the rest was but wild fire that sparkled or rather crackled a while, and soon went out with little pleasure or gazing of the beholders, those runers who could not raise admiration by the spirit of their poetry endeavored to do it by another, which was that of enchantments. This came in to supply the defect of that sublime and marvelous, which has been found both in poetry and prose among the learned ancients. The Gothic runers, to gain and establish the credit and admiration of their rhymes, turned the use of them very much to incantations and charms, pretending by them to raise storms, to calm the seas, to cause terror in their enemies, to transport themselves in the air, to conjure spirits, to cure diseases, and stanch bleeding wounds, to make women kind or easy, and men hard or invulnerable, as one of their most ancient runers affirms of himself and his own achievements, by force of these magical arms. The men or women who were

thought to perform such wonders or enchantments were, from *Vüses* or *Wises*, the name of those verses wherein their charms were conceived, called wizards or witches.[47]

Out of this quarry seem to have been raised all those trophies of enchantment that appear in the whole fabric of the old Spanish romances, which were the productions of the Gothic wit among them during their reign; and after the conquests of Spain by the Saracens they were applied to the long wars between them and the Christians. From the same may perhaps be derived all the visionary tribe of fairies, elves, and goblins, of sprites and of bulbeggars,[48] that serve not only to fright children into whatever their nurses please, but sometimes, by lasting impressions, to disquiet the sleeps and the very lives of men and women till they grow to years of discretion; and that, God knows, is a period of time which some people arrive to but very late, and perhaps others never. At least this belief prevailed so far among the Goths and their races that all sorts of charms were not only attributed to their runes or verses but to their very characters; so that about the eleventh century they were forbidden and abolished in Sweden, as they had been before in Spain, by civil and ecclesiastical commands or constitutions; and what has been since recovered of that learning or language has been fetched as far as Iceland itself.

How much of this kind and of this credulity remained even to our own age may be observed by any man that reflects so far as thirty or forty years how often avouched and how generally credited were the stories of fairies, sprites, witchcrafts, and enchantments. In some parts of France, and not longer ago, the common people believed certainly there were lougaroos,[49] or men turned into wolves; and I remember several Irish of the same mind. The remainders are woven into our very language: *Mara*,[50] in old Runic, was a goblin

47 Temple is correct in deriving *wizard* from *wise* (in the sense of possessing wisdom), but *witch* is from the Old English *wicca*, meaning one who practices the black art, or magic.

48 Hobgoblins. The etymology of the word is uncertain. It is hardly necessary to point out that fairies, elves, and other members of "the visionary tribe" are not peculiar to Britain, or to the literature of the runers.

49 *Loups-garous*, "wolf-men."

50 *Mare* in *nightmare* is an Old English word derived from a Teutonic root meaning *female monster. Nick* in "Old Nick" is popularly supposed to be a contraction of *Nicholas*, but the reason for the name as applied to the Devil is not clear. It has been suggested that the word may be connected with the archaic verb *nick*, meaning *to catch, trick, steal*, etc. *Bo* and *boo* are purely onomatopœic, and used to startle people. There

46 The dithyramb was a Greek choric hymn of wild character.

that seized upon men asleep in their beds, and took from them all speech and motion; *Old Nicka* was a sprite that came to strangle people who fell into the water; *Bo* was a fierce Gothic captain, son of Odin, whose name was used by his soldiers when they would fright or surprise their enemies; and the proverb of rhyming rats to death came, I suppose, from the same root.

There were, not longer since than the time I have mentioned, some remainders of the Runic poetry among the Irish. The great men of their septs,[51] among the many offices of their family, which continued always in the same races,[52] had not only a physician, a huntsman, a smith, and such like, but a poet and a tale-teller. The first recorded and sung the actions of their ancestors, and entertained the company at feasts. The latter amused them with tales when they were melancholy and could not sleep. And a very gallant gentleman of the north of Ireland has told me of his own experience, that, in his wolf-huntings there, when he used to be abroad in the mountains three or four days together, and lay very ill[53] o' nights so as he could not well sleep, they would bring him one of these taletellers, that, when he lay down, would begin a story of a king or a giant, a dwarf and a damosel, and such rambling stuff, and continue it all night long in such an even tone that you heard it going on whenever you awaked; and he believed nothing any physicians give could have so good and so innocent effect to make men sleep in any pains or distempers of body or mind. I remember in my youth some persons of our country, to have said grace in rhymes, and others their constant prayers; and 'tis vulgar enough that some deeds or conveyances of land have been so since the Conquest.

In such poor wretched weeds as these was poetry clothed during those shades of ignorance that overspread all Europe for so many ages after the sunset of the Roman learning and empire together, which were succeeded by so many new dominions or plantations of the Gothic swarms, and by a new face of customs, habit, language, and almost of nature. But upon the dawn of a new day, and the resurrection of other sciences, with the two learned languages, among us, this of poetry began to appear very early, though very un-

like itself, and in shapes as well as clothes, in humor and in spirit, very different from the ancient. It was now all in rhyme, after the Gothic fashion; for indeed none of the several dialects of that language or allay would bear the composure of such feet and measures as were in use among the Greeks and Latins; and some that attempted it soon left it off, despairing of success. Yet in this new dress poetry was not without some charms, especially those of grace and sweetness, and the ore begun to shine in the hands and works of the first refiners. Petrarch, Ronsard, Spenser, met with much applause upon the subjects of love, praise, grief, reproach. Ariosto and Tasso entered boldly upon the scene of heroic poems, but, having not wings for so high flights, began to learn of the old ones, fell upon their imitations, and chiefly of Virgil, as far as the force of their genius or disadvantage of new languages and customs would allow. The religion of the Gentiles had been woven into the contexture of all the ancient poetry with a very agreeable mixture, which made the moderns affect to give that of Christianity a place also in their poems. But the true religion was not found to become fiction so well as a false had done, and all their attempts of this kind seemed rather to debase religion than to heighten poetry.[54] Spenser endeavored to supply this with morality, and to make instruction instead of story the subject of an epic poem. His execution was excellent, and his flights of fancy very noble and high, but his design was poor, and his moral lay so bare that it lost the effect. 'Tis true, the pill was gilded, but so thin that the color and the taste were too easily discovered.

After these three I know none of the moderns that have made any achievements in heroic poetry worth recording. The wits of the age soon left off such bold adventures and turned to other veins, as if, not worthy to sit down at the feast, they contented themselves with the scraps, with songs and sonnets, with odes and elegies, with satires and panegyrics, and what we call copies of verses upon any subjects or occasions, wanting either genius or application for nobler or more

are many references to the power of Irish witches and rhymers to rhyme rats to death. See the commentaries on As You Like It, III, ii, 187–88.

51 Clans.

52 Temple uses *race* in the sense of *strain, breed* throughout his works.

53 Had a very uncomfortable bed.

54 An important feature of the "Quarrel of the Ancients and the Moderns," which Temple's Essay upon the Ancient and Modern Learning had inaugurated in England, was the controversy as to whether Christian doctrine and machinery were proper subjects for epic poetry. The great French critic Boileau had pronounced in his *Art Poétique* (Canto III) against their use, and Temple here follows the authority of Boileau. It is noteworthy that here as elsewhere Temple does not mention Milton, whose Paradise Lost is a sufficient refutation of the French critic's contentions.

laborious productions, as painters that cannot succeed in great pieces turn to miniature.

But the modern poets, to value this small coin, and make it pass, though of so much a baser metal than the old, gave it a new mixture from two veins which were little known or little esteemed among the ancients. There were indeed some fairies in the old regions of poetry, called epigrams, which seldom reached above the stature of two or four or six lines, and which, being so short, were all turned upon conceit, or some sharp hits of fancy or wit. The only ancient of this kind among the Latins were the *Priapeia*, which were little voluntaries or extemporaries written upon the ridiculous wooden statues of Priapus among the gardens of Rome. In the decays of the Roman learning and wit as well as language, Martial, Ausonius,[55] and others fell into this vein, and applied it indifferently to all subjects, which was before restrained to one, and dressed it something more cleanly than it was born. This vein of conceit seemed proper for such scraps or splinters into which poetry was broken, and was so eagerly followed as almost to overrun all that was composed in our several modern languages. The Italian, the French, the Spanish, as well as English, were for a great while full of nothing else but conceit. It was an ingredient that gave taste to compositions which had little of themselves. 'Twas a sauce that gave point to meat that was flat, and some life to colors that were fading; and, in short, those who could not furnish spirit supplied it with this salt, which may preserve things or bodies that are dead, but is, for aught I know, of little use to the living, or necessary to meats that have much or pleasing tastes of their own. However it were, this vein first overflowed our modern poetry, and with so little distinction or judgment, that we would have conceit as well as rhyme in every two lines, and run through all our long scribbles as well as the short, and the whole body of the poem, whatever it is. This was just as if a building should be nothing but ornament, or clothes nothing but trimming; as if a face should be covered over with black patches, or a gown with spangles; which is all I shall say of it.

Another vein which has entered and helped to corrupt our modern poesy is that of ridicule, as if nothing pleased but what made one laugh; which yet come from two very different affections of the mind. For as men have no disposition to laugh at things they are most pleased with, so they are very little pleased with many things they laugh at.

But this mistake is very general, and such modern poets as found no better way of pleasing thought they could not fail of it by ridiculing. This was encouraged by finding conversation run so much into the same vein, and the wits in vogue to take up with that part of it which was formerly left to those that were called fools, and were used in great families only to make the company laugh. What opinion the Romans had of this character appears in those lines of Horace:

> *Absentem qui rodit amicum,*
> *Qui non defendit alio culpante, solutos*
> *Qui captat risus hominum famamque dicacis,*
> *Fingere qui non visa potest, commissa tacere*
> *Qui nequit, hic niger est, hunc tu, Romane, caveto.*[56]

And 'tis pity the character of a wit in one age should be so like that of a black in another.

Rabelais[57] seems to have been father of the ridicule, a man of excellent and universal learning as well as wit; and though he had too much game given him for satire in that age by the customs of courts and of convents, of processes and of wars, of schools and of camps, of romances and legends, yet he must be confessed to have kept up his vein of ridicule by saying many things so malicious, so smutty, and so profane, that either a prudent, a modest, or a pious man could not have afforded, though he had never so much of that coin about him; and it were to be wished that the wits who have followed his vein had not put too much value upon a dress that better understandings would not wear, at least in public, and upon a compass they gave themselves which other men would not take. The matchless writer of Don Quixote[58] is much more to be admired for having made up so excellent a composition of satire or ridicule without those ingredients, and seems to be the best and highest strain that ever was or will be reached by that vein.

---

55 Martial, a Latin satiric poet, *c.* A.D. 40–104; Ausonius, a Latin poet, *c.* A.D. 309–394.

56 He who maligns an absent friend, who does not defend him when another blames him, who wins the silly laughter of people and thereby gets the reputation of a wit, who can feign things he never saw, who cannot keep a secret—such a one is a black sheep; beware of him, Roman. (Satires, I, iv, 81–85.)

57 François Rabelais, *c.* 1494–1553, whose mammoth satire dealing with Pantagruel and Gargantua was the greatest prose work of sixteenth-century France.

58 This greatest of Spanish prose works, by Cervantes, was published in 1605. A second part was completed in 1615, the year before his death.

It began first in verse with an Italian poem called *La Secchia Rapita*,[59] was pursued by Scarron[60] in French with his Virgil Travesty, and in English by Sir John Mince,[61] Hudibras,[62] and Cotton,[60] and with greater height of burlesque in the English than, I think, in any other language. But let the execution be what it will, the design, the custom, and example are very pernicious to poetry, and indeed to all virtue and good qualities among men, which must be disheartened by finding how unjustly and undistinguished they fall under the lash of raillery, and this vein of ridiculing the good as well as the ill, the guilty and the innocent together. 'Tis a very poor though common pretense to merit to make it appear by the faults of other men. A mean wit or beauty may pass in a room where the rest of the company are allowed to have none; 'tis something to sparkle among diamonds, but to shine among pebbles is neither credit nor value worth the pretending.

Besides these two veins brought in to supply the defects of the modern poetry, much application has been made to the smoothness of language or style, which has at the best but the beauty of coloring in a picture, and can never make a good one without spirit and strength. The Academy set up by Cardinal Richelieu[63] to amuse the wits of that age and country, and divert them from raking into his politics and ministry, brought this in vogue; and the French wits have for this last age been in a manner wholly turned to the refinement of their language, and indeed with such success that it can hardly be excelled, and runs equally through their verse and prose. The same vein has been likewise much cultivated in our modern English poetry, and by such poor recruits have the broken forces of this empire been of late made up; with what success

I leave to be judged by such as consider it in the former heights and the present declines both of power and of honor. But this will not discourage, however it may affect, the true lovers of this mistress, who must ever think her a beauty in rags as well as in robes.

Among these many decays there is yet one sort of poetry that seems to have succeeded much better with our moderns than any of the rest, which is dramatic, or that of the stage. In this the Italian, the Spanish, and the French have all had their different merit, and received their just applauses. Yet I am deceived if our English has not in some kind excelled both the modern and the ancient, which has been by force of a vein natural perhaps to our country, and which with us is called *humor*,[64] a word peculiar to our language, too, and hard to be expressed in any other; nor is it, that I know of, found in any foreign writers, unless it be Molière, and yet his itself has too much of the farce to pass for the same with ours. Shakespeare was the first that opened this vein upon our stage, which has run so freely and so pleasantly ever since that I have often wondered to find it appears so little upon any others, being a subject so proper for them, since humor is but a picture of particular life, as comedy is of general; and though it represents dispositions and customs less common, yet they are not less natural than those that are more frequently among men; for if humor itself be forced, it loses all the grace, which has been indeed the fault of some of our poets most celebrated in this kind.

It may seem a defect in the ancient stage that the characters introduced were so few, and those so common, as a covetous old man, an amorous young, a witty wench, a crafty slave, a bragging soldier. The spectators met nothing upon the stage but what they met in the streets and at every turn. All the variety is drawn only from different and uncommon events, whereas if the characters are so too, the diversity and the pleasure must needs be the more. But as of most general customs in a country, there is usually some ground from the nature of the people or the climate, so there may be amongst us for this vein of our stage, and a greater variety of humor in the picture, because there is a greater variety in the life. This may proceed from the native plenty of our soil, the unequalness of

---

59 The Rape of the Bucket, a mock-heroic poem by Alessandro Tassoni, was published in 1622. The subject is the war between the people of Modena and those of Bologna in the thirteenth century, occasioned by the carrying off by the Modenese of a bucket belonging to Bologna.

60 Paul Scarron, 1610–1660, a French poet whose *Virgile Travesti*, 1648–1652, is one of the wittiest of pseudo-epics of the day. It was paraphrased by Charles Cotton in *Scarronides*, 1664.

61 Sir John Mince (or Mennes), 1599–1671, was joint author of two collections of verse, Wit's Recreations, 1640, and *Musarum Deliciæ*, 1655.

62 Hudibras, the most famous of English burlesque poems, a satire on Puritanism, is by Samuel Butler, 1612–1680. Hudibras, in three parts, was published in 1663–1678.

63 The *Académie Française* had existed as a private literary society for eight years before it received Richelieu's official blessing in 1637.

64 Temple's comments on English comedy and his ascription of its superiority to its humor were commonplaces of literary criticism for many years. It has been noted that he uses the word *humor* in a sense intermediary between the Jonsonian and the modern, and implies by it the faculty or quality that gives rise to eccentric and amusing characters.

our climate, as well as the ease of our government, and the liberty of professing opinions and factions, which perhaps our neighbors may have about them, but are forced to disguise, and thereby they may come in time to be extinguished. Plenty begets wantonness and pride; wantonness is apt to invent, and pride scorns to imitate. Liberty begets stomach or heart, and stomach will not be constrained. Thus we come to have more originals, and more that appear what they are. We have more humor because every man follows his own, and takes a pleasure, perhaps a pride, to show it.

On the contrary, where the people are generally poor and forced to hard labor, their actions and lives are all of a piece; where they serve hard masters, they must follow his examples as well as commands, and are forced upon imitation in small matters as well as obedience in great. So that some nations look as if they were cast all by one mold, or cut out all by one pattern,—at least the common people in one and the gentlemen in another. They seem all of a sort in their habits, their customs, and even their talk and conversation, as well as in the application and pursuit of their actions and their lives.

Besides all this, there is another sort of variety amongst us, which arises from our climate and the dispositions it naturally produces. We are not only more unlike one another than any nation I know, but we are more unlike ourselves too at several times, and owe to our very air some ill qualities as well as many good. We may allow some distempers incident to our climate, since so much health, vigor, and length of life have been generally ascribed to it; for among the Greek and Roman authors themselves we shall find the Britons observed to live the longest, and the Egyptians the shortest, of any nations that were known in those ages. Besides, I think none will dispute the native courage of our men and beauty of our women, which may be elsewhere as great in particulars but nowhere so in general. They may be (what is said of diseases) as acute in other places, but with us they are epidemical. For my own part, who have conversed much with men of other nations, and such as have been both in great employments and esteem, I can say very impartially that I have not observed any so much true genius as among the English; nowhere more sharpness of wit, more pleasantness of humor, more range of fancy, more penetration of thought or depth of reflection among the better sort; nowhere more goodness of nature and of meaning, nor more plainness of sense and of life than among the common sort of country people; nor more blunt courage and honesty than among our seamen.

But with all this our country must be confessed to be what a great foreign physician called it, the Region of Spleen,[65] which may arise a good deal from the great uncertainty and many sudden changes of our weather in all seasons of the year. And how much these affect the heads and hearts, especially of the finest tempers, is hard to be believed by men whose thoughts are not turned to such speculations. This makes us unequal in our humors, inconstant in our passions, uncertain in our ends, and even in our desires. Besides, our different opinions in religion, and the factions they have raised or animated for fifty years past, have had an ill effect upon our manners and customs, inducing more avarice, ambition, disguise, with the usual consequences of them, than were before in our constitution. From all this it may happen that there is nowhere more true zeal in the many different forms of devotion, and yet nowhere more knavery under the shows and pretenses. There are nowhere so many disputers upon religion, so many reasoners upon government, so many refiners in politics, so many curious inquisitives, so many pretenders to business and state employments, greater porers upon books, nor plodders after wealth. And yet nowhere more abandoned libertines, more refined luxurists, extravagant debauchés, conceited gallants, more dabblers in poetry as well as politics, in philosophy and in chemistry. I have had several servants far gone in[66] divinity, others in poetry; have known, in the families of some friends, a keeper[67] deep in the Rosicrucian principles, and a laundress firm in those of Epicurus. What effect soever such a composition or medley of humors among us may have upon our lives or our government, it must needs have a good one upon our stage, and has given admirable play to our comical wits; so that, in my opinion, there is no vein of that sort, either ancient or modern, which excels or equals the humor of our plays. And for the rest, I cannot but observe, for the honor of our country, that the good qualities amongst us seem to be natural, and the ill ones more accidental and such as would be easily changed by the examples of princes and by the precepts of laws; such, I mean, as should be designed to form manners, to restrain excesses, to encourage industry, to prevent men's expenses beyond

65 The spleen was formerly supposed to be the seat of melancholy and kindred distempers.
66 Well advanced in the study of.
67 A gamekeeper.

their fortunes, to countenance virtue, and raise that true esteem due to plain sense and common honesty.

But to spin off this thread which is already grown too long: what honor and request the ancient poetry has lived in may not only be observed from the universal reception and use in all nations from China to Peru, from Scythia to Arabia, but from the esteem of the best and the greatest men as well as the vulgar. Among the Hebrews, David and Solomon, the wisest kings, Job and Jeremiah, the holiest men, were the best poets of their nation and language. Among the Greeks, the two most renowned sages and law-givers were Lycurgus and Solon, whereof the last is known to have excelled in poetry, and the first was so great a lover of it that to his care and industry we are said by some authors to owe the collection and preservation of the loose and scattered pieces of Homer in the order wherein they have since appeared. Alexander is reported neither to have traveled nor slept without those admirable poems always in his company. Phalaris, that was inexorable to all other enemies, relented at the charms of Stesichorus his muse. Among the Romans the last and great Scipio passed the soft hours of his life in the conversation of Terence, and was thought to have a part in the composition of his comedies. Cæsar was an excellent poet as well as orator, and composed a poem in his voyage from Rome to Spain, relieving the tedious difficulties of his march with the entertainments of his muse. Augustus was not only a patron but a friend and companion of Virgil and Horace, and was himself both an admirer of poetry and a pretender[68] too, as far as his genius would reach or his busy scene allow. 'Tis true, since his age we have few such examples of great princes favoring or affecting

poetry, and as few perhaps of great poets deserving it. Whether it be that the fierceness of the Gothic humors, or noise of their perpetual wars, frighted it away, or that the unequal mixture of the modern languages would not bear it, certain it is that the great heights and excellency both of poetry and music fell with the Roman learning and empire, and have never since recovered the admiration and applauses that before attended them. Yet such as they are amongst us, they must be confessed to be the softest and sweetest, the most general and most innocent amusements of common time and life. They still find room in the courts of princes and the cottages of shepherds. They serve to revive and animate the dead calm of poor or idle lives, and to allay or divert the violent passions and perturbations of the greatest and busiest men. And both these effects are of equal use to human life; for the mind of man is like the sea, which is neither agreeable to the beholder nor the voyager in a calm or in a storm, but is so to both when a little agitated by gentle gales; and so the mind, when moved by soft and easy passions or affections. I know very well that many who pretend to be wise by the forms of being grave are apt to despise both poetry and music as toys and trifles too light for the use of entertainment of serious men. But whoever find themselves wholly insensible to these charms would, I think, do well to keep their own counsel for fear of reproaching their own temper, and bringing the goodness of their natures, if not of their understandings, into question. It may be thought at least an ill sign, if not an ill constitution, since some of the Fathers went so far as to esteem the love of music a sign of predestination, as a thing divine, and reserved for the felicities of heaven itself. While this world lasts I doubt not but the pleasure and request of these two entertainments will do so too; and happy those that content themselves with those or any other so easy and so innocent, and do not trouble the world or other men, because they cannot be quiet themselves, though nobody hurts them!

When all is done, human life is, at the greatest and the best, but like a froward child, that must be played with and humored a little to keep it quiet till it falls asleep, and then the care is over.

---

68 He claimed to be a poet. With respect to Augustus and his patronage of poets, Pope remarks in the Advertisement to the First Epistle of the Second Book of Horace (To Augustus): "This epistle will show the learned world to have fallen into two mistakes: one, that Augustus was a patron of poets in general; whereas he not only prohibited all but the best writers to name him, but recommended that care even to the civil magistrate: . . . the other, that this piece was only a general discourse of poetry; whereas it was an apology for the poets, in order to render Augustus more their patron."

OF HEALTH AND LONG LIFE

[TEXT: *second collected edition of Temple's Works, 1731*]

I CAN truly say, that of all the paper I have blotted, which has been a great deal in my time, I have never written anything for the public without the intention of some public good. Whether I have succeeded or no is not my part to judge; and others, in what they tell me, may deceive either me or themselves. Good intentions are at least the seed of good actions; and every man ought to sow them, and leave it to the soil or the seasons whether they come up or no, and whether he or any other gather the fruit.

I have chosen those subjects of these essays wherein I take human life to be most concerned, and which are of most common use, or most necessary knowledge; and wherein, though I may not be able to inform men more than they know, yet I may perhaps give them the occasion to consider more than they do.

This is a sort of instruction that no man can dislike, since it comes from himself, and is made without envy or fear, constraint or obligation, which make us commonly dislike what is taught us by others. All men would be glad to be their own masters, and should not be sorry to be their own scholars, when they pay no more for their learning than their own thoughts, which they have commonly more store of about them than they know what to do with, and which, if they do not apply to something of good use, nor employ about something of ill, they will trifle away upon something vain or impertinent. Their thoughts will be but waking dreams, as their dreams are but sleeping thoughts. Yet, of all sorts of instructions, the best is gained from our own thoughts as well as experience. For though a man may grow learned by other men's thoughts, yet he will grow wise or happy only by his own; the use of other men's towards these ends is but to serve for one's own reflections. Otherwise they are but like meat swallowed down for pleasure or greediness, which only charges the stomach, or fumes into the brain, if it be not well digested, and thereby turned into the very mass or substance of the body that receives it.

Some writers, in casting up the goods most desirable in life, have given them this rank; health, beauty, and riches. Of the first I find no dispute, but to the two others much may be said. For beauty is a good that makes others happy rather than one's self; and how riches should claim so high a rank, I cannot tell, when so great, so wise, and so good a part of mankind have in all ages preferred poverty before them. The Therapeutæ and Ebionites among the Jews, and primitive monks and modern friars among Christians, so many dervishes among the Mahometans, the Brachmans among the Indians, and all the ancient philosophers; who, whatever else they differed in, agreed in this of despising riches, and at best esteeming them an unnecessary trouble or incumbrance of life; so that whether they are to be reckoned among goods or evils is yet left in doubt.

When I was young and in some idle company, it was proposed that everyone should tell what their three wishes should be, if they were sure to be granted. Some were vey pleasant, and some very extravagant; mine were health, and peace, and fair weather; which, though out of the way among young men, yet perhaps might pass well enough among old. They are all of a strain, for health in the body is like peace in the state and serenity in the air. The sun, in our climate at least, has something so reviving, that a fair day is a kind of sensual pleasure, and of all others the most innocent.

Peace is a public blessing, without which no man is safe in his fortunes, his liberty, or his life. Neither innocence or laws are a guard of defense; no possessions are enjoyed but in danger or fear, which equally lose the pleasure and ease of all that fortune can give us. Health is the soul that animates all enjoyments of life, which fade and are tasteless, if not dead, without it. A man starves at the best and the greatest tables, makes faces at the noblest and most delicate wines, is old and impotent in seraglios of the most sparkling beauties, poor and wretched in the midst of the greatest treasures and fortunes. With common diseases strength grows decrepit, youth loses all vigor, and beauty all charms; music grows harsh; and conversation disagreeable; palaces are prisons, or of equal confinement; riches are useless, honor and attendance are cumbersome, and crowns themselves are a burden. But if diseases are painful and violent, they equal all conditions of life, make no difference between a prince and a beggar; and a fit of the stone or the colic puts a king to the rack, and makes him as miserable as he can do the meanest, the worst, and most criminal of his subjects.

To know that the passions or distempers of the mind make our lives unhappy, in spite of all accidents and favors of fortune, a man perhaps must be a philosopher; and requires much thought, and study and deep reflections. To be a Stoic, and grow insensible of pain, as well as poverty or disgrace, one must be perhaps something more or less than a man, renounce common nature, oppose common truth and constant experience. But there needs little hearing or study, more than common thought and observation, to find out that ill health loses not only the enjoyments of fortune, but the pleasures of sense, and even of imagination, and hinders the common operations both of body and mind from being easy and free. Let the philosophers reason and differ about the chief good or happiness of man; let them find it where they can, and place it where they please; but there is no mistake so gross, or opinion so impertinent (how common soever), as to think pleasures arise from what is without us, rather than from what is within; from the impression given us of objects, rather than from the disposition of the organs that receive them. The various effects of the same objects upon different persons, or upon the same persons at different times, make the contrary most evident. Some distempers make things look yellow, others double what we see; the commonest alter our tastes and our smells, and the very foulness of ears changes sounds. The difference of tempers, as well as of age, may have the same effect, by the many degrees of perfection or imperfection in our original tempers, as well as of strength or decay, from the differences of health and of years. From all which 'tis easy, without being a great naturalist, to conclude, that our perceptions are formed, and our imaginations raised upon them, in a very great measure, by the dispositions of the organs through which the several objects make their impressions; and that these vary according to the different frame and temper of the others; as the sound of the same breath passing through an open pipe, a flute, or a trumpet.

But to leave philosophy, and return to health. Whatever is true in point of happiness depending upon the temper of the mind, 'tis certain that pleasures depend upon the temper of the body; and that, to enjoy them, a man must be well himself, as a vessel must

be sound to have your wine sweet; for otherwise, let it be never so pleasant and so generous, it loses the taste; and pour in never so much, it all turns sour, and were better let alone. Whoever will eat well, must have a stomach; who will relish the pleasure of drinks, must have his mouth in taste; who will enjoy a beautiful woman, must be in vigor himself; nay, to find any felicity, or take any pleasure in the greatest advantages of honor and fortune, a man must be in health. Who would not be covetous, and with reason, if this could be purchased with gold? Who not ambitious, if it were at the command of power, or restored by honor? But alas! a white staff will not help gouty feet to walk better than a common cane; nor a blue ribband bind up a wound so well as a fillet; the glitter of gold or of diamonds will but hurt sore eyes, instead of curing them; and an aching head will be no more eased by wearing a crown than a common night-cap.

If health be such a blessing, and the very source of all pleasure, it may be worth the pains to discover the regions where it grows, the springs that feed it, the customs and methods by which 'tis best cultivated and preserved. Towards this end, it will be necessary to consider the examples or instances we meet with of health and long life; which is the consequence of it; and to observe the places, the customs, and the conditions of those who enjoyed them in any degree extraordinary; from whence we may best guess at the causes, and make the truest conclusions.

Of what passed before the Flood, we know little from Scripture itself, besides the length of their lives; so as I shall only observe upon that period of time that men are thought neither to have eat flesh nor drunk wine before it ended. For to Noah first seems to have been given the liberty of feeding upon living creatures, and the prerogative of planting the vine. Since that time we meet with little mention of very long lives in any stories either sacred or profane, besides the Patriarchs of the Hebrews, the Brachmans among the old Indians, and the Brazilians at the time that country was discovered by the Europeans. Many of these were said then to have lived two hundred, some three hundred years. The same terms of life are attributed to the old Brachmans; and how long those of the Patriarchs were is recorded in Scripture. Upon all these I shall observe, that the Patriarchs' abodes were not in cities, but in open countries and fields: that their lives were pastoral, or employed in some sorts of agriculture: that they were of the same race to which their marriages were generally confined: that their diet was simple, as that of the ancients is generally represented, among whom flesh or wine was seldom used but at sacrifices or solemn feasts. The Brachmans were all of the same races, lived in fields and in woods, after the course of their studies were ended, and fed only upon rice, milk, or herbs. The Brazilians, when first discovered, lived the most natural original lives of mankind, so frequently described in ancient countries, before laws, or property, or arts made entrance among them; and so their customs may be concluded to have been yet more simple than either of the other two. They lived without business or labor, further than for their necessary food, by gathering fruits, herbs, and plants. They knew no drink but water; were not tempted to eat nor drink beyond common thirst or appetite; were not troubled with either public or domestic cares, nor knew any pleasures but the most simple and natural.

From all these examples and customs it may probably be concluded, that the common ingredients of health and long life (where births are not impaired from the conception by any derived infirmities of the race they come from) are great temperance, open air, easy labor, little care, simplicity of diet, rather fruits and plants than flesh, which easier corrupts; and water, which preserves the radical moisture, without too much increasing the radical heat: whereas sickness, decay, and death proceed commonly from the one preying too fast upon the other, and at length wholly extinguishing it.

I have sometimes wondered that the regions of so much health and so long lives were all under very hot climates; whereas the most temperate are allowed to produce the strongest and most vigorous bodies. But weaker constitutions may last as long as the strong, if better preserved from accidents; so Venice glass, as long as an earthen pitcher, if carefully kept; and, for one life that ends by mere decay of nature or age, millions are intercepted by accidents from without or diseases within; by untimely deaths or decays; from the effects of excess and luxury, immoderate repletion or exercise; the preying of our minds upon our bodies by long passions or consuming cares, as well as those accidents which are called violent. Men are perhaps most betrayed to all these dangers by great strength and vigor of constitution, by more appetite and larger fare in colder climates: in the warm, excesses are found more pernicious to health, and so more avoided; and, if experience and reflection do not cause temperance among them, yet it is forced upon them by the faint-ness of the appetite. I can find no better account of a story Sir Francis Bacon tells, of a very old man, whose customs and diet he inquired; but he said he observed none besides eating before he was hungry and drinking before he was dry; for by that rule he was sure never to eat nor drink much at a time. Besides, the warmth of air keeps the pores open, and by continual perspiration breathes out those humors, which breed most diseases, if in cooler climates it be not helped by exercise. And this I take to be the reason of our English constitutions finding so much benefit by the air of Montpelier, especially in long colds or consumptions, or rather lingering diseases; though I have known some who attributed the restoring of their health there as much to the fruits as the air of that place.

I know not whether there may be anything in the climate of Brazil more propitious to health than in other countries: for, besides what was observed among the natives upon the first European discoveries, I remember Don Francisco de Melo, a Portugal Ambassador in England, told me, it was frequent in his country for men spent with age or other decays, so as they could not hope for above a year or two of life, to ship themselves away in a Brazil fleet, and after their arrival there to go on a great length, sometimes of twenty or thirty years, or more, by the force of that vigor they recovered with that remove. Whether such an effect might grow from the air, or the fruits of that climate, or by approaching nearer the sun, which is the fountain of life and heat, when their natural heat was so far decayed; or whether the piecing out of an old man's life were worth the pains, I cannot tell; perhaps the play is not worth the candle.

I do not remember, either in story or modern observation, any examples of long life common to any parts of Europe, which the temper of the climate has probably made the scene of luxury and excesses in diet. Greece and Rome were of old celebrated, or rather defamed, for those customs, when they were not known in Asia nor Africa; and how guilty our colder climates are in this point, beyond the warmer of Spain and Italy, is but too well known. It is common among Spaniards of the best quality not to have tasted pure wine at forty years old. 'Tis an honor to their laws, that a man loses his testimony who can be proved once to have been drunk; and I never was more pleased with any reply than that of a Spaniard, who, having been asked whether he had a good dinner at a friend's house, said *Sí, señor, a via sabrado;* Yes, Sir, for there was something left. The great trade in Italy, and resort of strangers, especially of Germans, has made the use of wine something more frequent there, though not much among the persons of rank, who are observed to live longer at Rome and Madrid than in any other towns of Europe, where the qualities of the air force upon them the greatest temperance, as well as care and precaution. We read of many kings very long-lived in Spain, one I remember that reigned above seventy years. But Philip de Comines observes that none in France had lived to three score, from Charlemagne's time to that of Louis XI, whereas in England, from the Conquest to the end of Queen Elizabeth (which is a much shorter period of time), there have reigned five kings and one queen, whereof two lived sixty-five years, two sixty-eight, and two reached at least the seventieth year of their age. I wondered upon this subject when Monsieur Pompone, French Ambassador in my time at The Hague, a person of great worth and learning, as well as observation, told me there, that in his life he had never heard of any man in France that arrived at a hundred years; and I could imagine no reason for it, unless it be that the excellence of their climate, subject neither to much cold nor heat, gave them such a liveliness of temper and humor as disposed them to more pleasures of all kinds than any other countries. And, I doubt, pleasures too long continued, or rather too frequently repeated, may spend the spirits, and thereby life, too fast, to leave it very long; like blowing a fire too often, which makes it indeed burn the better, but last the less. For as pleasures perish themselves in the using, like flowers that fade with gathering, so it is neither natural nor safe to continue them long, to renew them without appetite, or ever to provoke them by arts or imagination where nature does not call, who can best tell us when and how much we need, or what is good for us, if we were so wise as to consult her. But a short life and a merry carries it, and is without doubt better than a long with sorrow and pain.

For the honor of our climate, it has been observed by ancient authors, that the Britons were longer-lived than any other nation to them known. And in modern times there have been more and greater examples of this kind than in any other countries of Europe. The story of old Parr is too late to be forgotten by many now alive, who was brought out of Derbyshire to the court in King Charles I's time, and lived to a hundred and fifty-three years old; and might have, as was thought, gone further, if the change of country air and diet for that of the town had not carried him off, perhaps un-

timely, at that very age. The late Robert Earl of Leicester, who was a person of great learning and observation, as well as of truth, told me several stories very extraordinary upon this subject; one, of a Countess of Desmond, married out of England in Edward IV's time, and who lived far in King James's reign, and was counted to have died some years above a hundred and forty; at which age she came from Bristol to London to beg some relief at court, having long been very poor by the ruin of that Irish family into which she was married.

Another he told me was of a beggar at a bookseller's shop, where he was some weeks after the death of Prince Henry; and observing those that passed by, he was saying to his company, that never such a mourning had he seen in England. This beggar said, No, never since the death of Prince Arthur. My Lord Leicester, surprised, asked what she meant, and whether she remembered it. She said, Very well; and upon his more curious inquiry, told him that her name was Rainsford, of a good family in Oxfordshire: that, when she was about twenty years old, upon the falseness of a lover, she fell distracted; how long she had been so, nor what passed in that time, she knew not; that, when she was thought well enough to go abroad, she was fain to beg for her living; that she was some time at this trade before she recovered any memory of what she had been, or where bred; that, when this memory returned, she went down into her country, but hardly found the memory of any of her friends she had left there; and so returned to a parish in Southwark, where she had some allowance among other poor, and had been for many years; and once a week walked into the city, and took what alms were given her. My Lord Leicester told me he sent to inquire at the parish, and found their account agree with the woman's: upon which he ordered her to call at his house once a week, which she did for some time; after which he heard no more of her. This story raised some discourse upon a remark of some in the company that mad people are apt to live long. They alleged examples of their own knowledge: but the result was, that, if it were true, it must proceed from the natural vigor of their tempers, which disposed them to passions so violent as ended in frenzies; and from the great abstinence and hardships of diet they are forced upon by the methods of their cure, and severity of those who had them in care; no other drink but water being allowed them, and very little meat.

The last story I shall mention from that noble

person, upon this subject, was of a morrice-dancer in Herefordshire; whereof, he said, he had a pamphlet still in his library, written by a very ingenious gentleman of that county, and which gave an account how such a year of King James's reign, there went about the country a set of morrice-dancers, composed of ten men who danced, a Maid Marian, and a tabor and pipe: and how these twelve, one with another, made up twelve hundred years. It is not so much that so many in one small county should live to that age as that they should be in vigor and in humor to travel and to dance.

I have, in my life, met with two of above a hundred and twelve; whereof the woman had passed her life in service, and the man in common labor, till he grew old, and fell upon the parish. But I met with one who had gone a much greater length, which made me more curious in my inquiries. 'Twas an old man, who begged usually at a lonely inn upon the road in Staffordshire, who told me he was a hundred twenty-four years old; that he had been a soldier in the Calais voyage, under the Earl of Essex, of which he gave me a sensible account. That, after his return, he fell to labor in his own parish, which was about a mile from the place where I met him; that he continued to work till a hundred and twelve, when he broke one of his ribs by a fall from a cart, and being thereby disabled, he fell to beg. This agreeing with what the master of the house told me was reported and believed by all his neighbors, I asked him what his usual food was; he said, milk, bread, and cheese, and flesh when it was given him. I asked him what he used to drink; he said, O, Sir, we have the best water in our parish that is in all the neighborhood. Whether he never drank anything else? he said, Yes, if anybody gave it him, but not otherwise. And the host told me, he had got many a pound in his house, but never spent one penny. I asked if he had any neighbors as old as he; and he told me but one, who had been his fellow-soldier at Calais, and was three years older; but he had been most of his time in a good service, and had something to live on now he was old.

I have heard, and very credibly, of many in my life, above a hundred years old, brought as witnesses upon trials of titles, and bounds of land: but I have observed most of them have been of Derbyshire, Staffordshire, or Yorkshire, and none above the rank of common farmers. The oldest I ever knew any persons of quality, or indeed any gentleman, either at home or abroad, was fourscore and twelve. This, added to all the former recites or observations, either of long-lived races or persons in any age or country, makes it easy to con-clude, that health and long life are usually blessings of the poor, not of the rich, and the fruits of temperance rather than of luxury and excess. And, indeed, if a rich man does not in many things live like a poor, he will certainly be the worse for his riches; if he does not use exercise, which is but voluntary labor; if he does not restrain appetite by choice, as the others do by necessity. If he does not practice sometimes even abstinence and fasting, which is the last extreme of want and poverty: if his cares and troubles increase with his riches, or his passions with his pleasures, he will certainly impair in health whilst he improves his fortunes, and lose more than he gains by the bargain; since health is the best of all human possessions, and without which the rest are not relished or kindly enjoyed.

It is observable in story that the ancient philosophers lived generally very long; which may be attributed to their great temperance, and their freedom from common passions as well as cares of the world. But the friars, in many orders, seem to equal them in all these, and yet are not observed to live long, so as some other reason may be assigned. I can give none, unless it be the great and constant confinement of the last, and liberty of the others. I mean not only that of their persons to their cloisters (which is not universal among them), but their condition of life, so tied to rules, and so absolutely subject to their superiors' commands, besides the very confinement of their minds and thoughts to a certain compass of notions, speculations, and opinions. The philosophers took the greatest liberty that could be, and allowed their thoughts, their studies, and inventions, the most unconfined range over the whole universe. They both began and continued their profession and condition of life at their own choice, as well as their abodes; whereas among the friars, though they may be voluntary at first, yet, after their vows made, they grow necessary and thereby constrained. Now 'tis certain that as nothing damps or depresses the spirits like great subjection or slavery, either of body or mind, so nothing nourishes, revives, and fortifies them like great liberty; which may possibly enter, among other reasons, of what has been observed about long life being found more in England than in others of our neighbor countries.

Upon the general and particular surveys already made, it may seem that the mountainous or barren countries are usually the scenes of health and long life; that they have been found rather in the hills of Palestine and Arcadia, than in the plains of Babylon or of Thessaly; and among us in England, rather upon the peak of Derbyshire, and the heaths of Staffordshire, than the fertile soils of other counties, that abound more in people and in riches. Whether this proceeds from the air being clearer of gross and damp exhalations, or from the meaner condition, and thereby harder fare, and more simple diet, or from the stronger nourishment of those grains and roots which grow in dry soils, I will not determine; but I think it is evident, from common experience, that the natives and inhabitants of hilly and barren countries have not only more health in general, but also more vigor, than those of the plains or fertile soils, and usually exceed them even in size and stature: so the largest bodies of men that are found in these parts of Europe are the Switzers, the Highlanders of Scotland, and the northern Irish. I remember King Charles the Second (a prince of much and various knowledge, and curious observation) upon this subject, falling in discourse, asked me, what could be the reason that in mountainous countries the men were commonly larger, and yet the cattle of all sorts smaller, than in others. I could think of none, unless it were that appetite being more in both, from the air of such places, it happened that, by the care of parents in the education of children, these seldom wanted food of some sort or other enough to supply nature and satisfy appetite during the age of their growth, which must be the greater by the sharpness of hunger and strength of digestion in drier airs: for milk, roots, and oats abound in such countries, though there may be scarcity of other food or grain. But the cattle, from the shortness of pasture and of fodder, have hardly enough to feed in summer; and very often want, in winter, even necessary food for sustenance of life; many are starved, and the rest stunted in their growth, which, after a certain age, never advances. Whether this be a good reason, or a better may be found, I believe one part of it will not be contested by any man that tries; which is, that the open dry air of hilly countries gives more stomach than that of plains and valleys, in which cities are commonly built, for the convenience of water, of trade, and the plenty of fruits and grains produced by the earth, with much greater increase and less labor in softer than in harder grounds. The faintness of appetite in such places, especially in great cities, makes the many endeavors to relieve and provoke it by art, where nature fails; and this is one great ground of luxury, and so many and various and extravagant inventions to heighten and improve it; which may serve perhaps for some refinement on pleasure, but not at all for any advantages of health or of life: on the con-

trary, all the great cities, celebrated most by the concourse of mankind, and by the inventions and customs of the greatest and most delicate luxury, are the scenes of the most frequent and violent plagues, as well as other diseases. Such are in our age Grand Cairo, Constantinople, Naples, and Rome; though the exact and constant care, in this last, helps them commonly to escape better than the others.

This introduces the use, and indeed the necessity, of physic in great towns and very populous countries, which remoter and more barren and desolate places are scarce acquainted with: for in the course of common life a man must often exercise, or fast, or take physic, or be sick; and the choice seems left to everyone as he likes. The two first are the best methods and means of preserving health; the use of physic is for restoring it, and curing those diseases which are generally caused by the want or neglect of the others; but is neither necessary, nor perhaps useful, for confirming the health, or to the length of life, being generally a force upon nature; though the end of it seems to be rather assisting nature than opposing it in its course.

How ancient, how general the study or profession of this science has been in the world, and how various the practice, may be worth a little inquiry and observation, since it so nearly concerns our healths and lives. Greece must be allowed to have been the mother of this, as much or more than of other sciences, most whereof are transplanted thither from more ancient and more eastern nations. But this seems to have first risen there, and with good reason; for Greece having been the first scene of luxury we meet with in story, and having thereby occasioned more diseases, seemed to owe the world that justice of providing the remedies. Among the more simple and original customs and lives of other nations it entered late, and was introduced by the Grecians. In ancient Babylon, how great and populous soever, no physicians were known, nor other methods for the cure of diseases, besides abstinence, patience, domestic care; or when these succeeded not, exposing the patient in the market, to receive the instructions of any persons that passed by, and pretended by experience or inquiries to have learned any remedies for such an illness. The Persian emperors sent into Greece for the physicians they needed, upon some extremity at first, but afterwards kept them residing with them. In old Rome they were long unknown; and, after having entered there, and continued for some time, they were all banished, and returned not in many years, till their fondness of all the Grecian arts and customs restored this, and introduced all the rest among them; where they continued in use and esteem during the greatness of that empire. With the rise and progress of the fierce northern powers and arms, this, as well as all other learning, was in a manner extinguished in Europe. But when the Saracen empire grew to such a height in the more eastern and southern parts of the world, all arts and sciences, following the traces of greatness and security in states or governments, began to flourish there, and this among the rest. The Arabians seem to have first retrieved and restored it in the Mahometan dominions; and the Jews in Europe, who were long the chief professors of it in the Gothic kingdoms; having been always a nation very mercurial, of great genius and application to all sorts of learning, after their dispersion; till they were discouraged by the persecutions of their religion and their persons among most of the Christian states. In the vast territories of India there are few physicians, or little esteemed, besides some European, or else of the race either of Jews or Arabs.

Through these hands and places this science has passed with greatest honor and applause: among others it has been less used or esteemed.

For the antiquity of it, and original in Greece, we must have recourse to Æsculapius, who lived in the age before the Trojan war, and whose son Macaon is mentioned to have assisted there; but whether as a physician or a surgeon, I do not find. How simple the beginnings of this art were, may be observed by the story of Æsculapius going about the country with a dog and a she-goat always following, both which he used much in his cures; the first for licking all ulcerated wounds, and the goat's milk for diseases of the stomach and lungs. We find little more recorded of either his methods or medicines; though he was so successful by his skill, or so admired for the novelty of his profession, as to have been honored with statues, esteemed son of Apollo, and worshipped as a god.

Whoever was accounted the god of physic, the prince of this science must be by all, I think, allowed to have been Hippocrates. He flourished in the time of the first renowned philosophers of Greece (the chief of whom was Democritus), and his writings are the most ancient of any that remain to posterity; for those of Democritus, and others of that age, are all lost, though many were preserved until the time of Antoninus Pius, and perhaps something later: and, it is probable, were suppressed by the pious zeal of some fathers, under the first Christian emperor. Those of

Hippocrates escaped this fate of his age by being esteemed so useful to human life, as well as the most excellent upon all subjects he treats: for he was a great philosopher and naturalist before he began the study of physic, to which both these are perhaps necessary. His rules and methods continued in practice as well as esteem without any dispute for many ages till the time of Galen; and I have heard a great physician say that his aphorisms are still the most certain and uncontrolled of any that science has produced. I will judge but of one, which, in my opinion, has the greatest race and height both of sense and judgment that I have read in few words, and the best expressed, *Ars longa, vita brevis, experientia fallax, occasio præceps, judicium difficile.*[1] By which alone, if no more remained of that admirable person, we may easily judge how great a genius he was, and how perfectly he understood both nature and art.

In the time of Adrian, Galen began to change the practice and methods of physic, derived to that age from Hippocrates; and those of his new institution continue generally observed in our time. Yet Paracelsus, about two hundred years ago, endeavored to overthrow the whole scheme of Galen, and introduce a new one of his own, as well as the use of chemical medicines; and has not wanted his followers and admirers ever since, who have, in some measure, compounded with the Galenists, and brought a mixed use of chemical medicines into the present practice.

Dr. Harvey gave the first credit, if not rise, to the opinion about the circulation of the blood, which was expected to bring in great and general innovations into the whole practice of physic, but has had no such effect. Whether the opinion has not had the luck to be so well believed as proved, sense and experience having not well agreed with reason and speculation; or whether the scheme has not been pursued so far as to draw it into practice; or whether it be too fine to be capable of it, like some propositions in mathematics, how true and demonstrative soever, I will not pretend to determine.

These great changes or revolutions in the physical empire have given ground to many attacks that have been made against it, upon the score of its uncertainty, by several wise and learned men, as well as by many ignorant and malicious. Montaigne has written a great deal, and very ingeniously, upon this point; and some sharp Italians; and many physicians are too free upon the subject, in the conversation of their friends. But,

---

[1] Art is long, life short, experiment deceptive, opportunity dangerous, and judgment difficult.

as the noble Athenian inscription told Demetrius, that he was in so much a god as he acknowledged himself to be a man; so we may say of physicians, that they are the greater in so much as they know and confess the weakness of their art. It is certain, however, that the study of physic is not achieved in any eminent degree, without very great advancements in other sciences; so that, whatever the profession is, the professors have been generally very much esteemed upon that account, as well as of their own art, as the most learned men of their ages, and thereby shared with the two other great professions in those advantages most commonly valued and most eagerly pursued; whereof the divines seem to have had the most honor, the lawyers the most money, and the physicians the most learning. I have known, in my time, at least five or six, that, besides their general learning, were the greatest wits in the compass of my conversation. And whatever can be said of the uncertainty of their art, or disagreement of its professors, they may, I believe, confidently undertake, that when divines arrive at certainty in their schemes of divinity, or lawyers in those of law, or politicians in those of civil government, the physicians will do it likewise in the methods and practice of physic; and have the honor of finding out the universal medicine, at least as soon as the chemists shall the philosopher's stone.

The great defects in this excellent science seem to me chiefly to have proceeded from the professors' application (especially since Galen's time) running so much upon method, and so little upon medicine; and in this to have addicted themselves so much to composition, and neglected too much the use of simples, as well as the inquiries and records of specific remedies.

Upon this occasion, I have sometimes wondered why a registry has not been kept in the colleges of physicians, of all such as have been invented by any professors of every age, found out by study or by chance, learned by inquiry, and approved by their practice and experience. This would supply the want of skill and study; arts would be improved by the experience of many ages, and derived by the succession of ancestors. As many professions are tied to certain races in several nations, so this of physic has been in some, by which parents were induced to the cares of improving and augmenting their knowledge, as others do their estates; because they were to descend to their posterity, and not die with themselves, as learning does in vulgar hands. How many methods as well as remedies are lost for want of this custom in the course of ages!

and which perhaps were of greater effect, and of more common benefit, than those that, succeeding in their places, have worn out the memory of the fomer, either by chance or negligence, or different humors of persons and times.

Among the Romans there were four things much in use, whereof some are so far out of practice in ours, and other late ages, as to be hardly known any more than by their names; these were bathing, fumigation, friction, and jactation. The first, though not wholly disused among us, yet is turned out of the service of health to that of pleasure; but may be of excellent effect in both. It not only opens the pores, provokes sweat, and thereby allays heat; supples the joints and sinews; unwearies and refreshes more than anything, after too great labor and exercise; but is of great effect in some acute pains, as of the stone and colic; and disposes to sleep, when many other remedies fail. Nor is it improbable that all good effects of any natural baths may be imitated by the artificial, if composed with care and skill of able naturalists or physicians.

Fumigation, or the use of scents, is not, that I know, at all practiced in our modern physic, nor the power and virtue of them considered among us; yet they may have as much to do good, for aught I know, as to do harm, and contribute to health as well as to diseases; which is too much felt by experience in all that are infectious, and by the operations of some poisons that are received only by the smell. How reviving as well as pleasing some scents of herbs or flowers are, is obvious to all: how great virtues they may have in diseases, especially of the head, is known to few, but may be easily conjectured by any thinking man. What is recorded of Democritus is worth remarking upon this subject; that being spent with age, and just at the point of death, and his sister bewailing that he should not live till the feast of Ceres, which was to be kept three or four days after; he called for loaves of new bread to be brought him, and with the steam of them under his nose prolonged his life till the feast was passed, and then died. Whether a man may live some time, or how long, by the steam of meat, I cannot tell; but the justice was great, if not the truth, in that story of a cook, who observing a man to use it often in his shop, and asking money, because he confessed to save his dinner by it, was adjudged to be paid by the chinking of his coin. I remember, that walking in a long gallery of the Indian House at Amsterdam, where vast quantities of mace, cloves, and nutmegs were kept in great open chests ranged all along one side of the room, I found something so reviving by the perfumed air, that I took notice of it to the company with me, which was a great deal, and they were all sensible of the same effect: which is enough to show the power of smells, and their operations both upon health and humor.

Friction is of great and excellent use, and of very general practice in the eastern countries, especially after their frequent bathings; it opens the pores, and is the best way of all forced perspiration; is very proper and effectual in all swellings and pains of the joints, or others in the flesh, which are not to be drawn to a head and break. It is a saying among the Indians that none can be much troubled with the gout who have slaves enough to rub them; and is the best natural account of some stories I have heard of persons who were said to cure several diseases by stroking.

Jactations were used for some amusement and allay in great and constant pains, and to relieve that intranquillity which attends most diseases, and makes men often impatient of lying still in their beds. Besides, they help or occasion sleep, as we find by the common use and experience of rocking froward children in cradles, or dandling them in their nurse's arms. I remember an old Prince Maurice of Nassau, who had been accustomed to hammocks in Brazil, and used them frequently all his life after, upon the pains he suffered by the stone or gout; and thought he found ease, and was allured to sleep by the constant motion or swinging of those airy beds, which was assisted by a servant, if they moved too little by the springs upon which they hung.

In Egypt of old, and at this time in Barbary, the general method of cures in most diseases is by burning with a hot iron; so as the bodies of their slaves are found often to have many scars upon them remaining of these operations. But this, and other uses and effects of fire, I have taken notice enough of, in an Essay upon the Indian Cure by Moxa in the Gout.

The ancient native Irish, and the Americans at the time of the first European discoveries and conquests there, knew nothing of physic beyond the virtues of herbs and plants. And, in this, the most polished nation agrees in a great measure with those that were esteemed most barbarous; and where the learning and voluptuousness are as great as were the native simplicity and ignorance of the others. For in China, though their physicians are admirable in the knowledge of the pulse, and by that, in discovering the causes of all inward diseases, yet their practice extends little further in the cures beyond the methods of diet, and the virtues of herbs and plants either inwardly taken or outwardly applied.

In the course of my life I have often pleased or entertained myself with observing the various and fantastical changes of the diseases generally complained of, and of the remedies in common vogue, which were like birds of passage, very much seen or heard of at one season, and disappeared at another, and commonly succeeded by some of a very different kind. When I was very young nothing was so much feared or talked of as rickets among children, and consumptions among young people of both sexes. After these the spleen came in play, and grew a formal disease: then the scurvy, which was the general complaint, and both were thought to appear in many various guises. After these, and for a time, nothing was so much talked of as the ferment of the blood, which passed for the cause of all sorts of ailments that neither physicians nor patients knew well what to make of. And to all these succeeded vapors, which serve the same turn, and furnish occasion of complaint among persons whose bodies or minds ail something, but they know not what; and, among the Chinese, would pass for mists of the mind or fumes of the brain, rather than indispositions of any other parts. Yet these employ our physicians perhaps more than other diseases, who are fain to humor such patients in their fancies of being ill, and to prescribe some remedies, for fear of losing their practice to others that pretend more skill in finding out the cause of diseases, or care in advising remedies, which neither they nor their patients find any effect of, besides some gains to one, and amusement to the other. This, I suppose, may have contributed much to the mode of going to the waters either cold or hot, upon so many occasions, or else upon none besides that of entertainment, and which commonly may have no other effect. And it is well if this be the worst of the frequent use of those waters, which, though commonly innocent, yet are sometimes dangerous, if the temper of the person or cause of the indisposition be unhappily mistaken, especially in people of age.

As diseases have changed vogue, so have remedies, in my time and observation. I remember at one time the taking of tobacco, at another the drinking of warm beer, proved for universal remedies; then swallowing of pebble stones, in imitation of falconers curing hawks. One doctor pretended to help all heats and fevers, by drinking as much cold spring water as the patient could bear; at another time, swallowing up a spoonful of powder of sea-biscuit after meals was infallible for all indigestion, and so preventing diseases: then coffee and tea began their successive reigns. The infusions of powder of steel have had their turns, and certain drops, of several names and compositions; but none that I find have established their authority, either long or generally, by any constant and sensible successes of their reign, but have rather passed like a mode, which everyone is apt to follow, and finds the most convenient or graceful while it lasts; and begins to dislike in both those respects when it goes out of fashion.

Thus men are apt to play with their healths and their lives, as they do with their clothes; which may be the better excused since both are so transitory, so subject to be spoiled with common use, to be torn by accidents, and at best to be so soon worn out. Yet the usual practice of physic among us runs still the same course, and turns, in a manner, wholly upon evacuation, either by bleeding, vomits, or some sorts of purgation; though it be not often agreed among physicians in what cases or what degrees any of these are necessary; nor among other men, whether any of them are necessary or no. Montaigne questions whether purging ever be so, and from many ingenious reasons: the Chinese never let blood; and, for the other, it is very probable that nature knows her own wants and times so well, and so easily finds her own relief that way, as to need little assistance, and not well to receive the common violences that are offered her. I remember three in my life and observation who were downright killed with vomits, as they could have been with daggers; and I can say for myself, upon an accident very near mortal, when I was young, that, sending for the two best physicians of the town, the first prescribed me a vomit, and immediately sent it me: I had the grace or sense to refuse it till the other came, who told me, if I had taken it, I could not have lived half an hour. I observed a consult of physicians, in a fever of one of my near friends, perplexed to the last degree whether to let him blood or no, and not able to resolve, till the course of the disease had declared itself, and thereby determined them. Another of my friends was so often let blood, by his first physician, that a second who was sent for questioned whether he would recover it; the first persisted the blood must be drawn till some good appeared; the other affirmed that in such diseases the whole mass was corrupted, but would purify again when the accident was past, like wine after a fermentation, which makes all in the vessel thick and foul for a season; but, when that is past, grows clear again of

itself. So much is certain, that it depends a great deal upon the temper of the patient, the nature of the disease in its first causes, upon the skill and care of the physician to decide whether any of these violences upon nature are necessary or no, and whether they are like to do good or harm.

The rest of our common practice consists in various compositions of innocent ingredients, which feed the hopes of the patient, and the apothecary's gains, but leave nature to her course, who is the sovereign physician in most diseases, and leaves little for others to do, further than to watch accidents; where they know no specific remedies, to prescribe diets; and, above all, to prevent disorders from the stomach, and take care that nature be not employed in the kitchen, when she should be in the field to resist her enemy; and that she should not be weakened in her spirits and strength, when they are most necessary to support and relieve her. It is true, physicians must be in danger of losing their credit with the vulgar, if they should often tell a patient he has no need of physic, and prescribe only rules of diet or common use; most people would think they had lost their fee; but the excellence of a physician's skill and care is discovered by resolving first whether it be best in the case to administer any physic or none, to trust to nature or to art; and the next, to give such prescriptions, as, if they do no good, may be sure to do no harm.

In the midst of such uncertainties of health and of physic, for my own part I have, in the general course of my life, and of many acute diseases, as well as some habitual, trusted to God Almighty, to nature, to temperance, or abstinence, and the use of common remedies, either vulgarly known and approved like proverbs by long observation and experience, either of my own or such persons as have fallen in the way of my observation or inquiry.

Among the plants of our soil and climate, those I esteem of greatest virtue and most friendly to health, are sage, rue, saffron, alehoof, garlic, and elder. Sage deserves not only the just reputation it has been always in of a very wholesome herb, in common uses and generally known, but is admirable in consumptive coughs, of which I have cured some very desperate, by a draft every morning of spring water, with a handful of sage boiled in it, and continued for a month. I do not question that, if it were used as tea, it would have at least in all kinds as good an effect upon health, if not of so much entertainment to the taste, being perhaps not so agreeable; and I had reason to believe when I was in Holland that vast quantities of sage were carried to the Indies yearly, as well as of tea brought over from those countries into ours.

Rue is of excellent use for all illnesses of the stomach that proceed from cold or moist humors; a great digester and restorer of appetite; dispels wind, helps perspiration, drives out ill humors, and thereby comes to be so much prescribed, and so commonly used in pestilential airs, and upon apprehensions of any contagion. The only ill of it lies in the too much or too frequent use, which may lessen or impair the natural heat of the stomach, by the greater heat of an herb very hot and dry; and therefore the juice made up with sugar into small pills, and swallowed only two or three at nights or mornings, and only when there is occasion, is the most innocent way of using it.

Saffron is, of all others, the safest and most simple cordial, the greatest reviver of the heart and cheerer of the spirits and cannot be of too common use in diet, any more than in medicine. The spirit of saffron is, of all others, the noblest and most innocent, and yet of the greatest virtue. I have known it restore a man out of the very agonies of death, when left by all physicians as wholly desperate. But the use of this and all spirits ought to be employed only in cases very urgent, either of decays or pains; for all spirits have the same effect with that mentioned of rue, which is, by frequent use, to destroy, and at last to extinguish the natural heat of the stomach; as the frequent drinking wine at meals does in a degree, and with time, but that of all strong waters more sensibly and more dangerously. Yet a long custom of either cannot be suddenly broken without danger, too, and must be changed with time, with lessening the proportions by degrees, with shorter first, and then with longer intermissions.

Alehoof, or ground-ivy is, in my opinion, of the most excellent and most general use and virtue of plants we have among us. It is allowed to be most sovereign for the eyes, admirable in frenzies, either taken inwardly or outwardly applied. Besides, if there be a specific remedy or prevention of the stone, I take it to be the constant use of alehoof ale, whereof I have known several experiences by others, and can, I thank God, allege my own for about ten years past. This is the plant with which all our ancestors made their common drink, when the inhabitants of this island were esteemed the longest livers of any in the known world; and the stone is said to have first come among us after hops were introduced here, and the staleness of beer brought into custom by preserving it long. It is known

enough, how much this plant has been decried, how generally soever it has been received in these maritime northern parts; and the chief reason, which I believe gave it vogue at first, was the preserving beer upon long sea voyages: but for common health, I am apt to think the use of heath or broom had been of much more advantage, though none yet invented of so great and general as that of alehoof, which is certainly the greatest cleanser of any plant known among us; and which in old England signified that which was necessary to the drinking of ale, the common or rather universal drink heretofore of our nation.

Garlic has of all our plants the greatest strength, affords most nourishment, and supplies most spirits to those who eat little flesh, as the poorer people seldom do in the hotter, and especially the more eastern climates: so that the labor of the world seems to be performed by the force and virtue of garlic, leeks, and onions, no other food or herbs or plants yielding strength enough for much labor. Garlic is of great virtue in all colics, a great strengthener of the stomach upon decays of appetite or indigestion, and I believe is (if at least there be any such) a specific remedy of the gout. I have known great testimonies of this kind within my acquaintance, and have never used it myself upon this occasion, without an opinion of some success or advantage. But I could never long enough bear the constraint of a diet I found not very agreeable myself, and at least fancied offensive to the company I conversed with.

Besides, this disease is to me so hereditary, and comes into my veins from so many ancestors, that I have reason to despair of any cure but the last, and content myself to fence against it by temperance and patience, without hopes of conquering such an inveterate enemy. Therefore I leave the use of garlic to such as are inveigled into the gout by the pleasure of too much drinking, the ill effects whereof are not more relieved by any other diet than by this plant, which is so great a drier and opener, especially by perspiration. Nor is it less used in many parts abroad as physic than as food. In several provinces of France it is usual to fall into a diet of garlic for a fortnight or three weeks, upon the first fresh butter of the spring; and the common people esteem it a preservative against the diseases of the ensuing year; and a broth of garlic or onions is so generally used the next day after a debauch as to be called *soupe à l'ivrogne*. This is enough to show the use as well as virtues of this northern spice, which is in mighty request among the Indians themselves, in the midst of so many others that enrich and perfume those noble regions.

Elder is of great virtue of all indispositions arising from any watery humors; and not only the flowers and berries, but even the green bark, are used with effect and perhaps equal success in their seasons. I have been told of some great cures of the gout by the succeeding use of all three throughout the year; but I have been always too libertine, for any great and long subjections, to make the trials. The spirit of elder is sovereign in colics; and the use of it, in general, very beneficial in scurvies and dropsies: though, in the last, I esteem broom yet of more virtue, either brewed in common drink, or the ashes taken in white wine every morning: which may perhaps pass for a specific remedy; whereof we may justly complain, that, after so long experience of so learned a profession as physic, we yet know so very few.

That which has passed of latter years for the most allowed in this kind, has been the quinquina, or Jesuits' powder, in fevers, but especially agues. I can say nothing of it upon any experience of my own, nor any within my knowledge. I remember its entrance upon our stage with some disadvantage, and the repute of leaving no cures without danger or worse returns. But the credit of it seems now to be established by common use and prescription, and to be improved by new and singular preparations; whereof I have very good and particular reasons to affirm that they are all amusements; and that what virtue there is in this remedy lies in the naked simple itself, as it comes over from the Indies, and in the choice of that which is least dried, or perished by the voyage.

The next specific I esteem to be that little insect called millepedes: the powder whereof, made up into little balls with fresh butter, I never knew fail of curing any sore throat: it must lie at the root of the tongue, and melt down at leisure upon going to bed. I have been assured that Doctor Mayerne used it as a certain cure for all cancers in the breast: and should be very tedious if I should tell you here how much the use of it has been extolled by several within my knowledge, upon the admirable effects for the eyes, the scurvy, and the gout; but there needs no more to value it, than what the ancient physicians affirm of it in those three words:

| *Digerit,* | *Aperit,* | *Abstergit.* |
| It digests, | It opens, | It cleanses. |

For rheums in the eyes and the head, I take a leaf of tobacco, put into the nostrils for an hour each morning, to be a specific medicine: or betony, if the other be too strong or offensive. The effect of both is to draw rheums off the head, through their proper and natural channel. And, as old Prince Maurice of Nassau told me, he had by this preserved his eyes, to so great an age, after the danger of losing them at thirty years old; and I have ever since used it with the same success, after great reasons near that age to apprehend the loss or decays of mine.

In times and places of great contagion, the strongest preservative yet known is a piece of myrrh held in the mouth when or where the danger is most apprehended; which I have both practiced and taught many others with success, in several places where cruel plagues have raged: though in such cases, after all, the best and safest is to run away as soon as one can. Yet, upon this occasion, I think myrrh may pass for a specific in prevention; and may, for aught I know, be of use in remedies, as the greatest remedy of corruption; which is known by the use of embalmings in the East.

For all illnesses of stomach, or indigestions, proceeding from hot or sharp humors, to which my whole family has been much subject, as well as very many of my acquaintance, and for which, powder of crabs' eyes and claws and burnt egg-shells are often prescribed as sweeteners of any sharp humors, I have never found anything of much or certain effect, besides the eating of strawberries, common cherries, white figs, soft peaches, or grapes, before every meal during their seasons; and when those are past, apples after meals; but all must be very ripe. And this, by my own and all my friends' experience who have tried it, I reckon for a specific medicine in this illness, so frequently complained of; at least, for the two first I never knew them fail; and the usual quantity is about forty cherries, without swallowing either skin or stone. I observe this the rather, because the recourse commonly made in this case to strong waters I esteem very pernicious, and which inevitably destroys the stomach with frequent use. The best, at least most innocent of all distilled liquors, is milk-water, made with balm, carduus, mint, and wormwood; which has many good effects in illnesses of the stomach, and none ill. The best and safest strong water, if any be so, for common use, I esteem to be that made of juniper berries especially in accidents of stone or colic.

Of all cordials, I esteem my Lady Kent's powder the best, the most innocent, and the most universal; though the common practice of physic abounds in nothing more, and the virtue seems to be little else, besides an allusion of the name to the heart.

Upon the gout I have writ what I had known or practiced, in an essay of moxa; and upon the spleen, what I had observed, in a chapter upon the dispositions of the people in the Netherlands. I shall only add for the help of my fellow-sufferers in the first, that, besides what is contained in the former essay, and since those pains have grown more diffused, and less fixed in one point, so as to be burned with moxa, which never failed of giving me present ease, I have found the most benefit from three methods. The first is, that of moving the joint where the pain begins as long as I am in my bed; which I have often done, and counted five or six hundred times or more, till I found first a great heat, and then perspiration, in the part; the heat spends or disperses the humor within, and the perspiration drives it out; and I have escaped many threats of ill fits by these motions. If they go on, the only poultice or plaster I have dealt with is wool from the belly of a fat sheep, which has often given me ease in a very little time. If the pains grow sharp and the swellings so diffused as not to be burned with moxa, the best remedy I have found is a piece of scarlet dipped in scalding brandy, laid upon the afflicted part, and the heat often renewed by dropping it upon the scarlet as hot as can be endured. And from this I have often found the same success as from moxa, and without breaking the skin or leaving any sore.

To what I have said in another place of the spleen, I shall only add here, that whatever the spleen is, whether a disease of the part so called, or of people that ail something, but they know not what; it is certainly a very ill ingredient into any other disease, and very often dangerous. For, as hope is the sovereign balsam of life, and the best cordial in all distempers both of body or mind; so fear, and regret, and melancholy apprehensions, which are the usual effects of the spleen, with the distractions, disquiets, or at least intranquillity they occasion, are the worst accidents that can attend any diseases; and make them often mortal, which would otherwise pass, and have had but a common course. I have known the most busy ministers of state, most fortunate courtiers, most vigorous youths, most beautiful virgins, in the strength or flower of their age, sink under common distempers, by the force of such weights, and the cruel damps and disturbances thereby given their spirits and their blood. It is no matter what is made the occasion, if well improved by spleen and melancholy apprehensions; a disappointed hope, a blot

of honor, a strain of conscience, an unfortunate love, an aching jealousy, a repining grief, will serve the turn, and all alike.

I remember an ingenious physician, who told me, in the fanatic times, he found most of his patients so disturbed by troubles of conscience that he was forced to play the divine with them, before he could begin the physician; whose greatest skill perhaps often lies in the infusing of hopes, and inducing some composure and tranquillity of mind, before they enter upon the other operations of their art; and this ought to be the first endeavor of the patient too; without which, all other medicines may lose their virtue.

The two greatest blessings of life are, in my opinion, health and good humor; and none contribute more to one another. Without health, all will allow life to be but a burden, and the several conditions of fortune to be all wearisome, dull, or disagreeable, without good humor; nor does any seem to contribute towards the true happiness of life but as it serves to increase that treasure or to preserve it. Whatever other differences are commonly apprehended in the several conditions of fortune, none perhaps will be found so true or so great as what is made by those two circumstances, so little regarded in the common course of pursuits of mortal men.

Whether long life be a blessing or no, God Almighty can only determine, who alone knows what length it is like to run, and how it is like to be attended. Socrates used to say that it was pleasant to grow old with good health and a good friend; and he might have reason. A man may be content to live while he is no trouble to himself or his friends; but, after that, it is hard if he be not content to die. I knew and esteemed a person abroad, who used to say, a man must be a mean wretch that desired to live after threescore years old. But so much, I doubt, is certain, that in life, as in wine, he that will drink it good must not draw it to dregs.

Where this happens, one comfort of age may be that whereas younger men are usually in pain when they are not in pleasure, old men find a sort of pleasure whenever they are out of pain. And, as young men often lose or impair their present enjoyments by raving after what is to come, by vain hopes, or fruitless fears, so old men relieve the wants of their age, by pleasing reflections upon what is past. Therefore men in the health and vigor of their age should endeavor to fill their lives with reading, with travel, with the best conversation, and the worthiest actions, either in their public or their private stations; that they may have something agreeable left to feed on when they are old, by pleasing remembrances.

But, as they are only the clean beasts which chew the cud, when they have fed enough; so they must be clean and virtuous men that can reflect with pleasure upon the past accidents or courses of their lives. Besides, men who grow old with good sense, or good fortunes, and good nature, cannot want the pleasure of pleasing others, by assisting with their gifts, their credit, and their advice, such as deserve it; as well as their care of children, kindness to friends, and bounty to servants.

But there cannot indeed live a more unhappy creature than an ill-natured old man, who is neither capable of receiving pleasures, nor sensible of doing them to others; and, in such a condition, it is time to leave them.

Thus have I traced in this essay whatever has fallen in my way or thoughts to observe concerning life and health, and which I conceive might be of any public use to be known or considered. The plainness wherewith it is written easily shows there could be no other intention; and it may at least pass like a Derbyshire charm, which is used among sick cattle, with these words, If it does thee no good, it will do thee no harm.

To sum up all, the first principle of health and long life is derived from the strength of our race of our birth; which gave occasion to that saying, *Gaudeant bene nati*, Let them rejoice that are happily born. Accidents are not in our power to govern; so that the best cares or provisions for life and health that are left us consist in the discreet and temperate government of diet and exercise: in both which all excess is to be avoided, especially in the common use of wine, whereof the first glass may pass for health, the second for good humor, the third for our friends, but the fourth is for our enemies.

For temperance in other kinds, or in general, I have given its character and virtues in the essay of moxa, so as to need no more upon that subject here.

When, in default or despite of all these cares, or by the effect of ill airs and seasons, acute or strong diseases may arise, recourse must be had to the best physicians that are in reach, whose success will depend upon thought and care, as much as skill. In all diseases of body or mind, it is happy to have an able physician for a friend, or discreet friend for a physician; which is so great a blessing that the wise man will have it to proceed only from God, where he says, "A faithful friend is the medicine of life and he that fears the Lord shall find him."

John Dryden

[1631–1700]

IN ADDITION to being, except for Milton, the greatest poet of the later seventeenth century, Dryden was also an eminent dramatist and the founder and first true master of modern English prose. Born in Aldwinkle, Northamptonshire, of a Puritan family, he was educated at Westminster School and at Trinity College, Cambridge, where he took his degree in 1654, after experiencing, like Bacon and Milton before him, some conflict with the academic authorities. His father died in the year Dryden received his degree, leaving him a modest patrimony, and a few years later, at the age of twenty-six, the poet went to London to seek his fortune. His first important work, the *Heroic Stanzas* in memory of Oliver Cromwell, appeared in 1659 and was followed the next year, with inconsistency but practicality, by *Astræa Redux*, a poem celebrating the restoration of Charles II. From 1666 to 1681, the year in which he wrote his great political satire *Absalom and Achitophel*, Dryden devoted his energies almost exclusively to the writing of plays, turning out no fewer than eighteen dramatic works in a wide variety of styles and genres.

Although Dryden earned his living as a dramatist, his commitment to the theater was more than merely commercial. Questions of dramatic art—the relative merits of classical, French, and English drama, the validity of the concept of tragicomedy, and the suitability of rhyme in tragic scenes—are the concern of his first major critical work, the *Essay of Dramatic Poesy* (1668). The *Essay* is written in dialogue form, one of the personages of the dialogue being Sir Robert Howard, the brother of Lady Elizabeth Howard, whom the poet had married in 1663. The *Essay* is a landmark in English criticism, and the *Defense of an Essay of Dramatic Poesy*, written later in the same year in answer to Howard's strictures, has a comparable significance. Throughout the 1670's Dryden continued his critical activity in a series of important prefaces to the published versions of his plays. Among the most striking are the prefaces to *The Conquest of Granada* and *All for Love*, both contained among the following selections.

Dryden is one of the forgers of the Neoclassical sensibility in English literature, and his influence was felt throughout the eighteenth century in both poetry and criticism. But although as a classicist he was deeply concerned with the establishment of rule and the maintenance of decorum, his qualities of flexibility, balance, and common sense make his literary criticism anything but narrow. No critic before him, for example, had displayed a comparable understanding of Shakespeare's genius, and his range of enthusiasms is impressively wide. For his critical writings Dryden forged a prose instrument of remarkable force and versatility: abandoning the exuberant and highly personalized devices of the Baroque prose artists, he developed a style in which clarity and precision are attained without the slightest loss of colloquial ease and naturalness. Dryden's bequest of such a style to the generation which followed him must count as one of his chief achievements.

The political events of the early 1680's—the so-called Popish Plot and the conspiracy of Monmouth—led him to turn his hand to verse satire, a genre in which he reached an almost definitive greatness. *Absalom and Achitophel* was followed by *The Medal* and *MacFlecknoe*, works which established him as one of the chief spokesmen and most able defenders of royal prerogative and Tory policy. In *Religio Laici* (1682) he applied his poetic genius to the defense of the Anglican Church, but in 1687, in *The Hind and the Panther*, he shifted his ground and urged the claims of the Church of Rome. Dryden's shift in religious allegiance has occasioned a good deal of controversy; he has been condemned as a time-server, and his conversion has been bluntly attributed to the accession to the throne of the Catholic James II. But it must be recognized that Dryden's entire spiritual development up to that time had taken the form of an ever more urgent search for authority—in politics, religion, letters, and life—and that his conversion to Catholicism was a logical conclusion to the development. In any case, the dethronement of James and the arrival of Protestant King William III did nothing to shake Dryden's faith, and his last years were rendered more difficult by his constancy.

Replaced as poet laureate by his old enemy Shadwell, whom he had held up to scorn in *MacFlecknoe*, Dryden was obliged during the last decade of his life to earn his living through translation. His work as a translator—of Ovid, Virgil, Horace, and Chaucer, among others—is of great distinction, and it also served as the occasion for two of the most important of his later critical works, the *Discourse Concerning the Original and Progress of Satire* (1692) and the *Preface to the Fables* (1700). During his last years, enthroned royally in Will's Coffee House, Dryden was the undisputed literary dictator of London. He died in 1700, the last literary giant in a century of giants.

J. DRYDEN. *Essays*, ed. W. P. Ker, 2 vols. (Oxford, 1900).
——————. *Works*, ed. E. N. Hooker and H. T. Swedenberg, Jr. (Berkeley, Calif., 1956–   ). The definitive edition.
——————. *The Best of Dryden*, ed. L. I. Bredvold (New York, 1933).
——————. *Poetry and Prose*, ed. D. N. Smith (Oxford, 1925).
K. YOUNG. *John Dryden* (London, 1954). A critical biography.
D. N. SMITH. *John Dryden* (Cambridge, 1950). A series of essays on Dryden.
C. E. WARD. *The Life of John Dryden* (Chapel Hill, N.C., and London, 1961).

AN ESSAY OF DRAMATIC POESY

[TEXT: *third edition, 1693*]

TO THE READER

THE drift of the ensuing discourse was chiefly to vindicate the honor of our English writers, from the censure of those who unjustly prefer the French before them. This I intimate, lest any should think me so exceedingly vain as to teach others an art which they understand much better than myself. But if this incorrect Essay, written in the country without the help of books or advice of friends, shall find any acceptance in the world, I promise to myself a better success of the Second Part, wherein I shall more fully treat of the virtues and faults of the English poets, who have written either in this, the epic, or the lyric way.

AN ESSAY OF DRAMATIC POESY

IT WAS that memorable day,[1] in the first summer of the late war, when our navy engaged the Dutch; a day wherein the two most mighty and best appointed fleets which any age had ever seen disputed the command of the greater half of the globe, the commerce of nations, and the riches of the universe: while these vast floating bodies, on either side, moved against each other in parallel lines, and our countrymen, under the happy conduct of his royal highness, went breaking, by little and little, into the line of the enemies; the noise of the cannon from both navies reached our ears about the city, so that all men being alarmed with it, and in a dreadful suspense of the event, which they knew was then deciding, everyone went following the sound as his fancy led him; and leaving the town almost empty, some took towards the park, some cross the river, others down it; all seeking the noise in the depth of silence.

Among the rest, it was the fortune of Eugenius,[2] Crites,[3] Lisideius,[4] and Neander,[5] to be in company together; three of them persons whom their wit and quality have made known to all the town; and whom I have chose to hide under these borrowed names, that they may not suffer by so ill a relation as I am going to make of their discourse.

Taking then a barge, which a servant of Lisideius had provided for them, they made haste to shoot the bridge, and left behind them that great fall of waters which hindered them from hearing what they desired: after which, having disengaged themselves from many vessels which rode at anchor in the Thames, and almost blocked up the passage towards Greenwich, they ordered the watermen to let fall their oars more gently; and then, everyone favoring his own curiosity with a strict silence, it was not long ere they perceived the air to break about them like the noise of distant thunder, or of swallows in a chimney: those little undulations of sound, though almost vanishing before

---

1 June 3, 1665.
2 Charles Sackville, Lord Buckhurst, later sixth Earl of Dorset.
3 Sir Robert Howard, brother of Dryden's wife.
4 Sir Charles Sedley.   5 Dryden.

they reached them, yet still seeming to retain somewhat of their first horror, which they had betwixt the fleets. After they had attentively listened till such time as the sound by little and little went from them, Eugenius, lifting up his head, and taking notice of it, was the first who congratulated to the rest that happy omen of our nation's victory: adding, that we had but this to desire in confirmation of it, that we might hear no more of that noise, which was now leaving the English coast. When the rest had concurred in the same opinion, Crites, a person of a sharp judgment, and somewhat too delicate a taste in wit, which the world have mistaken in him for ill-nature, said, smiling to us, that if the concernment of this battle had not been so exceeding great, he could scarce have wished the victory at the price he knew he must pay for it, in being subject to the reading and hearing of so many ill verses as he was sure would be made on that subject. Adding, that no argument could scape some of those eternal rhymers, who watch a battle with more diligence than the ravens and birds of prey; and the worst of them surest to be first upon the quarry: while the better able, either out of modesty writ not at all, or set that due value upon their poems, as to let them be often desired and long expected. "There are some of those impertinent people of whom you speak," answered Lisideius, "who to my knowledge are already so provided, either way, that they can produce not only a panegyric upon the victory, but, if need be, a funeral elegy on the duke; wherein, after they have crowned his valor with many laurels, they will at last deplore the odds under which he fell, concluding that his courage deserved a better destiny." All the company smiled at the conceit of Lisideius; but Crites, more eager than before, began to make particular exceptions against some writers, and said the public magistrate ought to send betimes to forbid them; and that it concerned the peace and quiet of all honest people, that ill poets should be as well silenced as seditious preachers. "In my opinion," replied Eugenius, "you pursue your point too far; for as to my own particular, I am so great a lover of poesy, that I could wish them all rewarded who attempt but to do well; at least, I would not have them worse used than one of their brethren was by Sylla the Dictator:— *Quem in concione vidimus* (says Tully), *cum ei libellum malus poeta de populo subjecisset, quod epigramma in eum fecisset tantummodo alternis versibus longiusculis, statim ex iis rebus quas tunc vendebat jubere ei præmium tribui, sub ea conditione ne quid postea scriberet.*" "I could wish with all my heart," replied Crites, "that many whom we know were as bountifully thanked upon the same condition,—that they would never trouble us again. For amongst others, I have a moral apprehension of two poets, whom this victory, with the help of both her wings, will never be able to escape." " 'Tis easy to guess whom you intend," said Lisideius; "and without naming them, I ask you, if one of them does not perpetually pay us with clenches[6] upon words, and a certain clownish kind of raillery? if now and then he does not offer at a catachresis or Clevelandism,[7] wresting and torturing a word into another meaning: in fine, if he be not one of those whom the French would call *un mauvais buffon;* one who is so much a well-willer to the satire, that he intends at least to spare no man; and though he cannot strike a blow to hurt any, yet he ought to be punished for the malice of the action, as our witches are justly hanged, because they think themselves to be such; and suffer deservedly for believing they did mischief, because they meant it."

"You have described him," said Crites, "so exactly, that I am afraid to come after you with my other extremity of poetry. He is one of those who, having had some advantage of education and converse, knows better than the other what a poet should be, but puts it into practice more unluckily than any man; his style and matter are everywhere alike: he is the most calm, peaceable writer you ever read: he never disquiets your passions with the least concernment, but still leaves you in as even a temper as he found you; he is a very leveler in poetry: he creeps along with ten little words in every line, and helps out his numbers with *For to,* and *Unto,* and all the pretty expletives he can find, till he drags them to the end of another line; while the sense is left tired halfway behind it: he doubly starves all his verses, first for want of thought, and then of expression; his poetry neither has wit in it, nor seems to have it; like him in Martial:

Pauper videri Cinna vult, et est pauper.

"He affects plainness, to cover his want of imagination: when he writes the serious way, the highest flight of his fancy is some miserable antithesis, or seeming contradiction; and in the comic he is still reaching at some thin conceit, the ghost of a jest, and that too flies before him, never to be caught; these swallows which we see before us on the Thames are the just resemblance

6 Puns.
7 John Cleveland, one of the Cavalier satirists, was noted for his harshness, as well as for his tortured ingenuity.

of his wit: you may observe how near the water they stoop, how many proffers they make to dip, and yet how seldom they touch it; and when they do, it is but the surface: they skim over it but to catch a gnat, and then mount into the air and leave it."

"Well, gentlemen," said Eugenius, "you may speak your pleasure of these authors; but though I and some few more about the town may give you a peaceable hearing, yet assure yourselves, there are multitudes who would think you malicious and them injured: especially him whom you first described; he is the very Withers[8] of the city: they have bought more editions of his works than would serve to lay under all their pies at the lord mayor's Christmas. When his famous poem first came out in the year 1660, I have seen them reading it in the midst of 'Change time; nay, so vehement they were at it, that they lost their bargain by the candles' ends;[9] but what will you say if he has been received amongst great persons? I can assure you this day he is the envy of one who is lord in the art of quibbling, and who does not take it well that any man should intrude so far into his province." "All I would wish," replied Crites, "is, that they who love his writings, may still admire him, and his fellow poet: *Qui Bavium non odit,* etc.,[10] is curse sufficient." "And farther," added Lisideius, "I believe there is no man who writes well, but would think he had hard measure, if their admirers should praise anything of his: *Nam quos contemnimus eorum quoque laudes contemnimus.*" "There are so few who write well in this age," said Crites, "that methinks any praises should be welcome; they neither rise to the dignity of the last age, nor to any of the ancients: and we may cry out of the writers of this time, with more reason than Petronius of his, *Pace vestra liceat dixisse, primi omnium eloquentium perdidistis:* you have debauched the true old poetry so far, that nature, which is the soul of it, is not in any of your writings."

"If your quarrel," said Eugenius, "to those who now write, be grounded only on your reverence to antiquity, there is no man more ready to adore those great Greeks and Romans than I am: but on the other side, I cannot think so contemptibly of the age in which I live, or so dishonorably of my own country,

8 George Wither, or Withers (1588–1667), a poet of the Spenserian School.
9 Bids for goods sold at auction were accepted so long as the candle-end kept burning.
10 "Who hates not Bavius, let him love thy songs." (Virgil, Eclogues iii. 90.)

as not to judge we equal the ancients in most kinds of poesy, and in some surpass them; neither know I any reason why I may not be as zealous for the reputation of our age as we find the ancients themselves were in reference to those who lived before them. For you hear your Horace saying,

> *Indignor quidquam reprehendi, non quia crassé*
> *Compositum, illepidève putetur, sed quia nuper.*[11]

And after:

> *Si meliora dies, ut vina, poemata reddit,*
> *Scire velim, pretim chartis quotus arroget annus?*[12]

"But I see I am engaging in a wide dispute, where the arguments are not like to reach close on either side; for poesy is of so large an extent, and so many both of the ancients and moderns have done well in all kinds of it, that in citing one against the other, we shall take up more time this evening than each man's occasions will allow him: therefore I would ask Crites to what part of poesy he would confine his arguments, and whether he would defend the general cause of the ancients against the moderns, or oppose any age of the moderns against this of ours?"

Crites, a little while considering upon this demand, told Eugenius, that if he pleased, he would limit their dispute to Dramatic Poesy; in which he thought it not difficult to prove, either that the ancients were superior to the moderns, or the last age of this of ours.

Eugenius was somewhat surprised, when he heard Crites make choice of that subject. "For aught I see," said he, "I have undertaken a harder province than I imagined; for though I never judged the plays of the Greek or Roman poets comparable to ours, yet, on the other side, those we now see acted come short of many which were written in the last age: but my comfort is, if we are overcome, it will be only by our own countrymen: and if we yield to them in this one part of poesy, we may surpass them in all the other: for in the epic or lyric way, it will be hard for them to show us one such amongst them, as we have many now living, or who lately were: they can produce nothing so courtly writ, or which expresses so much the conversation of a gentleman, as Sir John Suckling;

nothing so even, sweet, and flowing as Mr. Waller; nothing so majestic, so correct, as Sir John Denham; nothing so elevated, so copious, and full of spirit as Mr. Cowley; as for the Italian, French, and Spanish plays, I can make it evident, that those who now write surpass them; and that the drama is wholly ours."

All of them were thus far of Eugenius his opinion, that the sweetness of English verse was never understood or practiced by our fathers; even Crites himself did not much oppose it; and everyone was willing to acknowledge how much our poesy is improved by the happiness of some writers yet living; who first taught us to mold our thoughts into easy and significant words,—to retrench the superfluities of expression,—and to make our rhyme so properly a part of the verse, that it should never mislead the sense, but itself be led and governed by it.

Eugenius was going to continue this discourse, when Lisideius told him that it was necessary, before they proceeded further, to take a standing measure of their controversy; for how was it possible to be decided who writ the best plays, before we know what a play should be? But, this once agreed on by both parties, each might have recourse to it, either to prove his own advantages, or to discover the failings of his adversary.

He had no sooner said this, but all desired the favor of him to give the definition of a play; and they were the more importunate, because neither Aristotle, nor Horace, nor any other, who had writ of that subject, had ever done it.

Lisideius, after some modest denials, at last confessed he had a rude notion of it; indeed, rather a description than a definition; but which served to guide him in his private thoughts, when he was to make a judgment of what others writ: that he conceived a play ought to be, *A just and lively image of human nature, representing its passions and humors, and the changes of fortune to which it is subject, for the delight and instruction of mankind.*

This definition, though Crites raised a logical objection against it—that it was only *a genere et fine,* and so not altogether perfect, was yet well received by the rest; and after they had given order to the waterman to turn their barge, and row softly, that they might take the cool of the evening in their return, Crites, being desired by the company to begin, spoke on behalf of the ancients, in this manner:

"If confidence presage a victory, Eugenius, in his own opinion, has already triumphed over the ancients: nothing seems more easy to him than to overcome

---

11 Epistles II, i. 76–77.
  I lose my patience, and I own it, too,
    When works are censured not as bad but new. (Pope.)
12 *Ibid.* 34–35.
  If time improve our wits as well as wine,
    Say at what age a Poet grows divine. (Pope.)

those whom it is our greatest praise to have imitated well; for we do not only build upon their foundations, but by their models. Dramatic Poesy had time enough, reckoning from Thespis (who first invented it) to Aristophanes, to be born, to grow up, and to flourish in maturity. It has been observed of arts and sciences, that in one and the same century they have arrived to great perfection; and no wonder, since every age has a kind of universal genius, which inclines those that live in it to some particular studies: the work then, being pushed on by many hands, must of necessity go forward.

"Is it not evident, in these last hundred years, when the study of philosophy has been the business of all the Virtuosi in Christendom, that almost a new nature has been revealed to us? That more errors of the School have been detected, more useful experiments in philosophy have been made, more noble secrets in optics, medicine, anatomy, astronomy, discovered, than in all those credulous and doting ages from Aristotle to us?—so true it is, that nothing spreads more fast than science, when rightly and generally cultivated.

"Add to this, the more than common emulation that was in those times of writing well; which though it be found in all ages and all persons that pretend to the same reputation, yet poesy, being then in more esteem than now it is, had greater honors decreed to the professors of it, and consequently the rivalship was more high between them; they had judges ordained to decide their merit, and prizes to reward it; and historians have been diligent to record of Æschylus, Euripides, Sophocles, Lycophron, and the rest of them, both who they were that vanquished in these wars of the theatre, and how often they were crowned: while the Asian kings and Grecian commonwealths scarce afforded them a nobler subject than the unmanly luxuries of a debauched court, or giddy intrigues of a factious city:—*Alit æmulatio ingenia* (saith Paterculus), *et nunc invidia, nunc admiratio incitationem accendit:* Emulation is the spur of wit; and sometimes envy, sometimes admiration, quickens our endeavors.

"But now, since the rewards of honor are taken away, that virtuous emulation is turned into direct malice; yet so slothful, that it contents itself to condemn and cry down others, without attempting to do better: 'tis a reputation too unprofitable, to take the necessary pains for it; yet, wishing they had it, that desire is incitement enough to hinder others from it. And this, in short, Eugenius, is the reason why you have now so few good poets, and so many severe

judges. Certainly, to imitate the ancients well, much labor and long study is required; which pains, I have already shown, our poets would want encouragement to take if yet they had ability to go through the work. Those ancients have been faithful imitators and wise observers of that nature which is so torn and ill represented in our plays; they have handed down to us a perfect resemblance of her; which we, like ill copiers, neglecting to look on, have rendered monstrous, and disfigured. But, that you may know how much you are indebted to those your masters, and be ashamed to have so ill requited them, I must remember you, that all the rules by which we practice the drama at this day (either such as relate to the justness and symmetry of the plot, or the episodical ornaments, such as descriptions, narrations, and other beauties, which are not essential to the play) were delivered to us from the observations which Aristotle made of those poets who either lived before him, or were his contemporaries: we have added nothing of our own, except we have the confidence to say our wit is better; of which, none boast in this our age, but such as understand not theirs. Of that book which Aristotle has left us, περὶ τῆς Ποιητικῆς, Horace his Art of Poetry is an excellent comment, and, I believe, restores to us that second book of his concerning Comedy, which is wanting in him.

"Out of these two have been extracted the famous rules, which the French call *Des Trois Unités*, or, The Three Unities, which ought to be observed in every regular play; namely, of Time, Place, and Action.

"The unity of time they comprehend in twenty-four hours, the compass of a natural day, or as near as it can be contrived; and the reason of it is obvious to everyone,—that the time of the feigned action, or fable of the play, should be proportioned as near as can be to the duration of that time in which it is represented: since, therefore, all plays are acted on the theatre in the space of time much within the compass of twenty-four hours, that play is to be thought the nearest imitation of nature, whose plot or action is confined within that time; and, by the same rule which concludes this general proportion of time, it follows, that all the parts of it are (as near as may be) to be equally subdivided; namely, that one act take not up the supposed time of half a day, which is out of proportion to the rest; since the other four are then to be straitened within the compass of the remaining half: for it is unnatural that one act, which being spoke or written is not longer than the rest, should be supposed longer by the audience; it is therefore the poet's duty to take care that no act should be imagined to exceed the time in which it is represented on the stage; and that the intervals and inequalities of time be supposed to fall out between the acts.

"This rule of time, how well it has been observed by the ancients, most of their plays will witness; you see them in their tragedies (wherein to follow this rule is certainly most difficult), from the very beginning of their plays, falling close into that part of the story which they intend for the action or principal object of it, leaving the former part to be delivered by narration: so that they set the audience, as it were, at the post where the race is to be concluded; and, saving them the tedious expectation of seeing the poet set out and ride the beginning of the course, they suffer you not to behold him, till he is in sight of the goal, and just upon you.

"For the second unity, which is that of Place, the ancients meant by it, that the scene ought to be continued through the play, in the same place where it was laid in the beginning: for, the stage on which it is represented being but one and the same place, it is unnatural to conceive it many,—and those far distant from one another. I will not deny but, by the variation of painted scenes, the fancy, which in these cases will contribute to its own deceit, may sometimes imagine it several places, with some appearance of probability; yet it still carries the greater likelihood of truth if those places be supposed so near each other as in the same town or city; which may all be comprehended under the larger denominations of one place; for a greater distance will bear no proportion to the shortness of time which is allotted, in the acting, to pass from one of them to another; for the observation of this, next to the ancients, the French are to be most commended. They tie themselves so strictly to the unity of place that you never see in any of their plays a scene changed in the middle of an act: if the act begins in a garden, a street, or chamber, 'tis ended in the same place; and that you may know it to be the same, the stage is so supplied with persons, that it is never empty all the time: he who enters second, has business with him who was on before; and before the second quits the stage, a third appears who has business with him. This Corneille calls *la liaison des scènes*, the continuity or joining of the scenes; and 'tis a good mark of a well-contrived play, when all the persons are known to each other, and every one of them has some affairs with all the rest.

"As for the third unity, which is that of Action, the ancients meant no other by it than what the logicians do by their *finis*, the end or scope of any action; that which is the first in intention, and last in execution: now the poet is to aim at one great and complete action, to the carrying on of which all things in his play, even the very obstacles, are to be subservient; and the reason of this is as evident as any of the former. For two actions, equally labored and driven on by the writer, would destroy the unity of the poem; it would be no longer one play, but two: not but that there may be many actions in a play, as Ben Jonson has observed in his Discoveries; but they must be all subservient to the great one, which our language happily expresses in the name of *under-plots*: such as in Terence's Eunuch is the difference and reconcilement of Thais and Phædria, which is not the chief business of the play, but promotes the marriage of Chærea and Chremes's sister, principally intended by the poet. There ought to be but one action, says Corneille, that is, one complete action, which leaves the mind of the audience in a full repose; but this cannot be brought to pass but by many other imperfect actions, which conduce to it, and hold the audience in a delightful suspense of what will be.

"If by these rules (to omit many other drawn from the precepts and practice of the ancients) we should judge our modern plays, 'tis probable that few of them would endure the trial: that which should be the business of a day takes up in some of them an age; instead of one action, they are the epitomes of a man's life; and for one spot of ground, which the stage should represent, we are sometimes in more countries than the map can show us.

"But if we allow the ancients to have contrived well, we much acknowledge them to have written better. Questionless we are deprived of a great stock of wit in the loss of Menander among the Greek poets, and of Cæcilius, Afranius, and Varius, among the Romans; we may guess at Menander's excellency by the plays of Terence, who translated some of his; and yet wanted so much of him, that he was called by C. Cæsar the half-Menander; and may judge of Varius, by the testimonies of Horace, Martial, and Velleius Paterculus. 'Tis probable that these, could they be recovered, would decide the controversy; but so long as Aristophanes and Plautus are extant, while the tragedies of Euripides, Sophocles, and Seneca are in our hands, I can never see one of these plays which are now written but it increases my admiration of the ancients.

And yet I must acknowledge further, that to admire them as we ought, we should understand them better than we do. Doubtless many things appear flat to us, the wit of which depended on some custom or story, which never came to our knowledge; or perhaps on some criticism in their language, which being so long dead, and only remaining in their books, 'tis not possible they should make us understand perfectly. To read Macrobius, explaining the propriety and elegancy of many words in Virgil, which I had before passed over without consideration as common things, is enough to assure me that I ought to think the same of Terence; and that in the purity of his style (which Tully so much valued that he ever carried his works about him) there is yet left in him great room for admiration, if I knew but where to place it. In the meantime I must desire you to take notice that the greatest man of the last age, Ben Jonson, was willing to give place to them in all things: he was not only a professed imitator of Horace, but a learned plagiary of all the others; you track him everywhere in their snow: if Horace, Lucan, Petronius Arbiter, Seneca, and Juvenal had their own from him, there are few serious thoughts which are new in him: you will pardon me, therefore, if I presume he loved their fashion, when he wore their clothes. But since I have otherwise a great veneration for him, and you, Eugenius, prefer him above all other poets, I will use no farther arguments to you than his example: I will produce before you Father Ben, dressed in all the ornaments and colors of the ancients; you will need no other guide to our party, if you follow him; and whether you consider the bad plays of our age, or regard the good plays of the last, both the best and worst of the modern poets will equally instruct you to admire the ancients."

Crites had no sooner left speaking, but Eugenius, who had waited with some impatience for it, thus began:

"I have observed in your speech, that the former part of it is convincing as to what the moderns have profited by the rules of the ancients; but in the latter you are careful to conceal how much they have excelled them; we own all the helps we have from them, and want neither veneration nor gratitude, while we acknowledge that, to overcome them, we must make use of the advantages we have received from them: but to these assistances we have joined our own industry; for, had we sat down with a dull imitation of them, we might then have lost somewhat of the old

perfection, but never acquired any that was new. We draw not therefore after their lines, but those of nature; and having the life before us, besides the experience of all they knew, it is no wonder if we hit some airs and features which they have missed. I deny not what you urge of arts and sciences, that they have flourished in some ages more than others; but your instance in philosophy makes for me: for if natural causes be more known now than in the time of Aristotle, because more studied, it follows that poesy and other arts may, with the same pains, arrive still nearer to perfection; and, that granted, it will rest for you to prove that they wrought more perfect images of human life than we; which seeing in your discourse you have avoided to make good, it shall now be my task to show you some part of their defects, and some few excellencies of the moderns. And I think there is none among us can imagine I do it enviously, or with purpose to detract from them; for what interest of fame or profit can the living lose by the reputation of the dead? On the other side, it is a great truth which Velleius Paterculus affirms: *Audita visis libentius laudamus; et præsentia invidia præterita admiratione prosequimur; et his nos obrui, illis instrui credimus:* that praise or censure is certainly the most sincere, which unbribed posterity shall give us.

"Be pleased then in the first place to take notice that the Greek poesy, which Crites has affirmed to have arrived to perfection in the reign of the old comedy, was so far from it that the distinction of it into acts was not known to them; or if it were, it is yet so darkly delivered to us that we cannot make it out.

"All we know of it is from the singing of their Chorus; and that too is so uncertain, that in some of their plays we have reason to conjecture they sung more than five times. Aristotle indeed divides the integral parts of a play into four. First, the *Protasis*, or entrance, which gives light only to the characters of the persons, and proceeds very little into any part of the action. Secondly, the *Epitasis*, or working up of the plot, where the play grows warmer; the design or action of it is drawing on, and you see something promising that it will come to pass. Thirdly, the *Catastasis*, called by the Romans, *Status*, the height and full growth of the play: we may call it properly the counter-turn, which destroys that expectation, embroils the action in new difficulties, and leaves you far distant from that hope in which it found you; as you may have observed in a violent stream resisted by a narrow passage—it runs round to an eddy, and carries back the waters with more swiftness than it brought them on. Lastly, the *Catastrophe*, which the Grecians called λύσις the French *le dénouement*, and we the discovery, or unravelling of the plot: there you see all things settling again upon their first foundations; and, the obstacles which hindered the design or action of the play once removed, it ends with that resemblance of truth and nature that the audience are satisfied with the conduct of it. Thus this great man delivered to us the image of a play; and I must confess it is so lively, that from thence much light has been derived to the forming it more perfectly into acts and scenes: but what poet first limited to five the number of the acts, I know not; only we see it so firmly established in the time of Horace, that he gives it for a rule in comedy— *Neu brevior quinto, neu sit productior actu.* So that you see the Grecians cannot be said to have consummated this art; writing rather by entrances than by acts, and having rather a general indigested notion of a play, than knowing how and where to bestow the particular graces of it.

"But since the Spaniards at this day allow but three acts, which they call *Jornadas,* to a play, and the Italians in many of theirs follow them, when I condemn the ancients, I declare it is not altogether because they have not five acts to every play, but because they have not confined themselves to one certain number: 'tis building an house without a model; and when they succeeded in such undertakings, they ought to have sacrificed to Fortune, not to the Muses.

"Next, for the plot, which Aristotle called τό μῦθos, and often τῶν πραγμάτων σύνθεσις, [and from him the Romans *Fabula;*] it has already been judiciously observed by a late writer, that in their tragedies it was only some tale derived from Thebes or Troy, or at least something that happened in those two ages; which was worn so threadbare by the pens of all the epic poets, and even by tradition, itself of the talkative Greeklings (as Ben Jonson calls them), that before it came upon the stage it was already known to all the audience: and the people, so soon as ever they heard the name of Œdipus, knew as well as the poet, that he had killed his father by a mistake, and committed incest with his mother, before the play; that they were now to hear of a great plague, an oracle, and the ghost of Laius: so that they sat with a yawning kind of expectation, till he was to come with his eyes pulled out, and speak a hundred or more verses in a tragic tone, in complaint of his misfortunes. But one Œdipus, Hercules, or Medea, had been tolerable: poor people, they escaped not so good cheap; they had still the

chapon bouillé set before them, till their appetites were cloyed with the same dish, and, the novelty being gone, the pleasure vanished; so that one main end of Dramatic Poesy in its definition, which was to cause delight, was of consequence destroyed.

"In their comedies, the Romans generally borrowed their plots from the Greek poets; and theirs was commonly a little girl stolen or wandered from her parents, brought back unknown to the city, there got with child by some young fellow, who, by the help of his servant, cheats his father; and when her time comes, to cry, *Juno Lucina, fer opem,* one or other sees a little box or cabinet which was carried away with her, and so discovers her to her friends, if some god do not prevent it, by coming down in a machine, and taking the thanks of it to himself.

"By the plot you may guess much of the characters of the persons. An old father, who would willingly, before he dies, see his son well married; his debauched son, kind in his nature to his mistress, but miserably in want of money; a servant or slave, who has so much wit to strike in with him, and help to dupe his father; a braggadocio captain, a parasite, and a lady of pleasure.

"As for the poor honest maid, on whom the story is built, and who ought to be one of the principal actors in the play, she is commonly a mute in it: she has the breeding of the old Elizabeth way, which was for maids to be seen and not to be heard; and it is enough you know she is willing to be married when the fifth act requires it.

"These are plots built after the Italian mode of houses—you see through them all at once: the characters are indeed the imitation of nature, but so narrow, as if they had imitated only an eye or an hand, and did not dare to venture on the lines of a face, or the proportion of a body.

"But in how strait a compass soever they have bounded their plots and characters, we will pass it by, if they have regularly pursued them, and perfectly observed those three unities of time, place, and action; the knowledge of which you say is derived to us from them. But in the first place give me leave to tell you, that the unity of place, however it might be practiced by them, was never any of their rules: we neither find it in Aristotle, Horace, or any who have written of it, till in our age the French poets first made it a precept of the stage. The unity of time, even Terence himself, who was the best and most regular of them, has neglected: his *Heautontimoroumenos,* or Self-Punisher, takes up visibly two days, says Scaliger; the two first acts concluding the first day, the three last acts the day ensuing; and Euripides, in tying himself to one day, has committed an absurdity never to be forgiven him; for in one of his tragedies he has made Theseus go from Athens to Thebes, which was about forty English miles, under the walls of it to give battle, and appear victorious in the next act; and yet, from the time of his departure to the return of the Nuntius, who gives the relation of his victory, Æthra and the Chorus have but thirty-six verses; which is not for every mile a verse.

"The like error is as evident in Terence his Eunuch, when Laches, the old man, enters by mistake into the house of Thais; where, betwixt his exit and the entrance of Pythias, who comes to give an ample relation of the disorders he has raised within, Parmeno, who was left upon the stage, has not above five lines to speak. *C'est bien employer un temps si court*, says the French poet, who furnished me with one of the observations: and almost all their tragedies will afford us examples of the like nature.

" 'Tis true, they have kept the continuity, or, as you called it, *liaison des scènes*, somewhat better: two do not perpetually come in together, talk, and go out together; and other two succeed them, and do the same throughout the act, which the English call by the name of single scenes; but the reason is, because they have seldom above two or three scenes, properly so called, in every act; for it is to be accounted a new scene, not only every time the stage is empty, but every person who enters, though to others, makes it so; because he introduces a new business. Now the plots of their plays being narrow, and the persons few, one of their acts was written in a less compass than one of our well-wrought scenes; and yet they are often deficient even in this. To go no further than Terence; you find in the Eunuch, Antipho entering single in the midst of the third act, after Chremes and Pythias were gone off; in the same play you have likewise Dorias beginning the fourth act alone; and after she had made a relation of what was done at the Soldiers' entertainment (which by the way was very inartificial, because she was presumed to speak directly to the audience, and to acquaint them with what was necessary to be known, but yet should have been so contrived by the poet as to have been told by persons of the drama to one another, and so by them to have come to the knowledge of the people), she quits the stage, and Phædria enters next, alone likewise: he also gives you an account of himself, and of his returning from the country, in monologue; to which unnatural way of narration Terence is subject in all his plays. In his *Adelphi*, or Brothers, Syrus and Demea enter after the scene was broken by the departure of Sostrata, Geta, and Canthara; and indeed you can scarce look unto any of his comedies where you will not presently discover the same interruption.

"But as they have failed both in laying of their plots, and in the management, swerving from the rules of their own art by misrepresenting nature to us, in which they have ill satisfied one intention of a play, which was delight; so in the instructive part they have erred worse: instead of punishing vice and rewarding virtue, they have often shown a prosperous wickedness, and an unhappy piety: they have set before us a bloody image of revenge in Medea, and given her dragons to convey her safe from punishment; a Priam and Astyanax murdered, and Cassandra ravished, and the lust and murder ending in the victory of him who acted them: in short, there is no indecorum in any of our modern plays, which if I would excuse, I could not shadow with some authority from the ancients.

"And one farther note of them let me leave you: tragedies and comedies were not writ then as they are now, promiscuously, by the same person; but he who found his genius bending to the one, never attempted the other way. This is so plain that I need not instance to you, that Aristophanes, Plautus, Terence, never any of them writ a tragedy; Æschylus, Euripides, Sophocles, and Seneca never meddled with comedy: the sock and buskin were not worn by the same poet. Having then so much care to excel in one kind, very little is to be pardoned them if they miscarried in it; and this would lead me to the consideration of their wit, had not Crites given me sufficient warning not to be too bold in my judgment of it; because, the languages being dead, and many of the customs and little accidents on which it depended lost to us, we are not competent judges of it. But though I grant that here and there we may miss the application of a proverb or a custom, yet a thing well said will be wit in all languages; and though it may lose something in the translation, yet to him who reads it in the original, 'tis still the same: he has an idea of its excellency, though it cannot pass from his mind into any other expression or words than those in which he finds it. When Phædria, in the Eunuch, had a command from his mistress to be absent two days, and, encouraging himself to go through with it, said, *Tandem ego non illa caream, si sit opus, vel totum triduum?*—Parmeno, to mock the softness of his master, lifting up his hands and eyes, cries out, as it were in admiration, *Hui! universum triduum!* the elegancy of which *universum*, though it cannot be rendered in our language, yet leaves an impression on our souls: but this happens seldom in him; in Plautus oftener, who is infinitely too bold in his metaphors and coining words, out of which many times his wit is nothing; which questionless was one reason why Horace falls upon him so severely in those verses:

> *Sed proavi nostri Plautinos et numeros et*
> *Laudavere sales, nimium patienter utrumque.*
> *Ne dicam stolidè.*[13]

For Horace himself was cautious to obtrude a new word on his readers, and makes custom and common use the best measure of receiving it into our writings:

> *Multa renascentur quæ nunc cecidere, cadentque*
> *Quæ nunc sunt in honore vocabula, si volet usus,*
> *Quem penes arbitrium est, et jus, et norma loquendi.*[14]

"The not observing this rule is that which the world has blamed in our satirist, Cleveland: to express a thing hard and unnaturally, in his new way of elocution. 'Tis true, no poet but may sometimes use a catachresis: Virgil does it—

> *Mistaque ridenti colocasia fundet acantho*—[15]

in his eclogue of Pollio; and in his seventh Æneid:

> *mirantur et undæ,*
> *Miratur nemus insuetum fulgentia longe*
> *Scuta virum fluvio pictasque innare carinas.*

And Ovid once so modestly, that he asks leave to do it:

> *quem, si verbo audacia detur,*
> *Haud metuam summi dixisse Palatia cæli.*

calling the court of Jupiter by the name of Augustus his palace; though in another place he is more bold,

---

13 Our forefathers, good-natured, easy folks,
    Extolled the numbers and enjoyed the jokes
    Of Plautus, prompt both these and those to hear
    With tolerant—not to say with tasteless—ear.
        (*De Arte Poetica*, 270–71; Howes's translation.)
14 Full many a word, now lost, again shall rise,
    And many a word shall droop which now we prize,
    As shifting fashion stamps the doom of each,
    Sole umpire, arbitress, and guide of speech.
        (*De Arte Poetica*, 70–72; Howes.)
15 [The lavish earth] shall spread the lily, mingled with the laughing acanthus.

where he says,—*et longas visent Capitolia pompas.* But to do this always, and never be able to write a line without it, though it may be admired by some few pedants, will not pass upon those who know that wit is best conveyed to us in the most easy language; and is most to be admired when a great thought comes dressed in words so commonly received, that it is understood by the meanest apprehensions, as the best meat is the most easily digested: but we cannot read a verse of Cleveland's without making a face at it, as if every word were a pill to swallow: he gives us many times a hard nut to break our teeth, without a kernel for our pains. So that there is this difference betwixt his Satires and Doctor Donne's; that the one gives us deep thoughts in common language, though rough cadence; the other gives us common thoughts in abstruse words: 'tis true, in some places his wit is independent of his words, as in that of the rebel Scot:

Had Cain been Scot, God would have chang'd his doom;
Not forc'd him wander, but confin'd him home.

"*Si sic omnia dixisset!* This is wit in all languages: it is like Mercury, never to be lost or killed: —and so that other—

> For beauty, like white powder, makes no noise,
> And yet the silent hypocrite destroys.

You see the last line is highly metaphorical, but it is so soft and general, that it does not shock us as we read it.

"But, to return from whence I have digressed, to the consideration of the ancients' writing, and their wit (of which by this time you will grant us in some measure to be fit judges). Though I see many excellent thoughts in Seneca, yet he of them who had a genius most proper for the stage, was Ovid; he had a way of writing so fit to stir up a pleasing admiration and concernment, which are the objects of a tragedy, and to show the various movements of a soul combating betwixt two different passions, that, had he lived in our age, or in his own could have writ with our advantages, no man but must have yielded to him; and therefore I am confident the Medea is none of his: for, though I esteem it for the gravity and sententiousness of it, which he himself concludes to be suitable to a tragedy—*Omne genus scripti gravitate tragœdia vincit*— yet it moves not my soul enough to judge that he, who in the epic way wrote things so near the drama as the story of Myrrha, of Caunus and Biblis, and the rest, should stir up no more concernment where he most endeavored it. The masterpiece of Seneca I hold to be that scene in the *Troades*, where Ulysses is seeking for Astyanax to kill him: there you see the tenderness of a mother so represented in Andromache, that it raises compassion to a high degree in the reader, and bears the nearest resemblance of anything in the tragedies of the ancients to the excellent scenes of passion in Shakespeare, or in Fletcher: for love-scenes, you will find few among them; their tragic poets dealt not with that soft passion, but with lust, cruelty, revenge, ambition, and those bloody actions they produced; which were more capable of raising horror than compassion in an audience: leaving love untouched, whose gentleness would have tempered them; which is the most frequent of all the passions, and which, being the private concernment of every person, is soothed by viewing its own image in a public entertainment.

"Among their comedies, we find a scene or two of tenderness, and that where you would least expect it, in Plautus; but to speak generally, their lovers say little, when they see each other, but *anima mea vita mea; Ζωὴ καὶ ψυχῇ*, as the women in Juvenal's time used to cry out in the fury of their kindness. Any sudden gust of passion (as an ecstasy of love in an unexpected meeting) cannot better be expressed than in a word and a sigh, breaking one another. Nature is dumb on such occasions; and to make her speak would be to represent her unlike herself. But there are a thousand other concernments of lovers, as jealousies, complaints, contrivances, and the like, where not to open their minds at large to each other were to be wanting to their own love, and to the expectation of the audience; who watch the movements of their minds, as much as the changes of their fortunes. For the imaging of the first is properly the work of a poet; the latter he borrows from the historian."

Eugenius was proceeding in that part of his discourse, when Crites interrupted him. "I see," said he, "Eugenius and I are never like to have this question decided betwixt us; for he maintains the moderns have acquired a new perfection in writing; I can only grant they have altered the mode of it. Homer describes his heroes men of great appetites, lovers of beef broiled upon the coals, and good fellows; contrary to the practice of the French Romances, whose heroes neither eat, nor drink, nor sleep, for love. Virgil makes Æneas a bold avower of his own virtues:

Sum pius Æneas, fama super æthera notus;

which, in the civility of our poets is the character of a fanfaron or Hector: for with us the knight takes occasion to walk out, or sleep, to avoid the vanity of telling his own story, which the trusty 'squire is ever to perform for him. So in their love-scenes, of which Eugenius spoke last, the ancients were more hearty, were more talkative: they writ love as it was then the mode to make it; and I will grant thus much to Eugenius, that perhaps one of their poets, had he lived in our age, *si foret hoc nostrum fato delapsus in ævum* (as Horace says of Lucilius), he had altered many things; not that they were not natural before, but that he might accommodate himself to the age in which he lived. Yet in the meantime, we are not to conclude anything rashly against those great men, but preserve to them the dignity of masters, and give that honor to their memories, *quos Libitina sacravit*, part of which we expect may be paid to us in future times."

This moderation of Crites, as it was pleasing to all the company, so it put an end to that dispute; which Eugenius, who seemed to have the better of the argument, would urge no farther: but Lisideius, after he had acknowledged himself of Eugenius his opinion concerning the ancients, yet told him, he had forborne, till his discourse were ended, to ask him why he preferred the English plays above those of other nations? and whether we ought not to submit our stage to the exactness of our next neighbors?

"Though," said Eugenius, "I am at all times ready to defend the honor of my country against the French, and to maintain we are as well able to vanquish them with our pens, as our ancestors have been with their swords; yet, if you please," added he, looking upon Neander, "I will commit this cause to my friend's management; his opinion of our plays is the same with mine, and besides, there is no reason, that Crites and I, who have now left the stage, should re-enter so suddenly upon it; which is against the laws of comedy."

"If the question had been stated," replied Lisideius, "who had writ best, the French or English, forty years ago, I should have been of your opinion, and adjudged the honor to our own nation; but since that time" (said he, turning towards Neander), "we have been so long together bad Englishmen that we had not leisure to be good poets. Beaumont, Fletcher, and Jonson (who were only capable of bringing us to that degree of perfection which we have) were just then leaving the world; as if in an age of so much horror, wit and those milder studies of humanity had no farther business among us. But the Muses, who ever follow peace, went to plant in another country: it was then that the great Cardinal of Richelieu began to take them into his protection; and that, by his encouragement, Corneille, and some other Frenchmen, reformed their theater (which before was as much below ours, as it now surpasses it and the rest of Europe). But because Crites in his discourse for the ancients has prevented me, by observing many rules of the stage which the moderns have borrowed from them, I shall only, in short, demand of you, whether you are not convinced that of all nations the French have best observed them? In the unity of time you find them so scrupulous that it yet remains a dispute among their poets, whether the artificial day of twelve hours, more or less, be not meant by Aristotle, rather than the natural one of twenty-four; and consequently, whether all plays ought not to be reduced into that compass. This I can testify, that in all their dramas writ within these last twenty years and upwards, I have not observed any that have extended the time to thirty hours: in the unity of place they are full as scrupulous; for many of their critics limit it to that very spot of ground where the play is supposed to begin; none of them exceed the compass of the same town or city. The unity of action in all their plays is yet more conspicuous; for they do not burden them with under-plots, as the English do: which is the reason why many scenes of our tragi-comedies carry on a design that is nothing of kin to the main plot; and that we see two distinct webs in a play, like those in ill-wrought stuffs; and two actions, that is, two plays, carried on together, to the confounding of the audience, who, before they are warm in their concernments for one part, are diverted to another; and by that means espouse the interest of neither. From hence likewise it arises that the one half of our actors are not known to the other. They keep their distances, as if they were Montagues and Capulets, and seldom begin an acquaintance till the last scene of the fifth act, when they are all to meet upon the stage. There is no theatre in the world has anything so absurd as the English tragi-comedy; 'tis a drama of our own invention, and the fashion of it is enough to proclaim it so; here a course of mirth, there another of sadness and passion, and a third of honor and a duel: thus, in two hours and a half, we run through all the fits of Bedlam. The French affords you as much variety on the same day, but they do it not so unseasonably, or *mal à propos*, as we: our poets present you the play and the farce together; and our stages still retain somewhat of the original civility of the Red Bull:

Atque ursum et pugiles media inter carmina poscunt.[16]

The end of tragedies or serious plays, says Aristotle, is to beget admiration, compassion, or concernment; but are not mirth and compassion things incompatible? and is it not evident that the poet must of necessity destroy the former by intermingling of the latter? that is, he must ruin the sole end and object of his tragedy, to introduce somewhat that is forced into it, and is not of the body of it. Would you not think that physician mad, who, having prescribed a purge, should immediately order you to take restringents?

"But to leave our plays, and return to theirs. I have noted one great advantage they have had in the plotting of their tragedies; that is, they are always grounded upon some known history: according to that of Horace, *Ex noto fictum carmen sequar;* and in that they have so imitated the ancients that they have surpassed them. For the ancients, as was observed before, took for the foundation of their plays some poetical fiction, such as under that consideration could move but little concernment in the audience, because they already knew the event of it. But the French goes farther:

> *Atque ita mentitur, sic veris falsa remiscet*
> *Primo ne medium, medio ne discrepet imum.*[17]

He so interweaves truth with probable fiction that he puts a pleasing fallacy upon us; mends the intrigues of fate, and dispenses with the severity of history, to reward that virtue which has been rendered to us there unfortunate. Sometimes the story has left the success so doubtful that the writer is free, by the privilege of a poet, to take that which of two or more relations will best suit with his design: as for example, in the death of Cyrus, whom Justin and some others report to have perished in the Scythian war, but Xenophon affirms to have died in his bed of extreme old age. Nay, more, when the event is past dispute, even then we are willing to be deceived, and the poet, if he contrives it with appearance of truth, has all the audience of his party; at least during the time his play is acting: so naturally we are kind to virtue, when our own

16 In the midst of the verses they demand the bear and the pugilists.
17 And so adroitly mingles false with true,
   So with his fair illusions cheats the view,
   That all the parts—beginning, middle, end—
   In one harmonious compound sweetly blend.
                              (*De Arte Poetica*, 151–52; Howes.)

interest is not in question, that we take it up as the general concernment of mankind. On the other side, if you consider the historical plays of Shakespeare, they are rather so many chronicles of kings, or the business many times of thirty or forty years, cramped into a representation of two hours and a half; which is not to imitate or paint nature, but rather to draw her in miniature, to take her in little; to look upon her through the wrong end of a perspective, and receive her images not only much less, but infinitely more imperfect than the life: this, instead of making a play delightful, renders it ridiculous:

> *Quodcunque ostendis mihi sic, incredulus odi.*

For the spirit of man cannot be satisfied but with truth, or at least verisimility; and a poem is to contain, if not τὰ ἔτυμα, yet ἐτύμοισιν ὁμοῖα, as one of the Greek poets has expressed it.

"Another thing in which the French differ from us and from the Spaniards, is that they do not embarrass, or cumber themselves with too much plot; they only represent so much of a story as will constitute one whole and great action sufficient for a play; we, who undertake more, do but multiply adventures which, not being produced from one another, as effects from causes, but rarely following, constitute many actions in the drama, and consequently make it many plays.

"But by pursuing closely one argument, which is not cloyed with many turns, the French have gained more liberty for verse, in which they write; they have leisure to dwell on a subject which deserves it; and to represent the passions (which we have acknowledged to be the poet's work), without being hurried from one thing to another, as we are in the plays of Calderón, which we have seen lately upon our theatres under the name of Spanish plots. I have taken notice but of one tragedy of ours whose plot has that uniformity and unity of design in it which I have commended in the French; and that is Rollo, or rather, under the name of Rollo, the Story of Bassianus and Geta in Herodian: there indeed the plot is neither large nor intricate, but just enough to fill the minds of the audience, not to cloy them. Besides, you see it founded upon the truth of history—only the time of the action is not reducible to the strictness of the rules; and you see in some places a little farce mingled, which is below the dignity of the other parts, and in this all our poets are extremely peccant: even Ben Jonson himself, in Sejanus and Catiline, has given us this oleo of a play, this unnatural mixture of comedy and tragedy; which to me sounds just as ridiculously as the history of David with the merry humors of Golia's. In Sejanus you may take notice of the scene betwixt Livia and the physician which is a pleasant satire upon the artificial helps of beauty: in Catiline you may see the parliament of women; the little envies of them to one another; and all that passes betwixt Curio and Fulvia: scenes admirable in their kind, but of an ill mingle with the rest.

"But I return again to the French writers, who, as I have said, do not burden themselves too much with plot, which has been reproached to them by an ingenious person of our nation as a fault; for, he says, they commonly make but one person considerable in a play; they dwell on him, and his concernments, while the rest of the persons are only subservient to set him off. If he intends this by it—that there is one person in the play who is of greater dignity than the rest, he must tax, not only theirs, but those of the ancients, and which he would be loth to do, the best of ours; for it is impossible but that one person must be more conspicuous in it than any other, and consequently the greatest share in the action must devolve on him. We see it so in the management of all affairs; even in the most equal aristocracy, the balance cannot be so justly poised but someone will be superior to the rest, either in parts, fortune, interest, or the consideration of some glorious exploit; which will reduce the greatest part of business into his hands.

"But, if he would have us to imagine, that in exalting one character the rest of them are neglected, and that all of them have not some share or other in the action of the play, I desire him to produce any of Corneille's tragedies, wherein every person, like so many servants in a well-governed family, has not some employment, and who is not necessary to the carrying on of the plot, or at least to your understanding it.

"There are indeed some protatic persons in the ancients, whom they make use of in their plays, either to hear or to give the relation: but the French avoid this with great address, making their narrations only to, or by such, who are some way interested in the main design. And now I am speaking of relations, I cannot take a fitter opportunity to add this in favor of the French, that they often use them with better judgment and more *à propos* than the English do. Not that I commend narrations in general—but there are two sorts of them. One of those things which are antecedent to the play, and are related to make the conduct of it more clear to us. But 'tis a fault to choose such subjects for the stage as will force us on that rock because we see they are seldom listened to by the audience, and that is many times the ruin of the play; for, being once let pass without attention, the audience can never recover themselves to understand the plot: and indeed it is somewhat unreasonable that they should be put to so much trouble, as that, to comprehend what passes in their sight, they must have recourse to what was done, perhaps, ten or twenty years ago.

"But there is another sort of relations, that is, of things happening in the action of the play, and supposed to be done behind the scenes; and this is many times both convenient and beautiful; for by it the French avoid the tumult to which we are subject in England, by representing duels, battles, and the like; which renders our stage too like the theatres where they fight for prizes. For what is more ridiculous than to represent an army with a drum and five men behind it; all which the hero of the other side is to drive in before him; or to see a duel fought, and one slain with two or three thrusts of the foils, which we know are so blunted that we might give a man an hour to kill another in good earnest with them.

"I have observed that in all our tragedies, the audience cannot forbear laughing when the actors are to die; it is the most comic part of the whole play. All *passions* may be lively represented on the stage, if to the well-writing of them the actor supplies a good commanding voice, and limbs that move easily, and without stiffness; but there are many *actions* which can never be imitated to a just height: dying especially is a thing which none but a Roman gladiator could naturally perform on the stage, when he did not imitate or represent, but do it; and therefore it is better to omit the representation of it.

"The words of a good writer, which describe it lively, will make a deeper impression of belief in us than all the actor can insinuate into us, when he seems to fall dead before us; as a poet in the description of a beautiful garden, or a meadow, will please our imagination more than the place itself can please our sight. When we see death represented, we are convinced it is but fiction; but when we hear it related, our eyes, the strongest witnesses, are wanting, which might have undeceived us; and we are all willing to favor the sleight, when the poet does not too grossly impose on us. They therefore who imagine these relations would make no concernment in the audience, are deceived, by confounding them with the other, which are of things antecedent to the play: those are made often in cold blood, as I may say, to the audience; but these are warmed with our concernments, which were before awakened in the play. What the philosophers say of motion, that, when it is once begun, it continues of itself, and will do so to eternity, without some stop put to it, is clearly true on this occasion: the soul being already moved with the characters and fortunes of those imaginary persons, continues going of its own accord; and we are no more weary to hear what becomes of them when they are not on the stage, than we are to listen to the news of an absent mistress. But it is objected, that if one part of the play may be related, then why not all? I answer, some parts of the action are more fit to be represented, some to be related. Corneille says judiciously that the poet is not obliged to expose to view all particular actions which conduce to the principal: he ought to select such of them to be seen, which will appear with the greatest beauty, either by the magnificence of the show or the vehemence of the passions they produce, or some other charm which they have in them; and let the rest arrive to the audience by narration. 'Tis a great mistake in us to believe the French present no part of the action on the stage; every alteration or crossing of a design, every new-sprung passion, and turn of it, is a part of the action, and much the noblest, except we conceive nothing to be action till the players come to blows; as if the painting of the hero's mind were not more properly the poet's work than the strength of his body. Nor does this anything contradict the opinion of Horace, where he tells us,

Segnius irritant animos demissa per aurem,
Quam quæ sunt oculis subjecta fidelibus.[18]

For he says immediately after,

Non tamen intus
Digna geri promes in scenam; multaque; tolles
Ex oculis, quæ mox narret facundia præsens.[19]

18 Those which a tale shall through the ear impart,
   With fainter characters impress the heart
   Than those which, subject to the eye's broad gaze
   [The pleased spectator to himself conveys].
   (*De Arte Poetica*, 180–82.)
19 Yet drag not on the stage each horrid scene,
   Nor shock the sight with what should pass within.
   This let description's milder medium show,
   And leave to eloquence her tale of woe.
   (*Ibid.*, 182–84.)

Among which many he recounts some:

Nec pueros coram populo Medea trucidet,
Aut in avem Progne mutetur, Cadmus in anguem, etc.[20]

That is, those actions which by reason of their cruelty will cause aversion in us, or by reason of their impossibility, unbelief, ought either wholly to be avoided by a poet, or only delivered by narration. To which we may have leave to add, such as, to avoid tumult (as was before hinted), or to reduce the plot into a more reasonable compass of time, or for defect of beauty in them, are rather to be related than presented to the eye. Examples of all these kinds are frequent, not only among all the ancients, but in the best received of our English poets. We find Ben Jonson using them in his Magnetic Lady, where one comes out from dinner, and relates the quarrels and disorders of it, to save the undecent appearance of them on the stage, and to abbreviate the story; and this in express imitation of Terence, who had done the same before him in his Eunuch, where Pythias makes the like relation of what happened within at the soldiers' entertainment. The relations likewise of Sejanus's death, and the prodigies before it, are remarkable; the one of which was hid from sight, to avoid the horror and tumult of the representation; the other, to shun the introducing of things impossible to be believed. In that excellent play, The King and no King, Fletcher goes yet farther; for the whole unravelling of the plot is done by narration in the fifth act, after the manner of the ancients; and it moves great concernment in the audience, though it be only a relation, of what was done many years before the play. I could multiply other instances, but these are sufficient to prove that there is no error in choosing a subject which requires this sort of narrations; in the ill management of them, there may.

"But I find I have been too long in this discourse, since the French have many other excellencies not common to us; as that you never see any of their plays end with a conversion, or simple change of will, which is the ordinary way which our poets use to end theirs. It shows little art in the conclusion of a dramatic poem, when they who have hindered the felicity during the four acts, desist from it in the fifth, without some powerful cause to take them off their design; and though I deny not but such reasons may be found, yet it is a path that is cautiously to be trod, and the poet is to be sure he convinces the audience that the motive is strong enough. As for example, the conversion of the Usurer in The Scornful Lady seems to me a little forced; for, being an Usurer, which implies a lover of money to the highest degree of covetousness,—and such the poet has represented him,—the account he gives for the sudden change is, that he has been duped by the wild young fellow; which in reason might render him more wary another time, and make him punish himself with harder fare and coarser clothes, to get up again what he had lost: but that he should look on it as a judgment, and so repent, we may expect to hear in a sermon, but I should never endure it in a play.

"I pass by this; neither will I insist on the care they take that no person after his first entrance shall ever appear but the business which brings him upon the stage shall be evident; which rule, if observed, must needs render all the events in the play more natural; for there you see the probability of every accident, in the cause that produced it; and that which appears chance in the play will seem so reasonable to you, that you will there find it almost necessary: so that in the exit of the actor you have a clear account of his purpose and design in the next entrance (though, if the scene be well wrought, the event will commonly deceive you); for there is nothing so absurd, says Corneille, as for an actor to leave the stage only because he has no more to say.

"I should now speak of the beauty of their rhyme, and the just reason I have to prefer that way of writing in tragedies before ours in blank verse; but because it is partly received by us, and therefore not altogether peculiar to them, I will say no more of it in relation to their plays. For our own, I doubt not but it will exceedingly beautify them; and I can see but one reason why it should not generally obtain, that is, because our poets write so ill in it. This indeed may prove a more prevailing argument than all others which are used to destroy it, and therefore I am only troubled when great and judicious poets, and those who are acknowledged such, have writ or spoke against it: as for others, they are to be answered by that one sentence of an ancient author:—*Sed ut primo ad consequendos eos quos priores ducimus, accendimur, ita ubi aut praeteriri, aut aequari eos posse desperavimus, studium cum*

20 Let not the cruel Colchian mother slay
   Her smiling infants in the face of day; . . .
   Nor Procne's form the rising plumage take,
   Nor Cadmus sink into a slimy snake.

   (*Ibid.*, 185–87.)

spe senescit: quod, scilicet, assequi non potest, sequi desinit; . . . præteritoque eo in quo eminere non possumus, aliquid in quo nitamur, conquirimus."

Lisideius concluded in this manner; and Neander, after a little pause, thus answered him:

"I shall grant Lisideius, without much dispute, a great part of what he has urged against us; for I acknowledge that the French contrive their plots more regularly, and observe the laws of comedy and decorum of the stage (to speak generally) with more exactness than the English. Farther, I deny not but he has taxed us justly in some irregularities of ours, which he has mentioned; yet, after all, I am of opinion that neither our faults nor their virtues are considerable enough to place them above us.

"For the lively imitation of nature being in the definition of a play, those which best fulfill that law ought to be esteemed superior to the others. 'Tis true, those beauties of the French poesy are such as will raise perfection higher where it is, but are not sufficient to give it where it is not: they are indeed the beauties of a statue, but not of a man, because not animated with the soul of poesy, which is imitation of humor and passions: and this Lisideius himself, or any other, however biased to their party, cannot but acknowledge, if he will either compare the humors of our comedies, or the characters of our serious plays, with theirs. He who will look upon theirs which have been written till these last ten years, or thereabouts, will find it a hard matter to pick out two or three passable humors amongst them. Corneille himself, their arch-poet, what has he produced except The Liar, and you know how it was cried up in France; but when it came upon the English stage, though well translated, and that part of Durant acted to so much advantage as I am confident it never received in its own country, the most favorable to it would not put it in competition with many of Fletcher's or Ben Jonson's. In the rest of Corneille's comedies you have little humor; he tells you himself his way is first to show two lovers in good intelligence with each other; in the working up of the play to embroil them by some mistake, and in the latter end to clear it and reconcile them.

"But of late years Molière, the younger Corneille, Quinault, and some others, have been imitating afar off the quick turns and graces of the English stage. They have mixed their serious plays with mirth, like our tragi-comedies, since the death of Cardinal Richelieu; which Lisideius and many others not observing, have commended that in them for a virtue which they themselves no longer practice. Most of their new plays are, like some of ours, derived from the Spanish novels. There is scarce one of them without a veil, and a trusty Diego, who drolls much after the rate of The Adventures. But their humors, if I may grace them with that name, are so thin-sown, that never above one of them comes up in any play. I dare take upon me to find more variety of them in some one play of Ben Jonson's than in all theirs together; as he who has seen The Alchemist, The Silent Woman, or Bartholomew Fair, cannot but acknowledge with me.

"I grant the French have performed what was possible on the ground-work of the Spanish plays; what was pleasant before, they have made regular: but there is not above one good play to be writ on all those plots; they are too much alike to please often; which we need not the experience of our own stage to justify. As for their new way of mingling mirth with serious plot, I do not, with Lisideius, condemn the thing, though I cannot approve of their manner of doing it. He tells us, we cannot so speedily recollect ourselves after a scene of great passion and concernment, as to pass to another of mirth and humor, and to enjoy it with any relish: but why should he imagine the soul of man more heavy than his senses? Does not the eye pass from an unpleasant object to a pleasant in a much shorter time than is required to this? and does not the unpleasantness of the first commend the beauty of the latter? The old rule of logic might have convinced him, that contraries, when placed near, set off each other. A continued gravity keeps the spirit too much bent; we must refresh it sometimes, as we bait in a journey that we may go on with greater ease. A scene of mirth, mixed with tragedy, has the same effect upon us which our music has betwixt the acts; which we find a relief to us from the best plots and language of the stage, if the discourses have been long. I must therefore have stronger arguments, ere I am convinced that compassion and mirth in the same subject destroy each other; and in the meantime cannot but conclude, to the honor of our nation, that we have invented, increased, and perfected a more pleasant way of writing for the stage, than was ever known to the ancients or moderns of any nation, which is tragi-comedy.

"And this leads me to wonder why Lisideius and many others should cry up the barrenness of the French plots above the variety and copiousness of the English. Their plots are single; they carry on one design, which is pushed forward by all the actors, every scene in the play contributing and moving towards it. Our plays, besides the main design, have under-plots or by-concernments, of less considerable persons and intrigues, which are carried on with the motion of the main plot; as they say the orb of the fixed stars, and those of the planets, though they have motions of their own, are whirled about by the motion of the *primum mobile*, in which they are contained. That similitude expresses much of the English stage; for if contrary motions may be found in nature to agree; if a planet can go east and west at the same time;—one way by virtue of his own motion, the other by the force of the first mover;—it will not be difficult to imagine how the under-plot, which is only different, not contrary to the great design, may naturally be conducted along with it.

"Eugenius has already shown us, from the confessions of the French poets, that the unity of action is sufficiently preserved, if all the imperfect actions of the play are conducing to the main design; but when those petty intrigues of a play are so ill ordered that they have no coherence with the other, I must grant that Lisideius has reason to tax that want of due connection; for co-ordination in a play is as dangerous and unnatural as in a state. In the meantime he must acknowledge, our variety, if well ordered, will afford a greater pleasure to the audience.

"As for his other argument, that by pursuing one single theme they gain an advantage to express and work up the passions, I wish any example he could bring from them would make it good; for I confess their verses are to me the coldest I have ever read. Neither, indeed, is it possible for them, in the way they take, so to express passion, as that the effects of it should appear in the concernment of an audience, their speeches being so many declamations, which tire us with their length; so that instead of persuading us to grieve for their imaginary heroes, we are concerned for our own trouble, as we are in tedious visits of bad company; we are in pain till they are gone. When the French stage came to be reformed by Cardinal Richelieu, those long harangues were introduced to comply with the gravity of a churchman. Look upon the Cinna and the Pompey; they are not so properly to be called plays, as long discourses of reason of state; and Polieucte in matters of religion is as solemn as the long stops upon our organs. Since that time it is grown into a custom, and their actors speak by the hour-glass, like our parsons; nay, they account it the grace of their parts, and think themselves disparaged by the poet, if they may not twice or thrice in a play entertain the audience with a speech of an hundred lines. I deny not but this may suit well enough with the French; for as we, who are a more sullen people, come to be diverted at our plays, so they, who are of an airy and gay temper, come thither to make themselves more serious: and this I conceive to be one reason why comedies are more pleasing to us, and tragedies to them. But to speak generally: it cannot be denied that short speeches and replies are more apt to move the passions and beget concernment in us, than the other; for it is unnatural for anyone in a gust of passion to speak long together, or for another in the same condition to suffer him, without interruption. Grief and passion are like floods raised in little brooks by a sudden rain; they are quickly up; and if the concernment be poured unexpectedly in upon us, it overflows us: but a long sober shower gives them leisure to run out as they came in, without troubling the ordinary current. As for comedy, repartee is one of its chiefest graces; the greatest pleasure of the audience is a chase of wit, kept up on both sides, and swiftly managed. And this our forefathers, if not we, have had in Fletcher's plays, to a much higher degree of perfection than the French poets can reasonably hope to reach.

"There is another part of Lisideius his discourse, in which he rather excused our neighbors than commended them; that is, for aiming only to make one person considerable in their plays. 'Tis very true what he has urged, that one character in all plays, even without the poet's care, will have advantage of all the others; and that the design of the whole drama will chiefly depend on it. But this hinders not that there may be more shining characters in the play: many persons of a second magnitude, nay, some so very near, so almost equal to the first, that greatness may be opposed to greatness, and all the persons be made considerable, not only by their quality, but their action. 'Tis evident that the more the persons are, the greater will be the variety of the plot. If then the parts are managed so regularly, that the beauty of the whole be kept entire, and that the variety become not a perplexed and confused mass of accidents, you will find it infinitely pleasing to be led in a labyrinth of design, where you see some of your way before you, yet discern not the end till you arrive at it. And that all this is practicable, I can produce for examples many of our English plays: as The Maid's Tragedy, The Alchemist, The Silent Woman. I was going to have named The Fox, but that the unity of design seems not exactly observed in it; for there appear two actions in the play; the first naturally ending with the fourth act; the second forced from it in the fifth; which yet is the less to be condemned in him, because the disguise of Volpone, though it suited not with his character as a crafty or covetous person, agreed well enough with that of a voluptuary; and by it the poet gained the end at which he aimed, the punishment of vice, and the reward of virtue, both which that disguise produced. So that to judge equally of it, it was an excellent fifth act, but not so naturally proceeding from the former.

"But to leave this, and pass to the latter part of Lisideius his discourse, which concerns relations: I much acknowledge with him, that the French have reason to hide that part of the action which would occasion too much tumult on the stage, and to choose rather to have it made known by narration to the audience. Farther, I think it very convenient, for the reasons he has given, that all incredible actions were removed; but whether custom has so insinuated itself into our countrymen, or nature has so formed them to fierceness, I know not; but they will scarcely suffer combats and other objects of horror to be taken from them. And indeed, the indecency of tumults is all which can be objected against fighting: for why may not our imagination as well suffer itself to be deluded with the probability of it, as with any other thing in the play? For my part, I can with as great ease persuade myself that the blows are given in good earnest, as I can that they who strike them are kings or princes, or those persons which they represent. For objects of incredibility,—I would be satisfied from Lisideius, whether we have any so removed from all appearance of truth, as are those of Corneille's Andromède; a play which has been frequented the most of any he has writ. If the Perseus, or the son of a heathen god, the Pegasus, and the Monster, were not capable to choke a strong belief, let him blame any representation of ours hereafter. Those indeed were objects of delight; yet the reason is the same as to the probability: for he makes it not a ballet or masque, but a play, which is to resemble truth. But for death, that it ought not to be represented, I have, besides the arguments alleged by Lisideius, the authority of Ben Jonson, who has forborne it in his tragedies; for both the death of Sejanus and Catiline are related: though in the latter I cannot but observe one irregularity of that great poet; he has removed the scene in the same act from Rome to Catiline's army, and from thence again to Rome; and besides, has allowed a very inconsiderable time, after Catiline's speech, for the striking of the battle, and the return of Petreius, who is to relate the event of it to the senate: which I should not animadvert on him, who was otherwise a painful observer of τὸ πρέπον, or the *decorum* of the stage, if he had not used extreme severity in his judgment on the incomparable Shakespeare for the same fault.—To conclude on this subject of relations; if we are to be blamed for showing too much of the action, the French are as faulty for discovering too little of it: a mean betwixt both should be observed by every judicious writer, so as the audience may neither be left unsatisfied by not seeing what is beautiful, or shocked by beholding what is either incredible or undecent.

"I hope I have already proved in this discourse, that though we are not altogether so punctual as the French in observing the laws of comedy, yet our errors are so few, and little, and those things wherein we excel them so considerable, that we ought of right to be preferred before them. But what will Lisideius say, if they themselves acknowledge they are too strictly bounded by those laws, for breaking which he has blamed the English? I will allege Corneille's words, as I find them in the end of his Discourse of the Three Unities: *Il est facile aux spéculatifs d'estre sévères*, etc. ''Tis easy for speculative persons to judge severely; but if they would produce to public view ten or twelve pieces of this nature, they would perhaps give more latitude to the rules than I have done, when by experience they had known how much we are limited and constrained by them, and how many beauties of the stage they banished from it.' To illustrate a little what he has said: By their servile observations of the unities of time and place, and integrity of scenes, they have brought on themselves that dearth of plot, and narrowness of imagination, which may be observed in all their plays. How many beautiful accidents might naturally happen in two or three days, which cannot arrive with any probability in the compass of twenty-four hours? There is time to be allowed also for maturity of design, which, amongst great and prudent persons, such as are often represented in tragedy, cannot, with any likelihood of truth, be brought to pass at so short a warning. Farther; by tying themselves strictly to the unity of place, and unbroken scenes, they are forced many times to omit some beauties which cannot be shown where the act began; but might, if the scene were interrupted, and the stage cleared for the persons to enter in another place; and therefore the French poets are often forced upon absurdities; for if the act begins in a chamber, all the persons in the play must have some business or other to come thither, or else they are not to be shown that act; and sometimes their characters are very unfitting to appear there: as, suppose it were the king's bed-chamber; yet the meanest man in the tragedy must come and dispatch his business there, rather than in the lobby or courtyard (which is fitter for him), for fear the stage should be cleared, and the scenes broken. Many times they fall by it in a greater inconvenience; for they keep their scenes unbroken, and yet change the place; as in one of their newest plays, where the act begins in the street. There a gentleman is to meet his friend; he sees him with this man, coming out from his father's house; they talk together, and the first goes out: the second, who is a lover, has made an appointment with his mistress; she appears at the window, and then we are to imagine the scene lies under it. This gentleman is called away, and leaves his servant with his mistress; presently her father is heard from within; the young lady is afraid the serving-man should be discovered, and thrusts him into a place of safety, which is supposed to be her closet. After this, the father enters to the daughter, and now the scene is in a house; for he is seeking from one room to another for this poor Philipin, or French Diego, who is heard from within, drolling and breaking many a miserable conceit on the subject of his sad condition. In this ridiculous manner the play goes forward, the stage being never empty all the while: so that the street, the window, the houses, and the closet, are made to walk about, and the persons to stand still. Now what, I beseech you, is more easy than to write a regular French play, or more difficult than to write an irregular English one, like those of Fletcher, or of Shakespeare?

"If they content themselves, as Corneille did, with some flat design, which, like an ill riddle, is found out ere it be half proposed, such plots we can make every way regular, as easily as they; but whenever they endeavor to rise to any quick turns and counterturns of plot, as some of them have attempted, since Corneille's plays have been less in vogue, you see they write as irregularly as we, though they cover it more speciously. Hence the reason is perspicuous why no French plays, when translated, have, or ever can succeed on the English stage. For, if you consider the plots, our own are fuller of variety; if the writing, ours are more quick and fuller of spirit; and therefore 'tis a strange mistake in those who decry the way of writing plays in verse, as if the English therein imitated the French. We have borrowed nothing from them; our plots are weaved in English looms: we endeavor therein to follow the variety and greatness of characters which are derived to us from Shakespeare and Fletcher; the copiousness and well-knitting of the intrigues we have from Jonson; and for the verse itself we have English precedents of elder date than any of Corneille's plays. Not to name our old comedies before Shakespeare, which were all writ in verse of six feet, or Alexandrines, such as the French now use—I can show in Shakespeare many scenes of rhyme together, and the like in Ben Jonson's tragedies: in Catiline and Sejanus sometimes thirty or forty lines—I mean besides the Chorus, or the monologues; which, by the way, showed Ben no enemy to this way of writing, especially if you read his Sad Shepherd, which goes sometimes on rhyme, sometimes on blank verse, like an horse who eases himself on trot and amble. You find him likewise commending Fletcher's pastoral of The Faithful Shepherdess, which is for the most part in rhyme, though not refined to that purity to which it hath since been brought. And these examples are enough to clear us from a servile imitation of the French.

"But to return whence I have digressed: I dare boldly affirm these two things of the English drama; —First, that we have many plays of ours as regular as any of theirs, and which, besides, have more variety of plot and characters; and secondly, that in most of the irregular plays of Shakespeare or Fletcher (for Ben Jonson's are for the most part regular), there is a more masculine fancy and greater spirit in the writing than there is in any of the French. I could produce, even in Shakespeare's and Fletcher's works, some plays which are almost exactly formed; as The Merry Wives of Windsor, and The Scornful Lady: but because (generally speaking) Shakespeare, who writ first, did not perfectly observe the laws of comedy, and Fletcher, who came nearer to perfection, yet through carelessness made many faults; I will take the pattern of a perfect play from Ben Jonson, who was a careful and learned observer of the dramatic laws, and from all his comedies I shall select The Silent Woman; of which I will make a short examen, according to those rules which the French observe."

As Neander was beginning to examine The Silent Woman, Eugenius, earnestly regarding him; "I beseech you, Neander," said he, "gratify the company, and me in particular, so far, as before you speak of the play, to give us a character of the author; and tell us frankly your opinion, whether you do not think all writers, both French and English, ought to give place to him."

"I fear," replied Neander, "that in obeying your commands I shall draw some envy on myself. Besides, in performing them, it will be first necessary to speak somewhat of Shakespeare and Fletcher, his rivals in poesy; and one of them, in my opinion, at least his equal, perhaps his superior.

"To begin, then, with Shakespeare. He was the man who of all modern, and perhaps ancient poets, had the largest and most comprehensive soul. All the images of nature were still present to him, and he drew them, not laboriously, but luckily; when he describes anything, you more than see it, you feel it too. Those who accuse him to have wanted learning give him the greater commendation: he was naturally learned; he needed not the spectacles of books to read nature; he looked inwards, and found her there. I cannot say he is everywhere alike; were he so, I should do him injury to compare him with the greatest of mankind. He is many times flat, insipid; his comic wit degenerating into clenches, his serious swelling into bombast. But he is always great when some great occasion is presented to him; no man can say he ever had a fit subject for his wit, and did not then raise himself as high above the rest of poets,

Quantum lenta solent inter viburna cupressi.[21]

The consideration of this made Mr. Hales[22] of Eaton say, that there is no subject of which any poet ever writ, but he would produce it much better done in Shakespeare; and however others are now generally preferred before him, yet the age wherein he lived, which had contemporaries with him Fletcher and Jonson, never equalled them to him in their esteem: and in the last king's court, when Ben's reputation was at highest, Sir John Suckling, and with him the greater part of the courtiers, set our Shakespeare far above him.

"Beaumont and Fletcher, of whom I am next to speak, had, with the advantage of Shakespeare's wit, which was their precedent, great natural gifts, improved by study: Beaumont especially being so accurate a judge of plays, that Ben Jonson, while he lived, submitted all his writings to his censure, and, 'tis thought, used his judgment in correcting, if not contriving, all his plots. What value he had for him,

---

21 As the cypresses tower among the humbler trees of the wayside.

22 John Hales, author of The Golden Remains, 1659.

---

appears by the verses he writ to him; and therefore I need speak no farther of it. The first play that brought Fletcher and him in esteem was their Philaster: for before that, they had written two or three very unsuccessfully, as the like is reported of Ben Jonson, before he writ Every Man in His Humor. Their plots were generally more regular than Shakespeare's, especially those which were made before Beaumont's death; and they understood and imitated the conversation of gentlemen much better; whose wild debaucheries, and quickness of wit in repartees, no poet before them could paint as they have done. Humor, which Ben Jonson derived from particular persons, they made it not their business to describe: they represented all the passions very lively, but above all, love. I am apt to believe the English language in them arrived to its highest perfection: what words have since been taken in, are rather superfluous than ornamental. Their plays are now the most pleasant and frequent entertainments of the stage; two of theirs being acted through the year for one of Shakespeare's or Jonson's: the reason is, because there is a certain gaiety in their comedies, and pathos in their more serious plays, which suit generally with all men's humors. Shakespeare's language is likewise a little obsolete, and Ben Jonson's wit comes short of theirs.

"As for Jonson, to whose character I am now arrived, if we look upon him while he was himself (for his last plays were but his dotage), I think him the most learned and judicious writer which any theater ever had. He was a most severe judge of himself, as well as others. One cannot say he wanted wit, but rather that he was frugal of it. In his works you find little to retrench or alter. Wit, and language, and humor also in some measure we had before him; but something of art was wanting to the drama till he came. He managed his strength to more advantage than any who preceded him. You seldom find him making love in any of his scenes, or endeavoring to move the passions; his genius was too sullen and saturnine to do it gracefully, especially when he knew he came after those who had performed both to such an height. Humor was his proper sphere; and in that he delighted most to represent mechanic people. He was deeply conversant in the ancients, both Greek and Latin, and he borrowed boldly from them: there is scarce a poet or historian among the Roman authors of those times whom he has not translated in Sejanus and Catiline. But he has done his robberies so openly, that one may see he fears not to be taxed by any law.

He invades authors like a monarch; and what would be theft in other poets is only victory in him. With the spoils of these writers he so represents old Rome to us, in its rites, ceremonies, and customs, that if one of their poets had written either of his tragedies, we had seen less of it than in him. If there was any fault in his language, 'twas that he weaved it too closely and laboriously, in his comedies especially: perhaps, too, he did a little too much Romanize our tongue, leaving the words which he translated almost as much Latin as he found them: wherein, though he learnedly followed their language, he did not enough comply with the idiom of ours. If I would compare him with Shakespeare, I must acknowledge him the more correct poet, but Shakespeare the greater wit. Shakespeare was the Homer, or father of our dramatic poets; Jonson was the Virgil, the pattern of elaborate writing; I admire him, but I love Shakespeare. To conclude of him; as he has given us the most correct plays, so in the precepts which he has laid down in his Discoveries, we have as many and profitable rules for perfecting the stage, as any wherewith the French can furnish us.

"Having thus spoken of the author, I proceed to the examination of his comedy, The Silent Woman.

EXAMEN OF THE SILENT WOMAN

"To begin first with the length of the action; it is so far from exceeding the compass of a natural day, that it takes not up an artificial one. 'Tis all included in the limits of three hours and a half, which is no more than is required for the presentment on the stage: a beauty perhaps not much observed; if it had, we should not have looked on the Spanish translation of Five Hours with so much wonder. The scene of it is laid in London; the latitude of place is almost as little as you can imagine; for it lies all within the compass of two houses, and after the first act, in one. The continuity of scenes is observed more than in any of our plays, except his own Fox and Alchemist. They are not broken above twice or thrice at most in the whole comedy; and in the two best of Corneille's plays, the Cid and Cinna, they are interrupted once. The action of the play is entirely one; the end or aim of which is the settling Morose's estate on Dauphine. The intrigue of it is the greatest and most noble of any pure unmixed comedy in any language; you see in it many persons of various characters and humors, and all delightful. As first, Morose, or an old man, to whom all noise but his own talking is offensive. Some who would be thought critics, say this humor of his is forced: but to remove that objection, we may consider him first to be naturally of a delicate hearing, as many are, to whom all sharp sounds are unpleasant; and secondly, we may attribute much of it to the peevishness of his age, or the wayward authority of an old man in his own house, where he may make himself obeyed; and to this the poet seems to allude in his name Morose. Besides this, I am assured from divers persons, that Ben Jonson was actually acquainted with such a man, one altogether as ridiculous as he is here represented. Others say, it is not enough to find one man of such an humor; it must be common to more, and the more common the more natural. To prove this, they instance in the best of comical characters, Falstaff. There are many men resembling him; old, fat, merry, cowardly, drunken, amorous, vain, and lying. But to convince these people, I need but tell them that humor is the ridiculous extravagance of conversation, wherein one man differs from all others. If then it be common, or communicated to many, how differs it from other men's? or what indeed causes it to be ridiculous so much as the singularity of it? As for Falstaff, he is not properly one humor, but a miscellany of humors or images, drawn from so many several men: that wherein he is singular is his wit, or those things he says *præter expectatum*, unexpected by the audience; his quick evasions, when you imagine him surprised, which, as they are extremely diverting of themselves, so receive a great addition from his person; for the very sight of such an unwieldy old debauched fellow is a comedy alone. And here, having a place so proper for it, I cannot but enlarge somewhat upon this subject of humor into which I am fallen. The ancients had little of it in their comedies; for the τὸ γελοῖον of the old comedy, of which Aristophanes was chief, was not so much to imitate a man, as to make the people laugh at some odd conceit, which had commonly somewhat of unnatural or obscene in it. Thus, when you see Socrates brought upon the stage, you are not to imagine him made ridiculous by the imitation of his actions, but rather by making him perform something very unlike himself; something so childish and absurd, as by comparing it with the gravity of the true Socrates, makes a ridiculous object for the spectators. In their new comedy which succeeded, the poets sought indeed to express the ἦθος, as in their tragedies the πάθος of mankind. But this ἦθος contained only the general characters of men and manners; as old men, lovers, serving-men, courtezans, parasites, and such other persons as we see in their comedies; all which they made alike: that is, one old man or father, one lover, one courtezan, so like another, as if the first of them had begot the rest of every sort: *Ex homine hunc natum dicas.* The same custom they observed likewise in their tragedies. As for the French, though they have the word *humeur* among them, yet they have small use of it in their comedies or farces; they being but ill imitations of the *ridiculum*, or that which stirred up laughter in the old comedy. But among the English 'tis otherwise: where by humor is meant some extravagant habit, passion, or affection, particular (as I have said before) to some one person, by the oddness of which, he is immediately distinguished from the rest of men; which being lively and naturally represented, most frequently begets that malicious pleasure in the audience which is testified by laughter; as all things which are deviations from customs are ever the aptest to produce it: though by the way this laughter is only accidental, as the person represented is fantastic or bizarre; but pleasure is essential to it, as the imitation of what is natural. The description of these humors, drawn from the knowledge and observation of particular persons, was the peculiar genius and talent of Ben Jonson; to whose play I now return.

"Besides Morose, there are at least nine or ten different characters and humors in The Silent Woman; all which persons have several concernments of their own, yet are all used by the poet to the conducting of the main design to perfection. I shall not waste time in commending the writing of this play; but I will give you my opinion, that there is more wit and acuteness of fancy in it than in any of Ben Jonson's. Besides that he has here described the conversation of gentlemen in the persons of True-Wit, and his friends, with more gaiety, air, and freedom, than in the rest of his comedies. For the contrivance of the plot, 'tis extreme, elaborate, and yet withal easy; for the λύσις, or untying of it, 'tis so admirable, that when it is done, no one of the audience would think the poet could have missed it; and yet it was concealed so much before the last scene, that any other way would sooner have entered into your thoughts. But I dare not take upon me to commend the fabric of it, because it is altogether so full of art, that I must unravel every scene in it to commend it as I ought. And this excellent contrivance is still the more to be admired, because 'tis comedy, where the persons are only of common rank, and their business private, not elevated by passions or high concernments, as in serious plays. Here everyone is a

proper judge of all he sees, nothing is represented but that with which he daily converses: so that by consequence all faults lie open to discovery, and few are pardonable. 'Tis this which Horace has judiciously observed:

> *Creditur, ex medio quia res arcessit, habere*
> *Sudoris minimum; sed habet Comedia tanto*
> *Plus oneris, quanto veniæ minus.*

"But our poet who was not ignorant of these difficulties has made use of all advantages; as he who designs a large leap takes his rise from the highest ground. One of these advantages is that which Corneille has laid down as the greatest which can arrive to any poem, and which he himself could never compass above thrice in all his plays; *viz.*, the making choice of some signal and long-expected day, whereon the action of the play is to depend. This day was that designed by Dauphine for the settling of his uncle's estate upon him; which to compass, he contrives to marry him. That the marriage had been plotted by him long beforehand, is made evident by what he tells True-Wit in the second act, that in one moment he had destroyed what he had been raising many months.

"There is another artifice of the poet, which I cannot here omit, because by the frequent practice of it in his comedies he has left it to us almost as a rule; that is, when he has any character or humor wherein he would show a *coup de maistre*, or his highest skill, he recommends it to your observation by a pleasant description of it before the person first appears. Thus, in Bartholomew Fair he gives you the pictures of Numps and Cokes, and in this those of Daw, Lafoole, Morose, and the Collegiate Ladies; all which you hear described before you see them. So that before they come upon the stage, you have a longing expectation of them, which prepares you to receive them favorably; and when they are there, even from their first appearance you are so far acquainted with them, that nothing of their humor is lost to you.

"I will observe yet one thing further of this admirable plot; the business of it rises in every act. The second is greater than the first; the third than the second; and so forward to the fifth. There too you see, till the very last scene, new difficulties arising to obstruct the action of the play; and when the audience is brought into despair that the business can naturally be effected, then, and not before, the discovery is made. But that the poet might entertain you with more variety all this while, he reserves some new characters to show you, which he opens not till the second and third act; in the second Morose, Daw, the Barber, and Otter; in the third the Collegiate Ladies: all which he moves afterwards in by-walks, or under-plots, as diversions to the main design, lest it should grow tedious, though they are still naturally joined with it, and somewhere or other subservient to it. Thus, like a skillful chess-player, by little and little he draws out his men, and makes his pawns of use to his greater persons.

"If this comedy and some others of his were translated into French prose (which would now be no wonder to them, since Molière has lately given them plays out of verse, which have not displeased them), I believe the controversy would soon be decided betwixt the two nations, even making them the judges. But we need not call our heroes to our aid. Be it spoken to the honor of the English, our nation can never want in any age such who are able to dispute the empire of wit with any people in the universe. And though the fury of a civil war, and power for twenty years together abandoned to a barbarous race of men, enemies of all good learning, had buried the muses under the ruins of monarchy; yet, with the restoration of our happiness, we see revived poesy lifting up its head, and already shaking off the rubbish which lay so heavy on it. We have seen since his Majesty's return, many dramatic poems which yield not to those of any foreign nation, and which deserve all laurels but the English. I will set aside flattery and envy: it cannot be denied but we have had some little blemish either in the plot or writing of all those plays which have been made within these seven years; (and perhaps there is no nation in the world so quick to discern them, or so difficult to pardon them, as ours:) yet if we can persuade ourselves to use the candor of that poet, who, though the most severe of critics, has left us this caution by which to moderate our censures—

> *ubi plura nitent in carmine, non ego paucis*
> *Offendar maculis;* —[23]

if, in consideration of their many and great beauties, we can wink at some and little imperfections, if we, I say, can be thus equal to ourselves, I ask no favor from the French. And if I do not venture upon any particular judgment of our late plays, 'tis out of the consider-

ation which an ancient writer gives me: *vivorum ut magna admiratio, ita censura difficilis:* betwixt the extremes of admiration and malice, 'tis hard to judge uprightly of the living. Only I think it may be permitted me to say, that as it is no lessening to us to yield to some plays, and those not many, of our own nation in the last age, so can it be no addition to pronounce of our present poets, that they have far surpassed all the ancients, and the modern writers of other countries."

This was the substance of what was then spoken on that occasion; and Lisideius, I think, was going to reply, when he was prevented thus by Crites: "I am confident," said he, "that the most material things that can be said have been already urged on either side; if they have not, I must beg of Lisideius that he will defer his answer till another time: for I confess I have a joint quarrel to you both, because you have concluded, without any reason given for it, that rhyme is proper for the stage. I will not dispute how ancient it hath been among us to write this way; perhaps our ancestors knew no better till Shakespeare's time. I will grant it was not altogether left by him, and that Fletcher and Ben Jonson used it frequently in their Pastorals, and sometimes in other plays. Farther,—I will not argue whether we received it originally from our countrymen, or from the French; for that is an inquiry of as little benefit, as theirs who, in the midst of the great plague, were not so solicitous to provide against it, as to know whether we had it from the malignity of our own air, or by transportation from Holland. I have therefore only to affirm, that it is not allowable in serious plays; for comedies, I find you already concluding with me. To prove this, I might satisfy myself to tell you, how much in vain it is for you to strive against the stream of the people's inclination; the greatest part of which are prepossessed so much with those excellent plays of Shakespeare, Fletcher, and Ben Jonson, which have been written out of rhyme, that except you could bring them such as were written better in it, and those too by persons of equal reputation with them, it will be impossible for you to gain your cause with them, who will still be judges. This it is to which, in fine, all your reasons must submit. The unanimous consent of an audience is so powerful, that even Julius Cæsar (as Macrobius reports of him), when he was perpetual dictator, was not able to balance it on the other side; but when Laberius, a Roman Knight, at his request contended in the *Mime* with another poet, he was forced to cry out, *Etiam*

---

23   If then a poem charm me in the main,
    Slight faults I'll not too rigidly arraign.
                    (Horace, *De Arte Poetica*, 351–52.)

favente me victus es, Laberi. But I will not on this occasion take the advantage of the greater number, but only urge such reasons against rhyme, as I find in the writings of those who have argued for the other way. First, then, I am of opinion that rhyme is unnatural in a play, because dialogue there is presented as the effect of sudden thought: for a play is the imitation of nature; and since no man, without premeditation, speaks in rhyme, neither ought he to do it on the stage. This hinders not but the fancy may be there elevated to an higher pitch of thought than it is in ordinary discourse; for there is a probability that men of excellent and quick parts may speak noble things *extempore:* but those thoughts are never fettered with the numbers or sound of verse without study, therefore it cannot be but unnatural to present the most free way of speaking in that which is the most constrained. For this reason, says Aristotle, 'tis best to write tragedy in that kind of verse which is the least such, or which is nearest prose: and this amongst the ancients was the Iambic, and with us is blank verse, or the measure of verse kept exactly without rhyme. These numbers therefore are fittest for a play; the others for a paper of verses, or a poem; blank verse being as much below them as rhyme is improper for the drama. And if it be objected that neither are blank verses made *extempore,* yet, as nearest nature, they are still to be preferred.— But there are two particular exceptions, which many besides myself have had to verse; by which it will appear yet more plainly how improper it is in plays. And the first of them is grounded on that very reason for which some have commended rhyme; they say, the quickness of repartees in argumentative scenes receives an ornament from verse. Now what is more unreasonable than to imagine that a man should not only light upon the wit, but the rhyme too, upon the sudden? This nicking of him who spoke before both in sound and measure, is so great an happiness, that you must at least suppose the persons of your play to be born poets: *Arcades omnes, et cantare pares, et respondere parati:* they must have arrived to the degree of *quicquid conabar dicere;*—to make verses almost whether they will or no. If they are anything below this, it will look rather like the design of two, than the answer of one: it will appear that your actors hold intelligence together; that they perform their tricks like fortune-tellers, by confederacy. The hand of art will be too visible in it, against that maxim of all professions—*Ars est celare artem;* that it is the greatest perfection of art to keep itself undiscovered. Nor will it serve you to

object, that however you manage it, 'tis still known to be a play; and, consequently, the dialogue of two persons understood to be the labor of one poet. For a play is still an imitation of nature; we know we are to be deceived, and we desire to be so; but no man ever was deceived but with a probability of truth; for who will suffer a gross lie to be fastened on him? Thus we sufficiently understand that the scenes which represent cities and countries to us are not really such, but only painted on boards and canvas; but shall that excuse the ill painture or designment of them? Nay, rather ought they not be labored with so much the more diligence and exactness, to help the imagination? since the mind of man does naturally tend to truth; and therefore the nearer anything comes to the imitation of it, the more it pleases.

"Thus, you see, your rhyme is incapable of expressing the greatest thoughts naturally, and the lowest it cannot with any grace: for what is more unbefitting the majesty of verse, than to call a servant, or bid a door be shut in rhyme? and yet you are often forced on this miserable necessity. But verse, you say, circumscribes a quick and luxuriant fancy, which would extend itself too far on every subject, did not the labor which is required to well-turned and polished rhyme set bounds to it. Yet this argument, if granted, would only prove that we may write better in verse, but not more naturally. Neither is it able to evince that; for he who wants judgment to confine his fancy in blank verse, may want it as much in rhyme: and he who has it will avoid errors in both kinds. Latin verse was as great a confinement to the imagination of those poets as rhyme to ours; and yet you find Ovid saying too much on every subject. *Nescivit* (says Seneca) *quod bene cessit relinquere:* of which he gives you one famous instance in his description of the deluge:

Omnia pontus erat, deerant quoque litora ponto.
Now all was sea, nor had that sea a shore.

Thus Ovid's fancy was not limited by verse, and Virgil needed not verse to have bounded his.

"In our own language we see Ben Jonson confining himself to what ought to be said, even in the liberty of blank verse; and yet Corneille, the most judicious of the French poets, is still varying the same sense an hundred ways, and dwelling eternally on the same subject, though confined by rhyme. Some other exceptions I have to verse; but since these I have named are for the most part already public, I conceive it reasonable they should first be answered."

"It concerns me less than any," said Neander (seeing he had ended), "to reply to this discourse; because when I should have proved that verse may be natural in plays, yet I should always be ready to confess, that those which I have written in this kind come short of that perfection which is required. Yet since you are pleased I should undertake this province, I will do it, though with all imaginable respect and deference, both to that person from whom you have borrowed your strongest arguments, and to whose judgment, when I have said all, I finally submit. But before I proceed to answer your objections, I must first remember you, that I exclude all comedy from my defense; and next that I deny not but blank verse may be also used; and content myself only to assert, that in serious plays where the subject and characters are great, and the plot unmixed with mirth, which might allay or divert these concernments which are produced, rhyme is there as natural and more effectual than blank verse.

"And now having laid down this as a foundation—to begin with Crites—I must crave leave to tell him, that some of his arguments against rhyme reach no farther than, from the faults and defects of ill rhyme, to conclude against the use of it in general. May not I conclude against blank verse by the same reason? If the words of some poets who write in it are either ill chosen, or ill placed, which makes not only rhyme, but all kind of verse in any language unnatural, shall I, for their vicious affectations, condemn those excellent lines of Fletcher, which are written in that kind? Is there anything in rhyme more constrained than this line in blank verse?—*I heaven invoke, and strong resistance make;* where you see both the clauses are placed unnaturally, that is, contrary to the common way of speaking, and that without the excuse of a rhyme to cause it: yet you would think me very ridiculous, if I should accuse the stubbornness of blank verse for this, and not rather the stiffness of the poet. Therefore, Crites, you must either prove that words, though well chosen, and duly placed, yet render not rhyme natural in itself; or that, however natural and easy the rhyme may be, yet it is not proper for a play. If you insist on the former part, I would ask you, what other conditions are required to make rhyme natural in itself, besides an election of apt words, and a right disposition of them? For the due choice of your words expresses your sense naturally, and the due placing them adapts the rhyme to it. If you object that one verse may be made for the sake of another, though both the words

and rhyme be apt, I answer, it cannot possibly so fall out; for either there is a dependence of sense betwixt the first line and the second, or there is none: if there be that connection, then in the natural position of the words the latter line must of necessity flow from the former; if there be no dependence, yet still the due ordering of words makes the last line as natural in itself as the other: so that the necessity of a rhyme never forces any but bad or lazy writers to say what they would not otherwise. 'Tis true, there is both care and art required to write in verse. A good poet never establishes the first line till he has sought out such a rhyme as may fit the sense, already prepared to heighten the second: many times the close of the sense falls into the middle of the next verse, or farther off, and he may often prevail himself of the same advantages in English which Virgil had in Latin—he may break off in the hemistich, and begin another line. Indeed, the not observing these two last things makes plays which are writ in verse so tedious: for though, most commonly, the sense is to be confined to the couplet, yet nothing that does *perpetuo tenore fluere*, run in the same channel, can please always. 'Tis like the murmuring of a stream, which not varying in the fall, causes at first attention, at last drowsiness. Variety of cadences is the best rule; the greatest help to the actors, and refreshment to the audience.

"If then verse may be made natural in itself, how becomes it unnatural in a play? You say the stage is the representation of nature, and no man in ordinary conversation speaks in rhyme. But you foresaw when you said this, that it might be answered—neither does any man speak in blank verse, or in measure without rhyme. Therefore you concluded, that which is nearest nature is still to be preferred. But you took no notice that rhyme might be made as natural as blank verse, by the well placing of the words, etc. All the difference between them, when they are both correct, is, the sound in one, which the other wants; and if so, the sweetness of it, and all the advantage resulting from it, which are handled in the Preface to The Rival Ladies, will yet stand good. As for that place of Aristotle, where he says, plays should be writ in that kind of verse which is nearest prose, it makes little for you; blank verse being properly but measured prose. Now measure alone, in any modern language, does not constitute verse; those of the ancients in Greek and Latin consisted in quantity of words, and a determinate number of feet. But when, by the inundation of the Goths and Vandals into Italy, new languages were introduced, and barbarously mingled with the Latin, of which the Italian, Spanish, French, and ours (made out of them and the Teutonic) are dialects, a new way of poesy was practiced; new, I say, in those countries, for in all probability it was that of the conquerors in their own nations: at least we are able to prove, that the eastern people have used it from all antiquity (*vide* Daniel his Defense of Rhyme). This new way consisted in measure or number of feet, and rhyme; the sweetness of rhyme, and observation of accent, supplying the place of quantity in words, which could neither exactly be observed by those barbarians, who knew not the rules of it, neither was it suitable to their tongues, as it had been to the Greek and Latin. No man is tied in modern poesy to observe any farther rule in the feet of his verse, but that they be dissyllables; whether Spondee, Trochee, or Iambic, it matters not; only he is obliged to rhyme: neither do the Spanish, French, Italian, or Germans, acknowledge at all, or very rarely, any such kind of poesy as blank verse amongst them. Therefore, at most 'tis but a poetic prose, a *sermo pedestris;* and as such, most fit for comedies, where I acknowledge rhyme to be improper. Farther; as to that quotation of Aristotle, our couplet verses may be rendered as near prose as blank verse itself, by using those advantages I lately named—as breaks in an hemistich, or running the sense into another line—thereby making art and order appear as loose and free as nature: or not tying ourselves to couplets strictly, we may use the benefit of the Pindaric way practised in The Siege of Rhodes; where the numbers vary, and the rhyme is disposed carelessly, and far from often chiming. Neither is that other advantage of the ancients to be despised, of changing the kind of verse when they please, with the change of the scene, or some new entrance; for they confine not themselves always to iambics, but extend their liberty to all lyric numbers, and sometimes even to hexameter. But I need not go so far as to prove that rhyme, as it succeeds to all other offices of Greek and Latin verse, so especially to this of plays, since the custom of nations at this day confirms it; the French, Italian, and Spanish tragedies are generally writ in it; and sure the universal consent of the most civilized parts of the world ought in this, as it doth in other customs, to include the rest.

"But perhaps you may tell me, I have proposed such a way to make rhyme natural, and consequently proper to plays, as is unpracticable; and that I shall scarce find six or eight lines together in any play,

where the words are so placed and chosen as is required to make it natural. I answer, no poet need constrain himself at all times to it. It is enough he makes it his general rule; for I deny not but sometimes there may be a greatness in placing the words otherwise; and sometimes they may sound better; sometimes also the variety itself is excuse enough. But if, for the most part, the words be placed as they are in the negligence of prose, it is sufficient to denominate the way practicable; for we esteem that to be such, which in the trial oftener succeeds than misses. And thus far you may find the practice made good in many plays: where you do not, remember still, that if you cannot find six natural rhymes together, it will be as hard for you to produce as many lines in blank verse, even among the greatest of our poets, against which I cannot make some reasonable exception.

"And this, Sir, calls to my remembrance the beginning of your discourse, where you told us we should never find the audience favorable to this kind of writing, till we could produce as good plays in rhyme as Ben Jonson, Fletcher, and Shakespeare had writ out of it. But it is to raise envy to the living, to compare them with the dead. They are honored, and almost adored by us, as they deserve; neither do I know any so presumptuous of themselves as to contend with them. Yet give me leave to say thus much, without injury to their ashes; that not only we shall never equal them, but they could never equal themselves, were they to rise and write again. We acknowledge them our fathers in wit; but they have ruined their estates themselves, before they came to their children's hands. There is scarce an humor, a character, or any kind of plot, which they have not used. All comes sullied or wasted to us: and were they to entertain this age, they could not now make so plenteous treatments out of such decayed fortunes. This therefore will be a good argument to us, either not to write at all, or to attempt some other way. There is no bays to be expected in their walks: *tentanda via est, quà me quoque possum tollere humo.*

"This way of writing in verse they have only left free to us; our age is arrived to a perfection in it, which they never knew; and which (if we may guess by what of theirs we have seen in verse, as The Faithful Shepherdess, and Sad Shepherd) 'tis probable they never could have reached. For the genius of every age is different; and though ours excel in this, I deny not but to imitate nature in that perfection which they did in prose, is a greater commendation than to write in verse exactly. As for what you have added—that the people are not generally inclined to like this way,—if it were true, it would be no wonder, that betwixt the shaking off of an old habit, and the introducing of a new, there should be difficulty. Do we not see them stick to Hopkins' and Sternhold's psalms, and forsake those of David, I mean Sandys his translation of them? If by the people you understand the multitude, the oi πολλοί, 'tis no matter what they think; they are sometimes in the right, sometimes in the wrong: their judgment is a mere lottery. *Est ubi plebs rectè putat, est ubi peccat.* Horace says it of the vulgar, judging poesy. But if you mean the mixed audience of the populace and the noblesse, I dare confidently affirm that a great part of the latter sort are already favorable to verse; and that no serious plays written since the king's return have been more kindly received by them than The Siege of Rhodes, the Mustapha, The Indian Queen, and Indian Emperor.

"But I come now to the inference of your first argument. You said that the dialogue of plays is presented as the effect of sudden thought, but no man speaks suddenly, or *extempore*, in rhyme; and you inferred from thence, that rhyme, which you acknowledge to be proper to epic poesy, cannot equally be proper to dramatic, unless we could suppose all men born so much more than poets, that verses should be made in them, not by them.

"It has been formerly urged by you, and confessed by me, that since no man spoke any kind of verse *extempore*, that which was nearest nature was to be preferred. I answer you, therefore, by distinguishing betwixt what is nearest to the nature of comedy, which is the imitation of common persons and ordinary speaking, and what is nearest the nature of a serious play: this last is indeed the representation of nature, but 'tis nature wrought up to a higher pitch. The plot, the characters, the wit, the passions, the descriptions, are all exalted above the level of common converse, as high as the imagination of the poet can carry them, with proportion to verisimilitude. Tragedy, we know, is wont to image to us the minds and fortunes of noble persons, and to portray these exactly; heroic rhyme is nearest nature, as being the noblest kind of modern verse.

> *Indignatur enim privatis et prope socco*
> *Dignis carminibus narrari cæna Thyestæ,*[24]

[24] Thyestes' horrid feast disdains
    The Sock's light chit-chat and colloquial strains.
                                    (*De Arte Poetica*, 90–91.)

says Horace: and in another place,

> *Effutire leves indigna tragœdia versus.*[25]

Blank verse is acknowledged to be too low for a poem, nay more, for a paper of verses; but if too low for an ordinary sonnet, how much more for tragedy, which is by Aristotle, in the dispute betwixt the epic poesy and the dramatic, for many reasons he there alleges, ranked above it?

"But setting this defense aside, your argument is almost as strong against the use of rhyme in poems as in plays; for the epic way is everywhere interlaced with dialogue, or discoursive scenes; and therefore you must either grant rhyme to be improper here, which is contrary to your assertion, or admit it into plays by the same title which you have given it to poems. For though tragedy be justly preferred above the other, yet there is a great difficulty between them, as may easily be discovered in that definition of a play which Lisideius gave us. The *genus* of them is the same—a just and lively image of human nature, in its actions, passions, and traverses of fortune: so is the end— namely, for the delight and benefit of mankind. The characters and persons are still the same, *viz.*, the greatest of both sorts; only the manner of acquainting us with those actions, passions, and fortunes, is different. Tragedy performs it *viva voce*, or by action, in dialogue; wherein it excels the epic poem, which does it chiefly by narration, and therefore is not so lively an image of human nature. However, the agreement betwixt them is such, that if rhyme be proper for one, it must be for the other. Verse, 'tis true, is not the effect of sudden thought; but this hinders not that sudden thought may be represented in verse, since those thoughts are such as must be higher than nature can raise them without premeditation, especially to a continuance of them, even out of verse; and consequently you cannot imagine them to have been sudden either in the poet or in the actors. A play, as I have said, to be like nature, is to be set above it; as statues which are placed on high are made greater than the life, that they may descend to the sight in their just proportion.

"Perhaps I have insisted too long on this objection; but the clearing of it will make my stay shorter on the rest. You tell us, Crites, that rhyme appears most unnatural in repartees, or short replies: when he who answers (it being presumed he knew not what the

[25] The Tragic Muse, with bashfulness severe,
    Disdaining the base gibe and trivial jeer.
                                    (*Ibid.*, 230–31.)

other would say, yet) makes up that part of the verse which was left incomplete, and supplies both the sound and measure of it. This, you say, looks rather like the confederacy of two, than the answer of one.

"This, I confess, is an objection which is in every man's mouth, who loves not rhyme: but suppose, I beseech you, the repartee were made only in blank verse, might not part of the same argument be turned against you? for the measure is as often supplied there as it is in rhyme; the latter half of the hemistich as commonly made up, or a second line subjoined as a reply to the former; which any one leaf in Jonson's plays will sufficiently clear to you. You will often find in the Greek tragedians, and in Seneca, that when a scene grows up into the warmth of repartees, which is the close fighting of it, the latter part of the trimeter is supplied by him who answers; and yet it was never observed as a fault in them by any of the ancient or modern critics. The case is the same in our verse, as it was in theirs; rhyme to us being in lieu of quantity to them. But if no latitude is to be allowed a poet, you take from him not only his license of *quidlibet audendi*, but you tie him up in a straiter compass than you would a philosopher. This is indeed *Musas colere severiores*. You would have him follow nature, but he must follow her on foot: you have dismounted him from his Pegasus. But you tell us, this supplying the last half of a verse, or adjoining a whole second to the former, looks more like the design of two, than the answer of one. Suppose we acknowledge it: how comes this confederacy to be more displeasing to you, than in a dance which is well contrived? You see there the united design of many persons to make up one figure: after they have separated themselves in many petty divisions, they rejoin one by one into gross: the confederacy is plain amongst them, for chance could never produce anything so beautiful; and yet there is nothing in it that shocks your sight. I acknowledge the hand of art appears in repartee, as of necessity it must in all kinds of verse. But there is also the quick and poignant brevity of it (which is an high imitation of nature in those sudden gusts of passion) to mingle with it; and this, joined with the cadency and sweetness of the rhyme, leaves nothing in the soul of the hearer to desire. 'Tis an art which appears; but it appears only like the shadowings of painture, which being to cause the rounding of it, cannot be absent; but while that is considered, they are lost: so while we attend to the other beauties of the matter, the care and labor of the rhyme is carried from us, or at least drowned in its own sweetness, as bees are sometimes buried in their honey. When a poet has found the repartee, the last perfection he can add to it, is to put it into verse. However good the thought may be, however apt the words in which 'tis couched, yet he finds himself at a little unrest, while rhyme is wanting: he cannot leave it till that comes naturally, and then is at ease, and sits down contented.

"From replies, which are the most elevated thoughts of verse, you pass to those which are most mean, and which are common with the lowest of household conversation. In these, you say, the majesty of verse suffers. You instance in the calling of a servant, or commanding a door to be shut, in rhyme. This, Crites, is a good observation of yours, but no argument: for it proves no more but that such thoughts should be waived, as often as may be, by the address of the poet. But suppose they are necessary in the places where he uses them, yet there is no need to put them into rhyme. He may place them in the beginning of a verse, and break it off, as unfit, when so debased, for any other use: or granting the worst—that they require more room than the hemistich will allow, yet still there is a choice to be made of the best words, and least vulgar (provided they be apt), to express such thoughts. Many have blamed rhyme in general, for this fault, when the poet with a little care might have redressed it. But they do it with no more justice than if English poesy should be made ridiculous for the sake of the Water-poet's [26] rhymes. Our language is noble, full, and significant, and I know not why he who is master of it may not clothe ordinary things in it as decently as the Latin, if he use the same diligence in his choice of words: *delectus verborum origo est eloquentiæ.* It was the saying of Julius Cæsar, one so curious in his, that none of them can be changed but for a worse. One would think, *unlock the door*, was a thing as vulgar as could be spoken; and yet Seneca could make it sound high and lofty in his Latin:

Reserate clusos regii postes laris.
Set wide the palace gates.

"But I turn from this conception, both because it happens not above twice or thrice in any play that those vulgar thoughts are used; and then too (were there no other apology to be made, yet), the necessity of them, which is alike in all kinds of writing, may excuse them. For if they are little and mean in rhyme,

26 John Taylor the Water-Poet, the rudeness of whose verse had become proverbial.

they are of consequence such in blank verse. Besides that the great eagerness and precipitation with which they are spoken, makes us rather mind the substance than the dress; that for which they are spoken, rather than what is spoken. For they are always the effect of some hasty concernment, and something of consequence depends on them.

"Thus, Crites, I have endeavored to answer your objections; it remains only that I should vindicate an argument for verse, which you have gone about to overthrow. It had formerly been said that the easiness of blank verse renders the poet too luxuriant, but that the labor of rhyme bounds and circumscribes an over-fruitful fancy; the sense there being commonly confined to the couplet, and the words so ordered that the rhyme naturally follows them, not they the rhyme. To this you answered, that it was no argument to the question in hand; for the dispute was not which way a man may write best, but which is most proper for the subject on which he writes.

"First, give me leave, Sir, to remember you that the argument against which you raised this objection was only secondary: it was built on this hypothesis—that to write in verse was proper for serious plays. Which supposition being granted (as it was briefly made out in that discourse, by showing how verse might be made natural), it asserted, that this way of writing was an help to the poet's judgment, by putting bounds to a wild overflowing fancy. I think, therefore, it will not be hard for me to make good what it was to prove on that supposition. But you add, that were this let pass, yet he who wants judgment in the liberty of his fancy, may as well show the defect of it when he is confined to verse; for he who has judgment will avoid errors, and he who has it not will commit them in all kinds of writing.

"This argument, as you have taken it from a most acute person, so I confess it carries much weight in it; but by using the word judgment here indefinitely, you seem to have put a fallacy upon us. I grant, he who has judgment, that is, so profound, so strong, or rather so infallible a judgment, that he needs no helps to keep it always poised and upright, will commit no faults either in rhyme or out of it. And on the other extreme, he who has a judgment so weak and crazed that no helps can correct or amend it, shall write scurvily out of rhyme, and worse in it. But the first of these judg-

ments is nowhere to be found, and the latter is not fit to write at all. To speak therefore of judgment as it is in the best poets; they who have the greatest proportion of it, want other helps than from it, within. As for example, you would be loth to say that he who is endued with a sound judgment has no need of history, geography, or moral philosophy, to write correctly. Judgment is indeed the master-workman in a play; but he requires many subordinate hands, many tools to his assistance. And verse I affirm to be one of these; 'tis a rule and line by which he keeps his building compact and even, which otherwise lawless imagination would raise either irregularly or loosely; at least, if the poet commits errors with this help, he would make greater and more without it: 'tis, in short, a slow and painful, but the surest kind of working. Ovid, whom you accuse for luxuriancy in verse, had perhaps been farther guilty of it, had he writ in prose. And for your instance of Ben Jonson, who, you say, writ exactly without the help of rhyme; you are to remember, 'tis only an aid to a luxuriant fancy, which his was not: as he did not want imagination, so none ever said he had much to spare. Neither was verse then refined so much, to be an help to that age, as it is to ours. Thus then, the second thoughts being usually the best, as receiving the maturest digestion from judgment, and the last and most mature product of those thoughts being artful and labored verse, it may well be inferred, that verse is a great help to a luxuriant fancy; and this is what that argument which you opposed was to evince."

Neander was pursuing this discourse so eagerly that Eugenius had called to him twice or thrice, ere he took notice that the barge stood still, and that they were at the foot of Somerset-stairs, where they had appointed it to land. The company were all sorry to separate so soon, though a great part of the evening was already spent; and stood awhile looking back on the water, upon which the moonbeams played, and made it appear like floating quicksilver: at last they went up through a crowd of French people, who were merrily dancing in the open air, and nothing concerned for the noise of guns which had alarmed the town that afternoon. Walking thence together to the Piazze, they parted there; Eugenius and Lisideius to some pleasant appointment they had made, and Crites and Neander to their several lodgings.

A DEFENSE OF AN ESSAY OF DRAMATIC POESY[1]

[TEXT: *first edition, 1668*]

THE former edition of The Indian Emperor being full of faults, which had escaped the printer, I have been willing to overlook this second with more care; and though I could not allow myself so much time as was necessary, yet, by that little I have done, the press is freed from some gross errors which it had to answer for before. As for the more material faults of writing, which are properly mine, though I see many of them, I want leisure to amend them. 'Tis enough for those who make one poem the business of their lives, to leave that correct: yet excepting Virgil, I never met with any which was so in any language.

But while I was thus employed about this impression, there came to my hands a new printed play called The Great Favorite, or The Duke of Lerma; the author[2] of which, a noble and most ingenious person, has done me the favor to make some observations and animadversions upon my Dramatic Essay. I must confess he might have better consulted his reputation, than by matching himself with so weak an adversary. But if his honor be diminished in the choice of his antagonist, it is sufficiently recompensed in the election of his cause: which being the weaker, in all appearance, as combating the received opinions of the best ancient and modern authors, will add to his glory, if he overcome, and to the opinion of his generosity, if he be vanquished: since he engages at so great odds, and, so like a cavalier, undertakes the protection of the weaker party. I have only to fear on my own behalf that so good a cause as mine may not suffer by my ill management, or weak defense; yet I cannot in honor but take the glove, when 'tis offered me: though I am only a champion by succession; and no more able to defend the right of Aristotle and Horace than an infant Dimock[3] to maintain the title of a king.

For my own concernment in the controversy, it is

so small that I can easily be contented to be driven from a few notions of dramatic poesy; especially by one who has the reputation of understanding all things: and I might justly make that excuse for my yielding to him, which the philosopher made to the emperor— why should I offer to contend with him who is master of more than twenty legions of arts and sciences? But I am forced to fight, and therefore it will be no shame to be overcome.

Yet I am so much his servant, as not to meddle with anything which does not concern me in his Preface; therefore, I leave the good sense and other excellencies of the first twenty lines to be considered by the critics. As for the play of The Duke of Lerma, having so much altered and beautified it, as he has done, it can justly belong to none but him. Indeed, they must be extreme ignorant as well as envious, who would rob him of that honor; for you see him putting in his claim to it, even in the first two lines:

> Repulse upon repulse, like waves thrown back,
> That slide to hang upon obdurate rocks.

After this, let detraction do its worst; for if this be not his, it deserves to be. For my part, I declare for distributive justice; and from this and what follows, he certainly deserves *those advantages which he acknowledges to have received from the opinion of sober men.*

In the next place, I must beg leave to observe his great address in courting the reader to his party. For intending to assault all poets, both ancient and modern, he discovers not his whole design at once, but seems only to aim at me, and attacks me on my weakest side, my defense of verse.

To begin with me—he gives me the compellation of The Author of a Dramatic Essay, which is a little discourse in dialogue, for the most part borrowed from the observations of others: therefore, that I may not be wanting to him in civility, I return his compliment by calling him The Author of the Duke of Lerma.

But (that I may pass over his salute) he takes notice of my great pains to prove rhyme as natural in a serious play, and more effectual than blank verse. Thus, indeed, I did state the question; but he tells me, *I pursue that which I call natural in a wrong application: for 'tis not*

---

1 The Defense of an Essay of Dramatic Poesy was prefixed to the second edition of Dryden's The Indian Emperor, 1668.

2 The author was Sir Robert Howard, brother of Dryden's wife. He collaborated with Dryden in The Indian Queen.

3 The Dimocks of Scrivelsby, in Lincolnshire, had been since the time of William the Conqueror, the champions of the king, and in the ceremonies of the coronation they maintained the king's title. The custom has lapsed since the coronation of George IV.

the question whether rhyme or not rhyme be best or most natural for a serious subject, but what is nearest the nature of that it represents.

If I have formerly mistaken the question, I must confess my ignorance so far, as to say I continue still in my mistake: but he ought to have proved that I mistook it; for it is yet but *gratis dictum:* I still shall think I have gained my point, if I can prove that rhyme is best or most natural for a serious subject. As for the question as he states it, whether rhyme be nearest the nature of what it represents, I wonder he should think me so ridiculous as to dispute whether prose or verse be nearest to ordinary conversation.

It still remains for him to prove his inference—that, since verse is granted to be more remote than prose from ordinary conversation, therefore no serious plays ought to be writ in verse: and when he clearly makes that good, I will acknowledge his victory as absolute as he can desire it.

The question now is, which of us two has mistaken it; and if it appear I have not, the world will suspect *what gentleman that was, who was allowed to speak twice in Parliament, because he had not yet spoken to the question;* and perhaps conclude it to be the same, who, 'tis reported, maintained a contradiction *in terminis,* in the face of three hundred persons.

But to return to verse; whether it be natural or not in plays, is a problem which is not demonstrable of either side: 'tis enough for me that he acknowledges he had rather read good verse than prose: for if all the enemies of verse will confess as much, I shall not need to prove that it is natural. I am satisfied, if it cause delight: for delight is the chief, if not the only, end of poesy: instruction can be admitted but in the second place; for poesy only instructs as it delights. 'Tis true, that to imitate well is a poet's work; but to affect the soul, and excite the passions, and above all to move admiration, which is the delight of serious plays, a bare imitation will not serve. The converse, therefore, which a poet is to imitate, must be heightened with all the arts and ornaments of poesy, and must be such, as, strictly considered, could never be supposed spoken by any without premeditation.

As for what he urges, that a *play will still be supposed to be a composition of several persons speaking* ex tempore; *and that good verses are the hardest things which can be imagined to be so spoken;* I must crave leave to dissent from his opinion, as to the former part of it: for, if I am not deceived, a play is supposed to be the work of the poet, imitating or representing the conversation of several persons; and this I think to be as clear as he thinks the contrary.

But I will be bolder, and do not doubt to make it good, though a paradox, that one great reason why prose is not to be used in serious plays, is, because it is too near the nature of converse: there may be too great a likeness; as the most skillful painters affirm, that there may be too near a resemblance in a picture: to take every lineament and feature, is not to make an excellent piece; but to take so much only as will make a beautiful resemblance of the whole; and, with an ingenious flattery of nature, to heighten the beauties of some parts, and hide the deformities of the rest. For so says Horace:

> *Ut pictura poesis erit. . . .*
> *Hæc amat obscurum, vult hæc sub luce videri,*
> *Judicis argutum quæ non formidat acumen.*
> *. . . . . Et quæ*
> *Desperat tractata nitescere posse, relinquit.*[4]

In Bartholomew Fair, or the lowest kind of comedy, that degree of heightening is used, which is proper to set off that subject. 'Tis true the author was not there to go out of prose, as he does in his higher arguments of comedy, The Fox, and Alchemist; yet he does so raise his matter in that prose as to render it delightful; which he could never have performed had he only said or done those very things that are daily spoken or practiced in the Fair; for then the Fair itself would be as full of pleasure to an ingenious person as the play; which we manifestly see it is not. But he hath made an excellent lazar of it: the copy is of price, though the original be vile. You see in Catiline and Sejanus, where the argument is great, he sometimes ascends to verse, which shows he thought it not unnatural in serious plays; and had his genius been as proper for rhyme as it was for humor, or had the age in which he lived attained to as much knowledge in verse as ours, it is probable he would have adorned those subjects with that kind of writing.

Thus prose, though the rightful prince, yet is by common consent deposed, as too weak for the government of serious plays; and he failing, there now start up two competitors; one the nearer in blood, which is blank verse; the other more fit for the ends of

---

4 For poems are like pictures: . . .
This loves the shades, while that the light endures,
Nor shuns the nicest ken of connoisseurs. . . .
Much that he feels would tire, he lets alone.
                              (*De Arte Poetica,* 361–63, 140–50.)

government, which is rhyme. Blank verse is, indeed, the nearer prose, but he is blemished with the weakness of his predecessor. Rhyme (for I will deal clearly) has somewhat of the usurper in him; but he is brave and generous, and his dominion pleasing. For this reason of delight, the ancients (whom I will still believe as wise as those who so confidently correct them) wrote all their tragedies in verse, though they knew it most remote from conversation.

But I perceive I am falling into the danger of another rebuke from my opponent; for when I plead that the ancients used verse, I prove not that they would have admitted rhyme, had it then been written: all I can say is only this; that it seems to have succeeded verse by the general consent of poets in all modern languages: for almost all their serious plays are written in it: which, though it be no demonstration that therefore they ought to be so, yet at least the practice first, and then the continuation of it, shows that it attained the end—which was to please; and if that cannot be compassed here, I will be the first who shall lay it down. For I confess my chief endeavors are to delight the age in which I live. If the humor of this be for low comedy, small accidents, and raillery, I will force my genius to obey it, though with more reputation I could write in verse. I know I am not so fitted by nature to write comedy: I want that gaiety and humor which is required to it. My conversation is slow and dull, my humor saturnine and reserved: in short, I am none of those who endeavor to break jests in company, or make repartees. So that those who decry my comedies do me no injury, except it be in point of profit: reputation in them is the last thing to which I shall pretend. I beg pardon for entertaining the reader with so ill a subject; but before I quit that argument, which was the cause of this digression, I cannot but take notice how I am corrected for my quotation of Seneca, in my defense of plays in verse. My words are these: "Our language is noble, full, and significant; and I know not why he who is master of it, may not clothe ordinary things in it as decently as in the Latin, if he use the same diligence in his choice of words. One would think, *unlock a door*, was a thing as vulgar as could be spoken; yet Seneca could make it sound high and lofty in his Latin:

Reserate clusos regii postes laris."

But he says of me, *That being filled with the precedents of the ancients, who writ their plays in verse, I commend the thing; declaring our language to be full, noble, and* significant, *and charging all defects upon the* ill placing of words, *which I prove by quoting Seneca loftily expressing such an ordinary thing as* shutting a door.

Here he manifestly mistakes; for I spoke not of placing, but of the choice of words; for which I quoted that aphorism of Julius Cæsar:

Delectus verborum est origo eloquentiæ:

but *delectus verborum* is no more Latin for the placing of words than *reserate* is Latin for *shut the door*, as he interprets it, which I ignorantly construed *unlock* or *open* it.

He supposes I was highly affected by the sound of those words; and I suppose I may more justly imagine it of him; for if he had not been extremely satisfied with the sound, he would have minded the sense a little better.

But these are now to be no faults; for ten days after his book is published, and that his mistakes are grown so famous that they are come back to him, he sends his *Errata* to be printed, and annexed to his play; and desires, that instead of *shutting* you would read *opening;* which, it seems, was the printer's fault. I wonder at his modesty, that he did not rather say it was Seneca's or mine; and that in some authors, *reserare* was to *shut* as well as to *open*, as the word *barach*, say the learned, is both to *bless* and *curse*.

Well, since it was the printer, he was a naughty man to commit the same mistake twice in six lines: I warrant you *delectus verborum* for *placing of words* was his mistake too, though the author forgot to tell him of it: if it were my book, I assure you I should. For these rascals ought to be the proxies of every gentleman author, and to be chastised for him, when he is not pleased to own an error. Yet since he has given the *Errata*, I wish he would have enlarged them only a few sheets more, and then he would have spared me the labor of an answer: for this cursed printer is so given to mistakes, that there is scarce a sentence in the Preface without some false grammar or hard sense in it; which will all be charged upon the poet, because he is so good-natured as to lay but three errors to the printer's account, and to take the rest upon himself, who is better able to support them. But he needs not apprehend that I should strictly examine those little faults, except I am called upon to do it: I shall return therefore to that quotation of Seneca, and answer, not to what he writes, but to what he means. I never intended it as an argument, but only as an illustration of what I had said before concerning the election of words: and all he can charge me with is only this—that if Seneca could make an ordinary thing sound well in Latin by the choice of words, the same, with the like care, might be performed in English: if it cannot, I have committed an error on the right hand, by commending too much the copiousness and well-sounding of our language; which I hope my countrymen will pardon me. At least the words which follow in my Dramatic Essay will plead somewhat in my behalf; for I say there, that this objection happens but seldom in a play; and then, too, either the meanness of the expression may be avoided, or shut out from the verse by breaking it in the midst.

But I have said too much in the defense of verse; for after all, it is a very indifferent thing to me whether it obtain or not. I am content hereafter to be ordered by his rule, that is, to write it sometimes, because it pleases me; and so much the rather, because he has declared that it pleases him. But he has taken his last farewell of the muses, and he has done it civilly, by honoring them with the name of *his long acquaintances;* which is a compliment they have scarce deserved from him. For my own part, I bear a share in the public loss; and how emulous soever I may be of his fame and reputation, I cannot but give this testimony of his style,—that it is extreme poetical, even in oratory; his thoughts elevated sometimes above common apprehension; his notions politic and grave, and tending to the instruction of princes, and reformation of states; that they are abundantly interlaced with variety of fancies, tropes, and figures, which the critics have enviously branded with the name of obscurity and false grammar.

Well, he is now fettered in business of more unpleasant nature: the muses have lost him, but the commonwealth gains by it; the corruption of a poet is the generation of a statesman.

He will not venture again into the civil wars of censure; ubi . . . nullus habitura triumphos: if he had not told us he had left the muses, we might have half suspected it by that word *ubi,* which does not any way belong to them in that place; the rest of the verse is indeed Lucan's; but that *ubi,* I will answer for it, is his own. Yet he has another reason for this disgust of poesy; for he says immediately after, that *the manner of plays which are now in most esteem, is beyond his power to perform:* to perform the manner of a thing, I confess is new English to me. *However, he condemns not the satisfaction of others; but rather their unnecessary understanding, who, like Sancho Pança's doctor, prescribe too strictly to*

our appetites; for, says he, *in the difference of tragedy and comedy, and of farce itself, there can be no determination but by the taste, nor in the manner of their composure.*

We shall see him now as great a critic as he was a poet; and the reason why he excelled so much in poetry will be evident, for it will appear to have proceeded from the exactness of his judgment. *In the difference of tragedy, comedy, and farce itself, there can be no determination but by the taste.* I will not quarrel with the obscurity of his phrase, though I justly might; but beg his pardon if I do not rightly understand him. If he means that there is no essential difference betwixt comedy, tragedy, and farce, but what is only made by the people's taste, which distinguishes one of them from the other, that is so manifest an error that I need not lose time to contradict it. Were there neither judge, taste, nor opinion in the world, yet they would differ in their natures; for the action, character, and language of tragedy would still be great and high; that of comedy lower and more familiar; admiration would be the delight of one and satire of the other.

I have but briefly touched upon these things, because, whatever his words are, I can scarce imagine, that *he who is always concerned for the true honor of reason, and would have no spurious issue fathered upon her,* should mean anything so absurd as to affirm, *that there is no difference betwixt comedy and tragedy, but what is made by the taste only:* unless he would have us understand the comedies of my Lord L., where the first act should be pottages, the second fricassees, etc., and the fifth a *chère entière* of women.

I rather guess he means, that betwixt one comedy and tragedy and another, there is no other difference but what is made by the liking or disliking of the audience. This is indeed a less error than the former, but yet it is a great one. The liking or disliking of the people gives the play the denomination of good or bad; but does not really make or constitute it such. To please the people ought to be the poet's aim, because plays are made for their delight; but it does not follow that they are always pleased with good plays, or that the plays which please them are always good. The humor of the people is now for comedy; therefore, in hope to please them, I write comedies rather than serious plays; and so far their taste prescribes to me: but it does not follow from that reason that comedy is to be preferred before tragedy in its own nature; for that which is so in its own nature cannot be otherwise; as a man cannot but be a rational creature: but the opinion of the people may alter, and in another age, or perhaps in this, serious plays may be set up above comedies.

This I think a sufficient answer: if it be not, he has provided me of an excuse; it seems, in his wisdom, he foresaw my weakness, and has found out this expedient for me, *That it is not necessary for poets to study strict reason; since they are so used to a greater latitude than is allowed by that severe inquisition, that they must infringe their own jurisdiction, to profess themselves obliged to argue well.*

I am obliged to him for discovering to me this backdoor; but I am not yet resolved on my retreat: for I am of opinion that they cannot be good poets who are not accustomed to argue well. False reasonings and colors of speech are the certain marks of one who does not understand the stage; for moral truth is the mistress of the poet, as much as of the philosopher. Poesy must resemble natural truth, but it must be ethical. Indeed the poet dresses truth, and adorns nature, but does not alter them:

Ficta voluptatis causa sint proxima veris.

Therefore, that is not the best poesy which resembles notions of things that are not to things that are: though the fancy may be great, and the words flowing, yet the soul is but half satisfied when there is not truth in the foundation. This is that which makes Virgil be preferred before the rest of poets: in variety of fancy and sweetness of expression, you see Ovid far above him; for Virgil rejected many of these things which Ovid wrote. *A great wit's great work is to refuse,* as my worthy friend, Sir John Berkenhead, has ingeniously expressed it: you rarely meet with anything in Virgil but truth, which therefore leaves the strongest impression of pleasure in the soul. This I thought myself obliged to say in behalf of poesy; and to declare, though it be against myself, that when poets do not argue well, the defect is in the workman, not in the art.

And now I come to the boldest part of his discourse, wherein he attacks not me, but all the ancients and moderns; and undermines, as he thinks, the very foundations on which dramatic poesy is built. I could wish he would have declined that envy which must of necessity follow such an undertaking, and contented himself with triumphing over me in my opinions of verse, which I will never hereafter dispute with him; but he must pardon me, if I have that veneration for Aristotle, Horace, Ben Jonson, and Corneille, that I dare not serve him in such a cause, and against such

heroes, but rather fight under their protection, as Homer reports of little Teucer, who shot the Trojans from under the large buckler of Ajax Telamon:

Στῆ δ' ἄρ' ὑπ' Αἴαντος σάκεϊ Τελαμωνιάδαο.

He stood beneath his brother's ample shield,
And cover'd there, shot death through all the field.

The words of my noble adversary are these:
But if we examine the general rules laid down for plays by strict reason, we shall find the errors equally gross; for the great foundation which is laid to build upon, is nothing, as it is generally stated, as will appear upon the examination of the particulars.

These particulars, in due time, shall be examined: in the meanwhile, let us consider what this great foundation is, which he says is nothing, as it is generally stated. I never heard of any other foundation of dramatic poesy than the imitation of nature; neither was there ever pretended any other by the ancients, or moderns, or me, who endeavor to follow them in that rule. This I have plainly said in my definition of a play; that it is a just and lively image of human nature, etc. Thus the foundation, as it is generally stated, will stand sure, if this definition of a play be true; if it be not, he ought to have made his exceptions against it by proving that a play is not an imitation of nature, but somewhat else which he is pleased to think it.

But it is very plain that he has mistaken the foundation for that which is built upon it, though not immediately: for the direct and immediate consequence is this; if nature be to be imitated, then there is a rule for imitating nature rightly; otherwise there may be an end, and no means conducing to it. Hitherto I have proceeded by demonstration; but as our divines when they have proved a Deity, because there is order, and have inferred that this Deity ought to be worshiped, differ afterwards in the manner of the worship; so, having laid down that nature is to be imitated, and that proposition proving the next, that then there are means which conduce to the imitating of nature, I dare proceed no farther positively; but have only laid down some opinions of the ancients and moderns, and of my own, as means which they used, and which I thought probable for the attaining of that end. Those means are the same which my antagonist calls the foundations—how properly, the world may judge; and to prove that this is his meaning, he clears it immediately to you by enumerating those rules or propositions against which he makes his particular exceptions

—as namely, those of time, and place—in these words: *First, we are told the plot should not be so ridiculously contrived, as to crowd two several countries into one stage: secondly, to cramp the accidents of many years or days into the representation of two hours and an half; and lastly, a conclusion drawn, that the only remaining dispute is, concerning time, whether it should be contained in twelve or twenty-four hours; and the place to be limited to that spot of ground where the play is supposed to begin: and this is called nearest nature; for that is concluded most natural, which is most probable, and nearest to that which it presents.*

Thus he has only made a small mistake of the means conducing to the end, for the end itself; and of the superstructure for the foundation: but he proceeds: *To show, therefore, upon what ill grounds they dictate laws for Dramatic Poesy,* etc. He is here pleased to charge me with being magisterial, as he has done in many other places of his Preface. Therefore in vindication of myself, I must crave leave to say, that my whole discourse was skeptical, according to that way of reasoning which was used by Socrates, Plato, and all the Academics of old, which Tully and the rest of the ancients followed, and which is imitated by the modest inquisitions of the Royal Society. That it is so, not only the name will show, which is, *An Essay,* but the frame and composition of the work. You see, it is a dialogue sustained by persons of several opinions, all of them left doubtful, to be determined by the readers in general; and more particularly deferred to the accurate judgment of my Lord Buckhurst, to whom I made a dedication of my book. These are my words in my Epistle, speaking of the persons whom I introduced in my dialogue: " 'Tis true, they differed in their opinions, as 'tis probable they would; neither do I take upon me to reconcile, but to relate them, leaving your lordship to decide it in favor of that part which you shall judge most reasonable." And after that, in my Advertisement to the Reader, I said this: "The drift of the ensuing discourse is chiefly to vindicate the honor of our English writers from the censure of those who unjustly prefer the French before them. This I intimate, lest any should think me so exceeding vain, as to teach others an art which they understand much better than myself." But this is more than necessary to clear my modesty in that point; and I am very confident that there is scarce any man who has lost so much time as to read that trifle, but will be my compurgator as to that arrogance whereof I am accused. The truth is, if I had been naturally guilty of so much vanity as to dictate my opinions, yet I do not find that the char-

acter of a positive or self-conceited person is of such an advantage to any in this age, that I should labor to be publicly admitted of that order.

But I am not now to defend my own cause, when that of all the ancients and moderns is in question: for this gentleman, who accuses me of arrogance, has taken a course not to be taxed with the other extreme of modesty. Those propositions which are laid down in my discourse, as helps to the better imitation of nature, are not mine (as I have said) nor were ever pretended so to be, but derived from the authority of Aristotle and Horace, and from the rules and examples of Ben Jonson and Corneille. These are the men with whom properly he contends, and against *whom he will endeavor to make it evident, that there is no such thing as what they all pretend.*

His argument against the unities of place and time is this: *That 'tis as impossible for one stage to present two rooms or houses truly, as two countries or kingdoms; and as impossible that five hours or twenty-four hours should be two hours, as that a thousand hours or years should be less than what they are, or the greatest part of time to be comprehended in the less: for all of them being impossible, they are none of them nearest the truth or nature of what they present; for impossibilities are all equal, and admit of no degree.*

This argument is so scattered into parts that it can scarce be united into a syllogism; yet, in obedience to him, I will abbreviate and comprehend as much of it as I can in few words, that my answer to it may be more perspicuous. I conceive his meaning to be what follows, as to the unity of place (if I mistake, I beg his pardon, professing it is not out of any design to play the *Argumentative Poet*). If one stage cannot properly present two rooms or houses, much less two countries or kingdoms, then there can be no unity of place; but one stage cannot properly perform this: therefore there can be no unity of place.

I plainly deny his minor proposition; the force of which, if I mistake not, depends on this; that the stage being one place cannot be two. This, indeed, is as great a secret as that we are all mortal; but to requite it with another, I must crave leave to tell him, that though the stage cannot be two places, yet it may properly represent them, successively, or at several times. His argument is indeed no more than a mere fallacy, which will evidently appear, when we distinguish place, as it relates to plays, into real and imaginary. The real place is that theater, or piece of ground, on which the play is acted. The imaginary, that house, town, or country, where the action of the *Drama* is supposed to be; or more plainly, where the scene of the play is laid. Let us now apply this to that Herculean argument, *which, if strictly and duly weighed, is to make it evident that there is no such thing as what they all pretend.* It is impossible, he says, for one stage to present two rooms or houses: I answer, 'tis neither impossible, nor improper, for one real place to represent two or more imaginary places, so it be done successively; which in other words is no more than this: that the imagination of the audience, aided by the words of the poet, and painted scenes, may suppose the stage to be sometimes one place, sometimes another; now a garden, or wood, and immediately a camp: which, I appeal to every man's imagination, if it be not true. Neither the ancients nor moderns, as much fools as he is pleased to think them, ever asserted that they could make one place two; but they might hope, by the good leave of this author, that the change of a scene might lead the imagination to suppose the place altered: so that he cannot fasten those absurdities upon this scene of a play, or imaginary place of action, that it is one place, and yet two. And this being so clearly proved, that 'tis past any show of a reasonable denial, it will not be hard to destroy that other part of his argument which depends upon it; namely, that 'tis as impossible for a stage to represent two rooms or houses, as two countries or kingdoms; for his reason is already overthrown, which was, because both were alike impossible. This is manifestly otherwise; for 'tis proved that a stage may properly represent two rooms or houses; for the imagination being judge of what is represented, will in reason be less choked with the appearance of two rooms in the same house, or two houses in the same city, than with two distant cities in the same country, or two remote countries in the same universe. Imagination in a man or reasonable creature is supposed to participate of reason; and when that governs, as it does in the belief of fiction, reason is not destroyed, but misled, or blinded: that can prescribe to the reason, during the time of the representation, somewhat like a weak belief of what it sees and hears; and reason suffers itself to be so hoodwinked, that it may better enjoy the pleasures of the fiction: but it is never so wholly made a captive, as to be drawn headlong into a persuasion of those things which are most remote from probability: 'tis in that case a free-born subject, not a slave; it will contribute willingly its assent, as far as it sees convenient, but will not be forced. Now there is a greater vicinity in nature be-

twixt two rooms than betwixt two houses, betwixt two houses than betwixt two cities, and so of the rest; reason therefore can sooner be led by imagination to step from one room into another, than to walk to two distant houses, and yet rather to go thither, than to fly like a witch through the air, and be hurried from one region to another. Fancy and reason go hand in hand; the first cannot leave the last behind; and though fancy, when it sees the wide gulf, would venture over as the nimbler, yet it is withheld by reason, which will refuse to take the leap when the distance over it appears too large. If Ben Jonson himself will remove the scene from Rome into Tuscany in the same act, and from thence return to Rome, in the scene which immediately follows, reason will consider there is no proportionable allowance of time to perform the journey, and therefore will choose to stay at home. So, then, the less change of place there is, the less time is taken up in transporting the persons of the drama, with analogy to reason; and in that analogy, or resemblance of fiction to truth, consists the excellency of the play.

For what else concerns the unity of place, I have already given my opinion of it in my Essay;—that there is a latitude to be allowed to it—as several places in the same town or city, or places adjacent to each other in the same country, which may all be comprehended under the larger denomination of one place; yet with this restriction, that the nearer and fewer those imaginary places are, the greater resemblance they will have to truth; and reason, which cannot make them one, will be more easily led to suppose them so.

What has been said of the unity of place, may easily be applied to that of time: I grant it to be impossible that the greater part of time should be comprehended in the less, that twenty-four hours should be crowded into three: but there is no necessity of that supposition. For as place, so time relating to a play is either imaginary or real: the real is comprehended in those three hours, more or less, in the space of which the play is represented; the imaginary is that which is supposed to be taken up in the representation, as twenty-four hours more or less. Now no man ever could suppose that twenty-four real hours could be included in the space of three: but where is the absurdity of affirming that the feigned business of twenty-four imagined hours may not more naturally be represented in the compass of three real hours, than the like feigned business of twenty-four years in the same proportion of real time? For the proportions are always real, and much nearer, by his permission, of twenty-four to three, than of four thousand to it.

I am almost fearful of illustrating anything by similitude, lest he should confute it for an argument; yet I think the comparison of a glass will discover very aptly the fallacy of his argument, both concerning time and place. The strength of his reason depends on this, that the less cannot comprehend the greater. I have already answered, that we need not suppose it does: I say not that the less can comprehend the greater, but only that it may represent it: as in a glass or mirror of half a yard diameter, a whole room and many persons in it may be seen at once, not that it can comprehend that room or those persons, but that it represents them to the sight.

But the author of The Duke of Lerma is to be excused for his declaring against the unity of time; for, if I be not much mistaken, he is an interested person; the time of that play taking up so many years as the favor of the Duke of Lerma continued; nay, the second and third act including all the time of his prosperity, which was a great part of the reign of Philip the Third: for in the beginning of the second act he was not yet a favorite, and before the end of the third was in disgrace. I say not this with the least design of limiting the stage too servilely to twenty-four hours, however he be pleased to tax me with dogmatizing in that point. In my dialogue, as I before hinted, several persons maintained their several opinions: one of them, indeed, who supported the cause of the French poesy, said, how strict they were in that particular; but he who answered in behalf of our nation, was willing to give more latitude to the rule; and cites the words of Corneille himself, complaining against the severity of it, and observing what beauties it banished from the stage. In few words, my own opinion is this (and I willingly submit it to my adversary, when he will please impartially to consider it), that the imaginary time of every plot ought to be contrived into as narrow a compass as the nature of the plot, the quality of the persons, and variety of accidents will allow. In comedy I would not exceed twenty-four or thirty hours: for the plot, accidents, and persons of comedy are small, and may be naturally turned in a little compass: but in tragedy the design is weighty, and the persons great; therefore there will naturally be required a greater space of time in which to move them. And this, though Ben Jonson has not told us, yet 'tis manifestly his opinion: for you see that to his comedies

he allows generally but twenty-four hours; to his two tragedies, Sejanus and Catiline, a much larger time: though he draws both of them into as narrow a compass as he can: for he shows you only the latter end of Sejanus his favor, and the conspiracy of Catiline already ripe, and just breaking out into action.

But as it is an error on the one side, to make too great a disproportion betwixt the imaginary time of the play, and the real time of its representations; so on the other side, 'tis an oversight to compress the accidents of a play into a narrower compass than that in which they could naturally be produced. Of this last error the French are seldom guilty, because the thinness of their plots prevents them from it; but few Englishmen, except Ben Jonson, have ever made a plot with variety of design in it, included in twenty-four hours, which was altogether natural. For this reason, I prefer The Silent Woman before all other plays, I think justly; as I do its author, in judgment, above all other poets. Yet of the two, I think that error the most pardonable, which in too straight a compass crowds together many accidents; since it produces more variety, and consequently more pleasure to the audience; and because the nearness of proportion betwixt the imaginary and real time does speciously cover the compression of the accidents.

Thus I have endeavored to answer the meaning of his argument; for, as he drew it, I humbly conceive that it was none; as will appear by his proposition, and the proof of it: His proposition was this:

If strictly and duly weighed, 'tis as impossible for one stage to present two rooms or houses, as two countries or kingdoms, etc. And his proof this: *For all being impossible, they are none of them nearest the truth or nature of what they present.*

Here you see, instead of proof or reason, there is only *petitio principii;* for in plain words, his sense is this: Two things are as impossible as one another, because they are both equally impossible; but he takes those two things to be granted as impossible which he ought to have proved such, before he had proceeded to prove them equally impossible. He should have made out first, that it was impossible for one stage to represent two houses, and then have gone forward to prove that it was as equally impossible for a stage to present two houses as two countries.

After all this, the very absurdity to which he would reduce me is none at all: for he only drives at this, that if his argument be true, I must then acknowledge that there are degrees in impossibilities, which I easily grant him without dispute: and if I mistake not, Aristotle and the School are of my opinion. For there are some things which are absolutely impossible. and others which are only so *ex parte;* as it is absolutely impossible for a thing *to be*, and *not be*, at the same time; but for a stone to move naturally upward, is only impossible *ex parte materiæ;* but it is not impossible for the first mover to alter the nature of it.

His last assault, like that of a Frenchman, is most feeble: for whereas I have observed that none have been violent against verse, but such only as have not attempted it, or have succeeded ill in their attempt, he will needs, according to his usual custom, improve my observation to an argument, that he might have the glory to confute it. But I lay my observation at his feet, as I do my pen, which I have often employed willingly in his deserved commendations, and now most unwillingly against his judgment. For his person and parts, I honor them as much as any man living, and have had so many particular obligations to him, that I should be very ungrateful if I did not acknowledge them to the world. But I gave not the first occasion of this difference in opinions. In my Epistle Dedicatory before my Rival Ladies, I had said somewhat in behalf of verse, which he was pleased to answer in his Preface to his plays: that occasioned my reply in my Essay; and that reply begot this rejoinder of his in his Preface to The Duke of Lerma. But as I was the last who took up arms, I will be the first to lay them down. For what I have here written, I submit it wholly to him; and if I do not hereafter answer what may be objected against this paper, I hope the world will not impute it to any other reason than only the due respect which I have for so noble an opponent.

OF HEROIC PLAYS [1]

[TEXT: *second edition, 1673*]

WHETHER heroic verse ought to be admitted into serious plays is not now to be disputed: 'tis already in possession of the stage; and I dare confidently affirm that very few tragedies, in this age, shall be received without it. All the arguments which are formed against it can amount to no more than this, that it is not so near conversation as prose, and therefore not so natural. But it is very clear to all who understand poetry, that serious plays ought not to imitate conversation too nearly. If nothing were to be raised above that level, the foundation of poetry would be destroyed. And if you once admit of a latitude, that thoughts may be exalted, and that images and actions may be raised above the life, and described in measure without rhyme, that leads you insensibly from your own principles to mine: you are already so far onward on your way, that you have forsaken the imitation of ordinary converse. You are gone beyond it; and to continue where you are is to lodge in the open fields betwixt two inns. You have lost that which you call natural, and have not acquired the last perfection of art. But it was only custom which cozened us so long; we thought, because Shakespeare and Fletcher went no farther, that there the pillars of poetry were to be erected; that, because they excellently described passion without rhyme, therefore rhyme was not capable of describing it. But time has now convinced most men of that error. 'Tis indeed so difficult to write verse that the adversaries of it have a good plea against many who undertake that task, without being formed by art or nature for it. Yet, even they who have written worst in it would have written worse without it: they have cozened many with their sound, who never took the pains to examine their sense. In fine, they have succeeded; though, it is true, they have more dishonored rhyme by their good success, than they could have done by their ill. But I am willing to let fall this argument: 'tis free for every man to write, or not to write, in verse, as he judges it to be, or not to be, his talent; or as he imagines the audience will receive it.

For Heroic Plays (in which only I have used it without the mixture of prose), the first light we had of them, on the English theater, was from the late Sir William Davenant. It being forbidden him in rebellious times to act the tragedies and comedies, because they contained some matter of scandal to those good people, who could more easily dispossess their lawful sovereign than endure a wanton jest, he was forced to turn his thoughts another way, and to introduce the examples of moral virtue, writ in verse, and

1 Of Heroic Plays is the Prefatory Essay to the Conquest of Granada.

performed in recitative music. The original of this music, and of the scenes which adorned his work, he had from the Italian operas; but he heightened his characters (as I may probably imagine) from the example of Corneille and some French poets. In this condition did this part of poetry remain at his Majesty's return; when, growing bolder, as being now owned by a public authority, he reviewed his Siege of Rhodes, and caused it to be acted as a just drama. But as few men have the happiness to begin and finish any new project, so neither did he live to make his design perfect: there wanted the fullness of a plot, and the variety of characters to form it as it ought; and, perhaps, something might have been added to the beauty of the style. All which he would have performed with more exactness had he pleased to have given us another work of the same nature. For myself and others, who come after him, we are bound, with all veneration to his memory, to acknowledge what advantage we received from that excellent groundwork which he laid: and, since it is an easy thing to add to what already is invented, we ought all of us, without envy to him, or partiality to ourselves, to yield him the precedence in it.

Having done him this justice, as my guide, I may do myself so much, as to give an account of what I have performed after him. I observed then, as I said, what was wanting to the perfection of his Siege of Rhodes; which was design, and variety of characters. And in the midst of this consideration, by mere accident, I opened the next book that lay by me, which was an Ariosto in Italian; and the very first two lines of that poem gave me the light to all I could desire:

> Le donne, i cavalier, l'arme, gli amori,
> Le cortesie, l'audaci imprese io canto, etc.[2]

For the very next reflection which I made was this, that an heroic play ought to be an imitation, in little, of an heroic poem; and, consequently, that love and valor ought to be the subject of it. Both these Sir William Davenant had begun to shadow; but it was so, as first discoverers draw their maps, with headlands, and promontories, and some few outlines of somewhat taken at a distance, and which the designer saw not clearly. The common drama obliged him to a plot well formed and pleasant, or, as the ancients call it, one entire and great action. But this he afforded not himself

in a story, which he neither filled with persons, nor beautified with characters, nor varied with accidents. The laws of an heroic poem did not dispense with those of the other, but raised them to a greater height, and indulged him a further liberty of fancy, and of drawing all things as far above the ordinary proportion of the stage as that is beyond the common words and actions of human life; and, therefore, in the scanting of his images and design, he complied not enough with the greatness and majesty of an heroic poem.

I am sorry I cannot discover my opinion of this kind of writing, without dissenting much from his, whose memory I love and honor. But I will do it with the same respect to him, as if he were now alive, and overlooking my paper while I write. His judgment of an heroic poem was this: *That it ought to be dressed in a more familiar and easy shape; more fitted to the common actions and passions of human life; and, in short, more like a glass of nature, showing us ourselves in our ordinary habits, and figuring a more practicable virtue to us, than was done by the ancients or moderns.* Thus he takes the image of an heroic poem from the drama, or stage poetry; and accordingly intended to divide it into five books, representing the same number of acts; and every book into several cantos, imitating the scenes which compose our acts.

But this, I think, is rather a play in narration, as I may call it, than an heroic poem; if at least you will not prefer the opinion of a single man to the practice of the most excellent authors, both of ancient and latter ages. I am no admirer of quotations; but you shall hear, if you please, one of the ancients delivering his judgment on this question; it is Petronius Arbiter, the most elegant, and one of the most judicious authors of the Latin tongue; who, after he had given many admirable rules for the structure and beauties of an epic poem, concludes all in these following words:

Non enim res gestæ versibus comprehendendæ sunt, quod longe melius historici faciunt: sed, per ambages, deorumque ministeria, præcipitandus est liber spiritus, ut potius furentis animi vaticinatio appareat, quam religiosæ orationis, sub testibus, fides.[3]

In which sentence, and his own essay of a poem, which immediately he gives you, it is thought he

---

2 Of loves and ladies, knights and arms, I sing,
    Of courtesies, and many a daring feat. (Rose.)

3 For actual events are not to be recounted in verse, things which the historians do far better; but by means of digressions, and the good offices of the gods, the free spirit is to be urged on, that the prophesying of an inspired mind may appear in the poem, rather than the mere accuracy of a scrupulous discourse, under the control of witnesses.

taxes Lucan, who followed too much the truth of history, crowded sentences together, was too full of points, and too often offered at somewhat which had more of the sting of an epigram, than of the dignity and state of an heroic poem. Lucan used not much the help of his heathen deities: there was neither the ministry of the gods, nor the precipitation of the soul, nor the fury of a prophet (of which my author speaks), in his Pharsalia; he treats you more like a philosopher than a poet, and instructs you, in verse, with what he had been taught by his uncle Seneca in prose. In one word, he walks soberly afoot, when he might fly. Yet Lucan is not always this religious historian. The oracle of Appius, and the witchcraft of Erictho, will somewhat atone for him, who was, indeed, bound up by an ill-chosen and known argument, to follow truth with great exactness. For my part, I am of opinion that neither Homer, Virgil, Statius, Ariosto, Tasso, nor our English Spenser, could have formed their poems half so beautiful, without those gods and spirits, and those enthusiastic parts of poetry, which compose the most noble parts of all their writings. And I will ask any man who loves heroic poetry (for I will not dispute their tastes who do not), if the ghost of Polydorus in Virgil, the Enchanted Wood in Tasso, and the Bower of Bliss in Spenser (which he borrows from that admirable Italian) could have been omitted without taking from their works some of the greatest beauties in them. And if any man object the improbabilities of a spirit appearing, or of a palace raised by magic, I boldly answer him, that an heroic poet is not tied to a bare representation of what is true, or exceeding probable; but that he may let himself loose to visionary objects, and to the representation of such things as depending not on sense, and therefore not to be comprehended by knowledge, may give him a freer scope for imagination. 'Tis enough that, in all ages and religions, the greatest part of mankind have believed the power of magic, and that there are spirits or specters which have appeared. This, I say, is foundation enough for poetry; and I dare farther affirm that the whole doctrine of separated beings, whether those spirits are incorporeal substances (which Mr. Hobbes, with some reason, thinks to imply a contradiction), or that they are a thinner or more aërial sort of bodies (as some of the fathers have conjectured), may better be explicated by poets than by philosophers or divines. For their speculations on this subject are wholly poetical; they have only their fancy for their guide; and that, being sharper in an excellent poet, than it is likely it should

in a phlegmatic, heavy gownman, will see farther in its own empire, and produce more satisfactory notions on those dark and doubtful problems.

Some men think they have raised a great argument against the use of specters and magic poetry by saying they are unnatural; but whether they or I believe there are such things is not material; 'tis enough that, for aught we know, they may be in nature; and whatever is or may be, is not properly unnatural. Neither am I much concerned at Mr. Cowley's verses before Gondibert (though his authority is almost sacred to me): 'tis true, he has resembled the epic poetry to a fantastic fairy-land; but he has contradicted himself by his own example. For he has himself made use of angels and visions in his Davideis, as well as Tasso in his Godfrey.

What I have written on this subject will not be thought digression by the reader, if he please to remember what I said in the beginning of this essay, that I have modeled my heroic plays by the rules of an heroic poem. And if that be the most noble, the most pleasant, and the most instructive way of writing in verse and withal the highest pattern of human life, as all poets have agreed, I shall need no other argument to justify my choice in this imitation. One advantage the drama has above the other, namely, that it represents to view what the poem only does relate; and, *Segnius irritant animum demissa per aures, quam quæ sunt oculis subjecta fidelibus,*[4] as Horace tells us.

To those who object to my frequent use of drums and trumpets, and my representations of battles, I answer, I introduced them not on the English stage: Shakespeare used them frequently, and though Jonson shows no battle in his Catiline, yet you hear from behind the scenes the sounding of trumpets, and the shouts of fighting armies. But I add farther, that these warlike instruments, and even the representations of fighting on the stage, are no more than necessary to produce the effects of an heroic play; that is, to raise the imagination of the audience, and to persuade them, for the time, that what they behold on the theater is really performed. The poet is then to endeavor an absolute dominion over the minds of the spectators; for, though our fancy will contribute to its own deceit, yet a writer ought to help its operation: and that the Red Bull[5] has formerly done the same is no more an

---

4 Less keenly do those things affect us which come to us through the ears, than those which are subject to the trustworthy eyes. (*De Arte Poetica*, 180–81.)

5 A London theater of an unsavory reputation.

argument against our practice than it would be for a physician to forbear an approved medicine because a mountebank has used it with success.

Thus I have given a short account of heroic plays. I might now, with the usual eagerness of an author, make a particular defense of this. But the common opinion (how unjust soever) has been so much to my advantage, that I have reason to be satisfied, and to suffer with patience all that can be urged against it.

For, otherwise, what can be more easy for me than to defend the character of Almanzor, which is one great exception that is made against the play? 'Tis said, that Almanzor is no perfect pattern of heroic virtue, that he is a contemner of kings, and that he is made to perform impossibilities.

I must therefore avow, in the first place, from whence I took the character. The first image I had of him was from the Achilles of Homer; the next from Tasso's Rinaldo (who was a copy of the former), and the third from the Artaban of Monsieur Calprenède, who has imitated both. The original of these, Achilles, is taken by Homer for his hero; and is described by him as one who in strength and courage surpassed the rest of the Grecian army; but withal of so fiery a temper, so impatient of an injury, even from his king and general, that when his mistress was to be forced from him by the command of Agamemnon, he not only disobeyed it, but returned an answer full of contumely, and in the most opprobrious terms he could imagine. They are Homer's words which follow, and I have cited but some few amongst a multitude:

Οἰνοβαρές, κυνὸς ὄμματ' ἔχων, κραδίην δ' ἐλάφοιο,[6]
Δημοβόρος βασιλεύς, etc.[7]

Nay, he proceeded so far in his insolence, as to draw out his sword, with intention to kill him:

Ἕλκετο δ' ἐκ κολεοῖο μέγα ξίφας.[8]

And, if Minerva had not appeared, and held his hand he had executed his design; and it was all she could do to dissuade him from it. The event was, that he left the

army, and would fight no more. Agamemnon gives his character thus to Nestor:

Ἀλλ' ὅδ' ἀνὴρ ἐθέλει περὶ πάντων ἔμμεναι ἄλλων,
Πάντων μὲν κρέειν ἐθέλει, πάντεσσι δ' ἀνάσσειν.[9]

and Horace gives the same description of him in his Art of Poetry:

Honoratum si forte reponis Achillem,
Impiger, iracundus, inexorabilis, acer,
Jura neget sibi nata, nihil non arroget armis.[10]

Tasso's chief character, Rinaldo, was a man of the same temper; for, when he had slain Gernando in his heat of passion, he not only refused to be judged by Godfrey, his general, but threatened that if he came to seize him, he would right himself by arms upon him; witness these following lines of Tasso:

Venga egli, o mandi, io terrò fermo il piede:
Giudici fian tra noi la sorte, e l'arme;
Fera tragedia vuol che s'appresenti,
Per lor diporto, alle nemiche genti.[11]

You see how little these great authors did esteem the *point of honor*, so much magnified by the French, and so ridiculously aped by us. They made their heroes men of honor; but so as not to divest them quite of human passions and frailties: they contented themselves to show you what men of great spirits would certainly do when they were provoked, not what they were obliged to do by the strict rules of moral virtue. For my own part, I declare myself for Homer and Tasso, and am more in love with Achilles and Rinaldo, than with Cyrus and Oroöndates. I shall never subject my characters to the French standard, where love and honor are to be weighed by drachms and scruples. Yet

---

6 O monster! mix'd of insolence and fear,
　 Thou dog in forehead, but in heart a deer.
　　　　　　　　　　　　(Iliad I, 225; Pope.)
7 Scourge of thy people, violent and base.
　　　　　　　　　　　　(Ibid., 231; Pope.)
8 While half unsheathed appear'd the glittering blade.
　　　　　　　　　　　　(Ibid., 194; Pope.)

9 But that imperious, that unconquer'd soul,
　 No laws can limit, no respect control;
　 Before his pride must his superiors fall,
　 His word the law and he the lord of all?
　　　　　　　　　　　　(Ibid., 287–88; Pope.)
10 If haply to the stage you summon back
　 Great Peleus' son, adhere to Homer's track.
　 Proud, stern, relentless, brave, the hero draw,
　 His title conquest, and the sword his law.
　　　　　　　　　　　　(De Arte Poetica, 120–22; Howes.)
11 Here let him come in all his pomp of state;
　 I place my proud foot on the ground and wait
　 His unfeared presence and his scorned decree;
　 Sharp arms shall be our only jurors, Fate
　 Sole arbitress, and foemen flock to see
　 The sportful drama played,—a deep, deep tragedy.
　　　　　　　　　(Gerusalemme Liberata, v. 43; Wiffen's translation.)

where I have designed the patterns of exact virtues, such as in this play are the parts of Almahide, of Ozmyn, and Benzayda, I may safely challenge the best of theirs.

But Almanzor is taxed with changing sides: and what tie has he on him to the contrary? He is not born their subject whom he serves, and he is injured by them to a very high degree. He threatens them, and speaks insolently of sovereign power; but so do Achilles and Rinaldo, who were subjects and soldiers of Agamemnon and Godfrey of Bulloigne. He talks extravagantly in his passion; but, if I would take the pains to quote an hundred passages of Ben Jonson's Cethegus, I could easily show you that the rodomontades of Almanzor are neither so irrational as his, nor so impossible to be put in execution; for Cethegus threatens to destroy nature, and to raise a new one out of it; to kill all the Senate for his part of the action; to look Cato dead; and a thousand other things as extravagant he says, but performs not one action in the play.

But none of the former calumnies will stick: and, therefore, 'tis at last charged upon me, that Almanzor does all things; or, if you will have an absurd accusation, in their nonsense who make it, that he performs impossibilities. They say, that being a stranger, he appeases two fighting factions, when the authority of their lawful sovereign could not. This is indeed the most improbable of all his actions, but 'tis far from being impossible. Their king had made himself contemptible to his people, as the history of Granada tells us; and Almanzor, though a stranger, yet was already known to them by his gallantry, in the *juego de toros*, his engagement on the weaker side, and more especially by the character of his person and brave

actions, given by Abdalla just before; and, after all, the greatness of the enterprise consisted only in the daring, for he had the king's guards to second him. But we have read both of Cæsar, and many other generals, who have not only calmed a mutiny with a word, but have presented themselves single before an army of their enemies; which upon sight of them has revolted from their own leaders and come over to their trenches. In the rest of Almanzor's actions you see him for the most part victorious; but the same fortune has constantly attended many heroes who were not imaginary. Yet you see it no inheritance to him; for, in the first part, he is made a prisoner, and, in the last, defeated, and not able to preserve the city from being taken. If the history of the late Duke of Guise be true, he hazarded more and performed not less in Naples than Almanzor is feigned to have done in Granada.

I have been too tedious in this apology; but to make some satisfaction, I will leave the rest of my play exposed to the critics without defense.

The concernment of it is wholly passed from me, and ought to be in them who have been favorable to it, and are somewhat obliged to defend their own opinions. That there are errors in it, I deny not:

Ast opere in tanto fas est obrepere somnum.[12]

But I have already swept the stakes; and, with the common good fortune of prosperous gamesters, can be content to sit quietly; to hear my fortune cursed by some, and my faults arraigned by others, and to suffer both without reply.

12 Quoted incorrectly from Horace, *De Arte Poetica*, 360 –61.
    Howbeit, at times the noblest bard, I think,
    In works of long attempt may fairly wink.   (Howes.)

"ANTONY AND CLEOPATRA" AND
THE ART OF TRAGEDY[1]

[TEXT: *first edition, 1678*]

THE death of Antony and Cleopatra is a subject which has been treated by the greatest wits of our nation, after Shakespeare; and by all so variously that their example has given me the confidence to try myself in this bow of Ulysses amongst the crowd of suitors; and, withal, to take my own measures in aiming at the mark. I doubt not but the same motive has prevailed with all of us in this attempt; I mean the excellency of the moral: for the chief persons represented were famous patterns of unlawful love; and

1 Preface to Dryden's All for Love, or, The World Well Lost.

their end accordingly was unfortunate. All reasonable men have long since concluded, that the hero of the poem ought not to be a character of perfect virtue, for then he could not, without injustice, be made unhappy; nor yet altogether wicked, because he could not then be pitied. I have therefore steered the middle course; and have drawn the character of Antony as favorably as Plutarch, Appian, and Dion Cassius would give me leave; the like I have observed in Cleopatra. That which is wanting to work up the pity to a greater height was not afforded me by the story; for the crimes of love, which they both committed, were not occasioned by any necessity, or fatal ignorance, but were wholly voluntary; since our passions are, or ought to be, within our power. The fabric of the play is regular enough, as to the inferior parts of it; and the unities of time, place, and action, more exactly observed than perhaps the English theater requires. Particularly, the action is so much one that it is the only one of the kind without episode, or underplot; every scene in the tragedy conducing to the main design, and every act concluding with a turn of it. The greatest error in the contrivance seems to be in the person of Octavia; for, though I might use the privilege of a poet to introduce her into Alexandria, yet I had not enough considered that the compassion she moved to herself and children was destructive to that which I reserved for Antony and Cleopatra; whose mutual love, being founded upon vice, must lessen the favor of the audience to them, when virtue and innocence were oppressed by it. And, though I justified Antony in some measure, by making Octavia's departure to proceed wholly from herself; yet the force of the first machine[2] still remained; and the dividing of pity, like the cutting of a river into many channels, abated the strength of the natural stream. But this is an objection which none of my critics have urged against me; and therefore I might have let it pass, if I could have resolved to have been partial to myself. The faults my enemies have found are rather cavils concerning little and not essential decencies; which a master of the ceremonies may decide betwixt us. The French poets, I confess, are strict observers of these punctilios: they would not, for example, have suffered Cleopatra and Octavia to have met; or, if they had met, there must only have passed betwixt them some cold civilities, but no eagerness of repartee, for fear of offending against the greatness of their characters, and the modesty of their sex. This objection I foresaw, and at the

same time contemned; for I judged it both natural and probable that Octavia, proud of her new-gained conquest, would search out Cleopatra to triumph over her; and that Cleopatra, thus attacked, was not of a spirit to shun the encounter: and 'tis not unlikely that two exasperated rivals should use such satire as I have put into their mouths; for, after all, though the one were a Roman, and the other a queen, they were both women. 'Tis true, some actions, though natural, are not fit to be represented; and broad obscenities in words ought in good manners to be avoided: expressions therefore are a modest clothing of our thoughts, as breeches and petticoats are of our bodies. If I have kept myself within the bounds of modesty, all beyond is but nicety and affectation, which is no more but modesty depraved into a vice. They betray themselves who are too quick of apprehension in such cases, and leave all reasonable men to imagine worse of them than of the poet.

Honest Montaigne[3] goes yet further: *Nous ne sommes que cérémonie; la cérémonie nous emporte, et laissons la substance des choses. Nous nous tenons aux branches, et abandonnons le tronc et le corps. Nous avons appris aux dames de rougir, oyans seulement nommer ce qu'elles ne craignent aucunement à faire: nous n'osons appeler à droit nos membres, et ne craignons pas de les employer à toute sorte de débauche. La cérémonie nous défend d'exprimer par paroles les choses licites et naturelles, et nous l'en croyons; la raison nous défend de n'en faire point d'illicites et mauvaises, et personne ne l'en croit.* My comfort is, that by this opinion my enemies are but suckling critics, who would fain be nibbling ere their teeth are come.

Yet in this nicety of manners does the excellency of French poetry consist: their heroes are the most civil people breathing; but their good breeding seldom extends to a word of sense; all their wit is in their ceremony; they want the genius which animates our stage; and therefore 'tis but necessary, when they cannot please, that they should take care not to offend. But as the civilest man in the company is commonly the dullest, so these authors, while they are afraid to make you laugh or cry, out of pure good manners make you sleep. They are so careful not to exasperate a critic that they never leave him any work; so busy with the broom, and make so clean a riddance, that there is little left either for censure or for praise: for no part of a poem is worth our discommending where the whole is insipid; as when we have once tasted of palled wine, we stay not to examine it glass by glass. But

2 Literary or dramatic contrivance.

3 In his essay, *De la Présumption*.

while they affect to shine in trifles, they are often careless in essentials. Thus, their Hippolytus is so scrupulous in point of decency that he will rather expose himself to death than accuse his stepmother to his father; and my critics, I am sure, will commend him for it; but we of grosser apprehensions are apt to think that this excess of generosity is not practicable but with fools and madmen. This was good manners with a vengeance; and the audience is like to be much concerned at the misfortunes of this admirable hero: but take Hippolytus out of his poetic fit, and I suppose he would think it a wiser part to set the saddle on the right horse, and choose rather to live with the reputation of a plain-spoken, honest man, than to die with the infamy of an incestuous villain. In the meantime we may take notice that where the poet ought to have preserved the character as it was delivered to us by antiquity, when he should have given us the picture of a rough young man, of the Amazonian strain, a jolly huntsman, and both by his profession and his early rising a mortal enemy to love, he has chosen to give him the turn of gallantry, sent him to travel from Athens to Paris, taught him to make love, and transformed the Hippolytus of Euripides into Monsieur Hippolyte.[4] I should not have troubled myself thus far with French poets, but that I find our *Chedreux*[5] critics wholly form their judgments by them. But for my part, I desire to be tried by the laws of my own country; for it seems unjust to me that the French should prescribe here till they have conquered. Our little sonneteers, who follow them, have too narrow souls to judge of poetry. Poets themselves are the most proper, though I conclude not the only critics. But till some genius, as universal as Aristotle, shall arise, one who can penetrate into all arts and sciences, without the practice of them, I shall think it reasonable that the judgment of an artificer in his own art should be preferable to the opinion of another man; at least where he is not bribed by interest, or prejudiced by malice. And this, I suppose, is manifest by plain induction: for, first, the crowd cannot be presumed to have more than a gross instinct of what pleases or displeases them: every man will grant me this; but then, by a particular kindness to himself, he draws his own stake first, and will be distinguished from the multitude, of which other men may think him one. But, if I come closer to those who are allowed for witty men, either

by the advantage of their quality, or by common fame, and affirm that neither are they qualified to decide sovereignly concerning poetry, I shall yet have a strong party of my opinion; for most of them severally will exclude the rest, either from the number of witty men, or at least of able judges. But here again they are all indulgent to themselves; and everyone who believes himself a wit, that is, every man, will pretend at the same time to a right of judging. But to press it yet farther, there are many witty men, but few poets; neither have all poets a taste of tragedy. And this is the rock on which they are daily splitting. Poetry, which is a picture of nature, must generally please: but 'tis not to be understood that all parts of it must please every man; therefore is not tragedy to be judged by a witty man, whose taste is only confined to comedy. Nor is every man, who loves tragedy, a sufficient judge of it; he must understand the excellencies of it too, or he will only prove a blind admirer, not a critic. From hence it comes that so many satires on poets, and censures of their writings, fly abroad. Men of pleasant conversation (at least esteemed so), and endued with a trifling kind of fancy, perhaps helped out with some smattering of Latin, are ambitious to distinguish themselves from the herd of gentlemen, by their poetry—

> *Rarus enim ferme sensus communis in illa*
> *Fortuna.*[6]

And is not this a wretched affectation, not to be contented with what fortune has done for them, and sit down quietly with their estates, but they must call their wits in question, and needlessly expose their nakedness to public view? Not considering that they are not to expect the same approbation from sober men, which they have found from their flatterers after the third bottle. If a little glittering in discourse has passed them on us for witty men, where was the necessity of undeceiving the world? Would a man who has an ill title to an estate, but yet is in possession of it; would he bring it of his own accord to be tried at Westminster? We who write, if we want the talent, yet have the excuse that we do it for a poor subsistence; but what can be urged in their defense, who, not having the vocation of poverty to scribble, out of mere wantonness take pains to make themselves ridiculous? Horace was certainly in the right where he said *that no man is*

---

4 As in the *Phèdre* of Racine.
5 The name of the fashionable periwigs of the day, and, according to Scott, derived from their maker.

6 For "common sense" is very rare in that station of life. (Juvenal, viii. 73, 74.)

satisfied with his own condition.[7] A poet is not pleased because he is not rich; and the rich are discontented because the poets will not admit them of their number. Thus the case is hard with writers: if they succeed not, they must starve; and if they do, some malicious satire is prepared to level them, for daring to please without their leave. But while they are so eager to destroy the fame of others, their ambition is manifest in their concernment; some poem of their own is to be produced, and the slaves are to be laid flat with their faces on the ground, that the monarch may appear in the greater majesty.

Dionysius and Nero had the same longings, but with all their power they could never bring their business well about. 'Tis true, they proclaimed themselves poets by sound of trumpet; and poets they were, upon pain of death to any man who durst call them otherwise. The audience had a fine time on't, you may imagine; they sat in a bodily fear, and looked as demurely as they could: for 'twas a hanging matter to laugh unseasonably; and the tyrants were suspicious, as they had reason, that their subjects had 'em in the wind; so, every man, in his own defense, set as good a face upon the business as he could. 'Twas known beforehand that the monarchs were to be crowned laureates; but when the show was over, and an honest man was suffered to depart quietly, he took out his laughter which he had stifled, with a firm resolution never more to see an emperor's play, though he had been ten years a-making it. In the meantime the true poets were they who made the best markets, for they had wit enough to yield the prize with a good grace, and not contend with him who had thirty legions. They were sure to be rewarded if they confessed themselves bad writers, and that was somewhat better than to be martyrs for their reputations. Lucan's example was enough to teach them manners; and after he was put to death for overcoming Nero, the emperor carried it without dispute for the best poet in his dominions. No man was ambitious of that grinning honor; for if he heard the malicious trumpeter proclaiming his name before his betters, he knew there was but one way with him. Mæcenas took another course, and we know he was more than a great man, for he was witty too: but finding himself far gone in poetry, which Seneca assures us was not his talent, he thought it his best way to be well with Virgil and with Horace; that at least he might be a poet at the second hand; and we see how happily it has succeeded with him; for his own

bad poetry is forgotten, and their panegyrics of him still remain. But they who should be our patrons are for no such expensive ways to fame; they have much of the poetry of Mæcenas, but little of his liberality. They are for persecuting Horace and Virgil, in the persons of their successors; for such is every man who has any part of their soul and fire, though in a less degree. Some of their little zanies yet go farther; for they are persecutors even of Horace himself, as far as they are able, by their ignorant and vile imitations of him; by making an unjust use of his authority, and turning his artillery against his friends. But how would he disdain to be copied by such hands! I dare answer for him, he would be more uneasy in their company than he was with Crispinus, their forefather, in the Holy Way; and would no more have allowed them a place amongst the critics, than he would Demetrius the mimic, and Tigellius the buffoon:

> *Demetri, teque, Tigelli,*
> *Discipulorum inter jubeo plorare cathedras.*[8]

With what scorn would he look down on such miserable translators, who make doggerel of his Latin, mistake his meaning, misapply his censures, and often contradict their own? He is fixed as a landmark to set out the bounds of poetry—

> *Saxum antiquum, ingens,—*
> *Limes agro positus, litem ut discerneret arvis.*[9]

But other arms than theirs, and other sinews are required, to raise the weight of such an author; and when they would toss him against enemies—

> *Genua labant, gelidus concrevit frigore sanguis.*
> *Tum lapis ipse, viri vacuum per inane volutus,*
> *Nec spatium evasit totum, nec pertulit ictum.*[10]

For my part, I would wish no other revenge, either for myself, or the rest of the poets, from this rhyming

7 Satires, I. i. 1–3.

8 You, Demetrius and Tigellius, I bid go weep amidst the chairs of your pupils. (Horace, Satires, I. x. 90, 91.)
9 An antique stone he saw, the common bound Of neighb'ring fields, and barrier of the ground. (Virgil's Æneid, xii. 897–98. Dryden.)
10 Ibid., 905–07. Dryden translates it thus: His knocking knees are bent beneath the load, And shiv'ring cold congeals his vital blood. The stone drops from his arms, and, falling short For want of vigor, mocks his vain effort.

judge of the twelve-penny gallery, this legitimate son of Sternhold,[11] than that he would subscribe his name to his censure, or (not to tax him beyond his learning) set his mark: for, should he own himself publicly, and come from behind the lion's skin, they whom he condemns would be thankful to him, they whom he praises would choose to be condemned; and the magistrates, whom he has elected, would modestly withdraw from their employment, to avoid the scandal of his nomination. The sharpness of his satire, next to himself, falls most heavily on his friends, and they ought never to forgive him for commending them perpetually the wrong way, and sometimes by contraries. If he have a friend whose hastiness in writing is his greatest fault, Horace would have taught him to have minced the matter, and to have called it readiness of thought, and a flowing fancy; for friendship will allow a man to christen an imperfection by the name of some neighbor virtue—

> *Vellem in amicitia sic erraremus; et isti*
> *Errori nomen virtus posuisset honestum.*[12]

But he would never have allowed him to have called a slow man hasty, or a hasty writer a slow drudge, as Juvenal explains it—

> *Canibus pigris, scabieque vetusta*
> *Lævibus, et siccæ lambentibus ora lucernæ,*
> *Nomen erit, Pardus, Tigris, Leo; si quid adhuc est*
> *Quod fremit in terris violentius.*[13]

Yet Lucretius laughs at a foolish lover, even for excusing the imperfections of his mistress—

> *Nigra* μελίχροος *est, immunda et fœtida* ἄκοσμος . . . .
> *Balba loqui, non quit,* τραυλίζει; *muta pudens est, etc.*[14]

11 Referring to the famous metrical version of the Psalms by Sternhold, Hopkins, and others, which had become proverbial for the pedestrian quality of its verse.

12 Would that it were possible thus to err in matters of friendship, and that to such an error virtuous feeling would ascribe an honorable name. (Horace, Satires, I. iii. 41, 42.)

13 Lazy curs, hairless from inveterate mange, and licking the edges of a dry lamp, have for names, "Panther," "Tiger," "Lion,"—or if there be anything else which roars with greater fury in the world. (Juvenal, viii. 34–37. Translation by J. D. Lewis.)

14 The sallow skin is for the swarthy put,
And love can make a slattern of a slut. . . .
She stammers: O, what grace in lisping lies!
If she says nothing, to be sure she's wise.
(Lucretius, iv. 1160–64. Dryden's translation.)

But to drive it *ad Æthiopem cygnum*[15] is not to be endured. I leave him to interpret this by the benefit of his French version on the other side, and without farther considering him than I have the rest of my illiterate censors, whom I have disdained to answer, because they are not qualified for judges. It remains that I acquaint the reader that I have endeavored in this play to follow the practice of the ancients, who, as Mr. Rymer has judiciously observed, are and ought to be our masters. Horace likewise gives it for a rule in his Art of Poetry—

> *Vos exemplaria Græca*
> *Nocturna versate manu, versate diurna,*[16]

Yet though their models are regular, they are too little for English tragedy; which requires to be built in a larger compass. I could give an instance in the *Œdipus Tyrannus*,[17] which was the masterpiece of Sophocles; but I reserve it for a more fit occasion, which I hope to have hereafter. In my style, I have professed to imitate the divine Shakespeare; which that I might perform more freely, I have disencumbered myself from rhyme. Not that I condemn my former way, but that this is more proper to my present purpose. I hope I need not to explain myself, that I have not copied my author servilely: words and phrases must of necessity receive a change in succeeding ages; but it is almost a miracle that much of his language remains so pure; and that he who began dramatic poetry amongst us, untaught by any, and as Ben Jonson tells us, without learning, should by the force of his own genius perform so much, that in a manner he has left no praise for any who come after him. The occasion is fair, and the subject would be pleasant to handle the difference of styles betwixt him and Fletcher, and wherein, and how far they are both to be imitated. But since I must not be overconfident of my own performance after him, it will be prudence in me to be silent. Yet I hope I may affirm, and without vanity, that, by imitating him, I have excelled myself throughout the play; and particularly, that I prefer the scene betwixt Antony and Ventidius in the first act, to anything which I have written in this kind.

15 To call an Ethiopian a swan. (Juvenal, viii. 33.)

16 Your standard then be Greece! Her models bright
By day peruse, and reperuse by night. (Howes.)

17 Dryden wrote his Œdipus, in collaboration with Nathaniel Lee, in this same year, 1678. The theme is classical, but there are such Elizabethan elements as ghosts and incantations here and there in the play.

FROM

A DISCOURSE CONCERNING THE ORIGINAL
AND PROGRESS OF SATIRE[1]

[TEXT: *first edition, 1693*]

THERE has been a long dispute among the modern critics, whether the Romans derived their satire from the Grecians, or first invented it themselves. Julius Scaliger, and Heinsius, are of the first opinion; Casaubon, Rigaltius, Dacier, and the publisher of the Dauphin's Juvenal, maintain the latter. If we take satire in the general signification of the word, as it is used in all modern languages, for an invective, it is certain that it is almost as old as verse; and though hymns, which are praises of God, may be allowed to have been before it, yet the defamation of others was not long after it. After God had cursed Adam and Eve in Paradise, the husband and wife excused themselves, by laying the blame on one another; and gave a beginning to those conjugal dialogues in prose, which the poets have perfected in verse. The third chapter of Job is one of the first instances of this poem in holy Scripture; unless we will take it higher, from the latter end of the second where his wife advises him to curse his Maker.

This original, I confess, is not much to the honor of satire; but here it was nature, and that depraved; when it became art, it bore better fruit. Only we have learnt thus much already, that scoffs and revilings are of the growth of all nations; and, consequently, that neither the Greek poets borrowed from other people their art of railing, neither needed the Romans to take it from them. But, considering satire as a species of poetry, here the war begins amongst the critics. Scaliger the father will have it descend from Greece to Rome; and derives the word satire from *satyrus*, that mixed kind of animal, or, as the ancients thought him, rural god, made up betwixt a man and a goat; with a human head, hooked nose, pouting lips, a bunch, or struma, under the chin, pricked ears, and upright horns; the body shagged with hair, especially from the waist, and ending in a goat, with the legs and feet of that creature. But Casaubon, and his followers, with reason, con-

demn this derivation; and prove, that from *satyrus*, the word *satira*, as it signifies a poem, cannot possibly descend. For *satira* is not properly a substantive, but an adjective; to which the word *lanx* (in English, a charger, or large platter) is understood; so that the Greek poem made according to the manners of a satyr, and expressing his qualities, must properly be called satyrical, and not satire. And thus far 'tis allowed that the Grecians had such poems; but that they were wholly different *in specie* from that to which the Romans gave the name of satire.

This is what I have to say in general of satire: only, as Dacier has observed before me, we may take notice, that the word satire is of more general signification in Latin, than in French, or English. For amongst the Romans it was not only used for those discourses which decried vice, or exposed folly, but for others also, where virtue was recommended. But in our modern languages we apply it only to invective poems, where the very name of satire is formidable to those persons who would appear to the world what they are not in themselves; for in English to say satire, is to mean reflection, as we use that word in the worst sense; or as the French call it, more properly, *médisance*. In the criticism of spelling, it ought to be with *i* and not with *y*, to distinguish its true derivation from *satura*, not from *satyrus*. And if this be so, then it is false spelled throughout this book;[2] for here it is written *satyr*; which having not considered at the first, I thought it not worth correcting afterwards. But the French are more nice, and never spell it any other way than *satire*.

In a word, that former sort of satire, which is known in England by the name of lampoon, is a dangerous sort of weapon, and for the most part unlawful. We have no moral right on the reputation of other men.

---

1 The preface to The Satires of Juvenal and Persius, made English, dedicated to the Earl of Dorset.

2 The spelling is rectified in this edition.

'Tis taking from them what we cannot restore to them. There are only two reasons for which we may be permitted to write lampoons; and I will not promise that they can always justify us. The first is revenge, when we have been affronted in the same nature, or have been any ways notoriously abused, and can make ourselves no other reparation. And yet to know, that, in Christian charity, all offenses are to be forgiven, as we expect the like pardon for those which we daily commit against Almighty God. And this consideration has often made me tremble when I was saying our Saviour's prayer; for the plain condition of the forgiveness which we beg is the pardoning of others the offenses which they have done to us; for which reason I have many times avoided the commission of that fault, even when I have been notoriously provoked. Let not this, my lord, pass for vanity in me; for it is truth. More libels have been written against me than almost any man now living; and I had reason on my side, to have defended my own innocence. I speak not of my poetry, which I have wholly given up to the critics: let them use it as they please; posterity, perhaps, may be more favorable to me; for interest and passion will lie buried in another age, and partiality and prejudice be forgotten. I speak of my morals, which have been sufficiently aspersed; that only sort of reputation ought to be dear to every honest man, and is to me. But let the world witness for me, that I have been often wanting to myself in that particular; I have seldom answered any scurrilous lampoon, when it was in my power to have exposed my enemies; and, being naturally vindicative, have suffered in silence, and possessed my soul in quiet.

Anything, though never so little, which a man speaks of himself, in my opinion, is still too much; and therefore I will waive this subject, and proceed to give the second reason which may justify a poet when he writes against a particular person; and that is, when he is become a public nuisance. All those, whom Horace in his Satires, and Persius and Juvenal have mentioned in theirs, with a brand of infamy, are wholly such. 'Tis an action of virtue to make examples of vicious men. They may and ought to be upbraided with their crimes and follies; both for their own amendment, if they are not yet incorrigible, and for the terror of others, to hinder them from falling into those enormities which they see are so severely punished in the persons of others. The first reason was only an excuse for revenge; but this second is absolutely of a poet's office to perform; but how few lampooners are there

now living, who are capable of this duty! When they come in my way, 'tis impossible sometimes to avoid reading them. But, good God! how remote they are, in common justice, from the choice of such persons as are proper subject of satire! And how little wit they bring for the support of their injustice! The weaker sex is their most ordinary theme; and the best and fairest are sure to be the most severely handled. Amongst men, those who are prosperously unjust are entitled to a panegyric; but afflicted virtue is insolently stabbed with all manner of reproaches. No decency is considered, no fulsomeness omitted; no venom is wanting, as far as dullness can supply it. For there is a perpetual dearth of wit; a barrenness of good sense and entertainment. The neglect of the readers will soon put an end to this sort of scribbling. There can be no pleasantry where there is no wit; no impression can be made where there is no truth for the foundation. To conclude: they are like the fruits of the earth in this unnatural season; the corn which held up its head is spoiled with rankness; but the greater part of the harvest is laid along, and little of good income and wholesome nourishment is received into the barns.

.   .   .   .

Thus I have treated, in a new method, the comparison betwixt Horace, Juvenal, and Persius; somewhat of their particular manner belonging to all of them is yet remaining to be considered. Persius was grave, and particularly opposed his gravity to lewdness, which was the predominant vice in Nero's court, at the time when he published his satires, which was before that emperor fell into the excess of cruelty. Horace was a mild admonisher, a court-satirist, fit for the gentle times of Augustus, and more fit, for the reasons which I have already given. Juvenal was as proper for his times, as they for theirs; his was an age that deserved a more severe chastisement; vices were more gross and open, more flagitious, more encouraged by the example of a tyrant, and more protected by his authority. Therefore, wheresoever Juvenal mentions Nero, he means Domitian, whom he dares not attack in his own person, but scourges him by proxy. Heinsius urges in praise of Horace, that, according to the ancient art and law of satire, it should be nearer to comedy than tragedy; not declaiming against vice, but only laughing at it. Neither Persius nor Juvenal were ignorant of this, for they had both studied Horace. And the thing itself is plainly true. But as they had read Horace, they had likewise read Lucilius, of whom Persius says *secuit urbem; . . . et genuinum fregit in illis:* meaning Mutius and Lupus; and Juvenal also mentions him in these words: *Ense velut stricto, quoties Lucilius ardens infremuit,* etc. So that they thought the imitation of Lucilius was more proper to their purpose than that of Horace. "They changed satire" (says Holyday), "but they changed it for the better; for the business being to reform great vices, chastisement goes further than admonition; whereas a perpetual grin, like that of Horace, does rather anger than amend a man."

Thus far that learned critic, Barten Holyday,[3] whose interpretation and illustrations of Juvenal are as excellent as the verse of his translation and his English are lame and pitiful. For 'tis not enough to give us the meaning of a poet, which I acknowledge him to have performed most faithfully, but he must also imitate his genius and his numbers, as far as the English will come up to the elegance of the original. In few words, 'tis only for a poet to translate a poem. Holyday and Stapylton[4] had not enough considered this, when they attempted Juvenal: but I forbear reflections; only I beg leave to take notice of this sentence, where Holyday says, "a perpetual grin, like that of Horace, rather angers than amends a man." I cannot give him up the manner of Horace in low satire so easily. Let the chastisement of Juvenal be never so necessary for his new kind of satire; let him declaim as wittily and sharply as he pleases; yet still the nicest and most delicate touches of satire consist in fine raillery. This, my lord, is your particular talent, to which even Juvenal could not arrive. 'Tis not reading, 'tis not imitation of an author, which can produce this fineness; it must be inborn; it must proceed from a genius, and particular way of thinking, which is not to be taught; and therefore not to be imitated by him who has it not from nature. How easy is it to call rogue and villain, and that wittily! But how hard to make a man appear a fool, a blockhead, or a knave, without using any of those opprobrious terms! To spare the grossness of the names, and to do the thing yet more severely, is to draw a full face, and to make the nose and cheeks stand out, and and yet not to employ any depth of shadowing. This is the mystery of that noble trade, which yet no master can teach to his apprentice; he may give the rules,

but the scholar is never the nearer in his practice. Neither is it true that this fineness of raillery is offensive. A witty man is tickled while he is hurt in this manner, and a fool feels it not. The occasion of an offense may possibly be given, but he cannot take it. If it be granted, that in effect this way does more mischief; that a man is secretly wounded, and though he be not sensible himself, yet the malicious world will find it out for him; yet there is still a vast difference betwixt the slovenly butchering of a man, and the fineness of a stroke that separates the head from the body, and leaves it standing in its place. A man may be capable, as Jack Ketch's[5] wife said of his servant, of a plain piece of work, a bare hanging; but to make a malefactor die sweetly was only belonging to her husband. I wish I could apply it to myself, if the reader would be kind enough to think it belongs to me. The character of Zimri[6] in my Absalom is, in my opinion, worth the whole poem: it is not bloody, but it is ridiculous enough; and he, for whom it was intended, was too witty to resent it as an injury. If I had railed, I might have suffered for it justly; but I managed my own work happily, perhaps more dexterously. I avoided the mention of great crimes, and applied myself to the representing of blindsides, and little extravagancies; to which, the wittier a man is, he is generally the more obnoxious.[7] It succeeded as I wished; the jest went round, and he laughed at it in his turn who began the frolic.

. . . .

'Tis but necessary, that after so much has been said of satire some definition of it should be given. Heinsius, in his dissertations on Horace, makes it for me, in these words: "Satire is a kind of poetry, without a series of action, invented for the purging of our minds; in which human vices, ignorance, and errors, and all things besides, which are produced from them in every man, are severely reprehended; partly dramatically, partly simply, and sometimes in both kinds of speaking; but, for the most part, figuratively, and occultly; consisting in a low familiar way, chiefly in a sharp and pungent manner of speech; but partly, also, in a facetious and civil way of jesting; by which either hatred or laughter, or indignation, is moved." Where I cannot

3 Holyday, an Oxford scholar, had produced translations of both Persius and Juvenal which Dryden comments on here and elsewhere.
4 Sir Robert Stapylton's translation of the First Six Satires of Juvenal appeared in 1644, and a complete version was published three years later.

5 Jack Ketch, the most famous public executioner of the century, whose barbarity was notorious.
6 Zimri, in Dryden's "Absalom and Achitophel," is the second Duke of Buckingham.
7 Exposed, vulnerable.

but observe, that this obscure and perplexed definition, or rather description, of satire, is wholly accommodated to the Horatian way; and excluding the works of Juvenal and Persius, as foreign from that kind of poem. The clause in the beginning of it, *without a series of action*, distinguishes satire properly from stage-plays, which are all of one action, and one continued series of action. The end or scope of satire is to purge the passions; so far it is common to the satires of Juvenal and Persius. The rest which follows is also belonging to all three; till he comes upon us, with the excluding clause, *consisting in a low familiar way of speech*, which is the proper character of Horace; and from which the other two, their honor be it spoken, are far distant. But how come lowness of style, and the familiarity of words, to be so much the propriety of satire, that without them a poet can be no more a satirist, than without risibility he can be a man? Is the fault of Horace to be made the virtue and standing rule of this poem? Is the *grande sophos* of Persius, and the sublimity of Juvenal, to be circumscribed with the meanness of words and vulgarity of expression? If Horace refused the pains of numbers, and the loftiness of figures, are they bound to follow so ill a precedent? Let him walk afoot, with his pad in his hand, for his own pleasure; but let not them be accounted no poets, who choose to mount, and show their horsemanship. Holyday is not afraid to say, that there was never such a fall, as from his odes to his satires, and that he, injuriously to himself, untuned his harp. The majestic way of Persius and Juvenal was new when they began it, but 'tis old to us; and what poems have not, with time, received an alteration in their fashion? "Which alteration," says Holyday, "is to aftertimes as good a warrant as the first." Has not Virgil changed the manners of Homer's heroes in his *Æneis?* Certainly he has, and for the better: for Virgil's age was more civilized and better bred, and he writ according to the politeness of Rome, under the reign of Augustus Cæsar, not to the rudeness of Agememnon's age, or the time of Homer. Why should we offer to confine free spirits to one form, when we cannot so much as confine our bodies to one fashion of apparel? Would not Donne's Satires, which abound with so much wit, appear more charming, if he had taken care of his words, and of his numbers? But he followed Horace so very close that of necessity he must fall with him; and I may safely say it of this present age, that if we are not so great wits, as Donne, yet certainly we are better poets.

But I have said enough, and it may be too much, on this subject. Will your lordship be pleased to prolong my audience, only so far, till I tell you my own trivial thoughts, how a modern satire should be made? I will not deviate in the least from the precepts and examples of the ancients, who were always our best masters. I will only illustrate them, and discover some of the hidden beauties in their designs, that we thereby may form our own in imitation of them. Will you please but to observe, that Persius, the least in dignity of all the three, has notwithstanding been the first who has discovered to us this important secret, in the designing of a perfect satire; that it ought only to treat of one subject; to be confined to one particular theme; or at least, to one principally. If other vices occur in the management of the chief, they should only be transiently lashed, and not be insisted on, so as to make the design double. As in a play of the English fashion, which we call a tragi-comedy, there is to be but one main design; and though there be an underplot, or second walk of comical characters and adventures, yet they are subservient to the chief fable, carried along under it, and helping to it; so that the drama may not seem a monster with two heads. Thus, the Copernican system of the planets makes the moon to be moved by the motion of the earth, and carried about her orb, as a dependent of hers. Mascardi, in his discourse of the *Doppia Favola*, or double tale in plays, gives an instance of it in the famous pastoral of Guarini, called *Il Pastor Fido;* where Corsica and the Satyr are the under parts; yet we may observe, that Corsica is brought into the body of the plot, and made subservient to it. 'Tis certain that the divine wit of Horace was not ignorant of this rule, that a play, though it consists of many parts, must yet be one in the action, and must drive on the accomplishment of one design; for he gives this very precept, *sit quodvis simplex duntaxat et unum;* yet he seems not much to mind it in his satires, many of them consisting of more arguments than one; and the second without dependence on the first. Casaubon has observed this before me, in his preference of Persius to Horace; and will have his own beloved author to be the first who found out and introduced this method of confining himself to one subject. I know it may be urged in defense of Horace that this unity is not necessary; because the very word *satura* signifies a dish plentifully stored with all variety of fruit and grains. Yet Juvenal, who calls his poems a *farrago*, which is a word of the same signification with *satura*, has chosen to follow the same method of Persius, and not of Horace; and Boileau, whose example alone is a sufficient authority, has wholly confined himself, in all his satires, to this unity of design. That variety, which is not to be found in any one satire, is, at least, in many, written on several occasions. And if variety be of absolute necessity in every one of them, according to the etymology of the word, yet it may arise naturally from one subject, as it is diversely treated, in the several subordinate branches of it, all relating to the chief. It may be illustrated accordingly with variety of examples in the subdivisions of it, and with as many precepts as there are members of it; which, altogether, may complete that *olla*, or hotchpotch, which is properly a satire.

Under this unity of theme, or subject, is comprehended another rule for perfecting the design of true satire. The poet is bound, and that *ex officio*, to give his reader some one precept of moral virtue, and to caution him against some one particular vice or folly. Other virtues, subordinate to the first, may be recommended under that chief head; and other vices or follies may be scourged, besides that which he principally intends. But he is chiefly to inculcate one virtue, and insist on that. Thus Juvenal, in every satire excepting the first, ties himself to one principal instructive point, or to the shunning of moral evil. Even in the sixth, which seems only an arraignment of the whole sex of womankind, there is a latent admonition to avoid ill women, by showing how very few, who are virtuous and good, are to be found amongst them. But this, though the wittiest of all his satires, has yet the least of truth or instruction in it. He has run himself into his old declamatory way, and almost forgotten that he was not setting up for a moral poet.

Persius is never wanting to us in some profitable doctrine, and in exposing the opposite vices to it. His kind of philosophy is one which is the stoic; and every satire is a comment on one particular dogma of that sect, unless we will except the first, which is against bad writers; and yet even there he forgets not the precepts of the Porch. In general, all virtues are everywhere to be praised and recommended to practice; and all vices to be reprehended, and made either odious or ridiculous; or else there is a fundamental error in the whole design.

I have already declared who are the only persons that are the adequate object of private satire, and who they are that may properly be exposed by name for public examples of vices and follies; and therefore I will trouble your lordship no further with them. Of the best and finest manner of satire, I have said enough in the comparison betwixt Juvenal and Horace: 'tis that sharp, well-mannered way of laughing a folly out of countenance, of which your lordship is the best master in this age. I will proceed to the versification which is most proper for it, and add somewhat to what I have said already on that subject. The sort of verse which is called *burlesque*, consisting of eight syllables, or four feet, is that which our excellent Hudibras has chosen. I ought to have mentioned him before, when I spoke of Donne; but by a slip of an old man's memory he was forgotten. The worth of his poem is too well known to need my commendation, and he is above my censure. His satire is of the Varronian kind, though unmixed with prose. The choice of his numbers is suitable enough to his design, as he has managed it; but in any other hand, the shortness of his verse, and the quick returns of rhyme, had debased the dignity of style. And besides, the double rhyme (a necessary companion of burlesque writing) is not so proper for manly satire; for it turns earnest too much to jest, and gives us a boyish kind of pleasure. It tickles awkwardly with a kind of pain, to the best sort of readers: we are pleased ungratefully, and, if I may say so, against our liking. We thank him not for giving us that unseasonable delight, when we know he could have given us a better, and more solid. He might have left that task to others, who, not being able to put in thought, can only make us grin with the excrescence of a word of two or three syllables in the close. 'Tis, indeed, below so great a master to make use of such a little instrument. But his good sense is perpetually shining through all he writes; it affords us not the time of finding faults. We pass through the levity of his rhyme, and are immediately carried into some admirable useful thought. After all, he has chosen this kind of verse, and has written the best in it: and had he taken another, he would always have excelled; as we say of a court favorite, that whatsoever his office be, he still makes it uppermost, and most beneficial to himself.

The quickness of your imagination, my lord, has already prevented me; and you know beforehand, that I would prefer the verse of ten syllables, which we call the English heroic, to that of eight. This is truly my opinion. For this sort of number is more roomy; the thought can turn itself with greater ease in a larger compass. When the rhyme comes too thick upon us, it straitens the expression; we are thinking of the close, when we should be employed in adorning the thought. It makes a poet giddy with turning in a space too narrow for his imagination; he loses many beauties, without gaining one advantage. For a burlesque rhyme I have already concluded to be none; or, if it were, 'tis more easily purchased in ten syllables than in eight. In both occasions 'tis as in a tennis-court, when the strokes of greater force are given, when we strike out and play at length. Tassoni and Boileau have left us the best examples of this way, in the *Secchia Rapita*,[8] and the *Lutrin;*[9] and next them Merlin Coccaius in his *Baldus*. I will speak only of the two former, because the last is written in Latin verse. The *Secchia Rapita* is an Italian poem, a satire of the Varronian kind. 'Tis written in the stanza of eight, which is their measure for heroic verse. The words are stately, the numbers smooth, the turn both of thought and words is happy. The first six lines of the stanza seem majestical and severe; but the two last turn them all into a pleasant ridicule. Boileau, if I am not much deceived, has modeled from hence his famous *Lutrin*. He had read the burlesque poetry of Scarron, with some kind of indignation, as witty as it was, and found nothing in France that was worthy of his imitation: but he copied the Italian so well that his own may pass for an original. He writes it in the French heroic verse, and calls it an heroic poem; his subject is trivial, but his verse is noble. I doubt not but he had Virgil in his eye, for we find many admirable imitations of him, and some parodies; as particularly this passage in the fourth of the Æneids—

Nec tibi diva parens, generis nec Dardanus auctor,
Perfide; sed duris genuit te cautibus horrens
Caucasus; Hyrcanæque admorunt ubera tigres:[10]

which he thus translates, keeping to the words, but altering the sense—

Non, ton père à Paris, ne fut point boulanger:
Et tu n'es point du sang de Gervais, l'horloger;
Ta mère ne fut point la maitresse d'un coche:
Caucase dans ses flancs te forma d'une roche:
Une tigresse affreuse, en quelque antre écart
Te fit, avec son lait, sucer sa cruauté.

8 *La Secchia Rapita* (The Stolen Bucket) was declared by its author, Alessandro Tassoni (1565–1635), to be the first modern mock-heroic piece.

9 Boileau's *Le Lutrin* (The Reading-Desk), 1674, is the most successful French example of the mock epic.

10 Neither a goddess mother was to thee,
    Nor Dardanus, the founder of thy race.
    Traitor! but bred thee, jagged with flinty cliffs,
    The Caucasus, and Hyrcanian tigresses
    Their dugs approached.
                    (Translation by R. C. Singleton.)

And, as Virgil in his fourth Georgic, of the bees, perpetually raises the lowness of his subject, by the loftiness of his words, and ennobles it by comparisons drawn from empires, and from monarchs—

Admiranda tibi levium spectacula rerum,
Magnanimosque duces totiusque ordine gentis
Mores et studia, et populos, et prælia dicam.[11]

and again—

At genus immortale manet; multosque per annos
Stat fortuna domus, et avi numeratur avorum;[12]

we see Boileau pursuing him in the same flights, and scarcely yielding to his master. This, I think, my lord, to be the most beautiful and most noble kind of satire. Here is the majesty of the heroic, finely mixed with the venom of the other; and raising the delight which otherwise would be flat and vulgar, by the sublimity of the expression. I could say somewhat more of the delicacy of this and some other of his satires; but it might turn to his prejudice, if 'twere carried back to France.

I have given your lordship but this bare hint, in what verse and in what manner this sort of satire may be best managed. Had I time, I could enlarge on the beautiful turns of words and thoughts which are as requisite in this as in heroic poetry itself, of which the satire is undoubtedly a species. With these beautiful turns I confess myself to have been unacquainted, till about twenty years ago, in a conversation which I had with that noble wit of Scotland, Sir George Mackenzie, he asked me why I did not imitate in my verses the turns of Mr. Waller and Sir John Denham, of which he repeated many to me. I had often read with pleasure, and with some profit, those two fathers of our English poetry, but had not seriously enough considered those beauties which gave the last perfection to their works. Some sprinklings of this kind I had also formerly in my plays; but they were casual, and not designed. But this hint, thus seasonably given to me, first made me sensible of my own wants, and brought me afterwards to seek for the supply of them in other English authors. I looked over the darling of my youth, the famous Cowley; there I found, instead of them, the points of

11   Shows of pigmy things,
    That claim thy wonder,—both the high-souled chiefs,
    And habits, and pursuits, and clans, and wars,
    Of a whole nation duly will I sing. (Singleton.)

12   Yet imperishable lasts
    The lineage, and stands firm through many a year
    The fortune of the house, and ancestors
    Of ancestors are counted. (*Ibid.*)

wit, and quirks of epigram, even in the Davideis, an heroic poem, which is of an opposite nature to those puerilities; but no elegant turns, either on the word or on the thought. Then I consulted a greater genius (without offense to the *manes* of that noble author), I mean Milton. But as he endeavors everywhere to express Homer, whose age had not arrived to that fineness, I found in him a true sublimity, lofty thoughts, which were clothed with admirable Grecisms, and ancient words, which he had been digging from the mines of Chaucer and Spenser, and which, with all their rusticity, had somewhat of venerable in them; but I found not there neither that for which I looked. At last I had recourse to his master, Spenser, the author of that immortal poem called the Fairy Queen; and there I met with that which I had been looking for so long in vain. Spenser had studied Virgil to as much advantage as Milton had done Homer; and amongst the rest of his excellencies had copied that. Looking farther into the Italian, I found Tasso had done the same; nay more, that all the sonnets in that language are on the turn of the first thought; which Mr. Walsh, in his late ingenious preface to his poems, has observed. In short, Virgil and Ovid are the two principal fountains of them in Latin poetry. And the French at this day are so fond of them, that they judge them to be the first beauties; *délicat et bien tourné* are the highest commendations which they bestow on somewhat which they think a masterpiece.

An example of the turn on words, amongst a thousand others, is that in the last book of Ovid's *Metamorphoses*—

> *Heu! quantum scelus est, in viscera, viscera condi!*
> *Congestoque avidum pinguescere corpore corpus;*
> *Alteriusque animantem animantis vivere leto.*

An example on the turn both of thoughts and words is to be found in Catullus, in the complaint of Ariadne, when she was left by Theseus—

> *Tum jam nulla viro juranti fœmina credat;*
> *Nulla viri speret sermones esse fideles;*
> *Qui, dum aliquid cupiens animus prægestit apisci,*
> *Nil metuunt jurare, nihil promittere parcunt:*
> *Sed simul ac cupidæ mentis satiata libido est,*
> *Dicta nihil metuere, nihil perjuria curant.*

An extraordinary turn upon the words is that in Ovid's *Epistolæ Heroidum*, of Sappho to Phaon—

> *Si, nisi quæ forma poterit te digna videri,*
> *Nulla futura tua est, nulla futura tua est.*

Lastly, a turn, which I cannot say is absolutely on words, for the thought turns with them, is in the fourth Georgic of Virgil, where Orpheus is to receive his wife from Hell, on express condition not to look on her till she was come on earth—

> *Cum subita incautum dementia cepit amantem;*
> *Ignoscenda quidem, scirent si ignoscere Manes.*[13]

I will not burthen your lordship with more of them; for I write to a master who understands them better than myself. But I may safely conclude them to be great beauties. I might descend also to the mechanic beauties of heroic verse; but we have yet no English *prosodia*, not so much as a tolerable dictionary or a grammar; so that our language is in a manner barbarous; and what government will encourage any one, or more, who are capable of refining it, I know not: but nothing under a public expense can go through with it. And I rather fear a declination of the language, than hope an advancement of it in the present age.

I am still speaking to you, my lord, though, in all probability, you are already out of hearing. Nothing which my meanness can produce is worthy of this long attention. But I am come to the last petition of Abraham; if there be ten righteous lines, in this vast preface, spare it for their sake; and also spare the next city, because it is but a little one.

I would excuse the performance of this translation, if it were all my own; but the better, though not the greater part, being the work of some gentlemen, who have succeeded very happily in their undertaking, let their excellencies atone for my imperfections, and those of my sons. I have perused some of the satires, which are done by other hands; and they seem to me as perfect in their kind as anything I have seen in English verse. The common way which we have taken is not a literal translation, but a kind of paraphrase; or somewhat, which is yet more loose, betwixt a paraphrase and imitation. It was not possible for us, or any men, to have made it pleasant any other way. If rendering the exact sense of those authors, almost line for line, had been our business, Barton Holyday had done it already to our hands: and by the help of his learned notes and illustrations not only of Juvenal and Persius, but what yet is more obscure, his own verses, might be understood.

13   When sudden madness seized
     The heedless lover,—pardonable sure,
     If Manes knew how to pardon. (Singleton.)

But he wrote for fame, and wrote to scholars; we write only for the pleasure and entertainment of those gentlemen and ladies, who, though they are not scholars, are not ignorant; persons of understanding and good sense, who, not having been conversant in the original, or at least not having made Latin verse so much their business as to be critics in it, would be glad to find if the wit of our two great authors be answerable to their fame and reputation in the world. We have, therefore, endeavored to give the public all the satisfaction we are able in this kind.

And if we are not altogether so faithful to our author, as our predecessors Holyday and Stapylton, yet we may challenge to ourselves this praise, that we shall be far more pleasing to our readers. We have followed our authors at greater distance, though not step by step, as they have done; and oftentimes they have gone so close, that they have trod on the heels of Juvenal and Persius, and hurt them by their too near approach. A noble author would not be pursued too close by a translator. We lose his spirit, when we think to take his body. The grosser part remains with us, but the soul is flown away in some noble expression, or some delicate turn of words, or thought. Thus Holyday, who made this way his choice, seized the meaning of Juvenal; but the poetry has always escaped him.

They who will not grant me that pleasure is one of the ends of poetry, but that it is only a means of compassing the only end, which is instruction, must yet allow, that, without the means of pleasure, the instruction is but a bare and dry philosophy; a crude preparation of morals which we may have from Aristotle and Epictetus, with more profit than from any poet. Neither Holyday nor Stapylton have imitated Juvenal in the poetical part of him, his diction and his elocution. Nor had they been poets, as neither of them were, yet, in the way they took, it was impossible for them to have succeeded in the poetic part.

The English verse, which we call heroic, consists of no more than ten syllables; the Latin hexameter sometimes rises to seventeen; as, for example, this verse in Virgil—

Pulverulenta putrem sonitu quatit ungula campum.

Here is the difference of no less than seven syllables in a line, betwixt the English and the Latin. Now the medium of these is about fourteen syllables; because the dactyl is a more frequent foot in hexameters than the spondee. But Holyday, without considering that he wrote with the disadvantage of four syllables less in every verse, endeavors to make one of his lines to comprehend the sense of one of Juvenal's. According to the falsity of the proposition was the success. He was forced to crowd his verse with ill-sounding monosyllables, of which our barbarous language affords him a wild plenty; and by that means he arrived at his pedantic end, which was to make a literal translation. His verses have nothing of verse in them, but only the worst part of it, the rhyme; and that, into the bargain, is far from good. But, which is more intolerable, by cramming his ill-chosen, and worse-sounding monosyllables so close together, the very sense which he endeavors to explain is become more obscure than that of his author; so that Holyday himself cannot be understood, without as large a commentary as that which he makes on his two authors. For my own part, I can make a shift to find the meaning of Juvenal without his notes; but his translation is more difficult than his author. And I find beauties in the Latin to recompense my pains; but, in Holyday and Stapylton, my ears, in the first place, are mortally offended; and then their sense is so perplexed, that I return to the original, as the more pleasing task, as well as the more easy.

This must be said for our translation, that, if we give not the whole sense of Juvenal, yet we give the most considerable part of it; we give it, in general, so clearly, that few notes are sufficient to make us intelligible. We make our author at least appear in a poetic dress. We have actually made him more sounding, and more eloquent, than he was before in English; and have endeavored to make him speak that kind of English which he would have spoken had he lived in England, and had written to this age. If sometimes any of us (and 'tis but seldom) make him express the customs and manners of our native country rather than of Rome, 'tis either when there was some kind of analogy betwixt their customs and ours, or when, to make him more easy to vulgar understandings, we give him those manners which are familiar to us. But I defend not this innovation, 'tis enough if I can excuse it. For to speak sincerely, the manners of nations and ages are not to be confounded; we should either make them English, or leave them Roman. If this can neither be defended nor excused, let it be pardoned, at least, because it is acknowledged; and so much the more easily, as being a fault which is never committed without some pleasure to the reader.

Thus, my lord, having troubled you with a tedious visit, the best manners will be shown in the least ceremony. I will slip away while your back is turned, and while you are otherwise employed; with great confusion for having entertained you so long with this discourse, and for having no other recompense to make you, than the worthy labors of my fellow-undertakers in this work, and the thankful acknowledgments, prayers, and perpetual good wishes, of,

My Lord,
    Your Lordship's
        Most obliged, most humble,
           And most obedient Servant,

Aug. 18, 1692   JOHN DRYDEN

PREFACE TO THE "FABLES"[1]

[TEXT: *first edition, 1700*]

'TIS with a poet, as with a man who designs to build, and is very exact as he supposes, in casting up the cost beforehand; but, generally speaking, he is mistaken in his account, and reckons short of the expense he first intended. He alters his mind as the work proceeds, and will have this or that convenience more, of which he had not thought when he began. So has it happened to me; I have built a house, where I intended but a lodge; yet with better success than a certain nobleman,[2] who, beginning with a dog-kennel, never lived to finish the palace he had contrived.

From translating the first of Homer's Iliads (which I intended as an essay to the whole work), I proceeded to the translation of the twelfth book of Ovid's *Metamorphoses*, because it contains, among other things, the causes, the beginning, and ending of the Trojan war. Here I ought in reason to have stopped; but the speeches of Ajax and Ulysses lying next in my way, I could not balk 'em. When I had compassed them, I was so taken with the former part of the fifteenth book (which is the masterpiece of the whole *Metamorphoses*), that I enjoined myself the pleasing task of rendering it into English. And now I found by the number of my verses, that they began to swell into a little volume; which gave me an occasion of looking backward on some beauties of my author, in his former books; there occurred to me the Hunting of the Boar, Cinyras and Myrrha, the good-natured story of Baucis and Philemon, with the rest, which I hope I have translated closely enough, and given them the same turn of verse which they had in the original; and this, I may say, without vanity, is not the talent of every poet. He who has arrived the nearest to it, is the ingenious and learned Sandys,[3] the best versifier of the former age; if I may properly call it by that name, which was the former part of this concluding century. For Spenser and Fairfax[4] both flourished in the reign of Queen Elizabeth; great masters in our language, and who saw much further into the beauties of our numbers than those who immediately followed them. Milton was the poetical son of Spenser, and Mr. Waller of Fairfax; for we have our lineal descents and clans as well as other families. Spenser more than once insinuates that the soul of Chaucer was transfused into his body; and that he was begotten by him two hundred years after his decease. Milton has acknowledged to me that Spenser was his original; and many besides myself have heard our famous Waller own that he derived the harmony of his numbers from Godfrey of Bouillon, which was turned into English by Mr. Fairfax.

But to return: having done with Ovid for this time, it came into my mind, that our old English poet, Chaucer, in many things resembled him, and that with no disadvantage on the side of the modern author, as I shall endeavor to prove when I compare them; and as I am, and always have been, studious to promote the honor of my native country, so I soon resolved to put their merits to the trial, by turning some of the Canterbury Tales into our language, as it is now refined; for by this means, both the poets being sent in the same light, and dressed in the same English habit, story to be compared with story, a certain judgment may be made betwixt them by the reader, without obtruding my

---

1 Fables Ancient and Modern, translated into verse, from Homer, Ovid, Boccace, and Chaucer; with Original Poems.

2 The Duke of Buckingham, the Zimri of Absalom and Achitophel. The palace is Cliveden.

3 George Sandys (1578–1644), translator of Ovid's Metamorphoses.

4 Edward Fairfax's translation of Tasso's Godfrey of Bouillon, or the Recovery of Jerusalem, was published in 1604.

opinion on him. Or, if I seem partial to my countryman and predecessor in the laurel, the friends of antiquity are not few; and, besides many of the learned, Ovid has almost all the beaux, and the whole fair sex, his declared patrons. Perhaps I have assumed somewhat more to myself than they allow me, because I have adventured to sum up the evidence; but the readers are the jury, and their privilege remains entire, to decide according to the merits of the cause; or, if they please, to bring it to another hearing before some other court. In the meantime, to follow the thread of my discourse (as thoughts, according to Mr. Hobbes, have always some connection), so from Chaucer I was led to think on Boccace, who was not only his contemporary, but also pursued the same studies; wrote novels in prose, and many works in verse; particularly is said to have invented the octave rhyme, or stanza of eight lines, which ever since has been maintained by the practice of all Italian writers who are, or at least assume the title of, heroic poets. He and Chaucer, among other things, had this in common, that they refined their mother-tongues; but with this difference, that Dante had begun to file their language, at least in verse, before the time of Boccace, who likewise received no little help from his master Petrarch; but the reformation of their prose was wholly owing to Boccace himself, who is yet the standard of purity in the Italian tongue, though many of his phrases are become obsolete, as in process of time it must needs happen. Chaucer (as you have formerly been told by our learned Mr. Rymer)[5] first adorned and amplified our barren tongue from the Provençal, which was then the most polished of all the modern languages; but this subject has been copiously treated by that great critic, who deserves no little commendation from us his countrymen. For these reasons of time, and resemblance of genius, in Chaucer and Boccace, I resolved to join them in my present work; to which I have added some original papers of my own, which whether they are equal or inferior to my other poems, an author is the most improper judge; and therefore I leave them wholly to the mercy of the reader. I will hope the best, that they will not be condemned; but if they should, I have the excuse of an old gentleman, who, mounting on horseback before some ladies, when I was present, got up somewhat heavily, but desired of the fair spectators, that they would count fourscore and eight

before they judged him. By the mercy of God, I am already come within twenty years of his number; a cripple in my limbs, but what decays are in my mind the reader must determine. I think myself as vigorous as ever in the faculties of my soul, excepting only my memory, which is not impaired to any great degree: and if I lose not more of it, I have no great reason to complain. What judgment I had, increases rather than diminishes; and thoughts, such as they are, come crowding in so fast upon me, that my only difficulty is to choose or to reject, to run them into verse, or to give them the other harmony of prose; I have so long studied and practiced both, that they are grown into a habit, and become familiar to me. In short, though I may lawfully plead some part of the old gentleman's excuse, yet I will reserve it till I think I have greater need, and ask no grains of allowance for the faults of this my present work, but those which are given of course to human frailty. I will not trouble my reader with the shortness of time in which I writ it, or the several intervals of sickness. They who think too well of their own performances are apt to boast in their prefaces how little time their works have cost them, and what other business of more importance interfered; but the reader will be as apt to ask the question, why they allowed not a longer time to make their work more perfect? and why they had so despicable an opinion of their judges as to thrust their indigested stuff upon them, as if they deserved no better?

With this account of my present undertaking, I conclude the first part of this discourse; in the second part, as at a second sitting, though I alter not the draft, I must touch the same features over again, and change the dead-coloring of the whole. In general I will only say, that I have written nothing which savors of immorality or profaneness; at least, I am not conscious to myself of any such intention. If there happen to be found an irreverent expression, or a thought too wanton, they are crept into my verses through my inadvertency; if the searchers find any in the cargo, let them be staved[6] or forfeited, like counterbanded goods; at least, let their authors be answerable for them, as being but imported merchandise, and not of my own manufacture. On the other side, I have endeavored to choose such fables, both ancient and modern, as contain in each of them some instructive moral; which I could prove by induction, but the way is tedious, and they leap foremost into sight without the reader's

---

5 Thomas Rymer, Historiographer Royal, published in 1693 his famous Short View of Tragedy, in which among other things he praised Chaucer and attacked Shakespeare.

6 Broken up into staves, like so many contraband hogsheads.

trouble of looking after them. I wish I could affirm, with a safe conscience, that I had taken the same care in all my former writings; for it must be owned, that supposing verses are never so beautiful or pleasing, yet, if they contain anything which shocks religion or good manners, they are at best what Horace says of good numbers without good sense, *Versus inopes rerum, nugæque canoræ.* Thus far, I hope, I am right in court, without renouncing to my other right of self-defense, where I have been wrongfully accused, and my sense wire-drawn into blasphemy or bawdry, as it has often been by a religious lawyer,[7] in a late pleading against the stage; in which he mixes truth with falsehood, and has not forgotten the old rule of calumniating strongly, that something may remain.

I resume the thread of my discourse with the first of my translations, which was the first Iliad of Homer. If it shall please God to give me longer life, and moderate health, my intentions are to translate the whole Ilias; provided still that I meet with those encouragements from the public, which may enable me to proceed in my undertaking with some cheerfulness. And this I dare assure the world beforehand, that I have found, by trial, Homer a more pleasing task than Virgil, though I say not the translation will be less laborious; for the Grecian is more according to my genius than the Latin poet. In the works of the two authors we may read their manners, and natural inclinations, which are wholly different. Virgil was of a quiet, sedate temper; Homer was violent, impetuous and full of fire. The chief talent of Virgil was propriety of thoughts, and ornaments of words; Homer was rapid in his thoughts, and took all the liberties, both of numbers and of expressions, which his language, and the age in which he lived, allowed him. Homer's invention was more copious, Virgil's more confined; so that if Homer had not led the way, it was not in Virgil to have begun heroic poetry; for nothing can be more evident than that the Roman poem is but the second part of the Ilias; a continuation of the same story, and the persons already formed. The manners of Æneas are those of Hector, superadded to those which Homer gave him. The adventures of Ulysses in the Odysseis are imitated in the first six books of Virgil's Æneis; and though the accidents are not the same (which would have argued him of a servile copying, and total barrenness of invention), yet the seas were the same in which both the heroes wandered; and Dido cannot be denied to be the poetical daughter of Calypso. The six latter books of Virgil's poem are the four-and-twenty Iliads contracted; a quarrel occasioned by a lady, a single combat, battles fought, and a town besieged. I say not this in derogation to Virgil, neither do I contradict anything which I have formerly said in his just praise; for his episodes are almost wholly of his own invention, and the form which he has given to the telling makes the tale his own, even though the original story had been the same. But this proves, however, that Homer taught Virgil to design; and if invention be the first virtue of an epic poet, then the Latin poem can only be allowed a second place. Mr. Hobbes, in the preface to his own bald translation of the Ilias (studying poetry as he did mathematics, when it was too late), Mr. Hobbes, I say, begins the praise of Homer where he should have ended it. He tells us, that the first beauty of an epic poem consists in diction; that is, in the choice of words, and harmony of numbers. Now the words are the coloring of the work, which, in the order of nature, is last to be considered. The design, the disposition, the manners, and the thoughts, are all before it; where any of those are wanting or imperfect, so much wants or is imperfect in the imitation of human life, which is in the very definition of a poem. Words, indeed, like glaring colors, are the first beauties that arise and strike the sight; but, if the draft be false or lame, the figures ill disposed, the manners obscure or inconsistent, or the thoughts unnatural, then the finest colors are but daubing, and the piece is a beautiful monster at the best. Neither Virgil nor Homer were deficient in any of the former beauties; but in this last, which is expression, the Roman poet is at least equal to the Grecian, as I have said elsewhere; supplying the poverty of his language by his musical ear, and by his diligence.

But to return; our two great poets being so different in their tempers, one choleric and sanguine, the other phlegmatic and melancholic; that which makes them excel in their several ways is, that each of them has followed his own natural inclination, as well in forming the design, as in the execution of it. The very heroes show their authors: Achilles is hot, impatient, revengeful—

Impiger, iracundus, inexorabilis, acer, etc.[8]

---

7 Jeremy Collier, whose Short View of the Immorality and Profaneness of the English Stage, 1698, is the most famous attack on the stage in the language.

8 Horace, *De Arte Poetica*, 121.

Æneas patient, considerate, careful of his people, and merciful to his enemies; ever submissive to the will of heaven—

> . . . *quo fata trahunt retrahuntque, sequamur.*

I could please myself with enlarging on this subject, but am forced to defer it to a fitter time. From all I have said, I will only draw this inference, that the action of Homer, being more full of vigor than that of Virgil, according to the temper of the writer, is of consequence more pleasing to the reader. One warms you by degrees; the other sets you on fire all at once, and never intermits his heat. 'Tis the same difference which Longinus makes betwixt the effects of eloquence in Demosthenes and Tully. One persuades, the other commands. You never cool while you read Homer, even not in the second book (a graceful flattery to his countrymen); but he hastens from the ships, and concludes not that book till he has made you an amends by the violent playing of a new machine. From thence he hurries on his action with variety of events, and ends it in less compass than two months. This vehemence of his, I confess, is more suitable to my temper; and, therefore, I have translated his first book with greater pleasure than any part of Virgil; but it was not a pleasure without pains. The continual agitations of the spirits must needs be a weakening of any constitution, especially in age; and many pauses are required for refreshment betwixt the heats; the Iliad of itself being a third part longer than all Virgil's works together.

This is what I thought needful in this place to say of Homer. I proceed to Ovid and Chaucer, considering the former only in relation to the latter. With Ovid ended the Golden Age of the Roman tongue; from Chaucer the purity of the English tongue began. The manners of the poets were not unlike. Both of them were well-bred, well-natured, amorous, and libertine, at least in their writings; it may be also in their lives. Their studies were the same, philosophy and philology.[9] Both of them were knowing in astronomy; of which Ovid's books of the Roman Feasts, and Chaucer's Treatise of the Astrolabe, are sufficient witnesses. But Chaucer was likewise an astrologer, as were Virgil, Horace, Persius, and Manilius. Both writ with wonderful facility and clearness; neither were great inventors: for Ovid only copied the Grecian fables, and most of Chaucer's stories were taken from his Italian

contemporaries, or their predecessors. Boccace his Decameron was first published, and from thence our Englishman has borrowed many of his Canterbury Tales;[10] yet that of Palamon and Arcite was written, in all probability, by some Italian wit, in a former age, as I shall prove hereafter. The tale of Griselda was the invention of Petrarch;[11] by him sent to Boccace, from whom it came to Chaucer. Troilus and Criseyde was also written by a Lombard author,[12] but much amplified by our English translator, as well as beautified; the genius of our countrymen, in general, being rather to improve an invention than to invent themselves, as is evident not only in our poetry, but in many of our manufactures. I find I have anticipated already, and taken up from Boccace before I come to him; but there is so much less behind; and I am of the temper of most kings, who love to be in debt, are all for present money, no matter how they pay it afterwards; besides, the nature of a preface is rambling, never wholly out of the way, not in it. This I have learned from the practice of honest Montaigne, and return at my pleasure to Ovid and Chaucer, of whom I have little more to say.

Both of them built on the inventions of other men; yet since Chaucer had something of his own, as The Wife of Bath's Tale, The Cock and the Fox,[13] which I have translated, and some others, I may justly give our countryman the precedence in that part; since I can remember nothing of Ovid which was wholly his. Both of them understood the manners, under which name I comprehend the passions, and, in a larger sense, the descriptions of persons, and their very habits. For an example, I see Baucis and Philemon as perfectly before me, as if some ancient painter had drawn them; and all the pilgrims in the Canterbury Tales, their humors, their features, and the very dress, as distinctly as if I had supped with them at the Tabard in Southwark. Yet even there, too, the figures of Chaucer are much more lively, and set in a better light; which though I have not time to prove, yet I appeal to the

9 Philology here has not its present meaning, but connotes the study of literature, and polite learning in general.

10 Modern scholarship is not in agreement with Dryden on this point.

11 Dryden is also in error here. Petrarch, as is now well known, took the story of Griselda from the last *novella* of the Decameron, and Chaucer borrows it from Petrarch, or from some French translation of Petrarch's version.

12 Chaucer refers to "myn auctor called Lollius," whom scholars are unable to identify. Boccaccio's *Filostrato* is his chief source.

13 Chaucer may have borrowed this story from some now unknown French version.

reader, and am sure he will clear me from partiality. The thoughts and words remain to be considered in the comparison of the two poets, and I have saved myself one half of that labor, by owning that Ovid lived when the Roman tongue was in its meridian; Chaucer, in the dawning of our language; therefore that part of the comparison stands not on an equal foot, any more than the diction of Ennius and Ovid, or of Chaucer and our present English. The words are given up, as a post not to be defended in our poet, because he wanted the modern art of fortifying. The thoughts remain to be considered; and they are to be measured only by their propriety; that is, as they flow more or less naturally from the persons described, on such and such occasions. The vulgar judges, which are nine parts in ten of all nations, who call conceits and jingles wit, who see Ovid full of them, and Chaucer altogether without them, will think me little less than mad for preferring the Englishman to the Roman. Yet, with their leave, I must presume to say, that the things they admire are only glittering trifles, and so far from being witty, that in a serious poem they are nauseous, because they are unnatural. Would any man who is ready to die for love describe his passion like Narcissus? Would he think of *inopem me copia fecit*,[14] and a dozen more of such expressions, poured on the neck of one another, and signifying all the same thing? If this were wit, was this a time to be witty, when the poor wretch was in the agony of death? This is just John Littlewit, in Bartholomew Fair, who had a conceit (as he tells you) left him in his misery; a miserable conceit. On these occasions the poet should endeavor to raise pity; but, instead of this, Ovid is tickling you to laugh. Virgil never made use of such machines when he was moving you to commiserate the death of Dido: he would not destroy what he was building. Chaucer makes Arcite violent in his love, and unjust in the pursuit of it; yet when he came to die, he made him think more reasonably; he repents not of his love, for that had altered his character; but acknowledges the injustice of his proceedings, and resigns Emilia to Palamon. What would Ovid have done on this occasion? He would certainly have made Arcite witty on his deathbed; he had complained he was further off from possession, by being so near, and a thousand such boyisms, which Chaucer rejected as below the dignity of the subject. They who think otherwise, would, by the same reason, prefer Lucan and Ovid to Homer and

Virgil, and Martial to all four of them. As for the turn of words, in which Ovid particularly excels all poets, they are sometimes a fault, and sometimes a beauty, as they are used properly or improperly; but in strong passions always to be shunned, because passions are serious, and will admit no playing. The French have a high value for them; and, I confess, they are often what they call delicate, when they are introduced with judgment; but Chaucer writ with more simplicity, and followed nature more closely than to use them. I have thus far, to the best of my knowledge, been an upright judge betwixt the parties in competition, not meddling with the design nor the disposition of it; because the design was not their own; and in the disposing of it they were equal. It remains that I say somewhat of Chaucer in particular.

In the first place, as he is the father of English poetry, so I hold him in the same degree of veneration as the Grecians held Homer, or the Romans Virgil. He is a perpetual fountain of good sense; learned in all sciences; and, therefore, speaks properly on all subjects. As he knew what to say, so he knows also when to leave off; a continence which is practiced by few writers, and scarcely by any of the ancients, excepting Virgil and Horace. One of our late great poets[15] is sunk in his reputation, because he could never forgive any conceit which came in his way; but swept like a drag-net, great and small. There was plenty enough, but the dishes were ill sorted; whole pyramids of sweet-meats for boys and women, but little of solid meat for men. All this proceeded not from any want of knowledge, but of judgment. Neither did he want that in discerning the beauties and faults of other poets, but only indulged himself in the luxury of writing; and perhaps knew it was a fault, but hoped the reader would not find it. For this reason, though he must always be thought a great poet, he is no longer esteemed a good writer; and for ten impressions which his works have had in so many successive years, yet at present a hundred books are scarcely purchased once a twelvemonth; for, as my last Lord Rochester said, though somewhat profanely, Not being of God, he could not stand.

Chaucer followed nature everywhere, but was never so bold to go beyond her; and there is a great difference of being *poeta* and *nimis poeta*, if we may believe Catullus,[16] as much as betwixt a modest behavior and

14 Ovid, Metamorphoses, iii. 466.

15 Abraham Cowley.
16 Dryden is nodding here. He has in mind Martial's line, *Quid sit scire cupis: nimis poeta es.*" (Epigrams, iii. 44.)

affectation. The verse of Chaucer, I confess, is not harmonious to us; but 'tis like the eloquence of one whom
Tacitus commends, it was *auribus istius temporis accommodata:* they who lived with him, and some time after
him, thought it musical; and it continues so, even in
our judgment, if compared with the numbers of Lid-
gate and Gower, his contemporaries; there is the rude
sweetness of a Scotch tune in it, which is natural and
pleasing, though not perfect. 'Tis true, I cannot go so
far as he who published the last edition of him;[17] for
he would make us believe the fault is in our ears, and
that there were really ten syllables in a verse where we
find but nine; but this opinion is not worth confuting;
'tis so gross and obvious an error, that common sense
(which is a rule in everything but matters of faith and
revelation) must convince the reader, that equality of
numbers, in every verse which we call heroic, was
either not known, or not always practiced, in Chaucer's age. It were an easy matter to produce some
thousands of his verses, which are lame for want of half
a foot, and sometimes a whole one, and which no pronunciation can make otherwise. We can only say, that
he lived in the infancy of our poetry, and that nothing
is brought to perfection at the first. We must be children before we grow men. There was an Ennius, and in
process of time a Lucilius, and a Lucretius before Virgil
and Horace; even after Chaucer there was a Spenser, a
Harington,[18] a Fairfax, before Waller and Denham
were in being; and our numbers were in their nonage
till these last appeared. I need say little of his parentage,
life, and fortunes; they are to be found at large in all the
editions of his works. He was employed abroad, and
favored, by Edward the Third, Richard the Second,
and Henry the Fourth, and was poet, as I suppose, to
all three of them. In Richard's time, I doubt, he was a
little dipped in the rebellion of the Commons; and
being brother-in-law to John of Gaunt, it was no wonder if he followed the fortunes of that family; and was
well with Henry the Fourth when he had deposed his
predecessor. Neither is it to be admired, that Henry,
who was a wise as well as a valiant prince, who claimed
by succession, and was sensible that his title was not

17 It is but fair to Dryden to remember that, in the edition
of Chaucer with which he was familiar, the final *e* in most of
the words was omitted, so that he was not aware of the
melodious quality of Chaucer's verses as the poet wrote them,
and as we have them today. The edition he refers to is that of
Thomas Speght, reprinted 1687.
18 Sir John Harington, whose translation of Ariosto's
Orlando Furioso was published in 1591.

sound, but was rightfully in Mortimer, who had married the heir of York; it was not to be admired, I say,
if that great politician should be pleased to have the
greatest wit of those times in his interests, and to be
the trumpet of his praises. Augustus had given him the
example, by the advice of Mæcenas, who recommended Virgil and Horace to him; whose praises helped to
make him popular while he was alive, and after his
death have made him precious to posterity. As for the
religion of our poet, he seems to have some little bias
towards the opinions of Wycliffe, after John of Gaunt
his patron; somewhat of which appears in the tale
of Piers Plowman; yet I cannot blame him for inveighing so sharply against the vices of the clergy in
his age; their pride, their ambition, their pomp, their
avarice, their worldly interest, deserved the lashes
which he gave them, both in that, and in most of his
Canterbury Tales. Neither has his contemporary Boccace spared them: yet both those poets lived in much
esteem with good and holy men in orders; for the
scandal which is given by particular priests reflects not
on the sacred function. Chaucer's Monk, his Canon,
and his Friar, took not from the character of his Good
Parson. A satirical poet is the check of the laymen on
bad priests. We are only to take care that we involve
not the innocent with the guilty in the same condemnation. The good cannot be too much honored, nor
the bad too coarsely used; for the corruption of the
best becomes the worst. When a clergyman is whipped,
his gown is first taken off, by which the dignity of his
order is secured. If he be wrongfully accused, he has
his action of slander; and 'tis at the poet's peril if he
transgress the law. But they will tell us, that all kind of
satire, though never so well deserved by particular
priests, yet brings the whole order into contempt. Is
then the peerage of England anything dishonored when
a peer suffers for his treason? If he be libeled, or any
way defamed, he has his *scandalum magnatum* to punish
the offender. They who use this kind of argument,
seem to be conscious to themselves of somewhat
which has deserved the poet's lash, and are less concerned for their public capacity than for their private;
at least there is pride at the bottom of their reasoning.
If the faults of men in orders are only to be judged
among themselves, they are all in some sort parties;
for, since they say the honor of their order is concerned in every member of it, how can we be sure that
they will be impartial judges? How far I may be allowed to speak my opinion in this case, I know not;
but I am sure a dispute of this nature caused mischief

in abundance betwixt a King of England and an Archbishop of Canterbury; one standing up for the laws of
his land, and the other for the honor (as he called it) of
God's church; which ended in the murder of the prelate, and in the whipping of his Majesty from post to
pillar for his penance. The learned and ingenious Dr.
Drake has saved me the labor of inquiring into the
esteem and reverence which the priests have had of old;
and I would rather extend than diminish any part of it;
yet I must needs say, that when a priest provokes me
without any occasion given him, I have no reason, unless it be the charity of a Christian, to forgive him: *prior
læsit* is justification sufficient in the civil law. If I
answer him in his own language, self-defense I am
sure must be allowed me; and if I carry it further, even
to a sharp recrimination, somewhat may be indulged
to human frailty. Yet my resentment has not wrought
so far but that I have followed Chaucer in his character
of a holy man, and have enlarged on that subject with
some pleasure; reserving to myself the right, if I shall
think fit hereafter, to describe another sort of priests,
such as are more easily to be found than the Good
Parson; such as have given the last blow to Christianity in this age by a practice so contrary to their doctrine. But this will keep cold till another time. In the
meanwhile, I take up Chaucer where I left him.

He must have been a man of a most wonderful comprehensive nature, because, as it has been truly observed of him, he has taken into the compass of his
Canterbury Tales the various manners and humors (as
we now call them) of the whole English nation, in his
age. Not a single character has escaped him. All his
pilgrims are severally distinguished from each other;
and not only in their inclinations but in their very
physiognomies and persons. Baptista Porta [19] could not
have described their natures better, than by the marks
which the poet gives them. The matter and manner of
their tales, and of their telling, are so suited to their
different educations, humors, and callings, that each
of them would be improper in any other mouth. Even
the grave and serious characters are distinguished by
their several sorts of gravity: their discourses are such
as belong to their age, their calling, and their breeding;
such as are becoming of them, and of them only.
Some of his persons are vicious, and some virtuous;
some are unlearned, or (as Chaucer calls them) lewd,
and some are learned. Even the ribaldry of the low
characters is different: the Reeve, the Miller, and the
Cook, are several men, and distinguished from each

19 The famous Italian physiognomist (1538–1615).

other as much as the mincing Lady-Prioress and the
broad-speaking, gap-toothed Wife of Bath. But
enough of this; there is such a variety of game springing up before me, that I am distracted in my choice,
and know not which to follow. 'Tis sufficient to say, according to the proverb, that here is God's plenty. We
have our forefathers and great-grand-dames all before
us, as they were in Chaucer's days: their general characters are still remaining in mankind, and even in England, though they are called by other names than those
of monks, and friars, and canons, and lady-abbesses,
and nuns; for mankind is ever the same, and nothing
lost out of nature, though everything is altered. May I
have leave to do myself the justice (since my enemies
will do me none, and are so far from granting me to be
a good poet, that they will not allow me so much as to
be a Christian, or a moral man), may I have leave, I
say, to inform my reader, that I have confined my
choice to such tales of Chaucer as savor nothing of im-
modesty. If I had desired more to please than to instruct, the Reeve, the Miller, the Shipman, the Merchant, the Sumner, and, above all, the Wife of Bath, in
the prologue to her tale, would have procured me as
many friends and readers as there are beaux and ladies
of pleasure in the town. But I will no more offend
against good manners: I am sensible as I ought to be of
the scandal I have given by my loose writings; and
make what reparation I am able, by this public acknowledgment. If anything of this nature, or of profaneness
be crept into these poems, I am so far from defending
it, that I disown it. *Totum hoc indictum volo.* Chaucer
makes another manner of apology for his broad speaking, and Boccace makes the like, but I will follow
neither of them. Our countryman, in the end of
his Characters, before the Canterbury Tales, thus
excuses the ribaldry, which is very gross in many of
his novels—

> But firste, I pray you, of your courtesy,
> That ye ne arrete it not my villany,
> Though that I plainly speak in this mattere,
> To tellen you her words, and eke her chere;
> Ne though I speak her words properly,
> For this ye knowen as well as I,
> Who shall tellen a tale after a man,
> He mote rehearse as nye as ever he can:
> Everich word of it ben in his charge,
> All speke he, never so rudely, ne large:
> Or else he mote tellen his tale untrue,
> Or feine things, or find words new:
> He may not spare, altho he were his brother,
> He mote as wel say o word as another.

Crist spake himself full broad in holy Writ
And well I wote no villany is it,
Eke Plato saith, who so can him rede,
The words mote been cousin to the dede.[20]

Yet if a man should have enquired of Boccace or of Chaucer, what need they had of introducing such characters, where obscene words were proper in their mouths, but very indecent to be heard, I know not what answer they could have made; for that reason, such tales shall be left untold by me. You have here a specimen of Chaucer's language, which is so obsolete that his sense is scarce to be understood; and you have likewise more than one example of his unequal numbers, which were mentioned before. Yet many of his verses consist of ten syllables, and the words not much behind our present English; as for example, these two lines, in the description of the Carpenter's young wife—

Wincing she was, as is a jolly colt,
Long as a mast, and upright as a bolt.[21]

I have almost done with Chaucer, when I have answered some objections relating to my present work. I find some people are offended that I have turned these tales into modern English; because they think them unworthy of my pains, and look on Chaucer as a dry, old-fashioned wit, not worth reviving. I have often heard the late Earl of Leicester say, that Mr. Cowley himself was of that opinion; who, having read him over at my lord's request, declared he had no taste of him. I dare not advance my opinion against the judgment of so great an author; but I think it fair, however, to leave the decision to the public. Mr. Cowley was too modest to set up for a dictator, and being shocked perhaps with his old style, never examined into the depth of his good sense. Chaucer, I confess, is a rough diamond, and must first be polished, ere he shines. I deny not likewise, that, living in our early days of poetry, he writes not always of a piece; but sometimes mingles trivial things with those of greater moment. Sometimes also, though not often, he runs riot, like Ovid, and knows not when he has said enough. But there are more great wits besides Chaucer whose fault is their excess of conceits, and those ill sorted. An author is not to write all he can, but only all he ought. Having observed this redundancy in Chaucer (as it is an easy matter for a man of ordinary parts to find a fault in one of

greater), I have not tied myself to a literal translation; but have often omitted what I judged unnecessary, or not of dignity enough to appear in the company of better thoughts. I have presumed further, in some places, and added somewhat of my own where I thought my author was deficient, and had not given his thoughts their true luster, for want of words in the beginning of our language. And to this I was the more emboldened, because (if I may be permitted to say it myself) I found I had a soul congenial to his, and that I had been conversant in the same studies. Another poet, in another age, may take the same liberty with my writings; if at least they live long enough to deserve correction. It was also necessary sometimes to restore the sense of Chaucer, which was lost or mangled in the errors of the press. Let this example suffice at present; in the story of Palamon and Arcite, where the temple of Diana is described, you find these verses, in all the editions of our author:

There saw I Danè turned unto a tree,
I mean not the goddess Diane,
But Venus daughter, which that hight Danè.[22]

Which, after a little consideration, I knew was to be reformed into this sense, that Daphne, the daughter of Peneus, was turned into a tree. I durst not make thus bold with Ovid, lest some future Milbourne[23] should arise, and say, I varied from my author, because I understood him not.

But there are other judges, who think I ought not to have translated Chaucer into English, out of a quite contrary notion; they suppose there is a certain veneration due to his old language; and that it is little less than profanation and sacrilege to alter it. They are farther of opinion, that somewhat of his good sense will suffer in this transfusion, and much of the beauty of his thoughts will infallibly be lost, which appear with more grace in their old habit. Of this opinion was that excellent person, whom I mentioned, the late Earl of Leicester, who valued Chaucer as much as Mr. Cowley despised him. My lord dissuaded me from this attempt (for I was thinking of it for some years before his death), and his authority prevailed so far with me, as to defer my undertaking while he lived, in deference to him: yet my reason was not convinced with what he urged against it. If the first end of a writer be to be

20 Prologue to the Canterbury Tales, lines 725–42.
21 The Miller's Tale, lines 77–78.

22 The Knight's Tale, lines 1204–06.
23 Luke Milbourne published in 1698 a fierce attack, running to more than 200 pages, entitled Notes on Dryden's Virgil.

understood, then, as his language grows obsolete, his thoughts must grow obscure:

Multa renascentur, quæ nunc cecidere; cadentque
Quæ nunc sunt in honore vocabula, si volet usus,
Quem penes arbitrium est et jus et norma loquendi.[24]

When an ancient word, for its sound and significancy, deserves to be revived, I have that reasonable veneration for antiquity to restore it. All beyond this is superstition. Words are not like landmarks, so sacred as never to be removed; customs are changed, and even statutes are silently repealed, when the reason ceases for which they were enacted. As for the other part of the argument, that his thoughts will lose of their original beauty by the innovation of words; in the first place, not only their beauty, but their being is lost, where they are no longer understood, which is the present case. I grant that something must be lost in all transfusion, that is, in all translations; but the sense will remain, which would otherwise be lost, or at least be maimed, when it is scarce intelligible, and that but to a few. How few are there who can read Chaucer, so as to understand him perfectly! And if imperfectly, then with less profit, and no pleasure. 'Tis not for the use of some old Saxon friends,[25] that I have taken these pains with him: let them neglect my version, because they have no need of it. I made it for their sakes who understand sense and poetry as well as they, when that poetry and sense is put into words which they understand. I will go farther, and dare to add, that what beauties I lose in some places, I give to others which had them not originally: but in this I may be partial to myself; let the reader judge, and I submit to his decision. Yet I think I have just occasion to complain of them, who because they understand Chaucer, would deprive the greater part of their countrymen of the same advantage, and hoard him up, as misers do their grandam gold, only to look on it themselves, and hinder others from making use of it. In sum I seriously protest, that no man ever had, or can have, a greater veneration for Chaucer than myself. I have translated some part of his works, only that I might perpetuate his memory, or at least refresh it, amongst my countrymen. If I have altered him anywhere for the better, I must at the same time acknowledge, that I could have done nothing without him. *Facile est inventis addere* is no great commendation; and I am not so vain to think I deserved a greater. I will conclude what I have to say of him singly, with this one remark: a lady of my acquaintance who keeps a kind of correspondence with some authors of the fair sex in France, has been informed by them, that Mademoiselle de Scudery, who is as old as Sibyl, and inspired like her by the same God of Poetry, is at this time translating Chaucer into modern French. From which I gather, that he has been formerly translated into the old Provencal; for how she should come to understand Old English, I know not. But the matter of fact being true, it makes me think that there is something in it like fatality; that, after certain periods of time, the fame and memory of great wits should be renewed, as Chaucer is both in France and England. If this be wholly chance, 'tis extraordinary; and I dare not call it more, for fear of being taxed with superstition.

Boccace comes last to be considered, who, living in the same age with Chaucer, had the same genius, and followed the same studies. Both writ novels, and each of them cultivated his mother-tongue. But the greatest resemblance of our two modern authors being in their familiar style, and pleasing way of relating comical adventures, I may pass it over, because I have translated nothing from Boccace of that nature. In the serious part of poetry, the advantage is wholly on Chaucer's side; for though the Englishman has borrowed many tales from the Italian, yet it appears that those of Boccace were not generally of his own making, but taken from authors of former ages, and by him modeled; so that what there was of invention, in either of them, may be judged equal. But Chaucer has refined on Boccace, and has mended the stories which he has borrowed, in his way of telling; though prose allows more liberty of thought, and the expression is more easy when unconfined by numbers. Our countryman carries weight, and yet wins the race at disadvantage. I desire not the reader should take my word; and, therefore, I will set two of their discourses, on the same subject, in the same light, for every man to judge betwixt them. I translated Chaucer first, and, amongst the rest, pitched on The Wife of Bath's Tale; not daring, as I have said, to adventure on her Prologue, because 'tis too licentious. There Chaucer introduces an old woman, of mean parentage, whom a youthful knight, of noble blood, was forced to marry, and consequently loathed her. The crone being in bed with him on the wedding-night and finding his aversion,

24 Full many a word, now lost, again shall rise,
     And many a word shall droop which now we prize,
     As shifting fashion stamps the doom of each,
     Sole umpire, arbitress, and guide of speech.
     (Horace, *De Arte Poetica*, 70–72; Howes's translation.)
25 Friends who were acquainted with Old English.

endeavors to win his affection by reason, and speaks a good word for herself (as who could blame her?) in hope to mollify the sullen bridegroom. She takes her topics from the benefits of poverty, the advantages of old age and ugliness, the vanity of youth, and the silly pride of ancestry and titles, without inherent virtue, which is the true nobility. When I had closed Chaucer, I returned to Ovid, and translated some more of his fables; and, by this time, had so far forgotten The Wife of Bath's Tale, that, when I took up Boccace unawares I fell on the same argument, of preferring virtue to nobility of blood and titles, in the story of Sigismonda; which I had certainly avoided, for the resemblance of the two discourses, if my memory had not failed me. Let the reader weigh them both; and, if he thinks me partial to Chaucer, 'tis in him to right Boccace.

I prefer, in our countryman, far above all his other stories, the noble poem of Palamon and Arcite, which is of the epic kind, and perhaps not much inferior to the Ilias or the Æneis. The story is more pleasing than either of them, the manners as perfect, the diction as poetical, the learning as deep and various, and the disposition full as artful; only it includes a greater length of time, as taking up seven years at least; but Aristotle has left undecided the duration of the action; which yet is easily reduced into the compass of a year by a narration of what preceded the return of Palamon to Athens. I had thought, for the honor of our narration, and more particularly for his, whose laurel, though unworthy, I have worn after him, that this story was of English growth, and Chaucer's own; but I was undeceived by Boccace; for, casually looking on the end of his seventh *Giornata*, I found Dioneo (under which name he shadows himself), and Fiametta (who represents his mistress, the natural daughter of Robert, King of Naples), of whom these words are spoken: *Dioneo e Fiametta gran pezzo cantarono insieme d'Arcita, e di Palemone;* by which it appears, that this story was written before the time of Boccace but the name of its author being wholly lost, Chaucer is now become an original; and I question not but the poem has received many beauties by passing through his noble hands. Besides this tale there is another of his own invention, after the manner of the Provençals, called The Flower and the Leaf,[26] with which I was so particularly pleased, both for the invention and the moral, that I cannot hinder myself from recommending it to the reader.

As a corollary to this preface, in which I have done

26 Modern scholarship has shown that The Flower and the Leaf is not Chaucer's work.

justice to others, I owe somewhat to myself; not that I think it worth my time to enter the lists with one M——, or one B——, but barely to take notice, that such men there are, who have written scurrilously against me, without any provocation. M——, who is in orders, pretends, amongst the rest, this quarrel to me, that I have fallen foul on priesthood: if I have, I am only to ask pardon of good priests, and am afraid his part of the reparation will come to little. Let him be satisfied, that he shall not be able to force himself upon me for an adversary. I contemn him too much to enter into competition with him. His own translations of Virgil have answered his criticisms on mine. If (as they say he has declared in print) he prefers the version of Ogilby to mine, the world has made him the same compliment; for 'tis agreed, on all hands, that he writes even below Ogilby. That, you will say, is not easily to be done; but what cannot M—— bring about? I am satisfied, however, that, while he and I live together, I shall not be thought the worst poet of the age. It looks as if I had desired him underhand to write so ill against me; but upon my honest word I have not bribed him to do me this service, and am wholly guiltless of his pamphlet. 'Tis true, I should be glad if I could persuade him to continue his good offices, and write such another critique on anything of mine; for I find, by experience, he has a great stroke with the reader, when he condemns any of my poems, to make the world have a better opinion of them. He has taken some pains with my poetry; but nobody will be persuaded to take the same with his. If I had taken to the church, as he affirms, but which was never in my thoughts, I should have had more sense, if not more grace, than to have turned myself out of my benefice by writing libels on my parishioners. But his account of my manners and my principles are of a piece with his cavils and his poetry; and so I have done with him forever.

As for the city bard, or knight physician, I hear his quarrel to me is, that I was the author of Absalom and Achitophel, which, he thinks, is a little hard on his fanatic patrons in London.

But I will deal the more civilly with his two poems, because nothing ill is to be spoken of the dead; and therefore peace be to the *manes* of his Arthurs. I will only say, that it was not for this noble knight that I drew the plan of an epic poem on King Arthur, in my preface to the translation of Juvenal. The guardian angels of kingdoms were machines too ponderous for him to manage; and therefore he rejected them, as

Dares did the whirl-bats of Eryx when they were thrown before him by Entellus: yet from that preface, he plainly took his hint; for he began immediately upon the story, though he had the baseness not to acknowledge his benefactor, but instead of it, to traduce me in a libel.

I shall say the less of Mr. Collier, because in many things he has taxed me justly; and I have pleaded guilty to all thoughts and expressions of mine which can be truly argued of obscenity, profaneness, or immorality, and retract them. If he be my enemy, let him triumph; if he be my friend, as I have given him no personal occasion to be otherwise, he will be glad of my repentance. It becomes me not to draw my pen in the defense of a bad cause, when I have so often drawn it for a good one. Yet it were not difficult to prove, that in many places he had perverted my meaning by his glosses, and interpreted my words into blasphemy and bawdry, of which they were not guilty. Besides that, he is too much given to horse-play in his raillery, and comes to battle like a dictator from the plow. I will not say, "The zeal of God's house has eaten him up"; but I am sure it has devoured some part of his good manners and civility. It might also be doubted, whether it were altogether zeal which prompted him to this rough manner of proceeding; perhaps it became not one of his functions to rake into the rubbish of ancient and modern plays: a divine might have employed his pains to better purpose, than in the nastiness of Plautus and Aristophanes, whose examples, as they excuse not me, so it might be possibly supposed that he read them not without some pleasure. They who have written commentaries on those poets, or on Horace, Juvenal, and Martial, have explained some vices which, without their interpretation, had been unknown to modern times. Neither has he judged impartially betwixt the former age and us. There is more bawdry in one play of Fletcher's called The Custom of the Country, than in all ours together. Yet this has been often acted on the stage in my remembrance. Are the times so much more reformed now than they were five-and-twenty years ago? If they are, I congratulate the amendment of our morals. But I am not to prejudice the cause of my fellow poets, though I abandon my own defense: they have some of them answered for themselves; and neither they nor I can think Mr. Collier so formidable an enemy that we should shun him. He has lost ground, at the latter end of the day, by pursuing his point too far, like the Prince of Condé, at the battle of Senneph: from immoral plays to no plays, *ab abusu ad usum, non valet consequentia.* But, being a party, I am not to erect myself into a judge. As for the rest of those who have written against me, they are such scoundrels, that they deserve not the least notice to be taken of them. B—— and M—— are only distinguished from the crowd by being remembered to their infamy:

> . . . *Demetri, teque, Tigelli,*
> *Discipulorum inter jubeo plorare cathedras.*[27]

27 You, Demetrius and Tigellius, I bid go weep amidst the chairs of your pupils. (Horace, Satires, I. x. 90, 91.)

Anthony à Wood

[1632–1695]

WOOD was, like Burton, an Oxonian recluse, and, like Aubrey, an impassioned searcher after biographical facts, but he is a less attractive person and a less vigorous writer than either his great precursor or his busy contemporary. Massive accumulation of fact, rather than stylistic felicity or artistic form, gives his voluminous works their abiding value for the student of history or letters; the cranky, compulsive antiquarian who compiled them is almost lost behind his own piles of data.

Wood was born near Merton College, Oxford, and educated at that college; he spent his entire life in and around Oxford, died in the house in which he had been born, and was buried in Merton College Chapel. Not gifted with either gentleness or tact, he had few friends, and the same tactlessness reveals itself in his great biographical work, *Athenæ Oxonienses*, which aroused, in its outspoken comments on some of its subjects, a veritable storm of outrage and fury in some Oxford quarters. Indeed, some of Wood's observations on the Lord Chancellor Clarendon led to a lawsuit, the result of which was the public burning of certain portions of the work.

Three great works came from Wood's tireless efforts. The first is his *History and Antiquities of Oxon* (1669); the next is his most important work, the *Athenæ Oxonienses*, an account of all Oxford graduates who had distinguished themselves in any way. The third is his autobiography, on which he worked to the time of his death, an untidy but vivid work which gives us our clearest picture of the author himself.

The *Athenæ* is Wood's chief claim to fame. The brief lives contained in it are stiffer, less flexible than Aubrey's, and they supply more facts, but the living human being seldom emerges as vividly as in Aubrey's work. Nevertheless, the *Athenæ* is an impressive achievement, invaluable for a knowledge of seventeenth-century Oxford.

A. à WOOD. *Athenæ Oxonienses*, ed. P. Bliss, 4 vols. (Oxford, 1848).

————. *Life and Times*, collected from his diaries and other papers by A. Clark, 5 vols. (Oxford, 1891–1900).

————. *Life and Times*, intr. L. Powys (London, 1932). An abridged version of the preceding.

ATHENÆ OXONIENSES

[TEXT: *first edition, folio, 1692*]

EDWARD KELLEY, otherwise Talbot, was born in the City of Worcester at about 4 of the clock in the afternoon on the first day of Aug., 1555 (3 of Q. Mary), whose nativity being afterwards calculated, it did appear that he was born to be a man of clear understanding, quick apprehension, of an excellent wit, and of great propensity to philosophical studies and the mysteries of nature. This person, being about 17 years of age, at which time he had attained to a competency of grammar learning at Worcester and elsewhere, was sent to Oxon but to what house I cannot tell. . . .

Kelley having an unsettled mind left Oxon abruptly without being entered into the *matricula*, and in his rambles in Lancashire committing certain foul matters, lost both his ears at Lancaster, and about that time caused by his incantations a poor man that had been buried in the yard belonging to Lawchurch, near to Walton-in-the-Dale, to be taken out of his grave and to answer such questions that he then proposed to him. The story of which being to me incredible I shall refer you to the writer of it,[1] who is too credulous in many matters. About that time our author Kelley became intimate with Dr. John Dee, the famous mathematician, with whom continuing several years in philosophical studies and chemical experiments, they both became very famous among scholars and therefore noted by persons of high and noble extraction, one for the mathematics and the other for chemistry; for though Dee was the most eminent man of his time for the first, yet Kelley went far beyond him in the latter, as by the sequel it will appear. 'Tis reported by a certain Rosicrucian[2] that they were so strangely fortunate as to find a very large quantity of the *elixir* in some part of the ruins of Glastonbury Abbey, which was so incredibly rich in virtue that they lost much in making projection by way of trial before they found out the height of that medicine. In the beginning of 1583, Dr. J. Dee having contracted with certain spirits to act and converse with them, he appointed his friend Kelley to be his seer or skryer, or speculator, that is, to take notice what the spirits said and to tell it to Dee while he wrote down in a book what was dictated to him. Soon after Dee and Kelley being made known to and acquainted with the learned and most noble Polonian named Albert Alaskie, Prince of Sirad, who was come into England to see the fashions of the court and to admire the wisdom of the Queen, he thereupon had so great a respect for them, himself being a mathematician, that in Sept. following when he left England, he took them and their wives with him in the same ship, and traveling with him afterwards by land, he saw them safely conveyed to Cracow in Poland. Where continuing for some time, they removed to Prague; and at length, in Sept., 1586, to Trebona in Bohemia; at all which places tho' Kelley was several times troublesome, inconstant, and false to Dee, yet he mostly performed the office of skryer. And further, that notwithstanding Dee took the said spirits to be angelical, yet Kelley not, but rather mere delusions of the Devil. . . .

At Trebona, Kelley made projection, 9 Dec., 1586, with one small grain of the *elixir*, in proportion no bigger than the least grain of sand, upon one ounce and a quarter of common mercury, and it produced almost an ounce of pure gold. At another time he made projection upon a piece of metal cut out of a warming-pan, and without his touching or handling it or melting the metal—only warming it in the fire—the *elixir* being put thereon it was transmitted into pure silver. The said warming-pan and piece were sent to Q. Elizabeth by her ambassador then residing at Prague, that by fitting the piece with the place whence it was cut out it might exactly appear to be a part of the said warming-pan. At another time Kelley, who was openly profuse beyond the modest limits of a sober philosopher, did give away in gold-wire rings, or rings twisted with three gold wires, at the marriage of one of his maid-servants to the value of £4000, but this I think was acted after Dee had left him at Trebona, which was in May, 1589; otherwise it had not been done, and so consequently Rudolph II, Emperor of Germany, who had a great respect for him and Dee, would not for his prodigality or open management of the secret or

1 John Weever in his Discourse of Ancient Funeral Monuments, London, 1631.
2 Elias Ashmole.

rather, as some say, for a chemical cheat put upon him have committed him to close custody. . . .

At length our author Kelley—who had been knighted by the Emperor as it seems—being imprisoned the second time, at Prague, by the aforesaid Emperor, after he had been at liberty for some months and in a manner had crept into his favor, attempted an escape out of an high window by tying his sheets together after he had divided each into two parts at least; but he being too weighty for them fell to the ground before he was half way down; so that bruising his body and breaking his legs he died soon after, in Octob. as it seems, in fifteen hundred, ninety-and-five; for on the 25 Nov. following the news of his death came to Dr. Dee then in England, which he inserted in his Diary thus, "Nov. 25, *an.* 1595, news that Sir E. K. was slain."

NATHANIEL POWNOLL, a Kentish man born—in or near Canterbury—was entered a batler of Broadgate's Hall in Michaelmas term, *an.* 1599, aged 15, and two years after was made a student of Ch. Ch.,[3] where being an indefatigable plodder at his book and running through with wonderful diligence all the forms of philosophy, took the degree of M. of Arts, *an.* 1607. His life, as it deserved well of all so it was covetous of no man's commendation, himself being as far from pride as his desert was near it. He lived constantly in the university 10 years, in which time he learned eight languages, watched often, daily exercised, always studied, insomuch that he made an end of himself in an over-fervent desire to benefit others. And tho' he had out of himself sweat all his oil for his lamp and had laid the sun a-bed by his labors, yet he never durst adventure to do that, after all these studies done and ended, which our young novices, doing nothing, count nothing to do; but still thought himself as unfit, as he knew all men were unworthy, of so high an honor as to be the angels of God. And since in him so great examples of piety, knowledge, industry, and unaffected modesty have been long since fallen asleep, there is no other way left but to commend the titles of his monuments to posterity.[4]

WALTER RALEGH, a person in his time of a good natural wit, better judgment and of a plausible tongue, son of Walt. Ralegh, Esq., by Catharine his wife, daughter of Sir Philip Champernoon, Knt., was born at a place called Hayes in the parish of East Budleigh in Devonshire, *an* 1552. . . .

In 1568 or thereabouts, he became a commoner of Oriel Coll. at what time C. Champernoon, his kinsman, studied there, where his natural parts being strangely advanced by academical learning, under the care of an excellent tutor, became the ornament of the juniors and was worthily esteemed a proficient in oratory and philosophy. After he had spent about 3 years in that house where he had laid a good ground and sure foundation to build thereon, he left the university without a degree and went to the Middle Temple to improve himself in the intricate knowledge of the municipal laws. . . .

As for the remaining part of his life, it was sometimes low and sometimes in a middle condition and often tossed by fortune to and fro and seldom at rest. He was one that fortune had picked up out of purpose of whom to make an example or to use as her tennis ball thereby to show what she could do; for she tossed him up of nothing, and to and fro to greatness and from thence down to a little more than that wherein she found him, a bare gentleman, not that he was less, for he was well descended and of good alliance but poor in his beginnings. . . .

France was the first school wherein he learned the rudiments of war, and the Low Countries and Ireland, the military academies of those times, made him master of that discipline. For in both places he exposed himself afterwards to land service, but that in Ireland was a militia, which then did not yield him food and raiment, nor had he patience to stay there, tho' shortly after, in 1580, he went thither again and was a captain there under Arthur, Lord Grey, who succeeded Sir Will. Pelham in the deputyship of that kingdom. Afterwards gaining great credit, he was received into the court, became a person in favor, and had several boons bestowed on him afterwards, particularly the Castle of Sherburne in Dorsetshire, taken from the see of Salisbury. In the latter end of 1584 he discovered a new country, which he, in honor of the Queen, called Virginia, received the honor of knighthood from her, and was afterwards made captain of her Majesty's Guards, Seneschal of the Duchess of Cornwall and Exeter, Lord Warden of the Stannaries of Devon and Cornwall, Lord Lieutenant of Cornwall, and Governor of Jersey. In 1588 he showed himself active against the Invincible Armada of the Spaniards, and in 1592, being about that time a Parliament man wherein as in other Parliaments in the latter end of Q. Eliz. he was a

3 Christ Church.
4 There follows a list of the writings of this honest if obscure son of Oxford.

frequent speaker, he went to America with 15 men-of-war to possess himself of Panama, where the Spaniards ship their riches, or to intercept them in their passage homewards, but returned successless, and was out of favor for a time, not only for that but for devirginating a maid of honor, Elizabeth, daughter of Sir Nich. Throckmorton, whom he afterwards married, and for some months being kept under custody, was at length set free but banished the court. Afterwards to follow the direction of his own genius, that was always inclined to search out hidden regions and the secrets of nature, he undertook a navigation to Guiana that bears gold in 1595 purposely for the improvement and honor of his country both by getting store of wealth and by molesting the Spaniard within the inward coasts of America, which he thought would be more profitable than on the sea coasts where there are never any towns laden with any riches but when they are conveyed thither to be carried over into Spain. He set out from Plymouth on the 6th of Febr. and arrived at the Island Trinidad, 22 March. There he easily took a little city called St. Joseph, and the Governor thereof, Don Antonio de Bereo, but found not so much as a piece of silver there. Having inquired many things of this Antonio about the mines of gold in Guiana, he left his ship in Trinidad and entered the vast River Orinoco with little barks and some hundred soldiers. He searched up and down Guiana for the space of four miles among the crooked and short turnings of the water several ways. Where, being parched with the reflecting beams of the sun just over his head and too much wet sometimes with showers and having long wrestled with such like difficulties, he yet continued so long till that it growing wintry cold in Apr. the waters all overspread the earth; insomuch that now he could pass away in no less danger of the waters than he came thither in danger of his enemies. After his return he was constituted one of the chief persons in the expedition to Cadiz, where he performed notable service and obtained to himself at home a great name. In 1603 he presented to K. James at his entrance to the crown of England a manuscript of his own writing containing valid arguments against a peace to be made with Spain, which was then the common discourse. But the King being altogether for peace, 'twas rejected, and the same year, just after he had been deprived of the captainship of the Guard, which K. James bestowed on Sir Tho. Erskine, Viscount Fenton in Scotland, we find him in a plot against the King, generally called Sir Walter Ralegh's treason,

for which being brought to his trial, with others, at Winchester in 1603, was at length found guilty and condemned to die. But being reprieved, he was committed prisoner to the Tower of London for life, where he improved his confinement to the greatest advantage of learning and inquisitive men. In Apr. 1614, he published the History of the World, a book which for the exactness of its chronology, curiosity of its contexture, and learning of all sorts seems to be the work of an age. In 1617 power was granted to him to set forth ships and men for the undertaking an enterprise of a golden mine in Guiana in the southern parts of America, and on the 28th of March in the year following he left London in order for that voyage, notwithstanding Didacus Sarmiento de Acunna, Earl or Count of Gondomar, the Spanish ambassador to the K. of England, endeavored to hinder him with many arguments proposed to his Majesty. But at length Sir Walter going beyond his commission in taking and sacking the Town of St. Thome, belonging to the Spaniard, which was much aggravated by Gondomar, the King on the 9th of June, 1618, published his royal proclamation for the discovery of the truth of Ralegh's proceedings and for the advancement of justice. Whereupon, when Ralegh arrived at Plymouth, Sir Lewis Stucley, Vice-Admiral of the County of Devon, seized him and brought him up to London, 9, Aug. following. But Ralegh finding the court wholly guided by Gondomar, as 'tis said, notwithstanding I find elsewhere that he left England 16, July going before, he could hope for little mercy. Whereupon wisely contriving the design of an escape, was betrayed by Stucley, taken on the Thames, and committed to a close prison. . . .

On the 28th of the month of Oct. he was conveyed to the court called the King's Bench in Westminster, where it being proposed to him what he had to say for himself why the sentence of death, pronounced against him in 1603, should not be put in execution, he fell into a long discourse and vindicated himself so much that most wise men thought then, and all historians since, that his life could not be taken away upon that account. Afterwards being conveyed to the gatehouse, suffered death the next day, notwithstanding David Noion, Lord of Chesne, acted much to save him. Authors are perplexed, as some are pleased to say, under what topic to place him, whether of statesman, seaman, soldier, chemist, or chronologer, for in all these he did excel. And it still remains a dispute whether the age he lived in was more obliged to his pen or his sword, the one being busy in conquering the New, the other in so bravely describing the Old World.

ROBERT BURTON, known otherwise to scholars by the name of Democritus Junior, younger brother to Will. Burton, whom I shall mention under the year 1645, was born of an ancient and genteel family at Lindley in Leicestershire, 8 Feb., 1576, and therefore in the titles of several of his choice books which he gave to the public library he added to his surname *Lindliacus Leicestrensis*. He was educated in grammar learning in the free school of Sutton-Coldfield in Warwickshire, whence he was sent to Brasenose Coll, in the long vacation, *an.* 1593, where he made a considerable progress in logic and philosophy in the condition of a commoner. In 1599 he was elected student of Ch. Ch., and for form sake, tho' he wanted not a tutor, he was put under the tuition of Dr. John Bancroft, afterwards Bishop of Oxon. In 1614 he was admitted to the reading of the sentences, and on the 29 Nov., 1616, he had the vicarage of St. Thomas' parish in the west suburb of Oxon conferred on him by the Dean and canons of Ch. Church to the parishioners whereof he always gave the sacrament in wafers—which, with the rectory of Segrave in Leicester, given to him some years after by George, Lord Berkeley, he kept with much ado to his dying day. He was an exact mathematician, a curious calculator of nativities, a general read scholar, a thoro'-paced philologist, and one that understood the surveying of lands well. As he was by many accounted a severe student, a devourer of authors, a melancholy and humorous[5] person, so by others who knew him well a person of great honesty, plain dealing, and charity. I have heard some of the ancients of Ch. Ch. often say that his company was very merry, facete, and juvenile, and no man in his time did surpass him for his ready and dexterous interlarding his common discourses among them with verses from the poets or sentences from classical authors. Which being then all the fashion in the university made his company more acceptable. He hath written:

The Anatomy of Melancholy.—First printed in qu. and afterwards several times in fol., *an.* 1624, 1632, 38, and 1652, etc., to the greatest profit of the bookseller, who got an estate by it. 'Tis a book so full of variety of reading that gentlemen who have lost their rime and are put to a push for invention may furnish themselves with matter for common or scholastical discourse and writing. Several authors have unmercifully stolen matter from the said book without any acknowledgment, particularly one Will. Greenwood in his book entit., A Description of the Passion of Love, etc., Lond., 1657, oct., who, as others of the like humor do, sometimes takes his quotations without the least mention of Democritus Junior. He, the said R. Burton, paid his last debt to nature in his chamber in Ch. Ch. at or very near that time which he had some years before foretold from the calculation of his own nativity. Which being exact, several of the students did not forbear to whisper among themselves that, rather than there should be a mistake in the calculation, he sent up his soul to heaven thro' a slip about his neck. His body was afterwards with due solemnity buried near that of Dr. Rob. Weston in the north aisle which joins next to the choir of the Cath. of Ch. Church on the 27 of January in sixteen hundred thirty-and-nine. Over his grave was soon after erected a comely monument on the upper pillar of the said aisle, with his bust painted to the life. On the right hand of which is the calculation of his nativity and under the bust this inscription made by himself, all put up by the care of William Burton his brother. *Paucis notus, paucioribus ignotus, hic jacet Democritus junior, cui vitam dedit et mortem Melancholia. Obiit. viii, Id. A. C.* MDCXXXIX. He left behind him a very choice library of books, many of which he bequeathed to that of Bodley, and a hundred pounds to buy five pounds yearly for the supplying of Ch. Ch. library with books.

JEREMY TAYLOR tumbled out of his mother's womb into the lap of the Muses at Cambridge, was educated in Gonvil and Caius Coll. there till he was M. of A. Afterwards entering into holy orders, he supplied for a time the divinity lecturer's place in the Cath. of St. Paul in London, where behaving himself with great credit and applause far above his years came to the cognizance of that great encourager of learning, ingenuity, and virtue, Dr. Laud, Archb. of Cant., who thinking it for the advantage of the world that such mighty parts should be afforded better opportunities of study and improvement than a course of constant preaching would allow of, he caused him to be elected Fellow of Alls. Coll.,[6] *an.* 1636, where being settled, love and admiration still waited upon him, while he improved himself much in books. . . .

5 Full of humors.

6 All Souls' College, Oxford. Laud broke rules to put him in.

He became one of the chaplains to the said Archb. of Cant., who bestowed upon him the rectory of Uppingham in Rutlandshire, and other matters he would have done for him in order to his advance in the church, had not the rebellion unluckily broken out. In the year 1642 he was, with others, by virtue of his Maj. letters sent to this university, actually created D. of D. in that noted convocation held on the first day of Nov. the same year, he then being chaplain in ord. to his said Majesty and a frequent preacher before him and the court in Oxon. . . .

Upon the declining of the King's cause he retired into Wales, where he was suffered under the loyal Earl of Carbury of the Golden Grove in Caermarthenshire to officiate and keep school to maintain him and his children. From which, tho' it continued but a few years, were several youths most loyally educated and afterwards sent to the universities. In this solitude he began to write his excellent discourses, which are enough of themselves to furnish a library and will be famous to all succeeding generations for the exactness of wit, profoundness of judgment, richness of fancy, clearness of expression, copiousness of invention, and general usefulness to all the purposes of a Christian. By which he soon after got a great reputation among all persons of judgment and indifferences, and his name grew greater still as the world grew better and wiser. When he had spent some years in this retirement, in a private corner, as 'twere, of the world, his family was visited with sickness and thereby lost the dear pledges of God's favor, three sons of great hopes, within the space of two or three months. And tho' he had learned a quiet submission unto the divine will, yet this affliction touched him so sensibly that it made him desirous to leave the country. And going to London, he there for a time officiated in a private congregation of loyalists to his great hazard and danger. At length meeting with Edward, Lord Conway, a person of great honor and generosity, that lord, after he had understood his condition, made him a kind proffer; which our author Taylor embracing, it carried him over into Ireland and settled him at Portmore, a place made for study and contemplation; which he therefore dearly loved. And there he wrote his Cases of Conscience, a book that is able alone to give its author immortality. By this time the wheel of Providence brought about the King's happy restoration, and out of a confused chaos beauty and order began to appear, whereupon our loyal author went over to congratulate the Prince and people's happiness and bear a part in the universal triumph. It

was not long after his sacred Majesty began the settlement of the church, and Dr. Taylor being resolved upon the bishopric of Down and Connor, was consecrated thereunto at Dublin on the 27th of January, 1660, and on the 21st of June, 1661, he had the administration of the see of Dromore granted to him by his Majesty in consideration that he had been the church's champion and that he had suffered much in defense of its cause. With what care and faithfulness he discharged his office all upon the place knew well and what good rules and directions he gave to his clergy and how he taught them the practice of them by his own example. Upon his being made bishop, he was constituted a privy councilor, and the University of Dublin gave him their testimony by recommending him for their Vice-Chancellor, which honorable office he kept to his dying day. He was esteemed by the generality of persons a complete artist, accurate logician, exquisite, quick and acute in his reasonings, a person of great fluency in his language and of a prodigious readiness in his learning. . . .

But he had not only the accomplishments of a gentleman, but so universal were his parts that they were proportioned to everything. And tho' his spirit and humor were made up of smoothness and gentleness, yet he could bear with the harshness and roughness of the Schools[7] and was not unseen in their subtilties and spinosities. His skill was great both in the civil and canon law and casuistical divinity. And he was a rare conductor of souls and knew how to counsel and to advise, to solve difficulties, and determine cases, and quiet consciences. To these may be added his great acquaintance with the fathers and ecclesiastical writers and the doctors of the first and purest ages both of the Greek and Lat. church; which he hath made use of against the Rom. Catholics to vindicate the Church of England from the challenge of innovation and to prove her ancient, catholic, and apostolical. Add to all these, he was a person of great humility, had nothing in him of pride and humor, but was courteous and affable and of easy access. He was withal a person of great charity and hospitality; and whosoever compares his plentiful incomes with the inconsiderable estate he left at his death will be easily convinced that charity was steward for a great proportion of his revenue. To sum up all in a few words of another author:[8] "This great prelate had the good

7 The medieval Schoolmen.
8 George Rust, who succeeded Taylor as Bishop of Dromore.

humor of a gentleman, the eloquence of an orator, the fancy of a poet, the acuteness of a Schoolman, the profoundness of a philosopher, the wisdom of a chancellor, the sagacity of a prophet, the reason of an angel, and the piety of a saint. He had devotion enough for a cloister, learning enough for an university, and wit enough for a coll. of *virtuosi.* And had his parts and endowments been parceled out among his poor clergy that he left behind him, it would perhaps have made one of the best dioceses in the world." . . .⁹

He being overtaken with a violent fever surrendered up his pious soul to the Omnipotent at Lisburne, alias Lisnegarvy, on the thirteenth day of August in 1667, and was buried in a chapel of his own erection on the ruins of the old Cathedral of Dromore.

9 A list and description of Taylor's works follows.

Samuel Pepys

[1633–1703]

THE greatest of English diarists was born in London, the fifth child and second son of a tailor who later rose to be a landowner. After early education at St. Paul's School, he entered Trinity Hall, Cambridge, but later transferred as a sizar to Magdalene College in the same university. He received his B.A. in 1654 and his M.A. in 1660. In 1655 he married Elizabeth St. Michel, the daughter of a French Huguenot refugee, and, with the restoration of Charles II in 1660, he began a brilliant career in public affairs, a career which was to culminate in his service as Clerk of the Privy Seal and Secretary of the Admiralty. Pepys (he pronounced his name "Peeps") showed rare administrative and executive gifts in his economic reorganization of the British navy; he showed at the same time a shrewd capacity for improving his own affairs, for while establishing the navy on a sound financial basis he managed simultaneously to equip himself with a tidy fortune.

He pursued his avocations with as much energy and competence as his vocation: he was an inveterate play-goer and an amateur of music; he joined the Royal Society shortly after its foundation and served as its president in 1684; he was M.P. for Harwich in 1679. When his old naval associate James, Duke of York, ascended the throne as James II in 1685, Pepys's career reached its zenith, but with the Glorious Revolution of 1688 his days of public eminence were finished. Suspected of popery, he was imprisoned briefly in 1690 on an unfounded charge of Jacobite intrigue. He spent the remainder of his life in comfortable and bookish retirement in his mansion at Clapham and died in 1703—rich, respectable, successful, and honored.

Pepys the civil servant, the author of the monumental *Memoirs Relating to the State of the Royal Navy*, is an obscure figure in the dusty past. It is in a diary kept in code from 1660 to 1669 that Samuel Pepys is alive and immortal. Deciphered between the years 1819 and 1822 by the Reverend John Smith, the *Diary* presents, with an honesty which is so complete as to be frightening, a human personality. It seems never to occur to Pepys to falsify in any flattering way his own image of himself, any more than it occurs to him to trick out his descriptions of scenes or incidents with any self-conscious literary flourishes. Whether he is describing the Great Fire of London, or the latest court scandal, or the cost of new petticoats, or any desirable girl who has come into his line of vision, or the progress of an amour, it is the tangible reality which imposes itself on Pepys's sensibility and communicates itself in prose of incomparable raciness and vigor. Pepys is frightening because the very pulse of life—self-centered, rapacious, amoral—throbs in his sentences. His utter honesty, complete because it is unconscious, makes it difficult for his readers to maintain their own masks very securely.

Few writers are as little inclined to generalization or analysis as is Pepys, but few writers have such a fine eye for the miscellaneous details, physical and psychological, which make up the texture of experience. His complete indifference to analyzing his experience or abstracting from it makes it impossible for us to learn what compulsion drove him to the keeping of his journal, but it also makes him the most inimitable of diarists. The *Diary* ended in 1669, when the writer's difficulties with his eyes made it impossible for him to continue. As it stands it is, however inadvertently, a work of art, for its unity of tone and consistency of purpose end by making it in a very full sense what all art strives toward—a picture of reality.

S. PEPYS. *Diary*, ed. H. B. Wheatley, 10 vols. (London, 1893–99). Standard.

————. *Diary and Correspondence*, ed. R. Braybrooke, 5 vols. (London, 3d ed., 1848–49).

————. *Diary*, ed. J. Warrington, 3 vols. (London, 1953).

A. BRYANT. *Samuel Pepys*, 3 vols. (Cambridge, 1933–39). The most complete biography.

J. DRINKWATER. *Pepys: His Life and Character* (New York, 1930).

P. HUNT. *Samuel Pepys in the Diary* (Pittsburgh, 1958). A group of essays on various aspects of Pepys's work.

F R O M

THE DIARY OF SAMUEL PEPYS

[*Based on the text of the Everyman's Library* [*Braybrooke*] *edition, 1906*]

8th [MARCH, 1659/60]. At the Dog Tavern, Captain Philip Holland, with whom I advised how to make some advantage of my Lord's[1] going to sea, told me to have five or six servants entered on board as dead men, and I to give them what wages I pleased and so their pay to be mine; he also urged me to take the secretary's place that my Lord did proffer me.

8th (Lord's day) [APRIL, 1660[2]]. The lieutenant and I looked through his glass at two good merchantmen and at the women on board them, being pretty handsome.

18th [MAY[3]]. We got a smith's boy of the town to go along with us, and he showed us the church where Van Tromp lies entombed with a very fine monument. His epitaph is concluded thus:—*Tandem bello Anglico tantum non victor, certe invictus, vivere et vincere desiit.* There is a sea-fight cut in marble, with the smoke the best expressed that ever I saw in my life. From thence

to the great church that stands in a fine great market-place over against the Stadt-house, and there I saw a stately tomb of the old Prince of Orange, of marble and brass; wherein, among other rarities, there are the angels with their trumpets expressed as it were crying. Here were very fine organs in both the churches. It is a most sweet town, with bridges, and a river in every street. In every house of entertainment there hangs in every room a poor man's box, it being their custom to confirm all bargains by putting something into the box, and that binds as fast as anything. We also saw the guest-house, where it was pleasant to see what neat preparation there is for the poor. We saw one poor man a-dying there. We light by chance of an English house to drink in, where discourse of the town and the thing that hangs up in the Stadt-house like a bushel, which is a sort of punishment for offenders to carry through the streets over his head, which is a great weight. Back by water, where a pretty, sober, Dutch lass sat reading all the way, and I could not fasten any discourse upon her.

19th [JUNE]. Lady Pickering told me the story of her husband's case and desired my assistance with my Lord and did give me, wrapped up in paper, £5 in silver.

---

1 Sir Edward Montagu, afterwards Earl of Sandwich, the "my Lord" of the Diary, Pepys's employer, one of the two generals of the fleet.

2 Off the coast of Holland. Pepys went with Montagu to bring Charles II over to his throne.

3 At The Hague.

With my Lord to Whitehall, and my Lady Pickering.

23rd. To my Lord's lodgings, where Tom Guy come to me, and there stayed to see the King touch people for the king's evil. But he did not come at all, it rained so; and the poor people were forced to stand all the morning in the rain in the garden. Afterwards he touched them in the banquetting house.

18th [AUGUST]. Towards Westminster by water. I landed my wife at Whitefriars with £5 to buy her a petticoat, and my father persuaded her to buy a most fine cloth of 26s. a yard and a rich lace, that the petticoat will come to £5; but she doing it very innocently, I could not be angry.

25th [SEPTEMBER]. I did send for a cup of tea, a China drink, of which I never had drank before.

7th [OCTOBER] (Lord's day). To Whitehall on foot, calling at my father's to change my long black cloak for a short one, long cloaks being now quite out; but he being gone to church, I could not get one. I heard Dr. Spurstow preach before the King a poor dry sermon; but a very good anthem of Captain Cooke's afterwards. To my Lord's, and dined with him; he all dinner-time talking French to me and telling me the story how the Duke of York hath got my Lord Chancellor's daughter with child and that she do lay it to him and that for certain he did promise her marriage and had signed it with his blood but that he by stealth had got the paper out of her cabinet. And that the King would have him to marry her, but that he will not.[4]

13th. I went out to Charing Cross to see Major-General Harrison[5] hanged, drawn, and quartered; which was done there, he looking as cheerful as any man could do in that condition. He was presently cut down, and his head and heart shown to the people, at which there was great shouts of joy. It is said that he said he was sure to come shortly at the right hand of Christ to judge them that now had judged him; and that his wife do expect his coming again. Thus it was my chance to see the King beheaded at Whitehall and to see the first blood shed in revenge for the King at Charing Cross. Setting up shelves in my study.

20th. I dined with my Lord and Lady; he was very merry and did talk very high how he would have a French cook and a master of his horse and his lady and child to wear black patches; which methought was strange; but he is become a perfect courtier; and, among other things, my Lady saying that she could get

a good merchant for her daughter Jem, he answered that he would rather see her with a pedlar's pack at her back, so she married a gentleman, than she should marry a citizen. This afternoon, going through London and calling at Crowe's, the upholsterer's, in Saint Bartholomew's, I saw the limbs of some of our new traitors set upon Aldersgate, which was a sad sight to see; and a bloody week this and the last have been, there being ten hanged, drawn, and quartered.

21st (Lord's day). George Vines carried me up to the top of his turret, where there is Cooke's head set up for a traitor, and Harrison's set up on the other side of Westminster Hall. Here I could see them plainly, as also a very fair prospect about London.

12th [NOVEMBER]. My father and I discoursed seriously about my sister's coming to live with me, and yet I am much afraid of her ill nature. I told her plainly my mind was to have her come not as a sister but as a servant, which she promised me that she would, and with many thanks did weep for joy.

22nd. Mr. Fox come in presently and did receive us with a great deal of respect; and then did take my wife and I to the Queen's presence-chamber, where he got my wife placed behind the Queen's chair, and the two Princesses come to dinner. The Queen,[6] a very little, plain old woman, and nothing more in her presence in any respect nor garb than any ordinary woman. The Princess of Orange I had often seen before. The Princess Henrietta is very pretty, but much below my expectation; and her dressing of herself with her hair frizzed short up to her ears did make her seem so much the less to me. But my wife standing near her with two or three black patches on and well dressed, did seem to me much handsomer than she.

4th [DECEMBER]. This day the Parliament voted that the bodies of Oliver, Ireton, Bradshaw, and Thomas Pride should be taken up out of their graves in the Abbey and drawn to the gallows and there hanged and buried under it. Which, methinks, do trouble me that a man of so great courage as he was should have that dishonor, though otherwise he might deserve it enough.

10th [JANUARY, 1660/1]. Mr. Davis told us the particular examinations of these fanatics that are taken. And in short it is this, these fanatics that have routed all the train-bands that they met with, put the King's life-guards to the run, killed about twenty men, broke through the city gates twice; and all this in the daytime, when all the city was in arms—are not in all

---

4 He had married her on the 3d of September.

5 One of the judges of Charles I.

6 Henrietta Maria, Charles I's widow.

above 31. Whereas we did believe them—because they were seen up and down in every place almost in the city and had been in Highgate two or three days and in several other places—to be at least 500. A thing that never was heard of, that so few men should dare and do so much mischief. Their word was, "The King Jesus, and their heads[7] upon the gates!" Few of them would receive any quarter, but such as were taken by force and kept alive expecting Jesus to come here and reign in the world presently, and will not believe yet. The King this day come to town.

28th. I saw again The Lost Lady, which do now please me better than before; and here I sitting behind in a dark place, a lady spit backward upon me by a mistake, not seeing me; but after seeing her to be a very pretty lady, I was not troubled at it at all. At Mr. Holden's I bought a hat cost me 35s.

25th [MARCH, 1660/1]. Homewards, and took up a boy that had a lanthorn, that was picking up of rags, and got him to light me home, and had great discourse with him how he could get sometimes three or four bushels of rags in a day and got 3d. a bushel for them and many other discourses, what and how many ways there are for poor children to get their livings honestly.

10th [APRIL, 1661]. Here we had, for my sake, two fiddles, the one a bass viol, on which he that played, played well some lyra lessons, but both together made the worst music that ever I heard. We had a fine collation, but I took little pleasure in that for the illness of the music and for the intentness of my mind upon Mrs. Rebecca Allen. After we had done eating, the ladies went to dance, and among the men we had I was forced to dance, too; and did make an ugly shift. Mrs. R. Allen danced very well and seems the best humored woman that ever I saw. About nine o'clock Sir William and my Lady went home, and we continued dancing an hour or two, and so broke up very pleasant and merry, and so walked home, I leading Mrs. Rebecca, who seemed, I know not why, in that and other things, to be desirous of my favors, and would in all things show me respects. Going home, she would needs have me sing, and I did pretty well and was highly esteemed by them. So to Captain Allen's—where we was last night and heard him play on the harpsichord, and I found him to be a perfect good musician—and there, having no mind to leave Mrs. Rebecca, I did what with talk and singing (her father and I), Mrs. Turner and I stayed there till two o'clock in the morning, and was most

exceeding merry, and I had the opportunity of kissing Mrs. Rebecca very often.

11th. At two o'clock, with very great mirth, we went to our lodging and to bed, and lay till seven, and then called up by Sir W. Batten; so I rose, and we did some business, and then come Captain Allen, and he and I withdrew, and sang a song or two, and among others, took great pleasure in "Go and be hanged, that's twice good-bye." The young ladies come too, and so I did again please myself with Mrs. Rebecca; and about nine o'clock, after we had breakfasted, we set forth for London, and indeed I was a little troubled to part with Mrs. Rebecca, for which God forgive me. Thus we went away through Rochester. We baited at Dartford, and thence to London, but of all the journeys that ever I made this was the merriest and I was in a strange mood for mirth. Among other things, I got my Lady to let her maid, Mrs. Anne, to ride all the way on horseback, and she rides exceeding well; and so I called [her] my clerk, that she went to wait upon me. I met two little schoolboys going with pitchers of ale to their schoolmaster to break up against Easter, and I did drink of some of one of them, and gave him two-pence. By and by we come to two little girls keeping cows, and I saw one of them very pretty, so I had a mind to make her ask my blessing, and telling her that I was her godfather, she asked me innocently whether I was not Ned Warding, and I said that I was, so she kneeled down, and very simply called, "Pray, godfather, pray to God to bless me," which made us very merry, and I gave her two-pence. In several places I asked women whether they would sell me their children, but they denied me all, but said they would give me one to keep for them, if I would. Mrs. Anne and I rode under the man that hangs upon Shooter's Hill, and a filthy sight it was to see how his flesh is shrunk to his bones. So home, and I found all well, and a good deal of work done since I went. So to bed very sleepy for last night's work, concluding that it is the pleasantest journey in all respects that ever I had in my life.

23rd. About four I rose and got to the Abbey, where I followed Sir J. Denham, the surveyor, with some company he was leading in. And with much ado, by the favor of Mr. Cooper, his man, did get up into a great scaffold across the north end of the Abbey, where with a great deal of patience I sat from past four till eleven before the King come in. And a great pleasure it was to see the Abbey raised in the middle, all covered with red, and a throne—that is, a chair—and footstool on the top of it; and all the officers of all kinds, so much

7 The heads of the Regicides.

as the very fiddlers, in red vests. At last comes in the Dean and prebendaries of Westminster, with the bishops, many of them in cloth of gold copes, and after them the nobility all in their Parliament robes, which was a most magnificent sight. Then the Duke and the King with a scepter, carried by my Lord Sandwich, and sword and wand before him and the crown too. The King in his robes, bare-headed, which was very fine. And after all had placed themselves, there was a sermon and the service; and then in the quire at the high altar, the King passed through all the ceremonies of the Coronation, which to my great grief I and most in the Abbey could not see. The crown being put upon his head, a great shout begun, and he come forth to the throne, and there passed through more ceremonies: as taking the oath, and having things read to him by the Bishop; and his lords—who put on their caps as soon as the King put on his crown—and bishops come, and kneeled before him. And three times the King-at-Arms went to the three open places on the scaffold and proclaimed that if anyone could show any reason why Charles Stuart should not be King of England, that now he should come and speak. And a general pardon also was read by the Lord Chancellor, and medals flung up and down by my Lord Cornwallis, of silver, but I could not come by any. But so great a noise that I could make but little of the music; and indeed, it was lost to everybody. I went out a little while before the King had done all his ceremonies, and went round the Abbey to Westminster Hall, all the way within the rails, and 10,000 people with the ground covered with blue cloth, and scaffolds all the way. Into the hall I got, where it was very fine with hangings and scaffolds one upon another full of brave ladies; and my wife in one little one, on the right hand. Here I stayed walking up and down, and at last upon one of the side stalls I stood and saw the King come in with all the persons but the soldiers that were yesterday in the cavalcade; and a most pleasant sight it was to see them in their several robes. And the King come in with his crown on and his scepter in his hand, under a canopy borne up by six silver staves, carried by Barons of the Cinque Ports, and little bells at every end, And after a long time, he got up to the farther end, and all set themselves down at their several tables; and that was also a brave sight. And the King's first course carried up by the Knights of the Bath. And many fine ceremonies there was of the heralds leading up people before him, and bowing; and my Lord of Albemarle's going to the kitchen and eating a bit of the first dish that was to go to the King's

table. But, above all, was these three lords, Northumberland and Suffolk and the Duke of Ormond, coming before the courses on horseback, and staying so all dinnertime, and at last bringing up the King's champion, all in armor on horseback, with his spear and target carried before him. And a herald proclaims, "That if any dare deny Charles Stuart to be lawful King of England, here was a champion that would fight with him"; and with these words, the champion flings down his gauntlet, and all this he do three times in his going up towards the King's table. To which, when he is come, the King drinks to him, and then sends him the cup, which is of gold, and he drinks it off, and then rides back again with the cup in his hand. I went from table to table to see the bishops and all others at their dinner, and was infinitely pleased with it. And at the lords' table, I met with William Howe, and he spoke to my Lord for me, and he did give him four rabbits and a pullet, and so Mr. Creed and I got Mr. Minshell to give us some bread, and so we at a stall eat it, as everybody else did what they could get. I took a great deal of pleasure to go up and down and look upon the ladies and to hear the music of all sorts, but above all, the 24 violins. About six at night they had dined, and I went up to my wife. And strange it is to think that these two days have held up fair till now that all is done and the King gone out of the hall; and then it fell a-raining and thundering and lightening as I have not seen it do for some years. Which people did take great notice of, God's blessing of the work of these two days, which is a foolery to take too much notice of such things. I observed little disorder in all this, only the King's footmen had got hold of the canopy and would keep it from the Barons of the Cinque Ports, which they endeavored to force from them again but could not do it till my lord Duke of Albemarle caused it to be put into Sir R. Pye's hand till tomorrow to be decided. At Mr. Bowyer's; a great deal of company, some I knew, others I did not. Here we stayed upon the leads and below till it was late, expecting to see the fireworks, but they were not performed tonight. Only the city had a light like a glory round about it, with bonfires. At last, I went to King Street, and there sent Crockford to my father's and my house to tell them I could not come home tonight because of the dirt and a coach could not be had. And so I took my wife and Mrs. Frankleyn, who I proffered the civility of lying with my wife at Mrs. Hunt's tonight, to Axe-yard, in which, at the further end, there were three great bonfires, and a great many gallants, men and women; and they laid hold of us and would have us drink the King's health upon our knees, kneeling upon a faggot, which we all did, they drinking to us one after another, which we thought a strange frolic; but these gallants continued there a great while, and I wondered to see how the ladies did tipple. At last, I sent my wife and her bed-fellow to bed and Mr. Hunt and I went in with Mr. Thornbury, who did give the company all their wine, he being yeoman of the wine-cellar to the King; and there, with his wife and two of his sisters and some gallant sparks that were there, we drank the King's health and nothing else till one of the gentlemen fell down stark drunk and there lay; and I went to my Lord's pretty well. But no sooner a-bed with Mr. Shepley, but my head began to turn and I to vomit, and if ever I was foxed, it was now, which I cannot say yet, because I fell asleep and slept till morning. Thus did the day end with joy everywhere; and blessed be God, I have not heard of any mischance to anybody through it all, but only to Sergeant Glynne,[8] whose horse fell upon him yesterday, and is like to kill him, which people do please themselves to see how just God is to punish the rogue at such a time as this; he being now one of the King's sergeants, and rode in the cavalcade with Maynard,[9] to whom people wish the same fortune. There was also this night, in King Street, a woman had her eye put out by a boy's flinging a firebrand into the coach. Now, after all this, I can say that, besides the pleasure of the sight of these glorious things, I may now shut my eyes against any other objects nor for the future trouble myself to see things of state and show, as being sure never to see the like again in this world.

24th. Waked in the morning, with my head in a sad taking through the last night's drink, which I am very sorry for. So rose, and went out with Mr. Creed to drink our morning draught; which he did give me in chocolate to settle my stomach.

5th [JUNE]. This morning did give my wife £4 to lay out upon lace and other things for herself. Sir W. Penn[10] and I went out with Sir R. Slingsby to bowls in his alley, and there had good sport. I took my flageolet and played upon the leads in the garden, where Sir W. Penn come out in his shirt into his leads, and there we stayed talking and singing and drinking

great draughts of claret and eating botargo[11] and bread-and-butter till twelve at night, it being moon-shine; and so to bed, very near fuddled.

2nd [JULY]. My father writes that my uncle is by fits stupid and like a man that is drunk, and sometimes speechless. Went to Sir William Davenant's opera; this being the fourth day that it hath begun and the first that I have seen it. Today was acted the second part of The Siege of Rhodes. We stayed a very great while for the King and Queen of Bohemia; and by the breaking of a board over our heads we had a great deal of dust fell into the ladies' necks and the men's hair, which made good sport. The King being come, the scene opened, which indeed is very fine and magnificent, and well acted, all but the eunuch, who was so much out that he was hissed off the stage.

6th. Waked this morning with news, brought me by a messenger on purpose, that my Uncle Robert is dead; so I rose sorry in some respect, glad in my expectations in another respect. So I bought me a pair of boots in St. Martin's and got myself ready, and then to the post-house, and set out about eleven and twelve o'clock, taking the messenger with me that come to me, and so we rode, and got well by nine o'clock to Brampton, where I found my father well. My uncle's corpse in a coffin standing upon joint-stools in the chimney in the hall; but it begun to smell, and so I caused it to be set forth in the yard all night and watched by my aunt. My father and I lay together, I greedy to see the will, but did not ask to see it till tomorrow.

8th, 9th, 10th, 11th, 12th, 13th, I fell to work, and my father, to look over my uncle's papers and clothes, and continued all this week upon that business, much troubled with my aunt's base, ugly humors.

24th [AUGUST]. Called to Sir W. Batten's to see the strange creature that Captain Holmes hath brought with him from Guinea; it is a great baboon, but so much like a man in most things that, though they say there is a species of them, yet I cannot believe but that it is a monster got of man and she-baboon. I do believe that it already understands much English, and I am of the mind that it might be taught to speak or make signs. To the Opera, and there saw Hamlet, Prince of Denmark, done with scenes very well, but above all, Betterton did the Prince's part beyond imagination.

7th [SEPTEMBER]. Having appointed the young ladies at the Wardrobe[12] to go with them to the play

---

8 He lived to be knighted by Charles.

9 Sergeant to Cromwell; he also was knighted by the King.

10 Comptroller of the navy, father of the founder of Pennsylvania.

11 A kind of sausage.   12 Lord Sandwich's daughters.

today, my wife and I took them to the theater, where we seated ourselves close by the King and the Duke of York and Madame Palmer, which was great content; and, indeed, I can never enough admire her beauty. And here was Bartholomew Fair, with the puppet-show acted today, which had not been these forty years, it being so satirical against Puritanism they durst not till now, which is strange they should already dare to do it and the King to countenance it, but I do never a whit like it the better for the puppets, but rather the worse.

9th [DECEMBER]. At noon to dinner at the Wardrobe; where my Lady Wright was, who did talk much upon the worth and the desert of gallantry; and that there was none fit to be courtiers but such as have been abroad and know fashions; which I endeavored to oppose; and was troubled to hear her talk so, though she be a very wise and discreet lady in other things.

31st. To the office; and there late finishing our estimate of the debts of the navy to this day; and it come to near £374,000. So home and after supper and my barber had trimmed me, I sat down to end my journal for this year, and my condition at this time, by God's blessing, is that my health is very good, and so my wife's in all respects. My servants, W. Hewer, Sarah, Nell, and Wayneman; my house at the navy office. I suppose myself to be worth about £500 clear in the world, and my goods of my house my own, and what is coming to me from Brampton, when my father dies, which God defer. . . . I am upon writing a little treatise to present to the Duke, about our privilege in the seas, as to other nations striking their flags to us. But my greatest trouble is that I have for this last half year been a very great spendthrift in all manner of respects, that I am afraid to cast up my accounts, though I hope I am worth what I say above. But I will cast them up very shortly. I have newly taken a solemn oath about abstaining from plays and wine, which I am resolved to keep according to the letter of the oath which I keep by me.

18th [FEBRUARY, 1661/2]. Walking in the streets, which were everywhere full of brick-bats and tiles flung down by the extraordinary wind the last night, such as hath not been in memory before, unless at the death of the late Protector.

MARCH 1st. My wife and I by coach, first to see my little picture that is a-drawing and thence to the Opera, and there saw Romeo and Juliet, the first time it was ever acted, but it is a play of itself the worst that ever I heard, and the worst acted that ever I saw these people

do, and I am resolved to go no more to see the first time of acting, for they were all of them out more or less. I do find that I am £500 beforehand in the world, which I was afraid I was not, but I find that I had spent above £250 this last half year.

23rd [AUGUST, 1662]. But that which pleased me best was that my Lady Castlemaine [13] stood over against us upon a piece of Whitehall. But methought it was strange to see her lord and her upon the same place walking up and down without taking notice one of another, only at the first entry he put off his hat, and she made him a very civil salute, but afterwards took no notice one of another; but both of them now and then would take their child, which the nurse held in her arms, and dandle it. One thing more; there happened a scaffold below to fall, and we feared some hurt, but there was none, but she of all the great ladies only run down among the common rabble to see what hurt was done, and did take care of a child that received some little hurt, which methought was so noble. Anon there come one there booted and spurred, that she talked long with; and by and by, she being in her hair, she put on his hat, which was but an ordinary one, to keep the wind off; but it become her mightily, as everything else do. I went away, not weary with looking on her.

14th [SEPTEMBER]. To Whitehall chapel, where sermon almost done, and I heard Captain Cooke's new music. This the first day of having viols and other intruments to play a symphony between every verse of the anthems; but the music more full than it was last Sunday, and very fine it is.

29th. To the King's Theater, where we saw Midsummer's Night's Dream, which I had never seen before, nor shall ever again, for it is the most insipid, ridiculous play that ever I saw in my life.

26th [DECEMBER]. To the Wardrobe. Hither come Mr. Battersby; and we falling into discourse of a new book of drollery in use, called Hudibras, I would needs go find it out, and met with it at the Temple; cost me 2s. 6d. But when I come to read it, it is so silly an abuse of the Presbyter Knight going to the wars that I am ashamed of it; and by and by meeting at Mr. Townsend's at dinner, I sold it to him for 18d.

13th [JANUARY, 1662/3]. My poor wife rose by five o'clock in the morning, before day, and went to market and bought fowls and many other things for dinner, with which I was highly pleased, and the chine of beef was down also before six o'clock, and my own

13 One of the favorite mistresses of the King.

jack, of which I was doubtful, do carry it very well, things being put in order, and the cook come. By and by comes Dr. Clarke and his lady, his sister, and a she-cousin, and Mr. Pierce and his wife which was all my guests. I had for them, after oysters, at first course, a hash of rabbits and lamb, and a rare chine of beef. Next, a great dish of roasted fowl, cost me about 30s. and a tart, and then fruit and cheese. My dinner was noble, and enough. I had my house mighty clean and neat; my room below with a good fire in it; my dining-room above, and my chamber being made a with-drawing chamber; and my wife's a good fire also. I find my new table very proper, and will hold nine or ten people well, but eight with great room. At supper had a good sack posset and cold meat, and sent my guests away about ten o'clock at night, both them and myself highly pleased with our management of this day; and indeed their company was very fine, and Mrs. Clarke a very witty, fine lady, though a little conceited and proud. I believe this day's feast will cost me near £5.

14th. Examining part of my sea-manuscript with great pleasure, my wife sitting working by me.

15th. Mr. Coventry to dine with me, I having a wild goose roasted and a cold chine of beef and a barrel of oysters.

19th [APRIL, 1663]. (Easter Day) Up, and this day put on my close-kneed colored suit, which with new stockings of the color, with belt, and new gilt-handled sword, is very handsome. To church, where the young Scotchman preaching, I slept awhile. After supper, fell in discourse of dancing, and I find that Ashwell hath a very fine carriage, which makes my wife almost ashamed of herself to see herself so outdone, but to-morrow she begins to learn to dance for a month or two.

3rd [JULY]. Mr. Moore tells me great news that my Lady Castlemaine is fallen from court and this morning retired. He gives me no account of the reason but that it is so; for which I am sorry; and yet, if the King do it to leave off not only her but all mistresses, I should be heartily glad of it, that he may fall to look after business.[14]

4th. This day, in the Duke's chamber there being a Roman story in the hangings and upon the standard written these four letters—S. P. Q. R., Sir G. Carteret came to me to know what the meaning of those four letters were: which ignorance is not to be borne in a privy counsellor, methinks, what a schoolboy should be whipped for not knowing.

[14] The King did not break off with Castlemaine.

7th [SEPTEMBER]. To the Black Eagle in Bride Lane, and there had a chop of veal and some bread, cheese, and beer, cost me a shilling to my dinner; and so to Bartholomew Fair, where I met with Mr. Pickering, and he and I to see the monkeys at the Dutch house, which is far beyond the other that my wife and I saw the other day; and thence to see the dancing on the ropes, which was very poor and tedious. . . . By my letters from Tangier today I hear that it grows very strong by land and the mole goes on. They have lately killed about two hundred of the Moors and lost about forty or fifty. I am mightily afraid of laying out too much money in goods upon my house, but it is not money flung away, though I reckon nothing money but what is in the bank, till I have a good sum before-hand in the world.

9th. I met with Ned Pickering, he telling me the whole business of my Lord's folly with this Mrs. Becke, at Chelsea, of all which I am ashamed to see my Lord so grossly play the fool to the flinging off of all honor, friends, servants, and every thing and person that is good, with his carrying her abroad and playing on his lute under her window and forty other poor, sordid things, which I am grieved to hear; but believe it to no purpose for me to meddle with it, but let him go on till God Almighty and his own conscience and thoughts of his lady and family do it.

17th. With much ado through the fens, along dikes, where sometimes we were ready to have our horses sink to the belly, we go by night, with a great deal of stir and hard riding, to Parson's Drove, a heathen place, where I found my Uncle and Aunt Perkins and their daughters, poor wretches! in a sad, poor thatched cottage like a poor barn, or stable, peeling of hemp, in which I did give myself good content to see their manner of preparing of hemp; and in a poor condition of habit took them to our miserable inn, and there, after a long stay, and hearing of Frank, their son, the miller, play upon his treble, as he calls it, with which he earns part of his living, and singing of a country song, we set down to supper; the whole crew and Spankes's wife and child, a sad company of which I was ashamed, supped with us. By and by, news is brought to us that one of our horses is stole out of the stable, which proves my uncle's at which I am inwardly glad —I mean, that it was not mine; and at this we were at a great loss; and they doubting a person that lay at next door, a Londoner, some lawyer's clerk, we caused him to be secured in his bed and other care to be taken to seize the house; and so, about twelve at night or more, to bed in a sad, cold, stony chamber; and a little after I was asleep, they waked me to tell me that the horse was found, which was good news, and so to sleep, but was bit cruelly, and nobody else of our company, which I wonder at, by the gnats.

26th [OCTOBER]. Dr. Pierce tells me that the Queen is in a way to be pretty well again but that her delirium in her head continues still; that she talks idle, not by fits, but always, which in some lasts a week after so high a fever—in some more, and in some forever; that this morning she talked mightily that she was brought to bed and that she wondered that she should be delivered without pain and without being sick and that she was troubled that her boy was but an ugly boy. But the King being by, said, "No, it is a very pretty boy."—"Nay," says she, "if it be like you, it is a fine boy indeed, and I would be very well pleased with it."

31st. To my great sorrow find myself £43 worse than I was the last month, which was then £760, and now it is but £717. But it hath chiefly arisen from my layings-out in clothes for myself and wife; viz., for her about £12 and for myself £55, or thereabouts; having made myself a velvet cloak, two new cloth shirts, black, plain both, a new shag gown, trimmed with gold buttons and twist, with a new hat, and silk tops for my legs, and many other things, being resolved henceforward to go like myself. And also two periwigs, one whereof costs me £3 and the other 40s. I have worn neither yet, but will begin next week, God willing. I having laid out in clothes for myself and wife, and for her closet and other things without, these two months, this and the last, besides household expenses of victuals, etc., above £110. But I hope I shall with more comfort labor to get more, and with better success than when, for want of clothes, I was forced to sneak like a beggar. The Queen continues light-headed, but in hopes to recover. The plague is much in Amsterdam, and we in fear of it here, which God defend.[15] The Turk goes on mighty in the Emperor's dominions, and the princes cannot agree among themselves how to go against him.

3rd [NOVEMBER]. Home, and by and by comes Chapman, the periwig-maker, and upon my liking it, without more ado I went up, and there he cut off my hair, which went a little to my heart at present to part with it; but, it being over, and my periwig on, I paid him £3 for it; and away went he with my own hair to make up another of; and I, by and by, went abroad, after I had caused all my maids to look upon it; and they conclude it do become me; though Jane was

mightily troubled for my parting of my own hair, and so was Bess.

9th. He[16] tells me that the King by name, with all his dignities, is prayed for by them that they call fanatics as heartily and powerfully as in any of the other churches that are thought better. And that, let the King think what he will, it is them that must help him in the day of war. For so generally they are the most substantial sort of people and the soberest; and did desire me to observe it to my Lord Sandwich, among other things, that of all the old army now you cannot see a man begging about the streets; but what? You shall have this captain turned a shoemaker; the lieutenant, a baker; this a brewer; that a haberdasher; this common soldier a porter; and every man in his apron and frock, etc., as if they never had done anything else. Whereas, the others go with their belts and swords, swearing and cursing and stealing; running into people's houses, by force oftentimes, to carry away something; and this is the difference between the temper of one and the other; and concludes, and I think with some reason, that the spirits of the old Parliament soldiers are so quiet and contented with God's providences that the King is safer from any evil meant him by them one thousand times more than from his own discontented Cavalier.

21st [DECEMBER]. To Shoe Lane, to see a cockfighting at a new pit there, a spot I was never at in my life. But Lord! to see the strange variety of people, from Parliament man, by name Wildes, that was Deputy Governor of the Tower when Robinson was Lord Mayor, to the poorest 'prentices, bakers, brewers, butchers, draymen, and what not; and all these fellows one with another cursing and betting. I soon had enough of it. It is strange to see how people of this poor rank, that looks as if they had not bread to put in their mouths, shall bet three or four pounds at a time, and lose it, and yet bet as much the next battle.

3rd [FEBRUARY, 1663/4]. In Covent Garden tonight, going to fetch home my wife, I stopped at the great coffee-house there,[17] where I never was before; where Dryden, the poet, I knew at Cambridge, and all the wits of the town and Harris the player and Mr. Hoole of our college. And, had I had time then, or could at other times, it will be good coming thither, for there, I perceive, is very witty and pleasant discourse. But I could not tarry, and, as it was late, they were all ready to go away.

15 Forbid.

16 Mr. Blackburne, a Puritan friend of Pepys.
17 Will's.

13th [JUNE, 1664]. Spent the whole morning reading of some old navy books; wherein the order that was observed in the navy then, above what it is now, is very observable. Mr. Coventry did talk of a History of the Navy of England, how fit it were to be writ; and he did say that it hath been in his mind to propose to me the writing of the History of the late Dutch War, which I am glad to hear, it being a thing I much desire and sorts mightily with my genius; and, if done well, may recommend me much. So he says he will get me an order for making of searches to all records, etc., in order thereto, and I shall take great delight in doing of it.

2nd [SEPTEMBER]. To Bartholomew Fair, and our boy with us, and there showed them and myself the dancing on the ropes and several other the best shows; but pretty it is to see how our boy carries himself so innocently clownish as would make one laugh. Then up and down to buy combs for my wife to give her maids.

3rd. I have had a bad night's rest tonight, not sleeping well, as my wife observed; and I thought myself to be mightily bit by fleas, and in the morning she chid her maids for not looking the fleas a'days. But, when I rose, I found that it is only the change of the weather from hot to cold, which, as I was two winters ago, do stop my pores, and so my blood tingles and itches all day all over my body.

5th. Come W. Bowyer and dined with us; but strange to see how he could not endure onions in sauce to lamb but was overcome with the sight of it, and so was forced to make his dinner of an egg or two. To Woolwich, with a galley, all the way reading Sir J. Suckling's Aglaura, which, methinks, is but a mean play; nothing of design in it.

6th. Called upon Doll, our pretty 'Change woman, for a pair of gloves trimmed with yellow ribbon to [18] the petticoat my wife bought yesterday, which cost me 20*s*.; but she is so pretty that, God forgive me! I could not think it too much which is a strange slavery that I stand in to beauty, that I value nothing near it.

10th. This night, I received, by Will, £105, the first fruits of my endeavors in the late contract for victualing of Tangier, for which God be praised! for I can, with a safe conscience, say that I have therein saved the King £5,000 *per annum*, and yet got myself a hope of £300 *per annum*, without the least wrong to the King.

16th. Met Sir W. Warren, and afterwards to the Sun Tavern, where he brought to me, being all alone, a £100 in a bag, which I offered him to give him my receipt for, but he told me no, it was my own, which he had a little while since promised me; and so most kindly he did give it me, and I as joyfully, even out of myself, carried it home in a coach—he himself expressly taking care that nobody might see this business done, though I was willing enough to have carried a servant with me to have received it, but he advised me to do it myself.

13th [NOVEMBER]. (Lord's day) This morning to church, where mighty sport to hear our clerk sing out of tune, though his master sits by him that begins and keeps the time aloud for the parish. With my wife within doors and getting a speech out of Hamlet, "to be or not to be," without book. In the evening to sing psalms, and so to prayers and to bed.

9th [JANUARY, 1664/5]. Walked to Whitehall. In my way saw a woman that broke her thigh by her heels slipping up upon the frosty street. I saw the Royal Society bring their new book, wherein is nobly writ their charter and laws, and comes to be signed by the Duke as a Fellow; and all the Fellows are to be entered there, and lie as a monument; and the King hath put his, with the word Founder. Holmes was this day sent to the Tower, but I perceive it is made matter of jest only; but if the Dutch should be our masters, it may come to be of earnest to him, to be given over to them for a sacrifice, as Sir W. Ralegh was.

21st [FEBRUARY]. My wife busy in going with her woman to the hot-house to bathe herself after her long being within doors in the dirt, so that she now pretends to a resolution of being hereafter very clean. How long it will hold I can guess. . . . What mad freaks the maids of honor at court have! That Mrs. Jennings, one of the Duchess' maids, the other day dressed herself like an orange wench and went up and down and cried oranges; till, falling down, or by some accident, her fine shoes were discerned, and she put to a great deal of shame.

MARCH 1st. To Gresham College, where Mr. Hooke read a second very curious lecture about the late comet; among other things, proving very probably that this is the very same comet that appeared before in the year 1618 and that in such a time probably it will appear again, which is a very new opinion; but all will be in print. Then to the meeting, where Sir G. Carteret's two sons, his own and Sir N. Slanding, were admitted of the Society. And this day I did pay my admission

---

18 To match the color of.

money, 40s., to the Society. Here was very fine discourses and experiments, but I do lack philosophy enough to understand them, and so cannot remember them. Among others, a very particular account of the making of the several sorts of bread in France, which is accounted the best place for bread in the world.

5th [MAY, 1665]. After dinner to Mr. Evelyn's; he being abroad, we walked in his garden, and a lovely, noble ground he hath indeed. And, among other rarities, a hive of bees, so as, being hived in glass, you may see the bees making their honey and combs mighty pleasantly. This day, after I had suffered my own hair to grow long in order to wearing it, I find the convenience of periwigs is so great that I have cut off all short again and will keep to periwigs.

7th. [JUNE]. This day, much against my will, I did in Drury Lane see two or three houses marked with a red cross upon the doors and "Lord have mercy upon us!" writ there; which was a sad sight to me, being the first of the kind that, to my remembrance, I ever saw. It put me into an ill conception of myself and my smell, so that I was forced to buy some roll-tobacco to smell to and chaw, which took away the apprehension. By water home, where weary with walking and with the mighty heat of the weather and for my wife's not coming home, I stayed walking in the garden till twelve at night, when it begun to lighten exceedingly through the greatness of the heat.

8th. This day [19] they engaged, the Dutch neglecting greatly the opportunity of the wind they had of us; by which they lost the benefit of their fire-ships. The Earl of Falmouth, Muskerry, and Mr. Richard Boyle killed on board the Duke's ship, the Royal Charles, with one shot, their blood and brains flying in the Duke's face and the head of Mr. Boyle striking down the Duke, as some say. Earl of Marlborough, Portland, Rear Admiral Sansum, to Prince Rupert, killed, and Captain Kirby and Ableson. Sir John Lawson wounded on the knee. Hath had some bones taken out and is likely to be well again. Upon receiving the hurt, he sent to the Duke for another to command the Royal Oak. The Duke sent Jordan out of the St. George, who did brave things in her. Captain Jeremiah Smith of the Mary was second to the Duke, and stepped between him and Captain Seaton of the Urania, 76 guns and 400 men, who had sworn to board the Duke; killed him 200 men and took the ship; himself losing 99 men, and never an officer saved but himself and lieutenant. His

master indeed is saved, with his leg cut off. Admiral Opdam blown up, Tromp killed, and said by Holmes; all the rest of their admirals, as they say, but Everson, whom they dare not trust for his affection to the Prince of Orange, are killed. We have taken and sunk, as is believed, about twenty-four of their best ships; killed and taken near 8 or 10,000 men and lost, we think, not above 700. A greater victory never known in the world. They are all fled; some 43 got into the Texel and others elsewhere, and we in pursuit of the rest. Thence, with my heart full of joy, home. Then to my Lady Penn's, where they are all joyed, and not a little puffed up at the good success of their father; and good service indeed is said to have been done by him. Had a great bonfire at the gate; and I, with my Lady Penn's people and others, to Mrs. Turner's great room, and there down into the street. I did give the boys 4s. among them and mighty merry. So home to bed with my heart at great rest and quiet, saving that the consideration of the victory is too great for me presently to comprehend.

12th [AUGUST]. The people die so that now it seems they are fain to carry the dead to be buried by daylight, the nights not sufficing to do it in. And my Lord Mayor commands people to be within at nine at night all, as they say, that the sick may have liberty to go abroad for air. There is one also dead out of one of our ships at Deptford, which troubles us mightily—the Providence, fire-ship, which was just fitted to go to sea; but they tell me today no more sick on board.

31st. The plague having a great increase this week, beyond all expectation, of almost 2,000, making the general bill 7,000, odd 100; and the plague above 6,000. Thus this month ends with great sadness upon the public through the greatness of the plague everywhere through the kingdom almost. Every day sadder and sadder news of its increase. In the city died this week 7,496, and of them 6,102 of the plague. But it is feared that the true number of the dead this week is near 10,000; partly from the poor that cannot be taken notice of, through the greatness of the number, and partly from the Quakers and others that will not have any bell ring for them.

5th [OCTOBER]. To Mr. Evelyn's, to discourse of our confounded business of prisoners and sick and wounded seamen, wherein he and we are so much put out of order. And here he showed me his gardens, which are, for variety of evergreens and hedge of holly, the finest things I ever saw in my life. Thence in his coach to Greenwich, and there to my office, all the

19 June 3.

way having fine discourse of trees and the nature of vegetables.

5th [NOVEMBER]. Made a visit to Mr. Evelyn, who, among other things, showed me most excellent painting in little, in distemper, in Indian ink, water-colors, graving, and, above all, the whole secret of mezzotinto and the manner of it, which is very pretty, and good things done with it. He read to me very much also of his discourse, he hath been many years and now is about, about gardenage; which will be a most noble and pleasant piece. He read me part of a play or two of his making, very good, but not as he conceits them, I think, to be. He showed me his *Hortus Hiemalis*: leaves laid up in a book of several plants kept dry, which preserve color, however, and look very finely, better than an Herbal. In fine, a most excellent person he is, and must be allowed a little for a little conceitedness; but he may well be so, being a man so much above others. He read me, though with too much gusto, some little poems of his own, that were not transcendent, yet one or two very pretty epigrams; among others, of a lady looking in at a grate and being pecked at by an eagle that was there.

16th. Sir Edmund Pooly carried me down into the hold of the India ship, and there did show me the greatest wealth lie in confusion that a man can see in the world. Pepper scattered through every chink, you trod upon it; and in cloves and nutmegs I walked above the knees! whole rooms full. And silk in bales and boxes of copperplate, one of which I saw opened.

6th [DECEMBER]. Here the best company for music that I ever was in in my life, and wish I could live and die in it, both for music and the face of Mrs. Pierce and my wife and Knipp, who is pretty enough, but the most excellent, mad-humored thing, and sings the noblest that ever I heard in my life, and Rolt with her, some things together, most excellently. I spent the night in an ecstasy almost; and, having invited them to my house a day or two hence, we broke up.

25th. (Christmas Day) To church in the morning, and there saw a wedding in the church, which I have not seen many a day; and the young people so merry one with another! and strange to see what delight we married people have to see these poor fools decoyed into our condition, every man and woman gazing and smiling at them.

3rd [JANUARY, 1665/6]. Home, and find all my good company, I had bespoke, as Colman and his wife, and Lanier, Knipp and her surly husband; and good music we had, and among other things, Mr. Colman

sang my words I set, of "Beauty, retire,"[20] and they praise it mightily.

6th. To a great dinner and much company. Mr. Cuttle and his lady and I went, hoping to get Mrs. Knipp to us, having wrote a letter to her in the morning, calling myself "Dapper Dicky," in answer to hers of "Barbary Allen,"[21] but could not, and am told by the boy that carried my letter that he found her crying; and I fear she lives a sad life with that ill-natured fellow her husband. So we had a great, but I a melancholy dinner. After dinner to cards, and then comes notice that my wife is come unexpectedly to me to town. So I to her. It is only to see what I do and why I come not home; and she is in the right that I would have a little more of Mrs. Knipp's company before I go away.

28th. The King come to me of himself and told me, "Mr Pepys," says he, "I do give you thanks for your good service all this year, and I assure you I am very sensible of it." And the Duke of York did tell me with pleasure that he had read over my discourse about pursers and would have it ordered in my way, and so fell from one discourse to another.

10th [MARCH]. I find at home Mrs. Pierce and Knipp come to dine with me. We were mighty merry; and, after dinner, I carried them and my wife out by coach to the New Exchange, and there I did give my Valentine, Mrs. Pierce, a dozen pair of gloves and a pair of silk stockings, and Knipp for company, though my wife had, by my consent, laid out 20s. on her the other day, six pairs of gloves. The truth is, I do indulge myself a little the more in pleasure, knowing that this is the proper age of my life to do it and out of my observation that most men that do thrive in the world do forget to take pleasure during the time that they are getting their estate, but reserve that till they have got one, and then it is too late for them to enjoy it.

19th [AUGUST, 1666]. (Lord's day) Comes by agreement Mr. Reeves, bringing me a lanthorn, with pictures in glass, to make strange things appear on a wall, very pretty. We did also at night see Jupiter and his girdle and satellites, very fine, with my twelve-foot glass, but could not Saturn, he being very dark. Spong and I had also several fine discourses upon the globes this afternoon, particularly why the fixed stars do not

20 These words Pepys set to music are Solyman's in The Siege of Rhodes.
21 Mrs. Knipp chose her name from her "little Scotch song" Pepys had liked.

rise and set at the same hour all the year long, which he could not demonstrate nor I neither.

2nd [SEPTEMBER]. (Lord's day) Some of our maids sitting up late last night to get things ready against our feast today, Jane called us up about three in the morning to tell us of a great fire they saw in the city. So I rose and slipped on my nightgown and went to her window; and thought it to be on the back-side of Mark Lane at the farthest; but, being unused to such fires as followed, I thought it far enough off; and so went to bed again and to sleep. About seven rose again to dress myself, and there looked out at the window and saw the fire not so much as it was, and further off. So to my closet to set things to rights, after yesterday's cleaning. By and by Jane comes and tells me that she hears that above 300 houses have been burned down tonight by the fire we saw and that it is now burning down all Fish Street by London Bridge. So I made myself ready presently, and walked to the Tower; and there got upon one of the high places, Sir J. Robinson's little son going up with me; and there I did see the houses at that end of the bridge all on fire and an infinite great fire on this and the other side the end of the bridge; which, among other people, did trouble me for poor little Michell and our Sarah on the bridge. So down, with my heart full of trouble, to the lieutenant of the Tower, who tells me that it begun this morning in the King's baker's house in Pudding Lane and that it had burned down St. Magnus' Church and most part of Fish Street already. So I down to the water-side, and there got a boat, and through bridge, and there saw a lamentable fire. Poor Michell's house, as far as the Old Swan, already burned that way, and the fire running further, that in a very little time it got as far as the Steel-yard, while I was there. Everybody endeavoring to remove their goods, and flinging into the river or bringing them into lighters that lay off; poor people staying in their houses as long as till the very fire touched them, and then running into boats or clambering from one pair of stairs, by the water-side, to another. And among other things, the poor pigeons, I perceive, were loth to leave their houses, but hovered about the windows and balconies, till they burned their wings and fell down. Having stayed and in an hour's time seen the fire rage every way, and nobody, to my sight, endeavoring to quench it, but to remove their goods and leave all to the fire, and having seen it get as far as the Steel-yard, and the wind mighty high and driving it into the city; and everything, after so long a drought, proving combustible even the very stones of

churches; . . . I to Whitehall, with a gentleman with me, who desired to go off from the Tower, to see the fire, in my boat; and there up to the King's closet in the chapel, where people came about me, and I did give them an account dismayed them all, and word was carried in to the King. So I was called for, and did tell the King and the Duke of York what I saw; and that, unless his Majesty did command houses to be pulled down, nothing could stop the fire. They seemed much troubled, and the King commanded me to go to my Lord Mayor from him and command him to spare no houses, but to pull down before the fire every way. The Duke of York bid me to tell him that if he would have any more soldiers, he shall; and so did my Lord Arlington afterwards, as a great secret. Here meeting with Captain Cocke, I in his coach, which he lent me, and Creed with me to Paul's; and there walked along Watling Street, as well as I could, every creature coming away laden with goods to save, and, here and there, sick people carried away in beds. Extraordinary good goods carried in carts and on backs. At last met my Lord Mayor in Canning Street, like a man spent, with handkercher about his neck. To the King's message he cried, like a fainting woman, "Lord! what can I do? I am spent! people will not obey me. I have been pulling down houses; but the fire overtakes us faster than we can do it." That he needed no more soldiers and that, for himself, he must go and refresh himself, having been up all night. So he left me, and I him, and walked home; seeing people all almost distracted, and no manner of means used to quench the fire. The houses, too, so very thick thereabouts, and full of matter for burning, as pitch and tar, in Thames Street, and warehouses of oil and wines and brandy and other things. . . . Met with the King and Duke of York in their barge, and with them to Queenhithe, and there called Sir Richard Browne to them. Their order was only to pull down houses apace, and so below bridge at the water-side; but this little was or could be done, the fire coming upon them so fast. Good hopes there was of stopping it at the Three Cranes above and at Buttulph's Wharf below bridge, if care can be used; but the wind carries it into the city so as we know not, by the water-side, what it do there. River full of lighters and boats taking in goods, and good goods swimming in the water; and only I observed that hardly one lighter or boat in three that had the goods of a house in but there was a pair of virginals in it. Having seen as much as I could now, I away to Whitehall by appointment, and there walked to St. James's

Park; and there met my wife and Creed and Wood, and his wife, and walked to my boat; and there upon the water again, and to the fire up and down, it still increasing and the wind great. So near the fire as we could for smoke; and all over the Thames, with one's faces in the wind you were almost burned with a shower of fire-drops. This is very true, so as houses were burned by these drops and flakes of fire three or four, nay, five or six houses one from another. When we could endure no more upon the water, we to a little ale-house on the Bankside over against the Three Cranes, and there stayed till it was dark almost, and saw the fire grow; and as it grew darker, appeared more and more; and in corners and upon steeples and between churches and houses, as far as we could see up the hill of the city, in a most horrid, malicious, bloody flame, not like the fine flame of an ordinary fire. Barbary and her husband away before us. We stayed till, it being darkish, we saw the fire as only one entire arch of fire from this to the other side of the bridge and in a bow up the hill for an arch of above a mile long. It made me weep to see it. The churches, houses, and all on fire and flaming at once; and a horrid noise the flames made, and the cracking of houses at their ruin. So home with a sad heart, and there find everybody discoursing and lamenting the fire; and poor Tom Hater come with some few of his goods saved out of his house, which was burned upon Fish Street Hill. I invited him to lie at my house, and did receive his goods; but was deceived in his lying there, the news coming every moment of the growth of the fire; so as we were forced to begin to pack up our own goods and prepare for their removal; and did by moonshine, it being brave, dry, and moonshine and warm weather, carry much of my goods into the garden; and Mr. Hater and I did remove my money and iron chests into my cellar, as thinking that the safest place. And got my bags of gold into my office, ready to carry away, and my chief papers of accounts also there, and my tallies into a box by themselves.

4th. Sir W. Batten not knowing how to remove his wine, did dig a pit in the garden, and laid it in there; and I took the opportunity of laying all the papers of my office that I could not otherwise dispose of. And in the evening Sir W. Penn and I did dig another, and put our wine in it; and I my parmesan cheese as well as my wine and some other things. . . . This night, Mrs. Turner, who, poor woman, was removing her goods all this day, good goods, into the garden, and knows not how to dispose of them, and her husband supped

with my wife and me at night in the office upon a shoulder of mutton from the cook's without any napkin or anything in a sad manner, but were merry. Only now and then, walking into the garden, saw how horribly the sky looks, all on a fire in the night, was enough to put us out of our wits; and, indeed it was extremely dreadful, for it looks as if it was at us, and the whole heaven on fire. I after supper walked in the dark down to Tower Street, and there saw it all on fire, at the Trinity House on that side and the Dolphin Tavern on this side, which was very near us; and the fire with extraordinary vehemence. Now begins the practice of blowing up of houses in Tower Street, those next the Tower, which at first did frighten people more than anything; but it stopped the fire where it was done, it bringing down the houses to the ground in the same places they stood, and then it was easy to quench what little fire was in it, though it kindled nothing almost. W. Hewer this day went to see how his mother did, and comes late home, telling us how he hath been forced to remove her to Islington, her house in Pye Corner being burned; so that the fire is got so far that way and to the Old Bailey, and was running down to Fleet Street; and Paul's is burned and all Cheapside. I wrote to my father this night, but the post-house being burned, the letter could not go.

5th. I lay down in the office again upon W. Hewer's quilt, being mighty weary and sore in my feet with going till I was hardly able to stand. About two in the morning my wife calls me up and tells me of new cries of fire, it being come to Barking Church, which is the bottom of our lane. I up; and finding it so, resolved presently to take her away, and did, and took my gold, which was about £2,350, W. Hewer and Jane down by Proundy's boat to Woolwich. But, Lord! what a sad sight it was by moonlight to see the whole city almost on fire that you might see it as plain at Woolwich as if you were by it. There, when I come, I find the gates shut, but no guard kept at all; which troubled me, because of discourses now begun that there is a plot in it and that the French had done it. I got the gates open, and to Mr. Shelden's, where I locked up my gold and charged my wife and W. Hewer never to leave the room without one of them in it night or day. So back again, by the way seeing my goods well in the lighters at Deptford and watched well by people. Home, and whereas I expected to have seen our house on fire, it being now about seven o'clock, it was not. But to the fire, and there find greater hopes than I expected; for my confidence of finding our office on fire was such that I durst not ask anybody how it was with us till I come and saw it was not burned. But going to the fire, I find, by the blowing up of houses and the great help given by the workmen out of the King's yards, sent up by Sir W. Penn, there is a good stop given to it, as well at Mark Lane end as ours; it having only burned the dial of Barking Church and part of the porch, and was there quenched. I up to the top of Barking steeple, and there saw the saddest sight of desolation that I ever saw; everywhere great fires, oil-cellars and brimstone and other things burning. I became afraid to stay there long, and therefore down again as fast as I could, the fire being spread as far as I could see it; and to Sir W. Penn's and there eat a piece of cold meat, having eaten nothing since Sunday, but the remains of Sunday's dinner. Here I met with Mr. Young and Whistler; and, having removed all my things and received good hopes that the fire at our end is stopped, they and I walked into the town, and find Fenchurch Street, Gracious Street, and Lombard Street all in dust. The Exchange a sad sight, nothing standing there of all the statues or pillars but Sir Thomas Gresham's picture in the corner. Into Moorfields, our feet ready to burn walking through the town among the hot coals, and find that full of people and poor wretches carrying their goods there and everybody keeping his goods together by themselves; and a great blessing it is to them that it is fair weather for them to keep abroad night and day; drunk there, and paid two-pence for a plain penny loaf. Thence homeward, having passed through Cheapside and Newgate market, all burned; and seen Anthony Joyce's house in fire; and took up, which I keep by me, a piece of glass of the Mercers' Chapel in the street, where much more was, so melted and buckled with the heat of the fire like parchment. I also did see a poor cat taken out of a hole in a chimney, joining to the wall of the Exchange, with the hair all burnt off the body, and yet alive. So home at night, and find there good hopes of saving our office; but great endeavors of watching all night and having men ready; and so we lodged them in the office, and had drink and bread and cheese for them. And I lay down and slept a good night about midnight, though, when I rose, I heard that there had been a great alarm of French and Dutch being risen, which proved nothing.

14th [NOVEMBER]. To Knipp's lodging, whom I find not ready to go home with me; and there stayed reading of Waller's verses while she finished dressing, her husband being by. Her lodging very mean and the condition she lives in; yet makes a show without doors, God bless us!

25th [DECEMBER]. (Christmas Day) Lay pretty long in bed, and then rose, leaving my wife desirous to sleep, having sat up till four this morning seeing her maids make mince-pies. I to church, where our parson Mills made a good sermon. Then home, and dined well on some good ribs of beef roasted and mince-pies; only my wife, brother, and Barker, and plenty of good wine of my own, and my heart full of true joy; and thanks to God Almighty for the goodness of my condition at this day.

31st. Blessed be God! and I pray God make me thankful for it, I do find myself worth in money, all good, above £6,200; which is above £1,800 more than I was the last year: Thus ends this year of public wonder and mischief to this nation and therefore generally wished by all people to have an end. Myself and family well, having four maids and one clerk, Tom, in my house and my brother now with me to spend time in order to his preferment. Our health all well, public matters in a most sad condition; seamen discouraged for want of pay and are become not to be governed. Nor, as matters are now, can any fleet go out next year. Our enemies, French and Dutch, great, and grow more by our poverty. The Parliament backward in raising because jealous of the spending of the money; the city less and less likely to be built again, everybody settling elsewhere and nobody encouraged to trade. A sad, vicious, negligent court, and all sober men there fearful of the ruin of the whole kingdom this next year; from which, good God deliver us! One thing I reckon remarkable in my own condition is that I am come to abound in good plate so as at all entertainments to be served wholly with silver plates, having two dozen and a half.

7th [JANUARY, 1666/7]. To the Duke's House, and saw Macbeth, which, though I saw it lately, yet appears a most excellent play in all respects but especially in divertisement, though it be a deep tragedy; which is a strange perfection in a tragedy, it being most proper here and suitable.[22]

2nd [FEBRUARY]. This night comes home my new silver snuff-dish which I do give myself for my closet. I am very well pleased this night with reading a poem I brought home with me last night from Westminster Hall, of Dryden's, upon the present war;[23] a very good poem.

22 This was Davenant's adaptation, with the pretty witches.
23 *Annus Mirabilis.*

3rd. We fell to talking of the burning of the city; and my Lady Carteret herself did tell us how abundance of pieces of burnt papers were cast by the wind as far as Cranborn;[24] and among others she took up one, or had one brought her to see, which was a little bit of paper that had been printed, whereon there remained no more nor less than these words: "Time is, it is done."

12th [JUNE, 1667]. Home, where all our hearts do now ache; for the news is true that the Dutch have broke the chain[25] and burned our ships and particularly the Royal Charles; other particulars I know not, but it is said to be so. And, the truth is, I do fear so much that the whole kingdom is undone that I do this night resolve to study with my father and wife what to do with the little that I have in money by me, for I give up all the rest that I have in the King's hands, for Tangier, for lost. So God help us; and God knows what disorders we may fall into and whether any violence on this office or perhaps some severity on our persons, as being reckoned by the silly people, or perhaps may by policy of state be thought fit to be condemned by the King and Duke of York and so put to trouble, though, God knows! I have, in my own person, done my full duty, I am sure. Home, and to bed with a heavy heart.

29th [JULY]. Cousin Roger and Creed to dinner with me, and very merry. But among other things they told me of the strange, bold sermon of Dr. Creeton yesterday before the King; how he preached against the sins of the court and particularly against adultery, over and over instancing how for that single sin in David the whole nation was undone, and of our negligence in having our castles without ammunition and powder when the Dutch came upon us, and how we have no courage nowadays but let our ships be taken out of our harbor. . . . Among other discourse, my cousin Roger told us as a thing certain that the Archbishop of Canterbury,[26] that now is, do keep a wench and that he is as very a wencher as can be; and tells us it is a thing publicly known that Sir Charles Sedley had got away one of the Archbishop's wenches from him, and the Archbishop sent to him to let him know that she was his kinswoman and did wonder that he would offer any dishonor to one related to him. . . . Cousin Roger did acquaint me in private with an offer made of his marrying of Mrs. Elizabeth Wiles, whom I know; a kinswoman of Mr. Honiwood's, an ugly old maid but good housewife and is said to have £2,500 to her portion; but I can find that she hath but £2,000, which he prays me to examine; he says he will have her, she being one he hath long known intimately and a good housewife and discreet woman, though I am against it in my heart, she being not handsome at all. And it hath been the very bad fortune of the Pepyses that ever I knew never to marry an handsome woman, excepting Ned Pepys.

30th. With Creed to Whitehall; in our way meeting with Mr. Cooling, my Lord Chamberlain's secretary, on horseback, who stopped to speak with us, and he proved very drunk and did talk and would have talked all night with us, I not being able to break loose from him, he holding me so by the hand. But, Lord! to see his present humor, how he swears at every word and talks of the King and my Lady Castlemaine in the plainest words in the world. And from him I gather that the story I learned yesterday is true—that the King hath declared that he did not get the child of which she is conceived at this time. But she told him, "G—d d—n me, but you shall own it!" It seems, he is jealous of Jermyn, and she loves him so that the thoughts of his marrying of my Lady Falmouth puts her into fits of the mother; and he, it seems, hath been in her good graces from time to time continually for a good while; and once, as this Cooling says, the King had like to have taken him a-bed with her, but that he was fain to creep under the bed into her closet. . . . I never heard so much vanity from a man in my life. So, being now weary of him, we parted, and I took coach, and carried Creed to the Temple. There set him down, and to my office, till my eyes begun to ache, and then home to supper. A pullet with good sauce to my liking, and then to play on the flageolet with my wife, which she now does very prettily, and so to bed.

8th [AUGUST]. I to my bookseller's; where, by and by, I met Mr. Evelyn, and talked of several things but particularly of the times. And he tells me that wise men do prepare to remove abroad what they have for that we must be ruined, our case being past relief, the kingdom so much in debt, and the King minding nothing but his lust, going two days a week to see my Lady Castlemaine at Sir D. Harvey's.

18th. Into St. Dunstan's Church, where I heard an able sermon of the minister of the place; and stood by a pretty, modest maid, whom I did labor to take by the hand; but she would not, but get further and further

24 Over fifty miles from London.
25 Stretched across the Thames to protect the idle British fleet.
26 Gilbert Sheldon.

from me; and at last, I could perceive her to take pins out of her pocket to prick me if I should touch her again—which seeing, I did forbear, and was glad I did spy her design. And then I fell to gaze upon another pretty maid, in a pew close to me, and she on me; and I did go about to take her by the hand, which she suffered a little, and then withdrew. So the sermon ended, and the church broke up, and my amours ended also. Took coach and home, and there took up my wife, and to Islington.

26th. Dined at Sir W. Batten's, where Mr. Boreman was, who came from Whitehall; who tells us that he saw my Lord Chancellor come in his coach with some of his men, without his seal, to Whitehall to his chamber. And thither the King and Duke of York came and stayed together alone an hour or more. And it is said that the King do say that he will have the Parliament meet and that it will prevent much trouble by having of him out of their enmity by his place being taken away; for that all their enmity will be at him. It is said also that my Lord Chancellor answers that he desires he may be brought to his trial if he have done anything to lose his office; and that he will be willing and is most desirous to lose that and his head both together. Upon what terms they parted nobody knows. But the Chancellor looked sad, he says.

5th [OCTOBER]. To the King's House, and there, going in, met with Knipp, and she took us up into the tiring-rooms and to the women's shift, where Nell[27] was dressing herself and was all unready, and is very pretty, prettier than I thought. And into the scene-room, and there sat down, and she gave us fruit. And here I read the questions[28] to Knipp, while she answered me, through all her part of Flora Figarys, which was acted today. But, Lord! to see how they were both painted would make a man mad! and did make me loathe them; and what base company of men comes among them, and how lewdly they talk! and how poor the men are in clothes and yet what a show they make on the stage by candlelight is very observable. But to see how Nell cursed for having so few people in the pit was pretty, the other house carrying away all the people at the new play and is said nowadays to have generally most company as being better players. By and by into the pit, and there saw the play, which is pretty good.

2nd [NOVEMBER]. To the King's Playhouse, and there saw Henry the Fourth; and contrary to expectation, was pleased in nothing more than in Cartwright's

speaking of Falstaff's speech about "What is honor?" The house full of Parliament men, it being holiday with them. And it was observable how a gentleman of good habit, sitting just before us, eating of some fruit in the midst of the play, did drop down as dead, being choked; but with much ado Orange Moll did thrust her fingers down his throat and brought him to life again.

5th [MARCH, 1667/8]. I full of thoughts and trouble touching the issue of this day; and to comfort myself did go to the Dog and drink half a pint of mulled sack, and in the Hall[29] did drink a dram of brandy at Mrs. Hewlett's; and with the warmth of this did find myself in better order as to courage, truly. So we all up to the lobby, and, between eleven or twelve o'clock, were called in, with the mace before us, into the House, where a mighty full house. And we stood at the bar, namely, Brouncker, Sir J. Minnes, Sir T. Harvey, and myself, W. Penn being in the House as a member. I perceive the whole House was full of expectation of our defense what it would be, and with great prejudice. After the Speaker had told us the dissatisfaction of the House and read the report of the committee, I began our defense most acceptably and smoothly and continued at it without any hesitation or loss but with full scope and all my reason free about me, as if it had been at my own table, from that time till past three in the afternoon; and so ended, without any interruption from the Speaker; but we withdrew. And there all my fellow officers and all the world that was within hearing did congratulate me and cry up my speech as the best thing they ever heard; and my fellow officers were overjoyed in it.

15th [MARCH, 1668]. The Duke of York and all with him this morning were full of the talk of the 'prentices, who are not yet put down though the guards and militia of the town have been in arms all this night and the night before; and the 'prentices have made fools of them, sometimes by running from them and flinging stones at them. Some blood hath been spilt, but a great many houses pulled down; and, among others, the Duke of York was mighty merry at that of Daman Page's, the great bawd of the seamen; and the Duke of York complained merrily that he hath lost two tenants, by their houses being pulled down, who paid him for their wine licenses £15 a year. But these idle fellows have had the confidence to say that they did ill in contenting themselves in pulling down the little brothels and did not go and pull down the great one at Whitehall.

27 Nell Gwyn.　　　　　　　28 The cues.　　　　　　29 Westminster.

6th [APRIL]. I do hear that my Lady Castlemaine is horribly vexed at the late libel,[30] the petition of the poor prostitutes about the town, whose houses were pulled down the other day. I have got one of them, and it is not very witty, but devilish severe against her and the King. And I wonder how it durst be printed and spread abroad, which shows that the times are loose and come to a great disregard of the King or court or government.

9th [JUNE]. We came to Oxford, a very sweet place. Paid our guide £1 2s. 6d.; barber, 2s. 6d.; book, Stonehenge, 4s.; boy that showed me the colleges before dinner, 1s. To dinner; and then out with my wife and people and landlord. And to him that showed us the Schools and Library, 10s.; to him that showed us All Souls' College and Chicheley's[31] picture, 5s. So to see Christ Curch with my wife, I seeing several others very fine alone, before dinner, and did give the boy that went with me 1s. Strawberries, 1s. 2d. Dinner and servants, £1 0s. 6d. After coming home from the Schools, I out with the landlord to Brasenose College to the butteries, and in the cellar find the hand of the Child of Hale, . . . long.[32] Butler, 2s. Thence with coach and people to Physic-Garden, 1s. So to Friar Bacon's study. I up and saw it, and gave the man 1s. Bottle of sack for landlord, 2s. Oxford mighty fine place and well seated and cheap entertainment. At night came to Abingdon, where had been a fair of custard; and met many people and scholars going home; and there did get some pretty good music, and sang and danced till supper, 5s.

19th. My wife fell into her blubbering, and at length had a request to make to me, which was that she might go into France and live there out of trouble; and then all come out, that I loved pleasure and denied her any; and I find that there have been great fallings out between my father and her, whom, for ever hereafter, I must keep asunder, for they cannot possibly agree. And I said nothing, but, with very mild words and few, suffered her humor to spend, till we begun to be very quiet, and I think all will be over, and friends.

1st [SEPTEMBER]. To Bartholomew Fair, and there saw several sights; among others, the mare that tells[33] money and many things to admiration; and, among others, come to me, when she was bid to go to him of the company that most loved a pretty wench in a corner. And this did cost me 12d. to the horse, which I had flung him before, and did give me occasion to kiss a mighty *belle fille* that was exceedingly plain but *fort belle.*

21st [DECEMBER]. Went into Holborn, and there saw the woman that is to be seen with a beard. She is a little plain woman, a Dane; her name, Ursula Dyan; about forty years old; her voice like a little girl's; with a beard as much as any man I ever saw, black almost and grizzly; it began to grow at about seven years old and was shaved not above seven months ago and is now so big as any man's almost that ever I saw, I say, bushy and thick. It was a strange sight to me, I confess, and what pleased me mightily. Thence to the Duke's Playhouse, and saw Macbeth.

12th [JANUARY, 1668/9]. This evening I observed my wife mighty dull, and I myself was not mighty fond because of some hard words she did give me at noon out of a jealousy at my being abroad this morning, which God knows, it was upon the business of the office unexpectedly. But I to bed, not thinking but she would come after me. But waking by and by out of a slumber, which I usually fall into presently after my coming into the bed, I found she did not prepare to come to bed, but got fresh candles and more wood for her fire, it being mighty cold, too. At this being troubled, I after a while prayed her to come to bed; so, after an hour or two, she silent, and I now and then praying her to come to bed, she fell out into a fury, that I was a rogue and false to her. I did, as I might truly, deny it, and was mightily troubled, but all would not serve. At last, about one o'clock she come to my side of the bed and drew my curtain open and with the tongs red hot at the ends made as if she did design to pinch me with them, at which, in dismay, I rose up, and with a few words she laid them down; and did by little and little, very sillily, let all the discourse fall.

12th [FEBRUARY]. Home, and there Pelling hath got W. Penn's book against the Trinity.[34] I got my wife to read it to me; and I find it so well writ as, I think, it is too good for him ever to have writ it; and it is a serious sort of book and not fit for everybody to read.

10th [MAY, 1669]. Troubled, about three in the morning, with my wife's calling her maid up and

30 See Evelyn for 2nd of April, 1668.

31 The founder.

32 Pepys meant to fill in here the seventeen inches that the hand of John Middleton, the famous nine-foot-three Lancashire giant, measured. The picture of the "Child of Hale" is still at Brasenose College.

33 Counts.

34 This work, The Sandy Foundation Shaken, brought about the imprisonment of young Penn, the Quaker, in the Tower, whence he was delivered to his father to be transported.

rising herself to go with her coach abroad to gather May-dew, which she did, and I troubled for it for fear of any hurt, going abroad so betimes, happening to her; but I to sleep again, and she come home about six.

31st. Being called by my wife, we to the park, Mary Batelier and a Dutch gentleman, a friend of hers, being with us. Thence to the World's End, a drinking-house by the park; and there merry, and so home late. . . .

And thus ends all that I doubt I shall ever be able to do with my own eyes in the keeping of my Journal,[35] I being not able to do it any longer, having done now

35 Throughout the Diary, Pepys has complained of the trouble his work caused his eyes.

so long as to undo my eyes almost every time that I take a pen in my hand; and, therefore, whatever comes of it, I must forbear. And, therefore, resolve from this time forward to have it kept by my people in long-hand, and must be contented to set down no more than is fit for them and all the world to know; or, if there be anything, I must endeavor to keep a margin in my book open to add here and there a note in short-hand with my own hand.

And so I betake myself to that course which is almost as much as to see myself go into my grave. For which, and all the discomforts that will accompany my being blind, the good God prepare me!

George Savile

FIRST MARQUIS OF HALIFAX

[1633–1695]

THE name of the first Marquis of Halifax is met with much more often in the history of English politics than in that of English literature. No student of seventeenth-century history is unfamiliar with the handsome, witty, and urbane statesman who was adviser to kings and queens and upon whom, among many other interesting activities, devolved the duty of offering to William and Mary, in the banqueting room at Whitehall, the crown of England. Historians have always paid due tribute to his intellectual brilliance and his great gifts as orator and statesman, and he has been credited with an influence on public opinion of his day second to none. Halifax has not always received his due as a literary figure however, and the neglect of his writings is not easy to understand. As a master of aphorism he ranks almost with Bacon, Jonson, and John Selden, and his indebtedness to Montaigne, his favorite author, is readily perceptible in all his work.

Born in Thornhill, Yorkshire, Savile traveled in France and Italy in his youth. Elevated to the peerage as Viscount Halifax in 1668, he was admitted to the Privy Council in 1672, dismissed in 1676 because of a disagreement with Charles II, and readmitted in 1679, at the time of Sir William Temple's remodeling of the Council. In the same year he was made Earl of Halifax, and in 1682 he was made Marquis of Halifax and appointed Lord Privy Seal. Always a moderate in politics, he attempted consistently to mediate between the extreme positions represented by James, Duke of York, on the one hand and the radical Whigs on the other. In 1680 he was instrumental in defeating the Exclusion Bill, a Whig project which would have forbidden York's succession to the throne. In 1685, as James II, the ungrateful monarch dismissed his servant, but Halifax continued to attempt to maintain the Stuart monarchy until events made it clear that the House of Orange must be called in to preserve England's peace. He served William as faithfully and well as he had the two Stuart monarchs, and ended his days in honor and respect.

Halifax's most important work is *The Character of a Trimmer*, and it is as "the great trimmer" that he has effectively written himself down for future generations. Certainly in no other English work have the counsels of independence, reasonableness, moderation, and compromise been so persuasively set forth. The epithet "the great trimmer" had been applied to Halifax in 1684 by Sir Roger L'Estrange, a Tory extremist and one of the most capable pamphleteers of the day. Halifax rose to the occasion brilliantly, turning the epithet into a title of honor and arguing eloquently that the man who trims the boat is following a wiser course than those who unbalance it to one side or the other.

Among Halifax's other writings, the most important are *A Letter to a Dissenter*, *The Anatomy of an Equivalent*, and *The Lady's New-Year's Gift, or Advice to a Daughter*, the last-named being the least characteristic and most charming of his works, a late example of the Renaissance genre of the conduct-book.

Halifax's political counsels were seldom heeded in his own age of passion and intolerance, but they have earned for him a considerable reputation for wisdom in the centuries that have followed.

G. SAVILE. Marquis of Halifax. *Complete Works*, ed. W. Raleigh (Oxford, 1912).

H. C. FOXCROFT. *Life and Letters of Sir George Savile, Bart., First Marquis of Halifax*, 2 vols. (London, 1898). A monumental work, which includes an edition of Halifax's writings.

————. *A Character of the Trimmer* (Cambridge, 1946). A revised and abridged version of the foregoing.

THE CHARACTER OF A TRIMMER

[TEXT: *first collected edition, 1700*]

THE PREFACE

IT MUST be more than an ordinary provocation that can tempt a man to write in an age over-run with scribblers, as Egypt was with flies and locusts. That worst vermin of small authors hath given the world such a surfeit, that instead of desiring to write, a man would be more inclined to wish, for his own ease, that he could not read. But there are some things which do so raise our passions that our reason can make no resistance; and when madmen in two extremes shall agree to make common sense treason, and join to fix an ill character upon the only men in the nation who deserve a good one, I am no longer master of my better resolution to let the world alone, and must break loose from my more reasonable thoughts to expose these false coiners, who would make their copper wares pass upon us for good payment.

Amongst all the engines of dissension, there hath been none more powerful in all times than the fixing names upon one another of contumely and reproach; and the reason is plain, in respect of the people, who though generally they are uncapable of making a syllogism or forming an argument, yet they can pronounce a word; and that serveth their turn to throw it with their dull malice at the head of those they do not like. Such things even begin in jest and end in blood, and the same word which at first maketh the company merry groweth in time to a military signal to cut one another's throats.

These mistakes are to be lamented, though not easily cured, being suitable enough to the corrupted nature of mankind; but 'tis hard that men will not only invent ill names but they will wrest and misinterpret good ones; so afraid some are even of a reconciling sound, that they raise another noise to keep it from being heard, lest it should set up and encourage a dangerous sort of men, who prefer peace and agreement before violence and confusion.

Were it not for this, why, after we have played the fool with throwing Whig and Tory at one another, as boys do snowballs, do we grow angry at a new name, which by its true signification might do as much to put us into our wits as the other hath done to put us out of them?

This innocent word Trimmer signifieth no more than this: that if men are together in a boat, and one part of the company would weigh it down on one side, another would make it lean as much to the contrary; it happeneth there is a third opinion of those who conceive it would do as well if the boat went even, without endangering the passengers; now it is hard to imagine by what figure in language or by what rule in sense this cometh to be a fault, and it is much more a wonder it should be thought a heresy.

But so it happeneth, that the poor Trimmer hath now all the powder spent upon him alone, while the Whig is a forgotten, or at least a neglected enemy; there is no danger now to the state (if some men may be believed) but from the beast called a Trimmer; take heed of him, he is the instrument that must destroy church and state; a strange kind of monster, whose deformity is so exposed, that were it a true picture that is made of him, it would be enough to fright children and make women miscarry at the sight of it.

But it may be worth the examining whether he is such a beast as he is painted. I am not of that opinion, and am so far from thinking him an infidel either in church or state that I am neither afraid to expose the articles of his faith in relation to government, nor to say that I prefer them before any other political creed, that either our angry divines or our refined statesmen would impose upon us.

I have therefore in the following discourse endeavored to explain the Trimmer's principles and opinions, and then leave it to all discerning and impartial judges, whether he can with justice be so arraigned, and whether those who deliberately pervert a good name do not very justly deserve the worst that can be put upon themselves.

THE TRIMMER'S OPINION OF THE LAWS AND GOVERNMENT

OUR Trimmer, as he hath a great veneration for laws in general, so he hath a more particular for our own. He looketh upon them as the chains that tie up our unruly passions, which else, like wild beasts let loose, would reduce the world into its first state of barbarism and hostility; the good things we enjoy, we owe to them; and all the ill things we are freed from is by their protection.

God himself thought it not enough to be a creator, without being a lawgiver; and his goodness had been defective towards mankind in making them, if he had not prescribed rules to make them happy too.

All laws flow from that of Nature, and where that is not the foundation, they may be legally imposed, but they will be lamely obeyed. By this Nature is not meant that which fools and madmen misquote to justify their excesses; it is innocent and uncorrupted Nature, that which disposeth men to choose virtue, without its being prescribed, and which is so far from

inspiring ill thoughts into us, that we take pains to suppress the good ones it infuseth.

The civilized world hath ever paid a willing subjection to laws; even conquerors have done homage to them; as the Romans, who took patterns of good laws even from those they had subdued; and at the same time that they triumphed over an enslaved people, the very laws of that place did not only remain safe, but became victorious. Their new masters, instead of suppressing them, paid them more respect than they had from those who first made them; and by this wise method they arrived at such an admirable constitution of laws, that to this day they reign by them. This excellency of them triumpheth still, and the world payeth now an acknowledgment of their obedience to that mighty empire, though so many ages after it is dissolved. And by a later instance, the kings of France, who in practice use their laws pretty familiarly, yet think their picture is drawn with most advantage upon their seals, when they are placed in the seat of justice; and though the hieroglyphic is not there of so much use to the people as they would wish, yet it showeth that no prince is so great as not to think fit, for his own credit at least, to give an outward when he refuseth a real worship to the laws.

They are to mankind that which the sun is to plants, whilst it cherisheth and preserveth them. Where they have their force and are not clouded or suppressed, everything smileth and flourisheth; but where they are darkened and not suffered to shine out, it maketh everything to wither and decay.

They secure man not only against one another, but against themselves too; they are a sanctuary to which the Crown hath occasion to resort as often as the people, so that it is an interest as well as a duty to preserve them.

There would be no end of making a panegyric of laws; let it be enough to add that without laws the world would become a wilderness, and men little less than beasts; but with all this, the best things may come to be the worst, if they are not in good hands; and if it be true that the wisest men generally make the laws, it is true that the strongest do often interpret them. And as rivers belong as much to the channel where they run as to the spring from whence they first rise, so the laws depend as much upon the pipes through which they are to pass as upon the fountain from whence they flow.

The authority of a king who is head of the law, as well as the dignity of public justice, is debased when the clear stream of the law is puddled and disturbed by bunglers, or conveyed by unclean instruments to the people.

Our Trimmer would have them appear in their full luster, and would be grieved to see the day when, instead of speaking with authority from the seats of justice, they should speak out of a grate, with a lamenting voice like prisoners that desire to be rescued.

He wisheth that the Bench may have a natural as well as a legal superiority to the Bar; he thinketh men's abilities very much misplaced when the reason of him that pleadeth is visibly too strong for those who judge and give sentence.

When those from the Bar seem to dictate to their superiors upon the Bench, their furs will look scurvily about them, and the respect of the world will leave the bare character of a judge, to follow the essential knowledge of a lawyer, who may be greater in himself than the other can be with all his trappings.

An uncontested superiority in any calling will have the better of any discountenance[1] that authority can put upon it, and therefore if ever such an unnatural method should be introduced it is then that Westminster Hall might be said to stand upon its head, and though justice itself can never be so, yet the administration of it would be rendered ridiculous.

A judge hath such power lodged in him that the king will never be thought to have chosen well where the voice of mankind hath not beforehand recommended the man to his station; when men are made judges of what they do not understand, the world censureth such a choice, not out of ill will to the men, but fear for themselves.

If the king had the sole power of choosing physicians, men would tremble to see bunglers preferred, yet the necessity of taking physic from a doctor is generally not so great as that of receiving justice from a judge. And yet the inferences will be very severe in such cases, for either it will be thought that such men bought what they were not able to deserve, or, which is as bad, that obedience shall be looked upon as a better qualification in a judge than skill or integrity, when such sacred things as the laws are not only touched but guided by profane hands. Men will fear that out of the tree of the law, from whence we expect shade and shelter, such workmen will make cudgels to beat us with, or rather they will turn the cannon upon

our properties that were entrusted with them for their defense.

To see the laws mangled, disguised, speak quite another language than their own; to see them thrown from the dignity of protecting mankind to the disgraceful office of destroying them; and, notwithstanding their innocence in themselves, to be made the worst instruments that the most refined villainy can make use of, will raise men's anger above the power of laying it down again, and tempt them to follow the evil examples given them of judging without hearing, when so provoked by their desire of revenge. Our Trimmer therefore, as he thinketh the laws are jewels, so he believeth they are nowhere better set than in the constitution of our English government, if rightly understood and carefully preserved.

It would be too great partiality to say they are perfect or liable to no objection; such things are not of this world; but if they have more excellencies and fewer faults than any other we know, it is enough to recommend them to our esteem.

The dispute which is a greater beauty, a monarchy or a commonwealth, hath lasted long between their contending lovers, and they have behaved themselves so like lovers (who in good manners must be out of their wits), who used such figures to exalt their own idols on either side, and such angry aggravations to reproach one another in the contest, that moderate men have in all times smiled upon this eagerness, and thought it differed very little from a downright frenzy. We in England, by a happy use of the controversy, conclude them both in the wrong and reject them from being our pattern, not taking the words in the utmost extent, which is, monarchy, a thing that leaveth men no liberty, and a commonwealth, such a one as alloweth them no quiet.

We think that a wise mean between these barbarous extremes is that which self-preservation ought to dictate to our wishes; and we may say we have attained to this mean in a greater measure, than any nation now in being, or perhaps any we have read of, though never so much celebrated for the wisdom or felicity of their constitutions. We take from one the too great power of doing hurt and yet leave enough to govern and protect us; we take from the other the confusion, the parity, the animosities, and the license, and yet reserve a due care of such a liberty as may consist with men's allegiance; but it being hard, if not impossible, to be exactly even, our government hath much the stronger bias towards monarchy, which by the general consent

---

1 The text reads "distinct name." The reading, "discountenance," is Miss Foxcroft's emendation.

and practice of mankind seemeth to have the advantage in dispute against a commonwealth. The rules of a commonwealth are too hard for the bulk of mankind to come up to; that form of government requireth such a spirit to carry it on as doth not dwell in great numbers, but is restrained to so very few, especially in this age, that let the methods appear never so reasonable in paper, they must fail in practice, which will ever be suited more to men's nature as it is than as it should be.

Monarchy is liked by the people for the bells and tinsel, the outward pomp and gilding; and there must be milk for babes, since the greatest part of mankind are and ever will be included in that list; and it is approved by wise and thinking men (all circumstances and objections impartially considered) that it hath so great an advantage above all other forms, when the administration of that power falleth in good hands, that all other governments look out of countenance, when they are set in competition with it. Lycurgus might have saved himself the trouble of making laws if either he had been immortal, or that he could have secured to posterity a succeeding race of princes like himself; his own example was a better law than he could with all his skill tell how to make; such a prince is a living law that dictateth to his subjects, whose thoughts in that case never rise above their obedience; the confidence they have in the virtue and knowledge of the master preventing the scruples and apprehensions to which men are naturally inclined in relation to those that govern them. Such a magistrate is the life and soul of justice, whereas the law is but a body and a dead one, too, without his influence to give it warmth and vigor; and by the irresistible power of his virtue he doth so reconcile dominion and allegiance that all disputes between them are silenced and subdued. And indeed no monarchy can be perfect and absolute without exception but where the prince is superior by his virtue as well as by his character and his power. So that to screw out precedents of unlimited power is a plain diminution to a prince that nature hath made great, and who had better make himself a glorious example to posterity than borrow an authority from dark records raised out of the grave, which, besides their non-usage, have always in them matter of controversy and debate. And it may be affirmed that the instances are very rare of princes having the worst in the dispute with their people, if they were eminent for justice in time of peace or conduct in time of war; such advantage the Crown giveth

to those who adorn it by their own personal virtues.

But since for the greater honor of good and wise princes, and the better to set off their character by the comparison, Heaven hath decreed there must be a mixture, and that such as are perverse or insufficient, or perhaps both, are at least to have their equal turns in the government of the world; and besides, that the will of man is so various, and so unbounded a thing, and so fatal too when joined with power misapplied, it is no wonder if those who are to be governed are unwilling to have so dangerous as well as so uncertain a standard of their obedience.

There must be therefore rules and laws; for want of which, or at least the observation of them, it was as capital for a man to say that Nero did not play well upon the lute as to commit treason or blaspheme the Gods. And even Vespasian himself had like to have lost his life for sleeping whilst he should have attended and admired that emperor's impertinence upon the stage. There is a wantonness in great power that men are generally too apt to be corrupted with; and for that reason a wise prince, to prevent the temptation arising from common frailty, would choose to govern by rules for his own sake, as well as for his people's, since it only secureth him from errors, and doth not lessen the real authority that a good magistrate would care to be possessed of; for if the will of a prince is contrary either to reason itself, or to the universal opinion of his subjects, the law by a kind restraint rescueth him from a disease that would undo him; if his will on the other side is reasonable and well directed, that will immediately becometh a law, and he is arbitrary by an easy and natural consequence, without taking pains or overturning the world for it.

If princes consider laws as things imposed on them, they have the appearance of fetters of iron, but to such as would make them their choice as well as their practice they are chains of gold; and in that respect are ornaments, as in others they are a defense to them. And, by a comparison not improper for God's vicegerents upon earth, as our Maker never commandeth our obedience to anything that as reasonable creatures we ought not to make our own election, so a good and wise governor, though all laws were abolished would, by the voluntary direction of his own reason, do without restraint the very same things that they would have enjoined.

Our Trimmer thinketh that the king and kingdom ought to be one creature, not to be separated in their political capacity; and when either of them undertake to act apart, it is like the crawling of worms after they are cut in pieces, which cannot be a lasting motion, the whole creature not stirring at a time. If the body have a dead palsy, the head cannot make it move; and God hath not yet delegated such a healing power to princes as that they can in a moment say to a languishing people oppressed and in despair, Take up your bed and walk.

The figure of a king is so comprehensive and exalted a thing that it is a kind of degrading him to lodge that power separately in his own natural person, which can never be safely or naturally great but where the people are so united to him as to be flesh of his flesh and bone of his bone. For when he is reduced to the single definition of a man he sinketh into so low a character that it is a temptation upon men's allegiance, and an impairing that veneration which is necessary to preserve their duty to him; whereas a prince who is so joined to his people that they seem to be his limbs, rather than his subjects; clothed with mercy and justice rightly applied in their several places; his throne supported by love as well as by power; and the warm wishes of his devoted subjects, like never-failing incense, still ascending towards him, looketh so like the best image we can frame to ourselves of God Almighty that men would have much ado not to fall down and worship him, and would be much more tempted to the sin of idolatry than to that of disobedience.

Our Trimmer is of opinion, that there must be so much dignity inseparably annexed to the royal function as may be sufficient to secure it from insolence and contempt; and there must be condescensions from the Throne, like kind showers from Heaven, that the prince may look so much the more like God Almighty's deputy upon earth. For power without love hath a terrifying aspect, and the worship which is paid to it is like that which the Indians give out of fear to wild beasts and devils. He that feareth God only because there is an hell, must wish there were no God; and he who feareth the king only because he can punish, must wish there were no king. So that, without a principle of love, there can be no true allegiance; and there must remain perpetual seeds of resistance against a power that is built upon such an unnatural foundation as that of fear and terror. All force is a kind of foul play, and whosoever aimeth at it himself doth by implication allow it to those he playeth with; so that there will be ever matter prepared in the minds of people when they are provoked, and the prince, to secure himself, must live in the midst of his own sub-

jects as if he were in a conquered country, raise arms as if he were immediately to meet or resist an invasion, and all this while sleep as unquietly from the fear of the remedies, as he did before from that of the disease; it being hard for him to forget that more princes have been destroyed by the guards than by their people; and that even at the time when the rule was *Quod principi placuit lex esto*, the armies and Prætorian Bands which were the instruments of that unruly power were frequently the means made use of to destroy them who had it. There will ever be this difference between God and his vicegerents, that God is still above the instruments he useth, and out of the danger of receiving hurt from them. But princes can never lodge power in any hands which may not at some time turn it back upon them; for though it is possible enough for a king to have power to satisfy his ambition, yet no kingdom hath money enough to satisfy the avarice of underworkmen, who learn from that prince who will exact more than belongeth to him to expect from him much more than they deserve, and, growing angry upon the first disappointment, they are the devils which grow terrible to the conjurers themselves who brought them up, and can't send them down again. And besides that there can be no lasting radical security but where the governed are satisfied with the governors, it must be a dominion very unpleasant to a prince of an elevated mind to impose an abject and sordid servility instead of receiving the willing sacrifice of duty and obedience. The bravest princes in all times, who were incapable of any other kind of fear, have feared to grieve their own people; such a fear is a glory, and in this sense 'tis an infamy not to be a coward. So that the mistaken heroes who are void of this generous kind of fear need no other aggravation to complete their ill characters.

When a despotic prince hath bruised all his subjects with a slavish obedience, all the force he can use cannot subdue his own fears, enemies of his own creation, to which he can never be reconciled, it being impossible to do injustice and not to fear revenge. There is no cure for this fear but the not deserving to be hurt; and therefore a prince who doth not allow his thoughts to stray beyond the rules of justice hath always the blessing of an inward quiet and assurance as a natural effect of his good meaning to his people; and though he will not neglect due precautions to secure himself in all events, yet he is incapable of entertaining vain and remote suspicions of those of whom he resolveth never to deserve ill.

It is very hard for a prince to fear rebellion, who

neither doth, nor intendeth to do, anything to provoke it; therefore too great a diligence in the governors to raise and improve dangers and fears from the people is no very good symptom, and naturally begetteth an inference that they have thoughts of putting their subjects' allegiance to a trial; and therefore, not without some reason, fear beforehand that the irregularities they intend may raise men to a resistance.

Our Trimmer thinketh it no advantage to a government to endeavor the suppressing all kinds of right which may remain in the body of the people, or to employ small authors in it whose officiousness or want of money may encourage them to write, though it is not very easy to have abilities equal to such a subject. They forget that in their too high-strained arguments for the rights of princes, they very often plead against human nature, which will always give a bias to those reasons which seem of her side. It is the people that readeth those books and it is the people that must judge of them; and therefore no maxims should be laid down for the right of government to which there can be any reasonable objection; for the world hath an interest, and for that reason is more than ordinary discerning to find out the weak sides of such arguments as are intended to do them hurt; and it is a diminution to a government to promote or countenance such well-affected mistakes which are turned upon it with disadvantage whenever they are detected and exposed. And naturally the too earnest endeavors to take from men the right they have, tempt them, by the example, to claim that which they have not.

In power, as in most things, the way for princes to keep it, is not to grasp more than their arms can well hold; the nice and unnecessary inquiring into these things, or the licensing some books and suppressing some others without sufficient reason to justify the doing either, is so far from being an advantage to a government that it exposeth it to the censure of being partial, and to the suspicion of having some hidden designs to be carried on by these unusual methods.

When all is said, there is a natural reason of state, an undefinable thing, grounded upon the common good of mankind, which is immortal, and in all changes and revolutions still preserveth its original right of saving a nation, when the letter of the law perhaps would destroy it; and by whatsoever means it moveth, carrieth a power with it that admitteth of no opposition, being supported by Nature, which inspireth an immediate consent at some critical times into every individual member, to that which visibly tendeth to preservation of the whole; and this being so, a wise prince, instead of controverting the right of this reason of state, will by all means endeavor it may be of his side, and then he will be secure.

Our Trimmer cannot conceive that the power of any prince can be lasting, but where 'tis built upon the foundation of his own unborrowed virtue; he must not only be the first mover and the fountain from whence the great acts of state originally flow, but he must be thought so to his people that they may preserve their veneration for him; he must be jealous of his power, and not impart so much of it to any about him as that he may suffer an eclipse by it.

He cannot take too much care to keep himself up, for when a prince is thought to be led by those with whom he should only advise, and that the commands he giveth are transmitted through him, and are not of his own growth, the world will look upon him as a bird adorned with feathers that are not his own, or consider him rather as an engine[2] than a living creature; besides, 'twould be a contradiction for a prince to fear a commonwealth and at the same time create one himself, by delegating such a power to any number of men near him as is inconsistent with the figure of a monarch; it is the worst kind of coördination the Crown can submit to; for it is the exercise of power that draweth the respect along with it, and when that is parted with, the bare character of a king is not sufficient to keep it up. But though it is a diminution to a prince to parcel out so liberally his power amongst his favorites, it is worse to divide it with any other man, and to bring himself in competition with a single rival; a partner in government is so unnatural a thing that it is a squint-eyed allegiance that must be paid to such a double-bottomed monarchy. The two Czars of Muscovy[3] are an example that the most civilized part of the world will not be prone to follow. Whatsoever gloss may be put upon this method by those to whom it may be of some use, the prince will do well to remember and reflect upon the story of certain men who had set up a statue in honor of the sun, yet in a very little time they turned their backs to the sun, and their faces to the statue.

These mystical unions are better placed in the other world than they are in this, and we shall have much ado to find that in a monarchy God's vicegerency is delegated to more heads than that which is anointed.

2 A tool.
3 Peter (the Great) and his brother, Ivan, were joint Czars until the death of the latter.

Princes may lend some of their light to make another shine, but they must still preserve the superiority of being the brighter planet, and when it happeneth that the revetsion is in men's eyes, there is more care necessary to keep up the dignity of possession that men may not forget who is king, either out of their hopes or fears who shall be. If the sun should part with all his light to any other stars, the Indians would not know where to find their God, after he had so deposed himself, and would make the light (wherever it went) the object of their worship.

All usurpation is alike upon sovereignty, it is no matter from what hand it cometh, and crowned heads are to be the more circumspect in respect men's thoughts are naturally apt to ramble beyond what is present; they love to work at a distance, and in their greedy expectations which their minds may be filled with of a new master, the old one may be left to look a little out of countenance.

Our Trimmer owneth a passion for liberty, yet so restrained that it doth not in the least impair or taint his allegiance; he thinketh it hard for a soul that doth not love liberty ever to raise itself to another world; he taketh it to be the foundation of all virtue, and the only seasoning that giveth a relish to life; and though the laziness of a slavish subjection hath its charms for the more gross and earthly part of mankind, yet to men made of a better sort of clay, all that the world can give without liberty hath no taste. It is true nothing is sold so cheap by unthinking men; but that doth no more lessen the real value of it than a country fellow's ignorance doth that of a diamond in selling it for a pot of ale. Liberty is the mistress of mankind; she hath powerful charms which do so dazzle us that we find beauties in her which perhaps are not there, as we do in other mistresses. Yet if she was not a beauty, the world would not run mad for her; therefore, since the reasonable desire of it ought not to be restrained, and that even the unreasonable desire of it cannot be entirely suppressed, those who would take it away from a people possessed of it are likely to fail in the attempting, or be very unquiet in the keeping of it.

Our Trimmer admireth our blessed constitution, in which dominion and liberty are so well reconciled; it giveth to the prince the glorious power of commanding freemen, and to the subjects the satisfaction of seeing the power so lodged as that their liberties are secure. It doth not allow the Crown such a ruining power as that no grass can grow where'er it treadeth, but a cherishing and protecting power; such a one as hath a grim aspect only to the offending subjects, but is the joy and the pride of all the good ones; their own interest being so bound up in it as to engage them to defend and support it. And though in some instances the king is restrained, yet nothing in the government can move without him; our laws make a distinction between vassalage and obedience; between a devouring prerogative and a licentious ungovernable freedom; and as of all the orders of building the composite is the best, so ours by a happy mixture and a wise choice of what is best in others, is brought into a form that is our felicity who live under it, and the envy of our neighbors that cannot imitate it.

The Crown hath power sufficient to protect our liberties. The people have so much liberty as is necessary to make them useful to the Crown.

Our government is in a just proportion, no tympany, no unnatural swelling either of power or liberty; and whereas in all overgrown monarchies, reason, learning, and inquiry are hanged in effigy for mutineers, here they are encouraged and cherished as the surest friends to a government established upon the foundation of law and justice. When all is done, those who look for perfection in this world may look as the Jews have for their Messiah; and therefore our Trimmer is not so unreasonably partial as to free our government from all objections. No doubt there have been fatal instances of its sickness, and more than that, of its mortality for some time; though by a miracle it hath been revived again; but till we have another race of mankind, in all constitutions that are bounded there will ever be some matter of strife and contention, and, rather than want pretensions, men's passions and interests will raise them from the most inconsiderable causes.

Our government is like our climate. There are winds which are sometimes loud and unquiet; and yet, with all the trouble they give us, we owe part of our health unto them; they clear the air, which else would be like a standing pool, and instead of refreshment would be a disease unto us.

There may be fresh gales of asserting liberty without turning into such storms of hurricane as that the state should run any hazard of being cast away by them. These strugglings, which are natural to all mixed governments, while they are kept from growing into convulsions do by a mutual agitation from the several parts rather support and strengthen than weaken or maim the constitution; and the whole frame, instead of being torn or disjointed, cometh to be the better and closer knit by being thus exercised. But whatever faults our government may have, or a discerning critic may find in it, when he looketh upon it alone, let any other be set against it, and then it showeth its comparative beauty; let us look upon the most glittering outside of unbounded authority, and upon a nearer inquiry we shall find nothing but poor and miserable deformity within. Let us imagine a prince living in his kingdom, as if in a great galley, his subjects tugging at the oar, laden with chains, and reduced to real rags, that they may gain him imaginary laurels; let us represent him gazing among his flatterers, and receiving their false worship, like a child never contradicted, and therefore always cozened, or like a lady complimented only to be abused; condemned never to hear truth, and consequently never to do justice; wallowing in the soft bed of wanton and unbridled greatness, not less odious to the instruments themselves than to the objects of his tyranny; blown up into an ambitious dropsy, never to be satisfied by the conquest of other people or by the oppression of his own. By aiming to be more than a man, he falleth lower than the meanest of them, a mistaken creature, swelled with panegyrics, and flattered out of his senses, and not only an incumbrance, but a nuisance to mankind, a hardened and unrelenting soul; and, like some creatures that grow fat with poisons, he groweth great by other men's miseries; an ambitious ape of the Divine greatness, an unruly giant that would storm even heaven itself, but that his scaling-ladders are not long enough; in short, a wild and devouring creature in rich trappings, and with all his pride, no more than a whip in God Almighty's hand, to be thrown into the fire when the world hath been sufficiently scourged with it. This picture laid in right colors would not incite men to wish for such a government, but rather to acknowledge the happiness of our own, under which we enjoy all the privilege reasonable men can desire, and avoid all the miseries many others are subject to; so that our Trimmer would keep it with all its faults, and doth as little forgive those who give the occasion of breaking it, as he doth those that take it.

Our Trimmer is a friend to parliaments, notwithstanding all their faults and excesses, which of late have given such matter of objection to them; he thinketh that though they may at some times be troublesome to authority, yet they add the greatest strength to it under a wise administration; he believeth no government is perfect except a kind of omnipotence reside in it to exercise upon great occasions. Now this cannot be obtained by force alone upon people, let it be never so great; there must be their consent, too, or else a nation moveth only by being driven, a sluggish and constrained motion, void of that life and vigor which is necessary to produce great things, whereas the virtual consent of the whole being included in their representatives, and the king giving the sanction to the united sense of the people, every act done by such an authority seemeth to be an effect of their choice as well as a part of their duty; and they do, with an eagerness of which men are uncapable whilst under a force, execute whatsoever is so enjoined as their own wills, better explained by parliament, rather than from the terror of incurring the penalty of the law for omitting it. And by means of this political omnipotence, whatever sap or juice there is in a nation, may be to the last drop produced, whilst it riseth naturally from the root; whereas all power exercised without consent is like the giving wounds and gashes and tapping a tree at unseasonable times for the present occasion, which in a very little time must needs destroy it.

Our Trimmer believeth that by the advantage of our situation, there can hardly any such sudden disease come upon us, but that the king may have time enough left to consult with his physicians in parliament. Pretenses indeed may be made, but a real necessity so pressing that no delay is to be admitted is hardly to be imagined, and it will be neither easy to give an instance of any such thing for the time past, or reasonable to presume it will ever happen for the time to come. But if that strange thing should fall out, our Trimmer is not so strait-laced as to let a nation die or to be stifled rather than it should be helped by any but the proper officers. The cases themselves will bring the remedies along with them; and he is not afraid to allow that, in order to its preservation, there is a hidden power in government, which would be lost if it was defined, a certain mystery, by virtue of which a nation may at some critical times be secured from ruin; but then it must be kept as a mystery; it is rendered useless when touched by unskillful hands, and no government ever had, or deserved to have, that power which was so unwary as to anticipate their claim to it. Our Trimmer cannot help thinking it had been better if the Triennial Act had been observed; because 'tis the law, and he would not have the Crown by such an example teach the nation to break it; all irregularity is catching, it hath a contagion in it, especially in an age so much more inclined to follow ill patterns than good ones.

He would have had a parliament, because 'tis an essential part of the constitution, even without the law, it being the only provision in extraordinary cases in which there would be otherwise no remedy, and there can be no greater solecism in government than a failure of justice.

He would have had one because nothing else can unite and heal us; all other means are mere shifts and projects, houses of cards, to be blown down with the least breath, and cannot resist the difficulties which are ever presumed in things of this kind. And he would have had one because it might have done the king good, and could not possibly have done him hurt without his consent, which in that case is not to be supposed; and therefore for him to fear it is so strange and so little to be comprehended that the reasons can never be presumed to grow in our soil, or to thrive in it when transplanted from any other country. And no doubt there are such irresistible arguments for calling a parliament, that though it might be denied to the unmannerly mutinous petitions of men that are malicious and disaffected, it will be granted to the soft obsequious murmurs of his Majesty's best subjects, and there will be such rhetoric in their silent grief, that it will at last prevail against the artifices of those who, either out of guilt or interest, are afraid to throw themselves upon their country, knowing how scurvily they have used it. That day of judgment will come, though we know neither the day nor the hour. And our Trimmer will live so as to be prepared for it, with full assurance in the meantime that the lamenting voice of a nation cannot long be resisted, and that a prince who could so easily forgive his people when they had been in the wrong cannot fail to hear them when they are in the right.

THE TRIMMER'S OPINION CONCERNING THE PROTESTANT RELIGION

RELIGION hath such a superiority above other things, and that indispensable influence upon all mankind, that it is as necessary to our living happy in this world as it is to our being saved in the next. Without it man is an abandoned creature, one of the worst beasts nature hath produced, and fit only for the society of wolves and bears; therefore in all ages it hath been the foundation of government. And though false gods have been imposed upon the credulous part of the world, yet they were gods still in their opinion, and the awe and reverence men had to them and their oracles kept them within bounds towards one another, which the laws with all their authority could never have effected without the help of religion. The laws would not be able to subdue the perverseness of men's wills, which are wild beasts, and require a double chain to keep them down; for this reason 'tis said, that it is not a sufficient ground to make war upon a neighboring state, because they are of another religion, let it be never so differing; yet if they worship nor acknowledge no Deity at all, they may be invaded as public enemies of mankind, because they reject the only thing that can bind them to live well with one another. The consideration of religion is so twisted with that of government that it is never to be separated, and though the foundations of it ought to be eternal and unchangeable, yet the terms and circumstances of discipline are to be suited to the several climates and constitutions, so that they may keep men in a willing acquiescence unto them, without discomposing the world by nice disputes, which can never be of equal moment with the public peace.

Our religion here in England seemeth to be distinguished by a peculiar effect of God Almighty's goodness, in permitting it to be introduced, or rather restored, by a more regular method than the circumstances of most other reformed churches would allow them to do in relation to the government; and the dignity with which it hath supported itself since, and the great men our church hath produced, ought to recommend it to the esteem of all Protestants at least. Our Trimmer is very partial to it for these reasons and many more, and desireth that it may preserve its due jurisdiction and authority; so far he is from wishing it oppressed by the unreasonable and malicious cavils of those who take pains to raise objections against it.

The questions will then be, how and by what methods this church shall best support itself (the present circumstances considered) in relation to Dissenters of all sorts. I will first lay this for a ground, that as there can be no true religion without charity, so there can be no true human prudence without bearing and condescension. This principle doth not extend to oblige the church always to yield to those who are disposed to contest with her; the expediency of doing it is to be considered and determined according to the occasion, and this leads me to lay open the thoughts of our

Trimmer, in reference first to the Protestants, and then to the Popish recusants.

What hath lately happened among us maketh an apology necessary for saying anything that looketh like favor towards a sort of men who have brought themselves under such a disadvantage.

The late conspiracy[4] hath such broad symptoms of the disaffection of the whole party, that upon the first reflections, while our thoughts are warm, it would almost persuade us to put them out of the protection of our good nature, and to think that the Christian indulgence which our compassion for other men's sufferings cannot easily deny seemeth not only to be forfeited by the ill appearances that are against them, but even becometh a crime when it is so misapplied. Yet for all this, upon second and cooler thoughts, moderate men will not be so ready to involve a whole party in the guilt of a few, and to admit inferences and presumptions to be evidence in a case where the sentence must be so heavy as it ought to be against all those who have a fixed resolution against the government established. Besides, men who act by a principle grounded upon moral virtue can never let it be clearly extinguished by the most repeated provocations. If a right thing, agreeable to Nature and good sense, taketh root in the heart of a man that is impartial and unbiased, no outward circumstances can ever destroy it. It is true, the degree of a man's zeal for the prosecution of it may be differing; the faults of other men, the consideration of the public, and the reasonable prudence by which wise men will ever be directed, may give great allays; they may lessen, and for a time perhaps suppress, the exercise of that which in general proposition may be reasonable; but still whatever is so will inevitably grow and spring up again, having a foundation in Nature, which is never to be destroyed.

Our Trimmer therefore endeavoreth to separate the detestation of those who had either a hand or a thought in the late plot, from the principle of prudential as well as Christian charity towards mankind, and for that reason would fain use the means of reclaiming such of the Dissenters as are not incurable, and even of bearing to a degree those that are, as far as may consist with the public interest and security. He is far from justifying an affected separation from the communion of the church, and even in those that mean well and are mistaken, he looketh upon it as a

disease that hath seized upon their minds, very troublesome as well as dangerous, by the consequence it may produce. He doth not go about to excuse their making it an indispensable duty to meet in numbers to say their prayers; such meetings may prove mischievous to the state; at least the laws, which are the best judges, have determined that there is danger in them. He hath good nature enough to lament that the perverseness of a part should have drawn rigorous laws upon the whole body of the Dissenters, but when they are once made no private opinion must stand in opposition to them. If they are in themselves reasonable, they are in that respect to be regarded, even without being enjoined; if by the change of time and circumstances they should become less reasonable than when they were first made, even then they are to be obeyed too, because they are laws, till they are mended or repealed by the same authority that enacted them.

He hath too much deference to the constitution of our government to wish for more prerogative declarations in favor of scrupulous men, or to dispense with penal laws in such manner or to such an end that suspecting men might with some reason pretend that so hated a thing as persecution could never make way for itself with any hopes of success otherwise than by preparing the deluded world by a false prospect of liberty and indulgence. The inward springs and wheels whereby the engine moved are now so fully laid open and exposed that it is not supposable that such a baffled experiment should ever be tried again. The effect it had at the time, and the spirit it raised, will not easily be forgotten, and it may be presumed the remembrance of it may secure us from any more attempts of that nature for the future; we must no more break a law to give men ease than we are to rifle an house with a devout intention of giving the plunder to the poor. In this case our compassion would be as ill directed as our charity in the other.

In short, the veneration due to the laws is never to be thrown off, let the pretenses be never so specious. Yet with all this he cannot bring himself to think that an extraordinary diligence to take the uttermost penalty of laws upon the poor offending neighbor is of itself such an all-sufficient virtue that, without anything else to recommend men, it should entitle them to all kind of preferments and rewards. He would not detract from the merits of those who execute the laws, yet he cannot think such a piece of service as this can entirely change the man, and either make him a better divine, or a more knowing magistrate than he was

---

4 The so-called Rye House Plot, which had been discovered in 1683.

before, especially if it be done with a partial and un-equal hand in reverence to greater and more dangerous offenders.

Our Trimmer would have those mistaken men ready to throw themselves into the arms of the church, and he would have those arms as ready to receive them that shall come to us; he would have no supercilious look to fright those strayed sheep from coming into the fold again; no ill-natured maxims of an eternal suspicion, or a belief that those who have once been in the wrong can never be in the right again; but a visible preparation of mind to receive with joy all the prose-lytes that come amongst us, and much greater earnest-ness to reclaim than punish them. It is to be confessed there is a great deal to forgive, a hard task enough for the charity of a church so provoked; but that must not cut off all hopes of being reconciled. Yet if there must be some anger left still, let it break out into a Christian revenge, and by being kinder to the children of dis-obedience than they deserve, let the injured church triumph by throwing shame and confusion of face upon them. There should not always be storms and thunder; a clear sky would sometimes make the church look more like Heaven, and would do more towards the reclaiming those wanderers than a perpetual terror which seemeth to have no intermission. For there is in many, and particularly in Englishmen, a mistaken pleasure in resisting the dictates of rigorous authority; a stomach that riseth against a hard imposition, nay, in some, even a lust in suffering from a wrong point of honor, which doth not want the applause from the greater part of mankind, who have not learned to dis-tinguish. Constancy will be thought a virtue even where it is a mistake; and the ill-judging world will be apt to think that opinion most right which pro-duceth the greatest number of those who are willing to suffer for it. All this is prevented, and falleth to the ground, by using well-timed indulgence; and the stubborn adversary who valueth himself upon his re-sistance whilst he is oppressed, yieldeth insensibly to kind methods when they are applied to him; and the same man naturally melteth into conformity who perhaps would never have been beaten into it. We may be taught, by the compassion that attendeth the most criminal men when they are condemned, that faults are much more natural things than punishments, and that even the most necessary acts of severity do some kind of violence to our nature, whose indulgence will not be confined within the strait bounds of in-exorable justice. So that this should be an argument

for gentleness, besides that it is the likeliest way to make these men ashamed of their separation, whilst the pressing them too hard tendeth rather to make them proud of it.

Our Trimmer would have the clergy supported in their lawful rights, and in all the power and dignity that belongeth to them; and yet he thinketh that possibly there may be in some of them a too great eagerness to extend the ecclesiastical jurisdiction, which, though it may be well intended, yet the strain-ing of it too high hath an appearance of ambition that raiseth men's objections to it; and is so far unlike the apostolic zeal, which was quite otherwise employed, that the world draweth inferences from it which do the church no service.

He is troubled to see men of all sides sick of a calenture of a mistaken devotion, and it seemeth to him that the devout fire of mistaken charity with which the primitive Christians were inflamed is long since extinguished, and instead of it a devouring fire of anger and persecution breaketh out in the world. We wrangle now with one another about religion till the blood cometh, whilst the Ten Commandments have no more authority with us than if they were so many obsolete laws or proclamations out of date. He thinketh that a nation will hardly be mended by principles of religion where morality is made a heresy; and therefore, as he believeth devotion misplaced when it gets into a conventicle, he concludeth that loyalty is so too, when lodged in a drunken club; those virtues deserve a better seat of empire, and they are degraded when such men undertake their defense as have too great need of an apology themselves.

Our Trimmer wisheth that some knowledge may go along with the zeal on the right side, and that those who are in possession of the pulpit would quote at least so often the authority of the Scriptures as they do that of the state. There are many who borrow too often arguments from the government to use against their adversaries, and neglect those that are more pro-per and would be more powerful; a divine groweth less, and putteth a diminution on his own character, when he quoteth any law but that of God Almighty to get the better of those who contest with him. And as it is a sign of a decayed constitution when Nature with good diet cannot expel noxious humors without calling foreign drugs to her assistance, so it looketh like want of health in a church, when instead of de-pending upon the power of that truth which it holdeth, and the good examples of them that teach it, to support itself and to suppress errors, it should have a perpetual recourse to the secular authority, and even upon the slightest occasions.

Our Trimmer hath his objections to the too busy diligence and to the overdoing of some of the Dissenting clergy, and he doth as little approve of those of our church who wear God Almighty's liveries, as some old warders in the Tower do the king's who do nothing in their place but receive their wages for it. He thinketh that the liberty of the late times[5] gave men so much light and diffused it so universally amongst the people, that they are not now to be dealt with as they might have been in ages of less inquiry; and therefore, though in some well chosen and dearly beloved auditories good resolute nonsense backed with authority may prevail, yet generally men are become so good judges of what they hear that the clergy ought to be very wary how they go about to impose upon their understandings, which are grown less humble than they were in former times, when the men in black had made learning such a sin in the laity, that, for fear of offending, they made a conscience of being able to read. But now the world is grown saucy, and expecteth reasons, and good ones too, before they give up their own opinions to other men's dictates, though never so magisterially delivered to them.

Our Trimmer is far from approving the hypocrisy which seemeth to be the reigning vice amongst some of the Dissenting clergy; he thinketh it the most provoking sin men can be guilty of in relation to Heaven; and yet (which may seem strange) that very sin which shall destroy the soul of the man who preacheth may help to save those of the company that hear him, and even those who are cheated by the false ostentation of his strictness of life by that pattern be encouraged to the real practice of those Christian virtues which he doth so deceitfully profess; so that the detestation of this fault may possibly be carried on too far by our own orthodox divines, if they think it cannot be enough expressed without bending the stick another way; a dangerous method, and a worse extreme for men of that character, who by going to the outmost line of Christian liberty will certainly encourage others to go beyond it. No man doth less approve the ill-bred methods of some of the Dissenters in rebuking authority, who behave themselves as if they thought ill manners necessary to salvation; yet he cannot but distinguish and desire a mean between the sauciness of some of the Scotch apostles, and the undecent court-

5 The period of the Commonwealth.

ship of some of the silken divines, who, one would think, do practice to bow at the altar only to learn to make the better legs at court.

Our Trimmer approveth the principles of our church, that dominion is not founded in grace, and that our obedience is to be given to a Popish king in other things at the same time that our compliance with him in his religion is to be denied. Yet he cannot but think it a very extraordinary thing if a Protestant Church should by a voluntary election choose a Papist for their guardian, and receive directions for supporting their religion from one who must believe it a mortal sin not to endeavor to destroy it. Such a refined piece of breeding would not seem to be very well placed in the clergy, who will hardly find precedents to justify such an extravagant piece of courtship, and which is so unlike the primitive methods which ought to be our pattern. He hath no such unreasonable tenderness for any sorts of men as to expect their faults should not be impartially laid open as often as they give occasion for it; and yet he cannot but smile to see that the same man, who setteth up all the sails of his rhetoric to fall upon the Dissenters, when Popery is to be handled, he doth it so gingerly that he looketh like an ass mumbling of thistles, so afraid he is of letting himself loose where he may be in danger of letting his duty get the better of his discretion.

Our Trimmer is far from relishing the impertinent wanderings of those who pour out long prayers upon the congregation, and all from their own stock, which, God knoweth, for the most part is a barren soil, which produceth weeds instead of flowers, and by this means they expose religion itself rather than promote men's devotions. On the other side there may be too great restraint put upon men whom God and Nature hath distinguished from their fellow-laborers by blessing them with a happier talent, and by giving them not only good sense but a powerful utterance too, hath enabled them to gush out upon the attentive auditory with a mighty stream of devout and unaffected eloquence. When a man so qualified, endued with learning too, and above all, adorned with a good life, breaketh out into a warm and well-delivered prayer before his sermon, it hath the appearance of a divine rapture; he raiseth and leadeth the hearts of the assembly in another manner than the most composed or best studied form of set words can ever do; and the "Pray-we's," who serve up all their sermons with the same garnishing would look like so many statues or men of straw in the pulpit, compared with those who speak with such a powerful zeal that men are tempted at the moment to believe Heaven itself hath dictated their words to them.

Our Trimmer is not so unreasonably indulgent to the Dissenters as to excuse the irregularities of their complaints, and to approve their threatening styles, which are so ill suited to their circumstances as well as to their duty. He would have them to show their grief and not their anger to the government; and by such a submission to authority as becometh them, if they cannot acquiesce in what is imposed, let them deserve a legislative remedy to their sufferings, there being no other way to give them perfect redress. And either to seek it, or pretend to give it by any other method, would not only be vain but criminal too in those that go about it. Yet with all this, there may in the meantime be a prudential latitude left as to the manner of prosecuting the laws now in force against them. The government is in some degree answerable for such an administration of them as may be free from the censure of impartial judges; and in order to that, it would be necessary that one of these methods be pursued: either to let loose the laws to their utmost extent without any moderation or restraint, in which at least the equality of the government would be without objection, the penalties being exacted without remission from the Dissenters of all kinds; or, if that will not be done (and indeed there is no reason it should), there is a necessity of some connivance to the Protestant Dissenters to excuse that which in humanity must be allowed to the Papists, even without any leaning towards them, which must not be supposed in those who are or shall be in the administration of public business. And it will follow that, according to our circumstances, the distribution of such connivance must be made in such a manner that the greatest part of it may fall on the Protestant side; or else the objections will be so strong, and the inferences so clear, that the friends as well as the enemies of the Crown will be sure to take hold of them.

It will not be sufficient to say that the Papists may be connived at because they are good subjects, and that the Protestant Dissenters must suffer because they are ill ones. These general maxims will not convince discerning men, neither will any late instances make them forget what passed at other times in the world. Both sides have had their turns in being good and ill subjects, and therefore 'tis easy to imagine what suspicions would arise in the present conjuncture if such a partial argument as this should be imposed upon us.

The truth is, this matter speaks so much of itself that it is not only unnecessary but it may be unmannerly, to say any more of it.

Our Trimmer therefore could wish that since, notwithstanding the laws which deny churches to say mass in, not only the exercise but also the ostentation of Popery is as well or better performed in the chapels of so many foreign ministers, where the English openly resort in spite of proclamations and Orders of Council, which are grown to be as harmless things to them as the Pope's bulls and excommunications are to heretics who are out of his reach; I say, he could wish that by a seasonable as well as an equal piece of justice, there might be so much consideration had of the Protestant Dissenters, as that there might be at some times and at some places a veil thrown over an innocent and retired conventicle; and, that such an indulgence might be practiced with less prejudice to the church or diminution to the laws, it might be done so as to look rather like a kind omission to inquire more strictly than an allowed toleration of that which is against the rule established.

Such a skillful hand as this is very necessary in our circumstances, and the government by making no sort of men entirely desperate doth not only secure itself from villainous attempts but lay such a foundation for healing and uniting laws, whenever a Parliament shall meet, that the seeds of differences and animosities between the several contending sides may (Heaven consenting) be for ever destroyed.

THE TRIMMER'S OPINION CONCERNING THE PAPISTS

To speak of Popery leadeth me into such a sea of matter that it is not easy to forbear launching into it, being invited by such a fruitful theme, and by a variety never to be exhausted. But to confine it to the present subject, I will only say a short word of the religion itself, of its influence here at this time, and of our Trimmer's opinion in relation to our manner of living with them.

If a man would speak maliciously of this religion, one may say it is like those diseases where as long as one drop of the infection remaineth, there is still danger of having the whole mass of blood corrupted by it. In Swedeland[6] there was an absolute cure, and nothing of Popery heard of till Queen Christina

6 Sweden.

(whether moved by arguments of this or the other world may not be good manners to inquire) thought fit to change her religion and country, and to live at Rome, where she might find better judges of her virtues, and less ungentle censures of those princely liberties to which she was sometimes disposed, than she left at Stockholm, where the good breeding is as much inferior to that of Rome in general as the civility of the religion, the Cardinals having rescued the church from those clownish methods the fishermen had first introduced, and mended that pattern so effectually that a man of that age if he should now come into the world would not possibly know it.

In Denmark the reformation was entire; and in some states of Germany, as well as Geneva, the cure was universal; but in the rest of the world where the Protestant religion took place the Popish humor was too tough to be totally expelled. And so it was in England, though the change was made with all the advantage imaginable to the Reformation, it being countenanced and introduced by legal authority, and by that means might have been perhaps as perfect as in any other place, if the short reign of Edward the Sixth and the succession of a Popish Queen had not given such advantage to that religion that it hath subsisted ever since, under all the hardships that have been put upon it. It hath been a strong compact body, and made the more so by these sufferings. It was not strong enough to prevail, but it was able, with the help of foreign support, to carry on an interest which gave the Crown trouble, and to make a considerable (not to say dangerous) figure in the nation. So much as this could not have been done without some hopes, nor these hopes kept up without some reasonable grounds. In Queen Elizabeth's time the Spanish zeal for their religion, and the revenge for '88 gave warmth to the Papists here, and above all the right of the Queen of Scots to succeed was, while she lived, sufficient to give them a better prospect of their affairs. In King James's time their hopes were supported by the treaty of the Spanish Match, and his gentleness towards them, which they were ready to interpret more in their own favor than was either reasonable or became them, so little tenderness they have, even where it is most due, if the interest of their religion cometh in competition with it.

As for the late king, though he gave the most glorious evidence that ever man did of his being a Protestant, yet, by the more than ordinary influence the Queen was thought to have over him, and it so

happening that the greatest part of his anger was directed against the Puritans, there was such an advantage to men disposed to suspect, that they were ready to interpret it a leaning towards Popery, without which handle it was morally impossible that the ill-affected part of the nation could ever have seduced the rest into a rebellion.

That which helped to confirm many well meaning men in their misapprehensions of the king, was the long and unusual intermission of Parliaments; so that every year that passed without one made up a new argument to increase their suspicion, and made them presume that the Papists had a principal hand in keeping them off. This raised such heats in men's minds, to think that men who were obnoxious to the laws, instead of being punished, should have credit enough to secure themselves, even at the price of destroying the fundamental constitution, that it broke out into a flame, which, before it could be quenched, had almost reduced the nation to ashes.

Amongst the miserable effects of that unnatural war, none hath been more fatal to us than the forcing our princes to breathe in another air and to receive the early impressions of a foreign education. The barbarity of the English towards the king and the royal family might very well tempt him to think the better of everything he found abroad, and might naturally produce more gentleness at least towards a religion by which he was hospitably received, at the same time that he was thrown off and persecuted by the Protestants (though his own subjects), to aggravate the offense. The Queen Mother (as generally ladies do with age) grew most devout and earnest in her religion; and, besides the temporal rewards of getting larger subsidies from the French clergy, she had motives of another kind, to persuade her to show her zeal. And since by the Roman dispensatory a soul converted to the church is a sovereign remedy and layeth up a mighty stock of merit, she was solicitous to secure herself in all events, and therefore first set upon the Duke of Gloucester, who depended so much upon her good will that she might for that reason have been induced to believe the conquest would not be difficult. But it so fell out that he, either from his own constancy or that he had those near him by whom he was otherwise advised, chose rather to run away from her importunity than by staying to bear the continual weight of it. It is believed she had better success with another of her sons,[7] who, if he was not quite brought

7 The Duke of York, later James II.

off from our religion, at least such beginnings were made as made them very easy to be finished. His being of a generous and aspiring nature, and in that respect less patient in the drudgery of arguing, might probably help to recommend a church to him that exempts the laity from the vexation of inquiring. Perhaps he might (though by mistake) look upon that religion as more favorable to the enlarged power of kings, a consideration which might have its weight with a young prince in his warm blood and that was brought up in arms.

I cannot hinder myself from a small digression to consider with admiration that the Old Lady of Rome, with all her wrinkles, should yet have charms able to subdue great princes. So far from handsome, and yet so imperious; so painted, and yet so pretending; after having abused, deposed, and murdered so many of her lovers, she still findeth others glad and proud of their new chains; a thing so strange to indifferent judges, that those who will allow no other miracles in the Church of Rome must needs grant that this is one not to be contested. She sitteth in her shop, and selleth at dear rates her rattles and her hobby-horses, whilst the deluded world still continueth to furnish her with customers.

But whither am I carried with this contemplation? It is high time to return to my text, and to consider the wonderful manner of the king's coming home again, led by the hand of Heaven, and called by the voice of his own people, who received him, if possible, with joys equal to the blessing of peace and union which his restoration brought along with it. By this there was an end put to the hopes some might have abroad of making use of his less happy circumstances to throw him into foreign interests and opinions, which had been wholly inconsistent with our religion, our laws, and all other things that are dear to us; yet for all this some of those tinctures and impressions might so far remain as, though they were very innocent to him, yet they might have ill effects here by softening the animosity which seemeth necessary to the defender of the Protestant faith, in opposition to such a powerful and irreconcilable an enemy.

You may be sure that among all the sorts of men who applied themselves to the king at his first coming home for his protection the Papists were not the last, nor as they fain would have flattered themselves the least welcome, having their past sufferings as well as their present professions to recommend them; and there was something that looked like a particular consideration of them since it so happened that the indul-

gence promised to Dissenters at Breda was carried on in such a manner that the Papists were to divide with them. And though the Parliament, notwithstanding its resignation to the Crown in all things, rejected with scorn and anger a declaration framed for this purpose, yet the birth and steps of it gave such an alarm that men's suspicions once raised were not easily laid asleep again.

To omit other things, the breach of the Triple League, and the Dutch war with its appurtenances, carried jealousies to the highest pitch imaginable, and fed the hopes of one party and the fears of the other to such a degree that some critical revolutions were generally expected, when the ill success of that war, and the sacrifice France thought fit to make of the Papists here to their own interest abroad, gave them another check. And the act of enjoining the test to all in offices was thought to be no ill bargain to the nation, though bought at the price of 1,200,000 pounds, and the money applied to continue the war against the Dutch, than which nothing could be more unpopular or less approved. Notwithstanding these discouragements, Popery is a plant that may be mowed down, but the root will still remain; and, in spite of the laws, it will sprout up and grow again, especially if it should happen that there should be men in power, who, in weeding it out of our garden, will take care to cherish and keep it alive; and though the law for excluding them from places of trust was tolerably kept as to the outward form, yet there were many circumstances, which, being improved by the quick-sighted malice of ill-affected men, did help to keep up the world in their suspicions, and to blow up jealousies to such a height both in and out of Parliament that the remembrance of them is very unpleasant, and the example so extravagant, that it is to be hoped nothing in our age like it will be re-attempted. But to come closer to the case in question: in this condition we stand with the Papists, what shall now be done, according to our Trimmer's opinion, in order to the better bearing this grievance?—since as I have said before, there is no hope of being entirely free from it. Papists we must have among us, and if their religion keep them from bringing honey to the hive, let the government try at least by gentle means to take away the sting from them. The first foundation to be laid is that a distinct consideration is to be had of the Popish clergy, who have such an eternal interest against all accommodation that it is a hopeless thing to propose anything to them less than all; their stomachs have been set for it ever since the Reformation. They have pinned themselves to a principle that admits no mean; they believe Protestants will be damned, and therefore by an extraordinary effect of Christian charity they would destroy one half of England that the other might be saved. Then for this world they must be in possession of God Almighty, to receive his rents for him, not to account till the Day of Judgment, which is a good kind of tenure, and ye cannot well blame the good men that will stir up the laity to run any hazard in order to the getting them restored. What is it to the priest if the deluded zealot undoeth himself in the attempt? he singeth masses as jollily and with as good a voice at Rome or St. Omers as ever he did; is a single man and can have no wants but such as may be easily supplied. Yet that he may not seem altogether insensible or ungrateful to those that are his martyrs, he is ready to assure their executors, and if they please will procure a grant *sub annulo piscatoris*, that the good man by being hanged hath got a good bargain, and saved the singeing of some hundred of years, which he would else have had in Purgatory. There's no cure for this order of men, no expedient to be proposed, so that though the utmost severity of the laws against them may in some sort be mitigated, yet no treaty can be made with men who in this case have left themselves no free will, but are so muffled by zeal, tied by vows, and kept up by such unchangeable maxims of the priesthood, that they are to be left as desperate patients, and looked upon as men that will continue in an eternal state of hostility, till the nation is entirely subdued to them.

It is, then, only the lay Papists that are capable of being treated with, and we are to examine of what temper they are, and what arguments are the most likely to prevail upon them, and how far 'tis advisable for the government to be indulgent to them. The lay Papists generally keep their religion rather because they will not break company with those of their party than out of any settled zeal that hath root in them. Most of them do by the mediation of the priests marry amongst one another, to keep up an ignorant position by hearing only one side. Others by a mistake look upon it as they do upon escutcheons, the more ancient religion of the two; and as some men of a good pedigree will despise meaner men, though never so much superior to them by nature, so these undervalue Reformation as an upstart, and think there is more honor in supporting an old error than in embracing what seemeth to them to be a new truth. The laws have made them men of pleasure by excluding them

from public business, and it happeneth well they are so, since they will the more easily be persuaded by arguments of ease and conveniency to them. They have not put off the man in general, nor the Englishman in particular; those who in the late storm against them went into other countries, though they had all the advantages that might recommend them to a good reception, yet in a little time they chose to steal over again, and live here with hazard rather than abroad with security. There is a smell in our native earth better than all the perfumes in the East; there is something in a mother, though never so angry, that the children will more naturally trust her than the studied civilities of strangers, let them be never so hospitable; therefore 'tis not advisable nor agreeing with the rules of governing prudence to provoke men by hardships to forget that nature which else is sure to be of our side.

When these men by fair usage are put again into their right senses, they will have quite differing reflections from those which rigor and persecution had raised in them. A lay Papist will first consider his abbey lands, which, notwithstanding whatever hath or can be alleged, must sink considerably in the value the moment that Popery prevails; and it being a disputable matter whether zeal might not in a little time get the better of the law in that case, a considering man will admit that as an argument to persuade him to be content with things as they are, rather than run this or any other hazard by change, in which perhaps he may have no other advantage than that his now humble confessor may be raised to a bishopric, and from thence look down superciliously upon his patron, or which is worse, run to take possession for God Almighty of his abbey, in such a manner as the usurping landlord (as he will then be called) shall hardly be admitted to be so much as a tenant to his own lands, lest his title should prejudge that of the church, which will then be the landlord;[8] he will think what disadvantage 'tis to be looked upon as a separate creature, depending upon a foreign interest and authority, and for that reason, exposed to the jealousy and suspicion of his countrymen. He will reflect what an incumbrance it is to have his house a pasture for hungry priests to graze in, which have such a never-failing influence upon the foolish, which is the greatest part of every man's family, that a man's dominion even over his own

8 The text reads "language." The reading "landlord," which the sense seems to require, is Sir Walter Raleigh's emendation in his edition of Halifax.

children is mangled and divided, if not totally under-mined by them. Then to be subject to what arbitrary taxes the Popish convocation shall impose upon him for the carrying on the common interest of that reli-gion, under penalty of being marked out for an heretic by the rest of the party; to have no share in business, no opportunity of showing his own value to the world; to live at the best an useless, and by others to be thought a dangerous, member of the nation where he is born, is a burthen to a generous mind that cannot be taken off by all the pleasure of a lazy unmanly life, or by the nauseous enjoyment of a dull plenty, that pro-duceth no food for the mind, which will be considered in the first place by a man that hath a soul. When he shall think that if his religion, after his wading through a sea of blood, come at last to prevail it would infin-itely lessen if not entirely destroy the glory, riches, strength, and liberty of his own country, and what a sacrifice is this to make to Rome, where they are wise enough to wonder there should be such fools in the world as to venture, struggle, and contend, nay, even die martyrs, for that which, should it succeed, would prove a judgment instead of a blessing to them; he will conclude that the advantages of throwing some of their children back again to God Almighty, when they have too many of them, are not equal to the in-conveniences they may either feel or fear by continuing their separation from the religion established.

Temporal things will have their weight in the world, and though zeal may prevail for a time, and get the better in a skirmish, yet the war endeth generally on the side of flesh and blood, and will do so until man-kind is another thing than it is at present. And therefore a wise Papist, in cold blood considering these and many other circumstances, which 'twill be worth his pains to see if he can unmuffle himself from the mask of infallibility, will think it reasonable to set his im-prisoned senses at liberty, and that he hath a right to see with his own eyes, hear with his own ears, and judge by his own reason. The consequence of which might probably be that weighing things in a right scale, and seeing them in their true colors, he would distinguish between the merit of suffering for a good cause and the foolish ostentation of drawing incon-veniences upon himself; and therefore will not be unwilling to be convinced that our Protestant creed may make him happy in the other world, and the easier in this. A few of such wise proselytes would by their example draw so many after them that the party may insensibly melt away; and in a little time, without

any angry word, we should come to an union that all good men would have reason to rejoice at.

But we are not to presume upon these conversions without preparing men for them by kind and recon-ciling arguments; nothing is so against our nature as to believe those can be in the right who are too hard upon us. There is a deformity in everything that doth us hurt, it will look scurvily in our eye while the smart continueth, and a man must have an extraordinary measure of grace to think well of a religion that re-duceth him and his family to misery. In this respect our Trimmer would consent to the mitigation of such laws as were made (as it is said King Henry VIII got Queen Elizabeth) in a heat against Rome. It may be said that even States, as well as private men, are subject to passion; a just indignation of a villainous attempt produceth at the same time such remedies as perhaps are not without some mixture of revenge, and there-fore, though time cannot repeal a law, it may by a natural effect soften the execution of it. There is less danger to rouse a lion when at rest, than to awake laws that were intended to have their times of sleeping, nay, more than that, in some cases their natural periods of life, dying of themselves without the solemnity of being revoked any otherwise than by the common consent of mankind, who do cease to execute when the reasons in great measure fail that first created and justified the rigor of such unusual penalties.

Our Trimmer is not eager to pick out sore[9] places in history against this or any other party; quite con-trary, is very solicitous to find out anything that may be healing and tend to an agreement; but to prescribe the means of this gentleness so as to make it effectual must come from the only place that can furnish remedies for this cure, viz., a parliament. In the mean-time it is to be wished there may be such a mutual calmness of mind as that the Protestants might not be so jealous as still to smell the match that was to blow up the King and both Houses in the Gunpowder Treason, or to start at every appearance of Popery, as if it were just taking possession. On the other side, let not the Papists suffer themselves to be led by any hopes, though never so flattering, to a confidence or ostentation which must provoke men to be less kind to them; let them use modesty on their sides, and the Protestants indulgence on theirs; and by this means there would be an overlooking of all venial faults, a tacit connivance at all things that do not carry scandal

9 The text has "some places," and is thus emended by Miss Foxcroft.

with them, and would amount to a kind of natural dispensation with the severe laws, since there would be no more accusers to be found when the occasions of anger and animosity are once removed. Let the Papists in the meantime remember that there is a respect due from all lesser numbers to greater, a deference to be paid by an opinion that is exploded to one that is established. Such a thought, well digested, will have an influence upon their behavior and produce such a temper as must win the most eager adversaries out of their ill humor to them, and give them a title to all the favor that may be consistent with the public peace and security.

THE TRIMMER'S OPINION IN RELATION TO THINGS ABROAD

THE world is so composed that it is hard, if not impossible, for a nation not to be a great deal involved in the fate of their neighbors, and though, by the felicity of our situation, we are more independent than any other people, yet we have in all ages been concerned for our own sakes in the revolutions abroad. There was a time when England was the overbalancing power of Christendom, and that, either by inheritance or conquest, the better part of France received laws from us. After that, we being reduced into our own limits, France and Spain became the rivals for the universal monarchy, and our third power, though in itself less than either of the other, happened to be superior to any of them by that choice we had of throwing the scales on that side to which we gave our friendship. I do not know whether this figure did not make us as great as our former conquest; to be a perpetual umpire of two great contending powers, who gave us all their courtship, and offered all their incense at our altar, whilst the fate of either Prince seemed to depend upon the oracles we delivered; for the King of England to sit on his throne as in the Supreme Court of Justice (to which the two great monarchs appeal, pleading their cause, and expecting their sentence, declaring which side was in the right, or at least if we pleased which side should have the better of it) was a piece of greatness which was peculiar to us. And no wonder if we endeavored to preserve it, as we did for a considerable time, it being our safety as well as glory to maintain it. But by a fatality upon our councils, or by the refined policy of this latter age, we have thought fit to use industry to destroy this mighty power which

we have so long enjoyed; and that equality between the two monarchs which we might for ever have preserved hath been chiefly broken by us, whose interest it was above all others to maintain it. When one of them, like the overflowing of the sea, had gained more upon the other than our convenience or indeed our safety would allow, instead of mending the banks or making new ones, we ourselves with our own hands helped to cut them, to invite and make way for a farther inundation. France and Spain have had their several turns in making use of our mistakes, and we have been formerly as deaf to the instances of the then weaker part of the world to help them against the House of Austria, as we can now be to the earnestness of Spain that we would assist them against the power of France. Gondomar was as saucy, and as powerful too, in King James his court, as any French ambassador can have been at any time since; men talked as wrong then on the Spanish side, and made their court by it, as well as any can have done since by talking as much for the French; so that from that time, instead of weighing in a wise balance the power of either Crown, it looketh as if we had learned only to weigh the pensions and take the heaviest.

It would be tedious, as well as unwelcome, to recapitulate all our wrong steps, so that I will go no farther than the King's restoration, at which time the balance was on the side of France, and that by the means of Cromwell, who, for a separate interest of his own, had sacrificed that of the nation by joining with the stronger side to suppress the power of Spain, which he ought to have supported. Such a method was natural enough to an usurper, and showed he was not the lawful father of the people, by his having so little care of them; and the example, coming from that hand, one would think, should for that reason be less likely to be followed. But to go on; home cometh the king, followed with courtships from all nations abroad, of which some did it not only to make him forget how familiarly they had used him when he was in other circumstances, but to bespeak the friendship of a prince, who, besides his other greatness, was yet more considerable by being reëstablished by the love of his people. France had an interest either to dispose us to so much good will, or at least to put us into such a condition that we might give no opposition to their designs; and Flanders being a perpetual object in their eye, a lasting beauty for which they had an incurable passion, and not being kind enough to consent to them, they meditated to commit a rape upon her, which they thought would not be easy to do while England and Holland were agreed to rescue her whenever they should hear her cry out for help to them. To this end they put in practice seasonable and artificial whispers to widen things between us and the States. Amboyna and the fishery must be talked of here; the freedom of the seas and the preservation of trade must be insinuated there; and there being combustible matter on both sides, in a little time it took fire, which gave those that kindled it sufficient cause to smile and hug themselves, to see us both fall into the net they had laid for us. And it is observable and of good example to us, if we will take it, that their design being to set us together at cuffs to weaken us, they kept themselves lookers-on till our victories began to break the balance; then the king of France, like a wise prince, was resolved to support the beaten side, and would no more let the power of the sea than we ought to suffer the monarchy of Europe to fall into one hand. In pursuance to this he took part with the Dutch, and in a little time made himself umpire of the peace between us. Some time after, upon pretense of his Queen's title to part of Flanders by right of devolution, he falleth into it with a mighty force, for which the Spaniard was so little prepared that he made a very swift progress, and had such a torrent of undisputed victory, that England and Holland, though the wounds they had given one another were yet green, being struck with the apprehension of so near a danger to them, thought it necessary for their own defense to make up a sudden league, into which Sweden was taken to interpose for a peace between the two Crowns.

This had so good an effect that France was stopped in its career, and the Peace of Aix-la-Chapelle was a little after concluded. 'Twas a forced put; and though France wisely dissembled their inward dissatisfaction, yet from that very moment they resolved to untie the triple knot, whatever it cost them; for his Christian Majesty, after his conquering meals, ever riseth with a stomach; and he liked the pattern so well, that it gave him a longing desire to have the whole piece. Amongst the other means used for the attaining of this end, the sending over the Duchess of Orleans was not the least powerful. She was a very welcome guest here, and her own charms and dexterity, joined with other advantages that might help her persuasions, gave her such an ascendant that she should hardly fail of success. One of the preliminaries of her treaty, though a trivial thing in itself, yet was considerable in the consequence,

as very small circumstances often are in relation to the government of the world. About this time a general humor in opposition to France had made us throw off their fashion, and put on vests, that we might look more like a distinct people, and not be under the servility of imitation, which ever payeth a greater deference to the original than is consistent with the equality all independent nations should pretend to. France did not like this small beginning of ill humors, at least of emulation, and wisely considering that it is a natural introduction first to make the world their apes, that they may be afterwards their slaves, it was thought that one of the instructions Madam brought along with her was to laugh us out of these vests; which she performed so effectually, that in a moment, like so many footmen who had quitted their master's livery, we all took it again, and returned to our old service. So that the very time of doing it gave a very critical advantage to France, since it looked like an evidence of our returning to their interest, as well as to their fashion, and would give such a distrust of us to our new allies that it might facilitate the dissolution of the knot, which tied them so within their bounds that they were very impatient till they were freed from the restraint.

But the lady had a more extended commission than this, and, without doubt, laid the foundation of a new strict alliance, quite contrary to the other in which we had been so lately engaged. And of this there were such early appearances that the world began to look upon us as falling into apostasy from the common interest. Notwithstanding all this, France did not neglect at the same time to give good words to the Dutch, and even to feed them with hopes of supporting them against us, when on a sudden, that never-to-be-forgotten declaration of war against them cometh out, only to vindicate their own glory, and to revenge the injuries done to his brother in England, by which he became our second in this duel; so humble can this prince be, when at the same time he doth us more honor than we deserve, he layeth a greater share of the blame upon our shoulders than did naturally belong to us. The particulars of that war, our part in it while we stayed in it, and, when we were out of breath, our leaving the French to make an end of it, are things too well known to make it necessary, and too unwelcome in themselves to incite me, to repeat them. Only the wisdom of France is in this to be observed; that when we had made a separate peace which left them single to oppose the united force of the confederates, they were so far from being angry that they would not show so much as the least coldness, hoping to get as much by our mediation for a peace as they would have expected from our assistance in the war, our circumstances at that time considered.

This seasonable piece of indulgence in not reproaching us, but rather allowing those necessities of state which we gave for our excuse, was such an engaging method that it went a great way to keep us still in their chains, when, to the eye of the world, we had absolutely broke loose from them. And by what passed afterwards at Nimeguen, though the King's neutrality gave him the outward figure of a mediator, it appeared that his interposition was extremely suspected of partiality by the confederates, who upon that ground did, both at and before the conclusion of that treaty, treat his ministers there with a great deal of neglect. In this peace as well as in that of the Pyreneans and Aix-la-Chapelle, the king of France at the moment of making it had the thought of breaking it; for a very little time after he broached his pretensions upon Alost; which were things that if they had been offered by a less formidable hand would have been smiled at; but ill arguments, being seconded by good armies, carry such a power with them, that naked sense is a very unequal adversary. It was thought that these airy claims were chiefly raised with the prospect of getting Luxemburg for the equivalent; and this opinion was confirmed by the blocking it up afterwards, pretending to the county of Chimay that it might be entirely surrounded by the French dominions; and it was so pressed that it might have fallen in a little time, if the king of France had not sent orders to his troops to retire; and his Christian generosity, which was assigned for the reason of it, made the world smile since it is seen how differently his devout zeal worketh in Hungary. That specious reason was in many respects ill-timed, and France itself gave it so faintly, that at the very time it looked out of countenance. The true ground for his retiring is worth our observation; for at the instance of the confederates, offices were done and memorials given, but all ineffectual till the word *Parliament* was put into them. That powerful word had such an effect that even at that distance it raised the siege, which may convince us of what efficacy the king of England's words are when he will give them their full weight, and threaten with his Parliament. It is then that he appeareth that great figure we ought to represent him in our minds, the nation his body, he the head, and joined with that harmony that every word

he pronounceth is the word of a kingdom. Such words, as appeareth by this example, are as effectual as fleets and armies, because they can create them; and without this, his words sound abroad like a faint whisper, that is either not heard, or (which is worse) not minded.

But though France had made this step of forced compliance, it did not mean to leave off the pursuit of their pretensions and therefore immediately proposed the arbitration to the king; but it appeared that, notwithstanding his merit towards the confederates in saving Luxemburg, the remembrances of what had passed before had left such an ill taste in their mouths that they could not relish our being put into a condition to dispose of their interests, and therefore declined it by insisting upon a general treaty, to which France hath ever since continued to be averse. Our great earnestness also to persuade the confederates to consent to it was so unusual and so suspicious a method that it might naturally make them believe that France spake to them by our mouth, and for that reason, if there had been no other, might hinder the accepting it. And so little care hath been taken to cure this or other jealousies the confederates may have entertained, that, quite contrary, their ministers here every day take fresh alarms from what they observe in small, as well as in greater, circumstances; and they, being apt both to take and improve apprehensions of this kind, draw such inferences from them as make them entirely despair of us.

Thus we now stand, far from being innocent spectators of our neighbors' ruin, and by a fatal mistake forgetting what a certain forerunner it is to our own. And now it is time our Trimmer should tell something of his opinion upon this present state of things abroad. He first professeth to have no bias either for or against France, and that his thoughts are wholly directed by the interest of his own country. He alloweth, and hath read, that Spain used the same methods when it was in its height as France doth now; and therefore it is not partiality that moveth him, but the just fear, which all reasonable men must be possessed with, of an overgrowing power. Ambition is a devouring beast; when it hath swallowed one province, instead of being cloyed, it hath so much the greater stomach to another, and being fed becometh still more hungry; so that for the confederates to expect a security from anything but their own united strength is a most miserable fallacy; and, if they cannot resist the encroachments of France by their arms it is in vain for them to dream of any other means of preservation. It would have the better grace, besides the saving so much blood and ruin, to give up all at once; make a present of themselves, to appease this haughty monarch, rather than be whispered, flattered, or cozened out of their liberty.

Nothing is so soft as the first applications of a greater Prince to engage a weaker; but that smiling countenance is but a vizard, it is not the true face; for as soon as their turn is served, the courtship flies to some other prince or state, where the same part is to be acted over again; leaveth the old mistaken friend to neglect and contempt, and like an insolent lover to a cast-off mistress, reproaches her with that infamy of which he himself was the author. Sweden, Bavaria, Palatine, etc., may by their fresh examples teach other princes what they are reasonably to expect, and what snakes are hid under the flowers the court of France so liberally throweth upon them whilst they can be useful. The various methods and deep intrigues, with the differing notes in several countries, do not only give suspicion, but assurance that everything is put in practice by which universal monarchy may be obtained. Who can reconcile the withdrawing of his troops from Luxemburg in consideration of the war in Hungary which was not then declared, and presently after encouraging the Turk to take Vienna, and consequently to destroy the Empire? Or who can think that the persecution of the poor Protestants of France will be accepted of God as an atonement for hazarding the loss of the whole Christian faith? Can he be thought in earnest when he seemed to be afraid of the Spaniards and for that reason must have Luxemburg, and that he cannot be safe from Germany unless he is in possession of Strassburg? All injustice and violence must in itself be grievous, but the aggravations of supporting them by false arguments and insulting reasons has something in it yet more provoking than the injuries themselves; and the world hath ground enough to apprehend from such a method of arguing that even their senses are to be subdued as well as their liberties. Then the variety of arguments used by France in several countries is very observable. In England and Denmark nothing is insisted on but the greatness and authority of the Crown; on the other side the great men in Poland are commended who differ in opinion with the king, and they argue, like friends, to the privilege of the Diet against the separate power of the Crown. In Sweden they are troubled that the king should have changed something there of late, by his single authority, from the ancient and settled authority and constitutions. At Ratisbon the most Christian Majesty taketh the liberties of all the Electors and Free States into his protection, and telleth them the Emperor is a dangerous man, an aspiring hero, that would infallibly devour them, if he was not at hand to resist him on their behalf. But above all, in Holland, he hath the most obliging tenderness for the Commonwealth, and is in such disquiets lest it should be invaded by the Prince of Orange, that they can do no less in gratitude than undo themselves when he bids them, to show how sensible they are of his excessive good nature.

Yet, in spite of all these contradictions, there are in the world such refined statesmen as will upon their credit affirm the following paradoxes to be real truth; first, that France alone is sincere and keepeth its faith, and consequently that it is the only friend we can rely upon; that the king of France, of all men living, hath the least mind to be a conqueror; that he is a sleepy, tame creature, void of all ambition, a poor kind of a man, that hath no farther thoughts than to be quiet; that he is charmed[10] by his friendship to us; that it is impossible he should ever do us hurt, and therefore, though Flanders was lost, it would not in the least concern us; that he would fain help the Crown of England to be absolute, which would be to take pains to put it into a condition to oppose him, as it is, and must be, our interest as long as he continueth in such an overbalancing power and greatness.

Such a creed as this, if once received, might prepare our belief for greater things, and as he that taught men to eat a dagger began first with a penknife, so if we can be prevailed with to digest the smaller mistakes, we may at least make our stomachs strong enough for that of transubstantiation. Our Trimmer cannot easily be converted out of his senses by these state sophisters, and yet he hath no such peevish obstinacy as to reject all correspondence with France, because we ought to be apprehensive of the too great power of it. He would not have the king's friendship to the confederates extended to the involving him in any unreasonable or dangerous engagements, neither would he have him lay aside the consideration of his better establishment at home, out of his excessive zeal to secure his allies abroad; but, sure, there might be a mean between these two opposite extremes, and it may be wished that our friendship with France should at least be so bounded that it may consist with the honor[11] as well as the interest of England. There is no woman but hath her

10 Bewitched, rendered harmless.
11 The text reads "humor." The emendation, "honor," is Miss Foxcroft's.

fears of contracting too near an intimacy with a much greater beauty, because it exposeth her too often to a comparison that is not advantageous to her; and, sure, it may become a prince to be as jealous of his dignity as a lady can be of her good looks, and to be as much out of countenance to be thought an humble companion to so much a greater power. To be always seen in an ill light, to be so darkened by the brightness of a greater star, is somewhat mortifying; and when England might ride admiral at the head of the confederates, to look like the kitchen-yacht to the Grand Louis is but a scurvy figure for us to make in the map of Christendom. It would rise upon our Trimmer's stomach if ever (which God forbid) the power of calling and intermitting Parliaments here should be transferred to the Crown of France, and that all the opportunities of our own settlements at home should give way to their projects abroad, and that our interests should be so far sacrificed to our compliance, that all the omnipotence of France can never make us full amends for it. In the meantime, he shrinketh at the dismal prospect he can by no means drive away from his thoughts, that when France hath gathered all the fruit arising from our mistakes, and that we can bear no more for them, they will cut down the tree and throw it into the fire. All this while some superfine statesmen, to comfort us, would fain persuade the world that this or that accident may save us; and, for all that is or ought to be dear to us, would have us to rely wholly upon chance, not considering that fortune is wisdom's creature, and that God Almighty loves to be on the wisest as well as on the strongest side. Therefore, this is such a miserable shift, such a shameful evasion, that they would be laughed to death for it if the ruining consequence of this mistake did not more dispose men to rage and a detestation of it.

Our Trimmer is far from idolatry in other things; in one thing only he cometh near it, his country is in some degree his idol. He doth not worship the sun, because 'tis not peculiar to us; it rambles about the world, and is less kind to us than others. But for the earth of England, though perhaps inferior to that of many places abroad, to him there is divinity in it, and he would rather die than see a spire of English grass[12] trampled down by a foreign trespasser. He thinketh

there are a great many of his mind, for all plants are apt to taste of the soil in which they grow, and we that grow here have a root that produceth in us a stalk of English juice, which is not to be changed by grafting or foreign infusion; and I do not know whether anything less will prevail, than the modern experiment by which the blood of one creature is transmitted into another; according to which, before the French blood can be let into our bodies, every drop of our own must be drawn out of them.

Our Trimmer cannot but lament that by a sacrifice too great for one nation to make to another, we should be like a rich mine, made useless only for want of being wrought, and that the life and vigor which should move us against our enemies is miserably applied to tear our own bowels; that being made by our happy situation not only safer, but, if we please, greater too than other countries which far exceed us in extent; that having courage by nature, learning by industry, and riches by trade, we should corrupt all these advantages so as to make them insignificant, and, by a fatality which seemeth peculiar to us, misplace our active rage one against another, whilst we are turned into statues on that side where lieth our greatest danger; to be unconcerned not only at our neighbor's ruin but our own, and let our island lie like a great hulk in the sea, without rudder or sail, all the men cast away in her, or as if we were all children in a great cradle and rocked asleep to a foreign tune.

I say, when our Trimmer representeth to his mind our roses blasted and discolored, whilst the lilies triumph and grow insolent upon the comparison; when he considereth our own once flourishing laurel now withered and dying, and nothing left us but a remembrance of a better part in history than we shall make in the next age, which will be no more to us than an escutcheon hung upon our door when we are dead; when he forseeth, from hence growing, infamy from abroad, confusion at home, and all this without the possibility of a cure in respect of the voluntary fetters good men put upon themselves by their allegiance; without a good measure of preventing grace, he would be tempted to go out of the world like a Roman philosopher rather than endure the burthen of life under such a discouraging prospect.

But mistakes, as all other things, have their periods, and many times the nearest way to cure is not to oppose them, but stay till they are crushed with their own weight; for nature will not allow anything to continue long that is violent; violence is a wound, and

---

12 The text has "piece of English glass." The very happy emendation, "spire of English grass," is Miss Foxcroft's, and is supported by a contemporary copy of the essay in the possession of Mr. John Murray of University College, Exeter.

as a wound must be curable in a little time, or else 'tis mortal, but a nation comes near to be immortal, therefore the wound will one time or another be cured, though perhaps by such rough methods, if too long forborne, as may even make the best remedies we can prepare to be at the same time a melancholy contemplation to us. There is but one thing (God Almighty's Providence excepted) to support a man from sinking under these afflicting thoughts, and that is the hopes we draw singly from the king himself without the mixture of any other consideration.

Though the nation was lavish of their kindness to him at his first coming, yet there remaineth still a stock of warmth in men's hearts for him. Besides, the good influences of his happy planet are not yet all spent, and though the stars of men past their youth are generally declining and have less force, like the eyes of decaying beauties, yet by a blessing peculiar to himself we may yet hope to be saved by his autumnal fortune. He hath something about him that will draw down a healing miracle for his and our deliverance. A prince which seemeth fitted for such an offending age, in which men's crimes have been so general, that the not forgiving his people had been the destroying of them; whose gentleness giveth him a natural dominion that hath no bounds, with such a noble mixture of greatness and condescension, an engaging look that disarmeth men of their ill humors and their resentments; something in him that wanteth a name, and can be no more defined than it can be resisted; a gift of heaven of its last finishing, where it will be peculiarly kind; the only prince in the world that dares be familiar, or that hath right to triumph over those forms which were first invented to give awe to those who could not judge, and to hide defects from those that could; a prince that hath exhausted himself by his liberality, and endangered himself by his mercy; who outshineth by his own right and natural virtues all the varnish of studied acquisitions. His faults are like the shades to a good picture, or like alloy to gold, to make it the more useful; he may have some, but for any man to see them through so many reconciling virtues is a sacrilegious piece of ill nature, of which no generous mind can be guilty. A prince that deserveth to be loved for his own sake, even without the help of a comparison; our love, our duty, and our danger all join to cement our obedience to him. In short, whatever he can do, it is no more possible for us to be angry with him than with the bank that secureth us from the raging sea, the kind shade that hideth us from the scorching sun, the welcome hand that reacheth us a reprieve, or with the guardian angel that rescueth our souls from the devouring jaws of wretched eternity.

CONCLUSION

TO CONCLUDE, our Trimmer is so fully satisfied of the truth of those principles by which he is directed in reference to the public, that he will neither be bawled, threatened, laughed, nor drunk out of them; and instead of being converted by the arguments of his adversaries to their opinions, he is very much confirmed in his own by them. He professeth solemnly that were it in his power to choose, he would rather have his ambition bounded by the commands of a great and wise master, than let it range with a popular license, though crowned with success; yet he cannot commit such a sin against the glorious thing called liberty, nor let his soul stoop so much below itself, as to be content without repining to have his reason wholly subdued, or the privilege of acting like a sensible creature torn from him by the imperious dictates of unlimited authority, in what hand soever it happens to be placed. What is there in this that is so criminal as to deserve the penalty of that most singular apophthegm, *A Trimmer is worse than a rebel?* What do angry men ail to rail so against moderation? Doth it not look as if they were going to some very scurvy extreme that is too strong to be digested by the more considering part of mankind? These arbitrary methods, besides the injustice of them, are (God be thanked) very unskillful too, for they fright the birds, by talking so loud, from coming into the nets that are laid for them; and when men agree to rifle a house, they seldom give warning or blow a trumpet.

But there are some small statesmen who are so full charged with their own expectations that they cannot contain. And kind Heaven, by sending such a seasonable curse upon their undertakings, hath made their ignorance an antidote against their malice. Some of these cannot treat peaceably; yielding will not satisfy them; they will have men by storm. There are others that must have plots, to make their service more necessary, and have an interest to keep them alive, since they are to live upon them; and persuade the king to retrench his own greatness so as to shrink into the head of a party, which is the betraying him into such an unprincely mistake and to such a willful diminution of himself, that they are the last enemies he ought to allow himself to forgive. Such men, if they could, would prevail with the sun to shine only upon them and their friends, and to leave all the rest of the world in the dark. This is a very unusual monopoly, and may come within the equity of the law which maketh it treason to imprison the king. When such unfitting bounds are put to his favor, and he confined to the narrow limits of a particular set of men that would inclose him, these honest and only loyal gentlemen, if they may be allowed to bear witness for themselves, make a king their engine, and degrade him into a property at the very time that their flattery would make him believe they paid divine worship to him. Besides these, there is a flying squadron on both sides that are afraid the world should agree; small dabblers in conjuring that raise angry apparitions to keep men from being reconciled, like wasps that fly up and down, buzz and sting to keep men unquiet. But these insects are commonly short-lived creatures, and no doubt in a little time mankind will be rid of them. They were giants at least who fought once against Heaven, but for such pygmies as these to contend against it is such a provoking folly, that the insolent bunglers ought to be laughed and hissed out of the world for it. They should consider there is a soul in that great body of the people, which may for a time be drowsy and unactive, but when the leviathan is roused, it moveth like an angry creature, and will neither be convinced nor resisted. The people can never agree to show their united powers till they are extremely tempted and provoked to it; so that to apply cupping-glasses to a great beast naturally disposed to sleep, and to force the tame thing, whether it will or no, to be valiant, must be learnt out of some other book than Machiavelli, who would never have prescribed such a preposterous method. It is to be remembered that if princes have law and authority on their sides, the people on theirs may have nature, which is a formidable adversary. Duty, justice, religion, nay, even human prudence too, biddeth the people suffer anything rather than resist; but uncorrected nature, wherever it feels the smart, will run to the nearest remedy. Men's passions in this case are to be considered as well as their duty, let it be never so strongly enforced; for if their passions are provoked, they being as much a part of us as our limbs, they lead men into a short way of arguing, that admitteth no distinction, and from the foundation of self-defense they will draw inferences that will have miserable effects upon the quiet of a government.

Our Trimmer, therefore, dreads a general discontent, because he thinketh it differeth from a rebellion only as a spotted fever doth from the plague, the same species under a lower degree of malignity. It worketh several ways; sometimes like a slow poison that hath its effects at a great distance from the time it was given; sometimes like dry flax prepared to catch at the first fire; or like seed in the ground ready to sprout upon the first shower. In every shape 'tis fatal, and our Trimmer thinketh no pains or precaution can be so great as to prevent it.

In short, he thinketh himself in the right, grounding his opinion upon that truth which equally hateth to be under the oppressions of wrangling sophistry on the one hand, or the short dictates of mistaken authority on the other.

Our Trimmer adoreth the goddess Truth, though in all ages she hath been scurvily used, as well as those that worshiped her. 'Tis of late become such a ruining virtue that mankind seemeth to be agreed to commend and avoid it; yet the want of practice which repealeth the other laws hath no influence upon the law of Truth, because it hath root in Heaven, and an intrinsic value in itself, that can never be impaired. She showeth her greatness in this, that her enemies, even when they are successful, are ashamed to own it; nothing but powerful Truth hath the prerogative of triumphing, not only after victories, but in spite of them, and to put Conquest herself out of countenance. She may be kept under and suppressed, but her dignity still remaineth with her, even when she is in chains; Falsehood, with all her impudence, hath not enough to speak ill of her before her face. Such majesty she carrieth about her, that her most prosperous enemies are fain to whisper their treason; all the power upon earth can never extinguish her. She hath lived in all ages; and let the mistaken zeal of prevailing authority christen any opposition to it with what name they please, she maketh it not only an ugly and unmannerly but a dangerous thing to persist. She hath lived very retired indeed, nay, sometime so buried, that only some few of the discerning part of mankind could have a glimpse of her; with all that, she hath eternity in her, she knoweth not how to die; and from the darkest clouds that shade and cover her, she breaketh from time to time with triumph for her friends, and terror to her enemies.

Our Trimmer, therefore, inspired by this divine virtue thinketh fit to conclude with these assertions: that our climate is a Trimmer between that part of the world where men are roasted, and the other where they are frozen; that our church is a Trimmer between the frenzy of Platonic visions and the lethargic ignorance of Popish dreams; that our laws are Trimmers between the excess of unbounded power and the extravagance of liberty not enough restrained; that true virtue hath ever been thought a Trimmer, and to have its dwelling in the middle between the two extremes; that even God Almighty himself is divided between his two great attributes, his mercy and his justice.

In such company, our Trimmer is not ashamed of his name, and willingly leaveth to the bold champions of either extreme the honor of contending with no less adversaries than nature, religion, liberty, prudence, humanity, and common sense.

Thomas Traherne

[1637–1674]

THE belated discovery, in 1897, of the poetry and prose of Thomas Traherne presented to the literary world the last Metaphysical poet and one of the last voices of Renaissance Neoplatonism. The romantic aspect of this posthumous literary debut led at first to a certain overestimation of Traherne's poetry, which, though extremely interesting and fitfully inspired, is unquestionably minor. With the passage of the years his prose *Centuries of Meditations* have become the work on which his reputation chiefly rests, and there seems little doubt that that reputation will be secure.

Our skimpy knowledge of Traherne's life is derived almost exclusively from Anthony à Wood. The poet was the son of a Herefordshire shoemaker, descendant of an ancient Welsh family which had once been prominent. Despite his poverty, he was able to attend Oxford, and he took his degree at Brasenose College in 1656. He then took holy orders and retired to a country parish near Hereford, where he lived a peaceful and meditative life. Subsequently he enjoyed the patronage of Sir Orlando Bridgeman, Lord Keeper of the Great Seal, and he served as the Lord Keeper's chaplain first in London and later in Hereford.

In the seventeenth century only the following works of Traherne appeared: *Roman Forgeries* (1673), a theological polemic against the Roman Church; *Christian Ethics* (1675); and *A Serious and Pathetical Contemplation of the Mercies of God* (1699). Only the last-named shows real affinities with the works of private devotion for which he is remembered—the poems and the *Centuries*. These are similar in their subject matter, sometimes identical in their phrasing. Their common themes are the sanctity of childhood, the validity of intuition, and the immanence of God in Nature. The poems are often deficient in technique and imperfect in form, but the *Centuries* are expressed in a prose which has the individuality, the complexity, and the pulsating excitement of the great Baroque writers. The autobiographical passages of the *Third Century* have a particular interest and eloquence. In his sense of a mysteriously ordered and divinely directed cosmos surrounding us and active within us, Traherne looks back to the writers of the early seventeenth century, but in his obsession with infinity, his heroic aspiration toward the absolute, and his unbounded faith in the capacities of man he anticipates Blake, Wordsworth, and the Romantics. From his brief moment of time he uniquely fused the spirit of the past and the spirit of the future through a poetic sensibility which is as profound as it is curious.

T. TRAHERNE. *Poems, Centuries, and Thanksgivings*, ed. H. M. Margoliouth, 2 vols.
    (Oxford, 1958). The definitive edition, replacing Dobell's edition of 1908.
————. *A Serious and Pathetical Contemplation of the Mercies of God*, ed. R. Daniells
    (Toronto, 1941).
G. I. WADE. *Thomas Traherne* (Princeton, 1944). Biography.
G. E. WILLETT. *Traherne: An Essay* (Cambridge, 1919).

FROM

CENTURIES OF MEDITATIONS

[TEXT: *Margoliouth's edition, 1958*]

THE FIRST CENTURY

1

AN EMPTY book is like an infant's soul, in which anything may be written. It is capable of all things, but containeth nothing. I have a mind to fill this with profitable wonders. And since Love made you put it into my hands I will fill it with those Truths you love without knowing them: with those things which, if it be possible, shall show my Love; to you in communicating most enriching Truths: to Truth in exalting her beauties in such a Soul.

2

DO NOT wonder that I promise to fill it with those Truths you love but know not; for though it be a maxim in the schools *that there is no Love of a thing unknown*, yet I have found that things unknown have a secret influence on the soul, and like the center of the earth unseen violently attract it. We love we know not what, and therefore everything allures us. As iron at a distance is drawn by the loadstone, there being some invisible communications between them, so is there in us a world of Love to somewhat, though we know not what, in the world that should be. There are invisible ways of conveyance by which some great thing doth touch our souls, and by which we tend to it. Do you not feel yourself drawn by the expectation and desire of some Great Thing?

6

TRUE LOVE, as it intendeth the greatest gifts, intendeth also the greatest benefits. It contenteth not it-self in showing great things unless it can make them greatly useful. For Love greatly delighteth in seeing its object continually seated in the highest happiness. Unless therefore I could advance you higher by the uses of what I give, my Love could not be satisfied in giving you the whole world. But because, when you enjoy it, you are advanced to the throne of God, and may see His Love, I rest well pleased in bestowing it. It will make you to see your own greatness, the truth of the Scriptures, the amiableness of virtue, and the beauty of religion. It will enable you also to contemn the world and to overflow with praises.

7

TO CONTEMN the world, and to enjoy the world, are things contrary to each other. How then can we contemn the world which we are born to enjoy? Truly there are two worlds. One was made by God, the other by men. That made by God was great and beautiful. Before the fall, it was Adam's joy and the temple of his glory. That made by men is a Babel of confusions: invented riches, pomps and vanities, brought in by sin. Give all, saith Thomas à Kempis, for all. Leave the one that you may enjoy the other.

8

WHAT is more easy and sweet than meditation? Yet in this hath God commended his Love, that by meditation it is enjoyed. As nothing is more easy than to think, so nothing is more difficult than to think well. The easiness of thinking we received from God, the difficulty of thinking well proceeded from ourselves. Yet in truth, it is far more easy to think well than ill, because good thoughts be sweet and delightful. Evil thoughts are full of discontent and trouble. So that an evil habit and custom have made it difficult to think well, not Nature. For by nature nothing is so difficult as to think amiss.

9

IS IT NOT easy to conceive the world in your mind? To think the heavens fair? the sun glorious? the earth fruitful? the air pleasant? the sea profitable? and the Giver bountiful? Yet these are the things which it is difficult to retain. For could we always be sensible of their use and value, we should be always delighted with their wealth and glory.

10

TO THINK well is to serve God in the interior court: to have a mind composed of divine thoughts, and set in frame, to be like Him within. To conceive aright and to enjoy the world is to conceive the Holy Ghost and to see His Love, which is the mind of the Father. And this more pleaseth Him than many worlds, could we create as fair and great as this. For when you are once acquainted with the world, you will find the goodness and wisdom of God so manifest therein that it was impossible another or better would be made. Which being made to be enjoyed, nothing can please or serve Him more than the soul that enjoys it. For that soul doth accomplish the end of His desire in creating it.

11

LOVE is deeper than at first it can be thought. It never ceaseth but in endless things. It ever multiplies. Its benefits and its designs are always infinite. Were you not holy, divine, and blessed in enjoying the world, I should not care so much to bestow it. But now in this you accomplish the end of your creation, and serve God best, and please him most: I rejoice in giving it. For to enable you to please God, is the highest service a man can do you. It is to make you pleasing to the King of Heaven, that you may be the darling of his bosom.

15

SUCH endless depths live in the Divinity, and in the wisdom of God, that as he maketh one, so he maketh everyone the end of the world: and the supernumerary persons being enrichers of his inheritance. Adam and the world are both mine. And the posterity of Adam enrich it infinitely. Souls are God's jewels, every one of which is worth many worlds. They are his riches because his image, and mine for that reason. So that I alone am the end of the world: angels and men being all mine. And if others are so, they are made to enjoy it for my further advancement. God only being the Giver and I the Receiver. So that Seneca philosophized rightly when he said *"Deus me dedit solum toti mundi, et totum mundum mihi soli"*: God gave me alone to all the world, and all the world to me alone.

18

THE world is not this little cottage of heaven and earth. Though this be fair, it is too small a gift. When God made the world he made the heavens, and the heavens of heavens, and the angels, and the celestial powers. There also are parts of the world. So are all those infinite and eternal treasures that are to abide forever, after the Day of Judgment. Neither are these some here, and some there, but all everywhere, and at once to be enjoyed. The world is unknown, till the value and glory of it is seen: till the beauty and the serviceableness of its parts is considered. When you enter into it, it is an illimited field of variety and beauty: where you may lose yourself in the multitude of wonders and delights. But it is an happy loss to lose oneself in admiration at one's own felicity: and to find God in exchange for oneself. Which we then do when we see him in his gifts, and adore his glory.

19

YOU never know yourself till you know more than your body. The image of God was not seated in the features of your face but in the lineaments of your soul. In the knowledge of your powers, inclinations, and principles, the knowledge of yourself chiefly consisteth, which are so great that even to the most learned of men their greatness is incredible, and so divine that they are infinite in value. Alas, the world is but a little center in comparison to you. Suppose it millions of miles from the earth to the heavens, and millions of millions above the stars, both here and over the heads of our antipodes: it is surrounded with infinite and eternal space. And, like a gentleman's house to one that is traveling: it is a long time before you come unto it, you pass it in an instant, and leave it forever. The omnipresence and eternity of God are your fellows and companions. And all that is in them ought to be made your familiar treasures. Your understanding comprehends the world like the dust of a balance, measures heaven with a span, and esteems a thousand years but as one day. So that great endless eternal delights are only fit to be its enjoyments.

22

It is the nobility of man's soul that he is insatiable. For he hath a benefactor so prone to give that He delighteth in us for asking. Do not your inclinations tell you that the world is yours? Do you not covet it? Do you not long to have it? To enjoy it? To overcome it? To what end do men gather riches but to multiply more? Do they not, like Pyrrhus, the king of Epire, add house to house and lands to lands that they may get it all? It is storied of that prince that, having conceived a purpose to invade Italy, he sent for Cineas, a philosopher and the king's friend, to whom he communicated his design and desired his counsel. Cineas asked him to what purpose he invaded Italy. He said, To conquer it. And what will you do when you have conquered it? Go into France, said the king, and conquer that. And what will you do when you have conquered France? Conquer Germany. And what then, said the philosopher. Conquer Spain. I perceive, said Cineas, you mean to conquer all the world. What will you do when you have conquered all? Why then, said the king, we will return and enjoy ourselves at quiet in our own land. So you may now, said the philosopher, without all this ado. Yet could he not divert him till he was ruined by the Romans. Thus men get one hundred pounds a year that they may get another; and having two covet eight, and there is no end of all their labor, because the desire of their soul is insatiable. Like Alexander the Great, they must have all; and when they have got it all, be quiet. And may they not do all this before they begin? Nay, it would be well if they could be quiet. But if, after all, they shall be like the stars, that are seated on high but have no rest, what gain they more, but labor for their trouble? It was wittily fained that that young man sate down and cried for more worlds; so insatiable is man that millions will not please him. They are no more so than so many tennis-balls in comparison of the greatness and highness of his soul.

25

YOUR enjoyment of the world is never right till you so esteem it that everything in it is more your treasure than a king's exchequer full of gold and silver. And that exchequer yours also in its place and service. Can you take too much joy in your Father's works? He is himself in everything. Some things are little on the outside, and rough and common, but I remember the time when the dust of the streets were as pleasing as gold to my infant eyes, and now they are more precious to the eye of reason.

26

THE services of things and their excellencies are spiritual, being objects not of the eye but of the mind; and you more spiritual by how much more you esteem them. Pigs eat acorns, but neither consider the sun that gave them life nor the influences of the heavens by which they were nourished, nor the very root of the tree from which they came. This being the work of angels, who in a wide and clear light see even the sea that gave them moisture; and feed upon that acorn spiritually, while they know the ends for which it was created, and feast upon all these as upon a world of joys within it; while to ignorant swine that eat the shell it is an empty husk of no taste nor delightful savor.

27

YOU never enjoy the world aright till you see how a sand exhibiteth the wisdom and power of God: and prize in everything the service which they do you, by manifesting his glory and goodness to your soul, far more than the visible beauty on their surface, or the material services they can do your body. Wine by its moisture quencheth my thirst, whether I consider it or no: but to see it flowing from his love who gave it unto man, quencheth the thirst even of the holy angels. To consider it is to drink it spiritually. To rejoice in its diffusion is to be of a public mind. And to take pleasure in all the benefits it doth to all is heavenly, for so they do in heaven. To do so, is to be divine and good, and to imitate our infinite and eternal Father.

28

YOUR enjoyment of the world is never right till every morning you awake in heaven; see yourself in your Father's palace; and look upon the skies, the earth, and the air as celestial joys; having such a reverend esteem of all, as if you were among the angels. The bride of a monarch, in her husband's chamber, hath no such causes of delight as you.

29

YOU never enjoy the world aright till the sea itself floweth in your veins, till you are clothed with the heavens, and crowned with the stars: and perceive yourself to be the sole heir of the whole world, and more than so, because men are in it who are every one sole heirs as well as you. Till you can sing and rejoice and delight in God, as misers do in gold, and kings in scepters, you never enjoy the world.

30

TILL your spirit filleth the whole world, and the stars are your jewels: till you are as familiar with the ways of God in all ages as with your walk and table: till you are intimately acquainted with that shady nothing out of which the world was made: till you love men so as to desire their happiness, with a thirst equal to the zeal of your own: till you delight in God for being good to all: you never enjoy the world. Till you more feel it than your private estate, and are more present in the hemisphere, considering the glories and the beauties there, than in your own house. Till you remember how lately you were made, and how wonderful it was when you came into it: and more rejoice in the palace of your glory, than if it had been made but today morning.

31

YET further, you never enjoy the world aright till you so love the beauty of enjoying it that you are covetous and earnest to persuade others to enjoy it. And so perfectly hate the abominable corruption of men in despising it, that you had rather suffer the flames of hell than willingly be guilty of their error. There is so much blindness and ingratitude and damned folly in it. The world is a mirror of infinite beauty, yet no man sees it. It is a temple of majesty, yet no man regards it. It is a region of light and peace, did not men disquiet it. It is the Paradise of God. It is more to man since he is fallen than it was before. It is the place of angels and the Gate of Heaven. When Jacob waked out of his dream, he said "God is here, and I wist it not. How dreadful is this place! This is none other than the House of God, and the Gate of Heaven."

34

WOULD one think it possible for a man to delight in gauderies like a butterfly, and neglect the heavens? Did we not daily see it, it would be incredible. They rejoice in a piece of gold more than in the sun, and get a few little glimmering stones and call them jewels, and admire them because they be resplendent like the stars and transparent like the air and pellucid like the sea. But the stars themselves, which are ten thousand times more useful, great, and glorious, they disregard.

Nor shall the air itself be counted anything, though it be worth all the pearls and diamonds in ten thousand worlds, a work so divine by reason of its precious and pure transparency that all worlds would be nothing without such a treasure.

35

THE riches of the light are the works of God, which are the portion and inheritance of his sons, to be seen and enjoyed in heaven and earth, the sea, and all that is therein, the light and the day. Great and fathomless in use and excellency; true, necessary. Freely given; proceeding wholly from His infinite love. As worthy as they are easy to be enjoyed. Obliging us to love Him and to delight in Him, filling us with gratitude, and making us to overflow with praises and thanksgivings. The works of contentment and pleasure are of the day. So are the works which flow from the understanding of our mutual serviceableness to each other: arising from the sufficiency and excellency of our treasures, contentment, joy, peace, unity, charity, etc., whereby we are all knit together and delight in each other's happiness. For while everyone is heir of all the world and all the rest his superadded treasures, all the world serves him in himself and in them as his superadded treasures.

41

AS PICTURES are made curious by lights and shades, which without shades could not be, so is felicity composed of wants and supplies, without which mixture there could be no felicity. Were there no needs, wants would be wanting themselves, and supplies superfluous, want being the parent of celestial treasure. It is very strange: want itself is a treasure in heaven, and so great an one that without it there could be no treasure. God did infinitely for us, when he made us want like Gods, that like Gods we might be satisfied. The heathen deities wanted nothing, and were therefore happy, for they had no being. But the Lord God of Israel, the living and true God, was from all eternity, and from all eternity wanted like a God. He wanted the communication of His divine essence, and persons to enjoy it. He wanted worlds, He wanted spectators, He wanted joys, He wanted treasures. He wanted, yet He wanted not, for He had them.

42

THIS is very strange that God should want, for in Him is the fullness of all blessedness: He overfloweth eternally. His wants are as glorious as infinite: perfect needs that are in His nature, and ever blessed, because ever satisfied. He is from eternity full of want, or else He would not be full of treasure. Infinite want is the very ground and cause of infinite treasure. It is incredible, yet plain: want is the fountain of all His fullness. Want in God is a treasure to us. For had there been no need, He would not have created the world, nor made us, nor manifested His wisdom, nor exercised His power, nor beautified eternity, nor prepared the joys of heaven. But He wanted angels and men, images, companions, and these He had from all eternity.

43

INFINITE wants satisfied produce infinite joys, and, in the possession of joys, are infinite joys themselves. *The desire satisfied is a tree of life.* Desire imports something absent, and a need of what is absent. God was never without this tree of life. He did desire infinitely. Yet He was never without the fruits of this tree, which are the joys it produced. I must lead you out of this, into another world, to learn your wants. For till you find them you will never be happy, wants themselves being sacred occasions and means of felicity.

44

YOU must want like a God that you may be satisfied like God. Were you not made in his image? He is infinitely glorious, because all his wants and supplies are at the same time in his nature from eternity. He had, and from eternity he was without, all his treasures. From eternity he needed them, and from eternity he enjoyed them. For all eternity is at once in him, both the empty durations before the world was made, and the full ones after. His wants are as lively as his enjoyments: and always present with him. For his life is perfect, and he feels them both. His wants put a luster upon his enjoyments and make them infinite. His enjoyments being infinite crown his wants, and make them beautiful even to God himself. His wants and enjoyments being always present are delightful to each other, stable, immutable, perfective of each other, and delightful to him. Who being eternal and immutable, enjoyeth all his wants and treasures together. His wants never afflict him, his treasures never disturb him. His wants always delight him: his treasures never cloy him. The sense of his wants is always as great as if his treasures were removed: and as lively upon him. The

sense of his wants, as it enlargeth his life, so it infuseth a value and continual sweetness into the treasures he enjoyeth.

58

THE Cross is the abyss of wonders, the center of desires, the school of virtues, the house of wisdom, the throne of love, the theater of joys, and the place of sorrows. It is the root of happiness, and the Gate of Heaven.

THE SECOND CENTURY

6

THE consideration of this truth, that the world is mine, confirmeth my faith, God having placed the evidences of religion in the greatest and highest joys. For as long as I am ignorant that the world is mine, the love of God is defective to me. How can I believe that He gave His son to die for me, who, having power to do otherwise, gave me nothing but rags and cottages? But when I see once that He gave heaven and earth to me, and made me in His image to enjoy them in His similitude, I can easily believe that He gave His son also for me, especially since He commanded all angels and men to love me as Himself, and so highly honoreth me that whatsoever is done unto me He accounteth done unto Him.

7

PLACE yourself therefore in the midst of the world as if you were alone, and meditate upon all the services which it doth unto you. Suppose the sun were absent, and conceive the world to be a dungeon of darkness and death about you: you will then find his beams more delightful than the approach of angels, and loathe the abomination of that sinful blindness whereby you see not the glory of so great and bright a creature because the air is filled with its beams. Then you will think that all its light shineth for you, and confess that God hath manifested Himself indeed in the preparation of so divine a creature. You will abhor the madness of those who esteem a purse of gold more than it. Alas, what could a man do with a purse of gold in an everlasting dungeon? And shall we prize the sun less than it, which is the light and fountain of all our pleasures? You will then abhor the preposterous method of those who in an evil sense are blinded with its beams and to whom the presence of the light is the greatest darkness. For they who would repine at God without the sun are unthankful, having it, and therefore only despise it, because it is created.

40

IN ALL love there is a love begetting, and a love begotten, and a love proceeding. Which though they are one in essence subsist nevertheless in three several manners. For love is benevolent affection to another: which is of itself, and by itself relateth to its object. It floweth from itself and resteth in its object. Love proceedeth of necessity from itself, for unless it be o itself it is not love. Constraint is destructive and opposite to its nature. The love from which it floweth is the fountain of love. The love which streameth from it is the communication of love, or love communicated. The love which resteth in the object is the love which streameth to it. So that in all love the Trinity is clear. By secret passages without stirring, it proceedeth to its object; and is as powerfully present as if it did not proceed at all. The love that lieth in the bosom of the lover, being the love that is perceived in the spirit of the beloved: that is, the same in substance, though in the manner of substance, or subsistence different. Love in the bosom is the parent of love; love in the stream is the effect of love; love seen, or dwelling in the object, proceedeth from both. Yet are all these one and the selfsame love: though three loves.

41

LOVE in the fountain and love in the stream are both the same. And therefore are they both equal in time and glory. For love communicateth itself, and therefore love in the fountain is the very love communicated to its object. Love in the fountain is love in the stream, and love in the stream equally glorious with love in the fountain. Though it streameth to its object, it abideth in the lover and is the love of the lover.

42

WHERE love is the lover, love streaming from the lover is the lover; the lover streaming from himself, and existing in another person.

43

THIS person is the son of God, Who, as He is the wisdom of the Father, so is He the love of the Father.

For the Love of the Father is the wisdom of the Father. And this person did God by loving us beget, that He might be the means of our glory.

65

YOU are as prone to love as the sun is to shine; it being the most delightful and natural employment of the soul of man, without which you are dark and miserable. Consider therefore the extent of love, its vigor and excellency. For certainly he that delights not in love makes vain the universe, and is of necessity to himself the greatest burden. The whole world ministers to you as the theater of your love. It sustains you and all objects that you may continue to love them. Without which it were better for you to have no being. Life without objects is sensible emptiness, and that is a greater misery than death or nothing. Objects without love are a delusion of life. The objects of love are its greatest treasures: and without love it is impossible they should be treasures. For the objects which we love are the pleasing objects, and delightful things. And whatsoever is not pleasing and delightful to you can be no treasure: nay, it is distasteful, and worse than nothing, since we had rather it should have no being.

66

THAT violence wherewith sometimes a man doteth upon one creature is but a little spark of that love, even towards all, which lurketh in his nature. We are made to love: both to satisfy the necessity of our active nature and to answer the beauties in every creature. By love our souls are married and soldered to the creatures, and it is our duty like God to be united to them all. We must love them infinitely, but in God and for God, and God in them: namely all His excellencies manifested in them. When we dote upon the perfections and beauties of some one creature we do not love that too much, but other things too little. Never was anything in this world loved too much, but many things have been loved in a false way and all in too short a measure.

67

SUPPOSE a river or a drop of water, an apple or a sand, an ear of corn or an herb: God knoweth infinite excellencies in it more than we; He seeth how it relateth to angels and men, how it proceedeth from the most perfect lover to the most perfectly beloved, how it representeth all His attributes, how it conduceth in its place by the best of means to the best of ends; and for this cause it cannot be beloved too much. God the author and God the end is to be beloved in it; angels and men are to be beloved in it; and it is highly to be esteemed for all their sakes. O what a treasure is every sand when truly understood! Who can love any thing that God made too much? His infinite goodness and wisdom and power and glory are in it. What a world would this be, were every thing beloved as it ought to be!

68

SUPPOSE a curious and fair woman. Some have seen the beauties of heaven in such a person. It is a vain thing to say they loved too much. I dare say there are 10,000 beauties in that creature which they have not seen. They loved it not too much but upon false causes. Not so much upon false ones as only upon some little ones. They love a creature for sparkling eyes and curled hair, lily breasts and ruddy cheeks, which they should love moreover for being God's image, queen of the universe, beloved by angels, redeemed by Jesus Christ, an heiress of heaven and temple of the Holy Ghost; a mine and fountain of all virtues, a treasury of graces, and a child of God. But these excellencies are unknown. They love her perhaps, but do not love God more, nor men as much, nor heaven and earth at all; and so, being defective to other things, perish by a seeming excess to that. We should be all life and mettle and vigor and love to every thing; and that would poise us. I dare confidently say that every person in the whole world ought to be beloved as much as this, and, if there be any cause of difference, more than she is. But God, being beloved infinitely more, will be infinitely more our joy, and our heart will be more with Him. So that no man can be in danger by loving others too much, that loveth God as he ought.

81

FEW will believe the soul to be infinite, yet infinite is the first thing which is naturally known. Bounds and limits are discerned only in a secondary manner. Suppose a man were born deaf and blind. By the very feeling of his soul he apprehends infinite about him, infinite space, infinite darkness. He thinks not of wall and limits till he feels them and is stopped by them. That things are finite, therefore, we learn by our senses, but infinity we know and feel by our souls; and feel it so naturally as if it were the very essence and

being of the soul. The truth of it is, it is individually in the soul; for God is there, and more near to us than we are to ourselves. So that we cannot feel our souls but we must feel Him, in that first of properties, infinite space. And this we know so naturally that it is the only *primo et necessario cognitum in rerum natura:* Of all things the only first and most necessarily known; for we can unsuppose Heaven and Earth, and annihilate the world in our imagination, but the place where they stood will remain behind, and we cannot unsuppose or annihilate *that*, do what we can. Which without us is the chamber of our infinite treasures and within us the repository and recipient of them.

100

FELICITY is a thing coveted of all. The whole world is taken with the beauty of it, and he is no man, but a stock or stone, that does not desire it. Nevertheless, great offense hath been done by the philosophers, and scandal given through their blindness, many of them, in making Felicity to consist in negatives. They tell us it doth not consist in riches, it doth not consist in honors, it doth not consist in pleasures. Wherein then, saith a miserable man, doth it consist? Why, in contentment, in self-sufficiency, in virtues, in the right government of our passions, etc. Were it not better to show the amiableness of virtues and the benefit of the right government of our passions, the objects of contentment, and the grounds of self-sufficiency by the truest means? Which these never do. Ought they not to distinguish between true and false riches as our Saviour doth; between real and feigned honors? between clear and pure pleasures and those which are muddy and unwholesome? The honor that cometh from above, the true treasures, those rivers of pleasure that flow at His right hand for evermore are by all to be sought and by all to be desired. For it is the affront of Nature, a making vain the powers and a baffling the expectations of the soul, to deny it all objects, and a confining it to the grave and a condemning of it to death to tie it to the inward unnatural mistaken self-sufficiency and contentment they talk of. By the true government of our passions we disentangle them from impediments and fit and guide them to their proper objects. The amiableness of virtue consisteth in this: that by it all happiness is either attained or enjoyed. Contentment and rest ariseth from a full perception of infinite treasures; so that whosoever will profit in the mystery of felicity must see the objects of his happiness and the manner how they are to be enjoyed, and discern also the powers of his soul by which he is to enjoy them, and perhaps the rules that shall guide him in the way of enjoyment. All which you have here: God, the world, yourself, all things in time and eternity being the objects of your felicity, God the giver, and you the receiver.

THE THIRD CENTURY

1

WILL you see the infancy of this sublime and celestial greatness? Those pure and virgin apprehensions I had from the womb, and that divine light wherewith I was born are the best unto this day, wherein I can see the universe. By the gift of God they attended me into the world, and by his special favor I remember them till now. Verily they seem the greatest gifts his wisdom could bestow, for without them all other gifts had been dead and vain. They are unattainable by book, and therefore I will teach them by experience. Pray for them earnestly: for they will make you angelical, and wholly celestial. Certainly Adam in Paradise had not more sweet and curious apprehensions of the world than I when I was a child.

2

ALL appeared new, and strange at first, inexpressibly rare and delightful and beautiful. I was a little stranger, which at my entrance into the world was saluted and surrounded with innumerable joys. My knowledge was divine. I knew by intuition those things which since my apostasy I collected again by the highest reason. My very ignorance was advantageous. I seemed as one brought into the estate of innocence. All things were spotless and pure and glorious: yea, and infinitely mine, and joyful and precious. I knew not that there were any sins, or complaints, or laws. I dreamed not of poverties, contentions, or vices. All tears and quarrels were hidden from mine eyes. Everything was at rest, free and immortal. I knew nothing of sickness or death or rents or exaction, either for tribute or bread. In the absence of these I was entertained like an angel with the works of God in their splendor and glory, I saw all in the peace of Eden; heaven and earth did sing my Creator's praises, and could not make more melody to Adam than to me. All time was eternity, and a perpetual Sabbath. Is it not strange that an infant should be heir of the whole world, and see

those mysteries which the books of the learned never unfold?

3

THE corn was orient and immortal wheat, which never should be reaped, nor was ever sown. I thought it had stood from everlasting to everlasting. The dust and stones of the street were as precious as gold: the gates were at first the end of the world. The green trees when I saw them first through one of the gates transported and ravished me, their sweetness and unusual beauty made my heart to leap, and almost mad with ecstasy, they were such strange and wonderful things. The men! Oh what venerable and reverend creatures did the aged seem! Immortal cherubims! And young men glittering and sparkling angels, and maids strange seraphic pieces of life and beauty! Boys and girls tumbling in the street, and playing, were moving jewels. I knew not that they were born or should die; but all things abided eternally as they were in their proper places. Eternity was manifest in the light of the day, and something infinite behind everything appeared, which talked with my expectation and moved my desire. The city seemed to stand in Eden, or to be built in heaven. The streets were mine, the temple was mine, the people were mine, their clothes and gold and silver were mine, as much as their sparkling eyes, fair skins and ruddy faces. The skies were mine, and so were the sun and moon and stars, and all the world was mine; and I the only spectator and enjoyer of it. I knew no churlish proprieties,[1] nor bounds, nor divisions: but all proprieties and divisions were mine: all treasures and the possessors of them. So that with much ado I was corrupted, and made to learn the dirty devices of this world. Which now I unlearn, and become, as it were, a little child again that I may enter into the Kingdom of God.

6

EVERYONE provideth objects, but few prepare senses whereby and light wherein to see them. Since therefore we are born to be a burning and shining light, and whatever men learn of others they see in the light of others' souls, I will in the light of my soul show you the universe. Perhaps it is celestial, and will teach you how beneficial we may be to each other. I am sure it is a sweet and curious light to me, which, had I wanted,[2] I would have given all the gold and silver in all worlds to have purchased. But it was the gift of

1 Properties, private possessions.   2 Lacked.

God and could not be bought with money. And by what steps and degrees I proceeded to that enjoyment of all eternity which now I possess I will likewise show you. A clear and familiar light it may prove unto you.

7

THE first light which shined in my infancy in its primitive and innocent clarity was totally eclipsed: insomuch that I was fain to learn all again. If you ask me how it was eclipsed? Truly by the customs and manners of men, which like contrary winds blew it out: by an innumerable company of other objects, rude, vulgar and worthless things, that like so many loads of earth and dung did overwhelm and bury it: by the impetuous torrent of wrong desires in all others whom I saw or knew that carried me away and alienated me from it: by a whole sea of other matters and concernments that covered and drowned it: finally by the evil influence of a bad education that did not foster and cherish it. All men's thoughts and words were about other matters. They all prized new things which I did not dream of. I was a stranger and unacquainted with them; I was little and reverenced their authority; I was weak, and easily guided by their example; ambitious also, and desirous to approve myself unto them. And finding no one syllable in any man's mouth of those things, by degrees they vanished, my thoughts (as indeed what is more fleeting than a thought?) were blotted out; and at last all the celestial, great, and stable treasures to which I was born, as wholly forgotten as if they had never been.

8

HAD any man spoken of it, it had been the most easy thing in the world to have taught me, and to have made me believe that heaven and earth was God's house, and that he gave it me. That the sun was mine, and that men were mine, and that cities and kingdoms were mine also: that earth was better than gold, and that water, every drop of it, was a precious jewel. And that these were great and living treasures: and that all riches whatsoever else was dross in comparison. From whence I clearly find how docible our nature is in natural things, were it rightly entreated. And that our misery proceedeth ten thousand times more from the outward bondage of opinion and custom, than from any inward corruption or depravation of nature: And that it is not our parents' loins, so much as our parents' lives, that enthralls and blinds us. Yet is all our corruption derived from Adam, inasmuch as all the evil

examples and inclinations of the world arise from his sin. But I speak it in the presence of God and of our Lord Jesus Christ, in my pure primitive virgin light, while my apprehensions were natural, and unmixed, I cannot remember but that I was ten thousand times more prone to good and excellent things than evil. But I was quickly tainted and fell by others.

9

IT WAS a difficult matter to persuade me that the tinseled ware upon a hobby-horse was a fine thing. They did impose upon me, and obtrude their gifts, that made me believe a ribbon or a feather curious. I could not see where the curiousness or fineness; and to teach me that a purse of gold was of any value seemed impossible; the art by which it becomes so and the reasons for which it is accounted so were so deep and hidden to my inexperience. So that Nature is still nearest to natural things, and farthest off from preternatural, and to esteem that the reproach of Nature is an error in them only who are unacquainted with it. Natural things are glorious, and to know them glorious; but to call things preternatural natural, monstrous. Yet they all do it who esteem gold, silver, houses, lands, clothes, etc. the riches of Nature, which are indeed the riches of invention. Nature knows no such riches, but art and error makes them. Not the God of Nature, but Sin only was the parent of them. The Riches of Nature are our souls and bodies, with all their faculties, senses, and endowments. And it had been the easiest thing in the whole world, that all felicity consisted in the enjoyment of all the world, that it was prepared for me before I was born, and that nothing was more divine and beautiful.

12

BY THIS you may see who are the rude and barbarous Indians. For verily there is no savage nation under the cope of heaven, that is more absurdly barbarous than the Christian world. They that go naked and drink water and live upon roots are like Adam, or angels in comparison of us. But they indeed that call beads and glass buttons jewels, and dress themselves with feathers, and buy pieces of brass and broken hafts of knives of our merchants are somewhat like us. But we pass them in barbarous opinions and monstrous apprehensions, which we nick-name civility and the mode, amongst us. I am sure those barbarous people that go naked come nearer Adam, God, and angels in the simplicity of their wealth, though not in knowledge.

13

YOU would not think how these barbarous inventions spoil your knowledge. They put grubs and worms in men's heads that are enemies to all pure and true apprehensions, and eat out all their happiness. They make it impossible for them, in whom they reign, to believe there is any excellency in the works of God, or to taste any sweetness in the nobility of nature, or to prize any common, though never so great a blessing. They alienate men from the life of God, and at last make them to live without God in the world. To live the life of God is to live to all the works of God, and to enjoy them in his image, from which they are wholly diverted that follow fashions. Their fancies are corrupted with other jingles.

15

YET sometimes in the midst of these dreams I should come a little to myself, so far as to feel I wanted something, secretly to expostulate with God for not giving me riches, to long after an unknown happiness, to grieve that the world was so empty, and to be dissatisfied with my present state because it was vain and forlorn. I had heard of angels, and much admired that here upon earth nothing should be but dirt and streets and gutters. For as for the pleasures that were in great men's houses, I had not seen them, and it was my real happiness they were unknown, for because nothing deluded me I was the more inquisitive.

16

ONCE I remember (I think I was about four years old when) I thus reasoned with myself, sitting in a little obscure room in my father's poor house: If there be a God, certainly he must be infinite in goodness: and that I was prompted to by a real whispering instinct of nature. And if he be infinite in goodness, and a perfect being in wisdom and love, certainly he must do most glorious things, and give us infinite riches; how comes it to pass therefore that I am so poor? Of so scanty and narrow a fortune, enjoying few and obscure comforts? I thought I could not believe him a God to me unless all his power were employed to glorify me. I knew not then my soul, or body; nor did I think of the heavens and the earth, the rivers and the stars, the sun or the seas: all those were lost, and absent from me. But when I found them made out of nothing for me, then I had a God indeed, whom I could praise, and rejoice in.

17

SOMETIMES I should be alone, and without employment, when suddenly my soul would return to itself, and forgetting all things in the whole world which mine eyes had seen, would be carried away to the ends of the earth; and my thoughts would be deeply engaged with enquiries: how the earth did end? whether walls did bound it, or sudden precipices? Or whether the heavens by degrees did come to touch it; so that the face of the earth and heaven were so near, that a man with difficulty could creep under? Whatever I could imagine was inconvenient, and my reason being posed was quickly wearied. What also upheld the earth (because it was heavy) and kept it from falling; whether pillars or dark waters? And if any of these, what then upheld those, and what again those, of which I saw there would be no end? Little did I think that the earth was round, and the world so full of beauty, light, and wisdom. When I saw that, I knew by the perfection of the work there was a God, and was satisfied, and rejoiced. People underneath, and fields and flowers, with another sun and another day, pleased me mightily: but more when I knew it was the same sun that served them by night, that served us by day.

46

WHEN I came into the country, and being seated among silent trees, and meads and hills, had all my time in mine own hands, I resolved to spend it all, whatever it cost me, in the search of happiness, and to satiate that burning thirst which nature had enkindled in me from my youth. In which I was so resolute, that I chose rather to live upon ten pounds a year, and to go in leather clothes, and feed upon bread and water, so that I might have all my time clearly to myself, than to keep many thousands per annum in an estate of life where my time would be devoured in care and labor. And God was so pleased to accept of that desire, that from that time to this I have had all things plentifully provided for me, without any care at all, my very study of felicity making me more to prosper than all the care in the whole world. So that through his blessing I live a free and a kingly life as if the world were turned again to Eden, or much more, as it is at this day.

56

THEREFORE of necessity they must at first believe that Felicity is a glorious though an unknown thing.

And certainly it was the infinite wisdom of God that did implant by instinct so strong a desire of felicity in the soul, that we might be excited to labor after it, though we know it not, the very force wherewith we covet it supplying the place of understanding. That there is a felicity we all know by the desires after, that there is a most glorious felicity we know by the strength and vehemence of those desires, and that nothing but felicity is worthy of our labor, because all other things are the means only which conduce unto it. I was very much animated by the desires of philosophers, which I saw in heathen books aspiring after it. But the misery is, *It was unknown*. An altar was erected to it like that in Athens with this inscription: *To the Unknown God.*

THE FOURTH CENTURY

14

IN ORDER to this, he furnished himself with this maxim: *It is a good thing to be happy alone.* It is better to be happy in company, but good to be happy alone. Men owe me the advantage of their society, but if they deny me that just debt I will not be unjust to myself and side with them in bereaving me. I will not be discouraged, lest I be miserable for company. More company increases happiness, but does not lighten or diminish misery.

56

No man loves, but he loves another more than himself. In mean instances this is apparent. If you come into an orchard with a person you love and there be but one ripe cherry, you prefer it to the other. If two lovers delight in the same piece of meat, either takes pleasure in the other, and more esteems the beloved's satisfaction. What ails men, that they do not see it? In greater cases this is evident. A mother runs upon a sword to save her beloved. A father leaps into the fire to fetch out her beloved. Love brought Christ from Heaven to die for His beloved. It is in the nature of love to despise itself and to think only of its beloved's welfare. Look to it: it is not right love that is otherwise. Moses and St. Paul were no fools. God make me one of their number. I am sure nothing is more acceptable to Him than to love others so as to be willing to impart even one's own soul for their benefit and welfare.

83

WHETHER it be the soul itself, or God in the soul, that shines by love, or both, it is difficult to tell: but certainly the love of the soul is the sweetest thing in the world. I have often admired what should make it so excellent. If it be God that loves, it is the shining of his essence; if it be the soul, it is his image: if it be both, it is a double benefit.

THE FIFTH CENTURY

5

INFINITY of space is like a painter's table prepared for the ground and field of those colors that are to be laid thereon. Look how great he intends the picture, so great doth he make the table. It would be an absurdity to leave it unfinished, or not to fill it. To leave any part of it naked and bare and void of beauty would render the whole ungrateful to the eye and argue a defect of time or materials or wit in the limner. As the table is infinite, so are the pictures. God's wisdom is the art, his goodness the will, his word the pencil, his beauty and power the colors; His pictures are all His works and creatures, infinitely more real and more glorious, as well as more great and manifold, than the shadows of a landscape. But the life of all is, they are the spectator's own. He is in them as in His territories, and in all these views His own possessions.

7

ETERNITY is a mysterious absence of times and ages: an endless length of ages always present, and forever perfect. For as there is an immovable space wherein all finite spaces are enclosed, and all motions carried on and performed, so is there an immovable duration, that contains and measures all moving durations. Without which first the last could not be; no more than finite places, and bodies moving without infinite space. All ages being but successions correspondent to those parts of the eternity wherein they abide, and filling no more of it than ages can do. Whether they are commensurate with it or no, is difficult to determine. But the infinite immovable duration is eternity, the place and duration of all things, even of infinite space itself; the cause and end, the author and beautifier, the life and perfection of all.

POETRY

Seventeenth-Century Poetry

I

THE age of English poetry which begins with Donne and ends with Dryden confuses us with its variety almost as much as it impresses us with its greatness. The perception of the underlying unity of the literature of the age and the discrimination of the various stylistic categories into which this literature may be divided—two indispensable activities for the literary historian or for the reader who wants a clear conception of the period—are rendered more rather than less difficult by some of the practices of older historians and critics. The once familiar extension of the term "Elizabethan" to the entire period from 1600 to 1642, when coupled with the still customary application of the term "Augustan" to the segment from 1660 to 1700, leaves a meager span of eighteen years to which the term "seventeenth century" can be unequivocally applied. This drastic cropping of one of the major epochs of English poetry explains in part the currency of some extremely misleading literary categories: the fact that the heart of the century was the time of the Civil War and the Commonwealth, for example, probably accounts for the deceptive opposition of "Puritan" and "Cavalier" poets in many literary histories and handbooks. This opposition, however, ignores a number of important considerations—that the different royalist poets practiced a wide variety of styles; that Milton, surely the greatest of "Puritan" poets, cannot be seen as the center of any contemporaneous school; that "Puritan" poetry, as exemplified in the work of Wither, Milton, and Marvell, shows no coherent group characteristics at all; and that the general spirit we moderns are most inclined to label "Puritan" manifests itself most forcefully in the poems of Quarles—himself a fanatical royalist. Similarly, the traditional opposition of "Metaphysical" and "Cavalier" poets comes to grief when we recognize that many Cavaliers were profoundly influenced by Donne, the chief Metaphysical poet, and that Marvell—at one time at least tentatively Puritan in his political sympathies—combines a "Cavalier" polish with a deeply "Metaphysical" sensibility.

If these traditional literary-historical oppositions are of no value in describing the poetic situation of even the limited period 1642–60, can we use any more successfully the familiar division of the poets of the first two-thirds of the century into "schools" of Spenser, Donne, and Jonson? It seems to me that, if we exercise due caution and avoid rigidity, we can. Douglas Bush has remarked,[1] with reference to the schools of Jonson and Donne, that "the dichotomy is sound enough to be useful, and false enough to be troublesome," and his observation may justly be extended to embrace the school of Spenser. However misleading it may be if applied too mechanically, the initial separation

---

1 D. Bush, *English Literature in the Earlier Seventeenth Century* (New York, rev. ed., 1962), p. 104.

of seventeenth-century poets into these three categories recommends itself through its practical utility: Spenser was the greatest nondramatic poet of the sixteenth century, Jonson and Donne were the two schoolmasters of the new generations of seventeenth-century poets, and the influence exerted by the three men did in fact form rough groupings which serve as convenient points of departure for the study of the rich creations of the age.

The most essential cautions to be observed in viewing seventeenth-century poetry under the aspect of the great poets who influenced its course may be briefly summarized. To begin with, we should remember that, with the exception of Jonson, these poets did not really form "schools" in any strict sense of that term, and that even the most devoted of the "Sons of Ben" were alive to the vigorous example of Donne's technique. We should remember also that the various groups underwent an extensive kind of cross-fertilization; Thomas Carew, for example, fused the manners of Jonson and Donne in almost equal parts, retained something of the spirit of the Elizabethan lyric, and emerged with a poetic style which is fully individual, attributable to the exclusive influence of neither Donne nor Jonson, and yet unquestionably typical of the seventeenth-century sensibility as a whole. Finally, we should recognize that even the most conservatively devout followers of Spenser in the seventeenth century absorbed and reflected the concerns of their very different era: Drummond of Hawthornden and Giles Fletcher, Spenserians both, learned much from the Continental poets who had formed the highly colored, overwrought variety of High Baroque poetry—a poetic manner ultimately very different from Spenser's serene and controlled Renaissance style—and both departed from Spenserian subject matter in choosing to write on religious themes directly rather than allegorically.

Although the followers of Spenser, Jonson, and Donne may be seen as, respectively, emphasizing certain aspects of Renaissance tradition, reforming that tradition in the direction of a stricter, more restrained classicism, and revising that tradition in the name of a radical reliance on individual experience, all three share, to some extent, concerns and preoccupations which set them apart from their sixteenth-century predecessors. A sharpened awareness of the complex and contradictory nature of experience seems to be the feature which most generally characterizes the seventeenth-century poets. Paradox and antithesis, conceit and hyperbole, oxymoron and catachresis[2]—the rhetorical figures which dominate their poems are consistently those which focus attention on the perplexing nature of reality. And the general abandonment of such inherited fixed forms as sonnet and madrigal, ottava rima and rime royal, indicates the restlessness of temper which distinguishes the age, a restlessness which finds expression equally in the novel stanza forms of Donne and Herbert, the terse lyric patterns of Jonson and Carew, and the "picture" or "pattern" poems which constitute one of the more curious fashions of the time. Formal novelty, complexity of attitude, eccentricity of expression—these are all attributes of the kind of art which later centuries have labeled "Baroque," and the term may indeed serve as a convenient general designation for the generously varied poetic styles of the first two-thirds of the century. Like the prose of the age, the poetry may be conceived of as deriving its distinctive features either from the intellectual and spiritual ferment of the declining Renaissance, or from inevitable reaction against a

---

2 The last two figures are related in effect, *oxymoron* designating the union of contradictory terms (e.g., "living death") and *catachresis* the deliberate misuse of a term.

literary style which, established and cultivated for several generations, had outlived its vigor. It seems likely that both extraliterary and intraliterary forces combined to shape the Baroque styles and attitudes.

At the root of all Baroque expression is the intellectual capacity which the seventeenth century called "wit"—the ability to perceive similarities among dissimilar entities or experiences. Initially the term was used in English with approximately the meaning "intelligence"; in recent centuries it has taken on almost exclusively the meaning "mental alertness or verbal ingenuity enabling one to make amusing utterances." It was in the seventeenth century that the term underwent its semantic development from the early general meaning to the current specialized meaning, and during that century the term possessed simultaneously connotations of the most casual playfulness and the most profound seriousness. The opposed implications of the age's favorite critical term may be seen as symbolic of the tonal complexity which marks its poetry.

"Wit" unites the varied poets of seventeenth-century England, for it underlies equally the striking antitheses and surprising epithets of the brothers Giles and Phineas Fletcher, the pithy epigrams and epitaphs of Jonson, and the paradoxes, puns, and conceits of Donne and Herbert. It implies much more than playful verbal facility: in the most profound poetry of the age—in the lyrics of the major Metaphysical poets and in *Paradise Lost*, with its staggering cosmic ironies—it becomes a whole mode of vision in which individual emotional and spiritual experience is viewed in the light of infinite and total reality, and is judged and measured without being rejected. United by a common habit of mind, the seventeenth-century poets are united also by an ultimately religious center of concern and by a tendency to favor certain genres and forms which had not been especially popular among the Elizabethans.

II

ALTHOUGH the favorite Elizabethan genres and forms—eclogue, madrigal, sonnet, heroical epistle, and verse narrative—fell into relative disuse in the early years of the seventeenth century, a number of the more conservative poets—Drummond, Wither, Drayton, Browne, and others—continued to practice them. The epic muse of Spenser was courted fervently but, until *Paradise Lost*, unsuccessfully throughout the century: Phineas Fletcher (*The Purple Island*), Henry More (*Psychozoia*), and Edward Benlowes (*Theophila*) attempted to emulate Spenser's allegorical method. Such now forgotten poets as William Chamberlayne, William Bosworth, and John Chalkhill continued, without distinction, his fashion of romantic narrative. Probably the three most significant epic or quasi-epic poems between *The Faerie Queene* and *Paradise Lost* are Giles Fletcher's *Christ's Victory and Triumph* (1610), Sir William Davenant's *Gondibert* (1650), and Abraham Cowley's *Davideis* (1656). Of these, Fletcher's work strikes the modern reader as the most accessible—or, at any rate, as the least inaccessible—but all three have historical importance: *Gondibert* as an attempt to accommodate romantic material to the new criteria of rationalism and classicism, and *Christ's Victory* and *Davideis* as differing manifestations of the century's approach to religious material. Both of these latter works point, though at an enormous distance, in the direction of *Paradise Lost*.

Satire as the later sixteenth century had understood it—typified by the harsh, vituperative, general condemnations of Marston, Hall, and the young Donne—died out as a formal genre in the early 1600's (although the backward-looking Wither practiced it as late as 1621). When satire was revived by Cleveland and Butler in the middle years of the century, it had assumed a radically different character, influenced by the mock heroic spirit of Rabelais and Cervantes. Brought to perfection by Dryden in the 1680's, mock-heroic narrative satire was to become the dominant genre of the earlier eighteenth century.

Some other Elizabethan genres—the verse-letter and the epigram—continued in full strength, supported by the enormous prestige of Donne and Jonson respectively. The "topographical poem," which retained its symbolic and complimentary character in Jonson, Carew, and Waller, took on, in Denham's "Cooper's Hill," a discursive structure, pictorial texture, and moral-didactic purpose which point toward Pope's "Windsor Forest." Working within the same genre in "Upon Appleton House," Andrew Marvell achieved a cryptically puzzling but remarkably vivid blend of formal compliment, landscape description, and quasi-mystical contemplation of nature. The ode, at the beginning of the century vaguely conceived of as a dignified poem of elevated tone and indeterminate length, underwent considerable development at the hands of Jonson and Milton and, later, Cowley and Dryden. Cowley, in attempting to domesticate Pindar, founded the irregular English ode, and Dryden brought the form to its first pinnacle of achievement.

In form and genre, thus, seventeenth-century poetry is as varied as it is in tone and spirit. The dominant genre of the entire period, however, is certainly the personal lyric, either amorous or devotional. Whether composed in the manner of Donne or in that of Jonson, the seventeenth-century lyric differs from that of the sixteenth century in its more marked individuality of tone, its greater dramatic immediacy, and its consistent impulse to approach the condition of heightened conversation rather than that of quasi-musical incantation. Furthermore, the seventeenth-century abandonment of rigid traditional lyric forms in favor of original, often eccentric stanza patterns uniquely suited to the expression of a particular mood or insight gives the poetry of the age a quality which distinguishes it from that of both the century which preceded and the century which followed. If one excepts such giants as Spenser, Sidney, and Marlowe, it is often possible to mistake one sweet singer of the 1590's—a Nashe, a Lodge, or a Peele —for another. In the seventeenth century, however, even such a generally traditional poet as Herrick and even such minor poets as Suckling and Lovelace have their unmistakable accents. The personal lyrics of the Baroque age are personal in a very special sense.

III

THE shared qualities of the seventeenth-century lyric suggest that a kind of unity may be perceived in the poetic achievement of the age. The perception of unity ought not, however, to obscure the ever present fact of variety, a fact already pointed out with reference to the heirs of Spenser and the followers of Jonson and Donne who, among them, constitute the poets of the first two-thirds of the century. We have noted that such poets as Drayton and Drummond, Wither and Browne, Giles and Phineas Fletcher continued, in various ways, the pastoral, topographical, ethical, and patriotic traditions of Spenser. In the texture of their verse, too, these poets are faithful to their master: sensuous and conventional imagery, musical regularity of meter, consistent mythological reference—such are the features which dominate their practice. No one of them is the artistic equal of Spenser (Drayton perhaps comes closest, but he is still in no way comparable), and their minor stature shows itself, among other ways, in the relatively fragmentary nature of their total poetic utterances. Drayton's *Poly-Olbion* compares with *The Faerie Queene* in length and physical scope, but it scarcely challenges comparison as a sustained artistic whole. Giles Fletcher's *Christ's Victory and Triumph* recaptures something of Spenser's spiritual dignity and something of the melting beauty of his measure, but it is essentially a static poem, with nothing resembling narrative force or psychological interest. In reading it, one is inevitably aware of being at the end of a great tradition.

In the perspective of history, the seventeenth-century Spenserians unquestionably represent the end of High Renaissance poetry, but they had great importance in their own time. The popularity which the Metaphysical poets now enjoy can easily lead the incautious student into the historical error of believing that the circulation in manuscript of Donne's early songs and sonnets established, in the opening years of the century, the definitive triumph of the Metaphysical style. On the contrary, until at least the 1630's the Spenserians remained numerically dominant in English poetry. During the first third of the century, furthermore, they were the favorites of the general reading public, in contrast to such early Metaphysicals as Henry King and Lord Herbert of Cherbury, who were, like their master Donne, essentially the poets of a learned and courtly coterie —the "understanders," or people in the know, to whom Donne's publisher addressed the 1633 edition of the *Songs and Sonnets*.

Finally, in estimating the importance of Spenser's influence on seventeenth-century poetry, we must not forget that Milton, the greatest poet of the age, considered himself always the heir of "our sage and serious poet Spenser." The pre-eminence and originality of Milton's achievement in both lyric and epic genres leads us, quite properly, to stress his uniqueness, but even the towering genius of the poet of "Comus," "Lycidas," and *Paradise Lost* must build on the work of predecessors, and the "simple, sensuous and passionate" qualities toward which Milton aspired are clearly those which he found in *The Faerie Queene*. From the point of view of stylistic history, Milton's work is anomalous: he wrote "Lycidas," the crowning achievement of English Renaissance pastoral poetry, in 1637, when the "strong lines" of Donne and the other Metaphysicals were beginning to sweep all before them; he published *Paradise Lost* in 1667, after the emergence of Dryden and the establishment of the artistic norms of the Restoration period. More akin to Spenser than to any of his own great contemporaries, and opposed to most fashions of the time, Milton nevertheless shows the impact of his own age, not only in his concern with topical questions and in his direct treatment of religious themes, but also in the typically Baroque elaboration and complexity of the "Nativity Ode" and "Lycidas." Deeply involved with his age and yet faithful to an older poetic tradition, Milton finally defies categorization and demands that we read and judge him by only the standards established by his gigantic individuality.

IV

JOHN DONNE, Milton's great opposite in religious sensibility as in artistic attitude, possesses a comparable stature but stands in a very different relationship to the poetry of his time. Whereas Milton to a large extent remains outside the fashions of his day, Donne typifies and largely dictates those fashions. The style and attitudes of the *Songs and Sonnets* must be understood in part as youthful reactions against the poetic norms of the late sixteenth century. The Elizabethan sonneteers had celebrated an idealized sexual love in terms of a strict code inherited from the medieval troubadours by way of Petrarch and the Renaissance Platonists; Donne on the other hand presents love as an untidy and mysterious complex of physical desire and spiritual impulse. Repeatedly, in the *Songs and Sonnets*, he suggests the beloved as a human being rather than as an impossibly distant goddess-figure of the Petrarchan sort. The qualities of psychological and sexual realism are equally apparent in idealistic poems such as "The Good-Morrow" and cynical poems such as "The Indifferent"; beneath Donne's love poetry there lies always the awareness articulated in "The Ecstasy," the most complete expression of his philosophy of love:

> Love's mysteries in souls do grow,
> But yet the body is his book.

A similar reaction against the Elizabethan poets is found in the world of images conjured up by Donne; whereas the Elizabethans had bound themselves by relatively rigid rules of decorum to a distinct and limited stock of images—the precious metals, gems, heavenly bodies, flowers, swans, and larks dear to the sonneteers—Donne opens his poetry to the entire various world of human experience—lawsuits and voyages of discovery, scholastic learning and gunshot, mathematics, botany, and astronomy. *Gold* is a recurrent image in Spenser's world, used sometimes for its physical appearance as a representation of the beloved's hair, used at other times as a conventional symbol of value. When it appears in Donne it is likely, as in "A Valediction: Forbidding Mourning," to be used for its functional qualities:

> Our two souls therefore, which are one,
> Though I must go, endure not yet
> A breach but an expansion,
> Like gold to airy thinness beat.

The application brings us to the important question of Donne's typical figures of speech and rhetorical devices—conceit, paradox, pun, and irony. Although these figures of contradiction and surprise demonstrate further the extent of Donne's reaction against Elizabethan tradition, their more important function is a positive one. Essentially, the farfetched comparisons and tonal contrasts which dominate the *Divine Poems* as clearly as they do the *Songs and Sonnets* and *Elegies* are employed purposefully to reveal the complex and suprarational nature of emotional experience—whether that experience is the love of woman or the love of God. Occasionally, as in the verse-letters, Donne's "wit" seems to be the expression of an affected intellectual fashion; much more consistently, it operates as the instrument of a profound vision of life.

The important poets who are often grouped with Donne as the "Metaphysical poets" —George Herbert, Richard Crashaw, Henry Vaughan, Andrew Marvell, and Thomas Traherne—share with him a reliance on conceit, paradox, and irony, and a tendency toward colloquial diction, dramatic structure, and intellectual ingenuity, but in other respects they constitute a remarkably diverse group, as different from one another as they are from Donne. Herbert's effective restriction to the single theme of the religious quest may impress some modern readers as a limitation of the poet's total vision, but a thoughtful reading of *The Temple* reveals a coherent and ineffably sensitive account of man's varied spiritual states as recollected in the light of the supreme realization of union with God. Like Donne, Herbert is driven by a desire to recognize and identify himself with a divine principle of all-pervading unity; like him, he explores the diversity of experience in order to isolate and perceive that unity. The differences between the two poets—epitomized in Herbert's achieved serenity of tone and his tight formal perfection —derive from the more nearly complete success of the younger poet's quest rather than from an intrinsically narrower spiritual outlook. It is true that Donne gives us a wider frame of vision, that he poses, to a greater degree than Herbert, the unanswerable final questions which faith can surpass but never resolve. For these reasons, among others, Donne's unique position in English poetry remains secure. But Herbert too has his uniqueness; the moderation and sweetness of temper which breathe from his intricately fashioned lyrics give a voice to the best aspects of seventeenth-century Anglicanism and remind us that even the century of passion, ideology, and fanaticism could produce a saint of the middle way.

It has been common, in our century as in earlier times, to speak of "the school of Donne," implying that the major Metaphysical poets practiced their distinctive styles primarily because of that poet's influence. The present essay has, in attempting to classify the seventeenth-century poets, employed the same term, but it should be said at this point that our usage is, in reference to the chief poets of the Metaphysical style, merely conventional. For it seems probable that, had Donne never lived, the work not only of Herbert but also of Crashaw and Vaughan would have assumed much its present form. Although the homely images, ingenious conceits, conversational tone, and argumentative structure through which Herbert articulates his vision bear a family resemblance to analogous qualities in Donne's work, the resemblance is not one which suggests imitation: Herbert, for example, shows nothing of Donne's willful obscurity, and his references, though often learned, are never recondite. He knew Donne, and it is likely that the older poet's example confirmed some elements in his own practice, but essentially both poets were formed by the great currents of thought and taste which, all over Europe, created the Baroque style in the various arts. The more specific resemblances between the two poets may be traced to tendencies they have in common—an interest, for example, in the widespread devotional practice of formal meditation with its recommendations of concrete imaginative particularity, fusion of thought and feeling, and profound self-dramatization.

The forces which molded Crashaw and Vaughan can be identified with more preciseness: both poets, to begin with, launched their careers under the direct impetus of a reading of Herbert's *The Temple*, and echoes from that work persisted in Vaughan's poetry to the very end. (Vaughan had written secular poetry earlier, but his important verse all dates from his reading of Herbert.) Crashaw, despite his pious admiration for Herbert, is a very different sort of poet: he is the poet of frenzied extremes as Herbert is the poet of the quiet center, and he is, perhaps for that very reason, the most uneven of the Metaphysical poets, capable of ranging from the splendid ecstasies of the conclusion of the "Hymn to the Name and Honor of the Admirable Saint Teresa" to the bathetic horrors of parts of "The Weeper." Indeed, there is at least a case to be made for denying that Crashaw is a Metaphysical poet at all; his poetry, it is true, operates through conceit, paradox, and oxymoron, and it is notable for its witty ingenuity, but it consistently shows an associational rather than a logical type of structure, it is exclamatory rather than dramatic in method, and it employs a type of opulent sense-imagery totally alien to most Metaphysical poetry. In these latter respects, Crashaw is closer to Giles Fletcher and Joseph Beaumont than he is to Donne, Herbert, Marvell, or Vaughan; his style is, to some degree, that of the Continental High Baroque poets, and the admitted influence of the Italian Giambattista Marino (whom Crashaw translated) supports the classification.

Nevertheless, Crashaw's best poems—the hymns to Teresa, "Charitas Nimia," "To the Countess of Denbigh," and "In the Holy Nativity"—display, beside their High Baroque features, a psychological perceptiveness and a theological subtlety which suggest Herbert far more potently than they do Fletcher or Marino. The least typical, the most Italianate, of the Metaphysical poets, Crashaw is still most accurately designated by that term.

The work of the younger generation of Metaphysical poets—Marvell, Vaughan, and Traherne—differs significantly from that of the older practitioners of the style. The three poets, different as they are from each other, share a strong interest in external Nature, often interpreted mystically, together with strongly individualistic emphases which in some ways identify them as precursors of the Romantic poets. Marvell, one of the most complex and elusive figures in English literature, cannot be described simply, and his connections with the classical tradition make it advisable to postpone more extended consideration of him. In Vaughan, however, imitation of Herbert does not disguise a poetic temperament which is radically unlike that of the parson of Bemerton. Vaughan's loose poetic structure and uneven level of accomplishment underline the dissimilarity, and his use of esoteric doctrines to implement his orthodox Christian vision suggests the dissolution of the older world picture which had given Donne and Herbert their language and their technique. These tendencies are even more marked in the work of Vaughan's younger contemporary, Thomas Traherne, whose ecstatic syntax and un-orthodox theology seem distinctly proto-Romantic. These poets, however, share with their predecessors and with Marvell the central trait which ultimately defines Metaphysical poetry and which serves as the basis for its typical devices: like the earlier Metaphysical poets, the later ones consistently view their emotional experience in the light of a conception of absolute reality—a conception which is of necessity problematical and which establishes, by its very nature, a tense counterpoint to the expression of personal emotion.

Marvell exhibits all the relevant features of the Metaphysical poet: "The Garden" utilizes intellectual ingenuity and verbal play to arrive at a vision of the incommunicable, "The Definition of Love" operates through a series of brilliantly functional conceits, and "To His Coy Mistress" is a triumph of subtle modulation deriving from the witty examination of passionate feeling. But in both the terse control of his metrics and the polished urbanity of his phrasing, Marvell owes as much to Jonson as to Donne. There is, as T. S. Eliot has observed, an unusually strong element of sophisticated Latin culture in Marvell, and it makes him one of the most European of English poets. Essential to his impressive and very original achievement is his capacity for synthesizing and combining the more important of the diverse poetic traditions of the age.

But the very last echoes of English Metaphysical poetry were sounded across the Atlantic in the work of the Puritan clergyman Edward Taylor, who composed between 1682 and 1725 a body of devotional verse which reveals reminiscences of George Herbert and affinities with both Crashaw and Vaughan. For all his native endowments as a poet, however, Taylor does not attain anything like the stature of his predecessors in the mother-country; the cultural isolation which made his anachronistic work possible also made it inevitable that Metaphysical individualism should turn, in his case, into something like eccentricity. He remains a fascinating anomaly but a distinctly minor poet.

V

WHILE Marvell, Vaughan, and Traherne continued to write truly Metaphysical poetry in the second half of the seventeenth century, the style degenerated, in the hands of a whole group of lesser poets, into a fashionable kind of imitation of the surface of Donne's poetry. In John Cleveland the conceit becomes a purely decorative device, with no intrinsic connection to the poet's themes and values; in Abraham Cowley argumentative structure and intellectual play tend, at least in the early poems, to become the very subject of the poem rather than the terms in which a real subject is conceived. It is perhaps significant that the later work of both poets moves in directions altogether alien to the Metaphysical tradition: Cleveland's toward abusive political satire expressed in tight couplets, Cowley's toward odes and occasional verses in which the organizing principles are conceptual and discursive rather than metaphorical and argumentative. In both cases, it will be noted, an underlying belief in the supremacy of the purely rational is implied; the true Metaphysicals had employed reason as a vehicle for approaching the contemplation of ultimate mysteries beyond the reach of reason; Cleveland and Cowley employed poetry as an instrument for versifying narrowly rational propositions. In these poets, as clearly as in Denham and Waller, the accents of the Augustan age can already be heard.

The challenge offered the Renaissance world picture by late-Renaissance science had been a factor in forming both the Metaphysical and the High Baroque styles, for it had helped create a tentative, exploratory, and nervous poetic sensibility. The utter disintegration of the older world view, an accomplished fact by the 1650's, had the effect of making the Baroque styles unworkable as expressions of valid insight, except for powerful original geniuses such as Vaughan and Marvell, who were capable of adapting the older manner to the intricate demands of their own perceptions. In general, the spirit of the age, even before the restoration of Charles II ushered in a new intellectual climate, had come to demand a poetic style more commensurate with the requirements of science and inductive reasoning. It found its vehicle in the chastened classicism already adumbrated in the lyrics of Ben Jonson.

Jonson's influence on Jacobean and Caroline poetry was fully as great as Donne's, and in most cases the two influences coincided. We have already observed that Carew's poetry is a fusion of Jonsonian classicism and Donnesque wit, and a comparable amalgam supplies the substance of such poets as Waller, Suckling, and Lovelace: the earlier Jonsonians usually modify their classicism with a dash of the Metaphysical manner. Even Robert Herrick, most devout of the "Sons of Ben," has a capacity for smuggling into his verse hidden capsules of meaning—most notably, perhaps, in "Delight in Disorder," with its submerged condemnation of the Puritan ethic, and "Corinna's Going a-Maying," with its subtle and witty panegyric to pagan values. But the mention of these two poems also serves to remind us of another aspect of Herrick—that belated Elizabethan sensitivity to rural life and ritual which makes his work stand out amid the sophistication and intellectuality of its age. In Herrick, as in Milton and the great Metaphysicals, a strongly individualized personality transforms inherited form and matter.

But Jonsonian lyric poetry, with its restraint, precision, and decorum, with its reliance on a type of wit which elicits not the sense that some startling truth has been revealed but rather the sense that "what oft was thought" has been expressed more felicitously than ever before, points from the beginning in the direction of Dryden, Pope, and the other Augustans. Throughout the heyday of Metaphysical poetry this kind of Neoclassical verse continues its slow but steady rise to dominance: the poems of Waller (for the most part) and Denham exhibit a progressive tendency toward the closed heroic couplet, accompanied by a marked emphasis on a strictly rational and nonparadoxical kind of poetic statement. In their work, as in the later work of Cowley, one feels that the age of Dryden is already at hand.

VI

OF Dryden's impressive accomplishments as dramatist and critic, this is not the place to speak. His achievements as a nondramatic poet are striking in their range as well as their magnitude: in addition to the great political satires in heroic couplets—*Absalom and Achitophel*, *The Medal*, and *MacFlecknoe*—which are the most universally praised of his poems, he composed long discursive poems on religious issues (*Religio Laici*, *The Hind and the Panther*), songs of rare verve and polish (many of them occurring in his plays and masques), a group of splendid odes, and a body of occasional verse which ranks among the finest in our language. It should be noted that all the genres in which Dryden excelled have in common a kind of "public" quality—commentary, recommendation, commemoration, or panegyric—and that this quality is certainly related to the Augustan shifting of the direction of poetry from the private and the transcendent to the general and the practical. The matter of *Absalom and Achitophel* is local and topical; in the context of its Biblical paradigm, it becomes universal. But it is never personal in the sense in which Donne and Milton are always personal, and it is surely far from transcendent.

The public and general quality of Dryden's verse, as much as his regularization of meter and diction, gives him his historical importance as the father of Neoclassical poetry in England. But Dryden's function as norm-giver for the entire century which followed him should not blind us to the fact that, however much he prefigured the spirit of the eighteenth century, he remained a man and poet of the seventeenth. Even after the fashionable conceits of his youthful verse had yielded to the sharp common sense and rigorous decorum of his mature work, he retained the urbanely conversational manner and the witty ease of expression which had been shared by most of his predecessors. As close to his ancestor Jonson as to his descendant Pope, he often surprises us with a verse which suggests the insights of Donne, the great poet whom he in so many ways opposes. Like all the great artists of Baroque Europe, Dryden is aware of the cosmos and the unanswerable questions posed by finite man's position in it. When he chooses, as in "A Song for St. Cecilia's Day," to give voice to that awareness, we hear the accents of the century of Donne and Milton, Vaughan and Marvell:

> So, when the last and dreadful hour
> This crumbling pageant shall devour,
> The trumpet shall be heard on high,
> The dead shall live, the living die,
> And music shall untune the sky.

In any age Dryden would have stood out as a poet of the first magnitude. In the Restoration his pre-eminence was all but exclusive. For, apart from the aging Milton forging in blindness and solitude the greatest nondramatic poem in the language, England between 1660 and 1700 produced not a single poet worthy of comparison with him. Of the dissolute lyrists of the court of Charles II, only the Earl of Rochester possessed an impressive talent, and he died, a martyr to his own excesses, before he had done more than suggest his capacities. The others—Dorset, Sedley, and the rest— constitute a continuation of the traditions of Jacobean and Caroline song, but with a distinct coarsening of the conventional amorous attitudes underlying those traditions. These court poets, like Dryden and like Cleveland before them, introduced a number of metrical innovations, such as the replacement of the dominant iambic movement of the Caroline poets by anapestic measures, but in rhythm as in imagery there is a fatal facility and glibness in their work, a hardness which is essentially brittle. Outside the courtly circle, Charles Cotton wrote pleasant verses which continued the nature-meditation genre of Lovelace, Marvell, and Vaughan, but his work too has the tepid and uncommitted quality of decadence. If it were not for the genius of Dryden and the towering phenomenon of Milton, the Restoration would count as one of the lowest points in English poetry: the techniques of Baroque art had dissolved with the vision which had sustained them, and, apart from the prophetic achievement of Dryden, the attitudes and styles of the Neoclassical age had not yet taken firm shape.

VII

LOOKING back over the reaches of seventeenth-century poetry, the modern reader perceives a clear but complex historical pattern. During the first decades of the century the Renaissance style brought to perfection by Spenser remains statistically dominant but yields works of, at best, secondary importance until the genius of Milton gives it a new birth and a new definition. In the meantime, the spirit of the age finds more complete and typical expression in Donne and the other Metaphysical poets. The most important poets of the 1630's, 1640's, and 1650's Herbert, Crashaw, Vaughan, and Marvell—have some resemblance to Donne in their styles, and the most characteristic poets of those decades—Carew, Suckling, Lovelace, and Waller—effect individual fusions of the manner of Donne and the classical manner of Jonson. In the later work of Waller, Cleveland, and Cowley, the Metaphysical manner can be seen giving way to an opposed style, the Neoclassical style initiated by Jonson and destined to be perfected by Dryden.

In genre the same pattern may be recognized: the conventional forms of the Elizabethans give way to the highly personalized lyric forms of the Metaphysical and Jonsonian poets; these persist until late in the century, but even before the Restoration the formal satire and the pseudo-Pindaric ode emerge as the dominant genres of a new age. The history of poetic style and genre in the seventeenth century mirrors the deeper pattern of cultural history—the spiritual history of England during the crucial age in which modern Europe was born. Thus the development from Fletcher's *Christ's Victory and Triumph* through Herbert's *The Temple* to Dryden's *The Hind and the Panther* traces in microcosm the shift of the European consciousness from an exclusively and serenely religious orientation through a brief but perfect moment of balance between institutional and personal religious awareness to an orientation which is, even when dealing with religion, essentially political and social. Similarly, the movement from the sonnets of Drummond to the poems of Marvell to the later odes of Cowley parallels the movement from a mind securely rooted in inherited conventions through a mind which, for its tense moment, holds a variety of conventions in tentative and playful solution to a mind defined by a series of new conventions which are, however nominally classical, essentially sanctioned by a scientific world view.

The chief pattern in the spiritual history of the seventeenth century is the shift from a world view which is religious and mythic to one which is sociopolitical and scientific. Donne, for all the conscientious novelty of his technique, clearly holds to the older vision, and the fact that this vision was being challenged merely lends a note of eloquent urgency to his restatement of it. Dryden, just as clearly, is the voice of the triumphant modern vision. Between these two great poets lies the realm of seventeenth-century poetry: its chief figures—Jonson, Herbert, Herrick, Crashaw, Vaughan, Marvell—all present, as does Milton, the greatest figure of all, poems in which ancient religion and new science, tradition and innovation, humanism and devotion, flesh and spirit, coexist in a delicate but flawless balance. In their work, for perhaps the last time in the western world, poetry is a way of experiencing the totality of being. And when we turn to them we can, for the brief moment of the aesthetic experience, take on their complexity and wholeness.

BIBLIOGRAPHY
[A selective list]

J. BENNETT. *Five Metaphysical Poets* (New York, rev. ed., 1964).
D. BUSH. *English Literature in the Earlier Seventeenth Century, 1600–1660* (New York, rev. ed., 1962).
O. DE MOURGUES. *Metaphysical, Baroque and Précieux Poetry* (Oxford, 1953).
H. J. C. GRIERSON. *Cross Currents in English Literature of the Seventeenth Century* (London, 1929).
W. R. KEAST, ed. *Seventeenth-Century English Poetry*, rev. ed. (New York, 1971).
J. B. LEISHMAN. *The Metaphysical Poets* (Oxford, 1934).
L. L. MARTZ. *The Poetry of Meditation* (New Haven, 1954).
M. H. NICOLSON. *The Breaking of the Circle* (rev. ed., New York, 1960).
R. L. SHARP. *From Donne to Dryden* (Chapel Hill, N.C., 1940).
R. TUVE. *Elizabethan and Metaphysical Imagery* (Chicago, 1947).
R. WALLERSTEIN. *Studies in Seventeenth-Century Poetic* (Madison, Wis., 1950).
H. C. WHITE. *The Metaphysical Poets* (New York, 1936).
G. WILLIAMSON. *The Donne Tradition* (Cambridge, Mass., 1930).
———. *The Proper Wit of Poetry* (Chicago, 1961).
D. C. ALLEN. *Image and Meaning*, rev. ed. (Baltimore, 1968).
B. K. LEWALSKI. *Protestant Poetics and the Seventeenth-Century Religious Lyric* (Princeton, 1979).
L. L. MARTZ. *The Paradise Within* (New Haven, 1964).
———. *The Wit of Love* (South Bend, Ind., 1970).
J. A. MAZZEO. *Renaissance and Seventeenth-Century Studies* (New York, 1964).
E. MINER. *The Metaphysical Mode from Donne to Cowley* (Princeton, 1969).
———. *The Cavalier Mode from Jonson to Cotton* (Princeton, 1971).
———. *The Restoration Mode from Milton to Dryden* (Princeton, 1974).
L. NELSON, JR. *Baroque Lyric Poetry* (New Haven, 1961).
H. R. SWARDSON. *Poetry and the Fountain of Light* (Columbia, Mo., 1962).
F. J. WARNKE. *Versions of Baroque* (New Haven, 1972).
M. BRADBURY and D. PALMER, eds. *Metaphysical Poetry* (Stratford-upon-Avon Studies: No. 11) (London, 1970).

Michael Drayton

[1563–1631]

D RAYTON was, like Nicholas Breton, a writer whose creative period bridged the very different eras of Elizabeth and James. As he was also distinctly sensitive to the influence of other poets, his work may be divided into sixteenth- and seventeenth-century phases. Making his poetic debut in 1591 with *The Harmony of the Church*, a series of metrical paraphrases of scriptural passages, he proceeded to the composition of sonnets (*Idea's Mirror*, 1594), eclogues (*Idea, the Shepherd's Garland*, 1593), narrative poetry (*Mortimeriados*, 1596, revised and published as *The Barons' Wars*, 1603), and "complaints" (*England's Heroical Epistles*, 1597). In his latter phase he wrote, in addition to his massive *Polyolbion*, an encyclopedic historico-topographical poem celebrating England, songs, odes, and three groups of later sonnets which display ironic and colloquial traits which contrast with those of his earlier work. His Jacobean aspect is also manifested in his satiric recasting, as *The Man in the Moon* (1606), of his early pastoral *Endymion and Phoebe*.

For all of his sensitivity to the changing spirit of the age, however, Drayton seldom strikes the modern reader as anything but an Elizabethan poet who carries the traditions of Elizabethan lyricism and gusto into a very different time. *Polyolbion* is as Tudor in style and spirit as it is in conception, the two fine patriotic odes have the expansiveness we associate with Marlowe and the young Shakespeare, and *Nymphidia* (1627)—the crowning achievement of his later years—breathes the folkloristic spirit of the vanishing fairyland, whose departure Bishop Corbet was wryly to lament a few years later.

Born in Shakespeare's native county of Warwickshire, Drayton grew up as a page in the household of Sir Henry Goodere of Polesworth. Subsequently he wrote briefly for the stage, after which he depended on noble patrons for his support. To his disappointment, he never succeeded in attracting the patronage of King James, but Lucy, Countess of Bedford, and others enabled him to maintain both his independence and his productivity. He continued also his association with the Goodere family, and tradition holds that Anne, the daughter of Sir Henry, was the "Idea" celebrated in so much of his earlier poetry.

Despite the innate conservatism of his style and his stubbornly Spenserian conception of poetry, Drayton was an important figure in the literary circles of seventeenth-century London. He numbered in his extensive acquaintance such figures as Jonson (who, however, was severely critical of Drayton in his conversations with Drummond), Shakespeare, Chapman, Selden, Walton, Wither, Drummond, and Henry Reynolds. To the last-named he addressed, near the end of his life, an important verse epistle "Of Poets and Poesy."

Drayton's last poems were published posthumously in 1637, after which the poet's reputation fell into neglect for more than a century. For two centuries he has held an honored place in the history of English poetry, but he has never been subject to the kind of enthusiastic revival experienced by many of his less typical but greater contemporaries. Nevertheless, his imposing body of varied poetic work is still capable of eliciting delight from the modern reader who is willing to make the imaginative effort of reading his pastorals and his great topographical poem in the spirit in which the poet's original audience read them. And a few works—*Nymphidia*, for example, and the great sonnet "Since there's no help, come let us kiss and part"—are imperishable.

M. DRAYTON. *Works*, ed. J. W. Hebel, finished by K. Tillotson and B. H. Newdigate, 5 vols. (Oxford, 1931–41). The definitive edition.

B. H. NEWDIGATE. *Michael Drayton and His Circle* (Oxford, 1941). The standard biography.

S. A. TANNENBAUM. *Michael Drayton: A Concise Bibliography* (New York, 1941).

O. ELTON. *Michael Drayton: A Critical Study* (London, 1905).

R. L. SHARP. *From Donne to Dryden* (Chapel Hill, N.C., 1940). Contains a good treatment of Drayton.

FROM

POEMS [1619]

TO THE VIRGINIAN VOYAGE

You brave heroic minds
Worthy your country's name,
  That honor still pursue,
  Go, and subdue,
Whilst loit'ring hinds
Lurk here at home, with shame.

Britons, you stay too long;
Quickly aboard bestow you,
  And with a merry gale
  Swell your stretched sail,   10
With vows as strong
As the winds that blow you.

Your course securely steer,
West and by south forth keep,
  Rocks, lee shores, nor shoals,
  When Aeolus scowls,
You need not fear,
So absolute the deep.

And cheerfully at sea,
Success you still entice,   20
  To get the pearl and gold,
  And ours to hold,
Virginia,
Earth's only paradise,

Where nature hath in store
Fowl, venison, and fish,
  And the fruitful'st soil
  Without your toil
Three harvests more,
All greater than your wish.   30

And the ambitious vine
Crowns with his purple mass,
  The cedar reaching high
  To kiss the sky,
The cypress, pine,
And useful sassafras.

To whose the golden age
Still nature's laws doth give,
  No other cares that tend,
  But them to defend   40
From winter's age,
That long there doth not live.

Whenas the luscious smell
  Of that delicious land,
  Above the seas that flows,
  The clear wind throws,
Your hearts to swell
Approaching the dear strand,

In kenning of the shore,
Thanks to God first given,   50
   Oh you, the happi'st men,
   Be frolic then,
Let cannons roar,
Frighting the wide heaven.

And in regions far
Such heroes bring ye forth
   As those from whom we came,
   And plant our name
Under that star
Not known unto our north.   60

And as there plenty grows
Of laurel everywhere,
   Apollo's sacred tree,
   You it may see
A poet's brows
To crown, that may sing there.

Thy voyages attend,
Industrious Hakluyt,
   Whose reading shall enflame
   Men to seek fame,   70
And much commend
To after times thy wit.

TO THE CAMBRO-BRITONS AND THEIR HARP, HIS BALLAD OF AGINCOURT

Fair stood the wind for France,
When we our sails advance,
Nor now to prove our chance,
   Longer will tarry;
But putting to the main
At Kaux, the month of Seine,
With all his martial train,
   Landed King Harry.

And taking many a fort,
Furnished in warlike sort,   10
Marcheth towards Agincourt,
   In happy hour;

Skirmishing day by day
With those that stopped his way,
Where the French gen'ral lay
   With all his power.

Which in his height of pride,
King Henry to deride,
His ransom to provide
   To the King sending;   20
Which he neglects the while
As from a nation vile,
Yet with an angry smile
   Their fall portending.

And turning to his men,
Quoth our brave Henry then:
Though they to one be ten,
   Be not amazed.
Yet have we well begun,
Battles so bravely won   30
Have ever to the sun
   By fame been raised.

And for myself, quoth he,
This my full rest shall be,
England ne'er mourn for me,
   Nor more esteem me;
Victor I will remain,
Or on this earth lie slain,
Never shall she sustain
   Loss to redeem me.   40

Poitiers and Crecy tell,
When most their pride did swell,
Under our swords they fell;
   No less our skill is
Than when our grandsire great,
Claiming the regal seat
By many a warlike feat,
   Lopped the French lilies.

The Duke of York so dread
The eager vaward led;   50
With the main Henry sped
   Amongst his henchmen.
Excester had the rear,
A braver man not there,
Oh Lord, how hot they were
   On the false Frenchmen!

They now to fight are gone,
Armor on armor shone,
Drum now to drum did groan,
    To hear was wonder,   60
That with cries they make
The very earth did shake,
Trumpet to trumpet spake,
    Thunder to thunder.

Well it thine age became,
Oh noble Erpingham,
Which didst the signal aim
    To our hid forces;
When from a meadow by,
Like a storm suddenly,   70
The English archery
    Stuck the French horses.

With Spanish yew so strong,
Arrows a cloth-yard long,
That like to serpents stung,
    Piercing the weather;
None from his fellow starts,
But playing manly parts,
And like true English hearts,
    Stuck close together.   80

When down their bows they threw,
And forth their bilboes drew,
And on the French they flew,
    Not one was tardy;
Arms were from shoulders sent,
Scalps to the teeth were rent,
Down the French peasants went;
    Our men were hardy.

This while our noble King,
His broad sword brandishing,   90
Down the French host did ding,
    As to o'erwhelm it;
And many a deep wound lent,
His arms with blood besprent,
And many a cruel dent
    Bruised his helmet.

Gloster, that Duke so good,
Next of the royal blood,
For famous England stood
    With his brave brother;   100
Clarence, in steel so bright,
Though but a maiden knight,
Yet in that furious fight,
    Scarce such another.

Warwick in blood did wade,
Oxford the foe invade,
And cruel slaughter made,
    Still as they ran up;
Suffolk his ax did ply,
Beaumont and Willoughby   110
Bare them right doughtily,
    Ferrers and Fanhope.

Upon Saint Crispin's day
Fought was this noble fray,
Which fame did not delay
    To England to carry;
Oh, when shall English men
With such acts fill a pen,
Or England breed again
    Such a King Harry?   120

NYMPHIDIA, THE COURT OF FAIRY

[TEXT: *first edition, 1627*]

OLD Chaucer doth of Thopas tell,
    Mad Rabelais of Pantagruel,
A latter third of Dowsabell,
With such poor trifles playing;
Others the like have labored at
Some of this thing, and some of that,
And many of they know not what,
But that they must be saying.

Another sort there be that will
Be talking of the Fairies still,   10
Nor ever can they have their fill,
    As they were wedded to them;
No tales of them their thirst can slake,
So much delight therein they take,
And some strange thing they fain would make,
    Knew they the way to do them.

Then since no Muse hath been so bold,
Or of the later, or the old,
Those elvish secrets to unfold
Which lie from others' reading, 20
My active Muse to light shall bring
The court of that proud Fairy King,
And tell there of the reveling;
Jove prosper my proceeding.

And thou, Nymphidia, gentle fay,
Which meeting me upon the way
These secrets didst to me bewray,
Which I now am in telling;
My pretty light fantastic maid,
I here invoke thee to my aid, 30
That I may speak what thou hast said,
In numbers smoothly swelling.

This palace standeth in the air,
By necromancy placed there,
That it no tempests needs to fear,
Which way soe'er it blow it.
And somewhat southward toward the noon,
Whence lies a way up to the moon,
And thence the Fairy can as soon
Pass to the earth below it. 40

The walls of spiders' legs are made,
Well mortised and finely laid;
He was the master of his trade
It curiously that builded;
The windows of the eyes of cats,
And for the roof, instead of slats,
Is covered with the skins of bats,
With moonshine that are gilded.

Hence Oberon him sport to make
(Their rest when weary mortals take, 50
And none but only fairies wake)
Descendeth for his pleasure.
And Mab his merry queen by night
Bestrides young folks that lie upright,
In elder times the Mare that hight,
Which plagues them out of measure.

Hence shadows, seeming idle shapes
Of little frisking elves and apes
To earth do make their wanton 'scapes,
As hope of pastime hastes them, 60

Which maids think on the hearth they see
When fires well-near consumed be,
There dancing heys by two and three,
Just as their fancy casts them.

These make our girls their sluttery rue,
By pinching them both black and blue,
And put a penny in their shoe
The house for cleanly sweeping;
And in their courses make that round,
In meadows and in marshes found, 70
Of them so called the Fairy ground,
Of which they have the keeping.

These when a child haps to be got
Which after proves an idiot,
When folk perceive it thriveth not,
The fault therein to smother
Some silly doting brainless calf
That understands things by the half
Say that the fairy left this aufe
And took away the other. 80

But listen and I shall you tell
A chance in Fairy that befell,
Which certainly may please some well
In love and arms delighting;
Of Oberon that jealous grew
Of one of his own Fairy crew,
Too well, he feared, his queen that knew,
His love but ill requiting.

Pigwiggen was this Fairy knight,
One wondrous gracious in the sight 90
Of fair Queen Mab, which day and night
He amorously observed;
Which made King Oberon suspect
His service took too good effect,
His sauciness and often checked
And could have wished him starved.

Pigwiggen gladly would commend
Some token to Queen Mab to send,
If sea, or land, could aught him lend
Were worthy of her wearing; 100
At length this lover doth devise
A bracelet made of emmet's[1] eyes,
A thing he thought that she would prize,
No whit her state impairing,

1 Ants'.

And to the queen a letter writes,
Which he most curiously endites,
Conjuring her by all the rites
Of love, she would be pleased
To meet him, her true servant, where
They might without suspect or fear   110
Themselves to one another clear
And have their poor hearts eased.

"At midnight the appointed hour,
And for the queen a fitting bower"
Quoth he, "is that fair cowslip flower
On Hipcut Hill that groweth;
In all your train there's not a fay
That ever went to gather May
But she hath made it in her way,
The tallest there that groweth."   120

When by Tom Thumb, a Fairy page,
He sent it and doth him engage
By promise of a mighty wage
It secretly to carry;
Which done, the queen her maids doth call
And bids them to be ready all;
She would go see her summer hall,
She could no longer tarry.

Her chariot ready straight is made,
Each thing therein is fitting laid,   130
That she by nothing might be stayed,
For naught must her be letting;
Four nimble gnats the horses were,
Their harnesses of gossamer,
Fly Cranion [2] her charioteer
Upon the coach-box getting.

Her chariot of a snail's fine shell
Which for the colors did excel,
The fair Queen Mab becoming well
So lively was the limning;   140
The seat, the soft wool of the bee;
The cover, gallantly to see,
The wing of a pied butterfly,
I trow 'twas simple trimming.

The wheels composed of crickets' bones
And daintily made for the nonce,
For fear of rattling on the stones
With thistledown they shod it;

For all her maidens much did fear
If Oberon had chanced to hear   150
That Mab his queen should have been there
He would not have abode it.

She mounts her chariot with a trice,
Nor would she stay for no advice
Until her maids that were so nice
To wait on her were fitted,
But ran herself away alone,
Which when they heard, there was not one
But hasted after to be gone
As she had been diswitted.   160

Hop, and Mop, and Drop so clear,
Pip, and Trip, and Skip that were
To Mab their sovereign ever dear,
Her special maids of honor;
Fib and Tib, and Pink and Pin,
Tick and Quick, and Jill and Jin,
Tit and Nit, and Wap and Win,
The train that wait upon her.

Upon a grasshopper they got,
And what with amble and with trot,   170
For hedge nor ditch they spared not
But after her they hie them.
A cobweb over them they throw
To shield the wind if it should blow;
Themselves they wisely could bestow
Lest any should espy them.

But let us leave Queen Mab a while,
Through many a gate, o'er many a stile,
That now had gotten by this wile,
Her dear Pigwiggen kissing,   180
And tell how Oberon doth fare,
Who grew as mad as any hare
When he had sought each place with care
And found his queen was missing.

By grisly Pluto he doth swear,
He rent his clothes and tore his hair,
And as he runneth here and there
An acorn cup he greeteth,
Which soon he taketh by the stalk,
About his head he lets it walk,   190
Nor doth he any creature balk, [3]
But lays on all he meeteth.

2 Daddy long-legs.   3 Avoid.

The Tuscan poet[4] doth advance
The frantic paladin of France,
And those more ancient do enhance
Alcides[5] in his fury,
And others Ajax Telamon;[6]
But to this time there hath been none
So bedlam as our Oberon,
Of which I dare assure you.   200

And first encountering with a wasp,
He in his arms the fly doth clasp
As though his breath he forth would grasp,
Him for Pigwiggen taking;
"Where is my wife, thou rogue?" quoth he,
"Pigwiggen, she is come to thee;
Restore her, or thou diest by me!"
Whereat, the poor wasp quaking

Cries, "Oberon, great Fairy King,
Content thee, I am no such thing;   210
I am a wasp, behold my sting!"
At which the Fairy started;
When soon away the wasp doth go;
Poor wretch was never frighted so,
He thought his wings were much too slow,
O'erjoyed they so were parted.

He next upon a glow-worm light,
(You must suppose it now was night)
Which, for her hinder part was bright,
He took to be a devil,   220
And furiously her doth assail
For carrying fire in her tail;
He thrashed her rough coat with his flail;
The mad king feared no evil.

"Oh," quoth the glow-worm, "hold thy hand,
Thou puissant king of Fairyland,
Thy mighty strokes who may withstand;
Hold, or of life despair I!"
Together then herself doth roll,
And tumbling down into a hole   230
She seemed as black as any coal
Which vexed away the Fairy.

From thence he ran into a hive;
Amongst the bees he letteth drive,
And down their combs begins to rive,
All likely to have spoiled;

Which with their wax his face besmeared
And with their honey daubed his beard;
It would have made a man afeared
To see how he was moiled.[7]   240

A new adventure him betides;
He met an ant, which he bestrides
And post thereon away he rides
Which with his haste doth stumble
And came full over on her snout;
Her heels so threw the dirt about
For she by no means could get out
But over him doth tumble,

And being in this piteous case
And all beslurried,[8] head and face,   250
On runs he in this wild goose chase,
As here and there he rambles,
Half blind, against a molehill hit
And for a mountain taking it
For all he was out of his wit,
Yet to the top he scrambles.

And being gotten to the top
Yet there himself he could not stop
But down on th'other side doth chop,
And to the foot came rumbling,   260
So that the grubs therein that bred,
Hearing such turmoil overhead,
Thought surely they had all been dead,
So fearful was the jumbling.

And falling down into a lake,
Which him up to the neck doth take,
His fury somewhat it doth slake;
He calleth for a ferry;
Where you may some recovery note:
What was his club he made his boat,   270
And in his oaken cup doth float
As safe as in a wherry.

Men talk of the adventures strange
Of Don Quixote, and of their change,
Through which he armed oft did range,
Of Sancho Panza's travel;
But should a man tell every thing
Done by this frantic Fairy King
And them in lofty numbers sing,
It well his wits might gravel.   280

4 Ariosto, in his *Orlando Furioso*.   5 Hercules.
6 Hero of a tragedy by Sophocles.

7 Bedaubed.   8 Dirtied.

Scarce set on shore but therewithal
He meeteth Puck, which most men call
Hobgoblin, and on him doth fall
With words from frenzy spoken.
"Ho, Ho !" quoth Hob, "God save thy grace,
Who dressed thee in this piteous case?
He thus that spoiled my sovereign's face,
I would his neck were broken."

This Puck seems but a dreaming dolt,
Still walking like a ragged colt,   290
And oft out of a bush doth bolt
Of purpose to deceive us,
And leading us makes us to stray
Long winter's nights out of the way,
And when we stick in mire and clay,
Hob doth with laughter leave us.

"Dear Puck," quoth he, "my wife is gone;
As e'er thou lov'st King Oberon,
Let everything but this alone,
With vengeance and pursue her;   300
Bring her to me, alive or dead,
Or that vile thief Pigwiggen's head;
That villain hath defiled my bed;
He to this folly drew her."

Quoth Puck, "My liege, I'll never lin,
But I will thorough thick and thin,
Until at length I bring her in;
My dearest lord, ne'er doubt it;
Thorough brake, thorough brier,
Thorough muck, thorough mire,   310
Thorough water, thorough fire,
And thus goes Puck about it."

This thing Nymphidia overheard,
That on this mad king had a guard,
Not doubting of a great reward
For first this business broaching;
And through the air away doth go
Swift as an arrow from the bow,
To let her sovereign Mab to know
What peril was approaching.   320

The Queen, bound with love's powerful'st charm,
Sat with Pigwiggen arm in arm;
Her merry maids that thought no harm
About the room were skipping;

A humble-bee, their minstrel, played
Upon his hautboy; every maid
Fit for this revels was arrayed,
The hornpipe neatly tripping.

In comes Nymphidia and doth cry,
"My sovereign, for your safety, fly,   330
For there is danger but too nigh,
I posted to forewarn you;
The King hath sent Hobgoblin out
To seek you all the fields about,
And of your safety you may doubt,
If he but once discern you !"

When like an uproar in a town
Before them everything went down,
Some tore a ruff and some a gown,
'Gainst one another justling;   340
They flew about like chaff i'the wind;
For haste some left their masks behind;
Some could not stay their gloves to find;
There never was such bustling.

Forth ran they by a secret way
Into a brake that near them lay;
Yet much they doubted there to stay,
Lest Hob should hap to find them;
He had a sharp and piercing sight,
All one to him the day and night,   350
And therefore were resolved by flight
To leave this place behind them.

At length one chanced to find a nut
In th'end of which a hole was cut,
Which lay upon a hazel root,
There scattered by a squirrel
Which out the kernel gotten had,
When quoth this fay, "Dear Queen, be glad;
Let Oberon be ne'er so mad,
I'll set you safe from peril.   360

"Come all into this nut," quoth she,
"Come closely in; be ruled by me;
Each one may here a choser be;
For room ye need not wrastle,
Nor need ye be together heapt";
So one by one therein they crept
And lying down, they soundly slept,
As safe as in a castle.

Nymphidia that this while doth watch,
Perceived if Puck the queen should catch,   370
That he would be her over-match,
Of which she well bethought her;
Found it must be some powerful charm,
The Queen against him that must arm
Or surely he would do her harm,
For throughly he had sought her.

And listening if she aught could hear
That her might hinder or might fear,
But finding still the coast was clear,
Nor creature had descried her;   380
Each circumstance and having scanned,
She came thereby to understand
Puck would be with them out of hand,
When to her charms she hied her.

And first her fern seed doth bestow,
The kernel of the mistletoe,
And here and there, as Puck should go,
With terror to affright him,
She night-shade strews to work him ill,
Therewith her vervain and her dill,   390
That hindreth witches of their will,
Of purpose to despite him.

Then sprinkles she the juice of rue,
That groweth underneath the yew,
With nine drops of the midnight dew
From lunary distilling;
The moldwarp's brain mixed therewithal,
And with the same the pismire's gall,
For she in nothing short would fall,
The Fairy was so willing.   400

Then thrice under a briar doth creep,
Which at both ends was rooted deep,
And over it three times she leap,
Her magic much availing;
Then on Proserpina doth call,
And so upon her spell doth fall
Which here to you repeat I shall,
Not in one title failing:

By the croaking of the frog,
By the howling of the dog,   410
By the crying of the hog,
Against the storm arising;

By the evening curfew bell,
By the doleful dying knell,
Oh, let this my direful spell,
Hob, hinder thy surprising.

By the mandrake's dreadful groans,
By the lubrican's[9] sad moans,
By the noise of dead men's bones
In charnel houses rattling;   420
By the hissing of the snake,
The rustling of the fire-drake,
I charge thee thou this place forsake,
Nor of Queen Mab be prattling.

By the whirlwind's hollow sound,
By the thunder's dreadful stound,
Yells of spirits underground,
I charge thee not to fear us;
By the screech-owl's dismal note,
By the black night-raven's throat,   430
I charge thee, Hob, to tear thy coat
With thorns if thou come near us.

Her spell thus spoke, she stepped aside
And in a chink herself doth hide
To see thereof what would betide,
For she doth only mind him;
When presently she Puck espies,
And well she marked his gloating eyes
How under every leaf he pries
In seeking still to find them.   440

But once the circle got within,
The charms to work do straight begin,
And he was caught as in a gin;
For as he thus was busy,
A pain he in his headpiece feels,
Against a stubbed tree he reels
And up went poor Hobgoblin's heels,
Alas, his brain was dizzy.

At length upon his feet he gets;
Hobgoblin fumes, Hobgoblin frets,   450
And, as again he forward sets
And through the bushes scrambles,
A stump doth trip him in his pace,
Down comes poor Hob upon his face
And lamentably tore his case
Amongst the briars and brambles.

9 Leprechaun's.

"A plague upon Queen Mab," quoth he,
And all her maids, wheree'er they be!
I think the devil guided me
To see her so provoked."   460
Where, stumbling at a piece of wood,
He fell into a ditch of mud,
Where to the very chin he stood
In danger to be choked.

Now, worse than e'er he was before,
Poor Puck doth yell, poor Puck doth roar;
That waked Queen Mab, who doubted sore
Some treason hath been wrought her,
Until Nymphidia told the queen
What she had done, what she had seen,   470
Who then had well-near cracked her spleen
With very extreme laughter.

But leave we Hob to clamber out,
Queen Mab and all her Fairy rout,
And come again to have a bout
With Oberon yet madding;
And with Pigwiggen now distraught,
Who was much troubled in his thought,
That he so long the queen had sought
And through the fields was gadding.   480

And as he runs he still doth cry,
"King Oberon, I thee defy
And dare thee here in arms to try
For my dear Lady's honor,
For that she is a queen right good,
In whose defense I'll shed my blood,
And that thou in this jealous mood
Hast layed this slander on her."

And quickly arms him for the field,
A little cockle-shell his shield,   490
Which he could very bravely wield
Yet could it not be pierced;
His spear, a bent[10] both stiff and strong
And well-near of two inches long;
The pile[11] was of a horse-fly's tongue,
Whose sharpness naught reversed.

And puts him on a coat of mail,
Which was of a fish's scale,
That when his foe should him assail,
No point should be prevailing;   500

His rapier was a hornet's sting;
It was a very dangerous thing,
For, if he chanced to hurt the King,
It would be long in healing.

His helmet was a beetle's head,
Most horrible and full of dread,
That able was to strike one dead,
Yet did it well become him;
And, for a plume, a horse's hair,
Which, being tossed with the air   510
Had force to strike his foe with fear
And turn his weapon from him.

Himself he on an earwig set,
Yet scarce he on his back could get,
So oft and high he did corvet
Ere he himself could settle;
He made him turn and stop and bound,
To gallop, and to trot the round;
He scarce could stand on any ground
He was so full of mettle.   520

When soon he met with Thomalin,
One that a valiant knight had been,
And to King Oberon of kin.
Quoth he, "Thou manly Fairy,
Tell Oberon I come prepared,
Then bid him stand upon his guard;
This hand his baseness shall reward,
Let him be ne'er so wary.

"Say to him thus, that I defy
His slanders and his infamy,   530
And, as a mortal enemy
Do publicly proclaim him;
Withal, that if I had mine own,
He should not wear the Fairy crown,
But with a vengeance should come down,
Nor we a king should name him."

This Thomalin could not abide,
To hear his sovereign vilified,
But to the Fairy court him hied;
Full furiously he posted   540
With everything Pigwiggen said,
How title to the crown he laid
And in what arms he was arrayed,
As how himself he boasted.

10 Blade of grass.   11 Point.

'Twixt head and foot, from point to point
He told th'arming of each joint,
In every piece, how neat and quaint,
For Thomalin could do it;
How fair he sat, how sure he rid,
As of the courser he bestrid,   550
How managed and how well he did;
The king, which listened to it,

Quoth he, "Go, Thomalin, with speed,
Provide me arms, provide my steed
And everything that I shall need;
By thee I will be guided;
To straight account call thou thy wit,
See there be wanting not a whit
In everything see thou me fit,
Just as my foe's provided."   560

Soon flew this news through Fairyland,
Which gave Queen Mab to understand
The combat that was then in hand
Betwixt those men so mighty;
Which greatly she began to rue,
Perceiving that all Fairy knew
The first occasion from her grew
Of these affairs so weighty.

Wherefore, attended with her maids,
Through fogs and mists and damps she wades   570
To Proserpine, the Queen of Shades
To treat that it would please her
The cause into her hands to take
For ancient love and friendship's sake,
And soon thereof an end to make,
Which of much care would ease her.

A while there let we Mab alone,
And come we to King Oberon,
Who, armed to meet his foe, is gone
For proud Pigwiggen crying;   580
Who sought the Fairy king as fast,
And has so well his journies cast,
That he arrived at the last,
His puissant foe espying.

Stout Thomalin came with the king;
Tom Thumb doth on Pigwiggen bring,
That perfect were in everything
To single fights belonging;

And therefore they themselves engage
To see them exercise their rage   590
With fair and comely equipage,
Not one the other wronging.

So like in arms these champions were
As they had been a very pair,
So that a man would almost swear
That either had been either;
Their furious steeds began to neigh
That they were heard a mighty way;
Their staves upon their rests they lay;
Yet, e'er they flew together,   600

Their seconds minister an oath
Which was indifferent to them both
That on their knightly faith and troth
No magic them supplied,
And sought them that they had no charms
Wherewith to work each other's harms,
But came with simple open arms
To have their causes tried.

Together furiously they ran,
That to the ground came horse and man;   610
The blood out of their helmets span,
So sharp were their encounters.
And though they to the earth were thrown,
Yet quickly they regained their own;
Such nimbleness was never shown,
They were two gallant mounters.

When in a second course again
They forward came with might and main,
Yet which had better of the twain
The seconds could not judge yet;   620
Their shields were into pieces cleft,
Their helmets from their heads were reft,
And to defend them nothing left
These champions would not budge yet.

Away from them their staves they threw;
Their cruel swords they quickly drew,
And freshly they the fight renew,
That every stroke redoubled;
Which made Proserpina take heed
And make to them the greater speed,   630
For fear lest they too much should bleed,
Which wondrously her troubled.

When to th'infernal Styx she goes,
She takes the fogs from thence that rose,
And in a bag doth them enclose;
When well she had them blended,
She hies her then to Lethe spring,
A bottle and thereof doth bring
Wherewith she meant to work the thing
Which only she intended.   640

Now Proserpine with Mab is gone
Unto the place where Oberon
And proud Pigwiggen, one to one,
Both to be slain were likely;
And there themselves they closely hide
Because they would not be espied,
For Proserpine meant to decide
The matter very quickly,

And suddenly unties the poke
Which out of it sent such a smoke   650
As ready was them all to choke,
So grievous was the pother;
So that the knights each other lost
And stood as still as any post,
Tom Thumb nor Thomalin could boast
Themselves of any other.

But when the mist gan somewhat cease,
Proserpina commandeth peace,
And that a while they should release
Each other of their peril;   660
"Which here," quoth she, "I do proclaim
To all, in dreadful Pluto's name,
That, as ye will eschew his blame,
You let me hear the quarrel.

"But here yourselves you must engage
Somewhat to cool your spleenish rage;
Your grievous thirst and to assuage
That first you drink this liquor,

Which shall your understanding clear,
As plainly shall to you appear,   670
Those things from me that you shall hear,
Conceiving much the quicker."

This Lethe water, you must know,
The memory destroyeth so
That of our weal or of our woe
It all remembrance blotted;
Of it nor can you ever think;
For they no sooner took this drink
But naught into their brains could sink
Of what had them besotted.   680

King Oberon forgotten had
That he for jealousy ran mad,
But of his queen was wondrous glad
And asked how they came thither;
Pigwiggen likewise doth forget
That he Queen Mab had ever met,
Or that they were so hard beset
When they were found together.

Nor neither of them both had thought
That e'er they had each other sought,   690
Much less that they a combat fought,
But such a dream were loathing;
Tom Thumb had got a little sup,
And Thomalin scarce kissed the cup,
Yet had their brains so sure locked up,
That they remembered nothing.

Queen Mab and her light maids the while
Among themselves do closely smile
To see the king caught with this wile,
With one another jesting;   700
And to the Fairy court they went
With mickle joy and merriment,
Which thing was done with good intent,
And thus I left them feasting.

FROM

IDEA

[TEXT: *Poems, 1619*]

I

Like an adventurous seafarer am I,
Who hath some long and dangerous voyage been,
And called to tell of his discovery,
How far he sailed, what countries he had seen;
Proceeding from the port whence he put forth,
Shows by his compass how his course he steered,
When east, when west, when south, and when by
    north,
As how the pole to every place was reared,
What capes he doubled, of what continent,
The gulfs and straits that strangely he had passed,   10
Where most becalmed, where with foul weather spent,
And on what rocks in peril to be cast—
Thus, in my love, time calls me to relate
My tedious travels and oft-varying fate.

VI

How many paltry, foolish, painted things,
That now in coaches trouble every street,
Shall be forgotten, whom no poet sings,
Ere they be well wrapped in their winding sheet!
Where I to thee eternity shall give,
When nothing else remaineth of these days,
And queens hereafter shall be glad to live
Upon the alms of thy superfluous praise,
Virgins and matrons reading these my rhymes
Shall be so much delighted with thy story   10
That they shall grieve they lived not in these times,
To have seen thee, their sex's only glory.
So shalt thou fly above the vulgar throng,
Still to survive in my immortal song.

VIII

There's nothing grieves me but that age should haste
That in my days I may not see thee old;
That where those two clear, sparkling eyes are placed
Only two loopholes then I might behold.
That lovely arched, ivory, polished brow
Defaced with wrinkles that I might but see—
Thy dainty hair, so curled and crisped now
Like grizzled moss upon some aged tree;

Thy cheek, now flush with roses, sunk and lean;
Thy lips, with age as any wafer thin;   10
Thy pearly teeth out of thy head so clean,
That when thou feedst, thy nose shall touch thy
    chin.
These lines that now thou scornst, which should
    delight thee,
Then would I make thee read, but to despite thee.

IX

As other men, so I myself do muse
Why in this sort I wrest invention so,
And why these giddy metaphors I use,
Leaving the path the greater part do go.
I will resolve you. I am lunatic,
And ever this in madmen you shall find:
What they last thought of, when the brain grew sick,
In most distraction they keep that in mind.
Thus talking idly in this bedlam fit,
Reason and I, you must conceive, are twain;   10
'Tis nine years now since first I lost my wit,
Bear with me, then, though troubled be my brain.
With diet and correction, men distraught
(Not too far past) may to their wits be brought.

XXXVII

Dear, why should you command me to my rest,
When now the night doth summon all to sleep?
Methinks this time becometh lovers best;
Night was ordained together friends to keep.
How happy are all other living things,
Which though the day disjoin by several flight,
The quiet evening yet together brings,
And each returns unto his love at night!
Oh thou that art so courteous else to all,
Why shouldst thou, Night, abuse me only thus,   10
That every creature to his kind dost call,
And yet 'tis thou dost only sever us?
Well could I wish it would be ever day,
If when night comes you bid me go away.

LXI

Since there's no help, come let us kiss and part;
Nay, I have done, you get no more of me,
And I am glad, yea glad with all my heart
That thus so cleanly I myself can free;
Shake hands forever, cancel all our vows,
And when we meet at any time again,
Be it not seen in either of our brows
That we one jot of former love retain.
Now at the last gasp of love's latest breath,
When, his pulse failing, passion speechless lies,   10
When faith is kneeling by his bed of death,
And innocence is closing up his eyes,
Now if thou wouldst, when all have given him over,
From death to life thou mightst him yet recover.

Sir Henry Wotton

[1568–1639]

LTHOUGH poetry was an activity of minor concern to the diplomat and public servant Sir Henry Wotton, his small body of lyric and occasional verse displays a high degree of the polish and competence of which seventeenth-century courtiers were often capable. His song to Elizabeth of Bohemia, "You meaner beauties of the night," had a deserved popularity in its day.

The offspring of an old Kentish family, Wotton was educated at Winchester School and at New College and Queen's College, Oxford. While at Oxford he made the acquaintance of the young Donne, and the two were to remain close friends throughout their lives, although Wotton's poems show few signs of any influence of Donne. In 1595 he became agent and secretary to the Earl of Essex, but despite the closeness of their relationship he managed to avoid any suspicion of implication in the conspiracy against Elizabeth which cost that rash nobleman his head.

Knighted at the time of the accession of James I, Wotton served his royal master faithfully and skillfully, first as ambassador to Venice, then in important diplomatic posts in Germany and Holland. He spent most of his time between 1604 and 1624 abroad, and his experiences led him to the formulation of his famous epigrammatic definition of an ambassador as "an honest man, sent to lie [i.e., "reside"] abroad for the good of his country."

From 1624 until his death Wotton was provost of Eton College. In 1624 he published his *Elements of Architecture*. His poems were published posthumously in *Reliquiæ Wottonianæ* in 1651, with enlarged editions following in 1672 and 1685. Izaak Walton, the editor of the volume, also supplied it with a *Life* of Wotton.

J. HANNAH., ed. *The Poems of Sir Walter Raleigh . . . with Those of Sir Henry Wotton and Other Courtly Poets* (London, 1892). Still the best available source, among modern editions, for Wotton's poems.

L. P. SMITH. *Life and Letters of Sir Henry Wotton*, 2 vols. (Oxford, 1907).

A. W. WARD. *Sir Henry Wotton: A Biographical Sketch* (London, 1898).

H. H. ASQUITH. *Sir Henry Wotton* (London, 1919). A study of Wotton as a writer.

FROM

RELIQUIÆ WOTTONIANÆ [1651]

THE CHARACTER OF A HAPPY LIFE

How happy is he born and taught,
That serveth not another's will?
Whose armor is his honest thought,
And simple Truth his utmost skill?

Whose passions not his masters are,
Whose soul is still prepared for death,
Untied unto the world by care
Of public fame or private breath.

Who envies none that Chance doth raise,
Nor Vice hath ever understood,   10
How deepest wounds are given by praise,
Nor rules of state, but rules of good.

Who hath his life from rumors freed,
Whose conscience is his strong retreat,
Whose state can neither flatterers feed,
Nor ruin make oppressors great.

Who God doth late and early pray,
More of his grace than gifts to lend,
And entertains the harmless day
With a religious book or friend.   20

This man is freed from servile bands
Of hope to rise or fear to fall,
Lord of himself, though not of lands,
And having nothing yet hath all.

UPON THE DEATH OF SIR ALBERT MORTON'S WIFE

He first deceased; she for a little tried
To live without him, liked it not, and died.

ON HIS MISTRESS, THE QUEEN OF BOHEMIA[1]

You meaner beauties of the night,
    That poorly satisfy our eyes
More by your number than your light;
    You common people of the skies,
    What are you when the sun shall rise?

You curious chanters of the wood,
    That warble forth Dame Nature's lays,
Thinking your voices understood
    By your weak accents; what's your praise
    When Philomel her voice shall raise?   10

You violets, that first appear,
    By your pure purple mantles known,
Like the proud virgins of the year,
    As if the spring were all your own;
    What are you when the rose is blown?

So when my Mistress shall be seen
    In form and beauty of her mind,
By virtue first, then choice, a Queen,
    Tell me, if she were not designed
    The eclipse and glory of her kind?   20

ON HIS MISTRESS
1 The poem was written in 1619 to Elizabeth, daughter of James I, who married Frederic V, Elector Palatine, in 1613. In 1619 Frederic was made King of Bohemia, but Spanish and Austrian forces soon brought his reign to an end.

John Donne

[1572–1631]

ONNE has been a poet of major importance to our century. The rehabilitation of his reputation which took place between 1910 and 1930 played a role not only in revising the pantheon of English literature but also in shaping the style of much contemporary lyric poetry. Eliot, Pound, Auden, Thomas, Ransom, MacLeish, and scores of other twentieth-century poets have undergone his influence, and that influence continues to be a vital force in shaping the styles of younger poets. The dramatic and colloquial qualities of Donne's work, together with his acute psychological insights—all elements sought after by the modern idiom—make it easy to regard the poet as our own contemporary, as a strangely modern figure who speaks to us in our own accents across the centuries. But such an effect of contemporaneity, however much a part of Donne's greatness, can give rise to some faulty interpretations of his poetry. In approaching Donne's poems, whether the amorous *Songs and Sonnets*, the philosophical *Anniversaries*, or the passionate *Divine Poems*, the modern reader ought to bear in mind the fact that Donne is a man of the late Renaissance, steeped in scholastic, theological, and mystical learning alien to the twentieth century, and the fact that, as a poet of the Renaissance, he expresses himself not through the direct outpouring of his own feelings but through the projection of dramatic *personae* which emphasize separate aspects of his complex personality.

The earliest of Donne's poems—the amorous lyrics of the 1590's and the epistles, love elegies, and satires composed during the same period—thus constitute not the credo of a young profligate but the manifold explorations of a restless and devious sensibility determined to plumb the contradictory depths of sensuous and intellectual experience. These poems, taken as a whole, make it clear that, although the young Donne was no stranger to sexual passion, he was at the same time desperately concerned with the search for some principle of divine unity underlying both emotional experience and religious longing. The varied moods of the *Songs and Sonnets*—cynicism, coarseness, rapture, devotion—do not present any consistent pattern of development in the poet's conception of love; they represent rather his recognition of the complexities inherent in the most intense and perplexing of human experiences. "The Ecstasy" is perhaps the most coherent and profound exposition of Donne's philosophy of love, but its tentatively Platonic resolution—

> Love's mysteries in souls do grow,
> But yet the body is his book—

is incomplete without the consideration of the many other masks assumed by Eros in the *Songs and Sonnets*.

The early "Satire III: Of Religion" emphasizes the quality of spiritual quest which underlies all of Donne's early poetry and ought to be enough in itself to explode the myth formulated by some of Donne's admirers (among them Izaak Walton, the poet's first biographer), of the piratical young rake who, in the manner of St. Augustine, was metamorphosed into the saintly Dean of St. Paul's. Such a view, though pious, does violence to the unity and complexity of Donne's vision of experience. Recent research has established that, contrary to earlier belief, several of the *Holy Sonnets* were written as early as 1609 and some of the amorous verses as late as 1617. Such a confusing pattern is only to be expected in the work of a poet who felt compelled to view amorous experience under mystical metaphors and devotional experience under erotic metaphors; it may give us a sense of how we ought to approach the entire body of his work.

Very little of Donne's poetry was published during his lifetime: the *First Anniversary* appeared in 1611 and the *Second Anniversary* in 1612, the "Elegy upon the Death of Prince Henry" was published in Sylvester's collection entitled *Lachrymae Lachrymarum* in 1613, and a satiric poem of compliment by Donne preceded Thomas Coryat's *Crudities*, a travel book published in 1611. Both the amorous and the devotional lyrics were confined to circulation in manuscript, while the epistolary and commemorative verses of the early 1600's, designed for the delectation of patrons or prospective patrons, went, with varying degrees of success, to their destined recipients. The first collected edition of the poems appeared posthumously, in 1633, and was followed by many other editions in the seventeenth century.

Even before the publication of the collected poems, however, Donne had exerted a strong influence on younger poets who were familiar with his work through its manuscript circulation. Such poets as Lord Herbert of Cherbury, Henry King, and Thomas Carew gave early evidence of the growth of the "metaphysical" style, and Carew, in his "Elegy upon the Death of Dr. Donne," cited some of the qualities which his generation had found in the achievements of "a king who ruled as he thought fit / The universal monarchy of wit." Carew admired above all his master's "rich and pregnant fancy," "masculine expression," and "imperious wit"—in short, precisely those qualities of conversational roughness, conceited expression, and intellectual intricacy at which Dr. Johnson was to level his strictures in the eighteenth century, which Coleridge was to admire in the nineteenth, and which H. J. C. Grierson and T. S. Eliot were to praise in the twentieth.

What our age has most admired in Donne and his successors can be summed up in a phrase—the union of passion and intellect—and it is this quality which gives rise to Donne's distinguishing features. It is perhaps misleading to speak, as Eliot does, of Donne's "unified sensibility," for the phrase suggests a human being who has reconciled within himself the warring claims of flesh and spirit. The actual Donne, his greatest poetry tells us, was torn by the classic conflict in its most extreme form, and his vision of an all-surpassing unity of being was at best fragmentary and transient. But the poet within the troubled human being did at all times strive to articulate his vision honestly, without the facile aid of any wholly accepted tradition, either artistic or theological, and it is this fact, perhaps, which gives his work its enduring value.

J. DONNE. *Poetical Works*, ed. H. J. C. Grierson, 2 vols. (Oxford, 1912). The definitive edition.

————. *Songs and Sonnets*, ed. T. Redpath (London, 1956). A copiously annotated edition.

————. *Divine Poems*, ed. H. Gardner (Oxford, 1952). Contains much important information on the composition of these poems.

R. C. BALD. *Donne's Influence in English Literature* (Morpeth, 1932).

C. HUNT. *Donne's Poetry* (New Haven, 1954). Contains several valuable analyses.

G. KEYNES. *Bibliography of Dr. John Donne* (Cambridge, 3rd ed., 1958).

P. LEGOUIS. *Donne the Craftsman* (Paris, 1928).

J. B. LEISHMAN. *The Monarch of Wit* (London, rev. ed., 1962).

T. SPENCER, *et al.* *A Garland for John Donne* (Cambridge, Mass., 1931). A collection of essays.

L. UNGER. *Donne's Poetry and Modern Criticism* (Chicago, 1950).

B. K. LEWALSKI. *Donne's Anniversaries and the Poetry of Praise* (Princeton, 1973).

A. STEIN. *John Donne's Lyrics* (Minneapolis, 1962).

POEMS [1633]

SONGS AND SONNETS[1]

THE GOOD-MORROW

I wonder, by my troth, what thou and I
Did till we loved? were we not weaned till then,
But sucked on country pleasures, childishly?
Or snorted we in the seven sleepers' den?[2]
'Twas so; but this,[3] all pleasures fancies be.
If ever any beauty I did see,
Which I desired, and got, 'twas but a dream of thee.
And now good-morrow to our waking souls,
Which watch not one another out of fear;
For love all love of other sights controls,   10
And makes one little room an everywhere.
Let sea-discoverers to new worlds have gone;
Let maps to other, worlds on worlds have shown;
Let us possess one world; each hath one, and is one.

My face in thine eye, thine in mine appears,[4]
And true plain hearts do in the faces rest;
Where can we find two better hemispheres
Without sharp north, without declining west?
Whatever dies was not mixed equally;
If our two loves be one, or thou and I   20
Love so alike that none do slacken, none can die.

SONG

Go and catch a falling star,
    Get with child a mandrake root,[1]
Tell me where all past years are,
    Or who cleft the devil's foot,

Teach me to hear mermaids[2] singing,
    Or to keep off envy's stinging,
        And find
        What wind
Serves to advance an honest mind.

THE GOOD-MORROW

1 The section headings (Songs and Sonnets, Epigrams, Elegies, Satires, Letters, Divine Poems) did not appear in the edition of 1633, but were added in the edition of 1635.
2 Seven Christian youths of Ephesus, according to legend, hid in a cave during the persecution of the Christians by the emperor Decius, and slept on there for over two hundred years.
3 Except this love of ours.

4 The two lovers find their respective worlds, or hemispheres, in each other's eyes.

SONG

1 The forked root of the mandrake (mandragora) suggested the human body.
2 The mermaids are here identified, as in Spenser and other contemporary writers, with the sirens.

If thou be'st born to strange sights,   10
   Things invisible to see,
Ride ten thousand days and nights,
   Till age snow white hairs on thee,
Thou, when thou return'st, wilt tell me
   All strange wonders that befell thee,
      And swear
      Nowhere
Lives a woman true, and fair.

If thou find'st one, let me know;
   Such a pilgrimage were sweet.   20
Yet do not; I would not go,
   Though at next door we might meet.
Though she were true when you met her,
   And last till you write your letter,
      Yet she
      Will be
False, ere I come, to two or three.

WOMAN'S CONSTANCY

Now thou hast loved me one whole day,
Tomorrow when thou leav'st, what wilt thou say?
Wilt thou then antedate some new-made vow?
   Or say that now
We are not just those persons which we were?
Or, that oaths made in reverential fear
Of love, and his wrath, any may forswear?
Or, as true deaths true marriages untie,
So lovers' contracts, images of those,
Bind but till sleep, death's image, them unloose?   10
   Or, your own end to justify,
For having purposed change and falsehood, you
Can have no way but falsehood to be true?
Vain lunatic, against these 'scapes I could
   Dispute and conquer, if I would;
   Which I abstain to do,
For by tomorrow I may think so too.

THE UNDERTAKING

I have done one braver thing
   Than all the worthies did,
And yet a braver thence doth spring,
   Which is, to keep that hid.

It were but madness now t' impart
   The skill of specular stone,[1]
When he which can have learned the art
   To cut it, can find none.

So if I now should utter this,
   Others, because no more   10
Such stuff to work upon there is,
   Would love but as before.

But he who loveliness within
   Hath found, all outward loathes,
For he who color loves, and skin,
   Loves but their oldest clothes.

If, as I have, you also do
   Virtue attired in woman see,
And dare love that, and say so too,
   And forget the he and she;   20

And if this love, though placèd so,
   From prófane men you hide,
Which will no faith on this bestow,
   Or, if they do, deride,

Then you have done a braver thing
   Than all the worthies did;
And a braver thence will spring,
   Which is, to keep that hid.

THE SUN RISING

   Busy old fool, unruly sun,
     Why dost thou thus
Through windows and through curtains call on us?
Must to thy motions lovers' seasons run?
   Saucy pedantic wretch, go chide
   Late schoolboys and sour prentices,
  Go tell court-huntsmen that the king will ride,
  Call country ants to harvest offices;
Love, all alike, no season knows, nor clime,
Nor hours, days, months, which are the rags of
      time.   10

THE UNDERTAKING
  1 Probably a reference to the crystal in which the astrologer gazed.

Thy beams, so reverend and strong
   Why shouldst thou think?
I could eclipse and cloud them with a wink,
But that I would not lose her sight so long;
    If her eyes have not blinded thine,
    Look, and tomorrow late tell me
   Whether both the Indias of spice and mine [1]
   Be where thou left'st them, or lie here with me.
Ask for those kings whom thou saw'st yesterday,
And thou shalt hear, all here in one bed lay.   20

   She is all states, and all princes I;
    Nothing else is.
Princes do but play us; compared to this,
All honor's mimic, all wealth alchemy. [2]
   Thou, sun, art half as happy as we,
    In that the world's contracted thus;
   Thine age asks ease, and since thy duties be
   To warm the world, that's done in warming us.
Shine here to us, and thou art everywhere;
This bed thy center is, these walls thy sphere.   30

THE INDIFFERENT

I can love both fair and brown;
Her whom abundance melts, and her whom want
    betrays;
Her who loves loneness best, and her who masks and
    plays;
Her whom the country formed, and whom the town;
Her who believes, and her who tries; [1]
Her who still weeps with spongy eyes,
And her who is dry cork and never cries.
I can love her, and her, and you, and you;
I can love any, so she be not true.

Will no other vice content you?   10
Will it not serve your turn to do as did your mothers?
Or have you all old vices spent, and now would find
    out others?
Or doth a fear that men are true torment you?
Oh, we are not; be not you so;
Let me, and do you, twenty know.
Rob me, but bind me not, and let me go.

THE SUN RISING
  1 Mines of gold, silver, or precious stones.
  2 That is, "glittering dross" rather than real gold.

THE INDIFFERENT
  1 Tests, examines.

Must I, who came to travail thorough [2] you,
Grow your fixed subject because you are true?

Venus heard me sigh this song,
And by love's sweetest part, variety, she swore   20
She heard not this till now, and that it should be so no
    more.
She went, examined, and returned ere long,
And said, "Alas! some two or three
Poor heretics in love there be,
Which think to 'stablish dangerous constancy.
But I have told them, 'Since you will be true,
You shall be true to them who are false to you.' "

THE CANONIZATION

For God's sake hold your tongue, and let me love;
   Or chide my palsy, or my gout,
My five gray hairs, or ruined fortune flout;
   With wealth your state, your mind with arts
    improve,
    Take you a course, get you a place,
    Observe his Honor, or his Grace,
Or the king's real, or his stamped [1] face
   Contemplate; what you will, approve,
   So you will let me love.

Alas, alas, who's injured by my love?   10
   What merchant's ships have my sighs drowned?
Who says my tears have overflowed his ground?
   When did my colds a forward spring remove?
    When did the heats which my veins fill
    Add one more to the plaguy bill? [2]
Soldiers find wars, and lawyers find out still
   Litigious men, which quarrels move,
   Though she and I do love.

Call us what you will, we are made such by love;
   Call her one, me another fly,   20
We're tapers too, and at our own cost die,
   And we in us find the eagle and the dove.
    The phœnix riddle hath more wit
    By us; we two being one, are it.
So, to one neutral thing both sexes fit.
   We die and rise the same, and prove
   Mysterious by this love.

  2 Through.

THE CANONIZATION
  1 On coins.
  2 The list, published weekly, of the victims of the plague.

We can die by it, if not live by love,
   And if unfit for tombs and hearse
Our legend be, it will be fit for verse;   30
   And if no piece of chronicle we prove,
      We'll build in sonnets pretty rooms;
      As well a well-wrought urn becomes
The greatest ashes, as half-acre tombs,
   And by these hymns all shall approve
   Us canonized for love,

And thus invoke us: "You whom reverend love
   Made one another's hermitage;
You, to whom love was peace, that now is rage;
   Who did the whole world's soul contract, and
      drove   40
      Into the glasses of your eyes
      (So made such mirrors, and such spies,
That they did all to you epitomize)
   Countries, towns, courts; beg from above
   A pattern of your love!"

THE TRIPLE FOOL

     I am two fools, I know,
For loving, and for saying so
     In whining poetry.
But where's that wise man that would not be I
     If she would not deny?
Then as th' earth's inward, narrow, crooked lanes
   Do purge sea water's fretful salt away,
     I thought if I could draw my pains
Through rhyme's vexation, I should them allay.
Grief brought to numbers [1] cannot be so fierce,   10
For he tames it that fetters it in verse.

     But when I have done so,
Some man, his art and voice to show,
     Doth set and sing my pain,
And by delighting many, frees again
     Grief, which verse did restrain.
To love and grief tribute of verse belongs,
But not of such as pleases when 'tis read;
     Both are increasèd by such songs,
For both their triumphs so are publishèd,   20
And I, which was two fools, do so grow three.
Who are a little wise, the best fools be.

THE TRIPLE FOOL
   1 Verses.

LOVERS' INFINITENESS

If yet I have not all thy love,
Dear, I shall never have it all;
I cannot breathe one other sigh to move,
Nor can entreat one other tear to fall,
And all my treasure, which should purchase thee,
Sighs, tears, and oaths, and letters I have spent.
Yet no more can be due to me
Than at the bargain made was meant.
If then thy gift of love were partiàl,
That some to me, some should to others fall,   10
   Dear, I shall never have thee all.

Or if then thou gavest me all,
All was but all which thou hadst then;
But if in thy heart, since, there be or shall
New love created be, by other men
Which have their stocks entire, and can in tears,
In sighs, in oaths, and letters outbid me,
This new love may beget new fears,
For this love was not vowed by thee.
And yet it was, thy gift being general;   20
The ground, thy heart, is mine; whatever shall
   Grow there, dear, I should have it all.

Yet I would not have all yet.
He that hath all can have no more;
And since my love doth every day admit
New growth, thou shouldst have new rewards in
   store;
Thou canst not every day give me thy heart.
If thou canst give it, then thou never gavest it;
Love's riddles are, that though thy heart depart,
It stays at home, and thou with losing savest it: 30
But we will have a way more liberal
Than changing hearts, to join them; so we shall
   Be one, and one another's all.

SONG

   Sweetest love, I do not go [1]
     For weariness of thee,
   Nor in hope the world can show
     A fitter love for me;

SONG
   1 This song was probably written on the occasion of
Donne's going to the Continent in 1612 with his patron, Sir
Robert Drury, and Lady Drury. See A Valediction Forbidding Mourning below, which was written on the same
occasion.

But since that I
Must die at last, 'tis best
To use myself in jest
    Thus by feigned deaths to die.

Yesternight the sun went hence,
    And yet is here today;   10
He hath no desire nor sense,
    Nor half so short a way:
        Then fear not me,
But believe that I shall make
Speedier journeys, since I take
    More wings and spurs than he.

Oh how feeble is man's power,
    That if good fortune fall,
Cannot add another hour,
    Nor a lost hour recall!   20
        But come bad chance,[2]
And we join it to our strength,
And we teach it art and length,
    Itself o'er us to advance.

When thou sigh'st thou sigh'st not wind,
    But sigh'st my soul away,
When thou weep'st, unkindly kind,
    My life's blood doth decay.
        It cannot be
That thou lov'st me, as thou say'st,   30
If in thine my life thou waste,
    That art the best of me.

Let not thy divining heart[3]
    Forethink me any ill;
Destiny may take thy part,
    And may thy fears fulfill,
        But think that we
Are but turned aside to sleep;
They who one another keep
    Alive, ne'er parted be.   40

2 If bad chance come.
3 In his Life of Donne, Izaak Walton says that Mrs.
Donne's "divining soul boded her some ill in his absence."
Her forebodings were justified, for during her husband's
absence she gave birth to a dead child.

THE LEGACY

When I died last, and, dear, I die
    As often as from thee I go,
    Though it be but an hour ago,
And lovers' hours be full eternity,
I can remember yet that I
    Something did say, and something did bestow;
Though I be dead, which sent me, I should be
Mine own executor and legacy.

I heard me say, "Tell her anon
    That myself (that's you, not I)   10
    Did kill me, and when I felt me die,
I bid me send my heart when I was gone."
But I, alas, could there find none
    When I had ripped me and searched where hearts
        did lie.
It killed me again that I who still was true
In life, in my last will should cozen you.

Yet I found something like a heart,
    But colors it, and corners, had;
    It was not good, it was not bad,
It was entire to none, and few had part.   20
As good as could be made by art
    It seemed; and therefore, for our losses sad,
I meant to send this heart instead of mine,
But oh, no man could hold it, for 'twas thine.

A FEVER

Oh, do not die, for I shall hate
    All women so, when thou art gone,
That thee I shall not celebrate
    When I remember thou wast one.

But yet thou canst not die I know;
    To leave this world behind is death;
But when thou from this world wilt go,
    The whole world vapors with thy breath.

Or if, when thou, the world's soul, goest,
    It stay, 'tis but thy carcass then;   10
The fairest woman, but thy ghost;
    But corrupt worms, the worthiest men.

O wrangling schools that search what fire
    Shall burn this world, had none the wit
Unto this knowledge to aspire,
    That this her fever might be it?

And yet she cannot waste by this,
   Nor long bear this torturing wrong,
For much corruption needful is
   To fuel such a fever long.   20

These burning fits but meteors be,
   Whose matter in thee is soon spent.
Thy beauty, and all parts, which are thee,
   Are unchangeable firmament.

Yet 'twas of my mind, seizing thee,
   Though it in thee cannot persever;
For I had rather owner be
   Of thee one hour, than all else ever.

AIR AND ANGELS[1]

Twice or thrice had I loved thee
Before I knew thy face or name;
So in a voice, so in a shapeless flame,
Angels affect us oft, and worshiped be;
   Still when, to where thou wert, I came,
Some lovely glorious nothing I did see.
   But since my soul, whose child love is,
Takes limbs of flesh, and else could nothing do,
   More subtle than the parent is
Love must not be, but take a body too;   10
   And therefore what thou wert, and who,
      I bid love ask, and now
That it assume thy body I allow,
And fix itself in thy lip, eye, and brow.

Whilst thus to ballast love I thought,
And so more steadily to have gone,
With wares which would sink admiration,
I saw I had love's pinnace overfraught;
   Ev'ry thy hair[2] for love to work upon
Is much too much, some fitter must be sought; 20
   For, nor in nothing, nor in things
Extreme and scatt'ring bright, can love inhere.

Then as an angel, face and wings
Of air, not pure as it, yet pure doth wear,
   So thy love may be my love's sphere.
      Just such disparity
As is 'twixt air and angels' purity,
'Twixt women's love and men's will ever be.

THE ANNIVERSARY

All kings, and all their favorites,
   All glory of honors, beauties, wits,
The sun itself, which makes times as they pass,
Is elder by a year now than it was
When thou and I first one another saw;
All other things to their destruction draw,
   Only our love hath no decay;
This no tomorrow hath, nor yesterday;
Running, it never runs from us away,
But truly keeps his first, last, everlasting day.   10

Two graves must hide thine and my corse;
   If one might, death were no divorce.
Alas, as well as other princes, we,
Who prince enough in one another be,
Must leave at last in death these eyes and ears,
Oft fed with true oaths, and with sweet salt tears;
   But souls where nothing dwells but love,
All other thoughts being inmates, then shall prove
This, or a love increased there above,
When bodies to their graves, souls from their graves,
   remove.   20

And then we shall be throughly[1] blest,
   But we[2] no more than all the rest.
Here upon earth we are kings, and none but we
Can be such kings, nor of such, subjects be.
Who is so safe as we, where none can do
Treason to us, except one of us two?
   True and false fears let us refrain;
Let us love nobly, and live, and add again
Years and years unto years, till we attain
To write threescore; this is the second of our reign. 30

AIR AND ANGELS
  1 Donne's thought in this poem turns upon the medieval and the earlier Neoplatonic beliefs respecting the bodies of angels. The most commonly accepted theory was that angels in certain circumstances assumed bodies of air, which, though pure (ll. 23, 24), is not so pure as the angelic essence itself.
  2 That is, "thy ev'ry hair."

THE ANNIVERSARY
  1 Thoroughly.
  2 The 1633 edition reads "now no more."

TWICKENHAM GARDEN[1]

Blasted with sighs, and surrounded with tears,
    Hither I come to seek the spring,
    And at mine eyes, and at mine ears,
Receive such balms as else cure everything;
    But oh, self-traitor, I do bring
The spider love, which transubstantiates all,
    And can convert manna to gall;
And that this place may thoroughly be thought
    True Paradise, I have the serpent brought.

'Twere wholesomer for me that winter did   10
    Benight the glory of this place,
    And that a grave frost did forbid
These trees to laugh and mock me to my face;
    But that I may not this disgrace
Endure, nor yet leave loving, Love, let me
    Some senseless piece of this place be;
Make me a mandrake,[2] so I may groan here,
    Or a stone fountain weeping out my year.

Hither with crystal vials, lovers, come
    And take my tears, which are love's wine,   20
    And try your mistress' tears at home,
For all are false that taste not just like mine;
    Alas, hearts do not in eyes shine,
Nor can you more judge woman's thoughts by tears,
    Than by her shadow what she wears.
O perverse sex, where none is true but she,
    Who's therefore true, because her truth kills me.

THE DREAM

Dear love, for nothing less than thee
Would I have broke this happy dream;
    It was a theme
For reason, much too strong for fantasy,
Therefore thou wak'dst me wisely; yet
My dream thou brok'st not, but continuedst it,
Thou art so truth that thoughts of thee suffice
To make dreams truths, and fables histories;
Enter these arms, for since thou thought'st it best
Not to dream all my dream, let's act the rest.   10

TWICKENHAM GARDEN

1 The Countess of Bedford, Donne's patroness, had a
country house at Twickenham.

2 The mandrake was popularly believed to shriek when
pulled from the ground.

As lightning or a taper's light,
Thine eyes and not thy noise waked me;
    Yet I thought thee
(For thou lov'st truth) an angel, at first sight;
But when I saw thou saw'st my heart,
And knew'st my thoughts, beyond an angel's art,
When thou knew'st what I dreamt, when thou knew'st
    when
Excess of joy would wake me, and cam'st then,
I must confess it could not choose but be
Profane to think thee anything but thee.   20

Coming and staying showed thee, thee,
But rising makes me doubt that now
    Thou art not thou.
That love is weak where fear's as strong as he;
'Tis not all spirit, pure and brave,
If mixture it of fear, shame, honor, have.
Perchance as torches which must ready be,
Men light and put out, so thou deal'st with me:
Thou cam'st to kindle, go'st to come; then I
Will dream that hope again, but else would die.   30

LOVE'S GROWTH

I scarce believe my love to be so pure
    As I had thought it was,
    Because it doth endure
Vicissitude and season, as the grass;
    Methinks I lied all winter, when I swore
My love was infinite, if spring make it more.
But if this medicine, love, which cures all sorrow
With more, not only be no quintessence,
But mixed of all stuffs, paining soul or sense,
And of the sun his working vigor borrow,   10
Love's not so pure and abstract as they use
To say, which have no mistress but their Muse;
But as all else, being elemented too,
Love sometimes would contemplate, sometimes do.

And yet no greater, but more eminent,
    Love by the spring is grown;
    As, in the firmament,
Stars by the Sun are not enlarged, but shown,
Gentle love deeds, as blossoms on a bough,
From love's awakened root do bud out now.   20
If, as in water stirred more circles be
Produced by one, love such additions take,

Those like so many spheres, but one heaven make,
For they are all concentric unto thee.
And though each spring do add to love new heat,
As princes do in times of action get
New taxes, and remit them not in peace,
No winter shall abate the spring's increase.

A VALEDICTION OF WEEPING

Let me pour forth
My tears before thy face whilst I stay here,
For thy face coins them, and thy stamp they bear,
And by this mintage they are something worth,
    For thus they be
    Pregnant of thee;
Fruits of much grief they are, emblems of more—
When a tear falls, that thou fall'st which it bore,
So thou and I are nothing then, when on a diverse
        shore.

On a round ball   10
A workman that hath copies by, can lay
An Europe, Afric, and an Asia,
And quickly make that which was nothing, all;
    So doth each tear
    Which thee doth wear,
A globe, yea world, by that impression grow,
Till thy tears mixed with mine do overflow
This world; by waters sent from thee, my heaven
        dissolvèd so.

O more than moon,
Draw not up seas to drown me in thy sphere;   20
Weep me not dead, in thine arms, but forbear
To teach the sea what it may do too soon.
    Let not the wind
    Example find
To do me more harm than it purposeth;
Since thou and I sigh one another's breath,
Whoe'er sighs most is cruelest, and hastes the other's
        death.[1]

LOVE'S ALCHEMY

Some that have deeper digged love's mine than I,
Say where his centric happiness doth lie;
    I have loved, and got, and told,
But should I love, get, tell, till I were old,
I should not find that hidden mystery.
        Oh, 'tis imposture all!
And as no chemic[1] yet th' elixir[2] got,
    But glorifies his pregnant pot
    If by the way to him befall
Some odoriferous thing, or medicinal,[3]   10
    So lovers dream a rich and long delight,
    But get a winter-seeming summer's night.

Our ease, our thrift, our honor, and our day,
Shall we for this vain bubble's shadow pay?
    Ends love in this, that my man
Can be as happy as I can, if he can
Endure the short scorn of a bridegroom's play?
        That loving wretch that swears
'Tis not the bodies marry, but the minds,
    Which he in her angelic finds,   20
    Would swear as justly that he hears,
In that day's rude hoarse minstrelsy, the spheres.[4]
    Hope not for mind in women: at their best
    Sweetness and wit, they are but mummy possessed.

THE FLEA

Mark but this flea, and mark in this
How little that which thou deny'st me is;
It sucked me first, and now sucks thee,
And in this flea our two bloods mingled be;
Thou know'st that this cannot be said
A sin, nor shame, nor loss of maidenhead;
    Yet this enjoys before it woo,
    And pampered swells with one blood made of two,
    And this, alas, is more than we would do.

A VALEDICTION OF WEEPING
    1 A reference to the old belief that every sigh draws a drop
of blood from the heart.

LOVE'S ALCHEMY
    1 Alchemist.
    2 The elixir, or quintessence, was the preparation sought
by the alchemists whereby it was thought baser metals might
be transmuted into gold.
    3 Pronounced med'cinal.
    4 The music of the spheres.

Oh stay, three lives in one flea spare,   10
Where we almost, yea, more than married are.
This flea is you and I, and this
Our marriage bed and marriage temple is;
Though parents grudge, and you, we're met,
And cloistered in these living walls of jet.
   Though use make you apt to kill me,
   Let not to that, self-murder added be,
   And sacrilege: three sins in killing three.

Cruel and sudden, hast thou since
Purpled thy nail in blood of innocence?   20
Wherein could this flea guilty be,
Except in that drop which it sucked from thee?
Yet thou triumph'st and say'st that thou
Find'st not thyself nor me the weaker now;
   'Tis true. Then learn how false fears be:
   Just so much honor, when thou yield'st to me,
   Will waste, as this flea's death took life from thee.

THE MESSAGE

Send home my long strayed eyes to me,
Which, oh, too long have dwelt on thee;
Yet since there they have learned such ill,
   Such forced fashions,
   And false passions,
     That they be
     Made by thee
Fit for no good sight, keep them still.

Send home my harmless heart again,
Which no unworthy thought could stain;   10
But if it be taught by thine [1]
   To make jestings
   Of protestings,
     And break both
     Word and oath,
Keep it, for then 'tis none of mine.

Yet send me back my heart and eyes
That I may know and see thy lies,
And may laugh and joy, when thou
   Art in anguish   20
   And dost languish
     For someone
     That will none,
Or prove as false as thou art now.

THE MESSAGE
  1 The 1633 edition reads "Which if it be taught by thine";
the 1635 and subsequent editions read "But" etc.

A NOCTURNAL UPON SAINT LUCY'S DAY, BEING THE SHORTEST DAY [1]

'Tis the year's midnight, and it is the day's,
Lucy's, who scarce seven hours herself unmasks;
   The sun is spent, and now his flasks [2]
   Send forth light squibs, no constant rays;
     The whole world's sap is sunk;
The general balm th' hydroptic earth hath drunk,
Whither, as to the bed's feet, life is shrunk,
Dead and interred; yet all these seem to laugh,
Compared with me, who am their epitaph.

Study me then, you who shall lovers be   10
At the next world, that is, at the next spring;
   For I am every dead thing,
   In whom Love wrought new alchemy.
     For his art did express
A quintessence even from nothingness,
From dull privations, and lean emptiness,
He ruined me, and I am re-begot
Of absence, darkness, death—things which are not. [3]

All others from all things draw all that's good,
Life, soul, form, spirit, whence they being have;   20
   I, by Love's limbec, [4] am the grave
   Of all that's nothing. Oft a flood
     Have we two wept, and so
Drowned the whole world, us two; oft did we grow
To be two chaoses, when we did show
Care to aught else; and often absences
Withdrew our souls, and made us carcasses.

But I am by her death, which word wrongs her,
Of the first nothing the elixir grown;
   Were I a man, that I were one   30
   I needs must know; I should prefer,
     If I were any beast,

A NOCTURNAL
  1 St. Lucy's Day, December 13, was, according to the
calendar used in Donne's England, the shortest day in the
year.
  2 Powder-flasks.
  3 In this stanza and those which follow, Donne, in characteristically subtle fashion, is distinguishing between and
analyzing degrees of nothingness, and fancies himself the
elixir or quintessence of that nothingness which antedated the
creation of the world.
  4 The alembic or still of the alchemists.

Some ends, some means; yea plants, yea stones detest
And love; all, all some properties invest;
If I an ordinary nothing were,
As shadow, a light and body must be here.

But I am none; nor will my sun renew.
You lovers, for whose sake the lesser sun
    At this time to the Goat⁵ is run
    To fetch new lust, and give it you,   40
        Enjoy your summer all;
Since she enjoys her long night's festival,
Let me prepare towards her, and let me call
This hour her vigil, and her eve, since this
Both the year's and the day's deep midnight is.

THE BAIT¹

Come live with me, and be my love,
And we will some new pleasures prove,
Of golden sands, and crystal brooks,
With silken lines, and silver hooks.

There will the river whispering run,
Warmed by thy eyes more than the sun,
And there the enamored fish will stay,
Begging themselves they may betray.

When thou wilt swim in that live bath,
Each fish, which every channel hath,   10
Will amorously to thee swim,
Gladder to catch thee, than thou him.

If thou, to be so seen, beest loth,
By sun or moon, thou darkenest both;
And if myself have leave to see,
I need not their light, having thee.

Let others freeze with angling reeds,
And cut their legs with shells and weeds,
Or treacherously poor fish beset
With strangling snare, or windowy net.   20

A NOCTURNAL
5 Capricorn, one of the signs of the zodiac.

THE BAIT
1 A parody of Marlowe's The Passionate Shepherd to His
Love.

Let coarse bold hands from slimy nest
The bedded fish in banks out-wrest,
Or curious traitors, sleave-silk² flies,
Bewitch poor fishes' wand'ring eyes.

For thee, thou need'st no such deceit,
For thou thyself art thine own bait;
The fish that is not catched thereby,
Alas, is wiser far than I.

THE APPARITION

When by thy scorn, Oh murderess, I am dead,
And that thou thinkst thee free
From all solicitation from me,
Then shall my ghost come to thy bed,
And thee, fained vestal, in worse arms shall see;
Then thy sick taper will begin to wink,
And he whose thou art then, being tired before,
Will, if thou stir, or pinch to wake him, think
    Thou call'st for more,
And in false sleep will from thee shrink,   10
And then, poor aspen wretch, neglected thou
Bathed in a cold quicksilver sweat wilt lie
    A verier ghost than I;
What I will say, I will not tell thee now,
Lest that preserve thee; and since my love is spent,
I had rather thou shouldst painfully repent,
Than by my threatenings rest still innocent.

THE BROKEN HEART

He is stark mad, whoever says
    That he hath been in love an hour;
Yet not that love so soon decays,
    But that it can ten in less space devour;
Who will believe me, if I swear
That I have had the plague a year?
    Who would not laugh at me, if I should say,
    I saw a flask of powder burn a day?

Ah, what a trifle is a heart,
    If once into love's hands it come!   10
All other griefs allow a part
    To other griefs, and ask themselves but some;
They come to us; but us Love draws,
He swallows us, and never chaws.
    By him, as by chain'd shot, whole ranks do die,
    He is the tyrant pike, our hearts the fry.

2 Silk thread which can be separated into smaller filaments.

If 'twere not so, what did become
　Of my heart, when I first saw thee?
I brought a heart into the room,
　But from the room I carried none with me:　20
If it had gone to thee, I know
Mine would have taught thine heart to show
　More pity unto me; but Love, alas,
　At one first blow did shiver it as glass.

Yet nothing can to nothing fall,
　Nor any place be empty quite,
Therefore I think my breast hath all
　Those pieces still, though they be not unite;
And now as broken glasses show
A hundred lesser faces, so　　　　　　　30
　My rags of heart can like, wish, and adore,
　But after one such love can love no more.

A VALEDICTION FORBIDDING
MOURNING

As virtuous men pass mildly away,
　And whisper to their souls to go,
Whilst some of their sad friends do say,
　"The breath goes now," and some say
　　"No";

So let us melt, and make no noise,
　No tear-floods nor sigh-tempests move;
'Twere profanation of our joys
　To tell the laity our love.

Moving of the earth brings harm and fears;
　Men reckon what it did and meant;　　　10
But trepidation [1] of the spheres,
　Though greater far, is innocent.

Dull sublunary lovers' love
　(Whose soul is sense) cannot admit
Absence, because it doth remove
　Those things which elemented [2] it.

But we, by a love so much refined
　That ourselves know not what it is,
Inter-assurèd of the mind,
　Care less eyes, lips, and hands to miss.　　20

Our two souls, therefore, which are one,
　Though I must go, endure not yet
A breach, but an expansiòn,
　Like gold to airy thinness beat.

If they be two, they are two so
　As stiff twin compasses [3] are two;
Thy soul, the fixed foot, makes no show
　To move, but doth if the other do.

And though it in the center sit,
　Yet, when the other far doth roam,　　　30
It leans, and hearkens after it,
　And grows erect as that comes home.

Such wilt thou be to me, who must
　Like the other foot obliquely run:
Thy firmness draws my circle just, [4]
　And makes me end where I begun.

THE ECSTASY

Where, like a pillow on a bed,
　A pregnant bank swelled up to rest
The violet's reclining head,
　Sat we two, one another's best.
Our hands were firmly cémented
　With a fast balm, which thence did spring;
Our eye-beams twisted, and did thread
　Our eyes upon one double string.
So to intergraft our hands, as yet
　Was all the means to make us one;　　10
And pictures in our eyes to get
　Was all our propagation.
As, 'twixt two equal armies, fate
　Suspends uncertain victory,
Our souls, which, to advance their state,
　Were gone out, hung 'twixt her and me.
And whilst our souls negotiate there,
　We like sepulchral statues lay;
All day, the same our postures were,
　And we said nothing, all the day.　　20

A VALEDICTION
　1 A term from the Ptolemaic astronomy referring to the motion of the eighth (or ninth) sphere, which was thought to cause the "innocent" or harmless variation in the date of the equinox.
　2 Constituted.

3 A pair of dividers.　　　　　　　4 Perfect.

If any, so by love refined
    That he soul's language understood,
And by good love were grown all mind,
    Within convenient distance stood,
He, though he knew not which soul spake,
    Because both meant, both spake, the same,
Might thence a new concoction[1] take,
    And part far purer than he came.
This ecstasy doth unperplex
    (We said) and tell us what we love;   30
We see by this it was not sex;
    We see we saw not what did move;
But as all several souls contain
    Mixture of things, they know not what,
Love these mixed souls doth mix again
    And makes both one, each this and that.[2]
A single violet transplant,
    The strength, the color, and the size,
All which before was poor and scant,
    Redoubles still and multiplies.   40
When love with one another so
    Interinanimates two souls,
That abler soul, which thence doth flow,
    Defects of loneliness controls.
We then, who are this new soul, know
    Of what we are composed and made,
For the atomies[3] of which we grow
    Are souls, whom no change can invade.
But oh alas! so long, so far,
    Our bodies why do we forbear?   50
They are ours, though they are not we; we are
    The intelligences, they the spheres.[4]
We owe them thanks, because they thus
    Did us, to us, at first convey,
Yielded their forces, sense, to us,
    Nor are dross to us, but allay.[5]
On man heaven's influence works not so,
    But that it first imprints the air;[6]

For soul into the soul may flow,
    Though it to body first repair.   60
As our blood labors to beget
    Spirits, as like souls as it can,
Because such fingers need to knit
    That subtle knot which makes us man,
So must pure lovers' souls descend
    To affections, and to faculties,
Which sense may reach and apprehend;
    Else a great prince in prison lies.
To our bodies turn we then, that so
    Weak men on love revealed may look;   70
Love's mysteries in souls do grow,
    But yet the body is his book.
And if some lover, such as we,
    Have heard this dialogue of one,
Let him still mark us; he shall see
    Small change when we're to bodies gone.

THE ECSTASY
  1 Purification or sublimation.
  2 Grierson explains the passage, ll. 32–36, as follows: "We see now that we did not see before the true source of our love. What we thought was due to bodily beauty, we perceive now to have its source in the soul."
  3 Atoms.
  4 The heavenly bodies (spheres) were, according to the medieval schoolmen, moved and controlled by angels, or "intelligences."
  5 Alloy.
  6 The influence of the stars, according to astrology, was transmitted to man through the air. Donne thinks of the body as providing a similar medium between two souls.

LOVE'S DEITY

I long to talk with some old lover's ghost,
    Who died before the god of love was born:
I cannot think that he, who then loved most,
    Sunk so low as to love one which did scorn.
But since this god produced a destiny,
And that vice-nature,[1] custom, lets it be,
    I must love her that loves not me.

Sure, they which made him god meant not so much,
    Nor he in his young godhead practiced it.
But when an even flame two hearts did touch,   10
    His office was indulgently to fit
Actives to passives. Correspondency
Only his subject was; it cannot be
    Love till I love her that loves me.

But every modern god will now extend
    His vast prerogative as far as Jove.
To rage, to lust, to write to, to commend,
    All is the purlieu of the god of love.
Oh, were we wakened by this tyranny
To ungod this child again, it could not be   20
    I should love her who loves not me.

LOVE'S DEITY
  1 Substitute for nature.

Rebel and atheist too, why murmur I,
  As though I felt the worst that love could do?
Love might make me leave loving, or might try
  A deeper plague, to make her love me too;
Which, since she loves before,[2] I am loth to see.
Falsehood is worse than hate; and that must be
  If she whom I love should love me.

THE FUNERAL[1]

Whoever comes to shroud me, do not harm
  Nor question much
That subtle wreath of hair which crowns my arm;
The mystery, the sign you must not touch,
  For 'tis my outward soul,
Viceroy to that, which, then to heaven being gone,
  Will leave this to control,
And keep these limbs, her provinces, from dissolution.

For if the sinewy thread[2] my brain lets fall
  Through every part   10
Can tie those parts, and make me one of all,
These hairs which upward grew, and strength and art
  Have from a better brain,
Can better do it; except she meant that I
  By this should know my pain,
As prisoners then are manacled, when they're con-
    demned to die.

Whate'er she meant by it, bury it with me,
  For since I am
Love's martyr, it might breed idolatry
If into other hands these relics came;   20
  As 'twas humility
To afford to it all that a soul can do,
  So, 'tis some bravery,[3]
That since you would have none of me, I bury some
    of you.

THE RELIQUE

When my grave is broke up again
Some second guest to entertain
(For graves have learned that woman-head[1]
To be to more than one a bed),
  And he that digs it, spies
A bracelet of bright hair about the bone,
  Will he not let us alone,
And think that there a loving couple lies,
Who thought that this device might be some way
To make their souls, at the last busy day,   10
Meet at this grave, and make a little stay?

  If this fall in a time, or land,
  Where mis-devotion[2] doth command,
  Then he that digs us up will bring
  Us to the bishop, and the king,
    To make us reliques;[3] then
Thou shalt be a Mary Magdalen, and I
  A something else thereby;
All women shall adore us, and some men;
And since at such time miracles are sought,   20
I would have that age by this paper taught
What miracles we harmless lovers wrought.

  First, we loved well and faithfully,
  Yet knew not what we loved, nor why;
  Difference of sex no more we knew
  Than our guardian angels do;
    Coming and going, we
Perchance might kiss,[4] but not between those meals;
  Our hands ne'er touched the seals,
Which nature, injured by late law, sets free;   30
These miracles we did; but now alas,
All measure and all language I should pass,
Should I tell what a miracle she was.

FAREWELL TO LOVE

  Whilst yet to prove,
I thought there was some deity in love,

LOVE'S DEITY
  2 Already loves another.

THE FUNERAL
  1 Grierson thinks that this poem and the following may
have been addressed to Mrs. Magdalen Herbert, the mother
of George Herbert.
  2 The spinal cord.   3 Bravado, boldness.

THE RELIQUE
  1 Womanhood; womanly failing.
  2 Donne has in mind the custom of praying for the dead.
  3 A reference to the veneration of the relics of the saints,
a practice not approved of by the Protestant reformers.
  4 In Donne's England it was customary to kiss on meeting
and parting.

So did I reverence, and gave
Worship; as atheists at their dying hour
Call what they cannot name an unknown power,
   As ignorantly did I crave:
     Thus when
Things not yet known are coveted by men,
   Our desires give them fashion, and so
As they wax lesser, fall, as they size, grow.   10

     But, from late fair
His highness sitting in a golden chair,
   Is not less cared for after three days
By children, than the thing which lovers so
Blindly admire, and with such worship woo;
   Being had, enjoying it decays:
     And thence,
What before pleas'd them all, takes but one sense,
   And that so lamely, as it leaves behind
A kind of sorrowing dullness to the mind.   20

     Ah cannot we,
As well as cocks and lions jocund be,
   After such pleasures? Unless wise
Nature decreed (since each such act, they say,
Diminisheth the length of life a day)
   This, as she would man should despise
     The sport,
Because that other curse of being short,
   And only for a minute made to be,
Eagers desire to raise posterity.   30

     Since so, my mind
Shall not desire what no man else can find,
   I'll no more dote and run
To pursue things which had indamaged me.
And when I come where moving beauties be,
   As men do when the summer's sun
     Grows great,
Though I admire their greatness, shun their heat;
   Each place can afford shadows. If all fail,
'Tis but applying worm-seed to the tail.   40

THE COMPUTATION

For the first twenty years since yesterday
I scarce believed thou couldst be gone away;
For forty more I fed on favors past,
And forty on hopes that thou wouldst they might last.
Tears drowned one hundred, and sighs blew out two;
A thousand, I did neither think nor do,

Or not divide, all being one thought of you;
Or in a thousand more forgot that too.
Yet call not this long life, but think that I
Am, by being dead, immortal. Can ghosts die?

A LECTURE UPON THE SHADOW[1]

Stand still, and I will read to thee
A lecture, love, in love's philosophy.
   These three hours that we have spent
    Walking here, two shadows went
Along with us, which we ourselves produced;
But, now the sun is just above our head,
   We do those shadows tread,
    And to brave clearness all things are reduced.
So whilst our infant loves did grow,
   Disguises did, and shadows, flow   10
   From us and our cares; but now 'tis not so.

That love hath not attained the high'st degree
Which is still diligent lest others see.

Except our loves at this noon stay,
We shall new shadows make the other way.
   As the first were made to blind
    Others, these which come behind
Will work upon ourselves and blind our eyes.
If our loves faint and westwardly decline,   20
   To me thou falsely thine,
    And I to thee mine actions shall disguise.
The morning shadows wear away,
But these grow longer all the day.
But oh, love's day is short if love decay!

Love is a growing, or full constant light,
And his first minute after noon is night.

ELEGIES

ELEGY I.

Jealousy

Fond woman, which would'st have thy husband die,
And yet complain'st of his great jealousy;
If, swollen with poison, he lay in his last bed,
His body with a sere bark coverèd,

A LECTURE UPON THE SHADOW
  1 This poem was first printed in the 1635 edition.

Drawing his breath as thick and short as can
The nimblest crotcheting musician,
Ready with loathsome vomiting to spew
His soul out of one hell into a new,
Made deaf with his poor kindred's howling cries,
Begging with few feigned tears great legacies,   10
Thou would'st not weep, but jolly and frolic be,
As a slave which tomorrow should be free;
Yet weep'st thou, when thou see'st him hungerly
Swallow his own death, heart's-bane jealousy.
O give him many thanks, he is courteous,
That in suspecting kindly warneth us.
We must not, as we used, flout openly,
In scoffing riddles, his deformity,
Nor at his board together being sat,
With words, nor touch, scarce looks adulterate.   20
Nor when he swollen and pampered with great fare
Sits down and snorts, caged in his basket chair,
Must we usurp his own bed any more,
Nor kiss and play in his house as before.
Now I see many dangers, for that is
His realm, his castle, and his diocese.
But if, as envious men which would revile
Their prince or coin his gold themselves exile
Into another country and do it there,
We play in another house, what should we fear?   30
There we will scorn his household policies,
His silly plots and pensionary spies,
As the inhabitants of Thames' right side
Do London's mayor, or Germans the Pope's pride.[1]

ELEGY III.
Change

Although thy hand and faith, and good works too
Have sealed thy love, which nothing should undo,
Yea, though thou fall back, that apostasy
Confirm thy love, yet much, much I fear thee.
Women are like the arts, forced unto none,
Open to all searchers, unprized if unknown.
If I have caught a bird, and let him fly,
Another fowler using these means, as I,
May catch the same bird; and, as these things be,
Women are made for men, not him, nor me.   10

ELEGY I
  1 Those who lived on the right bank of the Thames were
beyond the authority of the mayor of London, as the inhabitants of the Protestant states of Germany were beyond that of
the Pope.

Foxes and goats, all beasts, change when they please;
Shall women, more hot, wily, wild than these,
Be bound to one man, and did nature then
Idly make them apter to endure than men?
They are our clogs, not their own; if a man be
Chained to a galley, yet the galley is free.
Who hath a plowland casts all his seed corn there,
And yet allows his ground more corn should bear;
Though Danuby into the sea must flow,
The sea receives the Rhene, Volga, and Po.   20
By nature, which gave it, this liberty
Thou lov'st; but oh! canst thou love it and me?
Likeness glues love; and if that thou so do,
To make us like and love, must I change too?
More than thy hate, I hate it; rather let me
Allow her change than change as oft as she,
And so not teach, but force my opinion
To love not anyone, nor everyone.
To live in one land is captivity,
To run all countries, a wild roguery;   30
Waters stink soon if in one place they bide,
And in the vast sea are more putrefied;
But when they kiss one bank, and leaving this
Never look back, but the next bank do kiss,
Then are they purest. Change is the nursery
Of music, joy, life, and eternity.

ELEGY VII.

Nature's lay idiot, I taught thee to love,
And in that sophistry, Oh, thou dost prove
Too subtle: Fool, thou didst not understand
The mystic language of the eye nor hand;
Nor couldst thou judge the difference of the air
Of sighs, and say, "This lies, this sounds despair;"
Nor by the eyes' water call a malady
Desperately hot or changing feverously.
I had not taught thee then the alphabet
Of flowers, how they devisefully being set   10
And bound up might with speechless secrecy
Deliver arrands mutely and mutually.
Remember since[1] all thy words used to be
To every suitor "Aye, if my friends agree,"
Since, household charms, thy husband's name to teach
Were all the love tricks that thy wit could reach;
And since, an hour's discourse could scarce have made
One answer in thee, and that ill-arrayed

ELEGY VII
  1 When.

In broken proverbs and torn sentences.
Thou art not by so many duties his,   20
That from the world's common having severed thee,
Inlaid² thee, neither to be seen nor see,
As mine, who have with amorous delicacies
Refined thee into a blissful Paradise.
Thy graces and good works my creatures be;
I planted knowledge and life's tree in thee,
Which, Oh, shall strangers taste? Must I, alas,
Frame and enamel plate and drink in glass?
Chafe wax for others' seals? Break a colt's force
And leave him then, being made a ready horse?   30

ELEGY IX.
The Autumnal¹

No spring nor summer beauty hath such grace
  As I have seen in one autumnal face.
Young beauties force our love, and that's a rape;
  This doth but counsel, yet you cannot 'scape.
If 'twere a shame to love, here 'twere no shame;
  Affection here takes reverence's name.
Were her first years the golden age? That's true;
  But now they are gold oft tried and ever new.
That was her torrid and inflaming time,
  This is her tolerable tropic clime.   10
Fair eyes! Who asks more heat than comes from hence,
  He in a fever wishes pestilence.
Call not these wrinkles graves; if graves they were,
  They were Love's graves, for else he is nowhere.
Yet lies not Love dead here, but here doth sit
  Vowed to this trench, like an anchorit;²
And here till hers, which must be his death, come,
  He doth not dig a grave, but build a tomb.
Here dwells he; though he sojourn everywhere
  In progress,³ yet his standing-house is here—   20
Here where still evening is, not noon nor night,
  Where no voluptuousness, yet all delight.
In all her words, unto all hearers fit,
  You may at revels, you at council sit.
This is Love's timber, youth his underwood;
  There he, as wine in June, enrages blood,

ELEGY VII
  2 Hid away.

ELEGY IX
  1 This poem is generally thought to have been addressed
to Mrs. Magdalen Herbert.
  2 Anchorite, hermit.
  3 The royal progress was a journey of state made by the
king or queen.

Which then comes seasonabliest when our taste
  And appetite to other things is past.
Xerxes' strange Lydian love, the platan tree,
  Was loved for age, none being so large as she;   30
Or else because, being young, nature did bless
  Her youth with age's glory, barrenness.
If we love things long sought, age is a thing
  Which we are fifty years in compassing;
If transitory things, which soon decay,
  Age must be loveliest at the latest day.
But name not winter faces, whose skin's slack,
  Lank as an unthrift's purse, but a soul's sack;
Whose eyes seek light within, for all here's shade;
  Whose mouths are holes, rather worn out than
    made;   40
Whose every tooth to a several place is gone,
  To vex their souls at resurrectiòn:
Name not these living death's-heads unto me,
  For these, not ancient, but antique be.
I hate extremes, yet I had rather stay
  With tombs than cradles, to wear out a day.
Since such love's natural lation⁴ is, may still
  My love descend, and journey down the hill.
Not panting after growing beauties; so
  I shall ebb out with them who homeward go.   50

ELEGY XVI.
On His Mistress¹

By our first strange and fatal interview,
By all desires which thereof did ensue,
By our long starving hopes, by that remorse
Which my words' masculine persuasive force
Begot in thee, and by the memory
Of hurts which spies and rivals threatened me,
I calmly beg; but by thy father's wrath,
By all pains which want and divorcement hath,
I conjure thee; and all the oaths which I
And thou have sworn to seal joint constancy,   10
Here I unswear, and overswear them thus:
Thou shalt not love by ways so dangerous.

  4 Motion from one place to another. Lation is one of the
many astronomical terms used in Donne's poetry.

ELEGY XVI
  1 This elegy appeared for the first time in print in 1635.
The poem purports to be the poet's remonstrance with his
mistress when she desired to disguise herself as a page and go
to the Continent with him. It has been thought by some to
have been addressed to Anne More.

Temper, O fair love, love's impetuous rage,
Be my true mistress still, not my feigned page.
I'll go, and by thy kind leave, leave behind
Thee, only worthy to nurse in my mind
Thirst to come back. Oh, if thou die before,
My soul from other lands to thee shall soar.
Thy else almighty beauty cannot move
Rage from the seas, nor thy love teach them love,   20
Nor tame wild Boreas' harshness; thou hast read
How roughly he in pieces shiverèd
Fair Orithea, whom he swore he loved.
Fall ill or good, 'tis madness to have proved
Dangers unurged; feed on this flattery,
That absent lovers one in th' other be.
Dissemble nothing: not a boy, nor change
Thy body's habit, nor mind's; be not strange
To thyself only; all will spy in thy face
A blushing womanly discovering grace.   30
Richly clothed apes are called apes; and as soon
Eclipsed as bright, we call the moon the moon.
Men of France, changeable chameleons,
Spitals[2] of diseases, shops of fashions,
Love's fuelers, and the rightest company
Of players which upon the world's stage be,
Will quickly know thee, and no less, alas!
Th' indifferent Italian, as we pass
His warm land, well content to think thee page,
Will hunt thee with such lust and hideous rage   40
As Lot's fair guests were vexed.[3] But none of these,
Nor spongy hydroptic Dutch shall thee displease,
If thou stay here. Oh, stay here! for, for thee,
England is only a worthy gallery[4]
To walk in expectation, till from thence
Our greatest King call thee to his presènce.
When I am gone, dream me some happiness,
Nor let thy looks our long hid love confess,
Nor praise, nor dispraise me, nor bless nor curse
Openly love's force, nor in bed fright thy nurse   50
With midnight's startings, crying out, "Oh, oh,
Nurse, oh, my love is slain; I saw him go
O'er the white Alps alone; I saw him, I,
Assailed, fight, taken, stabbed, bleed, fall, and die."
Augur me better chance, except dread Jove
Think it enough for me to have had thy love.

ELEGY XVI
  2 Hospitals.   3 Genesis 19.
  4 Corridor, serving as waiting room or entrance hall.

ELEGY XIX.
[*To His Mistress Going to Bed*]

Come, Madam, come! All rest my powers defy;
Until I labor, I in labor lie.
The foe ofttimes, having the foe in sight,
Is tired with standing though he never fight.
Off with that girdle, like heaven's zone glittering,
But a far fairer world encompassing.
Unpin that spangled breastplate which you wear,
That th' eyes of busy fools may be stopped there.
Unlace yourself, for that harmonious chime
Tells me from you that now it is bedtime.   10
Off with that happy busk, which I envy,
That still can be, and still can stand so nigh.
Your gown going off, such beauteous state reveals
As when from flow'ry meads th' hill's shadow steals.
Off with that wiry coronet, and show
The hairy diadem which on you doth grow.
Now off with those shoes, and then safely tread
In this, love's hallowed temple, this soft bed.
In such white robes heaven's angels used to be
Received by men; thou, angel, bring'st with thee   20
A heaven like Mahomet's paradise; and though
Ill spirits walk in white, we eas'ly know
By this these angels from an evil sprite:
Those set our hairs, but these our flesh upright.
    License my roving hands, and let them go
Before, behind, between, above, below.
O my America, my new-found-land!
My kingdom, safeliest when with one man manned,
My mine of precious stones, my empery,
How blest am I in this discovering thee!   30
To enter in these bonds is to be free;
Then where my hand is set my seal shall be.
    Full nakedness, all joys are due to thee!
As souls unbodied, bodies unclothed must be
To taste whole joys. Gems which you women use
Are like Atlanta's balls, cast in men's views
That, when a fool's eye lighteth on a gem,
His earthly soul may covet theirs, not them.
Like pictures, or like books' gay coverings made
For laymen, are all women thus arrayed;   40
Themselves are mystic books, which only we,
Whom their imputed grace will dignify,
Must see revealed. Then, since that I may know,
As liberally as to a midwife show
Thyself; cast all, yea, this white linen hence;
There is no penance due to innocence.
    To teach thee, I am naked first; why then,
What need'st thou have more covering than a man?

SATIRES

SATIRE III.
[*Of Religion*]

Kind pity chokes my spleen; brave scorn forbids
Those tears to issue which swell my eyelids;
I must not laugh, nor weep sins, and be wise;
Can railing then cure these worn maladies?
Is not our mistress, fair Religion,
As worthy of all our soul's devotion
As virtue was to the first blinded age?
Are not heaven's joys as valiant to assuage
Lusts as earth's honor was to them? Alas,
As we do them in means, shall they surpass   10
Us in the end? and shall thy father's spirit
Meet blind philosophers in heaven, whose merit
Of strict life may be imputed faith, and hear
Thee, whom he taught so easy ways and near
To follow, damned? O, if thou dar'st, fear this;
This fear great courage and high valor is.
Dar'st thou aid mutinous Dutch, and dar'st thou lay
Thee in ships, wooden sepulchers, a prey
To leaders' rage, to storms, to shot, to dearth?
Dar'st thou dive seas, and dungeons of the earth?   20
Hast thou courageous fire to thaw the ice
Of frozen North discoveries? and thrice
Colder than salamanders, like divine
Children in th' oven,[1] fires of Spain and the Line,
Whose countries limbecs to our bodies be,
Canst thou for gain bear? and must every he
Which cries not "Goddess!" to thy mistress draw
Or eat thy poisonous words? Courage of straw!
O desperate coward, wilt thou seem bold and
To thy foes and His, who made thee to stand   30
Sentinel in His world's garrison, thus yield,
And for forbidden wars leave th' appointed field?
Know thy foes: the foul devil, whom thou
Strivest to please, for hate, not love, would allow
Thee fain his whole realm to be quit;[2] and as
The world's all parts wither away and pass,

So the world's self, thy other loved foe, is
In her decrepit wane, and thou, loving this,
Dost love a withered and worn strumpet; last,
Flesh (itself's death) and joys which flesh can taste 40
Thou lovest; and thy fair goodly soul, which doth
Give this flesh power to taste joy, thou dost loathe.
   Seek true Religion. Oh where? Mirreus,
Thinking her unhoused here and fled from us,
Seeks her at Rome; there, because he doth know
That she was there a thousand years ago.
He loves her rags so, as we here obey
The statecloth where the prince sat yesterday.
Crantz to such brave loves will not be enthralled,
But loves her only who at Geneva is called   50
Religion, plain, simple, sullen, young,
Contemptuous, yet unhandsome; as among
Lecherous humors, there is one that judges
No wenches wholesome but coarse country drudges.
Graius stays still at home here, and because
Some preachers, vile ambitious bawds, and laws,
Still new like fashions, bid him think that she
Which dwells with us is only perfect, he
Embraceth her whom his godfathers will
Tender to him, being tender, as wards still   60
Take such wives as their guardians offer, or
Pay values. Careless Phrygius doth abhor
All, because all cannot be good; as one,
Knowing some women whores, dares marry none.
Gracchus loves all as one, and thinks that so
As women do in divers countries go
In divers habits, yet are still one kind,
So doth, so is Religion; and this blind-
    ness too much light breeds. But unmovèd, thou
Of force must one, and forced but one allow,   70
And the right. Ask thy father which is she;
Let him ask his. Though Truth and Falsehood be
Near twins, yet Truth a little elder is.
Be busy to seek her; believe me this,
He's not of none, nor worst, that seeks the best.
To adore, or scorn an image, or protest,
May all be bad. Doubt wisely; in strange way
To stand inquiring right is not to stray;
To sleep, or run wrong, is. On a huge hill,
Cragged and steep, Truth stands, and he that will 80
Reach her, about must and about must go;
And what the hill's suddenness resists, win so.
Yet strive so that before age, death's twilight,
Thy soul rest, for none can work in that night.
To will implies delay, therefore now do:
Hard deeds, the body's pains; hard knowledge, too,

---

1 See below, The Calm, ll. 27–35.
2 Certain manuscripts read "to be rid." Professor Grierson
says, "Whether we read 'quit' or 'rid,' the construction is
difficult. The phrase seems to mean 'to be free of his whole
Realm'—an unparalleled use of either adjective."

The mind's endeavors reach; and mysteries
Are like the sun, dazzling, yet plain to all eyes.
Keep the truth which thou has found; men do not
    stand
In so ill case here, that God hath with His hand   90
Signed kings blank charters to kill whom they hate;
Nor are they vicars, but hangmen, to Fate.
Fool and wretch, wilt thou let thy soul be tied
To man's laws, by which she shall not be tried
At the last day? Oh, will it then boot thee
To say a Philip or a Gregory,
A Harry or a Martin,[3] taught thee this?
Is not this excuse for mere contraries
Equally strong? Cannot both sides say so?
That thou mayest rightly obey power, her bounds
    know;   100
Those past, her nature and name is changed; to be
Then humble to her is idolatry.
As streams are, power is; those blest flowers that
    dwell
At the rough stream's calm head thrive and do well,
But having left their roots, and themselves given
To the stream's tyrannous rage, alas, are driven
Through mills and rocks and woods, and at last,
    almost
Consumed in going, in the sea are lost.
So perish souls, which more choose men's unjust
Power from God claimed, than God himself to
    trust.   110

LETTERS TO SEVERAL PERSONAGES

THE CALM[1]

Our storm is past, and that storm's tyrannous rage
A stupid calm, but nothing it, doth 'suage.
The fable is inverted, and far more
A block[2] afflicts now than a stork before.

Storms chafe, and soon wear out themselves, or us;
In calms, heaven laughs to see us languish thus.
As steady as I can wish that my thoughts were,
Smooth as thy mistress' glass, or what shines there,
The sea is now; and as the isles which we
Seek, when we can move, our ships rooted be.   10
As water did in storms, now pitch runs out,
As lead, when a fired church becomes one spout;
And all our beauty, and our trim, decays
Like courts removing, or like ended plays.
The fighting place now seamen's rags supply,
And all the tackling is a frippery.[3]
No use of lanterns;[4] and in one place lay
Feathers and dust, today and yesterday.[5]
Earth's hollownesses, which the world's lungs are,
Have no more wind than the upper vault of air.   20
We can nor lost friends nor sought foes recover,
But meteor-like, save that we move not, hover.
Only the calenture[6] together draws
Dear friends, which meet dead in great fishes' jaws;
And on the hatches, as on altars, lies
Each one, his own priest and own sacrifice;
Who[7] live, that miracle do multiply
Where walkers in hot ovens do not die.[8]
If in despite of these we swim, that hath
No more refreshing than our brimstone bath;   30
But from the sea into the ship we turn,
Like parboiled wretches, on the coals to burn.
Like Bajazet[9] encaged, the shepherd's scoff,
Or like slack-sinewed Samson, his hair off,

friend, Christopher Brooke. The Calm, a companion piece, described the doldrums which the fleet encountered later in the tropics. The poem was probably addressed, like The Storm, to Christopher Brooke.

2 The "block" is the log in Æsop's fable of King Log and King Stork.

3 "A place where cast-off clothes are sold." (Oxford English Dictionary.)

4 Grierson explains the phrase as a reference to the lanterns in the high sterns of the ships, used to keep the fleet together, now quite unnecessary in the doldrums.

5 In Ben Jonson's Conversations with William Drummond of Hawthornden we are told that Jonson knew these lines by heart.

6 A tropical fever or delirium in which sailors leap into the sea.

7 Those who.

8 A reference to the Biblical story of the three Hebrews in the fiery furnace (Daniel 3).

9 A reference to Marlowe's Tamburlaine, in which play Bajazet, the emperor of the Turks, is imprisoned in a cage by Tamburlaine.

SATIRE III

3 Philip II of Spain, the great defender of the Roman Catholic faith; Pope Gregory XIII or XIV; Henry VIII (Harry); Martin Luther.

THE CALM

1 Donne joined the Earl of Essex in the unsuccessful Islands Expedition in 1597, which was handicapped at the outset by a violent storm. Donne described the storm realistically in his verse letter, The Storm, which he addressed to his

Languish our ships. Now, as a myriad
Of ants durst the emperor's loved snake invade,[10]
The crawling galleys, sea-gaols, finny chips,
Might brave our pinnaces, now bed-rid ships.
Whether a rotten state, and hope of gain,
Or to disuse me from the queasy pain   40
Of being beloved, and loving, or the thirst
Of honor, or fair death, out-pushed me first,
I lose my end; for here, as well as I,
A desperate may live, and a coward die.
Stag, dog, and all which from or towards flies,
Is paid with life or prey, or doing, dies.
Fate grudges us all, and doth subtly lay
A scourge, 'gainst which we all forget to pray;
He that at sea prays for more wind, as well
Under the poles may beg cold, heat in hell.   50
What are we then? How little more, alas,
Is man now than before he was! He was
Nothing; for us, we are for nothing fit;
Chance or ourselves still disproportion it.
We have no power, no will, no sense. I lie;
I should not then thus feel this misery.

DIVINE POEMS

HOLY SONNETS

1

Thou hast made me, and shall Thy work decay?
Repair me now, for now mine end doth haste;
I run to death, and death meets me as fast,
And all my pleasures are like yesterday.
I dare not move my dim eyes any way,
Despair behind, and death before doth cast
Such terror, and my feeble flesh doth waste
By sin in it, which it towards hell doth weigh.

Only Thou art above, and when towards Thee
By Thy leave I can look, I rise again;   10
But our old subtle foe so tempteth me
That not one hour myself I can sustain.
Thy grace may wing me to prevent his art,
And Thou like adamant[1] draw mine iron heart.

2

As due by many titles I resign
Myself to Thee, O God; first I was made
By Thee, and for Thee, and when I was decayed
Thy blood bought that, the which before was Thine;
I am Thy sun, made with Thyself to shine,
Thy servant, whose pains Thou hast still repaid,
Thy sheep, Thine image, and, till I betrayed
Myself, a temple of Thy spirit divine;
Why doth the devil then usurp on me?
Why doth he steal, nay ravish that's Thy right?   10
Except Thou rise and for Thine own work fight,
Oh I shall soon despair when I do see
That Thou lov'st mankind well, yet wilt not choose me,
And Satan hates me, yet is loath to lose me.

5

I am a little world made cunningly
Of elements, and an angelic sprite;[1]
But black sin hath betrayed to endless night
My world's both parts, and, oh, both parts must die.
You which beyond that heaven which was most high
Have found new spheres, and of new lands can write,
Pour new seas in mine eyes, that so I might
Drown my world with my weeping earnestly,
Or wash it if it must be drowned no more:[2]
But oh it must be burnt![3] Alas, the fire   10
Of lust and envy have burnt it heretofore,
And made it fouler; let their flames retire,
And burn me, O Lord, with a fiery zeal[4]
Of Thee and Thy house, which doth in eating heal.

THE CALM
   10 According to Suetonius's Lives of the Cæsars, the emperor Tiberius had a pet snake which was devoured by ants
as the emperor was once about to enter Rome. The circumstance was accepted as a warning that he should beware the
fury of the mob, and Tiberius turned back without entering
the city.

HOLY SONNET 1
   1 The loadstone or magnet.

HOLY SONNET 5
   1 Spirit.
   2 A reference to the Divine promise (Genesis 9:11) that the
earth will not again be destroyed by a flood.
   3 That is, at the Day of Judgment. See II Peter 3:5–7.
   4 Compare Psalm 69:9, "For the zeal of thine house hath
eaten me up."

6

This is my play's last scene, here heavens appoint
My pilgrimage's last mile; and my race,
Idly yet quickly run, hath this last pace,
My span's last inch, my minute's latest point,
And gluttonous death will instantly unjoint
My body and soul, and I shall sleep a space;
But my ever-waking part shall see that face
Whose fear already shakes my every joint;
Then, as my soul to heaven her first seat takes flight,
And earth-born body in the earth shall dwell,   10
So fall my sins that all may have their right
To where they are bred and would press me, to hell.
Impute me righteous, thus purged of evil,
For thus I leave the world, the flesh, the devil.

7

At the round earth's imagined corners [1] blow
Your trumpets, angels, and arise, arise
From death, you numberless infinities
Of souls, and to your scattered bodies go;
All whom the flood did, and fire shall o'erthrow;
All whom war, dearth, age, agues, tyrannies,
Despair, law, chance, hath slain, and you whose eyes
Shall behold God, and never taste death's woe. [2]
But let them sleep, Lord, and me mourn a space,
For, if above all these, my sins abound,   10
'Tis late to ask abundance of Thy grace,
When we are there; here on this lowly ground,
Teach me how to repent; for that's as good
As if Thou hadst sealed my pardon, with Thy blood.

10

Death, be not proud, though some have callèd thee
Mighty and dreadful, for thou art not so;
For those whom thou think'st thou dost overthrow
Die not, poor Death, nor yet canst thou kill me.
From rest and sleep, which but thy pictures be,
Much pleasure, then from thee much more must flow,
And soonest our best men with thee do go,
Rest of their bones and souls' delivery.

HOLY SONNET 7
1 Donne has in mind Revelation 7:1: "And after these things, I saw four angels standing on the four corners of the earth, holding the four winds of the earth."
2 Compare St. Luke 9:27: "I tell you of a truth, there be some standing here which shall not taste of death till they see the kingdom of God."

Thou art slave to fate, chance, kings, and desperate
    men,
And dost with poison, war, and sickness dwell,   10
And poppy, or charms can make us sleep as well,
And better than thy stroke; why swell'st thou then?
One short sleep past, we wake eternally,
And Death shall be no more; Death, thou shalt die.

13

What if this present were the world's last night?
Mark in thy heart, O Soul, where thou dost dwell,
The picture of Christ crucified, and tell
Whether that countenance can thee affright;
Tears in his eyes quench the amazing light,
Blood fills his frowns, which from his pierced head fell.
And can that tongue adjudge thee unto hell,
Which prayed forgiveness for his foes' fierce spite?
No, no; but as in my idolatry
I said to all my profane mistresses,   10
"Beauty, of pity, foulness only is
A sign of rigor," so I say to thee,
"To wicked spirits are horrid shapes assigned,
This beauteous form assures a piteous mind."

14

Batter my heart, three-personed God; for You
As yet but knock, breathe, shine, and seek to mend;
That I may rise, and stand, o'erthrow me, and bend
Your force, to break, blow, burn, and make me new.
I, like an usurped town to another due,
Labor to admit You, but oh! to no end;
Reason, Your viceroy in me, me should defend,
But is captived and proves weak or untrue.
Yet dearly I love You, and would be lovèd fain,
But am betrothed unto Your enemy.   10
Divorce me, untie, or break that knot again,
Take me to You, imprison me, for I
Except You enthrall me, never shall be free,
Nor ever chaste, except You ravish me.

17

Since she whom I loved hath paid her last debt
To Nature and to hers, and my good is dead,
And her soul early into Heaven ravishèd,
Wholly on heavenly things my mind is set.
Here the admiring her my mind did whet
To seek Thee God, so streams do show their head;
But though I have found Thee, and Thou my thirst hast
    fed,
A holy thirsty dropsy melts me yet.

But why should I beg more love, whenas Thou
Dost woo my soul, for hers offering all Thine,
And dost not only fear lest I allow
My love to saints and angels, things divine,
But in Thy tender jealousy dost doubt
Lest the world, flesh, yea devil put Thee out?

18

Show me, dear Christ, Thy spouse so bright and clear.
What! is it she which on the other shore
Goes richly painted? or which, robbed and tore,
Laments and mourns in Germany and here?
Sleeps she a thousand, then peeps up one year?
Is she self-truth, and errs? now new, now outwore?
Doth she, and did she, and shall she evermore
On one, on seven, or on no hill appear?
Dwells she with us, or like adventuring knights
First travel we to seek, and then make love?   10
Betray, kind husband, Thy spouse to our sights,
And let mine amorous soul court Thy mild dove,
Who is most true and pleasing to Thee then
When she is embraced and open to most men.

GOODFRIDAY, 1613, RIDING WESTWARD

Let man's soul be a sphere, and then, in this,
The intelligence[1] that moves, devotion is,
And as the other spheres, by being grown
Subject to foreign motions, lose their own,
And being by others hurried every day,
Scarce in a year their natural form obey,
Pleasure or business, so, our souls admit
For their first mover, and are whirled by it.
Hence is't, that I am carried towards the west   9
This day, when my soul's form bends towards the east.
There I should see a sun, by rising, set,
And by that setting endless day beget:
But that Christ on this cross did rise and fall,
Sin had eternally benighted all.
Yet dare I almost be glad I do not see
That spectacle, of too much weight for me.
Who sees God's face, that is self-life, must die;
What a death were it then to see God die?
It made His own lieutenant, Nature, shrink;
It made His footstool crack, and the sun wink.   20

Could I behold those hands which span the poles,
And tune all spheres at once, pierced with those holes?
Could I behold that endless height which is
Zenith to us, and our antipodes,
Humbled below us? Or that blood which is
The seat of all our souls, if not of His,
Made dirt of dust, or that flesh which was worn
By God, for His apparel, ragg'd and torn?
If on these things I durst not look, durst I
Upon His miserable mother cast mine eye,   30
Who was God's partner here, and furnished thus
Half of that sacrifice which ransomed us?
Though these things, as I ride, be from mine eye,
They are present yet unto my memory,
For that looks towards them; and Thou look'st towards
          me,
O Saviour, as Thou hang'st upon the tree.
I turn my back to Thee but to receive
Corrections, till Thy mercies bid Thee leave.
O think me worth Thine anger; punish me;
Burn off my rusts and my deformity;   40
Restore Thine image so much, by Thy grace,
That Thou may'st know me, and I'll turn my face.

A HYMN TO CHRIST, AT THE AUTHOR'S LAST GOING INTO GERMANY[1]

In what torn ship soever I embark,
That ship shall be my emblem of Thy Ark;
What sea soever swallow me, that flood
Shall be to me an emblem of Thy blood;
Though Thou with clouds of anger do disguise
Thy face, yet through that mask I know those eyes,
     Which, though they turn away sometimes,
          They never will despise.

I sacrifice this island unto Thee,
And all whom I loved there, and who loved me;   10
When I have put our seas 'twixt them and me,
Put Thou Thy sea[2] betwixt my sins and Thee.
As the tree's sap doth seek the root below
In winter, in my winter now I go
     Where none but Thee, the eternal root
          Of true love I may know.

GOODFRIDAY, 1613
   1 According to beliefs inherited from the Middle Ages,
each of the cosmic spheres was guided by an angel, or
"intelligence."

A HYMN TO CHRIST
   1 The date of the voyage and the hymn was 1619.
   2 The blood of Christ.

Nor Thou nor Thy religion dost control
The amorousness of an harmonious soul,
But Thou would'st have that love Thyself: as Thou
Art jealous, Lord, so I am jealous now;   20
Thou lov'st not, till from loving more, Thou free
My soul; whoever gives, takes liberty:
    O, if Thou car'st not whom I love,
      Alas, Thou lov'st not me.

Seal then this bill of my divorce to all
On whom those fainter beams of love did fall;
Marry those loves, which in youth scattered be
On Fame, Wit, Hopes (false mistresses) to Thee.
Churches are best for prayer that have least light:
To see God only, I go out of sight;   30
    And to 'scape stormy days, I choose
      An everlasting night.

HYMN TO GOD, MY GOD, IN MY SICKNESS[1]

Since I am coming to that holy room
  Where, with Thy choir of saints for evermore
I shall be made Thy music, as I come
    I tune the instrument here at the door,
    And what I must do then, think here before.

Whilst my physicians by their love are grown
  Cosmographers, and I their map, who lie
Flat on this bed, that by them may be shown
    That this is my southwest discovery,
    Per fretum febris,[2] by these straits to die,   10

I joy that in these straits I see my west;
  For though their currents yield return to none,
What shall my west hurt me? As west and east
    In all flat maps[3] (and I am one) are one,
    So death doth touch the resurrection.

Is the Pacific Sea my home? Or are
  The eastern riches? Is Jerusalem?

Anyan,[4] and Magellan, and Gibraltàr,
  All straits, and none but straits, are ways to them,
Whether where Japhet dwelt, or Cham, or Shem.[5]

We think that Paradise and Calvary,   21
  Christ's cross and Adam's tree, stood in one place;
Look Lord, and find both Adams met in me;
  As the first Adam's sweat surrounds my face,
  May the last Adam's[6] blood my soul embrace.

So, in His purple wrapped receive me Lord,
  By these His thorns give me His other crown;
And as to others' souls I preached Thy word,
  Be this my text, my sermon to mine own:
  Therefore, that He may raise, the Lord throws
    down.   30

A HYMN TO GOD THE FATHER[1]

Wilt Thou forgive that sin where I begun,
  Which is my sin, though it were done before?
Wilt Thou forgive that sin through which I run,
  And do run still, though still I do deplore?
    When Thou hast done, Thou hast not done,
      For I have more.

Wilt Thou forgive that sin which I have won
  Others to sin? and make my sin their door?
Wilt Thou forgive that sin which I did shun
  A year, or two, but wallowed in a score?   10
    When Thou hast done, Thou hast not done,
      For I have more.

I have a sin of fear, that when I have spun
  My last thread, I shall perish on the shore;
But swear by Thyself, that at my death Thy Son
  Shall shine as He shines now, and heretofore;
    And, having done that, Thou hast done,[2]
      I fear no more.

4 Bering Strait.
5 The three sons of Noah, whose issue repopulated the world after the Flood. (See Genesis 9:18.)
6 Christ. (See I Corinthians 15:22, 45.)

HYMN TO GOD
1 Walton says that this poem was written eight days before the death of Donne. It does not appear in the 1633 edition, and was first printed in the edition of 1635.
2 Through the strait of fever. Donne is indulging in a pun on the word *fretum*, which means both *strait* and *raging*.
3 On a flat map of the world the points on the right edge correspond to those on the left.

A HYMN TO GOD THE FATHER
1 This hymn was written during a serious illness when Donne was about fifty. It was, as Walton tells us, set to music and sung in Donne's hearing in St. Paul's. The score is given in Grierson's edition of Donne, Oxford Press, 1912, Vol. II, pp. 252–54.
2 Here and elsewhere in the poem a pun is undoubtedly intended on the poet's name, which is pronounced "done."

Ben Jonson

[1572–1637]

AMID the imposing creations of Ben Jonson's life—the great comedies, the historically important tragedies, the significant critical utterances—his lyric poems occupy a special position. It is in his lyrics, achieved with an artistry so perfect as to leave an impression of effortlessness, that he is most alive for our time. Such jewels as "A Celebration of Charis," "Drink to me only with thine eyes," the epitaph "On my First Son," and almost any of the songs from the plays constitute a permanent testimony to the universal power of the classical ideal in art. The example of Jonson was immensely important in forging the style of the characteristic lyric of the first half of the seventeenth century: he inspired the whole group of gifted minor writers—Randolph, Cartwright, Godolphin, Suckling, and the rest—who delighted in calling themselves "the Tribe of Ben"; he bequeathed to his greatest "son," Robert Herrick, the classical sense of form which was an essential part of the younger poet's achievement; most importantly, he exerted an influence which combined with that of his great opposite Donne to supply a poetic idiom to artists as different as Carew, Lovelace, and Marvell.

Jonson may be compared with Donne not only in the significance of his innovations in the style of the lyric but also, to some degree, in the direction which those innovations took. Like Donne, Jonson curbed the sensuous fancy of the Elizabethan manner, introduced a crisper, less languorous rhythm, and achieved a more specifically intellectual type of structure. Despite these similarities, however, the differences between the two great Jacobean lyrists are more striking. Jonson remarked to Drummond of Hawthornden that Donne, although "the first poet in the world in some things," was one who "for not keeping of accent deserved hanging." In Jonson's own metrical practice, despite his clipped lines and his free use of anapestic substitutions, the Elizabethan accent is unmistakably kept. And "wit"—for Donne the capacity for forging relationships among the disparate phenomena of this plural world—is for Jonson essentially the ability to give terse and memorable expression to generally acknowledged truths—"what oft was thought but ne'er so well expressed."

The quotation from Pope is appropriate to a description of Jonson, for this first of English literary dictators was above all a classicist, an artist who gave expression not to the infinite aspirations and immortal longings of the race but rather to its practically attainable ambitions—human love, good friends, and the kind of workable virtue which is celebrated in "A Pindaric Ode to the Immortal Memory . . . of Sir Lucius Cary and Sir H. Morison." His is a limited, perhaps an earthbound, vision, but it is not an ignoble one. After the Baroque splendor of Donne and Crashaw had faded of its own intensity, Jonson's vision, like his style, had its long hour of triumph—in the poetry of Dryden and Pope and the criticism of Dr. Johnson. Together with his master Horace he provided Augustan England with its conception of the aim and nature of lyric poetry.

BEN JONSON, ed. C. H. Herford and P. Simpson, 11 vols. (Oxford, 1925–52). Definitive for the poetry as well as the prose.
————. *Poems*, ed. B. H. Newdigate (Oxford, 1936).
S. A. TANNENBAUM. *Ben Jonson: A Concise Bibliography* (New York, 1938).
E. C. DUNN. *Ben Jonson's Art* (Northampton, Mass., 1925).
K. A. McEUEN. *Classical Influences upon the Tribe of Ben* (Cedar Rapids, Iowa, 1939).
G. B. JOHNSTON. *Ben Jonson, Poet* (New York, 1945).
W. TRIMPI. *Ben Jonson's Poems: A Study of the Plain Style* (Stanford, 1962).

FROM

THE WORKS OF BENJAMIN JONSON [1616]

EPIGRAMS

TO WILLIAM CAMDEN

Camden,[1] most reverend head, to whom I owe
   All that I am in arts, all that I know
(How nothing's that!); to whom my country owes
   The great renown and name wherewith she goes;[2]
Than thee the age sees not that thing more grave,
   More high, more holy, that she more would crave.
What name, what skill, what faith hast thou in things!
   What sight in searching the most antique springs!
What weight and what authority in thy speech!
   Man scarce can make that doubt, but thou canst
      teach.   10
Pardon free truth and let thy modesty,
   Which conquers all, be once overcome by thee.
Many of thine this better could than I,
   But for their powers accept my piety.

ON MY FIRST DAUGHTER

Here lies, to each her parents' ruth,
Mary, the daughter of their youth;[1]
Yet all heaven's gifts being heaven's due,
It makes the father less to rue.
At six months' end she parted hence
With safety of her innocence;
Whose soul heaven's queen, whose name she bears,
In comfort of her mother's tears,
Hath placed amongst her virgin-train:
Where while that severed doth remain,
This grave partakes the fleshly birth,
Which cover lightly, gentle earth!

TO JOHN DONNE

Donne, the delight of Phœbus and each muse,
   Who, to thy one, all other brains refuse;
Whose every work of thy most early wit
   Came forth example, and remains so yet;
Longer a-knowing than most wits do live,
   And which no affection praise enough can give!
To it, thy language, letters, arts, best life,
   Which might with half mankind maintain a strife;
All which I mean to praise, and yet I would,
   But leave, because I cannot as I should.

TO WILLIAM CAMDEN
1 One of the most renowned of English antiquaries, and master of Westminster School when Jonson was there as a student.
2 A reference to Camden's chief work, the Latin poem *Britannia*, published in 1586, and translated by P. Holland in 1610.

ON MY FIRST DAUGHTER
1 From an entry in the parish register of St. Martin's in the Fields in London, it is supposed that Jonson's daughter died of the plague in November, 1593.

ON MY FIRST SON[1]

Farewell, thou child of my right hand, and joy;
　My sin was too much hope of thee, loved boy:
Seven years thou wert lent to me, and I thee pay,
　Exacted by thy fate, on the just day.
Oh, could I lose all father now! for why
Will man lament the state he should envy—
To have so soon 'scaped world's and flesh's rage,
　And if no other misery, yet age?
Rest in soft peace, and asked, say, "Here doth lie
　Ben Jonson his best piece of poetry;
For whose sake henceforth all his vows be such
　As what he loves may never like too much."

ON LUCY, COUNTESS OF BEDFORD[1]

This morning, timely rapt with holy fire,
　I thought to form unto my zealous muse
What kind of creature I could most desire
　To honor, serve, and love, as poets use.
I meant to make her fair, and free,[2] and wise,
　Of greatest blood, and yet more good than great;
I meant the day-star should not brighter rise,
　Nor lend like influence from his lucent seat;
I meant she should be courteous, facile, sweet,
　Hating that solemn vice of greatness, pride;　10
I meant each softest virtue there should meet,
　Fit in that softer bosom to reside.
Only a learned and a manly soul
　I purposed her; that should, with even powers,
The rock,[3] the spindle, and the shears control
　Of destiny, and spin her own free hours.
Such when I meant to feign, and wished to see,
　My muse bade, "Bedford write," and that was
　　she.

AN EPITAPH ON S. P., A CHILD OF QUEEN ELIZABETH'S CHAPEL[1]

Weep with me, all you that read
　This little story;
And know, for whom a tear you shed
　Death's self is sorry.
'Twas a child that so did thrive
　In grace and feature,
As heaven and nature seemed to strive
　Which owned the creature.
Years he numbered scarce thirteen
　When fates turned cruel,　　　　　10
Yet three filled zodiacs[2] had he been
　The stage's jewel;
And did act, what now we moan,
　Old men so duly,
As, sooth, the Parcæ[3] thought him one,
　He played so truly.
So, by error, to his fate
　They all consented;
But viewing him since, alas, too late!
　They have repented,　　　　　20
And have sought, to give new birth,
　In baths[4] to steep him;
But being so much too good for earth,
　Heaven vows to keep him.

EPITAPH ON ELIZABETH, L. H.[1]

Wouldst thou hear what man can say
　In a little? Reader, stay.

AN EPITAPH

1 In all modern books on the Elizabethan stage and in commentaries on this poem, it has been assumed that the initials "S. P." stand for "Salathiel" Pavy. Dr. Gerald Eades Bentley, of the University of Chicago, in an article entitled "A Good Name Lost" in the Times Literary Supplement (London) for May 30, 1942, offers conclusive evidence that the name of the boy-actor was not Salathiel but Solomon (or Salomon) Pavy. The boy had acted in two of Jonson's plays.
2 That is, the boy had acted for three full years.
3 The three Fates, who determine the duration of human life.
4 A reference to the story of Æson, the aged father of Jason, hero of the expedition for the Golden Fleece, who was made young again by a magic bath administered by Medea, wife of Jason.

EPITAPH ON ELIZABETH

1 "Elizabeth, L. H." has not been identified. It has been suggested that she may have been Elizabeth, Lady Hatton, wife of Sir Edward Coke.

ON MY FIRST SON

1 Jonson's son was born in 1596 and died of the plague in 1603. The poet, who was absent at the time of the boy's death, had a vision of his son in which, as he described it to William Drummond of Hawthornden, the lad appeared "of a manly shape," and of that growth "he shall be at the resurrection."

ON LUCY

1 The Countess of Bedford, one of the most celebrated patronesses of her day, was the inspiration of many poems by Jonson, Donne, and other contemporary poets.
2 Generous.　　　　　　　　　　　　　3 Distaff.

Underneath this stone doth lie
As much beauty as could die;
Which in life did harbor give
To more virtue than doth live.
If at all she had a fault,
Leave it buried in this vault.
One name was Elizabeth;
The other, let it sleep with death:
Fitter, where it died, to tell,
Than that it lived at all. Farewell!

THE FOREST

TO PENSHURST[1]

Thou art not, Penshurst, built to envious show
    Of touch[2] or marble, nor canst boast a row
Of polished pillars, or a roof of gold;
    Thou hast no lantern[3] whereof tales are told,
Or stairs or courts; but stand'st an ancient pile,
    And these, grudged at, art reverenced the while.
Thou joy'st in better marks, of soil, of air,
    Of wood, of water; therein thou art fair.
Thou hast thy walks for health as well as sport;
    Thy mount, to which the Dryads do resort,   10
Where Pan and Bacchus their high feasts have made
    Beneath the broad beech, and the chestnut shade,
That taller tree, which of a nut was set
    At his great birth,[4] where all the muses met.
There in the writhed bark are cut the names
    Of many a sylvan, taken with his flames;
And thence the ruddy satyrs oft provoke
    The lighter fauns to reach thy Lady's Oak.
Thy copse, too, named of Gamage,[5] thou hast there,
    That never fails to serve thee seasoned deer   20

When thou wouldst feast, or exercise thy friends.
    The lower land, that to the river bends,
Thy sheep, thy bullocks, kine, and calves do feed;
    The middle grounds thy mares and horses breed.
Each bank doth yield thee conies; and the tops,
    Fertile of wood, Ashore and Sidney's copse,
To crown thy open table, doth provide
    The purpled pheasant with the speckled side;
The painted partridge lies in every field,
    And, for thy mess, is willing to be killed.   30
And if the high-swollen Medway[6] fail thy dish,
    Thou hast thy ponds that pay thee tribute fish,
Fat aged carps that run into thy net,
    And pikes, now weary their own kind to eat,
As loth the second draught or cast to stay,
    Officiously at first themselves betray;
Bright eels that emulate them, and leap on land
    Before the fisher, or into his hand.
Then hath thy orchard fruit, thy garden flowers
    Fresh as the air, and new as are the hours.   40
The early cherry, with the later plum,
    Fig, grape, and quince, each in his time doth come;
The blushing apricot and woolly peach
    Hang on thy walls, that every child may reach.
And though thy walls be of the country stone,
    They are reared with no man's ruin, no man's groan;
There's none that dwell about them wish them down,
    But all come in, the farmer and the clown,
And no one empty-handed, to salute
    Thy lord and lady, though they have no suit.[7]   50
Some bring a capon, some a rural cake,
    Some nuts, some apples, some that think they make
The better cheeses bring 'em, or else send
    By their ripe daughters whom they would
        commend
This way to husbands, and whose baskets bear
    An emblem of themselves in plum or pear.
But what can this, more than express their love,
    Add to thy free provisions, far above
The need of such, whose liberal board doth flow
    With all that hospitality doth know?   60
Where comes no guest but is allowed to eat,
    Without his fear, and of thy lord's own meat;

TO PENSHURST

1 The home of the Sidney family in Kent. The head of the household at this time was Sir Robert Sidney, Viscount Lisle. He was the younger brother of Sir Philip Sidney and the father of Lady Dorothy Sidney, who was celebrated under the name of Sacharissa by the poet Waller. See Waller's poem, At Penshurst, p. 875.

2 Touchstone, a fine-grained dark stone.

3 A small tower on top of a dome or roof with glazed sides to admit light.

4 A chestnut tree, which stood until the end of the eighteenth century, was planted to commemorate the birth of Sir Philip Sidney in 1554.

5 Sir Robert Sidney had married, in rather romantic circumstances, Barbara Gamage, one of the wealthiest heiresses of the day. Her ability as a housekeeper is indicated throughout the poem, and particularly in ll. 76–88.

6 The river on which the estate is situated.

7 Petition, request for favors.

Where the same beer and bread, and self-same wine
  That is his lordship's shall be also mine.
And I not fain to sit, as some this day
  At great men's tables, and yet dine away.
Here no man tells [8] my cups, nor, standing by
  A waiter doth my gluttony envỳ,
But gives me what I call, and lets me eat;
  He knows below he shall find plenty of meat.   70
Thy tables hoard not up for the next day,
  Nor when I take my lodging need I pray
For fire or lights or livery; all is there
  As if thou then wert mine, or I reigned here;
There's nothing I can wish, for which I stay.
  That found King James, when hunting late this way
With his brave son, the prince, they saw thy fires
  Shine bright on every hearth as the desires
Of thy Penates had been set on flame
  To entertain them, or the country came   80
With all their zeal to warm their welcome here.
  What great I will not say, but sudden cheer
Didst thou then make 'em! and what praise was heaped
  On thy good lady then! who therein reaped
The just reward of her high housewifery;
  To have her linen, plate, and all things nigh
When she was far, and not a room but dressed
  As if it had expected such a guest!
These, Penshurst, are thy praise, and yet not all.
  Thy lady's noble, fruitful, chaste withal;   90
His children thy great lord may call his own,
  A fortune in this age but rarely known.
They are and have been taught religion; thence
  Their gentler spirits have sucked innocence.
Each morn and even they are taught to pray
  With the whole household, and may every day
Read, in their virtuous parents' noble parts,
  The mysteries of manners, arms, and arts.
Now, Penshurst, they that will proportion thee
  With other edifices when they see   100
Those proud ambitious heaps and nothing else,
May say, their lords have built, but thy lord dwells.

TO PENSHURST
8 Counts.

SONG, THAT WOMEN ARE BUT MEN'S SHADOWS

Follow a shadow, it still flies you;
  Seem to fly it, it will pursue:
So court a mistress, she denies you;
  Let her alone, she will court you.
Say, are not women truly, then,
  Styled but the shadows of us men?
At morn and even, shades are longest;
  At noon they are or short or none:
So men at weakest, they are strongest,
  But grant us perfect, they're not known.
Say, are not women truly, then,
  Styled but the shadows of us men?

SONG, TO CELIA [1]

Drink to me only with thine eyes,
  And I will pledge with mine;
Or leave a kiss but in the cup,
  And I'll not look for wine.
The thirst that from the soul doth rise
  Doth ask a drink divine;
But might I of Jove's nectar sup,
  I would not change for thine.
I sent thee late a rosy wreath,
  Not so much honoring thee   10
As giving it a hope, that there
  It could not withered be.
But thou thereon didst only breathe,
  And sent'st it back to me;
Since when it grows, and smells, I swear,
  Not of itself but thee.

SONG, TO CELIA
  1 This, the best known of Jonson's songs, is, like others of his lyrics, based on classical originals. It is a series of paraphrases of passages in four letters of Philostratus, a Greek rhetorician of the second and third centuries A.D. It has been conjectured that this and the other songs to Celia were written about the same time, and were addressed to some lady of Jonson's acquaintance.

FROM

THE WORKS OF BENJAMIN JONSON [1640-41]

UNDERWOODS

A HYMN ON THE NATIVITY OF MY SAVIOUR

I sing the birth was born tonight,
The Author both of life and light,
   The angels so did sound it;
And like the ravished shepherds said,
Who saw the light, and were afraid,
   Yet searched, and true they found it.

The Son of God, the eternal King,
That did us all salvation bring,
   And freed the soul from danger;
He whom the whole world could not take,   10
The Word which heaven and earth did make,
   Was now laid in a manger.

The Father's wisdom willed it so,
The Son's obedience knew no No,
   Both wills were in one stature;
And as that wisdom had decreed,
The Word was now made Flesh indeed,
   And took on him our nature.

What comfort by Him do we win,
Who made Himself the price of sin,   20
   To make us heirs of glory!
To see this Babe, all innocence,
A Martyr born in our defense,
   Can man forget this story?

A CELEBRATION OF CHARIS IN TEN LYRIC PIECES[1]

1. *His Excuse for Loving*

Let it not your wonder move,
Less your laughter, that I love.

Though I now write fifty years,
I have had, and have, my peers;
Poets though divine are men,
Some have loved as old again.
And it is not always face,
Clothes, or fortune, gives the grace,
Or the feature, or the youth;
But the language and the truth,   10
With the ardor and the passion,
Gives the lover weight and fashion.
If you then will read the story,
First prepare you to be sorry
That you never knew till now
Either whom to love, or how;
But be glad, as soon with me,
When you know that this is she
Of whose beauty it was sung:
She shall make the old man young,   20
Keep the middle age at stay,
And let nothing high decay;
Till she be the reason why
All the world for love may die.

4. *Her Triumph*[1]

See the chariot at hand here of love,
   Wherein my lady rideth!
Each that draws is a swan or a dove,
   And well the car love guideth.
As she goes, all hearts do duty
   Unto her beauty;
And, enamored, do wish, so they might
   But enjoy such a sight,
That they still were to run by her side,
Through swords, through seas, whither she would
   ride.   10

Do but look on her eyes; they do light
   All that love's world compriseth!
Do but look on her hair; it is bright
   As love's star when it riseth!

A CELEBRATION OF CHARIS
  1 Some of Jonson's finest lyrics were inspired by "Charis," who, if she was a real woman, has not been identified.

HER TRIUMPH
  1 These stanzas also appear as a song in Jonson's play, The Devil Is an Ass.

Do but mark, her forehead's smoother
   Than words that soothe her!
And from her arched brows, such a grace
   Sheds itself through the face,
As alone there triumphs to the life
All the gain, all the good, of the elements' strife.   20

Have you seen but a bright lily grow
   Before rude hands have touched it?
Ha' you marked but the fall o' the snow
   Before the soil hath smutched it?
Ha' you felt the wool of beaver
   Or swan's down ever?
Or have smelt o' the bud o' the brier?
   Or the nard² in the fire?
Or have tasted the bag of the bee?
O so white, O so soft, O so sweet is she!   30

A SONG

O do not wanton with those eyes,
   Lest I be sick with seeing;
Nor cast them down, but let them rise,
   Lest shame destroy their being.
O be not angry with those fires,
   For then their threats will kill me;
Nor look too kind on my desires,
   For then my hopes will spill me.
O do not steep them in thy tears,
   For so will sorrow slay me;
Nor spread them as distract with fears,
   Mine own enough betray me.

AN ELEGY

Though beauty be the mark of praise,
   And yours of whom I sing be such
   As not the world can praise too much,
Yet is 't your virtue now I raise.

A virtue, like allay,¹ so gone
   Throughout your form as, though that move
   And draw and conquer all men's love,
This subjects you to love of one.

Wherein you triumph yet; because
   'Tis of yourself, and that you use   10
   The noblest freedom, not to choose
Against or faith or honor's laws.

But who should less expect from you,
   In whom alone Love lives again,
   By whom he is restored to men,
And kept, and bred, and brought up true?

His falling temples you have reared,
   The withered garlands ta'en away;
    His altars kept from the decay
That envy wished, and nature feared;   20

And on them burn so chaste a flame,
   With so much loyalties' expense,
   As love, t' acquit such excellence,
Is gone himself into your name.

And you are he; the deity
   To whom all lovers are designed
   That would their better objects find;
Among which faithful troop am I.

Who, as an offspring at your shrine,
   Have sung this hymn, and here entreat   30
   One spark of your diviner heat
To light upon a love of mine.

Which, if it kindle not, but scant
   Appear, and that to shortest view,
   Yet give me leave t' adore in you
What I in her am grieved to want.

AN ODE TO HIMSELF

Where dost thou careless lie,
   Buried in ease and sloth?
Knowledge that sleeps doth die;
   And this security,¹
    It is the common moth
That eats on wits and arts, and destroys them both.

HER TRIUMPH
  2 An aromatic balsam.

AN ELEGY
  1 Alloy.

AN ODE TO HIMSELF
  1 Carelessness.

Are all the Aonian springs[2]
  Dried up? Lies Thespia[3] waste?
Doth Clarius' harp[4] want strings,
That not a nymph now sings?   10
  Or droop they as disgraced,
To see their seats and bowers by chattering pies[5]
    defaced?

If hence thy silence be,
  As 'tis too just a cause,
Let this thought quicken thee:
Minds that are great and free
  Should not on fortune pause;
'Tis crown enough to virtue still, her own applause.

What though the greedy fry
  Be taken with false baits   20
Of worded balladry,
And think it poesy?
  They die with their conceits,
And only piteous scorn upon their folly waits.

Then take in hand thy lyre;
  Strike in thy proper strain;
With Japhet's line aspire
Sol's chariot for new fire
  To give the world again;
Who aided him will thee, the issue of Jove's brain.[6] 30

And, since our dainty age
  Cannot endure reproof,
Make not thyself a page
To that strumpet the stage;
  But sing high and aloof,
Safe from the wolf's black jaw, and the dull ass's hoof.

A FIT OF RHYME AGAINST RHYME

  Rhyme, the rack of finest wits,
  That expresseth but by fits
    True conceit,

AN ODE TO HIMSELF
2 The springs on the Aonian mount, Helicon, the haunt
of the Muses.
3 A city near Helicon.
4 The harp of Apollo (called Clarius after his oracle at
Clarus), the god of song and music, and leader of the Muses.
5 Magpies.
6 Prometheus, the son of Japetus, aided by Minerva ("the
issue of Jove's brain"), stole fire from the sun and gave it to
man.

Spoiling senses of their treasure,
Cozening judgment with a measure,
  But false weight;
Wresting words from their true calling,
Propping verse for fear of falling
  To the ground;
Jointing syllabes,[1] drowning letters,   10
Fast'ning vowels as with fetters
  They were bound!
Soon as lazy thou wert known,
All good poetry hence was flown,
  And are banished.
For a thousand years together
All Parnassus' green did wither,
  And wit vanished.
Pegasus did fly away,
At the wells no Muse did stay,   20
  But bewailed
So to see the fountain dry,
And Apollo's music die,
  All lights failed!
Starveling rhymes did fill the stage;
Not a poet in an age
  Worth crowning;
Not a work deserving bays,[2]
Not a line deserving praise,
  Pallas frowning.   30
Greek was free from rhyme's infection,
Happy Greek by this protection
  Was not spoiled.
Whilst the Latin, queen of tongues,
Is not yet free from rhyme's wrongs,
  But rests foiled.
Scarce the hill again doth flourish,
Scarce the world a wit doth nourish
  To restore
Phœbus to his crown again,   40
And the Muses to their brain,
  As before.

Vulgar languages that want
Words and sweetness, and be scant
  Of true measure,
Tyrant rhyme hath so abusèd,
That they long since have refusèd
  Other cæsure.

A FIT OF RHYME
1 Syllables.
2 Poetic fame (from the wreath of bay leaves with which
poets were crowned).

He that first invented thee,
May his joints tormented be,   50
   Cramped for ever.
Still may syllables jar with time,
Still may reason war with rhyme,
   Resting never.
May his sense when it would meet
The cold tumor in his feet,
   Grow unsounder;
And his title be long fool,
That in rearing such a school
   Was the founder.   60

from [A PINDARIC ODE]

*To the Immortal Memory and Friendship of that
Noble Pair, Sir Lucius Cary and Sir H. Morison*

It is not growing like a tree
   In bulk, doth make man better be;
Or standing long an oak, three hundred year,
   To fall a log at last, dry, bald, and sear:
      A lily of a day
      Is fairer far, in May,
   Although it fall and die that night;
   It was the plant and flower of light.
In small proportions we just beauties see,
And in short measures life may perfect be.

FROM

MR. WILLIAM SHAKESPEARE'S COMEDIES, HISTORIES, AND TRAGEDIES [1623]

TO THE MEMORY OF MY BELOVED THE AUTHOR, MR. WILLIAM SHAKESPEARE, AND WHAT HE HATH LEFT US[1]

To draw no envy, Shakespeare, on thy name,
Am I thus ample[2] to thy book and fame,
While I confess thy writings to be such
As neither man nor Muse can praise too much.
'Tis true, and all men's suffrage.[3] But these ways[4]
Were not the paths I meant unto thy praise:
For seeliest[5] ignorance on these may light,
Which, when it sounds at best, but echoes right;
Or blind affection,[6] which doth ne'er advance
The truth, but gropes, and urgeth all by chance;   10
Or crafty malice might pretend this praise,
And think to ruin where it seemed to raise.
These are as some infamous bawd or whore
Should praise a matron—what could hurt her more?
But thou art proof against them, and, indeed,
Above the ill fortune of them, or the need.

I therefore will begin. Soul of the age,
The applause, delight, the wonder of our stage,
My Shakespeare, rise! I will not lodge thee by
Chaucer or Spenser, or bid Beaumont lie   20
A little further to make thee a room:[7]
Thou art a monument without a tomb,
And art alive still while thy book doth live,
And we have wits to read and praise to give.
That I not mix thee so, my brain excuses,
I mean with great, but disproportioned Muses;[8]
For, if I thought my judgment were of years,
I should commit[9] thee surely with thy peers,
And tell how far thou didst our Lyly outshine,
Or sporting Kyd, or Marlowe's mighty line.   30
And though thou hadst small Latin and less Greek,[10]
From thence to honor thee, I would not seek
For names, but call forth thundering Æschylus,
Euripides, and Sophocles to us,

TO THE MEMORY
  1 These lines were written for the First Folio of Shakespeare, 1623.
  2 Liberal.
  3 Vote, consensus of opinion.
  4 That is, by the conventional expressions of commendation.
  5 Most foolish.   6 Feeling.

  7 Chaucer, Spenser, and Beaumont were buried in Westminster Abbey.
  8 Poets of less merit.   9 Join.
  10 Jonson's famous line has resulted in the undue disparagement of Shakespeare's knowledge of Latin and Greek. In comparison with the monumental Classical learning of Jonson, Shakespeare's knowledge would be small, but from what we know of the curriculum of the grammar schools of his day, Shakespeare must have been master of more Latin, at least, than the ordinary college student of today.

Pacuvius, Accius,[11] him of Cordova dead,[12]
To life again, to hear thy buskin[13] tread
And shake a stage; or when thy socks were on,
Leave thee alone for the comparison
Of all that insolent Greece or haughty Rome
Sent forth, or since did from their ashes come.   40
Triumph, my Britain; thou hast one to show
To whom all scenes of Europe homage owe.
He was not of an age, but for all time!
And all the Muses still were in their prime
When like Apollo he came forth to warm
Our ears, or like a Mercury to charm.
Nature herself was proud of his designs,
And joyed to wear the dressing of his lines,
Which were so richly spun, and woven so fit,
As, since, she will vouchsafe no other wit: 50
The merry Greek, tart Aristophanes,[14]
Neat Terence, witty Plautus,[15] now not please,
But antiquated and deserted lie,
As they were not of nature's family.
Yet must I not give nature all; thy art,
My gentle Shakespeare, must enjoy a part:

TO THE MEMORY
   11 Early Roman tragic poets.
   12 Seneca, the philosopher, dramatist, and statesman, was
born at Cordova.
   13 The buskin, a high-heeled boot, worn by Greek tragic
actors, is used symbolically for Shakespeare's tragedies; the
sock, or light shoe, worn by comic actors, for his comedies.
   14 Aristophanes is as famous for the satire as for the humor
of his comedies.
   15 Terence and Plautus are the two best-known writers of
Latin comedy.

For though the poet's matter nature be,
His art doth give the fashion; and that he[16]
Who casts to write a living line must sweat
(Such as thine are) and strike the second heat   60
Upon the Muses' anvil, turn the same,
And himself with it, that he thinks to frame,
Or for the laurel he may gain a scorn;
For a good poet's made as well as born.
And such wert thou! Look how the father's face
Lives in his issue; even so the race
Of Shakespeare's mind and manners brightly shines
In his well-turnèd and true-filèd lines,
In each of which he seems to shake a lance,
As brandished at the eyes of ignorance.   70
Sweet swan of Avon, what a sight it were
To see thee in our waters yet appear,
And make those flights upon the banks of Thames
That so did take Eliza[17] and our James!
But stay; I see thee in the hemisphere
Advanced and made a constellation there!
Shine forth, thou star of poets, and with rage[18]
Or influence[19] chide or cheer the drooping stage,
Which, since thy flight from hence, hath mourned
     like night
And despairs day, but for thy volume's light.   80

   16 That man.
   17 Queen Elizabeth. At least a dozen of Shakespeare's
plays were acted at court during the reigns of Elizabeth and
King James I.
   18 Poetic rapture or prophetic enthusiasm.
   19 Of the stars.

SONGS FROM THE PLAYS AND MASQUES

[SLOW, SLOW, FRESH FOUNT]

Slow, slow, fresh fount, keep time with my salt tears;
   Yet slower, yet, oh, faintly, gentle springs;
List to the heavy part the music bears,
   Woe weeps out her division[1] when she sings.
     Droop herbs and flowers;
     Fall grief in showers,
     Our beauties are not ours;
      Oh, I could still,
Like melting snow upon some craggy hill,
     Drop, drop, drop, drop,
Since nature's pride is now a withered daffodil.
          —*Cynthia's Revels*, 1601

SLOW, SLOW
   1 Part of a musical composition.

[QUEEN AND HUNTRESS]

Queen and huntress,[1] chaste and fair,
Now the sun is laid to sleep,
Seated in thy silver chair,
State in wonted manner keep:
   Hesperus[2] entreats thy light,
   Goddess excellently bright.

QUEEN AND HUNTRESS
   1 Cynthia (Diana). A tribute to Queen Elizabeth, who, in
the masques that conclude the play, was represented by
Cynthia.
   2 The evening star.

Earth, let not thy envious shade
Dare itself to interpose;
Cynthia's shining orb was made
Heaven to clear [3] when day did close: 10
  Bless us, then, with wishèd sight,
  Goddess excellently bright.

Lay thy bow of pearl apart,
And thy crystal-shining quiver;
Give unto the flying hart
Space to breathe, how short soever:
  Thou that mak'st a day of night,
  Goddess excellently bright.
                              —*Cynthia's Revels*

[IF I FREELY MAY DISCOVER]

If I freely may discover [1]
What would please me in my lover:
  I would have her fair and witty,
  Savoring more of court than city;
  A little proud, but full of pity;
  Light and humorous in her toying,
  Oft building hopes and soon destroying;
  Long, but sweet, in the enjoying;
Neither too easy nor too hard,
All extremes I would have barred.   10

She should be allowed her passions,
So they were but used as fashions;
  Sometimes froward, and then frowning,
  Sometimes sickish, and then swowning,
  Every fit with change still crowning.
  Purely jealous I would have her;
  Then only constant when I crave her,
  'Tis a virtue should not save her.
Thus, nor her delicates would cloy me,
Neither her peevishness annoy me.   20
                              —*The Poetaster*, 1602

[THIS IS MAB, THE MISTRESS-FAIRY]

This is Mab, the mistress-fairy,
That doth nightly rob the dairy,

And can hurt or help the churning
As she please, without discerning.

She that pinches country wenches
If they rub not clean their benches,
And with sharper nails remembers
When they rake not up their embers;
But if so they chance to feast her,
In a shoe she drops a tester. [1]   10

This is she that empties cradles,
Takes out children, puts in ladles;
Trains forth midwives in their slumber
With a sieve the holes to number;
And then leads them from her boroughs
Home through ponds and water-furrows.

She can start our franklin's daughters
In their sleep with shrieks and laughters,
And on sweet Saint Anne's [2] night
Feed them with a promised sight,   20
Some of husbands, some of lovers,
Which an empty dream discovers.
                  —*A Particular Entertainment of the Queen
                    and Prince Their Highness at Althrope*,
                    1603

[FOOLS]

Fools, they are the only nation
Worth men's envy or admiration,
Free from care or sorrow-taking,
Selves and others merry making;
All they speak or do is sterling.
Your fool he is your great man's darling,
And your lady's sport and pleasure;
Tongue and babble are his treasure,
E'en his face begetteth laughter,
And he speaks truth free from slaughter;
He's the grace of every feast,   10
And sometimes the chiefest guest
Hath his trencher and his stool,
When wit waits upon the fool.
    Oh, who would not be
    He, he, he?
                  —*Volpone, Or, The Fox*, 1607

QUEEN AND HUNTRESS
  3 Make bright.

IF I FREELY
  1 Disclose.

THIS IS MAB
  1 Shilling.   2 Probably a misprint for "Saint Agnes."

[COME, MY CELIA, LET US PROVE[1]]

Come, my Celia, let us prove,[2]
While we can, the sports of love;
Time will not be ours for ever,
He, at length, our goods will sever.
Spend not then his gifts in vain:
Suns that set may rise again;
But if once we lose this light,
'Tis with us perpetual night.
Why should we defer our joys?
Fame and rumor are but toys.   10
Cannot we delude the eyes
Of a few poor household spies?
Or his easier ears beguile,
Thus removèd by our wile?
'Tis no sin love's fruits to steal,
But the sweet thefts to reveal;
To be taken, to be seen,
These have crimes accounted been.
                        —*Volpone, Or, The Fox*

[STILL TO BE NEAT[1]]

Still[2] to be neat, still to be dressed,
As you were going to a feast;
Still to be powdered, still perfumed:
Lady, it is to be presumed,
Though art's hid causes are not found,
All is not sweet, all is not sound.

Give me a look, give me a face,
That makes simplicity a grace;
Robes loosely flowing, hair as free:
Such sweet neglect more taketh me
Than all the adulteries of art;
They strike mine eyes, but not my heart.
            —*Epicœne, Or, The Silent Woman*, 1609

[HERE SHE WAS WONT TO GO]

Here she was wont to go, and here! and here!
Just where those daisies, pinks, and violets grow;

COME, MY CELIA
    1 This song is, in part, a paraphrase of the fifth ode of
Catullus.
    2 Experience.

STILL TO BE NEAT
    1 This poem is based on an anonymous late Latin poem.
    2 Always.

The world may find the spring by following her,
For other print her airy steps ne'er left;
Her treading would not bend a blade of grass,
Or shake the downy blow-ball from his stalk!
But like the soft west wind she shot along,
And where she went the flowers took thickest root,
As she had sowed 'em with her odorous foot.
                        —*The Sad Shepherd*, 1614

[THOUGH I AM YOUNG, AND CANNOT TELL]

Though I am young, and cannot tell
    Either that Death or Love is well,
Yet I have heard they both bear darts,
    And both do aim at human hearts.
And then again, I have been told
    Love wounds with heat, as Death with cold;
So that I fear they do but bring
    Extremes to touch, and mean one thing.

As in a ruin we it call
    One thing to be blown up, or fall;   10
Or to our end like way may have
    By a flash of lightning, or a wave;
So Love's inflamèd shaft or brand
    May kill as soon as Death's cold hand;
Except Love's fires the virtue have
    To fright the frost out of the grave.
                        —*The Sad Shepherd*

[THUS, THUS BEGIN THE YEARLY RITES]

1 *Nymph.* Thus, thus begin the yearly rites
            Are due to Pan on these bright nights;
            His morn now riseth, and invites
            To sports, to dances, and delights;
                All envious and profane away,
                This is the shepherds' holy-day.

2 *Nymph.* Strew, strew the glad and smiling ground
            With every flower, yet not confound
            The primrose-drop, the spring's own
                spouse,
            Bright daisies, and the lips of cows,   10
                The garden-star, the queen of May,
                The rose, to crown the holy-day.

3 *Nymph.* Drop, drop, you violets, change your hues,
　　　Now red, now pale, as lovers use,
　　　And in your death go out as well
　　　As when you lived unto the smell;
　　　　　That from your odor all may say,
　　　　　This is the shepherds' holy-day.
　　　　　　　　　—Pan's Anniversary, 1620

[THE FAERY BEAM UPON YOU]

　　The faery[1] beam upon you,
　　The stars to glister on you;
　　　A moon of light
　　　In the noon of night,
　　Till the fire-drake hath o'ergone you!

　　The wheel of fortune guide you,
　　The boy with the bow beside you;
　　　Run aye in the way
　　　Till the bird of day,
　　And the luckier lot betide you!
　　　　　—The Gipsies Metamorphosed, 1621

TO THE OLD, LONG LIFE AND TREASURE]

　　To the old, long life and treasure,
　　To the young, all health and pleasure;

　　To the fair, their face
　　　With eternal grace,
　　And the foul to be loved at leisure!
　　To the witty, all clear mirrors,
　　To the foolish, their dark errors;
　　　To the loving sprite,
　　　A secure delight;
　　To the jealous, his own false terrors!
　　　　　—The Gipsies Metamorphosed

[IT WAS A BEAUTY THAT I SAW]

　　It was a beauty that I saw
　　So pure, so perfect, as the frame
　　Of all the universe was lame,
　　To that one figure, could I draw,
　　Or give least line of it a law!

　　A skein of silk without a knot,
　　A fair march made without a halt,
　　A curious[1] form without a fault,
　　A printed book without a blot,
　　All beauty, and without a spot!
　　　　　—The New Inn, 1631

THE FAERY BEAM
1 Old plural of *fay.*

IT WAS A BEAUTY
1 Elegant.

John Fletcher

[1579–1625]

FLETCHER was born in Rye, Sussex, of a distinguished family. He was the grandson of the Elizabethan sonneteer Giles Fletcher, the first cousin of the religious poets Phineas Fletcher and Giles Fletcher the younger, and the son of the Reverend Richard Fletcher, who later became Bishop of Bristol and of London. Educated at Cambridge, Fletcher achieved his fame as a dramatist. His work with Francis Beaumont, in the most famous collaboration in English literary history, produced such masterpieces as *The Maid's Tragedy* and *Philaster* and led to the development of the genre tragicomedy, but Fletcher's independent work also produced much of value, such as the pastoral *The Faithful Shepherdess*. The influence of Jonson, particularly noticeable in the last-named play, can also be felt in Fletcher's masques and in the songs which, scattered so liberally throughout his dramatic works, give him a place in this anthology. Fletcher died of the plague in 1625.

F. BEAUMONT and J. FLETCHER. *Works*, ed. F. Glover and A. R. Waller, 10 vols. (Cambridge, 1905–12).

SONG

Care-charming Sleep, thou easer of all woes,
Brother to Death, sweetly thyself dispose
On this afflicted prince; fall like a cloud
In gentle showers, give nothing that is loud
Or painful to his slumbers; easy, sweet,
And as a purling stream, thou son of Night,
Pass by his troubled senses; sing his pain
Like hollow murmuring wind, or silver rain.
Into this prince gently, O gently slide,
And kiss him into slumbers like a bride.
            —*The Tragedy of Valentinian*, text 1697

ASPATIA'S SONG

Lay a garland on my hearse
    Of the dismal yew;
Maidens, willow branches bear,
    Say I dièd true.

My love was false, but I was firm
    From my hour of birth.
Upon my buried body lay
    Lightly, gently, earth.
            —*The Maid's Tragedy*, text 1622

[SLEEP]

Come, Sleep, and with thy sweet deceiving
    Lock me in delight awhile!
    Let some pleasing dreams beguile
    All my fancies; that from thence
    I may feel an influence,
All my powers of care bereaving!

Though but a shadow, but a sliding,
    Let me know some little joy!
    We that suffer long annoy
    Are contented with a thought
    Through an idle fancy wrought:
O let my joys have some abiding!
            —*The Woman-Hater*, text 1607

John Webster

[1580?–1634?]

ALMOST nothing is known of Webster's life, beyond the fact that he was the son of a London tailor. Primarily a writer for the theater, he collaborated with Dekker in a series of comedies, then found his proper vehicle in tragedy. His greatest works in that genre—*The White Devil* (*c.* 1612) and *The Duchess of Malfi* (*c.* 1614; published, 1623)—give him a rank only below that of Shakespeare and count among the supreme achievements of Jacobean drama. In 1612 Webster published an elegy on the death of Prince Henry, and in 1615 he contributed a notable series of characters to the sixth edition of the Overburian volume.

Webster, says T. S. Eliot, "saw the skull beneath the skin." The macabre sense of mortality which is so prominent in his plays finds expression in the famous dirge from *The White Devil*, a piece which suggests, when compared with those of Fletcher, the wide range of effects which could be achieved by interpolated song in the Jacobean drama.

J. WEBSTER. *Complete Works*, ed. F. L. Lucas, 4 vols. (London, 1927).

[A DIRGE]

Call for the robin-redbreast and the wren,
Since o'er shady groves they hover,
And with leaves and flowers do cover
The friendless bodies of unburied men.
Call unto his funeral dole
The ant, the field-mouse, and the mole,
To rear him hillocks that shall keep him warm,
And, when gay tombs are robbed, sustain no harm;
But keep the wolf far thence, that's foe to men,
For with his nails he'll dig them up again.
                    —*The White Devil*, 1612

[DEATH-SONG]

Hark, now everything is still;
The screech-owl and the whistler shrill
Call upon our dame aloud,
And bid her quickly don her shroud;

Much you had of land and rent,
Your length in clay's now competent.
A long war disturbed your mind;
Here your perfect peace is signed.
Of what is 't fools make such vain keeping?
Sin their conception, their birth weeping,   10
Their life a general mist of error,
Their death a hideous storm of terror.
Strew your hair with powders sweet,
Don clean linen, bathe your feet,
And, the foul fiend more to check,
A crucifix let bless your neck;
'Tis now full tide, 'tween night and day,
End your groan and come away.
                    —*The Duchess of Malfi*, 1623

THE MADMAN'S SONG

Oh, let us howl some heavy note,
    Some deadly-dogged howl,

Sounding as from the threatening throat
  Of beasts and fatal fowl!
As ravens, screech-owls, bulls, and bears,
  We'll bell, and bawl our parts,
Till irksome noise have cloyed your ears
  And còrrosived your hearts.
At last, whenas our quire wants breath,
  Our bodies being blest,
We'll sing like swans to welcome death,
  And die in love and rest.
                    —*The Duchess of Malfi*, 1623

Richard Corbet

[1582–1635]

CORBET enjoyed in his own time a reputation as a wit and *bon vivant*, which may strike modern sensibilities as being strangely at variance with the positions of high ecclesiastical dignity which he occupied. Born in Surrey, of a humble family, he distinguished himself at Westminster School and at Christ Church, Oxford. He was made Bishop of Oxford in 1628 and was translated to the see of Norwich in 1632. There he died a few years later.

The bishop was well known in the intellectual and artistic circles of Jacobean London, and he was, like so many literary men of the time, a friend of Jonson. His poems were published posthumously in 1647, and he was the subject of one of the most entertaining of Aubrey's *Brief Lives*. Corbet's humorous temperament would probably derive amusement from the fact that he is remembered today almost exclusively for his trivial but delightful "Farewell, rewards and fairies."

R. CORBET. *Poems*, ed. J. A. W. Bennett and H. R. Trevor-Roper (Oxford, 1955).

A PROPER NEW BALLAD, INTITULED THE FAIRIES' FAREWELL, OR GOD A MERCY WILL

To be sung or whistled, to the tune of Meadow Brow *by the learned, by the unlearned to the tune of* Fortune.

Farewell, rewards and fairies,
   Good housewives now may say,
For now foul sluts in dairies
   Do fare as well as they.
And though they sweep their hearths no less
   Than maids were wont to do,
Yet who of late for cleanliness
   Finds sixpence in her shoe?

Lament, lament, old abbeys,
   The fairies lost command;   10
They did but change priests' babies,
   But some have changed your land,

And all your children sprung from thence
   Are now grown Puritans;
Who live as changelings ever since,
   For love of your demesnes.

At morning and at evening both
   You merry were and glad,
So little care of sleep or sloth
   These pretty ladies had;   20
When Tom came home from labor,
   Or Ciss to milking rose,
Then merrily went their tabor,
   And nimbly went their toes.

Witness those rings and roundelays
   Of theirs, which yet remain,
Were footed in Queen Mary's days
   On many a grassy plain;

But since of late Elizabeth,
   And later James, came in,   30
They never danced on any heath
   As when the time hath been.

By which we note the fairies
   Were of the old profession;
Their songs were Ave Maries,
   Their dances were processions;
But now, alas, they all are dead,
   Or gone beyond the seas,
Or further from religion fled,
   Or else they take their ease.   40

A tell-tale in their company
   They never could endure,
And whoso kept not secretly
   Their mirth was punished sure;
It was a just and Christian deed
   To pinch such black and blue;
Oh, how the commonwealth doth need
   Such justices as you!

Now they have left our quarters,
   A register they have,   50
Who can preserve their charters,
   A man both wise and grave;
A hundred of their merry pranks
   By one that I could name
Are kept in store; con twenty thanks
   To William for the same.

To William Chourne of Staffordshire [1]
   Give land and praises due,
Who every meal can mend your cheer
   With tales both old and true;   60
To William all give audience,
   And pray ye for his noddle,
For all the fairies' evidence
   Were lost, if that were addle.
           —*Certain Elegant Poems*, 1647

A PROPER NEW BALLAD
1 Corbet's father-in-law.

Phineas Fletcher

[1582–1650]

P HINEAS FLETCHER is, like his brother Giles, chiefly important as an historical link between two of the greatest poets of England: Spenser and Milton. Strongly influenced by the former, they both exerted a modest influence on the latter, Phineas possibly giving Milton a few hints for the infernal scenes of *Paradise Lost* through the conception of Hell and Satan contained in his *Apollyonists*. In his own right he is, if taken in small doses, a curious and original poet, although certainly not a great one.

Educated at Eton and at King's College, Cambridge, Fletcher received his M.A. in 1608 and became a fellow of his college. In 1611 he was ordained and in 1615 he became chaplain to Sir Henry Willoughby, who later presented him with the living of Hilgay in Norfolk, where he remained from 1621 until his death. His first published poem, together with his brother's, appeared in *Sorrow's Joy* (1603), a Cambridge miscellany on the occasion of the death of Queen Elizabeth and the accession to the throne of James I. In around 1611 he wrote *Locustae vel Pietas Jesuitica*, a long narrative poem in Latin on the Gunpowder Plot of six years earlier. In 1627 he translated the poem into English in an expanded form as *The Locusts, or Apollyonists*. In its extravagant fancy and its militant Protestantism, *The Apollyonists* is a powerful, if uneven, poem. Its strangeness is overshadowed by that of *The Purple Island* (1633), surely one of the strangest poems in our language. In form an incredibly extended allegory of the human body conceived of in geographical terms, it derives from the anatomical allegory in *The Faerie Queene*, II, 9, but handles its material with a grotesqueness which was later to arouse the interest of James Joyce. Together with *The Purple Island* Fletcher published a series of *Piscatory Eclogues* on the model of those of the Italian poet Sannazzaro. An earlier work, *Britain's Ida, or Venus and Anchises*, was published in 1628 as Spenser's.

In his choice of genres, his faithful discipleship to Spenser, and his sensitivity to Continental influences, Phineas Fletcher is in many respects a belated sixteenth-century poet. In the detail of his style, however—its grotesqueness, its overwrought intensity, its religious concern—he is a poet of the seventeenth century, an exponent of one of the many varieties of that complex style which we call Baroque.

P. FLETCHER and G. FLETCHER. *Poetical Works*, ed. F. S. Boas, 2 vols. (Cambridge, 1908–09). Definitive.

P. FLETCHER. *Venus and Anchises*, ed. E. Seaton (London, 1926).

A. B. LANGDALE. *Phineas Fletcher, Man of Letters, Science, and Divinity* (New York, 1937).

M. H. NICHOLSON. (See under general poetry bibliography.)

J. H. HANFORD. *A Milton Handbook.* (See under Milton.) Assesses Milton's debt to the Fletchers.

H. E. CORY. *Spenser, the School of the Fletchers, and Milton* (Berkeley, Calif., 1912).

F R O M

THE APOLLYONISTS [1627]

CANTO I

1

OF MEN, nay beasts; worse, monsters; worst of all,
　Incarnate fiends, English Italianate;
Of priests, O no! mass-priests, priests-cannibal,
Who make their Maker, chew, grind, feed, grow fat
With flesh divine; of that great city's fall,
Which born, nursed, grown with blood, the earth's
　　empress sat,
　Cleansed, spoused to Christ, yet back to whoredom
　　fell,
　None can enough, something I fain would tell.
How black are quenched lights! Fallen heaven's a
　　double hell.

2

Great Lord, who graspest all creatures in Thy hand,
Who in Thy lap layest down proud Thetis' head,　11
And bindest her white curled locks in cauls of sand,
Who gatherest in Thy fist and layest in bed
The sturdy winds, who groundest the floating land
On fleeting seas, and over all hast spread
　Heaven's brooding wings to foster all below,
　Who makest the sun without all fire to glow,
The spring of heat and light, the moon to ebb and flow,

3

Thou world's sole Pilot, who in this poor isle
(So small a bottom) hast embarked Thy light,　20
And glorious Self and steerest it safe, the while
Hoarse drumming seas and winds' loud trumpets fight,
Who causest stormy heavens here only smile,
Steer me, poor ship-boy, steer my course aright;
　Breathe, gracious Spirit, breathe gently on these
　　lays;
　Be Thou my compass, needle to my ways;
Thy glorious work's my freight; my haven is Thy
　　praise.

4

Thou purple whore,[1] mounted on scarlet beast,
Gorged with the flesh, drunk with the blood of saints,
Whose amorous golden cup and charmed feast　30
All earthly kings, all earthly men attaints,
See thy live pictures, see thine own, thy best,
Thy dearest sons, and cheer thy heart that faints.
　Hark! thou saved island, hark! and never cease
　To praise that hand which held thy head in peace;
Else hadst thou swum as deep in blood as now in seas.

5

The cloudy night came whirling up the sky
And scatt'ring round the dews, which first she drew
From milky poppies, loads the drowsy eye.
The wat'ry moon, cold Vesper, and his crew　40
Light up their tapers; to the sun they fly
And at his blazing flame their sparks renew.
　Oh, why should earthly lights then scorn to tine
　Their lamps alone at that first Sun divine?
Hence as false as falling stars, as rotton wood, they
　　shine.

6

Her sable mantle was embroidered gay
With silver beams, with spangles round beset;
Four steeds her chariot drew: the first was gray,
The second blue, third brown, fourth black as jet.
The hollowing owl, her post,[2] prepares the way;　50
And winged dreams, as gnat swarms flutt'ring, let
　Sad sleep, who fain his eyes in rest would steep.
　Why then at death do weary mortals weep?
Sleep's but a shorter death; death's but a longer sleep.

1 The whore of Babylon, described in Rev. 17; it here represents the Roman Catholic Church.
2 Messenger.

7

And now the world, and dreams themselves, were
    drowned
In deadly sleep; the laborer snorteth fast,
His brawny arms unbent, his limbs unbound,
As dead, forget all toil to come, or past;
Only sad guilt and troubled greatness, crowned
With heavy gold and care, no rest can taste.   60
    Go then, vain man, go pill the live and dead,
    Buy, sell, fawn, flatter, rise, then couch thy head
In proud, but dangerous gold, in silk, but restless bed.

8

When lo! a sudden noise breaks the empty air:
A dreadful noise, which every creature daunts,
Frights home the blood, shoots up the limber hair;
For through the silent heaven hell's pursuivants,
Cutting their way, command foul spirits repair
With haste to Pluto, who their counsel wants.   69
    Their hoarse bass-horns like fenny bitterns sound;
    The earth shakes, dogs howl, and heaven itself,
      astound,
Shuts all his eyes; the stars in clouds their candles
    drowned.

9

Meantime, hell's iron gates by fiends beneath
Are open flung, which framed with wondrous art
To every guilty soul yields entrance eath;[3]
But never wight but He could thence depart,
Who dying once, was death to endless death.
So where the liver's channel to the heart
    Pays purple tribute, with their three-forked mace
    Three Tritons stand and speed his flowing race,   80
But stop the ebbing stream if once it back would pace.

10

The porter to the infernal gate is Sin,[4]
A shapeless shape, a foul deformed thing,
Nor nothing, nor a substance, as those thin
And empty forms which through the air fling
Their wandering shapes, at length they're fastened in
The crystal sight. It serves, yet reigns as king;
    It lives, yet's death; it pleases, full of pain;
    Monster! ah, who, who can thy being feign?
Thou shapeless shape, live death, pain pleasing, servile
    reign!   90

11

Of that first woman and the old serpent bred,
By lust and custom nursed, whom when her mother
Saw so deformed, how fain would she have fled
Her birth, and self! But she her dam would smother,
And all her brood, had not He rescued
Who was His mother's sire, His children's brother:
    Eternity, who yet was born and died;
    His own creator, earth's scorn, heaven's pride,
Who the Deity infleshed, and man's flesh deified.

12

Her former parts her mother seems resemble,
Yet only seems to flesh and weaker sight,   100
For she with art and paint could fine dissemble
Her loathsome face. Her back parts, black as night,
Like to her horrid sire, would force to tremble
The boldest heart. To the eye that meets her right
    She seems a lovely sweet, of beauty rare;
    But at the parting, he that shall compare,
Hell will more lovely deem, the devil's self more fair.

13

Her rosy cheek, quick eye, her naked breast,
And whatsoe'er loose fancy might entice,   110
She bare exposed to sight, all lovely dressed
In beauty's livery and quaint device.
Thus she bewitches many a boy unblest,
Who drenched in hell, dreams of all paradise:
    Her breasts, his spheres; her arms, his circling sky;
    Her pleasures, heaven; her love, eternity.
For her he longs to live; with her he longs to die.

14

But He that gave a stone power to descry
'Twixt natures hid, and check that metal's pride
That dares aspire to gold's fair purity,   120
Hath left a touchstone erring eyes to guide,
Which clears their sight and strips hypocrisy.
They see, they loathe, they curse her painted hide;
    Her as a crawling carrion they esteem;
    Her worst of ills, and worse than that, they deem,
Yet know her worse than they can think, or she can
    seem.

15

Close by her sat Despair, sad ghastly sprite,
With staring looks, unmoved, fast nailed to Sin;
Her body all of earth, her soul of fright,
About her thousand deaths, but more within;   130

---

3 Easy.   4 Cf. Paradise Lost II, 648–89.

Pale, pined cheeks, black hair, torn, rudely dight,
Short breath, long nails, dull eyes, sharp-pointed chin;
  Light, life, heaven, earth, herself, and all she fled.
  Fain would she die, but could not; yet half dead,
A breathing corse she seemed, wrapped up in living
    lead.

16

In the entrance Sickness and faint Languor dwelt,
Who with sad groans toll out their passing knell,
Late fear, fright, horror that already felt
The torturer's claws, preventing death and hell.
Within loud Grief and roaring Pangs that swelt   140
In sulphur flames, did weep and howl and yell.
  A thousand souls in endless dolors lie,
  Who burn, fry, hiss, and never cease to cry,
"Oh, that I ne'er had lived; oh, that I once could die!"

17

And now the infernal powers through the air driving,
For speed their leather pinions broad display;
Now at eternal death's wide gate arriving,
Sin gives them passage; still they cut their way
Till to the bottom of hell's palace diving,
They enter Dis'[5] deep conclave. There they stay,   150
  Waiting the rest, and now they all are met,
  A full foul senate; now they all are set,
The horrid court, big swoll'n with the hideous council
    sweat.

18

The midst, but lowest (in hell's heraldry
The deepest is the highest room) in state
Sat lordly Lucifer;[6] his fiery eye,
Much swoll'n with pride, but more with rage and hate,
As censor mustered all his company,
Who round about with awful silence sate.
  This do, this let rebellious spirits gain,   160
  Change God for Satan, heaven's for hell's sovereign:
O let him serve in hell, who scorns in heaven to reign![7]

19

Ah, wretch! who with ambitious cares oppressed,
Longest still for future, feelest no present good;
Despising to be better, wouldst be best,
Good never; who wilt serve thy lusting mood,

5 Pluto, ruler over Hades.
6 Cf. Paradise Lost II, 1–505.
7 Cf. Satan, in Paradise Lost I, 263: "Better to reign in hell
than serve in heaven."

Yet all command: not he who raised his crest,
But pulled it down, hath high and firmly stood.
  Fool! serve thy towering lusts, grow still, still crave,
  Rule, reign; this comfort from thy greatness have,
Now at thy top thou art a great commanding slave.

20

Thus fell this Prince of Darkness, once a bright   171
And glorious star; he willful turned away
His borrowed globe from that eternal light;
Himself he sought, so lost himself: his ray
Vanished to smoke, his morning sunk in night,
And never more shall see the springing day.
  To be in heaven the second he disdains;
  So now the first in hell and flames he reigns,
Crowned once with joy and light, crowned now with
    fire and pains.   180

21

As where the warlike Dane the scepter sways,
They crown usurpers with a wreath of lead,
And with hot steel, while loud the traitor brays,
They melt and drop it down into his head,—
Crowned he would live, and crowned he ends his days;
All so in heaven's courts this traitor sped,
  Who now, when he had overlooked his train,
  Rising upon his throne, with bitter strain
Thus 'gan to whet their rage and chide their frustrate
    pain.

22

"See, see, you Spirits (I know not whether more   190
Hated, or hating heaven) ah! see the earth
Smiling in quiet peace and plenteous store.
Men fearless live in ease, in love, and mirth;
Where arms did rage, the drum and cannon roar;
Where hate, strife, envy reigned, and meager dearth,
  Now lutes and viols charm the ravished ear;
  Men plow with swords; horse-heels their armors
    wear;
Ah! shortly scarce they'll know what war and armors
    were.

23

"Under their sprouting vines they sporting sit.
The old tell of evils past; youth laugh and play   200
And to their wanton heads sweet garlands fit,
Roses with lilies, myrtles weaved with bay.
The world's at rest; Erinnys, forced to quit
Her strongest holds, from earth is driven away.

Even Turks forget their empire to increase;
War's self is slain and whips of Furies cease.
We, we ourselves, I fear, will shortly live in peace.

24

"Meantime (I burn, I broil, I burst with spite)
In midst of peace that sharp two-edged sword   209
Cuts through our darkness, cleaves the misty night,
Discovers all our snares; that sacred word,
Locked up by Rome, breaks prison, spreads the light,
Speaks every tongue, paints, and points out the Lord,
    His birth, life, death, and cross; our gilded stocks,
    Our laymen's books, the boy and woman mocks;
They laugh, they fleer, and say, 'Blocks teach and
        worship blocks.'

25

"Springtides of light divine the air surround
And bring down heaven to earth; deaf Ignorance,
Vexed with the day, her head in hell hath drowned;
Fond Superstition, frighted with the glance   220
Of sudden beams, in vain hath crossed her round;
Truth and Religion everywhere advance
    Their conquering standards; Error's lost and fled;
    Earth burns in love to Heaven; Heaven yields her bed
To earth, and common grown, smiles to be ravished.

26

"That little swimming isle above the rest,
Spite of our spite and all our plots, remains
And grows in happiness: but late our nest,
Where we and Rome, and blood, and all our trains,
Monks, nuns, dead and live idols, safe did rest.   230
Now there, next the oath of God, that wrestler [8] reigns,
    Who fills the land and world with peace; his spear
    Is but a pen, with which he down doth bear
Blind ignorance, false gods, and superstitious fear.

27

"There God hath framed another paradise,
Fat olives dropping peace, victorious palms;
Nor in the midst, but everywhere doth rise
That hated tree of life, whose precious balms
Cure every sinful wound, give light to the eyes,
Unlock the ear, recover fainting qualms.   240
    There richly grows what makes a people blest,
    A garden planted by Himself and dressed,
Where He Himself doth walk, where He Himself doth
        rest.

8 The king, James I.

28

"There every star sheds his sweet influence
And radiant beams; great, little, old, and new,
Their glittering rays and frequent confluence
The milky path to God's high palace strew;
The unwearied pastors with steeled confidence,
Conquered and conquering, fresh their fight renew.
    Our strongest holds that thundering ordinance   250
    Beats down and makes our proudest turrets dance,
Yoking men's iron necks in His sweet governance.

29

"Nor can the old world content ambitious light;
Virginia, our soil, our seat, and throne,
(To which so long possession gives us right,
As long as hell's) Virginia's self is gone;
That stormy isle, which the Isle of Devils' [9] hight,
Peopled with faith, truth, grace, religion.
    What's next but hell? That now alone remains,   259
    And that subdued, even here He rules and reigns,
And mortals 'gin to dream of long, but endless pains.

30

"While we, good harmless creatures, sleep or play,
Forget our former loss and following pain,
Earth sweats for heaven, but hell keeps holiday.
Shall we repent, good souls, or shall we plain?
Shall we groan, sigh, weep, mourn, for mercy pray?
Lay down our spite, wash out our sinful stain?
    Maybe He'll yield, forget, and use us well,
    Forgive, join hands, restore us whence we fell;   269
Maybe He'll yield us heaven and fall Himself to hell.

31

"But me, O never let me, Spirits, forget
That glorious day when I your standard bore,
And scorning in the second place to sit,
With you assaulted heaven, His yoke forswore!
My dauntless heart yet longs to bleed and sweat
In such a fray; the more I burn, the more
    I hate: should He yet offer grace and ease,
    If subject we our arms and spite surcease,
Such offer should I hate, and scorn so base a peace.   279

32

"Where are those Spirits? Where that haughty rage
That durst with me invade eternal light?
What! Are our hearts fallen too? Droop we with age?
Can we yet fall from hell and hellish spite?

9 Bermuda.

Can smart our wrath, can grief out hate assuage?
Dare we with heaven, and not with earth to fight?
   Your arms, allies, yourselves as strong as ever;
   Your foes, their weapons, numbers, weaker never.
For shame, tread down this earth! What wants but
     your endeavor?

33

"Now by yourselves and thunder-daunted arms,
But never-daunted hate, I you implore,   290
Command, adjure, reinforce your fierce alarms;
Kindle, I pray, who never prayed before,
Kindle your darts, treble repay our harms.
Oh, our short time, too short, stands at the door!
   Double your rage; if now we do not ply
   We lone in hell, without due company,
And worse, without desert, without revenge shall lie.

34

"He, Spirits, (ah, that, that's our main torment!) He
Can feel no wounds, laughs at the sword and dart,
Himself from grief, from suffering wholly free;   300
His simple nature cannot taste of smart,
Yet in His members we Him grieved see;
For, and in them, He suffers; where His heart
   Lies bare and naked, there dart your fiery steel,
   Cut, wound, burn, sear, if not the head, the heel.
Let him in every part some pain and torment feel.

35

"That light comes posting on, that cursed light,
When they as He, all glorious, all divine,
(Their flesh clothed with the sun, and much more
     bright,
Yet brighter spirits) shall in His image shine,   310
And see Him as He is; there no despite,
No force, no art their state can undermine:
   Full of unmeasured bliss, yet still receiving,
   Their souls still childing joy, yet still conceiving,
Delights beyond the wish, beyond quick thoughts
     perceiving.

36

"But we fast pinioned with dark fiery chains,
Shall suffer every ill, but do no more;
The guilty spirit there feels extremest pains,
Yet fears worse than it feels; and finding store
Of present deaths, death's absence sore complains: 320
Oceans of ills without or ebb, or shore,

A life that ever dies, a death that lives,
   And, worst of all, God's absent presence gives
A thousand living woes, a thousand dying griefs.

37

"But when he sums his time and turns his eye
First to the past, then future pangs, past days
(And every day's an age of misery)
In torment spent, by thousands down he lays,
Future by millions, yet eternity
Grows nothing less, nor past to come allays.   330
   Through every pang and grief he wild doth run,
   And challenge coward death; doth nothing shun
That he may nothing be, does all to be undone.

38

"Oh, let our work equal our wages, let
Our Judge fall short, and when His plagues are spent,
Owe more than He hath paid, live in our debt;
Let heaven want vengeance, hell want punishment
To give our dues; when we with flames beset,
Still dying, live in endless languishment,
   This be our comfort: we did get and win   340
   The fires and tortures we are whelmed in;
We have kept pace, outrun His justice with our sin.

39

"And now you States of Hell, give your advice,
And to these ruins lend your helping hand."
This said and ceased; straight humming murmurs rise:
Some chafe, some fret, some sad and thoughtful stand,
Some chat, and some new stratagems devise;
And everyone heaven's stronger powers banned,
   And tear for madness their uncombed snakes;
   And everyone his fiery weapon shakes,   350
And everyone expects who first the answer makes.

40

So when the falling sun hangs o'er the main,
Ready to drop into the western wave
By yellow Cam, where all the Muses reign,
And with their towers his reedy head embrave,
The warlike gnat their flutt'ring armies train;
All have sharp spears, and all shrill trumpets have;
   Their files they double, loud their cornets sound,
   Now march at length, their troops now gather
     round;   359
The banks, the broken noise, and turrets fair rebound.

Lord Herbert of Cherbury

[1582–1648]

THE eldest offspring of one of the great families of the Welsh border, Herbert was the son of Richard Herbert and Magdalen Newport (who was to become, after her second marriage to Sir John Danvers, the friend and patroness of Donne) and the brother of George Herbert. He was born at Eyton-on-Severn and educated at University College, Oxford. While he was at Oxford, and shortly after his father's death, he married the heiress Mary Herbert, whose inheritance depended on her marrying someone with the same name. His domestic life seems to have been rather fragmentary, however; shortly after his marriage he traveled to the Continent on one of the many trips which occupied a large part of his earlier life. He had presented himself at Elizabeth's court in 1600, and he was made a Knight of the Bath on the occasion of James's coronation.

From 1619 to 1624 Herbert served as English ambassador at the French court, and he seems to have performed his duties with intelligence and devotion. Recalled after an altercation with the favorite of Louis XIII, he was rewarded for his service by being created Baron Herbert of Cherbury in 1629.

The years of his diplomatic service had been active in other respects as well. He had composed one of the most lively, and least accurate, autobiographies of the age, and he had engaged in much philosophical speculation. His treatise *De Veritate*, published in Paris in 1624, is the first purely metaphysical work written by an Englishman, and it gives him a position of some importance in the history of English thought. He has been labeled, although rather inaccurately, "the father of English deism."

In the early years of the century Herbert had made the acquaintance of John Donne, probably at his mother's house, and the poems which he began writing at that time show him to be the earliest disciple of that great poet. Herbert's satires and lyrics display the wit, the ingenuity, and the conversational tone characteristic of Donne, but they have almost nothing of the older poet's dramatic immediacy and passion. The distinctive note in Lord Herbert's verse is a kind of lyrical abstractness unique in the period.

Herbert's last years were rendered unhappy by quarrels with his children and by his inability to steer a neutral course between the royalist and parliamentary causes. In 1644, in order to save his library, he surrendered his castle at Montgomery to the Roundheads, and when he died a few years later he was still known to the Cavaliers as "the treacherous Lord Herbert." Not close to greatness as either poet, philosopher, or statesman, Herbert remains one of the more fascinating and versatile figures of a complex age.

LORD HERBERT OF CHERBURY. *Poems*, ed. G. C. Moore Smith (Oxford, 1923).
————. *Autobiography*, ed. S. Lee (London, rev. ed., 1906).
G. WILLIAMSON. (See under general poetry bibliography.)
B. WILLEY. (See under general poetry bibliography.) Has a good section on Herbert's thought.

FROM

OCCASIONAL VERSES [1665]

DITTY

Deep sighs, records of my unpitied grief,
  Memorials of my true though hopeless love,
Keep time with my sad thoughts, till wished relief
  My long despairs for vain and causeless prove.

Yet if such hap never to you befall,
I give you leave, break time, break heart and all.

UPON COMBING HER HAIR

Breaking from under that thy cloudy veil,
  Open and shine yet more, shine out more clear,
  Thou glorious golden-beam-darting hair,
Even till my wonder-strucken senses fail.

Shoot out in light and shine those rays on far,
  Thou much more fair than is the Queen of Love,
  When she doth comb her in her sphere above,
And from a planet turns a blazing-star.

Nay, thou art greater too, more destiny
  Depends on thee than on her influence;   10
  No hair thy fatal hand doth now dispense
But to some one a thread of life must be.

While gracious unto me, though both dost sunder
  Those glories which, if they united were,
  Might have amazèd sense, and shewest each hair,
Which if alone had been too great a wonder.

And now spread in their goodly length, she appears
  No creature which the earth might call her own,
  But rather one that in her gliding down   19
Heaven's beams did crown to shew us she was theirs.

And come from thence, how can they fear time's
    rage
  Which in his power else on earth most strange
  Such golden treasure doth to silver change
By that improper alchemy of age?

But stay, methinks new beauties do arise,
  While she withdraws these glories which were
    spread.
  Wonder of beauties, set thy radiant head
And strike out day from thy yet fairer eyes.

DITTY IN IMITATION OF THE SPANISH *ENTRE TANTO QUE L'AVRIL*

Now that the April of your youth adorns
  The garden of your face;
Now that for you each knowing lover mourns,
  And all seek to your grace:
Do nor repay affection with scorns.

What though you may a matchless beauty vaunt,
  And that all hearts can move
By such a power as seemeth to enchant?
  Yet without help of love
Beauty no pleasure to itself can grant.   10

Then think each minute that you lose a day;
  The longest youth is short,
The shortest age is long; time flies away,
  And makes us but his sport;
And that which is not youth's is age's prey.

See but the bravest horse, that prideth most,
  Though he escape the war,
Either from master to the man is lost,
  Or turned unto the car,
Or else must die with being ridden post.   20

Then lose not beauty, lovers, time, and all;
   Too late your fault you see,
When that in vain you would these days recall;
   Nor can you virtuous be
When without these you have not wherewithal.

ELEGY OVER A TOMB

Must I then see, alas, eternal night
   Sitting upon those fairest eyes,
And closing all those beams which once did rise
   So radiant and bright,
That light and heat in them to us did prove
   Knowledge and love?

Oh, if you did delight no more to stay
   Upon this low and earthly stage,
But rather chose an endless heritage,
   Tell us at least we pray   10
Where all the beauties that those ashes owed
   Are now bestowed.

Doth the sun now his light with yours renew?
   Have waves the curling of your hair?
Did you restore unto the sky and air
   The red and white and blue?
Have you vouchsafed to flowers since your death
   That sweetest breath?

Had not heaven's lights else in their houses slept,
   Or to some private life retired?   20
Must not the sky and air have else conspired,
   And in their regions wept?
Must not each flower else the earth could breed
   Have been a weed?

But thus enriched may we not yield some cause
   Why they themselves lament no more?
That must have changed the course they held before
   And broke their proper laws,
Had not your beauties given this second birth
   To heaven and earth.   30

Tell us, for oracles must still ascend,
   For those that crave them at your tomb:
Tell us, where are those beauties now become,
   And what they now intend;
Tell us, alas, that cannot tell our grief,
   Or hope relief.

TO HER HAIR

Black beamy hairs, which so seem to arise
   From the extraction of those eyes,
That into you she destin-like doth spin
The beams she spares, what time her soul retires,
   And by those hallowed fires,
   Keeps house all night within.

Since from within her awful front you shine,
   As threads of life which she doth twine,
And thence ascending with your fatal rays,
Do crown those temples, where Love's wonders
     wrought   10
   We afterwards see brought
   To vulgar light and praise.

Lighten through all your regions, till we find
   The causes why we are grown blind,
That when we should your glories comprehend
Our sight recoils, and turneth back again,
   And doth, as 'twere in vain,
   Itself to you extend.

Is it because past black there is not found
   A fixed or horizontal bound?   20
And so, as it doth terminate the white,
It may be said all colors to infold,
   And in that kind to hold
   Somewhat of infinite?

Or is it that the center of our sight
   Being veilèd in its proper night
Discerns your blackness by some other sense
Than that by which it doth pied colors see,
   Which only therefore be
   Known by their difference?   30

Tell us, when on her front in curls you lie
   So diaped[1] from that black eye.
That your reflected forms may make us know
That shining light in darkness all would find,
   Were they not upward blind
   With the sunbeams below.

TO HER HAIR
1 Irradiated.

SONNET OF BLACK BEAUTY

Black beauty, which above that common light,
  Whose power can no colors here renew
  But those which darkness can again subdue,
Dost still remain unvaried to the sight,
And like an object equal to the view
  Art neither changed with day nor hid with
     night;
  When all those colors which the world calls
     bright,
And which old poetry doth so pursue,
Are with the night so perishèd and gone
  That of their being there remains no mark,   10
Thou still abidest so entirely one.
  That we may know thy blackness is a spark
Of light ináccessible, and alone
  Our darkness which can make us think it dark.

ANOTHER SONNET, TO BLACK ITSELF

Thou Black, wherein all colors are composed,
  And unto which they all at last return,
  Thou color of the sun where it doth burn,
And shadow, where it cools, in thee is closed
Whatever nature can, or hath disposed
  In any other hue: from thee do rise
Those tempers and complexions, which disclosed,
  As parts of thee, do work as mysteries,
Of that thy hidden power; when thou dost reign
  The characters of fate shine in the skies,   10
And tell us what the heavens do ordain,
  But when earth's common light shines to our eyes,
Thou so retirest thyself that thy disdain
  All revelation unto man denies.

AN ODE UPON A QUESTION MOVED, WHETHER LOVE SHOULD CONTINUE FOREVER

Having interred her infant-birth,
  The watery ground that late did mourn,
  Was strewed with flowers for the return
Of the wished bridegroom of the earth.

The well-accorded birds did sing
  Their hymns unto the pleasant time,
  And in a sweet consorted chime
Did welcome in the cheerful spring.

To which, soft whistles of the wind,
  And warbling murmurs of a brook,   10
  And varied notes of leaves that shook,
An harmony of parts did bind.

While doubling joy unto each other,
  All in so rare consent was shown,
  No happiness that came alone,
Nor pleasure that was not another.

When with a love none can express,
  That mutually happy pair,
  Melander and Celinda fair,   20
The season with their loves did bless.

Walking towards a pleasant grove,
  Which did, it seemed, in new delight
  The pleasures of the time unite,
To give a triumph to their love,

They stayed at last, and on the grass
  Reposèd so, as o'er his breast
  She bowed her gracious head to rest,
Such a weight as no burden was.

While over either's compassed waist
  Their folded arms were so composed,   30
  As if in straitest bonds enclosed,
They suffered for joys they did taste.

Long their fixed eyes to heaven bent,
  Unchangèd, they did never move,
  As if so great and pure a love
No glass but it could represent.

When with a sweet though troubled look,
  She first brake silence, saying, "Dear friend,
  O, that our love might take no end,
Or never had beginning took!   40

I speak not this with a false heart,"
  (Wherewith his hand she gently strained)
  "Or that would change a love maintained
With so much faith on either part.

Nay, I protest, though death with his
  Worst counsel should divide us here,
  His terrors could not make me fear
To come where your loved presence is.

Only if love's fire with the breath
    Of life be kindlèd, I doubt[1]   50
    With our last air 'twill be breathed out,
And quenchèd with the cold of death.

That if affection be a line,
    Which is closed up in our last hour;
    O how 'twould grieve me, any power
Could force so dear a love as mine!"

She scarce had done, when his shut eyes
    An inward joy did represent,
    To hear Celinda thus intent
To a love he so much did prize.   60

Then with a look, it seemed, denied
    All earthly power but hers, yet so,
    As if to her breath he did owe
This borrowed life, he thus replied:

"O you, wherein they say souls rest,
    Till they descend pure heavenly fires,
    Shall lustful and corrupt desires
With your immortal seed be blessed?[2]

And shall our love, so far beyond
    That low and dying appetite,   70
    And which so chaste desires unite,
Not hold in an eternal bond?

Is it because we should decline
    And wholly from our thoughts exclude
    Objects that may the sense delude,
And study only the divine?

No sure, for if none can ascend
    Even to the visible degree
    Of things created, how should we
The invisible comprehend?   80

Or rather, since that Power expressed
    His greatness in his works alone,
    Being here best in his creatures known,
Why is he not loved in them best?

ODE UPON A QUESTION MOVED
  1 Fear.
  2 Melander is addressing the stars. Cf. Plato, *Timaeus*.

But is't not true, which you pretend,
    That since our love and knowledge here
    Only as parts of life appear,
So they with it should take their end.

O no, beloved, I am most sure,
    Those virtuous habits we acquire,   90
    As being with the soul entire,
Must with it evermore endure.

For if, where sins and vice reside,
    We find so foul a guilt remain,
    As never dying in his stain,
Still punished in the soul doth bide,

Much more that true and real joy,
    Which in a virtuous love is found,
    Must be more solid in its ground,
Than fate or death can e'er destroy.   100

Else should our souls in vain elect,
    And vainer yet were heaven's laws,
    When to an everlasting cause
They gave a perishing effect.

Nor here on earth then, nor above,
    Our good affection can impair,
    For where God doth admit the fair,
Think you that he excludeth love?

These eyes again then eyes shall see,
    And hands again these hands enfold,   110
    And all chaste pleasures can be told
Shall with us everlasting be.

For if no use of sense remain
    When bodies once this life forsake,
    Or they could no delight partake,
Why should they ever rise again?

And if every imperfect mind
    Make love the end of knowledge here,
    How perfect will our love be, where
All imperfection is refined!   120

Let then no doubt, Celinda, touch,
    Much less your fairest mind invade,
    Were not our souls immortal made,
Our equal loves can make them such.

So when one wing can make no way,
   Two joinèd can themselves dilate,
   So can two persons propagate,
When singly either would decay.

So when from hence we shall be gone,   130
   And be no more, nor you, nor I,
   As one another's mystery,
Each shall be both, yet both but one."

This said, in her uplifted face,
   Her eyes which did that beauty crown,
   Were like two stars, that having fallen down,
Look up again to find their place:

While such a moveless silent peace
   Did seize on their becalmèd sense,
   One would have thought some influence
Their ravished spirits did possess.   140

William Drummond

OF HAWTHORNDEN

[1585–1649]

THE most considerable Scottish poet between Sir David Lyndsay in the sixteenth century and Allan Ramsay in the eighteenth, the melancholy laird of
Hawthornden shows in his work a sensibility derived more from his great
library than from the experiences of actual life. Jonson said of his verses that
they "smelled too much of the schools and were not after the fancy of the time," and
the modern reader may occasionally agree. The fashion of Jonson's time now belongs
to history, however, and it is possible, in reading Drummond, to sense behind the
echoes of other poets the delicate and individual touch which is the poet's own.

Shortly after receiving his M.A. at Edinburgh University in 1605, Drummond went
to France for two years of further study. In 1610 he succeeded his father as laird, and a
few years later occurred the most significant episode in his emotional life: his fiancée,
Mary Cunningham, died shortly before their projected wedding. The experience seems
to have intensified permanently the melancholy, retiring, bookish qualities which had
always distinguished the poet's temperament. Even in bereavement Drummond found
a model for his expression; the amorous *Poems* (1616) fall, like the *Rime* of Petrarch,
into sections celebrating the life and mourning the death of the beloved. Drummond
also published *Forth Feasting* (1617), a panegyric on James I, and *A Cypress Grove* (1623),
a prose meditation on mortality. The latter was accompanied by *Flowers of Sion*,
Drummond's religious verses.

Drummond counts as a distinct conservative among seventeenth-century poets. His
models are primarily Sidney, Spenser, and Daniel among English poets and Petrarch,
Ronsard, Tasso, and Garcilaso de la Vega among Continental poets. His letters contain
an explicit expression of distaste for the "strong lines" of Donne and his followers, and
his entire work shows a fondness for the sonnet form, which had fallen out of favor
with most of his contemporaries. Undoubtedly, the conservative and derivative features
of Drummond's poetry come not only from his personality but also from the linguistic
situation in which he found himself. Living in an age when the once great tradition of
the Scots-English literary language was falling into decay, when the Scottish court had
removed to London to become the English court, he wrote his poems in standard
southern English, a language which was essentially foreign to him and which inevitably
assumed, in his hands, a kind of stilted artificiality which sometimes smothers his natural
eloquence.

In his last years Drummond wrote royalist pamphlets, and he died in the year of the
execution of Charles I.

W. DRUMMOND OF HAWTHORNDEN. *Poetical Works*, ed. L. E. Kastner, 2 vols. (Manchester, 1913).

D. MASSON. *Drummond of Hawthornden* (London, 1873). A monumental biography which is, despite its age, very useful.

F. R. FOGLE. *A Critical Study of William Drummond of Hawthornden* (New York, 1952).

F R O M

POEMS BY WILLIAM DRUMMOND OF HAWTHORNDEN [1616]

THE FIRST PART

SONNET 7

That learnèd Grecian,[1] who did so excel
In knowledge passing sense that he is named
Of all the after-worlds divine, doth tell
That at the time when first our souls are framed,
Ere in these mansions blind they come to dwell,
They live bright rays of that eternal light,
And others see, know, love, in heaven's great
    height;
Not toiled with aught to reason doth rebel.[2]
Most true it is, for straight at the first sight
My mind me told that in some other place   10
It elsewhere saw the idea of that face,
And loved a love of heavenly pure delight.
    No wonder now I feel so fair a flame,
    Sith[3] I her loved ere on this earth she came.

SONNET 9

Sleep, Silence' child, sweet father of soft rest,
Prince whose approach peace to all mortals brings,
Indifferent host to shepherds and to kings,
Sole comforter of minds with grief oppressed,
Lo, by thy charming rod all breathing things
Lie slumb'ring, with forgetfulness possessed;
And yet o'er me to spread thy drowsy wings
Thou spares, alas! who cannot be thy guest.

Since I am thine, O come, but with that face
To inward light which thou art wont to show,   10
With feignèd solace ease a true-felt woe;
Or if, deaf god, thou do deny that grace,
    Come as thou wilt, and what thou wilt bequeath;
    I long to kiss the image of my death.

SONG 2

Phœbus, arise,
And paint the sable skies
With azure, white, and red;
Rouse Memnon's mother from her Tithon's bed,[1]
That she thy cáreer may with roses spread;
The nightingales thy coming each where sing;
Make an eternal spring;
Give life to this dark world which lieth dead.
Spread forth thy golden hair
In larger locks than thou wast wont before,   10
And emperor-like, decore[2]
With diadem of pearl thy temples fair.
Chase hence the ugly night,
Which serves but to make dear thy glorious light.
This is that happy morn,
That day, long-wishèd day
Of all my life so dark
(If cruel stars have not my ruin sworn,
And fates not hope betray),
Which, only white, deserves   20
A diamond forever should it mark;
This is the morn should bring unto this grove
My love, to hear and recompense my love.

SONNET 7
1 Plato.
2 Not troubled with anything that rebels against reason.
3 Since.

SONG 2
1 Tithonus, a mortal who had been granted immortality, was the husband of Aurora (Memnon's mother), goddess of the dawn.
2 Decorate.

Fair king, who all preserves,
But show thy blushing beams,
And thou two sweeter eyes
Shalt see than those which by Peneus' streams
Did once thy heart surprise; [3]
Nay, suns, which shine as clear
As thou when two thou did to Rome appear.   30
Now, Flora, deck thyself in fairest guise;
If that ye, winds, would hear
A voice surpassing far Amphion's lyre,
Your stormy chiding stay;
Let Zephyr only breathe
And with her tresses play,
Kissing sometimes these purple ports of death.
The winds all silent are,
And Phœbus in his chair,
Ensaffroning sea and air,   40
Makes vanish every star;
Night like a drunkard reels,
Beyond the hills to shun his flaming wheels;
The fields with flowers are decked in every hue,
The clouds bespangle with bright gold their blue;
Here is the pleasant place,
And ev'ry thing save her, who all should grace.

THE SECOND PART

MADRIGAL 1

This life which seems so fair
Is like a bubble blown up in the air
By sporting children's breath,
Who chase it everywhere,
And strive who can most motion it bequeath;
And though it sometime seem of its own might,
Like to an eye of gold, to be fixed there,
And firm to hover in that empty height,
That only is because it is so light;
But in that pomp it doth not long appear,
    For even when most admired, it in a thought,
    As swelled from nothing, doth dissolve in
        nought.

SONG 2
3 Phœbus (Apollo) met and became enamored of Daphne
by the stream of the river-god Peneus, her father.

SONNET 8

My lute, be as thou wast when thou didst grow
With thy green mother in some shady grove,
When immelodious winds but made thee move,
And birds on thee their ramage [1] did bestow.
Sith that dear voice which did thy sounds approve,
Which used in such harmonious strains to flow,
Is reft from earth to tune those spheres above,
What art thou but a harbinger of woe?
Thy pleasing notes be pleasing notes no more,
But orphan wailings to the fainting ear,   10
Each stop a sigh, each sound draws forth a tear.
Be therefore silent as in woods before;
    Or if that any hand to touch thee deign,
    Like widowed turtle [2] still her loss complain.

URANIA, OR SPIRITUAL
POEMS

SONNET 2

Too long I followed have my fond desire,
And too long painted on the ocean streams;
Too long refreshment sought amidst the fire,
And hunted joys, which to my soul were blames.
Ah! when I had what most I did admire,
And seen of life's delights the last extremes,
I found all but a rose hedged with a brier,
A nought, a thought, a show of mocking dreams.
Henceforth on Thee mine only good I'll think,
For only Thou canst grant what I do crave;   10
Thy nail my pen shall be, Thy blood mine ink,
Thy winding-sheet my paper, study grave;
    And till that soul forth of this body fly,
    No hope I'll have but only only Thee.

MADRIGAL 2

Love which is here a care
That wit and will doth mar,
Uncertain truce and a most certain war,
A shrill tempestuous wind
Which doth disturb the mind,

And like wild waves our désigns all commove—
Among those sprites [1] above
Which see their Maker's face,
It a contentment is, a quiet peace,
  A pleasure void of grief, a constant rest,
  Eternal joy, which nothing can molest.

SONNET 7

Thrice happy he who by some shady grove
Far from the clamorous world doth live his own;
Though solitaire, yet who is not alone,
But doth converse with that Eternal Love.

MADRIGAL 2
1 Spirits.

Oh, how more sweet is birds' harmonious moan,
Or the soft sobbings of the widowed dove,
Than those smooth whisp'rings near a prince's
    throne,
Which good make doubtful, do the evil approve!
Oh, how more sweet is Zephyr's wholesome
    breath,   9
And sighs perfumed, which do the flowers unfold,
Than that applause vain honor doth bequeath!
How sweet are streams to poison drunk in gold!
  The world is full of horrors, falsehoods, slights;
  Woods' silent shades have only true delights.

FROM

FLOWERS OF SION [1630]

SONNET 3

Look how the flower which ling'ringly doth fade,
The morning's darling late, the summer's queen,
Spoiled of that juice which kept it fresh and green,
As high as it did raise, bows low the head;
Right so my life (contentments being dead,
Or in their contraries but only seen)
With swifter speed declines than erst it spread,
And, blasted, scarce now shows what it hath been.
As doth the pilgrim, therefore, whom the night
By darkness would imprison on his way,   10
Think on thy home, my soul, and think aright,
Of what yet rests thee of life's wasting day.
  Thy sun posts westward, passèd is thy morn,
  And twice it is not given thee to be born.

SONNET 11

The last and greatest herald [1] of heaven's King,
Girt with rough skins, hies to the deserts wild,
Among that savage brood the woods forth bring,
Which he than man more harmless found and mild;
His food was blossoms, and what young doth
    spring,
With honey that from virgin hives distilled;
Parched body, hollow eyes, some uncouth thing
Made him appear, long since from earth exiled.

SONNET 11
1 John the Baptist.

There burst he forth: "All ye whose hopes rely
On God, with me amidst these deserts mourn,   10
Repent, repent, and from old errors turn."
Who listened to his voice, obeyed his cry?
  Only the echoes which he made relent,
  Rung from their marble caves, "Repent, repent."

MADRIGAL 4

This world a hunting is:
The prey, poor man; the Nimrod fierce is death;
His speedy greyhounds are
Lust, sickness, envy, care,
Strife that ne'er falls amiss,
With all those ills which haunt us while we breathe.
Now if, by chance, we fly
Of these the eager chase,
Old age with stealing pace
Casts up his nets, and there we panting die.

SONNET 23

Sweet bird, that sing'st away the early hours,
Of winters past or coming void of care,
Well pleasèd with delights which present are,
Fair seasons, budding sprays, sweet-smelling
    flowers;

To rocks, to springs, to rills, from leavy bowers
Thou thy Creator's goodness dost declare,
And what dear gifts on thee He did not spare,
A stain to human sense in sin that lowers.
What soul can be so sick, which by thy songs,
Attired in sweetness, sweetly is not driven   10
Quite to forget earth's turmoils, spites, and wrongs,
And lift a reverend eye and thought to heaven?
    Sweet artless songster, thou my mind dost raise
    To airs of spheres, yes, and to angels' lays.

SONNET 25

More oft than once death whispered in mine ear:
Grave what thou hears in diamond and gold—
I am that monarch whom all monarchs fear,
Who hath in dust their far-stretched pride uprolled.
All, all is mine beneath moon's silver sphere,
And nought save virtue can my power withhold.
This, not believed, experience true thee told
By danger late when I to thee came near.
As bugbear then my visage I did show,   9
That of my horrors thou right use might'st make,
And a more sacred path of living take.
Now still walk armèd for my ruthless blow;
    Trust flattering life no more, redeem time past,
    And live each day as if it were the last.

Giles Fletcher

[c. 1585–1623]

LIKE his elder brother Phineas, Giles Fletcher was a follower of Spenser and a forerunner of Milton. In his own right, however, he is a more considerable poet than his brother; his masterpiece, *Christ's Victory and Triumph*, has some monotonous passages, but it also has a good number of passages of breathtaking beauty and originality. It shows the influence of Spenser in its allegorical technique, its richly sensuous texture, and its stanza form—a modified version of the Spenserian stanza—but in its reliance on paradox, conceit, and oxymoron it has an affinity to the work of Du Bartas and other Continental poets who first formulated the Baroque poetic style. Fletcher's style, though markedly different from Donne's, constitutes a parallel development away from the sustained naturalness and ease of Renaissance style; Fletcher's concentration on certain Spenserian features at the expense of others leads ultimately to an effect very different from that of his master.

Giles Fletcher received his B.A. from Trinity College, Cambridge, in 1606, and became reader in Greek there in 1615. In 1617 an ecclesiastical living was bestowed on him—by Francis Bacon, according to one story—and in 1619 he received another living, at Alderton in Suffolk, where he spent the remainder of his short life. That life was, according to Fuller, made unhappy by the low-church proclivities of his "clownish, low-parted parishioners."

Christ's Victory and Triumph, published in 1610, while the poet was still at Cambridge, is a religious epic divided into four cantos dealing with, respectively, the nativity, temptation, crucifixion, and ascension of Christ. Canto II, in its evocation of Christ in the wilderness and its characterization of Satan, provided Milton with more than a few hints for *Paradise Regained,* but Canto IV supplies perhaps the best example of Fletcher's distinctive and at times dazzling poetic gifts.

(For bibliography, see under Phineas Fletcher.)

F R O M

CHRIST'S TRIUMPH AFTER DEATH [1610]

CANTO IV
Christ's Victory and Triumph

1

BUT now the second morning from her bower
Began to glister in her beams; and now
The roses of the day began to flower
In the eastern garden, for heaven's smiling brow
Half insolent for joy began to show.
　　The early sun came lively dancing out,
　　And the brag lambs ran wantoning about,
That heaven and earth might seem in triumph both
　　　　to shout.

2

The engladded spring, forgetful now to weep,
Began to eblazon from her leafy bed;　　　　　10
The waking swallow broke her half-year's sleep;
And every bush lay deeply purpured
With violets; the wood's late-wintry head
　　Wide flaming primroses set all on fire,
　　And his bald trees put on their green attire,
Among whose infant leaves the joyous birds
　　　　conspire.

3

And now the taller sons, whom Titan warms,
Of unshorn mountains, blown with easy winds,
Dandled the morning's childhood in their arms;
And if they chanced to slip the prouder pines,　　20
The under corylets did catch the shines
　　To gild their leaves; saw never happy year
　　Such joyful triumph and triumphant cheer,
As though the aged world anew created were.

4

Say, earth, why has thou got thee new attire
And stickest thy habit full of daisies red?
Seems that thou dost to some high thought aspire,
And some new-found-out bridegroom meanest
　　　　to wed.

Tell me ye trees, so fresh appareled,
　　So never let the spiteful canker waste you,　　30
　　So never let the heavens with lightning blast you,
Why go you now so trimly dressed, or whither
　　　　haste you?

5

Answer me, Jordan, why thy crooked tide
So often wanders from his nearest way,
As though some other way thy stream would slide,
And fain salute the place where something lay?
And you sweet birds, that, shaded from the ray,
　　Sit caroling and piping grief away,
　　The while the lambs to hear you dance and play,
Tell me, sweet birds, what it is you so fain would
　　　　say?　　　　　　　　　　　　　　40

6

And thou fair spouse of earth that every year
Gettest such a numerous issue of thy bride,
How chance thou hotter shinest, and drawest more
　　　　near?
Sure thou somewhere some worthy sight hast spied,
That in one place for joy thou canst not bide.
　　And you dead swallows, that so lively now
　　Through the flit air your winged passage row,
How could new life into your frozen ashes flow?

7

Ye primroses and purple violets,
Tell me why blaze ye from your leafy bed,　　　50
And woo men's hands to rend you from your sets,
As though you would somewhere be carrièd,
With fresh perfumes and velvets garnishèd?
　　But ah! I need not ask; 'tis surely so:
　　You all would to your Saviour's triumphs go;
There would ye all wait and humble homage do.

8

There should the earth herself with garlands new
And lovely flowers embellished adore;
Such roses never in her garland grew,
Such lilies never in her breast she wore,　　　　60

Like beauty never yet did shine before.
　　There should the sun another sun behold,
　　From whence himself borrows his locks of gold
That kindle heaven and earth with beauties
　　manifold.

9

There might the violet and the primrose sweet
Beams of more lively and more lovely grace,
Arising from their beds of incense meet;
There should the swallow see new life embrace
Dead ashes, and the grave unheal his face
　　To let the living from his bowels creep,　　70
　　Unable longer his own dead to keep;
There heaven and earth should see their Lord
　　awake from sleep.

10

Their Lord, before by other judged to die,
Now judge of all Himself; before forsaken
Of all the world, that from His aid did fly,
Now by the saints into their armies taken;
Before for an unworthy man mistaken,
　　Now worthy to be God confessed; before
　　With blasphemies by all the basest tore,
Now worshipèd by angels, that Him low adore.　　80

11

Whose garment was before indipped in blood,
But now imbrightened into heavenly flame,
The sun itself outglitters, though he should
Climb to the top of the celestial frame
And force the stars go hide themselves for shame;
　　Before that under earth was burièd,
　　But now about the heavens is carrièd,
And there forever by the angels herièd.[1]

12

So fairest Phosphor, the bright morning star,
But newly washed in the green element,　　90
Before the drowsy night is half aware,
Shooting his flaming locks with dew besprent,
Springs lively up into the orient;
　　And the bright drove, fleeced in gold, he chases
　　To drink, that on the Olympic mountain grazes,
The while the minor planets forfeit all their faces.

13

So long He wandered in our lower sphere
That heaven began his cloudy stars despise,
Half envious, to see on earth appear
A greater light than flamed in his own skies.　　100
At length it burst for spite, and out there flies
　　A globe of wingèd angels, swift as thought,
　　That on their spotted feathers lively caught
The sparkling earth, and to their azure fields it
　　brought.

14

The rest, that yet amazèd stood below,
With eyes cast up, as greedy to be fed,
And hands upheld, themselves to ground did
　　throw;
So when the Trojan boy[2] was ravishèd,
As through the Idalian woods they say he fled,
　　His aged guardians stood all dismayed,　　110
　　Some lest he should have fallen back afraid,
And some their hasty vows and timely prayers
　　said.

15

Toss up your heads, ye everlasting gates,
And let the Prince of glory enter in!
At whose brave volley of siderial states,
The sun to blush, and stars grow pale were seen,
When leaping first from earth, He did begin
　　To climb His angel's wings; "Then open hang
　　Your crystal doors," so all the chorus sang
Of heavenly birds, as to the stars they nimbly
　　sprang.　　120

16

Hark! how the floods clap their applauding hands,
The pleasant valleys singing for delight;
The wanton mountains dance about the lands;
The while the fields, struck with the heavenly light,
Set all their flowers a-smiling at the sight;
　　The trees laugh with their blossoms; and the
　　sound
　　Of the triumphant shout of praise that crowned
The flaming Lamb, breaking through heaven, hath
　　passage found.

1 Cf. Old English, *herian*, to praise.

2 Ganymede, cup-bearer to the gods, carried to Olympus by Zeus.

17

Out leap the antique patriarchs all in haste,
To see the powers of hell in triumph led,   130
And with small stars a garland interchased
Of olive leaves they bore, to crown His head,
That was before with thorns degloried.
     After them flew the prophets, brightly stoled
     In shining lawn, and wimpled manifold,
Striking their ivory harps, strung all in chords of gold.

18

To which the saints victorious carols sung,
Ten thousand saints at once, that with the sound
The hollow vaults of heaven for triumph rung;
The cherubim their clamors did confound   140
With all the rest, and clapt their wings around;
     Down from their thrones the dominations flow,
     And at His feet their crowns and scepters throw;
And all the princely souls fell on their faces low.

19

Nor can the martyrs' wounds them stay behind,
But out they rush among the heavenly crowd,
Seeking their heaven out of their heaven to find,
Sounding their silver trumpets out so loud
That the shrill noise broke through the starry
          cloud;
     And all the virgin souls in pure array   150
     Came dancing forth and making joyous play:
So Him they lead along into the courts of day.

20

So Him they lead into the courts of day,
Where never war, nor wounds abide Him more;
But in that house eternal peace doth play,
Acquieting the souls, that new before
Their way to heaven through their own blood did
          score,
     But now, estrangèd from all misery,
     As far as heaven and earth discoasted lie,
Swelter in quiet waves of immortality.   160

21

And if great things by smaller may be guessed,
So in the midst of Neptune's angry tide
Our Britain Island, like the weedy nest
Of true halcyon,[3] on the waves doth ride,

3 The kingfisher, popularly believed to nest upon the
waves and to impose calm on the waters during its period of
nesting.

And softly sailing, scorns the water's pride;
     While all the rest, drowned on the Continent
     And tost in bloody waves, their wounds lament,
And stand to see our peace, as struck with
          wonderment.

22

The ship of France religious waves do toss,
And Greece itself is now grown barbarous;   170
Spain's children hardly dare the ocean cross,
And Belge's field lies waste and ruinous,
That unto those the heavens are envious,
     And unto them, themselves are strangers grown,
     And unto these, the seas are faithless known,
And unto her, alas! her own is not her own.

23

Here only shut we Janus' iron gates,
And call the welcome Muses to our springs,
And are but pilgrims from our heavenly states,
The while the trusty earth sure plenty brings,   180
And ships through Neptune safely spread their
          wings.
     Go, blessed Island, wander where thou please,
     Unto thy God, or men, heaven, lands, or seas;
Thou canst not lose thy way; thy king with all
          hath peace.

24

Dear Prince, thy subject's joy, hope of their heirs,
Picture of peace, or breathing image rather,
The certain argument of all our prayers,
Thy Harry's and thy country's lovely father,
Let peace in endless joys forever bathe her
     Within thy sacred breast, that at thy birth   190
     Brought'st her with thee from heaven to dwell
          on earth,
Making our earth a heaven, and paradise of mirth.

25

Let not my liege misdeem these humble lays,
As licked with soft and supple blandishment,
Or spoken to disparagon his praise;
For though pale Cynthia near her brother's tent
Soon disappears in the white firmament,
     And gives him back the beams before were his,
     Yet when he verges, or is hardly riz,
She the vive[4] image of her absent brother is.   200

4 Lively.

26

Nor let the Prince of Peace his beadsman blame,
That with his Stewart⁵ dares his Lord compare,
And heavenly peace with earthly quiet shame;
So pines to lowly plants compared are,
And lightning Phœbus to a little star.
    And well I wot, my rhyme, albe unsmooth,
    Ne says but what it means, ne means but sooth,
Ne harms the good, ne good to harmful person
    doth.

27

Gaze but upon the house where man embowers:
With flowers and rushes paved is his way,   210
Where all the creatures are his servitors;
The winds do sweep his chambers every day,
And clouds do wash his rooms; the ceiling gay,
    Starred aloft, the gilded knobs embrave.
    If such a house God to another gave,
How shine those glittering courts He for Himself
    will have?

28

And if a sullen cloud as sad as night,
In which the sun may seem embodied,
Depured of all his dross, we see so white,
Burning in melted gold his wat'ry head,   220
Or round with ivory edges silvered,
    What luster super-excellent will he
    Lighten on those that all his sunshine see,
In that all-glorious court in which all glories be?

29

If but one sun, with his diffusive fires,
Can paint the stars and the whole world with light,
And joy and life in each heart inspires,
And every saint shall shine in heaven as bright
As doth the sun in his transcendent might,   229
    (As faith may well believe what truth once says)
    What shall so many suns united rays
But dazzle all the eyes, that now in heaven we
    praise?

30

Here let my Lord hang up His conquering lance
And bloody armor with late slaughter warm,

⁵ A play on the name of the royal house of Stuart.

And looking down on His weak militants,
Behold His saints, midst of their hot alarm,
Hang all their golden hopes upon His arm;
    And in this lower field dispacing wide,
    Through windy thoughts that would their nails
      misguide,
Anchor their fleshly ships fast in His wounded
    side.   240

31

Here may the band that now in triumph shines,
And that, before they were invested thus,
In earthly bodies carried heavenly minds,
Pitched round about in order glorious,
Their sunny tents and houses luminous;
    All the eternal day in songs employing,
    Joying their end, without end of their joying,
While their Almighty Prince destruction is
    destroying.

32

Full, yet without satiety, of that
Which whets and quiets greedy appetite,   250
Where never sun did rise, nor ever set;
But one eternal day and endless light
Gives time to those who time is infinite;
    Speaking with thought, obtaining without fee,
    Beholding Him whom never eye could see,
And magnifying Him that cannot greater be.

33

How can such joy as this want words to speak?
And yet what words can speak such joy as this?
Far from the world, that might their quiet break,
Here the glad souls the face of beauty kiss,   260
Poured out in pleasure on their beds of bliss;
    And drunk with nectar torrents, ever hold
    Their eyes on Him, whose graces manifold,
The more they do behold, the more they would
    behold.

34

Their sight drinks lovely fires in at their eyes;
Their brain sweet incense with fine breath accloys,
That on God's sweating altar burning lies;
Their hungry ears feed on their heavenly noise
That angels sing, to tell their untold joys;
    Their understanding naked truth, their wills   270
    The all, and self-sufficient Goodness fills,
That nothing here is wanting, but the want of ills.

35

No sorrow now hangs clouding on their brow,
No bloodless malady empales their face,
No age drops on their hairs his silver snow,
No nakedness their bodies doth embase,
No poverty themselves and theirs disgrace,
  No fear of death the joy of life devours,
  No unchaste sleep their precious time deflowers,
No loss, no grief, no change wait on their winged
      hours.   280

36

But now their naked bodies scorn the cold,
And from their eyes joy looks, and laughs at pain;
The infant wonders how he came so old,
And old man how he came so young again;
Still resting, though from sleep they still refrain,
  Where all are rich, and yet no gold they owe,
  And all are kings, and yet no subjects know.
All full, and yet no time on food they do bestow.

37

For things that pass are past, and in this field
The indeficient spring no winter fears;   290
The trees together fruit and blossom yield;
The unfading lily leaves of silver bears,
And crimson rose a scarlet garment wears.
  And all of these on the saints' bodies grow,
  Not, as they wont, on baser earth below;
Three rivers here of milk and wine and honey flow.

38

About the holy city rolls a flood
Of molten crystal, like a sea of glass,
On which weak stream a strong foundation
      stood;
Of living diamond the building was,   300
That all things else besides itself did pass;
  Her streets, instead of stones, the stars did pave,
  And little pearls for dust, it seemed to have,
On which soft-streaming manna, like pure snow,
      did wave.

39

In midst of this city celestial,
Where the eternal temple should have rose,[6]
Lightened the Idea Beatifical:
End and beginning of each thing that grows,

6 Cf. Revelation 21:22.

Whose self no end, nor yet beginning knows;
  That hath no eyes to see, nor ears to hear,   310
  Yet sees and hears and is all eye, all ear;
That nowhere is contained and yet is everywhere.

40

Changer of all things, yet immutable;
Before and after all, the first and last,
That moving all, is yet immovable;
Great without quantity, in whose forecast
Things past are present, things to come are past;
  Swift without motion, to whose open eye
  The hearts of wicked men unbreasted lie,   319
At once absent and present to them, far and nigh.

41

It is no flaming luster made of light,
No sweet consent, or well-timed harmony,
Ambrosia for to feast the appetite,
Or flowery odor mixed with spicery,
No soft embrace or pleasure bodily;
  And yet it is a kind of inward feast,
  A harmony that sounds within the breast,
An odor, light, embrace, in which the soul doth
      rest.

42

A heavenly feast, no hunger can consume,
A light unseen, yet shines in every place,   330
A sound no time can steal, a sweet perfume
No winds can scatter, an entire embrace
That no satiety can e'er unlace;
  Ingraced into so high a favor, there
  The saints with their beau-peers whole worlds
      outwear,
And things unseen do see, and things unheard do
      hear.

43

Ye blessed souls, grown richer by your spoil,
Whose loss, though great, is cause of greater gains.
Here may your weary spirits rest from toil.
Spending your endless evening that remains,   340
Among those white flocks and celestial trains
  That feed upon their Shepherd's eyes, and frame
  That heavenly music of so wondrous frame,
Psalming aloud the holy honors of His name.

44

Had I a voice of steel to tune my song,
Were every verse as smoothly filed as glass,

And every member turnèd to a tongue,
And every tongue were made of sounding brass,
Yet all that skill and all this strength, alas!
   Should it presume to gild, were misadvisèd   350
   The place where David hath new songs devisèd,
As in his burning throne he sits emparadisèd.

45

Most happy prince, whose eyes those stars behold,
Treading ours under feet, now mayest thou pour
That overflowing skill wherewith of old
Thou wont'st to comb rough speech; now mayest
    thou shower
Fresh streams of praise upon that holy bower,
   Which well we heaven call, not that it rolls,
   But that it is the haven of our souls:
Most happy prince, whose sight so heavenly sight
    beholds!   360

46

Ah, foolish shepherds, that were wont esteem
Your God all rough and shaggy-haired to be;
And yet far wiser shepherds than ye deem,
For who so poor (though who so rich) as He,
When, with us hermiting in low degree,
   He washed His flocks in Jordan's spotless tide;
   And, that His dear remembrance ay might bide,
Did to us come and with us lived and for us died?

47

But now so lively colors did embeam
His sparkling forehead, and so shiny rays   370
Kindled His flaming locks that down did stream
In curls along His neck, where sweetly plays
(Singing His wounds of love in sacred lays)
   His dearest spouse, spouse of the dearest Lover,
   Knitting a thousand knots over and over,
And dying still for love, but they her still recover.

48

Fair Egliset, that at His eyes doth dress
Her glorious face, those eyes from whence are shed

Infinite bel-amours, where to express
His love, high God all heaven as captive leads,   380
And all the banners of His grace dispreads,
   And in those windows doth His arms englaze,
   And on those eyes the angels all do gaze,
And from those eyes the lights of heaven do glean
    their blaze.

49

But let the Kentish lad that lately taught
His oaten reed the trumpet's silver sound,
Young Thyrsilis,[7] and for his music brought
The willing spheres from heaven to lead a round
Of dancing nymphs and herds, that sung and
    crowned
   Eclecta's hymen with ten thousand flowers   390
   Of choicest praise, and hung her heavenly bowers
With saffron garlands, dressed for nuptial
    paramours,

50

Let his shrill trumpet with her silver blast,
Of fair Eclecta and her spousal bed,
Be the sweet pipe and smooth encomiast;
But my green Muse, hiding her younger head
Under old Camus' flaggy banks, that spread
   Their willow locks abroad, and all the day
   With their own wat'ry shadows wanton play,
Dares not those high amours and love-sick songs
    assay.   400

51

Impotent words, weak lines, that strive in vain,
In vain, alas, to tell so heavenly sight!
So heavenly sight as none can greater feign,
Feign what he can that seems of greatest might,
   Might any yet compare with Infinite?
   Infinite sure those joys, my words but light;
Light is the palace where she dwells—O blessed
    wight!

7 Thirsil, Phineas Fletcher's pastoral pseudonym.

George Wither

[1588–1667]

ITHER is, like Drummond, an essentially conservative poet who carries the traditions of the Elizabethan age into the seventeenth century. As Drummond cultivated the unfashionable forms of sonnet and canzone, so Wither wrote pastorals and general satires in an age which had turned its primary attention to other types of literature. Wither's old-fashioned qualities did not, however, diminish either his immense popularity or his extraordinary productivity.

Born of a well-to-do family in Brentworth, Hampshire, Wither attended Magdalen College, Oxford, but did not graduate. He is next heard of as a student of law at Lincoln's Inn in London, where he wrote his satire *Abuses Stripped and Whipped* (1613), the frankness of which led to his being imprisoned for several months in the Marshalsea. Little dismayed by the experience, he occupied his time by writing a sequence of pastorals, *The Shepherd's Hunting* (published in 1615), into which he introduced, under pastoral names, both himself and his friend William Browne of Tavistock, with whom he had collaborated earlier on *The Shepherd's Pipe*. In 1622 appeared the collection *Fair Virtue, the Mistress of Philarete*, which contains the best of his lyric verse.

At some point in the 1620's Wither's talent seems to have run dry, and that fact may be related to his fervent espousal of the moral and political aims of Puritanism. At any rate, the poems he continued to pour forth throughout the rest of his long life are monotonously didactic and have little interest for the modern reader. Of some historical significance is his *Collection of Emblems, Ancient and Modern*, which appeared in 1635, the year of Quarles' *Emblems*, and ranks with that work as an example of emblem poetry.

Wither served as an officer in Cromwell's army, and it is said that, being captured, he was saved from hanging by the intercession of Sir John Denham, who held that, as long as Wither was alive, he himself would not be accounted the worst poet in England. Later critics, among them Charles Lamb, have been kinder to Wither's modest virtues and have admired the virile lyricism which is the dominant trait of his earlier work.

G. WITHER. *Poetry*, ed. F. Sidgwick, 2 vols. (London, 1902). Contains most of the early lyrics.

FROM

FAIR VIRTUE, THE MISTRESS OF PHILARETE [1622]

SONNET 4[1]

Shall I, wasting in despair
Die because a woman's fair?
Or make pale my cheeks with care
'Cause another's rosy are?
Be she fairer than the day,
Or the flow'ry meads in May,
   If she be not so to me,
    What care I how fair she be?

Shall my heart be grieved or pined
'Cause I see a woman kind?   10
Or a well-disposèd nature
Joinèd with a lovely feature?[2]
Be she meeker, kinder than
Turtledove or pelican,[3]
   If she be not so to me,
    What care I how kind she be?

Shall a woman's virtues move
Me to perish for her love?
Or, her well-deserving known,
Make me quite forget mine own?   20
Be she with that goodness blest
Which may gain her name of best,
   If she be not such to me,
    What care I how good she be?

'Cause her fortune[4] seems too high,
Shall I play the fool and die?
Those that bear a noble mind,
Where they want of riches find,
Think what with them they would do
That without them dare to woo;   30
   And unless that mind I see,
    What care I how great she be?

Great or good, or kind, or fair,
I will ne'er the more despair;
If she love me, this believe,
I will die ere she shall grieve;
If she slight me when I woo,
I can scorn and let her go;
   For if she be not for me,
    What care I for whom she be?   40

SONNET 5

I wandered out a while agone,
And went I know not whither;
But there do beauties many a one
Resort and meet together,
And Cupid's power will there be shown
If ever you come thither.

For like two suns, two beauties bright
I shining saw together,
And tempted by their double light
My eyes I fixed on either;   10
Till both at once so thralled my sight,
I loved, and knew not whether.[1]

Such equal sweet Venus gave,[2]
That I preferred not either;
And when for love I thought to crave,
I knew not well of whether,
For one while this I wished to have,
And then I that had liefer.

A lover of the curious't eye
Might have been pleased in either,   20
And so, I must confess, might I,
Had they not been together.
Now both must love or both deny,
In one enjoy I neither.

SONNET 4
  1 "Sonnet" here means *song*, as often in the sixteenth and
early seventeenth centuries.
  2 Form.
  3 The pelican was believed to feed her young with blood
from her own breast.
  4 Birth, position.

SONNET 5
  1 Which.
  2 The line is obviously defective. Perhaps it should read,
"Such equal sweetness Venus gave."

But yet at last I 'scaped the smart
  I feared at coming hither;
For seeing my divided heart—
  I, choosing, knew not whether—
Love angry grew and did depart,
And now I care for neither.   30

A CHRISTMAS CAROL

So now is come our joyful'st feast,
  Let every man be jolly;
Each room with ivy leaves is drest,
  And every post with holly.
    Though some churls at our mirth repine,
    Round your foreheads garlands twine,
    Drown sorrow in a cup of wine,
And let us all be merry.

Now all our neighbors' chimneys smoke,
  And Christmas blocks[1] are burning;   10
Their ovens they with baked meats choke,
  And all their spits are turning.
    Without the door let sorrow lie,
    And if for cold it hap to die,
    We'll bury it in a Christmas pie,
And evermore be merry.

Now every lad is wondrous trim,
  And no man mind his labor;
Our lasses have provided them
  A bagpipe and a tabor.   20
    Young men and maids, and girls and boys
    Give life to one another's joys;
    And you anon shall by their noise
Perceive that they are merry.

Rank misers now do sparing shun,
  Their hall of music soundeth;
And dogs thence with whole shoulders run,
  So all things there aboundeth.
    The country-folk themselves advance,   29
    For Crowdy-Mutton's[2] come out of France,
    And Jack shall pipe and Jill shall dance,
And all the town be merry.

Ned Swash hath fetched his bands[3] from pawn,
  And all his best apparel;
Brisk Nell hath bought a ruff of lawn
  With droppings of the barrel.
    And those that hardly all the year
    Had bread to eat or rags to wear,
    Will have both clothes and dainty fare,
And all the day be merry.   40

Now poor men to the justices
  With capons make their arrants,[4]
And if they hap to fail of these,
  They plague them with their warrants.
    But now they feed them with good cheer,
    And what they want they take in beer,
    For Christmas comes but once a year,
And then they shall be merry.

Good farmers in the country nurse
  The poor, that else were undone;   50
Some landlords spend their money worse,
  On lust and pride at London.
    There the roisters[5] they do play,
    Drab and dice their land away,
    Which may be ours another day;
And therefore let's be merry.

The client now his suit forbears,
  The prisoner's heart is easèd;
The debtor drinks away his cares,
  And for the time is pleasèd.   60
    Though others' purses be more fat,
    Why should we pine or grieve at that?
    Hang sorrow, care will kill a cat,
And therefore let's be merry.

Hark how the wags abroad do call
  Each other forth to rambling;
Anon you'll see them in the hall,
  For nuts and apples scrambling.
    Hark how the roofs with laughters sound!
    Anon they'll think the house goes round;   70
    For they the cellar's depths have found,
And there they will be merry.

A CHRISTMAS CAROL
  1 Logs.
  2 Possibly a musician, or perhaps a musical instrument, with a joking reference to its nasal sound.

3 Ruffs.
4 Errands. That is, they seek out excuses for going.
5 Roisterers.

The wenches with their wassail bowls
  About the streets are singing;
The boys are come to catch the owls,[6]
  The wild mare[7] in is bringing.[8]
    Our kitchen boy hath broke his box,[9]
    And to the dealing[10] of the ox
    Our honest neighbors come by flocks,
And here they will be merry.   80

Now kings and queens poor sheep-cotes have,
  And mate[11] with everybody;
The honest now may play the knave,
  And wise men play at noddy.[12]
    Some youths will now a-mumming[13] go,
    Some others play at rowland-hoe,[14]
    And twenty other gameboys[15] moe;[16]
Because they will be merry.

6 A game.   7 The seesaw.
8 Is being brought in.
9 Has opened his Christmas collection-box.
10 Dividing.   11 Associate.
12 A pun on the word. "Noddy" is a card game and also
a simpleton.
13 Masquerading.   14 A game.
15 Gambols.   16 More.

Then wherefore in these merry days
  Should we, I pray, be duller?   90
No, let us sing some roundelays
  To make our mirth the fuller.
    And while we thus inspirèd sing,
    Let all the streets with echoes ring;
    Woods and hills and everything
Bear witness we are merry.

A SONNET UPON A STOLEN KISS

Now gentle sleep hath closèd up those eyes
Which waking kept my boldest thoughts in awe,
And free access unto that sweet lip lies,
From whence I long the rosy breath to draw;
Methinks no wrong it were if I should steal
From those two melting rubies one poor kiss;
None sees the theft that would the thief reveal,
Nor rob I her of aught which she can miss;
Nay, should I twenty kisses take away,
There would be little sign I had done so;   10
Why then should I this robbery delay?
Oh! she may wake and therewith angry grow.
    Well, if she do, I'll back restore that one,
    And twenty hundred thousand more for loan.

F R O M

A COLLECTION OF EMBLEMS [1635]

THE MARIGOLD

When with a serious musing I behold
The grateful and obsequious marigold,
How duly every morning she displays
Her open breast, when Titan spreads his rays;
How she observes him in his daily walk,
Still bending towards him her tender stalk;
How, when he down declines, she droops and
              mourns,
Bedewed, as 'twere, with tears, till he returns;
And how she veils her flowers when he is gone,
As if she scornèd to be lookèd on   10
By an inferior eye, or did contemn
To wait upon a meaner light than him;
When this I meditate, methinks the flowers
Have spirits far more generous than ours,

And give us fair examples to despise
The servile fawnings and idolatries
Wherewith we court these earthly things below,
Which merit not the service we bestow.
    But, O my God! though groveling I appear
Upon the ground, and have a rooting here   20
Which hales me downward, yet in my desire
To that which is above me I aspire,
And all my best affections I profess
To him that is the sun of righteousness.
Oh, keep the morning of His incarnation,
The burning noontide of His bitter passion,
The night of His descending and the height
Of His ascension ever in my sight,
    That imitating Him in that I may,
    I never follow an inferior way.   30

William Browne
OF TAVISTOCK
[1591?–1643?]

LIKE his friend George Wither, William Browne continued the tradition of Sidneyan and Spenserian pastoral well into the seventeenth century. Born in the town of Tavistock in Devon, he always displayed a fervent local patriotism which has led to the association of his birthplace with his name. He was educated at Exeter College, Oxford, and at the Inner Temple, after which for several years he practiced law in London. The first book of his *Britannia's Pastorals* appeared in 1613, the second book in 1616. Between these dates he collaborated with Wither, Christopher Brooke, and John Davies of Hereford on a pastoral volume entitled *The Shepherd's Pipe*, published in 1614. From around 1624 he was in the service of the Earls of Pembroke.

Browne's talent is minor but very real, and his characteristic charm can be found not only in his shorter lyrics but also in many lyric passages of his pastoral narratives.

W. BROWNE. *Poetical Works*, ed. G. Goodwin, 2 vols. (London, 2d ed., 1904).

F. W. MOORMAN. *William Browne: His Britannia's Pastorals and the Pastoral Poetry of the Elizabethan Age* (Strasbourg, 1897). The most complete study.

ON THE DEATH OF MARIE, COUNTESS OF PEMBROKE (1621)

Underneath this sable hearse
Lies the subject of all verse:
Sidney's sister, Pembroke's mother;
Death, ere thou has slain another,
Fair, and learned, and good as she,
Time shall throw a dart at thee.

Marble piles let no man raise
To her name for after days;
Some kind woman borne as she,
Reading this, like Niobe
Shall turn marble and become
Both her mourner and her tomb.

SONG OF THE SIRENS

Steer hither, steer, your wingèd pines,
    All beaten mariners,
Here lie Love's undiscovered mines,
    A prey to passengers;
Perfumes far sweeter than the best
Which make the phœnix' urn and nest.
    Fear not your ships,
Nor any to oppose you, save our lips;
    But come on shore,
Where no joy dies till Love hath gotten more.   10
For swelling waves, our panting breasts
    Where never storms arise,
Exchange; and be awhile our guests:
    For stars gaze on our eyes.

The compass Love shall hourly sing,
And as he goes about the ring,
   We will not miss
To tell each point he nameth with a kiss.
                    —*The Inner Temple Masque,* 1615
                         (Emmanuel College MS.)

These, with many more, methought, complained
That nature should those needless things produce,
Which not alone the sun from others gained,   11
But turn it wholly to their proper use.
   I could not choose but grieve that nature made
   So glorious flowers to live in such a shade.

SONG

For her gait if she be walking,
   Be she sitting I desire her
   For her state's sake, and admire her
For her wit if she be talking:
   Gait and state and wit approve her;
   For which all and each I love her.

Be she sullen, I commend her
   For a modest; be she merry,
   For a kind one her prefer I.
Briefly, everything doth lend her
   So much grace and so approve her
   That for everything I love her.

[DOWN IN A VALLEY]

Down in a valley, by a forest's side,
Near where the crystal Thames rolls on her waves,
I saw a mushroom stand in haughty pride,
As if the lilies grew to be his slaves.
The gentle daisy, with her silver crown,
Worn in the breast of many a shepherd's lass;
The humble violet, that lowly down
Salutes the gay nymphs as they trimly pass:

Robert Herrick

[1591–1674]

O F T H E influences which shaped the poetry of Robert Herrick, Latin classicism as mediated by Ben Jonson was unquestionably the most important. But, although Herrick expresses his veneration for "Saint Ben" in a number of his poems, the note struck most consistently in his work is a highly original and beautifully sustained one. Less intellectually rigorous than the poems of Donne and the other metaphysicals, less ethically conceived than the poems of his master Jonson, Herrick's lyrics have qualities of grace, immediacy, and sensitivity to the cyclic movement of nature which assure him a degree of immortality equal to that of many more ambitious poets. Swinburne has called him, with some justice, "the first in rank and station of English song-writers."

A Londoner by birth, Herrick was the son of a goldsmith who died while the poet was still in infancy. He was apprenticed to an uncle who was also a goldsmith, but he left this seemingly uncongenial trade and entered St. Catherine's College, Cambridge, in 1613, at the relatively late age of twenty-two. He received his B.A. in 1617 and his M.A. in 1620, after which he returned to London, ostensibly to study law but actually to frequent Jonson's favorite taverns and there to learn the rudiments of his true craft, poetry. Among his other acquaintances during these London years were the courtiers Endymion Porter and Henry Herbert (the younger brother of Edward and George Herbert, later Master of the Revels to Charles I), the composers William and Henry Lawes, and the all-powerful royal favorite, the Duke of Buckingham. At some point during these years he must have given up all pretense of a legal career, for he was in holy orders by 1627, the year in which he accompanied Buckingham as chaplain on the unsuccessful military expedition against the Isle of Rhé in France. Two years later, after the Duke's assassination, Herrick sought and obtained the ecclesiastical living of Dean Prior in distant Devonshire.

During his eighteen years as a rural minister in the west of England, Herrick achieved a miniature but wholly genuine artistic greatness. He applied to the materials of his observation and imagination the lessons of brevity, conciseness, and formal perfection which he had learned from Jonson and, behind Jonson, from Horace and Catullus. Beneath the high classical polish of his verse, however, there is a pagan, primitive awareness of the worship of the soil implicit in the folk ceremonies marking the passage of the rural year—despite the ostensibly Christian nature of those ceremonies. The jubilant celebration of natural fertility underlies all of Herrick's work—not only the poems on the festivities of Christmas, Candlemas, and Harvest Home, but also the lovely *carpe diem* address to Corinna on May Day, the haunting laments for the annual disappearance of earthly beauty, and the exuberant celebrations of the beauties of his imaginary mistresses. It is a measure of Herrick's ultimate richness that this pagan sensibility coexists quite amiably with the simple and sincere Christianity expressed in his *Noble Numbers*. The quality which the seventeenth century called *wit*—essentially the capacity for entertaining simultaneously opposed notions—explains Herrick's richness as it does that of the more profound and complex poets of his day.

Expelled by the Puritans in 1647, Herrick returned to London to see through the press the single book of poems on which his entire fame rests. *Hesperides*, together with *Noble Numbers*, was published in 1648. Although the song "Gather ye rosebuds while ye may" became one of the most popular poems of the century, the volume as a whole did not enjoy extraordinary popularity, partly because its manner was too Elizabethan, partly because the turmoil of the day left scant room for sympathy with Herrick's rural and Arcadian subjects. He was obliged to wait until the late nineteenth century to receive his full measure of fame.

Herrick wrote nothing of importance after *Hesperides*, but lived on well into the Restoration. In 1662 his vicarage at Dean Prior was restored to him, and there, in the country which had inspired him, he died.

R. HERRICK. *Poetical Works.* ed. L. C. Martin (Oxford, 1956). Definitive.

F. W. MOORMAN. *Robert Herrick* (London, 1910). A biographical and critical study.

F. DELATTRE. *Robert Herrick* (Paris, 1912). In French; the most exhaustive critical biography.

M. CHUTE. *Two Gentle Men* (New York, 1959). A shorter biography, coupled with a biography of George Herbert.

C. BROOKS. "What Does Poetry Communicate?" in *The Well Wrought Urn* (New York, 1947). A brilliant discussion of "Corinna's Going a-Maying."

K. A. McEUEN. (See under Jonson bibliography.)

R. MACAULAY. *The Shadow Flies* (New York, 1932). A novel in which Herrick is the central figure.

FROM

HESPERIDES [1648]

THE ARGUMENT[1] OF HIS BOOK

I sing of brooks, of blossoms, birds, and bowers:
Of April, May, of June, and July flowers.
I sing of May-poles, hock-carts,[2] wassails, wakes,[3]
Of bridegrooms, brides, and of their bridal cakes.
I write of youth, of love, and have access
By these, to sing of cleanly wantonness.
I sing of dews, of rains, and piece by piece
Of balm, of oil, of spice, and ambergris.[4]

THE ARGUMENT

1 "Argument" is the term formerly used for a brief summary of the contents of a book, poem, etc.

2 The hock-cart was the cart that brought in the last load of the harvest. The celebration of "harvest home" followed upon its arrival. See Herrick's poem, The Hock-Cart, p. 815.

3 Times of merrymaking, formerly held on the anniversary of the dedication of a church, or on the day of the patron saint of the church.

4 A substance secreted by the sperm whale, and used in making perfumes.

I sing of times trans-shifting; and I write
How roses first came red, and lilies white.   10
I write of groves, of twilights, and I sing
The court of Mab,[5] and of the Fairy King.[6]
I write of hell; I sing (and ever shall)
Of heaven, and hope to have it after all.

WHEN HE WOULD HAVE HIS
VERSES READ

In sober mornings do not thou rehearse
The holy incantation of a verse;
But when that men have both well drunk and fed,
Let my enchantments then be sung or read.
When laurel spirts i' th' fire, and when the hearth
Smiles to itself, and gilds the roof with mirth;
When up the thyrse[1] is raised, and when the sound
Of sacred orgies[2] flies—A round, a round![3]
When the rose reigns, and locks with ointments
        shine,
Let rigid Cato read these lines of mine.

HIS ANSWER TO A QUESTION

Some would know
        Why I so
Long still do tarry,
        And ask why
        Here that I
Live, and not marry?
        Thus I those
        Do oppose:
What man would be here
        Slave to thrall,
        If at all
He could live free here?

THE ARGUMENT
5 For an account of Mab see Shakespeare's Romeo and
Juliet, Act I, sc. 4, ll. 88 ff., and Jonson's This Is Mab, the
Mistress-Fairy, p. 770.
6 Oberon. See Shakespeare's Midsummer Night's Dream,
Herrick's Oberon's Feast, p. 816, and Drayton's Nymphidia,
p. 722.

WHEN HE WOULD
1 "A javelin twined with ivy." (Herrick.)
2 "Songs to Bacchus." (Herrick.) Strictly speaking, the
word is used of all the ceremonial rites in honor of Bacchus,
or of other deities.
3 A song by three or more persons, each taking up the
tune in turn.

UPON THE LOSS OF HIS
MISTRESSES

I have lost, and lately, these
Many dainty mistresses:
Stately Julia, prime of all;
Sappho next, a principal;
Smooth Anthea, for a skin
White, and heaven-like crystalline;
Sweet Electra, and the choice
Myrrha, for the lute, and voice.
Next, Corinna, for her wit,
And for the graceful use of it;   10
With Perilla—all are gone;
Only Herrick's left alone,
For to number sorrow by
Their departures hence, and die.

TO ROBIN REDBREAST

Laid out for dead, let thy last kindness be
With leaves and moss-work for to cover me;
And while the wood-nymphs my cold corpse inter,
Sing thou my dirge, sweet-warbling chorister!
For epitaph, in foliage, next write this:
    Here, here the tomb of Robin Herrick is.

DISCONTENTS IN DEVON

More discontents I never had
    Since I was born, than here;
Where I have been, and still am, sad,
    In this dull Devonshire;
Yet justly too I must confess,
    I ne'er invented such
Ennobled numbers for the press
    Than where I loathed so much.

CHERRY-RIPE

Cherry-ripe, ripe, ripe, I cry,
Full and fair ones; come and buy.
If so be you ask me where
They do grow, I answer: There,
Where my Julia's lips do smile;
There's the land, or cherry-isle:
Whose plantations fully show
All the year where cherries grow.

HIS REQUEST TO JULIA

Julia, if I chance to die
Ere I print my poetry,
I most humbly thee desire
To commit it to the fire;
Better 'twere my book were dead,
Than to live not pérfected.

THE CHEAT OF CUPID: OR, THE UNGENTLE GUEST

One silent night of late,
　When every creature rested,
Came one unto my gate,
　And knocking me molested.

"Who's that," said I, "beats there,
　And troubles thus the sleepy?"
"Cast off," said he, "all fear,
　And let not locks thus keep ye.

"For I a boy am, who
　By moonless nights have swervèd;　　10
And all with showers wet through,
　And e'en with cold half starvèd."

I pitiful arose,
　And soon a taper lighted;
And did myself disclose
　Unto the lad benighted.

I saw he had a bow,
　And wings, too, which did shiver;
And looking down below,
　I spied he had a quiver.　　20

I to my chimney's shine
　Brought him, as love professes,
And chafed his hands with mine,
　And dried his dropping tresses.

But when he felt him warmed,
　"Let's try this bow of ours
And string if they be harmed,"
　Said he, "with these late showers."

Forthwith his bow he bent,
　And wedded string and arrow,　　30
And struck me that it went
　Quite through my heart and marrow.

Then laughing loud, he flew
　Away, and thus said flying,
"Adieu, mine host, adieu!
　I'll leave thy heart a-dying."

DELIGHT IN DISORDER

A sweet disorder in the dress
Kindles in clothes a wantonness;[1]
A lawn[2] about the shoulders thrown
Into a fine distraction;[3]
An erring lace, which here and there
Enthralls the crimson stomacher;[4]
A cuff neglectful, and thereby
Ribands to flow confusèdly;
A winning wave (deserving note)
In the tempestuous petticoat;　　10
A careless shoe-string, in whose tie
I see a wild civility:[5]
Do more bewitch me, than when art
Is too precise in every part.

DEAN-BOURN, A RUDE RIVER IN DEVON, BY WHICH SOMETIMES HE LIVED

Dean-bourn, farewell; I never look to see
Dean, or thy warty incivility.
Thy rocky bottom that doth tear thy streams
And makes them frantic, ev'n to all extremes,
To my content I never should behold,
Were thy streams silver, or thy rocks all gold.
Rocky thou art, and rocky we discover
Thy men and rocky are thy ways all over.
O men, O manners, now and ever known
To be a rocky generatiòn!　　10
A people currish, churlish as the seas,
And rude, almost, as rudest salvages.
With whom I did, and may re-sojourn, when
Rocks turn to rivers, rivers turn to men.

DELIGHT IN DISORDER
　1 Mirthfulness.　　　　2 A scarf of lawn or linen.
　3 Confusion.
　4 Part of the dress forming the lower section of the bodice in front.
　5 Order, good breeding.

TO DIANEME [2]

Sweet, be not proud of those two eyes,
Which, star-like, sparkle in their skies;
Nor be you proud that you can see
All hearts your captives, yours yet free;
Be you not proud of that rich hair
Which wantons with the love-sick air;
Whenas[1] that ruby which you wear,
Sunk from the tip of your soft ear,
Will last to be a precious stone
When all your world of beauty's gone.

CORINNA'S GOING A-MAYING

Get up, get up, for shame, the blooming morn
Upon her wings presents the god unshorn.[1]
  See how Aurora[2] throws her fair
  Fresh-quilted colors[3] through the air!
  Get up, sweet slug-a-bed, and see
  The dew bespangling herb and tree.
Each flower has wept, and bowed toward the East,
Above an hour since; yet you not dressed,
  Nay! not so much as out of bed?
  When all the birds have matins said,   10
  And sung their thankful hymns: 'tis sin,
  Nay, profanation to keep in;
Whenas[4] a thousand virgins on this day
Spring, sooner than the lark, to fetch in may.[5]

Rise, and put on your foliage, and be seen
To come forth, like the spring-time, fresh and
    green
  And sweet as Flora. Take no care
  For jewels for your gown, or hair;
  Fear not, the leaves will strew
  Gems in abundance upon you;   20
Besides, the childhood of the day has kept,
Against[6] you come, some orient[7] pearls unwept;

Come, and receive them while the light
Hangs on the dew-locks of the night:
  And Titan[8] on the eastern hill
  Retires himself, or else stands still
Till you come forth. Wash, dress, be brief in
    praying:
Few beads are best, when once we go a-maying.

Come, my Corinna, come; and, coming, mark
How each field turns a street, each street a park   30
  Made green, and trimmed with trees; see how
  Devotion gives each house a bough,
  Or branch; each porch, each door, ere this,
  An ark, a tabernacle is,
Made up of white-thorn neatly interwove;
As if here were those cooler shades of love.
  Can such delights be in the street,
  And open fields, and we not see't?
  Come, we'll abroad; and let's obey
  The proclamation made for May: 40
And sin no more, as we have done, by staying;
But, my Corinna, come, let's go a-maying.

There's not a budding boy or girl this day
But is got up, and gone to bring in may.
  A deal of youth, ere this, is come
  Back, and with white-thorn laden home.
  Some have dispatched their cakes and cream,
  Before that we have left[9] to dream;
And some have wept, and wooed, and plighted
    troth,
And chose their priest, ere we can cast off sloth.   50
  Many a green-gown[10] has been given;
  Many a kiss, both odd and even:
  Many a glance too has been sent
  From out the eye, love's firmament;
Many a jest told of the keys betraying
This night, and locks picked, yet we're not
    a-maying.

Come, let us go, while we are in our prime,
And take the harmless folly of the time.
  We shall grow old apace and die
  Before we know our liberty.   60

TO DIANEME
 1 When.

CORINNA'S GOING A-MAYING
 1 Apollo.   2 Goddess of the dawn.
 3 Freshly mingled, like colors in a newly made quilt.
 4 When.   5 The blossoms of the white hawthorn.
 6 Until.   7 Shining.

 8 The sun.
 9 Ceased.
 10 That is, many a gown made green by rolling on the
grass.

Our life is short, and our days run
    As fast away as does the sun;
And as a vapor, or a drop of rain,
Once lost, can ne'er be found again:
    So when or you or I are made
    A fable, song, or fleeting shade,
All love, all liking, all delight
Lies drowned with us in endless night.
Then while time serves, and we are but decaying,
Come, my Corinna, come, let's go a-maying.   70

TO LIVE MERRILY, AND TO TRUST TO GOOD VERSES

Now is the time for mirth,
    Nor check or tongue be dumb;
For with the flow'ry earth
    The golden pomp is come.

The golden pomp is come;
    For now each tree does wear,
Made of her pap[1] and gum,
    Rich beads of amber here.

Now reigns the rose, and now
    Th' Arabian dew besmears   10
My uncontrollèd brow
    And my retorted hairs.

Homer, this health to thee,
    In sack of such a kind
That it would make thee see
    Though thou wert ne'er so blind.

Next, Virgil I'll call forth
    To pledge this second health
In wine, whose each cup's worth
    An Indian commonwealth.   20

A goblet next I'll drink
    To Ovid, and suppose,
Made he the pledge, he'd think
    The world had all one nose.[2]

Then this immensive cup
    Of aromatic wine,

Catullus, I quaff up
    To that terse muse of thine.

Wild I am now with heat;
    O Bacchus! cool thy rays!   30
Or frantic, I shall eat
    Thy thyrse, and bite the bays.

Round, round the roof does run;
    And being ravished thus,
Come, I will drink a tun
    To my Propertius.

Now, to Tibullus, next,
    This flood I drink to thee;
But stay, I see a text
    That this presents to me.   40

Behold, Tibullus lies
    Here burnt, whose small return
Of ashes scarce suffice
    To fill a little urn.

Trust to good verses then;
    They only will aspire,
When pyramids, as men,
    Are lost i' th' funeral fire.

And when all bodies meet,
    In Lethe to be drowned,   50
Then only numbers sweet
    With endless life are crowned.

TO THE VIRGINS, TO MAKE MUCH OF TIME

Gather ye rosebuds while ye may,
    Old Time is still a-flying;
And this same flower that smiles today,
    Tomorrow will be dying.

The glorious lamp of heaven, the sun,
    The higher he's a-getting,
The sooner will his race be run,
    And nearer he's to setting.

That age is best which is the first,
    When youth and blood are warmer;   10
But being spent, the worse, and worst
    Times still succeed the former.

TO LIVE MERRILY
  1 Pulp.
  2 A pun on Ovid's full name, Publius Ovidius *Naso*
("nose").

Then be not coy, but use your time;
  And while ye may, go marry:
For having lost but once your prime,
  You may forever tarry.

HIS POETRY HIS PILLAR

Only a little more
  I have to write;
    Then I'll give o'er,
And bid the world good night.

'Tis but a flying minute
  That I must stay,
    Or linger in it;
And then I must away.

O Time, that cut'st down all,
  And scarce leav'st here   10
    Memorial
Of any men that were!

How many lie forgot
  In vaults beneath,
    And piecemeal rot
Without a fame in death!

Behold this living stone
  I rear for me,
    Ne'er to be thrown
Down, envious Time, by thee.   20

Pillars let some set up,
  If so they please;
    Here is my hope,
And my pyramides.

LYRIC FOR LEGACIES

Gold I've none, for use or show,
Neither silver to bestow
At my death; but thus much know,
That each lyric here shall be
Of my love a legacy,
Left to all posterity.
Gentle friends, then, do but please
To accept such coins as these
As my last remembrances.

TO MUSIC, TO BECALM HIS FEVER

Charm me asleep, and melt me so
  With thy delicious numbers,
That being ravished, hence I go
  Away in easy slumbers.
    Ease my sick head,
    And make my bed,
Thou power that canst sever
    From me this ill,
    And quickly still,
  Though thou not kill   10
    My fever.

Thou sweetly canst convert the same
  From a consuming fire
Into a gentle-licking flame,
  And make it thus expire.
    Then make me weep
    My pains asleep,
And give me such reposes
    That I, poor I,
    May think thereby   20
    I live and die
      'Mongst roses.

Fall on me like a silent dew,
  Or like those maiden showers
Which by the peep of day do strew
  A baptime ¹ o'er the flowers.
    Melt, melt my pains
    With thy soft strains,
That having ease me given,
    With full delight   30
    I leave this light
    And take my flight
      For heaven.

TO THE ROSE
Song

Go, happy rose, and interwove
With other flowers, bind my love.
  Tell her, too, she must not be
  Longer flowing, longer free,
  That so oft has fettered me.

TO MUSIC
1 Baptism.

Say, if she's fretful, I have bands
Of pearl and gold, to bind her hands;
  Tell her, if she struggle still,
  I have myrtle rods at will,
  For to tame, though not to kill.   10

Take thou my blessing thus, and go
And tell her this—but do not so,
  Lest a handsome anger fly
  Like a lightning from her eye,
  And burn thee up, as well as I.

THE HOCK-CART,[1] OR HARVEST HOME:

To the Right Honorable Mildmay, Earl of Westmorland

Come, sons of summer, by whose toil
We are the lords of wine and oil;
By whose tough labors and rough hands
We rip up first, then reap our lands.
Crowned with the ears of corn, now come,
And to the pipe sing harvest home.
Come forth, my lord, and see the cart
Dressed up with all the country art.
See here a maukin,[2] there a sheet
As spotless pure as it is sweet;   10
The horses, mares, and frisking fillies,
Clad all in linen, white as lilies;
The harvest swains and wenches bound
For joy to see the hock-cart crowned.
About the cart hear how the rout
Of rural younglings raise the shout,
Pressing before, some coming after:
Those with a shout, and these with laughter.
Some bless the cart; some kiss the sheaves;
Some prank them up with oaken leaves;   20
Some cross the fill-horse;[3] some with great
Devotion stroke the home-borne wheat;
While other rustics, less attent
To prayers than to merriment,
Run after with their breeches rent.

Well on, brave boys, to your lord's hearth,
Glitt'ring with fire, where for your mirth
Ye shall see first the large and chief
Foundation of your feast, fat beef,
With upper stories, mutton, veal,   30
And bacon, which makes full the meal;
With sev'ral dishes standing by,
As here a custard, there a pie,
And here all-tempting frumenty.
And for to make the merry cheer,
If smirking wine be wanting here,
There's that which drowns all care, stout beer,
Which freely drink to your lord's health;
Then to the plow, the commonwealth,
Next to your flails, your fans, your fats;[4]   40
Then to the maids with wheaten hats;
To the rough sickle and crook'd scythe,
Drink, frolic boys, till all be blithe.
Feed and grow fat, and as ye eat
Be mindful that the lab'ring neat,[5]
As you, may have their fill of meat.[6]
And know, besides, ye must revoke
The patient ox unto his yoke,
And all go back unto the plow
And harrow, though they're hanged up now.   50
And, you must know, your lord's word's
    true:
Feed him you must, whose food fills you,
And that this pleasure is like rain,
Not sent ye for to drown your pain
But for to make it spring again.

TO THE WESTERN WIND

Sweet western wind, whose luck it is,
  Made rival with the air,
To give Perenna's lip a kiss,
  And fan her wanton hair,
Bring me but one, I'll promise thee,
  Instead of common showers,
Thy wings shall be embalmed by me
  And all beset with flowers.

HOW ROSES CAME RED [1]

Roses at first were white,
  Till they could not agree
Whether my Sappho's breast
  Or they more white should be.

THE HOCK-CART
  1 See note on The Argument of His Book, p. 809.
  2 Malkin; a rough, colored cloth.
  3 The horse that draws the cart. The fills are the shafts of
the cart.

4 Vats.   5 Cattle.   6 Food.

But being vanquished quite,
    A blush their cheeks bespread;
Since which, believe the rest,
    The roses first came red.

HOW VIOLETS CAME BLUE

Love on a day, wise poets tell,
    Some time in wrangling spent,
Whether the violets should excel,
    Or she, in sweetest scent.

But Venus having lost the day,
    Poor girls, she fell on you
And beat ye so, as some dare say,
    Her blows did make ye blue.

TO ANTHEA, WHO MAY COMMAND HIM ANYTHING

Bid me to live, and I will live
    Thy protestant to be:
Or bid me love, and I will give
    A loving heart to thee.

A heart as soft, a heart as kind,
    A heart as sound and free
As in the whole world thou canst find,
    That heart I'll give to thee.

Bid that heart stay, and it will stay,
    To honor thy decree;   10
Or bid it languish quite away,
    And't shall do so for thee.

Bid me to weep, and I will weep,
    While I have eyes to see;
And having none, yet I will keep
    A heart to weep for thee.

Bid me despair, and I'll despair,
    Under that cypress tree;
Or bid me die, and I will dare
    E'en death, to die for thee.   20

Thou art my life, my love, my heart,
    The very eyes of me;
And hast command of every part,
    To live and die for thee.

TO MEADOWS

Ye have been fresh and green,
    Ye have been filled with flowers;
And ye the walks have been
    Where maids have spent their hours.

Ye have beheld how they
    With wicker arks[1] did come,
To kiss, and bear away
    The richer cowslips home.

Ye've heard them sweetly sing,
    And seen them in a round;[2]   10
Each virgin, like a spring,
    With honeysuckles crowned.

But now we see none here
    Whose silv'ry feet did tread,
And, with disheveled hair,
    Adorned this smoother mead.

Like unthrifts, having spent
    Your stocks, and needy grown,
Ye're left here to lament
    Your poor estates, alone.   20

OBERON'S FEAST[1]

Shapcot,[2] to thee the fairy state
I with discretion dedicate,
Because thou prizest things that are
Curious and unfamiliar.
Take first the feast; these dishes gone,
We'll see the fairy court anon.

A little mushroom table spread,
After short prayers, they set on bread;
A moon-parched grain of purest wheat,
With some small glitt'ring grit[3] to eat   10

TO MEADOWS
1 Baskets.   2 A dance in a circle.

OBERON'S FEAST
1 This was the first of Herrick's poems to appear in print. A briefer version of it, with many variants from the text given here, was published in 1635.
2 Herrick wrote another poem To His Peculiar [*i.e.*, particular, intimate] Friend, Master Thomas Shapcot, Lawyer. Very little is known of Shapcot.
3 To serve as knife or spoon.

His choice bits with; then in a trice
They make a feast less great than nice.
But all this while his eye is served,
We must not think his ear was starved,
But that there was in place to stir
His spleen,[4] the chirring grasshopper,
The merry cricket, puling[5] fly,
The piping gnat, for minstrelsy.
And now we must imagine first
The elves present to quench his thirst   20
A pure seed-pearl of infant dew,
Brought and besweetened in a blue
And pregnant violet; which done,
His kitling[6] eyes begin to run
Quite through the table, where he spies
The horns of papery butterflies,
Of which he eats, and tastes a little
Of that we call the cuckoo's spittle.
A little fuzz-ball pudding stands
By, yet not blessed by his hands;   30
That was too coarse, but then forthwith
He ventures boldly on the pith
Of sugared rush, and eats the sag[7]
And well-bestrutted[8] bee's sweet bag,
Gladding his palate with some store
Of emmets' eggs, what would he more?
But beards of mice, a newt's stewed thigh,
A bloated earwig, and a fly,
With the red-capped worm that's shut
Within the conclave of a nut,   40
Brown as his tooth. A little moth,
Late fattened in a piece of cloth;
With withered cherries, mandrakes' ears,
Moles' eyes; to these, the slain stag's tears,
The unctuous dewlaps of a snail;
The broke heart of a nightingale
O'ercome in music; with a wine
Ne'er ravished from the flattering vine,
But gently pressed from the soft side
Of the most sweet and dainty bride,   50
Brought in a dainty daisy, which
He fully quaffs up to bewitch
His blood to height; this done, commended
Grace by his priest; the feast is ended.

THE BELLMAN [1]

From noise of scare-fires[1] rest ye free,
From murders *Benedicite!*[2]
From all mischances that may fright
Your pleasing slumbers in the night
Mercy secure ye all, and keep
The goblin from ye while ye sleep.
Past one o'clock, and almost two,
My masters all, good day to you!

UPON PRUDENCE BALDWIN HER SICKNESS

Prue, my dearest maid, is sick,
Almost to be lunatic;
Æsculapius![1] come and bring
Means for her recovering,
And a gallant cock shall be
Offered up by her to thee.

UPON A CHILD THAT DIED

Here she lies, a pretty bud,
Lately made of flesh and blood,
Who as soon fell fast asleep
As her little eyes did peep.
Give her strewings, but not stir
The earth that lightly covers her.

CONTENT, NOT CATES

'Tis not the food but the content
That makes the table's merriment;
Where trouble serves the board, we eat
The platters there as soon as meat.
A little pipkin with a bit
Of mutton or of veal in it
Set on my table, trouble-free,
More than a feast contenteth me.

THE BELLMAN
  1 Sudden conflagrations.
  2 God bless you! Cf. Milton's Il Penseroso, ll. 83, 84 on p. 890.

UPON PRUDENCE
  1 The Roman god of medicine.

OBERON'S FEAST
  4 That is, to arouse his laughter.   5 Droning.
  6 Diminutive.   7 Sagging.
  8 Swollen.

TO DAFFODILS

Fair daffodils, we weep to see
  You haste away so soon;
As yet the early-rising sun
  Has not attained his noon.
    Stay, stay,
  Until the hasting day
    Has run
  But to the even-song;
And, having prayed together, we
  Will go with you along.   10

We have short time to stay, as you;
  We have as short a spring;
As quick a growth to meet decay,
  As you, or any thing.
    We die,
  As your hours do, and dry
    Away
  Like to the summer's rain;
Or as the pearls of morning's dew,
  Ne'er to be found again.   20

THE MAD MAID'S SONG

Good morrow to the day so fair;
  Good morning, sir, to you;
Good morrow to mine own torn hair,
  Bedabbled with the dew.

Good morning to this primrose too;
  Good morrow to each maid,
That will with flowers the tomb bestrew
  Wherein my love is laid.

Ah woe is me, woe, woe is me,
  Alack and welladay!   10
For pity, sir, find out that bee,
  Which bore my love away.

I'll seek him in your bonnet brave;
  I'll seek him in your eyes;
Nay, now I think they've made his grave
  I' the bed of strawberries.

I'll seek him there; I know, ere this,
  The cold, cold earth doth shake [1] him;

THE MAD MAID'S SONG
  1 Chill.

But I will go, or send a kiss
  By you, sir, to awake him.   20

Pray hurt him not; though he be dead,
  He knows well who do love him,
And who with green turfs rear his head,
  And who do rudely move him.

He's soft and tender; pray take heed;
  With bands of cowslips bind him,
And bring him home;—but 'tis decreed
  That I shall never find him.

TO DAISIES, NOT TO SHUT SO SOON

Shut not so soon! the dull-eyed night
  Has not as yet begun
To make a seizure on the light
  Or to seal up the sun.

No marigolds yet closèd are,
  No shadows great appear;
Nor doth the early shepherd's star
  Shine like a spangle here.

Stay but till my Julia close
  Her life-begetting eye,
And let the whole world then dispose
  Itself to live or die.

TO BLOSSOMS

Fair pledges of a fruitful tree,
  Why do ye fall so fast?
  Your date is not so past
But you may stay yet here a while,
  To blush and gently smile,
    And go at last.

What, were ye born to be
  An hour or half's delight,
  And so to bid good night?
'Twas pity nature brought ye forth   10
  Merely to show your worth,
    And lose you quite.

But you are lovely leaves, where we
  May read how soon things have
  Their end, though ne'er so brave;[1]
And after they have shown their pride,
  Like you a while, they glide
    Into the grave.

TO THE WATER NYMPHS, DRINKING AT THE FOUNTAIN

Reach with your whiter[1] hands to me
  Some crystal of the spring,
And I about the cup shall see
  Fresh lilies flourishing.

Or else, sweet nymphs, do you but this—
  To the glass your lips incline,
And I shall see by that one kiss
  The water turned to wine.

[MISTRESS SUSANNA SOUTHWELL] UPON HER FEET

    Her pretty feet
    Like snails did creep
    A little out, and then,
As if they started at bo-peep,[1]
    Did soon draw in again.

MEAT WITHOUT MIRTH

Eaten I have, and though I had good cheer,
I did not sup, because no friends were there.
Where mirth and friends are absent when we dine
Or sup, there wants the incense and the wine.

HIS CONTENT IN THE COUNTRY

Here, here I live with what my board
Can with the smallest cost afford;

Though ne'er so mean the viands be,
They well content my Prue[1] and me.
Or pea, or bean, or wort,[2] or beet,
Whatever comes, content makes sweet.
Here we rejoice because no rent
We pay for our poor tenement,
Wherein we rest, and never fear
The landlord or the usurer.   10
The quarter-day does ne'er affright
Our peaceful slumbers in the night.
We eat our own, and batten more
Because we feed on no man's score;
But pity those whose flanks grow great
Swelled with the lard of others' meat.
We bless our fortunes when we see
Our own belovèd privacy;
And like our living, where we're known
To very few, or else to none.   20

THE FAIRIES

If ye will with Mab find grace,
Set each platter in his place;
Rake the fire up, and get
Water in ere sun be set.
Wash your pails and cleanse your dairies:
Sluts are loathsome to the fairies.
Sweep your house; who doth not so,
Mab will pinch her by the toe.

HIS PRAYER TO BEN JONSON[1]

  When I a verse shall make,
    Know I have prayed thee,
  For old religion's sake,
    Saint Ben, to aid me.

  Make the way smooth for me,
    When I, thy Herrick,
  Honoring thee, on my knee
    Offer my lyric.

HIS CONTENT IN THE COUNTRY
  1 Prudence Baldwin, the faithful servant of the poet during his residence at Dean Prior. She is the subject of several poems by Herrick.
  2 A potherb.

HIS PRAYER
  1 This is one of half a dozen poems in which Herrick expresses his affection and admiration for Ben Jonson.

TO BLOSSOMS
  1 Beautiful.

TO THE WATER NYMPHS
  1 Very white.

UPON HER FEET
  1 Peekaboo.

Candles I'll give to thee,
And a new altar;
And thou, Saint Ben, shalt be
Writ in my psalter.

THE NIGHT-PIECE, TO JULIA[1]

Her eyes the glow-worm lend thee;
The shooting stars attend thee;
  And the elves also,
  Whose little eyes glow
Like the sparks of fire, befriend thee.

No will-o'-the-wisp mis-light thee;
Nor snake or slow-worm[2] bite thee;
  But on, on thy way,
  Not making a stay,
Since ghost there's none to affright thee.   10

Let not the dark thee cumber;[3]
What though the moon does slumber?
  The stars of the night
  Will lend thee their light,
Like tapers clear without number.

Then, Julia, let me woo thee,
Thus, thus to come unto me;
  And when I shall meet
  Thy silv'ry feet,
My soul I'll pour into thee.   20

THE HAG

The hag is astride
This night for to ride,
The devil and she together;
  Through thick and through thin,
  Now out and then in,
Though ne'er so foul be the weather.

A thorn or a burr
She takes for a spur;
With a lash of a bramble she rides now;
  Through brakes and through briers,   10
  O'er ditches and mires,
She follows the spirit that guides now.

No beast for his food
Dares now range the wood,
But hushed in his lair he lies lurking;
  While mischiefs by these,
  On lands and on seas,
At noon of night are a-working.

The storm will arise
And trouble the skies;   20
This night, and more for the wonder,
  The ghost from the tomb
  Affrighted shall come,
Called out by the clap of the thunder.

THE COUNTRY LIFE, TO THE HONORED MR. END. PORTER,[1] GROOM OF THE BEDCHAMBER TO HIS MAJESTY

Sweet country life, to such unknown
Whose lives are others', not their own!
But, serving courts and cities, be
Less happy less enjoying thee.
Thou never plow'st the ocean's foam
To seek and bring rough pepper home;
Nor to the Eastern Ind dost rove
To bring from thence the scorchèd clove;
Nor, with the loss of thy loved rest,
Bring'st home the ingot from the West.   10
No, thy ambition's masterpiece
Flies no thought higher than a fleece;
Or how to pay thy hinds, and clear
All scores, and so to end the year;
But walk'st about thine own dear bounds,
Not envying others' larger grounds,
For well thou know'st 'tis not the extent
Of land makes life, but sweet content.

THE NIGHT-PIECE
  1 The stanzaic pattern of this poem seems to have been suggested by that of Jonson's The Faery Beam Upon You, p. 772.
  2 A small snakelike lizard.   3 Trouble.

THE COUNTRY LIFE
  1 Endymion Porter, a friend of both James I and Charles I, was the most prominent patron of Herrick and of many other literary men of the day.

When now the cock, the plowman's horn,
Calls forth the lily-wristed morn, 20
Then to thy corn-fields thou dost go,
Which, though well soiled,[2] yet thou dost
    know
That the best compost for the lands
Is the wise master's feet and hands.
There at the plow thou find'st thy team,
With a hind whistling there to them,
And cheer'st them up by singing how
The kingdom's portion is the plow.
This done, then to th' enameled meads
Thou go'st, and as thy foot there treads 30
Thou seest a present godlike power
Imprinted in each herb and flower,
And smell'st the breath of great-eyed kine,
Sweet as the blossoms of the vine.
Here thou behold'st thy large, sleek neat
Unto the dewlaps up in meat;
And as thou look'st, the wanton steer,
The heifer, cow, and ox draw near
To make a pleasing pastime there;
These seen, thou go'st to view thy flocks 40
Of sheep, safe from the wolf and fox,
And find'st their bellies there as full
Of short, sweet grass as backs with wool,
And leav'st them, as they feed and fill,
A shepherd piping on a hill.
For sports, for pageantry, and plays,
Thou hast thy eves and holydays,
On which the young men and maids meet
To exercise their dancing feet,
Tripping the comely country round, 50
With daffodils and daisies crowned.
Thy wakes, thy quintals,[3] here thou hast,
Thy Maypoles, too, with garlands graced,
Thy morris-dance, thy Whitsun-ale,
Thy shearing-feast, which never fail;
Thy harvest-home, thy wassail bowl,
That's tossed up after fox-i'-the-hole,[4]
Thy mummeries,[5] thy Twelfth-tide kings
And queens, the Christmas revelings,
Thy nut-brown mirth, thy russet wit, 60
And no man pays too dear for it.

To these thou hast thy times to go,
And trace the hare i' the treacherous snow;
Thy witty wiles to draw, and get
The lark into the trammel net;
Thou hast thy cockrood[6] and thy glade,
To take the precious pheasant made;
Thy lime-twigs, snares, and pitfalls then,
To catch the pilfering birds, not men.
O happy life! if that their good 70
The husbandmen but understood,
Who all the day themselves do please,
And younglings, with such sports as these;
And, lying down, have naught to affright
Sweet sleep, that makes more short the night.

Cætera desunt—[7]

TO ELECTRA [4]

I dare not ask a kiss,
    I dare not beg a smile,
Lest having that or this,
    I might grow proud the while.

No, no, the utmost share
    Of my desire shall be
Only to kiss that air
    That lately kissèd thee.

HIS RETURN TO LONDON

From the dull confines of the drooping west,
To see the day spring from the pregnant east,
Ravished in spirit, I come, nay more, I fly
To thee, blest place of my nativity!
Thus, thus, with hallowed foot I touch the ground
With thousand blessings by thy fortune crowned.
O fruitful genius! that bestowest here
An everlasting plenty, year by year.
O place! O people! Manners framed to please
All nations, customs, kindreds, languages! 10
I am a free-born Roman, suffer then
That I amongst you live a citizen.
London my home is, though by hard fate sent
Into a long and irksome banishment;
Yet since called back, henceforward let me be,
O native country, repossessed by thee!

THE COUNTRY LIFE
  2 Manured.
  3 A quintal or quintain was an object to be tilted at.
  4 An old game "wherein boys lift up one leg and hop on the other." (Oxford English Dictionary.)
  5 Performances by mummers, or disguised actors.

  6 "A broad way or glade in a wood, through which wood-cocks, etc., might dart . . . so as to be caught by nets stretched across the opening." (Oxford English Dictionary.)
  7 "The rest is wanting."

For rather than I'll to the west return,
I'll beg of thee first here to have mine urn.
Weak I am grown, and must in short time fall;
Give thou my sacred relics burial.   20

HIS GRANGE, OR PRIVATE WEALTH

Though clock,
To tell me how night draws hence, I've none,
A cock
I have, to sing how day draws on.
I have
A maid, my Prue, by good luck sent
To save
That little Fates me gave or lent.
A hen
I keep, which creaking[1] day by day,   10
Tells when
She goes her long white egg to lay.
A goose
I have, which with a jealous ear,
Lets loose
Her tongue to tell what danger's near.
A lamb
I keep, tame, with my morsels fed,
Whose dam
An orphan left him, lately dead.   20
A cat
I keep, that plays about my house,
Grown fat
With eating many a miching[2] mouse.
To these
A Tracy[3] I do keep, whereby
I please
The more my rural privacy.
Which are
But toys to give my heart some ease: 30
Where care
None is, slight things do lightly please.

A TERNARY OF LITTLES, UPON A PIPKIN OF JELLY SENT TO A LADY

A little saint best fits a little shrine,
A little prop best fits a little vine,
As my small cruse best fits my little wine.

A little seed best fits a little soil,
A little trade best fits a little toil,
As my small jar best fits my little oil.

A little bin best fits a little bread,
A little garland fits a little head,
As my small stuff best fits my little shed.

A little hearth best fits a little fire,   10
A little chapel fits a little quire,
As my small bell best fits my little spire.

A little stream best fits a little boat,
A little lead best fits a little float,
As my small pipe best fits my little note.

A little meat best fits a little belly,
As sweetly, lady, give me leave to tell ye,
This little pipkin fits this little jelly.

UPON JULIA'S CLOTHES

Whenas[1] in silks my Julia goes,
Then, then, methinks, how sweetly flows
That liquefaction of her clothes.

Next, when I cast mine eyes and see
That brave[2] vibration each way free,
Oh, how that glittering taketh me!

UPON PRUE, HIS MAID[1]

In this little urn is laid
Prudence Baldwin, once my maid,
From whose happy spark here let
Spring the purple violet.

UPON JULIA'S CLOTHES
    1 When.   2 Bright.

UPON PRUE
    1 This little epitaph is playful and premature, as Prudence
Baldwin survived her master four years.

HIS GRANGE
    1 Clucking.   2 Pilfering.
    3 Herrick's spaniel.

CEREMONIES FOR CHRISTMAS

Come, bring with a noise,[1]
My merry, merry boys,
The Christmas log to the firing;
While my good dame, she
Bids ye all be free,
And drink to your hearts' desiring.

With the last year's brand
Light the new block, and
For good success in his spending,
On your psalteries[2] play,   10
That sweet luck may
Come while the log is a-teending.[3]

Drink now the strong beer,
Cut the white loaf here,
The while the meat is a-shredding;
For the rare mince-pie
And the plums stand by
To fill the paste that's a-kneading.

THE AMBER BEAD

I saw a fly within a bead
Of amber cleanly burièd;
The urn was little, but the room
More rich than Cleopatra's tomb.

CEREMONIES FOR CANDLEMAS EVE

Down with the rosemary and bays,
  Down with the mistletoe;
Instead of holly, now upraise
  The greener box, for show.

The holly hitherto did sway;
  Let box now domineer
Until the dancing Easter Day
  Or Easter's Eve appear.

Then youthful box which now hath grace
  Your houses to renew,   10
Grown old, surrender must his place
  Unto the crispèd yew.

When yew is out, then birch comes in
  And many flowers beside,
Both of a fresh and fragrant kin
  To honor Whitsuntide.

Green rushes then, and sweetest bents,
  With cooler oaken boughs,
Come in for comely ornaments,
  To re-adorn the house.   20
Thus times do shift, each thing his turn does hold;
New things succeed, as former things grow old.

THE CEREMONIES FOR CANDLEMAS DAY

Kindle the Christmas brand, and then
  Till sunset let it burn;
Which quenched, then lay it up again
  Till Christmas next return.
Part must be kept, wherewith to teend[1]
  The Christmas log next year;
And where 'tis safely kept, the fiend
  Can do no mischief there.

UPON BEN JONSON

Here lies Jonson with the rest
Of the poets, but the best.
Reader, wouldst thou more have known?
Ask his story, not this stone.
That will speak what this can't tell
Of his glory. So farewell.

AN ODE FOR HIM

Ah, Ben!
Say how or when
Shall we, thy guests,
Meet at those lyric feasts
Made at the Sun,
The Dog, the Triple Tun,[1]
Where we such clusters[2] had
As made us nobly wild, not mad;
And yet each verse of thine
Outdid the meat, outdid the frolic wine.   10

CEREMONIES FOR CHRISTMAS
  1 That is, a joyful noise, a melodious sound.
  2 The psaltery was a medieval stringed instrument.
  3 Kindling.

THE CEREMONIES
  1 Kindle.

AN ODE FOR HIM
  1 Taverns in London where Jonson and his group gathered.
  2 Of grapes; *i.e.*, wine.

My Ben!
Or come again,
Or send to us
Thy wit's great overplus;
But teach us yet
Wisely to husband it,
Lest we that talent spend,
And having once brought to an end
That precious stock, the store   19
Of such a wit the world should have no more.

HIS WISH [2]

Fat be my hind; unlearned be my wife;
Peaceful my night; my day devoid of strife:
To these a comely offspring I desire,
Singing about my everlasting fire.

UPON HIS SPANIEL TRACY

Now thou art dead, no eye shall ever see,
For shape and service, spaniel like to thee.
This shall my love do, give thy sad death one
Tear, that deserves of me a million.

THE PILLAR OF FAME[1]

Fame's pillar here at last we set,
Out-during marble, brass or jet;
  Charmed and enchanted so
  As to withstand the blow
    Of   overthrow;
    Nor shall the seas,
    O r   o u t r a g e s
    Of storms, o'erbear
    What we uprear;
    Tho' kingdoms fall,   10
  This   pillar   never   shall
  Decline or waste at all;
But stand for ever by his own
Firm and well-fixed foundatìon.

To his book's end this last line he'd have placed:
Jocund his Muse was, but his life was chaste.

THE PILLAR
1 This is one of the "shaped poems" of the period.

F R O M

HIS NOBLE NUMBERS [1647]

Published with *Hesperides*, 1648

HIS PRAYER FOR ABSOLUTION

For those my unbaptizèd rhymes,
Writ in my wild unhallowed times;
For every sentence, clause, and word,
That's not inlaid with Thee, my Lord,
Forgive me, God, and blot each line
Out of my book that is not Thine.
But if, 'mongst all, Thou find'st here one
Worthy Thy benediction,
That one of all the rest shall be
The glory of my work and me.

TO FIND GOD

Weigh me the fire; or canst thou find
A way to measure out the wind?

Distinguish all those floods that are
Mixed in that wat'ry theater,[1]
And taste thou them as saltless there
As in their channel first they were.
Tell[2] me the people that do keep[3]
Within the kingdoms of the deep;
Or fetch me back that cloud again,
Beshivered into seeds of rain.   10
Tell[2] me the motes, dust, sands, and spears
Of corn, when summer shakes his ears.
Show me that world of stars, and whence
They noiseless spill their influence.
This if thou canst; then show me Him
That rides the glorious cherubim.

TO FIND GOD
1 The ocean.   2 Count.   3 Dwell.

HIS LITANY TO THE HOLY SPIRIT

In the hour of my distress,
When temptations me oppress,
And when I my sins confess,
    Sweet Spirit, comfort me!

When I lie within my bed,
Sick in heart and sick in head,
And with doubts discomforted,
    Sweet Spirit, comfort me!

When the house doth sigh and weep,
And the world is drowned in sleep,   10
Yet mine eyes the watch do keep,
    Sweet Spirit, comfort me!

When the artless [1] doctor sees
No one hope, but of his fees,
And his skill runs on the lees,
    Sweet Spirit, comfort me!

When his potion and his pill
Has or none or little skill,
Meet for nothing but to kill,
    Sweet Spirit, comfort me!   20

When the passing bell doth toll,
And the furies in a shoal
Come to fright, a parting soul,
    Sweet Spirit, comfort me!

When the tapers now burn blue,
And the comforters are few,
And that number more than true,
    Sweet Spirit, comfort me!

When the priest his last hath prayed,
And I nod to what is said,   30
'Cause my speech is now decayed,
    Sweet Spirit, comfort me!

When, God knows, I'm tossed about,
Either with despair or doubt,
Yet, before the glass be out,
    Sweet Spirit, comfort me!

When the Tempter me pursu'th
With the sins of all my youth,
And half damns me with untruth,
    Sweet Spirit, comfort me!   40

When the flames and hellish cries
Fright mine ears and fright mine eyes,
And all terrors me surprise,
    Sweet Spirit, comfort me!

When the Judgment is revealed,
And that opened which was sealed,
When to Thee I have appealed,
    Sweet Spirit, comfort me!

A THANKSGIVING TO GOD FOR HIS HOUSE

Lord, Thou hast given me a cell
    Wherein to dwell,
A little house, whose humble roof
    Is weather-proof;
Under the spars of which I lie
    Both soft and dry;
Where Thou, my chamber for to ward,
    Hast set a guard
Of harmless thoughts, to watch and keep
    Me while I sleep.   10
Low is my porch, as is my fate,
    Both void of state;
And yet the threshold of my door
    Is worn by the poor,
Who thither come and freely get
    Good words, or meat.
Like as my parlor, so my hall
    And kitchen's small;
A little buttery, and therein
    A little bin,   20
Which keep my little loaf of bread
    Unchipped, unflead; [1]
Some brittle sticks of thorn or brier
    Make me a fire,
Close by whose living coal I sit,
    And glow like it.
Lord, I confess too, when I dine,
    The pulse [2] is Thine,
And all those other bits that be
    There placed by Thee;   30

HIS LITANY
1 Unskilled.

A THANKSGIVING
1 Unflayed, unbroken.   2 Peas, beans, etc.

The worts, the purslane,[3] and the mess
  Of watercress,
Which of Thy kindness Thou hast sent;
  And my content
Makes those, and my belovèd beet
  To be more sweet.
'Tis Thou that crown'st my glittering
    hearth
  With guiltless mirth,
And giv'st me wassail bowls to drink,
  Spiced to the brink.   40
Lord, 'tis Thy plenty-dropping hand
  That soils[4] my land,
And giv'st me, for my bushel sown,
  Twice ten for one;
Thou mak'st my teeming hen to lay
  Her egg each day;
Besides my healthful ewes to bear
  Me twins each year;
The while the conduits of my kine
  Run cream for wine.   50
All these, and better, Thou dost send
  Me, to this end,
That I should render for my part
  A thankful heart;
Which, fired with incense, I resign
  As wholly Thine;
But the acceptance, that must be,
  My Christ, by Thee.

TO DEATH

Thou bid'st me come away,
And I'll no longer stay
Than for to shed some tears
For faults of former years,
And to repent some crimes
Done in the present times;
And next, to take a bit
Of bread, and wine with it;
To don my robes of love,
Fit for the place above;   10
To gird my loins about
With charity throughout,
And so to travel hence
With feet of innocence:
These done, I'll only cry
God mercy, and so die.

A THANKSGIVING
3 An herb formerly used for salads.   4 Fertilizes.

ANOTHER GRACE FOR A CHILD

Here a little child I stand,
Heaving up my either hand;
Cold as paddocks[1] though they be,
Here I lift them up to Thee,
For a benison to fall
On our meat and on us all. Amen.

THE BELLMAN [2]

Along the dark and silent night,
With my lantern, and my light,
And the tinkling of my bell,
Thus I walk, and this I tell:
Death and dreadfulness call on
To the general Sessiòn;[1]
To whose dismal bar, we there
All accounts must come to clear.
Scores of sins we've made here many,
Wiped out few, God knows, if any.   10
Rise ye debtors then, and fall
To make payment, while I call.
Ponder this when I am gone;
By the clock 'tis almost one.

THE WHITE ISLAND, OR PLACE OF THE BLEST

In this world, the isle of dreams,
While we sit by sorrow's streams,
Tears and terrors are our themes,
  Reciting;

But when once from hence we fly,
More and more approaching nigh
Unto young eternity,
  Uniting

In that whiter island, where
Things are evermore sincere;   10
Candor[1] here and luster there
  Delighting:

ANOTHER GRACE
1 Toads or frogs.

THE BELLMAN
1 The Last Judgment.

THE WHITE ISLAND
1 Dazzling whiteness.

There no monstrous fancies shall
Out of hell an horror call,
To create, or cause at all,
    Affrighting.

There, in calm and cooling sleep
We our eyes shall never steep,
But eternal watch shall keep,
    Attending   20

Pleasures, such as shall pursue
Me immortalized, and you;
And fresh joys, as never, too,
    Have ending.

TO KEEP A TRUE LENT

Is this a fast, to keep
    The larder lean,
        And clean
From fat of veals and sheep?

Is it to quit the dish
    Of flesh, yet still
        To fill
The platter high with fish?

Is it to fast an hour
    Or ragg'd to go,   10
        Or show
A downcast look, and sour?

No; 'tis a fast to dole
    Thy sheaf of wheat
        And meat
Unto the hungry soul.

It is to fast from strife,
    From old debate
        And hate;
To circumcise thy life;   20

To show a heart grief-rent;
    To starve thy sin,
        Not bin.
And that's to keep thy Lent.

Francis Quarles

[1592–1644]

ORACE WALPOLE remarked, in the late eighteenth century, that Milton "had to wait until the world had done admiring Quarles." It is surely a comment on the universal inadequacy of popular taste that Quarles, a mediocre poet, should have been the most widely read poet in a century which included not only Milton but also such giants as Donne, Jonson, and Herbert. But if Quarles has interested subsequent centuries more as a literary curiosity than anything else, he is still worthy of something better than contempt, for he was a careful workman, capable of an occasional somber power. Born in Essex of a prosperous family, Quarles was educated at Christ's College, Cambridge, and at Lincoln's Inn. He acted as cup-bearer at the wedding of the Princess Elizabeth to the Elector Palatine in 1613, and he then accompanied that ill-starred lady to Germany as a member of her retinue. In 1620 he returned to England and published his first poetic work, a grim Scriptural paraphrase entitled *A Feast for Worms Set Forth in a Poem of the History of Jonah*. It was fully typical of the direction his talent was to take.

In 1626 Quarles became secretary to James Ussher, Archbishop of Armagh in Ireland; in 1633 he returned to England, where, in 1635, he published his most important work, the *Emblems, Divine and Moral*. It soon achieved a phenomenal popularity, especially among the Puritans—ironically enough, for the author was one of the most fervently devoted royalists who ever lived. The emblem is a curious literary form which was first developed in the sixteenth century but reached the height of its fashion in the earlier seventeenth. It consists of a print illustrating some moral or divine truth followed by an appropriate Scriptural citation, a poem analyzing and commenting on the picture, a further quotation, or quotations, from Fathers of the Church or other authorities, and, usually, a concluding epigram. In its quality as a kind of *Gesamtkunstwerk*, breaking down the normal barriers of the various artistic media, the emblem is fully characteristic of the sensibility of the Baroque age, but pure emblem poetry, as practiced by Quarles and Wither, seldom rises to real distinction, the presence of the picture acting perhaps as a kind of curb on the imagination of the poet. It is in certain poems of Herbert and Crashaw, not strictly emblem poems but inspired by the emblematic habit of mind, that the form makes its greatest contribution to literature.

F. QUARLES. *Collected Works*, ed. A. B. Grosart, 3 vols. (Edinburgh, 1880–81). Old, but still the only edition of the complete works.

G. S. HAIGHT. "The Sources of Quarles's Emblems," *Library*, Ser. 4, XVI (1935).

R. FREEMAN. *English Emblem Books* (London, 1948). The definitive study of emblem literature in England.

FROM

EMBLEMS, DIVINE AND MORAL [1635][1]

THE FIRST BOOK

EMBLEM XIV

Phosphere redde diem.

Will: Marshall Sculpsit.

PSALM 13:3

Lighten mine eyes, O Lord, lest I sleep the sleep of death.

Will it ne'er be morning? Will that promised light
  Ne'er break, and clear those clouds of night?

PSALM 13:3

1 Most of the engravings in Quarles's Emblems are copies
or adaptations of those in two Jesuit emblem books: Herman
Hugo's *Pia Desideria*, published at Antwerp in 1624, and
Typus Mundi, compiled by members of the College of the

Sweet Phosphor,[2] bring the day,
  Whose conquering ray
May chase these fogs. Sweet Phosphor, bring the day.

How long! How long shall these benighted eyes
  Languish in shades, like feeble flies

Expecting spring? How long shall darkness soil
  The face of earth, and thus beguile
Our souls of rightful action? When, when will day 10
  Begin to dawn, whose new-born ray
May gild the weather-cocks of our devotion,
  And give our unsouled souls new motion?
    Sweet Phosphor, bring the day;
      Thy light will fray
These horrid mists. Sweet Phosphor, bring the day.

Let those have night that slyly love to immure
  Their cloistered crimes, and sin secure;
Let those have night that blush to let men know
  The baseness they ne'er blush to do; 20
Let those have night that love to have a nap,
  And loll in Ignorance's lap;
Let those whose eyes, like owls', abhor the light,
  Let those have night that love the night.
    Sweet Phosphor, bring the day;
      How sad delay
Afflicts dull hopes! Sweet Phosphor, bring the day.

Alas! my light-in-vain-expecting eyes
  Can find no objects but what rise
From this poor mortal blaze, a dying spark 30
  Of Vulcan's forge, whose flames are dark
And dangerous; a dull, blue-burning light,
  As melancholy as the night;
Here's all the suns that glister in the sphere
  Of earth. Ah me! What comfort's here?
    Sweet Phosphor, bring the day;
      Haste, haste away
Heaven's loitering lamp. Sweet Phosphor, bring the
  day.

Society of Jesus at Antwerp and published at Antwerp in
1627. The originals of most of the illustrations in Books I
and II of Quarles's Emblems are in *Typus Mundi*. All the
plates of Books III, IV, and V of Quarles's volume were
copied or adapted from *Pia Desideria*. The poems are
Quarles's own.
  2 Phosphorus, the morning star.

Blow, Ignorance! O thou whose idle knee
    Rocks earth into a lethargy,   40
And with thy sooty fingers has benight
    The world's fair cheeks, blow, blow thy spite;
Since thou hast puffed our greater taper, do
    Puff on, and out the lesser too.
If e'er that breath-exilèd flame return,
    Thou hast not blown as it will burn.
        Sweet Phosphor, bring the day;
          Light will repay
The wrongs of night. Sweet Phosphor, bring the day.

Epigram 14

My soul, if Ignorance puff out this light,
She'll do a favor that intends a spite;
'T seems dark abroad, but take this light away,
Thy windows will discover break o' day.

EMBLEM XV[1]

Debilitata fides : Terbras Astræa reliquit

REVELATION 12:12
  1 The engraving for this emblem is one of the ten in the

REVELATION 12:12

The devil is come unto you, having a great wrath, because he knoweth that he hath but a short time.

Lord, canst Thou see and suffer? Is thy hand
    Still bound to the peace? Shall earth's black
        monarch take
A full possession of thy wasted land?
    Oh, will Thy slumbering vengeance never wake
    Till full-aged, law-resisting custom shake
The pillars of Thy right, by false command?
    Unlock Thy clouds, great Thunderer, and come
        down;
    Behold whose temples wear Thy sacred crown;
Redress, redress our wrongs; revenge, revenge
        Thy own.

See how the bold usurper mounts the seat   10
    Of royal majesty; how overstrawing
Perils with pleasure, pointing every threat
    With bugbear death, by torments over-awing
    Thy frighted subjects; or by favors drawing
Their tempted hearts to his unjust retreat;
    Lord, canst Thou be so mild, and he so bold?
    Or can Thy flocks be thriving, when the fold
Is governed by the fox? Lord, canst Thou see and
    hold?

That swift-winged advocate that did commence
    Our welcome suits before the King of kings,   20
That sweet ambassador that hurries hence
    What airs the harmonious soul or sighs or sings,
    See how she flutters with her idle wings;
Her wings are clipt, and eyes put out by sense;
    Sense-conquering Faith is now grown blind and
        cold,
    And basely cravened, that in times of old
Did conquer heaven itself, do what the Almighty
    could.

Behold, how double Fraud does scourge and tear
    Astræa's[2] wounded sides, plowed up and rent
With knotted cords, whose fury has no ear;   30

Emblems for which no originals have been found. It has been assumed, however, that all ten were probably copied from other plates.
  2 Astræa was the goddess of justice.

See how she stands a prisoner, to be sent
   A slave into eternal banishment,
I know not whither, oh, I know not where;
   Her patent must be canceled in disgrace;
   And sweet-lipped Fraud, with her divided face,
Must act Astræa's part, must take Astræa's place.

Faith's pinions clipt? and fair Astræa gone?
   Quick-seeing Faith now blind? and Justice see?
Has Justice now found wings? And has Faith none?
   What do we here? Who would not wish to be 40
   Dissolved from earth, and with Astræa flee
From this blind dungeon to that sun-bright throne?
   Lord, is Thy scepter lost, or laid aside?
   Is hell broke loose, and all her fiends untied?
Lord, rise, and rouse, and rule, and crush their
      furious pride.

Epigram 15

My soul, sit thou a patient looker on;
Judge not the play before the play be done:
Her plot has many changes; every day
Speaks a new scene; the last act crowns the play.

Wherefore hidest thou thy face, or holdest mee for thine Enemy. Job: 13.24
W.S.Sc:

THE THIRD BOOK

EMBLEM VII

JOB 13:24

Wherefore hidest thou thy face, and holdest me for thine enemy?

Why dost Thou shade Thy lovely face? Oh why
Does that eclipsing hand so long deny
The sunshine of Thy soul-enlivening eye?

Without that light, what light remains in me?
Thou art my life, my way, my light; in Thee
I live, I move, and by Thy beams I see.

Thou art my life: if Thou but turn away,
My life's a thousand deaths; Thou art my way:
Without Thee, Lord, I travel not, but stray.

My light Thou art: without Thy glorious sight, 10
My eyes are darkened with perpetual night.
My God, Thou art my way, my life, my light.

Thou art my way: I wander if Thou fly;
Thou art my light: if hid, how blind am I!
Thou art my life: if Thou withdraw, I die.

Mine eyes are blind and dark, I cannot see;
To whom, or whither, should my darkness flee,
But to the light? and who's that light but Thee?

My path is lost, my wandering steps do stray;
I cannot safely go, nor safely stay; 20
Whom should I seek but Thee, my path, my way?

Oh, I am dead: to whom shall I, poor I,
Repair: to whom shall my sad ashes fly
But life? and where is life but in Thine eye?

And yet Thou turn'st away Thy face, and fly'st me;
And yet I sue for grace, and Thou deny'st me;
Speak, art Thou angry, Lord, or only try'st me?

Unscreen those heavenly lamps, or tell me why
Thou shad'st thy face; perhaps Thou think'st no eye
Can view those flames, and not drop down and die.

If that be all, shine forth and draw Thee nigher;   31
Let me behold and die, for my desire
Is, phœnix-like, to perish in that fire.

Death-conquered Lazarus [1] was redeemed by Thee;
If I am dead, Lord, set death's prisoner free;
Am I more spent, or stink I worse than he?

If my puffed life be out, give leave to tine [2]
My shameless snuff at that bright lamp of Thine;
Oh, what's Thy light the less for lightening mine?

If I have lost my path, great Shepherd, say,   40
Shall I still wander in a doubtful way?
Lord, shall a lamb of Israel's sheepfold stray?

Thou art the pilgrim's path, the blind man's eye,
The dead man's life; on Thee my hopes rely;
If Thou remove, I err, I grope, I die.

Disclose Thy sunbeams, close Thy wings and stay;
See, see how I am blind and dead, and stray,
O Thou that art my light, my life, my way.

Epigram 7

If heaven's all-quickening eyes vouchsafe to shine
Upon our souls, we slight; if not, we whine:
Our equinoctial hearts can never lie
Secure beneath the tropics of that eye.

THE FOURTH BOOK

EMBLEM III

Stay my stepps in thy Pathes that my feet do not slide. Ps. 17. 5.
W. M. Sc:

PSALM 17:5

Stay my steps in thy paths, that my feet do not slide.

Whene'er the old exchange of profit rings
    Her silver saints-bell of uncertain gains,
My merchant-soul can stretch both legs and wings;
    How I can run, and take unwearied pains!
      The charms of profit are so strong that I,
      Who wanted legs to go, [1] find wings to fly.

JO[1] 13:24
  [1] See St. John 11:32–44.   2 To light.

PSALM 17:5
  1 Walk.

If time-beguiling Pleasure but advance
  Her lustful trump, and blow her bold alarms,
Oh how my sportful soul can frisk and dance,
    And hug that siren in her twinèd arms!   10
      The sprightly voice of sinew-strengthening
        Pleasure
      Can lend my bedrid soul both legs and leisure.

If blazing Honor chance to fill my veins
  With flattering warmth, and flash of courtly fire,
My soul can take a pleasure in her pains;
    My lofty strutting steps disdain to tire;
      My antic² knees can turn upon the hinges
      Of compliment, and screw a thousand cringes.

But when I come to Thee, my God, that art
  The royal mine of everlasting treasure,   20
The real honor of my better part,
    And living fountain of eternal pleasure,
      How nerveless are my limbs! how faint and
        slow!
      I have nor wings to fly, nor legs to go.

So when the streams of swift-foot Rhine convey
  Her upland riches to the Belgic shore,
The idle vessel slides the wat'ry way,
    Without the blast or tug of wind or oar;
      Her slippery keel divides the silver foam
      With ease: so facile is the way from home!   30

But when the home-bound vessel turns her sails
  Against the breast of the resisting stream,
Oh then she slugs; nor sail nor oar prevails!
    The stream is sturdy, and her tide's extreme:
      Each stroke is loss, and ev'ry tug is vain;
      A boat-length's purchase is a league of pain.

Great All in All, that art my rest, my home;
  My way is tedious, and my steps are slow:
Reach forth Thy helpful hand, or bid me come;
  I am Thy child, O teach Thy child to go;   40
    Conjoin Thy sweet commands to my desire,
    And I will venture, though I fall or tire.

Epigram 3

Fear not, my soul, to lose for want of cunning;
Weep not; heaven is not always got by running:
Thy thoughts are swift, although thy legs be slow;
True love will creep, not having strength to go.

2 Like those of a buffoon.

THE FIFTH BOOK

EMBLEM III

*My Beloved is mine and I am his, He
feedeth among the Lillies. Cant: 2.16.*

Will: Simpson: sculp:

CANTICLES¹ 2:16

*My beloved is mine, and I am his; he feedeth among the
lilies.*

Ev'n like two little bank-dividing brooks
  That wash the pebbles with their wanton streams,
And having ranged and searched a thousand nooks,
  Meet both at length in silver-breasted Thames,
    Where in a greater current they conjoin,
So I my best beloved's am; so He is mine.

CANTICLES 2:16
1 The Song of Solomon.

Ev'n so we met, and after long pursuit,
  Ev'n so we joined; we both became entire.
No need for either to renew a suit,
  For I was flax, and He was flames of fire.   10
    Our firm-united souls did more than twine;
So I my best beloved's am; so He is mine.

If all those glitt'ring monarchs that command
  The servile quarters of this earthly ball
Should tender, in exchange, their shares of land,
  I would not change my fortunes for them all;
    Their wealth is but a counter to my coin;
The world's but theirs; but my beloved's mine.

Nay more, if the fair Thespian ladies [2] all
  Should heap together their diviner treasure,   20
That treasure should be deemed a price too small
  To buy a minute's lease of half my pleasure.
    'Tis not the sacred wealth of all the Nine
Can buy my heart from Him, or His from being
  mine.

Nor time, nor place, nor chance, nor death, can bow
  My least desires unto the least remove;
He's firmly mine by oath, I His by vow;
  He's mine by faith, and I am His by love;
    He's mine by water, I am His by wine;
Thus I my best beloved's am; thus He is mine.   30

He is my altar; I His holy place;
  I am His guest, and He my living food;
I'm His by penitence, He mine by grace;
  I'm His by purchase, He is mine by blood.
    He's my supporting elm, and I His vine;
Thus I my best beloved's am; thus He is mine.

He gives me wealth, I give him all my vows;
  I give Him songs, He gives me length of days;
With wreaths of grace He crowns my conq'ring
  brows,
  And I His temples with a crown of praise;   40
    Which He accepts as an everlasting sign
That I my best beloved's am, that He is mine.

Epigram 3

Sing, Hymen, to my soul: what, lost and found?
Welcomed, espoused, enjoyed so soon and crowned!
He did but climb the cross, and then came down
To th' gates of hell; triumphed, and fetched a crown.

  2 The nine Muses.

EMBLEM IV

*I am my beloveds, & his Desire is
towards mee. Cant: 7.10. W: Simpson
Sc:*

CANTICLES 7:10

I am my beloved's, and his desire is towards me.

Like to the arctic needle, that doth guide
  The wand'ring shade by his magnetic power,
And leaves his silken gnomon to decide
  The question of the controverted hour,
First frantics up and down from side to side,
    And restless beats his crystalled iv'ry case
    With vain impatience; jets from place to place,
And seeks the bosom of his frozen bride;
    At length he slacks his motion, and doth rest
His trembling point at his bright pole's belovèd
  breast.   10

Ev'n so my soul, being hurried here and there,
  By ev'ry object that presents delight,
Fain would be settled, but she knows not where;
  She likes at morning what she loathes at night:

She bows to honor, then she lends an ear
    To that sweet swan-like voice of dying pleasure,
    Then tumbles in the scattered heaps of
        treasure;
Now flattered with false hope, now foiled with fear:
    Thus finding all the world's delight to be
But empty toys, good God, she points to Thee.   20

But hath the virtued steel a power to move?
    Or can the untouched needle point aright?
Or can my wand'ring thoughts forbear to rove,
    Unguided by the virtue of Thy sp'rit?
Oh hath my laden soul the art to improve
    Her wasted talent, and, unraised, aspire
    In this sad moulting time of her desire?
Not first belov'd, have I the power to love?
    I cannot stir but as Thou please to move me,
Nor can my heart return Thee love until Thou
        love me.   30

The still commandress of the silent night
    Borrows her beams from her bright brother's eye;
His fair aspect fills her sharp horns with light,
    If he withdraw, her flames are quenched and die:
Ev'n so the beams of Thy enlight'ning sp'rit,
    Infused and shot into my dark desire,
    Inflame my thoughts, and fill my soul with fire,
That I am ravished with a new delight;
    But if Thou shroud Thy face, my glory fades,
And I remain a nothing, all composed of shades.   40

Eternal God! O Thou that only art,
    The sacred fountain of eternal light,
And blessed loadstone of my better part,
    O Thou, my heart's desire, my soul's delight!
Reflect upon my soul, and touch my heart,
    And then my heart shall prize no good above
        Thee;
    And then my soul shall know Thee; knowing,
        love Thee;
And then my trembling thoughts shall never start
    From Thy commands, or swerve the least   49
        degree,
Or once presume to move, but as they move in Thee.

Epigram 4

My soul, thy love is dear; 'twas thought a good
And easy penn'worth of thy Saviour's blood;
But be not proud; all matters rightly scanned,
'Twas over-bought: 'twas sold at second hand.

EMBLEM VI[1]

*Whom haue I in heauen but thee or what
desire I on earth in respect of thee. Ps: 73.*
    W. S. fe:

PSALM 73:25

*Whom have I in heaven but thee? and what desire I on
earth in respect of thee?*

I love, and have some cause to love, the earth:
    She is my Maker's creature, therefore good;
She is my mother, for she gave me birth;
    She is my tender nurse; she gives me food.
But what's a creature, Lord, compared with Thee?
Or what's my mother or my nurse to me?

PSALM 73:25
    1 Robert Browning commented on this illustration in a
letter to Elizabeth Barrett, dated August 19, 1846. He calls
Quarles's Emblems "my childhood's pet book," and mentions
the "squat little woman-figure with a loose gown, hair in a
coil, and bare feet," who sits on a "terrestrial ball." The
original of this plate is in *Pia Desideria* (III, 6). For the names
of the cities on the original plate have been substituted
London, Roxwell, Finchingfield ("Finchfield"), and Hilgay,
towns associated with Quarles and his friends.

I love the air; her dainty sweets refresh
   My drooping soul, and to new sweets invite me;
Her shrill-mouthed choir sustain me with their
     flesh,
   And with their Polyphonian[2] notes delight me. 10
But what's the air, or all the sweets that she
Can bless my soul withal, compared to Thee?

I love the sea; she is my fellow-creature,
   My careful purveyor; she provides me store;[3]
She walls me round; she makes my diet greater;
   She wafts my treasure from a foreign shore.
But, Lord of oceans, when compared with Thee,
What is the ocean or her wealth to me?

To heaven's high city I direct my journey,
   Whose spangled suburbs entertain mine eye;   20
Mine eye, by contemplation's great attorney,
   Transcends the crystal pavement of the sky.
But what is heaven, great God, compared to Thee?
Without Thy presence, heaven's no heaven to me.

Without Thy presence, earth gives no refection;
   Without Thy presence, sea affords no treasure;
Without Thy presence, air's a rank infection;
   Without Thy presence, heaven itself's no
     pleasure.
If not possessed, if not enjoyed in Thee,   30
What's earth, or sea, or air, or heaven, to me?

2 Many-sounding.   3 Abundance.

The highest honors that the world can boast
   Are subjects far too low for my desire;
The brightest beams of glory are, at most,
   But dying sparkles of Thy living fire.
The proudest flames that earth can kindle be
But nightly glowworms, if compared to Thee.

Without Thy presence, wealth are bags of cares;
   Wisdom but folly; joy, disquiet sadness;
Friendship is treason, and delights are snares;
   Pleasure's but pain, and mirth but pleasing
     madness.   40
Without Thee, Lord, things be not what they be;
Nor have they being, when compared with Thee.

In having all things, and not Thee, what have I?
   Not having Thee, what have my labors got?
Let me enjoy but Thee, what farther crave I?
   And having Thee alone, what have I not?
I wish no sea, nor land; nor would I be
Possessed of heaven, heaven unpossessed of Thee.

Epigram 6

Who would not throw his better thoughts about him,
And scorn this dross within him; that, without him?
Cast up, my soul, thy clearer eye; behold,
If thou be fully melted, there's the mold.

FROM

DIVINE FANCIES [1632]

A GOOD-NIGHT

Close now thine eyes and rest secure;
Thy soul is safe enough, thy body sure;
   He that loves thee, He that keeps
And guards thee, never slumbers, never sleeps.

The smiling conscience in a sleeping breast
   Has only peace, has only rest;
   The music and the mirth of kings
Are all but very discords, when she sings;
   Then close thine eyes and rest secure;
No sleep so sweet as thine, no rest so sure.

Henry King

[1592–1669]

HENRY KING is remembered primarily for a single poem, the great elegy "The Exequy," in which the manner introduced by Donne is adapted with impressive skill and individuality to lamenting the death of the poet's wife. Among his poems, however, may be found several others of comparable distinction, in which a kind of Jonsonian polish is joined with a very Donnesque indulgence in wit and conceit. King, indeed, ranks with Herbert of Cherbury as one of the earliest disciples of Donne, who was his close friend and whose literary executor he became.

King was the eldest son of John King, who was chaplain to Sir Thomas Egerton, Lord Keeper of the Great Seal, and who later became Bishop of London. After receiving his early education at Westminster School, King entered Christ Church, Oxford, at a time when his father was Dean of that college and also Vice-Chancellor of the University. Taking his B.A. in 1611 and his M.A. in 1614, the poet proceeded to an ecclesiastical career which the prominence of his father rendered notably successful. As Prebendary of St. Paul's and Archdeacon of Colchester he was in close association with Donne; in 1639 he was made Dean of Rochester and in 1642 Bishop of Chichester, but the Puritan capture of that city promptly deprived him of his post and he was not restored to it until the return of Charles II. In 1617 King had married Anne Berkeley; her death a scant seven years later moved him to the composition of the elegy which gives him his special importance among the minor poets of the century.

HENRY KING. *English Poems*, ed. L. Mason (New Haven, 1914).
————. *The Poems*, ed. J. Sparrow (London, 1925).
————. *Poems*, ed. M. C. Crum (Oxford, 1965).
L. MASON. *The Life and Works of Henry King* (New Haven, 1913).
G. WILLIAMSON. (See under general poetry bibliography.)

FROM

POEMS, ELEGIES, PARADOXES, AND SONNETS [1657]

SONNET

Tell me no more how fair she is,
   I have no mind to hear
The story of that distant bliss
   I never shall come near;
By sad experience I have found
That her perfection is my wound.

And tell me not how fond I am
   To tempt a daring fate,
From whence no triumph ever came
   But to repent too late;   10
There is some hope ere long I may
In silence dote myself away.

I ask no pity, Love, from thee,
   Nor will thy justice blame,
So that thou wilt not envy me
   The glory of my flame,
Which crowns my heart whene'er it dies,
In that it falls her sacrifice.

THE EXEQUY[1]

Accept, thou shrine of my dead saint,
Instead of dirges, this complaint;
And for sweet flowers to crown thy hearse,
Receive a strew of weeping verse
From thy grieved friend, whom thou
   might'st see
Quite melted into tears for thee.

Dear loss! since thy untimely fate
My task hath been to meditate
On thee, on thee; thou art the book,
The library whereon I look,   10
Though almost blind. For thee, loved clay,
I languish out, not live, the day,

Using no other exercise
But what I practice with mine eyes;
By which wet glasses I find out
How lazily time creeps about
To one that mourns; this, only this,
My exercise and business is.
So I compute the weary hours
With sighs dissolvèd into showers.   20

Nor wonder if my time go thus
Backward and most preposterous;
Thou hast benighted me; thy set
This eve of blackness did beget,
Who wast my day, though overcast
Before thou hadst thy noontide passed;
And I remember must in tears,
Thou scarce hadst seen so many years
As day tells hours. By thy clear sun
My love and fortune first did run;   30
But thou wilt never more appear
Folded within my hemisphere,
Since both thy light and motion
Like a fled star is fall'n and gone;
And 'twixt me and my soul's dear wish
An earth now interposèd is,
Which such a strange eclipse doth make
As ne'er was read in almanac.

I could allow thee for a time
To darken me and my sad clime;   40
Were it a month, a year, or ten,
I would thy exile live till then,
And all that space my mirth adjourn,
So thou wouldst promise to return,
And putting off thy ashy shroud,
At length disperse this sorrow's cloud.

But woe is me! the longest date
Too narrow is to calculate
These empty hopes; never shall I
Be so much blest as to descry   50
A glimpse of thee, till that day come
Which shall the earth to cinders doom,
And a fierce fever must calcine
The body of this world like thine,

THE EXEQUY
  1 The poem was composed in memory of Anne, the first
wife of the author, who died about 1624.

My little world. That fit of fire
Once off, our bodies shall aspire
To our souls' bliss; then we shall rise
And view ourselves with clearer eyes
In that calm region where no night
Can hide us from each other's sight.   60

Meantime, thou hast her, earth; much good
May my harm do thee. Since it stood
With Heaven's will I might not call
Her longer mine, I give thee all
My short-lived right and interest
In her whom living I loved best;
With a most free and bounteous grief,
I give thee what I could not keep.
Be kind to her, and prithee look
Thou write into thy doomsday book   70
Each parcel of this rarity
Which in thy casket shrined doth lie.
See that thou make thy reck'ning straight,
And yield her back again by weight;
For thou must audit on thy trust
Each grain and atom of this dust,
As thou wilt answer Him that lent,
Not gave thee, my dear monument.

So close the ground, and 'bout her shade
Black curtains draw; my bride is laid.   80

Sleep on, my love, in thy cold bed,
Never to be disquieted!
My last good-night! Thou wilt not wake
Till I thy fate shall overtake;
Till age, or grief, or sickness must
Marry my body to that dust
It so much loves, and fill the room
My heart keeps empty in thy tomb.
Stay for me there, I will not fail
To meet thee in that hollow vale.   90
And think not much of my delay;
I am already on the way,
And follow thee with all the speed
Desire can make, or sorrows breed.
Each minute is a short degree,
And ev'ry hour a step towards thee.
At night when I betake to rest,
Next morn I rise nearer my west
Of life, almost by eight hours' sail,
Than when sleep breathed his drowsy gale.   100

Thus from the sun my bottom steers,
And my day's compass downward bears;
Nor labor I to stem the tide
Through which to thee I swiftly glide.

'Tis true, with shame and grief I yield,
Thou like the van first took'st the field,
And gotten hath the victory
In thus adventuring to die
Before me, whose more years might crave
A just precedence in the grave.   110
But hark! my pulse like a soft drum
Beats my approach, tells thee I come;
And slow howe'er my marches be,
I shall at last sit down by thee.

The thought of this bids me go on,
And wait my dissolution
With hope and comfort. Dear, forgive
The crime, I am content to live
Divided, with but half a heart,
Till we shall meet and never part.   120

THE SURRENDER

My once dear love, hapless that I no more
Must call thee so, the rich affection's store
That fed our hopes lies now exhaust and spent,
Like sums of treasure unto bankrupts lent.

We that did nothing study but the way
To love each other, with which thoughts the day
Rose with delight to us, and with them set,
Must learn the hateful art how to forget.

We that did nothing wish that Heav'n could give
Beyond ourselves, nor did desire to live   10
Beyond that wish, all these now cancel must
As if not writ in faith, but words and dust.

Yet witness those clear vows which lovers make,
Witness the chaste desires that never brake
Into unruly heats; witness that breast
Which in thy bosom anchored his whole rest;
'Tis no default in us, I dare acquite
Thy maiden faith, thy purpose fair and white
As thy pure self, Cross planets did envy
Us to each other, and Heav'n did untie   20
Faster than vows could bind. Oh, that the stars,
When lovers meet, should stand opposed in wars!

Since, then, some higher destinies command,
Let us not strive, nor labor to withstand
What is past help. The longest date of grief
Can never yield a hope of our relief;
And though we waste ourselves in moist laments,
Tears may drown us, but not our discontents.

Fold back our arms, take home our fruitless loves,
That must new fortunes try, like turtledoves   30
Dislodgèd from their haunts. We must in tears
Unwind a love knit up in many years.
In this last kiss I here surrender thee
Back to thyself, so thou again art free;
Thou in another, sad as that, resend
The truest heart that lover e'er did lend.

Now turn from each. So fare our severed hearts
As the divorced soul from her body parts.

UPON THE DEATH OF MY EVER-DESIRED FRIEND, DOCTOR DONNE OF PAUL'S

To have lived eminent, in degree
Beyond our loftiest flights, that is, like thee,
Or to have had too much merit is not safe;
For such excesses find no epitaph.
At common graves we have poetic eyes
Can melt themselves in easy elegies;
Each quill can drop his tributary verse,
And pin it with the hatchments to the hearse.
But at thine, poem or inscriptiòn,
Rich soul of wit and language, we have none;   10
Indeed a silence does that tomb befit
Where is no herald left to blazon it.
Widowed invention justly doth forbear
To come abroad, knowing thou art not here,
Late her great patron; whose prerogative
Maintained and clothed her so, as none alive
Must now presume to keep her at thy rate,
Though he the Indies for her dower estate:
Or else that awful fire which once did burn
In thy clear brain, now fall'n into thy urn,   20
Lives there to fright rude empirics from thence,
Which might profane thee by their ignorance.
Whoever writes of thee, and in a style
Unworthy such a theme, does but revile
Thy precious dust, and wake a learned spirit
Which may revenge his rapes upon thy merit.

For all a low-pitched fancy can devise
Will prove at best but hallowed injuries.

Thou, like the dying swan, didst lately sing
Thy mournful dirge in audience of the King;   30
When pale looks and faint accents of thy breath
Presented so to life that piece of death [1]
That it was feared and prophesied by all
Thou hither cam'st to preach thy funeral. [2]
Oh, hadst thou in an elegiac knell
Rung out unto the world thine own farewell,
And in thy high victorious numbers beat
The solemn measure of thy grieved retreat,
Thou might'st the poet's service now have missed,
As well as then thou didst prevent [3] the priest, 40
And never to the world beholden be
So much as for an epitaph for thee!

I do not like the office. Nor is't fit,
Thou, who didst lend our age such sums of wit,
Shouldst now reborrow from her bankrupt mine
That ore to bury thee which once was thine.
Rather, still leave us in thy debt; and know,
Exalted soul, more glory 'tis to owe
Unto thy hearse what we can never pay
Than with embasèd coin those rites defray.   50

Commit we then thee to thyself. Nor blame
Our drooping loves, which thus to thine own fame
Leave thee executor, since, but by thy own,
No pen could do thee justice, nor bays crown
Thy vast desert; save that, we nothing can
Depute to be thy ashes' guardian.

So jewelers no art or metal trust
To form the diamond but the diamond's dust.

SIC VITA

Like to the falling of a star,
Or as the flights of eagles are,
Or like the fresh spring's gaudy hue,
Or silver drops of morning dew,

UPON THE DEATH

1 The portrait which Donne had painted of himself in his shroud.

2 Donne's last sermon, Death's Duel, was preached, after a severe illness, before the King at Whitehall in 1630.

3 Anticipate.

Or like a wind that chafes the flood,
Or bubbles which on water stood:
Even such is man, whose borrowed light
Is straight called in, and paid to night.

The wind blows out, the bubble dies;
The spring entombed in autumn lies;
The dew dries up, the star is shot;
The flight is past, and man forgot.

FROM

HARLEIAN MS. 6917, BRITISH MUSEUM

A CONTEMPLATION UPON FLOWERS

Brave flowers, that I could gallant it like you,
And be as little vain;
You come abroad, and make a harmless show,
And to your beds of earth again;
You are not proud, you know your birth,
For your embroidered garments are from earth.

You do obey your months and times, but I
Would have it ever spring;

My fate would know no winter, never die,
Nor think of such a thing;   10
Oh that I could my bed of earth but view,
And smile, and look as cheerfully as you.

Oh teach me to see death and not to fear,
But rather to take truce;
How often have I seen you at a bier,
And there look fresh and spruce;
You fragrant flowers then teach me that my
        breath
Like yours may sweeten and perfume my death.

George Herbert

[1593–1633]

OF THE many seventeenth-century poets revalued and exalted by our own century, none, not even Donne, has achieved a more striking elevation than has George Herbert. Scorned by the Augustan age for his exercises in "false wit" (the phrase is Addison's), tolerated by the nineteenth century for his piety and "quaintness," Herbert is now generally recognized as a towering figure in Baroque poetry and as perhaps the finest devotional poet in our language.

Almost all of Herbert's poetry is contained in *The Temple*, which was probably composed in its entirety during the last years of his life, when he was parson of the country parish of Bemerton near Salisbury. Just before his death Herbert sent the manuscript of *The Temple* to his friend Nicholas Ferrar with the request that "if he can think it may turn to the advantage of any dejected poor soul, let it be made public; if not, let him burn it; for I and it are less than the least of God's mercies." The exemplary piety for which the work is famous breathes in the quoted statement, but the heroic and saintly quality of that piety only appears when we recognize what consummate and painstaking artistry had gone into the making of Herbert's book. The death-bed sacrifice of his life's work of art takes its meaning from the fact that the work is not a random set of private prayers but an ineffably complex and marvelously unified poetic whole: as the poet had written, "My God must have my best, even all I had."

Influenced by Sir Philip Sidney, influenced by John Donne (although to a smaller degree than has sometimes been maintained), Herbert is as remarkable for his artistic originality as for anything else. Perhaps no other English poet of the age develops to as intense a degree as he the identification of matter and manner characteristic of much Baroque art. His pattern poems, "The Altar" and "Easter-Wings," are the most famous examples of this tendency, but subtler and more effective examples may be found in "Denial," with its emblematic use of rime, or "The Thanksgiving," with its brutally ironic rhetoric. The variety within *The Temple* is astounding: formal celebrations of feasts of the Church stand beside divine love songs parodied from secular verse; miniature allegories such as "The Pilgrimage" have their place beside miniature spiritual autobiographies such as "Affliction" [1] and miniature dramas such as "Dialogue." Herbert's subject is single and simple, but in his treatment he marshals all the poetic techniques known to the most various age of English poetry.

The artistry of *The Temple* is as admirable in its totality as in its detail: the over-all structure is so complex as to defy schematization, but there is a definite progression from "The Church Porch," with its homely, didactic, and low-keyed counsels, to what a recent critic has called "the sacramental introduction" which we meet inside "The

Church" proper. The progression continues from this introduction through the varied personal conflicts, aspirations, disappointments, and reassurances which make up the body of the work to the final invitation to partake of the meal of love ("Love" [3]) which closes the work by drawing together the threads of Eucharistic imagery which have run through it. Herbert was a lover of music, and one finds in *The Temple* something perhaps analogous to the contrapuntal structure of the music of the poet's age. Immensely popular throughout the seventeenth century, Herbert's poetry fell into almost complete neglect during the eighteenth. Revival began when Coleridge noted that Herbert was "a true poet." It has remained for our age to perceive, beside the saint, and great poet and true artist.

G. HERBERT. *Works*, ed. F. E. Hutchinson (Oxford, rev. ed., 1945). The definitive edition.

A. G. HYDE. *George Herbert and His Times* (London, 1906).

M. BOTTRALL. *George Herbert* (London, 1954).

S. A. AND D. TANNENBAUM. *George Herbert: A Concise Bibliography* (New York, 1946).

J. SUMMERS. *George Herbert: His Religion and His Art* (Cambridge, Mass., 1954).

R. TUVE. *A Reading of George Herbert* (London, 1952).

M. CHUTE. (See under Herrick bibliography.)

A. CHARLES. *A Life of George Herbert* (Ithaca, N.Y., 1977).

S. FISH. *The Living Temple: Catechizing in Herbert* (Berkeley, Calif., 1978).

C. FREER. *Music for a King* (Baltimore, 1972).

M. E. RICKEY. *Utmost Art: Complexity in the Verse of George Herbert* (Lexington, Ky., 1966).

A. STEIN. *George Herbert's Lyrics* (Baltimore, 1968).

H. VENDLER. *The Poetry of George Herbert* (Cambridge, Mass., 1974).

F R O M

IZAAK WALTON'S LIFE OF MR. GEORGE HERBERT

[1670]

[TO HIS MOTHER]

My God, where is that ancient heat towards Thee
  Wherewith whole shoals of martyrs once did burn,
  Besides their other flames? Doth poetry
Wear Venus' livery, only serve her turn?
Why are not sonnets made of Thee, and lays
  Upon Thine altar burnt? Cannot Thy love
  Heighten a spirit to sound out Thy praise
As well as any she? Cannot Thy Dove
Outstrip their Cupid easily in flight?
  Or, since Thy ways are deep and still the same,   10
  Will not a verse run smooth that bears Thy name?
Why doth that fire, which by Thy power and might
  Each breast does feel, no braver fuel choose
  Than that which one day worms may chance refuse?

Sure, Lord, there is enough in Thee to dry
  Oceans of ink; for, as the deluge did
  Cover the earth, so doth Thy majesty:
Each cloud distills Thy praise, and doth forbid
Poets to turn it to another use.
  Roses and lilies speak Thee; and to make   20
  A pair of cheeks of them is Thy abuse.
Why should I women's eyes for crystal take?
Such poor invention burns in their low mind
  Whose fire is wild, and doth not upward go
  To praise, and on Thee, Lord, some ink bestow.
Open the bones, and you shall nothing find
  In the best face but filth; when, Lord, in Thee
  The beauty lies in the discovery.

FROM

THE TEMPLE [1633]

THE CHURCH PORCH[1]

1

Thou, whose sweet youth and early hopes enhance
Thy rate and price, and mark thee for a treasure,
Hearken unto a verser who may chance
Rhyme thee to good, and make a bait of pleasure.
    A verse may find him who a sermon flies,
    And turn delight into a sacrifice.

5

Drink not the third glass, which thou canst not tame,
When once it is within thee; but before,
Mayst rule it as thou list; and pour the shame,
Which it would pour on thee, upon the floor.
    It is most just to throw that on the ground
    Which would throw me there if I keep the round.

7

Shall I, to please another's wine-sprung mind,
Lose all mine own? God hath giv'n me a measure
Short of his can and body; must I find
A pain in that wherein he finds a pleasure?
    Stay at the third glass: if thou lose thy hold,
    Then thou art modest, and the wine grows bold.

11

When thou dost tell another's jest, therein
Omit the oaths, which true wit cannot need;
Pick out of tales the mirth, but not the sin;
He pares his apple, that will cleanly feed.
    Play not away the virtue of that name
    Which is thy best stake when griefs make thee
      tame.

14

Fly idleness, which yet thou canst not fly
By dressing, mistressing, and compliment.
If those take up thy day, the sun will cry
Against thee, for his light was only lent.
    God gave thy soul brave wings; put not those
      feathers
    Into a bed, to sleep out all ill weathers.

THE CHURCH PORCH
  1 The stanzas were not numbered in the 1633 edition.

16

O England! full of sin, but most of sloth;
Spit out thy phlegm, and fill thy breast with glory;
Thy gentry bleats, as if thy native cloth
Transfused a sheepishness into thy story;
    Not that they all are so, but that the most
    Are gone to grass, and in the pasture los+

17

This loss springs chiefly from our education
Some till their ground, but let weeds choke
Some mark a partridge, never their child's f;
Some ship them over, and the thing is done.
    Study this art, make it thy great design;
    And if God's image move thee not, let tł

18

Some great estates provide, but do not breed
A mastering mind; so both are lost thereby;
Or else they breed them tender, make them need
All that they leave; this is flat poverty.
    For he that needs five thousand pound to live
    Is full as poor as he that needs but five.

19

The way to make thy son rich is to fill
His mind with rest, before his trunk with riches;
For wealth without contentment climbs a hill
To feel those tempests which fly over ditches.
    But if thy son can make ten pounds his measure,
    Then all thou addest may be called his treasure.

22

Look to thy mouth; diseases enter there.
Thou hast two sconces,[2] if thy stomach call:
Carve or discourse; do not a famine fear.
Who carves, is kind to two; who talks, to all.
    Look on meat, think it dirt, then eat a bit;
    And say withal, "Earth to earth I commit."

25

By all means use sometimes to be alone.
Salute thyself; see what thy soul doth wear.

  2 Safeguards, protections.

Dare to look in thy chest, for 'tis thine own,
And tumble up and down what thou find'st there.
    Who cannot rest till he good fellows find,
    He breaks up house, turns out of doors his mind.

27

Never exceed thy income. Youth may make
Ev'n with the year, but age, if it will hit,
Shoots a bow short, and lessens still his stake
As the day lessens, and his life with it.
    Thy children, kindred, friends, upon thee call;
    Before thy journey, fairly part with all.

29

What skills it if a bag of stones or gold
About thy neck do drown thee? Raise thy head,
Take stars for money; stars not to be told[3]
By any art, yet to be purchased.
    None is so wasteful as the scraping dame.
    She loseth three for one: her soul, rest, fame.

30

By no means run in debt: take thine own measure.
Who cannot live on twenty pound a year
Cannot on forty; he's a man of pleasure,
A kind of thing that's for itself too dear.
    The curious unthrift makes his clothes too wide,
    And spares himself, but would his tailor chide.

32

In clothes, cheap handsomeness doth bear the bell.[4]
Wisdom's a trimmer thing than shop e'er gave.
Say not, then, "This with that lace will do well,"
But, "This with my discretion will be brave."[5]
    Much curiousness[6] is a perpetual wooing
    Nothing with labor, folly long a-doing.

33

Play not for gain, but sport. Who plays for more
Than he can lose with pleasure, stakes his heart;
Perhaps his wife's, too, and whom she hath bore;
Servants and churches also play their part.
    Only a herald, who that way doth pass,
    Finds his cracked name at length in the church-
        glass.

34

If thou love game at so dear a rate,
Learn this, that hath old gamesters dearly cost:
Dost lose? rise up; dost win? rise in that state.
Who strive to sit out losing hands, are lost.
    Game is a civil gunpowder; in peace
    Blowing up houses with their whole increase.

59

Scorn no man's love, though of a mean degree;
Love is a present for a mighty king.
Much less make anyone thine enemy.
As guns destroy, so may a little sling.
    The cunning workman never doth refuse
    The meanest tool that he may chance to use.

63

In alms regard thy means, and others' merit.
Think heaven a better bargain than to give
Only thy single market-money for it.
Join hands with God to make a man to live.
    Give to all something; to a good poor man,
    Till thou change names, and be where he began.

65

Restore to God his due in tithe and time;
A tithe purloined cankers the whole estate.
Sundays observe; think when the bells do chime,
'Tis angels' music, therefore come not late.
    God then deals blessings; if a king did so,
    Who would not haste, nay give, to see the show?

68

When once thy foot enters the church, be bare.
God is more there than thou, for thou art there
Only by His permission. Then beware,
And make thyself all reverence and fear.
    Kneeling ne'er spoiled silk stocking; quit thy
        state.
    All equal are within the church's gate.

69

Resort to sermons, but to prayers most;
Praying's the end of preaching. O be dressed!
Stay not for the other pin: why, thou hast lost
A joy for it worth worlds. Thus hell doth jest
    Away thy blessings, and extremely flout thee,
    Thy clothes being fast, but thy soul loose about
        thee.

---

3 Counted, valued.   4 Win the prize.
5 Handsome.   6 Fastidiousness.

72

Judge not the preacher, for he is thy judge.
If thou mislike him, thou conceiv'st him not.
God calleth preaching folly. Do not grudge
To pick out treasures from an earthen pot.
　　The worst speak something good; if all want
　　　sense,
　　God takes a text, and preacheth patience.

76

Sum up at night what thou hast done by day,
And in the morning what thou hast to do.
Dress and undress thy soul; mark the decay
And growth of it. If, with thy watch, that too
　　Be down, then wind up both; since we shall be
　　Most surely judged, make thy accounts agree.

77

In brief, acquit thee bravely; play the man.
Look not on pleasures as they come, but go.
Defer not the least virtue: life's poor span
Make not an ell by trifling in thy woe.
　　If thou do ill, the joy fades, not the pains;
　　If well, the pain doth fade, the joy remains.

THE ALTAR[1]

A broken altar, Lord, Thy servant rears,
Made of a heart and cémented with tears;
　　Whose parts are as Thy hand did frame;
　　No workman's tool hath touched the same.
　　　　A　heart　alone
　　　　Is　such　a　stone
　　　　As　nothing　but
　　　　Thy　power　doth　cut.
　　　　Wherefore each part
　　　　Of my hard heart
　　　　Meets in this frame　　　10
　　　　To praise Thy name;
　　That if I chance to hold my peace,
　　These stones to praise Thee may not cease.
Oh, let Thy blessed sacrifice be mine,
And　sanctify　this　altar　to　be　Thine.

THE ALTAR

　1 Poems in which the lines are arranged to form figures, and emblematic verse in general, were much in favor in the seventeenth century. Altars, crosses, and pyramids were especially popular in religious poetry. See Herbert's poem, Easter Wings, and Herrick's The Pillar of Fame, p. 824.

EASTER WINGS[1]

Lord, who createdst man in wealth and store,[2]
　　Though foolishly he lost the same,
　　　　Decaying more and more
　　　　　　Till he became
　　　　　　　Most poor:
　　　　　　　With Thee
　　　　　　O let me rise
　　　　As larks, harmoniously,
　　And sing this day Thy victories:
Then shall the fall further the flight in me.　　10

My tender age in sorrow did begin:
　　And still with sicknesses and shame
　　　　Thou didst so punish sin
　　　　　　That I became
　　　　　　　Most thin.
　　　　　　　With Thee
　　　　　　Let me combine,
　　　　And feel this day Thy victory;
　　For, if I imp[3] my wing on Thine,
Affliction shall advance the flight in me.　　20

THE THANKSGIVING

Oh King of grief! (a title strange yet true,
　　To Thee of all kings only due)
Oh King of wounds! How shall I grieve for Thee,
　　Who in all grief preventest me?
Shall I weep blood? Why Thou hast wept such store
　　That all Thy body was one door.
Shall I be scourgèd, flouted, boxèd, sold?
　　'Tis but to tell the tale is told.
My God, my God, why dost Thou part from me?
　　Was such a grief as cannot be.　　10
Shall I then sing, skipping Thy doleful story,
　　And side with Thy triumphant glory?
Shall Thy strokes be my stroking? Thorns, my flower?
　　Thy rod, my posy? Cross, my bower?
But how then shall I imitate Thee, and
　　Copy Thy fair though bloody hand?
Surely I will revenge me on Thy love,
　　And try who shall victorious prove.

EASTER WINGS

　1 In the early editions of The Temple, the lines of Easter Wings were printed vertically, the first stanza on the left-hand page facing the second on the right-hand page.
　2 Abundance.
　3 A term from falconry: to mend the damaged wing of a hawk by grafting to it feathers from another bird.

If Thou dost give me wealth, I will restore
    All back unto Thee by the poor.   20
If Thou dost give me honor, men shall see,
    The honor doth belong to Thee.
I will not marry; or, if she be mine,
    She and her children shall be Thine.
My bosom friend, if he blaspheme Thy name,
    I will tear thence his love and fame.
One half of me being gone, the rest I give
    Unto some chapel, die or live.
As for Thy passion—But of that anon,
    When with the other I have done.   30
For Thy predestination I'll contrive,
    That three years hence, if I survive,
I'll build a spittle [1] or mend common ways,
    But mend mine own without delays.
Then I will use the works of Thy creation,
    As if I used them but for fashion.
The world and I will quarrel; and the year
    Shall not perceive that I am here.
My music shall find thee, and every string
    Shall have his attribute to sing;   40
That all together may accord in Thee,
    And prove one God, one harmony.
If Thou shalt give me wit, it shall appear,
    If Thou hast given it me, 'tis here.
Nay, I will read Thy book, and never move
    Till I have found therein Thy love,
Thy art of love, which I'll turn back on Thee:
    O my dear Saviour, victory!
Then for Thy passion—I will do for that—
    Alas, my God, I know not what.   50

THE REPRISAL

I have considered it and find
There is no dealing with Thy mighty passion;
For though I die for Thee I am behind;
    My sins deserve the condemnation.

O make me innocent, that I
May give a disentangled state and free;
And yet Thy wounds still my attempts defy,
    For by Thy death I die for Thee.

THE THANKSGIVING
  1 Hospital.

Ah, was it not enough that Thou
By Thy eternal glory didst outgo me?   10
Couldst Thou not grief's sad conquests me allow,
    But in all victories overthrow me?

Yet by confession will I come
Into Thy conquest: though I can do nought
Against Thee, in Thee I will overcome
    The man who once against Thee fought.

THE AGONY

Philosophers have measured mountains,
Fathomed the depths of seas, of states, and kings,
Walked with a staff to heaven, and traced fountains;
    But there are two vast, spacious things,
The which to measure it doth more behoove,
Yet few there are that sound them: Sin and Love.

Who would know Sin, let him repair
Unto Mount Olivet; there shall he see
A man so wrung with pains that all his hair,
    His skin, his garments bloody be.   10
Sin is that press and vice which forceth pain
To hunt his cruel food through every vein.

Who knows not love, let him assay
And taste that juice which on the cross a pike
Did set again abroach; then let him say
    If ever he did taste the like.
Love is that liquor sweet and most divine,
Which my God feels as blood, but I as wine.

REDEMPTION

Having been tenant long to a rich lord,
    Not thriving, I resolvèd to be bold,
    And make a suit unto him, to afford
A new small-rented lease and cancel th'old.
In heaven at his manor I him sought:
    They told me there that he was lately gone
    About some land which he had dearly bought
Long since on earth, to take possession.
I straight returned, and knowing his great birth,
    Sought him accordingly in great resorts;   10
    In cities, theaters, gardens, parks, and courts:
At length I heard a ragged noise and mirth
    Of thieves and murderers; there I him espied,
    Who straight, "Your suit is granted" said, and died.

EASTER

Rise, heart, thy Lord is risen; sing His praise
   Without delays,
Who takes thee by the hand, that thou likewise
   With Him mayst rise;
That, as His death calcinèd thee to dust,
His life may make thee gold, and, much more, just.

Awake, my lute, and struggle for thy part
   With all thy art;
The cross taught all wood to resound His name
   Who bore the same;   10
His stretched sinews taught all strings what key
Is best to celebrate this most high day.

Consort both heart and lute, and twist a song
   Pleasant and long;
Or, since all music is but three parts vied
   And multiplied,
O, let Thy blessed spirit bear a part,
And make up our defects with His sweet art.

I got me flowers to straw Thy way;   20
I got me boughs off many a tree:
But Thou wast up by break of day,
And brought'st Thy sweets along with Thee.

The sun arising in the east,
Though he give light, and the east perfume,
If they should offer to contest
With Thy arising, they presume.

Can there be any day but this,
Though many suns to shine endeavor?
We count three hundred, but we miss:
There is but one, and that one ever.   30

AFFLICTION [1]

When first Thou didst entice to Thee my heart,
   I thought the service brave;
So many joys I writ down for my part,
   Besides what I might have
Out of my stock of natural delights,
Augmented with Thy gracious benefits.

I lookèd on Thy furniture so fine,
   And made it fine to me;
Thy glorious household-stuff did me entwine,
   And 'tice me unto Thee.   10
Such stars I counted mine: both heav'n and earth
Paid me my wages in a world of mirth.

What pleasures could I want, whose King I served,
   Where joys my fellows were?
Thus argued into hopes, my thoughts reserved
   No place for grief or fear.
Therefore my sudden soul caught at the place,
And made her youth and fierceness seek Thy face.

At first Thou gav'st me milk and sweetnesses;
   I had my wish and way;   20
My days were strawed with flowers and happiness,
   There was no month but May.
But with my years, sorrows did twist and grow,
And made a party unawares for woe.

My flesh began [1] unto my soul in pain:
   Sicknesses cleave my bones;
Consuming agues dwell in ev'ry vein,
   And tune my breath to groans.
Sorrow was all my soul; I scarce believed,
Till grief did tell me roundly, that I lived.   30

When I got health, Thou took'st away my life,
   And more, for my friends die.
My mirth and edge was lost; a blunted knife
   Was of more use than I.
Thus thin and lean, without a fence or friend,
I was blown through with ev'ry storm and wind.

Whereas my birth and spirit rather took
   The way that takes the town,
Thou didst betray me to a ling'ring book,
   And wrap me in a gown.   40
I was entangled in the world of strife
Before I had the power to change my life.

Yet, for I threatened oft the siege to raise,
   Not simp'ring all mine age,
Thou often didst with academic praise
   Melt and dissolve my rage.
I took the sweetened pill till I came near;
I could not go away, nor persevere.

AFFLICTION
1 Complained, threatened.

Yet lest perchance I should too happy be
  In my unhappiness,   50
Turning my purge to food, Thou throwest me
  Into more sicknesses.
Thus doth Thy power cross-bias me, not making
Thine own gift good, yet me from my ways taking.

Now I am here, what Thou wilt do with me
  None of my books will show.
I read and sigh and wish I were a tree,
  For sure then I should grow
To fruit or shade. At least some bird would trust
Her household to me, and I should be just.   60

Yet, though Thou troublest me, I must be meek;
  In weakness must be stout.
Well, I will change the service and go seek
  Some other master out.
Ah, my dear God! though I am clean forgot,
Let me not love Thee if I love Thee not.

PRAYER [1]

Prayer, the church's banquet, angels' age,
  God's breath in man returning to his birth,
  The soul in paraphrase, heart in pilgrimage,
The Christian plummet sounding heaven and earth;
Engine against the Almighty, sinner's tower,
  Reversèd thunder, Christ-side-piercing spear,
  The six days' world-transposing in an hour,
A kind of tune, which all things hear and fear;
Softness, and peace, and joy, and love, and bliss,
  Exalted manna, gladness of the best,   10
  Heaven in ordinary, man well dressed,
The Milky Way, the bird of Paradise,
  Church bells beyond the stars heard, the soul's
    blood,
The land of spices, something understood.

THE TEMPER [1]

How should I praise Thee, Lord! How should my
    rhymes
  Gladly engrave Thy love in steel,
If what my soul doth feel sometimes,
  My soul might ever feel!

Although there were some forty heavens, or more,
  Sometimes I peer above them all;
Sometimes I hardly reach a score,
  Sometimes to hell I fall.

O rack me not to such a vast extent;
  Those distances belong to Thee.   10
The world's too little for Thy tent,
  A grave too big for me.

Wilt Thou meet arms with man, that Thou dost
    stretch
  A crumb of dust from heaven to hell?
Will great God measure with a wretch?
  Shall He thy stature spell?

O let me, when Thy roof my soul hath hid,
  O let me roost and nestle there;
Then of a sinner Thou art rid,
  And I of hope and fear.   20

Yet take Thy way, for sure Thy way is best;
  Stretch or contract me, Thy poor debtor.
This is but tuning of my breast,
  To make the music better.

Whether I fly with angels, fall with dust,
  Thy hands made both, and I am there.
Thy power and love, my love and trust,
  Make one place everywhere.

JORDAN [1][1]

Who says that fictions only and false hair
  Become a verse? Is there in truth no beauty?
Is all good structure in a winding stair?
May no lines pass except they do their duty
    Not to a true, but painted chair?

Is it no verse except enchanted groves
And sudden arbors shadow coarse-spun lines?
Must purling streams refresh a lover's loves?
Must all be veiled, while he that reads, divines,
    Catching the sense at two removes?   10

JORDAN [1]
  1 It has been suggested that the winding course of the
River Jordan is used in this and in Jordan [2] as an emblem
of the intricacies and meanderings of the kind of poetry he
is describing.

Shepherds are honest people; let them sing.
Riddle who list for me, and pull for prime;[2]
I envy no man's nightingale or spring,
Nor let them punish me with loss of rhyme,
Who plainly say, My God, my King.

MATINS

I cannot ope mine eyes,
But Thou art ready there to catch
My morning soul and sacrifice;
Then we must needs for that day make a match.

My God, what is a heart?
Silver, or gold, or precious stone,
Or star, or rainbow, or a part
Of all these things, or all of them in one?

My God, what is a heart,
That Thou shouldst it so eye, and woo,   10
Pouring upon it all Thy art,
As if that Thou hadst nothing else to do?

Indeed, man's whole estate
Amounts, and richly, to serve Thee;
He did not heaven and earth create,
Yet studies them, not Him by whom they be.

Teach me Thy love to know,
That this new light, which now I see,
May both the work and workman show,
Then by a sunbeam I will climb to Thee.   20

CHURCH MONUMENTS

While that my soul repairs to her devotion,
Here I entomb my flesh, that it betimes
May take acquaintance of this heap of dust,
To which the blast of Death's incessant motion,
Fed with the exhalation of our crimes,
Drives all at last. Therefore I gladly trust

My body to this school, that it may learn
To spell his elements, and find his birth
Written in dusty heraldry and lines;
Which dissolution sure doth best discern,   10
Comparing dust with dust, and earth with earth.
These laugh at jet and marble, put for signs,

JORDAN [1]
2 Draw for a winning hand in a card game.

To sever the good fellowship of dust,
And spoil the meeting: what shall point out them,
When they shall bow and kneel and fall down flat
To kiss those heaps which now they have in trust?
Dear flesh, while I do pray, learn here thy stem
And true descent, that, when thou shalt grow fat,

And wanton in thy cravings, thou mayst know
That flesh is but the glass which holds the dust   20
That measures all our time; which also shall
Be crumbled into dust. Mark here below
How tame these ashes are, how free from lust,
That thou mayst fit thyself against thy fall.

CHURCH MUSIC

Sweetest of sweets, I thank you! When displeasure
    Did through my body wound my mind,
You took me thence, and in your house of pleasure
    A dainty lodging me assigned.

Now I in you without a body move,
    Rising and falling with your wings.
We both together sweetly live and love,
    Yet say sometimes, God help poor kings!

Comfort, I'll die; for if you post from me,
    Sure I shall do so and much more.
But if I travel in your company,
    You know the way to heaven's door.

THE WINDOWS

Lord, how can man preach Thy eternal word?
    He is a brittle, crazy glass;
Yet in Thy temple Thou dost him afford
    This glorious and transcendent place,
    To be a window, through Thy grace.

But when Thou dost anneal in glass Thy story,
    Making Thy life to shine within
The holy preachers, then the light and glory
    More reverend grows, and more doth win,
    Which else shows waterish, bleak, and thin.   10

Doctrine and life, colors and light, in one
    When they combine and mingle, bring
A strong regard and awe; but speech alone
    Doth vanish like a flaring thing,
    And in the ear, not conscience ring.

THE QUIDDITY

My God, a verse is not a crown;
No point of honor, or gay suit;
No hawk, or banquet, or renown,
Nor a good sword, nor yet a lute.

It cannot vault, or dance, or play;
It never was in France or Spain;
Nor can it entertain the day
With a great stable or demesne.

It is no office, art, or news;
Nor the Exchange, or busy Hall;
But it is that which, while I use,
I am with Thee, and *Most take all*.

EMPLOYMENT [2]

He that is weary, let him sit.
    My soul would stir
And trade in courtesies and wit
    Quitting the fur
To cold complexions needing it.

Man is no star, but a quick coal
    Of mortal fire;
Who blows it not, nor doth control
    A faint desire,
Lets his own ashes choke his soul.   10

When the elements did for place contest
    With Him, whose will
Ordained the highest to be best,
    The earth sat still,
And by the others is oppressed.

Life is a business, not good cheer;
    Ever in wars.
The sun still shineth there or here,
    Whereas the stars
Watch an advantage to appear.   20

Oh that I were an orange tree,
    That busy plant!
Then should I ever laden be,
    And never want
Some fruit for him that dressed me.

But we are still too young or old;
    The man is gone
Before we do our wares unfold:
    So we freeze on,
Until the grave increase our cold.   30

DENIAL

When my devotions could not pierce
    Thy silent ears,
Then was my heart broken, as was my verse;
    My breast was full of fears
        And disorder.

My bent thoughts, like a brittle bow,
    Did fly asunder.
Each took his way; some would to pleasures go,
    Some to the wars and thunder
        Of alarms.   10

As good go anywhere, they say,
    As to benumb
Both knees and heart, in crying night and day,
    "Come, come, my God, O come,"
        But no hearing.

Oh that Thou shouldst give dust a tongue
    To cry to Thee,
And then not hear it crying! All day long
    My heart was in my knee,
        But no hearing.   20

Therefore my soul lay out of sight,
    Untuned, unstrung;
My feeble spirit, unable to look right,
    Like a nipped blossom hung
        Discontented.

O cheer and tune my heartless breast,
    Defer no time;
That so Thy favors granting my request,
    They and my mind may chime,
        And mend my rhyme.   30

VANITY

The fleet astronomer can bore
And thread the spheres with his quick-piercing mind.
He views their stations, walks from door to door,
    Surveys as if he had designed

To make a purchase there. He sees their dances,
    And knoweth long before
Both their full-eyed aspects and secret glances.

    The nimble diver with his side
Cuts through the working waves, that he may fetch
His dearly-earnèd pearl, which God did hide   10
    On purpose from the venturous wretch;
That he might save his life, and also hers
      Who with excessive pride
Her own destruction and his danger wears.

    The subtle chymic[1] can divest
And strip the creature[2] naked, till he find
The callow principles within their nest.
    There he imparts to them his mind,
Admitted to their bed-chamber, before
      They appear trim and dressed   20
To ordinary suitors at the door.

    What hath not man sought out and found,
But his dear God? who yet His glorious law
Embosoms in us, mellowing the ground
    With showers and frosts, with love and awe,
So that we need not say, "Where's this command?"
      Poor man, thou searchest round
To find out death, but missest life at hand.

VIRTUE

Sweet day, so cool, so calm, so bright,
    The bridal of the earth and sky;
The dew shall weep thy fall tonight,
    For thou must die.

Sweet rose, whose hue, angry and brave,
    Bids the rash gazer wipe his eye;
Thy root is ever in its grave,
    And thou must die.

Sweet spring, full of sweet days and roses,
    A box where sweets compacted lie;   10
My music shows ye have your closes,[1]
    And all must die.

Only a sweet and virtuous soul,
    Like seasoned timber, never gives;
But though the whole world turn to coal,[2]
    Then chiefly lives.

THE PEARL[1]

I know the ways of learning: both the head
And pipes that feed the press,[2] and make it run;
What reason hath from nature borrowed,
Or of itself, like a good housewife, spun
In laws and policy; what the stars conspire;[3]
What willing nature speaks, what forced by fire;[4]
Both the old discoveries, and the new-found seas,
The stock and surplus, cause and history;
All these stand open, or I have the keys;
    Yet I love Thee.   10

I know the ways of honor: what maintains
The quick returns of courtesy and wit;
In vies of favors whether[5] party gains
When glory[6] swells the heart, and moldeth it
To all expressions both of hand and eye,
Which on the world a true-love-knot[7] may tie,
And bear the bundle wheresoe'er it goes;
How many drams of spirit there must be
To sell my life unto my friends or foes;
    Yet I love Thee.   20

I know the ways of pleasure: the sweet strains,
The lullings and the relishes of it;
The propositions of hot blood and brains;
What mirth and music mean; what love and wit
Have done these twenty hundred years and more;
I know the projects of unbridled store;[8]

2 Be burned to cinders, at the Day of Judgment. See II Peter 3:10.

THE PEARL
  1 Herbert's poem is based upon St. Matthew 13:45, "Again, the kingdom of heaven is likened unto a merchant man, seeking goodly pearls, who, when he had found one pearl of great price, went and sold all that he had, and bought it."
  2 The printing press to which the poet refers was apparently operated by water. It has been conjectured that the line may also contain an oblique reference to the winepress.
  3 Astrological knowledge.
  4 The teachings of natural science, and the operations of alchemy.
  5 Which.   6 Desire for glory, ambition.
  7 A knot or bow of ribbon used as a token of fidelity in love.
  8 Abundance, wealth.

VANITY
  1 Alchemist, or chemist.   2 Any created thing.

VIRTUE
  1 "Close" is a technical term for the conclusion or resolution of a musical phrase.

My stuff is flesh, not brass; my senses live,
And grumble oft that they have more in me
Than he that curbs them, being but one to five;
    Yet I love Thee.   30

I know all these, and have them in my hand;
Therefore not seelèd,[9] but with open eyes
I fly to Thee, and fully understand
Both the main sale and the commodities;[10]
And at what rate and price I have Thy love,
With all the circumstances that may move.
Yet through these labyrinths, not my groveling wit,
But Thy silk twist let down from heaven to me
Did both conduct and teach me how by it
    To climb to Thee.   40

MAN

    My God, I heard this day
That none doth build a stately habitation
    But he that means to dwell therein.
    What house more stately hath there been,
Or can be, than is man, to whose creation
    All things are in decay?

    For man is everything,
And more: he is a tree, yet bears more fruit;
    A beast, yet is, or should be, more;
    Reason and speech we only bring;   10
Parrots may thank us if they are not mute,
    They go upon the score.

    Man is all symmetry,
Full of proportions, one limb to another,
    And all to all the world besides.
    Each part may call the farthest brother,
For head with foot hath private amity,
    And both with moons and tides.

    Nothing hath got so far
But man hath caught and kept it as his prey: 20
    His eyes dismount the highest star;
    He is in little all the sphere;
Herbs gladly cure our flesh, because that they
    Find their acquaintance there.

For us the winds do blow,
The earth doth rest, heav'n move, and fountains flow.
    Nothing we see but means our good,
    As our delight, or as our treasure;
The whole is either our cupboard of food,
    Or cabinet of pleasure.   30

    The stars have us to bed;
Night draws the curtain, which the sun withdraws;
    Music and light attend our head;
    All things unto our flesh are kind
In their descent and being, to our mind
    In their ascent and cause.

    Each thing is full of duty:
Waters united are our navigation;
    Distinguishèd, our habitation;
    Below, our drink; above, our meat;[1]   40
Both are our cleanliness. Hath one such beauty?
    Then how are all things neat!

    More servants wait on man
Than he'll take notice of; in every path
    He treads down that which doth befriend him
    When sickness makes him pale and wan.
Oh, mighty love! Man is one world and hath
    Another to attend him.

    Since then, my God, Thou hast
So brave a palace built, O dwell in it,   50
    That it may dwell with Thee at last!
    Till then afford us so much wit
That as the world serves us we may serve Thee,
    And both Thy servants be.

LIFE

I made a posy[1] while the day ran by:
"Here will I smell my remnant out, and tie
    My life within this band."[2]
But Time did beckon to the flowers, and they
By noon most cunningly did steal away,
    And withered in my hand.

MAN
  1 See Genesis 1:6–10.

LIFE
  1 Nosegay.
  2 "I will give the rest of my life to enjoying these flowers
I have here."

THE PEARL
  9 A term in falconry; the eyelids of young falcons were
seeled, or sewn up, during the period of training.
  10 Both what he gives up and what he gains in surrendering
to God.

My hand was next to them, and then my heart;
I took, without more thinking, in good part
              Time's gentle admonition;
Who did so sweetly death's sad taste convey,   10
Making my mind to smell my fatal day,
              Yet sug'ring the suspicion.

Farewell, dear flowers; sweetly your time ye spent,
Fit, while ye lived, for smell or ornament,
              And after death for cures.
I follow straight, without complaints or grief;
Since, if my scent be good, I care not if
              It be as short as yours.

JORDAN [2]¹

When first my lines of heav'nly joys made mention,
Such was their luster, they did so excel,
That I sought out quaint words and trim invention;
My thoughts began to burnish,² sprout, and swell,
Curling with metaphors a plain intention,
Decking the sense as if it were to sell.

Thousands of notions in my brain did run,
Off'ring their service, if I were not sped.³
I often blotted⁴ what I had begun:
This was not quick⁵ enough, and that was dead.   10
Nothing could seem too rich to clothe the sun,
Much less those joys which trample on his head.

As flames do work and wind when they ascend,
So did I weave myself into the sense.
But while I bustled, I might hear a friend
Whisper, "How wide⁶ is all this long pretense!⁷
There is in love a sweetness ready penned,
Copy out only that, and save expense."

CONSCIENCE

      Peace, prattler, do not lower:
Not a fair look, but thou dost call it foul:
Not a sweet dish, but thou dost call it sour:
      Music to thee doth howl.
   By listening to thy chatting fears
   I have both lost mine eyes and ears.

      Prattler, no more, I say:
My thoughts must work, but like a noiseless sphere;
Harmonious peace must rock them all the day:
      No room for prattlers there.   10
   If thou persistest, I will tell thee,
   That I have physic to expel thee.

      And the receipt shall be
My Saviour's blood: whenever at his board
I do but taste it, straight it cleanseth me,
      And leaves thee not a word;
   No, not a tooth or nail to scratch,
   And at my actions carp or catch.

      Yet if thou talkest still,
Besides my physic, know there's some for thee: 20
Some wood and nails to make a staff or bill
      For those that trouble me:
   The bloody cross of my dear lord
   Is both my physic and my sword.

THE QUIP¹

   The merry World did on a day
      With his train-bands² and mates agree
   To meet together where I lay,
      And all in sport to jeer at me.

   First Beauty crept into a rose;
      Which when I plucked not, "Sir," said she,
   "Tell me, I pray, whose hands are those?"³
      But Thou shalt answer, Lord, for me.

   Then Money came, and chinking still,
      "What tune is this, poor man?" said he;
   "I heard in music you had skill."   10
      But Thou shalt answer, Lord, for me.

   Then came brave⁴ Glory puffing by
      In silks that whistled, who but he?
   He scarce allowed me half an eye.
      But Thou shalt answer, Lord, for me.

JORDAN [2]
   1 See note on Jordan [1], p. 849.   2 Spread out.
   3 Had not accomplished the desired end.
   4 Blotted out, effaced.   5 Lively, vigorous.
   6 Wide of the mark.   7 Striving.

THE QUIP
   1 "Quip" here means "sharp retort." See ll. 23, 24.
   2 Citizen soldiers; here used in the sense of comrades.
   3 "Why do they not pluck the rose?"
   4 Finely dressed.

Then came quick Wit and Conversation,
    And he would needs a comfort be,
And, to be short, make an oration.
    But Thou shalt answer, Lord, for me.   20

Yet when the hour of Thy design
    To answer these fine things shall come,
Speak not at large; say I am Thine;
    And then they have their answer home.

THE DAWNING

Awake sad heart, whom sorrow ever drowns;
    Take up thine eyes, which feed on earth;
Unfold thy forehead gathered into frowns;
    Thy saviour comes, and with Him mirth.
        Awake, awake;
And with a thankful heart His comforts take.
    But thou dost still lament and pine and cry;
    And feel His death, but not His victory.

Arise sad heart; if thou do not withstand,
    Christ's resurrection thine may be;   10
Do not by hanging down break from the hand,
    Which as it riseth raiseth thee.
        Arise, arise;
And with His burial-linen dry thine eyes:
    Christ left His grave-clothes, that we might, when
        grief
Draws tears or blood, not want a handkerchief.

JESU

Jesu is in my heart, His sacred name
Is deeply carvèd there, but th'other week
A great affliction broke the little frame,
Even all to pieces, which I went to seek:
And first I found the corner, where was *J*,
After, where *ES*, and next, where *U* was graved.
When I had got these parcels, instantly
I sat me down to spell them and perceived
That to my broken heart he was "I ease you,"
        And to my whole is *JESU*.

DIALOGUE

Sweetest Saviour, if my soul
    Were but worth the having,
Quickly should I then control
    Any thought of waving.

But when all my care and pains
Cannot give the name of gains
To Thy wretch so full of stains,
    What delight or hope remains?

"What, Child, is the balance thine,
    Thine the poise and measure?   10
If I say, 'Thou shalt be Mine,'
    Finger not My treasure.
What the gains in having thee
Do amount to, only He
Who for man was sold can see;
    That transferred th'accounts to me."

But as I can see no merit
    Leading to this favor;
So the way to fit me for it
    Is beyond my savor.   20
As the reason then is Thine,
So the way is none of mine;
I disclaim the whole design;
Sin disclaims and I resign.

"That is all, if that I could
    Get without repining;
And My clay, My creature, would
    Follow My resigning;
That as I did freely part
With My glory and desert,   30
Left all joys to feel all smart—"
    Ah, no more; Thou break'st my heart.

TIME

Meeting with Time: "Slack thing," said I,
"Thy scythe is dull; whet it for shame."
"No marvel, Sir," he did reply,
"If it at length deserve some blame;
    But where one man would have me grind it,
    Twenty for one too sharp do find it."

"Perhaps some such of old did pass,
Who above all things loved this life;
To whom thy scythe a hatchet was,
Which now is but a pruning-knife.   10
    Christ's coming hath made man thy debtor,
    Since by thy cutting he grows better.

"And in his blessing thou art blest;
For where thou only wert before
An executioner at best,
Thou art a gardener now, and more,
   An usher to convey our souls
   Beyond the utmost stars and poles.

"And this is that makes life so long,
While it detains us from our God.   20
Even pleasures here increase the wrong,
And length of days lengthen the rod.
   Who wants the place where God doth dwell
   Partakes already half of hell.

"Of what strange length must that needs be,
Which even eternity excludes!"
Thus far Time heard me patiently;
Then chafing said, "This man deludes:
   What do I here before his door?
   He doth not crave less time but more."   30

At length I got unto the Gladsome Hill,
   Where lay my hope,   20
Where lay my heart; and climbing still,
   When I had gained the brow and top,
A lake of brackish waters on the ground
   Was all I found.

With that abashed, and struck with many a sting
   Of swarming fears,
I fell and cried, "Alas, my King,
   Can both the way and end be tears?"
Yet taking heart I rose, and then perceived
   I was deceived.   30

My hill was further, so I flung away,
   Yet heard a cry,
Just as I went, "None goes that way
   And lives." "If that be all," said I,
"After so foul a journey death is fair,
   And but a chair."

THE PILGRIMAGE

I traveled on, seeing the hill, where lay
   My expectation.
A long it was and weary way:
   The gloomy Cave of Desperation
I left on th' one, and on the other side
   The Rock of Pride.

And so I came to Fancy's Meadow, strowed
   With many a flower;
Fain would I here have made abode,
   But I was quickened by my hour.   10
So to Care's Copse I came, and there got through
   With much ado.

That led me to the Wild of Passion, which
   Some call the Wold;
A wasted place, but sometimes rich.
   Here I was robbed of all my gold,
Save one good angel,[1] which a friend had tied
   Close to my side.

THE COLLAR

I struck the board,[1] and cried, "No more!
   I will abroad!
What? Shall I ever sigh and pine?
My lines and life are free, free as the road,
   Loose as the wind, as large as store.[2]
      Shall I be still in suit?[3]
Have I no harvest but a thorn
To let me blood, and not restore
What I have lost with cordial[4] fruit?
      Sure there was wine   10
Before my sighs did dry it. There was corn
   Before my tears did drown it.
Is the year only lost to me?
      Have I no bays[5] to crown it?
No flowers, no garlands gay? All blasted?
      All wasted?
Not so, my heart! But there is fruit,
   And thou hast hands.

THE PILGRIMAGE
1 A gold coin of the value of ten shillings. Herbert is playing upon the word, of course.

THE COLLAR
1 Table.   2 As large as abundance itself.
3 In attendance, as a suitor, for preferment or award.
4 Restorative.
5 The poet's wreaths of bay, or laurel.

Recover all thy sigh-blown age
On double pleasures. Leave thy cold dispute   20
Of what is fit and not. Forsake thy cage,
    Thy rope of sands,
Which petty thoughts have made, and made to thee
  Good cable, to enforce and draw,
    And be thy law,
While thou didst wink and wouldst not see.
    Away! Take Heed!
    I will abroad!
Call in thy death's head there![6] Tie up thy fears!
    He that forbears   30
    To suit and serve his need
    Deserves his load."
But as I raved, and grew more fierce and wild
    At every word,
Methoughts I heard one calling, "Child!"
    And I replied, "My Lord!"

THE PULLEY

When God at first made man,
Having a glass of blessings standing by,
"Let us," said He, "pour on him all we can.
Let the world's riches, which dispersèd lie,
    Contract into a span."

So strength first made a way;
Then beauty flowed, then wisdom, honor,
    pleasure.
When almost all was out, God made a stay,
Perceiving that, alone of all His treasure,
    Rest in the bottom lay.   10

"For if I should," said He,
"Bestow this jewel also on My creature,
He would adore My gifts instead of Me
And rest in nature, not the God of nature;
    So both should losers be.

"Yet let him keep the rest,
But keep them with repining restlessness.
Let him be rich and weary, that at last,
If goodness lead him not, yet weariness
    May toss him to My breast."   20

THE COLLAR
6 "Take away the mementos of mortality!"

THE FLOWER

How fresh, O Lord, how sweet and clean
Are Thy returns! Even as the flowers in spring,
  To which, besides their own demean,[1]
The late-past frosts tributes of pleasure bring.
    Grief melts away
    Like snow in May,
As if there were no such cold thing.

Who would have thought my shriveled heart
Could have recovered greenness? It was gone
  Quite underground, as flowers depart   10
To see their mother-root, when they have blown;[2]
    Where they together
    All the hard weather,
Dead to the world, keep house unknown.

These are Thy wonders, Lord of power,
Killing and quickening, bringing down to hell
  And up to heaven in an hour;
Making a chiming of a passing bell.[3]
    We say amiss
    This or that is;   20
Thy word is all, if we could spell.[4]

Oh, that I once past changing were,
Fast in Thy paradise, where no flower can wither!
  Many a spring I shoot up fair,
Offering[5] at heav'n, growing and groaning
    thither;
    Nor doth my flower
    Want a spring shower,
My sins and I joining together.[6]

But while I grow in a straight line,
Still upwards bent, as if heaven were mine own,
  Thy anger comes, and I decline.   31
What frost to that? What pole is not the zone
    Where all things burn,
    When Thou dost turn,
And the least frown of Thine is shown?[7]

THE FLOWER
  1 Demeanor.   2 Bloomed.
  3 The bell rung at the time of death to call for prayers for
the departing soul.
  4 Comprehend.   5 Aiming.
  6 To produce tears of contrition.
  7 The frown of God brings to a sensitive soul like Herbert
a coldness so intense as to make even the poles seem like the
torrid zone.

And now in age I bud again;
After so many deaths I live and write;
I once more smell the dew and rain,
And relish versing. O my only Light,
　　It cannot be   40
　　That I am he
On whom Thy tempests fell all night.

These are Thy wonders, Lord of love,
To make us see we are but flowers that glide;
Which when we once can find and prove,
Thou hast a garden for us where to bide.
　　Who would be more,
　　Swelling through store,[8]
Forfeit their paradise by their pride.

THE FORERUNNERS

The harbingers[1] are come. See, see their mark;
White is their color, and behold my head.
But must they have my brain? must they dispark[2]
Those sparkling notions which therein were bred?
　　Must dullness turn me to a clod?
Yet have they left me, "Thou art still my God."

Good men ye be to leave me my best room,
Ev'n all my heart, and what is lodged there;
I pass not,[3] I, what of the rest become,
So "Thou art still my God" be out of fear.   10
　　He will be pleased with that ditty;
And if I please Him, I write fine and witty.

Farewell, sweet phrases, lovely metaphors.
But will ye leave me thus? when ye before
Of stews and brothels only knew the doors,
Then did I wash you with my tears, and more,
　　Brought you to church well-drest and clad:
My God must have my best, ev'n all I had.

Lovely enchanting language, sugar-cane,
Honey of roses, whither wilt thou fly?   20

THE FLOWER
　8 Abundance.

THE FORERUNNERS
　1 The reference is to the custom of sending servants ahead
of a royal progress in order to claim accommodations by
making chalk marks on the doors of desired houses.
　2 Remove from a park.   3 Care not.

Hath some fond lover 'ticed thee to thy bane?
And wilt thou leave the Church, and love a sty?
　　Fie! thou wilt soil thy broidered coat,
And hurt thyself and him that sings the note.

Let foolish lovers, if they will love dung,
With canvas, not with arras, clothe their shame;
Let Folly speak in her own native tongue.
True Beauty dwells on high; ours is a flame
　　But borrowed thence to light us thither.
Beauty and beauteous words should go together.

Yet if you go, I pass not; take your way.   31
For "Thou art still my God" is all that ye
Perhaps with more embellishment can say.
Go, birds of spring; let winter have his fee;
　　Let a bleak paleness chalk the door,
So all within be livelier than before.

DISCIPLINE

Throw away Thy rod,
Throw away Thy wrath.
　　O my God,
Take the gentle path.

For my heart's desire
Unto Thine is bent;
　　I aspire
To a full consent.

Not a word or look
I affect to own,   10
　　But by book,
And Thy book alone.

Though I fail, I weep;
Though I halt in pace,
　　Yet I creep
To the throne of grace.

Then let wrath remove;
Love will do the deed,
　　For with love
Stony hearts will bleed.   20

Love is swift of foot.
Love's a man of war,
　　And can shoot,
And can hit from far.

Who can 'scape his bow?
    That which wrought on Thee,
        Brought Thee low,
    Needs must work on me.

Throw away Thy rod;
    Though man frailties hath,
        Thou art God.   30
    Throw away Thy wrath.

A servant with this clause
    Makes drudgery divine;
Who sweeps a room as for Thy laws
    Makes that and the action fine.   20

This is the famous stone
    That turneth all to gold;
For that which God doth touch and own
    Cannot for less be told.[5]

THE ELIXIR[1]

Teach me, my God and King,
    In all things Thee to see;
And what I do in anything,
    To do it as for Thee.

Not rudely, as a beast,
    To run into an action;
But still to make Thee prepossessed,[2]
    And give it his[3] perfection.

A man that looks on glass
    On it may stay his eye,   10
Or, if he pleaseth, through it pass,
    And then the heaven espy.

All may of Thee partake;
    Nothing can be so mean
Which with his[3] tincture,[4] "for Thy sake,"
    Will not grow bright and clean.

THE ELIXIR
1 See Note 2 on Donne's Love's Alchemy, p. 744.
2 "Always to make Thee possessed of me in advance."
3 Its.
4 Essential quality; used here to mean the philosopher's
stone, with which Herbert identifies the elixir in the last
stanza.

LOVE [3]

Love bade me welcome; yet my soul drew back,
    Guilty of dust and sin.
But quick-eyed Love, observing me grow slack
    From my first entrance in,
Drew nearer to me, sweetly questioning
    If I lacked anything.

"A guest," I answered, "worthy to be here."
    Love said, "You shall be he."
"I, the unkind, ungrateful? Ah my dear,
    I cannot look on Thee."   10
Love took my hand, and smiling, did reply,
    "Who made the eyes but I?"

"Truth, Lord, but I have marred them; let my shame
    Go where it doth deserve."
"And know you not," says Love, "who bore the
                                        blame?"
    "My dear, then I will serve."
"You must sit down," says Love, "and taste my meat."
    So I did sit and eat.

5 Counted, valued.

Thomas Carew

[1594?–1640]

WHAT we are told of the character of Carew the man affords a striking contrast to what his work tells us of Carew the poet: it is the contrast between a frivolous and irresponsible ne'er-do-well on the one hand and a singularly devoted and careful craftsman on the other. Most of Carew's virtue may have been confined to his work, but that work shows him to be perhaps the finest artist among the Tribe of Ben. The second son of the prominent lawyer and official Sir Matthew Carew, the poet entered Merton College, Oxford, in 1608, and received his B.A. there in 1611. Thereafter he studied law at the Middle Temple, although with a noticeable lack of enthusiasm. Through his father's influence he obtained a post as secretary to Sir Dudley Carleton, ambassador to Venice and later to the Netherlands. He was in Carleton's service from 1613 until 1616, when he was dismissed for writing a satire against the ambassador and Lady Carleton. When, in 1619, he became secretary to Lord Herbert of Cherbury on the latter's undertaking his embassy to Paris, he seems to have found a more congenial employer, one who appreciated his wit and his talent. From around 1630 until his death, Carew was attached to the court of Charles I in a number of positions of honor. In addition to Jonson, Donne, and Herbert of Cherbury, he numbered among his friends Howell, Suckling, Davenant, Townshend, and Sandys, all of whom admired his gifts.

"His Muse was hide-bound, and the issue of 's brain/ Was seldom brought forth but with trouble and pain," wrote Sir John Suckling of his friend's poetry in "A Sessions of the Poets." But the gifted and careless Suckling's satiric barb turns back upon him, for it is precisely Carew's artistic seriousness which makes his polished and elegant lyrics superior to those of Suckling and the minor Jonsonians. Limited in scope to amorous commonplace and occasional compliment or lament, Carew's poetry nevertheless attains something like perfection as an expression of the poetic norms of the Caroline era. These norms are based on roughly equal proportions of the influences of Donne and Jonson, but the tact and individuality with which Carew combines the accents of his masters reveal both a sure instinct and a fine critical intelligence—an intelligence which displays itself most clearly in the poet's elegy on the death of Donne, which counts as one of the more perceptive critical documents of the age.

Carew's genius for assimilation can be seen also in his utilization of Italian influences, particularly that of Marino, whom he makes completely his own. His versatility shows itself further in his masque *Coelum Britannicum*, written and presented at court in 1634. He wrote, too, his share of religious verse, and though it is easy to be amused at the pieties of the author of such inspired erotica as "The Rapture," such a poem as his compliment to George Sandys on his translation of the Psalms has an unmistakable sincerity and force.

It is too easy, finally, to underestimate Carew. Unquestionably a minor poet, he has the distinction of being one of the best in an age when minor poetry frequently touched greatness.

T. CAREW. *Poems*, ed. R. Dunlap (Oxford, 1949).

E. SELIG. *The Flourishing Wreath* (New Haven, 1958). A youthful but perceptive essay.

F. R. LEAVIS. *Revaluation* (Cambridge, 1936). Contains good analysis and appreciation of Carew.

G. WILLIAMSON. (See under general poetry bibliography.)

K. A. McEUEN. (See under Jonson bibliography.)

FROM

POEMS [1640]

THE SPRING

Now that the winter's gone, the earth hath lost
Her snow-white robes; and now no more the frost
Candies the grass, or casts an icy cream
Upon the silver lake or crystal stream:
But the warm sun thaws the benumbèd earth,
And makes it tender; gives a sacred birth
To the dead swallow; wakes in hollow tree
The drowsy cuckoo and the humblebee.
Now do a choir of chirping minstrels bring,
In triumph to the world, the youthful spring.   10
The valleys, hills, and woods in rich array
Welcome the coming of the longed-for May.
Now all things smile; only my love doth lour;
Nor hath the scalding noonday sun the power
To melt that marble ice, which still doth hold
Her heart congealed, and makes her pity cold.
The ox, which lately did for shelter fly
Into the stall, doth now securely lie
In open fields; and love no more is made
By the fireside; but in the cooler shade   20
Amyntas now doth with his Chloris sleep
Under a sycamore, and all things keep
Time with the season: only she doth carry
June in her eyes, in her heart January.

A BEAUTIFUL MISTRESS

If when the sun at noon displays
        His brighter rays,
        Thou but appear,
He then, all pale with shame and fear,

Quencheth his light,
Hides his dark brow, flies from thy sight,
        And grows more dim,
Compared to thee, than stars to him.
If thou but show thy face again,
When darkness doth at midnight reign,   10
The darkness flies, and light is hurled
Round about the silent world:
So as alike thou driv'st away
Both light and darkness, night and day.

A PRAYER TO THE WIND

Go, thou gentle whispering wind,
Bear this sigh, and if thou find
Where my cruel fair doth rest,
Cast it in her snowy breast;
So, inflamed by my desire,
It may set her heart afire.
Those sweet kisses thou shalt gain
Will reward thee for thy pain.
Boldly light upon her lip,
There suck odors, and thence skip   10
To her bosom; lastly fall
Down, and wander over all.
Range about those ivory hills,
From whose every part distills
Amber dew; there spices grow,
There pure streams of nectar flow;
There perfume thyself, and bring
All those sweets upon thy wing.
As thou return'st, change by thy power
Every weed into a flower;   20

Turn each thistle to a vine,
Make the bramble eglantine;
For so rich a booty made,
Do but this, and I am paid.
Thou canst with thy powerful blast
Heat apace, and cool as fast;
Thou canst kindle hidden flame,
And again destroy the same:
Then, for pity, either stir
Up the fire of love in her,   30
That alike both flames may shine,
Or else quite extinguish mine.

MEDIOCRITY IN LOVE REJECTED

Give me more love or more disdain:
   The torrid or the frozen zone
Bring equal ease unto my pain,
   The temperate affords me none;
Either extreme, of love or hate,
Is sweeter than a calm estate.

Give me a storm; if it be love,
   Like Danaë in that golden shower,
I swim in pleasure; if it prove
   Disdain, that torrent will devour   10
My vulture-hopes; and he's possessed
Of heaven, that's but from hell released.
   Then crown my joys, or cure my pain:
   Give me more love or more disdain.

PERSUASIONS TO ENJOY

If the quick[1] spirits in your eye
   Now languish, and anon must die;
If every sweet and every grace
Must fly from that forsaken face;
   Then, Celia, let us reap our joys
   Ere Time such goodly fruit destroys.

Or, if that golden fleece must grow
Forever free from aged snow;
If those bright suns must know no shade,
Nor your fresh beauties ever fade;   10
Then fear not, Celia, to bestow
What, still being gathered, still must grow.
   Thus, either Time his sickle brings
   In vain, or else in vain his wings.

PERSUASIONS
1 Lively.

INGRATEFUL BEAUTY THREATENED

Know, Celia, since thou art so proud,
   'Twas I that gave thee thy renown;
Thou hadst in the forgotten crowd
   Of common beauties lived unknown,
Had not my verse exhaled thy name,
And with it imped[1] the wings of fame.

That killing power is none of thine,
   I gave it to thy voice and eyes;
Thy sweets, thy graces, all are mine;
   Thou art my star, shin'st in my skies;   10
Then dart not from thy borrowed sphere
Lightning on him that fixed thee there.

Tempt me with such affrights no more,
   Lest what I made I uncreate;
Let fools thy mystic forms adore,
   I'll know thee in thy mortal state;
Wise poets that wrapped truth in tales
Knew her themselves through all her veils.

DISDAIN RETURNED

He that loves a rosy cheek,
   Or a coral lip admires,
Or from star-like eyes doth seek
   Fuel to maintain his fires;
As old Time makes these decay,
So his flames must waste away.

But a smooth and steadfast mind,
   Gentle thoughts and calm desires,
Hearts with equal love combined,
   Kindle never-dying fires.   10
Where those are not, I despise
Lovely cheeks, or lips, or eyes.

No tears, Celia, now shall win
   My resolved heart to return;
I have searched thy soul within,
   And find nought but pride and scorn;
I have learned thy arts, and now
Can disdain as much as thou.
   Some power, in my revenge, convey
   That love to her I cast away.   20

INGRATEFUL BEAUTY
1 A technical term in falconry; to repair the injured wing
of a hawk by grafting to it feathers from another bird.

ETERNITY OF LOVE PROTESTED

How ill doth he deserve a lover's name,
    Whose pale weak flame
    Cannot retain
His heat in spite of absence or disdain,
But doth at once, like paper set on fire,
    Burn and expire;
True love can never change his seat,
Nor did he ever love that could retreat.

That noble flame, which my breast keeps alive,
    Shall still survive   10
    When my soul's fled;
Nor shall my love die when my body's dead,
That shall wait on me to the lower shade,
    And never fade;
My very ashes in their urn
Shall like a hallowed lamp forever burn.

UPON A RIBBON

This silken wreath, which circles in mine arm,
Is but an emblem of that mystic charm
Wherewith the magic of your beauties binds
My captive soul, and round about it winds
Fetters of lasting love. This hath entwined
My flesh alone; that hath empaled my mind.
Time may wear out these soft weak bands, but those
Strong chains of brass Fate shall not discompose.
This holy relic may preserve my wrist,
But my whole frame doth by that power subsist;   10
To that my prayers and sacrifice, to this
I only pay a superstitious kiss.
This but the idol, that's the deity;
Religion there is due; here, ceremony;
That I receive by faith, this but in trust;
Here I may tender duty, there I must;
This order as a layman I may bear,
But I become Love's priest when that I wear;
This moves like air; that as the center stands;
That knot your virtue tied, this but your hands;   20
That, nature framed; but this was made by art;
This makes my arm your prisoner; that, my heart.

EPITAPH ON THE LADY MARY VILLIERS [3]

This little vault, this narrow room,
Of love and beauty is the tomb;

The dawning beam that 'gan to clear
Our clouded sky, lies darkened here,
Forever set to us, by death
Sent to inflame the world beneath.
'Twas but a bud, yet did contain
More sweetness than shall spring again;
A budding star that might have grown
Into a sun, when it had blown.   10
This hopeful beauty did create
New life in Love's declining state;
But now his empire ends, and we
From fire and wounding darts are free;
His brand, his bow, let no man fear—
The flames, the arrows, all lie here.

AN ELEGY UPON THE DEATH OF DOCTOR DONNE, DEAN OF PAUL'S[1]

Can we not force from widowed poetry,
Now thou art dead, great Donne, one elegy
To crown thy hearse? Why yet did we not trust,
Though with unkneaded dough-baked prose, thy dust,
Such as the unscissored[2] lect'rer from the flower
Of fading rhet'ric, short-lived as his hour,
Dry as the sand that measures it, might lay
Upon the ashes, on the funeral day?
Have we nor tune nor voice? Didst thou dispense
Through all our language both the words and sense? 10
'Tis a sad truth. The pulpit may her plain
And sober Christian precepts still retain;
Doctrines it may, and wholesome uses, frame;
Grave homilies and lectures, but the flame
Of thy brave soul, that shot such heat and light,
As burnt our earth and made our darkness bright,
Committed holy rapes upon the will,
Did through the eye the melting heart distill,
And the deep knowledge of dark truths so teach
As sense might judge where fancy could not reach, 20
Must be desired forever. So the fire
That fills with spirit and heat the Delphic choir,
Which, kindled first by thy Promethean breath,
Glowed here a while, lies quenched now in thy death.
The Muses' garden, with pedantic weeds
O'erspread, was purged by thee; the lazy seeds
Of servile imitation thrown away,
And fresh invention planted; thou didst pay

AN ELEGY
1 First printed in Donne's Poems, 1633.
2 With hair uncut.

The debts of our penurious bankrupt age;
Licentious thefts, that make poetic rage   30
A mimic fury, when our souls must be
Possessed, or with Anacreon's ecstasy
Or Pindar's, not their own; the subtle cheat
Of sly exchanges, and the juggling feat
Of two-edged words, or whatsoever wrong
By ours was done the Greek or Latin tongue,
Thou hast redeemed, and opened us a mine
Of rich and pregnant fancy; drawn a line
Of masculine expression, which had good
Old Orpheus seen, or all the ancient brood   40
Our superstitious fools admire and hold
Their lead more precious than thy burnished gold,
Thou hadst been their exchequer, and no more
They in each other's dung had searched for ore.
Thou shalt yield no precedence, but of time
And the blind fate of language, whose tuned chime
More charms the outward sense; yet thou mayst claim
From so great disadvantage greater fame,
Since to the awe of thy imperious wit
Our troublesome language bends, made only fit   50
With her tough thick-ribbed hoops to gird about
Thy giant fancy, which had proved too stout
For their soft melting phrases. As in time
They had the start, so did they cull the prime
Buds of invention many a hundred year,
And left the rifled fields, besides the fear
To touch their harvest; yet from those bare lands
Of what was only thine, thy only hands,
And that their smallest work, have gleanèd more
Than all those times and tongues could reap before.   60
     But thou art gone, and thy strict laws will be
Too hard for libertines in poetry;
They will recall the goodly exiled train
Of gods and goddesses, which in thy just reign
Was banished nobler poems; now with these,
The silenced tales i' th' *Metamorphoses*,[3]
Shall stuff their lines, and swell the windy page,
Till verse, refined by thee in this last age,
Turn ballad-rhyme, or those old idols be
Adored again with new apostasy.   70
     O, pardon me, that break with untuned verse
The reverend silence that attends thy hearse,
Whose solemn awful murmurs were to thee,
More than these rude lines, a loud elegy,
That did proclaim in a dumb eloquence,
The death of all the arts; whose influence,

AN ELEGY
  3 Of Ovid.

Grown feeble, in these panting numbers lies,
Gasping short-winded accents, and so dies.
So doth the swiftly turning wheel not stand
In the instant we withdraw the moving hand,   80
But some short time retain a faint weak course,
By virtue of the first impulsive force;
And so, whilst I cast on thy funeral pile
The crown of bays, oh, let it crack awhile,
And spit disdain, till the devouring flashes
Suck all the moisture up, then turn to ashes.
     I will not draw thee envy to engross
All thy perfections, or weep all the loss;
Those are too numerous for one elegy,
And this too great to be expressed by me.   90
Let others carve the rest; it shall suffice
I on thy grave this epitaph incise:
     Here lies a king that ruled as he thought fit
     The universal monarchy of wit;
     Here lies two flamens, and both those the best,
     Apollo's first, at last the true God's priest.

TO A LADY THAT DESIRED I WOULD LOVE HER

Now you have freely given me leave to love,
          What will you do?
Shall I your mirth or passion move
          When I begin to woo?
Will you torment, or scorn, or love me too?

Each petty beauty can disdain, and I,
          Spite of your hate,
Without your leave can see, and die;
          Dispense a nobler fate:
'Tis easy to destroy, you may create.   10

Then give me leave to love, and love me too;
          Not with design
To raise, as love's curst rebels do
          When puling poets whine,
Fame to their beauty from their blubbered eyne.

Grief is a puddle, and reflects not clear
          Your beauty's rays;
Joys are pure streams, your eyes appear
          Sullen in sadder lays;
In cheerful numbers they shine bright with praise,

Which shall not mention, to express you fair,   21
    Wounds, flames, and darts,
Storms in your brow, nets in your hair,
    Suborning all your parts,
Or to betray or torture captive hearts.

I'll make your eyes like morning suns appear,
    As mild and fair,
Your brow as crystal, smooth and clear,
    And your disheveled hair
Shall flow like a calm region of the air.   30

Rich nature's store, which is the poet's treasure,
    I'll spend to dress
Your beauties, if your mine of pleasure
    In equal thankfulness
You but unlock, so we each other bless.

TO MY WORTHY FRIEND, MASTER GEORGE SANDYS ON HIS TRANS-LATION OF THE PSALMS

I press not to the choir, nor dare I greet
The holy place with my unhallowed feet;
My unwashed muse pollutes not things divine,
Nor mingles her profaner notes with thine;
Here humbly at the porch she stays,
And with glad ears sucks in thy sacred lays.
So devout penitents of old were wont,
Some without door and some beneath the font,
To stand and hear the Church's liturgies,
Yet not assist the solemn exercise.   10
Sufficeth her that she a lay-place gain,
To trim thy vestments, or but bear thy train;
Though not in tune or wing she reach thy lark,
Her lyric feet may dance before the Ark.
Who knows but that her wand'ring eyes that run
Now hunting glowworms, may adore the sun?
A pure flame may, shot by almighty power
Into her breast, the earthly flame devour.
My eyes in penitential dew may steep
That brine which they for sensual love did weep.   20
So, though 'gainst nature's course, fire may be quenched
With fire, and water be with water drenched,
Perhaps my restless soul, tired with pursuit
Of mortal beauty, seeking without fruit

Contentment there, which hath not, when enjoyed,
Quenched all her thirst, nor satisfied though cloyed,
Weary of her vain search below, above
In the first fair may find the immortal love.
Prompted by thy example then, no more
In molds of clay will I my God adore;   30
But tear those idols from my heart, and write
What His blest sp'rit, no fond love, shall indite.
Then I no more shall court the verdant bay,
But the dry leafless trunk on Golgothà;
And rather strive to gain from thence one thorn,
Than all the flourishing wreaths by laureates worn.

A SONG

Ask me no more where Jove bestows,
When June is past, the fading rose;
For in your beauty's orient deep [1]
These flowers, as in their causes,[2] sleep.

Ask me no more whither doth stray
The golden atoms of the day;
For in pure love heaven did prepare
Those powders to enrich your hair.

Ask me no more whither doth haste
The nightingale, when May is past;   10
For in your sweet dividing [3] throat
She winters, and keeps warm her note.

Ask me no more where those stars light
That downwards fall in dead of night;
For in your eyes they sit, and there
Fixèd become, as in their sphere.

Ask me no more if east or west
The phœnix builds her spicy nest;
For unto you at last she flies,
And in your fragrant bosom dies.   20

A SONG
  1 Lustrous depth.
  2 Technically, the material cause of the Aristotelian philosophy; here, the roots, seeds, or buds.
  3 Singing, articulating harmoniously. A technical term in music for the "execution of a rapid passage, originally conceived of as the dividing of each of a succession of long notes into several short ones." (Oxford English Dictionary.)

James Shirley

[1596–1666]

A N Y anthology of nondramatic poetry in the seventeenth century must, if it hopes to be truly representative, take some account of the vast quantity of excellent verse written by men who are undistinguished save for one or two lyrics—or are primarily distinguished in fields other than poetry. In the latter category belongs the dramatist James Shirley, whose place in the history of the seventeenth-century lyric is assured by a single poem, his great dirge, "The Glories of Our Blood and State."

Born in London, and educated at St. John's, Oxford, and at St. Catharine's Hall, Cambridge, where he took his degree, Shirley followed the profession of schoolmaster during most of his life, except for the period 1625–39, when he enjoyed considerable court favor in London as the purveyor of plays which were admirably suited to the taste of the time. Shirley owes much to Jonson, both as poet and playwright, but his long Ovidian poem *Narcissus* (c. 1618) has a distinctly Elizabethan flavor. His earlier poems appeared in 1646; "The Glories of Our Blood and State" in a dramatic entertainment published in 1659.

J. SHIRLEY. *Poems*, ed. R. L. Armstrong (New York, 1941).

[OF DEATH]

The glories of our blood and state
  Are shadows, not substantial things;
There is no armor against fate;
  Death lays his icy hand on kings:
    Scepter and crown
    Must tumble down,
And in the dust be equal made
With the poor crooked scythe and spade.

Some men with swords may reap the field,
  And plant fresh laurels where they kill;   10
But their strong nerves at last must yield;
  They tame but one another still:

    Early or late,
    They stoop to fate,
And must give up their murmuring breath,
When they, pale captives, creep to death.

The garlands wither on your brow,
  Then boast no more your mighty deeds;
Upon death's purple altar now,
  See where the victor-victim bleeds: 20
    Your heads must come
    To the cold tomb;
Only the actions of the just
Smell sweet and blossom in their dust.
      —*The Contention of Ajax and Ulysses*, 1659

Owen Felltham

[1602?–1668]

LIKE Shirley, Felltham is the poet of a single poem. His "When, Dearest, I but Think on Thee" was sufficiently popular in its own day to be erroneously attributed to Suckling in an early edition of that worthy's works, and it has remained popular with modern lovers of seventeenth-century verse. Some account of what little is known of Felltham's life may be found in the headnote to the selection from his prose in this volume.

[WHEN, DEAREST, I BUT THINK ON THEE]

When, dearest, I but think on thee,
Methinks all things that lovely be
Are present, and my soul delighted:
   For beauties that from worth arise
   Are, like the grace of deities,
Still present with us, though unsighted.

Thus while I sit and sigh the day
With all his spreading lights away,
Till night's black wings do overtake me:
   Thinking on thee, thy beauties then,   10
   As sudden lights do sleeping men,
So they by their bright rays awake me.

Thus absence dies, and dying proves
No absence can consist with loves
That do partake of fair perfection:
   Since in the darkest night they may
   By their quick motion find a way
To see each other by reflection.

The waving sea can with such flood
Bathe some high palace that hath stood   20
Far from the main up in the river:
   O think not then but love can do
   As much, for that's an ocean too,
That flows not every day, but ever.

                         —*Lusoria,* 1661

Thomas Randolph

[1605–1635]

EXORBITANTLY admired in his own day, the short-lived Thomas Randolph has not attracted the attention of posterity to any great degree. His poems and plays have their share of the wit and charm common to the school of Jonson, but they lack an individual note, any of that "unexpressible addition of comeliness" which makes unforgettable so much seventeenth-century literature, sacred and secular alike.

Born in Newnham-cum-Badby, near Daventry in Northamptonshire, Randolph was educated at Westminster School and at Trinity College, Cambridge, where he received his B.A. in 1628 and his M.A. in 1632. Shortly thereafter he went to London, where he was already known to the circle of Jonson as a wit and writer of their own persuasion. His death was bemoaned in language which coupled his name with those of Jonson and Shakespeare, but his true position is rather with Cartwright, Godolphin, and others of the more derivative of Ben's disciples.

T. RANDOLPH. *Poems*, ed. G. Thorn-Drury (London, 1929).
E. BLUNDEN. *Votive Tablets* (London, 1931). Contains a good essay on Randolph.
G. C. MOORE SMITH. *Thomas Randolph* (Oxford, 1927).

FROM

POEMS [1638]

UPON HIS PICTURE

When age hath made me what I am not now,
And every wrinkle tells me where the plow
Of time hath furrowed; when an ice shall flow
Through every vein, and all my head wear snow;
When death displays his coldness in my cheek,
And I myself in my own picture seek,
Not finding what I am, but what I was,
In doubt which to believe, this or my glass:
Yet though I alter, this remains the same
As it was drawn, retains the primitive frame   10
And first complexion; here will still be seen
Blood on the cheek, and down upon the chin;

Here the smooth brow will stay, the lively eye,
The ruddy lip, and hair of youthful dye.
Behold what frailty we in man may see,
Whose shadow is less given to change than he!

AN ELEGY

Love, give me leave to serve thee and be wise,
To keep thy torch in but restore blind eyes.
I will a flame into my bosom take
That martyrs court when they embrace the stake:
Not dull and smoky fires, but heat divine,
That burns not to consume but to refine.

I have a mistress for perfections rare
In every eye, but in my thoughts most fair.
Like tapers on the altar shine her eyes;
Her breath is the perfume of sacrifice.   10
And wheresoe'er my fancy would begin,
Still her perfection lets religion in.
I touch her like my beads with devout care,
And come unto my courtship as my prayer.
We sit and talk and kiss away the hours,
As chastely as the morning dews kiss flowers.
Go, wanton lover, spare thy sighs and tears,
Put on the livery which thy dotage wears,
And call it love; where heresy gets in
Zeal's but a coal to kindle greater sin.   20
We wear no flesh, but one another greet,
As blessed souls in separation meet.
Were't possible that my ambitious sin
Durst commit rapes upon a Cherubin,
I might have lustful thoughts to her, of all
Earth's heavenly quire the most angelical.

Looking into my breast, her form I find
That like my guardian angel keeps my mind
From rude attempts; and when affections stir,
I calm all passions with one thought of her.   30
Thus they whose reasons love, and not their sense,
The spirits love: thus one intelligence
Reflects upon his like, and by chaste loves
In the same sphere this and that angel moves.
Nor is this barren love; one noble thought
Begets another, and that still is brought
To bed of more; virtues and grace increase,
And such a numerous issue ne'er can cease,
Where children, though great blessings, only be
Pleasures reprieved to some posterity.   40
Beasts love like men, if men in lust delight,
And call that love which is but appetite.
When essence meets with essence, and souls join
In mutual knots, that's the true nuptial twine:
Such, Lady, is my love, and such is true;
All other love is to your sex, not you.

Sir William Davenant

[1606–1668]

D AVENANT, or "D'Avenant," as he often spelled his name, was born in Oxford, the son of a tavern-keeper who ultimately became mayor of the town. His parents were friends of Shakespeare, and legend maintains that the great poet was Davenant's godfather (a more bizarre legend holds that Shakespeare was in fact his father!). At an early age Davenant went to London, where he served as a page in two noble houses. After some military service on the Continent, he returned to London, where he studied law at the Middle Temple, became the friend of Endymion Porter and Edward Hyde (later Earl of Clarendon), and began writing extensively for the theater, as well as for representations at court. At the death of Jonson in 1637 he became poet laureate.

During the Civil War Davenant fought for the king, and after the execution of Charles I he followed his new master into exile. Charles II rewarded him by making him governor of Maryland, but on the way to his post he was captured by the Cromwellians and imprisoned in the Tower. Released and eventually pardoned (legend, active again, ascribes his release to the intercession of Milton), he returned to his literary and theatrical pursuits. Since drama as such had been prohibited, he devoted his energies to the new genre of opera, and with the *Siege of Rhodes* (1656) did much to pave the way for characteristic forms of Restoration theater—both the opera proper and the "heroic play" perfected by Dryden.

Davenant's colorful and varied career did not prevent him from attaining some distinction in a number of literary areas. His long poem *Gondibert* (1650) has not appealed to posterity, but it has historical importance as an attempt to lead epic traditions in directions agreeable to the growing rationalistic and scientific concerns of the time. A more significant document for the intellectual history of the age is the critical debate between Davenant and Hobbes which was published with the epic.

Davenant's lyric poetry does not rank with the finest of the 1640's and 1650's, but it has considerable polish and variety.

SIR W. DAVENANT. *Selected Poems*, ed. D. Bush (Cambridge, Mass., 1943).

A. HARBAGE. *Sir William Davenant, Poet-Venturer, 1606–1668* (Philadelphia, 1935). Has a good treatment of *Gondibert*.

A. H. NETHERCOT. *Sir William Davenant, Poet Laureate and Playwright-Manager* (Chicago, 1938). Focuses more on Davenant's work as a dramatist.

R. L. SHARP. (See under general poetry bibliography.)

FROM

WORKS [1673]

SONG

The lark now leaves his wat'ry nest,
    And climbing shakes his dewy wings;
He takes this window for the east,
    And to implore your light he sings:
Awake, awake! the morn will never rise
Till she can dress her beauty at your eyes.

The merchant bows unto the seaman's star,
    The plowman from the sun his season takes;
But still the lover wonders what they are
    Who look for day before his mistress wakes.
Awake, awake, break through your veils of lawn!
Then draw your curtains, and begin the dawn.

TO THE QUEEN, ENTERTAINED AT NIGHT BY THE COUNTESS OF ANGLESEY

Fair as unshaded light, or as the day
In its first birth, when all the year was May;
Sweet as the altar's smoke, or as the new
Unfolded bud, swelled by the early dew;
Smooth as the face of waters first appeared,
E'er tides began to strive or winds were heard;
Kind as the willing saints, and calmer far
Than in their sleeps forgiven hermits are:
You that are more than our discreeter fear   9
Dares praise with such full art, what make you here?
Here, where the summer is so little seen,
That leaves (her cheapest wealth) scarce reach at green,
You come, as if the silver planet were
Misled a while from her much injured sphere,
And to ease the travails of her beams tonight,
In this small lantern would contract her light.

ENDYMION PORTER AND OLIVIA[1]

Olivia:
    Before we shall again behold
In his diurnal race the world's great eye,

We may as silent be and cold,
As are the shades where buried lovers lie.

Endymion:
    Olivia, 'tis no fault of love
To lose ourselves in death, but O, I fear,
    When life and knowledge is above
Restored to us, I shall not know thee there.   10

Olivia:
    Call it not heaven, my love, where we
Ourselves shall see and yet each other miss:
    So much of heaven I find in thee
As, thou unknown, all else privation is.

Endymion:
    Why should we doubt, before we go
To find the knowledge which shall ever last,
    That we may there each other know?
Can future knowledge quite destroy the past?   20

Olivia:
    When at the bowers in the Elysian shade
I first arrive, I shall examine where
    They dwell, who love the highest virtue made;
For I am sure to find Endimion there.

Endymion:
    From this vexed world when we shall both retire,
Where all are lovers and where all rejoice;
    I need not seek thee in the heavenly quire;
For I shall know Olivia by her voice.   30

SONG

O thou that sleepst like pig in straw,
    Thou lady dear, arise;
Open, to keep the sun in awe,
    Thy pretty pinking eyes;
And, having stretched each leg and arm,
    Put on your clean white smock,
And then, I pray, to keep you warm,
    A petticoat or dock.[1]

ENDYMION
    1 Porter was a prominent courtier and patron of poets.

SONG
    1 Bustle.

Arise, arise! Why should you sleep,
  When you have slept enough?   10
Long since, French boys cried "Chimney-sweep,"
  And damsels "Kitching-stuff."

The shops were opened long before,
  And youngest prentice goes
To lay at's master's chamber door
  His master's shining shoes.

Arise, arise; your breakfast stays,
  Good water-gruel warm,
Or sugar-sops, which Galen says
  With mace will do no harm.   20
Arise, arise; when you are up,
  You'll find more to your cost,
For morning's draught in caudle-cup,[2]
  Good nutbrown ale, and toast.

2 A warm drink of spiced ale or wine.

Edmund Waller

[1606–1687]

GREATLY admired in his own century, and regarded in the eighteenth century as the greatest of English lyric poets, Waller has not worn very well; of his copious production of verse, only a handful of graceful amorous lyrics are likely still to give pleasure. Nevertheless, he counts as an important figure in the history of English poetic style, for, together with Sir John Denham, he gave nearly definitive form to the closed couplet, which was to become the chief vehicle of the poets of the Augustan age. Apart from his cultivation of the couplet (in which he was anticipated by Sir John Beaumont, George Sandys, and Edward Fairfax), Waller was largely a conventional Caroline poet—that is to say, a follower of Jonson who employs some touches of Donne. This character he essentially maintained until his death on the eve of the Glorious Revolution of 1688.

The son of a rich father, Waller was born in Coleshill, Buckinghamshire, and was educated at Eton and at King's College, Cambridge. Leaving Cambridge without a degree, he studied law at Lincoln's Inn. In 1631 he married an heiress, and, though his motive seems to have been love, he increased thereby his already remarkable fortune. She died three years later, and some time thereafter the poet began his unsuccessful courtship of Lady Dorothy Sidney, the "Sacharissa" of his early poems, which were published in 1645.

Although initially a moderate parliamentarian in his sympathies, Waller shifted his allegiance to the royalist party in 1643 and was deeply involved in what became known as "Waller's Plot" to capture London for the king. He escaped with a fine and banishment, probably because of his wealth and influence, and went to Paris, where John Evelyn was his friend and Thomas Hobbes was the tutor of his son.

Pardoned in 1651, he returned to England and wrote a *Panegyric* to Cromwell. At the time of the Restoration he composed an address of welcome to Charles II. When the king observed that the poem was inferior in quality to the panegyric to Oliver, Waller made his famous reply: "Sire, we poets never succeed so well in writing truth as in fiction." He spent his old age as a Member of Parliament and a vigorous spokesman for a policy of tolerance, respected by all for his wit and genius.

E. WALLER. *Poems*, ed. G. Thorn-Drury (London, 1893). Old, but still the standard edition.

SAMUEL JOHNSON. "Life of Waller," in *Lives of the English Poets* (London, 1779–81). A perceptive critique, one of the more brilliant to be found in the *Lives*. (The *Lives* are available in several modern editions.)

R. WALLERSTEIN. "The Rhetoric and Metre of the Heroic Couplet," *PMLA*, 50 (1935).

W. L. CHERNAIK. *The Poetry of Limitation: a Study of Edmund Waller* (New Haven, 1968).

FROM

POEMS [1686]

TO THE KING, ON HIS NAVY[1]

Where'er thy navy spreads her canvas wings,
Homage to thee, and peace to all she brings;
The French and Spaniard, when thy flags appear,
Forget their hatred, and consent to fear.
So Jove from Ida did both hosts survey,
And when he pleased to thunder, part the fray.
Ships heretofore in seas like fishes sped,
The mighty still upon the smaller fed;
Thou on the deep imposest nobler laws,
And by that justice hast removed the cause   10
Of those rude tempests, which for rapine sent,
Too oft, alas! involved the innocent.
Now shall the ocean, as thy Thames, be free
From both those fates, of storms and piracy.
But we most happy, who can fear no force
But wingèd troops, or Pegasean horse.
'Tis not so hard for greedy foes to spoil
Another nation, as to touch our soil.
Should nature's self invade the world again,
And o'er the center spread the liquid main,   20
Thy power were safe, and her destructive hand
Would but enlarge the bounds of thy command;
Thy dreadful fleet would style thee lord of all,
And ride in triumph o'er the drownèd ball;
Those towers of oak o'er fertile plains might go,
And visit mountains where they once did grow.
    The world's Restorer never could endure
That finished Babel should those men secure,
Whose pride designed that fabric to have stood
Above the reach of any second flood;   30
To thee, His chosen, more indulgent, He
Dares trust such power with so much piety.

TO MR. HENRY LAWES,[1] WHO HAD THEN NEWLY SET A SONG OF MINE, IN THE YEAR 1635

Verse makes heroic virtue live;
But you can life to verses give.
As, when in open air we blow,
The breath, though strained, sounds flat and low;
But if a trumpet take the blast,
It lifts it high, and makes it last:
So in your airs our numbers dressed,
Make a shrill sally from the breast
Of nymphs, who, singing what we penned,
Our passions to themselves commend;   10
While love, victorious with thy art,
Governs at once their voice and heart.
    You, by the help of tune and time,
Can make that song which was but rhyme.
Noy[2] pleading, no man doubts the cause;
Or questions verses set by Lawes.
    As a church window, thick with paint,
Lets in a light but dim and faint,
So others, with division,[3] hide
The light of sense, the poet's pride;   20
But you alone may truly boast
That not a syllable is lost:
The writer's and the setter's skill
At once the ravished ears do fill.
Let those which only warble long,
And gargle in their throats a song,
Content themselves with *ut, re, mi:*[4]
Let words, and sense, be set by thee.

TO MR. HENRY LAWES

1 Lawes was one of the most accomplished English musical composers of the seventeenth century, and a member of the King's Music, the orchestra at Whitehall. In 1634 he had composed the music for Milton's masque, Comus. He set to music many of the finest lyrics of the day. Milton has a sonnet to Lawes in which he, like Waller, praises him for his skill in setting verse so that the music accords with the poet's meaning.
2 William Noy, one of the ablest lawyers of his day, became attorney-general in 1631.
3 Less tasteful composers disguise the "sense" of the poem by their setting.
4 The vocal scale.

TO THE KING
1 G. Thorn-Drury thinks the poem belongs to the year 1627, when Buckingham was engaged in the preparation of the fleet.

AT PENSHURST[1] [1]

Had Sacharissa[2] lived when mortals made
Choice of their deities, this sacred shade
Had held an altar to her power, that gave
The peace and glory which these alleys have;
Embroidered so with flowers where she stood,
That it became a garden of a wood.
Her presence has such more than human grace
That it can civilize the rudest place;
And beauty too, and order, can impart,
Where nature ne'er intended it, nor art.   10
The plants acknowledge this, and her admire
No less than those of old did Orpheus' lyre;
If she sit down, with tops all towards her bowed,
They round about her into arbors crowd;
Or if she walk, in even ranks they stand,
Like some well marshaled and obsequious band.
Amphion[3] so made stones and timber leap
Into fair figures from a confused heap;
And in the symmetry of her parts is found
A power like that of harmony in sound.   20
    Ye lofty beeches, tell this matchless dame
That if together ye fed all one flame,
It could not equalize the hundredth part
Of what her eyes have kindled in my heart!
Go, boy, and carve this passion on the bark
Of yonder tree,[4] which stands the sacred mark
Of noble Sidney's birth; when such benign,
Such more than mortal-making stars did shine,
That there they cannot but forever prove
The monument and pledge of humble love;   30
His humble love whose hopes shall ne'er rise higher
Than for a pardon that he dares admire.

SONG

Say, lovely dream, where couldst thou find
    Shadows to counterfeit that face?
    Colors of this glorious kind
    Come not from any mortal place.

In heaven itself thou sure wert drest
    With that angel-like disguise;
    Thus deluded am I blest,
And see my joy with closèd eyes.

But, ah, this image is too kind
    To be other than a dream!   10
    Cruel Sacharissa's mind
Never put on that sweet extreme.

Fair dream, if thou intend'st me grace,
    Change that heavenly face of thine;
    Paint despised love in thy face,
And make it to appear like mine.

Pale, wan, and meager let it look,
    With a pity-moving shape,
    Such as wander by the brook
Of Lethe, or from graves escape.   20

Then to that matchless nymph appear,
    In whose shape thou shinest so,
    Softly in her sleeping ear,
With humble words express my woe.

Perhaps from greatness, state, and pride,
    Thus surprisèd she may fall:
    Sleep does disproportion hide,
And, death resembling, equals all.

TO A VERY YOUNG LADY[1]

Why came I so untimely forth
Into a world which, wanting thee,
Could entertain us with no worth
Or shadow of felicity,
That time should me so far remove
From that which I was born to love?

Yet, fairest blossom! do not slight
That age which you may know so soon;
The rosy morn resigns her light,
And milder glory, to the noon: 10
And then what wonders shall you do,
Whose dawning beauty warms us so?

AT PENSHURST
    1 See Jonson's To Penshurst, p. 763.
    2 Under this name Lady Dorothy Sidney, daughter of the
second Earl of Leicester, was paid poetical courtship in many
of Waller's verses.
    3 At the building of Thebes, Amphion, the son of Zeus,
played with such magic skill on the lyre, which he had received from Hermes, that the stones moved of their own
accord and formed the wall.
    4 The tree that had been planted in honor of the birth of
Sir Philip Sidney.

TO A VERY YOUNG LADY
    1 The title in the 1645 edition is "To my young Lady
Lucy Sidney."

Hope waits upon the flowery prime;
And summer, though it be less gay,
Yet is not looked on as a time
Of declination or decay;
For with a full hand that does bring
All that was promised by the spring.

THE BATTLE OF THE SUMMER ISLANDS[1]

CANTO I

What fruits they have, and how heaven smiles
Upon those late-discovered isles.

Aid me, Bellona,[2] while the dreadful fight
Betwixt a nation and two whales I write.
Seas stained with gore I sing, adventurous toil,
And how these monsters did disarm an isle.
  Bermudas, walled with rocks, who does not know?
That happy island where huge lemons grow,
And orange trees, which golden fruit do bear,
The Hesperian garden boasts of none so fair;
Where shining pearl, coral, and many a pound,
On the rich shore, of ambergris is found.   10
The lofty cedar, which to heaven aspires,
The prince of trees, is fuel for their fires;
The smoke by which their loaded spits do turn,
For incense might on sacred altars burn;
Their private roofs on odorous timber borne,
Such as might palaces for kings adorn.
The sweet palmettos a new Bacchus yield,
With leaves as ample as the broadest shield,
Under the shadow of whose friendly boughs
They sit, carousing where their liquor grows.   20
Figs there unplanted through the fields do grow,
Such as fierce Cato did the Romans show,
With the rare fruit inviting them to spoil
Carthage, the mistress of so rich a soil.
The naked rocks are not unfruitful there,
But, at some constant seasons, every year

Their barren tops with luscious food abound,
And with the eggs of various fowls are crowned.
Tobacco is the worst of things which they
To English landlords, as their tribute, pay.   30
Such is the mold, that the blest tenant feeds
On precious fruits, and pays his rent in weeds.
With candied plantains, and the juicy pine,[3]
On choicest melons, and sweet grapes, they dine,
And with potatoes fat their wanton swine.
Nature these cates with such a lavish hand
Pours out among them, that our coarser land
Tastes of that bounty, and does cloth return,
Which not for warmth but ornament is worn;
For the kind spring, which but salutes us here,   40
Inhabits there, and courts them all the year.
Ripe fruits and blossoms on the same trees live;
At once they promise what at once they give.
So sweet the air, so moderate the clime,
None sickly lives, or dies before his time.
Heaven sure has kept this spot of earth uncursed
To show how all things were created first.
The tardy plants in our cold orchards placed
Reserve their fruit for the next age's taste.
There a small grain in some few months will be   50
A firm, a lofty, and a spacious tree.
The palma-christi,[4] and the fair papaw,
Now but a seed, preventing[5] nature's law,
In half the circle of the hasty year
Project a shade, and lovely fruit do wear.
And as their trees, in our dull region set,
But faintly grow, and no perfection get,
So in this northern tract our hoarser throats
Utter unripe and ill-constrainèd notes,
Where the supporter of the poets' style,   60
Phœbus, on them eternally does smile.
Oh! how I long my careless limbs to lay
Under the plantain's shade, and all the day
With amorous airs my fancy entertain,
Invoke the Muses, and improve my vein!
No passion there in my free breast should move,
None but the sweet and best of passions, love.
There while I sing, if gentle love be by,
That tunes my lute, and winds the strings so high,
With the sweet sound of Sacharissa's name   70
I'll make the listening savages grow tame—
But while I do these pleasing dreams indite,
I am diverted from the promised fight.

THE BATTLE
  1 The description of the battle occurs in the last two of the
three cantos of the poem, which are omitted here. The
Bermudas, discovered by the Spaniards in the early sixteenth
century, and named for Juan de Bermudez, a Spanish navi-
gator, were long called Somers Islands (or "the Summer
Islands") after Sir George Somers, who settled them in 1609.
  2 Roman goddess of war.

3 Pineapple.   4 The castor oil plant.
5 Anticipating.

TO PHYLLIS

Phyllis! why should we delay
Pleasures shorter than the day?
Could we (which we never can)
Stretch our lives beyond their span,
Beauty like a shadow flies,
And our youth before us dies.
Or, would youth and beauty stay,
Love hath wings, and will away.
Love hath swifter wings than Time;
Change in love to heaven does climb.   10
Gods, that never change their state,
Vary oft their love and hate.
    Phyllis! to this truth we owe
All the love betwixt us two.
Let not you and I inquire
What has been our past desire;
On what shepherds you have smiled,
Or what nymphs I have beguiled;
Leave it to the planets, too,
What we shall hereafter do;   20
For the joys we now may prove,
Take advice of present love.

ON A GIRDLE

That which her slender waist confined
Shall now my joyful temples bind;
No monarch but would give his crown,
His arms might do what this has done.

It was my heaven's extremest[1] sphere,
The pale[2] which held that lovely deer;
My joy, my grief, my hope, my love,
Did all within this circle move.

A narrow compass, and yet there
Dwelt all that's good and all that's fair;
Give me but what this riband bound,
Take all the rest the sun goes round!

TO A LADY SINGING A SONG OF HIS COMPOSING

Chloris! yourself you so excel,
When you vouchsafe to breathe my thought,
That, like a spirit, with this spell
Of my own teaching, I am taught.

That eagle's fate and mine are one,
Which, on the shaft that made him die,
Espied a feather of his own,
Wherewith he wont to soar so high.

Had Echo, with so sweet a grace,
Narcissus' loud complaints returned,
Not for reflection of his face,
But of his voice, the boy had burned.

SONG

Stay, Phœbus, stay!
The world to which you fly so fast,
Conveying day
From us to them, can pay your haste
With no such object, nor salute your rise
With no such wonder, as De Mornay's[1] eyes.

Well does this prove
The error of those antique books,
Which made you move
About the world; her charming looks
Would fix your beams, and make it ever day,
Did not the rolling earth snatch her away.

WHILE I LISTEN TO THY VOICE

While I listen to thy voice,
Chloris, I feel my life decay;
That powerful noise[1]
Calls my flitting soul away.
Oh! suppress that magic sound,
Which destroys without a wound.

Peace, Chloris, peace! or singing die,
That together you and I
To heaven may go;
For all we know
Of what the blessed do above
Is, that they sing and that they love.

SONG
1 It has been suggested that the lady, as yet unidentified, was one of the French attendants of Queen Henrietta Maria.

ON A GIRDLE
1 Outermost.   2 Enclosure.

WHILE I LISTEN
1 Harmonious sound.

GO, LOVELY ROSE

Go, lovely rose,
Tell her that wastes her time and me
    That now she knows,
When I resemble her to thee,
    How sweet and fair she seems to be.

Tell her that's young,
And shuns to have her graces spied,
    That hadst thou sprung
In deserts, where no men abide,
    Thou must have uncommended died.   10

Small is the worth
Of beauty from the light retired;
    Bid her come forth,
Suffer herself to be desired,
    And not blush so to be admired.

Then die, that she
The common fate of all things rare
    May read in thee;
How small a part of time they share,
    That are so wondrous sweet and fair.   20

OF ENGLISH VERSE

Poets may boast, as safely vain,
Their works shall with the world remain;
Both, bound together, live or die,
The verses and the prophecy.

But who can hope his lines should long
Last in a daily changing tongue?
While they are new, envy prevails;
And as that dies, our language fails.

When architects have done their part,
The matter may betray their art;   10
Time, if we use ill-chosen stone,
Soon brings a well-built palace down.

Poets that lasting marble seek
Must carve in Latin or in Greek;

We write in sand, our language grows,
And, like the tide, our work o'erflows.

Chaucer his sense can only boast,
The glory of his numbers lost!
Years have defaced his matchless strain,
And yet he did not sing in vain.   20

The beauties which adorned that age,
The shining subjects of his rage,[1]
Hoping they should immortal prove,
Rewarded with success his love.

This was the generous poet's scope,
And all an English pen can hope,
To make the fair approve his flame,
That can so far extend their fame.

Verse, thus designed, has no ill fate
If it arrive but at the date   30
Of fading beauty; if it prove
But as long-lived as present love.

OF THE LAST VERSES IN THE BOOK

When we for age could neither read nor write,
The subject made us able to indite;
The soul, with nobler resolutions decked,
The body stooping, does herself erect.
No mortal parts are requisite to raise
Her that, unbodied, can her Maker praise.
    The seas are quiet when the winds give o'er;
So, calm are we when passions are no more!
For then we know how vain it was to boast
Of fleeting things, so certain to be lost.   10
Clouds of affection from our younger eyes
Conceal that emptiness which age descries.
    The soul's dark cottage, battered and decayed,
Lets in new light through chinks that time has made;
Stronger by weakness, wiser, men become
As they draw near to their eternal home.
Leaving the old, both worlds at once they view,
That stand upon the threshold of the new.

OF ENGLISH VERSE
  1 Poetic ardor.

John Milton

[1608–1674]

ARLIER in our century the poetry of John Milton was subjected to a formidable series of attacks by a number of prominent poets and critics, chief among them T. S. Eliot and Ezra Pound, who felt that the discrepancies between Milton's practice and that of Donne and the Metaphysicals served to symbolize the deleterious effect which Milton's influence had had upon later English poets and might still have on the poets of the present. The controversies thus stirred up in the 1920's and 1930's belong now to history, and it is possible to evaluate them as cultural phenomena in their own right. One thing, however, is certain: now that the tumult and the shouting have died away, Milton serenely retains his position as one of the two supreme poets of the English language. Recent critical appraisals, along with the reactions of new generations of common readers, indicate that Milton, in the manner of the very greatest poets, continues to convey new depths and shades of meanings to the human race.

Milton poses a special problem for the editors of a volume of selections from the whole range of seventeenth-century poetry. It is by definition impossible to include *Paradise Lost*, and it is effectively impossible to include either *Paradise Regained* or *Samson Agonistes* in its entirety. And the representation of any of these great and complex works by selected passages is inevitably misleading. It is best, perhaps, to direct the reader to any of the easily available and excellent modern editions of the complete Milton and to let the poet stand among his fellows in this volume as represented by his lesser works— several of which, such as the ode "On the Morning of Christ's Nativity" and "Lycidas," rank with the glories of our literature.

If it is difficult to excerpt Milton, it is equally difficult to comment in short space upon his works. Paradoxically, although he stands alone among seventeenth-century poets, isolated by his genius, his intellect, and his character alike, he at the same time sums up in his work the total traditions of Renaissance art and Christian humanism which lie behind him—and also, in his unique way, gives permanent expression to most of the intellectual concerns and stylistic tendencies of his complicated age. Untouched by the stylistic revolution of the Metaphysicals, equally untouched by the subsequent reaction of the Restoration poets, he owes his allegiance to Spenser and before Spenser to Tasso and Ariosto, and before them, ultimately, to the great poets of the classical world: to Virgil and Ovid, to Theocritus and Homer. And yet, as several modern critics have demonstrated, the world of "Lycidas" and *Paradise Lost* is not a simple though perplexing re-creation of the world of ancient poetry or that of high Renaissance poetry. In its violent dramatic tensions, in its radical use of space and time, it is fully expressive of the contorted world of Baroque Europe—the Europe of Donne and Marino, of Bernini,

Rembrandt, and Monteverdi. Only a firm yet flexible sense of decorum, rooted in a powerful mind and an extraordinary erudition, enables Milton to absorb the tension and turmoil of his age and to derive from them forms of immutable balance and permanence.

Milton was the son of a well-to-do London scrivener, an amateur musician and a man of considerable culture. Introduced to intellectual pursuits at a very early age, the poet received his formal education at St. Paul's School in London and at Christ's College, Cambridge, which he entered in 1625 and from which he received his B.A. (1629) and his M.A. (1632). His poetic creation may be divided into four well-defined periods. The first extends from his juvenilia (he was composing verse at the age of fifteen) to the works of his years at Cambridge, which include the ode "On the Morning of Christ's Nativity" and, in all probability, "L'Allegro" and "Il Penseroso." The second embraces the years 1632–38, often called the "Horton Period" from his residence during most of that time at his father's estate at Horton in Buckinghamshire. To this time belong "Comus," "Lycidas," and the effective coming to maturity of Milton's genius. After Milton's return from his European journey of 1638–39, he launched into twenty years of politics and public service during which he ignored poetry almost altogether. To this third period belong most of the sonnets, including those remarkable sonnets on public men and public affairs which stand midway between the nonamorous sonnets of Petrarch and the sonnets of Wordsworth and have almost no connection with the erotic delicacies of the Elizabethans. The year 1645 saw the publication of Milton's collected earlier poems; "Comus" and "Lycidas" had made their appearance previously, "Comus" being printed in 1637 as *A Masque Presented at Ludlow Castle* and "Lycidas" being included in the memorial volume *Justa Edouardo King Naufrago* in 1638.

Milton's fourth period, of course, extends from the Restoration of 1660 to his death and embraces the composition of the great works in the major genres. *Paradise Lost* was published in 1667 and again in 1674, the second edition being preceded by a noble complimentary poem by Andrew Marvell. The "brief epic" *Paradise Regained*, together with the tragedy *Samson Agonistes*, appeared in 1671. Blind and isolated, Milton had achieved in these last years the aim which had been his since childhood—to "leave something so written to aftertimes as they should not willingly let it die."

J. MILTON. *Works*, general ed. F. A. Patterson, 18 vols. (New York, 1931–38). Followed by 2 index vols., ed. F. A. Patterson, assisted by F. R. Fogle (New York, 1940). The great Columbia edition; definitive.

————. *Complete Poems and Major Prose*, ed. M. Y. Hughes (New York, 1957). This is, like the entry which follows, an excellent edition for most purposes. Contains valuable commentary.

————. *Poems*, ed. J. H. Hanford (New York, 2nd ed., 1953).

————. *The Poems of Mr. John Milton, with Essays in Analysis*, ed. C. Brooks and J. Hardy (New York, 1951). An edition of the *Poems* of 1645, with excellent analyses by the editors.

D. MASSON. *The Life of John Milton*, 7 vols. (London, rev. ed., 1881–96). This massive work retains great value.

J. H. Hanford. *John Milton, Englishman* (New York, 1949). A good biography.

————. *A Milton Handbook* (New York, 4th ed., 1946). A very useful biographical, bibliographical, and critical compendium.

E. M. W. TILLYARD. *Milton* (London, 2nd ed., 1949). A critical biography.

————. *The Miltonic Setting* (Cambridge, 1938). Essays on various aspects.

D. M. WOLFE. *Milton in the Puritan Revolution* (New York, 1941).

W. R. PARKER. *Milton's Contemporary Reputation* (Columbus, Ohio, 1940).

———. *Milton's Debt to Greek Tragedy in "Samson Agonistes"* (Baltimore, 1937).

K. SVENDSEN. *Milton and Science* (Cambridge, 1956).

D. C. ALLEN. *The Harmonious Vision* (Baltimore, 1954). Essays on *Paradise Lost* and other of Milton's poems.

C. S. LEWIS. *A Preface to Paradise Lost* (London, 1942).

D. BUSH. *Paradise Lost in Our Time* (New York, 1945).

A. STEIN. *Answerable Style: Essays on "Paradise Lost"* (Minneapolis, 1953).

———. *Heroic Knowledge* (Minneapolis, 1957). On *Paradise Regained*.

J. S. DIEKHOFF. *Milton's "Paradise Lost": A Commentary on the Argument* (New York, 1946).

B. RAJAN. *"Paradise Lost" and the Seventeenth-Century Reader* (London, 1947).

I. G. MacCAFFREY. *Paradise Lost as "Myth"* (Cambridge, Mass., 1959).

J. SUMMERS. *The Muse's Method* (Cambridge, Mass., 1962).

E. M. POPE. *"Paradise Regained:" The Tradition and the Poem* (Baltimore, 1957).

L. NELSON. *Baroque Lyric Poetry* (New Haven, 1961). Has interesting studies of the "Nativity Ode" and "Lycidas."

R. TUVE. *Images and Themes in Five Poems by Milton* (Cambridge, Mass., 1957).

C. A. PATRIDES, ed. *Milton's Lycidas: The Tradition and the Poem* (New York, 1961). An anthology of critical essays.

L. L. MARTZ. *Poet of Exile* (New Haven, 1980).

M. A. RADZINOWICZ. *Toward Samson Agonistes* (Princeton, 1978).

J. M. WEBBER. *Milton and His Epic Tradition* (Seattle, 1979).

FROM

POEMS [1673]

from

AT A VACATION EXERCISE IN THE COLLEGE, PART LATIN, PART ENGLISH[1]

The Latin Speeches ended, the English thus began:

Hail, Native Language, that by sinews weak
Didst move my first endeavoring tongue to speak,
And mad'st imperfect words with childish trips,
Half unpronounced, slide through my infant lips,
Driving dumb Silence from the portal door,
Where he had mutely sat two years before:
Here I salute thee, and thy pardon ask
That now I use thee in my latter[2] task!
Small loss it is that thence can come unto thee;
I know my tongue but little grace can do thee.   10

Thou need'st not be ambitious to be first;
Believe me, I have thither packed the worst:
And, if it happen as I did forecast,
The daintiest dishes shall be served up last.
I pray thee then deny me not thy aid,
For this same small neglect that I have made;
But haste thee straight to do me once a pleasure,
And from thy wardrobe bring thy chiefest treasure,
Not those new-fangled toys,[3] and trimming slight
Which takes[4] our late fantastics with delight;   20
But cull those richest robes and gay'st attire,
Which deepest spirits and choicest wits desire.
I have some naked thoughts that rove about,
And loudly knock to have their passage out,
And, weary of their place, do only stay
Till thou hast decked them in thy best array;
That so they may, without suspect[5] or fears,
Fly swiftly to this fair assembly's ears.
Yet I had rather, if I were to choose,
Thy service in some graver subject use,   30

AT A VACATION
1 Milton adds the annotation, *"Anno Ætatis 19."* This poem was published for the first time in the 1673 edition of Milton's poems.
2 Present.

3 Trifles.   4 Bewitches, pleases.
5 Suspicion.

Such as may make thee search thy coffers round,
Before thou clothe my fancy in fit sound:
Such where the deep⁶ transported mind may soar
Above the wheeling poles, and at Heaven's door
Look in, and see each blissful deity
How he before the thunderous throne doth lie,
Listening to what unshorn Apollo sings
To the touch of golden wires, while Hebe brings
Immortal⁷ nectar to her kingly sire;
Then, passing through the spheres of watchful fire,   40
And misty regions of wide air next under,
And hills of snow and lofts of pilèd thunder,
May tell at length how green-eyed Neptune raves,
In Heaven's defiance mustering all his waves;
Then sing of secret things that come to pass
When beldam⁸ Nature in her cradle was;
And last of kings and queens and heroes old,
Such as the wise Demodocus once told
In solemn songs at King Alcinous' feast,
While sad Ulysses' soul and all the rest   50
Are held, with his melodious harmony,
In willing chains, and sweet captivity. . . .

ON THE MORNING OF
CHRIST'S NATIVITY¹

This is the month, and this the happy morn,
Wherein the Son of Heaven's eternal King,
Of wedded Maid and Virgin Mother born,
Our great redemption from above did bring;
For so the holy sages² once did sing,
   That he our deadly forfeit should release,³
And with his Father work us a perpetual peace.

That glorious form, that light unsufferable,
And that far-beaming blaze of majesty,

AT A VACATION
   6 In the Latin sense of *high.*
   7 Conferring immortality.   8 Grandmother.

ON THE MORNING
   1 Composed in December, 1629, as a "birthday gift to
Christ." Milton had come of age in that month, and was in
his fourth year at Cambridge. It is the finest production of his
early maturity, and the first example of the serious and lofty
style of which he was later to be the master.
   2 The Old Testament prophets.
   3 Remit the fine or penalty of death which resulted from
Adam's sin.

Wherewith he wont⁴ at Heaven's high council-table
To sit the midst of Trinal Unity,   11
He laid aside, and, here with us to be,
   Forsook the courts of everlasting day,
And chose with us a darksome house of mortal clay.

Say, Heavenly Muse, shall not thy sacred vein
Afford a present to the Infant God?
Hast thou no verse, no hymn, or solemn strain,
To welcome him to this his new abode,
Now while the heaven, by the sun's team untrod,
   Hath took no print of the approaching light,   20
And all the spangled host keep watch in squadrons
      bright?

See how from far upon the eastern road
The star-led wizards⁵ haste with odors sweet!
Oh! run; prevent⁶ them with thy humble ode,
And lay it lowly at his blessèd feet;
Have thou the honor first thy Lord to greet,
   And join thy voice unto the angel quire,
From out his secret altar touched with hallowed fire.⁷

THE HYMN

It was the winter wild,
While the Heaven-born child   30
   All meanly wrapped in the rude manger lies;
Nature in awe to him
Had doffed her gaudy trim,
   With her great Master so to sympathize:
It was no season then for her
To wanton with the sun her lusty paramour.

Only with speeches fair
She woos the gentle air
   To hide her guilty front⁸ with innocent snow,
And on her naked shame,   40
Pollute with sinful blame,
   The saintly veil of maiden white to throw,
Confounded, that her Maker's eyes
Should look so near upon her foul deformities.

   4 Was wont, accustomed.
   5 The Wise Men from the East.   6 Anticipate.
   7 See Isaiah 6:6. The poet's lips, purified by the hallowed
fire, would join the "angel quire" in greeting the infant
Christ.
   8 Nature is, like man, thought of as under a curse as the
result of the Fall of man.

But he, her fears to cease,
Sent down the meek-eyed Peace;
   She crowned with olive green came softly sliding
Down through the turning sphere,[9]
His ready harbinger,
   With turtle[10] wing the amorous clouds dividing, 50
And waving wide her myrtle wand,
She strikes a universal peace through sea and land.

No war, or battle's sound,
Was heard the world around;
   The idle spear and shield were high uphung;
The hookèd[11] chariot stood,
Unstained with hostile blood;
   The trumpet spake not to the armèd throng;
And kings sate still with awful[12] eye,
As if they surely knew their sovran Lord was by. 60

But peaceful was the night
Wherein the Prince of Light
   His reign of peace upon the earth began.
The winds, with wonder whist,[13]
Smoothly the waters kissed,
   Whispering new joys to the mild ocean,
Who now hath quite forgot to rave,
While birds of calm[14] sit brooding on the charmèd
      wave.

The stars, with deep amaze,[15]
Stand fixed in steadfast gaze, 70
   Bending one way their precious influence,[16]
And will not take their flight,
For all the morning light,
   Or Lucifer[17] that often warned them thence;
But in their glimmering orbs did glow,
Until their Lord himself bespake, and bid them go.

And, though the shady gloom
Had given day her room,
   The sun himself withheld his wonted speed,
And hid his head for shame, 80
As his inferior flame
   The new-enlightened world no more should need:
He saw a greater Sun appear
Than his bright throne or burning axletree could bear.

The shepherds on the lawn,[18]
Or ere the point of dawn,
   Sat simply chatting in a rustic row;
Full little thought they than[19]
That the mighty Pan[20]
   Was kindly come to live with them below; 90
Perhaps their loves, or else their sheep,
Was all that did their silly[21] thoughts so busy keep.

When such music sweet
Their hearts and ears did greet,
   As never was by mortal finger strook,[22]
Divinely warbled voice
Answering the stringèd noise,[23]
   As all their souls in blissful rapture took:[24]
The air such pleasure loth to lose,
With thousand echoes still prolongs each heavenly
      close.[25] 100

Nature that heard such sound
Beneath the hollow round[26]
   Of Cynthia's seat, the airy region thrilling,[27]
Now was almost won
To think her part was done,
   And that her reign had here its last fulfilling;
She knew such harmony alone[28]
Could hold all Heaven and Earth in happier union.

At last surrounds their sight
A globe of circular light, 110

---

9 The whole globe of the stars, which, in the Ptolemaic cosmology, revolved daily about the earth.
  10 Turtledove.
  11 Having hooks, or scythes, projecting from the axles.
  12 Full of awe.   13 Hushed.
  14 The halcyons, which, according to Classical mythology, bred during a calm period at the winter solstice.
  15 Amazement, wonder.
  16 The stars were supposed, in astrology, to affect or "influence" the lives of human beings. Milton represents their influence at the time of the birth of Christ as altogether beneficent.
  17 Literally, "light-bearer." Either the morning star or the sun.

  18 Field or pasture.   19 Then.
  20 Christ. The Greek god Pan, the deity of universal nature, was frequently identified in Renaissance poetry with Christ.
  21 Simple, innocent.   22 Struck.
  23 Harmonious sound.   24 Captivated, bewitched.
  25 Cadence.   26 The sphere of the moon.
  27 Penetrating.
  28 Of itself, without the aid of Nature and her system of spheres, etc.

That with long beams the shame-faced night arrayed,
The helmèd cherubim
And swordèd seraphim
　Are seen in glittering ranks with wings displayed,
Harping in loud and solemn quire,
With unexpressive[29] notes to Heaven's new-born Heir.

Such music (as 'tis said)
Before was never made,
　But when of old the Sons of Morning sung,[30]
While the Creator great　　　　　　　　　　120
His constellations set,
　And the well-balanced world on hinges hung,
And cast the dark foundations deep,
And bid the weltering waves their oozy channel keep.

Ring out, ye crystal spheres!
Once bless our human ears,
　If ye have power to touch our senses so;
And let your silver chime
Move in melodious time;
　And let the bass of heaven's deep organ blow;　130
And with your ninefold harmony
Make up full consort[31] to the angelic symphony.

For, if such holy song
Enwrap our fancy long,
　Time will run back and fetch the Age of Gold;[32]
And speckled[33] Vanity
Will sicken soon and die;
　And leprous Sin will melt from earthly mold;
And Hell itself will pass away,
And leave her dolorous mansions to the peering day.

Yea, Truth and Justice then　　　　　　　141
Will down return to men,
　Orbed in a rainbow; and, like[34] glories wearing,
Mercy will sit between,
Throned in celestial sheen,
　With radiant feet the tissued[35] clouds down
　　　steering;

And Heaven, as at some festival,
Will open wide the gates of her high palace-hall.

But wisest Fate says No,
This must not yet be so,　　　　　　　　150
　The Babe lies yet in smiling infancy,
That on the bitter cross
Must redeem our loss,
　So both himself and us to glorify:
Yet first to those ychained[36] in sleep,
The wakeful trump[37] of doom must thunder through
　the deep,

With such a horrid[38] clang
As on Mount Sinai rang,[39]
　While the red fire and smold'ring clouds outbrake:
The agèd Earth aghast　　　　　　　　　160
With terror of that blast
　Shall from the surface to the center shake;
When at the world's last sessiòn,
The dreadful Judge in middle air shall spread his
　throne.

And then at last our bliss
Full and perfect is,
　But now begins; for from this happy day
The old Dragon[40] under ground
In straiter limits bound,
　Not half so far casts his usurpèd sway,　　170
And, wroth to see his kingdom fail,
Swinges[41] the scaly horror of his folded tail.

The oracles are dumb,[42]
No voice or hideous hum
　Runs through the archèd roof in words deceiving.
Apollo from his shrine
Can no more divine,
　With hollow shriek the steep of Delphos[43] leaving.
No nightly trance or breathèd spell
Inspires the pale-eyed priest from the prophetic cell.

29 Inexpressible.　30 See Job 38:7.　31 Union with.
32 Milton here makes a composite picture of the Christian millennium at the end of the world (Revelation 20–22) and the Golden Age of Classical mythology, in which Astræa, goddess of justice, will return to earth.
33 Plague-spotted.
34 Similar. The first version (1645) of this line reads, "Th' enameled arras of the rainbow wearing."
35 As if made of "tissue," a cloth interwoven with silver.

36 The prefix y-, as often in Chaucer, is a survival of the Old English past-participial prefix ge-.
37 The awakening trumpet of the Day of Doom.
38 Terrifying.　　　　　　　39 See Exodus 19:16.
40 Satan. See Revelation 12:9.　　　　41 Lashes.
42 A reference to the legend that at the time of Christ's birth pagan oracles ceased to make prophecies.
43 Delphi, the seat of the famous oracle of Apollo.

The lonely mountains o'er,   181
And the resounding shore,
    A voice of weeping heard, and loud lament;
From haunted spring and dale,
Edged with poplar pale,
    The parting Genius[44] is with sighing sent,
With flower-inwoven tresses torn
The Nymphs in twilight shade of tangled thickets
        mourn.

In consecrated earth,
And on the holy hearth,   190
    The Lars[45] and Lemures[45] moan with midnight
        plaint;
In urns and altars round,
A drear and dying sound
    Affrights the Flamens at their service quaint;[46]
And the chill marble[47] seems to sweat,[48]
While each peculiar power forgoes his wonted seat.

Peor and Baälim[49]
Forsake their temples dim,
    With that twice-battered god[50] of Palestine;
And mooned Ashtaroth,[51]   200
Heaven's queen and mother both,
    Now sits not girt with tapers' holy shine;
The Libyc Hammon[52] shrinks his horn,
In vain the Tyrian maids their wounded Thammuz[53]
        mourn.

And sullen Moloch[54] fled,
Hath left in shadows dread

His burning idol all of blackest hue;
In vain with cymbals' ring
They call the grisly king,
    In dismal dance about the furnace blue;   210
The brutish gods[55] of Nile as fast,
Isis and Orus, and the dog Anubis, haste.

Nor is Osiris seen
In Memphian grove or green,
    Trampling the unshowered[56] grass with lowings
        loud;
Nor can he be at rest
Within his sacred chest;[57]
    Nought but profoundest Hell can be his shroud;
In vain, with timbreled anthems dark,
The sable-stolèd sorcerers bear his worshiped ark.

He feels from Juda's land   221
The dreaded Infant's hand;
    The rays of Bethlehem blind his dusky eyne;
Nor all the gods beside
Longer dare abide,
    Not Typhon,[58] huge, ending in snaky twine:
Our Babe, to show his Godhead true,
Can in his swaddling bands control the damnèd crew.

So, when the sun in bed,
Curtained with cloudy red,   230
    Pillows his chin upon an orient[59] wave,
The flocking shadows pale
Troop to the infernal jail,
    Each fettered ghost slips to his several grave,
And the yellow-skirted fays
Fly after the night-steeds, leaving their moon-loved
        maze.[60]

44 The guardian spirit of a locality.
45 In Roman mythology the household gods and spirits
of the dead.
46 The priests at their curious (or elaborate) service.
47 Statue.
48 As a portent of the ill fate about to overtake the god.
49 One of the sun gods, called Baals or Baälim (the Hebrew
masculine plural), whose shrine was on Mount Peor in Moab.
See Numbers 23:28.
50 Dagon, the fish-god, whose image was thrown down
twice before the Ark of the Covenant. See I Samuel 5:4.
51 The Hebrew feminine plural of Ashtoreth, or Astarte,
identified with the moon.
52 Ammon, the Egyptian deity, whose shrine was in the
Libyan desert.
53 A Syrian god identified by the Greeks with Adonis,
who was slain by a boar.
54 A god of the Ammonites, in whose idol children were
burned.

55 Isis was the sister and wife of Osiris, and mother of
Orus (or Horus). Isis was represented with cow's horns with
the disk of the moon between them; Orus, with a hawk's
head; and Osiris, the chief Egyptian deity, whose shrine was
at Memphis, as a bull.
56 A reference to the lack of rain in Egypt.
57 The small ark or chest in which a figure of the god was
kept and carried in processions.
58 The monster of Greek mythology, half man and half
serpent, who was vanquished by Zeus and Hercules.
59 Lustrous, pearl-like.
60 The forests loved by Diana and the other gods.

But see! the Virgin blest
Hath laid her Babe to rest.
    Time is our tedious song should here have ending:
Heaven's youngest-teemèd star [61]   240
Hath fixed her polished car,
    Her sleeping Lord with handmaid lamp attending;
And all about the courtly [62] stable
Bright-harnessed [63] angels sit in order serviceable.

ON TIME [1]

Fly, envious Time, till thou run out thy race:
Call on the lazy leaden-stepping Hours,
Whose speed is but the heavy plummet's pace; [2]
And glut thyself with what thy womb devours,
Which is no more than what is false and vain,
And merely mortal dross;
So little is our loss,
So little is thy gain!
For, when as each thing bad thou hast entombed,
And, last of all, thy greedy self consumed,   10
Then long Eternity shall greet our bliss
With an individual kiss;
And Joy shall overtake us as a flood,
When every thing that is sincerely good
And perfectly divine,
With Truth, and Peace, and Love, shall ever shine
About the supreme throne
Of him, to whose happy-making sight alone
When once our heavenly-guided soul shall climb,
Then, all this earthy grossness quit, [3]   20
Attired with stars we shall for ever sit,
    Triumphing over Death, and Chance, and thee, O
        Time!

ON THE MORNING
  61 Newest-born star (the star of Bethlehem).
  62 Since it serves as a king's residence.
  63 In bright armor.

ON TIME
  1 In the Cambridge Manuscript of Milton's poems, where
this poem is written in Milton's hand, a subtitle, later crossed
out, states that the lines were "to be set on a clock case."
  2 An allusion to the weight of lead suspended on a string,
which operated the works of the clock.
  3 Having been discarded.

AT A SOLEMN MUSIC [1]

Blest pair of Sirens, pledges of Heaven's joy,
Sphere-born harmonious sisters, Voice and Verse, [2]
Wed your divine sounds, and mixed power employ,
Dead things with inbreathed sense able to pierce;
And to our high-raised phantasy [3] present
That undisturbèd song of pure concent, [4]
Aye sung before the sapphire-colored throne [5]
To him that sits thereon,
With saintly shout and solemn jubilee;
Where the bright Seraphim in burning [6] row   10
Their loud uplifted angel-trumpets blow,
And the Cherubic host in thousand quires
Touch their immortal harps of golden wires,
With those just Spirits that wear victorious palms, [7]
Hymns devout and holy psalms
Singing everlastingly: [8]
That we on Earth, with undiscording voice,
May rightly answer [9] that melodious noise;
As once we did, till disproportioned sin
Jarred against nature's chime, and with harsh din   20
Broke the fair music that all creatures made
To their great Lord, whose love their motion swayed
In perfect diapason, [10] whilst they stood
In first obedience, and their state of good.
O may we soon again renew that song,
And keep in tune with Heaven, till God ere long
To his celestial consort [11] us unite,
To live with him, and sing in endless morn of light!

SONG ON MAY MORNING

Now the bright morning star, day's harbinger,
Comes dancing from the east, and leads with her

AT A SOLEMN MUSIC
  1 The theme of the poem is essentially that of the Platonic
doctrine of the music of the spheres, which was sung by the
celestial Sirens, but which cannot be heard by the gross ears
of sinful humanity. With the Platonic elements are mingled
the mythology and mysticism of both the Old and the New
Testaments.
  2 Milton mentions only two of the eight Sirens described
by Plato at the close of his Republic, and gives them names
of his own devising.
  3 Imagination.   4 Harmony.
  5 See the vision described in Ezekiel 1:26.
  6 Shining.   7 See Revelation 7:9.
  8 See Revelation 14:3-4.
  9 Sing in complete accord with.
  10 The "concord of the octave"; the entire compass of
harmonious tones.
  11 Company of musicians.

The flowery May, who from her green lap throws
The yellow cowslip and the pale primrose.
  Hail, bounteous May, that dost inspire
  Mirth, and youth, and warm desire!
  Woods and groves are of thy dressing;
  Hill and dale doth boast thy blessing.
Thus we salute thee with our early song,
And welcome thee, and wish thee long.

ON SHAKESPEARE[1]

What needs my Shakespeare for his honored bones
The labor of an age in pilèd stones?
Or that his hallowed reliques should be hid
Under a star-ypointing[2] pyramid?
Dear son of memory, great heir of fame,
What need'st thou such weak witness of thy name?
Thou in our wonder and astonishment
Has built thyself a livelong monument.
For whilst, to the shame of slow-endeavoring art,
Thy easy numbers flow, and that each heart   10
Hath from the leaves of thy unvalued[3] book
Those Delphic[4] lines with deep impression took,
Then thou, our fancy of itself bereaving,
Dost make us marble with too much conceiving,[5]
And so sepùlchred in such pomp dost lie
That kings for such a tomb would wish to die.

L'ALLEGRO[1]

Hence, loathèd Melancholy,
  Of Cerberus and blackest Midnight born[2]
In Stygian cave forlorn,
  'Mongst horrid shapes, and shrieks, and sights
      unholy!

ON SHAKESPEARE
  1 This poem, dated 1630 by Milton, was the first of his compositions to appear in print. It was among the commendatory poems prefixed to the Second Folio of Shakespeare's plays in 1632.
  2 See note on "ychained," p. 884. Milton has here prefixed the "y" to the present participle for the sake of the rhythm.
  3 Invaluable.
  4 Inspired (as by the oracle of Apollo at Delphi).
  5 Thinking, imagining.

L'ALLEGRO
  1 The title is Italian for "The Cheerful Man." The structure of the two companion lyrics, L'Allegro and Il Penseroso follows the same general plan. The poems represent two contrasting, but not mutually exclusive or incompatible, poetic moods, and the poet obviously takes as keen delight in depicting one series of experiences as the other.
  2 The genealogy is invented by Milton.

Find out some uncouth[3] cell,
  Where brooding Darkness spreads his jealous wings,
And the night-raven sings;
  There, under ebon shades and low-browed rocks,
As ragged as thy locks,
  In dark Cimmerian[4] desert ever dwell.   10
But come, thou Goddess fair and free,
In heaven yclept Euphrosyne,
And by men, heart-easing Mirth;
Whom lovely Venus, at a birth,
With two sister Graces more,
To ivy-crownèd Bacchus bore:
Or whether (as some sager sing)
The frolic wind that breathes the spring,
Zephyr, with Aurora playing,
As he met her once a-Maying,   20
There, on beds of violets blue,
And fresh-blown roses washed in dew,
Filled her with thee, a daughter fair,
So buxom,[5] blithe, and debonair.[6]
Haste thee, Nymph, and bring with thee
Jest, and youthful Jollity,
Quips and Cranks[7] and wanton Wiles,
Nods and Becks and wreathèd Smiles,
Such as hang on Hebe's cheek,
And love to live in dimple sleek;   30
Sport that wrinkled Care derides,
And laughter holding both his sides.
Come, and trip it as ye go,
On the light fantastic toe;
And in thy right hand lead with thee
The mountain nymph, sweet Liberty;
And, if I give thee honor due,
Mirth, admit me of thy crew,
To live with her, and live with thee,
In unreprovèd[8] pleasures free;   40
To hear the lark begin his flight,
And, singing, startle the dull night,
From his watch-tower in the skies,
Till the dappled dawn doth rise;
Then to come,[9] in spite of sorrow,
And at my window bid good-morrow,

  3 Unfamiliar, uncanny.
  4 The Cimmerians, according to Homer, dwelt in "eternal cloud and darkness" beyond the "ocean-stream."
  5 Gracious, lively.   6 Courteous.
  7 Witty turns of speech.   8 Innocent.
  9 A much-disputed passage. "To come" would seem to be coordinate with "To live," in l. 39, "To hear," in l. 41, and "oft listening," in l. 53.

Through the sweetbrier or the vine,
Or the twisted eglantine;[10]
While the cock, with lively din,
Scatters the rear of darkness thin;   50
And to the stack or the barn door,
Stoutly struts his dames before:
Oft listening how the hounds and horn
Cheerly rouse the slumbering morn,
From the side of some hoar[11] hill,
Through the high wood echoing shrill:
Sometime walking, not unseen,
By hedgerow elms, on hillocks green,
Right against[12] the eastern gate
Where the great sun begins his state,[13]   60
Robed in flames and amber light,
The clouds in thousand liveries dight;[14]
While the plowman, near at hand,
Whistles o'er the furrowed land,
And the milkmaid singeth blithe,
And the mower whets his scythe,
And every shepherd tells his tale[15]
Under the hawthorn in the dale.
Straight mine eye hath caught new pleasures,
Whilst the lantskip[16] round it measures: 70
Russet lawns, and fallows[17] gray,
Where the nibbling flocks do stray;
Mountains on whose barren breast
The laboring clouds do often rest;
Meadows trim with daisies pied;
Shallow brooks, and rivers wide;
Towers and battlements it sees
Bosomed high in tufted trees,
Where perhaps some beauty lies,
The cynosure of neighboring eyes.   80
Hard by a cottage chimney smokes
From betwixt two aged oaks,
Where Corydon[18] and Thyrsis met
Are at their savory dinner set
Of herbs and other country messes,
Which the neat-handed Phillis dresses;

And then in haste her bower[19] she leaves,
With Thestylis to bind the sheaves;
Or, if the earlier season lead,
To the tanned haycock in the mead.   90
Sometimes, with secure delight,
The upland hamlets will invite,
When the merry bells ring round,
And the jocund rebecks[20] sound
To many a youth and many a maid
Dancing in the chequered shade,
And young and old come forth to play
On a sunshine holiday,
Till the livelong daylight fail:
Then to the spicy nut-brown ale,   100
With stories told of many a feat,
How Faery Mab the junkets[21] eat.
She was pinched and pulled, she said;
And he, by friar's lantern[22] led,
Tells how the drudging goblin[23] sweat
To earn his cream-bowl duly set,
When in one night, ere glimpse of morn,
His shadowy flail hath threshed the corn
That ten day-laborers could not end;
Then lies him down, the lubbar[24] fiend,   110
And, stretched out all the chimney's[25] length,
Basks at the fire his hairy strength,
And crop-full out of doors he flings,
Ere the first cock his matin rings.
Thus done the tales, to bed they creep,
By whispering winds soon lulled asleep.
Towered cities please us then,
And the busy hum of men,
Where throngs of knights and barons bold,
In weeds[26] of peace, high triumphs[27] hold,   120
With store[28] of ladies, whose bright eyes
Rain influence,[29] and judge the prize
Of wit or arms, while both contend
To win her grace whom all commend.
There let Hymen[30] oft appear
In saffron robe, with taper clear,

19 Cottage.   20 Primitive fiddles.
21 Sweet curds. "Eat" is the past tense of the verb; pronounced "ett."
22 Jack-o'-lantern, will-o'-the-wisp. The 1673 edition reads, "And by the friar's lantern led."
23 The Robin Goodfellow of the country legends, referred to frequently as Hobgoblin.
24 Clumsy, drudging.   25 The fireplace's.
26 Garments.   27 Festivals.   28 Abundance.
29 An astrological term, referring to the power of the stars over human beings.
30 The god of marriage, a common figure in masques.

10 Since eglantine is another name for the sweetbrier, it is commonly assumed that Milton here means the woodbine or honeysuckle.
11 "Grey, from absence of foliage." (Oxford English Dictionary.)
12 Towards.   13 Stately progress.
14 Arrayed.   15 Counts his number (of sheep).
16 Landscape.   17 Plowed fields.
18 Corydon, Thyrsis, Phillis, and Thestylis are type names of shepherds and shepherdesses.

And pomp, and feast, and revelry,
With masque and antique pageantry;
Such sights as youthful poets dream
On summer eves by haunted stream.   130
Then to the well-trod stage anon,
If Jonson's learnèd sock[31] be on,
Or sweetest Shakespeare, Fancy's child,
Warble his native wood-notes wild.
And ever, against eating cares,
Lap me in soft Lydian[32] airs,
Married to immortal verse,
Such as the meeting[33] soul may pierce,
In notes with many a winding bout[34]
Of linkèd sweetness long drawn out   140
With wanton heed and giddy cunning,
The melting voice through mazes running,
Untwisting all the chains that tie
The hidden soul of harmony;
That Orpheus' self may heave his head
From golden slumber on a bed
Of heaped Elysian flowers, and hear
Such strains as would have won the ear
Of Pluto to have quite set free
His half-regained Eurydice.   150
    These delights if thou canst give,
Mirth, with thee I mean to live.

IL PENSEROSO[1]

Hence, vain deluding Joys,
    The brood of Folly without father bred!
How little you bested,[2]
    Or fill the fixèd mind with all your toys;
Dwell in some idle brain,
    And fancies fond[3] with gaudy shapes possess,
As thick and numberless
    As the gay motes that people the sunbeams,
Or likest hovering dreams,
    The fickle pensioners[4] of Morpheus' train.   10

But, hail! thou Goddess sage and holy,
Hail, divinest Melancholy!
Whose saintly visage is too bright
To hit the sense of human sight,
And therefore to our weaker view
O'erlaid with black, staid Wisdom's hue;
Black, but such as in esteem
Prince Memnon's sister[5] might beseem,
Or that starred Ethiop queen[6] that strove
To set her beauty's praise above   20
The Sea-Nymphs, and their powers offended.
Yet thou art higher far descended:
Thee bright-haired Vesta long of yore
To solitary Saturn bore;
His daughter she; in Saturn's reign
Such mixture was not held a stain.
Oft in glimmering bowers and glades
He met her, and in secret shades
Of woody Ida's[7] inmost grove,
Whilst yet there was no fear of Jove.   30
Come, pensive Nun, devout and pure,
Sober, steadfast, and demure,
All in a robe of darkest grain,[8]
Flowing with majestic train,
And sable stole of cypress lawn[9]
Over thy decent[10] shoulders drawn.
Come; but keep thy wonted state,
With even step, and musing gait,
And looks commercing[11] with the skies,
Thy rapt soul sitting in thine eyes: 40
There, held in holy passion still,
Forget thyself to marble, till
With a sad[12] leaden downward cast
Thou fix them on the earth as fast.
And join with thee calm Peace and Quiet,
Spare Fast, that oft with gods doth diet,
And hears the Muses in a ring
Aye round about Jove's altar sing;
And add to these retirèd Leisure,
That in trim gardens takes his pleasure;   50

L'ALLEGRO
  31 See note 13 on p. 769.
  32 The Lydian "mode" of ancient music was characterized by softness and delicacy, in contrast to the Dorian (of stateliness) and the Phrygian (of liveliness).
  33 Responsive.   34 Turn, passage.

IL PENSEROSO
  1 The title is seventeenth-century Italian for "The Meditative Man."
  2 Bestead, avail.   3 Foolish.   4 Retinue.

  5 Hemera, sister of the beautiful Ethiopian prince who fought with the Trojans. See the Odyssey, XI, 552.
  6 Cassiopeia, mother of Andromeda, whose boasts about her beauty and that of her daughter led to a feud with the Nereids. After death Cassiopeia and her daughter were translated to the constellations that bear their names.
  7 Mt. Ida on the island of Crete, home of Saturn and birthplace of Jupiter.
  8 Color; in this case probably dark purple.
  9 Black linen or crape.   10 Comely.
  11 Communing.   12 Sober, serious.

But, first and chiefest, with thee bring
Him that yon soars on golden wing,
Guiding the fiery-wheelèd throne,
The Cherub Contemplation;
And the mute Silence hist [13] along,
'Less Philomel [14] will deign a song,
In her sweetest saddest plight,
Smoothing the rugged brow of Night,
While Cynthia [15] checks her dragon yoke,
Gently o'er the accustomed oak.   60
Sweet bird that shunn'st the noise of folly,
Most musical, most melancholy!
Thee, chauntress, oft the woods among
I woo, to hear thy even-song;
And, missing thee, I walk unseen
On the dry smooth-shaven green
To behold the wandering moon,
Riding near her highest noon,
Like one that had been led astray
Through the heaven's wide pathless way,   70
And oft, as if her head she bowed,
Stooping through a fleecy cloud.
Oft, on a plat [16] of rising ground,
I hear the far-off curfew sound,
Over some wide-watered shore,
Swinging slow with sullen roar;
Or, if the air will not permit,
Some still removèd place will fit,
Where glowing embers through the room
Teach light to counterfeit a gloom,   80
Far from all resort of mirth,
Save the cricket on the hearth,
Or the bellman's drowsy charm
To bless the doors from nightly harm.
Or let my lamp, at midnight hour,
Be seen in some high lonely tower,
Where I may oft outwatch the Bear,
With thrice great Hermes,[17] or unsphere
The spirit of Plato, to unfold
What worlds or what vast regions hold   90
The immortal mind that hath forsook
Her mansion in this fleshly nook;
And of those Dæmons that are found
In fire, air, flood, or underground,

Whose power hath a true consent[18]
With planet or with element.
Sometime let gorgeous Tragedy
In sceptred pall [19] come sweeping by,
Presenting Thebes, or Pelops' line,
Or the tale of Troy divine,   100
Or what (though rare) of later age
Ennobled hath the buskined [20] stage,
But, O sad Virgin! that thy power
Might raise Musæus [21] from his bower;
Or bid the soul of Orpheus sing
Such notes as, warbled to the string,
Drew iron tears down Pluto's cheek,
And made Hell grant what love did seek;
Or call up him [22] that left half-told
The story of Cambuscan bold,   110
Of Camball, and of Algarsife,
And who had Canace to wife,
That owned the virtuous ring and glass,
And of the wondrous horse of brass
On which the Tartar king did ride;
And if aught else great bards beside
In sage and solemn tunes have sung,
Of tourneys, and of trophies hung,
Of forests, and enchantments drear,
Where more is meant than meets the ear.   120
Thus, Night, oft see me in thy pale career,
Till civil-suited Morn appear,
Not tricked and frounced, as she was wont
With the Attic boy [23] to hunt,
But kerchieft in a comely cloud,
While rocking winds are piping loud,
Or ushered with a shower still,
When the gust hath blown his fill,
Ending on the rustling leaves,
With minute-drops [24] from off the eaves.   130
And, when the sun begins to fling
His flaring beams, me, Goddess, bring
To archèd walks of twilight groves,
And shadows brown, that Sylvan [25] loves,

18 Complete agreement; another reference to astrology.
19 Royal robe.
20 See the note on Jonson's To the Memory of . . .
Shakespeare, p. 769.
21 A mythical Greek poet, sometimes referred to as the
son of Orpheus.
22 Chaucer, who left unfinished his Squire's Tale.
23 Cephalus of Attica, of whom Eos, goddess of the dawn.
became enamored.
24 Drops falling at intervals of a minute.
25 The woodland god, Sylvanus.

13 Bring silently.   14 The nightingale.
15 The moon.   16 Plot.
17 Hermes Trismegistus, as the Greeks called the Egyptian
Thoth, the god of wisdom.

Of pine, or monumental oak,
Where the rude axe with heavèd stroke
Was never heard the nymphs to daunt,
Or fright them from their hallowed haunt.
There, in close covert, by some brook,
Where no profaner eye may look,   140
Hide me from day's garish eye,
While the bee with honeyed thigh,
That at her flowery work doth sing,
And the waters murmuring,
With such consort[26] as they keep,
Entice the dewy-feathered Sleep.
And let some strange mysterious dream
Wave at his wings, in airy stream
Of lively portraiture displayed,
Softly on my eyelids laid;   150
And, as I wake, sweet music breathe
Above, about, or underneath,
Sent by some Spirit to mortals good,
Or the unseen Genius[27] of the wood.
But let my due feet never fail
To walk the studious cloister's pale,[28]
And love the high embowèd roof,
With antique pillars massy-proof,[29]
And storied windows richly dight,
Casting a dim religious light.   160
There let the pealing organ blow,
To the full-voiced quire below,
In service high and anthems clear,
As may with sweetness, through mine ear,
Dissolve me into ecstasies,
And bring all Heaven before mine eyes.
And may at last my weary age
Find out the peaceful hermitage,
The hairy gown and mossy cell,
Where I may sit and rightly spell[30]   170
Of every star that heaven doth shew,
And every herb that sips the dew,
Till old experience do attain
To something like prophetic strain.
   These pleasures, Melancholy, give;
And I with thee will choose to live.

SONNET VII
[On his having arrived at the age of twenty-three]

How soon hath Time, the subtle thief of youth,
   Stolen on his wing my three-and-twentieth year!
My hasting days fly on with full career,
   But my late spring no bud or blossom shew'th.
Perhaps my semblance might deceive the truth
   That I to manhood am arrived so near;
   And inward ripeness doth much less appear,
   That some more timely-happy spirits endu'th.[1]
Yet, be it less or more, or soon or slow,
   It shall be still[2] in strictest measure even[3]   10
   To that same lot, however mean or high,
Toward which Time leads me, and the will of Heaven.
   All is, if I have grace to use it so,
   As ever in my great Task-Master's eye.

SONNET VIII[1]
[When the assault was intended to the city]

Captain or Colonel,[2] or Knight in Arms,
   Whose chance on these defenseless doors may seize,
   If deed of honor did thee ever please,
   Guard them, and him within protect from harms.
He can requite thee; for he knows the charms
   That call fame on such gentle acts as these,
   And he can spread thy name o'er lands and seas,
   Whatever clime the sun's bright circle warms.
Lift not thy spear against the Muses' bower:
   The great Emathian conqueror[3] bid spare   10
   The house of Pindarus, when temple and tower
Went to the ground; and the repeated air
   Of sad Electra's poet had the power
   To save the Athenian walls from ruin bare.[4]

SONNET VII
   1 Endows.   2 Always.   3 Conformable to.

SONNET VIII
   1 Composed in November, 1642, when London was expecting an assault by the Royalists after their partial victory at Edgehill. London was saved by the forces of the Earl of Essex at Turnham Green.
   2 The word "Colonel" has three syllables here.
   3 Alexander the Great. According to the legend, the conqueror spared only one house, that of the poet Pindar, when his army sacked Thebes.
   4 According to Plutarch, in his life of the Spartan general, Lysander, one of the Spartan officers dissuaded his fellows from destroying Athens by his singing of a chorus from Euripides' Electra.

IL PENSEROSO
   26 Company.   27 Guardian spirit.
   28 Enclosure.
   29 Proof against mass, strong enough to support the roof.
   30 Study, ponder.

LYCIDAS[1]

In this Monody the Author bewails a learned Friend, unfortunately drowned in his passage from Chester on the Irish Seas, 1637; and, by occasion, foretells the ruin of our corrupted clergy, then in their height.

Yet once more, O ye laurels,[2] and once more,
Ye myrtles brown,[3] with ivy never sere,
I come to pluck your berries harsh and crude,
And with forced fingers rude
Shatter your leaves before the mellowing year.[4]
Bitter constraint, and sad occasion dear[5]
Compels me to disturb your season due;
For Lycidas[6] is dead, dead ere his prime,
Young Lycidas, and hath not left his peer.
Who would not sing for Lycidas? he knew   10
Himself to sing, and build the lofty rhyme.
He must not float upon his watery bier
Unwept, and welter[7] to the parching wind,
Without the meed of some melodious tear.
    Begin, then, Sisters[8] of the sacred well
That from beneath the seat of Jove doth spring;
Begin, and somewhat loudly sweep the string.
Hence with denial vain and coy[9] excuse:
So may some gentle Muse
With lucky words favor my destined urn,   20
And as he passes turn,
And bid fair peace be to my sable shroud!
For we were nursed upon the selfsame hill,
Fed the same flock, by fountain, shade, and rill.
    Together both, ere the high lawns appeared
Under the opening eyelids of the Morn,
We drove a-field, and both together heard
What time[10] the gray-fly winds her sultry horn,
Battening our flocks with the fresh dews of night,
Oft till the star that rose, at evening, bright   30
Toward Heaven's descent had sloped his westering
    wheel.

Meanwhile the rural ditties were not mute,
Tempered to the oaten flute;
Rough Satyrs danced, and Fauns with cloven heel
From the glad sound would not be absent long;
And old Damœtas[11] loved to hear our song.
    But, oh! the heavy change, now thou art gone,
Now thou art gone and never must return!
Thee, Shepherd, thee the woods and desert caves,
With wild thyme and the gadding vine o'er-
    grown,   40
And all their echoes, mourn.
The willows, and the hazel copses green,
Shall now no more be seen
Fanning their joyous leaves to thy soft lays.
As killing as the canker[12] to the rose,
Or taint-worm to the weanling herds that graze,
Or frost to flowers, that their gay wardrobe wear,
When first the white-thorn[13] blows;
Such, Lycidas, thy loss to shepherd's ear.
    Where were ye, Nymphs,[14] when the remorse-
    less deep   50
Closed o'er the head of your loved Lycidas?
For neither were ye playing on the steep[15]
Where your old bards, the famous Druids, lie,
Nor on the shaggy top of Mona[16] high,
Nor yet where Deva[17] spreads her wizard stream.
Ay me! I fondly[18] dream
"Had ye been there," . . . for what could that
    have done?
What could the Muse[19] herself that Orpheus bore,
The Muse herself, for her enchanting son,
Whom universal nature did lament,   60
When, by the rout[20] that made the hideous roar,
His gory visage down the stream was sent,
Down the swift Hebrus to the Lesbian shore?

LYCIDAS

1 Lycidas was first published in 1638 in *Justa Edovardo King,* a volume of memorial verses on Edward King, a college mate of Milton, who was drowned off the coast of Wales, on August 10, 1637.
2 Laurel, myrtle, and ivy are evergreens with which poets were traditionally crowned.
3 Dark.
4 Before the poet's genius has been matured by time.
5 Keenly felt.
6 A typical shepherd's name in pastoral elegies.
7 Toss about. King's body was never recovered.
8 The Muses, to whom certain springs (wells) were sacred.
9 Modest.   10 Heard the gray-fly when.

11 Another type name from pastoral poetry. Possibly the reference is to some tutor at the university.
12 The canker worm.   13 The hawthorn.
14 The sea nymphs are here identified, as in other pastoral elegies, with the Muses.
15 Mountain.
16 The Roman name of the isle of Anglesey, off the Welsh coast.
17 The river Dee, which flows between England and Wales into the Irish Sea. The adjective "wizard" indicates the supernatural associations connected with the stream.
18 Foolishly.   19 Calliope, the Muse of epic poetry.
20 The band of frenzied women of Thrace who, because of Orpheus' slight to them after his loss of Eurydice, tore him in pieces.

Alas! what boots [21] it with uncessant care
To tend the homely, slighted, shepherd's trade, [22]
And strictly meditate the thankless Muse?
Were it not better done, as others use,
To sport with Amaryllis in the shade,
Or with the tangles of Neæra's hair?
Fame is the spur that the clear [23] spirit doth raise
(That last infirmity of noble mind)   71
To scorn delights, and live laborious days;
But the fair guerdon when we hope to find,
And think to burst out into sudden blaze,
Comes the blind Fury [24] with the abhorrèd shears,
And slits the thin-spun life. "But not the praise,"
Phœbus [25] replied, and touched my trembling
          ears: [26]
"Fame is no plant that grows on mortal soil,
Nor in the glistering [27] foil
Set off to the world, nor in broad rumor lies,   80
But lives and spreads aloft by those pure eyes
And perfect witness of all-judging Jove;
As he pronounces lastly on each deed,
Of so much fame in heaven expect thy meed."
O fountain Arethuse, [28] and thou honored flood,
Smooth-sliding Mincius, crowned with vocal
          reeds,
That strain I heard was of a higher mood.
But now my oat [29] proceeds,
And listens to the Herald of the Sea [30]
That came in Neptune's plea.   90
He asked the waves, and asked the felon winds,
What hard mishap hath doomed this gentle
          swain?

And questioned every gust of rugged wings
That blows from off each beakèd promontory.
They knew not of his story;
And sage Hippotades [31] their answer brings,
That not a blast was from his dungeon strayed,
The air was calm, and on the level brine
Sleek Panope [32] with all her sisters played.
It was that fatal and perfidious bark,   100
Built in the eclipse, [33] and rigged with curses dark,
That sunk so low that sacred head of thine.
    Next, Camus, [34] reverend sire, went footing
          slow,
His mantle hairy, and his bonnet sedge,
Inwrought with figures dim, and on the edge
Like to that sanguine [35] flower inscribed with woe.
"Ah! who hath reft," quoth he, "my dearest
          pledge?"
Last came, and last did go,
The Pilot of the Galilean Lake; [36]
Two massy keys he bore of metals twain   110
(The golden opes, the iron shuts amain [37]).
He shook his mitred [38] locks, and stern bespake:
"How well could I have spared for thee, young
          swain,
Anow [39] of such as, for their bellies' sake,
Creep, and intrude, and climb into the fold!
Of other care they little reckoning make
Than how to scramble at the shearers' feast,
And shove away the worthy bidden guest.
Blind mouths! that scarce themselves know
          how to hold
A sheep-hook, or have learnt aught else the
          least   120
That to the faithful herdman's art belongs!
What recks it them? What need they? They are
          sped; [40]

21 Profits.   22 The writing of poetry.
23 Pure, noble.
24 In Classical mythology it is Atropos, one of the three
Fates, who cuts the thread of life. Milton has purposely
identified the Fates with the Furies here to reinforce the idea
of the blind and senseless working of the forces which carried
young King off.
25 Apollo, god of poetic inspiration.
26 A Virgilian figure meaning to recall something to one's
mind.
27 Glittering gold or silver leaf, placed under transparent
gems to enhance their brilliance.
28 Arethusa, a spring in Sicily, the country of Theocritus,
symbolizes the Greek tradition of pastoral poetry, as Mincius,
the river near which Virgil was born, does the Latin.
29 The shepherd's pipe of oat straw.
30 Triton, the herald and agent of Neptune, who came to
present Neptune's plea of innocence of the guilt of having
drowned Lycidas.

31 Æolus, son of Hippotes, god of the winds.
32 One of the fifty Nereids, or sea nymphs.
33 The proverbial omen of ill fortune.
34 A personification of the river Cam, which flows
through Cambridge.
35 Literally, bloody. The flower referred to is the purple
hyacinth, named for the youth Hyacinthus, slain by Apollo.
The hyacinth was reputed to be marked αι, αι (Woe! Woe!).
36 St. Peter, the legendary keeper of the keys of heaven.
See St. Matthew 16:19. He is introduced here as the earthly
founder and chief pastor (shepherd) of the church, of which
young King was to have been a pastor.
37 With force.   38 Wearing a miter (as a bishop).
39 Enough.
40 They have succeeded in getting what they wanted.

And, when they list, their lean and flashy songs
Grate on their scrannel[41] pipes of wretched straw;
The hungry sheep look up, and are not fed,
But, swoln with wind and the rank mist they
    draw,
Rot inwardly, and foul contagion spread;
Besides what the grim wolf[42] with privy paw
Daily devours apace, and nothing said.
But that two-handed engine[43] at the door   130
Stands ready to smite once, and smite no more."
    Return, Alpheus;[44] the dread voice is past
That shrunk thy streams; return, Sicilian Muse,
And call the vales, and bid them hither cast
Their bells and flowerets of a thousand hues.

Ye valleys low, where the mild whispers use[45]
Of shades, and wanton winds, and gushing brooks,
On whose fresh lap the swart star[46] sparely
    looks,
Throw hither all your quaint enameled eyes,
That on the green turf suck the honeyed
    showers,   140
And purple all the ground with vernal flowers.
Bring the rathe[47] primrose that forsaken dies,
The tufted crow-toe, and pale jessamine,
The white pink, and the pansy freaked with jet,
The glowing violet,
The musk rose, and the well-attired woodbine,
With cowslips wan that hang the pensive head,
And every flower that sad embroidery wears;
Bid amaranthus all his beauty shed,
And daffadillies fill their cups with tears,   150
To strew the laureate hearse where Lycid lies.
For so, to interpose a little ease,
Let our frail thoughts dally with false surmise.

Ay me! whilst thee the shores and sounding seas
Wash far away, where'er thy bones are hurled;
Whether beyond the stormy Hebrides,
Where thou perhaps under the whelming tide
Visit'st the bottom of the monstrous world;
Or whether thou, to our moist vows denied,
Sleep'st by the fable of Bellerus old,[48]   160
Where the great Vision of the guarded mount[49]
Looks toward Namancos[50] and Bayona's hold.[50]
Look homeward, Angel, now, and melt with ruth:
And, O ye dolphins, waft the hapless youth.
    Weep no more, woeful shepherds, weep no
      more,
For Lycidas, your sorrow, is not dead,
Sunk though he be beneath the watery floor.
So sinks the day-star[51] in the ocean bed,
And yet anon repairs his drooping head,
And tricks[52] his beams, and with new-spangled
    ore   170
Flames in the forehead of the morning sky:
So Lycidas, sunk low, but mounted high,
Through the dear might of Him that walked the
    waves,
Where, other groves and other streams along,
With nectar pure his oozy locks he laves,
And hears the unexpressive[53] nuptial song,[54]
In the blest kingdoms meek of joy and love.
There entertain him all the Saints above,
In solemn troops, and sweet societies,
That sing, and singing in their glory move,   180
And wipe the tears forever from his eyes.
Now, Lycidas, the shepherds weep no more;
Henceforth thou art the Genius[55] of the shore,
In thy large recompense, and shalt be good
To all that wander in that perilous flood.
    Thus sang the uncouth[56] swain to the oaks and
      rills,
While the still Morn went out with sandals gray:
He touched the tender stops of various quills,
With eager thought warbling his Doric[57] lay:

41 Thin, harsh.   42 The Roman Catholic Church.
43 The most celebrated crux in Milton's poetry. Just what particular "engine" or instrument of reform Milton had in mind is not known. The two Houses of Parliament have been suggested, among many possible sources of reform. The figure seems to imply a sword or ax, and may have been suggested by such Biblical passages as St. Matthew 3:10 and Revelation 1:16.
44 A river whose god was the lover of Arethusa, referred to in l. 85. The invocation to Alpheus and the "Sicilian Muse" signifies the poet's return to the pastoral strain after the digression on the corruption of the church.
45 Are accustomed to dwell.
46 The Dog Star, Sirius, whose baleful influence blasts or makes "swart" the summer's flowers.
47 Early.

48 The abode of the fabulous Bellerus was Land's End, the southwestern extremity of England.
49 St. Michael's Mount in Cornwall, under the protection of the sword of St. Michael the Archangel.
50 In Spain. (Hold = stronghold).   51 The sun.
52 Dresses.   53 Inexpressible.
54 At "the marriage supper of the Lamb." See Revelation 19:9.
55 Guardian spirit.
56 In the original sense of unknown, or rustic.
57 The dialect in which the Sicilian pastoral poets wrote.

And now the sun had stretched out all the hills,
And now was dropt into the western bay;   191
At last he rose, and twitched his mantle blue:
Tomorrow to fresh woods, and pastures new.

SONGS FROM *COMUS*[1]

THE LADY

Sweet Echo, sweetest nymph, that liv'st unseen   230
    Within thy airy shell
By slow Meander's margent green,
    And in the violet-embroidered vale
    Where the love-lorn nightingale
Nightly to thee her sad song mourneth well:
Canst thou not tell me of a gentle pair
    That likest thy Narcissus are?
      O, if thou have
    Hid them in some flowery cave,
      Tell me but where,   240
    Sweet queen of parley, daughter of the sphere!
So may'st thou be translated to the skies,
And give resounding grace to all heaven's harmonies!

THE SPIRIT

    Sabrina fair,
      Listen where thou art sitting   860
    Under the glassy, cool, translucent wave,
      In twisted braids of lilies knitting
    The loose train of thy amber-dropping hair;
      Listen for dear honor's sake,
      Goddess of the silver lake,
                Listen and save!
    Listen, and appear to us,
    In name of great Oceanus.
    By the earth-shaking Neptune's mace,[2]
    And Tethys' grave majestic pace;   870
    By hoary Nereus' wrinkled look,
    And the Carpathian wizard's[3] hook;[4]
    By scaly Triton's winding shell,
    And old soothsaying Glaucus' spell;
    By Leucothea's lovely hands,
    And her son that rules the strands;

    By Thetis' tinsel-slippered feet,
    And the songs of Sirens sweet;
    By dead Parthenope's dear tomb,
    And fair Ligea's golden comb,   880
    Wherewith she sits on diamond rocks
    Sleeking her soft alluring locks;
    By all the Nymphs that nightly dance
    Upon thy streams with wily glance;
    Rise, rise, and heave thy rosy head
    From thy coral-paven bed,
    And bridle in thy headlong wave,
    Till thou our summons answered have.
                Listen and save!

Sabrina rises, attended by Water-Nymphs, and sings.

    By the rushy-fringèd bank,   890
    Where grows the willow and the osier dank,
      My sliding chariot stays,
    Thick set with agate, and the azurn sheen
    Of turkis[5] blue, and emerald green,
      That in the channel strays;
    Whilst from off the waters fleet
    Thus I set my printless feet
    O'er the cowslip's velvet head,
      That bends not as I tread.
    Gentle swain, at thy request   900
      I am here!

THE SPIRIT

    Goddess dear,
    We implore thy powerful hand
    To undo the charmèd band
    Of true virgin here distressed
    Through the force and through the wile
    Of unblest enchanter vile.

SABRINA

    Shepherd, 'tis my office best
    To help ensnarèd chastity.
    Brightest Lady, look on me.   910
    Thus I sprinkle on thy breast
    Drops that from my fountain pure
    I have kept of precious cure,
    Thrice upon thy finger's tip,
    Thrice upon thy rubied lip:

COMUS
  1 Milton entitled the poem simply, "A Mask Presented at Ludlow Castle, 1634."
  2 His trident.   3 Proteus.   4 Crook.   5 Turquoise.

Next this marble venomed seat,
Smeared with gums of glutinous heat,
I touch with chaste palms moist and cold;
Now the spell hath lost his hold;
And I must haste ere morning hour   920
To wait in Amphitrite's bower.

Sabrina descends, and the Lady rises out of her seat.

THE SPIRIT

Virgin, daughter of Locrine,
Sprung of old Anchises' line,
May thy brimmèd waves for this
Their full tribute never miss
From a thousand petty rills,
That tumble down the snowy hills;
Summer drouth or singèd air
Never scorch thy tresses fair,
Nor wet October's torrent flood   930
Thy molten crystal fill with mud;
May thy billows roll ashore
The beryl, and the golden ore;
May thy lofty head be crowned
With many a tower and terrace round,
And here and there thy banks upon
With groves of myrrh and cinnamon!

The dances ended, the Spirit epiloguizes.

To the ocean now I fly,
And those happy climes that lie
Where day never shuts his eye,
Up in the broad fields of the sky.
There I suck the liquid air,   980
All amidst the gardens fair
Of Hesperus, and his daughters three
That sing about the golden tree.
Along the crispèd[6] shades and bowers
Revels the spruce and jocund Spring;
The Graces and the rosy-bosomed Hours
Thither all their bounties bring.
That there eternal Summer dwells,
And west winds with musky wing
About the cedarn alleys fling   990
Nard[7] and cassia's balmy smells.
Iris there with humid bow
Waters the odorous banks, that blow

Flowers of more mingled hue
Than her purfled[8] scarf can shew,
And drenches with Elysian dew
(List, mortals, if your ears be true)
Beds of hyacinth and roses,
Where young Adonis oft reposes,
Waxing well of his deep wound,   1000
In slumber soft, and on the ground
Sadly sits the Assyrian queen.
But far above, in spangled sheen,
Celestial Cupid, her famed son, advanced
Holds his dear Psyche, sweet entranced
After her wandering labors long,
Till free consent the gods among
Make her his eternal bride,
And from her fair unspotted side
Two blissful twins are to be born,   1010
Youth and Joy; so Jove hath sworn.

But now my task is smoothly done,
I can fly, or I can run
Quickly to the green earth's end,
Where the bowed welkin[9] slow doth bend;
And from thence can soar as soon
To the corners of the moon.

Mortals, that would follow me,
Love Virtue; she alone is free.
She can teach ye how to climb   1020
Higher than the sphery chime;[10]
Or, if Virtue feeble were,
Heaven itself would stoop to her.

SONNET XV

On the Late Massacre in Piemont[1]

Avenge, O Lord, thy slaughtered saints, whose bones
Lie scattered on the Alpine mountains cold;
Even them who kept thy truth so pure of old,
When all our fathers worshiped stocks and stones,

---

6 Ruffled by the breeze.   7 Spikenard.

8 Decorated.   9 Sky.   10 The music of the spheres.

SONNET XV

1 "Piemont" is the French form of "Piedmont," now a part of Italy. In 1655, the Waldensians, a Protestant religious sect living in the Piedmontese Alps, were cruelly persecuted by the Duke of Savoy. A wave of indignation swept over England, which elicited official protests from Cromwell, and called forth this most vigorous of Milton's sonnets.

Forget not: in thy book record their groans
  Who were thy sheep, and in their ancient fold
  Slain by the bloody Piemontese, that rolled
  Mother with infant down the rocks. Their moans
The vales redoubled to the hills, and they
  To Heaven. Their martyred blood and ashes sow   10
  O'er all the Italian fields, where still doth sway
The triple Tyrant;[2] that from these may grow
  A hundredfold, who, having learnt thy way,
  Early may fly the Babylonian woe.[3]

SONNET XVI[1]
[On his Blindness]

When I consider how my light is spent
  Ere half my days in this dark world and wide,
  And that one talent[2] which is death to hide
  Lodged with me useless, though my soul more bent
To serve there with my Maker, and present
  My true account, lest He returning chide,
  "Doth God exact day-labor, light denied?"
  I fondly[3] ask. But Patience, to prevent

SONNET XV
  2 The Pope, who wears a tiara with three crowns.
  3 The punishment reserved for the Church of Rome. The early Protestants identified the Babylon of the Book of Revelation with the Roman Catholic Church. See Revelation 14:8, 17:5, and 18:2.

SONNET XVI
  1 This sonnet seems to have been written in the early days of Milton's blindness, and has therefore been assigned by Professor Tillyard and others to 1652, or a slightly later date.
  2 See St. Matthew 25:14-30.   3 Foolishly.

That murmur, soon replies, "God doth not need
  Either man's work or His own gifts. Who best   10
  Bear His mild yoke, they serve Him best. His state
Is kingly: thousands at His bidding speed,
  And post o'er land and ocean without rest;
  They also serve who only stand and wait."

SONNET XIX[1]
[On his Deceased Wife]

Methought I saw my late espousèd saint
  Brought to me like Alcestis from the grave,[2]
  Whom Jove's great son to her glad husband gave,
  Rescued from death by force, though pale and faint.
Mine, as whom washed from spot of child-bed taint
  Purification in the Old Law did save,[3]
  And such as yet once more I trust to have
  Full sight of her in Heaven without restraint,
Came vested all in white, pure as her mind.
  Her face was veiled; yet to my fancied sight   10
  Love, sweetness, goodness, in her person shined
So clear as in no face with more delight.
  But, oh! as to embrace me she inclined,
  I waked, she fled, and day brought back my night.

SONNET XIX
  1 This, Milton's last sonnet, has been supposed for more than two centuries to have been written about his second wife, Katherine Woodcock. Professor W. R. Parker, however, in the Review of English Studies, July, 1945, argues persuasively that Milton's first wife, Mary Powell, is the subject of the sonnet. See also Fitzroy Pyle in the Review of English Studies, XXV, 1949.
  2 Alcestis, the wife of Admetus, king of Thessaly, offered to die for her husband, but was rescued from death by Hercules, son of Zeus. Milton is thought to have had in mind the Alcestis of Euripides.
  3 See Leviticus 12:2-8.

FROM

THE CAMBRIDGE MANUSCRIPT OF MILTON'S POEMS[1]

ON THE LORD GENERAL FAIRFAX AT THE SIEGE OF COLCHESTER

Fairfax,[2] whose name in arms through Europe rings,
   Filling each mouth with envy or with praise,
   And all her jealous monarchs with amaze,
   And rumors loud that daunt remotest kings,
Thy firm unshaken virtue[3] ever brings
   Victory home, though new rebellions raise
   Their Hydra heads, and the false North[4] displays
   Her broken league to imp[5] their serpent wings.
O yet a nobler task awaits thy hand;
   For what can war but endless war still breed?   10
   Till Truth and Right from violence be freed,
And public Faith cleared from the shameful brand
   Of public Fraud. In vain doth Valor bleed,
   While Avarice and Rapine share the land.

TO THE LORD GENERAL CROMWELL, MAY, 1652

On the proposals of certain ministers at the Committee for Propagation of the Gospel

Cromwell, our chief of men, who through a cloud,
   Not of war only, but detractions rude,
   Guided by faith and matchless fortitude,
   To peace and truth thy glorious way hast plowed,

And on the neck of crownèd Fortune[1] proud
   Hast reared God's trophies, and his work pursued,
   While Darwen stream,[2] with blood of Scots imbrued,
   And Dunbar field,[3] resounds thy praises loud,
And Worcester's laureate wreath: yet much remains
   To conquer still; peace hath her victories   10
   No less renowned than war: new foes[4] arise,
Threatening to bind our souls with secular chains.
   Help us to save free conscience from the paw
   Of hireling wolves,[5] whose gospel is their maw.

TO MR. CYRIACK SKINNER UPON HIS BLINDNESS[1]

Cyriack, this three years' day[2] these eyes, though clear
   To outward view of blemish or of spot,
   Bereft of light, their seeing have forgot;
   Nor to their idle orbs doth sight appear
Of sun, or moon, or star, throughout the year,
   Or man, or woman. Yet I argue not
   Against Heaven's hand or will, nor bate a jot
   Of heart or hope; but still bear up[3] and steer

ON THE LORD GENERAL FAIRFAX

1 The three following sonnets were not published until 1694, when they appeared in imperfect versions in Edward Phillips's Life of Milton. The text of the sonnets here printed is from the Cambridge Manuscript of Milton's Poems, now preserved in the library of Trinity College, Cambridge. Many of the poems in the Manuscript are in Milton's own hand, among them the sonnet to Fairfax.

2 Sir Thomas Fairfax won decisive victories over the Royalists at Marston Moor on July 2, 1644, and at Naseby, June 14, 1645. After a siege of seventy-five days, he won the city of Colchester in August, 1648. He retired from active participation in the war shortly thereafter.

   3 Manly courage.   4 Scotland.

   5 To mend the injured wing of a falcon by grafting feathers to it.

TO THE LORD GENERAL CROMWELL

   1 A reference to the Stuarts.

   2 Cromwell defeated the Scots at the battle of Preston, which was fought on the banks of the river Darwen nearby.

   3 Cromwell defeated the Scots at Dunbar, Scotland, on September 3, 1650, and on September 3, 1651, defeated the Scottish invaders at Worcester.

   4 The Presbyterians.

   5 See St. Matthew 7:15 and Lycidas, 114–122, p. 154.

TO MR. CYRIACK SKINNER

   1 Written probably in 1655, to Cyriack Skinner, a former pupil of Milton's, who had become one of his most intimate friends.

   2 For the past three years.

   3 A nautical term: "to put the helm 'up' so as to bring the vessel into the direction of the wind." (Oxford English Dictionary.)

Right onward. What supports me, dost thou ask?
    The conscience,[4] friend, to have lost them overplied
    In Liberty's defense, my noble task,[5]   11
Of which all Europe talks from side to side.
    This thought might lead me through the world's
        vain mask
    Content, though blind, had I no better guide.

4 Consciousness.
5 The writing of his Defense of the English People, 1651, to which he had given his days and nights, despite his physicians' warnings.

Sir John Suckling

[1609–1642]

I N HIS witty "A Sessions of the Poets," Suckling describes himself as one who "loved not the Muses so well as his sport," and the casually unconcerned attitude toward both art and life reflected in the phrase accounts for the qualities of his poetry—both its intrinsic triviality and its irresistible charm. In his verse as in his life (an account of which precedes the selection from his prose), Suckling epitomizes one aspect of the Cavalier temperament as fully as his friend Lovelace epitomizes the opposed aspect. Like most of the Caroline court poets, Suckling was essentially a follower of Jonson in his poetic style, but in his work as in Carew's there is also a significant degree of imitation of Donne. Whereas Carew, however, had learned from Donne such basic elements of the Metaphysical style as argumentative structure, the intellectual conceit, and the trick of learned reference, Suckling borrowed from him—in addition to a good many lines and phrases—the tone of libertine cynicism which Donne had affected in the early elegies and the more "outrageous" of the *Songs and Sonnets*.

Suckling's witty libertinism, however, is not fully explained by influence, either Donnesque or French. Any thorough reading of his poetry reveals a restless and inquiring but skeptical mind, coming to rest finally in a radical naturalism modified only by an aristocrat's unquestioned sense of *noblesse oblige*. His mind challenges everything except his own code, and it is the persistence of that code, perhaps, which explains why his poetry is so often moving as well as amusing, and why his character is attractive as well as fascinating.

The friend of Carew and Davenant as well as of Jonson and Lovelace, Suckling achieved considerable fame in his own century, both as a poet and as a symbol. His extravagantly staged drama *Aglaura* was published in 1638, and his lyric poems appeared in two posthumous publications, the *Fragmenta Aurea* of 1646 and the *Last Remains* of 1659. The oft-quoted phrase applied to him by Millamant in Congreve's *Way of the World* remains the best summary of both the man and his verse: "Natural, easy Suckling."

SIR J. SUCKLING. *Works*, ed. A. H. Thompson (London, 1910).

F. O. HENDERSON. "Traditions of *Précieux* and *Libertin* in Suckling's Poetry," *ELH*, 4 (1937). A useful article.

K. A. McEUEN. (See under Jonson bibliography.)

FROM

FRAGMENTA AUREA [1646]

SONNET I

Dost see how unregarded now
   That piece of beauty passes?
There was a time when I did vow
     To that alone;
   But mark the fate of faces,
That red and white works now no more on me
Than if it could not charm, or I not see.

And yet the face continues good,
   And I have still desires,
Am still the selfsame flesh and blood,   10
     As apt to melt
   And suffer from those fires;
Oh! some kind power unriddle where it lies,
Whether my heart be faulty, or her eyes?

She every day her man does kill,
   And I as often die;
Neither her power, then, nor my will
     Can questioned be.
   What is the mystery?   20
Sure beauty's empires, like to greater states,
Have certain periods set, and hidden fates.

SONNET II

Of thee, kind boy, I ask no red and white,
   To make up my delight;
   No odd becoming graces,
Black eyes, or little know-not-whats in faces;
Make me but mad enough, give me good store
   Of love for her I court;
     I ask no more,
'Tis love in love that makes the sport.

There's no such thing as that we beauty call,
   It is mere cozenage all;   10
   For though some, long ago,
Liked certain colors mingled so and so,

That doth not tie me now from choosing new;
   If I a fancy take
     To black and blue,
That fancy doth it beauty make.

'Tis not the meat, but 'tis the appetite
   Makes eating a delight;
     And if I like one dish
More than another, that a pheasant is;   20
What in our watches, that in us is found,
   So to the height and nick
     We up be wound,
No matter by what hand or trick.

SONNET III

Oh! for some honest lover's ghost,[1]
     Some kind unbodied post[2]
     Sent from the shades below!
     I strangely long to know
Whether the nobler chaplets wear,
Those that their mistress' scorn did bear,
     Or those that were used kindly.

For whatsoe'er they tell us here
     To make those sufferings dear,
     'Twill there, I fear, be found   10
     That to the being crowned
To have loved alone will not suffice,
Unless we also have been wise
     And have our loves enjoyed.

What posture can we think him in,
     That here unloved again
     Departs, and is thither gone
     Where each sits by his own?
Or how can that Elysium be,
Where I my mistress still must see   20
     Circled in other's arms?

SONNET III
   1 For the inspiration of Suckling's first line see the beginning of Donne's Love's Deity, p. 748.
   2 Messenger.

For there the judges all are just,
 And Sophonisba[3] must
 Be his whom she held dear,
 Not his who loved her here;
The sweet Philoclea,[4] since she died,
Lies by her Pyrocles his side,
 Not by Amphialus.

Some bays, perchance, or myrtle bough,
 For difference crowns the brow   30
 Of those kind souls that were
 The noble martyrs here;
And if that be the only odds
(As who can tell?), ye kinder gods,
 Give me the woman here.

[THE LOVER'S CLOCK]

That none beguilèd be by Time's quick flowing,
Lovers have in their hearts a clock still going;
 For, though Time be nimble, his motions
  Are quicker
  And thicker
 Where Love hath his notions.

Hope is the mainspring on which moves desire,
And these do the less wheels, fear, joy, inspire;
 The balance is thought, evermore
  Clicking   10
  And striking,
 And ne'er giving o'er.

Occasion's the hand which still's moving round,
Till by it the critical hour may be found;
 And, when that falls out, it will strike
  Kisses,
  Strange blisses,
 And what you best like.

SONNET III
3 Daughter of the Carthaginian general Hasdrubal. She
had been betrothed by her father to the Numidian prince
Masinissa, but was later married by her father to Masinissa's
rival, Syphax. Masinissa conquered Syphax, married Sophonisba, and upon Scipio's demand for the surrender of the
lady, sent her poison, with which she immediately ended her
life.
4 In Sidney's Arcadia the Arcadian princess Philoclea is
beloved by her cousin Amphialus, but she loves and is later
wedded to the Thracian prince Pyrocles.

[THE SIEGE]

'Tis now, since I sat down before
 That foolish fort, a heart,
(Time strangely spent) a year and more,
 And still I did my part:

Made my approaches, from her hand
 Unto her lip did rise,
And did already understand
 The language of her eyes;

Proceeded on with no less art—
 My tongue was engineer;   10
I thought to undermine the heart
 By whispering in the ear.

 When this did nothing, I brought down
  Great cannon-oaths, and shot
A thousand thousand to the town;
 And still it yielded not.

I then resolved to starve the place
 By cutting off all kisses,
Praising and gazing on her face,
 And all such little blisses.   20

To draw her out, and from her strength,
 I drew all batteries in,
And brought myself to lie at length
 As if no siege had been.

When I had done what man could do
 And thought the place mine own,
The enemy lay quiet too,
 And smiled at all was done.

I sent to know from whence and where
 These hopes and this relief;   30
A spy informed, Honor was there,
 And did command in chief.

"March, march," quoth I; "the word straight give;
 Let's lose no time, but leave her;
That giant upon air will live,
 And hold it out for ever.

"To such a place our camp remove
 As will no siege abide;
I hate a fool that starves her love,
 Only to feed her pride."   40

A BALLAD UPON A WEDDING[1]

I tell thee, Dick,[2] where I have been,
Where I the rarest things have seen,
   Oh, things without compare!
Such sights again cannot be found
In any place on English ground,
   Be it at wake[3] or fair.

At Charing Cross, hard by the way
Where we (thou know'st) do sell our hay
   There is a house with stairs;
And there I did see coming down   10
Such folk as are not in our town,
   Vorty,[4] at least, in pairs.

Amongst the rest, one pestilent fine
(His beard no bigger, though, than thine)
   Walked on before the rest.
Our landlord looks like nothing to him;
The King (God bless him!), 'twould undo him
   Should he go still[5] so dressed.

At course-a-park,[6] without all doubt,
He should have been the first taken out   20
   By all the maids i' the town,
Though lusty Roger there had been,
Or little George upon the Green,
   Or Vincent of the Crown.

But wot you what? the youth was going
To make an end of all his wooing;
   The parson for him stayed.
Yet by his leave, for all his haste,
He did not so much wish all past,
   Perchance, as did the maid.   30

The maid—and thereby hangs a tale;
For such a maid no Whitsun-ale[7]
   Could ever yet produce;
No grape, that's kindly[8] ripe, could be
So round, so plump, so soft as she,
   Nor half so full of juice.

Her finger was so small the ring
Would not stay on, which they did bring;
   It was too wide a peck:
And to say truth (for out it must),   40
It looked like the great collar (just)
   About our young colt's neck.

Her feet beneath her petticoat,
Like little mice stole in and out,
   As if they feared the light;
But oh, she dances such a way,
No sun upon an Easter day
   Is half so fine a sight!

He would have kissed her once or twice,
But she would not, she was so nice,   50
   She would not do't in sight;
And then she looked as who should say,
"I will do what I list today,
   And you shall do't at night."

Her cheeks so rare a white was on,
No daisy makes comparison
   (Who sees them is undone),
For streaks of red were mingled there,
Such as are on a Katherne[9] pear
   (The side that's next the sun).   60

Her lips were red, and one was thin
Compared to that was next her chin
   (Some bee had stung it newly);
But, Dick, her eyes so guard her face
I durst no more upon them gaze
   Than on the sun in July.

A BALLAD

1 This poem was probably written for the marriage of Roger Boyle, Baron Broghill, and the Lady Margaret Howard in 1641. The artistry and ingenuity with which the courtly author has identified himself with a naïve and hearty rustic have delighted readers for three centuries.

2 It has been suggested that "Dick" may be Suckling's friend, Richard Lovelace, but it is more likely a type name for a rustic.

3 See note on p. 809.   4 Rustic dialect for *forty*.

5 Always.

6 "A country game in which a girl called out one of the other sex to chase her." (Oxford English Dictionary.)

7 A country merry-making held at Whitsuntide, fifty days after Easter.

8 Naturally, fully, ripe.

9 The Catherine pear, a small and early variety.

Her mouth so small, when she does speak,
Thou'dst swear her teeth her words did break,
   That they might passage get;
But she so handled still the matter,   70
They came as good as ours, or better,
   And are not spent a whit.

If wishing should be any sin,
The parson himself had guilty been
   (She looked that day so purely);
And did the youth so oft the feat
At night, as some did in conceit,
   It would have spoiled him, surely.

Passion o' me, how I run on![10]
There's that that would be thought upon,   80
   I trow, besides the bride.
The business of the kitchen's great,
For it is fit that man should eat,
   Not was it there denied.

Just in the nick the cook knocked thrice,
And all the waiters in a trice
   His summons did obey;
Each serving-man, with dish in hand,
Marched boldly up, like our trained band,[11]
   Presented, and away.   90

When all the meat was on the table,
What man of knife or teeth was able
   To stay to be entreated?
And this the very reason was—
Before the parson could say grace,
   The company was seated.

Now hats fly off, and youths carouse;
Healths first go round, and then the house;
   The bride's[12] came thick and thick:
And when 'twas named another's health,   100
Perhaps he made it hers by stealth;
   And who could help it, Dick?

O' the sudden up they rise and dance;
Then sit again and sigh and glance;
   Then dance again and kiss;
Thus several ways the time did pass,
Whilst every woman wished her place,
   And every man wished his!

By this time all were stolen aside
To counsel and undress the bride,   110
   But that he must not know;
But yet 'twas thought he guessed her mind,
And did not mean to stay behind
   Above an hour or so.

When in he came, Dick, there she lay
Like new-fallen snow melting away
   ('Twas time, I trow, to part);
Kisses were now the only stay,
Which soon she gave, as who would say,
   "God be with ye, with all my heart."   120

But just as heavens would have, to cross it,
In came the bridesmaids with the posset.
   The bridegroom eat in spite,
For had he left the women to't,
It would have cost two hours to do't,
   Which were too much that night.

At length the candle's out, and now
All that they had not done, they do.
   What that is, who can tell?
But I believe it was no more   130
Than thou and I have done before
   With Bridget and with Nell.

10 The order of the 1648 and other later editions is followed here. In the 1646 edition this stanza with the two halves inverted appears after l. 96.
11 The militia.
12 The bride's health.

FROM

THE LAST REMAINS OF SIR JOHN SUCKLING [1659]

[OUT UPON IT! I HAVE LOVED]

Out upon it! I have loved
  Three whole days together;
And am like to love three more,
  If it prove fair weather.

Time shall moult away his wings,
  Ere he shall discover
In the whole wide world again
  Such a constant lover.

But the spite on't is, no praise
  Is due at all to me: 10
Love with me had made no stays
  Had it any been but she.

Had it any been but she,
  And that very face,
There had been at least ere this
  A dozen dozen in her place.

SONG

I prithee send me back my heart,
  Since I cannot have thine;
For if from yours you will not part,
  Why then shouldst thou have mine?

Yet now I think on't, let it lie,
  To find it were in vain;
For th' hast a thief in either eye
  Would steal it back again.

Why should two hearts in one breast lie,
  And yet not lodge together?   10
O love, where is thy sympathy,
  If thus our breasts thou sever?

But love is such a mystery
  I cannot find it out;
For when I think I'm best resolved,
  I then am most in doubt.

Then farewell care, and farewell woe,
  I will no longer pine;
For I'll believe I have her heart
  As much as she hath mine.   20

A SOLDIER

I am a man of war and might,
And know thus much, that I can fight,
Whether I am in the wrong or right,
      Devoutly.

No woman under heaven I fear,
New oaths I can exactly swear,
And forty healths my brain will bear
      Most stoutly.

I cannot speak, but I can do
As much as any of our crew,   10
And, if you doubt it, some of you
      May prove me.

I dare be bold thus much to say,
If that my bullets do but play,
You would be hurt so night and day,
      Yet love me.

SONGS FROM THE PLAYS

SONG

Why so pale and wan, fond lover?
    Prithee, why so pale?
Will, when looking well can't move her,
    Looking ill prevail?
    Prithee, why so pale?

Why so dull and mute, young sinner?
    Prithee, why so mute?
Will, when speaking well can't win her,
    Saying nothing do't?
    Prithee, why so mute?   10

Quit, quit, for shame; this will not move,
    This cannot take her.
If of herself she will not love,
    Nothing can make her:
    The devil take her!
                —Aglaura, 1646

SONG

No, no, fair heretic, it needs must be
    But an ill love in me,
    And worse for thee.
For were it in my power
To love thee now this hour
    More than I did the last,
'Twould then so fall
    I might not love at all.
Love that can flow, and can admit increase,
Admits as well an ebb, and may grow less.   10

True love is still the same; the torrid zones
    And those more frigid ones,
    It must not know;
For love, grown cold or hot,
Is lust or friendship, not
    The thing we have;
For that's a flame would die,
    Held down or up too high.
Then think I love more than I can express,
And would love more, could I but love thee
    less.   20
                —Aglaura

A SONG TO A LUTE[1]

Hast thou seen the down in the air,
    When wanton blasts have tossed it?
Or the ship on the sea,
    When ruder waves have crossed it?
Hast thou marked the crocodile's weeping
    Or the fox's sleeping?
Or hast viewed the peacock in his pride,
    Or the dove by his bride,
    When he courts for his lechery?
O, so fickle, O, so vain, O, so false, so false is she!
                —The Sad One, 1659

SONG TO A LUTE
1 The poem is a parody on the third stanza of Jonson's
Her Triumph, p. 765.

James Graham,

FIRST MARQUIS OF MONTROSE

[1612–1650]

T
O AN even greater extent than Shirley or Felltham, the Marquis of Montrose is remembered for a single lyric—"My dear and only Love," which surely counts as the definitive expression of royalist fervor, the personal devotion of the aristocrat to his feudal liege lord.

Montrose's few lyrics are sparks struck off from a gallant and chivalrous life of action. The leading royalist general in Scotland, he was for some time astonishingly successful in defeating the parliamentary forces. After the execution of Charles I, he led an unsuccessful counterrebellion for the exiled Charles II. On its suppression, he was hanged, drawn, and quartered in Edinburgh.

J. GRAHAM, Marquis of Montrose. *Poems*, ed. J. L. Weir (London, 1938).

J. BUCHAN. *The Life of Montrose* (Boston, rev. ed., 1928).

[MY DEAR AND ONLY LOVE]

My dear and only Love, I pray
  This noble world of thee
Be governed by no other sway
  But purest monarchy;
For if confusion have a part,
  Which virtuous souls abhor,
And hold a synod in thy heart,
  I'll never love thee more.

Like Alexander I will reign,
  And I will reign alone: 10
My thoughts shall evermore disdain
  A rival on my throne.
He either fears his fate too much,
  Or his deserts are small,
That puts it not unto the touch
  To win or lose it all.

But I must rule and govern still,
  And always give the law,
And have each subject at my will,
  And all to stand in awe.   20
But 'gainst my battery, if I find
  Thou shunn'st the prize so sore
As that thou sett'st me up a blind,
  I'll never love thee more.

Or in the empire of thy heart,
  Where I should solely be,
Another do pretend a part
  And dares to vie with me;
Or if committees thou erect,
  And go on such a score,   30
I'll sing and laugh at thy neglect,
  And never love thee more.

But if thou wilt be constant then,
  And faithful of thy word,
I'll make thee glorious by my pen
  And famous by my sword:
I'll serve thee in such noble ways
  Was never heard before;
I'll crown and deck thee all with bays,
  And love thee evermore.   40
  —*A Choice Collection of Comic and Serious*
  Scots Poems, III, 1711

Samuel Butler

[1612–1680]

IT IS easy to see the weaknesses of *Hudibras*, the single work for which Samuel Butler is remembered. Much too long, this satirical verse narrative lacks both form and focus; modeled on *Don Quixote*, it has not a trace of the wisdom and humanity of Cervantes' masterpiece. Indeed, even if it is compared with the other work which influenced it, Cleveland's "The Rebel Scot," it seems crude in both attitude and technique. And the objects of its satire seem arbitrarily thrown together: there is, after all, no intrinsic connection among Puritanism, mystical philosophy, and chivalric love; they are related only to the extent that all three phenomena struck Butler as ridiculous and pernicious.

Nevertheless, *Hudibras* counts as the most important English political satire before Dryden—perhaps because of the sheer intensity of its high-spirited comic invention, perhaps because the author's eccentric rhyming technique raises doggerel itself to the level of art. To England in the 1660's, reacting against a decade of civil war and a decade of Puritan rule, none of its defects were obvious; Charles II enjoyed heartily this blunderbuss attack on his enemies, and court and country followed suit. Despite the quantity of necessary footnotes, the modern reader can share their enjoyment—provided that he takes his *Hudibras* in small doses.

Butler was born in Worcestershire and is said to have attended Cambridge briefly. Subsequently he served in the household of the Countess of Kent, then as clerk to a Presbyterian justice of the peace named Sir Samuel Luke, the alleged model for Sir Hudibras. Part I of the satire was published in 1663, Part II in 1664, and Part III in 1678. Butler wrote nothing else of significance except for a group of excellent prose characters which were not collected and published until the eighteenth century. Despite a pension from the king and the admiration of the court wits, Butler died in relative want. He has his final historical importance as one of the transitional figures between the age of Metaphysical poetry and the age of Augustan satire.

S. BUTLER. *Hudibras*, ed. A. R. Waller (Cambridge, 1905).
J. VELDKAMP. *Samuel Butler, The Author of Hudibras* (Hilversum, 1923).
E. A. RICHARDS. *Hudibras and the Burlesque Tradition* (New York, 1937).
I. JACK. *Augustan Satire* (Oxford, 1952). Contains a good essay on *Hudibras*.

FROM

HUDIBRAS [1678]

PART I

from CANTO I

WHEN civil fury first grew high,
    And men fell out, they knew not why;
When hard words, jealousies, and fears
Set folks together by the ears
And made them fight, like mad or drunk,
For Dame Religion as for punk,
Whose honesty they all durst swear for,
Though not a man of them knew wherefore;
When gospel-trumpeter, surrounded
With long-eared rout, to battle sounded,   10
And pulpit, drum ecclesiastic,
Was beat with fist instead of a stick;—
Then did Sir Knight abandon dwelling,
And out he rode a-coloneling.
    A wight he was whose very sight would
Entitle him Mirror of Knighthood;
That never bent his stubborn knee [1]
To anything but chivalry,
Nor put up blow but that which laid
Right Worshipful on shoulder-blade; [2]   20
Chief of domestic knights and errant,
Either for chartel [3] or for warrant;
Great on the bench, great in the saddle,
That could as well bind o'er as swaddle: [4]
Mighty he was at both of these,
And styled of war as well as peace.
(So some rats of amphibious nature
Are either for the land or water.)
But here our authors make a doubt
Whether he were more wise or stout.   30

CANTO I

1 An allusion to the refusal of the Presbyterians to kneel
at the Sacrament of the Lord's Supper.
2 I.e., he would permit no blow to pass unrevenged except
the one on his shoulder by which the king knighted him.
3 A challenge.
4 The meaning probably is that he could either make peace
by settling disputes among his neighbors, or, if they could
not agree, bind them over to the court for trial.

Some hold the one and some the other;
But howsoe'er they make a pother,
The difference was so small his brain
Outweighed his rage but half a grain;
Which made some take him for a tool
That knaves do work with, called a fool.
And offer to lay wagers that
As Montaigne, playing with his cat,
Complains she thought him but an ass,
Much more she would Sir Hudibras   40
(For that's the name our valiant knight
To all his challenges did write);
But they're mistaken very much,
'Tis plain enough he was no such.
We grant, although he had much wit,
He was very shy of using it;
As being loth to wear it out,
And therefore bore it not about,
Unless on holidays, or so
As men their best apparel do.   50
Beside, 'tis known he could speak Greek
As naturally as pigs squeak;
That Latin was no more difficile
Than to a blackbird 'tis to whistle.
Being rich in both, he never scanted
His bounty unto such as wanted,
But much of either would afford
To many that had not one word.
For Hebrew roots, although they're found
To flourish most in barren ground,   60
He had such plenty as sufficed
To make some think him circumcised;
And truly so perhaps he was,
'Tis many a pious Christian's case.
He was in logic a great critic,
Profoundly skilled in analytic:
He could distinguish and divide
A hair 'twixt south and southwest side;
On either which he would dispute,
Confute, change hands, and still confute: 70
He'd undertake to prove, by force
Of argument, a man's no horse;
He'd prove a buzzard is no fowl,
And that a lord may be an owl,

A calf an alderman, a goose a justice,
And rooks committee-men and trustees.[5]
He'd run in debt by disputation,
And pay with ratiocination.
All this by syllogism true,
In mood and figure, he would do.   80
      For rhetoric, he could not ope
His mouth but out there flew a trope;
And when he happened to break off
In the middle of his speech, or cough,
He had hard words ready to show why,
And tell what rules he did it by.
Else, when with greatest art he spoke,
You'd think he talked like other folk;
For all a rhetorician's rules
Teach nothing but to name his tools.   90
His ordinary rate of speech
In loftiness of sound was rich,
A Babylonish dialect,
Which learned pedants much affect.
It was a parti-colored dress
Of patched and piebald languages:
'Twas English cut on Greek and Latin,
Like fustian heretofore on satin.[6]
It had an odd promiscuous tone,
As if he'd talked three parts in one;   100
Which made some think, when he did gabble,
They'd heard three laborers of Babel,
Or Cerberus himself pronounce
A leash of languages at once.
This he as volubly would vent
As if his stock would ne'er be spent;
And truly, to support that charge,
He had supplies as vast and large.
For he could coin or counterfeit
New words with little or no wit;   110
Words so debased and hard no stone
Was hard enough to touch them on.
And when with hasty noise he spoke 'em,
The ignorant for current took 'em;
That had the orator,[7] who once
Did fill his mouth with pebble-stones
When he harangued, but known his phrase,
He would have used no other ways.

In mathematics he was greater
Than Tycho Brahe or Erra Pater:[8]   120
For he, by geometric scale,
Could take the size of pots of ale;
Resolve by sines and tangents, straight,
If bread or butter wanted weight;
And wisely tell what hour o' the day
The clock does strike, by algebra.
      Beside, he was a shrewd philosopher,
And had read every text and gloss over;
Whate'er the crabbed'st author hath,
He understood by implicit faith;   130
Whatever sceptic could inquire for;
For every why he had a wherefore;
Knew more than forty of them do,
As far as words and terms could go:
All which he understood by rote
And, as occasion served, would quote,
No matter whether right or wrong;
They might be either said or sung.
His notions fitted things so well
That which was which he could not tell,   140
But oftentimes mistook the one
For th' other, as great clerks have done.
He could reduce all things to acts,
And knew their natures by abstracts;
Where entity and quiddity,
The ghosts of defunct bodies, fly;[9]
Where truth in person does appear,
Like words congealed in northern air.
He knew what's what, and that's as high
As metaphysic wit can fly.   150
In school-divinity as able
As he that hight Irrefragable;[10]
Profound in all the nominal
And real ways beyond them all;
And with as delicate a hand
Could twist as tough a rope of sand,
And weave fine cobwebs, fit for skull
That's empty when the moon is full;
Such as take lodgings in a head
That's to be let unfurnishèd.   160

5 Persons appointed by Parliament to act in certain matters pertaining to property and lands in the counties.
6 The coarse fustian had holes cut in it so that the satin underneath might show through.
7 Demosthenes cured the defect in his speech by practicing speaking with pebbles in his mouth.

8 Butler's name for the famous astrologer, William Lilly, who was held in high esteem by the House of Commons.
9 Butler is satirizing the over-subtle distinctions of medieval philosophers with respect to body, entity, and substance; particularly of those who maintained that entity and substance may remain after the body has perished.
10 Alexander Hales, an English metaphysician of the thirteenth century, was called the "Irrefragable (i.e., invincible) Doctor" because of his irresistible arguments.

He could raise scruples dark and nice,
And after solve 'em in a trice;
As if divinity had catched
The itch, of purpose to be scratched,
Or, like a mountebank, did wound
And stab herself with doubts profound,
Only to show with how small pain
The sores of faith are cured again;
Although by woeful proof we find
They always leave a scar behind.   170
He knew the seat of Paradise,
Could tell in what degree it lies;
And, as he was disposed, could prove it
Below the moon, or else above it;
What Adam dreamt of when his bride
Came from her closet in his side;
Whether the devil tempted her
By a High Dutch interpreter;[11]
If either of them had a navel;
Who first made music malleable:[12]   180
Whether the serpent at the Fall
Had cloven feet or none at all:
All this without a gloss or comment
He would unriddle in a moment,
In proper terms, such as men smatter
When they throw out, and miss the matter.
    For his religion, it was fit
To match his learning and his wit:
'Twas Presbyterian true blue,
For he was of that stubborn crew   190
Of errant saints whom all men grant
To be the true church militant:
Such as do build their faith upon
The holy text of pike and gun;
Decide all controversies by
Infallible artillery,
And prove their doctrine orthodox
By apostolic blows and knocks;
Call fire, and sword, and desolation
A godly, thorough reformation,   200
Which always must be carried on
And still be doing, never done;
As if religion were intended
For nothing else but to be mended.

A sect whose chief devotion lies
In odd, perverse antipathies;
In falling out with that or this,
And finding somewhat still amiss;
More peevish, cross, and splenetic
Than dog distract or monkey sick;   210
That with more care keep holy day
The wrong, than others the right way;
Compound for sins they are inclined to
By damning those they have no mind to;
Still so perverse and opposite
As if they worshiped God for spite.
The selfsame thing they will abhor
One way and long another for.
Free will they one way disavow,
Another, nothing else allow;   220
All piety consists therein
In them, in other men all sin.
Rather than fail, they will defy
That which they love most tenderly;
Quarrel with minced pies, and disparage
Their best and dearest friend, plum porridge;
Fat pig and goose itself oppose,
And blaspheme custard through the nose.
Th' apostles of this fierce religion,
Like Mahomet's, were ass[13] and widgeon,[14] 230
To whom our knight by fast instinct
Of wit and temper was so linked,
As if hypocrisy and nonsense
Had got the advowson of his conscience.

   .   .   .   .

A squire he had whose name was Ralph,   455
That in the adventure went his half.
Though writers, for more statelier tone,
Do call him *Ralpho*, 'tis all one;
And when we can with meter safe
We'll call him so, if not plain *Raph;*   460
For rhyme the rudder is of verses,
With which, like ships, they steer their courses.
An equal stock of wit and valor
He had laid in, by birth a tailor.

---

11 A satirical thrust at the theory of Goropius Becanus
that High Dutch was the language spoken by Adam and Eve.

12 A reference to Pythagoras's experiments on sounds,
first suggested to him by his hearing the sounds from the
hammer (Lat., *malleus*) in a smith's shop.

13 "Ass" refers to the *alborach*, the creature upon which
Mahomet said he rode on his night journey to heaven.

14 The reference is, presumably, to the tame pigeon that
Mahomet taught to pick seeds out of his ear, and so cause it
to be believed that he was inspired by the Holy Spirit.

The mighty Tyrian queen[15] that gained
With subtle shreds a tract of land,
Did leave it, with a castle fair,
To his great ancestor, her heir.
From him descended cross-legged knights,[16]
Famed for their faith and warlike fights 470
Against the bloody cannibal,
Whom they destroyed, both great and small.
This sturdy squire had as well
As the bold Trojan knight, seen hell,
Not with a counterfeited pass
Of golden bough,[17] but true gold lace.
His knowledge was not far behind
The knight's, but of another kind,
And he another way came by it;
Some call it *Gift*, and some *New Light*,[18] 480
A liberal art, that costs no pains
Of study, industry, or brains.
His wits were sent him for a token,
But in the carriage cracked and broken
Like commendation ninepence,[19] crookt
With—*To and from my Love*—it looked.
He ne'er considered it, as loth
To look a gift-horse in the mouth;
And very wisely would lay forth
No more upon it than 'twas worth. 490
But as he got it freely, so
He spent it frank and freely too;
For saints themselves will sometimes be,
Of gifts that cost them nothing, free.
By means of this, with hem and cough,
Prolongers to enlightened snuff,
He could deep mysteries unriddle
As easily as thread a needle;

For as of vagabonds we say
That they are ne'er beside their way, 500
Whate'er men speak by this *New Light*,
Still they are sure to be i' the right.
'Tis a dark lantern of the spirit,
Which none see by but those that bear it;
A light that falls down from on high
For spiritual trades to cozen by;
An *ignis fatuus* that bewitches,
And leads men into pools and ditches
To make them dip themselves, and sound
For Christendom in dirty pond; 510
To dive, like wild fowl, for salvation,
And fish to catch regeneration.
This light inspires, and plays upon
The nose of saint like bagpipe drone,
And speaks through hollow, empty soul
As through a trunk or whispering hole,
Such language as no mortal ear
But spiritual eavesdroppers can hear.
So Phœbus or some friendly Muse
Into small poets song infuse, 520
Which they at second hand rehearse
Through reed or bagpipe, verse for verse.
Thus Ralph became infallible
As three- or four-legged oracle,[20]
The ancient cup,[21] or modern chair,[22]
Spoke truth point-blank, though unaware
For mystic learning, wondrous able
In magic, talisman, and cabal,
Whose primitive tradition reaches
As far as Adam's first green breeches;[23] 530
Deep-sighted in intelligences,
Ideas, atoms, influences,
And much of *terra incognita*,
The intelligible world,[24] could say;
A deep occult philosopher,
As learned as the wild Irish are,

15 The allusion is to Dido, Queen of Carthage, who, in Virgil's Æneid, purchased as much land as she could surround with an ox's hide. She shrewdly cut the hide into thin strips and· obtained a tract with a circumference of more than twenty furlongs.

16 Knights who had been on the Crusades had effigies with legs crossed on their tombs; tailors usually sit with crossed legs at their work.

17 Æneas, "the Trojan knight," gave a golden bough to Proserpine to gain admittance to Hades to see his father Anchises. The tailor repaired frequently to a container, called hell, under the board on which he sat, where he kept pieces of stolen gold lace, etc.

18 References to the special inspiration claimed by Independents and Anabaptists.

19 A bent ninepenny piece of silver was a common love token.

20 A reference to the three-legged stool, or *tripos*, upon which the priestess at Delphi sat when she uttered her oracles. The "four-legged oracle" may refer to divination by quadrupeds.

21 Joseph's divining cup. See Genesis 44:5.

22 The Pope's chair.

23 In the Geneva Bible, the version commonly used by the Puritans, Genesis 3:7 reads, "And they sewed fig-tree leaves together, and made themselves breeches."

24 A satirical jibe at the world of the philosophers, in which, like parrots, men talk of what they do not understand.

Or Sir Agrippa,[25] for profound
And solid lying much renowned.
He Anthroposophus,[26] and Fludd,[27]
And Jacob Behmen[28] understood;   540
Knew many an amulet and charm
That would do neither good nor harm;
In Rosicrucian lore[29] as learned
As he that *verè adeptus*[30] earned.
He understood the speech of birds
As well as they themselves do words:
Could tell what subtlest parrots mean,
That speak and think contrary clean;
What member 'tis of whom they talk
When they cry "Rope," and "Walk, knave,
     walk."   550
He'd extract numbers out of matter
And keep them in a glass, like water
Of sovereign power to make men wise:
For, dropped in blear thick-sighted eyes,
They'd make them see in darkest night,
Like owls, though purblind in the light.
By help of these, as he professed,
He had first matter seen undressed.
He took her naked, all alone,
Before one rag of form was on.   560
The chaos, too, he had decried
And seen quite through, or else he lied:

Not that of pasteboard, which men show
For groats at fair of Barthol'mew;[31]
But its great grandsire, first o' the name,
Whence that and Reformation came;
Both cousin-germans, and right able
T' inveigle and draw in the rabble.
But Reformation was, some say,
O' the younger house to puppet-play.[32]   570
He could foretell whatsoever was
By consequence to come to pass:
As death of great men, alterations,
Diseases, battles, inundations,
All this without th' eclipse of sun,
Or dreadful comet, he hath done
By inward light, a way as good,
And easy to be understood,
But with more lucky hit than those
That use to make the stars depose,   580
Like knights o' the post,[33] and falsely charge
Upon themselves what others forge,
As if they were consenting to
All mischief in the world men do;
Or, like the devil, did tempt and sway 'em
To rogueries and then betray 'em.
They'll search a planet's house to know
Who broke and robbed a house below;
Examine Venus and the moon,
Who stole a thimble and a spoon;   590
And though they nothing will confess,
Yet by their very looks can guess
And tell what guilty aspect bodes,
Who stole, and who received the goods.
They'll question Mars, and by his look
Detect who 'twas that nimmed a cloak;
Make Mercury confess and 'peach
Those thieves which he himself did teach.[34]
They'll find in the physiognomies
O' the planets all men's destinies;   600

25 Cornelius Agrippa, an occult philosopher, who became secretary to the Emperor Maximilian and counselor to the Emperor Charles V.

26 *Anthroposophus*, meaning "one wise in the knowledge of men," was a nickname given to Thomas Vaughan, brother of Henry Vaughan the poet, who was the author of an exceedingly occult treatise on the state of man after death called *Anthroposophia Theomagica*. Thomas Vaughan was an ardent student of Cornelius Agrippa. Butler is referring to Vaughan in ll. 529, 530 above, with respect to Vaughan's maintaining in his *Magia Adamica* that the learning of the Magi was derived from the knowledge that God had imparted to Adam in Paradise. Thomas Vaughan had considerable influence on the philosophy of Henry Vaughan.

27 Robert Fludd, an occult philosopher of wide learning, wrote an apology for the Rosicrucians.

28 Jacob Behmen (or Boehme), a mystical philosopher, was the founder of a sect called the Behmenists.

29 The Rosicrucians were members of a secret and occult philosophical society, the origins of which are disputed but certainly of great antiquity, and certain branches or societies of which still exist.

30 The title assumed by certain alchemists who pretended to have found the philosopher's stone. They were commonly called Adept Philosophers.

31 Bartholomew Fair, held in West Smithfield, London, was the most famous of the medieval fairs, and continued, with many changes for the worse, until 1855. Among its most popular exhibits in the seventeenth century were the puppet-shows, portraying Biblical scenes and ideas such as the chaos, the creation, the flood, etc.

32 *I.e.*, those who claimed to act by inner light were like puppets moved by a superior force.

33 Dishonest persons who waited around courts of justice to be hired to give evidence about matters of which they knew nothing.

34 Mercury was the patron or god of thieves, and was represented often with a purse in his hand.

Like him that took the doctor's bill
And swallowed it instead o' the pill;
Cast the nativity o' the question,
And from positions to be guessed on,
As sure as if they knew the moment
Of native's birth, tell what will come on't.[35]
They'll feel the pulses of the stars
To find out agues, coughs, catarrhs,
And tell what crisis does divine
The rot in sheep, or mange in swine;   610
In men what gives or cures the itch,
What makes them cuckolds, poor or rich;

35 Astrologers, when inquired of concerning the future of
a child, were thought to be able to forecast the future from
the position of the stars at the moment the question was
asked if the inquirer did not know the exact moment of the
child's birth.

What gains or loses, hangs or saves;
What makes men great, what fools or knaves;
But not what wise, for only of those
The stars, they say, cannot dispose,
No more than can the astrologians:
There they say right, and like true Trojans.
This Ralpho knew, and therefore took
The other course, of which we spoke.   620
    Thus was th' accomplished knight endued
With gifts and knowledge per'lous shrewd.
Never did trusty squire with knight,
Or knight with squire, jump more right.
Their arms and equipage did fit,
As well as virtues, parts, and wit.
Their valors, too, were of a rate,
And out they sallied at the gate. . . .

Richard Crashaw

[1612?–1649]

RICHARD CRASHAW is unique among the major English Metaphysical poets, both in his Roman Catholic faith and in his consistent adherence to a set of artistic conventions more Continental than English. In particular, he is the chief English exponent of the poetic style variously known as *marinismo*, *secentismo*, and "High Baroque," which resembles the more familiar Metaphysical style in its ingenuity, theatricality, and reliance on surprise, but which differs from it in its emphasis on sensuous imagery, its associational structure, and its heavy use of oxymoron and catachresis. It is a style which is historically linked with Counter-Reformation Catholicism, and Crashaw's ultimate conversion to that religion may be regarded as the fulfillment of a sensibility which had always been implicitly Catholic.

Born in London, Crashaw was the son of the fiercely anti-Catholic clergyman William Crashaw. He was educated at the Charterhouse School and at Pembroke College, Cambridge, from which he received his B.A. in 1634, becoming a fellow of Peterhouse College in the next year. While still an undergraduate he became a close friend of the poet Cowley, and his fellowship at Peterhouse, noted as a center of High Church feeling, led to his becoming familiar with Nicholas Ferrar and the lay religious community at Little Gidding, anathematized by the Puritans as "the Arminian nunnery."

With the triumph of the Parliamentarians, Crashaw, together with many others of the High Church persuasion, was expelled from his fellowship and went into exile on the Continent. After a brief and unhappy residence in Leiden in Holland and after a return to England, he went to Paris, where he embraced Catholicism. Through the good offices of the exiled queen of Charles I, he was introduced to the Pope and eventually received an ecclesiastical post at the shrine of Loreto in Italy. Here, shortly after his appointment, he died.

Crashaw's first important English poems appeared in *Steps to the Temple, with Other Delights of the Muses*, first published in 1646, and reissued in an expanded and revised edition in 1648. The posthumous *Carmen Deo Nostro* (Paris, 1652) consists largely of revisions of the earlier poems, for Crashaw was a tireless polisher of his work, and the work itself, with its sensuous and decorative texture, lends itself to almost unlimited expansion.

Despite the tribute to Herbert expressed in the title of his first volume, Crashaw's poems owe almost nothing to the parson of Bemerton, with his moderation, control, and sense of structure. Indeed, Crashaw's poems, in their bold application of sexual imagery to devotional themes and in their frequent expression of a kind of sado-masochistic rapture, are liable to tempt the twentieth-century reader into psychological conjectures scarcely supported by our slender knowledge of Crashaw's emotional life. The cautious reader will be wary of such conjectures—not only because of the relative absence of external data but also because of the nature of Crashaw's self-conscious and sophisticated art, an art which, as a study of the Continental literatures will convince us, was capable of going deliberately to emotional extremes in order to give tangible form to its spiritual and intellectual visions.

Crashaw is an uneven poet, and even at his best he is likely to offend the sensibility of a reader trained exclusively in the traditions of English and American poetry. For the sophisticated reader, however, or for the reader who will absorb imaginatively the frame of reference within which Crashaw works, the best of his poems—"Charitas Nimia," "To the Countess of Denbigh," or the great hymns to Saint Teresa—constitute an inimitable and unforgettable fusion of the traditions of Metaphysical devotional verse with the wider traditions of European Baroque art.

R. CRASHAW. *Poems*, ed. L. C. Martin (Oxford, 1927).

A. WARREN. *Richard Crashaw: A Study in Baroque Sensibility* (Baton Rouge, La., 1939; paperback: Ann Arbor, Mich., 1957).

R. C. WALLERSTEIN. *Richard Crashaw: A Study in Style and Poetic Development* (Madison, Wis., 1935; paperback, 1959).

M. PRAZ. *The Flaming Heart* (New York, 1958). Contains an excellent essay on Crashaw.

F. J. WARNKE. *European Metaphysical Poetry* (New Haven, 1961). Examines some of the relations between Metaphysical and High Baroque poetry.

N. F. BERTONASCO. *Crashaw and the Baroque* (University, Ala., 1971).

R. T. PETERSSON. *The Art of Ecstasy* (New York, 1970).

M. E. RICKEY. *Rhyme and Meaning in Richard Crashaw* (Lexington, Ky., 1961).

G. W. WILLIAMS. *Image and Symbol in the Sacred Poetry of Richard Crashaw* (Columbia, S.C., 1963).

F R O M

THE DELIGHTS OF THE MUSES [1648]

WISHES TO HIS (SUPPOSED) MISTRESS

Whoe'er she be,
That not impossible she,
That shall command my heart and me;

Where'er she lie,
Locked up from mortal eye,
In shady leaves of destiny,

Till that ripe birth
Of studied fate stand forth,
And teach[1] her fair steps to our earth;

Till that divine   10
Idea take a shrine
Of crystal flesh, through which to shine;

Meet you her, my wishes,
Bespeak her to my blisses,
And be ye called my absent kisses.

I wish her beauty,
That owes not all his[2] duty
To gaudy tire,[3] or glist'ring shoe-tie;

Something more than
Taffeta or tissue can,   20
Or rampant feather, or rich fan;

More than the spoil
Of shop, or silkworm's toil,
Or a bought blush, or a set smile;

A face that's best
By its own beauty dressed,
And can alone command the rest;

A face made up
Out of no other shop
Than what nature's white hand sets ope;   30

A cheek where youth
And blood, with pen of truth
Write what the reader sweetly ru'th;

A cheek where grows
More than a morning rose,
Which to no box his being owes;

Lips where all day
A lover's kiss may play,
Yet carry nothing thence away;

Looks that oppress 4   40
Their richest tires, but dress
And clothe their simplest nakedness.

Eyes that displace
The neighbor diamond, and out-face
That sunshine by their own sweet grace;

Tresses that wear
Jewels but to declare
How much themselves more precious are;

Whose native ray
Can tame the wanton day   50
Of gems, that in their bright shades play—

Each ruby there,
Or pearl that dare appear,
Be its own blush, be its own tear;

A well-tamed heart,
For whose more noble smart
Love may be long choosing a dart;

Eyes that bestow
Full quivers on love's bow,
Yet pay less arrows than they owe;   60

Smiles that can warm
The blood, yet teach a charm,
That chastity shall take no harm;

Blushes that bin 5
The burnish of no sin,
Nor flames of aught too hot within;

Joys that confess
Virtue their mistress,
And have no other head to dress;

Fears, fond and flight, 6   70
As the coy bride's, when night
First does the longing lover right;

Tears, quickly fled
And vain, as those are shed
For a dying maidenhead;

Days that need borrow
No part of their good morrow
From a fore-spent night of sorrow;

Days that, in spite
Of darkness, by the light   80
Of a clear mind are day all night;

Nights sweet as they,
Made short by lover's play,
Yet long by the absence of the day;

Life that dares send
A challenge to his end,
And, when it comes, say, "Welcome, friend!"

Sidneian showers
Of sweet discourse, 7 whose powers
Can crown old winter's head with flowers;   90

Soft silken hours,
Open suns, shady bowers;
'Bove all, nothing within that lowers;

---

5 Be, are.   6 Foolish and fleeting.
7 A reference to the elegant conversations of Sir Philip
Sidney's Arcadia, which still retained its popularity as a
ladies' book.

WISHES TO HIS MISTRESS
4 Overpower by contrast.

Whate'er delight
Can make day's forehead bright,
Or give down to the wings of night.

In her whole frame
Have nature all the name,[8]
Art and ornament the shame.

Her flattery,   100
Picture and poesy:
Her counsel her own virtue be.[9]

I wish her store
Of worth may leave her poor
Of wishes;[10] and I wish—no more.

Now if time knows
That her whose radiant brows
Weave them a garland of my vows;

Her whose just bays[11]
My future hopes can raise,   110
A trophy to her present praise;

Her that dares be
What these lines wish to see:
I seek no further—it is she.

'Tis she, and here
Lo! I unclothe and clear
My wishes' cloudy character.

May she enjoy it
Whose merit dare apply it,
But modesty dares still deny it.   120

Such worth as this is
Shall fix my flying wishes,
And determine them to[12] kisses.

Let her full glory,
My fancies, fly before ye!
Be ye my fictions, but her story.

WISHES TO HIS MISTRESS
8 Repute.
9 I.e., however others may flatter her, let her take counsel only of her own virtue.
10 Without need of wishes.   11 Laurels.
12 Terminate, or resolve, them into.

MUSIC'S DUEL[1]

Now westward Sol had spent the richest beams
Of noon's high glory, when hard by the streams
Of Tiber, on the scene of a green plat,
Under protection of an oak, there sat
A sweet lutes-master, in whose gentle airs
He lost the day's heat and his own hot cares.
    Close in the covert of the leaves there stood
A nightingale, come from the neighboring wood
(The sweet inhabitant of each glad tree,
Their muse, their siren, harmless siren she).   10
There stood she listening, and did entertain
The music's soft report; and mold the same
In her own murmurs, that whatever mood
His curious fingers lent, her voice made good.
The man perceived his rival and her art,
Disposed to give the light-foot lady sport,
Awakes his lute, and 'gainst the fight to come
Informs it in a sweet præludium
Of closer strains, and ere the war begin,
He lightly skirmishes on every string   20
Charged with a flying touch; and straightway she
Carves out her dainty voice as readily
Into a thousand sweet distinguished tones,
And reckons up in soft divisions
Quick volumes of wild notes, to let him know
By that shrill taste she could do something too.
    His nimble hands instinct then taught each string
A cap'ring cheerfulness, and made them sing
To their own dance; now negligently rash
He throws his arm, and with a long-drawn dash   30
Blends all together; then distinctly trips
From this to that; then quick returning skips
And snatches this again, and pauses there.
She measures every measure, everywhere
Meets art with art; sometimes as if in doubt
Not perfect yet, and fearing to be out
Trails her plain ditty in one long-spun note
Through the sleek passage of her open throat.
A clear unwrinkled song then doth she point it
With tender accents, and severely joint it   40
By short diminutives, that being reared
In controverting warbles evenly shared,
With her sweet self she wrangles; he amazed
That from so small a channel should be raised

MUSIC'S DUEL
1 Based on a Latin poem by the Jesuit Famianus Strada (1572–1649).

The torrent of a voice whose melody
Could melt into such sweet variety
Strains higher yet, that tickled with rare art
The tatling strings (each breathing in his part)
Most kindly do fall out; the grumbling bass
In surly groans disdains the treble's grace.   50
The high-perched treble chirps at this, and chides,
Until his finger (moderator) hides
And closes the sweet quarrel, rousing all
Hoarse, shrill, at once, as when the trumpets call
Hot Mars to the harvest of death's field, and woe
Men's hearts into their hands; this lesson too
She gives him back; her supple breast thrills out
Sharp airs, and staggers in a warbling doubt
Of dallying sweetness, hovers o'er her skill,
And folds in waved notes with a trembling bill   60
The pliant series of her slippery song.
Then starts she suddenly into a throng
Of short, thick sobs, whose thund'ring volleys
                float
And roll themselves over her lubric throat
In panting murmurs, stilled out of her breast,
That ever-bubbling spring, the sugared nest
Of her delicious soul, that there does lie,
Bathing in streams of liquid melody,
Music's best seed-plot, whence in ripened airs
A golden-headed harvest fairly rears   70
His honey-dropping tops, plowed by her breath,
Which there reciprocally laboreth
In that sweet soil. It seems a holy quire,
Founded to the name of great Apollo's lyre,
Whose silver roof rings with the sprightly notes
Of sweet-lipped angel-imps, that swill their throats
In cream of morning-Helicon [2] and then
Prefer soft anthems to the ears of men,
To woo them from their beds, still murmuring
That men can sleep while they their matins sing,   80
(Most divine service), whose so early lay
Prevents [3] the eyelids of the blushing day.
There might you hear her kindle her soft voice
In the close murmur of a sparkling noise,
And lay the groundwork of her hopeful song,
Still keeping in the forward stream, so long,
Till a sweet whirlwind (striving to get out)
Heaves her soft bosom, wanders round about,
And makes a pretty earthquake in her breast,
Till the fledged notes at length forsake their nest, 90

Fluttering in wanton shoals, and to the sky
Winged with their own wild echoes pratling fly.
She opes the floodgate and lets loose a tide
Of streaming sweetness, which in state doth ride
On the waved back of every swelling strain,
Rising and falling in a pompous train.
And while she thus discharges a shrill peal
Of flashing airs, she qualifies their zeal
With the cool epode of a graver note,
Thus high, thus low, as if her silver throat   100
Would reach the brazen voice of war's hoarse bird;
Her little soul is ravished, and so poured
Into loose ecstasies that she is placed
Above herself, music's enthusiast.
    Shame now and anger mixed a double stain
In the musician's face; "Yet once again,
Mistress, I come; now reach a strain, my lute,
Above her mock, or be forever mute.
Or tune a song of victory to me,
Or to thyself sing thine own obsequy."   110
So said, his hands sprightly as fire he flings,
And with a quavering coyness tastes the strings.
The sweet-lipped sisters musically frighted
Singing their fears are fearfully delighted.
Trembling as when Apollo's golden hairs
Are fanned and frizzled in the wanton airs
Of his own breath, which married to his lyre
Doth tune the spheres, and make heaven's self look
                higher.
From this to that, from that to this he flies,
Feels music's pulse in all her arteries;   120
Caught in a net which there Apollo spreads,
His fingers struggle with the vocal threads;
Following those little rills, he sinks into
A sea of Helicon; his hand does go
Those parts of sweetness which with nectar drop,
Softer than that which pants in Hebe's cup.
The humorous strings expound his learned touch,
By various glosses; now they seem to grutch [4]
And murmur in a buzzing din, then jingle
In shrill-tongued accents, striving to be single. 130
Every smooth turn, every delicious stroke
Gives life to some new grace; thus doth he invoke
Sweetness by all her names; thus, bravely thus,
(Fraught with a fury so harmonious)
The lute's light genius now does proudly rise,
Heaved on the surge of swollen rhapsodies,

2 Mythical residence of Apollo and the Muses.
3 Anticipates.

4 Complain.

Whose flourish, meteor-like, doth curl the air
With flash of high-born fancies, here and there
Dancing in lofty measures, and anon
Creeps on the soft touch of a tender tone,   140
Whose trembling murmurs melting in wild airs
Runs to and fro, complaining his sweet cares
Because those precious mysteries that dwell
In music's ravished soul he dare not tell,
But whisper to the world; thus do they vary
Each string his note, as if they meant to carry
Their master's blest soul (snatched out at his ears
By a strong ecstasy) through all the spheres
Of music's heaven, and seat it there on high
In the Empyræum of pure harmony.   150
At length (after so long, so loud a strife
Of all the strings, still breathing the best life

Of blest variety attending on
His fingers' fairest revolution
In many a sweet rise, many as sweet a fall)
A full-mouth diapason swallows all.
  This done, he lists what she would say to this,
And she, although her breath's late exercise
Had dealt too roughly with her tender throat,
Yet summons all her sweet powers for a note;   160
Alas, in vain! For while, sweet soul, she tries
To measure all those wild diversities
Of chattering strings by the small size of one
Poor simple voice, raised in a natural tone,
She fails, and failing grieves, and grieving dies.
She dies, and leaves her life the victor's prize,
Falling upon his lute; O fit to have
(That lived so sweetly) dead, so sweet a grave!

F R O M

CARMEN DEO NOSTRO [1652]

TO THE NOBLEST AND BEST OF LADIES, THE COUNTESS OF DENBIGH[1]

Persuading her to resolution in religion, and to render herself without further delay into the communion of the Catholic Church

What Heaven entreated heart is this,
Stands trembling at the gate of bliss?
Holds fast the door, yet dares not venture
Fairly to open it, and enter;
Whose definition is a doubt
'Twixt life and death, 'twixt in and out.
Say, lingering fair, why comes the birth
Of your brave soul so slowly forth?
Plead your pretenses, O you strong
In weakness, why you choose so long   10
In labor of yourself to lie,
Not daring quite to live nor die.
Ah, linger not, loved soul! A slow
And late consent was a long no;

Who grants at last, long time tried
And did his best to have denied.
What magic bolts, what mystic bars
Maintain the will in these strange wars!
What fatal, yet fantastic bands
Keep the free heart from its own hands!   20
So when the year takes cold we see
Poor waters their own prisoners be;
Fettered and locked up fast they lie
In a sad self-captivity.
The astonished nymphs their flood's strange
    fate deplore,
To see themselves their own severer shore.
Thou that alone canst thaw this cold,
And fetch the heart from its stronghold,
Almighty Love! end this long war,
And of a meteor make a star.   30
Oh, fix this fair indefinite,
And 'mongst Thy shafts of sovereign light
Choose out that sure decisive dart
Which has the key of this close heart,
Knows all the corners of 't, and can control
The self-shut cabinet of an unsearched soul.
Oh, let it be at last Love's hour;
Raise this tall trophy of Thy power;
Come once the conquering way, not to confute
But kill this rebel-word, "irresolute,"   40

TO THE NOBLEST AND BEST OF LADIES
  1 The Countess of Denbigh, a patron of Crashaw, was one of the ladies of the bedchamber to Queen Henrietta Maria. The volume *Carmen Deo Nostro* was dedicated to her.

That so, in spite of all this peevish strength
Of weakness, she may write, "Resolved at
    length."
Unfold at length, unfold, fair flower,
And use the season of Love's shower;
Meet His well-meaning wounds, wise heart!
And haste to drink the wholesome dart,
That healing shaft, which Heaven till now
Hath in Love's quiver hid for you.
O dart of Love! arrow of light!
O happy you, if it hit right!   50
It must not fall in vain, it must
Not mark the dry regardless dust.
Fair one, it is your fate, and brings
Eternal worlds upon its wings.
Meet it with wide-spread arms, and see
Its seat your soul's just center be.
Disband dull fears, give faith the day;
To save your life, kill your delay.
It is Love's siege, and sure to be
Your triumph, through His victory.   60
'Tis cowardice that keeps this field,
And want of courage not to yield.
Yield then, O yield, that Love may win
The fort at last, and let life in;
Yield quickly, lest perhaps you prove
Death's prey, before the prize of Love.
This fort of your fair self, if 't be not won,
He is repulsed indeed, but you're undone.

IN THE HOLY NATIVITY OF OUR
LORD GOD

A Hymn Sung as by the Shepherds

CHORUS

Come, we shepherds whose blest sight
Hath met love's noon in nature's night;
Come, lift we up our loftier song
And wake the sun that lies too long.

To all our world of well-stol'n joy
    He slept, and dreamed of no such thing,
While we found out Heaven's fairer eye,
    And kissed the cradle of our King.
Tell him he rises now too late
To show us aught worth looking at.   10

Tell him we now can show him more
    Than he e'er showed to mortal sight,
Than he himself e'er saw before,
    Which to be seen needs not his light.
Tell him, Tityrus, where th' hast been;
Tell him, Thyrsis, what th' hast seen.

TITYRUS

Gloomy night embraced the place
    Where the noble Infant lay;
The Babe looked up and showed His face:
    In spite of darkness, it was day.   20
It was Thy day, Sweet, and did rise
Not from the east, but from Thine eyes.

    Chorus. It was Thy day, Sweet, [etc.]

THYRSIS

Winter chid aloud, and sent
    The angry north to wage his wars;
The north forgot his fierce intent,
    And left perfumes instead of scars.
By those sweet eyes' persuasive powers,
Where he meant frost, he scattered flowers.

    Chorus. By those sweet eyes' [etc.]   30

BOTH

We saw Thee in Thy balmy nest,
    Young Dawn of our eternal day!
We saw Thine eyes break from Their east
    And chase the trembling shades away.
We saw Thee, and we blessed the sight;
We saw Thee by Thine own sweet light.

TITYRUS

"Poor world," said I, "what wilt thou do
    To entertain this starry Stranger?
Is this the best thou canst bestow,
    A cold and not too cleanly manger?   40
Contend, ye powers of heav'n and earth,
To fit a bed for this huge birth!"

    Chorus. Contend, ye powers [etc.]

THYRSIS

"Proud world," said I, "cease your contest,
    And let the mighty Babe alone—
The phœnix builds the phœnix' nest,
    Love's architecture is His own;
The Babe whose birth embraves this morn
Made His own bed ere He was born."

Chorus. The Babe whose birth [etc.]   50

TITYRUS

I saw the curled drops, soft and slow,
    Come hovering o'er the place's head,
Off'ring their whitest sheets of snow
    To furnish the fair Infant's bed.
"Forbear," said I, "be not too bold;
Your fleece is white, but 'tis too cold."

Chorus. "Forbear," said I, [etc.]

THYRSIS

I saw the obsequious seraphims
    Their rosy fleece of fire bestow;
For well they now can spare their wings,   60
    Since Heav'n itself lies here below.
"Well done," said I, "but are you sure
Your down so warm will pass for pure?"

Chorus. "Well done," said I, [etc.]

TITYRUS

No, no, your King's not yet to seek
    Where to repose His royal head;
See, see, how soon His new-bloomed cheek
    'Twixt mother's breasts is gone to bed.
"Sweet choice!" said we, "no way but so,
Not to lie cold, yet sleep in snow."   70

Chorus. "Sweet choice!" said we, [etc.]

BOTH

We saw Thee in Thy balmy nest,
    Bright Dawn of our eternal day!
We saw Thine eyes break from Their east,
    And chase the trembling shades away.
We saw Thee, and we blessed the sight;
We saw Thee by Thine own sweet light.

Chorus. We saw Thee, [etc.]

FULL CHORUS

Welcome, all wonders in one sight!
    Eternity shut in a span,   80
Summer in winter, day in night,
    Heaven in earth, and God in man!
Great little One, whose all-embracing birth
Lifts earth to Heaven, stoops Heav'n to earth.

Welcome, though nor to gold nor silk,
    To more than Cæsar's birthright is;
Two sister-seas of virgin-milk,
    With many a rarely tempered kiss,
That breathes at once both maid and mother,
Warms in the one, cools in the other.   90

Welcome, though not to those gay flies
    Gilded i' th' beams of earthly kings,
Slippery souls in smiling eyes;
    But to poor shepherds, homespun things,
Whose wealth's their flock, whose wit, to be
    Well read in their simplicity.
Yet when young April's husband-showers
    Shall bless the fruitful Maia's bed,
We'll bring the first-born of her flowers
    To kiss Thy feet and crown Thy head.   100
To Thee, dread Lamb, whose love must keep
    The shepherds more than they the sheep;
To Thee, meek Majesty! soft King
    Of simple graces and sweet loves,
Each of us his lamb will bring,
    Each his pair of silver doves;
Till burnt at last in fire of Thy fair eyes,
    Ourselves become our own best sacrifice.

CHARITAS NIMIA; OR, THE DEAR
BARGAIN

Lord, what is man? why should he cost Thee
So dear? what had his ruin lost Thee?
Lord, what is man, that Thou hast over-bought
So much a thing of naught?

Love is too kind, I see, and can
Make but a simple merchant-man.
'Twas for such sorry merchandise
Bold painters have put out his eyes.

Alas, sweet Lord! what were't to Thee
If there were no such worms as we? 10
Heav'n ne'er the less still Heav'n would be,
 Should mankind dwell
 In the deep hell.
What have his woes to do with Thee?

 Let him go weep
 O'er his own wounds;
 Seraphims will not sleep,
Nor spheres let fall their faithful rounds.

 Still would the youthful spirits sing,
And still Thy spacious palace ring; 20
Still would those beauteous ministers of light
 Burn all as bright,
And bow their flaming heads before Thee;
Still thrones and dominations[1] would adore Thee.
Still would those ever-wakeful sons of fire
 Keep warm Thy praise
 Both nights and days,
And teach Thy loved name to their noble lyre.

Let froward dust then do its kind,
And give itself for sport to the proud wind. 30
Why should a piece of peevish clay plead shares
In the eternity of Thy old cares?
Why shouldst Thou bow Thy awful breast to see
What mine own madnesses have done with me?

Should not the king still keep his throne
Because some desperate fool's undone?
Or will the world's illustrious eyes
Weep for every worm that dies?

 Will the gallant sun
 E'er the less glorious run? 40
Will he hang down his golden head,
Or e'er the sooner seek his western bed,
 Because some foolish fly
 Grows wanton, and will die?

If I were lost in misery,
What was it to Thy heaven and Thee?
What was it to Thy precious blood
If my foul heart called for a flood?

CHARITAS NIMIA
1 Thrones and dominations are two orders of the angelic hierarchy.

What if my faithless soul and I
 Would needs fall in 50
 With guilt and sin;
What did the Lamb that He should die?
What did the Lamb that He should need,
When the wolf sins, Himself to bleed?

 If my base lust
Bargained with death and well-beseeming dust,
 Why should the white
 Lamb's bosom write
 The purple name
 Of my sin's shame? 60
Why should His unstained breast make good
My blushes with His own heart-blood?

O my Saviour, make me see
How dearly Thou has paid for me;
That, lost again, my life may prove,
As then in death, so now in love,

SAINT MARY MAGDALENE; OR, THE WEEPER

Lo! where a wounded heart with bleeding eyes conspire,
Is she a flaming fountain, or a weeping fire?

 Hail, sister springs!
 Parents of silver-footed rills!
 Ever-bubbling things!
 Thawing crystal! snowy hills,
Still spending, never spent! I mean
Thy fair eyes, sweet Magdalene!

 Heavens thy fair eyes be,
 Heavens of ever-falling stars;
 'Tis seed-time still with thee,
 And stars thou sow'st, whose harvest dares
Promise the earth to countershine 11
Whatever makes heav'n's forehead fine.

 But we're deceivèd all.
 Stars indeed they are, too true,
 For they but seem to fall,
 As heav'n's other spangles do.
It is not for our earth and us
To shine in things so precious.

Upwards thou dost weep;
Heav'n's bosom drinks the gentle stream;
Where the milky rivers creep,   21
Thine floats above, and is the cream.
Waters above th' heav'ns, what they be
We're taught best by thy tears and thee.

Every morn from hence
A brisk cherub something sips,
Whose sacred influence
Adds sweetness to his sweetest lips;
Then to his music, and his song
Tastes of this breakfast all day long.   30

Not in the evening's eyes,
When they red with weeping are
For the sun that dies,
Sits sorrow with a face so fair;
Nowhere but here did ever meet
Sweetness so sad, sadness so sweet.

When sorrow would be seen
In her brightest majesty,
For she is a queen,
Then is she dressed by none but thee;   40
Then, and only then, she wears
Her proudest pearls; I mean thy tears.

The dew no more will weep
The primrose's pale cheek to deck;
The dew no more will sleep,
Nuzzled in the lily's neck;
Much rather would it be thy tear,
And leave them both to tremble here.

There's no need at all
That the balsam-sweating bough   50
So coyly should let fall
His med'cinable tears, for now
Nature hath learnt t' extract a dew
More sovereign and sweet from you.

Yet let the poor drops weep,
Weeping is the ease of woe;
Softly let them creep,
Sad that they are vanquished so;
They, though to others no relief,
Balsam may be for their own grief.   60

Such the maiden gem
By the purpling vine put on,
Peeps from her parent stem
And blushes at the bridegroom sun;
This wat'ry blossom of thy eyne,
Ripe, will make the richer wine.

When some new bright guest
Takes up among the stars a room,
And Heav'n will make a feast,
Angels with crystal vials come   70
And draw from these full eyes of thine
Their Master's water, their own wine.

Golden though he be,
Golden Tagus murmurs though;
Were his way by thee,
Content and quiet he would go;
So much more rich would he esteem
Thy silver, than his golden stream.

Well does the May that lies
Smiling in thy cheeks confess   80
The April in thine eyes;
Mutual sweetness they express:
No April e'er lent kinder showers,
Nor May returned more faithful flowers.

O cheeks! beds of chaste loves
By your own showers seasonably dashed;
Eyes! nests of milky doves
In your own wells decently washed;
O wit of Love! that thus could place
Fountain and garden in one face.   90

O sweet contest, of woes
With loves, of tears with smiles disputing!
O fair and friendly foes,
Each other kissing and confuting!
While rain and sunshine, cheeks and eyes,
Close in kind contrarieties.

But can these fair floods be
Friends with the bosom fires that fill thee?
Can so great flames agree
Eternal tears should thus distill thee?   100
O floods, O fires, O suns, O showers!
Mixed and made friends by Love's sweet
                                    powers.

'Twas his well-pointed dart
That digged these wells and dressed this
   vine;
And taught the wounded heart
The way into these weeping eyne.
Vain loves, avaunt! bold hands, forbear!
The Lamb hath dipped His white foot here.

And now where'er He strays
Among the Galilean mountains,   110
Or more unwelcome ways,
He's followed by two faithful fountains,
Two walking baths, two weeping motions,
Portable and compendious oceans.

O thou, thy Lord's fair store!
In thy so rich and rare expenses,
Even when He showed most poor,
He might provoke the wealth of
   princes;
What prince's wanton'st pride e'er could
Wash with silver, wipe with gold?   120

Who is that King, but He
Who call'st His crown to be called thine,
That thus can boast to be
Waited on by a wand'ring mine,
A voluntary mint, that strows
Warm silver showers where'er He goes!

O precious prodigal!
Fair spendthrift of thyself! thy measure,
Merciless love, is all,
Even to the last pearl in thy treasure;   130
All places, times, and objects be
Thy tears' sweet opportunity.

Does the day-star rise?
Still thy tears do fall and fall.
Does day close his eyes?
Still the fountain weeps for all.
Let night or day do what they will,
Thou hast thy task, thou weepest still.

Does thy song lull the air?
Thy falling tears keep faithful time.   140
Does thy sweet-breathèd prayer
Up in clouds of incense climb?
Still at each sigh, that is, each stop,
A bead, that is, a tear, does drop.

At these thy weeping gates,
Watching their wat'ry motiòn,
Each wingèd moment waits,
Takes his tear and gets him gone;
By thine eye's tinct ennobled thus,
Time lays him up, he's precious.   150

Not, "So long she lived,"
Shall thy tomb report of thee;
But, "So long she grieved,"
Thus must we date thy memory.
Others by moments, months and years,
Measure their ages, thou by tears.

So do perfumes expire;
So sigh tormented sweets, oppressed
With proud unpitying fire;
Such tears the suff'ring rose that's vexed 160
With ungentle flames does shed,
Sweating in a too warm bed.

Say, ye bright brothers,
The fugitive sons of those fair eyes,
Your faithful mothers,
What make you here? What hopes can
   'tice
You to be born? What cause can borrow
You from those nests of noble sorrow?

Whither away so fast?
For sure the sordid earth   170
Your sweetness cannot taste,
Nor does the dust deserve your birth.
Sweet, whither haste you then? O say
Why you trip so fast away!

"We go not to seek
The darlings of Aurora's bed,
The rose's modest cheek,
Nor the violet's humble head;
Though the field's eyes, too, weepers be
Because they want such tears as we.   180

"Much less mean we to trace
The fortune of inferior gems,
Preferred to some proud face,
Or perched upon feared diadems:
Crowned heads are toys. We go to meet
A worthy object, our Lord's feet."

A HYMN TO THE NAME AND HONOR OF THE ADMIRABLE SAINT TERESA[1]

Foundress of the Reformation of the Discalced[2] Carmelites, both men and women. A woman for angelical height of speculation, for masculine courage of performance, more than a woman; who yet a child outran maturity, and durst plot a martyrdom.

Love, thou art absolute sole lord
Of life and death. To prove the word,
We'll now appeal to none of all
Those thy old soldiers, great and tall,
Ripe men of martyrdom, that could reach down
With strong arms their triumphant crown;
Such as could with lusty breath
Speak loud into the face of death
Their great Lord's glorious name; to none   9
Of those whose spacious bosoms spared a throne
For love at large to fill. Spare blood and sweat,
And see Him take a private seat,
Making His mansion in the mild
And milky soul of a soft child.

    Scarce has she learnt to lisp the name
Of martyr, yet she thinks it shame
Life should so long play with that breath
Which spent can buy so brave a death.
She never undertook to know
What death with Love should have to do;   20
Nor has she e'er yet understood
Why to show love she should shed blood;
Yet though she cannot tell you why,
She can love and she can die.

    Scarce has she blood enough to make
A guilty sword blush for her sake;
Yet has she a heart dares hope to prove
How much less strong is death than Love.

    Be Love but there, let poor six years
Be posed with the maturest fears   30
Man trembles at, you straight shall find
Love knows no nonage, nor the mind.
'Tis Love, not years or limbs, that can
Make the martyr or the man.

Love touched her heart, and lo it beats
High, and burns with such brave heats,
Such thirsts to die, as dares drink up
A thousand cold deaths in one cup.
Good reason, for she breathes all fire;
Her weak[3] breast heaves with strong desire   40
Of what she may with fruitless wishes
Seek for amongst her mother's kisses.

    Since 'tis not to be had at home,
She'll travel to a martyrdom.
No home for hers confesses she
But where she may a martyr be.

    She'll to the Moors, and trade with them
For this unvalued[4] diadem.
She'll offer them her dearest breath,
With Christ's name in 't, in change for death.
She'll bargain with them, and will give   51
Them God, teach them how to live
In Him; or, if they this deny,
For Him she'll teach them how to die.
So shall she leave amongst them sown
Her Lord's blood, or at least her own.

    Farewell then, all the world, adieu!
Teresa is no more for you.
Farewell, all pleasures, sports, and joys,
Never till now esteemèd toys;   60
Farewell, whatever dear may be,[5]
Mother's arms, or father's knee;
Farewell house and farewell home,
She's for the Moors and martyrdom!

    Sweet, not so fast! lo, thy fair Spouse
Whom thou seek'st with so swift vows
Calls thee back, and bids thee come
T' embrace a milder martyrdom.

    Blest powers forbid thy tender life
Should bleed upon a barbarous knife;   70
Or some base hand have power to rase[6]
Thy breast's chaste cabinet, and uncase
A soul kept there so sweet; oh no,
Wise Heav'n will never have it so:
Thou art Love's victim, and must die
A death more mystical and high;
Into Love's arms thou shalt let fall
A still surviving funeral.

A HYMN
1 Crashaw's devotion to the great Spanish mystic Saint Teresa (1515–1582) inspired two of the best-known religious poems in the language.
2 Barefoot.

3 The 1652 edition reads "what"; the 1648 edition, "weak."
4 Invaluable.
5 This line, missing in the 1652 edition, is supplied from that of 1648.
6 Cut, slash.

His is the dart [7] must make the death
Whose stroke shall taste thy hallowed breath;
A dart thrice dipped in that rich flame   81
Which writes thy Spouse's radiant name
Upon the roof of Heav'n, where aye
It shines, and with a sovereign ray
Beats bright upon the burning faces
Of souls which in that name's sweet graces
Find everlasting smiles. So rare,
So spiritual, pure, and fair
Must be th' immortal instrument
Upon whose choice point shall be sent   90
A life so loved; and that there be
Fit executioners for thee,
The fair'st and first-born sons of fire,
Blest seraphim, shall leave their choir
And turn Love's soldiers, upon thee
To exercise their archery.
   Oh, how oft shalt thou complain
Of a sweet and subtle pain,
Of intolerable joys,
Of a death in which who dies   100
Loves his death, and dies again,
And would forever so be slain,
And lives and dies, and knows not why
To live, but that he thus may never leave to die!
   How kindly will thy gentle heart
Kiss the sweetly killing dart!
And close in his embraces keep
Those delicious wounds, that weep
Balsam to heal themselves with. Thus
When these thy deaths, so numerous,   110
Shall all at last die into one,
And melt thy soul's sweet mansion;
Like a soft lump of incense, hasted
By too hot a fire, and wasted
Into perfuming clouds, so fast
Shalt thou exhale to Heav'n at last
In a resolving sigh; and then,
Oh, what? Ask not the tongues of men;
Angels cannot tell; suffice,
Thyself shall feel thine own full joys   120
And hold them fast forever. There
So soon as thou shalt first appear, [8]

The moon of maiden stars, thy white
Mistress, attended by such bright
Souls as thy shining self, shall come
And in her first ranks make thee room;
Where 'mongst her snowy family
Immortal welcomes wait for thee.
   Oh, what delight when revealed life shall
      stand
And teach thy lips heav'n with his hand,   130
On which thou now mayst to thy wishes
Heap up thy consecrated kisses.
What joys shall seize thy soul when she,
Bending her blessed eyes on thee,
Those second smiles of heaven, shall dart
Her mild rays through thy melting heart!
   Angels, thy old friends, there shall greet thee,
Glad at their own home now to meet thee.
   All thy good works which went before
And waited for thee at the door   140
Shall own thee there, and all in one
Weave a constellation
Of crowns, with which the King, thy Spouse,
Shall build up thy triumphant brows.
   All thy old woes shall now smile on thee,
And thy pains sit bright upon thee;
All thy sorrows here shall shine, [9]
All thy sufferings be divine;
Tears shall take comfort and turn gems,
And wrongs repent to diadems.   150
Even thy deaths shall live, and new
Dress the soul that erst they slew;
Thy wounds shall blush to such bright scars
As keep account of the Lamb's wars.
   Those rare works where thou shalt leave writ
Love's noble history, with wit
Taught thee by none but Him, while here
They feed our souls, shall clothe thine there.
Each heav'nly word by whose hid flame
Our hard hearts shall strike fire, the same   160
Shall flourish on thy brows, and be
Both fire to us and flame to thee,
Whose light shall live bright in thy face
By glory, in our hearts by grace.
   Thou shalt look round about and see
Thousands of crowned souls throng to be
Themselves thy crown; sons of thy vows,
The virgin-births with which thy sovereign
      Spouse

---

7 One of Teresa's visions was of an angel appearing with
a dart of gold, which he thrust into her heart several times,
causing thereby intense pain but inflaming her with an even
greater love of God.

8 This line in the 1652 edition reads, "So soon as you first
appear."

9 This line, omitted in the 1652 edition, is supplied from
that of 1648.

Made fruitful thy fair soul, go now
And with them all about thee, bow   170
To Him. "Put on," He'll say, "put on,
My rosy love, that thy rich zone
Sparkling with the sacred flames
Of thousand souls whose happy names
Heav'n keeps upon thy score. Thy bright
Life brought them first to kiss the light
That kindled them to stars." And so
Thou with the Lamb, thy Lord, shalt go,
And whereso'er He sets His white
Steps, walk with Him those ways of light   180
Which who in death would live to see
Must learn in life to die like thee.

THE FLAMING HEART

Upon the book and picture of the seraphical Saint Teresa,
as she is usually expressed with a seraphim beside her.

Well-meaning readers, you that come as friends
And catch the precious name this piece pretends;
Make not too much haste to admire
That fair-cheeked fallacy of fire.
That is a seraphim, they say,
And this the great Teresia.
Readers, be ruled by me, and make
Here a well-placed and wise mistake;
You must transpose the picture quite,
And spell it wrong to read it right;   10
Read him for her and her for him;
And call the saint the seraphim
    Painter, what didst thou understand,
To put her dart into his hand?
See, even the years and size of him
Shows this the mother seraphim.
This is the mistress-flame; and duteous he
Her happy fireworks, here, comes down to see.
O most poor-spirited of men!
Had thy cold pencil kissed her pen,   20
Thou couldst not so unkindly [1] err
To show us this faint shade for her.
Why man, this speaks pure mortal frame;
And mocks with female frost love's manly flame.
One would suspect thou meant'st to paint
Some weak, inferior, woman saint.

But had thy pale-faced purple took
Fire from the burning cheeks of that bright book,
Thou wouldst on her have heaped up all
That could be found seraphical;   30
Whate'er this youth of fire wears fair,
Rosy fingers, radiant hair,
Glowing cheek, and glistering wings,
All those fair and flagrant things,
But before all that fiery dart
Had filled the hand of this great heart.
    Do then as equal right requires,
Since his the blushes be, and hers the fires,
Resume and rectify thy rude design;
Undress thy seraphim into mine.   40
Redeem this injury of thy art;
Give him the veil, give her the dart.
    Give him the veil, that he may cover
The red cheeks of a rivaled lover,
Ashamed that our world now can show
Nests of new seraphims here below.
    Give her the dart, for it is she
(Fair youth) shoots both thy shaft and thee.
Say, all ye wise and well-pierced hearts
That live and die amidst her darts,   50
What is it your tasteful spirits prove
In that rare life of her, and love?
Say and bear witness. Sends she not
A seraphim at every shot?
What magazines of immortal arms there shine!
Heaven's great artillery in each love-spun line.
Give then the dart to her who gives the flame;
Give him the veil, who kindly takes the shame.
    But if it be the frequent fate
Of worse faults to be fortunate;   60
If all's prescription; and proud wrong
Harkens not to an humble song;
For all the gallantry of him,
Give me the suffering seraphim.
His be the bravery of all those bright things,
The glowing cheeks, the glistering wings;
The rosy hand, the radiant dart;
Leave her alone the flaming heart.
    Leave her that; and thou shalt leave her
Not one loose shaft, but love's whole quiver.   70
For in love's field was never found
A nobler weapon than a wound.
Love's passives are his activ'st part.
The wounded is the wounding heart.
O heart! the equal poise of love's both parts,
Big like with wounds and darts,

THE FLAMING HEART
  1 Unnaturally.

Live in these conquering leaves; live all the same,
And walk through all tongues one triumphant
    flame;
Live here, great heart, and love and die and kill,
And bleed and wound, and yield and conquer still.
Let this immortal life, where'er it comes,   81
Walk in a crowd of loves and martyrdoms.
Let mystic deaths wait on 't, and wise souls be
The love-slain witnesses of this life of thee.
O sweet incendiary! show here thy art,
Upon this carcass of a hard cold heart;
Let all thy scattered shafts of light, that play
Among the leaves of thy large books of day,
Combined against this breast, at once break in
And take away from me myself and sin!   90
This gracious robbery shall thy bounty be,
And my best fortunes such fair spoils of me.
O thou undaunted daughter of desires!
By all thy dower of lights and fires;
By all the eagle in thee, all the dove;
By all thy lives and deaths of love;
By thy large draughts of intellectual day,
And by thy thirsts of love more large than they;
By all thy brim-filled bowls of fierce desire,
By thy last morning's draught of liquid fire;   100
By the full kingdom of that final kiss
That seized thy parting soul, and sealed thee His;

By all the heav'ns thou hast in Him,
Fair sister of the seraphim,
By all of Him we have in thee,
Leave nothing of myself in me!
Let me so read thy life that I
Unto all life of mine may die!

A SONG

Lord, when the sense of Thy sweet grace
Sends up my soul to seek Thy face,
Thy blessed eyes breed such desire
I die in Love's delicious fire.
    O Love, I am Thy sacrifice!
Be still triumphant, blessed eyes!
Still shine on me, fair suns! that I
Still may behold, though still I die.

SECOND PART

Though still I die, I live again,
Still longing so to be still slain;   10
So gainful is such loss of breath,
I die even in desire of death.
    Still live in me this loving strife
Of living death and dying life;
For while Thou sweetly slayest me,
Dead to myself, I live in Thee.

John Cleveland

[1613–1658]

METAPHYSICAL poetry was a relatively short-lived literary phenomenon, partly because its complexity and difficulty demanded practitioners of a very distinguished sort, partly because the new scientific world view and the new classicism required a different kind of vehicle for their expression. Whatever the reason, signs of decadence in the style can be perceived as early as the late 1640's, nowhere more markedly than in the poems of John Cleveland, whose love lyrics and occasional pieces use the intellectual conceit and the witty paradox in an affected, nonfunctional manner which has neither the psychological profundity of Donne nor the emotional appropriateness of King and Lord Herbert. Devices which were for them instruments of vision were used by Cleveland merely as ornaments of fashion. But, although Cleveland represents the decadence of one literary movement, he foreshadows the emergence of another: the anti-Puritan satires which he wrote during the Civil War ("The Rebel Scot" being the best known of them) anticipate the Augustan temper as clearly as do the couplets of Waller and Denham.

The son of a Leicestershire clergyman and teacher, Cleveland studied at Christ's College, Cambridge, receiving his B.A. in 1631 and his M.A. in 1635. He had, in 1634, become a fellow of St. John's College, but was, like Crashaw, ousted from his position by the Puritans in the early 1640's. Removing to Oxford, he devoted all his energies to the doomed royalist cause; he was imprisoned briefly in 1655 by Commonwealth men who had forgotten neither the potency nor the popularity of his satirical verse, but he was released after a personal appeal to Cromwell. In declining health, he spent his last years at Gray's Inn, where he became a close friend of Samuel Butler, who was destined to perfect the satirical instrument Cleveland had designed.

Cleveland enjoyed an enormous vogue in his own day, both as amorous lyrist and as satirist. He survives as a curiosity of literature, but he remains an intriguing one.

J. CLEVELAND. *Poems*, ed. J. M. Berdan (New Haven, 1911).

G. SAINTSBURY, ed. *Minor Poets of the Caroline Period*, 3 vols. (Oxford, 1921). Volume III contains Cleveland's poems.

A. ALVAREZ. *The School of Donne* (New York, 1961). Has a good chapter on Cleveland and the decline of Metaphysical style.

G. WILLIAMSON. (See under general poetry bibliography.)

JOHN CLEVELAND

F R O M

JONSONUS VIRBIUS [1638]

AN ELEGY ON BEN JONSON

Who first reformed our stage with justest laws,
And was the first best judge in his own cause;
Who, when his actors trembled for applause,

Could with a noble confidence prefer
His own, by right, to a noble theater,
From principles which he knew could not err;

Who to his fable did his persons fit,
With all the properties of art and wit,
And above all that could be acted, writ;

Who public follies did to covert drive,   10
Which he again could cunningly retrive,
Leaving them no ground to rest on and thrive:

Here Jonson lies, whom, had I named before,
In that one word alone I had paid more
Than can be now, when plenty makes me poor.

F R O M

CLIEVELANDI VINDICIÆ; OR, CLIEVELAND'S
GENUINE POEMS [1677]

FUSCARA; OR, THE BEE ERRANT

Nature's confectioner, the bee
(Whose suckets¹ are moist alchemy,
The still of his refining mold
Minting the garden into gold),
Having rifled all the fields
Of what dainties Flora yields,
Ambitious now to take excise
Of a more fragrant paradise,
At my Fuscara's sleeve arrived,
Where all delicious sweets are hived.   10
The airy freebooter distrains
First on the violets of her veins,
Whose tincture, could it be more pure,
His ravenous kiss had made it bluer.
Here did he sit and essence quaff
Till her coy pulse had beat him off,
That pulse which he that feels may know
Whether the world's long-lived or no.

The next he preys on is her palm
(That almoner of transpiring balm),   20
So soft, 'tis air but once removed,
Tender as 'twere a jelly gloved.
Here, while his canting drone-pipe scanned
The mystic figures of her hand,
He tipples palmistry and dines
On all her fortune-telling lines.
He bathes in bliss and finds no odds
Betwixt this nectar and the gods'.
He perches now upon her wrist,
A proper hawk for such a fist,   30
Making that flesh his bill of fare
Which hungry cannibals would spare;
Where lilies in a lovely brown
Inoculate² carnation,
Her *argent* skin with *or*³ so streamed
As if the Milky Way were creamed.

2 To insert a bud in. The "lovely brown" is a poetic
indication that Fuscara is freckled.

3 *Argent* and *or* are heraldic terms for silver and gold
respectively.

FUSCARA
1 Sweetmeats.

From hence he to the woodbine bends
That quivers at her fingers' ends,
That runs division on the tree
Like a thick-branching pedigree.   40
So 'tis not her the bee devours,
It is a pretty maze of flowers;
It is the rose that bleeds when he
Nibbles his nice phlebotomy.
About her finger he doth cling
I' th' fashion of a wedding ring,
And bids his comrades of the swarm
Crawl like a bracelet 'bout her arm.
Thus when the hovering publican[4]
Had sucked the toll of all her span,   50
Tuning his draughts with drowsy hums
As Danes carouse by kettle-drums,
It was decreed, that posy gleaned,
The small familiar should be weaned.
At this the errant's courage quails,
Yet aided by his native sails
The bold Columbus still designs
To find her undiscovered mines.
To th' Indies of her arm he flies,
Fraught both with east and western prize;   60
Which when he had in vain essayed,
Armed like a dapper lancepresade[5]
With Spanish pike, he broached a pore
And so both made and healed the sore;
For as in gummy trees there's found
A salve to issue at the wound,
Of this her breach the like was true,
Hence trickled out a balsam, too.
But oh, what wasp was 't that could prove
Ravaillac[6] to my Queen of Love?   70
The King of Bees, now jealous grown
Lest her beams should melt his throne,
And finding that his tribute slacks,
His burgesses and state of wax
Turned to a hospital, the combs
Built rank and file like beadsmen's rooms,
And what they bleed but tart and sour
Matched with my Danaë's golden shower,
Live honey all—the envious elf
Stung her, 'cause sweeter than himself.   80
    Sweetness and she are so allied
    The bee committed parricide.

FUSCARA
4 Toll-gatherer.   5 Lance corporal.
6 The assassin of Henry of Navarre.

UPON PHILLIS WALKING IN A MORNING BEFORE SUN-RISING

The sluggish morn as yet undressed,
My Phillis brake from out her east,
As if she'd made a match to run
With Venus, usher to the sun.
The trees, like yeomen of the guard,
Serving her more for pomp than ward,
Ranked on each side, with loyal duty
Weaved branches to enclose her beauty.
The plants, whose luxury was lopped,
Or age with crutches underpropped,   10
Whose wooden carcasses were grown
To be but coffins of their own,
Revive, and at her general dole
Each receives his ancient soul.
The wingèd choristers began
To chirp their matins, and the fan
Of whistling winds like organs played,
Until their voluntaries made
The weakened earth in odors rise
To be her morning sacrifice.   20
The flowers, called out of their beds,
Start and raise up their drowsy heads,
And he that for their color seeks
May see it vaulting to her cheeks,
Where roses mix—no civil war
Divides her York and Lancaster.
The marigold (whose courtier's face
Echoes the sun and doth unlace
Her at his rise, at his full stop
Packs and shuts up her gaudy shop)   30
Mistakes her cue and doth display:
Thus Phillis antedates the day.
These miracles had cramped the sun,
Who, fearing that his kingdom's won,
Powders with light his frizzled locks
To see what saint his luster mocks.
The trembling leaves through which he played,
Dappling the walk with light and shade
Like lattice-windows, give the spy
Room but to peep with half an eye,   40
Lest her full orb his sight should dim
And bid us all good night in him,
Till she should spend a gentle ray
To force us a new-fashioned day.
    But what religious palsy's this
Which makes the boughs divest their bliss,

And that they might her footsteps straw,
Drop their leaves with shivering awe?
Phillis perceived, and (lest her stay
Should wed October unto May,   50
And, as her beauty caused a spring,
Devotion might an autumn bring)
Withdrew her beams, yet made no night,
But left the sun her curate-light.

MARK ANTONY

Whenas the nightingale chanted her vespers,
And the wild forester couched on the ground,
Venus invited me in th' evening whispers
Unto a fragrant field with roses crowned,
    Where she before had sent
    My wishes' complement;
    Unto my heart's content
    Played with me on the green.
        Never Mark Antony
        Dallied more wantonly   10
        With the fair Egyptian Queen.

First on her cherry cheeks I mine eyes feasted,
Thence fear of surfeiting made me retire;
Next on her warmer lips, which when I tasted
My duller spirits made active as fire.
    Then we began to dart
    Each at another's heart,
    Arrows that knew no smart,
    Sweet lips and smiles between.
        Never Mark, etc.   20

Wanting a glass to plait her amber tresses,
Which like a bracelet rich deckèd mine arm,
Gaudier than Juno wears whenas she graces
Jove with embraces more stately than warm;
    Then did she peep in mine
    Eyes' humor crystalline;
    I in her eyes was seen,
    As if we one had been.
        Never Mark, etc.

Mystical grammar of amorous glances;   30
Feeling of pulses, the physic of love;
Rhetorical courtings and musical dances;
Numb'ring of kisses arithmetic prove;
    Eyes like astronomy;
    Straight-limbed geometry;
    In her art's ingeny [1]
    Our wits were sharp and keen.
        Never Mark Antony
        Dallied more wantonly
        With the fair Egyptian Queen.   40

THE REBEL SCOT [1]

How, Providence? and yet a Scottish crew?
Then Madam Nature wears black patches too!
What, shall our nation be in bondage thus
Unto a land that truckles under us?
Ring the bells backward! I am all on fire.
Not all the buckets in a country quire
Shall quench my rage. A poet should be feared
When angry, like a comet's flaming beard.
And where's the stoic can his wrath appease,
To see his country sick of Pym's [2] disease?   10
By Scotch invasion to be made a prey
To such pigwidgeon [3] myrmidons as they?
But that there's charm in verse, I would not quote
The name of Scot without an antidote;
Unless my head were red, that I might brew
Invention there that might be poison too.
Were I a drowsy judge whose dismal note
Disgorgeth halters as a juggler's throat
Doth ribbons; could I in Sir Empiric's [4] tone
Speak pills in phrase and quack destruction;   20

MARK ANTONY
1 Ingenuity, wit.

THE REBEL SCOT
1 Cleveland's most famous poem. From this and others of
Cleveland's satires Samuel Butler learned many of the devices
of satire and burlesque which he employed in his Hudibras.
Cleveland's poem is inspired by the Royalists' hatred of the
Scots after their invasion of England in 1643, to fight on the
side of the Parliament.
2 John Pym ("King Pym"), one of the greatest of the
leaders of the Parliamentary group. His last act of statesman-
ship was to secure the aid of Scottish arms for the Parliament
in the war with the King.
3 A kind of cant term for anything petty or small.
4 I.e., "Sir Quack's."

Or roar like Marshall,[5] that Geneva bull,
Hell and damnation a pulpit full;
Yet to express a Scot, to play that prize,
Not all those mouth-grenadoes can suffice.
Before a Scot can properly be curst,
I must like Hocus swallow daggers first.
Come, keen iambics, with your badgers' feet,
And badger-like bite till your teeth do meet.
Help, ye tart satirists, to imp my rage
With all the scorpions[6] that should whip this age.   30
Scots are like witches; do but whet your pen,
Scratch till the blood come, they'll not hurt you
        then.
Now, as the martyrs were enforced to take
The shape of beasts, like hypocrites at stake,
I'll bait my Scot so, yet not cheat your eyes:
A Scot within a beast is no disguise.
    No more let Ireland brag; her harmless nation
Fosters no venom since the Scot's plantation;
Nor can our feigned antiquity obtain:
Since they came in, England hath wolves again.   40
The Scot that kept the Tower might have shown,
Within the grate of his own breast alone,
The leopard and the panther, and engrossed
What all those wild collegiates had cost
The honest high-shoes[7] in their termly fees;
First to the salvage[8] lawyer, next to these.
Nature herself doth Scotchmen beasts confess,
Making their country such a wilderness:
A land that brings in question and suspense   49
God's omnipresence, but that Charles came thence,
But that Montrose[9] and Crawford's[10] loyal band
Atoned their sin and christened half their land.

Nor is it all the nation hath these spots:
There is a Church as well as Kirk of Scots,
As in a picture where the squinting paint
Shows fiend on this side, and on that side saint.
He that saw hell in 's melancholy dream
And in the twilight of his fancy's theme,
Scared from his sins, repented in a fright,
Had he viewed Scotland, had turned proselyte.   60
A land where one may pray with curst intent,
Oh may they never suffer banishment!
Had Cain been Scot, God would have changed
        his doom:[11]
Not forced him wander, but confined him home!
Like Jews they spread, and as infection fly,
As if the devil had ubiquity.
Hence 'tis they live at rovers[12] and defy
This or that place, rags of geography.
They're citizens of the world; they're all in all;
Scotland's a nation epidemical.   70
And yet they ramble not to learn the mode,
How to be dressed, or how to lisp abroad;
To return knowing in the Spanish shrug,
Or which of the Dutch states a double jug
Resembles most in belly or in beard
(The card by which the mariners are steered).
No, the Scots-errant fight and fight to eat;
Their ostrich stomachs make their swords their
        meat.
Nature with Scots as tooth-drawers hath dealt,
Who use to string their teeth upon their belt.   80
    Yet wonder not at this their happy choice,
The serpent's fatal still to Paradise.
Sure, England hath the hemorrhoids, and these
On the north postern of the patient seize
Like leeches; thus they physically thirst
After our blood, but in the cure shall burst!
    Let them not think to make us run o' the score
To purchase villenage, as once before
When an act passed to stroke them on the head,
Call them good subjects, buy them gingerbread.[13]   90
    Not gold, nor acts of grace, 'tis steel must tame
The stubborn Scot; a prince that would reclaim
Rebels by yielding, doth like him, or worse,
Who saddled his own back to shame his horse.

---

5 Stephen Marshall, a leading Puritan preacher. His initials furnished the first two letters of the word "Smectymnuus," used as the signature of the group of Puritan ministers who wrote the famous pamphlet against episcopacy in 1641. Marshall is said to have preached before the House of Commons for more than seven hours without ceasing.

6 Whips with metal points at the ends.

7 Rustics, plain men.   8 Savage.

9 James Graham, Marquis of Montrose, was leader of the Covenanters and famed for his gallantry as a soldier. He aided in suppressing the supporters of Charles I and the Episcopalians in Aberdeenshire, but after the Pacification of Berwick in 1639 he became an ardent supporter of the King. After ten years of eventful service in the Royalist cause, he was captured and hanged.

10 Ludovic Lindsay, Earl of Crawford, was the associate of Montrose in the Civil War. He was more fortunate than Montrose, and survived until after the Restoration.

11 See Genesis 4:1–15.

12 "At rovers" is a term in archery meaning a mark chosen to shoot at for distance only; at random.

13 A reference to the voting of the gratuity of 300,000 pounds as a testimony of the friendship of the English to the Scots after their invasion in 1641.

Was it for this you left your leaner soil,
Thus to lard Israel with Egypt's spoil?
They are the Gospel's life-guard; but for them,
The garrison of New Jerusalem,
What would the brethen do? The Cause! The
    Cause!
Sack-possets and the fundamental laws!   100
  Lord! What a godly thing is want of shirts!
How a Scotch stomach and no meat converts!
They wanted food and raiment; so they took
Religion for their seamstress and their cook.
Unmask them well; their honors and estate,
As well as conscience, are sophisticate.
Shrive but their titles and their moneys poise,[14]
A laird and twenty pence pronounced with noise,
When contrued, but for a plain yeoman go,
And a good sober twopence, and well so.   110
Hence, then, you proud impostors; get you gone,
You Picts in gentry and devotiòn;
You scandal to the stock of verse, a race
Able to bring the gibbet in disgrace.
Hyperbolus[15] by suffering did traduce
The ostracism and shamed it out of use.
The Indian that Heaven did forswear
Because he heard some Spaniards were there,
Had he but known what Scots in hell had been,
He would, Erasmus-like, have hung between.   120
My Muse hath done. A voider for the nonce,
I wrong the devil should I pick their bones.
That dish is his; for when the Scots decease,
Hell, like their nation, feeds on barnacles.
A Scot, when from the gallow-tree got loose,
Drops into Styx and turns a solan goose.[16]

THE REBEL SCOT
  14 Balance, weigh.
  15 Hyperbolus, an Athenian demagogue of the fifth
century B.C., calling for the exercise of the ostracism against
two political enemies, was himself ostracized when the two
parties united against him and voted to expel him. As a result
of this debasing of the system, the use of the ostracism was
never again resorted to.
  16 An allusion to the old belief that certain trees bore
barnacles each of which contained a perfectly formed goose,
known as the solan goose.

ON THE MEMORY OF MR. EDWARD KING, DROWNED IN THE IRISH SEAS[1]

I like not tears in tune, nor do I prize
His artificial grief who scans his eyes.
Mine weep down pious beads, but why should I
Confine them to the Muse's rosary?
I am no poet here; my pen's the spout
Where the rain-water of mine eyes runs out
In pity of that name, whose fate we see
Thus copied out in grief's hydrography.
The Muses are not mermaids, though upon
His death the ocean might turn Helicon.   10
The sea's too rough for verse: who rhymes upon't
With Xerxes strives to fetter the Hellespont.
My tears will keep no channel, know no laws
To guide their streams, but like the waves, their
    cause,
Run with disturbance till they swallow me
As a description of his misery.
But can his spacious virtue find a grave
Within th' imposthumed bubble of a wave?
Whose learning if we found, we must confess
The sea but shallow and him bottomless.   20
Could not the winds, to countermand thy death,
With their whole card of lungs redeem thy breath?
Or some new island in thy rescue peep
To heave thy resurrection from the deep,
That so the world might see thy safety wrought
With no less wonder than thyself was thought?
The famous Stagirite,[2] who in his life
Had Nature as familiar as his wife,
Bequeathed his widow to survive with thee,
Queen Dowager of all philosophy—   30
An ominous legacy, that did portend
Thy fate and predecessor's second end.
Some have affirmed that what on earth we find,
The sea can parallel in shape and kind.
Books, arts, and tongues were wanting, but in thee
Neptune hath got an university.
We'll dive no more for pearls; the hope to see
Thy sacred reliques of mortality

ON THE MEMORY
  1 First published in *Justa Edovardo King*, 1638, the volume
of verses in memory of Edward King. The volume is famed
chiefly for containing Milton's Lycidas, with which, of
course, Cleveland's poem should be compared.
  2 Aristotle.

Shall welcome storms, and make the seaman prize
His shipwreck now more than his merchandise.   40
He shall embrace the waves and to thy tomb
As to a royaler exchange shall come.
What can we now expect? Water and fire,
Both elements our ruin do conspire,
And that dissolves us which doth us compound.
One Vatican was burnt, another drowned.

We of the gown our libraries must toss
To understand the greatness of our loss;
Be pupils to our grief, and so much grow
In learning as our sorrows overflow.   50
When we have filled the runlets of our eyes,
We'll issue it forth and vent such elegies
As that our tears shall seem the Irish Seas,
We floating islands, living Hebrides.

Sir John Denham

[1615–1669]

BORN in Ireland of noble parents, Sir John Denham studied at Trinity College, Oxford, but failed to take a degree, being even then subject to the weakness for gambling and other forms of excess which was to manifest itself throughout his life. In 1634 he was studying law at Lincoln's Inn, and in the same year he married. In 1638 he inherited his father's large fortune. His drama *The Sophy* (1641) was widely admired, and his long, discursive "Cooper's Hill," published in a pirated edition of 1642, went through some five printings before the authorized edition appeared, with enlargements, in 1665.

"Cooper's Hill" gave definitive form to the hitherto amorphous genre of the "topographical poem," a loosely organized piece of descriptive verse in which landscape serves as a series of cues to sententious generalization and moralization. The poem is the ancestor of Pope's "Windsor Forest," and Denham reveals a kinship to Pope both in his closed couplets and in his distinctly proto-Augustan penchant for parallelism, antithesis, and chiasmus.

After fighting for the king during the Civil War, Denham went into exile in Paris, whence he undertook several missions for Charles II. He returned to England in 1652 and remained there until 1659. He was knighted at the Restoration, in 1663 became a member of the Royal Society, and in 1665 married for the second time. His second wife shortly thereafter became the mistress of the Duke of York, a fact which contemporary opinion regarded as the cause of the temporary madness which afflicted the poet toward the end of his life.

Denham's reputation, like Waller's, has not worn well, but Dryden, Pope, and Johnson all considered him one of the major poets of his age.

SIR J. DENHAM. *Poetical Works*, ed. T. H. Banks, Jr. (New Haven, 1928).

S. JOHNSON, in *Lives of the English Poets*. (See under Waller bibliography.)

G. WILLIAMSON. "The Rhetorical Pattern of Neo-classical Wit," *MP*, 33 (1935–36). (Reprinted in his *Seventeenth-Century Contexts*, Chicago, 1961.)

E. R. WASSERMAN, in *The Subtler Language* (Baltimore, 1959). An excellent essay on "Cooper's Hill."

FROM
POEMS AND TRANSLATIONS [1668]

COOPER'S HILL

SURE there are poets which did never dream
Upon Parnassus, nor did taste the stream
Of Helicon; we therefore may suppose
Those made not poets, but the poets those.
And as courts make not kings, but kings the court,
So where the Muses and their train resort,
Parnassus stands: if I can be to thee
A poet, thou Parnassus art to me.
Nor wonder, if (advantaged in my flight,
By taking wing from thy auspicious height)   10
Through untraced ways and airy paths I fly,
More boundless in my fancy than my eye:
My eye, which swift as thought contracts the space
That lies between, and first salutes the place
Crowned with that sacred pile, so vast, so high,
That whether 'tis a part of earth or sky
Uncertain seems, and may be thought a proud
Aspiring mountain, or descending cloud,
Paul's, the late theme of such a Muse whose flight
Has bravely reached and soared above thy height; [1]
Now shalt thou stand though sword, or time, or
      fire,   20
Or zeal more fierce than they, thy fall conspire,
Secure, whilst thee the best of poets sings,
Preserved from ruin by the best of kings.
Under his proud survey the city lies,
And like a mist beneath a hill doth rise,
Whose state and wealth, the business and the crowd,
Seems at this distance but a darker cloud;
And is to him who rightly things esteems
No other in effect than what it seems.   30
Where, with like haste, through several ways they
      run,
Some to undo and some to be undone;
While luxury and wealth, like war and peace,
Are each the other's ruin and increase,
As rivers lost in seas, some secret vein
Thence reconveighs, there to be lost again.
Oh, happiness of sweet retired content!
To be at once secure and innocent.

Windsor the next (where Mars with Venus dwells,
Beauty with strength) above the valley swells   40
Into my eye and doth itself present
With such an easy and unforced ascent
That no stupendous precipice denies
Access, no horror turns away our eyes;
But such a rise as doth at once invite
A pleasure and a reverence from the sight.
Thy mighty master's emblem, in whose face
Sat meekness, heightened with majestic grace;
Such seems thy gentle height, made only proud
To be the basis of that pompous load,   50
Than which a nobler weight no mountain bears,
But Atlas only that supports the spheres.
When nature's hand this ground did thus advance,
'Twas guided by a wiser power than chance,
Marked out for such a use as if 'twere meant
T'invite the builder, and his choice prevent.
Nor can we call it choice when what we choose,
Folly or blindness only could refuse.
A crown of such majestic towers doth grace
The gods' great mother [2] when her heavenly race 60
Do homage to her; yet she cannot boast
Amongst that numerous and celestial host
More heroes than can Windsor, nor doth fame's
Immortal book record more noble names.
Not to look back so far, to whom this isle
Owes the first glory of so brave a pile,
Whether to Cæsar, Albanact, or Brute, [3]
The British Arthur, or the Danish Canute
(Though this of old no less contest did move
Than when for Homer's birth seven cities strove; 70
Like him in birth, thou shouldst be like in fame,
As thine his fate, if mine had been his flame);
But whose'er it was, nature designed
First a brave place, and then as brave a mind.
Not to recount those several kings, to whom
It gave a cradle, or to whom a tomb,
But thee, great Edward, and thy greater son, [4]
(The lilies which his father wore, he won)
And thy Bellona, who the consort came
Not only to thy bed, but to thy fame;   80

COOPER'S HILL
1 Waller, Upon His Majesty's Repairing of Paul's.
2 Cybele, a Near Eastern nature goddess.
3 Brutus, the legendary founder of Britain.
4 Edward III and the Black Prince, his son.

She to thy triumph led one captive king
And brought that son, which did the second bring.[5]
Then didst thou found that Order [6] (whether love
Or victory thy royal thoughts did move).
Each was a noble cause, and nothing less
Than the design has been the great success,
Which foreign kings and emperors esteem
The second honor to their diadem.
Had thy great destiny but given thee skill
To know, as well as power to act her will,   90
That from those kings, who then thy captives were
In after-times should spring a royal pair [7]
Who should possess all that thy mighty power,
Or thy desires more mighty, did devour,
To whom their better fate reserves whate'er
The victor hopes for, or the vanquished fear;
That blood, which thou and thy grandsire shed,
And all that since these sister nations bled,
Had been unspilt, had happy Edward known
That all the blood he spilt had been his own.   100
When he that patron chose [8] in whom are joined
Soldier and martyr, and his arms confined
Within the azure circle, he did seem
But to foretell and prophesy of him
Who to his realms that azure round hath joined,
Which nature for their bound at first designed;
That bound, which to the world's extremest ends,
Endless itself, its liquid arms extends:
Nor doth he need those emblems which we paint,
But is himself the soldier and the saint.   110
Here should my wonder dwell, and here my praise;
But my fixed thoughts my wandering eye betrays,
Viewing a neighboring hill, whose top of late
A chapel crowned, till in the common fate
The adjoining Abbey [9] fell (may no such storm
Fall on our times, where ruin must reform).
Tell me, my Muse, what monstrous dire offense,
What crime could any Christian king incense
To such a rage? Was't luxury, or lust?
Was he so temperate, so chaste, so just?   120
Were these their crimes? They were his own much
      more;
But wealth is crime enough to him that's poor,

Who having spent the treasures of his crown,
Condemns their luxury to feed his own.
And yet this act, to varnish o'er the shame
Of sacrilege, must bear devotion's name.
No crime so bold but would be understood
A real, or at least a seeming good.
Who fears not to do ill, yet fears the name,
And free from conscience, is a slave to fame.   130
Thus he the church at once protects and spoils;
But Prince's swords are sharper than their styles.[10]
And thus to the ages past he makes amends,
Their charity destroys, their faith defends.
Then did religion in a lazy cell,
In empty, airy contemplations dwell,
And like the block, unmoved, lay; but ours,
As much too active, like the stork devours.
Is there no temperate region can be known,
Betwixt their frigid, and our torrid zone?   140
Could we not wake from that lethargic dream,
But to be restless in a worse extreme?
And for that lethargy was there no cure,
But to be cast into a calenture?[11]
Can knowledge have no bound, but must advance
So far, to make us wish for ignorance?
And rather in the dark to grope our way
Than led by a false guide to err by day?
Who sees these dismal heaps, but would demand
What barbarous invader sacked the land?   150
But when he hears no Goth, no Turk did bring
This desolation, but a Christian king,
When nothing but the name of zeal appears
'Twixt our best actions and the worst of theirs,
What does he think our sacrilege would spare,
When such the effects of our devotions are?
Parting from thence 'twixt anger, shame, and fear,
Those for what's past, and this for what's too near,
My eye, descending from the hill, surveys
Where Thames amongst the wanton valleys
      strays.   160
Thames, the most loved of all the ocean's sons,
By his old sire, to his embraces runs,
Hasting to pay his tribute to the sea,
Like mortal life to meet eternity.
Though with those streams he no resemblance
      hold,
Whose foam is amber and their gravel gold;
His genuine, and less guilty wealth to explore,
Search not his bottom, but survey his shore,

5 Queen Phillippa is *Bellona*; the first "captive king" is King David II of Scotland and the second, King John II of France.
6 The Order of the Garter.
7 Charles I and Henrietta Maria.
8 St. George.   9 Chertsey Abbey.

10 Titles. In reference to Henry VIII's book against Luther.
11 A tropical fever.

O'er which he kindly spreads his spacious wing,
And hatches plenty for the ensuing spring.   170
Nor then destroys it with too fond a stay,
Like mothers which their infants overlay;
Nor with a sudden and impetuous wave,
Like profuse kings, resumes the wealth he gave.
No unexpected inundations spoil
The mower's hopes, nor mock the plowman's toil;
But God-like his unwearied bounty flows;
First loves to do, then loves the good he does.
Nor are his blessings to his banks confined,
But free and common as the sea or wind;   180
When he to boast, or to disperse his stores,
Full of the tributes of his grateful shores,
Visits the world, and in his flying towers
Brings home to us, and makes the Indies ours;
Finds wealth where 'tis, bestows it where it wants,
Cities in deserts, woods in cities plants,
So that to us no thing, no place is strange,
While his fair bosom is the world's exchange.
O could I flow like thee, and make thy stream
My great example, as it is my theme!   190
Though deep, yet clear, though gentle, yet not dull,
Strong without rage, without o'er-flowing full.
Heaven her Eridanus[12] no more shall boast,
Whose fame in thine, like lesser currents lost,
Thy nobler streams shall visit Jove's abodes,
To shine amongst the stars and bathe the gods.
Here nature, whether more intent to please
Us or herself with strange varieties
(For things of wonder give no less delight
To the wise Maker's, than beholder's sight,   200
Though these delights from several causes move;
For so our children, thus our friends we love),
Wisely she knew the harmony of things,
As well as that of sounds, from discords springs.
Such was the discord which did first disperse
Form, order, beauty through the universe.
While dryness moisture, coldness heat resists,
All that we have, and that we are, subsists;
While the steep horrid roughness of the wood
Strives with the gentle calmness of the flood,   210
Such huge extremes when nature doth unite,
Wonder from thence results, from thence delight.
The stream is so transparent, pure, and clear,
That had the self-enamored youth[13] gazed here,
So fatally deceived he had not been,
While he the bottom, not his face had seen.

But his proud head the airy mountain hides
Among the clouds; his shoulders and his sides
A shady mantle clothes; his curled brows   219
Frown on the gentle stream, which calmly flows,
While winds and storms his lofty forehead beat,
The common fate of all that's high or great.
Low at his foot a spacious plain is placed,
Between the mountain and the stream embraced,
Which shade and shelter from the hill derives,
While the kind river wealth and beauty gives;
And in the mixture of all these appears
Variety, which all the rest indears.
This scene had some bold Greek, or British bard
Beheld of old, what stories had we heard   230
Of fairies, satyrs, and the nymphs, their dames,
Their feasts, their revels, and their amorous flames.
'Tis the same still, although their airy shape
All but the quick poetic sight escape.
There Faunus and Sylvanus keep their courts,
And thither all the horned host resorts
To graze the ranker mead; that noble herd
On whose sublime and shady fronts is reared
Nature's great masterpiece, to show how soon
Great things are made, but sooner are undone.   240
Here have I seen the king, when great affairs
Give leave to slacken and unbend his cares,
Attended to the chase by all the flower
Of youth, whose hopes a nobler prey devour.
Pleasure with praise and danger they would buy,
And wish a foe that would not only fly.
The stag now conscious of his fatal growth,
At once indulgent to his fear and sloth,
To some dark covert his retreat had made,
Where no man's eye, nor heaven's should invade
His soft repose; when the unexpected sound   251
Of dogs and men his wakeful ear doth wound.
Roused with the noise, he scarce believes his ear,
Willing to think the illusions of his fear
Had given this alarm; but straight his view
Confirms that more than all he fears is true.
Betrayed in all his strengths, the wood beset,
All instruments, all arts of ruin met,
He calls to mind his strength and then his speed,
His winged heels, and then his armed head;   260
With these to avoid, with that his fate to meet;
But fear prevails and bids him thrust his feet.
So fast he flies that his reviewing eye
Has lost the chasers, and his ear the cry;
Exulting, till he finds their nobler sense
Their disproportioned speed does recompense.

12 A mythical river.   13 Narcissus.

Then curses his conspiring feet, whose scent
Betrays that safety which their swiftness lent.
Then tries his friends: among the baser herd,
Where he so lately was obeyed and feared,   270
His safety seeks; the herd, unkindly wise,
Or chases him from thence, or from him flies.
Like a declining statesman left forlorn
To his friends' pity and pursuers' scorn,
With shame remembers, while himself was one
Of the same herd, himself the same had done.
Thence to the coverts and the conscious groves,
The scenes of his past triumphs and his loves,
Sadly surveying where he ranged alone,
Prince of the soil and all the herd his own,   280
And like a bold knight errant did proclaim
Combat to all, and bore away the dame,
And taught the woods to echo to the stream
His dreadful challenge and his clashing beam;
Yet faintly now declines the fatal strife,
So much his love was dearer than his life.
Now every leaf and every moving breath
Presents a foe, and every foe a death.
Wearied, forsaken, and pursued, at last
All safety in despair of safety placed,   290
Courage he thence resumes, resolved to bear
All their assaults, since 'tis in vain to fear.
And now too late he wishes for the fight
That strength he wasted in ignoble flight.
But when he sees the eager chase renewed,
Himself by dogs, the dogs by men pursued,
He straight revokes his bold resolve, and more
Repents his courage than his fear before;
Finds that uncertain ways unsafest are,
And doubt a greater mischief than despair.   300
Then to the stream, when neither friends, nor force,
Nor speed, nor art avail, he shapes his course;
Thinks not their rage so desperate to assay
An element more merciless than they.
But fearless they pursue, nor can the flood
Quench their dire thirst; alas, they thirst for blood.
So toward a ship the oarfin'd galleys ply,
Which wanting sea to ride, or wind to fly,
Stands but to fall revenged on those that dare
Tempt the last fury of extreme despair.   310
So fares the stag among the enraged hounds,
Repels their force, and wounds returns for wounds.
And as a hero, whom his baser foes
In troops surround, now these assails, now those,
Though prodigal of life, disdains to die,
By common hands; but if he can descry

Some nobler foe's approach, to him he calls
And begs his fate, and then contented falls:
So when the king a mortal shaft lets fly
From his unerring hand, then glad to die,   320
Proud of the wound, to it resigns his blood
And stains the crystal with a purple flood.
This a more innocent and happy chase
Than when of old, but in the self-same place,[14]
Fair liberty pursued, and meant a prey
To lawless power, here turned and stood at bay,
When in that remedy all hope was placed
Which was, or should have been at least, the last.
Here was that Charter sealed wherein the crown
All marks of arbitrary power lays down.   330
Tyrant and slave, those names of hate and fear,
The happier style of king and subject bear:
Happy when both to the same center move
When kings give liberty, and subjects love.
Therefore not long in force this Charter stood;
Wanting that seal, it must be sealed in blood.
The subjects armed, the more the princes gave,
The advantage only took the more to crave.
Till kings by giving, give themselves away,
And even that power that should deny, betray.   340
"Who gives constrained, but his own fear reviles,
Not thanked, but scorned; nor are they gifts, but
        spoils."
Thus kings, by grasping more than they could hold,
First made their subjects by oppression bold;
And popular sway, by forcing kings to give
More than was fit for subjects to receive,
Ran to the same extremes; and one excess
Made both, by striving to be greater, less.
When a calm river, raised with sudden rains,   349
Or snows dissolved, o'erflows the adjoining plains,
The husbandmen with high-raised banks secure
Their greedy hopes, and this he can endure.
But if with bays and dams they strive to force
His channel to a new or narrow course,
No longer then within his banks he dwells;
First to a torrent, then a deluge swells;
Stronger and fiercer by restraint he roars,
And knows no bound, but makes his power his
        shores.

14 Runnymede, where King John was forced to sign the
Magna Charta.

SOMNUS, THE HUMBLE GOD

Somnus, the humble god that dwells
In cottages and smoky cells,
Hates gilded roofs and beds of down;
And, though he fears no prince's frown,
Flies from the circle of a crown.

Come, I say, thou powerful god,
And thy leaden charming rod,
Dipped in the Lethean lake,
O'er his wakeful temples shake,
Lest he should sleep and never wake.   10

Nature, alas, why art thou so
Obliged to thy greatest foe?
Sleep, that is thy best repast,
Yet of death it bears the taste,
And both are the same thing at last.

Richard Lovelace

[1618–1657]

L ITERARY history has coupled Lovelace and Suckling as twin stereotypes of the seventeenth-century cavalier, and in both life and art the two men justify the grouping. The consistent emphases of Lovelace's poetry, however, underline a set of cavalier ideals quite different from those epitomized by his friend's work: where Suckling is brittle and flippant, Lovelace is serious; where Suckling exalts fickleness, Lovelace praises constancy. Both poets exhibit the usual Caroline fusion of the influences of Donne and Jonson, but Lovelace sometimes adds to it a strain of melting sensuousness almost suggestive of Crashaw.

Born of a prominent Kentish family, Lovelace was educated at the Charterhouse and at Gloucester Hall, Oxford, where, in 1636, he was granted an M.A. at the request of the king and queen, who had visited the University and were struck by his beauty. Lovelace had written a play while at Oxford, and he distinguished himself as an amateur of painting and music. His quiet life as a connoisseur and country gentleman was interrupted by the troubles of the 1640's: after presenting to the Long Parliament a petition for the restoration of the rights of the king, he was imprisoned in 1642, and on his release he went to France, where he fought for the French against the Spanish. Back in England again, he was imprisoned for ten months in 1648. His poems were published in the volume *Lucasta* (1649), with a commendatory poem by Andrew Marvell. Lovelace's last years are obscure, and he is said to have died in poverty.

Like that of other gifted dilettantes of the age, Lovelace's work is extremely uneven, but at its best, as in the handful of anthology pieces which have given him immortality, it displays the extraordinary sureness of touch and tone which distinguishes the minor poetry of the seventeenth century.

R. LOVELACE. *Poems*, ed. C. H. WILKINSON, 2 vols. (Oxford, 1925; 2nd ed. in one vol., 1930).

C. H. HARTMANN. *The Cavalier Spirit and Its Influence on the Life and Work of Richard Lovelace* (London, 1925). The most complete study.

FROM

LUCASTA [1649]

SONG

To Lucasta. Going Beyond the Seas

If to be absent were to be
　　Away from thee;
Or that when I am gone,
You or I were alone,
Then, my Lucasta, might I crave
Pity from blustering wind or swallowing
　　　　wave.

But I'll not sigh one blast or gale
　　To swell my sail,
Or pay a tear to 'suage
The foaming blow-god's[1] rage;　　　　10
For whether he will let me pass
Or no, I'm still as happy as I was.

Though seas and land betwixt us both,
　　Our faith and troth,
Like separated souls,
All time and space controls;
Above the highest sphere we meet,
Unseen, unknown, and greet as angels greet.

So then we do anticipate
　　Our after-fate,　　　　20
And are alive i' the skies,
　If thus our lips and eyes
Can speak like spirits unconfined
In Heaven, their earthly bodies left behind.

SONG

To Lucasta. Going to the Wars

Tell me not, sweet, I am unkind,
　　That from the nunnery
Of thy chaste breast and quiet mind
　　To war and arms I fly.

True, a new mistress now I chase,
　　The first foe in the field;
And with a stronger faith embrace
　　A sword, a horse, a shield.

Yet this inconstancy is such
　　As you too shall adore;
I could not love thee, dear, so much,
　　Loved I not honor more.

SONG

*To Amarantha, That She Would Dishevel Her
Hair*

Amarantha sweet and fair,
Ah, braid no more that shining hair!
　As my curious hand or eye,
Hovering round thee, let it fly.

Let it fly as unconfined
As its calm ravisher, the wind,
　Who hath left his darling, th' East,
To wanton o'er that spicy nest.

Ev'ry tress must be confessed
But neatly tangled at the best,　　　10
　Like a clue of golden thread,
Most excellently ravelèd.

Do not then wind up that light
In ribands, and o'ercloud in night;
　Like the sun in's early ray,
But shake your head and scatter day.

See, 'tis broke! Within this grove,
The bower, and the walks of love,
　Weary lie we down and rest,
And fan each other's panting breast.　　　20

Here we'll strip and cool our fire
In cream below, in milk-baths higher;
　And when all wells are drawen dry,
I'll drink a tear out of thine eye.

SONG TO LUCASTA. GOING BEYOND THE SEAS
　1 The text reads "blew-god's," but the reference is probably to the "blow-god," Æolus, god of the winds.

Which our very joys shall leave,
That sorrows thus we can deceive;
    Or our very sorrows weep,
    That joys so ripe, so little keep.

ODE

To Lucasta. The Rose

Sweet, serene sky-like flower,
Haste to adorn her bower;
    From thy long cloudy bed
    Shoot forth thy damask head.

New-startled blush of Flora!
The grief of pale Aurora,
    Who will contest no more,
    Haste, haste, to strow her floor.

Vermilion ball that's given
From lip to lip in heaven,   10
    Love's couch's coverled,
    Haste, haste, to make her bed.

Dear offspring of pleased Venus
And jolly plump Silenus,
    Haste, haste, to deck the hair
    Of th' only sweetly fair.

See! rosy is her bower,
Her floor is all this flower;
    Her bed a rosy nest
    By a bed of roses pressed.   20

But early as she dresses,
Why fly you her bright tresses?
    Ah! I have found, I fear—
    Because her cheeks are near.

GRATIANA DANCING AND SINGING

See! with what constant motiòn,
Even and glorious as the sun,
    Gratiana steers that noble frame,
Soft as her breast, sweet as her voice,
That gave each winding law and poise,
    And swifter than the wings of fame.

She beat the happy pavëment
By such a star made firmament,
    Which now no more the roof envies,
But swells up high with Atlas ev'n,   10
Bearing the brighter, nobler heav'n,
    And in her all the deities.

Each step trod out a lover's thought
And the ambitious hopes he brought,
    Chained to her brave feet with such arts,
Such sweet command and gentle awe,
As when she ceased, we sighing saw
    The floor lay paved with broken hearts.

So did she move; so did she sing
Like the harmonious spheres that bring   20
    Unto their rounds their music's aid;
Which she performèd such a way
As all th' enamored world will say
    The Graces dancèd, and Apollo played.

THE SCRUTINY

SONG

Why should you swear I am forsworn,
    Since thine I vowed to be?
Lady, it is already morn,
    And 'twas last night I swore to thee
    That fond impossibility.

Have I not loved thee much and long,
    A tedious twelve hours' space?
I must all other beauties wrong,
    And rob thee of a new embrace,
    Could I still dote upon thy face.   10

Not but all joy in thy brown hair
    By others may be found;
But I must search the black and fair,
    Like skillful mineralists that sound
For treasure in unplowed-up ground.

Then, if when I have loved my round,
    Thou prov'st the pleasant she,
With spoils of meaner beauties crowned
    I laden will return to thee,
    Ev'n sated with variety.   20

THE GRASSHOPPER

To My Noble Friend, Mr. Charles Cotton [1]

ODE

O thou that swing'st upon the waving hair
    Of some well-fillèd oaten beard,
Drunk ev'ry night with a delicious tear
    Dropped thee from heav'n, where now th'art
        reared;

The joys of earth and air are thine entire,
    That with thy feet and wings dost hop and fly;
And, when thy poppy works, thou dost retire
    To thy carved acorn-bed to lie.

Up with the day, the sun thou welcom'st then,
    Sport'st in the gilt plats [2] of his beams,   10
And all these merry days mak'st merry, men,
    Thyself, and melancholy streams.

But ah, the sickle! Golden ears are cropped;
    Ceres and Bacchus bid good night;
Sharp frosty fingers all your flowers have topped,
    And what scythes spared, winds shave off quite.

Poor verdant fool! and now green ice! thy joys
    Large and as lasting as thy perch of grass,
Bid us lay in 'gainst winter, rain, and poise
    Their floods with an o'erflowing glass.   20

Thou best of men and friends! we will create
    A genuine summer in each other's breast,
And spite of this cold time and frozen fate,
    Thaw us a warm seat to our rest.

Our sacred hearths shall burn eternally
    As vestal flames; the North Wind, he
Shall strike his frost-stretched wings, dissolve, and
        fly
    This Ætna in epitome.

Dropping December shall come weeping in,
    Bewail th' usurping of his reign;   30
But when in show'rs of old Greek [3] we begin,
    Shall cry he hath his crown again.

THE GRASSHOPPER
  1 The elder Cotton, father of the poet.
  2 In the braids of sunbeams; cf. l. 1.
  3 Old Greek wine.

Night as clear Hesper shall our tapers whip
    From the light casements where we play,
And the dark hag from her black mantle strip,
    And stick there everlasting day.

Thus richer than untempted kings are we,
    That asking nothing, nothing need:
Though lord of all what seas embrace, yet he
    That wants himself is poor indeed.   40

TO LUCASTA. FROM PRISON

AN EPODE

Long in thy shackles, liberty
I ask, not from these walls but thee
(Left for a while another's bride),
To fancy all the world beside.

Yet ere I do begin to love,
See! how I all my objects prove;
Then my free soul to that confine
'Twere possible I might call mine.

First I would be in love with Peace,
And her rich swelling breasts' increase;   10
But how, alas! how may that be,
Despising earth, she will love me?

Fain would I be in love with War,
As my dear just avenging star;
But War is loved so everywhere,
Ev'n he disdains a lodging here.

Thee and thy wounds I would bemoan,
Fair thorough-shot [1] Religiòn;
But he lives only that kills thee,
And whoso binds thy hands is free.   20

I would love a Parliament
As a main prop from Heaven sent;
But ah! who's he that would be wedded
To th' fairest body that's beheaded?

TO LUCASTA
  1 Shot through.

Next would I court my Liberty,
And then my birthright, Property;
But can that be, when it is known
There's nothing you can call your own?

A Reformation I would have,
As for our griefs a sov'reign salve;   30
That is, a cleansing of each wheel
Of state that yet some rust doth feel;

But not a Reformation so
As to reform were to o'erthrow;
Like watches by unskillful men
Disjointed, and set ill again.

The Public Faith I would adore,
But she is bankrupt of her store;
Nor how to trust her can I see,
For she that cozens all, must me.   40

Since then none of these can be
Fit objects for my love and me,
What then remains but th'only spring
Of all our loves and joys, the King?

He who, being the whole ball
Of day on earth, lends it to all;
When seeking to eclipse his right,
Blinded, we stand in our own light.

And now an universal mist
Of error is spread o'er each breast,   50
With such a fury edged as is
Not found in th'inwards of th'Abyss.

Oh, from thy glorious starry wain,
Dispense on me one sacred beam,
To light me where I soon may see
How to serve you, and you trust me.

TO ALTHEA. FROM PRISON

SONG

When Love with unconfinèd wings
    Hovers within my gates,
And my divine Althea brings
    To whisper at the grates;
When I lie tangled in her hair
    And fettered to her eye,
The gods [1] that wanton in the air
    Know no such liberty.

When flowing cups run swiftly round,
    With no allaying Thames,   10
Our careless heads with roses bound,
    Our hearts with loyal flames;
When thirsty grief in wine we steep,
    When healths and draughts go free,
Fishes that tipple in the deep
    Know no such liberty.

When, like committed [2] linnets, I
    With shriller throat shall sing
The sweetness, mercy, majesty,
    And glories of my King;   20
When I shall voice aloud how good
    He is, how great should be,
Enlargèd winds that curl the flood
    Know no such liberty.

Stone walls do not a prison make,
    Nor iron bars a cage:
Minds innocent and quiet take
    That for an hermitage.
If I have freedom in my love,
    And in my soul am free,   30
Angels alone, that soar above,
    Enjoy such liberty.

TO ALTHEA
1 Most seventeenth-century manuscripts read "birds."
2 To prison; caged.

Abraham Cowley

[1618–1667]

C OWLEY'S poetry, like that of Waller and Cleveland, manifests the transition between the Baroque and Neoclassical styles. Born in London of middle-class parents, Cowley studied at Westminster School and revealed his precocity by publishing, at the age of fifteen, a volume of creditable verse entitled *Poetical Blossoms* (1633). In 1639 he received his B.A. from Trinity College, Oxford, where he had become a close friend of Crashaw, and thereafter he became a fellow. With the coming of the Puritans to Cambridge, he removed to royalist Oxford, and was formally ejected from his fellowship in 1644.

Between 1644 and 1654 Cowley was in France, where he served the exiled king and the queen mother on a number of secret missions. In 1654 he returned to England, possibly as a royalist agent, an hypothesis which is lent credence by the fact that he was imprisoned in the next year and released on making submission to the Commonwealth. He then studied medicine at Oxford, receiving his M.D. in 1657. At the Restoration, Cowley did not enjoy the kind of reward he may have merited, Charles II regarding his submission to Cromwell as a defection. Through the offices of the queen mother he did receive a pension, however, and he led a retired life until his death in 1667. He was buried in Westminster Abbey.

The Mistress, Cowley's collection of Metaphysical love poems, was published in 1647 without his permission. It enjoyed great popularity, as its conceited and witty manner exploited the fashion for "strong lines" without making on its readers the intellectual demands of Donne. His Christian epic, *Davideis* (1656), largely conceived in the 1640's, makes it clear that his poetic assumptions are only superficially Metaphysical: its closed couplets and its correct classicism anticipate the Restoration manner, and his later poems —especially the Pindaric odes and occasional pieces such as the ode addressed to the Royal Society—point in the same direction. In general, Cowley's "wit," however Metaphysical in appearance, is conceived in Hobbesian terms, as "begetting the ornaments of a poem" rather than as constituting its structure and its meaning.

Cowley's *Poems* were published in 1656, and his reputation remained high during the Restoration, waning, however, throughout the eighteenth century. He has not shared in the general revival enjoyed by many Metaphysical poets in our century.

A. COWLEY. *English Writings*, ed. A. R. Waller, 2 vols. (Cambridge, 1905–06).
————. *The Mistress and Other Select Poems*, ed. J. Sparrow (London, 1926).
S. JOHNSON, in *Lives of the English Poets*. (See under Waller bibliography.) Johnson's "Life of Cowley" contains the famous analysis of the Metaphysical poets. See appendix.

A. H. NETHERCOT. *Abraham Cowley: the Muses' Hannibal* (Oxford, 1931). Biography.

R. B. HINMAN. *Abraham Cowley's World of Order* (Cambridge, Mass., 1960). A detailed study, with an unusually sympathetic appreciation.

A. ALVAREZ. (See under Cleveland bibliography.) Has a good chapter on Cowley.

F R O M

LOVE'S RIDDLE [1638]

SPORT

The merry waves dance up and down, and play,
    Sport is granted to the sea;
Birds are the choristers of the empty air,
    Sport is never wanting there.
The ground doth smile at the spring's flowery birth,
    Sport is granted to the earth;

The fire its cheering flame on high doth rear,
    Sport is never wanting there.
If all the elements, the earth, the sea,
    Air, and fire, so merry be,
Why is man's mirth so seldom and so small,
    Who is compounded of them all?

F R O M

THE WORKS OF MR. ABRAHAM COWLEY [1668]

MISCELLANIES

ON THE DEATH OF MR. WILLIAM HERVEY[1]

Immodicis brevis est ætas, & rara senectus. Mart.[2]

It was a dismal and a fearful night;
Scarce could the morn drive on the unwilling light,
When sleep, death's image, left my troubled breast,
    By something liker death possessed.
My eyes with tears did uncommanded flow,
    And on my soul hung the dull weight
    Of some intolerable fate.
What bell was that? Ah me! Too much I know.

My sweet companion, and my gentle peer,
Why hast thou left me thus unkindly here,   10
Thy end forever, and my life to moan?
    Oh, thou hast left me all alone!

Thy soul and body, when death's agony
    Besieged around thy noble heart,
    Did not with more reluctance part
Than I, my dearest friend, do part from thee.

My dearest friend, would I had died for thee![3]
Life and this world henceforth will tedious be.
Nor shall I know hereafter what to do
    If once my griefs prove tedious too.   20
Silent and sad I walk about all day,
    As sullen ghosts stalk speechless by
    Where their hid treasures lie;
Alas, my treasure's gone; why do I stay?

He was my friend, the truest friend on earth;
A strong and mighty influence joined our birth.
Nor did we envy the most sounding name
    By friendship given of old to fame.
None but his brethren he, and sisters, knew
    Whom the kind youth preferred to me;   30
    And even in that we did agree,
For much above myself I loved them too.

MR. WILLIAM HERVEY

1 Of Hervey, a friend of Cowley's Cambridge days, we know only what the elegy tells us.

2 The line from Martial (6.29) may be rendered, "To those extraordinarily gifted, life is short, and old age rare."

3 David's lament for his son Absalom, II Samuel 18:33.

Say, for you saw us, ye immortal lights,
How oft unwearied have we spent the nights?
Till the Ledæan stars, so famed for love,[4]
   Wondered at us from above.
We spent them not in toys,[5] in lusts, or wine,
   But search of deep philosophy,
   Wit, eloquence, and poetry,   39
Arts which I loved, for they, my friend, were thine.

Ye fields of Cambridge, our dear Cambridge, say,
Have ye not seen us walking every day?
Was there a tree about, which did not know
   The love betwixt us two?
Henceforth, ye gentle trees, forever fade;
   Or your sad branches thicker join,
   And into darksome shades combine,
Dark as the grave wherein my friend is laid.

Henceforth no learned youths beneath you sing
Till all the tuneful birds to your boughs they bring;
No tuneful birds play with their wonted cheer,   51
   And call the learned youths to hear;
No whistling winds through the glad branches fly,
   But all with sad solemnity
   Mute and unmovèd be,
Mute as the grave wherein my friend does lie.

To him my Muse made haste with every strain
Whilst it was new, and warm yet from the brain;
He loved my worthless rhymes, and like a friend
   Would find out something to commend.   60
Hence now, my Muse; thou canst not me delight;
   Be this my latest verse
   With which I now adorn his hearse,
And this my grief without thy help shall write.

Had I a wreath of bays about my brow,
I should contemn that flourishing honor now,
Condemn it to the fire, and joy to hear
   It rage and crackle there.
Instead of bays, crown with sad cypress me,
   Cypress which tombs does beautify;   70
   Not Phœbus grieved so much as I
For him who first was made that mournful tree.[6]

4 Castor and Pollux, the twin sons of Leda and the Swan (Zeus in disguise) were, because of their great love for each other, placed in the heavens as "the Twins" (Gemini).
5 Trifling diversions.
6 Cyparissus, a beautiful youth loved by Apollo, died of grief because he had accidentally killed a pet stag. He was metamorphosed by Apollo into a cypress.

Large was his soul; as large a soul as e'er
Submitted to inform a body here;
High as the place 'twas shortly in Heaven to have,
   But low and humble as his grave;
So high that all the virtues there did come
   As to their chiefest seat,
   Conspicuous and great;
So low that for me, too, it made a room.   80

He scorned this busy world below, and all
That we, mistaken mortals, pleasure call;
Was filled with innocent gallantry and truth,
   Triumphant o'er the sins of youth.
He, like the stars, to which he now is gone,
   That shine with beams like flame,
   Yet burn not with the same,
Had all the light of youth, of the fire none.

Knowledge he only sought, and so soon caught,
As if for him knowledge had rather sought;   90
Nor did more learning ever crowded lie
   In such a short mortality.
Whene'er the skillful youth discoursed or writ,
   Still did the notions throng
   About his eloquent tongue,
Nor could his ink flow faster than his wit.

So strong a wit did nature to him frame
As all things but his judgment overcame;
His judgment like the heavenly moon did show,
   Tempering that mighty sea below.   100
Oh, had he lived in learning's world, what bound
   Would have been able to control
   His overpowering soul?
We have lost in him arts that not yet are found.

His mirth was the pure spirits of various wit,
Yet never did his God or friends forget,
And, when deep talk and wisdom came in view,
   Retired and gave to them their due.
For the rich help of books he always took,
   Though his own searching mind before   110
   Was so with notions written o'er
As if wise nature had made that her book.

So many virtues joined in him as we
Can scarce pick here and there in history,
More than old writers' practice e'er could reach,
   As much as they could ever teach.

These did religion, queen of virtues, sway,
    And all their sacred motions steer,
    Just like the first and highest sphere,
Which wheels about, and turns all heaven one way.[7]

With as much zeal, devotion, piety,   121
He always lived, as other saints do die.
Still[8] with his soul severe account he kept,
    Weeping all debts out ere he slept.
Then down in peace and innocence he lay,
    Like the sun's laborious light,
    Which still in water sets at night,
Unsullied with his journey of the day.

Wondrous young man, why wert thou made so
        good,
To be snatched hence ere better understood,   130
Snatched before half of thee enough was seen!
    Thou ripe, and yet thy life but green!
Nor could thy friends take their last sad farewell,
    But danger and infectious death
    Maliciously seized on that breath,
Where life, spirit, pleasure always used to dwell.

But happy thou, ta'en from this frantic age,
Where ignorance and hypocrisy does rage!
A fitter time for Heaven no soul e'er chose,
    The place now only free from those.   140
There 'mong the blest thou dost forever shine,
    And wheresoe'er thou casts thy view
    Upon that white and radiant crew,
Seest not a soul clothed with more light than thine.

And if the glorious saints cease not to know
Their wretched friends who fight with life below,
Thy flame to me does still the same abide,
    Only more pure and rarefied.
There whilst immortal hymns thou dost rehearse,
    Thou dost with holy pity see   150
    Our dull and earthly poesy,
Where grief and misery can be joined with verse.

ON THE DEATH OF MR. CRASHAW[1]

Poet and saint! to thee alone are given
The two most sacred names of earth and heaven,
The hard and rarest union which can be,
Next that of Godhead with humanity.
Long did the Muses banished slaves abide,
And built vain pyramids to mortal pride;
Like Moses thou—though spells and charms
        withstand—
Hast brought them nobly home back to their Holy
        Land.
    Ah wretched we, poets of earth! but thou
Wert, living, the same poet which thou'rt now.   10
Whilst angels sing to thee their airs divine,
And joy in an applause so great as thine,
Equal society with them to hold,
Thou need'st not make new songs, but say the old.
And they, kind spirits, shall all rejoice to see
How little less than they exalted man may be.
Still the old heathen gods in numbers dwell;
The heavenliest thing on earth still keeps up hell.
Nor have we yet quite purged the Christian land;
Still idols here like calves at Bethel[2] stand.   20
And though Pan's death long since all oracles broke,
Yet still in rhyme the fiend Apollo spoke:[3]
Nay, with the worst of heathen dotage we,
Vain men, the monster woman deify;
Find stars, and tie our fates there, in a face,
And Paradise in them by whom we lost it place.
What different faults corrupt our Muses thus?
Wanton as girls; as old wives, fabulous![4]
Thy spotless Muse, like Mary, did contain
The boundless Godhead; she did well disdain   30
That her eternal verse employed should be
On a less subject than eternity;
And for a sacred mistress scorned to take
But her whom God himself scorned not His spouse
        to make.
It, in a kind, her miracle did do;
A fruitful mother was, and virgin too.

MR. CRASHAW
    1 For an account of Crashaw's life, see p. 916.
    2 After the division of the Hebrew nation, Jeroboam, ruler
of the northern kingdom of Israel, in order to prevent his
people from going to worship at Jerusalem, the capital of the
southern kingdom of Judah, set up two golden calves at
Bethel and made a shrine there. See I Kings 12:25-33.
    3 Apollo, the patron of the Muses and of poetry, spoke
through love poems.
    4 Given to fables, gossipy.

MR. WILLIAM HERVEY
    7 The *primum mobile*, the outermost sphere of the universe
according to the older cosmology, which set in motion the
other spheres.
    8 Always.

How well, blest swan, did fate contrive thy death;
And made thee render up thy tuneful breath
In thy great mistress' arms, thou most divine
And richest offering of Loretto's shrine!   40
Where, like some holy sacrifice to expire,
A fever burns thee, and love lights the fire.[5]
Angels, they say, brought the famed chapel there,
And bore the sacred load in triumph through the
    air.
'Tis surer much they brought thee there; and they
And thou, their charge, went singing all the way.
    Pardon, my Mother Church, if I consent
That angels led him when from thee he went,
For even in error sure no danger is
When joined with so much piety as his.   50
Ah, mighty God, with shame I speak it, and grief,
Ah that our greatest faults were in belief!
And our weak reason were even weaker yet,
Rather than thus our wills too strong for it.
His faith perhaps in some nice[6] tenets might
Be wrong; his life, I'm sure, was in the right.
And I myself a Catholic will be
So far at least, great saint, to pray to thee.
    Hail, bard triumphant, and some care bestow
On us, the poets militant below!   60
Opposed by our old enemy, adverse chance,
Attacked by envy, and by ignorance,
Enchained by beauty, tortured by desires,
Exposed by tyrant love to savage beasts and fires.
Thou from low earth in nobler flames didst rise,
And, like Elijah,[7] mount alive the skies.
Elisha-like[8] (but with a wish much less,
More fit thy greatness and my littleness),
Lo, here I beg (I whom thou once didst prove
So humble to esteem, so good to love)   70
Not that thy spirit might on me doubled be,
I ask but half thy mighty spirit for me;
And when my Muse soars with so strong a wing,
'Twill learn of things divine, and first of thee to
    sing.

ANACREONTICS; OR, SOME COPIES OF VERSES TRANSLATED PARAPHRASTICALLY OUT OF ANACREON

II. DRINKING

The thirsty earth soaks up the rain,
And drinks, and gapes for drink again.
The plants suck in the earth, and are
With constant drinking fresh and fair.
The sea itself, which one would think
Should have but little need of drink,
Drinks ten thousand rivers up,
So filled that they o'erflow the cup.
The busy sun—and one would guess
By his drunken, fiery face no less—   10
Drinks up the sea, and when he's done,
The moon and stars drink up the sun.
They drink and dance by their own light;
They drink and revel all the night.
Nothing in nature's sober found,
But an eternal health goes round.
Fill up the bowl then, fill it high,
Fill all the glasses there, for why
Should every creature drink but I?
Why, man of morals, tell me why?   20

VIII. THE EPICURE

Fill the bowl with rosy wine,
Around our temples roses twine,
And let us cheerfully a while
Like the wine and roses smile.
Crowned with roses, we contemn
Gyges'[1] wealthy diadem.
Today is ours; what do we fear?
Today is ours; we have it here.
Let's treat it kindly, that it may
Wish, at least, with us to stay.
Let's banish business, banish sorrow;
To the gods belongs tomorrow.

MR. CRASHAW
  5 Cowley's note: "Mr. Crashaw died of a fever at Loretto,
being newly chosen canon of that church."
  6 Subtle.   7 See II Kings 2:11.
  8 See II Kings 2:9.

ANACREONTICS
  1 The riches of Gyges, king of Lydia in the seventh
century B.C., like those of Crœsus, became a proverb.

X. The Grasshopper

Happy insect, what can be
In happiness compared to thee?
Fed with nourishment divine,
The dewy morning's gentle wine!
Nature waits upon thee still,
And thy verdant cup does fill;
'Tis filled wherever thou dost tread,
Nature's self's thy Ganymede.
Thou dost drink and dance and sing,
Happier than the happiest king!   10
All the fields which thou dost see,
All the plants, belong to thee;
All that summer hours produce,
Fertile made with early juice.
Man for thee does sow and plow,
Farmer he, and landlord thou!
Thou dost innocently joy,
Nor does thy luxury destroy;
The shepherd gladly heareth thee,
More harmonious than he.   20
Thee country hinds with gladness hear,
Prophet of the ripened year!
Thee Phœbus loves and does inspire;
Phœbus is himself thy sire.
To thee of all things upon earth
Life is no longer than thy mirth.
Happy insect, happy thou,
Dost neither age nor winter know.
But when thou'st drunk and danced and sung
Thy fill the flowery leaves among,   30
Voluptuous and wise withal,
Epicurean animal!
Sated with thy summer feast,
Thou retir'st to endless rest.

THE MISTRESS

THE WISH

Well then; I now do plainly see,
This busy world and I shall ne'er agree;
The very honey of all earthly joy
   Does of all meats the soonest cloy;
     And they, methinks, deserve my pity
Who for it can endure the stings,
The crowd, and buzz, and murmurings
     Of this great hive, the city.

     Ah, yet, ere I descend to the grave
May I a small house and large garden have!   10
And a few friends, and many books, both true,
   Both wise, and both delightful too!
     And since love ne'er will from me flee,
A mistress moderately fair,
And good as guardian angels are,
     Only beloved, and loving me!

     O fountains, when in you shall I
Myself, eased of unpeaceful thoughts, espy?
O fields! O woods! when, when shall I be made
     The happy tenant of your shade?   20
     Here's the spring-head of pleasure's flood,
   Where all the riches lie that she
     Has coined and stamped for good.

     Pride and ambition here
Only in far-fetched metaphors appear;
Here naught but winds can hurtful murmurs
         scatter,
     And naught but Echo flatter.
     The gods, when they descended, hither
From heaven did always choose their way;
And therefore we may boldly say   30
     That 'tis the way, too, thither.

     How happy here should I
And one dear she live and, embracing, die!
She who is all the world, and can exclude
     In deserts, solitude.
     I should have then this only fear,
Lest men, when they my pleasures see,
Should hither throng to live like me,
     And so make a city here.

PINDARIC ODES[1]

THE PRAISE OF PINDAR IN IMITATION OF HORACE HIS SECOND ODE, BOOK 4

Pindarum quisquis studet æmulari, &c.

1

Pindar is imitable by none;
  The phœnix Pindar is a vast species alone.
Whoe'er but Dædalus with waxen wings could fly
And neither sink too low nor soar too high?
    What could he who followed claim
But of vain boldness the unhappy fame,
    And by his fall a sea to name?
    Pindar's unnavigable song,
Like a swollen flood from some steep mountain,
    pours along;
  The ocean meets with such a voice   10
From his enlarged mouth as drowns the ocean's
    noise.

2

So Pindar does new words and figures roll
Down his impetuous dithyrambic tide,
    Which in no channel deigns to abide,
    Which neither banks nor dikes control.
    Whether the immortal gods he sings
    In a no less immortal strain,
Or the great acts of god-descended kings,
Who in his numbers still survive and reign,
    Each rich embroidered line,   20
    Which their triumphant brows around
    By his sacred hand is bound,
Does all their starry diadems outshine.

3

Whether at Pisa's race[2] he please
To carve in polished verse the conquerors' images,
Whether the swift, the skillful, or the strong
Be crownèd in his nimble, artful, vigorous song,

Whether some brave young man's untimely fate
In words worth dying for he celebrate,
    Such mournful and such pleasing words   30
As joy to his mother's and his mistress' grief affords,
    He bids him live and grow in fame;
    Among the stars he sticks his name;
The grave can but the dross of him devour,
So small is death's, so great the poet's power.

Lo, how the obsequious wind and swelling air
    The Theban swan does upwards bear
Into the walks of clouds, where he does play,
And with extended wings opens his liquid way,
    Whilst, alas, my timorous Muse   40
    Unambitious tracks pursues;
    Does, with weak, unballast wings,
    About the mossy brooks and springs,
    About the trees' new-blossomed heads,
    About the gardens' painted beds,
    About the fields and flowery meads,
    And all inferior beauteous things,
      Like the laborious bee,
    For little drops of honey flee,
And there with humble sweets contents her
    industry.   50

from DAVIDEIS, BOOK III

[AWAKE, AWAKE, MY LYRE][1]

  Awake, awake, my lyre,
And tell thy silent master's humble tale
    In sounds that may prevail,
  Sounds that gentle thoughts inspire;
    Though so exalted she
    And I so lowly be,
Tell her such different notes make all thy harmony.

PINDARIC ODES
  1 Whether or not Cowley was ignorant of the regular structure of Pindar's odes, his odes are more "Pindaric" in spirit and manner than in form. He is the originator in English of the so-called "irregular ode."
  2 The Olympic games. Pisa, near Olympia, was often identified in poetry, as here, with the scene of the games.

AWAKE, AWAKE, MY LYRE
  1 Davideis, A Sacred Poem of the Troubles of David, Cowley's most ambitious work, is an epic poem of which only four books of a projected twelve were completed. The poem is in heroic couplets. The song here printed is sung beneath the window of Michol, daughter of King Saul, by the young David, who is in love with her.

Hark how the strings awake,
And though the moving hand approach not near,
    Themselves with awful fear   10
  A kind of numerous trembling make.
    Now all thy forces try,
    Now all thy charms apply,
Revenge upon her ear the conquests of her eye.

    Weak lyre! thy virtue sure
Is useless here, since thou art only found
    To cure but not to wound,
  And she to wound but not to cure.
    Too weak, too, wilt thou prove
    My passion to remove;   20
Physic to other ills, thou'rt nourishment to love.

    Sleep, sleep again, my lyre,
For thou canst never tell my humble tale
    In sounds that will prevail,
  Nor gentle thoughts in her inspire;
    All thy vain mirth lay by,
    Bid thy strings silent lie;
Sleep, sleep again, my lyre, and let thy master die.

VERSES ON SEVERAL
OCCASIONS

HYMN. TO LIGHT

First-born of Chaos, who so fair didst come
  From the old Negro's darksome womb!
  Which, when it saw the lovely child,
The melancholy mass put on kind looks and smiled,

Thou tide of glory which no rest dost know,
  But ever ebb and ever flow!
  Thou golden shower of a true Jove,[1]
Who does in thee descend, and heaven to earth
    make love!

Hail, active nature's watchful life and health,
  Her joy, her ornament and wealth!   10

Hail to thy husband Heat, and thee!
Thou the world's beauteous bride, the lusty bride-
    groom he!

Say, from what golden quivers of the sky
  Do all thy wingèd arrows fly?
  Swiftness and power by birth are thine:
From thy great Sire they came, thy Sire the Word
    divine.[2]

'Tis, I believe, this archery to show,
  That so much cost in colors thou,
  And skill in painting, dost bestow
Upon thy ancient arms, the gaudy heavenly bow. 20

Swift as light thoughts their empty career run,
  Thy race is finished when begun;
  Let a post-angel[3] start with thee,
And thou the goal of earth shalt reach as soon as he.

Thou in the moon's bright chariot, proud and gay,
  Dost thy bright wood of stars survey,
  And all the year dost with thee bring,
Of thousand flowery lights, thine own nocturnal
    spring.

Thou Scythian-like[4] dost round thy lands, above
  The sun's gilt tent, forever move,   30
  And still, as thou in pomp dost go,
The shining pageants of the world attend thy show.

Nor amidst all these triumphs dost thou scorn
  The humble glowworms to adorn,
  And with those living spangles gild—
O greatness without pride!—the bushes of the field.

Night and her ugly subjects thou dost fright,
  And sleep, the lazy owl of night;
  Ashamed and fearful to appear,
They screen their horrid shapes with the black
    hemisphere.   40

With 'em there hastes, and wildly takes the alarm,
  Of painted dreams, a busy swarm;
  At the first opening of thine eye,
The various clusters break, the antic atoms fly.

HYMN
  1 A reference to Jove's assuming the form of a shower of
gold to visit Danaë, daughter of the King of Argos, who had
imprisoned her in a tower of brass.

  2 Genesis 1:3, "And God said, Let there be light: and there
was light."
  3 Angel-messenger.
  4 An allusion to the nomadic life of the Scythians.

The guilty serpents and obscener beasts
   Creep conscious to their secret rests;
   Nature to thee does reverence pay;
Ill omens and ill sights removes out of thy way.

At thy appearance, Grief itself is said
   To shake his wings and rouse his head.   50
   And cloudy Care has often took
A gentle beamy smile reflected from thy look.

At thy appearance, Fear itself grows bold;
   Thy sunshine melts away his cold.
   Encouraged at the sight of thee,
To the cheek color comes, and firmness to the knee.

Even Lust, the master of a hardened face,
   Blushes if thou beest in the place;
   To darkness' curtains he retires;
In sympathizing night he rolls his smoky fires.   60

When, goddess, thou lift'st up thy wakened head
   Out of the morning's purple bed,
   Thy quire of birds about thee play,
And all the joyful world salutes the rising day.

The ghosts and monster spirits that did presume
   A body's privilege to assume
   Vanish again invisibly,
And bodies gain again their visibility.

All the world's bravery that delights our eyes
   Is but thy several liveries;   70
   Thou the rich dye on them bestow'st;
Thy nimble pencil paints this landscape as thou
     go'st.

A crimson garment in the rose thou wear'st;
   A crown of studded gold thou bear'st;
   The virgin lilies in their white
Are clad but with the lawn of almost naked light.

The violet, spring's little infant, stands
   Girt in thy purple swaddling-bands;
   On the fair tulip thou dost dote;
Thou cloth'st it in a gay and parti-colored coat.   80

With flame condensed thou dost the jewels fix,
   And solid colors in it mix;
   Flora herself envies to see
Flowers fairer than her own, and durable as she.

Ah, goddess! would thou couldst thy hand with-
     hold
   And be less liberal to gold;
   Didst thou less value to it give,
Of how much care, alas! mightst thou poor man
     relieve!

To me the sun is more delightful far,
   And all fair days much fairer are,   90
   But few, ah wondrous few, there be
Who do not gold prefer, O goddess, even to thee.

Through the soft ways of heaven, and air, and sea,
   Which open all their pores to thee,
   Like a clear river thou dost glide,
And with thy living stream through the close
     channels slide.

But where firm bodies thy free course oppose,
   Gently thy source the land o'erflows,[5]
   Takes there possession, and does make   99
Of colors mingled, light, a thick and standing lake.

But the vast ocean of unbounded day
   In the empyrean heaven does stay.[6]
   Thy rivers, lakes, and springs below
From thence took first their rise, thither at last
     must flow.

TO THE ROYAL SOCIETY[1]

I

Philosophy, the great and only heir
   Of all that human knowledge which has been
Unforfeited by man's rebellious sin,
   Though full of years he do appear

HYMN
5 The physicists of Cowley's day thought of light as a stream of material particles, which could penetrate air or water, but were unable to pass through a solid substance.
6 The highest heaven, conceived of as a region of pure fire and light.

TO THE ROYAL SOCIETY
1 Cowley had been asked by Thomas Sprat to compose an ode for his history of the Royal Society, and he responded with this hymn. It was first printed in 1667 in Sprat's History of the Royal Society. The Royal Society, which was founded in 1660, had been formally incorporated in 1662, with the King as a member. Cowley was keenly interested in the new experimental philosophy, as natural science was then called, and published in 1661 A Proposition for the Advancement of Experimental Philosophy.

(Philosophy, I say, and call it "he,"
For whatsoe'er the painters' fancy be,
　It a male virtue seems to me),
Has still been kept in nonage till of late,
Nor managed or enjoyed his vast estate:
Three or four thousand years, one would have
　　　thought,　　　　　　　　　　　　　10
To ripeness and perfection might have brought
　A science so well bred and nursed,
And of such hopeful parts, too, at the first.
But oh, the guardians and the tutors then,
Some negligent and some ambitious men,
　Would ne'er consent to set him free,
　Or his own natural powers to let him see,
Lest that should put an end to their authority.

2

That his own business he might quite forget,
They amused him with the sports of wanton wit;　20
With the desserts of poetry they fed him,
Instead of solid meats to increase his force;
Instead of vigorous exercise, they led him
Into the pleasant labyrinths of ever-fresh discourse;[2]
　Instead of carrying him to see
The riches which do hoarded for him lie
　In nature's endless treasury,
　They chose his eye to entertain,
　His curious but not covetous eye,
With painted scenes, and pageants of the brain.　30
Some few exalted spirits this latter age has shown,
That labored to assert the liberty,
From guardians who were now usurpers grown,
Of this old minor still, captived philosophy;
　But 'twas rebellion called to fight
　For such a long-oppressèd right.
Bacon at last, a mighty man, arose,
　Whom a wise king and nature chose
　Lord Chancellor of both their laws,
And boldly undertook the injured pupil's cause.　40

3

Authority, which did a body boast.
Though 'twas but air condensed, and stalked about
Like some old giant's more gigantic ghost
　To terrify the learned rout,

With the plain magic of true reason's light
　He chased out of our sight,
Nor suffered living men to be misled
　By the vain shadows of the dead:
To graves, from whence it rose, the conquered
　　　phantom fled.
He broke that monstrous god which stood　　50
In midst of the orchard, and the whole did claim,
　Which, with a useless scythe of wood
　And something else not worth a name—
　Both vast for show, yet neither fit
　Or to defend or to beget;
　Ridiculous and senseless terrors!—made
Children and superstitious men afraid.
　The orchard's open now and free;
Bacon has broke that scarecrow deity;
　Come, enter, all that will;
Behold the ripened fruit; come gather now your fill.
　Yet still, methinks, we fain would be　　61
　Catching at the forbidden tree;[3]
　We would be like the Deity
When truth and falsehood, good and evil, we
Without the senses' aid, within ourselves would see;
　For 'tis God only who can find
　All nature in His mind.

4

From words, which are but pictures of the thought
(Though we our thoughts from them perversely
　　　drew),　　　　　　　　　　　　　70
To things, the mind's right object, he it brought:
Like foolish birds to painted grapes we flew;
He sought and gathered for our use the true;
And when on heaps the chosen bunches lay,
He pressed them wisely the mechanic way,
Till all their juice did in one vessel join,
Ferment into a nourishment divine,
　The thirsty soul's refreshing wine.
Who to the life an exact piece would make,
Must not from others' work a copy take;　　80
　No, not from Rubens or Vandyck;
Much less content himself to make it like
The ideas and the images which lie
In his own fancy or his memory.

---

2 A reference to the methods of the medieval schoolmen.

3 "The forbidden tree" of logic, an unsound method of arriving at scientific truth, still has a fascination for man in spite of Bacon's having thrown open the "orchard" of experimental science.

No, he before his sight must place
The natural and living face;
The real object must command
Each judgment of his eye and motion of his hand.

5

From these and all long errors of the way
In which our wandering predecessors went,   90
And like the old Hebrews many years did stray
      In deserts but of small extent,
Bacon, like Moses, led us forth at last;
      The barren wilderness he passed,
      Did on the very border stand
      Of the best promised land,
And, from the mountain's top of his exalted wit,
      Saw it himself, and showed us it.
But life did never to one man allow
Time to discover worlds, and conquer too;   100
Nor can so short a line sufficient be
To fathom the vast depths of nature's sea.
      The work he did we ought to admire,
And were unjust if we should more require
From his few years, divided 'twixt the excess
Of low affliction and high happiness.
For who on things remote can fix his sight
That's always in a triumph or a fight?

6

From you, great champions, we expect to get
These spacious countries but discovered yet,   110
Countries where yet instead of nature we
Her images and idols worshiped see.
These large and wealthy regions to subdue,
Though learning has whole armies at command
      Quartered about in every land,
A better troop she ne'er together drew.
      Methinks, like Gideon's little band,[4]
      God with design has picked out you,
To do these noble wonders by a few: 119
When the whole host He saw, "They are," said He,
      "Too many to o'ercome for Me."
      And now He chooses out His men
      Much in the way that He did then:
      Not those many whom He found
      Idly extended on the ground,

To drink with their dejected head
The stream just so as by their mouths it fled;
      No, but those few who took the waters up,
      And made of their laborious hands the cup.

7

Thus you prepared; and in the glorious fight   130
      Their wondrous pattern, too, you take:
Their old and empty pitchers first they brake,
And with their hands then lifted up the light.
      Io! Sound too the trumpets here!
Already your victorious lights appear;
New scenes of heaven already we espy,
And crowds of golden worlds on high,
Which, from the spacious plains of earth and sea,
      Could never yet discovered be
By sailor's or Chaldean's[5] watchful eye.   140
Nature's great works no distance can obscure;
No smallness her near objects can secure.[6]
      You've taught the curious sight to press
      Into the privatest recess
Of her imperceptible littleness.
      You've learned to read her smallest hand,
And well begun her deepest sense to understand.

8

Mischief and true dishonor fall on those
Who would to laughter or to scorn expose
So virtuous and so noble a design,[7]   150
So human for its use, for knowledge so divine.
The things which these proud men despise, and call
      Impertinent, and vain, and small,
Those smallest things of nature let me know,
Rather than all their greatest actions do.
Whoever would deposèd truth advance
      Into the throne usurped from it,
Must feel at first the blows of ignorance
      And the sharp points of envious wit.
So when, by various turns of the celestial dance,   160
      In many thousand years
      A star, so long unknown, appears,

4 For the story of Gideon's band see Judges 7:4–7.

5 The Chaldeans, or Babylonians, were famous as astrologers.
6 Great strides were made in developing the telescope and the microscope in the seventeenth century, and the Royal Society was particularly interested in experiments with lenses and optical instruments.
7 Sprat's history was written in large part as a vindication of the Royal Society, and attempted to win over some of the critics of the new experimental philosophy.

Though heaven itself more beauteous by it grow,
It troubles and alarms the world below,
Does to the wise a star, to fools a meteor show.

9

With courage and success, you the bold work begin;
   Your cradle has not idle been:
None e'er but Hercules and you could be
At five years' age worthy a history.
     And ne'er did fortune better yet   170
     The historian to the story fit:
     As you from all old errors free
And purge the body of philosophy,

So from all modern follies he
Has vindicated eloquence and wit.
His candid style like a clean stream does slide,
   And his bright fancy all the way
   Does, like the sunshine, in it play;
It does, like Thames, the best of rivers, glide,
Where the god does not rudely overturn,   180
   But gently pour the crystal urn,
And with judicious hand does the whole current
   guide.
It has all the beauties nature can impart,
And all the comely dress without the paint of art.

Andrew Marvell

[1621–1678]

ANDREW MARVELL is one of the most elusive of poets. His small but very great body of lyric poetry, in which Metaphysical ingenuity and Jonsonian smoothness combine with a Latin clarity and perfection of form, presents the reader with observations on nature, love, and God which seem on the surface easy, urbane, and fluent but which prove on closer inspection to be both profound and problematical. In Marvell's lyrics the total experience of a sensitive, subtle, and sophisticated mind is rendered into pure art—a kind of art which challenges the analytic intellect of his readers but at the same time remains serenely and cryptically above it, finally accessible, like the work of Shakespeare and Keats, only to the sympathetic imagination.

Marvell was born in Yorkshire, the son of a clergyman who had become headmaster of the Hull Alms-house. The poet received his early education in Hull, after which, at the age of twelve, he entered Trinity College, Cambridge. He took his B.A. in 1639 and, after a rumored period of dalliance with Roman Catholicism, spent some four years in travel on the Continent, where he added French, Italian, Spanish, and Dutch to his already formidable knowledge of languages.

Being absent on his travels, Marvell took no appreciable part in the struggle between king and parliament. Both his Anglican faith and his friendship with Lovelace and other royalists, however, suggest that his initial sympathies must have lain with Charles. But the years 1650–52 found him serving as tutor to the daughter of Lord Fairfax, the retired parliamentary general, at the latter's estate, Nunappleton House, and during the decade of the Commonwealth and the Protectorate he developed the balanced admiration for Cromwell which he expressed definitively in his great "Horatian Ode." In 1653 Milton recommended him for a governmental post; he did not receive it at that time, but in 1657 he became one of Milton's assistants in the Latin Secretaryship. In 1659 he became a Member of Parliament for Hull, a post which he retained until his death. He is reputed to have been influential in saving Milton from prolonged imprisonment and possible execution at the time of the Restoration; during the reign of Charles II he proved himself to be an eloquent spokesman for policies of toleration (especially in his prose work *The Rehearsal Transprosed*, 1672–73), and he wrote a series of vicious verse satires against Charles and his ministers.

The satires constitute Marvell's only poetic efforts after 1660; the great lyric poems were all composed during the 1650's, and most scholars attribute the greater part of them to the Nunappleton period celebrated in Marvell's longest poem, "Upon Appleton House," in which his characteristic descriptive and philosophical themes find their fullest expression. Marvell belongs to the second generation of Metaphysical poets, and by the time he wrote, the style was already in the state of decadence typified by the work of Cleveland and Cowley. The short span of Marvell's creativity may possibly be explained by his adherence to a historically outmoded poetic style; it may, on the other hand, be explained by the triumph of the political and social aspect of his complex sensibility. There is, in any event, no trace of decadence in Marvell's lyric work: the poems of the early 1650's, first published in the posthumous *Miscellaneous Poems* (1681), are one of the supreme achievements of the English Metaphysical style and of European Baroque poetry in general.

A. MARVELL. *Poems and Letters*, ed. H. M. Margoliouth, 2 vols. (Oxford, 2nd ed., 1952). Definitive.

————. *Poems*, ed. H. Macdonald (Cambridge, Mass., 1952).

P. LEGOUIS. *Andrew Marvell: Poet, Puritan, Patriot* (Oxford, 1965). The standard biography.

M. C. BRADBROOK and M. G. LLOYD THOMAS. *Andrew Marvell* (Cambridge, 1940).

W. H. BAGGULEY, ed. *Tercentenary Tributes to Andrew Marvell* (Oxford, 1922). Contains appreciative essays by T. S. Eliot and others.

D. C. ALLEN. *Image and Meaning* (Baltimore, 1960). Has a useful analysis of "Upon Appleton House," as well as a study of "The Nymph Complaining."

A. BERTHOFF. *The Resolved Soul* (Princeton, 1970).

R. COLIE. *My Ecchoing Song* (Princeton, 1970).

J. B. LEISHMAN. *The Art of Marvell's Poetry* (London, 1966).

C. A. PATRIDES, ed. *Approaches to Marvell* (London, 1978).

J. WALLACE. *Destiny His Choice* (London, 1968).

F R O M

MISCELLANEOUS POEMS [1681]

ON A DROP OF DEW

See how the orient dew,
Shed from the bosom of the morn
  Into the blowing roses,
Yet careless of its mansion new,
For the clear region where 'twas born
  Round in itself incloses,
  And in its little globe's extent
Frames as it can its native element;
  How it the purple flow'r does slight,
  Scarce touching where it lies,   10
But gazing back upon the skies,
  Shines with a mournful light,
    Like its own tear,
Because so long divided from the sphere.
  Restless it rolls and unsecure,
  Trembling lest it grow impure,

  Till the warm sun pity its pain,
And to the skies exhale it back again.
  So the soul, that drop, that ray
Of the clear fountain of eternal day, 20
Could it within the human flower be seen,
  Rememb'ring still its former height,
  Shuns the sweet leaves and blossoms green;
  And recollecting its own light,
Does, in its pure and circling thoughts, express
The greater heaven in an heaven less.
  In how coy a figure wound,
  Every way it turns away;
  So the world excluding round,
  Yet receiving in the day; 30
  Dark beneath but bright above,
  Here disdaining, there in love;

How loose and easy hence to go,
How girt and ready to ascend;
Moving but on a point below,
It all about does upwards bend.
Such did the manna's sacred dew distill,
White and entire, though congealed and chill;[1]
Congealed on earth, but does, dissolving, run
Into the glories of th' almighty sun.   40

THE CORONET

When for the thorns with which I long, too long,
    With many a piercing wound,
    My Saviour's head have crowned,
I seek with garlands to redress that wrong;
    Through every garden, every mead,
    I gather flowers (my fruits are only flowers)
    Dismantling all the fragrant towers[1]
That once adorned my shepherdess's head.
And now when I have summed up all my store,
    Thinking (so I myself deceive)   10
    So rich a chaplet thence to weave
As never yet the king of glory wore;
    Alas I find the serpent old
    That, twining in his speckled breast,
    About the flowers disguised does fold,
    With wreaths of fame and interest.
Ah, foolish man, that wouldst debase with them,
And mortal glory, heaven's diadem!
    But Thou who only couldst the serpent tame,
    Either his slippery knots at once untie,   20
And disentangle all his winding snare;
Or shatter too with him my curious frame,[2]
And let these wither, so that he may die,
Though set with skill and chosen out with care,
That they, while Thou on both their spoils dost
        tread,
May crown Thy feet, that could not crown Thy
        head.

ON A DROP OF DEW
    1 See Exodus 16:4–15.

THE CORONET
    1 Elaborate headdresses for ladies.
    2 The floral frame designed by the poet.

BERMUDAS[1]

Where the remote Bermudas ride,
In the ocean's bosom unespied,
From a small boat that rowed along,
The listening winds received this song:
    "What should we do but sing His praise
That led us through the watery maze
Unto an isle so long unknown,
And yet far kinder than our own?
Where He the huge sea-monsters wracks,[2]
That lift the deep upon their backs;   10
He lands us on a grassy stage,
Safe from the storms' and prelates' rage.
He gave us this eternal spring
Which here enamels everything,
And sends the fowls to us in care,
On daily visits through the air;
He hangs in shades the orange bright,
Like golden lamps in a green night,
And does in the pomegranates close
Jewels more rich than Ormus[3] shows;   20
He makes the figs our mouths to meet,
And throws the melons at our feet;
But apples[4] plants of such a price,
No tree could ever bear them twice;
With cedars, chosen by His hand,
From Lebanon, He stores the land;
And makes the hollow seas, that roar,
Proclaim the ambergris on shore;
He cast (of which we rather boast)
The Gospel's pearl upon our coast,   30
And in these rocks for us did frame
A temple, where to sound His name.
Oh! let our voice His praise exalt,
Till it arrive at heaven's vault,
Which thence (perhaps) rebounding, may
Echo beyond the Mexique Bay."
    Thus sung they in the English boat,
An holy and a cheerful note;
And all the way, to guide their chime,
With falling oars they kept the time.   40

BERMUDAS
    1 The Bermudas were settled in the early seventeenth
century by religious exiles from England, who are represented as singing the song. For another description of the
Bermudas see Waller's Battle of the Summer Islands, p. 876.
    2 Wrecks.
    3 Ormuz, an island in the Persian Gulf, famous for its
diamond mart and proverbial for its wealth.
    4 Pineapples.

A DIALOGUE BETWEEN THE SOUL
AND BODY

SOUL

Oh, who shall from this dungeon raise
A soul enslaved so many ways?
With bolts of bones; that fettered stands
In feet, and manacled in hands;
Here blinded with an eye, and there
Deaf with the drumming of an ear;
A soul hung up, as 'twere, in chains
Of nerves and arteries and veins;
Tortured, besides each other part,
In a vain head and double heart.   10

BODY

Oh, who shall me deliver whole
From bonds of this tyrannic soul?
Which stretched upright, impales me so
That mine own precipice I go;
And warms and moves this needless frame,
A fever could but do the same.
And, wanting where its spite to try,
Has made me live to let me die.
A body that could never rest,
Since this ill spirit it possessed.   20

SOUL

What magic could me thus confine
Within another's grief to pine?
Where whatsoever it complain,
I feel, that cannot feel, the pain.
And all my care itself employs,
That to preserve which me destroys.
Constrained not only to endure
Diseases, but, what's worse, the cure;
And ready oft the port to gain,
Am shipwrecked into health again.   30

BODY

But physic yet could never reach
The maladies thou me dost teach:
Whom first the cramp of hope does tear,
And then the palsy shakes of fear;
The pestilence of love does heat,
Or hatred's hidden ulcer eat.
Joy's cheerful madness does perplex,
Or sorrow's other madness vex;
Which knowledge forces me to know,
And memory will not forgo.   40

What but a soul could have the wit
To build me up for sin so fit?
So architects do square and hew
Green trees that in the forest grew.

THE NYMPH COMPLAINING FOR
THE DEATH OF HER FAWN

The wanton troopers riding by
Have shot my fawn, and it will die.
Ungentle men! They cannot thrive
To kill thee. Thou ne'er didst alive
Them any harm, alas, nor could
Thy death yet do them any good.
I'm sure I never wished them ill,
Nor do I for all this, nor will;
But if my simple prayers may yet
Prevail with heaven to forget   10
Thy murder, I will join my tears
Rather than fail. But oh, my fears!
It cannot die so. Heaven's King
Keeps register of everything,
And nothing may we use in vain.
Ev'n beasts must be with justice slain,
Else men are made their deodands; [1]
Though they should wash their guilty hands,
In this warm life-blood, which doth part
From thine, and wound me to the heart,   20
Yet could they not be clean, their stain
Is dyed in such a purple grain. [2]
There is not such another in
The world to offer for their sin.
    Unconstant Sylvio, when yet
I had not found him counterfeit,
One morning (I remember well)
Tied in this silver chain and bell,
Gave it to me: nay, and I know
What he said then; I'm sure I do: 30
Said he, "Look how your huntsman here
Hath taught a fawn to hunt his dear."
But Sylvio soon had me beguiled;
This waxèd tame, while he grew wild,
And quite regardless of my smart,
Left me his fawn, but took his heart.

THE NYMPH
    1 Literally, "given or forfeited to God." In old English law,
a thing which had been the direct cause of the death of a
person, was given to God, that is, forfeited to the Crown for
pious purposes.
    2 A powerful red dye, made from the dried bodies of
certain insects.

Thenceforth I set myself to play
My solitary time away
With this, and very well content,
Could so mine idle life have spent;   40
For it was full of sport and light
Of foot and heart, and did invite
Me to its game: it seemed to bless
Itself in me; how could I less
Than love it? Oh, I cannot be
Unkind to a beast that loveth me.

    Had it lived long, I do not know
Whether it too might have done so
As Sylvio did; his gifts might be
Perhaps as false, or more, than he;   50
But I am sure, for aught that I
Could in so short a time espy,
Thy love was far more better than
The love of false and cruel men.

    With sweetest milk and sugar, first
I it at mine own fingers nursed;
And as it grew, so every day
It waxed more white and sweet than they.
It had so sweet a breath! And oft
I blushed to see its foot more soft   60
And white, shall I say than my hand?
Nay, any lady's of the land.

    It is a wondrous thing how fleet
'Twas on those little silver feet;
With what a pretty skipping grace
It oft would challenge me the race;
And when it had left me far away,
'Twould stay, and run again, and stay;
For it was nimbler much than hinds,
And trod as if on the four winds.   70

    I have a garden of my own,
But so with roses overgrown,
And lilies, that you would it guess
To be a little wilderness;
And all the springtime of the year
It only lovèd to be there.
Among the beds of lilies I
Have sought it oft, where it should lie,
Yet could not, till itself would rise,
Find it, although before mine eyes;   80
For, in the flaxen lilies' shade,
It like a bank of lilies laid.
Upon the roses it would feed,
Until its lips e'en seemed to bleed;
And then to me 'twould boldly trip,
And print those roses on my lip.

But all its chief delight was still
On roses thus itself to fill,
And its pure virgin limbs to fold
In whitest sheets of lilies cold: 90
Had it lived long, it would have been
Lilies without, roses within.

    O help! O help! I see it faint
And die as calmly as a saint!
See how it weeps! the tears do come
Sad, slowly dropping like a gum.
So weeps the wounded balsam; so
The holy frankincense doth flow;
The brotherless Heliades[3]
Melt in such amber tears as these.   100

    I in a golden vial will
Keep these two crystal tears, and fill
It till it do o'erflow with mine;
Then place it in Diana's shrine.

    Now my sweet fawn is vanished to
Whither the swans and turtles go,
In fair Elysium to endure,
With milk-white lambs and ermines pure.
O do not run too fast; for I
Will but bespeak thy grave, and die.   110

    First, my unhappy statue shall
Be cut in marble, and withal
Let it be weeping, too; but there
Th' engraver sure his art may spare;
For I so truly thee bemoan
That I shall weep, though I be stone,
Until my tears, still dropping, wear
My breast, themselves engraving there.
There at my feet shalt thou be laid,
Of purest alabaster made;   120
For I would have thine image be
White as I can, though not as thee.

---

3 Phaëton, the brother of the Heliades (daughters of Helios,
the sun) while attempting unsuccessfully to drive the chariot
of the sun, was killed by a thunderbolt from Zeus, to avert
the destruction of the world. His sisters, bewailing his death
immoderately, were turned into poplars, and their still falling
tears were transformed into amber.

TO HIS COY[1] MISTRESS

Had we but world enough, and time,
This coyness, Lady, were no crime.
We would sit down, and think which way
To walk, and pass our long love's day.
Thou by the Indian Ganges' side
Shouldst rubies find; I by the tide
Of Humber[2] would complain. I would
Love you ten years before the Flood,
And you should, if you please, refuse
Till the conversion of the Jews.   10
My vegetable[3] love should grow
Vaster than empires and more slow;
An hundred years should go to praise
Thine eyes, and on thy forehead gaze;
Two hundred to adore each breast,
But thirty thousand to the rest;
An age at least to every part,
And the last age should show your heart.
For, Lady, you deserve this state,[4]
Nor would I love at lower rate.   20
    But at my back I always hear
Time's wingèd chariot hurrying near;
And yonder all before us lie
Deserts of vast eternity.
Thy beauty shall no more be found,
Nor, in thy marble vault, shall sound
My echoing song; then worms shall try
That long-preserved virginity,
And your quaint[5] honor turn to dust,
And into ashes all my lust: 30
The grave's a fine and private place,
But none, I think, do there embrace.
    Now therefore, while the youthful hue
Sits on thy skin like morning lew,[6]
And while thy willing soul transpires[7]
At every pore with instant[8] fires,
Now let us sport us while we may,
And now, like amorous birds of prey,

Rather at once our time devour
Than languish in his slow-chapped[9] power.   40
Let us roll all our strength and all
Our sweetness up into one ball,
And tear our pleasures with rough strife
Thorough the iron gates of life;
Thus, though we cannot make our sun
Stand still, yet we will make him run.

THE GALLERY

Clora, come view my soul, and tell
Whether I have contrived it well:
Now all its several lodgings lie,
Composed into one gallery,
And the great arras-hangings, made
Of various facings, by are laid,
That, for all furniture, you'll find
Only your picture in my mind.

Here thou art painted in the dress
Of an inhuman murderess;   10
Examining[1] upon our hearts
Thy fertile shop of cruel arts,
Engines more keen than ever yet
Adornèd tyrant's cabinet,
Of which the most tormenting are,
Black eyes, red lips, and curlèd hair.

But, on the other side, thou'rt drawn,
Like to Aurora in the dawn;
When in the east she slumbering lies,
And stretches out her milky thighs,   20
While all the morning choir does sing
And manna falls and roses spring,
And, at thy feet the wooing doves
Sit perfecting their harmless loves.

Like an enchantress here thou show'st,
Vexing thy restless lover's ghost;
And, by a light obscure, dost rave
Over his entrails, in the cave,
Divining thence, with horrid care,
How long thou shalt continue fair;   30
And (when informed) them throw'st away
To be the greedy vulture's prey.

TO HIS COY MISTRESS
  1 "Coy" here has the older meaning of modest, reserved, inaccessible.
  2 The river on which is situated Marvell's town of Hull.
  3 Growing in the manner of plants.
  4 Dignified treatment.
  5 Fastidious; there is, also, a suggestion of "old-fashioned."
  6 Warmth, according to Margoliouth, who thus emended the "glew" of the original edition. Another suggested emendation is "dew."
  7 Comes forth.   8 Eager.

9 Slow-jawed; i.e., slowly devouring.

THE GALLERY
  1 Testing.

But, against that, thou sitt'st afloat,
Like Venus in her pearly boat;
The halcyons, calming all that's nigh,
Betwixt the air and water fly;
Or, if some rolling wave appears,
A mass of ambergris it bears,
Nor blows more wind than what may well
Convoy the perfume to the smell.   40

These pictures, and a thousand more,
Of thee, my gallery do store,
In all the forms thou canst invent,
Either to please me, or torment;
For thou alone, to people me,
Art grown a numerous colony,
And a collection choicer far
Than or Whitehall's, or Mantua's[2] were.

But of these pictures, and the rest,
That at the entrance likes me best,   50
Where the same posture and the look
Remains with which I first was took;
A tender shepherdess, whose hair
Hangs loosely playing in the air,
Transplanting flowers from the green hill
To crown her head and bosom fill.

THE FAIR SINGER

To make a final conquest of all me,
Love did compose so sweet an enemy,
In whom both beauties to my death agree,
Joining themselves in fatal harmony;
That while she with her eyes my heart does bind,
She with her voice might captivate my mind.

I could have fled from one but singly fair;
My disentangled soul itself might save,
Breaking the curlèd trammels of her hair.
But how should I avoid to be her slave,   10
Whose subtle art invisibly can wreathe
My fetters of the very air I breathe?

THE DEFINITION OF LOVE

My love is of a birth as rare
As 'tis, for object, strange and high;
It was begotten by Despair
Upon Impossibility.

Magnanimous Despair alone
Could show me so divine a thing,
Where feeble Hope could ne'er have flown,
But vainly flapped its tinsel wing.

And yet I quickly might arrive
Where my extended soul is fixed;   10
But Fate does iron wedges drive,
And always crowds itself betwixt.

For Fate with jealous eyes does see
Two perfect loves, nor lets them close;[1]
Their union would her ruin be,
And her tyrannic power depose.

And therefore her decrees of steel
Us as the distant poles have placed
(Though Love's whole world on us doth
          wheel),
Not by themselves to be embraced;   20

Unless the giddy heaven fall,
And earth some new convulsion tear,
And, us to join, the world should all
Be cramped into a planisphere.[2]

As lines, so loves, oblique may well
Themselves in every angle greet;
But ours, so truly parallel,
Though infinite, can never meet.

THE GALLERY
  2 Famous art galleries.

THE DEFINITION OF LOVE
  1 Unite.
  2 A map of the globe projected on a plane surface; a "flat globe."

Therefore the love which us doth bind,
But Fate so enviously debars, 30
Is the conjunction of the mind,
And opposition of the stars.

THE PICTURE OF LITTLE T. C.[1]
IN A PROSPECT OF FLOWERS

See with what simplicity
This nymph begins her golden days!
In the green grass she loves to lie,
And there with her fair aspect tames
The wilder flowers, and gives them names;
But only with the roses plays,
 And them does tell
What color best becomes them, and what smell.

Who can foretell for what high cause
This darling of the gods was born? 10
Yet this is she whose chaster laws
The wanton Love shall one day fear,
And under her command severe
See his bow broke and ensigns torn.
 Happy, who can
Appease this virtuous enemy of man!

Oh then let me in time compound,
And parley with those conquering eyes,
Ere they have tried their force to wound;
Ere with their glancing wheels they drive 20
In triumph over hearts that strive,
And them that yield but more despise.
 Let me be laid
Where I may see thy glories from some shade.

Meantime, whilst every verdant thing
Itself does at thy beauty charm,
Reform the errors of the spring:
Make that the tulips may have share
Of sweetness, seeing they are fair;
And roses of their thorns disarm; 30
 But most procure
That violets may a longer age endure.

THE PICTURE
1 Professor Margoliouth identifies "T. C." as "possibly
Theophila Cornewall," who was born in 1644.

But, O young beauty of the woods,
Whom nature courts with fruits and flowers,
Gather the flowers, but spare the buds,
Lest Flora, angry at thy crime,
To kill her infants in their prime,
Do quickly make th' example yours;
 And ere we see,
Nip in the blossom all our hopes and thee. 40

THE MOWER AGAINST GARDENS

Luxurious[1] man, to bring his vice in use,
 Did after him the world seduce,
And from the fields the flowers and plants allure,
 Where Nature was most plain and pure.
He first enclosed within the gardens square
 A dead and standing pool of air,
And a more luscious earth for them did knead,
 Which stupefied them while it fed.
The pink grew then as double as his mind;
 The nutriment did change the kind. 10
With strange perfumes he did the roses taint;
 And flowers themselves were taught to paint.
The tulip white did for complexion seek,
 And learned to interline its cheek;
Its onion root they then so high did hold,
 That one was for a meadow sold:[2]
Another world was searched through oceans new,
 To find the marvel of Peru;[3]
And yet these rarities might be allowed
 To man, that sovereign thing and proud, 20
Had he not dealt between the bark and tree,
 Forbidden mixtures there to see.
No plant now knew the stock from which it came;
 He grafts upon the wild the tame,
That the uncertain and adulterate fruit
 Might put the palate in dispute.
His green seraglio has its eunuchs too,
 Lest any tyrant him outdo;
And in the cherry he does Nature vex,
 To procreate without a sex.[4] 30
'Tis all enforced, the fountain and the grot,
 While the sweet fields do lie forgot,

THE MOWER AGAINST GARDENS
1 Lecherous.
2 A reference to the tulip mania in Holland in the 1630's.
3 Mirabilia Peruviana, a species of flower.
4 Macdonald explains these lines as a reference to the
propagation of cherries through grafting.

Where willing Nature does to all dispense
   A wild and fragrant innocence;
And fauns and fairies do the meadows till
   More by their presence than their skill.
Their statues polished by some ancient hand,
   May to adorn the gardens stand;
But, howsoe'er the figures do excel,
   The Gods themselves with us do dwell.   40

THE MOWER TO THE GLOWWORMS

Ye living lamps, by whose dear light
The nightingale does sit so late,
And studying all the summer night,
Her matchless songs does meditate;

Ye country comets, that portend
No war nor prince's funeral,[1]
Shining unto no higher end
Than to presage the grass's fall;

Ye glowworms, whose officious[2] flame
To wandering mowers shows the way,   10
That in the night have lost their aim,[3]
And after foolish fires[4] do stray;

Your courteous lights in vain you waste,
Since Juliana here is come,
For she my mind hath so displaced
That I shall never find my home.

THE MOWER'S SONG

My mind was once the true survey
Of all these meadows fresh and gay,
And in the greenness of the grass
Did see its hopes as in a glass;
When Juliana came, and she,
What I do to the grass, does to my thoughts and me.

But these, while I with sorrow pine,
Grew more luxuriant still and fine,
That not one blade of grass you spied,
But had a flower on either side;   10
When Juliana came, and she,
What I do to the grass, does to my thoughts and me.

Unthankful meadows, could you so
A fellowship so true forgo,
And in your gaudy May-games meet,
While I lay trodden under feet?
When Juliana came, and she,
What I do to the grass, does to my thoughts and me.

But what you in compassion ought,
Shall now by my revenge be wrought;   20
And flowers, and grass, and I, and all
Will in one common ruin fall;
For Juliana comes, and she,
What I do to the grass, does to my thoughts and me.

And thus, ye meadows, which have been
Companions of my thoughts more green,
Shall now the heraldry become
With which I shall adorn my tomb;
For Juliana comes, and she,   29
What I do to the grass, does to my thoughts and me.

THE GARDEN

How vainly men themselves amaze
To win the palm, the oak, or bays,
And their incessant labors see
Crowned from some single herb, or tree,
Whose short and narrow-vergèd shade
Does prudently their toils upbraid;
While all flowers and all trees do close[1]
To weave the garlands of repose!

Fair Quiet, have I found thee here,
And Innocence, thy sister dear?   10
Mistaken long, I sought you then
In busy companies of men.
Your sacred plants, if here below,
Only among the plants will grow;
Society is all but rude
To[2] this delicious solitude.

THE MOWER TO THE GLOWWORMS
1 A reference to the old superstition that comets, meteors, etc., were portents of evil.
2 Not in the modern sense of meddlsome, but with the older meaning of obliging, serviceable.
3 Destination.   4 Will-o'-the-wisps.

THE GARDEN
1 Unite.   2 In comparison to.

No white nor red [3] was ever seen
So amorous as this lovely green.
Fond lovers, cruel as their flame,
Cut in these trees their mistress' name: 20
Little, alas, they know or heed
How far these beauties hers exceed!
Fair trees, wheresoe'er your barks I wound,
No name shall but your own be found.

When we have run our passion's heat,
Love hither makes his best retreat.
The gods, that mortal beauty chase,
Still in a tree did end their race:
Apollo hunted Daphne so,
Only that she might laurel grow;   30
And Pan did after Syrinx speed,
Not as a nymph, but for a reed.

What wondrous life in this I lead!
Ripe apples drop about my head;
The luscious clusters of the vine
Upon my mouth do crush their wine;
The nectarine and curious [4] peach
Into my hands themselves do reach;
Stumbling on melons, as I pass,
Ensnared with flowers, I fall on grass.   40

Meanwhile the mind from pleasure less
Withdraws into its happiness;
The mind, that ocean where each kind
Does straight its own resemblance find;
Yet it creates, transcending these,
Far other worlds and other seas,
Annihilating all that's made
To a green thought in a green shade.

Here at the fountain's sliding foot,
Or at some fruit-tree's mossy root,   50
Casting the body's vest aside,
My soul into the boughs does glide:
There, like a bird, it sits and sings,
Then whets [5] and combs its silver wings,
And, till prepared for longer flight,
Waves in its plumes the various light.

Such was that happy garden-state,
While man there walked without a mate:
After a place so pure and sweet,
What other help could yet be meet!   60
But 'twas beyond a mortal's share
To wander solitary there:
Two paradises 'twere in one
To live in Paradise alone.

How well the skillful gardener drew,
Of flowers and herbs, this dial new; [6]
Where, from above, the milder sun
Does through a fragrant zodiac run;
And, as it works, the industrious bee
Computes its time as well as we!   70
How could such sweet and wholesome hours
Be reckoned but with herbs and flowers?

from

UPON APPLETON HOUSE, TO MY LORD FAIRFAX

Within this sober frame expect
Work of no foreign architect
That unto caves the quarries drew,
And forests did to pastures hew;
Who, of his great design in pain,
Did for a model vault his brain;
Whose columns should so high be raised,
To arch the brows which on them gazed.

Why should, of all things, man, unruled,
Such unproportioned dwellings build?   10
The beasts are by their dens expressed,
And birds contrive an equal nest;
The low-roofed tortoises do dwell
In cases fit of tortoise-shell;
No creature loves an empty space;
Their bodies measure out their place.

But he, superfluously spread,
Demands more room alive than dead;
And in his hollow palace goes
Where winds, as he, themselves may lose.   20
What need of all this marble crust
To impark the wanton mote of dust,
That thinks by breadth the world to unite,
Though the first builders failed in height?

THE GARDEN
3 The white and red of a lady's complexion.
4 Rare, exquisite.   5 Preens.

6 The garden plot, designed in the form of a sundial.

But all things are composèd here,
Like nature, orderly, and near;
In which we the dimensions find
Of that more sober age and mind,
When larger-sizèd men did stoop   30
To enter at a narrow loop,
As practicing, in doors so strait,
To strain themselves through Heaven's gate.

And surely, when the after-age
Shall hither come in pilgrimage,
These sacred places to adore,
By Vere¹ and Fairfax trod before,
Men will dispute how their extent
Within such dwarfish confines went;
And some will smile at this, as well
As Romulus his bee-like cell.²   40

Humility alone designs
Those short but admirable lines
By which, ungirt and unconstrained,
Things greater are in less contained.
Let others vainly strive t' immure
The circle in the quadrature!
These holy mathematics can
In every figure equal man.

Yet thus the laden house does sweat,
And scarce endures the master great;   50
But, where he comes, the swelling hall
Stirs, and the square grows spherical;
More by his magnitude distressed,
Than he is by its straitness pressed:
And too officiously it slights
That in itself, which him delights.

So honor better lowness bears,
Than that unwonted greatness wears;
Height with a certain grace does bend,
But low things clownishly ascend.   60
And yet what needs there here excuse,
Where everything does answer use?
Where neatness nothing can condemn,
Nor pride invent what to contemn?

. . . .

UPON APPLETON HOUSE
  1 The family name of Fairfax's wife.
  2 The thatched hut in Rome in which Romulus was
reputed to have lived.

When in the east the morning ray
Hangs out the colors of the day,   290
The bee through these known alleys hums,
Beating the dian³ with its drums.
Then flowers their drowsy eyelids raise,
Their silken ensigns each displays,
And dries its pan yet dank with dew,
And fills its flask with odors new.

These, as their governor goes by,
In fragrant volleys they let fly,
And to salute their governess
Again as great a charge they press: 300
None for the virgin nymph;⁴ for she
Seems, with the flowers, a flower to be.
And think so still! though not compare
With breath so sweet, or cheek so fair!

Well shot, ye firemen! Oh how sweet
And round your equal fires do meet;
Whose shrill report no ear can tell,
But echoes to the eye and smell!
See how the flowers, as at parade,
Under their colors stand displayed;   310
Each regiment in order grows,
That of the tulip, pink, and rose.

But when the vigilant patrol
Of stars walks round about the pole,
Their leaves that to the stalks are curled
Seem to their staves the ensigns furled.
Then in some flower's belovèd hut,
Each bee, as sentinel, is shut,
And sleeps so too, but, if once stirred,
She runs you through, nor asks the word.   320

Oh thou, that dear and happy isle,
The garden of the world erewhile,
Thou Paradise of the four seas,
Which Heaven planted us to please,
But, to exclude, the world, did guard
With watery, if not flaming sword,—
What luckless apple did we taste,
To make us mortal, and thee waste?

Unhappy! shall we never more
That sweet militia restore,   330
When gardens only had their towers
And all the garrisons were flowers;

3 Reveille.   4 Maria, the daughter of Lord Fairfax.

When roses only arms might bear,
And men did rosy garlands wear?
Tulips, in several colors barred,
Were then the Switzers of our guard;

The gardener had the soldier's place,
And his more gentle forts did trace;
The nursery of all things green
Was then the only magazine;   340
The winter quarters were the stoves,
Where he the tender plants removes.
But war all this doth overgrow:
We ordnance plant, and powder sow.

And yet there walks one on the sod,
Who, had it pleasèd him and God,
Might once have made our gardens spring
Fresh as his own, and flourishing.
But he preferred to the Cinque Ports
These five imaginary forts,   350
And, in those half-dry trenches, spanned
Power which the ocean might command.

For he did, with his utmost skill,
Ambition weed, but conscience till;
Conscience, that heaven-nursèd plant,
Which most our earthly gardens want.
A prickling leaf it bears, and such
As that which shrinks at every touch,
But flowers eternal, and divine,
That in the crowns of Saints do shine.   360
  .   .   .   .
And now to the abyss I pass
Of that unfathomable grass,   370
Where men like grasshoppers appear,
But grasshoppers are giants there;
They, in their squeaking laugh, contemn
Us as we walk more low than them,
And from the precipices tall
Of the green spires to us do call.

To see men through this meadow dive,
We wonder how they rise alive,
As under water none does know
Whether he fall through it or go.   380
But, as the mariners that sound,
And show upon their lead the ground,
They bring up flowers so to be seen,
And prove they've at the bottom been.

No scene that turns with engines strange
Does oftener than these meadows change.
For, when the sun the grass hath vexed,
The tawny mowers enter next;
Who seem like Israelites to be,
Walking on foot through a green sea.   390
To them the grassy deeps divide,
And crowd a lane to either side.
  .   .   .   .
    Thus I, easy philosopher,
Among the birds and trees confer,
And little now to make me wants,
Or of the fowls or of the plants:
Give me but wings as they, and I
Straight floating on the air shall fly;
Or turn me but, and you shall see
I was but an inverted tree.

Already I begin to call
In their most learned original;   570
And, where I language want, my signs
The bird upon the bough divines,
And more attentive there doth sit
Than if she were with lime-twigs knit.
No leaf does tremble in the wind,
Which I returning cannot find.

Out of these scattered Sibyl's leaves,
Strange prophecies my fancy weaves,
And in one history consumes,
Like Mexique painting, all the plumes;   580
What Rome, Greece, Palestine, e'er said,
I in this light mosaic read.
Thrice happy he, who, not mistook,
Hath read in nature's mystic book!

And see how chance's better wit
Could with a mask my studies hit!
The oak-leaves me embroider all,
Between which caterpillars crawl;
And ivy, with familiar trails,
Me licks and clasps and curls and hales.   590
Under this antic cope I move,
Like some great prelate of the groove.

Then, languishing with ease, I toss
On pallets swoln of velvet moss,
While the wind, cooling through the boughs,
Flatters with air my panting brows.

Thanks for my rest, ye mossy banks,
And unto you, cool zephyrs, thanks,
Who, as my hair, my thoughts too shed,
And winnow from the chaff my head!   600

How safe, methinks, and strong behind
These trees, have I encamped my mind;
Where beauty, aiming at the heart,
Bends in some tree its useless dart,
And where the world no certain shot
Can make, or me it toucheth not,
But I on it securely play,
And gall its horsemen all the day.

Bind me, ye woodbines, in your twines;
Curl me about, ye gadding vines;   610
And oh, so close your circles lace,
That I may never leave this place!
But, lest your fetters prove too weak,
Ere I your silken bondage break,
Do you, O brambles, chain me too,
And, courteous briars, nail me through!

Here in the morning tie my chain,
Where the two woods have made a lane,
While, like a guard on either side,
The trees before their lord divide;   620
This, like a long and equal thread,
Betwixt two labyrinths does lead.
But, where the floods did lately drown,
There at the evening stake me down.

For now the waves are fallen and dried,
And now the meadows fresher dyed,
Whose grass, with moisture color dashed,
Seems as green silks but newly washed.
No serpent new, or crocodile,
Remains behind our little Nile;   630
Unless itself you will mistake,
Among these meads the only snake.

See in what wanton harmless folds
It everywhere the meadow holds,
And its yet muddy back doth lick,
Till as a crystal mirror slick,
Where all things gaze themselves, and doubt
If they be in it, or without;
And for his shade which therein shines,
Narcissus-like, the sun too pines.   640

Oh what a pleasure 'tis to hedge
My temples here with heavy sedge;
Abandoning my lazy side,
Stretched as a bank unto the tide;
Or to suspend my sliding foot
On the osier's undermined root,
And in its branches tough to hang,
While at my lines the fishes twang!

But now away my hooks, my quills,⁵
And angles, idle utensils!   650
The young Maria walks to-night:
Hide, trifling youth, thy pleasures slight;
'Twere shame that such judicious eyes
Should with such toys a man surprise;
She that already is the law
Of all her sex, her age's awe.

See how loose Nature, in respect
To her, itself doth recollect,
And every thing so whisht⁶ and fine,
Starts forthwith to its bonne mine.   660
The sun himself of her aware,
Seems to descend with greater care,
And, lest she see him go to bed,
In blushing clouds conceals his head.

So when the shadows laid asleep,
From underneath these banks do creep,
And on the river, as it flows,
With ebon shuts begin to close,
The modest halcyon comes in sight,
Flying betwixt the day and night;   670
And such a horror calm and dumb,
Admiring Nature does benumb;

The viscous air, wheres'er she fly,
Follows and sucks her azure dye;
The jellying stream compacts below,
If it might fix her shadow so;
The stupid fishes hang, as plain
As flies in crystal overta'en.
And men the silent scene assist,
Charmed with the sapphire-wingèd mist.   680

5 Floats.   6 Quiet.

Maria such, and so doth hush
The world, and through the evening rush.
No new-born comet such a train
Draws through the sky, nor star new slain.
For straight those giddy rockets fail,
Which from the putrid earth exhale;
But by her flames, in Heaven tried,
Nature is wholly vitrified.

'Tis she that to these gardens gave
That wondrous beauty which they have;　690
She straightness on the woods bestows;
To her the meadow sweetness owes;
Nothing could make the river be
So crystal pure, but only she,
She yet more pure, sweet, straight, and fair
Than gardens, woods, meads, rivers are.

Therefore what first she on them spent,
They gratefully again present;
The meadow carpets where to tread,
The garden flowers to crown her head,　700
And for a glass the limpid brook,
Where she may all her beauties look;
But, since she would not have them seen,
The wood about her draws a screen.

For she to higher beauties raised,
Disdains to be for lesser praised.
She counts her beauty to converse
In all the languages as hers;
Nor yet in those herself employs,
But for the wisdom, not the noise;　710
Nor yet that wisdom would affect,
But as 'tis Heaven's dialect.

.　.　.　.　.　.　.　.

Meantime, ye fields, springs, bushes, flowers,
Where yet she leads her studious hours,
(Till Fate her worthily translates,
And find a Fairfax for our Thwaites)[7]
Employ the means you have by her,
And in your kind yourselves prefer;　750
That, as all virgins she precedes,
So you all woods, streams, gardens, meads.

For you, Thessalian Tempe's seat
Shall now be scorned as obsolete;
Aranjuez, as less, disdained;
The Bel-Retiro,[8] as constrained;
But name not the Idalian grove,
For 'twas the seat of wanton love;
Much less the dead's Elysian fields;
Yet nor to them your beauty yields.　760

'Tis not, what once it was, the world,
But a rude heap together hurled;
All negligently overthrown,
Gulfs, deserts, precipices, stone;
Your lesser world contains the same,
But in more decent order tame;
You, Heaven's center, Nature's lap,
And Paradise's only map.

But now the salmon-fishers moist
Their leathern boats begin to hoist;　770
And, like Antipodes in shoes,
Have shod their heads in their canoes.
How tortoise-like, but not so slow,
These rational amphibii go!
Let's in; for the dark hemisphere
Does now like one of them appear.

AN HORATIAN ODE UPON CROMWELL'S RETURN FROM IRELAND[1]

The forward[2] youth that would appear[3]
Must now forsake his Muses dear,
　Nor in the shadows sing
　His numbers languishing:
'Tis time to leave the books in dust,
And oil th' unusèd armor's rust,
　Removing from the wall
　The corslet of the hall.
So restless Cromwell could not cease
In the inglorious arts of peace,　10
　But through adventurous war
　Urgèd his active star;

8 Aranjuez and Bel-Retiro were both famous resorts of Spanish royalty.

UPON APPLETON HOUSE
　7 In a passage of the poem omitted from this selection, Marvell tells of how one of Fairfax's ancestors won the beautiful and virtuous Isabella Thwaites.

AN HORATIAN ODE
　1 Cromwell returned from Ireland at the close of May, 1650, and prepared to direct the campaign in Scotland.
　2 Ambitious.　　　　3 Win public recognition.

And like the three-forked lightning, first
Breaking the clouds where it was nursed,
   Did thorough his own side [4]
   His fiery way divide.
For 'tis all one to courage high,
The emulous or enemy;
   And with such to inclose
   Is more than to oppose.   20
Then burning through the air he went,
And palaces and temples rent;
   And Cæsar's head at last
   Did through his laurels blast.
'Tis madness to resist or blame
The force of angry heaven's flame;
   And, if we would speak true,
   Much to the man is due,
Who, from his private gardens, where
He lived reservèd and austere   30
   (As if his highest plot
   To plant the bergamot),[5]
Could by industrious valor climb
To ruin the greatest work of time,
   And cast the kingdoms old
   Into another mold;
Though Justice against Fate complain,
And plead the ancient rights in vain;
   But those do hold or break,
   As men are strong or weak.   40
Nature, that hateth emptiness,
Allows of penetration [6] less,
   And therefore must make room
   Where greater spirits come.
What field of all the civil wars,
Where his were not the deepest scars?
   And Hampton [7] shows what part
   He had of wiser art;
Where, twining subtle fears with hope,
He wove a net of such a scope   50
   That Charles himself might chase
   To Carisbrooke's narrow case,

That thence the royal actor borne
The tragic scaffold might adorn;
   While round the armèd bands
   Did clap their bloody hands.
He nothing common did, or mean,
Upon that memorable scene,
   But with his keener eye
   The axe's edge did try;   60
Nor called the gods with vulgar spite
To vindicate his helpless right;
   But bowed his comely head
   Down, as upon a bed.
This was that memorable hour
Which first assured the forcèd power;
   So, when they did design
   The Capitol's first line,
A bleeding head,[8] where they begun,
Did fright the architects to run;   70
   And yet in that the state
   Foresaw its happy fate.
And now the Irish are ashamed
To see themselves in one year tamed;
   So much one man can do
   That does both act and know.
They can affirm his praises best,
And have, though overcome, confessed
   How good he is, how just,
   And fit for highest trust,   80
Nor yet grown stiffer with command,
But still in the republic's hand—
   How fit is he to sway
   That can so well obey!
He to the Commons' feet presents
A kingdom for his first year's rents;
   And, what he may, forbears
   His fame, to make it theirs;
And has his sword and spoils ungirt,
To lay them at the public's skirt: 90
   So when the falcon high
   Falls heavy from the sky,
She, having killed, no more does search
But on the next green bough to perch;
   Where, when he first does lure,
   The falconer has her sure.
What may not, then, our isle presume,
While victory his crest does plume?

---

4 Party.   5 A species of pear.
6 A term from scholastic philosophy, meaning here "occupation of the same space by two bodies at the same time." (Oxford English Dictionary.)
7 Hampton Court Palace, where Charles was detained. During the negotiations between Cromwell and the King, the latter escaped to Carisbrooke Castle on the Isle of Wight. Marvell's implication that Cromwell permitted the escape in order to use it later against the King is not credited by most present-day historians.

8 The temple of Jupiter in Rome was said to have been called the Capitol because a human head [caput] was found while the workmen were digging the foundations. The discovery was hailed as a favorable omen.

What may not others fear,
If thus he crown each year? 100
A Cæsar he, ere long, to Gaul,
To Italy an Hannibal,
    And to all states not free
    Shall climactèric be.
The Pict⁹ no shelter now shall find
Within his part-colored¹⁰ mind,
    But from this valor sad¹¹
    Shrink underneath the plaid;

9 The Scot.
10 Changeable. A pun on the Latin word, *picti*, painted, from which *Pict* was thought to be derived. There may be also a reference to the tartan pattern of the Highland costume.
11 Firm, resolute.

Happy if in the tufted brake
The English hunter him mistake, 110
    Nor lay his hounds in near
    The Caledonian¹² deer.
But thou, the war's and fortune's son,
March indefatigably on!
    And for the last effect,
    Still keep thy sword erect;
Besides the force it has to fright
The spirits of the shady night,¹³
    The same arts that did gain
    A power must it maintain. 120

12 Scottish.
13 "The cross-hilt of the sword would avert *the spirits of the shady night.*" (Margoliouth.)

Henry Vaughan

[1621–1695]

ALTHOUGH the Metaphysical poetic style yielded in the latter half of the seventeenth century to the burgeoning Neoclassicism adumbrated in Waller and Denham, it continued to produce some poets of great importance, chief among them Marvell, Vaughan, and Traherne. The work of this younger generation of Metaphysical poets is, however, distinctly different from that of Donne and Herbert: Marvell's statements are frequently veiled in a cool and inscrutable ambiguity, Traherne gives himself over to radically individualistic doctrines which almost anticipate Romanticism, and Vaughan expresses a religious attitude which is, if basically orthodox, couched in a strikingly esoteric symbolic scheme. Vaughan's work, especially, suggests that the later Baroque sensibility, faced with a triumphant new cosmology which threatened to render its terms obsolete, was capable of a final flowering rooted in personal and subjective mysticism.

Henry Vaughan was born in Breconshire, Wales, and he retained throughout his life strong feelings of local patriotism, affixing to his name the title "the Silurist" in honor of the Celtic tribe (*Silures*) which had once inhabited his native region. Like many Welshmen, he was educated at Jesus College, Oxford, which, together with his twin brother Thomas, he entered in 1638, but he left without taking a degree in order to pursue the study of law in London. His studies were interrupted by the Civil War, and it is reasonably certain that he served with the royalist forces. At some point after the war he studied medicine, and he spent the rest of his life as a country doctor in his native Wales.

As a student in London, Vaughan had begun an inconclusive dalliance with the Muse, producing, in *Poems, with the Tenth Satire of Juvenal Englished* (1646) and *Olor Iscanus* (1651), a body of conventional secular verse in which the fashionable influences of Donne and Jonson are strongly in evidence. During the late 1640's, however, a number of experiences conspired to bring about in him a religious awakening which made him a great poet. Of these experiences—the sorrows of the war, a serious illness, the death of a beloved younger brother—it is impossible to say which was crucial, but the entire emotional complex was galvanized into high art by a reading of George Herbert, to whom Vaughan pays noble tribute in the preface to *Silex Scintillans* (1650; Part II, 1655), the work on which his reputation wholly rests. Few great poets have been as heavily influenced by a predecessor as was Vaughan by Herbert, but very few poets have transformed their influences so completely; despite the countless echoes of *The Temple* in *Silex Scintillans*, the effect of the work is utterly different. Herbert's greatness is inseparable from his flawless craftsmanship; he is a poet of entire artistic structures. Vaughan's greatness lies in his occasional and incomplete felicities; he is a poet of stanzas, single lines, or even isolated phrases. Furthermore, whereas Herbert's poems derive always from the great central traditions of Christianity, Vaughan's frequently utilize as a frame of reference the kind of recondite learning cultivated by his brother Thomas, who was famous as an alchemist and mystical philosopher.

Like Marvell, Vaughan wrote all his best work during a brief period. (His last volume, *Thalia Rediviva*, 1678, is made up of undistinguished early and occasional pieces.) And, though his achievement lacks the polished perfection of either Herbert's or Marvell's, it contains individual passages which are the equal of anything in English devotional poetry.

H. VAUGHAN. *Works*, ed. L. C. Martin (Oxford, 2nd ed., 1957). Definitive; also contains the poet's prose works.

F. E. HUTCHINSON. *Henry Vaughan* (Oxford, 1947). The standard biography.

E. BLUNDEN. *On the Poems of Henry Vaughan* (London, 1927).

E. HOLMES. *Henry Vaughan and the Hermetic Philosophy* (Oxford, 1932). Stresses Vaughan's esoteric sources.

R. GARNER. *Henry Vaughan: Experience and the Tradition* (Chicago, 1959). In opposition to Holmes, stresses the orthodoxy of Vaughan's religious thought.

E. C. PETTET. *Of Paradise and Light* (Cambridge, 1960). A useful recent study.

R. A. DURR. *On the Mystical Poetry of Henry Vaughan* (Cambridge, Mass., 1962).

F R O M

OLOR ISCANUS[1] [1651]

[BOETHIUS, *DE CONSOLATIONE PHILOSOPHIÆ*]

LIBER 2. METRUM 5

Happy that first white age when we
Lived by the earth's mere charity!
No soft luxurious diet then
Had effeminated men:
No other meat, nor wine, had any
Than the coarse mast, or simple honey;
And by the parents' care laid up,
Cheap berries did the children sup.

No pompous wear was in those days,
Of gummy silks or scarlet baize.   10
Their beds were on some flow'ry brink,
And clear spring-water was their drink.
The shady pine in the sun's heat
Was their cool and known retreat,
For then 'twas not cut down, but stood
The youth and glory of the wood.
The daring sailor with his slaves
Then had not cut the swelling waves,
Nor for desire of foreign store
Seen any but his native shore.   20
No stirring drum scarred that age,
Nor the shrill trumpet's active rage,
No wounds by bitter hatred made,
With warm blood soiled the shining blade;
For how could hostile madness arm
An age of love to public harm,
When common justice none withstood,
Nor sought rewards for spilling blood?

LIBER 2
1 Vaughan's favorite cognomen was *Olor Iscanus*, the Swan of Usk, the river near his birthplace.

Oh that at length our age would raise
  Into the temper of those days!   30
But—worse than Etna's fires!—debate
And avarice inflame our state.

Alas! who was it that first found
Gold, hid of purpose under ground,
That sought out pearls, and dived to find
Such precious perils for mankind!

FROM

SILEX SCINTILLANS [1655]

REGENERATION

A ward, and still in bonds, one day
  I stole abroad;
It was high spring, and all the way
  Primrosed and hung with shade;
    Yet was it frost within,
      And surly winds
Blasted my infant buds, and sin
  Like clouds eclipsed my mind.

Stormed thus, I straight perceived my spring
  Mere stage and show,   10
My walk a monstrous mountained thing,
  Rough-cast with rocks and snow;
    And as a pilgrim's eye,
      Far from relief,
Measures the melancholy sky,
  Then drops and rains for grief,

So sighed I upwards still, at last
  'Twixt steps and falls
I reached the pinnacle, where placed
  I found a pair of scales;   20
    I took them up and laid
      In th' one, late pains;
The other smoke and pleasures weighed,
  But proved the heavier grains.

With that some cried, "Away!" Straight I
  Obeyed, and led
Full east, a fair, fresh field could spy;
  Some called it Jacob's bed,[1]

A virgin soil which no
  Rude feet ere trod,   30
Where, since he stepped there, only go
  Prophets and friends of God.

Here I reposed; but scarce well set,
  A grove descried
Of stately height, whose branches met
  And mixed on every side;
    I entered, and once in,
      Amazed to see 't,
Found all was changed, and a new spring
  Did all my senses greet.   40

The unthrift sun shot vital gold,
  A thousand pieces,
And heaven its azure did unfold,
  Checkered with snowy fleeces;
    The air was all in spice,
      And every bush
A garland wore; thus fed my eyes,
  But all the ear lay hush.

Only a little fountain lent
  Some use for ears,   50
And on the dumb shades language spent,
  The music of her tears;
    I drew her near, and found
      The cistern full
Of divers stones, some bright and round,
  Others ill-shaped and dull.

The first, pray mark, as quick as light
  Danced through the flood,
But the last, more heavy than the night,
  Nailed to the center stood;   60

REGENERATION
1 See Genesis 28:10–22.

I wondered much, but tired
    At last with thought,
My restless eye that still desired
    As strange an object brought.

It was a bank of flowers where I descried,
    Though 'twas midday,
Some fast asleep, others broad-eyed
    And taking in the ray;
    Here musing long, I heard
      A rushing wind   70
Which still increased, but whence it stirred
    No where I could not find.

I turned me round, and to each shade
    Dispatched an eye
To see if any leaf had made
    Least motion or reply,
    But while I list'ning sought
      My mind to ease
By knowing where 'twas, or where not,
    It whispered, "Where I please."   80

"Lord," then said I, "on me one breath,
And let me die before my death!"

VANITY OF SPIRIT

Quite spent with thoughts, I left my cell and lay
Where a shrill spring tuned to the early day.
    I begged here long, and groaned to know
    Who gave the clouds so brave a bow,
    Who bent the spheres, and circled in
    Corruption with this glorious ring;
    What is His name, and how I might
    Descry some part of His great light.
I summoned nature: pierced through all her store,
Broke up some seals which none had touched
        before: 10
    Her womb, her bosom, and her head
    Where all her secrets lay abed,
    I rifled quite; and having passed
    Through all her creatures, came at last
    To search myself, where I did find
    Traces and sounds of a strange kind.
Here of this mighty spring I found some drills,
With echoes beaten from the eternal hills;
    Weak beams and fires flashed to my sight,
    Like a young east, or moonshine night,   20

Which showed me in a nook cast by
A piece of much antiquity,
With hieroglyphics quite dismembered,
And broken letters scarce remembered.
I took them up and, much joyed, went about
To unite those pieces, hoping to find out
    The mystery; but this ne'er done,
    That little light I had was gone:
    It grieved me much. At last, said I,
    Since in these veils my eclipsèd eye   30
    May not approach Thee (for at night
    Who can have commerce with the light?),
    I'll disapparel, and to buy
    But one half glance, most gladly die.

THE RETREAT

Happy those early days, when I
Shined in my angel infancy;
Before I understood this place
Appointed for my second race,
Or taught my soul to fancy aught
But a white, celestial thought;
When yet I had not walked above
A mile or two from my first Love,
And looking back, at that short space,
Could see a glimpse of His bright face;   10
When on some gilded cloud or flower
My gazing soul would dwell an hour,
And in those weaker glories spy
Some shadows of eternity;
Before I taught my tongue to wound
My conscience with a sinful sound,
Or had the black art to dispense
A several sin to every sense,
But felt through all this fleshly dress
Bright shoots of everlastingness.   20
    Oh, how I long to travel back,
And tread again that ancient track!
That I might once more reach that plain
Where first I left my glorious train;
From whence the enlightened spirit sees
That shady city of palm trees.
But, ah! my soul with too much stay
Is drunk, and staggers in the way.
Some men a forward motion love;
But I by backward steps would move,   30
And when this dust falls to the urn,
In that state I came, return.

[JOY OF MY LIFE WHILE LEFT ME HERE!][1]

Joy of my life while left me here!
    And still my love!
How in thy absence thou dost steer
    Me from above!
    A life well led
    This truth commends,
    With quick or dead
    It never ends.

Stars are of mighty use; the night
    Is dark, and long;   10
The road foul; and where one goes right,
    Six may go wrong.
    One twinkling ray,
    Shot o'er some cloud,
    May clear much way,
    And guide a crowd.

God's saints are shining lights: who stays
    Here long must pass
O'er dark hills, swift streams, and steep ways
    As smooth as glass;   20
    But these all night,
    Like candles, shed
    Their beams, and light
    Us into bed.

They are, indeed, our pillar-fires,[2]
    Seen as we go;
They are that city's shining spires
    We travel to:
    A swordlike gleam[3]
    Kept man for sin   30
    First *out;* this beam
    Will guide him *in.*

[SILENCE AND STEALTH OF DAYS!]

Silence and stealth of days! 'Tis now,
    Since thou art gone,
Twelve hundred hours, and not a brow
    But clouds hang on.

JOY OF MY LIFE
    1 This is one of a group of poems that seems to have been
inspired by the death of a favorite brother, William. Others
of the group are Silence and Stealth of Days, and I Walked
the Other Day to Spend My Hour.
    2 See Exodus 13:21.   3 See Genesis 3:24.

As he that in some cave's thick damp,
    Locked from the light,
Fixeth a solitary lamp
    To brave the night,
And walking from his sun, when past
    That glimmering ray,   10
Cuts through the heavy mists in haste
    Back to his day;
So o'er fled minutes I retreat
    Unto that hour,
Which showed thee last, but did defeat
    Thy light and power.
I search, and rack my soul to see
    Those beams again;
But nothing but the snuff to me
    Appeareth plain: 20
That, dark and dead, sleeps in its known
    And common urn;
But those, fled to their Maker's throne,
    There shine, and burn.
Oh, could I track them! but souls must
    Track one the other;
And now the spirit, not the dust,
    Must be thy brother.
But I have one Pearl, by whose light
    All things I see;   30
And in the heart of earth and night
    Find Heaven, and thee.

PEACE

My soul, there is a country
    Far beyond the stars,
Where stands a wingèd sentry
    All skillful in the wars.
There, above noise and danger,
    Sweet Peace sits crowned with smiles,
And One born in a manger
    Commands the beauteous files.
He is thy gracious friend,
    And—O my soul awake!—   10
Did in pure love descend
    To die here for thy sake.
If thou canst get but thither,
    There grows the flower of peace,
The rose that cannot wither,
    Thy fortress and thy ease.

Leave, then, thy foolish ranges;
　　For none can thee secure
But One who never changes,
　　Thy God, thy life, thy cure.   20

[AND DO THEY SO?]

ROMANS 8:19

*Etenim res creatæ exerto capite observantes
expectant revelationem Filiorum Dei.*[1]

And do they[2] so? Have they a sense
　　Of aught but influence?
Can they their heads lift, and expect,
　　And groan too? Why the elect
Can do no more; my volumes said
　　They were all dull, and dead;
They judged them senseless, and their state
　　Wholly inanimate.
　　　　Go, go, seal up thy looks,
　　　　And burn thy books.   10

I would I were a stone, or tree,
　　Or flower, by pedigree,
Or some poor highway herb, or spring
　　To flow, or bird to sing!
Then should I, tied to one sure state,
　　All day expect my date;
But I am sadly loose, and stray
　　A giddy blast each way;
　　　　O let me not thus range,
　　　　Thou canst not change!   20

Sometime I sit with Thee and tarry
　　An hour or so, then vary;
Thy other creatures in this scene
　　Thee only aim and mean;
Some rise to seek Thee, and with heads
　　Erect, peep from their beds;
Others, whose birth is in the tomb,
　　And cannot quit the womb,
　　　　Sigh there, and groan for Thee,
　　　　Their liberty.   30

O let me not do less! Shall they
　　Watch, while I sleep or play?
Shall I thy mercies still abuse
　　With fancies, friends, or news?
O brook[3] it not! Thy blood is mine,
　　And my soul should be Thine;
O brook it not! why wilt Thou stop,
　　After whole showers, one drop?
　　　　Sure Thou wilt joy to see
　　　　Thy sheep with Thee.   40

CORRUPTION

Sure it was so. Man in those early days
　　Was not all stone and earth;
He shined a little, and by those weak rays
　　Had some glimpse of his birth.
He saw Heaven o'er his head, and knew from
　　　　whence
　　He came, condemnèd hither;
And, as first love draws strongest, so from hence
　　His mind sure progressed thither.
Things here were strange unto him: sweat and till,
　　All was a thorn or weed: 10
Nor did those last, but—like himself—died still
　　As soon as they did seed.
They seemed to quarrel with him, for that act
　　That felled him foiled them all:
He drew the curse upon the world, and cracked
　　The whole frame with his fall.
This made him long for home, as loth to stay
　　With murmurers and foes;
He sighed for Eden, and would often say,
　　"Ah! what bright days were those!"   20
Nor was Heaven cold unto him; for each day
　　The valley or the mountain
Afforded visits, and still paradise lay
　　In some green shade or fountain.
Angels lay lieger[1] here; each bush and cell,
　　Each oak and highway knew them;
Walk but the fields, or sit down at some well,
　　And he was sure to view them.

AND DO THEY SO?
　1 "For created things, watching with head erect, await the revelation of the Sons of God." Professor A. C. Howell points out that Vaughan's quotation is from Theodore Beza's Latin translation of the New Testament, not from the Vulgate.
　2 Supposedly inanimate things, stones, trees, etc.

3 Tolerate, endure.

CORRUPTION
1 To act as an ambassador-lieger, *i.e.*, a resident as opposed to an extraordinary ambassador. (From Old English *liegan*, to lie.)

Almighty Love! where art Thou now? Mad man
   Sits down and freezeth on;   30
He raves, and swears to stir nor fire, nor fan,
   But bids the thread be spun.
I see, Thy curtains are close-drawn; Thy bow
   Looks dim, too, in the cloud;
Sin triumphs still, and man is sunk below
   The center, and his shroud.
All's in deep sleep and night: thick darkness lies
   And hatcheth o'er Thy people—
But hark! what trumpet's that? what angel cries,
   "Arise! thrust in Thy sickle"?   40

THE DAWNING

Ah! what time wilt Thou come? when shall
       that cry,[1]
"The bridegroom's coming," fill the sky?
Shall it in the evening run,
When our words and works are done?
Or will Thy all-surprising light
     Break at midnight,
When either sleep or some dark pleasure
Possesseth mad man without measure?
Or shall these early fragrant hours
     Unlock Thy bowers,   10
And with their blush of light descry
Thy locks crowned with eternity?
Indeed, it is the only time
That with Thy glory doth best chime;
All now are stirring, every field
     Full hymns doth yield,
The whole creation shakes off night,
And for Thy shadow looks the light;
Stars now vanish without number,
Sleepy planets set and slumber,   20
The pursy clouds disband and scatter,
All expect some sudden matter;
Not one beam triumphs, but from far
     That morning star.
Oh, at what time soever, Thou,
Unknown to us, the heavens wilt bow,
And with Thy angels in the van
Descend to judge poor careless man,
Grant I may not like puddle lie
In a corrupt security,   30
Where, if a traveler water crave,
He finds it dead and in a grave;

THE DAWNING
  1 See St. Matthew 25:10.

But as this restless vocal spring
All day and night doth run and sing,
And though here born, yet is acquainted
Elsewhere, and flowing keeps untainted,
So let me all my busy age
In Thy free services engage;
And though while here of force I must
Have commerce sometimes with poor dust,   40
And in my flesh, though vile and low,
As this doth in her channel flow,
Yet let my course, my aim, my love,
And chief acquaintance be above;
So when that day and hour shall come
In which Thyself will be the sun,
Thou'lt find me dressed and on my way,
Watching the break of Thy great Day.

LOVE AND DISCIPLINE

Since in a land not barren still
(Because Thou dost Thy grace distill)
My lot is fallen, blest be Thy will!

And since these biting frosts but kill
Some tares in me which choke or spill
That seed Thou sow'st, blest be Thy skill!

Blest be Thy dew, and blest Thy frost,
And happy I to be so crossed,
And cured by crosses at Thy cost.

The dew doth cheer what is distressed,   10
The frosts ill weeds nip and molest;
In both Thou work'st unto the best.

Thus while Thy several mercies plot,
And work on me now cold, now hot,
The work goes on and slacketh not;

For as Thy hand the weather steers,
So thrive I best, 'twixt joys and tears,
And all the year have some green ears.

THE WORLD

I saw eternity the other night
Like a great ring of pure and endless light,
   All calm as it was bright;
And round beneath it, time, in hours, days, years,
   Driven by the spheres,

Like a vast shadow moved, in which the world
  And all her train were hurled.[1]
The doting lover in his quaintest[2] strain
  Did there complain;
Near him, his lute, his fancy, and his flights,   10
  Wit's sour delights,
With gloves and knots,[3] the silly snares of pleasure,
  Yet his dear treasure,
All scattered lay, while he his eyes did pour
  Upon a flower.

The darksome statesman,[4] hung with weights and
    woe,
Like a thick midnight fog, moved there so slow
  He did not stay nor go;
Condemning thoughts, like mad eclipses, scowl
  Upon his soul,   20
And crowds of crying witnesses without
  Pursued him with one shout.
Yet digged the mole, and lest his ways be found,
  Worked under ground,
Where he did clutch his prey. But one did see
  That policy:[5]
Churches and altars fed him; perjuries
  Were gnats and flies;[6]
It rained about him blood and tears; but he
  Drank them as free.[7]   30

The fearful miser on a heap of rust
Sat pining all his life there, did scarce trust
  His own hands with the dust;
Yet would not place one piece[8] above, but lives
  In fear of thieves.
Thousands there were as frantic as himself,
  And hugged each one his pelf:
The downright epicure placed heaven in sense,
  And scorned pretense;
While others, slipped into a wide excess,   40
  Said little less;

THE WORLD
  1 The poet is contrasting the great calm, unchanging ring
of light above and the constantly revolving spheres of the
Ptolemaic universe below.
  2 Decorated with the most elaborate conceits and fancies.
  3 Love knots.   4 Unscrupulous politician.
  5 Stratagem.   6 Of no importance.
  7 As freely and liberally as they rained about him.
  8 Invest one coin. See St. Matthew 6:20.

The weaker sort, slight trivial wares enslave,
  Who think them brave;[9]
And poor, despisèd Truth sat counting by[10]
  Their victory.

Yet some, who all this while did weep and sing,
And sing and weep, soared up into the ring;
  But most would use no wing.
"O fools!" said I, "thus to prefer dark night
  Before true light!   50
To live in grots and caves, and hate the day
  Because it shows the way,
The way which from this dead and dark abode
  Leads up to God;
A way where you might tread the sun and be
  More bright than he!"
But, as I did their madness so discuss,
  One whispered thus:
"This ring the Bridegroom[11] did for none provide,
  But for His bride."   60

MAN

Weighing the steadfastness and state
Of some mean things which here below reside,
Where birds like watchful clocks the noiseless date
  And intercourse of times divide;
Where bees at night get home and hive, and
    flowers
    Early, as well as late,
Rise with the sun, and set in the same bowers;

  I would, said I, my God would give
The staidness of these things to man! for these
To His divine appointments ever cleave,   10
  And no new business breaks their peace;
The birds nor sow nor reap, yet sup and dine;
    The flowers without clothes live,
Yet Solomon was never dressed so fine.

  Man hath still either toys or care;
He hath no root, nor to one place is tied,
But ever restless and irregular
  About this earth doth run and ride;
He knows he hath a home, but scarce knows where;
  He says it is so far
That he hath quite forgot how to go there.   20

  9 Fine, beautiful.   10 Observing, taking note of.
11 See Revelation 21:9.

He knocks at all doors, strays and roams,
Nay, hath not so much wit as some stones have,
Which in the darkest nights point to their homes
By some hid sense their Maker gave;
Man is the shuttle, to whose winding quest
And passage through these looms
God ordered motion, but ordained no rest.

[I WALKED THE OTHER DAY TO SPEND MY HOUR][1]

I walked the other day, to spend my hour,
Into a field,
Where I sometimes had seen the soil to yield
A gallant flower;
But winter now had ruffled all the bower
And curious store
I knew there heretofore.

Yet I, whose search loved not to peep and peer
I' the face of things,
Thought with myself, there might be other
springs   10
Besides this here,
Which, like cold friends, sees us but once a year;
And so the flower
Might have some other bower.

Then taking up what I could nearest spy,
I digged about
That place where I had seen him to grow out;
And by and by
I saw the warm recluse alone to lie,
Where, fresh and green,   20
He lived of us unseen.

Many a question intricate and rare
Did I there strow;
But all I could extort was, that he now
Did there repair
Such losses as befell him in this air,
And would ere long
Come forth most fair and young.

This past, I threw the clothes quite o'er his head;
And, stung with fear   30
Of my own frailty, dropped down many a tear
Upon his bed;
Then, sighing, whispered, "Happy are the dead!
What peace doth now
Rock him asleep below!"

And yet, how few believe such doctrine springs
From a poor root,
Which all the winter sleeps here under foot,
And hath no wings
To raise it to the truth and light of things,   40
But is still trod
By every wandering clod.

O Thou! whose spirit did at first inflame
And warm the dead,
And by a sacred incubation fed
With life this frame,
Which once had neither being, form, nor name,
Grant I may so
Thy steps track here below,

That in these masques and shadows I may see 50
Thy sacred way;
And by those hid ascents climb to that day
Which breaks from Thee,
Who art in all things, though invisibly;
Show me Thy peace,
Thy mercy, love, and ease.

And from this care, where dreams and sorrows
reign;
Lead me above
Where light, joy, leisure, and true comforts move
Without all pain;   60
There, hid in Thee, show me his life again,
At whose dumb urn
Thus all the year I mourn!

[THEY ARE ALL GONE INTO THE WORLD OF LIGHT]

They are all gone into the world of light,
And I alone sit lingering here!
Their very memory is fair and bright,
And my sad thoughts doth clear.[1]

I WALKED THE OTHER DAY
1 See note to "Joy of My Life While Left Me Here!",
p. 981.

THEY ARE ALL GONE
1 Brighten.

It[2] glows and glitters in my cloudy breast,
  Like stars upon some gloomy grove,
Or those faint beams in which this hill is
      dressed
    After the sun's remove.

I see them walking in an air of glory,
  Whose light doth trample on my days;   10
My days, which are at best but dull and hoary,
  Mere glimmerings and decays.

O holy hope, and high humility,
  High as the heavens above!
These are your walks, and you have showed
      them me
    To kindle my cold love.

Dear, beauteous death! the jewel of the just,
  Shining nowhere but in the dark;
What mysteries do lie beyond thy dust,
  Could man outlook that mark![3]   20

He that hath found some fledged bird's nest
      may know
  At first sight if the bird be flown;
But what fair well or grove he sings in now,
  That is to him unknown.

And yet, as angels in some brighter dreams
  Call to the soul when man doth sleep,
So some strange thoughts transcend our
      wonted themes,
    And into glory peep.

If a star were confined into a tomb,
  Her captive flames must needs burn there;   30
But when the hand that locked her up gives
      room,
    She'll shine through all the sphere.

O Father of eternal life, and all
  Created glories under Thee!
Resume Thy spirit[4] from this world of thrall
  Into true liberty!

Either disperse these mists, which blot and fill
  My pèrspective[5] still as they pass;
Or else remove me hence unto that hill
  Where I shall need no glass.   40

THE MORNING WATCH

Oh joys! Infinite sweetness! With what flowers
And shoots of glory my soul breaks and buds!
    All the long hours
    Of night, and rest
    Through the still shrouds
    Of sleep, and clouds,
    This dew fell on my breast.
    Oh how it bloods
And spirits all my earth! Hark! In what rings
And hymning circulations the quick world   10
    Awakes and sings;
    The rising winds
    And falling springs,
    Birds, beasts,—all things
    Adore Him in their kinds.
    Thus all is hurled
In sacred hymns and order: the great chime
And symphony of nature. Prayer is
    The world in tune,
    A spirit-voice   20
    And vocal joys
    Whose echo is heaven's bliss.
    Oh let me climb
When I lie down! The pious soul by night
Is like a clouded star whose beams, though said
    To shed their light
    Under some cloud
    Yet are above
    And shine and move   30
    Beyond that misty shroud;
    So, in my bed,
That curtained grave, though sleep, like ashes, hide
My lamp and life, both shall in Thee abide.

UNPROFITABLENESS

How rich, O Lord, how fresh Thy visits are!
'Twas but just now my bleak leaves hopeless hung,
  Sullied with dust and mud;

THEY ARE ALL GONE
  2 The memory of departed friends.   3 Boundary.
  4 Take back my spirit which Thou hast created.

5 Telescope.

Each snarling blast shot through me, and did shear
Their youth, and beauty; cold showers nipped and
         wrung
    Their spiciness and blood;
But since Thou didst in one sweet glance survey
Their sad decays, I flourish, and once more
    Breathe all perfumes and spice;
I smell a dew like myrrh, and all the day   10
Wear in my bosom a full sun; such store
    Hath one beam from Thy eyes.
But, ah, my God! what fruit hast Thou of this?
What one poor leaf did ever I yet fall
    To wait upon Thy wreath?
Thus Thou all day a thankless weed dost dress,
And when Thou hast done, a stench, a fog is all
    The odor I bequeath.

COCK-CROWING

Father of lights! what sunny seed,
What glance of day hast Thou confined
Into this bird? To all the breed
This busy ray Thou hast assigned;
    Their magnetism works all night,
    And dreams of paradise and light.

Their eyes watch for the morning hue;
Their little grain, expelling night,
So shines and sings as if it knew
The path unto the house of light.   10
    It seems their candle, howe'er done,
    Was tinned[1] and lighted at the sun.

If such a tincture, such a touch,
So firm a longing can empower,
Shall Thy own image think it much
To watch for Thy appearing hour?
    If a mere blast so fill the sail,
    Shall not the breath of God prevail?

O Thou immortal Light and Heat!
Whose hand so shines through all this frame   20
That, by the beauty of the seat,
We plainly see who made the same,
    Seeing Thy seed abides in me,
    Dwell Thou in it, and I in Thee!

To sleep without Thee is to die;
Yea, 'tis a death partakes of hell:
For where Thou dost not close the eye,
It never opens, I can tell.
    In such a dark Egyptian border,[2]
    The shades of death dwell, and disorder.   30

If joys, and hopes, and earnest throes,
And hearts whose pulse beats still for light
Are given to birds, who but Thee knows
A love-sick soul's exalted flight?
    Can souls be tracked by any eye
    But His who gave them wings to fly?

Only this veil which Thou hast broke,
And must be broken yet in me,
This veil, I say, is all the cloak
And cloud which shadows Thee from me.   40
    This veil Thy full-eyed love denies,
    And only gleams and fractions spies.

O take it off! make no delay;
But brush me with Thy light that I
May shine unto a perfect day,
And warm me at Thy glorious eye!
    O take it off, or till it flee,
    Though with no lily, stay with me!

THE BIRD

Hither thou com'st: the busy wind all night
Blew through thy lodging, where thy own warm wing
Thy pillow was. Many a sullen storm
(For which coarse man seems much the fitter born)
    Rained on thy bed
    And harmless head.

And now, as fresh and cheerful as the light,
Thy little heart in early hymns doth sing
Unto that Providence, whose unseen arm
Curbed them, and clothed thee well and warm.   10
    All things that be, praise Him, and had
    Their lesson taught them when first made.

COCK-CROWING
1 Teened, kindled.

2 Land. The reference is to the plague of darkness in
Egypt. See Exodus 10:21–23.

So hills and valleys into singing break;
And though poor stones have neither speech nor
    tongue,
While active winds and streams both run and speak,
Yet stones are deep in admiratiòn.[1]
Thus praise and prayer here beneath the sun
Make lesser mornings, when the great are done.

For each inclosèd spirit is a star
    Enlight'ning his own little sphere,   20
Whose light, though fetched and borrowèd from far,
    Both mornings makes and evenings there.

But as these birds of light make a land glad,
Chirping their solemn matins on each tree,
So in the shades of night some dark fowls be,
Whose heavy notes make all that hear them sad.

    The turtle[2] then in palm trees mourns,
        While owls and satyrs howl;
    The pleasant land to brimstone turns,
        And all her streams grow foul.   30

Brightness and mirth, and love and faith, all fly,
Till the day-spring breaks forth again from high.

THE TIMBER

Sure thou didst flourish once! and many springs,
Many bright mornings, much dew, many showers
Passed o'er thy head; many light hearts and wings,
Which now are dead, lodged in thy living bowers.

And still a new succession sings and flies;
Fresh groves grow up, and their green branches shoot
Towards the old and still enduring skies,
While the low violet thrives at their root.

But thou beneath the sad and heavy line
Of death, doth waste all senseless, cold, and dark;   10
Where not so much as dreams of light may shine,
Nor any thought of greenness, leaf, or bark.

THE BIRD
  1 Wonder.   2 Turtledove.

And yet (as if some deep hate and dissent,
Bred in thy growth betwixt high winds and thee,
Were still alive) thou dost great storms resent
Before they come, and know'st how near they be.

Else all at rest thou liest, and the fierce breath
Of tempests can no more disturb thy ease;
But this thy strange resentment after death
Means only those who broke in life thy peace.   20

So murdered man, when lovely life is done,
And his blood freezed, keeps in the center still
Some secret sense, which makes the dead blood run
At his approach that did the body kill.

And is there any murderer worse than sin?
Or any storms more foul than a lewd life?
Or what resentient can work more within
Than true remorse, when with past sins at strife?

He that hath left life's vain joys and vain care,
And truly hates to be detained on earth,   30
Hath got an house where many mansions are,
And keeps his soul unto eternal mirth.

But though thus dead unto the world, and ceased
From sin, he walks a narrow, private way;
Yet grief and old wounds make him sore displeased,
And all his life a rainy, weeping day.

For though he would forsake the world, and live
As mere a stranger, as men long since dead;
Yet joy itself will make a right soul grieve
To think he should be so long vainly led.   40

But as shades set off light, so tears and grief
(Though of themselves but a sad blubbered story)
By showing the sin great, show the relief
Far greater, and so speak my Saviour's glory.

If my way lies through deserts and wild woods,
Where all the land with scorching heat is curst,
Better the pools should flow with rain and floods
To fill my bottle, than I die with thirst.

Blest showers they are, and streams sent from above
Begetting virgins where they used to flow;   50
And trees of life no other water love;
These upper springs, and none else make them grow.

But these chaste fountains flow not till we die;
Some drops may fall before, but a clear spring
And ever running, till we leave to fling
Dirt in her way, will keep above the sky.

ROMANS 6:7
He that is dead is freed from sin.

THE DWELLING-PLACE
ST. JOHN 1:38–39

What happy secret fountain,
  Fair shade or mountain,
Whose undiscovered virgin glory
Boasts it this day, though not in story,
Was then thy dwelling? Did some cloud,
Fixed to a tent, descend and shroud
My distressed Lord? Or did a star,
Beckoned by Thee, though high and far,
In sparkling smiles haste gladly down
To lodge light and increase her own?   10
My dear, dear God! I do not know
What lodged Thee then, nor where, nor how;
But I am sure Thou dost now come
Oft to a narrow, homely room,
Where Thou too hast but the least part:
My God, I mean my sinful heart.

CHILDHOOD

I cannot reach it; and my striving eye
Dazzles at it, as at eternity.
  Were now that chronicle alive,
Those white designs which children drive,[1]
And the thoughts of each harmless hour,
With their content, too, in my power,
Quickly would I make my path even,
And by mere playing go to heaven.

  Why should men love
A wolf more than a lamb or dove?   10
Or choose hell-fire and brimstone streams
Before bright stars and God's own beams?
Who kisseth thorns will hurt his face,
But flowers do both refresh and grace,
And sweetly living—fie on men!—
Are, when dead, medicinal then;
If seeing much should make staid eyes,
And long experience should make wise,
Since all that age doth teach is ill,
Why should I not love childhood still?   20
Why, if I see a rock or shelf,
Shall I from thence cast down myself?
Or by complying with the world,
From the same precipice be hurled?
Those observations are but foul
Which make me wise to lose my soul.

And yet the practice worldlings call
Business, and weighty action all,
Checking the poor child for his play,
But gravely cast themselves away.

  Dear, harmless age! the short, swift span
Where weeping Virtue parts with man;
Where love without lust dwells, and bends   30
What way we please without self-ends.

An age of mysteries! which he
Must live twice that would God's face see;
Which angels guard, and with it play,
Angels! which foul men drive away.

How do I study now, and scan
Thee more than e'er I studied man,   40
And only see through a long night
Thy edges and thy bordering light!
Oh for thy center and midday!
For sure that is the narrow way!

THE NIGHT

Through that pure virgin shrine,
That sacred veil drawn o'er Thy glorious noon,
That men might look and live, as glowworms shine,
  And face the moon,
  Wise Nicodemus saw such light
  As made him know his God by night.[1]

CHILDHOOD
1 Project.

THE NIGHT
1 See St. John 3:2.

Most blest believer he!
Who in that land of darkness and blind eyes
Thy long-expected healing wings could see,
        When Thou didst rise!   10
    And, what can never more be done,
    Did at midnight speak with the Sun!

    Oh who will tell me where
He found Thee at that dead and silent hour?
What hallowed solitary ground did bear
        So rare a flower,
    Within whose sacred leaves did lie
    The fullness of the Deity?

    No mercy-seat of gold,
No dead and dusty cherub, nor carved stone,   20
But His own living works did my Lord hold
        And lodge alone;
    Where trees and herbs did watch and peep
    And wonder, while the Jews did sleep.

    Dear night! this world's defeat;
The stop to busy fools; care's check and curb;
The day of spirits; my soul's calm retreat
        Which none disturb!
    Christ's progress, and His prayer time;[2]
    The hours to which high Heaven doth chime;   30

    God's silent, searching flight;
When my Lord's head is filled with dew, and all
His locks are wet with the clear drops of night;
        His still, soft call;
    His knocking time;[3] the soul's dumb watch,
    When spirits their fair kindred catch.

    Were all my loud, evil days
Calm and unhaunted as is thy dark tent,
Whose peace but by some angel's wing or voice
        Is seldom rent,   40
    Then I in heaven all the long year
    Would keep, and never wander here.

    But living where the sun
Doth all things wake, and where all mix and tire
Themselves and others, I consent and run
        To every mire,
    And by this world's ill-guiding light,
    Err more than I can do by night.

THE NIGHT
2 See St. Mark 1:35, St. Luke 21:37, and St. Luke 22:39–44.
3 See Revelation 3:20.

There is in God—some say—
A deep but dazzling darkness, as men here   50
Say it is late and dusky, because they
        See not all clear.
    Oh for that night, where I in Him
    Might live invisible and dim!

THE WATERFALL

With what deep murmurs through time's
        silent stealth
Doth thy transparent, cool, and watery wealth
        Here flowing fall,
        And chide, and call,
As if his liquid, loose retinue stayed
Lingering, and were of this steep place afraid,
        The common pass
        Where, clear as glass,
        All must descend—
        Not to an end,   10
But quickened by this steep and rocky grave,
Rise to a longer course more bright and brave.

        Dear stream! dear bank! where often I
        Have sat and pleased my pensive eye,
        Why, since each drop of thy quick store
        Runs thither whence it flowed before,
        Should poor souls fear a shade or night,
        Who came, sure, from a sea of light?
        Or since those drops are all sent back
        So sure to thee, that none doth lack,   20
        Why should frail flesh doubt any more
        That what God takes He'll not restore?

        O useful element and clear!
        My sacred wash and cleanser here,
        My first consigner unto those
Fountains of life where the Lamb goes!
What sublime truths and wholesome themes
Lodge in thy mystical deep streams!
Such as dull man can never find
Unless that Spirit lead his mind   30
Which first upon thy face did move,
And hatched all with His quickening love.
As this loud brook's incessant fall
In streaming rings restagnates all,

Which reach by course the bank, and then
Are no more seen, just so pass men.
O my invisible estate,
My glorious liberty, still late!
Thou art the channel my soul seeks,
Not this with cataracts and creeks.   40

QUICKNESS

False life, a foil and no more, when
    Wilt thou be gone?
Thou foul deception of all men
That would not have the true come on.

Thou art a moon-like toil, a blind
    Self-posing state,
A dark contest of waves and wind,
A mere tempestuous debate.

Life is a fixed, discerning light,
    A knowing joy;   10
No chance or fit, but ever bright
And calm and full, yet doth not cloy.

'Tis such a blissful thing that still
    Doth vivify
And shine and smile and hath the skill
To please without eternity.

Thou art a toilsome mole, or less;
    A moving mist;
But life is what none can express:
A quickness which my God hath kissed.   20

THE BOOK

Eternal God! Maker of all
That have lived here since the man's fall;
The Rock of Ages! in whose shade
They live unseen, when here they fade;

Thou knew'st this paper when it was
Mere seed, and after that but grass;
Before 'twas dressed or spun, and when
Made linen, who did wear it then:
What were their lives, their thoughts, and
    deeds,
Whether good corn or fruitless weeds.   10

Thou knew'st this tree when a green shade
Covered it, since a cover made,
And where it flourished, grew, and spread,
As if it never should be dead.

Thou knew'st this harmless beast when he
Did live and feed by Thy decree
On each green thing; then slept—well fed—
Clothed with this skin which now lies spread
A covering o'er this aged book;
Which makes me wisely weep, and look   20
On my own dust; mere dust it is,
But not so dry and clean as this.
Thou knew'st and saw'st them all, and though
Now scattered thus, dost know them so.

O knowing, glorious Spirit! when
Thou shalt restore trees, beasts, and men,
When Thou shalt make all new again,
Destroying only death and pain,
Give him amongst Thy works a place
Who in them loved and sought Thy face!   30

Charles Cotton

[1630–1687]

SON OF THE Charles Cotton who was the friend of such literary men as Donne, Jonson, Carew, and Lovelace, the poet Cotton was educated privately and traveled in France. Taking no active part in the Civil War, he led the life of a retired country gentleman until some time around 1665, when he seems to have encountered financial difficulties which obliged him to write for his living. His works include *Scarronides, or Virgil Travestied* (1664–65), a burlesque poem which enjoyed great popularity in its day, a translation of Montaigne (1685–86), and a continuation of Walton's *Complete Angler*, included in the fifth edition of that work (1676). The last-mentioned effort was at least in part a labor of love, for Cotton was as impassioned an angler as his friend Walton.

Cotton's *Poems on Several Occasions*, on which his present modest but secure reputation rests, were published posthumously in 1689.

C. COTTON. *Poems*, ed. J. Beresford (London, 1923).
————. *Poems*, ed. J. Buxton (London, 1958). Includes some manuscript poems not found in Beresford.
C. J. SEMBOWER. *The Life and the Poetry of Charles Cotton* (Philadelphia, 1911).

FROM

POEMS ON SEVERAL OCCASIONS [1689]

NOON QUATRAINS

The day grows hot, and darts his rays
From such a sure and killing place,
That this half world are fain to fly
The danger of his burning eye.

His early glories were benign,
Warm to be felt, bright to be seen,
And all was comfort, but who can
Endure him when meridian?

Of him we as of kings complain,
Who mildly do begin to reign,   10
But to the zenith got of power,
Those whom they should protect devour.

Has not another Phaëton
Mounted the chariot of the sun,
And, wanting art to guide his horse,
Is hurried from the sun's due course?

If this hold on, our fertile lands
Will soon be turned to parchèd sands,
And not an onion that will grow
Without a Nile to overflow.   20

The grazing herds now droop and pant,
Ev'n without labor fit to faint,
And willingly forsook their meat,
To seek out cover from the heat.

The lagging ox is now unbound,
From larding the new-turned-up ground,
Whilst Hobbinol alike o'erlaid
Takes his coarse dinner to the shade.

Cellars and grottoes now are best
To eat and drink in, or to rest,   30
And not a soul above is found
Can find a refuge under ground.

When pagan tyranny grew hot,
Thus persecuted Christians got
Into the dark but friendly womb
Of unknown subterranean Rome.

And as that heat did cool at last,
So a few scorching hours o'erpassed,
In a more mild and temp'rate ray
We may again enjoy the day.   40

EVENING QUATRAINS

The day's grown old, the fainting sun
Has but a little way to run,
And yet his steeds, with all his skill,
Scarce lug the chariot down the hill,

With labor spent and thirst oppressed,
Whilst they strain hard to gain the west,
From fetlocks hot drops melted light,
Which turn to meteors in the night.

The shadows now so long do grow
That brambles like tall cedars show,   10
Molehills seem mountains, and the ant
Appears a monstrous elephant.

A very little, little flock
Shades thrice the ground that it would stock;
Whilst the small stripling following them
Appears a mighty Polypheme.[1]

These being brought into the fold,
And by the thrifty master told,[2]
He thinks his wages are well paid,
Since none are either lost or strayed.   20

Now lowing herds are each-where heard,
Chains rattle in the villein's yard,[3]
The cart's on tail set down to rest,
Bearing on high the cuckold's crest.

The hedge is stripped, the clothes brought in,
Nought's left without should be within;
The bees are hived and hum their charm,
Whilst every house does seem a swarm.

The cock now to the roost is pressed,
For he must call up all the rest;   30
The sow's fast pegged within the sty,
To still her squeaking progeny.

Each one has had his supping mess,
The cheese is put into the press,
The pans and bowls clean scalded all,
Reared up against the milk-house wall.

And now on benches all are sat
In the cool air to sit and chat,
Till Phœbus, dipping in the west,
Shall lead the world the way to rest.   40

EVENING QUATRAINS
1 Polyphemus, one of the Cyclopes, fed his flocks on Mt.
Ætna. See the Odyssey for the story of Ulysses' encounter
with him.
   2 Counted.   3 Farmyard.

Katherine Philips

[1631–1664]

KATHERINE PHILIPS, known to her literary friends as "the matchless Orinda," was the first Englishwoman to write poetry of real value. The daughter of John Fowler, a London merchant, she married in 1648 and established a "Society of Friendship" for the discussion of literature. Her translation of Corneille's *Pompée* was produced in Dublin in 1663, with considerable success. An unauthorized edition of her poems appeared in the year of her death; an enlarged edition, containing also her Corneille translations, *Pompey* and *Horace*, was published in 1667.

Orinda's acquaintance included such distinguished names as Cowley, Cartwright, Vaughan, and Jeremy Taylor. She exchanged complimentary verses with Vaughan, and Taylor dedicated to her his *Discourse on the Nature of Friendship*.

The poem "To my Excellent Lucasia" is typical of Orinda's verse in its Platonism, its Metaphysical conceits, and its attenuated prettiness.

K. PHILIPS. *Selected Poems*, ed. J. R. Tutin (Cottingham near Hull, 1904).

G. SAINTSBURY, ed. *Minor Poets of the Caroline Period*, 3 vols. (Oxford, 1905). Vol. I contains the poems.

P. W. SOUERS. *The Matchless Orinda* (Cambridge, Mass., 1931). A thorough critical biography.

F R O M

POEMS [1667]

TO MY EXCELLENT LUCASIA, ON OUR FRIENDSHIP

I did not live until this time
  Crowned my felicity,
When I could say without a crime
  I am not thine, but thee.

This carcass breathed and walked and slept,
  So that the world believed
There was a soul the motions kept,
  But they were all deceived.

For as a watch by art is wound
  To motion, such was mine;   10
But never had Orinda found
  A soul till she found thine;

Which now inspires, cures, and supplies,
  And guides my darkened breast;
For thou art all that I can prize,
  My joy, my life, my rest.

No bridegroom's nor crown-conqueror's mirth
  To mine compared can be;
They have but pieces of this earth,
  I've all the world in thee.   20

Then let our flames still light and shine,
  And no false fear control,
As innocent as our design,
  Immortal as our soul.

John Dryden

[1631–1700]

THE conception of John Dryden as the true founder of English Neoclassicism, as a poet and critic whose spirit dominates the entire Augustan age, is both familiar and just. It has sometimes led, however, to the assumption that he was a kind of eighteenth-century poet before-the-fact, an assumption which is dangerously inaccurate. For Dryden was as fully a man and poet of the seventeenth century as his dates indicate—in his all-pervasive wit, in his religious orientation, and, most of all perhaps, in the extraordinary range and scope of his poetic activity.

The first efforts of the young Dryden are typified by his elegy "Upon the Death of the Lord Hastings" (1650), an extravagant example of the Metaphysical style in its decadent, or Clevelandesque, phase. His "Heroic Stanzas on the Death of Cromwell" (1658), like the politically reversed *Astræa Redux* (1660) which was composed in celebration of the restoration of Charles II, showed a remarkable growth in technical mastery, and his long and skillful *Annus Mirabilis* (1666) made it evident that the great poet of the new age had emerged. All three of these poems are occasional and thus manifest that shift from the personal and private mode to the official and public which serves, more than any other literary development of the time, to epitomize the difference between pre-Restoration and Restoration verse. Dryden, the greatest poet of the Restoration, is the greatest occasional poet in our language.

The neatly end-stopped couplets of *Astræa Redux* brought to perfection a technique which had been slowly developing throughout the century—in the work of Sir John Beaumont, Waller, and Denham. Dryden had been active as a playwright since early in the 1660's, and his introduction of the pentameter couplet into the "heroic" plays of love and honor which he had made the fashion gave rise to the term "heroic couplet," which has since served as the designation for the chief poetic instrument of the Augustans.

Dryden's function as a public poet was ratified in 1668 by his appointment as poet laureate, an appointment which was largely due to the skill with which he had defended Charles' interests in *Annus Mirabilis*. It was as the literary spokesman of the government that Dryden reached what probably must be accounted the summit of his achievement —the great political satires elicited by the hysteria attendant on the Popish Plot and the attempt to exclude the Duke of York from the succession to the throne. *Absalom and Achitophel* (1681), *The Medal* (1682), and *MacFlecknoe* (1682) owe something to the example of Cleveland and Butler, but in their polish, their urbanity, and their deadly aim they constitute something wholly new in English satire. In particular, the brilliant but restrained portraits which adorn *Absalom* served as a model for all subsequent verse satire. The doctrinal poems *Religio Laici* (1682) and *The Hind and the Panther* (1687), the first defending the Anglican position, the second written after the poet's conversion to Catholicism, make a less immediate appeal to the modern reader, but both poems show Dryden at the height of his extraordinary powers as a poet of the intellect.

Deprived of his laureateship at the Glorious Revolution of 1688, Dryden was obliged to devote himself to the drama once more, and to those translations which represent (especially his Virgil) yet another facet of his varied genius. Out of favor at the court of Protestant William and Mary, he retained his position as absolute literary dictator of England, and ruled his domain from Will's Coffee House, which his presence had made the literary center of the country. (A more detailed account of Dryden's life appears in the introduction to the selection from his prose in this volume.)

As satirist, dramatist, and occasional poet, Dryden is best approached through a study of his long poems. His lyric gifts, however, ought not to be overlooked—the graceful songs interspersed throughout his plays, and, most of all, the great odes with which he stabilized the form in English. Dryden's position as the father of eighteenth-century literature is obvious; a reading of the poem to Mistress Anne Killigrew or the odes to St. Cecilia reminds us that his influence reaches beyond the Augustans to Wordsworth and the Romantics, to the entire nineteenth century and beyond.

J. DRYDEN. *Works*, ed. Sir W. Scott, rev. by G. Saintsbury, 18 vols. (Edinburgh, 1882–92).
    Until now, the definitive and complete edition.
————. *Works*, ed. E. N. Hooker and H. T. Swedenberg, Jr. (Berkeley, Calif., 1956–).
    When completed, will be definitive.
————. *The Poems of John Dryden*, ed. James Kinsley, 4 vols. (London, 1958).
————. *Poetical Works*, ed. G. R. Noyes (Boston, rev. ed., 1950).
D. NICHOL SMITH. *John Dryden* (Cambridge, 1950).
M. VAN DOREN. *The Poetry of John Dryden* (New York, 3rd ed., 1946).
T. S. ELIOT. *Homage to John Dryden* (London, 1924).
————. *John Dryden* (New York, 1932).
L. I. BREDVOLD. *The Intellectual Milieu of John Dryden* (Ann Arbor, Mich., 1934).
J. M. OSBORN. *John Dryden: Some Biographical Facts and Problems* (New York, 1940).
I. JACK. (See under Butler bibliography).
R. NEVO. *The Dial of Virtue* (Princeton, 1963).
B. N. SCHILLING. *Dryden and the Conservative Myth* (New Haven, 1961).
E. MINER. *Dryden's Poetry* (Bloomington, Ind., 1967).

SONGS FROM THE PLAYS

[AH, FADING JOY]

Ah, fading joy, how quickly art thou past!
  Yet we thy ruin haste.
As if the cares of human life were few,
  We seek out new;
And follow fate, that does too fast pursue.

See how on every bough the birds express
  In their sweet notes their happiness.
  They all enjoy and nothing spare,
But on their Mother Nature lay their care:

Why then should man, the lord of all below,   10
  Such troubles choose to know
As none of all his subjects undergo?

Hark, hark, the waters fall, fall, fall,
  And with a murmuring sound
  Dash, dash, upon the ground,
    To gentle slumbers call.
          —*The Indian Emperor*, 1665

[YOU PLEASING DREAMS]

You pleasing dreams of love and sweet delight,
Appear before this slumbering virgin's sight;
Soft visions, set her free
From mournful piety.
Let her sad thoughts from Heaven retire;
And let the melancholy love
Of those remoter joys above
Give place to your more sprightly fire.
Let purling streams be in her fancy seen,
And flowery meads, and vales of cheerful green; 10
And in the midst of deathless groves
Soft sighing wishes lie,
And smiling hopes fast by,
And just beyond 'em ever-laughing loves.
                              —*Tyrannic Love*, 1670

[AH, HOW SWEET IT IS TO LOVE!]

Ah, how sweet it is to love!
Ah, how gay is young desire!
And what pleasing pains we prove
When we first approach love's fire!
    Pains of love be sweeter far
    Than all other pleasures are.

Sighs which are from lovers blown
Do but gently heave the heart;
Ev'n the tears they shed alone
Cure, like trickling balm, their smart.   10
    Lovers, when they lose their breath,
    Bleed away in easy death.

Love and time with reverence use,
Treat them like a parting friend;
Nor the golden gifts refuse,
Which in youth sincere they send,
    For each year their price is more,
    And they less simple than before.

Love, like spring-tides full and high,
Swells in every youthful vein,   20
But each tide does less supply,
Till they quite shrink in again.
    If a flow in age appear,
    'Tis but rain, and runs not clear.
                              —*Tyrannic Love*

[YOU CHARMED ME NOT WITH THAT FAIR FACE]

You charmed me not with that fair face,
    Though it was all divine:
To be another's is the grace
    That makes me wish you mine.

The gods and fortune take their part
    Who, like young monarchs, fight,
And boldly dare invade that heart
    Which is another's right.

First, and with hope, we undertake
    To pull up every bar;   10
But, once possessed, we faintly make
    A dull defensive war.

Now every friend is turned a foe,
    In hope to get our store;
And passion makes us cowards grow,
    Which made us brave before.
                              —*An Evening's Love*, 1671

[WHEREVER I AM]

Wherever I am, and whatever I do,
    My Phyllis is still in my mind;
When angry, I mean not to Phyllis to go,
    My feet of themselves the way find;
Unknown to myself I am just at her door,
    And when I would rail, I can bring out no more
    Than "Phyllis, too fair and unkind!"

When Phyllis I see, my heart bounds in my breast,
    And the love I would stifle is shown;
But asleep or awake, I am never at rest   10
    When from my eyes Phyllis is gone.
Sometimes a sad dream does delude my sad mind,
But alas! when I wake, and no Phyllis I find,
    How I sigh to myself all alone!

Should a king be my rival in her I adore,
    He should offer his treasure in vain.
O let me alone to be happy and poor,
    And give me my Phyllis again!
Let Phyllis be mine, and but ever be kind
    I could to a desert with her be confined
    And envy no monarch his reign.   20

Alas! I discover too much of my love,
   And she too well knows her own power;
She makes me each day a new martyrdom prove,
   And makes me grow jealous each hour;
But let her each minute torment my poor mind,
I had rather love Phyllis, both false and unkind,
   Than ever be freed from her power.
           —*The Conquest of Granada, Part I*, 1672

[FAREWELL, UNGRATEFUL TRAITOR]

Farewell, ungrateful traitor,
   Farewell, my perjured swain,
Let never injured creature
   Believe a man again.
The pleasure of possessing
Surpasses all expressing,
But 'tis too short a blessing,
   And love too long a pain.

'Tis easy to deceive us
   In pity of your pain,   10
But when we love, you leave us
   To rail at you in vain.
Before we have descried it,
There is no bliss beside it,
But she that once has tried it,
   Will never love again.

The passion you pretended
   Was only to obtain;
But when the charm is ended
   The charmer you disdain.   20
Your love by ours we measure,
Till we have lost our treasure,
But dying is a pleasure,
   When loving is a pain.
           —*The Spanish Friar*, 1681

[OLD FATHER OCEAN CALLS MY TIDE][1]

Old Father Ocean calls my tide,
Come away, come away;
The barks upon the billows ride,
The master will not stay.

The merry bo'sun from his side
His whistle takes, to check and chide
The ling'ring lads' delay,
And all the crew aloud has cried,
"Come away, come away."

See, the god of seas attends thee,   10
Nymphs divine, a beauteous train;
All the calmer gales befriend thee,
In thy passage o'er the main.
Every maid her locks is binding,
Every Triton's horn is winding,
Welcome to the watery plain!
          —*Albion and Albanius*, 1685

MERCURY'S SONG TO PHÆDRA

Fair Iris I love, and hourly I die,
But not for a lip, nor a languishing eye;
She's fickle and false, and there we agree;
But I am as false and as fickle as she.
We neither believe what either can say;
And, neither believing, we neither betray.

'Tis civil to swear, and say things of course;
We mean not the taking for better or worse.
When present, we love; when absent, agree;
I think not of Iris, nor Iris of me.
The legend of love no couple can find,
So easy to part, or so equally joined.
          —*Amphitryon*, 1690

SONG TO A MINUET

How happy the lover,
   How easy his chain,
   How pleasing his pain!
How sweet to discover
   He sighs not in vain!
For love every creature
Is formed by his nature;
   No joys are above
   The pleasures of love.

OLD FATHER OCEAN
1 Spoken by the River Thames, whose tide is to bear James, Duke of York (Albanius), out to sea on his journey to Brussels. The play portrays allegorically the triumph of Charles II (Albion) and James II over their enemies. James's retirement to the Continent in 1679 was made advisable by the anti-Catholic feeling engendered by the circumstances of the Popish Plot.

In vain are our graces,   10
    In vain are your eyes,
    If love you despise;
When age furrows faces,
    'Tis time to be wise.
Then use the short blessing
That flies in possessing:
    No joys are above
    The pleasures of love.

                                —*King Arthur,* 1691

[SONG SUNG BY VENUS IN HONOR OF BRITANNIA]

Fairest isle, all isles excelling,
    Seat of pleasures and of loves;
Venus here will choose her dwelling,
    And forsake her Cyprian groves.

Cupid from his favorite nation
    Care and envy will remove;
Jealousy, that poisons passion,
    And despair, that dies for love.

Gentle murmurs, sweet complaining,
    Sighs that blow the fire of love;   10
Soft repulses, kind disdaining,
    Shall be all the pains you prove.

Every swain shall pay his duty,
    Grateful every nymph shall prove;
And as these excel in beauty,
    Those shall be renowned for love.

                                —*King Arthur*

FROM

ANNUS MIRABILIS[1] [1667]

[THE NEW LONDON]

Yet, London, empress of the northern clime,   845
By an high fate thou greatly didst expire:
Great as the world's, which, at the death of time,
Must fall, and rise a nobler frame by fire.

. . . .

Methinks already, from this chymic flame,
I see a city of more precious mold;   1170
Rich as the town[2] which gives the Indies name,
With silver paved, and all divine with gold.

Already laboring with a mighty fate,
She shakes the rubbish from her mounting brow,
And seems to have renewed her charter's date,
Which Heav'n will to the death of time allow.

More great than human now, and more August,[3]
New deified she from her fire does rise;
Her widening streets on new foundations trust,
And, opening, into larger parts she flies.   1180

Before, she like some shepherdess did show,
Who sate to bathe her by a river's side,
Not answering to her fame, but rude and low,
Nor taught the beauteous arts of modern pride.

Now, like a maiden queen, she will behold
From her high turrets hourly suitors come;
The East with incense, and the West with gold,
Will stand like suppliants to receive her doom.

The silver Thames, her own domestic flood,
Shall bear her vessels, like a sweeping train,   1190
And often wind, as of his mistress proud,
With longing eyes to meet her face again.

ANNUS MIRABILIS

1 Of Dryden's poem Annus Mirabilis: The Year of Wonders, 1666, we print here stanzas 212, 293–98, in which he describes a new and finer London rising out of the ashes of the Great Fire of that year.

2 "Mexico" (note by Dryden).

3 "The old name of London" (note by Dryden).

FROM

ABSALOM AND ACHITOPHEL[1] [1682]

PART I

IN PIOUS times, ere priestcraft did begin,
Before polygamy was made a sin;
When man on many multiplied his kind,
Ere one to one was cursedly confined;
When nature prompted, and no law denied
Promiscuous use of concubine and bride;
Then Israel's monarch after heaven's own heart,
His vigorous warmth did variously impart
To wives and slaves; and, wide as his command,
Scattered his Maker's image through the land.   10
Michal, of royal blood, the crown did wear,
A soil ungrateful to the tiller's care:
Not so the rest; for several mothers bore
To godlike David several sons before.
But since like slaves his bed they did ascend,
No true succession could their seed attend.
Of all this numerous progeny was none
So beautiful, so brave, as Absalom:
Whether, inspired by some diviner lust,
His father got him with a greater gust;   20
Or that his conscious destiny made way,
By manly beauty, to imperial sway.
Early in foreign fields he won renown
With kings and states allied to Israel's crown;
In peace the thoughts of war he could remove,
And seemed as he were only born for love.
Whate'er he did, was done with so much ease,
In him alone 'twas natural to please:
His motions all accompanied with grace,
And Paradise was opened in his face.   30

With secret joy indulgent David viewed
His youthful image in his son renewed:
To all his wishes nothing he denied;
And made the charming Annabel[2] his bride.
What faults he had (for who from faults is free?)
His father could not, or he would not see.
Some warm excesses which the law forbore,
Were construed youth that purged by boiling o'er,
And Amnon's murder,[3] by a specious name,
Was called a just revenge for injured fame.   40
Thus praised and loved, the noble youth remained,
While David, undisturbed, in Sion[4] reigned.
But life can never be sincerely blest:
Heaven punishes the bad, and proves[5] the best.
The Jews, a headstrong, moody, murmuring race,
As ever tried the extent and stretch of grace;
God's pampered people, whom, debauched with
    ease,
No king could govern, nor no God could please
(Gods they had tried of every shape and size
That god-smiths could produce, or priests devise);
These Adam-wits,[6] too fortunately free,   51
Began to dream they wanted liberty;
And when no rule, no precedent was found,
Of men by laws less circumscribed and bound,
They led their wild desires to woods and caves,
And thought that all but savages were slaves.
They too, when Saul[7] was dead, without a blow,
Made foolish Ishbosheth[8] the crown forgo;
Who banished David did from Hebron[9] bring,
And with a general shout proclaimed him King: 60
Those very Jews, who, at their very best,
Their humor more than loyalty expressed,
Now wondered why so long they had obeyed
An idol monarch, which their hands had made;

ABSALOM AND ACHITOPHEL

1 This, Dryden's earliest satire, first published in 1681, is
also his greatest. With great ingenuity he applies the Biblical
story of the revolt of Absalom, the much-loved son of King
David, against his father (II Samuel 13–18) to the plot of the
handsome young Duke of Monmouth, the illegitimate and
greatly loved son of Charles II, against his father's brother,
James, Duke of York, heir to the throne and a Roman
Catholic. The Earl of Shaftesbury, the leader of the Whigs,
who instigated the plot, is Achitophel; Charles II is David;
England is Israel; the English, the Jews; and so on. Dryden's
poem constitutes a defense of the King, at whose request he
wrote the poem, and the Tories.

2 Anne Scott, Countess of Buccleuch.
3 No convincing explanation of the allusion has yet been
found.
4 London.   5 Tests.
6 Persons, like Adam in Paradise, not contented with their
fortunate lot.
7 Oliver Cromwell.
8 Richard Cromwell, the son and successor of Oliver.
9 Probably Scotland, where Charles was crowned king
before his coronation in London (Jerusalem, Sion).

Thought they might ruin him they could create,
Or melt him to that golden calf,[10] a State.
But these were random bolts; no formed design,
Nor interest made the factious crowd to join:
The sober part of Israel, free from stain,
Well knew the value of a peaceful reign;   70
And, looking backward with a wise affright,
Saw seams of wounds, dishonest to the sight:
In contemplation of whose ugly scars
They cursed the memory of civil wars.
The moderate sort of men, thus qualified,[11]
Inclined the balance to the better side;
And David's mildness managed it so well,
The bad found no occasion to rebel.
But when to sin our biased nature leans,
The careful Devil is still at hand with means;   80
And providently pimps for ill desires:
The Good Old Cause[12] revived, a plot requires.
Plots, true or false, are necessary things,
To raise up commonwealths and ruin kings.
　　The inhabitants of old Jerusalem[13]
Were Jebusites;[14] the town so called from them;
And theirs the native right—
But when the chosen people[15] grew more strong,
The rightful cause at length became the wrong,
And every loss the men of Jebus bore,   90
They still were thought God's enemies the more.
Thus worn or weakened, well or ill content,
Submit they must to David's government:
Impoverished and deprived of all command,
Their taxes doubled as they lost their land;
And, what was harder yet to flesh and blood,
Their gods disgraced, and burnt like common
　　wood.
This set the heathen priesthood in a flame;
For priests of all religions are the same:
Of whatsoe'er descent their godhead be,   100
Stock, stone, or other homely pedigree,
In his defense his servants are as bold
As if he had been born of beaten gold.
The Jewish rabbins,[16] though their enemies,
In this conclude them honest men and wise;
For 'twas their duty, all the learnèd think,
To espouse his cause by whom they eat and drink.

From hence began that Plot,[17] the nation's curse,
Bad in itself, but represented worse,
Raised in extremes, and in extremes decried,   110
With oaths affirmed, with dying vows denied,
Not weighed or winnowed by the multitude,
But swallowed in the mass, unchewed and crude.
Some truth there was, but dashed and brewed with
　　lies
To please the fools and puzzle all the wise:
Succeeding times did equal folly call
Believing nothing or believing all.
The Egyptian[18] rites the Jebusites embraced,
Where gods were recommended by their taste;
Such savory deities must needs be good   120
As served at once for worship and for food.[19]
By force they could not introduce these gods,
For ten to one in former days was odds;
So fraud was used, the sacrificer's trade—
Fools are more hard to conquer than persuade.
Their busy teachers mingled with the Jews
And raked for converts even the Court and stews;
Which Hebrew priests[20] the more unkindly took
Because the fleece accompanies the flock.
Some thought they God's Anointed[21] meant to
　　slay   130
By guns, invented since full many a day:
Our author swears it not; but who can know
How far the Devil and Jebusites may go?
　　This Plot, which failed for want of common
　　　　sense,
Had yet a deep and dangerous consequence;
For as, when raging fevers boil the blood,
The standing lake soon floats into a flood,
And every hostile humor which before
Slept quiet in its channels bubbles o'er,
So several factions from this first ferment   140
Work up to foam and threat the government.
Some by their friends, more by themselves thought
　　wise,
Opposed the power to which they could not rise.

---

10 See Exodus 32:1–6.　　　11 Of such a disposition.
12 That of the Commonwealth.
13 The old name of Jerusalem was Jebusi.
14 Roman Catholics.　　　　15 The Protestants.
16 Anglican clergymen.

17 The alleged Popish Plot of 1678, about which the
Whigs were, or pretended to be, so concerned. It was invented by Titus Oates and was supposed to have as its aim
the murder of the King and the placing of the government
in the hands of the Jesuits.
　18 French.
　19 A contemptuous reference to the Roman Catholic
doctrine of transubstantiation.
　20 The Anglican clergy.　　　21 King Charles II.

Some had in courts been great, and, thrown from
        thence,
Like fiends were hardened in impertinence.
Some, by their Monarch's fatal mercy, grown
From pardoned rebels kinsmen to the throne,
Were raised in power and public office high;
Strong bands, if bands ungrateful men could tie.
Of these the false Achitophel[22] was first;   150
A name to all succeeding ages curst;
For close[23] designs and crooked counsels fit;
Sagacious, bold, and turbulent of wit;
Restless, unfixed in principles and place;
In power unpleased, impatient of disgrace:
A fiery soul, which, working out its way,
Fretted the pigmy body to decay,
And o'er-informed the tenement of clay.
A daring pilot in extremity;
Pleased with the danger, when the waves went
        high,   160
He sought the storms; but, for a calm unfit,
Would steer too near the sands, to boast his wit.
Great wits are sure to madness near allied,
And thin partitions do their bounds divide;
Else why should he, with wealth and honor blest,
Refuse his age the needful hours of rest?
Punish a body which he could not please;
Bankrupt of life, yet prodigal of ease?
And all to leave what with his toil he won,
To that unfeathered two-legged thing, a son;   170
Got,[24] while his soul did huddled[25] notions try,
And born a shapeless lump, like anarchy.
In friendship false, implacable in hate;
Resolved to ruin or to rule the State.
To compass this the triple bond[26] he broke,
The pillars of the public safety shook,
And fitted Israel for a foreign yoke;
Then seized with fear, yet still affecting fame,
Usurped a patriot's all-atoning name.
So easy still it proves in factious times,   180
With public zeal to cancel private crimes.
How safe is treason, and how sacred ill,
Where none can sin against the people's will!
Where crowds can wink, and no offense be known,
Since in another's guilt they find their own!

Yet fame deserved no enemy can grudge;
The statesman we abhor, but praise the judge.
In Israel's courts ne'er sat an Abbethdin[27]
With more discerning eyes, or hands more clean;
Unbribed, unsought, the wretched to redress;   190
Swift of despatch, and easy of access.
Oh, had he been content to serve the Crown,
With virtues proper only to the gown;[28]
Or had the rankness of the soil been freed
From cockle,[29] that oppressed the noble seed!
David for him his tuneful harp had strung,
And Heaven had wanted[30] one immortal song.
But wild Ambition loves to slide, not stand,
And Fortune's ice prefers to Virtue's land.
Achitophel, grown weary to possess   200
A lawful fame, and lazy happiness,
Disdained the golden fruit to gather free,
And lent the crowd his arm to shake the tree.
Now, manifest of[31] crimes contrived long since,
He stood at bold defiance with his Prince;
Held up the buckler of the people's cause
Against the crown, and skulked behind the laws.
The wished occasion of the Plot he takes;
Some circumstances finds, but more he makes.
By buzzing emissaries fills the ears   210
Of listening crowds with jealousies and fears
Of arbitrary counsels brought to light,
And proves the King himself a Jebusite.
Weak arguments! which yet he knew full well
Were strong with people easy to rebel.
For, governed by the moon, the giddy Jews
Tread the same track when she the prime renews;
And once in twenty years, their scribes record,
By natural instinct they change their lord.
Achitophel still wants a chief, and none   220
Was found so fit as warlike Absalom:
Not that he wished his greatness to create
(For politicians neither love nor hate),
But, for he knew his title not allowed,
Would keep him still depending on the crowd,
That kingly power, thus ebbing out, might be
Drawn to the dregs of a democracy.
Him he attempts with studied arts to please,
And sheds his venom with such words as these:

22 Anthony Ashley Cooper, Earl of Shaftesbury, had once
been a trusted adviser of the King.
    23 Secret.   24 Begotten.   25 Confused.
    26 The alliance of England, Holland, and Sweden against
France in 1667, which was broken by the war with France
against Holland, 1670.

27 The head of the Jewish court. Shaftesbury had been
Lord Chancellor.
    28 Judge.   29 Weeds.
    30 Lacked, i.e., David would have sung his praises instead
of writing a psalm, and Heaven would have had one song
the less.
    31 Having evident signs of.

"Auspicious Prince, at whose nativity   230
Some royal planet ruled the southern sky;
Thy longing country's darling and desire;
Their cloudy pillar and their guardian fire,
Their second Moses, whose extended wand
Divides the seas and shows the promised land;
Whose dawning day in every distant age
Has exercised the sacred prophet's rage:
The people's prayer, the glad diviners' theme,
The young men's vision, and the old men's dream!
Thee, Savior, thee, the nation's vows confess, 240
And, never satisfied with seeing, bless:
Swift unbespoken pomps thy steps proclaim,
And stammering babes are taught to lisp thy name.
How long wilt thou the general joy detain,
Starve and defraud the people of thy reign?
Content ingloriously to pass thy days
Like one of virtue's fools that feeds on praise;
Till thy fresh glories, which now shine so bright,
Grow stale and tarnish with our daily sight.
Believe me, royal youth, thy fruit must be   250
Or gathered ripe, or rot upon the tree.
Heaven has to all allotted, soon or late,
Some lucky revolution of their fate;
Whose motions if we watch and guide with skill
(For human good depends on human will),
Our fortune rolls as from a smooth descent,
And from the first impression takes the bent;
But if unseized she glides away like wind,
And leaves repenting folly far behind.
Now, now she meets you with a glorious prize,
And spreads her locks before her as she flies. 261
Had thus old David, from whose loins you spring,
Not dared, when fortune called him, to be King,
At Gath[32] an exile he might still remain,
And heaven's anointing oil had been in vain.
Let his successful youth your hopes engage;
But shun the example of declining age:
Behold him setting in his western skies,
The shadows lengthening as the vapors rise.
He is not now, as when on Jordan's sand[33]   270
The joyful people thronged to see him land,
Covering the beach, and blackening all the strand;
But, like the Prince of Angels, from his height
Comes tumbling downward with diminished light;

Betrayed by one poor Plot to public scorn
(Our only blessing since his curst return),
Those heaps of people which one sheaf did bind,
Blown off and scattered by a puff of wind.
What strength can he to your designs oppose,
Naked of friends, and round beset with foes?   280
If Pharaoh's[34] doubtful succor he should use,
A foreign aid would more incense the Jews;
Proud Egypt would dissembled friendship bring,
Foment the war, but not support the King:
Nor would the royal party e'er unite
With Pharaoh's arms to assist the Jebusite;
Or if they should, their interest soon would break,
And with such odious aid make David weak.
All sorts of men by my successful arts,
Abhorring kings, estrange their altered hearts   290
From David's rule: and 'tis the general cry,
'Religion, commonwealth, and liberty.'
If you, as champion of the public good,
Add to their arms a chief of royal blood,
What may not Israel hope, and what applause
Might such a general gain by such a cause?
Not barren praise alone, that gaudy flower
Fair only to the sight, but solid power;
And nobler is a limited command,
Given by the love of all your native land,   300
Than a successive title, long and dark,
Drawn from the moldy rolls of Noah's ark."
      What cannot praise effect in mighty minds,
When flattery soothes, and when ambition blinds!
Desire of power, on earth a vicious weed,
Yet, sprung from high, is of celestial seed;
In God 'tis glory; and when men aspire,
'Tis but a spark too much of heavenly fire.
The ambitious youth, too covetous of fame,
Too full of angels' metal in his frame,   310
Unwarily was led from virtue's ways,
Made drunk with honor, and debauched with
      praise.
Half loth and half consenting to the ill
(For loyal blood within him struggled still),
He thus replied: "And what pretense have I
To take up arms for public liberty?
My father governs with unquestioned right;
The faith's defender, and mankind's delight;
Good, gracious, just, observant of the laws: 319
And Heaven by wonders has espoused his cause.

---

32 Brussels.
33 A reference to the landing of Charles at Dover, May 1, 1660.

34 Charles was a pensioner of Louis XIV (Pharaoh), whose financial aid helped to make him independent of Parliament.

Whom has he wronged in all his peaceful reign?
Who sues for justice to his throne in vain?
What millions has he pardoned of his foes
Whom just revenge did to his wrath expose?
Mild, easy, humble, studious of our good,
Inclined to mercy, and averse from blood;
If mildness ill with stubborn Israel suit,
His crime is God's belovèd attribute.
What could he gain, his people to betray
Or change his right for arbitrary sway?   330
Let haughty Pharaoh curse with such a reign
His fruitful Nile, and yoke a servile train.
If David's rule Jerusalem displease,
The Dog Star heats their brains to this disease.
Why then should I, encouraging the bad,
Turn rebel and run popularly mad?
Were he a tyrant, who by lawless might
Oppressed the Jews and raised the Jebusite,
Well might I mourn; but nature's holy bands
Would curb my spirits and restrain my hands: 340
The people might assert their liberty,
But what was right in them were crime in me.
His favor leaves me nothing to require,
Prevents my wishes, and outruns desire.
What more can I expect while David lives?
All but his kingly diadem he gives:
And that"—but there he paused; then sighing said—
"Is justly destined for a worthier head.
For when my father from his toils shall rest
And late augment the number of the blest,   350
His lawful issue shall the throne ascend,
Or the collateral line, where that shall end.
His brother, though oppressed with vulgar spite,
Yet dauntless, and secure of native right,
Of every royal virtue stands possessed;
Still dear to all the bravest and the best.
His courage foes, his friends his truth proclaim;
His loyalty the King, the world his fame.
His mercy even the offending crowd will find,
For sure he comes of a forgiving kind.   360
Why should I then repine at Heaven's decree,
Which gives me no pretense to royalty?
Yet oh that fate, propitiously inclined,
Had raised my birth, or had debased my mind;
To my large soul not all her treasure lent,
And then betrayed it to a mean descent!
I find, I find my mounting spirits bold,
And David's part disdains my mother's mold.
Why am I scanted by a niggard birth?
My soul disclaims the kindred of her earth   370

And, made for empire, whispers me within,
'Desire of greatness is a godlike sin.' "
    Him staggering so when hell's dire agent found,
While fainting Virtue scarce maintained her
      ground,
He pours fresh forces in, and thus replies:
    "The eternal God, supremely good and wise,
Imparts not these prodigious gifts in vain:
What wonders are reserved to bless your reign!
Against your will, your arguments have shown,
Such virtue's only given to guide a throne.   380
Not that your father's mildness I contemn;
But manly force becomes the diadem.
'Tis true he grants the people all they crave
And more, perhaps, than subjects ought to have:
For lavish grants suppose a monarch tame,
And more his goodness than his wit proclaim.
But when should people strive their bonds to break,
If not when kings are negligent or weak?
Let him give on till he can give no more,
The thrifty Sanhedrin [35] shall keep him poor;   390
And every shekel which he can receive,
Shall cost a limb of his prerogative.
To ply him with new plots shall be my care;
Or plunge him deep in some expensive war;
Which when his treasury can no more supply,
He must, with the remains of kingship, buy.
His faithful friends, our jealousies and fears
Call Jebusites, and Pharaoh's pensioners;
Whom when our fury from his aid has torn,
He shall be naked left to public scorn.   400
The next successor, whom I fear and hate,
My arts have made obnoxious to the State;
Turned all his virtues to his overthrow,
And gained our elders to pronounce a foe.
His right, for sums of necessary gold,
Shall first be pawned, and afterward be sold;
Till time shall ever-wanting David draw
To pass your doubtful title into law:
If not, the people have a right supreme
To make their kings; for kings are made for them.
All empire is no more than power in trust,   411
Which, when resumed, can be no longer just.
Succession, for the general good designed,
In its own wrong a nation cannot bind;
If altering that the people can relieve,
Better one suffer than a nation grieve.

35 The supreme council in ancient Jerusalem; here, of
course, the British Parliament.

The Jews well know their power: ere Saul they
    chose,
God was their king, and God they durst depose.
Urge now your piety, your filial name,
A father's right, and fear of future fame;   420
The public good, that universal call,
To which even Heaven submitted, answers all.
Nor let his love enchant your generous mind;
'Tis nature's trick to propagate her kind.
Our fond begetters, who would never die,
Love but themselves in their posterity.
Or let his kindness by the effects be tried,
Or let him lay his vain pretense aside.
God said he loved your father; could he bring
A better proof, than to anoint him king?   430
It surely showed he loved the shepherd well,
Who gave so fair a flock as Israel.
Would David have you thought his darling son?
What means he, then, to alienate the crown?
The name of godly he may blush to bear:
'Tis after God's own heart to cheat his heir.
He to his brother gives supreme command;
To you a legacy of barren land,
Perhaps the old harp, on which he thrums his lays,
Or some dull Hebrew ballad in your praise.   440
Then the next heir, a prince severe and wise,
Already looks on you with jealous eyes;
Sees through the thin disguises of your arts,
And marks your progress in the people's hearts.
Though now his mighty soul its grief contains,
He meditates revenge who least complains;
And, like a lion, slumbering in the way,
Or sleep dissembling, while he waits his prey,
His fearless foes within his distance draws,
Constrains his roaring, and contracts his paws; 450
Till at the last, his time for fury found,
He shoots with sudden vengeance from the ground;
The prostrate vulgar passes o'er and spares,
But with a lordly rage his hunter tears.
Your case no tame expedients will afford:
Resolve on death, or conquest by the sword,
Which for no less a stake than life you draw;
And self-defense is nature's eldest law.
Leave the warm people no considering time;
For then rebellion may be thought a crime.   460
Prevail yourself of what occasion gives,
But try your title while your father lives;
And that your arms may have a fair pretense,
Proclaim you take them in the King's defense;

Whose sacred life each minute would expose
To plots, from seeming friends, and secret foes.
And who can sound the depth of David's soul?
Perhaps his fear his kindness may control.
He fears his brother, though he loves his son,
For plighted vows too late to be undone.   470
If so, by force he wishes to be gained,
Like women's lechery, to seem constrained:
Doubt not; but when he most affects the frown,
Commit a pleasing rape upon the crown.
Secure his person to secure your cause:
They who possess the prince, possess the laws."
    He said, and this advice above the rest
With Absalom's mild nature[36] suited best:
Unblamed of life (ambition set aside),
Not stained with cruelty, nor puffed with pride,
How happy had he been, if destiny   481
Had higher placed his birth, or not so high!
His kingly virtues could have claimed a throne,
And blessed all other countries but his own.
But charming greatness since so few refuse,
'Tis juster to lament him than accuse.
Strong were his hopes a rival to remove,
With blandishments to gain the public love;
To head the faction while their zeal was hot,
And popularly prosecute the plot.   490
To further this, Achitophel unites
The malcontents of all the Israelites;
Whose differing parties he could wisely join,
For several ends, to serve the same design:
The best (and of the princes some were such),
Who thought the power of monarchy too much;
Mistaken men, and patriots in their hearts;
Not wicked, but seduced by impious arts.
By these the springs of property were bent,   499
And wound so high, they cracked the government.
The next for interest sought to embroil the State,
To sell their duty at a dearer rate;
And make their Jewish markets of the throne,
Pretending public good to serve their own.
Others thought kings an useless, heavy load,
Who cost too much and did too little good.
These were for laying honest David by
On principles of pure good husbandry.

---

36 Dryden was forced to treat Monmouth as gently as
possible, as the King was very fond of him. He was, also, a
popular favorite, and his wife was a patron of Dryden. He is
therefore portrayed as the tool of Shaftesbury, and a victim
of circumstances rather than as a villain.

With them joined all the haranguers of the throng
That thought to get preferment by the tongue. 510
Who follow next a double danger bring,
Not only hating David, but the King:
The Solymæan [37] rout,[38] well versed of old
In godly faction, and in treason bold;
Cowering and quaking at a conqueror's sword,
But lofty [39] to a lawful prince restored;
Saw with disdain an Ethnic [40] plot begun,
And scorned by Jebusites to be outdone.
Hot Levites [41] headed these; who, pulled before
From the ark, which in the Judges' days they bore,
Resumed their cant, and with a zealous cry   521
Pursued their old beloved theocracy,
Where Sanhedrin [42] and priest enslaved the nation
And justified their spoils by inspiration;
For who so fit to reign as Aaron's race [43]
If once dominion they could found in grace!
These led the pack; though not of surest scent,
Yet deepest-mouthed against the government.
A numerous host of dreaming saints succeed,
Of the true old enthusiastic breed;   530
'Gainst form and order they their power employ,
Nothing to build and all things to destroy.
But far more numerous was the herd of such,
Who think too little, and who talk too much.
These out of mere instinct, they knew not why,
Adored their fathers' God and property;
And, by the same blind benefit of fate,
The Devil and the Jebusite did hate:
Born to be saved, even in their own despite,
Because they could not help believing right.[44]   540
Such were the tools; but a whole Hydra more
Remains, of sprouting heads too long to score.
Some of their chiefs were princes of the land:
In the first rank of these did Zimri [45] stand;
A man so various, that he seemed to be
Not one, but all mankind's epitome:
Stiff in opinions, always in the wrong;
Was everything by starts, and nothing long;
But, in the course of one revolving moon,
Was chemist, fiddler, statesman, and buffoon: 550

Then all for women, painting, rhyming, drinking,
Besides ten thousand freaks that died in thinking.
Blest madman, who could every hour employ,
With something new to wish, or to enjoy!
Railing and praising were his usual themes;
And both (to show his judgment) in extremes:
So over-violent, or over-civil,
That every man, with him, was God or Devil.
In squand'ring wealth was his peculiar art:
Nothing went unrewarded but desert.   560
Beggared by fools, whom still he found too late,
He had his jest, and they had his estate.
He laughed himself from Court; then sought relief
By forming parties, but could ne'er be chief;
For, spite of him, the weight of business fell
On Absalom and wise Achitophel:
Thus, wicked but in will, of means bereft,
He left not faction, but of that was left.
     Titles and names 'twere tedious to rehearse
Of lords, below the dignity of verse.   570
Wits, warriors, Commonwealth's men, were the
     best;
Kind husbands, and mere nobles, all the rest.
And therefore, in the name of dullness, be
The well-hung Balaam [46] and cold Caleb,[47] free;
And canting Nadab [48] let oblivion damn,
Who made new porridge for the paschal lamb.
Let friendship's holy band some names assure;
Some their own worth, and some let scorn secure.
Nor shall the rascal rabble here have place,
Whom kings no titles gave, and God no grace: 580
Not bull-faced Jonas,[49] who could statutes draw
To mean rebellion, and make treason law.
But he, though bad, is followed by a worse,
The wretch who heaven's anointed dared to curse:
Shimei,[50] whose youth did early promise bring
Of zeal to God and hatred to his King,
Did wisely from expensive sins refrain,
And never broke the Sabbath, but for gain;

37 Of London (Solyma = Jerusalem).
38 Rabble.   39 Haughty.
40 Heathen, Gentile; here, Papist.
41 The Presbyterian ministers.
42 Parliament.   43 The clergy.
44 Believers in election and predestination.
45 George Villiers, the Second Duke of Buckingham, and
son of Charles I's favorite.

46 The Earl of Huntingdon, a turncoat from the party of
Monmouth to that of the Duke of York. For an account of
Balaam see Numbers 22–24.
47 Lord Grey of Werk, who had permitted an intrigue
between Monmouth and his own wife.
48 Lord Howard of Escrick.
49 Sir William Jones, the prosecutor of those accused of
complicity in the Popish Plot, who later turned against the
Court party.
50 Slingsby Bethel, a Whig, chosen by poll sheriff of
London, 1680.

Nor ever was he known an oath to vent,
Or curse, unless against the government.   590
Thus heaping wealth, by the most ready way
Among the Jews, which was to cheat and pray,
The city, to reward his pious hate
Against his master, chose him magistrate.
His hand a vare[51] of justice did uphold;
His neck was loaded with a chain of gold.
During his office, treason was no crime;
The sons of Belial had a glorious time;
For Shimei, though not prodigal of pelf,
Yet loved his wicked neighbor as himself.   600
When two or three were gathered to declaim
Against the monarch of Jerusalem,
Shimei was always in the midst of them;
And if they cursed the King when he was by,
Would rather curse than break good company.
If any durst his factious friends accuse,
He packed a jury of dissenting Jews;
Whose fellow-feeling in the godly cause
Would free the suff'ring saint from human laws.
For laws are only made to punish those   610
Who serve the King, and to protect his foes.
If any leisure time he had from power
(Because 'tis sin to misemploy an hour),
His business was, by writing, to persuade
That kings were useless, and a clog to trade;
And that his noble style he might refine,
No Rechabite[52] more shunned the fumes of wine.
Chaste were his cellars, and his shrieval[53] board
The grossness of a city feast abhorred:
His cooks, with long disuse, their trade forgot;   620
Cool was his kitchen, though his brains were hot.
Such frugal virtue malice may accuse,
But sure 'twas necessary to the Jews;
For towns once burnt such magistrates require
As dare not tempt God's providence by fire.
With spiritual food he fed his servants well,
But free from flesh that made the Jews rebel;
And Moses' laws he held in more account,
For forty days of fasting on the mount.
To speak the rest, who better are forgot,   630
Would tire a well-breathed witness of the Plot.

Yet, Corah,[54] thou shalt from oblivion pass:
Erect thyself, thou monumental brass,[55]
High as the serpent of thy metal made,
While nations stand secure beneath thy shade.
What though his birth were base, yet comets rise
From earthy vapors, ere they shine in skies.
Prodigious actions may as well be done
By weaver's issue,[56] as by prince's son.
This arch-attestor for the public good   640
By that one deed ennobles all his blood.
Who ever asked the witnesses' high race,
Whose oath with martyrdom did Stephen grace?
Ours was a Levite, and as times went then,
His tribe were God Almighty's gentlemen.
Sunk were his eyes, his voice was harsh and loud,
Sure signs he neither choleric was nor proud:
His long chin proved his wit; his saintlike grace
A church vermilion, and a Moses' face.
His memory, miraculously great,   650
Could plots, exceeding man's belief, repeat;
Which therefore cannot be accounted lies,
For human wit could never such devise.
Some future truths are mingled in his book;
But where the witness failed, the prophet spoke:
Some things like visionary flights appear;
The spirit caught him up, the Lord knows where;
And gave him his rabbinical degree,
Unknown to foreign university.
His judgment yet his memory did excel;   660
Which pieced his wondrous evidence so well,
And suited to the temper of the times,
Then groaning under Jebusitic crimes.
Let Israel's foes suspect his heavenly call,
And rashly judge his writ apocryphal;
Our laws for such affronts have forfeits made:
He takes his life, who takes away his trade.
Were I myself in witness Corah's place,
The wretch who did me such a dire disgrace,
Should whet my memory, though once forgot,
To make him an appendix of my plot.   671
His zeal to Heav'n made him his Prince despise,
And load his person with indignities;
But zeal peculiar privilege affords,
Indulging latitude to deeds and words;

54 Titus Oates, chief figure in the Popish Plot. For the Biblical account of the insurrection of Corah (Korah) against Moses, see Numbers 16.
55 An allusion to the serpent of brass made by Moses and set up on a pole for the Israelites to look at and be healed of their serpent bites. See Numbers 21.
56 Oates was the son of a weaver.

51 Wand.
52 For an account of the Rechabites, who were forbidden to use wine, see Jeremiah 35.
53 Sheriff's.

And Corah might for Agag's murder call,
In terms as coarse as Samuel used to Saul.[57]
What others in his evidence did join
(The best that could be had for love or coin),
In Corah's own predicament will fall;   680
For *witness* is a common name to all.

    Surrounded thus with friends of every sort,
Deluded Absalom forsakes the Court;
Impatient of high hopes, urged with renown,
And fired with near possession of a crown,
The admiring crowd are dazzled with surprise,
And on his goodly person feed their eyes.
His joy concealed, he sets himself to show,
On each side bowing popularly low;
His looks, his gestures, and his words he frames,
And with familiar ease repeats their names.   691
Thus formed by nature, furnished out with arts,
He glides unfelt into their secret hearts.
Then, with a kind compassionating look,
And sighs, bespeaking pity ere he spoke,
Few words he said, but easy those and fit,
More slow than Hybla-drops,[58] and far more
        sweet.

    "I mourn, my countrymen, your lost estate;
Though far unable to prevent your fate:
Behold a banished man, for your dear cause   700
Exposed a prey to arbitrary laws!
Yet oh! that I alone could be undone,
Cut off from empire, and no more a son!
Now all your liberties a spoil are made;
Egypt and Tyrus[59] intercept your trade,
And Jebusites your sacred rites invade.
My father, whom with reverence yet I name,
Charmed into ease, is careless of his fame;
And, bribed with petty sums of foreign gold,
Is grown in Báthsheba's[60] embraces old;   710
Exalts his enemies, his friends destroys,
And all his power against himself employs.
He gives, and let him give, my right away;
But why should he his own and yours betray?

He, only he, can make the nation bleed,
And he alone from my revenge is freed.
Take then my tears" (with that he wiped his eyes);
" 'Tis all the aid my present power supplies:
No court-informer can these arms accuse;
These arms may sons against their fathers use: 720
And 'tis my wish, the next successor's reign
May make no other Israelite complain."

    Youth, beauty, graceful action seldom fail;
But common interest always will prevail;
And pity never ceases to be shown
To him who makes the people's wrongs his own.
The crowd, that still[61] believe their kings oppress,
With lifted hands their young Messiah bless:
Who now begins his progress to ordain
With chariots, horsemen, and a num'rous train;[62]
From east to west his glories he displays,   731
And, like the sun, the promised land surveys.
Fame runs before him as the morning star,
And shouts of joy salute him from afar.
Each house receives him as a guardian god,
And consecrates the place of his abode.
But hospitable treats did most commend
Wise Issachar,[63] his wealthy western friend.
This moving court, that caught the people's eyes,
And seemed but pomp, did other ends disguise:
Achitophel had formed it, with intent   741
To sound the depths, and fathom, where it went,
The people's hearts; distinguish friends from foes,
And try their strength, before they came to blows.
Yet all was colored with a smooth pretense
Of specious love, and duty to their prince.
Religion and redress of grievances,
Two names that always cheat and always please,
Are often urged; and good King David's life
Endangered by a brother and a wife.[64]   750
Thus in a pageant show a plot is made,
And peace itself is war in masquerade.
O foolish Israel! never warned by ill!
Still the same bait, and circumvented still!

---

57 See I Samuel 15. Agag is Sir Edmund Berry Godfrey, a Westminster justice of the peace, before whom Oates made his first formal deposition with respect to the alleged Plot. Godfrey was found dead in October, 1678, and his murder is still considered the most mysterious crime in English history because of the contradictory character of the evidence.

58 The honey of Hybla, in Sicily, was proverbial for its excellence.

59 France and Holland.

60 The Duchess of Portsmouth, mistress of Charles II.

61 Always.

62 In August, 1680, Monmouth made a progress through central and western England, and at Taunton in Somerset he was met by nearly 30,000 persons.

63 Thomas Thynne, who had been ordered to leave the country, entertained Monmouth while on his progress.

64 Catherine of Braganza, whom Charles II had married in 1662, had failed to provide her husband with an heir to the throne, thus leaving his brother, the Duke of York, next in line of succession, and paving the way for the Popish Plot.

Did ever men forsake their present ease,
In midst of health imagine a disease;
Take pains contingent mischiefs to foresee,
Make heirs for monarchs, and for God decree?
What shall we think! Can people give away,
Both for themselves and sons, their native sway?
Then they are left defenseless to the sword 761
Of each unbounded, arbitrary lord:
And laws are vain, by which we right enjoy,
If kings unquestioned can those laws destroy.
Yet if the crowd be judge of fit and just,
And kings are only officers in trust,
Then this resuming cov'nant was declared
When kings were made, or is forever barred.
If those who gave the scepter could not tie
By their own deed their own posterity, 770
How then could Adam bind his future race?
How could his forfeit on mankind take place?
Or how could heavenly justice damn us all,
Who ne'er consented to our father's fall?
Then kings are slaves to those whom they
      command,
And tenants to their people's pleasure stand.
Add, that the power for property allowed
Is mischievously seated in the crowd;
For who can be secure of private right,
If sovereign sway may be dissolved by might? 780
Nor is the people's judgment always true:
The most may err as grossly as the few;
And faultless kings run down, by common cry,
For vice, oppression, and for tyranny.
What standard is there in a fickle rout,
Which, flowing to the mark, runs faster out?
Nor only crowds, but Sanhedrins may be
Infected with this public lunacy,
And share the madness of rebellious times,
To murder monarchs for imagined crimes. 790
If they may give and take whene'er they please,
Not kings alone (the Godhead's images),
But government itself at length must fall
To nature's state, where all have right to all.
Yet, grant our lords the people kings can make,
What prudent men a settled throne would shake?
For whatsoe'er their sufferings were before,
That change they covet makes them suffer more.
All other errors but disturb a state,
But innovation is the blow of fate. 800
If ancient fabrics nod, and threat to fall,
To patch up the flaws, and buttress up the wall,

Thus far 'tis duty: but here fix the mark;
For all beyond it is to touch our ark.
To change foundations, cast the frame anew,
Is work for rebels who base ends pursue,
At once divine and human laws control,
And mend the parts by ruin of the whole.
The tamp'ring world is subject to this curse,
To physic their disease into a worse. 810
   Now what relief can righteous David bring?
How fatal 'tis to be too good a king!
Friends he has few, so high the madness grows:
Who dare be such, must be the people's foes.
Yet some there were, ev'n in the worst of days;
Some let me name, and naming is to praise.
   In this short file Barzillai [65] first appears;
Barzillai, crowned with honor and with years.
Long since, the rising rebels he withstood
In regions waste, beyond the Jordan's flood: 820
Unfortunately brave to buoy the State;
But sinking underneath his master's fate.
In exile with his godlike prince he mourned;
For him he suffered, and with him returned.
The Court he practiced,[66] not the courtier's art;
Large was his wealth, but larger was his heart,
Which well the noblest objects knew to choose,
The fighting warrior and recording Muse.
His bed could once a fruitful issue boast;
Now more than half a father's name is lost. 830
His eldest hope, with every grace adorned,
By me (so heaven will have it) always mourned,
And always honored, snatched in manhood's
      prime
By unequal fates, and Providence's crime;
Yet not before the goal of honor won,
All parts fulfilled of subject and of son:
Swift was the race, but short the time to run.
O narrow circle, but of power divine,
Scanted in space, but perfect in thy line!
By sea, by land, thy matchless worth was known,
Arms thy delight, and war was all thy own: 841
Thy force, infused, the fainting Tyrians [67] propped;
And haughty Pharaoh found his fortune stopped.
O ancient honor! O unconquered hand,
Whom foes unpunished never could withstand!

---

65 James Butler, Duke of Ormond, Lord Lieutenant of
Ireland at the beginning of the Civil War, and again after the
Restoration.
66 Frequented.   67 The Dutch.

But Israel was unworthy of thy name;
Short is the date of all immoderate fame.
It looks as Heaven our ruin had designed,
And durst not trust thy fortune and thy mind.
Now, free from earth, thy disencumbered soul 850
Mounts up, and leaves behind the clouds and
              starry pole:
From thence thy kindred legions may'st thou bring,
To aid the guardian angel of thy king.
Here stop, my Muse, here cease thy painful flight;
No pinions can pursue immortal height:
Tell good Barzillai thou canst sing no more,
And tell thy soul she would have fled before:
Or fled with his life, and left this verse
To hang on her departed patron's hearse?
Now take thy steepy flight from heaven, and see
If thou canst find on earth another *he*:   861
Another *he* would be too hard to find;
See then whom thou canst see not far behind.
Zadoc,[68] the priest, whom, shunning power and
              place,
His lowly mind advanced to David's grace.
With him the Sagan of Jerusalem,[69]
Of hospitable soul and noble stem;
Him of the western dome,[70] whose weighty sense
Flows in fit words and heavenly eloquence.
The prophet's sons, by such example led,   870
To learning and to loyalty were bred:
For colleges on bounteous kings depend,
And never rebel was to arts a friend.
To these succeed the pillars of the laws,
Who best could plead, and best can judge a cause.
Next them a train of loyal peers ascend:
Sharp-judging Adriel,[71] the Muses' friend,
Himself a Muse—in Sanhedrin's debate
True to his prince, but not a slave of state,
Whom David's love with honors did adorn,   880
That from his disobedient son were torn.
Jotham[72] of piercing wit and pregnant thought,
Endued by nature, and by learning taught

To move assemblies, who but only tried
The worse a while, then chose the better side:
Nor chose alone, but turned the balance too;
So much the weight of one brave man can do.
Hushai,[73] the friend of David in distress;
In public storms, of manly steadfastness:
By foreign treaties he informed his youth,   890
And joined experience to his native truth.
His frugal care supplied the wanting throne;
Frugal for that, but bounteous of his own:
'Tis easy conduct when exchequers flow,
But hard the task to manage well the low;
For sovereign power is too depressed or high,
When kings are forced to sell, or crowds to buy.
Indulge one labor more, my weary Muse,
For Amiel:[74] who can Amiel's praise refuse?
Of ancient race by birth, but nobler yet   900
In his own worth, and without title great:
The Sanhedrin long time as chief he ruled,
Their season guided, and their passion cooled:
So dext'rous was he in the crown's defense,
So formed to speak a loyal nation's sense,
That, as their band was Israel's tribes in small,
So fit was he to represent them all.
Now rasher charioteers the seat ascend,
Whose loose careers his steady skill commend:
They, like the unequal ruler[75] of the day,   910
Misguide the seasons, and mistake the way;
While he withdrawn at their mad labor smiles,
And safe enjoys the sabbath of his toils.
     These were the chief, a small but faithful band
Of worthies, in the breach who dared to stand
And tempt the united fury of the land.
With grief they viewed such powerful engines bent
To batter down the lawful government:
A numerous faction, with pretended frights,
In Sanhedrins to plume the regal rights;   920
The true successor from the Court removed;
The Plot, by hireling witnesses, improved.
These ills they saw, and, as their duty bound,
They showed the King the danger of the wound;
That no concessions from the throne would please,
But lenitives fomented the disease;
That Absalom, ambitious of the crown,
Was made the lure to draw the people down;

68 William Sancroft, Archbishop of Canterbury.
69 Henry Compton, Bishop of London.
70 The Dean of Westminster. The college referred to in l. 872 is Westminster School, which was founded by Queen Elizabeth.
71 John Sheffield, Earl of Mulgrave, and later Duke of Buckinghamshire, was Dryden's patron and friend.
72 George Savile, Marquis of Halifax, author of The Character of a Trimmer and himself a master of the art of "trimming" the political boat.

73 Laurence Hyde, son of the great Lord Chancellor Hyde, later Earl of Rochester, and holder of many political offices.
74 Edward Seymour, Speaker of the House of Commons, 1673–1679.
75 Phaëton. See note on p. 965.

That false Achitophel's pernicious hate
Had turned the Plot to ruin Church and State;   930
The council violent, the rabble worse;
That Shimei taught Jerusalem to curse.

　　With all these loads of injuries oppressed,
And long revolving in his careful breast
The event of things, at last, his patience tired,
Thus from his royal throne, by heaven inspired,
The godlike David spoke; with awful fear
His train their Maker in their master hear.

　　"Thus long have I, by native mercy swayed,
My wrongs dissembled, my revenge delayed: 940
So willing to forgive the offending age;
So much the father did the king assuage.
But now so far my clemency they slight,
The offenders question my forgiving right.
That one was made for many, they contend;
But 'tis to rule, for that's a monarch's end.
They call my tenderness of blood, my fear;
Though manly tempers can the longest bear.
Yet since they will divert my native course,
'Tis time to show I am not good by force.   950
Those heaped affronts that haughty subjects bring
Are burdens for a camel, not a king.
Kings are the public pillars of the State,
Born to sustain and prop the nation's weight;
If my young Samson will pretend a call
To shake the columns, let him share the fall:
But oh that he would yet repent and live!
How easy 'tis for parents to forgive!
With how few tears a pardon might be won
From nature, pleading for a darling son!   960
Poor pitied youth, by my paternal care
Raised up to all the height his frame could bear!
Had God ordained his fate for empire born,
He would have given his soul another turn:
Gulled with a patriot's name, whose modern sense
Is one that would by law supplant his prince;
The people's brave, the politician's tool;
Never was patriot yet but was a fool.
Whence comes it that religion and the laws
Should more be Absalom's than David's cause? 970
His old instructor, ere he lost his place,
Was never thought indued with so much grace.
Good heavens, how faction can a patriot paint!
My rebel ever proves my people's saint.
Would *they* impose an heir upon the throne?
Let Sanhedrins be taught to give their own.[76]

A king's at least a part of government,
And mine as requisite as their consent;
Without my leave a future king to choose
Infers a right the present to depose.   980
True, they petition me to approve their choice,
But Esau's hands suit ill with Jacob's voice.
My pious subjects for my safety pray,
Which to secure, they take my power away.
From plots and treasons heaven preserve my years,
But save me most from my petitioners!
Unsatiate as the barren womb or grave;
God cannot grant so much as they can crave.
What then is left, but with a jealous eye
To guard the small remains of royalty?   990
The law shall still direct my peaceful sway,
And the same law teach rebels to obey.
Votes shall no more established power control,
Such votes as make a part exceed the whole:
No groundless clamors shall my friends remove,
Nor crowds have power to punish ere they prove;
For gods and godlike kings their care express,
Still to defend their servants in distress.
Oh that my power to saving were confined!
Why am I forced, like heaven, against my mind,
To make examples of another kind?   1001
Must I at length the sword of justice draw?
Oh curst effects of necessary law!
How ill my fear they by my mercy scan!
Beware the fury of a patient man!
Law they require, let Law then show her face;
They could not be content to look on Grace,
Her hinder parts, but with a daring eye
To tempt the terror of her front, and die.
By their own arts, 'tis righteously decreed,   1010
Those dire artificers of death shall bleed.
Against themselves their witnesses will swear,
Till viper-like their mother Plot they tear,
And suck for nutriment that bloody gore
Which was their principle of life before.
Thus Belial with their Belzebub will fight;
Thus on my foes, my foes shall do me right.
Nor doubt the event;[77] for factious crowds engage
In their first onset all their brutal rage.
Then let 'em take an unresisted course;   1020
Retire, and traverse, and delude their force;
But, when they stand all breathless, urge the fight,
And rise upon 'em with redoubled might;

76 *I.e.*, what is theirs to give.

77 Outcome.

For lawful power is still superior found:
When long driven back, at length it stands the
     ground."
     He said. The Almighty, nodding, gave consent,
And peals of thunder shook the firmament.

Henceforth a series of new time began,
The mighty years in long procession ran:
Once more the godlike David was restored,   1030
And willing nations knew their lawful lord.

FROM

THRENODIA AUGUSTALIS

A Funeral-Pindaric Poem to the Happy Memory of King Charles II

[1685]

15

A warlike prince[1] ascends the regal state,
A prince long exercised by fate: 430
Long may he keep, though he obtains it late.
Heroes in Heaven's peculiar mold are cast,
They and their poets are not formed in haste;
Man was the first in God's design, and man was made
     the last.
False heroes, made by flattery so,
Heaven can strike out, like sparkles, at a blow;

THRENODIA AUGUSTALIS
1 James II, who succeeded his brother, Charles II, in 1685.

But ere a prince is to perfection brought,
He costs Omnipotence a second thought.
     With toil and sweat,
     With hardening cold and forming heat   440
     The Cyclops[2] did their strokes repeat,
Before the impenetrable shield was wrought.
     It looks as if the Maker would not own
          The noble work for His,
Before 'twas tried and found a masterpiece.

2 The Cyclopes are represented in various legends as
assistants of Hephæstus (Vulcan), and makers of metal armor
and ornaments for gods and heroes.

MEMORIAL POEMS

TO THE MEMORY OF MR. OLDHAM[1]

Farewell, too little and too lately known!
Whom I began to think and call my own;
For sure our souls were near allied, and thine
Cast in the same poetic mold with mine.
One common note on either lyre did strike,
And knaves and fools we both abhorred alike.
To the same goal did both our studies drive;
The last set out, the soonest did arrive.
Thus Nisus[2] fell upon the slippery place,
While his young friend performed and won the race.

TO THE MEMORY
1 First printed in John Oldham's Remains in Verse and
Prose, 1684. Oldham died at the age of thirty in 1683.
2 Nisus, slipping on the spot where steers had been slain
for sacrifice, threw himself in front of another runner, Salius,
and thus made it possible for his friend Euryalus to win.
(Virgil, Æneid v. 327 ff.).

O early ripe! to thy abundant store   11
What could advancing age have added more?
It might (what nature never gives the young)
Have taught the numbers of thy native tongue.
But satire needs not those, and wit will shine
Through the harsh cadence of a rugged line:
A noble error, and but seldom made,
When poets are by too much force betrayed.
The generous fruits, though gathered ere their prime,
Still showed a quickness; and maturing time   20
But mellows what we write to the dull sweets of
     rhyme.
Once more, hail and farewell! farewell, thou young,
But, ah too short! Marcellus[3] of our tongue!
Thy brows with ivy, and with laurels bound;
But fate and gloomy night encompass thee around.

3 The son of Octavia, sister of Augustus, whose death
Virgil predicts in the Æneid (vi. 860 ff.).

TO THE PIOUS MEMORY OF THE ACCOMPLISHED YOUNG LADY MRS. ANNE KILLIGREW, EXCELLENT IN THE TWO SISTER ARTS OF POESY AND PAINTING

AN ODE[1]

1

Thou youngest virgin-daughter of the skies,
  Made in the last promotion of the blest,
Whose palms, new plucked from Paradise,
In spreading branches more sublimely rise,
  Rich with immortal green above the rest;
Whether, adopted to some neighboring star,[2]
Thou roll'st above us in thy wandering race,
  Or in procession fixed and regular,
  Moved with the heaven's majestic pace,
  Or called to more superior bliss,   10
Thou tread'st with seraphim the vast abyss:
Whatever happy region is thy place,
Cease thy celestial song a little space;
Thou wilt have time enough for hymns divine,
  Since Heaven's eternal year is thine.
Hear, then, a mortal Muse thy praise rehearse
    In no ignoble verse,
But such as thy own voice did practise here,
  When thy first-fruits of poesy were given,
  To make thyself a welcome inmate there,   20
    While yet a young probationer,
    And candidate of Heaven.

2

If by traduction[3] came thy mind,
  Our wonder is the less to find
A soul so charming from a stock so good;
Thy father was transfused into thy blood:
So wert thou born into the tuneful strain,
An early, rich, and inexhausted vein.

But if thy pre-existing soul
  Was formed at first with myriads more,   30
It did through all the mighty poets roll
  Who Greek or Latin laurels wore,
And was that Sappho last, which once it was before.
  If so, then cease thy flight, O Heaven-born mind!
Thou hast no dross to purge from thy rich ore,
  Nor can thy soul a fairer mansion find
  Than was the beauteous frame she left behind:
Return,[4] to fill or mend the quire of thy celestial kind!

3

May we presume to say that at thy birth
New joy was sprung in Heaven as well as here on
    earth?   40
For sure the milder planets did combine
On thy auspicious horoscope to shine,
And even the most malicious were in trine.[5]
    Thy brother-angels at thy birth
    Strung each his lyre, and tuned it high,
    That all the people of the sky
Might know a poetess was born on earth;
  And then, if ever, mortal ears
  Had heard the music of the spheres.
  And if no clustering swarm of bees   50
On thy sweet mouth distilled their golden dew,
    'Twas that such vulgar miraclès
    Heaven had not leisure to renew;
For all the blest fraternity of love
Solémnized there thy birth, and kept thy holiday
    above.

4

O gracious God! how far have we
Profaned Thy heavenly gift of poesy!
Made prostitute and profligate the Muse,
Debased to each obscene and impious use,
Whose harmony was first ordained above   60
For tongues of angels and for hymns of love!
Oh wretched we! why were we hurried down
    This lubric and adulterate age
(Nay, added fat pollutions of our own)
    To increase the steaming ordures of the stage?
What can we say to excuse our second fall?
Let this thy vestal, Heaven, atone for all:

MRS. ANNE KILLIGREW

1 First published in the volume of poems by Anne Killigrew that appeared after her death, 1686. The title *Mrs.* was applied in the seventeenth and eighteenth centuries to an unmarried woman (as in this instance) as well as to a married one.

2 One of the planets, in contrast with the fixed stars alluded to in l. 8.

3 Inheritance.

4 *I.e.*, to Heaven, the original home of the soul.

5 The "aspect" of two planets distant from each other by 120°, a third of the zodiac; a benign aspect.

Her Arethusian[6] stream remains unsoiled,
Unmixed with foreign filth, and undefiled;
Her wit was more than man; her innocence, a child. 70

5

Art she had none, yet wanted none,
    For nature did that want supply;
So rich in treasures of her own,
    She might our boasted stores defy:
Such noble vigor did her verse adorn
That it seemed borrowed where 'twas only born.
Her morals, too, were in her bosom bred,
    By great examples daily fed,
What in the best of books, her father's life, she read.
And to be read herself she need not fear;   80
Each test and every light her Muse will bear,
Though Epictetus[7] with his lamp were there.
Even love (for love sometimes her Muse expressed)
Was but a lambent flame which played about her
            breast,
    Light as the vapors of a morning dream;
So cold herself, whilst she such warmth expressed,
    'Twas Cupid bathing in Diana's stream.

6

Born to the spacious empire of the Nine,
    One would have thought she should have been
            content
To manage with that mighty government;   90
But what can young, ambitious souls confine?
    To the next realm she stretched her sway,
    For Painture near adjoining lay,
A plenteous province and alluring prey:
A chamber of dependencies was framed
(As conquerors will never want pretense,
    When armed, to justify the offense),
And the whole fief in right of Poetry she claimed.
The country open lay without defense,
For poets frequent inroads there had made,   100
    And perfectly could represent
The shape, the face, with every lineament;
And all the large demesnes which the dumb sister
            swayed,

All bowed beneath her government,
Received in triumph wheresoe'er she went.
Her pencil drew whate'er her soul designed,
And oft the happy draught surpassed the image in her
            mind:
    The sylvan scenes of herds and flocks
    And fruitful plains and barren rocks;
    Of shallow brooks that flowed so clear   110
    The bottom did the top appear;
    Of deeper too and ampler floods,
    Which, as in mirrors, showed the woods;
    Of lofty trees, with sacred shades
    And pérspectives of pleasant glades,
    Where nymphs of brightest form appear,
    And shaggy satyrs standing near,
    Which them at once admire and fear;
The ruins, too, of some majestic piece,
Boasting the power of ancient Rome or Greece, 120
Whose statues, friezes, columns, broken lie,
And, though defaced, the wonder of the eye.
What nature, art, bold fiction, e'er durst frame,
Her forming hand gave feature to the name;
So strange a concourse ne'er was seen before
But when the peopled ark the whole creation bore.

7

The scene then changed: with bold, erected look
Our martial King[8] the sight with reverence strook,
For, not content to express his outward part,
Her hand called out the image of his heart;   130
His warlike mind, his soul devoid of fear,
His high designing thoughts were figured there,
As when by magic, ghosts are made appear.
Our phœnix Queen was portrayed, too, so bright
Beauty alone could beauty take so right:
Her dress, her shape, her matchless grace,
Were all observed, as well as heavenly face;
With such a peerless majesty she stands
As in that day she took the crown from sacred hands;
Before, a train of heroines was seen—   140
In beauty foremost, as in rank, the Queen.
Thus nothing to her genius was denied,
    But, like a ball of fire, the farther thrown,
    Still with a greater blaze she shone,
And her bright soul broke out on every side.
What next she had designed, Heaven only knows:
To such immoderate growth her conquest rose
That fate alone its progress could oppose.

6 See note 28, p. 893.
7 Epictetus, the Greek Stoic philosopher and moralist, had
an earthenware lamp which was sold after his death for a
huge sum of money, but it has been suggested that Dryden
probably had in mind here the more famous lamp of
Diogenes, used in the search for an honest man.

8 James II.

8

Now all those charms, that blooming grace,
The well-proportioned shape, and beauteous face,
Shall never more be seen by mortal eyes;   151
In earth the much-lamented virgin lies.
Not wit nor piety could fate prevent;
Nor was the cruel destiny content
To finish all the murder at a blow,
To sweep at once her life and beauty too;
But, like a hardened felon, took a pride
    To work more mischievously slow,
    And plundered first, and then destroyed.
Oh, double sacrilege on things divine,   160
To rob the relic and deface the shrine!
    But thus Orinda died:[9]
Heaven, by the same disease, did both translate;
As equal were their souls, so equal was their fate.

9

Meantime her warlike brother[10] on the seas
His waving streamers to the winds displays,
And vows for his return with vain devotion pays.
    Ah, generous youth, that wish forbear;
    The winds too soon will waft thee here!
    Slack all thy sails, and fear to come;   170
Alas! thou know'st not thou art wrecked at home!
No more shalt thou behold thy sister's face;
Thou hast already had her last embrace.
But look aloft, and if thou kenn'st from far,
Among the Pleiads, a new-kindled star,
If any sparkles than the rest more bright,
'Tis she that shines in that propitious light.

10

When in mid-air the golden trump shall sound,
    To raise the nations under ground;[11]
When in the Valley of Jehoshaphat[12]   180
The judging God shall close the book of fate,
    And there the last assizes keep
    For those who wake and those who sleep;
    When rattling bones together fly[13]
    From the four corners of the sky;
When sinews o'er the skeletons are spread,
Those clothed with flesh, and life inspires the dead;
The sacred poets first shall hear the sound,
    And foremost from the tomb shall bound,
For they are covered with the lightest ground,   190
And straight, with inborn vigor, on the wing,
Like mournful larks, to the new morning sing.
There thou, sweet saint, before the quire shalt go,
As harbinger of Heaven, the way to show,
The way which thou so well hast learned below.

[LINES PRINTED UNDER THE EN-
GRAVED PORTRAIT OF MILTON][1]

    Three poets, in three distant ages born,
    Greece,[2] Italy,[3] and England did adorn.
    The first in loftiness of thought surpassed,
    The next in majesty, in both the last:
    The force of Nature could no farther go;
    To make a third she joined the former two.

11 I Corinthians 15:52.   12 Joel 3:12.
13 Ezekiel 37:1–14.

MRS. ANNE KILLIGREW
9 The poetess, Katherine Philips, known as "the matchless Orinda." Both Katherine Philips and Anne Killigrew died of smallpox.
10 She had two brothers in the navy: Henry, later an admiral, and James, a captain.

LINES PRINTED
1 The lines appeared without the author's name, under the portrait of Milton which served as the frontispiece of Tonson's folio edition (the fourth edition) of Paradise Lost, 1688.
2 Homer.   3 Virgil.

POEMS IN HONOR OF SAINT CECILIA[1]

A SONG FOR ST. CECILIA'S DAY
November 22, 1687

1

From harmony, from heavenly harmony
   This universal frame began;
    When Nature underneath a heap
     Of jarring atoms lay,
    And could not heave her head,
The tuneful Voice was heard from high,
    "Arise, ye more than dead."
Then cold and hot and moist and dry
   In order to their stations leap,
    And music's power obey.   10
From harmony, from heavenly harmony
   This universal frame began:
    From harmony to harmony
Through all the compass of the notes it ran,
The diapason closing full in Man.

2

What passion cannot music raise and quell?
   When Jubal[2] struck the corded shell,
   His listening brethren stood around,
    And, wondering, on their faces fell
To worship that celestial sound: 20
Less than a God they thought there could not dwell
    Within the hollow of that shell,
    That spoke so sweetly and so well.
What passion cannot music raise and quell?

3

   The trumpet's loud clangor
    Excites us to arms
   With shrill notes of anger
    And mortal alarms.
   The double, double, double beat
    Of the thund'ring drum   30
   Cries "Hark, the foes come;
Charge, charge, 'tis too late to retreat."

4

   The soft complaining flute
   In dying notes discovers[3]
   The woes of hopeless lovers,
Whose dirge is whispered by the warbling lute.

5

   Sharp violins proclaim
Their jealous pangs and desperation,
Fury, frantic indignation,
Depth of pains and height of passion,   40
   For the fair, disdainful dame.

6

   But Oh! What art can teach,
   What human voice can reach,
   The sacred organ's praise?
Notes inspiring holy love,
Notes that wing their heavenly ways
   To mend the choirs above.

7

Orpheus could lead the savage race,
And trees unrooted left their place,
   Sequaceous of the lyre;   50
But bright Cecilia raised the wonder higher;
When to her organ vocal breath was given,
An angel heard and straight appeared,
   Mistaking earth for heaven.

GRAND CHORUS

As from the power of sacred lays
   The spheres began to move,
And sung the great Creator's praise
   To all the blest above;
So when the last and dreadful hour
This crumbling pageant shall devour,   60
The trumpet shall be heard on high,
The dead shall live, the living die,
And music shall untune the sky.

SONG
  1 Cecilia is the patron saint of music.
  2 See Genesis 4:21.

3 Reveals.

ALEXANDER'S FEAST;
OR, THE POWER OF MUSIC

An Ode in Honor of St. Cecilia's Day, 1697

I

'Twas at the royal feast for Persia won
　　By Philip's warlike son:[1]
　　　Aloft in awful state
　　　The godlike hero sate
　　On his imperial throne;
His valiant peers were placed around,
Their brows with roses and with myrtles bound
(So should desert in arms be crowned);
　　The lovely Thais,[2] by his side,
Sate like a blooming Eastern bride,　　　　　10
　　In flower of youth and beauty's pride.
　　　Happy, happy, happy pair!
　　　　None but the brave,
　　　　None but the brave,
　　None but the brave deserves the fair.

CHORUS

　　Happy, happy, happy pair!
　　　None but the brave,
　　　None but the brave,
　None but the brave deserves the fair.

2

　　Timotheus,[3] placed on high　　　　20
　　　Amid the tuneful quire,
　With flying fingers touched the lyre;
　The trembling notes ascend the sky,
　　And heavenly joys inspire.
The song began from[4] Jove,
Who left his blissful seats above
(Such is the power of mighty love):
A dragon's fiery form belied[5] the god;
　Sublime on radiant spires[6] he rode,
When he to fair Olympia[7] pressed;　　　30
And while he sought her snowy breast;
Then round her slender waist he curled,
And stamped an image of himself, a sovereign of the
　　　　world.

The listening crowd admire the lofty sound:
"A present deity!" they shout around;
"A present deity!" the vaulted roofs rebound.
　　　With ravished ears
　　　The monarch hears;
　　　Assumes the god,
　　　Affects to nod,　　　　　40
　And seems to shake the spheres.

CHORUS

　　　With ravished ears
　　　The monarch hears;
　　　Assumes the god,
　　　Affects to nod,
　And seems to shake the spheres.

3

The praise of Bacchus then the sweet musician sung,
　Of Bacchus ever fair and ever young.
　　The jolly god in triumph comes:　　49
　Sound the trumpets, beat the drums!
　　Flushed with a purple grace,
　　He shows his honest[8] face:
Now give the hautboys breath! he comes, he comes!
　Bacchus, ever fair and young,
　　Drinking joys did first ordain:
　Bacchus' blessings are a treasure;
　Drinking is the soldier's pleasure;
　　　Rich the treasure,
　　　Sweet the pleasure,
　Sweet is pleasure after pain.　　　　60

CHORUS

　Bacchus' blessings are a treasure;
　Drinking is the soldier's pleasure;
　　　Rich the treasure,
　　　Sweet the pleasure;
　Sweet is pleasure after pain.

4

Soothed with the sound, the King grew vain,
　Fought all his battles o'er again,
And thrice he routed all his foes, and thrice he slew
　　　the slain.
The master saw the madness rise,
His glowing cheeks, his ardent eyes;　　　70
And while he heaven and earth defied,
Changed his hand and checked his pride.[9]

He chose a mournful Muse,
  Soft pity to infuse:
He sung Darius [10] great and good,
  By too severe a fate,
Fallen, fallen, fallen, fallen,
  Fallen from his high estate,
And weltering in his blood;
Deserted at his utmost need   80
By those his former bounty fed,
On the bare earth exposed he lies,
With not a friend to close his eyes.
With downcast looks the joyless victor sate.
  Revolving in his altered soul
  The various turns of chance below;
And now and then a sigh he stole,
  And tears began to flow.

CHORUS

  Revolving in his altered soul
    The various turns of chance below;
  And now and then a sigh he stole,   91
    And tears began to flow.

5

The mighty master smiled to see
That love was in the next degree;
'Twas but a kindred sound to move,
For pity melts the mind to love.
  Softly sweet, in Lydian [11] measures,
  Soon he soothed his soul to pleasures.
"War," he sung, "is toil and trouble;
Honor, but an empty bubble;   100
  Never ending, still beginning,
Fighting still, and still destroying:
  If the world be worth thy winning,
  Think, O think it worth enjoying.
    Lovely Thais sits beside thee,
    Take the good the gods provide thee."
The many rend the skies with loud applause;
So Love was crowned, but Music won the cause.
  The prince, unable to conceal his pain,
    Gazed on the fair,   110
    Who caused his care,

10 Darius, king of Persia, conquered by Alexander, was stabbed by one of his companions as Alexander was on the point of capturing him.
  11 See note 32, p. 889.

    And sighed and looked, sighed and looked,
    Sighed and looked, and sighed again;
At length, with love and wine at once oppressed,
The vanquished victor sunk upon her breast.

CHORUS

  The prince, unable to conceal his pain,
    Gazed on the fair,
    Who caused his care,
    And sighed and looked, sighed and looked,   119
    Sighed and looked, and sighed again;
At length, with love and wine at once oppressed,
The vanquished victor sunk upon her breast.

6

  Now strike the golden lyre again:
  A louder yet, and yet a louder strain.
  Break his bands of sleep asunder,
  And rouse him, like a rattling peal of thunder.
    Hark, hark! the horrid [12] sound
      Has raised up his head;
      As awaked from the dead,
    And amazed, he stares around.   130
  "Revenge, revenge!" Timotheus cries;
    "See the Furies arise!
    See the snakes that they rear,
    How they hiss in their hair,
  And the sparkles that flash from their eyes!
    Behold a ghastly band,
    Each a torch in his hand!
Those are Grecian ghosts, that in battle were slain,
      And unburied remain
      Inglorious on the plain: 140
      Give the vengeance due
      To the valiant crew!
Behold how they toss their torches on high,
  How they point to the Persian abodes,
And glittering temples of their hostile gods!"
The princes applaud with a furious joy;
And the King seized a flambeau with zeal to destroy;
      Thais led the way,
      To light him to his prey,   149
And, like another Helen, fired another Troy.

CHORUS

  And the King seized a flambeau with zeal to destroy;
      Thais led the way,
      To light him to his prey,
  And, like another Helen, fired another Troy.

  12 Rude, rough.

7

Thus, long ago,
Ere heaving bellows learned to blow,
   While organs yet were mute,
   Timotheus, to his breathing flute
      And sounding lyre,
Could swell the soul to rage or kindle soft desire.   160
   At last divine Cecilia came,
   Inventress of the vocal frame:[13]
The sweet enthusiast,[14] from her sacred store,
   Enlarged the former narrow bounds,
   And added length to solemn sounds,
With nature's mother-wit, and arts unknown before.

ALEXANDER'S FEAST
   13 Although St. Cecilia had long been associated with the organ ("the vocal frame") in art and legend, no one before Dryden seems to have credited her with its invention.
   14 One divinely inspired.

Let old Timotheus yield the prize,
   Or both divide the crown:
He raised a mortal to the skies;
   She drew an angel down.   170

GRAND CHORUS

   At last divine Cecilia came,
   Inventress of the vocal frame:
The sweet enthusiast, from her sacred store,
   Enlarged the former narrow bounds,
   And added length to solemn sounds,
With nature's mother-wit, and arts unknown before.
Let old Timotheus yield the prize,
   Or both divide the crown:
He raised a mortal to the skies;
   She drew an angel down.   180

FROM

THE SECULAR MASQUE[1] [1700]

[HUNTING SONG]

DIANA

With horns and hounds I waken the day,
And hie to the woodland walks away;
I tuck up my robe and am buskined soon,
And tie to my forehead a wexing[2] moon;
I course the fleet stag and unkennel the fox,
And chase the wild goats o'er the summits of rocks;
With shouting and hooting we pierce through the sky,
And Echo turns hunter and doubles the cry.

HUNTING SONG
   1 The masque was written by the poet for his benefit performance at Drury Lane on March 25, 1700, that being New Year's Day by the system then in use. The day was mistakenly supposed to be the beginning of the eighteenth century, and the theme of the masque was the seventeenth century, supposed to have ended. The deities of the chase, of war, and of love, together with other mythological and allegorical figures, are introduced as representing the various changes and activities of the century.
   2 Waxing.

CHORUS

With shouting and hooting we pierce through the sky,
And Echo turns hunter and doubles the cry.   10

[THE SEVENTEENTH CENTURY]

Momus. All, all of a piece throughout:
   Pointing to Diana, Thy chase had a beast in view;
         to Mars, Thy wars brought nothing about;
      to Venus, Thy lovers were all untrue.
Janus. 'Tis well an old age is out.
Chronos. And time to begin a new.

CHORUS OF ALL

All, all of a piece throughout:
Thy chase had a beast in view;
Thy wars brought nothing about;
Thy lovers were all untrue.   10
'Tis well an old age is out,
And time to begin a new.

Thomas Traherne

[1637–1674]

THE last of the English Metaphysical poets was born in Hereford of humble antecedents, and educated at Oxford. He led a quiet and withdrawn life (recounted in more detail in the introduction to the selection from his prose), and none of his poems were printed during his lifetime or even during his century, with the exception of the curious free-verse "Thanksgivings" contained in *A Serious and Pathetical Contemplation of the Mercies of God* (1699).

The story of the discovery of Traherne's manuscript poems at the turn of our century is well known, and its inherently fascinating quality led at first to an overestimation of the poet's great but flawed abilities. The poems, included in a manuscript book discovered in 1897 by W. T. Brooke, were initially attributed to Vaughan by Grosart, but were identified as Traherne's by the publisher Bertram Dobell. The latter's inspired detection was verified in 1910 when the Burney Ms. was found in the British Museum. This manuscript is a copy of Traherne's poems prepared for the press by the poet's brother Philip but not published at that time. Unfortunately, Philip combined a heavy editorial hand with a distinct lack of poetic ability, and the poems which are not duplicated from the Dobell Ms. suffer badly from his emendations.

Like Vaughan and Marvell, Traherne restates the complex and paradoxical vision of the earlier Metaphysicals in terms which indicate the extent of the seventeenth-century revolution in thought and attitude, but his view of experience is more radically individualistic and intuitive than that of his lyric contemporaries. His handling of his obsessive theme of childhood, in particular, is striking in its vigorous (and, from a seventeenth-century point of view, heretical) denial of the doctrine of original sin. Traherne has often been compared to Blake and Wordsworth, and his work does, indeed, suggest a surprising affinity with that of the great Romantics.

Traherne's poetry is as uneven in quality as it is original in impact. To an even greater degree than Vaughan, he is a poet of single lines rather than whole artistic structures, and he frequently presents us with a limping bit of doggerel redeemed forever by a passage of unforgettable beauty. There are enough such passages to assure him a permanent place in the history of English lyric poetry.

T. TRAHERNE. *Centuries, Poems, and Thanksgivings*, ed. H. M. Margoliouth, 2 vols. (Oxford, 1958). Definitive.
————. *Poems, Centuries, and Three Thanksgivings*, ed. A. Ridler (Oxford, 1966).
G. I. WADE. *Thomas Traherne* (Princeton, 1944). A full critical biography.
G. E. WILLETT. *Traherne, An Essay* (Cambridge, 1919).
K. W. SALTER. *Thomas Traherne: Mystic and Poet* (London, 1964).
S. STEWART. *The Expanded Voice* (San Marino, Calif., 1970).

POEMS [DOBELL FOLIO MS.]

THE SALUTATION

These little limbs,
These eyes and hands which here I find,
These rosy cheeks wherewith my life begins,
    Where have ye been? behind
What curtain were ye from me hid so long?
Where was, in what abyss, my speaking tongue?

    When silent I
So many thousand, thousand years
Beneath the dust did in a chaos lie,
    How could I smiles or tears,   10
Or lips or hands or eyes or ears perceive?
Welcome ye treasures which I now receive.

    I that so long
Was nothing from eternity,
Did little think such joys as ear or tongue
    To celebrate or see:
Such sounds to hear, such hands to feel, such feet,
Beneath the skies on such a ground to meet.

    New burnished joys,
Which yellow gold and pearls excel!   20
Such sacred treasures are the limbs in boys,
    In which a soul doth dwell;
Their organized joints and azure veins
More wealth include than all the world contains.

    From dust I rise,
And out of nothing now awake;
These brighter regions which salute mine eyes,
    A gift from God I take.
The earth, the seas, the light, the day, the skies,
The sun and stars are mine if those I prize.   30

    Long time before
I in my mother's womb was born,
A God, preparing, did this glorious store,
    The world, for me adorn.
Into this Eden so divine and fair,
So wide and bright, I come His son and heir.

    A stranger here
Strange things doth meet, strange glories see;
Strange treasures lodged in this fair world appear,
    Strange all and new to me;   40
But that they mine should be, who nothing was,
That strangest is of all, yet brought to pass.

WONDER

How like an angel came I down!
    How bright are all things here!
When first among His works I did appear
    Oh, how their glory me did crown!
The world resembled His eternity,
    In which my soul did walk;
And everything that I did see
    Did with me talk.

The skies in their magnificence,
    The lively, lovely air,   10
Oh, how divine, how soft, how sweet, how fair!
    The stars did entertain my sense,
And all the works of God, so bright and pure,
    So rich and great did seem,
As if they must endure
    In my esteem.

A native health and innocence
    Within my bones did grow;
And while my God did all His glories show,
    I felt a vigor in my sense   20
That was all spirit. I within did flow
    With seas of life, like wine;
I nothing in the world did know
    But 'twas divine.

Harsh ragged objects were concealed,
    Oppressions, tears, and cries,
Sins, griefs, complaints, dissensions, weeping eyes
    Were hid, and only things revealed
Which heavenly spirits and the angels prize.
    The state of innocence   30
And bliss, not trades and poverties,
    Did fill my sense.

The streets were paved with golden stones;
  The boys and girls were mine,
Oh, how did all their lovely faces shine!
  The sons of men were holy ones,
In joy and beauty they appeared to me,
    And everything which here I found,
  While like an angel I did see,
    Adorned the ground.   40

Rich diamond and pearl and gold
  In every place was seen;
Rare splendors, yellow, blue, red, white, and green,
  Mine eyes did everywhere behold.
Great wonders clothed with glory did appear,
    Amazement was my bliss,
  That and my wealth was everywhere;
    No joy to this!

Cursed and devised proprieties,
  With envy, avarice,   50
And fraud, those fiends that spoil even Paradise,
  Flew from the splendor of mine eyes;
And so did hedges, ditches, limits, bounds:
    I dreamed not aught of those,
  But wandered over all men's grounds,
    And found repose.

Proprieties[1] themselves were mine,
  And hedges, ornaments;
Walls, boxes, coffers, and their rich contents
  Did not divide my joys, but all combine.   60
Clothes, ribbons, jewels, laces, I esteemed
  My joys by others worn:
  For me they all to wear them seemed
    When I was born.

INNOCENCE

1

But that which most I wonder at, which most
I did esteem my bliss, which most I boast,
  And ever shall enjoy, is that within
    I felt no stain nor spot of sin.

WONDER
  1 Proprietorships, ownerships.

No darkness then did overshade,
But all within was pure and bright;
No guilt did crush nor fear invade,
But all my soul was full of light.

A joyful sense and purity
  Is all I can remember;   10
The very night to me was bright,
'Twas summer in December.

2

A serious meditation did employ
My soul within, which, taken up with joy
Did seem no outward thing to note, but fly
  All objects that do feed the eye.

While if those very objects did
Admire and prize and praise and love,
Which in their glory most are hid,
Which presence only doth remove.   20

Their constant daily presence I
  Rejoicing at, did see,
And that which takes them from the eye
Of others offered them to me.

3

No inward inclination did I feel
To avarice or pride; my soul did kneel
In admiration all the day. No lust, nor strife,
  Polluted then my infant life.

No fraud nor anger in me moved,
No malice, jealousy, or spite;   30
All that I saw I truly loved:
Contentment only and delight

Were in my soul. O Heaven! what bliss
  Did I enjoy and feel!
What powerful delight did this
Inspire! for this I daily kneel.

4

Whether it be that nature is so pure,
And custom only vicious; or that sure
God did by miracle the guilt remove,
  And made my soul to feel His love   40

So early; or that 'twas one day
Wherein this happiness I found,
Whose strength and brightness so do ray,
That still it seems me to surround—

Whate'er it is, it is a light
    So endless unto me
That I a world of true delight
Did then, and to this day do see.

5

That prospect was the gate of Heaven, that day
The ancient light of Eden did convey   50
Into my soul: I was an Adam there,
    A little Adam in a sphere

Of joys! Oh, there my ravished sense
Was entertained in Paradise,
And had a sight of innocence,
Which was beyond all bound and price.

An antepast of Heaven sure!
    I on the earth did reign;
Within, without me, all was pure:
I must become a child again.   60

DESIRE

For giving me desire,
An eager thirst, a burning ardent fire,
    A virgin infant flame,
A love with which into the world I came,
    An inward hidden heavenly love,
    Which in my soul did work and move,
    And ever, ever me inflame
With restless longing, heavenly avarice,
    That never could be satisfied,
That did incessantly a paradise   10
Unknown suggest, and something undescribed
    Discern, and bear me to it; be
    Thy name forever praised by me.

My parched and withered bones
Burnt up did seem; my soul was full of groans;
    My thoughts extensions were:
Like paces, reaches, steps they did appear;
    They somewhat hotly did pursue,
    Knew that they had not all their due,
    Nor ever quiet were.   20

But made my flesh like hungry, thirsty ground,
    My heart a deep profound abyss,
And every joy and pleasure but a wound,
    So long as I my blessedness did miss.
    Oh happiness! A famine burns,
    And all my life to anguish turns!

    Where are the silent streams,
The living waters and the glorious beams,
    The sweet reviving bowers,
The shady groves, the sweet and curious flowers,   30
    The springs and trees, the heavenly days,
    The flow'ry meads, and glorious rays,
    The gold and silver towers?
Alas! all these are poor and empty things!
    Trees, waters, days, and shining beams,
Fruits, flowers, bowers, shady groves, and springs,
No joy will yield, no more than silent streams;
    Those are but dead material toys,
    And cannot make my heavenly joys.

    O love! Ye amities,   40
And friendships that appear above the skies!
    Ye feasts and living pleasures!
Ye senses, honors, and imperial treasures!
    Ye bridal joys! ye high delights
    That satisfy all appetites!
    Ye sweet affections, and
Ye high respects! Whatever joys there be
    In triumphs, whatsoever stand
In amicable sweet society,
Whatever pleasures are at His right hand,   50
    Ye must before I am divine
    In full propriety be mine.

    This soaring, sacred thirst,
Ambassador of bliss, approachèd first,
    Making a place in me
That made me apt to prize, and taste, and see.
    For not the objects but the sense
    Of things doth bliss to our souls dispense,
    And make it, Lord, like Thee.
Sense, feeling, taste, complacency, and sight,   60
    These are the true and real joys,
The living, flowing, inward, melting, bright,
And heavenly pleasures; all the rest are toys;
    All which are founded in desire,
    As light in flame and heat in fire.

THE RECOVERY

To see us but receive, is such a sight
As makes His treasures infinite!
Because His goodness doth possess
In us, His own, and our own blessedness.
  Yea, more, His love doth take delight
  To make our glory infinite;
    Our blessedness to see
    Is even to the Deity
A beatific vision! He attains
His ends while we enjoy. In us He reigns.   10

For God enjoyed is all His end.
Himself He then doth comprehend
When He is blessed, magnified,
Extolled, exalted, praised, and glorified,
  Honored, esteemed, beloved, enjoyed,
  Admired, sanctified, obeyed,
    That is received. For He
    Doth place His whole felicity
In that: who is despised and defied,
Undeified almost if once denied.   20

In all His works, in all His ways,
We must His glory see and praise;
And since our pleasure is the end,
We must His goodness and His love attend.
  If we despise His glorious works,
  Such sin and mischief in it lurks
    That they are all made in vain;
    And this is even endless pain
To Him that sees it: whose diviner grief
Is hereupon (ah me!) without relief.   30

We please His goodness that receive;
Refusers Him of all bereave,
As bridegrooms know full well that build
A palace for their bride. It will not yield
Any delight to him at all
If she for whom he made the hall
  Refuse to dwell in it,
  Or plainly scorn the benefit.
Her act that's wooed yields more delight and pleasure
If she receives, than all the pile of treasure.   40

But we have hands, and lips, and eyes,
And hearts and souls can sacrifice;
And souls themselves are made in vain
If we our evil stubbornness retain.
  Affections, praises, are the things
  For which He gave us all those springs;
    They are the very fruits
    Of all those trees and roots,
The fruits and ends of all His great endeavors,
Which he abolisheth whoever severs.   50

'Tis not alone a lively sense,
A clear and quick intelligence,
A free, profound, and full esteem;
Though these elixirs all and ends do seem:
  But gratitude, thanksgiving, praise,
  A heart returned for all those joys,
    These are the things admired,
    These are the things by Him desired:
These are the nectar and the quintessence,
The cream and flower that most affect His sense.   60

The voluntary act whereby
These are repaid is in His eye
More precious than the very sky.
All gold and silver is but empty dross,
  Rubies and sapphires are but loss,
  The very sun, and stars, and seas
    Far less His spirit please:
    One voluntary act of love
Far more delightful to His soul doth prove,
And is above all these as far as love.   70

POEMS OF FELICITY [BURNEY MS. 392]

NEWS

News from a foreign country came,
As if my treasures and my joys lay there;
So much it did my heart inflame,
'Twas wont to call my soul into mine ear,
    Which thither went to meet
      Th' approaching sweet,
    And on the threshold stood
    To entertain the secret good;
      It hovered there
    As if 'twould leave mine ear,   10
And was so eager to embrace
Th' expected tidings as they came,
That it could change its dwelling-place
    To meet the voice of fame.

As if new tidings were the things
Which did comprise my wishèd unknown treasure
Or else did bear them on their wings,
With so much joy they came, with so much pleasure.
    My soul stood at the gate
      To re-create   20
    Itself with bliss, and woo
    Its speedier approach; a fuller view
      It fain would take,
    Yet journeys back would make
Unto my heart, as if 'twould fain
Go out to meet, yet stay within,
Fitting a place to entertain
    And bring the tidings in.

What sacred instinct did inspire
My soul in childhood with an hope so strong?   30
What secret force moved my desire
T' expect my joys beyond the seas, so young?
    Felicity I knew
      Was out of view;
    And being left alone,
I thought all happiness was gone
      From earth; for this
    I longed for absent bliss,
Deeming that sure beyond the seas,
Or else in something near at hand   40
Which I knew not, since nought did please
    I knew, my bliss did stand.

But little did the infant dream
That all the treasures of the world were by,
    And that himself was so the cream
And crown of all which round about did lie.
    Yet thus it was! The gem,
      The diadem,
    The ring enclosing all
That stood upon this earthen ball,   50
    The heav'nly eye,
    Much wider than the sky,
Wherein they all included were,
The love, the soul, that was the king
Made to possess them, did appear
    A very little thing.

THE APOSTASY

    One star
    Is better far
    Than many precious stones;
One sun, which is by its own luster seen,
    Is worth ten thousand golden thrones;
    A juicy herb, or spire of grass,
    In useful virtue, native green,
      An em'rald doth surpass,
    Hath in 't more value, though less seen.

    No wars,   10
    Nor mortal jars,
    Nor bloody feuds, nor coin,
Nor griefs which these occasion, saw I then;
    Nor wicked thieves which this purloin;
    I had no thoughts that were impure;
    Esteeming both women and men
      God's work, I was secure,
    And reckoned peace my choicest gem.

    As Eve,
    I did believe   20
    Myself in Eden set,
Affecting neither gold nor ermined crowns,
    Nor aught else that I need forget;
    No mud did foul my limpid streams,
    No mist eclipsed my sun with frowns;
      Set off with heav'nly beams,
    My joys were meadows, fields, and towns.

Those things
Which cherubins
Did not at first behold   30
Among God's works, which Adam did not see—
As robes, and stones enchased in gold,
Rich cabinets, and such-like fine
Inventions—could not ravish me;
I thought not bowls of wine
Needful for my felicity.

All bliss
Consists in this,
To do as Adam did,
And not to know those superficial joys   40
Which were from him in Eden hid,
Those little new-invented things,
Fine lace and silks, such childish toys
As ribands are, and rings,
Or worldly pelf that us destroys.

For God,
Both great and good,
The seeds of melancholy
Created not, but only foolish men,
Grown mad with customary folly,   50
Which doth increase their wants, so dote
As when they elder grow they then
Such baubles chiefly note;
More fools at twenty years than ten.

But I,
I know not why,
Did learn among them too,
At length; and when I once with blemished eyes
Began their pence and toys to view,
Drowned in their customs, I became   60
A stranger to the shining skies,
Lost as a dying flame,
And hobby-horses brought to prize.

The sun
And moon forgone
As if unmade, appear
No more to me; to God and Heaven dead
I was, as though they never were;
Upon some useless gaudy book,
When what I knew of God was fled,   70
The child being taught to look,
His soul was quickly murthered.

O fine!
O most divine!
O brave! they cried; and showed
Some tinsel thing whose glittering did amaze,
And to their cries its beauty owed;
Thus I on riches, by degrees,
Of a new stamp did learn to gaze,
While all the world for these   80
I lost, my joy turned to a blaze.

POVERTY

As in the house I sate,
Alone and desolate,
No creature but the fire and I,
The chimney and the stool, I lift mine eye
Up to the wall,
And in the silent hall
Saw nothing mine
But some few cups and dishes shine,
The table and the wooden stools
Where people used to dine;   10
A painted cloth there was,
Wherein some ancient story wrought
A little entertained my thought,
Which light discovered through the glass.

I wondered much to see
That all my wealth should be
Confined in such a little room,
Yet hope for more I scarcely durst presume.
It grieved me sore
That such a scanty store   20
Should be my all;
For I forgot my ease and health,
Nor did I think of hands or eyes,
Nor soul nor body prize;
I neither thought the sun,
Nor moon, nor stars, nor people, mine,
Though they did round about me shine;
And therefore was I quite undone.

Some greater things, I thought,
Must needs for me be wrought,   30
Which till my craving mind could see
I ever should lament my poverty;
I fain would have
Whatever bounty gave.
Nor could there be
Without or love or Deity;

For should not He be infinite
Whose hand created me?
Ten thousand absent things
Did vex my poor and wanting mind,   40
Which, till I be no longer blind,
Let me not see the King of kings.

His love must surely be
Rich, infinite, and free;
Nor can He be thought a God
Of grace and power, that fills not His abode,
His holy court,
In kind and liberal sort;
Joys and pleasures,
Plenty of jewels, goods, and treasures,   50
To enrich the poor, cheer the forlorn,
His palace must adorn,
And given all to me;
For till His works my wealth became,
No love or peace did me inflame:
But now I have a Deity.

RIGHT APPREHENSION [1]

Give but to things their true esteem,
And those which now so vile and worthless seem
Will so much fill and please the mind
That we shall there the only riches find.
How wise was I
In infancy!
I then saw in the clearest light;
But corrupt custom is a second night.

Custom, that must a trophy be
When wisdom shall complete her victory;   10
For trades, opinions, errors, are
False lights, but yet received to set off ware
More false; we're sold
For worthless gold.
Diana was a goddess made
That silversmiths might have the better trade.

But give to things their true esteem,
And then what's magnified most vile will seem;
What's commonly despised will be
The truest and the greatest rarity.   20
What men should prize
They all despise:
The best enjoyments are abused;
The only wealth by madmen is refused.

A globe of earth is better far
Than if it were a globe of gold; a star
More brighter than a precious stone;
The sun more glorious than a costly throne—
His warming beam,
A living stream   30
Of liquid pearl, that from a spring
Waters the earth, is a most precious thing.

What newness once suggested to,
Now clearer reason doth improve my view;
By novelty my soul was taught
At first, but now reality my thought
Inspires; and I
Perspicuously
Each way instructed am by sense,
Experience, reason, and intelligence.   40

A globe of gold must barren be,
Untilled and useless; we should neither see
Trees, flowers, grass, or corn
Such a metálline massy globe adorn;
As splendor blinds
So hardness binds,
No fruitfulness it can produce;
A golden world can't be of any use.

Ah me! this world is more divine;
The wisdom of a God in this doth shine.   50
What ails mankind to be so cross?
The useful earth they count vile dirt and dross,
And neither prize
Its qualities
Nor Donor's love. I fain would know
How or why men God's goodness disallow.

The earth's rare ductile soil,
Which duly yields unto the plowman's toil
Its fertile nature, gives offense,
And its improvement by the influence   60
Of Heav'n; for these
Do not well please,
Because they do upbraid men's hardened hearts,
And each of them an evidence imparts

Against the owner; whose design
It is that nothing be reputed fine,
Nor held for any excellence
Of which he hath not in himself the sense.

He too well knows
That no fruit grows   70
In him, obdurate wretch, who yields
Obedience to Heav'n less than the fields.

But being, like his lovèd gold,
Stiff, barren, and impen'trable, though told
He should be otherwise, he is
Uncapable of any heav'nly bliss.
His gold and he
Do well agree,
For he's a formal hypocrite,
Like that, unfruitful, yet on th' outside bright.   80

Ah, happy infant! wealthy heir!
How blessed did the heaven and earth appear
Before thou knew'st there was a thing
Called gold! barren of good, of ill the spring
Beyond compare!
Most quiet were
Those infant days when I did see
Wisdom and wealth couched in simplicity.

ON LEAPING OVER THE MOON

I saw new worlds beneath the water lie,
New people; yea, another sky
And sun, which seen by day
Might things more clear display.
Just such another
Of late my brother
Did in his travel see, and saw by night
A much more strange and wondrous sight;
Nor could the world exhibit such another
So great a sight but in a brother.   10

Adventure strange! No such in story we
New or old, true or feignèd, see.
On earth he seemed to move,
Yet heaven went above;
Up in the skies
His body flies
In open, visible, yet magic, sort;
As he along the way did sport,
Over the flood he takes his nimble course
Without the help of feignèd horse.   20

As he went tripping o'er the king's highway,
A little pearly river lay,
O'er which, without a wing
Or oar, he dared to swim,
Swim through the air
On body fair;
He would not trust Icarian wings,
Lest they should prove deceitful things;
For had he fall'n, it had been wondrous high,
Not from, but from above, the sky.   30

He might have dropped through that thin element
Into a fathomless descent;
Unto the nether sky
That did beneath him lie,
And there might tell
What wonders dwell
On earth above. Yet doth he briskly run,
And, bold, the danger overcome;
Who, as he leapt, with joy related soon
How happy he o'erleapt the moon.   40

What wondrous things upon the earth are done
Beneath, and yet above, the sun!
Deeds all appear again
In higher spheres; remain
In clouds as yet,
But there they get
Another light, and in another way
Themselves to us *above* display.
The skies themselves this earthly globe surround;
We're even here within them found.   50

On heav'nly ground within the skies we walk,
And in this middle center talk:
Did we but wisely move,
On earth in heav'n above,
Then soon should we
Exalted be
Above the sky; from whence whoever falls,
Through a long dismal precipice
Sinks to the deep abyss where Satan crawls,
Where horrid death and déspair lies.   60

As much as others thought themselves to lie
Beneath the moon, so much more high
Himself he thought to fly
Above the starry sky,
As *that* he spied
Below the tide.

Thus did he yield me in the shady night
    A wondrous and instructive light,
Which taught me that under our feet there is,
    As o'er our heads, a place of bliss.   70

SHADOWS IN THE WATER

In unexperienced infancy
Many a sweet mistake doth lie:
Mistake though false, intending true;
A seeming somewhat more than view;
    That doth instruct the mind
    In things that lie behind,
And many secrets to us show
Which afterwards we come to know.

Thus did I by the water's brink
Another world beneath me think;   10
And while the lofty spacious skies
Reversèd there, abused mine eyes,
    I fancied other feet
    Came mine to touch or meet;
As by some puddle I did play
Another world within it lay.

Beneath the water people drowned,
Yet with another heaven crowned,
In spacious regions seemed to go
As freely moving to and fro: 20
    In bright and open space
    I saw their very face;
Eyes, hands, and feet they had like mine;
Another sun did with them shine.

'Twas strange that people there should walk,
And yet I could not hear them talk:
That through a little wat'ry chink,
Which one dry ox or horse might drink,
    We other worlds should see,
    Yet not admitted be;   30
And other confines there behold
Of light and darkness, heat and cold.

I called them oft, but called in vain;
No speeches we could entertain:
Yet did I there expect to find
Some other world, to please my mind.
    I plainly saw by these
    A new Antipodes,
Whom, though they were so plainly seen,
A film kept off that stood between.   40

By walking men's reversed feet
I chanced another world to meet;
Though it did not to view exceed
A phantom, 'tis a world indeed,
    Where skies beneath us shine,
    And earth by art divine
Another face presents below,
Where people's feet against ours go.

Within the regions of the air,
Compassed about with heavens fair,   50
Great tracts of land there may be found
Enriched with fields and fertile ground;
    Where many numerous hosts
    In those far distant coasts,
For other great and glorious ends
Inhabit, my yet unknown friends.

O ye that stand upon the brink,
Whom I so near me through the chink
With wonder see: what faces there,
Whose feet, whose bodies, do ye wear?   60
    I my companions see
    In you, another me.
They seemèd others, but are we;
Our second selves these shadows be.

WALKING

To walk abroad is, not with eyes
But thoughts, the fields to see and prize;
    Else may the silent feet,
        Like logs of wood,
Move up and down, and see no good,
    Nor joy nor glory meet.

Ev'n carts and wheels their place do change,
But cannot see, though very strange
    The glory that is by;
        Dead puppets may   10
Move in the bright and glorious day,
    Yet not behold the sky.

And are not men than they more blind,
Who, having eyes, yet never find
    The bliss in which they move?
        Like statues dead
They up and down are carrièd,
    Yet neither see nor love.

To *walk* is by a thought to go;
To move in spirit to and fro;   20
     To mind the good we see;
       To taste the sweet;
Observing all the things we meet,
     How choice and rich they be.

To note the beauty of the day,
And golden fields of corn survey;
     Admire each pretty flower
       With its sweet smell;
To praise their Maker, and to tell
     The marks of His great power.   30

To fly abroad like active bees,
Among the hedges and the trees,
     To cull the dew that lies
       On ev'ry blade,
From ev'ry blossom; till we lade
     Our minds as they their thighs.

Observe those rich and glorious things,
The rivers, meadows, woods, and springs,
     The fructifying sun;
       To note from far   40
The rising of each twinkling star,
     For us his race to run.

A little child these well perceives,
Who, tumbling in green grass and leaves,
     May rich as kings be thought;
       But there's a sight
Which perfect manhood may delight,
     To which we shall be brought.

While in those pleasant paths we talk,
'Tis *that* tow'rds which at last we walk;   50
     For we may by degrees
       Wisely proceed
Pleasures of love and praise to heed,
     From viewing herbs and trees.

FROM

A SERIOUS AND PATHETICAL CONTEMPLATION OF THE MERCIES OF GOD [1699]

from

A THANKSGIVING AND PRAYER FOR THE NATION

O Lord, the children of my people are Thy peculiar
     treasures,
Make them mine, O God, even while I have them,
My lovely companions, like Eve in Eden!
So much my treasure that all other wealth is without
     them
       But dross and poverty.
Do they not adorn and beautify the World,
     And gratify my Soul which hateth Solitude!
Thou, Lord, hast made Thy servant a sociable creature,
       for which I praise Thy name;
A lover of company, a delighter in equals;
     Replenish the inclination which Thyself hath im-
       planted,   10
And give me eyes
To see the beauty of that life and comfort

Wherewith those by their actions
     Inspire the nations.
Their Markets, Tillage, Courts of Judicature, Mar-
     riages, Feasts and Assemblies, Navies, Armies,
Priests and Sabbaths, Trades and Business, the voice of
     the Bridegroom, Musical Instruments, the light
     of Candles, and the grinding of Mills
Are comfortable. O Lord, let them not cease.
The riches of the land are all the materials of my felicity
     in their hands:
They are my Factors, Substitutes, and Stewards;
Second Selves, who by Trade and Business animate
     my wealth,   20
Which else would be dead and rust in my hands;
But when I consider, O Lord, how they come unto Thy
     temples, fill Thy Courts, and sing Thy praises,

O how wonderful they then appear !
  What Stars,
  Enflaming Suns,
  Enlarging Seas
   Of Divine Affection,
  Confirming Patterns,
  Infusing Influence,

  Do I feel in these !   30
Who are the shining light
Of all the land (to my very soul):
  Wings and Streams
  Carrying me unto Thee,
The Sea of Goodness from whence they
  came.

Charles Sackville
EARL OF DORSET
[1638–1706]

CHARLES SACKVILLE, Lord Buckhurst, who succeeded to the earldom of Dorset in 1677, ranks with his friends Sedley and Rochester as one of the licentious luminaries of a licentious age, a worthy companion to the "merry monarch" whose wit and immorality set the tone for an era. Typical of the Restoration court poets in his cynicism and brittleness, Dorset nevertheless was gifted with critical and creative abilities which won the respect of Dryden, who presents him under the name "Eugenius" as one of the participants in his *Essay of Dramatic Poesy*. A great patron of literature, Dorset supported, in addition to Dryden, such figures as Wycherly, Tate, and Shadwell.

Dorset took time from his dissipations to write a number of charming, although unquestionably minor, lyrics. His later life was relatively respectable; he championed the Protestant cause in the Glorious Revolution of 1688, was active in Parliament, and ultimately rose to the post of Lord Chamberlain of the kingdom.

Dorset's most famous poem, the light lyric "To all you ladies now at land," was written (at least according to the poet) on the eve of a naval engagement with the Dutch. Its wit and insouciance are as typical of the age as of the author.

B. HARRIS. *Charles Sackville, Sixth Earl of Dorset, Patron and Poet of the Restoration* (Urbana, Ill., 1940).

[SONG, WRITTEN AT SEA, IN THE FIRST DUTCH WAR][1]

To all you ladies now at land,
  We men at sea do write;
But first I hope you'll understand
  How hard 'tis to indite:
The Muses now, and Neptune too,
We must implore, to write to you.

For though the Muses should be kind,
  And fill our empty brain;
Yet when rough Neptune calls the wind
  To rouse the azure main,
Our paper, ink, and pen, and we
Roll up and down our ship at sea.   10

Then, if we write not by each post,
  Think not we are unkind,
Nor yet conclude that we are lost
  By Dutch or else by wind;
Our tears we'll send a speedier way:
The tide shall bring them twice a day.

SONG

1 The date of the poem is November, 1664, according to Norman Ault (*Seventeenth Century Lyrics*, rev. ed., New York: William Sloane Associates, pp. 508–09). The lines were written, presumably, while Dorset was serving under the Duke of York in his first cruise. The version here given is that of Mr. Ault, from the British Museum Harleian Ms. 3991, first transcribed by him, and corrected, in a few cases, by the 1721 text.

With wonder and amaze the King
   Will vow his seas grow bold;   20
Because the tides more water bring
   Than they were wont of old:
But you must tell him that our cares
Send floods of grief to Whitehall Stairs.

To pass the tedious hours away,
   We throw the merry main;[2]
Or else at serious ombre play:
   But why should we in vain
Each other's ruin thus pursue?
We were undone when we left you.   30

If foggy[3] Opdam[4] did but know
   Our sad and dismal story,
The Dutch would scorn so weak a foe,
   And leave the port of Goree;[5]
And what resistance can they find
From men that left their hearts behind?

Let wind and weather do their worst,
   Be you to us but kind;
Let Frenchmen vapor,[6] Dutchmen curse,
   No sorrow shall we find: 40
'Tis then no matter how things go,
Nor who's our friend, nor who's our foe.

In justice, you cannot refuse
   To think of our distress,
Since we in hope of honor lose
   Our certain happiness;
All our designs are but to prove
Ourselves more worthy of your love.

Alas! our tears tempestuous grow
   And cast our hopes away;   50
While you unmindful of our woe,
   Sit careless at a play:
And now permit some happier man
To kiss your busk, and wag your fan.

When any mournful tune you hear,
   That dies in every note
As if it sighed for each man's care
   For being so remote,
Think then how oft our love we made
To you, while all those tunes were played.   60

And now we have told all our love,
   And also all our tears,
We hope our declarations move
   Some pity for our cares;
Let's hear of no unconstancy,
We have too much of that at sea.

[THE ADVICE][1]

Phyllis, for shame! let us improve
   A thousand several ways
These few short minutes stol'n by love
   From many tedious days.

Whilst you want courage to despise
   The censure of the grave,
For all the tyrants in your eyes,
   Your heart is but a slave.

My love is full of noble pride,
   And never will submit   10
To let that fop, Discretion, ride
   In triumph over wit.

False friends I have, as well as you,
   That daily counsel me
Vain frivolous trifles to pursue,
   And leave off loving thee.

When I the least belief bestow
   On what such fools advise,
May I be dull enough to grow
   Most miserably wise.   20

SONG
  2 A hand at dice (Johnson).   3 Befuddled.
  4 The Dutch admiral.
  5 An island off the Dutch coast.   6 Boast.

THE ADVICE
  1 The text is from Westminster Drollery, I, 1671.

[DORINDA][1]

Dorinda's sparkling wit and eyes,
  Uniting, cast too fierce a light,
Which blazes high, but quickly dies,
  Pains not the heart, but hurts the sight.

Love is a calmer, gentler joy,
  Smooth are his looks and soft his pace;
Her Cupid is a blackguard boy
  That runs his link[2] full in your face.

[1] Dorinda is thought to have been Katherine Sedley, Countess of Dorchester, daughter of Sir Charles Sedley. She was a mistress of James II. The text is that of C. Gildon's A New Miscellany, 1701.
[2] Torch.

Sir Charles Sedley

[1639?–1701]

THE life and works of Sedley closely parallel those of his friend Dorset. Like the notorious earl, he was, at least in his earlier years, a violent and dissolute man, given to indecent public pranks from the consequences of which only his good friend the king could save him. But, again like Dorset, he was also a gifted lyric poet and a critic so astute that Dryden gave him a place (as "Lisideius") in the *Essay of Dramatic Poesy*.

The posthumous son of a Kentish baronet, Sedley studied at Oxford and, in 1657, removed to London, where he immediately became active in literary and court circles. His first play, *The Mulberry Garden*, was presented in 1668, and in general he pursued literature with more intensity than did Dorset. His less reputable pursuits included Nell Gwynn, who became his mistress before she attracted the attention of the king (in consequence of which court wits gave the poet the appellation "Charles the First"). Sedley's daughter became the mistress of James, Duke of York, and that fact may have contributed to the hostility which led Sedley to support the claims of William in 1688.

After the Glorious Revolution, Sedley led a quieter life and served in the House of Commons. He ranks second only to Rochester among the Restoration court poets, but in comparison with the lyrics of the earlier part of the century his seem shallow and contrived.

SIR C. SEDLEY. *Poetical and Dramatic Works*, ed. V. de Sola Pinto, 2 vols. (London, 1928).
V. DE SOLA PINTO. *Sir Charles Sedley: 1639–1701* (London, 1927). The most complete study.

[TO CHLORIS][1]

Ah, Chloris! that I now could sit
  As unconcerned as when
Your infant beauty could beget
  No pleasure, nor no pain.

When I the dawn used to admire,
  And praised the coming day,
I little thought the growing fire
  Must take my rest away.

Your charms in harmless childhood lay
  Like metals in the mine: 10
Age from no face took more away
  Than youth concealed in thine.

But as your charms insensibly
  To their perfection pressed,
Fond Love, as unperceived, did fly,
  And in my bosom rest.

[1] From The Mulberry Garden, 1668.

My passion with your beauty grew,
　　And Cupid at my heart,
Still as his mother favored you,
　　Threw a new flaming dart.　　　　　　20

Each gloried in their wanton part:
　　To make a lover, he
Employed the utmost of his art;
　　To make a beauty, she.

Though now I slowly bend to love,
　　Uncertain of my fate,
If your fair self my chains approve,
　　I shall my freedom hate.

Lovers, like dying men, may well
　　At first disordered be,　　　　　　　30
Since none alive can truly tell
　　What fortune they must see.

F R O M

THE MISCELLANEOUS WORKS [1702]

[LOVE STILL HAS SOMETHING]

Love still has something of the sea,
　　From whence his mother rose;
No time his slaves from doubt can free,
　　Nor give their thoughts repose;

They are becalmed in clearest days,
　　And in rough weather tossed;
They wither under cold delays,
　　Or are in tempests lost.

One while they seem to touch the port,
　　Then straight into the main　　　　10
Some angry wind in cruel sport
　　The vessel drives again.

At first disdain and pride they fear,
　　Which if they chance to 'scape,
Rivals and falsehood soon appear
　　In a more dreadful shape.

By such degrees to joy they come,
　　And are so long withstood,
So slowly they receive the sum,
　　It hardly does them good.　　　　　20

'Tis cruel to prolong a pain,
　　And to defer a joy,
Believe me, gentle Celemene,
　　Offends the wingèd boy.

An hundred thousand oaths your fears
　　Perhaps would not remove;
And if I gazed a thousand years
　　I could no deeper love.

[TO CELIA]

Not, Celia, that I juster am
　　Or better than the rest;
For I would change each hour, like them,
　　Were not my heart at rest.

But I am tied to very thee,
　　By every thought I have;
Thy face I only care to see,
　　Thy heart I only crave.

All that in woman is adored
　　In thy dear self I find,　　　　　　10
For the whole sex can but afford
　　The handsome and the kind.

Why then should I seek farther store,[1]
　　And still make love anew?
When change itself can give no more,
　　'Tis easy to be true.

[THE KNOTTING SONG]

"Hears not my Phyllis how the birds
　　Their feathered mates salute?
They tell their passion in their words:
　　Must I alone be mute?"
Phyllis, without frown or smile,
Sat and knotted all the while.

TO CELIA
1 Abundance.

"The god of love in thy bright eyes
   Does like a tyrant reign;
But in thy heart a child he lies,
   Without his dart or flame."   10
Phyllis, without frown or smile,
Sat and knotted all the while.

"So many months in silence past,
   And yet in raging love,
Might well deserve one word at last
   My passion should approve."
Phyllis, without frown or smile,
Sat and knotted all the while.

"Must then your faithful swain expire,
   And not one look obtain,   20
Which he, to soothe his fond desire,
   Might pleasingly explain?"
Phyllis, without frown or smile,
Sat and knotted all the while.

[PHYLLIS IS MY ONLY JOY]

Phyllis is my only joy,
   Faithless as the winds or seas;
Sometimes coming, sometimes coy,
   Yet she never fails to please;
     If with a frown
     I am cast down,
     Phyllis smiling,
     And beguiling,
Makes me happier than before.

Though, alas! too late I find   10
   Nothing can her fancy fix,
Yet the moment she is kind
   I forgive her all her tricks;
     Which, though I see,
     I can't get free;
     She deceiving,
     I believing;
What need lovers wish for more?

Edward Taylor

[1642?–1729]

THE foremost poet of colonial America, Edward Taylor was born in the vicinity of Coventry and emigrated to Massachusetts Bay Colony in 1668, presumably because of the disabilities under which nonconformists suffered in Restoration England. Little is known of his early life, but it is possible that he studied for some time at Cambridge University. Settling in Boston, Taylor continued his education at Harvard, where he shared rooms with the Samuel Sewall who later attained fame as judge and diarist, and, on his graduation in 1671, he accepted the pastorate of Westfield, Massachusetts, at that time a village on the very borders of civilization.

Taylor remained pastor of Westfield for nearly fifty years, devoting his life to the needs of his parishioners—both as spiritual guide and as physician, for his library, an unusually large one for frontier America, contained numerous medical books. At the same time, however, he led an inner life of extraordinary devotional intensity, and this life is recorded in the poems which he composed during his Westfield years but specific-ally forbade his heirs to publish, thus manifesting an attitude which curiously anticipates that of a later and greater New England poet who in some ways resembles him—Emily Dickinson.

Taylor's work, apart from some miscellaneous and occasional poems and a curious *Metrical History of Christianity*, consists of the religious allegory *God's Determinations Touching His Elect, Christographia*, a series of sermons, and over 200 *Preparatory Meditations before my Approach to the Lord's Supper*. The latter poems, Taylor's most personal and intense, are those on which his fame chiefly rests. That fame dates only from 1937, when Thomas H. Johnson unearthed the collection of manuscript poems which had long lain unknown in the Yale University Library.

If Taylor counts as the first considerable American poet, he counts also as the last representative of the English Metaphysical style, for the poems, with their bold conceits, colloquial tone, and dramatic urgency, are clearly in the tradition of Donne and Herbert, as well as in the related but gaudier tradition of the French poet Du Bartas and his English imitators. Indeed, Taylor's work shows occasional affinities with that of many of the major English Metaphysicals—not only Herbert (and Taylor's echoes indicate con-clusively that he was familiar with *The Temple*) but also Crashaw, whom he resembles in his sensuous metaphor, and Vaughan, whom he resembles in his hieroglyphic approach to observed nature. Like these predecessors, Taylor was a learned poet, and this quality is evident both in his use of the traditional practice of formal meditation and in his recurrent emphasis on the drama of election as conceived of by strict Calvinistic theology. Learned also is a particular type of devotional lyric to which Taylor was especially addicted—the "typological" poem, in which an episode from the Old Testament is rigorously analyzed as a foreshadowing of an incident in the life and ministry of Christ. Examples of such poems are Meditations 7 and 12 of the second series among the following selections.

Transatlantic cultural lag, a phenomenon often to be noted in later centuries, probably accounts for Taylor's practice of a literary style which had become extinct in the mother country. Isolation, both geographical and chronological—an isolation which in Taylor's case was deliberate—probably accounts for the unevenness of his achievement: for the faulty structure, uncertain tone, wrenched rhythms, and hysterical images which mar many of even his best poems. These traits, which ally Taylor more closely with Benlowes than with Herbert or Vaughan, are sufficient to warn us from the kind of overestimation to which his historical interest might easily lead, but they do not prevent the modern reader from recognizing Taylor as a compelling and often exciting poet.

E. TAYLOR. *Poems,* ed. D. E. Stanford (New Haven, 1960). This, the standard edition, contains the complete *Preparatory Meditations* and *God's Determinations,* together with selections from the *Metrical History* and the miscellaneous poems. It is preceded by an excellent critical essay by L. L. Martz.

————. *Poetical Works,* ed. T. H. Johnson (Princeton, 1943). The pioneer edition. Contains *God's Determinations* and a selection from the *Meditations* and miscellaneous poems.

————. *Christographia,* ed. N. S. Grabo (New Haven, 1962). First publication of a series of sermons on Christ. The sermons are based on the same biblical texts as many of the *Preparatory Meditations,* with which they coordinate.

W. C. BROWN. "Edward Taylor: An American Metaphysical," *AL,* XVI (1944).

R. H. PEARCE. *The Continuity of American Poetry* (Princeton, 1961).

————. "Edward Taylor: the Poet as Puritan," *NEQ,* XXIII (1950).

H. BLAU. "Heaven's Sugar Cake: Theology and Imagery in the Poetry of Edward Taylor," NEQ, XXVI (1953).

A. WARREN. "Edward Taylor," in *Rage for Order* (Chicago, 1948).

FROM

THE POEMS OF EDWARD TAYLOR [1960]

from

GOD'S DETERMINATIONS TOUCHING HIS ELECT

THE PREFACE

Infinity, when all things it beheld
In Nothing, and of Nothing all did build,

Upon what base was fixed the lath wherein
He turned this globe and rigalled it so trim?
Who blew the bellows of His furnace vast?
Or held the mold wherein the world was cast?
Who laid its cornerstone? Or whose command?
Where stand the pillars upon which it stands?
Who laced and filleted[1] the earth so fine,
With rivers like green ribbons smaragdine?
Who made the seas its selvedge[2] and it locks   10

1 Bound.   2 Border, edge.

Like a quilt ball within a silver box?
Who spread its canopy? Or curtains spun?
Who in this bowling alley bowled the sun?
Who made it always when it rises set,
To go at once both down, and up to get?
Who the curtain rods made for this tapestry?
Who hung the twinkling lanterns in the sky?
Who? Who did this? Or who is He? Why, know
It's only Might Almighty this did do.   20
His hand hath made this noble work which stands,
His glorious handiwork not made by hands.
Who spake all things from nothing; and with ease
Can speak all things to nothing, if He please.
Whose little finger at His pleasure can
Out mete ten thousand worlds with half a span:
Whose Might Almighty can by half a looks
Root up the rocks and rock the hills by the roots.
Can take this mighty world up in His hand,
And shake it like a squitchen³ or a wand.   30
Whose single frown will make the heavens shake
Like as an aspen-leaf the wind makes quake.
Oh, what a might is this Whose single frown
Doth shake the world as it would shake it down?
Which All from Nothing fet,⁴ from Nothing, All:
Hath All on Nothing set, lets Nothing fall.
Gave All to nothing-man indeed, whereby
Through nothing-man all might him glorify.
In Nothing then embossed the brightest gem
More precious than all preciousness in them.   40
But nothing-man did throw down all by sin:
And darkenèd that lightsome gem in him.
     That now his brightest diamond is grown
     Darker by far than any coal-pit stone.

THE JOY OF CHURCH FELLOWSHIP RIGHTLY ATTENDED

In Heaven soaring up, I dropped an ear
     On earth: and Oh, sweet melody:
And listening, found it was the saints who were
     Encoached for Heaven that sang for joy.
     For in Christ's coach they sweetly sing,
     As they to glory ride therein.

Oh, joyous hearts! Enfired with holy flame!
     Is speech thus tasslèd with praise?
Will not your inward fire of joy contain;
     That it in open flames doth blaze?   10
     For in Christ's coach saints sweetly sing,
     As they to glory ride therein.

And if a string do slip by chance, they soon
     Do screw it up again, whereby
They set it in a more melodious tune
     And a diviner harmony.
     For in Christ's coach they sweetly sing,
     As they to glory ride therein.

In all their acts, public and private, nay,
     And secret too, they praise impart.   20
But in their acts divine and worship, they
     With hymns do offer up their heart.
     Thus in Christ's coach they sweetly sing,
     As they to glory ride therein.

Some few not in; and some whose time and place
     Block up this coach's way do go
As travelers afoot, and so do trace
     The road that gives them right thereto,
     While in this coach these sweetly sing,
     As they to glory ride therein.   30

TWO POEMS

HUSWIFERY

Make me, O Lord, Thy spinning-wheel complete.
     Thy holy word my distaff make for me.
Make mine affections Thy swift flyers¹ neat
     And make my soul Thy holy spool to be.
     My conversation make to be Thy reel
     And reel the yarn thereon spun of Thy wheel.

Make me Thy loom then, knit therein this twine:
     And make Thy Holy Spirit, Lord, wind quills:
Then weave the web Thyself. The yarn is fine.
     Thine ordinances make my fulling-mills.   10
     Then dye the same in heavenly colors choice,
     All pinked with varnished flowers of paradise.

THE PREFACE
     3 Of doubtful meaning, possibly "a piece of bark used in grafting" (Stanford).
     4 Fetched.

HUSWIFERY
     1 The part of a spinning-wheel that twists the thread and leads it to the bobbin (Stanford).

Then clothe therewith mine understanding, will,
Affections, judgment, conscience, memory,
My words and actions, that their shine may fill
My ways with glory and Thee glorify.
Then mine apparel shall display before Ye
That I am clothed in holy robes for glory.

THE EBB AND FLOW

When first Thou on me, Lord, wroughtst Thy sweet
    print,
    My heart was made Thy tinder-box.
    My 'ffections were Thy tinder in 't,
        Where fell Thy sparks by drops.
Those holy sparks of heavenly fire that came
Did ever catch and often out would flame.

But now my heart is made Thy censer trim,
    Full of Thy golden altar's fire,
    To offer up sweet incense in
        Unto Thyself entire: 10
I find my tinder scarce Thy sparks can feel
That drop from out Thy holy flint and steel.

Hence doubts out bud for fear Thy fire in me
    'S a mocking ignis fatuus,
    Or lest Thine altar's fire out be,
        It's hid in ashes thus.
Yet when the bellows of Thy spirit blow
Away mine ashes, then Thy fire doth glow.

from

PREPARATORY MEDITATIONS BEFORE MY APPROACH TO THE LORD'S SUPPER

THE PROLOGUE

Lord, can a crumb of dust the earth outweigh,
    Outmatch all mountains, nay the crystal sky?
Imbosom in 't designs that shall display
    And trace into the boundless deity?
    Yea, hand a pen whose moisture doth gild o'er
    Eternal glory with a glorious glore.[1]

THE PROLOGUE
  1 Glory.

If it is pen had of an angel's quill,
    And sharpened on a precious stone ground tight,
And dipped in liquid gold, and moved by skill
    In crystal leaves should golden letters write,   10
    It would but blot and blur, yea, jag and jar,
    Unless Thou mak'st the pen and scribener.

I am this crumb of dust which is designed
    To make my pen unto Thy praise alone,
And my dull fancy I would gladly grind
    Unto an edge on Zion's precious stone;
    And write in liquid gold upon Thy name
    My letters till Thy glory forth doth flame.

Let not th' attempts break down my dust I pray,
    Nor laugh Thou them to scorn, but pardon give.   20
Inspire this crumb of dust till it display
    Thy glory through 't: and then Thy dust shall live.
    Its failings then Thou'lt overlook, I trust,
    They being slips slipped from Thy crumb of dust.

Thy crumb of dust breathes two words from its breast,
    That Thou wilt guide its pen to write aright
To prove Thou art and that Thou art the best
    And shew Thy properties to shine most bright.
    And then Thy works will shine as flowers on stems
    Or as in jewelary shops do gems.   30

from

PREPARATORY MEDITATIONS
First Series

1. MEDITATION

What love is this of Thine that cannot be
    In Thine infinity, O Lord, confined,
Unless it in Thy very person see
    Infinity and finity conjoined?
    What hath Thy godhead, as not satisfied,
    Married our manhood, making it its bride?

Oh matchless love! Filling heaven to the brim!
    O'errunning it: all running o'er beside
This world! Nay, overflowing hell; wherein
    For Thine elect there rose a mighty tide!   10
    That there our veins might through Thy person bleed,
    To quench those flames that else would on us feed.

Oh! that Thy love might overflow my heart!
　To fire the same with love: for love I would.
But oh! my straitened breast! my lifeless spark!
　My fireless flame! What chilly love, and cold?
　In measure small! In manner chilly! See.
　Lord, blow the coal: Thy love enflame in me.

6. MEDITATION

(Cant. 2:1. The Lily of the Valleys)

Am I Thy gold? Or purse, Lord, for Thy wealth;
　Whether in mine or mint refined for Thee?
I'm counted so, but count me o'er Thyself,
　Lest gold-washed face, and brass in heart I be.
　I fear my touchstone touches when I try
　Me, and my counted gold too overly.

Am I new-minted by Thy stamp indeed?
　Mine eyes are dim; I cannot clearly see.
Be Thou my spectacles that I may read
　Thine image and inscription stamped on me.　10
　If Thy bright image do upon me stand,
　I am a golden angel[1] in Thy hand.

Lord, make my soul Thy plate: Thine image bright
　Within the circle of the same enfoil.
And on its brims in golden letters write
　Thy superscription in an holy style.
　Then I shall be Thy money, Thou my hoard:
　Let me Thy angel be, be Thou my Lord.

29. MEDITATION

(Joh. 20:17. My Father, and your Father, to my God, and your God)

My shattered fancy stole away from me
　(Wits run a-wooling over Eden's park)
And in God's garden saw a golden tree,
　Whose heart was all divine, and gold its bark.
　Whose glorious limbs and fruitful branches strong
　With saints and angels bright are richly hung.

6. MEDITATION
1 A gold coin.

Thou! Thou! my dear dear Lord, art this rich tree,
　The tree of life within God's Paradise.
I am a withered twig, dried fit to be
　A chat[1] cast in Thy fire, writh[2] off by vice.　10
　Yet if Thy milk-white gracious hand will take me
　And graft me in this golden stock, Thou'lt make me.

Thou'lt make me then its fruit, and branch to spring,
　And though a nipping east wind blow, and all
Hell's nymphs with spite their dog's sticks thereat
　　ding[3]
　To dash the graft off, and its fruits to fall,
　Yet I shall stand Thy graft, and fruits that are
　Fruits of the tree of life Thy graft shall bear.

I being graft in Thee, there up do stand
　In us relations all that mutual are.　20
I am Thy patient, pupil, servant, and
　Thy sister, mother, dove, spouse, son, and heir.
　Thou art my priest, physician, prophet, king,
　Lord, brother, bridegroom, father, everything.

I being graft in Thee am grafted here
　Into Thy family, and kindred claim
To all in heaven, God, saints, and angels there.
　I Thy relations my relations name.
　Thy father's mine, Thy God my God, and I
　With saints and angels draw affinity.　30

My Lord, what is it that Thou dost bestow?
　The praise on this account fills up, and throngs
Eternity brimful, doth overflow
　The heavens vast with rich angelic songs.
　How should I blush? How tremble at this thing,
　Not having yet my gam-ut[4] learned to sing.

But, Lord, as burnished sunbeams forth out fly,
　Let angel-shine forth in my life outflame,
That I may grace Thy graceful family
　And not to Thy relations be a shame.　40
　Make me Thy graft, be Thou my golden stock.
　Thy glory then I'll make my fruits and crop.

29. MEDITATION
1 Branch used for kindling (Stanford).　2 Wrenched.
3 Throw.　4 Musical scale.

32. MEDITATION
(1 Cor. 3:22. Whether Paul or Apollos, or Cephas)

Thy grace, dear Lord, 's my golden wrack, I find,
  Screwing my fancy into ragged rhymes,
Tuning Thy praises in my feeble mind
  Until I come to strike them on my chimes.
  Were I an angel bright, and borrow could
  King David's harp, I would them play on gold.

But plunged I am, my mind is puzzlèd,
  When I would spin my fancy thus unspun,
In finest twine of praise I'm muzzlèd,
  My tazzled [1] thoughts twirled into snick-snarls run.
  Thy grace, my Lord, is such a glorious thing,   11
  It doth confound me when I would it sing.

Eternal love an object mean did smite,
  Which by the prince of darkness was beguiled,
That from this love it ran and swelled with spite,
  And in the way with filth was all defiled,
  Yet must be reconciled, cleansed, and begraced,
  Or from the fruits of God's first love displaced.

Then grace, my Lord, wrought in Thy heart a vent,
  Thy soft soft hand to this hard work did go,   20
And to the milk-white throne of justice went
  And entered bond that grace might overflow.
  Hence did Thy person to my nature tie
  And bleed through human veins to satisfy.

Oh! grace, grace, grace! This wealthy grace doth lay
  Her golden channels from Thy father's throne,
Into our earthen pitchers to convey
  Heaven's aqua vitae to us for our own.
  O! Let Thy golden gutters run into
  My cup this liquor till it overflow.   30

Thine ordinances, grace's wine-fats [2] where
  Thy spirit walks, and grace's runs do lie,
And angels waiting stand with holy cheer
  From grace's conduit head, with all supply.
  These vessels full of grace are, and the bowls
  In which their taps do run are precious souls.

Thou to the cups dost say (that catch this wine)
  "This liquor, golden pipes, and wine-fats plain,
Whether Paul, Apollos, Cephas, all are thine."
  Oh golden word! Lord, speak it o'er again.   40
  Lord, speak it home to me, say these are mine.
  My bells shall then Thy praises bravely chime.

38. MEDITATION
(1 Joh. 2:1. An Advocate with the Father)

Oh! What a thing is man? Lord, who am I?
  That Thou shouldst give him law (Oh! golden line)
To regulate his thoughts, words, life thereby;
  And judge him wilt thereby too in Thy time.
  A court of justice Thou in heaven holdst
  To try his case while he's here housed on mold.

How do Thy angels lay before Thine eye
  My deeds both white and black I daily do?
How doth Thy court Thou pannel'st there them try?
  But flesh complains: "What right for this? Let's
    know.   10
  For, right or wrong, I can't appear unto't.
  And shall a sentence pass on such a suit?"

Soft; blemish not this golden bench, or place.
  Here is no bribe, nor colorings to hide,
Nor pettifogger to befog the case,
  But justice hath her glory here well tried.
  Her spotless law all spotted cases tends;
  Without respect or disrespect them ends.

God's judge himself; and Christ attorney is;
  The Holy Ghost registerer is found.   20
Angels the sergeants are; all creatures kiss
  The book, and do as evidences abound.
  All cases pass according to pure law,
  And in the sentence is no fret nor flaw.

What say'st, my soul? Here all thy deeds are tried.
  Is Christ thy advocate to plead thy cause?
Art thou His client? Such shall never slide.
  He never lost His case: He pleads such laws
  As carry do the same, nor doth refuse
  The vilest sinner's case that doth Him choose.   30

32. MEDITATION
  1 Tangled.   2 Wine-vats.

This is His honor, not dishonor: nay,
    No habeas corpus gainst His clients came;
For all their fines His purse doth make down pay.
    He non-suits Satan's suit or casts the same.
    He'll plead thy case, and not accept a fee.
    He'll plead *sub forma pauperis* for thee.

My case is bad. Lord, be my advocate.
    My sin is red: I'm under God's arrest.
Thou hast the hint of pleading; plead my state.
    Although it's bad, Thy plea will make it best.   40
    If Thou wilt plead my case before the king,
    I'll wagon-loads of love and glory bring.

39. MEDITATION

(*From* 1 *Joh.* 2:1. *If any Man Sin, We Have an
Advocate*)

My sin! My sin, my God, these cursed dregs,
    Green, yellow, blue-streaked poison hellish, rank,
Bubs hatched in nature's nest on serpents' eggs,
    Yelp, chirp, and cry; they set my soul a-cramp.
    I frown, chide, strike, and fight them, mourn and
      cry
    To conquer them, but cannot them destroy.

I cannot kill nor coop them up: my curb
    'S less than a snaffle in their mouth: my reins
They as a twine thread snap: by hell they're spurred:
    And load my soul with swagging loads of pains.   10
    Black imps, young devils, snap, bite, drag to bring
    And pick me headlong hell's dread whirlpool in.

Lord, hold Thy hand: for handle me Thou mayst
    In wrath: but oh, a twinkling ray of hope
Methinks I spy Thou graciously display'st.
    There is an advocate: a door is ope.
    Sin's poison swell my heart would till it burst,
    Did not a hope hence creep in 't thus and nurse 't.

Joy, joy, God's son's the sinner's advocate,
    Doth plead the sinner guiltless, and a saint.   20
But yet attornies' pleas spring from the state,
    The case is in: if bad, it's bad in plaint.
    My papers do contain no pleas that do
    Secure me from, but knock me down to, woe.

I have no plea mine advocate to give:
    What now? He'll anvil arguments great store
Out of His flesh and blood to make thee live.
    O dear-bought arguments: good pleas therefore.
    Nails made of heavenly steel, more choice than gold
    Drove home, well-clenched, eternally will hold.   30

Oh! Dear-bought plea, dear Lord, what buy 't so dear?
    What with Thy blood purchase Thy plea for me?
Take argument out of Thy grave t' appear
    And plead my case with, me from guilt to free.
    These maul both sin and devils, and amaze
    Both saints and angels; wreathe their mouths with
      praise.

What shall I do, my Lord? What do, that I
    May have Thee plead my case? I fee Thee will
With faith, repentance, and obediently
    Thy service gainst Satanic sins fulfill.   40
    I'll fight Thy fields while live I do, although
    I should be hacked in pieces by Thy foe.

Make me Thy friend, Lord, be my surety: I
    Will be Thy client, be my advocate:
My sins make Thine, Thy pleas make mine hereby.
    Thou wilt me save, I will Thee celebrate.
    Thou'lt kill my sins that cut my heart within:
    And my rough feet shall Thy smooth praises sing.

from

PREPARATORY MEDITATIONS
Second Series

3. MEDITATION

(*Rom.* 5:14. *Who is the Figure of Him that was to
Come*)

Like to the marigold, I blushing close
    My golden blossoms when Thy sun goes down:
Moist'ning my leaves with dewy sighs, half froze
    By the nocturnal cold, that hoars my crown.
    Mine apples ashes are in apple-shells
    And dirty too: strange and bewitching spells!

When, Lord, mine eye doth spy Thy grace to beam
  Thy mediatorial glory in the shine
Out-spouted so from Adam's typic stream
  And emblemized in Noah's polished shrine,   10
  Thine theirs outshines so far it makes their glory
  In brightest colors, seem a smoky story.

But when mine eye, full of these beams, doth cast
  Its rays upon my dusty essence thin,
Impregnate with a spark divine, defaced,
  All candied o'er with leprosy of sin,
  Such influences on my spirit light,
  Which them as bitter gall or cold ice smite.

My bristled sins hence do so horrid 'pear,
  None but Thyself (and Thou decked up must be
In Thy transcendent glory sparkling clear)   21
  A mediator unto God for me.
  So high they rise, Faith scarce can toss a sight
  Over their head upon Thyself to light.

Is't possible such glory, Lord, e'er should
  Center its love on me, sin's dunghill else?
My case up take? Make it its own? Who would
  Wash with His blood my blots out? Crown His
    shelf
  Or dress His golden cupboard with such ware?
  This makes my pale-faced hope almost despair.   30

Yet let my titimouse's quill suck in
  Thy grace's milk-pails some small drop: or cart
A bit, or splinter of some ray, the wing
  Of grace's sun sprindged[1] out, into my heart:
  To build there wonder's chapel where Thy praise
  Shall be the psalms sung forth in gracious lays.

7. MEDITATION

(Ps. 105:17. He sent a Man before Them, even
Joseph, who was Sold, etc.)

All dull, my Lord, my spirits flat, and dead,
  All water-soaked and sapless to the skin.
Oh! Screw me up and make my spirit's bed
  Thy quickening virtue, for my ink is dim,
  My pencil blunt. Doth Joseph type out Thee?
  Heralds of angels sing out, "Bow the knee."

Is Joseph's glorious shine a type of Thee?
  How bright art Thou? He envied was as well.
And so was Thou. He's stripped and picked, poor he,
  Into the pit. And so was Thou. They shell   10
  Thee of Thy kernel. He by Judah's sold
  For twenty bits; thirty for Thee he'd told.

Joseph was tempted by his mistress vile.
  Thou by the devil, but both shame the foe.
Joseph was cast into the jail awhile.
  And so was Thou. Sweet apples mellow so.
  Joseph did from his jail to glory run.
  Thou from death's pallet rose like morning sun.

Joseph lays in against the famine, and
  Thou dost prepare the bread of life for Thine.   20
He bought with corn for Pharoah th' men and land.
  Thou with Thy bread mak'st such themselves
    consign
  Over to Thee, that eat it. Joseph makes
  His brethren bow before him. Thine too quake.

Joseph constrains his brethren till their sins
  Do gall their souls. Repentance babbles fresh.
Thou treatest sinners till repentance springs,
  Then with him send'st a Benjamin-like mess.[1]
  Joseph doth cheer his humble brethren. Thou   29
  Dost stud with joy the mourning saints that bow.

Joseph's bright shine th' Eleven Tribes must preach.
  And Thine Apostles now eleven, Thine.
They bear his presents to his friends: Thine reach
  Thine unto Thine, thus now behold a shine.
  How hast Thou penciled out, my Lord, most bright
  Thy glorious image here, on Joseph's light.

This I bewail in me under this shine,
  To see so dull a color in my skin.
Lord, lay Thy brightsome colors on me Thine.
  Scour Thou my pipes, then play Thy tunes therein.
  I will not hang my harp in willows by,   41
  While Thy sweet praise my tunes doth glorify.

---

3. MEDITATION
  1 Sprinkled.

7. MEDITATION
  1 Feast.

12. MEDITATION

(Ezek. 37:24. David my Servant shall be their King)

Dull, dull indeed! What, shall it e'er be thus?
  And why? Are not Thy promises, my Lord,
Rich, quick'ning things? How should my full cheeks
    blush
    To find me thus? And those a lifeless word?
  My heart is heedless: unconcerned hereat:
  I find my spirits spiritless and flat.

Thou court'st mine eyes in sparkling colors bright,
  Most bright indeed, and soul-enamoring,
With the most shining sun, whose beams did smite
  Me with delightful smiles to make me spring.   10
  Embellished knots of love assault my mind,
  Which still is dull, as if this sun n'er shined.

David in all his gallantry now comes,
  Bringing, to tend Thy shrine, his royal glory,
Rich prowess, prudence, victories, sweet songs,
  And piety to pencil out Thy story;
  To draw my heart to Thee in this brave shine
  Of typic beams, most warm. But still I pine.

Shall not this lovely beauty, Lord, set out
  In dazzling shining flashes 'fore mine eye,   20
Enchant my heart, love's golden mine, till 't spout
  Out streams of love refin'd that on Thee lie?
  Thy glory's great: Thou David's kingdom shalt
  Enjoy for aye. I want and that's my fault.

Spare me, my Lord, spare me, I greatly pray,
  Let me Thy gold pass through Thy fire until
Thy fire refine, and take my filth away.
  That I may shine like gold, and have my fill
  Of love for Thee; until my virginal
  Chime out in changes sweet Thy praises shall.   30

Wipe off my rust, Lord, with Thy wisp me scour,
  And make Thy beams perch on my strings their
    blaze.
My tunes clothe with Thy shine, and quavers pour
  My cursing strings on, loaded with Thy praise.
  My fervent love with music in her hand,
  Shall then attend Thyself, and Thy command.

143. MEDITATION

*(Can. 6:10. Who is She that Looks Forth as the Morning.
Fair as the Moon, Clear as the Sun, Terrible as an Army
with Banners)*

Wonders amazed! Am I espoused to Thee?
  My glorious Lord? What! Shall my bit of clay
Be made more bright than brightest angels be,
  Look forth like as the morning every way?
  And shall my lump of dirts wear such attire?
  Rise up in heavenly ornaments thus, higher?

But still the wonders stand, shall I look like
  The glorious morning that doth gild the sky
With golden beams that make all day grow light,
  And view the world o'er with its golden eye?   10
  And shall I rise like fair as the fair moon,
  And bright as is the sun, that lights each room?

When we behold a piece of China clay
  Formed up into a China dish complete,
All spicèd o'er as with gold sparks display
  Their beauty all under a glass robe neat,
  We gaze thereat, and wonder rise up will,
  Wond'ring to see the Chinese art and skill.

How then should we and angels but admire
  Thy skill and vessel Thou hast made bright thus   20
Out for to look like to the morning tire
  That shineth out in all bright heavenly plush?
  Whose golden beams all varnish o'er the skies
  And gild our canopy in golden wise?

Wonders are nonplussed to behold Thy spouse
  Look forth like to the morning whose sweet rays
Gild o'er our skies as with transparent boughs
  Like orient gold of a celestial blaze.
  Fair as the moon, bright as the sun, most clear,
  Gilding with spiritual gold grace's bright sphere.

O blessed! Virgin spouse, shall thy sharp looks   31
  Gild o'er the objects of thy shining eyes
Like fairest moon and brightest sun do th' fruits
  Even as that make the morning shining rise?
  The fairest moon in 'ts socket's candle-light
  Unto the night and th' sun's day's candle bright.

Thy spouse's robes all made of spiritual silk
  Of th' web wove in the heaven's bright loom indeed,
By the Holy Spirit's hand more white than milk
  And fitted to attire thy soul that needs.   40
    As th' morning bright's made of the sun's bright
       rays,
    So th' Spirit's web thy soul's rich loom o'erlays.

Oh! Spouse adornèd like the morning clear,
  Chasing the night out from its hemisphere.
And like the fair face of the moon, whose cheer
  Is very brave and like the bright sun 'pear,
    Thus gloriously fitted in brightest story
    Of grace espoused to be the king of glory.

And thus decked up methinks my ear attends
  Kings', queens' and ladies' query, "Who is this?   50
Enravished at her sight, how she out sends
  Her looks like to the morning filled with bliss,
    Fair as the moon, clear as the sun in 'ts costs [1]
    And terrible as is a bannered host?"

And all in grace's colors thus bedight,
  That do transcend with glory's shine the sun
And moon for fairness and for glorious light,
  As doth the sun a glowworm's shine outrun.
    No wonder then and if the Bridegroom say,
    "Thou art all fair, my Love, Yea, everway."   60

May I a member be, my Lord, once made
  Here of Thy spouse in truest sense, though it be
The meanest of all, a toe, or finger 'rayd,[2]
  I'st[3] have enough of bliss, espoused to Thee.
    Then I in brightest glory ere 't be long
    Will honor Thee singing that wedden[4] song.

143. MEDITATION
  1 Course.   2 Arrayed.   3 I shall.   4 Wedding.

146. MEDITATION

(*Cant. 6:13. Return, oh Shulamite, Return, Return*)

My dear, dear Lord, I know not what to say:
  Speech is too coarse a web for me to clothe
My love to Thee in or it to array
  Or make a mantle. Would'st Thou not such loathe?
    Thy love to me's too great for me to shape
    A vesture for the same at any rate.

When as Thy love doth touch my heart down-tossed
  It tremblingly runs, seeking Thee its all,
And as a child when it his nurse hath lost
  Runs seeking her, and after her doth call.   10
    So when Thou hid'st from me, I seek and sigh.
    Thou sayest, "Return, return, Oh Shulamite."

Rent out on use Thy love, Thy love I pray.
  My love to Thee shall be Thy rent, and I
Thee use on use, int'rest on int'rest pay.
  There's none extortion in such usury.

I'll pay Thee use on use for 't and therefore
  Thou shalt become the greatest usurer.
But yet the principal I'll ne'er restore.
  The same is Thine and mine. We shall not jar.   20
    And so this blessed usury shall be
    Most profitable both to Thee and me.

And shouldst Thou hide Thy shining face most fair
  Away from me. And in a sinking wise
My trembling beating heart brought nigh t' despair
  Should cry to Thee and in a trembling guise,
    Lord, quicken it. Drop in its ears delight,
    Saying, "Return, return, my Shulamite."

John Wilmot

EARL OF ROCHESTER

[1647–1680]

ROCHESTER, the third member of the libertine triumvirate of the Restoration, was by far the most gifted member of the group, and it is regrettable that his more or less complete cynicism—more metaphysically based than that of Dorset or Sedley—committed him to a career of triviality for which his graceful lyrics and effective satires do not really compensate. The son of a Royalist general who was created earl for his services, Rochester displayed precocity and entered Wadham College, Oxford, at an early age. After the customary grand tour of the Continent, he returned to England to take up a life of epic dissipation, interrupted by distinguished service in the Dutch wars of 1665–66, but resumed again and terminated only on his deathbed by the conversion recorded by Bishop Burnet.

Rochester was the inseparable companion of Charles II, but the poet's scandalous exploits obliged the king to banish him from court at regular intervals. One such exploit involved the kidnapping of an heiress, Elizabeth Malet, who later was so enthralled by Rochester's heroism during the war that she accepted his proposal of marriage. Subsequently the earl took as his mistress the actress Elizabeth Barry, and his patronage assisted her to become one of the most prominent figures of the Restoration stage.

During his short life of frivolity and debauchery, Rochester found time to write a number of brittle but melodious love lyrics, a vast quantity of pornographic verse, and a number of satires, of which *A Satire against Mankind* (1675) is the best.

J. WILMOT, Earl of Rochester. *Collected Works*, ed. J. Hayward (London, 1926).
———. *Poems*, ed. V. de Sola Pinto (London, 1953).
———. *Complete Poems*, ed. D. M. Vieth (New Haven, 1968).
V. DE SOLA PINTO. *Rochester: Portrait of a Restoration Poet* (London, 1935).
C. WILLIAMS. *Rochester* (London, 1935).

FROM

POEMS ON SEVERAL OCCASIONS [1680]

UPON DRINKING IN A BOWL

Vulcan, contrive me such a cup
  As Nestor[1] used of old:
Show all thy skill to trim it up;
  Damask it round with gold.

Make it so large that, filled with sack
  Up to the swelling brim,
Vast toasts on the delicious lake,
  Like ships at sea, may swim.

Engrave not battle on his cheek;
  With war I've nought to do: 10
I'm none of those that took Maestrick,[2]
  Nor Yarmouth[3] leaguer[4] knew.

Let it no name of planets tell,
  Fixed stars, or constellations;
For I am no Sir Sidrophel,[5]
  Nor none of his relations.

But carve thereon a spreading vine;
  Then add two lovely boys;
Their limbs in amorous folds entwine,
  The type of future joys.   20

Cupid and Bacchus my saints are;
  May drink and love still reign:
With wine I wash away my cares,
  And then to love again.

CONSTANCY

A Song

I cannot change as others do,
  Though you unjustly scorn,
Since that poor swain that sighs for you,
  For you alone was born.
No, Phyllis, no; your heart to move
  A surer way I'll try;
And to revenge my slighted love,
  Will still love on, will still love on, and die.

When killed with grief Amyntas lies,
  And you to mind shall call   10
The sighs that now unpitied rise,
  The tears that vainly fall,
That welcome hour that ends this smart,
  Will then begin your pain:
For such a faithful tender heart
  Can never break, can never break in vain.

LOVE AND LIFE

All my past life is mine no more,
  The flying hours are gone,
Like transitory dreams given o'er,
Whose images are kept in store,
  By memory alone.

The time that is to come, is not:
  How can it then be mine?
The present moment's all my lot,
And that, as fast as it is got,
  Phyllis, is wholly thine.   10

Then talk not of inconstancy,
  False hearts, and broken vows;
If I, by miracle, can be
This livelong minute true to thee,
  'Tis all that heaven allows.

UPON DRINKING
  1 A reference to the Iliad, xi. 632 ff.
  2 Taken by the French and English, 1673.
  3 An English man-of-war.   4 A besieging force.
  5 An astrologer portrayed in Butler's Hudibras, Part II,
Canto 3.

FROM

POEMS [1696]

[ABSENT FROM THEE]

Absent from thee I languish still;
  Then ask me not when I return.
The straying fool 'twill plainly kill,
  To wish all day, all night to mourn.

Dear, from thine eyes then let me fly,
  That my fantastic mind may prove[1]
The torments it deserves to try,
  That tears my fixed heart from my love.

When wearied with a world of woe
  To thy safe bosom I retire;   10
Where love, and peace, and truth does flow,
  May I contented there expire:

Lest once more wandering from that heaven,
  I fall on some base heart unblessed,
Faithless to thee, false, unforgiven,
  And lose my everlasting rest.

ABSENT FROM THEE
1 Experience.

[MY DEAR MISTRESS]

My dear mistress has a heart
  Soft as those kind looks she gave me,
When with love's resistless art,
  And her eyes, she did enslave me;
But her constancy's so weak,
  She's so wild and apt to wander,
That my jealous heart would break
  Should we live one day asunder.

Melting joys about her move,
  Killing pleasures, wounding blisses;   10
She can dress her eyes in love,
  And her lips can arm with kisses;
Angels listen when she speaks;
  She's my delight, all mankind's wonder;
But my jealous heart would break
  Should we live one day asunder.

APPENDIX

Appendix

A CRITICAL MISCELLANY

THE literature of the seventeenth century in England has, since its own time, inspired much literary criticism and theory, and the following selections only hint at the extent and quality of the work thus inspired. Dr. Johnson's famous remarks in the "Life of Cowley" constitute a perceptive, if hostile, analysis of the style of Metaphysical poetry, and modern criticism has frequently accepted Johnson's terms while revising his judgment. H. J. C. Grierson's introduction to his 1921 anthology of Metaphysical verse, and the essay in which T. S. Eliot reviewed that volume, are both to a certain degree elaborations of Johnson's analysis. These two essays were among the most influential in effecting the twentieth-century revival of a taste for Donne and the other Metaphysicals.

Criticism and scholarship in other areas of seventeenth-century studies have been equally active: Milton studies have been extensive and varied, and a new examination of seventeenth-century prose style (typified by the work of Morris W. Croll) has been carried out. Such scholars as Louis L. Martz and Joseph A. Mazzeo have reinterpreted seventeenth-century poetry in the light of the thought of the age, and many critics (among them Mario Praz, Austin Warren, and Frank J. Warnke) have attempted to place seventeenth-century English poetry more clearly in its perspective amid the other European literatures and the other arts.

Samuel Johnson
[1709–1784]

[THE METAPHYSICAL POETS][1]

WIT, like all other things subject by their nature to the choice of man, has its changes and fashions, and at different times takes different forms. About the beginning of the seventeenth century appeared a race of writers that may be termed the *metaphysical poets*, of whom, in a criticism on the works of Cowley, it is not improper to give some account.

[1] From "Abraham Cowley," *The Lives of the Poets,* 1779.

The metaphysical poets were men of learning, and to show their learning was their whole endeavor; but, unluckily resolving to show it in rhyme, instead of writing poetry they only wrote verses, and very often such verses as stood the trial of the finger better than of the ear; for the modulation was so imperfect, that they were only found to be verses by counting the syllables.

If the father of criticism[2] has rightly denominated poetry τέχνη μιμητική, *an imitative art*, these writers will, without great wrong, lose their right to the name of poets, for they cannot be said to have imitated anything; they neither copied nature for life, neither

[2] Aristotle.

painted the forms of matter, nor represented the operations of intellect.

Those, however, who deny them to be poets, allow them to be wits. Dryden confesses of himself and his contemporaries, that they fall below Donne in wit, but maintains that they surpass him in poetry.

If wit be well described by Pope, as being "that which has been often thought, but was never before so well expressed," they certainly never attained, nor ever sought it; for they endeavored to be singular in their thoughts, and were careless of their diction. But Pope's account of wit is undoubtedly erroneous: he depresses it below its natural dignity, and reduces it from strength of thought to happiness of language.

If by a more noble and more adequate conception that be considered as wit which is at once natural and new, that which, though not obvious, is, upon its first production, acknowledged to be just; if it be that which he that never found it wonders how he missed, to wit of this kind the metaphysical poets have seldom risen. Their thoughts are often new, but seldom natural; they are not obvious, but neither are they just; and the reader, far from wondering that he missed them, wonders more frequently by what perverseness of industry they were ever found.

But wit, abstracted from its effects upon the hearer, may be more rigorously and philosophically considered as a kind of *discordia concors;* a combination of dissimilar images, or discovery of occult resemblances in things apparently unlike. Of wit, thus defined, they have more than enough. The most heterogeneous ideas are yoked by violence together; nature and art are ransacked for illustrations, comparisons, and allusions; their learning instructs, and their subtlety surprises; but the reader commonly thinks his improvement dearly bought, and, though he sometimes admires, is seldom pleased.

From this account of their compositions it will be readily inferred that they were not successful in representing or moving the affections. As they were wholly employed on something unexpected and surprising, they had no regard to that uniformity of sentiment which enables us to conceive and to excite the pains and the pleasure of other minds: they never inquired what, on any occasion, they should have said or done, but wrote rather as beholders than partakers of human nature; as beings looking upon good and evil, impassive and at leisure; as Epicurean deities, making remarks on the actions of men, and the vicissitudes of life, without interest and without emotion. Their

courtship was void of fondness, and their lamentation of sorrow. Their wish was only to say what they hoped had been never said before.

Nor was the sublime more within their reach than the pathetic; for they never attempted that comprehension and expanse of thought which at once fills the whole mind, and of which the first effect is sudden astonishment, and the second rational admiration. Sublimity is produced by aggregation, and littleness by dispersion. Great thoughts are always general, and consist in positions not limited by exceptions, and in descriptions not descending to minuteness. It is with great propriety that subtlety, which in its original import means exility of particles, is taken in its metaphorical meaning for nicety of distinction. Those writers who lay on the watch for novelty could have little hope of greatness; for great things cannot have escaped former observation. Their attempts were always analytic; they broke every image into fragments; and could no more represent, by their slender conceits and labored particularities, the prospects of nature, or the scenes of life, than he who dissects a sunbeam with a prism can exhibit the wide effulgence of a summer noon.

What they wanted however of the sublime, they endeavored to supply by hyperbole; their amplification had no limits; they left not only reason but fancy behind them; and produced combinations of confused magnificence, that not only could not be credited, but could not be imagined.

Yet great labor, directed by great abilities, is never wholly lost: if they frequently threw away their wit upon false conceits, they likewise sometimes struck out unexpected truth; if their conceits were far-fetched, they were often worth the carriage. To write on their plan, it was at least necessary to read and think. No man could be born a metaphysical poet, nor assume the dignity of a writer, by descriptions copied from descriptions, by imitations borrowed from imitations, by traditional imagery, and hereditary similes, by readiness of rhyme, and volubility of syllables.

In perusing the works of this race of authors, the mind is exercised either by recollection or inquiry; either something already learned is to be retrieved, or something new is to be examined. If their greatness seldom elevates, their acuteness often surprises; if the imagination is not always gratified, at least the powers of reflection and comparison are employed; and in the mass of materials which ingenious absurdity has thrown together, genuine wit and useful knowledge may be sometimes found buried perhaps in grossness of expression, but useful to those who know their value; and such as, when they are expanded to perspicuity, and polished to elegance, may give luster to works which have more propriety though less copiousness of sentiment.

This kind of writing, which was, I believe, borrowed from Marino and his followers, had been recommended by the example of Donne, a man of a very extensive and various knowledge; and by Jonson, whose manner resembled that of Donne more in the ruggedness of his lines than in the cast of his sentiments.

When their reputation was high, they had undoubtedly more imitators than time has left behind. Their immediate successors, of whom any remembrance can be said to remain, were Suckling, Waller, Denham, Cowley, Cleveland, and Milton. Denham and Waller sought another way to fame, by improving the harmony of our numbers. Milton tried the metaphysic style only in his lines upon Hobson the Carrier. Cowley adopted it, and excelled his predecessors, having as much sentiment and more music. Suckling neither improved versification, nor abounded in conceits. The fashionable style remained chiefly with Cowley; Suckling could not reach it, and Milton disdained it.

Critical remarks are not easily understood without examples; and I have therefore collected instances of the modes of writing by which this species of poets, for poets they were called by themselves and their admirers, was eminently distinguished.

As the authors of this race were perhaps more desirous of being admired than understood, they sometimes drew their conceits from recesses of learning not very much frequented by common readers of poetry. Thus Cowley on *Knowledge*:

The sacred tree midst the fair orchard grew;
 The phœnix Truth did on it rest,
 And built his perfum'd nest,
That right Porphyrian tree which did true logic show.
 Each leaf did learned notions give,
 And th' apples were demonstrative:
So clear their color and divine,
The very shade they cast did other lights outshine.

On Anacreon continuing a lover in his old age:

 Love was with thy life entwin'd,
 Close as heat with fire is join'd,

 A powerful brand prescrib'd the date
 Of thine, like Meleager's fate,
 Th' antiperistasis of age
 More inflam'd thy amorous rage.
 Elegy upon Anacreon.

In the following verses we have an allusion to a Rabbinical opinion concerning Manna:

 Variety I ask not: give me one
 To live perpetually upon.
 The person Love does to us fit,
 Like manna, has the taste of all in it.

Thus Donne shows his medicinal knowledge in some encomiastic verses:

 In every thing there naturally grows
 A balsamum to keep it fresh and new,
 If 't were not injur'd by extrinsique blows;
 Your birth and beauty are this balm in you.
 But you, of learning and religion,
 And virtue, and such ingredients, have made
 A mithridate, whose operation
Keeps off, or cures what can be done or said.
 DONNE, *To the Countess of Bedford.*

Though the following lines of Donne, on the last night of the year, have something in them too scholastic, they are not inelegant:

This twilight of two years, not past nor next,
 Some emblem is of me, or I of this,
Who, meteor-like, of stuff and form perplext,
 Whose what and where in disputation is,
 If I should call me anything, should miss.
I sum the years and me, and find me not
 Debtor to th' old, nor creditor to th' new;
That cannot say, my thanks I have forgot,
 Nor trust I this with hopes; and yet scarce true
This bravery is, since these times show'd me you.
 DONNE, *To the Countess of Bedford.*

Yet more abstruse and profound is Donne's reflection upon man as a microcosm:

 If men be worlds, there is in every one
 Something to answer in some proportion
 All the world's riches: and in good men, this
 Virtue, our form's form, and our soul's soul is.

Of thoughts so far-fetched, as to be not only un-expected but unnatural, all their books are full.

To a Lady, who made posies for rings

They, who above do various circles find,
Say, like a ring th' equator heaven does bind.
When heaven shall be adorn'd by thee,
(Which then more heaven than 'tis, will be,)
'Tis thou must write the poesy there,
For it wanteth one as yet,
Though the sun pass through 't twice a year,
The sun, who is esteem'd the god of wit.
COWLEY.

The difficulties which have been raised about identity in philosophy, are by Cowley with still more perplexity applied to love:

Five years ago (says story) I lov'd you,
For which you call me most inconstant now:
Pardon me, madam, you mistake the man;
For I am not the same that I was then;
No flesh is now the same 'twas then in me,
And that my mind is chang'd yourself may see.
The same thoughts to retain still, and intents,
Were more inconstant far: for accidents
Must of all things most strangely inconstant prove,
If from one subject they t' another move:
My members then, the father members were
From whence these take their birth, which now are
    here.
If then this body love what th' other did,
'Twere incest, which by nature is forbid.
                                    Inconstancy.

The love of different women is, in geographical poetry, compared to travels through different countries:

Hast thou not found each woman's breast
    (The land where thou hast traveled)
Either by savages possest,
    Or wild, and uninhabited?
What joy could'st take, or what repose,
In countries so uncivilis'd as those?

        .   .   .   .   .   .

Lust, the scorching dog-star, here
    Rages with immoderate heat;
Whilst Pride, the rugged Northern Bear
    In others makes the cold too great.

And where these are temperate known,
The soil's all barren sand, or rocky stone.
                        COWLEY, *The Welcome.*

A lover, burnt up by his affection, is compared to Egypt:

        The fate of Egypt I sustain,
        And never feel the dew of rain
From clouds which in the head appear;
        But all my too much moisture owe
        To overflowings of the heart below.
                                COWLEY, *Sleep.*

The lover supposes his lady acquainted with the ancient laws of augury and rites of sacrifice:

        And yet this death of mine, I fear,
        Will ominous to her appear:
        When, sound in every other part,
        Her sacrifice is found without an heart.
        For the last tempest of my death
        Shall sigh out that too, with my breath.
                        COWLEY, *The Concealment.*

That the chaos was harmonised, has been recited of old; but whence the different sounds arose remained for a modern to discover:

Th' ungovern'd parts no correspondence knew;
An artless war from thwarting motions grew;
Till they to number and fixt rules were brought.
Water and air he for the tenor chose;
Earth made the base; the treble, flame arose.
                                        COWLEY.

The tears of lovers are always of great poetical account; but Donne has extended them into worlds. If the lines are not easily understood, they may be read again:
                    On a round ball
        A workman, that hath copies by, can lay
        An Europe, Afric, and an Asia,
And quickly make that, which was nothing, All.
        So doth each tear,
        Which thee doth wear,
A globe, yea would, by that impression grow.
Till thy tears mixt with mine do overflow
This world, by waters sent from thee my heaven
        dissolvèd so.
                        A Valediction of Weeping.

On reading the following lines, the reader may perhaps cry out—*Confusion worse confounded:*

> Here lies a she sun, and a he moon there,
>   She gives the best light to his sphere,
>   Or each is both, and all, and so
> They unto one another nothing owe.
>   DONNE, *Epithalamion on the Count Palatine, etc.*

Who but Donne would have thought that a good man is a telescope?

> Though God be our true glass through which we see
> All, since the being of all things is he,
> Yet are the trunks, which do to us derive
> Things in proportion fit, by perspective
> Deeds of good men; for by their living here,
> Virtues, indeed remote, seem to be near.

Who would imagine it possible that in a very few lines so many remote ideas could be brought together?

> Since 'tis my doom, Love's undershrieve,
>   Why this reprieve?
> Why doth my she advowson fly
>   Incumbency?
> To sell thyself dost thou intend
>   By candle's end,
> And hold the contrast thus in doubt,
>   Life's taper out?
> Think but how soon the market fails,
> Your sex lives faster than the males;
> And if to measure age's span,
> The sober Julian were th' account of man,
> Whilst you live by the fleet Gregorian.
>   CLEVELAND, *To Julia to expedite her Promise.*

Of enormous and disgusting hyperboles, these may be examples:

> By every wind that comes this way,
>   Send me at least a sigh or two,
> Such and so many I'll repay
> As shall themselves make winds to get to you.
>   COWLEY.

> In tears I'll waste these eyes,
>   By Love so vainly fed;
> So lust of old the Deluge punished.
>   COWLEY.

> All arm'd in brass, the richest dress of war,
> (A dismal glorious sight,) he shone afar.
> The sun himself started with sudden fright,
> To see his beams return so dismal bright.
>   COWLEY.

An universal consternation:

> His bloody eyes he hurls round, his sharp paws
> Tear up the ground; then runs he wild about,
> Lashing his angry tail and roaring out.
> Beasts creep into their dens, and tremble there:
> Trees, though no wind is stirring, shake with fear;
> Silence and horror fill the place around;
> Echo itself dares scarce repeat the sound.
>   COWLEY.

Their fictions were often violent and unnatural.

Of his Mistress bathing

> The fish around her crowded, as they do
> To the false light that treacherous fishes show,
> And all with as much ease might taken be,
>   As she at first took me:
>   For ne'er did light so clear
>   Among the waves appear,
> Though every night the sun himself set there.
>   COWLEY.

The poetical effect of a lover's name upon glass:

>   My name engrav'd herein
> Doth contribute my firmness to this glass;
>   Which, ever since that charm, hath been
>   As hard as that which grav'd it was.
> DONNE, *A Valediction of my Name in the Window.*

Their conceits were sentiments slight and trifling.

On an inconstant Woman

> He enjoys thy calmy sunshine now,
>   And no breath stirring hears,
> In the clear heaven of thy brow
>   No smallest cloud appears.
> He sees thee gentle, fair, and gay,
> And trusts the faithless April of thy May.
>   COWLEY, *in imitation of Horace.*

Upon a paper written with the juice of lemon, and read by the fire:

> So, nothing yet in thee is seen,
> But when a genial heat warms thee within,
> A new-born wood of various lines there grows;
>   Here buds an A, and there a B,
>   Here sprouts a V, and there a T,
> And all the flourishing letters stand in rows.
>   COWLEY.

As they sought only for novelty, they did not much inquire whether their allusions were to things high or low, elegant or gross; whether they compared the little to the great, or the great to the little.

Physics and Chirurgery for a Lover

> Gently, ah gently, madam, touch
>   The wound which you yourself have made;
> That pain must needs be very much,
>   Which makes me of your hand afraid.
> Cordials of pity give me now,
>   For I too weak for purgings grow.
>   COWLEY, *Counsel*.

The World and a Clock

> Mahol, th' inferior world's fantastic face
> Thro' all the turns of matter's maze did trace,
> Great Nature's well-set clock in pieces took;
> On all the springs and smallest wheels did look
> Of life and motion, and with equal art
> Made up again the whole of every part.
>   COWLEY, *Davideis*, book i.

A coal-pit has not often found its poet; but that it may not want its due honor, Cleveland has paralleled it with the sun:

> The moderate value of our guiltless ore
> Makes no man atheist, nor no woman whore;
> Yet why should hallow'd vestal's sacred shrine
> Deserve more honor than a flaming mine?
> These pregnant wombs of heat would fitter be,
> Than a few embers, for a deity.
> Had he our pits, the Persian would admire
> No sun, but warm 's devotion at our fire:
> He'd leave the trotting whipster, and prefer
> Our profound Vulcan 'bove that waggoner.
> For wants he heat, or light? or would have store,
> Of both? 'tis here: and what can suns give more?

> Nay, what's the sun but, in a different name,
> A coal-pit rampant, or a mine on flame?
> Then let this truth reciprocally run,
> The sun 's heaven's coalery, and coals our sun.
>   CLEVELAND, *News from Newcastle*.

Death, a Voyage

> No family
> E'er rigg'd a soul for heaven's discovery,
> With whom more venturers might boldly dare
> Venture their stakes, with him in joy to share.
>   DONNE.

Their thoughts and expressions were sometimes grossly absurd, and such as no figures or license can reconcile to the understanding.

A Lover neither dead nor alive

> Then down I laid my head,
> Down on cold earth; and for a while was dead,
> And my freed soul to a strange somewhere fled;
>   "Ah, sottish soul," said I,
>   When back to its cage again I saw it fly;
>   "Fool to resume her broken chain,
>   And row her galley here again!
>   Fool to that body to return
> Where it condemn'd and destin'd is to burn!
>   Once dead, how can it be,
> Death should a thing so pleasant seem to thee,
> That thou should'st come to live it o'er again in me?"
>   COWLEY, *The Despair*.

A Lover's Heart, a hand grenado

> Woe to her stubborn heart, if once mine come
>   Into the self-same room,
>   'Twill tear and blow up all within,
> Like a grenado shot into a magazine.
> Then shall Love keep the ashes, and torn parts,
>   Of both our broken hearts:
>   Shall out of both one new one make;
> From her's th' allay; from mine, the metal take.
>   COWLEY, *The Given Heart*.

The poetical propagation of light:

> The prince's favor is diffus'd o'er all,
> From which all fortunes, names, and natures fall;
> Then from those wombs of stars, the bride's bright
>   eyes,
>   At every glance a constellation flies

And sowes the court with stars, and doth prevent
　In light and power, the all-ey'd firmament:
First her eye kindles other ladies' eyes,
　Then from their beams their jewels lusters rise;
And from their jewels torches do take fire,
And all is warmth, and light, and good desire.

DONNE.

They were in very little care to clothe their notions with elegance of dress, and therefore miss the notice and the praise which are often gained by those who think less, but are more diligent to adorn their thoughts.

That a mistress beloved is fairer in idea than in reality, is by Cowley thus expressed:

Thou in my fancy dost much higher stand
Than women can be plac'd by Nature's hand;
And I must needs, I'm sure, a loser be,
To change thee, as thou'rt there, for very thee.

COWLEY, *Against Fruition.*

That prayer and labor should co-operate, are thus taught by Donne:

In none but us are such mixt engines found,
As hands of double office; for the ground
We till with them; and them to heaven we raise:
Who prayerless labors, or, without this, prays,
Doth but one half, that's none.

By the same author, a common topic, the danger of procrastination, is thus illustrated:

──────That which I should have begun
In my youth's morning, now late must be done;
And I, as giddy travelers must do,
Which stray or sleep all day, and having lost
Light and strength, dark and tir'd, must then ride
　post.

DONNE, *To M. B. B.*

All that man has to do is to live and die: the sum of humanity is comprehended by Donne in the following lines:

Think in how poor a prison thou didst lie;
After enabled but to suck and cry.
Think, when 'twas grown to most, 'twas a poor inn,
A province pack'd up in two yards of skin,

And that usurp'd, or threaten'd with a rage
Of sicknesses, or their true mother, age.
But think that death hath now enfranchis'd thee;
Thou hast thy expansion now, and liberty;
Think, that a rusty piece discharg'd is flown
In pieces, and the bullet is his own,
And freely flies: this to thy soul allow,
Think thy shell broke, think thy soul hatch'd but now.

DONNE, *The Progress of the Soul.*

They were sometimes indelicate and disgusting. Cowley thus apostrophises beauty:

──────Thou tyrant, which leav'st no man free!
Thou subtle thief, from whom nought safe can be!
Thou murtherer, which hast kill'd, and devil which
　　would'st damn me!

COWLEY, *Beauty.*

Thus he addresses his mistress:

Thou who, in many a propriety,
So truly art the sun to me,
Add one more likeness, which I'm sure you can,
And let me and my sun beget a man.

COWLEY, *The Parting.*

Thus he represents the meditations of a lover:

Though in thy thoughts scarce any tracts have been
So much as of original sin,
Such charms thy beauty wears as might
Desires in dying confest saints excite.
　Thou with strange adultery
Dost in each breast a brothel keep;
　Awake, all men do lust for thee,
And some enjoy thee when they sleep.

COWLEY.

The true Taste of Tears

Hither with crystal vials, lovers, come,
　And take my tears, which are love's wine,
And try your mistress' tears at home;
　For all are false, that taste not just like mine.

DONNE, *Twickenham Garden.*

This is yet more indelicate:

As the sweet sweat of roses in a still,
As that which from chaf'd musk-cat's pores doth trill,

As the almighty balm of th' early East;
Such are the sweat drops of my mistress' breast.
And on her neck her skin such luster sets,
They seem no sweat drops, but pearl coronets:
Rank, sweaty froth thy mistress' brow defiles.

DONNE, Elegie VIII.

Their expressions sometimes raise horror, when they intend perhaps to be pathetic:

> As men in hell are from diseases free,
>   So from all other ills am I,
>   Free from their known formality:
> But all pains eminently lie in thee.

COWLEY, The Usurpation.

They were not always strictly curious, whether the opinions from which they drew their illustrations were true; it was enough that they were popular. Bacon remarks, that some falsehoods are continued by tradition, because they supply commodious allusions.

> It gave a piteous groan, and so it broke:
> In vain it something would have spoke:
> The love within too strong for 't was,
> Like poison put into a Venice-glass.

COWLEY, The Heartbreaking.

In forming descriptions, they looked out, not for images, but for conceits. Night has been a common subject which poets have contended to adorn. Dryden's *Night* is well known; Donne's is as follows:

> Thou seest me here at midnight, now all rest:
> Time's dead low-water; when all minds divest
> To-morrow's business, when the laborers have
> Such rest in bed, that their last church-yard grave,
> Subject to change, will scarce be a type of this,
> Now when the client, whose last hearing is
> To-morrow, sleeps; when the condemned man,
> Who, when he opes his eyes, must shut them then
> Again by death, although sad watch he keep,
> Doth practice dying by a little sleep,
> Thou at this midnight seest me.

It must be however confessed of these writers, that if they are upon common subjects often unnecessarily and unpoetically subtle, yet where scholastic speculation can be properly admitted, their copiousness and acuteness may justly be admired. What Cowley has written upon Hope shows an unequaled fertility of invention:

> Hope, whose weak being ruin'd is,
> Alike if it succeed, and if it miss;
> Whom good or ill does equally confound,
> And both the horns of Fate's dilemma wound;
>   Vain shadow! which dost vanquish quite,
>   Both at full noon and perfect night!
>   The stars have not a possibility
>   Of blessing thee;
> If things then from their end we happy call,
> 'Tis Hope is the most hopeless thing of all.
>   Hope, thou bold taster of delight,
>   Who, whilst thou should'st but taste, devour'st it
>   quite!
> Thou bring'st us an estate, yet leav'st us poor,
> By clogging it with legacies before!
> The joys which we entire should wed,
> Come deflower'd virgins to our bed;
> Good fortunes without gain imported be,
>   Such mighty custom's paid to thee:
> For joy, like wine kept close, does better taste,
> If it take air before its spirits waste.

COWLEY, Against Hope.

To the following comparison of a man that travels, and his wife that stays at home, with a pair of compasses, it may be doubted whether absurdity or ingenuity has the better claim:

> Our two souls therefore, which are one,
>   Though I must go, endure not yet
> A breach, but an expansion,
>   Like gold to airy thinness beat.
> If they be two, they are two so
>   As stiff twin-compasses are two;
> Thy soul the fixt foot, makes no show
>   To move, but doth, if th' other do.
> And though it in the center sit,
>   Yet, when the other far doth roam,
> It leans, and hearkens after it,
>   And grows erect, as that comes home.
> Such wilt thou be to me, who must
>   Like th' other foot obliquely run.
> Thy firmness makes my circle just,
>   And makes me end, where I begun.

DONNE, A Valediction forbidding Mourning.

In all these examples it is apparent, that whatever is improper or vicious is produced by a voluntary deviation from nature in pursuit of something new and strange; and that the writers fail to give delight, by their desire of exciting admiration.

T. S. Eliot

THE METAPHYSICAL POETS

BY COLLECTING these poems[1] from the work of a generation more often named than read, and more often read than profitably studied, Professor Grierson has rendered a service of some importance. Certainly the reader will meet with many poems already preserved in other anthologies, at the same time that he discovers poems such as those of Aurelian Townshend or Lord Herbert of Cherbury here included. But the function of such an anthology as this is neither that of Professor Saintsbury's admirable edition of Caroline poets nor that of the *Oxford Book of English Verse*. Mr. Grierson's book is in itself a piece of criticism and a provocation of criticism; and we think that he was right in including so many poems of Donne, elsewhere (though not in many editions) accessible, as documents in the case of "metaphysical poetry." The phrase has long done duty as a term of abuse or as the label of a quaint and pleasant taste. The question is to what extent the so-called metaphysicals formed a school (in our own time we should say a "movement"), and how far this so called school or movement is a digression from the main current.

Not only is it extremely difficult to define metaphysical poetry, but difficult to decide what poets practice it and in which of their verses. The poetry of Donne (to whom Marvell and Bishop King are sometimes nearer than any of the other authors) is late Elizabethan, its feeling often very close to that of Chapman. The "courtly" poetry is derivative from Jonson, who borrowed liberally from the Latin; it expires in the next century with the sentiment and witticism of Prior. There is finally the devotional verse of Herbert, Vaughan, and Crashaw (echoed long after by Christina Rossetti and Francis Thompson); Crashaw, sometimes more profound and less sectarian

[1] *Metaphysical Lyrics and Poems of the Seventeenth Century: Donne to Butler.* Selected and edited, with an Essay, by Herbert J. C. Grierson (Oxford: Clarendon Press. London: Milford).

than the others, has a quality which returns through the Elizabethan period to the early Italians. It is difficult to find any precise use of metaphor, simile, or other conceit, which is common to all the poets and at the same time important enough as an element of style to isolate these poets as a group. Donne, and often Cowley, employ a device which is sometimes considered characteristically "metaphysical"; the elaboration (contrasted with the condensation) of a figure of speech to the farthest stage to which ingenuity can carry it. Thus Cowley develops the commonplace comparison of the world to a chess-board through long stanzas (*To Destiny*), and Donne, with more grace, in *A Valediction*, the comparison of two lovers to a pair of compasses. But elsewhere we find, instead of the mere explication of the content of a comparison, a development by rapid association of thought which requires considerable agility on the part of the reader.

> On a round ball
> A workman that hath copies by, can lay
> An Europe, Afrique, and an Asia,
> And quickly make that, which was nothing, All,
> So doth each teare,
> Which thee doth weare,
> A globe, yea, world by that impression grow,
> Till thy tears mixt with mine doe overflow
> This world, by waters sent from thee, my heaven
> dissolved so.

Here we find at least two connections which are not implicit in the first figure, but are forced upon it by the poet: from the geographer's globe to the tear, and the tear to the deluge. On the other hand, some of Donne's most successful and characteristic effects are secured by brief words and sudden contrasts:

> A bracelet of bright hair about the bone,

where the most powerful effect is produced by the sudden contrast of associations of "bright hair" and of "bone." This telescoping of images and multiplied associations is characteristic of the phrase of some of the dramatists of the period which Donne knew: not to mention Shakespeare, it is frequent in Middleton, Webster, and Tourneur, and is one of the sources of the vitality of their language.

Johnson, who employed the term "metaphysical poets," apparently having Donne, Cleveland, and Cowley chiefly in mind, remarks of them that "the most heterogeneous ideas are yoked by violence together." The force of this impeachment lies in the failure of the conjunction, the fact that often the ideas are yoked but not united; and if we are to judge of styles of poetry by their abuse, enough examples may be found in Cleveland to justify Johnson's condemnation. But a degree of heterogeneity of material compelled into unity by the operation of the poet's mind is omnipresent in poetry. We need not select for illustration such a line as:

Notre âme est un trois-mâts cherchant son Icarie;

we may find it in some of the best lines of Johnson himself (*The Vanity of Human Wishes*):

His fate was destined to a barren strand,
A petty fortress, and a dubious hand;
He left a name at which the world grew pale,
To point a moral, or adorn a tale.

where the effect is due to a contrast of ideas, different in degree but the same in principle, as that which Johnson mildly reprehended. And in one of the finest poems of the age (a poem which could not have been written in any other age), the *Exequy* of Bishop King, the extended comparison is used with perfect success: the idea and the simile become one, in the passage in which the Bishop illustrates his impatience to see his dead wife, under the figure of a journey:

Stay for me there; I will not faile
To meet thee in that hollow Vale.
And think not much of my delay;
I am already on the way,
And follow thee with all the speed
Desire can make, or sorrows breed.
Each minute is a short degree,
And ev'ry houre a step towards thee.
At night when I betake to rest,
Next morn I rise nearer my West
Of life, almost by eight houres sail,
Than when sleep breath'd his drowsy gale. . . .
But heark! My Pulse, like a soft Drum
Beats my approach, tells *Thee* I come;
And slow howere my marches be,
I shall at last sit down by *Thee*.

(In the last few lines there is that effect of terror which is several times attained by one of Bishop King's admirers, Edgar Poe.) Again, we may justly take these quatrains from Lord Herbert's Ode, stanzas which

would, we think, be immediately pronounced to be of the metaphysical school:

So when from hence we shall be gone,
And be no more, nor you, nor I,
As one another's mystery,
Each shall be both, yet both but one.

This said, in her up-lifted face,
Her eyes, which did that beauty crown,
Were like two starrs, that having faln down,
Look up again to find their place:

While such a moveless silent peace
Did seize on their becalmed sense,
One would have thought some influence
Their ravished spirits did possess.

There is nothing in these lines (with the possible exception of the stars, a simile not at once grasped, but lovely and justified) which fits Johnson's general observations on the metaphysical poets in his essay on Cowley. A good deal resides in the richness of association which is at the same time borrowed from and given to the word "becalmed"; but the meaning is clear, the language simple and elegant. It is to be observed that the language of these poets is as a rule simple and pure; in the verse of George Herbert this simplicity is carried as far as it can go—a simplicity emulated without success by numerous modern poets. The *structure* of the sentences, on the other hand, is sometimes far from simple, but this is not a vice; it is a fidelity to thought and feeling. The effect, at its best, is far less artificial than that of an ode by Gray. And as this fidelity induces variety of thought and feeling, so it induces variety of music. We doubt whether, in the eighteenth century, could be found two poems in nominally the same meter, so dissimilar as Marvell's *Coy Mistress* and Crashaw's *Saint Teresa;* the one producing an effect of great speed by the use of short syllables, and the other an ecclesiastical solemnity by the use of long ones:

Love, thou art absolute sole lord
Of life and death.

If so shrewd and sensitive (though so limited) a critic as Johnson failed to define metaphysical poetry by its faults, it is worth while to inquire whether we may not have more success by adopting the opposite method: by assuming that the poets of the seventeenth century (up to the Revolution) were the direct and normal development of the precedent age; and, without prejudicing their case by the adjective "metaphysical," consider whether their virtue was not something permanently valuable, which subsequently disappeared, but ought not to have disappeared. Johnson has hit, perhaps by accident, on one of their peculiarities, when he observes that "their attempts were always analytic"; he would not agree that, after the dissociation, they put the material together again in a new unity.

It is certain that the dramatic verse of the later Elizabethan and early Jacobean poets expresses a degree of development of sensibility which is not found in any of the prose, good as it often is. If we except Marlowe, a man of prodigious intelligence, these dramatists were directly or indirectly (it is at least a tenable theory) affected by Montaigne. Even if we except also Jonson and Chapman, these two were notably erudite, and were notably men who incorporated their erudition into their sensibility: their mode of feeling was directly and freshly altered by their reading and thought. In Chapman especially there is a direct sensuous apprehension of thought, or a recreation of thought into feeling, which is exactly what we find in Donne:

> in this one thing, all the discipline
> Of manners and of manhood is contained;
> A man to join himself with th' Universe
> In his main sway, and make in all things fit
> One with that All, and go on, round as it;
> Not plucking from the whole his wretched part,
> And into straits, or into nought revert,
> Wishing the complete Universe might be
> Subject to such a rag of it as he;
> But to consider great Necessity.

We compare this with some modern passage:

> No, when the fight begins within himself,
> A man's worth something. God stoops o'er his head,
> Satan looks up between his feet—both tug—
> He's left, himself, i' the middle; the soul wakes
> And grows. Prolong that battle through his life!

It is perhaps somewhat less fair, though very tempting (as both poets are concerned with the perpetuation of love by offspring), to compare with the stanzas already quoted from Lord Herbert's Ode the following from Tennyson:

> One walked between his wife and child,
> With measured footfall firm and mild,
> And now and then he gravely smiled.
>   The prudent partner of his blood
>   Leaned on him, faithful, gentle, good,
>   Wearing the rose of womanhood.
> And in their double love secure,
> The little maiden walked demure,
> Pacing with downward eyelids pure.
>   These three made unity so sweet,
>   My frozen heart began to beat,
>   Remembering its ancient heat.

The difference is not a simple difference of degree between poets. It is something which had happened to the mind of England between the time of Donne or Lord Herbert of Cherbury and the time of Tennyson and Browning; it is the difference between the intellectual poet and the reflective poet. Tennyson and Browning are poets, and they think; but they do not feel their thought as immediately as the odor of a rose. A thought to Donne was an experience; it modified his sensibility. When a poet's mind is perfectly equipped for its work, it is constantly amalgamating disparate experience; the ordinary man's experience is chaotic, irregular, fragmentary. The latter falls in love, or reads Spinoza, and these two experiences have nothing to do with each other, or with the noise of the typewriter or the smell of cooking; in the mind of the poet these experiences are always forming new wholes.

We may express the difference by the following theory: The poets of the seventeenth century, the successors of the dramatists of the sixteenth, possessed a mechanism of sensibility which could devour any kind of experience. They are simple, artificial, difficult, or fantastic, as their predecessors were; no less nor more than Dante, Guido Cavalcanti, Guinizelli, or Cino. In the seventeenth century a dissociation of sensibility set in, from which we have never recovered; and this dissociation, as is natural, was aggravated by the influence of the two most powerful poets of the century, Milton and Dryden. Each of these men performed certain poetic functions so magnificently well that the magnitude of the effect concealed the absence of others. The language went on and in some respects improved; the best verse of Collins, Gray, Johnson, and even Goldsmith satisfies some of our fastidious demands better than that of Donne or Marvell or King. But while the language became more refined, the feeling became more crude. The feeling, the sensibility, expressed in the *Country Churchyard* (to say nothing of Tennyson and Browning) is cruder than that in the *Coy Mistress*.

The second effect of the influence of Milton and Dryden followed from the first, and was therefore slow in manifestation. The sentimental age began early in the eighteenth century, and continued. The poets revolted against the ratiocinative, the descriptive; they thought and felt by fits, unbalanced; they reflected. In one or two passages of Shelley's *Triumph of Life*, in the second *Hyperion*, there are traces of a struggle toward unification of sensibility. But Keats and Shelley died, and Tennyson and Browning ruminated.

After this brief exposition of a theory—too brief, perhaps, to carry conviction—we may ask, what would have been the fate of the "metaphysical" had the current of poetry descended in a direct line from them, as it descended in a direct line to them? They would not, certainly, be classified as metaphysical. The possible interests of a poet are unlimited; the more intelligent he is the better; the more intelligent he is the more likely that he will have interests: our only condition is that he turn them into poetry, and not merely meditate on them poetically. A philosophical theory which has entered into poetry is established, for its truth or falsity in one sense ceases to matter, and its truth in another sense is proved. The poets in question have, like other poets, various faults. But they were, at best, engaged in the task of trying to find the verbal equivalent for states of mind and feeling. And this means both that they are more mature, and that they wear better, than later poets of certainly not less literary ability.

It is not a permanent necessity that poets should be interested in philosophy, or in any other subject. We can only say that it appears likely that poets in our civilization, as it exists at present, must be *difficult*. Our civilization comprehends great variety and complexity, and this variety and complexity, playing upon a refined sensibility, must produce various and complex results. The poet must become more and more comprehensive, more allusive, more indirect, in order to force, to dislocate if necessary, language into his meaning. (A brilliant and extreme statement of this view, with which it is not requisite to associate oneself, is that of M. Jean Epstein, *La Poésie d'aujourd-hui*.)

Hence we get something which looks very much like the conceit—we get, in fact, a method curiously similar to that of the "metaphysical poets," similar also in its use of obscure words and of simple phrasing.

> O géraniums diaphanes, guerroyeurs sortilèges,
> Sacrilèges monomanes !
> Emballages, dévergondages, douches ! O pressoirs
> Des vendanges des grands soirs !
> Layettes aux abois,
> Thyrses au fond des bois !
> Transfusions, représailles,
> Relevailles, compresses et l'éternal potion,
> Angélus ! n'en pouvoir plus
> De débâcles nuptiales ! de débâcles nuptiales !

The same poet could write also simply:

> Elle est bien loin, elle pleure,
> Le grand vent se lamente aussi . . .

Jules Laforgue, and Tristan Corbière in many of his poems, are nearer to the "school of Donne" than any modern English poet. But poets more classical than they have the same essential quality of transmuting ideas into sensations, of transforming an observation into a state of mind.

> Pour l'enfant, amoureux de cartes et d'estampes,
> L'univers est égal à son vaste appétit.
> Ah, que le monde est grand à la clarté des lampes !
> Aux yeux du souvenir que le monde est petit !

In French literature the great master of the seventeenth century—Racine—and the great master of the nineteenth—Baudelaire—are in some ways more like each other than they are like any one else. The greatest two masters of diction are also the greatest two psychologists, the most curious explorers of the soul. It is interesting to speculate whether it is not a misfortune that two of the greatest masters of diction in our language, Milton and Dryden, triumph with a dazzling disregard of the soul. If we continued to produce Miltons and Drydens it might not so much matter, but as things are it is a pity that English poetry has remained so incomplete. Those who object to the "artificiality" of Milton or Dryden sometimes tell us to "look into our hearts and write." But that is not looking deep enough; Racine or Donne looked into a good deal more than the heart. One must look into the cerebral cortex, the nervous system, and the digestive tracts.

May we not conclude, then, that Donne, Crashaw, Vaughan, Herbert and Lord Herbert, Marvell, King, Cowley at his best, are in the direct current of English poetry, and that their faults should be reprimanded by this standard rather than coddled by antiquarian affection? They have been enough praised in terms which are implicit limitations because they are "metaphysical" or "witty," "quaint" or "obscure," though at their best they have not these attributes more than other serious poets. On the other hand, we must not reject the criticism of Johnson (a dangerous person to disagree with) without having mastered it, without having assimilated the Johnsonian canons of taste. In reading the celebrated passage in his essay on Cowley we must remember that by wit he clearly means something more serious than we usually mean today; in his criticism of their versification we must remember in what a narrow discipline he was trained, but also how well trained; we must remember that Johnson tortures chiefly the chief offenders, Cowley and Cleveland. It would be a fruitful work, and one requiring a substantial book, to break up the classification of Johnson (for there has been none since) and exhibit these poets in all their difference of kind and of degree, from the massive music of Donne to the faint, pleasing tinkle of Aurelian Townshend—whose *Dialogue between a Pilgrim and Time* is one of the few regrettable omissions from the excellent anthology of Professor Grierson.

Morris W. Croll

THE BAROQUE STYLE IN PROSE

I. INTRODUCTION

IN THE latter years of the sixteenth century a change declared itself in the purposes and forms of the arts of Western Europe for which it is hard to find a satisfactory name. One would like to describe it, because of some interesting parallels with a later movement, as the first modern manifestation of the Romantic Spirit; and it did, in fact, arise out of a revolt against the classicism of the high Renaissance. But the terms "romantic" and "classical" are both perplexing and unphilosophical; and their use should not be extended.

It would be much clearer and more exact to describe the change in question as a radical effort to adapt traditional modes and forms of expression to the uses of a self-conscious modernism; and the style that it produced was actually called in several of the arts— notably in architecture and prose-writing—the "modern" or "new" style. But the term that most conveniently describes it is "baroque." This term, which was at first used only in architecture, has lately been extended to cover the facts that present themselves at the same time in sculpture and in painting; and it may now properly be used to describe, or at least to name, the characteristic modes of expression in all the arts during a certain period—the period, that is, between the high Renaissance and the eighteenth century; a period that begins in the last quarter of the sixteenth century, reaches a culmination at about 1630, and thenceforward gradually modifies its character under new influences.

Expressiveness rather than formal beauty was the pretension of the new movement, as it is of every movement that calls itself modern. It disdained complacency, suavity, copiousness, emptiness, ease, and in avoiding these qualities sometimes obtained effects of contortion or obscurity, which it was not always willing to regard as faults. It preferred the forms that express the energy and labor of minds seeking the truth, not without dust and heat, to the forms that express a contented sense of the enjoyment and possession of it. In a single word, the motions of souls, not their states of rest, had become the themes of art.

The meaning of these antitheses may be easily illustrated in the history of Venetian painting, which passes, in a period not longer than one generation, from the self-contained and relatively symmetrical designs of Titian, through the swirls of Tintoretto, to the contorted and aspiring lines that make the paintings of El Greco so restless and exciting. Poetry moves in the same way at about the same time; and we could metaphorically apply the terms by which we distinguish El Greco from Titian to the contrast between the rhythms of Spenser and the Petrarcans, on one hand, and the rhythms of Donne, on the other, between the style of Ariosto and the style of Tasso. In the sculptures of Bernini (in his portrait busts as well as in his more famous and theatrical compositions) we may again observe how ideas of motion take the place of ideas of rest; and the operation of this principle is constantly to be observed also in the school of architecture associated with the same artist's name. "In the façade of a Baroque church," says Geoffrey Scott, "a movement, which in the midst of a Bramantesque design would be destructive and repugnant, is turned to account and made the basis of a more dramatic, but not less satisfying treatment, the motive of which is not peace, but energy." [1]

And finally the change that takes place in the prose style of the same period—the change, that is, from Ciceronian to anti-Ciceronian forms and ideas—is exactly parallel with those that were occurring in the other arts, and is perhaps more useful to the student of the baroque impulse than any of the others, because it was more self-conscious, more definitely theorized by its leaders, and more clearly described by its friends and foes. In some previous studies I have considered the triumph of the anti-Ciceronian movement at considerable length; but I have been concerned chiefly with the theory of the new style; and my critics have complained, justly, that I have been too difficult, or even abstract. In the present study I hope to correct this defect. Its purpose is to describe the *form* of anti-Ciceronian, or baroque, prose.

There are of course several elements of prose technique: diction, or the choice of words; the choice of figures; the principle of balance or rhythm; the form of the period, or sentence; and in a full description of baroque prose all of these elements would have to be considered. The last-mentioned of them—the form of the period—is, however, the most important and the determinant of the others; and this alone is to be the subject of discussion in the following pages.

The anti-Ciceronian period was sometimes described in the seventeenth century as an "exploded" period; and this metaphor is very apt if it is taken as describing solely its outward appearance, the mere fact of its form. For example, here is a period from Sir Henry Wotton, a typical expression of the political craft of the age:

Men must beware of running down steep places with weighty bodies; they once in motion, *suo feruntur pondere;* steps are not then voluntary.

The members of this period stand farther apart one from another than they would in a Ciceronian sentence; there are no syntactic connectives between them whatever; and semicolons or colons are necessary to its proper punctuation. In fact, it has the appearance of having been disrupted by an explosion within.

[1] *The Architecture of Humanism*, p. 225.

The metaphor would be false, however, if it should be taken as describing the manner in which this form has been arrived at. For it would mean that the writer first shaped a round and complete oratorical period in his mind and then partly undid his work. And this, of course, does not happen. Wotton gave this passage its form, not by demolishing a Ciceronian period, but by omitting several of the steps by which roundness and smoothness of composition might have been attained. He has deliberately avoided the processes of mental revision in order to express his idea when it is nearer the point of its origin in his mind.

We must stop for a moment on the word *deliberately*. The negligence of the anti-Ciceronian masters, their disdain of revision, their dependence upon casual and emergent devices of construction, might sometimes be mistaken for mere indifference to art or contempt of form; and it is, in fact, true that Montaigne and Burton, even Pascal and Browne, are sometimes led by a dislike of formality into too licentious a freedom. Yet even their extravagances are purposive, and express a creed that is at the same time philosophical and artistic. Their purpose was to portray, not a thought, but a mind thinking, or, in Pascal's words, *la peinture de la pensée*. They knew that an idea separated from the act of experiencing it is not the idea that was experienced. The ardor of its conception in the mind is a necessary part of its truth; and unless it can be conveyed to another mind in something of the form of its occurrence, either it has changed into some other idea or it has ceased to be an idea, to have any existence whatever except a verbal one. It was the latter fate that happened to it, they believed, in the Ciceronian periods of sixteenth-century Latin rhetoricians. The successive processes of revision to which these periods had been submitted had removed them from reality by just so many steps. For themselves, they preferred to present the truth of experience in a less concocted form, and deliberately chose as the moment of expression that in which the idea first clearly objectifies itself in the mind, in which, therefore, each of its parts still preserves its own peculiar emphasis and an independent vigor of its own—in brief, the moment in which truth is still *imagined*.

The form of a prose period conceived in such a theory of style will differ in every feature from that of the conventional period of an oratorical, or Ciceronian, style; but its most conspicuous difference will appear in the way it connects its members or clauses one with another. In the period quoted above from Wotton the members are syntactically wholly free; there are no ligatures whatever between one and another. But there is another type of anti-Ciceronian period, in which the ordinary marks of logical succession—conjunctions, pronouns, etc.—are usually present, but are of such a kind or are used in such a way as to bind the members together in a characteristically loose and casual manner. The difference between the two types thus described may seem somewhat unimportant; and it is true that they run into each other and cannot always be sharply distinguished. The most representative anti-Ciceronians, like Montaigne and Browne, use them both and intermingle them. But at their extremes they are not only distinguishable; they serve to distinguish different types, or schools, of seventeenth-century style. They derive from different models, belong to different traditions, and sometimes define the philosophical affiliations of the authors who prefer them.

They will be considered here separately; the first we will call, by a well-known seventeenth-century name, the *période coupé*, or, in an English equivalent, the "curt period" (so also the *stile coupé*, or the "curt style"); the other by the name of the "loose period" (and the "loose style"); though several other appropriate titles suggest themselves in each case.[2]

II. STILE COUPÉ

I

ONE example of the *période coupé* has already been given. Here are others:[3]

Pour moy, qui ne demande qu'à devenir plus sage, non plus sçavant ou éloquent, ces ordonnances logiciennes et aristoteliques ne sont pas à propos; je veulx qu'on commence par le dernier poinct: j'entends assez que c'est que Mort et Volupté; qu'on ne s'amuse pas à les anatomizer.—MONTAIGNE, II, 10, "Des Livres."

'Tis not worth the reading, I yield it, I desire thee not to lose time in perusing so vain a subject, I should peradventure be loth myself to read him or thee so writing; 'tis not *operae pretium*.—BURTON, *Anatomy of Melancholy*, "To the Reader."

2 For example, the *stile coupé* was sometimes called *stile serré* ("serried style"), and Francis Thompson has used this term in describing a kind of period common in Browne. For synonyms of "loose style" see a succeeding section of this paper [p. 1071].

3 The punctuation in all cases is that of editions which profess to follow in this respect good seventeenth-century editions or manuscripts.

No armor can defend a fearful heart. It will kill itself within.—FELLTHAM, *Resolves*, "Of Fear and Cowardice."

Mais il faut parier; cela n'est pas volontaire; vous êtes embarqués.—PASCAL, *Pensées*, Article II.

L'éloquence continue ennuie.

Les princes et les rois jouent quelquefois. Ils ne sont pas toujours sur leurs trônes; ils s'y ennuient: la grandeur a besoin d'être quittée pour être sentie.—PASCAL, *Pensées*, "Sur l'Éloquence."

The world that I regard is myself; it is the microcosm of my own frame that I cast mine eye on: for the other, I use it but like my globe, and turn it round sometimes for my recreation.—BROWNE, *Religio Medici*, II, 11.

Il y a des hommes qui attendent a être dévots et religieux que tout le monde se déclare impie et libertin: ce sera alors le parti du vulgaire; ils sauront s'en dégager. —LA BRUYÈRE, *Des Esprits Forts*.

In all of these passages, as in the period quoted from Wotton, there are no two main members that are syntactically connected. But it is apparent also that the characteristic style that they have in common contains several other features besides this.

In the first place, each member is as short as the most alert intelligence would have it. The period consists, as some of its admirers were wont to say, of the nerves and muscles of speech alone; it is as hard-bitten, as free of soft or superfluous flesh, as "one of Caesar's soldiers."[4]

Second, there is a characteristic order, or mode of progression, in a curt period that may be regarded either as a necessary consequence of its omission of connectives or as the causes and explanation of this. We may describe it best by observing that the first member is likely to be a self-contained and complete statement of the whole idea of the period. It is so because writers in this style like to avoid prearrangements and preparations; they begin, as Montaigne puts it, at *le dernier poinct*, the point aimed at. The first member therefore exhausts the mere fact of the idea; logically there is nothing more to say. But it does not exhaust its imaginative truth or the energy of its conception. It is followed, therefore, by other members, each with a new tone or emphasis, each expressing a new apprehension of the truth expressed in the first.

4 The phrase comes from a midseventeenth-century work on prose style (*Precetti*, repr. Milan, 1822) by Daniello Bartoli, and is there applied to *il dir moderno*.

We may describe the progress of a curt period, therefore, as a series of imaginative moments occurring in a logical pause or suspension. Or—to be less obscure—we may compare it with successive flashes of a jewel or prism as it is turned about on its axis and takes the light in different ways.

It is true, of course, that in a series of propositions there will always be some logical process; the truth stated will undergo some development or change. For example, in the sentence from Montaigne on page 1067, the later members add something to the idea; and in the quotation from Pascal's *Pensées sur l'Éloquence*, on the same page, the thought suddenly enlarges in the final member. Yet the method of advance is not logical; the form does not express it. Each member, in its main intention, is a separate act of imaginative realization.

In the third place, one of the characteristics of the curt style is deliberate asymmetry of the members of a period; and it is this trait that especially betrays the modernistic character of the style. The chief mark of a conventional, or "classical," art, like that of the sixteenth century, is an approximation to evenness in the size and form of the balanced parts of a design; the mark of a modernistic art, like that of the seventeenth, and the nineteenth and twentieth, centuries, is the desire to achieve an effect of balance or rhythm among parts that are obviously not alike—the love of "some strangeness in the proportions."

In a prose style asymmetry may be produced by varying the length of the members within a period. For example, part of the effect of a sentence from Bishop Hall is due to a variation in this respect among members which nevertheless produce the effect of balance or rhythmic design.

What if they [crosses and adversities] be unpleasant? They are physic; it is enough if they be wholesome.[5]— HALL, *Heaven upon Earth*, XIII.

But the desired effect is more characteristically produced by conspicuous differences of form, either with or without differences of length. For instance, a characteristic method of the seventeenth century was to begin a succession of members with different kinds of subject-words. In the sentence from Wotton (page 1066) the first two members have personal subjects, the third the impersonal "steps"; in the following from Pascal the opposite change is made.

Mais il faut parier; cela n'est pas volontaire; vous êtes embarqués.

In both of these periods, moreover, each of the three members has a distinct and individual turn of phrase, meant to be different from the others. Again, in the period of La Bruyère quoted on page 1067 each new member involves a shift of the mind to a new subject. (Observe also the asymmetry of the members in point of length.)

Sometimes, again, asymmetry is produced by a change from literal to metaphoric statement, or by the reverse, or by a change from one metaphor to another, as in the last example quoted from Pascal, where the metaphor of one embarked upon a ship abruptly takes the place of that of a man engaged in a bet. Or there may be a leap from the concrete to the abstract form; and this is an eminently characteristic feature of the *stile coupé* because this style is always tending toward the aphorism, or *pensée*, as its ideal form. The second passage quoted from Pascal on page 1067 illustrates this in a striking way. It is evident that in the first three members—all concrete, about kings and princes—the author's mind is turning toward a general truth, which emerges complete and abstract in the last member: *La grandeur a besoin d'être quittée pour être sentie.*

The curt style, then, is not characterized only by the trait from which it takes its name, its omission of connectives. It has the four marks that have been described: first, studied brevity of members; second, the hovering, imaginative order; third, asymmetry; and fourth, the omission of the ordinary syntactic ligatures. None of these should, of course, be thought of separately from the others. Each of them is related to the rest and more or less involves them; and when they are all taken together they constitute a definite rhetoric, which was employed during the period from 1575 to 1675 with as clear a knowledge of its tradition and its proper models as the sixteenth-century Ciceronians had of the history of the rhetoric that they preferred.

In brief, it is a Senecan style; and, although the imitation of Seneca never quite shook off the imputation of literary heresy that had been put upon it by the Augustan purism of the preceding age, and certain

---

5 Note how exactly this reproduces a movement characteristic of Seneca: "Quid tua, uter [Caesar or Pompey] vincat? Potest melior vincere: non potest non pejor esse qui vicerit."

amusing cautions and reservations were therefore felt to be necessary, yet nearly all of the theorists of the new style succeeding in expressing their devotion to their real master in one way or another. Moreover, they were well aware that the characteristic traits of Seneca's style were not his alone, but had been elaborated before him in the Stoic schools of the Hellenistic period; and all the earlier practitioners of the *stile coupé*, Montaigne (in his first phase), Lipsius, Hall, Charron, etc., write not only as literary Senecans, but rather more as philosophical Stoics.

Senecanism and Stoicism are, then, the primary implications of *stile coupé*. It must be observed, however, that a style once established in general use may cast away the associations in which it originated; and this is what happened in the history of the curt style. Montaigne, for instance, confessed that he had so thoroughly learned Seneca's way of writing that he could not wholly change it even when his ideas and tastes had changed and he had come to prefer other masters. And the same thing is to be observed in many writers of the latter part of the century: St. Evrémond, Halifax, and La Bruyère, for instance. Though these writers are all definitely anti-Stoic and anti-Senecan, all of them show that they had learned the curt style too well ever to unlearn it or to avoid its characteristic forms; and there was no great exaggeration in Shaftesbury's complaint, at the very end of the century, that no other movement of style than Seneca's—what he calls the "Senecan amble"—had been heard in prose for a hundred years past.

2

The curt or serried style depends for its full effect upon the union of the several formal traits that have been described in the preceding section. We have assumed hitherto that these traits are as rigorous and unalterable as if they were prescribed by a rule; and in the examples cited there have been no significant departures from any of them. But of course slight variations are common even in passages that produce the effect of *stile coupé;* and some searching is necessary to discover examples as pure as those that have been cited. This is so evidently true that it would need no illustration except for the fact that certain kinds of period eminently characteristic of seventeenth-century prose arise from a partial violation of the "rules" laid down. Two of these may be briefly described.

a) In a number of writers (Browne, Felltham, and South, for example) we often find a period of two members connected by *and, or,* or *nor,* which evidently has the character of *stile coupé* because the conjunction has no logical *plus* force whatever. It merely connects two efforts of the imagination to realize the same idea; two as-it-were synchronous statements of it. The following from Browne will be recognized as characteristic of him:

'Tis true, there is an edge in all firm belief, and with an easy metaphor we may say the sword of faith.— *Religio Medici,* I, 10.

Again:

Therefore I perceive a man may be twice a child before the days of dotage; and stand in need of Aeson's bath before threescore.—*Ibid.,* I, 42.

Often, too, in a period consisting of a larger number of members the last two are connected by an *and* or the like. But this case can be illustrated in connection with the one that immediately follows.

b) The rule that the successive members of a *période coupé* are of different and often opposed forms, are asymmetrical instead of symmetrical, is sometimes partly violated inasmuch as these members begin with the same word or form of words, for example, with the same pronoun-subject, symmetry, parallelism, and some regularity of rhythm thus introducing themselves into a style that is designed primarily and chiefly to express a dislike of these frivolities. It is to be observed, however, that the members that begin with this suggestion of oratorical pattern usually break it in the words that follow. Except for their beginnings they are as asymmetrical as we expect them to be, and reveal that constant novelty and unexpectedness that is so characteristic of the "baroque" in all the arts.

One illustration is to be found in the style of the "character" writings that enjoyed so great a popularity in the seventeenth century. The frequent recurrence of the same subject-word, usually *he* or *they,* is the mannerism of this style, and is sometimes carried over into other kinds of prose in the latter part of the century, as, for instance, in writings of La Bruyère that are not included within the limits of the character genre,[6] and in passages of Dryden. It is indeed so conspicuous a mannerism that it may serve to conceal what is after all the more significant feature of the

6 For instance, in the famous passage "De l'Homme" describing the beastlike life of the peasants of France.

"character" style, namely, the constant variation and contrast of form in members that begin in this formulistic manner.

The style of the "character," however, is that of a highly specialized genre; and the form of the period with reiterated introductory formula can be shown in its more typical character in other kinds of prose, as, for example, in a passage from Browne describing the Christian Stoicism of his age:

Let not the twelve but the two tables be thy law: let Pythagoras be thy remembrancer, not thy textuary and final instructor: and learn the vanity of the world rather from Solomon than Phocylides.[7]—*Christian Morals,* p. xxi.

Browne touches lightly on these repetitions, and uses them not too frequently. Balzac[8] uses them characteristically and significantly. A paragraph from his *Entretiens* (No. XVIII, "De Montaigne et de ses Escrits") may be quoted both in illustration of this fact and for the interest of its subject matter:

Nous demeurasmes d'accord que l'Autheur qui veut imiter Seneque commence par tout et finit par tout. Son Discours n'est pas un corps entier: c'est un corps en pieces; ce sont des membres couppez; et quoy que les parties soient proches les unes des autres, elles ne laissent pas d'estre separées. Non seulement il n'y a point de nerfs qui les joignent; il n'y a pas mesme de cordes ou d'aiguillettes qui les attachent ensemble: tant cet Autheur est ennemy de toutes sortes de liaisons, soit de la Nature, soit de l'Art: tant il s'esloigne de ces bons exemples que vous imitez si parfaitement.

The passage illustrates exactly Balzac's position in the prose development of the seventeenth century. Montaigne is indeed—in spite of his strictures upon him—his master. He aims, like Montaigne, at the philosophic ease and naturalness of the *genus humile;* he has his taste for aphorism, his taste for metaphor; he is full of "points," and loves to make them show; in short, he is "baroque." But by several means, and chiefly by the kinds of repetition illustrated in this passage (*c'est . . . ce sont; il n'a point . . . il n'y a pas mesme; tant . . . tant*), he succeeds in introducing that effect of art, of form, of rhythm, for which Descartes

and so many other of his contemporaries admired him. He combines in short the "wit" of the seventeenth century with at least the appearance of being "a regular writer," which came, in the forties and fifties, to be regarded in France as highly desirable. In his political writings, and especially in *Le Prince*, his iterated opening formula becomes too evident a mannerism, and on page after page one reads periods of the same form: two or three members beginning alike and a final member much longer and more elaborate than the preceding that may or may not begin in the same way. The effect is extremely rhetorical.

3

Finally, we have to observe that the typical *période coupé* need not be so short as the examples of it cited at the beginning of the present section. On the contrary, it may continue, without connectives and with all its highly accentuated peculiarities of form, to the length of five or six members. Seneca offered many models for this protracted aphoristic manner, as in the following passage from the *Naturales Quæstiones* (vii. 31):

There are mysteries that are not unveiled the first day: Eleusis keepeth back something for those who come again to ask her. Nature telleth not all her secrets at once. We think we have been initiated: we are still waiting in her vestibule. Those secret treasures do not lie open promiscuously to every one: they are kept close and reserved in an inner shrine.

Similar in form is this six-member period from Browne's *Religio Medici* (I, 7):

To see ourselves again we need not look for Plato's year: every man is not only himself; there have been many Diogeneses, and as many Timons, though but few of that name; men are lived over again; the world is now as it was in ages past; there was none then but there hath been some one since that parallels him, and is, as it were, his revived self.[9]

What has been said in a previous section of the characteristic mode of progression in *stile coupé* is

---

7 The period occurs in the midst of a paragraph in which each main member of each period begins with a verb in the imperative mood.

8 Jean Louis Guez de Balzac (1597?–1654). [Editors.]

9 Felltham uses this manner with too much self-consciousness. See, for instance, a passage on the terse style (*Resolves*, I, 20) beginning: "They that speak to Children assume a pretty lisping."

strikingly illustrated in such passages as these. Logically they do not move. At the end they are saying exactly what they were at the beginning. Their advance is wholly in the direction of a more vivid imaginative realization: a metaphor revolves, as it were, displaying its different facets; a series of metaphors flash their lights; or a chain of "points" and paradoxes reveals the energy of a single apprehension in the writer's mind. In the latter part of the seventeenth century a number of critics satirize this peculiarity of the Senecan form. Father Bouhours, for instance, observed that with all its pretensions to brevity and significance this style makes less progress in five or six successive statements than a Ciceronian period will often make in one long and comprehensive construction. The criticism is, of course, sound if the only mode of progression is the logical one; but in fact there is a progress of imaginative apprehension, a revolving and upward motion of the mind as it rises in energy, and views the same point from new levels; and this spiral movement is characteristic of baroque prose.

III. THE LOOSE STYLE

1

IN THE preceding pages we have been illustrating a kind of period in which the members are in most cases syntactically disjunct, and we have seen that in this style the members are characteristically short. It is necessary now to illustrate the other type of anti-Ciceronian style spoken of at the beginning, in which the members are usually connected by syntactic ligatures, and in which, therefore, both the members and the period as a whole may be, and in fact usually are, as long as in the Ciceronian style, or even longer.

It is more difficult to find an appropriate name for this kind of style than for the other. The "trailing" or "linked" style would describe a relation between the members of the period that is frequent and indeed characteristic, but is perhaps too specific a name. "Libertine" indicates exactly both the form of the style and the philosophical associations that it often implies; but it is wiser to avoid these implications in a purely descriptive treatment. There is but one term that is exact and covers the ground: the term "loose period" or "loose style"; and it is this that we will usually employ. In applying this term, however, the reader must be on his guard against a use of it that slipped into many rhetorical treatises of the nineteenth century. In these works the "loose sentence" was defined as one that has its main clause near the beginning;

and an antithetical term "periodic sentence"—an improper one—was devised to name the opposite arrangement. "Loose period" is used here without reference to this confusing distinction.

In order to show its meaning we must proceed by means of examples; and we will take first a sentence—if, indeed, we can call it a sentence—in which Bacon contrasts the "Magistral" method of writing works of learning with the method of "Probation" appropriate to "induced knowledge," "the latter whereof [he says] seemeth to be *via deserta et interclusa.*"

> For as knowledges are now delivered, there is a kind of contract of error between the deliverer and the receiver: for he that delivereth knowledge desireth to deliver it in such form as may be best believed, and not as may be best examined; and he that receiveth knowledge desireth rather present satisfaction than expectant inquiry; and so rather not to doubt than not to err: glory making the author not to lay open his weakness, and sloth making the disciple not to know his strength. —*Advancement of Learning*, Book I.

The passage is fortunate because it states the philosophy in which anti-Ciceronian prose has its origin and motive. But our present business is with its form; and in order to illustrate this we will place beside it another passage from another author.

> Elle [l'Imagination] ne peut rendre sages les fous; mais elle les rend heureux à l'envi de la raison, qui ne peut rendre ses amis que miserables, l'une les couvrant de gloire, l'autre de honte.[10]—PASCAL, *Pensées*, "L'Imagination."

There is a striking similarity in the way these two periods proceed. In each case an antithesis is stated in the opening members; then the member in which the second part of the antithesis is stated puts out a dependent member. The symmetrical development announced at the beginning is thus interrupted and cannot be resumed. The period must find a way out, a syntactic way of carrying on and completing the idea it carries. In both cases the situation is met in the same way, by a concluding member having the form of an absolute-participle construction, in which the antithetical idea of the whole is sharply, aphoristically resumed.

---

10 There should, rhetorically speaking, be semicolons, not commas, after *raison* and *miserables*.

The two passages, in short, are written as if they were meant to illustrate in style what Bacon calls "the method of induced knowledge"; either they have no predetermined plan or they violate it at will; their progression adapts itself to the movements of a mind discovering truth as it goes, thinking while it writes. At the same time, and for the same reason, they illustrate the character of the style that we call "baroque." See, for instance, how symmetry is first made and then broken, as it is in so many baroque designs in painting and architecture; how there is constant swift adaptation of form to the emergencies that arise in an nergetic and unpremeditated forward movement; and observe, further, that these signs of spontaneity and improvisation occur in passages loaded with as heavy a content as rhetoric ever has to carry. That is to say, they combine the effect of great mass with the effect of rapid motion; and there is no better formula than this to describe the ideal of the baroque design in all the arts.

But these generalizations are beyond our present purpose. We are to study the loose period first, as we did the curt period, by observing the character of its syntactic links. In the two sentences quoted there are, with a single exception, but two modes of connection employed. The first is by co-ordinating conjunctions, the conjunctions, that is, that allow the mind to move straight on from the point it has reached. They do not necessarily refer back to any particular point in the preceding member; nor do they commit the following member to a predetermined form. In other words, they are the loose conjunctions, and disjoin the members they join as widely as possible. *And*, *but*, and *for* are the ones employed in the two sentences; and these are of course the necessary and universal ones. Other favorites of the loose style are *whereas*, *nor* (= *and not*), and the correlatives *though* . . . . *yet*, *as* . . . . *so*. Second, each of the two periods contains a member with an absolute-participle construction. In the loose style many members have this form, and not only (as in the two periods quoted) at the ends of periods, but elsewhere. Sir Thomas Browne often has them early in a period, as some passages to be cited in another connection will show. This is a phenomenon easily explained. For the absolute construction is the one that commits itself least and lends itself best to the solution of difficulties that arise in the course of a spontaneous and unpremeditated progress. It may state either a cause, or a consequence, or a mere attendant circumstance; it may be concessive or justificatory; it may be

a summary of the preceding or a supplement to it; it may express an idea related to the whole of the period in which it occurs, or one related only to the last preceding member.

The co-ordinating conjunctions and the absolute-participle construction indicate, then, the character of the loose period. Like the *stile coupé*, it is meant to portray the natural, or thinking, order; and it expresses even better than the curt period the anti-Ciceronian prejudice against formality of procedure and the rhetoric of the schools. For the omission of connectives in the *stile coupé* implies, as we have seen, a very definite kind of rhetorical form, which was practiced in direct imitation of classical models, and usually retained the associations that it had won in the Stoic schools of antiquity. The associations of the loose style, on the other hand, are all with the more skeptical phases of seventeenth-century thought—with what was then usually called "Libertinism"; and it appears characteristically in writers who are professed opponents of determined and rigorous philosophic attitudes. It is the style of Bacon and of Montaigne (after he has found himself), of La Mothe le Vayer, and of Sir Thomas Browne. It appears always in the letters of Donne; it appears in Pascal's *Pensées;* and, in the latter part of the century, when Libertinism had positively won the favor of the world away from Stoicism, it enjoyed a self-conscious revival, under the influence of Montaigne, in the writings of St. Évremond, Halifax, and Temple. Indeed, it is evident that, although the Senecan *stile coupé* attracted more critical attention throughout the century, its greatest achievements in prose were rather in the loose or Libertine manner. But it must also be said that most of the skeptics of the century had undergone a strong Senecan influence; and the styles of Montaigne, Browne, Pascal, and Halifax, for instance, can only be described as displaying in varying ways a mingling of Stoic and Libertine traits.

2

Besides the two syntactic forms that have been mentioned—the co-ordinating conjunctions and the absolute construction—there are no others that lend themselves by their nature to the loose style, except the parenthesis, which we need not illustrate here. But it must not be supposed that it tends to exclude other modes of connection. On the contrary, it obtains its characteristic effects from the syntactic forms that are logically more strict and binding, such as the relative pronouns and the subordinating conjunctions, by using them in a way peculiar to itself. That is to say, it uses them as the necessary logical means of advancing the idea, but relaxes at will the tight construction which they seem to impose; so that they have exactly the same effect as the loose connections previously described and must be punctuated in the same way. In other words, the parts that they connect are no more closely knit together than it chooses they shall be; and the reader of the most characteristic seventeenth-century prose soon learns to give a greater independence and autonomy to subordinate members than he would dare to do in reading any other.

The method may be shown by a single long sentence from Sir Thomas Browne:

I could never perceive any rational consequence from those many texts which prohibit the children of Israel to pollute themselves with the temples of the heathens; we being all Christians, and not divided by such detested impieties *as* might profane our prayers, or the place wherein we make them; *or that* a resolved conscience may not adore her Creator anywhere, *especially* in places devoted to his service; *where,* if their devotions offend him, mine may please him; if theirs profane it, mine may hallow it.[11]—*Religio Medici,* I, 3.

The period begins with a statement complete in itself, which does not syntactically imply anything to follow it; an absolute participle carries on, in the second member. Thereafter the connectives are chiefly subordinating conjunctions. Observe particularly the use of *as, or that,* and *where:* how slight these ligatures are in view of the length and mass of the members they must carry. They are frail and small hinges for the weights that turn on them; and the period abounds and expands in nonchalant disregard of their tight, frail logic.

This example displays the principle; but of course a single passage can illustrate only a few grammatical forms. Some of those used with a characteristic looseness in English prose of the seventeenth century are: relative clauses beginning with *which,* or with *whereto, wherein,* etc.; participial constructions of the kind scornfully called "dangling" by the grammarians; words in a merely appositional relation with some noun or pronoun preceding, yet constituting a semi-independent member of a period; and of course such

subordinating conjunctions as are illustrated above. It is unnecessary to illustrate these various cases.

3

The connections of a period cannot be considered separately from the order of the connected members; and, in fact, it is the desired order of development that determines the character of the connections rather than the reverse. In the oratorical period the arrangement of the members is "round" or "circular," in the sense that they are all so placed with reference to a central or climactic member that they point forward or back to it and give it its appropriate emphasis. This order is what is meant by the names *periodos, circuitus,* and "round composition," by which the oratorical period has been variously called; and it is the chief object of the many revisions to which its form is submitted.

The loose period does not try for this form, but rather seeks to avoid it. Its purpose is to express, as far as may be, the order in which an idea presents itself when it is first experienced. It begins, therefore, without premeditation, stating its idea in the first form that occurs; the second member is determined by the situation in which the mind finds itself after the first has been spoken; and so on throughout the period, each member being an emergency of the situation. The period—in theory, at least—is not made; it becomes. It completes itself and takes on form in the course of the motion of mind which it expresses. Montaigne, in short, exactly described the theory of the loose style when he said: "J'ecris volontiers sans project; le premier trait produit le second."

The figure of a circle, therefore, is not a possible description of the form of a loose period; it requires rather the metaphor of a chain, whose links join end to end. The "linked" or "trailing" period is, in fact, as we have observed, an appropriate name for it. But there is a special case for which this term might better be reserved, unless we should choose to invent a more specific one, such as "end-linking," or "terminal linking," to describe it. It is when a member depends, not upon the general idea, or the main word, of the preceding member, but upon its final word or phrase alone. And this is, in fact, a frequent, even a characteristic, kind of linking in certain authors, notably Sir Thomas Browne and his imitators. The sentence last quoted offers two or three illustrations of it: the connective words *as, especially,* and *where* all refer to the immediately preceding words or phrases; and in

---

11 Italics are mine.

another period by the same author there is one very conspicuous and characteristic instance.

As there were many reformers, so likewise many reformations; every country proceeding in a particular way and method, according as their national interest, together with their constitution and clime, inclined them: some angrily and with extremity; others calmly and with mediocrity, not rending, but easily dividing, the community, and leaving an honest possibility of a reconciliation;—*which* though peaceable spirits do desire, and may conceive that revolution of time and the mercies of God may effect, yet that judgment that shall consider the present antipathies between the two extremes,—their contrarities in condition, affection, and opinion,—may with the same hopes expect a union in the poles of heaven.—*Religio Medici*, I, 4.

Here the word *which* introduces a new development of the idea, running to as much as five lines of print; yet syntactically it refers only to the last preceding word *reconciliation*. The whole long passage has been quoted, however, not for this reason alone, but because it illustrates so perfectly all that has been said of the order and connection of the loose period. It begins, characteristically, with a sharply formulated complete statement, implying nothing of what is to follow. Its next move is achieved by means of an absolute-participle construction.[12] This buds off a couple of appositional members; one of these budding again two new members by means of dangling participles. Then a *which* picks up the trail, and at once the sentence becomes involved in the complex, and apparently tight, organization of a *though . . . . yet* construction. Nevertheless it still moves freely, digressing as it will, extricates itself from the complex form by a kind of *anacoluthon* (in the *yet* clause), broadening its scope, and gathering new confluents, till it ends, like a river, in an opening view.

The period, that is, moves straight onward everywhere from the point it has reached; and its construction shows ideally what we mean by the linked or trailing order. It is Browne's peculiar mastery of this construction that gives his writing constantly the effect of being, not the result of a meditation, but an actual meditation in process. He writes like a philosophical scientist making notes of his observation as it occurs. We see his pen move and stop as he thinks. To write thus, and at the same time to create beauty of cadence

12 Observe that the period from Browne quoted on p. 1070 begins with movements of the same kind.

in the phrases and rhythm in the design—and so Browne constantly does—is to achieve a triumph in what Montaigne called "the art of being natural"; it is the eloquence, described by Pascal, that mocks at formal eloquence.

4

The period just quoted serves to introduce a final point concerning the form of the loose period. We have already observed that the second half of this period, beginning with *which*, has a complex suspended syntax apparently like that of the typical oratorical sentence. The anti-Ciceronian writer usually avoids such forms, it is true; most of his sentences are punctuated by colons and semicolons. But, of course, he will often find himself involved in a suspended construction from which he cannot escape. It remains to show that even in these cases he still proceeds in the anti-Ciceronian manner, and succeeds in following, in spite of the syntactic formalities to which he commits himself, his own emergent and experimental order. Indeed, it is to be observed that the characteristic quality of the loose style may appear more clearly in such difficult forms than in others. For baroque art always displays itself best when it works in heavy masses and resistant materials; and out of the struggle between a fixed pattern and an energetic forward movement often arrives at those strong and expressive disproportions in which it delights.

We shall return to Browne in a moment in illustration of the point, but we shall take up a simpler case first. In a well-known sentence, Pascal, bringing out the force of imagination, draws a picture of a venerable magistrate seated in church, ready to listen to a worthy sermon. *Le voilà prêt à l'ouir avec un respect exemplaire.*

Que le prédicateur vienne a paraître: si la nature lui a donné une voix enrouée et un tour de visage bizarre, que son barbier l'ait mal rasé, si le hasard l'a encore barbouillé de surcroît, quelque grandes vérités qu'il annonce, je parie la perte de la gravité de notre sénateur.

Unquestionably a faulty sentence by all the school-rules! It begins without foreseeing its end, and has to shift the reader's glance from the preacher to the magistrate in the midst of its progress by whatever means it can. Observe the abruptness of the form of the member *quelques grandes vérités*. Observe the sudden appearance of the first person in the last member. Yet the critic who would condemn its rhetorical form would have also to declare that there is no art in those vivid dramatic narratives that so often appear in the conversation of animated talkers; for this period moves in an order very common in such conversation.[13]

In this passage the free and anti-Ciceronian character of the movement is chiefly due to its dramatic vividness and speed. It follows the order of life. Sometimes, however, we can see plainly that it is the mystical speculation of the seventeenth century that changes the regular form of the period and shapes it to its own ends. Sir Thomas Browne provides many interesting illustrations, as, for instance, in the period quoted in the preceding section, and in the following:

I would gladly know how Moses, with an actual fire, calcined or burnt the golden calf into powder: for that mystical metal of gold, whose solary and celestial nature I admire, exposed unto the violence of fire, grows only hot, and liquefies, but consumeth not; so when the consumable and volatile pieces of our bodies shall be refined into a more impregnable and fixed temper, like gold, though they suffer from the action of flames, they shall never perish, but lie immortal in the arms of fire. —*Religio Medici*, I, 50.

With the first half of this long construction we are not now concerned. In its second half, however, beginning with *so when*, we see one of those complex movements that have led some critics to speak of Browne as—of all things!—a Ciceronian. It is in fact the opposite of that. A Ciceronian period closes in at the end; it reaches its height of expansion and emphasis at the middle or just beyond, and ends composedly. Browne's sentence, on the contrary, opens constantly outward; its motions become more animated and vigorous as it proceeds; and it ends, as his sentences are likely to do, in a vision of vast space or time, losing itself in an *altitudo*, a hint of infinity. As, in a previously quoted period, everything led up to the phrase, "a union in the poles of heaven," so in this everything leads up to the concluding phrase, "but lie immortal in the arms of fire." And as we study the form of the structure we can even observe where this ending re-

vealed itself, or, at least, how it was prepared. The phrase "like gold" is the key to the form of the whole. After a slow expository member, this phrase, so strikingly wrenched from its logical position, breaks the established and expected rhythm, and is a signal of more agitated movement, of an ascending effort of imaginative realization that continues to the end. In a different medium, the period closely parallels the technique of an El Greco composition, where broken and tortuous lines in the body of the design prepare the eye for curves that leap upward beyond the limits of the canvas.

The forms that the loose period may assume are infinite, and it would be merely pedantic to attempt a classification of them. In one of the passages quoted we have seen the dramatic sense of reality triumphing over rhetorical formalism; in another, the form of a mystical exaltation. For the purpose of description— not classification—it will be convenient to observe still a third way in which a loose period may escape from the formal commitments of elaborate syntax. It is illustrated in a passage in Montaigne's essay "Des Livres" (II, 10), praising the simple and uncritical kind of history that he likes so much. In the course of the period he mentions *le bon Froissard* as an example, and proceeds so far (six lines of print) in a description of his method that he cannot get back to his general idea by means of his original syntactic form, or at least cannot do so without very artificial devices. He completes the sentence where it is; but completes his idea in a pair of curt (*coupés*) sentences separated by a colon from the preceding: "C'est la matière de l'histoire nue et informe; chascun en peult faire son proufit autant qu'il a d'entendement." This is a method often used by anti-Ciceronians to extricate themselves from the coils of a situation in which they have become involved by following the "natural" order. A better example of it is to be seen in a passage from Pascal's essay on "Imagination," from which another passage has already been cited.

Le plus grand philosophe du monde, sur une planche plus large qu'il ne faut, s'il y a au-dessous un précipice, quoique sa raison le convainque de sa sureté, son imagination prévaudra. Plusieurs n'en sauroient soutenir la pensée sans pâlir et suer.—*Pensées*, "L'Imagination."

Nothing could better illustrate the "order of nature"; writing, that is, in the exact order in which the matter presents itself. It begins by naming the

---

13 It may be said that Pascal's *Pensées* should not be cited in illustration of prose form because they were written without revision and without thought of publication. But a good deal of characteristic prose of the time was so written; and the effect at which Bacon, Burton, Browne, and many others aimed was of prose written in that way.

subject, *le plus grand philosophe*, without foreseeing the syntax by which it is to continue. Then it throws in the elements of the situation, using any syntax that suggests itself at the moment, proceeding with perfect dramatic sequence, but wholly without logical sequence, until at last the sentence has lost touch with its stated subject. Accordingly, this subject is merely left hanging, and a new one, *son imagination*, takes its place. It is a violent, or rather a nonchalant, *anacoluthon*. The sentence has then, after a fashion, completed itself. But there is an uneasy feeling in the mind. After all, *le plus grand philosophe* has done nothing; both form and idea are incomplete. Pascal adds another member (for, whatever the punctuation, the *plusieurs* sentence is a member of the period), which completely meets the situation, though a grammatical purist may well object that the antecedent of *plusieurs* was in the singular number.

Pascal is usually spoken of as a "classical" writer; but the term means nothing as applied to him except that he is a writer of tried artistic soundness. He is, in fact, as modernistic, as bold a breaker of the rules and forms of rhetoric, as his master Montaigne, though he is also a much more careful artist. *La vraie éloquence*, he said, *se moque de l'éloquence*.

5

Two kinds of style have been analyzed in the preceding pages: the concise, serried, abrupt *stile coupé*, and the informal, meditative, and "natural" loose style. It is necessary to repeat—once more—that in the best writers these two styles do not appear separately in passages of any length, and that in most of them they intermingle in relations far too complex for description. They represent two sides of the seventeenth-century mind: its sententiousness, its penetrating wit, its Stoic intensity, on the one hand, and its dislike of formalism, its roving and self-exploring curiosity, in brief, its skeptical tendency, on the other. And these two habits of mind are generally not separated one from the other; nor are they even always exactly distinguishable. Indeed, as they begin to separate or to be opposed to each other in the second half of the century we are aware of the approach of a new age and a new spirit. The seventeenth century, as we are here considering it, is equally and at once Stoic and Libertine; and the prose that is most characteristic of it expresses these two sides of its mind in easy and natural relations one with the other.

IV. THE PUNCTUATION OF THE SEVENTEENTH-CENTURY PERIOD

THE "long sentence" of the anti-Ciceronian age has received a remarkable amount of attention ever since it began to be corrected and go out of use; and there have been two conflicting views concerning it. The older doctrine—not yet quite extinct—was that the long sentences of Montaigne, Bacon, Browne, and Taylor were sentences of the same kind as those of Cicero and his sixteenth-century imitators; only they were badly and crudely made, monstrosities due to some wave of ignorance that submerged the syntactic area of the seventeenth-century mind. Their true character, it was thought, would be shown by substituting commas for their semicolons and colons; for then we should see that they are quaint failures in the attempt to achieve sentence-unity.

The other view is the opposite of this, namely, that we should put periods in the place of many of its semicolons and colons. We should then see that what look like long sentences are really brief and aphoristic ones. The contemporary punctuation of our authors is again to be corrected, but now in a different sense. This is the view urged by Faguet in writing of Montaigne, and by Sir Edmund Gosse concerning the prose of Browne and Taylor.

This later view is useful in correcting some of the errors of the earlier one. But, in fact, one of them is just as false as the other; and both of them illustrate the difficulties experienced by minds trained solely in the logical and grammatical aspects of language in interpreting the forms of style that prevailed before the eighteenth century. In order to understand the punctuation of the seventeenth century we have to consider the relation between the grammatical term *sentence* and the rhetorical term *period*.

The things named by these terms are identical. *Period* names the rhetorical, or oral, aspect of the same thing that is called in grammar a *sentence;* and in theory the same act of composition that produces a perfectly logical grammatical unit would produce at the same time a perfectly rhythmical pattern of sound. But, in fact, no utterance ever fulfills both of these functions perfectly, and either one or the other of them is always foremost in a writer's mind. One or the other is foremost also in every theory of literary education; and the historian may sometimes distinguish literary periods by the relative emphasis they put upon grammatical and rhetorical considerations. In general we may say, though there may be exceptions, that before the eighteenth century rhetoric occupied much more attention than grammar in the minds of teachers and their pupils. It was so, for instance, in the Middle Ages, as is clear from their manuals of study and the curricula of their schools. It was still true in the sixteenth century; and the most striking characteristic of the literary prose of that century, both in Latin and in the vernacular tongues, was its devotion to the conventional and formal patterns of school-rhetoric.

The laws of grammatical form, it is true, were not at all disturbed or strained at this time by the predominance of rhetorical motives. There was no difficulty whatever in saying what these rhetoricians had to say in perfect accordance with logical syntax because they had, in fact, so little to say that only the most elementary syntax was necessary for its purposes. Furthermore, the rhetorical forms they liked were so symmetrical, so obvious, that they almost imposed a regular syntax by their own form.

But a new situation arose when the leaders of seventeenth-century rationalism—Lipsius, Montaigne, Bacon—became the teachers of style. The ambition of these writers was to conduct an experimental investigation of the moral realities of their time, and to achieve a style appropriate to the expression of their discoveries and of the mental effort by which they were conducted. The content of style became, as it were, suddenly greater and more difficult; and the stylistic formalities of the preceding age were unable to bear the burden. An immense rhetorical complexity and license took the place of the simplicity and purism of the sixteenth century; and, since the age had not yet learned to think much about grammatical propriety, the rules of syntax were made to bear the expenses of the new freedom. In the examples of seventeenth-century prose that have been discussed in the preceding pages some of the results are apparent. The syntactic connections of a sentence become loose and casual; great strains are imposed upon tenuous, frail links; parentheses are abused; digression becomes licentious; *anacoluthon* is frequent and passes unnoticed; even the limits of sentences are not clearly marked, and it is sometimes difficult to say where one begins and another ends.

Evidently the process of disintegration could not go on forever. A stylistic reform was inevitable, and it must take the direction of a new formalism or "correctness." The direction that it actually took was determined by the Cartesian philosophy, or at least by

the same time-spirit in which the Cartesian philosophy had its origin. The intellect, that is to say, became the arbiter of form, the dictator of artistic practice as of philosophical inquiry. The sources of error, in the view of the Cartesians, are imagination and dependence upon sense-impressions. Its correctives are found in what they call "reason" (which here means "intellect"), and an exact distinction of categories.

To this mode of thought we are to trace almost all the features of modern literary education and criticism, or at least of what we should have called modern a generation ago: the study of the precise meaning of words; the reference to dictionaries as literary authorities; the study of the sentence as a logical unit alone; the careful circumscription of its limits and the gradual reduction of its length; the disappearance of semicolons and colons; the attempt to reduce grammar to an exact science; the idea that forms of speech are always either correct or incorrect; the complete subjection of the laws of motion and expression in style to the laws of logic and standardization—in short, the triumph, during two centuries, of grammatical over rhetorical ideas.

This is not the place to consider what we have gained or lost by this literary philosophy, or whether the precision we have aimed at has compensated us for the powers of expression and the flexibility of motion that we have lost; we have only to say that we must not apply the ideas we have learned from it to the explanation of seventeenth-century style. In brief, we must not measure the customs of the age of semicolons and colons by the customs of the age of commas and periods. The only possible punctuation of seventeenth-century prose is that which it used itself. We might sometimes reveal its grammar more clearly by repunctuating it with commas or periods, but we should certainly destroy its rhetoric.

Austin Warren

BAROQUE ART AND THE EMBLEM

TRIDENTINE Catholicism found graphic and plastic embodiment in the painting of Correggio, Murillo, El Greco, Rembrandt, Rubens, Guido Reni, and the Carracci, in the sculptures of Bernini, in the emblem books of the Jesuits and Benedictines; it transformed Rome into a city of magnificent churches, where the *Seicento* still lingers.

Here, in this pictorial world, will be found, urged with sensual power, all the themes which compelled the baroque imagination: angels and cherubs, the Infant Jesus, the shepherds and kings doing homage to the Nativity, the Circumcision, the crucified Saviour from whose wounds flow water and blood, the Sacred Heart, the Pietà, *quem transivit gladius*, the Assumption of the *Mater Dei*, the weeping Magdalen, the ecstatic Teresa, the Holy Innocents, the ripe men of martyrdom, the mystics receiving the stigmata or swooning in trances or carried into the seventh heaven, hearing the music of the angels, and, finally, the Day of Judgment when this miraculous globe dissolves into ashes and the trumpet of doom, *mirum spargens sonum*, calls the souls to final separation.[1]

In the painting of the Counter-Reformation, under the close surveillance of theologians, who assigned the artists their subjects, and, in considerable measure, prescribed the treatment,[2] lie incarnate the religious life of the age, its attitudes and its themes. Everywhere in Italian churches one sees depicted the new devotions—the angels, who float rosily among the clouds of Jesuit frescoes; the Holy Family; St. Joseph; the Infant Jesus, devotion particularly dear to the cloister. Traditional themes assume untraditional treatment. The uncovering of the Catacombs and the missionary deaths in India, South America, and Protestant Europe magnified the cult of martyrdom; but, whereas, in the Middle Ages, the martyrs had been depicted triumphant of countenance, they were now represented writhing in the agony of torture or enduring ingeniously cruel death; they struggle before our eyes, roasting in flames or streaming with blood.[3] Under the influence of Bernini, whose statue of Alexander VII was immediately felt to be a master work, the

skeleton became a familiar equipage of mortuary monuments, while the tense and sometimes agitated effigies of the dead seem remote from the serene sleep with which the thirteenth century endowed them.[4] The saints, ordinarily visualized by medieval art in the performance of miracles, now appear as recipients of miraculous grace; and the composure of their faces and figures, the tranquil amenity of Raphael's Virgins, has yielded to the physically contorted pattern of the trance or the rapture.[5] The contraventions of law and reason which Protestantism sought to minimize are everywhere selected for celebration. Common sense and sober judgment, the "wisdom of this world," are flagrantly violated; and prudence is made to seem a paltry thing in comparison to the extremes, often united, of pain and ecstasy.

The baroque style is exuberant, rhetorical, sensual, grandiose. The repose and symmetry of Renaissance art have yielded to agitation, aspiration, ambition, an intense striving to transcend the limits of each genre. Sculpture and architecture would elicit the effects of painting; painting—weary of exact draftsmanship, clearly outlined masses, grouping within the plane, and the architectural fitting of the design to the square or circle of the canvas—would move upward or backward, would anticipate the agility of the cinema, would flow, would disappear into modulated glooms or dissolve into luminosity. In architecture, all is splendor and surprise: polychrome marble, gold coffering, life-size and untranquil statues, ceilings frescoed so as to open the basilican horizontal into a firmament of floating angels, ingenious perspectives, façades designed not to reveal the construction but to be, in themselves, impressive.[6]

The baroque was the Catholic counterstatement to the reformer's attacks on the wealth of the Church and her use of painting and sculpture. Uncommitted to any single style in architecture or the fine arts, the Church found in the baroque appeal to the senses a mode compatible with her tradition.

Protestant and Catholic attitudes towards the arts differ significantly. The one will have no "graven images" of the supernatural; probably Hebrew in its origin, it reappears in Mohammedanism, in iconoclastic movements, in Calvinism; for it, the senses are

1 My characterization of baroque art is based chiefly upon three masterly books: Mâle's *L'Art Religieux après le Concile de Trente;* G. Scott's *The Architecture of Humanism;* and Wölfflin's *Principles of Art History.* Copious reproductions of the ecclesiastical architecture, painting, and sculpture are to be found in C. Ricci's *Baroque Architecture and Sculpture in Italy* (London, 1912); G. Magni's *Il Barocco a Roma e nella Scultura decorativa* (Turin, 1911)—of which Vol. I is devoted to churches; A. E. Brinckmann's *Barockskulptur . . .* (Berlin, 1919); and W. Pinder's *Deutsche Barockplastik* (Leipzig, 1933); cf. also W. Hausenstein's fully illustrated *Vom Geist des Barock* (Munich, 1924).

2 Mâle, chap. I, "L'art et les artistes après le concile de Trente," especially pp. 15–17.

3 *Ibid.,* chap. III, "Le Martyre," especially pp. 116–26.

4 *Ibid.,* chap. V, "La Mort," especially pp. 220–21.

5 *Ibid.,* chap. IV, "La Vision et l'extase."

6 The Jesuits "furent les premiers probablement à faire peindre sur la voûte de la nef un ciel qui la fit disparaître" (Mâle, *op. cit.,* 197–98). Cf. Hausenstein, plates 48–50.

seductive—instruments of the flesh, enemies of the spirit. The other—more ancient, more indulgent—incorporates elements of Greek polytheism and Platonism; it sees a ladder of ascent from beautiful things to beautiful minds and beautiful souls, and, finally, to that unchanging Beauty which is, if not God, then in God. It sees the Incarnation not only as an event in time but as a sanctification of the body and the senses.

Catholicism has persistently affirmed that, as the body, the senses, the affections, and the imagination are integral parts of man, they must all collaborate in God's service; that the lower may officiate as instruments to the higher. Inner humility is not hindered but assisted by genuflection; kissing the crucifix, while the imagination engages itself upon Calvary, stirs the emotions of pity and penitence and habituates the devout to patience in their own pains.

God transcends all fitting homage, to be sure, as He transcends all human comprehension. What, for devotion and for worship, follows? Should men therefore relinquish all efforts at a theology or a cultus? Catholicism has long ago given its negative. God stands in no need of human gifts; but, since men would avow their gratitude, express their aspirations and their homage, let them offer of their best, as, to the Infant Jesus, the shepherds presented lambs, and the kings, gold, frankincense, and myrrh. If the heavenly palaces unimaginably surpass all houses built by human hands, let men, at any rate, rear for God a cathedral to overtop their cottages; let all the arts enrich and adorn the sanctuary.

What Catholicism desired for homage to God, the Renaissance desired for its witness to the dignity of man. It coveted splendor in the ceremonial of court: parades, pageants, theatric spectacles, the monumental and magnificent in architecture.[7]

It was the office of the Counter-Reformation to gratify all Renaissance appetites not directly pagan and to extend still further, in opposition to Protestant censure, the traditional Catholic employment of the arts.

In this extension, the Jesuits, exponents of the new Catholicism, had dominance; and the *Spiritual Exercises* of St. Ignatius, the influence of which was, throughout Europe, profound, authorized the "Application of the Senses" to all the themes of religion. The *Exercises*, designed to occupy a month, devote successive weeks to meditation upon sin and the hell

which awaits the impenitent, the life of Christ, His sufferings and crucifixion, and the Resurrection and Ascension into the heaven where eternal joy awaits the holy. At the beginning of each meditation, the imagination is invited to see, hear, smell, taste, and feel the outward lineaments of that which it contemplates. For example, the prelude to the fifth day's exercise, *meditatio de Inferno*, is a "compositio": the envisaging of Hell in its length, breadth, and depth. Then, in turn, the senses are invoked: "The first point consists in this, that I see with the eye of the imagination those enormous fires, and the souls as it were in bodies of fire. The second point consists in this, that I hear with the ears of the imagination the lamentations, howlings, cries, the blasphemies against our Lord and against all His Saints. The third point consists in this, that I smell with the sense of smell of the imagination the smoke, brimstone, refuse and rotting things of hell. The fourth point consists in this, that I taste with the sense of taste of the imagination the bitter things, the tears, sorrow, and the worm of conscience in hell. The fifth point consists in feeling with the sense of touch of the imagination how these fires fasten upon and burn souls."[8]

Not to all the themes of contemplation could the complete range of the senses be applied; and naturally, the sight took preëminence, since, for truths purely abstract, it alone could devise symbols. If the theme be the birth of Christ, then the scene must be visualized: the stable, the manger; but if it be the misery of sin, then the imagination may picture a soul imprisoned in the body, banished among animals, in the vale of tears.[9] The Ignatian method thus seeks to localize both the historic and the psychological, to realize, in pictorial or symbolic form, the whole of religion.

From such a method, the transition to emblems, *tableaux vivants*, and paintings designed to stir the pious emotions is but slight. An early edition of the *Exercitia* was illustrated with engravings visualizing not only Heaven and Hell but the states of the soul, the virtues and vices, the warfare between good and evil. To illustrate the Seven Deadly Sins, the engraver depicts a man, nearly naked, sitting in a circular stone dungeon, beneath which yawns the bottomless pit of

7 Burckhardt, *The Civilization of the Renaissance in Italy*, Part V, chap. VIII, "The Festivals."

8 *Exercitia Spiritualia*, I Hebdomada, Exercitium quintum.

9 "In meditatione de re invisibili, ut est hic de peccatis, compositio erit videre visu imaginationis et considerare animam meam esse in hoc corpore corruptibili tamquam carcere inclusam, et totum compositum in hoc valle tamquam exsulans inter bruta animalia" (I Hebdomada, Exercitium primum).

perdition; the culprit is pierced with seven swords, each entering the part of anatomy which is propense to a particular sin, each ending, beyond the hilt, in the head of the bird, beast, or reptile to which the sin is natural—e.g., the goat for *luxuria,* for *superbia* the peacock. The former of the emblems makes palpable and objective a series of abstract processes; the latter brings to the sinner, incapable of realizing the moral horror of sin, a vivid consciousness of how ugly and bestial it is, visualizes the insecurity which is now his, the pains which await him. The lesson addresses the imagination.[10]

Admirably suited to Jesuit use were those Renaissance and *Seicento* arts, the emblem and the *impresa,* two small genres habitually confounded outside of Italy. As distinguished by specialists in definition, the *impresa* or "heroic symbol" was the more esoteric: it might not contain the human form; might not be obvious enough so that ordinary folk could interpret it; its accompanying motto must be in a language other than that spoken by the owner; and it was designed for the use of an individual. In function, it symbolized the character or purpose of an eminent person or gave visual expression to his motto.[11]

The emblem, on the other hand, addressed humanity at large—particularly children, women, citizens; it sought to convey moral and spiritual truths through the medium of pictures drawn not from the life of Christ or the saints but from the inner life of man, bodied forth in metaphors and short allegories. Far less restricted than the *impresa,* it ordinarily portrayed human figures in some symbolic action against a minutely and realistically delineated background; but the whole aim is nonnaturalistic: the figures personify such "faculties" as the soul, such virtues as love; and there is a free use of such palpable properties as the globe, the cross, the heart.[12]

For their art, the emblematists could claim a long ancestry, reaching back to the Egyptian hieroglyphics and, for Christian precedent, to the burning bush and Gideon's fleece and the parables. "An emblem," affirmed Quarles, chief of the English practitioners, "is but a silent Parable. Let not the tender Eye checke, to see the allusion to our blessed Saviour figured, in these Types. In holy Scripture, He is sometimes called a Sower; sometimes a Fisher; sometimes a Physitian: And why not presented so, as well to the eye, as to

the eare? Before the knowledge of letters, God was knowne by *Hierogliphicks;* And, indeed, what are the Heaven, the Earth, nay every Creature, but *Hierogliphicks* and *Emblems* of His Glory?"[13]

Inaugurated by Alciati, whose collection appeared in 1531 and went through a hundred and forty editions during the sixteenth century, the emblem became, in the seventeenth century, a favorite medium of religious instruction. It had long served the purposes of profane love, with Cupid as its prime figure; in 1615, Vaenius issued *Amoris Divini Emblemata,* in which Cupid has yielded to a winged figure very like that of Christ conceived, according to the devotional wont of the Counter-Reformation, as a child. By a similar metamorphosis, the Cyprian goddess of love gives place to the Blessed Virgin or to Anima, the soul desired by Christ.[14]

Jesuits led the other religious orders in exploiting the happy blend of *dulce et utile.* While, for princes and potentates, at whose flattery they excelled, they devised *impresa,* for popular consumption they produced book after book of sacred emblems—accompanied with epigrams, Latin elegiacs, prose commentaries, and patristic quotations.[15] Representative are the *Pia Desideria* of Hermannus Hugo, the *Typus Mundi* of the Antwerp Jesuits, *Cor Jesu Amanti Sacrum, Partheneia Sacra* by the English Jesuit, Henry Hawkins, and *Cardiomorphoseos* by Francesco Pona. From Antwerp, renowned for its engravers, came the *Schola Cordis* and the *Regia Via Crucis,* both by a Benedictine, van Haeften.

The volumes show a propensity either to group the innumerable emblems under a common theme or to include in each design a common symbol, thus affording scope for metaphorical gymnastic. Chesneau's *Orpheus Eucharisticus* limits its theme to Christ in the Holy Communion; but, as Orpheus by his song drew all creatures, animate and inanimate, to follow him, so the new and divine Orpheus must be represented as commanding and bodying himself forth in all things. The illustrative emblems therefore range through a hundred types, arranged under the general headings of *humana sacra, humana profana, aves* (Chesneau's favorites), *quadrupes, pisces, serpentes,* and so on down to flowers, plants, and fruits. As symbols of the

---

10 Füllöp-Miller, *The Power and Secret of the Jesuits,* illustrations opp. pp. 6 and 7.

11 Praz, *Studi sul Concettismo,* 42.   12 *Ibid.,* 134–35.

13 "To the Reader," *Emblemes,* 1635.

14 Praz, *op. cit.,* 105.

15 *Ibid.,* chap. IV, "L'utile e il dolce" (on the Jesuit employment of the *impresa* and the emblem), especially pp. 135–39, 158–62.

Blessed Virgin, the *Partheneia Sacra* offers, and illustrates, the garden, the rose, the lily, the violet, the sunflower, the dew, the bee, the heavens, the rainbow, the moon, the star, the olive, the nightingale, the palm, the house, the hen, the pearl, the dove, the fountain, the mountain, the sea, the ship, the phoenix, and the swan. Equal versatility can be displayed by variations upon a reiterated symbol. In *Typus Mundi*, the mundane globe appears in each design; in Quarles' *Hieroglyphicks of the Life of Man*, a candle; in the *Regia Via*, a cross.

In the *Schola Cordis* and the *Cardiomorphoseos*, a fleshly, palpable heart undergoes all manner of strangely wonderful operations and transformations. The *Schola* depicts the soul offering Jesus half a heart, while her companion, her worldly self, retains the other; depicts the soul trying in vain to fit the round world into the triangular heart; depicts the heart being plowed, tilled, seeded. Frequently the design translates into bluntly visual terms a scriptural metaphor. "Pour out thine heart like water before the face of the Lord" becomes a young woman, the soul, emptying her heart-shaped bottle into a brook, while the divine Eros stands by attentively. "I sleep, but my heart waketh" takes form in the recumbent figure of a virgin who, though the eyes of her body are closed, holds at arm's length a large heart centrally occupied by a large and wide-open eye. The hundred designs in the *Cardiomorphoseos*, among the most grotesque of emblems, show the heart with one eye or, Argus-like, with many eyes; the heart pierced with arrows; the heart as a fortress surmounted by a crucifix and assailed by warrior demons; the heart streaming blood from its pores and refreshing a subjacent garden of flowers; the Sacred Heart exuding drops of blood which fall upon the human heart; the heart as a fountain: streams of water outline a face with nose and eyebrows, from under which large eyes emit tears. An art of bizarre ingenuity, the sacred emblem does not hesitate to translate into visual form any metaphor offered, in poetry, to the ear.[16]

Ut pictura poesis. The connection of the emblem with poetry was, from the start, close: indeed the term often transferred itself from the picture to the epigram which ordinarily accompanied it. Sometimes the epigram prompted the design; frequently—and this must always have been the case with English emblem books, which, like Quarles', only reproduced the plates from Continental collections—the design inspired the verses.[17] For example, under the emblem, from *Schola Cordis*, of the soul endeavoring to fit the globe into the heart, Christopher Harvey, who used the same designs in his *School of the Heart*, wrote:

> The whole round world is not enough to fill
>   The heart's three corners, but it craveth still;
> Only the Trinity, that made it, can
>   Suffice the vast triangled heart of man.[18]

In any case, the same kind of fancy produced both.[19]

Thus the arts reinforced one another. The influence on poetry was not only to encourage the metaphorical habit but to impart to the metaphors a hardness, a palpability which, merely conceived, they were unlikely to possess. And yet the metaphors ordinarily analogized impalpabilities—states of the soul, concepts, abstractions. The effect was a strange tension between materiality and spirituality which almost defines the spirit of the Counter-Reformation; and from this attempt to prove to St. Thomas' fingers the substance of the substantial, baroque drawing and painting take their inception. Many emblems owe their undeniable grotesqueness to the visualization of metaphors, often scriptural, which were not intended so to be visualized. But having received this embodiment, the sensibility becomes acclimated to them, and the consequence is the production of analogous metaphors in poetry.

The emblem books lent themselves both to the extended and the contracted conceit, to the elaborate development of one figure or the phantasmagorical succession of many. If one meditated upon a single emblem and sought to express it in poetry, the consequence might be a short allegory; if, on the other hand, one felt the method of such books as the *Orpheus* or the *Partheneia*, one would seek a hundred

---

16 The representative volumes I describe are all in the Widener Library at Harvard, which has an excellent collection of emblematists.

17 Praz, "The English Emblem Literature," *English Studies*, XVI (1934), 129–40.

18 *School of the Heart*, Epigram 10.

19 The design might prompt a longer poem as well as an epigram; and, with Quarles, it often does, especially if the design be elaborate. Emblem 14 of Book III depicts the Body (a naked and fleshly female) turning her back upon the prospect in order to look through a prism at the shifting colors of appearances, while, seated by her, the modestly garbed Soul peers intently through a telescope at the realities, a skeletal Death and a triangular Trinity. To develop the design requires a lyric of some length.

metaphors to body forth the same object or conception.

Both the emblem and the "conceit" proceed from the wit, the faculty which discerns analogies, and shows itself the more witty as the things analogized are the more separate one from the other. In all this there may be more prestidigitation, the virtuoso's desire to amaze:

> È del poeta il fin la meraviglia . . .
> Chi non sa far stupir, vada alla striglia![20]

But the method, employed by the pens of the philosophical or the pious, may own another rationale. The wit of the poet, that too must be consecrated to God; *le jongleur* may perform his feats of agility to honor the Queen of Heaven. But wit may be more than an offering: it may be an instrument of vision. With its discovery of occult couplings, it perhaps penetrates to the center of the universe, where, however dissimilar they appear to the unobservant, all things unite. "What are all creatures but hieroglyphics and emblems of His glory?" As with Quarles, so with the Catholic emblematists, we may be sure, the conception that the universe is ultimately but a vast system of correspondences, a *Mondo Simbolico*, gave coherence and sanctification to the leaps of the devout wit. The wonder which poetry must produce may be not at the wit of its author but at the wit of God, at the fearful and wonderful nature of His creation, at His miracles which change water into wine and sinners into saints, at the divine power of metamorphosis.

Louis L. Martz

MEDITATION

THE poetry included in the present volume has been described by a remarkable variety of terms: it has been called "metaphysical," "devotional," "meditative," "mystical," or, in terms drawn from the world of visual art, "mannerist" and "baroque." The complexity and range of the poems deserve such a wealth of terminology, and every one of these terms may be found helpful in illuminating certain aspects of the poetry. This Introduction will concentrate upon two of these terms, "metaphysical" and "meditative," in order to explore the inner working of the poetry and to suggest some of its relationships to the age in which it was composed.

I

The term "metaphysical poetry," as used by literary critics over the past fifty or sixty years, has come to include poetry, notably that of Herbert or Donne, which possesses the following characteristics. First, abrupt and dramatic openings, often with a vivid image or exclamation: "For Godsake hold your tongue, and let me love." Secondly, a colloquial, familiar manner of speech, used in the most adored and sanctified presences, whether it be the presence of a Lady, or the presence of the Lord. Thirdly, a firm argumentative construction, which makes the last line of the poem implicit in the first and gives to the whole poem a peculiar tautness and concentration. Fourthly, an introspective quality, an element of self-analysis, particularly when the poet is dealing with the nature of love, whether sacred or profane. And finally, most distinctively, the quality that Samuel Johnson described when he found in this poetry "a combination of dissimilar images, or discovery of occult resemblances in things apparently unlike." "The most heterogeneous ideas are yoked by violence together; nature and art are ransacked for illustrations, comparisons, and allusions; their learning instructs, and their subtilty surprises; but the reader commonly thinks his improvement dearly bought, and, though he sometimes admires, is seldom pleased."[1] Modern readers, more often pleased by this daring use of metaphor, have come to accept the "metaphysical conceit" as a valid and significant mode of poetical action.

Metaphysical poems tend to begin in the midst of an occasion; and the meaning of the occasion is explored and grasped through this peculiar use of metaphor. The old Renaissance conceit, the ingenious comparison, is developed into a device by which the extremes of abstraction and concreteness, the extremes of unlikeness, may be woven together into a fabric of

---

20 "The aim of the poet is the marvelous. . . . He who knows not how to astonish deserves the cudgel!" *La Murtoleide*, Fischiata 33 (Marino, *Poesie Varie*, ed. Croce [Bari, 1913], 395).

1 Samuel Johnson, "Life of Cowley," in *Lives of the English Poets*, 2 vols., Oxford University Press ("World's Classics"), 1952; see I, 12–16, for Johnson's account of the metaphysical poets.

argument unified by the prevailing force of "wit." *Wit*, in all the rich and varied senses that the word held in this era: intellect, reason, powerful mental capacity, cleverness, ingenuity, intellectual quickness, inventive and constructive ability, a talent for uttering brilliant things, the power of amusing surprise.

One way of using this metaphysical, "conceited" style may be represented by Thomas Carew's poem, "To my inconstant Mistris," a poem that shows the strong influence of Donne:

> When thou, poore excommunicate
>   From all the joyes of love, shalt see
> The full reward, and glorious fate,
>   Which my strong faith shall purchase me,
>   Then curse thine owne inconstancy.
>
> A fayrer hand than thine, shall cure
>   That heart, which thy false oathes did wound;
> And to my soul, a soul more pure
>   Than thine, shall by Loves hand be bound,
>   And both with equall glory crown'd.
>
> Then shalt thou weepe, entreat, complain
>   To Love, as I did once to thee;
> When all thy teares shall be as vain
>   As mine were then, for thou shalt bee
>   Damn'd for thy false Apostasie.

The poem is built upon an original use of the familiar conceit by which the experience of human love is rendered in religious terms. Here the faithless lady is excommunicated as an apostate from the religion of love, while her lover will receive the reward of his "strong faith" by being crowned in glory, like the saints in heaven. But, paradoxically, his faith will be demonstrated, his constancy in love rewarded, by the act of turning to another lady, with a "fayrer hand" and "a soul more pure." Inconstancy is thus met with the threat of counter-inconstancy; and all the rich religious terms take on in the end a swagger of bravado. The poem thus presents a brief episode in erotic frustration, a vignette in which the backlash of the lover's bitterness is conveyed by the immediacy of his language, by the conversational flexibility of actual speech working within a strict stanza-form.

One should, however, note that this poem contains certain elements that are not peculiar to "metaphysical poetry," but are discernible throughout the poetry of the English Renaissance. Abrupt openings and the use of conversational speech are also found, for example,

in Wyatt, Sidney, and Ben Jonson, the last of whom, as a practicing dramatist, knew all about the use of colloquial idiom in poetry. The voice of living speech is everywhere in the poetry of Donne's time; it is not a distinguishing quality of metaphysical poetry, but rather a part of the whole Elizabethan heritage of song and sonnet and drama. Conversely, the quality of introspection and self-analysis, so characteristic of Donne and Herbert, plays no significant part in Carew's love-song. It seems clear that this quality does not form an indispensable part of a definition of metaphysical poetry, since certain poems by Suckling, Carew, Lovelace, Waller, and Davenant are often included under this term. Consider, for example, the following poem by Thomas Carew, "Boldnesse in Love":

> Marke how the bashfull morne, in vaine
>   Courts the amorous Marigold,
> With sighing blasts, and weeping raine;
>   Yet she refuses to unfold.
> But when the Planet of the day,
>   Approacheth with his powerfull ray,
> Then she spreads, then she receives
> His warmer beames into her virgin leaves.
> So shalt thou thrive in love, fond Boy;
>   If thy teares, and sighes discover
> Thy griefe, thou never shalt enjoy
>   The just reward of a bold lover:
> But when with moving accents, thou
>   Shalt constant faith, and service vow,
> Thy *Celia* shall receive those charmes
> With open eares, and with unfolded armes.

Such a poem as this is clearly not metaphysical by any definition that would include an introspective quality; this and many other poems like it have been called metaphysical because of their intricate manipulation of imagery and their employment of the argued metaphor, the metaphysical conceit. This use of metaphor is a common quality in nearly all the poems usually included under the term metaphysical poetry; it is, I think, the prime distinguishing quality of this poetry.

In many poems, though not perhaps in Carew's, this peculiar use of metaphor may be called "metaphysical" in a sense approaching the philosophical use of that word. This point has been made clear by the recent studies of Mazzeo and Bethell, which have had the effect of extending, enriching, and giving a positive emphasis to Samuel Johnson's view of the metaphysical use of imagery, through a careful examination of the theories of poetic wit developed on the Continent during the seventeenth century by critical writers such as Gracián and Tesauro.[2] From the standpoint of these seventeenth-century critics, the witty use of the conceit, when properly developed, had a truly metaphysical significance, for it arose from the philosophic doctrine of correspondences. As Mazzeo sums up the view: "Thus God created a world full of metaphors, analogies and conceits, and so far from being ornamentation, they are the law by which creation was effected. God wrote the book of nature in metaphor, and so it should be read. . . . The universe is a vast net of correspondences which unites the whole multiplicity of being. The poet approaches and creates his reality by a series of more or less elaborate correspondences." "God created such a world for the purpose of arousing the wonder of men, and man himself made conceits because he alone of all the creatures of God needed to seek out the variety of the universe and express it."[3] In short, the metaphysical use of metaphor derives from a belief in the existence of a universal harmony of being, based upon the Renaissance doctrine of hierarchies, wherein all created things, from angels down to minerals, are arranged in classes, with each class having its corresponding items in a class above or below. The result is that from this point of view all classes or planes of being, all links in the chain, were seen as being connected by what Tillyard calls a "network of correspondences."[4] Renaissance man lived in a universe of analogy which was for him not a fiction but a scientific fact. The primary function of the intellect of man was to discover these analogies, for they were the clues to a unity created by the greatest intellect of all, the mind of God. Thus the use of man's intellect corresponds to the divine power of creation.

2 See Joseph Anthony Mazzeo, "A Seventeenth-Century Theory of Metaphysical Poetry," and "Metaphysical Poetry and the Poetic of Correspondence," originally published in 1951 and 1953 and now collected in Mazzeo's *Renaissance and Seventeenth-Century Studies* (Columbia University Press, 1964), pp. 29–59. Much the same view has been independently presented by S. L. Bethell, "The Nature of Metaphysical Wit," *Northern Miscellany of Literary Criticism*, I (1953), 19–40; more easily available in Frank Kermode's collection, *Discussions of John Donne* (Boston, Heath, 1962), pp. 136–49.
3 Mazzeo, *Renaissance and Seventeenth-Century Studies*, pp. 54–56.
4 E. M. W. Tillyard, *The Elizabethan World Picture* (New York, Macmillan, 1944), p. 77.

One example from the poetry of Henry Vaughan may serve to illustrate the search for correspondences: "The Showre":

'Twas so, I saw thy birth: That drowsie Lake
From her faint bosome breath'd thee, the disease
Of her sick waters, and Infectious Ease.
　　But, now at Even
　　Too grosse for heaven,
Thou fall'st in teares, and weep'st for thy mistake.

Ah! it is so with me; oft have I prest
Heaven with a lazie breath, but fruitles this
Peirc'd not; Love only can with quick accesse
　　Unlock the way,
　　When all else stray
The smoke, and Exhalations of the breast.

Yet, if as thou doest melt, and with thy traine
Of drops make soft the Earth, my eyes could weepe
O're my hard heart, that's bound up, and asleepe,
　　Perhaps at last
　　(Some such showres past,)
My God would give a Sun-shine after raine.

Vaughan has trained himself to see analogies between himself and the outer universe. He has trained himself to find the moral and spiritual application of outer images to his inner being. "I see the use," he cries in another poem, as he watches a raging storm; that is, he sees the correspondence between the storm and his own turbulent state of mind. In such poems the chosen image is thoroughly explored to bear out the principle of the network of analogies. Such poems then are deservedly called metaphysical through their use of metaphor: they seek through images drawn from the *many* to discover the *One*. By unifying man's inner being, such a quest becomes metaphysical in the true and basic sense of the word "metaphysics": "That branch of speculative inquiry which treats of the first principles of things, including such concepts as being, substance, essence, time, space, cause, identity, etc.; theoretical philosophy as the ultimate science of Being and Knowing" (OED).

This is the sense in which John Dryden used the word when he wrote that Donne "affects the metaphysics" (that is to say, inclines toward the metaphysics) "not only in his satires, but in his amorous verses, where nature only should reign; and perplexes the minds of the fair sex with nice speculations of philosophy, when he should engage their hearts, and entertain them with the softnesses of love."[5] Dryden there expresses the difference between a social poet, who sees nature in terms of the human community,[6] and the metaphysical poet, who sees nature as the key to a transcendent truth alive in the entire universe. Samuel Johnson, evidently picking up the term metaphysical from Dryden, then went on to give his own classic definition of the method of the metaphysical poets: "Their attempts were always analytick; they broke every image into fragments: and could no more represent, by their slender conceits and laboured particularities, the prospects of nature, or the scenes of life, than he, who dissects a sun-beam with a prism, can exhibit the wide effulgence of a summer noon." But the wide effulgence of a summer noon had for Donne and Herbert and Vaughan its major interest as a field of imagery where analytic attempts could discover some hint of a higher principle, the principle of universal analogy, by which all created things are bound together in the mind of God, and secondarily, within the mind of man.

Poetry is metaphysical, then, when it seeks by complex analogies to find a central principle of being, within the bounds of a given situation. That situation may involve the relationship between a man and a woman, at various levels of seriousness, or it may involve the relationship between man and the Deity. One may find a metaphysical correspondence presented by Richard Lovelace in his poem, "Gratiana dauncing and singing":

See! with what constant Motion
Even, and glorious, as the Sunne,
  Gratiana steers that Noble Frame,
Soft as her breast, sweet as her voyce
That gave each winding Law and poyze,
  And swifter than the wings of Fame.

She beat the happy Pavement
By such a Starre made Firmament,
  Which now no more the Roofe envies;
But swells up high with Atlas ev'n,
Bearing the brighter, nobler Heav'n,
  And in her, all the Deities.

Different as they are, Lovelace and Vaughan are both using the universe of correspondences to seek their central principle of being, whether it lies in a Lady or in God. The basic quality of metaphysical poetry, then, is that long ago described by James Smith in an essay too often neglected, where he argues that the central impulse of such poetry "is given by an overwhelming concern with metaphysical problems; with problems either deriving from, or closely resembling in the nature of their difficulty, the problem of the Many and the One."[7]

2

In his interesting anthology, *European Metaphysical Poetry*, Frank Warnke has made an important distinction between the terms meditative and metaphysical. He suggests that "the meditation is a genre—one which recurs at intervals in our history and which, in the sixteenth and seventeenth centuries, assumed a special importance." "Metaphysical poetry is a particular style, an historically limited manner of writing in various genres. At the same time, one must recognize the important relationship which this genre and this style bear to one another."[8] I would agree with Warnke that the roots of this relationship lie in the spirit of the age; meditative action and the metaphysical style reflect a kindred response to the same basic conditions.

The metaphysical style of writing arose, it seems, in response to a widespread reaction against the efflorescent, expansive, highly melodious mode of the earlier Renaissance, as found in Edmund Spenser; it arose also, I believe, in response to a widespread feeling that the manifold expansions of human outlook were rapidly moving out of control: expansions through recovery of the classics, through access to the Bible in vernacular languages, through a new emphasis upon the early fathers of the Church, through the fierce religious controversies that rocked the age, through the advance of science in all areas, and through the vigorous exploration of the earth by seamen, traders, and conquistadors. As a result, in the latter part of the sixteenth century poetry showed a tendency to coalesce and concentrate its powers towards the sharp

---

5 *Essays of John Dryden*, ed. W. P. Ker, 2 vols. (Oxford, Clarendon Press, 1926), II, 19.
6 For the tradition of social poetry in the seventeenth century, see Sylvester's Introduction to Volume 2 of this collection.

7 James Smith, "On Metaphysical Poetry," in *Determinations*, ed. F. R. Leavis (London, Chatto, 1934), p. 24.
8 *European Metaphysical Poetry*, tr. and ed. by Frank J. Warnke (Yale University Press, 1961), p. 56, n. 72.

illumination and control of carefully selected moments in experience.

The widespread practice of methodical religious meditation during the same era may be traced, I believe, to the same causes: religious meditation was a way of finding order within the self, a way of controlling the chaos of wordly experience, by concentrating the mind's powers upon a single image, event, or problem. Since the process of meditation, as practiced in this era, was an intensely imaginative action of the mind, it inevitably bears a close relationship to the writing of poetry. The relationship is shown by the poem's own internal action, as the mind engages in acts of interior dramatization. The speaker accuses himself; he talks to God within the self; he approaches the love of God through memory, understanding, and will; he sees, hears, smells, tastes, touches by imagination the scenes of Christ's life as they are represented on a mental stage. Essentially, the meditative action consists of an interior drama, in which a man projects a self upon an inner stage, and there comes to know that self in the light of a divine presence.

To understand the "art of meditation" as it was taught and practiced in Donne's time, one may turn to the compact treatise printed as an appendix in this volume: "The Practical Methode of Meditation," written by the Jesuit Edward Dawson for an English audience, and published on the Continent in 1614.[9] Dawson's treatise, written at the peak of the period's intense concern with the "method" of meditation, sums up the principles that had gradually come to dominate the meditative life of the Continent, primarily through the influence of the *Spiritual Exercises* of Ignatius Loyola. Dawson's handbook is in fact a paraphrase of the *Spiritual Exercises*, with adaptations and extensions prompted, as he says, by "approved Authors and experience." He gives the essence of the advice for meditation that was being offered by spiritual counselors throughout Europe, as well as by the numerous underground priests in England. At the same time this advice was being offered in dozens of popular treatises on meditation that were circulating in thousands of copies throughout Europe, and in England as well.

Dawson shows by his blunt, simple, "practical" manner the way in which the art of meditation might become part of the everyday life of everyman. The

matter-of-fact tone of the treatise, indeed, helps to convey its central and pervasive assumptions: that man, whether he will or not, lives in the intimate presence of God, and that his first duty in life is to cultivate an awareness of that presence. Thus arises the whole elaborate ceremony of meditation: the careful preparation of materials the night before; the "practice of the presence of God," as it was called, before actual meditation; the preparatory prayers; the preludes; the deliberate, orderly operation of the "three powers of the soul"—memory, understanding, will; and the conclusion in "some affectionate speach" or colloquy with God or the saints, in which "wee may talke with God as a servant with his Maister, as a sonne with his Father, as one friend with another, as a spouse with her beloved bridgrome, or as a guilty prisoner with his Judge, or in any other manner which the holy Ghost shall teach us." The aim of meditation is to apprehend the reality and the meaning of the presence of God with every faculty at man's command. The body must first learn its proper behavior during the ceremony: hence we have detailed advice on whether to kneel, or walk, or sit, or stand. The five senses must learn how to bend their best efforts toward this end: hence the elaborately detailed explanation of the Jesuit "application of the senses" to the art of meditation. Everyday life must come to play its part, for the meditative man must feel that the presence of God is here, now, on his own hearth, in his own stable, and in the deep center of the mind: thus "we may help our selves much to the framing of spirituall conceites [thoughts], if we apply unto our matter familiar similitudes, drawne from our ordinary actions, and this as well in historicall, as spirituall meditations." That is to say, analogies from the world of daily actions must be brought to bear upon the history of the life of Christ, as well as upon such matters as the problem of sin and the excellence of the virtues.

Among all the varied ways of using the senses and physical life in meditation, the most important, most effective, and most famous is the prelude known as the "composition of place." This brilliant Ignatian invention, to which the Jesuit *Exercises* owe a large part of their power, is given its full and proper emphasis by Dawson: "for on the well making of this *Preludium* depends both the understanding of the mystery, and attention in our meditation." Whatever the subject may be, the imagination, the image-making power of man, must endeavor to represent it "so lively, as though we saw [it] indeed, with our corporall eyes." For historical matters, such as events in the life of

---

9 Unless otherwise noted, all the subsequent quotations concerning the practice of meditation are taken from this treatise.

Christ or a saint, we must visualize the scene in the most vivid and exact detail, "by imagining our selves to be really present at those places." In treating spiritual subjects we must gain the same end by creating "some similitude, answerable to the matter." Thus, for the Last Things, Death, Judgment, Hell, and Heaven, the similitude may be created by imagining the scene in detail, by creating, for example, a likeness of one's self on the deathbed, "forsaken of the Physitians, compassed about with our weeping friends, and expecting our last agony." But the similitude may also be much more figurative: the word "similitude," in seventeenth-century usage, could refer to any kind of parable, allegory, simile, or metaphor. Dawson, discussing the preparation for meditation, suggests that we should "begin to take some tast of our meditation" before the actual performance begins, by stirring up the "affections," the emotions, appropriate to each meditation: "Which we may perform more easily," he adds, "yf we keep in our mind some similitude answering to the affection we would have." And later he suggests that, among several dramatic ways of strengthening these affections, we may sometimes proceed by "faygning [imagining] the very vertues in some venerable shape bewayling their neglect." Thus too he notes that, in the opening similitude for the meditation on sins, "we may imagine our soule to be cast out of Paradise, and to be held prisoner in this body of ours, fettered with the chaines of disordinate Passions, and affections, and clogged with the burden of our owne flesh." In short, this insistence upon "seeing the place" and upon the frequent use of "similitudes" in meditation invites every man to use his image-making faculty with the utmost vigor, in order to ensure a concrete, dramatic setting within which the meditative action may develop. Upon the inward stage of that scene or similitude, the memory, the understanding, and the will may then proceed to explore and understand and feel the proper role of the self in relation to the divine omnipotence and charity. Thus heaven and earth are brought together in the mind; and human action is placed in a responsive, intimate relation with the supernatural.

An important qualification, however, needs to be added to the advice of Dawson. In the Ignatian way, he insists that every meditation must begin with some vivid "composition," but we should not be led to expect that every meditative poem will begin with some vivid scene or symbol. Many do so, directly or implicitly, with the speaker present, for example, at some scene in the life of Christ; but many meditative

poems also begin simply with a brief, terse statement of the problem or theme to be explored:

Why are wee by all creatures waited on?

Why do I languish thus, drooping and dull . . .

Come, come, what doe I here?

I Sing the *Name* which none can say,
But touch't with an interiour *Ray*,
The *Name* of our *New Peace*, our *Good*,
Our *Blisse*, and supernaturall *Blood*,
The *Name* of all our Lives, and Loves.

Such openings, though not mentioned by Dawson, are advised by other writers for abstract topics, particularly by St. François de Sales, who notes, "It is true that we may use some similitude or comparison to assist us in the consideration of these subjects," but he fears that the making of "such devices" may prove burdensome, and thus for the meditation of "invisible things" he advises one to begin with "a simple proposal" of the theme.[10] A meditative poem, then, will tend to open in any one of three ways: (1) with a vivid participation in some scene in the life of Christ or a saint; (2) with a "similitude, answerable to the matter," that is, with some imaginary setting or metaphorical representation; (3) with a "simple proposal" of the issue to be considered.

With the event or theme thus firmly presented within a "recollected" mind fully aware of the presence of God, the meditative action of the three powers of the soul begins to develop each "point" (usually three) into which the long process of meditation (usually lasting an hour) has been divided during the period of preparation. It is evident from Dawson's account that the operation of the memory is inseparable from and continuous with the opening composition or proposal; for the role of memory is to set forth the subject with all its necessary "persons, wordes, and workes." The understanding then proceeds to analyze ("discourse" upon) the meaning of the topic, in relation to the individual self, until gradually the will takes fire and the appropriate

10 See St. Francis de Sales, *Introduction to the Devout Life* (1609), tr. and ed. by John K. Ryan (Image Books, 1955), pp. 83–84. The whole treatise, especially the second part, is of the utmost interest to anyone concerned with studying the details of meditative practice in this era.

personal affections arise. It is clear too from Dawson's account that these affections of the will inevitably lead into the colloquy, where the speaker utters his fears and hopes, his sorrows and joys, in "affectionate speach" before God. The full process of meditation always ends with such a colloquy, but, as Dawson points out, "We may make such manner of speaches in other places of our meditation, and it will be best, and almost needfull so to do."

At the same time, the interior drama will tend to have a firm construction, for the process of meditation, in treating each "point," will tend to display a three-fold movement, according with the action of that interior trinity, memory, understanding, and will. Now and then we may find this threefold process echoed or epitomized within the borders of a short poem; or we may find the process suggested at length in a long poem such as Southwell's "Saint Peters Complaint" or Crashaw's "On the name of Jesus"; or we may find it suggested by a sequence of short poems, as in the poems of Traherne in the Dobell manuscript.[11] But what one should expect to find, more often, is some part of the whole meditative action, set down as particularly memorable, perhaps in accordance with the kind of self-examination advised by Dawson under the heading: "What is to be done after Meditation." One is urged here to scrutinize carefully the manner in which one has performed every part of the meditative process, from preparation through colloquy; to examine closely the distractions, consolations, or desolations that one may have experienced; and finally, to "note in some little booke those thinges which have passed in our Meditation, or some part of them, if we think, them worth the, paynes." Meditative poems present such memorable moments of self-knowledge, affections of sorrow and love, colloquies with the divine presence, recollected and preserved through the aid of the kindred art of poetry.

Meditation points towards poetry in its use of images, in its technique of arousing the passionate affections of the will, in its suggestion that the ultimate reach of meditation is found in the advice of Paul to the Ephesians: "Be filled with the Spirit; speaking to yourselves in psalms and hymns and spiritual songs, singing and making melody in your heart to the Lord." A meditative poem, then, represents the con-

vergence of two arts upon a single object: in English poetry of the late Renaissance the art of meditation entered into and transformed its kindred art of poetry. To express its highest reaches, the art of meditation drew upon all the poetical resources available in the culture of its day. Southwell, writing in an era dominated by the uninspired verse of the poetical miscellanies—with their heavy-footed, alliterative style and their doggerel ballad-stanzas—could use his meditative techniques, along with his knowledge of Italian poetry, to impart a new and startling vigor even to a moribund poetical mode. Alabaster, writing near the end of the 1590's, at the close of the great era of English sonneteering, could use his meditative art to transform the Elizabethan sonnet. Donne, knowing all the devices of current poetry—whether in satire, love song, sonnet, Ovidian elegy, funeral elegy, courtly compliment, or religious hymn—attained many of his greatest creations in those poems where his mastery of the meditative art could add a new dimension to these modes of poetic art. Herbert, master of music, adept in every form of Elizabethan song or sonnet, could turn all these varied forms into a temple of praise for his Master's presence. And Crashaw, drawn to the extravagant modes of the Continental baroque, could nevertheless, at his best, tame and control his extravaganzas by the firm structure of a meditation.

3

To illustrate this convergence of the arts, let us look closely at one great poem that may be said to represent an epitome of the art of meditation, as Dawson has explained the process. It is Donne's "Hymn to God my God, in my sicknesse," written in 1623 (or perhaps in 1631), when Donne was in his fifties: it is thus a poem that may be regarded as the culmination of a lifetime's practice in the arts of poetry and meditation.

Its opening stanza recalls the careful preparation that preceded meditation: preparation in which the end and aim of the process was fully plotted and foreseen, and in which the speaker placed himself securely in the presence of God:

Since I am comming to that Holy roome,
    Where, with thy quire of Saints for evermore,
I shall be made thy Musique; As I come
    I tune the instrument here at the dore,
And what I must doe then, thinke here before.

11 See John Malcolm Wallace, "Thomas Traherne and the Structure of Meditation," *A Journal of English Literary History*, 25 (1958), 79–89.

The emphasis falls upon the deliberate process of *thinking*: the meditation will proceed by rational, articulated stages. First comes the "composition of place," in which the speaker, lying upon what he believes will be his deathbed, works out a careful "similitude" that will enable him to understand himself:

> Whilst my Physitians by their love are growne
> Cosmographers, and I their Mapp, who lie
> Flat on this bed, that by them may be showne
> That this is my Southwest discoverie
> *Per fretum febris*, by these streights to die . . .

The doctors are charting forth upon his outstretched body a "discoverie" such as Magellan made; but the "streights" through which this passage will be made are the straits, the difficulties and pains, of death: *Per fretum febris*, "through the straits of fever." The witty play on words shows a remarkable equanimity, that striking ability of Donne to view his own situation from a distance, to hold his own body and soul off at arm's length and study his situation in objective detail, as the art of meditation encouraged one to do.

So Donne sees that he is now upon his westward passage, toward sundown, but as he questions himself, he finds joy in the prospect, for he knows that a flat map is only an illusory diagram. At the far edge, West becomes East, sundown becomes sunrise:

> I joy, that in these straits, I see my West;
> For though theire currants yeeld returne to none,
> What shall my West hurt me? As West and East
> In all flatt Maps (and I am one) are one,
> So death doth touch the Resurrection.

Donne's questioning in the middle stanzas of the poem indicates a process of analysis bent upon understanding the goal of his passage, and indeed the very questions imply the goal:

> Is the Pacifique Sea my home? Or are
> The Easterne riches? Is *Jerusalem*?
> *Anyan*, and *Magellan*, and *Gibraltare*,
> All streights, and none but streights, are wayes to them,
> Whether where *Japhet* dwelt, or *Cham*, or *Sem*.

The traveler to the peaceful ocean, or to the wealth of the Orient, or to that holy city whose name means "Vision of Peace," may move through the "Straits of Anyan" (supposed to separate Asia and America), or the Straits of Magellan, or the Straits of Gibraltar. But however one goes, the voyage is full of pain and difficulty. And this is true whatever regions of the earth he may sail from or sail between, "Whether where *Japhet* dwelt, or *Cham*, or *Sem*." In thus recalling the ancient division of the earth into the inheritance given to the three sons of Noah, Donne suggests the universality and the inevitability of those straits which face every man who seeks his ultimate home.

In the geography of Donne's present moment there is only one goal, the heavenly Paradise made possible by Calvary, redemption by the sacrifice of Christ. In the outer world this singleness of aim is suggested by the fact that the Paradise of Eden (usually set in Mesopotamia) and Calvary have both been located in the same region of the earth, the Near East. In the same way Adam and Christ now meet in the sick man on his bed. The sweat of his fever fulfills the curse laid upon the first Adam, but the blood of Christ will, the speaker hopes, redeem his soul:

> We thinke that *Paradise* and *Calvarie*,
> *Christs* Crosse, and *Adams* tree, stood in one place;
> Looke Lord, and finde both *Adams* met in me;
> As the first *Adams* sweat surrounds my face,
> May the last *Adams* blood my soule embrace.

He prays in familiar colloquy that, for his funeral shroud, he may be wrapped in the blood of Christ, a royal garment of purple, and that thus he may be granted the Crown of Glory in Heaven. So the poem ends with a recapitulation of the central paradox: death is the passage of life, West and East are one, flatness leads to rising:

> So, in his purple wrapp'd receive mee Lord,
> By these his thornes give me his other Crowne;
> And as to others soules I preach'd thy word,
> Be this my Text, my Sermon to mine owne,
> Therfore that he may raise the Lord throws down.

The closing colloquy reminds us that the whole poem has been spoken in the presence of God: it is all a testimony of faith presented as a hymn of gratitude to the Creator.

The poem, then, reveals in miniature all the essential components of a full religious meditation: preparation, composition, discourse (in the old sense of analytic reasoning), and colloquy; or, to use other terms of the time, memory, understanding, and will, the three powers of the soul which are unified in the process of meditation, forming an interior trinity that represents an image, although defaced, of the greater Trinity. The poem thus becomes the ultimate tuning of that "Instrument" which was John Donne himself: poet, theologian, voyager, preacher, meditative man. If one wonders to find such wit and ingenuity manifested even on the deathbed, the answer is clear: here is the instrument that God has made, and at the last, it is proper that the unique timbre and tone of the instrument should be heard.

4

At the same time, this meditative poem is also a work in the metaphysical style, since it displays the characteristic use of the conceit, as described by Dame Helen Gardner: "In a metaphysical poem the conceits are instruments of definition in an argument or instruments to persuade."[12] In secular love-poetry the conceits form part of an argument or a process of persuasion addressed to a lady. In religious poetry the conceits are used by a voice that is speaking inwardly, to the self, or to God, or to the self in the presence of God, for the purpose of defining the relation of the self to God, persuading the self to accept and love that relationship and its creator, or persuading God to accept that human self, with all its faults.

There is thus a natural affinity between the meditative action and the metaphysical style, an affinity that may be seen quite clearly in a sonnet written, it seems, about ten years before John Donne's Holy Sonnets: one of William Alabaster's poems dealing with "the ensignes of Christes Crucifyinge." The sonnet begins with a direct address to the symbols of the Crucifixion, which the speaker appears to have directly before his eyes; crying out to them, fully aware of the paradoxes that they represent, he proposes the question of his own proper response:

O sweete and bitter monuments of paine,
bitter to Christ who all the paine endured,
butt sweete to mee, whose Death my life procured,
how shall I full express such loss, such gaine?

Turning to consider the faculties that lie within himself, his tongue, his eyes, his soul, he proceeds to

12 *The Metaphysical Poets*, ed. Helen Gardner, Penguin (rev. ed., 1966), p. 21.

explain to himself how these may be led toward their proper end, by writing in the book of his soul the record of his sin:

My tonge shall bee my penne, mine eyes shall raine
teares for my inke, the place where I was cured
shall bee my booke, where haveing all abjured
and calling heavens to record in that plaine,
thus plainely will I write, noe sinne like mine;

And finally, holding fast with tenacious logic to his previous images, he closes in colloquy with the Lord, whose presence has been implicit throughout:

when I have done, doe thou, Jesue divine,
take upp the tarte spunge of thy passione
and blott itt forth: then bee thy spiritt the Quill,
thy bloode the Inke, and with compassione
write thus upon my soule: thy Jesue still.

Abrupt opening, condensed and compact phrasing, with touches of colloquial speech, witty development of central conceits, coalescing the abstract and the concrete, logic, paradox—all the qualities of the European metaphysical style are there—yet something more creates the poem's modest success. The speaker has learned how to make himself present before the "monuments" of the Passion, how to concentrate memory, understanding, and will upon these symbols of Christ's suffering, how to develop the personal meaning of the Passion through the use of appropriate similitudes, how to drive home the meaning for the self in affectionate colloquy with God. The art of meditation has provided the techniques by which Alabaster could create a brief interior drama. It is, I believe, in these techniques of self-dramatization that we find the peculiar contribution of the art of meditation to poetry. They are techniques which find a most congenial alliance with the metaphysical style, but which may also combine with a variety of other styles: early Elizabethan, Jonsonian, baroque, or Miltonic.

This effort to distinguish between the meditative and the metaphysical may help to solve the problem of Donne's relation to later poets of the seventeenth century. Specific debts to Donne are obvious in some of the secular poetry of the period, such as Carew's, but in the religious poetry of Herbert, Crashaw, or Vaughan, where one somehow feels a more essential kinship, such debts are much more elusive, indeed almost nonexistent. To some it has seemed possible to argue that in general Herbert descends from Donne, and that since Herbert influenced Crashaw and Vaughan, the two latter poets are thus at least the grandsons of Donne. But recent studies have shown Herbert's deep-rooted independence of Donne: his use of medieval forms and symbols, his mastery of all varieties of Elizabethan poetry and song, his mastery of the meditative techniques. What Herbert passed on to Vaughan was his own great and original creation, which Vaughan proceeded to use in his own highly original way, combining Herbert's example with the example of the Sons of Ben Jonson, to whose line he displays his allegiance in his early secular poems. The few echoes of Donne that we meet in Vaughan's first volume (1646) are overwhelmed by his dominant experiments in the Jonsonian mode of couplet-rhetoric, as the opening poem of the volume clearly testifies, a poem addressed to a certain friend, R.W.:

When we are dead, and now, no more
Our harmles mirth, our wit, and score
Distracts the Towne; when all is spent
That the base niggard world hath lent
Thy purse, or mine, when the loath'd noise
Of Drawers, Prentises, and boyes
Hath left us, and the clam'rous barre
Items no pints i'th'Moone, or Starre . . .
When all these Mulets are paid, and I
From thee, deare wit, must part, and dye;
Wee'le beg the world would be so kinde,
To give's one grave, as wee'de one minde;
There (as the wiser few suspect,
That spirits after death affect)
Our soules shall meet, and thence will they
(Freed from the tyranny of clay)
With equall wings, and ancient love
Into the Elysian fields remove,
Where in those blessed walkes they'le find,
More of thy Genius, and my mind:
    First, in the shade of his owne bayes,
Great *BEN* they'le see, whose sacred Layes,
The learned Ghosts admire, and throng,
To catch the subject of his Song.
Then *Randolph* in those holy Meades,
His Lovers, and *Amyntas* reads,[13]

13 Thomas Randolph (1605–1635), a follower of Ben Jonson; his pastoral drama *Amyntas* was published in 1638; the next two lines refer to Randolph's poem "On the Death of a Nightingale." See the selection from Randolph in Volume 2 of this collection.

Whilst his Nightingall close by,
Sings his, and her owne Elegie;
From thence dismiss'd by subtill roades,
Through airie paths, and sad aboads;
They'le come into the drowsie fields
Of Lethe, which such vertue yeelds,
That (if what Poets sing be true)
The streames all sorrow can subdue.

This steady, terse, and easy handling of the tetrameter couplet is a hallmark of the Jonsonian mode, and it is a form into which many of Vaughan's finest poems in *Silex Scintillans* are cast. Yet poems in the tetrameter couplet are not at all characteristic of Donne or Herbert. It is worth noting, too, in passing, that this Jonsonian use of the tetrameter couplet is found in Crashaw's poems on St. Teresa (along with variations into the pentameter); and it is also one of Andrew Marvell's favorite forms. This does not mean that we should substitute Jonson for Donne as the prime poetical model for these writers; in fact, the influence of Jonson and that of Donne are almost inseparably intermingled throughout the seventeenth century, and particularly in Marvell, the most eclectic of poets. But the appearance of a Jonsonian style in these poets will provide striking evidence of the way in which the art of meditation could and did combine with any available mode in poetry.

5

At the same time, in dealing with Vaughan, Marvell, or Traherne, one should remember that the strict Ignatian method of meditation, as outlined by Dawson, was itself an outgrowth of ancient ways of meditation that had been developing since the days of Augustine, and earlier. In fact, the Augustinian mode of meditation was still highly influential in the seventeenth century, through the widespread circulation of the works of Augustine and his followers. The Augustinian way of meditation was less formal and less logical in its procedures, since it consisted in a roving quest for the traces, the vestiges of God, first in external nature and then, most importantly, within the mind of man. As Augustine explains the quest in the tenth book of his *Confessions* (chapters 6 through 27), it consists of a search for the image of God within the mind of man, an image defaced by sin, but nevertheless restored in its essential powers through the sacrifice of Christ. It is man's duty, according to Augustinian thought, to advance as far as he can towards a renewal of this image, with the help of divine grace.

A superb account of the entire process is given in Henry Vaughan's poem, "Vanity of Spirit," Here the meditative man has apparently been studying in his room, which has come to seem oppressive to him, and so the poem begins:

> Quite spent with thoughts I left my Cell, and lay
> Where a shrill spring tun'd to the early day.

In the presence of this active, vital aspect of nature the speaker begins his quest for the divine light:

> I beg'd here long, and gron'd to know
> Who gave the Clouds so brave a bow,
> Who bent the spheres, and circled in
> Corruption with this glorious Ring.
> What is his name, and how I might
> Descry some part of his great light.

First he turns to external nature in the effort to find the vestiges of divinity:

> I summon'd nature: peirc'd through all her store,
> Broke up some seales, which none had touch'd before,
>   Her wombe, her bosome, and her head
>   Where all her secrets lay a bed
>   I rifled quite, and having past
>   Through all the Creatures, came at last
>   To search my selfe, where I did find
>   Traces, and sounds of a strange kind.

The word "traces" is simply a translation of the Augustinian term *vestigia*, vestiges of divinity. As he finds those traces of the divine within himself, he discovers that they are in fact closely related to external nature, as he goes on to say: "Here of this mighty spring, I found some drills," that is, some trickles or small streams of the spring with which the poem has opened. The same forces appear to be working within himself as are at work in outer nature, with an implication perhaps that one "mighty spring" lies behind all:

> Here of this mighty spring, I found some drills,
> With Ecchoes beaten from th' eternall hills;
>   Weake beames, and fires flash'd to my sight,

> Like a young East, or Moone-shine night,
> Wich shew'd me in a nook cast by
> A peece of much antiquity,
> With Hyerogliphicks quite dismembred,
> And broken letters scarce remembred.

This is a symbol of the image of God within man, the defaced image which the speaker wishes to restore:

> I tooke them up, and (much Joy'd), went about
> T' unite those peeces, hoping to find out
>   The mystery; but this neer done,
>   That little light I had was gone:
>   It griev'd me much. At last, said I,
>   *Since in these veyls my Ecclips'd Eye*
>   *May not approach thee, (for at night*
>   *Who can have commerce with the light?)*
>   *I'le disapparell, and to buy*
>   *But one half glaunce, most gladly dye.*

One should note that the mysterious, roving action represented in this poem is an action different from the method of meditation set forth by Dawson's treatise. The Ignatian method shows the powerful impact of medieval thought, with its emphasis upon analysis by the human understanding, and also upon the principle central to the philosophy of Thomas Aquinas: that all human knowledge must be drawn from sensory experience. The method of meditation set forth by Dawson is, as we have seen, a precise, carefully designed process, moving from the composition of place into the threefold movement of the memory, understanding, and will. But in what may be called the Augustinian mode of meditation, we can find no exact method; it consists rather of a groping movement into areas of the mind that lie beyond the knowledge gained through the senses, areas which contain a knowledge deriving from the vestiges of the image of God, which has never been totally destroyed in man. This is the view of the soul's interior action represented in a passage of Andrew Marvell's "On a Drop of Dew," where the word "recollecting" is used in its basic sense, to indicate an act of "collecting together again" the divine light within the mind or soul of man:

> So the Soul, that Drop, that Ray
> Of the clear Fountain of Eternal Day,
> Could it within the humane flow'r be seen,
>   Remembring still its former height,

Shuns the sweat leaves and blossoms green;
　And, recollecting its own Light,
Does, in its pure and circling thoughts, express
The greater Heaven in an Heaven less.

Such a view of the sources of human knowledge is of course strongly influenced by platonic and neo-platonic thought, which enjoyed a powerful revival during the Renaissance, first among the platonists of Florence, and later among the group of seventeenth-century English philosophers known as the Cambridge Platonists. Vaughan and Traherne were both deeply influenced by these currents of platonism, including the strange, occult variant of neoplatonism associated with alchemy and known as the "Hermetic Philosophy," from its attribution to the mythical writer, Hermes Trismegistus. As the last selection in this volume we have included some passages from the prose meditations of Traherne which illustrate these tendencies toward Christian platonism that flourished in England in the middle of the seventeenth century.

Thus the ways in which a meditative action may be found in poetry are manifold: the meditative art is as changing, resourceful, and elusive as the mind in which the meditation is enacted. Now and then, as in the case of Donne's Hymn, one may say that the poem is a meditation: Donne himself uses the term to describe his fifteenth Holy Sonnet:

Wilt thou love God, as he thee! then digest,
　My Soule, this wholsome meditation . . .

But, for the most part, it is better to speak of meditative poems, that is to say, poems in which some aspects of the meditative art may be discerned. From this standpoint, a poem such as Marvell's "Dialogue, between the Resolved Soul, and Created Pleasure" might be called meditative, since it enacts an interior drama; but it is not, of course, a meditation of the kind that Dawson describes. One may also, in poets such as Donne or Marvell, find some reflection of meditative habits in poems that are secular ("The Garden") or in poems that are cleverly profane ("The Funerall"). If, as Wallace Stevens suggests, meditation is the mind's "essential exercise," one would expect the results to ramify throughout a poet's career.

Finally, whatever terms we may prefer to use in discussing this poetry, it is wise to remember the advice of Kenneth Burke: "As, in musical theory, one chord is capable of various analyses, so in literature the appeal of one event may be explained by various principles. The important thing is not to confine the explanation to *one* principle, but to formulate sufficient principles to make an explanation possible."[14]

Joseph A. Mazzeo

METAPHYSICAL POETRY AND THE POETIC OF CORRESPONDENCE

THE inquiry into the nature of metaphor remains a vital intellectual problem in our time, and the development of science and philosophy since the time of Kant has tended to make ever more evident the important role which metaphors and analogies play in the sciences as well as in the arts. Morris Cohen in his *Preface to Logic* says:

. . . metaphors are not merely artificial devices for making discourse vivid and poetical, but are also necessary for the apprehension and communication of new ideas. This is confirmed by the history of language and of early poetry as well as by the general results of modern psychology.

The prevailing view since Aristotle's *Rhetoric* regards metaphor as an analogy from which the words of comparison, *like* or *as*, etc. are omitted. This presupposes that the recognition of the literal truth precedes the metaphor, which is always a conscious transference of the properties of one thing to another. But history shows that metaphors are generally older than expressed analogies. If intelligence grows from the vague and confused to the more definite by a process of discrimination, we may well expect that the mere motion common to animate and inanimate beings should impress us even before we have made a clear distinction between these two kinds of being . . . metaphors may thus be viewed as expressing the vague and confused but primal perception of identity which subsequent processes of discrimination transform into a clear assertion of an identity or a common element (or relation) which the two different things possess. This helps us to explain the proper function of

14 Kenneth Burke, *Counter-Statement*, 2nd ed. (Phoenix Books, 1957), p. 129.

metaphors in science as well as in relation and art, and cautions us against fallacious arguments for or against views expressed in metaphorical language.[1]

Cohen goes on to say that metaphor may be, and often is, the way in which any creative mind perceives new relationships, and that the awareness of dealing with an analogy rather than with an identity comes later, if at all.[2] We must bear in mind, however, that Cohen is primarily interested in the function of analogical thinking in philosophical and scientific investigation. His analysis does not apply with equal validity to the function of metaphor in poetry, where metaphor exists as a final kind of statement and not as statement in need of further intellectual clarification or organization. However, he does establish the cardinal point about metaphorical statement and its relationship to literal and mathematical statement with considerable clarity, demonstrating the present-day reversal of the prevailing view of metaphor. In any case, his kind of approach is essential for a thorough understanding of past investigations of the nature of metaphor.

The seventeenth century witnessed a revival of interest in metaphor among literary critics and rhetoricians similar in intensity to that of our own time. The major seventeenth-century theorists of metaphor or conceit were all continental Europeans: Baltasar Gracián in Spain and Emmanuele Tesauro, Cardinal Sforza-Pallavicino, Pierfrancesco Minozzi, and Matteo Pellegrini in Italy. These critics faced a problem that some seventeenth-century English critics might have faced, but never so far as I can find, did face: what was the theoretical basis of the "metaphysical" style so widespread in the poetry of the seventeenth century?

If, in the seventeenth century, literature in Italy and elsewhere in Europe rebelled against the old forms and struck out along new paths, the criticism, in spite of its opposition to the Aristotle of the *Cinquecento*, remained in some essentials the same as that of the preceding century. This would seem to be true in investigations concerning metaphor, for our theorists generally *defined* it as a modification of literal statement or its ornamentation.[3] This conception of metaphor was not their only one, but it is the one most easily discerned

and the only conception of metaphor which would emerge from a superficial reading of their works. Whenever they define, they take their cue from Aristotle and describe metaphor as the pleasant ornamentation of a literal statement of fact. This adornment helps us to learn the "plain" truth easily and pleasantly.[4] Metaphor was such a great good that the theorists felt that the accumulation of conceits in abundance was also a great good. Other elements in written expression which were theoretically found to be good, elements such as rhythm, "invention" and stylistic traits, were duly praised and their development in abundance was encouraged.[5] The foregoing characterization is fairly typical of the evaluation of the tractates given by Borinski, Croce, and Menéndez y Pelayo.[6]

Although it is true that there was often discussion of metaphor in terms of ornament in the tractates on the conceit, Gracián and his Italian followers as well made the attempt to separate the poetic faculty of *ingegno* from any subservience to rhetorical notions of ornamentation. Gracián in particular often explicitly affirmed that *ingegno* does not serve to ornament thought but to create beauty (beauty in the sense that "wit" is poetic beauty for our theorists).[7] However, in developing this conception Gracián ended with an analogy between "wit" and architecture in which the solidity of a structure was compared to literal statement while "wit" furnished the ornamentation. If this analogy from architecture is compared to the analogy

1 Morris R. Cohen, *A Preface to Logic* (New York, 1944), p. 83.

2 *Ibid.*, p. 85.

3 B. Croce, *Problemi di estetica*, 4th ed. (Bari, 1949), p. 313.

4 E. Tesauro, *Il cannochiale aristotelico*, 2nd ed. (Venezia, 1663), p. 112.

5 Croce, *Problemi*, pp. 313–14.

6 Marcellino Menéndez y Pelayo, *Historia de las ideas esteticas en España*, 9 vols. (Madrid, 1928–1933), vol. II, part II, p. 536. Karl Borinski, *Baltasar Gracián und die Hofliteratur in Deutschland* (Halle, 1894), 39. Croce, *Problemi*, p. 315. Menéndez y Pelayo calls the work of Gracián a more or less unsuccessful attempt to substitute an "ideological" rhetoric for the purely formal, ornamental conception of rhetoric which dominated literary theory in Gracián's time. Karl Borinski saw in Gracián's conception of *gusto* a special faculty of aesthetic judgment distinct from logical judgment; he calls it the major single contribution to aesthetics in modern times. Benedetto Croce, though he is in partial agreement with Borinski, regards the work of Gracián and of most of his Italian followers as specimens of seventeenth-century preciosity rather than critical works concerned with poetic theory. This general estimate of the theorists seems to be that, although they foreshadowed certain aesthetic and philosophical theories, they really never transcended the traditional ideas of their own time.

7 Croce, *Problemi*, pp. 315–16.

from harmony quoted below, it will be noticed that the two analogies are quite different in meaning.

lo que es para los ojos la hermosura y para los oídos la consonancia, eso es para el entendimiento el concepto [i.e. la correspondencia que se halla entre los objetos.]

In the one case we have wit defined as the ornamentation of plain and literal statements, in the other case, the analogy from harmony, we have wit as the faculty which seeks out and realizes the hidden resemblances between things.[8]

This antithesis is to be found in one way or another in all the theorists and is based on the inability to transcend the distinction between plain and metaphorical speech. The idea that "plain" expression is studied by the science of grammar while rhetoric rules the domain of all ornate or non-literal expression was still dominant. The hegemony of this idea in all thinking about literary criticism made it inevitable that, when discussing all "ornate" expression including poetry, the theorists should fall back on the abstract schemes and definitions of traditional rhetoric.

Tesauro as well as Gracián fell into this same kind of difficulty. For him the essence of wit resided in the "figure," or in all that raised expression above the level of plain discourse.[9] The same raising of expression also constituted the distinction between prose and poetry.[10] Tesauro further divided the notion of "figure" into three separate classifications: those that delight the ear by mellifluous periods, those that delight the affections by the vivacity of the images they present, and those that delight the intellect by their wit. The essence of "witty" figures was metaphor, and Tesauro distinguished eight species in the course of his analysis of "witty" expression.[11] It is obvious that Tesauro's elaboration of the kinds of figures did not transcend the antithesis between "plain" and "ornate" speech.

A similar antithesis is revealed by the difficulty

our critics had in formulating a criterion for determining what constitutes excess in the use of the conceit, a difficulty especially present to those critics like Matteo Pellegrini who had a more temperate view of *Concettismo* than his colleagues. They failed to solve this problem because the determination of excess in the use of the conceit demanded other critical principles than the ones with which they were working. On the one hand, as we have seen, it was necessary to transcend the distinction between plain and metaphorical speech, and on the other, to acquire a functional conception of metaphor. These changes would have established poetry as a unique form of statement irreducible to any prose paraphrase. The criterion of excess would then have become a function of whether all the statements in a poem succeed together in giving a "coherent and powerful structure of attitudes."[12] But the theorists accepted the conventional distinction between plain and metaphorical speech and were therefore committed, at least in theory, to a conception of poetry as the accumulation of ornamental metaphor; and the more metaphor one could accumulate the better the poem.

It was these theoretical difficulties that led to the covert introduction of other aesthetic faculties by the side of *ingegno*, faculties which were to judge deficiencies and excesses in poetry. There was an appeal to *furore*, poetic genius, and *gusto*, all concepts which served to deny the omnipotence of the rules in the production of a work of art. When Pellegrini ultimately renounced the attempt to formulate rules for the production of good *concetti* he could only come up with the statement that they must be *leggieri* or graceful, and regretted not being able to say how remote the analogies of a conceit can be before they become excessive.[13] The very fact that he posed the question in this matter is further evidence of the inadequacy of the critical criteria with which he was working.

Minozzi, a minor theorist of the conceit, who staunchly defended *concettismo* against the mild criticism of Pellegrini, was compelled to admit that the extravagant conceits Pellegrini condemned were after all best used in treating the lives of the saints, because unlike profane subjects, religious subjects cannot be praised to excess. He says:

---

8 Cf. Tesauro, *op. cit.*, p. 248; Baltasar Gracián, *Arte de ingenio* (Madrid, 1944), pp. 40 and 46.

9 Tesauro, *op. cit.*, p. 112.

10 G. Cesareo, *Storia delle teorie estetiche in Italia* (Bologna, 1924), p. 37.

11 Tesauro, *op. cit.*, pp. 113 *et seq.* See also pp. 278–79 for the subdivision of the class of "witty" figures into the following eight: Hiperbole, Hipotiposi, Metafora di Somiglianza, Equivoco, Opposito, Decettione, Metafora di Attributione, Laconismo. Tesauro devotes a chapter to each of these subdivisions.

12 I have borrowed the phrase "a coherent and powerful structure of attitudes" from Mr. Cleanth Brooks' *The Well Wrought Urn* (New York, 1947), p. 225.

13 Cf. Croce, *Problemi*, p. 332.

. . . essi Santi sono meritevole d'ogni qualunque artifizioso ingrandimento, e di loro sempre favellasi daddovero, ed eglino stessi per tanto sono superiori ad ogni umana adulazione. Onde nelle vite de'santi eziando gli scherzi hanno forza di persuadere e di commuovere, essendo presi per serietà non per ischerzi. Ed alle volte è più atto a commuovere uno scherzo perchè dilette che una semplice purità perchè non ha del lusinghiero.[14]

It is clear, then, that this theory of poetry tended, as the theorists themselves realized, to fall on the one hand into a purely legalistic conception of poetry, and on the other into an exclusively intellectualistic account of the process of literary creation. They attempted to avoid the first pitfall by the formulation of concepts like *furore*, and to avoid the second by attempting to distinguish between logical and aesthetic judgments, *ingegno* and intellect.

Although the theorists tried to distinguish *ingegno* from intellect, they always finished up by finding a kind of intellectual truth in the conceit. This was a logical conclusion drawn from their purely intellectualistic definition of the conceit itself.[15] As long as the product of the *ingegno* was defined in exclusively intellectualistic terms, there was scant hope of considering the *ingegno* a faculty sharply divorced from the intellect and its operations. The inability to distinguish between the function of metaphor in poetry and the function of metaphor in philosophy and science is at the root of this particular dilemma. The attempted solution of this problem introduced a modified notion of the *ingegno* as a kind of creative or super-intellect distinct from ratiocinative intellect. But a final solution of the problem awaited the realization of the way in which all metaphors are alike as well as the way in which they differ in function when metaphorical thought occurs in poetry, science, and religion.[16]

The thought of our theorists on the distinctions between logical and aesthetic judgments deserves some scrutiny. Pallavicino, Tesauro, and Minozzi all warn that there is a difference between the syllogism

as it functions in logic and the rhetorical syllogism. Tesauro adapted the enthymeme to describe the notion of the expanded conceit.[17] He then discussed the difference in purpose that distinguished these two kinds of syllogism, a distinction which, for Croce, foreshadowed the later distinction between logic and aesthetics, the one ratiocinative and the other expressive. Thus the enthymeme, equivalent for Tesauro to the expanded conceit in some contexts, aimed at producing aesthetic pleasure, while the logical syllogism arrived at the truth through dialectic. The *enthymema urbanum* had the function of delighting; also called *cavillazione retorica*, it proceeded by leaps and bounds which delighted the reader whereas *cavillazione dialettica* proceeded by regular intervals.[18]

In Tesauro's view, it was not proper to consider a literary statement as a logical affirmation. It is possible to say that poems are ugly or beautiful, but not that they are false or sophistic. The nature of *cavillazione retorica* tells us that one does not inquire into truth with literary statement, but simply states that which is to be enjoyed.[19] One should combat false philosophers, but leave orators alone to adopt splendid and eloquent forms.[20] The positive aspect of this analysis of Tesauro lies in the attempt to distinguish between aesthetic and logical judgments. On the other hand, the distinction between plain and metaphorical speech leads to an inadequate conception of the truth by identifying it with plain expression; the inevitable conclusion from this is that poetry is either the embellished "truth" or a pleasant but total "lie," both of which opinions Tesauro held at different times. In practice his distinctions became two purely empirical distinctions between plain and dialectical expression and ornate or witty expression. Thus in the final analysis, he returned to the conventional enthymeme and syllogism.[21] The adherence to the conventional divisions of grammar, rhetoric, and logic always interfered with the conception of poetry as a unique form of statement.[22]

For Croce the theorists are especially important in the history of thought because of their effect on the philosophy of Vico. He finds that Vico invigorated

---

14 Pierfrancesco Minozzi, *Gli sfogamenti dell'ingegno* (Venezia, 1641), cited in Croce, *Problemi*, 334.

15 Croce, *Estetica*, Bari, 1945, 8th ed., p. 216.

16 Cf. Wilbur Marshall Urban, *Language and Reality* (New York, 1939), for a general discussion of the philosophy of language and the rôle of metaphor in the various branches of creation and inquiry.

17 Tesauro, *op. cit.*, pp. 110–13, 450–52.

18 *Ibid.*, pp. 451 and 445; Croce, *Problemi*, p. 330.

19 Tesauro, *op. cit.*, p. 450.

20 Tesauro, *op. cit.*., p. 451; Croce, *Problemi*, p. 341.

21 Croce, *Storia dell'età barocca*, 2nd ed. (Bari, 1946), p. 188.

22 Croce, *Problemi*, p. 343, cf. Tesauro, *op. cit.*, pp. 449 and 452.

the theory of Pallavicino concerning "first apprehension" (a notion Croce believes similar to his "aesthetic intuition") and changed the Tesaurian interpretation of the rhetorical syllogism, analogous to the logical syllogism, into the conception of a "poetic logic" prior and analogous to a logic of "developed mind" (*mente spiegata*).[23] This concept of Vico later formed the basis for the aesthetic of Baumgarten.[24] Tesauro also extended the categories of rhetoric to pictorial and sculptural forms of expression, as well as to drama and pantomime, in which expression is accomplished by means of gestures. These various types of expression are extensively discussed in the *Cannochiale*, and Tesauro carefully explained the various sensible modes by which an interior image may be externalized.[25] There are (1) the signs of speech, (2) mute signs, as in sculpture or painting, or (3) mixed signs, by which he meant the drama (gestures and words) and the emblem and *impresa* (picture with accompanying motto). A second classification is into (1) spoken and written expression (*acutezze verbali*); (2) the emblem, *impresa* or other pictorial and sculptural forms (*acutezze simboliche o figurative*); and (3) a classification which refers to the drama and pantomime, called that of *acutezze sensibili*. Tesauro was able to classify any form of expression by means of these two sets of concepts. It is of the greatest importance to observe that all these forms of expression are called *acutezze* or witty metaphorical expressions, and this included the mute forms as well.[26] The implication is clear that all expression, linguistic and symbolic, is basically metaphorical; although Tesauro was working with the conventional categories of rhetoric, in this instance he clearly tried to transcend the old distinctions between rhetoric, grammar, and logic or between plain and metaphorical expression. As far as I know, Tesauro's analysis of the forms of expression constitutes one of the earliest extensive attempts to formulate a unified theory of the arts.

Vico took the interpretation of rhetorical categories that Tesauro made and changed them into the categories by which the imagination states itself. The category of mute signs and mixed types became one of the Viconian *linguaggi mutoli* of the imagination, a faculty which expressed itself not only in words but

also in lines and colours.[27] Vico's mute and mixed categories included emblems, impresas, heraldic figures, military ensigns, etc., symbolic modes of expression evidently analogous to Tesauro's *acutezze simboliche o figurate*.[28]

In spite of all this the theorists of the conceit were so bound to the authority of what was conceived to be the Aristotelian theory that when they faced any situation requiring a new definition of metaphor they invariably fell back on ornamental conceptions in spite of their attempt to respond to the theoretical exigencies of their new inquiries. However, when our theorists were free to discuss metaphor without any precision of definition, we find a substantially different conception of metaphor by the side of the old one. This is especially true of Tesauro, and it is in his curious researches on the efficient causes of wit that we find some of his most fruitful ideas about metaphor, ideas which were as much as variance with the traditional conception of metaphor as his analysis and extention of rhetorical categories.

Wit was a topic which the ancients had not exhausted or even investigated thoroughly, and Tesauro's opinions fell freely; it is here that we see his link with some of the important currents of Renaissance thought most clearly.

Tesauro maintained that *acutezze* or conceits were not created by men only but by God, his angels, and by animals. The universe was created by a God who was a "witty creator," an *arguto favellatore*, a witty writer or talker.[29] The world was a poem made up of conceits. The notion that the world is a poem of God is old enough as a conception and, in various forms, goes back at least to Plotinus.[30] However, the important difference for Tesauro is that the world is a "metaphysical" poem and God a "metaphysical" poet. He conceived *ingegno* as the faculty in man analogous to God's creative power. It is a small particle of the divine nature, for it can create "being" where there was no "being" before.[31] As God created a "meta-

23 Croce, *Storia*, p. 288.
24 Croce *Problemi*, p. 345.
25 Tesauro, *op. cit.*, pp. 14–54.
26 Tesauro, *op. cit.*, pp. 50–53.

27 Croce, *Estetica*, p. 254.
28 Croce, *La filosophia di Giambattista Vico*, 4th ed. (Bari, 1947), p. 54.
29 Cf. Croce, *Problemi*, 345, where Croce maintains that this concept of nature as made up of *acutezze* prepared the way for the study of the concept of the beautiful in nature.
30 Rosamund Tuve, *Elizabethan and Metaphysical Imagery* (Chicago, 1946), p. 159. The Stoics also speak of the world-poem or world-drama.
31 Tesauro, *op. cit.*, p. 76.

physical" world, so the poet creates "metaphysical" poems. God is:

arguto favellatore, mottegiando agli Uomini et agli Angeli, con varie Imprese eroiche e Simboli figurati, gli altissimi suoi concetti.[32]

The sky is

un vasto ceruleo scudo, ove l'ingegnosa Natura disegna ciò che medita: formando eroiche Imprese e Simboli misteriosi e arguti dei suoi segreti.[33]

Thunder is really nothing but an *acutezza* of the mixed type, picture and motto together, and the whole of nature speaks in conceits. They are:

formidabile Argutie et Simboliche
Cifere della natura, mute insieme e vocali;
avendo La Saetta per corpo e il Tuono per motto.[34]

The conventional idea of the book of nature is implied in all of Tesauro's speculation on this matter. This idea is old and traditional, but Tesauro sees the book of nature written in conceits, in witty metaphors. This book was read in many ways during the lifetime of the concept. Its most fruitful reading was by Tesauro's contemporary Galileo, who read it mathematically.[35]

Sig. Mario Praz finds Tesauro's conception of the world as *acutezze* bizarre, and it might seem so at first glance. The apparent strangeness of this conception is increased when we are told that angels and demons (identified with pagan deities) all spoke in witty oracles and communicated with men in dreams which themselves were nothing but *acutezze*.[36] The song of the nightingale presented a pattern of verse, revealing one aspect of the rhythmic pulse of the "world-poem." The bestiary traditions were made "metaphysical," and all animals and plants revealed witty significance to the observer with *ingegno*. As the *acutezze* of poets are called "flowers," so flowers are the *acutezze* of nature.[37]

Thus God created a world full of metaphors, analogies and conceits, and so far from being ornamentation, they are the law by which creation was effected. God wrote the book of nature in metaphor, and so it should be read. The arts, the creation of men, are also *acutezze*, and painters are nothing but mute poets.[38] Now the poetic involved in this view of the world is not the poetic of ornamental metaphor, but what I call "the poetic of correspondences." When the conceit is said to have those properties which enable it to pierce the intellect or to arouse sensations of marvel and wonder, we do wrong to think, as some critics have, of the more excessive kinds of Baroque art. What is meant is that quality of vision which the discovery of correspondences can bring, the "thrill" which the awareness of an analogy gives the intellect when it first becomes aware of the identity between things formerly believed unconnected. The universe is a vast net of correspondences which unites the whole multiplicity of being. The poet approaches and creates his reality by a series of more or less elaborate correspondences.

Pallavicino, in a very illuminating passage, said that the function of *ingegno*—we must remember that *ingegno* is the poetic faculty *par excellence*—is precisely the power to search out these correspondences. He also speculated upon Homer's "golden chain," suggesting that it may have been a mythological representation of this world of correspondences.

Poichè quel dono di natura che si chiama ingegno consiste appunto in congiungere per mezzo di scaltre apprensioni oggetti che pareano affatti sconessi, rintracciando in essi gli occulti vestigi d'amicizia fra la stessa contrarietà, la non avvertita unità di special somiglianza nella somma dissimilitudine, qualche vincolo, qualche parentela, qualche confederazione dove altri non l'avrebbe mai sospettato. Annadò la natura maestrevolmente fra loro tutti i suoi effetti, e ciò fu per avventura il misterio di quell'aurea catena omerica. Nè v'ha nel mondo verun oggetto sì solitario e sì sciolto che frà laberinti della filosofia non somministri qualche aureo filo per giungere alla notizia d'ogni altro oggetto quanto si voglia lontano ed ascoso. Ma queste fila quanto son lucide per la nobiltà del metallo tanto sono invisibili per la sottigliezza della mole. L'arte di ben ravvisarle contiensi principalmente negli otto libri meravigliosi della Topica di Aristotile,

32 *Ibid.*, p. 54.
33 *Ibid.*, p. 68.
34 *Ibid.*, p. 69.
35 See Galileo Galilei, *I massimi sistemi*, in *Opere*, I (Milan-Rome, 1946).
36 Tesauro, *op. cit.*, p. 72–75.
37 *Ibid.*, p. 75.

38 *Ibid.*, pp. 53 and 306.

in cui si mostra la maniera di indagar le ragioni per disputar probabilmente in ogni maniera ed a favor di ciascuna parte . . . [Ma] che giovano i precetti dell'arte dove manca l'abilita dell'ingegno? Perciò la più vera topica e più sagace è la perspicacia che ne dà la natura.[39]

Nature then was not the object of simple observation and enjoyment; it was the "matter" in which man discovered and read the metaphors of divine wisdom, for the world itself was a "metaphysical" poem. God created such a world for the purpose of arousing the wonder of men, and man himself made conceits because he alone of all the creatures of God needed to seek out the variety of the universe and express it. Man cannot remain on the level of plain perception and plain discourse.[40] Wit was, as Mr. Austin Warren states, "more than an offering," which is to say more than a technique of ornamentation and decoration:

. . . it was also an instrument of vision. With its occult couplings, it penetrates to the centre of the universe, where, however dissimilar they may appear to the unobservant, all things unite.[41]

The theorists have both these conceptions of wit. Wit is, on the one hand, the exploration of a universe made up of a series of correspondences; and yet there is praise of wit as ornamentation, praise of the kind of wit that is not vision and whose occult couplings do not reveal a higher unity.

The desire to discover cosmic affinities and to draw and develop universal correspondence and analogies indicates an attempt to deepen the value of words; it is a sign of awareness in poets and critics of situations in the multiplicity of being that had not yet been individualized and which they were trying to realize by verbal suggestions and by what seemed to be strange and hybrid analogies. The conceit was the instrument for this poetic exploration of reality. Pallavicino says of the nature of the conceit:

. . . la principal dilettazione dell'intelletto consiste nel meravigliarsi . . . Ma intanto la meraviglia è scaturigine d'un sommo piacere intellettuale, in quanto è sempre congiunta col saper ciò che prima era ignoto; E Quanto più era ignoto, o più eziando contrario alla nostra credenza, tanto è maggior la meraviglia.[42]

The notion of the *mirabile* is in this passage clearly related to the conceit conceived as an instrument of insight, not to the conceit as an ornamentation of knowledge. Tesauro also defined the metaphor as a means of vision:

La metafora tutti [gli obietti] a stretta li rinzeppa in un Vocabulo: e quasi in miraculoso modo gli ti fa travedere l'uno dentro all'altro. Onde maggiore è il tuo diletto: nella maniera, che più curiosa e piacevol cosa e mirar molti obietti per un istraforo di perspettiva, che se gli originali medesimi successivamente ti venisser passando dinanzi agli occhi.[43]

This statement is buttressed elsewhere when Tesauro says that any obscurity in the conceit is justified only as the revelation of a little mystery (*un piccolo mistero*). After all, the whole of reality for Tesauro made up of *acutezze* or the revelation of little mysteries, of which his work treats only those *acutezze* which deal with words and figures.[44]

Thus, by seeking out and establishing correspondences, the *ingegno* makes order out of disorder and brings clarity where there had been only darkness and mystery. Nature to those of little *ingegno* seemed like an obvious thing, but to the man of *ingegno* it was a mystery to be investigated, an obstacle to be overcome. Nature really worked against art, for our theorists, and it had to be probed to reveal Pallavicino's "golden thread."

Two conceptions of metaphor, and therefore two poetics, existed side by side in the work of our theorists, and we see them shifting from one to the other, a sign that the problems they raised were not capable of full solution in the terms in which they were stated. One of these poetics, the one built on metaphor as ornament, is negative; the other, which I call the "poetic of correspondences," is positive. This does not imply that one theory was responsible for bad and the other for good poetry, for a theory of poetry never creates

39 Sforza-Pallavicino, *Del Bene* (Milan, 1831), book III, part 2, chapt. 55. 1st ed. (Rome, 1644). This passage suggests a connection between the poetic of correspondences and the renewed importance of the doctrine of the *coincidentia oppositorum* in the Renaissance, although it is an interpretation of the doctrine rather than a restatement of it if, indeed, there is any direct connection.

40 Tesauro, *op. cit.*, pp. 54 and 111.

41 Austin Warren, *Richard Crashaw: A Study in Baroque Sensibility* (University, La., 1939), p. 75.

42 Sforza-Pallavicino, *Trattato*, pp. 77–78.

43 Tesauro, *op. cit.*, p. 276.

44 *Ibid.*, p. 53.

works of art. A poetic is only the theoretical expression of a living art, of a concrete poetic reality found in the work of the poets whose art elicits observations from critics and aestheticians. What I mean by the terms "positive" and "negative" is that the theory of the conceit as ornament was not capable of further development, while the theory of universal correspondences, conceived as a poetic, was revived and culminated in the poetic of Baudelaire. In his essay on Victor Hugo he clearly defined this position:

Chez les excellents poètes il n'y a pas de métaphore de comparaison ou d'épithète qui ne soit d'une adaptation mathématiquement exacte dans la circonstance actuelle, parce que ces comparaisons, ces métaphores et ces épithètes sont puisées dans l'inépuisable fonds de l'universelle analogie, et qu'elles ne peuvent être puisées ailleurs.[45]

Although the treatises on the conceit appear to have been little read after the seventeenth century, the theory of metaphor which they developed was kept alive through the occult tradition, and reached Baudelaire through the agency of Swedenborg. It is not an accident that the great analogical complexity of much modern poetry should have been largely the work of Yeats and Baudelaire, two poets who studied the occult sciences and who revived the conception of the poet as one who approaches reality through the discovery of the analogies latent in nature.

If, as Cassirer maintains, the Renaissance theory of mathematical physics is linked to the Renaissance theory of art by the formulation of the problem of form, the positive aspects of the theory of the conceit are linked to Renaissance science by the theories of correspondence and universal analogy. There is then a parallelism between Renaissance scientific and philosophical thought on the one hand, and the theory of the conceit on the other, which helps to account for the way in which "metaphysical" poetry was able to digest so much scientific and technical imagery.[46] The poetic of correspondences implies an underlying belief in the unity and connection of all things. Such

a view simplifies the assimilation of all kinds of unusual images in poetry, for such a universe—unlike the universe of Samuel Johnson and other neo-classical critics—has no class of objects which can be considered "unpoetic."

The negative notion of metaphor stated by these theorists is closely allied to the general change in ways of feeling that accompanied the change from "Renaissance" to "Baroque." Many theories have been advanced to explain the emphasis on the Baroque in the seventeenth century, but there is little doubt that, from the point of view of the historian of culture, it may best be understood as the exaggeration of tendencies already present in the Renaissance. Croce suggests that the Renaissance preoccupation with form became the Baroque preoccupation with ornament.

The critics of the eighteenth and nineteenth centuries often ignored the literary productions of *Concettismo*, or, as it was called in England, the "metaphysical" school. When they read them, it was usually to hold them up as warnings and examples of what poets should avoid. The most important single objection levelled against the "metaphysicals" and the *concettisti* was that they were unfaithful to nature. In the light of the *Weltanschaung* implied by the poetic of correspondences, this particular objection has less foundation than it might seem to have. The metaphysical poets of the seventeenth century may have been unfaithful to the eighteenth-century Lockean or Cartesian nature, but not to the nature of their own times. I do not mean to imply that *Concettismo* did not display exaggerations. Even the greatest writers have written inferior works, and every literary movement becomes mannered and exaggerated, in time. The best poets of this kind, a Marvell or a Donne, occasionally strained after a figure of speech. But this seems to be the exception rather than the rule. Many images we today would call "artificial conceits"—in Dr. Johnson's meaning of the term—were really faithful and accurate images. This universe contained relationships which no longer exist for us; they have been eliminated from our perception by Baconianism and Cartesianism. What may seem to us strange and far-fetched similitudes were often truths, even commonplaces, in their world of insight. The theorists of the conceit envisaged the poet's universe as a complex system of universal analogical relationships which the poets expressed and revealed. The critics of subsequent times no longer understood this view of the

45 Charles Baudelaire, Essay on "Victor Hugo," in *Oeuvres*, 2 vols. (Paris, 1938), vol. II.
46 Mario Praz, *Studi sul Concettismo* (Florence, 1946), p. 136. This aspect of metaphysical poetry has often been noticed. Sig. Praz attributes the prevalence of scientific imagery in metaphysical poetry to a shift in taste. For Ernst Cassirer's thesis see *Individuum und Kosmos in der Philosophie der Renaissance* (Leipzig, 1927), especially ch. 4.

world. Although we may, if we choose, agree with Johnson's conclusion about the "metaphysicals," we cannot accept his basis for that judgment. This truth by no means reflects on Johnson's critical powers. Bradley's Pickwickian definition of metaphysics might be applied in the same sense to literary criticism: both fields of endeavour are at least partially concerned with inventing "bad reasons for what we believe upon instinct."

Frank J. Warnke

ART AS PLAY

THE preceding chapter has remarked on the Baroque preoccupation with the idea of the world as a theatre and life as a play, an idea which is, as we have seen, an inversion of the more obvious perception of conventional mimesis, in terms of which the theatre is the world and the play is life. The topos "life is a play" is, it was suggested, one of the typical forms in which the Baroque vision of life is communicated, by essayist and lyric poet as well as by dramatist. It is to be expected that the world-view implied by a governing metaphor of such wide prevalence would give rise to a specific conception of art significantly different, at least in its emphases, from those of some other ages. In Sir Thomas Browne, as in Gracián and the other theorists of the conceit, the ancient idea of God as artist and the creation as work of art receives striking elaboration, and Calderón never tires of making use of the same idea.[1] The theatre-metaphor, one might say, is a special instance of the literally held ontological theory of creation as art.

That theory in itself, if it inspired little in the way of overt literary speculation, permeated a great deal of the creative literature of the Baroque age. It is difficult to respond as fully as is desirable to a great many characteristic Baroque works of literary art if one has not developed a sense of the very mode of artistic being of those works, a mode of being which has little to do with simple didacticism and still less to do with simple mimesis. It has, I believe, a great deal to do with the phenomenon of *play*—that vast and crucial area of human activity of which *a* play is a particular local division. If the entire creation is literally a work of art, then that creation has of its very nature something of that attractively and gently spurious quality which adheres to any artifact as soon as it is consciously felt *as* artifact, and much of that quality, that complex of jocosity, make-believe, and ambivalence which makes up the concept of *play*, will characterize creation at one remove, that is to say, the art of man.

In *Homo Ludens*, his profound study of the play-element in culture, Johan Huizinga defines his subject in the following terms: "play is a voluntary activity or occupation executed within certain fixed limits of time and place, according to rules freely accepted but absolutely binding, having its aim in itself and accompanied by a feeling of tension, joy and the consciousness that it is 'different' from 'ordinary life'." In the course of his study Huizinga attempts to establish the important connections which he believes exist between this activity and the phenomena of myth and ritual, those phenomena which embody man's attempt to understand—or, better, to participate in—the incomprehensible mystery of existence. To the mind of "the savage, the child and the poet," reality presents itself as an "agonistic structure," and the "processes in life and the cosmos are seen as the eternal conflict of opposites which is the root-principle of existence."[2] Such a confrontation of existence is perhaps the defining feature of all art which is truly successful as art; it is, I think, surely the defining feature of the art of the Baroque age, an age which, in spite of its utilitarian, didactic, and polemic concerns, lived in constant awareness of the specific qualities of art. This awareness may supply a shadow of an answer to the questions posed at the end of chapter 1: How is it that typical Baroque literary works combine utilitarian purpose with mannered and self-conscious style? How is it that they fuse, in a manner astounding to modern naïveté, the presumably opposed qualities of formality and individuality? How is it that they express, in forms of the greatest sophistication, a life-experience which is primitive in its intensity?

The sense of life as the conflict of opposites supplies

1 See E. R. Curtius, *European Literature and the Latin Middle Ages*, trans. W. R. Trask (New York, 1953), pp. 544–70. Also J. A. Mazzeo, *Renaissance and Seventeenth-Century Studies* (New York, 1964), pp. 54–59; and cf. Sir Thomas Browne, "Religio Medici", in *Religio Medici and Other Writings*, ed. F. L. Huntley (New York, 1951), pp. 17–18.

2 J. Huizinga, *Homo Ludens*, Eng. trans. (Boston: Beacon Press, 1955), pp. 28, 116.

a clear spiritual basis for the seventeenth-century pre-occupation with the drama: on an unconscious level, presumably, the agon of fictional characters reenacts, as did that of the ancient Greeks, the universal agon of the cosmos. The all-embracing conflict of opposites includes also a specific conflict which is central to the theatre-topos examined in the preceding chapter, as well as to a wide variety of other literary phenomena of the age. That is the conflict between the self and the non-self, or, more precisely, between the concept of the self as the self and the concept of the self as other-than-the-self. One might consider in this connection John Donne's obsessive preoccupation with the conflict in his *Songs and Sonets*:

> Loves riddles are, that though thy heart depart,
>   It stayes at home, and thou with losing savest it:
> But wee will have a way more liberall,
>   Then changing hearts, to joyne them, so wee shall
>   Be one, and one anothers All.[3]

But one might also consider a wide range of other manifestations—the creation of the self as a dramatic character in the prose works of Montaigne, Burton, and Browne, and the central role played by dramatic projection of the self in formal meditation and in the religious poetry related to such meditation.[4] Agon and make-believe, two of the constituents of the play-attitude, lead inevitably to that experience of almost vertiginous levity, of extravagant release, which one associates with the phenomenon of play. All three elements—agon, make-believe, and levity—are conspicuously present in Baroque literature. Their presence—and to a degree that perhaps warrants the overall conception of Baroque art as played art—does not in any sense mean that Baroque literature is not serious. It is intensely serious, profoundly in touch with the sacred, precisely because it *is* played.[5]

The efflorescence of the dramatic lyric in the Baroque age is one of the most striking manifestations of the play-spirit in art, and it is undoubtedly significant that a large number of those dramatic lyrics are devotional in nature: one need only think of Donne's *Divine Poems*, of Herbert's *The Temple*, and, on the Continent, of the religious poems of Huygens and Fleming, of La Ceppède and Quevedo. In such poems a concern with the divine is by definition primary, but that concern expresses itself neither through simple pious praise nor through formal exhortation but rather through the acting out of a tense dramatic situation, an agon in which the contestants may be God and the soul, the soul and some personified abstraction, opposed aspects of the soul, or some other dramatis personae projected outward from inner experience. Baroque devotional poetry is saturated with the spirit of play in a larger sense as well: the Victorian parsons who kept alive Herbert's modest reputation throughout the nineteenth century, excusing his "quaintness" for the sake of his piety, erred in the same direction as some modern critics who insist that we see the poet's wit solely as an instrument of sober spiritual vision. Neither recognizes just how funny much of the poetry is, and just how necessary an appreciation of its funniness is to an appreciation of its profound, personality-transforming seriousness.

"Funny" may be the wrong adjective, but some equally extreme element of the play-spirit hovers constantly over *The Temple*. "The Collar" has often, and justly, been praised for the intensity and gravity with which it gives voice to religious experience, and yet the poem operates on the basis of extravagant wit, extending from the multiple puns of the title ("collar" in general, clerical "collar," "caller," and "choler") through the Eucharistic imagery which persistently and ironically dominates the blasphemous language of the rebellious speaker, to the intentionally ludicrous peripeteia of the final line. The experience of a sympathetic reading of "The Collar" is a curiously ironic and strangely invigorating one: as the images of liberation accumulate, the reader, identifying with the rebellious speaker, feels not release but rather something like a progressive strangulation as the objects of material desire close in around him. With the final turn of the poem, submission is experienced as true liberation; the collar is revealed as the way to freedom.

---

3 John Donne, *Poetical Works*, ed. H. J. C. Grierson, 2 vols. (Oxford, 1912), 1:18. Further citations of Donne in this chapter are to this edition and will be given in the text.

4 L. L. Martz, *The Poetry of Meditation*, rev. ed. (New Haven, 1962).

5 Huizinga, pp. 16–27; R. Caillois, *Man, Play, and Games*, trans. M. Barash (New York, 1961); F. J. Warnke, "Sacred Play: Baroque Poetic Style," *JAAC* 22, no. 4 (Summer 1964): 455–64, and "Play and Metamorphosis in Marvell's Poetry," *SEL* 5, no. 1 (Winter 1965): 23–30.

> But as I rav'd and grew more fierce and wilde
>   At every word,
> Me thoughts I heard one calling, *Child*!
>   And I reply'd, *My Lord*.

The poem is, in part, an artistic rendering of the kind of experience Herbert refers to in the words which he spoke on his deathbed to his friend Mr. Duncon, describing the poems of *The Temple* as "a picture of the many spiritual Conflicts that have past betwixt God and my Soul, before I could subject mine to the will of Jesus my Master, in whose service I have now found perfect freedom."[6]

Relevant here is the connection between the experience of paradoxical liberation embodied in "The Collar" and the account of the play-spirit as we find it in Huizinga: "a voluntary activity . . . executed within certain fixed limits . . . according to rules freely accepted but absolutely binding, having its aim in itself and accompanied by a feeling of tension, joy and the consciousness that it is 'different' from 'ordinary life'."[7] There is something theological-sounding about Huizinga's definition, as there is much playful about the experience of "The Collar"; one is reminded of the lines from a poem on childhood by Herbert's disciple Henry Vaughan: "Quickly would I make my path even, / And by meer playing go to Heaven."[8]

Intellectual play is the very essence of Herbert's formidable technique, not only in such obvious examples as his "shaped" or "pattern" poems, "The Altar" and "Easter Wings," but also, more subtly, in such poems as "Deniall," in which the breakdown of the speaker's contact with God reflects itself in the breakdown of the rhyme-scheme, "Trinitie Sunday," which is made up of three stanzas of three lines each, and "Paradise," in which the central metaphor of pruning is reinforced by lopping off letters progressively to form the rhyme-words:

> When thou dost greater judgements SPARE,
> And with thy knife but prune and PARE,
> Ev'n fruitfull trees more fruitfull ARE.
>
> [p. 133]

"My God must have my best, ev'n all I had," writes Herbert in "The Forerunners" (pg. 176), the finest of the many poems on poetry scattered throughout *The Temple*. His best, the best of a Baroque poet, is his wit, his tricks with language; and his volume becomes, from one point of view, an offering like that of the jongleur of Notre Dame.

Herbert's devotional poetry, with its play-aesthetic behind it, is in no sense unique in the Baroque age. In England, in their various ways, the other devotional poets of the Metaphysical succession—Crashaw, Vaughan, and Traherne—display similar emphases, and Continental devotional poetry exhibits a similar fusion of intense religious emotion and intellectual play. The religious lyrics of the German Paul Fleming and the Dutchman Constantijn Huygens abound especially in examples of such fusion.[9] The Baroque devotional poets were often struck by the same divine jokes, and one can find numerous examples of identical witty motifs turning up all over Europe in the seventeenth century. One such motif is that which describes the good thief who was crucified beside Christ as having "stolen" his salvation: Giles Fletcher, in *Christ's Victory and Triumph*, writes: "And with him stood the happy theefe, that stole / By night his owne salvation . . ."[10] On the Continent, Jean de la Ceppède writes of the repentant thief "dont aujourd'huy l'invincible valeur, / Le Christ mesme a volé"; the Dutch poet Heiman Dullaert observes that he "komt het Hemelryk tot roofgoet te verrassen" ("he seizes Heaven as a robber's prey"); Giuseppe Artale introduces the same jest; and both Quevedo and Lope de Vega have poems based on it.[11] In every case the jest operates as a mechanism of psychological release— both in the general sense in which any jest effects a kind of release, and in the more special religious sense in which the participant is released from mundane life into a spiritual world dominated by norms of value which are utterly different from the mundane (the paradoxes which occur so heavily in Donne's *Holy Sonnets* work in much the same way).

Thus far, then, there are two respects in which the typical Baroque devotional poem gives evidence of the play-element: it is agonistic in mode, and it employs a kind of serious jocularity, expressed in witty metaphor, pun, and elaborate formalism, with the final effect of achieving a break-through into a kind of solemn lightheartedness, the result of a transcendence of or liberation from the mundane and secular. (The mundane itself, so prominent in the diction and imagery of Herbert and Donne, is spiritually transformed by being viewed in the context of the divine.)

---

6 George Herbert, *Works*, ed. F. E. Hutchinson (Oxford, 1941), pp. 153–54, xxxvii. Further citations from Herbert are to this edition and are given in the text.

7 *Homo Ludens*, p. 28.

8 Henry Vaughan, *Works*, ed. L. C. Martin, 2nd ed. (Oxford, 1957), p. 520.

9 See my *European Metaphysical Poetry* (New Haven, 1961).

10 Giles and Phineas Fletcher, *Poetical Works*, ed. F. S. Boas, 2 vols. (Cambridge, 1908), 1:71.

11 See my *European Metaphysical Poetry*, p. 64.

If the contentions made early in this chapter have any validity, the play-attitude should be noticeably present in types of literature other than the devotional. Such is, I am convinced, the case. To choose only two examples, such massive—and profoundly serious—prose works as *The Anatomy of Melancholy* and the *Religio Medici* habitually joke with the reader, sometimes gravely, sometimes with an almost carnival-like abandon. Even more consistently, both works operate through the projection of a persona, an image of the author's self which some other aspect of the author regards with a curious combination of delight, astonishment, trepidation, and bemused fascination. The splitting of the self characteristic of both Burton and Browne bestows on their masterpieces something of the agonistic quality already noted in the work of the devotional poets.

The *Anatomy* and the *Religio* are both simultaneously religious and scientific works. If we turn to Baroque works of an avowedly secular character, we shall find the play attitude expressed with comparable force and thoroughgoingness.

There is a lot of playing in the love lyrics of the seventeenth century—most obviously in the more lighthearted of Donne's *Songs and Sonets* and poems written under their influence by Thomas Carew, Sir John Suckling, and other English poets, and in several of the lyrics of Théophile de Viau, Marc-Antoine de Saint-Amant, and other of the French *libertins*. But play is also present in love poems which cannot be classified as merely jocular. In such passionate and profound utterances as "The Good-Morrow," "Lovers Infinitenesse," "The Anniversarie," and "The Extasie," Donne creates an atmosphere of play, almost of joke, without in the least degree compromising the seriousness of his statements, all of which, significantly, have as part of their subject the transcendence of the individual identity through participation in a mutual love. In Donne's love poetry as in his, or Herbert's, devotional poetry, the fact that the poem exists in the sphere of play relates at once to its dramatic and agonistic qualities, its powerful emotional effect, and its manifestation of the theme of transcendence.

The playfulness of Baroque love poetry shows itself in four distinct but related features: the imposition of a double view, through which the speaker simultaneously voices his personal passion and distances himself from it in a half-amused way; the formulation of the speaker's relation to the beloved in quasi-dramatic terms; the use of comic hyperbole; and the practice of insulting or showing aggression toward the beloved, with the consequent creation of a kind of amorous agon, or erotic flyting. Conspicuously present in Donne's love poetry, these features almost define the practice of many other important Baroque love poets both in England and on the Continent. Distancing, usually jocular and frequently dramatic, is as characteristic of Carew, Suckling, and Lovelace as it is of Donne. In Suckling's "I prithee send me back my heart," or Carew's "Mediocrity in Love Rejected," the speaker's passion, protested to his beloved in direct address, is coupled with an attitude of levity conveyed through extravagant wit and a tone which might be described as tenderly jesting. Much of Suckling's work takes the form of unequivocal joke, as in the familiar songs "Why so pale and wan, fond lover" and "Out upon it, I have loved," but he is equally capable of the typically Baroque combination of the playful and the passionate.

The combination continues throughout the period. John Cleveland's hyperbolic spoofs are not devoid of a certain intense, however paradoxical, emotional involvement, and Dryden's songs, composed when the Baroque style was moribund, still operate on a basis of combined passion and levity which recalls both Carew and Ben Jonson. Many of the Continental poets project their amorous avowals to the accompaniment of the same kind of ironic distancing—Paul Fleming and Hofmann von Hofmannswaldau in Germany, Constantijn Huygens in Holland, Marino in Italy, and Etienne Durand, Théophile de Viau, and Marc-Antoine de Saint-Amant in France. The accompaniment seems obligatory in such French lyrists as Jean Bertaut and Pierre Motin. The latter is particularly fond of erotic jokes which depend on religious associations, as in one sonnet in which he begs his lady's favor on the grounds that faith without "good works" is insufficient to salvation, or another in which he points out to a certain Mademoiselle La Croix that her name implies more mercy than she has hitherto shown her frustrated lover.[12] More trivial than Donne's, Motin's lyrics nevertheless demonstrate the same compulsion to transfer both amorous and devotional materials to the realm of play, a realm in which, strangely, the seriousness of those materials is ratified rather than compromised.

The devices of comic hyperbole and amorous agon

12 *Ibid.*, pp. 122–25.

are sufficiently important to demand separate consideration. Comic hyperbole constitutes one special form of ironic distancing, but its relation to the play-spirit is not limited to such distancing, or, rather, the distancing which it induces relates not only to the irony of obvious exaggeration but also to more mysterious potentialities for transformation inherent in the figure of hyperbole itself. There is nothing inevitably comic or playful in extreme hyperbole of the sort that marks the Petrarchan tradition, as one may see by turning to Petrarch himself: the desperate exaggeration and tormented ingenuity of his metaphors operate as fully accurate correlatives for the lover's psychological condition, and it is on that condition that our attention, with sympathy and fascination, is centered. Typical Baroque hyperbole, even among the heirs of Petrarch, operates rather differently. One type, frequently encountered in Marino, Herrick, Carew, and Cleveland, is frankly and obviously playful. In poems employing such hyperbole, it is clear that the poet-speaker in no sense intends his protestations to be taken seriously—even as indications, on the psychological level, of the speaker's passion (one might note, for example, Cleveland's "Fuscara; or, the Bee Errant" and "Upon Phyllis").

Another type of Baroque hyperbole is more complex in its effects, more serious, one might say, in its playfulness. In Donne's "The Canonization," for example, the burlesque of conventional Petrarchan hyperbole functions simultaneously as a humorous parody, a modest affirmation of the truth of the speaker's emotion, and a highly sophisticated placing of that emotion in a context of recognition of the world outside his amorous sufferings. By virtue of conceding that his sorrows do not affect the external world, the speaker at once admits the existence of that world and asserts the substantial, if limited, validity of his amorous protestations:

Alas, alas, who's injur'd by my love?
　What merchants ships have my sighs drown'd?
Who saies my teares have overflow'd his ground?
　When did my colds a forward spring remove?
　　When did the heats which my veines fill
　Adde one more to the plaguie Bill?
Soldiers finde warres, and Lawyers finde out still
　Litigious men, which quarrels move,
　Though she and I do love.

[1:14]

"The Canonization" depends for a part of its effect on the reader's awareness of the tension between the convention of Petrarchan hyperbole and the poet's simultaneous burlesque and rehabilitation of that convention. There is another variety of Baroque hyperbole which operates on principles radically different from those inherited from Petrarch. In the lyrics of Góngora, typically, images drawn from nature are applied to the speaker's beloved with a hyperbolic stress on the superiority of the girl's beauties to those of nature. There is nothing seemingly novel or distinctive about this device: such hyperbolic comparisons are as old as amorous poetry itself. What distinguishes Góngora's practice as characteristically Baroque is his emphasis on the vehicle of the hyperbole to the virtual exclusion of the tenor—a paradoxical exclusion, in view of his ostensible motive. In his sonnet "Mientras por competir con tu cabello," for example, the speaker declares that his mistress's charms excel the beauty of the sun, the lily, the pink, and the crystal water.[13] But the reader's attention is directed not, as it would be by Petrarch or the Elizabethans, toward a visualization of the girl's beauty, but rather towards a visualization of natural beauties in themselves. Moreover, those natural beauties are presented in a manner not representational or picturesque but quasi-abstract. We are aware not of the pictorially presented sun, lily, pink, and water, but of gold, white, red, and crystal as qualities in themselves, abstracted from the objects in which they have their being. The sonnet concludes with the poet's reminder to the beloved that her beauties will ultimately dissolve into earth, smoke, dust, shade, nothing: "En tierra, en humo, en polvo, en sombra, en nada." As in Donne and Andreas Gryphius, the *carpe diem* theme, with its conventional reminder that beauty will age, die, and decay, is heightened to an assertion that beauty will turn to nothing at all. Góngora's hyperboles express the obsessive Baroque concern with the illusoriness of the phenomenal and the transitoriness of all earthly experience.

Another sonnet, "O claro honor del liquido elemento," manifests the same concentration on the hyperbolic vehicle and the same tendency toward abstraction.[14] Although the poem hyperbolically places the beloved in a position of superiority to the river, the superfluous admonition to the river that it

13 Luis de Góngora y Argote, *Obras en verso del Homero español*, ed. D. Alonso (Madrid, 1963), p. 12, recto.
14 *Ibid.*, p. 15, verso. See above, pp. 38–39.

continue to flow reminds us of the inexorable passage of time which will destroy the lady's beauty. The effect of the poem is surely not comic, but both its evocation of metamorphosis and its strangely dispassionate awareness of illusion relate it generally to the phenomenon of play.

The Italian Marino's exaltation of female beauty above the beauty of landscape works with a more simple playfulness, as in "La bella schiava," in which the beauty of a lovely Negress is presented as surpassing that of the sun—with incidental puns on the various meanings of "sole" in Italian:

> La 've più ardi, o Sol, sol per tuo scorno
> un sole è nato; un Sol, che nel bel volto
> porta la notte ed ha negli occhi il giorno.[15]

In "Vergänglichkeit der Schönheit," a sonnet by the German Marinist Christian Hofmann von Hofmannswaldau, a fusion of Marino's lightheartedness and Góngora's somber thoughtfulness occurs: the beauties of the beloved, analogized to the beauties of nature, will ultimately turn to complete nothingness—except for her heart, which, being as hard as diamond, will endure forever:

> Dein Herze kann allein zu aller Zeit bestehen,
> Dieweil es die Natur aus Diamant gemacht.[16]

The lover's sufferings do not dampen his sense of humor.

A final type of comic hyperbole might be perceived in some of the amorous poems of Góngora's countryman Don Francisco de Quevedo, several of whose sonnets go beyond the traditional Petrarchan exaggeration of the lover's suffering to achieve something like the grotesque: the speaker becomes ludicrous, even if his emotion does not, and the poems establish a tension between his real and painful emotion and his self-conscious perception of the state to which he has been reduced.

Donne, Góngora, Marino, Hofmannswaldau, and Quevedo thus demonstrate some of the more complex uses of hyperbole. What unites the various uses is a recognition that hyperbole, through its arbitrarily and absolutely aesthetic mode of existence, can enable the poet simultaneously to give utterance to intense

passion and to stand outside that passion as an observer. Baroque hyperbole, in short, tends toward the sphere of play and toward the curious transcendence of normal concerns and values which typically occurs within that sphere.

Another stock device of Petrarchan poetry retained and strikingly elaborated by the Baroque amorous poets is the assumption of a state of enmity between lover and beloved. Petrarchan poetry abounds in *dolci nemiche*—"dear enemies" and "sweet warriors"— the lady's obligatory rigor causing her lover such pain that he must regard her as his enemy. The conventional attitude assumes some bizarre twists in the Baroque age. In the insolent banter of many of Suckling's anti-Petrarchan lyrics, as in the aggressive arrogance of some of Carew's poems, the pose of hostility has been transformed from one signifying abject complaint to one signifying the cheerful acceptance of combat with an hereditary enemy. Donne, whose *Songs and Sonets* constitute a compendium of Baroque amorous attitudes, exemplifies the pose of agonistic insult in such poems as "Womans Constancy," "The Indifferent," and "The Apparition." The consistent implication, for these seventeenth-century poets, is that woman is the "sweet enemy" not simply because of her rigor toward her suitor but rather because she is man's opposite—necessary and desirable, but nevertheless (or perhaps therefore) opposite. The mood of these agonistic poems, and of even more extreme examples provided by such French *libertin* poets as Théophile de Viau and Marc-Antoine de Saint-Amant, is that of much amorous comedy, the mood of the flytings between Beatrice and Benedick in *Much Ado About Nothing*, between Rosalind and Orlando in *As You Like It*, and between Millamant and Mirabell in *The Way of the World* (not for nothing is "natural, easy Suckling" Millament's favorite poet). The condition of playful sexual agon, so emphasized by the Baroque love poets and so underplayed by most of their Renaissance predecessors, is a recurrent psychological constant. It underlies the Saturnalian and Fescennine rites of the ancients, as it underlies in our own day the convention of initial antipathy between boy and girl which turns up in so much popular fiction and theatre, the primitive quality of which is suggested by the forms it sometimes assumes—the comic-strip cliché of the wife armed with a rolling pin, and the Hollywood comedy cliché of the girl who receives a spanking from her irate suitor. What is involved, and stressed particularly in the Baroque version of the

---

15 G. B. Marino, *Poesie Varie*, ed. B. Croce (Bari, 1913), p. 105.

16 My *European Metaphysical Poetry*, pp. 188–89.

constant, is the celebration of "the eternal conflict of opposites which is the root principle of existence," which Huizinga sees as central to the play-element in culture.[17]

Agonistic insult as a convention in Baroque love poetry ranges from playful but still basically Petrarchan complaint in such a poem as Hofmannswaldau's "Vergänglichkeit der Schönheit," through the bantering but often tender animosities of Donne, Carew, and Suckling, to the outright slanders of Saint-Amant. Implicit in all versions of the attitude is the quasi-mythic sense of the playful agon as a participation in reality—another instance of the curious Baroque tendency to incorporate into forms of great elegance and sophistication a profoundly primitive sense of nature and of man's place in it. The feeling for nature in Baroque amorous poetry seldom issues as a sense of the picturesque. Donne shows almost no interest in nature as picture, Marino's confections have more to do finally with the poet's wit than with his senses, and Góngora's use of landscape, as we have seen, breaks natural imagery down analytically into its abstract constituents. Nevertheless, the amorous agon often takes place in a setting of nature, with a consequently implied identification of human sexuality with the processes of the earth.

Saint-Amant's long erotic poem "La Jouissance" opens with the careful staging of a natural scene against the background of which the protagonist and his mistress consummate their love. The evocation of the landscape, though relatively detailed and specific, is not mere descriptive ornament, for it is clear that in the ecstasy of love the participants become a part of the landscape: their bodies stretched out on the earth become in a sense a part of that earth (as they do also in Théophile's "La Solitude"). Possessed by nature, the lovers in Saint-Amant possess nature in turn, and the French poet makes use of one of Donne's favorite tropes: that in owning each other the lovers own more than all the kings of earth. Shortly thereafter, as Saint-Amant celebrates the consummation of love, he introduces the agon-motif in one of its most playful and paradoxical forms:

La langue, estant de la partie,
Sitost qu'un baiser l'assiégeait,
Au bord des lèvres se rangeait,
Afin de faire une sortie;

L'ennemy, recevant ses coups,
Souffrait un martyre si doux,
Qu'il en bénissait les atteintes;
Et mille longs soupirs, servant en mesme temps
De chants de victoire et de plaintes,
Montraient que les vaincus estoient les plus contents.[18]

The inherent association among the theme of love, the motif of agon, and the setting in nature is suggested by the fact that even John Donne, Londoner and scorner of the country, provides both a landscape and a muted version of the agon-motif for his most profound exploration of the metaphysics of love, "The Extasie":

> Where, like a pillow on a bed,
> A Pregnant banke swel'd up, to rest
> The violets reclining head,
> Sat we two, one anothers best.
>
> [1:51]

A few stanzas later the rapt lovers are presented as adversaries:

> As 'twixt two equall Armies, Fate
> Suspends uncertaine victorie,
> Our soules, (which to advance their state,
> Were gone out,) hung 'twixt her, and mee.
> And whil'st our soules negotiate there,
> Wee like sepulchrall statues lay;
> All day, the same our postures were,
> And wee said nothing, all the day.
>
> [1:51–52]

In these Baroque love poems, ironic distancing, dramatic form, comic hyperbole, and jocular aggression, either separately or in combination, enable the lover-protagonist to experience sexual passion as simultaneously the transcendence of his individual identity and the condition of existence of that identity at its highest and truest level. In Donne and in the German Paul Fleming the lover finds his heart only through losing it. In such poems as "La Jouissance," "La Solitude," and Herrick's "Corinna's Going a-Maying," nature and sexual love are assimilated to each other, and the self is asserted by virtue of the fact that it is provisionally annihilated in contact with the totality of nature. The pattern suggested here reminds one of some aspects of Shakespeare's comedies:

---

[17] Huizinga, *Homo Ludens*, p. 116.

[18] Marc-Antoine de Saint-Amant, *Oeuvres Poétiques*, ed. L. Vérane (Paris, 1930), p. 44.

disguise, particularly disguise of sex, as a symbolic expression of the capacity for metamorphosis, for the loss of self, which is in turn the indispensable condition and infallible sign of a self of the truest and most fully differentiated sort.

It reminds one also of the uses made of the themes of withdrawal and engagement in much Baroque poetry. In such poems as "La Solitude" or Marvell's "The Garden" and "Upon Appleton House" withdrawal into nature constitutes a quasi-mystical loss of the sense of individual identity—not, however, in the manner of Romantic nature poetry, largely because of the invariable presence of the play-element. The seventeenth-century gentleman's encounter with nature leads not to a state of permanent pantheistic trance but rather to a witty recognition of a temporary state in which the identity, by being compromised, is paradoxically affirmed. The basic pattern is one of alternating withdrawal and engagement—withdrawal from social and passionate life and engagement with nature, followed by withdrawal from nature and re-engagement with society and passion. The pattern appears at its clearest and most complete in the poems of Marvell, but it underlies poems by Saint-Amant, Théophile, Lovelace, and Herrick as well.

No Baroque lyric poet explores the themes of nature, love, and metamorphosis more cogently than does Andrew Marvell, and no poet is more committed to the devices of play. An examination of his work in the love lyric may bring more clarity to a consideration of play as a central mode in such poetry. Comic hyperbole is the principal feature of "The Unfortunate Lover"; and "The Gallery" and "The Fair Singer" supply amusing examples of neo-Petrarchan love-agon with a new twist. "The Gallery" presents tableaux of the speaker's mistress in the various contradictory poses she assumes in his mind—as murderess and Aurora, as witch and Venus. All versions of the lady are accurate, for her nature as the erotic focus identifies her with the metamorphic principle of nature, as the poem's last picture makes clear. All the transformations of which she is capable have their origin in her role as Shepherdess:

> But, of these Pictures and the rest,
> That at the Entrance likes me best:
> Where the same Posture, and the Look
> Remains, with which I first was took.
> A tender Shepherdess, whose Hair
> Hangs loosely playing in the Air,

> Transplanting Flow'rs from the green Hill,
> To crown her Head and Bosome fill.[19]

"The Fair Singer" has fun with the Petrarchan trope of the sweet enemy by the simple expedient of turning the amorous agon into a full-scale military campaign:

> To make a final conquest of all me.
> Love did compose so sweet an Enemy,
> In whom both Beauties to my death agree,
> Joyning themselves in fatal Harmony;
> That while she with her Eyes my Heart does bind,
> She with her Voice might captivate my Mind.

> I could have fled from One but singly fair:
> My dis-intangled Soul it self might save,
> Breaking the curled trammels of her hair.
> But How should I avoid to be her Slave,
> Whose subtile Art invisibly can wreath
> My fetters of the very Air I breath?

> It had been easie fighting in some plain,
> Where Victory might hang in equal choice,
> But all resistance against her is vain,
> Who has th' advantage both of Eyes and Voice,
> And all my Forces needs must be undone,
> She having gained both the Wind and Sun.
> [1:31]

Other poets of the age, notably Herrick, Carew, and Lovelace in England, and Joost van den Vondel in Holland, were fond of the situation celebrated here—the singing of a beautiful woman—but Marvell's stress on the agonistic and jocular potentialities exemplifies very completely the Baroque tendency to make of the play-attitude an instrument for controlling and understanding emotion without losing or disarming it. . . .

There ought to be a better word than *play* to denote the cast of mind underlying the work of Marvell and so many other Baroque figures, but our language does not seem to have one. One might, to try to delineate it further, suggest that this cast of mind has something to do with a radical sense of the power of an aesthetic conception to hold in solution all manner of opposed conceptions which are, however opposed, mutually valid. Such a sense informs the conceits, paradoxes, and ironies of the Metaphysical poets, but it informs

19 Andrew Marvell, *Poems and Letters*, ed. H. M. Margoliouth, 2 vols., 2d ed. (Oxford, 1952), 1:26. Further citations are to this edition and are given in the text.

also much of the work of John Milton, a poet who is, despite the occasional grim humor of *Paradise Lost*, scarcely to be thought of as playful. Nevertheless, the play-spirit, with its dynamic potentiality for synthesis, fills "L'Allegro" and "Il Penseroso," and, though it would require a perverse love of paradox to classify "Lycidas" as a "playful" poem, there is a sense in which that great elegy operates through an awareness of the power of an aesthetic conception to achieve resolutions which neither faith nor philosophy can reach.

Those critics are probably all extinct who once taught that Milton really had more sympathy with his thoughtful man than with his joyful man, as proven by the fact that "Il Penseroso" is some twenty-four lines longer than "L'Allegro." The absurdity of such an approach is obvious; what is less obvious, perhaps, is that any approach to these poems which aims at the sober determination of "meanings" or "attitudes" is doomed to founder. Both poems (or, more accurately, both movements of the single poem) remain with flawless tact on the aesthetic surface of things—appropriately enough, since their concern is with the aesthetic surface of things and with the re-creation of a specifically aesthetic joy.[20]

The connection between this aesthetic joy and the spirit of play should be made clear by the gusty humor of the opening of "L'Allegro," with its burlesque diction, its comic hyperbole, and its amusingly inappropriate heaviness of tone:

Hence loathed Melancholy
   Of *Cerberus*, and blackest midnight born,
In *Stygian* Cave forlorn
  'Mongst horrid shapes, and shreiks, and sights
      unholy,
Find out some uncouth cell,
  Wher brooding darknes spreads his jealous wings,
And the night-Raven sings;
  There under *Ebon* shades, and low-brow'd Rocks,
As ragged as thy Locks,
  In dark *Cimmerian* desert ever dwell.[21]

The mood of "Il Penseroso" renders its parallel opening dismissal of "vain deluding joyes" less obvious in its playfulness, but it is impossible to read much gravity into the lines[22] if we recognize that the thoughtful man is having every bit as much fun in his activities as is the joyful man, and that he is quite as hedonistically single-minded in his pursuit of pleasure, even at the end of the poem when the speaker, with a kind of luxuriant sentimentality, pictures his old age:

And may at last my weary age
Find out the peacefull hermitage,
The Hairy Gown and Mossy Cell,
Where I may sit and rightly spell,
Of every Star that Heav'n doth shew,
And every Herb that sips the dew;
Till old experience do attain
To somthing like Prophetic strain.
                        [p. 428]

The careful way in which the activities of the two men (or the two moods) are balanced reminds us constantly that both poems are about pleasure: the difference finally is no more than the difference between enjoying tragedy and enjoying comedy—two different kinds of play. Structural balance also has the effect of modulating the tone, preventing it from ever becoming so intense as to exceed the purely aesthetic. The matched references to the myth of Orpheus (always one of Milton's favorites) supply an example of such modulation. In "L'Allegro," near the very end of that joyful poem, the reference is to the myth in its most pathetic aspect: the epithet in the last line of the ensuing passage renders that pathos with great poignancy:

Untwisting all the chains that ty
The hidden soul of harmony.
That *Orpheus* self may heave his head
From golden slumber on a bed
Of heapt *Elysian* flowres, and hear
Such streins as would have won the ear
Of *Pluto*, to have quite set free
His half regain'd Eurydice.
                        [p. 424]

20 The central thesis of Susan Sontag's essay "Against Interpretation" (in her *Against Interpretation* [New York, 1965]) is, though somewhat overstated, basically just. It is a healthy corrective to the conception of criticism as translation or paraphrase which afflicts so many different critical schools.

21 John Milton, *Poetical Works*, ed. H. Darbishire (London, 1958), p. 420. Further citations are to this edition and are given in the text.

22 For a discussion of the comic aspects of these openings, see E. M. W. Tillyard, *The Miltonic Setting* (Cambridge, 1938), pp. 1–28.

In the melancholy context of "Il Penseroso," on the other hand, the poet chooses a very different moment in the myth, the moment at which, however precariously, love has triumphed over death:

> But, O sad Virgin, that thy power
> Might raise *Musaeus* from his bower,
> Or bid the soul of *Orpheus* sing
> Such notes as warbled to the string,
> Drew Iron tears down *Pluto's* cheek,
> And made Hell grant what Love did seek.
>
> [p. 426]

In each case the tension between the mood of the poem and the mood of the reference prevents the overall mood from becoming either exclusively cheerful or exclusively melancholy, and the effect is to keep both poems within the realm of the aesthetic, another word, perhaps, for the realm of play within which the poems have their being. Hence, though the emotions they evoke are exquisitely moving, those emotions are always aesthetic.

To describe "L'Allegro" and "Il Penseroso" as "purely aesthetic" works is, in a sense, to describe them as impersonal, or rather suprapersonal, works. Such works expose themselves to the charge of insincerity as their opposites, confessional works, expose themselves to the charge of sentimentality. Insincerity is the charge historically brought against "Lycidas." The charge, whether it presents itself in its classicistic or its romantic form,[23] is almost automatically refuted by a consideration of literary traditions and systems of decorum larger than those of Dr. Johnson or of the nineteenth century, and such were, of course, the traditions and systems from within which Milton wrote. The death by drowning of Milton's classmate Edward King is as clearly an "occasion" for an artistic work as is the untimely death of Elizabeth Drury (Donne's "Anniversaries"), and the work which it occasions is a pastoral elegy—by definition a kind of poem in which a distinct aesthetic distancing occurs, a variety of material is encompassed, and a certain psychological pattern, wider than the strictly individual, is accomplished.[24]

Pastoral elegiac tradition itself also refutes the charge of diffuseness which has been leveled against the poem. The alleged "digressions" on fame and on the corrupt clergy are not only conventional for the Renaissance pastoralist; they are firmly integrated into the poem by the fact that they have reference to the two symbolic functions of the shepherd-figure for the Christian humanist: the shepherd as poet and the shepherd as priest.[25] If the poem presents problems of interpretation, they derive not from any supposed lack of unity or sincerity but from complex ambiguities which lie at its very heart. One might examine, for example, the question of where Lycidas is at the climax of the poem, in the passages immediately preceding and constituting the consolation experienced by the speaker. At the conclusion of the great flower catalog, the speaker recognizes with pain that even the consolation of decorating the poet's corpse is denied his mourners by the fact that the corpse has been lost at sea. The recognition leads at once to the lowest spiritual point of the poem, but that point is immediately transcended, illogically and mysteriously, in the apostrophe to St. Michael and the dolphins:

> Ay me! Whilst thee the shores, and sounding Seas
> Wash far away, where ere thy bones are hurld,
> Whether beyond the stormy *Hebrides*,
> Where thou perhaps under the whelming tide
> Visit'st the bottom of the monstrous world;
> Or whether thou to our moist vows deny'd,
> Sleep'st by the fable of *Bellerus* old,
> Where the great vision of the guarded Mount
> Looks toward *Namancos* and *Bayona's* hold;
> Look homeward Angel now, and melt with ruth,
> And, O ye *Dolphins*, waft the haples youth.
>
> [p. 451]

The puzzling swiftness of the consolation is intensified by the lines which follow:

23 The definitive version of the classicistic charge is leveled by Dr. Johnson in his "Life of Milton" (1778), in *Lives of the English Poets*, ed. L. Archer-Hind, 2 vols. (London, 1925), 1:95–96. The romantic charge may be encountered in the response of the average untutored modern reader.

24 J. H. Hanford, "The Pastoral Elegy and Milton's *Lycidas*," *PMLA* 25 (1910): 403–47, gives perhaps the best account of Milton's relation to the tradition from which "Lycidas" derives. See also N. Frye, "Literature as Context: Milton's *Lycidas*," in his *Fables of Identity* (New York, 1963), pp. 119–29.

25 M. H. Nicolson, *John Milton: A Reader's Guide to His Poetry* (New York, 1963), pp. 87–111.

Weep no more, woful Shepherds, weep no more,
For *Lycidas* your sorrow is not dead,
Sunk though he be beneath the watry floar,
So sinks the day-star in the Ocean bed,
And yet anon repairs his drooping head,
And tricks his beams, and with new spangled Ore,
Flames in the forehead of the morning sky:
So *Lycidas* sunk low, but mounted high,
Through the dear might of him that walk'd the
        waves;
Where other groves, and other streams along,
With *Nectar* pure his oozy Locks he laves,
And hears the unexpressive nuptiall Song,
In the blest Kingdoms meek of joy and love.
There entertain him all the Saints above,
In solemn troops, and sweet Societies
That sing, and singing in their glory move,
And wipe the tears for ever from his eyes.
Now *Lycidas* the Shepherds weep no more;
Henceforth thou art the Genius of the shore,
In thy large recompense, and shalt be good
To all that wander in that perilous flood.

                                    [p. 451]

We are told that Lycidas has been carried away by the ocean tides, that he is among the blessed in heaven, and that he has been appointed the genius of the shore of the sea in which he was drowned. The mutual opposition of the assertions is perplexing, even if we regard the first assertion as one which is retracted by the other two (and, in view of the forceful conviction of the lines, it is difficult to do so with much confidence). The point is, I think, that the multiplicity of assertions as to the whereabouts of Lycidas constitutes in itself the consolation. Liberated from the restrictions of his finiteness, the dead poet can now be simultaneously absorbed into the element of his death, alive forever in heaven, and present as a guardian spirit by the shores of the Irish Sea.

The abruptness of the speaker's reversal from dejection to joy is also justified by the ambiguity of the water-symbol itself. In the course of the vision of the lost corpse, the weight of the symbolic meaning shifts from water-as-death to water-as-rebirth.[26] For Milton, as for so many poets before and after him, water as symbol inevitably carries both associations, and so it is that what we thought was the low point of the poem is revealed, at the moment of the appeal to the archangel, as the high point. Water imagery has, of course, been conspicuously present since the beginning of the poem—in the invocation to the "Sisters of the sacred well," in the reference to the head of Orpheus sent "Down the Swift *Hebrus*," in the apostrophes to "Fountain *Arethuse*" and "Smooth-sliding *Mincius*," in the appearances of Camus and St. Peter ("The pilot of the *Galilean* lake"), and elsewhere—and it is supremely appropriate that at the climax of the poem, after Lycidas's death has been revealed as his life, Christ should make his appearance as he "that walk'd the waves."[27]

The point I am making, of course, is that the effective resolution of "Lycidas" derives not from religious doctrine or philosophical conviction per se but rather from the recapitulation of a mythic pattern of death and rebirth; and such mythic patterns, one might suggest, are the ultimate source of all literary conventions. The resolution of "Lycidas" derives from its literary form: the basis of the speaker's consolation may be Christian faith, but that faith operates within the poem under a larger, nonspecific aspect—one which is mythic, conventional, literary, artistic.

"Lycidas" is not a playful poem in the sense of "The Garden" or "Upon Appleton House," but it is in a sense a "played" poem. Perhaps it would have been more accurate to entitle this chapter "art as art," for the eminence of the art of the seventeenth century rests upon the artist's radical awareness of the authority which his art by its very nature possesses, as a form of knowledge and a variety of spiritual achievement.

26 *Ibid.*
27 Nicolson, *John Milton*, p. 102. For a consideration of "Lycidas" as a Baroque poem on rather different grounds, see L. Nelson, *Baroque Lyric Poetry* (New Haven, 1961), pp. 64–76, 138–52.

INDEX OF AUTHORS

Prose
INDEX OF TITLES

(For a complete listing of all subtitles of prose selections, see the table of contents, pp. vii–xiv.)

Poetry
INDEX OF TITLES AND FIRST LINES

(Titles of poems are printed in italics, and first lines of poems in roman.)